IPA Symbol	Example	as in
		English Consonants
b	'bid	**bid**
d	'did	**did**
dʒ	'dʒet	**jet**
ð	'ðis	**this**
f	'fit	**fit**
g	'get	**get**
h	'hed	**head**
hw	'hwet	**whet**
j	'jes	**yes**
k	'ke:k	**cake**
l	'leg	**leg**
ļ	'midļ	**middle**
m	'men	**men**
m̩	'o:pm̩	**open** (some pronunciations)
n	'net	**net**
ņ	'kitņ	**kitten**
ŋ	'riŋ, 'riŋk	**ring, rink**
p	'pin	**pin**
r	'red, 'meri·	**red, merry**
ʳ (raised r)	'kaʳd (= 'kard, 'ka:d)	**card**
s	'sit	**sit**
ʃ	'ʃo:	**show**
t	'to:, 'to:t	**toe, tote**
ţ	'siţiŋ, 'hi:ţəd	**sitting, heated** (most U. S. pronunciations)
tʃ	'tʃip	**chip**
θ	'θiŋk	**think**
v	'vet	**vet**
w	'wet	**wet**
z	'zip	**zip**
ʒ	'viʒən, 'be:ʒ	**vision, beige**

IPA Symbol	Example	as in
		English Vowels
ə	bə'nænə, 'bəd	**banana, bud**
əʳ	'bəʳd, 'bəţəʳ	**bird, butter**
æ	'fæd, 'æsk	**fad, ask**
ɑ	'baðəʳ, 'k...	
ɑ:	'fɑ:ðəʳ, 'ɑ...	
ai	'bai, 'raid	
au	'bau, 'nau	
e	'fed	
e:	'fe:d	
i	'bid	**bid**
i:	'bi:d	**bead**
o:	'ko:t	**coat**
ɔ:	'kɔ:t, 'lɔ:	**caught, law**
ɔi	'bɔi, 'kɔin	**boy, coin**
u	'gud, 'put, puʳ	**good, put, poor**
u:	'mu:d, 'mju:zik	**mood, music**
		Non-English Vowels
œ	'hœlə, bœf	German **Hölle**, French **boeuf**
œ:	'hœ:lə, fœ:	German **Höhle**, French **feu**
y	'fylən	German **füllen**
y:	'fy:lən, ry:	German **fühlen**, French **rue**
		Non-English Consonants
β	aβ'lar	Spanish **hablar**
ç	'iç	German **ich**
ɣ	a'mi:ɣo:	Spanish **amigo**
ł	'tʃesłaf	Polish **Czesław**
ļ	ļa'neļi·	Welsh **Llanelli**
ɲ	'di:ɲ	French **digne**
ɾ	'ɾanðə	Welsh **Rhondda**
x	'lax, 'bax	Scottish **loch**, German **Bach**
ɥ	lɥi:	French **lui**
ʗ	'ʗxū	**!Kung** (an implosive click)
ʖ	'ʖhɔ:sa:	**Xhosa** (an implosive click)

Diacritics used in IPA transcriptions

IPA Symbol	Example	as in	Explanation
'	'æpəl	**apple**	primary stress
ˌ	'æpəlˌsɔ:s	**applesauce**	secondary stress
:	'ni:t	**neat**	an augmented vowel
·	'hæpi·	**happy**	variation between simple and augmented
~	bɔ̃		...f a vowel
˘	'siţiŋ, 'h...		...sually unvoiced consonant
ₒ	ļa'neļi·		...equivalent of a voiced
ˌ	'kitņ		...onant
ˎ	mə'ţildə		...onsonant

Pronouncing Dictionary

of

Proper Names

Pronouncing Dictionary

of

Proper Names

Pronunciations for more than 28,000 Proper Names,
Selected for Currency, Frequency, or Difficulty of Pronunciation

*Including Place Names; Given Names; Names of Famous
Individuals; Cultural, Literary, Historical, and Biblical Names;
Mythological Names; Names of Peoples and Tribes; Company
Names and Product Names; with Pronunciations Transcribed into
the International Phonetic Alphabet and a Simplified Phonetic
Respelling; and Including an Explanatory Introduction*

Editor:

John K. Bollard

Associate Editors:

Frank R. Abate
Katherine M. Isaacs
Rima McKinzey

Omnigraphics, Inc.
Penobscot Building • Detroit, Michigan 48226

Editorial Staff

John K. Bollard, *Editor*

Frank R. Abate, Katherine M. Isaacs,
and Rima McKinzey, *Associate Editors*

Elaine Chasse, Jennifer Feola, Terri Finkeldey, Jacquelyn Goodwin,
Elizabeth Jewell, Jane Wozniak, *Editorial Assistants*

Design Consultant: John F. Kallio
Computer Consultant: Stephen Bladey
Data Processing and Typesetting: GAC/Shepard Poorman
Indianapolis, Ind.

Omnigraphics, Inc.

Matthew P. Barbour, *Production Manager*
Laurie Lanzen Harris, *Vice President, Editorial Director*
Peter E. Ruffner, *Vice President, Administration*
James A. Sellgren, *Vice President, Operations & Finance*

Frederick G. Ruffner, Jr., *Publisher*

Copyright © 1998 Omnigraphics, Inc.

Library of Congress Cataloging-in-Publication Data

Pronouncing dictionary of proper names : pronunciations for more than 28,000 proper names, selected for
currency, frequency, or difficulty of pronunciation / edited by John K. Bollard : associate editors, Frank R.
Abate, Katherine M. Isaacs and Rima McKinzey.
   p. cm.
   "Including place names; given names; names of famous individuals; cultural, literary, historical and
Biblical names; mythological names; names of peoples and tribes; company names and product names; with
pronunciations transcribed into the International Phonetic Alphabet and a simplified phonetic respelling and
including an explanatory introduction."
   ISBN 0-7808-0098-2 (lib. bdg. : alk. paper)
   1. English language—Pronunciation—Dictionaries.   2. Names—Pronunciation.   I. Bollard, John K.
II. Abate, Frank R.   III. Isaacs, Katherine M.   IV. McKinzey, Rima.
PE1137.P822   1997   97-23664
423'.1—dc21   CIP

Printed in the United States of America

Contents

Preface

In this world of instantaneous global communication, where national and international affairs are matters of daily concern and discussion, we find that our knowledge of geography, of well-known personages, and of other peoples and cultures can no longer be confined to the familiar. As a result, especially in the realm of names and proper nouns, we are often confronted with an uncertainty about pronunciation. How is a name to be pronounced, particularly if we have never heard it spoken aloud or if we are not sure of what we heard? English spelling is notorious for being only an approximate, often ambiguous indication of pronunciation, and proper names are particularly troublesome in this regard. Couple this with the need to talk about people, places, things, and ideas from around the world and it would seem that to sound well informed we ought to know not only English, but the rules for pronouncing more than a few other languages as well.

This *Pronouncing Dictionary of Proper Names* is designed to lessen this uncertainty by indicating acceptable pronunciations for a wide range of names that may not easily be found in other reference sources. Pronunciations appear both in a respelling system that should be "user-friendly" to the non-specialist, and in a version of the International Phonetic Alphabet (IPA), widely employed by linguists and other specialists.

The pronunciations shown in the *Pronouncing Dictionary of Proper Names* reflect the major variations in American dialects, and to the best of our ability we have represented the local or personal pronunciations used by those who live in a particular place or who themselves bear a particular name. We have drawn on a wide range of current reference books, studies of pronunciation in English and other languages, and on the actual pronunciations of those familiar with the person, place, or subject in question. Thus, we are confident that the users of the *Pronouncing Dictionary of Proper Names* will find it a reliable guide to the pronunciation of more than 28,000 names. Both common and unusual names may be found here, making this dictionary useful to native English speakers as well as to those who have learned or are learning English as a second or additional language.

I have enjoyed working with Frank Abate and Katherine Isaacs of Omnigraphics, who selected the bulk of the names for inclusion and who spent many hours refining the conception, layout, and design of this dictionary. A considerable debt of gratitude is also owed to Rima McKinzey, who read through and corrected the pronunciations with great skill and dispatch and made many valuable suggestions. Further improvements were made through an innovation used, we believe, for the first time in the preparation of any dictionary—pronunciations were actually "proof-listened." Through facilities made available by AT & T Bell Laboratories of Murray Hill, New Jersey, all pronunciations were actually *heard* using speech-synthesis technology. We are particularly grateful to Ken Church and Richard Sproat of Bell Labs for making the necessary arrangements.

Thanks also go to Dick Doll, Chuck Lacy, and the staff of GAC/Shepard Poorman of Indianapolis, Ind., who, besides typesetting, developed the programming that automatically generated drafts of the simplified respellings used in this dictionary from formal IPA transcriptions (for further details, consult the **Introduction**). Their work transformed a collection of raw data into the pages you see here, and they accepted with graceful equanimity all the quirks, complexities, and problems we presented them with. Many friends and colleagues tolerated my frequent requests for information about pronunciations in their fields of knowledge or about places they have lived in or visited. Craig Davis of Smith College has freely shared his knowledge, linguistic expertise, and time in discussions of many names in a number of areas. Special thanks in this regard go to Dennis Hudson, also of Smith College, whose interests and understanding are wide-ranging and who has made both freely available to me; his contribution to this book is not limited to advice on the terminology of those world religions in which he is recognized as expert.

Finally, while living with any writer is trying, living with a lexicographer—who may seem more interested in words and isolated names rather than whole sentences or coherent ideas—must be doubly so. For her contribution to this book, for her patience, for her understanding of me if not always of my often obscure queries, and for her encouragement, mere thanks seem woefully inadequate, but they are offered here to my wife, Margaret Lloyd, as small recompense.

John K. Bollard
May 1993 *Florence, Massachusetts*

Preface to the Second Edition

For this second edition of the *Pronouncing Dictionary of Proper Names* a wide selection of over 5,000 geographical, biographical and other proper names have been added to the corpus of the first edition. Many names were included that have come into prominence in recent years through current events, popular culture, and sports. Here you may now find **Zalata Filipovic** and **Brett Favre, Srebrenica** and **Arab,** Alabama. In addition to adding many placenames around the world, a particular effort has been made to extend our coverage of US placenames with difficult or unpredictable pronunciations; thus, we have added such places as **Mexia,** Texas, the **Oquirrh** Mountains, Utah, and **Vienna,** Georgia. The editors have also added all names from the Old and New Testaments not found in the first edition. Rather than giving specific identifications to these names and their varients, they are usually labeled simply *Biblical name.* As a minor departure in style for these scriptural names, an approximation of the Hebrew pronunciation is given *after* the Anglicized pronunciation.

I owe many thanks to my associate editors, Frank Abate, Katherine Isaacs and especialy Rima McKinzey, who produced with great care the IPA transcriptions for most of the new entries. Thanks, too, to Dick Doll, Chuck Lacy and the staff of GAC Shepard Poorman, who have again wrestled our complex electronic data into a book. The editors offer this second edition confident that it will continue to be a useful and reliable addition to the library, school, and home reference shelf.

John K. Bollard
March 1997 *Florence, Massachusetts*

Introduction

The *Pronouncing Dictionary of Proper Names* (*PDPN*) provides pronunciations for some 28,000 names that are frequently encountered in speech and reading. Entries are briefly identified and current English pronunciations are shown both in a simplified phonetic respelling and in a formal transcription. In many cases alternative or variant pronunciations that may be considered as acceptable variants are also shown.

For foreign names not as widely known in English, it is assumed that the English-speaking users of this book will be interested in approximating the pronunciation of the language of origin, without being required to learn the intricacies of pronunciation for many different languages. The pronunciations given for such names enable the reader to do just this. Careful use of the transcriptions should result in an intelligent, acceptable English pronunciation of the name in question.

Selection Criteria

With the universe of proper names numbering in the many millions, clearly some criteria are needed to select the most useful entries and maintain a convenient size.

Frequency and Currency

Certain classes of items considered of primary interest for their frequency or currency are covered in depth. These include:

> Countries of the world (and terms for inhabitants)
> National capitals and other important cities
> Principal landmarks
> U.S. states, state capitals, and important cities
> Common given names and surnames
> Principal religions of the world
> Principal languages of the world
> Principal ethnic groups of the world

Names "Difficult to Pronounce"

For many of the entries in *PDPN*, inclusion was on the grounds of difficulty. The spelling of a name, even a fairly common American English name, is not always a clear indication of how it is pronounced. Certain names, those of foreign origin to a native speaker of English, perhaps many names to someone learning English, may be problematic. This is true especially when a name that one wishes to say has been encountered only in writing. Some of the more unusual or foreign-sounding names may cause difficulty or uncertainty even after one has heard them. *PDPN* provides a handy resource in such instances, providing a fully acceptable pronunciation—in an easy to use form—for thousands of troublesome names.

Categories of Names Covered

The following categories of names are covered in *PDPN*. In selecting individual entries for these categories, emphasis was on the criteria noted above—frequency, currency, and variation or troublesomeness of pronunciation for many speakers of English:

Given Names and Surnames: about 3,000 of the most common given names (including their non-English forms), and some 1,000 commonly encountered surnames

Geographic Names: historically and culturally significant cities, regions, provinces, states; noted buildings, streets, neighborhoods, stadiums; historical and cultural sites of importance

Geographical Features: mountains and mountain ranges, valleys, oceans and seas, rivers, lakes, deserts, etc.

People: famous and infamous individuals, both living and dead, particularly those whose names may be considered "difficult to pronounce"

Nature and the Environment: breeds of animals (dogs, cats, horses, etc.); major taxonomic groups (Arthropods, Echinoderms, etc.); names of dinosaurs; natural phenomena

History: peoples, cultures, tribes; dynasties and royal houses, kings, rulers

Politics and Current Affairs: national legislative bodies; parties and factions; news agencies and services; newspapers and magazines

Literature: authors and their works; settings, both fictional and real; literary characters

Religion: sects and denominations; sacred books; all Biblical names; founders, prophets; popes; shrines and holy places

Philosophy: schools; philosophers; "-ologies & -isms"

Culture and the Arts: museums and works of art; musical works; groups, orchestras, ensembles; concert halls; holidays around the world; art/musical/cultural festivals; awards

Company and Product Names: especially if "difficult to pronounce"

Popular Culture: celebrities, products, and designers, especially if "difficult to pronounce"

Food and Drink: wines and spirits; brands of beer; famous dishes

Science and Technology: chemical elements; subatomic particles; units of measure; theories; "-ologies & -isms"; eponymic phrases, as for apparatus (e.g., Petri dish); aircraft; pronounced computer acronyms; computer languages; satellites; stars, planets, constellations, astronomical features and phenomena.

Cross References and Variant Spellings

Many names, especially foreign place names, appear in various forms, depending for instance on the source language and the manner in which the name has been anglicized, as in **Kraków/Cracow**. Some places, entities, and a number of people, too, have more than one name; **Beijing/Peiping/Peking**, **Cambodian/Khmer**, and *Kareem* **Abdul-Jabbar**/*Lew* **Alcindor** are familiar examples. Two types of cross reference are used to direct the reader to alternative names and variant spellings of names.

Cross references for alternative names are given in square brackets following the boldface headword:

Beijing [Peiping, Peking]
  city, China
Peiping [Beijing]
  city, China
Peking [Beijing]
  city, China

In some cases the cross reference is given only at the less common form, directing the reader to a more common or more fully anglicized form:

Makkah [Mecca]
  city, Saudi Arabia
Mecca
  city, Saudi Arabia, center of Islam

Square-bracketed cross-references always lead to entries with a different pronunciation. Many names, however, have variant spellings which represent the same pronunciation. Such variants are given at the main entry, separated by commas:

Betsey, Betsy
  pers. name

Sometimes only a part of the name is shown in order to indicate a spelling variation:

Tchaikovsky, Tsch-
  Peter Ilyich, *Russian composer*

If spelling variants do not fall in close alphabetical proximity, the variant spelling will be entered at its own place with a cross reference to the main entry given in the entry identification:

Tschaikovsky
  See **Tchaikovsky**

Entry Identifications

Each entry has brief entry identification on the line below. These identifications are intentionally very concise, and are meant only to specify the name being pronounced, not to define the name in detail.

Some abbreviated identifications are used, especially *pl. name*, for particularly common place (geographic) names. The identification *pers. name* is used for personal names, that is, both given names and surnames of people. For many non-English given names, the identification states the foreign language in which the name is so pronounced. Entries for surnames may also specify in the identification a particular individual (by given name) who has that surname. Entries for some unusual given names specify in the identification the surname of the individual who uses the given name being pronounced. The identification *pert. to* is used to refer not only to the adjectival forms of proper names, but also to indicate "demonyms" (names that are used for residents or inhabitants), or other relationships.

References to states of the United States use the standard two-letter postal abbreviations.

Variant Pronunciations

The pronunciations given in this book may be considered acceptable in American English, as judged by the editors. Where there are two or more pronunciations for a given entry, a more common pronunciation is given first, if that may be confidently determined. However, the widespread variation in the speech of American and other English speakers makes it difficult to assess the relative frequency of common, acceptable variants. In many cases pronunciation differences between two or more widely used dialects (for example, the dialects of the north-central U.S., eastern New England, the upper and lower South, and the Southwest—each spoken by millions of Americans) require the representation of two or more equally acceptable variants. A classic example is the name **Mary**.

In cases of foreign names, transcriptions that represent the pronunciation of the language of origin are given first, followed by anglicized versions, as at **Bach**. In cases where the first pronunciation shown for a non-English name differs markedly from or is not as common as other anglicized pronunciations, the subsequent anglicized variant or variants are preceded by a dollar sign, ⓢ, to indicate that they are common U.S. pronunciations:

Cortés
Hernán *or* Hernando; *Spanish*   kawr-TĀS, ⓢ kawr-TEZ, KAWR-tez   kɔːrˈteɪs, ⓢ kɔːrˈtez,
conquistador   ˈkɔːrˌtez

A number of names are pronounced significantly differently in the U.S. and Britain. In these cases a U.S. pronunciation is given first and the British version or versions are preceded by a pound sign, Ⓔ:

Davies
family name   DĀ-vēz, Ⓔ DĀ-vis   ˈdeɪviːz, Ⓔ ˈdeɪvis

Two Pronunciation Systems

The *Pronouncing Dictionary of Proper Names* shows pronunciations in two different systems. A simplified pronunciation system, based on familiar conventions of English spelling, is shown in the middle (second) column of the text. The second system employs the alphabet of the International Phonetic Association (IPA), widely used by linguists and found in several standard dictionaries. Considerable attention has been given to making these systems comparable and compatible. Both show the same basic information, though the IPA provides more phonetic detail for those who are interested.

In the body of the book the two pronunciation respellings or transcriptions are shown in side-by-side columns. In the explanation of each system that follows, pairs of uprights | . . . | set off the simplified respellings; slash marks or virgules / . . . / enclose IPA transcriptions.

Simplified Pronunciation System

The simplified pronunciation system uses ordinary letters or combinations of letters to represent sounds. Diacritical marks and unusual symbols or combinations of letters are kept to a minimum; only a macron and an underline are used. As will be familiar to many from traditional practice, the macron | ¯ | is used above vowels to represent the "long" vowels *e, i, o,* and *oo* (as in *beat, bite, boat,* and *boot*). Of course, as with any system, it will help to spend a few minutes learning the conventions used to represent sounds in *PDPN.* The simplified symbols are explained below.

Pronunciation Key

For quick reference, a summarized key to the simplified pronunciation system appears at the bottom of every text page in *PDPN.* The key indicates with an example word the sound represented by each of the simplified symbols. A fuller form of the key also appears on the inside front and back covers of *PDPN* and is also given below.

Stress

In simplified respellings, heavily stressed syllables are indicated by full-size capital letters: **Daisy** | DĀ-zē |, **Decatur** | di-KĀT-uhr |, **Arness** |ahr-NES |. Entries with one syllable are shown as stressed, that is, in all uppercase symbols. Though by its very nature stress is relative, any syllable spoken without context, as in a dictionary citation form, must be given some degree of stress. Thus, an isolated utterance of the name *Smith* is closer in sound to the first (stressed) syllable of *smithy* than to the second (unstressed) syllable of the phrase *blacksmith shop.* Thus, to show the pronunciation of *smithy* as |SMITH-ē| but *Smith* as |smith| would be both phonetically inconsistent and possibly confusing; hence the entry **Smith** |SMITH|.

Secondary, or lighter, stress is shown in small capital letters: **Stonehenge** | STŌN-HENJ|, **Alamo** |AL-uh-MŌ|.

In accordance with international usage, no stress is shown for languages such as Korean and Japanese, which have relatively equal stress on each syllable. Though French dictionaries generally show no stress, pronunciations of French names in *PDPN* are shown with stress indicated in the simplified version. This is in accord with the general impression of French pronunciation on the native English speaker's ear. No stress is shown in the corresponding IPA transcription of French names.

Simplified Pronunciation Symbols

The following lists, arranged more or less "alphabetically," include all of the symbols used in the simplified system. The list of English vowels and consonants is followed by a list of some non-English sounds. It is helpful to think of these characters as just symbols and not as letters of the alphabet. While a single letter of the alphabet may represent several different sounds in ordinary English spelling (for example, *a* in *act, ape, all, above; g* in *go, gin, beige*), each simplified pronunciation symbol has just the single sound value indicated below.

Symbol	Example	as in
a A	FAD, ASK	f<u>a</u>d, <u>a</u>sk } Some speakers use |ah| in *ask*.
ā Ā	FĀD	f<u>a</u>de
ah AH	FAH-<u>th</u>uhr, AHSK	f<u>a</u>ther, <u>a</u>sk ⌐ Many U.S. speakers do not
		} rhyme *father* and *bother*;
	BAH-<u>th</u>uhr, KAHT	b<u>o</u>ther, c<u>o</u>t ⌐ see the IPA chart.
aw AW	KAWT, LAW	c<u>au</u>ght, l<u>aw</u> } Many U.S. speakers use |ah|
		in these words, rhyming *caught* with *cot*.
b B	BID	<u>b</u>id
ch CH	CHIP	<u>ch</u>ip
d D	DID	<u>d</u>id
e E	FED	f<u>e</u>d
ē Ē	BĒD	b<u>ea</u>d
f F	FIT	<u>f</u>it
g G	GET	<u>g</u>et
h H	HED	<u>h</u>ead
hw HW	HWET, HWICH	<u>wh</u>et, <u>wh</u>ich } Many U.S. and British
		speakers pronounce these the same as *wet* and *witch*.
i I	BID	b<u>i</u>d
ī Ī	BĪ, RĪD, LĪ	b<u>uy</u>, r<u>i</u>de, l<u>ie</u>
j J	JET	<u>j</u>et
k K	KIK, KUK	<u>k</u>i<u>ck</u>, <u>c</u>oo<u>k</u>
l L	LEG, MID-l	<u>l</u>eg, midd<u>le</u>
m M	MEN	<u>m</u>en
n N	NET, KIT-n	<u>n</u>et, kitt<u>en</u>
ng NG	RING, RINGK	ri<u>ng</u>, ri<u>n</u>k
ō Ō	KŌT	c<u>oa</u>t
oi OI	BOI, KOIN	b<u>oy</u>, c<u>oi</u>n
o͞o O͞O	MO͞OD	m<u>oo</u>d
ow OW	OWT, NOW	<u>ou</u>t, n<u>ow</u>
p P	PIN, LIP	<u>p</u>in, li<u>p</u>
r R	RED, KAHRD	<u>r</u>ed, ca<u>r</u>d
s S	SIT	<u>s</u>it
t T	TŌ, SIT-ing	<u>t</u>oe, si<u>tt</u>ing
th TH	THIN	<u>th</u>in
<u>th</u> <u>TH</u>	THIS	<u>th</u>is
u U	GUD, PUT, PUR	g<u>oo</u>d, p<u>u</u>t, p<u>oo</u>r
uh UH	buh-NAN-uh, BUHD	b<u>a</u>nan<u>a</u>, b<u>u</u>d
uhr UHR	BET-uhr, BUHRD	bett<u>er</u>, b<u>ir</u>d
v V	VET	<u>v</u>et
w W	WET, WICH	<u>w</u>et, <u>w</u>itch
y Y	YES	<u>y</u>es
z Z	ZIP	<u>z</u>ip
zh ZH	MEZH-uhr	mea<u>s</u>ure

Simplified Vowel Symbols

Most of the traditional "short" vowel sounds are represented by single letters. (There is no plain "o" symbol, as explained in the section on |ah| below.)

|a| as in *bat*.
|e| as in *bed*.
|i| as in *bid*.
|u| as in *good, put, full*.

The traditional "long" vowels are represented by single characters with macrons or by double characters.

|ā| as in *bake*.
|ē| as in *bead*.
|ī| as in *bide, lie*.
|ō| as in *boat*.
|ōō| as in *food*. (The macron is used here to avoid confusion with the *oo* in *look*.)

A few additional vowel sounds are represented by double characters:

|ah| as in *father* and *bother*. The combination |ah| is used, rather than |o| because: (1) It avoids the misleading use of different symbols for the same sound. For example, for most Americans *Mach* rhymes with *mock*; hence |MAHK| for both, not |MAHK| for one and |MOK| for the other, as in some dictionaries. (2) It conforms to actual phonetic fact—for most U.S. speakers this is an unrounded vowel, that is, it is pronounced without a rounding of the lips associated with the letter "o". (3) It is more consistent with the spelling and pronunciation of a high percentage of names in *PDPN*, especially non-English names.

Most U.S. speakers rhyme the stressed vowels of *father* and *bother*. For those who do not rhyme these vowels, the distinction is shown in the IPA transcriptions. For example, the simplified respellings for these words would be |FAHTH-uhr| and |BAHTH-uhr|, whereas the IPA transcriptions would be /'fɑ·ðəʳ/ (= /'faðəʳ, 'fɑːðəʳ/) versus /'bɑðəʳ/, thus allowing for both rhyming and non-rhyming pronunciations. In any case, users of this book are simply recommended to use the sound suggested by the simplified respelling that is natural to their own speech and no confusion should occur.

|aw| as in *law* and *bought*. Many speakers in the U.S. do not rhyme *cot* and *caught*; we represent their differing pronunciations as |KAHT| and |KAWT|. But a great number of U.S. speakers (in eastern New England, western Pennsylvania, and increasingly elsewhere, particularly in the midwest, west, and southwest) do not distinguish between |ah| and |aw|. That is, they regularly rhyme such pairs as *cot—caught, collar—caller, hock—hawk, wok—walk*, and *stocking—stalking*. Such speakers will quite naturally interpret both |ah| and |aw| as the single sound they normally use.

|uh, UH| as in *banana* and *bud*. This symbol is used to represent the most frequent vowel sound in English, sometimes called the "neutral vowel." It is the vowel of the unstressed syllables in such words as <u>A</u>meri<u>ca</u>, b<u>a</u>nan<u>a</u>, cab<u>i</u>net, nati<u>o</u>n, comp<u>u</u>t<u>e</u>d, and <u>be</u>liev<u>a</u>ble. In such unstressed syllables in the actual speech of many Americans this sound may vary from the vowel |uh| usually heard at the end of *sofa* to an unstressed version of the |i| sound in *sit*, as often heard in the last syllable of *habit*.

In some dictionaries the symbol /ə/, called "schwa," pronounced |SHWAH|, is used to represent this sound.

In stressed syllables |UH| represents the sound of the vowel of *bud* and *glove*. In most U.S. speech the quality of this stressed vowel is much the same as it is in unstressed positions, thus the simplified system uses the same symbol to represent this vowel in both situations.

|uhr, UHR| represents a vowel-consonant combination that has a vowel similar to |uh| and |UH|, but the presence of |r| changes the vowel sound to that heard in *sister, bird, work,* and *hurry.*

Familiar combinations are also used to show diphthongs:

|oi| as in *boy.*
|ow| as in *now.*

Simplified Consonant Symbols

The following characters represent the familiar and usual English sounds of the corresponding letter of the alphabet: |b, d, f, h, m, n, p, s, t, v, z|.

The remaining consonant symbols may be described as follows:

|ch| as in *chip.* (This is actually a combination of two sounds: |t| + |sh|.)

|g| as in *get, game* (never as in *gem*). See |j|.

|hw| as in *whet, which* when pronounced differently than *wet, witch.* Many U.S. and British speakers do not have |hw| in their speech; such speakers pronounce both *wet* and *whet* as |WET|.

|j| as in *jet, gem.* (This is actually a combination of two sounds: |d| + |zh|.)

|l| as in *leg, miller,* and *middle.*

In Polish there are two distinct |l| sounds. The simplified system represents both of these as |l|. Polish names spelled with an ordinary *l* are pronounced with the tongue-tip |l| heard in English *lily;* Polish names spelled with the slant-crossed *ł* (called barred l) are pronounced with an |l| produced farther back on the tongue, as in some pronunciations of English *pool.* The latter sound may be approximated in Polish names by using a |w|, as in **Czesław** |CHES-lahf| or |CHES-wahf|, and **Wałesa** |vah-LEⁿ-suh| or |vah-WEⁿ-suh|. This Polish back *ł* is represented as /ł/ in IPA.

|ng| as in *ring, rink.* This is actually a single sound, not two; compare *singer* |SING-uhr| and *finger* |FING-guhr|.

|r| as in *red, card.* The pronunciation of speakers who do not pronounce |r| before another consonant or a pause is not represented in the simplified respellings, though it is indicated in the IPA transcriptions. See /r/ in the IPA section below. In French and Portuguese, |r| is frequently made with the uvula, at the back of the mouth. In many other languages it is trilled or is pronounced by tapping the tip of the tongue just once behind the teeth, as it is in Spanish and in many British and Scots dialects. To indicate the tapped |r|, as opposed to the usual U.S. retroflex |r|, some American cartoonists spell the British pronunciation of *very* as "veddy." This is similar to the voiced tap of the tongue heard in both *ladder* and *latter* in most U.S. dialects.

|sh| as in *show*. This is actually a single sound, not two.

|th| as in *thin*. This is actually a single sound, not two. It is an "unvoiced" *th*, that is, the *th* sound is made without vibration of the vocal cords.

|t͟h| as in *this*. This is actually a single sound, not two. It is a "voiced" *th*, that is, the *th* sound is made with vibration of the vocal cords. Note the use of the underline to indicate voicing, as distinct from unvoiced |th| without the underline.

|w| as in *wet*. When shown without a vowel symbol preceding it in the same syllable, this symbol represents consonantal *w*. There is no consonantal |w| in the simplified symbols |aw| and |ow|.

|y| as in *yes*. Always represents the consonant *y*, never a vowel sound as in the *y* at the end of *city*.

|zh| as in *measure*. This is actually a single sound, not two.

Some Non-English Vowels and Consonants

Special symbols or combinations of symbols, some with macrons or underlining, are used to indicate several sounds that are present in foreign names, though not commonly used in English.

Simplified	Examples	
ḡ Ḡ	ah-ME-ḡō	Span. **amiḡo**; *Anglicized alternative:* |g|.
hl HL	hlah-NEHL-ē	Welsh **Llanelli**; *Anglicized alternative:* |l| *or* |thl|.
k͟h K͟H	BAHK͟H, IK͟H, LAHK͟H	Ger. **Bach**, **ich**, Scottish **loch**.
n	BAWⁿ	*after a nasalized vowel, as in* Fr. **bon**; *Anglicized alternative:* |n|.
ue UE	rue, FUE-luhn	Fr. **rue**, Ger. **fühlen**.
	FUEL-uhn	Ger. **füllen**.
uh(r) UH(R)	BUH(R)F, HUH(R)L-uh	*Anglicization of* Fr. **boeuf**, Ger. **Hölle**.
	FUH(R), HUH(R)-luh	*Anglicization of* Fr. **feu**, Ger. **Höhle**.
v̠ V̠	ahv̠-LAHR	Span. **hablar**; *Anglicized alternative:* |b| *or* |v|.

Non-English Sounds

|ḡ| as in Spanish *amigo*. This consonant is pronounced much like |g|, except that the flow of air is never completely stopped as it is with English |g|. It is similar to |kh| but with vibration of the vocal cords. In most English contexts |g| is an acceptable alternative.

|hl| as in Welsh *Llanelli*. This is a voiceless *l* produced by placing the tongue in the position for |l| and simply blowing air past the side of the tongue; the |l| of English *clean* is very similar. Many English speakers substitute either a regular English |l| or the combination |thl|; thus *Llanelli* |hlah-NEHL-ē| could be anglicized as |thlah-NETH-lē| or |la-NEL-ē|

|kh| as in Ger. *Bach, ich,* Scots *loch.* In German there are two distinct phonemes (sounds that differentiate words) in *Bach* and *ich,* but the distinction is not usually maintained in English. In *PDPN* the difference is indicated only in the IPA transcriptions. These consonants are pronounced much like the |k| in *book* and *beak,* except that the flow of air is never completely stopped as it is with |k|. In most English contexts |k| is an acceptable alternative; when spelled *H* or *Ch* at the beginning of a word, as in *Hanukkah* or *Chanukah,* |h| is an acceptable alternative.

|ⁿ| as in French *bon* or *Mont Blanc.* The raised *n* does not itself stand for a sound; rather it indicates that the preceding vowel (or occasionally diphthong) is nasalized—that is, pronounced with the nasal passages open.

|ue, UE| The vowel shown as /yː/ in IPA, represented by the *ue* of French *rue* and the *üh* of German *fühlen,* is shown as |ue, UE| in the simplified system. It can be approximated in English by pronouncing the *ee* of *feel* while keeping the lips fully rounded as in the vowel sound of *fool.*

The vowel shown as /y/ in IPA, represented by the *ü* of German *füllen,* is also shown as |ue, UE| in the simplified system. It can be approximated by pronouncing the *i* of *fill* while keeping the lips somewhat rounded as in the vowel sound of *full.*

Some common anglicizations of these sounds are |ē|, |i|, |u|, |yōō|, and |yu|.

|uh(r), UH(R)| The vowel shown as /œ/ in IPA, as in French *boeuf,* German *Hölle,* is similar to the vowel of English *bird,* without the |r| sound. In the simplified respellings it is anglicized to |uh(r), UH(R)|. It can be more closely approximated by pronouncing the *e* of *bed* with the lips somewhat rounded as in *bought.*

The vowel shown as /œː/ in IPA, as in French *feu,* German *Höhle,* is similar to the sound above and is similarly anglicized. It can be approximated by pronouncing the *ay* of *hay* while keeping the lips fully rounded as in the vowel sound of *hoe.*

|v̲| as in Spanish *hablar* is produced with the two lips, rather than with the upper teeth and lower lip as in English |v|. In most English contexts either a |b| or a |v| is an acceptable alternative.

Pronunciations in the
International Phonetic Alphabet (IPA)

In 1888 the International Phonetic Association (IPA) was formed and its members devised a phonetic alphabet for representing the pronunciation of any language. The basic principles for this alphabet are that each symbol stands for only one sound, each sound is represented by only one symbol, and the symbols are based on the shapes of characters in the Roman alphabet (insofar as is possible). The transcriptions appearing in the third column in the text of *PDPN* employ a version of the IPA alphabet that is familiar to many linguists. In this introduction, IPA transcriptions are enclosed in slant lines / . . . /; square brackets [. . .] are occasionally used to discuss a degree of phonetic or dialectal variation implied by the IPA symbols as they are used in *PDPN*.

While the basic pronunciation information provided by both the simplified and IPA systems is compatible, the IPA transcriptions show more phonetic detail and dialectal variation than is possible in the simplified versions. These differences are outlined below, as are the particular conventions of IPA transcriptions used in *PDPN*.

The IPA transcriptions in *PDPN* are *broadly phonemic;* that is, each symbol represents a sound that is a phoneme (a meaningfully significant unit of sound) in some or all dialects of English. By the very nature of a wide-ranging dictionary of names, it is also necessary to include a few symbols to represent sounds not commonly found as phonemes in English words or names but that are phonemes in other languages. These have been kept to a minimum, and anglicized equivalents are either shown explicitly in both IPA and simplified columns, or the IPA symbols may be rendered as anglicizations in the simplified respelling column.

Regional or Dialectal Variation

In the IPA transcriptions in *PDPN*, variation in the regional or dialectal use or distribution of phonemes is explicitly shown, for there is no single variety of speech in the U.S. that is standard for the whole country. For example, **Quincy** is pronounced /ˈkwin(t)siˑ/ in some parts of the U.S. and /ˈkwinziˑ/ in others; **Gary** is pronounced /ˈgæriˑ/ by some speakers and /ˈgeriˑ/ by others. In such cases, variant pronunciations are shown in *PDPN*. However, regional or dialectal differences in the actual *sound* of each phoneme usually remain implicit. A native speaker of English using *PDPN* will interpret each symbol in phonetic accord with his or her natural speech, depending on the context. For example, the pronunciation of the phoneme /i/ in *bid* varies regionally in American English. Millions of speakers, especially in the northern half of the U.S., pronounce *bid* as a simple monophthong: /ˈbid/. But millions of other speakers, especially in the southeastern states, pronounce *bid* as a single syllable with a diphthongal glide: [ˈbiəd]. The IPA transcription for *bid* in *PDPN* would be /ˈbid/, which users will naturally and automatically interpret appropriately for their own dialects. Non-native speakers of English, of course, will approximate the pronunciation of whatever variety of English they have learned or are learning to use.

Such phonetic differences are part of what gives our language the rich variety and range of character that it enjoys. *Any* transcription can only be a partial representation of the living sounds of the language. Even though *PDPN* does not explicitly represent variation at this level of narrow phonetic detail, users still will be able to reproduce pronunciations that are both widely acceptable and consistent with their own natural speech.

Stress in IPA Transcriptions

In IPA, primary stress is indicated by a raised mark and secondary stress by a lowered one: **Daisy** /'deːziˑ/, **Decatur** /diˈkeːʈəʳ/, **Alamo** /'æləˌmoː/, **Stonehenge** /'stoːnˌhendʒ/. Single syllable entries are generally transcribed with primary stress on the understanding that, though stress is relative, the utterance of an isolated form without the context of running speech requires a degree of stress comparable to that of a relatively stressed syllable in context, as in *Smith* /'smiθ/ and *smithy* /'smiθiˑ/. In accord with international practice, no stress is shown in those languages, such as French, Japanese, and Korean, which have relatively level stress or stress that is variable according to context in a sentence.

Vowels in IPA Transcriptions

The following discussion of vowels will outline briefly the phonetic production of vowel sounds and will note the significance of any relevant IPA diacritic marks used with them.

IPA	Example	as in
æ	'fæd, 'æsk	f<u>a</u>d, <u>a</u>sk
ɑ	'bɑðəʳ, 'kɑt, 'fɑðəʳ	b<u>o</u>ther, c<u>o</u>t, f<u>a</u>ther
ɑː	'fɑːðəʳ, 'ɑːsk	f<u>a</u>ther, <u>a</u>sk
ɑi	'bɑi, 'rɑid	b<u>uy</u>, r<u>i</u>de
ɑu	'bɑu, 'nɑu	b<u>ough</u>, n<u>ow</u>
e	'fed	f<u>e</u>d
eː	'feːd	f<u>a</u>de
i	'bid	b<u>i</u>d
iː	'biːd	b<u>ea</u>d
oː	'koːt	c<u>oa</u>t
ɔː	'kɔːt, 'lɔː	c<u>augh</u>t, l<u>aw</u>
ɔi	'bɔi, 'kɔin	b<u>oy</u>, c<u>oi</u>n
u	'gud, 'put, puʳ	g<u>oo</u>d, p<u>u</u>t, p<u>oor</u>
uː	'muːd, 'mjuːzik	m<u>oo</u>d, m<u>u</u>sic
ə	bə'nænə, 'bəd	b<u>a</u>nan<u>a</u>, b<u>u</u>d
əʳ	'bəʳd, 'bəʈəʳ	b<u>ir</u>d, butt<u>er</u>

IPA Vowel Symbols

A vowel is produced when sound generated by the vocal cords passes through the mouth without significant obstruction. The sound of a particular vowel is determined by a number of factors, among the more important of which are the shape of the mouth cavity and the position of the tongue and lips. The height of the tongue within the central mouth area plays a major role in the differing pronunciation of vowels. Thus, the vowels are usually classified as low, mid, or high, and as front, central, or back, according to the position of the highest part of the tongue when the vowel is sounded.

For example, in the high front vowel of *beat* the tongue is raised close to the upper front of the mouth cavity. For the low front vowel of *bat* the mouth is open wider and the tongue lowered; for *bought* the tongue is low and moved farther toward the back of the mouth. In English the back vowels are generally accompanied by some degree of lip-rounding. Thus, a doctor asks a patient to say "Ah" in order to examine the patient's throat, for in pronouncing that low central vowel the mouth is open wide, the tongue is lowered, and the lips are unrounded.

This can be elucidated by the use of a diagram. **Diagram 1** represents a schematic vertical cross-section of the central mouth cavity. The front of the mouth is toward the left of the diagram; the back is toward the right. (For ease of reference, the diagram is divided accordingly and the resulting boxes are numbered from 1 to 9.)

For the present discussion, the vowels of American English are classified into two broad categories: simple vowels, as in *bit, bet, bat, pot, put,* and *but,* and augmented

Diagram 1: The Vowel Chart

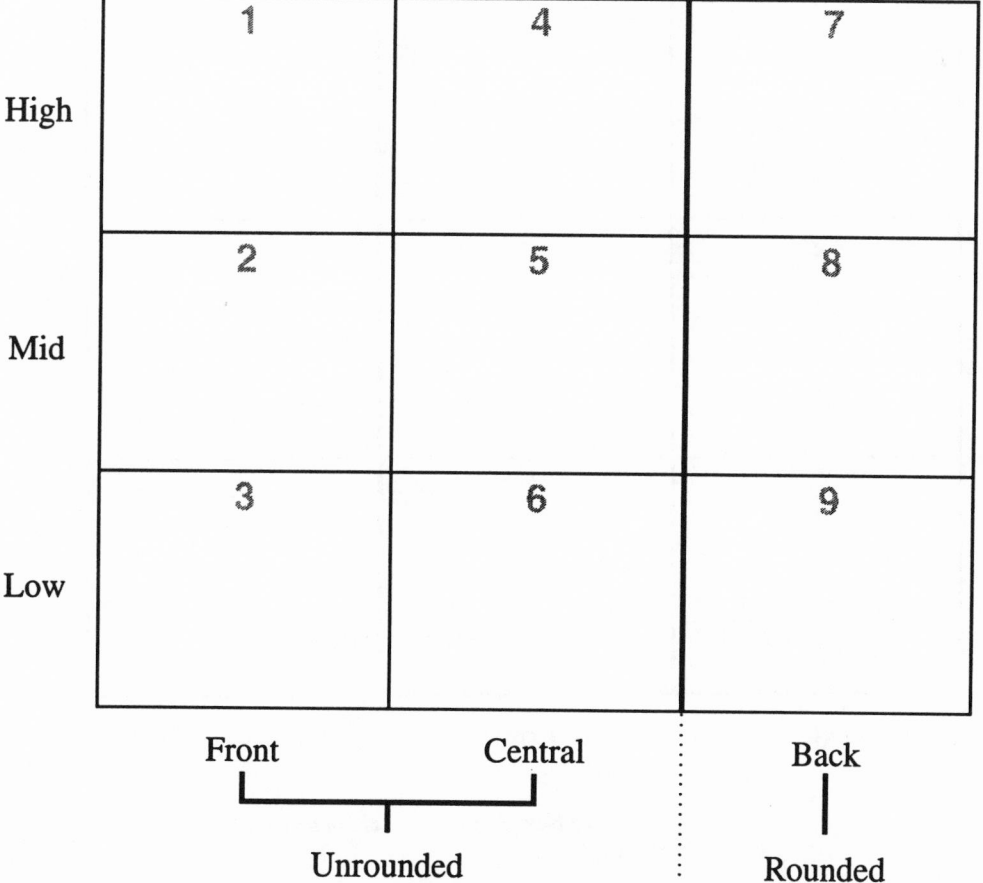

vowels, as in *beat, bait, bought, boat, boot,* and *bird.* These two categories are discussed below.

Simple Vowels

The simple vowels, traditionally called "short vowels," are sometimes called *lax vowels* because the muscle of the tongue is relatively relaxed when they are spoken. They are also called *checked vowels* because, with the exception of /ə/, they do not usually occur at the end of a word or syllable. That is, checked vowels are almost always followed by a consonant, as in *bit, bet, bat, hot,* and *put.* **Diagram 2** shows the relative positions of the simple vowels.

1. /i/ as in *bit.*

2. /e/ as in *bet.* The symbol /ẽ/ with the tilde indicating nasalization is used to represent the nasalized vowel heard in French *vin* /'vẽ/; to American ears this vowel might sound closer to the vowel of *bat,* as in ['vǣ], but since in *PDPN* this vowel occurs most frequently in French names, the symbol /ẽ/ is used to accord with French practice.

Diagram 2: The Simple Vowels

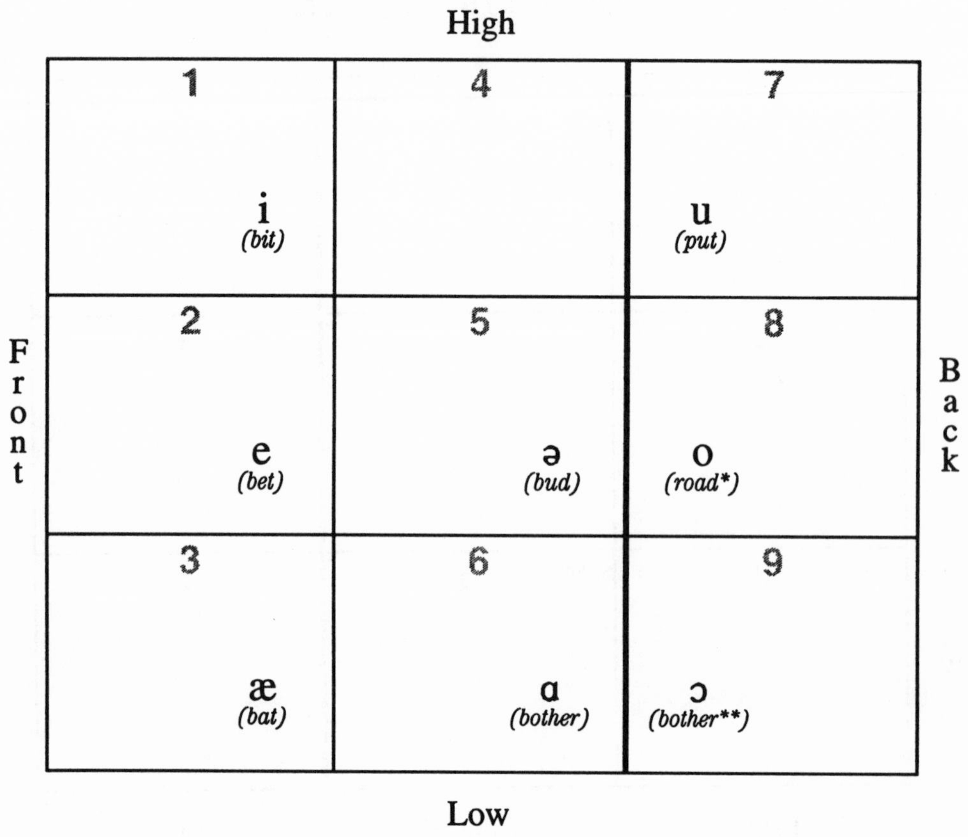

High

1	4	7
i *(bit)*		u *(put)*
2	**5**	**8**
e *(bet)*	ə *(bud)*	o *(road*)*
3	**6**	**9**
æ *(bat)*	ɑ *(bother)*	ɔ *(bother**)*

F r o n t ←→ B a c k

Low

* eastern New England (in certain names)
** British

3. /æ/ as in *bat.*

4. The high central vowel, represented in IPA by [ɨ], is not phonemic in English; that is, it does not contrast with other vowel sounds to make different English words. Nor is it necessary to show a distinction in *PDPN* for languages in which [ɨ] may be phonemic, for the distinction would be lost on English speakers, who regularly and quite adequately anglicize and interpret it as /i/ or /ə/. Therefore, no high central vowel symbol is used in *PDPN.*

5. /ə/ as in *but* and the second vowel of *sofa.* Some transcribers use /ʌ/ to represent the mid-central stressed vowel and reserve /ə/ for the so-called "neutral" vowel in unstressed positions. However, in most American speech the quality of the mid-central vowel does not vary significantly as a result of stress alone and the single symbol /ə/ is sufficient. Thus, in *PDPN* /ə/ is used to represent the mid-central vowel in both stressed and unstressed syllables. Because of its frequency in unstressed syllables, the vowel /ə/ is the most common vowel in American English. The actual phonetic realization of unstressed /ə/ varies considerably depending both on dialect and on the sounds it occurs in conjunction with. For example, the final vowel of *pages* may range from [ə] to [i], though a transcription in *PDPN* would show only /ˈpeɪdʒəz/.

6. /ɑ/ as in *hot, cod.* Those speakers, particularly in eastern New England and southern Britain, who have a low, back, somewhat rounded vowel [ɔ] for these words will automatically interpret the symbol /ɑ/ as [ɔ] in accordance with their own speech; see /ɔ/ below. The symbol /ɑ/ also represents the sound of *â* in French *château* and of *a* in Spanish *hablar.*

   The symbol /ɑ̃/ with the tilde indicating nasalization is used to represent the nasalized vowel heard in French *blanc* /blɑ̃/.

7. /u/ as in *put, good.*

8. /o/ is phonemic American English only in the older speech of New England, where it distinguishes *road* /ˈrod/ from *rode* /ˈroːd/. Even in New England this distinction is rapidly disappearing, and it is reflected in *PDPN* transcriptions only occasionally (as at the entry for **Holyoke**) in names where it is fairly common locally, but even there only in free variation with /oː/.

9. /ɔ/ as in eastern New England or British *pot, cod, bother.* This rounded low back vowel occurs as a phoneme in some English dialects, resulting in distinct vowels in *cart* /ˈkɑːt/ and *cot* /ˈkɔt/. The great majority of U.S. speakers, however, have only one vowel, /ɑ/, in these words *cart* /ˈkɑrt/ and *cot* /ˈkɑt/; hence /ɔ/ is not used in *PDPN.* Speakers with the rounded [ɔ] in their speech will interpret /ɑ/ as [ɔ] where appropriate for their dialect—usually where it is spelled with an *o.* However, the phonemic vowel contrast in such pairs as *cart—cot, heart—hot,* and *father—bother* for such speakers is, indeed, represented in *PDPN* as explained below in the discussions of /ɑː/ and /r/. Some other languages do contrast /ɔ/ and /ɔː/ phonemically, but since most U.S. speakers do not have such a contrast /ɔː/ is used throughout *PDPN;* see /ɔː/ below.

   The symbol /ɔ̃/ with the tilde indicating nasalization is used to represent the nasalized vowel heard in French *bon* /bɔ̃/.

Augmented Vowels

The augmented vowels, many of which are traditionally called "long vowels," may be thought of as similar to the corresponding simple vowels with the addition of one or more features. This augmentation is indicated by the use of a special colon /ː/ in conjunction with a simple vowel symbol. In general, the augmented vowels are produced with the tongue more tense than for the simple vowels. Hence the augmented vowels are often referred to as *tense vowels*. They may also be referred to as *free vowels,* because they occur at the end of words or syllables, as in *play, see,* and *blue.* Another common feature in English is some degree of diphthongization or movement of the tongue from one position to another. Also, the augmented front vowels are usually produced farther forward in the mouth than the corresponding simple vowels. The back vowels are usually pronounced farther back, with the addition of greater lip-rounding.

NOTE: In *PDPN* the half-colon /ˑ/ is used to indicate that in some speech a simple vowel is heard and in other speech the corresponding augmented vowel is heard. It might be thought of as the shorthand equivalent of an IPA colon in parenthesis. Thus, transcriptions such as /ˈsɪţiˑ/ for *city* (=/ˈsɪţi(ː)/) indicate that some speakers say /ˈsɪţiː/ and others say /ˈsɪţi/.

Diagram 3 adds the augmented vowels to the schematic outline of simple vowels. This shows the relative positions of the augmented vowels both to each other and to the simple vowels.

The augmented vowels in English are often diphthongal; that is, the vowel begins with the mouth and tongue in one position and ends after a change in their position. When it occurs, this movement begins at or near the position for the corresponding simple vowel and moves upward and toward the front or back as indicated in **Diagram 3.** For instance the vowel of *late* /ˈleːt/ is actually [ei] in most (but not all) U.S. speech, beginning at the position of /e/ and moving toward /i/ or even /iː/. This diphthongization is shown in square brackets in the explanations below. In many other languages the augmented vowels are true monophthongs, articulated at a higher and/or more tense position than the corresponding simple vowel.

1. /iː/ as in *beat.*

2. /eː/ as in *bait.* Often pronounced in English as [ei], in other languages as monophthongal [eː].

3. /æː/ as in *cab* or *can* ("to preserve") in dialects that distinguish the two senses of *can* in "Let's can [ˈkæːn] what we can [ˈkæn]." This vowel is often realized as [æə] or [æi]. /æː/ is not used in *PDPN* because its phonemic status is uncertain and limited in its geographic distribution and even there restricted to a very few items (and perhaps then only in careful speech), such as *can* "to preserve" vs. *can* "to be able" and *halve* vs. *have.* In most U.S. speech [æː] occurs as a positional variant of /æ/ in certain phonetic contexts—most notably before nasals, as in *man* and *ham.*

4. The high central augmented vowel, represented in IPA by /ɨː/, is not phonemic in English and is, therefore, not used in *PDPN*; see the note on the simple vowel 4 /ɨ/ above.

5. /ɜː/ as in *bird.* The presence of *r* after a vowel and before a consonant or pause has the effect of constricting the tongue (drawing it back or lowering it and bending back the tongue tip), thus affecting the quality of the preceding vowel. In dialects in which preconsonantal or prepausal *r* is not pronounced as /r/, the mid-central vowel

Diagram 3: The Augmented & Simple Vowels

High

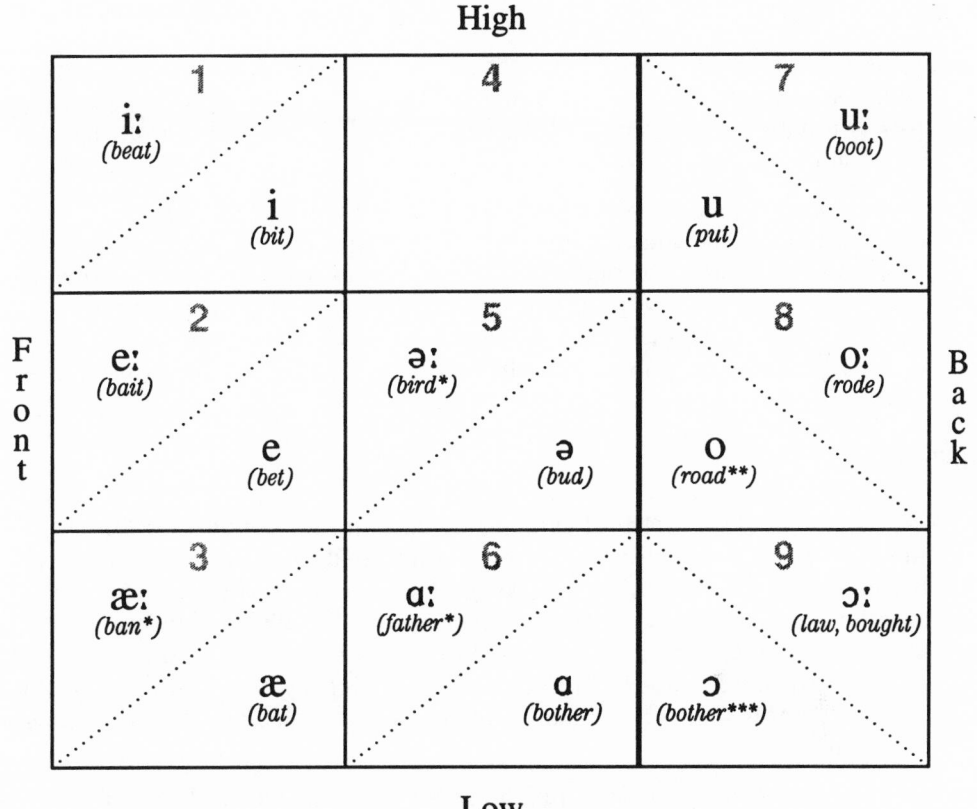

Low

*   in some dialects
**   eastern New England (in certain names)
***   British

of *bird* /ˈbɜːd/ is distinct from the vowel of *bud* /ˈbəd/; in comparison with the latter, the vowel of *bird* /ˈbɜːd/ is raised and/or lengthened in duration, as well as affected by the shift in the position and tenseness of the tongue. The pronunciation of those who do pronounce this *r* may be represented simply as /ˈbərd/. In *PDPN* a transcription such as /ˈbərd/ for *Byrd* indicates that many speakers pronounce /ˈbərd/, and many others pronounce /ˈbɜːd/; see /ʳ/ below.

In some New York City speech and in parts of the southeastern U.S., /ɜː/ may be diphthongized in the direction of /i/, resulting in [əi]. Those who do not use this diphthongized vowel often comment on it or satirize it as *boid* or *Boyd* for *bird*, though only for a very small and diminishing number of New Yorkers is *bird* actually realized as /ˈbɔid/; other New Yorkers will differentiate *Boyd* /ˈbɔid/ and *bird* [ˈbəid] = /ˈbɜːd/. In the southeastern U.S. *Boyd* and *bird* are always distinct.

6. /ɑː/ as in *father* in the speech of those who do not rhyme it with *bother* and in *ask* in the speech of those who use a vowel distinct from that in *black*. This is also the vowel of French *patte.* The vowel /ɑː/ is also to be understood as the alternative to

/ɑr/ for those speakers who do not pronounce preconsonantal or prepausal *r.* Thus /ˈpɑʳk/ for *park* indicates that some speakers say /ˈpɑrk/ and others say /ˈpɑːk/; see /ʳ/ below.

7. /uː/ as in *boot.*

8. /oː/ as in *slow, coat.* Usually pronounced as diphthongal [ou] in U.S. speech. In educated southern British speech /oː/ is often realized as [əu]. In other languages /oː/ is usually monophthongal [oː], i.e., a rounded mid back vowel that does not move in the direction of /u/.

9. /ɔː/ as in *bought, caught, caller* in the speech of those who do not rhyme these with *cot* and *collar.* The growing number of U.S. speakers in eastern New England, western Pennsylvania, the midwest, west, and southwest who *do* rhyme such pairs as *cot—caught* and *collar—caller* will interpret /ɔː/ as their own appropriate variety of /ɑ/. In some dialects, such as in the southeastern U.S., /ɔː/ is often diphthongal [ɔu]; in some northeastern dialects it is often strongly rounded and sometimes diphthongized as [ɔːə].

Diphthongs

1. /ɑi/ as in *sigh, night, buy.* This diphthong begins in the area of box 6 in **Diagram 4** and moves toward or into that of box 1. In some southeastern U.S. speech, especially before voiced consonants such as /d/ or /z/ in contrast to unvoiced /t/ or /s/, the diphthongal movement is minimal or even absent, though in compensation the onset vowel [ɑ] is either lengthened or raised to /ɑː/ or both lengthened and raised. Thus, in such speech *tide* /ˈtɑid/ (= [ˈtɑˑd,ˈtɑːd]) does not rhyme with either *Tod* /ˈtɑd/ or *Tad* /ˈtæd/. This southern version of /ɑi/ is often parodied or satirized by those who do not use it.

2. /ɑu/ as in *now, house, out.* This diphthong begins in the area of box 6 in **Diagram 4** and moves toward or into that of box 7. In some dialects, such as parts of Canada and the upper midwestern U.S., and parts of Virginia, when it occurs before voiceless consonants such as /s/ or /t/ (e.g. in *house* and *out*), this diphthong is realized as [əu], which others may interpret as /oː/. The symbol /ɑũ/ with the tilde indicating nasalization is used to represent the nasalized diphthong in Portuguese *são* /ˈsɑũ/.

3. /ɔi/ as in *boy, coin.* This diphthong begins in the area of box 9 in **Diagram 4** and moves toward or into that of box 1. In dialects or utterances where the diphthongal movement does not actually reach the position of /i/ in box 1, this diphthong may be realized as [ɔə] or [ɔːə].

Diagram 4: The Diphthongs

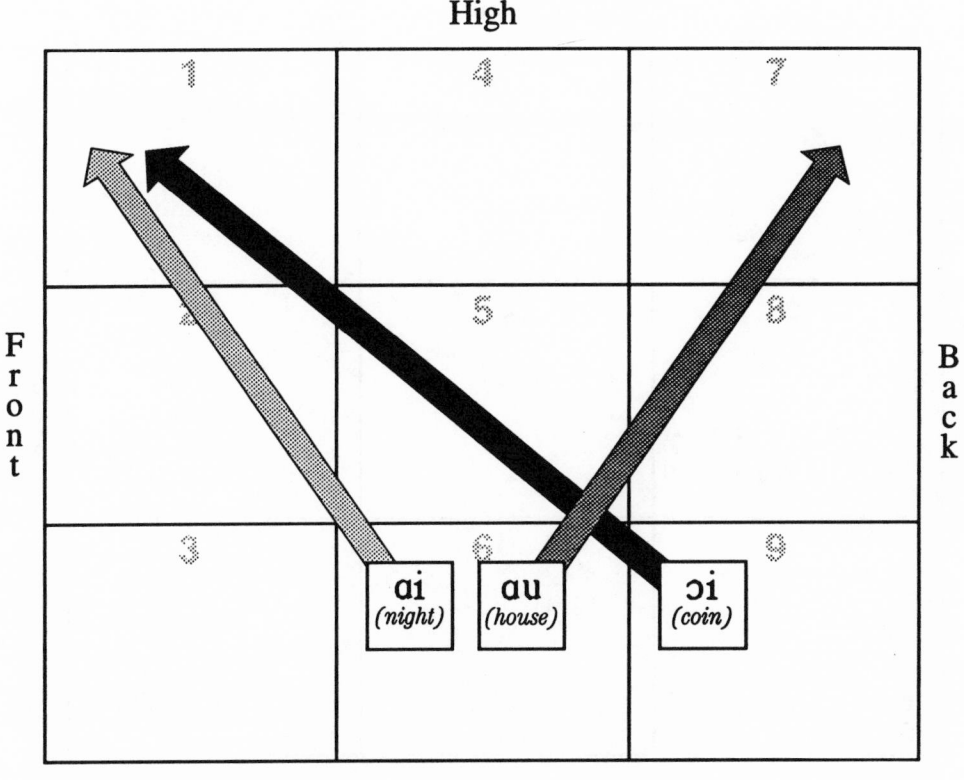

Four Non-English Vowels

As shown in **Diagram 5** below, the non-English vowels used in *PDPN* are front rounded vowels, i.e., vowels pronounced in approximately the same position as the corresponding unrounded English vowels, but accompanied by lip rounding. The simple front rounded vowels are accompanied by slight lip rounding; the augmented front rounded vowels are accompanied by rather more, tense lip rounding.

1. /yː/ as in German *fühlen,* French *rue.* A high, tense front vowel, fully rounded.

2. /y/ as in German *füllen.* A high, lax front vowel, somewhat rounded.

3. /œː/ as in German *Höhle,* French *feu.* A mid, tense front vowel, fully rounded.

4. /œ/ as in German *Hölle,* French *boeuf.* A mid, lax front vowel, somewhat rounded. The symbol /œ̃/ with the tilde indicating nasalization is used to represent the nasalized vowel in French *un* / œ̃/.

Diagram 5: Non-English Front Rounded Vowels

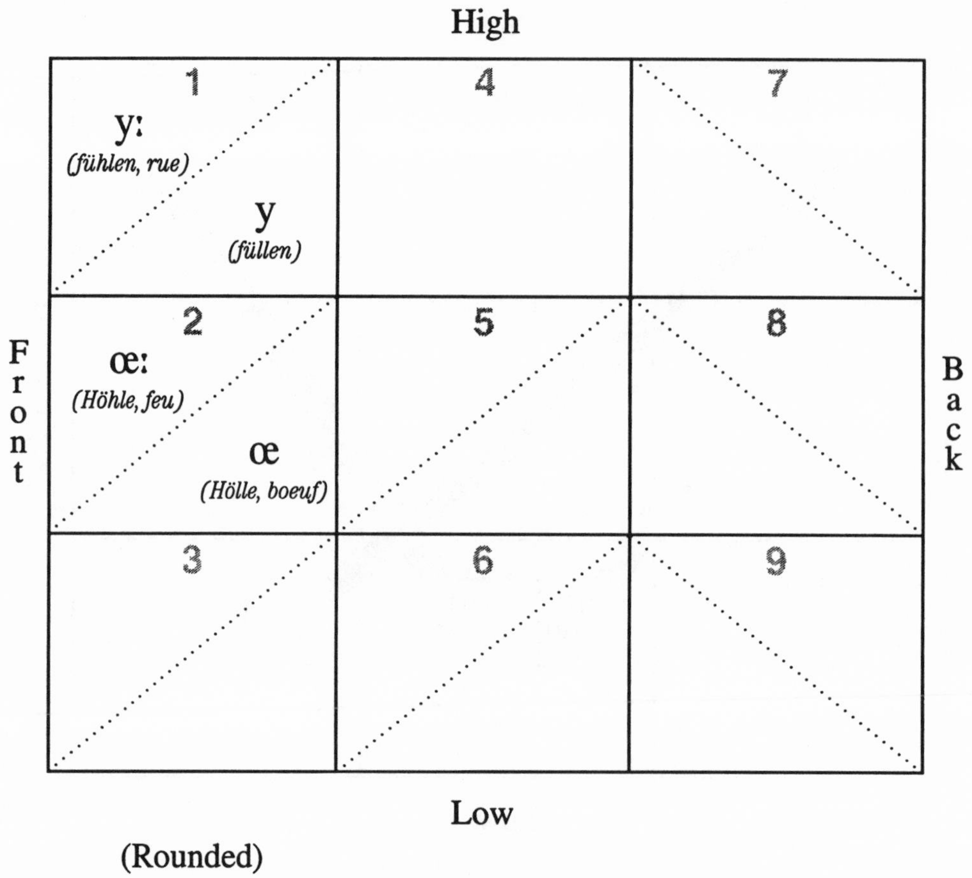

High

1 **y:** *(fühlen, rue)* **y** *(füllen)*	4	7
2 **œ:** *(Höhle, feu)* **œ** *(Hölle, boeuf)*	5	8
3	6	9

F r o n t   B a c k

Low

(Rounded)

German: fühlen, füllen, Höhle, Hölle
French: rue, feu, boeuf

Consonants in IPA Transcription

In contrast to vowels, a consonant is produced when the flow of air is partly or fully obstructed at some point in the throat or mouth or by the tongue or lips. The particular nature of a consonant is determined by the place in which the flow of air is obstructed and by the presence or absence of voicing from the vocal cords.

Following is a table of the IPA consonant symbols used in *PDPN*. The table is followed by a few notes on sounds which deserve some commentary in their English contexts and on sounds that are not English consonant phonemes. Consonants not discussed in the notes should be easily understood from the examples given in the table itself.

IPA Consonant Symbols

IPA	Example	as in
b	'bid	**b**i**d**
β	aβ'lɑr	Spanish ha**bl**ar
ç	'iç	German i**ch**
d	'did	**d**i**d**
dʒ	'dʒet	**j**et
ð	'ðis	**th**is
f	'fit	**f**i**t**
g	'get	**g**et
ɣ	ɑ'miːɣoː	Spanish ami**g**o
h	'hed	**h**ead
hw	'hwet	**wh**et
j	'jes	**y**es
k	'keːk	**c**a**k**e
l	'leg	**l**eg
l̦	'midl̦	mid**dle**
ɫ	'tʃesɫɑːf	Polish Czes**ł**aw
l̥	l̥ɑ'nel̥iˑ	Welsh **Ll**ane**ll**i
m	'men	**m**e**n**
m̩	'oːpm̩	some pronunciations of o**pen**
n	'net	**n**e**t**
n̩	'kitn̩	kit**ten**
ŋ	'riŋ, 'riŋk	ri**ng**, ri**nk**
ɲ	'diːɲ	French di**gne**
p	'pin	**p**in
r	'red, 'meriˑ	**r**ed, me**rr**y
ʳ (raised r)	'kɑʳd, = 'kɑrd, 'kɑːd	ca**r**d
ɹ	'ɹɑnðə	Welsh **Rh**ondda
s	'sit	**s**i**t**
ʃ	'ʃoː	**sh**ow
t	'toː, 'toːt	**t**oe, **t**o**t**e
t̬	'sit̬iŋ, 'hiːt̬əd	most U. S. pronunciations of si**tt**ing, hea**t**ed
tʃ	'tʃip	**ch**ip
θ	'θiŋk	**th**ink
v	'vet	**v**e**t**
w	'wet	**w**e**t**
x	'lɑx, 'bɑx	Scottish lo**ch**, German Ba**ch**
ɥ	lɥiː	French l**ui**
z	'zip	**z**ip
ʒ	'viʒən, 'beːʒ	vi**s**ion, bei**g**e
ʗ	'ʗxū	**!**Kung (an implosive click)
ʖ	'ʖhɔːsɑː	**X**hosa (an implosive click)

IPA Consonant Symbols

/β/ as in Spanish *hablar.* This represents a voiced bilabial fricative. It is a fricative sound like /v/, but it is pronounced with the two lips like /b/, rather than with the upper teeth and lower lip. In most contexts where it occurs, /b/ and /v/ are acceptable alternatives in English.

/ç/ as in German *ich.* In some languages the palatal fricative /ç/, heard in German *ich,* contrasts phonemically with the velar fricative /x/, heard in German *Bach.* English speakers, who generally have neither sound as a significant feature of their speech, may find it difficult to distinguish between the two. In general, this is not a problem; /ç/ usually occurs before or after front vowels and English speakers will produce the appropriate sound automatically in such positions, because the tongue is moved forward to produce the neighboring vowel. In contrast, /x/ usually occurs before or after central or back vowels in which the tongue is positioned farther back.

   For both /ç/ and /x/ the sound /k/ is an acceptable anglicization in the middle and at the end of words, as in *Joachim* and *loch;* /h/ is an acceptable variant at the beginning of words, as in *chutzpah* and *Chanukah.*

/dʒ/ as in *judge.* Many linguists interpret the consonants of *judge* as a combination of /d/ + /ʒ/, giving /'dʒədʒ/. This is the method adopted in *PDPN.* Other linguists interpret these as single fricative consonants, represented by the single symbol /ǰ/.

/ɣ/ as in Spanish *amigo.* This symbol represents a voiced fricative that is pronounced like /x/ but with the addition of voicing. In English, /g/ is an acceptable alternative.

/hw/ as in *whet.* In *PDPN* the pronunciation of *whet* is indicated as /'hwet/ when it is pronounced differently than *wet* /'wet/. Some linguists analyze the sound preceding the vowel in *whet* as a single consonant, represented as /ʍ/.

/l/ as in *leg, pool.* See /l̩, m̩, n̩/ and /ɫ/ below.

/l̩, m̩, n̩/ as in *middle, open,* and *kitten.* The mark /ˌ/ under /l, m, n/ indicates that the consonant so marked is syllabic; that is, the consonant alone forms the nucleus of a syllable with no vowel. Thus, for *buttoning* the transcription /'bətn̩iŋ/ represents a three-syllable pronunciation /'bət-n̩-iŋ/, while /'bətniŋ/ represents a two syllable pronunciation /'bət-niŋ/. The incidence of syllabic consonants varies somewhat in English dialects and at different stylistic levels; the usual alternatives are /əl, əm, ən/. Syllabic /m̩/ is heard much less frequently than /l̩/ and /n̩/; it occurs most frequently between two bilabial consonants in casual speech, as in *an open boat* /ən 'oːpm̩ 'boːt/ in contrast with *an open eye* /ən 'oːpən 'ɑi/ or *an open sea* /ən 'oːpən 'siː/.

/ɬ/ as in Welsh *Llanelli.* This is a voiceless *l* produced by placing the tongue in the position for /l/ and simply blowing air past the side of the tongue; the /l/ of English *clean* is very similar. Many English speakers substitute either a regular English /l/ or the combination /θl/; thus *Llanelli* /ɬɑ'neɬiˑ/ could be anglicized as /θlɑ'neθliˑ/ or /lɑ'neliˑ/

/ɫ/ as in Polish *Czesław, Wałesa.* In English the /l/ of *leg* and the /l/ of *pool* are actually pronounced in different parts of the mouth. The /l/ of *pool* is farther back than that of *leg.* But these variants of /l/ belong to the same English phoneme and need only one symbol because there are no English words distinguished solely by such a difference. In Polish, on the other hand, these two variations of /l/ are phonemic. In

PDPN the symbol /ł/ is used to represent the sound represented in the Polish spelling by an *l* with a slanted bar through it. This Polish phoneme is similar to the /l/ of English *pool,* and it may be approximated either with /l/ or with the phonetically similar /w/.

/m/ as in *men, home.* See also /ḷ, m̩, ṇ/ above.

/n/ as in *none.* See also /ḷ, m̩, ṇ/ above.

/ŋ/ as in *ring, singer, sink, finger.* Note that this is a single sound and that in words such as *ring, singer,* and *sink* there is no following /g/ sound. In some other words, such as *finger, longer,* and *stronger,* the /ŋ/ is followed by /g/ in most English dialects. Compare *singer* /'siŋər/ and *finger* /'fiŋgər/.

/ɲ / as in French *digne.* This is a palatal nasal consonant pronounced farther back on the tongue than /n/. In French it is frequently represented by *gn.*

/r/ as in *red, merry.* Most consonants are produced in a particular way in one particular part of the mouth. However, the consonant represented by /r/ may be pronounced in different ways in different languages and in different dialects and varieties of English. In U.S. English /r/ is most frequently pronounced with the tongue in a retroflex position, with the tip of the tongue turned up or back. In some varieties of American and British English, and in other languages, such as Spanish, /r/ may be a trill or a single tap of the tongue tip on the alveolar ridge behind the teeth. This is similar to the sound heard for *dd* in *ladder* and for *tt* in *latter* in most U.S. dialects; see the note on /t/ below. To indicate a British pronunciation which uses this tapped /r/, as opposed to the retroflex or trilled /r/, some American cartoonists spell "very" as "veddy."

/ʳ/ the raised *r,* as in *card.* In most U.S. speech /r/ before another consonant or a pause is pronounced with the tongue in a retroflex position as outlined in the previous section. However, in some U.S. speech (primarily in eastern New England, the New York metropolitan area, and the southeastern states) and in educated southern British speech, an *r* in the spelling is not pronounced /r/ when it occurs before another consonant (as in *card, burn,* or *Can you hear me?*), or before a pause (as in *Who took my car?*). This feature is often referred to as *r*-dropping, though the *r* is not always completely dropped. In many cases *r* may be realized as a lengthening of the preceding vowel (e.g. *arms* may be homophonous with *alms* /'ɑːmz/), or as a diphthongization by the addition of an unstressed, non-syllabic /ə/ to the preceding vowel (e.g. *hire Lear* may sound similar to *Hialeah*). The raised /ʳ/ in *PDPN* indicates that some speakers pronounce a consonantal /r/ while others augment the preceding vowel by lengthening or diphthongizing it, or (especially after unstressed syllables) by simply dropping the /r/ altogether.

Some "*r*-dropping" dialects pronounce a word-final /r/ when the next word begins with a vowel, as in *your apple,* and others do not. This is known as a "linking *r*"; it occurs consistently in southern British speech, frequently in the *r*-dropping speech of eastern New England, and often in that of New York City, though it is less common in other *r*-dropping American English. A related development is the occurrence of an "intrusive *r*" between a word ending in /ə/ or /ɔː/ (and occasionally /ɑ/) and another word beginning in a vowel, but where there is no *r* in the spelling, as in the phrase *law and order,* which may be pronounced /ˌlɔːrənˈɔːdə/ by British and some American *r*-droppers. This intrusive *r* occasions much comment from those who do not use it, but it is simply an extended application of the rule for linking *r*. Intrusive *r* is most frequent among British and eastern New England *r*-droppers. This is the feature that accounts for /r/ the heard at the end of the word *Cuba* as often remarked on in the speech of President John F. Kennedy. Intrusive *r* is not shown in *PDPN* or, indeed, in most general dictionaries.

The following examples illustrate the types of variation implied by the raised /ʳ/; in these examples the raised dot [˙] is used to indicate a lengthening or prolongation of the vowel without diphthongization.

beard	/ˈbiʳd/	=	[ˈbird]	*or* [ˈbiəd, ˈbi˙d]
bear	/ˈbæʳ, ˈbeʳ/	=	[ˈbær, ˈber]	*or* [ˈbæə, ˈbæ˙, ˈbeə, ˈbe˙]
bird	/ˈbɚd/	=	[ˈbɚd]	*or* [ˈbɜːd]
bard	/ˈbɑʳd/	=	[ˈbɑrd]	*or* [ˈbɑːd]
bored	/ˈbɔːʳd, ˈbɔːʳd/	=	[ˈbɔːrd, ˈbɔːrd]	*or* [ˈbɔːəd, ˈbɔːəd, ˈbɔː˙d]
moored	/ˈmuʳd/	=	[ˈmurd]	*or* [ˈmuəd, ˈmu˙d]
better	/ˈbeṭəʳ/	=	[ˈbeṭər]	*or* [ˈbeṭə]

NOTE: In *PDPN* these distinctions are indicated in the IPA transcriptions with raised r but are not reflected in the simplified respellings.

/r̥/ as in Welsh *Rhondda*. This is actually an unvoiced /r/, though some linguists may interpret it as /hr/. In Welsh it is usually a voiceless tapped or trilled /r/. A plain voiced /r/ is an acceptable English equivalent, as is /hr/.

/t/ as in *tight, kitten*.

/ṭ/ as in *sitting*. As with most consonants, the sound of /t/ varies according to its position in the word. For instance, the plosive /t/ in *team* is aspirated or released, whereas in *meet* the /t/ is stopped but often not aspirated or released. In most U.S. speech a /t/ between vowels is pronounced as a voiced tap of the tongue. This voiced /ṭ/ does not usually occur at the beginning of a stressed syllable, as in *potato* /pəˈteːṭoː/, though in some New England speech one may indeed hear /bəˈteːṭə/. In *PDPN* the voiced /t/ is indicated as /ṭ/ in positions where U.S. speakers commonly use it, with the understanding that in some dialects—and especially in British and other non-American varieties of English—intervocalic /t/ is usually the voiceless and aspirated stop /t/ rather than a voiced tap.

/tʃ/ as in *church*. Many linguists interpret the sounds spelled with *ch* in *church* as a combination of /t/ + /ʃ/, giving /ˈtʃɚtʃ/. This is the method adopted in *PDPN*. Other linguists interpret these as single fricative consonants, represented by the single symbol /č/.

/x/ as in Scottish *loch*, German *Bach*. See also /ç/ above. For both /ç/ and /x/ the sound /k/ is an acceptable anglicization in the middle and at the end of words, as in *Joachim* and *loch;* /h/ is an acceptable variant at the beginning of words, as in *chutzpah* and *Chanukah*.

/ɥ/ as in French *lui*. This sound, actually a rounded /j/, is difficult for native English speakers to reproduce; it may be approximated by pronouncing /w/. Note, however, that in French *lui* /lɥiː/ is distinct from *Louis* /lwiː/.

/ʇ/, /ʖ/ as in *!Kung* and *Xhosa* respectively. These represent sounds used in some African languages that are clicks or implosive consonants. The first is similar to the palatal sound made to imitate a popping cork; the second is similar to the sound English speakers make on the side of the tongue to gee up a horse.

Diacritics Used in IPA transcriptions

IPA	Example	as in	Explanation
/ˈ/	/ˈæpəl/	**apple**	primary stress
/ˌ/	/ˈæpəlˌsɔːs/	**applesauce**	secondary stress
/ː/	/ˈniːt/	**neat**	an augmented vowel
/ˑ/	/ˈhæpiˑ/	**happy**	variation between simple and augmented vowels
/˜/	/bɔ̃/	French **bon**	nasalization of a vowel
/ˬ/	/ˈsi̬ti̬ŋ, ˈhiːti̬əd/	**si**tt**ing, hea**t**ed**	voicing of a usually unvoiced consonant
/˳/	/l̥ɑˈnel̥iˑ/	Welsh **Ll**ane**ll**i	the voiceless equivalent of a voiced consonant
/ˌ/	/ˈkitn̩/	**kitt**en	a syllabic consonant
/ˌ/	/məˈt̡ildə/	Russian **Ma**t**hilde**	a palatalized consonant

Note on palatalization: In some languages, such as Russian and Irish Gaelic, a consonant is sometimes palatalized, that is, pronounced with the tongue touching or moving toward the palate, adding a /j/-like sound to the consonant. This palatalization is indicated by the addition of a hook to the bottom right of the character, e.g. /r̡, t̡, z̡, m̡/ in Russian *Lavrenti* /ˌləvˈr̡ent̡ij/, *Kuzmich* /kuːz̡ˈm̡iːtʃ/. In *PDPN* palatalization is shown only in the IPA transcriptions and not in the simplified respellings.

Abbreviations

States of the United States are identified with the standard two-letter postal abbreviations.

cent.	century	*pert.*	pertaining
co.	company	*pl.*	plural
corp.	corporation	*pl. name*	place name
dept.	department	*prov.*	province
E	East	*S*	South
lang.	language	*sg.*	singular
mtn.	mountain	*tdmk*	trademark
mts.	mountains	*US*	United States
N	North	*W*	West
pers. name	personal name		

Simplified Pronunciation Symbols

(See the Introduction for detailed explanation)

Symbol	Example	as in
a A	FAD, ASK	fad, ask
ā Ā	FĀD	fade
ah AH	BAH-thuhr, KAHT;	bother, cot;
	FAH-thuhr, AHSK	father, ask
aw AW	KAWT, LAW	caught, law
b B	BID	bid
ch CH	CHIP	chip
d D	DID	did
e E	FED	fed
ē Ē	BĒD	bead
f F	FIT	fit
g G	GET	get
ğ Ğ	ah-ME-ğō	Span. amigo (*Anglicized alternative* g)
h H	HED	head
hl HL	hlah-NEHL-ē	Welsh **Llanelli** (*Anglicized alternative* l *or* thl)
hw HW	HWET, HWICH	whet, which
i I	BID	bid
ī Ī	BĪ, RĪD, LĪ	buy, ride, lie
j J	JET	jet
k K	KIK, KUK	kick, cook
kh KH	BAHKH, IKH, LAHKH	Ger. **Bach**, **ich**, Scottish **loch**.
l L	LEG, MID-l	leg, middle
m M	MEN	men
n N	NET, KIT-n	net, kitten
ng NG	RING, RINGK	ring, rink
ō Ō	KŌT	coat
oi OI	BOI, KOIN	boy, coin
o͞o O͞O	MO͞OD	mood
ow OW	OWT, NOW	out, now
p P	PIN, LIP	pin, lip
r R	RED, KAHRD	red, card
s S	SIT	sit
t T	TŌ, SIT-ing	toe, sitting
th TH	THIN	thin
th TH	THIS	this
u U	GUD, PUT, PUR	good, put, poor
ue UE	RUE, FUE-luhn;	Fr. **rue**, Ger. **fühlen**;
	FUEL-uhn	Ger. **füllen**
uh UH	buh-NAN-uh, BUHD	banana, bud
uhr UHR	BET-uhr, BUHRD	better, bird
uh(r) UH(R)	BUH(R)F,	*Anglicization of* Fr. **boeuf**, Ger. **Hölle**.
	HUH(R)L-uh	
	FUH(R),	*Anglicization of* Fr. **feu**, Ger. **Höhle**.
	HUH(R)-luh	
v V	VET	vet
v̱ V̱	ahv̱-LAHR	Span. **hablar** (*Anglicized alternative* b *or* v)
w W	WET, WICH	wet, witch
y Y	YES	yes
z Z	ZIP	zip
zh ZH	MEZH-uhr	measure

International Phonetic Alphabet Symbols

IPA Symbol	Example	as in
English Consonants		
b	'bid	**b**id
d	'did	**d**i**d**
dʒ	'dʒet	**j**et
ð	'ðis	**th**is
f	'fit	**f**it
g	'get	**g**et
h	'hed	**h**ead
hw	'hwet	**wh**et
j	'jes	**y**es
k	'keːk	**c**a**k**e
l	'leg	**l**eg
ļ	'midļ	mi**ddle**
m	'men	**m**e**n**
m̩	'oːpm̩	o**pen** (some pronunciations)
n	'net	**n**e**t**
ņ	'kitņ	ki**tten**
ŋ	'riŋ, 'riŋk	ri**ng**, ri**n**k
p	'pin	**p**in
r	'red, 'meriˑ	**r**ed, me**rr**y
ʳ (raised r)	'kaʳd (= 'kard, 'kaːd)	ca**r**d
s	'sit	**s**it
ʃ	'ʃoː	**sh**ow
t	'toː, 'toːt	**t**oe, **t**o**t**e
ţ	'siţiŋ, 'hiːţəd	si**tt**ing, hea**t**ed (most U. S. pronunciations)
tʃ	'tʃip	**ch**ip
θ	'θiŋk	**th**ink
v	'vet	**v**et
w	'wet	**w**et
z	'zip	**z**ip
ʒ	'viʒən, 'beːʒ	vi**s**ion, bei**g**e

IPA Symbol	Example	as in
English Vowels		
ə	bə'nænə, 'bəd	b**a**n**a**n**a**, b**u**d
əʳ	'bəʳd, 'bəţəʳ	b**ir**d, butt**er**
æ	'fæd, 'æsk	f**a**d, **a**sk
ɑ	'baðəʳ, 'kat, 'faðəʳ	b**o**ther, c**o**t, f**a**ther
ɑː	'faːðəʳ, 'ɑːsk	f**a**ther, **a**sk
ai	'bai, 'raid	b**uy**, r**i**de
au	'bau, 'nau	b**ou**gh, n**ow**
e	'fed	f**e**d
eː	'feːd	f**a**de
i	'bid	b**i**d
iː	'biːd	b**ea**d
oː	'koːt	c**oa**t
ɔː	'kɔːt, 'lɔː	c**au**ght, l**aw**
ɔi	'bɔi, 'kɔin	b**oy**, c**oin**
u	'gud, 'put, puʳ	g**oo**d, p**u**t, p**oor**
uː	'muːd, 'mjuːzik	m**oo**d, m**u**sic
Non-English Vowels		
œ	'hœlə, bœf	German H**ö**lle, French b**oeu**f
œː	'hœːlə, fœː	German H**öh**le, French f**eu**
y	'fylən	German f**ü**llen
yː	'fyːlən, ryː	German f**üh**len, French r**u**e
Non-English Consonants		
β	aβ'lar	Spanish ha**b**lar
ç	'iç	German i**ch**
ɣ	a'miːɣoː	Spanish ami**g**o
ł	'tʃesłaːf	Polish Czes**ł**aw
ļ	ļa'neļiˑ	Welsh **Ll**ane**ll**i
ɲ	'diːɲ	French di**gn**e
ʀ	'ʀanðə	Welsh **Rh**ondda
x	'lax, 'bax	Scottish lo**ch**, German Ba**ch**
ɥ	lɥiː	French l**u**i
ʗ	'ʗxū	**!**Kung (an implosive click)
ʖ	'ʖɔːsɑː	**X**hosa (an implosive click)

Diacritics used in IPA transcriptions

IPA Symbol	Example	as in	Explanation
'	'æpəl	**a**pple	primary stress
ˌ	'æpəlˌsɔːs	**a**pple**s**auce	secondary stress
ː	'niːt	n**ea**t	an augmented vowel
ˑ	'hæpiˑ	happ**y**	variation between simple and augmented vowels
~	bɔ̃	French b**on**	nasalization of a vowel
ˬ	'siţiŋ, 'hiːţəd	si**tt**ing, hea**t**ed	voicing of a usually unvoiced consonant
ₒ	ļa'neļiˑ	Welsh **Ll**ane**ll**i	the voiceless equivalent of a voiced consonant
ˌ	'kitņ	ki**tten**	a syllabic consonant
ˎ	mə'ţildə	Russian Ma**th**ilde	a palatalized consonant

A

AAA
    American Automobile Assoc.   TRIP-uhl Ā; Ā-Ā-Ā   ,tripəl 'eː; ,eː,eː'eː

AAAS
    American Assoc. for the Advancement   TRIP-uhl Ā ES   ,tripəl ,eː 'es
        of Science

Aabenraa
    see Åbenrå

Aachen
    city, Germany   AH<u>KH</u>-uhn   'ɑxən

Aage
    pers. name   AW-guh   'ɔːgə

Aaiu'n, El [Aiun, Laayoune]
    town, W Sahara   EL Ī-OON   ,el ɑi'uːn

Aalborg, Ålborg
    port, Denmark   AWL-BAWRG   'ɔːl,bɔːʳg

Aalsmeer
    commune, Netherlands   AHLS-MER   'ɑls,meʳ

Aalst
    city, district, Belgium   AHLST   'ɑːlst

Aalto
    Alvar, Finnish designer   AHL-tō   'ɑltoː

Aarau
    commune, Switzerland   AHR-ow   'ɑːrɑu

Aare
    river, Switzerland   AHR-uh   'ɑrə

Aargau
    canton, Switzerland   AHR-gow   'ɑːʳgɑu

Aarhus
    see Århus

Aaron
    1. pers. name   AR-uhn, ER-uhn   'ærən, 'erən
    2. Danish, German   AHR-AWN   'ɑr,ɔːn
    3. French   ah-RAW^n ɑrɔ̃

Aaronic
    pert. to Aaron   ar-AHN-ik, er-AHN-ik   ær'ɑnik, er'ɑnik

Aaronite
    descendent of Aaron   AR-uh-NĪT, ER-uh-NĪT   'ærə,nɑit, 'erə,nɑit

Aart
    pers. name, Dutch   AHRT   'ɑːʳt

Aasen
    Ivar Andreas, *Norwegian philologist*   AH-suhn   'ɑːsən

Aass
    Norwegian beer   AHS   'ɑs

Aat [Ath]
  district, Belgium   AHT   ˈɑːt

Abaco
  island, British Virgin Islands   AB-uh-KŌ   ˈæbəˌkoː

Ābādān
  port, Iran   AHB-uh-DAHN, AB-uh-DAN   ˌɑbəˈdɑn, ˌæbəˈdæn

Abaddon
  destroying angel   uh-BAD-n   əˈbædn̩

Abadía
  pers. name, Spanish   ahv-ah-T̲H̲Ē-ah   ɑβaˈðiːɑ

Abagtha
  Biblical name   uh-BAG-thuh, uh-VAHG-tuh   əˈbægθə, əˈvɑgtə

Abahai
  Manchu emperor, China   AH-BAH-HĪ   ˈɑːbɑːˈhai

Abakan
  river, town, Russia   AH-buh-KAHN, UH-buh-KAHN   ˌɑbəˈkan, ˌəbəˈkan

Abana
  Biblical name   AB-uh-nuh   ˈæbənə

Abancay
  town, Peru   AHB-ahng-KĪ   ˌɑbaŋˈkai

Abarbanel [Abravanel]
  Judah, *Spanish philosopher;* Isaac   ah-V̲AHR-v̲ah-NEL   ɑˌβɑrβaˈnel
    ben Judah, *Jewish religious*
    writer in Spain

Abarim
  Mtns., *ancient name, Jordan*   AB-uh-RIM, AHB-ah-RIM   ˈæbəˌrim, ˌɑbaˈrim

Abas
  Perseus's great-grandfather   AB-uhs   ˈæbəs

Abasiyanuk
  Sait Faik, *Turkish writer*   ahb-AHS-ē-(y)ah-NUK   ɑbˌɑsiː(j)ɑˈnuk

Abate
  family name   uh-BAHT-ē, uh-BĀT   əˈbɑti·, əˈbeːt

Abauzit
  Firmin, *French theologian*   ah-bō-ZĒT   ɑboːziːt

Abba
  1. Swedish rock group; pers. name   AB-uh   ˈæbə
  2. Hebrew title   AHB-bah   ˈɑːbbɑ

Abba Arika [Rab]
  Babylonian rabbi   AHB-uh uh-RĒ-kuh, uh-RĒ-k̲h̲uh   ˌɑbə əˈriːkə, əˈriːxə

'Abbādid
  Muslim dynasty, Spain   AB-uh-DID   ˈæbəˌdid

Abbado
  Claudio, *Italian conductor*   uh-BAHD-ō, ahb-BAHD-ō   əˈbadoː, ɑbˈbadoː

Abbasid
  Islamic dynasty   AB-uh-sid, uh-BAS-id   ˈæbəsid, əˈbæsid

Abbé
  lake, Ethiopia   ah-BĀ   ɑˈbeː

Abbe
  Cleveland, *American meteorologist;*   AB-ē   ˈæbi·
    Ernst, *German physicist*

Abbeville
  1. US pl. name; US publisher   AB-ē-VIL   ˈæbi·ˌvil
  2. commune, France   ahb-VĒL, ah-buh-VĒL   ɑːbviːl, ɑːbəviːl

Abda
  Biblical name   AB-duh   ˈæbdə

Key (col. 2):   a: fad   ā: fade   ah: father   ar: marry   aw: law   e: fed   ē: feed   er: merry   i: hid   ī: hide   ō: coat   o͞o: boot
oi: boy   ow: now   u: put   uh: above   uhr: bird   ch: chop   ng: ring   sh: show   th: thick   th: this   zh: measure

Abd al-Hamid
   sultans, Ottoman Empire   AHB-duhl-hah-MĒD   'abdəlha'miːd

Abdallah
   1. pers. name   ab-DAL-uh   æb'dælə
   2. Arabic, Persian   AHB-dah-LAH   ˌɑːbdɑːˈlɑː

'Abd al-Malik ibn Marwān
   Muslim caliph   AHB-duhl-mah-LĒK ɪʙ-uhn   'abdəlma'liːk ˌibən mar'wan
              mahr-WAHN

'Abd al-Mu'min
   Berber founder of Almohad dynasty,   AHB-duhl-mo͞o-MĒN   'abdəlmuː'miːn
   Spain & Morocco

'Abd al-Qādir al-Jīlānī
   Persian religious leader   AHB-duhl-KAH-ᴅɪʀ ᴀʜʟ-jē-LAHN-ē   'abdəl'ka,dir ˌaldʒiːˈlaniː

Ābdānān
   town, Iran   AHB-duh-NAHN   ˌɑːbdəˈnɑːn

Abd ar-Rahman
   Muslim rulers of Spain   ahb-DAHR-rahkh-MAHN   ab,darrax'maːn

Abdel
   pers. name, Arabic   uhb-DUL   əb'dul

Abdeel
   Biblical name   AB-dē-ᴇʟ, AHV-dē-ᴇʟ   'æbdiːˌel, 'avdiːˌel

Abdelkader
   Algerian leader   AB-duhl-KAHD-uhr   ˌæbdəl'kadəʳ

Abdera [Avdira]
   city, ancient Thrace   ab-DIR-uh   æb'dirə

Abdi
   Biblical name   AB-DĪ, AHV-dē   'æbˌdai, 'avdiː

Abdias
   Old Testament book   ab-DĪ-uhs   æb'daiəs

Abdiel
   Biblical name   AB-dē-ᴇʟ, AHV-dē-ᴇʟ   'æbdiːˌel, 'avdiːˌel

'Abd ol-Bahā'
   Persian religious leader   AHB-duhl-bah-HAH   'abdəlba'ha

Abdon
   pers. name   AB-dahn   'æbdan

'Abdorrahmān Khān
   Afghani ruler   AHB-dawr-(R)AHᴋʜ-mahn ᴋʜAHN,   ˌabdɔːr'(r)axman 'xan, 'kan
              KAHN

Abdul
   1. pers. name; Paula, *US pop*   ab-DO͞OL, AB-dul   æb'duːl, 'æbdul
   entertainer
   2. Arabic   uhb-DUL   əb'dul

Abdülaziz
   Ottoman sultan   AHB-due-lahz-ĒZ   ˌabdyːlaz'iːz

Abdülhamid
   Ottoman sultan   AHB-duel-hahm-ĒD   ˌabdyːlham'iːd

Abdul Aziz, King
   airport, Jeddah, Saudi Arabia   KING ahb-DO͞OL ah-ZĒZ   ˌkiŋ ab,duːl a'ziːz

Abdul-Jabbar
   Kareem, *US basketball player*   ab-DO͞OL-juh-BAHR   æb,du·ldʒə'baʳ

Abdullah
   1. pers. name   ab-DUHL-uh   æb'dələ
   2. Arabic, Persian   AHB-dul-AH   ˌaːbdul'aː

Abdülmecid
   Ottoman sultan   AHB-duel-mej-ĒD   ˌabdyːlmedʒ'iːd

Foreign Sounds: ue: *Fr.* **rue**, *Ger.* **füllen**   uh(r): *Fr.* **boeuf**, *Ger.* **Höhle**   kh: *Ger.* **ich**, *Scot.* **loch**   ḡ: *Sp.* **amigo**   v: *Sp.* **hablar**
hl: *Welsh* **Llanelli**.   CAPITALS: primary stress.   SMALL CAPS: secondary stress.   Ⓢ: U.S. pron.   Ⓔ: British pron.

Abdus
　pers. name, Punjabi　　ahb-DUS　　ɑbˈdus

Abe
　1. pers. name　　ĀB　　ˈeːb
　2. lang., Ivory Coast　　AHB-ā　　ˈɑbeː

Abéché
　city, Chad　　AHB-ā-SHĀ　　ˌɑbeːˈʃeː

Abednego
　Biblical name　　uh-BED-ni-gō　　əˈbednigoː

Abe Kōbō
　Japanese novelist, playwright　　ahb-ā kō-bō　　ɑbeː koːboː

Abel
　1. pers. name　　Ā-buhl　　ˈeːbəl
　2. Danish, Dutch, Norwegian　　AHB-uhl　　ˈɑːbəl
　3. French　　ah-BEL　　ɑːbel

Abelam
　Papuan people, New Guinea　　uh-BEL-uhm　　əˈbeləm

Abelard
　Peter, *French philosopher*　　AB-uh-LAHRD　　ˈæbəˌlɑʳd

Abelardo
　pers. name, Spanish　　ahv̱-ā-LAHR-tẖō　　ɑβeːˈlɑrðoː

Abelbethmaachah
　Biblical name　　Ā-buhl-beth-MĀ-uh-kuh,　　ˌeːbəlbeθˈmeːəkə,
　　　　AHV-el-BET-mā-uh-KH̱AH　　ˌɑvelˌbetmeːəˈxɑ

Abelcheramim
　Biblical name　　Ā-buhl-KER-uh-MIM, Ā-vel-krah-MĒM　　ˌeːbəlˈkerəˌmim,
　　　　　　ˌeːvelkrɑˈmiːm

Abelian
　mathematics system　　uh-BḖ-lē-uhn, uh-BḔL-yuhn　　əˈbiːliːən, əˈbiːljən

Abelmayim
　Biblical name　　Ā-buhl-MĀ-im, -MAH-yim　　ˌeːbəlˈmeːim, -ˈmɑjim

Abelmeholah
　Biblical name　　Ā-buhl-me-HŌ-luh, -muh-kẖō-LAH　　ˌeːbəlmeˈhoːlə, -məxoːˈlɑ

Abelshitim
　Biblical name　　Ā-buhl-SHIT-im, -shuh-TḔM　　ˌeːbəlˈʃițim, -ʃəˈtiːm

Abelson
　Philip Hauge, *US physical chemist*　　Ā-buhl-suhn　　ˈeːbəlsən

Abe Isoo
　Japanese politician　　ahb-ā ē-sōō　　ɑbeː iːsuː

Abe Masahiro
　Japanese politician　　ahb-ā mahs-ah-hē-rō　　ɑbeː mɑsɑhiːroː

Abenaki [Abnaki]
　N. American people　　AB-uh-NAHK-ē, AB-uh-NAK-ē,　　ˌæbəˈnɑki·, ˌæbəˈnæki·,
　　　　AHB-uh-NAHK-ē　　ˌɑbəˈnɑki·

Abencerrajes
　feuding Moorish family in Granada,　　ah-v̱en-thār-RAH-kẖās　　ɑβenθeːrˈrɑxeːs
　Spain

Abengourou
　dept., Ivory Coast　　ah-BEN-gōō-rōō　　ɑˈbenguːruː

Åbenrå, Aabenraa
　town, fjord, Denmark　　AW-buhn-RAW　　ˈɔːbənˌrɔː

Abeokuta
　town, Nigeria　　ah-BĀ-ō-kōō-TAH　　ɑˈbeːoːkuːˌtɑ

Abercrombie, -by
　pers. name　　AB-uhr-KRAHM-bē, -KRUHM-bē　　ˈæbəʳˌkrɑmbi·, -ˌkrəmbi·

Key (col. 2):　a: fad　ā: fade　ah: father　ar: marry　aw: law　e: fed　ē: feed　er: merry　i: hid　ī: hide　ō: coat　ōō: boot
oi: boy　ow: now　u: put　uh: above　uhr: bird　ch: chop　ng: ring　sh: show　th: thick　tẖ: this　zh: measure

Aberdare
  town, Wales; mtn. range, Kenya   AB-uhr-DAR, AB-uhr-DER   ˌæbəʳˈdæʳ, ˌæbəʳˈdeʳ
Aberdeen
  1. seaport, Scotland   AB-uhr-DĒN   ˌæbəʳˈdiːn
  2. US pl. name   AB-uhr-DĒN   ˈæbəʳˌdiːn
Aberdonian
  pert. to Aberdeen   AB-uhr-DŌ-nē-uhn, AB-uhr-DŌN-yuhn   ˌæbəʳˈdoːniːən, ˌæbəʳˈdoːnjən
Abergavenny
  1. borough, Wales   AB-uhr-guh-VEN-ē   ˌæbəʳgəˈveniˑ
  2. British title & family name   AB-uhr-guh-VEN-ē, AB-uhr-GEN-ē   ˌæbəʳgəˈveniˑ, ˌæbəʳˈgeniˑ
Aberystwyth
  town, Wales   AB-uh-RIS-TWITH, AB-uh-RUHS-TWITH   ˌæbəˈrisˌtwiθ, ˌæbəˈrəsˌtwiθ
Abez
  Biblical name   Ā-BEZ   ˈeːˌbez
Abhá
  town, Saudi Arabia   AHB-hah   ˈabhɑ
Abi
  Biblical name   Ā-BĪ, AHV-ē   ˈeːˌbɑi, ˈɑviː
Abia, Abiah
  Biblical name   uh-BĪ-uh, ah-VĒ-yah   əˈbɑiə, ɑˈviːjɑ
Abiasaph
  Biblical name   uh-BĪ-uh-SAF, uh-VĪ-uh-SAHF   əˈbɑiəˌsæf, əˈvɑiəˌsɑf
Abiathar
  Biblical name   uh-BĪ-uh-THAHR, AHV-ē-ah-TAHR   əˈbɑiəˌθɑʳ, ˌɑviːɑˈtɑʳ
Abida, Abidah
  Biblical name   uh-BĪD-uh, ah-VĒ-dah   əˈbɑidə, ɑˈviːdɑ
Abidan
  Biblical name   AB-uh-DAN, AH-vē-DAHN   ˈæbəˌdæn, ˌɑviːˈdɑn
Abidjan
  seaport, Ivory Coast   AB-i-JAHN   ˌæbiˈdʒɑn
Abidjanaise, L'
  see L'Abidjanaise
Abiel
  pers. name   AHB-ē-uhl, Ā-bē-uhl, uh-BĪ-uhl   ˈabiːəl, ˈeːbiːəl, əˈbɑiəl
Abiezer
  Biblical name   Ā-BĪ-Ē-zuhr, AHV-ē-EZ-er   ˌeːˌbɑiˈiːzəʳ, ˌɑviːˈezeʳ
Abiezrite
  Biblical name   Ā-BĪ-EZ-RĪT   ˌeːˌbɑiˈezˌrɑit
Abigail
  pers. name   AB-uh-GĀL   ˈæbəˌgeːl
Abihail
  Biblical name   AB-uh-HĀL, AHV-ē-KHAH-yil   ˈæbəˌheːl, ˌɑviːˈxɑjil
Abihu
  Biblical name   uh-BĪ-H(Y)OO   əˈbɑiˌh(j)uː
Abijah
  pers. name   uh-BĪ-juh   əˈbɑidʒə
Abilene
  1. city, TX   AB-uh-LĒN   ˈæbəˌliːn
  2. region, Syria   AB-uh-LĒ-nē   ˌæbəˈliːniˑ
Abílio
  pers. name   ah-BĒL-yoo   ɑːˈbiːljuː
Abimael
  Biblical name   uh-BIM-ē-EL, ah-VĒ-mah-EL   əˈbimiˑˌel, ɑˌviːmɑˈel
Abimelech
  Biblical name   uh-BIM-uh-LEK   əˈbiməˌlek

Abinadab
Biblical name   uh-BIN-uh-DAB, ah-VĒ-nah-DAHV   ə'binə‚dæb, ɑ‚viːnɑ'dɑv

Abingdon
town, England   AB-ing-duhn   'æbiŋdən

Abinoam
Biblical name   uh-BIN-uh-wuhm, uh-BIN-uh-WAM   ə'binəwəm, ə'binə‚wæm

Abipón
S. American people   AB-uh-PAHN, AB-uh-PAHN, AB-uh-PŌN   'æbə‚pɑn, ‚æbə'pɑn, ‚æbə'poːn

Abiram
Biblical name   uh-BĪ-RAM, AHV-ē-RAHM   ə'bai‚ræm, ‚ɑviː'rɑm

Abishag
Biblical name   AB-i-SHAG   'æbi‚ʃæg

Abishai
Biblical name   uh-BISH(-ē)-Ī, AB-uh-SHĪ   ə'biʃ(iˑ)‚ai, 'æbə‚ʃai

Abishalom [Absalom]
Biblical name   uh-BISH-uh-luhm, ahv-Ē-shah-LŌM   ə'biʃələm, ɑv‚iːʃɑ'loːm

Abishua
Biblical name   uh-BISH-uh-wuh, ahv-Ē-shuh-WAH   ə'biʃəwə, ɑv‚iːʃə'wɑ

Abishur
Biblical name   uh-BĪ-shuhr, AHV-ē-SHUR   ə'baiʃə^r, ‚aviː'ʃu^r

Abital
Biblical name   uh-BĪ-TAL, AB-uh-TAL, AHV-ē-TAHL   ə'bai‚tæl, 'æbə‚tæl, ‚aviː'tal

Abitibi
lake, Canada   AB-uh-TIB-ē   ‚æbə'tibiˑ

Abitub
Biblical name   uh-BĪ-tuhb, AB-uh-TUHB   ə'baitəb, 'æbə‚təb

Abiud
Biblical name   uh-BĪ-uhd   ə'baiəd

Abkhaz
lang., people, Georgia   ahb-KAHZ, ahb-KAHS   ɑb'kɑz, ɑb'kɑs

Abnaki [Abenaki]
N. American people   ab-NAHK-ē, ab-NAK-ē, ahb-NAHK-ē   æb'nɑkiˑ, æb'nækiˑ, ɑb'nɑkiˑ

Abner
pers. name   AB-nuhr   'æbnə^r

Aboisso
dept., Ivory Coast   AHB-wahs-Ō, uh-BOI-sō   ‚abwɑs'oː, ə'bɔisoː

Abolhassan
pers. name, Arabic (A. Bani-Sadr)   AHB-uhl-khah-SAHN, Ⓢ AHB-uhl-hah-SAHN   ‚abəlxɑ'san, Ⓢ ‚abəlhɑ'san

Abomey
town, Benin   AB-uh-MĀ, uh-BŌ-mē   ‚æbə'meː, ə'boːmiˑ

About
Edmond François Valentin, *French*   ah-BOO   aːbuː
writer

Abra
province, river, Philippines   AHB-ruh   'abrə

Abraham
1. pers. name   Ā-bruh-HAM   'eːbrə‚hæm
2. Danish, Norwegian   AH-brah-HAHM   'aːbrɑ‚haːm
3. French   ah-brah-AHM   aːbraːaːm
4. German   AHB-rah-HAHM   'abrɑ‚ham
5. Spanish   ahv-RAHN, ahv-rah-AHN   aβ'ran, aβra'an
6. Swedish   AHB-rah-HAHM   'abraː‚ham

Key (col. 2):   a: fad   ā: fade   ah: father   ar: marry   aw: law   e: fed   ē: feed   er: merry   i: hid   ī: hide   ō: coat   ōō: boot
oi: boy   ow: now   u: put   uh: above   uhr: bird   ch: chop   ng: ring   sh: show   th: thick   th̲: this   zh: measure

Abrahán
  pers. name   ahv-RAHN, ahv-rah-AHN   aβ'rɑn, aβrɑ'ɑn
Abram
  1. pers. name   Ā-bruhm   'eːbrəm
  2. Russian   uh-BRAHM   ə'brɑːm
Abramovich
  Shalom Jacob, *Russian Jewish*   uh-BRAHM(-uh)-VICH   ə'brɑːm(ə),vitʃ
   writer
Abrams
  Talber, *US aviator, explorer*   Ā-bruhmz   'eːbrəmz
Abravanel [Abarbanel]
  Judah, *Spanish philosopher;* Isaac   ah-VRAH-vah-NEL   ɑ,βrɑβɑ'nel
   ben Judah, *Jewish religious*
   writer in Spain
Abrohnah
  Biblical name   uh-BRŌ-nuh   ə'broːnə
Abruzzi
  region, Italy   ah-BROOT-sē, uh-BROOT-sē   ɑ'bruːtsiˑ, ə'bruːtsiˑ
Abruzzi e Molise
  former region, Italy   ah-BROOT-sē ā MAW-lē-SĀ   ɑ'bruːtsiˑ eː 'mɔːliːˌseː
Absalom
  pers. name   AB-suh-luhm   'æbsələm
absinthe
  liquor   AB-sinth   'æbsinθ
Absolut
  vodka brand   AHP-sō-LOOT   ˌɑpsoː'luːt
Abt
  Franz, *German composer*   AHPT   'ɑpt
Abu
  1. pers. name, Arabic   ah-BOO   ɑ'buː
  2. Persian   AHB-oo   'ɑːbuː
Abu Alaa [Ahmed Korei]
  Palestinian politician   ah-BOO ah-LAH   ɑ'buː ɑ'lɑ
Abu al-Ala al-Maari
  Arabic poet   ah-BOO ahl-AHL-ah ahl-MAH-AHR-ē   ɑ'buː ɑlˌɑlɑ ɑl'mɑˌariː
Abū al-Fidā', Abulfeda
  Arab historian & geographer   uh-BOO(-uh)l-fē-DAH   ə,buː(ə)lfiː'dɑ
Abū al-Qāsim [Abul Kasim, Albucasis]
  Spanish Arab physician   uh-BOO(-uh)l-KAHS-im   ə,buː(ə)l'kɑsim
Abū Bakr
  First Muslim caliph   uh-BOO BAK-uhr   ə,buː 'bækər
Abu Dhabi
  state & town, United Arab Emirates   AHB-oo THAHB-ē, AHB-oo DAHB-ē   ˌɑbuː 'ðabiˑ, ˌɑbuː 'dabiˑ
Abu Hanifa
  Muslim theologian   ah-BOO hah-NĒ-fuh   ɑ'buː hɑ'niːfə
Abuja
  capital, Nigeria   ah-BOO-yah   ɑ'buːjɑ
Abulfeda
  see Abū al-Fidā'
Abul Kasim [Abū al-Qāsim]
  Spanish Arab physician   uh-BUL-KAHS-im   ə,bul'kɑsim
Abū Ma'shar [Albumazar]
  Muslim astrologer   uh-BOO-MAHSH-uhr   ə,buː'mɑʃər

Abu Simbel
  site, Egypt   AHB-o͞o SIM-buhl   ˌɑbuː 'simbəl
Abū Ẓabī [Abu Dhabi]
  state & town, United Arab Emirates   AHB-o͞o T̲H̲AHB-ē   ˌɑbuː 'ðɑbiˑ
Abyán
  governorate, Yemen   ab-YAHN, ahb-YAHN   æb'jɑn, ɑb'jɑn
Abydos
  town, Egypt   uh-BĪD-uhs   ə'bɑidəs
Abyssinia [Ethiopia]
  country, Africa   AB-uh-SIN-ē-uh, AB-uh-SIN-yuh   ˌæbə'siniːə, ˌæbə'sinjə
Abzug
  Bella, *US politician*   AB-zug   'æbzug
Academus
  legendary Attic hero   AK-uh-DĒ-muhs, AK-uh-DĀ-muhs   ˌækə'diːməs, ˌækə'deːməs
Acadia
  National Park, *ME; region, Canada*   uh-KĀD-ē-uh   ə'keːdiːə
Acadian
  pert. to Acadia; *French-Canadian*   uh-KĀD-ē-uhn   ə'keːdiːən
  exile
Acadie
  French form of Acadia   ah-kah-DĒ   ɑːkɑːdiː
Acapulco
  town, Mexico   AHK-uh-PUL-kō, AK-, -PŌŌL-kō   ˌɑkə'pulkoː, ˌæk-, -'puːlkoː
Acapulco de Juárez
  town, Mexico   ahk-uh-PŌŌL-kō t̲h̲ā K̲H̲WAHR-es   ɑkə'puˑlkoː ðeː 'xwɑres
Acaraí, Serra
  mtn. range, Brazil & Guyana   SER-ah AH-kah-rah-Ē   ˌserɑ ˌɑkɑrɑ'iː
Acarnania
  dept, Greece   AK-uhr-NĀ-nē-uh   ˌækə^r'neːniːə
Acastus
  Argonaut   uh-KAS-tuhs   ə'kæstəs
Açba [Assaba]
  region, Mauritania   AHK-bah, AHK̲H̲-bah   'ɑkbɑ, 'ɑçbɑ
Accad
  Biblical name   AHK-AHD, AK-AD   'ɑkˌɑd, 'ækˌæd
Accho, Acco, Acho, 'Akko [Acre,
  Ptolemais]
  town, district, Israel   AHK-ō   'ɑkoː
Accipiter
  hawk genus   ak-SIP-uht-uhr   æk'sipət̮ə^r
Accomack
  county, VA   AK-uh-MAK   'ækəˌmæk
Accra
  seaport, Ghana   uh-KRAH   ə'krɑ
Aceh
  see Atjeh
Aceldama [Akeldama]
  potter's field   uh-SEL-duh-muh   ə'seldəmə
Acestes
  host of Aeneas in Sicily   uh-SES-tēz   ə'sestiːz
Achaea [Achaia]
  dept, Greece   uh-KĒ-uh   ə'kiːə
Achaea Phthiotis
  region, Greece   uh-KĒ-uh thī-ŌT-uhs   ə'kiːə θɑi'oːt̮əs

Key (col. 2):   a: fad ā: fade ah: father ar: marry aw: law e: fed ē: feed er: merry i: hid ī: hide ō: coat o͞o: boot
oi: boy ow: now u: put uh: above uhr: bird ch: chop ng: ring sh: show th: thick t̲h̲: this zh: measure

Achaean League
 ancient Greek alliance   uh-KĒ-uhn   əˈkiːən

Achaemenid
 Persian dynasty   uh-KĒ-muh-nid   əˈkiːmənid

Achaemenides
 companion of Odysseus   AK-uh-MEN-uh-DĒZ   ˌækəˈmenəˌdiːz

Achaia [Achaea]
 region, ancient Greece   uh-KĪ-uh, uh-KĀ-uh   əˈkɑiə, əˈkeːə

Achan [Achar]
 Biblical name   Ā-kuhn, AH<u>KH</u>-ahn   ˈeːkən, ˈɑxɑn

Achar [Achan]
 Biblical name   Ā-kahr, AH<u>KH</u>-ahr   ˈeːkɑr, ˈɑxɑʳ

Achates
 1. friend of Aeneas; pers. name   uh-KĀT-ēz   əˈkeːțiːz
 2. Swedish   ah-KAHT-uhs   ɑːˈkɑțəs

Achbor
 Biblical name   AK-bawr, AH<u>KH</u>-   ˈækbɔːʳ, ˈɑx-

Achebe
 Chinua, *Nigerian writer*   ah-CHĀ-bā   ɑˈtʃeːbeː

Acheen
 see Achin

Achelous
 Boeotian river god   AK-uh-LŌ-uhs   ˌækəˈloːəs

Achernar
 star   AK-uhr-NAHR, Ā-kuhr-NAHR   ˈækəʳˌnɑʳ, ˈeːkəʳˌnɑʳ

Acheron
 river in Hades   AK-uh-RAHN, AK-uh-ruhn   ˈækəˌrɑn, ˈækərən

Acheson
 Dean, *US statesman*   ACH-uh-suhn   ˈætʃəsən

Achille
 1. pers. name, French   ah-SHĒL   ɑːʃiːl
 2. Italian   ah-KĒL-lā   ɑˈkiːlleː

Achille Lauro
 hijacked Italian cruise ship   ah-KĒL-lā LOWR-ō   ɑˈkiːlleː ˈlɑuroː

Achilles
 1. Homeric hero; pers. name   uh-KIL-ēz   əˈkiliːz
 2. German   ah-<u>KH</u>IL-uhs   ɑˈçiləs

Achim
 Biblical name   Ā-kim, YAH<u>KH</u>-im   ˈeːkim, ˈjɑxim

Achin, Atchin, Acheen [Atjeh]
 province, Indonesia   ah-CHĒN   ɑˈtʃiːn

Achinese
 see Atjehnese

Achiote
 plant   AHK-ē-ŌT-ē   ˌɑkiːˈoːțiˑ

Achitophel
 Biblical name   uh-KIT-uh-FEL   əˈkițəˌfel

Achish
 Biblical name   Ā-kish, ah<u>kh</u>-ĒSH   ˈeːkiʃ, ɑxˈiːʃ

Achmed
 pers. name   AH<u>KH</u>-med, ah<u>kh</u>-MET   ˈɑxmed, ɑxˈmet

Acholi [Akoli]
 lang., people, Uganda, Sudan   uh-KŌ-lē, uh-CHŌ-lē   əˈkoːliˑ, əˈtʃoːliˑ

Acho
 see Accho

Foreign Sounds: ue: *Fr.* **rue**, *Ger.* **füllen**   uh(r): *Fr.* b**oeuf**, *Ger.* H**öh**le   <u>kh</u>: *Ger.* i**ch**, *Scot.* lo**ch**   ḡ: *Sp.* ami**g**o   v̲: *Sp.* ha**b**lar
hl: *Welsh* **Ll**anelli.   CAPITALS: primary stress.   SMALL CAPS: secondary stress.   Ⓢ: U.S. pron.   Ⓔ: British pron.

Achor
  Biblical name — Ā-KAWR, ah-<u>KH</u>AWR — 'eːˌkɔːʳ, ɑ'xɔːʳ
Achsa, Achsah
  Biblical name — AK-suh, AH<u>KH</u>- — 'æksə, 'ɑx-
Achshaph
  Biblical name — AK-SHAF, ah<u>kh</u>-SHAHF — 'ækˌʃæf, ɑx'ʃɑf
Achzib
  Biblical name — AK-zib — 'ækzib
Acis
  lover of Galatea — Ā-suhs — 'eːsəs
Acisclo
  pers. name, Spanish — ah-THĒS-klō, ah-SĒS-klō — ɑ'θiːsklɔː, ɑ'siːsklɔː
Acislo
  pers. name, Spanish — ah-THĒ-slō, ah-SĒ-slō — ɑ'θiːslɔː, ɑ'siːslɔː
Ackerman
  Bettye Louise, *US actress* — AK-uhr-muhn — 'ækəʳmən
Acoma
  N. American people — AHK-uh-MAW, AK-uh-MAW — 'ɑkəˌmɔː, 'ækəˌmɔː
Aconcagua
  Mount, *Argentina* — AHK-uhn-KAHG̃-wah,   Ⓢ AK-uhn-KAHG-wuh, AHK- — ˌɑkən'kɑɣwɑ,   Ⓢ ˌækən'kɑgwə, ˌɑk-
Aconite
  plant — AK-uh-NĪT — 'ækəˌnɑit
Açores, Ilhas dos [Azores]
  island archipelago, Portugal — IL-yuhz duz uh-SAWR-ish, uh-SAWR-is — 'iljəz duz ə'sɔːriʃ, ə'sɔːris
Acor, Serra de
  mtn. range, Portugal — SER-uh dā ah-KAWR — ˌserə deː ɑː'kɔːʳ
Acre [Accho, Ptolemais]
  1. state, Brazil — AHK-ruh, AH-krā — 'ɑkrə, 'ɑkreː
  2. town, district, Israel — AHK-uhr, Ā-kuhr — 'ɑkəʳ, 'eːkəʳ
Acquaviva
  castle, San Marino — AHK-wuh-VĒ-vuh — ˌɑkwə'viːvə
Acrisius
  grandfather of Perseus — uh-KRISH-(ē-)uhs — ə'kriʃ(iː)əs
Acropolis
  Athenian citadel — uh-KRAHP-uh-luhs — ə'krɑpələs
Actaeon
  mythical Greek hunter — ak-TĒ-uhn — æk'tiːən
Acte [Aktí]
  peninsula, Greece — AHK-tē — 'ɑkti·
actinium
  element — ak-TIN-ē-uhm — æk'tiniːəm
Actium
  promontory, battlesite, Greece — AK-shē-uhm, AK-tē-uhm — 'ækʃiːəm, 'æktiːəm
Acuff
  Roy, *US country singer* — Ā-KUHF — 'eːˌkəf
Acura
  car make — AK-yuh-ruh — 'ækjərə
Acushnet
  US golf equipment co. — uh-KUSH-nuht, -NET — ə'kuʃnət, -ˌnet
Ada
  1. programming lang.; pers. name — ĀD-uh — 'eːdə
  2. French — ah-DAH — ɑːdɑː
  3. Italian — AH-dah — 'ɑdɑ

Key (col. 2):   a: fad   ā: fade   ah: father   ar: marry   aw: law   e: fed   ē: feed   er: merry   i: hid   ī: hide   ō: coat   o͞o: boot
oi: boy   ow: now   u: put   uh: above   uhr: bird   ch: chop   ng: ring   sh: show   th: thick   <u>th</u>: this   zh: measure

Adadah
   Biblical name   AD-uh-duh, uh-DĀD-uh   'ædədə, ə'deːdə

Adad-nirari
   name, Assyrian kings   uh-DAHD-nuh-RAHR-ē, -nē-RAHR-ē   ə,dadnə'rari', -niː'rari'

Adah
   wife of Lamech; pers. name   ĀD-uh   'eːdə

Adaiah
   Biblical name   uh-DĀ-uh, uh-DĪ-uh   ə'deːə, ə'daiə

Adaiah
   Biblical name   uh-DĀ-uh, uh-DĪ-uh   ə'deːə, ə'daiə

Adair
   county, IA, KY, MO, OK; pers. name   uh-DAR, uh-DER   ə'dæ^r, ə'de^r

Adak
   Alaskan island   Ā-DAK   'eː,dæk

Adalbert
   1. pers. name, Danish   AHD-ahl-BERT   'aːdaːl,bert
   2. German   AHD-ahl-BERT   'adal,be^rt

Adalia
   1. Biblical name   AD-l-Ī-uh, ah-DAHL-yuh   ,ædḷ'aiə, a'daljə
   2. former name for Antalya, *port,*   AHD-l-ē-AH   ,adḷiː'a
     Turkey

Adam
   1. pers. name   AD-uhm   'ædəm
   2. Danish, Polish, Serbo-Croatian   AHD-ahm   'aːdaːm
   3. Dutch   AHD-ahm   'aːdam
   4. French   ah-DAHⁿ   aːdã
   5. German   AHD-ahm   'adam
   6. Russian   uh-DAHM   ə'daːm
   7. Swedish   AH-dahm   'adaːm

Adamah
   Biblical name   AD-uh-muh, AHD-uh-MAH   'ædəmə, ,adə'ma

Adamaoua, Adamawa
   province, Cameroon   AHD-uh-MAH-wuh   ,adə'mawə

Adams
   John, *2nd US president;* John   AD-uhmz   'ædəmz
    Quincy, *6th US president*

Adam's Peak [Samanala]
   sacred mtn., Sri Lanka   AD-uhmz PĒK   'ædəmz 'piːk

'Adan
   governorate, Aden   AHD-ahn   'adan

Adán
   pers. name, Spanish   ah-<u>TH</u>AHN   a'ðan

Adana
   province, city, Turkey   AHD-uh-NAH   ,adə'na

Adapazarı
   city, Turkey   AHD-uh-PAHZ-uh-RUH   ,adə,pazə'rə

Adar
   Jewish month   ah-DAHR, AHD-AHR   a'da^r, 'ad,a^r

Adar Sheni [Veadar]
   Jewish month   ah-DAHR shā-NĒ, SHĀ-nē   a,da^r ʃeː'niː, 'ʃeːni'

Adbeel
   Biblical name   AD-bē-EL, AHD-buh-EL   'ædbiː,el, ,adbə'el

Addams
   Jane, *US social worker (Nobel l931)*   AD-uhmz   'ædəmz

Foreign Sounds: ue: *Fr.* **rue**, *Ger.* **füllen**   uh(r): *Fr.* **boeuf**, *Ger.* **Höhle**   <u>kh</u>: *Ger.* i<u>ch</u>, *Scot.* lo<u>ch</u>   ḡ: *Sp.* ami**g**o   <u>v</u>: *Sp.* ha**b**lar
hl: *Welsh* **Ll**anelli.   CAPITALS: primary stress.   SMALL CAPS: secondary stress.   ⑤: U.S. pron.   ⑥: British pron.

Addan, Addon
Biblical name   AD-ahn, uh-DAHN   'ædɑn, ə'dɑn
Addar
Biblical name   AD-AHR, uh-DAHR   'æd,ɑ^r, ə'dɑ^r
Addi
Biblical name   AD-Ī   'æd,ɑi
Addington
1. pers. name   AD-ing-tuhn   'ædiŋtən
2. Henry, *English politician*   AD-ing-tuhn   'ædiŋtən
Addis Ababa
city, Ethiopia   AD-uhs AB-uh-buh   ˌædəs 'æbəbə
Addison
Joseph, *English author; pers. name*   AD-uh-suhn   'ædəsən
Addon
see Addan
Adela
1. pers. name   AD-l-uh, uh-DĀ-luh, uh-DEL-uh   'ædḷə, ə'deːlə, ə'delə
2. Spanish   ah-T͟HĀ-lah   ɑ'ðeːlɑ
Adelaide
1. port, Australia; pers. name   AD-l-ĀD   'ædḷ,eːd
2. Italian   AHD-ā-LAH-ē-dā   ˌɑde:'lɑi:de:
Adélaïde
pers. name, French   ah-dā-lah-ĒD   ɑːde:lɑːi:d
Adelard
of Bath, English philosopher   AD-l-AHRD   'ædḷ,ɑ^rd
Adelard [Aethelheard]
Mercian cleric   AD-l-AHRD   'ædḷ,ɑ^rd
Adelbert
1. pers. name   AD-l-buhrt, uh-DEL-   'ædḷbə^rt, ə'del-
2. German   AHD-uhl-BERT   'ɑdəl,be^rt
Adele
1. pers. name   uh-DEL   ə'del
2. German   ah-DĀ-luh   ɑ'de:lə
Adèle
1. pers. name   uh-DEL   ə'del
2. French   ah-DEL   ɑːdel
Adélie [Terre Adélie]
Coast *or* Land, *region, Antarctica*   uh-DĀ-lē, ah-DĀ-lē   ə'de:liˑ, ɑ'de:liˑ
Adeline
1. pers. name   AD-l-ĪN, -ĒN, -uhn   'ædḷ,ɑin, -,i:n, -ən
2. Danish   AHD-uh-LĒ-nuh   ˌɑːdə'li:nə
Adelphi
University, *NY*   uh-DEL-FĪ   ə'del,fɑi
Adelung
Johann Christoph, *German grammarian & philologist*   AHD-l-UNG   'ɑdḷ,uŋ
Aden
seaport, gulf, Yemen   AHD-n, ĀD-n, AD-n   'ɑdṇ, 'e:dṇ, 'ædṇ
Adenauer
Konrad, *German statesman*   AHD-n-OW(-uh)r, AD-n-OW(-uh)r   'ɑdṇ,ɑu(ə)^r, 'ædṇ,ɑu(ə)^r
Adeodato
pers. name   AHD-Ā-ō-DAH-tō   ˌɑd,e:oː'dɑtoː
Adeodatus
Christian saint; pope   ĀD-ē-AHD-uht-uhs   ˌe:di:'ɑdəțəs

Key (col. 2):   a: fad   ā: fade   ah: father   ar: marry   aw: law   e: fed   ē: feed   er: merry   i: hid   ī: hide   ō: coat   ōō: boot
oi: boy   ow: now   u: put   uh: above   uhr: bird   ch: chop   ng: ring   sh: show   th: thick   th: this   zh: measure

Ader
1. Clément, French inventor	ah-DER	ɑːder
2. Biblical name	ĀD-uhr, ah-DER	'eːdəʳ, ɑ'deʳ

Adhémar de Monteil [Aimar de Le Puy]
French cleric	ah-dā-MAHR duh mawⁿ-TĀ(Y)	ɑːdeːmɑːr də mɔ̃teː(j)

Adherbal
Numidian ally of Rome	ad-HUHR-buhl	æd'həʳbəl

Adhola
lang., people, Uganda, Kenya	uh-DŌ-luh	ə'doːlə

Adidas
tdmk, athletic wear	uh-DĒD-uhs	ə'diːdəs

Adiel
Biblical name	AD-ē-EL, ĀD-; AHD-ē-EL	'ædiː,el, 'eːd-; ,ɑdiː'el

Adige
river, Italy	AHD-uh-JĀ	'ɑdə,dʒeː

Adin
Biblical name	ĀD-n, Ā-din, ah-DĒN	'eːdn̩, 'eːdin, ɑ'diːn

Adina
Biblical name	AD-n-uh, uh-DĪ-nuh, ah-DĒ-nuh	'ædnə, ə'dainə, ɑ'diːnə

Adirondack
mtn. range, NY	AD-uh-RAHN-DAK	,ædə'rɑn,dæk

Adithaim
Biblical name	AD-uh-THĀ-uhm, AHD-ē-TAH-yim	,ædə'θeːəm, ,ɑdiː'tɑjim

Adjar
see Adzhar

Adlai
pers. name	AD-lā, -lē, -LĪ	'ædleː, -liˑ, -,lai

Adler
pers. name	AD-luhr	'ædləʳ

Admah
Biblical name	AD-mah, AD-muh, ahd-MAH	'ædmɑ, 'ædmə, ɑd'mɑ

Admatha
Biblical name	ad-MĀ-thuh, AD-muh-thuh	æd'meːθə, 'ædməθə

Admete
Samian legendary heroine	ad-MĒT-ē	æd'miːţiˑ

Admetus
Argonaut	ad-MĒT-uhs	æd'miːţəs

Adna
Biblical name	AD-nuh, ahd-NAH	'ædnə, ɑd'nɑ

Adnah
Biblical name	AD-nuh, ahd-NAH	'ædnə, ɑd'nɑ

Adolf
1. pers. name	AD-AHLF, ĀD-AHLF, -AWLF; uh-DAHLF, uh-DAWLF	'æd,ɑlf, 'eːd,ɑlf, -,ɔːlf; ə'dɑlf, ə'dɔːlf
2. Czech, Danish	AH-DAWLF	'ɑː,dɔːlf
3. Dutch, German, Norwegian, Polish, Swedish	AHD-AWLF	'ɑd,ɔːlf
4. Russian	uh-DAWLF	ə'dɔːl̩f

Adolfo
1. pers. name, Italian	ah-DAWL-fō	ɑ'dɔːlfoː
2. Spanish	ah<u>th</u>-AWL-fō	ɑð'ɔːlfoː

Foreign Sounds: ue: *Fr.* **rue**, *Ger.* **füllen**   uh(r): *Fr.* **boeuf**, *Ger.* **Höhle**   kh: *Ger.* **ich**, *Scot.* **loch**   ḡ: *Sp.* **amigo**   v: *Sp.* **hablar**
hl: *Welsh* **Llanelli**.   CAPITALS: primary stress.   SMALL CAPS: secondary stress.   ⑤: U.S. pron.   ⑥: British pron.

Adolph

  1. pers. name — AD-AHLF, ĀD-AHLF, -AWLF; uh-DAHLF, uh-DAWLF — 'æd‚ɑlf, 'eːd‚ɑlf, -‚ɔːlf; ə'dɑlf, ə'dɔːlf

  2. Danish, German — AHD-AWLF — 'ɑd‚ɔːlf

Adolphe

  1. pers. name — AD-AHLF, ĀD-AHLF, -AWLF; uh-DAHLF, uh-DAWLF — 'æd‚ɑlf, 'eːd‚ɑlf, -‚ɔːlf; ə'dɑlf, ə'dɔːlf

  2. French — ah-DAWLF — ɑːdɔːlf

Adolpho

  pers. name, Portuguese — ah-<u>TH</u>AWL-fo͞o — ɑːˈðɔːlfuː

Adolphus

  king of Germany, pers. name — uh-DAWL-fuhs, -DAHL-fuhs — ə'dɔːlfəs, -'dɑlfəs

Adonai

  Hebrew title for God — AD-uh-NĪ, AHD-uh-NOI — ‚ædə'nɑi, ‚ɑdə'nɔi

Adonais

  elegy on Keats by Shelley — AD-n-Ā-uhs, AD-uh-NĀ-uhs — ‚ædņ'eːəs, ‚ædə'neːəs

Adoni-bezek

  Biblical name — AD-uh-NĪ-BĒ-ZEK, AHD-aw-NĒ-BEZ-EK — 'ædə‚nɑi'biː‚zek, ‚ɑdɔː'niː'bez‚ek

Adonijah

  pers. name — AD-uh-NĪ-juh, AD-n-Ī-juh — ‚ædə'nɑidʒə, ‚ædņ'ɑidʒə

Adonikam

  Biblical name — AD-uh-NĪ-kuhm — ‚ædə'nɑikəm

Adoniram

  Biblical name — AD-uh-NĪ-ruhm — ‚ædə'nɑirəm

Adonis

  handsome youth of Greek myth — uh-DAHN-uhs, uh-DŌ-nuhs — ə'dɑnəs, ə'doːnəs

Adoni-zedek

  Biblical name — AD-uh-NĪ-ZĒ-DEK, AHD-aw-NĒT-SED-EK — 'ædə‚nɑi'ziː‚dek, ‚ɑdɔː'niːt'sed‚ek

Adoraim

  Biblical name — AD-uh-RĀ-uhm, AHD-ō-RAH-yim — ‚ædə'reːəm, ‚ɑdɔː'rɑjim

Adoram

  Biblical name — uh-DAWR-ahm, uh-DŌR-ahm — ə'dɔːrɑm, ə'doːrɑm

Adrammelech

  Biblical name — uh-DRAM-uh-LEK, AH-drah-MEL-e<u>kh</u> — ə'dræmə‚lek, ‚ɑdrɑ'melex

Adramyttium

  Biblical name — A-druh-MIT-ē-uhm — ‚ædrə'miṭiːəm

Adrar

  dept., Algeria; region, Mauritania — ah-DRAHR — ɑ'drɑʳ

Adrastus

  Argive king — uh-DRAS-tuhs — ə'dræstəs

Adria

  Biblical name — Ā-drē-uh — 'eːdriːə

Adriaan, Adriaen

  pers. name, Dutch — AH-drē-AHN — 'ɑːdriː‚ɑːn

Adrian

  1. E. D., English physiologist (Nobel 1932); pers. name — Ā-drē-uhn — 'eːdriːən

  2. Dutch — AH-drē-AHN — 'ɑːdriː‚ɑn

  3. German — AHD-rē-AHN — 'ɑdriː‚ɑn

Adriani

  John, *US physician* — Ā-drē-AHN-ē, Ā-drē-AN-ē — ‚eːdriː'ɑni·, ‚eːdriː'æni·

Key (col. 2):   a: f**a**d   ā: f**a**de   ah: f**a**ther   ar: m**a**rry   aw: l**a**w   e: f**e**d   ē: f**ee**d   er: m**e**rry   i: h**i**d   ī: h**i**de   ō: c**oa**t   o͞o: b**oo**t   oi: b**oy**   ow: n**ow**   u: p**u**t   uh: **a**bove   uhr: b**ir**d   ch: **ch**op   ng: ri**ng**   sh: **sh**ow   th: **th**ick   <u>th</u>: **th**is   zh: mea**s**ure

Adriano
  1. pers. name, Italian   AHD-rē-AHN-ō   ˌɑdriːˈɑnoː
  2. Spanish   ah-thrē-AHN-ō   aðriːˈɑnoː
Adrias
  Biblical name   Ā-drē-uhs   ˈeːdriːəs
Adriatic
  Sea, Mediterranean   Ā-drē-AT-ik   ˌeːdriːˈæʈik
Adriel
  Biblical name   Ā-drē-uhl   ˈeːdriːəl
Adrienne
  1. pers. name   Ā-drē-EN, -uhn; Ā-drē-EN   ˈeːdriːˌen, -ən; ˌeːdriːˈen
  2. French   ah-drē-EN   aːdriːen
Adullam
  Biblical name   uh-DUHL-uhm, ah-DŌŌ-LAHM   əˈdələm, aˈduːˌlɑm
Adullamite
  Biblical name   uh-DUHL-uh-MĪT   əˈdələˌmɑit
Adummim
  Biblical name   uh-DUHM-im, AHD-ōō-MĒM   əˈdəmim, ˌɑduːˈmiːm
Adventism
  religion   AD-vent-IZ-uhm, uhd-VENT-IZ-uhm   ˈædventˌizəm, ədˈventˌizəm
Adıyaman
  province, Turkey   AHD-uh-yuh-MAHN   ˌɑdəjəˈmɑn
Adyghe, Adygei
  lang., Europe   UH-DŌŌG-yuh, Ⓢ AHD-uh-GĀ,   ˌəˈduːgjəi, Ⓢ ˈɑdəˌgeː,
                                    AHD-uh-GĀ   ˌɑd̪əˈgeː
Adyukru
  lang., Ivory Coast   uh-DYŌŌ-krōō   əˈdjuːkruː
Adzhar, Adjar
  autonomous republic, Georgia   uh-JAHR   əˈdʒɑ^r
Adzopé
  dept., Ivory Coast   AHD-zō-PĀ, ahd-ZŌ-pä   ˌɑdzoːˈpeː, ɑdˈzoːpeː
Aeacus
  ruler of Myrmidons   Ē-uh-kuhs   ˈiːəkəs
Aeaea
  island home of Circe in the Odyssey   ē-Ē-uh   iːˈiːə
Aechmagoras
  beloved of Heracles   ēk-MAG-uh-ruhs, ek-   iːkˈmægərəs, ek-
Aedilfrid [Aethelfrith]
  Anglo-Saxon ruler   AD-l-FRID, ATH-uhl-   ˈædl̩ˌfrid, ˈæðəl-
Aedon
  woman transformed into nightingale   Ē-DAHN, ā-ĒD-n   ˈiːˌdɑn, eːˈiːdn̩
Aeetes
  father of Medea   ē-Ē-TĒZ, ē-ĒT-ēz   iːˈiːˌtiːz, iːˈiːʈiːz
Aegaeon
  hundred-headed giant   ē-JĒ-uhn, ē-JĒ-AHN   iˈˈdʒiːən, iˈˈdʒiːˌɑn
Aegaleos
  Mt., Greece   ē-GAHL-ē-ŌS, ā-   iˈˈgɑliːˌoːs, eː-
Aegean
  Sea, Mediterranean   i-JĒ-uhn, ē-JĒ-uhn   iˈdʒiːən, iːˈdʒiːən
Aegestes
  son of Aegesta   ē-JES-TĒZ   iˈˈdʒesˌtiːz
Aegeus
  father of Theseus   ē-JĒ-uhs, Ē-JŌŌS   iˈˈdʒiːəs, ˈiːˌdʒuːs

---

Foreign Sounds: ue: *Fr.* **rue**, *Ger.* **füllen**   uh(r): *Fr.* **boeuf**, *Ger.* **Höhle**   kh: *Ger.* **ich**, *Scot.* **loch**   g̃: *Sp.* amigo   v̲: *Sp.* hablar
hl: *Welsh* **Llanelli**.   CAPITALS: primary stress.   SMALL CAPS: secondary stress.   Ⓢ: U.S. pron.   Ⓔ: British pron.

Aegidius
   pers. name   e-GĒD-yus, e-GĒD-ē-us, i-JID-ē-uhs   e'giːdjus, e'giːdiːus, i'dʒidiːəs

Aegina
   Greek island   i-JĪ-nuh   i'dʒainə

Aegir
   Scandinavian sea god   Ā-GIR   'eːˌgiʳ

Aegisthus
   lover of Clytemnestra   ē-JIS-thuhs   iˑ'dʒisθəs

Aegospotami
   ancient battlesite, Thrace   Ē-guh-SPAHT-uh-MĪ   ˌiːgə'spɑṭəˌmɑi

Aegyptus
   ruler of Egypt   ē-JIP-tuhs   iˑ'dʒiptəs

Aelfheah [Alphege, Elphege, Alphage]
   English martyr   ALF-HA-uh<u>kh</u>   'ælfˌhæəx

Aelfled [Aethelflaed]
   Anglo-Saxon ruler, daughter of Alfred the Great   AL-fled   'ælfled

Aelfric
   English abbot   AL-frik, AL-frich   'ælfrik, 'ælfritʃ

Aelius
   pers. name   Ē-lē-uhs   'iːliːəs

Aelius Aristides
   Greek rhetorician   Ē-lē-uhs AR-uh-STĪD-ĒZ   'iːliːəs ˌærə'stɑidˌiːz

Aelle
   Anglo-Saxon ruler   AL-uh   'ælə

Aemilianus
   pers. name   i-MIL-ē-Ā-nuhs   iˌmiliː'eːnəs

Aemilius
   pers. name   i-MIL-ē-uhs, -MIL-yuhs   i'miliːəs, -'miljəs

Aeneas
   Trojan hero; ancestor of Romans   i-NĒ-uhs, ⓔ ē-NĒ-uhs   i'niːəs, ⓔ iː'niːəs

Aeneid
   epic, Vergil   i-NĒ-uhd, ⓔ Ē-nē-uhd   i'niːəd, ⓔ 'iːniːəd

Aenon
   Biblical name   Ē-nuhn, Ē-NAHN   'iːnən, 'iːˌnɑn

Aeolia
   island of Aeolus   ē-Ō-lē-uh, ā-Ō-lē-uh   iː'oːliːə, eː'oːliːə

Aeolian
   musical mode; ancient Greek people   ē-Ō-lē-uhn, ā-Ō-lē-uhn   iː'oːliːən, eː'oːliːən

Aeolic
   Aeolian   ē-AHL-ik   iː'ɑlik

Aeolis
   coastal region, Asia Minor   Ē-uh-luhs   'iːələs

Aeolus
   Greek god of wind   Ē-uh-luhs   'iːələs

Aepytus
   son of Merope   ē-PĒT-uhs   iˑ'piːṭəs

Aerhatai Shan [Altay]
   town, Mongolia   AH-UHR-HAH-TĪ SHAHN   'ɑ'əʳha'tai 'ʃan

A-erh-chin Shan-mo [Altun Shan]
   mtn. range, Tibet, China   AH-UHR-JIN-SHAHN-MŌ   'ɑ'əʳ'dʒin'ʃan'moː

Aer Lingus
   Irish airline   AR-LING-guhs, ER-   ˌæʳ'liŋgəs, ˌeʳ-

Key (col. 2):   a: fad   ā: fade   ah: father   ar: marry   aw: law   e: fed   ē: feed   er: merry   i: hid   ī: hide   ō: coat   ōō: boot
oi: boy   ow: now   u: put   uh: above   uhr: bird   ch: chop   ng: ring   sh: show   th: thick   <u>th</u>: this   zh: measure

Aeroflot
   Russian airline   AR-uh-FLAWT, ER-, -FLŌT   'ærə͵flɔːt, 'er-, -͵flɔːt
Aeromexico
   Mexican airline   Ī-rō-MĀ-hi-kō   ͵airoː'meˑhikoː
Aerope
   mother of Agamemnon and Menelaus   ā-ER-uh-pē, IR-uh-pē   eː'erəpiˑ, 'irəpiˑ
Aerospatiale
   French aircraft co.   ah-ā-raw-spahs-YAHL   aːeːrɔːspaːsjaːl
Aeschines
   Athenian orator   ES-ki-NĒZ, ⓔ Ē-ski-   'eski͵niːz, ⓔ 'iːski-
Aeschylus
   Greek tragedian   ES-kuh-luhs, ⓔ Ē-skuh-   'eskələs, ⓔ 'iːskə-
Aesculapian
   pert. to Aesculapius   ES-k(y)uh-LĀ-pē-uhn, ⓔ ĒS-   ͵esk(j)ə'leːpiːən, ⓔ ͵iːs-
Aesculapius [Asclepius]
   Greek god of medicine   ES-k(y)uh-LĀ-pē-uhs, ⓔ ĒS-   ͵esk(j)ə'leːpiːəs, ⓔ ͵iːs-
Æsir
   Scandinavian gods   Ā-ZIR, Ā-SIR   'eː͵ziʳ, 'eː͵siʳ
Aeson
   father of Jason   Ē-suhn   'iːsən
Aesop
   Greek fablist   Ē-SAHP, Ē-suhp   'iː͵sɑp, 'iːsəp
Aesopian
   pert. to Aesop   ē-SŌ-pē-uhn, ē-SAHP-ē-uhn   iː'soːpiːən, iː'sɑpiːən
Aethalides
   Argonaut   ē-THAL-uh-DĒZ   iˑ'θælə͵diːz
Aethelbald
   Anglo-Saxon king of Mercia   ATH-uhl-BAWLD, ATH-   'æðəl͵bɔːld, 'æθ-
Aethelflaed [Ethelfleda, Aelfled]
   Anglo-Saxon ruler, daughter of Alfred   ATH-uhl-FLAD, ATH-   'æðəl͵flæd, 'æθ-
   the Great
Aethelfrith [Ethelfrith, Etelfrid, Aedilfrid]
   Anglo-Saxon ruler   ATH-uhl-FRITH, ATH-   'æðəl͵friθ, 'æθ-
Aethelheard [Ethelhard, Adelard, Edelred]
   Mercian cleric   ATH-uhl-HA(-uh)rd, ATH-   'æðəl͵hæ(ə)ʳd, 'æθ-
Aether
   personification of the upper sky   Ē-thuhr   'iːθəʳ
Aethra
   mother of Theseus   Ē-thruh   'iːθrə
Aëtius
   Syrian heretic   ā-Ē-shē-uhs   eː'iːʃiːəs
Aetna
   1. US insurance co.   ET-nuh   'etnə
   2. see Etna
Aetolia
   dept, Greece   ē-TŌL-yuh, ē-TŌ-lē-uh   iː'toːljə, iː'toːliːə
Aetolian League
   ancient Greek alliance   ē-TŌ-lē-uhn   iː'toːliːən
Aetolus
   son of Endymion   ē-TŌ-luhs, ĒT-l-uhs   iˑ'toːləs, 'iːtləs
Afar [Danakil]
   lang., people, E. Africa   AH-FAHR   'ɑ͵fɑʳ

Foreign Sounds: ue: *Fr.* **rue**, *Ger.* **füllen**   uh(r): *Fr.* **bœuf**, *Ger.* **Höhle**   <u>kh</u>: *Ger.* i<u>ch</u>, *Scot.* lo<u>ch</u>   g̱: *Sp.* ami**g**o   <u>v</u>: *Sp.* ha**b**lar
hl: *Welsh* **Ll**anelli.   CAPITALS: primary stress.   SMALL CAPS: secondary stress.   ⓢ: U.S. pron.   ⓔ: British pron.

Afars and Issas		
former name for Djibouti	AHF-AHRZ uhn(d) ē-SAHZ	'af₁aʳz ən(d) iː'sɑz
Affenpinscher		
dog breed	AF-uhn-PIN-chuhr	'æfən₁pintʃəʳ
Affleck		
Thomas, *American cabinetmaker*	AF-LEK	'æf₁lek
Affligem Tripel		
Belgian beer	AHF-liğ-uhm TRIP-uhl	'afliɣəm 'tripəl
Afghan		
resident of Afghanistan; lang.	AF-GAN	'æf₁gæn
Afghanistan		
republic, Asia	af-GAN-uh-STAN	æf'gænə₁stæn
AFL-CIO		
labor organization	Ā-EF-EL-SĒ-Ī-Ō	₁eː₁ef'el₁siː₁ai'oː
Afonso		
king of Portugal	uh-FAWⁿ(N)-sōō	ə'fɔ̃(n)suː
Afra		
pers. name	AF-ruh	'æfrə
Afrânio		
pers. name, Portuguese	uh-FRAHN-yōō, ah-	ə'frɑːnjuː, ɑː-
Africa		
continent	AF-ri-kuh	'æfrikə
African		
pert. to Africa	AF-ri-kuhn	'æfrikən
Africanus		
pers. name	AF-ri-KĀ-nuhs	₁æfri'keːnəs
Afrikaans		
lang., S. Africa	AF-ri-KAHN(T)S, AF-ri-KAHNZ	₁æfri'kan(t)s, ₁æfri'kɑnz
Afrikander, Africander		
cattle	AF-ri-KAN-duhr	₁æfri'kændəʳ
Afrikaner		
speaker of Afrikaans	AF-ri-KAHN-uhr	₁æfri'kɑnəʳ
Afro-		
a combining form meaning African	AF-rō	'æfroː
AFSCME		
American Federation of State,	AF-skmē	'æfskmi·
County, and Municipal Employees		
Afusare		
lang., Nigeria	AF-yōō-SAHR-ē	₁æfjuˑ'sɑri·
Afyon		
city, Turkey	ahf-YŌN	ɑf'joːn
Afyonkarahısar		
prov., Turkey	ahf-YŌN-KAHR-uh-huh-SAHR	ɑf'joːn₁kɑrəhə'sɑːʳ
Afzelius		
Arvid August, *Swedish folklorist*	ahv-SĀ-lē-uhs	ɑːv'seːliːəs
Agabus		
Biblical name	AG-uh-buhs	'ægəbəs
Agadez		
city, dept., Niger	AG-uh-DES	₁ægə'des
Agadir		
port, prefecture, Morocco	AHG-uh-DIR	₁agə'diʳ
Agag		
Amelekite king	Ā-GAG	'eː₁gæg
Agagite		
Biblical name	Ā-guh-GĪT	'eːgə₁gait

Key (col. 2):   a: fad   ā: fade   ah: father   ar: marry   aw: law   e: fed   ē: feed   er: merry   i: hid   ī: hide   ō: coat   ōō: boot
oi: boy   ow: now   u: put   uh: above   uhr: bird   ch: chop   ng: ring   sh: show   th: thick   th̲: this   zh: measure

Aga Khan
head of Shi'ism   AHG-uh K͟HAHN, KAHN   ˌɑgə ˈxɑn, ˈkɑn

Agamedes
legendary architect   AG-uh-MĒ-DĒZ   ˌægəˈmiːˌdiːz

Agamemnon
leader of Greeks against Trojans   AG-uh-MEM-NAHN, AG-uh-MEM-nuhn   ˌægəˈmemˌnɑn, ˌægəˈmemnən

Agaña
town, Guam   uh-GAHN-yuh   əˈgɑnjə

Agapetus, Agapitus
papal name   AG-uh-PĒT-uhs   ˌægəˈpiːʈəs

Agar
1. *lang., Sudan, Ethiopia*   AH-GAHR   ˈɑˌgɑʳ
2. Herbert Sebastian, *American writer*   Ā-GAHR   ˈeːˌgɑʳ
3. *Biblical name*   Ā-GAHR   ˈeːˌgɑʳ
4. *seaweed derivative*   AHG-uhr   ˈɑgəʳ

Agartala
city, India   UHG-uhr-tuh-LAH   ˌəgəʳtəˈlɑ

Agassi
Andre, *US tennis player*   AG-uh-sē   ˈægəsiˑ

Agassiz
Louis, *US naturalist; lake, Canada*   AG-uh-sē   ˈægəsiˑ

Agatha
pers. name   AG-uh-thuh   ˈægəθə

Agathe
1. *pers. name, French*   ah-GAHT   ɑːgɑːt
2. *German*   ah-GAH-tuh   ɑˈgatə

Agatho
pope   AG-uh-THŌ   ˈægəˌθoː

Agathocles
tyrant of Syracuse   uh-GATH-uh-KLĒZ   əˈgæθəˌkliːz

Agathon
1. *Greek poet, playwright*   AG-uh-THAHN   ˈægəˌθɑn
2. *pers. name, French*   ah-gah-TAW[n]   ɑːgɑːtɔ̃

Agave
daughter of Cadmus   uh-GAHV-ē   əˈgɑviˑ

Agboville
dept., Ivory Coast   AHG-bō-VĒL   ˌɑgboːˈviːl

Agdistis
hermaphrodite in Greek myth   ag-DIS-tuhs   ægˈdistəs

Agee
James, *US writer*   Ā-jē   ˈeːdʒiˑ

Agen
city, France   ah-ZHE[n]   ɑʒẽ

Agenais [Agenois]
historical region, France   ah-zhuh-NĀ   ɑʒəneˑ

Agenois [Agenais]
historical region, France   ah-zhuhn-WAH   ɑʒənwɑ

Agenor
1. *father of Europa, Cadmus, Phoenix, Cilix*   uh-GEN-AWR, uh-GĀ-NAWR   əˈgenˌɔːʳ, əˈgeːˌnɔːʳ
2. *pers. name, German*   ah-GĀ-NAWR   ɑˈgeːˌnɔːʳ

Agénor
pers. name, French   ah-zhā-NAWR   ɑːʒeːnɔːr

Ager
  Milton, *American songwriter*   Ā-juhr   'eːdʒəʳ
Ageratum
  plant   AJ-uh-RĀT-uhm   ˌædʒəˈreːţəm
Agesilaus
  name, Spartan kings   ˌ uh-JES-uh-LĀ-uhs   əˌdʒesəˈleːəs
Agfa
  tdmk for photographic film   AG-fuh   'ægfə
Aggada, the [Haggadah]
  part of Jewish Talmud   uh-GAHD-uh, uh-GAWD-uh, ah-;   əˈgɑdə, əˈgɔːdə, ɑ-; ɑgəˈdɑ
                                              ahg-uh-DAH
Aggershus
  see Akershus
Aggeus
  Old Testament book   a-GĒ-uhs   æˈgiːəs
Aggies
  Texas A&M team   AG-ēz   'ægiˑz
Āghā Mohammad Khān
  shah, Iran, founder of Qājār dynasty   ah-GAH mō-HAM-uhd K̲HAHN,   ɑˈgɑː moːˈhæməd 'xɑn,
                                              mō-HAH-mahd, KAHN   moːˈhɑːmɑːd, 'kɑn
Agheila, El [Al-Agheila]
  town, Libya; WWII battle site   EL uh-GĀ-luh   ˌel əˈgeːlə
Aghlabid
  Arab dynasty   AHG̲-luh-BID   'ɑɣləˌbid
Aghrim
  see Aughrim
Agin-Buryat
  district, Russia   uh-GYĒN-bur-YAHT   əˌgjiːnburˈjɑt
Agincourt
  village, France, battle site, 1415   AJ-uhn-KAWR(T), AZH-   'ædʒənˌkɔːʳ(t), 'æʒ-
Aginnum
  ancient name for Agen   uh-JIN-uhm   əˈdʒinəm
Aginskoye
  town, Russia   uh-GĒN-skuh-yuh   əˈgiːnskəjə
Agis
  Spartan king   Ā-juhs   'eːdʒəs
Aglaia
  one of the Graces   uh-GLĪ-uh, uh-GLĀ-uh   əˈglɑiə, əˈgleːə
Agnes
  1. pers. name   AG-nuhs   'ægnəs
  2. German   AHG-nes   'ɑgnes
  3. Norwegian   AHNG-nuhs   'ɑŋnəs
Agnès
  pers. name, French   ahn-YES   ɑːnjes
Agnesi
  Maria Gaetana, *Italian*   ahn-YĀ-zē   ɑnˈjeːziˑ
    mathematician
Agnew
  Spiro T., *US politician*   AG-N(Y)O̅O̅   'ægˌn(j)uː
Agnoetism
  early Christian sect   AG-nō-ĒT-IZ-uhm, AG-nō-ĒT-IZ-uhm   ˌægnoːˈiːţˌizəm,
                                                                                             'ægnoːˌiːţˌizəm
Agno
  river, Philippines   AHG-nō   'ɑgnoː

Key (col. 2):   a: fad ā: fade ah: father ar: marry aw: law e: fed ē: feed er: merry i: hid ī: hide ō: coat o̅o̅: boot
oi: boy ow: now u: put uh: above uhr: bird ch: chop ng: ring sh: show th: thick <u>th</u>: this zh: measure

Agnolo
  pers. name   AHN-yō-lō   'anjoːloː

Agnon
  S. Y., *Israeli author (Nobel 1966)*   AG-NAHN, AHG-NAHN   'ægˌnɑn, 'ɑgˌnɑn

Agnus Dei
  Christian symbol ("Lamb of God");   AHG-NUS DĀ(-ē), AHG-N$\overline{OO}$S,   ˌɑgˌnus 'deː(iː), ˌɑgˌnuːs,
    section of the Mass   AHN-Y$\overline{OO}$S, AG-nuhs   ˌɑnˌjuːs, ˌægnəs

Agobard
  saint, Frankish cleric   ah-gō-BAHR   ɑːgoːbɑːr

Agonistes
  see Samson Agonistes

Agostinho
  pers. name, Portuguese   uh-g$\overline{oo}$sh-TĒN-y$\overline{oo}$, AH-g$\overline{oo}$s-   əguːʃ'tiːnjuː, ˌɑːguːs-

Agostino
  pers. name, Italian   AHG-ō-STĒ-nō   ˌagoː'stiːnoː

Agoult
  Marie Catherine Sophie d',   ah-G$\overline{OO}$ ɑːguː
    (pseudonym Daniel Stern*), French*
    writer

Agra
  city, India, site of Taj Mahal   AHG-ruh   'agrə

Agricola
  pers. name   uh-GRIK-uh-luh   ə'grikələ

Ağrı Dağı [Ararat]
  mtn., Turkey   AHĞ-rē dah-ḠĒ   ˌɑɣriː dɑ'ɣiː

Agrigenetics
  US corp.   AG-ruh-juh-NET-iks, AG-rē-   ˌægrədʒə'neţiks, ˌægriˈ-

Agrigento
  town, prov, Italy   AHG-ri-JEN-tō   ˌagri'dʒentoː

Agrippa
  1. Marcus Vipsanius, *Roman*   uh-GRIP-uh   ə'gripə
    statesman; pers. name
  2. French   ah-grē(p)-PAH   ɑːgriː(p)pɑː

Agrippina
  Roman pers. name   AG-ruh-PĒ-nuh, AG-ruh-PĪ-nuh   ˌægrə'piːnə, ˌægrə'painə

Agronsky
  Martin, *TV commentator*   uh-GRAHN-skē   ə'grɑnskiˈ

Agua Caliente Band
  N. American people   AHG-wuh kahl-YEN-tā   'ɑgwə kɑl'jenteː

Aguacatec
  lang., Guatemala   uh-GWAH-kuh-TEK   ə'gwɑkəˌtek

Aguascalientes
  city, state, Mexico   ahğ-wah-skahl-YEN-tās   ɑɣwɑskɑl'jenteːs

Aguecheek
  Sir Andrew, *character in* Twelfth   Ā-gy$\overline{oo}$-CHĒK   'eːgjuˈˌtʃiːk
    Night, *Shakespeare*

Aguila
  Spanish beer   ah-GĒ-lah   ɑ'giːla

Aguinaldo
  Emilio, *Philippine leader*   ah-gē-NAHL-dō   ɑgiː'nɑldoː

Agung, Gunung
  volcano, Indonesia   G$\overline{OO}$-nung AH-gung   'guːnuŋ 'ɑːguŋ

Agur
  Biblical name   Ā-guhr, AHG-$\overline{oo}$r   'eːgəʳ, 'aguːʳ

Foreign Sounds: ue: *Fr.* rue, *Ger.* füllen   uh(r): *Fr.* boeuf, *Ger.* Höhle   <u>kh</u>: *Ger.* ich, *Scot.* loch   ğ: *Sp.* amigo   y: *Sp.* hablar
hl: *Welsh* Llanelli.   CAPITALS: primary stress.   SMALL CAPS: secondary stress. $: U.S. pron.   £: British pron.

Agusan
river, former province, Philippines   ah-G$\overline{OO}$-SAHN   ɑ'guː‚sɑn

Agulhas
cape, southern tip of Africa   uh-GUHL-uhs   ə'gələs

Agustín
pers. name   ah-g$\overline{oo}$s-TĒN   ɑguːs'tiːn

Ahab
king of Israel; character in Moby Dick, *H. Melville*   Ā-HAB   'eː‚hæb

Ahad Ha-Am
pseudonym of Asher Ginsberg, *Zionist leader*   ah<u>kh</u>-AHD <u>kh</u>ah-AHM   ɑx‚ɑd xɑ'ɑm

Ahaggar [Hoggar]
mtn. range, Algeria   uh-HAHG-uhr, AH-huh-GAHR   ə'hɑgər, ‚ɑhə'gɑr

Aha of Shabḥa
rabbi & scholar   AH<u>KH</u>-ah uhv SHAHB-<u>KH</u>AH   'ɑxɑ əv 'ʃɑb‚xɑ

Aharah
Biblical name   uh-HER-uh, AH<u>KH</u>-RAH<u>KH</u>   ə'herə, 'ɑx‚rɑx

Aharhel
Biblical name   uh-HAHR-huhl, AH<u>KH</u>-ahr-<u>KH</u>EL   ə'hɑrhəl, ‚ɑxɑr'xel

Ahasai
Biblical name   uh-HĀ-SĪ, -SĀ; AH<u>KH</u>-ZĪ   ə'heː‚sɑi, -‚seː; 'ɑx‚zɑi

Ahasbai
Biblical name   uh-HAZ-BĪ, ah-<u>KH</u>AHS-BĪ   ə'hæz‚bɑi, ɑ'xɑs‚bɑi

Ahasuerus [Xerxes]
King of Persia   Ā-HAZ-y$\overline{oo}$-IR-uhs, Ā-HAZ-y$\overline{oo}$-ER-uhs   ‚eː‚hæzjuː'irəs, ‚eː‚hæzjuː'erəs

Ahava
Biblical name   uh-HĀ-vuh, AH-hahv-AH   ə'heːvə, ‚ɑhɑv'ɑ

Ahaz
King of Judah   Ā-HAZ   'eː‚hæz

Ahaziah [Ochozias]
Biblical king   Ā-(h)uh-ZĪ-uh, AH<u>KH</u>-ahz-YAH-h$\overline{oo}$ ‚eː(h)ə'zaiə, ‚ɑxɑz'jɑhuː

Ahban
Biblical name   AHB-AN, AH<u>KH</u>-BAHN   'ɑb‚æn, 'ɑx‚bɑn

Ahenobarbus
Roman cognomen   uh-HĒ-nuh-BAHR-buhs, uh-HEN-uh-, uh-HĀ-nuh-   ə‚hiːnə'bɑʳbəs, ə‚henə-, ə‚heːnə-

Aher
Biblical name   Ā-(h)uhr, ah-<u>KH</u>ER   'eː(h)əʳ, ɑ'xeʳ

Aherne
pers. name   uh-HUHRN, Ā-HUHRN   ə'həʳn, 'eː‚həʳn

Ahi
Biblical name   Ā-HĪ, ah-<u>KH</u>Ē   'eː‚hɑi, ɑ'xiː

Ahiah, Ahijah
Biblical name   uh-HĪ-uh, ah-<u>KH</u>Ē-yuh   ə'hɑiə, ɑ'xiːjə

Ahiam
Biblical name   uh-HĪ-uhm, AH<u>KH</u>-ē-AHM   ə'hɑiəm, ‚ɑxiː'ɑm

Ahian
Biblical name   uh-HĪ-uhn, ah<u>kh</u>-YAHN   ə'hɑiən, ɑx'jɑn

Ahiezer
Biblical name   Ā-HĪ-Ē-zuhr, ah-HĪ-uh-ZER, ah<u>kh</u>-ē-EZ-er   ‚eː‚hɑi'iːzəʳ, ɑ'hɑiə‚zeʳ, ɑxiː'ezer

Ahihud
Biblical name   uh-HĪ-HUD, AH<u>KH</u>-ē-H$\overline{OO}$D   ə'hɑi‚hud, ‚ɑxiː'huːd

---

Key (col. 2):   a: fad   ā: fade   ah: father   ar: marry   aw: law   e: fed   ē: feed   er: merry   i: hid   ī: hide   ō: coat $\overline{oo}$: boot
oi: boy   ow: now   u: put   uh: above   uhr: bird   ch: chop   ng: ring   sh: show   th: thick   <u>th</u>: this   zh: measure

Ahikam
Biblical name   uh-HĪ-KAM, AH<u>KH</u>-ē-KAHM   ə'hai͵kæm, ͵axiː'kɑm

Ahilud
Biblical name   uh-HĪ-luhd, AH<u>KH</u>-ē-L̄OOD   ə'hailəd, ͵axiː'luːd

Ahimaaz
Biblical name   uh-HIM-uh-AZ, Ā-hī-MAH-AZ, AH<u>KH</u>-ē-MAH-AHTS   ə'himə͵æz, ͵eːhai'mɑ͵æz, ͵axiː'mɑ͵ats

Ahiman
Biblical name   uh-HĪ-muhn, AH<u>KH</u>-ē-MAHN   ə'haimən, ͵axiː'mɑn

Ahimelech
Biblical name   uh-HIM-uh-LEK, AH<u>KH</u>-ē-MEL-E<u>KH</u>   ə'himə͵lek, ͵axiː'mel͵ex

Ahimoth
Biblical name   uh-HĪ-muhth, uh-HĪ-MAWTH ah<u>kh</u>-ē-MŌT   ə'haiməθ, ə'hai͵mɔːθ axiː'moːt

Ahinadab
Biblical name   uh-HIN-uh-DAB, AH<u>KH</u>-ē-nah-DAHV   ə'hinə͵dæb, ͵axiːnɑ'dɑv

Ahinoam
Biblical name   uh-HIN-ō-AM, AH<u>KH</u>-ē-nō-AHM   ə'hinoː͵æm, ͵axiːnoː'ɑm

Ahio
Biblical name   uh-HĪ-ō, AH<u>KH</u>-yō   ə'haioː, 'axjoː

Ahira
Biblical name   uh-HĪ-ruh, ah-<u>KHĒ</u>-rah   ə'hairə, ɑ'xiːrɑ

Ahiram
Biblical name   uh-HĪ-ruhm, ah-<u>KHĒ</u>-RAHM   ə'hairəm, ɑ'xiː͵rɑm

Ahiramite
Biblical name   uh-HĪ-ruh-MĪT   ə'hairə͵mait

Ahisamach
Biblical name   uh-HIZ-uh-MAK, ah-<u>KHĒ</u>-sah-MAH<u>KH</u>   ə'hizə͵mæk, ɑ'xiːsɑ͵mɑx

Ahishahar
Biblical name   uh-HĪ-shā-HAHR, uh-HISH-uh-HAHR, ah-<u>KHĒ</u>-shah-<u>KH</u>AHR   ə'haiʃeː͵haʳ, ə'hiʃə͵haʳ, ɑ'xiːʃɑ͵xar

Ahishar
Biblical name   uh-HĪ-SHAHR, ah-<u>KHĒ</u>-SHAHR   ə'hai͵ʃaʳ, ɑ'xiː͵ʃar

Ahithophel
Biblical name   uh-HITH-uh-FEL, ah-<u>KHĒ</u>T-ō-FEL   ə'hiθə͵fel, ɑ'xiːțoː͵fel

Ahitub
Biblical name   uh-HĪT-uhb, ah-<u>KHĒ</u>-TUV   ə'haițəb, ɑ'xiː͵tuv

Ahlab
Biblical name   AHL-AB, AH<u>KH</u>-LAHV   'al͵æb, 'ax͵lav

Ahlai
Biblical name   AHL-ā-Ī, AH<u>KH</u>-LĪ   'aleː͵ai, 'ax͵lai

Ahmad
pers. name, Arabic   AHM-ahd, AHM-ad   'amɑd, 'amæd

Ahmadabad
city, state, India   AHM-uhd-uh-BAHD   'amədə͵bad

Aḥmad Khān Abdāli
orig. name of Aḥmad Shāh Durrānī   AH<u>KH</u>-mahd <u>KH</u>AHN ahb-DAHL-ē, KAHN   ͵axmad ͵xan ab'dali·, ͵kan

Ahmadnagar, Ahmednagar
district, city, India   AH-muhd-NUHG-uhr   ͵aːməd'nəgəʳ

Ahmadpur East
city, Pakistan   AH-muhd-PUR ĒST   'aːməd͵pur 'iːst

Aḥmad Shāh Durrāni
founder, Afghanistan   AH<u>KH</u>-mahd SHAH dur-AHN-ē   ͵axmad ͵ʃa dur'ɑni·

Foreign Sounds: ue: *Fr.* **rue**, *Ger.* **füllen**   uh(r): *Fr.* **boeuf**, *Ger.* **Höhle**   kh: *Ger.* **ich**, *Scot.* **loch**   g̱: *Sp.* ami**g**o   v̱: *Sp.* ha**b**lar
hl: *Welsh* **Ll**anelli.   CAPITALS: primary stress.   SMALL CAPS: secondary stress.   Ⓢ: U.S. pron.   Ⓔ: British pron.

Ahmed

1. pers. name	AHM-uhd	'aməd
2. Albanian	ah<u>kh</u>-MED	ax'med
3. Arabic	AHM-ed	'amed
4. Turkish	ah-MET	a'met

Ahmed Korei [Abu Alaa]

Palestinian politician	AH<u>KH</u>-med kawr-Ā	'axmed kɔːr'eː

Ahmet

pers. name, Turkish	ah-MET	a'met

Ahmose

Egyptian pharaoh	AHM-ŌS	'am‚oːs

Ahoah

Biblical name	uh-HŌ-uh, ah<u>kh</u>-Ō-AH<u>KH</u>	ə'hoːə, ax'oː‚ax

Ahohite

Biblical name	uh-HŌ-HĪT	ə'hoː‚hait

Aholah

Biblical name	uh-HŌ-luh, AH-hō-LAH	ə'hoːlə, ‚ahoː'la

Aholiab

Biblical name	uh-HŌ-lē-AB, ah-HŌ-lē-AHV	ə'hoːliː‚æb, a‚hoːliː'av

Aholibah [Aholah]

Biblical name	uh-HŌ-lē-buh, ah-HŌ-lē-VAH	ə'hoːli·bə, a'hoːliː‚va

Aholibamah

Biblical name	uh-HŌ-lē-BĀ-muh, ah-HŌ-li-VAHM-ah	ə‚hoːli·'beːmə, a‚hoːli'vama

Ahuachapán

department, El Salvador	AH-wuh-chuh-PAHN	‚awətʃə'pan

Ahumai

Biblical name	uh-H(Y)OO̅-MĪ, uh-H(Y)OO̅-mā-Ī, ah-<u>KH</u>OO̅-MĪ	ə'h(j)uː‚mai, ə'h(j)uːmeː‚ai, a'xu‚mai

Ahuntsic

College, CT	uh-HUHN(T)-sik	ə'hən(t)sik

Ahura Mazda

Zoroastrian god	uh-HUR-uh MAHZ-duh, AH-HUR-uh	ə'hurə 'mazdə, 'a‚hurə

Ahuzam, Ahuzzam

Biblical name	uh-H(Y)OO̅-ZAM, AH<u>KH</u>-oo̅-ZAHM	ə'h(j)uː‚zæm, ‚axuː'zam

Ahuzzath

Biblical name	uh-HUHZ-uhth, AH<u>KH</u>-oo̅-ZAHT	ə'həzəθ, ‚axuː'zat

Ahvāz, Ahwaz

city, district, Iran	ah-WAHZ	a'waz

Ahvenanmaa [Åland]

Finnish islands, Baltic Sea	AH<u>KH</u>-vuh-nahn-MAH	'axvənan‚ma

Ahzai

Biblical name	AHZ-Ī, AH<u>KH</u>-Ī	'az‚ai, 'ax‚ai

Ai

Biblical name	Ā-Ī, Ī	'eː‚ai, 'ai

Aiah, Aijah [Ajah]

Biblical name	ā-Ī-(y)uh, Ī-(Y)AH, AH-yah	eː'ai(j)ə, 'ai‚(j)a, 'aja

Aiaru

Babylonian month	Ī-AHR-oo̅	ai'aruː

Aiath

Biblical name	ā-Ī-uhth, Ā-YATH, Ī-yaht	eː'aiəθ, 'eː‚jæθ, 'aijat

Aibak

see Āybak		

Aichi

prefecture, Japan	Ī-chē	aitʃiː

Key (col. 2):   a: f**a**d   ā: f**a**de   ah: f**a**ther   ar: m**a**rry   aw: l**a**w   e: f**e**d   ē: f**ee**d   er: m**e**rry   i: h**i**d   ī: h**i**de   ō: c**oa**t   oo̅: b**oo**t
oi: b**oy**   ow: n**ow**   u: p**u**t   uh: **a**bove   uhr: b**i**rd   ch: **ch**op   ng: ri**ng**   sh: **sh**ow   th: **th**ick   <u>th</u>: **th**is   zh: mea**s**ure

Aïda
  opera, Verdi   ī-ĒD-uh   ɑiˈiːdə

Aidan
  pers. name   ĀD-n   ˈeːdn̩

Aidin
  see Aydın

AIDS
  Acquired Immune Deficiency   ĀDZ   ˈeːdz
    Syndrome

Aiello
  Danny, *US entertainer*   ī-(Y)EL-ō   ɑiˈ(j)eloː

Ai-hui [Taheiho]
  town, China   Ī-HWĒ   ˈɑiˈhwiː

Aija
  Biblical name   ā-Ī-juh, Ī-juh, AH-yah   eːˈɑidʒə, ˈɑidʒə, ˈɑja

Aijalon
  Biblical name   Ā-juh-LAHN, AH-yah-LŌN   ˈeːdʒəˌlɑn, ˌɑjaˈloːn

Aijeleth shahar
  Biblical name   Ā-je-LETH SHĀ-HAHR, ah-YEL-et   ˈeːdʒeˌleθ ˈʃeːˌhɑʳ, aˈjelet
     shah-<u>KH</u>AHR   ʃaˈxɑʳ

Aiken
  Howard H., *scientist; county, city,*   Ā-kuhn   ˈeːkən
    SC; Technical College, *SC; pers.*
    name

Aikins
  Claude, *US actor*   Ā-kuhnz   ˈeːkənz

Aikman
  Troy, *US football player*   ĀK-muhn   ˈeːkmən

Aileen
  pers. name   ī-LĒN   ɑiˈliːn

Ailette
  river, France   ā-LET   eːlet

Ailey
  Alvin, Jr., *US dancer, choreographer*   Ā-lē   ˈeːliˑ

Aimar de Le Puy [Adhémar de Monteil]
  French cleric   em-ahr duh luh PWĒ   emɑr də lə pɥiː

Aimé, Aimee, Aimée
  1. pers. name   ā-MĀ, em-Ā   eːˈmeː, emˈeː
  2. French   em-Ā   emeː

Ain
  1. department, river, France   Eⁿ   ẽ
  2. Biblical name   Ā-in, ĀN   ˈeːin, ˈeːn

Aino
  1. lang., people, Japan   Ī-nō   ˈɑinoː
  2. pers. name, Finnish   Ī-naw   ˈɑinɔː

Ainslie
  Hew, *Scottish-born American poet*   ĀNZ-lē   ˈeːnzliˑ

Ainsworth
  city, IA, NE   ĀNZ-WUHRTH   ˈeːnzˌwəʳθ

Aintree
  town, England; site of Grand   ĀN-trē   ˈeːntriˑ
    National steeplechase

Ainu [Aino]
  lang., people, Japan   Ī-no͞o   ˈɑinuː

Foreign Sounds: ue: *Fr.* r**ue**, *Ger.* f**ü**llen   uh(r): *Fr.* b**oeuf**, *Ger.* H**öh**le   <u>kh</u>: *Ger.* i**ch**, *Scot.* lo**ch**   ḡ: *Sp.* ami**g**o   v̱: *Sp.* ha**b**lar
hl: *Welsh* L**l**anelli.   CAPITALS: primary stress.   SMALL CAPS: secondary stress.   Ⓢ: U.S. pron.   Ⓔ: British pron.

Aïoun el Atrous		
city, Mauritania	ah-Y$\overline{OO}$N el ah-TR$\overline{OO}$S	ɑ'juːn el ɑ'truːs
Aïr [Asben, Azbine]		
region, Niger	ah-IR, ER, AR	ɑ'i^r, 'e^r, 'æ^r
Aird		
Sir John, *British builder of Aswan dam*	ERD, ARD	'e^{r}d, 'æ^{r}d
Aire		
1. river, England	AR, ER	'æ^r, 'e^r
2. river, France	ER, [S] AR	er, [S] 'æ^r, 'e^r
Airedale		
dog breed	AR-DĀL, ER-DĀL	'æ^{r}ˌdeːl, 'e^{r}ˌdeːl
Aisén, Aysen		
region, former province, Chile	Ī-SĀN, Ī-SEN	ɑi'seːn, ɑi'sen
Aisha		
pers. name	Ā-shuh, Ī-shuh, ah-Ē-shuh	'eːʃə, 'ɑiʃə, ɑ'iːʃə
Aisne		
river, dept, France	EN, [S] ĀN	en, [S] 'eːn
Aitken, Aitkin		
pers. name	ĀT-kuhn, Ā-kuhn	'eːtkən, 'eːkən
Aitkin		
county, MN	Ā-kuhn	'eːkən
Aiun, Aaiun [Aaiu'n, El]		
town, W Sahara	Ī-$\overline{OO}$N	ɑi'uːn
Aius Locutius		
a divine voice	Ā-(y)uhs lō-KY$\overline{OO}$-shuhs	'eː(j)əs loː'kjuːʃəs
Aiwa		
audio equipment co.	Ī-wuh, Ā-wuh	'ɑiwə, 'eːwə
Aix-en-Provence		
city, France	ĀK-SAH^n-prō-VAH^{n}S	ˌe·kˌsɑ̃proː'vɑ̃s
Aix-la-Chapelle		
city, Germany	ĀK-slah-shuh-PEL	ˌe·kslɑʃə'pel
Aix-les-Bains		
town, France	āk-slā-BE^n	e·ksleː'bɛ̃
Aizawl		
town, India	Ī-ZOWL	ɑi'zɑul
Ajaccio		
seaport, Corsica	ah-YAHCH-ō, ah-ZHAHK-syō	ɑ'jɑtʃoː, ɑːʒɑːksjoː
Ajah, Ayyah [Aiah]		
Biblical name	Ā-juh, AH-yah	'eːdʒə, 'ɑjɑ
Ajaigarh		
former state, India	uh-JĪ-GAHR, uh-JĪ-guhr	ə'dʒɑiˌgɑ^r, ə'dʒɑigə^r
Ajalon		
Biblical name	AJ-uh-LAHN, A-yuh-LAHN, ah-yah-LŌN	'ædʒəˌlɑn, 'æjəˌlɑn, ɑjɑ'loːn
Ajanta		
village, mtn. range, India, site of cave paintings	uh-JUHNT-uh	ə'dʒəntə
Ajax		
the Great, *son of Telamon;* the Lesser, *leader of Locrians against Trojans*	Ā-JAKS	'eːˌdʒæks
Ajmān		
town, state, United Arab Emirates	aj-MAHN, aj-MAN	ædʒ'mɑn, ædʒ'mæn
Ajmer, Ajmere		
district, city, India	uhj-MIR	ədʒ'mi^r

Key (col. 2): a: **fad** ā: **fade** ah: **father** ar: **marry** aw: **law** e: **fed** ē: **feed** er: **merry** i: **hid** ī: **hide** ō: **coat** $\overline{oo}$: **boot** oi: **boy** ow: **now** u: **put** uh: **above** uhr: **bird** ch: **chop** ng: **ring** sh: **show** th: **thick** th: **this** zh: **measure**

Akaba
see 'Aqaba

Akai
audio equipment co.   uh-KĪ, AK-Ī   ə'kɑi, 'æk‚ɑi

Akalkot
former state, India   uh-KAHL-KŌT   ə'kɑl‚koːt

Akan
Biblical name   Ā-kuhn, AH-kahn   'eːkən, 'ɑkɑn

Akan [Twi]
lang., Ghana, Ivory Coast   AHK-AHN   'ɑk‚ɑn

Akaroa
borough, New Zealand   A-kuh-RŌ-uh   ‚ækə'roːə

Akbar
emperor of India   AK-buhr, AK-BAHR   'ækbəʳ, 'æk‚bɑʳ

Ak-Chin
Indian reservation, US   ak-CHIN   æk'tʃin

Akeldama [Aceldama]
potter's field   uh-KEL-duh-muh   ə'keldəmə

Aker
Egyptian earth god   AK-uhr, Ā-kuhr, AHK-uhr   'ækəʳ, 'eːkəʳ, 'ɑkəʳ

Akershus, Aggershus
county, Norway   AHK-uhrs-HOOS   'ɑkəʳs‚huːs

Akhaltsikhe
town, Georgia; capital, Turkish Armenia   uh-<u>KHAH</u>LT-si-<u>kh</u>uh   ə'xɑltsixə

Akhenaton [Ikhnaton]
Egyptian king   AHK(-uh)-NAHT-n   ‚ɑk(ə)'nɑtṇ

Aki
former province, Japan   ah-kē   ɑki·

Akiba ben Joseph
Jewish sage & martyr   ah-KĒ-bah ben JŌ-zuhf, ah-KĒ-vuh, JŌ-suhf   ɑ'kiːbɑ ben 'dʒoːzəf, ɑ'kiːvə, 'dʒoːsəf

Akihito
Japanese emperor   ah-kē-hē-tō   ɑkiːhiːtoː

Akim
1. pers. name, Polish   AH-kēm   'ɑːkiːm
2. Russian   UHK-YĒM   ‚ək'jiːm

Akita
port, Japan; dog breed   uh-KĒT-uh, ah-KĒT-uh   ə'kiːṭə, ɑ'kiːṭə

Akitsune
pers. name, Japanese   ah-kēt-sun-e   ɑkiːtsune

Akjoujt
city, Mauritania   ahk-ZHOO-zhuht   ɑk'ʒuːʒət

Akkad
ancient Asian region   AHK-AHD, AK-AD   'ɑk‚ɑd, 'æk‚æd

Akkadian
ancient lang.   uh-KAD-ē-uhn, ak-AD-ē-uhn, uh-KĀD-ē-uhn   ə'kædiːən, æk'ædiːən, ə'keːdiːən

'Akko
see Acre

Akkub
Biblical name   AK-uhb, AHK-OOV   'ækəb, 'ɑk‚uːv

Aklan
province, Philippines   ahk-LAHN   ɑk'lɑn

Foreign Sounds: ue: *Fr.* **rue**, *Ger.* **füllen**   uh(r): *Fr.* **boeuf**, *Ger.* **Höhle**   <u>kh</u>: *Ger.* **ich**, *Scot.* **loch**   g̃: *Sp.* a**m**igo   v: *Sp.* ha**b**lar
hl: *Welsh* **Ll**anelli.   CAPITALS: primary stress.   SMALL CAPS: secondary stress.   Ⓢ: U.S. pron.   Ⓔ: British pron.

Akola
district, India — uh-KŌ-luh — əˈkoːlə

Akoli [Acholi]
lang., people, Uganda, Sudan — uh-KŌ-lē — əˈkoːliˑ

Akrabbim
Biblical name — ak-RAB-im, ahk-RAHB-im, ahk-rah-BIM — ækˈræbim, akˈrɑbim, ɑkrɑˈbim

Akron
city, OH — AK-ruhn — ˈækrən

Aksel
pers. name — AHK-SEL — ˈɑːkˌsel

Aktí [Acte]
peninsula, Greece — ahk-TĒ — akˈtiː

Aktyubinsk
town, division, Kazakhstan — uhk-TYOO-B(Y)INSK — əkˈtjuːˌb(j)insk

Akure
city, Nigeria — ah-KUR-ē — ɑˈkuriˑ

Akureyri
town, Iceland — AHK-uer-Ā-rē, ⑤ AH-kuh-RER-ē — ˌɑkyrˈeːriˑ, ⑤ ˌɑkəˈreriˑ

Akutagawa Ryūnosuke [Chokodo Shujin, Gaki]
Japanese writer — ah-kōōt-ah-gah-wah ryōo-nō-suk-e — ɑkuːtɑgɑwɑ rjuːnoːsuke

Akvavit
liquor — AHK-wuh-VĒT, AHK-vah-VĒT — ˌɑkwəˈviːt, ˈɑkvɑˈviːt

Akyab [Sittwe]
town, Burma — ak-YAB — ækˈjæb

Al
pers. name — AL — ˈæl

Alabama
state, US — AL-uh-BAM-uh — ˌæləˈbæmə

Alabama-Coushatta
Indian reservation, US — AL-uh-BAM-uh-ku-SHAHT-uh — ˌæləˈbæməkuˈʃɑʈə

Alabaman
pert. to Alabama — AL-uh-BAM-uhn — ˌæləˈbæmən

Alabamian
pert. to Alabama — AL-uh-BAM-ē-uhn — ˌæləˈbæmiːən

Alacaluf
S. American people — AL-uh-kuh-LOOF, AL-uh-kuh-LOOF — ˌæləkəˈluːf, ˈæləkəˌluːf

Alachua
county, FL — uh-LAHCH-uh-WĀ, uh-LACH-uh-WĀ, -uh-wuh — əˈlɑtʃəˌweː, əˈlætʃəˌweː, -əwə

Alacoque
Saint Marguerite Marie, French nun — ah-lah-KAWK — ɑːlɑːkɔːk

Aladdin
hero, Arabian Nights — uh-LAD-n — əˈlædn̩

Al-Agheila [El Agheila, Al-'Uqaylah]
town, Libya; WWII battle site — AHL-uh-GĀ-luh, AL- — ˌɑləˈgeːlə, ˌæl-

Alagoas
state, Brazil — AL-uh-GŌ-uhs — ˌæləˈgoːəs

Alain
1. pers. name — AL-uhn — ˈælən
2. French — ah-LEⁿ — ɑːlẽ

Alajuela
province, Costa Rica — AHL-ah-HWĀ-lah — ˌɑlɑˈhweːlɑ

Key (col. 2):   a: fad   ā: fade   ah: father   ar: marry   aw: law   e: fed   ē: feed   er: merry   i: hid   ī: hide   ō: coat   ōō: boot
oi: boy   ow: now   u: put   uh: above   uhr: bird   ch: chop   ng: ring   sh: show   th: thick   <u>th</u>: this   zh: measure

Alamán
   Lucas, *Mexican historian &*   ahl-ah-MAHN   ɑlɑˈmɑn
     politician
Alamance
   stream, county, NC   AL-uh-MAN(T)S   ˈælə͵mæn(t)s
Alamannia
   region, France & Germany   AL-uh-MAN-ē-uh   ͵æləˈmæniːə
Alameda
   city, county, CA   AL-uh-MĒD-uh   ͵æləˈmiːdə
Alamein
   see El Alamein
Alaminos
   Antonio, *early Spanish navigator*   ahl-ah-MĒ-nōs   ɑlɑˈmiːnoːs
Alammelech, Allammelech
   Biblical name   uh-LAM-uh-LEK, AH-lah-MEL-E<u>KH</u>   əˈlæmə͵lek, ͵ɑlɑˈmel͵ex
Alamo
   mission, San Antonio, TX   AL-uh-MŌ   ˈælə͵moː
Alamogordo
   county, dam, NM   AL-uh-muh-GAWR-dō   ͵æləməˈgɔːʳdoː
Alamosa
   county, city, CO   AL-uh-MŌ-suh, AL-uh-M$\overline{OO}$-suh ͵æləˈmoːsə, ͵æləˈmuːsə
Alamoth
   Biblical name   AL-uh-MAWTH   ˈælə͵mɔːθ
Alamut
   Rock of, *medieval fortress, Iran*   AL-uh-M$\overline{OO}$T   ͵æləˈmuːt
Alan
   pers. name   AL-uhn   ˈælən
Alana
   pers. name   uh-LAHN-uh, uh-LAN-uh   əˈlɑnə, əˈlænə
Al-Anbār
   governorate, Iraq   ahl-AHN-BAHR   ɑlˈɑn͵bɑʳ
Åland [Ahvenanmaa]
   Finnish islands, Baltic Sea   AW-luhnd   ˈɔːlənd
Al-Anon
   US organization   AL-uh-NAHN   ˈælə͵nɑn
Alaotra
   lake, Madagascar   AL-uh-Ō-truh, AL-ē-Ō-truh   ͵æləˈoːtrə, ͵æliːˈoːtrə
Alaouite, Alawite Druze
   people, Syria   AL-uh-WĒT DR$\overline{OO}$Z, AL-uh-WĒT ˈælə͵wiːt ˈdruːz, ͵æləˈwiːt
Alar
   tdmk for a pesticide   AL-AHR   ˈæl͵ɑʳ
Alarcón
   Pedro Antonio de, *Spanish writer &* ahl-ahr-KAWN   ɑlɑʳˈkɔːn
    diplomat
Alaric
   1. pers. name   AL-uh-rik   ˈælərik
   2. French   ah-lah-RĒK   ɑːlɑːriːk
Al-'Arīsh ['Arīsh, El]
   town, Sinai   AHL-ah-RĒSH, AL-   ͵ɑlɑˈriːʃ, ͵æl-
Alasdair
   pers. name   AL-uh-stuhr   ˈæləstəʳ
Alaska
   state, US   uh-LAS-kuh   əˈlæskə
Alaskan malamute
   dog breed   uh-LAS-kuhn MAL-uh-MY$\overline{OO}$T ə͵læskən ˈmælə͵mjuːt

Foreign Sounds: ue: *Fr.* **rue**, *Ger.* **füllen** uh(r): *Fr.* **boeuf**, *Ger.* **Höhle** <u>kh</u>: *Ger.* **ich**, *Scot.* **loch** ḡ: *Sp.* **amigo** v̱: *Sp.* **hablar**
hl: *Welsh* **Llanelli**.   CAPITALS: primary stress.   SMALL CAPS: secondary stress.   Ⓢ: U.S. pron.   Ⓔ: British pron.

al-Assad

   Hafez, *president, Syria*   AHL-uh-SAHD, Ⓢ AL-uh-SAD   ˌɑːləˈsɑːd, Ⓢ ˌæləˈsæd

Alastair

   pers. name   AL-uh-STAR, -STER; AL-uh-stuhr   ˈæləˌstærʳ, -ˌsteʳ; ˈæləstəʳ

Alava

   Cape, *WA, most westerly point of*   AL-uh-vuh   ˈæləvə
      contiguous US

Álava

   Basque province, Spain   AHL-uh-vuh   ˈɑləvə

Alayskiy Khrebet

   mtn. range, Kirgizstan   ah-LĪ-skyiy K͟HRIB-yawt   ɑˌlɑiskjij ˈxribjɔːt

Alba

   pers. name   AHL-bah   ˈɑlbɑ

Albacete

   prov, Spain   ahl-v̲ah-SĀ-tā   ɑlβɑˈseːteː

Al-Bahra Al-Ahmar

   governorate, Egypt   ahl-BAH-huhr ahl-AHM-AHR   ɑlˌbɑhər ɑlˈɑm₎ɑʳ

Alba Iulia

   city, Romania   AHL-buh YŌOL-yuh   ˌɑlbə ˈjuːljə

Alba Longa

   ancient city, Latium   AL-buh LAWNG-guh   ˌælbə ˈlɔːŋgə

Alban

   1. pers. name   AWL-buhn, AL-   ˈɔːlbən, ˈæl-
   2. French   ahl-BAHⁿ   ɑːlbɑ̃
   3. German   ahl-BAHN, AHL-BAHN   ɑlˈbɑn, ˈɑlˌbɑn

Albani

   Danish beer   AHL-bah-nē   ˈɑːlbɑːniˑ

Albania

   republic, Europe   al-BĀ-nē-uh, awl-, -nyuh   ælˈbeːniːə, ɔːl-, -njə

Albanian

   lang., Albania   al-BĀ-nē-uhn, awl-, -nyuhn   ælˈbeːniːən, ɔːl-, -njən

Alban League

   ancient Latin confederation   AL-buhn, AWL-   ˈælbən, ˈɔːl-

Albano

   lake, Italy   al-BAHN-ō, ahl-   ælˈbɑnoː, ɑl-

Albany

   1. city, county, NY; river, Canada   AWL-buh-nē   ˈɔːlbəniˑ
   2. city, Australia   AL-buh-nē   ˈælbəniˑ
   3. city, GA   awl-BE-nē   ɔːlˈbeniˑ

Albatross

   sea bird   AL-buh-TRAWS, -TRAHS   ˈælbəˌtrɔːs, -ˌtrɑs

Albay

   province, Philippines   ahl-BĪ   ɑlˈbai

Albee

   Edward, *US writer*   AWL-bē, AL-bē   ˈɔːlbiˑ, ˈælbiˑ

Albemarle

   George Monck, Duke of, *English*   AL-buh-MAHRL   ˈælbəˌmɑʳl
      general; county, VA; town, sound,
      college, NC

Albéniz

   Isaac, *Spanish pianist & composer*   ahl-V̲Ā-nēth, ahl-V̲Ā-nēs   ɑlˈβeːniːθ, ɑlˈβeːniːs

Alberdi

   Juan Bautista, *Argentine statesman*   ahl-V̲ER-t͟hē   ɑlˈβerðiː
      & philosopher

Key (col. 2): a: fad ā: fade ah: father ar: marry aw: law e: fed ē: feed er: merry i: hid ī: hide ō: coat ōō: boot
oi: boy ow: now u: put uh: above uhr: bird ch: chop ng: ring sh: show th: thick t͟h: this zh: measure

Alberghetti		
Anna Maria, *US entertainer*	AL-buhr-GET-ē	ˌælbəʳˈgeṭiˑ
Alberic		
pers. name	AL-buh-rik	ˈælbərik
Alberich		
king of the dwarves in Teutonic myth; pers. name	AHL-buh-RIKH	ˈɑlbəˌriç
Albericus		
pers. name	AL-buh-RĪ-kuhs	ˌælbəˈrɑikəs
Albert		
1. pers. name	AL-buhrt	ˈælbəʳt
2. Danish, Finnish, Hungarian	AHL-BERT	ˈɑːlˌbert
3. Dutch	AHL-BERT	ˈɑlˌbert
4. French	ahl-BER	ɑːlber
5. German	AHL-BERT	ˈɑlˌbeʳt
6. Norwegian	AHL-buhrt, AHL-BERT	ˈɑlbərt, ˈɑlˌbert
7. Swedish	AHL-buhrt	ˈɑːlbərt
Albers		
Josef, *German-born US artist*	AHL-BERS, [$] AL-buhrz	ˈɑlˌbers, [$] ˈælbəʳz
Alberta		
province, Canada; pers. name	al-BUHRT-uh	ælˈbəʳtə
Alberti		
Leon Battista, *Italian Renaissance man*	ahl-BER-tē	ɑlˈbeʳtiː
Alberto		
1. pers. name, Italian	ahl-BER-tō	ɑlˈbertoː
2. Portuguese	ahl-BER-too	ɑlˈbertuː
3. Spanish	ahl-VER-tō	ɑlˈβertoː
Albertus		
1. pers. name	al-BUHRT-uhs	ælˈbəʳṭəs
2. Dutch	ahl-BER-tues	ɑlˈbertys
Albertus Magnus		
German philosopher, saint; college, CT	al-BUHRT-uhs MAG-nuhs	ælˈbəʳṭəs ˈmægnəs
Albertville		
1. city, AL	AL-buhrt-VIL	ˈælbəʳtˌvil
2. village, France	ahl-ber-VĒL, [$] AL-buhr-VIL	ɑːlberviːl, [$] ˈælbəʳˌvil
Albi		
city, France	ahl-BĒ	ɑːlbiː
Albi		
city, France	ahl-BĒ	ɑːlbiː
Albigenses		
medieval Christian sect	AL-buh-JEN-SĒZ	ˌælbəˈdʒenˌsiːz
Albigensian		
pert. to Albigenses	AL-buh-JEN-sē-uhn	ˌælbəˈdʒensiːən
Albigensianism		
tenets of the Albigenses	AL-buh-JEN-sē-uh-NIZ-uhm	ˌælbəˈdʒensiːəˌnizəm
Albigeois		
former region, France	ahl-bē-ZHWAH	ɑːlbiːʒwɑː
Albinoni		
Tomaso Giovanni, *Italian composer*	AHL-bē-NŌ-nē, [$] AL-buh-NŌ-nē	ˌɑlbiːˈnoːniː, [$] ˌælbəˈnoːniˑ
Albinus		
Roman cognomen	al-BĪ-nuhs	ælˈbɑinəs

Foreign Sounds: ue: *Fr.* **rue**, *Ger.* **füllen** uh(r): *Fr.* **boeuf**, *Ger.* **Höhle** kh: *Ger.* **ich**, *Scot.* **loch** g̃: *Sp.* **amigo** v: *Sp.* **hablar** hl: *Welsh* **Llanelli**. CAPITALS: primary stress. SMALL CAPS: secondary stress. [$]: U.S. pron. [£]: British pron.

Albion
   ancient name of Gt. Britain; US pl.   AL-bē-uhn   'ælbiːən
   name; College, *MI; pers. name*

Alborán Basin
   Mediterranean Sea   AL-buh-RAHN   ,ælbə'rɑn

Ålborg
   see Aalborg

Ålborg-Nørresundby [Aalborg]
   port, Denmark   AWL-BAWR(Y)-NUH(R)R-uh-SUN-bue   'ɔːl,bɔːr(j)'nœrə,sunbyː

Albrecht
   1. pers. name, Danish   AHL-BREKHT   'ɑːl,breçt
   2. German   AHL-BREKHT   'al,breçt

Albret
   Gascon family   ahl-BRE   ɑːlbre

Albright
   pers. name   AWL-BRĬT   'ɔːl,brɑit

Albucasis [Abū al-Qāsim]
   Spanish Arab physician   AL-byu-KĀ-suhs   ,ælbju'keːsəs

Albufeira
   resort, Portugal   AHL-bo͞o-FĀ-ruh, -FER-uh   ,ɑlbuː'feːrə, -'ferə

Albula
   mtn. pass, river, Switzerland   AL-b(y)uh-luh   'ælb(j)ələ

Albumazar [Abū Ma'shar]
   Muslim astrologer   AL-byu-MAZ-uhr   ,ælbju'mæzər

Albuquerque
   city, NM   AL-buh-KUHR-kē, AL-byuh-KUHR-kē   'ælbə,kərkiˑ, 'ælbjə,kərkiˑ

Āl Bū Saʿīd
   Muslim dynasty in Oman & Zanzibar   AHL BŌO sah-ĒD   'ɑl 'buː sa'iːd

Alcaeus
   Greek poet   al-SĒ-uhs   æl'siːəs

Alcalá Zamora
   Niceto, *Spanish politician*   ahl-kah-LAH thah-MAWR-ah   ɑlkɑ'lɑ θɑ'mɔːrɑ

Alcan
   highway, Alaska-Canada   AL-KAN   'æl,kæn

Alcántara
   commune, Spain   ahl-KAHNT-uh-ruh, al-KANT-uh-ruh   ɑl'kɑnʈərə, æl'kænʈərə

Alcatraz
   island, prison, San Francisco Bay   AL-kuh-TRAZ   'ælkə,træz

Alcazar
   Moorish palace   AL-kuh-ZAHR, al-KAZ-uhr   ,ælkə'zɑr, æl'kæzər

Alceste
   opera, Gluck   al-SEST   æl'sest

Alcestis
   tragedy, Euripides   al-SES-tuhs   æl'sestəs

Alcibiades
   Athenian leader   AL-suh-BĪ-uhd-ēz   ,ælsə'bɑiədiːz

Alcide
   1. pers. name, French   ahl-SĒD   ɑːlsiːd
   2. Italian   ahl-SĒ-dā   ɑl'siːdeː

Alcides
   pers. name, Spanish   ahl-SĒ-thās, ahl-THĒ-thās   ɑl'siːðeːs, ɑl'θiːðeːs

Alcindor
   Lew, *former name of* Kareem   al-SIN-duhr   æl'sindər
   Abdul-Jabbar

Key (col. 2):   a: fad ā: fade ah: father ar: marry aw: law e: fed ē: feed er: merry i: hid ī: hide ō: coat o͞o: boot
oi: boy ow: now u: put uh: above uhr: bird ch: chop ng: ring sh: show th: thick th̲: this zh: measure

Alcinoüs
   king of Phaeacia, host to Odysseus,   al-SIN-uh-wuhs   æl'sinəwəs
   Jason, and Medea

Alcmaeon
   son of Amphiaraus   alk-MĒ-uhn   ælk'miːən

Alcmene
   wife of Amphitryon, mother of   alk-MĒ-nē   ælk'miːni·
   Heracles

Alcoa
   city, TN; US aluminum co.   al-KŌ-uh   æl'koːə

Alcona
   county, MI   al-KŌ-nuh   æl'koːnə

Alcorn
   county, MS   AWL-KAWRN   'ɔːl,kɔː^rn → 'ɔːl,kɔːʳn

Alcott
   Louisa May, *US writer;* Bronson,   AWL-kuht, AL-kuht, AWL-KAHT,   'ɔːlkət, 'ælkət, 'ɔːl,kɑt,
   US educator, philosopher   AL-KAHT   'æl,kɑt

Alcova
   Dam, *WY*   al-KŌ-vuh   æl'koːvə

Alcuin
   English scholar   AL-kwuhn   'ælkwən

Alcyone
   wife of Ceyx; star in Pleiades   al-SĪ-uh-nē   æl'sɑiəni·

Alcyoneus
   giant defeated by Hercules   al-SĪ-uh-NĒ-uhs, al-SĪ-uh-NO͞OS   æl,sɑiə'niːəs, æl'sɑiə,nuːs

Alda
   Alan, *US actor, writer, director*   AWL-duh   'ɔːldə

Aldabra
   island group, Seychelles   al-DAB-ruh   æl'dæbrə

Aldan
   river, mtns., Yakutsk, Siberia   ul-DAHN   ul'dɑn

Aldebaran
   star   al-DEB-uh-ruhn   æl'debərən

Alder
   Kurt, *German chemist (Nobel 1950)*   AHL-duhr   'ɑldəʳ

Alderney
   Channel Island   AWL-duhr-nē   'ɔːldəʳni·

Aldershot
   borough, Hampshire, England   AWL-duhr-SHAHT   'ɔːldəʳ,ʃɑt

Alderson Broaddus
   College, *WV*   AWL-duhr-suhn BRAWD-uhs   'ɔːldəʳsən 'brɔːdəs

Aldine
   print types by A. Manutius   AWL-DĪN, AWL-DĒN   'ɔːl,dɑin, 'ɔːl,diːn

Aldo
   pers. name   AHL-dō   'ɑldoː

Aldous
   pers. name (A. Huxley)   AWL-duhs   'ɔːldəs

Aldredge
   Theoni, *Greek costume designer*   AWL-drij   'ɔːldridʒ

Aldobrandini
   Florentine noble family   AHL-dō-brahn-DĒ-nē   ,aldoːbrɑn'diːni·

Aldrin
   Edwin E. 'Buzz', *US astronaut*   AWL-druhn   'ɔːldrən

Aldwinckle
   village, England   AH-nik-uhl   'ɑːnikəl

Alec, Aleck
  pers. name   AL-uhk   'ælək
Alecost
  herb   ĀL-KAHST   'eːlˌkɑst
Alecto
  see Allecto
Aleg
  city, Mauritania   ah-LEG   ɑ'leg
Aleichem
  Shalom, *pseudonym of* Sholem   uh-LĀ-kuhm, uh-LĀ-<u>kh</u>uhm   ə'leːkəm, ə'leːxəm
    Rabinowitz, *US author*
Aleixandre
  Vicente, *Spanish poet (Nobel 1977)*   ahl-ek-SAHN-dre   ɑlek'sɑndre
Alejandro
  pers. name, Spanish   ahl-ā-<u>KHAHN</u>-drō   ɑleː'xɑndroː
Alejo
  pers. name, Portuguese   ahl-Ā-zh$\overline{oo}$ ɑl'eːʒuː
Alekhine, Alekhin
  Alexander, *Russian chess master*   UHL-YŌ<u>KH</u>-yin   ˌəl'joːxjin
Aleksander
  pers. name, Polish   AH-lek-SAHN-der   ˌɑːlek'sɑːnder
Aleksandr
  pers. name, Russian   UHL-yik-SAHN-duhr   ˌəljik'sɑːndər
Aleksandra
  pers. name, Russian   UHL-yik-SAHN-druh   ˌəljik'sɑːndrə
Aleksey
  pers. name, Russian   UHL-yik-SYĀ(-ē)   ˌəljik'sjeː(iː)
Alekseyevich
  pers. name, Russian   UHL-yik-SYĀ(-yiv)-yich   ˌəljik'sjeː(jiv)jitʃ
Alekseyevna
  pers. name, Russian   UHL-yik-SYĀ(-yuh)v-nuh   ˌəljik'sjeː(jə)vnə
Alemán
  Miguel, *president, Mexico;* Mateo,   ahl-ā-MAHN   ɑleː'mɑn
    Spanish writer
Alemanni
  Germanic tribes   AL-uh-MAN-ē   ˌælə'mæniˑ
Alemannic
  German dialect   AL-uh-MAN-ik   ˌælə'mænik
Alembert, d'
  Jean Le Rond, *French*   dah-lahⁿ-BER   dɑːlɑ̄ber
    mathematician, scientist, & scholar
Alemeth, Allemeth
  Biblical name   AL-uh-METH   'æləˌmeθ
Alençon
  city, France   ah-lahⁿ-SAWⁿ   ɑːlɑ̄sɔ̄
Alentejo
  ancient province, Portugal   uh-LEⁿ(N)-TEZH-$\overline{oo}$ əˌlẽ(n)'teʒuː
Alenuihaha
  channel, HI   AHL-uh-N$\overline{OO}$-ē-HAH-hah   ˌɑləˌnuːiːˈhɑhɑ
Aleppo
  city, Syria   uh-LEP-ō   ə'lepoː
Ales
  pers. name   ĀLZ   'eːlz
Alessandria
  province, Italy   AH-les-SAHN-drē-uh   ˌɑles'sɑndriːə

Key (col. 2):   a: fad   ā: fade   ah: father   ar: marry   aw: law   e: fed   ē: feed   er: merry   i: hid   ī: hide   ō: coat $\overline{oo}$: boot
oi: boy   ow: now   u: put   uh: above   uhr: bird   ch: chop   ng: ring   sh: show   th: thick   <u>th</u>: this   zh: measure

Alessandro
  pers. name — AH-lās-SAHN-drō — ˌaleːsˈsandroː

Aletsch
  glacier, Switzerland — AHL-ich — ˈalitʃ

Aleut
  N. American people — AL-ē-OOT, AL-ē-OOT, uh-LOOT — ˌæliːˈuːt, ˈæliːˌuːt, əˈluːt

Aleutians
  island chain, AK — uh-LOO-shuhnz — əˈluːʃənz

Alex
  pers. name — AL-uhks — ˈæləks

Alexa
  pers. name — uh-LEK-suh — əˈleksə

Alexander
  1. pers. name — AL-ig-ZAN-duhr, EL-, Ⓔ ZAHN-duhr — ˌæligˈzændəʳ, ˌel-, Ⓔ -ˈzɑːndəʳ
  2. Dutch — AH-lek-SAHN-duhr — ˌɑːlekˈsandər
  3. Finnish, Polish — AH-lek-SAHN-der — ˌɑːlekˈsaːnder
  4. German — AHL-ek-SAHN-duhr — ˌalekˈsandəʳ
  5. Norwegian — AHL-uhk-SAHN-duhr — ˌaləkˈsandər
  6. Russian — uhl-yik-SAHN-duhr — əljikˈsaːndər
  7. Swedish — AH-luhk-SAHN-duhr — ˌɑːləkˈsaːndər

Alexandra
  1. pers. name — AL-ig-ZAN-druh, EL-, Ⓔ -ZAHN- — ˌæligˈzændrə, ˌel-, Ⓔ -ˈzɑːn-
  2. Danish — AH-lek-SAHN-druh — ˌɑːlekˈsaːndrə

Alexandre
  1. pers. name — AL-ig-ZAN-duhr, EL-, Ⓔ -ZAHN- — ˌæligˈzændəʳ, ˌel-, Ⓔ -ˈzɑːn-
  2. French — ah-lek-SAHⁿDR, -SAHⁿ-druh — aːleksãdr, -sãdrə

Alexandretta [İskenderun]
  gulf, Mediterranean Sea; city, Turkey — AL-ig-zan-DRET-uh, EL-, Ⓔ -zahn-DRET-uh — ˌæligzænˈdrețə, ˌel-, Ⓔ -zɑːnˈdretə

Alexandria
  Egyptian seaport; US pl. name — AL-ig-ZAN-drē-uh, EL- — ˌæligˈzændriːə, ˌel-

Alexandroúpolis [Dedé Agach]
  city, Greece — AHL-ik-sahn-DROO-paw-lēs — ˌaliksanˈdruːpɔːliːs

Alexei, Alexey
  1. pers. name — uh-LEK-sā — əˈlekseː
  2. Russian — UHL-yiks-YĀ(-ē) — ˌəljiksˈjeː(iː)

Alexis
  1. pers. name — uh-LEK-suhs — əˈleksəs
  2. Finnish — AH-LEK-sis — ˈɑːˌleksis

Alfa
  Dutch beer — AHL-fuh — ˈalfə

Alfalfa
  character in Little Rascals — al-FAL-fuh — ælˈfælfə

Alfaro
  Eloy, *Ecuadorian politician &
  general;* Ricardo Joaquín,
  Panamanian politician — ahl-FAHR-ō — alˈfaroː

Alfa Romeo
  tdmk for a car — AL-fuh ruh-MĀ-ō — ˌælfə rəˈmeːoː

Al-Fashir [Fasher, El]
  town, Sudan — ahl FAHSH-IR — al ˈfaʃˌiʳ

Al Fatah
  Palestinian group — AHL fah-TAH, fuh-TAH, FAH-TAH, AL — ˌɑːl faˈta, fəˈta, ˈfaˌta, ˌæl

---

Alföld

plains region, SE Europe	AWL-FUH(R)LD	'ɔːlˌfœːld

Alfonse

pers. name	AL-FAHNS, -FAHNZ; AL-FAHNS, -FAHNZ	'ælˌfɑns, -ˌfɑnz; ˌæl'fɑns, -'fɑnz

Alfonsin

Raul R., *president, Argentina*	ahl-fawn-SĒN	ɑlfɔːn'siːn

Alfonso

1. pers. name	al-FAHN-sō, -zō	æl'fɑnsoː, -zoː
2. German	ahl-FAWN-zō	ɑl'fɔːnzoː
3. Italian, Spanish	ahl-FAWN-sō	ɑl'fɔːnsoː

Alfred

1. pers. name	AL-fruhd, AL-fuhrd	'ælfrəd, 'ælfəʳd
2. Dutch	AHL-FRET	'ɑlˌfret
3. Finnish, Swedish	AHL-FRED	'ɑːlˌfred
4. French	ahl-FRED	ɑːlfred
5. German	AHL-FRĀT	'ɑlˌfreːt
6. Norwegian	AHL-FRED	'ɑlˌfred
7. Polish	AHL-FRET	'ɑːlˌfret

Alfreda

pers. name	al-FRĒD-uh	æl'friːdə

Alfredo

1. pers. name, Italian	ahl-FRĀ-dō	ɑl'freːdoː
2. Spanish	ahl-FRĀ-<u>th</u>ō	ɑl'freːðoː

Alfsborg

see Älvsborg

Al-Fung [Fung, El]

former province, Sudan	ahl FUNG	ɑl 'fuŋ

Alfvén

Hannes Olof, *Swedish physicist (Nobel 1970)*	al(f)-VĀN, AL(F)-VEN	æl(f)'veːn, ˌæl(f)'ven

Algarve

ancient kingdom, region, province, Portugal	ahl-GAHR-vuh, ahl-GAHRV	ɑl'gɑʳvə, ɑl'gɑʳv

Algäu, Allgäu

region, Bavaria, Germany; Alps, *mtn. range, Germany & Austria*	AHL-GOI	'ɑlˌgɔi

Algäuer Alpen

see Allgäuer Alpen

Algeciras

resort, Spain	ahl-<u>kh</u>ā-THĒ-rahs, -SĒ-rahs	ɑlxeː'θiːrɑs, -'siːrɑs

Alger

1. Horatio, *writer*	AL-juhr	'ældʒəʳ
2. department, Algeria	ahl-ZHĀ	ɑːlʒeː

Alger [Algerus Magister]

of Liège, *French priest & writer*	ahl-ZHĀ	ɑːlʒeː

Algeria

republic, Africa	al-JIR-ē-uh	æl'dʒiriːə

Algerian

pert. to Algeria *or* Algiers	al-JIR-ē-uhn	æl'dʒiriːən

Algernon

1. pers. name	AL-juhr-nuhn, -NAHN	'ældʒəʳnən, -ˌnɑn
2. French	ahl-zher-NAWⁿ	ɑːlʒernɔ̃

Algerus Magister [Alger]

French priest & writer	AL-juh-ruhs MAJ-uh-stuhr	'ældʒərəs 'mædʒəstəʳ

Key (col. 2):   a: fad   ā: fade   ah: father   ar: marry   aw: law   e: fed   ē: feed   er: merry   i: hid   ī: hide   ō: coat   ōō: boot
oi: boy   ow: now   u: put   uh: above   uhr: bird   ch: chop   ng: ring   sh: show   th: thick   th: this   zh: measure

Algiers
  city, Algeria   al-JIRZ   æl'dʒiᴿz

ALGOL
  programming lang.   AL-GAWL, AL-GAHL   'æl,gɔːl, 'æl,gɑl

Algol
  binary star   AL-GAWL, AL-GAHL   'æl,gɔːl, 'æl,gɑl

Algoma
  University, *Canada*   al-GŌ-muh   æl'goːmə

Algonkin [Algonquin]
  N. American people   al-GAHNG-kuhn   æl'gaŋkən

Algonquin
  N. American people   al-GAHN-kwuhn, al-GAHNG-kwuhn   æl'gɑnkwən, æl'gaŋkwən

Alhambra
  1. city, CA   al-HAM-bruh   æl'hæmbrə
  2. Moorish palace, Granada, Spain   ahl-AHM-brah, Ⓢ al-HAM-bruh, al-HAHM-bruh   al'ɑmbra, Ⓢ æl'hæmbrə, æl'hɑmbrə

Al-Hasa [Hasa, El]
  province, Saudi Arabia   ahl-HAHS-uh   al'hasə

Alhazen
  Arab mathematician   AL-huh-ZEN   ,ælhə'zen

Ali
  1. Muhammad, *US boxer; pers. name*   ah-LĒ; AL-ē, AHL-ē   ɑ'liː; 'æliˑ, 'aliˑ
  2. Arabic   ah-LĒ, a-LĒ   ɑː'liː, æ'liː
  3. Persian   ah-LĒ   ɑː'liː
  4. Turkish   ah-LĒ   ɑ'liː

Aliah
  Biblical name   uh-LĪ-uh, AL-ē-uh   ə'laiə, 'æliːə

Aliákmon [Vistritsa]
  river, Greece, Macedonia   ahl-YAHK-mawn   al'jakmɔːn

Alian
  Biblical name   uh-LĪ-uhn, AL-ē-uhn   ə'laiən, 'æliːən

Alianza Republicana Nacionalista [Arena]
  political party, El Salvador   ahl-ē-AHN-sah rā-p͞oo-blē-KAHN-ah nah-sē-ō-nah-LĒ-stah   ɑliː'ɑnsa reːpuːbliː'kɑna nasiːoːnɑ'liːstɑ

Ali Baba
  hero, Arabian Nights   AL-ē BAHB-uh   ,æliː 'babə

Alicante
  town, prov, Spain   ahl-ē-KAHN-tā, Ⓢ AL-i-KANT-ē   ɑliː'kanteː, Ⓢ ,æli'kæntiˑ

Alice
  1. pers. name   AL-uhs   'æləs
  2. French   ah-LĒS   ɑːliːs
  3. German   ah-LĒ-suh   ɑ'liːsə
  4. Italian   ah-LĒ-chā   ɑ'liːtʃeː

Alicia
  1. pers. name   uh-LISH(-ē)-uh, uh-LĒ-shuh   ə'liʃ(iː)ə, ə'liːʃə
  2. Italian   ah-LĒ-chah   ɑ'liːtʃa
  3. Spanish   ah-LĒS-yah, ah-LĒTH-yah   ɑ'liːsja, ɑ'liːθja

Al-'id al-Kabir
  Islamic festival   ahl-ID AHL-kahb-IR   al'id ,ɑlkɑb'ir

Aligarh
  district, India   AHL-ē-GUHR, -GAHR   ,ɑliː'gəᴿ, -'gɑᴿ

Alija
  pers. name (A. Izetbegovic)   uh-LĒ-(y)uh, ah-   ə'liː(j)ə, ɑ-

---

Foreign Sounds: ue: *Fr.* **rue**, *Ger.* **füllen**   uh(r): *Fr.* **boeuf**, *Ger.* **Höhle**   <u>kh</u>: *Ger.* **ich**, *Scot.* **loch**   g̱: *Sp.* **amigo**   <u>v</u>: *Sp.* **hablar** hl: *Welsh* **Llanelli.**   CAPITALS: primary stress.   SMALL CAPS: secondary stress.   Ⓢ: U.S. pron.   Ⓔ: British pron.

Ali Pasha, Ali Paşa		
Turkish governor	ah-LĒ pah-SHAH, [$] ah-LĒ PAHSH-uh, AHL-ē, PASH-uh, puh-SHAH	ɑ'liː pɑ'ʃɑ, [$] ɑˌliː 'pɑʃə, 'ɑliˑ, 'pæʃə, pə'ʃɑ
Alirajpur		
former state, India	AHL-i-RAHJ-PUR	ˌɑli'rɑdʒˌpuʳ
Alison		
pers. name	AL-uh-suhn	'æləsən
Alistair		
pers. name	AL-uh-STAR, AL-uh-STER, AL-uh-stuhr	'æləˌstæʳ, 'æləˌsteʳ, 'æləstəʳ
Alitalia		
Italian airline	AL-i-TAL-yuh, AL-i-TAL-ē-uh	ˌæli'tæljə, ˌæli'tæliːə
Al-Karak [Kerak, El]		
town, fortress, Jordan	ahl-KAHR-ahk	ɑl'kɑrɑk
Alka-Seltzer		
tdmk for an over-the-counter medicine	AL-kuh-SELT-suhr	'ælkəˌseltsəʳ
Allah		
Islamic name for God	AHL-uh, AL-uh, AHL-AH, ah-LAH	'ɑlə, 'ælə, 'ɑlˌɑ, ɑ'lɑ
Allahabad		
city, district, India	AL-uh-huh-BAD, -BAHD	'æləhəˌbæd, -ˌbɑd
Allais		
Maurice, *French economist, engineer (Nobel 1988)*	ah-LE	ɑːle
Allamakee		
county, IA	AL-uh-muh-KĒ	ˌæləmə'kiː
Allammelech		
see Alammelech		
Allan		
pers. name	AL-uhn	'ælən
Allardice, -dyce		
pers. name	AL-uhr-DĪS	'æləʳˌdɑis
All-Bran		
tdmk for a brand of cereal	AWL-BRAN	'ɔːlˌbræn
Allecto, Alecto		
one of the Greek Furies	uh-LEK-tō	ə'lektoː
Allegan		
county, city, MI	AL-i-guhn	'æligən
Allegheny		
county, PA; river, mts., US	AL-uh-GĀ-nē, AL-uh-GEN-ē	ˌælə'geːniˑ, ˌælə'geniˑ
Allegri		
pers. name (A. A. Correggio)	uh-LEG-rē, uh-LĀ-grē	ə'legriˑ, ə'leːgriˑ
Allegro, L'		
see L'Allegro		
Allemande		
dance	AL-uh-MAND, AL-uh-MAND	'æləˌmænd, ˌælə'mænd
Allemeth		
see Alemeth		
Allen		
pers. name	AL-uhn	'ælən
Allende Gossens		
Salvador, *president, Chile*	ah-YEN-dā GAW-sens	ɑ'jendeː 'gɔːsens
Allentown		
city, PA	AL-uhn-TOWN	'ælənˌtɑun
Allergan		
US personal products co.	AL-uhr-GAN	'æləʳˌgæn

Key (col. 2): a: fad ā: fade ah: father ar: marry aw: law e: fed ē: feed er: merry i: hid ī: hide ō: coat o͞o: boot oi: boy ow: now u: put uh: above uhr: bird ch: chop ng: ring sh: show th: thick t͟h: this zh: measure

Alleyn
Edward, *English actor*   AL-uhn, al-ĒN, al-ĀN   'ælən, æl'iːn, æl'eːn

Allgäu [Allgäuer Alpen]
Alps, *mtn. range, Germany, Austria;*   AHL-GOI, AL-GOI   'ɑlˌɡɔi, 'ælˌɡɔi
cattle breed

Allgäuer Alpen, Algäuer Alpen
mtn. range, Germany, Austria   AHL-GOI-uhr AHL-puhn   'ɑlˌɡɔiəʳ 'ɑlpən

Allhallows Eve
Oct. 31   awl-HAL-ōz   ɔːl'hæloːz

Allie, Ally
pers. name   AL-ē   'æliˑ

Allier
dept., river, France   ahl-YĀ   ɑːljeː

Allison
pers. name   AL-uh-suhn   'æləsən

Allium
genus of onions and garlic   AL-ē-uhm   'æliːəm

Alliluyeva
Svetlana, *Russian writer, daughter*   AHL-uh-LOO-yuh-vuh   ˌɑlə'luːjəvə
of Stalin

Allingham
Margery Louise, *English writer*   AL-ing-uhm, Ⓢ -HAM   'æliŋəm, Ⓢ -ˌhæm

Alloa
town, Scotland   AL-uh-wuh   'æləwə

Allon
Biblical name   AL-AHN, ā-LŌN, ah-LŌN   'ælˌɑn, eː'loːn, ɑ'loːn

Allon-bachuth, Allon-bacuth
Biblical name   AL-AHN-BAHK-uhth,   'ælˌɑn'bɑkəθ, ɑˌloːnbɑ'xuːt
    ah-LŌN-bah-KHOOT

Allora
town, Australia   AL-uh-ruh   'ælərə

Allosaurus
dinosaur   AL-uh-SAWR-uhs   ˌælə'sɔːrəs

Allouez
Claude Jean, *French missionary in*   ahl-WĀ   ɑːlweː
America

Allsop, Allsopp
pers. name   AWL-SAHP   'ɔːlˌsɑp

All Souls
college, Oxford Univ.   AWL SŌLZ   ˌɔːl 'soːlz

Allvar
pers. name, Swedish   AHL-VAHR   'ɑːlˌvɑːʳ

Alma
1. *Crimean river; US pl. name; pers.*   AL-muh   'ælmə
name
2. *German*   AHL-mah   'ɑlmɑ

Alma-Ata
city, Kazakhstan   AL-muh-uh-TAH   ˌælmə-ə'tɑ

Almadén
tdmk for wine   AL-muh-DEN, AL-muh-DEN   ˌælmə'den, 'ælməˌden

Almadies
Cape, *westernmost point of Africa*   AL-muh-DĒ-uhs   ˌælmə'diːəs

Almagest
Ptolemaic work on astronomy   AL-muh-JEST   'ælməˌdʒest

Foreign Sounds: ue: *Fr.* **rue**, *Ger.* **füllen**   uh(r): *Fr.* **boeuf**, *Ger.* **Höhle**   kh: *Ger.* **ich**, *Scot.* **loch**   g̱: *Sp.* **amigo**   v: *Sp.* **hablar** hl: *Welsh* **Llanelli.**   CAPITALS: primary stress.   SMALL CAPS: secondary stress.   Ⓢ: U.S. pron.   Ⓔ: British pron.

Al-Mansūra [Mansūra, El]
   city, Egypt   AHL-mahn-SUR-uh   ˌɑlmɑnˈsurə

Alma-Tadema
   Sir Lawrence, *British painter*   AL-muh-TAD-uh-muh   ˈælməˈtædəmə

Almaty
   new name of Alma-Ata, *Kazakhstan*   uhl-MAHT-ē   əlˈmɑːṭiː

Almeida
   1. pers. name, Spanish   ahl-MĀ-<u>th</u>ah   ɑlˈmeːða
   2. Portugese   awl-MĀD-uh   ɔːlˈmeːdə

Almería
   province, town, Spain   AHL-mā-RĒ-uh   ˌɑlmeːˈriːə

Al Mina
   Syria, *site of ancient trading post*   ahl MĒ-nuh, al   ɑːl ˈmiːnə, æl

Al-Minya [Minya, El]
   city, Egypt   ahl-MIN-yuh   ɑlˈminjə

Almodad
   Biblical name   ahl-MŌ-DAD   ɑlˈmoːˌdæd

Almohad
   Muslim dynasty, Spain & Morocco   AL-muh-HAD   ˌælməˈhæd

Almon
   Biblical name   AL-MAHN, ahl-MŌN   ˈælˌmɑn, ɑlˈmoːn

Almon-diblathaim
   Biblical name   AL-MAHN-DIB-luh-THĀ-im   ˈælˌmɑnˌdibləˈθeːim

Almora
   district, India   ahl-MŌR-uh   ɑlˈmoːrə

Almoravid
   Muslim dynasty, Spain & Morocco   AL-muh-RAHV-id, ahl-MAWR-uh-vid   ˌælməˈrɑvid, ɑlˈmɔːrəvid

Al-Muthanna
   governorate, Iraq   AHL-moo-THAN-uh, AL-   ˌɑːlmuːˈθænə, ˌæl-

Alnu
   people   AL-N(Y)OO   ˈælˌn(j)uː

Alnwick
   castle, England   AN-ik   ˈænik

Aloadae
   sons of Poseidon   al-Ō-uh-dē, AL-uh-WĀD-ē   ælˈoːədiˑ, ˌæləˈweːdiˑ

Aloha
   Stadium, *Honolulu, HI; Hawaiian*   uh-LŌ-HAH   əˈloːˌhɑ
   greeting

Alois
   1. pers. name   uh-LOIS   əˈlɔis
   2. Czech   AH-LOIS   ˈɑːˌlɔis
   3. German   AHL-ō-ĒS, AHL-OIS   ˈɑloːˌiːs, ˈɑlˌɔis

Aloisius
   1. pers. name   AL-uh-WISH-uhs   ˌæləˈwiʃəs
   2. German   AHL-ō-ĒZ-yus, -Ē-zē-us   ˌɑloːˈiːzjus, -ˈiːziːus

Aloïsius
   pers. name, French   ah-lō-ēz-YUES   ɑːloːiːzjyːs

Alonso
   1. pers. name   uh-LAHN-zō   əˈlɑnzoː
   2. Italian, Spanish   ah-LAWN-sō   ɑˈlɔːnsoː

Alonzo
   pers. name   uh-LAHN-zō   əˈlɑnzoː

Alor
   Islands, *Strait, Indonesia*   AL-AWR, AHL-   ˈælˌɔːʳ, ˈɑl-

---

Key (col. 2):   a: fad   ā: fade   ah: father   ar: marry   aw: law   e: fed   ē: feed   er: merry   i: hid   ī: hide   ō: coat   oo: boot
oi: boy   ow: now   u: put   uh: above   uhr: bird   ch: chop   ng: ring   sh: show   th: thick   <u>th</u>: this   zh: measure

Alor Setar [Alur Setar]
  town, Malaysia — AL-AWR sē-TAHR, AHL- — ˌæl‚ɔːʳ siː'taʳ, ˌɑl-

Alor Star [Alor Setar]
  town, Malaysia — AL-AWR STAHR, AHL- — ˌæl‚ɔːʳ 'staʳ, ˌɑl-

Aloys
  1. pers. name, French — ah-law-ĒS — ɑːlɔːiːs
  2. German — AHL-aw-ues, AHL-OIS — 'alɔːys, 'al‚ɔis

Aloyse
  pers. name, French — ah-law-ĒZ — ɑːlɔːiːz

Aloysius
  pers. name — AL-uh-WISH-uhs — ˌælə'wiʃəs

Alp Arslan
  Persian sultan — AHLP ahr-SLAHN — ˌalp aʳ'slan

Alpe Adria
  regional association, S Europe — ALP(-uh) Ā-drē-uh — ˌælp(ə) 'eːdriːə

Alpena
  city, county, MI — al-PĒ-nuh — æl'piːnə

Alpenziger
  cheese — AL-puhn-ZĒ-guhr — 'ælpən‚ziːgəʳ

Alpert
  Herb, *US musician* — AL-puhrt — 'ælpəʳt

Alpes Bernoises [Bernese Alps]
  mtn. range, Switzerland — ahl-puh bern-WAHZ — ɑːlpə bernwaːz

Alpes Cottiennes [Cottian Alps]
  Alpine mtn. range — ahl-puh kaw-TYEN — ɑːlpə kɔːtjen

Alpes-de-Haute-Provence
  dept., France — ahlpuh duh ōt pruh-VAHⁿS — ɑːlpə də oːt prəvɑ̃s

Alpes de Savoie [Savoy Alps]
  Alpine mtn. range — ahl-puh duh sahv-WAH — ɑːlpə də saːvwaː

Alpes du Dauphiné [Dauphiné Alps]
  Alpine mtn. range — ahl-puh due dō-fē-NĀ — ɑːlpə dy doːfiːneː

Alpes Graies [Graian Alps]
  Alpine mtn. range — ahl-puh GRĀ — ɑːlpə greː

Alpes-Maritimes
  Alpine mtn. range — ahl-puh-mah-rē-TĒM — ɑːlpəmaːriːtiːm

Alpha Boötes [Arcturus]
  star — AL-fuh bō-ŌT-ēz — ˌælfə boː'oːʈiːz

Alpha Centauri
  triple star — AL-fuh sen-TAWR-ē — ˌælfə sen'tɔːriˑ

Alphaeus
  Biblical name — al-FĒ-uhs, AL-fē-uhs — æl'fiːəs, 'ælfiːəs

Alphage [Aelfheah]
  English martyr — AL-FĀJ — 'æl‚feːdʒ

Alpharabius [Fārābī, al-]
  Muslim philosopher — AL-fuh-RĀ-bē-uhs — ˌælfə're:biːəs

Alphege [Aelfheah]
  English martyr — AL-FEJ — 'æl‚fedʒ

Alpheus
  Greek river god — al-FĒ-uhs — æl'fiːəs

Alphonse
  1. pers. name — AL-FAHNS, -FAHNZ; al-FAHNS, -FAHNZ — 'æl‚fɑns, -‚fɑnz; æl'fɑns, -'fɑnz
  2. French — ahl-FAWⁿS, ahl-FAWⁿ-suh — ɑːlfɔ̃s, ɑːlfɔ̃sə

Foreign Sounds: ue: *Fr.* **rue**, *Ger.* **füllen**   uh(r): *Fr.* **boeuf**, *Ger.* **Höhle**   <u>kh</u>: *Ger.* i**ch**, *Scot.* lo**ch**   g̱: *Sp.* ami**g**o   <u>v</u>: *Sp.* ha**b**lar
hl: *Welsh* **Ll**anelli.   CAPITALS: primary stress.   SMALL CAPS: secondary stress.   Ⓢ: U.S. pron.   Ⓔ: British pron.

Alphonso
  pers. name   al-FAHN-sō, al-FAHN-zō   æl'fɑnsoː, æl'fɑnzoː
Alpi Liguri [Ligurian Alps]
  Alpine mtn. range   AHL-pē LĒ-gur-ē   ˌɑlpiː 'liːguriː
Alpine
  county, CA; town, TX; pert. to the   AL-PĪN   'ælˌpɑin
    Alps
Alpi Pennine [Pennine Alps]
  Alpine mtn. range   AHL-pē pān-NĒ-nā   ˌɑlpiː peːn'niːneː
Alpi Reti [Rhaetian Alps]
  Alpine mtn. range   AHL-pē RĀ-tē   ˌɑlpiː 'reːtiː
Alps
  mtn. range, Europe   ALPS   'ælps
Alpujarras, Alpuxaras, Las
  mountainous region, Spain   lahs ahl-po͞o-KHAHR-uhs   lɑs ɑlpuː'xɑrəs
Al-Qa-disiyah
  governorate, Iraq   ahl-KAH-di-SĒ-yuh, al-   ɑːlˌkɑdi'siːjə, æl-
Alsace
  province, France   al-SAS, al-SĀS   æl'sæs, æl'seːs
Alsacienne
  quiche with onions   ahl-sahs-YEN   ɑːlsɑːsjen
al-Sadat
  Anwar, *see* Sadat, al-
Alsatian
  European people; dog breed   al-SĀ-shuhn   æl'seːʃən
Alsop
  pers. name   AWL-SAHP   'ɔːlˌsɑp
Alston
  pers. name   AWL-stuhn   'ɔːlstən
Altadena
  city, CA   AL-tuh-DĒ-nuh   ˌæltə'diːnə
Altai
  lang., Russia; mts., Asia   AL-TĪ   'ælˌtɑi
Altai
  see Altay
Altaic
  lang. family   al-TĀ-ik   æl'teːik
Altai Krai
  territory, Russia   UHL-TĪ KRĪ   ˌəl'tɑi 'krɑi
Altair
  star   al-TĪR, al-TAR   æl'tɑir, æl'tær
Altai Shan
  mtn. range, Asia   AL-TĪ SHAHN   'ælˌtɑi 'ʃɑn
Altamaha
  river, sound, GA   AWL-tuh-muh-HAW   'ɔːltəməˌhɔː
Altamira
  caverns, Spain   AHL-tuh-MIR-uh, AL-tuh-MIR-uh   ˌɑltə'mirə, ˌæltə'mirə
Altamont
  city, IL, OR, TN   AL-tuh-MAHNT   'æltəˌmɑnt
Altan Khan [Anda]
  Mongol chief   AHL-tahn KHAHN, KAHN   'ɑltɑn 'xɑn, 'kɑn
Altar [Capac-Urcu]
  extinct volcano, Ecuador   ahl-TAHR   ɑl'tɑr
Altaschith
  Biblical name   al-TAS-kith, AHL-tahsh-KHET   æl'tæskiθ, ˌɑltɑʃ'xet

Key (col. 2):   aː fad   ā: fade   ah: father   ar: marry   aw: law   e: fed   ē: feed   er: merry   i: hid   ī: hide   ō: coat   o͞o: boot
oi: boy   ow: now   u: put   uh: above   uhr: bird   ch: chop   ng: ring   sh: show   th: thick   th: this   zh: measure

Alta Verapaz
   department, Guatemala   ahl-tah v̲ā-rah-PAHS   ɑltɑ βeːra'pɑs

Altay, Altai [Aerhatai Shan]
   town, Mongolia   UHL-TĪ   ˌəl'tɑi

Altbairisch
   German beer   ahlt-BĪ-rish   ɑlt'bɑiriʃ

Altdorf [Altorf]
   commune, Switzerland   AHLT-DAWRF   'ɑltˌdɔːʳf

Altdorfer
   Albrecht, *German artist*   AHLT-DAWR-fuhr   'ɑltˌdɔːʳfəʳ

Alteelva
   river, Norway   AHL-tuh-EL-vuh   ˌɑltə'elvə

Altenburg
   city, Germany; German name of   AHLT-n-BURK, Ⓢ AHLT-n-BUHRG,   'ɑltn̩buʳk, Ⓢ 'ɑltn̩bəʳg,
   Mosonmagyaróvár   AHL-tuhn-, -BURG   'ɑltən-, -ˌbuʳg

Altenmünster
   German beer   AHL-tuhn-MUEN-stuhr   'ɑltənˌmyːnstəʳ

Althaea
   mother of Meleager   al-THẼ-uh   æl'θiːə

Althea
   pers. name   al-THẼ-uh   æl'θiːə

Althing
   ancient Icelandic legislative body   AWL-THING, AHL-THING   'ɔːlˌθiŋ, 'ɑlˌθiŋ

Althorp
   town, England   AWL-truhp, AWL-THAWRP   'ɔːltrəp, 'ɔːlˌθɔːʳp

Altman
   Sidney, *US biologist (Nobel 1989)*   AWLT-muhn   'ɔːltmən

Alto, Pico
   highest peak, Azores   PẼ-ko͞o AHL-to͞o   'piːkuː 'ɑːltuː

Alto Adige
   Italy, former admin. district   AHL-tō AHD-uh-jā   ˌɑltoː 'ɑdədʒeː

Alto Alentejo
   province, Portugal   AHL-to͞o uh-leⁿ(n)-TEZH-o͞o   ˌɑːltuː əlẽ(n)'teʒuː

Altoona
   town, PA   al-TO͞O-nuh   æl'tuːnə

Alto Paraguay
   dept., Paraguay   AHL-tō PAHR-ah-GWĪ, AL-tō   ˌɑltoː 'pɑrɑˌgwɑi, ˌæltoː
         PAR-uh-GWĪ, -GWĀ   'pærəˌgwɑi, -ˌgweː

Alto Paraná
   river, dept., Paraguay   AHL-tō PAHR-ah-NAH, AL-tō   ˌɑltoː ˌpɑrɑ'nɑ, ˌæltoː
         PAR-uh-NAH   ˌpærə'nɑ

Altorf [Altdorf]
   commune, Switzerland   AHL-TAWRF   'ɑlˌtɔːʳf

Altrincham
   town, England   AWL-tring-uhm   'ɔːltriŋəm

Altun Shan
   mtn. range, China   AHL-TUN SHAHN, Ⓢ AL-tuhn   'ɑl'tun 'ʃɑn, Ⓢ 'æltən

Alturas Rancheria
   Indian reservation, US   al-TUR-uhs RAN-chuh-RẼ-uh   æl'turəs ˌræntʃə'riːə

Altyn Tagh [Altun Shan]
   mtn. range, Tibet, China   AHL-TIN-TAH(G)   'ɑl'tin'tɑ(g)

Al-'Uqaylah [Al-Agheila]
   town, Libya; WWII battle site   AHL-uh-KĪ-luh   ˌɑlə'kɑilə

aluminium
   British variant of aluminum   AL-yuh-MIN-ē-uhm   ˌæljə'miniːəm

---

Foreign Sounds: ue: *Fr.* **rue**, *Ger.* **füllen**   uh(r): *Fr.* **boeuf**, *Ger.* **Höhle**   k̲h̲: *Ger.* **ich**, *Scot.* **loch**   g̃: *Sp.* **amigo**   v̲: *Sp.* **hablar**
hl: *Welsh* **Llanelli.**   CAPITALS: primary stress.   SMALL CAPS: secondary stress.   Ⓢ: U.S. pron.   Ⓔ: British pron.

aluminum		
element	uh-L$\overline{OO}$-muh-nuhm	əˈluːmənəm
Alur		
lang., people, Uganda, Zaire, Sudan	AH-LUR, ah-LUR	ˈɑˌluʳ, aˈluʳ
Alured		
pers. name	AL-yuh-RED	ˈæljəˌred
Alur Setar [Alor Setar]		
city, Malaysia	AL-UR sē-TAHR, AHL-	ˌælˌuʳ siːˈtɑʳ, ˌɑl-
Alush		
Biblical name	Ā-luhsh, AHL-$\overline{oo}$sh	ˈeːləʃ, ˈɑluːʃ
Alva		
1. pers. name	AL-vuh	ˈælvə
2. Spanish	AHL-vah	ˈɑlβɑ
Alvah		
Biblical name	AL-vuh, AHL-vah	ˈælvə, ˈɑlvɑ
Alvan		
Biblical name	AL-vuhn, AH-luh-VAHN	ˈælvən, ˌɑləˈvɑn
Alvar		
pers. name, Finnish	AHL-VAHR	ˈɑːlˌvɑːʳ
Álvar		
pers. name, Spanish	AHL-vahr	ˈɑlβɑr
Alvarado, Paso de		
mtn. pass, Andes, between Argentina & Chile	PAHS-ō thā AHL-vah-RAHTH-ō	ˈpɑsoː ðeː ˌɑlβɑˈrɑðoː
Álvares		
pers. name, Portuguese	AHL-vuh-rish, AHL-vahr-is	ˈɑlvəriʃ, ˈɑlvɑːris
Alvarez		
Luis W., US physicist (Nobel 1968)	AL-vuh-REZ	ˈælvəˌrez
Álvarez		
pers. name, Spanish	AHL-vahr-ās, -āth	ˈɑlvareːs, -eːθ
Alvaro		
pers. name, Spanish	ahl-VAHR-ō	alˈβaroː
Alvensleben-Erxleben		
Gustav, Prussian general	AHL-vuhn-SLĀ-buhn-ERK-SLĀ-buhn	ˈɑlvənˌsleːbənˈerkˌsleːbən
Alvernia		
College, PA	al-VUHR-nē-uh	ælˈvəʳniːə
Alverno		
College, WI	al-VUHR-nō	ælˈvəʳnoː
Alvin		
pers. name	AL-vuhn	ˈælvən
Älvsborg, Alfsborg, Elfsborg		
county, Sweden	ELFS-BAWR, ⓢ ELFS-BAWR(-ē)	ˈelfsˌbɔːɹ, ⓢ ˈelfsˌbɔːr(i·)
Al-Wadi Al-Jadid		
governorate, Egypt	ahl-WAHD-ē AHL-jah-DĒD	alˌwadiː ˌɑldʒɑˈdiːd
Alwar, Alwur		
former state, India	UHL-wuhr	ˈəlwəʳ
Alyattes		
Lydian king	AL-ē-AT-ēz	ˌæliːˈæt̪iːz
Alypius		
Greek musical theorist	uh-LIP-ē-uhs	əˈlipiːəs
Alyssum		
plant	uh-LIS-uhm	əˈlisəm
Alzado		
Lyle, US football player	al-ZĀD-ō	ælˈzeːdoː

Key (col. 2):   a: fad   ā: fade   ah: father   ar: marry   aw: law   e: fed   ē: feed   er: merry   i: hid   ī: hide   ō: coat $\overline{oo}$: boot
oi: boy   ow: now   u: put   uh: above   uhr: bird   ch: chop   ng: ring   sh: show   th: thick   th̲: this   zh: measure

Alzheimer's
   disease of progressive dementia   AHLTS-HĪ-muhrz   'ɑlts₁haiməʳz

Amad
   Biblical name   Ā-MAD, ahm-AHD   'eː₁mæd, ɑm'ɑd

Amadeo
   1. Italian   AHM-ah-DĀ-ō   ₁ɑmɑ'deːoː
   2. Spanish   ahm-ah-T͟HĀ-ō   ɑmɑ'ðeːoː

Amadeus
   1. pers. name   AM-uh-DĒ-uhs, AHM-, -DĀ-uhs   ₁æmə'diːəs, ₁ɑm-, -'deːəs
   2. German   AH-mah-DĀ-us   ₁ɑmɑ'deːus
   3. Swedish   AH-mah-DĀ-uhs   ₁ɑmɑː'deːəs

Amadis
   1. pers. name   AM-uhd-uhs   'æmədəs
   2. French   ah-mah-DĒS   ɑːmɑːdiːs

Amadjuak
   Lake, *Baffin Island, Canada*   uh-MAJ-uh-WAK   ə'mædʒə₁wæk

Amado
   pers. name   ah-MAHT͟H-ō   ɑ'mɑðoː

Amador
   county, CA   AM-uh-DAWR   'æmə₁dɔːʳ

Amagasaki
   city, Japan   ahm-ah-gah-sahk-ē   ɑmɑgɑsɑkiː

Amahuaca
   S. American people   AHM-uh-WAHK-uh, AM-   ₁ɑmə'wɑkə, ₁æm-

Amakusa
   island group, sea, Japan   ahm-ah-ko͞o-sah   ɑmɑkuːsɑ

Amal
   Biblical name   Ā-MAL, ahm-AHL   'eː₁mæl, ɑm'ɑl

Amalek
   Biblical name   AM-uh-LEK, AHM-ah-LEK   'æmə₁lek, ₁ɑmɑ'lek

Amalekite
   Biblical name   AM-uh-LEK-ĪT, uh-MAL-uh-KĪT   'æmə₁lek₁ait, ə'mælə₁kait

Amalekites
   ancient Middle Eastern people   AM-uh-LEK-ĪTS, uh-MAL-uh-KĪTS   'æmə₁lek₁aits, ə'mælə₁kaits

Amalfi
   town, Italy   uh-MAHL-fē   ə'mɑlfiˑ

Amalric [Amaury]
   king of Jerusalem   uh-MAL-rik   ə'mælrik

Amalthea
   nurse of the infant Zeus; satellite of   AM-uhl-THĒ-uh, uh-mal-THĒ-uh   ₁æməl'θiːə, əmæl'θiːə
   Jupiter

Amam
   Biblical name   Ā-MAM, ahm-AHM   'eː₁mæm, ɑm'ɑm

Amambay
   department, Paraguay   ahm-ahm-BĪ   ɑmɑm'bai

Amami, Amami Gunto [Oshima]
   island group, Japan   ah-mah-mē (gun-tō)   ɑmɑmiː (guntoː)

Aman
   Folk Ensemble, *dance co., CA*   AH-MAHN, uh-MAHN   'ɑ₁mɑn, ə'mɑn

Amana
   city; IA; tdmk for an appliance brand   uh-MAN-uh   ə'mænə

Amanda
   1. pers. name   uh-MAN-duh   ə'mændə
   2. German   ah-MAHN-duh   ɑ'mɑndə

Foreign Sounds: ue: *Fr.* **rue**, *Ger.* **füllen**   uh(r): *Fr.* **boeuf**, *Ger.* **Höhle**   <u>kh</u>: *Ger.* i<u>ch</u>, *Scot.* lo<u>ch</u>   g̱: *Sp.* ami**g**o   y: *Sp.* ha**b**lar
hl: *Welsh* **Ll**anelli.   CAPITALS: primary stress.   SMALL CAPS: secondary stress.   Ⓢ: U.S. pron.   Ⓔ: British pron.

Amandine
  pers. name, French   ah-mah^n-DĒN   ɑːmɑ̃diːn

Amānollah Khān
  Afghan ruler   UHM-uhn-UL-uh <u>KH</u>AHN, KAHN   ˌəmən'ulə 'xɑn, 'kɑn

Amapá
  territory, Brazil   AHM-ah-PAH   ˌɑmɑ'pɑ

Amaranth
  plant   AM-uh-RANTH   'æməˌrænθ

Amarapura
  former capital of kingdom of Burma   UHM-uh-RAHP-uh-RAH, AHM-   ˌəməˌrɑpə'rɑ, ˌɑm-

Amara Simha
  Sanskrit grammarian   UHM-uh-ruh SI^n-huh   ˌəmərə 'sĩhə

Amaravati
  ruined city, India   UHM-uh-RAHV-uht-ē   ˌəmə'rɑvəti·

Amar Dās
  Sikh guru   uh-MAHR DAHS   ə'mɑʳ 'dɑs

Amaretto di Saronno
  liqueur brand   AM-uh-RET-ō dē suh-RAWN-ō, AHM-   ˌæmə'reto: di· sə'rɔːnoː, ˌɑm-

Amargosa
  river, NV, CA; mtn. range, CA   AM-AHR-GŌ-suh   ˌæmˌɑr'goːsə

Amariah
  Biblical name   AM-uh-RĪ-uh, ahm-AHR-yah   ˌæmə'raiə, ɑm'ɑrjɑ

Amarillo
  city, TX   AM-uh-RIL-ō, AM-uh-RIL-uh   ˌæmə'riloː, ˌæmə'rilə

Amarit
  Thai beer   AHM-uh-rit   'ɑmərit

Amaryllis
  pers. name   AM-uh-RIL-uhs   ˌæmə'riləs

Amasa
  Biblical name   uh-MĀ-suh, AM-uh-suh   ə'meːsə, 'æməsə

Amasai
  Biblical name   uh-MĀ-SĪ, AM-uh-SĪ, AHM-ah-SĪ   ə'meːˌsai, 'æməˌsai, ˌɑmɑ'sai

Amashsai
  Biblical name   uh-MASH-SĪ, uh-MASH-Ī, ahm-AHSH-SĪ   ə'mæʃˌsai, ə'mæʃˌai, ɑm'ɑʃˌsai

Amasiah
  Biblical name   AM-uh-SĪ-uh, ah-MAHS-yah   ˌæmə'saiə, ɑ'mɑsjɑ

Amasias [Amaziah]
  king of Judah   AM-uh-SĪ-uhs   ˌæmə'saiəs

Amasis
  Egyptian king   uh-MĀ-suhs   ə'meːsəs

Amasya
  province, Turkey   AHM-uhs-YAH   ˌɑməs'jɑ

Amata
  wife of Latinus in Virgil's Aeneid   uh-MAHT-uh   ə'mɑtə

Amati
  Italian family of violin makers   ah-MAHT-ē, uh-MAHT-ē   ɑ'mɑti·, ə'mɑti·

Amaury
  1. king of Jerusalem; pers. name   uh-MAWR-ē, AM-uhr-ē, Ā-muhr-ē   ə'mɔːri·, 'æməri·, 'eːməri·
  2. French   ah-maw-RĒ   ɑːmɔːriː

Amaziah
  Biblical name   AM-uh-ZĪ-uh, ahm-AHTS-yah   ˌæmə'zaiə, ɑm'ɑtsjɑ

Key (col. 2):   aː fad   āː fade   ah: father   ar: marry   aw: law   e: fed   ēː feed   er: merry   i: hid   īː hide   ōː coat   ōōː boot
oi: boy   ow: now   u: put   uh: above   uhr: bird   ch: chop   ng: ring   sh: show   th: thick   <u>th</u>: this   zh: measure

Amaziah [Amasias]
  king of Judah — AM-uh-ZĪ-uh — ˌæməˈzɑiə

Amazon
  river, S. America; female warrior — AM-uh-ZAHN, AM-uh-zuhn — ˈæməˌzɑn, ˈæməzən

Amazonas
  state, Brazil; commissary, Colombia; — AM-uh-ZŌ-nuhs — ˌæməˈzoːnəs
  department, Peru; territory,
  Argentina; territory, Venezuela

Amba
  lang., people, Africa — AHM-buh, AM-buh — ˈɑmbə, ˈæmbə

Ambala
  division, district, India — uhm-BAHL-uh — əmˈbɑlə

Ambato
  city, Ecuador — ahm-BAHT-ō — amˈbɑt̪oː

Ambedkar
  Bhimrao Ramji, *Indian lawyer &* — ahm-BED-kahr — amˈbedkɑʳ
  activist

Amber
  1. pers. name — AM-buhr — ˈæmbəʳ
  2. ruined city, India — UHM-buhr, AHM-buhr — ˈəmbəʳ, ˈɑmbəʳ

Ambergris Cay
  island, Belize — AM-buhr-GRĒS KĒ, -GRIS, KĀ — ˌæmbəʳˌgriːs ˈkiː, -ˌgris, ˈkeː

Ambergris Cays
  island group, West Indies — AM-buhr-GRĒS KĒZ, -GRIS, KĀZ — ˈæmbəʳˌgriːs ˈkiːz, -ˌgris, ˈkeːz

Ambo [Avamba]
  lang., people, Angola, Namibia — AHM-bō, AM-bō — ˈɑmboː, ˈæmboː

Amboina
  island, district, town, Indonesia — am-BOI-nuh — æmˈbɔinə

Amboise
  commune, France — ahⁿ-BWAHZ — ɑ̃bwɑːz

Ambon
  island, district, port, Moluccas — AM-BAHN — ˈæmˌbɑn

Ambos Camarines
  fomer province, Philippines — AHM-bōs KAHM-uh-RĒ-nuhs — ˈɑmboːs ˌkaməˈriːnəs

Ambracian Gulf [Arta]
  inlet, Ionian Sea, Greece — am-BRĀ-shuhn GUHLF — æmˌbreːʃən ˈgəlf

Ambrim, Ambrym
  island, Vanuatu — AM-BRIM — ˈæmˌbrim

Ambrogini [Politian, Poliziano]
  Angelo, *Italian poet & scholar* — AHM-brō-JĒ-nē — ˌambroːˈdʒiːniˑ

Ambrogio
  pers. name — ahm-BRŌ-jō — amˈbroːdʒoː

Ambrose
  1. pers. name — AM-BRŌZ, -BRŌS — ˈæmˌbroːz, -ˌbroːs
  2. Dutch — AHM-BRŌS — ˈɑmˌbroːs

Ambrosian
  pert. to Ambrose — am-BRŌ-zhuhn, am-BRŌ-zē-uhn — æmˈbroːʒən, æmˈbroːziːən

Ambrosius
  1. pers. name — am-BRŌ-zhuhs, am-BRŌ-zē-uhs — æmˈbroːʒəs, æmˈbroːziːəs
  2. Dutch — ahm-BRŌ-sē-ues — amˈbroːsiːys
  3. German — ahm-BRŌZ-yus, ahm-BRŌ-zē-us — amˈbroːzjus, amˈbroːziːus

Amburayan
  river, region, Philippines — AHM-bur-Ī-AHN — ˌamburˈɑiˌan

Foreign Sounds: ue: *Fr.* **rue**, *Ger.* **füllen** uh(r): *Fr.* **boeuf**, *Ger.* **Höhle** <u>kh</u>: *Ger.* **ich**, *Scot.* **loch** g̃: *Sp.* **amigo** <u>v</u>: *Sp.* **hablar**
hl: *Welsh* **Llanelli**. CAPITALS: primary stress. SMALL CAPS: secondary stress. Ⓢ: U.S. pron. Ⓔ: British pron.

Amdahl		
US computer co.	AM-DAHL, AHM-DAHL	'æmˌdɑl, 'ɑmˌdɑl
Amda Tseyon		
founder of Ethiopian state	AHM-daht-SĪ-AHN	ˌɑmdɑt'sɑiˌɑn
Ameche		
Don, *US entertainer;* Alan, *US football player*	uh-MĒ-chē	ə'miːtʃiˑ
Amedeo		
pers. name, Italian	AHM-ā-DE-ō	ˌɑmeː'deoː
Amelia		
1. pers. name	uh-MĒL-yuh	ə'miːljə
2. Italian	ah-MEL-yah	ɑ'meljɑ
3. Spanish	ah-MĀL-yah	ɑ'meːljɑ
Ameling		
Elly, *Dutch soprano*	AHM-uh-ling	'ɑməliŋ
Amen [Amon]		
Egyptian god of the air	AHM-uhn, Ā-muhn	'ɑmən, 'eːmən
Amenemhat [Amenemhet]		
Egyptian king	AHM-uhn-em-HAHT	ˌɑmənem'hɑt
Amenemhet		
Egyptian king	AHM-uhn-em-HET	ˌɑmənem'het
Amenhotep		
king of Egypt	AHM-uhn-HŌ-TEP	ˌɑmən'hoːˌtep
Amenophis		
name, Egyptian pharaohs	AHM-uh-NŌ-fuhs	ˌɑmə'noːfəs
Amen-Ra		
Egyptian sun god	AHM-uhn-RAH	ˌɑmən'rɑ
Amerasian		
Asian American	AM-uh-RĀ-zhuhn, AM-uh-RĀ-shuhn	ˌæmə'reːʒən, ˌæmə'reːʃən
America		
Western Hemisphere, esp. US	uh-MER-uh-kuh, uh-MUHR-uh-kuh, uh-MAR-uh-kuh	ə'merəkə, ə'mərəkə, ə'mærəkə
American		
pert. to America	uh-MER-uh-kuhn, uh-MUHR-uh-kuhn, uh-MAR-uh-kuhn	ə'merəkən, ə'mərəkən, ə'mærəkən
Americana		
things pert. to America	uh-MER-uh-KAHN-uh, uh-MER-uh-KAN-uh	əˌmerə'kɑnə, əˌmerə'kænə
American Cyanamid		
US biotechnology co.	sī-AN-uh-muhd	sɑi'ænəməd
Americanism		
American English usage	uh-MER-uh-kuh-NIZ-uhm, uh-MUHR-uh-kuh-NIZ-uhm, uh-MAR-uh-kuh-NIZ-uhm	ə'merəkəˌnizəm, ə'mərəkəˌnizəm, ə'mærəkəˌnizəm
americium		
element	AM-uh-RISH-ē-uhm, AM-uh-RIS-ē-uhm	ˌæmə'riʃiːəm, ˌæmə'risiːəm
Américo		
pers. name	ah-MĀ-rē-kō	ɑ'meːriːkoː
Americus		
1. pers. name	uh-MER-i-kuhs	ə'merikəs
2. Dutch	ah-MĀ-rē-kuhs	ɑː'meːriːkəs
Amerigo		
pers. name, Italian	AHM-ā-RĒ-gō, Ⓢ uh-MER-uh-GŌ	ˌɑmeː'riːgoː, Ⓢ ə'merəˌgoː
Amerind		
American Indian people or lang.	AM-uh-RIND	'æməˌrind

Key (col. 2): a: **fad** ā: **fade** ah: **father** ar: **marry** aw: **law** e: **fed** ē: **feed** er: **merry** i: **hid** ī: **hide** ō: **coat** o͞o: **boot** oi: **boy** ow: **now** u: **put** uh: **above** uhr: **bird** ch: **chop** ng: **ring** sh: **show** th: **thick** t͟h: **this** zh: **measure**

Amerindian
  pert. to American Indians — AM-uh-RIN-dē-uhn — ˌæməˈrindiːən
Amerrique, Sierra de
  mtn. range, Nicaragua — sē-ER-rah <u>th</u>ā AHM-er-RĒ-kā — siːˈɛrɑ ðeː ˌamerˈriːkeː
Amery
  Leopold, *British journalist &* — Ā-muh-rē, ĀM-rē — ˈeːməriˑ, ˈeːmriˑ
  politician
Amhara
  former kingdom, Ethiopia — ahm-HAHR-uh — amˈhɑrə
Amharic
  lang., Ethiopia — am-HAR-ik, ahm-HAHR-ik — æmˈhærik, amˈhɑrik
Amharinya [Amharic]
  lang., Ethiopia — AM-huh-RĒN-yuh — ˌæmhəˈriːnjə
Amherst
  town, MA, NY, Canada; county, VA; — AM-uhrst, AM-HUHRST — ˈæməʳst, ˈæmˌhəʳst
  peninsula, district, Burma
Amhet Paşa Bursali
  Turkish writer — ah-MET pah-SHAH BUR-sah-LĒ — ɑˈmet pɑˈʃɑ ˌbuʳsɑˈliː
Amhrán na bhFiann
  Irish natl. anthem — AHV-rawn nah VĒ-uhn — ˈɑvrɔːn nɑ ˈviːən
Ami
  pers. name — ah-MĒ — ɑːmiː
Amici
  Giovanni Battista, *Italian* — ah-MĒ-chē — ɑˈmiːtʃiˑ
  astronomer & inventor
Amidism
  Buddhist sect — AM-uhd-IZ-uhm — ˈæmədˌizəm
Amiens
  town, France — ahm-YEⁿ — ɑːmjē
Amilcare
  pers. name, Italian — ah-MĒL-KAHR-ā — ɑˈmiːlˌkɑreː
Amin
  Idi, *ruler, Uganda* — ah-MĒN — ɑˈmiːn
Aminadab, Amminadab
  Biblical name — uh-MIN-uh-DAB, ahm-IN-ah-DAHV — əˈminəˌdæb, amˌinɑˈdɑv
Amintore
  pers. name, Italian — ah-MĒN-TAWR-ā — ɑˈmiːnˌtɔːreː
Amirante
  Islands, *dependency of Seychelles* — AM-uh-RANT — ˈæməˌrænt
Amiri
  pers. name — ah-MIR-ē — ɑˈmiriˑ
Amis
  Kingsley, *British author* — Ā-muhs — ˈeːməs
Amish
  Christian sect — AHM-ish, AM-ish, Ā-mish — ˈɑmiʃ, ˈæmiʃ, ˈeːmiʃ
Amite
  county, MS — ā-MĒT — eːˈmiːt
Amittai
  Biblical name — uh-MIT-Ī — əˈmitˌai
Amity
  pers. name — AM-uht-ē — ˈæməṭiˑ
Amityville
  town, NY — AM-uht-ē-VIL — ˈæməṭiˑˌvil
Amizabad
  see Ammizabad

Foreign Sounds: ue: *Fr.* **rue**, *Ger.* **füllen**   uh(r): *Fr.* **boeuf**, *Ger.* **Höhle**   <u>kh</u>: *Ger.* **ich**, *Scot.* **loch**   ḡ: *Sp.* **amigo**   <u>v</u>: *Sp.* **hablar**
hl: *Welsh* **Llanelli**.   CAPITALS: primary stress.   SMALL CAPS: secondary stress.   Ⓢ: U.S. pron.   Ⓔ: British pron.

Ammah		
Biblical name	AM-uh, AHM-ah	'æmə, 'ɑmɑ
Amman		
city, Jordan	ah-MAHN, uh-MAHN, uh-MAN	ɑ'mɑn, ə'mɑn, ə'mæn
Ammenemes		
name, Egyptian pharaohs	AHM-uh-NĀ-mēz, AM-uh-NĒ-mēz	ˌɑmə'neːmiːz, ˌæmə'niːmiːz
Ammi		
Biblical name	AM-Ī, ahm-Ē	'æmˌɑi, ɑm'iː
Ammianus Marcellinus		
Roman historian	AM-ē-Ā-nuhs MAHR-suh-LĪ-nuhs	ˌæmiː'eːnəs ˌmɑ^{r}sə'lɑinəs
Ammiel		
Biblical name	AM-ē-EL, AHM-ē-EL	'æmiːˌel, ˌɑmiː'el
Ammihud		
Biblical name	uh-MĪ-HUHD, uh-MĪ-HUD, AHM-ē-HO͞OD	ə'mɑiˌhəd, ə'mɑiˌhud, ˌɑmiː'huːd
Amminadab		
see Aminadab		
Ammi-shaddai		
Biblical name	AM-ē-SHAD-Ī, ah-MĒ-shahd-Ī	ˌæmiː'ʃædˌɑi, ɑˌmiːʃɑd'ɑi
Ammizabad, Amizabad		
Biblical name	uh-MIZ-uh-BAD, uh-MĪ-zuh-BAD, ah-MĒ-zahv-AHD	ə'mizəˌbæd, ə'mɑizəˌbæd, ɑ'miːzɑvˌɑd
Ammon		
Field, *ballpark, Pittsburgh, PA*	AM-uhn	'æmən
Ammon [Amon]		
Egyptian god of the air	AHM-uhn, AM-uhn	'ɑmən, 'æmən
Ammonite		
ancient Semitic people, lang.	AM-uh-NĪT	'æməˌnɑit
Ammonitess		
a female Ammonite	AM-uh-NĪT-uhs, AM-uh-NĪT-uhs	ˌæmə'nɑiţəs, 'æməˌnɑiţəs
Ammonius Saccas		
Alexandrian philosopher, founder of Neoplatonism	uh-MŌ-nē-uhs SAK-uhs	ə'moːniːəs 'sækəs
Ammonoosuc		
river, NH	AM-uh-NO͞O-sik, -suhk	ˌæmə'nuːsik, -sək
Amne Machin Shan		
mtn. range, China	AM-nē muh-JIN SHAHN	'æmniː mə'dʒin 'ʃɑn
Amnon		
Biblical name	AM-NAHN, AHM-NŌN	'æmˌnɑn, 'ɑmˌnoːn
Amoco		
American Oil Co.	AM-uh-KŌ	'æməˌkoː
Amok		
Biblical name	Ā-MAHK, Ā-muhk, ah-MŌK	'eːˌmɑk, 'eːmək, ɑ'moːk
Amon		
Egyptian god of the air	AHM-uhn, AM-uhn, Ā-muhn	'ɑmən, 'æmən, 'eːmən
Amon-Re		
Egyptian sun god	AHM-uhn-RĀ, AM-uhn-RĀ, Ā-muhn-RĀ	ˌɑmən'reː, ˌæmən'reː, ˌeːmən'reː
Amontillado		
wine	ah-MAHN-tē-YAHTH-ō, Ⓢ uh-MAHN-tuh-LAHD-ō	ɑˌmɑntiː'jɑðoː, Ⓢ əˌmɑntə'lɑdoː
Amorite		
Biblical name	AM-uh-RĪT	'æməˌrɑit
Amorites		
Mesopotamian desert people	AM-uh-RĪTS	'æməˌrɑits

Key (col. 2): a: fad ā: fade ah: father ar: marry aw: law e: fed ē: feed er: merry i: hid ī: hide ō: coat o͞o: boot oi: boy ow: now u: put uh: above uhr: bird ch: chop ng: ring sh: show th: thick th: this zh: measure

Amory

pers. name — Ā-muh-rē — 'eːməriˑ

Amos

1. *Old Testament book; pers. name* — Ā-muhs — 'eːməs
2. *Czech* — AH-maws — 'amɔːs

Amoy [Xiamen]

city, China — ah-MOI — ɑ'mɔi

Amoz

Biblical name — Ā-MAHZ, ah-MŌTS — 'eːˌmɑz, ɑ'moːts

Ampara [Amparai]

district, city, Sri Lanka — AHM-puh-RAH — ˌɑmpə'rɑ

Amparai

district, city, Sri Lanka — AHM-puh-RĪ — ˌɑmpə'rai

Ampére

André-Marie, *French physicist* — ah^n-PER — ɑ̃per

Amphiaraus

legendary Greek seer & Argonaut — AM-fē-uh-RĀ-uhs — ˌæmfiːə'reːəs

Amphictyon

legendary king of Athens — am-FIK-tē-AHN, am-FIK-tē-uhn — æm'fiktiːˌɑn, æm'fiktiːən

Amphion

son of Zeus and Antiope — am-FĪ-uhn, AM-fē-uhn — æm'faiən, 'æmfiːən

Amphipolis

ancient Macedonian city — am-FIP-uh-luhs — æm'fipələs

Amphitrite

queen of the sea, wife of Poseidon — AM-fuh-TRĪT-ē — ˌæmfə'traiţiˑ

Amphitryon

husband of Alcmene & stepfather to Heracles — am-FI-trē-uhn, -trē-AHN — æm'fitriːən, -triːˌɑn

Ampliatus

Biblical name — am-PLĪ-uht-uhs — æm'plaiəţəs

Amram

Biblical name — AM-RAM, AHM-RAHM — 'æmˌræm, 'amˌram

Amramite

Biblical name — AM-ruh-MĪT, AM-RAM-ĪT — 'æmrəˌmait, 'æmˌræmˌait

Amraphel

Biblical name — AM-ruh-FEL, AHM-rah-FEL — 'æmrəˌfel, ˌamra'fel

Amravati

district, India — uhm-RAH-vuht-ē, ahm- — əm'ravəţiˑ, am-

Amreli

district, India — uhm-RĀ-lē, ahm- — əm'reːliˑ, am-

Amritsar

city, district, India — UHM-RIT-suhr, ahm-RIT-suhr — ˌəm'ritsə^r, am'ritsə^r

Amstel

Dutch beer — AHM-stuhl — 'amstəl

Amsterdam

city, Netherlands; US pl. name — AM-stuhr-DAM — 'æmstə^{r}ˌdæm

Amstetten

city, Austria — AHM-SHTET-n — 'amˌʃtetn̩

Am-Timan

city, Chad — AHM-tē-MAHN — ˌamtiː'man

Amtrak

US railroad — AM-TRAK — 'æmˌtræk

Amu Darya

river, central & western Asia — AHM-o͞o DAHR-yuh — ˌamuː 'darjə

Foreign Sounds: ue: *Fr.* **rue**, *Ger.* **füllen**   uh(r): *Fr.* **boeuf**, *Ger.* **Höhle**   kh: *Ger.* **ich**, *Scot.* **loch**   ḡ: *Sp.* **amigo**   v: *Sp.* **hablar**
hl: *Welsh* **Llanelli**.   CAPITALS: primary stress.   SMALL CAPS: secondary stress.   ⓢ: U.S. pron.   ⓔ: British pron.

Amuesha
lang., people, Peru   ahm-WĀ-shuh   ɑmˈweːʃə

Amun [Amon]
Egyptian god of the air   AHM-uhn, AM-uhn, Ā-muhn   ˈɑmən, ˈæmən, ˈeːmən

Amundsen
Roald, *Norwegian explorer*   AHM-uhn-suhn   ˈɑmənsən

Amur
river, Asia   ah-MUR   ɑˈmuʳ

Amuzgo
lang., people, Mexico   ah-MO͞OS-gō, uh-MO͞OZ-gō   ɑˈmuːsgoː, əˈmuːzgoː

Amway
trademark for housewares   AM-WĀ   ˈæmˌweː

Amy
pers. name   Ā-mē   ˈeːmiˑ

Amymone
daughter of Danaus and Europa   AM-Ī-MŌ-nē   ˌæmˌɑiˈmoːniˑ

Amyraldism
Christian sect   AM-uh-RAL-DIZ-uhm   ˌæməˈrælˌdizəm

Amzi
Biblical name   AM-ZĪ, AHM-tsē   ˈæmˌzɑi, ˈɑmtsiˑ

An
pers. name   ahn, an   ɑn, æn

Anab
Biblical name   Ā-NAB, ahn-AHV   ˈeːˌnæb, ɑnˈɑv

Anabaptism
Christian sect   AN-uh-BAP-TIZ-uhm   ˌænəˈbæpˌtizəm

Anabaptist
believer in Anabaptism   AN-uh-BAP-tuhst   ˌænəˈbæptəst

Anacin
pain reliever, tdmk   AN-uh-suhn   ˈænəsən

Anacletus
pope   AN-uh-KLĒT-uhs   ˌænəˈkliːʈəs

Anaconda
city, MT; S. American snake   AN-uh-KAHN-duh   ˌænəˈkɑndə

Anacreon
Greek writer   uh-NAK-rē-uhn, -rē-AHN   əˈnækriːən, -riːˌɑn

Anacostia
river, District of Columbia; suburb,   AN-uh-KAW-stē-uh, -KAHS-tē-uh   ˌænəˈkɔːstiːə, -ˈkɑstiːə
Washington, DC

Anadolu [Anatolia]
region, Turkey   AHN-uhd-ō-LO͞O   ˌɑnədoːˈluː

Anadyr
river, town, gulf, Russia   AHN-uh-DĒR   ˌɑnəˈd̦iːr

Anah
Biblical name   Ā-nuh, AHN-ah   ˈeːnə, ˈɑnɑ

Anaharath
Biblical name   uh-NĀ-huh-RATH, ah-NAH<u>KH</u>-ah-RAHT   əˈneːhəˌræθ, ɑˈnɑxɑˌrɑt

Anaheim
city, CA   AN-uh-HĪM   ˈænəˌhɑim

Anáhuac
plateau, Mexico   ah-NAH-wahk   ɑˈnɑwɑk

Anaiah
Biblical name   uh-NĪ-uh, ah-NAH-yah   əˈnɑiə, ɑˈnɑjɑ

Anaïs
pers. name (A. Nin)   uh-NĪ-uhs, uh-NĀ-uhs   əˈnɑiəs, əˈneːəs

---

Key (col. 2): a: fad ā: fade ah: father ar: marry aw: law e: fed ē: feed er: merry i: hid ī: hide ō: coat o͞o: boot
oi: boy ow: now u: put uh: above uhr: bird ch: chop ng: ring sh: show th: thick <u>th</u>: this zh: measure

Anak
  Biblical name   Ā-NAK, ah-NAHK   'eːˌnæk, ɑ'nɑk
Anakim
  Biblical name   AN-uh-kim, AHN-ah-KĒM   'ænəkim, ˌɑnɑ'kiːm
Anam
  see Annam
Anambra
  state, Nigeria   uh-NAHM-bruh   ə'nɑmbrə
Anammelech
  Biblical name   uh-NAM-uh-LEK, AHN-ah-MEL-EKH   ə'næməˌlek, ˌɑnɑ'melˌex
Anan
  Biblical name   Ā-NAN, AHN-ahn   'eːˌnæn, 'ɑnɑn
Anani
  Biblical name   uh-NĀ-nē, ah-NAHN-ē   ə'neːni·, ɑ'nɑni·
Ananiah
  Biblical name   AN-uh-NĪ-uh, ah-NAHN-yah   ˌænə'naiə, ɑ'nɑnjɑ
Ananias
  Biblical name   AN-uh-NĪ-uhs   ˌænə'naiəs
Ananke
  Greek goddess of necessity; satellite   uh-NANG-kē, uh-NAN-KĒ   ə'næŋki·, ə'nænˌkiː
  of Jupiter
Anantapur
  district, India   uh-NUHNT-uh-PUR   ə'nəntəˌpuʳ
Anasazi
  N. American people   AHN-uh-SAHZ-ē   ˌɑnə'sɑzi·
Anastas
  pers. name, Russian   uh-NUHS-TAHS   əˌnəs'tɑːs
Anastasia
  1. pers. name   AN-uh-STĀ-zh(ē-)uh, -sh(ē-)uh   ˌænə'steːʒ(iː)ə, -ʃ(iː)ə
  2. German   AHN-ah-STAHZ-yuh, -STAHZ-ē-uh   ˌɑnɑ'stɑzjə, -'stɑziːə
Anastasio
  1. pers. name, Italian   AHN-ahs-TAHZ-yō   ˌɑnɑs'tɑzjoː
  2. Spanish   ahn-ahs-TAHS-yō   ɑnɑs'tɑsjoː
Anastasius
  1. pers. name   AN-uh-STĀ-zh(ē-)uhs, -sh(ē-)uhs   ˌænə'steːʒ(iː)əs, -ʃ(iː)əs
  2. German   AHN-ah-STAHZ-yus, -STAHZ-ē-us   ˌɑnɑ'stɑzjus, -'stɑziːus
Anat
  1. Egyptian goddess of war   AHN-uht   'ɑnət
  2. pers. name   uh-NAHT   ə'nɑt
Anath
  Biblical name   Ā-NATH, ah-NAHT   'eːˌnæθ, ɑ'nɑt
Anathoth
  Biblical name   AN-uh-THAWTH, AHN-ah-TŌT   'ænəˌθɔːθ, ˌɑnɑ'toːt
Anathothite
  Biblical name   AN-uh-THAW-THĪT   'ænəˌθɔːˌθait
Anatol
  pers. name, Russian   uh-NUH-TAWL   əˌnə'tɔːl
Anatole
  1. pers. name   AN-uh-TŌL, -TAWL   'ænəˌtoːl, -ˌtɔːl
  2. French   ah-nah-TAWL   ɑːnɑːtɔːl
Anatoli, Anatoly
  pers. name, Russian   uh-NUH-TAWL-yi, Ⓢ AN-uh-TŌ-lē   əˌnə'tɔːljij, Ⓢ ˌænə'toːli·
Anatolia
  region, Turkey   AN-uh-TŌ-lē-uh, AN-uh-TŌL-yuh   ˌænə'toːliːə, ˌænə'toːljə

Foreign Sounds: ue: *Fr.* **rue**, *Ger.* **füllen**   uh(r): *Fr.* **boeuf**, *Ger.* **Höhle**   <u>kh</u>: *Ger.* **ich**, *Scot.* **loch**   g̱: *Sp.* **amigo**   y: *Sp.* **hablar**
hl: *Welsh* **Llanelli.**   CAPITALS: primary stress.   SMALL CAPS: secondary stress.   Ⓢ: U.S. pron.   Ⓔ: British pron.

Anatolian
  lang. family   AN-uh-TŌ-lē-uhn, AN-uh-TŌL-yuhn   ˌænəˈtoːliːən, ˌænəˈtoːljən

Anatosaurus
  dinosaur   uh-NAT-uh-SAWR-uhs,   əˌnætəˈsɔːrəs, ˌænˌætəˈsɔːrəs
       AN-AT-uh-SAWR-uhs

Anawrahta [Aniruddha]
  first king of Burma   AHN-ow-RAHT-uh   ˌɑnɑuˈrɑṭə

Anaxagoras
  Greek philosopher   AN-AK-SAG-uh-ruhs   ˌænˌækˈsægərəs

Anaximander
  Greek philosopher   uh-NAK-suh-MAN-duhr,   əˈnæksəˌmændəʳ,
       uh-NAK-suh-MAN-duhr   əˌnæksəˈmændəʳ

Anaximenes
  Greek philosopher   AN-ak-SIM-uh-NĒZ   ˌænækˈsiməˌniːz

Ancash
  dept., Peru   AHNG-KAHSH   ˈɑŋˌkɑʃ

Anchieta
  José de, *Portuguese missionary*   AHⁿ(N)-shē-ET-uh   ˌɑ̃(n)ʃiːˈeṭə

Anchises
  father of Aeneas   an-KĪ-zēz, ang-KĪ-zēz   ænˈkɑiziːz, æŋˈkɑiziːz

Anchorage
  division, city, AK   ANG-k(uh-)rij   ˈæŋk(ə)ridʒ

Ancilla Domini
  College, *IN*   an-SIL-uh DAHM-uh-nē   ænˌsilə ˈdaməniˑ

Ancona
  city, Italy   ahng-KŌ-nuh, ang-KŌ-nuh   ɑŋˈkoːnə, æŋˈkoːnə

Ancre
  river, France   AHⁿKR, Ⓢ AHⁿ(N)-kruh   ɑ̃kr, Ⓢ ˈɑ̃(n)krə

Ancud
  port, gulf, Chile   ahng-KO͞OTH   ɑŋˈkuːð

Ancyra
  ancient name of Ankara   an-SĪ-ruh   ænˈsɑirə

Anda [Altan Khan]
  Mongol chief   AHN-dah   ˈɑndɑ

Andalucía
  region, Spain   ahn-duh-lo͞o-SĒ-uh,   ɑndəluːˈsiːə, ɑndəluːˈθiːə
       ahn-duh-lo͞o-THĒ-uh

Andalusia
  city, AL   AN-duh-LO͞O-zhuh,   ˌændəˈluːʒə, ˌændəˈluːʒiːə
       AN-duh-LO͞O-zhē-uh

Andaman
  islands, sea, Asia   AN-duh-muhn, AN-duh-MAN   ˈændəmən, ˈændəˌmæn

Andean
  pert. to Andes Mts.   an-DĒ-uhn, AN-dē-uhn   ænˈdiːən, ˈændiːən

Anders
  1. Danish   AHN-uhrs   ˈɑːnərs
  2. Swedish   AHN-duhrs   ˈɑːndərs
  3. Władysław, Polish soldier   AHN-ders   ˈɑnders

Andersen
  1. pers. name   AN-duhr-suhn   ˈændəʳsən
  2. Hans Christian, Danish author   AHN-uhr-suhn; Ⓢ AN-duhr-suhn   ˈɑːnərsən; Ⓢ ˈændəʳsən

Andersen Nexø
  Martin, *Danish novelist*   AH-nuhr-suhn NIK-suh(r)   ˈɑnərsən ˈniksœ

Key (col. 2):   a: fad   ā: fade   ah: father   ar: marry   aw: law   e: fed   ē: feed   er: merry   i: hid   ī: hide   ō: coat   o͞o: boot
oi: boy   ow: now   u: put   uh: above   uhr: bird   ch: chop   ng: ring   sh: show   th: thick   th̲: this   zh: measure

Anderson

  C. D., *US physicist (Nobel 1936);*   AN-duhr-suhn   'ændəʳsən
  Philip W., *US physicist (Nobel*
  1977); pers. name

Andes

  mtn. range, S. America   AN-dēz   'ændiːz

Andhra Pradesh

  state, India   AHN-druh pruh-DĀSH, pruh-DESH   ˌɑndrə prə'deːʃ, prə'deʃ

Andina

  region, Argentina   ahn-DĒ-nah   ɑn'diːnɑ

Andizhan

  city, division, Uzbekistan   UHN-di-ZHAHN, Ⓢ AHN-di-ZHAHN   ˌənd̺i'ʒɑn, Ⓢ ˌandi'ʒɑn

Ando

  pers. name, Japanese   ahn-dō   ɑndoː

Andoni

  lang., Nigeria   an-DŌ-nē   æn'doːniˑ

Andorra

  principality, Europe   an-DAWR-uh, an-DAHR-uh   æn'dɔːrə, æn'dɑrə

Andorran

  pert. to Andorra   an-DAWR-uhn, an-DAHR-uhn   æn'dɔːrən, æn'dɑrən

Andover

  town, MA; town, Canada; borough,   AN-DŌ-vuhr, AN-duh-vuhr   'ænˌdoːvəʳ, 'ændəvəʳ
  England

André

  1. pers. name   AHN-drā   'ɑndreː
  2. French   ahⁿ-DRĀ   ɑ̃dreː
  3. Swedish   ahn-DRĀ   ɑːn'dreː

András

  pers. name, Hungarian   AHN-DRAHSH   'ɑnˌdrɑːʃ

Andre

  pers. name; wine brand   AHN-drā   'ɑndreː

Andrea

  1. pers. name   AN-drē-uh, AHN-   'ændriːə, 'ɑn-
  2. Italian   ahn-DRE-ah   ɑn'dreɑ

Andrea del Sarto

  see Sarto, del

Andrea Doria

  ship, sunk 1956   AN-drē-uh DŌR-ē-uh, DAWR-ē-uh   ˌændriːə 'doːriːə, 'dɔːriːə

Andreanof

  Islands, *AK*   AN-drē-AN-AWF, -AN-uhf   ˌændriː'ænˌɔːf, -'ænəf

Andreas

  1. pers. name   AN-drē-uhs, AN-drā-uhs; an-DRĀ-uhs   'ændriːəs, 'ændreːəs;
                                  æn'dreːəs
  2. Danish   ahn-DRI-ahs   ɑːn'driɑːs
  3. Dutch, German, Norwegian   ahn-DRĀ-ahs   ɑn'dreːas
  4. Latin   AN-drē-uhs, an-DRĒ-uhs   'ændriːəs, æn'driːəs
  5. Mod. Greek   ahn-<u>THRE</u>-ahs   ɑn'ðreɑs
  6. Swedish   ahn-DRĀ-ahs   ɑːn'dreːɑːs

Andreevich, Andreyevich

  pers. name, Russian   UHN-DRĀ(-yiv)-YICH   ˌən'dreː(jiv)ˌjitʃ

Andrei, Andrey

  pers. name, Russian   UHN-DRĀ(-ē), Ⓢ AHN-DRĀ   ˌən'dreː(iː), Ⓢ 'ɑnˌdreː

Andreotti

  Giulio, *Italian politician*   AHN-drā-AWT-tē, Ⓢ AN-drē-AHT-ē   ˌɑndreː'ɔːttiˑ, Ⓢ ˌændriː'ɑt̺iˑ

Foreign Sounds: ue: *Fr.* **rue**, *Ger.* **füllen**   uh(r): *Fr.* **boeuf**, *Ger.* **Höhle**   <u>kh</u>: *Ger.* **ich**, *Scot.* **loch**   ḡ: *Sp.* **amigo**   <u>y</u>: *Sp.* **hablar**
hl: *Welsh* **Llanelli**.   CAPITALS: primary stress.   SMALL CAPS: secondary stress.   Ⓢ: U.S. pron.   Ⓔ: British pron.

Andress
  Ursula, *US actress*   AN-druhs   'ændrəs

Andretti
  Mario, *US race car driver*   an-DRET-ē, ahn-DRET-ē   æn'dreṭi·, an'dreṭi·

Andrew
  pers. name   AN-dr$\overline{oo}$ 'ændruː

Andrić
  Ivo, *Serbo-Croatian author (Nobel 1961)*   AHN-drich, AHN-drēch   'aːndritʃ, 'aːndriːtʃ

Andries
  pers. name, Dutch   AHN-drēs   'andriːs

Andrija
  pers. name, Serbo-Croatian   ahn-DRĒ-yah   aːn'driːjaː

Androcles
  fabled Roman slave who helped a lion   AN-druh-KLĒZ   'ændrə‚kliːz

Androgeos
  son of Minos and Pasiphae   an-DRAHJ-ē-uhs   æn'dradʒiːəs

Andromache
  wife of Hector in Greek legend   an-DRAHM-uh-kē   æn'draməki·

Andromeda
  wife of Perseus in Greek legend; constellation & galaxy   an-DRAHM-uhd-uh   æn'dramədə

Andronicus
  1. name, Eastern Roman emperors   AN-druh-NĪ-kuhs, an-DRAHN-i-kuhs   ‚ændrə'naikəs, æn'dranikəs
  2. see Titus Andronicus

Andropov
  Yuri, *president, USSR*   ahn-DRAW-puhf, ⑤ an-DRŌ-PAWF   an'drɔːpəf, ⑤ æn'droː‚pɔːf

Andros
  1. island, Bahamas   AN-druhs   'ændrəs
  2. island, Greece   AHN-DRAWS, AN-druhs   'an‚drɔːs, 'ændrəs
  3. Sir Edmund, *British governor in colonial America*   AN-druhs   'ændrəs

Androscoggin
  river, county, ME   AN-druh-SKAHG-uhn   ‚ændrə'skagən

Andrzej
  pers. name, Polish   AHN-jā   'aːndʒeː

Andvari, Andwari
  Scandinavian mythological dwarf   ahnd-VAHR-ē   and'vari·

Andy
  pers. name   AN-dē   'ændi·

Anem
  Biblical name   Ā-NEM, Ā-nuhm, ah-NEM   'eː‚nem, 'eːnəm, a'nem

Aner
  Biblical name   Ā-nuhr, ahn-ER   'eːnə^r, an'e^r

Anethothite
  Biblical name   AN-uh-THAW-THĪT   'ænə‚θɔː‚θait

Aneto, Pico de
  highest peak in the Pyrenees, Spain   PĒ-kō thā ah-NĀT-ō   'piːkoː ðeː a'neːṭoː

Aneurin
  ancient Welsh poet; pers. name   uh-NĪ-ruhn   ə'nairən

Anfinsen
  Christian B., *US biochemist (Nobel 1972)*   AN-fuhn-suhn   'ænfənsən

---

Key (col. 2): a: fad ā: fade ah: father ar: marry aw: law e: fed ē: feed er: merry i: hid ī: hide ō: coat ōō: boot
oi: boy ow: now u: put uh: above uhr: bird ch: chop ng: ring sh: show th: thick <u>th</u>: this zh: measure

Anga
  ancient name for Bihar, *India*   UHNG-guh   'əŋgə

Angami
  lang., people, India, Burma   an-GAHM-ē   æn'gɑmiˑ

Angara
  river, Russia   AHNG-guh-RAH   ˌɑːŋgə'rɑː

Angaran
  continental shield, Asia   ahng-GAR-uhn   ɑŋ'gærən

Angas
  lang., Nigeria   AHNG-guhs   'ɑŋgəs

Angel
  pers. name   ĀN-juhl   'eːndʒəl

Ángel, Angel
  pers. name, Spanish   AHNG-k͟hāl, ĀN-juhl, AHN-hel   'ɑŋçeːl, 'eːndʒəl, 'ɑnhel

Angela
  1. pers. name   AN-juh-luh   'ændʒələ
  2. Italian   ahn-JĀ-lah   ɑn'dʒeːlɑ
  3. German   ahng-GĀ-luh   ɑŋ'geːlə

Angelena
  river, county, TX; pers. name   AN-juh-LĒ-nuh   ˌændʒə'liːnə

Angeleno
  resident of Los Angeles   AN-juh-LĒ-nō   ˌændʒə'liːnoː

Angel Falls [Churún Merú]
  waterfall, Venezuela   ĀN-juhl   'eːndʒəl

Angelica
  1. pers. name   an-JEL-i-kuh   æn'dʒelikə
  2. German   ahng-GĀ-lē-kah   ɑŋ'geːliːkɑ
  3. Italian   ahn-JEL-ē-kah   ɑn'dʒeliːkɑ

Angelico
  1. Fra, *Italian painter*   ahn-JEL-i-kō   ɑn'dʒelikoː
  2. pers. name   an-JEL-ē-kō, ahn-   æn'dʒeliːkoː, ɑn-

Angélique
  pers. name   ahⁿ-zhā-LĒK   ɑ̃ʒeːliːk

Angell
  Sir Norman, *English author,*   ĀN-juhl   'eːndʒəl
  politician (Nobel 1933); Roger,
  US baseball writer

Angeln
  region, Schleswig-Holstein, Germany   AHNG-uhln   'ɑŋəln

Angelo
  1. State University, *TX; pers. name*   AN-juh-lō   'ændʒəloː
  2. German, Italian   ahn-JĀ-lō   ɑn'dʒeːloː

Angelou
  Maya, *US writer*   AHN-juh-LOO, AN-zhuh-LOO,   'ɑndʒəˌluː, 'ɑnʒəˌluː,
                        AN-juh-LŌ *(her own pron.)*   'ændʒəˌlo *(her own pron.)*

Angelus
  prayer   AN-juh-luhs   'ændʒələs

Angennes [Rambouillet]
  Catherine d', *French hostess*   ahⁿ-ZHEN   ɑ̃ʒen

Angers
  city, France   ahⁿ-ZHĀ   ɑ̃ʒeː

Angevin
  pert. to Anjou   AN-juh-vuhn   'ændʒəvən

Anghiera
  Pietro, *Italian historian*   ahng-GYER-ah   ɑŋ'gjerɑ

Foreign Sounds: ue: *Fr.* **rue**, *Ger.* **füllen**   uh(r): *Fr.* **boeuf**, *Ger.* **Höhle**   k͟h: *Ger.* **ich**, *Scot.* **loch**   g̱: *Sp.* **amigo**   v̱: *Sp.* **hablar**
hl: *Welsh* **Llanelli**.   CAPITALS: primary stress.   SMALL CAPS: secondary stress.   ⑨: U.S. pron.   ⑥: British pron.

Angie
  pers. name   AN-jē   'ændʒi·

Angkor Wat
  Khmer temple, Cambodia   AHNG-kuhr WAHT, AHNG-KAWR   'aŋkə^r 'wɑt, 'aŋ,kɔː^r 'wɑt
                                       WAHT

Angles
  European people   ANG-guhlz   'æŋgəlz

Anglesey
  island, former county, Wales   ANG-guhl-sē   'æŋgəlsi·

Anglia
  Latin for England   ANG-glē-uh   'æŋgliːə

Anglican
  pert. to Church of England   ANG-gli-kuhn   'æŋglikən

Anglicanism
  Christian denomination   ANG-gli-kuh-NIZ-uhm   'æŋglikə,nizəm

Anglo
  pert. to England; *non-Hispanic*   ANG-glō   'æŋgloː

Anglo-American
  English and American   ANG-glō-uh-MER-uh-kuhn,   ,æŋgloːə'merəkən,
                                       -uh-MUHR-uh-kuhn,   -ə'mɜrəkən, -ə'mærəkən
                                       -uh-MAR-uh-kuhn

Anglo-Catholic
  high church Anglican   ANG-glō-KATH-(uh-)lik   ,æŋgloː'kæθ(ə)lik

Anglo-Indian
  pert. to India *and* England *or* ANG-glō-IN-dē-uhn   ,æŋgloː'indiːən
  English

Anglo-Irish
  pert. to Ireland *and* England *or* ANG-glō-Ī-rish   ,æŋgloː'airiʃ
  English

Anglophile
  admirer of England   ANG-gluh-FĪL   'æŋglə,fail

Anglophilia
  admiration for England   ANG-gluh-FIL-ē-uh   ,æŋglə'filiːə

Anglophobe
  one who dislikes England   ANG-gluh-FŌB   'æŋglə,foːb

Anglophobia
  dislike of England   ANG-gluh-FŌB-ē-uh   ,æŋglə'foːbiːə

Anglophone
  English-speaking   ANG-gluh-FŌN   'æŋglə,foːn

Anglo-Saxon
  European lang. (Old English)   ANG-glō-SAK-suhn   ,æŋgloː'sæksən

Angola
  republic, Africa   ang-GŌ-luh, an-   æŋ'goːlə, æn-

Angmagssalik
  settlement, Greenland   ah(ng)-MAH(K)-suh-LIK   ɑ(ŋ)'mɑ(k)sə,lik

Angol
  city, Chile   ahng-GŌL   aŋ'goːl

Angolan
  pert. to Angola   ang-GŌ-luhn, an-   æŋ'goːlən, æn-

Angora
  former name of Ankara; *breed of* ang-GŌR-uh, an-GŌR-uh, -GAWR-uh   æŋ'goːrə, æn'goːrə, -'gɔːrə
  cat, goat, or rabbit

Key (col. 2): a: **fad** ā: **fade** ah: **father** ar: **marry** aw: **law** e: **fed** ē: **feed** er: **merry** i: **hid** ī: **hide** ō: **coat** ōō: **boot**
oi: **boy** ow: **now** u: **put** uh: **above** uhr: **bird** ch: **chop** ng: **ring** sh: **show** th: **thick** <u>th</u>: **this** zh: **measure**

Angostura
    former name of Ciudad Bolivar,   ANG-guh-ST(Y)UR-uh   ˌæŋgəˈst(j)urə
    Venezuela; aromatic bark used in
    bitters

Angoulême
    city, France; French noble title   ahⁿ-gōō-LEM   ɑ̃guːlem

Angoumois
    historical region, France   ahⁿ-gōōm-WAH   ɑ̃guːmwɑ

Ångström
    Anders Jonas, *Swedish scientist*   AWNG-struhm, ⓢ ANG-struhm   ˈɔːŋstrəm, ⓢ ˈæŋstrəm

Angra do Heroísmo
    former district, Portugal; port, Azores   AHNG-gruh dōō ER-ōō-ĒZH-mōō   ˈɑŋgrə duː ˌeruːˈiːʒmuː

Ang Thong, Angthong
    province, Thailand   ahng-TAWNG   ɑŋˈtɔːŋ

Anguier
    François & Michel André, *French*   ahⁿ-GYĀ   ɑ̃gjeː
    sculptors

Anguilla
    island, West Indies   ang-GWIL-uh, an-   æŋˈgwilə, æn-

Angus
    pers. name   ANG-guhs   ˈæŋgəs

Anhalt
    state, Germany   AHN-HAHLT   ˈɑnˌhɑlt

Anheuser-Busch
    US beer co.   AN-HĪ-zuhr-BUSH   ˌænˌhɑizəʳˈbuʃ

anhinga
    bird   an-HING-guh   ænˈhiŋgə

Anhui, Anhwei
    province, China   AHN-(H)WĀ   ˈɑnˈ(h)weː

Anhur
    Egyptian sun god   AHN-HUR   ˈɑnˌhuʳ

Anhwei
    see Anhui

ANI
    automatic number identification   AN-ē, Ā-EN-Ī   ˈæniˑ, ˌeːˌenˈɑi

ani
    bird   ah-NĒ   ɑˈniː

Aniakchak
    crater, national monument, AK   AN-ē-AK-chak   ˌæniːˈæktʃæk

Aniam
    Biblical name   uh-NĪ-uhm, Ā-nē-uhm   əˈnɑiəm, ˈeːniːəm

Anicetus
    pope   AN-i-SĒT-uhs   ˌæniˈsiːʈəs

Anim
    Biblical name   Ā-nim   ˈeːnim

Aniruddha [Anawrahta]
    first king of Burma   AN-uh-RŌŌD-uh   ˌænəˈruːdə

Anita
    1. pers. name   uh-NĒT-uh   əˈniːʈə
    2. Danish, German, Spanish   ah-NĒ-tah   ɑˈniːtɑ

Anjelica
    pers. name (A. Huston)   an-JEL-i-kuh   ænˈdʒelikə

Anjou
    province, France; town, Canada   ahⁿ-ZHŌŌ; ⓢ AHN-JŌŌ, ahn-ZHŌŌ,   ɑ̃ʒuː; ⓢ ˈɑnˌdʒuː, ɑnˈʒuː,
         AN-JŌŌ   ˈænˌdʒuː

Foreign Sounds: ue: *Fr.* **rue**, *Ger.* **füllen**   uh(r): *Fr.* **boeuf**, *Ger.* **Höhle**   <u>kh</u>: *Ger.* i**ch**, *Scot.* lo**ch**   ḡ: *Sp.* ami**g**o   v: *Sp.* ha**b**lar
hl: *Welsh* **Ll**anelli.   CAPITALS: primary stress.   SMALL CAPS: secondary stress.   ⓢ: U.S. pron.   Ⓔ: British pron.

Ankara
  city, province, Turkey | AHNG-kuh-ruh, ANG-kuh-ruh | 'aŋkərə, 'æŋkərə
Ankole
  plateau, Uganda | ahng-KŌ-lā, -lē | aŋ'koːleː, -liˑ
Ankwe
  lang., Nigeria | AHNG-kwā | 'aŋkweˑ
Ankylosaurus
  dinosaur | AN-kuh-luh-SAWR-ē-uh | ˌænkələ'sɔːriːə
Ann
  pers. name | AN | 'æn
Anna
  1. pers. name | AN-uh | 'ænə
  2. Dutch | AHN-ah | 'anaː
  3. French | ahn-NAH | aːnnaː
  4. German | AHN-ah | 'ana
  5. Italian, Latvian | AHN-nah | 'anna
  6. Polish, Swedish | AHN-nah | 'aːnnaː
  7. Russian | AHN-nuh | 'aːnnə
Annaba
  department, port, Algeria | an-AHB-uh | æn'abə
Annabella
  pers. name | AN-uh-BEL-uh | ˌænə'belə
Anna Karénina
  novel, L. Tolstoy | AHN-uh kuh-REN-uh-nuh | 'anə kə'renənə
Annam, Anam
  historic kingdom, Vietnam | uh-NAM | ə'næm
Annamarie, Anna-Marie
  pers. name | AN-uh-muh-RĒ | ˌænəmə'riː
Annan
  city, Scotland | AN-uhn | 'ænən
Anna Perenna
  Roman goddess | AN-uh puh-REN-uh | ˌænə pə'renə
Annapolis
  city, MD | uh-NAP-(uh-)luhs | ə'næp(ə)ləs
Annapurna
  mtn. range, Nepal | AN-uh-PUR-nuh | ˌænə'purnə
Ann Arbor
  city, MI | an AHR-buhr | æn 'aʳbəʳ
Annan
  city, Scotland | AN-uhn | 'ænən
Annas
  Biblical name | AN-uhs | 'ænəs
Anne
  1. pers. name | AN | 'æn
  2. French | AHN | an, aːn
  3. Swedish | AHN | 'aːn
  4. German | AHN-uh | 'anə
Anne Arundel
  county, MD | AN uh-RUHN-dl, *locally* AN uh-RUHN-l, AN uh-RAN-l | ˌæn ə'rəndl̩, *locally* ˌæn ə'rənl̩, ˌæn ə'rænl̩
Annecy
  city, lake, France | ahn-SĒ, ah-nuh-SĒ | aːnsiː, aːnəsiː
Annelida
  worm phylum | uh-NEL-uhd-uh | ə'nelədə

Key (col. 2): a: fad ā: fade ah: father ar: marry aw: law e: fed ē: feed er: merry i: hid ī: hide ō: coat ōō: boot
oi: boy ow: now u: put uh: above uhr: bird ch: chop ng: ring sh: show th: thick <u>th</u>: this zh: measure

Annemarie		
1. pers. name	AN-muh-RĒ	ˌænmə'riː
2. German	AHN-uh-mah-RĒ	ˌɑnəmɑ'riː
Annenberg		
Walter, *founder* TV Guide *magazine, US ambassador to England*	AN-uhn-BUHRG	'ænənˌbə^{r}g
Annette		
1. Islands Reserve, *Indian reservation, US*	a-NET, uh-NET	æ'net, ə'net
2. pers. name	uh-NET	ə'net
3. French	ah-NET	ɑːnet
4. German	ah-NET-uh	ɑ'net̯ə
Annibale		
pers. name, Italian	AHN-nē-BAH-lā	ˌɑnniː'bɑleː
Annie		
pers. name	AN-ē	'æniˑ
Annil el Azraq		
region, Sudan	ah-NIL EL ahz-RAHK	ɑˌnil ˌel ɑz'rɑk
Anno		
Japanese writer, illustrator	ahn-nō	ɑnnoː
Anno Domini		
'in the year of the Lord'	AN-ō DAHM-uh-nē, DAHM-uh-NĪ	ˌænoː 'dɑməniˑ, 'dɑməˌnɑi
Annunzio		
pers. name, Italian	ahn-NO͞ONT-sē-ō	ɑn'nuːntsiːoː
Anoka		
county, MN	uh-NŌ-kuh	ə'noːkə
Anoka-Ramsey		
Community College, *MN*	uh-NŌ-kuh-RAM-zē	ə'noːkə'ræmziˑ
Anouilh		
Jean, *French author*	ah-NO͞O, [$] a-NO͞O-ē	ɑːnuːj, [$] æ'nuːiˑ
Anpu [Anubis]		
Egyptian god of the dead	AHN-PO͞O	'ɑnˌpuː
Anqet [Anuket]		
Egyptian goddess	AHNG-kuht	'ɑŋkət
Anquetil-Duperron		
Abraham Hyacinthe, *French scholar*	ah^{n}k-TĒL-duh(r)-puh-RAW^{n}	ɑ̃ktiːldœːpərɔ̃
Ansbach		
former principality, Germany	AHN(T)S-BAHKH	'ɑn(t)sˌbɑx
Anschluss		
political union of Austria, Germany	AHN-SHLUS	'ɑnˌʃlus
Anse, L'		
see L'Anse		
Ansel		
pers. name	AN-suhl	'ænsəl
Anselm		
1. Christian saint, philosopher; pers. name	AN-SELM	'ænˌselm
2. German	AHN-ZELM	'ɑnˌzelm
3. Swedish	AHN-selm, AHN-suhlm	'ɑːnselm, 'ɑːnsəlm
An-Shan		
city, China	AHN-SHAHN	'ɑn'ʃɑn
Anshan [Anzan]		
region, ancient Persia	AHN-SHAHN	'ɑnˌʃɑn

Foreign Sounds: ue: *Fr.* **rue**, *Ger.* **füllen** uh(r): *Fr.* **boeuf**, *Ger.* **Höhle** kh: *Ger.* **ich**, *Scot.* **loch** g̃: *Sp.* amigo v̱: *Sp.* hablar hl: *Welsh* **Ll**anelli. CAPITALS: primary stress. SMALL CAPS: secondary stress. [$]: U.S. pron. [£]: British pron.

ANSI
   American National Standards   AN-zē, AN(T)-sē   'ænzi·, 'æn(t)si·
   Institute

Antaeus
   1. Libyan giant in Greek myth   an-TĒ-uhs, an-TĀ-uhs   æn'tiːəs, æn'teːəs
   2. US literary magazine   an-TĀ-uhs   æn'teːəs

Antakya [Antioch]
   city, Turkey   ANT-uhk-YAH   ˌæntək'jɑ

Antal
   pers. name (A. Dorati)   AHN-TAHL   'ɑnˌtɑl

Antalcidas
   King's Peace of, Spartan-Persian   an-TAL-suh-duhs   æn'tælsədəs
   pact

Antalya
   province, gulf, port, Turkey   AHNT-l-YAH   ˌɑntļ'jɑ

Antananarivo
   city, Madagascar   AHN-tuh-NAHN-uh-RĒ-vō, AN-tuh-NAN-   ˌɑntəˌnɑnə'riːvoː, ˌæntəˌnæn-

Antarctica
   continent   ant-AHRK-ti-kuh, ant-AHRT-i-kuh   ænt'ɑʳktikə, ænt'ɑʳtikə

Antares
   star   an-TAR-ĒZ   æn'tærˌiːz

Antenor
   adviser to Priam   an-TEN-uhr, an-TEN-AWR, an-TĒ-nawr   æn'tenəʳ, æn'tenˌɔːʳ,
        æn'tiːnɔːʳ

Anterus
   pope   ANT-uh-ruhs   'æntərəs

Antheil
   George, American composer   AN-TĪL   'ænˌtail

Anthony
   1. pers. name   AN-thuh-nē, Ⓔ AN-tuh-nē   'ænθəni·, Ⓔ 'æntəni·
   2. Dutch   ahn-TŌ-nē   ɑn'toːniː

Anthothijah [Antothijah]
   Biblical name   AN-thō-THĪ-juh, ahn-TAW-tē-YAH   ˌænθoː'θaidʒə, ɑnˌtɔːtiː'jɑ

Antibes
   city, French Riviera   ahⁿ-TĒB   ɑ̃tiːb

Antichrist
   antagonist of Christ   ANT-ē-KRĪST, AN-TĪ-KRĪST   'ænti·ˌkraist, 'ænˌtaiˌkraist

Anticleia
   wife of Laertes, mother of Odysseus   ANT-i-KLĒ-uh, ANT-i-KLĀ-uh   ˌænti'kliːə, ˌænti'kleːə

Anticosti
   island, Canada   ANT-i-KAWS-tē   ˌænti'kɔːsti·

Antietam
   village, creek, battle site, MD   an-TĒT-uhm   æn'tiːṭəm

Antigone
   daughter of Oedipus; play, Sophocles   an-TIG-uh-nē   æn'tigəni·

Antigonish
   county, town, Nova Scotia, Canada   ANT-i-guh-NISH   ˌæntigə'niʃ

Antigonus Doson
   Macedonian regent   an-TIG-uh-nuhs DŌ-SAHN   æn'tigənəs 'doːˌsɑn

Antigonus Gonatas
   Macedonian king   an-TIG-uh-nuhs GAHN-uht-uhs   æn'tigənəs 'gɑnəṭəs

Antigua
   1. island, Caribbean   an-TĒ-gwuh, an-TIG-wuh   æn'tiːgwə, æn'tigwə
   2. city, Guatemala   ahn-TĒG-wah; Ⓢ an-TĒ-gwuh,   ɑn'tiːɣwɑ; Ⓢ æn'tiːgwə,
        an-TIG-wuh   æn'tigwə

Key (col. 2):   a: fad   ā: fade   ah: father   ar: merry   aw: law   e: fed   ē: feed   er: merry   i: hid   ī: hide   ō: coat   ōō: boot
oi: boy   ow: now   u: put   uh: above   uhr: bird   ch: chop   ng: ring   sh: show   th: thick   th̲: this   zh: measure

Antigua and Barbuda
  island nation, Caribbean   an-TĒ-gwuh uhn(d) bahr-B$\overline{OO}$-duh,   æn'tiːgwə ən(d) bɑ^r'buːdə,
                                              an-TIG-wuh   æn'tigwə
Antiguan
  pert. to Antigua   an-TĒ-gwuhn, an-TIG-wuhn   æn'tiːgwən, æn'tigwən
Antillean
  pert. to Antilles   an-TIL-ē-uhn   æn'tiliːən
Antilles
  islands, West Indies   an-TIL-ēz   æn'tiliːz
Antillian
  College, *Puerto Rico*   an-TIL-ē-uhn   æn'tiliːən
Antilochus
  son of Nestor   an-TIL-uh-kuhs   æn'tiləkəs
antimony
  element   ANT-uh-MÕ-nē   'æntəˌmoːniˑ
Antinous
  suitor of Penelope   an-TIN-uh-wuhs   æn'tinəwəs
Antioch
  ancient Syrian city; city, CA;   ANT-ē-AHK   'æntiːˌɑk
    university, OH
Antiochus
  son of Heracles; ancient Syrian kings   an-TĪ-uh-kuhs   æn'tɑiəkəs
Antiope
  mother of Amphion and Zethus;   an-TĪ-uh-pē   æn'tɑiəpiˑ
    queen of the Amazons
Antioquia
  department, Colombia   ahn-tē-Õ-kē-uh   ɑntiː'oːkiːə
Antipas
  epithet, Herod   ANT-uh-PAS, ANT-uh-puhs   'æntəˌpæs, 'æntəpəs
Antipater
  Macedonian general   an-TIP-uht-uhr   æn'tipətə^r
Antipatris
  Biblical name   ANT-i-PAH-truhs, an-TIP-uh-truhs   ˌænti'pɑtrəs, æn'tipətrəs
Antiphanes
  Greek playwright   an-TIF-uh-NĒZ   æn'tifəˌniːz
Antipodes
  Australia and New Zealand   an-TIP-uhd-ĒZ   æn'tipədˌiːz
Antique
  province, Philippines   ahn-TĒ-kā   ɑn'tiːkeː
Antisana
  volcano, Ecuador   ANT-i-SAHN-uh   ˌænti'sɑnə
Antisthenes
  Greek philosopher   an-TIS-thuh-NĒZ   æn'tisθəˌniːz
Antlia
  constellation   ANT-lē-uh   'æntliːə
Antofagasta
  former province, region, Chile   AHN-tō-fuh-GAHS-tuh   ˌantoːfə'gɑstə
Antofalla
  mtn., Argentina   AHN-tō-FĪ-uh, -FAH-zhuh   ˌantoː'faiə, -'faʒə
Antoine
  1. pers. name   AN-TWAHN, an-TWAHN   'ænˌtwan, æn'twan
  2. French   ah^n-TWAHN   ãtwaːn
Antoinette
  1. pers. name   AN-twuh-NET, AN-tuh-NET   ˌæntwə'net, ˌæntə'net
  2. French   ah^n-twah-NET   ãtwaːnet

Foreign Sounds: ue: *Fr.* **rue**, *Ger.* **füllen**   uh(r): *Fr.* **boeuf**, *Ger.* **Höhle**   <u>kh</u>: *Ger.* **ich**, *Scot.* **loch**   ḡ: *Sp.* amigo   v̲: *Sp.* hablar
hl: *Welsh* **Llanelli**.   CAPITALS: primary stress.   SMALL CAPS: secondary stress.   Ⓢ: U.S. pron.   Ⓔ: British pron.

Antommarchi

  Francesco, *Corsican physician to*   AHN-tawm-MAHR-kē   ˌɑntɔːmˈmɑʳkiː
  Napolean

Antón

  pers. name, Spanish   ahn-TAWN   ɑnˈtɔːn

Anton

  1. pers. name   AN-TAHN, AN-TŌN, ANT-n   ˈænˌtɑn, ˈænˌtɔːn, ˈæntn̩
  2. Czech, Swedish   AHN-TAWN   ˈɑːnˌtɔːn
  3. Dutch, Estonian, Norwegian,   AHN-TAWN   ˈɑnˌtɔːn
  Polish
  4. German   AHN-TŌN   ˈɑːnˌtɔːn
  5. Italian   ahn-TAWN   ɑnˈtɔːn
  6. Russian   UHN-TAWN   ˌənˈtɔːn

Antonescu

  Ion, *Romanian general & leader*   AHN-taw-NES-ko͞o   ˌɑntɔːˈneskuː

Antoni

  pers. name   ahn-TAW-nē   ɑːnˈtɔːniː

Antonia

  1. pers. name   an-TŌ-nē-uh, an-TŌN-yuh   ænˈtɔːniːə, ænˈtɔːnjə
  2. French   ahⁿ-tawn-YAH   ɑ̃tɔːnjɑː
  3. Italian   ahn-TAWN-yah   ɑnˈtɔːnjɑ
  4. Spanish   ahn-TŌN-yah   ɑnˈtɔːnjɑ

Antonie

  pers. name, German   ahn-TŌN-yuh, ahn-TŌ-nē-uh   ɑnˈtɔːnjə, ɑnˈtɔːniːə

Antonin

  pers. name, French   ahⁿ-taw-NEⁿ   ɑ̃tɔːnẽ

Antonín

  pers. name, Czech   AHN-tawn-YĒN   ˈɑntɔːnˌjiːn

Antonines

  Roman imperial family   AN-tuh-NĪNZ   ˈæntəˌnɑinz

Antoninus

  pers. name   AN-tuh-NĪ-nuhs   ˌæntəˈnɑinəs

Antoninus Pius

  Roman emperor   AN-tuh-NĪ-nuhs PĪ-uhs   ˌæntəˈnɑinəs ˈpɑiəs

Antonio

  1. pers. name   an-TŌ-nē-ō, an-TŌN-yō   ænˈtɔːniːˌoː, ænˈtɔːnjoː
  2. French   ahⁿ-tawn-YŌ   ɑ̃tɔːnjoː
  3. German   ahn-TŌN-yō, ahn-TŌ-nē-ō   ɑnˈtɔːnjoː, ɑnˈtɔːniːˌoː
  4. Italian   ahn-TAWN-yō   ɑnˈtɔːnjoː
  5. Portuguese   ahⁿ(n)-TAWN-yo͞o   ɑ̃(n)ˈtɔːnjuː
  6. Spanish   ahn-TŌN-yō   ɑnˈtɔːnjoː

Antônio

  pers. name, Portuguese   ahⁿ(n)-TAWN-yo͞o   ɑ̃(n)ˈtɔːnjuː

Antonioni

  Michelangelo, *Italian film director*   AN-TŌ-nē-Ō-nē   ˌænˌtɔːniːˈoːniˑ

Antonius

  1. pers. name   an-TŌ-nē-uhs, an-TŌN-yuhs   ænˈtɔːniːəs, ænˈtɔːnjəs
  2. Dutch   ahn-TŌ-nē-ues   ɑnˈtɔːniːys

Antony

  1. Mark, Roman general; pers. name   AN-tuh-nē   ˈæntəniˑ
  2. Dutch   ahn-TŌ-nē   ɑnˈtɔːniː
  3. French   ahⁿ-taw-NĒ   ɑ̃tɔːniː

Antothijah [Anthothijah]

  Biblical name   ANT-uh-THĪ-juh, ahn-TAW-tē-YAH   ˌæntəˈθɑidʒə, ɑnˌtɔːtiːˈjɑ

Key (col. 2):   a: f**a**d   ā: f**a**de   ah: f**a**ther   ar: m**a**rry   aw: l**a**w   e: f**e**d   ē: f**ee**d   er: m**e**rry   i: h**i**d   ī: h**i**de   ō: c**oa**t   o͞o: b**oo**t
oi: b**oy**   ow: n**ow**   u: p**u**t   uh: **a**bove   uhr: b**ir**d   ch: **ch**op   ng: ri**ng**   sh: **sh**ow   th: **th**ick   t̲h̲: **th**is   zh: mea**s**ure

Antrim
    city, N. Ireland; county, MI   AN-truhm   ˈæntrəm

Antsiranana
    port, province, Madagascar   ANT-suh-RAHN-uh-nuh   ˌæntsəˈranənə

Antung
    former province, city, China   AHN-DUNG   ˈɑnˈduŋ

Antwerp
    city, Belgium   ANT-WUHRP, AN-TWUHRP   ˈæntˌwəʳp, ˈænˌtwəʳp

Antwerpen [Anvers]
    province, Belgium   AHNT-VER-puh(n)   ˈɑntˌverpə(n)

Anub
    Biblical name   Ā-nuhb, ah-NOOV   ˈeːnəb, ɑˈnuːv

Anubis
    Egyptian god of the dead   uh-N(Y)OO-buhs   əˈn(j)uːbəs

Anuket
    Egyptian goddess   AHN-(y)oo-kuht   ˈɑn(j)uːkət

Anukis [Anuket]
    Egyptian goddess   AHN-(y)oo-kuhs   ˈɑn(j)uːkəs

Anuradhapura
    city, district, Sri Lanka   UHN-uh-RAHD-uh-PUR-uh   ˌənəˌrɑdəˈpurə

Anvers [Antwerpen]
    province, Belgium   ahⁿ-VER(S)   ɑ̃ver(s)

Anville
    Jean Baptiste, *French geographer*   ahⁿ-VĒL   ɑ̃viːl
    & cartographer

Anwar
    pers. name (A. Sadat)   AHN-WAHR   ˈɑnˌwɑʳ

Anyi
    lang., Ghana, Ivory Coast   AHN-yē   ˈɑnjiˑ

Anytus
    Athenian politician who convicted   ahn-ĒT-uhs   ɑnˈiːʈəs
    Socrates

Anzac
    Australian & New Zealand armed   AN-ZAK   ˈænˌzæk
    forces, WW2

Anzan [Anshan]
    region, ancient Persia   AHN-ZAHN   ˈɑnˌzɑn

Anzio
    town, Italy   AN-zē-ō   ˈænziːoː

Anzoátegui
    state, Venezuela   ahn-sō-AH-teg-ē   ɑnsoːˈɑtegiː

ANZUS
    treaty between Australia, New   AN-zuhs   ˈænzəs
    Zealand, US

Ao
    lang., Burma   OW   ˈɑu

Aomori
    prefecture, city, Japan   ah-ō-mōr-ē   ɑoːmoːriː

Aonia
    district, Greece   ā-Ō-nē-uh   eːˈoːniːə

Aosta
    province, Italy   ah-AW-stuh   ɑˈɔːstə

Aoudad
    wild sheep breed   OW-DAD, AH-u-DAD   ˈɑuˌdæd, ˈɑ-uˌdæd

Foreign Sounds: **ue**: *Fr.* **rue**, *Ger.* **füllen**   **uh(r)**: *Fr.* **boeuf**, *Ger.* **Höhle**   **kh**: *Ger.* i**ch**, *Scot.* lo**ch**   **ḡ**: *Sp.* ami**g**o   **v̱**: *Sp.* ha**b**lar
hl: *Welsh* **Ll**anelli.   CAPITALS: primary stress.   SMALL CAPS: secondary stress.   ⑤: U.S. pron.   ⑥: British pron.

Apache
N. American people uh-PACH-ē ə'pætʃi·
Apalachee
N. American people AP-uh-LACH-ē ˌæpə'lætʃi·
Apalachicola
river, bay, city, FL AP-uh-LACH-i-KŌ-luh ˌæpəˌlætʃi'koːlə
Apamea
several ancient cities, Mesopotamia, AP-uh-MĒ-uh ˌæpə'miːə
Syria, Phrygia
Apaporis
river, Colombia AHP-uh-PŌR-ēs, -PAWR-ēs ˌɑpə'poːriːs, -'pɔːriːs
Aparri
port, Philippines uh-PAHR-ē ə'pɑri·
Apatosaurus
dinosaur (Brontosaurus) AP-uht-uh-SAWR-uhs, ˌæpəţə'sɔːrəs, ˌeːˌpæţə'sɔːrəs
 Ā-PAT-uh-SAWR-uhs
Apeldoorn
commune, Netherlands AHP-uhl-DAWRN 'ɑpəlˌdɔːʳn
Apelles
Greek painter; Biblical name uh-PEL-ēz ə'peliːz
Apellicon of Teos
Athenian bibliophile uh-PEL-i-KAHN uhv TĒ-AHS ə'peliˌkɑn əv 'tiːˌɑs
Apennines
mtn. range, Italy AP-uh-NĪNZ 'æpəˌnɑinz
Apgar score
rating of infant health AP-GAHR 'æpˌgɑʳ
ap Gwilym
see Dafydd ap Gwilym
Apharsathchites
Biblical name uh-fahr-SATH-KĪTS əfɑr'sæθˌkɑits
Aphek
Biblical name Ā-FEK, ah-FEK 'eːˌfek, ɑ'fek
Aphekah
Biblical name uh-FĒ-kuh ə'fiːkə
Aphiah
Biblical name uh-FĪ-uh ə'fɑiə
Aphra
pers. name AF-ruh 'æfrə
Aphrodite
Greek goddess of love AF-ruh-DĪT-ē ˌæfrə'dɑiţi·
Aphrodite Terra
highland on planet Venus AF-ruh-DĪT-ē TER-uh ˌæfrə'dɑiţi· 'terə
Apia
city, Samoa uh-PĒ-uh, ah-PĒ-uh ə'piːə, ɑ'piːə
Apicocomplexa
phylum of protozoans Ā-pi-KŌ-kuhm-PLEK-suh, AP-i-KŌ- ˌeːpiˌkoːkəm'pleksə,
ˌæpiˌkoː-
Apis
Egyptian god; mythical Greek king Ā-puhs 'eːpəs
Apo
Mount, *highest mtn. in the* AHP-ō 'ɑpoː
Philippines
Apocalypse
New Testament book uh-PAHK-uh-LIPS ə'pɑkəˌlips

Apocrypha
  non-canonical books of the Bible uh-PAHK-ruh-fuh əˈpɑkrəfə
Apollinaire
  Guillaume, *French poet* ah-paw-lē-NER ɑːpɔːliːner
Apollinarianism
  beliefs of Bishop Apollinaris uh-PAHL-uh-NAR-ē-uh-NIZ-uhm əˌpɑləˈnæriːəˌnizəm
Apollinaris
  Syrian prelate; Wilhelm, *French* uh-PAHL-uh-NAR-uhs əˌpɑləˈnærəs
  poet, aka G. Apollinaire
Apollo
  Greek god of prophecy and music uh-PAHL-ō əˈpɑloː
Apollonia
  lake, Turkey; several ancient towns, AP-uh-LŌ-nē-uh, -LŌN-yuh ˌæpəˈloːniːə, -ˈloːnjə
  Cyrenaica, Illyria, Macedonia,
  Thrace; Biblical name
Apollonius
  1. pers. name AP-uh-LŌ-nē-uhs ˌæpəˈloːniːəs
  2. German AHP-ō-LŌN-yus, AHP-ō-LŌ-nē-uhs ˌɑpoːˈloːnjus, ˌɑpoːˈloːniːəs
Apollonius Rhodius
  Greek epic poet AP-uh-LŌ-nē-uhs RŌD-ē-uhs ˌæpəˈloːniːəs ˈroːdiːəs
Apollos
  Biblical name uh-PAHL-uhs əˈpɑləs
Apollyon
  angel of the bottomless pit uh-PAHL-yuhn, uh-PAHL-ē-uhn əˈpɑljən, əˈpɑliːən
Apophis
  Egyptian snake-demon AP-uh-fuhs ˈæpəfəs
Apopka
  city, lake, FL uh-PAHP-kuh əˈpɑpkə
Apostles' Creed
  Christian prayer uh-PAHS-uhlz KRĒD əˌpɑsəlz ˈkriːd
Appaim
  Biblical name AP-ā-uhm, ah-PAH-yim ˈæpeːəm, ɑˈpɑjim
Appalachia
  region, eastern US AP-uh-LĀ-ch(ē-)uh, ˌæpəˈleːtʃ(iː)ə, ˌæpəˈlætʃ(iː)ə
  AP-uh-LACH(-ē)-uh *(usual local* *(usual local pron.),*
  pron.), AP-uh-LĀ-sh(ē-)uh ˌæpəˈleːʃ(iː)ə
Appalachian
  mtn. range, US AP-uh-LĀ-ch(ē-)uhn, ˌæpəˈleːtʃ(iː)ən,
  AP-uh-LACH(-ē)-uhn, ˌæpəˈlætʃ(iː)ən,
  AP-uh-LĀ-sh(ē-)uhn ˌæpəˈleːʃ(iː)ən
Appaloosa
  horse AP-uh-LOO-suh ˌæpəˈluːsə
Appanoose
  county, IA AP-uh-NOOS ˈæpəˌnuːs
Appassionata, The
  sonata, Beethoven uh-PASH-uh-NAHT-uh əˌpæʃəˈnɑtə
Appenines
  mtn. range, Italy AP-uh-NĪNZ ˈæpəˌnɑinz
Appennino [Appenines]
  mtn. range, Italy AHP-pen-NĒ-nō ˌɑppenˈniːnoː
Appenzell
  canton, Switzerland AHP-uhn(t)-SEL, Ⓢ AP-uhn-ZEL ˈɑpən(t)ˌsel, Ⓢ ˈæpənˌzel
Appian Way [Via Appia]
  ancient Roman road AP-ē-uhn WĀ ˌæpiːən ˈweː

Appert

Nicolas François, *French inventor*   ah-PER   ɑːper
& *chef*

Apphia

Biblical name   AF-ē-uh, AP-fē-uh   'æfiːə, 'æpfiːə

Appii Forum

Roman forum   AP-ē-Ī FŌR-uhm, AP-ē-Ē, FAWR-uhm   'æpiːˌɑi 'foːrəm, 'æpiːˌiː,
                                                                                 'foːrəm

Appius

pers. name   AP-ē-uhs   'æpiːəs

Appius Claudius

Roman patrician name   AP-ē-uhs KLAWD-ē-uhs   'æpiːəs 'kloːdiːəs

Appleton

Sir Edward V., *English physicist*   AP-uhl-tuhn, AP-uhlt-n   'æpəltən, 'æpəltn̩
(*Nobel 1947*)

Appollonia

US actress, singer   AP-uh-LŌ-nē-uh, -LŌN-yuh   ˌæpə'loːniːə, -'loːnjə

Appollonius

Greek mathematician   AP-uh-LŌ-nē-uhs   ˌæpə'loːniːəs

Appomattox

river, county, town (site of Civil War AP-uh-MAT-iks   ˌæpə'mætiks
surrender),VA

Apraksin, Apraxin

Fyodor Matveyevich, *Russian*   uh-PRAHK-syin   ə'prɑksjin
admiral

Apries

Egyptian king   AP-rē-ĒZ   'æpriːˌiːz

April

month; pers. name   Ā-pruhl   'eːprəl

Apteryx

bird genus   AP-tuh-riks   'æptəriks

Apthorp

pers. name   AP-THAWRP   'æpˌθoːʳp

Apuania

province, Italy   ah-PWAHN-yuh   ɑ'pwɑnjə

Apuleius

Lucius, *N. African philosopher,*   AP-yuh-LĒ-(y)uhs   ˌæpjə'liː(j)əs
author

Apulia

prov, Italy   uh-P(Y)O͞OL-yuh   ə'p(j)uːljə

Apure

river, state, Venezuela   ah-PUR-ā   ɑ'pureː

Apurímac

river, department, Peru   AHP-uh-RĒ-MAHK   ˌɑpə'riːˌmɑk

Apus

constellation   Ā-puhs   'eːpəs

'Aqaba

Gulf of, *Red Sea*   AHK-uh-buh, AK-uh-buh   'ɑkəbə, 'ækəbə

'Aqaba, Akaba

seaport, Jordan   AHK-uh-buh, AK-uh-buh   'ɑkəbə, 'ækəbə

Aquarian

pert. to Aquarius   uh-KWAR-ē-uhn, uh-KWER-ē-uhn   ə'kwæriːən, ə'kweriːən

Aquarids

meteor shower   uh-KWAR-idz, uh-KWER-idz   ə'kwæridz, ə'kweridz

---

Key (col. 2): a: fad ā: fade ah: father ar: marry aw: law e: fed ē: feed er: merry i: hid ī: hide ō: coat o͞o: boot
oi: boy ow: now u: put uh: above uhr: bird ch: chop ng: ring sh: show th: thick t͟h: this zh: measure

Aquarius
  constellation, sign of the zodiac   uh-KWAR-ē-uhs, uh-KWER-ē-uhs   ə'kwæriːəs, ə'kweriːəs
Aquascutum
  retail apparel firm   ak-wuh-SKYOOT-uhm, ahk-   ækwə'skjuːʈəm, ɑk-
Aquavit
  Scandinavian liquor   AHK-wuh-VĒT   'ɑkwə,viːt
Aqua Vitae
  alcoholic drink   AK-wuh VĪT-ē, VĒT-ē, VĒT-Ī   ,ækwə 'vaiʈiˈ, 'viːʈiˈ, 'viːʈ,ai
Aquila
  constellation   AK-wuh-luh   'ækwələ
Aquila, L'
  province, commune, Italy   LAHK-wil-uh   'lɑkwilə
Aquilegia [Columbine]
  plant   AK-wuh-LĒ-j(ē-)uh   ,ækwə'liːdʒ(iː)ə
Aquinas
  St. Thomas, Italian philosopher   uh-KWĪ-nuhs   ə'kwɑinəs
Aquino
  Corazon & Benigno, Philippine   ah-KĒ-nō, Ⓢ uh-KĒ-nō   ɑ'kiːnoː, Ⓢ ə'kiːnoː
  leaders
Aquitaine
  region, France   AK-wuh-TĀN   'ækwə,teːn
Aquitania
  Latin for Aquitaine   AK-wuh-TĀ-nē-uh, -TĀN-yuh   ,ækwə'teːniːə, -'teːnjə
Ara
  constellation   AR-uh, ER-uh   'ærə, 'erə
Arab [Arabian]
  1. a member of a Semitic people of   AR-uhb, ER-uhb, *in some dialects and*   'ærəb, 'erəb, *in some dialects*
  the Arabian peninsula; breed of   *esp. formerly* Ā-RAB   *and esp. formerly* 'eː,ræb
  horse
  2. Biblical name   AR-uhb, ER-uhb, Ā-RAB, AHR-ahv   'ærəb, 'erəb, 'eː,ræb, 'ɑrɑv
  3. town, AL   Ā-RAB   'eː,ræb
'Araba, Wadi al-
  valley between Israel & Jordan   WAHD-ē ahl AHR-uh-buh, al   ,wɑdiː ɑːl 'ɑrəbə, æl 'ærəbə
                                          AR-uh-buh
Arabah
  Biblical name   AR-uh-buh, ER-uh-buh, AHR-ah-VAH   'ærəbə, 'erəbə, ,ɑrɑ'vɑ
Arabia
  peninsula, Asia   uh-RĀ-bē-uh   ə'reːbiːə
Arabian [Arab]
  a member of a Semitic people of the   uh-RĀ-bē-uhn   ə'reːbiːən
  Arabian peninsula; breed of horse
Arabic
  lang., N Africa, Middle East, Arabian   AR-uh-bik   'ærəbik
  Peninsula
Araby
  literary term for Arabia; story, J.   AR-uh-bē   'ærəbiˈ
  Joyce
Aracaju
  city, port, Brazil   AHR-uh-kuh-ZHOO   ,ɑrəkə'ʒuː
Arachne
  mythological weaver changed into a   uh-RAK-nē   ə'rækniˈ
  spider
Arad
  1. county, city, Romania   ah-RAHD   ɑ'rɑd
  2. Biblical name   Ā-RAD, ahr-AHD   'eː,ræd, ɑr'ɑd

Foreign Sounds: ue: *Fr.* **rue**, *Ger.* **füllen**   uh(r): *Fr.* **boeuf**, *Ger.* **Höhle**   kh: *Ger.* **ich**, *Scot.* **loch**   g̃: *Sp.* **amigo**   v: *Sp.* **hablar**
hl: *Welsh* **Llanelli**.   CAPITALS: primary stress.   SMALL CAPS: secondary stress.   Ⓢ: U.S. pron.   Ⓔ: British pron.

Arafat
    Yasir, *PLO leader*   AR-uh-FAT   'ærə‚fæt
Arafura
    sea, Australia   AR-uh-FUR-uh   ‚ærə'furə
Aragón, Aragon
    river, ancient kingdom, Spain   ahr-ah-ḠAWN; ⑤ AR-uh-GAHN,   aᴿɑ'ɣɔːn; ⑤ 'ærə‚gɑn,
                                   AR-uh-guhn   'ærəgən
Aragua
    state, Venezuela   ah-RAHḠ-wuh   ɑ'rɑɣwə
Araguaia, Araguaya
    natl. park, river, Brazil   AR-uh-GWĪ-(y)uh   ‚ærə'gwɑi(j)ə
Arah
    Biblical name   Ā-ruh, ahr-AH<u>KH</u>   'eːrə, ɑr'ɑx
Arahsamnu
    Babylonian month   AHR-ah<u>kh</u>-SAHM-noo   ‚ɑrɑx'sɑmnuː
Arāk
    city, Iran   uh-RAHK   ə'rɑk
Arakan [Rakhine]
    state, Burma   AHR-uh-KAHN, AR-uh-KAN   ‚ɑrə'kɑn, ‚ærə'kæn
Arakan Yoma
    mtn. range, Burma   AHR-uh-KAHN YŌ-muh, AR-uh-KAN   ‚ɑrə'kɑn 'joːmə, ‚ærə'kæn
Araks
    river, Turkey, Armenia, & Azerbaijan   ah-RAHKS   ɑ'rɑks
Aral
    inland sea, Asia   AR-uhl   'ærəl
Aralskoye More [Aral]
    inland sea, Asia   uh-RAL-skuh-yuh MAWR-(y)uh   ə‚rælskəjə 'mɔːr(j)ə
Aram
    1. pers. name, Armenian   ahr-AHM   ɑr'ɑm
    2. Eugene, English philologist &   AR-uhm, ER-   'ærəm, 'er-
       murderer; ancient country, SW
       Asia
Aramaeans
    ancient Semitic people   AR-uh-MĀ-uhnz, AR-uh-MĒ-uhnz   ‚ærə'meːənz, ‚ærə'miːənz
Aramaic
    ancient Semitic lang.   AR-uh-MĀ-ik   ‚ærə'meːik
Aramis
    1. character in The Three   ah-rah-MĒS, ⑤ AR-uh-muhs,   ɑːrɑːmiːs, ⑤ 'ærəməs,
      Musketeers, *A. Dumas*   AR-uh-MĒS   ‚ærə'miːs
    2. cologne brand   AR-uh-muhs, ER-uh-muhs   'ærəməs, 'erəməs
Aram-Maacah
    Biblical name   Ā-RAM MĀ-uh-kuh, ahr-AHM   'eː‚ræm 'meːəkə, ɑr'ɑm
                              MAH-ah-<u>KHAH</u>   ‚mɑɑ'xɑ
Aram-Naharaim
    Biblical name   Ā-RAM NĀ-(h)uh-RĀ-uhm, ah-RAHM   'eː‚ræm ‚neː(h)ə're:əm,
                              NAH-hah-RAH-yim   ɑ'rɑm ‚nɑhɑ'rɑjim
Aram-Zobah
    Biblical name   Ā-RAM ZŌ-buh, ahr-AHM tsō-VAH   'eː‚ræm 'zoːbə, ɑr'ɑm tsoː'vɑ
Aran
    Irish island   AR-uhn   'ærən
Aranha
    Oswaldo, *Brazilian diplomat*   ah-RAHN-yah   ɑː'rɑːnjɑː
Aran Mawddwy, Aran Mowddwy
    mtn., Wales   AHR-ahn MOW<u>TH</u>-wē, ⑤ AR-uhn   ‚ɑrɑn 'mɑuðwiˑ, ⑤ ‚ærən
                              MOW<u>TH</u>-wē   'mɑuðwiˑ

Key (col. 2):   a: fad   ā: fade   ah: father   ar: marry   aw: law   e: fed   ē: feed   er: merry   i: hid   ī: hide   ō: coat   o͞o: boot
oi: boy   ow: now   u: put   uh: above   uhr: bird   ch: chop   ng: ring   sh: show   th: thick   <u>th</u>: this   zh: measure

Aransas
　county, TX　　　uh-RAN-suhs　　　ə'rænsəs
Arantxa
　pers. name (A. Sánchez Vicario)　ah-RAHNT-sah, Ⓢ ah-RAHN-chuh　a'rantsa, Ⓢ a'rantʃə
Arányi
　Jelly Eva d', *Hungarian violinist*　ah-RAHN-yē　a'ranji·
Arapaho
　N. American people　uh-RAP-uh-HŌ　ə'ræpə‚hoː
Arapahoe
　county, CO　uh-RAP-uh-HŌ　ə'ræpə‚hoː
Arapesh
　lang., people, New Guinea　AHR-uh-PESH　'arə‚peʃ
Arara
　S. American people　uh-RAHR-uh　ə'rarə
Ararat [Ağrı Dağı]
　mtn.,Turkey　AR-uh-RAT　'ærə‚ræt
Aras
　Turkish name for Araks　ah-RAHS　a'ras
Aratus
　Greek general　uh-RĀT-uhs　ə'reːṭəs
Arauca
　town, Colombia; river, Venezuela　uh-ROW-kuh　ə'raukə
Araucanía, La
　region, Chile　lah ahr-ow-kahn-Ē-uh　la araukan'iːə
Araucanian
　lang., people, S. America　uh-ROW-KAHN-ē-uhn,　ə‚rau'kaniːən, ‚ærɔː'keːniːən
　　　　　AR-aw-KĀ-nē-uhn
Araukan [Araucanian]
　lang., people, S. America　uh-ROW-kuhn　ə'raukən
Araucanía, La
　region, Chile　lah ahr-ow-kahn-Ē-uh　la araukan'iːə
Arauco
　gulf, former province, Chile　uh-ROW-kō　ə'raukoː
Araunah
　Biblical name　uh-R‾OO-nuh, uh-RAW-nuh,　ə'ruːnə, ə'rɔːnə, ar'avna
　　　　　ahr-AHV-nah
Arausio
　ancient name of Orange, *France*　uh-RAW-zhē-ō　ə'rɔːʒiː‚oː
Arawak
　S. American people　AR-uh-WAHK, AR-uh-WAK　'ærə‚wak, 'ærə‚wæk
Arba
　Biblical name　AHR-buh, AHR-BAH　'aʳbə, 'aʳ‚ba
Arba Minch
　town, Ethiopia　AHR-buh MINCH　‚aʳbə 'mintʃ
Arbat
　district, Moscow　ahr-BAHT　aʳ'bat
Arbathite
　Biblical name　AHR-buh-THĬT　'aʳbə‚θait
Arber
　Werner, *Swiss microbiologist (Nobel 1978)*　AHR-buhr　'aʳbəʳ
Arbīl [Erbil, Irbīl]
　governorate, city, Iraq　AHR-BĒL　'aʳ‚biːl
Arbite
　Biblical name　AHR-BĪT　'aʳ‚bait

Foreign Sounds: ue: *Fr.* **rue**, *Ger.* **füllen**　uh(r): *Fr.* **boeuf**, *Ger.* **Höhle**　kh: *Ger.* **ich**, *Scot.* **loch**　ḡ: *Sp.* **amigo**　v̲: *Sp.* **hablar**
hl: *Welsh* **Llanelli.**　CAPITALS: primary stress.　SMALL CAPS: secondary stress.　Ⓢ: U.S. pron.　Ⓔ: British pron.

Arbitron
  media ratings   AHR-buh-TRAHN   ˈɑʳbəˌtrɑn

Arborvitae
  plant   AHR-buhr-VĪT-ē   ˌɑʳbəʳˈvaiţiˑ

Arbour
  Bernie, Stadium, *Hamilton, Ontario*   AHR-buhr   ˈɑʳbəʳ

Arbroath
  port, Scotland   ahr-BRŌTH   ɑʳˈbroːθ

Arbuthnot
  pers. name   ahr-BUHTH-nuht, AHR-buhth-NAHT   ɑʳˈbəθnət, ˈɑʳbəθˌnɑt

Arbutus
  town, MD   ahr-BYO͞OT-uhs   ɑʳˈbjuːţəs

Arcadia
  1. city, CA, FL; ancient country, Greece   ahr-KĀD-ē-uh   ɑʳˈkeːdiːə
  2. region, Greece   AHR-kuh-THḔ-uh   ˌɑrkəˈðiːə

Arcadian
  pert. to Arcadia   ahr-KĀD-ē-uhn   ɑʳˈkeːdiːən

Arcady
  ancient name for Arcadia, *Greece*   AHR-kuhd-ē   ˈɑʳkədiˑ

Arcaro
  George 'Eddie', *US jockey*   ahr-KAR-ō, ahr-KER-ō   ɑʳˈkæroː, ɑʳˈkeroː

Arcas
  son of Zeus and Callisto   AHR-kuhs   ˈɑʳkəs

Arc de Triomphe
  monument, Paris, France   ahrk duh trē-AWⁿF   ɑːrk də triːɔf

Arce
  Manuel José, *Salvadoran politician*   AHR-sā   ˈɑʳseː

Archaeopteryx
  prehistoric bird   AHR-kē-AHP-tuh-riks   ˌɑʳkiːˈɑptəriks

Archaeozoic
  see Archeozoic

Archangel [Arkhangelsk]
  city, Russia   AHR-KĀN-juhl   ˈɑʳˌkeːndʒəl

Archbold
  Stadium, *Syracuse, NY*   AHRCH-BŌLD, AHRCH-BAWLD   ˈɑʳtʃˌboːld, ˈɑʳtʃˌbɔːld

Archelaus
  ethnarch of Judea   AHR-kuh-LĀ-uhs   ˌɑʳkəˈleːəs

Archeozoic, Archaeozoic
  geologic period   AHR-kē-uh-ZŌ-ik   ˌɑʳkiːəˈzoːik

Archerd
  Army, *entertainment columnist*   AHR-chuhrd   ˈɑʳtʃəʳd

Archevites
  Biblical name   AHR-kuh-VĪTS   ˈɑʳkəˌvaits

Archibald
  pers. name   AHR-chuh-BAWLD, -buhld   ˈɑʳtʃəˌbɔːld, -bəld

Archidamus
  name, Spartan kings   AHR-kuh-DĀ-muhs   ˌɑʳkəˈdeːməs

Archie
  pers. name   AHR-chē   ˈɑʳtʃiˑ

Archilochus
  Greek poet   ahr-KIL-uh-kuhs   ɑʳˈkiləkəs

Archimède
  pers. name, French   ahr-shē-MED   ɑːrʃiːmed

Key (col. 2): a: fad ā: fade ah: father ar: marry aw: law e: fed ē: feed er: merry i: hid ī: hide ō: coat oͦ: boot
oi: boy ow: now u: put uh: above uhr: bird ch: chop ng: ring sh: show th: thick th: this zh: measure

Archimedean screw		
water-raising device	AHR-kuh-MĒD-ē-uhn SKRO͞O	ˌaʳkə'miːdiːən 'skruː
Archimedes		
Greek scientist; pers. name	AHR-kuh-MĒD-ēz	ˌaʳkə'miːdiːz
Archipenko		
Alexsandr, *Ukrainian-born US*	AHR-kyi-PYENG-kō,	ˌaʳkji'pjeŋkoː,
sculptor	Ⓢ AHR-ki-PENG-kō	Ⓢ ˌaʳki'peŋkoː
Archippus		
Biblical name	ahr-KIP-uhs	aʳ'kipəs
Archite		
Biblical name	AHR-KĪT	'aʳˌkait
Archosauria		
dinosaur subclass	AHR-kuh-SAWR-ē-uh	ˌaʳkə'sɔːriːə
Archuleta		
county, CO	AHR-chuh-LET-uh	ˌaʳtʃə'letə
Archy		
literary cockroach	AHR-chē	'aʳtʃiˑ
Archytas		
Greek philosopher	ahr-KĪT-uhs	aʳ'kaiţəs
Arciniegas		
Germán, *Colombian author*	ahr-sēn-YĀ-ḡahs	arsiːn'jeːɣas
Arcite		
lover in "The Knight's Tale,"	ahr-SĒT-uh, AHR-SĪT	aʳ'siːţə, 'aʳˌsait
Chaucer		
Arctic		
pert. to polar north	AHRK-tik, AHRT-ik	'aʳktik, 'aʳtik
Arcturus [Alpha Boötes]		
star	ahrk-T(Y)UR-uhs	aʳk't(j)urəs
Ard		
Biblical name	AHRD	'aʳd
Ardashir		
name, kings of Persia	AHRD-uh-shuhr	'aʳdəʃəʳ
Ardèche		
river, dept., France	ahr-DESH	aːrdeʃ
Arden		
English forest	AHRD-n	'aʳdn̩
Ardennes		
region, Luxembourg & France	ahr-DEN	arden, Ⓢ aʳ'den
Ardite		
Biblical name	AHR-DĪT	'aʳˌdait
Ardjuno		
volcano, Indonesia	ahr-JO͞O-nō	aʳ'dʒuːnoː
Ardnamurchan		
Point, *extreme western point of Great*	AHRD-nuh-MUHR-k͟huhn, -kuhn	'aʳdnəˌməʳxən, -kən
Britain, Scotland		
Ardon		
Biblical name	AHR-DAHN, ahr-DŌN	'aʳˌdan, aʳ'doːn
Ardrey		
Robert, *American writer*	AHR-drē	'aʳdriˑ
Ards		
county, Northern Ireland	AHRDZ	'aʳdz
Arduino		
Giovanni, *Italian geologist*	AHR-duh-WĒ-nō	ˌardə'wiːnoː
Arecibo		
port, Puerto Rico	ahr-uh-SĒ-v̠ō	arə'siːβoː

Areli
  Biblical name   uh-RĒ-LĬ, ahr-EL-ē   ə'riːˌlai, ɑr'eliː

Arelite
  Biblical name   uh-RĒ-LĪT   ə'riːˌlait

Arena [Alianza Republicana Nacionalista]
  political party, El Salvador   ah-RĀ-nah   ɑ'reːnɑ

Arenac
  county, MI   AR-uh-NAK   'ærəˌnæk

Arenal
  volcano, Costa Rica   AHR-uh-NAHL   ˌɑrə'nɑl

Arendal
  port, Norway   AHR-uhn-DAHL   'ɑrənˌdɑl

Arendt
  Hannah, *German-born US political scientist*   uh-RENT, AHR-uhnt, AR-uhnt   ə'rent, 'ɑrənt, 'ærənt

Arensky
  Anton Stepanovich, *Russian composer*   UHR-YEN-skyiy, ⓢ uh-REN-skē   ˌər'jenskjij, ⓢ ə'renskiˑ

Areopagite
  member of the Areopagus   AR-ē-AHP-uh-JĬT, -GĪT   ˌæriː'ɑpəˌdʒait, -ˌgait

Areopagitica
  treatise, J. Milton   AR-ē-uh-puh-JIT-i-kuh   ˌæriːəpə'dʒiṭikə

Areopagus
  hill, Athens; Athenian tribunal   AR-ē-AHP-uh-guhs   ˌæriː'ɑpəgəs

Arequipa
  department, city, Peru   AHR-uh-KĒ-puh   ˌɑrə'kiːpə

Ares
  Greek god of war   AR-ĒZ, ER-ĒZ   'ærˌiːz, 'erˌiːz

Aretaeus
  Greek physician   AR-uh-TĒ-uhs   ˌærə'tiːəs

Aretas
  Biblical name   ER-i-TAS   'eriˌtæs

Aretha
  pers. name (A. Franklin)   uh-RĒ-thuh   ə'riːθə

Arethusa
  mythological nymph   AR-uh-TH(Y)OO-zuh   ˌærə'θ(j)uːzə

Arezzo
  prov, Italy   ah-RET-sō, uh-RET-sō   ɑ'retsoː, ə'retsoː

Argand
  Aimé, *Swiss physicist & inventor;* Jean Robert, *Swiss mathematician*   ahr-GAHⁿ, ⓢ AHR-GAND, -guhnd   ɑːrgã, ⓢ 'ɑrˌgænd, -gənd

Argead
  ruling house of Macedonia   ahr-GĒ-uhd   ɑrˈgiːəd

Argenteuil
  county, Quebec, Canada; city, France   ahr-zhahⁿ-TUH(R)Y, ⓢ AHR-zhuhn-TWĒ   ɑrʒãtœj, ⓢ ˌɑrʒən'twiː

Argentina
  republic, S. America   AHR-juhn-TĒ-nuh   ˌɑrdʒən'tiːnə

Argentine
  pert. to Argentina   AHR-juhn-TĒN, -TĪN   'ɑrdʒənˌtiːn, -ˌtain

Argentine, The
  alternate name for Argentina   AHR-juhn-TĒN, -TĪN   'ɑrdʒənˌtiːn, -ˌtain

Argentino
  lake, Argentina; pers. name   ahr-ğān-TĒ-nō   ɑrɣeːn'tiːnoː

Key (col. 2):   a: fad   ā: fade   ah: father   ar: marry   aw: law   e: fed   ē: feed   er: merry   i: hid   ī: hide   ō: coat   oo: boot
oi: boy   ow: now   u: put   uh: above   uhr: bird   ch: chop   ng: ring   sh: show   th: thick   th: this   zh: measure

Argeș
   river, county, Romania   AHR-JESH   'aʳˌdʒeʃ
Argive
   pert. to Argos   AHR-JĪV, AHR-GĪV   'aʳˌdʒaiv, 'aʳˌgaiv
Argo
   Jason's ship; island, Nile River,   AHR-gō   'aʳgoː
   Sudan
Argob
   Biblical name   AHR-GAHB, ahr-GAWV   'aʳˌgab, aʳ'gɔːv
Argolis
   district, Greece   AHR-guh-luhs   'aʳgələs
argon
   element   AHR-GAHN   'aʳˌgan
Argonauts
   Jason's companions on the Argo   AHR-guh-NAWTS   'aʳgəˌnɔːts
Argonne
   region, forest, France   ahr-GAWN, Ⓢ ahr-GAHN, AHR-GAHN   aːrgɔːn, Ⓢ aʳ'gan, 'aʳˌgan
Argos
   city, Greece   AHR-GAWS, AHR-guhs   'aʳˌgɔːs, 'aʳgəs
Argostolion
   city, Greece   AHR-guh-STAWL-YAWN   ˌaʳgə'stɔːljɔːn
Arguedas
   Alcides, Bolivian writer & diplomat   ahr-GWĀ-thahs   ar'gweːðas
Argun [O-erh-ku-na]
   river, Asia, between China & Russia   ahr-GŌŌN   aʳ'guːn
Argus
   Odysseus's dog; many-eyed guardian   AHR-guhs   'aʳgəs
   of Io
Argyle, Argyll
   Scottish pl. name; knitting pattern;   ahr-GĪL, AHR-GĪL   aʳ'gail, 'aʳˌgail
   pers. name
Argyll and Bute
   district, Scotland   ahr-GĪL uhn(d) BYŌŌT   aʳ'gail ən(d) 'bjuːt
Arhangay
   county, Mongolia   AHR-khahn-GĪ   'arxanˌgai
Århus, Aarhus
   county, city, bay, Denmark   AWR-HŌŌS   'ɔːʳˌhuːs
Ari
   lang., Ethiopia; pers. name   AHR-ē   'ariˑ
Aria
   province, ancient Persia   AR-ē-uh, ER-, uh-RĪ-uh   'æriːə, 'er-, ə'raiə
Ariadne
   daughter of Minos and Pasiphae   AR-ē-AD-nē   ˌæriː'ædniˑ
Arian
   adherent of Arianism   AR-ē-uhn, ER-ē-uhn   'æriːən, 'eriːən
Ariana
   region, ancient Persia   AR-ē-AH-nuh, AHR-ē-   ˌæriː'anə, ˌariː-
Ariane
   French-built rocket   ahr-YAHN, Ⓢ AHR-ē-AHN, AR-ē-AN   aːrjaːn, Ⓢ ˌariː'an, ˌæriː'æn
Arianism
   Christian heresy   AR-ē-uh-NIZ-uhm, ER-   'æriːəˌnizəm, 'er-
Ariarathes
   Persian ruler of Cappadocia   AR-ē-uh-RĀ-thēz   ˌæriːə'reːθiːz

---

Arias Sanchez

Oscar, *Costa Rican politician (Nobel 1987)* — AHR-ē-ahs SAHN-chās — ˈɑriːɑs ˈsɑntʃeːs

Arica

port, prov., Chile — ah-RĒ-kah — aˈriːkɑ

Ariccia

town, Italy — ah-RĒ(T)-chah — aˈriː(t)tʃɑ

Aricia

former name of Ariccia — uh-RISH(-ē)-uh — əˈriʃ(iː)ə

Aridatha

Biblical name — AR-uh-DĀ-thuh, uh-RID-uh-thuh, ahr-Ē-dah-TAH — ˌærəˈdeːθə, əˈridəθə, arˌiːdɑˈtɑ

Ariège [La Riège]

river, department, France — ahr-YEZH — arjeʒ

Arieh

Biblical name — uh-RĪ-uh, AR-ē-uh, ER-ē-uh, AHR-ye — əˈraiə, ˈæriːə, ˈeriːə, ˈarje

Ariel

spirit in The Tempest, *Shakespeare; satellite of Uranus; British research satellite* — AR-ē-uhl, ER- — ˈæriːəl, ˈer-

Aries

constellation, sign of the zodiac — AR-(ē-)-ĒZ, ER- — ˈær(iː)ˌiːz, ˈer-

Arikara

N. American people — uh-RIK-uh-ruh — əˈrikərə

Arimathaea, Arimathea

town, ancient Palestine — AR-uh-muh-THĒ-uh, ER- — ˌærəməˈθiːə, ˌer-

Arioch

Biblical name — AR-ē-AHK, ER-ē-AHK, ahr-YŌKH — ˈæriːˌɑk, ˈeriːˌɑk, arˈjoːx

Arion

semilegendary Greek poet & musician; winged horse of Adrastus — uh-RĪ-uhn — əˈraiən

Ariosto

Ludovico, *Italian poet* — AHR-ē-AHS-tō, AHR-ē-Ō-stō — ˌariːˈastoː, ˌariːˈoːstoː

Arisai

Biblical name — uh-RIZ-ē-Ī, AHR-uh-sĪ, AHR-ē-SĪ — əˈriziːˌai, ˈarəˌsai, ˌariːˈsai

ˈArīsh, El [Al-ˈArīsh]

town, Sinai — EL-ah-RĒSH — ˌelaˈriːʃ

Aristaeus

Greek mythological bee-keeper — AR-uh-STĒ-uhs, ER- — ˌærəˈstiːəs, ˌer-

Aristagoras

ancient Ionian revolutionary — AR-uh-STAG-uh-ruhs — ˌærəˈstægərəs

Aristarchus

1. crater on Moon — AR-uh-STAHR-kuhs, ER- — ˌærəˈstɑrkəs, ˌer-

2. Biblical name — AR-uh-STAHR-kuhs, ER- — ˌærəˈstɑrkəs, ˌer-

Aristide

1. Jean Bertrand, *Haitian priest, politician; pers. name, French* — ah-rē-STĒD, ⑤ AR-uh-STĒD, ER- — aːriːstiːd, ⑤ ˌærəˈstiːd, ˌer-

2. Italian — ah-RĒ-stē-dā — aˈriːstiːdeː

Aristides

1. Athenian statesman; pers. name — AR-uh-STĪD-ēz — ˌærəˈstaidiːz

2. Spanish — ah-rē-STĒ-thās — ariːˈstiːðeːs

Aristippus

Greek philosopher — AR-uh-STIP-uhs, ER- — ˌærəˈstipəs, ˌer-

Key (col. 2): a: fad ā: fade ah: father ar: marry aw: law e: fed ē: feed er: merry i: hid ī: hide ō: coat ōō: boot oi: boy ow: now u: put uh: above uhr: bird ch: chop ng: ring sh: show th: thick th̲: this zh: measure

Aristobulus
  Biblical name — uh-RIS-tuh-BYOO-luhs — ə,ristə'bjuːləs
Aristogiton
  see Harmodius and Aristogiton
Aristophanes
  Greek comic playwright — AR-uh-STAHF-uh-NĒZ, ER- — ,ærə'stɑfə,niːz, ,er-
Aristophanic
  pert. to Aristophanes — uh-RIS-tuh-FAN-ik, AR-uh-stuh-FAN-ik, ER-uh-stuh- — ə,ristə'fænik, ,ærəstə'fænik, ,erəstə-
Aristotelian
  pert. to Aristotle — AR-uh-stuh-TĒL-yuhn, -TĒ-lē-uhn — ,ærəstə'tiːljən, -'tiːliːən
Aristotelianism
  philosophy of Aristotle — AR-uh-stuh-TĒL-yuh-NIZ-uhm, -TĒ-lē-uh-NIZ-uhm — ,ærəstə'tiːljə,nizəm, -'tiːliːə,nizəm
Aristotle
  Greek philosopher — AR-uh-STAHT-l, AR-uh-STAHT-l — 'ærə,stɑtl̩, ,ærə'stɑtl̩
Ari Thorgilsson
  Icelandic cleric & historian — AHR-ē THAWR-gyils-SAWN — ,ɑri· 'θɔːrgjils,sɔːn
Arius
  Greek ecclesiastic — uh-RĪ-uhs, AR-ē-uhs — ə'raiəs, 'æriːəs
Arizona
  state, US — AR-uh-ZŌ-nuh — ,ærə'zoːnə
Arkadhía [Arcadia]
  region, Greece — AHR-kuh-THĒ-uh, AHR-kuh-DĒ-uh — ,ɑrkə'ðiːə, ,ɑʳkə'diːə
Arkadi, Arkady
  pers. name, Russian — UHR-KAHD-yi — ,ər'kɑːdjij
Arkansan
  person from AR — ahr-KAN-zuhn — ɑʳ'kænzən
Arkansas
  1. US river — ahr-KAN-zuhs *(usual in KS, often in CO)*, AHR-kuhn-SAW *(usual elsewhere)* — ɑr'kænzəs *(usual in KS, often in CO)*, 'ɑʳkən,sɔː *(usual elsewhere)*
  2. state, US — AHR-kuhn-SAW — 'ɑʳkən,sɔː
Arkhangelsk [Archangel]
  city, Russia — ahr-KAN-GELSK — ɑʳ'kæn,gelsk
Arkite
  Biblical name — AHR-KĪT — 'ɑʳ,kait
Arlanda
  airport, Stockholm — AHR-LAHN-duh — 'ɑr,lɑndə
Arlberg
  mtn. pass, Austria; skiing technique — AHRL-BERK, AHRL-BUHRG — 'ɑʳl,beʳk, 'ɑʳl,bəʳg
Arledge
  Roone, *US television executive* — AHR-lij — 'ɑʳlidʒ
Arlen
  pers. name — AHR-luhn — 'ɑʳlən
Arlene
  pers. name — ahr-LĒN, ⓔ AHR-LĒN — ɑʳ'liːn, ⓔ 'ɑʳ,liːn
Arles
  town, France — AHRL — ɑːrl
Arlin
  pers. name — AHR-luhn — 'ɑʳlən
Arlington
  city, TX; town, MA; natl. cemetery, VA; pers. name — AHR-ling-tuhn — 'ɑʳliŋtən

Arlo		
pers. name	AHR-lō	ˈɑʳloː
Arlon		
district, town, Belgium	ahr-LAW^{n}	ɑrlɔ̃
Arlyn		
pers. name	AHR-luhn	ˈɑʳlən
Armada		
Spanish fleet	ahr-MAHD-uh, ahr-MĀD-uh, ahr-MAD-uh	ɑʳˈmɑdə, ɑʳˈmeːdə, ɑʳˈmædə
Armageddon		
Christian final battle	AHR-muh-GED-n	ˌɑʳməˈgedn̩
Armagh		
county, Ireland	ahr-MAH, AHR-MAH	ɑʳˈmɑ, ˈɑʳˌmɑ
Armagnac		
district, France; brandy	ahr-mahn-YAHK, [$] AHR-muhn-YAK	ɑːrmɑːnjɑːk, [$] ˌɑʳmənˈjæk
Armand		
1. pers. name	AHR-muhnd, AHR-MAHND, ahr-MAHND	ˈɑʳmənd, ˈɑrˌmɑnd, ɑrˈmɑnd
2. French	ahr-MAH^{n}	ɑːrmɑ̃
3. German	AHR-MAHNT	ˈɑʳˌmɑnt
4. Romanian	ahr-MAHND	ɑrˈmɑnd
Armande		
pers. name, French	ahr-MAH^{n}D	ɑːrmɑ̃d
Armando		
pers. name, Italian, Spanish	ahr-MAHN-dō	ɑrˈmɑndoː
Armani		
Giorgio, *Italian designer*	ahr-MAHN-ē	ɑʳˈmɑniˑ
Armatrading		
Joan, *US singer*	AHR-muh-TRĀD-ing	ˈɑʳməˌtreːdiŋ
Armenia		
1. republic, Asia	ahr-MĒ-nē-uh	ɑʳˈmiːniːə
2. city, Colombia	ahr-MĀN-yuh	ɑʳˈmeːnjə
Armenian		
lang., W. Asia; pert. to Armenia	ahr-MĒ-nē-uhn, -nyuhn	ɑʳˈmiːniːən, -njən
Armentieres, Armentières		
city, France	ahr-mah^{n}-TYER, [$] AHR-muhn-tē-ER, [£] AHR-muhn-TIRZ	ɑːrmɑ̃tjer, [$] ˌɑʳməntiːˈeʳ, [£] ˈɑʳmənˌtiʳz
Arminianism		
teachings of J. Arminius	ahr-MIN-ē-uh-NIZ-uhm	ɑʳˈminiːəˌnizəm
Arminius		
Jacobus, *Dutch theologian; Germanic hero*	ahr-MIN-ē-uhs	ɑʳˈminiːəs
Armistead		
pers. name	AHR-muh-STED, -stuhd	ˈɑʳməˌsted, -stəd
Armitage		
Ballet, *dance co., NY*	AHR-muht-ij	ˈɑʳmət̬idʒ
Armoni		
Biblical name	ahr-MŌ-NĪ, -nē	ɑʳˈmoːˌnɑi, -niˑ
Armorica		
ancient region, France	ahr-MAWR-i-kuh, ahr-MAHR-	ɑʳˈmɔːrikə, ɑʳˈmɑr-
Armstrong		
Louis, *US musician;* Neil, *US astronaut; pers. name*	AHRM-STRAWNG	ˈɑʳmˌstrɔːŋ
Army		
pers. name (A. Archerd)	AHR-mē	ˈɑʳmiˑ

Key (col. 2): a: **fad** ā: **fade** ah: **father** ar: **marry** aw: **law** e: **fed** ē: **feed** er: **merry** i: **hid** ī: **hide** ō: **coat** o͞o: **boot** oi: **boy** ow: **now** u: **put** uh: **above** uhr: **bird** ch: **chop** ng: **ring** sh: **show** th: **thick** th: **this** zh: **measure**

Arnan
  Biblical name | AHR-NAHN, ahr-NAHN | 'ɑʳˌnɑn, ɑʳˈnɑn
Arnaud, Arnault
  pers. name, French | ahr-NŌ | ɑːrnoː
Arnaz
  Desi, *US entertainer* | ahr-NEZ | ɑʳˈnez
Arne
  1. Thomas, *English composer* | AHRN | 'ɑʳn
  2. pers. name | AHR-nē | 'ɑʳniˑ
  3. Czech | AHR-ne | 'ɑrne
  4. Norwegian | AHR-nuh | 'ɑrnə
Arness
  James, *US actor* | ahr-NES | ɑʳˈnes
Arnhem
  city, Netherlands | AHRN-HEM, AHR-nuhm | 'ɑʳnˌhem, 'ɑʳnəm
Arnhem Land, Arnhemland
  region, Australia | AHR-nuhm-LAND | 'ɑʳnəmˌlænd
Árni
  pers. name, Icelandic | OWD-nē *[sic]* | 'ɑudniː *[sic]*
arnica
  herb | AHR-ni-kuh | 'ɑʳnikə
Arno
  river, Italy; pers. name, German | AHR-nō | 'ɑʳnoː
Arnold
  1. pers. name | AHR-nuhld | 'ɑʳnəld
  2. Danish, Norwegian | AHR-nawl | 'ɑrnɔːl
  3. Dutch | AHR-NAWLT | 'ɑrˌnɔːlt
  4. French | ahr-NAWLD | ɑːrnɔːld
  5. German | AHR-NAWLT | 'ɑʳˌnɔːlt
Arnoldson
  K. P., *Swedish author, politician* | AHRN-l-suhn, AHR-nuhld-suhn | 'ɑʳnl̩sən, 'ɑʳnəldsən
  (Nobel 1908)
Arnon
  Biblical name | AHR-NAHN, ahr-NŌN | 'ɑʳˌnɑn, ɑʳˈnoːn
Arnsberg
  district, city, Germany | AHRNS-BERK | 'ɑʳnsˌbeʳk
Arnulf
  Holy Roman Emperor | AHR-NULF | 'ɑʳˌnulf
Arod
  Biblical name | Ā-RAHD, AR-AHD, ER-AHD, ah-RŌD | 'eːˌrɑd, 'ærˌɑd, 'erˌɑd, ɑˈroːd
Arodi
  Biblical name | uh-RŌD-Ī, AR-uh-DĪ, ER-uh-DĪ | əˈroːdˌɑi, 'ærəˌdɑi, 'erəˌdɑi
Arodite
  Biblical name | Ā-RAHD-ĪT, AR-uh-DĪT, ER-uh-DĪT | 'eːˌrɑdˌɑit, 'ærəˌdɑit, 'erəˌdɑit
Aroer
  Biblical name | uh-RŌ-uhr, AHR-aw-ER | əˈroːəʳ, ˌɑrɔːˈeʳ
Aroerite
  Biblical name | uh-RŌ-uh-RĪT | əˈroːəˌrɑit
Arolsen
  town, Germany | AHR-uhl-zuhn | 'ɑrəlzən
Aron
  Raymond Claude Ferdinand, | ah-RAWⁿ | ɑrɔ̃
  French philosopher

Foreign Sounds: ue: *Fr.* **rue**, *Ger.* **füllen**   uh(r): *Fr.* **boeuf**, *Ger.* **Höhle**   <u>kh</u>: *Ger.* **ich**, *Scot.* **loch**   g̱: *Sp.* **amigo**   v: *Sp.* **hablar**
hl: *Welsh* **Llanelli**.   CAPITALS: primary stress.   SMALL CAPS: secondary stress. $: U.S. pron.   £: British pron.

Aroostook
  county, ME — uh-R͞OOS-tuhk, uh-RUS-tuhk, -tik — ə'ruːstək, ə'rustək, -tik

Arouet
  pers. name, French (F. M. A. de Voltaire) — ahr-WE — aːrwe

Arp
  1. Bill, *US humorist* — AHRP — 'ɑʳp
  2. Jan, *French artist, poet* — AHRP — aːrp

Arpachshad [Arphaxad]
  Biblical name — ahr-PAK-SHAD, AHR-pah<u>kh</u>-SHAHD — aʳ'pæk,ʃæd, ˌɑrpɑx'ʃɑd

Arpad
  1. pers. name — AHR-pad — 'ɑʳpæd
  2. Biblical name — AHR-PAD — 'ɑr,pæd

Árpád
  pers. name, Hungarian — AHR-pahd — 'ɑrpɑd

ARPANET
  Advanced Research Projects Agency Network, computer network — AHR-puh-NET — 'ɑʳpə,net

Arphaxad [Arpachshad]
  Biblical name — ahr-FAK-sad, AHR-pah<u>kh</u>-SHAHD — ar'fæksæd, ˌɑrpɑx'ʃɑd

Arpino
  Italian town, home of Cicero — ahr-PĒ-no — aʳ'piːno

Arpinum
  Latin form of Arpino — ahr-PĪ-nuhm — aʳ'painəm

Arquette
  Rosanna, *US actress* — ahr-KET — aʳ'ket

Arran
  island, Scotland — AR-uhn — 'ærən

Arras
  town, France — ah-RAHS, ⑤ uh-RAHS, AR-uhs — aːras, ⑤ ə'ras, 'ærəs

Arrau
  Claudio, *Chilean pianist* — ahr-ROW, ⑤ uh-ROW — ar'rau, ⑤ ə'rau

Arrecife de Lanzarote
  port, Canary Islands — AHR-ā-TH͞E-fā <u>th</u>ā LAHN-thah-RAW-tā, AHR-e-S͞E-fā — ˌareː'θiːfeː ðeː ˌlanθa'rɔːteː, ˌareː'siːfeː

Arrhenius
  S. A., *Swedish physicist, chemist (Nobel 1903)* — uh-RĀ-nē-uhs, uh-RĒ-nē-uhs — ə'reːniːəs, ə'riːniːəs

Arrol
  Sir William, *Scottish bridge builder* — AR-uhl — 'ærəl

Arrow
  Kenneth J., *US economist (Nobel 1972)* — AR-ō — 'æroː

arsenic
  element — AHRS-nik, AHRS-n-ik — 'ɑʳsnik, 'ɑʳsn̩ik

Arsenio
  1. pers. name — ahr-SIN-ē-ō, ahr-SIN-yō, ahr-SEN- — aʳ'siniːoː, aʳ'sinjoː, aʳ'sen-
  2. Italian — ahr-SEN-yō — ar'senjoː
  3. Spanish — ahr-SĀN-yō — ar'seːnjoː

Arshile
  pers. name (A. Gorky) — ahr-SH͞E-luh — aʳ'ʃiːlə

Ārsī [Arusi]
  region, Ethiopia — AHR-sē — 'aːʳsiː

Key (col. 2): a: f**a**d ā: f**a**de ah: f**a**ther ar: m**a**rry aw: l**a**w e: f**e**d ē: f**ee**d er: m**e**rry i: h**i**d ī: h**i**de ō: c**oa**t ōō: b**oo**t
oi: b**oy** ow: n**ow** u: p**u**t uh: **a**bove uhr: b**i**rd ch: **ch**op ng: ri**ng** sh: **sh**ow th: **th**ick <u>th</u>: **th**is zh: mea**s**ure

Arsinoë [Crocodilopolis]
    ancient town, Cyrenaica; city,   ahr-SIN-uh-WĒ   ɑʳˈsinəˌwiː
      feminine pers. name, ancient Egypt

Art
    pers. name   AHRT   ˈɑʳt

Arta [Ambracian Gulf]
    Gulf of, inlet, Ionian Sea, Greece   AHRT-uh   ˈɑrtə

Árta
    river, city, department, Greece   AHRT-uh   ˈɑʳʈə

Artaxata
    ancient city, Armenia   ahr-TAK-suht-uh   ɑʳˈtæksəʈə

Artaxerxes
    king, Persia   AHRT-uh(g)-ZUHRK-SĒZ   ˌɑʳʈə(g)ˈzəʳkˌsiːz

Art Deco
    design style   AHR(T) dā-KŌ, DĀ-kō, DEK-ō   ˌɑʳ(t) deːˈkoː, ˈdeːkoː, ˈdekoː

Artemas
    Biblical name   AHRT-uh-muhs   ˈɑʳʈəməs

Artemis
    Greek goddess of the moon; pers.   AHRT-uh-muhs   ˈɑʳʈəməs
      name

Artemision
    ancient wonder at Ephesus   AHRT-uh-MIZH-uhn   ˌɑʳʈəˈmiʒən

Artemisium
    cape, Euboea   AHRT-uh-MĒ-zē-uhm, -MĒ-zh(ē-)uhm   ˌɑʳʈəˈmiːziːəm, -ˈmiːʒ(iː)əm

Artemus
    pers. name   AHRT-uh-muhs   ˈɑʳʈəməs

Arthabaska
    county, Quebec, Canada   AHR-thuh-BAS-kuh   ˌɑʳθəˈbæskə

Arthropods
    segmented invertebrates   AHR-thruh-PAHDZ   ˈɑʳθrəˌpɑdz

Arthur
    1. Chester A., 21st US president;   AHR-thuhr   ˈɑʳθəʳ
      legendary British ruler; pers. name
    2. French   ahr-TUER   aːrtyːr
    3. German   AHR-tur   ˈɑʳtuʳ
    4. Hungarian   AHR-tur   ˈɑrtur
    5. Portuguese   uhr-TŌOR, ahr-   ərˈtuːr, ɑːr-
    6. Welsh   AHR-thir   ˈɑrθir

Arthurian
    pert. to King Arthur   ahr-TH(Y)UR-ē-uhn   ɑʳˈθ(j)uriːən

Artigas
    José Gervasio, father of Uruguayan   ahr-TĒ-ḡahs   ɑrˈtiːɣas
      independence; department, town,
      Uruguay

Artiodactyla
    hoofed animals   AHRT-ē-ō-DAK-tuh-luh   ˌɑʳʈiːoːˈdæktələ

Artis
    pers. name   AHRT-uhs   ˈɑʳʈəs

Artium Baccalaureus
    bachelor of arts, A.B. or B.A.   AHRT-ē-uhm BAK-uh-LŌR-ē-uhs,   ˈɑʳʈiːəm ˌbækəˈloːriːəs,
       -LAWR-ē-uhs   -ˈloːriːəs

Artium Magister
    master of arts, M.A.   AHRT-ē-uhm MAJ-uh-stuhr   ˈɑʳʈiːəm ˈmædʒəstəʳ

Art Nouveau
    design style   AHR(T) nŌŌ-VŌ   ˌɑʳ(t) nuːˈvoː

Foreign Sounds: ue: *Fr.* **rue**, *Ger.* **füllen** uh(r): *Fr.* **boeuf**, *Ger.* **Höhle** kh: *Ger.* **ich**, *Scot.* **loch** ḡ: *Sp.* **amigo** v̠: *Sp.* **hablar** hl: *Welsh* **Llanelli**. CAPITALS: primary stress. SMALL CAPS: secondary stress. Ⓢ: U.S. pron. Ⓔ: British pron.

Artois
former province, France	ahr-TWAH	ɑːɾtwɑː

Artôt
Belgian family of musicians	ahr-TŌ	ɑːɾtoː

Artur
1. pers. name, German	AHR-tur	'ɑʳtur
2. Polish	AHR-tōōr	'ɑːɾtuːr
3. Portuguese	uhr-TŌŌR, ahr-	ər'tuːr, ɑːr-
4. Russian	UHR-TŌŌR	ˌər'tuːr
5. Swedish	AHR-tuhr	'ɑːɾtər

Arturi
pers. name, Finnish	AHR-tur-ē	'ɑːʳturi·

Arturo
1. pers. name, Italian, Spanish	ahr-TŌŌ-rō	ɑr'tuːroː
2. Portuguese	uhr-TŌŌ-roo, ahr-	ər'tuːruː, ɑːr-

Artus
1. pers. name, Dutch	AHR-tues	'ɑrtys
2. French	ahr-TUES	ɑːɾtys

Artvin [Çoruh]
province, city, Turkey	ahrt-VĒN	ɑʳt'viːn

Artzybasheff
Mikhail, *Russian novelist*	UHRT-si-BAH-shif	ˌəʳtsi'bɑːʃif

Arua
S. American people	AHR-uh-WAH, AHR-uh-WAH	'ɑrəˌwɑ, ˌɑrə'wɑ

Aruba
island, Caribbean	uh-RŌŌ-buh	ə'ruːbə

Aruboth, Arubboth
Biblical name	uh-RŌŌ-BŌTH, uh-RŌŌ-buhth, AHR-ōō-BŌT	ə'ruːˌboːθ, ə'ruːbəθ, ˌɑruː'boːt

Arumah
Biblical name	uh-RŌŌ-muh, AHR-ōō-MAH	ə'ruːmə, ˌɑruː'mɑ

Arumanian [Romanian]
lang., Europe	AHR-ōō-MĀ-nē-uhn	ˌɑru·'meːniːən

Arunachal Pradesh
state, India	AHR-uh-NAHCH-uhl pruh-DĀSH, pruh-DESH	ˌɑrəˌnɑtʃəl prə'deːʃ, prə'deʃ

Arundel
borough, England	AR-uhn-duhl	'ærəndəl

Arusha
region, Tanzania	uh-RŌŌ-shuh	ə'ruːʃə

Arusi, Arussi [Ārsī]
region, Ethiopia	uh-RŌŌ-sē	ə'ruːsiː

Arvad
Biblical name	AHR-VAD, ahr-VAHD	'ɑʳˌvæd, ɑʳ'vɑd

Arvadites
Biblical name	AHR-vuh-DĪTS	'ɑʳvəˌdaits

Arvayheer
town, Mongolia	AHR-vā-KHIR	ˌɑʳveː'xiʳ

Arvid
pers. name, Swedish	AHR-vid	'ɑːʳvid

ARVN
Army, Republic of (South) Vietnam	AHR-vuhn	'ɑʳvən

Āryabhaṭa
Indian mathematician & astronomer	AHR-yuh-BUHT-uh	ˌɑrjə'bəʈə

Key (col. 2):   a: fad ā: fade ah: father ar: marry aw: law e: fed ē: feed er: merry i: hid ī: hide ō: coat ōō: boot
oi: boy ow: now u: put uh: above uhr: bird ch: chop ng: ring sh: show th: thick th̲: this zh: measure

Aryan		
Indo-European people or lang.	AR-ē-uhn, ER-ē-uhn, AHR-yuhn	'æriːən, 'eriːən, 'ɑrjən
Arza		
Biblical name	AHR-zuh, AHRT-suh, ahrt-SAH	'ɑ^{r}zə, 'ɑ^{r}tsə, ɑ^{r}t'sɑ
Arzawa		
ancient Luwian city	ahr-ZAH-wuh	ɑ^{r}'zawə
Asa		
pers. name	Ā-suh	'eːsə
Asadābād		
city, Afghanistan	uh-SAHD-uh-BAHD	əˌsɑdə'bɑd
asafetida, asafoetida		
plant	AS-uh-FIT-uhd-ē, AS-uh-FET-uhd-uh	ˌæsə'fiţədiˑ, ˌæsə'feţədə
Asahara		
Shoko, *leader of Aum Shinrikyo*	ahs-ah-hahr-ah, [$] AHS-uh-HAHR-uh	ɑsɑhɑrɑ, [$] ˌɑsə'hɑrə
Asahel		
Biblical name	AS-uh-HEL, Ā-suh-HEL, AHS-ah-HEL	'æsəˌhel, 'eːsəˌhel, ˌɑsɑ'hel
Asahi		
Japanese beer	ah-sah-hē	ɑsɑhiː
Asahiah		
Biblical name	AS-uh-HĪ-uh, ah-SAH-yah	'æsəˌhɑiə, ɑ'sɑjɑ
Asaiah		
Biblical name	uh-ZĀ-uh, ah-SAH-yah	ə'zeːə, ɑ'sɑjɑ
Asama [Asamayama]		
volcano, Japan	ah-sahm-ah	ɑsɑmɑ
Asamayama [Asama]		
volcano, Japan	ah-sahm-ah-yahm-ah	ɑsɑmɑjɑmɑ
Asaph		
pers. name	AS-uhf, Ā-suhf	'æsəf, 'eːsəf
Asareel		
Biblical name	uh-SĀ-rē-EL, AS-uh-RĒL, AHS-ah-REL	ə'seːriːˌel, 'æsəˌriːl, ˌɑsɑ'rel
Asarel		
Biblical name	uh-SĀ-REL, AHS-ah-REL	ə'seːˌrel, ˌɑsɑ'rel
Asarelah		
Biblical name	AS-uh-RĒ-luh, AHS-ah-RĀ-lah	ˌæsə'riːlə, ˌɑsɑ'reːlɑ
Asben [Azbine, Aïr]		
region, Niger	as-BEN	æs'ben
Asbury		
Ball Park, *Chicago, IL; pers. name*	AZ-BER-ē, AZ-b(uh-)rē	'ævzˌberiˑ, 'æzb(ə)riˑ
Asbury Park		
city, NJ	AZ-BER-ē PAHRK, AZ-b(uh-)rē PAHRK	ˌæzˌberiˑ 'pɑ^{r}k, ˌæzb(ə)riˑ 'pɑ^{r}k
Ascalon [Ashqelon]		
archaeological site, former city-state, Israel	AHS-kuh-LAWN, AS-kuh-LAHN	'ɑskəˌlɔːn, 'æskəˌlɑn
Ascanius [Iulus]		
son of Aeneas	as-KĀ-nē-uhs	æs'keːniːəs
Ascension		
parish, LA; island, Atlantic	uh-SEN-chuhn	ə'sentʃən
Asch		
Sholem, *Polish writer*	AHSH, ASH	'ɑːʃ, 'æʃ
Ascham		
Roger, *English writer*	AS-kuhm	'æskəm
ASCII		
American Standard Code for Information Interchange	AS-kē	'æskiˑ

Foreign Sounds: ue: *Fr.* **rue**, *Ger.* **füllen** uh(r): *Fr.* **boeuf**, *Ger.* **Höhle** kh: *Ger.* **ich**, *Scot.* **loch** g̃: *Sp.* **amigo** v̲: *Sp.* **hablar** hl: *Welsh* **Llanelli**. CAPITALS: primary stress. SMALL CAPS: secondary stress. [$]: U.S. pron. [£]: British pron.

Asclepius [Aesculapius]
  Greek god of medicine   as-KLĀ-pē-uhs, as-KLĒ-pē-uhs   æs'kleːpiːəs, æs'kliːpiːəs
Ascoli Piceno
  province, commune, Italy   AS-kuh-lē pē-CHĀ-nō   'æskəliː pi·'tʃeːnoː
Ascot
  village, race track, England   AS-kuht, AS-kaht   'æskət, 'æskat
Asculum Picenum
  ancient name of commune of Ascoli   AS-kyuh-luhm pī-SĒ-nuhm   'æskjələm paiˈsiːnəm
  Piceno
Asea Brown Bovari
  multi-national power systems corp.   uh-SĀ-(y)uh BROWN bō-VER-ē   əˈseː(j)ə 'braun boːˈveri·
ASEAN
  Southeast Asian treaty organization   AHS-ē-AHN, AS-ē-AHN, AS-ē-uhn   'asiːˌan, 'æsiːˌan, 'æsiːən
Āsela [Aselle]
  city, Ethiopia   ah-SĀ-luh   ɑ'seːlə
Aselle
  city, Ethiopia   ah-SEL   ɑ'sel
Asenath
  Biblical name   AS-e-NATH, AHS-uh-NAHT   'æseˌnæθ, ˌɑsə'nɑt
Aser
  Biblical name   Ā-suhr   'eːsər
Asgard
  abode of Scandinavian gods   AS-GAHRD, AZ-GAHRD   'æsˌgɑrd, 'æzˌgɑrd
Asgeir
  pers. name, Icelandic   AHS-GĀR   'asˌgeːr
Asgeirsson
  Asgeir, *Icelandic statesman*   AHS-gār-SAWN   'asgeːrˌsɔːn
Ashan
  Biblical name   Ā-shuhn, ah-SHAHN   'eːʃən, ɑ'ʃɑn
Ashanti
  African people; region, Ghana   uh-SHANT-ē, uh-SHAHNT-ē   ə'ʃænti·, ə'ʃɑnti·
Ashbea
  Biblical name   ash-BĒ-uh, ahsh-BĒ-ah   æʃ'biːə, ɑʃ'biːɑ
Ashbel
  Biblical name   ASH-BEL, ahsh-BEL   'æʃˌbel, ɑʃ'bel
Ashbelite
  Biblical name   ASH-BEL-ĪT   'æʃˌbelˌait
Ashby
  pers. name   ASH-bē   'æʃbi·
Ashby-de-la-Zouch
  town, England   ASH-bē duh lah ZO͞OSH   'æʃbi· də lɑ 'zuːʃ
Ashdod
  town, Israel; Biblical name   ASH-DAHD, ahsh-DŌD   'æʃˌdad, ɑʃ'doːd
Ashdodite
  Biblical name   ASH-DAHD-ĪT   'æʃˌdadˌait
Ashdoth-Pisgah
  Biblical name   ASH-DŌTH-PIZ-guh,   'æʃˌdoːθ'pizgə, ɑʃ'dɔːtpis'gɑ
                                             ahsh-DAWT-pis-GAH
Ashe
  Arthur, *US tennis player*   ASH   'æʃ
Asher
  pers. name   ASH-uhr   'æʃər
Asherah
  Biblical name   uh-SHĒ-ruh, uh-SHIR-uh, ASH-uh-ruh, ə'ʃiːrə, ə'ʃirə, 'æʃərə,
                                             AHSH-ā-RAH   ˌaʃeː'ra

---

Key (col. 2): a: fad ā: fade ah: father ar: marry aw: law e: fed ē: feed er: merry i: hid ī: hide ō: coat o͞o: boot
oi: boy   ow: now   u: put   uh: above   uhr: bird   ch: chop   ng: ring   sh: show   th: thick   <u>th</u>: this   zh: measure

Asheville
city, NC ASH-vuhl, ASH-VIL 'æʃvəl, 'æʃˌvil

Ashhur
Biblical name ASH-uhr, ahsh-KHUR 'æʃəʳ, aʃ'xuʳ

Ashikaga
city, Japan; Japanese dynasty ah-shē-kahg-ah aʃiːkaga

Ashikei
pers. name, Japanese ah-shē-kā aʃiːkeː

Ashima
Biblical name uh-SHĪ-muh, uh-SHĒ-muh, ə'ʃaimə, ə'ʃiːmə, 'æʃəmə,
ASH-uh-muh, AHSH-ē-MAH ˌaʃiː'ma

Ashkelon
see Ashqelon

Ashkenaz
Biblical name ASH-kuh-NAZ, AHSH-kuh-NAHZ 'æʃkəˌnæz, ˌaʃkə'naz

Ashkenazi
Jew of Eastern & Central Europe ASH-kuh-NAZ-ē, AHSH-kuh-NAHZ-ē ˌæʃkə'næziˑ, ˌaʃkə'naziˑ

Ashkenazim
pl. of Ashkenazi ASH-kuh-NAZ-uhm, ˌæʃkə'næzəm, ˌaʃkə'nazəm
AHSH-kuh-NAHZ-uhm

Ashkhabad
city, Turkmenistan ASH-kuh-BAD, ASH-kuh-BAHD 'æʃkəˌbæd, 'æʃkəˌbad

Ashland
US pl. name ASH-luhnd 'æʃlənd

Ashleigh, Ashley, Ashlie
pers. name ASH-lē 'æʃliˑ

Ashluslay
S. American people AHSH-luh-SLĪ ˌaʃlə'slai

Ashmole
Elias, *English antiquary* ASH-MŌL 'æʃˌmoːl

Ashmolean
museum, library, Oxford, England ash-MŌ-lē-uhn, ash-MŌL-yuhn æʃ'moːliːən, æʃ'moːljən

Ashnah
Biblical name ASH-nuh, ahsh-NAH 'æʃnə, aʃ'na

Ashpenaz
Biblical name ASH-puh-NAZ, AHSH-puh-NAHZ 'æʃpəˌnæz, ˌaʃpə'naz

Ashqelon, Ashkelon [Ascalon]
archaeological site, former city-state, AHSH-kuh-LŌN, ASH-kuh-LAHN 'aʃkəˌloːn, 'æʃkəˌlan
Israel

Ashrawi
Hanan, *Palestinian spokeswoman* ahsh-RAH-wē aʃ'rawiˑ

Ashriel
Biblical name ASH-rē-EL, AHS-rē-EL 'æʃriːˌel, ˌasriː'el

Ash-Shaqra [Shaqra]
town, Saudi Arabia ahsh shuhk-RAH aʃ ʃək'ra

Ashtabula
county, OH ASH-tuh-BYOO-luh ˌæʃtə'bjuːlə

Ashtaroth
Biblical name ASH-tuh-RAHTH, ASH-tuh-RŌTH, 'æʃtəˌraθ, 'æʃtəˌroːθ,
AHSH-tuh-RAHT ˌaʃtə'rat

Ashtoreth [Astarte]
Mesopotamian goddess of love ASH-tuh-RETH 'æʃtəˌreθ

Ashteroth Karnaim
  Biblical name　　ASH-tuh-RAHTH kahr-NĀ-uhm,　　'æʃtə,raθ kar'neːəm,
　　　　　　　　　　ASH-tuh-RŌTH; AHSH-tuh-RAHT　　'æʃtə,roːθ; ,aʃtə'rat
　　　　　　　　　　kahr-NAH-yim　　　　　　　　　kar'najim

Ashur
  Biblical name　　ASH-uhr, ahsh-UR　　'æʃəʳ, aʃ'uʳ

Ashura
  Islamic fast day　　uh-SHUR-uh　　ə'ʃurə

Ashurbanipal
  Assyrian king　　AHSH-ur-BAHN-i-PAHL　　,aʃur'bani,pal

Ashurite
  Biblical name　　ASH-uh-RĪT　　'æʃə,rait

Ashur-nasir-pal
  name, Assyrian kings　　AHSH-ur-NAHZ-uhr-PAHL　　,aʃuʳ'nazəʳ,pal

Ashvath
  Biblical name　　ASH-VATH, ahsh-VAHT　　'æʃ,væθ, aʃ'vat

Asia
  continent; daughter of Oceanus　　Ā-zhuh, Ā-shuh　　'eːʒə, 'eːʃə

Asiago
  Italian cheese　　AHS-ē-AHG-ō　　,asiː'agoː

Asia Minor
  ancient region　　Ā-zhuh MĪ-nuhr, Ā-shuh　　,eːʒə 'mainəʳ, ,eːʃə

Asian
  pert. to Asia　　Ā-zhuhn, Ā-shuhn　　'eːʒən, 'eːʃən

Asiarchs
  Biblical name　　Ā-zē-AHRKS　　'eːziː,aʳks

Asiatic
  pert. to Asia　　Ā-zhē-AT-ik, Ā-shē-, Ā-zē-　　,eːʒiː'æṭik, ,eːʃiː-, ,eːziː-

Asiel
  Biblical name　　AS-ē-EL, Ā-sē-EL, AH-sē-EL　　'æsiː,el, 'eːsiː,el, ,asiː'el

Asimov
  Isaac, *US author*　　AZ-uh-MAWF, AZ-uh-MAWV　　'æzə,mɔːf, 'æzə,mɔːv

Askew
  pers. name　　AS-kyōō　　'æskjuː

Askin
  Leon, *US director, actor, producer, writer*　　AS-kuhn　　'æskən

Asmara
  capital of Eritrea, *Ethiopia*　　ahs-MAHR-uh　　as'marə

Asmat
  lang., New Guinea　　AHZ-MAHT, AHS-MAHT　　'az,mat, 'as,mat

Asīr
  prov., Saudi Arabia　　ah-SIR　　a'siʳ

Asnah
  Biblical name　　AS-nuh, ahs-NAH　　'æsnə, as'na

Asnapper
  Biblical name　　as-NAP-uhr　　æs'næpəʳ

Asmodeus
  devil　　az-muh-DĒ-uhs, as-MŌD-ē-uhs; *(in Paradise Lost)* AS-muh-DĒ-uhs, az-　　æzmə'diːəs, æs'moːdiːəs; *(in Paradise Lost)* ,æsmə'diːəs, æz-

Asnuntuck
  Community College, *CT*　　uh-SNUHN-tuhk　　ə'snəntək

Aso [Asosan]
  volcano, Japan　　ah-sō　　asoː

Key (col. 2):　a: fad　ā: fade　ah: father　ar: marry　aw: law　e: fed　ē: feed　er: merry　i: hid　ī: hide　ō: coat　ōō: boot
oi: boy　ow: now　u: put　uh: above　uhr: bird　ch: chop　ng: ring　sh: show　th: thick　th: this　zh: measure

Ašo
   lang., Burma   AHSH-ō, AHS-ō   'aʃoː, 'asoː

Aśoka
   king of India   uh-SŌ-kuh   ə'soːkə

Aśoka, Ashoka
   Indian emperor   uh-SHŌ-kuh   ə'ʃoːkə

Asosan [Aso]
   volcano, Japan   ah-sō-sahn   asoːsɑn

Asotin
   county, WA   uh-SŌT-n   ə'soːtn̩

Aspartame
   artificial sweetener   AS-puhr-TĀM, uh-SPAHR-TĀM   'æspəʳˌteːm, ə'spaʳˌteːm

Aspasia
   Greek consort of Pericles   as-PĀ-sh(ē-)uh, as-PĀ-zh(ē-)uh   æs'peːʃ(iː)ə, æs'peːʒ(iː)ə

Aspatha
   Biblical name   as-PĀ-thuh, AHS-pah-TAH   æs'peːθə, ˌaspɑ'tɑ

Aspen
   city, CO   AS-puhn   'æspən

Asperges
   rite of sprinkling with holy water   a-SPUHR-jēz   æ'spəʳdʒiːz

Asphodel
   plant   AS-fuh-DEL   'æsfəˌdel

Aspidistra
   plant   AS-puh-DIS-truh   ˌæspə'distrə

Asplund
   Erik Gunnar, *Swedish architect*   AHS-pluhnd   'aːsplənd

Asriel
   Biblical name   AS-rē-EL, AHS-rē-EL   'æsriːˌel, ˌasriː'el

Asrielite
   Biblical name   AS-rē-uh-LĪT   'æsriːəˌlait

Assaba [Açba]
   region, Mauritania   uh-SAHB-uh   ə'sabə

Assad, al-
   see al-Assad

Assal
   lake, Djibouti   ah-SAHL   ɑ'sal

Assam
   state, India   ah-SAHM, uh-SAM, AS-AM   ɑ'sɑm, ə'sæm, 'æsˌæm

Assamese
   pert. to Assam   AS-uh-MĒZ, -MĒS   ˌæsə'miːz, -'miːs

Assateague
   Island, *MD & VA*   AS-uh-TĒG   'æsəˌtiːg

Assen
   commune, Netherlands   AHS-uhn   'asən

Asser
   1. Welsh monk, tutor to Alfred the Great   AS-uhr   'æsəʳ
   2. T. M. C., Dutch jurist, law professor (Nobel 1911)   AHS-uhr   'asəʳ

Asshur
   Biblical name   ASH-uhr, ahsh-UR   'æʃəʳ, aʃ'uʳ

Asshurim
   Biblical name   uh-SHUR-im, AHSH-ur-IM   ə'ʃurim, ˌaʃur'im

Assiniboia
   region, Canada   uh-SIN-uh-BOI-uh   əˌsinə'bɔiə

Assiniboin, -ne
   N. American people   uh-SIN-uh-BOIN   ə'sinə,bɔin

Assiniboine
   river, mtn., Canada   uh-SIN-uh-BOIN   ə'sinə,bɔin

Assiout
   see Asyūt

Assir
   Biblical name   AZ-uhr, ah-SIR   'æzə^r, ɑ'si^r

Assisi
   commune, Italy   uh-SĒ-sē, uh-SĒ-zē   ə'siːsiˑ, ə'siːziˑ

Assiut
   see Asyūt

Assos
   Biblical name   AS-AHS   'æs,ɑs

Assouan, Assuan
   see Aswān

Assyria
   ancient Near Eastern kingdom uh-SIR-ē-uh   ə'siriːə

Assyrian
   lang., pert. to Assyria   uh-SIR-ē-uhn   ə'siriːən

Assyriologist
   student of Assyria   uh-SIR-ē-AHL-uh-juhst   ə,siriː'ɑlədʒəst

Assyriology
   study of Assyria   uh-SIR-ē-AHL-uh-jē   ə,siriː'ɑlədʒiˑ

Asta
   pers. name   AST-uh   'æstə

Astaire
   Fred, *US dancer, actor*   uh-STAR, uh-STER   ə'stæ^r, ə'ste^r

Astarte [Ashtoreth]
   Mesopotamian goddess of love uh-STAHRT-ē, a-STAHRT-ē ə'stɑ^{r}ţiˑ, æ'stɑ^{r}ţiˑ

astatine
   element   AS-tuh-TĒN   'æstə,tiːn

Asti
   prov & town, Italy   AHS-tē   'ɑstiˑ

Astin
   Patty Duke, *US actress*   AS-tuhn   'æstən

Astin Tagh [Altun Shan]
   mtn. range, Tibet, China   AHS-TIN-TAH(G)   'ɑs'tin'tɑ(g)

Asti Spumante
   wine   AHS-tē spu-MAHN-tā, AS-, -MAHNT-ē ,ɑstiˑ spu'manteː, ,æs-,
                                                  -'manti·

Aston
   F. W., *English physicist (Nobel* AS-tuhn   'æstən
   1922); pers. name

Aston Martin
   car make   AS-tuhn MAHRT-n   ,æstən 'mɑ^{r}tṇ

Astor
   pers. name   AS-tuhr   'æstə^r

Astoria
   district, New York City   uh-STŌR-ē-uh, uh-STAWR-ē-uh, a- ə'stoːriːə, ə'stoːriːə, æ-

Astraea
   daughter of Zeus and Themis as-TRĒ-uh   æs'triːə

Astrakhan
   city, Russia   AS-truh-KAN, AS-truh-kuhn 'æstrə,kæn, 'æstrəkən

---

Key (col. 2): a: fad ā: fade ah: father ar: marry aw: law e: fed ē: feed er: merry i: hid ī: hide ō: coat ōō: boot
oi: boy ow: now u: put uh: above uhr: bird ch: chop ng: ring sh: show th: thick <u>th</u>: this zh: measure

Astrid
  1. pers. name, Danish   AHS-trē<u>th</u>   'ɑːstriːð
  2. Swedish   AHS-trid   'ɑstrid

Astrodome
  stadium, Houston, TX   AS-truh-DŌM   'æstrə,doːm

Astrophel
  Sir Philip Sidney's poetic name for himself   AS-truh-FEL   'æstrə,fel

Astroturf
  tdmk for artificial grass   AS-trō-TUHRF   'æstroː,təʳf

Asturias
  Miguel Angel, Guatemalan author (Nobel 1967); region Spain   ahs-TUR-yahs; Ⓢ uh-ST(Y)UR-ē-uhs, a-   ɑs'turjɑs; Ⓢ ə'st(j)uriːəs, æ-

Astyages
  Median king   a-STĪ-uh-JĒZ   æ'stɑiə,dʒiːz

Astyanax
  son of Hector and Andromache   a-STĪ-uh-NAKS   æ'stɑiə,næks

Asu
  lang., Africa   AHS-o͞o   'ɑsuː

Asunción
  city, dept., Paraguay; pers. name, Spanish   ah-so͞on-SYŌN, -THYŌN, Ⓢ ah-SO͞ON(T)-sē-ŌN   ɑsuːn'sjoːn, -'θjoːn, Ⓢ ɑ,suːn(t)siː'oːn

Asuncion
  island, Micronesia   ah-SO͞ON-sē-ŌN   ɑ,suːnsiː'oːn

Aśvaghosa
  Indian philosopher & poet   AHSH-vuhg-HŌ-suh   'aʃvəg,hoːsə

Aswān, Assuan
  city, dam, Egypt   a-SWAHN, ah-SWAHN   æ'swɑn, ɑ'swɑn

Aswān Dam
  dam, Egypt   a-SWAHN DAM, AS-WAHN DAM   æ,swɑn 'dæm, ,æs,wɑn 'dæm

Asyncritus
  Biblical name   uh-SIN-krit-uhs   ə'sinkriţəs

Asyūt, Assiout, Assiut [Siut]
  governorate, Egypt   ahs-YO͞OT   ɑs'juːt

Atabapo
  river, Colombia & Venezuela   ah-tah-<u>V</u>AHP-ō, Ⓢ AHT-uh-BAHP-ō   atɑ'βapoː, Ⓢ ,aţə'bapoː

Atacama
  desert, people, prov, Chile   AHT-uh-KAHM-uh, AT-   ,aţə'kamə, ,æţ-

Atacameño
  S. American people   AHT-uh-kuh-MĀN-yō   ,aţəkə'meːnjoː

Atacazo
  volcano, Ecuador   AHT-uh-KAHS-ō   ,aţə'kɑsoː

Atad
  Biblical name   Ā-TAD, ah-TAHD   'eː,tæd, ɑ'tɑd

Atahualpa, Atahuallpa
  Incan king   AHT-uh-WAHL-puh   ,aţə'wɑlpə

Atakapa
  N. American people   uh-TAK-uh-puh, uh-TAHK-uh-puh, -PAW, -PAH   ə'tækəpə, ə'takəpə, -,pɔː, -,pɑ

Atalanta
  mythological heroine who raced her suitors   AT-l-ANT-uh   ,ætḷ'æntə

Atar
  city, Mauritania   AH-TAHR   'a,tɑʳ

Foreign Sounds: ue: *Fr.* **rue**, *Ger.* **füllen**   uh(r): *Fr.* **boeuf**, *Ger.* **Höhle**   <u>kh</u>: *Ger.* i**ch**, *Scot.* lo**ch**   ḡ: *Sp.* ami**g**o   <u>v</u>: *Sp.* ha**b**lar
hl: *Welsh* **Ll**anelli.   CAPITALS: primary stress.   SMALL CAPS: secondary stress.   Ⓢ: U.S. pron.   Ⓔ: British pron.

Atarah
   Biblical name   AT-uh-RAH, uh-tah-RAH   'æṭə‚rɑ, əta'rɑ
Atari
   US toy brand   uh-TAHR-ē   ə'tari·
Ataroth
   Biblical name   AT-uh-RAWTH, AHT-ah-RŌT   'æṭə‚rɔːθ, ‚atɑ'roːt
Ataroth-Addar
   Biblical name   AT-uh-RAWTH-AD-AHR,   'æṭə‚rɔːθ'æd‚ɑʳ,
                            AHT-ah-RŌT-ah-DAHR   ‚atɑ'roːtɑ'dɑr
Atascosa
   county, TX   AT-uh-SKŌ-suh   ‚æṭə'skoːsə
Ataturk, Atatürk
   see Kemal Atatürk
Atayal [Tayal]
   Malayasian people, lang.   AHT-uh-YAHL   ‚aṭə'jal
Atchafalaya
   river, bay, LA   (uh-)CHAF-uh-LĪ-uh   (ə)‚tʃæfə'lɑiə
Atchin
   see Achin
Atchison
   county, KS, MO   ACH-uh-suhn   'ætʃəsən
Ate
   Greek goddess of error &   AHT-ē, ĀT-ē, AH-TĀ, Ā-TĒ   'aṭi·, 'eːṭi·, 'a‚teː, 'eː‚tiː
    foolhardiness
Aten [Aton]
   Egyptian god   AHT-n, ĀT-n   'atn̩, 'eːtn̩
Ater
   Biblical name   ĀT-uhr, ah-TER   'eːṭəʳ, a'ter
Atget
   Eugène, *French photographer*   aht-ZHE   aːtʒe
Ath [Aat]
   district, Belgium   AHT   aːt
Athabasca, -ka
   lake, river, univ., Canada   ATH-uh-BAS-kuh   ‚æθə'bæskə
Athabascan
   people, lang., N. America   ATH-uh-BAS-kuhn   ‚æθə'bæskən
Athach
   Biblical name   Ā-THAK, ah-TAHKH   'eː‚θæk, a'tax
Athaiah
   Biblical name   uh-THĪ-uh, AH-TAH-YAH   ə'θɑiə, ‚a‚tɑ'jɑ
Athaliah
   Biblical name   ATH-uh-LĪ-uh, AH-TAHL-YAH   ‚æθə'lɑiə, ‚a‚tɑl'jɑ
Athamania
   district, ancient Epirus   ATH-uh-MĀ-nē-uh   ‚æθə'meːniːə
Athamas
   father of Phrixus and Helle   ATH-uh-muhs   'æθəməs
Athan
   English Christian saint   ATH-uhn   'æθən
Athanase
   pers. name, French   ah-tah-NAHZ   aːtɑːnɑːz
Athanasian
   Christian creed   ATH-uh-NĀ-zhuhn, -NĀ-shuhn   ‚æθə'neːʒən, -'neːʃən
Athanasius
   Christian saint; pers. name   ATH-uh-NĀ-sh(ē-)uhs, -sē-uhs,   ‚æθə'neːʃ(iː)əs, -siːəs, -ziːəs
                            -zē-uhs

Key (col. 2):   a: fad   ā: fade   ah: father   ar: merry   aw: law   e: fed   ē: feed   er: merry   i: hid   ī: hide   ō: coat   ōō: boot
oi: boy   ow: now   u: put   uh: above   uhr: bird   ch: chop   ng: ring   sh: show   th: thick   <u>th</u>: this   zh: measure

Atharva-Veda		
Hindu magic spells	uh-TAHR-vuh-VĀD-uh	ə'tɑrvə've:də
Athelney		
historical refuge of King Alfred, England	ATH-uhl-nē	'æθəlni·
Athelstan		
English king	ATH-uhl-STAN, A̱TH-uhl-, -STAHN	'æθəl,stæn, 'æðəl-, -,stɑn
Athelstane		
pers. name	ATH-uhl-STĀN	'æθəl,ste:n
Athena		
Greek goddess of wisdom	uh-THĒ-nuh	ə'θi:nə
Athenaeum		
gentlemen's club, London	ATH-uh-NĒ-uhm	,æθə'ni:əm
Athene [Athena]		
Greek goddess of wisdom	uh-THĒ-nē, uh-THĒ-nuh	ə'θi:ni·, ə'θi:nə
Athenian		
pert. to Athens	uh-THĒ-nē-uhn	ə'θi:ni:ən
Athenodorus		
Greek sculptor	uh-THĒ-nuh-DŌR-uhs, -DAWR-uhs	ə,θi:nə'do:rəs, -'dɔ:rəs
Athens		
city, Greece; US pl. name	ATH-uhnz	'æθənz
Athgarh		
former state, India	UHT-GAHR, AHT-	'ət,gɑr, 'ɑt-
Athínai [Athens]		
city, Greece	ah-THĒ-nā	ɑ'θi:ne:
Athlai		
Biblical name	ATH-LĪ, ATH-lē-Ī, aht-LĪ	'æθ,lai, 'æθli:,ai, ɑt'lai
Athmallik		
former state, India	UHT-MUHL-ik, aht-MAHL-ik	,ət'məlik, ɑt'mɑlik
Athol		
city, MA	ATH-AWL	'æθ,ɔ:l
Athol, Athole		
pers. name	ATH-uhl	'æθəl
Atholl		
mtn. district, Scotland	ATH-uhl	'æθəl
Athos		
1. one of The Three Musketeers, *A. Dumas*	ah-TŌS, ⑤ ATH-ŌS, Ā-THŌS	ɑ:to:s, ⑤ 'æθ,o:s, 'e:,θo:s
2. mtn., Greece	ATH-AHS, Ā-THAHS	'æθ,ɑs, 'e:,θɑs
Ati		
city, Chad	ah-TĒ	ɑ'ti:
Atitlán		
lake, volcano, town, Guatemala	AHT-ēt-LAHN	,ɑt̬i·t'lɑn
Atjeh, Aceh [Achin]		
province, Indonesia	AHCH-Ā	'atʃ,e:
Atjehnese, Achinese		
lang., people, North Sumatra	ACH-uh-NĒZ, -NĒS	,ætʃə'ni:z, -'ni:s
Atkins		
Chet, *US guitarist; pers. name*	AT-kuhnz	'ætkənz
Atkinson		
pers. name	AT-kuhn-suhn	'ætkənsən
Atlanta		
city, GA	uht-LANT-uh, at-LANT-uh	ət'læntə, æt'læntə
Atlantic		
ocean	uht-LANT-ik, at-LANT-ik	ət'læntik, æt'læntik

Foreign Sounds: ue: *Fr.* **rue**, *Ger.* **füllen**   uh(r): *Fr.* **boeuf**, *Ger.* **Höhle**   kh: *Ger.* **ich**, *Scot.* **loch**   ḡ: *Sp.* **amigo**   v̱: *Sp.* **hablar**
hl: *Welsh* **Llanelli**.   CAPITALS: primary stress.   SMALL CAPS: secondary stress.   ⑤: U.S. pron.   ⓔ: British pron.

Atlántida
  department, Honduras   aht-LAHN-tē-<u>th</u>ah   ɑt'lɑntiːðɑ
Atlantis
  mythical island   uht-LANT-uhs, at-LANT-uhs   ət'læntəs, æt'læntəs
Atlas
  mtn. system, Africa; giant who   AT-luhs   'ætləs
    supports the heavens
Atlee
  pers. name   AT-lē   'ætliˈ
Atli
  Old Norse form of Atilla   AHT-lē   'ɑtliˈ
Atman
  Hindu individual soul; the universal   AHT-muhn, AHT-MAHN   'ɑtmən, 'ɑtˌmɑn
    self
Atoka
  county, OK   uh-TŌ-kuh   ə'toːkə
Aton [Aten]
  Egyptian god   AHT-n, AH-TŌN, ĀT-n, Ā-TAHN   'ɑtn̩, 'ɑˌtoːn, 'eːtn̩, 'eːˌtɑn
Atraf-i-Balda
  former district, India   uh-TRAHF-ē-BUHL-duh, -BAHL-duh   əˌtrɑfiː'bəldə, -'bɑldə
Atrak [Atrek]
  river, Iran & Turkmenistan   uh-TRAK   ə'træk
Atrek [Atrak]
  river, Iran & Turkmenistan   uh-TREK   ə'trek
Atreus
  father of Agamemnon and Menelaus   Ā-trē-uhs, Ā-TR$\overline{OO}$S   'eːtriːəs, 'eːˌtruːs
Atropos
  one of the Fates   A-truh-PAHS   'ætrəˌpɑs
Atroth-beth-Joab
  Biblical name   A-TRAHTH-BETH-JŌ-AB,   'æˌtrɑθˌbeθ'dʒoː,æb,
                                              aht-RŌT-BET-yō-AHV   ɑt'roːtˌbetjoː'ɑv
Atroth-shophan
  Biblical name   A-TRAHTH-SHŌ-FAN,   'æˌtrɑθ'ʃoːˌfæn,
                                              ah-TRŌT-shō-FAHN   ɑ'troːtʃoː'fɑn
Attai
  Biblical name   AT-ē-Ī, AT-Ī, ah-TĪ   'æt̪iːˌai, 'æt̪ˌai, ɑ'tai
Attala
  county, MS   uh-TAL-uh   ə'tælə
Attaleia
  ancient name for Antalya,   AT-l-Ī-uh   ˌæt̪l'aiə
Attalia
  Biblical name for Antalya   ATL-Ī-uh   ˌæt̪l'aiə
Attalus
  king of Pergamum   AT-l-uhs   'æt̪ləs
At-Tamīm
  governorate, Iraq   aht-TAHM-ĒM   ɑt'tɑmˌiːm
Attapu [Attopeu]
  province, Laos   ah-TŌ-p$\overline{oo}$, ah-TAHP-$\overline{oo}$ ɑ'toːpuː, ɑ'tɑpuː
Attenborough
  Sir Richard, British actor, director;   AT-n-b(uh-)ruh   'ætn̩b(ə)rə
    David, *British naturalist*
Attica
  region, Greece; city, IN; village,   AT-i-kuh   'æt̪ikə
    prison, NY

Key (col. 2): a: fad ā: fade ah: father ar: marry aw: law e: fed ē: feed er: merry i: hid ī: hide ō: coat $\overline{oo}$: boot
oi: boy ow: now u: put uh: above uhr: bird ch: chop ng: ring sh: show th: thick <u>th</u>: this zh: measure

Atticism		
expression from Attic Greek	AT-uh-SIZ-uhm	'æṭə,sizəm
Atticus		
pers. name	AT-uh-kuhs	'æṭəkəs
Attikí [Attica]		
region, Greece	AHT-i-K(Y)Ē	ˌaṭi'k(j)iː
Attila		
1. king of the Huns; pers. name	AT-l-uh, uh-TIL-uh	'æṭlə, ə'tilə
2. Hungarian	ah-TIL-ah	a'tilɑ
Attis		
companion of Cybele	AT-uhs	'æṭəs
Attleboro		
city, MA	AT-l-buhr-uh, -buh-ruh, -buh-rō	'æṭlbər-ə, -bə-rə, -bəroː
Attopeu [Attapu]		
province, Laos	ah-TŌ-poo	a'toːpuː
Attu		
Alaskan island	A-too	'ætuː
Attucks		
Crispus, *Black American patriot*	AT-uhks	'æṭəks
Atum		
Egyptian creator god	AHT-uhm	'aṭəm
Atuona		
village, Marquesas Islands	AHT-uh-WŌ-nuh	ˌaṭə'woːnə
Aube		
river, France	ŌB	oːb
Aube Nouvelle, L'		
see L'Aube Nouvelle		
Auberjonois		
René, *US actor*	Ō-buhr-zhahn-WAH	ˌoːbərˤʒan'wa
Auberon		
pers. name	AW-buh-ruhn, Ō-buh-ruhn, -RAHN	'ɔːbərən, 'oːbərən, -ˌran
Aubervilliers		
commune, France	ō-ber-vēl-YĀ	oːberviːljeː
Aubigné [Maintenon]		
Françoise d', *French noblewoman*	ō-bēn-YĀ	oːbiːnjeː
Aubrey		
pers. name	AWB-rē	'ɔːbriˑ
Auburn		
US pl. name	AW-buhrn	'ɔːbəˤn
Aubusson		
1. Piérre d', French soldier, cardinal; commune, France	ō-bue-SAW^n	oːbyːsɔ̃
2. rug	ō-bue-SAW^n, ⓢ Ō-buh-SAHN	oːbyːsɔ̃, ⓢ 'oːbəˌsan
Aubyn		
Christian saint	AW-buhn	'ɔːbən
Auch		
town, France	ŌSH	oːʃ
Auchentoshan		
Scotch distillery	AW<u>KH</u>-uhn-TAW-shuhn, -TAHSH-uhn	'ɔːxənˌtɔːʃən, -ˌtaʃən
Auchincloss		
Louis, *US writer*	AW-kuhn-KLAHS	'ɔːkənˌklas

Foreign Sounds: **ue**: *Fr.* **rue**, *Ger.* **füllen** **uh(r)**: *Fr.* **boeuf**, *Ger.* **Höhle** **kh**: *Ger.* **ich**, *Scot.* **loch** **ḡ**: *Sp.* **amigo** **v**: *Sp.* **hablar** **hl**: *Welsh* **Llanelli**. CAPITALS: primary stress. SMALL CAPS: secondary stress. ⓢ: U.S. pron. Ⓔ: British pron.

Auchinleck

   1. Sir Claude, British field marshall   AW-kuhn-LEK, AW-kuhn-LEK,   ˌɔːkənˈlek, ˈɔːkənˌlek,
          ahkh-uhn-LEK   ɑxənˈlek

   2. parish, Scotland   AHKH-uhn-LEK, AW-kuhn-LEK,   ˌɑxənˈlek, ˌɔːkənˈlek,
          AW-khuhn-LEK   ˈɔːxənˌlek

   3. James Boswell's estate, Scotland   AF-LEK   ˈæfˌlek

Auchmuty

   Sir Samuel, *British general*   awk-MYOOT-ē   ɔːkˈmjuːṭiˑ

Auckland

   city, New Zealand   AW-kluhnd   ˈɔːklənd

Aude

   river, France   ŌD   oːd

Auden

   Wystan Hugh, *English poet in US*   AWD-n   ˈɔːdn̩

Audi

   car co.   OWD-ē   ˈɑudiˑ

Audie

   pers. name   AWD-ē   ˈɔːdiˑ

Audley

   Thomas, *English lord chancellor*   AWD-lē   ˈɔːdliˑ

Audrain

   county, MO   aw-DRĀN, AW-DRĀN   ɔːˈdreːn, ˈɔːˌdreːn

Audran

   French family of artists   ō-DRAHⁿ   oːdrɑ̃

Audrey

   pers. name   AW-drē   ˈɔːdriˑ

Audubon

   John James, *US naturalist*   AWD-uh-buhn, AWD-uh-BAHN   ˈɔːdəbən, ˈɔːdəˌbɑn

Audubon's caracara

   hawk   AWD-uh-buhnz KAR-uh-KAR-uh,   ˈɔːdəbənz ˌkærəˈkærə,
          AWD-uh-BAHNZ, KAR-uh-kuh-RAH   ˈɔːdəˌbɑnz, ˌkærəkəˈrɑ

Auel

   Jean M., *US writer*   OW(-uh)l   ˈɑu(ə)l

Auer

   Carl, *Austrian chemist;* Leopold,   OW(-uh)r   ˈɑu(ə)ʳ
       Hungarian violinist

Auerbach

   1. Berthold, German writer   OW(-uh)r-BAHKH, -BAHK   ˈɑu(ə)ʳˌbax, -ˌbak
   2. Red, sports personality   OW(-uh)r-BAK, -BAHK   ˈɑu(ə)ʳˌbæk, -ˌbak

Auge

   1. mother of Telephus in Greek myth   OW-gē, OW-jē, AW-jē   ˈɑugiˑ, ˈɑudʒiˑ, ˈɔːdʒiˑ
   2. pers. name, French   ŌZH   oːʒ

Augean stables

   filthy stables cleaned by Heracles   aw-JĒ-uhn   ɔːˈdʒiːən

Augeas

   owner of Augean stables   aw-JĒ-uhs   ɔːˈdʒiːəs

Aughrim, Aghrim

   parish, town, battle site, Ireland   AW-gruhm   ˈɔːgrəm

Augier

   pers. name, French   ōzh-YĀ   oːʒjeː

Auglaize

   county, OH   aw-GLĀZ   ɔːˈgleːz

Augrabies Falls, Aughrabies Falls

   waterfall, national park, South Africa   aw-GRAHB-ēz FAWLZ   ɔːˌgrɑbiːz ˈfɔːlz

---

Key (col. 2):   a: fad ā: fade ah: father ar: **marry** aw: **law** e: fed ē: feed er: **merry** i: hid ī: hide ō: coat ōō: boot
oi: **boy**   ow: **now** u: put uh: **above** uhr: bird ch: chop ng: ring sh: **show** th: thick th: this zh: measure

Augsburg

   1. city, Germany   OWKS-BURK, Ⓢ AWGZ-BUHRG,   'ɑuks,buʳk, Ⓢ 'ɔːgz,bəʳg,
                                   OWGZ-BURG   'ɑugz,buʳg

   2. College, MN   AWGZ-BUHRG   'ɔːgz,bəʳg

August

   1. month; pers. name   AW-guhst   'ɔːgəst

   2. Danish, Finnish, German OW-gust   'ɑugust

   3. Polish   OW-gōost   'ɑuguːst

   4. Swedish   OW-guhst   'ɑugəst

Augusta

   1. US pl. name; pers. name aw-GUHST-uh, uh-   ɔːˈgəstə, ə-

   2. French   aw-gue-STAH, ō-   ɔːgyːstɑː, oː-

   3. German   ow-GUS-tah   ɑuˈgustɑ

   4. region, Sicily; pers. name, Italian ow-GŌŌ-stah   ɑuˈguːstɑ

   5. Spanish   ow-ḠŌŌ-stah   ɑuˈɣuːstɑ

Augustan

   pert. to Augustus   uh-GUHS-tuhn, aw-   əˈgəstən, ɔː-

Augustana

   College, IL, SD   AW-guhs-TAN-uh   ,ɔːgəsˈtænə

Auguste

   1. pers. name, French   aw-GUST, ō-   ɔːgyːst, oː-

   2. German   ow-GUS-tuh   ɑuˈgustə

Augustijn

   Belgian beer   OW-ḡuhs-TĪN   'ɑuɣəs,tɑin

Augustín

   pers. name, Spanish   ow-gōō-STĒN   ɑuguːˈstiːn

Augustin

   1. pers. name   aw-GUHS-tuhn, uh-   ɔːˈgəstən, ə-

   2. Czech   OW-gust-YIN   'ɑugust,jin

   3. Dutch   OW-gue-STĪN   'ɑugyː,stɑin

   4. French   aw-gue-STEⁿ, ō-   ɔːgyːstẽ, oː-

   5. German   OW-gus-TĒN   ,ɑugusˈtiːn

   6. Swedish   OW-guh-STĒN   ,ɑugəˈstiːn

Augustine

   1. pers. name   AW-guhs-TĒN, aw-GUHS-tuhn,   'ɔːgəs,tiːn, ɔːˈgəstən,
                                   uh-GUHS-tuhn   əˈgəstən

   2. French   aw-gues-TĒN, ō-   ɔːgyːstiːn, oː-

Augustine, St.

   see St. Augustine

Augustinerbräu München

   German beer   OW-gus-TĒ-nuhr-BROI MUEN-<u>kh</u>uhn   ,ɑugusˈtiːnəʳ,brɔi 'mynçən

Augustinians

   religious order   AW-guh-STIN-ē-uhnz   ,ɔːgəˈstiniːənz

Augusto

   1. pers. name, Italian   ow-GŌŌ-stō   ɑuˈguːstoː

   2. Portuguese   ow-GŌŌSH-tōō, -GŌŌS-tōō   ɑuˈguːʃtuː, -ˈguːstuː

   3. Spanish   ow-GŌŌ-stō   ɑuˈguːstoː

Augustus

   1. Roman emperor; pers. name aw-GUHS-tuhs, uh-   ɔːˈgəstəs, ə-

   2. German   ow-GUS-tus   ɑuˈgustus

Aulard

   François Alphonse, French ō-LAHR   oːlɑr
     historian

Foreign Sounds: ue: *Fr.* r**ue**, *Ger.* f**ü**llen uh(r): *Fr.* b**oeu**f, *Ger.* H**öh**le <u>kh</u>: *Ger.* i**ch**, *Scot.* lo**ch** ḡ: *Sp.* ami**g**o <u>v</u>: *Sp.* ha**b**lar
hl: *Welsh* **Ll**anelli. CAPITALS: primary stress. SMALL CAPS: secondary stress. Ⓢ: U.S. pron. Ⓔ: British pron.

Auld Lang Syne
  Scottish song   ŌL-(D)ANG-ZĪN, -ŌL-(D)LANG-, -SĪN   ˌoːlˌ(d)æŋˈzain, ˌoːlˌ(d)læŋ-, -ˌsain

Aulis
  ancient Greek city   AW-luhs, OW-luhs   ˈɔːləs, ˈauləs

Aulus
  Roman praenomen   OW-luhs, AW-luhs   ˈauləs, ˈɔːləs

Aumale
  French noble family; county, duchy,   ō-MAHL   oːmɑːl
    France

Aum Shinrikyo
  Japanese cult   ōm-shin-rik-yō   oːmʃinrikjoː

Aundh
  former state, India   OWND   ˈaund

Aungerville, Aungervyle [de Bury]
  Richard, *English bibliophile*   AWN-juhr-VIL, -vuhl   ˈɔːndʒəʳˌvil, -vəl

Aung San Suu Kyi
  Burmese opposition leader   OWNG SAHN SOO CHĒ   ˈauŋ ˈsɑn ˈsuː ˈtʃiː

Aunis
  historical region, France   ō-NĒS   oːniːs

Aura
  mother of Inachus   AWR-uh   ˈɔːrə

Aurangabad
  city, India   ow-RUHNG-(g)uh-BAHD   auˈrəŋ(g)əˌbad

Aurèle
  pers. name   aw-REL, ō-   ɔːrel, oː-

Aurelia
  pers. name   aw-RĒ-lē-uh   ɔːˈriːliːə

Aurelian
  Roman emperor   aw-RĒ-lē-uhn   ɔːˈriːliːən

Aureliano
  pers. name   ow-rāl-YAHN-ō   aureːlˈjanoː

Aurelio
  1. pers. name, Italian   ow-REL-yō   auˈreljoː
  2. Spanish   ow-RĀL-yō   auˈreːljoː

Aurelius
  1. pers. name   aw-RĒ-lē-uhs, aw-RĒL-yuhs   ɔːˈriːliːəs, ɔːˈriːljəs
  2. German   ow-RĀL-yus, ow-RĀ-lē-us   auˈreːljus, auˈreːliːus

Aureomycin
  tdmk for chlortetracycline   AW-rē-ō-MĪS-n   ˌɔːriːoːˈmaisn̩

Auriga
  constellation   aw-RĪ-guh   ɔːˈraigə

Aurignac
  commune, paleolithic caves, France   aw-rēn-YAHK   ɔːriːnjɑːk

Aurillac
  town, France   aw-rē-(Y)AHK   ɔːriː(j)ɑːk

Auriol
  Vincent, *French politician*   awr-YAWL   ɔːrjɔːl

Aurora
  1. Roman dawn goddess; pers. name   uh-RŌR-uh, aw-, -RAWR-   əˈroːrə, ɔː-, -ˈrɔːr-
  2. German, Spanish   ow-RŌ-rah   auˈroːra

Aurora Australis
  'Southern Lights'   uh-RŌR-uh aw-STRĀ-luhs,   əˈroːrə ɔːˈstreːləs, əˈrɔːrə,
                           uh-RAWR-uh, ahs-TRĀ-luhs   asˈtreːləs

---

Key (col. 2):   a: fad   ā: fade   ah: father   ar: marry   aw: law   e: fed   ē: feed   er: merry   i: hid   ī: hide   ō: coat   ōō: boot
oi: boy   ow: now   u: put   uh: above   uhr: bird   ch: chop   ng: ring   sh: show   th: thick   th̲: this   zh: measure

Aurora Borealis
  'Northern Lights' — uh-RŌR-uh BŌR-ē-AL-uhs, uh-RAWR-uh, BAWR-, ⓔ -Ā-luhs — ə'rɔːrə ˌbɔːriː'æləs, ə'rɔːrə, ˌbɔːr-, ⓔ -'eːləs

Aurore
  pers. name, French — aw-RAWR, ō-RAWR — ɔːrɔːr, oːrɔːr

Ausangate, Nevado
  mtn., Peru — nä-VAH<u>TH</u>-ō ow-sahn-GAHT-ä — neː'vaðoː ausan'gaʈeː

Ausangate Knot [Ausangate, Nevado]
  mtn., Peru — OW-suhng-GAHT-ē NAHT — ˌausəŋˌgaʈiˑ 'nat

Auschwitz [Oświęcim]
  Nazi concentration camp, Poland — OWSH-VITS, OWSH-WITS — 'auʃˌvits, 'auʃˌwits

Aushi
  lang., Africa — OW-shē — 'auʃiˑ

Auslander
  Joseph, *American poet* — AW-SLAN-duhr — 'ɔːˌslændəʳ

Ausone
  French wine — ō-ZAWN — oːzɔːn

Ausonio
  pers. name — ow-ZAWN-yō — au'zɔːnjoː

Aussie
  an Australian — aw-sē, AHS-ē; ⓔ *& Austral.* AW-zē — ɔːsiˑ, 'asiˑ; ⓔ *& Austral.* 'ɔːziˑ

Aust-Agder
  county, Norway — OWST-AHG-duhr — 'austˌagdər

Austen
  pers. name — AWS-tuhn — 'ɔːstən

Auster
  literary, South Wind — AW-stuhr — 'ɔːstəʳ

Austerlitz
  battle site, Czech republic; Frederick, *orig. surname of* Fred Astaire — OW-stuhr-LITS, AW- — 'austəʳˌlits, 'ɔː-

Auteuil
  district, Paris — ō-TUH(R)Y, Ⓢ ō-TWĒ — oːtœj, Ⓢ oː'twiː

Austin
  city, TX; pers. name — AW-stuhn — 'ɔːstən

Australasia
  portion of Oceania — AWS-truh-LĀ-zhuh, AHS-, -LĀ-shuh — ˌɔːstrə'leːʒə, ˌas-, -'leːʃə

Australe, Mare
  see Mare Australe

Australia
  continent, nation — aw-STRĀL-yuh, ahs-TRĀL-yuh, uh-STRĀL-yuh — ɔː'streːljə, as'treːljə, ə'streːljə

Australian
  pert. to Australia — aw-STRĀL-yuhn, uh-; ahs-TRĀL-yuhn — ɔː'streːljən, ə-; as'treːljən

Australopithecus
  genus of hominids — aw-STRĀ-lō-PITH-i-kuhs, AW-struh-lō-PITH-i-kuhs — ɔːˌstreːloˑ'piθikəs, ˌɔːstrəloː'piθikəs

Austria
  republic, Europe — AWS-trē-uh, AHS- — 'ɔːstriːə, 'as-

Austrian
  pert. to Austria — AWS-trē-uhn, AHS- — 'ɔːstriːən, 'as-

Austro-
  combining form for Austria — AW-strō, AW-strō — 'ɔːstroː, ˌɔːstroː

Austro-Hungarian
  European empire   AW-strō-huhng-GAR-ē-uhn,   ˌɔːstroːhəŋˈgæriːən,
                         -huhng-GER-ē-uhn   -həŋˈgeriːən

Austronesia
  region, S. Pacific   AW-struh-NĒ-zhuh, AHS-truh-,   ˌɔːstrəˈniːʒə, ˌɑstrə-, -ˈniːʃə
                         -NĒ-shuh

Autauga
  county, AL   aw-TAW-guh   ɔːˈtɔːgə

Autolycus
  Argonaut; grandfather of Odysseus   aw-TAHL-i-kuhs   ɔːˈtɑlikəs

Automedon
  charioteer of Achilles; Greek poet   aw-TAHM-uhd-uhn,   ɔːˈtɑmədən, ɔːˈtɑməˌdɑn
                         aw-TAHM-uh-DAHN

Autry
  Orvon Gene, *US singer, actor,*   AW-trē   ˈɔːtriˑ
  executive

Auvergne
  province, France   aw-VERN-yuh; Ⓢ ō-VERN(-yuh),   ɔːverɲ ; Ⓢ oːˈveʳn(jə),
                      ō-VUHRN   oːˈvəʳn

Auxerre
  town, France   ō-SER   oːser

Auxerrois
  medieval countship, France   aw-ser-WAH   ɔːserwɑː

Auyuittuq
  National Park, *Northwest Territories,*   ow-Y͞OO-uht-uhk, -uh-TUHK   auˈjuːətək, -əˌtək
  Canada

Ava
  pers. name   Ā-vuh, AHV-uh   ˈeːvə, ˈɑvə

Avalon
  Frankie, *US pop singer; Celtic island*   AV-uh-LAHN   ˈævəˌlan
  paradise

Avamba [Ambo]
  lang., people, Angola, Namibia   uh-VAHM-buh   əˈvambə

Avar
  lang., people, Caucasus Mts.   AH-VAHR   ˈɑˌvɑʳ

Avanti
  early kingdom, India   uh-VUHNT-ē, uh-VAHNT-ē   əˈvəntiˑ, əˈvɑntiˑ

Avarua
  village, port, Cook Islands   AHV-uh-R͞OO-uh   ˌɑvəˈruːə

Avdira
  Mod. Greek name for Abdera   ahv-DIR-uh   avˈdirə

Avebury
  village, England, site of henge type   Ⓔ ĀV-b(uh-)rē, Ⓢ ĀV-BER-ē   Ⓔ ˈeːvb(ə)riˑ,Ⓢ ˈeːvˌberiˑ
  megalithic remains

Aveiro
  district, lagoon, port, Portugal   uh-VĀ-r͞oo, uh-VER-͞oo   əˈveːruː, əˈveruː

Avellaneda
  1. Alonso Fernández de, *Spanish*   ahv̠-ā(l)-yah-NĀ-t̠hah   aβeː(l)jaˈneːða
  writer
  2. Nicolás, *Argentine politician*   ahv̠-ā-zhah-NĀ-t̠hah   aβeːʒaˈneːða

Avellino
  prov & town, Italy   AHV-el-LĒ-nō, Ⓢ AHV-uh-LĒ-nō   ˌavelˈliːnoː, Ⓢ ˌavəˈliːnoː

Ave Maria
  prayer   AHV-ā muh-RĒ-uh   ˌaveː məˈriːə

Key (col. 2):   a: fad   ā: fade   ah: father   ar: marry   aw: law   e: fed   ē: feed   er: merry   i: hid   ī: hide   ō: coat   o͞o: boot
oi: boy   ow: now   u: put   uh: above   uhr: bird   ch: chop   ng: ring   sh: show   th: thick   t̠h: this   zh: measure

Aven
   Biblical name   Ā-vuhn, AHV-en   'eːvən, 'ɑven

Avennasar [Fārābī, al-]
   Muslim philosopher   AV-uh-NĀ-suhr   ˌævə'neːsəʳ

Avenol
   Joseph, *French diplomat,*   ahv-NAWL   ɑːvnɔːl
     secretary-general of the League of
     Nations

Aventine
   hill, Rome, Italy   AV-uhn-TĪN, AV-uhn-TĒN   'ævən₊tain, 'ævən₊tiːn

Averell
   pers. name   Ā-v(uh-)ruhl   'eːv(ə)rəl

Averett
   College, *VA*   Ā-v(uh-)ruht   'eːv(ə)rət

Averroes
   Arab philosopher   uh-VER-uh-WĒZ, AV-uh-RŌ-ēz   ə'verəˌwiːz, ˌævə'roːiːz

Averroism, Averrhoism
   philosophy of Averroes   uh-VER-uh-WIZ-uhm,   ə'verəˌwizəm, ˌævə'roːˌizəm
                    AV-uh-RŌ-IZ-uhm

Avery
   pers. name   Ā-vuh-rē, ĀV-rē   'eːvəriˑ, 'eːvriˑ

Aveyron
   river, department, France   ah-vā-RAWⁿ   ɑːveːrɔ̃

Avi [Wortis]
   US children's author; pers. name   AHV-ē   'ɑviˑ

Avia
   sportswear brand   Ā-vē-uh   'eːviːə

Avianca
   Colombian airline   ahv-yahng-kuh   ɑβjɑŋkə

Avicenna
   Islamic philosopher   AV-uh-SEN-uh   ˌævə'senə

Avignon
   prov & town, France   ah-vēn-YAWⁿ   ɑːviːnjɔ̃

Avila
   College, *MO*   AV-uh-luh   'ævələ

Ávila
   prov, city, Spain   AHV-ē-lah, Ⓢ AHV-i-luh   'aβiːla, Ⓢ 'avilə

Ávila Camacho
   Manuel, *Mexican soldier &*   AH-vē-lah kah-MAHCH-ō   'aβiːla ka'matʃoː
     politician

Avim, Avvim
   Biblical name   Ā-vim, ahv-ĒM   'eːvim, ɑv'iːm

Avis
   car rental co.   Ā-vuhs   ˌeːvəs

Avith
   Biblical name   Ā-vith, ahv-ĒT   'eːviθ, ɑv'iːt

Avogadro's number
   chemical constant   AV-uh-GAHD-rōz, AHV-   ˌævə'gɑdroːz, ˌɑv-

Avon
   1. town, CT, MA; city, OH; brand of   Ā-VAHN   'eːˌvɑn
     cosmetics
   2. county, various rivers, England   Ā-vuhn   'eːvən
   3. village, NY; river, Devonshire,   AV-uhn   'ævən
     England
   4. loch, river, Scotland   AHN   'ɑːn

Foreign Sounds: ue: *Fr.* **rue**, *Ger.* **füllen**   uh(r): *Fr.* **boeuf**, *Ger.* **Höhle**   kh: *Ger.* **ich**, *Scot.* **loch**   ḡ: *Sp.* **amigo**   v̱: *Sp.* **hablar**
hl: *Welsh* **Llanelli**.   CAPITALS: primary stress.   SMALL CAPS: secondary stress.   Ⓢ: U.S. pron.   Ⓔ: British pron.

Avoyelles
  parish, LA   uh-VOI-uhlz, AV-wah-YEL   ə'vɔiəlz, ˌævwɑ'jel

Avraam
  pers. name, Russian   uhv-RUH-AHM   əvˌrɑ'ɑːm

Avvim
  see Avim

AWACS
  surveillance system   Ā-WAKS   'eːˌwæks

Awaji
  island, Japan   ah-wahj-ē   ɑwadʒiˈ

Awami
  League, political party, Pakistan &   uh-WAHM-ē   ə'wɑmiˈ
    Bangladesh

Awa Odori
  Japanese holiday   ah-wah ō-dawr-ē   ɑwɑ oːdɔːriː

Awasa
  town, Ethiopia   ah-WAH-suh   ɑ'wɑsə

Awlad'Ali
  people, Africa   OW-lahd-al-Ē   'ɑulɑdæl'iː

AWOL
  absent without leave   Ā-WAWL   'eːˌwɔːl

Awu, Gunung
  volcano, Indonesia   GOO-NUNG AH-woo   'guːˌnuŋ 'ɑwuː

Axel
  1. pers. name   AK-suhl   'æksəl
  2. Danish, Swedish   AHK-suhl   'ɑːksəl
  3. German, Norwegian   AHK-suhl   'ɑksəl

Axelrod
  Julius, US pharmacologist (Nobel   AK-suhl-RAHD   'æksəlˌrɑd
    1970)

Axl
  pers. name   AK-suhl   'æksəl

Axminster
  town, England; carpet   AK-SMIN(T)-stuhr   'ækˌsmin(t)stəʳ

Axton
  Hoyt, US singer, composer   AK-stuhn   'ækstən

Ayacucho
  department, Peru   Ī-uh-KOO-chō   ˌɑiə'kuːtʃoː

Ayaida
  people, Africa   ah-YĪD-uh   ɑ'jɑidə

Ayala
  Eusebio, Paraguayan politician;   Ī-AHL-ah   ɑi'ɑlɑ
    Juan Manuel de, Spanish
    explorer

Aya Sofia [Hagia Sophia, Santa
Sophia]
  museum, mosque, church, Istanbul   Ī-(y)uh sō-FĒ-uh   ˌɑi(j)ə soː'fiːə

Ayatollah
  Shiite Muslim title   Ī-uh-TŌ-luh, Ī-uh-TAHL-uh,   ˌɑiə'toːlə, ˌɑiə'tɑlə, ˌɑiə'tələ,
                          Ī-uh-TUHL-uh, Ī-uh-tuh-LAH   ˌɑiətə'lɑ

Āybak, Aibak [Samangān]
  city, Afghanistan   Ī-BAK   'ɑiˌbæk

Aydelotte
  Frank, American educator   ĀD-l-AHT   'eːdlˌɑt

Key (col. 2):   a: fad   ā: fade   ah: father   ar: marry   aw: law   e: fed   ē: feed   er: merry   i: hid   ī: hide   ō: coat   ōō: boot
oi: boy   ow: now   u: put   uh: above   uhr: bird   ch: chop   ng: ring   sh: show   th: thick   th̲: this   zh: measure

Aydın, Aidin [Tralles]
   province, town, Turkey   Ī-DIN   ɑi'din

Ayer
   pers. name   Ā(-uh)r, ER, AR   'eː(ə)ʳ, 'eʳ, 'æʳ

Ayers Rock [Uluru]
   outcrop, Australia   ERZ RAHK, ARZ, Ā-uhrz   'eʳz 'rɑk, 'æʳz, 'eːəʳz

Ayinger Altbairisch
   German beer   Ī-ing-uhr ahlt-BĪ-rish   'ɑi-iŋəʳ ɑlt'bɑiriʃ

Ayinger Export-Weissbier
   German beer   Ī-ing-uhr ek-SPAWRT-VĪS-BIR   'ɑi-iŋəʳ ek‚spɔːʳt'vɑis‚biʳ

Ayinger Fest-Märzen
   German beer   Ī-ing-uhr FEST-MERT-suhn   'ɑi-iŋəʳ 'fest‚meʳtsən

Ayinger Jahrhundert-Bier
   German beer   Ī-ing-uhr YAHR-HUN-duhrt-BIR   'ɑi-iŋəʳ 'jaʳ‚hundəʳt‚biʳ

Ayinger Maibock
   German beer   Ī-ing-uhr MĪ-BAHK   'ɑi-iŋəʳ 'mɑi‚bɑk

Ayinger Ur-Weizen
   German beer   Ī-ing-uhr UR-VĪT-suhn   'ɑi-iŋəʳ 'uʳ‚vɑitsən

Aykroyd
   Dan, *US actor, comedian*   AK-ROID   'æk‚rɔid

Aylesbury
   town, England   ĀLZ-b(uh-)rē, ĀLZ-BER-ē   'eːlzb(ə)ri·, 'eːlz‚beri·

Aymara
   lang., people, S. America   Ī-muh-RAH, Ī-MAHR-uh   ‚ɑimə'rɑ, ɑi'mɑrə

Ayn
   pers. name (A. Rand)   ĪN, ĀN   'ɑin, 'eːn

Ayodhya
   city, India   uh-YUHD-yuh   ə'jədjə

Ayr
   town, Australia; town, river, Scotland   AR, ER   'æʳ, 'eʳ

Ayres
   Lew, *US actor*   ARZ, ERZ   'æʳz, 'eʳz

Ayrshire
   county, Scotland   AR-shuhr, ER-shuhr, -SHIR   'æʳʃəʳ, 'eʳʃəʳ, -‚ʃiʳ

Ayrton
   William Edward, *English inventor;*   ERT-n, ART-n   'eʳtn̩, 'æʳtn̩
      Hertha Marks, *his wife, English*
      inventor

Aysén
   see Aisén

Ayyah
   see Ajah

Ayyūbid
   Muslim dynasty in Egypt   Ī-(Y)OO-bid   ɑi'(j)uːbid

Azal
   Biblical name   Ā-zal, aht-SAHL   'eːzæl, ɑt'sɑl

Azalea Bowl
   stadium, Palatka, FL   uh-ZĀL-yuh BŌL   ə'zeːljə ‚boːl

Azaliah
   Biblical name   AZ-uh-LĪ-uh, uht-sahl-YAH-hoo   ‚æzə'lɑiə, ətsɑl'jɑhuː

Azamgarh
   district, India   AHZ-uhm-GAHR   'ɑzəm‚gɑr

Azaña y Díaz
   Manuel, *Spanish politician*   ahs-AHN-yah ē THĒ-ahs,   ɑs'ɑnjɑ iː 'ðiːɑs, ɑθ'ɑnjɑ iː
                          ahth-AHN-yah ē THĒ-ahth   'ðiːɑθ

Foreign Sounds: ue: *Fr.* **r**u**e**, *Ger.* f**ü**llen uh(r): *Fr.* b**oeu**f, *Ger.* H**öh**le kh: *Ger.* i**ch**, *Scot.* lo**ch** ğ: *Sp.* ami**g**o v: *Sp.* ha**b**lar
hl: *Welsh* L**l**anelli. CAPITALS: primary stress. SMALL CAPS: secondary stress. Ⓢ: U.S. pron. Ⓔ: British pron.

Azande [Zande]
lang., Africa   uh-ZAN-dē   əˈzændiˑ

Azaniah
Biblical name   AZ-uh-NĪ-uh, uh-zahn-YAH   ˌæzəˈnɑiə, əzanˈja

Āẕarbāyān-e Gharbī
prov., Iran   AH-zuhr-bī-YAHN-e ĞAHR-ṿē   ˈazərbaiˌjane ˈɣɑʳβiː

Āẕarbāyān-e Sharqī
prov., Iran   AH-zuhr-bī-YAHN-e SHAHR-kē   ˈazərbaiˌjane ˈʃɑʳkiː

Azareel [Azarel]
Biblical name   AZ-uh-RĒL, uh-zahr-EL   ˈæzəˌriːl, əzarˈel

Azarel [Azareel]
Biblical name   AZ-uh-REL, uh-zahr-EL   ˈæzəˌrel, əzarˈel

Azariah
1. Biblical name   AZ-uh-RĪ-uh, uh-zahr-YAH   ˌæzəˈrɑiə, əzarˈja
2. Apocryphal book; pers. name   AZ-uh-RĪ-uh   ˌæzəˈrɑiə

Azaz
Biblical name   Ā-ZAZ, ahz-AHZ   ˈeːˌzæz, azˈaz

Azazel
evil spirit   uh-ZĀ-zuhl   əˈzeːzəl

Azaziah
Biblical name   AZ-uh-ZĪ-uh, uh-zahz-YAH-ho͞o   ˌæzəˈzɑiə, əzazˈjahuː

Azbine [Aïr]
region, Niger   az-BĒN   æzˈbiːn

Azbuk
Biblical name   AZ-BUHK, ahz-BO͞OK   ˈæzˌbək, azˈbuːk

Azcapotzalco
city, Mexico   AHS-kuh-puht-SAHL-kō   ˌɑskəpətˈsalkoː

Azekah
Biblical name   uh-ZĒ-kuh, ā-ZĒ-kuh, uh-zē-KAH   əˈziːkə, eːˈziːkə, əziːˈka

Azel
Biblical name   Ā-ZEL, Ā-zuhl, AHT-sel   ˈeːˌzel, ˈeːzəl, ˈatsel

Azenberg
Emanuel, theatrical producer   Ā-zuhn-BUHRG   ˈeːzənˌbəʳg

Azerbaijan, Azerbaidzhan
republic, Asia   AZ-uhr-bī-ZHAHN, -JAHN   ˌæzəʳbaiˈʒan, -ˈdʒan

Azerbaijani
lang., people, Asia   AZ-uhr-BĪ-JAHN-ē, AZ-uhr-BĪ-ZHAHN-ē   ˌæzəʳˌbaiˈdʒaniˑ, ˌæzəʳˌbaiˈʒaniˑ

Azeri [Azerbaijani]
lang., Asia   ah-ZER-ē   ɑˈzeriˑ

Azgad
Biblical name   AZ-GAD, ahz-GAHD   ˈæzˌgæd, azˈgad

Aziel
Biblical name   Ā-zē-EL, Ā-zē-uhl, YAH-AH-zē-EL   ˈeːziːˌel, ˈeːziːəl, ˌjɑ-aziːˈel

Aziz
Tariq, Iraqi politician   ah-ZĒZ   ɑˈziːz

Aziza
Biblical name   uh-ZĪ-zuh, uh-zē-ZAH   əˈzɑizə, əziːˈza

Azmaveth
Biblical name   az-MĀ-VETH, az-MĀ-vuhth, ahz-MAH-vet   æzˈmeːˌveθ, æzˈmeːvəθ, azˈmavet

Azmon
Biblical name   AZ-MAHN, aht-SMŌN   ˈæzˌman, atˈsmoːn

Aznoth-Tabor
Biblical name   AZ-NAHTH-TĀ-BAWR, -TĀ-buhr   ˈæzˌnɑθˈteːˌbɔːʳ, -ˈteːbəʳ

Key (col. 2):   a: fad   ā: fade   ah: father   ar: marry   aw: law   e: fed   ē: feed   er: merry   i: hid   ī: hide   ō: coat   o͞o: boot
oi: boy   ow: now   u: put   uh: above   uhr: bird   ch: chop   ng: ring   sh: show   th: thick   <u>th</u>: this   zh: measure

Azogues

   city, Ecuador   uh-SŌ-guhs, uh-ZŌ-guhs   ə'soːgəs, ə'zoːgəs

Azor

   Biblical name   Ā-ZAWR   'eːˌzɔːʳ

Azores

   islands, Atlantic   Ā-ZŌRZ, Ā-ZAWRZ, uh-ZŌRZ,   'eːˌzoːʳz, 'eːˌzɔːʳz, ə'zoːʳz,
                             uh-ZAWRZ   ə'zɔːʳz

Azotus [Ashdod]

   Biblical name; town, Israel   uh-ZŌT-uhs   ə'zoːʈəs

Azov

   sea, Europe   AZ-AWF, ĀZ-AWF, -AHV   'æz,ɔːf, 'eːz,ɔːf, -,ɑv

Azriel

   Biblical name   AZ-rē-EL, AHZ-rē-EL   'æzriːˌel, ˌɑzriː'el

Azrikam

   Biblical name   az-RĪ-KAM, AZ-ri-KAM, AHZ-rē-KAHM   æz'rɑiˌkæm, 'æzriˌkæm,
                                                  ˌɑzriː'kɑm

AZT [Zidovudine]

   AIDS drug   Ā-ZĒ-TĒ   ˌeːˌziː'tiː

Aztec

   N. American people   AZ-TEK   'æz,tek

Azteca [Aztec]

   N. American people   az-TĀ-kuh   æz'teːkə

Aztec-Tanoan

   ancient lang., N. America   AZ-TEK-TAHN-uh-wuhn   ˌæzˌtek'tɑnəwən

Azua

   province, Dominican Republic   AHS-wuh, AHZ-wuh   'ɑswə, 'ɑzwə

Azuay

   province, Ecuador   ah-SWĪ   ɑ'swɑi

Azubah

   Biblical name   uh-ZOO-buh, AH-zoo-VAH   ə'zuːbə, ˌɑzuː'vɑ

Azuma

   volcano, Japan   ah-zum-ah   ɑzumɑ

Azur, Azzur

   Biblical name   Ā-zuhr, ahz-UR   'eːzəʳ, ɑz'ur

Azusa

   city, CA   uh-ZOO-suh   ə'zuːsə

Azzah

   Biblical name   AZ-uh, ahz-AH   'æzə, ɑz'ɑ

Azzan

   Biblical name   AZ-uhn, ahz-AHN   'æzən, ɑz'ɑn

B

Baader-Meinhof
  German terrorist group   BAHD-uhr-MĪN-HAWF   ˌbɑdəʳˈmɑɪnˌhɔːf
Baakpe
  lang., Africa   BAHK-pā, BAK-pā   ˈbɑkpeˈ, ˈbækpeˈ
Baal
  Semitic storm god; idol   BĀ(-uh)l, BAHL   ˈbeː(ə)l, ˈbɑl
Baalah
  Biblical name   BĀ-uh-luh, BAH-ah-LAH   ˈbeːələ, ˌbɑ-aˈlɑ
Baalath
  Biblical name   BĀ-uh-LATH, BAH-ah-LAHT   ˈbeːəˌlæθ, ˌbɑ-aˈlɑt
Baalathbeer
  Biblical name   BĀ-uh-luhth-BIR,   ˈbeːələθˈbiʳ, ˌbɑ-aˈlɑtbəˈer
        BAH-ah-LAHT-buh-ER
Baalbek
  town, Lebanon   BAHL-BEK, BĀ-uhl-BEK, BAL-BEK   ˈbɑlˌbek, ˈbeːəlˌbek, ˈbælˌbek
Baal-berith
  Biblical name   BĀ(-uh)l-BĒR-uhth, BAH-ahl-BRĒT   ˈbeː(ə)lˈbiːrəθ, ˈbɑ-alˈbriːt
Baalejudah
  Biblical name   BĀ(-uh)-lē-JOOD-uh,   ˈbeː(ə)liˈdʒuːdə,
        BAH-ah-LĀ-(y)uh-hoō-DAH   ˈbɑ-aˌleː(j)əhuːˈda
Baal-gad
  Biblical name   BĀ(-uh)l-GAD, BAH-ahl-GAHD   ˈbeː(ə)lˈgæd, ˈbɑ-alˈgad
Baal-hamon
  Biblical name   BĀ(-uh)l-HĀ-muhn   ˈbeː(ə)lˈheːmən
Baal-hanan
  Biblical name   BĀ(-uh)l-HĀ-NAN,   ˈbeː(ə)lˈheːˌnæn,
        BAH-ahl-khah-NAHN   ˈbɑ-alxaˈnan
Baal-hazor
  Biblical name   BĀ(-uh)l-HĀ-ZAWR,   ˈbeː(ə)lˈheːˌzɔːʳ,
        BAH-ahl-khaht-sawr   ˈbɑ-alxatsɔːr
Baal-herman
  Biblical name   BĀ(-uh)l-HUHR-muhn,   ˈbeː(ə)lˈhəʳmən,
        BAH-ahl-kher-MAWN   ˈbɑ-alxerˈmɔːn
Baalis
  Biblical name   BĀ(-uh)-lis, BAH-ah-LĒS   ˈbeː(ə)lis, ˌbɑ-aˈliːs
Baalism
  religion   BĀL-ɪz-uhm   ˈbeːlˌizəm
Baal-meon
  Biblical name   BĀ(-uh)l-MĒ-uhn, BAH-ahl-muh-ŌN   ˈbeː(ə)lˈmiːən, ˈbɑ-almə'oːn
Baal-peor
  Biblical name   BĀ(-uh)l-PĒ-awr, BAH-ahl-pi-AWR   ˈbeː(ə)lˈpiːɔːʳ, ˈbɑ-alpiˈɔːr

Key (col. 2):   a: fad ā: fade ah: father ar: marry aw: law e: fed ē: feed er: merry i: hid ī: hide ō: coat oō: boot
oi: boy   ow: now   u: put   uh: above   uhr: bird   ch: chop   ng: ring   sh: show   th: thick   <u>th</u>: this   zh: measure

Baal-perazim
  Biblical name BĀ(-uh)l-PER-uh-ZIM, -puh-RĀ-zim, 'beː(ə)l'perə,zim, -pə'reːzim,
    BAH-ahl-praht-SĒM 'bɑ-ɑlprɑt'siːm

Baal-shalishah
  Biblical name BĀ(-uh)l-SHAL-i-shuh, 'beː(ə)l'ʃæliʃə, 'bɑ-ɑlʃa'liːʃɑ
    BAH-ahl-shah-LĒ-shah

Ba'al Shem-Tov [Besht]
  cognomen of Israel ben Eliezer BAHL SHEM TŌV 'bɑl 'ʃem 'toːv

Baal-tamar
  Biblical name BĀ(-uh)l-TĀ-MAHR, 'beː(ə)l'teː,mɑr, 'bɑ-ɑltɑ'mɑr
    BAH-ahl-tah-MAHR

Baal-zebub [Beelzebub]
  devil BĀ(-uh)l-ZĒ-BUHB, BAH-ahlts-VŌŌV 'beː(ə)l'ziː,bəb, 'bɑ-ɑlts'vuːv

Baal-zephon
  Biblical name BĀ(-uh)l-ZĒ-fuhn, BAH-ahlt-sef-ŌN 'beː(ə)l'ziːfən, 'bɑ-ɑltsef'oːn

Baana, Baanah
  Biblical name BĀ-uh-nuh, BAH-ah-NAH 'beːənə, ˌbɑ-ɑ'nɑ

Baara
  Biblical name BĀ-uh-ruh, BAR-uh, BER-uh, 'beːərə, 'bærə, 'berə,
    BAH-AH-RAH ˌbɑ-ɑ'rɑ

Baaseiah
  Biblical name BĀ-e-SĪ-uh, BAH-ah-se-YAH ˌbeːe'sɑiə, ˌbɑ-ase'jɑ

Baasha
  Biblical name BĀ-uh-shuh, BAH-uh-SHAH 'beːəʃə, ˌbɑə'ʃɑ

Babar
  elephant in books by Jean de bah-BAHR, Ⓢ buh-BAHR, BAHB-AHR, bɑːbɑːr, Ⓢ bə'bɑr, 'bɑb,ɑr,
    Brunhoff BĀ-BAHR 'beː,bɑr

Babbitt
  novel & character, S. Lewis; pers. BAB-uht 'bæbət
    name

Babbitt
  Bruce, *US politician* BAB-uht 'bæbət

Babbittry
  attitude of Babbit BAB-uh-trē 'bæbətriˑ

Babe
  pers. name BĀB 'beːb

Babel
  1. Biblical city, tower BĀ-buhl, BAB-uhl 'beːbəl, 'bæbəl
  2. Isaac, *Russian writer* BAH-byil, Ⓢ BAB-uhl 'bɑːbjil̦, Ⓢ 'bæbəl

Babette
  pers. name ba-BET, buh- bæ'bet, bə-

Babilonia
  Tai, *US figure skater* BAB-uh-LŌ-nē-uh, -LŌN-yuh ˌbæbə'loːniːə, -'loːnjə

Babism
  doctrine of 19th century Iranian BAHB-IZ-uhm 'bɑb,izəm
    religious sect

Babs
  pers. name BABZ 'bæbz

Babycham
  tdmk for a beverage BĀ-bē-SHAM 'beːbiˑˌʃæm

Babylon
  ancient city, Iraq; village, NY BAB-uh-luhn, -LAHN 'bæbələn, -ˌlɑn

Babylonia
  ancient Asian empire BAB-uh-LŌ-nē-uh, -nyuh ˌbæbə'loːniːə, -njə

Foreign Sounds: **ue:** *Fr.* **rue**, *Ger.* **füllen** **uh(r):** *Fr.* **boeuf**, *Ger.* **Höhle** <u>kh</u>: *Ger.* i<u>ch</u>, *Scot.* lo<u>ch</u> ḡ: *Sp.* ami**g**o ⱱ: *Sp.* ha**b**lar
hl: *Welsh* **Ll**anelli. CAPITALS: primary stress. SMALL CAPS: secondary stress. Ⓢ: U.S. pron. £: British pron.

Babylonian
  pert. to Babylon   BAB-uh-LŌ-nē-uhn   ˌbæbə'loːniːən
Baca
  county, CO   BĀ-kuh   'beːkə
Bacall
  Lauren, *US actress*   buh-KAWL, buh-KAHL   bə'kɔːl, bə'kɑl
Bacardi
  tdmk for rum   buh-KAHRD-ē   bə'kɑʳdiˑ
Baccarat
  game; glassmakers   BAHK-uh-RAH, BAK-uh-RAH,   ˌbɑkə'rɑ, ˌbækə'rɑ, 'bɑkəˌrɑ,
                                      BAHK-uh-RAH, BAK-uh-RAH   'bækəˌrɑ
Bacchae
  attendants of Bacchus   BAK-ē, BAK-Ī   'bækiː, 'bækˌɑi
Bacchanalia
  ancient Greek festival   BAK-uh-NĀL-yuh, -NĀ-lē-uh   ˌbækə'neːljə, -'neːliːə
Bacchic
  pert. to Bacchus   BAK-ik   'bækik
Bacchus
  Greco-Roman god of wine; pers.   BAK-uhs, BAHK-uhs   'bækəs, 'bɑkəs
  name
Bach
  family of German composers &   BAHKH, BAHK   'bɑx, 'bɑk
  musicians
Bachama
  lang., Nigeria   bah-SHAHM-uh, bah-CHAHM-uh   bɑ'ʃɑmə, bɑ'tʃɑmə
Bacharach
  Burt, *US composer; former ballpark,* BAK(-uh)-RAK   'bæk(ə)ˌræk
  Atlantic City, NJ
Bacon
  Francis, *English philosopher;*   BĀ-kuhn   'beːkən
  Roger, *English philosopher*
Bacone
  College, *OK*   buh-KŌN   bə'koːn
Baconian
  pert. to F. Bacon   bā-KŌ-nē-uhn, bā-KŌN-yuhn   beː'koːniːən, beː'koːnjən
Bactria
  ancient Asian country   BAK-trē-uh   'bæktriːə
Bactrian camel
  Asian two-humped camel   BAK-trē-uhn KAM-uhl   ˌbæktriːən 'kæməl
Bad
  German place-name element   BAHT, BAHD   'bɑt, 'bɑd
Badaga
  lang., people, South India   buh-DAHG-uh   bə'dɑgə
Bade
  lang., Nigeria   BAHD-ā   'bɑdeˑ
Baden
  1. city, Austria; former state,   BAHD-n   'bɑdn̩
  Germany
  2. pers. name, English   BĀD-n   'beːdn̩
Baden-Baden
  city, Germany   BAHD-n-BAHD-n   ˌbɑdn̩'bɑdn̩
Baden-Powell
  Robert, *founder of Boy Scouts*   BĀD-n-PŌ-uhl, BĀD-n-POW(-uh)l   ˌbeːdn̩'poːəl, ˌbeːdn̩'pau(ə)l

---

Key (col. 2):   a: fad   ā: fade   ah: father   ar: marry   aw: law   e: fed   ē: feed   er: merry   i: hid   ī: hide   ō: coat   ōō: boot
oi: boy   ow: now   u: put   uh: above   uhr: bird   ch: chop   ng: ring   sh: show   th: thick   th: this   zh: measure

Baden-Württemberg *province, Germany*	BAHD-n-VURT-uhm-BERK, Ⓢ -WUHRT-uhm-BUHRG, -WIRT-uhm-BUHRG	'bɑdn̩'vyʳtəm,beʳk, Ⓢ -'wəʳtəm,bəʳg, -'wiʳtəm,bəʳg
Bader *pers. name (Ruth B. Ginsburg)*	BĀD-uhr	'beːdəʳ
Badham John, *US film director*	BAD-uhm	'bædəm
Bad Lands *arid region, SD, NE*	BAD LAN(D)Z	'bæd ,læn(d)z
Baedeker *German publisher; guidebook*	BĀD-i-kuhr, BED-i-kuhr	'beːdikəʳ, 'bedikəʳ
Baekeland Leo Hendrick, *US chemist*	BAK-uh-LAHNT, Ⓢ BĀK-(uh-)luhnd	'bækə,lɑnt, Ⓢ 'beːk(ə)lənd
Baeyer Adolf von, *German organic chemist (Nobel 1905)*	BĀ-(y)uhr	'beː(j)əʳ
Baez Joan, *US singer-songwriter*	BĪ-EZ, BAH-EZ, bī-EZ, BĪZ *(her own pron.)*	'bɑi,ez, 'bɑ,ez, bɑi'ez, 'bɑiz *(her own pron.)*
Bafang *lang., Cameroon*	bah-FAHNG	bɑ'fɑŋ
Baffin *bay, island, Arctic Ocean*	BAF-uhn	'bæfən
Bafou *lang., Cameroon*	bah-FOO	bɑ'fuː
Bagehot Walter, *English economist*	BAJ-uht	'bædʒət
Baggins *see* Bilbo Baggins		
Baghdad *city, Iraq*	BAG-DAD, bag-DAD	'bæg,dæd, bæg'dæd
Bagirmi *lang., people, Chad*	buh-GIR-mē	bə'giʳmiˑ
Bagnold Enid, *English writer*	BAG-nuhld	'bægnəld
Bagobo *lang., people, Philippine Islands*	buh-GŌ-bō	bə'goːboː
Bagration Petr, *Russian general*	BUH-GRUH-tyi-YAWN	,bə,grətji'jɔːn
Baguio *city, Philippines*	BAHG-ē-ō	'bɑɣiːoː
Bahá'í *religion*	buh-HĪ	bə'hɑi
Baha'ism *religion*	bah-HAH-IZ-uhm, buh-, -HĪ-IZ-uhm	bɑ'hɑ,izəm, bə-, -'hɑi,izəm
Bahamas, The *islands, Atlantic*	buh-HAHM-uhz, buh-HĀ-muhz *(not used by residents)*	bə'hɑməz, bə'heːməz *(not used by residents)*
Bahamian *pert. to* the Bahamas	buh-HĀ-mē-uhn, buh-HAHM-ē-uhn	bə'heːmiːən, bə'hɑmiːən
Bahasa Indonesian *lang., Indonesia*	buh-HAHS-uh IN-duh-NĒ-zhuhn, -NĒ-shuhn	bə'hɑsə ,ində'niːʒən, -'niːʃən

Foreign Sounds: ue: *Fr.* **rue**, *Ger.* **füllen** uh(r): *Fr.* **boeuf**, *Ger.* **Höhle** kh: *Ger.* **ich**, *Scot.* **loch** g̃: *Sp.* **amigo** v̱: *Sp.* **hablar** hl: *Welsh* **Llanelli**. CAPITALS: primary stress. SMALL CAPS: secondary stress. Ⓢ: U.S. pron. [£]: British pron.

Bahia		
state, Brazil	bah-Ē-uh, [$] buh-HĒ-uh	ba'iːə, [$] bə'hiːə
Bahnar		
lang., people, South Vietnam	buh-NAHR, BAH-NAHR, bah-NAHR	bə'nɑ^{r}, 'bɑˌnɑ^{r}, bɑ'nɑ^{r}
Bahrain		
island, country, Persian Gulf	bah-RĀN, bahkh-RĀN	bɑ'reːn, bɑx'reːn
Bahraini		
pert. to Bahrain	bah-RĀN-ē, bahkh-RĀN-ē	bɑ'reːniˑ, bɑx'reːniˑ
Bahurim		
Biblical name	buh-H(Y)UR-im, buh-YUR-im, BAHKH-O͞O-RĒM	bə'h(j)urim, bə'jurim, ˌbɑxuː'riːm
Bai, Pai		
lang., China	BĪ	'bɑi
Baiae		
ancient Roman resort	BĪ-Ē, BĀ(-Ē)	'bɑiˌiː, 'beː(ˌiː)
Baikal		
lake, Siberia	bī-KAHL, bī-KAWL, bī-KAL	bɑi'kɑl, bɑi'kɔːl, bɑi'kæl
Baika-sai		
Japanese festival	bī-kah-sī	bɑikɑsɑi
Baines		
pers. name (L. B. Johnson)	BĀNZ	'beːnz
Baio		
Scott, *US actor*	BĀ-ō	'beːoː
Baird		
Bil, *US puppeteer, author*	BARD, BERD	'bæ^{r}d, 'be^{r}d
Baisak		
Hindu New Year	VĪ-SHAHK	'βɑiˌʃɑk
Baiul		
Oksana, *Ukrainian figure skater*	bī-O͞OL	bɑi'uːl
Baja California		
peninsula, Mexico	BAH-hah KAL-uh-FAWRN-yuh, KAL-uh-FAWR-nē-uh	'bɑhɑ ˌkælə'fɔː^{r}njə, ˌkælə'fɔː^{r}niːə
Baja California Norte		
state, Mexico	NAWR-tā	'nɔː^{r}teː
Baja California Sur		
state, Mexico	SUR	'su^{r}
Bajer		
Fredrik, *Danish politician, author (Nobel 1908)*	BĪ(-uh)r	'bɑi(ə)^{r}
Bakbakkar		
Biblical name	bak-BAK-AHR, BAHK-bah-KAHR	bæk'bækˌɑ^{r}, ˌbɑkbɑ'kɑr
Bakbuk		
Biblical name	BAK-BUK, BAK-BUHK, bahk-BO͝OK	'bækˌbuk, 'bækˌbək, bɑk'buːk
Bakbukiah		
Biblical name	BAK-b(y)o͞o-KĪ-uh, BAHK-BO͝OK-YAH	ˌbækb(j)uː'kɑiə, ˌbɑkˌbuːk'jɑ
Bakelite		
tdmk for plastic	BĀ-kuh-LĪT, BĀ-KLĪT	'beːkəˌlɑit, 'beːˌklɑit
Bakerloo		
London underground line	BĀ-kuhr-LO͞O	ˌbeːkə^{r}'luː
Bakewell		
town, England	BĀK-WEL, BĀK-wuhl	'beːkˌwel, 'beːkwəl
Bakhtiari		
Iranian people	BAHK-tē-AHR-ē, bahk-TYAHR-ē	ˌbɑktiː'ɑriˑ, bɑk'tjɑriˑ

Key (col. 2): a: fad ā: fade ah: father ar: marry aw: law e: fed ē: feed er: merry i: hid ī: hide ō: coat o͞o: boot oi: boy ow: now u: put uh: above uhr: bird ch: chop ng: ring sh: show th: thick th: this zh: measure

Bakke case
US Supreme Court case   BAHK-ē, BAK-ē   'bɑki', 'bæki'
Bakker
1. James, *US TV evangelist*   BĀ-kuhr   'beːkəʳ
2. Robert T., *US paleontologist*   BAHK-uhr   'bakəʳ
Bakr
Abu, *political leader*   BAHK-uhr   'bakəʳ
Bakshi
Ralph, *US film producer, director*   BAK-shē   'bækʃi'
Bakst
Leon, *Russian painter/designer*   BAHKST   'baːkst
Baku
city, Azerbaijan   bah-KOO   bɑ'kuː
Bakue
lang., Liberia, Ivory Coast   buh-KOO-ā   bə'kuːeː
Bakunin
Mikhail, *Russian anarchist*   buh-KOON-yin   bə'kuːnjin
Bala
lake, Wales   BAHL-uh   'balə
Balaam
Old Testament prophet   BĀ-luhm   'beːləm
Bala-Cynwyd
1. *town, Wales*   BAHL-uh-KUHN-wid   ˌbalə'kənwid
2. *town, PA*   BAL-uh-KIN-wid   ˌbælə'kinwid
Baladan
Biblical name   BAL-uh-DAN, BAH-lah-DAHN   'bæləˌdæn, ˌbalɑ'dan
Balah
Biblical name   BĀ-luh, bah-LAH   'beːlə, bɑ'lɑ
Balak
Biblical name   BĀ-LAK, bah-LAHK   'beːˌlæk, bɑ'lak
Balanchine
George, *US choreographer*   BAL-uhn-CHĒN, -SHĒN;   ˌbælən'tʃiːn, -'ʃiːn;
                 BAL-uhn-CHĒN, -SHĒN   'bælənˌtʃiːn, -ˌʃiːn
Balanta
lang., people, Guinea-Bissau, Senegal   buh-LAHNT-uh, buh-LANT-uh   bə'lantə, bə'læntə
Balantak
lang., South Sulawesi (Celebes)   BAL-uhn-TAHK   'bælənˌtak
Balatón
lake, Hungary   BAW-luh-TŌN, BAL-uh-TAHN   'bɔːləˌtoːn, 'bæləˌtan
Balboa
Vasco Nuñez de, *Spanish explorer*   bal-BŌ-uh   bæl'boːə
Balch
Emily G., *US economist, sociologist*   BAWLCH   'bɔːltʃ
   (*Nobel 1946*)
Balcom
pers. name   BAL-kuhm, BAWL-kuhm   'bælkəm, 'bɔːlkəm
Baldassare
pers. name   BAHL-dahs-SAHR-ā   ˌbaldas'sareː
Baldr, Balder
Scandinavian hero-god   BAWL-duhr   'bɔːldəʳ
Balduin
pers. name   BAHL-duh-WĒN   ˌbaldə'wiːn
Baldung Grien
Hans, *artist*   BAHL-dung GRĒN   'balduŋ 'griːn

Foreign Sounds: **ue**: *Fr.* **rue**, *Ger.* **füllen**   **uh(r)**: *Fr.* **boeuf**, *Ger.* **Höhle**   <u>kh</u>: *Ger.* **ich**, *Scot.* lo**ch**   ḡ: *Sp.* ami**g**o   <u>v</u>: *Sp.* ha**b**lar
hl: *Welsh* **Ll**anelli.   CAPITALS: primary stress.   SMALL CAPS: secondary stress.   Ⓢ: U.S. pron.   Ⓔ: British pron.

Baldwin
   pers. name   BAWLD-wuhn   'bɔːldwən
Bâle
   French form of Basel, *Switzerland*   BAHL   bɑl
Baleares, Islas
   island group, Mediterranean   ĒZ-lahs bahl-ē-AHR-uhs   'iːzlɑs bɑliː'ɑrəs
Balearic Islands [Baleares, Islas]
   island group, Mediterranean   BAL-ē-AR-ik   ˌbæliː'ærik
Balenciaga
   Cristóbal, *Spanish fashion designer*   bahl-en-THYAHḠ-ah   bɑlen'θjɑɣɑ
Balfour Declaration
   British support for Israel   BAL-fuhr, BAL-FŌR, BAL-FAWR   'bælfəʳ, 'bælˌfoːʳ, 'bælˌfɔːʳ
Bali
   Indonesian island; lang., Africa   BAHL-ē, BAL-ē   'bɑliˑ, 'bæliˑ
Balikpapan
   port, Borneo   BAHL-ik-PAHP-AHN   ˌbɑlik'pɑpˌɑn
Balinese
   lang., people, Bali   BAHL-uh-NĒZ, BAL-, -NĒS   ˌbɑlə'niːz, ˌbæl-, -'niːs
Baliol
   pers. name   BĀL-yuhl   'beːljəl
Balkan
   peninsula, mts., eastern Europe   BAWL-kuhn   'bɔːlkən
Balkans
   countries on Balkan Peninsula   BAWL-kuhnz   'bɔːlkənz
Balkar [Karachay]
   lang., people, Caucasus Mts.   bahl-KAHR, BAHL-KAHR   bɑl'kɑʳ, 'bɑlˌkɑʳ
Balkhash
   lake, Kazakhstan   bal-KASH, bahl-KAHSH   bæl'kæʃ, bɑl'kɑʃ
Ballantine
   US brewery, US publisher   BAL-uhn-TĪN   'bælənˌtɑin
Ballarat
   city, Australia   BAL-uh-RAT   'bæləˌræt
Ballater
   village, Scotland   BAL-uht-uhr   'bælətəʳ
Ballesteros
   Seve, *Spanish golfer*   bah(l)-yes-TĀ-rōs, BAHL-uh-STER-ōs   bɑ(l)jes'teːroːs, 'bɑləˌsteroːs
Ballet Folklórico de México
   Mexican dance troupe   bah-LĀ fōl-KLAWR-ē-kō thā MĀ-hē-kō   bɑ'leː foːl'klɔːriːkoː ðeː
                                                                                           'meˑhiːkoː
Ballet Russe
   dance company   ba-LĀ RUS, R͞OOS   bæ'leː 'rus, 'ruːs
Ballina
   city, Australia   BAL-uh-nuh   'bælənə
Balliol
   college, Oxford Univ.   BĀL-ē-uhl   'beːliːəl
Ballo in Maschera
   opera, Verdi   BAHL-lō in mahs-KĀ-rah   'bɑlloː in mɑs'keːrɑ
Bally
   Swiss shoe co.; game mfg. co.   bah-YĒ; Ⓢ BAL-ē, BAHL-ē   bɑːjiː; Ⓢ 'bæliˑ, 'bɑliˑ
Balmoral
   castle, Scotland   bal-MAWR-uhl, bal-MAHR-uhl   bæl'mɔːrəl, bæl'mɑrəl
Balochi [Baluchi]
   lang., Middle & Near East   buh-LŌ-chē   bə'loːtʃiˑ
Balor
   evil Irish god   BĀ-luhr, BĀ-LAWR   'beːləʳ, 'beːˌlɔːʳ

Key (col. 2):   a: fad   ā: fade   ah: father   ar: marry   aw: law   e: fed   ē: feed   er: merry   i: hid   ī: hide   ō: coat   o͞o: boot
oi: boy   ow: now   u: put   uh: above   uhr: bird   ch: chop   ng: ring   sh: show   th: thick   t̲h̲: this   zh: measure

Balranald		
town, Australia	bal-RAN-ld	bæl'rænl̩d
Baltasar, Baltazar		
pers. name, Spanish	bahl-tah-SAHR, -THAHR	bɑltɑ'sɑr, -'θɑr
Baltasare		
pers. name, Italian	BAHL-tah-ZAHR-ā	ˌbɑltɑ'zɑreː
Balthasar		
1. pers. name	BAL-thuh-ZAHR; bal-THĀ-zuhr, -THAZ-uhr	'bælθəˌzɑ^r; bæl'θeːzə^r, -'θæzə^r
2. Dutch	BAHL-tah-SAHR	'bɑltɑːˌsɑr
3. French	bahl-tah-ZAHR	bɑːltɑːzɑːr
4. German	BAHL-tah-ZAHR	'bɑltɑˌzɑ^r
Balthazar		
1. pers. name	BAL-thuh-ZAHR; BAL-THĀ-zuhr, -THAZ-uhr	'bælθəˌzɑ^r; bæl'θeːzə^r, -'θæzə^r
2. French	bahl-tah-ZAHR	bɑːltɑːzɑːr
Baltic		
Sea, *N. Atlantic; region, N. Europe*	BAWL-tik	'bɔːltik
Baltimore		
1. city, MD	BAWL-tuh-MŌR, BAWL-tuh-MAWR, *(esp. by residents)* BAWL-(uh-)muhr	'bɔːltəˌmoː^r, 'bɔːltəˌmɔː^r, *(esp. by residents)* 'bɔːl(ə)mə^r
2. David, *US microbiologist (Nobel 1975)*	BAWL-tuh-MŌR, -MAWR, -muhr	'bɔːltəˌmoː^r, -ˌmɔː^r, -mə^r
Baluchi [Balochi]		
lang., Middle & Near East	buh-LOO-chē	bə'luːtʃiˑ
Balúchistán		
province, Pakistan	buh-LOO-chuh-STAHN, -STAN	bəˌluːtʃə'stɑn, -'stæn
Balzac		
Honoré de, *French novelist*	bahl-ZAHK, [$] BAWL-ZAK, BAL-ZAK	bɑːlzɑːk, [$] 'bɔːlˌzæk, 'bælˌzæk
Bamah		
Biblical name	BĀ-muh, bah-MAH	'beːmə, bɑ'mɑ
Bamako		
city, Mali	BAM-uh-KŌ	'bæməˌkoː
Bambara		
lang., Africa	bam-BAHR-uh	bæm'bɑrə
Bamber		
pers. name	BAM-buhr	'bæmbə^r
Bamberg		
city, Germany	BAHM-BERK, [$] BAM-BUHRG	'bɑmˌbe^{r}k, [$] 'bæmˌbə^{r}g
Bambi		
deer, Disney character; pers. name	BAM-bē	'bæmbiˑ
Bamileke		
lang., Cameroon	BAHM-uh-LĀ-kā	ˌbɑmə'leːkeː
Bamoth		
Biblical name	BĀ-MAHTH, BĀ-MAWTH, BĀ-muhth, bah-MŌT	'beːˌmɑθ, 'beːˌmɔːθ, 'beːməθ, bɑ'moːt
Bamoth-baal		
Biblical name	BĀ-MAHTH-BĀ(-uh)l, BĀ-MAWTH-, BĀ-muhth-; bah-MŌT-BAH-ahl	'beːˌmɑθ'beː(ə)l, 'beːˌmɔːθ-, 'beːməθ-; bɑ'moːt'bɑ-ɑl
Banbury		
town, England	BAN-b(uh-)rē, BAM-b(uh-)rē	'bænb(ə)riˑ, 'bæmb(ə)riˑ
Banda		
islands, sea, Pacific; lang., Africa	BAN-duh, BAHN-duh	'bændə, 'bɑndə

Foreign Sounds: ue: *Fr.* **rue**, *Ger.* **füllen** uh(r): *Fr.* **boeuf**, *Ger.* **Höhle** kh: *Ger.* **ich**, *Scot.* **loch** g̃: *Sp.* **amigo** v̲: *Sp.* **hablar** hl: *Welsh* **Llanelli**. CAPITALS: primary stress. SMALL CAPS: secondary stress. [$]: U.S. pron. [£]: British pron.

Band-Aid
  tdmk for bandages   BAN-DĀD, ban-DĀD   'bæn,deːd, bæn'deːd

Bandaranaike
  Sirimavo, *Sri Lankan politician*   BUHN-duh-ruh-NĪ-kuh   ,bəndərə'naikə

Bandera
  county, TX   ban-DER-uh   bæn'derə

Banderas
  Antonio, *Spanish-born US actor*   bahn-DER-uhs   ban'derəs

Bandjabi
  lang., Cen. Africa   bahn-JAHB-ē   ban'dʒabiˑ

Bandoeng, Bandung
  city, Java   BAHN-DUNG, BAN-DUNG, -DUHNG   'ban,duŋ, 'bæn,duŋ, -,dəŋ

Bandundu
  prov & town, Zaire   bahn-DOON-doo   ban'duːnduː

Baneasa
  airport, Romania   BAHN-ā-AHS-uh   ,bane'asə

Banff
  city, former county, Scotland; town,   BAMF   'bæmf
    Canada

Bangalore
  city, India   BAHNG-guh-LŌR, -LAWR   'baŋgə,loːʳ, -,lɔːʳ

Banghāzī [Benghazi]
  city, former province, Libya   bahn-GAHZ-ē, bahng-GAHZ-ē,   ban'gaziˑ, baŋ'gaziˑ,
         bang-GAHZ-ē, -GAZ-ē   bæŋ'gaziˑ, -'gæziˑ

Bangkok
  city, Thailand   BANG-KAHK, bang-KAHK   'bæŋ,kak, bæŋ'kak

Bangla
  lang., India   BAHNG-gluh, BANG-gluh,   'baŋglə, 'bæŋglə, 'bəŋglə
         BUHNG-gluh

Bangladesh
  republic, Asia   BAHNG-gluh-DESH, BANG-, BUHNG-,   ,baŋglə'deʃ, ,bæŋ-, ,bəŋ-,
         -DĀSH   -'deːʃ

Bangladeshi
  pert. to Bangladesh   BAHNG-gluh-DESH-ē, BANG-, BUHNG-,   ,baŋglə'deʃiˑ, ,bæŋ-, ,bəŋ-,
         -DĀ-shē   -'deːʃiˑ

Bangor
  1. town, N. Ireland   BANG-guhr   'bæŋgəʳ
  2. city, Wales   BANG-guhr, BANG-gawr   'bæŋgəʳ, 'bæŋgɔːʳ
  3. city, ME, PA   BANG-GAWR, BAN-GAWR, BANG-guhr   'bæŋ,gɔːʳ, 'bæn,gɔːʳ,
                  'bæŋgəʳ

Bang Pla Soi
  former name of Chon Buri   BAHNG PLAH SOI   'baŋ 'pla 'sɔi

Bangui
  1. city, Central African Republic   bahng-GĒ, BAHNG-GĒ   baŋ'giː, 'baŋ,giː
  2. city, Philippines; bay, South China   BAHNG-gē   'baŋgiˑ
    Sea

Bangweulu
  lake, Zambia   BANG-wē-OO-loo   ,bæŋwiː'uːluː

Bani
  Biblical name   BĀ-NĪ, bah-NĒ   'beː,nai, ba'niː

Bani-Sadr
  Abolhassan, *former Iranian*   BAHN-ē-SAHD-uhr   ,baniˑ'sadəʳ
    president

Banja Luka
  city, Bosnia   BAHN-yuh-LOO-kuh   ,banjə'luːkə

Key (col. 2):   a: fad   ā: fade   ah: father   ar: marry   aw: law   e: fed   ē: feed   er: merry   i: hid   ī: hide   ō: coat   ōō: boot
oi: boy   ow: now   u: put   uh: above   uhr: bird   ch: chop   ng: ring   sh: show   th: thick   <u>th</u>: this   zh: measure

Banjermasin, Bandjarmasin
town, Indonesia   BAN-juhr-MAHS-n, BAHN-   ˌbændʒəʳˈmɑsn̩, ˌbɑn-

Banjul
city, Gambia   BAHN-JŌŌL   ˈbɑnˌdʒuːl

Bankim
pers. name, Bengali   BAWNG-kim   ˈbɔːŋkim

Bann
Irish river   BAN   ˈbæn

Banna
lang., Ethiopia   BAHN-uh, BAN-uh   ˈbɑnə, ˈbænə

Bannock
N. American people   BAN-uhk, BAN-ik   ˈbænək, ˈbænik

Bannockburn
village, Scotland   BAN-uhk-BUHRN, BAN-uhk-BUHRN   ˈbænəkˌbəʳn, ˌbænəkˈbəʳn

Banquo
character in Macbeth, *Shakespeare*   BANG-kwō, BAN-kwō   ˈbæŋkwoː, ˈbænkwoː

Banting
Sir Frederick G., *Canadian physician (Nobel 1923)*   BANT-ing   ˈbæntiŋ

Bantu
lang., people, Africa   BAN-tōō, BAHN-tōō   ˈbæntuː, ˈbɑntuː

Banyuwangi, Banjuwangi
port, Indonesia   BAHN-yuh-WAHNG-ē   ˌbɑnjəˈwɑŋiˑ

Banzan
pers. name, Japanese   bahn-zahn   bɑnzɑn

Bao Dai
Vietnamese politician   BOW DĪ, BAH-ō DĪ   ˈbau ˈdai, ˈbaoː ˈdai

Baptist
1. pers. name   BAP-tuhst, BAB-tuhst   ˈbæptəst, ˈbæbt̪əst
2. Dutch, German   bahp-TIST   bɑpˈtist

Baptista
1. pers. name   bap-TIS-tuh   bæpˈtistə
2. Flemish   bahp-TIS-tah   bɑpˈtistɑ
3. Portuguese   buh-TĒSH-tuh, bah-TĒ-stah   bəˈtiːʃtə, bɑːˈtiːstɑː

Baptiste
pers. name, French   bah-TĒST   bɑːtiːst

Bara
Theda, *US actress*   BAR-uh   ˈbærə

Barabbas
Jewish prisoner in New Testament   buh-RAB-uhs   bəˈræbəs

Barachel
Biblical name   BAHR-uh-KEL, BAR-uh-KEL, buh-RĀ-kuhl, BAH-rah<u>kh</u>-EL   ˈbɑrəˌkel, ˈbærəˌkel, bəˈreːkəl, ˌbɑrɑxˈel

Barachias
Biblical name   BAHR-uh-KĪ-uhs, BAR-uh-   ˌbɑrəˈkaiəs, ˌbærə-

Baraga
county, MI   BAR-uh-guh   ˈbærəgə

Barajas
airport, Madrid   BAHR-ah-hahs, -hah   ˈbɑrɑhɑs, -hɑ

Barak
Biblical name   BĀ-RAK, bah-RAHK   ˈbeːˌræk, bɑˈrɑk

Baraka
Imamu Amiri, *US poet*   BAHR-uh-kuh, buh-RAHK-uh   ˈbɑrəkə, bəˈrɑkə

Barambu
lang., Sudan, Congo   buh-RAHM-bōō   bəˈrɑmbuː

Foreign Sounds: ue: *Fr.* **rue**, *Ger.* **füllen**   uh(r): *Fr.* **boeuf**, *Ger.* **Höhle**   <u>kh</u>: *Ger.* **ich**, *Scot.* **loch**   g̃: *Sp.* **amigo**   v: *Sp.* **hablar**
hl: *Welsh* **Llanelli**.   CAPITALS: primary stress.   SMALL CAPS: secondary stress.   Ⓢ: U.S. pron.   Ⓑ: British pron.

Baranof
　island, AK　　　　　　　　BAR-uh-NAWF, BAR-uh-NAHF,　　'bærə,nɔːf, 'bærə,nɑf,
　　　　　　　　　　　　　　　　buh-RAHN-uhf　　　　　　　　bə'rɑnəf

Bárány
　Robert, *Austrian physician (Nobel*　　BAHR-AHN-yuh　　　　　'bɑr,ɑnjə
　　1914)

Barat
　College, *IL*　　　　　　　buh-RAT　　　　　　　　　　bə'ræt

Barbacoa
　S. American people　　　　BAHR-buh-KŌ-uh　　　　　　,bɑʳbə'koːə

Barbadian
　pert. to Barbados　　　　　bahr-BĀD-ē-uhn　　　　　　bɑʳ'beːdiːən

Barbados
　island, West Indies　　　　bahr-BĀD-uhs, -ōz, -ōs, -ahs　　bɑʳ'beːdəs, -oːz, -oːs, -ɑs

Barbara
　1. pers. name　　　　　　BAHR-b(uh-)ruh　　　　　　'bɑʳb(ə)rə
　2. German　　　　　　　BAHR-bahr-ah　　　　　　　'bɑʳbɑrɑ
　3. Italian　　　　　　　　BAHR-bahr-ah　　　　　　　'barbɑrɑ
　4. Russian　　　　　　　BUHR-BAH-ruh　　　　　　　,bər'baːrə

Barbarossa
　epithet, Frederick I, Germany　　BAHR-buh-RAHS-uh　　　　,bɑʳbə'rɑsə

Barbary
　region, West Africa　　　　BAHR-buh-rē　　　　　　　'bɑʳbəriˑ

Barbeau
　Adrienne, *US actress*　　　bahr-BŌ　　　　　　　　　bɑʳ'boː

Barbee
　Victor, *US ballet dancer*　　BAHR-bē　　　　　　　　　'bɑʳbiˑ

Barbera
　Joe, *US cartoonist*　　　　bahr-BER-uh　　　　　　　bɑʳ'berə

Barbie
　Klaus, *Nazi war criminal; tdmk for a*　BAHR-bē　　　　　　　　'bɑʳbiˑ
　　toy doll; pers. name

Barbiere di Siviglia
　opera, Rossini　　　　　　bahr-BYER-ā dē si-VĒL-yah　　bɑʳ'bjereː diː si'viːljɑ

Barbirolli
　Sir John, *British conductor*　　BAHR-buh-RAHL-ē　　　　　,bɑʳbə'rɑliˑ

Barbizon
　school of painting　　　　BAHR-buh-ZAHN　　　　　　'bɑʳbə,zɑn

Barbour
　county, AL, WV　　　　　BAHR-buhr　　　　　　　　'bɑʳbəʳ

Barbra
　pers. name　　　　　　　BAHR-bruh　　　　　　　　'bɑʳbrə

Barbuda
　see Antigua and Barbuda

Barcelona
　prov & town, Spain　　　BAHR-thuh-LŌ-nuh, BAHR-suh-LŌ-nuh　　,bɑʳθə'loːnə, ,bɑʳsə'loːnə

Barclaycard
　tdmk for a bank card　　　BAHR-klē-KAHRD　　　　　'bɑʳkliˑ,kɑʳd

Barclays
　bank, United Kingdom　　BAHR-klēz　　　　　　　　'bɑʳkliˑz

Barcoo
　river, Australia　　　　　bahr-KOO　　　　　　　　bɑʳ'kuː

Bardeen
　John, *US physicist (Nobel 1956,*　　bahr-DĒN　　　　　　　　bɑʳ'diːn
　　1972)

Key (col. 2):　a: fad　ā: fade　ah: father　ar: marry　aw: law　e: fed　ē: feed　er: merry　i: hid　ī: hide　ō: coat　ōō: boot
oi: boy　ow: now　u: put　uh: above　uhr: bird　ch: chop　ng: ring　sh: show　th: thick　tẖ: this　zh: measure

Bardolino
   wine   BAHRD-l-Ē-nō, BAHRD-uh-LĒ-nō   ˌbaʳdḷˈiːnoː, ˌbaʳdəˈliːnoː

Bardot
   Brigitte, *French actress*   bahr-DŌ   baːrdoː

Bare'e
   lang., Central Sulawesi (Celebes)   buh-RĀ-Ā   bəˈreːˌeː

Barenboim
   Daniel, *US pianist, conductor*   BAR-uhn-BOIM   ˈbærənˌbɔim

Barents Sea
   Arctic   BAR-uhn(t)s, BAHR-uhn(t)s   ˈbærən(t)s, ˈbaːrən(t)s

Barhumite
   Biblical name   bahr-(H)YOO̅-MĪT   baʳˈ(h)juːˌmait

Bari
   lang., people, Africa; prov & town,   BAHR-ē   ˈbariˑ
      Italy

Bariah
   Biblical name   buh-RĪ-uh, bah-RĒ-ah<u>kh</u>   bəˈraiə, baˈriːax

barium
   element   BAR-ē-uhm, BER-ē-uhm   ˈbæriːəm, ˈberiːəm

Bar-jesus
   Biblical name   bahr-JĒ-zuhs   baʳˈdʒiːzəs

Bar-jona
   Biblical name   bahr-JŌ-nuh   baʳˈdʒoːnə

Barking and Dagenham
   industrial borough, England   BAHR-king uhn DAG-nuhm,   ˈbaʳkiŋ ən ˈdægnəm, ˈbɔːkiŋ
                          BAW-king

Barkla
   C. G., *English physicist (Nobel 1917)*   BAHR-kluh   ˈbaʳklə

Barkley
   Charles, *US basketball player*   BAHR-klē   ˈbaʳkliˑ

Barkos
   Biblical name   BAHR-KAHS, bahr-KŌS   ˈbaʳˌkas, baʳˈkoːs

Barlach
   Ernst, *artist*   BAHR-LAH<u>KH</u>   ˈbaʳˌlax

Bar-le-Duc
   commune, France   bahr-luh-DUEK   baːrlədyːk

Barlow, Barlowe
   pocket knife; pers. name   BAHR-lō   ˈbaʳloː

Barmecide feast
   incident, Arabian Nights   BAHR-muh-SĪD FĒST   ˌbaʳməˌsaid ˈfiːst

Barnabas
   pers. name   BAHR-nuh-buhs   ˈbaʳnəbəs

Barnaby
   pers. name   BAHR-nuh-bē   ˈbaʳnəbiˑ

Barnard
   Dr. Christiaan, *South African*   BAHR-nuhrd   ˈbaʳnəʳd
      surgeon; College, *NY; pers. name*

Barnegat
   inlet, bay of Atlantic Ocean, NJ   BAHR-ni-GAT, BAHR-ni-guht   ˈbaʳniˌgæt, ˈbaʳnigət

Barnet
   borough, England   BAHR-nuht   ˈbaʳnət

Barney
   pers. name   BAHR-nē   ˈbaʳniˑ

Barnouw
   Erik, *US author, educator*   BAHR-NŌ   ˈbaʳˌnoː

Foreign Sounds: ue: *Fr.* **rue**, *Ger.* **füllen**   uh(r): *Fr.* **boeuf**, *Ger.* **Höhle**   <u>kh</u>: *Ger.* **ich**, *Scot.* **loch**   g̱: *Sp.* **amigo**   v: *Sp.* **hablar**
hl: *Welsh* **Llanelli**.   CAPITALS: primary stress.   SMALL CAPS: secondary stress.   Ⓢ: U.S. pron.   Ⓔ: British pron.

Barnstable
  county, MA   BAHRN-stuh-buhl   'bɑʳnstəbəl
Barnstaple
  bay, borough, England   BAHRN-stuh-puhl, BAHRN-stuh-buhl   'bɑʳnstəpəl, 'bɑʳnstəbəl
Barnum
  P. T., US showman   BAHR-nuhm   'bɑʳnəm
Barnwell
  city, county, SC   BAHRN-wuhl   'bɑʳnwəl
Baron, Barron
  pers. name   BAR-uhn   'bærən
Barona
  Indian reservation, US   buh-RŌ-nuh   bə'roːnə
Baroque art
  elaborately ornamented style   buh-RŌK, ba-RŌK, -RAHK, -RAWK   bə'roːk, bæ'roːk, -'rɑk, -'rɔːk
Barranquilla
  city, Colombia   bahr-rahn-KĒ(L)-yuh,   barran'kiː(l)jə,
                 ⑤ BAR-uhn-KĒ-(y)uh   ⑤ ˌbærən'kiː(j)ə
Barre
  town, MA, VT   BAR-ē   'bæriˑ
Barrett
  pers. name   BAR-uht   'bærət
Barry
  pers. name; island, Wales   BAR-ē   'bæriˑ
Barrymore
  US acting family   BAR-ē-MŌR, BAR-ē-MAWR   'bæriˑˌmoːʳ, 'bæriˑˌmɔːʳ
Barsabas
  Biblical name   BAHR-suh-buhs   'bɑʳsəbəs
Barsabbas
  Biblical name   bahr-SAB-uhs, BAHR-suh-buhs   bɑʳ'sæbəs, 'bɑʳsəbəs
Barstow
  College, CA   BAHR-stō   'bɑʳstoː
Bart
  pers. name   BAHRT   'bɑʳt
Barth
  1. Karl, *Swiss theologian*   BAHRT   'bɑʳt
  2. John, *US author*   BAHRTH   'bɑʳθ
Barthes
  Roland, *French critic/author*   BAHRT   bɑːrt
Barthold
  1. pers. name, Dutch   BAHR-TAWLT   'bar‚tɔːlt
  2. German   BAHR-TAWLT   'bɑʳ‚tɔːlt
Bartholdi
  Frédéric Auguste, *French sculptor*   bahr-tawl-DĒ, ⑤ bahr-TAWL-dē,   bɑːrtɔːldiː, ⑤ bɑʳ'tɔːldiˑ,
                 bahr-TAHL-dē   bɑʳ'tɑldiˑ
Bartholomaeus
  pers. name, Latin   bahr-TAHL-uh-MĒ-uhs, -THAHL-   bɑʳ‚tɑlə'miːəs, -‚θɑl-
Bartholomaus
  1. pers. name, Dutch   BAHR-TŌ-lō-MĀ-ues   ˌbar‚to:loː'meːys
  2. German   BAHR-TŌ-lō-ME-us   ˌbɑʳ‚toːloː'meus
Bartholomeu
  pers. name, Portuguese   BAHR-tōō-lōō-MĀ-u   ˌbɑːrtuːluː'meːu
Bartholomeus
  pers. name, Dutch   BAHR-TŌ-lō-MĀ-ues   ˌbar‚toːloː'meːys
Bartholomew
  pers. name   bahr-THAHL-uh-MYŌŌ   bɑʳ'θɑlə‚mjuː

Key (col. 2):   a: **fad**   ā: **fade**   ah: **father**   ar: **marry**   aw: **law**   e: **fed**   ē: **feed**   er: **merry**   i: **hid**   ī: **hide**   ō: **coat**   ōō: **boot**
oi: **boy**   ow: **now**   u: **put**   uh: **above**   uhr: **bird**   ch: **chop**   ng: **ring**   sh: **show**   th: **thick**   <u>th</u>: **this**   zh: **measure**

Bartimeus
Biblical name BAHRT-uh-MĒ-uhs ˌbɑʳṭə'miːəs
Bartleby
story, H. Melville BAHRT-l-bē 'bɑʳt̬l̩biˑ
Bartlesville Wesleyan
College, *OK* BAHRT-uhlz-VIL WEZ-lē-uhn, 'bɑʳt̬lz̩ˌvil 'wezliːən,
WES-lē-uhn 'wesliːən
Bartlett
pers. name BAHRT-luht 'bɑʳtlət
Bartók
Bela, *Hungarian composer* BAHR-TAHK, BAHR-TAWK 'bɑʳˌtɑk, 'bɑʳˌtɔːk
Bartolomé
pers. name, Spanish bahr-tō-lō-MĀ bɑrtoːloːˈmeː
Bartolomeo
1. pers. name, Italian BAHR-tō-lō-ME-ō ˌbɑrtoːloːˈmeoː
2. Spanish bahr-tō-lō-MĀ-ō bɑrtoːloːˈmeːoː
Bartolommeo
pers. name, Italian BAHR-tō-lōm-ME-ō ˌbɑrtoːloːmˈmeoː
Barton
Clara, *US founder of Red Cross;* BAHRT-n 'bɑʳtn̩
Derek H. R., *English organic*
chemist (Nobel 1969)
Baruch
1. Old Testament book; pers. name buh-ROOK, BAHR-OOK bə'ruːk, 'bɑrˌuːk
2. Bernard, US statesman buh-ROOK bə'ruːk
Baruj
pers. name, Spanish BAHR-ookh 'bɑruːx
Baryshnikov
Mikhail, *ballet dancer* buh-RISH-ni-kuhf, bə'riʃn̩ikəf, ⓢ bə'riʃniˌkɔːf,
ⓢ buh-RISH-ni-KAWF, -KAWV -ˌkɔːv
Barzillai
Biblical name bahr-ZIL-ē-Ī, BAHR-zuh-LĪ bɑʳ'ziliːˌai, ˌbɑʳzə'lai
Barzun
Jacques, *US author* bahr-ZUHN bɑʳ'zən
Basa
lang., Africa BAHS-uh 'bɑsə
Basant Panchami
Hindu festival VUHS-uhnt PUHN-chuh-mē 'βəsənt 'pəntʃəmiˑ
Basari
lang., Guinea, Senegal, Gambia buh-SAHR-ē bə'sɑriˑ
Bascomb
pers. name BAS-kuhm 'bæskəm
Basel
city, Switzerland BAHZ-uhl 'bɑzəl
Basemath
Biblical name BAS-uh-MATH, BAZ-; BAH-suh-MAHT 'bæsəˌmæθ, 'bæz-; ˌbɑsə'mɑt
Basenji
dog breed buh-SEN-jē, buh-ZEN-jē bə'sendʒiˑ, bə'zendʒiˑ
Bashan
Biblical name BĀ-SHAN, bah-SHAHN 'beːˌʃæn, bɑ'ʃɑn
Bashan-havoth-jair
Biblical name BĀ-SHAN-HĀ-VAHTH-JĀ-IR, 'beːˌʃæn'heːˌvɑθ'dʒeːˌiʳ,
bah-SHAHN-khah-VŌT-yah-IR bɑ'ʃɑnxɑ'voːtjɑ'ir
Bashemath
Biblical name BASH-uh-MATH, BAH-suh-MAHT 'bæʃəˌmæθ, ˌbɑsə'mɑt

Basherawa
   lang., Nigeria   buh-SHER-uh-wuh   bə'ʃerəwə

Bashevis
   pers. name (I. B. Singer)   buh-SHEV-uhs   bə'ʃevəs

Bashkir
   republic, Asia   bash-KIR   bæʃ'kiʳ

Bashō
   poetic name of Matsuo Munefusa,   bah-shō   baʃoː
      Japanese poet

Basie
   Count, *US bandleader*   BĀ-sē   'beːsi·

Basil
   pers. name   BAZ-uhl, BĀ-zuhl   'bæzəl, 'beːzəl

Basilius
   1. pers. name, German   bah-ZĒL-yus, bah-ZĒ-lē-us;   ba'ziːljus, ba'ziːliːus;
                         BAHZ-i-LĒ-us   ˌbazi'liːus
   2. Latin   buh-SIL-ē-uhs, buh-ZIL-ē-uhs   bə'siliːəs, bə'ziliːəs

Basingstoke
   town, England   BĀ-zing-STŌK   'beːziŋˌstoːk

Baskerville
   John, *English typographer; typefont*   BAS-kuhr-VIL   'bæskəʳˌvil

Basle
   alternate spelling for Basel,   BAHL   'bal
      Switzerland

Basotho
   people, Lesotho (pl. Masotho)   bah-SŌT-ō, bah-SŌŌT-ōō   ba'soːṭoː, ba'suːṭu

Basov
   Nikolai Gennadiyevich, *Russian*   BAH-SAWF, BAHS-AWV   'baːˌsɔːf, 'bas,ɔːv
      physicist (Nobel 1964)

Basque
   lang., people, Europe   BASK   'bæsk

Basra
   prov & town, Iraq   BAHS-ruh, BAHZ-ruh   'basrə, 'bazrə

Basrah, Al [Basra]
   prov & town, Iraq   ahl BAHS-ruh, ahl BUHS-ruh, al   aːl 'basrə, aːl 'bəsrə, æl
                         BAS-ruh   'bæsrə

Bas-Rhin
   dept, France   BAH-REⁿ   barẽ

Bass
   Saul, *graphic designer, filmmaker;*   BAS   'bæs
      tdmk for English ale; tdmk for
      shoes

Basse-Normandie
   region, France   BAHS nawr-mahⁿ-DĒ   bas nɔːrmãdiː

Bassist
   College, *OR*   BAS-uhst   'bæsəst

Bast
   Egyptian sun goddess   BAST, BAHST   'bæst, 'bast

Bastet [Bast]
   Egyptian sun goddess   BAS-tuht, BAHS-tuht   'bæstət, 'bastət

Bastiano
   pers. name   bahs-TYAHN-ō   bas'tjanoː

Bastille
   French prison   bah-STĒL   baːstiːl

Key (col. 2):   a: **fad**   ā: **fade**   ah: **father**   ar: **marry**   aw: **law**   e: **fed**   ē: **feed**   er: **merry**   i: **hid**   ī: **hide**   ō: **coat**   ōō: **boot**
oi: **boy**   ow: **now**   u: **put**   uh: **above**   uhr: **bird**   ch: **chop**   ng: **ring**   sh: **show**   th: **thick**   th̲: **this**   zh: **measure**

Bastogne
   district, Belgium   bah-STAWN-yuh, ⑤ bas-TŌN(-yuh)   bɑːstɔːɲ , ⑤ bæs'toːn(jə)
Bastrop
   county, TX   BAS-truhp   'bæstrəp
Basutoland
   former name of Lesotho   buh-SO͞OT-ō-LAND   bə'suːṭoːˌlænd
Bataan
   prov, Philippines   buh-TAN, buh-TAHN   bə'tæn, bə'tɑn
Batak [Toba]
   lang., people, Sumatra   buh-TAHK, bah-TAHK   bə'tɑk, bɑ'tɑk
Batang
   town, Indonesia   BAH-TAHNG   'bɑˌtɑŋ
Batavia
   city, Indonesia; US pl. name   buh-TĀ-vē-uh   bə'teːviːə
Bateke
   lang., Cen. Africa   buh-TĀ-kā   bə'teːkeː
Bateman
   Jason, *actor;* Justine, *actress*   BĀT-muhn   'beːtmən
Ba'th
   political party, Iraq and Syria   BAHTH, BATH   'bɑ·θ, 'bæθ
Bath-rabbim
   Biblical name   bath-RAB-im   bæθ'ræbim
Bathsheba
   consort of King David   bath-SHĒ-buh   bæθ'ʃiːbə
Bathshua
   Biblical name   BATH-SHO͞O-uh, bath-SHO͞O-uh,   'bæθˌʃuːə, bæθ'ʃuːə,
        BAHT-sho͞o-AH   ˌbɑtʃuː'ɑ
Batista
   1. Fulgencio, *Cuban leader*   bah-TĒ-stah, ⑤ buh-TĒ-stuh   bɑ'tiːsta, ⑤ bə'tiːstə
   2. pers. name, Portuguese   bah-TĒSH-tuh, -tah   bɑː'tiːʃtə, -tɑː
Batman
   comic-book hero   BAT-MAN   'bætˌmæn
Baton Rouge
   city, LA   BAT-n RO͞OZH   ˌbætn̩ 'ruːʒ
Bats
   lang., Georgia   BAHTS, BATS   'bɑts, 'bæts
Batswana
   people, Botswana   baht-SWAHN-uh   bɑt'swɑnə
Batta
   lang., Cameroon   BAT-uh   'bæṭə
Battenberg
   town, Germany   BAHT-n-BERK, ⑤ BAT-n-BUHRG   'bɑtn̩ˌbeʳk, ⑤ 'bætn̩ˌbəʳg
Battersea
   English district   BAT-uhr-sē   'bæṭəʳsi·
Battista
   pers. name, Italian   baht-TĒ-stah   bɑt'tiːsta
Battus
   founder of Cyrene in Libya   BAT-uhs   'bæṭəs
Baubo
   hostess of Demeter   BAW-bō   'bɔːboː
Bauchi
   state, town, Nigeria   BOW-chē   'bautʃi·
Baucis
   hostess of Zeus and Hermes   BAW-suhs   'bɔːsəs

Foreign Sounds: ue: *Fr.* **rue**, *Ger.* **füllen**   uh(r): *Fr.* **boeuf**, *Ger.* **Höhle**   <u>kh</u>: *Ger.* **ich**, *Scot.* **loch**   ğ: *Sp.* **amigo**   y̆: *Sp.* **hablar**
hl: *Welsh* **Llanelli**.   CAPITALS: primary stress.   SMALL CAPS: secondary stress.   ⑤: U.S. pron.   Ⓔ: British pron.

Baudelaire
Charles, *French poet*   bōd(-uh)-LER, ⑤ bōd-LAR, bōd-LER   boːd(ə)ler, ⑤ boːdlæ^r,
                                                                            boːd'le^r

Baudouin
king of Belgium   bō-DWE^n boːdwẽ

Bauer
Martin, *theatrical producer*   BOW(-uh)r   'bau(ə)^r

Bauhaus
design school   BOW-HOWS   'bau‚haus

Baumé
Antoine, *French chemist;*   bō-mā, ⑤ bō-MĀ   boːmeː, ⑤ boː'meː
hydrometric scale

Bausch & Lomb
US optics co.   BOWSH uhn(d) LAHM   ‚bauʃ ən(d) 'lam

Bautista
pers. name, Spanish   bow-TĒ-stah   bau'tiːsta

Bavai, Bavvai
Biblical name   BĀ-vē-Ī, bah-VĪ   'beːviː‚ai, ba'vai

Bavaria
prov, Germany   buh-VER-ē-uh, buh-VAR-ē-uh   bə'veriːə, bə'væriːə

Bavarian
Alps, *mtn. range, Germany*   buh-VER-ē-uhn, buh-VAR-ē-uhn   bə'veriːən, bə'væriːən

Baya
Bantu people   BĪ-(y)uh   'bai(j)ə

Bayamesa, La
see La Bayamesa

Bayamo
river, city, Cuba   buh-YAHM-ō   bə'jamoː

Bayamón
river, city, Puerto Rico   BĪ-uh-MŌN   ‚baiə'moːn

Bayard
pers. name   BĪ-uhrd, BĀ-uhrd   'baiə^{r}d, 'beːə^{r}d

Bay de Noc
Community College, *MI*   BĀ duh NAHK   'beː də 'nak

Bayer
tdmk, aspirin   BĀ-uhr, BER   'beːə^r, 'be^r

Bayerische Alpen
mtn. range, Germany   BĪ-uh-RISH-uh AHL-puhn   'baiə‚riʃə 'alpən

Bayerische Motoren Werke
German car co. (BMW)   BĪ-uh-RISH-uh MŌT-uh-ruhn VER-kuh   'baiə‚riʃə 'moːʈərən 've^{r}kə

Bayerische Wald
Bavarian forest   BĪ-uh-RISH-uh VAHLT   'baiə‚riʃə 'valt

Bayern [Bavaria]
prov, Germany   BĪ-uhrn   'baiə^{r}n

Bayern Munich
German soccer team   BĪ-uhrn MYŌŌ-nik, MYŌŌ-ni<u>kh</u>   'baiə^{r}n 'mjuːnik, 'mjuːnix

Bayeux Tapestry
12th c. tapestry   bah-YUH(R), ⑤ bī-(Y)ŌŌ, bā-(Y)ŌŌ   baːjœː, ⑤ bai'(j)uː, beː'(j)uː

Bayh
political family, IN   BĪ   'bai

Baykal, Ozero [Baikal]
lake, Siberia   ōz-YER-uh bī-KAHL   oːz'jerə bai'kal

Bayonne
1. *city, NJ*   bā-ŌN   beː'oːn
2. *town, France*   bah-YAWN, ⑤ bā-ŌN   baːjɔːn, ⑤ beː'oːn

Key (col. 2): a: fad ā: fade ah: father ar: marry aw: law e: fed ē: feed er: merry i: hid ī: hide ō: coat ōō: boot
oi: boy ow: now u: put uh: above uhr: bird ch: chop ng: ring sh: show th: thick <u>th</u>: this zh: measure

Bayreuth
   city, Germany; music festival   bī-ROIT, BĪ-ROIT   bɑi'rɔit, 'bɑi,rɔit

Bazlith
   Biblical name   BAZ-lith, baht-SLĒT   'bæzliθ, bɑt'sli:t

Bazluth
   Biblical name   BAZ-luhth, baht-SLŌOT   'bæzləθ, bɑt'slu:t

Beach-la-Mar [Bêche-de-Mer]
   lang., Vanuatu, Solomon Islands   BĒCH-luh-MAHR   ˌbi:tʃlə'mɑʳ

Beaconsfield
   1. district, England   BEK-uhnz-FĒLD, BĒ-kuhnz-FĒLD   'bekənzˌfi:ld, 'bi:kənzˌfi:ld
   2. pl. name, Australia, Canada, S.   BĒ-kuhnz-FĒLD   'bi:kənzˌfi:ld
     Africa

Beadle
   G. W., US biochemical geneticist   BĒD-l   'bi:dl̩
     (Nobel 1958)

Bealiah
   Biblical name   BĒ-uh-LĪ-uh, buh-AHL-YAH   ˌbi:ə'lɑiə, bə,ɑl'jɑ

Bealoth
   Biblical name   BĒ-uh-LAHTH, BĒ-uh-LAWTH,   'bi:əˌlɑθ, 'bi:əˌlɔ:θ, bəɑ'lo:t
      buh-ah-LŌT

Beard
   Charles A., historian   BĒRD   'biʳd

Beardsley
   pers. name   BĒRDZ-lē   'biʳdzli·

Béarn
   region, France   bā-AHRN   be:ɑ:rn

Béarnaise
   egg-based sauce   BĀ-uhr-NĀZ, BĀ-ahr-NĀZ, ber-NĀZ   ˌbe:əʳ'ne:z, ˌbe:ɑʳ'ne:z,
      beʳ'ne:z

Beatles, the
   English rock group   BĒT-lz   'bi:tl̩z

Beatrice
   1. pers. name   BĒ-uh-truhs, BĒ-truhs, bē-A-truhs,   'bi:ətrəs, 'bi:trəs, bi:'ætrəs,
      BĀ-uh-truhs   'be:ətrəs
   2. German   BĀ-ah-TRĒ-suh   ˌbe:ɑ'tri:sə
   3. Italian   BĀ-ah-TRĒ-chā   ˌbe:ɑ'tri:tʃe:
   4. city, NE   bē-A-truhs   bi:'ætrəs

Beatrix
   1. pers. name   BĒ-uh-triks, BĒ-triks; bē-A-triks,   'bi:ətriks, 'bi:triks; bi:'ætriks,
      BĀ-uh-triks   'be:ətriks
   2. German   bā-AH-triks   be:'ɑtriks
   3. Latin   bē-Ā-triks   bi:'e:triks

Beatty
   1. Clyde, US circus owner   BĒT-ē   'bi:ṭi·
   2. Ned, US actor; Warren, *US actor*   BĀT-ē, BĒT-ē   'be:ṭi·, 'bi:ṭi·

Beatus
   1. pers. name, German   bā-AH-tus   be:'ɑtus
   2. Latin   bē-ĀT-uhs, bā-AH-tus   bi:'e:ṭəs, be:'ɑtus

Beau
   pers. name (B. Brummell)   BŌ   'bo:

Beauchamp
   pers. name, English   BĒ-chuhm   'bi:tʃəm

Beauclerk
   Topham, English dandy   BŌ-KLER   'bo:ˌkleʳ

Foreign Sounds: ue: *Fr.* **rue,** *Ger.* **füllen**   uh(r): *Fr.* **boeuf,** *Ger.* **Höhle**   <u>kh</u>: *Ger.* **ich,** *Scot.* **loch**   ğ: *Sp.* **amigo**   <u>v</u>: *Sp.* **hablar**
hl: *Welsh* **Llanelli.**   CAPITALS: primary stress.   SMALL CAPS: secondary stress.   Ⓢ: U.S. pron.   Ⓔ: British pron.

Beaufort
   1. county, town, NC   BŌ-fuhrt, BŌŌ-fuhrt, BŌŌ-fuhrd   'boːfəʳt, 'buːfəʳt, 'buːfəʳd
   2. county, city, SC   BYŌŌ-fuhrt, -fuhrd   'bjuːfəʳt, -fəʳd
   3. scale of wind force   BŌ-fuhrt   'boːfəʳt
   4. Sea, Arctic   BŌ-fuhrt   'boːfəʳt
   5. pers. name   BŌ-fuhrt, BYŌŌ-fuhrt   'boːfəʳt, 'bjuːfəʳt
Beaujolais
   region, wine, France   bō-zhaw-LE, Ⓢ BŌ-zhuh-LĀ, -zhō-LĀ   boːʒɔːle, Ⓢ ˌboːʒəˈleː,
                                                      -ʒɔːˈleː

Beaulieu
   1. parish, abbey, England   BYŌŌ-lē   'bjuːliˑ
   2. US winery   bōl-YUH(R), BŌL-yōō   boːlˈjə(r), 'boːljuː
Beaumes de Venise
   wine   BŌM duh vuh-NĒZ   boːm də vəniːz
Beaumont
   pers. name   BŌ-MAHNT, -muhnt   'boːˌmɑnt, -mənt
Beaune
   wine   BŌN   boːn
Beauséjour
   town, Manitoba   BŌ-SĀ-ZHUHR, BŌ-zuh-ZHUHR   ˌboːˌseːˈʒəʳ, 'boːzəˌʒəʳ
Beauvoir
   Simone de, *French writer*   bōv-WAHR   boːvwɑːr
Beaver
   N. American people   BĒ-vuhr   'biːvəʳ
Bebai
   Biblical name   BĒ-bē-Ī, BEB-ē-Ī, be-VĪ   'biːbiːˌɑi, 'bebiːˌɑi, be'vɑi
Béchamel
   white sauce   BĀ-shuh-MEL   ˌbeːʃəˈmel
Bêche-de-Mer [Beach-la-Mar, Bislama]
   lang., Vanuatu, Solomon Islands   BĀSH-duh-MER   ˌbeːʃdəˈmeʳ
Becher
   Biblical name   BĒ-kuhr, BEK-uhr, bekh-ER   'biːkəʳ, 'bekəʳ, bex'er
Becherite
   Biblical name   BĒ-kuh-RĪT, BEK-uh-RĪT   'biːkəˌrɑit, 'bekəˌrɑit
Bechet
   Sidney, *jazz soprano saxophonist*   buh-SHĀ   bəˈʃeː
Bechorath, Becorath
   Biblical name   bē-KŌR-ATH, -KAWR-ATH,   biˑˈkoːrˌæθ, -ˈkoːrˌæθ,
                         buh-KHŌ-RAHT   bəˌxoːˈrat
Bechtel
   Group, Inc., US co.   BEK-TEL, bek-TEL   'bekˌtel, bek'tel
Bechuana
   Bantu people, lang.   BECH(-uh)-WAHN-uh   ˌbetʃ(ə)'wɑnə
Bechuanaland [Botswana]
   republic, Africa   BECH(-uh)-WAHN-uh-LAND   ˌbetʃ(ə)'wɑnəˌlænd
Becker
   Boris, *tennis player*   BEK-uhr   'bekəʳ
Becket
   Thomas à, *English saint*   BEK-uht   'bekət
Beckett
   Samuel, *Irish author (Nobel 1969)*   BEK-uht   'bekət
Beckmann
   Max, *German artist*   BEK-MAHN   'bekˌmɑn

Key (col. 2): a: fad ā: fade ah: father ar: marry aw: law e: fed ē: feed er: merry i: hid ī: hide ō: coat ōō: boot
oi: boy ow: now u: put uh: above uhr: bird ch: chop ng: ring sh: show th: thick th: this zh: measure

Becky
  pers. name BEK-ē 'beki·
Becquerel
  A. H., French physicist (Nobel 1903) bek(-uh)-REL bek(ə)rel
Bedad
  Biblical name BĒ-DAD, buh-DAHD 'biː,dæd, bə'dɑd
Bedan
  Biblical name BĒ-DAN, buh-DAHN 'biː,dæn, bə'dɑn
Bede
  Anglo-Saxon scholar; pers. name BĒD 'biːd
Bedell
  pers. name buh-DEL bə'del
Bedford
  pers. name; pl. name BED-fuhrd 'bedfəʳd
Bedfordshire
  county, English BED-fuhrd-shuhr, -SHIR 'bedfəʳdʃəʳ, -,ʃiʳ
Bediah
  Biblical name bi-DĒ-uh, BED-uh-YAH bi'diːə, ,bedə'jɑ
Bedivere
  Arthurian hero BED-uh-VIR 'bedə,viʳ
Bedloe's Island
  former name, Liberty Island, NY BED-lōz 'bedloːz
Bednorz
  J. Georg, German crystallographer BED-NAWRTS 'bed,nɔːʳts
  (Nobel 1987)
Bedouin
  nomadic Arab BED(-uh)-wuhn 'bed(ə)wən
Bedřich
  pers. name, Czech BED-rzhi<u>kh</u>, Ⓢ BED-uhr-ZHI<u>KH</u> 'bedrʒiç, Ⓢ 'bedəʳ,ʒix
Beecham
  Sir Thomas, English conductor BĒ-chuhm 'biːtʃəm
Beecher
  family of US clergy; pers. name BĒ-chuhr 'biːtʃəʳ
Beeliada
  Biblical name bē-LĪ-uh-duh, buh-EL-yah-DAH bi·'laiədə, bə,eljɑ'dɑ
Beelzebub
  devil; fallen angel in Paradise Lost, bē-EL-zuh-BUHB; BĒL-zuh-BUHB, BEL- biː'elzə,bəb; 'biːlzə,bəb, 'bel-
  Milton
Beer
  Biblical name BĒ-uhr, BIR, buh-ER 'biːəʳ, 'biʳ, bə'er
Beera, Beerah
  Biblical name bē-IR-uh, BIR-uh, buh-ER-AH biː'irə, 'birə, bə,er'ɑ
Beerbohm
  Max, English critic BIR-BŌM, BIR-buhm 'biʳ,boːm, 'biʳbəm
Beer-elim
  Biblical name BĒ-uh-RĒ-luhm, BIR-Ē-luhm, 'biːə'riːləm, 'bir'iːləm,
  buh-ER-el-ĒM bə'erel'iːm
Beeri
  Biblical name bē-IR-Ī, BIR-Ī, buh-ER-Ē biː'ir,ai, 'bir,ai, bə,er'iː
Beer-lahairoi
  Biblical name BĒ-uhr-luh-HĪ-ROI, BIR-; 'biːəʳlə'hai,rɔi, 'biʳ-;
  buh-ER-lah<u>kh</u>-Ī-raw-Ē bə,eʳlax,airɔː'iː
Beernaert
  Auguste, Belgian politician (Nobel BER-NAHRT 'beʳ,nɑʳt
  1909)

Beeroth
Biblical name   bē-IR-AHTH, -AWTH; buh-ER-ŌT   biːˈirˌɑθ, -ˌɔːθ; bəˌerˈoːt
Beeroth-bene-jaakan
Biblical name   bē-IR-AHTH-BĒ-nē-JĀ-uh-kuhn,   biːˈirˌɑθˈbiːniːˈdʒeːəkən,
                                     BIR-AHTH-;   ˈbirˌɑθ-; bəˌerˈoːtbəˌneːjɑɑ
                                     buh-ER-ŌT-buh-NĀ-yuh-ah-KAHN

Beerothite
Biblical name   bē-IR-uh-THĬT, BIR-uh-THĬT   biːˈirəˌθait, ˈbirəˌθait
Beersheba
district, Israel   bir-SHĒ-buh, ber-SHĒ-buh,   birˈʃiːbə, berˈʃiːbə, bərˈʃiːbə
                                     buhr-SHĒ-buh
Beery
Noah, *US actor*   BIR-ē   ˈbiriˑ
Beeshterah
Biblical name   bē-ESH-tuh-ruh, buh-ESH-tuh-RAH   biːˈeʃtərə, bəˌeʃtəˈrɑ
Beethoven
Ludwig van, *German composer*   BĀT-HŌ-vuhn, ⑤ BĀ-TŌ-vuhn,   ˈbeːtˌhoːvən, ⑤ ˈbeːˌtoːvən,
                                     BĀT-Ō-vuhn   ˈbeːˌt̩oːvən
Beeton
pers. name   BĒT-n   ˈbiːtn̩
Begin
Menachem, *Israeli prime minister*   buh-GĒN, BĀ-gin   bəˈgiːn, ˈbeːgin
  (Nobel 1978)
Begley
Ed, Jr., *US producer, actor*   BEG-lē   ˈbegliˑ
Beguine
dance   buh-GĒN   bəˈgiːn
Behan
Brendan, *Irish writer*   BĒ-uhn   ˈbiːən
Behar
see Bihar
Behemoth
legendary Biblical animal   bi-HĒ-muhth, BĒ-uh-muhth, -MAWTH,   biˈhiːməθ, ˈbiːəməθ, -ˌmɔːθ,
                                     -MAHTH   -ˌmɑθ
Behistun [Bīsitūn]
town, Iran   BĀ-his-TOON   ˌbeːhisˈtuːn
Behn
Aphra, *English writer*   BEN, ⑤ BĀN   ˈben, ⑤ ˈbeːn
Behring
E. A. von, *German bacteriologist*   BER-ing   ˈberiŋ
  (Nobel 1901)
Beiden, Pete
Field, *ballpark, Fresno, CA*   PĒT BĪD-n   ˈpiːt ˈbaidn̩
Beiderbecke
Bix, *US jazz musician*   BĪD-uhr-BEK   ˈbaidərˌbek
Beijing [Peiping, Peking]
city, China   BĀ-JING, BĀ-ZHING   ˈbeːˈdʒiŋ, ˈbeːˈʒiŋ
Beirut
city, Lebanon   bā-ROOT   beːˈruːt
Beja
lang., people, Sudan, Ethiopia   BĀ-juh   ˈbeːdʒə
Bekaa
valley, Lebanon   buh-KAH, bek-AH   bəˈkɑ, bekˈɑ

Key (col. 2):   a: **f**a**d   ā: **f**a**de   ah: **f**a**ther   ar: **marry**   aw: **l**a**w   e: **f**e**d   ē: **f**ee**d   er: **merry**   i: **h**i**d   ī: **h**i**de   ō: **c**oa**t   ōō: **b**oo**t
oi: **boy**   ow: **now**   u: **p**u**t   uh: **above**   uhr: **bird**   ch: **chop**   ng: **ring**   sh: **show**   th: **thick**   <u>th</u>: **this**   zh: **measure**

Békésy
  Georg von, *US physiologist (Nobel 1961)*   BĀ-kuh-shē   'beːkəʃiˑ

Bekka, The
  governorate, Lebanon   <u>th</u>uh be-KAH   ðə be'kɑ

Bel & the Dragon
  Apocryphal book   BEL   'bel

Bel
  Biblical name   BEL   'bel

Bela
  pers. name   BEL-uh, BĀ-luh, BĒ-luh   'belə, 'beːlə, 'biːlə

Béla
  pers. name, Hungarian   BĀ-lah   'beːlɑ

Bela, Belah
  Biblical name   BĒ-luh, BEL-uh, BEL-ah   'biːlə, 'belə, 'belɑ

Belafonte
  Harry, *US singer*   BEL-uh-FAHNT-ē   'beləˌfɑntiˑ

Belaite
  Biblical name   BĒ-luh-ĪT, BEL-uh-ĪT   'biːləˌait, 'beləˌait

Belarus [Byelorussia]
  republic, E. Europe   BEL-uh-R̄O͞OS, BĀ-luh-R̄O͞OS   ˌbelə'ruːs, ˌbeːlə'ruːs

Belasco
  David, *US playwright/producer*   buh-LAS-kō   bə'læskoː

Belau [Palau]
  islands, Pacific   buh-LOW   bə'lau

Belding
  pers. name   BEL-ding   'beldiŋ

Belém
  city, Brazil   be-LĀ ⓢ buh-LEM   be'leː ⓢ bə'lem

Belfast
  city, N. Ireland   BEL-FAST, bel-FAST   'belˌfæst, bel'fæst

Bel Geddes
  US acting family   bel GED-ēz   bel 'gediˑz

Belgian
  pert. to Belgium   BEL-juhn   'beldʒən

Belgian Malinois
  dog breed   MAL-uhn-WAH   ˌmælən'wɑ

Belgian Tervuren
  dog breed   TUHR-VYUR-uhn, ter-   ˌtəʳ'vjurən, teʳ-

Belgium
  country, Europe   BEL-juhm   'beldʒəm

Belgrade [Beograd]
  city, Serbia   BEL-GRĀD, -GRAHD, -GRAD; bel-GRĀD, -GRAHD, -GRAD   'belˌgreːd, -ˌgrɑd, -ˌgræd; bel'greːd, -'grɑd, -'græd

Belgravia
  district, London, England   bel-GRĀ-vē-uh   bel'greːviːə

Belial
  devil; fallen angel in Paradise Lost, *J. Milton*   BĒ-lē-uhl, BĒL-yuhl   'biːliːəl, 'biːljəl

Belinda
  pers. name   buh-LIN-duh   bə'lində

Belisarius
  general, Eastern Roman Empire   BEL-uh-SAR-ē-uhs, BEL-uh-SAHR-ē-uhs   ˌbelə'særiːəs, ˌbelə'sɑriːəs

Belize
  country, river, city, Cen. America   buh-LĒZ   bə'liːz

Foreign Sounds: ue: *Fr.* r**ue**, *Ger.* f**ü**llen   uh(r): *Fr.* b**oeu**f, *Ger.* H**öh**le   <u>kh</u>: *Ger.* i**ch**, *Scot.* lo**ch**   ḡ: *Sp.* ami**g**o   v̲: *Sp.* ha**b**lar
hl: *Welsh* **Ll**anelli.   CAPITALS: primary stress.   SMALL CAPS: secondary stress.   ⓢ: U.S. pron.   ⓔ: British pron.

Belizean		
pert. to Belize	buh-LĒ-zē-uhn	bə'liːziːən
Belkin		
Boris David, *Russian violinist*	BYEL-kyin	'bjel̥kjin
Belknap		
county, NH	BEL-NAP	'belˌnæp
Bell & Howell		
US camera co.	BEL uhn(d) HOW(-uh)l	ˌbel ən(d) 'hau(ə)l
Bella		
1. pers. name	BEL-uh	'belə
2. German	BEL-ah	'belɑ
3. Italian	BEL-lah	'bellɑ
Bella Coola		
N. American people	BEL-uh KŌŌ-luh	ˌbelə 'kuːlə
Bellamy		
Ralph, *US actor; pers. name*	BEL-uh-mē	'beləmiˑ
Bellarmine		
College, *KY*	BEL-AHR-muhn, BEL-AHR-MĒN	'belˌɑʳmən, 'belˌɑʳˌmiːn
Belleau		
village, France	be-LŌ	beloː
Belleek		
town, Ireland; porcelain	buh-LĒK	bə'liːk
Bellerophon		
Greek mythological hero	buh-LER-uh-fuhn, -FAHN	bə'lerəfən, -ˌfɑn
Belle Strasbourgeoise, La		
see La Belle Strasbourgeoise		
Bellevue		
College, *NE; hospital, New York City*	BEL-vyōō	'belvjuː
Belle-Vue Kriek		
Belgian beer	bel-VUH(R) KRĒK	bel'vœː 'kriːk
Belli		
Melvin, *US attorney*	BEL-Ī	'belˌɑi
Bellingshausen		
sea, South Pacific Ocean	BEL-ingz-HOWZ-n	'beliŋzˌhɑuzn
Bellini		
family of Italian painters; Vincenzo, *Italian composer*	bāl-LĒ-nē, [$] be-LĒ-nē, buh-	beˑl'liːniˑ, [$] be'liːniˑ, bə-
Bellona		
Roman goddess of war	buh-LŌ-nuh	bə'loːnə
Bellow		
Saul, *US author (Nobel 1976)*	BEL-ō	'beloː
Belmopan		
town, Belize	BEL-mō-PAN	ˌbelmoː'pæn
Belo Horizonte		
city, Brazil	BĀ-lō HAWR-uh-ZAHNT-ē, BEL-ō, HAHR-	'beːloː ˌhɔːrə'zɑntiˑ, 'beloː, ˌhɑr-
Beloit		
College, *WI; city, KS, WI*	buh-LOIT	bə'loit
Belorussia		
republic, Europe	BEL-o-RUHSH-uh	ˌbelo'rəʃə
Belorussian [Bielo-, Byelo-]		
lang., Belorussia, Poland	BEL-ō-RUHSH-uhn	ˌbeloː'rəʃən
Bel Paese		
tdmk for a soft cheese	BEL pah-Ā-zuh, pah-Ā-zē	ˌbel pɑ'eːzə, pɑ'eːziˑ

Key (col. 2): a: **fad** ā: **fade** ah: **father** ar: **marry** aw: **law** e: **fed** ē: **feed** er: **merry** i: **hid** ī: **hide** ō: **coat** ōō: **boot** oi: **boy** ow: **now** u: **put** uh: **above** uhr: **bird** ch: **chop** ng: **ring** sh: **show** th: **thick** th: **this** zh: **measure**

Belshazzar
  king of Babylon — bel-SHAZ-uhr — bel'ʃæzəʳ

Beltane
  Celtic pagan festival — BEL-TĀN, BEL-tuhn, BEL-tuh-nuh — 'bel‚teːn, 'beltən, 'beltənə

Belteshazzar
  Biblical name — BEL-tuh-SHAZ-uhr, BEL-tuh-SHAHT-SAHR — ‚beltə'ʃæzəʳ, ‚beltə‚ʃat'sɑr

Beltrami
  county, MN — bel-TRAM-ē — bel'træmiˑ

Beluga
  sturgeon; caviar; whale — buh-LOO-guh — bə'luːgə

Belus
  father of Egyptus and Danaus — BEL-uhs — 'beləs

Belushi
  James, John, US entertainers — buh-LOO-shē — bə'luːʃiˑ

Belva
  pers. name — BEL-vuh — 'belvə

Belvoir
  1. castle, pl. name, England — BĒ-vuhr — 'biːvəʳ
  2. street, London, England — BEL-VWAWR — 'bel‚vwɔːʳ
  3. see Fort Belvoir

Bemba
  lang., Africa — BEM-buh — 'bembə

Bemidji
  city, MN — buh-MIJ-ē — bə'midʒiˑ

Bemis
  US industrial products co. — BĒ-muhs — 'biːməs

Ben
  pers. name — BEN — 'ben

Bena
  lang., people, Africa — BEN-uh, BĀ-nuh — 'benə, 'beːnə

Ben-abinadab
  Biblical name — BEN-uh-BIN-uh-DAB, BEN-ah-VĒ-nah-DAHV — ‚benə'binə‚dæb, ‚benɑ‚viːnɑ'dav

Benacerraf
  Baruj, US immunologist (Nobel 1980) — ben-AS-uh-ruhf — ben'æsərəf

Benadryl
  tdmk for a medication — BEN-uh-DRIL — 'benə‚dril

Benaiah
  Biblical name — bē-NĪ-uh, bē-NĀ-uh, buh-; buh-NAH-YAH-hoo — biːˈnɑiə, biːˈneːə, bə-; bə‚nɑ'jɑhuː

Benalla
  city, Australia — buh-NAL-uh — bə'nælə

Ben-ammi
  Biblical name — ben-AM-Ī, BEN-ah-MĒ — ben'æm‚ɑi, ‚benɑ'miː

Benares [Varanasi]
  city, India — buh-NAHR-uhs — bə'nɑʳəs

Benatar
  Pat, rock singer — BEN-uh-TAHR — 'benə‚tɑʳ

Benavente y Martínez
  Jacinto, Spanish playwright (Nobel 1922) — bān-ah-VĀN-tā ē mahr-TĒ-nāth, mahr-TĒ-nās; Ⓢ BEN-uh-VENT-ē ē mahr-TĒ-nuhs — beːnɑ'veːnteː iː mɑr'tiːneːθ, mɑr'tiːneːs; Ⓢ ‚benə'ventiː iː mɑʳ'tiːnəs

---

Foreign Sounds: ue: *Fr.* **rue**, *Ger.* **füllen**   uh(r): *Fr.* **boeuf**, *Ger.* **Höhle**   kh: *Ger.* **ich**, *Scot.* **loch**   g̃: *Sp.* **amigo**   v̲: *Sp.* **hablar**
hl: *Welsh* **Llanelli**.   CAPITALS: primary stress.   SMALL CAPS: secondary stress.   Ⓢ: U.S. pron.   Ⓔ: British pron.

Benazir
  pers. name (B. Bhutto)   BEN-uh-ZIR, BEN-uh-ZIR   ˌbenə'ziʳ, 'benəˌziʳ

Benchley
  Peter, *US author*   BENCH-lē   'bentʃli·

Ben-deker
  Biblical name   ben-DĒ-kuhr, ben-DEK-uhr,   ben'diːkəʳ, ben'dekəʳ,
         ben-DEK-ER   ben'dekˌer

Bendigo
  city, Australia   BEN-duh-gō   'bendəgoː

Bene-berak
  Biblical name   BEN-uh-BIR-AK, buh-NĀ-BRAHK   'benə'birˌæk, bəˌneː'brɑk

Benedetto
  pers. name   BĀ-nā-DĀT-tō   ˌbeːneː'deːttoː

Benedict
  1. pers. name   BEN-uh-DIKT, Ⓔ *also* BEN-it   'benəˌdikt, Ⓔ *also* 'benit
  2. Dutch   BĀ-nuh-dikt   'beːnədikt
  3. German   BĀ-nā-dikt   'beːneːdikt

Bénédict
  pers. name, French   bā-nā-DĒKT   beːneːdiːkt

Benedictine
  monk; liqueur   BEN-uh-DIK-tuhn, -TĒN   ˌbenə'diktən, -ˌtiːn

Benedictus
  section of the Mass; pers. name,   BEN-i-DIK-tuhs   ˌbeni'diktəs
    Latin

Benedikt
  pers. name, German   BĀ-nā-dikt   'beːneːdikt

Bene-jaakan
  Biblical name   BEN-uh-JĀ-uh-kuhn,   ˌbenə'dʒeːəkən,
         buh-NĀ-yuh-ah-KAHN   bəˌneːjɑɑ'kɑn

Benelux countries
  Belgium, Luxembourg, and the   BEN-uh-LUHKS   'benəˌləks
    Netherlands

Benét
  Stephen Vincent & William Rose,   buh-NĀ   bə'neː
    US writers

Benetton
  clothing retailer   BEN-uh-TAHN, BEN-uh-tuhn   'benəˌtɑn, 'benətən

Benevento
  prov & town, Italy   BEN-uh-VEN-tō   ˌbenə'ventoː

Benewah
  county, ID   BEN-WAH, BEN-WAW   'benˌwɑ, 'benˌwɔː

Bengal
  region, India; bay, Indian Ocean   ben-GAWL, beng-GAWL, -GAHL   ben'gɔːl, beŋ'gɔːl, -'gɑl

Bengalese
  pert. to Bengal   BENG-guh-LĒZ, BENG-guh-LĒS, BEN-   ˌbeŋgə'liːz, ˌbeŋgə'liːs, ˌben-

Bengali
  lang., people, Bangladesh, India   ben-GAW-lē, ben-GAHL-ē, beng-   ben'gɔːli·, ben'gɑli·, beŋ-

Ben-geber
  Biblical name   ben-JĒ-buhr, ben-GEV-ER   ben'dʒiːbəʳ, ben'gevˌer

Benghazi [Banghāzī]
  city, former province, Libya   ben-GAHZ-ē, beng-GAHZ-ē, -GAZ-ē   ben'gɑzi·, beŋ'gɑzi·, -'gæzi·

Bengt
  pers. name, Swedish   BENGT   'beŋt

Benguela
  region, city, Angola; Atlantic current   ben-G(W)EL-uh, beng-G(W)EL-uh   ben'g(w)elə, beŋ'g(w)elə

Key (col. 2):   a: fad   ā: fade   ah: father   ar: marry   aw: law   e: fed   ē: feed   er: merry   i: hid   ī: hide   ō: coat   ōō: boot
oi: boy   ow: now   u: put   uh: above   uhr: bird   ch: chop   ng: ring   sh: show   th: thick   th: this   zh: measure

Ben Gurion
    David, *Israeli leader; airport, Tel*   BEN gur-YAWN, ⑤ ben GUR-ē-uhn   ˌben gurˈjɔːn, ⑤ ben ˈguriːən
    Aviv

Ben-hadad
    Biblical name   ben-HĀ-DAD, BEN-hah-DAHD   benˈheːˌdæd, ˌbenhɑˈdad

Ben-hail
    Biblical name   ben-HĀ(-uh)l, ben-<u>KH</u>AH-yil   benˈheː(ə)l, benˈxɑjil

Ben-hanan
    Biblical name   ben-HĀ-NAN, BEN-<u>kh</u>ah-NAHN   benˈheːˌnæn, ˌbenxɑˈnɑn

Ben-hur
    Biblical name   ben-HUHR, ben-<u>KH</u>UR   benˈhəʳ, benˈxur

Bénigne
    pers. name, French   bā-nēn-yuh   beːniːɲ

Benigno
    pers. name, Spanish   bā-NĒG-nō   beːˈniːgnoː

Benihana
    Japanese restaurant chain   BEN-ē-HAHN-uh   ˌbeniˈhɑnə

Benin
    country, river, city, bight, Africa   buh-NĒN, buh-NIN   bəˈniːn, bəˈnin

Beninese
    pert. to Benin   BEN-uh-NĒZ, -NĒS   ˌbenəˈniːz, -ˈniːs

Beninu
    Biblical name   bi-NĪ-N(Y)O͞O, buh-NĒ-N(Y)O͞O   biˈnɑiˌn(j)uː, bəˈniːˌn(j)uː

Beni Suef
    city, Egypt   BEN-ē su-ĀF   ˌbeniˈ suˈeːf

Benito
    pers. name, Italian, Spanish   bā-NĒT-ō   beːˈniː̬toː

Benito Cereno
    story, H. Melville   buh-NĒT-ō suh-RĒ-nō   bəˈniː̬toː səˈriːnoː

Benjamim
    pers. name, Portuguese   BĀ-zhuh-MIⁿ, -zhah-MIⁿ   ˌbẽːʒəˈmĩ, -ʒɑˈmˈĩ

Benjamin
    1. pers. name   BEN-juh-muhn, BENJ-muhn   ˈbendʒəmən, ˈbendʒmən
    2. Dutch   BEN-yah-muhn   ˈbenjɑːmən
    3. French   beⁿ-zhah-MEⁿ   bẽʒɑːmẽ
    4. German   BEN-yah-mēn   ˈbenjɑmiːn
    5. Hungarian   BEN-yah-min   ˈbenjɑːmin

Benjamite
    Biblical name   BEN-juh-MĪT   ˈbendʒəˌmɑit

Ben Macdhui
    mountain, Britain   BEN muhk-DO͞O-ē   ˈben məkˈduːiˈ

Benne Seed
    sesame seed   BEN-ē   ˈbeniˈ

Bennett
    pers. name   BEN-uht   ˌbenət

Ben Nevis
    mtn., Scotland   ben NEV-uhs   ben ˈnevəs

Benno
    1. pers. name, German   BEN-ō   ˈbenoː
    2. Russian   BEN-nuh   ˈbennə

Benny
    pers. name   BEN-ē   ˈbeniˈ

Beno
    Biblical name   BĒ-nō, BĀ-nō, BEN-ō, buh-NŌ   ˈbiːnoː, ˈbeːnoː, ˈbenoː, bəˈnoː

Foreign Sounds: ue: *Fr.* **rue**, *Ger.* f**ü**llen   uh(r): *Fr.* b**oeu**f, *Ger.* H**öh**le   <u>kh</u>: *Ger.* i**ch**, *Scot.* lo**ch**   g̃: *Sp.* ami**g**o   v̲: *Sp.* ha**b**lar
hl: *Welsh* **Ll**anelli.   CAPITALS: primary stress.   SMALL CAPS: secondary stress.   ⑤: U.S. pron.   ⓔ: British pron.

Benoît *pers. name, French*	buhn-WAH	bənwaː
Benoit Samuelson Joan, *US marathoner*	buh-NOIT SAM-yuh(-wuh)l-suhn	bə'nɔit 'sæmjə(wə)lsən
Benoni *Biblical name*	buh-NŌ-NĪ, BEN-ō-NĒ	bə'noːˌnɑi, ˌbenoː'niː
Bentham Jeremy, *English jurist, philosopher*	BEN-thuhm	'benθəm
Benthamism *philosophy of Bentham*	BEN-thuh-MIZ-uhm	'benθəˌmizəm
Benthamite *adherent of Benthamism*	BEN-thuh-MĪT	'benθəˌmɑit
Bentley *tdmk for an English car*	BENT-lē	'bentliˑ
Benvenuto *pers. name*	BĀN-vā-NO͞O-tō	ˌbeːnveː'nuːtoː
Benz Karl Friedrich, *German engineer*	BENTS, [$] BENZ	'bents, [$] 'benz
Benzedrine *tdmk for amphetamine*	BEN-zuh-DRĒN	'benzəˌdriːn
Benzoheth *Biblical name*	ben-ZŌ-HETH, ben-ZŌ-uhth, BEN-zō-KHET	ben'zoːˌheθ, ben'zoːəθ, ˌbenzoː'xet
Beograd [Belgrade] *city, Serbia*	BĀ-uh-GRAHD	'beːəˌgrɑːd
Beon *Biblical name*	BĒ-AHN, buh-AWN	'biːˌɑn, bə'ɔːn
Beor *Biblical name*	BĒ-AWR, BĒ-ŌR, buh-ŌR	'biːˌɔː^r, 'biːˌoː^r, bə'oːr
Beothuk *N. American people*	BĀ-uh-THUK	'beːəˌθuk
Beowulf *Old English poem*	BĀ-uh-WULF	'beːəˌwulf
Beqa'a, El [The Bekka] *governorate, Lebanon*	EL be-KAH	ˌel be'kɑ
Bera *Biblical name*	BIR-uh, BĒ-ruh, BER-ah	'birə, 'biːrə, 'berɑ
Beracah, Berachah *Biblical name*	BER-uh-KAH, brah-KHAH	'berəˌkɑ, brɑ'xɑ
Berachiah *Biblical name*	BER-uh-KĪ-uh, BER-ekh-YAH-ho͞o	ˌberə'kɑiə, ˌberex'jɑhuː
Beraiah *Biblical name*	buh-RĪ-uh, BER-ē-Ī-uh, buh-RĪ-yah	bə'rɑiə, ˌberiː'ɑiə, bə'rɑijɑ
Berba *lang., Benin*	BUHR-buh	'bə^{r}bə
Berber *lang., people, Africa*	BUHR-buhr	'bə^{r}bə^r
Berceuse *lullaby*	ber-SUH(R)Z	bersœːz
Berchtesgaden *town, Bavaria*	BERKH-tuhs-GAHD-n	'berxtəsˌgɑdn̩
Berchtoldstag *Jan. 2nd holiday, Switzerland*	BERKH-TŌLT-STAHG	'berxˌtoːltˌstɑg
Berdyaev, Berdyayev Nicolai, *Russian philosopher*	byird-YAH-yif	bjird'jɑːjif

Key (col. 2): a: **fad** ā: **fade** ah: **father** ar: **marry** aw: **law** e: **fed** ē: **feed** er: **merry** i: **hid** ī: **hide** ō: **coat** o͞o: **boot** oi: **boy** ow: **now** u: **put** uh: **above** uhr: **bird** ch: **chop** ng: **ring** sh: **show** th: **thick** th: **this** zh: **measure**

Berea
  College, *KY; city, OH*   buh-RĒ-uh   bə'riːə

Berechiah
  Biblical name   BER-uh-KĪ-uh, BER-e<u>kh</u>-YAH   ˌberə'kɑiə, ˌberex'jɑ

Bered
  Biblical name   BIR-ED, BĒ-RED, BER-ed   'birˌed, 'biːˌred, 'bered

Beregovoy
  Pierre, *prime minister, France*   ber-uh-gōv-WAH   berəgoːvwɑ

Berenice
  pers. name   BER-uh-NĪ-sē, -NĪ-kē, -NĒ-chā, -NĒS   ˌberə'nɑisiˈ, -'nɑikiˈ, -'niːtʃeː, -'niːs

Berenice's Hair [Coma Berenices]
  constellation   BER-uh-NĪ-sēz HAR, HER   ˌberə'nɑisiˈz 'hærʳ, 'heʳ

Beresford
  Bruce, *Australian film director*   BER-uhz-fuhrd, BER-uhs-fuhrd   'berəzfəʳd, 'berəsfəʳd

Berg
  Paul, *US molecular biologist (Nobel 1980)*   BUHRG   'bəʳg

Bergama
  town, Turkey   buhr-GAHM-uh   bəʳ'gɑmə

Bergamo
  prov & town, Italy   BER-guh-MŌ   'beʳgəˌmoː

Bergen
  1. Community College, *county, NJ*   BUHR-guhn   'bəʳgən
  2. city, Norway   BUHR-guhn, BER-guhn   'bəʳgən, 'beʳgən

Berger
  Richard L., *US film executive*   BUHR-guhr   'bəʳgəʳ

Bergerac
  commune, France   ber-zhuh-RAHK   berʒərɑːk

Bergisch-Gladbach
  city, Germany   BER-gish-GLAHT-BAH<u>KH</u>   ˌbergiʃ'glɑtˌbɑx

Bergius
  Friedrich, *German chemist (Nobel 1931)*   BER-gē-us   'beʳgiːus

Bergman
  Ingmar, *Swedish film director*   BER-mahn, ⑤ BUHRG-muhn   'beɽmɑːn, ⑤ 'bəʳgmən

Bergson
  Henri, *French philosopher (Nobel 1927)*   berk-SAWⁿ, berk-SAWN, ⑤ BERG-suhn   berksɔ̃, berksɔːn, ⑤ 'beʳgsən

Bergsonism
  philosophy of Bergson   BERG-suh-NIZ-uhm   'beʳgsəˌnizəm

Bergström
  Sune K., *Swedish biochemist (Nobel 1982)*   BER(Y)-STRUH(R)M, ⑤ BUHRG-STRUHM   'ber(j)ˌstrœm, ⑤ 'bəʳgˌstrəm

Beri
  Biblical name   BIR-Ī, BĒ-rī, bā-RĒ   'birˌɑi, 'biːrɑi, beː'riː

Beriah
  Biblical name   buh-RĪ-uh, buh-rē-AH   bə'rɑiə, bəriː'ɑ

Beriite
  Biblical name   buh-RĪ-ĪT   bə'rɑiˌɑit

Bering
  Sea, *Strait, N. Pacific*   BIR-ing, BER-ing   'biriŋ, 'beriŋ

Beringer
  tdmk for a wine   BER-in-juhr   'berindʒəʳ

Foreign Sounds: ue: *Fr.* **rue**, *Ger.* **füllen**   uh(r): *Fr.* **boeuf**, *Ger.* **Höhle**   <u>kh</u>: *Ger.* **ich**, *Scot.* **loch**   ḡ: *Sp.* **amigo**   v̲: *Sp.* **hablar** hl: *Welsh* **Llanelli.**   CAPITALS: primary stress.   SMALL CAPS: secondary stress.   ⑤: U.S. pron.   ⓔ: British pron.

Berisha

Sali, *president, Albania*   buh-RISH-uh, buh-RĒ-shuh   bə'riʃə, bə'riːʃə

Berith

Biblical name   BIR-ith, BĒ-rith, buh-RĒT   'biriθ, 'biːriθ, bə'riːt

Berke

pers. name (B. Breathed)   BUHRK   'bəʳk

Berkeleianism

philosophy of G. Berkeley   BAHRK-lē-uh-NIZ-uhm, ⑤ BUHRK-;   'baʳkliːə,nizəm, ⑤ 'bəʳk-;
     BAHR-KLĒ-uh-NIZ-uhm, ⑤ BUHR-   ˌbaʳ'kliːə,nizəm, ⑤ ˌbəʳ-

Berkeley

1. US pl. name   BUHR-klē   'bəʳkliˑ

2. pers. name   BUHR-klē, Ⓔ BAHR-klē   'bəʳkliˑ, Ⓔ 'baʳkliˑ

3. George, *British philosopher*   BAHR-klē, ⑤ BUHR-klē   'baʳkliˑ, ⑤ 'bəʳkliˑ

berkelium

element   BUHR-klē-uhm, Ⓔ *also*   'bəʳkliːəm, Ⓔ *also*
     buhr-KĒ-lē-uhm   bəʳ'kiːliːəm

Berkhamsted

town, England   BUHR-kuhm-stuhd,   'bəʳkəmstəd, 'baʳkəmstəd,
     BAHR-kuhm-stuhd, -STED   -ˌsted

Berks [Berkshire]

county, England   BAHRKS   'baʳks

Berkshire

1. hills, county, MA   BUHRK-SHIR, BUHRK-shuhr   'bəʳkˌʃiʳ, 'bəʳkʃəʳ

2. county, England   BAHRK-shuhr, BUHRK-shuhr, -SHIR   'baʳkʃəʳ, 'bəʳkʃəʳ, -ˌʃiʳ

Berle

1. Adolf Augustus, *US diplomat*   BUHR-lē   'bəʳliˑ

2. Milton, *US actor, comedian*   BUHRL, BUHR-uhl   'bəʳl̩, 'bərəl

Berlin

1. city, Germany   ber-LĒN, ⑤ buhr-LIN   beʳ'liːn, ⑤ bəʳ'lin

2. US pl. name   BUHR-luhn, BUHR-LIN   'bəʳlən, 'bəʳˌlin

Berliner Kindl Weisse

German beer   ber-LIN-uhr KIN-dl VĪ-suh   beʳ'linəʳ 'kindl̩ 'vɑisə

Berlioz

Hector, *French composer*   ber-LYŌZ, ⑤ BER-lē-ŌZ   berljoːz, ⑤ 'beʳliːˌoːz

Berlitz

lang. schools   BUHR-luhts   'bəʳləts

Berlusconi

Silvio, *Italian politician, businessman*   BER-luh-skō-nē   ˌbeʳləskoːniˑ

Bermagui

town, Australia   BUHR-muh-GYŌŌ-ē   ˌbəʳmə'gjuːiˑ

Bermuda

islands, Atlantic   buhr-MYŌŌD-uh   bəʳ'mjuːdə

Bermudan

pert. to Bermuda   buhr-MYŌŌD-n   bəʳ'mjuːdn̩

Bern, Berne

canton, city, Switzerland   BERN, BUHRN   'beʳn, 'bəʳn

Bernadette

pers. name   BUHR-nuh-DET   ˌbəʳnə'det

Bernalillo

county, NM   BUHRN-l-Ē-ō   ˌbəʳnl̩'iːoː

Key (col. 2):   a: fad   ā: fade   ah: father   ar: marry   aw: law   e: fed   ē: feed   er: merry   i: hid   ī: hide   ō: coat   ōō: boot
oi: boy   ow: now   u: put   uh: above   uhr: bird   ch: chop   ng: ring   sh: show   th: thick   <u>th</u>: this   zh: measure

Bernard
  1. pers. name   buhr-NAHRD, BUHR-NAHRD,   bərˈnɑʳd, ˈbəʳˌnɑʳd, ˈbəʳnəʳd
            BUHR-nuhrd
  2. Dutch   BER-NAHRT   ˈberˌnɑrt
  3. French   ber-NAHR   bernɑːr
  4. Polish   BER-nahrt   ˈbernɑːrt

Bernarde
  pers. name, French   ber-NAHRD   bernɑːrd

Bernardine
  Christian monastic order   BUHR-nuhr-DĒN   ˌbəʳnəʳˈdiːn

Bernardino
  1. pers. name, Italian   BĀR-nahr-DĒ-nō   ˌbeːrnarˈdiːnoː
  2. Portuguese   BUHR-nuhr-DĒ-noo, buhr-nahr-   ˌbəʳnəʳˈdiːnuː, bənɑːr-
  3. Spanish   ber-nahr-T͟HĒ-nō   bernarˈðiːnoː

Bernardo
  1. pers. name, Italian   ber-NAHR-dō   berˈnardoː
  2. Portuguese   buhr-NAHR-doo, ber-   bərˈnaːrduː, ber-
  3. Spanish   ber-NAHR-t͟hō   berˈnarðoː

Bernardus
  1. pers. name   buhr-NAHR-duhs   bəʳˈnaʳdəs
  2. Dutch   ber-NAHR-dues   berˈnardys

Bernay
  pers. name   BER-nā, buhr-NĀ   ˈberneː, bərˈneː

Berner Alpen [Bernese Alps]
  mtn. range, Switzerland   BER-nuhr AHL-puhn   ˌbeʳnər ˈɑlpən

Bernese Alps
  mtn. range, Switzerland   BUHR-NĒZ ALPS, BUHR-NĒS   ˌbəʳˈniːz ˈælps, ˈbəʳˌniːs

Bernese Oberland [Bernese Alps]
  mtn. range, Switzerland   buhr-NĒZ Ō-buhr-LAHNT,   bəʳˈniːz ˈoːbəʳˌlant,
            Ō-buhr-LAND   ˈoːbəʳˌlænd

Bernhard
  1. pers. name, Danish, Dutch   BERN-HAHRT   ˈbernˌhart
  2. German   BERN-HAHRT   ˈbeʳnˌhaʳt

Bernhardt
  Sarah, *French actress*   ber-NAHR, ⑧ BUHRN-HAHRT   bernɑːr, ⑧ ˈbəʳnˌhart

Bernice
  1. pers. name   buhr-NĒS, BUHR-nuhs   bəʳˈniːs, ˈbəʳnəs
  2. Biblical name   buhr-NĒS, buhr-NĒ-suh   bəʳˈniːs, bəʳˈniːsə

Bernie
  pers. name   BUHR-nē   ˈbəʳniˑ

Bernina
  Italian sewing machine co.   buhr-NĒ-nuh   bəʳˈniːnə

Bernina, Piz
  peak, Switzerland   PĒTS buhr-NĒ-nuh   ˌpiːts bəʳˈniːnə

Bernini
  Giovanni Lorenzo, *Italian artist*   buhr-NĒ-nē   bəʳˈniːniˑ

Bernkasteler
  German beer   BERN-kahs-TEL-uhr   ˌbeʳnkɑsˈteləʳ

Bernoulli
  Jacques, *Swiss mathematician*   ber-noo-(Y)Ē, ⑧ buhr-NOO-lē,   bernu:(j)iː, ⑧ bəʳˈnuːliˑ,
            ber-NOO-ē   berˈnuːiˑ

Bernstein
  1. Carl, US journalist   BUHRN-STĒN, BUHRN-STĪN   ˈbəʳnˌstiːn, ˈbəʳnˌstain
  2. Leonard, US conductor, composer   BUHRN-STĪN, BUHRN-STĒN   ˈbəʳnˌstain, ˈbəʳnˌstiːn

---

Foreign Sounds: ue: *Fr.* **rue**, *Ger.* **füllen**   uh(r): *Fr.* **boeuf**, *Ger.* **Höhle**   kh: *Ger.* **ich**, *Scot.* **loch**   g̃: *Sp.* **amigo**   v: *Sp.* **hablar**
hl: *Welsh* **Llanelli**.   CAPITALS: primary stress.   SMALL CAPS: secondary stress.   ⑧: U.S. pron.   ⑥: British pron.

Berodach Baladan
   Biblical name   buh-RŌ-DAK BAL-uh-DAN,   bə'roː₁dæk 'bælə₁dæn,
       buh-rō-DAH<u>KH</u> BAHL-ah-DAHN   bəroː'dɑx ₁bɑlɑ'dɑn

Berothah [Berothai]
   Biblical name   buh-RŌ-thuh, BER-ō-TĪ   bə'roːθə, ₁beroː'tɑi

Berothai
   Biblical name   buh-RŌ-THĪ, BER-ō-TĪ   bə'roː₁θɑi, ₁beroː'tɑi

Berothite
   Biblical name   BIR-uh-THĪT   'birə₁θɑit

Berra
   Yogi, *US baseball player*   BER-uh   'berə

Berrien
   county, GA, MI   BER-ē-uhn   'beriːən

Berrima
   town, Australia   BER-uh-muh   'berəmə

Berry
   Halle, *US actress*   BER-ē   'beriˑ

Bert
   1. pers. name   BUHRT   'bəʳt
   2. German   BERT   'beʳt

Berta
   lang., Ethiopia, Sudan   BUHRT-uh   'bəʳʈə

Bertha
   1. pers. name   BUHR-thuh   'bəʳθə
   2. German   BER-tah   'beʳtɑ

Berthe
   pers. name, French   BERT   bert

Berthold
   1. pers. name, French   ber-TAWLD   bertɔːld
   2. German   BER-TAWLT   'beʳ₁tɔːlt

Bertie
   1. county, NC   buhr-TĒ, BUHR-TĒ   bəʳ'tiː, 'bəʳ₁tiː
   2. pers. name   BUHRT-ē   'bəʳʈiˑ

Bertil
   pers. name, Swedish   BER-tuhl   'beʳtəl

Bertillon
   1. Alphonse, French anthropologist   ber-tē-YAWⁿ   bertiːjɔ̃
   2. system of identification   BUHRT-l-AHN, BER-tē-YAWⁿ   'bəʳtl̩₁ɑn, ₁beʳtiː'jɔ̃

Bertinelli
   Valerie, *US actress*   BUHRT-n-EL-ē   ₁bəʳtn̩'eliˑ

Bertolt
   pers. name, German   BER-TAWLT   'beʳ₁tɔːlt

Bertolucci
   Bernardo, *Italian film director*   BERT-l-OO-chē   ₁beʳtl̩'uːtʃiˑ

Bertram
   pers. name   BUHR-truhm   'bəʳtrəm

Bertrand
   1. pers. name   BUHR-truhnd   'bəʳtrənd
   2. French   ber-TRAHⁿ   bertrɑ̃

Berwick
   1. pers. name   BUHR-wik, Ⓔ BER-ik   'bəʳwik, Ⓔ 'berik
   2. US pl. name   BUHR-wik   'bəʳwik

Berwickshire
   county, Scotland   BER-ik-shuhr, -SHIR, -SHĪR   'berikʃəʳ, -₁ʃiʳ, -₁ʃɑiʳ

Key (col. 2):   a: fad   ā: fade   ah: father   ar: marry   aw: law   e: fed   ē: feed   er: merry   i: hid   ī: hide   ō: coat   ōō: boot
oi: boy   ow: now   u: put   uh: above   uhr: bird   ch: chop   ng: ring   sh: show   th: thick   <u>th</u>: this   zh: measure

Berwick-upon-Tweed
  town, England   BER-ik-uh-pahn-TWĒD   ˈberikəpɑnˈtwiːd

Beryl
  pers. name   BER-uhl   ˈberəl

beryllium
  element   buh-RIL-ē-uhm   bəˈriliːəm

Berzelius
  Jöns Jakob, Swedish scientist   buhr-ZĀ-lē-uhs, buhr-ZĒ-lē-uhs   bəʳzeːliːəs, bəʳziːliːəs

Bes
  Egyptian god   BES, BĀS   ˈbes, ˈbeːs

Besai
  Biblical name   BĒ-SĪ, be-SĪ   ˈbiːˌsɑi, beˈsɑi

Besançon
  town, France   buh-zahⁿ-SAWⁿ, buh-ZAN(T)-suhn   bəzɑ̃sɔ̃, bəˈzæn(t)sən

Besht
  acronym of Ba'al Shem-Tov   BESHT   ˈbeʃt

Besodeiah
  Biblical name   BES-uh-DĪ-uh, -DĀ-uh, -DĒ-uh; buh-sōd-YAH   ˌbesəˈdɑiə, -ˈdeːə, -ˈdiːə; bəsoːdˈja

Besor
  Biblical name   BĒ-SŌR, BĒ-SAWR, buh-SŌR   ˈbiːˌsoːʳ, ˈbiːˌsɔːʳ, bəˈsoːr

Bess
  pers. name   BES   ˈbes

Bessarabia
  region, Europe; former prov, Romania   BES-uh-RĀ-bē-uh   ˌbesəˈreːbiːə

Bessemer
  city, AL, MI; borough, PA; steel-making process   BES-uh-muhr   ˈbesəməʳ

Bessie
  pers. name   BES-ē   ˈbesiˑ

Bessmertnykh
  Alexander, government official, USSR   buhsh-MERT-nikh   bəʃˈmeʳtnix

Bestia
  Roman cognomen   BES-chē-uh, BESH-chē-uh, BES-tē-uh   ˈbestʃiːə, ˈbeʃtʃiːə, ˈbestiːə

Betah
  Biblical name   BĒT-uh, BE-TAHKH   ˈbiːʈə, ˈbeˌtɑx

Betamax
  tdmk for a videotape system   BĀT-uh-MAKS   ˈbeːʈəˌmæks

Betelgeuse
  star   BET-l-JOOZ, BĒT-l-JOOZ, -JOOS   ˈbetl̩ˌdʒuːz, ˈbiːtl̩ˌdʒuːz, -ˌdʒuːs

Beten
  Biblical name   BĒT-n, BE-TEN   ˈbiːtn̩, ˈbeˌten

Beth-abara
  Biblical name   beth-AB(-uh)-ruh   beθˈæb(ə)rə

Beth-anath
  Biblical name   beth-Ā-NATH, BE-tah-NAHT   beθˈeːˌnæθ, ˌbetɑˈnɑt

Beth-anoth
  Biblical name   beth-Ā-NAHTH, BĀ-tah-NŌT   beθˈeːˌnɑθ, ˌbeːtɑˈnoːt

Bethany
  US pl. name; town, Jordan; pers. name   BETH-uh-nē   ˈbeθəniˑ

Beth-arabah
Biblical name — beth-AR-uh-buh, BĀT-HAH-AH-rah-VAH — beθ'ærəbə, ˌbeːt-hɑ-ɑrɑ'vɑ

Beth-aram
Biblical name — beth-Ā-RAM, beth-AR-uhm, BĀT-HAH-RAHM — beθ'eː̩ræm, beθ'ærəm, ˌbeːt-hɑ'ram

Beth-arbel
Biblical name — beth-AHR-bel, BĀ-TAHR-BEL — beθ'ɑʳbel, ˌbeːˌtɑr'bel

Beth-ashbea
Biblical name — beth-ASH-bē-uh, BĀ-TAHSH-BĀ-ah — beθ'æʃbiːə, ˌbeːˌtaʃ'beːɑ

Beth-aven
Biblical name — beth-Ā-vuhn, bā-TAH-ven — beθ'eːvən, beːˈtaven

Beth-azmaveth
Biblical name — BETH-AZ-MĀ-vuhth, -AZ-MĀ-vuhth; BĀ-tahz-MAHV-et — ˌbeθˌæz'meːvəθ, -'æzˌmeːvəθ; ˌbeːtaz'mavet

Beth-baal-meon
Biblical name — beth-BĀ(-uh)l-MĒ-AHN, bāt-BAH-AHL-muh-ŌN — beθ'beː(ə)l'miːˌan, beːt'bɑˌɑlmə'oːn

Beth-birei
Biblical name — beth-BIR-ē-Ī, BĀT-bir-Ē — beθ'biriːˌɑi, ˌbeːtbir'iː

Beth-biri [Beth-birei]
Biblical name — beth-BIR-Ī, BĀT-bir-Ē — beθ'birˌɑi, ˌbeːtbir'iː

Beth-car
Biblical name — BETH-KAHR, BĀT-KAHR — 'beθˌkɑʳ, 'beːt'kɑr

Beth-dagon
Biblical name — beth-DĀ-GAHN, BĀT-dah-GŌN — beθ'deːˌgan, ˌbeːtdɑ'goːn

Beth-diblathaim
Biblical name — BETH-DIB-luh-THĀ-im, BĀT-DIV-lah-TAH-yim — ˌbeθˌdiblə'θeːim, ˌbeːtˌdivlɑ'tajim

Bethe
Hans Albrecht, *US physicist (Nobel 1967)* — BĀT-uh — 'beːʈə

Beth-eden
Biblical name — beth-ĒD-n, bā-TED-en — beθ'iːdn̩, beːˈteden

Bethel
division, AK; archaeological site, Jordan — BETH-uhl — 'beθəl

Bethelite
Biblical name — BETH-uh-LĪT — 'beθəˌlɑit

Beth-emek
Biblical name — beth-Ē-MEK, bā-TEM-ek — beθ'iːˌmek, beːˈtemek

Bether
Biblical name — BĒ-thuhr — 'biːθəʳ

Bethesda
district, MD — buh-THEZ-duh — bə'θezdə

Beth-ezel
Biblical name — beth-Ē-zuhl, BĀT-HAH-ET-sel — beθ'iːzəl, ˌbeːt-hɑ'etsel

Beth-gader
Biblical name — beth-GĀD-uhr, bāt-GED-er — beθ'geːdəʳ, beːt'geder

Beth-gamul
Biblical name — beth-GĀ-muhl, BĀT-gah-MOOL — beθ'geːməl, ˌbeːtgɑ'muːl

Beth-Gilgal
Biblical name — beth-GIL-GAL, BĀT-gil-GAHL — beθ'gilˌgæl, ˌbeːtgil'gɑl

---

Key (col. 2):   a: fad   ā: fade   ah: father   ar: marry   aw: law   e: fed   ē: feed   er: merry   i: hid   ī: hide   ō: coat   ōō: boot
oi: boy   ow: now   u: put   uh: above   uhr: bird   ch: chop   ng: ring   sh: show   th: thick   th̲: this   zh: measure

Beth-haccerem, Beth-haccherem
   Biblical name   beth-HAK-uh-REM, -ha-KIR-uhm;   beθ'hækə,rem, -hæ'kirəm;
                                   BĀT-HAH-KER-em   ,beːt-ha'kerem

Beth-haggan
   Biblical name   beth-HAG-uhn, BĀT-HAH-GAHN   beθ'hægən, ,beːt-ha'gɑn

Beth-haran [Beth-heran]
   Biblical name   beth-HĀ-ruhn, -HAR-uhn, -HER-uhn;   beθ'heːrən, -'hærən, -'herən;
                                     BĀT-HAH-RAHN   ,beːt-ha'rɑn

Beth-heran
   Biblical name   beth-HĒ-ruhn, -HER-uhn;   beθ'hiːrən, -'herən;
                                     BĀT-HAH-RAHN   ,beːt-ha'rɑn

Beth-hoglah
   Biblical name   beth-HAHG-luh, -HAW-gluh;   beθ'haglə, -'hɔːglə;
                                     BĀT-khahg-LAH   ,beːtxag'la

Beth-horon
   Biblical name   beth-HŌR-AHN, -HAWR-AHN;   beθ'hoːr,ɑn, -'hɔːr,ɑn;
                                     BĀT-khaw-RŌN   ,beːtxɔː'roːn

Beth-Jeshimoth
   Biblical name   beth-JESH-i-MAHTH, -MAWTH;   beθ'dʒeʃi,maθ, -,mɔːθ;
                                     BĀT-HAH-yuh-shi-MAWT   ,beːt-hajəʃi'mɔːt

Beth-lebaoth
   Biblical name   beth-LEB-ā-AHTH, BETH-luh-BĀ-AHTH,   beθ'lebeː,ɑθ, ,beθlə'beː,ɑθ,
                                     -AWTH; BĀT-luh-vah-ŌT   -,ɔːθ; ,beːtləva'oːt

Bethlehem
   town, Jordan; city, PA;   BETH-li-HEM, BETH-lē-(h)uhm   'beθli,hem, 'beθliː(h)əm
Bethlehemite
   Biblical name   BETH-luh-HEM-ĪT, BETH-lē-uh-MĪT   'beθlə,hem,ait, 'beθliːə,mait
Beth-marcaboth
   Biblical name   beth-MAHR-kuh-BAHTH, -BŌTH;   beθ'maʳkə,baθ, -,boːθ;
                                     BĀT-HAH-MAHR-kah-VAWT   ,beːt-ha,marka'vɔːt

Beth-meon
   Biblical name   beth-MĒ-AHN, BĀT-muh-ŌN   beθ'miː,ɑn, ,beːtmə'oːn
Beth-Millo
   Biblical name   beth-MIL-ō, -MĒ-lō; BĀT-mi-LŌ   beθ'miloː, -'miːloː;
                                                             ,beːtmi'loː

Beth-nimrah
   Biblical name   beth-NIM-ruh, BĀT-nim-RAH   beθ'nimrə, ,beːtnim'ra
Beth-palet [Beth-pelet]
   Biblical name   beth-PĀ-luht, bāt-PAH-let   beθ'peːlət, beːt'palet
Beth-pazzez
   Biblical name   beth-PAZ-EZ, BĀT-paht-SETS   beθ'pæz,ez, ,beːtpat'sets
Beth-pelet, Beth-phelet
[Beth-palet]
   Biblical name   beth-PĒ-luht, bāt-PEL-et   beθ'piːlət, beːt'pelet
Beth-peor
   Biblical name   beth-PĒ-AWR, -PĒ-ŌR; BĀT-puh-ŌR   beθ'piː,ɔːʳ, -'piː,oːʳ;
                                                             ,beːtpə'oːr

Beth-phage
   Biblical name   BETH-fuh-jē, BETH-FĀJ, beth-FAHJ-ē   'beθfədʒiː, 'beθ,feːdʒ,
                                                             beθ'fadʒiː

Beth-rapha
   Biblical name   beth-RĀ-fuh, BĀT-rah-FAH   beθ're:fə, ,beːtra'fa
Beth-rehob
   Biblical name   beth-RĒ-HAHB, BĀT-ruh-KHŌV   beθ'riː,hab, ,beːtrə'xoːv

---

Foreign Sounds: ue: *Fr.* **rue**, *Ger.* **füllen**   uh(r): *Fr.* **boeuf**, *Ger.* **Höhle**   kh: *Ger.* **ich**, *Scot.* lo**ch**   ğ: *Sp.* amigo   v: *Sp.* hablar
hl: *Welsh* **Llanelli.**   CAPITALS: primary stress.   SMALL CAPS: secondary stress.   Ⓢ: U.S. pron.   Ⓔ: British pron.

Bethsaida		
ancient city, possibly in Galilee	beth-SĀ-uhd-uh	beθ'seːədə
Bethsaida		
Biblical name	beth-SĀ-uhd-uh	beθ'seːədə
Bethshan		
Biblical name	beth-SHAHN, bāt-SHAHN	beθ'ʃan, beːt'ʃan
Beth-shean		
Biblical name	beth-SHĒ-uhn, BĀT-shuh-AHN	beθ'ʃiːən, ˌbeːtʃə'an
Beth-shemesh		
Biblical name	beth-SHĒ-MESH, bāt-SHEM-ESH	beθ'ʃiːˌmeʃ, beːt'ʃemˌeʃ
Beth-shittah		
Biblical name	beth-SHIT-uh, BĀT-hahsh-i-TAH	beθ'ʃiţə, ˌbeːthaʃi'ta
Beth-tappuah		
Biblical name	beth-TAP-(y)uh-wuh, BĀT-tah-POO-ahkh	beθ'tæp(j)əwə, ˌbeːtta'puːax
Bethuel		
Biblical name	beth-YOO-uhl, BETH-yuh-wuhl, buh-too-EL	beθ'juːəl, 'beθjəwəl, bətuː'el
Bethul		
Biblical name	BĒ-THUL, BETH-uhl, buh-TOOL	'biːˌθul, 'beθəl, bə'tuːl
Bethune		
1. Mary McLeod, US educator	buh-TH(Y)OON	bə'θ(j)uːn
2. British pers. name	BĒT-n	'biːtṇ
Bethune-Cookman		
College, FL	buh-TH(Y)OON-KUK-muhn	bə'θ(j)uːn'kukmən
Beth-zur		
Biblical name	beth-ZUR, bāt-TSOOR	beθ'zuʳ, beːt'tsuːr
Betje		
pers. name	BECH-uh	'betʃə
Betjeman		
Sir John, English poet	BECH-uh-muhn	'betʃəmən
Betonim		
Biblical name	BET-uh-NIM, buh-TŌ-nim, buh-TŌ-NIM	'betəˌnim, bə'toːnim, bəˌto:'nim
Betsey, Betsy		
pers. name	BET-sē	'betsi·
Bette		
pers. name	BET	'bet
Bettina		
1. pers. name	buh-TĒ-nuh, be-	bə'tiːnə, be-
2. German	be-TĒ-nah	be'tiːna
Bettino		
pers. name, Italian	bāt-TĒ-nō	beːt'tiːnoː
Betty, Bettye		
pers. name	BET-ē	'beţi·
Beulah		
pers. name	BYOO-luh	'bjuːlə
Bevan		
Aneurin, British politician; pers. name	BEV-uhn	'bevən
Beverley, -ly		
pers. name	BEV-uhr-lē	'bevəʳli·
Beverly Hills		
city, CA	BEV-uhr-lē HILZ	'bevəʳli· 'hilz

Key (col. 2):   a: fad ā: fade ah: father ar: marry aw: law e: fed ē: feed er: merry i: hid ī: hide ō: coat ōō: boot
oi: boy   ow: now   u: put   uh: above   uhr: bird   ch: chop   ng: ring   sh: show   th: thick   th: this   zh: measure

Beverwijk
   commune, Netherlands   BĀ-vuhr-VĪK   'beːvəʳˌvɑik

Bewick
   Thomas, *English artist*   BYOO-ik   'bjuːik

Bexar
   county, TX   BAR, BER   'bæʳ, 'beʳ

Bexley
   borough, England; city, OH   BEKS-lē   'beksliˑ

Beyle [Stendhal]
   Marie Henri, *French writer*   BEL   bel

Bezai
   Biblical name   BĒ-zē-Ī, bē-ZĀ-Ī, bet-SĪ   'biːziː,ɑi, biː'zeː,ɑi, bet'sɑi

Bezalel [Bezalul]
   Biblical name   BEZ-uh-LEL, -uh-luhl; buht-sahl-EL   'bezə,lel, -ələl; bətsɑl'el

Bezalul
   Biblical name   BEZ-uh-luhl, buht-sahl-EL   'bezələl, bətsɑl'el

Bezek
   Biblical name   BĒ-ZEK, BAHT-sek, BET-sek   'biː,zek, 'bɑtsek, 'betsek

Bezer
   Biblical name   BĒ-zuhr, BET-ser   'biːzəʳ, 'betser

Bézique, Be-
   game   buh-ZĒK   bə'ziːk

Bhadgaon
   former name of Bhaktapur, *Nepal*   BUHD-GOWN   'bəd,gɑun

Bhagavad Gita
   Hindu text   BAHG-uh-VAHD GĒT-uh,   ˌbɑgə,vɑd 'giːṭə, ˌbəgə,vəd
                 BUHG-uh-VUHD GĒ-tuh   'giːtə

Bhaktapur
   city, Nepal   BUHK-tuh-PUR   'bəktə,puʳ

Bharat
   Sanskrit name of India   BUH-ruht   'bərət

Bhil
   people, India   BĒL   'biːl

Bhili
   lang., India   BĒ-lē   'biːliˑ

Bhimrao
   pers. name   BĒM-ROW   'biːm,rɑu

Bhojpuri
   lang., India   BAHJ-puh-rē   'bɑdʒpəriˑ

Bhopal
   state, city, India   bō-PAHL   boː'pɑl

Bhotia
   Asian people   BŌT-ē-uh   'boːṭiːə

Bhumibol Adulyadej
   king, Thailand   POO-mē-PŌN ah-DOON-luh-DĀT *[sic]*   'puːmiːˌpoːn a'duːnlə,deːt
                                      [sic]

Bhután
   kingdom, Himalayas   bu-TAN, boo-TAHN   bu'tæn, buː'tɑn

Bhutanese
   pert. to Bhutan   BOOT-n-ĒZ, -ĒS   ˌbuːtn̩'iːz, -'iːs

Bhutia [Murmi]
   lang., India (Sikkim), Nepal   BOOT-ē-uh   'buːṭiːə

Bhutto
   Benazir Ali, *Pakistani politician*   BOO-tō   'buːtoː

Foreign Sounds: ue: *Fr.* **rue**, *Ger.* **füllen** uh(r): *Fr.* **boeuf**, *Ger.* **Höhle** kh: *Ger.* **ich**, *Scot.* **loch** ḡ: *Sp.* **amigo** v̱: *Sp.* **hablar**
hl: *Welsh* **Llanelli**. CAPITALS: primary stress. SMALL CAPS: secondary stress. Ⓢ: U.S. pron. Ⓔ: British pron.

Biafra
  former region, Nigeria; Bight of, *bay, Africa*   bē-AF-ruh, bē-AHF-ruh, bī-AF-ruh   biːˈæfrə, biːˈɑfrə, baiˈæfrə

Bialik
  Mayim, *US actress*   bē-AL-ik, BYAL-ik   biːˈælik, ˈbjælik

Białystok
  city, Poland   bē-AHL-ē-STAWK   biːˈaɫiˌstɔːk

Bianca
  1. pers. name   bē-AHNG-kuh, -ANG-kuh   biːˈɑŋkə, -ˈæŋkə
  2. Italian   BYAHNG-kah   ˈbjɑŋkɑ

Biarritz
  commune, France   byah-RĒTS, ⑤ BĒ-uh-RITS, BĒ-uh-RITS   bjɑːriːts, ⑤ ˌbiːəˈrits, ˈbiːəˌrits

Bible
  Christian holy book   BĪ-buhl   ˈbaibəl

Bibliothecarius
  antipope   BIB-lē-ō-te-KAR-ē-uhs, -KER-   ˌbibliːoːteˈkæriːəs, -ˈker-

Bibliothèque nationale
  library, Paris   bē-blē-aw-TEK nahs-yaw-NAHL   biːbliːɔːtek nɑːsjɔːnɑːl

Bic
  tdmk for pens, cigarette lighters   BIK   ˈbik

Bicester
  town, England   BIS-tuhr   ˈbistəʳ

Bichon frise
  dog breed   bē-SHAWⁿ frē-ZĀ   biːˌʃɔ̃ friːˈzeː

Bichri
  Biblical name   BIK-RĪ, bikh-RĒ   ˈbikˌrai, bixˈriː

Biddeford
  town, ME   BID-uh-fuhrd   ˈbidəfəʳd

Biddulph
  town, England   BID-UHLF, BID-l   ˈbidˌəlf, ˈbidl̩

Bideford
  town, England   BID-uh-fuhrd   ˈbidəfəʳd

Biden
  Joseph R., Jr., *US politician*   BĪD-n   ˈbaidn̩

Bidkar
  Biblical name   BID-KAHR, bid-KAHR   ˈbidˌkɑʳ, bidˈkɑʳ

Bieckert
  Argentinian beer   BĒ-kuhrt   ˈbiːkəʳt

Biederman
  Charles Joseph, *US artist*   BĒD-uhr-muhn   ˈbiːdəʳmən

Biedermeier
  style of furnishings   BĒD-uhr-MĪ(-uh)r   ˈbiːdəʳˌmai(ə)ʳ

Bielorussian [Belo-, Byelo-]
  lang., Belorussia, Poland   bē-EL-ō-RUHSH-uhn, BYEL-ō-   biːˌeloˈrəʃən, ˌbjeloː-

Bienaimé
  pers. name, French   byeⁿ-ne-MĀ   bjɛ̃nemeː

Bien Hoa
  province, Vietnam   byen hō-uh   bjen hoːə

Bienvenu
  pers. name, French   byeⁿv(-uh)-NUE   bjɛ̃v(ə)nyː

Bienville
  1. parish, LA   bē-EN-vuhl, bē-EN-VIL   biːˈenvəl, biːˈenˌvil
  2. lake, Canada   bē-EN-VIL, byahⁿ-VIL   biːˈenˌvil, bjɑ̃vil

---

Key (col. 2):   a: fad   ā: fade   ah: father   ar: marry   aw: law   e: fed   ē: feed   er: merry   i: hid   ī: hide   ō: coat   ōō: boot
oi: boy   ow: now   u: put   uh: above   uhr: bird   ch: chop   ng: ring   sh: show   th: thick   th̲: this   zh: measure

Bierstadt		
Albert, *artist*	BIR-STAT, BIR-SHTAHT	ˈbi^{r}ˌstæt, ˈbi^{r}ˌʃtɑt
Bigelow		
US carpet co.	BIG-uh-LŌ	ˈbigəˌloː
Big Foot [Sasquatch]		
legendary manlike creature	BIG FUT	ˈbig ˌfut
Bigtha		
Biblical name	BIG-thuh, big-TAH	ˈbigθə, bigˈtɑ
Bigthan		
Biblical name	BIG-THAN, big-TAHN	ˈbigˌθæn, bigˈtɑn
Bigthana [Bigthan]		
Biblical name	big-THĀ-nuh, BIG-thuh-nuh	bigˈθeːnə, ˈbigθənə
Bigvai		
Biblical name	BIG-vē-Ī, BIG-VĪ, big-VĪ	ˈbigviːˌɑi, ˈbigˌvɑi, bigˈvɑi
Bihać		
town, Bosna-Hercegovina	BĒ-HAHCH	ˈbiːˌhɑtʃ
Bihar, Behar		
state, India	bi-HAHR	biˈhɑ^{r}
Bihari		
lang., India, Nepal	bē-HAHR-ē	biˑˈhɑriˑ
Bikaner		
state, city, India	BIK-uh-NER, BĒ-kuh-NER, -NIR	ˌbikəˈne^{r}, ˌbiːkəˈne^{r}, -ˈni^{r}
Bikel		
Theodore, *US entertainer*	bi-KEL	biˈkel
Bikini		
atoll, Marshall Islands	buh-KĒ-nē	bəˈkiːniˑ
Biko		
Stephen, *S. African activist*	BĒ-kō	ˈbiːkoː
Bikol		
lang., people, Philippine Islands	bē-KŌL	biːˈkoːl
Bilaan		
lang., people, Philippine Islands	bē-LAH-AHN, bē-LAHN	biːˈlɑˌɑn, biːˈlɑn
Bilbao		
city, Spain	bil-V̲AH-ō, [$] bil-BOW, bil-BĀ-ō	bilˈβɑoː, [$] bilˈbɑu, bilˈbeːoː
Bilbo Baggins		
character in The Hobbit, *J. R. R. Tolkien*	BIL-bō BAG-inz	ˈbilboː ˈbæginz
Bildad		
Biblical name	BIL-DAD	ˈbilˌdæd
Bileam		
Biblical name	BIL-ē-uhm, BĪ-lē-uhm, bi-LAHM	ˈbiliːəm, ˈbɑiliːəm, biˈlɑm
Bilgah		
Biblical name	BIL-guh, bil-GAH	ˈbilgə, bilˈgɑ
Bilgai		
Biblical name	BIL-gē-Ī, BIL-GĪ, bil-GĪ	ˈbilgiːˌɑi, ˈbilˌgɑi, bilˈgɑi
Bilhah		
Biblical name	BIL-HAH, bil-HAH	ˈbilˌhɑ, bilˈhɑ
Bilhan		
Biblical name	BIL-HAN, bil-HAHN	ˈbilˌhæn, bilˈhɑn
Bilin		
lang., Ethiopia	buh-LĒN	bəˈliːn
Bill		
pers. name	BIL	ˈbil
Billie		
pers. name	BIL-ē	ˈbiliˑ

Foreign Sounds: ue: *Fr.* **rue**, *Ger.* **füllen** uh(r): *Fr.* **boeuf**, *Ger.* **Höhle** k̲h̲: *Ger.* **ich**, *Scot.* **loch** ḡ: *Sp.* **amigo** v̲: *Sp.* **hablar** hl: *Welsh* **Llanelli**. CAPITALS: primary stress. SMALL CAPS: secondary stress. [$]: U.S. pron. [£]: British pron.

Billingsgate
London fish market   BIL-ingz-GĀT   'bilɪŋz͵geːt
Billy
pers. name   BIL-ē   'biliˑ
Biloxi
town, MS; N. American people   buh-LUHK-sē, buh-LAHK-sē   bə'ləksiˑ, bə'lɑksiˑ
Bilshan
Biblical name   BIL-SHAN, bil-SHAHN   'bil͵ʃæn, bil'ʃɑn
Bimhal
Biblical name   BIM-HAL, bim-HAHL   'bim͵hæl, bim'hɑl
Bimini
islands, British Virgin Islands   BIM-uh-nē   'biməniˑ
Biminis
pl. form of Bimini   BIM-uh-nēz   'biməniˑz
Binea
Biblical name   BIN-ē-uh, bi-NAH   'biniːə, bi'nɑ
Binet
  1. Alfred, French psychologist   bē-NE, ⑤ buh-NĀ   biːne, ⑤ bə'neː
  2. intelligence test   buh-NĀ   bə'neː
Bing
pers. name; cherries   BING   'biŋ
Bingen
city, Germany   BING-uhn   'biŋən
Binghamton
city, NY   BING-uhm-tuhn   'biŋəmtən
Bing Yin
Chinese year (Tiger)   BING YIN   'biŋ 'jin
Bini [Edo]
lang., people, Nigeria   buh-NĒ   bə'niː
Binnig
Gerd, *German physicist (Nobel 1986)* BIN-i<u>kh</u>   'biniç
Binnui
Biblical name   BIN-yuh-WĪ, bi-N(Y)OO̅-ē   'binjə͵wai, bi'n(j)uːiː
Binyamin
pers. name, Hebrew   BEN-yuh-MĒN   'benjə͵miːn
Biographia Literaria
prose work, Coleridge   BĪ-uh-GRAF-ē-uh LIT-uh-RAR-ē-uh   ͵baiə'græfiːə ͵litə'ræriːə
Bioko
island, Equatorial Guinea   bē-Ō-kō   biː'oːkoː
Biola
University, *CA*   bī-Ō-luh   bɑi'oːlə
Bion
Greek pastoral poet   BĪ-AHN   'bai͵ɑn
BIOS
basic input-output system   BĪ-AHS, BĪ-ŌS   'bai͵ɑs, 'bai͵oːs
Bios Copper
Belgian beer   BĒ-ahs KAHP-uhr, BĪ-ahs   'biːas 'kapəʳ, 'baias
Birgit
pers. name, Swedish   BIR-yit   'biʳjit
Birgitta
pers. name, Swedish   bir-GIT-uh   biʳ'giṯə
Birmingham
  1. city, AL   BUHR-ming-HAM   'bəʳmiŋ͵hæm
  2. city, England   BUHR-ming-uhm, BRUHM-uh-juhm   'bəʳmiŋəm, 'brəmədʒəm

---

Key (col. 2): a: fad ā: fade ah: father ar: ma**rry** aw: **law** e: fed ē: feed er: me**rry** i: hid ī: hide ō: coat ō̅o̅: boot
oi: **boy** ow: **now** u: put uh: above uhr: b**ir**d ch: **chop** ng: ri**ng** sh: **show** th: **thick** <u>th</u>: **this** zh: measure

Birnam Wood
  former forest, Scotland   BUHR-nuhm WUD   'bəʳnəm 'wud

Birobidzhan
  city, admin. div., Russia   BIR-ō-buh-JAHN   ˌbiroːbə'dʒɑn

Bisaya [Sebuano]
  lang., people, Philippine Islands   buh-SĪ-(y)uh   bə'sɑi(j)ə

Birsha
  Biblical name   BIR-shuh, bir-SHAH   'biʳʃə, bir'ʃɑ

Birzaith [Birzavith]
  Biblical name   bir-ZĀ-uhth, bir-ZAH-yit   biʳ'zeːəθ, bir'zajit

Birzavith [Birzaith]
  Biblical name   bir-ZĀ-vuhth, bir-ZAH-yit   biʳ'zeːvəθ, bir'zajit

Biscay
  bay of Atlantic, W France & N   BIS-kā   'biskeː
    Spain; prov, Spain

Biscayne
  bay, FL; car model   bis-KĀN, BIS-KĀN   bis'keːn, 'bisˌkeːn

Bishlam
  Biblical name   BISH-LAM, BISH-luhm, bish-LAHM   'biʃˌlæm, 'biʃləm, biʃ'lɑm

Bisho
  town, S. Africa   BĒ-shō   'biːʃoː

Bishop
  Elizabeth, US poet; J. Michael, US   BISH-uhp   'biʃəp
    microbiologist (Nobel 1989)

Bīsitūn [Behistun]
  town, Iran   BĒ-suh-TO͞ON   ˌbiːsə'tuːn

Bislama [Bêche-de-Mer]
  lang., Vanuatu, Solomon Islands   BĒ-sluh-MAH   ˌbiːslə'mɑˑ

Bismarck
  1. Otto von, German statesman   BIS-MAHRK, Ⓢ BIZ-MAHRK   'bisˌmɑʳk, Ⓢ 'bizˌmɑʳk
  2. city, ND; archipelago, sea, Pacific   BIZ-MAHRK   'bizˌmɑʳk

bismuth
  element   BIZ-muhth   'bizməθ

Bissau
  seaport, Guinea-Bissau   bis-OW, bis-OWⁿ   bis'au, bis'aū

Bisset
  Jacqueline, US entertainer   BIS-uht   'bisət

Bisu [Bes]
  Egyptian god   BIS-o͞o   'bisuː

Bitburg
  town, Germany   BIT-BURK, Ⓔ BIT-BUHRG   'bitˌburk, Ⓔ 'bitˌbəʳg

Bitburger
  German beer   BIT-BUR-guhr, Ⓔ BIT-BUHR-guhr   'bitˌbuʳgəʳ, Ⓔ 'bitˌbəʳgəʳ

Bithiah
  Biblical name   BITH-ē-uh, bi-THĪ-uh, bit-YAH   'biθiːə, bi'θaiə, bit'ja

Bithron
  Biblical name   BITH-RAHN, bit-RŌN   'biθˌrɑn, bit'roːn

Bithynia
  ancient state, Asia Minor   buh-THIN-ē-uh   bə'θiniːə

Bitlis
  prov, Turkey   bit-LĒS   bit'liːs

Bix
  pers. name (B. Biederbecke)   BIKS   'biks

Bizerte
  port, Tunisia   buh-ZERT-ē, bi-ZERT   bə'zeʳʈiˑ, bi'zeʳt

Bizet
  Georges, *French composer*   bē-ZE, ⓢ bē-ZĀ   biːze, ⓢ biːˈzeː

Biziothiah
  Biblical name   BIZ-ē-uh-THĪ-uh, biz-YŌT-uh-uh-YAH   ˌbiziːəˈθaiə, bizˈjoːtə-əˌjɑ

Bizjothjah [Biziothiah]
  Biblical name   biz-JAHTH-yuh, biz-YŌT-uh-uh-YAH   bizˈdʒɑθjə, bizˈjoːtə-əˌjɑ

Biztha
  Biblical name   BIZ-thuh, biz-TAH   ˈbizθə, bizˈtɑ

Bjarni
  pers. name   BYAHD-nē   ˈbjɑdniː

Bjørn, Björn
  pers. name   BYUHRN   ˈbjœːrn

Bjørnson
  Bjørnstjerne, *Norwegian author*   BYUHRN-suhn   ˈbjœːrnsən
  (Nobel 1903)

Bjørnstjerne
  pers. name, Norwegian   BYUHRN-STYER-nuh   ˈbjœːrnˌstjernə

Black
  James, *British pharmacologist*   BLAK   ˈblæk
  (Nobel 1988); Sea, *Europe, Asia;*
  various rivers, US

Blackett
  P. M. S., *British physicist (Nobel*   BLAK-uht   ˈblækət
  1948)

Blackfeet
  pl. of Blackfoot   BLAK-FĒT   ˈblækˌfiːt

Blackfoot
  N. American people   BLAK-FUT   ˈblækˌfut

Blackfriars
  district, 16th-century theater, London,   blak-FRĪ-uhrz, BLAK-FRĪ-uhrz   blækˈfraiə[r]z, ˈblækˌfraiə[r]z
  England

Black Maria
  patrol wagon   BLAK muh-RĪ-uh   ˌblæk məˈraiə

Blackpool
  town, Lancashire   BLAK-PŌŌL   ˈblækˌpuːl

Blair
  pers. name   BLAR, BLER   ˈblæ[r], ˈble[r]

Blaise
  1. pers. name   BLĀZ   ˈbleːz
  2. French   BLEZ   blez

Blakeney
  Sir Percival, *hero of* The Scarlet   BLĀK-nē   ˈbleːkniˑ
  Pimpernel

Blanc
  1. Louis, *French historian*   BLAH[n]   blɑ̃
  2. Mel, *US cartoon voice*   BLANGK   ˈblæŋk
  3. Cape, *Africa*   BLAH[n], ⓢ BLANGK   blɑ̃, ⓢ ˈblæŋk

Blanc, Mont
  see Mont Blanc

Blanc fumé
  wine   BLAH[n] fue-MĀ   blɑ̃ fyːmeː

Blanchard
  James J., *US politician*   BLAN-chuhrd   ˈblæntʃə[r]d

Key (col. 2): a: fad ā: fade ah: father ar: marry aw: law e: fed ē: feed er: merry i: hid ī: hide ō: coat ōō: boot
oi: boy ow: now u: put uh: above uhr: bird ch: chop ng: ring sh: show th: thick <u>th</u>: this zh: measure

Blanche
1. pers. name	BLANCH	'blæntʃ
2. French	BLAHⁿSH	blɑ̃ʃ

Blarney
town, Ireland	BLAHR-nē	'blɑʳniˑ

Blasco-Ibáñez
Vincente, Spanish novelist	BLAHS-kō-ē-VAHN-yāth, -ē-VAHN-yās	'blɑskoːiːˈβanjeːθ, -iːˈβanjeːs

Blastus
Biblical name	BLAS-tuhs	'blæstəs

Blaupunkt
German audio co.	BLOW-PUNG(K)T	'blau,puŋ(k)t

Blavatsky
Madame Helena, *founder of* Theosophy	bluh-VAT-skē, bluh-VAHT-skē	blə'vætskiˑ, blə'vɑtskiˑ

Bleecker
street, New York City; stadium, Albany, NY	BLĒ-kuhr	'bliːkəʳ

Blenheim
town, palace, England; borough, New Zealand; English/French form of Blindheim	BLEN-uhm	'blenəm

Blériot
Louis, *French aviator/inventor*	blār-YŌ, Ⓢ BLER-ē-ō	bleːrjoː, Ⓢ 'bleriːˌoː

Bleu cheese
cheese	BLUH(R), BLOO	'blœː, 'bluː

Blindheim [Blenheim]
village, Germany	BLINT-HĪM	'blintˌhaim

Blitz Weinhard
beer	BLITS VĪN-HAHRT, WĪN-HAHRT	'blits 'vainˌhaʳt, 'wainˌhaʳt

Bloch
1. Felix, *US physicist (Nobel 1952)*	BLAHK	'blɑk
2. Konrad E., *US biochemist (Nobel 1964)*	BLAHK, BLAWK, BLAWKH	'blɑk, 'blɔːk, 'blɔːx

Block
Herbert Lawrence, *US cartoonist (penname* Herblock*)*	BLAHK	'blɑk

Bloembergen
Nicolaas, *US physicist (Nobel 1981)*	BLOOM-BUHR-guhn	'bluːmˌbəʳgən

Bloemfontein
city, South Africa	BLOOM-FAHN-TEN	'bluːmˌfanˌten

Blois
city, France	BLWAH, Ⓢ bluh-WAH	blwɑː, Ⓢ blə'wɑ

Blood
N. American people	BLUHD	'bləd

Bloom
pers. name	BLOOM	'bluːm

Bloomfield
US pl. name; pers. name	BLOOM-FĒLD	'bluːmˌfiːld

Bloomingdales
US department store	BLOO-ming-DĀLZ	'bluːmiŋˌdeːlz

Bloomington
city, IN	BLOO-ming-tuhn	'bluːmiŋtən

Bloomsbury
district, London	BLOOMZ-b(uh-)rē	'bluːmzb(ə)riˑ

Foreign Sounds: ue: *Fr.* **rue**, *Ger.* **füllen** uh(r): *Fr.* **boeuf**, *Ger.* **Höhle** <u>kh</u>: *Ger.* **ich**, *Scot.* **loch** ğ: *Sp.* **amigo** ᵥ: *Sp.* **hablar**   hl: *Welsh* **Llanelli**. CAPITALS: primary stress. SMALL CAPS: secondary stress. Ⓢ: U.S. pron. Ⓔ: British pron.

Blount		
county, AL, TN; pers. name	BLUHNT	'blənt
Blücher		
Gebhard von, *Prussian militarist*	BLUE-k͟huhr, Ⓢ BLO͞O-kuhr	'bly:xəʳ, Ⓢ 'blu:kəʳ
Bluebeard		
fairy tale character	BLO͞O-BĒRD	'blu:ˌbiʳd
Blumberg		
Baruch Samuel, *US biochemist (Nobel 1976)*	BLUHM-BUHRG, BLO͞OM-BUHRG	'bləmˌbəʳg, 'blu:mˌbəʳg
Blume		
Judy, *US author*	BLO͞OM	'blu:m
Blyth		
1. Edward, *English naturalist*	BLĪ, BLĪTH, BLĪT͟H	'blɑi, 'blɑiθ, 'blɑið
2. borough, England	BLĪT͟H	'blɑið
Blythe		
pers. name	BLĪT͟H	'blɑið
Blyton		
Enid, *British author*	BLĪT-n	'blɑitn̩
BMW		
German car marque	BĒ-em-DUHB-uh(l-)yo͞o	ˌbi:em'dəbə(l)juˑ
B'nai B'rith		
international Jewish organization	buh-NĀ BRITH	bəˌne: 'briθ
Bo		
1. pers. name	BŌ	'bo:
2. Swedish	BO͞O	'bu:
Boabdil		
Spanish name of Muhammad XI, sultan of Granada	bō-ahv̲-DĒL	bo:ɑβ'di:l
Boadicea [Boudicca]		
ancient British queen	BŌ-uhd-uh-SĒ-uh	ˌbo:ədə'si:ə
Boal		
town, Spain	BWAHL	'bwɑl
Boanerges		
Biblical name	BŌ-uh-NUHR-jēz	ˌbo:ə'nəʳdʒi:z
Boas		
Franz, *US anthropologist*	BŌ-AZ	'bo:ˌæz
Boaz, [Booz]		
Biblical name	BŌ-AZ	'bo:ˌæz
Bob		
pers. name	BAHB	'bɑb
Bobby		
pers. name	BAHB-ē	'bɑbiˑ
Bobko		
Karol J., *US astronaut, shuttle pilot*	BAHB-kō	'bɑbko:
Bobo		
lang., Mali, Burkina Faso	BŌ-bō	'bo:bo:
Bobst		
Elmer Holmes, Library, *New York City*	BAHBST, BAHPST	'bɑbst, 'bɑpst
Boca Raton		
town, FL	BŌ-kuh-ruh-TŌN	ˌbo:kərə'to:n
Boccaccio		
1. Giovanni, *medieval Italian author*	bōk-KAHT-chō, Ⓢ buh-KAHCH-(ē-)ō	bo:k'kɑttʃo:, Ⓢ bə'kɑtʃ(i:)o:
2. pers. name; game	buh-KAHCH-(ē-)ō	bə'kɑtʃ(i:)o:

Key (col. 2): a: **fad** ā: **fade** ah: **father** ar: **marry** aw: **law** e: **fed** ē: **feed** er: **merry** i: **hid** ī: **hide** ō: **coat** o͞o: **boot** oi: **boy** ow: **now** u: **put** uh: **above** uhr: **bird** ch: **chop** ng: **ring** sh: **show** th: **thick** t͟h: **this** zh: **measure**

Boche
  disparaging term for a German   BAWSH, BAHSH   'bɔːʃ, 'baʃ
  soldier

Bocheru
  Biblical name   BAHK-uh-ROO, BŌ-kuh-; bawkh-ROO   'bakə‚ruː, 'boːkə-; bɔːx'ruː

Bochim
  Biblical name   BŌ-kim, baw-KHĒM   'boːkim, bɔː'xiːm

Bodensee
  lake, Swiss Alps   BŌD-n-ZĀ   'boːdn̩‚zeː

Bodhisattva
  Buddhist holy one   BŌD-uh-SUHT-vuh, -SAHT-vuh   ‚boːdə'sʌtvə, -'sɑtvə

Bodhran
  Irish drum   BAWR-uhn, BAWTH-ruhn   'bɔːrən, 'bɔːðrən

Bodie
  island, NC   BAHD-ē   'badiː

Bodleian
  library, Oxford Univ., England   bahd-LĒ-uhn, BAHD-lē-uhn   bad'liːən, 'badliːən

Bodo
  lang., people, India   BŌD-ō   'boːdoː

Bodoni
  type style   buh-DŌ-nē, bō-DŌ-nē   bə'doːniˑ, boː'doːniˑ

Boehm
  Richard Wood, US ambassador   BŌM   'boːm

Boeing
  US aerospace co.   BŌ-ing   'boːiŋ

Boeotia
  prov, Greece   bē-Ō-shuh   biː'oːʃə

Boeotian
  pert. to Boeotia   bē-Ō-sh(ē-)uhn   biː'oːʃ(iː)ən

Boer
  War, S. Africa   BŌR, BAWR, BUR   'boːr, 'bɔːr, 'bur

Boerne
  city, TX   BUHR-nē   'bərniˑ

Boethius
  medieval philosopher   bō-Ē-thē-uhs   boː'iːθiːəs

Boeuf Bourguignon
  stew with wine   buh(r)f bur-gē-NYAWⁿ, BĒF   bœf burgiːɲ ɔ̃, ‚biːf
     bur-gēn-YAWⁿ   burgiˑn'jɔ̃

Bogalusa
  city, LA   BŌ-guh-LOO-suh   ‚boːgə'luːsə

Bogart
  Humphrey, US actor   BŌ-GAHRT   'boː‚garˑt

Bogdan
  1. pers. name, Bulgarian, Polish   BAWG-DAHN   'bɔːg‚dɑːn
  2. Romanian   bawg-DAHN   bɔːg'dɑn
  3. Russian   BUHG-DAHN   ‚bəg'dɑːn

Boggabilla
  town, Australia   BAHG-uh-BIL-uh   ‚bagə'bilə

Boghaz-Koy
  Hittite ruins, Turkey   BŌ-(G)AHZ-KOI   ‚boː‚(g)az'kɔi

Bognor Regis
  town, England   BAHG-nuhr RĒ-juhs   ‚bagnər 'riːdʒəs

Bogotá
  river, city, Colombia   BŌ-guh-TAW, -TAH   ‚boːgə'tɔː, -'ta

---

Foreign Sounds: ue: *Fr.* **rue**, *Ger.* füllen   uh(r): *Fr.* **boeuf**, *Ger.* Höhle   kh: *Ger.* ich, *Scot.* loch   g̱: *Sp.* amigo   v̱: *Sp.* hablar
hl: *Welsh* Llanelli.   CAPITALS: primary stress.   SMALL CAPS: secondary stress.   Ⓢ: U.S. pron.   Ⓔ: British pron.

Bogota		
city, NJ	buh-GŌT-uh	bə'goːt̬ə
Bogumil		
pers. name, German	BŌ-gum-ĒL	'boːgumˌiːl
Bogumił		
pers. name, Polish	baw-GO͞O-mēl	bɔː'guːmiːɫ
Bohai		
see Po Hai		
Bohan		
Marc, *French fashion designer*	baw-AH^{n}	bɔːɑ̃
Bohan		
Biblical name	BŌ-HAN, BAW-HAHN	'boːˌhæn, 'bɔːˌhɑn
Bohème, La		
opera, Puccini	LAH bō-EM	ˌlɑ boː'em
Bohemia		
prov, Czech republic	bō-HĒ-mē-uh	boː'hiːmiːə
Bohol		
island, strait, Philippines	bō-HAWL	boː'hɔːl
Bohr		
Aage N., *Danish physicist (Nobel 1975); his father* Niels H. D., *Danish physicist (Nobel 1922)*	BŌR, BAWR	'boːʳ, 'bɔːʳ
Bohun, de		
Anglo-Norman family in Welsh Marches	duh BO͞ON	də 'buːn
Bohuslav		
pers. name	BAW-hus-lahf	'bɔːhuslɑːf
Boipatong		
township, South Africa	BOI-puh-TAWNG, BOI-puh-TAWNG	ˌbɔipə'tɔːŋ, 'bɔipəˌtɔːŋ
Bois de Boulogne		
park, Paris, France	bwah duh bo͞o-LAWN-yuh, [$] BWAH duh bo͞o-LŌN, bo͞o-LOIN	bwɑː də buːlɔːɲ , [$] 'bwɑ də buˑ'loːn, buˑ'lɔin
Bois de Vincennes		
park, Vincennes, France	bwahd ve^{n}-SEN	bwɑːd vẽsen
Boise		
county, ID	BOI-sē *(local pron.)*, BOI-zē	'bɔisiˑ *(local pron.)*, 'bɔiziˑ
Bojaxhiu [Mother Teresa]		
Agnes Gonxha, *Albanian religious (Nobel 1979)*	bō-yahkh-YO͞O	boːjɑx'juː
Bokaro		
city, Bihar, India	bō-KAHR-ō	boː'kɑroː
Bokhara		
1. rug	bo͞o-KHAHR-uh, bō-KAHR-uh	buː'xɑrə, boː'kɑrə
2. see Bukhara		
Bokmål [Dano-Norwegian]		
literary Norwegian	BO͞OK-MAWL, [$] BUK-MAWL, -MAHL	'buːkˌmɔːl, [$] 'bukˌmɔːl, -ˌmɑl
Bolero		
dance	buh-LER-ō	bə'leroː
Boleslav		
Bohemian ruler; pers. name	BŌ-luh-SLAHF	'boːləˌslɑf
Bolesław		
Polish ruler; pers. name	baw-LES-lahf	bɔː'lesɫɑːf

Key (col. 2): a: **fad** ā: **fade** ah: **father** ar: **marry** aw: **law** e: **fed** ē: **feed** er: **merry** i: **hid** ī: **hide** ō: **coat** o͞o: **boot** oi: **boy** ow: **now** u: **put** uh: **above** uhr: **bird** ch: **chop** ng: **ring** sh: **show** th: **thick** th: **this** zh: **measure**

Boleyn
 Anne, *wife of Henry VIII, mother of*   bu-LIN, BUL-uhn   bu'lin, 'bulən
 Elizabeth I
Bolger
 Ray, *US actor*   BŌL-juhr   'boːldʒəʳ
Bolingbroke
 Henry of, *King Henry IV*   ⒺBAHL-ing-BRUK, BUL-ing-BRUK,   Ⓔ'baliŋ,bruk, 'buliŋ,bruk,
                             ⓈBŌ-ling-BRUK, -BRŌK   Ⓢ'boːliŋ,bruk, -,broːk
Bolinger
 Dwight, *US linguist*   BAHL-uhn-juhr   'baləndʒəʳ
Bolívar
 Simón, *S. American leader; S.*   bō-LĒ-vahr, ⒮ buh-LĒ-VAHR,   boː'liːβar, Ⓢ bə'liː,vaʳ,
 American pl. name   BAHL-uh-vuhr   'baləvəʳ
Bolivar
 US pl. name; pers. name   BAHL-uh-vuhr   'baləvəʳ
Bolivia
 republic, S. America   buh-LIV-ē-uh   bə'liviːə
Bolivian
 pert. to Bolivia   buh-LIV-ē-uhn   bə'liviːən
Böll
 Heinrich, *German author (Nobel*   BUH(R)L   'bœːl
 1972)
Bolla
 tdmk for Italian wine   BŌ-luh   'boːlə
Bollard
 John K., *US lexicographer*   BAHL-uhrd, ⒺBAHL-AHRD   'baləʳd, Ⓔ'bal,aʳd
Bologna
 prov & town, Italy   buh-LŌN-yuh, buh-LŌ-nuh   bə'loːnjə, bə'loːnə
Bolognese
 1. pert. to Bologna, Italy   BŌ-luhn-(Y)ĒZ, BŌ-luhn-(Y)ĒS   ,boːlən'(j)iːz, ,boːlən'(j)iːs
 2. pasta sauce   BŌ-luhn-(Y)ĒZ, BŌ-luhn-(Y)ĒS,   ,boːlən'(j)iːz, ,boːlən'(j)iːs,
                             BŌ-luhn-YĀZ   ,boːlən'jeːz
Bolshevik
 communist   BŌL-shuh-vik, BAWL-, BAHL-   'boːlʃəvik, 'boːl-, 'bal-
Bolshevism
 doctrines of Bolsheviks   BŌL-shuh-VIZ-uhm, BAWL-, BAHL-   'boːlʃə,vizəm, 'boːl-, 'bal-
Bolshevist
 follower of Bolsheviks   BŌL-shuh-vuhst, BAWL-, BAHL-   'boːlʃəvəst, 'boːl-, 'bal-
Bolshoi
 ballet, Moscow   BŌL-SHOI, BAWL-SHOI   'boːl,ʃɔi, 'bɔːl,ʃɔi
Bolt Beranek and Newman
 US high-technology co.   BŌLT buh-RAN-ik uhn(d)   'boːlt bə'rænik ən(d)
                             N(Y)OO-muhn   'n(j)uːmən
Bolzano
 Bernhard, *Austrian theologian*   bawlt-SAHN-ō   bɔːlt'sanoː
Bombay
 city, India   bahm-BĀ   bam'beː
Bon
 Buddhist festival   BAHN   'ban
Bona [Bône]
 former name of Annaba, *Algeria*   BŌ-nuh   'boːnə
Bona Dea
 Roman divinity   BŌ-nuh DĀ-uh   ,boːnə 'deːə
Bonaire
 island, Netherlands Antilles   buh-NAR, buh-NER   bə'næʳ, bə'neʳ

Foreign Sounds: ue: *Fr.* **rue**, *Ger.* **füllen** uh(r): *Fr.* **boeuf**, *Ger.* **Höhle** <u>kh</u>: *Ger.* **ich**, *Scot.* **loch** ḡ: *Sp.* **amigo** v̱: *Sp.* **hablar**
hl: *Welsh* **Llanelli**. CAPITALS: primary stress. SMALL CAPS: secondary stress. Ⓢ: U.S. pron. Ⓔ: British pron.

Bonamy
  pers. name   BAHN-uh-mē   'banəmi·

Bonaparte [Buonaparte]
  Corsican family, incl. Napoléon   baw-nah-PAHRT, Ⓢ BŌ-nuh-PAHRT   bɔːnɑːpɑrt, Ⓢ 'bɔːnə,pɑʳt

Bonaventura
  1. pers. name, German   BŌ-nah-ven-TOO̅-rah   ,bɔːnɑven'tuːrɑ
  2. Italian   BAW-nahv-en-TOO̅-rah   ,bɔːnɑven'tuːrɑ

Bonaventure
  1. pers. name   BAHN-uh-VEN-chuhr, BAHN-uh-VEN-   ,banə'ventʃəʳ, 'banə,ven-
  2. French   baw-nah-vahⁿ-TUER   bɔːnɑːvãtyːr

Bondi
  beach, Australia   BAHN-DĪ, bahn-DĪ   'ban,dai, ban'dai

Bône [Bona]
  former name of Annaba, *Algeria*   BŌN   'bɔːn

Bone [Boni]
  gulf, Indonesia   BŌ-nē   'bɔːni·

Bonheur
  Rosa, *French painter*   baw-NUHR   bɔːnœr

Bon Homme
  county, SD   BAHN-uhm   'banəm

Boni [Bone]
  gulf, Indonesia   BŌ-nē   'bɔːni·

Boniface
  pers. name   BAHN-uh-fuhs, -FĀS   'banəfəs, -,feːs

Bonifacius
  1. pers. name   BAHN-uh-FĀ-sh(ē-)uhs   ,banə'feːʃ(iː)əs
  2. German   BŌ-nē-FAHTS-yus, -FAHT-sē-us   ,bɔːniː'fatsjus, -'fatsiːus

Bonin
  Islands, *Pacific*   BŌ-nuhn   'bɔːnən

Bonior
  David, *US politician*   BAHN-yuhr   'banjəʳ

Bonjour Tristesse
  novel, Françoise Sagan   bawⁿ-ZHOO̅R trēs-TES   bõʒuʳr triːstes

Bon Jovi
  rock group   bahn JŌ-vē   ban 'dʒɔːvi·

Bonn
  former capital, W. Germany   BAHN, BAWN   'ban, 'bɔːn

Bonnard
  Pierre, *French artist*   baw-NAHR   bɔːnɑːr

Bonneville
  1. Benjamin, *American explorer;*   BAHN-uh-VIL   'banə,vil
    county, ID
  2. US car model   BAHN-uh-VIL, BAHN-ē-VIL   'banə,vil, 'bani·,vil

Bonnezeaux
  French wine   bawn-ZŌ   bɔːnzɔː

Bonnie, Bonny
  pers. name   BAHN-ē   'bani·

Bono
  1. Sonny, *US entertainer, politician*   BŌ-nō   'bɔːnɔː
  2. Irish rock singer   BAW-nō, BAHN-ō   'bɔːnɔː, 'banɔː

Bontok
  lang., people, Philippine Islands   bahn-TAHK   ban'tak

Bonynge
  Richard, *Austrian conductor*   BAHN-ing   'baniŋ

Key (col. 2):   a: f**a**d   ā: f**a**de   ah: f**a**ther   ar: m**a**rry   aw: l**a**w   e: f**e**d   ē: f**ee**d   er: m**e**rry   i: h**i**d   ī: h**i**de   ō: c**oa**t   oo̅: b**oo**t
oi: b**oy**   ow: n**ow**   u: p**u**t   uh: **a**bove   uhr: b**i**rd   ch: **ch**op   ng: ri**ng**   sh: **sh**ow   th: **th**ick   <u>th</u>: **th**is   zh: mea**s**ure

Boogie-woogie
 musical style   BUG-ē-WUG-ē, BŌŌ-gē-WŌŌ-gē   ˌbugi·ˈwugi·, ˌbuːgiˈwuːgi·

Booker
 pers. name   BUK-uhr   ˈbukəʳ

Boole
 George, *English mathematician*   BŌŌL   ˈbuːl

Boolean
 pert. to G. Boole; algebra   BŌŌ-lē-uhn   ˈbuːliːən

Boorman
 John, *British film producer, director*   BUR-muhn, BAWR-muhn   ˈbuʳmən, ˈbɔːʳmən

Boorstin
 Daniel J., *US author*   BUR-stuhn, BAWR-stuhn   ˈbuʳstən, ˈbɔːʳstən

Boötes
 constellation   bō-ŌT-ēz   boːˈoːʈiːz

Booz [Boaz]
 Biblical name   BŌ-AHZ   ˈboːˌɑz

Bop
 local name for Bophuthatswana   BAHP   ˈbɑp

Bophuthatswana
 Black enclaves, South Africa   BŌ-pŌŌ-taht-SWAHN-uh   ˌboːpuːtɑtˈswɑnə

Bora-Bora
 island, French Polynesia   BŌR-uh-BŌR-uh, BAWR-uh-BAWR-uh   ˌboːrəˈboːrə, ˌbɔːrəˈbɔːrə

Borach
 Fanny, *orig. name of* Fanny Brice   BŌR-uhk, BAWR-uhk   ˈboːrək, ˈbɔːrək

Borah
 William E., *US political leader*   BŌR-uh, BAWR-uh   ˈboːrə, ˈbɔːrə

Borchert
 Field, *ballpark, Milwaukee, WI*   BAWR-chuhrt   ˈbɔːʳtʃəʳt

Bordeaux
 city, France; wine   bawr-DŌ   bɔːʳˈdoː

Bordelaise
 brown sauce   BAWRD-l-ĀZ   ˌbɔːʳdl̩ˈeːz

Bordet
 Jules, *Belgian bacteriologist (Nobel 1919)*   bawr-DĀ   bɔːrdeː

Boreades
 children of the North Wind   BŌR-ē-AD-ēz, BAWR-ē-AD-ēz   ˌboːriːˈædiːz, ˌbɔːriːˈædiːz

Boreal owl
 bird   BŌR-ē-uhl OWL, BAWR-   ˈboːriːəl ˈɑul, ˈbɔːr-

Boreas
 Greek god of the North Wind   BŌR-ē-uhs, BAWR-ē-uhs   ˈboːriːəs, ˈbɔːriːəs

Borg
 Bjorn, *Swedish tennis player*   BAWR-yuh, Ⓢ BAWRG   ˈbɔːrj, Ⓢ ˈbɔːʳg

Borge
 Victor, *US comedian, pianist*   BAWR-guh   ˈbɔːʳgə

Borges
 Jorge Luis, *Argentinian author*   BAWR-ḡās, Ⓢ BAWR-HĀS   ˈbɔːrɣeːs, Ⓢ ˈbɔːʳˌheːs

Borghese, Galleria
 picture gallery, Rome, Italy   GAHL-uh-RĒ-uh bawr-GĀ-zā   ˌgɑləˈriːə bɔːʳˈgeːzeː

Borgia
 Italian family   BAWR-jah, BAWR-juh, BAWR-zhuh   ˈbɔːʳdʒɑ, ˈbɔːʳdʒə, ˈbɔːʳʒə

Borglum
 Gutzon, *US sculptor*   BAWR-gluhm   ˈbɔːʳgləm

Borgnine
 Ernest, *US actor*   BAWRG-NĪN   ˈbɔːʳgˌnain

Borgoña
  red Iberian wine — bawr-GŌN-yuh — bɔːˈrˈgoːnjə

Boris
  1. pers. name — BŌR-uhs, BAWR-uhs, BAHR-uhs — ˈboːrəs, ˈbɔːrəs, ˈbɑrəs
  2. Bulgarian — BAWR-ēs, baw-RĒS — ˈbɔːriːs, bɔːˈriːs
  3. Russian — BUHR-YĒS — ˌbərˈjiːs

Boris Godunov
  Mussorgsky opera — BŌR-uhs GŌD-n-AWF, BAWR-uhs, GAWD-n-AWF, guh-dōō-NAWF — ˌboːrəs ˈgoːdn̩ˌɔːf, ˌboːrəs, ˈgoːdn̩ˌɔːf, gəduːˈnɔːf

Borisoglebsk
  city, Russia — buh-RIS-uh-GLEPSK — bəˌrisəˈglepsk

Borlaug
  Norman E., US agricultural scientist (Nobel 1970) — BAWR-LAWG — ˈbɔːrˌlɔːg

Born
  Max, German physicist (Nobel 1954) — BAWRN — ˈbɔːrn

Borneo
  island, Asia — BAWR-nē-ō — ˈbɔːrniːoː

Bornholm
  island, Denmark — BAWRN-HŌ(L)M — ˈbɔːrn̩ˌhoː(l)m

Borodin
  Aleksandr, Russian composer, chemist — buh-RUHD-YĒN, ⑤ BAWR-uh-DĒN — bəˌrədˈjiːn, ⑤ ˌbɔːrəˈdiːn

boron
  element — BŌR-AHN, BAWR-AHN — ˈboːrˌɑn, ˈbɔːrˌɑn

Bororo
  S. American people — BŌR-uh-RŌ — ˌboːrəˈroː

Borscht Belt
  Jewish resorts, Catskill Mts., NY — BAWRSHT BELT — ˈbɔːrʃt ˌbelt

Borzoi
  dog; publisher's imprint — BAWR-ZOI — ˈbɔːrˌzɔi

Boscath
  see Bozkath

Bosch
  1. Carl, German chemist (Nobel 1931) — BAWSH, BAHSH — ˈbɔːʃ, ˈbaʃ
  2. Hieronymus, Dutch painter — BAWS, ⑤ BAHSH, BAWSH — ˈbɔːs, ⑤ ˈbaʃ, ˈbɔːʃ
  3. manufacturing co. — BAHSH, BAWSH — ˈbaʃ, ˈbɔːʃ

Bosco
  Philip Michael, *US actor* — BAHS-kō — ˈbaskoː

Bose
  1. Satyendranath, Indian scientist — BŌS, BAWS, BAWSH, BŌZ — ˈboːs, ˈbɔs, ˈbɔːʃ, ˈboːz
  2. US audio co. — BŌZ — ˈboːz

Bosley
  Tom, *US actor; pers. name* — BAHZ-lē — ˈbazliˑ

Bosna-Hercegovina
  republic, E Europe — BAHS-nuh-HERT-suh-GŌ-vē-nuh, -GŌ-vuh-nuh — ˈbasnəˈheˈrtsəˌgoːviːnə, -ˌgoːvənə

Bosnia and Herzegovina
  republic, E Europe — BAHZ-nē-uh uhn(d) HERT-suh-gō-VĒ-nuh, HERT-suh-GŌ-vuh-nuh, HUHRT- — ˈbazniːə ən(d) ˌheˈrtsəgoːˈviːnə, ˌheˈrtsəˈgoːvənə, ˌhəˈrt-

Bosor
  Biblical name — BŌ-SAWR, BŌ-SŌR — ˈboːˌsɔːr, ˈboːˌsoːr

Key (col. 2):   a: fad ā: fade ah: father ar: marry aw: law e: fed ē: feed er: merry i: hid ī: hide ō: coat ōō: boot oi: boy ow: now u: put uh: above uhr: bird ch: chop ng: ring sh: show th: thick th: this zh: measure

Bosporus
   strait, Turkey   BAHS-p(uh-)ruhs   ˈbɑsp(ə)rəs

Bosque
   county, TX   BAHS-kē   ˈbɑskiˑ

Bosque Redondo
   Indian reservation, US   BAHSK ri-DAHN-dō   ˈbɑsk riˈdɑndoː

Bosse
   Field, ballpark, Evansville, IL   BAWS, BAHS   ˈbɔːs, ˈbɑs

Bossier
   parish, LA   BŌ-zhuhr   ˈboːʒəʳ

Boston
   city, MA; mts., AR; borough, England   BAW-stuhn   ˈbɔːstən

Boston Camerata
   chamber orchestra and chorus, MA   BAW-stuhn KAHM-uh-RAHT-uh   ˌbɔːstən ˌkɑməˈrɑtə

Bostwick
   Barry, US actor   BAHS-twik   ˈbɑstwik

Boswell
   pers. name   BAHZ-WEL, -wuhl   ˈbɑzˌwel, -wəl

Bosworth Field
   English battlefield   BAHZ-wuhrth FĒLD   ˌbɑzwəʳθ ˈfiːld

Botany Bay
   inlet, former penal colony, Australia   BAHT-n-ē BĀ, BAHT-nē   ˈbɑtn̩iˑ ˈbeː, ˈbɑtniˑ

Botetourt
   county, VA   BAHT-uh-TAHT, BŌT-uh-TAWRT   ˈbɑtəˌtɑt, ˈboːtəˌtɔːʳt

Botha
   P. W., S. African political leader   BU-uh-tah, Ⓢ BŌT-uh   ˈbuətaː, Ⓢ ˈboːtə

Bothe
   Walther, German physicist (Nobel 1954)   BŌT-uh   ˈboːtə

Bothnia
   gulf, Baltic Sea   BAHTH-nē-uh   ˈbɑθniːə

Botswana
   republic, Africa   baht-SWAHN-uh   bɑtˈswɑnə

Botticelli
   Sandro, Italian artist; game   BAHT-uh-CHEL-ē   ˌbɑtəˈtʃeliˑ

Botticino
   Italian wine   BAHT-uh-CHĒ-nō   ˌbɑtəˈtʃiːnoː

Bottineau
   county, ND   BAHT-n-Ō, BAHT-uh-NŌ   ˌbɑtn̩ˈoː, ˌbɑtəˈnoː

Boubou
   bird   B̄OO-B̄OO   ˈbuːˌbuː

Boucher
   François, French painter   b̄oo-SHĀ   buːʃeː

Bouches-du-Rhône
   dept, France   b̄oosh-(uh-)due-RŌN   buːʃ(ə)dyːroːn

Boudicca [Boadicea]
   ancient British queen   b̄oo-DIK-uh   buːˈdikə

Bougainville
   island, Pacific   B̄OO-guhn-VIL, BŌ-guhn-, BUG-uhn-   ˈbuːgənˌvil, ˈboːgən-, ˈbugən-

Bougainvillea
   plant   B̄OO-guhn-VIL-yuh, BŌ-, BUG-uhn-, -VĒ-(y)uh   ˌbuːgənˈviljə, ˌboː-, ˌbugən-, -ˈviː(j)ə

Bouguereau
   Adolphe-William, French painter   b̄oo-GRŌ, b̄oo-guh-RŌ   buːgroː, buːgəroː

Boulanger
  Nadia, *French music teacher/*   bo͞o-lahⁿ-ZHĀ   buːlãʒeː
    conductor
Boulder
  city, CO   BŌL-duhr   'boːldə^r
Boule
  ancient Athenian council   BO͞O-lē, bo͞o-LĀ   'buːliˑ, buː'leː
Bouleuterion
  ancient Athenian council building   BO͞O-L(Y)O͞O-TIR-ē-AHN   ˌbuːˌl(j)uː'tiriːˌɑn
Boulez
  Pierre, *French composer, conductor*   bo͞o-LEZ   buːlez
Boulogne
  seaport, France   bo͞o-LAWN-yuh, ⓢ bo͞o-LŌN,   buːlɔːɲ , ⓢ buˑ'loːn, buˑ'lɔin
                                          bo͞o-LOIN
Boulogne-sur-Mer
  seaport, France   bo͞o-lawn-yuh-suer-MER   buːlɔːɲ syːrmer
Boult
  Sir Adrian, *English conductor*   BŌLT   'boːlt
Boumédienne
  Mohammed, *Algerian politician*   bo͞o-mād-YEN   buːmeːdjen
Boun Pimay
  Laotian festival   BŌN pim-Ī   'boːn pim'ɑi
Bourbon
  1. county, KA, KY; alcoholic   BUHR-buhn   'bɚbən
    beverage
  2. French royal family   bo͞or-BAWⁿ   buˑrbɔ̃
Bourbonnais
  prov, France   bo͞or-baw-NE, ⓢ BUR-buh-NĀ   buːrbɔːne, ⓢ ˌbu^rbə'neː
Bourgeois
  Léon, *French politician (Nobel 1920)* bur-ZHWAH   buːrʒwɑː
Bourgogne [Burgundy]
  former kingdom, region, France   bo͞or-GAWN-yuh   buːrgɔːɲ
Bourgueil
  French wine   bur-GUH(R)-yuh, ⓢ bawr-GĪ, bur-   burgœj, ⓢ bɔː^r'gɑi, bu^r-
Bourguiba
  Habib, *president, Tunisia*   bur-GĒ-buh   bu^rgiːbə
Bourj Barajneh
  Palestinian refugee camp, Beirut   BURZH buh-RAHZH-nuh   'bu^rʒ bə'rɑʒnə
Bournemouth
  town, England   BAWRN-muhth, BURN-muhth   'bɔː^rnməθ, 'bu^rnməθ
Bourse
  European stock exchange   BURS, BŌRS, BAWRS   'bu^rs, 'boː^rs, 'bɔː^rs
Bouterse
  Desire, *Surinam politician*   bo͞o-TERS   buːters
Boutros
  pers. name (B. Boutros-Ghali)   BO͞O-trōs, BO͞O-truhs   'buːtroːs, 'buːtrəs
Boutros-Ghali
  Boutros, *UN Secretary General*   BO͞O-trōs-ĠAHL-ē,   ˌbuːtroːs'ɣaliˑ,
                                          ⓢ BO͞O-trōs-GAHL-ē, BO͞O-truhs-   ⓢ ˌbuːtroːs'galiˑ, ˌbuːtrəs-
Bouvet
  Norwegian island, Atlantic   BO͞O-vā   'buːveː
Bouvier
  family name   BO͞O-vē-Ā, bo͞ov-YĀ   'buːviːˌeː, buːv'jeː
Bouvier des Flandres
  dog breed   BO͞O-vē-Ā duh FLAN-duhrz, FLAHⁿDR ˌbuːviːˑeː də 'flændə^rz, 'flɑ̃dr

---

Key (col. 2):   a: fad   ā: fade   ah: father   ar: marry   aw: law   e: fed   ē: feed   er: merry   i: hid   ī: hide   ō: coat   o͞o: boot
oi: boy   ow: now   u: put   uh: above   uhr: bird   ch: chop   ng: ring   sh: show   th: thick   <u>th</u>: this   zh: measure

Bovary

Madame, *character, G. Flaubert*   bō-vah-RĒ, ⑤ BŌ-v(uh-)rē   boːvɑːriː, ⑤ 'boːv(ə)ri·

Bovet

Daniel, *Italian pharmacologist*   bō-VĀ   boː've:
(Nobel 1957)

Bowdoin

College, *ME*   BŌD-n   'boːdn̩

Bowery

district, New York City   BOW-(uh-)rē   'bɑu(ə)ri·

Bowie

1. Jim, *American soldier & pioneer;*   BOO̅-ē, BŌ-ē   'buːi·, 'boːi·
knife

2. David, *British rock musician*   BŌ-ē   'boːi·

Bowral

town, Australia   BOW-ruhl   'bɑurəl

Bowyer

pers. name   BŌ-yuhr, BOI-(y)uhr   'boːjəʳ, 'bɔi(j)əʳ

Box Butte

county, NE   BAHKS-BYOO̅T   'bɑksˌbjuːt

Boxer

dog breed   BAHK-suhr   'bɑksəʳ

Boyacá

dept, Colombia   boi-yuh-KAH   bɔijə'kɑ

Boyanup

town, Australia   BOI-(y)uh-NUHP   'bɔi(j)əˌnəp

Boyd

pers. name   BOID   'bɔid

Boyd Orr

John, *Scottish nutritionist (Nobel*   BOID AWR   'bɔid 'ɔːʳ
1949)

Boylan

John Patrick, *US record producer,*   BOI-luhn   'bɔilən
songwriter

Boyne

Irish river, battle site   BOIN   'bɔin

Boynton

pers. name   BOINT-n   'bɔintn̩

Boz

pen name of C. Dickens   BAHZ, BŌZ *(Dickens' pronunc.)*   'bɑz, 'boːz *(Dickens'*
                                                                  pronunc.)

Bozcaada

Turkish island, Aegean   BŌZ-jah-DAH   ˌboːzdʒɑ'dɑ

Bozez

Biblical name   BŌ-ZEZ, BŌ-zuhz, bōt-SETS   'boːˌzez, 'boːzəz, boːt'sets

·Bozkath, Boscath

Biblical name   BAHZ-KATH, BAHS-KATH,   'bɑzˌkæθ, 'bɑsˌkæθ, bɑt'skɑt
                   baht-SKAHT

Bozrah

1. town, CT   BAHZ-ruh   'bɑzrə
2. Biblical name   BAHZ-ruh, bahts-RAH   'bɑzrə, bɑts'rɑ

Brabançonne, La

see La Brabançonne

Brabant

former duchy of Netherlands; prov,   bruh-BANT, bruh-BAHNT   brə'bænt, brə'bɑnt
Belgium

Foreign Sounds: ue: *Fr.* **rue**, *Ger.* **füllen**   uh(r): *Fr.* **boeuf**, *Ger.* **Höhle**   <u>kh</u>: *Ger.* **ich**, *Scot.* **loch**   ḡ: *Sp.* **amigo**   v̠: *Sp.* **hablar**
hl: *Welsh* **Llanelli**.   CAPITALS: primary stress.   SMALL CAPS: secondary stress.   ⑤: U.S. pron.   ⑥: British pron.

Brabantio
  character in Othello, *Shakespeare*   bruh-BANT-ē-ō, bruh-BAN(T)-shē-ō   brə'bænti:o:, brə'bæn(t)ʃi:o:
Brachiosaurus
  dinosaur   BRAK-ē-uh-SAWR-uhs   ˌbræki:ə'sɔ:rəs
Bracknell
  Lady, *character in* The Importance   BRAK-nl, BRAK-nuhl   'bræknḷ, 'bræknəl
  of Being Earnest, *O. Wilde*
Bradbury
  Ray, *US author*   BRAD-BER-ē, BRAD-b(uh-)rē   'bræd,beri·, 'brædb(ə)ri·
Bradenton
  city, FL   BRĀD-n-tuhn   'bre:dn̩tən
Bradford
  city, PA; pers. name   BRAD-fuhrd   'brædfəʳd
Bradley
  pers. name   BRAD-lē   'brædli·
Braemar
  village, Scotland   brā-MAHR   bre:'maʳ
Braga
  prov & town, Portugal   BRAHG-uh   'bra:gə
Bragança
  prov & town, Portugal; city, Brazil   bruh-GAHⁿN-suh   brə'gãnsə
Bragg
  Sir William H. *& his son* Sir W.   BRAG   'bræg
  Lawrence, *English physicists*
  (Nobel 1915)
Brahe
  Tycho, *Danish astronomer*   BRAH-huh, Ⓢ BRAH(-hē)   'bra:hə, Ⓢ 'bra(hi:)
Brahma
  1. Hindu universal soul; Hindu god,   BRAHM-uh   'bramə
  member of supreme triad
  2. breed of cattle and fowl   BRĀ-muh, BRAHM-uh, BRAM-uh   'bre:mə, 'bramə, 'bræmə
Brahman, -min
  1. high caste Hindu   BRAHM-uhn   'bramən
  2. breed of cattle and fowl   BRĀ-muhn, BRAHM-uhn, BRAM-uhn   'bre:mən, 'bramən, 'bræmən
Brahmanic
  pert. to Brahman Hindus   bruh-MAHN-ik, bruh-MAN-ik   brə'manik, brə'mænik
Brahmanism
  religion   BRAHM-uh-NIZ-uhm, BRAH-muh-   'bramə,nizəm, 'bra:mə-
Brahmaputra
  river, Tibet, China   BRAHM-uh-P(Y)O̅O̅-truh   ˌbramə'p(j)u:trə
Brahmin
  high caste Hindu; upper-class New   BRAHM-uhn, BRAH-muhn   'bramən, 'bra:mən
  Englander
Brahmoism
  Hindu doctrine   BRAHM-uh-WIZ-uhm,   'bramə,wizəm,
       BRAH-muh-WIZ-uhm   'bra:mə,wizəm
Brahms
  Johannes, *German composer*   BRAHMS, Ⓢ BRAHMZ   'brams, Ⓢ 'bramz
Brahui
  lang., people, Pakistan   brah-HO̅O̅-ē   bra'hu:i·
Braille
  Louis, *French teacher of the blind;*   BRAH-yuh, Ⓢ BRĀL   braj, Ⓢ 'bre:l
  system of writing for the blind
Brainerd
  Community College, *MN*   BRĀ-nuhrd   'bre:nəʳd

Key (col. 2):   a: fad   ā: fade   ah: father   ar: marry   aw: law   e: fed   ē: feed   er: merry   i: hid   ī: hide   ō: coat   o̅o̅: boot
oi: boy   ow: now   u: put   uh: above   uhr: bird   ch: chop   ng: ring   sh: show   th: thick   t͟h: this   zh: measure

Braintree
  town, MA   BRĀN-trē   'breːntriː

Bramwell
  pers. name   BRAM-wuhl, -WEL   'bræmwəl, -ˌwel

Branagan
  Laura, *US singer*   BRAN-uh-guhn   'brænəgən

Branagh
  Kenneth, *Irish actor and director*   BRAN-uh, BRAN-AW   'brænə, 'brænˌɔː

Brancacci
  chapel, Italy   brahn-KAHT-chē   brɑn'kɑttʃiˑ

Branchus
  founder of the oracle at Didymas   BRANG-kuhs   'bræŋkəs

Brancusi
  Constantin, *Romanian sculptor*   BRAHN-ko͞osh, ⑤ bran-KO͞O-sē   'brɑnkuːʃ, ⑤ bræn'kuːsiˑ

Brandeis
  University, *MA*   BRAN-DĬS   'brænˌdɑis

Brandenburg
  city, Germany   BRAHN-duhn-BURK, ⑤ BRAN-duhn-BUHRG   'brɑndənˌbuʳk, ⑤ 'brændənˌbəʳg

Brandi
  pers. name   BRAN-dē   'brændiˑ

Brandis
  Jonathan, *US actor*   BRAN-duhs   'brændəs

Brando
  Marlon, *US actor*   BRAN-dō   'brændoː

Brandon
  pers. name   BRAN-duhn   'brændən

Brandt
  Willy, *W. German chancellor (Nobel 1971)*   BRAHNT, BRANT   'brɑnt, 'brænt

Brandy
  alcoholic beverage; pers. name   BRAN-dē   'brændiˑ

Branford
  pers. name   BRAN-fuhrd   'brænfəʳd

Braniff
  US airline   BRAN-uhf   'brænəf

Brant [Thayendanegea]
  Joseph, *Mohawk Indian chief*

Branting
  Karl Hjalmar, *Swedish statesman (Nobel 1921)*   BRAHNT-ing, ⑤ BRANT-ing   'brɑːntiŋ, ⑤ 'bræntiŋ

Branwen
  pers. name   BRAN-wuhn, BRAHN-, -WEN   'brænwən, 'brɑˑn-, -ˌwen

Braque
  Georges, *French painter*   BRAHK   brɑːk

Brasenose
  college, Oxford Univ.   BRĀZ-NŌZ   'breːzˌnoːz

Brasidas
  Spartan general   BRAS-uhd-uhs   'bræsədəs

Brasilia
  capital city, Brazil   bruh-ZIL-yuh, bruh-ZĒL-yuh   brə'ziljə, brə'ziːljə

Brasseurs Biere de Paris
  French beer   brah-SUHR BYER-uh duh pah-RĒ   brɑːsœr bjerə də pɑːriː

Foreign Sounds: ue: *Fr.* **rue**, *Ger.* f**ü**llen   uh(r): *Fr.* b**oeu**f, *Ger.* H**ö**hle   <u>kh</u>: *Ger.* i**ch**, *Scot.* lo**ch**   ḡ: *Sp.* ami**g**o   v̲: *Sp.* ha**b**lar
hl: *Welsh* **Ll**anelli.   CAPITALS: primary stress.   SMALL CAPS: secondary stress.   ⑤: U.S. pron.   ⓔ: British pron.

Brassin de Garde Saint Leonard
  French beer — brah-SE^n duh GAHRD se^n lā-aw-NAHR — brɑːsē də gɑːrd sē leːɔːnɑːr

Bratislava
  capital, Slovakia — BRAHT-uh-SLAHV-uh, BRAT- — ˌbratə'slavə, ˌbræt̪-

Bratsk
  city, Russia — BRAHTSK — 'brɑːtsk

Brattain
  Walter, *US physicist (Nobel 1956)* — BRAT-n — 'brætn̩

Brattleboro
  town, VT — BRAT-l-BUHR-uh, BRAT-l-BUH-ruh — 'brætl̩ˌbər-ə, 'brætl̩ˌbə-rə

Braun
  1. C. F., *German physicist (Nobel 1909);* Wernher von, *US engineer* — BROWN, ⑤ BRAWN — 'braun, ⑤ 'brɔːn
  2. housewares co. — BRAWN — 'brɔːn

Brauneberg
  German wine — BROWN-uh-BERK — 'braunəˌbeʳk

Braunschweig
  prov & town, Germany — BROWN-SHFĪK, ⑤ BROWN-SHWĪG — 'braunˌʃfaik, ⑤ 'braunˌʃwaig

Braverman
  Charles Dell, *US film producer, director* — BRĀ-vuhr-muhn — 'breːvəʳmən

Brazil
  republic, S. America — bruh-ZIL — brə'zil

Brazilian
  pert. to Brazil — bruh-ZIL-yuhn — brə'ziljən

Brazoria
  county, TX — bruh-ZŌR-ē-uh, bruh-ZAWR-ē-uh — brə'zoːriːə, brə'zɔːriːə

Brazos
  river, county, TX — BRAZ-uhs — 'bræzəs

Brazosport
  College, *TX* — BRAZ-uh-SPAWRT — 'bræzəˌspɔːʳt

Brazzaville
  city, Congo — BRAZ-uh-VIL, BRAHZ-uh-VĒL — 'bræzəˌvil, 'brazəˌviːl

Brcko
  city, Bosnia — BUHRT-skō — 'bəʳtskoː

Bream
  Julian, *British guitarist* — BRĒM — 'briːm

Breathalyser
  tdmk for an alcohol tester — BRETH-uh-LĪ-zuhr — 'breθəˌlaizəʳ

Breathed
  Berke, *US cartoonist* — BRETH-uhd — 'breθəd

Breathitt
  county, KY — BRETH-uht — 'breθət

Brébeuf
  Jean de, *French explorer* — brā-BUH(R)F — breːbœf

Brecht
  Bertolt, *German playwright/poet* — BRE<u>KHT</u>, BREKT — 'breçt, 'brekt

Breckinridge
  John C., *US vice president* — BREK-uhn-RIJ — 'brekənˌridʒ

Brecknockshire
  former county, Wales — BREK-nuhk-shuhr, BREK-NAHK-, -SHIR — 'breknəkʃəʳ, 'brekˌnak-, -ˌʃiʳ

Breda
  city, Netherlands — brā-DAH — breː'da

Key (col. 2):   a: fad   ā: fade   ah: father   ar: marry   aw: law   e: fed   ē: feed   er: merry   i: hid   ī: hide   ō: coat   ōō: boot
oi: boy   ow: now   u: put   uh: above   uhr: bird   ch: chop   ng: ring   sh: show   th: thick   <u>th</u>: this   zh: measure

Bremen
   1. city, GA, IN   BREM-uhn   'bremən
   2. city, state, Germany   BRĀ-muhn, ⓢ BREM-uhn,   'breːmən, ⓢ 'bremən,
Bremerhaven
   seaport, Germany   BRĀ-muhr-HAHF-uhn,   'breːməʳˌhafən,
                         ⓢ BREM-uhr-HAHV-uhn   ⓢ 'breməʳˌhavən
Brenau
   College, GA   BREN-OW   'brenˌɑu
Brenda
   pers. name   BREN-duh   'brendə
Brendan
   pers. name   BREN-duhn   'brendən
Bren gun
   submachine gun   BREN GUHN   'bren ˌgən
Brennan
   William Joseph, Jr., US Supreme BREN-uhn   'brenən
      Court justice
Brenner
   mtn. pass, Tirol Alps   BREN-uhr PAS   'brenəʳ 'pæs
Brent
   borough, England   BRENT   'brent
Brenton
   pers. name   BRENT-n   'brentṇ
Brescia
   1. College, KY   BRESH-uh   'breʃə
   2. prov & town, Italy   BRĀ-shuh, BRESH-uh   'breːʃə, 'breʃə
Breslau [Wrocław]
   city , Poland   BRES-LOW   'bresˌlɑu
Brest
   port, France   BREST   brest
Brest-Litovsk
   city, Belorussia   BREST-luh-TAWFSK   ˌbrestlə'tɔːfsk
Bret, Brett
   pers. name   BRET   'bret
Bretagne [Brittany]
   prov, France   bruh-TAHN-yuh   brətɑːɲ
Breton
   Celtic people, lang., Brittany BRET-n   'bretṇ
Brett
   pers. name   BRET   'bret
Breuer
   Marcel, US architect, furniture BROI(-uh)r   'brɔi(ə)ʳ
      designer
Breughel
   see Brueghel
Brevard
   county, FL; town, college, NC bruh-VAHRD   brə'vɑʳd
Brewarrina
   town, Australia   bruh-WAHR-uh-nuh   brə'warənə
Brewster
   pers. name   BROO-stuhr   'bruːstəʳ
Brezhnev
   Leonid, president, USSR   BREZH-nyuhf, BREZH-NEF   'breʒnjəf, 'breʒˌnef

---

Foreign Sounds: **ue**: *Fr.* **rue**, *Ger.* **füllen**   **uh(r)**: *Fr.* **boeuf**, *Ger.* **Höhle**   <u>kh</u>: *Ger.* i**ch**, *Scot.* lo**ch**   ḡ: *Sp.* ami**go**   v̱: *Sp.* ha**b**lar
hl: *Welsh* **Ll**anelli.   CAPITALS: primary stress.   SMALL CAPS: secondary stress.   ⓢ: U.S. pron.   ⓔ: British pron.

Brian

1. pers. name	BRĪ-uhn	'braɪən
2. Irish Gaelic	BRĒ-uhn	'briːən

Brian Boru

Irish king	BRĒ-uhn buh-ROO, BRĪ-uhn	ˌbriːən bə'ruː, ˌbraɪən

Briand

Aristide, *French statesman (Nobel 1926)*	brē-AHⁿ	briːɑ̃

Briard

dog breed	brē-AHR(D)	briː'ɑʳ(d)

Briareus

hundred-armed monster in Greek mythology	brē-AR-ē-uhs, brī-	briː'æriːəs, braɪ-

Brice

Fanny, *US entertainer; pers. name*	BRĪS	'braɪs

Bridalveil

waterfall, Yosemite National Park	BRĪD-l-VĀL	'braɪdl̩ˌveːl

Brideshead

estate in E. Waugh novels	BRĪDZ-HED	'braɪdzˌhed

Bridgeport

city, AL, CT	BRIJ-PŌRT, BRIJ-PAWRT	'brɪdʒˌpoːʳt, 'brɪdʒˌpɔːʳt

Bridget

pers. name	BRIJ-uht	'brɪdʒət

Bridgetown

city, Barbados; town, Canada	BRIJ-TOWN	'brɪdʒˌtaʊn

Bridgman

P. W., *US physicist (Nobel 1946)*	BRIJ-muhn	'brɪdʒmən

Bridlington

town, England	BRID-ling-tuhn, *(locally)* BUHR-ling-tuhn, BAW-ling-tuhn	'brɪdlɪŋtən, *(locally)* 'bəʳlɪŋtən, 'bɔːlɪŋtən

Bridport

town, England	BRID-PAWRT	'brɪdˌpɔːʳt

Brie

region, France; cheese	BRĒ	'briː

Brienz

lake, Switzerland	brē-EN(T)S	briː'en(t)s

Brienzer See [Brienz]

lake, Switzerland	brē-EN(T)-suhr ZĀ	briː'en(t)səʳ ˌzeː

Brigadoon

Lerner & Loewe musical	BRIG-uh-DOON	ˌbrɪgə'duːn

Brighton

town, England	BRĪT-n	'braɪtn̩

Brigid

pers. name	BRIJ-uhd	'brɪdʒəd

Brigitta

1. pers. name, Italian	brē-JET-tah	briː'dʒiːttɑ
2. Swedish	bri-GĒ-tah	bri'giːtɑː

Brigitte

1. pers. name	BRIJ-uht, BRIZH-uht, bruh-ZHĒT	'brɪdʒət, 'brɪʒət, brə'ʒiːt
2. French	brē-ZHĒT	briːʒiːt

Brill

E.J., *Dutch publishing co.*	BRIL	'brɪl

Brillo

tdmk for a cleaning pad	BRIL-ō	'brɪloː

Key (col. 2): a: fad ā: fade ah: father ar: marry aw: law e: fed ē: feed er: merry i: hid ī: hide ō: coat ōō: boot oi: boy ow: now u: put uh: above uhr: bird ch: chop ng: ring sh: show th: thick <u>th</u>: this zh: measure

Brindisi
   prov & town, Italy   BRIN-duh-zē, BRĒN-duh-zē   'brindəzi·, 'briːndəzi·

Brinell number/test/hardness
   measurements for metals & alloys   bruh-NEL   brə'nel

Brinkley
   David, *US news commentator*   BRING-klē   'briŋkli·

Brinley
   pers. name   BRIN-lē   'brinli·

Brinsley
   pers. name   BRINZ-lē   'brinzli·

Brisa Cerveza Ligera
   Mexican beer   BRĒ-sah ser-VĀ-sah lē-KHER-ah   'briːsɑ ser've:sɑ liː'xerɑ

Brisbane
   city, Australia   BRIZ-buhn, BRIZ-BĀN   'brizbən, 'briz‚beːn

Brisco-Hooks
   Valerie, *US Olympic track and field athlete*   BRIS-kō-HUKS   ‚briskoː'huks

Briseis
   favorite slave of Achilles   bruh-SĀ-uhs   brə'seːəs

Brises
   father of Briseis   BRĪ-sēz   'brɑisiːz

Bristol
   city, England   BRIST-l   'bristl̩

Bristol-Myers Squibb
   US pharmaceutical co.   BRIST-l-MĪ(-uh)r(z) SKWIB   ‚bristl̩‚mɑi(ə)ʳ(z) 'skwib

Britain
   kingdom, Europe   BRIT-n   'britn̩

Britannia
   literary term for Great Britain   bruh-TAN-yuh, bruh-TAN-ē-uh   brə'tænjə, brə'tæniːə

Britannic
   pert. to Britain   bruh-TAN-ik   brə'tænik

Briticism
   British English usage   BRIT-uh-SIZ-uhm, BRIT-uh-SHIZ-uhm   'briṭə‚sizəm, 'briṭə‚ʃizəm

British
   pert. to Britain   BRIT-ish   'briṭiʃ

British Columbia
   province, Canada   BRIT-ish kuh-LUHM-bē-uh   ‚briṭiʃ kə'ləmbiːə

Britisher
   person from Britain   BRIT-uh-shuhr   'briṭəʃəʳ

Britomartis
   Cretan goddess   BRIT-uh-MAHRT-uhs   ‚briṭə'mɑʳṭəs

Briton
   inhabitant of Britain   BRIT-n   'britn̩

Brittanica
   encyclopedia   bri-TAN-i-kuh   bri'tænikə

Brittany [Bretagne]
   prov, France; pers. name   BRIT-n-ē, BRIT-nē   'britn̩i·, 'britni·

Brixham
   town, England   BRIK-suhm   'briksəm

Brno
   city, Czech republic   BUHR-nō   'bəʳnoː

Brobdingnag
   fictional land created by Jonathan Swift   BRAHB-ding-NAG, BRAHB-dig-NAG   'brɑbdiŋ‚næg, 'brɑbdig‚næg

---

Foreign Sounds: ue: *Fr.* **rue**, *Ger.* f**ü**llen   uh(r): *Fr.* b**oeuf**, *Ger.* H**ö**hle   <u>kh</u>: *Ger.* i**ch**, *Scot.* lo**ch**   g̱: *Sp.* ami**g**o   v̱: *Sp.* ha**b**lar
hl: *Welsh* **Ll**anelli.   CAPITALS: primary stress.   SMALL CAPS: secondary stress.   ($): U.S. pron.   (£): British pron.

Brobdingnagian
   inhabitant of Brobdingnag   BRAHB-ding-NAG-ē-uhn,   ˌbrɑbdiŋ'næɡiːən,
                             BRAHB-dig-NAG-ē-uhn   ˌbrɑbdig'næɡiːən

Broca
   Pierre Paul, *French surgeon*   braw-KAH, ⓢ brō-KAH   brɔːkɑː, ⓢ broː'kɑ

Broca's area
   speech center of brain   brō-KAHZ   broː'kɑz

Broccoli
   Albert Romolo, *US film producer*   BRAHK-(uh-)lē   'brɑk(ə)liˑ

Brock
   Karena Diane, *ballerina*   BRAHK   'brɑk

Brodie
   pers. name   BRŌD-ē   'broːdiˑ

Brodsky
   Joseph, *Russian-born US poet*   BRAWT-ski; ⓢ BRAHT-skē,   'brɔːtsk̮ij; ⓢ 'brɑtskiˑ,
     (Nobel 1987)   BRAHD-skē   'brɑdskiˑ

Broederbond
   Afrikaner group   BRO͞OD-uhr-BAWNT,   'bruːdəʳˌbɔːnt,
                 ⓢ BRO͞OD-uhr-BAHNT, -BAHND   ⓢ 'bruˑdəʳˌbɑnt, -ˌbɑnd

Broglie, de
   Louis, *French physicist (Nobel 1929)*   duh BRAW-yuh, duh BROI   də brɔːj, də brɔi

Brokaw
   Tom, *US broadcast journalist*   BRŌ-KAW   'broːˌkɔː

Broke
   Arthur, *English poet;* Sir Philip,   BRUK   'bruk
     English naval officer

Brolin
   James, *US actor*   BRŌ-luhn   'broːlən

Brolio
   Italian wine   BRŌL-yō   'broːljoː

bromine
   element   BRŌ-MĒN   'broːˌmiːn

Bromley
   borough, England   BRUHM-lē, BRAHM-lē   'brəmliˑ, 'brɑmliˑ

Bronislaw
   pers. name   brahn-Ē-slahf, BRAHN-uhs-LAHF   brɑn'iːslɑf, 'brɑnəsˌlɑf

Bronisław
   pers. name, Polish   braw-NĒ-slahf   brɔː'niːsłɑːf

Bronowski
   Jacob, *British mathematician*   bruh-NAWF-skē, bruh-NAHF-skē   brə'nɔːfskiˑ, brə'nɑfskiˑ

Bronstein
   Arthur J., *US phonetician; pers.*   BRAHN-STĒN   'brɑnˌstiːn
     name

Brontë
   family of English authors   BRAHNT-ē, BRAHN-tā   'brɑntiˑ, 'brɑnteː

Brontosaurus
   dinosaur (Apatosaurus)   BRAHNT-uh-SAWR-uhs   ˌbrɑntə'sɔːrəs

Bronwen
   pers. name   BRAHN-wuhn, -WEN   'brɑnwən, -ˌwen

Bronwyn
   pers. name   BRAHN-wuhn   'brɑnwən

Bronx
   river, NY; borough, New York City   BRAHNGKS   'brɑŋks

Brook, Brooke
   pers. name   BRUK   'bruk

Key (col. 2):   a: **fad**   ā: **fade**   ah: **father**   ar: **marry**   aw: **law**   e: **fed**   ē: **feed**   er: **merry**   i: **hid**   ī: **hide**   ō: **coat**   o͞o: **boot**
oi: **boy**   ow: **now**   u: **put**   uh: **above**   uhr: **bird**   ch: **chop**   ng: **ring**   sh: **show**   th: **thick**   th: **this**   zh: **measure**

Brooklyn		
borough, New York City	BRUK-luhn	'bruklən
Brooks		
Van Wyck, *historian; pers. name*	BRUKS	'bruks
Broome		
county, NY	BRO͞OM, BRUM	'bruːm, 'brum
Brothers Karamazov, The		
novel, Dostoyevsky	KAR-uh-MAHD-ZAWF	ˌkærə'mɑdˌzɔːf
Brougham		
1. Henry Peter, *English statesman*	BRUM, BRO͞O(-uh)m, BRŌ(-uh)m, BRAWM	'brum, 'bruː(ə)m, 'broː(ə)m, 'brɔːm
2. carriage or automoblie	BRO͞O(-uh)m, BRŌ(-uh)m, BRAWM	'bruː(ə)m, 'broː(ə)m, 'brɔːm
Brouilly		
wine region, France	bro͞o-YĒ	bruːjiː
Broward		
county, FL	BROW-uhrd	'brɑuəʳd
Brower		
David Ross, *US conservationist*	BROW(-uh)r	'brɑu(ə)ʳ
Brown		
pers. name	BROWN	'brɑun
Browne		
Sir Thomas, *English author*	BROWN	'brɑun
Brownie		
fictional elf; pers. name	BROW-nē	'brɑuniˑ
Browning		
Robert & Elizabeth Barrett, *English poets; pers. name*	BROW-ning	'brɑuniŋ
Broz [Tito]		
Josip, *Yugoslav statesman*	BRAWZ, BRŌZ	'brɔːz, 'broːz
Brubeck		
Dave, *US jazz musician*	BRO͞O-BEK	'bruːˌbek
Bruce		
pers. name	BRO͞OS	'bruːs
Bruckner		
Anton, *Austrian composer/organist*	BRUK-nuhr	'bruknəʳ
Brueghel, Bruegel, Breughel		
family of Flemish painters	BRUH(R)-g̃uhl, [$] BROI-guhl	'brœːɣəl, [$] 'brɔigəl
Bruges		
town, Belgium	BRUEZH, BRO͞OZH	'bryːʒ, 'bruːʒ
Brugge [Bruges]		
town, Belgium	BRUEG-uh	'bryːgə
Brugh na Boinne		
prehistoric burial site, Ireland	BRO͞O nuh BOIN	ˌbruː nə 'bɔin
Bruichladdich		
Scotch whiskey	BRO͞O-ich-LAD-ē	ˌbruːitʃ'lædiˑ
Brule		
county, SD	BRO͞OL, BRO͞O-lē	'bruːl, 'bruːliˑ
Brumaire		
month, French Revolutionary calendar	brue-MER	bryːmer
Brummell		
George Bryan (Beau), *English dandy*	BRUHM-uhl	'brəməl
Brundisium		
ancient name of Brindisi	BRUHN-DIZH(-ē)-uhm	ˌbrən'diʒ(iː)əm

Foreign Sounds: ue: *Fr.* **rue**, *Ger.* **füllen** uh(r): *Fr.* **boeuf**, *Ger.* **Höhle** kh: *Ger.* **ich**, *Scot.* **loch** g̃: *Sp.* **amigo** v̲: *Sp.* **hablar** hl: *Welsh* **Llanelli**. CAPITALS: primary stress. SMALL CAPS: secondary stress. [$]: U.S. pron. [£]: British pron.

Brunei
   river, sultanate, Borneo   bru-NĪ, BROO̅-NĪ   bruˈnɑi, ˈbruːˌnɑi

Bruneian
   pert. to Brunei   bru-NĪ-uhn, BROO̅-NĪ-uhn   bruˈnɑiən, ˈbruːˌnɑiən

Brunei Darussalam
   official name for Brunei   bru-NĪ DAHR-uh-suh-LAHM   bruˈnɑi ˌdɑrəsəˈlɑm

Brunelleschi
   Filippo, *Florentine architect*   BROO̅-l-ES-kē   ˌbruːnḷˈeskiˑ

Brunhild
   German legendary heroine   BROO̅N-HILT   ˈbruːnˌhilt

Brunhilde, Brunnhilde
   German legendary heroine   broo̅n-HIL-duh   bruˑnˈhildə

Brünnhilde
   German form of Brunhilde   bruen-HIL-duh, ⑤ broo̅n-HIL-duh   bryːnˈhildə, ⑤ bruˑnˈhildə

Bruno
   1. pers. name   BROO̅-nō   ˈbruːnoː
   2. French   brue-NŌ   brynoː
   3. German, Italian, Swedish   BROO̅-nō   ˈbruːnoː
   4. Lithuanian   BRUN-aw   ˈbrunɔː

Brunswick
   city, GA, OH; prov & town, Germany   BRUHNZ-wik   ˈbrənzwik

Brussel [Brussels]
   city, Belgium   BRUES-uhl   ˈbrysəl

Brussels
   city, Belgium   BRUHS-uhlz   ˈbrəsəlz

Brussels griffon
   dog breed   BRUHS-uhlz GRIF-uhn   ˈbrəsəlz ˈgrifən

Brut
   1. cologne brand; English or French   BROO̅T   ˈbruːt
      Arthurian chronicle
   2. Welsh chronicle   BRUED, BRID, ⑤ BRIT   ˈbryd, ˈbrid, ⑤ ˈbrit

Brutus
   pers. name   BROO̅T-uhs   ˈbruːʈəs

Bruxelles [Brussels]
   city, Belgium   brue-SEL   bryːsel

Bryan
   William Jennings, *US lawyer,*   BRĪ-uhn   ˈbrɑiən
      politician; pers. name

Bryansk
   city, Russia   brē-AHN(T)SK   briːˈɑn(t)sk

Bryant
   pers. name   BRĪ-uhnt   ˈbrɑiənt

Brylcreem
   tdmk for a hair product   BRIL-KRĒM   ˈbrilˌkriːm

Bryn
   pers. name   BRIN   ˈbrin

Brynhild
   Valkyrie in Scandinavian legend   BRIN-HILD   ˈbrinˌhild

Brynley
   pers. name   BRIN-lē   ˈbrinliˑ

Bryn Mawr
   College, *town, PA*   BRIN MAWR, BRIN MAHR   ˌbrin ˈmɔːʳ, ˌbrin ˈmɑʳ

Brynmawr
   town, Wales   brin-MOWR, ⑤ brin-MOW(-uh)r   brinˈmɑur, ⑤ brinˈmɑu(ə)ʳ

Key (col. 2):   a: fad ā: fade ah: father ar: marry aw: law e: fed ē: feed er: merry i: hid ī: hide ō: coat oo̅: boot
oi: boy ow: now u: put uh: above uhr: bird ch: chop ng: ring sh: show th: thick th: this zh: measure

Brynner
  Yul, *US actor* — BRIN-uhr — 'brinə^r

Brythonic
  branch of Celtic langs — brith-AHN-ik — briθ'ɑnik

Brzezinski
  Zbigniew, *US statesman* — bruh-ZHIN-skē, bruh-ZIN-skē, buhr- — brə'ʒinskiˑ, brə'zinskiˑ, bə^r-

B'Shevat
  Jewish holiday — buh-shuh-VAHT, buhsh-VAHT — bəʃə'vɑt, bəʃ'vɑt

Bual
  Portuguese wine grape — BWAHL — 'bwɑl

Buart Nark, Buat Nak
  Buddhist holy day — BWAHT NAHK, buh-WAHT NAHK — 'bwɑˑt 'nɑk, bə'wɑˑt 'nɑk

Buber
  Martin, *philosopher* — B$\overline{OO}$-buhr — 'buːbə^r

Bucaramanga
  city, Colombia — B$\overline{OO}$-kuh-ruh-MAHNG-guh — ˌbuːkərə'mɑŋgə

Bucephalus
  horse of Alexander the Great — by$\overline{oo}$-SEF-uh-luhs — bjuː'sefələs

Buchan
  John, *Scottish author* — BUH<u>KH</u>-uhn, BUHK-uhn — 'bəxən, 'bəkən

Buchanan
  1. James, *15th US president;* James M., *US economist (Nobel 1986)* — by$\overline{oo}$-KAN-uhn, byuh- — bjuˑ'kænən, bjə-
  2. *US pl. name* — by$\overline{oo}$-KAN-uhn, buh-, byuh- — bjuˑ'kænən, bə-, bjə-

Bucharest
  city, Romania — B(Y)$\overline{OO}$-kuh-REST — 'b(j)uːkəˌrest

Buchenwald
  Nazi concentration camp, Germany — B$\overline{OO}$-<u>kh</u>uhn-VAHLT, ⑤ B$\overline{OO}$-kuhn-WAWLD — 'buːxənˌvɑlt, ⑤ 'buːkənˌwɔːld

Buchmanism
  principles of Moral Rearmament — BUHK-muh-NIZ-uhm — 'bəkməˌnizəm

Buchmanite
  one who believes in Buchmanism — BUHK-muh-NĪT — 'bəkməˌnɑit

Buchner
  Eduard, *German chemist (Nobel 1907)* — B$\overline{OO}$K-nuhr, BUK-nuhr — 'buːknə^r, 'buknə^r

Buchwald
  Art, *US columnist* — BUHK-WAWLD, BUK-WAWLD — 'bəkˌwɔːld, 'bukˌwɔːld

Buck
  Pearl S., *US author (Nobel 1938)* — BUHK — 'bək

Buckingham
  1. *borough, palace, England; county, VA* — BUHK-ing-uhm, BUHK-ing-HAM — 'bəkiŋəm, 'bəkiŋˌhæm
  2. Lindsey, *US rock musician* — BUHK-ing-HAM — 'bəkiŋˌhæm

Buckinghamshire
  county, England — BUHK-ing-uhm-shuhr, BUHK-ing-uhm-SHIR — 'bəkiŋəmʃə^r, 'bəkiŋəmˌʃi^r

Buckley
  William F., Jr., *US columnist, editor, commentator* — BUHK-lē — 'bəkliˑ

Buckminster
  pers. name — BUHK-MIN(T)-stuhr — 'bəkˌmin(t)stə^r

Buckner
  Bill, *US baseball player* — BUHK-nuhr — 'bəknə^r

Foreign Sounds: **ue**: *Fr.* **rue**, *Ger.* **füllen**   **uh(r)**: *Fr.* **boeuf**, *Ger.* **Höhle**   <u>kh</u>: *Ger.* **ich**, *Scot.* **loch**   ḡ: *Sp.* **amigo**   <u>v</u>: *Sp.* **hablar**
hl: *Welsh* **Llanelli**.   CAPITALS: primary stress.   SMALL CAPS: secondary stress.   ⑤: U.S. pron.   ⓔ: British pron.

Bucovina, Bukovina
   region, Eastern/Central Europe   B̅O̅O-kuh-V̅E-nuh   ˌbuːkə'viːnə

Bucyrus
   city, OH   byu-S̅I-ruhs   bju'sɑirəs

Bud
   pers. name   BUHD   'bəd

Budapest
   city, Hungary   B̅O̅OD-uh-PEST, B̅O̅OD-uh-PESHT,   'buːdəˌpest, 'buːdəˌpeʃt,
                 BY̅O̅OD-   'bjuːd-

Buddha
   founder of Buddhism   BUD-uh, B̅O̅OD-uh   'budə, 'buːdə

Buddha Visakha
   Buddhist holiday   BUD-uh V̲ISH-uh-kuh, B̅O̅OD-uh   'budə 'βiʃəkə, 'buːdə

Buddhism
   religion   B̅O̅OD-ɪZ-uhm, BUD-ɪZ-uhm   'buːdˌizəm, 'budˌizəm

Buddleia
   plant   BUHD-lē-uh   'bədliːə

Buddy
   pers. name   BUHD-ē   'bədiˈ

Budé
   French publisher   bue-D̅A   byːdeː

Budějovice
   see Českė Budějovice

Buduma
   lang., people, Chad   buh-D̅O̅O-muh   bə'duːmə

Budweis
   German name of Českė Budějovice   BUT-V̅IS   'butˌvais

Budweiser
   US beer   BUHD-W̅I-zuhr   'bədˌwaizəʳ

Buel, Buell
   pers. name   BY̅O̅OL, BY̅O̅O-uhl   'bjuːl, 'bjuːəl

Buena
   borough, NJ   BY̅O̅O-nuh   'bjuːnə

Buena Park
   city, CA   BY̅O̅O-nuh PAHRK   ˌbjuːnə 'pɑʳk

Buenaventura
   city, Colombia   bwā-nah-v̲ān-TY̅O̅O-rah,   bweːnaβeːn'tjuːrɑ,
                 Ⓢ BWEN-uh-ven-T(Y)UR-uh,   Ⓢ ˌbwenəven't(j)urə,
                 BWĀ-nuh-   ˌbweːnə-

Buena Vista
   1. college, county, IA; lake, mtn., CA;   BY̅O̅O-nuh VIS-tuh   ˌbjuːnə 'vistə
     city, GA, VA
   2. mtn., Costa Rica; island, Pacific   BWĀ-nuh V̅ES-tuh   ˌbweːnə 'viːstə

Buena Vista Rancheria
   Indian reservation, US   BWĀ-nuh VIS-tuh RAN-chuh-R̅E-uh   ˌbweːnə 'vistə ˌræntʃə'riːə

Buenos Aires
   prov & city, Argentina   BWĀ-nuhs AR-ēz, ER-ēz, ̅IR-ēz;   ˌbweːnəs 'æriːz, 'eriːz,
                 B̅O-nuhs   'airiːz; ˌboːnəs

Bufadora, La
   port, Mexico   lah b̅o̅o-fah-TH̅O-rah   lɑ buːfɑ'ðoːrɑ

Buffalo
   US pl. name   BUHF-uh-L̅O   'bəfəˌloː

Buffkins
   Archie Lee, *US performing arts*   BUHF-kuhnz   'bəfkənz
    administrator

Key (col. 2):   a: fad   ā: fade   ah: father   ar: marry   aw: law   e: fed   ē: feed   er: merry   i: hid   ī: hide   ō:\coat   o̅o̅: boot
oi: boy   ow: now   u: put   uh: above   uhr: bird   ch: chop   ng: ring   sh: show   th: thick   th: this   zh: measure

Bug
  river, Poland   B͞O͞OG, Ⓢ BUHG   'buːg, Ⓢ 'bəg

Buganda
  native kingdom, Uganda   b(y)o͞o-GAHN-duh   b(j)uː'gɑndə

Bugatti
  Italian car co.   bu-GAHT-ē   bu'gɑṭiˑ

Buginese
  lang., people, South Sulawesi   BUHG-uh-NĒZ, -NĒS   ˌbəgə'niːz, -'niːs
    (Celebes)

Bugloss
  plant   BY͞O͞O-GLAHS, BY͞O͞O-GLAWS   'bjuːˌglɑs, 'bjuːˌglɔːs

Buhl
  city, ID   BY͞O͞OL   'bjuːl

Buick
  US car co.   BY͞O͞O-ik   'bjuːik

Buidhe
  pers. name, Irish   B͞O͞O-uh(-_thuh_)   'buːə(ðə)

Buisson
  F. É., French educator (Nobel 1927)   bwē-SAWⁿ   bwiːsɔ̃

Buitenzorg
  city, Indonesia   BĪT-n-ZAWRG   'baitn̩ˌzɔːʳg

Bujumbura
  city, Burundi   B͞O͞O-juhm-BUR-uh   ˌbuːdʒəm'burə

Bukhara, Bokhara
  city, Uzbekistan   bo͞o-_KHAHR_-uh   buː'xɑrə

Bukharin
  Nikolai, *Russian political leader*   bo͞o-KAHR-yin   buː'kɑrjin

Bukidnon
  lang., people, Philippine Islands   bo͞o-KID-NAHN   buː'kidˌnɑn

Bukki
  Biblical name   BUK-Ī, bo͞o-KĒ   'bukˌɑi, buː'kiˑ

Bukkiah
  Biblical name   buh-KĪ-uh, B͞O͞O-kē-YAH-ho͞o   bə'kɑiə, ˌbuːkiː'jɑhuː

Bukovina
  see Bucovina

Bul
  Biblical name   BUL, B͞O͞OL   'bul, 'buːl

Bulahdelah
  town, Australia   BUL-uh-DĒ-luh   ˌbulə'diːlə

Bulbul
  bird   BUL-BUL   'bulˌbul

Bulgakov
  Mikhail, *writer*   bo͞ol-GAH-kuhf   buːl'gɑːkəf

Bulganin
  Nikolai A., *Premier, USSR*   buhl-GAHN-yēn, Ⓢ bul-GAN-uhn   bəl'gɑːnjiˑn, Ⓢ bul'gænən

Bulgar
  Bulgarian   BUHL-GAHR, BUHL-guhr   'bəlˌgɑʳ, 'bəlgəʳ

Bulgaria
  republic, Europe   buhl-GAR-ē-uh, bul-, -GER-   bəl'gæriːə, bul-, -'ger-

Bulgarian
  lang., Bulgaria; pert. to Bulgaria   BUHL-GAR-ē-uhn, bul-, -GER-   ˌbəl'gæriːən, bul-, -'ger-

Bull
  1. John, *personification of England*   BUL   'bul
  2. Olaf, *Norwegian poet;* Ole,   B͞O͞OL   'buːl
    Norwegian violinist

Foreign Sounds: ue: *Fr.* **rue**, *Ger.* **füllen**   uh(r): *Fr.* **boeuf**, *Ger.* **Höhle**   <u>kh</u>: *Ger.* **ich**, *Scot.* **loch**   ḡ: *Sp.* **amigo**   <u>v</u>: *Sp.* **hablar**
hl: *Welsh* **Llanelli.**   CAPITALS: primary stress.   SMALL CAPS: secondary stress.   Ⓢ: U.S. pron.   Ⓔ: British pron.

Bulli

   town, Australia   BUL-Ī   'bul‚aı

Bull Moose

   member of Progressive Party   bul MOOS   bul 'muːs

Bulloch

   county, GA   BUL-uhk   'bulək

Bullock

   county, AL   BUL-uhk   'bulək

Bulova

   tdmk for watches and clocks   BUL-uh-vuh   'buləvə

Bulu

   lang., people, Africa   BOO-loo   'buːluː

Bulwer-Lytton

   Edward, *English novelist*   BUL-wuhr-LIT-n   ‚bulwəʳ'lɪtn̩

Buna

   village, New Guinea   BOO-nuh   'buːnə

Bunah

   Biblical name   B(Y)OO-nuh, boo-NAH   'b(j)uːnə, buːˈnɑ

Bunche

   Ralph, *US diplomat (Nobel 1950)*   BUHNCH   'bənt∫

Buncombe

   county, NC   BUHNG-kuhm   'bəŋkəm

Bund

   pro-Nazi organization in US   BUNT, BUND, BUHND   'bunt, 'bund, 'bənd

Bundesbank

   German bank   BUN-duhs-BAHNGK, -BANGK   'bundəs‚baŋk, -‚bæŋk

Bundesliga

   German soccer league   BUN-duhs-LĒ-guh   'bundəs‚liːgə

Bundesrat

   German upper house of Parliament   BUN-duhs-RAHT   'bundəs‚rɑt

Bundestag

   German lower house of Parliament   BUN-duh-STAHG   'bundə‚stɑg

Bundesversammlung

   Austrian federal assembly   BUN-duhs-fer-ZAHM-lung   ‚bundəsferˈzɑmluŋ

Bundeswehr

   armed forces, W. Germany   BUN-duhs-VER   'bundəs‚veʳ

Bundt

   type of cake pan   BUHNT   'bənt

Bunin

   I. A., *Russian author (Nobel 1933)*   BOON-yuhn, BOON-YĒN   'buːnjən, 'buːn‚jiːn

Bunnahabhain

   distillery, Scotland   BUHN-uh-HAHV-uhn   ‚bənəˈhɑvən

Bunni

   Biblical name   BUHN-Ī, bun-Ē   'bən‚aı, bun'iː

Bunraku

   Japanese puppet theater   bun-rahk-oo   bunrɑkuː

Buñuel

   Luis, *Spanish film director*   bun-WEL   bun'wel

Bunyan

   John, *English writer;* Paul, *US*   BUHN-yuhn   'bənjən

     legendary woodsman

Bunyanesque

   pert. to Bunyan   BUHN-yuh-NESK   ‚bənjəˈnesk

Key (col. 2):   a: fad   ā: fade   ah: father   ar: marry   aw: law   e: fed   ē: feed   er: merry   i: hid   ī: hide   ō: coat   ōō: boot
oi: boy   ow: now   u: put   uh: above   uhr: bird   ch: chop   ng: ring   sh: show   th: thick   th: this   zh: measure

Buonaparte

Italian form of Bonaparte — BWAW-nah-PAHR-tā, Ⓢ BŌ-nuh-PAHRT — ˌbwɔːnɑˈpɑrteː, Ⓢ ˈboːnəˌpɑrt

Burbank

city, CA — BUHR-BANGK — ˈbərˌbæŋk

Burberry

English clothing co. — BUHR-buh-rē, BUHR-buhr-ē, Ⓢ BUHR-BER-ē — ˈbərbə-riˑ, ˈbərbər-iˑ, Ⓢ ˈbərˌberiˑ

Burdett

pers. name — buhr-DET — bərˈdet

Burdock

plant — BUHRD-uhk — ˈbərdək

Bureau

county, IL — BYOOR-ō, BYUR-ō — ˈbjuːroː, ˈbjuroː

Burger

Warren Earl, US Supreme Court justice — BUHR-guhr — ˈbərgər

Burgerbräu

German beer — BUR-guhr-BROI — ˈburgərˌbrɔi

Burgess

Anthony, British writer; pers. name — BUHR-juhs — ˈbərdʒəs

Burghardt

pers. name — BUHRG-HAHRT — ˈbərgˌhɑrt

Burghoff

Gary, US actor — BUHR-GAWF, BUHR-GAHF — ˈbərˌgɔːf, ˈbərˌgɑf

Burgos

city, Spain; cheese — BUR-ḡōs, BUR-GŌS — ˈburɣoːs, ˈburˌgoːs

Burgoyne

John, British general — BUHR-GOIN, buhr-GOIN — ˈbərˌgɔin, bərˈgɔin

Burgundian

pert. to Burgundy — buhr-GUHN-dē-uhn — bərˈgəndiːən

Burgundy

region, France; wine — BUHR-guhn-dē — ˈbərgəndiˑ

Burkina Faso

republic, Africa — bur-KĒ-nuh FAHS-ō — burˈkiːnə ˈfɑsoː

Burl

pers. name — BUHRL — ˈbərl

Burleigh

county, ND — BUHR-lē — ˈbərliˑ

Burley

city, ID — BUHR-lē — ˈbərliˑ

Burlingame

city, CA — BUHR-luhn-GĀM — ˈbərlənˌgeːm

Burma [Myanmar]

republic, Asia — BUHR-muh — ˈbərmə

Burmese

lang., Burma — BUHR-MĒZ, -MĒS — ˌbərˈmiːz, -ˈmiːs

Burnet

Sir Macfarlane, Australian virologist (Nobel 1960) — buhr-NET, BUHR-nuht — bərˈnet, ˈbərnət

Burnett

Carol, US actress, comedienne — BUHR-NET — ˌbərˈnet

Burnham

pers. name — BUHRN-uhm — ˈbərnəm

Foreign Sounds: ue: *Fr.* **rue**, *Ger.* **füllen** uh(r): *Fr.* **boeuf**, *Ger.* **Höhle** kh: *Ger.* **ich**, *Scot.* **loch** ḡ: *Sp.* **amigo** v: *Sp.* **hablar**
hl: *Welsh* **Llanelli**. CAPITALS: primary stress. SMALL CAPS: secondary stress. Ⓢ: U.S. pron. Ⓔ: British pron.

Burnham-on-Sea		
town, England	BUHR-nuhm-ahn-SĒ, -awn-SĒ	ˌbəʳnəmɑn'siː, -ɔːn'siː
Burns		
George, *US comedian; pers. name*	BUHRNZ	'bəʳnz
Burrhus		
pers. name (B. F. Skinner)	BUHR-uhs, BUH-ruhs	'bər-əs, 'bə-rəs
Burroughs		
Edgar Rice, *US writer;* William S., *US writer*	BUHR-ōz, BUH-rōz, BUHR-uhz, BUH-ruhz	'bər-oːz, 'bə-roːz, 'bər-əz, 'bə-rəz
Burroughs Wellcome		
British pharmaceutical co.	BUH-rōz WEL-kuhm, BUHR-ōz, BUH-ruhz, BUHR-uhz	'bə-roːz 'welkəm, 'bər-oːz, 'bə-rəz, 'bər-əz
Bursa		
prov & town, Turkey	bur-SAH	buʳ'sɑ
Burstyn		
Ellen, *US actress*	BUHR-stuhn	'bəʳstən
Burt		
pers. name	BUHRT	'bəʳt
Burton		
pers. name	BUHRT-n	'bəʳtn̩
Burundi		
republic, Africa	buh-RO͞ON-dē	bə'ruːndiˑ
Burundian		
pert. to Burundi	buh-RO͞ON-dē-uhn	bə'ruːndiːən
Burushaski		
lang., India, Pakistan	BUR-uh-SHAHS-kē	ˌburə'ʃɑskiˑ
Buryat		
lang., people, Russia	bur-YAHT, BUR-ē-AHT	buʳ'jɑt, 'buriːˌɑt
Bury St. Edmunds		
town, England	BER-ē suhnt ED-muhn(d)z, sānt	ˌberiː sənt 'edmən(d)z, seːnt
Buscaglia		
Leo, *US physician*	buh-SKAL-ē-uh	bə'skæliːə
Busch		
US beer; stadium, St. Louis, MO	BUSH	'buʃ
Busey		
Gary, *US actor, musician*	BYO͞O-zē, BYO͞O-sē	'bjuːziˑ, 'bjuːsiˑ
Bush		
George, *41st US president*	BUSH	'buʃ
Bushido		
code of samurai	bush-(i-)dō, [S] BUSH-i-DŌ, BO͞O-shi-DŌ	buʃ(i)doː, [S] 'buʃiˌdoː, 'buːʃiˌdoː
Bushman [San]		
lang., people, Angola	BUSH-muhn	'buʃmən
Busiris		
mythical king of Egypt	byo͞o-SĪ-ruhs	bjuː'sɑirəs
Busoni		
Ferruccio, *Italian pianist, composer*	b(y)o͞o-ZŌ-nē	b(j)uː'zoːniˑ
Busuanga		
island, Philippines	bo͞o-SWAHNG-uh	buː'swɑŋə
Butch		
pers. name	BUCH	'butʃ
Butenandt		
Adolf, *German biochemist (Nobel 1939)*	BO͞OT-n-AHNT	'buːtn̩ˌɑnt

Key (col. 2): a: fad ā: fade ah: father ar: marry aw: law e: fed ē: feed er: merry i: hid ī: hide ō: coat o͞o: boot oi: boy ow: now u: put uh: above uhr: bird ch: chop ng: ring sh: show th: thick t͟h: this zh: measure

Buteo

   hawk genus   BYOO̅T-ē-ō   'bjuːʈiː,oː

Butes

   son of Boreas   BYOO̅T-ēz   'bjuːʈiːz

Buthelezi

   Mangosuthu, *S. African leader*   BOO̅T-l-Ā-zē, BOO̅-tuh-LĀ-zē   ,buːtlˈeːziˈ, ,buːtəˈleːziˈ

Butler

   Nicholas Murray, *US educator*   BUHT-luhr   'bətləʳ
     (*Nobel 1931*); Samuel, *English*
     poet

Buto [Edjo]

   Egyptian guardian goddess   B(Y)OO̅T-ō   'b(j)uːʈoː

Butte

   city, MT; county, CA, ID, SD   BYOO̅T   'bjuːt

Buxtehude

   Dietrich, *Danish composer*   BUKS-duh-HOO̅-thuh, *Ger.*   ,buksdəˈhuːðə, *Ger.*
                                  BUK-stuh-HOO̅D-uh,   ,bukstəˈhuːdə,
                              Ⓢ BUK-stuh-HOO̅D-uh   Ⓢ 'bukstə,huːdə

Buyi [Puyi]

   lang., China   BOO̅-YĒ   'buːˈjiː

Buys Ballot

   Christoph, *Dutch meteorologist*   BUH(R)IS buh-LAWT   'bœis bəˈlɔːt

Buys Ballot's law

   air pressure principle   BĪS buh-LAHTS LAW, BĪZ   ,bais bə,lats 'lɔː, ,baiz

Buz

   Biblical name   BUHZ, BOO̅Z   'bəz, 'buːz

Buzi

   Biblical name   B(Y)OO̅-ZĪ, boo̅-ZĒ   'b(j)uː,zai, buːˈziː

Buzite

   Biblical name   B(Y)OO̅-ZĪT   'b(j)uː,zait

Buzyges

   mythical inventor of the yoke   byoo̅-ZĪ-jēz   bjuˈzaidʒiːz

Buzz

   pers. name   BUHZ   'bəz

Buzzards Bay

   inlet, town, MA   BUHZ-uhrdz BĀ   ,bəzəʳdz 'beː

BVD

   brand of underwear   BĒ-vē-DĒ   ,biːviːˈdiː

Byblis

   daughter of Miletus   BIB-luhs   'bibləs

Byblos

   ancient Phoenician seaport   BIB-luhs   'bibləs

Bydgoszcz

   prov & town, Poland   BID-GAWSH(CH)   'bid,gɔːʃ(tʃ)

Byelorussia [Belarus]

   republic, E. Europe   BYEL-ō-RUHSH-uh, bē-EL-ō-   ,bjeloːˈrəʃə, biːˌeloː-

Byelorussian [Belo-, Bielo-]

   lang., Belorussia, Poland   bē-EL-ō-RUHSH-uhn, BYEL-ō-   biːˌeloːˈrəʃən, ,bjeloː-

Byerly Turk

   racehorse   BĪ(-uh)r-lē TUHRK   'bai(ə)ʳliˈ 'təʳk

Byng

   Julian H.G., *English general*   BING   'biŋ

Foreign Sounds: ue: *Fr.* **rue**, *Ger.* **füllen** uh(r): *Fr.* **boeuf**, *Ger.* **Höhle** kh: *Ger.* **ich**, *Scot.* **loch** ḡ: *Sp.* **amigo** v: *Sp.* **hablar**
hl: *Welsh* **Llanelli**. CAPITALS: primary stress. SMALL CAPS: secondary stress. Ⓢ: U.S. pron. Ⓔ: British pron.

Byrd
    Richard E., *US explorer;* Robert C.,   BUHRD   'bəʳd
       US fiddler; William, *English*
       composer; pers. name

Byrne
    David, *US musician, composer*   BUHRN   'bəʳn

Byron
    George Gordon, Lord, *English*   BĪ-ruhn   'bairən
       poet; pers. name

Byronic
    pert. to Lord Byron   bī-RAHN-ik   bai'ranik

Bysshe
    pers. name (P. B. Shelley)   BISH   'biʃ

Byzantine Empire
    Eastern Roman Empire   BIZ-n-TĒN, buh-ZAN-, BĪZ-n-;   'bizn̩,tiːn, bə'zæn-, 'baizn̩-;
                       BIZ-n-TĪN   'bizn̩,tain

Byzantinism
    political doctrine   buh-ZAN-tuh-NIZ-uhm,   bə'zæntə,nizəm,
                       -ZANT-n-IZ-uhm   -'zæntn̩,izəm

Byzantium
    ancient name for Istanbul   buh-ZAN-sh(ē-)uhm, -ZANT-ē-uhm   bə'zænʃ(iː)əm, -'zæntiːəm

Byzas
    founder of Byzantium   BĪ-zuhs, BĒ-zuhs   'baizəs, 'biːzəs

C

Cadca
    town, Slovakia   CHAHT-sah   'tʃatsa

Caacupé
    town, Paraguay   kah-ah-ko͞o-PĀ   ka-akuː'peː

Caaguazú
    department, Paraguay   kah-ah-gwah-SO͞O   ka-agwa'suː

Caamaño
    José María Plácido, *Ecuadorian*   kah-ahm-AHN-yō   ka-am'anjoː
       politician

Caan
    James, *US actor, director*   KAHN   'kan

Caazapá
    department, Paraguay   kah-ah-sah-PAH   ka-asa'pa

Cab
    pers. name (C. Calloway)   KAB   'kæb

Cabañas
    department, El Salvador; city, Cuba   kah-V̲AHN-yahs   ka'βanjas

Cabanatuan
    municipality, Philippines   kah-v̲ah-nah-TWAHN   kaβana'twan

---

Key (col. 2):   a: fad   ā: fade   ah: father   ar: marry   aw: law   e: fed   ē: feed   er: merry   i: hid   ī: hide   ō: coat   o͞o: boot
oi: boy   ow: now   u: put   uh: above   uhr: bird   ch: chop   ng: ring   sh: show   th: thick   th̲: this   zh: measure

Cabarroquis
  municipality, Philippines kah-<u>v</u>ahr-RŌ-kēs kaβɑr'roːkiːs

Cabarrus
  county, NC kuh-BAR-uhs, kuh-BER-uhs kə'bærəs, kə'berəs

Cabazon Band
  N. American people KAB-uh-ZŌN, KAB-uh-ZŌN 'kæbə¸zoːn, ¸kæbə'zoːn

Cabbo Delgado
  province, Mozambique KAHB-o͞o del-GAHD-o͞o 'kɑbuː del'gɑduː

Cabbon
  Biblical name KAB-uhn, kah-BŌN 'kæbən, kɑ'boːn

Cabeço Rainha
  mountain, Portugal kuh-BĀ-so͞o RĨN-yuh kə'beːsuː 'rɑinjə

Cabell
  James Branch, *US author; county,* KAB-uhl 'kæbəl
  WV; *pers. name*

Cabernet
  wine variety KAB-uhr-NĀ, -NE ¸kæbə^r'neː, -'ne

Cabeza de Vaca
  Álvar Núñez, *Spanish explorer* kah-VĀ-thah thā VAHK-ah kɑ'βeːθɑ ðeː 'βɑkɑ

Cabinda [Kabinda]
  district, province, region, Angola kuh-BIN-duh kə'bində

Cabiri, Cabeiri
  mysterious Greek divinities kuh-BIR-ē kə'biri·

Cabo Delgado
  cape, province, Mozambique KAH-bō del-GAHD-ō 'kaboː del'gadoː

Cabot
  notable American family; pers. name KAB-uht 'kæbət

Cabral
  Pedro, *Portuguese navigator* kuh-BRAHL kə'brɑl

Cabreira
  mtn. peak, Portugal kahb-RĀ-ruh kɑb'reːrə

Cabrillo
  College, *CA* kuh-BRĒ-(y)ō kə'briː(j)oː

Cabrini
  Frances X. (Mother), *US nun;* kuh-BRĒ-nē, ka- kə'briːni·, kæ-
  College, *PA*

Cabul
  Biblical name KĀ-buhl, kahv-O͞OL 'keːbəl, kav'uːl

Caca
  pre-Roman goddess of the hearth KĀ-kuh, KAHK-uh 'keːkə, 'kakə

Čačak, Cjachak
  town, Serbia CHAH-CHAHK 'tʃaˌtʃak

Cacao
  plant kuh-KOW, kuh-KĀ-ō kə'kau, kə'keːoː

Caccia
  cape, Italy KAHCH-uh 'katʃə

Cáceres
  prov & town, Spain KAHTH-uh-rās, KAHS-uh-rās 'kaθəreːs, 'kasəreːs

Cachalote
  South American bird KASH-uh-LŌT 'kæʃəˌloːt

Cacharel
  perfume KASH-uh-REL ¸kæʃə'rel

Cache
  river, AR; county, UT KASH 'kæʃ

Foreign Sounds: ue: *Fr.* **rue**, *Ger.* **füllen** uh(r): *Fr.* **boeuf**, *Ger.* **Höhle** <u>kh</u>: *Ger.* **ich**, *Scot.* **loch** ḡ: *Sp.* **amigo** <u>v</u>: *Sp.* **hablar**
hl: *Welsh* **Llanelli**. CAPITALS: primary stress. SMALL CAPS: secondary stress. ⑤: U.S. pron. ⑥: British pron.

Cache la Poudre
　river, Colorado　　　KASH luh POOD-uhr　　　ˌkæʃ lə 'puːdəʳ

Cacheu
　region, Guinea-Bissau　　　KAHSH-oo　　　'kaʃuː

Cachí, Nevado de
　peak, Argentina　　　nä-VAHTH-ō the kah-CHĒ　　　neː'vaðoː ðe kaˈtʃiː

Caciocavallo
　Italian cheese　　　KAH-chō-kuh-VAHL-ō　　　ˌkatʃoːkəˈvaloː

Cacique
　Native American chief or political　　　kuh-SĒK　　　kəˈsiːk
　　boss in the Hispanic Americas

Cacus
　pre-Roman fire god　　　KĀ-kuhs　　　'keːkəs

Cadbury
　British candy co.　　　KAD-b(uh-)rē, ⑤ KAD-BER-ē　　　'kædb(ə)riˑ, ⑤ 'kædˌberiˑ

CAD-CAM
　computer design system　　　KAD-KAM　　　'kædˌkæm

Caddo
　N. American people; parish, LA;　　　KAD-ō　　　'kædoː
　　county, OK

Caddom
　N. American people　　　KAD-uhm　　　'kædəm

Cadillac
　1. city, MI; US car make　　　KAD-l-AK　　　'kædl̩ˌæk
　2. Antoine de La Mothe, Sieur de,　　　kah-dē-YAHK, ⑤ KAD-l-AK　　　kaːdiˑjaːk, ⑤ 'kædl̩ˌæk
　　French colonialist

Cadiz
　1. city, KY　　　KĀD-iz　　　'keːdiz
　2. village, OH　　　KAD-iz　　　'kædiz
　3. city, Philippines　　　KAHD-ēs　　　'kadiːs

Cádiz, Cadiz
　prov & town, Spain　　　KAH-thēth, KAH-thēs, ⑤ kuh-DIZ,　　　'kaðiːθ, 'kaðiːs, ⑤ kəˈdiz,
　　　　　　KĀD-iz, KAHD-iz, KAD-iz　　　　　'keːdiz, 'kadiz, 'kædiz

Cadmean
　pert. to Cadmus　　　KAD-mē-uhn　　　'kædmiːən

cadmium
　element　　　KAD-mē-uhm　　　'kædmiːəm

Cadmus
　mythical founder of Thebes; pers.　　　KAD-muhs　　　'kædməs
　　name

Cadogan
　pers. name　　　kuh-DUHG-uhn　　　kəˈdəgən

Cadwallader
　pers. name　　　kad-WAHL-uhd-uhr, kuhd-　　　kædˈwalədəʳ, kəd-

Caecilius
　Roman name　　　suh-SIL-ē-uhs, kī-KIL-ē-uhs　　　səˈsiliːəs, kaiˈkiliːəs

Caeculus
　founder of Praeneste　　　SĒ-kyuh-luhs　　　'siːkjələs

Caecus
　Roman cognomen　　　SĒ-kuhs, KĪ-kuhs　　　'siːkəs, 'kaikəs

Caedmon
　Anglo-Saxon poet　　　KAD-muhn　　　'kædmən

Caedmonian
　pert. to Caedmon　　　kad-MŌ-nē-uhn　　　kædˈmoːniːən

Key (col. 2): a: fad ā: fade ah: father ar: marry aw: law e: fed ē: feed er: merry i: hid ī: hide ō: coat oo: boot
oi: boy ow: now u: put uh: above uhr: bird ch: chop ng: ring sh: show th: thick th: this zh: measure

Caelian		
hill, Rome, Italy	SĒ-lē-uhn	'siːliːən
Caelius		
Roman name	SĒ-lē-uhs, KĪ-lē-uhs	'siːliːəs, 'kɑiliːəs
Caelum		
constellation	SĒ-luhm	'siːləm
Caelus		
personification of the sky	SĒ-luhs, KĪ-luhs	'siːləs, 'kɑiləs
Caen		
city, France	KAH^{n}, [$] KAHN	kɑ̃, [$] 'kɑn
Caerdydd [Cardiff]		
city, Wales	kīr-DĒTH	kɑir'diːð
Caerleon		
district, Wales	kahr-LĒ-uhn	kɑ^{r}'liːən
Caernarfon, -von		
town, Wales	kahr-NAHR-vuhn, kuhr-NAHR-vuhn	kɑ^{r}'nɑ^{r}vən, kə^{r}'nɑ^{r}vən
Caernarvonshire		
former county, Wales	kuhr-NAHR-vuhn-shuhr, kahr-, -SHIR	kə^{r}'nɑ^{r}vənʃə^{r}, kɑ^{r}-, -ˌʃi^{r}
Caerphilly		
town, Wales; cheese	kīr-FIL-ē	kɑi^{r}'fili·
Caesar		
Julius, *Roman general & statesman; pers. name*	SĒ-zuhr	'siːzə^{r}
Caesarea		
ancient city, Middle East	SĒ-zuh-RĒ-uh, SES-uh-RĒ-uh, SEZ-uh-RĒ-uh	ˌsiːzə'riːə, ˌsesə'riːə, ˌsezə'riːə
Caesarean		
pert. to Caesar; *surgical birth*	si-ZAR-ē-uhn, si-ZER-ē-uhn	si'zæriːən, si'zeriːən
Caesarea Philippi		
Biblical name	SĒ-zuh-RĒ-uh FIL-uh-PĪ, SES-uh-, SEZ-uh-, fuh-LIP-Ī	ˌsiːzə'riːə 'filəˌpɑi, ˌsesə-, ˌsezə-, fə'lipˌɑi
Cagayan		
river, Philippines	KAHG-uh-YAHN	ˌkɑgə'jɑn
Cagayan de Oro		
city, Philippines	KAHG-uh-YAHN dā ŌR-ō	ˌkɑgə'jɑn deː 'oːroː
Cagliari		
prov & town, Italy	KAHL-yuh-rē	'kɑljəri·
Cagliostro		
Alessandro di Conte, *Italian adventurer*	kahl-YŌ-strō, kal-YŌ-strō	kɑl'joːstroː, kæl'joːstroː
Cagney		
James, *US actor*	KAG-NĒ	'kægˌni·
Caguas		
city, Puerto Rico	KAHḠ-WAHS	'kɑɣˌwɑs
Cahenslyism		
Catholic ethnic-group plan	kuh-HENZ-lē-IZ-uhm, -HENS-	kə'henzliːˌizəm, -'hens-
Cahil Dehe Band		
N. American people	kuh-HĒL DĀ-hā	kə'hiːl 'deːheː
Cahn		
Sammy, *US lyric songwriter*	KAHN	'kɑn
Cahors		
town, France	kah-AWR	kɑɔːr
Cahto		
N. American people	KAHT-ō	'kɑtoː

Foreign Sounds: ue: *Fr.* **rue**, *Ger.* **füllen** uh(r): *Fr.* **boeuf**, *Ger.* **Höhle** kh: *Ger.* **ich**, *Scot.* **loch** ḡ: *Sp.* amigo v̲: *Sp.* **hablar** hl: *Welsh* **Llanelli**. CAPITALS: primary stress. SMALL CAPS: secondary stress. [$]: U.S. pron. [£]: British pron.

Cahuilla
  N. American people   kuh-WĒ-uh   kə'wiːə

Caiaphas
  Biblical name   KĪ-uh-fuhs   'kaiəfəs

Caicos
  islands, Bahamas   KĀ-kuhs, KĪ-kōs   'keːkəs, 'kaikoːs

Caillié, Caillé
  René Auguste, *French explorer*   kah-YĀ   kaːjeː

Cain
  Biblical name   KĀN, KAH-yin   'keːn, 'kajin

Cainan
  Biblical name   kā-Ī-nuhn, KĀ-nuhn, kā-NAHN   keː'ainən, 'keːnən, keː'nan

Caingang
  S. American people   KĪN-GANG   'kain,gæŋ

Cainism
  Gnostic heresy   KĀ-NIZ-uhm   'keː,nizəm

Cairngorm
  mtn. & mtn. range, Scotland   KARN-GAWRM, KERN-GAWRM   'kæʳn,gɔːʳm, 'keʳn,gɔːʳm

Cairns
  seaport, Australia   KARNZ, KERNZ   'kæʳnz, 'keʳnz

Cairo
  1. city, Egypt   KĪ-rō   'kairoː
  2. city, GA, IL   KER-ō, KĀ-rō   'keroː, 'keːroː

Cair Paravel
  fictional castle, C.S. Lewis   KĪR PAR-uh-VEL   ,kaiʳ ,pærə'vel

Caithness
  district, Scotland   KĀTH-nes, KĀTH-nuhs, kāth-NES   'keːθnes, 'keːθnəs, keːθ'nes

Caitlin
  pers. name   KĀT-luhn   'keːtlən

Caius
  1. pers. name   KĀ-uhs, KĪ-uhs   'keːəs, 'kaiəs
  2. Gonville and Caius College,   KĒZ   'kiːz
    Cambridge University

Cajamarca, Caxamarca
  department, Peru   KAH-huh-MAHR-kuh   ,kahə'maʳkə

Cajun
  French Catholic from Arcadia, in LA   KĀ-juhn   'keːdʒən

Cakchiquel
  lang.. Cen. America   KAHK-chi-KEL, KAHK-chi-KEL   ,kaktʃi'kel, 'kaktʃi,kel

Çakmak
  Fevzi, *Turkish soldier and politician*   chahk-MAHK   tʃak'mak

Čakste
  Janis, *president of Latvia*   CHAHK-stuh   'tʃakstə

Calabar
  port, Nigeria   KAL-uh-BAHR, KAL-uh-BAHR   'kælə,baʳ, ,kælə'baʳ

Calabria
  region, Italy   kuh-LĀ-brē-uh, kuh-LAHB-rē-uh   kə'leːbriːə, kə'labriːə

Caladium
  plant   kuh-LĀD-ē-uhm   kə'leːdiːəm

Calah
  Biblical name   KĀ-luh, KAL-uh, KAHL-ah<u>kh</u>   'keːlə, 'kælə, 'kalax

Calais
  1. seaport, France   kah-LE, ⑤ ka-LĀ, KAL-ā   kaˑle, ⑤ kæ'leː, 'kæleː
  2. city, ME   KAL-uhs   'kæləs

Key (col. 2):   a: fad   ā: fade   ah: father   ar: marry   aw: law   e: fed   ē: feed   er: merry   i: hid   ī: hide   ō: coat   ōō: boot
oi: boy   ow: now   u: put   uh: above   uhr: bird   ch: chop   ng: ring   sh: show   th: thick   <u>th</u>: this   zh: measure

Calamus
plant   KAL-uh-muhs   'kæləməs

Calapan
municipality, Philippines   KAHL-uh-PAHN   ˌkɑlə'pɑn

Călăraşi
county, Romania   kuh-luh-RAHSH(-ē)   kələ'raʃ(iˑ)

Calaveras
river, county, CA; warbler   KAL-uh-VER-uhs   ˌkælə'verəs

Calcasieu
river, parish, LA   KAL-kuh-SHOO   'kælkəˌʃuː

Calceolaria
plant   KAL-sē-uh-LAR-ē-uh   ˌkælsiːə'læriːə

Calchas
Greek seer during Trojan War   KAL-kuhs   'kælkəs

calcium
element   KAL-sē-uhm   'kælsiːəm

Calcol
Biblical name   KAL-KAHL, KAL-KAWL, kahl-KAWL   'kælˌkɑl, 'kælˌkɔːl, kɑl'kɔːl

Calcutta
city, India   kal-KUHT-uh   kæl'kətə

Caldas
department, Colombia   KAHL-duhs   'kɑldəs

Caldecott
children's book award for illustrators   KAWL-duh-KAHT   'kɔːldəˌkɑt

Caldecott
Randolph, *English artist and illustrator*   KAWL-duh-kuht   'kɔːldəkət

Calder
Alexander Milne, *US sculptor*   KAWL-duhr   'kɔːldəʳ

Calderón de la Barca
Pedro, *Spanish dramatist and poet*   KAHL-duh-RŌN dā lah VAHR-kah   ˌkɑldə'roːn deː la 'βaʳka

Caldus
Roman cognomen   KAWL-duhs   'kɔːldəs

Caleb
pers. name   KĀ-luhb   'keːləb

Caledonia
ancient name for Scotland; US pl. name   KAL-uh-DŌN-yuh, KAL-uh-DŌ-nē-uh   ˌkælə'doːnjə, ˌkælə'doːniːə

Caledonian
pert. to Caledonia   KAL-uh-DŌN-yuhn, KAL-uh-DŌ-nē-uhn   ˌkælə'doːnjən, ˌkælə'doːniːən

Calendula
plant   kuh-LEN-juh-luh   kə'lendʒələ

Calfee Park
Pulaski, VA   KAF-ē   'kæfiˑ

Calgary
city, Canada   KAL-guh-rē   'kælgəriˑ

Calgon
US cleaning products co.   KAL-GAHN, KAL-guhn   'kælˌgɑn, 'kælgən

Calhoun
John C., *US politician; US pl. name; pers. name*   kal-HOON, KAL-HOON, kuh-HOON   kæl'huːn, 'kælˌhuːn, kə'huːn

Cali
city, Colombia   KAHL-ē   'kɑliˑ

Caliari [Veronese]
Paolo, *Venetian painter*   kahl-YAHR-ē   kɑl'jɑriˑ

Foreign Sounds: ue: *Fr.* **rue**, *Ger.* **füllen**   uh(r): *Fr.* **boeuf**, *Ger.* **Höhle**   kh: *Ger.* **ich**, *Scot.* **loch**   ḡ: *Sp.* **amigo**   v̲: *Sp.* **hablar**
hl: *Welsh* **Llanelli**.   CAPITALS: primary stress.   SMALL CAPS: secondary stress.   Ⓢ: U.S. pron.   Ⓔ: British pron.

Caliban
   slave in The Tempest, *Shakespeare*   KAL-uh-BAN   'kælə‚bæn
Calicut
   city, India   KAL-i-kuht   'kælikət
California
   state, US; gulf, Mexico   KAL-uh-FAWRN-yuh   ‚kælə'fɔːᶦnjə
Californio
   resident of California   KAL-uh-FAWRN-yō   ‚kælə'fɔːᶦnjoː
californium
   element   KAL-uh-FAWR-nē-uhm   ‚kælə'fɔːᶦniːəm
Caligula
   Roman emperor   kuh-LIG-yuh-luh   kə'ligjələ
Călinescu
   Armand, *Romanian politician*   kuh-lē-NES-kōō   kəliː'neskuː
Calixto
   pers. name   kah-LĒ(K)S-tō   kɑ'liː(k)stoː
Calixtus
   pope   kuh-LIK-stuhs   kə'likstəs
Calla
   plant   KAL-uh   'kælə
Callao
   prov & town, Peru   kuh-YAH-ō, kuh-YOW   kə'jɑoː, kə'jɑu
Callao
   city, constitutional province, Peru   kuh-YOW, kuh-YAH-ō   kə'jɑu, kə'jɑoː
Callas
   Maria, *US soprano*   KAL-uhs   'kæləs
Calles
   Plutarco Elías, *Mexican politician*   KAH-yās   'kɑjeːs
Calley
   William L., Jr., *US officer at My Lai*   KA-lē   'kæli·
Callias
   Peace of, *Athenian-Persian pact*   KAL-ē-uhs   'kæliːəs
Callimachus
   Greek poet   kuh-LIM-uh-kuhs   kə'liməkəs
Calliope
   1. muse of epic poetry; hummingbird   kuh-LĪ-uh-pē   kə'lɑiəpi·
   2. street, New Orleans   KAL-ē-ŌP   'kæliː‚oːp
Callirhoe
   mother of Geryon and Echidna   kuh-LIR-uh-wē   kə'lirəwi·
Callisto
   nymph loved by Zeus; satellite of   kuh-LIS-tō   kə'listoː
      Jupiter
Callistus
   pope   kuh-LIS-tuhs   kə'listəs
Callot
   Jacques, *French painter/engraver*   kah-LŌ   kɑːloː
Calloway
   Cab, *US jazz singer*   KAL-uh-WĀ   'kælə‚weː
Calneh
   Biblical name   KAL-nuh, kahl-NE   'kælnə, kɑl'ne
Calno
   Biblical name   KAL-nō, kahl-NŌ   'kælnoː, kɑl'noː
Caloosahatchee
   National Wildlife Refuge, river, FL   kuh-LŌŌ-suh-HACH-ē   kə‚luːsə'hætʃi·

Key (col. 2): a: fad ā: fade ah: father ar: marry aw: law e: fed ē: feed er: merry i: hid ī: hide ō: coat ōō: boot
oi: boy   ow: now   u: put   uh: above   uhr: bird   ch: chop   ng: ring   sh: show   th: thick   <u>th</u>: this   zh: measure

Caloris
  basin on Mercury kuh-LŌR-uhs, -LAWR- kə'lo:rəs, -'lɔ:r-
Calotrope
  plant KAL-uh-TRŌP 'kælə,tro:p
Calphalon
  tdmk for cookware KAL-fuh-LAHN 'kælfə,lɑn
Calpurnia
  Julius Caesar's wife kal-PUHR-nē-uh kæl'pəʳni:ə
Calpurnius
  pers. name, Latin kal-PUHR-nē-uhs kæl'pəʳni:əs
Caltanissetta
  province, Italy KAHL-tuh-ni-SET-uh ,kɑltəni'seţə
Calumet
  river, lake, harbor, Chicago, IL; KAL-yuh-MET, KAL-yuh-muht 'kæljə,met, 'kæljəmət
  county, WI; industrial area, IN, IL
Calumet City
  city, IL KAL-yuh-MET SIT-ē, KAL-yuh-muht ,kæljə,met 'siţi·, ,kæljəmət
Calumet Farm
  horse-breeding farm, KY KAL-yuh-MET FAHRM, KAL-yuh-muht ,kæljə,met 'fɑʳm, ,kæljəmət
Calusa
  N. American people kuh-LOO-suh kə'lu:sə
Calvados
  dept, France; apple brandy kahl-vah-DŌS, Ⓢ KAL-vuh-DŌS, kɑ:lvɑ:do:s, Ⓢ ,kælvə'do:s,
  -DAWS, -DAHS -'dɔ:s, -'dɑs
Calvary [Golgotha]
  site of Christ's crucifixion KAL-v(uh-)rē 'kælv(ə)ri·
Calvert
  pers. name KAL-vuhrt 'kælvəʳt
Calvin
  John, *French theologian;* Melvin, *US* KAL-vuhn 'kælvən
  chemist (Nobel 1961); pers. name
Calvinism
  religion KAL-vuh-NIZ-uhm 'kælvə,nizəm
Calvinist
  one who adheres to Calvinism KAL-vuh-nuhst 'kælvənəst
Calvino
  Italo, *writer* kahl-VĒ-nō, kal-VĒ-nō kɑl'vi:no:, kæl'vi:no:
Calvo
  Paul MacDonald, *US governor,* KAL-vō 'kælvo:
  Guam
Calvus
  Roman cognomen KAL-vuhs 'kælvəs
Calydon
  ancient city, Greece KAL-uh-DAHN, KAL-uhd-n 'kælə,dɑn, 'kælədṇ
Calypso
  lover of Odysseus; style of West kuh-LIP-sō kə'lipso:
  Indian music
Cam
  river, Cambridgeshire, England KAM 'kæm
Cam
  see Cão
Camacan
  S. American people KAHM-uh-KAHN ,kɑmə'kɑn
Camagüey
  prov & town, Cuba KAHM-uh-GWĀ, KAM-uh-GWĀ ,kɑmə'gwe:, ,kæmə'gwe:

Foreign Sounds: ue: *Fr.* **rue**, *Ger.* **füllen** uh(r): *Fr.* **boeuf**, *Ger.* **Höhle** kh: *Ger.* **ich**, *Scot.* **loch** g̅: *Sp.* **amigo** v̄: *Sp.* **hablar**
hl: *Welsh* **Llanelli**. CAPITALS: primary stress. SMALL CAPS: secondary stress. Ⓢ: U.S. pron. Ⓔ: British pron.

Camaldolites
   religious order   kuh-MAL-duh-LĪTS   kə'mældə,laits

Camarasaurus
   dinosaur   KAM-uh-ruh-SAWR-uhs   ˌkæmərə'sɔːrəs

Camargue, La
   island, Rhone river, France   lah kah-MAHRG   lɑː kɑːmɑːrg

Camas
   county, ID; city, WA   KAM-uhs   'kæməs

Camarines Norte
   province, Philippines   KAHM-uh-RĒ-nuhs NŌR-tā   ˌkaməˌriːnəs 'noːʳteː

Camarines Sur
   province, Philippines   KAHM-uh-RĒ-nuhs SUR   ˌkaməˌriːnəs 'suʳ

Cambodia [Kampuchea]
   republic, SE Asia   kam-BŌD-ē-uh   kæm'boːdiːə

Cambodian [Khmer]
   lang., people, Indochina   kam-BŌD-ē-uhn   kæm'boːdiːən

Cambrai
   city, France   kahⁿ-BRE   kãbre

Cambria
   county, PA; Latin & poetic name for   KAM-brē-uh   'kæmbriːə
     Wales

Cambria Heights
   Queens, New York City   KĀM-brē-uh HĪTS   ˌkeːmbriːə 'haits

Cambrian
   mtn. range, Wales; geologic period   KAM-brē-uhn, KĀM-brē-uhn   'kæmbriːən, 'keːmbriːən

Cambridge
   city, MA; city, university, England   KĀM-brij   'keːmbridʒ

Cambridgeshire
   county, England   KĀM-brij-shuhr, -SHIR   'keːmbridʒʃəʳ, -ˌʃiʳ

Cambunian
   Mountains, *mtn. range, Greece*   kam-BYŌŌ-nē-uhn   kæm'bjuːniːən

Cambyses
   Persian king   kam-BĪ-SĒZ   kæm'baiˌsiːz

Camden
   city, NJ, ME; borough, England   KAM-duhn   'kæmdən

Camelia
   pers. name   kuh-MĒL-yuh   kə'miːljə

Camellia
   flower   kuh-MĒL-yuh   kə'miːljə

Camelopardalis
   constellation   kuh-MEL-uh-PAHRD-l-uhs, KAM-uh-lō-   kəˌmelə'paʳdl̩əs, ˌkæməloː-

Camelot
   site of King Arthur's court   KAM-uh-LAHT   'kæməˌlat

Camembert
   village, France; cheese   kah-mem-BER, ⓢ KAM-uhm-BER   kɑːmember, ⓢ 'kæməmˌbeʳ

Camenae
   prophetic nymphs of Roman springs   kuh-MĒ-nē   kə'miːniˑ

Camerata Bern
   chamber orchestra, Switzerland   KAHM-uh-RAHT-uh BERN   ˌkamə'raṭə 'beʳn

Cameron
   univ., OK; pl. name, US; pers. name   KAM-(uh-)ruhn   'kæm(ə)rən

Cameroon
   republic, Africa   KAM-uh-RŌŌN   ˌkæmə'ruːn

Cameroonian
   pert. to Cameroon   KAM-uh-RŌŌ-nē-uhn   ˌkæmə'ruːniːən

Key (col. 2):   a: **fad**   ā: **fade**   ah: **father**   ar: **marry**   aw: **law**   e: **fed**   ē: **feed**   er: **merry**   i: **hid**   ī: **hide**   ō: **coat**   ōō: **boot**
oi: **boy**   ow: **now**   u: **put**   uh: **above**   uhr: **bird**   ch: **chop**   ng: **ring**   sh: **show**   th: **thick**   <u>th</u>: **this**   zh: **measure**

Camiguin		
island, volcano, Philippines	KAHM-uh-GWĒN, KAM-	ˌkaməˈgwiːn, ˌkæm-
Camilla		
1. female warrior who fought Aeneas; pers. name	kuh-MIL-uh	kəˈmilə
2. Italian	kah-MĒL-lah	kaˈmiːlla
3. Norwegian	kah-MIL-lah	kaˈmilla
Camille		
1. pers. name	kuh-MĒL	kəˈmiːl
2. French	kah-MĒ	kaːmiːj
Camillo		
1. pers. name, German	kah-MIL-ō	kaˈmiloː
2. Italian	kah-MĒL-lō	kaˈmiːlloː
3. Portuguese	kuh-MĒ-loo͞, kah-	kəˈmiːluː, kaː-
Camillus		
Roman cognomen	kuh-MIL-uhs	kəˈmiləs
Cammaerts		
Émile, *Belgian author*	KAHM-ahrts	kaːmaː^{r}ts
Camões, Camoëns		
Luiz de, *Portuguese poet*	kuh-MOI^{n}SH	kəˈmɔĩʃ
Camorra		
Italian secret society	kuh-MAWR-uh	kəˈmɔːrə
Camp		
pers. name	KAMP	ˈkæmp
Campa		
S. American people	KAHM-puh	ˈkampə
Campagna		
region, Italy	kahm-PAHN-yuh, kam-	kamˈpanjə, kæm-
Campanella		
Roy, *US baseball executive*	KAM-puh-NEL-uh	ˌkæmpəˈnelə
Campania		
region, Italy	kahm-PAHN-yuh, kam-PĀN-yuh, kam-PĀ-nē-uh	kamˈpanjə, kæmˈpeːnjə, kæmˈpeːniːə
Campari		
tdmk for an alcoholic drink	kahm-PAHR-ē	kamˈpa^{r}iˑ
Campbell		
ancient Scottish family; US place name; pers. name	KAM-buhl, [$] *also* KAM-uhl	ˈkæmbəl, [$] *also* ˈkæməl
Campeche		
state, city, Mexico; bay, Gulf of Mexico	kahm-PĀ-chā, [$] kam-PĒ-chē	kamˈpeːtʃeː, [$] kæmˈpiːtʃiː
Campina Grande		
city, Brazil	kah^n(m)-PĒ-nuh GRAH^n(N)-duh	kã(m)ˈpiːnə ˈgrã(n)də
Campinas		
city, Brazil	kah^n(m)-PĒ-nuhs	kã(m)ˈpiːnəs
Campion		
Thomas, *English poet & composer*	KAM-pē-uhn, KAM-pyuhn	ˈkæmpiːən, ˈkæmpjən
Campobasso		
province, Italy	KAHM-pō-BAHS-sō	ˌkampoːˈbassoː
Campobello		
island, New Brunswick, Canada	KAM-puh-BEL-ō	ˌkæmpəˈbeloː
Campo Grande		
city, Brazil	KAH^n(M)-poo͞ GRAH^n(N)-duh	ˈkã(m)puː ˈgrã(n)də
Camptosaurus		
dinosaur	KAM(P)-tuh-SAWR-uhs	ˌkæm(p)təˈsɔːrəs

Camp Verde		
Indian reservation, US	kamp VUHRD-ē, VERD-ē	kæmp 'vəʳdiˑ, 'veʳdiˑ
Cam Ranh Bay		
military base, Vietnam	KAM rahn BĀ	ˌkæm rɑn 'beː
Camrose Lutheran		
College, *Canada*	KAM-RŌZ LO͞O-th(uh-)ruhn	'kæmˌroːz 'luːθ(ə)rən
Camus		
Albert, *French author (Nobel 1957)*	kah-MUE, [S] ka-MO͞O	kɑːmyː, [S] kæ'muː
Cana		
Biblical town	KĀ-nuh	'keːnə
Canaan		
Biblical name, Palestine	KĀ-nuhn	'keːnən
Canaanites		
ancient Palestinian people	KĀ-nuh-NĪTS	'keːnəˌnɑits
Canace		
daughter of Aeolus and Aenarete	KAN-uh-sē	'kænəsiˑ
Cañada		
College, *CA*	kuhn-YAHD-uh, kan-	kən'jɑdə, kæn-
Canada		
country, N. America	KAN-uhd-uh, kah-nah-DAH	'kænədə, kɑːnɑːdɑː
Canadian		
pert. to Canada	kuh-NĀD-ē-uhn	kə'neːdiːən
Çanakkale		
province, Turkey	CHAHN-uh-kuh-LĀ	ˌtʃɑnəkə'leː
Çanakkale Boğazı [Dardanelles]		
strait, Turkey	CHAHN-uh-kuh-LĀ bō-ḠAHZ-ē	ˌtʃɑnəkə'leː boː'ɣɑziˑ
Canal [Canaletto]		
Giovanni Antonio, *Venetian painter*	kah-NAHL	kɑ'nɑl
Canaletto [Canal]		
Venetian painter	KAHN-ah-LET-tō, [S] KAN-l-ET-ō	ˌkɑnɑ'lettoː, [S] ˌkænl̩'eţoː
Canandaigua		
city, lake, NY	KAN-uhn-DĀ-gwuh	ˌkænən'deːgwə
Cañar		
Ecuador	kuhn-YAHR	kən'jɑʳ
Canarias, Islas [Canary Islands]		
islands, Atlantic	ĒZ-lahs kuh-NAHR-ē-ahs	'iːzlɑs kə'nɑriːɑs
Canaries [Canary Islands]		
islands, Atlantic	kuh-NER-ēz	kə'neriˑz
Canary Islands		
islands, Atlantic	kuh-NER-ē Ī-luhn(d)z	kəˌneriˑ 'ɑilən(d)z
Canaveral		
cape, FL	kuh-NAV-(uh-)ruhl	kə'næv(ə)rəl
Canberra		
city, Australia	KAN-b(uh-)ruh, [S] KAN-BER-uh	'kænb(ə)rə, [S] 'kænˌberə
Canby		
city, MN, OR	KAN-bē	'kænbiˑ
Cancer		
constellation, sign of the zodiac	KAN-suhr	'kænsəʳ
Cancún		
city, Mexico	kan-KO͞ON	kæn'kuːn
Candace		
1. Biblical name	KAN-duh-sē, KAN-duhs, KAN-DĀS	'kændəsiː, 'kændəs, 'kænˌdeːs
2. pers. name	KAN-duhs	'kændəs

Candice
   pers. name   KAN-duhs   'kændəs
Candida
   play, G.B. Shaw   kan-DĒD-uh   kæn'diːdə
Candide
   novel, Voltaire   kahⁿ-DĒD, Ⓢ kan-DĒD   kɑ̃diːd, Ⓢ kæn'diːd
Cándido
   1. pers. name, Spanish   KAHN-dē-t͟hō   'kɑndiːðoː
   2. pers. name, Portuguese   KAHN-dē-t͟hoo   'kɑːndiːðuː
Candlemas
   Christian holy day (Feb. 2)   KAN-dl-muhs   'kændl̩məs
Canea
   town, Greece   kuh-NĒ-uh   kə'niːə
Canelones
   department, Uruguay   KAHN-uh-LŌ-nuhs, KAN-l-Ō-nuhs   ˌkanə'loːnəs, ˌkænl̩'oːnəs
Canendiyú
   department, Paraguay   KAHN-EN-dē-YOO   ˌkan,endiː'juː
Canens
   personification of song   KĀ-nuhnz   'keːnənz
Canes Venatici
   constellation   KĀ-NĒZ vuh-NĀT-uh-SĪ   'keːˌniːz və'neːṭəˌsɑi
Canetti
   Elias, *Bulgarian author (Nobel 1981)*   kuh-NET-ē   kə'neṭiˑ
Caniff
   Milton, *US cartoonist*   kuh-NIF   kə'nif
Canisius
   College, *NY*   kuh-NISH-(ē-)uhs   kə'niʃ(iː)əs
Canis Major
   constellation   KĀ-nuhs MĀ-juhr   ˌkeːnəs 'meːdʒəʳ
Canis Minor
   constellation   KĀ-nuhs MĪ-nuhr   ˌkeːnəs 'mɑinəʳ
Cankar
   Ivan, *Slovene writer and patriot*   TSAHN-KAHR   'tsɑːnˌkɑːʳ
Çankırı, Chankiri
   province, Turkey   CHAHNG-kuh-RĒ   ˌtʃɑŋkə'riː
Canna
   plant   KAN-uh   'kænə
Cannae
   Italy, site of Hannibal's victory   KAN-ē   'kæniː
Cannanore
   city, islands, India   KAN-uh-NŌR, KAN-uh-NAWR   'kænəˌnoːʳ, 'kænəˌnɔːʳ
Canneh
   Biblical name   KAN-uh, kah-NE   'kænə, kɑ'ne
Cannes
   town, France; film festival   KAHN, Ⓢ KAN   kɑːn, Ⓢ 'kæn
Cañon
   wren   KAN-yuhn   'kænjən
Cañon de Colca
   canyon, Peru   kahn-yawn dā KŌL-kah   kɑnjɔːn deː 'koːlkɑ
Canoncito
   Indian reservation, US   KAN-yuhn-SĒT-ō   ˌkænjən'siːṭoː
Canonicus
   Native American leader   kuh-NAHN-i-kuhs   kə'nɑnikəs
Canopus
   steersman of the Argo; star   kuh-NŌ-puhs   kə'noːpəs

Foreign Sounds: ue: *Fr.* **rue**, *Ger.* **füllen**   uh(r): *Fr.* **boeuf**, *Ger.* **Höhle**   k͟h: *Ger.* **ich**, *Scot.* **loch**   g̱: *Sp.* **amigo**   v̱: *Sp.* **hablar**
hl: *Welsh* **Llanelli**.   CAPITALS: primary stress.   SMALL CAPS: secondary stress.   Ⓢ: U.S. pron.   Ⓔ: British pron.

Canossa
　village, Italy　　　　　　　kuh-NAHS-uh　　　　　　　　　　kəˈnɑsə

Canowindra
　town, Australia　　　　　　kuh-NOWN-druh　　　　　　　　kəˈnɑundrə

Canseco
　Jose, *US baseball player*　kuhn-SĀ-kō, kan-SĀ-kō　　　kənˈseːkoː, kænˈseːkoː

Cantab
　abbreviation for Cantabrigian　KAN-TAB　　　　　　　　ˈkænˌtæb

Cantabria
　region, Spain　　　　　　　kahn-TAHV̲-rē-ah　　　　　　　kɑnˈtɑβriːɑ

Cantabrigia
　Latin form of Cambridge　　KANT-uh-BRIJ-(ē-)uh　　　　ˌkæntəˈbridʒ(iː)ə

Cantabrigian
　student at or graduate of Cambridge　KANT-uh-BRIJ-ē-uhn　ˌkæntəˈbridʒiːən
　　Univ.

cantata
　choral composition　　　　kuhn-TAHT-uh　　　　　　　　kənˈtɑt̪ə

Cantenac-Margaux
　French wine　　　　　　　　kahⁿt-NAHK-mahr-GŌ　　　　kɑtnɑːkmɑːrgoː

Canterbury
　town, England　　　　　　KANT-uhr-b(uh-)rē, KANT-uhr-BER-ē　ˈkæntəʳb(ə)riˑ, ˈkæntəʳˌberiˑ

Canticle of Canticles
　Old Testament book　　　　KANT-i-kuhl(z)　　　　　　　ˈkæntikəl(z)

Cantinflas
　Mexican entertainer　　　　KAN-tuhn-FLAHS　　　　　　　ˈkæntənˌflas

Canton
　town, MA; city, OH; atoll, Pacific　KANT-n　　　　　　ˈkæntn̩

Canton [Guangzhou]
　city, China　　　　　　　　KAN-TAHN, kan-TAHN　　　　ˈkænˌtɑn, kænˈtɑn

Cantonese
　lang., China; pert. to Canton, *China*　KANT-n-ĒZ, -ĒS　ˌkæntn̩ˈiːz, -ˈiːs

Cantor
　Eddie, *US comedian*　　　　KANT-uhr　　　　　　　　　ˈkæntəʳ

Canuck
　slang for French Canadian　kuh-NUHK　　　　　　　　kəˈnək

Canucks
　Vancouver, B.C., hockey team　kuh-NUHKS　　　　　　kəˈnəks

Canute, Cnut
　early king of England, Denmark,　kuh-N(Y)O͞OT　　　　kəˈn(j)uːt
　　Norway

Canyon de Chelly
　National Monument, AZ　　KAN-yuhn duh SHĀ-lē　　　ˈkænjən də ˈʃeːliˑ

Cão, Cam
　Diogo, *Portuguese navigator*　KOWⁿ　　　　　　　　　ˈkaũ

Caodaism
　East Asian religion　　　　kow-DĪ-IZ-uhm　　　　　　　kauˈdaiˌizəm

Caol Ila
　Scotch whiskey distillery　KLĒ-luh　　　　　　　　　ˈkliːlə

Capac-Urcu [Altar]
　extinct volcano, Ecuador　　KAHP-ahk-UR-ko͞o　　　　ˌkɑpɑkˈuʳkuː

Capaneus
　one of the Seven against Thebes　KAP-uh-NĒ-uhs　　　ˌkæpəˈniːəs

Cap-de-Mourlin
　French wine　　　　　　　　kahp-duh-mur-LEⁿ　　　　kɑːpdəmurlẽ

Key (col. 2):　a: fad　ā: fade　ah: father　ar: marry　aw: law　e: fed　ē: feed　er: merry　i: hid　ī: hide　ō: coat　o͞o: boot
oi: boy　ow: now　u: put　uh: above　uhr: bird　ch: chop　ng: ring　sh: show　th: thick　th̲: this　zh: measure

Cape Cod
peninsula, MA kāp KAHD keːp 'kɑd

Cape Girardeau
county, city, MO KĀP juh-RAHRD-ō ˌkeːp dʒə'rɑʳdoː

Čapek
Karel, *Czech playwright* CHAH-pek 'tʃɑːpek

Capella
star kuh-PEL-uh kə'pelə

Cape Province
province, South Africa kāp PRAHV-ins keːp 'prɑvins

Capercaillie
bird (fowl) KAP-uhr-KAL-(y)ē ˌkæpəʳ'kæl(j)iˑ

Capernaum
Biblical town kuh-PUHR-nē-uhm kə'pəʳniːəm

Capetian
French royal dynasty kuh-PĒ-shuhn kə'piːʃən

Capetown
city, S. Africa KĀP-TOWN 'keːpˌtɑun

Cape Verde
islands, Atlantic KĀP VUHRD ˌkeːp 'vəʳd

Cape Verdean
pert. to Cape Verde KĀP VUHRD-ē-uhn ˌkeːp 'vəʳdiːən

Capezio
shoe mfr. kuh-PĒ-zē-ō kə'piːziːoː

Caphtor
Biblical name KAF-TAWR, KAF-TŌR, kahf-TAWR 'kæfˌtɔːʳ, 'kæfˌtoːʳ, kɑf'tɔːr

Caphtorim
plural of Caphtor KAF-TAWR-im, -TŌR-; kahf-tawr-ĒM 'kæfˌtɔːrim, -ˌtoːr-; kɑftɔːr'iːm

Capilano
Stadium, *Vancouver, Canada* KAP-uh-LAHN-ō, -LAN-ō ˌkæpə'lɑnoː, -'lænoː

Capistrano
mission, CA, site of swallows' return KAP-uh-STRAHN-ō ˌkæpə'strɑnoː

Capitan Grande
Indian reservation, US KAP-uh-TAN GRAND(-ē) 'kæpəˌtæn 'grænd(iˑ)

Capitoline
hill, Rome, Italy KAP-uht-l-ĪN, ⓔ kuh-PIT-l-ĪN 'kæpətlˌɑin, ⓔ kə'pitlˌɑin

Capiz
province, Philippines KAHP-ēs 'kɑpiːs

Capodimonte
Italian town; ceramic ware KAHP-ō-dē-MAHN-TĀ ˌkɑpoːdiˑ'mɑnˌteː

Capo Ferrato
Sardinian wine KAHP-ō fer-AH-tō ˌkɑpoː fer'ɑtoː

Capone
Al 'Scarface', *US gangster* kuh-PŌN kə'poːn

Caporetto
Italian form of Kobarid KAP-uh-RET-ō ˌkæpə'reʈoː

Capote
Truman, *US author* kuh-PŌT-ē kə'poːʈiˑ

Capote Ute
N. American people kuh-PŌT-ē Y͞OOT kə'poːʈiˑ 'juːt

Cappadocia
region, Turkey KAP-uh-DŌ-sh(ē-)uh ˌkæpə'doːʃ(iː)ə

Capra
Frank, *US film producer, director* KAP-ruh 'kæprə

Capreae
   Latin form of Capri   KAP-rē-Ē   'kæpriː‚iː

Capri
   island, Italy   ka-PRĒ, kuh-PRĒ, KAHP-rē, KAP-rē   kæ'priː, kə'priː‚, 'kɑpriˑ, 'kæpriˑ

Capricorn
   constellation, sign of the zodiac   KAP-ri-KAWRN   'kæpri‚kɔːʳn

Capricornus
   constellation   KAP-ri-KAWR-nuhs   ‚kæpri'kɔːʳnəs

Caproni
   Giovanni Battista, *Italian airplane builder*   kah-PRŌ-nē   ka'proːniˑ

Capshaw
   Kate, *US actress*   KAP-SHAW   'kæp‚ʃɔː

Capua
   town, Italy   KAP-yuh-wuh   'kæpjəwə

Capucci
   shoe mfr.   kah-P͞OOT-chē, kuh-P͞OO-chē   ka'puːttʃiˑ, kə'puːtʃiˑ

Capuchins
   religious order   KAP-(y)uh-shuhnz, kuh-PY͞OO-shuhnz   'kæp(j)əʃənz, kə'pjuːʃənz

Capucine
   French entertainer   kah-pue-SĒN   kaːpyːsiːn

Capulet
   Juliet's family in Romeo & Juliet   KAP-yuh-luht   'kæpjələt

Caquetá
   department, Colombia   KAHK-uh-TAH   ‚kɑkə'tɑ

Carabobo
   state, Venezuela   KAHR-ah-V̱Ō-v̱ō   ‚kɑrɑ'βoːβoː

Caracalla
   Roman emperor   KAR-uh-KAL-uh   ‚kærə'kælə

Caracara
   bird   KAR-uh-KAR-uh, KAR-uh-kuh-RAH   ‚kærə'kærə, ‚kærəkə'rɑ

Caracas
   city, Venezuela   kuh-RAK-uhs, kuh-RAHK-uhs   kə'rækəs, kə'rɑkəs

Caracul
   sheep breed   KAR-uh-kuhl   'kærəkəl

Caradoc
   1. pers. name   kuh-RAHD-awg, -uhk   kə'rɑdɔːg, -ək
   2. Welsh   kah-RAH-dawg   kɑːˈrɑːdɔːg

Caraş-Severin
   county, Romania   KAHR-AHSH-SEV-uh-RĒN   'kɑr‚aʃ‚sevə'riːn

Caravaggio
   Michelangelo da, *Italian painter*   KAR-uh-VAHJ-ō, KAR-uh-VAHZH-ō, -VAHJ-ē-ō, -VAHZH-ē-ō   ‚kærə'vadʒoː, ‚kærə'vaʒoː, -'vadʒiː‚oː, -'vaʒiː‚oː

Caravanche [Karawanken]
   Alpine mtn. range   KAH-re-VAHNG-kā   ‚kɑre'vaŋkeː

Caraway
   Hattie Ophelia, *US politician*   KAR-uh-WĀ, KER-   'kærə‚weː, 'ker-

Carazo
   department, Nicaragua   kuh-RAHS-ō   kə'rɑsoː

Carbo
   Roman cognomen   KAHR-bō   'kɑʳboː

carbon
   element   KAHR-buhn   'kɑʳbən

Key (col. 2):   a: fad ā: fade ah: father ar: marry aw: law e: fed ē: feed er: merry i: hid ī: hide ō: coat o͞o: boot
oi: boy ow: now u: put uh: above uhr: bird ch: chop ng: ring sh: show th: thick <u>th</u>: this zh: measure

Carbonari
  European secret political party   KAHR-buh-NAHR-ē   ˌkɑʳbə'nɑri·

Carbonnieux
  French wine   kahr-bawn-YUH(R)   kɑːrbɔːnjœː

Carcas
  Biblical name   KAHR-kuhs, kahr-KAHS   'kɑʳkəs, kɑr'kɑs

Carcassonne
  city, France   kahr-kah-SAWN, ⑤ kahr-kuh-SAWN, -SŌN   kɑːrkɑːsɔːn, ⑤ kɑʳkə'sɔːn, -'soːn

Carchemish
  ancient Hittite capital, Turkey   KAHR-kuh-MISH, kahr-KĒ-mish   'kɑʳkəˌmiʃ, kɑʳ'kiːmiʃ

Carchemish
  Biblical name   KAHR-KEM-ish, kahr-KĒ-mish, KAHR-kuh-MISH   'kɑʳˌkemiʃ, kɑʳ'kiːmiʃ, ˌkɑrkə'miʃ

Carchi
  province, Ecuador   KAHR-chē   'kɑʳtʃi·

Cardamom
  mtn. range, Thailand; spice   KAHRD-uh-muhm, KAHRD-uh-MAHM   'kɑʳdəməm, 'kɑʳdəˌmɑm

Cárdenas
  Lázaro, *president, Mexico*   KAHR-THĀ-nahs, ⑤ KAHRD-n-AHS   'kɑʳˌðeːnɑs, ⑤ 'kɑʳdn̩ˌɑs

Cárdenas Solórzano
  Cuauhtémoc, *Mexican politician*   KAHR-thā-nahs sō-LAWR-sahn-ō   'kɑʳðeːnɑs soː'lɔːʳsɑnoː

Cardiff [Caerdydd]
  city, Wales   KAHR-duhf   'kɑʳdəf

Cardiganshire
  former county, Wales   KAHRD-uh-guhn-shuhr, -SHIR, -SHĪR   'kɑʳdəgənʃəʳ, -ˌʃiʳ, -ˌʃaiʳ

Cardin
  Pierre, *French fashion designer*   kahr-DEⁿ, ⑤ kahr-DAN, kahr-DAⁿ   kɑːrdẽ, ⑤ kɑʳ'dæn, kɑʳ'dæ

Cardinale
  Claudia, *Italian entertainer*   KAHRD-n-AHL-ā   ˌkɑʳdn̩'ɑleː

Cardinal Stritch
  College, *WI*   KAHRD-n-uhl STRICH, KAHRD-nuhl   'kɑʳdn̩əl 'stritʃ, 'kɑʳdnəl

Cardozo
  Benjamin Nathan, *justice, US Supreme Court*   kahr-DŌ-zō   kɑʳ'doːzoː

Carducci
  Giosuè, *Italian poet (Nobel 1906)*   kahr-DOOT-chē; ⑤ kahr-DOO-chē   kɑr'duːttʃiː; ⑤ kɑʳ'duːtʃi·

Carew
  1. Thomas, *English poet; pers. name*   kuh-ROO   kə'ruː
  2. town, castle, Wales   KAR-oo, KAR-ē, KER-   'kæruː, 'kæri·, 'ker-

Carey
  pers. name   KAR-ē, KER-ē   'kæri·, 'keri·

Caria
  ancient district, Asia Minor   KAR-ē-uh, KER-ē-uh   'kæriːə, 'keriːə

Carib
  S. & Cen. American people   KAR-uhb   'kærəb

Caribbean
  sea   KAR-uh-BĒ-uhn, kuh-RIB-ē-uhn   ˌkærə'biːən, kə'ribiːən

Caribou
  N. American people   KAR-uh-BOO   'kærəˌbuː

Carignan
  wine grape variety   kahr-ēn-YAHⁿ   kɑːriːnjã

Cariñena
  Spanish wine   KAHR-ē-NĀN-yuh   ˌkɑriː'neːnjə

Foreign Sounds: ue: *Fr.* **rue**, *Ger.* **füllen**   uh(r): *Fr.* **boeuf**, *Ger.* **Höhle**   <u>kh</u>: *Ger.* **ich**, *Scot.* **loch**   g̱: *Sp.* **amigo**   v̱: *Sp.* **hablar**
hl: *Welsh* **Llanelli**.   CAPITALS: primary stress.   SMALL CAPS: secondary stress.   ⑤: U.S. pron.   Ⓔ: British pron.

Carinthia
state, Austria	kuh-RIN-thē-uh	kəˈrinθiːə

Carioca
dance	KAR-ē-Ō-kuh	ˌkæriːˈoːkə

Cariri
S. American people	KAR-uh-RĒ	ˌkærəˈriː

Carl
1. pers. name	KAHRL, KAHR-uhl	ˈkɑʳl, ˈkɑrəl
2. Danish, Norwegian, Swedish	KAHRL	ˈkɑrl
3. Finnish	KAHRL	ˈkɑːrl
4. German	KAHRL	ˈkɑʳl

Carla
pers. name	KAHR-luh	ˈkɑʳlə

Carle
Eric, *US children's author, illustrator*	KAHRL	ˈkɑʳl

Carleton
College, *MN; pers. name*	KAHRL-tuhn, KAHRLT-n	ˈkɑʳltən, ˈkɑʳltn̩

Carlin
George, *US comedian*	KAHR-luhn	ˈkɑʳlən

Carlisle
John, *US politician; pl. name; pers. name*	kahr-LĪL, KAHR-LĪL, kuhr-LĪL	kɑʳˈlail, ˈkɑʳˌlail, kəʳˈlail

Carlo
1. pers. name	KAHR-lō	ˈkɑʳloː
2. Italian	KAHR-lō	ˈkarloː
3. Swedish	KAHR-lō	ˈkɑːrloː

Carlo Rossi
wine	KAHR-lō RAWS-ē	ˌkɑʳloː ˈrɔːsiˑ

Carlos
1. pers. name	KAHR-lōs, KAHR-luhs	ˈkɑʳloːs, ˈkɑʳləs
2. German	KAHR-LAWS	ˈkaʳˌloːs
3. Portuguese	KAHR-lōōsh, -lōōs	ˈkaːrluːʃ, -luːs
4. Spanish	KAHR-lōs	ˈkarloːs

Carlota
pers. name, Spanish	kahr-LŌ-tah	karˈloːta

Carlotta
1. pers. name	kahr-LAHT-uh	kɑʳˈlaṭə
2. Italian	kahr-LAWT-tah	karˈlɔːtta

Carlovingian [Carolingian]
Frankish dynasty of Charlemagne	KAHR-luh-VINJ-(ē-)uhn	ˌkɑʳləˈvindʒ(iː)ən

Carlsbad
city, CA, NM; caverns, NM	KAHRLZ-BAD, KAHR-uhlz-BAD	ˈkɑʳlzˌbæd, ˈkarəlzˌbæd

Carlsberg
Danish beer	KAHRLS-BERG̃, ⓢ KAHRLZ-BUHRG	ˈkarlsˌberɣ, ⓢ ˈkɑʳlzˌbəʳg

Carlstadt
borough, NJ	KAHRL-STAT	ˈkɑʳlˌstæt

Carlton
pers. name	KAHRL-tuhn, KAHRLT-n	ˈkɑʳltən, ˈkɑʳltn̩

Carly
pers. name	KAHR-lē	ˈkɑʳliˑ

Carlyle
city, IL	kahr-LĪL, KAHR-LĪL	kɑʳˈlail, ˈkɑʳˌlail

Carmarthenshire
former county, Wales	kuhr-MAHR-thuhn-shuhr, kahr-, -SHIR	kəʳˈmɑʳðənʃəʳ, kɑʳ-, -ˌʃiʳ

Key (col. 2): a: fad ā: fade ah: father ar: marry aw: law e: fed ē: feed er: merry i: hid ī: hide ō: coat ōō: boot
oi: boy ow: now u: put uh: above uhr: bird ch: chop ng: ring sh: show th: thick th: this zh: measure

Carme
   satellite of Jupiter   KAHR-mā   'kaʳmeː

Carmel
  1. city, CA   kahr-MEL   kaʳmel
  2. town, IN, NY; Mount, *Israel*   KAHR-muhl   'kaʳməl

Carmela
  pers. name   kahr-MEL-uh   kaʳmelə

Carmelites
  religious order   KAHR-muh-LĪTS   'kaʳmə‚laits

Carmen
  pers. name   KAHR-muhn   'kaʳmən

Carmenta
  Roman nymph, mother of Evander   kahr-MEN-tuh   kaʳmentə

Carmichael
  1. Hoagy, *US songwriter*   KAHR-MĪ-kuhl, kahr-MĪ-kuhl   'kaʳ‚maikəl, kaʳmaikəl
  2. community, CA   KAHR-MĪ-kuhl   'kaʳ‚maikəl

Carmi
  Biblical name   KAHR-MĪ, kahr-MĒ   'kaʳ‚mai, karˈmiː

Carmina Burana
  collection of medieval songs; choral   KAHR-MĒ-nuh b(y)u-RAHN-uh,   ‚kaʳ‚miːnə b(j)uˈranə,
    work, Orff   kahr-muh-nuh   kaʳmənə

Carmite
  Biblical name   KAHR-MĪT   'kaʳ‚mait

Carmona
  commune, Spain   kahr-MŌ-nuh   kaʳmoːnə

Carmona
  António Óscar de Fragoso,   kuhr-MŌ-nuh   kəʳmoːnə
    Portuguese general, politician

Carna
  virgin huntress in Greek myth   KAHR-nuh   'kaʳnə

Carnac
  commune, France (megalithic site) KAHR-NAK   'kaʳ‚næk

Carnap
  Rudolf, *German-US philosopher* KAHR-NAP   'kaʳ‚næp

Carnarvon
  fishing port, Western Australia kahr-NAHR-vuhn, kuhr-NAHR-vuhn kaʳnaʳvən, kəʳnaʳvən

Carnauba
  palm   kahr-NAW-buh, kahr-NOW-buh,   kaʳnɔːbə, kaʳnaubə,
                                KAHR-nah-OO-buh   ‚kaʳnaˈuːbə

Carnaval-Souvenir de Chicoutimi
  Quebec festival   kahr-nah-VAHL-soov(-uh)-NIR duh kaːrnaːvaːlsuːv(ə)nir də
                                shē-koo-tē-MĒ   ʃiːkuːtiːmiː

Carnegie
  Andrew, *US industrialist; concert* KAHR-nuh-gē, kahr-NEG-ē   'kaʳnəgiˑ, kaʳnegiˑ
    hall, New York City; pers. name

Carnegie-Mellon
  univ., Pittsburgh, PA   KAHR-nuh-gē-MEL-uhn,   ‚kaʳnəgiˑˈmelən,
                                kahr-NEG-ē-MEL-uhn   kaʳ‚negiˑˈmelən

Carnelian
  chalcedony   kahr-NĒL-yuhn   kaʳniːljən

Carner
  Joanne Gunderson, *US golfer*   KAHR-nuhr   'kaʳnəʳ

Carnes
  Kim, *rock singer*   KAHRNZ   'kaʳnz

Carney		
Art, *US actor*	KAHR-nē	'kɑʳniˑ
Carnic		
Alps, *Alpine mtn. range*	KAHR-nik	'kɑʳnik
Carnivora		
meat-eaters	kahr-NIV-uh-ruh	kɑʳ'nivərə
Carnosauria		
dinosaur infraorder	KAHR-nuh-SAWR-ē-uh	ˌkɑʳnə'sɔːriːə
Carol, Carole		
pers. name	KAR-uhl, KER-uhl	'kærəl, 'kerəl
Carolina		
1. early American colony	KAR-uh-LĪ-nuh	ˌkærə'lɑinə
2. city, Puerto Rico	KAHR-uh-LĒ-nuh, KAR-uh-LĒ-nuh	ˌkɑrə'liːnə, ˌkærə'liːnə
Caroline		
1. archipelago, Pacific; pers. name	KAR-uh-LĪN, KAR-uh-luhn, KER-	'kærəˌlɑin, 'kærələn, 'ker-
2. French	kah-raw-LĒN	kɑˑrɔːliːn
3. county, MD, VA	KAR-uh-LĪN, KER-	'kærəˌlɑin, 'ker-
Carolingian		
Frankish dynasty of Charlemagne	KAR-uh-LIN-j(ē-)uhn	ˌkærə'lindʒ(iː)ən
Carolinian		
pert. to the Carolinas *or* Carolingian	KAR-uh-LIN-ē-uhn, KAR-uh-LĒN-yuhn	ˌkærə'liniːən, ˌkærə'liːnjən
Carolus		
1. pers. name, French	kah-raw-LUES	kɑːrɔːlyːs
2. Latin	KAR-uh-luhs	'kærələs
Carolus Magnus		
Latin form of Charlemagne	KAR-uh-luhs MAG-nuhs	'kærələs 'mægnəs
Carolyn		
pers. name	KAR-uh-luhn	'kærələn
Caron		
Leslie, *entertainer*	kuh-RŌN	kə'roːn
Caroní		
river, Venezuela	KAHR-uh-NĒ	ˌkɑrə'niː
Carotene		
pigment	KAR-uh-TĒN	'kærəˌtiːn
Carothers		
Wallace Hume, *US chemist*	kuh-RUHTH-uhrz	kə'rəðəʳz
Carpaccio		
Vittore, *Italian painter*	kahr-PAHCH-ō, kahr-PAHCH-ē-ō	kɑʳ'patʃoː, kɑʳ'patʃiːˌoː
Carpathian		
mtn. range, Europe	kahr-PĀ-thē-uhn	kɑʳ'peːθiːən
Carpatho-Ukraine		
region in Ukraine	KAHR-puh-thō-yōō-KRĀN	'kɑʳpəθoːjuˑ'kreːn
Carpentaria		
Gulf of, *inlet, Australia*	KAHR-puhn-TER-ē-uh, -TAR-ē-uh	ˌkɑʳpən'teriːə, -'tæriːə
Carpus		
Biblical name	KAHR-puhs	'kɑʳpəs
Carracci		
Annibale, *Italian painter*	kahr-RAHCH-ē	kɑr'ratʃiˑ
Carradine		
David, Keith & John, *US actors*	KAR-uh-DĒN, KER-uh-DĒN	'kærəˌdiːn, 'kerəˌdiːn
Carrageen		
seaweed	KAR-uh-GĒN	'kærəˌgiːn
Carrantuohill, Carrantual		
peak, Ireland	KAR-uhn-TŌŌ-uhl	ˌkærən'tuːəl

Key (col. 2):   a: fad   ā: fade   ah: father   ar: marry   aw: law   e: fed   ē: feed   er: merry   i: hid   ī: hide   ō: coat   ōō: boot
oi: boy   ow: now   u: put   uh: above   uhr: bird   ch: chop   ng: ring   sh: show   th: thick   th: this   zh: measure

Carranza
  Venustiano, *politician, Mexico*   kahr-RAHN-sah   kɑr'rɑnsɑ
Carrara
  commune, Italy   kuh-RAHR-uh   kə'rɑrə
Carrara
  14th century Italian ruling family   kah-RAHR-ah   kɑ'rɑrɑ
Carrefour
  French retailer   kahr-F$\overline{OO}$R, ⑤ kahr-FŌR, kahr-FAWR   kɑːrfuːr, ⑤ kɑʳ'foːʳ, kɑʳ'fɔːʳ
Carrel
  Alexis, *French surgeon, biologist*   kah-REL, ⑤ kuh-REL, KAR-uhl   kɑːrel, ⑤ kə'rel, 'kærəl
  (Nobel 1912)
Carrera
  Barbara, *actress*   kuh-RER-uh   kə'rerə
Carreras
  Jose, *Spanish tenor*   kahr-RER-ahs   kɑr'rerɑs
Carrhae
  site of Roman defeat, 53 B.C.   KAR-ē, KER-ē   'kæri·, 'keri·
Carrickfergus, Carraig Fhearghais
  seaport, county, Northern Ireland   KAR-ik-FUHR-guhs   ˌkærik'fəʳgəs
Carrie
  pers. name   KAR-ē, KER-ē   'kæri·, 'keri·
Carrier
  N. American people   KAR-ē-uhr, KER-ē-uhr   'kæriːəʳ, 'keriːəʳ
Carrier
  Willis Haviland, *US engineer and*   KAR-ē-uhr   'kæriːəʳ
  inventor
Carroll
  Lewis, *pseudonym of* C. L.   KAR-uhl, KER-uhl   'kærəl, 'kerəl
  Dodgson, *English writer; pers.*
  name
Carruades de Château Lafite
  wine   kahr-WAHD duh shah-TŌ lah-FĒT   kɑːrwɑːd də ʃɑtoː lɑːfiːt
Carruth
  Gorton, *US author*   kuh-R$\overline{OO}$TH   kə'ruːθ
Carruthers
  pers. name   kuh-RUH<u>TH</u>-uhrz   kə'rəðəʳz
Carshena
  Biblical name   kahr-SHĒ-nuh, KAHR-shuh-nuh,   kɑʳ'ʃiːnə, 'kɑʳʃənə,
      KAHR-shuh-NAH   ˌkɑrʃə'nɑ
Carson
  pers. name   KAHR-suhn   'kɑʳsən
Carta Blanca
  Mexican beer   KAHR-tah BLAHNG-kah   'kɑrtɑ 'blɑŋkɑ
Cartagena
  city, Spain, Colombia   kahr-tah-GĀ-nah,   kɑrtɑ'yeːnɑ, ⑤ ˌkɑʳţə'geːnə,
      ⑤ KAHRT-uh-GĀ-nuh, -JĒ-nuh,   -'dʒiːnə, -'heːnə
      -HĀ-nuh
Cartago
  province, Costa Rica   kahr-TAHG-ō   kɑʳ'tɑgoː
Carte
  Richard D'Oyly, *English impresario*   KAHRT   'kɑʳt
Carter
  Jimmy, *39th US president; pers.*   KAHRT-uhr   'kɑʳţəʳ
  name

Foreign Sounds: ue: *Fr.* **rue**, *Ger.* **füllen**   uh(r): *Fr.* **boeuf**, *Ger.* **Höhle**   <u>kh</u>: *Ger.* i**ch**, *Scot.* lo**ch**   ḡ: *Sp.* ami**g**o   y̱: *Sp.* ha**b**lar
hl: *Welsh* **Ll**anelli.   CAPITALS: primary stress.   SMALL CAPS: secondary stress.   ⑤: U.S. pron.   ⑥: British pron.

Carteret		
1. borough, NJ; county, NC	KAHRT-uh-RET	ˌkɑ^{r}t̬ə'ret
2. village, France	kahr-TRE, kahr-tuh-RE, [$] KAHRT-uh-RĀ	kɑːrtre, kɑrtəre, [$] ˌkɑ^{r}t̬ə'reː
Cartesian		
pert. to Descartes	kahr-TĒ-zhuhn, [£] kahr-TĒ-zē-uhn	kɑ^{r}'tiːʒən, [£] kɑ^{r}'tiːziːən
Cartesianism		
philosophy of Descartes	kahr-TĒ-zhuh-NIZ-uhm	kɑ^{r}'tiːʒəˌnizəm
Carthage		
ancient African city; US pl. name	KAHR-thij	'kɑ^{r}θidʒ
Carthaginian		
pert. to Carthage	KAHR-thuh-JIN-ē-uhn	ˌkɑ^{r}θə'dʒiniːən
Carthusians		
religious order	kahr-TH(Y)O͞O-zhuhnz	kɑ^{r}'θ(j)uːʒənz
Cartier		
1. jewelry retailer; pers. name	KAHRT-ē-Ā, kahr-TYĀ	'kɑ^{r}t̬iːˌeː, kɑ^{r}'tjeː
2. French	kahr-TYĀ	kɑːrtjeː
Cartier-Bresson		
Henri, *French photographer*	kahr-tyā-brā-SAW^{n}	kɑːrtjeːbreːsɔ̃
Cartland		
Barbara, *British author*	KAHRT-luhnd	'kɑ^{r}tlənd
Caruso		
Enrico, *Italian tenor*	kuh-RO͞O-sō, kuh-RO͞O-zō	kə'ruːsoː, kə'ruːzoː
Carvalho		
pers. name, Portuguese	kuhr-VAHL-yo͞o	kər'vɑljuː
Casablanca		
seaport, Morocco; movie	KAS-uh-BLANG-kuh, KAZ-; KAHS-uh-BLAHNG-kuh, KAHZ-	ˌkæsə'blæŋkə, ˌkæz-; ˌkɑsə'blɑŋkə, ˌkɑz-
Casa Grande		
National Monument, *AZ*	KAHS-uh GRAHN-dē, GRAHN-dā	'kɑsə 'grɑndiˑ, 'grɑndeː
Casals		
Pablo, *Spanish cellist/composer*	kuh-SAHLZ	kə'sɑlz
Casamance [Kasamansa]		
river, region, Senegal	KAZ-uh-MAH^{n}S	ˌkæzə'mɑ̃s
Casanare		
intendancy, Colombia	KAHS-uh-NAHR-ā	ˌkɑsə'nɑreː
Casanova		
Francesco, *Italian artist;* Giovanni Giacomo, *Italian adventurer & sensualist*	KAS-uh-NŌ-vuh, KAZ-uh-NŌ-vuh	ˌkæsə'noːvə, ˌkæzə'noːvə
Cäsar		
pers. name, German	TSEZ-AHR	'tsezˌɑ^{r}
Casaubon		
The Rev. Edward, *character in George Eliot's* Middlemarch	kuh-SAW-buhn	kə'sɔːbən
Casbah		
see Kasbah		
Cascais		
fishing port, Portugal	kahsh-KĪSH	kɑʃ'kaiʃ
Caserta		
province, town, Italy	kuh-ZERT-uh	kə'zert̬ə
Casey		
pers. name	KĀ-sē	'keːsiˑ
Cashmere		
see Kashmir		

Key (col. 2): a: **fad** ā: **fade** ah: **father** ar: **marry** aw: **law** e: **fed** ē: **feed** er: **merry** i: **hid** ī: **hide** ō: **coat** o͞o: **boot** oi: **boy** ow: **now** u: **put** uh: **above** uhr: **bird** ch: **chop** ng: **ring** sh: **show** th: **thick** th: **this** zh: **measure**

Casimir
   1. pers. name   KAZ-uh-MIR   'kæzə₁miʳ
   2. French   kah-zē-MĒR   kɑːziːmiːr

Casino
   town, Australia   kuh-SĒ-nō   kə'siːnoː

Casio
   electronics co.   KAS-ē-ō   'kæsiː₁oː

Casiphia
   Biblical name   kuh-SIF-ē-uh, KAHS-if-YAH   kə'sifiːə, ₁kɑsif'jɑ

Casiquiare
   waterway, Venezuela   KAHS-i-KYAHR-ē   ₁kɑsi'kjɑriː

Caslon
   William, *English typefounder*   KAZ-luhn   'kæzlən

Casluhim
   Biblical name   KAS-lōō-HIM, kas-LŌŌ-HIM,   'kæsluː₁him, kæs'luː₁him,
                                KAHS-lōō-<u>KHIM</u>   ₁kɑsluː'xim

Caspar
   1. comic book ghost; pers. name   KAS-puhr   'kæspəʳ
   2. Danish   KAHS-PAHR   'kɑːs₁par
   3. Dutch, Norwegian   KAHS-PAHR   'kɑs₁pɑr
   4. German   KAHS-PAHR   'kɑs₁pɑʳ

Casper
   city, WY; pers. name   KAS-puhr   'kæspəʳ

Caspian
   inland sea, Europe & Asia; character,   KAS-pē-uhn   'kæspiːən
     C.S. Lewis

Cass
   county, IN; pers. name   KAS   'kæs

Cassaba [Cassava]
   edible root   kuh-SAHB-uh   kə'sɑbə

Cassandra
   Trojan prophetess; pers. name   kuh-SAN-druh   kə'sændrə

Cassatt
   Mary, *US painter*   kuh-SAT   kə'sæt

Cassava
   edible root   kuh-SAHV-uh   kə'sɑvə

Cassavetes
   John, *US actor*   KAS-uh-VET-ēz, KAS-uh-VĒT-ēz   ₁kæsə'vetiːz, ₁kæsə'viːt̬iːz

Cassell
   reference book publisher   KAS-uhl   'kæsəl

Cassia
   1. county, ID   KASH-(ē-)uh   'kæʃ(iː)ə
   2. spice   KASH-uh   'kæʃə

Cassidy
   Fred, *US lexicographer*   KAS-uhd-ē   'kæsədiˑ

Cassin
   René, *French jurist, statesman*   kah-SEⁿ   kɑːsē
     (Nobel 1968)

Cassini
   Oleg, *US fashion designer*   kuh-SĒ-nē   kə'siːniˑ

Cassiodorus
   Flavius Magnus Aurelius, *Roman*   KAS-ē-uh-DŌR-uhs, -DAWR-uhs   ₁kæsiːə'doːrəs, -'dɔːrəs
    statesman and writer

Cassiopeia
   mother of Andromeda; constellation   KAS-ē-uh-PĒ-(y)uh   ₁kæsiːə'piː(j)ə

Foreign Sounds: **ue**: *Fr.* **rue**, *Ger.* **füllen**   **uh(r)**: *Fr.* **boeuf**, *Ger.* **Höhle**   <u>kh</u>: *Ger.* i<u>ch</u>, *Scot.* lo<u>ch</u>   g̱: *Sp.* ami**g**o   v̲: *Sp.* ha**b**lar
hl: *Welsh* **Ll**anelli.   CAPITALS: primary stress.   SMALL CAPS: secondary stress.   Ⓢ: U.S. pron.   Ⓔ: British pron.

Cassiphone
  daughter of Odysseus and Circe   kuh-SIF-uh-nē   kə'sifəni·

Cassirer
  Ernst, *German philosopher*   kah-SIR-uhr   kɑ'sirəʳ

Cassis
  French wine   ka-SĒ   kæ'si:

Cassius
  pers. name   KASH-(ē-)uhs, KAS-ē-uhs   'kæʃ(i:)əs, 'kæsi:əs

Cassowary
  Australian bird   KAS-uh-WER-ē   'kæsə‚weri·

Cassubian [Kashubian]
  lang., Europe   kas-YOO-bē-uhn, kash-OO-bē-uhn   kæs'ju:bi:ən, kæʃ'u:bi:ən

Castalia
  town, OH   kas-TĀ-lē-uh   kæs'te:li:ə

Castel Gandolfo
  site of papal palace   KAS-TEL gahn-DAHL-fō, KAHS-TEL, gahn-DAWL-fō   ‚kæs‚tel gɑn'dɑlfo:, ‚kɑs‚tel, gɑn'dɔ:lfo:

Castellón de la Plana
  province, Spain   KAHS-tuh(l)-YŌN duh lah PLAHN-uh   ‚kɑstə(l)'jo:n də lɑ 'plɑnə

Castelo Branco
  Humberto, *Brazilian politician; district, Portugal*   kah-STĀ-loo BRAHⁿ(NG)-koo   kɑ:'ste:lu: 'brɑ̃(ŋ)ku:

Castiglione
  Conte Baldassare, *Italian diplomat & writer*   KAHS-tēl-YŌ-nā   ‚kɑsti:l'jo:ne:

Castile
  region, NY; region, Spain [Castilla]   ka-STĒL   kæ'sti:l

Castilian
  Spanish dialect   kas-TIL-yuhn   kæs'tiljən

Castilla [Castile]
  region, Spain   kah-STĒ(L)-yah   kɑ'sti:(l)jɑ

Castilla-La Mancha
  region, Spain   kah-STĒ(L)-yah-lah-MAHN-chuh   kɑ'sti:(l)jɑlɑ'mantʃə

Castilla-León
  region, Spain   kah-STĒ(L)-yah-lā-ŌN   kɑ'sti:(l)jɑle:'o:n

Castlereagh
  Robert Stewart, Viscount, *British statesman; county, Northern Ireland*   KAS-uhl-RĀ   'kæsəl‚re:

Castor
  twin of Pollux in Greek myth; star Alpha Geminorum   KAS-tuhr   'kæstəʳ

Castries
  capital, St. Lucia   ka-STRĒ, KAHS-TRĒS   kæ'stri:, 'kɑs‚tri:s

Castro
  Fidel, *president, Cuba*   KAS-trō   'kæstro:

Castrol
  motor oil brand   KAS-TRŌL, KAS-TRAHL   'kæs‚tro:l, 'kæs‚trɑl

Castruccio
  pers. name   kahs-TROOT-chō   kɑs'tru:ttʃo:

Caswell
  county, NC   KAZ-wuhl, KAZ-WEL   'kæzwəl, 'kæz‚wel

Catahoula
  lake, parish, LA   KAT-uh-HOO-luh   ‚kæțə'hu:lə

Key (col. 2):   a: fad   ā: fade   ah: father   ar: marry   aw: law   e: fed   ē: feed   er: merry   i: hid   ī: hide   ō: coat   ōo: boot
oi: boy   ow: now   u: put   uh: above   uhr: bird   ch: chop   ng: ring   sh: show   th: thick   <u>th</u>: this   zh: measure

Catalan
  lang., Spain   KAT-l-uhn, KAT-l-AN, KAT-l-AN   'kætlən, 'kætl̩,æn, ,kætl̩'æn

Çatal Huyuk
  Neolithic site, central Turkey   CHAHT-l HŌŌ-yuk   'tʃɑtl̩ 'huˑjuk

Catalonia
  region, Spain   KAT-l-ŌN-yuh, KAT-l-Ō-nē-uh   ,kætl̩'oːnjə, ,kætl̩'oːniːə

Catalonian [Catalan]
  lang., Spain   KAT-l-Ō-nē-uhn   ,kætl̩'oːniːən

Catalpa
  tree genus   kuh-TAL-puh, kuh-TAH(L)-puh, kuh-TAW(L)-puh, -buh   kə'tælpə, kə'tɑ(l)pə, kə'tɔː(l)pə, -bə

Cataluña, -lunya [Catalonia]
  region, Spain   KAHT-uh-LŌŌN-yuh, KAT-l-ŌŌN-yuh   ,kɑtə'luːnjə, ,kætl̩'uːnjə

Catamarca
  province, Argentina   KAHT-ah-MAHR-kuh   ,kɑtɑ'mɑʳkə

Catanduanes
  island, province, Philippines   KAHT-uhn-DWAHN-uhs   ,kɑtən'dwɑnəs

Catania
  prov & town, Italy   kuh-TAHN-yuh, kuh-TĀN-yuh   kə'tɑnjə, kə'teːnjə

Catanzaro
  province, Italy   KAHT-ahn(d)-ZAHR-ō   ,kɑtɑn(d)'zɑroː

Catarman
  municipality, Philippines   KAHT-ahr-MAHN   ,kɑtɑʳ'mɑn

Catawba
  river, US; N. American people; college, NC; grape variety   kuh-TAW-buh, kuh-TAHB-uh   kə'tɔːbə, kə'tɑbə

Catbalogan
  municipality, Philippines   KAHT-buh-LŌ-guhn   ,kɑtbə'loːgən

Caterham and Warlingham
  town, England   KĀT-uh-ruhm uhn(d) WAWR-ling-uhm   'keːʈərəm ən(d) 'wɔːʳliŋəm

Caterina
  pers. name, Italian   KAH-tā-RĒ-nah   ,kɑteː'riːnɑ

Cates
  pers. name   KĀTS   'keːts

Cathar
  medieval Christian sect   KATH-AHR   'kæθ,ɑʳ

Catharine
  pers. name   KATH-(uh-)ruhn   'kæθ(ə)rən

Catharism
  religion   KATH-uh-RIZ-uhm, KATH-AHR-IZ-uhm   'kæθə,rizəm, 'kæθ,ɑr,izəm

Cathay
  literary term for China   kuh-THĀ, ka-THĀ   kə'θeː, kæ'θeː

Cather
  Willa, *US author*   KATH-uhr   'kæðəʳ

Catherine
  1. pers. name   KATH-(uh-)ruhn   'kæθ(ə)rən
  2. French   kah-tuh-RĒN, kah-TRĒN   kɑːtəriːn, kɑːtriːn

Cathleen ni Houlihan
  play, W. B. Yeats   kath-LĒN nē HŌŌ-luh-HAN   kæθ'liːn niˑ 'huːlə,hæn

Catholic
  Christian religion   KATH-(uh-)lik   'kæθ(ə)lik

Catholicism
  Christian religion   kuh-THAHL-uh-SIZ-uhm   kə'θɑlə,sizəm

Foreign Sounds: ue: *Fr.* **rue**, *Ger.* **füllen**   uh(r): *Fr.* **boeuf**, *Ger.* **Höhle**   kh: *Ger.* **ich**, *Scot.* **loch**   ḡ: *Sp.* **amigo**   y: *Sp.* **hablar**   hl: *Welsh* **Llanelli**.   CAPITALS: primary stress.   SMALL CAPS: secondary stress.   ⑤: U.S. pron.   ⑥: British pron.

Cathrine
  pers. name   KATH-ruhn   'kæθrən

Cath's
  nickname of St. Catherine's   KATS   'kæts
    College, *Cambridge Univ.*

Cathy
  pers. name   KATH-ē   'kæθiˑ

Catiline
  Roman conspirator   KAT-l-ĪN   'kætl̩ˌɑin

Cato
  M. Porcius, *Roman statesman* KĀT-ō   'keːt̯oː

Catoosa
  county, GA   kuh-TOO-suh   kə'tuːsə

Catreus
  son of Minos and Pasiphae KA-trē-uhs, KA-TROOS   'kætriːəs, 'kæˌtruːs

Catrin
  pers. name   KA-truhn   'kætrən

Catrina
  pers. name   kuh-TRĒ-nuh   kə'triːnə

Catrine
  pers. name   KA-TRĒN   'kæˌtriːn

Catron
  county, NM   kuh-TRAHN   kə'trɑn

Catskill
  mtn. range, village, NY   KAT-SKIL   'kætˌskil

Cattaraugus
  county, Indian reservation, NY KAT-uh-RAW-guhs, KAT-uh-RAW-guhs   'kætəˌrɔːgəs, ˌkætə'rɔːgəs

Cattegat
  see Kattegat

Cattell
  James McKeen, *US psychologist* kuh-TEL   kə'tel

Catton
  Bruce, *US historian*   KAT-n   'kætn̩

Catulle
  pers. name, French   kah-TUEL   kɑːtyːl

Catullus
  Roman poet   kuh-TUHL-uhs   kə'tələs

Cauca
  river, department, Colombia KOW-kuh   'kɑukə

Caucasia [Caucasus]
  region, mtn. range, between Europe kaw-KĀ-zhuh, kaw-KĀ-shuh   kɔː'keːʒə, kɔː'keːʃə
    and Asia

Caucasian
  pert. to Caucasus; *Indo-European* kaw-KĀ-zhuhn, kaw-KAZH-uhn, ⓔ   kɔː'keːʒən, kɔː'kæʒən, ⓔ
    race   kaw-KĀ-zē-uhn   kɔ'keːziːən

Caucasus
  region, mtn. range, between Europe KAW-kuh-suhs   'kɔːkəsəs
    and Asia

Caunus
  son of Miletus   KAW-nuhs   'kɔːnəs

Caura
  river, Venezuela   KOW-ruh   'kɑurə

Cauthen
  Steve, *US-born jockey*   KAW-thuhn, KAHTH-uhn   'kɔːθən, 'kɑθən

---

Key (col. 2):   a: **f**a**d** ā: **f**a**de** ah: **f**a**ther** ar: **ma**rry aw: **l**a**w** e: **f**e**d** ē: **f**ee**d** er: **me**rry i: **h**i**d** ī: **h**i**de** ō: **c**oa**t** oo: **b**oo**t**
oi: **b**oy ow: **n**ow u: **p**u**t** uh: **a**bove uhr: **bi**rd ch: **ch**op ng: ri**ng** sh: **sh**ow th: **th**ick <u>th</u>: **th**is zh: mea**s**ure

Cauvery
   waterfall, river, India   KAW-vuh-rē   ˈkɔːvəriˑ

Cavafy
   pseudonym of Konstantínos Kaváfis   kah-VAH-fē   kɑˈvɑfiˑ

Cavalleria Rusticana
   opera, Mascagni   KAV-uh-luh-RĒ-uh RUS-ti-KAHN-uh   ˌkævələˈriːə ˌrustiˈkɑnə

Cavatina
   simple melody   KAV-uh-TĒ-nuh, KAHV-uh-TĒ-nuh   ˌkævəˈtiːnə, ˌkɑvəˈtiːnə

Cavell
   Edith, *English nurse, WWI*   KAV-uhl, kuh-VEL   ˈkævəl, kəˈvel

Cavendish
   William, *British prime minister*   KAV-uhn-dish   ˈkævəndiʃ

Cavett
   Dick, *US talk show host*   KAV-uht   ˈkævət

Cavite
   prov, port, Philippines   kuh-VĒT-ē   kəˈviː̝iˑ

Cawdor
   parish, Scotland   KAWD-uhr   ˈkɔːdəʳ

Cawley
   Evonne Goolagong, *Australian*   KAW-lē   ˈkɔːliˑ
     tennis player

Caxamarca
   see Cajamarca

Caxton
   William, *English printer*   KAK-stuhn   ˈkækstən

Cayapa
   S. American people   kuh-YAHP-uh, kī-AHP-uh   kəˈjɑpə, kɑiˈɑpə

Cayapo
   S. American people   KAH-yuh-PŌ, KĪ-uh-PŌ   ˌkajəˈpoː, ˌkɑiəˈpoː

Cayenne
   city, French Guiana; spice   kī-EN, kā-EN   kɑien, keːˈen

Cay Lobos
   island, British Virgin Islands   KĒ LŌ-bōs, KĀ, LŌ-bōz, LŌ-buhs   ˌkiː ˈloːboːs, ˈkeː, ˈloːboːz,
                                                 ˈloːbəs

Cayman
   islands, West Indies   kā-MAN, *attributively (as in "C.*   keːˈmæn, *attributively (as in*
                         Islands") KĀ-muhn   *"C. Islands")* ˈkeːmən

Caymus
   winery, CA   KĀ-muhs   ˈkeːməs

Cayo
   district, Belize   KĪ-(y)ō   ˈkɑi(j)oː

Cayo Verde
   lime liqueur   KĪ-ō VERD-ē, VUHRD-ē   ˌkɑioː ˈveʳdiˑ, ˈvəʳdiˑ

Cay Sal
   island, British Virgin Islands   KĒ SAL, KĀ   ˈkiː ˈsæl, ˈkeː

Cayuga
   lake, county, NY; N. American people kuh-YOO-guh, KYOO-guh,   kəˈjuːgə, ˈkjuːgə, keːˈ(j)uːgə
                          kā-(Y)OO-guh

Cayuse
   N. American people   KĪ-(Y)OOS, kī-(Y)OOS   ˈkɑiˌ(j)uːs, kɑiˈ(j)uːs

Cazenovia
   village, NY (birthplace of Hiawatha) KAZ-uh-NŌ-vē-uh   ˌkæzəˈnoːviːə

CD-ROM
   compact disk-read-only memory   SĒ-dē-RAHM   ˌsiːdiːˈrɑm

Ceará
  state, Brazil   SĀ-uh-RAH   ˌseːəˈrɑ

Ceausescu
  Nicolae, *former president, Romania*   chow-SHESH-koo   tʃauˈʃeʃkuː

Cebu
  island & seaport, Philippines   sā-BOO   seːˈbuː

Cebu
  island, city, province, Philippines   sā-VOO   seːˈβuː

Cebuano
  see Sebuano

Cecchetti
  Enrico, *Italian dancer and teacher*   chāk-KĀT-tē   tʃeːkˈkeːtti

Cech
  Thomas R., *US biochemist (Nobel*   CHEKH, CHEK   ˈtʃex, ˈtʃek
  1989)

Cecil
  1. E. A. R., *English statesman*   SES-uhl, SIS-uhl   ˈsesəl, ˈsisəl
  (Nobel 1937)
  2. pers. name   SĒ-suhl, ⓔ SES-uhl, SIS-uhl   ˈsiːsəl, ⓔ ˈsesəl, ˈsisəl
  3. county, MD   SIS-uhl, SĒ-suhl   ˈsisəl, ˈsiːsəl

Cecile
  pers. name   suh-SĒL, ⓔ SES-ĒL, SES-uhl, SIS-uhl   səˈsiːl, ⓔ ˈsesˌiːl, ˈsesəl,
                                                                                 ˈsisəl

Cécile
  1. pers. name, French   sā-SĒL   seːsiːl
  2. Canadian French   sā-SIL   seːsil

Cecilia
  pers. name   suh-SIL-ē-uh, suh-SIL-yuh,   səˈsiliːə, səˈsiljə, səˈsiːljə
                                          suh-SĒL-yuh

Cecillo Village
  Indian reservation, US   suh-SĒ(L)-yō   səˈsiː(l)joː

Cecily
  pers. name   SIS-(uh-)lē, SES-(uh-)lē   ˈsis(ə)liˑ, ˈses(ə)liˑ

Cecrops
  mythical king of Attica   SEK-RAHPS   ˈsekˌrɑps

Cedalion
  instructor of Hephaestus   si-DĀ-lē-uhn   siˈdeːliːən

Čedomilj
  pers. name   CHED-aw-MĒL   ˈtʃedɔːˌmiːl̩

Cedric
  pers. name   SED-rik, SĒ-drik   ˈsedrik, ˈsiːdrik

Cegelec
  French electric power co.   sej-el-EK   sedʒelek

Ceilidh
  Trail, *Cape Breton Island, Nova*   KĀ-lē   ˈkeːliˑ
  Scotia; Irish & Scottish evening of
  musical entertainment

Ceiriog
  pers. name, Welsh   KER-yawg   ˈkerjɔːg

Cela
  Camilo José, *Spanish author (Nobel*   thā-LAH, sā-LAH   θeːˈlɑ, seːˈlɑ
  1989)

Celandine
  plant   SEL-uhn-DĪN, SEL-uhn-DĒN   ˈselənˌdɑin, ˈselənˌdiːn

---

Celanese
  tdmk for a synthetic fiber   SEL-uh-NĒZ, SEL-uh-NĒZ   ˌselə'niːz, 'seləˌniːz

Celebes [Sulawesi]
  island, sea, Indonesia   SEL-uh-BĒZ, suh-LĒ-bez   'seləˌbiːz, sə'liːbiːz

Celebrator Doppelbock
  German beer   CHĀ-lā-BRAH-TAWR DAHP-uhl-BAHK   ˌtʃeːleː'braˌtɔʳ 'dapəlˌbak

Celest, Celeste
  pers. name   suh-LEST   sə'lest

Céleste
  pers. name, French   sā-LEST   seːlest

Celestine
  pope   SEL-uh-STĪN; suh-LES-tin, -TĪN   'seləˌstain; sə'lestin, -ˌtain

Celeus
  king of Eleusis   SĒ-lē-uhs, SĒL-YO͞OS   'siːliːəs, 'siːlˌjuːs

Celia
  pers. name   SĒL-yuh   'siːljə

Cellini
  Benvenuto, *Florentine artist;*   chuh-LĒ-nē   tʃə'liːni·
  jewelers

Cello
  musical instrument   CHEL-ō   'tʃeloː

Celluloid
  tdmk for a thermoplastic   SEL-yuh-LOID   'seljəˌlɔid

Celsius
  Anders, *Swedish astronomer;*   SEL-sē-uhs, SEL-shuhs   'selsiːəs, 'selʃəs
  temperature scale

Celtic
  lang. family   KEL-tik, SEL-tik   'keltik, 'seltik

Celtics
  basketball team, Boston; soccer team,   SEL-tiks   'seltiks
  Scotland

Celtic Sea
  sea, Atlantic Ocean   KEL-tik SĒ, SEL-tik   ˌkeltik 'siː, ˌseltik

Celts
  people, Europe   KELTS, SELTS   'kelts, 'selts

Celtus
  son of Heracles and Celtine   SEL-tuhs   'seltəs

Cemal
  pers. name, Turkish   ke-MAHL   ke'mal

Cenchreae
  Biblical name   ken-KRĒ-uh, sen-KRĒ-Ī, SEN-krē-uh   ken'kriːə, sen'kriːˌai, 'senkriːə

Cenci, The
  tragedy, P. B. Shelley   CHEN-chē   'tʃentʃi·

Cenis, Mont
  Alpine pass   mawⁿ SNĒ, mawⁿ suh-NĒ   mɔ̃ sniː, mɔ̃ səniː

Cenozoic
  geologic era   SĒ-nuh-ZŌ-ik, SEN-uh-   ˌsiːnə'zoːik, ˌsenə-

Centaur
  mythical creature; constellation   SEN-TAWR   'senˌtɔːʳ

Centaurus
  constellation   sen-TAWR-uhs   sen'tɔːrəs

Centel
  US telephone co.   SEN-TEL, sen-TEL   'senˌtel, sen'tel

Foreign Sounds: ue: *Fr.* **rue**, *Ger.* **füllen**   uh(r): *Fr.* **boeuf**, *Ger.* **Höhle**   <u>kh</u>: *Ger.* **ich**, *Scot.* **loch**   g̱: *Sp.* **amigo**   <u>v</u>: *Sp.* **hablar** hl: *Welsh* **Llanelli**.   CAPITALS: primary stress.   SMALL CAPS: secondary stress.   Ⓢ: U.S. pron.   Ⓔ: British pron.

Centex
   US construction co.   SEN-TEKS   'sen͵teks
Centlivre
   Susannah, *English dramatist and*   sent-LIV-uhr, -LĒ-vuhr   sent'livəʳ, -'liːvəʳ
   actress
Centre
   1. county, PA; town, AL   SENT-uhr   'sentəʳ
   2. region, France   SAHⁿTR   sãtr
Centre Pompidou
   city, France   sahⁿ-truh pawⁿ-pē-D$\overline{\text{OO}}$ sãtrə pɔ̃piːduː
Centro-Oeste
   region, Brazil   SEⁿ(N)-tr$\overline{\text{oo}}$ ō-ES-tuh   'sẽ(n)truː oːˈestə
Centuriate assembly
   Roman legislative body   sen-T(Y)UR-ē-uht uh-SEM-blē   sen'tʃuriːət̬ əˈsembliˑ
Cephalonia
   region, Greece   SEF-uh-LŌN-yuh, -LŌ-nē-uh   ͵sefəˈloːnjə, -ˈloːniːə
Cephalus
   husband of Procris   SEF-uh-luhs   'sefələs
Cephas
   Biblical name   SĒ-fuhs   'siːfəs
Cepheids
   type of variable star   SĒ-fē-uhdz, SEF-ē-uhdz   'siːfiːədz, 'sefiːədz
Cepheus
   Argonaut, husband of Cassiopeia;   SĒ-FY$\overline{\text{OO}}$S, SĒ-fē-uhs   'siː͵fjuːs, 'siːfiːəs
   constellation
Ceram, Seram
   island, Indonesia; sea, Pacific   SĀ-RAHM   'seː͵rɑm
Ceramus
   mythical inventor of pottery   suh-RAM-uhs   səˈræməs
Ceratopsia
   dinosaur suborder   SER-uh-TAHP-sē-uh   ͵serəˈtɑpsiːə
Ceratosaurus
   dinosaur   SER-uht-ō-SAWR-uhs   ͵serət̬oːˈsɔːrəs
Ceraunian
   Mountains, *mtn. range, Greece*   suh-RAW-nē-uhn   səˈrɔːniːən
Cerberus
   3-headed dog of Hades   SUHR-b(uh-)ruhs   'səʳb(ə)rəs
Cercopes
   mythical dwarves who robbed   suhr-KŌ-pēz   səʳˈkoːpiːz
   Heracles
Cerenkov
   see Cherenkov
Cerenkov effect, Che-
   light emission caused by a charged   chuh-RENG-kawf, -kuhf   tʃəˈreŋkɔːf, -kəf
   particle
Ceres
   1. Roman harvest goddess; asteroid   SIR-ēz   'siriːz
   2. Danish beer   SE-räs   'sereːs
Cerf
   Bennett, *US publisher*   SUHRF   'səʳf
Cerigo [Cythera]
   Mediterranean island   CHER-i-GŌ   'tʃeri͵goː
cerium
   element   SIR-ē-uhm   'siriːəm

Key (col. 2):   a: fad   ā: fade   ah: father   ar: marry   aw: law   e: fed   ē: feed   er: merry   i: hid   ī: hide   ō: coat $\overline{\text{oo}}$: boot
oi: boy   ow: now   u: put   uh: above   uhr: bird   ch: chop   ng: ring   sh: show   th: thick   th: this   zh: measure

CERN
  acronym, European particle physics   SUHRN   'sə^{r}n
    laboratory

Cerritos
  city, College, *CA*   suh-RĒT-uhs   sə'riːţəs

Cerro Coso
  Community College, *CA*   SER-ō KŌ-sō   'seroː 'koːsoː

Cerro de Pasco
  mtn., town, Peru   SER-ō the PAHS-kō   'seroː ðe 'paskoː

Cerro de Punta
  see Punta, Cerro de

Cerro Gordo
  county, IA   SER-uh GAWRD-ō   ˌserə 'gɔːᵣdoː

Cerro Largo
  department, Uruguay   SER-ō LAHR-gō   'seroː 'laᵣgoː

Cerulean warbler
  bird   suh-R$\overline{OO}$-lē-uhn WAWR-bluhr   sə'ruːliːən 'wɔːᵣbləᵣ

Cervantes Saavedra
  Miguel de, *Spanish novelist*   ther-<u>V</u>AHN-tās sah-ah-<u>VATH</u>-rah,   θerˈβanteːs sa-aˈβeːðra,
                   ⓢ suhr-VAN-tēz SAH(-uh)-VĀ-druh,   ⓢ səᵣ'væntiːz
                   ser-VAHN-TĀS   ˌsa(ə)'veːdrə, seᵣ'van,teːs

Cervin, Mont [Matterhorn]
  mtn. range, Switzerland, Italy   maw^n ser-VE^n mɔ̃ servɛ̃

Cervino, Monte [Matterhorn]
  mtn. range, Switzerland, Italy   MŌN-tā cher-VĒ-nō   ˌmoːnte: tʃer'viːnoː

Césaire
  pers. name, French   sā-ZER   seːzer

Cesar
  pers. name, Spanish   SĀ-sahr, THĀ-sahr, ⓢ SĀ-zahr   'seːsaᵣ, 'θeːsaᵣ, ⓢ 'seːzaᵣ

César
  1. pers. name, French   sā-ZAHR   seːzaːr
  2. Spanish   SĀ-sahr, THĀ-   'seːsar, 'θeː-

Cesare
  pers. name, Italian   CHĀ-zahr-ā   'tʃeːzareː

Cesareo
  pers. name, Spanish   sā-SAHR-ā-ō, thā-   seː'sareːoː, θeː-

cesium
  element   SĒ-zē-uhm   'siːziːəm

České Budějovice [Budweis]
  city, port, Czech Republic   CHES-kā BUD-uh-YAW-vit-SĀ   'tʃeskeː 'budəˌjoːvitˌseː

České Zemé
  republic, Czech Republic   CHES-ke ZEM-e   'tʃeske 'zeme

Cessna
  US aircraft co.   SES-nuh   'sesnə

Cetacea
  order of whales & porpoises   sē-TĀ-sh(ē-)uh   siː'teːʃ(iː)ə

Cetatea Alba
  city, Ukraine   che-TAHT-yuh AHL-buh   tʃe'tatjə 'albə

Cetewayo, Cetywayo, [Cetshwayo, Ketchwayo]
  Zulu king   KECH-WAH-yō, ⓢ SET-uh-WĀ-ō,   ˌketʃ'waːjoː, ⓢ ˌseţə'weːoː,
                   KET-uh-, -WĪ-ō   ˌkeţə-, -'waioː

Foreign Sounds: ue: *Fr.* **rue**, *Ger.* füllen   uh(r): *Fr.* **boeuf**, *Ger.* Höhle   kh: *Ger.* **ich**, *Scot.* loch   ḡ: *Sp.* amigo   v: *Sp.* hablar
hl: *Welsh* **Ll**anelli.   CAPITALS: primary stress.   SMALL CAPS: secondary stress.   ⓢ: U.S. pron.   ⓔ: British pron.

Cetshwayo, Ketchwayo [Cetewayo]
Zulu king   KECH-WAH-yō, ⑤ KECH-WĀ-ō, -WĪ-ō   ˌketʃˈwɑːjoː, ⑤ ˌketʃˈweːoː, -ˈwɑioː

Ceto
mother of the Graeae   SĒT-ō   ˈsiːțoː

Cetus
constellation   SĒT-uhs   ˈsiːțəs

Ceuta
Spanish military station, port, Morocco   THĀ-ōōT-uh, SĀ-ōōT-uh   ˈθeːˌuːțə, ˈseːˌuːțə

Cévennes
mtn. range, France   sā-VEN   seːven

Ceylon [Sri Lanka]
island, state, Indian Ocean   si-LAHN, sā-LAHN   siˈlɑn, seːˈlɑn

Ceyx
friend of Heracles   SĒ-iks   ˈsiːiks

Cézanne
Paul, French painter   sā-ZAHN   seːzɑːn

Chaadayev
Pyotr Yakovlevich, Russian writer   chuh-UH-DAH-yiv   tʃə,əˈdɑːjiv

Chablis
wine   shuh-BLĒ, shah-, sha-   ʃəˈbliː, ʃɑ-, ʃæ-

Chabot
College, CA   shuh-BŌ   ʃəˈboː

Cha-cha
dance   CHAH-CHAH   ˈtʃɑˌtʃɑ

Chachalaca
S. & Cen. American bird   CHAH-chuh-LAHK-uh   ˌtʃɑtʃəˈlɑkə

Chachapoyas
town, Peru   CHAH-chuh-PŌ-yuhs   ˌtʃɑtʃəˈpoːjəs

Chaco
region, central S. America   CHAHK-ō   ˈtʃɑkoː

Chachoengsao, Chaxerngsao
province, Thailand   CHAH-CHUHNG-SOW   ˈtʃɑˌtʃəŋˈsɑu

Chaconne
dance   shah-KAWN, shah-KAHN, shah-KUHN, sha-   ʃɑˈkɔːn, ʃɑˈkɑn, ʃɑˈkən, ʃæ-

Chad
country, Africa; pers. name   CHAD   ˈtʃæd

Chadian
pert. to Chad   CHAD-ē-uhn   ˈtʃædiːən

Chadron
State College, NE   SHAD-ruhn   ˈʃædrən

Chadwick
Sir James, English physicist (Nobel 1935)   CHAD-wik   ˈtʃædwik

Chaeronea
ancient city, Greece   KER-uh-NĒ-uh, KIR-   ˌkerəˈniːə, ˌkir-

Chafee
John H., US politician   CHĀ-fē   ˈtʃeːfiˑ

Chaffee
county, CO   CHAF-ē, CHĀ-fē   ˈtʃæfiˑ, ˈtʃeːfiˑ

Chaffey
College, CA   CHAF-ē   ˈtʃæfiˑ

Key (col. 2):   a: fad ā: fade ah: father ar: marry aw: law e: fed ē: feed er: merry i: hid ī: hide ō: coat ōō: boot
oi: boy   ow: now   u: put   uh: above   uhr: bird   ch: chop   ng: ring   sh: show   th: thick   th̲: this   zh: measure

Chaffinch
   songbird — CHAF-inch — 'tʃæfintʃ

Chagall
   Marc, *Russian painter in France* — shah-GAHL — ʃɑːgɑːl

Chagang, Jagang
   province, N. Korea — chah-gahng — tʃagaŋ

Chagres
   river, Panama — CHAHG-ruhs, CHAG-ruhs — 'tʃagrəs, 'tʃægrəs

Chagrin
   river, OH — shuh-GRIN, SHUG-ruhn, SHAG-ruhn — ʃə'grin, 'ʃugrən, 'ʃægrən

Chahar
   prov, Mongolia — CHAH-HAHR — 'tʃɑ'hɑʳ

Chahar Mahall va Bakhtiari
   province, Iran — chah-HAHR mah-HAHL vah BAHKH-tyah-RĒ — tʃɑˌhɑʳ mɑˌhɑl vɑː ˌbɑːxtjɑ'riː

Chaibasa
   town, India — chi-BAHS-uh — tʃi'bɑsə

Chaim
   1. pers. name, Hebrew — khī-(Y)IM, KHĪ-(y)im — xai'(j)im, 'xɑi(j)im
   2. Yiddish — KHĪ-(y)im — 'xai(j)im

Chain
   E. B., *British biochemist (Nobel 1945)* — CHĀN — 'tʃeːn

Chainat, Jainat, Jayanath
   province, Thailand — CHĪ-NAHT — 'tʃai'nɑt

Chaiyaphum, Jayabum
   province, Thailand — CHĪ-(y)uh-P̄OOM — ˌtʃai(j)ə'puːm

Chalatenango
   department, El Salvador — CHAHL-uh-tuh-NAHNG-gō, chuh-LAH-tuh- — ˌtʃalətə'naŋgoː, tʃəˌlɑtə-

Chalcedon
   ancient city, Asia Minor — KAL-suh-DAHN, kal-SĒD-n — 'kælsəˌdɑn, kæl'siːdn̩

Chalcedony
   quartz — kal-SED-n-ē, chal-SED-n-ē; KAL-suh-DŌ-nē, CHAL-suh-DŌ-nē — kæl'sednĭˑ, tʃæl'sednĭˑ; 'kælsəˌdoːnĭˑ, 'tʃælsəˌdoːnĭˑ

Chalcidice
   peninsula, Greece — chal-SID-uh-sē — tʃæl'sidəsĭˑ

Chalciope
   second wife of Aegeus — kal-SĪ-uh-pē — kæl'saiəpĭˑ

Chalcis
   city, Greece — KAL-suhs, KAL-kuhs — 'kælsəs, 'kælkəs

Chalcodon
   father of Chalciope and Elephenor — KAL-kuh-DAHN — 'kælkəˌdɑn

Chalcolithic Age
   latter Neolithic period, Near East — KAL-kuh-LITH-ik — ˌkælkə'liθik

Chalcopyrite
   mineral — KAL-kuh-PĪ-RĪT — ˌkælkə'paiˌrait

Chaldea, Chaldaea
   region of Babylonia — kal-DĒ-uh — kæl'diːə

Chaldean
   pert. to Chaldea — kal-DĒ-uhn — kæl'diːən

Chaldee [Chaldean]
   pert. to Chaldea — kal-DĒ — kæl'diː

Chaliapin

Fëdor, *Russian opera star*   shuhl-YAHP-yin   ʃəl'jaːpjin

Chalma

Mexico   CHAHL-mah   'tʃalma

Chalmers

pers. name   CHAL-muhrz, CHAHL-   'tʃælməᵉz, 'tʃal-

Chalons-sur-Marne

commune, France   shah-LAWⁿ-suer-MAHRN   ʃaːlõsyːrmaːrn

Cham

lang., people, Indochina   CHAHM   'tʃam

Chamaeleon, Chameleon

constellation   kuh-MĒL-yuhn, kuh-MĒ-lē-uhn   kə'miːljən, kə'miːliːən

Chamberlain

Sir Austen, *British statesman (Nobel*   CHĀM-buhr-luhn   'tʃeːmbəᵉlən
    1925) & his brother Neville,
    British statesman; Owen, *US*
    physicist (Nobel 1959)

Chambéry

city, France   shahⁿ-bā-RĒ   ʃãbeːriː

Chambezi

river, Africa   cham-BĒ-zē   tʃæm'biːziˑ

Chambly

city, Quebec, Canada   shahⁿ-BLĒ, ⑤ SHAM-blē   ʃãbliː, ⑤ 'ʃæmbliː

Chamois

antelope; fabric   SHAM-ē, sham-WAH   'ʃæmiˑ, ʃæm'wa

Chamonix

mtn. valley, France   shah-maw-NĒ   ʃaːmɔːniː

Chamorro

Violetta, *Nicaraguan politician;*   chuh-MAWR-ō   tʃə'mɔːroː
    lang., people, Guam

Chamorro Vargas

Emiliano, *Nicaraguan general and*   chah-MAWR-rō V̲AHR-g̲ahs   tʃa'mɔːrroː 'βarɣas
    politician

Champagne

region, France   shahⁿ-PAHN-yuh, ⑤ sham-PĀN   ʃãpaːɲ , ⑤ ʃæm'peːn

Champagne-Ardenne

region, France   shahⁿ-pahn-yahr-DEN   ʃãpaːnjaːrden

Champaign

county, IL, OH; city, IL   sham-PĀN   ʃæm'peːn

Champaquí

peak, Argentina   CHAHM-puh-KĒ   ˌtʃampə'kiː

Champasak

province, Laos   CHAHM-puh-SAHK   ˌtʃampə'sak

Champigny

French wine   shahⁿ-pēn-YĒ   ʃãpiːnjiː

Champlain

1. *lake, NY, VT, & Quebec*   sham-PLĀN   ʃæm'pleːn
2. Samuel de, *French explorer*   shahⁿ-PLEⁿ; ⑤ sham-PLĀN   ʃãpleː; ⑤ ʃæm'pleːn

Champollion

Jean-François, *French Egyptologist*   shah-pawl-YAWⁿ   ʃaːpɔːljõ

Champs Élysées

boulevard, Paris, France   SHAHⁿZ ā-lē-ZĀ   ʃãz eːliːzeː

Chancellor

John William, *US news*   CHAN(T)-s(uh-)luhr   'tʃæn(t)s(ə)ləᵉ
    correspondent

Key (col. 2):   a: fad   ā: fade   ah: father   ar: marry   aw: law   e: fed   ē: feed   er: merry   i: hid   ī: hide   ō: coat   ōō: boot
oi: boy   ow: now   u: put   uh: above   uhr: bird   ch: chop   ng: ring   sh: show   th: thick   th̲: this   zh: measure

Chandigarh
   city, India   CHUHN-dē-guhr   'tʃəndiːgəʳ

Chandra
   1. pers. name, Bengali   CHAWN-draw   'tʃɔːndrɔː
   2. Sanskrit   CHUHN-druh   'tʃəndrə

Chandragupta
   1st emperor of India   CHUHN-druh-GUP-tuh   ˌtʃəndrə'guptə

Chandrasekhar
   Subrahmanyan, *US astrophysicist*   CHUHN-druh-SĀ-kuhr   ˌtʃəndrə'seːkəʳ
   (Nobel 1983)

Chandrasekhara
   pers. name, Bengali   CHUHN-druh-SHĀ-kuh-ruh   ˌtʃəndrə'ʃeːkərə

Chanel
   fragrance   shuh-NEL   ʃə'nel

Chanell
   pers. name   shuh-NEL   ʃə'nel

Chaney
   Lon, *US actor*   CHĀ-nē   'tʃeːni·

Changan [Xian]
   city, China   CHAHNG-AHN   'tʃaŋ'an

Changchun, Ch'ang-ch'ung
   city, China   CHAHNG-CHUN   'tʃaŋ'tʃun

Chang-hua
   county, Taiwan   CHAHNG-HWAH   'tʃaŋ'hwɑ

Changi
   airport, Singapore   JAHNG-GĒ   'dʒaŋ'giː

Chang Jiang [Yangtze]
   river, China   CHAHNG jē-AHNG   'tʃaŋ dʒiː'aŋ

Changsha, Ch'ang-sha
   city, China   CHAHNG-SHAH   'tʃaŋ'ʃa

Chang Tso-lin
   see Zhang Zuolin

Ch'ang-won
   city, S. Korea   chahng-wahn   tʃaŋwan

Chankiri
   see Çankırı

Chantabun
   province, Thailand   CHAHN-tah-B̄OO̅N   ˌtʃɑntɑ'buːn

Chantal
   town, Haiti   shahⁿ-TAHL, ⑤ shahn-TAHL   ʃɑ̃tɑːl, ⑤ ʃɑn'tɑl

Chant de Railliemant
   national anthem, Cameroon   SHAHⁿ duh rī-yē-MAHⁿT   ʃɑ̃ də raijiːmɑ̃t

Chanthaburi, Chantaburi
   [Chantabun]
   province, Thailand   chahn-TAH-bu-RĒ   tʃɑn,tɑbu'riː

Chanticleer
   rooster; US vocal ensemble   CHANT-i-KLIR, SHANT-i-KLIR   ˌtʃænti'kliʳ, ˌʃænti'kliʳ

Chantilly
   1. town, France   shahⁿ-tē-YĒ   ʃɑ̃tiːjiː
   2. village, VA   shan-TIL-ē   ʃæn'tili·

Chanukah
   Jewish holiday   K̲H̲AHN-uh-kuh, HAHN-uh-kuh   'xɑnəkə, 'hɑnəkə

Chao
   1. Chinese family of Sung dynasty   JOW   'dʒɑu
   2. pers. name   CHOW   'tʃɑu

Foreign Sounds: ue: *Fr.* **rue**, *Ger.* **füllen**   uh(r): *Fr.* **boeuf**, *Ger.* **Höhle**   k̲h̲: *Ger.* **ich**, *Scot.* **loch**   ḡ: *Sp.* **amigo**   v̲: *Sp.* **hablar**
hl: *Welsh* **Llanelli**.   CAPITALS: primary stress.   SMALL CAPS: secondary stress.   ⑤: U.S. pron.   ⑥: British pron.

Ch'ao-an [Chaozhou]
  city, China — CHOW-AHN — ˈtʃauˈan

Chao Phraya
  river, Thailand — chow PRĪ-uh — tʃau ˈpraiə

Chaos
  void preceding the Greek gods; — KĀ-AHS — ˈkeːˌɑs
    computer network protocol

Chaozhou [Ch'ao-an]
  city, China — CHOW-JŌ — ˈtʃauˈdʒoː

Chapellet
  California wine — SHAP-uh-LĀ — ˌʃæpəˈleː

Chaplin
  Charlie, *US actor* — CHAP-luhn — ˈtʃæplən

Chappaquiddick
  island, MA — CHAP-uh-KWID-ik — ˌtʃæpəˈkwidik

Chapultepec
  fortress, park, Mexico City — chuh-POOL-tuh-PEK — tʃəˈpuːltəˌpek

Charashim
  Biblical name — KAHR-uh-SHIM, KHAHR-ah-SHIM — ˈkarəˌʃim, ˌxaraˈʃim

Charcot
  Jean M., *French scientist* — shahr-KŌ — ʃaːrkoː

Chardin
  Jean, *French traveler* — shahr-DE^n — ʃaːrdẽ

Chardonnay
  wine — SHAHRD-n-Ā, SHAHR-duh-NĀ, SHAHRD-n-Ā — ˌʃɑʳdn̩ˈeː, ˌʃɑʳdəˈneː, ˈʃɑʳdn̩ˌeː

Chardzhou
  subdivision, Turkmenistan — chahr-JŌ — tʃɑʳˈdʒoː

Charente
  river, dept, France — shah-RAH^{n}T — ʃaːrãt

Chargoggagoggman-
chaugagogg-
chaubunagungamaug
[Chaubunagungamaug]
  lake, MA — chahr-GAHG-uh-GAHG-man-CHAW-guh-GAHG-chaw-BUHN-uh-GUHNG-guh-MAWG — tʃɑʳˈgagəˌgagmæn ˈtʃɔːgəˌgagtʃɔː ˌbənəˈgəŋgəˌmɔːg

Chargui, Hodh ech
  region, Mauritania — HAWD ekh shahr-GĒ — ˌhɔːd ex ʃɑʳˈgiː

Chari-Baguirmi
  prefecture, Chad — shah-RĒ-bah-GĒR-mē — ʃaˌriːbaˈgiːʳmiˑ

Chārikār
  town, Afghanistan — CHAHR-ē-KAHR — ˌtʃariːˈkɑʳ

Chari, Shari
  river, Africa — SHAHR-ē — ˈʃariˑ

Chariclo
  mother of Tiresias — KAR-i-KLŌ — ˈkæriˌkloː

Charing Cross
  district, London — CHAR-ing KRAWS, CHER-ing — ˌtʃæriŋ ˈkrɔːs, ˌtʃeriŋ

Charis
  singular of Charites — KAR-uhs — ˈkærəs

Charisse
  Cyd, *US actress* — shuh-RĒS — ʃəˈriːs

Charites
  Roman goddesses of beauty — KAR-uht-ēz — ˈkærətiːz

Key (col. 2): a: fad ā: fade ah: father ar: marry aw: law e: fed ē: feed er: merry i: hid ī: hide ō: coat ōō: boot
oi: boy ow: now u: put uh: above uhr: bird ch: chop ng: ring sh: show th: thick th: this zh: measure

Chariton
    county, MO; river, US   SHAR-uht-n   'ʃærətn̩

Charlemagne
    1. Frankish king; pers. name   SHAHR-luh-MĀN   'ʃɑʳləˌmeːn
    2. French   shahr-luh-MAHN-yuh   ʃaːrləmaːɲ

Charles
    1. pers. name   CHAHRLZ   'tʃɑʳlz
    2. Dutch   SHAHRL   'ʃɑrl
    3. French   SHAHRL   ʃaːrl

Charles de Gaulle [Roissy]
    airport, Paris   SHAHRL duh GŌL   ʃaːrl də goːl

Charleston
    city, county, SC   CHAHRL-stuhn, CHAHRLZ-tuhn   'tʃɑʳlstən, 'tʃɑʳlztən

Charlevoix
    county, MI   SHAHR-luh-VOI   'ʃɑʳləˌvɔi

Charlevoix-Est
    county, Quebec, Canada   shahr-luh-VWAH-EST   ʃaːrləvwɑest

Charlevoix-Ouest
    county, Quebec, Canada   shahr-luh-VWAH-WEST   ʃarləvwawest

Charley, Charlie
    pers. name   CHAHR-lē   'tʃɑʳiˑ

Charlot
    André Eugene Maurice, *British*   shahr-LŌ, Ⓢ SHAHR-LŌ   ʃaːrloː, Ⓢ 'ʃɑʳˌloː
    theatrical manager and producer

Charlotte
    1. city, MI   shahr-LAHT, SHAHR-luht   ʃɑʳ'lɑt, 'ʃɑʳlət
    2. city, NC; county, FL, VA; pers.   SHAHR-luht   'ʃɑʳlət
    name
    3. French   shahr-LAWT   ʃaːrlɔːt
    4. German   shahr-LAW-tuh   ʃɑʳ'lɔːtə
    5. Swedish   shahr-LAWT   ʃaːr'lɔːt

Charlotte Amalie
    city, US Virgin Islands   SHAHR-luht uh-MAHL-yuh   'ʃɑʳlət ə'maljə

Charlton
    pers. name   CHAHRLT-n, CHAHRL-tuhn   'tʃɑʳltn̩, 'tʃɑʳltən

Charmat
    sparkling wine production method   shahr-MAH   ʃaːrmaː

Charmides
    dialogue of Plato   KAHR-muh-DĒZ   'kɑʳməˌdiːz

Charo
    US entertainer   CHAHR-ō, CHAR-ō, CHER-ō   'tʃaroː, 'tʃæroː, 'tʃeroː

Charolais
    breed of cattle   SHAR-uh-LĀ   ˌʃærə'leː

Charon
    ferryman of Hades; satellite of Pluto   KAR-uhn, KER-uhn   'kærən, 'kerən

Charro Days
    Mexican border fiesta   CHAHR-ō   'tʃaroː

Charrúa
    S. American people   chuh-ROO-uh   tʃə'ruːə

Chartism
    political movement   CHAHRT-ɪz-uhm   'tʃɑʳt̩ˌizəm

Chartres
    city, France   SHAHRTR, Ⓢ SHAHRT, SHAHR-truh   ʃaːrtr, Ⓢ 'ʃɑʳt, 'ʃɑʳtrə

Foreign Sounds: ue: *Fr.* rue, *Ger.* füllen   uh(r): *Fr.* boeuf, *Ger.* Höhle   <u>kh</u>: *Ger.* ich, *Scot.* loch   g̃: *Sp.* amigo   <u>v</u>: *Sp.* hablar
hl: *Welsh* Llanelli.   CAPITALS: primary stress.   SMALL CAPS: secondary stress.   Ⓢ: U.S. pron.   Ⓔ: British pron.

Chartreuse
  French liqueur   shahr-TRUH(R)Z, ⑤ shahr-TRŌŌZ,   ʃɑːrtrœːz, ⑤ ʃɑrˈtruːz, -ˈtruːs
                                           -TRŌŌS
Charybdis
  personified whirlpool off Sicily   kuh-RIB-duhs, shuh-, chuh-   kəˈribdəs, ʃə-, tʃə-
Chasid
  see Hasid
Chassagne-Montrachet
  French wine   shah-SAHN-yuh-mawⁿ-rah-SHE   ʃaːsaːɲ mɔ̃raːʃe
Chassahowitzka
  National Wildlife Refuge, *FL*   CHAS-uh-HOW-(w)uht-skuh   ˌtʃæsəˈhɑu(w)ətskə
Chateaubriand
  François, *French statesman &*   shah-tō-brē-AHⁿ   ʃaːtoːbriːɑ̃
    author
Château-Chalon
  wine   shah-TŌ-shah-LAWⁿ   ʃatoːʃaːlɔ̃
Chateau Chevalier
  wine   sha-TŌ SHEV-uh-LIR, shuh-val-YĀ   ʃæˈtoː ˌʃevəˈlir, ʃəvælˈjeː
Château-Couhins
  wine   shah-TŌ-kōō-EⁿS   ʃatoːkuːẽs
Chateauguay, Chât-
  town, Canada; river, US & Canada   SHAT-uh-GĀ, ⑤ SHAT-uh-gē,   ˌʃæʔəˈgeː, ⑤ ˈʃæʔəgiˈ,
                                           SHAT-uh-GĀ   ˈʃæʔəˌgeː
Château-Haut-Brion
  wine   shah-TŌ-ō-brē-AWⁿ   ʃatoːoːbriːɔ̃
Château-Lafite
  wine   shah-TŌ-lah-FĒT   ʃatoːlaːfiːt
Château-Latour
  wine   shah-TŌ-lah-TŌŌR   ʃatoːlaːtuːr
Chateau Leonay
  wine   sha-TŌ LĒ-uh-NĀ, -NĪ   ʃæˈtoː ˌliːəˈneː, -ˈnɑi
Château-Margaux
  wine   shah-TŌ-mahr-GŌ   ʃatoːmaːrgoː
Chateau Montelena
  wine   sha-TŌ MAHNT-l-Ā-nuh   ʃæˈtoː ˌmɑntl̩ˈeːnə
Château-Mouton-Rothschild
  wine   shah-TŌ-mōō-TAWⁿ-rawt-SHĒLD   ʃatoːmuːtɔ̃rɔːtʃiːld
Châteauneuf-du-Pape
  wine   shah-tō-NUH(R)F-due-PAHP   ʃatoːnœfdyːpaːp
Chateau St. Jean
  winery, CA   sha-TŌ sānt JĒN   ʃæˈtoː seːnt ˈdʒiːn
Chateau Souverain
  winery, CA   sha-TŌ SŌŌ-vuh-REN, SŌŌ-vuh-RĀN   ʃæˈtoː ˌsuːvəˈren, ˈsuːvəˌreːn
Chateau Yaldara
  wine   sha-TŌ YAL-duh-ruh   ʃæˈtoː ˈjældərə
Châtelet
  Gabrielle Émilie Le Tonnelier de   shaht-LE   ʃaːtle
    Breteuil, Marquise du, *French*
    mathematician, physicist, and
    philosopher, mistress of Voltaire
Chatham
  College, *PA, county, GA, NC; city,*   CHAT-uhm   ˈtʃæʔəm
    Canada; borough, England;
    islands, New Zealand

Key (col. 2):   a: f**a**d   ā: f**a**de   ah: f**a**ther   ar: m**a**rry   aw: l**a**w   e: f**e**d   ē: f**ee**d   er: m**e**rry   i: h**i**d   ī: h**i**de   ō: c**oa**t   ōō: b**oo**t
oi: b**oy**   ow: n**ow**   u: p**u**t   uh: **a**bove   uhr: b**ir**d   ch: **ch**op   ng: ri**ng**   sh: **sh**ow   th: **th**ick   <u>th</u>: **th**is   zh: mea**s**ure

Chatila
    Palestinian refugee camp, Lebanon   shah-TĒ-luh   ʃɑˈtiːlə

Chatino
    lang., people, Mexico   chuh-TĒ-nō   tʃəˈtiːnoː

Chattahoochee
    river, US; county, GA   CHAT-uh-H$\overline{\text{OO}}$-chē   ˌtʃæʈəˈhuːtʃiˑ

Chattanooga
    city, TN   CHAT-uh-N$\overline{\text{OO}}$-guh, CHAT-n-$\overline{\text{OO}}$-guh,   ˌtʃæʈəˈnuːgə, ˌtʃæʈnˈuːgə,
                         CHAT-uh-NU-guh   ˌtʃæʈəˈnugə

Chatterjee, Chatterji
    Bankim Chandra, *Indian novelist*   CHAT-uhr-jē   ˈtʃæʈəˑrdʒiˑ

Chatterley
    Connie, *character in* Lady   CHAT-uhr-lē   ˈtʃæʈəˑrliˑ
      Chatterley's Lover, *D.H.*
      Lawrence

Chattooga
    county, GA   chuh-T$\overline{\text{OO}}$-guh   tʃəˈtuːgə

Chaubunagungamaug
[Chargoggagoggman-
chaugagoggchau-
bunagungamaug]
    lake, MA   chaw-BUHN-uh-GUHNG-guh-MAWG   tʃɔːˌbənəˈgəŋgəˌmɔːg

Chaucer
    Geoffrey, *English poet*   CHAW-suhr   ˈtʃɔːsəʳ

Chaucerian
    pert. to Chaucer   chaw-SIR-ē-uhn, chaw-SER-ē-uhn   tʃɔːˈsiriːən, tʃɔːˈseriːən

Chaudet
    Denis-Antoine, *French sculptor*   shaw-DE   ʃɔːde

Chaulmoogra
    tree   chawl-M$\overline{\text{OO}}$-gruh   tʃɔːlˈmuːgrə

Chaumont
    commune, France   shō-MAW^n ʃoːmɔ̃

Chauncey
    pers. name   CHAWN-sē, CHAHN-   ˈtʃɔːnsiˑ, ˈtʃɑn-

Chautauqua
    county, KA, NY; lake, town, NY;   shuh-TAWK-wuh   ʃəˈtɔːkwə
      National Wildlife Refuge, *IL*

Chaves
    1. county, NM   CHAV-uhs, SHAV-uhs   ˈtʃævəs, ˈʃævəs
    2. commune, Portugal   SHAHV-ēsh   ˈʃɑːviːʃ

Chavez
    Cesar, *US union official*   SHAHV-EZ, CHAH-VEZ   ˈʃavˌez, ˈtʃɑˌvez

Chavin
    S. American people   chuh-VĒN   tʃəˈviːn

Chavis
    Benjamin Franklin, Jr., *US civil*   CHAV-uhs, CHĀ-vuhs   ˈtʃævəs, ˈtʃeːvəs
      rights leader

Chaxernsao
    see Chachoengsao

Chayefsky
    Paddy, *US author*   chī-EF-skē, chī-EV-skē   tʃaiˈefskiˑ, tʃaiˈevskiˑ

Chayim
    1. pers. name, Hebrew   k<u>h</u>ī-(Y)IM, <u>KHĪ</u>-(y)im   xaiˈ(j)im, ˈxai(j)im
    2. Yiddish   <u>KHĪ</u>-(y)im   ˈxai(j)im

Foreign Sounds: ue: *Fr.* **rue**, *Ger.* **füllen** uh(r): *Fr.* **boeuf**, *Ger.* **Höhle** <u>kh</u>: *Ger.* **ich**, *Scot.* **loch** ḡ: *Sp.* **amigo** v̲: *Sp.* **hablar**
hl: *Welsh* **Llanelli.**   CAPITALS: primary stress. SMALL CAPS: secondary stress. ($): U.S. pron. (£): British pron.

Chaz
  perfume brand   CHAZ   'tʃæz
Che
  pers. name, Spanish   CHĀ   'tʃeː
Cheatham
  county, TN   CHĒT-uhm   'tʃiːtəm
Cheb
  town, Czech Republic   K͟HEP, Ⓢ KEP, HEP   'xep, Ⓢ 'kep, 'hep
Chebar
  Biblical name   KĒ-BAHR, kuh-VAHR   'kiːˌbɑʳ, kə'vɑr
Cheboksary
  city, Russia   CHEB-ahk-SAHR-yi, -SAHR-ē   ˌtʃebɑk'sɑːrjij, -'sɑriˑ
Cheboygan
  river, county, city, MI   shi-BOI-guhn   ʃi'bɔigən
Chechen
  lang., people, Georgia and   chuh-CHEN   tʃə'tʃen
    Kazakhstan
Chechnya
  region, Russia   chech-NYAH, Ⓢ CHECH-nē-uh   tʃetʃ'njɑ, Ⓢ 'tʃetʃniːə
Cheddar
  town, England; cheese   CHED-uhr   'tʃedər
Chedor-laomer
  Biblical name   KED-AWR-LĀ-uh-muhr,   ˌkedˌɔːʳ'leːəməʳ,
                                     kuh-DAWR-lah-AW-mer   kəˌdɔːrlɑ'ɔːmer
Chehalis
  N. American people   chuh-HĀ-luhs   tʃə'heːləs
Cheju
  island, S. Korea   chā-jōō   tʃeːdʒuː
Cheka
  secret police, USSR   CHEK-uh   'tʃekə
Chekhov
  Anton, *Russian writer*   CHEK͟H-uhf, Ⓢ CHEK-AWF,   'tʃexəf, Ⓢ 'tʃekˌɔːf, 'tʃekˌɔːv
                                     CHEK-AWV
Chekiang
  see Zhejiang
Chekov
  Pavel, *character, Star Trek*   CHEK-AWF, CHEK-AWV   'tʃekˌɔːf, 'tʃekˌɔːv
Chelal
  Biblical name   KĒ-LAL, kuh-LAHL   'kiːˌlæl, kə'lɑl
Chelan
  county, WA   shuh-LAN   ʃə'læn
Chéliff [Sheliff]
  river, Algeria   shā-LĒF   ʃeːliːf
Chelm
  province, Poland   K͟HELM, Ⓢ KELM, HELM   'xeɫm, Ⓢ 'kelm, 'helm
Chelone
  girl changed into a tortoise   kē-LŌ-nē   kiː'loːniˑ
Chelsea
  city, MA; London borough; pers. CHEL-sē   'tʃelsiˑ
    name
Cheltenham
  city, England; type font   CHELT-n-uhm   'tʃeltn̩əm
Chelub
  Biblical name   KĒ-LUHB, kuh-LŌŌV   'kiːˌləb, kə'luːv

Key (col. 2):   a: f**a**d   ā: f**a**de   ah: f**a**ther   ar: m**a**rry   aw: l**a**w   e: f**e**d   ē: f**ee**d   er: m**e**rry   i: h**i**d   ī: h**i**de   ō: c**oa**t   ōō: b**oo**t
oi: b**oy**   ow: n**ow**   u: p**u**t   uh: **a**bove   uhr: b**i**rd   ch: **ch**op   ng: ri**ng**   sh: **sh**ow   th: **th**ick   t͟h: **th**is   zh: mea**s**ure

Chelubai
   Biblical name   kuh-L$\overline{OO}$-BĪ, kuh-l$\overline{oo}$-VĪ   kə'luː‚bɑi, kəluː'vɑi

Chelyabinsk
   city, Russia   chel-YAH-buhn(t)sk   tʃel'jɑːbən(t)sk

Chemarim
   Biblical name   KEM-uh-RIM, kuh-mahr-ĒM   'kemə‚rim, kəmɑr'iːm

Chemehuevi
   N. American people   CHEM-uh-WĀ-vē   ‚tʃemə'weːviˑ

Chemin-de-fer
   game   shuh-MAN-duh-FER   ʃə‚mændə'feʳ

Chemnitz [Karl Marx Stadt]
   city, Germany   <u>KH</u>EM-nits   'çemnits

Chemosh
   Biblical name   KĒ-MAHSH, KĒ-MŌSH, kuh-MŌSH   'kiː‚mɑʃ, 'kiː‚moːʃ, kə'moːʃ

Chemung
   river, US; county, NY   shi-MUHNG   ʃi'məŋ

Ch'en
   Chinese dynasty   CHUHN   'tʃən

Chenaanah
   Biblical name   kuh-NĀ-uh-nuh, kuh-NAH-ah-NAH   kə'neːənə, kə‚nɑɑ'nɑ

Chenango
   river, county, NY   shuh-NANG-gō   ʃə'næŋgoː

Ch'en Ch'eng
   Chinese soldier and politician   CHUHN CHUHNG   'tʃən 'tʃəŋ

Chen-chiang
   see Zhejiang

Cheney
   Richard B., *US politician;* Stadium,   CHĀ-nē   'tʃeːniˑ
       Tacoma, WA

Chengchow
   see Zhengzhou

Chengdu, Ch'ung-tu
   city, China   CHUHNG-D$\overline{OO}$ 'tʃəŋ'duː

Cheng [Shih Hwang-ti]
   Chinese emperor   JUHNG   'dʒəŋ

Chénier
   André, *French poet*   shān-YĀ   ʃeːnjeː

Chenin Blanc
   wine   shuh-neⁿ-BLAHⁿ, Ⓢ SHEN-in   ʃənēblɑ̃, Ⓢ ‚ʃenin 'blɑŋk
       BLAHNGK

Chennault
   Claire, *US militarist*   shuh-NAWLT   ʃə'nɔːlt

Chennault
   Claire Lee, *US aviator*   shuh-NAWLT   ʃə'nɔːlt

Cheops [Khufu]
   Egyptian pharoah   KĒ-AHPS   'kiː‚ɑps

Chephar-ammoni [Chephar Haammonai]
   Biblical name   KĒ-fahr-AM-uh-NĪ, KFAHR   'kiːfɑr'æmə‚nɑi, ‚kfɑʳ
       hah-AHM-ō-NĪ   hɑ‚amoː'nɑi

Chephar Haammonai
   Biblical name   KĒ-FAHR huh-AM-uh-NĪ, KFAHR   'kiː‚fɑʳ hə'æmə‚nɑi, ‚kfɑʳ
       hah-AHM-ō-NĪ   hɑ‚amoː'nɑi

Chephirah
   Biblical name   kuh-FĪ-ruh, kuh-FĒ-RAH   kə'fɑirə, kə‚fiː'rɑ

Foreign Sounds: ue: *Fr.* rue, *Ger.* füllen   uh(r): *Fr.* boeuf, *Ger.* Höhle   <u>kh</u>: *Ger.* ich, *Scot.* loch   g̵: *Sp.* amigo   v̶: *Sp.* hablar
hl: *Welsh* Llanelli.   CAPITALS: primary stress.   SMALL CAPS: secondary stress.   Ⓢ: U.S. pron.   Ⓔ: British pron.

Cher		
1. US entertainer	SHER	'ʃeʳ
2. river, dept, France	SHER	ʃer
Cheran		
Biblical name	KĒ-ruhn, KIR-uhn, kuh-RAHN	'kiːrən, 'kirən, kə'rɑn
Cherbourg		
seaport, France	sher-BO͞OR, [$] SHER-BUR(G), SHUHR-BUR(G)	ʃerbuːr, [$] 'ʃeʳˌbuʳ(g), 'ʃəʳˌbuʳ(g)
Cheremis [Mari]		
lang., people, Russia	CHER-uh-MIS, CHER-uh-MĒS	ˌtʃerə'mis, ˌtʃerə'miːs
Cherenkov, Ce-		
Pavel Alekseevich, *Russian physicist (Nobel 1958)*	chir-yin-KAWF, [$] chuh-RENG-kawf, -kuhf	tʃirjin'kɔːf, [$] tʃə'reŋkɔːf, -kəf
Cherenkov effect		
see Cerenkov effect		
Cherepovets		
city, Russia	chi-ri-PUH-VYETS, [$] CHER-uh-puh-VETS	tʃiriˌpə'vjets, [$] ˌtʃerəpə'vets
Cherethites		
Biblical name	KER-uh-THĪTS, KIR-	'kerəˌθɑits, 'kir-
Cherie, Chérie		
pers. name	shuh-RĒ, sher-Ē, SHER-ē	ʃə'riː, ʃer'iː, 'ʃeriˑ
Cheri-Suisse		
Swiss liqueur	shā-RĒ-SWĒS	ʃeːriːswiːs
Cherith		
Biblical name	KĒ-ruhth, KIR-uhth, kuh-RĒT	'kiːrəθ, 'kirəθ, kə'riːt
Cherkassy, Cherkasi		
city, Ukraine	chir-KAHS-ē, [$] CHUHR-KAHS-ē, -KAS-ē	tʃir'kɑsiː, [$] ˌtʃəʳ'kɑsiˑ, -'kæsiˑ
Cherkessk		
town, Russia	chir-KYESK, [$] CHUHR-KESK	tʃir'kjesk, [$] ˌtʃəʳ'kesk
Cherna [Crna]		
river, Macedonia	CHER-nuh	'tʃeʳnə
Chernenko		
Konstantin, *gen. secy. USSR*	chern-YENG-kō	tʃeʳn'jeŋkoː
Chernigov		
medieval principality, Russia	chir-NYĒ-guhf	tʃir'njiːgəf
Chernobyl		
city, Ukraine	chir-NŌ-bil, [$] chuhr-NŌ-buhl	tʃir'noːbil̥, [$] tʃəʳ'noːbəl
Chernomyrdin		
Viktor S., *Russian prime minister*	CHUHR-nuh-MIRD-n, CHER-	ˌtʃəʳnə'miʳdn̩, ˌtʃeʳ-
Chernovtsy		
city, Ukraine	CHIR-nuhft-SĒ, [$] chuhr-NŌFT-sē	ˌtʃirnəft'siː, [$] tʃəʳ'noːftsiˑ
Chernyshevsky		
Nikolay Gavrilovich, *Russian radical*	CHUHR-nyi-SHEF-skyiy	ˌtʃərnji'ʃefskjij
Cherokee		
N. American people	CHER-uh-kē	'tʃerəkiˑ
Chersonese, The		
any of several European & Asian peninsulas	KUHR-suh-NĒZ, -NĒS; KUHR-suh-NĒZ, -NĒS	'kəʳsəˌniːz, -ˌniːs; ˌkəʳsə'niːz, -'niːs
Cherub		
Biblical name	CHER-uhb, kuh-RO͞OV	'tʃerəb, kə'ruːv
Cherubim		
order of angels	CHER-(y)uh-BIM	'tʃer(j)əˌbim

Key (col. 2): a: fad ā: fade ah: father ar: marry aw: law e: fed ē: feed er: merry i: hid ī: hide ō: coat o͞o: boot oi: boy ow: now u: put uh: above uhr: bird ch: chop ng: ring sh: show th: thick <u>th</u>: this zh: measure

Cherubini
   Luigi Carlo Zenobi Salvadore   KĀ-rōō-BĒ-nē   ˌkeːruːˈbiːniˑ
     Maria, *Italian composer*

Cherwell
   river, district, Oxfordshire   CHAHR-wuhl   ˈtʃɑʳwəl

Cheryl
   pers. name   SHER-uhl   ˈʃerəl

Chesalon
   Biblical name   KES-uh-LAHN, kuh-SAH-LŌN   ˈkesəˌlɑn, kəˌsɑˈloːn

Chesapeake Bay
   inlet, Atlantic Ocean   CHES-uh-PĒK BĀ   ˈtʃesəˌpiːk ˈbeː

Chesebrough-Pond's
   US cosmetics co.   CHĒZ-bruh-PAHN(D)Z   ˌtʃiːzbrəˈpɑn(d)z

Chesed
   Biblical name   KĒ-SED, KĒ-suhd, KES-ED   ˈkiːˌsed, ˈkiːsəd, ˈkesˌed

Cheshire
   county, England; cheese; cat   CHESH-uhr, CHESH-IR   ˈtʃeʃəʳ, ˈtʃeʃˌiʳ

Cheshunt
   town, England   CHES-uhnt   ˈtʃesənt

Chesil
   Biblical name   KĒ-suhl, kuh-SĒL   ˈkiːsəl, kəˈsiːl

Chessline Park
   Philadelphia, PA   CHES-LĪN   ˈtʃesˌlɑin

Chester
   pl. name, US & England; pers. name   CHES-tuhr   ˈtʃestəʳ

Chesulloth
   Biblical name   kuh-SUL-AHTH, -uhth; kuh-SŌŌ-LŌT   kəˈsulˌɑθ, -əθ; kəˌsuːˈloːt

Chet
   pers. name   CHET   ˈtʃet

Chetnik
   member, Serbian nationalist group   chet-NĒK   tʃetˈniːk

Chetumal
   town, Mexico   CHĀ-tōō-MAHL   ˌtʃeːtuːˈmɑl

Cheval Blanc
   wine   shuh-vahl BLAHⁿ   ʃəvɑːl blɑ̃

Chevalier
   Maurice, French-born entertainer   sh(uh-)vahl-YĀ, ⓢ shuh-VAL-yā   ʃ(ə)vɑːljeː, ⓢ ʃəˈvæljeː

Chevaliers du Tastevin
   French wine order   sh(uh-)vahl-YĀ due tahs-tuh-VEⁿ   ʃ(ə)vɑːljeː dyː tɑːstəvẽ

Cheviot
   1. county, OH   SHIV-ē-uht, SHEV-ē-uht   ˈʃiviːət, ˈʃeviːət
   2. range of hills, English-Scottish   CHĒ-vē-uht *(local pron.)*, CHEV-ē-uht,   ˈtʃiːviːət *(local pron.)*,
     border   CHIV-ē-uht, ⓢ SHEV-ē-uht   ˈtʃeviːət, ˈtʃiviːət,
                                              ⓢ ˈʃeviːət

Chevrolet
   US car make   SHEV-ruh-LĀ   ˌʃevrəˈleː

Chevy
   1. nickname for Chevrolet   SHEV-ē   ˈʃeviˑ
   2. pers. name   CHEV-ē   ˈtʃeviˑ

Chevy Chase
   urban district, MD; US comedian   CHEV-ē CHĀS   ˈtʃeviˑ ˈtʃeːs

Chewa [Nyanja]
   lang., people, Africa   CHĀ-wah   ˈtʃeːwɑ

Cheyenne
   N. American people; city, WY   shī-AN, shī-EN   ʃɑiˈæn, ʃɑiˈen

---

Foreign Sounds: ue: *Fr.* **rue**, *Ger.* **füllen**   uh(r): *Fr.* **boeuf**, *Ger.* **Höhle**   <u>kh</u>: *Ger.* i<u>ch</u>, *Scot.* lo<u>ch</u>   g̃: *Sp.* ami**g**o   <u>v</u>: *Sp.* ha**b**lar
hl: *Welsh* **Ll**anelli.   CAPITALS: primary stress.   SMALL CAPS: secondary stress.   ⓢ: U.S. pron.   ⓔ: British pron.

Cheyney
  town, PA   CHĀ-nē   'tʃeːniˑ

Chezib
  Biblical name   KĒ-zuhb, kuh-ZĒV   'kiːzəb, kə'ziːv

Ch'i
  Chinese dynasty   CHĒ   'tʃiː

Chiang Ch'ing
  see Jiang Qing

Chiang Kai-shek
  Chinese leader; airport, Taipei   jē-AHNG KĪ-SHEK, Ⓢ CHANG kī-SHEK   dʒiː'aŋ 'kai'ʃek, Ⓢ ˌtʃæŋ kai'ʃek

Chiang Mai [Chiengmai, Kiangmai]
  province, Thailand   jē-AHNG MĪ   dʒiː'aŋ 'mai

Chiang Rai [Chiengrai]
  province, Thailand   jē-AHNG RĪ   dʒiː'aŋ 'rai

Chianti
  wine   kē-AHNT-ē, kē-ANT-ē   kiː'antiˑ, kiː'æntiˑ

Chiapas
  state, Mexico   chē-AHP-uhs   tʃiː'apəs

Chiari
  commune, Italy   kē-AHR-ē   kiː'ariˑ

Chiat-Day
  US advertising co.   SHĪ-uht-DĀ   ˌʃaiət'deː

Chiba
  prefecture, Japan   chē-buh   tʃiːbə

Chibcha
  S. American people   CHIB-chah   'tʃibtʃa

Chic
  French beer   SHĒK   ʃiːk

Chicago
  city, IL   shuh-KAHG-ō, shuh-KAW-gō, chuh-   ʃə'kagoː, ʃə'kɔːgoː, tʃə-

Chicana
  Mexican-American (fem.)   chi-KAHN-uh, shi-KAHN-uh   tʃi'kanə, ʃi'kanə

Chicano
  Mexican-American (masc.)   chi-KAHN-ō, shi-KAHN-ō   tʃi'kanoː, ʃi'kanoː

Ch'i-ch'i-ha-erh
  see Qiqihar

Chichén Itzá
  village, archaeological site, Mexico   chi-CHEN ēt-SAH   tʃiˌtʃen iˑt'sa

Chichester
  town, England   CHICH-uh-stuhr   'tʃitʃəstərˡ

Chichewa
  lang., SE Africa   CHĒ-chuh-WAW   'tʃiːtʃəˌwɔː

Chichibu
  city, Japan   chē-chē-bōō   tʃiːtʃiːbuː

Chick
  pers. name   CHIK   'tʃik

Chickadee
  songbird   CHIK-uh-dē   'tʃikədiː

Chickamauga
  city, dam, Georgia   CHIK-uh-MAW-guh   ˌtʃikə'mɔːgə

Chickasaw
  N. American people   CHIK-uh-SAW   'tʃikəˌsɔː

Chiclayo
  city, Peru   chē-KLĪ-(y)ō   tʃiː'klai(j)oː

Key (col. 2):   aː **fad**   ā: **fade**   ah: **father**   ar: **marry**   aw: **law**   e: **fed**   ē: **feed**   er: **merry**   i: **hid**   ī: **hide**   ō: **coat**   ōō: **boot**
oi: **boy**   ow: **now**   u: **put**   uh: **above**   uhr: **bird**   ch: **chop**   ng: **ring**   sh: **show**   th: **thick**   <u>th</u>: **this**   zh: **measure**

Chico
city, CA; rivers, Argentina, CHĒ-kō 'tʃiːkoː
Phillipines; pers. name

Chicopee
town, MA CHIK-uh-pē 'tʃikəpiˑ

Chicot
county, AR SHĒ-kō 'ʃiːkoː

Chicoutimi
river, county, Quebec, Canada shi-kōō-tē-MĒ, ⑤ shuh-KŌŌT-uh-MĒ ʃikuːtiːmiː, ⑤ ʃə'kuːʈəˌmiˑ

Chicxulub
town, Mexico chē(k)-sōō-LŌŌB tʃiː(k)suː'luːb

Chidon
Biblical name KĪD-n, KĪ-DAHN, kē-DAWN 'kɑidn̩, 'kɑiˌdɑn, kiː'dɔːn

Chiengmai [Chiang Mai]
province, Thailand jē-ENG-MĪ dʒiː'eŋ'mɑi

Chiengrai [Chiang Rai]
province, Thailand jē-ENG-RĪ dʒiː'eŋ'rɑi

Chieti
province, Italy kē-ET-ē kiː'eʈiː

Chigha Sarai
town, Afghanistan chuh-GAH suh-RĪ tʃə'gɑ sə'rɑi

Chihli [Po Hai]
gulf, Yellow Sea JIR-LĒ, CHĒ-LĒ 'dʒirˈliː, 'tʃiːˈliː

Chihuahua
state, city, Mexico; dog chuh-WAH-wah, shuh-, -wuh tʃə'wɑwɑ, ʃə-, -wə

Chikamatsu Monzaemon
Japanese dramatist chē-kah-maht-sōō mawn-zah-em-awn tʃiːkɑmɑtsuː mɔːnzɑ-emɔːn

Chilcotin
N. American people chil-KŌT-n tʃil'koːtn̩

Childe
pers. name (C. Hassam) CHĪLD 'tʃɑild

Childress
Alice, US author, playwright CHIL-druhs 'tʃildrəs

Chile
republic, S. America CHĒ-lā, CHIL-ē 'tʃiːleː, 'tʃiliˑ

Chileab
Biblical name KIL-ē-AB, KĪ-lē-AB, kil-AHV 'kiliːˌæb, 'kɑiliːˌæb, kil'ɑv

Chilean
pert. to Chile CHIL-ē-uhn, chuh-LĀ-uhn 'tʃiliːən, tʃə'leːən

Chili
town, NY CHĪ-LĪ 'tʃɑiˌlɑi

Chilion
Biblical name KIL-ē-AHN, kil-YŌN 'kiliːˌɑn, kil'joːn

Chilkat, -cat
N. American people CHIL-KAT 'tʃilˌkæt

Chillagoe
town, Australia CHIL-uh-gō 'tʃiləgoː

Chillicothe
US pl. name CHIL-uh-KAHTH-ē, CHIL-uh-KAW-thē ˌtʃilə'kɑθiˑ, ˌtʃilə'kɔːθiˑ

Chillon
castle, Switzerland shē-YAWn, ⑤ shil-AHN, SHIL-AHN, ʃiːjɔ̃, ⑤ ʃil'ɑn, 'ʃilˌɑn, 'ʃilən
SHIL-uhn

Chilmad
Biblical name KIL-MAD, kil-MAHD 'kilˌmæd, kil'mɑd

Foreign Sounds: ue: *Fr.* **rue**, *Ger.* **füllen** uh(r): *Fr.* **boeuf**, *Ger.* **Höhle** kh: *Ger.* **ich**, *Scot.* **loch** ḡ: *Sp.* **amigo** v: *Sp.* **hablar**
hl: *Welsh* **Llanelli**. CAPITALS: primary stress. SMALL CAPS: secondary stress. ⑤: U.S. pron. Ⓔ: British pron.

Chilpancingo do los Bravos
   town, Mexico   chēl-pahn-SING-gō tho̱ lōs BRAHV̱-ōs   tʃiːlpɑn'siŋgoː ðoː loːs
                                                 'braβoːs

Chiltern Hills
   hill range, England   CHIL-tuhrn HILZ   'tʃiltərn 'hilz

Chimaera, Chimera
   monster in Greek mythology   kī-MIR-uh, kuh-MIR-uh   kai'mirə, kə'mirə

Chimaltenango
   department, Guatemala   chē-mahl-tā-NAHNG-gō   tʃiːmɑlteː'nɑŋgoː

Chimay
   Belgian beer   chē-MĪ   tʃi:'mai

Chimborazo
   mtn., Ecuador   CHIM-buh-RAHZ-ō, SHIM-   ˌtʃimbə'razoː, ˌʃim-

Chimbote
   port, Peru   chēm-BŌ-tā   tʃiːm'boːteː

Chimbu
   province, Papua New Guinea   CHIM-bo͞o   'tʃimbuː

Chimham
   Biblical name   KIM-HAM, kim-HAHM   'kimˌhæm, kim'hɑm

Chimkent
   town, Kazakhstan   chim-KENT   tʃim'k̩ent

Chimu
   S. American people   chē-MO͞O   tʃiː'muː

Chin
   hills, people, Burma; pers. name   CHIN   'tʃin

Ch'in
   Chinese dynasty (source of name   CHĒN   'tʃiːn
     China)

Chin
   Chinese dynasties   JIN   'dʒin

China
   republic, Asia   CHĪ-nuh   'tʃainə

Chi-nan
   see Jinan

Chinandega
   department, Nicaragua   CHIN-uhn-DĀ-guh   ˌtʃinən'deːgə

Chinantec
   lang., people, Mexico   CHIN-uhn-TEK   'tʃinənˌtek

Chinatown
   urban district designator   CHĪ-nuh-TOWN   'tʃainəˌtaun

Chincoteague
   town, VA; bay, MD, VA   SHING-kuh-TĒG, CHING-kuh-TĒG;   ˌʃiŋkə'tiːg, ˌtʃiŋkə'tiːg;
                        SHING-kuh-TĒG, CHING-kuh-TĒG   'ʃiŋkə'tiːg, 'tʃiŋkə'tiːg

Chindwin
   river, Burma   CHIN-DWIN   'tʃin'dwin

Chinese
   lang., people, Asia   chī-NĒZ, -NĒS   tʃai'niːz, -'niːs

Ch'ing
   Chinese dynasty   CHING   'tʃiŋ

Ching Hai
   see Tsing Hai

Chinghai
   see Qinghai

Chingpaw
   lang., people, Burma, South China   CHING-PAW   'tʃiŋˌpɔː

Key (col. 2):   a: fad   ā: fade   ah: father   ar: marry   aw: law   e: fed   ē: feed   er: merry   i: hid   ī: hide   ō: coat   o͞o: boot
oi: boy   ow: now   u: put   uh: above   uhr: bird   ch: chop   ng: ring   sh: show   th: thick   t̲h̲: this   zh: measure

Ching Sen
  Chinese ceremony   CHING SUHN   'tʃiŋ 'sən
Chinh
  Truong, *president, Vietnam*   CHIN   'tʃin
Chinhoyi
  town, caves, Zimbabwe   chin-HŌ-yē, chin-HOI   chin'hoːjiˑ, chin'hɔi
Chinkiang [Zhenjiang]
  city, China   JIN-yē-AHNG   'dʒinjiː'aŋ
Chinnereth
  Biblical name   KIN-uh-RETH, ki-NER-et   'kinə,reθ, ki'neret
Chinneroth [Chinnereth]
  Biblical name   KIN-uh-RAHTH, ki-NER-ōt   'kinə,rɑθ, ki'neroːt
Chino
  city, CA   CHĒ-nō   'tʃiːnoː
Chinook
  N. American people   shuh-NUK, chuh-NUK, -NO͞OK   ʃə'nuk, tʃə'nuk, -'nuːk
Ch'in Shih Huang Ti [Shih Hwang-ti]
  Chinese emperor   CHIN SHIR HWAHNG DĒ   'tʃin 'ʃiʳ 'hwaŋ 'diː
Chinua
  pers. name (C. Achebe)   CHIN-yuh-wuh   'tʃinjəwə
Chios
  island, Greece   KĒ-AHS, KĪ-AHS   'kiː,as, 'kai,as
Chipewyan
  N. American people   CHIP-uh-WĪ-uhn   ,tʃipə'waiən
Chipola
  river, US, college, FL   chuh-PŌ-luh   tʃə'poːlə
Chippendale
  furniture style   CHIP-uhn-DĀL   'tʃipən,deːl
Chippewa [Ojibwa]
  N. American people   CHIP-uh-WAW, -WAH, -WĀ, -wuh   'tʃipə,wɔː, -,wɑ, -,weː, -wə
Chiquimula
  department, Guatemala   chē-kē-MO͞O-lah   tʃiːkiˑ'muːla
Chiquita
  tdmk for bananas   chi-KĒT-uh   tʃi'kiːʈə
Chirac
  Jacques, *French politician*   shē-RAHK   ʃiːrɑːk
Chi Rho
  Christian symbol   KĪ RŌ, KĒ RŌ   'kai 'roː, 'kiː 'roː
Chiricahua
  N. American people   CHIR-e-KAH-wuh   ,tʃire'kɑwə
Chirico
  Giorgio de, *Italian painter*   KĒ-ri-KŌ, KIR-i-KŌ   'kiːri,koː, 'kiri,koː
Chiriguano
  S. American people   CHIR-uh-GWAHN-ō   ,tʃiʳə'gwanoː
Chiriqui
  province, Panama   chir-ē-KĒ   tʃiriː'kiː
Chiron
  Centaur who reared Achilles and Jason   KĪ-ruhn   'kairən
Chiroptera
  order of bats   kī-RAHP-tuh-ruh   kai'rɑptərə
Chirripó Grande
  peak, Costa Rica   CHIR-rē-PŌ GRAHN-dā   ,tʃirriː'poː 'grɑndeː

Foreign Sounds: **ue:** *Fr.* **rue**, *Ger.* **füllen**   **uh(r):** *Fr.* **boeuf**, *Ger.* **Höhle**   <u>**kh**</u>: *Ger.* **ich**, *Scot.* **loch**   **g̃:** *Sp.* **amigo**   **v:** *Sp.* **hablar**   **hl:** *Welsh* **Llanelli**.   CAPITALS: primary stress.   SMALL CAPS: secondary stress.   Ⓢ: U.S. pron.   Ⓔ: British pron.

Chisago
county, MN	shi-SAW-gō	ʃi'sɔːgoː

Chisholm
cattle trail	CHIZ-uhm	'tʃizəm

Chişinău [Kishinev]
capital, Moldova	KĒ-shuh-NOW	ˌkiːʃə'nɑu

Chislon
Biblical name	KIZ-LAHN, KIS-LAHN, kis-LŌN	'kizˌlɑn, 'kisˌlɑn, kis'loːn

Chisloth-tabor
Biblical name	KIS-LAHTH-TĀ-BAWR, -BŌR, -buhr; kis-LAWT-tah-VAWR	'kisˌlɑθ'teːˌbɔː^r, -ˌboː^r, -bə^r; kis'lɔːtta'vɔːr

Chita
1. pers. name (C. Rivera)	CHĒT-uh	'tʃiːtə
2. city, Russia	chi-TAH	tʃi'tɑ

Chitimacha
N. American people	CHIT-uh-MAHSH-uh	ˌtʃitə'mɑʃə

Chitradurga
town, India	CHIT-ruh-DUHR-guh	ˌtʃitrə'də^rgə

Chitral
river, Afghanistan	chi-TRAHL	tʃi'trɑl

Chitré
town, Panama	chē-TRĀ	tʃiː'treː

Chitta
pers. name, Bengali	CHIT-tuh	'tʃittə

Chittagong
region, Bangladesh	CHIT-uh-GAHNG, CHIT-uh-GAWNG	'tʃitəˌgɑŋ, 'tʃitəˌgɔːŋ

Chittim
Biblical name	KIT-im, ki-TĒM	'kitim, ki'tiːm

Ch'iung-shan [Kiungshan, Kiungchow]
city, China	chē-UNG-SHAHN	tʃiː'uŋ'ʃɑn

Chivas Regal
Scotch liquor	SHIV-uhs RĒ-guhl	ˌʃivəs 'riːgəl

Chlodowech [Clovis]
Frankish king	KLŌD-ō-VE<u>KH</u>	'kloːdoːˌveç

Chlodwig [Clovis]
Frankish king	KLŌT-vi<u>kh</u>	'kloːtviç

Chloe, Chloë
pers. name	KLŌ-ē	'kloːiˑ

chlorine
element	KLŌR-ĒN, KLAWR-ĒN	'kloːrˌiːn, 'klɔːrˌiːn

Chloris
Greek flower goddess	KLŌR-uhs, KLAWR-uhs	'kloːrəs, 'klɔːrəs

Chlotaire
French form of Chlotar	klō-TER	kloːter

Chlotar
Frankish king of Merovingian line	KLŌ-TAHR	'kloːˌtɑ^r

Chlothar
German form of Chlotar	KLŌ-TAHR	'kloːˌtɑ^r

Chlotilde
1. pers. name, French	klaw-TĒLD	klɔːtiːld
2. German	klō-TIL-duh	kloː'tildə

Choate
US prep school	CHŌT	'tʃoːt

Key (col. 2):   a: fad   ā: fade   ah: father   ar: marry   aw: law   e: fed   ē: feed   er: merry   i: hid   ī: hide   ō: coat   ōō: boot
oi: boy   ow: now   u: put   uh: above   uhr: bird   ch: chop   ng: ring   sh: show   th: thick   <u>th</u>: this   zh: measure

Chobe
  district, national park, Botswana   CHŌ-bā, -bē   'tʃoːbeː, -biˑ
Chocano
  José Santos, *Peruvian poet*   chō-KAHN-ō   tʃoːˈkɑnoː
Chocó
  S. American people   chuh-KŌ   tʃəˈkoː
Choctaw
  N. American people   CHAHK-taw   'tʃɑktɔː
Choiseul
  Solomon Islands   shwah-ZUH(R)L   ʃwɑzœl
Chokodo Shujin [Akutagawa
  Ryūnosuke]
  Japanese writer   chō-kō-dō shōō-jin tʃoːkoːdoː ʃuːdʒin
Chokwe
  see Ciokwe
Chol
  lang., people, Mexico   CHŌL   'tʃoːl
Chŏllanam
  prov, Korea   chuhl-lah-nahm   tʃəllɑnɑm
Chŏllapuk
  prov, Korea   chuhl-lah-puk   tʃəllɑpuk
Cholmondeley
  town, England; British family name   CHUHM-lē   'tʃəmliˑ
Choluteca
  river, department, Honduras   CHAW-lōō-TĀ-kuh   ˌtʃɔːluːˈteːkə
Chomsky
  Noam, *US linguist*   CHAHM(P)-skē   'tʃɑm(p)skiˑ
Chomskyan
  pert. to Chomsky   CHAHM(P)-skē-uhn   'tʃɑm(p)skiːən
Chon Buri [Bang Pla Soi]
  province, Thailand   CHUHN bu-RĒ   'tʃən buˈriː
Chondokyo
  religion   chahn-DŌK-yō   tʃanˈdoːkjoː
Chongjin
  prov, N. Korea   chuhng-jēn   tʃəŋdʒiːn
Chongqing, Chungking
  town, China   CHUHNG-KING   'tʃəŋ'kiŋ
Chono
  S. American people   CHŌ-nō   'tʃoːnoː
Chontal
  lang., people, Mexico   chawn-TAHL   tʃɔːnˈtɑl
Chontales
  department, Nicaragua   chawn-TAHL-ās, chahn-   tʃɔːnˈtɑleːs, tʃɑn-
Choosuk
  Korean festival   chōō-suk   tʃuːsuk
Cho Oyu
  Mount, *Himalayas*   CHŌ ō-YŌŌ   ˌtʃoː oːˈjuː
Chopicolqui
  peak, Peru   chō-pē-KŌL-kē   tʃoːpiˑˈkoːlkiː
Chopin
  1. Frédéric, *Polish composer, pianist*   *Polish* KHAWP-yin, *French* shaw-PEⁿ,   *Polish* 'xɔːpjin, *French*
                                          ⓢ SHŌ-PAN, SHŌ-PAⁿ   ʃɔːpẽ, ⓢ 'ʃoːˌpæn, 'ʃoːˌpæ̃
  2. Katherine, *US writer*   SHŌ-PAN, shō-PAN, SHŌ-puhn   'ʃoːˌpæn, ʃoːˈpæn, 'ʃoːpən
Chorazin
  Biblical name   kawr-Ā-zin, kōr-   kɔːrˈeːzin, koːr-

Foreign Sounds: ue: *Fr.* **rue**, *Ger.* **füllen**   uh(r): *Fr.* **bœuf**, *Ger.* **Höhle**   <u>kh</u>: *Ger.* **ich**, *Scot.* lo**ch**   ğ: *Sp.* amigo   v̯: *Sp.* hablar
hl: *Welsh* **Ll**anelli.   CAPITALS: primary stress.   SMALL CAPS: secondary stress.   ⓢ: U.S. pron.   ⓔ: British pron.

Chortí
  lang., people, Guatemala, Honduras   CHAWRT-ē   ˈtʃɔːʳtiˑ
Chorum
  see Çorum
Choteau
  city, MT   SHŌ-tō   ˈʃoːtoː
Chou
  Chinese dynasty   JŌ   ˈdʒoː
Chou En-Lai, Jou Enlai, Zhou Enlai
  premier, China   JŌ EN-LĪ   ˈdʒoː ˈenˈlɑi
Chough
  type of crow   CHUHF   ˈtʃəf
Chou-shan, Chu Shan, Chusan
  archipelago, East China Sea   JŌO-SHAHN, JŌ-   ˈdʒuːˈʃɑn, ˈdʒoː-
Chouteau
  county, MT   SHŌ-tō   ˈʃoːtoː
Chowan
  river, county, NC   chuh-WAHN   tʃəˈwɑn
Chow chow
  dog   CHOW CHOW   ˈtʃau ˌtʃau
Choxo-no-Sekku
  Chrysanthemum Day *(Sept. 9),* *Japan*   chōk-sō-nō-sek-kōo   tʃoːksoːnoːsekkuː
Choybalsan
  city, Mongolia   CHOI-bahl-SAHN   ˌtʃɔibɑlˈsɑn
Chremonidean War
  Athens-Sparta conflict   KRĒ-muh-NID-ē-uhn   ˌkriːməˈnidiːən
Chrétien
  Jean, *prime minister, Canada; pers. name, French*   krā-TYEⁿ, Ⓢ krā-TYEN   kreːtjē, Ⓢ kreːˈtjen
Chrétien de Troyes, Chrestien de Troyes
  medieval French poet   krā-TYEⁿ duh TRWAH   kreːtjē də trwɑː
Chris
  pers. name   KRIS   ˈkris
Chrissie, Chrissy
  pers. name   KRIS-ē   ˈkrisiˑ
Christ
  see Jesus Christ
Christabel
  poem, Coleridge; pers. name   KRIS-tuh-BEL, -buhl   ˈkristəˌbel, -bəl
Christadelphianism
  Christian sect   KRIS-tuh-DEL-fē-uh-NIZ-uhm   ˌkristəˈdelfiːəˌnizəm
Christ Church
  college, Oxford Univ.   KRĪS(T) CHUHRCH   ˈkrɑis(t) ˌtʃəʳtʃ
Christchurch
  city, New Zealand   KRĪS(T)-CHUHRCH   ˈkrɑis(t)ˌtʃəʳtʃ
Christen
  1. pers. name, Danish   KRIS-tuhn   ˈkristən
  2. Norwegian   KRIS-tn   ˈkristn̩
Christendom
  the Christian world   KRIS-n-duhm   ˈkrisn̩dəm
Christiaan
  pers. name, Dutch   KRIS-tē-AHN   ˈkristiːˌɑːn

Key (col. 2):   a: fad   ā: fade   ah: father   ar: marry   aw: law   e: fed   ē: feed   er: merry   i: hid   ī: hide   ō: coat   ōō: boot
oi: boy   ow: now   u: put   uh: above   uhr: bird   ch: chop   ng: ring   sh: show   th: thick   <u>th</u>: this   zh: measure

Christian
1. pert. to Christianity; *pers. name*	KRIS-chuhn, KRISH-	'kristʃən, 'kriʃ-
2. Danish	KRĒ-styahn	'kriːstjaːn
3. Dutch	KRIS-tē-AHN	'kristiːˌɑn
4. French	krē-STYAH^n	kriːstjɑ̃
5. German	KRIS-tyahn, -tē-AHN	'kristjɑn, -tiːˌɑn
6. Norwegian	KRIS-tyahn	'kristjɑn
7. Swedish	KRIS-tē-ahn, KRISH-ahn	'kristiːɑːn, 'kriʃɑːn

Christiana
pers. name, German	kris-TYAHN-ah, -tē-AHN-ah	kris'tjɑnɑ, -tiː'ɑnɑ

Christianity
religion	KRIS-chē-AN-uht-ē, KRISH-chē-, KRIS-tē-	ˌkristʃiː'ænəţi·, ˌkriʃtʃiː-, ˌkristiː-

Christiansted
town, Virgin Is.	KRIS-chuhn-STED, KRISH-	'kristʃən,sted, 'kriʃ-

Christie
pers. name	KRIS-tē	'kristi·

Christina
pers. name	kris-TĒ-nuh	kris'tiːnə

Christine
1. pers. name	kris-TĒN, KRIS-TĒN	kris'tiːn, 'krisˌtiːn
2. French	krē-STĒN	kriːstiːn
3. German	kris-TĒ-nuh	kris'tiːnə
4. Swedish	kri-STĒN	kri'stiːn

Christmas
1. Christian holiday; island, Indian Ocean; island, Pacific, see Kiritimati Atoll	KRIS-muhs	'krisməs

Christmastide
Christmas season	KRIS-muh-STĪD	'krismə,staid

Christmastime
Christmas season	KRIS-muh-STĪM	'krismə,staim

Christo
Bulgarian artist	KRIS-TŌ	'kris,toː

Christobel
pers. name	KRIS-tuh-BEL	'kristə,bel

Christofer
pers. name, Norwegian, Swedish	kris-TAW-fuhr	kris'tɔːfər

Christoff
pers. name, German	KRIS-TAWF	'kris,tɔːf

Christoffer
pers. name, Swedish	kris-TAWF-fuhr	kris'tɔːffər

Christoph
1. pers. name, Dutch, German, Swedish	KRIS-TAWF	'kris,tɔːf
2. Hungarian	KRIS-tawf	'kristɔːf

Christophe
pers. name, French	krē-STAWF	kriːstɔːf

Christopher
1. pers. name	KRIS-tuh-fuhr	'kristəfə^r
2. Swedish	kris-TAW-fuhr	kris'tɔːfər

Christovão
pers. name, Portuguese	KRĒSH-tōō-VOW^n, KRĒS-	ˌkriːʃtuː'vaũ, ˌkriːs-

Christ's College
college, Cambridge Univ.	KRĪS(TS) KAHL-ij	'krais(ts) ˌkɑlidʒ

Christy
pers. name	KRIS-tē	'kristi·

chromium
element	KRŌ-mē-uhm	'kroːmiːəm

Chrysaor
son of Poseidon and Medusa	krī-SĀ-AWR	krɑiˈseːˌɔːʳ

Chryseis
Trojan woman given to Agamemnon in Iliad	krī-SĒ-uhs, krī-SĀ-uhs	krɑiˈsiːəs, krɑiˈseːəs

Chryses
father of Chryseis	KRĪ-sēz	'krɑisiːz

Chrysippus
son of Pelops and Axioche	krī-SIP-uhs	krɑiˈsipəs

Chrysler
US car mfr.; building, New York City	KRĪ-sluhr	'krɑisləʳ

Chrysopelia
tree nymph in Arcadia	KRĪ-suh-PĒ-lē-uh, -PĒL-yuh	ˌkrɑisəˈpiːliːə, -ˈpiːljə

Chrysostom
John, *Christian saint*	KRIS-uhs-tuhm, kris-AHS-tuhm	'krisəstəm, krisˈɑstəm

Chrystal
pers. name	KRIS-tl	'kristl̩

Chu
1. family name of Ming dynasty of China	JŌO	'dʒuː
2. river, Kazakhstan	CHŌO	'tʃuː

Chuang-tzu
Chinese philosopher and teacher	JWAHNG-DZU, -DZŌO	'dʒwɑŋ'dzu, -'dzuː

Chub
Biblical name	KUHB, CHUHB, KŌOV	'kəb, 'tʃəb, 'kuːv

Chūbu
region, Honshu Island, Japan	chōo-bōo	tʃuːbuː

Chubu
region, Japan	chōo-bōo	tʃuːbuː

Chubut
river, province, Argentina	chōo-VŌOT	tʃuːˈβuːt

Chuck
pers. name	CHUHK	'tʃək

Ch'ü-fou [Kufow]
town, China, residence of Confucius	CHUE-FŌ, CHŌO-	'tʃyˈfoː, 'tʃuː-

Chugach
National Forest, *AK*	CHŌO-gach	'tʃuːgætʃ

Chūgoku
region, Honshu Island, Japan	chōo-gō-kōo	tʃuːgoːkuː

Chugoku
region, Japan	chōo-gō-kōo	tʃuːgoːkuː

Chuj
lang., people, Guatemala	CHŌO(KH), CHŌA-ē	'tʃuː(x), 'tʃuːi·

Chukchi
Sea, *part of Arctic ocean; lang., Russia*	CHUHK-chē, CHUK-chē	'tʃəktʃi·, 'tʃuktʃi·

Chukot
peninsula, mtn. range, Russia	chuh-KAHT	tʃəˈkɑt

Chula Vista
city, CA	CHŌO-luh VIS-tuh	ˌtʃuːlə 'vistə

Key (col. 2):   a: fad   ā: fade   ah: father   ar: marry   aw: law   e: fed   ē: feed   er: merry   i: hid   ī: hide   ō: coat   ōo: boot
oi: boy   ow: now   u: put   uh: above   uhr: bird   ch: chop   ng: ring   sh: show   th: thick   th̲: this   zh: measure

Chulym, Chulim
   river, Russia   chuh-LIM   tʃə'lim
Chumash
   N. American people   CHOO-mash   'tʃuːmæʃ
Chumphon, Jumporn
   province, Thailand   CHUM-PAWN   'tʃum'pɔːn
Chun
   Biblical name   KUHN, CHUHN, KOON   'kən, 'tʃən, 'kuːn
Ch'unch'on
   town, S. Korea   choon-chuhn   tʃuːntʃən
Chun Doo Hwan
   Korean military leader, politician juh(r)n dō hwahn   dʒœn doː hwɑn
Chung
   pers. name   CHUNG, CHUHNG   'tʃuŋ, 'tʃəŋ
Ch'ungch'ŏngnam
   prov, S. Korea   chung-chahng-nahm   tʃuŋtʃɑŋnɑm
Ch'ungch'ŏngpuk
   prov, S. Korea   chung-chahng-puk   tʃuŋtʃɑŋpuk
Chung-chia [Puyi]
   lang., people, China   JUNG-JAH, JUNG-jē-AH   'dʒuŋ'dʒɑ, 'dʒuŋdʒiː'ɑ
Chungking
   see Chongqing
Ch'ung-te
   Manchu reign of emperor Abahai CHUNG-DUH   'tʃuŋ'də
Ch'ung-tu
   see Chengdu
Chung Yeung
   Chinese festival   JUNG yuh-UNG   'dʒuŋ jə'uŋ
Chuquisaca
   department, Bolivia   choo-kē-SAHK-uh   tʃuːkiː'sɑkə
Chur
   town, Switzerland   KUR   'kuʳ
Churchill
   Sir Winston L. S., British statesman, author (Nobel 1953); college, Cambridge Univ.; pl. name CHUHR-CHIL, Ⓢ *also* CHUHRCH-HIL   'tʃəʳˌtʃil, Ⓢ *also* 'tʃəʳtʃˌhil
Churún Merú [Angel Falls]
   waterfall, Venezuela   chu-ROON mā-ROO   tʃu'ruːn meː'ruː
Chu Shan, Chusan
   see Chou-shan
Chushan-rishathaim
   see Cushan-rishathaim
Chust
   see Khust
Chuvash
   lang., people, Russia   CHOO-VAHSH, chu-VAHSH   'tʃuːˌvaʃ, tʃu'vaʃ
Chuza
   Biblical name   K(Y)OO-zuh   'k(j)uːzə
Chuzzlewit
   Martin, character in Martin Chuzzlewit, *C. Dickens* CHUHZ-uhl-WIT   'tʃəzəlˌwit
Ciao!
   shoe co.; Italian greeting   CHOW   'tʃau
Ciaran [Kieran]
   Irish saint   KYAHR-uhn   'kjɑrən

Foreign Sounds: ue: *Fr.* **rue**, *Ger.* **füllen**   uh(r): *Fr.* **boeuf**, *Ger.* **Höhle** <u>kh</u>: *Ger.* **ich**, *Scot.* **loch** g̃: *Sp.* **amigo** <u>v</u>: *Sp.* **hablar**
hl: *Welsh* **Llanelli**. CAPITALS: primary stress. SMALL CAPS: secondary stress. Ⓢ: U.S. pron. Ⓔ: British pron.

Ciardi
  John, *US poet*   CHAHRD-ē   'tʃɑʳdiˑ

Ciba-Geigy
  pharmaceutical co.   SĒB-uh-GĪ-gē   ˌsiːbəˈgaigiˑ

Cibber
  Colley, *English poet, actor*   SIB-uhr   'sibəʳ

Cibola
  Stadium, *McCook, NE*   SĒ-buh-luh   'siːbələ

Cibola
  county, New Mexico   SIB-uh-luh   'sibələ

Cibolo
  river, Texas   SIB-uh-LŌ   'sibəˌloː

Ciboney
  Cuban people   SĒ-buh-NĀ   ˌsiːbəˈneː

Ciccone
  Madonna Louise, *original name of*   chi-KŌ-nē   tʃiˈkoːniˑ
  Madonna, *US entertainer*

Cicely
  fictional town, AK; pers. name   SIS-(uh-)lē   'sis(ə)liˑ

Cicero
  Roman orator & statesman; town, IL   SIS-uh-RŌ   'sisəˌroː

Cicéron
  pers. name, French   sē-sā-RAWⁿ   siːseːrɔ̃

Ciceronian
  pert. to Cicero   SIS-uh-RŌ-nē-uhn, SIS-uh-RŌN-yuhn   ˌsisəˈroːniːən, ˌsisəˈroːnjən

Cicily
  pers. name   SIS-(uh-)lē   'sis(ə)liˑ

Cicones
  allies of the Trojans   si-KŌ-NĒZ   si'koːˌniːz

Cid, El
  cognomen of Rodrigo Diaz de Vivar   el THĒTH, Ⓢ el SID   el 'θiːð, Ⓢ el 'sid

Ciechanów
  province, Poland   chuh-<u>KH</u>AH-nōof   tʃəˈxɑːnuːf

Ciego de Avila
  province, Cuba   sē-Ā-ḡō <u>th</u>ā ah-V<u>Ē</u>-luh   siːˈeːɣoː ðeː ɑˈβiːlə

Cienfuegos
  port, Cuba   sē-en-FWĀ-ḡōs   siːenˈfweːɣoːs

Cilicia
  ancient country, Asia Minor   suh-LISH-(ē-)uh   səˈliʃ(iː)ə

Cilix
  founder of Cilicia   SIL-iks   'siliks

Cillas
  charioteer of Pelops   SIL-uhs   'siləs

Cimabue
  Giovanni, *Italian painter*   CHĒ-muh-BŌO-ā   ˌtʃiːməˈbuːeː

Cimarron
  US river; county, OK; city, KS   SIM-uh-RŌN, SIM-uh-RAHN,   'siməˌroːn, 'siməˌrɑn,
             SIM-uh-ruhn   'simərən

Cimbri
  Germanic or Celtic people   SIM-BRĪ, KIM-brē   'simˌbrɑi, 'kimbriˑ

Cimmerians
  mythical people dwelling in darkness   suh-MER-ē-uhnz   səˈmeriːənz

Cimon
  Athenian leader   SĪ-muhn   'sɑimən

Key (col. 2):   a: fad   ā: fade   ah: father   ar: marry   aw: law   e: fed   ē: feed   er: merry   i: hid   ī: hide   ō: coat   ōō: boot
oi: boy   ow: now   u: put   uh: above   uhr: bird   ch: chop   ng: ring   sh: show   th: thick   <u>th</u>: this   zh: measure

Cinchona
  plant   sing-KŌ-nuh, sin-CHŌ-nuh   siŋ'koːnə, sin'tʃoːnə

Cincinnati
  city, OH   SIN-suh-NAT-ē, SIN-suh-NAT-uh   ˌsinsə'nætiˑ, ˌsinsə'nætə

Cincinnatian
  pert. to Cincinnati   SIN-suh-NAT-ē-uhn   ˌsinsə'nætiːən

Cincinnatus
  Roman general; pers. name   SIN-suh-NAT-uhs   ˌsinsə'nætəs

Cinco de Mayo
  May 5th holiday, Mexico   SING-kō thā MĪ-ō   'siŋkoː ðeː 'mɑioː

Cinderella
  fairy tale character   SIN-duh-REL-uh   ˌsində'relə

Cindy
  pers. name   SIN-dē   'sindiˑ

Cinerama
  tdmk for a movie process   SIN-uh-RAM-uh, SIN-uh-RAHM-uh   ˌsinə'ræmə, ˌsinə'rɑmə

Cinna
  Roman leader   SIN-uh   'sinə

Cinnabar
  mineral   SIN-uh-BAHR   'sinəˌbɑʳ

Cinnamon
  spice   SIN-uh-muhn   'sinəmən

Cinneroth
  Biblical name   SIN-uh-RAHTH, KIN-uh-RŌT   'sinəˌrɑθ, ˌkinə'roːt

Cinquefoil
  plant   SINGK-foil, SANGK-foil   'siŋkˌfɔil, 'sæŋkˌfɔil

Cinque Ports
  port association, England   SINGK PŌRTS, PAWRTS   'siŋk ˌpoːʳts, ˌpɔːʳts

Cinqueterre
  coastal region, Italy   CHING-kwuh-TER-ā   ˌtʃiŋkwə'tereː

Cinyras
  first king of Cyprus   SIN-uh-ruhs   'sinərəs

Cinzano
  wine   chin-ZAHN-ō   tʃin'zɑnoː

Ciokwe, Chokwe
  lang., Africa   CHAWK-wā   'tʃɔːkweː

Circassian
  lang., SE Europe   suhr-KASH-uhn   səʳ'kæʃən

Circe
  sorceress in Odyssey   SUHR-sē   'səʳsiˑ

Circinus
  constellation   SUHRS-n-uhs   'səʳsn̩əs

Cirencester
  town, England   SĪ-ruhn-SES-tuhr, SIS-it-uhr   'sɑirənˌsestəʳ, 'sisitəʳ

Cis
  Biblical name   SIS   'sis

Cisalpine Gaul
  Roman province   sis-AL-PĪN GAWL   sis'ælˌpɑin 'gɔːl

Cisco
  Junior College, *TX*   SIS-kō   'siskoː

Ciskei
  Black enclave, South Africa   SIS-KĪ   'sisˌkɑi

Cisneros
  Sandra, *US novelist*   sis-NER-ōs   sis'neroːs

Foreign Sounds: ue: *Fr.* r**ue**, *Ger.* f**ü**llen   uh(r): *Fr.* b**oeuf**, *Ger.* H**öh**le   <u>kh</u>: *Ger.* i**ch**, *Scot.* lo**ch**   ḡ: *Sp.* ami**g**o   <u>v</u>: *Sp.* ha**b**lar
hl: *Welsh* L**l**anelli.   CAPITALS: primary stress.   SMALL CAPS: secondary stress.   ⑤: U.S. pron.   ⑥: British pron.

Cisneros
Henry, *US government official*   sis-NER-ōs   sis'neroːs
Cissie
pers. name   SIS-ē   'sisiˑ
Cistercians
religious order   sis-TUHR-shuhnz   sis'təʳʃənz
Citadel, The
military college, SC   SIT-uhd-l, SIT-uh-DEL   'siţədl̩, 'siţə,del
Cithaeron
king of Plataea   suh-THIR-AHN, suh-THĒ-RAHN   sə'θir,an, sə'θiː,ran
Citibank
US bank   SIT-ē-BANGK   'siţiˑ,bæŋk
Citicorp
US financial co.   SIT-ē-KAWRP   'siţiˑ,kɔːʳp
Citium
ancient city, Cyprus   SISH-(ē-)uhm   'siʃ(iː)əm
Citlaltépetl [Orizaba]
mtn., city, Mexico   sēt-LAHL-TĀ-PET-l   siːt,lal'teː,petl̩
Citroën
French car co.   sē-traw-EN   siːtrɔːen
Citron
fruit   SI-truhn   'sitrən
Città Vecchia
city, Malta   chi-TAH VEK-yah   tʃi'ta 'vekja
Ciudad Bolívar [Angostura]
port, Venezuela   syo͞o-THAH(TH) vō-LĒ-vahr   sjuː'ða(ð) βoː'liːβar
Ciudad de México
city, Mexico   syo͞o-THAH(TH) thuh MĀ-hē-kō   sjuː'ða(ð) ðə 'meˑhiːkoː
Ciudad Real
prov & town, Spain   syo͞o-THAH(TH) rā-AHL   sjuː'ða(ð) reː'al
Ciudad Trujillo
city, Dominican Republic   syo͞o-THAH(TH) tro͞o-KHĒ(L)-yō   sjuː'ða(ð) tru'çiː(l)joː
Ciudad Victoria
town, Mexico   syo͞o-THAH(TH) vēk-TAWR-yah   sjuː'ða(ð) βiːk'tɔːrja
Cjachak
see Cacak
Clackamas
river, county, OR   KLAK-uh-muhs   'klækəməs
Claflin
College, SC   KLAF-luhn   'klæflən
Claiborne
1. Liz, US fashion designer   KLĀ-BAWRN   'kleː,bɔːʳn
2. pers. name   KLĀ-buhrn, KLĀ-BAWRN   'kleːbəʳn, 'kleː,bɔːʳn
Clair, Claire
1. pers. name   KLAR, KLER   'klæʳ, 'kleʳ
2. René, French film writer and   KLER   kler
   director; pers. name, French
3. German   KLER   'kleʳ
Clairette
wine grape   kler-ET   kler'et
Clairol
hair-products brand   KLAR-AWL, KLER-AWL   'klær,ɔːl, 'kler,ɔːl
Clallam
county, WA   KLAL-uhm   'klæləm

Key (col. 2):   a: fad   ā: fade   ah: father   ar: marry   aw: law   e: fed   ē: feed   er: merry   i: hid   ī: hide   ō: coat   o͞o: boot
oi: boy   ow: now   u: put   uh: above   uhr: bird   ch: chop   ng: ring   sh: show   th: thick   th: this   zh: measure

Clallam, Klallam

    N. American people   KLAL-uhm   'klæləm

Clara

    1. pers. name   KLAR-uh   'klærə

    2. French   klah-RAH   klɑːrɑː

    3. German, Spanish   KLAHR-ah   'klɑrɑ

Clare

    pers. name   KLAR, KLER   'klær^r, 'kle^r

Clare Hall

    college, Cambridge Univ.   KLER HAWL, ⓢ *also* KLAR   'kle^r ˌhɔːl, ⓢ *also* 'klæ^r

Clarence

    1. pers. name   KLAR-uhns   'klærəns

    2. French   klah-RAH^{n}S   klɑːrɑ̄s

Clarendon

    county, SC; city, AR, TX; Oxford   KLAR-uhn-duhn   'klærəndən
      printing press

Claret

    red wine   KLAR-uht   'klærət

Claretian

    religious order   kluh-RĒ-shuhn   klə'riːʃən

Clarice

    pers. name   KLAR-uhs, KLER-uhs   'klærəs, 'klerəs

Clarinet

    musical instrument   KLAR-uh-NET, KLAR-uh-NET   ˌklærə'net, 'klærəˌnet

Clarissa

    pers. name   kluh-RIS-uh   klə'risə

Clark

    Petula, British actress; pers. name   KLAHRK   'klɑ^{r}k

Clarke

    pers. name   KLAHRK   'klɑ^{r}k

Clarkson

    pers. name   KLAHRK-suhn   'klɑ^{r}ksən

Clatsop

    county, Community College, OR   KLAT-suhp   'klætsəp

Claud

    pers. name   KLAWD   'klɔːd

Clauda

    Biblical name   KLAWD-uh   'klɔːdə

Claude

    1. Albert, Belgian biologist (Nobel   KLŌD   kloːd
      1974)

    2. pers. name   KLAWD   'klɔːd

    3. French   KLŌD   kloːd

Claudel

    Paul Louis Charles Marie, French   klō-DEL   kloːdel
      writer and diplomat

Claudette

    pers. name   klaw-DET   klɔː'det

Claudia

    pers. name   KLAWD-ē-uh   'klɔːdiːə

Claudian

    pert. to Claudius   KLAWD-ē-uhn   'klɔːdiːən

Claudine

    pers. name   klō-DĒN   kloːdiːn

Foreign Sounds: ue: *Fr.* **rue**, *Ger.* **füllen**   uh(r): *Fr.* **boeuf**, *Ger.* **Höhle**   <u>kh</u>: *Ger.* **ich**, *Scot.* **loch**   ḡ: *Sp.* **amigo**   v̱: *Sp.* **hablar**
hl: *Welsh* **Llanelli**.   CAPITALS: primary stress.   SMALL CAPS: secondary stress.   ⓢ: U.S. pron.   ⓔ: British pron.

Claudio		
1. pers. name, Italian	KLOWD-yō	'klaudjoː
2. Spanish	KLOWTH-yō	'klauðjoː
Cláudio		
pers. name, Portuguese	KLOWTH-yo͞o	'klauðjuː
Claudius		
1. Roman emperor; pers. name	KLAWD-ē-uhs	'klɔːdiːəs
2. German	KLOWD-yus, KLOW-dē-us	'klaudjus, 'klaudiːus
Claudius Gothicus		
Roman emperor	KLAWD-ē-uhs GAHTH-i-kuhs	'klɔːdiːəs 'gɑθikəs
Claus		
pers. name, Dutch, Norwegian	KLOWS	'klaus
Clausewitz		
Karl von, *Prussian militarist*	KLOW-zuh-VITS	'klauzəˌvits
Clavell		
James, *US writer*	kluh-VEL	klə'vel
Claxton		
pers. name	KLAK-stuhn	'klækstən
Clayburgh		
Jill, *US actress*	KLĀ-BUHRG	'kleːˌbə^{r}g
Clayton		
pers. name	KLĀT-n	'kleːtn̩
Clazomenae		
ancient city, Asia Minor	kluh-ZAHM-uh-NĒ	klə'zɑməˌniː
Cleanthes		
Greek philosopher	klē-AN-THĒZ	kliː'ænˌθiːz
Clearasil		
tdmk for a skin care product	KLIR-uh-SIL	'klirəˌsil
Cleary		
Beverly Atlee, *US author*	KLIR-ē	'kliriˑ
Cleburne		
county, AL, AR; city, TX	KLĒ-buhrn	'kliːbə^{r}n
Cleese		
John, *British actor*	KLĒZ	'kliːz
Cleeve Cloud		
highest point in Cotswold Hills, England	KLĒV KLOWD	'kliːv 'klaud
Cleisthenes		
tyrant of Sicyon; Athenian statesman	KLĪS-thuh-NĒZ	'klaisθəˌniːz
Cleland		
John, *English novelist*	KLEL-uhnd	'klelənd
Clem		
pers. name	KLEM	'klem
Clematis		
plant	KLEM-uht-uhs, kli-MAT-uhs, kli-MAHT-uhs	'kleməţəs, kli'mæţəs, kli'mɑţəs
Clémence		
pers. name, French	klā-MAH^{n}S	kleːmɑ̃s
Clemence		
pers. name	KLEM-uhns	'kleməns
Clemenceau		
Georges, *political leader*	klā-mah^n-SŌ, [S] KLEM-uhn-SŌ	kleːmɑ̃soː, [S] ˌklemən'soː

Key (col. 2): a: fad ā: fade ah: father ar: marry aw: law e: fed ē: feed er: merry i: hid ī: hide ō: coat o͞o: boot oi: boy ow: now u: put uh: above uhr: bird ch: chop ng: ring sh: show th: thick th: this zh: measure

Clemens		
1. Samuel, *US author, aka* Mark Twain; *pers. name*	KLEM-uhnz	'klemənz
2. German	KLĀ-mens	'kleːmens
3. Latin	KLEM-uhnz, KLĒ-muhnz	'klemənz, 'kliːmənz
Clement		
pers. name	KLEM-uhnt	'klemənt
Clément		
pers. name, French	klā-MAH^{n}	kleːmɑ̃
Clemente		
1. Roberto, *US baseball player*	kluh-MENT-ē	klə'mentiˑ
2. pers. name, Italian	klā-MEN-tā	kleː'menteː
3. Spanish	klā-MĀN-tā	kleː'meːnteː
Clementi		
Muzio, *Italian pianist and composer*	klā-MEN-tē, [$] kluh-MENT-ē	kleː'mentiː, [$] klə'mentiˑ
Clémentine		
pers. name, French	klā-mah^{n}-TĒN	kleːmɑ̃tiːn
Clementine		
pers. name	KLEM-uhn-TĪN	'klemən,tɑin
Cleo		
pers. name	KLĒ-ō	'kliːoː
Cleomenes		
name, Spartan kings	klē-AHM-uh-NĒZ	kliː'ɑmə,niːz
Cleon		
Athenian general & politician	KLĒ-AHN	'kliː,ɑn
Cleone		
Athenian general	klē-Ō-nē	kliː'oːniˑ
Cleopas		
Biblical name	KLĒ-uh-puhs, klē-Ō-puhs	'kliːəpəs, kliː'oːpəs
Cleopatra		
Egyptian queen	KLĒ-uh-PA-truh, -PĀ-truh, -PAH-truh	,kliːə'pætrə, -'peːtrə, -'pɑtrə
Cleophas		
Biblical name	KLĒ-uh-fuhs, klē-Ō-puhs	'kliːəfəs, kliː'oːpəs
Clerc-Milon-Mondon		
wine	KLER-mē-LAW^{n}-maw^{n}-DAW^{n}	klermiːlɔ̃mɔ̃dɔ̃
Clerihew		
quatrain rhyming aabb; pers. name	KLER-i-HYOO	'kleri,hjuː
Clerkes of Oxenford		
choral ensemble, England	KLAHRKS uhv AHK-suhn-fuhrd, AHK-suhn-FAWRD	'klɑ^{r}ks əv 'ɑksənfə^{r}d, 'ɑksən,fɔː^{r}d
Clermont		
Fulton's steamboat	KLER-MAHNT	'kle^{r},mɑnt
Clermont-Ferrand		
city, France	kler-maw^{n}-fuh-RAH^{n}	klermɔ̃fərɑ̃
Clete		
nurse to Penthesilea	KLĒT-ē	'kliːt̬iˑ
Clevedon		
town, England	KLĒV-duhn	'kliːvdən
Cleveland		
Grover, *22d & 24th US president; city, OH; county, AR, NC, OK; county, England; pers. name*	KLĒV-luhnd	'kliːvlənd
Cliburn		
Van, *US pianist*	KLĪ-buhrn	'klɑibə^{r}n

Foreign Sounds: ue: *Fr.* **rue**, *Ger.* **füllen** uh(r): *Fr.* **boeuf**, *Ger.* **Höhle** kh: *Ger.* **ich**, *Scot.* **loch** g: *Sp.* **amigo** v: *Sp.* **hablar** hl: *Welsh* **Llanelli**. CAPITALS: primary stress. SMALL CAPS: secondary stress. [$]: U.S. pron. [£]: British pron.

Clichy
suburb of Paris, France　　klē-SHĒ　　　　kliːʃiː
Clicquot
champagne　　klē-KŌ　　　　kliːkoː
Cliff
pers. name　　KLIF　　　　'klif
Clifford
pers. name　　KLIF-uhrd　　　　'klifəʳd
Clifton
pers. name　　KLIF-tuhn　　　　'kliftən
Clinelish
Scotch whisky　　KLĪN-LĒSH　　　　'klɑin‚liːʃ
Clinique
skincare products　　kluh-NĒK　　　　klə'niːk
Clinton
Bill, *US president;* Hillary Rodham,　　KLINT-n　　　　'klintn̩
　US first lady
Clio
1. muse of history　　KLĪ-ō, KLĒ-ō　　　　'klɑioː, 'kliːoː
2. street, New Orleans; advertising　　KLĒ-ō　　　　'kliːoː
　award
Clive
pers. name　　KLĪV　　　　'klɑiv
Clodius
pers. name　　KLŌD-ē-uhs　　　　'kloːdiːəs
Cloncurry
town, Australia　　klahn-KUH-rē　　　　klɑn'kəriˑ
Clootie
the Devil　　KLOOT-ē　　　　'kluːʈiˑ
Cloris
pers. name　　KLŌR-uhs, KLAWR-uhs　　　　'kloːrəs, 'klɔːrəs
Clos de Bèze
wine　　KLŌ duh BEZ　　　　kloː də bez
Clos de Tart
wine　　KLŌ duh TAHR　　　　kloː də tɑr
Clos de Vougeot
wine　　KLŌ duh voo-ZHŌ　　　　kloː də vuːʒoː
Clos du Bois
winery, CA　　KLŌ duh BWAH　　　　‚kloː də 'bwɑ
Clos du Roi
wine　　KLŌ duer WAH　　　　kloː dyːr wɑː
Clos Fourtet
wine　　KLŌ fur-TE　　　　kloː furte
Close
Glenn, *US actress*　　KLŌS　　　　'kloːs
Clotho
one of the Fates　　KLŌ-thō　　　　'kloːθoː
Clotilde
1. pers. name, French　　klaw-TĒLD　　　　klɔːtiːld
2. Italian　　klō-TĒL-dä　　　　kloː'tiːldeː
Clough
1. Arthur Hugh, *English poet*　　KLUHF　　　　'kləf
2. pers. name　　KLUHF, KLŌ　　　　'kləf, 'kloː
Clouseau
fictional French police inspector　　kloo-ZŌ　　　　kluːzoː

Key (col. 2):　a: fad　ã: fade　ah: father　ar: marry　aw: law　e: fed　ē: feed　er: merry　i: hid　ī: hide　ō: coat　ōō: boot
oi: boy　ow: now　u: put　uh: above　uhr: bird　ch: chop　ng: ring　sh: show　th: thick　th: this　zh: measure

Clovis
  pers. name — klaw-VĒS, KLŌ-vis — klɔːviːs, 'kloːvis

Clovis [Chlodwig, Chlodowech]
  Frankish king — klaw-VĒS; ⑤ KLŌ-vuhs — klɔːviːs; ⑤ 'kloːvəs

Cluett
  Sanford Lockwood, *US engineer* — KLOO-uht — 'kluːət

Cluj
  county, Romania — KLOOZH — 'kluːʒ

Cluj-Napoca
  city, Romania — KLOOZH-NAHP-ō-kuh, -nah-PŌ-kuh — 'kluːʒ'napoːkə, -na'poːkə

Clumber
  spaniel — KLUHM-buhr — 'kləmbəʳ

Cluny
  commune, abbey, France; lace — klue-NĒ, ⑤ kloo-NĒ — klyːniː, ⑤ kluː'niː

Clurman
  Harold, *US theatrical director and* — KLUR-muhn — 'kluʳmən
  critic

Clutha
  river, New Zealand — KLOO-thuh — 'kluːθə

Clwyd
  river, county, Wales — KLOO-id, ⑤ KLOO-ēd — 'klu·id, ⑤ 'kluːi·d

Clwydian
  pert. to Clwyd — kloo-ID-ē-uhn — kluː'idiːən

Clyde
  river, Scotland; pers. name — KLĪD — 'klɑid

Clydesdale
  horse breed — KLĪDZ-DĀL — 'klɑidz,deːl

Clymene
  mother of Atlas, Prometheus, — KLIM-uh-nē — 'kliməni·
  Epimetheus

Clymenus
  founder of the Olympic Games — KLIM-uh-nuhs — 'klimənəs

Clytemnestra
  wife of Agamemnon — KLĪT-uhm-NES-truh, ⑥ — ,klɑitəm'nestrə, ⑥
  KLĪ-tuhm-NĒ-struh — ,klɑitəm'niːstrə

CMOS
  complementary metal oxide silicon — SĒ-MAHS — 'siː,mɑs
  semiconductor

Cnaeus, Cneius
  Roman praenomen — NĒ-uhs — 'niːəs

Cnidus
  ancient Greek city — NĪD-uhs, kuh-NĪD-uhs — 'nɑidəs, kə'nɑidəs

Cnossus
  ancient Cretan city — NAHS-uhs — 'nasəs

Cnut
  see Canute

Coahoma
  county, MS — kō-HŌ-muh — koː'hoːmə

Coahuila
  state, Mexico — KŌ-uh-WĒ-luh — ,koːə'wiːlə

Coahuiltec
  N. American people — KŌ-uh-WĒL-TEK — ,koːə'wiːl,tek

Coalinga
  city, CA — KŌ-uh-LING-guh — ,koːə'liŋgə

Foreign Sounds: ue: *Fr.* **rue**, *Ger.* **füllen** uh(r): *Fr.* **boeuf**, *Ger.* **Höhle** kh: *Ger.* **ich**, *Scot.* **loch** g̃: *Sp.* amigo v: *Sp.* hablar hl: *Welsh* **Llanelli**. CAPITALS: primary stress. SMALL CAPS: secondary stress. ⑤: U.S. pron. ⑥: British pron.

Coase
　Ronald H., *British-born US*　　　　KŌS　　　　　　　　　　　　'koːs
　　economist
Coatlicue
　Mayan earth goddess　　　　kō-AHT-li-KWĀ, kō-AT-li-KWĀ　　koː'ɑtliˌkweː, koː'ætliˌkweː
Cobá
　ancient Mayan city, Mexico　kō-V̲AH, Ⓢ kō-BAH　　　　koː'βɑ, Ⓢ koː'bɑ
cobalt
　element　　　　　　　KŌ-BAWLT, KŌ-buhlt　　　　'koːˌbɔːlt, 'koːbəlt
Cobán
　city, Guatamala　　　kō-V̲AHN, Ⓢ kō-BAHN　　　　koː'βɑn, Ⓢ koː'bɑn
Cobar
　town, Australia　　　KŌ-BAHR　　　　　　　　'koːˌbɑ^r
COBE
　Cosmic Background Explorer　KŌ-bē　　　　　　　　'koːbiˑ
Coblenz
　see Koblenz
COBOL
　programming lang.　　KŌ-BAWL, KŌ-BAHL　　　　'koːˌbɔːl, 'koːˌbɑl
Coburn
　James, *US actor*　　　KŌ-buhrn　　　　　　　　'koːbə^rn
Coca-Cola
　soft drink brand & co.　KŌ-kuh-KŌ-luh, *in rapid speech*　ˌkoːkə'koːlə, *in rapid speech*
　　　　　　　　　　　　kō-KŌ-luh　　　　　　　　koː'koːlə
Cocama
　see Kokama
Cochabamba
　dept, Bolivia　　　　KŌ-chuh-BAHM-buh　　　　ˌkoːtʃə'bɑmbə
Cochimi
　N. American people　KŌ-chuh-MĒ　　　　　　ˌkoːtʃə'miː
Cochin
　seaport, India　　　kō-CHIN　　　　　　　　koː'tʃin
Cochise
　1. Apache leader　　kō-CHĒS　　　　　　　　koː'tʃiːs
　2. county, AZ　　　kuh-CHĒS, kō-CHĒS　　　kə'tʃiːs, koː'tʃiːs
Cochiti
　N. American people　kō-CHĒT-ē　　　　　　　koː'tʃiːt̪iˑ
Cochoa
　song bird　　　　　kuh-CHŌ-uh　　　　　　kə'tʃoːə
Cockaigne, Cockayne
　Land of, *fabled land of luxury*　kah-KĀN　　　　　　　kɑ'keːn
Cockburn
　British family name　KŌ-buhrn　　　　　　　'koːbə^rn
Cockcroft
　Sir John D., *British physicist (Nobel*　KAHK-(K)RAWFT　　　'kakˌ(k)rɔːft
　1951)
Cockney
　person from east end of London,　KAHK-nē　　　　　　　'kakniˑ
　　England
Coclé
　province, Panama　　kō-KLĀ　　　　　　　　koː'kleː
Coconino
　county, AZ　　　　KŌ-kuh-NĒ-nō　　　　　ˌkoːkə'niːnoː
Cocopah
　N. American people　KŌ-kuh-PAH, kō-kuh-PAH　'koːkəˌpɑ, ˌkoːkə'pɑ

Key (col. 2):　a: fad　ā: fade　ah: father　ar: marry　aw: law　e: fed　ē: feed　er: merry　i: hid　ī: hide　ō: coat　o͞o: boot
oi: boy　ow: now　u: put　uh: above　uhr: bird　ch: chop　ng: ring　sh: show　th: thick　t̲h̲: this　zh: measure

Cocos Islands
atolls, Indian Ocean   KŌ-kuhs   'koːkəs

Cocteau
Jean, French writer   kawk-TŌ, Ⓢ kahk-TŌ   kɔːktoː, Ⓢ kɑk'toː

Codex Juris Canonici
Roman Catholic Church law   KŌD-EKS JUR-uhs KAN-uh-NĪ-sē, YUR-uhs, KAN-uh-NĒ-sē   'koːd,eks 'dʒurəs ,kænə'nɑisi', 'jurəs, ,kænə'niːsi'

Codington
county, SD   KAHD-ing-tuhn   'kɑdiŋtən

Codona
Alfredo, Mexican aerialist   kō-<u>TH</u>Ō-nah   koː'ðoːnɑ

Codrus
son of Melanthus; king of Athens   KAHD-ruhs   'kɑdrəs

Cody
William "Buffalo Bill", US scout, entertainer   KŌD-ē   'koːdi'

Coelenterates
marine invertebrates   sē-LENT-uh-RĀTS, suh-   siː'lentə,reːts, sə-

Coeliris
dinosaur   SĒ-luh-ruhs   'siːlərəs

Coelophysis
dinosaur   sē-LŌ-fuh-zuhs, sē-LAHF-uh-zuhs, -suhs; SĒ-luh-FĪ-suhs   siː'loːfəzəs, siː'lɑfəzəs, -səs; ,siːlə'faisəs

Coelurosauria
dinosaur infraorder   SĒL-yuh-rō-SAWR-ē-uh   ,siːljəroː'sɔːriːə

Coelus
Roman name for Uranus   SĒ-luhs   'siːləs

Coetzee
S. African family name   ko͞ot-SI-uh, ko͞ot-SĒ   kuːt'siə, kuːt'siː

Coeur d'Alene
river, city, lake, ID; N. American people   KAWRD-l-ĀN   ,kɔːʳdļ'eːn

Coeur de Lion
Richard I of England, "lionhearted"   kuhr duh LYAWⁿ, Ⓢ KUHR duh LĪ-uhn, LĒ-uhn   kœr də ljɔ̃, Ⓢ ,kəʳ də 'lɑiən, 'liːən

Coeus
son of Uranus and Gaia   SĒ-uhs   'siːəs

Coffee
county, AL, GA, TN   KAW-fē, KAHF-ē   'kɔːfi', 'kɑfi'

Coggan
Frederick Donald, archbishop of Canterbury   KAHG-uhn   'kɑgən

Cognac
brandy   KŌN-YAK, KAWN-YAK, KAHN-YAK   'koːn,jæk, 'kɔːn,jæk, 'kɑn,jæk

Cohan
George M., composer   KŌ-HAN   'koː,hæn

Cohen
Stanley, US biochemist (Nobel 1986)   KŌ-uhn   'koːən

Cohn
Sam, US film and theatrical agent   KŌN   'koːn

Cohoes
city, NY   kuh-HŌZ   kə'hoːz

Foreign Sounds: **ue**: *Fr.* **rue**, *Ger.* f**ü**llen   **uh**(r): *Fr.* b**oeu**f, *Ger.* H**ö**hle   <u>kh</u>: *Ger.* i**ch**, *Scot.* lo**ch**   <u>g</u>: *Sp.* ami**g**o   <u>v</u>: *Sp.* ha**b**lar
hl: *Welsh* **Ll**anelli.   CAPITALS: primary stress.   SMALL CAPS: secondary stress.   Ⓢ: U.S. pron.   Ⓔ: British pron.

Cohosh
herb   KŌ-HAHSH   'koːˌhɑʃ

Coimbatore
city, India   KOIM-buh-TUR   'kɔimbəˌtuʳ

Coimbra
district, Portugal   ku-IM-bruh, kō-IM-bruh   ku'imbrə, koː'imbrə

Cointreau
liqueur   kweⁿ-TRŌ   kwẽ'troː

Cointrin
airport, Geneva   kweⁿ-TREⁿ   kwẽtrẽ

Cojedes
state, Venezuela   kō-HĀ-<u>th</u>uhs   koː'heːðəs

Cojutepeque
city, El Salvador   kō-HŌŌT-uh-PĀ-kā, -kē   koːˌhuːṭə'peːkeː, -kiˑ

Coke
British family name   KUK, KŌŌK, KŌK   'kuk, 'kuːk, 'koːk

Coke, Cooke
Sir Edward, English jurist   KUK   'kuk

Colbert
1. Claudette, US actress   kawl-BER, KŌL-BER   kɔːl'beʳ, 'koːlˌbeʳ
2. county, AL   KAHL-buhrt   'kɑlbəʳt

Colby
College, ME; city, KS, WI; cheese   KŌL-bē   'koːlbiˑ

Colchester
1. town, CT, VT; county, Nova Scotia, Canada   KŌL-CHES-tuhr, KŌL-chuh-stuhr   'koːlˌtʃestəʳ, 'koːltʃəstəʳ
2. town, England   KŌL-chuh-stuhr   'koːltʃəstəʳ

Colchicum
plant   KAHL-chi-kuhm, KAHL-ki-kuhm   'kɑltʃikəm, 'kɑlkikəm

Colchis
ancient country, Asia   KAHL-kuhs   'kɑlkəs

Coldstream Guards
British royal regiment   KŌL(D)-STRẼM GAHRDZ   ˌkoːl(d)ˌstriːm 'gɑʳdz

Cole
pers. name   KŌL   'koːl

Cölemerık [Hakkâri, Hakâri]
town, Turkey   CHUH(R)-luh-muh-RUHK, -RIK   ˌtʃœːləmə'rək, -'rik

Coleridge
Samuel Taylor, English poet   KŌL-rij, KŌ-luh-rij   'koːlridʒ, 'koːləridʒ

Colet
John, English educator   KAHL-uht   'kɑlət

Colet
Louise, French writer   kō-LE   koːle

Colette
1. pers. name   kuh-LET   kə'let
2. French   kaw-LET   kɔːlet
3. Sidonie, French writer   kaw-LET, Ⓢ kuh-LET, kahl-ET   kɔːlet, Ⓢ kə'let, kɑl'et

Coleus
plant   KŌ-lē-uhs   'koːliːəs

Colgate
University, NY   KŌL-GĀT   'koːlˌgeːt

Colhozeh
Biblical name   kahl-HŌ-zuh, KAHL-<u>kh</u>ah-ZE   kɑl'hoːzə, ˌkɑlxɑ'ze

---

Key (col. 2):   a: fad   ā: fade   ah: father   ar: marry   aw: law   e: fed   ē: feed   er: merry   i: hid   ī: hide   ō: coat   ōō: boot
oi: boy   ow: now   u: put   uh: above   uhr: bird   ch: chop   ng: ring   sh: show   th: thick   <u>th</u>: this   zh: measure

Colijn
  Hendrikus, *Dutch anti-Fascist*   kuh-LĬN   kəˈlɑin
    politician
Colima
  state, Mexico   kuh-LĒ-muh   kəˈliːmə
Colima warbler
  songbird   kuh-LĒ-muh WAWR-bluhr   kəˈliːmə ˈwɔːʳbləʳ
Colin
  1. pers. name   KAHL-uhn, KŌ-luhn   ˈkɑlən, ˈkoːlən
  2. French   kaw-LEⁿ   kɔːlẽ
  3. German   KŌ-lin, -lēn   ˈkoːlin, -liːn
Collarenebri
  town, Australia   KAHL-uh-REN-uh-BRĬ   ˌkɑləˈrenəˌbrɑi
Colleen
  pers. name   kahl-ĒN   kɑlˈiːn
College Misericordia
  college, PA   KAHL-ij MIZ-uh-ri-KAWR-dē-uh,   ˈkɑlidʒ ˌmizəriˈkɔːʳdiːə,
                          MIZ-ER-i-KAWR-dē-uh   ˌmizˌeriˈkɔːʳdiːə
Colleton
  county, SC   KAHL-uht-n   ˈkɑlətn̩
Colley
  pers. name (C. Cibber)   KAHL-ē   ˈkɑliˑ
Colli Albani
  Italian wine   KAHL-ē ahl-BAHN-ē   ˈkɑliː ɑlˈbɑniˑ
Colli Piacentini
  Italian wine   KAHL-ē PYAH-chen-TĒ-nē   ˈkɑliː ˌpjɑtʃenˈtiːniː
Collossae, Colosse
  Biblical name   kuh-LAHS-ē   kəˈlɑsiː
Colmar [Kolmar]
  city, France   kōl-MAHR, ⑤ KŌL-MAHR   koːlmɑːʳ, ⑤ ˈkoːlˌmɑʳ
Cologne [Köln]
  city, Germany   kuh-LŌN   kəˈloːn
Colombia
  republic, S. America   kuh-LUHM-bē-uh, kuh-LŌM-bē-uh kəˈləmbiːə, kəˈloːmbiːə
Colombian
  pert. to Colombia   kuh-LUHM-bē-uhn, kuh-LŌM-bē-uhn kəˈləmbiːən, kəˈloːmbiːən
Colombo
  city, Sri Lanka   kuh-LUHM-bō   kəˈləmboː
Colón
  Cristóbal, *Spanish name for*   kuh-LŌN   kəˈloːn
    Christopher Columbus; *prov., city,*
    Panama; town, Argentina; town,
    Cuba
Colonia
  department, Uruguay   kuh-LŌN-yuh   kəˈloːnjə
Colonna
  Roman noble family   kuh-LŌ-nuh   kəˈloːnə
Colonus
  Sophoclean setting   kuh-LŌ-nuhs   kəˈloːnəs
Colorado
  1. river, state, & desert, US   KAHL-uh-RAD-ō, KAHL-uh-RAHD-ō ˌkɑləˈrædoː, ˌkɑləˈrɑdoː
  2. river, Argentina; S. American KAHL-uh-RAHD-ō   ˌkɑləˈrɑdoː
    people
Colosseum
  ampitheater, Rome   KAHL-uh-SĒ-uhm   ˌkɑləˈsiːəm

Foreign Sounds: ue: *Fr.* **rue**, *Ger.* **füllen** uh(r): *Fr.* **boeuf**, *Ger.* **Höhle** <u>kh</u>: *Ger.* i**ch**, *Scot.* lo**ch** g̃: *Sp.* ami**g**o <u>v</u>: *Sp.* ha**b**lar
hl: *Welsh* L**l**anelli. CAPITALS: primary stress. SMALL CAPS: secondary stress. ⑤: U.S. pron. Ⓔ: British pron.

Colossians

New Testament book   kuh-LAHSH-(ē-)uhnz,   kə'laʃ(iː)ənz, kə'lɑsiːənz
kuh-LAHS-ē-uhnz

Colossus of Rhodes

ancient wonder   kuh-LAHS-uhs uhv RŌDZ   kə'lɑsəs əv 'roːdz

Colquhoun

Patrick, *Scottish merchant, police*   kuh-H$\overline{OO}$N   kə'huːn
reformer

Colquitt

county, GA   KAHL-kwit   'kɑlkwit

Colton

city, CA   KŌLT-n   'koːltn̩

Coltrane

John, *US jazz musician*   kōl-TRĀN, KŌL-TRĀN   koːl'treːn, 'koːl,treːn

Colum

Padraic, *Irish poet and playwright*   KAHL-uhm   'kɑləm

Columba

constellation   kuh-LUHM-buh   kə'ləmbə

Columbia

river, US & Canada; District of, *US;*   kuh-LUHM-bē-uh   kə'ləmbiːə
University, *NY*

Columbiana

county, OH   kuh-LUHM-bē-AN-uh   kə,ləmbiː'ænə

Columbine [Aquilegia]

plant   KAHL-uhm-BĪN   'kaləm,bain

columbium

element   kuh-LUHM-bē-uhm   kə'ləmbiːəm

Columbus

Christopher, *Italian-born Spanish*   kuh-LUHM-buhs   kə'ləmbəs
explorer; city, OH; pers. name

Colusa

county, CA   kuh-L$\overline{OO}$-suh   kə'luːsə

Colusa Rancheria

Indian reservation, US   kuh-L$\overline{OO}$-suh RAN-chuh-RĒ-uh   kə'luːsə ,ræntʃə'riːə

Coma Berenices [Berenice's Hair]

constellation   KŌ-muh BER-uh-NĪ-sēz   'koːmə ,berə'naisiːz

Comal

county, TX   kuh-MAHL   kə'mɑl

Comanche

N. American people; county, KS, OK,   kuh-MAN-chē   kə'mæntʃiˑ
TX

Comaneci

Nadia, *Romanian gymnast*   KŌ-muh-NĀCH, KŌ-muh-NĒCH   ,koːmə'neːtʃ, ,koːmə'niːtʃ

Comayagua

department, Honduras   kō-mah-YAHG̃-wuh   koːmɑ'jaɣwə

Comecon

Eastern bloc trade group   KAHM-i-KAHN   'kami,kɑn

Comédie Française

French national theater   kaw-mā-DĒ frah^n-SEZ   kɔːmeːdiː frɑsez

Comenius

John Amos, *Moravian bishop*   kuh-MĀ-nē-uhs, kuh-MĒ-nē-uhs   kə'meːniːəs, kə'miːniːəs

COMEX

commodities exchange   KAHM-EKS, KAHM-iks   'kam,eks, 'kamiks

Comfrey

plant   KUHM(P)-frē   'kəm(p)friˑ

Key (col. 2):   a: fad   ā: fade   ah: father   ar: marry   aw: law   e: fed   ē: feed   er: merry   i: hid   ī: hide   ō: coat $\overline{oo}$: boot
oi: boy   ow: now   u: put   uh: above   uhr: bird   ch: chop   ng: ring   sh: show   th: thick   th̲: this   zh: measure

Comilla, Kumilla
   region, Bangladesh   kuh-MIL-uh, ku-   kəˈmilə, ku-

Comines, Commines, Commynes
   Philippe de, *French politician*   kaw-MĒN   kɔːmiːn

Cominform
   Communist organization   KAHM-uhn-FŌRM, KAHM-uhn-FAWRM   ˈkamənˌfoːʳm, ˈkamənˌfɔːʳm

Comintern
   Communist organization   KAHM-uhn-TUHRN   ˈkamənˌtəʳn

Comiskey
   Park, *ballpark, Chicago, IL*   kuh-MIS-kē   kəˈmiski·

Comitia centuriata
   Roman legislative assembly   kō-MISH-(ē-)uh SEN-T(Y)UR-ē-ĀT-uh, -AHT-uh   kɔːˈmiʃ(iː)ə ˌsenˌt(j)uriːˈeːʈə, -ˈaʈə

Comitia curiata
   early Roman legislative assembly   kō-MISH-(ē-)uh KYUR-ē-ĀT-uh, -AHT-uh   kɔːˈmiʃ(iː)ə ˌkjuriːˈeːʈə, -ˈaʈə

Comitia tributa
   Roman legislative assembly   kō-MISH-(ē-)uh trī-BYŌŌT-uh   kɔːˈmiʃ(iː)ə traiˈbjuːʈə

Commagene
   ancient district, Syria   KAHM-uh-JĒ-nē   ˌkaməˈdʒiːni·

Commager
   Henry Steele, *US historian*   KAHM-i-juhr   ˈkamidʒəʳ

Commander [Komandorskiye]
   Islands, *island group, Bering Sea*   kuh-MAN-duhr   kəˈmændəʳ

Commedia dell' Arte
   early Italian comedy   kuh-MĀD-ē-uh DEL AHRT-ē, kuh-MED-ē-uh   kəˈmeːdiːə ˌdel ˈaʳʈi·, kəˈmediːə

Commercy
   commune, France; small cupcakes   kaw-mer-SĒ, Ⓢ KAHM-uhr-SĒ   kɔːmersiː, Ⓢ ˌkaməʳˈsiː

Commewijne
   district, Surinam   KAW-muh-VĪ-nuh   ˌkɔːməˈvainə

Commines
   see Comines

Commodus
   Roman emperor   KAHM-uhd-uhs   ˈkamədəs

Commynes
   see Comines

Comneni [Comnenus]
   Byzantine noble family   kahm-NEN-ē   kamˈneni·

Comnenus [Comneni]
   Byzantine noble family   kahm-NĒ-nuhs   kamˈniːnəs

Como
   prov & lake, Italy   KŌ-mō   ˈkoːmoː

Comoran
   pert. to or inhabitant of Comoros   KAHM-uh-ruhn, kuh-MAWR-uhn   ˈkamərən, kəˈmɔːrən

Comoros
   islands   KAHM-uh-RŌZ, -RŌS; kuh-MAWR-ōz, -ōs   ˈkaməˌroːz, -ˌroːs; kəˈmɔːroːz, -oːs

Compadre
   Stadium, *Chandler, AZ*   kuhm-PAH-drā   kəmˈpadreː

Compaq
   US computer co.   KAHM-PAK   ˈkamˌpæk

Compiègne
   city, France   kawⁿ-PYEN   kɔ̃pjen

Foreign Sounds: ue: *Fr.* **rue**, *Ger.* **füllen**   uh(r): *Fr.* **b**oeuf, *Ger.* **Höhle**   kh: *Ger.* i**ch**, *Scot.* lo**ch**   g̃: *Sp.* ami**g**o   y: *Sp.* ha**b**lar   hl: *Welsh* **Ll**anelli.   CAPITALS: primary stress.   SMALL CAPS: secondary stress.   Ⓢ: U.S. pron.   Ⓔ: British pron.

Compsognathus
  dinosaur   kahmp-SAHG-nuh-thuhs   kɑmp'sɑgnəθəs
Compton
  A. H., *US physicist (Nobel 1927)*   KAHM(P)-tuhn   'kɑm(p)tən
Compton-Burnett
  Dame Ivy, *English writer*   KAHM(P)-tuhn-BUHR-nuht   'kɑm(p)tən'bərnət
Comstock Lode
  US silver deposit   KAHM-STAHK LŌD   'kɑm,stɑk 'loːd
Comtat Venaissin
  historical region, France   kawⁿ-TAH vuh-ne-SEⁿ   kɔ̃tɑː vənesẽ
Comte
  Auguste, *French philosopher*   KAWⁿT   kɔ̃t
Comtism
  philosophy of Comte   KAHM-TIZ-uhm, KAWⁿ(N)-TIZ-uhm   'kɑm,tizəm, 'kɔ̃(n),tizəm
Comus
  Roman god of mirth; masque, J.   KŌ-muhs   'koːməs
    Milton
ConAgra
  US farm products co.   KAHN-AG-ruh, kahn-AG-ruh   'kɑn,ægrə, kɑn'ægrə
Conakry, Konakri
  city, Guinea   KAHN-uh-krē   'kɑnəkriˑ
Conan
  1. pers. name   KAWN-uhn, KŌ-nuhn   'kɔːnən, 'koːnən
  2. the Barbarian, *film character* KŌ-NAN, KŌ-nuhn   'koː,næn, 'koːnən
Conaniah
  Biblical name   KAHN-uh-NĪ-uh, KŌ-nuh-;   ,kɑnə'naiə, ,koːnə-;
                                       KAW-nahn-YAH-hoo   ,kɔːnan'jɑhuː
Concepción
  city, Chile; dept., Paraguay; pers. kawn-seps-YAWN,   kɔːnseps'jɔːn, kɔːnθep'θjɔːn
    name   kawn-thep-THYAWN
Concepcion
  David Ismael, *US baseball player*   kuhn-SEP-sē-ŌN   kən,sepsiː'oːn
Concepción, La
  see La Concepción
Concertgebouw
  orchestra, Netherlands   kawn-SERT-ḡuh-BOW,   kɔːn'serᵗtɣə,bau,
                                       Ⓢ kuhn-SERT-guh-BOW,   Ⓢ kən'serᵗtgə,bau,
                                       kuhn-SUHRT-   kən'səᵗt-
Concertina
  musical instrument   KAHN-suhr-TĒ-nuh   ,kɑnsəᵗ'tiːnə
Concertino
  short concerto   KAHN-chuhr-TĒ-nō   ,kɑntʃəᵗ'tiːnoː
Conchagua
  volcano, El Salvador   kawn-CHAHḠ-wuh   kɔːn'tʃɑɣwə
Concho
  river, county, TX   KAHN-chō   'kɑntʃoː
Conchobor
  legendary Irish king   KAHNG-khuh-vuhr, KAHNG-khuhr,   'kɑŋxəvər, 'kɑŋxər,
                                       Ⓢ KAHNG-kuh-vuhr   Ⓢ 'kɑŋkəvər
Concilium plebus tributum
  Roman plebeian assembly   kuhn-SIL-ē-uhm PLĀ-buhs   kən'siliəm 'pleːbəs
                                       tri-BYOOT-uhm, PLĒ-buhs   tri'bjuːʈəm, 'pliːbəs

---

Key (col. 2):   a: fad   ā: fade   ah: father   ar: marry   aw: law   e: fed   ē: feed   er: merry   i: hid   ī: hide   ō: coat   oo: boot
oi: boy   ow: now   u: put   uh: above   uhr: bird   ch: chop   ng: ring   sh: show   th: thick   <u>th</u>: this   zh: measure

Concord
  1. river, town, MA, city, CA, NH;   KAHNG-kuhrd, KAHN-, -KAWRD   'kaŋkə^rd, 'kan-, -,kɔː^rd
  grape
  2. city, NC   KAHN-KAWRD, KAHNG-KAWRD   'kan,kɔː^rd, 'kaŋ,kɔː^rd
Concorde
  supersonic passenger plane   KAHNG-KAWRD, KAHN-KAWRD   'kaŋ,kɔː^rd, 'kan,kɔː^rd
Condé
  French noble family   kawⁿ-DĀ   kɔ̃deː
Condé Nast
  publishing co.   KAHN-dā NAST, KAHN-dē   ,kandeː 'næst, ,kandiˑ
Condillac
  Étienne Bonnot de, French   kawⁿ-dē-YAHK   kɔ̃diːjaːk
  philosopher
Condobolin
  town, Australia   kuhn-DŌ-bluhn   kən'doːblən
Condoleezza
  pers. name   KAHN-duh-LĒ-zuh   'kandə,liːzə
Condor
  vulture   KAHN-duhr, KAHN-DAWR   'kandə^r, 'kan,dɔː^r
Conecuh
  river, county, AL   kuh-NĀ-kuh   kə'neːkə
Conejos
  county, CO   kuh-NĀ-uhs, kuh-NĀ-huhs   kə'neːəs, kə'neːhəs
Conestoga [Susquehanna]
  N. American people   KAHN-uh-STŌ-guh   ,kanə'stoːgə
Coney Island
  resort, NY   KŌ-nē Ī-luhnd   'koːniː 'ailənd
Confucian
  pert. to Confucius   kuhn-FYŌŌ-shuhn   kən'fjuːʃən
Confucianism
  doctrines of Confucius   kuhn-FYŌŌ-shuh-NIZ-uhm   kən'fjuːʃə,nizəm
Confucius
  Chinese philosopher   kuhn-FYŌŌ-shuhs   kən'fjuːʃəs
Conga
  dance; drum   KAHNG-guh   'kaŋgə
Congo [Zaire]
  river, republic, Africe   KAHNG-gō   'kaŋgoː
Congolese
  pert. to the Congo   KAHNG-guh-LĒZ, -LĒS   ,kaŋgə'liːz, -'liːs
Congregational
  Christian church   KAHNG-gri-GĀ-shuhn-l,   ,kaŋgri'geːʃənl,
                                            KAHNG-gri-GĀSH-nuhl   ,kaŋgri'geːʃnəl
Congregationalism
  system of church governance   KAHNG-gri-GĀ-shuhn-l-IZ-uhm,   ,kaŋgri'geːʃənḷ,izəm,
                                            KAHNG-gri-GĀSH-nuh-LIZ-uhm   ,kaŋgri'geːʃnə,lizəm
Congreve
  William, English dramatist   KAHN-GRĒV, KAHNG-GRĒV   'kan,griːv, 'kaŋ,griːv
Coniston Water
  lake, England   KAHN-uh-stuhn WAWT-uhr,   'kanəstən ,wɔːtə^r, 'watə^r
                                            WAHT-uhr
Connacht, Connaught
  prov, Irish Republic   KAHN-AWT, kuh-NAWT   'kan,ɔːt, kə'nɔːt
Connecticut
  river, state, US   kuh-NET-i-kuht   kə'neţikət

Foreign Sounds: ue: *Fr.* **rue,** *Ger.* **füllen** uh(r): *Fr.* **boeuf,** *Ger.* **Höhle** kh: *Ger.* **ich,** *Scot.* **loch** g̅: *Sp.* amigo v̲: *Sp.* hablar
hl: *Welsh* **Llanelli.** CAPITALS: primary stress. SMALL CAPS: secondary stress. ⑤: U.S. pron. ⑥: British pron.

Connemara
   region, Irish Republic   KAHN-uh-MAHR-uh, KAHN-uh-MAR-uh   ˌkanə'marə, ˌkanə'mærə
Connery
   Sean, *British actor*   KAHN-uh-rē   'kanəri·
Connie
   pers. name   KAHN-ē   'kani·
Conniff
   Ray, *US conductor, composer*   KAHN-if   'kanif
CONOCO
   oil co.   KAHN-uh-KŌ   'kanəˌkoː
Conon
   pope   KŌ-NAHN, KŌ-nuhn   'koːˌnan, 'koːnən
Conor
   pers. name   KAHN-uhr   'kanəʳ
Conquian
   game   KAHNG-kē-uhn   'kaŋkiːən
Conrad
   1. pers. name   KAHN-RAD, -ruhd   'kanˌræd, -rəd
   2. Danish   KAWN-RAH<u>TH</u>   'kɔːnˌrað
   3. Dutch, German   KAWN-RAHT   'kɔːnˌrat
Conrad Grebel
   College, *Canada*   KAHN-RAD GRĀ-buhl   'kanˌræd 'greːbəl
Conrail, ConRail
   US rail freight carrier   KAHN-RĀL   'kanˌreːl
Conroy
   pers. name   KAHN-ROI   'kanˌrɔi
Consentes
   the twelve major Roman deities   kuhn-SEN-tēz   kən'sentiːz
Considine
   Bob, *US journalist*   KAHN-suh-DĪN   'kansəˌdain
Consilium
   Roman imperial cabinet   kuhn-SIL-ē-uhm   kən'siliːəm
Constable
   John, *English painter*   KAHN-stuh-buhl   'kanstəbəl
Constance
   1. lake, Swiss Alps; pers. name   KAHN-stuhn(t)s   'kanstən(t)s
   2. French   kawⁿ-STAHⁿS   kɔ̃stɑ̃s
   3. see Konstanz
Constanta, Constantsa
   county, port, Romania   kuhn-STAHN(T)-suh   kən'stan(t)sə
Constantin
   1. pers. name   KAHN-stuhn-TIN   'kanstənˌtin
   2. French   kawⁿ-stahⁿ-TEⁿ   kɔ̃stɑ̃tɛ̃
   3. German, Romanian   KAWN-stahn-TĒN   ˌkɔːnstan'tiːn
Constantine
   1. Roman emperor; pers. name   KAHN-stuhn-TĒN, -TĪN   'kanstənˌtiːn, -ˌtain
   2. town, Algeria   KAHN-stuhn-TĒN   'kanstənˌtiːn
Constantinople
   former name of Istanbul   KAHN-STANT-n-Ō-puhl   ˌkanˌstæntn̩'oːpəl
Constantius
   name, Roman emperors   kahn-STAN-chē-uhs, -STAN-shē-uhs   kan'stæntʃiːəs, -'stænʃiːəs
Consus
   Roman harvest god   KAHN-suhs   'kansəs
Contac
   tdmk for a cold medicine   KAHN-TAK   'kanˌtæk

Key (col. 2):   a: f**a**d   ā: f**a**de   ah: f**a**ther   ar: m**a**rry   aw: l**a**w   e: f**e**d   ē: f**ee**d   er: m**e**rry   i: h**i**d   ī: h**i**de   ō: c**oa**t   ōō: b**oo**t
oi: b**oy**   ow: n**ow**   u: p**u**t   uh: **a**bove   uhr: b**i**rd   ch: **ch**op   ng: ri**ng**   sh: **sh**ow   th: **th**ick   <u>th</u>: **th**is   zh: mea**s**ure

Contadina
  food co. KAHNT-uh-DĒ-nuh ˌkɑntəˈdiːnə

Contadora
  C. American political process kōn-tah-DAWR-ah, koːntɑˈdɔːrɑ, ˌkɑntəˈdɔːrə
    KAHNT-uh-DAWR-uh

Contadora, Isla
  island, Panama ĒZ-lah kōn-tah-DAWR-ah ˈiːzlɑ koːntɑˈdɔːrɑ

Conte
  Silvio, *US politician* KAHNT-ē ˈkɑntiˑ

Contra
  anti-Sandinista group KAHN-truh, KŌN-truh ˈkɑntrə, ˈkoːntrə

Contra Costa
  county, CA KAHN-truh KAHS-tuh, KAW-stuh ˌkɑntrə ˈkɑstə, ˈkɔːstə

Conure
  parrot KAHN-yuhr ˈkɑnjəʳ

Converse
  Frederick Shepherd, *US composer;* KAHN-VUHRS ˈkɑnˌvəʳs
    brand name, shoes

Conway
  English form of Conwy; *pers. name* KAHN-WĀ ˈkɑnˌweː

Conwy
  town, Wales KAHN-wē ˈkɑnwiˑ

Cooder
  Ry, *US guitarist, recording artist* KOOD-uhr ˈkuːdəʳ

Cooke
  Alistair, *Anglo-American journalist* KUK ˈkuk

Coolabah
  Australian tree KOO-luh-BAH ˈkuːləˌbɑː

Coolangatta
  town, Australia KOOL-uhn-GAT-uh ˌkuˑlənˈgætə

Coolgardie
  town, Australia kool-GAHRD-ē kuˑlˈgɑʳdiˑ

Coolidge
  Calvin, *30th US president* KOO-lij ˈkuːlidʒ

Coonabarabran
  town, Australia KOO-nuh-BAR-uh-BRAN, KUN-uh- ˌkuːnəˈbærəˌbræn, ˌkunə-

Coonamble
  town, Australia koo-NAM-buhl kuˑˈnæmbəl

Coonatto
  Australia koo-NAT-ō kuˑˈnætoː

Cooper
  James Fenimore, *US writer;* Leon KOO-puhr, KUP-uhr ˈkuːpəʳ, ˈkupəʳ
    N., *US physicist (Nobel 1972)*

Coorg [Kodagu]
  lang., people, India KURG ˈkuʳg

Coors
  US beer KURZ ˈkuʳz

Coos
  1. *county, OR; N. American people* KOOS ˈkuːs
  2. *county, NH* kō-AHS, KŌ-ahs koːˈɑs, ˈkoːɑs

Coosa
  river, county, AL KOO-suh ˈkuːsə

Cootamundra
  town, Australia KOOT-uh-MUHN-druh ˌkuˑʈəˈməndrə

Foreign Sounds: ue: *Fr.* **rue**, *Ger.* **füllen** uh(r): *Fr.* **boeuf**, *Ger.* **Höhle** **kh**: *Ger.* **ich**, *Scot.* **loch** g̃: *Sp.* **amigo** ṿ: *Sp.* **hablar**
hl: *Welsh* **Llanelli**. CAPITALS: primary stress. SMALL CAPS: secondary stress. ⑤: U.S. pron. ⑥: British pron.

Copacabana
  beach, Rio de Janeiro, Brazil   KŌ-puh-kuh-BAN-uh   ˌkoːpəkə'bænə

Copán
  department, Honduras   kō-PAHN   koː'pɑn

Copenhagen [København]
  city, Denmark   KŌ-puhn-HAHG-uhn,   ˌkoːpən'hɑgən,
         KŌ-puhn-HĀ-guhn   'koːpənˌheːgən

Copernicus [Kopernik,
Koppernigk]
  Nicolaus, *Polish astronomer*   kuh-PUHR-ni-kuhs, kō-PUHR-ni-kuhs   kə'pəʳnikəs, koː'pəʳnikəs

Copiah
  county, MS   kuh-PĪ-uh   kə'paiə

Copiah-Lincoln
  Junior College, *MS*   kuh-PĪ-uh-LING-kuhn   kə'paiə'liŋkən

Copiapó
  river, town, Chile   kō-pyah-PŌ, ⑤ KŌ-pē-uh-PŌ   koːpja'poː, ⑤ ˌkoːpiːə'poː

Copland
  Aaron, *US composer*   KŌP-luhnd   'koːplənd

Copley
  John Singleton, *US painter; square,*   KAHP-lē   'kɑpliˑ
    Boston, MA

Coppélia
  ballet, Delibes   kō-pāl-YAH   koːpeːljaː

copper
  element   KAHP-uhr   'kapəʳ

Copperfield
  David, *Dickens character;* David, *US*   KAHP-uhr-FĒLD   'kapəʳˌfiːld
    magician

Coppin
  State College, *MD*   KAHP-uhn   'kapən

Coppola
  Francis Ford, *US film director*   KAHP-uh-luh   'kapələ

Copt
  member of Coptic *church*   KAHPT   'kapt

Coptic
  Afro-Asiatic lang.; Christian sect.   KAHP-tik   'kaptik

Coqueiros, Point
  easternmost point of South America   POINT kō-KĀ-uh-ro͞os   ˌpɔint koː'keːəruːs

Coquilhatville
  province, Zaire   kaw-kē-ah-VĒL, ⑤ kō-KĒ-uh-VIL,   kɔːkiːɑːviːl, ⑤ koː'kiːəˌvil,
         KŌ-kē-AT-VIL   ˌkoːkiː'ætˌvil

Coquilles St. Jacques
  scallop dish   kaw-KĒ seⁿ ZHAHK, ⑤ kō-KĒL sa(n)   kɔkiːj sē ʒɑːk, ⑤ koː'kiːl
         ZHAHK   sæ(n) 'ʒɑk

Coquimbo
  region, port, Chile   kō-KĒM-bō   koː'kiːmboː

Cora
  pers. name   KŌR-uh, KAWR-uh   'koːrə, 'kɔːrə

Coral
  Sea, *South Pacific*   KAWR-uhl SĒ, KAHR-uhl   ˌkɔːrəl 'siː, ˌkɑrəl

Corantijn
  see Courantyne

Corazon
  pers. name, Spanish   KAWR-uh-ZŌN   ˌkɔːrə'zoːn

Key (col. 2):   a: fad   ā: fade   ah: father   ar: marry   aw: law   e: fed   ē: feed   er: merry   i: hid   ī: hide   ō: coat   o͞o: boot
oi: boy   ow: now   u: put   uh: above   uhr: bird   ch: chop   ng: ring   sh: show   th: thick   t͟h: this   zh: measure

Corban
  Biblical name — KAWR-BAN, kahr-BAHN — 'kɔː^rˌbæn, kɑr'bɑn
Corbières
  district, France; wine — kawr-BYER — kɔːrbjer
Corbulo
  Roman general & conspirator — KAWR-byuh-LŌ — 'kɔː^rbjəˌloː
Corbusier, Le
  pseudonym of J. C. Jeanneret, *Swiss architect* — luh kawr-buez-YĀ — lə kɔːrbyːzjeː
Corcoran
  School of Art, *Washington, D. C.* — KAWR-kuh-ruhn — 'kɔː^rkərən
Corcovado
  peak, Rio de Janeiro, Brazil — KAWR-kō-VAHD-o͞o — ˌkɔː^rkoː'vɑduː
Corcyra
  ancient name of Corfu — kawr-SĪ-ruh — kɔː^r'sɑirə
Cordelia
  youngest daughter in King Lear, Shakespeare — kawr-DĒL-yuh, kawr-DĒ-lē-uh — kɔː^rdiːljə, kɔː^rdiːliːə
Cordeliers
  French revolutionary organization — kawr-duhl-YĀ, Ⓢ KAWRD-l-ĒRZ — kɔːrdəljeː, Ⓢ ˌkɔː^rdl̩'iː^rz
Cordell
  pers. name — kawr-DEL — kɔː^r'del
Cordero
  Angel, *US jockey* — kawr-DER-ō — kɔː^r'deroː
Cordial Médoc
  wine — kawrd-YAHL mā-DAWK — kɔːrdjaːl meːdɔːk
Cordillera Central
  mtn. range, Andes — KAWRD-l-(Y)ER-uh SEN-TRAHL, KAWRD-ē-ER-uh — ˌkɔː^rdl̩'(j)erə ˌsen'trɑl, ˌkɔː^rdiː'erə
Cordillera de Carabaya
  Andean range, Peru — KAWRD-l-(Y)ER-uh thā KAHR-uh-BĪ-(y)uh, KAWR-dē-ER-uh — ˌkɔː^rdl̩'(j)erə ðeː ˌkɑrə'bɑi(j)ə, ˌkɔː^rdiː'erə
Cordillera Mérida
  mtn. range, Venezuela — KAWRD-l-(Y)ER-uh MER-uhd-uh, KAWRD-ē-ER-uh — ˌkɔː^rdl̩'(j)erə 'merədə, ˌkɔː^rdiː'erə
Córdoba, Cordova
  pl. name, Argentina, Colombia, Mexico, Spain — KAWR-dō-vah; Ⓢ KAWR-duh-buh, KAWR-duh-vuh — 'kɔːrdoːβɑ; Ⓢ 'kɔː^rdəbə, 'kɔː^rdəvə
Cordon Bleu
  1. attributive, used of excellent cooking (esp. French) — kawr-DAWⁿ BLUH(R) — kɔːrdō blœː
  2. African songbird — KAWRD-n BLO͞O — ˌkɔː^rdn̩ 'bluː
Cordova
  see Córdoba
CORE
  Congress of Racial Equality — KŌR, KAWR — 'koː^r, 'kɔː^r
Corea
  Chick, *jazz musician* — kuh-RĒ-uh — kə'riːə
Coreopsis
  plant — KAWR-ē-AHP-suhs — ˌkɔːriː'ɑpsəs
Corey
  Elias James, *US chemist (Nobel 1990); pers. name* — KŌR-ē, KAWR-ē — 'koːriˑ, 'kɔːriˑ
Corfam
  tdmk for a synthetic leather — KAWR-FAM — 'kɔː^rˌfæm

Foreign Sounds: ue: *Fr.* **rue**, *Ger.* **füllen** uh(r): *Fr.* **bœuf**, *Ger.* **Höhle** kh: *Ger.* **ich**, *Scot.* **loch** g̱: *Sp.* **amigo** v: *Sp.* **hablar** hl: *Welsh* **Llanelli**. CAPITALS: primary stress. SMALL CAPS: secondary stress. Ⓢ: U.S. pron. Ⓔ: British pron.

Corfu
   island, Greece   kawr-F$\overline{OO}$, K$\bar{O}$R-f(y)$\overline{oo}$ kɔːˈfuː, ˈkɔːf(j)uː

Corgi
   dog breed   KAWR-gē   ˈkɔːgi·

Cori
   Carl F. *& his wife* Gerty, *US*   K$\bar{O}$R-ē, KAWR-ē   ˈkoːri·, ˈkɔːri·
       biochemists (Nobel 1947)

Corinna
   pers. name   kuh-RIN-uh, -R$\bar{E}$-nuh   kəˈrinə, -ˈriːnə

Corinne
   pers. name   kuh-RIN, -R$\bar{E}$N   kəˈrin, -ˈriːn

Corinnus
   legendary Trojan poet   kawr-IN-uhs   kɔːrˈinəs

Corinth
   city, Greece   KAWR-inth, KAHR-   ˈkɔːrinθ, ˈkɑr-

Corinthian
   architectural order   kuh-RIN-thē-uhn   kəˈrinθiːən

Corinthians
   New Testament book   kuh-RIN-thē-uhnz   kəˈrinθiːənz

Corinthus
   king of Corinth   kuh-RIN-thuhs   kəˈrinθəs

Coriolanus
   play, Shakespeare   K$\bar{O}$R-ē-uh-L$\bar{A}$-nuhs,   ˌkoˈriːəˈleːnəs, ˌkɔːriːəˈleːnəs
       KAWR-ē-uh-L$\bar{A}$-nuhs

Coriolis effect
   phenomenon   K$\bar{O}$R-ē-$\bar{O}$-luhs, K$\bar{O}$R-ē-uh-L$\bar{E}$S, KAWR-   ˌkoːriːˈoːləs, ˌkoːriːəˈliːs,
                                               ˌkɔːr-

Cork
   county, borough, Eire   KAWRK   ˈkɔːk

Corliss
   pers. name (C. Lamont)   KAWR-luhs   ˈkɔːləs

Cormack
   Allan MacLeod, *South African-born*   KAWR-muhk   ˈkɔːmək
       US physicist (Nobel 1979)

Cormier
   Robert, *US author*   KAWRM-yā, KAWR-mē-uhr   ˈkɔːmjeː, ˈkɔːmiːər

Corneille
   Pierre, *French writer; pers. name*   kawr-NE, ⑤ kawr-N$\bar{A}$(L)   kɔːrnej, ⑤ kɔːˈneː(l)

Cornejo
   Mariano Harlan, *Peruvian statesman*   kawr-N$\bar{A}$-hō   kɔːrˈneːhoː
       and jurist

Cornel
   pers. name (C. Wilde)   kawr-NEL   kɔːˈnel

Cornelia
   pers. name   kawr-N$\bar{E}$L-yuh, -N$\bar{E}$-lē-uh   kɔːˈniːljə, -ˈniːliːə

Cornelis
   pers. name, Dutch   kawr-N$\bar{A}$-luhs   kɔːˈneːləs

Cornelius
   pers. name   kawr-N$\bar{E}$L-yuhs, -N$\bar{E}$-lē-uhs   kɔːˈniːljəs, -ˈniːliːəs

Cornell
   University, *NY*   kawr-NEL   kɔːˈnel

Cornell
   Ezra, *US financier and*   kawr-NEL   kɔːˈnel
       philanthropist; university, NY; pers.
       name

Key (col. 2):   a: fad   ā: fade   ah: father   ar: marry   aw: law   e: fed   ē: feed   er: merry   i: hid   ī: hide   ō: coat $\overline{oo}$: boot
oi: boy   ow: now   u: put   uh: above   uhr: bird   ch: chop   ng: ring   sh: show   th: thick   <u>th</u>: this   zh: measure

Cornforth
John Warcup, *Australian-born*   KAWRN-fuhrth, -FŌRTH, -FAWRTH   'kɔːᶦnfəᶦθ, -ˌfoːᶦθ, -ˌfɔːᶦθ
British chemist (Nobel 1975)

Cornish
Celtic lang.   KAWR-nish   'kɔːᶦniʃ

Cornwall
former county, England; pers. name   KAWRN-WAWL, KAWRN-wuhl   'kɔːᶦnˌwɔːl, 'kɔːᶦnwəl

Cornwallis
Charles, *British general*   kawrn-WAHL-uhs   kɔːᶦn'wɑləs

Coro
town, gulf, Venezuela   KŌR-ō   'koːroː

Coromandel
channel, New Zealand   KAWR-uh-MAN-dl, KAHR-   ˌkɔːrə'mændl̩, ˌkɑr-

Corona
Puerto Rican beer   kō-rō-NAH, ⓢ kuh-RŌ-nuh   koːroː'nɑ, ⓢ kə'roːnə

Corona Australis
constellation   kuh-RŌ-nuh aw-STRĀ-luhs, ahs-TRĀ-luhs   kə'roːnə ɔː'streːləs, ɑs'treːləs

Corona Borealis
constellation   kuh-RŌ-nuh BŌR-ē-AL-uhs, BAWR-   kə'roːnə ˌboːriː'æləs, ˌbɔːr-

Coronel Oviedo
city, Paraguay   kō-ruh-NEL ō-VYĀ-thō   koːrə'nel oː'vjeːðoː

Coronides
daughters of Orion   kuh-RAHN-uhd-ēz   kə'rɑnədiːz

Coronis
mother of Asclepius by Apollo   kuh-RŌ-nuhs   kə'roːnəs

Coronus
Argonaut   kuh-RŌ-nuhs   kə'roːnəs

Corot
Jean Baptiste Camille, *French*   kaw-RŌ   kɔːroː
painter

Corovodë
town, Albania   CHAWR-uh-VŌ-duh   ˌtʃɔːrə'voːdə

Corowa
town, Australia   KAHR-uh-wuh, KAWR-uh-wuh   'kɑrəwə, 'kɔːrəwə

Corozal
district, Belize   KAWR-uh-ZAHL, KAHR-uh-ZAHL   ˌkɔːrə'zɑl, ˌkɑrə'zɑl

Corpus Christi
city, TX; Christian festival   KAWR-puhs KRIST-ē   ˌkɔːᶦpəs 'kristiˑ

Correggio
Antonio Allegri, *Italian painter*   kuh-REJ-ō, kuh-REJ-ē-Ō   kə'redʒoː, kə'redʒiːˌoː

Corregidor
island, Philippines   kuh-REG-uh-DAWR   kə'regəˌdɔːᶦ

Corrèze
department, France   kaw-REZ   kɔːrez

Corriedale
sheep breed   KAWR-ē-DĀL   'kɔːriˑˌdeːl

Corrientes
prov & town, Argentina   kawr-rē-EN-tās   kɔːrriː'enteːs

Corrigan
Mairead, *Irish peace activist (Nobel 1976)*   KAWR-i-guhn   'kɔːrigən

Corryvreckan, Corrievrechan, Corrievrekin
whirlpool, strait, Scotland   KAWR-ē-VREK-uhn, KAHR-   ˌkɔːriˑ'vrekən, ˌkɑr-

---

Foreign Sounds: **ue**: *Fr.* **rue**, *Ger.* **füllen**   **uh(r)**: *Fr.* **boeuf**, *Ger.* **Höhle**   **kh**: *Ger.* **ich**, *Scot.* **loch**   **g̃**: *Sp.* **amigo**   **v̱**: *Sp.* **hablar**
hl: *Welsh* **Llanelli.**   CAPITALS: primary stress.   SMALL CAPS: secondary stress.   ⓢ: U.S. pron.   ⓔ: British pron.

Corse [Corsica]
Mediterranean island   KAWRS   kɔːrs

Corsica
Mediterranean island   KAWR-si-kuh   'kɔːʳsikə

Corsican
pert. to Corsica   KAWR-si-kuhn   'kɔːʳsikən

Cortaillod
wine   kawr-tī-YŌ   kɔːrtɑijoː

Cortes
parliament in Spain & Portugal   KAWR-TES, KAWR-TEZ   'kɔːʳˌtes, 'kɔːʳˌtez

Cortés
1. Hernán *or* Hernando, *Spanish conquistador*   kawr-TĀS, ⑤ kawr-TEZ, KAWR-TEZ   kɔːr'teːs, ⑤ kɔːʳ'tez, 'kɔːʳˌtez
2. *region, Honduras*   kawr-TĀS   kɔːr'teːs

Cortese
wine   kawr-TĀ-zā   kɔːʳ'teːzeː

Cortina d'Ampezzo
village, ski resort, Italy   kawr-TĒ-nuh dahm-PET-sō   kɔːʳ'tiːnə dɑm'petsoː

Cortina Rancheria
Indian reservation, US   kawr-TĒ-nuh RAN-chuh-RĒ-uh   kɔːʳ'tiːnə ˌræntʃə'riːə

Çoruh [Artvin]
province, Turkey   chō-RUK   tʃoː'ruk

Çorum, Chorum
province, Turkey   chaw-ROOM   tʃɔː'ruːm

Coruña, La
see La Coruña

Corvallis
city, OR   kawr-VAL-uhs   kɔːʳ'væləs

Corvina
wine   kawr-VĒ-nuh   kɔːʳ'viːnə

Corvo
tdmk for an Italian wine   KAWR-vō   'kɔːʳvoː

Corvus
constellation   KAWR-vuhs   'kɔːʳvəs

Cory
pers. name   KŌR-ē, KAWR-ē   'koːriˑ, 'kɔːriˑ

Corydon
pers. name   KŌR-uh-duhn, KAWR-uh-duhn, -DAHN   'koːrədən, 'kɔːrədən, -ˌdɑn

Cos
see Kós

Cosam
Biblical name   KŌ-SAM   'koːˌsæm

Cosa Nostra
organized crime group   KŌ-suh NŌ-struh, KŌ-zuh   ˌkoːsə 'noːstrə, ˌkoːzə

Cosby
Bill, *US entertainer*   KAHZ-bē   'kɑzbiˑ

Cos d'Estournel
wine   kaws des-tur-NEL   kɔːs desturnel

Cosell
Howard, *US sportscaster*   kō-SEL   koː'sel

Cosenza
province, Italy   kō-ZEN(T)-suh   koː'zen(t)sə

Cosgrave
William Thomas, *Irish politician*   KAHZ-GRĀV   'kɑzˌgreːv

Key (col. 2): a: fad ā: fade ah: father ar: marry aw: law e: fed ē: feed er: merry i: hid ī: hide ō: coat ōō: boot oi: boy ow: now u: put uh: above uhr: bird ch: chop ng: ring sh: show th: thick th: this zh: measure

Coshocton
   county, OH   kuh-SHAHK-tuhn   kə'ʃɑktən

Cosi fan tutte
   opera, Mozart   kō-SĒ FAHN T͞OOT-tā, T͞OOT-ē   koːˌsiː ˌfan 'tuːtteː, 'tuːʈiˑ

Cosigüina Volcán
   volcano, Nicaragua   KŌ-si-GWĒ-nah vawl-KAHN   ˌkoːsi'gwiːnɑ vɔːl'kɑn

Cosima
   pers. name, German   KŌ-zē-mah   'koːziːmɑ

Cosimo
   pers. name, Italian   KAW-zē-mō   'kɔːziːmoː

Cosmas
   pers. name (C. Ndeti)   KAHZ-muhs, KAHZ-MAHS   'kɑzməs, 'kazˌmɑs

Cosmo
   1. nickname for Cosmopolitan   KAHZ-mō   'kɑzmoː
     magazine; pers. name
   2. Italian   KAWZ-mō   'kɔːzmoː

Cosmos
   1. the universe; PBS television series   KAHZ-muhs, KAHZ-MŌS, KAHZ-MAHS   'kɑzməs, 'kazˌmoːs, 'kazˌmɑs
   2. flower   KAHZ-muhs, KAHZ-muhz   'kɑzməs, 'kazməz

Cossack
   elite corps of Russian horsemen   KAHS-AK, KAHS-uhk   'kɑsˌæk, 'kɑsək

Costa Blanca
   resort, Spain   KŌ-stuh BLAHNG-kuh   ˌkoːstə 'blaŋkə

Costa Brava
   resort, Spain   KŌ-stuh BRAHV-uh   ˌkoːstə 'brɑvə

Costa de Almería
   resort, Spain   KŌ-stuh th̲ā AHL-mā-RĒ-uh   ˌkoːstə ðeː ˌalmeː'riːə

Costa de la Luz
   resort, Spain   KŌ-stuh th̲ā lah L͞OOS   ˌkoːstə ðeː lɑ 'luːs

Costa del Azahar
   resort, Spain   KŌ-stuh th̲el AHZ-ah-<u>KHAHR</u>   ˌkoːstə ðel ˌaza'xɑr

Costa de Lisboa
   region, Portugal   KŌ-stuh dā lēzh-VŌ-uh   ˌkoːstə deː liːʒ'voːə

Costa del Sol
   region, Spain   KŌS-tah th̲el SŌL   'koːstɑ ðel 'soːl

Costa de Prata
   region, Portugal   KŌ-stuh dā PRAHT-uh   ˌkoːstə deː 'prɑːʈə

Costa do Algarve
   region, Portugal   KŌ-stuh dō ahl-AHR-vā   ˌkoːstə doː al'aːʳveː

Costa Dorada
   resort, Spain   KŌ-stuh dō-RAH<u>TH</u>-uh   ˌkoːstə doː'rɑðə

Costa do Sol
   region, Portugal   KŌ-stuh dō SŌL   ˌkoːstə doː 'soːl

Costa Dourada
   region, Portugal   KŌ-stuh DŌ-o͞o-RAHD-uh   ˌkoːstə 'doːuːˌrɑːdə

Costa Mesa
   city, CA   KŌ-stuh MĀ-suh, KAHS-tuh   ˌkoːstə 'meːsə, ˌkastə

Costa Rica
   republic, S. America   KAHS-tuh RĒ-kuh, KAWS-tuh, KŌS-tuh   ˌkastə 'riːkə, ˌkɔːstə, ˌkoːstə

Costa Rican
   pert. to Costa Rica   KAHS-tuh RĒ-kuhn, KAWS-tuh,   ˌkastə 'riːkən, ˌkɔːstə,
                                KŌS-tuh   ˌkoːstə

Costa Verde
   region, Portugal   KŌ-stuh VERD-uh   ˌkoːstə 'verdə

Foreign Sounds: ue: *Fr.* **rue,** *Ger.* f**ü**llen   uh(r): *Fr.* b**oeu**f, *Ger.* H**öh**le   <u>kh</u>: *Ger.* i**ch,** *Scot.* lo**ch**   g̱: *Sp.* ami**g**o   v: *Sp.* ha**b**lar   hl: *Welsh* **Ll**anelli.   CAPITALS: primary stress.   SMALL CAPS: secondary stress.   Ⓢ: U.S. pron.   Ⓔ: British pron.

Costello Elvis, *British musician, songwriter;* Lou, *US actor*	kahs-TEL-ō	kɑs'teloː
Costes Dieudonné, *French aviator*	KAWST	kɔːst
Costilla *county, CO*	kahs-TĒ-uh	kɑs'tiːə
Cosumnes River College, *CA*	kuh-SUHM-nuhs RIV-uhr	kə'səmnəs 'rivəʳ
Cotabato del Norte *province, Philippines*	KŌT-uh-BAHT-ō <u>th</u>el NAWR-tā, NAWRT-ē	ˌkoːʈə'baʈoː ðel 'nɔːʳteː, 'nɔːʳʈiː
Cotabato del Sur *province, Philippines*	KŌT-uh-BAHT-ō <u>th</u>el SUR	ˌkoːʈə'baʈoː ðel 'suʳ
Côte, La *region, France*	lah KŌT	lɑː koːt
Côte Blonde *region, France*	kōt BLAWⁿD	koːt blɔ̃d
Côte Brune *region, France*	kōt BRUEN	koːt bryːn
Côte Chalonnaise *region, France*	kōt shah-law-NEZ	koːt ʃaːlɔːnez
Côte d'Azur *French Riviera*	kōt dah-ZUER, ⓢ KŌT duh-ZUR	koːt daːzyːr, ⓢ ˌkoːt də'zuʳ
Côte de Beaune *region, France; wine*	kōt duh BŌN	koːt də boːn
Côte de Beaune Villages *wine*	kōt duh BŌN vē-LAHZH	koːt də boːn viːlɑːʒ
Côte de Bourg *region, France*	kōt duh BO̅O̅R	koːt də buːr
Côte de Brouilly *region, France*	kōt duh broo̅-YĒ	koːt də bruːjiː
Côte de Nuits *region, France*	kōt duh NWĒ, ⓢ KŌT duhn WĒ	koːt də nɥiː, ⓢ ˌkoːt dən 'wiː
Côte des Blancs *region, France*	kōt duh BLAHⁿ	koːt də blɑ̃
Côte d'Ivoire [Ivory Coast] *republic, Africa*	KŌT dēv-WAHR	ˌkoːt diːv'waʳ
Côte d'Or *region, French*	kōt DAWR	koːt dɔːr
Côte Rôtie *region, France*	kōt raw-TĒ, rō-TĒ	koːt rɔːtiː, roːtiː
Côtes de Castillon *region, France*	kōt duh kah-stē-YAWⁿ	koːt də kaːstiːjɔ̃
Côtes de Provence *region, France*	kōt duh praw-VAHⁿS	koːt də prɔːvãs
Côtes-du-Nord *dept, France*	kōt-due-NAWR	koːtdyːnɔːr
Côtes du Rhône *region, France*	kōt due RŌN	koːt dyː roːn
Cotinga *South American bird*	kō-TING-guh, kuh-	koː'tiŋgə, kə-
Cotonou *port, Africa*	KŌT-n-OO̅	ˌkoːtn̩'uː

Cotopaxi
volcano, prov, Ecuador   KŌT-uh-PAHK-sē, -PAK-sē   ˌkoːʈə'pɑksiˑ, -ˈpæksiˑ

Cotswolds
hills, England   KAHT-swuhldz, KAHT-SWÕLDZ   'kɑtswəldz, 'kɑtˌswoːldz

Cotta
Roman cognomen   KAHT-uh   'kɑʈə

Cottbus
county, Germany   KAHT-bus   'kɑtbus

Cottey
College, MO   KAHT-ē   'kɑʈiˑ

Cottian
Alps, Alpine mtn. range   KAHT-ē-uhn   'kɑʈiːən

Cotton
pers. name   KAHT-n   'kɑtn̩

Cotuí
town, Dominican Republic   kō-TWĒ   koː'twiː

Cotuit
town, MA   kuh-T(Y)OO-uht   kə't(j)uːət

Coty
René Jules Gustave, *French politician*   kaw-TĒ   kɔːtiː

Coucal
type of cuckoo   KOO-kuhl   'kuːkəl

Coué
Emile, *French psychotherapist*   KWĀ   kweː

Coues's
flycatcher   KOWZ   'kɑuz

Cougar
pers. name   KOO-guhr, KOO-GAHR   'kuːgə[r], 'kuːˌgɑ[r]

Coughlin
Charles Edward, *US clergyman*   KAWG-lin, KAHG-lin   'kɔːglin, 'kɑglin

Coulee Dam
town, WA   KOO-lē DAM   'kuːliˑ 'dæm

Coulomb
Charles Augustin de, *French physicist*   koo-LAW[n], ⓢ KOO-LAHM, KOO-LŌM, koo-LŌM   kuːlɔ̃, ⓢ 'kuːˌlɑm, 'kuːˌloːm, kuː'loːm

Count
title; pers. name (C. Basie)   KOWNT   'kɑunt

Couperin
François, *French composer*   koo-PRE[n], koo-puh-RE[n]   kuːprẽ, kuːpərẽ

Courant
newspaper, Hartford, CT   KUHR-uhnt, KUH-ruhnt   'kər-ənt, 'kə-rənt

Courantyne, Corantijn
river, Guyana and Suriname   KŌR-uhn-TĪN, KAWR-   'koːrənˌtain, 'kɔːr-

Courbet
Gustave, *French painter*   kur-BE   kurbe

Cournand
A. F., *US physician (Nobel 1956)*   kur-NAH[n]   ku[r]'nɑ̃

Courtenay
pers. name   KŌRT-nē, KAWRT-nē, -n-ā   'koː[r]tniˑ, 'kɔː[r]tniˑ, -ṇeː

Courteney, Courtney
pers. name   KŌRT-nē, KAWRT-nē   'koː[r]tniˑ, 'kɔː[r]tniˑ

Courvoisier
cognac   KURV-WAHZ-YĀ   ˌku[r]vˌwɑz'jeː

Foreign Sounds: ue: *Fr.* **rue**, *Ger.* **füllen**   uh(r): *Fr.* **boeuf**, *Ger.* **Höhle**   k͟h: *Ger.* **ich**, *Scot.* **loch**   ḡ: *Sp.* **amigo**   v̱: *Sp.* **hablar**
hl: *Welsh* **Llanelli**.   CAPITALS: primary stress.   SMALL CAPS: secondary stress.   ⓢ: U.S. pron.   ⓔ: British pron.

Coushatta
N. American people   ku-SHAHT-uh   kuˈʃaʈə

Cousteau
Jacques, *undersea explorer*   ko͞o-STŌ   kuːstoː

Cousy
Bob, *US sports personality*   KO͞O-zē   ˈkuːziˑ

Coutet
wine   ku-TE, ⑤ ko͞o-TĀ   kute, ⑤ kuːteː

Covarrubias
Miguel, *Mexican artist*   kō-y̱ahr-RO͞OB-yahs   koːβarˈruːbjɑs

Coveleski
Stanley, Regional Stadium, *South Bend, IN*   STAN-lē KŌ-vuh-LES-kē   ˈstænliˑ ˌkoːvəˈleskiˑ

Covent Garden
district, London   KUHV-uhnt GAHRD-n   ˌkəvənt ˈgɑʳdn̩

Coventry
1. city, England   KAHV-uhn-trē, KUHV-uhn-trē   ˈkɑvəntriˑ, ˈkəvəntriˑ
2. town, CT, RI   KUHV-uhn-trē, KAHV-uhn-trē   ˈkəvəntriˑ, ˈkɑvəntriˑ

Covina
city, CA   kō-VĒ-nuh   koːˈviːnə

Covington
US pl. name   KUHV-ing-tuhn   ˈkəviŋtən

Cowdrey
pers. name   KOW-drē, KOW-drā   ˈkɑudriˑ, ˈkɑudreː

Cowes
town, England   KOWZ   ˈkɑuz

Coweta
county, GA   kuh-WĒT-uh   kəˈwiːtə

Cowley Fathers
religious order   KOW-lē, KO͞O-lē   ˈkɑuliˑ, ˈkuːliˑ

Cowlitz
county, WA   KOW-luhts   ˈkɑuləts

Cowper
1. William, English poet   KO͞O-puhr, KUP-uhr, KOW-puhr   ˈkuːpəʳ, ˈkupəʳ, ˈkɑupəʳ
2. pers. name   KOW-puhr, KO͞O-puhr   ˈkɑupəʳ, ˈkuːpəʳ

Coxsackie
village, NY   kuk-SAHK-ē, kahk-SAK-ē   kukˈsɑkiˑ, kɑkˈsækiˑ

Coz
Biblical name   KAHZ, KŌTS   ˈkɑz, ˈkoːts

Cozbi
Biblical name   KAHZ-BĪ, kahz-BĒ   ˈkɑzˌbɑi, kɑzˈbiː

Cozumel, Isla
island, Caribbean   ĒZ-lah KŌ-zuh-MEL   ˈiːzlɑ ˌkoːzəˈmel

Cozzens
James Gould, *US novelist*   KUHZ-uhnz   ˈkəzənz

Crac, Le [Kerak, El]
crusaders' name for El Kerak   luh KRAHK, ⑤ luh KRAK   lə krɑːk, ⑤ lə ˈkræk

Cracow
see Kraków

Craig
pers. name   KRĀG, KREG   ˈkreːg, ˈkreg

Craigavon
county, Northern Ireland   krā-GAV-uhn   kreːˈgævən

Craighead
county, AR   KRĀG-HED   ˈkreːgˌhed

Key (col. 2):   a: f**a**d   ā: f**a**de   ah: f**a**ther   ar: m**a**rry   aw: l**a**w   e: f**e**d   ē: f**ee**d   er: m**e**rry   i: h**i**d   ī: h**i**de   ō: c**oa**t   o͞o: b**oo**t
oi: b**oy**   ow: n**ow**   u: p**u**t   uh: **a**bove   uhr: b**ir**d   ch: **ch**op   ng: ri**ng**   sh: **sh**ow   th: **th**ick   <u>th</u>: **th**is   zh: mea**s**ure

Craigie
  William, *Scottish linguist* ... KRĀ-gē ... 'kreːgiˑ
Craiova
  city, Romania ... krī-(Y)Ō-vuh ... krɑiˈ(j)oːvə
Cram
  Donald J., *US chemist (Nobel 1987)* ... KRAM ... 'kræm
Cranach
  Lucas (the Elder), *German painter* ... KRAHN-uh<u>kh</u> ... 'krɑnəx
Cranbrook
  city, British Columbia, Canada ... KRAN-BRUK, KRAM-BRUK ... 'krænˌbruk, 'kræmˌbruk
Crangi
  airport, Singapore ... KRAHNG-gē, KRANG-gē ... 'krɑŋgiˑ, 'kræŋgiˑ
Cranmer
  Thomas, *Protestant archbishop* ... KRAN-muhr ... 'krænməʳ
Crashaw
  Richard, *English poet* ... KRASH-AW ... 'kræʃˌɔː
Crassus
  Roman general ... KRAS-uhs ... 'kræsəs
Crater
  constellation ... KRĀT-uhr ... 'kreːtəʳ
Cratylus
  dialogue of Plato ... KRAT-l-uhs ... 'krætɬəs
Craveri's murrelet
  sea bird ... kruh-VER-ēz MUHR-luht ... krəˈveriˑz 'məʳlət
Craxi
  Bettino, *Italian politician* ... KRAHK-sē ... 'krɑksiˑ
Crayola
  tdmk for crayons ... krā-Ō-luh ... kreˈoːlə
Crécy
  village, France ... krā-SĒ ... kreːsiː
Crécy, potage
  cream of carrot soup ... pō-TAHZH krā-SĒ ... poːˈtɑˑʒ kreːˈsiː
Credit Lyonnais
  French bank ... krā-DĒ lyaw-NE ... kreːdiː ljoːne
Cree
  N. American people ... KRĒ ... 'kriː
Creek
  N. American people ... KRĒK ... 'kriːk
Creighton
  1. family name ... KRĀT-n, Ⓔ KRĪT-n ... 'kreːtn̩, Ⓔ 'krɑitn̩
  2. University, NE ... KRĀT-n ... 'kreːtn̩
Creme Chantilly
  sweetened whipped cream ... krem shahⁿ-tē-YĒ ... krem ʃɑ̃tiːjiː
Crème de Menthe
  liqueur ... KREM duh MEN(T)TH, KRĒM, MINT ... ˌkrem də 'men(t)θ, ˌkriːm, 'mint
Cremer
  Sir William R., *English pacifist (Nobel 1903)* ... KRĒ-muhr ... 'kriːməʳ
Cremona
  prov, city, Italy ... kruh-MŌ-nuh ... krəˈmoːnə
Creole
  lang., Haiti ... KRĒ-ŌL ... 'kriːˌoːl

Foreign Sounds: ue: *Fr.* **rue**, *Ger.* **füllen**   uh(r): *Fr.* **boeuf**, *Ger.* **Höhle**   <u>kh</u>: *Ger.* **ich**, *Scot.* **loch**   g̃: *Sp.* **amigo**   v̰: *Sp.* **hablar**
hl: *Welsh* **Llanelli**.   CAPITALS: primary stress.   SMALL CAPS: secondary stress.   Ⓢ: U.S. pron.   Ⓔ: British pron.

Creon
    king of Corinth, host to Jason and　　KRĒ-AHN　　　　　　　　　　'kriː₁ɑn
    Medea; king of Thebes
Crépy
    region, France　　　　　　　　　　krä-PĒ　　　　　　　　　　　　kreːpiː
Cres
    early king of Crete　　　　　　　　KRES　　　　　　　　　　　　　'kres
Crescens
    Biblical name　　　　　　　　　　KRES-uhnz　　　　　　　　　　'kresənz
Cresphontes
    king of Messenia　　　　　　　　kres-FAHN-TĒZ　　　　　　　　kres'fɑn₁tiːz
Crespigny
    street, London　　　　　　　　　kres-PĒ-nē　　　　　　　　　　kres'piːniˑ
Crespin
    Régine, *opera star*　　　　　　　kres-PE^n　　　　　　　　　　krespē
Cressida [Criseyde]
    legendary lover in Shakespeare's　KRES-uhd-uh　　　　　　　　　'kresədə
    Troilus & Cressida
Cresson
    Edith, *French prime minister*　　krä-SAW^n　　　　　　　　　kreˑsɔ̃
Cressy
    English form of Crécy　　　　　KRES-ē　　　　　　　　　　　'kresiˑ
Cresta Blanca
    wine　　　　KRES-tuh BLANG-kuh, BLAHNG-kuh　　₁krestə 'blæŋkə, 'blɑŋkə
Creswick
    pers. name　　　　　　　　　　KREZ-ik　　　　　　　　　　　'krezik
Cret
    Paul Philippe, *US architect*　　KRĀ　　　　　　　　　　　　　'kreː
Cretaceous
    geologic period　　　　　　　　kri-TĀ-shuhs, krē-　　　　　　kri'teːʃəs, kriː-
Cretan
    pert. to Crete　　　　　　　　　KRĒT-n　　　　　　　　　　　'kriːtn̩
Crete
    island, Greece　　　　　　　　　KRĒT　　　　　　　　　　　　'kriːt
Creus, Cabo
    cape, Spain　　　　　　KAHV̠-ō krä-O͞OS　　　　　　₁kɑβoː kreː'uːs
Creusa
    wife of Aeneas; mother of Ion by　krē-(Y)O͞O-suh, krä-(Y)O͞O-suh　kriː'(j)uːsə, kreː'(j)uːsə
    Apollo
Creuse
    region, France　　　　　　　　KRUH(R)Z　　　　　　　　　krœːz
Creutzfeldt-Jakob
    brain disorder　　　　　　KROITS-felt-YAHK-ōb　　　　₁krɔitsfelt'jɑkoːb
Crichton
    James, *Scottish prodigy;* Michael,　KRĪT-n　　　　　　　　　　　'kraitn̩
    US writer
Crick
    F. H. C., *English molecular biologist*　KRIK　　　　　　　　　　　'krik
    (Nobel 1962)
Crimea
    peninsula, Ukraine　　　　　　krī-MĒ-uh, kruh-MĒ-uh　　　krɑi'miːə, krə'miːə
Crimean
    pert. to Crimea　　　　　　　　krī-MĒ-uhn　　　　　　　　　krɑi'miːən
Criolo
    lang., W. Africa　　　　　　　　krē-Ō-lō　　　　　　　　　　kriː'oːloː

Key (col. 2):　a: fad　ā: fade　ah: father　ar: marry　aw: law　e: fed　ē: feed　er: merry　i: hid　ī: hide　ō: coat　oo̅: boot
oi: boy　ow: now　u: put　uh: above　uhr: bird　ch: chop　ng: ring　sh: show　th: thick　t̲h̲: this　zh: measure

Crioulo		
lang., W. Africa	krē-Ō-lō, krē-O͞O-lō	kriː'oːloː, kriː'uːloː
Crisco		
tdmk for shortening	KRIS-kō	'kriskoː
Criseyde [Cressida]		
legendary lover in Chaucer's Troilus & Criseyde	kruh-SĀD-uh	krə'seːdə
Crisium, Mare		
see Mare Crisium		
Crispian		
pers. name	KRIS-pē-uhn	'krispiːən
Crispin		
pers. name	KRIS-puhn	'krispən
Crispus		
pers. name	KRIS-puhs	'krispəs
Crist		
Judith, *US film, drama critic*	KRIST	'krist
Cristal		
Portuguese beer	krē-STAHL	kriː'stɑl
Cristina		
pers. name, Italian	krē-STĒ-nah	kriː'stiːnɑ
Cristóbal		
town, Panama; pers. name, Spanish	krē-STŌ-vahl, [$] kris-TŌ-buhl	kriː'stoːβɑl, [$] kris'toːbəl
Cristoforo		
pers. name	krē-STAW-fō-rō	kriː'stɔːfoːroː
Critheis		
mother of Homer	kri-THĀ-uhs	kri'θeːəs
Critias		
Athenian despot; dialogue of Plato	KRISH-(ē-)uhs, KRIT-ē-uhs	'kriʃ(iː)əs, 'kritiːəs
Crito		
dialogue of Plato	KRĪT-ō	'krɑitoː
Crittenden		
county, AR	KRIT-n-duhn	'kritn̩dən
Crittenton		
Charles Nelson, *US businessman and philanthropist*	KRIT-n-tuhn, -duhn	'kritn̩tən, -dən
Crna [Cherna]		
river, Macedonia	TSUHR-nuh, SUHR-nuh	'tsərnə, 'sərnə
Crna Gora [Montenegro]		
republic, E. Europe (former kingdom)	TSUHR-nuh GŌR-uh, SUHR-nuh, GAWR-uh	ˌtsərnə 'goːʳə, ˌsərnə, 'gɔːrə
Croagh Patrick		
mountain, Ireland	KRŌ PA-trik	ˌkroː 'pætrik
Croat [Croatian]		
inhabitant of Croatia	KRŌT, KRŌ-AT, KRŌ-AHT	'kroːt, 'kroːˌæt, 'kroːˌɑt
Croatia [Hrvatska]		
republic, E. Europe	krō-Ā-sh(ē-)uh	kroː'eːʃ(iː)ə
Croatian [Croat]		
inhabitant of or pert. to Croatia	krō-Ā-shuhn	kroː'eːʃən
Croce		
1. Benedetto, *Italian historian*	KRŌ-chā	'kroːtʃeː
2. Jim, *US singer*	KRŌ-chē	'kroːtʃiˑ
Crockett		
Davy, *US frontiersman*	KRAHK-uht	'krɑkət

Foreign Sounds: ue: *Fr.* **rue**, *Ger.* **füllen** uh(r): *Fr.* **boeuf**, *Ger.* **Höhle** kh: *Ger.* **ich**, *Scot.* **loch** g: *Sp.* **amigo** v: *Sp.* **hablar** hl: *Welsh* **Llanelli**. CAPITALS: primary stress. SMALL CAPS: secondary stress. [$]: U.S. pron. [£]: British pron.

Crocodilopolis

   early name of city of Arsinoë   KRAHK-uh-duh-LAHP-uh-luhs,   ˌkrakədə'lapələs,
                                 KRAHK-uhd-l-AHP-uh-luhs   ˌkrakəd̩'apələs

Crocodylia

   reptilian order   KRAHK-uh-DIL-ē-uh   ˌkrakə'diliːə

Croesus

   Lydian king of legendary wealth   KRĒ-suhs   'kriːsəs

Croghan

   George, *US trader and Indian agent*   KRŌ-uhn   'kroːən

Crohn's disease

   bowel disorder   KRŌNZ duh-ZĒZ   'kroːnz dəˌziːz

Croix de Guerre

   French military award   krwah duh GER, Ⓢ K(R)WAH duh   krwaː də ger, Ⓢ ˌk(r)wɑ də
                             GER   'geʳ

Cro-Magnon

   early homo sapiens   krō-MAG-nuhn, krō-MAN-yuhn   kroː'mægnən, kroː'mænjən

Crommelin's

   comet   KRAHM-uh-linz   'kramәlinz

Cromwell

   1. Oliver *& his son* Richard, *English*   KRAHM-WEL, KRUHM-WEL,   'kram ˌwel, 'krəm ˌwel,
      statesmen   KRAHM-wuhl, KRUHM-wuhl   'kramwəl, 'krəmwəl
   2. town, CT; town, New Zealand   KRAHM-WEL, KRAHM-wuhl   'kram ˌwel, 'kramwəl

Cronin

   James W., *US physicist (Nobel*   KRŌ-nuhn   'kroːnən
     1980)

Cronkite

   Walter, *US journalist*   KRAHNG-KĪT, KRAHN-   'kraŋ ˌkait, 'kran-

Cronus

   Greek god, father of Zeus   KRŌ-nuhs   'kroːnəs

Crosby

   Bing, *US entertainer*   KRAWZ-bē   'krɔːzbiˑ

Crotalaria

   plant   KRŌT-l-AR-ē-uh   ˌkroːtl̩'æriːə

Croteau

   Gary, *hockey player*   kruh-TŌ   krə'toː

Croton

   1. river, NY   KRŌT-n   'kroːtn̩
   2. founder of Crotona   KRŌT-n, KRŌ-TAHN   'kroːtn̩, 'kroːˌtɑn

Crotona

   Greek colony in Italy   kruh-TŌ-nuh   krə'toːnə

Croton-on-Hudson

   village, NY   KRŌT-n-AHN-HUHD-suhn, -AWN-   ˌkroːtn̩ˌɑn'hədsən, -ˌɔːn-

Crotus

   foster-brother of the Muses   KRŌT-uhs   'kroːʈəs

Crow

   N. American people   KRŌ   'kroː

Crowe

   1. Adm. William James, Jr., *former*   KROW   'krɑu
     Chair, US Joint Chiefs of Staff
   2. Catherine, *English novelist;* Sir   KRŌ   'kroː
     Joseph Archer, *English critic*

Crowell

   Thomas Y., *US publisher*   KRŌ-uhl   'kroːəl

Crowfoot

   pers. name   KRŌ-FUT   'kroːˌfut

Key (col. 2):   a: f**a**d   ā: f**a**de   ah: f**a**ther   ar: m**a**rry   aw: l**aw**   e: f**e**d   ē: f**ee**d   er: m**e**rry   i: h**i**d   ī: h**i**de   ō: c**oa**t   oo: b**oo**t
oi: b**oy**   ow: n**ow**   u: p**u**t   uh: **a**bove   uhr: b**ir**d   ch: **ch**op   ng: ri**ng**   sh: **sh**ow   th: **th**ick   <u>th</u>: **this**   zh: mea**s**ure

Croydon		
borough, England	KROID-n	'krɔidn̩
Cruickshank		
Andrew, *Scottish actor*	KRUK-SHANGK	'kruk͵ʃæŋk
Cruikshank		
George, *English illustrator*	KRUK-SHANGK	'kruk͵ʃæŋk
Crusoe, Robinson		
see Robinson Crusoe		
Crux		
constellation	KRUHKS	'krəks
Cruz		
pers. name	KRŌŌZ	'kruːz
Crystal		
pers. name	KRIS-tl	'kristl̩
Csongrád		
county, city, Hungary	CHAWN-GRAHD	'tʃɔːn͵grad
Ctesias		
Greek explorer	TĒ-zē-uhs	'tiːziːəs
Ctesiphon		
ancient city, Iraq	TES-uh-FAHN, TĒ-suh-FAHN	'tesə͵fan, 'tiːsə͵fan
Ctesiphon		
ancient city, Parthia	TES-uh-FAHN	'tesə͵fan
Ctimene		
sister of Odysseus	TIM-uh-nē	'timəniˑ
Cua		
lang., South Vietnam	KWAH	'kwɑ
Cuajimalpa		
municipality, Mexico	kwah-hē-MAHL-puh	kwɑhiː'mɑlpə
Cuauh-témoc, Cuauhtémoc, [Guatimozin]		
last emperor of the Aztecs; pers. name, Mexico	kwow-TEM-ōk	kwɑu'temoːk
Cuanza, Kwanza		
river, Africa	KWAHN-zuh	'kwɑnzə
Cuba		
island, West Indies	KYŌŌ-buh	'kjuːbə
Cuba Libre		
cocktail	K(Y)ŌŌ-buh LĒ-bruh	'k(j)uːbə 'liːbrə
Cuban		
pert. to or from Cuba	KYŌŌ-buhn	'kjuːbən
Çubuk		
river, Turkey	chuh-BUK	tʃə'buk
Cucamonga		
city, CA	KŌŌ-kuh-MAHNG-guh	͵kuːkə'mɑŋgə
Cuchulainn		
legendary Irish hero	ku-KHUL-uhn, ⓢ kuh-HUL-uhn, kuh-HŌŌ-luhn	ku'xulən, ⓢ kə'hulən, kə'huːlən
Cúcuta		
city, Colombia	KŌŌ-kŌŌ-TAH	'kuːkuː͵tɑ
Cudahy		
Michael, *US meat packer*	KUHD-uh-HĒ	'kədə͵hiː
Cuenca		
city, Ecuador	KWENG-kuh	'kweŋkə

Foreign Sounds: ue: *Fr.* **rue**, *Ger.* **füllen**   uh(r): *Fr.* **boeuf**, *Ger.* **Höhle**   k̲h̲: *Ger.* **ich**, *Scot.* **loch**   g̅: *Sp.* **amigo**   v̲: *Sp.* **hablar**
hl: *Welsh* **Llanelli**.   CAPITALS: primary stress.   SMALL CAPS: secondary stress.   ⓢ: U.S. pron.   ⓔ: British pron.

Cuernavaca
> *town, Mexico*   kwer-nah-V̲AHK-ah,   kwerna'βaka,
>   ⑤ KWER-nuh-VAHK-uh, -VAK-uh   ⑤ ˌkweᶉnə'vakə, -'vækə

Cuernos
> *highest peak in Negros, Philippines*   KWER-nuhs   'kweᶉnəs

Cuervo Gold
> *brand of tequila*   KWER-vō GŌLD   ˌkweᶉvoː 'goːld

Cuesta
> *College, CA*   KWĀS-tuh, KWES-tuh   'kweːstə, 'kwestə

Cugat
> *Xavier, US bandleader*   KO͞O-GAHT   'kuːˌgat

Cuiabá, Cuyabá
> *river, Brazil*   KO͞O-yuh-BAH   ˌkuːjə'ba

Cuicatec
> *lang., people, Mexico*   KWĒ-kuh-TEK   'kwiːkəˌtek

Cuisinart
> *food processor*   KWĒ-zuh-NAHRT, KWĒ-zuh-NAHRT   'kwiːzəˌnaᶉt, ˌkwiːzə'naᶉt

Cuíto
> *river, Africa*   KWĒ-tō   'kwiːtoː

Cukor
> *George, US film director*   KO͞O-KAWR   'kuːˌkoːᶉ

Culgoa
> *river, Australia*   KUHL-GŌ-uh   'kəlˌgoːə

Culiacán
> *river, city, Mexico*   KO͞OL-yuh-KAHN   ˌkuːljə'kan

Culkin
> *Macaulay, US actor*   KUHL-kuhn   'kəlkən

Cullman
> *county, AL*   KUHL-muhn   'kəlmən

Culver
> *town, IN*   KUHL-vuhr   'kəlvəᶉ

Culver City
> *city, CA*   KUHL-vuhr SIT-ē   ˌkəlvəᶉ 'sitiˑ

Culver-Stockton
> *College, MO*   KUHL-vuhr-STAHK-tuhn   'kəlvəᶉ'staktən

Culzean
> *bay, Scotland*   kuh-LĀN *[sic]*   kə'leːn *[sic]*

Cumae
> *ancient city, Italy*   KYO͞O-mē   'kjuːmiː

Cumaean
> *pert. to Cumae*   KYO͞O-mē-uhn, kyo͞o-MĀ-uhn   'kjuːmiːən, kjuˑ'meːən

Cumaná
> *city, Venezuela*   ko͞o-mah-NAH   kuːma'na

Cumberland
> *former county, England*   KUHM-buhr-luhnd   'kəmbəᶉlənd

Cumbria
> *ancient Celtic kingdom; county,* KUHM-brē-uh   'kəmbriːə
>   *England*

Cumin
> *spice*   KUHM-uhn, KYO͞O-muhn   'kəmən, 'kjuːmən

Cuminapanema
> *river, Brazil*   KO͞O-mē-nuh-PAHN-ā-MAH   ˌkuːmiːnəˌpaneː'ma

Cuna
> *Central American people*   KO͞O-nuh   'kuːnə

Key (col. 2):   a: fad   ā: fade   ah: father   ar: **m**a**rry**   aw: law   e: fed   ē: feed   er: **m**e**rry**   i: hid   ī: hide   ō: coat   o͞o: boot
oi: **boy**   ow: **now**   u: **put**   uh: **above**   uhr: **bird**   ch: **chop**   ng: ri**ng**   sh: **show**   th: **thick**   t̲h̲: **this**   zh: mea**sure**

Cunard
British steamship co. | k(y)u-NAHRD | k(j)u'nɑʳd

Cunaxa
town, ancient Babylonia | kyo͞o-NAK-suh | kjuː'næksə

Cunctator
agnomen of Q. Fabius Maximus | KUHNGK-TĀT-uhr, KUNGK-TĀT-uhr | 'kəŋkˌteːʈəʳ, 'kuŋkˌteːʈəʳ

Cundinamarca
department, Colombia | KO͞ON-di-nuh-MAHR-kuh | ˌkuːndinə'mɑʳkə

Cunene
river, Africa | ko͞o-NĀ-nuh | kuː'neːnə

Cunha, da
Tristão, Portuguese explorer | duh KO͞ON-yuh | də 'kuːnjə

Cunnamulla
town, Australia | KUHN-uh-MUHL-uh | ˌkənə'mələ

CUNY
City University of New York | KYO͞O-nē | 'kjuːni·

Cuomo
Mario, US politician | KWŌ-mō | 'kwoːmoː

Cupertino
city, CA | K(Y)O͞O-puhr-TĒ-nō | ˌk(j)uːpəʳ'tiːnoː

Cupid
Roman god of love | KYO͞O-puhd | 'kjuːpəd

Cupido
Belgian beer | ko͞o-PĒ-dō | kuː'piːdoː

Cuprinol
tdmk for a wood preservative | K(Y)O͞O-pruh-NAWL | 'k(j)uːprəˌnɔːl

Curaçao
island, Netherlands Antilles; liqueur | K(Y)UR-uh-SŌ, -SOW | ˌk(j)urə'soː, -'sɑu

Curaray
river, Ecuador | KUR-uh-RĪ | ˌkurə'rɑi

Curassow
South & Central American bird | K(Y)UHR-uh-SŌ | 'k(j)ərəˌsoː

Cures
ancient town, Italy | KYUR-ēz | 'kjuriːz

Curetes
attendants of the goddess Rhea; guardians of Zeus on Crete | kyu-RĒT-ēz | kju'riːʈiːz

Curia
ancient senate house, Rome | KYUR-ē-uh | 'kjuriːə

Curiae
early Roman political-social divisions | KYUR-ē-Ē, -ē-Ī | 'kjuriːˌiː, -iːˌɑi

Curiate
early Roman assembly | KYUR-ē-uht | 'kjuriːət

Curie
Marie S., French physicist (Nobel 1903, 1911); her husband Pierre, French physicist (Nobel 1903) | kue-RĒ, Ⓢ kyu-RĒ, KYUR-ē | kyːriː, Ⓢ kju'riː, 'kjuri·

Curitiba
city, Brazil | KUR-uh-TĒ-buh | ˌkurə'tiːbə

curium
element | KYUR-ē-uhm | 'kjuriːəm

Curll
Edmund, English bookseller | KUHRL, KUHR-uhl | 'kəʳl, 'kərəl

Curran
pers. name | KUHR-uhn, KUH-ruhn | 'kərən, 'kəˌrən

Foreign Sounds: ue: *Fr.* **rue**, *Ger.* **füllen** uh(r): *Fr.* **boeuf**, *Ger.* **Höhle** kh: *Ger.* **ich**, *Scot.* **loch** g̱: *Sp.* **amigo** v̱: *Sp.* **hablar** hl: *Welsh* **Llanelli.** CAPITALS: primary stress. SMALL CAPS: secondary stress. Ⓢ: U.S. pron. Ⓔ: British pron.

Current
   river, MO, AR   KUHR-uhnt, KUH-ruhnt   'kərənt, 'kərənt

Currituck
   county, NC   KUHR-uh-ᴛᴜʜK, KUHR-uh-TUHK   'kərə,tək, ,kərə'tək

Curruá
   river, Brazil   kur-WAH   kuʳ'wa

Curruapanema
   river, Brazil   kur-WAH-PAHN-ā-MAH   kuʳ,wa,pane:'ma

Cursus Honorum
   Roman political career path   KUR-suhs ahn-AWR-uhm, KUHR-   'kuʳsəs an'ɔːrəm, 'kəʳ-

Curt
   1. pers. name   KUHRT   'kəʳt
   2. German   KURT   'kuʳt

Curtis
   pers. name   KUHRT-uhs   'kəʳt̬əs

Curtius
   1. Ernst, German historian   KURT-sē-uhs   'kuʳtsiːəs
   2. early Roman hero   KUHR-sh(ē-)uhs   'kəʳʃ(iː)əs

Curzon
   pers. name   KUHR-zuhn   'kəʳzən

Cuscatlán
   department, El Salvador   KOO-skaht-LAHN   ,kuːskat'lan

Cush
   see Kush

Cushan-rishathaim,
Chushan-rishathaim
   Biblical name   KUSH-ᴀɴ-ʀɪsʜ-uh-THĀ-im,   'kuʃˌænˌriʃə'θeːim,
                   K(Y)OO-SHAN-;   'k(j)uːˌʃæn-;
                   koo-SHAHN-ri-shah-TAH-yim   kuː'ʃanriʃa'tajim

Cushi
   Biblical name   KUSH-ɪ, K(Y)OO-SHĪ, koo-SHĒ   'kuʃˌai, 'k(j)uːˌʃai, kuː'ʃiː

Cushite
   Biblical name   KUSH-ɪᴛ, K(Y)OO-SHĪT, koo-SHĒT   'kuʃˌait, 'k(j)uːˌʃait, kuː'ʃiːt

Cushitic
   Afro-Asiatic lang. group   ku-SHIT-ik, koo-SHIT-ik   ku'ʃit̬ik, kuː'ʃit̬ik

Cutex
   tdmk for nail care products   KYOO-TEKS   'kjuːˌteks

Cuth [Cuthah]
   Biblical name   KUHTH, KUTH, KOO-TAH   'kəθ, 'kuθ, 'kuːˌta

Cuthah
   Biblical name   K(Y)OO-thuh, KOO-TAH   'k(j)uːθə, 'kuːˌta

Cuthbert
   pers. name   KUHTH-buhrt   'kəθbəʳt

Cuttack
   city, India   KUHT-uhk   'kət̬ək

Cuttyhunk
   island, MA   KUHT-ē-HUHNGK   'kət̬iːˌhəŋk

Cutty Sark
   ship; Scotch brand   KUHT-ē SAHRK, Ⓔ KUHT-ē SAHRK   'kət̬iˑ ˌsaʳk, Ⓔ ˌkət̬iˑ 'saʳk

Cuvaison
   winery, CA   KOO-vā-SAHN   ˌkuːveː'san

Cuvette
   province, Congo   koo-VET   kuː'vet

Cuvier
   Georges, *French naturalist*   kue-VYĀ   kyːvjeː

Key (col. 2):   a: fad   ā: fade   ah: father   ar: marry   aw: law   e: fed   ē: feed   er: merry   i: hid   ī: hide   ō: coat   oo: boot
oi: boy   ow: now   u: put   uh: above   uhr: bird   ch: chop   ng: ring   sh: show   th: thick   th: this   zh: measure

Cuyabá
  see Cuiabá

Cuyahoga
  river, county, OH   KĪ-uh-HŌ-guh, kuh-HŌ-guh,   ˌkɑiəˈhɔːgə, kəˈhɔːgə,
                         -HAW-guh, -HAHG-uh   -ˈhɔːgə, -ˈhɑgə

Cuyapaipe Band
  N. American people   KĪ-uh-PĪ-pā   ˌkɑiəˈpɑipeː

Cuyuni
  river, Venezuela   ku-YŌŌ-nē   kuˈjuːniˑ

Cuzco
  city, beer, Peru   KŌŌ-skō   ˈkuːskoː

Cwmbran
  town, Wales   kŌŌm-BRAHN   kuˑmˈbrɑn

Cybele
  Phrygian earth goddess   SIB-uh-lē   ˈsibəliˑ

Cyclades
  Aegean islands   SIK-luh-DĒZ   ˈsikləˌdiːz

Cycladic [Cyclades]
  Islands, *Aegean sea*   si-KLAD-ik, -KLĀD-   siˈklædik, -ˈkleːd-

Cyclamen
  flower   SĪ-kluh-muhn, SIK-luh-muhn   ˈsɑikləmən, ˈsikləmən

Cyclopean
  pert. to Cyclops   SĪ-kluh-PĒ-uhn, sī-KLŌ-pē-uhn,   ˌsɑikləˈpiːən, sɑiˈkloːpiːən,
                      sī-KLAHP-ē-uhn   sɑiˈklɑpiːən

Cyclopes
  pl. of Cyclops   sī-KLŌ-pēz   sɑiˈkloːpiːz

Cyclops
  one-eyed giant in Greek mythology;   SĪ-KLAHPS   ˈsɑiˌklɑps
    play, Euripides

Cycnus
  son of Ares, killed by Heracles; son   SIK-nuhs   ˈsiknəs
    of Poseidon, strangled by Achilles

Cyd
  pers. name (C. Charisse)   SID   ˈsid

Cydnus
  historic river, Turkey   SID-nuhs   ˈsidnəs

Cygnet
  baby swan   SIG-nuht   ˈsignət

Cygnus
  constellation   SIG-nuhs   ˈsignəs

Cyllene [Killíni, Ziria, Zeria]
  mountain, Greece   suh-LĒ-nē   səˈliːniˑ

Cylon
  Athenian tyrant   SĪ-LAHN   ˈsɑiˌlɑn

Cymbeline
  play, Shakespeare   SIM-buh-LĒN   ˈsimbəˌliːn

Cymraeg [Welsh]
  lang., Wales   kuhm-RĪG   kəmˈrɑig

Cymric
  pert. to British Celts, *esp.* Welsh   KUHM-rik   ˈkəmrik

Cymru [Wales]
  principality, Gt. Britain   KUHM-rē   ˈkəmriˑ

Cymry [Welsh]
  people, Wales   KUHM-rē   ˈkəmriˑ

Foreign Sounds: ue: *Fr.* **rue**, *Ger.* **füllen**   uh(r): *Fr.* **boeuf**, *Ger.* **Höhle**   kh: *Ger.* **ich**, *Scot.* **loch**   ḡ: *Sp.* **amigo**   v̲: *Sp.* **hablar**
hl: *Welsh* **Llanelli.**   CAPITALS: primary stress.   SMALL CAPS: secondary stress.   ⑤: U.S. pron.   £: British pron.

Cynar

wine	CHĒ-nahr	'tʃiːnɑʳ

Cyndi

pers. name	SIN-dē	'sindi·

Cynewulf

Anglo-Saxon poet	KIN-uh-WULF, KUN-uh-WULF	'kinə,wulf, 'kunə,wulf

Cynthia

pers. name	SIN-thē-uh	'sinθiːə

Cyparissus

son of Telephus, became a cypress tree	SIP-uh-RIS-uhs	ˌsipə'risəs

Cyprian

1. pers. name	SIP-rē-uhn	'sipriːən
2. Polish	TSIP-ryahn	'tsiprjɑːn

Cypriano

pers. name	thē-prē-AH-nō, sē-	θiːpriː'ɑnoː, siː-

Cyprien

pers. name, French	sē-prē-Eⁿ	siːpriːē

Cypriot

pert. to Cyprus	SIP-rē-uht	'sipriːət

Cyprjan

pers. name, Polish	TSIP-ryahn, ⑤ SIP-rē-uhn	'tsiprjɑːn, ⑤ 'sipriːən

Cyprus

Mediterranean island	SĪ-pruhs	'sɑiprəs

Cypselus

tyrant of Corinth, one of the Seven Sages	SIP-suh-luhs	'sipsələs

Cyrano de Bergerac

Savinien de, French soldier, satirist	sē-rah-NŌ duh ber-zhuh-RAHK, ⑤ SIR-uh-NŌ duh BER-zhuh-RAK, BUHR-zhuh-RAK	siːrɑːnoː də berʒərɑːk, ⑤ 'sirə,noː də 'berʒə,ræk, 'bəʳʒə,ræk

Cyrenaica

region, Libya	SIR-uh-NĀ-uh-kuh, SĪ-ruh-	ˌsirə'neːəkə, ˌsɑirə-

Cyrenaicism

ancient philosophical school	SIR-uh-NĀ-uh-SIZ-uhm, SĪ-ruh-	ˌsirə'neːə,sizəm, ˌsɑirə-

Cyrenaics

followers of Aristippus of Cyrene	SIR-uh-NĀ-iks, SĪ-ruh-NĀ-iks	ˌsirə'neːiks, ˌsɑirə'neːiks

Cyrene

nymph loved by Apollo; ancient African city	sī-RĒ-nē	sɑi'riːni·

Cyrenian

pert. to Cyrene	sī-RĒ-nē-uhn	sɑi'riːniːən

Cyrenius

Biblical name	sī-RĒ-nē-uhs	sɑi'riːniːəs

Cyril

pers. name	SIR-uhl	'sirəl

Cyrillianism

Christian heresy	suh-RIL-ē-uh-NIZ-uhm	sə'riliːə,nizəm

Cyrillic

pert. to Cyril; Russian alphabet	suh-RIL-ik	sə'rilik

Cyrus

1. Persian king; pers. name	SĪ-ruhs	'sɑirəs
2. French	sē-RUES	siːryːs

Cythera [Cerigo]

Mediterranean island	suh-THIR-uh	sə'θirə

Key (col. 2):   a: fad ā: fade ah: father ar: marry aw: law e: fed ē: feed er: merry i: hid ī: hide ō: coat ōo: boot
oi: boy   ow: now   u: put   uh: above   uhr: bird   ch: chop   ng: ring   sh: show   th: thick   th̲: this   zh: measure

Cytherea
   name for Aphrodite   SITH-uh-RĒ-uh   ˌsiθəˈriːə

Cytissorus
   grandson of King Athamas of Alos   suh-TIS-uh-ruhs   səˈtisərəs

Cyzicus
   king of the Doliones; killed by Jason   SIZ-i-kuhs   ˈsizikəs

Czardas
   dance   CHAHR-DAHSH, CHAHR-DASH   ˈtʃɑrˌdɑʃ, ˈtʃɑrˌdæʃ

Częstochowa
   city, Poland   CHEⁿ-stuh-K<u>H</u>Ō-vah,   ˌtʃɛ̃stəˈxoːvɑː,
           Ⓢ CHEN-stuh-KŌ-vuh   Ⓢ ˌtʃɛnstəˈkoːvə

Czech
   lang., people, republic, Europe   CHEK   ˈtʃek

Czechoslovak
   inhabitant of or pert. to   CHEK-uh-SLŌ-VAHK, -VAK   ˌtʃekəˈsloːˌvɑk, -ˌvæk
   Czechoslovakia

Czechoslovakia
   republic, Europe   CHEK-uh-sluh-VAHK-ē-uh, -VAK-ē-uh   ˌtʃekəsləˈvɑkiːə, -ˈvækiːə

Czeladz
   commune, Poland   CHEL-AHJ   ˈtʃelˌɑːdʒ

Czerny
   Karl, *Austrian pianist/composer*   CHER-nē   ˈtʃeʳniˑ

Czesław
   pers. name, Polish   CHES-lahf   ˈtʃesłɑːf

Czolgosz
   Leon F., *US anarchist, assassin of*   CHAWL-GAWSH   ˈtʃɔːlˌgɔːʃ
   William McKinley

D

DAB
   German beer   DĀ-AH-BĀ, DAHP   ˌdeːɑˈbeː, ˈdɑp

Dabareh [Daberath]
   Biblical name   DAB-uh-ruh, DAHV-uh-RAHT   ˈdæbərə, ˌdɑvəˈrat

Dabbasheth, Dabbesheth
   Biblical name   DAB-uh-SHETH, dah-BAH-shet   ˈdæbəˌʃeθ, dɑˈbɑʃet

Daberath [Dabareh]
   Biblical name   DAB-uh-RATH, DAHV-uh-RAHT   ˈdæbəˌræθ, ˌdɑvəˈrat

Dabney
   pers. name   DAB-nē   ˈdæbniˑ

Dacca, Dhaka
   city, Bangladesh   DAHK-uh, DAK-uh   ˈdɑkə, ˈdækə

Dachau
   Nazi concentration camp, Germany   DAH<u>KH</u>-ow, Ⓢ DAHK-OW   ˈdɑxɑu, Ⓢ ˈdɑkˌɑu

Daché
   Lilly, *US milliner*   da-SHĀ   dæˈʃeː

Dachshund

   dog breed   DAHKS-HUNT, -HUND; DAHK-suhnt, -suhnd   'dɑks,hunt, -,hund; 'dɑksənt, -sənd

Dacia

   ancient kingdom, Roman province   DĀ-sh(ē-)uh   'deːʃ(iː)ə

Dacian

   pert. to Dacia   DĀ-sh(ē-)uhn, DĀ-sē-uhn   'deːʃ(iː)ən, 'deːsiːən

Dacron

   tdmk for polyester fiber   DĀ-KRAHN, DAK-RAHN   'deː,krɑn, 'dæk,rɑn

Dactyls

   companions to Rhea or Cybele   DAK-tuhlz   'dæktḷz

Dad

   informal for father   DAD   'dæd

Dada

   wife of Samon   DĀD-uh, DAD-uh   'deːdə, 'dædə

Dada [Dadaism]

   artistic movement   DAHD-ah   'dɑdɑ

Dadaism [Dada]

   artistic movement   DAHD-ah-IZ-uhm   'dɑdɑ,izəm

Daddah

   Moktar, *Mauritanian statesman*   DAHD-ah   'dɑdɑ

Daddy

   informal for father   DAD-ē   'dædiˑ

Daedalion

   father of Chione   duh-DĀ-lē-uhn   də'deːliːən

Daedalus

   legendary builder of labyrinth   DED-l-uhs, DĒD-l-uhs   'dedḷəs, 'diːdḷəs

Daemen

   College, *NY*   DĀ-muhn   'deːmən

Daewoo

   South Korean manufacturing co.   dā-(w)o͞o   deː(w)uː

Daffin Park

   Savannah, GA   DAF-uhn   'dæfən

Dafydd

   pers. name, Welsh   DAHV-i<u>th</u>   'dɑvið

Dafydd ap Gwilym

   Welsh poet   DAHV-i<u>th</u> ahp GWIL-im   'dɑvið ɑp 'gwilim

Dag

   pers. name, Swedish   DAHG   'dɑg

da Gama, Vasco

   see Vasco da Gama

Dagbani

   lang., people, Ghana, Togo   dahg-BAHN-ē   dɑg'bɑniˑ

Dagestan, Daghestan

   republic, southwestern Russia   duh-gyi-STAHN, ⑤ DAHG-uh-STAHN, DAG-uh-STAN   dəgji'stɑn, ⑤ ,dɑgə'stɑn, ,dægə'stæn

Daghur, Dagur

   lang., people, Manchuria   dah-GUR   dɑ'guʳ

Dagmar

   1. pers. name   DAG-MAHR   'dæg,mɑʳ

   2. Danish   DAHG-mahr   'dɑːgmɑr

Dagobert

   1. pers. name, French   dah-gaw-BER   dɑːgɔːber

   2. German   DAHG-ō-BERT   'dɑgoː,beʳt

Key (col. 2):   a: fad   ā: fade   ah: father   ar: marry   aw: law   e: fed   ē: feed   er: merry   i: hid   ī: hide   ō: coat   o͞o: boot
oi: boy   ow: now   u: put   uh: above   uhr: bird   ch: chop   ng: ring   sh: show   th: thick   <u>th</u>: this   zh: measure

Dagobert *Merovingian king*	dah-gō-BER, [$] DAG-uh-BUHRT	dɑgoːber, [$] 'dægəˌbə^{r}t
Dagomba *lang., Ghana*	duh-GAHM-buh	də'gɑmbə
Dagon *Biblical name*	DĀ-GAHN, dah-GŌN	'deːˌgɑn, dɑ'goːn
Dago Peak *mountain, ID*	DĀ-gō PĒK	'deːgoː 'piːk
Daguerre Louis Jacques Mandé, *French inventor*	dah-GER, [$] duh-GER	dɑːger, [$] də'ge^r
Dagur *see* Daghur		
Dagwood *comic strip figure; large sandwich*	DAG-WUD	'dægˌwud
Da Hinggan Ling *mountain range, China*	DAH KHING-AHN LING, HING-AHN	'dɑː 'xiŋ'ɑn 'liŋ, 'hiŋ'ɑn
Dahl Roald, *British writer*	DAHL	'dɑˑl
Dahlia *plant*	DAL-yuh, DAHL-yuh, [£] DĀL-yuh	'dæljə, 'dɑljə, [£] 'deːljə
Dahlonega *city, GA*	duh-LAHN-uh-guh	də'lɑnəgə
Dahomey *republic, Africa*	duh-HŌ-mē, dah-	də'hoːmiˑ, dɑ-
Daihatsu *Japanese car co.*	dī-HAHT-so͞o	dɑi'hɑtsuː
Dai Ichi Kangyo *Japanese bank*	dī ē-chē kahng-(g)yō	dɑi iːtʃiː kɑŋ(g)joː
Dáil Eireann *legislature, Ireland*	DOIL ER-(y)uhn	'dɔil 'er(j)ən
Daimler Gottlieb, *German engineer*	DĪM-luhr, [$] DĀM-luhr	'dɑimlə^r, [$] 'deːmlə^r
Dai Nippon *Japanese printing co.*	dī nip-ahn	dɑi nipɑn
Daiquiri *1. alcoholic drink*	DĪ-kuh-rē, DAK(-uh)-rē	'dɑikəriˑ, 'dæk(ə)riˑ
2. commune, Cuba	DĪ-kuh-RĒ	ˌdɑikə'riː
Dairen [Dalian] *city, China*	DĪ-RUHN, DĪ-REN	'dɑi'rən, 'dɑi'ren
Daisy *pers. name*	DĀ-zē	'deːziˑ
Daiwa *Japanese bank*	dī-wah	dɑiwɑ
Dakar *city, Senegal*	duh-KAHR, DAK-AHR	də'kɑ^r, 'dækˌɑ^r
Dakota, Dakotah *N. American people*	duh-KŌT-uh	də'koːt̬ə
Dakotan *pert. to* Dakota	duh-KŌT-n	də'koːtn̩
Daladier Edouard, *French statesman*	dah-lahd-YĀ	dɑːlɑːdjeː
Dalaiah *Biblical name*	duh-LĪ-uh, duh-LĀ-uh, DAL-ē-Ī-uh, duh-lah-YAH	də'lɑiə, də'leːə, ˌdæliː'ɑiə, dəlɑ'jɑ

Dalai Lama
  Tibetan spiritual leader   DAHL-ī LAHM-uh   'dɑlˌɑi 'lɑmə
Dalandzadgad
  provincial capital, Mongolia   DAHL-ahn-JAHD-GAHD   ˌdɑlɑn'dʒɑdˌgɑd
Dale
  pers. name   DĀL   'deːl
Dalén
  Nils Gustaf, *Swedish inventor (Nobel*   duh-LĀN   də'leːn
  1912)
Dalgliesh
  Adam, *fictional police inspector, P.*   dal-GLĒSH, dahl-GLĒSH   dæl'gliːʃ, dɑl'gliːʃ
  D. James
Dalhousie
  town, Canada   dal-HOW-zē   dæl'hɑuziˑ
Dali
  Salvador, *Spanish artist*   DAHL-ē, dah-LĒ *(his own pron.)*   'dɑliˑ, dɑ'liː *(his own pron.)*
Dalian, Dalien [Dairen]
  city, China   DAH-lē-EN   'dɑliː'en
Dallas
  city, TX   DAL-uhs   'dæləs
Dalles, The
  city, OR   <u>thuh</u> DALZ   ðə 'dælz
Dalmanutha
  Biblical name   DAL-muh-N(Y)O̅O̅-thuh   ˌdælmə'n(j)uːθə
Dalmatia
  coastal region, Croatia   dal-MĀ-sh(ē-)uh   dæl'meːʃ(iː)ə
Dalmatian
  dog breed   dal-MĀ-shuhn   dæl'meːʃən
Dalmaticus
  Roman cognomen   dal-MAT-i-kuhs   dæl'mæṭikəs
Dalphon
  Biblical name   DAL-FAHN, dahl-FŌN   'dælˌfɑn, dɑl'foːn
Dalton
  John, *English chemist and physicist*   DAWL-tn   'dɔːltn̩
Daltry
  Roger, *British rock singer*   DAWL-trē, DAHL-trē   'dɔːltriˑ, 'dɑltriˑ
Daly
  Tyne, *US actress;* Tim, *US actor*   DĀ-lē   'deːliˑ
Dalziel
  James Henry, *British newspaper*   DAL-zēl, dē-EL   'dælziːl, diː'el
  owner
Dam
  Henrik, *Danish biochemist (Nobel*   DAHM   'dɑm
  1943)
Damanhūr
  city, Egypt   DAH-mahn-HUR   ˌdɑːmɑn'huʳ
Damaris
  Biblical name   DAM-uh-ruhs   'dæmərəs
Damascene
  Biblical name   DAM-uh-SĒN   'dæməˌsiːn
Damaschke
  E.C. "Dutch," Field, *ballpark,*   duh-MAS-kē   də'mæskiˑ
  Oneonta, NY
Damascus
  capital, Syria   duh-MAS-kuhs   də'mæskəs

Key (col. 2): a: fad ā: fade ah: father ar: marry aw: law e: fed ē: feed er: merry i: hid ī: hide ō: coat o̅o̅: boot
oi: boy ow: now u: put uh: above uhr: bird ch: chop ng: ring sh: show th: thick <u>th</u>: this zh: measure

Dámaso
   pers. name   DAH-mah-sō, T̲H̲AH-   'damasoː, 'ða-

Damasus
   pope   DAM-uh-suhs   'dæməsəs

D'Amato
   Alfonse, *US politician*   duh-MAHT-ō   də'maṭoː

D'Amboise
   Jacques, *US ballet dancer*   dahm-BWAHZ   dam'bwɑz

Damián
   pers. name, Spanish   dahm-YAHN, t̲h̲ahm-   dam'jan, ðam-

Damian
   1. pers. name   DĀM-yuhn, DĀ-mē-uhn   'deːmjən, 'deːmiːən
   2. German   dahm-YAHN, DAHM-ē-AHN   dam'jan, ˌdamiː'an

Damiano
   pers. name, Italian   dahm-YAHN-ō   dam'janoː

Damião
   pers. name, Portuguese   duhm-YOW[n], t̲h̲uhm-, dahm-, t̲h̲ahm-   dəm'jaũ, ðəm-, daːm-, ðaːm-

Damien
   1. pers. name   DĀ-mē-uhn   'deːmiːən
   2. French   dahm-YE[n]   daːmjɛ̃

Damietta
   city, Egypt   DAM-ē-ET-uh   ˌdæmiː'eṭə

Damm
   Spanish beer   DAHM   'dam

Damocles
   legendary figure (sword of D.)   DAM-uh-KLĒZ   'dæməˌkliːz

Damodar
   river, India   DAHM-uh-DAHR   'daməˌdaʳ

Damon
   pers. name   DĀ-muhn   'deːmən

Damone
   Vic, *US entertainer*   duh-MŌN   də'moːn

Dampier
   William, *English buccaneer and explorer*   DAM-pē-uhr, DAMP-yuhr   'dæmpiːəʳ, 'dæmpjəʳ

Damson
   fruit   DAM-zuhn   'dæmzən

Dan
   1. river, VA; Biblical village; pers. name   DAN   'dæn
   2. lang., people, Liberia, Ivory Coast   DAN, DAHN   'dæn, 'dɑn

Dana
   pers. name   DĀ-nuh   'deːnə

Danae, Danaë
   mother of Perseus   DAN-uh-Ē, DĀ-nuh-Ē   'dænəˌiː, 'deːnəˌiː

Danaid
   daughter of Danaus; Monarch butterfly   DAN-ē-ID, DAN-ā-ID   'dæniːˌid, 'dæneːˌid

Danaides, Danaïdes
   daughters of Danaus; family of butterflies   duh-NĀ-uhd-ĒZ   də'neːədˌiːz

Danakil [Afar]
   lang., people, desert, Ethiopia, Djibouti   DAN-uh-KIL, DAN-uh-KĒL   'dænəˌkil, 'dænəˌkiːl

---

Foreign Sounds: **ue**: *Fr.* **rue**, *Ger.* **füllen**   **uh(r)**: *Fr.* **boeuf**, *Ger.* **Höhle**   **kh**: *Ger.* **ich**, *Scot.* **loch**   **ḡ**: *Sp.* **amigo**   **v**: *Sp.* **hablar**
hl: *Welsh* **Llanelli**.   CAPITALS: primary stress.   SMALL CAPS: secondary stress.   Ⓢ: U.S. pron.   Ⓔ: British pron.

Da Nang		
seaport, Vietnam	DAH NAHNG, Ⓢ duh-NANG	ˈdɑ ˈnɑŋ, Ⓢ dəˈnæŋ
Danaus		
ruler of Argos, brother of Aegyptus	DAN-ē-uhs, DAN-ā-UHS	ˈdæniːəs, ˈdæneːˌəs
Danbury		
city, CT, NC	DAN-BER-ē, DAN-b(uh-)rē	ˈdænˌberiˑ, ˈdænb(ə)riˑ
Danceteller		
dance co., PA	DAN(T)S-TEL-uhr	ˈdæn(t)sˌteləʳ
Dandenong		
Ranges, *mtn., Australia*	DAN-duh-NAHNG, DAN-duh-NAWNG	ˈdændəˌnɑŋ, ˈdændəˌnɔːŋ
Dandie Dinmont		
terrier breed	DAN-dē DIN-MAHNT	ˈdændiˑ ˈdinˌmɑnt
Dane		
inhabitant of Denmark; pers. name	DĀN	ˈdeːn
Danegeld		
ancient tax, England	DĀN-GELD	ˈdeːnˌgeld
Danelaw, Danelagh		
English laws	DĀN-LAW	ˈdeːnˌlɔː
Danforth		
pers. name	DAN-FAWRTH	ˈdænˌfɔːʳθ
Dangla, Dang-la		
mountain range, Tibet	dahng-LAH	dɑŋˈlɑː
Dania		
city, FL	DĀ-nē-uh	ˈdeːniːə
Dániel		
pers. name, Hungarian	DAH-nē-el	ˈdɑːniːel
Daniel		
1. Old Testament book; pers. name	DAN-yuhl	ˈdænjəl
2. Dutch	DAH-nē-EL	ˈdɑːniːˌel
3. French	dahn-YEL	dɑːnjel
4. German	DAHN-yel, DAHN-ē-el	ˈdɑnjel, ˈdɑniːel
5. Spanish	<u>th</u>ahn-YEL, dahn-	ðɑnˈjel, dɑn-
6. Swedish	DAH-nē-el	ˈdɑniːel
Daniele		
pers. name, Italian	dahn-YEL-e	dɑnˈjele
Danielle		
pers. name	dan-YEL	dænˈjel
Daniello		
pers. name, Italian	dahn-YEL-lō	dɑnˈjelloː
Danilova		
Alexandra, *Russian ballet dancer*	duh-NĒ-luh-vuh	dəˈniːləvə
Danish		
lang., people, Europe	DĀ-nish	ˈdeːniʃ
Danite		
Biblical name	DAN-ĪT	ˈdænˌɑit
Danjaan		
Biblical name	dan-JĀ-uhn, DAHN-uh-YAH-AHN	dænˈdʒeːən, ˌdɑnəˈjɑˌɑn
Dannah		
Biblical name	DAN-uh, dahn-AH	ˈdænə, dɑnˈɑ
D'Annunzio		
Gabriele, *Italian writer*	dah-NO͞ONT-sē-ō	dɑˈnuːntsiːoː
Danny		
pers. name	DAN-ē	ˈdæniˑ
Dano-Norwegian [Bokmål]		
literary Norwegian	DĀ-nō-nawr-WĒ-juhn	ˌdeːnoːnɔːʳˈwiːdʒən

Key (col. 2): a: fad ā: fade ah: father ar: marry aw: law e: fed ē: feed er: merry i: hid ī: hide ō: coat o͞o: boot oi: boy ow: now u: put uh: above uhr: bird ch: chop ng: ring sh: show th: thick <u>th</u>: this zh: measure

Dante
   pers. name   DAHN-TĀ, DAN-TĀ, DANT-ē,   'dɑn͵teː, 'dæn͵teː, 'dænti·,
                           DAHNT-ē   'dɑnti·

Dante Alighieri
   Italian poet   DAHN-TĀ AL-uhg-YER-ē, DAN-TĀ,   'dɑn͵teː ͵æləg'jeri·, 'dæn͵teː,
                           DANT-ē, DAHNT-ē   'dænti·, 'dɑnti·

Dantean
   pert. to Dante Alighieri   DANT-ē-uhn, DAHNT-ē-uhn,   'dæntiːən, 'dɑntiːən,
                           dan-TĒ-uhn, dahn-TĒ-uhn   dæn'tiːən, dɑn'tiːən

Dantesque
   pert. to Dante Alighieri   dan-TESK, dahn-TESK   dæn'tesk, dɑn'tesk

Danton
   Georges, *French revolutionary*   dahⁿ-TAWⁿ   dɑ̃tɔ̃

Danube
   river, Europe   DAN-yo͞ob   'dænju·b

Danubian
   pert. to the Danube   dan-YO͞O-bē-uhn, duhn-YO͞O-bē-uhn   dæn'juːbiːən, dən'juːbiːən

Danvers
   city, MA   DAN-vuhrz   'dænvəʳz

Danya
   pers. name (D. Krupske)   DAN-yuh, DAHN-yuh   'dænjə, 'dɑnjə

Danzig [Gdańsk]
   city, Poland   DAHNT-sig, DANT-sig   'dɑntsig, 'dæntsig

Daphne
   nymph loved by Apollo; pers. name   DAF-nē   'dæfni·

Daphnis
   beautiful son of Hermes   DAF-nuhs   'dæfnəs

Daphnis and Chloë
   novel, Longus   DAF-nuhs uhn(d) KLŌ-ē   'dæfnəs ən(d) 'kloːi·

Daphnis et Chloé
   ballet, Ravel   dahf-NĒS ā klaw-Ā   dɑːfniːs eː klɔːeː

Da Ponte
   Lorenzo, *Italian poet*   dah PAWN-tā, Ⓢ duh-PAHN-tē   dɑː 'pɔːnteː, Ⓢ də'pɑnti·

Daqing
   city, China   DAH-CHING   'dɑ'tʃiŋ

Dara [Darda]
   Biblical name   DAR-uh, DER-uh, DAHR-ah   'dærə, 'derə, 'dɑrɑ

Darcy, D'Arcy
   pers. name   DAHR-sē   'dɑʳsi·

Darda [Dara]
   Biblical name   DAHR-duh, dahr-DAH   'dɑʳdə, dɑr'dɑ

Dardanelles [Çanakkale Boğazı,
Hellespont]
   strait, Turkey   DAHRD-n-ELZ   ͵dɑʳdn̩'elz

Dardanus
   Trojan ancestor   DAHRD-n-uhs   'dɑʳdn̩əs

Dardic
   lang. family   DAHRD-ik   'dɑʳdik

Dar es Salaam
   city, Tanzania   DAHR ES suh-LAHM   ͵dɑr ͵es sə'lɑm

Darién
   Spanish colony, isthmus, Panama   dahr-YEN   dɑr'jen

Darien
   city, CT; city, GA; village, IL   DAR-ē-EN, DER-ē-EN   ͵dæriː'en, ͵deriː'en

---

Foreign Sounds: ue: *Fr.* **rue**, *Ger.* **füllen**   uh(r): *Fr.* **boeuf**, *Ger.* **Höhle**   <u>kh</u>: *Ger.* **ich**, *Scot.* **loch**   ḡ: *Sp.* **amigo**   <u>v</u>: *Sp.* **hablar**
hl: *Welsh* **Llanelli**.   CAPITALS: primary stress.   SMALL CAPS: secondary stress.   Ⓢ: U.S. pron.   Ⓔ: British pron.

Darin

Bobby, James, *US entertainers*	DAR-uhn, DER-uhn	'dærən, 'derən

Darío

Rubén, *Nicaraguan poet and diplomat*	dah-RĒ-ō	dɑ'riːoː

Darius

1. *name, Persian kings; pers. name*	duh-RĪ-uhs	də'rɑiəs
2. *French*	dahr-YUES	dɑːrjyːs

Darjeeling, Darjiling

district, India; tea	dahr-JĒ-ling	dɑʳ'dʒiːliŋ

Darkon

Biblical name	DAHR-KAHN, dahr-KŌN	'dɑʳ‚kɑn, dɑr'koːn

Darlene

pers. name	dahr-LĒN	dɑʳ'liːn

Darley Arabian

horse	DAHR-lē uh-RĀ-bē-uhn	'dɑʳliˑ ə'reːbiːən

Darlington

county, town, SC; borough, England; pers. name	DAHR-ling-tuhn	'dɑʳliŋtən

Darmstadt

prov & town, Germany	DAHRM-SHTAHT, ⓢ DAHRM-STAT	'dɑʳm‚ʃtat, ⓢ 'dɑʳm‚stæt

Darrell

pers. name	DAR-uhl, DER-uhl	'dærəl, 'derəl

Darren

pers. name	DAR-uhn, DER-uhn	'dærən, 'derən

Darrow

Clarence Seward, *US lawyer*	DAR-ō	'dæroː

Darryl

pers. name	DAR-uhl, DER-uhl	'dærəl, 'derəl

D'Artagnan

character in The Three Musketeers, *A. Dumas*	dahr-tahn-YAHⁿ, ⓢ dahr-TAN-yuhn	dɑːrtɑːnjã, ⓢ dɑʳ'tænjən

Darth Vader

Star Wars villain	DAHRTH VĀD-uhr	‚dɑʳθ 'veːdəʳ

Dartmoor

natl. park, prison, England	DAHRT-MUR, -MŌR, -MAWR	'dɑʳt‚muʳ, -‚moːʳ, -‚mɔːʳ

Dartmouth

borough, England; town, Nova Scotia; college, NH	DAHRT-muhth	'dɑʳtməθ

Darwin

Charles, *Brit. scientist; pl. name; college, Cambridge Univ.*	DAHR-wuhn	'dɑʳwən

Darwinian

pert. to Charles Darwin	dahr-WIN-ē-uhn	dɑʳ'winiːən

Darwinism

origin of species theory	DAHR-wuh-NIZ-uhm	'dɑʳwə‚nizəm

Das

Chitta Ranjan, *Indian politician*	DAHS	'dɑs

Dasain

Nepalese festival	DAH-SHĪN	'dɑ‚ʃain

Dashiell

pers. name	duh-SHĒL *(pron. of D. Hammett)*, DASH-uhl	də'ʃiːl *(pron. of D. Hammett)*, 'dæʃəl

Key (col. 2):   a: fad ā: fade ah: father ar: marry aw: law e: fed ē: feed er: merry i: hid ī: hide ō: coat ōō: boot
oi: boy   ow: now   u: put   uh: above   uhr: bird   ch: chop   ng: ring   sh: show   th: thick   th̲: this   zh: measure

da Silva

  1. pers. name   duh SIL-vuh   də 'silvə

  2. Portuguese   t͟huh SIL-vuh, duh; t͟hah SIL-vah, dah   ðə 'silvə, də; ðɑː 'silvɑː, dɑː

Dassault

  French aircraft co.   dah-SŌ   dɑːsoː

Dassin

  Jules, *US director*   DAS-uhn   'dæsən

Dathan

  Biblical name   DĀ-thuhn, dah-TAHN   'deːθən, dɑ'tɑn

Datil Range

  mountain range, NM   DAT-l RĀNJ   'dætl̩ ˌreːndʒ

Datong, Ta-t'ung

  city, China   DAH-TUNG   'dɑ'tuŋ

Datsun

  Japanese car make   DAHT-suhn, DAT-suhn   'dɑtsən, 'dætsən

Daudet

  Alphonse, *French writer*   daw-DE, Ⓢ dō-DĀ   dɔːde, Ⓢ doː'deː

Daud Khan

  Sardar Mohammad, *Afghan politician*   dah-O͞OD K͟HAHN, KAHN   dɑ'uːd 'xɑn, 'kɑn

Daumier

  Honoré, *French artist*   dōm-YĀ   doːm'jeː

Daunus

  brother of Iapyx and Peucetius   DAW-nuhs   'dɔːnəs

Dauphin

  1. county, PA; river, Canada   DAW-fuhn   'dɔːfən

  2. title, French prince   dō-FEⁿ   doːfẽ

Dauphiné

  prov, France; Alps, *Alpine mtn. range*   dō-fē-NĀ   doːfi'neː

Dauphinoise

  cookery preparation   dō-fēn-WAHZ   doːfiːnwɑːz

Dausset

  Jean, *French immunologist (Nobel 1980)*   dō-SE   doːse

Davallia

  plant   duh-VAL-yuh   də'væljə

Davao

  seaport, Philippines   DAHV-ow, dah-VOW   'dɑvˌau, dɑ'vau

Dave

  pers. name   DĀV   'deːv

D'Avenant

  Sir William, *British poet laureate*   DAV-(uh-)nuhnt   'dæv(ə)nənt

Davenant, D'Avenant

  Sir William, *English poet and dramatist*   DAV-(uh-)nuhnt   'dæv(ə)nənt

Davenport

  city, Iowa   DAV-uhn-PAWRT, DAV-m-PAWRT   'dævənˌpɔːʳt, 'dævm̩ˌpɔːʳt

---

David
1. pers. name	DĀ-vuhd	'deːvəd
2. Dutch	DAH-vuht	'daːvət
3. French	dah-VĒD	daːviːd
4. German	DAHV-ēt, DAHF-ēt, -it	'daviːt, 'dafiːt, -it
5. Hebrew	dahv-ĒD, DAW-vuhd	dav'iːd, 'dɔːvəd
6. Italian	DAHV-ēd	'daviːd
7. Russian	DUHV-YĒD	ˌdəv'jiːd

David Lipscomb
College, *TN*	DĀ-vuhd LIP-skuhm	'deːvəd 'lipskəm

Davies
family name	DĀ-vēz, ⓔ DĀ-vis	'deːviːz, ⓔ 'deːvis

Daviess
counties, IN, KY, MO	DĀ-vuhs, DĀ-vēz	'deːvəs, 'deːˌviːz

da Vinci
see Leonardo da Vinci

Davis
family name	DĀ-vis	'deːvis

Davison
pers. name	DĀ-vuh-suhn	'deːvəsən

Davisson
C. J., *US physicist (Nobel 1937)*	DĀ-vuh-suhn	'deːvəsən

Davos
Swiss resort	dah-VŌS	da'voːs

Davy
pers. name	DĀ-vē	'deːviˑ

Dawes
Charles G., *US vice president* *(Nobel 1925)*	DAWZ	'dɔːz

Dawn
pers. name	DAWN, DAHN	'dɔːn, 'dɑn

Dayak [Dyak]
people, lang., Sarawak & Borneo	DĪ-AK	'daiˌæk

Dayan
Moshe, *Israeli leader*	dī-AHN, dah-YAHN	dai'an, da'jan

Dayna
pers. name	DĀ-nuh	'deːnə

Dayton
city, OH	DĀT-n	'deːtn̩

Daytona Beach
town, FL	dā-TŌ-nuh BĒCH	deːˌtoːnə 'biːtʃ

Da Yunhe
canal, China	DAH YUN-HUH	'da 'jun'hə

Dayyan
pers. name	dī-(Y)AHN	dai'(j)an

Dazai Osamu
pseudonym of Shuji Tsushima, *Japanese novelist*	dahz-ī ō-sahm-ōō	dazai oːsamuː

Dazu
town, China	DAHD-ZŌŌ, DAH-ZŌŌ	'dad'zuː, 'da'zuː

Deaf Smith
county, TX	DEF SMITH, DĒF	ˌdef 'smiθ, ˌdiːf

Dean, Deane
pers. name	DĒN	'diːn

Key (col. 2):   a: fad   ā: fade   ah: father   ar: marry   aw: law   e: fed   ē: feed   er: merry   i: hid   ī: hide   ō: coat   ōō: boot
oi: boy   ow: now   u: put   uh: above   uhr: bird   ch: chop   ng: ring   sh: show   th: thick   th: this   zh: measure

DeAndre
pers. name   dē-AN-drā, dē-AHN-drā   diːˈændreː, diːˈɑndreː

Dearborn
county, IN; city, MI   DIR-BAWRN, DIR-buhrn   ˈdiʳˌbɔːʳn, ˈdiʳbəʳn

Deauville
resort, France   dō-VĒL, ⑤ DŌ-VIL   doːviːl, ⑤ ˈdoːˌvil

De Baca
county, NM   dē BAHK-uh   diː ˈbɑkə

DeBakey
Michael Ellis, *US cardiovascular*   duh-BĀ-kē   dəˈbeːkiˑ
surgeon

de Balzac
see Balzac

DeBeers
S. African diamond mining co.   duh-BIRZ   dəˈbiʳz

Debir
Biblical name   DĒ-buhr, duh-vi-RAH   ˈdiːbəʳ, dəviˈrɑ

Deborah
pers. name   DEB-(uh-)ruh   ˈdeb(ə)rə

Debrecen
city, Hungary   DEB-ruht-SEN   ˈdebrətˌsen

Debrett
British publisher, peerage   duh-BRET   dəˈbret

Debreu
Gerard, *French-born US economist*   duh-BROO   dəˈbruː
(Nobel 1983)

de Bury [Aungerville]
Richard, *English bibliophile*   duh BER-ē   də ˈberiˑ

Debussy
Claude, *French composer*   duh-bue-SĒ, ⑤ DEB-yuh-SĒ,   dəbyːsiː, ⑤ ˌdebjəˈsiː,
                                     DĀ-byuh-SĒ   ˌdeːbjəˈsiː

Debye
P. J. W., *Dutch-born US physicist* duh-BĪ   dəˈbɑi
(Nobel 1936)

DEC
US computer co.   DEK   ˈdek

Decalogue
the Ten Commandments   DEK-uh-LAWG, DEK-uh-LAHG   ˈdekəˌlɔːg, ˈdekəˌlɑg

Decameron
Boccaccio work   duh-KAM-uh-ruhn, -RAHN   dəˈkæmərən, -ˌrɑn

Decapolis
Biblical name   duh-KAP-uh-lis   dəˈkæpəlis

Decatur
Stephen, *US naval officer; pl. name,* di-KAT-uhr   diˈkeːʈəʳ
US

Decca
US record co.   DEK-uh   ˈdekə

Deccan, Dekkan
southern Indian peninsula   DEK-uhn, DEK-AN   ˈdekən, ˈdekˌæn

December
month   di-SEM-buhr   diˈsembəʳ

Decimus
pers. name   DES-uh-muhs   ˈdesəməs

Decius
Roman emperor; pers. name   DĒ-sh(ē-)uhs   ˈdiːʃ(iː)əs

Foreign Sounds: ue: *Fr.* **r**ue, *Ger.* f**ü**llen   uh(r): *Fr.* b**oeu**f, *Ger.* H**öh**le   <u>kh</u>: *Ger.* i**ch**, *Scot.* lo**ch**   ḡ: *Sp.* ami**g**o   v: *Sp.* ha**b**lar
hl: *Welsh* **Ll**anelli.   CAPITALS: primary stress.   SMALL CAPS: secondary stress.   ⑤: U.S. pron.   ⑥: British pron.

DeConcini
  Dennis, *US politician* — DĒ-kuhn-SĒ-nē — ˌdiːkən'siːniˑ
Decorah
  city, IA — duh-KŌR-uh, duh-KAWR-uh — də'koːrə, də'kɔːrə
Dedan
  Biblical name — DĒD-n, duh-DAHN — 'diːdn̩, də'dɑn
Dedanim
  Biblical name — DED-n-IM, DĒD-n-IM, duh-dah-NĒM — 'dedn̩ˌim, 'diːdn̩ˌim, dədɑ'niːm
Dedanite
  Biblical name — DED-n-ĪT, DĒD-n-ĪT — 'dedn̩ˌait, 'diːdn̩ˌait
Dedé Agach
  Turkish name of Alexandroúpolis — ded-Ā uh-ḠAHCH — dedˌeː ə'ɣɑtʃ
Dedeaux
  Field, *ballpark, Los Angeles, CA* — DĀ-DŌ — 'deːˌdoː
Dedham
  town, MA — DED-uhm — 'dedəm
Deems
  pers. name (D. Taylor) — DĒMZ — 'diːmz
Deepavali
  Hindu festival — DĒ-PAHV-uh-lē — 'diːˌpɑvəliˑ
Def Leppard
  rock group — def LEP-uhrd — def 'lepərd
Defoe
  Daniel, *English writer* — di-FŌ — di'foː
Deforest, DeForest
  pers. name — di-FAWR-uhst, di-FAHR-uhst — di'fɔːrəst, di'fɑrəst
De Funiak Springs
  town, FL — duh F(Y)O͞O-nē-AK SPRINGZ — də 'f(j)uːniːˌæk 'spriŋz
Degas
  Edgar, *French artist* — duh-GAH, Ⓢ dā-GAH — dəgɑ, Ⓢ də'gɑ, deːˈgɑ
de Gaulle
  Charles, *president, France* — duh GŌL, Ⓢ di GŌL, di GAWL — də goːl, Ⓢ di 'goːl, di 'gɔːl
Degeneres
  Ellen, *US actress* — di-JEN-uh-ruhs — di'dʒenərəs
Degh
  river, India, Pakistan — DĀG — 'deːg
De Havilland
  Geoffrey, *English aircraft designer;* Olivia, *US actress* — duh HAV-uh-luhnd — də 'hævələnd
Dehmelt
  Hans G., *German-born US physicist* (Nobel 1989) — DĀ-MELT, DĀ-muhlt — 'deːˌmelt, 'deːməlt
Deianeira, Deianira
  wife of Hercules — DĀ-uh-NĪ-ruh, DĒ-uh-NĪ-ruh, -nē-ruh — ˌdeːə'nairə, ˌdiːə'nairə, -niːrə
Deil
  the Devil — DĒL — 'diːl
Deimos
  satellite of Mars — DĀ-mōs, DĀ-muhs — 'deːmoːs, 'deːməs
Deinodon
  dinosaur — DĪ-nuh-DAHN — 'dainəˌdɑn
Deioces
  legendary first king of the Medes — DĒ-uh-SĒZ — 'diːəˌsiːz

Key (col. 2): a: fad ā: fade ah: father ar: marry aw: law e: fed ē: feed er: merry i: hid ī: hide ō: coat o͞o: boot
oi: boy ow: now u: put uh: above uhr: bird ch: chop ng: ring sh: show th: thick th̲: this zh: measure

Deiphobus
   son of Priam and Hecuba   DĀ-uh-FŌ-buhs   ˌdeːəˈfoːbəs

Deiphontes
   husband of Hyrnetho   DĒ-uh-FAHN-TĒZ   ˌdiːəˈfɑnˌtiːz

Deira
   ancient British kingdom   DĀ-ruh   ˈdeːrə

Deirdre
   pers. name   DIR-druh, DIR-drē   ˈdiʳdrə, ˈdiʳdriˑ

Deir-el-Bahri
   Egyptian site, near Thebes   DER-al-BAHR-ē   ˈderælˈbɑriˑ

Deisenhofer
   Johann, *German biochemist (Nobel 1988)*   DĪ-zuhn-HŌ-fuhr   ˈdaizənˌhoːfəʳ

De Kalb
   pl. name, US; college, GA   di KALB, *esp. southeastern US* di KAB   di ˈkælb, *esp. southeastern US* di ˈkæb

Dekar
   Biblical name   DĒ-KAHR, DEK-AHR, DEK-ER   ˈdiːˌkɑʳ, ˈdekˌɑʳ, ˈdekˌer

De Klerk
   F. W., *S. African politician*   duh KLERK, di KLUHRK   də ˈkleʳk, di ˈkləʳk

De Koninck
   Belgian beer   duh KAW-ningk   də ˈkɔːniŋk

de Kooning
   Willem, *US painter*   duh KOO-ning   də ˈkuːniŋ

de Kruif
   Paul Henry, *US bacteriologist and writer*   duh KRĪF   də ˈkrɑif

DeKuyper
   brand of schnapps   di-KĪ-puhr   diˈkaipəʳ

Delacroix
   Eugène, *French painter*   duh-lah-KRWAH, Ⓢ DEL-uh-K(R)WAH   dəlɑːkrwɑː, Ⓢ ˌdeləˈk(r)wɑ

de la Garza
   E(kika), *US politician*   DEL uh GAHR-zuh   ˌdel ə ˈgɑrzə

Delaiah
   Biblical name   duh-LĪ-uh, duh-LĀ-uh, duh-lah-YAH-hoo   dəˈlaiə, dəˈleːə, dəlaˈjɑhuː

de la Madrid Hurtado
   Miguel, *president, Mexico*   dā lah mah-<u>THRĒTH</u> <u>oo</u>r-TAH-<u>th</u>ō   deː lɑ mɑˈðriːð uːrˈtɑðoː

De la Mare
   Walter, *English writer*   DEL-uh-MAR, DEL-uh-MER   ˌdeləˈmæʳ, ˌdeləˈmeʳ

de la Mer
   pers. name   DEL-uh-muhr, DEL-uh-MIR   ˈdeləməʳ, ˈdeləˌmiʳ

Delamere
   pers. name   DEL-uh-MIR   ˈdeləˌmiʳ

Delano
   1. *pers. name*   DEL-uh-NŌ   ˈdeləˌnoː
   2. *city, CA*   duh-LĀ-NŌ   dəˈleːˌnoː

de la Renta
   Oscar, *fashion designer*   duh luh RAHⁿ(N)-tuh, DĒ, REN-tuh   də lə ˈrɑ(n)tə, ˌdiː, ˈrentə

Delaunay
   Robert, *French painter*   duh-law-NE   dəlɔːne

De Laurentiis
   Dino, *film producer*   dā law-REN-tis, Ⓢ duh luh-RENT-uhs, DĒ   deː lɔːˈrentis, Ⓢ də ləˈrentəs, ˌdiː

Foreign Sounds: ue: *Fr.* **rue**, *Ger.* **füllen**   uh(r): *Fr.* **boeuf**, *Ger.* **Höhle**   <u>kh</u>: *Ger.* **ich**, *Scot.* **loch**   ḡ: *Sp.* **amigo**   v̲: *Sp.* **hablar** hl: *Welsh* **Llanelli**.   CAPITALS: primary stress.   SMALL CAPS: secondary stress.   Ⓢ: U.S. pron.   Ⓔ: British pron.

Delavan		
city, WI	DEL-uh-VAN	'delə,væn
Delaware		
river, state, US; N. American people [Lenni-Lenape]	DEL-uh-WAR, -WER, -wuhr	'delə,wær, -,we^{r}, -wə^{r}
Delbrück		
Max, *German-born US biologist (Nobel 1969)*	DEL-BRUEK, DEL-BRUK	'del,bryk, 'del,bruk
Deledda		
Grazia, *Italian author (Nobel 1926)*	dā-LED-dah, [S] duh-LED-uh	deː'ledda, [S] də'ledə
De Leon		
city, TX	DEL-ē-AHN, DĒ lē-AHN	'deliː,ɑn, ,diː liː'ɑn
Delft		
city, Netherlands	DELFT	'delft
Delhi		
1. city, India	DEL-ē	'deliˑ
2. town, LA, NY, OH, Ontario	DEL-HĪ	'del,hɑi
Delia		
pers. name	DĒ-lē-uh, DĒL-yuh	'diːliːə, 'diːljə
Delian League		
Athenian alliance	DĒ-lē-uhn	'diːliːən
Delibes		
Léo, *French composer*	duh-LĒB	də'liːb
Delilah		
Biblical name	di-LĪ-luh	di'lɑilə
Delius		
Frederick, *English composer*	DĒ-lē-uhs, DĒL-yuhs	'diːliːəs, 'diːljəs
Dell		
pers. name	DEL	'del
Della		
pers. name (D. Reese)	DEL-uh	'delə
della Robbia		
family of Italian artists	DEL-uh RŌ-bē-uh, DEL-uh RAHB-ē-uh	,delə 'roːbiːə, ,delə 'rɑbiːə
Dell'Olio		
Louis, *US fashion designer*	del-Ō-lē-ō	del'oːliːoː
Delmarva		
Peninsula, *east coast, US*	del-MAHR-vuh	del'mɑ^{r}və
Delmonico		
steak cut	del-MAHN-i-kō	del,mɑnikoː
Del Monte		
US food processing co.	del MAHNT-ē	del 'mɑntiˑ
Del Norte		
county, CA; city, CO	del NŌRT-ā, del NAWRT-ā	del 'noː^{r}t̪eː, del 'nɔː^{r}teː
Delorimier		
Downs, *Montreal, Canada*	duh-LAWR-uhm-YĀ	də,lɔːrəm'jeː
Delos		
Aegean island	DĒ-LAHS, DEL-ōs	'diː,lɑs, 'deloːs
De Los Angeles		
Victoria, *Spanish opera star*	dā laws AHNG-hel-ās	deː lɔːs 'ɑŋheleːs
De Lourdes		
College, *IL*	duh LURD(Z)	də 'lu^{r}d(z)
Delphi		
ancient Greek city, site of oracle	DEL-FĪ	'del,fɑi
Delphian		
pert. to Delphi	DEL-fē-uhn, DELF-yuhn	'delfiːən, 'delfjən

Key (col. 2): a: **fad** ā: **fade** ah: **father** ar: **marry** aw: **law** e: **fed** ē: **feed** er: **merry** i: **hid** ī: **hide** ō: **coat** ōō: **boot** oi: **boy** ow: **now** u: **put** uh: **above** uhr: **bird** ch: **chop** ng: **ring** sh: **show** th: **thick** th: **this** zh: **measure**

Delphic
   pert. to Delphi   DEL-fik   'delfik

Delphinium
   plant   del-FIN-ē-uhm   del'fini:əm

Delphinus
   constellation   del-FĪ-nuhs   del'fainəs

Delphus
   hero of Delphi   DEL-fuhs   'delfəs

Delphos
   city, OH   DEL-fuhs   'delfəs

Del Rio
   city, TX   del RĒ-ō   del 'ri:o:

del Sarto
   see Sarto, del

DeLuise
   Dom, *US actor*   DEL-uh-WĒZ   ˌdelə'wi:z

De Man
   Paul, *Belgian-born literary critic*   duh-MAHN   dəman

Demas
   Biblical name   DĒ-muhs, DĀ-muhs   'di:məs, 'de:məs

de Maupassant
   see Maupassant

Demavend
   mtn., Iran   DEM-uh-VEND   'deməˌvend

Demerara
   raw sugar   DEM-uh-RER-uh, DEM-uh-RAHR-uh   ˌdemə'rerə, ˌdemə'rarə

Demerara
   river, Guyana; type of brown sugar   DEM-uh-RAHR-uh, -RER-uh   ˌdemə'rarə, -'rerə

Demorest
   town, GA   DEM-uh-REST   'deməˌrest

Demerol
   tdmk for a sedative   DEM-uh-RAWL, -RŌL   'deməˌrɔ:l, -ˌro:l

Demeter
   Greek earth and fertility goddess   di-MĒT-uhr   di'mi:ʈə^r

Demetrios
   pers. name, Mod. Greek   <u>th</u>ē-MĒ-trē-AWS   ði:'mi:tri:ˌɔ:s

Demetrius
   pers. name   duh-MĒ-trē-uhs   də'mi:tri:əs

Demetrius Poliorcetes
   Macedonian king   duh-MĒ-trē-uhs PAHL-ē-awr-SET-ēz   də'mi:tri:əs ˌpali:ɔ:^{r}'si:ʈi:z

Demi
   pers. name (D. Moore)   duh-MĒ, DEM-ē   də'mi:, 'demi·

de Mille
   Cecil B., *US movie producer*   duh MIL   də 'mil

Demiphon
   king of Eleonte   DEM-uh-FAHN   'deməˌfan

Democrat
   member of Democratic party   DEM-uh-KRAT   'deməˌkræt

Democratic
   US political party   DEM-uh-KRAT-ik   ˌdemə'kræʈik

Democritus
   Greek philosopher   di-MAHK-ruht-uhs   di'makrətəs

Demodice
   aunt of Phrixus   duh-MAHD-uh-sē   də'madəsi·

Demodocus
  Homeric bard   dē-MAHD-uh-kuhs   di·ˈmɑdəkəs
Demophon
  son of Theseus   DEM-uh-FAHN   ˈdemə͵fɑn
Demopolis
  city, AL   dem-AH-puh-luhs   demˈɑpələs
Demosthenes
  Athenian orator   di-MAHS-thuh-NĒZ   diˈmɑsθə͵niːz
Dempsey
  Jack, US boxer   DEM(P)-sē   ˈdem(p)si·
Demuth
  Charles, US painter   duh-MOOTH   dəˈmuːθ
Denali [McKinley]
  mtn., National Park and Preserve,   duh-NAHL-ē   dəˈnɑli·
    AK
Denbigh
  town, Wales   DEN-bē   ˈdenbi·
Denbighshire [Clwyd]
  former county, Wales   DEN-bē-shuhr, -SHIR   ˈdenbi·ʃəʳ, -͵ʃiʳ
Dendritis
  name used by Helen in Rhodes   den-DRĬT-uhs, den-DRĒT-uhs   denˈdrɑiʈəs, denˈdriːʈəs
Dene, Déné
  Canadian Indian people   DEN-ē, DEN-Ā   ˈdeni·, ˈden͵eː
Deneb
  star   DEN-EB, DEN-uhb   ˈden͵eb, ˈdenəb
Deneuve
  Catherine, French actress   duh-NUH(R)V   dənœːv
Deng Xiaoping, Teng Hsiao-p'ing
  Chinese leader   DUHNG SHOW-PING   ˈdəŋ ˈʃɑuˈpiŋ
Denham
  Sir John, English poet   DEN-uhm   ˈdenəm
Denikin
  Anton, Russian militarist   dyin-YĒK-yin   djinˈjiːkjin
Deniliquin
  town, Australia   duh-NIL-i-kwuhn   dəˈnilikwən
De Niro
  Robert, US actor   duh NIR-ō   də ˈniroː
Denis
  1. pers. name   DEN-uhs   ˈdenəs
  2. Dutch   duh-NĒS   dəˈniːs
  3. French   duh-NĒ   dəniː
  4. Russian   din-YES   ḍinˈjiːs
Denise
  1. pers. name   duh-NĒS, -NĒZ   dəˈniːs, -ˈniːz
  2. French   duh-NĒZ   dəniːz
Denison
  city, IA, TX; univ., OH   DEN-uh-suhn   ˈdenəsən
Denizli
  prov & town, Turkey   DEN-uhz-LĒ   ͵denəzˈliː
Denmark
  kingdom, Europe   DEN-MAHRK   ˈden͵mɑʳk
Dennie, Denny
  pers. name   DEN-ē   ˈdeni·
Dennis
  pers. name   DEN-uhs   ˈdenəs

Key (col. 2):   a: **fad**   ā: **fade**   ah: **father**   ar: **marry**   aw: **law**   e: **fed**   ē: **feed**   er: **merry**   i: **hid**   ī: **hide**   ō: **coat**   oo: **boot**
oi: **boy**   ow: **now**   u: **put**   uh: **above**   uhr: **bird**   ch: **chop**   ng: **ring**   sh: **show**   th: **thick**   <u>th</u>: **this**   zh: **measure**

Denny's
   US restaurant chain   DEN-ēz   ˈdeniːz

Denpasar
   city, Indonesia   duhn-PAHS-AHR   dənˈpɑsˌɑʳ

D'Entrecasteaux
   Islands, *Pacific Ocean*   deⁿ-truh-kah-STŌ   dētrəkɑstoː

Denver
   city, CO; pers. name   DEN-vuhr   ˈdenvəʳ

Denys
   pers. name, French   duh-NĒ   dəniː

Déodat
   pers. name, French   dā-aw-DAH(T)   deːɔːdɑː(t)

De Palma
   Brian Russel, *US film writer,*   duh PAHL-muh, duh PAWL-muh   də ˈpɑlmə, də ˈpɔːlmə
      director

Depardieu
   Gerard, *French actor*   dā-pahr-DYUH(R)   deːpɑːrdjœː

DePauw
   University, *IN*   duh-PAW   dəˈpɔː

Depeche Mode
   rock group   duh-PESH MŌD   dəˈpeʃ ˈmoːd

Depo-Provera
   tdmk for a progesterone drug   DEP-ō-pruh-VER-uh, -VIR-uh   ˌdepoːprəˈverə, -ˈvirə

De Quincey
   Thomas, *English essayist*   duh KWIN(T)-sē   də ˈkwin(t)siˑ

DeQuindre
   Park, *stadium, Detroit, MI*   di-KIN-druh   diˈkindrə

Derain
   André, *French painter*   duh-REⁿ   dərẽ

Derbe
   Biblical name   DUHR-buh   ˈdəʳbə

Derby
   1. city, CT, KS; town, VT   DUHR-bē   ˈdəʳbiˑ
   2. city, horse race, England   DAHR-bē   ˈdɑʳbiˑ

Derby Line
   village, VT   DUHR-bē LĪN   ˌdəʳbiˑ ˈlain

Derbyshire
   county, England   DAHR-bē-shuhr, -SHIR   ˈdɑʳbiˑʃəʳ, -ˌʃiʳ

Derdriu
   legendary Irish heroine   DER-dr͞oo   ˈderdruː

Derek
   pers. name   DER-ik   ˈderik

Deringer
   Henry, *US gunsmith*   DER-uhn-juhr   ˈderəndʒəʳ

Dermoptera
   colugos or flying lemurs   DUHR-MAHP-tuh-ruh   ˌdəʳˈmɑptərə

Dermot
   pers. name   DUHR-muht   ˈdəʳmət

Deroyce
   pers. name (F. D. Etheredge)   duh-ROIS   dəˈrɔis

Derrick
   pers. name   DER-ik   ˈderik

Derrida
   Jacques, *French literary critic*   der-ē-DAH, Ⓢ duhr-ē-DAH   deriːdɑ, Ⓢ dəriːˈdɑ

Derry
  town, Ireland   DER-ē   ˈderiˑ

Dershowitz
  Alan, *US lawyer, writer*   DUHR-shuh-WITS   ˈdəʳʃəˌwits

Der Spiegel
  German newspaper   der SHPĒ-guhl   deʳ ˈʃpiːgəl

Derwent
  river, England   DUHR-wuhnt   ˈdəʳwənt

Derwent Water
  lake, England   DUHR-wuhnt WAWT-uhr, WAHT-uhr   ˈdəʳwənt ˌwɔːʈəʳ, ˌwɑʈəʳ

Desai
  Morarji Ranchhodji, *prime minister, India*   duh-SĪ   dəˈsɑi

de Sales
  St. Francis, *French ecclesiastic*   duh SAHL, Ⓢ duh SAHL(Z), duh SĀLZ   də sɑːl, Ⓢ də ˈsɑl(z), də ˈseːlz

Des Allemands, Lake
  lake, LA   LĀK des AL-muhn   ˌleːk des ˈælmən

Des Arc
  town, AR   DEZ AHRK   ˈdez ˌɑrk

Descartes
  René, *French philosopher*   dā-KAHRT   deːkɑːrt, Ⓢ deːˈkɑʳt

Deschutes
  river, county, OR   di-SHŌŌTS   diˈʃuːts

Desdemona
  wife of Othello   DEZ-duh-MŌ-nuh   ˌdezdəˈmoːnə

Deseret News
  Salt Lake City newspaper   DEZ-uh-RET N(Y)ŌŌZ   ˌdezəˈret ˈn(j)uːz

Desha
  county, AR   duh-SHĀ   dəˈʃeː

Desi
  pers. name (D. Arnaz)   DEZ-ē   ˈdeziˑ

De Sica
  Vittorio, *Italian director*   di SĒ-kuh   di ˈsiːkə

Desiderius
  1. *pers. name, German*   DĀ-zē-DĀR-yus, -DĀ-rē-us   ˌdeːziˈdeːrjus, -ˈdeːriːus
  2. *Latin*   DES-i-DIR-ē-uhs   ˌdesiˈdiriːəs

Désiré, Désirée
  pers. name, French   dā-zē-RĀ   deːziːreː

Des Moines
  river, city, IA   di-MOIN   diˈmɔin

Desmond
  pers. name   DEZ-muhnd   ˈdezmənd

de Soto
  Hernando, *Spanish explorer*   duh SŌT-ō   də ˈsoːʈoː

Des Peres
  city, MO   duh PER(Z)   də ˈper(z)

Des Plaines
  river, city, IL   des PLĀNZ   des ˈpleːnz

des Prez, Desprez
  see Josquin des Prez

Dessalines
  Jean Jacques, *emperor, Haiti*   dā-sah-LĒN   deːsɑːliːn

Dessalinienne, La
  see La Dessalinienne

Key (col. 2):   a: fad   ā: fade   ah: father   ar: marry   aw: law   e: fed   ē: feed   er: merry   i: hid   ī: hide   ō: coat   ōō: boot
oi: boy   ow: now   u: put   uh: above   uhr: bird   ch: chop   ng: ring   sh: show   th: thick   <u>th</u>: this   zh: measure

Dessau
  city, Germany   DES-ow   'des₁ɑu

de Stijl
  Dutch school of art   duh STĪL   də 'stɑil

d'Estournelles de Constant
  Paul, French diplomat (Nobel 1909)   dā-tur-NEL duh kawⁿ-STAHⁿ   deːturnel də kɔ̃stɑ̃

Detlev
  1. pers. name   DET-luhf   'detləf
  2. German   DET-lef   'detlef

de Tocqueville
  see Tocqueville, de

Detroit
  city, MI; river, US & Canada   di-TROIT, DĒ-TROIT   di'trɔit, 'diːˌtrɔit

Dettifoss
  waterfall, Iceland   DET-ē-FAWS   'deti·ˌfɔːs

Deucalion
  son of Prometheus, husband of   d(y)o͞o-KĀL-yuhn   d(j)uː'keːljən
    Pyrrha

Deuel
  county, NE, SD   D(Y)o͞o-uhl   'd(j)uːəl

Deukmejian
  George, governor, CA   d(y)o͞ok-MĀ-j(ē-)uhn   d(j)uːk'meːdʒ(iː)ən

Deus
  Latin for 'God'   DĀ-us, DĒ-uhs   'deːus, 'diːəs

Deusdedit
  pope   DĒ-uhs-DED-uht, -DĒD-uht   ˌdiːəs'dedət, -'diːdət

Deuteronomy
  Old Testament book   D(Y)o͞oT-uh-RAHN-uh-mē   ˌd(j)uːtə'rɑnəmi·

Deutsch
  German (lang.)   DOICH   'dɔitʃ

Deutsche Mark
  German currency   DOICH(-uh)-MAHRK,   ˌdɔitʃ(ə)'mɑʳk,
                      DOICH(-uh)-MAHRK   'dɔitʃ(ə)ˌmɑʳk

Deutschland
  Germany   DOICH-LAHNT, Ⓢ DOICH-luhnd,   'dɔitʃˌlɑnt, Ⓢ 'dɔitʃlənd,
                      DOICH-LAND   'dɔitʃˌlænd

Deutschland über Alles
  German anthem   DOICH-lahnt ue-buhr AHL-uhs   'dɔitʃlɑːnt yːbər 'aːləs

Deux-Sèvres
  department, France   duh(r)-SEVR, –SEV-ruh   dœːsevr, -sevrə

De Valera
  Eamon, Irish political leader   DEV-uh-LER-uh, DEV-uh-LIR-uh   ˌdevə'lerə, ˌdevə'lirə

Devanagari
  Sanskrit script   DĀ-vuh-NAHG-uh-rē   ˌdeːvə'nɑgəri·

Devane
  William, US actor   duh-VĀN   də'veːn

Devault
  Memorial Stadium, Bristol, VA   duh-VŌ   də'voː

Deventer
  city, Netherlands   DĀ-vuhn-tuhr   'deːvəntəʳ

Devereaux Meadow
  Raleigh, NC   DEV-uh-RŌ MED-ō, MED-uh   'devəˌroː 'medoː, 'medə

Devereux
  English family, earls of Essex   DEV-uh-Ro͞oKS, -Ro͞o, -REKS, -ruh, -RŌ   'devəˌruːks, -ˌruː, -ˌreks, -rə,
                                                         -ˌroː

Devito
   Danny Michael, *US actor*   duh-VĒT-ō   də'viːțoː

Devon
   1. former county, England; river,   DEV-uhn   'devən
      Scotland
   2. river, Nottinghamshire, England   DĒ-vuhn   'diːvən
   3. pers. name   DEV-uhn, di-VAHN *(D. White)*   'devən, di'vɑn *(D. White)*

Devonian
   geologic period   di-VŌ-nē-uhn   di'voːniːən

Devonshire
   county, England   DEV-uhn-shuhr, -SHIR   'devənʃərᵉ, -,ʃirᵉ

De Voto
   Bernard A., *US historian*   di VŌT-ō   di 'voːțoː

De Vries
   Peter, *US writer*   di VRĒS   di 'vriːs

DeVries
   Dr. William C., *US surgeon*   duh-VRĒS, duh-VRĒZ   də'vriːs, də'vriːz

de Waart
   Edo, *Dutch conductor*   duh VAHRT   də 'vɑːʳt

Dewar's
   Scotch whiskey   D(Y)OO-uhrz, DURZ   'd(j)uːəʳz, 'duʳz

Dewey
   John, *US educator;* Melvil, *US*   D(Y)OO-ē   'd(j)uːiˑ
      librarian; Thomas, *US politician;*
      pers. name

Dewhurst
   Colleen, *Canadian actress*   D(Y)OO-HUHRST   'd(j)uː,həʳst

Dexedrine
   tdmk for an appetite suppressant   DEK-suh-DRĒN, -DRIN   'deksə,driːn, -,drin

Dexter
   pers. name   DEKS-tuhr   'dekstəʳ

Dezhnev
   cape, Russia   dezh-NYAWF, desh-NYAWF   deʒ'njɔːf, deʃ'njɔːf

Dezhneva, Mys [Dezhnev]
   cape, Russia   MIS dezh-NYAW-vuh,   'mis deʒ'njɔːvə, deʃ'njɔːvə
                         desh-NYAW-vuh

Dhahran
   city, Saudi Arabia   dah-RAHN, DAH-huh-RAHN   dɑ'rɑn, ,dɑhə'rɑn

Dhaka
   see Dacca

Dharma Bums, The
   novel, Jack Kerouac   thuh DAHR-muh BUHMZ   ðə 'dɑʳmə 'bəmz

Dhaulagiri
   mtn., Nepal   DOW-luh-GIR-ē   ,dɑulə'giriˑ

Dhelfoi [Delphi]
   village, Greece   thel-FĒ   ðel'fiː

Dhu'l-Hijja
   Islamic month   dool-HI-yah   duːl'hijɑ

Dhu'l-Qa'dah
   Islamic month   dool-KAH-dah   duːl'kɑdɑ

Diabelli
   Anton, *Austrian composer and music*   DĒ-ah-BEL-ē   ,diːɑ'beliː
      publisher

Diablo
   Stadium, *Tempe, AZ*   dē-AB-lō, dī-AB-lō   diː'æbloː, dɑi'æbloː

Key (col. 2):   a: fad   ā: fade   ah: father   ar: marry   aw: law   e: fed   ē: feed   er: merry   i: hid   ī: hide   ō: coat   ōō: boot
oi: boy   ow: now   u: put   uh: above   uhr: bird   ch: chop   ng: ring   sh: show   th: thick   th: this   zh: measure

Diablo Valley
  College, *CA*   dē-AB-lō, dī-AB-lō   diːˈæbloː, daiˈæbloː

Diaghilev
  Sergei Pavlovich, *Russian ballet*   DYAHG-yil-yif, Ⓢ dē-AHG-uh-LEF   ˈdjɑːgjiljif, Ⓢ diːˈɑgəˌlef
    producer

Diaguita
  S. American people   DĒ-uh-GĒT-uh   ˌdiːəˈgiːʈə

Dialo
  lang., Senegal   dē-AL-ō   diːˈæloː

Diamantina
  river, Australia   DĪ-uh-muhn-TĒ-nuh   ˌdaiəmənˈtiːnə

Diana
  Roman moon goddess and virgin   dī-AN-uh   daiˈænə
    huntress; pers. name

Diane
  pers. name   dī-AN, dē-AN   daiˈæn, diːˈæn

Dianetics
  movement founded by L. Ron   DĪ-uh-NET-iks   ˌdaiəˈneʈiks
    Hubbard

Dianthus
  plant   dī-AN(T)-thuhs   daiˈæn(t)θəs

Diarmaid, Diarmid
  1. pers. name   DUHR-muhd, DUHR-muht   ˈdərməd, ˈdərmət
  2. Irish Gaelic   DYUHR-mit   ˈdjərmit

Dias
  Bartholomeu, *Portuguese navigator*   DĒ-AHSH   ˈdiːˌɑːʃ

Diaspora
  dispersal of people from their   dī-AS-p(uh-)ruh   daiˈæsp(ə)rə
    homeland

Diaz
  1. pers. name   DĒ-ahs   ˈdiːɑs
  2. Portuguese   DĒ-uhsh   ˈdiːəʃ
  3. Spanish   DĒ-ahs, DĒ-ahth   ˈdiːɑs, ˈdiːɑθ

Diaz de Vivar
  Rodrigo, *Spanish hero, aka* El Cid   DĒ-ahth thā vē-VAHR   ˈdiːɑθ ðeː βiːˈβɑr

Díaz Ordaz
  Gustavo, *Mexican politician*   DĒ-ahs awr-THAHS   ˈdiːɑs ɔːrˈðɑs

Diblah [Diblath]
  Biblical name   DIB-luh   ˈdiblə

Diblaim
  Biblical name   dib-LĀ-uhm, DIB-LĀ-uhm,   dibˈleːəm, ˈdibˌleːəm,
    div-LAH-yim   divˈlajim

Diblath [Diblah]
  Biblical name   DIB-LATH, div-LAHT   ˈdibˌlæθ, divˈlat

Dibon
  Biblical name   DĪ-BAHN, dē-VAWN   ˈdaiˌbɑn, diːˈvɔːn

Dibon-gad
  Biblical name   DĪ-BAHN-GAD, dē-VAWN-GAHD   ˈdaiˌbanˈgæd, diːˈvɔːnˈgad

Dibri
  Biblical name   DIB-RĪ, DIB-rē, div-RĒ   ˈdibˌrai, ˈdibriˑ, divˈriː

Dick
  pers. name   DIK   ˈdik

Dickcissel
  songbird   dik-SIS-uhl, DIK-SIS-uhl   dikˈsisəl, ˈdikˌsisəl

---

Foreign Sounds: ue: *Fr.* **rue**, *Ger.* f**ü**llen   uh(r): *Fr.* b**oeuf**, *Ger.* H**ö**hle   <u>kh</u>: *Ger.* i**ch**, *Scot.* lo**ch**   g̱: *Sp.* ami**g**o   <u>v</u>: *Sp.* ha**b**lar
hl: *Welsh* **Ll**anelli.   CAPITALS: primary stress.   SMALL CAPS: secondary stress.   Ⓢ: U.S. pron.   Ⓔ: British pron.

Dickens
　Charles, *English novelist*　　　　DIK-uhnz　　　　　　　　　'dikənz
Dickensian
　pert. to Dickens　　　　　　　　di-KEN-zē-uhn　　　　　di'kenziːən
Dictys
　protector of Danae and Perseus　DIK-tuhs　　　　　　　　'diktəs
Diderik
　pers. name, Dutch　　　　　　　DĒ-duh-RIK　　　　　　'diːdəˌrik
Diderot
　Denis, *French philosopher*　　　　dē-DRŌ, ⑤ DĒD-uh-RŌ　diːdroː, ⑤ 'diːdəˌroː
Didion
　Joan, *US writer*　　　　　　　　DID-ē-uhn　　　　　　　'didiːən
Dido
　queen of Carthage　　　　　　DĪD-ō　　　　　　　　　'daidoː
Didrikson
　pers. name (B. D. Zaharias)　　DĒ-drik-suhn　　　　　　'diːdriksən
Didymus
　Biblical name　　　　　　　　DID-uh-muhs　　　　　　'didəməs
Diederich
　pers. name, German　　　　　　DĒ-duh-RIKH　　　　　　'diːdəˌriç
Diedrich
　pers. name　　　　　　　　　DĒ-drik　　　　　　　　'diːdrik
Diefenbaker
　John, *Canadian statesman*　　　DĒ-fuhn-BĀ-kuhr　　　　'diːfənˌbeːkəʳ
Diefenbaker
　John George, *Canadian politician*　DĒ-fuhn-BĀ-kuhr　　　'diːfənˌbeːkəʳ
Dieffenbachia
　plant　　　　　　　　　　　DĒ-fuhn-BAK-ē-uh,　　　ˌdiːfən'bækiːə, ˌdiːfən'bɑkiːə
　　　　　　　　　　　　　　　DĒ-fuhn-BAHK-ē-uh
Die Fledermaus
　operetta, J. Strauss　　　　　dē FLĀD-uhr-MOWS　　　diː 'fleːdəʳˌmɑus
Diego
　pers. name, Spanish　　　　　DYĀ-ḡō, THYĀ-, ⑤ dē-Ā-ḡō　'djeːɣoː, 'ðjeː-, ⑤ diː'eːgoː
Diego Garcia
　island, Indian Ocean　　　　　dē-Ā-ḡō gahr-SĒ-uh　　　diːˌeːgoː gɑʳ'siːə
Diegueño
　N. American people　　　　　DĒ-uh-GĀN-yō　　　　　ˌdiːə'geːnjoː
Diekirch
　town, beer, Luxembourg　　　DĒ-KIRKH, DĒ-KIRK　　'diːˌkiʳx, 'diːˌkiʳk
Diels
　Otto, *German chemist (Nobel 1950)*　DĒLS, DĒLZ　　　　　'diːls, 'diːlz
Diem
　see Ngo Dinh Diem
Dien Bien Phu
　Vietnam　　　　　　　　　DYEN BYEN FŌŌ　　　ˌdjen ˌbjen 'fuː
Dieppe
　seaport, France　　　　　　DYEP, ⑤ dē-EP　　　　　djep, ⑤ diː'ep
Diesel
　Rudolf, *German engineer*　　　DĒ-zuhl　　　　　　　'diːzəl
Dies Irae
　Latin hymn　　　　　　　DĒ-ās IR-ā, DĒ-āz, Ē-RĀ, IR-Ī, Ē-RĪ　ˌdiːeːs 'ireː, ˌdiːeːz, 'iːˌreː,
　　　　　　　　　　　　　　　　　　　　　　　　　　'irˌai, 'iːˌrɑi
Diest
　town, Belgium　　　　　　DĒST　　　　　　　　'diːst

Key (col. 2): a: fad ā: fade ah: father ar: marry aw: law e: fed ē: feed er: merry i: hid ī: hide ō: coat ōō: boot
oi: boy ow: now u: put uh: above uhr: bird ch: chop ng: ring sh: show th: thick th: this zh: measure

Die Stem van Suid-Afrika

national anthem, South Africa   dē SHTĀM fahn suid-AHF-rē-kuh   diː ˈʃteːm faːn syidˈɑːfriːkə

Diet

legislature (e.g. Japanese parliament)   DĪ-uht   ˈdɑiət

Dieter

pers. name   DĒT-uhr   ˈdiːṭəʳ

Dietrich

1. pers. name, French   dē-TRĒK   diːtriːk

2. German   DĒ-tri<u>kh</u>   ˈdiːtriç

Dietz

Howard, US lyricist   DĒTS   ˈdiːts

Dieudonné

pers. name, French   dyuh(r)-daw-NĀ   djœdɔːneː

Die Walküre

opera, R. Wagner   DĒ vahl-KUE-ruh   ˌdiː valˈkyːrə

Dighton

city, KS; town, MA   DĪT-n   ˈdɑitn̩

Dihevi

lang., Maldives   duh-HĀ-vē   dəˈheːviˑ

Dijon

city, France; mustard   dē-ZHAWⁿ; dē-ZHAHN   diːʒɔ̃; diːˈʒɑn

Dijonnaise

mustard sauce   dē-zhaw-NEZ   diːʒɔːnez

Diklah

Biblical name   DIK-luh, DIK-LAH, dik-LAH   ˈdiklə, ˈdikˌlɑ, dikˈlɑ

Dilean

Biblical name   DĪ-lē-uhn, DIL-ē-uhn, dil-AHN   ˈdɑiliːən, ˈdiliːən, dilˈɑn

Dillingham

division, AK   DIL-ing-HAM   ˈdiliŋˌhæm

Dillon

pers. name   DIL-uhn   ˈdilən

DiMaggio

Joe, US baseball player   duh-MAJ-ē-ō, duh-MAJ-ō   dəˈmædʒiːˌoː, dəˈmædʒoː

Dimashq [Damascus]

city, Syria   di-MAHSHK   diˈmɑʃk

Dimitri

1. pers. name   duh-MĒ-trē   dəˈmiːtriˑ

2. Mod. Greek   <u>th</u>ē-MĒ-trē   ðiːˈmiːtriː

3. Russian   dim-YĒ-tri   ḍimˈjiːtrij

Dimitrie

pers. name, Romanian   di-MĒ-tri-(y)e   diˈmiːtri(j)e

Dimitrije

pers. name, Serbo-Croatian   dē-MĒ-trē-ye   diːˈmiːtriːje

Dimitry

1. pers. name, Romanian   di-MĒ-tri   diˈmiːtri

2. Russian   dim-YĒ-tri   ḍimˈjiːtrij

Dimnah

Biblical name   DIM-nuh, dim-NAH   ˈdimnə, dimˈnɑ

Dimoetes

brother of Troezen   DĪ-muh-WĒT-ēz   ˌdɑiməˈwiːṭiːz

Dimon

Biblical name   DĪ-MAHN, DĪ-muhn, dē-MŌN   ˈdɑiˌmɑn, ˈdɑimən, diːˈmoːn

Dimonah

Biblical name   dī-MŌ-nuh, duh-; DĒ-mō-NAH   dɑiˈmoːnə, də-; ˌdiːmoːˈnɑ

Foreign Sounds: ue: *Fr.* **rue**, *Ger.* **füllen**   uh(r): *Fr.* **boeuf**, *Ger.* **Höhle**   <u>kh</u>: *Ger.* **ich**, *Scot.* **loch**   g̅: *Sp.* **amigo**   v̠: *Sp.* **hablar** hl: *Welsh* **Llanelli**.   CAPITALS: primary stress.   SMALL CAPS: secondary stress.   Ⓢ: U.S. pron.   Ⓔ: British pron.

Dina
  pers. name   DĒ-nuh, DĪ-nuh   'diːnə, 'dainə

Dinah
  pers. name   DĪ-nuh   'dainə

Dinant
  resort, Belgium   dē-NAH[n]   diːnã

Dinara Planina [Dinaric Alps]
  Alpine mtn. range   DĒ-nuh-rah plah-NĒ-nuh   'diːnɑrɑ plɑ'niːnə

Dinaric
  Alps, Alpine mtn. range   duh-NAR-ik   də'nærik

Dinesen
  Isak, Danish writer   DĒ-nuh-suhn, DIN-uh-suhn   'diːnəsən, 'dinəsən

Dingell
  John D., US politician   DING-guhl   'diŋgəl

Ding Mao
  Chinese year (Hare)   DING MOW   'diŋ 'mɑu

Dinhabah
  Biblical name   DIN-(h)uh-buh, din-HĀ-buh,   'din(h)əbə, din'heːbə,
                    din-HAHV-ah   din'hɑvɑ

Dinis [Diniz]
  king of Portugal   dē-NĒSH   di:'niːʃ

Diniz [Dinis]
  king of Portugal   dē-NĒZH, dē-NĒZ   di:'niːʒ, di:'niːz

Dinka
  people, Africa   DING-kuh   'diŋkə

Dinkelacker
  German beer   DING-kuh-LAHK-uhr   'diŋkə,lɑkəʳ

Dinkelacker Weizenkrone
  German beer   DING-kuh-LAHK-uhr   'diŋkə,lɑkəʳ 'vaitsən,kroːnə
                    VĪT-suhn-KRŌ-nuh

Dinnyés
  Lajos, Hungarian politician DIN-YĀSH   'din,jeːʃ

Dino
  pers. name   DĒ-nō   'diːnoː

Dinwiddie
  county, VA   DIN-WID-ē, din-WID-ē   'din,widiˑ, din'widiˑ

Dio Cassius
  Roman historian   DĪ-ō KASH-(ē-)uhs, KAS-ē-uhs ,daioː 'kæʃ(iː)əs, 'kæsiːəs

Dio Chrysostom
  Greek rhetorician   DĪ-Ō kris-AHS-tuhm   'dai,oː kris'ɑstəm

Diocletian
  Roman emperor   DĪ-uh-KLĒ-shuhn   ,daiə'kliːʃən

Diodorus Siculus
  Greek historian   DĪ-uh-DAWR-uh(s) SIK-yuh-luhs ,daiə,dɔːrə(s) 'sikjələs

Diogenes
  Greek philosopher   dī-AHJ-uh-NĒZ   dai'adʒə,niːz

Diogenes Laertius
  ancient Greek writer   dī-AHJ-uh-NĒZ lā-UHR-sh(ē-)uhs dai'adʒə,niːz leː'ərʃ(iː)əs

Diogo
  pers. name, Portuguese DYŌ-goo, <u>TH</u>YŌ-goo   'djoːguː, 'ðjoːguː

Diomede
  islands, Bering Strait; English form DĪ-uh-MĒD   'daiə,miːd
    of Diomedes

Diomedes
  name of two Greek heroes DĪ-uh-MĒD-ēz   ,daiə'miːdiːz

Key (col. 2): a: fad ā: fade ah: father ar: marry aw: law e: fed ē: feed er: merry i: hid ī: hide ō: coat o͞o: boot
oi: boy ow: now u: put uh: above uhr: bird ch: chop ng: ring sh: show th: thick <u>th</u>: this zh: measure

Dion
  Laconian king; pers. name DĒ-AHN, DĪ-AHN, -uhn 'diː,ɑn, 'dɑi,ɑn, -ən
Dione
  mother of Aphrodite; mother of Niobe dī-Ō-nē, dē-Ō-nē dɑi'oːniˑ, diː'oːniˑ
  & Pelops; satellite of Saturn
Dionisio
  1. pers. name, Italian DĒ-ō-NĒZ-yō ˌdiːoː'niːzjoː
  2. Spanish dyō-NĒS-yō, thyō- djo'niːsjoː, ðjoː-
Dionne
  pers. name dē-AHN diː'ɑn
Dionysia
  festival of Dionysus DĪ-uh-NISH-uh, -NIZ-ē-uh, -NIS-ē-uh ˌdɑiə'niʃə, -'niziːə, -'nisiːə
Dionysiac
  pert. to Dionysia DĪ-uh-NISH-ē-AK, -NIZ-ē-AK, -NIS-ē-AK ˌdɑiə'niʃiːˌæk, -'niziːˌæk,
  -'nisiːˌæk
Dionysian
  pert. to Dionysus DĪ-uh-NISH-uhn, -NĪ-sē-uhn, ˌdɑiə'niʃən, -'nɑisiːən,
  -NIZ-ē-uhn -'niziːən
Dionysios
  pers. name, Mod. Greek thyawn-YĒS-yaws ðjoːn'jiːsjoːs
Dionysius
  tyrants of Syracuse; pers. name DĪ-uh-NISH-(ē-)uhs, -NIS-ē-uhs, ˌdɑiə'niʃ(iː)əs, -'nisiːəs,
  -NĪ-sē-uhs -'nɑisiːəs
Dionysus
  Greek god of wine DĪ-uh-NĪ-suhs, DĪ-uh-NĒ-suhs ˌdɑiə'nɑisəs, ˌdɑiə'niːsəs
Diop
  David, *Senegalese poet* DYAWP 'djoːp
Dior
  Christian, *fashion designer* dē-AWR, DĒ-AWR diː'oːr, 'diːˌoːr
Dioscorus
  pope dī-AHS-kuh-ruhs dɑi'ɑskərəs
Dioscuri
  the twins Castor and Pollux DĪ-uhs-KYUR-Ī, dī-AHS-kyuh-RĪ ˌdɑiəs'kjur,ɑi, dɑi'ɑskjəˌrɑi
Diosdado
  pers. name, Spanish dē-ōs-THAHTH-ō diːoːs'ðɑðoː
Diotrephes
  Biblical name dī-AH-truh-FĒZ dɑi'ɑtrəˌfiːz
Dioula
  lang., Ivory Coast dē-Ō-luh, dē-OO-luh diː'oːlə, diː'uːlə
Diplodocus
  dinosaur duh-PLAHD-uh-kuhs də'plɑdəkəs
·Dirac
  P. A. M., *British physicist (Nobel* di-RAK di'ræk
  1933)
Directoire
  French Directory dē-rek-TWAHR diːrektwɑːr
Dirk
  1. pers. name DUHRK 'dərk
  2. Dutch DIRK 'dirk
Dis [Orcus]
  Roman god of the Underworld DIS 'dis
Disch-Falk
  Field, *ballpark, Austin, TX* DISH-FAW(L)K 'diʃ'fɔː(l)k
Dishan
  Biblical name DĪ-SHAN, di-SHAHN 'dɑiˌʃæn, di'ʃɑn

Foreign Sounds: ue: *Fr.* **rue,** *Ger.* **füllen** uh(r): *Fr.* **boeuf,** *Ger.* **Höhle** kh: *Ger.* **ich,** *Scot.* **loch** ḡ: *Sp.* **amigo** ṿ: *Sp.* **hablar**
hl: *Welsh* **Llanelli.** CAPITALS: primary stress. SMALL CAPS: secondary stress. Ⓢ: U.S. pron. Ⓔ: British pron.

Dishon
  Biblical name   DĪ-SHAHN, di-SHŌN   'dɑiˌʃɑn, di'ʃoːn
Dísir
  Scandinavian goddesses of battle and   DIS-IR   'disˌiʳ
  fate
Disney
  Walt, *US cartoon pioneer*   DIZ-nē   'dizniˑ
Dis Pater
  Roman Father of Riches, ruler of the   DIS PĀT-uhr, PAHT-uhr   ˌdis 'peːʈəʳ, 'pɑʈəʳ
  Underworld
Disraeli
  Benjamin, *English statesman*   diz-RĀ-lē   diz'reːliˑ
District of Columbia
  see Columbia
Dives
  Roman god of riches   DĪ-vēz   'dɑiviːz
Divinitatis Baccalaureus
  bachelor of divinity, D.B.   duh-VIN-uh-TĀT-uhs   dəˌvinə'teːʈəs ˌbækə'loːriːəs,
                                           BAK-uh-LŌR-ē-uhs, -LAWR-ē-uhs   -'loːriːəs
Divinitatis Doctor
  doctor of divinity, D.D.   duh-VIN-uh-TĀT-uhs DAHK-TAWR   dəˌvinə'teːʈəs 'dɑkˌtoːʳ
Divinyls
  rock group   di-VĪ-nlz   di'vainl̩z
Diwali
  Hindu festival   DIV-AHL-ē   'divˌɑliˑ
Dixie
  nickname for the southeastern US;   DIK-sē   'diksiˑ
  pers. name
Dixieland
  nickname for the southeastern US   DIK-sē-LAND   'diksiˑˌlænd
Dizahab
  Biblical name   DIZ-uh-HAB, DĪ-zuh-HAB,   'dizəˌhæb, 'daizəˌhæb,
                                           DĒT-sah-HAHV   ˌdiːtsɑ'hɑv
Djajawidjaja
  Range, *mtn. range, Indonesia*   JAH-yuh-wuh-JAH-yuh   ˌdʒɑjəwə'dʒɑjə
Djakarta, Jakarta
  city, Indonesia   juh-KAHRT-uh   dʒə'kɑʳʈə
Djambi, Jambi
  river, province, town, Indonesia   JAHM-BĒ   'dʒɑmˌbiˑ
Django
  pers. name   JANG-gō   'dʒæŋgoː
Djawa
  see Java
Djerma
  African people   dē-ER-muh, DYER-muh   diː'eʳmə, 'djeʳmə
Djhowtey [Thoth]
  Egyptian god of wisdom   JŌ-tā   'dʒoːteː
Djibouti, Jibuti
  republic, Africa   juh-BOOT-ē   dʒə'buːʈiˑ
Djilas
  Milovan, *Yugoslav politician*   JĒ-lahs   'dʒiːlɑs
Djoser
  Egyptian king   ZHŌ-suhr, ZŌ-suhr   'ʒoːsəʳ, 'zoːsəʳ
Dmitri
  pers. name   di-MĒ-trē   di'miːtriː

Key (col. 2): a: fad ā: fade ah: father ar: marry aw: law e: fed ē: feed er: merry i: hid ī: hide ō: coat oo̅: boot
oi: boy ow: now u: put uh: above uhr: bird ch: chop ng: ring sh: show th: thick th̲: this zh: measure

Dmitry
    pers. name, Russian   DMĒ-tri   'dm̪iːtrij

Dmowski
    Roman, *Polish statesman*   DMAWF-SKĒ, ⓢ duh-MAWF-skē   'dmɔːfˌskiˑ, ⓢ dəˈmɔːfskiˑ

Dnepr [Dnieper]
    river, Europe   duhn-YEPR   dənˈjepr̪

Dnepropetrovsk
    city, Ukraine   duhn-YEP-rō-pyuh-TRAWFSK, NEP-rō-puh-TRAWFSK   dənˌjeproːpjəˈtrɔːfsk, ˌneproːpəˈtrɔːfsk

Dnestr [Dniester]
    river, Ukraine   duh-NYESTR   dəˈnjestr

Dnieper [Dnepr]
    river, Europe   NĒ-puhr, duh-NĒ-puhr   'niːpəʳ, dəˈniːpəʳ

Dniester [Dnestr]
    river, Ukraine   NĒ-stuhr, duh-NĒ-stuhr   'niːstəʳ, dəˈniːstəʳ

Doberman Pinscher
    dog breed   DŌ-buhr-muhn PIN-chuhr   ˌdoːbəʳmən 'pintʃəʳ

Dobie
    pers. name   DŌ-bē   'doːbiˑ

Döblin
    Alfred, *German physician and writer*   DUH(R)-BLĒN   'dœːˌbliːn

Dobrynin
    Anatoly, *Russian diplomat*   duh-BRIN-yin   dəˈbrinjin

Doc
    short for doctor; pers. name   DAHK   'dɑk

Docetism
    early Christian doctrine   dō-SĒT-ɪz-uhm, DŌ-suh-TɪZ-uhm   doːˈsiːtˌizəm, 'doːsəˌtizəm

Doctorow
    E. L., *US writer*   DAHK-tuh-RŌ   'dɑktəˌroː

Doctor Zhivago
    novel by Boris Pasternak   DAHK-tuhr zhuh-VAHG-ō   'dɑktər ʒəˈvɑgoː

Dodai
    Biblical name   DŌ-DĪ, DŌD-ē-Ī, dō-DĪ   'doːˌdai, 'doːdiːˌai, doːˈdai

Dodanim
    Biblical name   DŌD-n-ɪM, dō-DĀ-nim, DAW-dah-NĒM   'doːdn̪ˌim, doːˈdeːnim, ˌdoːdɑˈniːm

Dodavah [Dodavahu]
    Biblical name   DAHD-uh-vuh, DŌD-uh-vuh, dō-DĀ-vuh, DŌ-dah-VAH-hoo   'dadəvə, 'doːdəvə, doːˈdeːvə, ˌdoːdɑ'vahuː

Dodavahu
    Biblical name   dō-DAV-uh-H(Y)OO, DŌD-uh-VĀ-H(Y)OO, DŌ-dah-VAH-hoo   doːˈdævəˌh(j)uː, ˌdoːdəˈveːˌh(j)uː, ˌdoːdɑ'vahuː

Dodecanese
    island group, Greece   dō-DEK-uh-NĒZ, -NĒS   doːˈdekəˌniːz, -ˌniːs

Dodgson
    Charles, *English writer, aka* Lewis Carroll   DAHJ-suhn, DAHD-suhn   'dadʒsən, 'dadsən

Dodie
    pers. name   DŌD-ē   'doːdiˑ

Dodo
    Biblical name   DŌD-ō, DŌD-uh, dō-DŌ   'doːdoː, 'doːdə, doːˈdoː

Dodoma
    city, Tanzania   DŌD-uh-muh, -MAH   'doːdəmə, -ˌmɑ

Foreign Sounds: ue: *Fr.* **rue**, *Ger.* f**ü**llen   uh(r): *Fr.* b**oeuf**, *Ger.* H**ö**hle   <u>kh</u>: *Ger.* i**ch**, *Scot.* lo**ch**   g̱: *Sp.* ami**g**o   v̱: *Sp.* ha**b**lar
hl: *Welsh* **Ll**anelli.   CAPITALS: primary stress.   SMALL CAPS: secondary stress.   ⓢ: U.S. pron.   ⓔ: British pron.

Dodona
   ancient town, Greece   duh-DŌ-nuh, dō-   də'doːnə, doː-

Doeg
   Biblical name   DŌ-EG, daw-EG   'doː,eg, dɔː'eg

Doenitz
   see Dönitz

Dogon
   lang., people, Mali, Burkina Faso   DŌ-GAHN   'doː,gɑn

Dogrib
   N. American people   DAW-GRIB, DAHG-RIB   'dɔː,grib, 'dɑg,rib

Doha
   city, Qatar   DŌ-huh   'doːhə

Doheny
   Edward L., Memorial Library, *Los*   duh-HĒ-nē   də'hiːni·
     Angeles, CA

Doherty
   Joseph, *Irish nationalist*   DAW(-uh)rt-ē, DAH(-uh)rt-ē,   'dɔː(ə)ʳʈi·, 'dɑ(ə)ʳʈi·,
                                 DAWR-uht-ē   'dɔːʳəʈi·

Dohnányi
   Ernő, *Hungarian composer*   daw(kh)-NAHN-yē, dahk-NAHN-yē   dɔː(x)'nɑːnji·, dɑk'nɑnji·

Dohnanyi, von
   Christoph, *German conductor;*   FAWN dawkh-NAHN-yē   ,fɔːn dɔːx'nanji·
     Ernst, *German composer*

Doisy
   E. A., *US biochemist (Nobel 1943)*   DOI-zē   'dɔizi·

Dolby
   tdmk for an audio recording system   DŌL-bē, DAHL-bē   'doːlbi·, 'dɑlbi·

Dolgoruky
   Russian noble family   DUHL-guh-ROO-kyiy   ,dəlgə'ruːkjij

Dolius
   gardener for Odysseus   DŌ-lē-uhs, DŌL-yuhs   'doːliːəs, 'doːljəs

Dolly
   pers. name   DAHL-ē   'dɑli·

Dolmetsch
   Arnold, *British musician*   DAHL-MECH   'dɑl,metʃ

Dolomites
   Alpine mtn. range   DŌ-luh-MĪTS, DAHL-uh-MĪTS   'doːlə,mɑits, 'dɑlə,mɑits

Dolomitiche, Alpi [Dolomites]
   Alpine mtn. range   AHL-pē DŌ-luh-mē-TĒ-kā   'ɑlpiː ,doːləmiː'tiːkeː

Dolomiti [Dolomites]
   Alpine mtn. range   DŌ-luh-MĒ-tē   ,doːlə'miːti·

Dolon
   Trojan killed by Diomedes   DŌ-luhn, DŌ-LAHN   'doːlən, 'doː,lɑn

Dolores
   pers. name   duh-LŌR-uhs, duh-LAWR-uhs   də'loːrəs, də'lɔːrəs

Dom
   pers. name   DAHM   'dɑm

Domagk
   Gerhard, *German bacteriologist,*   DŌ-MAHK   'doː,mɑk
     pathologist (Nobel 1939)

Domain Chandon
   winery, CA   dō-MĀN shan-DAHN, duh-MĀN,   doː,meːn ʃæn'dɑn, də,meːn,
                              shan-DAWN   ʃæn'dɔːn

Domenichino [Zampieri]
   Bolognese painter   dō-MĀ-ni-KĒ-nō   doː,meːni'kiːnoː

Key (col. 2): a: fad ā: fade ah: father ar: marry aw: law e: fed ē: feed er: merry i: hid ī: hide ō: coat ōō: boot
oi: boy ow: now u: put uh: above uhr: bird ch: chop ng: ring sh: show th: thick <u>th</u>: this zh: measure

Domenici
  Pete V., *US politician*   duh-MEN-uh-chē, DAHM-uh-NĒ-chē   də'menətʃi˙, ˌdamə'niːtʃi˙

Domenico
  1. pers. name   duh-MEN-i-kō   də'menikoː
  2. Italian   dō-MĀ-nē-kō   doː'meːniːkoː

Doménikos
  pers. name, Greek   dō-MĀ-nē-kaws   doː'meːniːkɔːs

Domesday Book, Doomsday Book
  11th c. survey of English land   DOOMZ-DĀ, DŌMZ-DĀ   'duːmzˌdeː, 'doːmzˌdeː

Domfürsten
  German beer   DAWM-FUR-stuhn   'dɔːmˌfyʳstən

Dómhnall
  pers. name, Irish   THUV-nuhl, THUN-uhl, DAHN-uhl   'ðuvnəl, 'ðunəl, 'danəl

Dominate
  term for Late Roman Empire   DAHM-uh-NĀT   'daməˌneːt

Domingo
  1. Placido, Mexican tenor   duh-MING-gō, dō-   də'miŋgoː, doː-
  2. pers. name, Portuguese   doo-MI(NG)-goo, thoo-   duː'mĩ(ŋ)guː, ðuː-
  3. Spanish   dō-MING-gō, thō-   doː'miŋgoː, ðoː-

Domingos
  pers. name, Portuguese   du-MĒ(NG)-goosh, thoo-, -goos   du'miː(ŋ)guːʃ, ðuː-, -guːs

Dominic
  pers. name   DAHM-uh-nik   'damənik

Dominica
  island, West Indies   DAHM-uh-NĒ-kuh, duh-MIN-uh-kuh   ˌdamə'niːkə, də'minəkə

Dominican
  pert. to Dominica *or* Dominican Republic   DAHM-uh-NĒ-kuhn, duh-MIN-uh-kuhn   ˌdamə'niːkən, də'minəkən

Dominican Republic
  republic, West Indies   duh-MIN-uh-kuhn   də'minəkən

Dominicus
  1. pers. name   duh-MIN-i-kuhs   də'minikəs
  2. German   dō-MĒ-nē-kus   doː'miːniːkus

Dominique
  pers. name, French   daw-mē-NĒK   dɔːmiːniːk

Dominus
  Latin for 'Lord'   DAHM-i-nuhs, DAHM-i-NUS, DŌ-mi-NOOS   'daminəs, 'damiˌnus, 'doːmiˌnuˑs

Domitian
  Roman emperor   duh-MISH-uhn   də'miʃən

Domitius
  Roman name   duh-MISH-(ē-)uhs   də'miʃ(iː)əs

Dom Pérignon
  French monk; champagne   dawⁿ pā-rēn-YAWⁿ, ⓢ DAHM PER-uhn-YAWN   dɔ̃ peːriːnjɔ̃, ⓢ ˌdam ˌperən'jɔːn

Domrémy
  brandy   dawⁿ-rā-MĒ   dɔ̃reːmiː

Don
  river, Russia; river, Yorkshire; river, Scotland; pers. name   DAHN   'dan

Dona Ana
  county, NM   DŌN-yuh AN-uh   ˌdoːnjə 'ænə

Donagh
  pers. name, Irish   THUHN-uh, DUHN-uh   'ðənə, 'danə

Foreign Sounds: ue: *Fr.* **rue**, *Ger.* **füllen**   uh(r): *Fr.* **boeuf**, *Ger.* **Höhle**   kh: *Ger.* **ich**, *Scot.* **loch**   g̱: *Sp.* **amigo**   v̱: *Sp.* **hablar**
hl: *Welsh* **Llanelli.**   CAPITALS: primary stress.   SMALL CAPS: secondary stress.   ⓢ: U.S. pron.   ⓔ: British pron.

Donal
  pers. name   THŌO-nuhl, DAHN-uhl   'ðuːnəl, 'dɑnəl

Donald
  pers. name   DAHN-ld   'dɑnl̩d

Donatello
  Donato, *Italian sculptor*   DAHN-uh-TEL-ō   ˌdɑnə'teloː

Donatism
  Christian heresy   DAHN-uh-TIZ-uhm, DŌ-nuh-   'dɑnəˌtizəm, 'doːnə-

Donato
  pers. name, Italian   dō-NAH-tō   doː'nɑtoː

Donatus
  pers. name   do-NAH-tus   do'nɑtus

Donau [Danube]
  river, Europe   DŌ-NOW   'doːˌnɑu

Doncaster
  county borough, England   DAHNG-kuh-stuhr   'dɑŋkəstəʳ

Donegal
  city, Irish Republic   DAHN-i-GAWL, DUHN-i-GAWL   ˌdɑni'gɔːl, ˌdəni'gɔːl

Donets
  river, Russia and Ukraine   duh-NETS, duh-NYETS   də'nets, də'njets

Donetsk
  city, Ukraine   duh-NETSK, duh-NYETSK   də'netsk, də'njetsk

Don Giovanni
  opera, Mozart   DAHN JŌ-VAHN-nē, DAHN   ˌdɑn dʒoː'vɑnniː, ˌdɑn
                jē-uh-VAHN-ē   dʒiːə'vɑni·

Dönitz, Doenitz
  Karl, *German admiral*   DUH(R)-nits   'dœːnits

Dongting Hu, Tung-t'ing Hu
  lake, China   DUNG-TING HŌO   'duŋ'tiŋ 'huː

Doniphan
  county, KA   DAHN-uh-fuhn   'dɑnəfən

Donizetti
  Gaetano, *Italian composer*   DŌN-uh(d)-ZET-ē, DAHN-uh(d)-ZET-ē   ˌdoːnə(d)'zeʈi·, ˌdɑnə(d)'zeʈi·

Don Juan
  legendary Spanish lover   dahn (H)WAHN; *in Byron's poem* dahn   dɑn '(h)wɑn; *in Byron's*
                JŌO-uhn   *poem* dɑn 'dʒuːən

Donleavy
  J. P., *US writer*   dahn-LĒ-vē, DUHN-; DAHN-LĒ-vē,   dɑn'liːvi·, ˌdən-; 'dɑnˌliːvi·,
                DUHN-   'dən-

Donna
  pers. name   DAHN-uh   'dɑnə

Donnall
  pers. name   DAHN-l   'dɑnl̩

Donne
  John, *English poet*   DUHN   'dən

Donnelly, R.R.
  US printing co.   DAHN-l-ē   'dɑnl̩i·

Donny
  pers. name   DAHN-ē   'dɑni·

Donnybrook
  suburb, Dublin, Ireland   DAHN-ē-BRUK   'dɑni·ˌbruk

Donovan
  Scottish rock singer; pers. name   DAHN-uh-vuhn   'dɑnəvən

Don Pasquale
  opera, Donizetti   DAWN pahs-KWAHL-ā, DAHN   ˌdɔːn pɑs'kwɑleː, ˌdɑn

---

Key (col. 2): a: fad ā: fade ah: father ar: marry aw: law e: fed ē: feed er: merry i: hid ī: hide ō: coat ōō: boot
oi: boy ow: now u: put uh: above uhr: bird ch: chop ng: ring sh: show th: thick th̲: this zh: measure

Don Quixote
   novel, Cervantes   dahng kē-<u>KHŌ</u>-tä, Ⓢ DAHNG kē-HŌT-ē, DAHN, kē-HŌ-TÄ; Ⓔ dahng KWIK-suht, dahn   dɑŋ kiːˈxoːteː, Ⓢ ˌdɑŋ kiːˈhoːt̯iˑ, ˌdɑn, kiːˈhoːˌteː, Ⓔ dɑŋ ˈkwiksət, dɑn

Donus
   pope   DŌ-nuhs   ˈdoːnəs

Doomsday Book
   see Domesday Book

Doonesbury
   Trudeau comic strip   DOONZ-BER-ē, DOONZ-b(uh-)rē   ˈduːnzˌberiˑ, ˈduːnzb(ə)riˑ

Door
   county, WI   DŌR, DAWR   ˈdoːʳ, ˈdɔːʳ

Dophkah
   Biblical name   DAHF-kuh, dahf-KAH   ˈdɑfkə, dɑfˈka

Doppelgänger
   ghostly double   DAW-puhl-GENG-uhr, DUHB-uhl-GANG-uhr   ˈdɔːpəlˌgeŋəʳ, ˈdəbəlˌgæŋəʳ

Doppler effect
   change in frequency relative to speed   DAHP-luhr   ˈdɑpləʳ

Dor
   Biblical name   DAWR, DŌR   ˈdɔːʳ, ˈdoːʳ

Dora
   pers. name   DŌR-uh, DAWR-uh   ˈdoːrə, ˈdɔːrə

Dorado
   constellation   duh-RAHD-ō   dəˈrɑdoː

Dorati
   Antal, US composer and conductor   dawr-AHT-ē   dɔːrˈɑt̯iˑ

Dorcas
   pers. name   DAWR-kuhs   ˈdɔːʳkəs

Dorchester
   borough, England; county, MD, SC   DAWR-chuh-stuhr, DAWR-CHES-tuhr   ˈdɔːʳtʃəstəʳ, ˈdɔːʳˌtʃestəʳ

Dordogne
   dept., France   dawr-DAWN-yuh   dɔːrdɔːɲ

Dordrecht
   city, Netherlands   DAWR-DRE<u>KH</u>T   ˈdɔːʳˌdrext

Dordt
   College, IA   DAWRT   ˈdɔːʳt

Doré
   Gustave, French illustrator   daw-RĀ   dɔːreː

Doreen
   pers. name   daw-RĒN, duh-; DŌR-ēn, DAWR-   dɔːˈriːn, də-; ˈdoːriːn, ˈdɔːr-

Doria
   Andrea, Italian political leader   DAWR-yah, Ⓢ DŌR-ē-uh, DAWR-ē-uh   ˈdɔːrjɑ, Ⓢ ˈdoːriːə, ˈdɔːriːə

Dorian
   musical mode; pers. name   DŌR-ē-uhn, DAWR-ē-uhn   ˈdoːriːən, ˈdɔːriːən

Dorians
   ancient invaders of Greece   DŌR-ē-uhnz, DAWR-   ˈdoːriːənz, ˈdɔːr-

Doric order
   architectural order   DAWR-ik, DAHR-ik   ˈdɔːrik, ˈdɑrik

Doris
   mother of Nereids; pers. name   DAWR-uhs, DAHR-uhs   ˈdɔːrəs, ˈdɑrəs

Dorothea
   pers. name   DAWR-uh-TH<u>Ē</u>-uh, DAHR-   ˌdɔːrəˈθiːə, ˌdɑr-

Dorothée
   pers. name, French   daw-raw-TĀ   dɔːrɔːteː

Foreign Sounds: ue: *Fr.* **rue**, *Ger.* **füllen** uh(r): *Fr.* **boeuf**, *Ger.* **Höhle** <u>kh</u>: *Ger.* **ich**, *Scot.* **loch** ḡ: *Sp.* **amigo** v̱: *Sp.* **hablar** hl: *Welsh* **Llanelli**. CAPITALS: primary stress. SMALL CAPS: secondary stress. Ⓢ: U.S. pron. Ⓔ: British pron.

Dorothy
　pers. name　　　　　　　　DAWR-uh-thē, DAHR-　　　　　'dɔːrəθiˑ, 'dɑr-
Dorrigo
　town, Australia　　　　　　DAHR-i-gō, DAWR-i-gō　　　　'dɑrigoː, 'dɔːrigoː
Dorset
　county, England　　　　　　DAWR-suht　　　　　　　　　'dɔːʳsət
Dorsey
　James, Thomas, *US band leaders*　DAWR-sē　　　　　　　'dɔʳsiˑ
Dort
　city, Netherlands　　　　　DAWRT　　　　　　　　　　'dɔːʳt
Dortmund
　city, Germany　　　　　　DAWRT-MUNT, ⓢ DAWRT-muhnd　'dɔːʳt,munt, ⓢ 'dɔːʳtmənd
Dortmunder-Actien Alt
　German beer　　　　　　　DAWRT-MUN-duhr-AHK-tē-uhn AHLT　'dɔːʳt,mundəʳˌaktiːən 'alt
Dortmunder Kronen
　German beer　　　　　　　DAWRT-MUN-duhr KRŌ-nuhn　　'dɔːʳt,mundəʳ 'kroːnən
Dorus
　mythical ancestor of the Dorians　DŌR-uhs, DAWR-uhs　　　'doːrəs, 'dɔːrəs
Dorval
　airport, Montreal　　　　　dawr-VAHL　　　　　　　　dɔːr'vaˑl
DOS
　disk operating system (computer　DAHS　　　　　　　　　'das
　software)
Dos Equis (XX)
　Mexican beer　　　　　　　dōs EK-ēs　　　　　　　　doːs 'ekiːs
Dos Passos
　John, *US novelist*　　　　　duhs PAS-uhs　　　　　　　dəs 'pæsəs
Dostoyevsky
　Feodor, *Russian author*　　　duhs-TUH-YĀF-ski,　　　　dəs,təˈjeːfskij,
　　　　　　　　　　　　　ⓢ DAHS-tuh-YEF-skē,　　　　ⓢ ˌdastəˈjefskiˑ,
　　　　　　　　　　　　　DAHS-tuh-YEV-skē　　　　　ˌdastəˈjevskiˑ
Dothan
　city, AL　　　　　　　　　DŌ-thuhn　　　　　　　　　'doːθən
Dothan
　Biblical name　　　　　　DŌ-thuhn, daw-TAHN　　　　'doːθən, dɔː'tan
Dottie
　pers. name　　　　　　　DAHT-ē　　　　　　　　　'datiˑ
Douai, Douay
　city, France　　　　　　　DWE, du-Ā　　　　　　　　dwe, du'eː
Douala
　city, Cameroon　　　　　du-AHL-uh　　　　　　　　du'alə
Douay Bible
　English translation of Vulgate　dōo-Ā, DŌO-Ā　　　　　　du'ˑeː, 'duːˌeː
Doubleday
　Abner, *reputed US inventor of*　DUHB-uhl-DĀ　　　　　　'dəbəlˌdeː
　baseball
Doubs
　river, France　　　　　　DŌO　　　　　　　　　　'duː
Doug
　pers. name　　　　　　　DUHG　　　　　　　　　'dəg
Dougal
　pers. name　　　　　　　DŌO-guhl　　　　　　　　'duːgəl
Doughty
　Charles Montagu, *English poet and*　DOWT-ē　　　　　'dautiˑ
　traveler

Key (col. 2):　a: fad　ā: fade　ah: father　ar: marry　aw: law　e: fed　ē: feed　er: merry　i: hid　ī: hide　ō: coat　ōo: boot
oi: boy　ow: now　u: put　uh: above　uhr: bird　ch: chop　ng: ring　sh: show　th: thick　t͟h: this　zh: measure

Douglas		
pers. name, pl. name	DUHG-luhs	ˈdəgləs
Douglas-Home		
Alexander, *British statesman*	DUHG-luhs-HYO͞OM, [$] *also* DUHG-luhs-YO͞OM	ˌdəgləsˈhjuːm, [$] *also* ˌdəgləsˈjuːm
Doukas		
see Ducas		
Doukhobors, Dukhobors		
Russian religious sect	DO͞O-kuh-BAWRZ	ˈduːkəˌbɔːʳz
Doulton		
Sir Henry, *English potter*	DŌLT-n	ˈdoːltn̩
Dover		
DE, NH, NJ, OH; city, England	DŌ-vuhr	ˈdoːvəʳ
Dow		
lake, Africa; US chemical co.	DOW	ˈdɑu
Dow-Jones		
US financial publisher	DOW-JŌNZ	ˌdɑuˈdʒoːnz
Dowland		
John, *English lutenist, composer*	DOW-luhnd, DŌ-luhnd	ˈdɑulənd, ˈdoːlənd
Downing		
college, Cambridge Univ.	DOWN-ing	ˈdɑuniŋ
Doxiadis		
Konstantínos Apostolos, *Greek architect and planner*	dahks-YAH-thēs	dɑksˈjɑðiːs
D'Oyly Carte		
English light opera company	DOI-lē KAHRT	ˌdɔiliˑ ˈkɑʳt
Draco		
Athenian lawgiver; constellation	DRĀ-kō	ˈdreːkoː
Draconian		
pert. to Draco	drā-KŌ-nē-uhn, druh-KŌ-nē-uhn	dreːˈkoːniːən, drəˈkoːniːən
Draconids		
meteor shower	druh-KAHN-idz, druh-KŌ-nidz	drəˈkɑnidz, drəˈkoːnidz
Dracula		
novel, Bram Stoker	DRAK-yuh-luh	ˈdrækjələ
Drakensberg [Quathlamba]		
mtn. range, S. Africa	DRAHK-uhnz-BUHRG	ˈdrɑkənzˌbəʳg
Dramamine		
tdmk for a motion-sickness remedy	DRAM-uh-MĒN, DRAM-uh-min	ˈdræməˌmiːn, ˈdræməmin
Drambuie		
liqueur	dram-B(Y)O͞O-ē	dræmˈb(j)uːiˑ
Drammen		
port, Norway	DRAHM-uhn	ˈdrɑmən
Drava		
river, Europe	DRAHV-uh	ˈdrɑvə
Dravidian		
lang. family, India	druh-VID-ē-uhn	drəˈvidiːən
Dravidic		
pert. to Dravidian	druh-VID-ik	drəˈvidik
Dravosburg		
borough, PA	druh-VŌZ-BUHRG	drəˈvoːzˌbəʳg
Dred		
pers. name	DRED	ˈdred
Dreher		
Italian beer	DRĀ-(h)uhr	ˈdreː(h)əʳ

Dreiser
  Theodore, *US author* — DRĪ-zuhr — 'drɑizəʳ
Dresden
  city, Germany — DREZ-duhn — 'drezdən
Drew
  pers. name — DR‾OO — 'druː
Drexel
  University, *PA* — DREK-suhl — 'dreksəl
Dreyfus
  Alfred, *French army officer* — dre-FUES, ⓢ DRĪ-fuhs, DRĀ-fuhs — drefyːs, ⓢ 'drɑifəs, 'dreːfəs
Dreyfuss
  Richard Stephan, *US actor* — DRĪ-fuhs — 'drɑifəs
Drogheda
  port, Republic of Ireland — DROI-uhd-uh, DRAW-uhd-uh, DROID-uh — 'drɔiədə, 'drɔːədə, 'drɔidə
Druid
  one of a pre-Christian Celtic learned class — DR‾OO-uhd, DR‾OO-id — 'druːəd, 'druːid
Druidism
  beliefs & tenets of the Druids — DR‾OO-uhd-IZ-uhm — 'druːəd,izəm
Drury Lane
  English theatre — DRUR-ē LĀN — 'druri· 'leːn
Drusilla
  pers. name — dru-SIL-uh — dru'silə
Drusus
  Roman cognomen — DR‾OO-suhs — 'druːsəs
Druze
  religion — DR‾OOZ — 'druːz
Dryas
  son of Ares — DRĪ-uhs — 'drɑiəs
Dryden
  John, *English poet* — DRĪD-n — 'drɑidn̩
Dryer
  Fred, *US actor, football player* — DRĪ(-uh)r — 'drɑi(ə)ʳ
Dryope
  companion to the Hamadryad nymphs — DRĪ-uh-pē — 'drɑiəpi·
Dryops
  father of Dryope — DRĪ-AHPS — 'drɑi,ɑps
Drysdale
  pers. name — DRĪZ-DĀL — 'drɑiz,deːl
Dry Tortugas
  islands, FL — DRĪ tawr-T‾OO-guhz — ˌdrɑi tɔːʳ'tuːgəz
Duala
  lang., people, Africa — d(y)‾oo-AHL-uh — d(j)uː'ɑlə
Duane
  pers. name — DWĀN, duh-WĀN — 'dweːn, də'weːn
Duarte
  1. pers. name, Portuguese — DWAHR-tuh, THWAHR-, -tā — 'dwɑːrtə, 'ðwɑːr-, -teː
  2. Spanish — DWAHR-tā — 'dwɑrteː
Duarte
  José Napoleón, *Salvadoran politician* — DWAHR-TĀ — 'dwɑr,teː
Dubai, Dubayy
  city, United Arab Emirates — duh-BĪ, d‾oo-BĪ — də'bɑi, du·'bɑi

---

Dubbo
  city, Australia   DUHB-ō   'dəboː

Dubcek
  Alexander, *Czech politician*   DŌOB-CHEK   'duːb,t∫ek

Dublin
  Ireland   DUHB-lin   'dəblin

Dubliner
  resident of Dublin   DUHB-luh-nuhr   'dəblənəʳ

Duboeuf, Georges
  wine shipper   ZHAWRZH due-BUH(R)F   ʒɔːrʒ dybœf

Du Bois
  1. William Edward Burghardt, *US* d(y)ōo BOIS   d(j)uˑ 'bɔis
     educator
  2. city, PA   du-BOIS, DŌO-BOIS   du'bɔis, 'duː,bɔis

Dubois
  county, IN   du-BOIS, DŌO-BOIS   du'bɔis, 'duː,bɔis

Dubonnet
  aperitif   D(Y)ŌO-buh-NĀ   ,d(j)uːbəˈneː

Dubos
  René Jules, *US bacteriologist*   due-BŌ(S), ⑤ dōo-BŌS   dyːboː(s), ⑤ duːˈboːs

DuBose
  pers. name   d(y)ōo-BŌZ   d(j)uːˈboːz

Dubrovnik
  city, Croatia   DŌO-BRAWV-nik, du-BRAWV-nik   'duː,brɔːvnik, du'brɔːvnik

Dubs
  Jakob, *Swiss politician*   DUPS   'dups

Dubuffet
  Jean, *French artist*   due-bue-FE   dyːbyːfe

Dubuque
  city, Iowa   duh-BYŌOK   dəˈbjuːk

Ducas, Dukas, Doukas
  family name of Byzantine rulers of D(Y)ŌO-kuhs   'd(j)uːkəs
     the Eastern Roman Empire

Ducati
  Italian motorcycle co.   d(y)ōo-KAHT-ē   d(j)uːˈkɑ̈ţiˑ

Duchamp
  Marcel, *French painter*   due-SHAHⁿ   dyː∫ɑ̃

Duchesne
  river, county, UT   du-SHĀN   du'∫eːn

Duchin
  Peter, *US entertainer*   DŌO-chuhn   'duːt∫ən

Duchovny
  David, *US actor*   dōo-CHAHV-nē, -CHŌV-nē   duːˈt∫ɑvniˑ, -ˈt∫oːvniˑ

Ducommun
  Elie, *Swiss journalist (Nobel 1902)* due-kaw-MUHⁿ   dyːkɔmœ̃ː

Dudevant
  Amandine, *married name of* George   dued(-uh)-VAHⁿ   dyːd(ə)vɑ̃
  Sand

Dudley
  pers. name   DUHD-lē   'dədliˑ

Duesenberg
  US automobile   DŌO-zuhn-BUHRG   'duːzən,bəʳg

Duesseldorf
  airport, Düsseldorf   DUES-uhl-DAWRF,   'dysəl,dɔːʳf,
                                       ⑤ D(Y)ŌOS-uhl-DAWRF   ⑤ 'd(j)uːsəl,dɔːʳf

---

Foreign Sounds: ue: *Fr.* **rue**, *Ger.* **fü**llen uh(r): *Fr.* b**oeu**f, *Ger.* H**öh**le kh: *Ger.* i**ch**, *Scot.* lo**ch** ḡ: *Sp.* ami**g**o v̱: *Sp.* ha**b**lar
hl: *Welsh* **Ll**anelli. CAPITALS: primary stress. SMALL CAPS: secondary stress. ⑤: U.S. pron. ⑥: British pron.

Dufay
   Guillaume, *Burgundian composer*   due-FE, ⑤ dōō-FĪ   dyːfe, ⑤ duːˈfɑi

Dufy
   Raoul, *French artist*   due-FĒ   dyːfiː

Dugonics
   András, *Hungarian novelist*   DUG-aw-nich   ˈdugɔːnitʃ

Duisburg
   city, Germany   D(Y)ŌŌS-BURG, D(Y)ŌŌZ-BURG,   ˈd(j)uːs,buʳg, ˈd(j)uːz,buʳg,
                       -BUHRG   -,bəʳg

Dukakis
   Michael S., *US politician*   dōō-KAHK-uhs   duˑˈkɑkəs

Dukas
   Paul, *French composer*   due-KAHS   dyːkɑːs

Duke
   title; pers. name   D(Y)ŌŌK   ˈd(j)uːk

Dukeries, The
   region of Nottinghamshire, England   t̲h̲uh D(Y)ŌŌ-kuh-rēz   ðə ˈd(j)uːkəriˑz

Dukhobors
   see Doukhobors

Dulbecco
   Renato, *Italian-born US molecular*   DUHL-BEK-ō   ,dəlˈbekoː
     biologist (Nobel 1975)

Dulcinea
   beloved of Don Quixote   DUHL-suh-NĒ-uh, DUHL-suh-NĀ-uh   ,dəlsəˈniːə, ,dəlsəˈneːə

Dullea
   Keir, *US entertainer*   duh-LĀ   dəˈleː

Dulles
   John Foster, *US statesman*   DUHL-uhs   ˈdələs

Duluth
   city, MN   duh-LŌŌTH   dəˈluːθ

Duma
   Russian council   DŌŌ-muh, DŌŌ-MAH   ˈduːmə, ˈduː,mɑ

Dumah
   Biblical name   D(Y)ŌŌ-muh, dōō-MAH   ˈd(j)uːmə, duːˈmɑ

Dumas
   1. pers. name   d(y)ōō-MAH, D(Y)ŌŌ-MAH   d(j)uːˈmɑ, ˈd(j)uː,mɑ
   2. French   due-MAH   dyːmɑː

Du Maurier
   Dame Daphne, *English author*   d(y)u-MAWR-ē-Ā, d(y)u-MAHR-ē-Ā   d(j)uˈmɔːriː,eː, d(j)uˈmɑriː,eː

Dumbo
   Disney animated character   DUHM-bō   ˈdəmboː

Dum Dum
   city, India   DUHM DUHM   ˈdəm ,dəm

Dumfries and Galloway
   region, Scotland   DUHM-FRĒS uhn(d) GAL-uh-WĀ   ,dəmˈfriːs ən(d) ˈgælə,weː

Du Mont
   Allen Balcom, *US engineer*   D(Y)ŌŌ-MAHNT, d(y)ōō-MAHNT   ˈd(j)uː,mɑnt, d(j)uːˈmɑnt

Dunant
   J. H., *Swiss philanthropist (Nobel*   due-NAH^n dyːnɑ̄
     1901)

Dunaway
   Faye, *US actress*   DUHN-uh-WĀ   ˈdənə,weː

Dunbar
   John, *Scottish poet*   DUHN-BAHR, DUHM-BAHR   ˈdən,bɑʳ, ˈdəm,bɑʳ

Key (col. 2):   aː fad   āː fade   ahː father   arː **marry**   awː **law**   eː fed   ēː feed   erː **merry**   iː hid   īː hide   ōː coat   ōōː boot
oiː **boy**   owː **now**   uː put   uhː above   uhrː bird   chː chop   ngː ring   shː show   thː thick   t̲h̲ː this   zhː measure

Duncan		
pers. name	DUHNG-kuhn	'dəŋkən
Dunciad		
poem, A. Pope	DUHN-sē-AD	'dənsiː,æd
Dundalk		
1. seaport, Ireland	DUHN-DAWK, DUHN-DAWLK	ˌdən'dɔːk, ˌdən'dɔːlk
2. city, MD	DUHN-DAWK	'dənˌdɔːk
Dundee		
city, Scotland	DUHN-DĒ	ˌdən'diː
Dunedin		
city, FL; city, New Zealand	DUH-NĒD-n	ˌdə'niːdn̩
Dungeness		
National Wildlife Refuge, *WA; headland, England*	DUHN-juh-NES, DUHNJ-NES, DUHN-juh-NES	ˌdəndʒə'nes, ˌdəndʒ'nes, 'dəndʒəˌnes
Dungog		
town, Australia	duhn-GAHG, duhn-GAWG	dən'gɑg, dən'gɔːg
Dunhill		
tobacco products co.	DUHN-HIL	'dənˌhil
Dunkerque, Dunkirk		
seaport, France	duh^{n}-KERK, [$] DUHN-KUHRK, DUHN-KUHRK	dœ̃kerk, [$] 'dənˌkə^{r}k, ˌdən'kə^{r}k
Dunkirk		
city, IN, NY	DUHN-KUHRK	'dənˌkə^{r}k
Dun Laoghaire [Dunleary]		
port of Dublin, Ireland	DOON LER-uh, DUHN LER-uh, DUHN LIR-ē	ˌduˑn 'lerə, ˌdən 'lerə, ˌdən 'liriˑ
Dunleary [Dun Laoghaire]		
port of Dublin, Ireland	DUHN-LIR-ē	ˌdən'liriˑ
Dunlop		
1. tire co.	DUHN-LAHP	'dənˌlɑp
2. British family name	DUHN-LAHP	ˌdən'lɑp
Dunnachie		
pers. name	DUHN-uh-khē, -kē	'dənəçiˑ, -kiˑ
Dunsinane		
1. fortified hill, Scotland	DUHN-SIN-uhn	ˌdən'sinən
2. in Macbeth, *Shakespeare*	DUHN-suh-NĀN, DUHN-suh-NĀN	ˌdənsə'neːn, 'dənsəˌneːn
Duns Scotus		
John, *Scottish philosopher*	DUHN SKŌT-uhs	ˌdən 'skoːt̬əs
Dunstan		
pers. name	DUHN-stuhn	'dənstən
Du Page		
College, *county, IL*	d(y)oo PĀJ	d(j)uː 'peːdʒ
Duparc		
Henri, *French composer*	due-PAHRK	dyːpɑrk
Dupin		
Amandine, *maiden name of A. Dudevant (pseudonym George Sand);* Chevalier Auguste, *fictional detective of E. A. Poe*	due-PE^{n}	dyːpẽ
Duplessis		
Maurice Le Noblet, *Canadian politician*	due-plā-SĒ	dyːpleˑsiː
Duplin		
county, NC	D(Y)OO-pluhn	'd(j)uːplən

Foreign Sounds: ue: *Fr.* **rue**, *Ger.* **füllen** uh(r): *Fr.* **boeuf**, *Ger.* **Höhle** kh: *Ger.* **ich**, *Scot.* **loch** g̃: *Sp.* **amigo** v: *Sp.* **hablar** hl: *Welsh* **Llanelli**. CAPITALS: primary stress. SMALL CAPS: secondary stress. [$]: U.S. pron. [£]: British pron.

Du Pont, Dupont
   US chemical co.; Pierre Samuel IV,   d(y)o͞o-PAHNT, D(Y)O͞O-PAHNT   d(j)uˈpɑnt, ˈd(j)uːˌpɑnt
   US politician

duPont de Nemours
   E. I., *US chemical co. founder*   d(y)o͞o-PAHNT dā nä-MAWRZ   d(j)uˈˌpɑnt deː neːˈmɔːʳz

Dupree
   J. J. M. M. W. G., *character in*   d(y)u-PRḖ   d(j)uˈpriː
   Milne poem

Duquesne
   University, *PA*   d(y)u-KĀN   d(j)uˈkeːn

Du Quoin
   city, IL   do͞o-KOIN   duːˈkɔin

Dura
   Biblical name   D(Y)UR-uh, do͞o-RAH   ˈd(j)urə, duːˈrɑ

Duracell
   tdmk for batteries   D(Y)UR-uh-SEL   ˈd(j)urəˌsel

Dura-Europus
   ancient Seleucid city   D(Y)UR-uh-yu-RŌ-puhs   ˌd(j)urəjuˈroːpəs

Durand
   city, MI; city, WI   d(y)u-RAND   d(j)uˈrænd

Duran Duran
   rock group   d(y)u-RAN d(y)u-RAN   d(j)uˈræn d(j)uˈræn

Durango
   state, Mexico   d(y)u-RANG-gō   d(j)uˈræŋgoː

Durant
   Will *and* Ariel, *US historians*   d(y)u-RANT   d(j)uˈrænt

Durante
   Jimmy, *US entertainer*   duh-RANT-ē   dəˈrænţiˈ

Duras
   French dukedom   due-RAHS   dyːrɑːs

Durban
   seaport, South Africa   DUHR-buhn   ˈdəʳbən

Durenberger
   David Ferdinand, *US politician*   D(Y)UR-uhn-BUHR-guhr   ˈd(j)urənˌbəʳgəʳ

Dürer
   Albrecht, *German painter/engraver*   DUER-uhr, Ⓢ D(Y)UR-uhr   ˈdyːrəʳ, Ⓢ ˈd(j)urəʳ

Durga Puja
   Indian festival   DUR-guh PO͞O-juh   ˈdurgə ˈpuːdʒə

Durham
   US pl. name; city, county, England   DUHR-uhm, DUH-ruhm, DUR-uhm   ˈdər-əm, ˈdə-rəm, ˈdurəm

Durian
   tasty, foul-smelling fruit   D(Y)UR-ē-uhn, D(Y)UR-ē-AHN   ˈd(j)uriːən, ˈd(j)uriːˌɑn

Dürkheim
   1. Emile, *French sociologist*   duer-KEM   dyːrkem
   2. town, Germany   DURK-HĪM, Ⓢ DIRK-HĪM, DUHRK-   ˈdyʳkˌhaim, Ⓢ ˈdiʳkˌhaim, ˈdəʳk-

Durning
   Charles, *US actor*   DUHR-ning   ˈdəʳniŋ

Durocher
   Leo, *US baseball player, manager*   duh-RŌ-shuhr   dəˈroːʃəʳ

Durrell
   Lawrence, Gerald, *English authors*   DUH-ruhl, DUR-uhl, DUHR-uhl   ˈdə-rəl, ˈdurəl, ˈdər-əl

Dürrenmatt
   Friedrich, *Swiss writer*   DUER-uhn-MAHT   ˈdyrənˌmɑt

Key (col. 2):   aː fad   ā: fade   ah: father   ar: marry   aw: law   e: fed   ē: feed   er: merry   i: hid   ī: hide   ō: coat   o͞o: boot
oi: boy   ow: now   u: put   uh: above   uhr: bird   ch: chop   ng: ring   sh: show   th: thick   <u>th</u>: this   zh: measure

Dur-Sharrukin
 ancient Assyrian city   DUR-shah-R͞OO-kuhn   ˌdu^rʃɑˈruːkən

Duryea
 Charles Edgar *and* James Frank,   DUR-YĀ, DUR-ē-Ā   ˈdurˌjeː, ˈduriːˌeː
  US inventors and manufacturers

Duse
 Eleanora, *Italian actress*   D͞OO-zā   ˈduːzeː

Dushanbe
 city, Tadzhikistan   d(y)͞oo-SHAHM-buh,   d(j)uːˈʃambə,
      Ⓢ d(y)͞oo-SHAHM-bā   Ⓢ d(j)uˈˈʃambeː

Dussault
 Nancy, *US entertainer*   D(Y)͞OO-SAWLT   ˈd(j)uːˌsɔːlt

Dussehra
 Indian festival   DUHS-uh-ruh   ˈdəsərə

Düsseldorf
 city, Germany   DUES-uhl-DAWRF,   ˈdysəlˌdɔː^rf,
      Ⓢ D(Y)͞OO-suhl-DAWRF   Ⓢ ˈd(j)uːsəlˌdɔː^rf

Dustin
 pers. name   DUHS-tuhn   ˈdəstən

Dutchess
 county, NY   DUHCH-uhs   ˈdətʃəs

Dutch [Netherlandic]
 lang., Netherlands, Belgium,   DUHCH   ˈdətʃ
  Suriname, Antilles

Dutoit
 Charles, *Swiss conductor*   due-TWAH, Ⓢ duh-TWAH   dyːtwaː, Ⓢ dəˈtwɑ

Dutra
 Eurico, *president, Brazil*   D͞OO-trah   ˈduːtrɑ

Du'uzu
 Babylonian month   du-͞OO-z͞oo   duˈuːzuː

Duval
 county, FL, TX   d͞oo-VAWL, duh-VAWL, -VAL   duːˈvɔːl, dəˈvɔːl, -ˈvæl

Duvalier
 Jean-Claude, *dictator, Haiti*   due-vahl-YĀ, Ⓢ d(y)u-VAL-yā   dyːvaːljeː, Ⓢ d(j)uˈvæljeː

Duvall
 Robert, *US actor*   d(y)u-VAWL, d(y)u-VAL   d(j)uˈvɔːl, d(j)uˈvæl

Duve
 Christian de, *Belgian chemist,*   D͞OO-vuh   ˈduːvə
  biologist (Nobel 1974)

Du Vigneaud
 Vincent, *US biochemist (Nobel 1955)*   d(y)͞oo VĒN-yō   d(j)uː ˈviːnjoː

Duwamish, Dwamish
 river, WA   duh-WAHM-ish, DWAHM-ish   dəˈwamiʃ, ˈdwamiʃ

Dvina
 river, gulf, Belorussia, Latvia, Russia   DVYĒ-nah, Ⓢ duh-VĒ-nuh   ˈdvjiːnɑː, Ⓢ dəˈviːnə

Dvinsk
 city, Latvia   DVYINSK, Ⓢ duh-VINSK   ˈdvjiṇsk, Ⓢ dəˈvinsk

Dvorak
 1. Antonin, *Bohemian composer*   (duh-)-VAWR-ZHAHK   (də)ˈvɔːrˌʒɑk
 2. US pers. name; keyboard layout   (duh-)-VAWR-AK, (duh-)-VAWR-ZHAK   (də)ˈvɔːrˌæk, (də)ˈvɔːrˌʒæk

Dwayne
 pers. name   DWĀN, duh-WĀN   ˈdweːn, dəˈweːn

Dwight
 pers. name   DWĪT, duh-WĪT   ˈdwait, dəˈwait

Foreign Sounds: ue: *Fr.* **rue**, *Ger.* **füllen**   uh(r): *Fr.* **boeuf**, *Ger.* **Höhle**   kh: *Ger.* **ich**, *Scot.* **loch**   g̱: *Sp.* **amigo**   v̱: *Sp.* **hablar** hl: *Welsh* **Llanelli**.   CAPITALS: primary stress.   SMALL CAPS: secondary stress.   Ⓢ: U.S. pron.   Ⓔ: British pron.

Dyak [Dayak]
   people, lang., Sarawak & Borneo   DĪ-AK   'dɑi̩æk

Dyckman Oval
   New York City site   DĪK-muhn Ō-vuhl   'dɑikmən 'oːvəl

Dyersburg
   State Jr. College, TN   DĪ(-uh)rz-BUHRG   'dɑi(ə)ʳz̩bəʳg

Dyfed
   county, ancient kingdom, Wales   DUHV-ed, DUHV-id   'dəved, 'dəvid

Dylan
   1. pers. name   DIL-uhn   'dilən
   2. Welsh   DUHL-ahn, -uhn   'dələːn, -ən

Dymo
   tdmk for a labeling machine   DĪ-mō   'dɑimoː

Dymoke
   English family of Lincolnshire   DIM-uhk   'dimək
      holding office of king's champion

D'Youville
   College, NY   DYŌO-VIL, DYŌO-vuhl   'djuː̩vil, 'djuːvəl

Dysart
   Richard, US actor   DĪ-SAHRT   'dɑi̩sɑʳt

dysprosium
   element   dis-PRŌ-zē-uhm, dis-PRŌ-zh(ē-)uhm   dis'proːziːəm, dis'proːʒ(iː)əm

Dyula
   lang., people, Ivory Coast, Burkina   dē-ŌO-luh, DYŌO-luh   diː'uːlə, 'djuːlə
      Faso, Ghana

Dzhugashvili
   Iosif, orig. name of Joseph Stalin   jōo-guhsh-VYĒL-yē   dʒuːgəʃ'vjiːljiˑ

Dzerzhinsky, Dzerzhinski
   Feliks Edmundovich, Russian   dyir-ZHEN-skyiy, (d)zir-   djiʳ'ʒiːnskjij, (d)ziʳ-
      politician

Dzindza
   lang., Africa   (D)ZIN-(d)zuh   '(d)zin(d)zə

Dzongkha
   lang., Bhutan   DZAWNG-kuh   'dzɔːŋkə

Dzungarian Ala Tau
   mtn. range, Kazakhstan, China   (d)zung-GER-ē-uhn ᴀʜ-lah TOW,   (d)zuŋ'geriːən ̩ɑlɑ 'tɑu,
       (d)zung-GAR-ē-uhn   (d)zuŋ'gæriːən

Key (col. 2):   a: fad ā: fade ah: father ar: marry aw: law e: fed ē: feed er: merry i: hid ī: hide ō: coat ōō: boot
oi: boy ow: now u: put uh: above uhr: bird ch: chop ng: ring sh: show th: thick th̲: this zh: measure

E

E. coli
    bacteria Escherichia coli   Ē KŌ-LĪ   ˌiː ˈkoːˌlɑi

Eadbert, Eadberht
    Anglo-Saxon king   ED-buhrt, A-uhd-BUHRT   ˈedbəʳt, ˈædˌbəʳt

Eadweard
    pers. name   ED-wuhrd   ˈedwəʳd

Eagleton
    Thomas Francis, *US politician*   Ē-guhl-tuhn   ˈiːgəltən

Eaker
    Ira Clarence, *US general*   Ā-kuhr   ˈeːkəʳ

Eakins
    Thomas, *US painter and sculptor* Ā-kinz   ˈeːkinz

Ealing
    borough, England   Ē-ling   ˈiːliŋ

Eames
    pers. name   ĀMZ, ĒMZ   ˈeːmz, ˈiːmz

Eames
    Charles, *US designer*   ĒMZ   ˈiːmz

Eamon, Eamonn
    pers. name   Ā-muhn   ˈeːmən

Eannatum
    Sumerian king   Ē-uh-NĀT-uhm, Ā-uh-NAHT-uhm   ˌiːəˈneːʈəm, ˌeːəˈnɑʈəm

Earhart
    Amelia, *US aviator*   ER-HAHRT, IR-HAHRT   ˈeʳˌhɑʳt, ˈiʳˌhɑʳt

Earl, Earle
    pers. name   UHRL, UHR-uhl   ˈəʳl, ˈərəl

Early
    Jubal, *American militarist*   UHR-lē   ˈəʳliˑ

Earnest
    pers. name   UHR-nuhst   ˈəʳnəst

Earp
    Wyatt, *US law officer*   UHRP   ˈəʳp

Eartha
    pers. name   UHR-thuh   ˈəʳθə

Earvin
    pers. name   UHR-vin   ˈəʳvin

Eastcheap
    street, market area, London   ĒS(T)-CHĒP   ˈiːs(t)ˌtʃiːp

Eastern Nazarene
    College, *MA*   Ē-stuhrn NAZ-uh-RĒN, NAZ-uh-RĒN   ˈiːstəʳn ˌnæzəˈriːn, ˈnæzəˌriːn

East Feliciana
    parish, LA   ĒST fuh-LISH-ē-AN-uh   ˌiːst fəˌliʃiːˈænə

Eastham
  town, MA   Ē-STAM   'iː‚stæm

Easthampton
  town, MA   ē-STAM(P)-tuhn, ēst-HAM(P)-tuhn   iː'stæm(p)tən, iːst'hæm(p)tən

Easton
  Sheena, *pop singer*   Ē-stuhn   'iːstən

East Sussex
  county, England   ēs(t) SUHS-iks   iːs(t) 'səsiks

Eau Claire
  city, county, WI   ō KLAR, ō KLER   oː 'klæʳ, oː 'kleʳ

Ebal
  Biblical name   Ē-buhl, ā-VAHL   'iːbəl, eː'vɑl

Ebbets
  Field, *ballpark, Brooklyn, NY*   EB-uhts   'ebəts

Ebbw Vale
  town, Wales   EB-o͞o VĀL   ‚ebuː 'veːl

EBCDIC
  extended binary coded decimal   EP-suh-DIK, EB-suh-DIK   'epsə‚dik, 'ebsə‚dik
    interchange code

Ebed
  Biblical name   Ē-BED, EV-ed   'iː‚bed, 'eved

Ebed-melech
  Biblical name   Ē-BED-MEL-EK, EV-ed-MEL-E<u>KH</u>   'iː‚bed'mel‚ek, 'eved'mel‚ex

Ebel
  jewelers   ā-BEL, Ā-buhl   eː'bel, 'eːbəl

Eben
  pers. name   EB-uhn   'ebən

Ebenezer
  1. pers. name   EB-uh-NĒ-zuhr   ‚ebə'niːzəʳ
  2. French   ā-bā-nā-ZER   eːbeːneːzer

Eber
  Biblical name   Ē-buhr, EB-uhr, EV-er   'iːbəʳ, 'ebəʳ, 'ever

Eberhard, -hardt
  pers. name, German   Ā-buhr-HAHRT   'eːbəʳ‚hɑʳt

Eberhart
  Richard, *US poet*   EB-uhr-HAHRT   'ebəʳ‚hɑʳt

Ebert
  Roger Joseph, *US film critic*   Ē-buhrt   'iːbəʳt

Ebez
  Biblical name   Ē-BEZ, EV-ETS   'iː‚bez, 'ev‚ets

Ebiasaph
  Biblical name   i-BĪ-uh-SAF, EV-yah-SAHF   i'bɑiə‚sæf, ‚evjɑ'sɑf

Ebionism
  Gnostic heresy   Ē-bē-uh-NIZ-uhm, EB-   'iːbiːə‚nizəm, 'eb-

Ebla
  ancient city, Syria   EB-luh, Ē-bluh   'eblə, 'iːblə

Ebony
  magazine; pers. name   EB-uh-nē   'ebəniˑ

Eboracum
  Latin name for York, England   i-BAWR-uh-kuhm, i-BAHR-uh-kuhm,   i'bɔːrəkəm, i'bɑrəkəm,
                    Ē-buh-RAHK-uhm   ‚iːbə'rɑkəm

Ebro
  river, Spain   Ā-<u>v</u>rō   'eːβroː

Écarté
  game   Ā-kahr-TĀ   ‚eːkɑʳ'teː

Key (col. 2):   a: fad   ā: fade   ah: father   ar: marry   aw: law   e: fed   ē: feed   er: merry   i: hid   ī: hide   ō: coat   o͞o: boot
oi: boy   ow: now   u: put   uh: above   uhr: bird   ch: chop   ng: ring   sh: show   th: thick   <u>th</u>: this   zh: measure

Ecbatana
   capital city of Median dynasty   ek-BAT-n-uh   ek'bætŋə

Ecce Homo
   depiction of Christ crowned with   EK-ā HŌ-mō, EK-ē   ‚eke· 'hoːmoː, ‚eki·
     thorns

Eccles
   Sir John Carew, *Australian*   EK-uhlz   'ekəlz
     neurophysiologist (Nobel 1963)

Ecclesia
   Athenian assembly   i-KLĀ-zh(ē-)uh, i-KLĒ-, -ZĒ-uh   i'kleːʒ(iː)ə, i'kliː-, -ziːə

Ecclesiastes
   Old Testament book   ik-LĒ-zē-AS-tēz, ek-   ik‚liːziː'æstiːz, ek-

Ecclesiasticus
   Old Testament book   ik-LĒ-zē-AS-ti-kuhs, ek-   ik‚liːziː'æstikəs, ek-

Echegaray y Eizaguirre
   José, *Spanish dramatist,*   ā-chā-ḡah-RĪ ē ā-thah-ḠWIR-ā,   eːtʃeːɣaˈrai iː eːθaˈɣwireː,
     mathematician (Nobel 1904)   ā-sah-ḠWIR-ā   eːsaˈɣwireː

Echeverría
   Esteban, *Argentine poet*   Ā-chā-ver-RĒ-ah   ‚eːtʃeːverˈriːɑ

Echidna
   half-female, half-serpent monster in   i-KID-nuh   i'kidnə
     Greek mythology; spiny anteater

Echinoderms
   marine invertebrates   i-KĪ-nuh-DUHRMZ   i'kɑinə‚dəʳmz

Echlin
   US motor vehicle parts co.   EK-luhn   'eklən

Echo
   nymph rejected by Narcissus   EK-ō   'ekoː

Echuca
   town, Australia   uh-CHOO-kuh   ə'tʃuːkə

Eck, Rusty
   Stadium, *Wichita, KS*   RUHS-tē EK   'rəsti· 'ek

Eckerd
   College, *FL*   EK-uhrd   'ekəʳd

Eckhard
   pers. name, German   EK-HAHRT   'ek‚hɑʳt

Eckstine
   Billy (William Clarence), *US singer*   EK-STĪN   'ek‚stɑin

Eco
   Umberto, *Italian author*   EK-ō   'ekoː

Ecorse
   city, MI   Ē-KAWRS   'iː‚kɔːʳs

Ector
   pers. name   EK-tuhr   'ektəʳ

Ecuador
   republic, S. America   EK-wuh-DAWR, EK-wuh-DAWR   'ekwə‚dɔːʳ, ‚ekwə'dɔːʳ

Ecuadorean
   pert. to Ecuador   EK-wuh-DAWR-ē-uhn   ‚ekwə'dɔːriːən

Ed
   pers. name   ED   'ed

Edam
   town, Netherlands; cheese   ĒD-uhm, Ē-DAM   'iːdəm, 'iː‚dæm

Edar
   Biblical name   Ē-DAHR, ED-er   'iː‚dɑʳ, 'eder

Foreign Sounds: ue: *Fr.* **rue**, *Ger.* **füllen** uh(r): *Fr.* **boeuf**, *Ger.* **Höhle** kh: *Ger.* **ich**, *Scot.* **loch** ḡ: *Sp.* **amigo** v: *Sp.* **hablar** hl: *Welsh* **Llanelli**. CAPITALS: primary stress. SMALL CAPS: secondary stress. ⑤: U.S. pron. £: British pron.

Edda
   Icelandic saga   ED-uh   'edə
Eddie, Eddy
   pers. name   ED-ē   'edi·
Edelman
   Gerald M., *US biochemist (Nobel*   ED-l-muhn   'edḷmən
      1972); Marian Wright, *children's*
      rights activist
Edelman
   Marian Wright, *US children's*   ĀD-l-muhn   'eːdḷmən
      advocate
Edelred [Aethelheard]
   Mercian cleric   E<u>TH</u>-uhl-RED, ED-l-   'eðəl‚red, 'edḷ-
Eden
   paradise; US pl. name   ĒD-n   'iːdṇ
Edentata
   toothless mammals   Ē-DEN-TAHT-uh, Ē-DEN-TĀT-uh   ‚iː‚den'taʈə, ‚iː‚den'teːʈə
Eder
   German river   ĀD-uhr   'eːdəʳ
Ederle
   Gertrude, *sports personality*   ED-uhr-lē   'edəʳliˑ
Edessa
   ancient city, Mesopotamia   i-DES-uh   i'desə
Edgar
   pers. name   ED-guhr   'edgəʳ
Edgard
   pers. name, French   ed-GAHR   edgaːr
Edgerton
   Harold E. "Doc", *US scientist,*   EJ-uhr-tuhn   'edʒəʳtən
      inventor
Edgerton
   city, WI   EJ-uhr-tuhn   'edʒəʳtən
Edie
   pers. name   ĒD-ē   'iːdiˑ
Edina
   city, MN, MO   i-DĪ-nuh   i'daɪnə
Edinboro
   University, *PA*   ED-uhn-BUHR-uh   'edən‚bərə
Edinburg
   city, TX; town, IN   ED-n-BUHRG   'edṇ‚bəʳg
Edinburgh
   city, Scotland   ED-n-BUHR-uh, ED-n-BUH-ruh,   'edṇ‚bər-ə, 'edṇ‚bə-rə,
                                           ED-n-b(uh-)ruh   'ednb(ə)rə
Edison
   Thomas, *US inventor*   ED-uh-suhn   'edəsən
Edisto
   river, SC   ED-uh-STŌ   'edə‚stoː
Edith
   1. pers. name   ĒD-uhth   'iːdəθ
   2. French   ā-DĒT   eːdiːt
   3. German   Ā-dit   'eːdit
Edjo [Buto]
   Egyptian guardian goddess   EJ-ō   'edʒoː

Key (col. 2): a: fad ā: fade ah: father ar: marry aw: law e: fed ē: feed er: merry i: hid ī: hide ō: coat ōō: boot
oi: boy ow: now u: put uh: above uhr: bird ch: chop ng: ring sh: show th: thick <u>th</u>: this zh: measure

Edmond
1. pers. name	ED-muhnd	'edmənd
2. French	ed-MAW^n	edmɔ̃

Edmonton
city, Alberta, Canada	ED-muhn-tuhn	'edməntən

Edmund
1. pers. name	ED-muhnd	'edmənd
2. German	ET-MUNT	'et,munt

Edna
pers. name	ED-nuh	'ednə

Edo
1. former name, Tokyo	ed-ō	edoː
2. pers. name, Dutch	Ā-dō	'eːdoː

Edoardo
pers. name, Italian	Ā-dō-AHR-dō	,eːdoː'ɑrdoː

Edo [Bini]
lang., people, Nigeria	ED-ō	'edoː

Edom [Idumea]
Biblical name	ĒD-uhm, ed-ŌM	'iːdəm, ed'oːm

Edomite
Biblical name	ĒD-uh-MĪT	'iːdə,mɑit

Édouard
pers. name, French	ā-DWAHR	eːdwɑːr

Edrei
Biblical name	ED-rē-Ī, e-DRĀ-ē	'edriː,ɑi, e'dreːiː

Edsel
car make; pers. name	ED-suhl	'edsəl

Eduard
1. pers. name, Czech	ED-u-ahrt	'eduɑːrt
2. Dutch	Ā-due-ahrt	'eːdyɑrt
3. German	Ā-dōō-ahrt	'eːduːɑ^{r}t
4. Russian	id-ōō-AHRT	iduː'ɑːrt
5. Danish	ID-vahrd	'idvɑrd

Eduardo
1. pers. name, Italian	ād-WAHR-dō	eːd'wardoː
2. Portuguese	ēth-WAHR-dōō	iːð'waːrduː
3. Spanish	ā-THWAHR-thō	eː'ðwarðoː

Eduskunta
Finnish parliament	ED-us-KUN-tah	'edus,kuntɑ

Edvard
1. pers. name, Danish	ID-VAHRD	'id,vɑrd
2. Czech	ED-vahrt	'edvɑːrt
3. Norwegian	ED-VAHRT, ĀD-	'ed,vɑrt, 'eːd-
4. Swedish	ĀD-VAHRD	'eːd,vɑːrd

Edward
1. pers. name	ED-wuhrd	'edwə^{r}d
2. Danish	ID-VAHRD	'id,vɑrd
3. German	ET-VAHRT	'et,vɑ^{r}t
4. Polish	ED-VAHRT	'ed,vɑːrt

Edwardian
pert. to Edward VII of England	ed-WAWRD-ē-uhn, ed-WAHRD-ē-uhn	ed'wɔː^{r}diːən, ed'wɑ^{r}diːən

Edwards
Jonathan, *US clergyman;* Sir O. M., *Welsh scholar; pers. name*	ED-wuhrdz	'edwə^{r}dz

---

Foreign Sounds: ue: *Fr.* **rue**, *Ger.* **füllen**   uh(r): *Fr.* **boeuf**, *Ger.* **Höhle**   kh: *Ger.* **ich**, *Scot.* **loch**   g̃: *Sp.* amigo   v: *Sp.* hablar
hl: *Welsh* **Llanelli.**   CAPITALS: primary stress.   SMALL CAPS: secondary stress.   ⑤: U.S. pron.   ⑥: British pron.

Edwin
  1. pers. name   ED-wuhn   'edwən
  2. German   ET-VĒN   'et‚viːn
Edwina
  pers. name   ed-WĒ-nuh, -WIN-uh   ed'wiːnə, -'winə
Eemil
  pers. name, Finnish   EM-il   'emil
Eero
  pers. name, Finnish   ER-ō   'eroː
Eeyore
  character in Winnie the Pooh,   Ē-AWR   'iː‚ɔːʳ
  Milne
Efes [Ephesus]
  ancient Ionian city, Asia Minor   EF-uhs   'efəs
Effingham
  county, GA; county, city, IL   EF-ing-HAM   'efiŋ‚hæm
Efi Deild
  Icelandic legislative body   EP-ē DĀLD *[sic]*   'epiː 'deːld *[sic]*
Efik
  lang., people, Nigeria   EF-ik   'efik
Efim
  pers. name   yi-FĒM   ji'fiːm
Efrem
  pers. name   EF-ruhm   'efrəm
Egas Moniz
  António, *Portuguese neurologist*   Ā-gahs mō-NĒZ   'eːgɑːs moː'niːz
  (Nobel 1949)
Egbert
  pers. name   EG-buhrt   'egbəʳt
Eger
  German river   EG-er   'egeʳ
Egeria
  advisor to Numa Pompilius; Roman   ē-JIR-ē-uh   i·'dʒiriːə
  goddess of springs
Egger
  Austrian beer   EG-uhr   'egəʳ
Eggleton
  Arthur C., *Canadian politician*   EG-uhl-tuhn   'egəltən
Eglah
  Biblical name   EG-luh, eg-LAH   'eglə, eg'lɑ
Eglaim
  Biblical name   EG-lē-uhm, eg-LAH-yēm   'egliːəm, eg'lɑjiːm
Eglantine
  bush   EG-luhn-TĪN, EG-luhn-TĒN   'eglən‚tɑin, 'eglən‚tiːn
Eglevsky
  André Yevgenyevich, *US dancer*   i-GLEF-skē, EG-luhf-skē   i'glefskiː, 'egləfski·
Eglon
  Biblical name   EG-LAHN, eg-LŌN   'eg‚lɑn, eg'loːn
Egmont
  1. Beethoven overture; pers. name   EG-MAHNT   'eg‚mɑnt
  2. German   EG-MAWNT   'eg‚mɔːnt
Egon
  pers. name, Dutch   Ā-GAWN   'eː‚gɔːn
Egri Bikavér
  wine   EG-rē BIK-uh-vuhr   'egri· 'bikəvəʳ

Key (col. 2):　a: fad　ā: fade　ah: father　ar: marry　aw: law　e: fed　ē: feed　er: merry　i: hid　ī: hide　ō: coat　ōō: boot
oi: boy　ow: now　u: put　uh: above　uhr: bird　ch: chop　ng: ring　sh: show　th: thick　th̲: this　zh: measure

Egypt
 republic, Africa   Ē-juhpt, Ē-jipt   'iːdʒəpt, 'iːdʒipt
Egyptian
 pert. to Egypt   i-JIP-shuhn   i'dʒipʃən
Egyptology
 study of Egyptian antiquities   Ē-juhp-TAHL-uh-jē   ˌiːdʒəp'tɑlədʒiˑ
Ehi
 Biblical name   Ē-HĪ, e-KHĒ   'iːˌhɑi, e'xiː
Ehrenburg
 Ilya G., *Russian writer*   Ā-rin-BŌŌRKH, ⑤ ER-uhn-BURG,   'eːrin,buːʳx, ⑤ 'erən,buʳg,
    -BURK   -ˌbuʳk
Ehrenfels
 Christian von Freiherr, *German*   Ā-ruhn-FELS   'eːrən,fels
  philosopher
Ehricke
 Krafft A., *US aeronautical engineer*   ER-i-kuh   'erikə
  and physicist
Ehrlich
 Paul, *German chemist, bacteriologist*   ER-likh, ⑤ ER-lik   'eʳliç, ⑤ 'eʳlik
  (Nobel 1908)
Ehrlichman
 John Daniel, *US author, former*   ER-lik-muhn, UHR-lik-muhn   'eʳlikmən, 'əʳlikmən
  presidential assistant
Ehud
 Biblical name   Ē-HUHD, Ā-H(Y)ŌŌD, e-HŌŌD   'iːˌhəd, 'eːˌh(j)uːd, e'huːd
Eichmann
 Adolf, *Nazi official*   ĪKH-MAHN, ⑤ ĪK-muhn   'aiç,man, ⑤ 'aikmən
Eiffel Tower
 Paris, France   Ī-fuhl   'aifəl
Eigen
 Manfred, *German chemist (Nobel*   Ī-guhn   'aigən
  1967)
Eiger
 mtn. range, Switzerland   Ī-guhr   'aigəʳ
Eigg
 island, Scotland   EG, ĀG   'eg, 'eːg
Eijkman
 Christian, *Dutch physician,*   ĀK-MAHN; ⑤ ĪK-muhn, ĀK-muhn   'eːk,man; ⑤ 'aikmən,
  pathologist (Nobel 1929)   'eːkmən
Eikenberry
 Jill, *actress*   Ī-kuhn-BER-ē   'aikən,beriˑ
Eiki
 pers. name, Japanese   ā-kē   eːkiˑ
Eikonoklastes
 treatise, J. Milton   Ī-KAHN-uh-KLAS-tēz   ˌai,kanə'klæstiːz
Eilat
 port, Israel   ā-LAHT   eː'lat
Eileen
 pers. name   ī-LĒN, Ī-LĒN, Ā-LĒN   ai'liːn, 'ai,liːn, 'eːˌliːn
Eilhard, -hardt
 pers. name, German   ĪL-HAHRT   'ail,haʳt
Einar
 1. pers. name, Danish   Ī-NAHR   'ai,nɑr
 2. Icelandic   Ā-NAHR   'eːˌnɑr
 3. Swedish   Ā-NAHR   'eːˌnɑːr

Foreign Sounds: ue: *Fr.* **rue**, *Ger.* **füllen**   uh(r): *Fr.* **boeuf**, *Ger.* **Höhle**   kh: *Ger.* **ich**, *Scot.* **loch**   g̃: *Sp.* **amigo**   y: *Sp.* **hablar**
hl: *Welsh* **Llanelli**.   CAPITALS: primary stress.   SMALL CAPS: secondary stress.   ⑤: U.S. pron.   ⑥: British pron.

Einbecker Ur-Bock
   German beer   ĪN-BEK-uhr UR-BAHK   'ain‚bekə^r 'u^r‚bɑk

Eindhoven
   city, Netherlands   ĪNT-HŌ-vuhn, ĀNT-HŌ-vuhn   'aint‚hoːvən, 'eːnt‚hoːvən

Einer
   pers. name   Ā-nuhr   'eːnər

Einstein
   Albert, *German-born US physicist*   ĪN-STĪN, ĪN-SHTĪN   'ain‚stain, 'ain‚ʃtain
   (Nobel 1921)

einsteinium
   element   ĪN-STĪ-nē-uhm, īn-STĪ-nē-uhm   'ain‚stainiːəm, ain'stainiːəm

Einthoven
   Willem, *Dutch physiologist (Nobel*   ĀNT-HŌ-vuhn, ĪNT-HŌ-vuhn   'eːnt‚hoːvən, 'aint‚hoːvən
   1924)

Eire [Ireland]
   republic, Europe   AR-uh, ER-uh, Ī-ruh   'ærə, 'erə, 'airə

EISA
   extended industry standard   Ā-suh   'eːsə
   architecture

Eisaku
   pers. name, Japanese   ā-sah-kōō   eːsɑkuː

Eisenhower
   Dwight D., *34th US president*   ĪZ-n-HOW(-uh)r   'aizn̩‚hau(ə)^r

Eisenstaedt
   Alfred, *photographer*   Ī-zuhn-SHTAT, -SHTET, -STAT   'aizən‚ʃtæt, -‚ʃtet, -‚stæt

Eisenstein
   Sergey Mikhaylovich, *Russian*   IZ-yin-SHTĪN, ⓢ Ī-zuhn-STĪN   ‚izjin'ʃtain, ⓢ 'aizən‚stain
   theater and motion-picture director

Eisteddfod
   Welsh arts festival   ī-STETH-vuhd, -vawd   ai'steðvəd, -vɔːd

Eisteddfodau
   pl. of Eisteddfod   Ī-STETH-VAWD-Ī   ‚ai‚steð'vɔːd‚ai

Ekaterina
   pers. name (E. Gordeeva)   yuh-KAHT-uh-RĒ-nuh   jə‚kɑtə'riːnə

Ekaterinburg
   see Yekaterinburg

Ekelöf
   Gunnar, *Swedish poet*   Ā-kuh-LUH(R)F   'eːkə‚lœf

Eker
   Biblical name   Ē-kuhr, EK-er   'iːkə^r, 'eker

Ekoi
   lang., people, Cameroon, Nigeria   Ā-KOI   'eː‚kɔi

Ekron
   Biblical name   EK-RAHN, ek-RŌN   'ek‚rɑn, ek'roːn

Ekronite
   Biblical name   EK-ruh-NĪT   'ekrə‚nait

Ektachrome
   tdmk for a color film   EK-tuh-KRŌM   'ektə‚kroːm

Eku Bavaria
   German beer   Ā-kōō buh-VAHR-ē-uh   'eːkuː bə'vɑriːə

Eku Edelbock
   German beer   Ā-kōō ĀD-l-BAHK   'eːkuː 'eːdl̩‚bak

Eku Hefe-Weizen
   German beer   Ā-kōō HĀ-fuh-VĪT-suhn   'eːkuː 'heːfə‚vaitsən

---

Key (col. 2):   a: f**a**d   ā: f**a**de   ah: f**a**ther   ar: m**a**rry   aw: l**a**w   e: f**e**d   ē: f**ee**d   er: m**e**rry   i: h**i**d   ī: h**i**de   ō: c**oa**t   ōō: b**oo**t
oi: b**oy**   ow: n**ow**   u: p**u**t   uh: **a**bove   uhr: b**ir**d   ch: **ch**op   ng: ri**ng**   sh: **sh**ow   th: **th**ick   <u>th</u>: **th**is   zh: mea**s**ure

Eku Jubiläumsbier		
German beer	Ā-kōō YŌŌ-bil-OIMS-BIR	'eːkuː 'juːbil‚ɔims‚biᵉ
Eku Kulminator Urtyp Hell 28		
German beer	Ā-kōō KUL-min-AH-TAWR UR-TUEP HEL AH<u>KH</u>-tunt-SVAHNT-si<u>kh</u>	'eːkuː 'kulmin‚ɑ‚tɔᵉ 'ur‚tyːp 'hel ‚ɑxtunt'svɑntsiç
Eku Weizen		
German beer	Ā-kōō VĪT-suhn	'eːkuː 'vɑitsən
Ela		
highest note; Guido's note	ā-LAH	eːˈlɑ
Elagabalus		
Roman emperor	EL-uh-GAB-uh-luhs	‚eləˈgæbələs
Elah		
Biblical name	Ē-luh, EL-uh, el-AH	'iːlə, 'elə, el'ɑ
Elaine		
pers. name	i-LĀN	iˈleːn
El Al		
Israeli airline co.	el AL, el AHL	el 'æl, el 'ɑːl
El Alamein		
village, Egypt	EL AL-uh-MĀN	‚el ‚æləˈmeːn
Elam		
ancient Near Eastern kingdom	Ē-luhm	'iːləm
El-Amarna		
ancient Egyptian city	EL-uh-MAHR-nuh	‚eləˈmɑᵉnə
Elamite		
lang., native of Elam	Ē-luh-MĪT	'iːlə‚mɑit
Elara		
satellite of Jupiter	uh-LAR-uh, uh-LER-uh, uh-LAHR-uh	əˈlærə, əˈlerə, əˈlɑrə
Elasah		
Biblical name	el-Ā-suh, EL-uh-suh, EL-ah-SAH	elˈeːsə, 'eləsə, ‚elɑˈsɑ
Elath		
ancient name of 'Aqaba; seaport, Israel	Ā-LAHT, Ē-LATH	'eː‚lɑt, 'iː‚læθ
Elba		
island, Mediterranean	EL-buh	'elbə
Elbe		
river, Europe	EL-buh, ELB	'elbə, 'elb
Elberfeld		
city, Germany	EL-buhr-FELT	'elbəᵉ‚felt
Elbrus		
mtn., mtn. range, Caucasus Mts.	el-BRŌŌZ	elˈbruːz
El-bethel		
Biblical name	el-BETH-uhl, EL-bā-TEL	elˈbeθəl, ‚elbeːˈtel
Elbing		
German form of Elblag	EL-bing	'elbiŋ
Elblag [Elbing]		
province, city, Poland	EL-BLAWNGK	'el‚blɔːŋk
Elbridge		
pers. name	EL-brij	'elbridʒ
Elburz		
mtn. range, Iran	el-BURZ	elˈbuᵉz
El Cajon		
city, CA	EL kuh-HŌN	‚el kəˈhoːn
El Camino		
College, CA	EL kuh-MĒ-nō	‚el kəˈmiːnoː

Eldaah
  Biblical name   el-DĀ-uh, EL-dah-AH   el'deːə, ˌelda'a
Eldad
  Biblical name   EL-DAD, el-DAHD   'elˌdæd, el'dɑd
Eldon
  pers. name   EL-duhn   'eldən
El Dorado
  1. city, AR, KS   EL duh-RĀD-ō   ˌel də're:do:
  2. county, CA   EL duh-RAHD-ō   ˌel də'rado:
  3. city of gold   EL duh-RAHD-ō, EL duh-RĀD-ō   ˌel də'rado:, ˌel də're:do:
Eldorado
  city, IL, TX   EL-duh-RĀD-ō   ˌeldə're:do:
El Dorado Springs
  city, NV   EL duh-RĀD-ō SPRINGZ   ˌel dəˌre:do: 'spriŋz
Eldridge
  pers. name   EL-drij   'eldridʒ
Elea
  ancient town, Italy   Ē-lē-uh   'i:li:ə
Elead
  Biblical name   EL-ē-uhd, Ē-lē-AD, el-AHD   'eli:əd, 'i:li:ˌæd, el'ɑd
Elealeh
  Biblical name   Ē-lē-Ā-luh, EL-ē-Ā-luh, el-Ā-uh-luh, EL-ah-LE   ˌi:li:'e:lə, ˌeli:'e:lə, el'e:ələ, ˌela'le
Eleanor
  pers. name   EL-uh-nuhr, -NAWR, -NŌR   'elənəʳ, -ˌnɔːʳ, -ˌnoːʳ
Eleanora
  pers. name, Italian   el-ā-uh-NŌR-uh   ele:ə'no:rə
El-easah
  Biblical name   EL-ē-Ā-suh, i-LĒ-uh-suh, EL-ah-SAH   ˌeli:'e:sə, i'li:əsə, ˌela'sɑ
Eleaticism
  beliefs of the Eleatics   EL-ē-AT-uh-SIZ-uhm   ˌeli:'æṭəˌsizəm
Eleatics
  school of Greek philosophers   EL-ē-AT-iks   ˌeli:'æṭiks
Eleazar
  pers. name   EL-ē-Ā-zuhr   ˌeli:'e:zəʳ
Eleázar
  pers. name, Spanish   ā-lā-AH-sahr, -thahr   e:le:'ɑsar, -θar
El-eazar
  Biblical name   EL-ē-Ā-zuhr, EL-ah-ZAHR   ˌeli:'e:zəʳ, ˌela'zar
Eleazar ben Azariah
  Rabbinic scholar   EL-ē-Ā-zuhr ben AZ-uh-RĪ-uh, BEN uh-ZAHR-yuh   ˌeli:'e:zəʳ ben ˌæzə'raiə, 'ben ə'zarjə
Electra
  daughter of Agamemnon   uh-LEK-truh, ē-LEK-truh   ə'lektrə, i·'lektrə
Electrolux
  tdmk for a vacuum cleaner   i-LEK-truh-LUHKS   i'lektrəˌləks
El-elohe-Israel
  Biblical name   EL-uh-LŌ-hā-IZ-rē-uhl, -IZ-RĀ-uhl; EL-el-aw-HĀ-yis-rah-EL   ˌelə'lo:heː'izri:əl, -'izˌre:əl; ˌelelɔː,he:jisra'el
Elen
  1. pers. name   EL-uhn   'elən
  2. Welsh   EL-en   'elen

Key (col. 2):   a: fad   ā: fade   ah: father   ar: marry   aw: law   e: fed   ē: feed   er: merry   i: hid   ī: hide   ō: coat   ōō: boot
oi: boy   ow: now   u: put   uh: above   uhr: bird   ch: chop   ng: ring   sh: show   th: thick   th: this   zh: measure

Elena
1. pers. name	EL-uh-nuh, i-LĀ-nuh, i-LĒ-nuh	'elənə, i'leːnə, i'liːnə
2. German	Ā-lā-nah	'eːleːnɑ
3. Italian	EL-ā-NAH	'eleːˌnɑ
4. Romanian	e-LEN-ah	e'lenɑ

Eleonora
1. pers. name	EL-uh-NAWR-uh, -NŌR-uh	ˌelə'nɔːrə, -'noːrə
2. Italian	Ā-lā-ō-NAWR-ah	ˌeːleːoː'nɔːrɑ

Eleonore
pers. name, German	Ā-lā-ō-NŌ-ruh	ˌeːleːoː'noːrə

Éleonore
pers. name, French	ā-lā-aw-NAWR	eːleːɔːnɔːr

Eleph
Biblical name	Ē-LEF, EL-EF	'iːˌlef, 'elˌef

Eleusinian
pert. to Eleusis	EL-yu-SIN-ē-uhn	ˌelju'siniːən

Eleusis [Elevsis]
ancient Greek city	i-LOO-suhs	i'luːsəs

Eleuthera
island, Bahamas	i-LOO-thuh-ruh	i'luːθərə

Eleutherios
pers. name, Mod. Greek	EL-YEF-THER-yaws	ˌelˌjef'θerjɔːs

Eleutherius
pope	EL-yuh-THIR-ē-uhs	ˌeljə'θiriːəs

Elevsis [Eleusis]
town, Greece	EL-uhf-SĒS	ˌeləf'siːs

Elfsborg
see Älvsborg

Elgar
Sir Edward, *English composer*	EL-GAHR, EL-guhr	'elˌgɑʳ, 'elgəʳ

Elgin
1. city, IL; US pers. name	EL-juhn	'eldʒən
2. city, TX	EL-guhn	'elgən
3. Marbles, Parthenon frieze; town, Scotland; British pers. name	EL-gin, EL-guhn	'elgin, 'elgən

El Greco
see Greco, El

El-hanan
Biblical name	el-HĀ-nuhn, el-khah-NAHN	el'heːnən, elxɑ'nɑn

Eli
1. pers. name	Ē-LĪ	'iːˌlai
2. Welsh	Ā-lēˑ	'eːliˑ
3. Biblical name	Ē-LĪ, el-Ē	'iːˌlai, el'iː

Elia
1. pen name of Charles Lamb	Ē-lē-uh, ĒL-yuh	'iːliːə, 'iːljə
2. pers. name (E. Kazan)	i-LĪ-uh	i'laiə

Eliab
Biblical name	i-LĪ-AB, EL-ē-AHV	i'laiˌæb, ˌeliːˈɑv

Eliada
Biblical name	i-LĪ-uhd-uh, EL-yah-DAH	i'laiədə, ˌelja'dɑ

Eliade
Mircea, *US religious scholar*	EL-ē-AHD-uh	ˌeliː'ɑdə

Eliah
Biblical name	i-LĪ-uh, EL-ē-YAH	i'laiə, ˌeliːˈja

Foreign Sounds: ue: *Fr.* **rue**, *Ger.* **füllen** uh(r): *Fr.* **boeuf**, *Ger.* **Höhle** kh: *Ger.* **ich**, *Scot.* **loch** ḡ: *Sp.* **amigo** v̱: *Sp.* **hablar**
hl: *Welsh* **Llanelli**. CAPITALS: primary stress. SMALL CAPS: secondary stress. Ⓢ: U.S. pron. Ⓔ: British pron.

Eliahba, Eliahbah
  Biblical name   i-LĪ-uh-buh, EL-yah<u>kh</u>-BAH   i'laiəbə, ˌeljɑx'bɑ
Eliakim
  Biblical name   i-LĪ-uh-kim, el-yah-KĒM   i'laiəkim, eljaˈkiːm
Eliam
  Biblical name   i-LĪ-uhm, EL-ē-AHM   i'laiəm, ˌeliːˈɑm
Elias
  1. pers. name   i-LĪ-uhs   i'laiəs
  2. Finnish   EL-YAHS   'elˌjɑːs
  3. German   ā-LĒ-ahs   eːˈliːɑs
  4. Swedish   el-Ē-ahs   el'iːɑːs
Elías
  pers. name, Spanish   ā-LĒ-ahs   eːˈliːɑs
Eliasaph
  Biblical name   i-LĪ-uh-SAF, EL-yah-SAHF   i'laiəˌsæf, ˌeljaˈsaf
Eliashib
  Biblical name   i-LĪ-uh-SHIB, EL-yah-SHĒV   i'laiəˌʃib, ˌeljaˈʃiːv
Eliathah
  Biblical name   i-LĪ-uh-thuh, EL-ē-AH-tah   i'laiəθə, ˌeliːˈɑtɑ
Elidad
  Biblical name   i-LĪ-DAD, EL-ē-DAHD   i'laiˌdæd, ˌeliːˈdɑd
Elie
  pers. name   Ē-lē   'iːliˑ
Élie
  pers. name, French   ā-LĒ   eːliː
Eliel
  Biblical name   i-LĪ-uhl, Ē-lē-EL   i'laiəl, 'iːliːˌel
Elienai
  Biblical name   EL-ē-Ē-NĪ, EL-ē-Ā-NĪ, el-Ē-en-Ī   ˌeliːˈiːˌnɑi, ˌeliːˈeːˌnɑi,
                                                                           elˌiːenˈɑi
Eliezer
  1. Biblical name   EL-ē-Ē-zuhr, EL-ē-Ā-zuhr, EL-ē-EZ-er ˌeliːˈiːzəʳ, ˌeliːˈeːzəʳ,
                                                                           ˌeliːˈezer
  2. see Israel ben Eliezer
Elihoenai
  Biblical name   EL-ē-HŌ-Ē-NĪ, -Ē-nē-Ī; EL-yuh-HŌ-ā-NĪ ˌeliːˌhoˈiːˌnɑi, -'iːniːˌɑi;
                                                                           ˌeljəˌhoːeːˈnɑi
Eli-horeph
  Biblical name   EL-ē-HŌR-EF, -HAWR-EF;   'eliːˈhoːrˌef, -'hɔːrˌef;
                                     EL-ē-<u>KH</u>Ō-REF   ˌeliːˈxoːˌref
Elihu
  pers. name   EL-uh-HYŌŌ, i-LĪ-HYŌŌ   'eləˌhjuː, i'laiˌhjuː
Elijah
  Hebrew prophet; pers. name   i-LĪ-juh   i'laidʒə
Elika
  Biblical name   i-LĪ-kuh, EL-i-kuh, EL-ē-KAH   i'laikə, 'elikə, ˌeliːˈkɑ
Elim
  Biblical name   Ē-luhm, ā-LĒ-mah   'iːləm, eːˈliːmɑ
Elimelech
  Biblical name   i-LIM-uh-LEK, EL-i-MEL-E<u>KH</u>   i'liməˌlek, ˌeli'melˌex
Elinor
  pers. name   EL-uh-nuhr, -NAWR   'elənəʳ, -ˌnɔːʳ
Elioenai
  Biblical name   EL-ē-uh-WĒ-NĪ, i-LĪ-uh-; el-YŌ-en-Ī   ˌeliːəˈwiːˌnɑi, iˌlaiə-;
                                                                           elˌjoːenˈɑi

---

Key (col. 2):   a: fad ā: fade ah: father ar: marry aw: law e: fed ē: feed er: merry i: hid ī: hide ō: coat ōō: boot
oi: boy   ow: now   u: put   uh: above   uhr: bird   ch: chop   ng: ring   sh: show   th: thick   <u>th</u>: this   zh: measure

Elion
> Gertrude B., *US chemist (Nobel 1988)* EL-ē-uhn 'eliːən

Eliot
> George (*pseudonym of* Mary Ann Evans), *English novelist;* T. S. *US-born British poet (Nobel 1948); pers. name* EL-ē-uht, EL-yuht 'eliːət, 'eljət

Eliotic
> *"of Eliot" (esp. T. S. Eliot), adj.* EL-ē-AHT-ik ˌeli'aṭik

Eliphal
> *Biblical name* i-LĪ-FAL, EL-ē-FAL, EL-ē-FAHL i'laiˌfæl, 'eliːˌfæl, ˌeliː'fal

Eliphalet
> *pers. name* i-LIF-uh-luht, -LET i'lifələt, -ˌlet

Eliphaz
> *Biblical name* EL-ē-FAZ, i-LĪ-FAZ, EL-ē-FAHZ 'eliːˌfæz, i'laiˌfæz, ˌeliː'faz

Elipheleh [Eliphelehu]
> *Biblical name* i-LIF-uh-LĀ, EL-ē-FLE i'lifəˌleˑ, ˌeliː'fle

Eliphelehu
> *Biblical name* i-LIF-uh-LĒ-H(Y)OO, e-LIF-uh-lē-H(Y)OO, EL-ē-FLE-HOO iˌlifə'liːˌh(j)uː, e'lifəliːˌh(j)uː, ˌeliː'fleˌhu

Eliphelet
> *Biblical name* i-LIF-uh-LET, EL-i-FEL-uht i'lifəˌlet, ˌeli'felət

Elis [Ilía]
> *dept, Greece* Ē-luhs 'iːləs

Elisabeth
> *1. pers. name* i-LIZ-uh-buhth i'lizəbəθ
> *2. German* ā-LĒ-zah-BET eːˈliːzaˌbet
> *3. Swedish* el-Ē-sah-BET el'iːsaːˌbet

Élisabeth
> *pers. name, French* ā-lē-zah-BET eːliːzaːbet

Eliseus
> *Biblical name* EL-uh-SĒ-uhs ˌelə'siːəs

Elisha
> *pers. name* i-LĪ-shuh i'laiʃə

Elishah
> *Biblical name* i-LĪ-shuh, EL-ē-SHAH i'laiʃə, ˌeliː'ʃa

Elishama
> *Biblical name* i-LISH-uh-muh, EL-i-SHĀ-muh, Ē-LĪ-SHAHM-ah, el-Ē-shah-MAH i'liʃəmə, ˌeli'ʃeːmə, ˌiːˌlai'ʃama, el,iːʃa'ma

Elishaphat
> *Biblical name* i-LISH-uh-FAT, Ē-LĪ-SHĀ-FAT, el-Ē-shah-FAHT i'liʃəˌfæt, ˌiːˌlai'ʃeːˌfæt, el,iːʃa'fat

Elisheba
> *Biblical name* i-LISH-uh-buh, i-LĪ-shuh-buh, EL-ē-SHEV-ah i'liʃəbə, i'laiʃəbə, ˌeliː'ʃeva

Eli-shua
> *Biblical name* EL-ē-SHOO-uh, i-LISH-uh-wuh, EL-ē-SHOO-ah ˌeliː'ʃuːə, i'liʃəwə, ˌeliː'ʃuːa

Elisir d'Amore
> *opera, Donizetti* Ā-lē-ZIR dah-MŌ-rā ˌeːliː'zi^r da'moːreː

Eliud
> *Biblical name* i-LĪ-uhd i'laiəd

Elixir Végétale
> *Carthusian tonic* ā-lēk-SĒR vā-zhā-TAHL eːliːksiːr veːʒeːtaːl

---

Foreign Sounds: ue: *Fr.* **rue,** *Ger.* **füllen** uh(r): *Fr.* **boeuf,** *Ger.* **Höhle** <u>kh</u>: *Ger.* **ich,** *Scot.* **loch** ḡ: *Sp.* **amigo** v: *Sp.* **hablar** hl: *Welsh* **Llanelli.** CAPITALS: primary stress. SMALL CAPS: secondary stress. ⑤: U.S. pron. ⑥: British pron.

Eliza
1. pers. name	i-LĪ-zuh	iˈlaizə
2. Polish	ā-LĔ-zah	eːˈliːzaː

Elizabeth
1. pers. name	i-LIZ-uh-buhth	iˈlizəbəθ
2. Dutch	ā-LĔ-zah-BET	eːˈliːzaːˌbet

Eli-zaphan
Biblical name	EL-ē-ZĀ-fuhn, Ĕ-LĪ-; ELT-sah-FAHN	ˌeliˈzeːfən, ˌiːˌlai-; ˌeltsaˈfan

Elizaveta
pers. name, Russian	yuhl-YĔ-zah-VE-tah	jəlˌjiːzaːˈvetaː

Elizur
Biblical name	i-LĪ-zuhr, EL-ēt-SUR	iˈlaizəʳ, ˌeliːtˈsur

Elkanah
Biblical name	el-KĀ-nuh, EL-kuh-nuh, EL-kah-NAH	elˈkeːnə, ˈelkənə, ˌelkaˈna

Elke
pers. name, German	EL-kuh	ˈelkə

Elkin
town, NC; pers. name	EL-kuhn	ˈelkən

Elko
county, NV; Indian reservation, US	EL-kō	ˈelkoː

Elkosh
Biblical name	EL-KAHSH	ˈelˌkaʃ

Elkoshite
Biblical name	el-KAHSH-ĪT, el-KŌ-SHĪT	elˈkaʃˌait, elˈkoːˌʃait

Ella
pers. name	EL-uh	ˈelə

El Lago
city, TX	el LAHG-ō	el ˈlagoː

Ellás [Greece]
country, Europe	e-LAHS	eˈlas

Ellasar
Biblical name	el-Ā-SAHR, el-AHS-AHR, EL-ahs-AHR, EL-ah-SAHR	elˈeːˌsaʳ, elˈasˌaʳ, ˈelasˌaʳ, ˌelaˈsar

Ellen
1. pers. name	EL-uhn	ˈelən
2. Swedish	EL-luhn	ˈellən

Ellery
pers. name	EL-uh-rē	ˈeləriˑ

Ellesmere
island, Canada; lake, port, England; lake, New Zealand; Chaucer manuscript	ELZ-MIR	ˈelzˌmiʳ

Ellesse
US footwear co.	EL-ES-Ā	ˌelˌesˈeː

Ellice
island group, Pacific Ocean	EL-uhs	ˈeləs

Ellis
Albert, US psychologist, author, educator; Havelock, English physician; island, NY; pers. name	EL-uhs	ˈeləs

Ellison
Harlan Jay, US author; Ralph, US author	EL-uh-suhn	ˈeləsən

Elly
pers. name	EL-ē	ˈeliˑ

Elman
   Mischa, *US violinist*   EL-muhn   'elmən

Elmer
   pers. name   EL-muhr   'elmə^r

Elmira
   city, NY   el-MĪ-ruh   el'mairə

Elmo
   Christian saint; pers. name   EL-mō   'elmoː

Elmodam
   Biblical name   el-MŌ-DAM   el'moː‚dæm

El Monte
   city, CA   el MAHNT-ē   el 'manţiˑ

Elmore
   county, AL, ID   EL-MŌR, EL-MAWR   'el‚moː^r, 'el‚mɔː^r

Elnaam
   Biblical name   el-NĀ-uhm, el-NAH-AHM   el'neːəm, el'na‚am

Elnathan
   Biblical name   el-NĀ-thuhn, EL-nah-TAHN   el'neːθən, ‚elna'tan

El Niño
   current, Pacific Ocean   el NĒN-yō   el 'niːnjoː

Elohim
   Hebrew name for God   EL-ō-HĒM, el-Ō-HIM   ‚eloː'hiːm, el'oː‚him

Elohistic
   referring to God as Elohim   EL-uh-HIS-tik   ‚elə'histik

Eloi
   1. Biblical name   i-LŌ-Ī   i'loː‚ai
   2. characters in The Time Machine,   Ē-LOI   'iː‚lɔi
      H. G. Wells

Elon
   Biblical name   Ē-LAHN, el-ŌN   'iː‚lan, el'oːn

Elon-beth-hanan
   Biblical name   Ē-LAHN-beth-HĀ-nuhn,   'iː‚lanbeθ'heːnən,
                          el-ŌN-BET-khah-NAHN   el'oːn‚betxa'nan

Elon College
   town, college, NC   Ē-LAHN KAHL-ij   'iː‚lan 'kalidʒ

Elonite
   Biblical name   Ē-LAHN-ĪT, EL-uh-NĪT   'iː‚lan‚ait, 'elə‚nait

Eloth
   Biblical name   Ē-LAHTH, ā-LŌT   'iː‚laθ, eː'loːt

Eloy
   pers. name, Spanish   ā-LOI   eː'lɔi

El-paal
   Biblical name   el-PĀ-AL, el-PAH-AHL   el'peː‚æl, el'pa‚al

El-paran
   Biblical name   el-PĀ-ruhn, EL-pahr-AHN   el'peːrən, ‚elpar'an

El Paso
   city, TX   el PAS-ō   el 'pæsoː

El Paso de Robles [Paso Robles]
   city, CA   el-PAS-uhd-uh-RŌ-buhlz el‚pæsədə'roːbəlz

El-pelet
   Biblical name   el-PEL-uht   el'pelət

Elpenor
   companion of Odysseus   el-PĒ-NAWR   el'piː‚nɔː^r

Elphege [Aelfheah]
   English martyr   EL-FEJ   'el‚fedʒ

Foreign Sounds: ue: *Fr.* **rue**, *Ger.* f**ü**llen   uh(r): *Fr.* b**oeu**f, *Ger.* H**öh**le   kh: *Ger.* i**ch**, *Scot.* lo**ch**   ḡ: *Sp.* ami**g**o   v: *Sp.* ha**b**lar
hl: *Welsh* **Ll**anelli.   CAPITALS: primary stress.   SMALL CAPS: secondary stress.   Ⓢ: U.S. pron.   Ⓔ: British pron.

Elroy

pers. name	EL-ROI	'elˌrɔi

Elsa

1. pers. name	EL-suh	'elsə
2. French	el-SAH	elsɑː
3. German	EL-zah	'elzɑ
4. Swedish	EL-sah	'elsɑː

El Salvador

country, Cen. America	el sahl-vah-<u>TH</u>AWR, ⑤ el SAL-vuh-DAWR	el sɑlvɑ'ðɔːr, ⑤ el 'sælvəˌdɔːʳ

Elsevier

Dutch publishing co.	EL-suh-VIR	ˌelsə'viʳ

Elsie

pers. name	EL-sē	'elsiˑ

Elsinore

city, lake, CA; seaport, Denmark (setting for Hamlet, *Shakespeare)* [Helsingør]	EL-suh-NŌR, -NAWR	'elsəˌnoːʳ, -ˌnɔːʳ

Elspeth

pers. name	EL-SPETH, EL-spuhth	'elˌspeθ, 'elspəθ

Eltekeh

Biblical name	EL-tek-uh, EL-tuh-KE	'eltekə, ˌeltə'ke

Eltinge

Julian, *US entertainer*	EL-ting	'eltiŋ

Eltolad

Biblical name	el-TŌ-LAD, EL-tō-LAHD	el'toːˌlæd, ˌeltoː'lɑd

Elton

pers. name	ELT-n	'eltn̩

Éluard

Paul, *pseudonym of* Eugène Grindel, *French poet*	āl-WAHR, ⑤ Ā-luh-WAHR	eːlɥɑːr, ⑤ ˌeːlə'waʳ

Elul

Jewish month	el-O͞OL, EL-ul	el'uːl, 'elul

Eluzai

Biblical name	i-L(Y)O͞O-zē-Ī, i-L(Y)O͞O-ZĪ, EL-o͞o-ZĪ	i'l(j)uːziːˌɑi, i'l(j)uːˌzɑi, ˌeluː'zɑi

Elvira

pers. name	el-VĪ-ruh, -VIR-uh	el'vɑirə, -'virə

Elvis

pers. name	EL-vuhs, EL-vis	'elvəs, 'elvis

Elway

John, *US football player*	EL-WĀ	'elˌweː

Elwood

pers. name	EL-wud	'elwud

Ely

pers. name; pl. name	Ē-lē	'iːliˑ

Elymas

Biblical name	EL-uh-MAS	'eləˌmæs

Elyria

city, OH	i-LIR-ē-uh	i'liriːə

Elysée

palace, Paris, France	ā-lē-ZĀ	eːliːzeː

Key (col. 2): a: **fad** ā: **fade** ah: **father** ar: **marry** aw: **law** e: **fed** ē: **feed** er: **merry** i: **hid** ī: **hide** ō: **coat** o͞o: **boot**
oi: **boy** ow: **now** u: **put** uh: **above** uhr: **bird** ch: **chop** ng: **ring** sh: **show** th: **thick** <u>th</u>: **this** zh: **measure**

Elysian Fields

   Greek mythological realm of dead;   i-LIZH-uhn FĒL(D)Z, i-LĒ-zhuhn   i'liʒən 'fiːl(d)z, i'liːʒən
   ballpark, Hoboken, NJ; street, New
   Orleans

Elysium

   Elysian Fields   i-LIZH-uhm, i-LIZ-ē-uhm   i'liʒəm, i'liziːəm

Elytis

   Odysseus, *Greek poet (Nobel 1979)*   EL-ē-TĒS   'eliːˌtiːs

Elzabad

   Biblical name   el-ZĀ-BAD, EL-zā-BAD, EL-zah-VAHD   el'zeːˌbæd, 'elzeːˌbæd, ˌelzɑ'vɑd

Elzaphan

   Biblical name   el-ZĀ-fuhn, EL-zuh-fuhn, ELT-sah-FAHN   el'zeːfən, 'elzəfən, ˌeltsɑ'fɑn

Emanuel

   1. pers. name   i-MAN-yuh(-wuh)l   i'mænjə(wə)l
   2. Czech   EM-AH-nuh-WEL   'emˌɑːnəˌwel
   3. Danish   i-MAH-nuh-wuhl   i'mɑːnəwəl
   4. Dutch   ā-MAH-nue-EL   eː'mɑːnyːˌel
   5. Finnish   e-MAH-nuh-WEL   e'mɑːnəˌwel
   6. French   ā-mah-NWEL   eːmɑ'nɥel
   7. German   ā-MAHN-o͞o-EL   eː'mɑnuːˌel
   8. Swedish   e-MAH-nuh-wuhl   e'mɑnəwəl

Emanuele

   pers. name, Italian   Ā-mahn-WEL-e   ˌeːmɑn'wele

Embarras, Embarrass

   river, IL   AM-BRAW   'æmˌbrɔː

Embo

   lang., Africa   EM-bō   'emboː

Embry-Riddle

   Aeronautical University, *FL*   EM-brē-RID-l   'embriˈridl̩

Emerich

   1. pers. name   EM-uh-rik   'emərik
   2. German   Ā-muh-RIKH   'eːməˌriç

Emerson

   Ralph Waldo, *US writer; pers. name*   EM-uhr-suhn   'eməʳsən

Emil

   1. pers. name   Ē-muhl, Ā-muhl, EM-uhl   'iːməl, 'eːməl, 'eməl
   2. Czech, Finnish, Hungarian   EM-il   'emil
   3. Danish   i-MĒL   i'miːl
   4. German   Ā-mēl   'eːmiːl
   5. Polish   EM-ēl   'emiːl
   6. Swedish   Ā-mil   'eːmil

Émil

   pers. name, French   ā-MĒL   eːmiːl

Emile

   pers. name   ā-MĒL, Ā-muhl   eː'miːl, 'eːməl

Émile

   1. pers. name, Dutch   ā-MĒL   eː'miːl
   2. French   ā-MĒL   eːmiːl

Emilia

   1. pers. name   uh-MIL-ē-uh, -MIL-yuh   ə'miliːə, -'miljə
   2. Spanish   ā-MĒL-yah   eː'miːljɑ

Emiliano

   pers. name, Spanish   ā-mēl-YAHN-ō   eːmiːl'jɑnoː

Foreign Sounds: ue: *Fr.* **rue**, *Ger.* **füllen**   uh(r): *Fr.* **boeuf**, *Ger.* **Höhle**   <u>kh</u>: *Ger.* **ich**, *Scot.* **loch**   ḡ: *Sp.* **amigo**   <u>v</u>: *Sp.* **hablar**
hl: *Welsh* **Llanelli**.   CAPITALS: primary stress.   SMALL CAPS: secondary stress.   Ⓢ: U.S. pron.   Ⓔ: British pron.

Emilia-Romagna
  province, Italy　　　　　ā-MĒL-yuh-rō-MAHN-yuh　　　　　eːˈmiːljəroːˈmɑnjə
Emilio
  pers. name, Italian, Spanish　　　ā-MĒL-yō　　　　　eːˈmiːljoː
Emily
  pers. name　　　　　EM-uh-lē　　　　　ˈeməliˑ
Emim
  Biblical name　　　　　Ē-MIM, ā-MĒM　　　　　ˈiːˌmim, eːˈmiːm
Emirian
  inhabitant of United Arab Emirates　　　i-MIR-ē-uhn　　　　　iˈmiriːən
Emlyn
  pers. name　　　　　EM-luhn　　　　　ˈemlən
Emma
  1. pers. name　　　　　EM-uh　　　　　ˈemə
  2. Dutch　　　　　EM-ah　　　　　ˈemɑː
  3. French　　　　　em-MAH　　　　　emmɑː
  4. German　　　　　EM-ah　　　　　ˈemɑ
  5. Italian　　　　　EM-mah　　　　　ˈemmɑ
Emmanuel
  1. pers. name; college, GA, MA,　　i-MAN-yuh(-wuh)l　　　　iˈmænjə(wə)l
    Cambridge Univ.
  2. French　　　　　ā-mahn-WEL, em-ahn-　　　　eːmɑːnɥel, emɑːn-
  3. German　　　　　e-MAHN-o͞o-EL　　　　　eˈmɑnuːˌel
  4. Mod. Greek　　　　　EM-ahn-WEL　　　　　ˌemɑnˈwel
Emmanuele
  pers. name, Italian　　　ĀM-mahn-WEL-ā　　　　ˌeːmmɑːnˈweleː
Emmaus
  town, Palestine; borough, PA　　e-MĀ-uhs　　　　　eˈmeːəs
Emmaus
  Biblical name　　　　　i-MĀ-uhs　　　　　iˈmeːəs
Emmeline
  pers. name　　　　　EM-uh-LĪN, EM-uh-LĒN　　　ˈeməˌlɑin, ˈeməˌliːn
Emmentaler
  original Swiss cheese　　EM-uhn-TAHL-uhr　　　ˈemənˌtɑləʳ
Emmet, Emmett
  pers. name　　　　　EM-uht　　　　　ˈemət
Emmie
  pers. name　　　　　EM-ē　　　　　ˈemiˑ
Emmor
  Biblical name　　　　　EM-AWR, EM-ŌR　　　ˈemˌɔːʳ, ˈemˌoːʳ
Emmuska
  pers. name, Hungarian　　EM-MUSH-KAH　　　ˈemˌmuʃˌkɑ
Emmy
  television award; pers. name　　EM-ē　　　　　ˈemiˑ
Emory
  pers. name　　　　　EM-uh-rē　　　　　ˈeməriˑ
Empedocles
  Greek philosopher　　em-PED-uh-KLĒZ　　　emˈpedəˌkliːz
Emporia
  city, KS, VA　　em-PŌR-ē-uh, em-PAWR-ē-uh　　emˈpoːriːə, emˈpɔːriːə
Empusa
  cannibalistic she-monster in Greek　　em-PYO͞O-suh, em-PYO͞O-zuh　　emˈpjuːsə, emˈpjuːzə
    myth
Ems
  river, Germany　　　EM(P)S, EMZ　　　　　ˈem(p)s, ˈemz

Key (col. 2):　a: fad　ā: fade　ah: father　ar: marry　aw: law　e: fed　ē: feed　er: merry　i: hid　ī: hide　ō: coat　o͞o: boot
oi: boy　ow: now　u: put　uh: above　uhr: bird　ch: chop　ng: ring　sh: show　th: thick　t͟h: this　zh: measure

Enaim
   Biblical name   i-NĀ-uhm, ā-NAH-YĒM   i'neːəm, eː'nɑˌjiːm
Enam
   Biblical name   Ē-NAM, ā-NAHM   'iːˌnæm, eː'nɑm
Enan
   Biblical name   Ē-NAN, ā-NAHN   'iːˌnæn, eː'nɑn
Enberg
   Dick, *US sportscaster*   EN-BUHRG   'enˌbəʳg
Enceladus
   satellite of Saturn   en-SEL-uhd-uhs   en'selədəs
Encke's
   comet   ENG-kuhz   'eŋkəz
Encratism
   early Christian asceticism   ENG-kruh-TIZ-uhm, EN-   'eŋkrəˌtizəm, 'en-
Enders
   J. F., *US microbiologist (Nobel 1954)*   END-uhrz   'endəʳz
Endicott
   College, *MA*   EN-di-kuht, EN-di-KAHT   'endikət, 'endiˌkɑt
Endor
   town, Israel   EN-DAWR   'enˌdɔːʳ
Endymion
   shepherd loved by Selene in Greek   en-DIM-ē-uhn   en'dimiːən
     mythology; poem, Keats; pers.
     name
Eneas
   Biblical name   i-NĒ-uhs   i'niːəs
En-eglaim
   Biblical name   en-EG-lē-uhm, Ā-NEG-LAH-yēm   en'egliːəm, ˌeːˌneg'lɑjiːm
Enesco
   Georges, *French form of* Gheorge   ā-nes-KŌ, Ⓢ uh-NES-kō   eːneskoː, Ⓢ ə'neskoː
     Enescu
Enescu
   Gheorghe, *Romanian composer/*   uh-NES-ko͞o   ə'neskuː
     conductor
Enewetak
   atoll, Pacific   EN-uh-WĒ-TAHK, e-NĒ-wuh-TAHK   ˌenə'wiːˌtɑk, e'niːwəˌtɑk
Enfant, L'
   see L'Enfant
Enfield
   town, CT, NH, NC; borough, England   EN-FĒLD   'enˌfiːld
En-gannim
   Biblical name   en-GAN-im, ĀN-gah-NĒM   en'gænim, ˌeːngɑ'niːm
En-gedi
   Biblical name   en-GED-ē, en-GĒ-DĪ, ān-GED-ē   en'gediː, en'giːˌdɑi, eːn'gediː
Engelbert
   1. pers. name   ENG-guhl-buhrt   'eŋgəlbəʳt
   2. Finnish   ENG-el-BERT   'eŋelˌbert
   3. German   ENG-uhl-BERT   'eŋəlˌbeʳt
Engels
   Friedrich, *German political theorist*   ENG-uhls, ENG-(g)uhlz   'eŋəls, 'eŋ(g)əlz
England
   kingdom, Gt. Britain   ING-gluhnd, ING-luhnd   'iŋglənd, 'iŋlənd
Engle, L'
   see L'Engle

Foreign Sounds: ue: *Fr.* **rue**, *Ger.* **füllen**   uh(r): *Fr.* b**oeu**f, *Ger.* H**öh**le   <u>kh</u>: *Ger.* i**ch**, *Scot.* lo**ch**   g̱: *Sp.* ami**g**o   v̲: *Sp.* ha**b**lar
hl: *Welsh* **Ll**anelli.   CAPITALS: primary stress.   SMALL CAPS: secondary stress.   Ⓢ: U.S. pron.   Ⓔ: British pron.

English
lang., Europe, N. America   ING-glish, ING-lish   'ɪŋglɪʃ, 'ɪŋlɪʃ

English Channel [La Manche]
strait between England & France   ING-glish CHAN-l, ING-lish   ˌɪŋglɪʃ 'tʃænl, ˌɪŋlɪʃ

Enguerrand
pers. name, French   ahⁿ-guh-RAHⁿ   ɑ̃gərɑ̃

En-haddah
Biblical name   en-HAD-uh, ĀN-khah-DAH   en'hædə, ˌeːnxɑ'dɑ

En-hakkore
Biblical name   en-HAK-uh-ruh, EN-HAK-AWR-uh, ĀN-HAHK-ō-RE   en'hækərə, ˌenˌhæk'ɔːrə, ˌeːnˌhɑkoː're

En-hazor
Biblical name   en-HĀ-ZAWR, ĀN-khaht-SŌR   en'heːˌzɔːʳ, ˌeːnxɑt'soːr

ENIAC
vacuum-tube computer   Ē-nē-AK, EN-ē-AK   'iːniːˌæk, 'eniːˌæk

Enid
1. city, OK; pers. name   Ē-nuhd   'iːnəd
2. Welsh   EN-id   'enid

Enlil
supreme Sumerian god   EN-LIL   'enˌlil

En-mishpat
Biblical name   en-MISH-PAT, ĀN-mish-PAHT   en'miʃˌpæt, ˌeːnmiʃ'pɑt

Enna
Sicilian city   EN-uh   'enə

Ennius
Roman poet   EN-ē-uhs   'eniːəs

Eno
Brian, *British composer, musician*   Ē-nō   'iːnoː

Enoch
pers. name   Ē-nuhk, Ē-nik, Ē-NAHK   'iːnək, 'iːnik, 'iːˌnɑk

Enos
Seth's son; pers. name   Ē-nuhs   'iːnəs

Enosh [Enos]
Biblical name   Ē-NAHSH, en-ŌSH   'iːˌnɑʃ, en'oːʃ

Enrico
pers. name, Italian   en-RĒ-kō   en'riːkoː

En-rimmon
Biblical name   en-RIM-uhn, ĀN-ri-MŌN   en'rimən, ˌeːnri'moːn

Enrique
pers. name, Spanish   ān-RĒ-kā   eˑn'riːkeː

Enriquez
Rene, *US actor*   en-RĒ-kez   en'riːkez

En-rogel
Biblical name   en-RŌ-guhl, ĀN-raw-GEL   en'roːgəl, ˌeːnrɔː'gel

Ensenada
city, Mexico; town, Argentina   en-se-NAHTH-ah, ⑤ EN(T)-se-NAHD-uh   ense'nɑða, ⑤ ˌen(t)se'nɑdə

En-shemesh
Biblical name   en-SHĒ-MESH, ān-SHEM-ESH   en'ʃiːˌmeʃ, eːn'ʃemˌeʃ

Ensi
title of Sumerian city governor   EN-sē   'ensiˑ

En-tappuah
Biblical name   en-TAP-yuh-wuh, ĀN-tah-POO-AHKH   en'tæpjəwə, ˌeːntɑ'puːˌɑx

Entebbe
town, Uganda   en-TEB-uh, en-TEB-ē   en'tebə, en'tebiˑ

Key (col. 2):   a: fad   ā: fade   ah: father   ar: marry   aw: law   e: fed   ē: feed   er: merry   i: hid   ī: hide   ō: coat   ōō: boot
oi: boy   ow: now   u: put   uh: above   uhr: bird   ch: chop   ng: ring   sh: show   th: thick   <u>th</u>: this   zh: measure

Entre-Deux-Mers
  wine — ahⁿ-truh-duh(r)-MER — ãtrədœːmer

Enver
  pers. name, Albanian — EN-ver — 'enveʳ

Enver Paşa
  Turkish soldier and leader of Young Turks — en-VER pah-SHAH — en'veʳ pɑ'ʃɑː

Enyo
  Greek goddess of war — en-Ē-ō, en-Ī-ō — en'iːoː, en'ɑioː

Eocene
  geologic epoch — Ē-uh-SĒN — 'iːə,siːn

Eoin
  pers. name, Irish — YŌ(-uh)n, Ō-uhn — 'joː(ə)n, 'oːən

Eolian
  pert. to rock or sand carried by wind — ē-Ō-lē-uhn — iː'oːliːən

Eolithic
  geologic period — Ē-uh-LITH-ik — ,iːə'liθik

Eolus
  mtn., CO — ē-Ō-luhs — iː'oːləs

Eos
  Greek dawn goddess — Ē-AHS — 'iː,ɑs

Epaenetus
  see Epenetus

Epaminondas
  Theban general — i-PAM-uh-NAHN-duhs — i,pæmə'nɑndəs

Epaphras
  Biblical name — EP-uh-FRAS — 'epə,fræs

Epaphroditus
  Biblical name — i-PAF-ruh-DĪT-uhs — i,pæfrə'dɑiʈəs

Epcot
  Disneyworld attraction — EP-KAHT — 'ep,kɑt

Epeius
  builder of the Trojan horse — e-PĀ-(y)uhs — e'peː(j)əs

Epenetus, Epaenetus, Epœnetus
  Biblical name — i-PĒ-nuht-uhs — i'piːnəʈəs

Épernay
  wine — ā-per-NE — eːperne

Ephah
  Biblical name — Ē-fuh, ā-FAH — 'iːfə, eː'fɑ

Ephai
  Biblical name — Ē-FĪ, Ē-fē-Ī, ē-FĒ — 'iː,fɑi, 'iːfiː,ɑi, iː'fiː

Epher
  Biblical name — Ē-fuhr, EF-ER — 'iːfəʳ, 'ef,er

Ephes-dammim
  Biblical name — Ē-fuhs-DAM-uhm, EF-es-dah-MIM — 'iːfəs'dæməm, 'efesdɑ'mim

Ephesians
  New Testament book — i-FĒ-zhuhnz — i'fiːʒənz

Ephesus [Efes]
  ancient Ionian city, Asia Minor — EF-uh-suhs — 'efəsəs

Ephialtes
  Athenian statesman — EF-ē-AL-TĒZ — ,efiː'æl,tiːz

Ephlal
  Biblical name — EF-LAL, ef-LAHL — 'ef,læl, ef'lɑl

Ephod
  Biblical name — Ē-FAHD, ef-AWD — 'iː,fɑd, ef'ɔːd

Ephor
   Spartan official   Ē-fuhr, Ē-FAWR   'iːfəʳ, 'iːˌfɔːʳ

Ephphatha
   Biblical name   EF-uh-thuh   'efəθə

Ephraim
   1. city, UT; pers. name   Ē-frā-uhm, -frē-uhm; EF-ruhm   'iːfriːəm, 'iːfrəm
   2. mountain range, Jordan; Biblical   Ē-frē-uhm, Ē-fruhm, e-FRAH-yim   'iːfriːəm, 'iːfrəm, e'frajim
     name

Ephraimite
   Biblical name   Ē-frē-uh-MĪT, EF-ruh-MĪT   'iːfriːəˌmait, 'efrəˌmait

Ephrata
   1. borough, PA   EF-ruht-uh   'efrəʈə
   2. city, WA   i-FRĀT-uh   i'freːʈə

Ephratah, Ephrathah
   Biblical name   EF-ruht-uh, ef-RAH-tah   'efrəʈə, ef'rɑtɑ

Ephrath
   Biblical name   Ē-FRATH, ef-RAHT   'iːˌfræθ, ef'rɑt

Ephrathite
   Biblical name   EF-ruh-THĪT   'efrəˌθait

Ephron
   Nora *and* Delia, *US writers*   EF-ruhn   'efrən

Epictetus
   Greek philosopher; Greek potter &   EP-ik-TĒT-uhs   ˌepik'tiːʈəs
     painter

Epicureanism
   philosophy of Epicurus   EP-i-kyu-RĒ-uh-NIZ-uhm,   ˌepikju'riːəˌnizəm,
                            EP-i-KYUR-ē-uh-NIZ-uhm   ˌepi'kjuriːəˌnizəm

Epicurus
   Greek philosopher   EP-i-KYUR-uhs   ˌepi'kjurəs

Epidaurus
   ancient Greek seaport   EP-uh-DAWR-uhs   ˌepə'dɔːrəs

Epigoni
   sons of Seven against Thebes   i-PIG-uh-NĪ, i-PIG-uh-nē   i'pigəˌnɑi, i'pigəniˑ

Epimetheus
   brother of Atlas & Prometheus;   EP-uh-MĒ-thē-uhs   ˌepə'miːθiːəs
     satellite of Saturn

Epinomis
   dialogue of Plato   EP-uh-NŌ-muhs   ˌepə'noːməs

Epione
   wife of Asclepius   uh-PĪ-uh-nē   ə'paiəniˑ

Epiphany
   Christian season   i-PIF-uh-nē   i'pifəniˑ

Epirus [Ipiros]
   region, Greece   i-PĪ-ruhs   i'pairəs

Episcopalianism
   religion   i-PIS-kuh-PĀ-lē-uh-NIZ-uhm   iˌpiskə'peːliːəˌnizəm

Epœnetus
   See Epenetus

Epithalamion
   bridal poem, E. Spenser   EP-uh-thuh-LĀ-mē-uhn   ˌepəθə'leːmiːən

Epopeus
   king of Sicyon and Corinth   i-PŌ-pē-uhs   i'poːpiːəs

EPROM
   computer memory chip   Ē-PRAHM   'iːˌprɑm

Key (col. 2):   a: fad   ā: fade   ah: father   ar: marry   aw: law   e: fed   ē: feed   er: merry   i: hid   ī: hide   ō: coat   ōō: boot
oi: boy   ow: now   u: put   uh: above   uhr: bird   ch: chop   ng: ring   sh: show   th: thick   <u>th</u>: this   zh: measure

Epsom
  town, England   EP-suhm   ˈepsəm

Epson
  computer co.   EP-suhn   ˈepsən

Epstein
  Sir Jacob, *British sculptor*   EP-STĪN   ˈepˌstain

Epstein-Barr
  mononucleosis virus   EP-STĪN-BAHR   ˌepˌstainˈbaʳ

Equator
  great circle at latitude 0°   i-KWĀT-uhr, Ē-KWĀT-uhr   iˈkweːṭəʳ, ˈiːˌkweːṭəʳ

Equatorial Guinea
  republic, Africa   Ē-kwuh-TŌR-ē-uhl GIN-ē, EK-wuh-, -TAWR-ē-uhl   ˌiːkwəˌtoːriːəl ˈginiˑ, ˌekwə-, -ˌtoːriːəl

Equatorial Guinean
  pert. to Equatorial Guinea   Ē-kwuh-TŌR-ē-uhl GIN-ē-uhn, EK-wuh-, -TAWR-ē-uhl   ˌiːkwəˌtoːriːəl ˈginiːən, ˌekwə-, -ˌtoːriːəl

Equites
  Roman social class   EK-wuh-TĀS, EK-wuh-TĒZ   ˈekwəˌteːs, ˈekwəˌtiːz

Equuleus
  constellation   e-KWOO-lē-uhs   eˈkwuːliːəs

Er
  myth, Plato's Republic   ER, UHR   ˈeʳ, ˈəʳ

Eran
  Biblical name   IR-AN, Ē-RAN, er-AHN   ˈirˌæn, ˈiːˌræn, erˈɑn

Eranite
  Biblical name   IR-uhn-ĪT, Ē-ruh-NĪT   ˈirənˌait, ˈiːrəˌnait

Erasistratus
  Greek physician   ER-uh-SIS-truht-uhs   ˌerəˈsistrəṭəs

Érasme
  pers. name, French   ā-RAHSM   eːraːsm

Erasmo
  pers. name, Italian   ā-RAHZ-mō   eːˈrazmoː

Erasmus
  1. Desiderius *Dutch humanist; pers. name*   i-RAZ-muhs   iˈræzməs
  2. Danish   i-RAHS-mus   iˈrɑsmus
  3. German   ā-RAHS-mus   eːˈrɑsmus

Erastus
  pers. name   i-RAS-tuhs   iˈræstəs

Erath
  county, TX   Ē-RATH   ˈiːˌræθ

Erato
  1. muse of lyric poetry   ER-uh-TŌ   ˈerəˌtoː
  2. street, New Orleans   i-RAHT-ō, i-RAT-ō   iˈrɑṭoː, iˈræṭoː

Eratosthenes
  Greek scientist   ER-uh-TAHS-thuh-NĒZ   ˌerəˈtɑsθəˌniːz

Erawan
  oil & gas field, Gulf of Thailand   ER-uh-WAHN, ER-uh-WAHN   ˈerəˌwɑn, ˌerəˈwɑn

Erbil [Arbīl, Irbīl]
  governorate, city, Iraq   ER-BĒL   ˈeʳˌbiːl

erbium
  element   UHR-bē-uhm   ˈəʳbiːəm

Ercilla y Zúñiga
  Alonso de, *Spanish epic poet and soldier*   er-THĒ(L)-yah ē THOON-yē-gah   erˈθiː(l)ja iː ˈθuːnjiːga

---

Foreign Sounds: ue: *Fr.* **rue**, *Ger.* **füllen** uh(r): *Fr.* **boeuf**, *Ger.* **Höhle** kh: *Ger.* **ich**, *Scot.* **loch** ḡ: *Sp.* **amigo** v̱: *Sp.* **hablar** hl: *Welsh* **Llanelli**. CAPITALS: primary stress. SMALL CAPS: secondary stress. Ⓢ: U.S. pron. Ⓑ: British pron.

Erda

  Norse earth goddess   ERD-uh   'eʳdə

Erdenet

  city, Mongolia   ERD-n-ET   ˌeʳdn̩'et

Erebus

  personification of the infernal shades   ER-uh-buhs   'erəbəs
    in Greek mythology; James Ross's
    ship; volcano, Antarctica

Erech

  Biblical name   Ē-REK, ER-EK, ER-E<u>KH</u>   'iːˌrek, 'erˌek, 'erˌex

Erechtheum

  temple, Athens   ER-uhk-THĒ-uhm, ER-EK-   ˌerək'θiːəm, ˌerˌek-

Erechtheus

  king of Athens   uh-REK-thē-uhs, uh-REK-TH(Y)O͞OS   ə'rekθiːəs, ə'rekˌθ(j)uːs

Eretria

  ancient Greek city   e-RĒ-trē-uh   e'riːtriːə

Erewhon

  utopian work, S. Butler   ER-uh-(H)WAHN   'erəˌ(h)wɑn

Erfurt

  city, Germany   ER-FURT, ER-fuhrt   'eʳˌfuʳt, 'eʳfəʳt

Erginus

  king of the Minyans; Argonaut   er-JĪ-nuhs   eʳ'dʒɑinəs

Erhard

  Ludwig, *German politician; pers.*   ER-HAHRT, ĀR-HAHRT   'eʳˌhɑʳt, 'eːʳˌhɑʳt
    name

Eri

  Biblical name   IR-Ī, Ē-RĪ, er-Ē   'irˌai, 'iːˌrai, er'iː

Eric

  1. pers. name   ER-ik   'erik
  2. Danish   IR-ēk   'iriːk
  3. Norwegian   Ā-rēk   'eːriːk
  4. Swedish   Ā-rik   'eːrik

Erica

  pers. name   ER-i-kuh   'erikə

Erich

  pers. name, German   Ā-ri<u>kh</u>   'eːriç

Erichthonius

  king of Athens   ER-ik-THŌ-nē-uhs   ˌerik'θoːniːəs

Ericsson

  Leif, *Norse explorer*   ER-ik-suhn   'eriksən

Eridanus

  legendary river into which Phaethon   i-RID-n-uhs   i'ridn̩əs
    fell; constellation

Eridu

  Sumerian seaport   ER-uh-DO͞O   'erəˌduː

Erie

  lake; city, PA; canal, NY; county, NY,   IR-ē   'iri·
    OH, PA; North American people

Erigone

  mother of Staphylus; daughter of   i-RIG-uh-nē   i'rigəni·
    Aegisthus and Clytemnestra

Key (col. 2):   a: fa**d**   ā: fa**d**e   ah: f**a**ther   ar: m**a**rry   aw: l**a**w   e: f**e**d   ē: f**ee**d   er: m**e**rry   i: h**i**d   ī: h**i**de   ō: c**oa**t   o͞o: b**oo**t
oi: b**oy**   ow: n**ow**   u: p**u**t   uh: **a**bove   uhr: b**i**rd   ch: **ch**op   ng: ri**ng**   sh: **sh**ow   th: **th**ick   <u>th</u>: **th**is   zh: mea**s**ure

Erik

1. pers. name	ER-ik	ˈerik
2. Danish	IR-ēk	ˈiriːk
3. French	ā-RĒK	eːriːk
4. German, Swedish	Ā-rik	ˈeːrik
5. Norwegian	Ā-rēk	ˈeːriːk

Erika

1. pers. name	ER-i-kuh	ˈerikə
2. German	Ā-rē-KAH	ˈeːriːˌkɑ

Erin

Ireland; pers. name	AR-uhn, ER-uhn	ˈærən, ˈerən

Erinyes

the Eumenides or Furies	i-RIN-ē-ĒZ	iˈriniːˌiːz

Erinys

singular of Erinyes	i-RIN-uhs, i-RĪ-nuhs	iˈrinəs, iˈrainəs

Eriphyle

sister of Adrastus & wife of Amphiaraus	ER-uh-FĪ-lē	ˌerəˈfaili·

Eris

Greek goddess, personification of strife	ER-uhs, IR-uhs	ˈerəs, ˈirəs

Erite

Biblical name	IR-ĪT, Ē-RĪT	ˈirˌait, ˈiːˌrait

Eritrea

region, Ethiopia	ER-uh-TRĒ-uh, ER-uh-TRĀ-uh	ˌerəˈtriːə, ˌerəˈtreːə

Erlander

Tage, *Swedish statesman*	er-LAHN-duhr	eʳˈlandəʳ

Erlanger

Joseph, *US physiologist (Nobel 1944)*	UHR-LANG-uhr	ˈəʳˌlæŋəʳ

Erlau

Hungarian commune	ER-LOW	ˈeʳˌlau

Erle

pers. name	UHRL, UHR-uhl	ˈəʳl, ˈərəl

Ermitage

wine	er-mē-TAHZH	ermiːtaːʒ

Ernani

opera, Verdi	er-NAHN-ē	eʳˈnani·

Ernest

1. pers. name	UHR-nuhst	ˈəʳnəst
2. French	er-NEST	ernest
3. German	er-NEST	eʳˈnest
4. Swedish	ER-nuhst	ˈernəst

Ernestine

1. pers. name	UHR-nuh-STĒN	ˈəʳnəˌstiːn
2. German	ER-nes-TĒ-nuh	ˌeʳnesˈtiːnə
3. French	er-nes-TĒN	ernestiːn

Ernesto

1. pers. name, Italian	ār-NES-tō	eːrˈnestoː
2. Portuguese	ēr-NESH-tōo, -NES-tōo	iːrˈneʃtuː, -ˈnestuː
3. Spanish	er-NĀ-stō	erˈneːstoː

Ernie

pers. name	UHR-nē	ˈəʳni·

Ernő

pers. name, Hungarian	ER-nuh(r)	ˈernœː

Foreign Sounds: ue: *Fr.* **rue**, *Ger.* **füllen** uh(r): *Fr.* **boeuf**, *Ger.* **Höhle** k̲h̲: *Ger.* i**ch**, *Scot.* lo**ch** ğ: *Sp.* ami**g**o v̲: *Sp.* ha**b**lar hl: *Welsh* **Ll**anelli. CAPITALS: primary stress. SMALL CAPS: secondary stress. ⑧: U.S. pron. ⑧: British pron.

Ernst
  1. Richard R., *Swiss chemist*   ERNST   'eᵣnst
  2. pers. name   UHRNST, ERNST   'əᵣnst, 'eᵣnst
  3. Dutch, Norwegian, Swedish   ERNST   'ernst
  4. German   ERNST   'eᵣnst

Eroica
  Beethoven's 3rd symphony   i-RŌ-ik-uh, e-RŌ-ik-uh   i'roːikə, e'roːikə

Eros
  Greek god of love; asteroid 433   ER-AHS, IR-AHS   'er‚ɑs, 'ir‚ɑs

Erroll
  pers. name   ER-uhl   'erəl

Erse
  Gaelic   UHRS   'əᵣs

Érsekújvár [Nové Zámky]
  town, Slovakia   ER-SHEK-O͞OI-VAHR   ‚eᵣ‚ʃek'uːi‚vɑᵣ

Erskine
  College & Seminary, SC; pers. name   UHR-skuhn   'əᵣskən

Erté
  costume designer   er-TĀ, ER-TĀ   eᵣ'teː, 'eᵣ‚teː

Ēr'tra [Eritrea]
  region, Ethiopia   ER-truh   'ertrə

Ervine
  St. John Greer, *Irish playwright and novelist*   UHR-vin   'əᵣvin

Erving
  Julius Winfield, *US basketball player*   UHR-ving   'əᵣviŋ

Erwin
  1. pers. name   UHR-wuhn   'əᵣwən
  2. German   ER-vēn   'eᵣviːn

Erymanthus
  son of Apollo   ER-uh-MAN-thuhs   ‚erə'mænθəs

Erysichthon
  Thessalian autophage punished by Demeter   ER-uh-SIK-THAHN   ‚erə'sik‚θɑn

Erysimum
  plant   ir-IS-uh-muhm   ir'isəməm

Eryx
  son of Aphrodite   ER-iks   'eriks

Erzgebirge
  mountain range, Germany, Czech Republic   ERTS-guh-BIR-guh   'eᵣtsgə‚biᵣgə

Erzquell Edelbräu
  German beer   ERTS-KVEL ĀD-l-BROI   'eᵣts‚kvel 'eːdl̩‚brɔi

Esaias
  1. pers. name, Dutch   ā-SAH-YAHS, -SĪ-(Y)AHS   eː'saː‚jas, -'sai‚(j)ɑs
  2. Swedish   e-SĪ-ahs   e'saiɑːs

Esaki
  Leo, *Japanese physicist (Nobel 1973)*   es-ah-kē   esɑki·

Esala Perahera
  Sri Lankan festival   ES-uh-luh PER-uh-HER-uh   'esələ 'perə‚herə

Esarhaddon
  Assyrian king   Ē-SAHR-HAD-n   ‚iː‚sɑᵣ'hædn̩

Esau
  Biblical name   Ē-SAW   'iː‚sɔː

Key (col. 2):   a: fad   ā: fade   ah: father   ar: marry   aw: law   e: fed   ē: feed   er: merry   i: hid   ī: hide   ō: coat   o͠o: boot
oi: boy   ow: now   u: put   uh: above   uhr: bird   ch: chop   ng: ring   sh: show   th: thick   th: this   zh: measure

Escalante
  river, UT — ES-kuh-LANT-ē — ˌeskə'lænt̬i·

Escambia
  river, US; county, AL, FL — e-SKAM-bē-uh — e'skæmbiːə

Escambia
  river, SE United States — e-SKAM-bē-uh — e'skæmbiːə

Escanaba
  river, MI — ES-kuh-NAHB-uh — ˌeskə'nɑbə

Eschenbach
  Christoph, *German pianist,* — ESH-uhn-BAHKH — 'eʃənˌbɑx
  conductor

Escher
  Maurits Corneille (*or* Cornelis), — ES-khuhr, Ⓢ ESH-uhr — 'esxər, Ⓢ 'eʃər
  Dutch artist

Escoffier
  Auguste, *French chef* — es-kawf-YĀ — eskɔːfjeː

Escondido
  city, CA — ES-kuhn-DĒD-ō — ˌeskən'diːdoː

Escondido
  city, CA — ES-kuhn-DĒD-ō — ˌeskən'diːdoː

Escorial
  building outside Madrid, Spain — es-kōr-YAHL, Ⓢ es-KAWR-ē-uhl — eskoːr'jɑl, Ⓢ es'kɔːriːəl

ESDI
  enhanced small device interface — ES-dē — 'esdi·

Esdraelon
  plain, Israel — EZ-druh-Ē-luhn — ˌezdrə'iːlən

Esdras
  Old Testament book, pers. name — EZ-druhs — 'ezdrəs

Esek
  Biblical name — Ē-SEK, ES-EK — 'iːˌsek, 'esˌek

Esfahān
  prov & town, Iran — ES-fuh-HAHN — ˌesfə'hɑn

Eshkol
  Levi, *Israeli politician* — esh-KAWL — eʃ'kɔːl

Eshowe
  village, S. Africa — ESH-uh-WĀ — 'eʃəˌweː

Eshtaol
  Biblical name — ESH-tā-AHL, ESH-tah-ŌL — 'eʃteːˌɑl, ˌeʃtɑ'oːl

Eshtaolites
  Biblical name — ESH-tā-uh-LĪTS — 'eʃteːəˌlaits

Eshtemoa [Eshtemoh]
  Biblical name — ESH-ti-MŌ-uh — ˌeʃti'moːə

Eshtemoh
  Biblical name — ESH-tuh-MŌ, ESH-tuh-MAW — 'eʃtəˌmoː, ˌeʃtə'mɔː

Eshton
  Biblical name — ESH-TAHN, esh-TŌN — 'eʃˌtan, eʃ'toːn

Eskimo
  N. American & Siberian peoples — ES-kuh-MŌ — 'eskəˌmoː

Esli
  Biblical name — ES-lē — 'esliː

Esmeralda
  county, NV; pers. name — EZ-muh-RAL-duh — ˌezmə'rældə

Espérance
  1. pers. name, French — es-pā-RAHⁿS — espeːrɑ̃s
  2. German — ES-pā-RAHNS — ˌespeː'rans

Foreign Sounds: ue: *Fr.* **rue**, *Ger.* **füllen** uh(r): *Fr.* **boeuf**, *Ger.* **Höhle** kh: *Ger.* **ich**, *Scot.* **loch** ḡ: *Sp.* **amigo** v: *Sp.* **hablar**
hl: *Welsh* **Llanelli**. CAPITALS: primary stress. SMALL CAPS: secondary stress. Ⓢ: U.S. pron. Ⓔ: British pron.

Esperantist

  advocate of Esperanto   ES-puh-RAHNT-uhst,   ˌespə'rɑntəst, ˌespə'ræntəst
                              ES-puh-RANT-uhst

Esperanto

  artificial lang.   ES-puh-RAHN-tō, ES-puh-RANT-ō   ˌespə'rɑntoː, ˌespə'ræntoː

Espírito Santo

  island, state, Brazil   uh-SPIR-uh-TOO SAHN-too   ə'spirəˌtuː 'sɑntuː

Espíritu Santo

  state, Vanuatu; island off Baja uh-SPIR-uh-TOO SAHN-tō   ə'spirəˌtuː 'sɑntoː
    California

Esposito

  Phil, Tony, *ice hockey players* ES-puh-ZĒT-ō   ˌespə'ziːt̥oː

Esquiline

  hill, Rome, Italy   ES-kwuh-LĪN, ES-kwuh-luhn   'eskwəˌlain, 'eskwələn

Esquipulas

  town, Guatemala   ES-ki-POO-luhs   ˌeski'puːləs

Esquivel

  Adolfo Pérez, *Argentine human* ā-skē-VEL   eːskiː'βel
    rights activist (Nobel 1980)

Esrom

  Biblical name   ES-RAHM   'esˌrɑm

Essaouira [Mogador]

  city, Morocco   ES-uh-WIR-uh   ˌesə'wirə

Essen

  city, Germany   ES-n   'esn̩

Essene

  Jewish ascetic sect   i-SĒN, ES-ĒN   i'siːn, 'esˌiːn

Essequibo

  river, county, Guyana   ES-uh-KWĒ-bō   ˌesə'kwiːboː

Essex

  pl. name, US, England   ES-iks   'esiks

Esso

  tdmk for oil products   ES-ō   'esoː

Est! Est!! Est!!!

  wine   EST EST EST   ˌest ˌest 'est

Este

  city, Italy   ES-tā   'esteː

Esteban

  pers. name, Spanish   ā-STĀ-vahn   eː'steːβɑn

Estée Lauder

  cosmetics   EST-Ā LAWD-uhr   ˌestˌeː 'lɔːdəʳ

Estefan

  Gloria, *US rock singer*   es-TEF-uhn, es-TEF-AHN   es'tefən, es'tefˌɑn

Estella

  pers. name   uh-STEL-uh, es-TEL-uh   ə'stelə, es'telə

Estelle

  pers. name   es-TEL, ES-tl, uh-STEL   es'tel, 'estl̩, ə'stel

Esterházy

  noble Hungarian family   ES-tuhr-HAH-zē   'estəʳˌhɑːzi·

Estes

  1. pers. name   ES-tuhs   'estəs
  2. park, CO   ES-tēz, ES-tuhs   'estiːz, 'estəs

Estevanico

  US explorer   ES-tuh-VAHN-i-kō   ˌestə'vɑnikoː

Key (col. 2): a: fad ā: fade ah: father ar: marry aw: law e: fed ē: feed er: merry i: hid ī: hide ō: coat oo: boot
oi: boy ow: now u: put uh: above uhr: bird ch: chop ng: ring sh: show th: thick th: this zh: measure

Esther
   Old Testament book; pers. name   ES-tuhr   'estəʳ

Estonia
   Baltic republic   e-STŌ-nē-uh, e-STŌN-yuh   e'stoːniːə, e'stoːnjə

Estonian
   pert. to Estonia   es-TŌ-nē-uhn, -nyuhn   es'toːniːən, -njən

Estoril
   town, Portugal   ĒSH-tuh-RIL   ˌiːʃtə'ril

Estragon
   herb   ES-truh-GAHN   'estrəˌgɑn

Estremadura
   former prov, Portugal   ES-truh-muh-DUR-uh   ˌestrəmə'durə

Estremadura, Extremadura
   region, Spain   es-trā-mah-<u>THUR</u>-ah,   estreːmɑ'ðurɑ,
            Ⓢ E(K)S-truh-muh-DUR-uh   Ⓢ ˌe(k)strəmə'durə

ETA
   Basque separatist movement   ET-uh   'eţə

Etam
   Biblical name   Ē-TAM, ā-TAHM   'iːˌtæm, eː'tɑm

Étaples
   commune, France   ā-TAHPL   eːtɑːpl

Etchebaster
   Pierre, *French Basque athlete*   ich-i-bahsh-TER   itʃibɑːʃter

Etelfrid [Aethelfrith]
   Anglo-Saxon ruler   E<u>TH</u>-uhl-FRID, ETH-   'eðəlˌfrid, 'eθ-

Eteocles
   son of Oedipus; brother of Polynices   i-TĒ-uh-KLĒZ   i'tiːəˌkliːz

Etham
   Biblical name   Ē-THAM, e-TAHM   'iːˌθæm, e'tɑm

Ethan
   pers. name   Ē-thuhn   'iːθən

Ethanim
   Biblical name   ETH-uh-NIM, ET-ah-NĒM   'eθəˌnim, ˌetɑ'niːm

Eth-baal
   Biblical name   eth-BĀ-uhl, et-BAH-AHL   eθ'beːəl, et'bɑˌɑl

Ethel
   pers. name   ETH-uhl   'eθəl

Ethelbald
   Anglo-Saxon king of Mercia   ETH-uhl-BAWLD, ETH-   'eðəlˌbɔːld, 'eθ-

Ethelbert
   pers. name   ETH-uhl-BUHRT   'eðəlˌbəʳt

Ethelfleda [Aethelflaed]
   Anglo-Saxon ruler, daughter of Alfred   E<u>TH</u>-uhl-FLED-uh, ETH-   'eðəlˌfledə, 'eθ-
   the Great

Ethelfrith [Aethelfrith]
   Anglo-Saxon ruler   E<u>TH</u>-uhl-FRITH, ETH-   'eðəlˌfriθ, 'eθ-

Ethelhard [Aethelheard]
   Mercian cleric   E<u>TH</u>-uhl-HA(-uh)rd, ETH-   'eðəlˌhæ(ə)ʳd, 'eθ-

Ethelred
   English king   ETH-uhl-RED   'eθəlˌred

Ether
   Biblical name   Ē-thuhr, ET-er   'iːθəʳ, 'eter

Etheredge
   Forest Deroyce, *US politician*   ETH-(uh-)rij   'eθ(ə)ridʒ

Foreign Sounds: ue: *Fr.* **rue**, *Ger.* **füllen**   uh(r): *Fr.* **boeuf**, *Ger.* **Höhle**   <u>kh</u>: *Ger.* **ich**, *Scot.* **loch**   ḡ: *Sp.* **amigo**   <u>v</u>: *Sp.* **hablar**
hl: *Welsh* **Llanelli.**   CAPITALS: primary stress.   SMALL CAPS: secondary stress.   Ⓢ: U.S. pron.   Ⓔ: British pron.

Etherege
Sir George, *English dramatist*   ETH(-uh)-RIJ   'eθ(ə)ˌridʒ

Ethiop
person from Ethiopia   Ē-thē-ŌP   'iːθiːˌoːp

Ethiopia [Abyssinia]
country, Africa   Ē-thē-Ō-pē-uh   ˌiːθiː'oːpiːə

Ethiopian
pert. to Ethiopia   Ē-thē-Ō-pē-uhn   ˌiːθiː'oːpiːən

Ethiopic
pert. to Ethiopia   Ē-thē-Ō-pik   ˌiːθiː'oːpik

Ethkazin, Eth-Kazin
Biblical name   eth-KĀ-zuhn, et-kaht-SIN   eθ'keːzən, etkɑt'sin

Ethnan
Biblical name   ETH-NAN, et-NAHN   'eθˌnæn, et'nɑn

Ethni
Biblical name   ETH-NĪ, et-NĒ   'eθˌnɑi, et'niː

Étienne
pers. name, French   ā-TYEN   eːtjen

Etna, Aetna
Mount, *volcano, Sicily*   ET-nuh   'etnə

Étoile
wine   ā-TWAHL   eː'twɑːl

Eton
1. British school   ĒT-n   'iːtn
2. lang., Africa   ĒT-n, Ē-TAHN, ē-TŌN   'iːtn̩, 'iːˌtɑn, iː'toːn

Etonian
pert. to Eton   ē-TŌ-nē-uhn   iː'toːniːən

Etowah
river, GA; county, AL; town, TN   ET-uh-WAW, ĒT-ē-WAW, -WAH   'eţəˌwɔː, 'iːţiˈˌwɔː, -ˌwɑ

Etruria
region of ancient Italy   i-TRUR-ē-uh   i'truriːə

Etrurian
pert. to Etruria   i-TRUR-ē-uhn   i'truriːən

Etruscan
ancient lang.; native of or pert. to Etruria   i-TRUHS-kuhn   i'trəskən

Ettie, Etty
pers. name   ET-ē   'eţiˈ

Eubanks
Bob, *US TV entertainer*   YOO-BANGKS   'juːˌbæŋks

Euboea
island, Greece   yu-BĒ-uh   ju'biːə

Eubouleus
legendary swineherd   yoo-BOO-lē-uhs   juˈ'buːliːəs

Eubulus
Biblical name   yu-BYOO-luhs, YOO-byuh-luhs   juˈ'bjuːləs, 'juːbjələs

Eucharist
Holy Communion   YOO-kuh-ruhst, YOO-kruhst   'juːkərəst, 'juːkrəst

Euchre
game   YOO-kuhr   'juːkəʳ

Eucken
R. C., *German philosopher (Nobel 1908)*   OI-kuhn   'ɔikən

Euclid
Greek mathematician; city, OH   YOO-kluhd   'juːkləd

Key (col. 2):   a: fad   ā: fade   ah: father   ar: marry   aw: law   e: fed   ē: feed   er: merry   i: hid   ī: hide   ō: coat   ōō: boot
oi: boy   ow: now   u: put   uh: above   uhr: bird   ch: chop   ng: ring   sh: show   th: thick   <u>th</u>: this   zh: measure

Euclidean
  pert. to Euclid   yu-KLID-ē-uhn   juˈklidiːən

Euclides
  pers. name, Portuguese   āu-KLĒ-dāsh, -dās   eːuˈkliːdeːʃ, -deːs

Eudes
  pers. name, French   UH(R)D   œːd

Eudora
  pers. name   yōō-DŌR-uh, DAWR-uh   juːˈdoːrə, -ˈdoːrə

Eudoxus
  Greek explorer; Greek astronomer,   yu-DAHK-suhs   juˈdɑksəs
    mathematician

Eufaula
  city, AL; city, OK   yu-FAW-luh   juˈfoːlə

Eugen
  pers. name, German   oi-GĀN   ɔiˈgeːn

Eugene
  city, OR; pers. name   yōō-JĒN, YŌŌ-JĒN   juːˈdʒiːn, ˈjuːˌdʒiːn

Eugène
  pers. name, French   uh(r)-ZHEN   œːʒen

Eugene Onegin
  opera, Tchaikovsky   yu-JĒN awn-YĀ-guhn   juˈdʒiːn ɔːnˈjeːgən

Eugenia
  pers. name   yōō-JĒ-nē-uh, yōō-JĒN-yuh   juˑˈdʒiːniːə, juˑˈdʒiːnjə

Eugenie
  pers. name, German   oi-GĀ-nē-uh, oi-GĀN-yuh   ɔiˈgeːniːə, ɔiˈgeːnjə

Eugénie
  pers. name, French   uh(r)-zhā-NĒ   œːʒeːniː

Eugenio
  1. pers. name, Italian   āu-JEN-yō   eːuˈdʒenjoː
  2. Spanish   āu-<u>KH</u>ĀN-yō   eːuˈçeːnjoː

Eugénio
  pers. name, Portuguese   āu-ZHĀN-yōō   eːuˈʒeːnjuː

Eugenius
  name of four popes   yōō-JĒ-nē-uhs, yōō-JĒN-yuhs   juːˈdʒiːniːəs, juːˈdʒiːnjəs

Eulalie
  pers. name   YŌŌ-luh-lē   ˈjuːləliˑ

Eulalius
  antipope   yu-LĀ-lē-uhs, yu-LĀL-yuhs   juˈleːliːəs, juˈleːljəs

Euler
  Ulf von, *Swedish physiologist (Nobel*   OI-luhr   ˈɔiləʳ
  1970)

Euler-Chelpin
  Hans von, *German-born Swedish*   OI-luhr-KEL-puhn   ˌɔiləʳˈkelpən
  chemist (Nobel 1929)

Euler Landpils
  German beer   OI-luhr LAHNT-PILS   ˈɔiləʳ ˈlɑntˌpils

Euless, John
  Park, *ballpark, Fresno, CA*   JAHN YŌŌ-luhs   ˈdʒɑn ˈjuːləs

Eumaeus
  swineherd of Odysseus   yōō-MĀ-uhs   juˑˈmeːəs

Eumenides
  the Greek Furies or Erinyes; tragedy,   yu-MEN-uh-DĒZ   juˈmenəˌdiːz
  Aeschylus

Eumolpus
  founder of Eleusian mysteries   yōō-MAWL-puhs, yōō-MAHL-puhs   juˑˈmoːlpəs, juˑˈmɑlpəs

---

Euneus		
son of Jason and Hypsipyle	YO͞O-nē-uhs	'juːniːəs
Eunice		
1. pers. name	YO͞O-nuhs	'juːnəs
2. Latin	yu-NĪ-sē	ju'nɑisiˑ
Eunomus		
cup-bearer killed by Heracles	yo͞o-NŌ-muhs	juˑ'noːməs
Euodia		
Biblical name	yo͞o-ŌD-ē-uh	juː'oːdiːə
Euodias [Euodia]		
Biblical name	yo͞o-ŌD-ē-uhs	juː'oːdiːəs
Euparkeria		
dinosaur	YO͞O-pahr-KER-ē-uh, YO͞O-pahr-KIR-ē-uh	ˌjuːpɑʳ'keriːə, ˌjuːpɑʳ'kiriːə
Eupatrids		
Athenian aristocracy	yo͞o-PA-truhdz, YO͞O-puh-TRIDZ	juː'pætrədz, 'juːpəˌtridz
Euphemus		
Argonaut, son of Poseidon and Europa	yo͞o-FĒ-muhs	juˑ'fiːməs
Euphonia		
songbird	yo͞o-FŌ-nē-uh	juˑ'foːniːə
Euphorbia		
plant	yo͞o-FAWR-bē-uh	juˑ'fɔːʳbiːə
Euphrates		
river, Asia	yo͞o-FRĀT-ēz	juˑ'freːt̬iːz
Euphrosyne		
pers. name	yu-FRAHS-n-ē, yu-FRAHZ-uh-nē	ju'frɑsn̩iˑ, ju'frɑzəniˑ
Euphues		
character, J. Lyly	YO͞O-fyuh-WĒZ	'juːfjəˌwiːz
Eurailpass		
European train discount fare	YUR-ĀL-PAS, -PAHS	'jurˌeːlˌpæs, -ˌpɑːs
Eurasia		
Europe & Asia	yu-RĀ-zhuh, yu-RĀ-shuh	ju'reːʒə, ju'reːʃə
Euratom		
European nuclear regulating organization	yur-AT-uhm	jur'æt̬əm
Eure		
river, department, France	UH(R)R, [$] UHR	'œr, [$] 'əʳ
Eurico		
pers. name, Portuguese	āu-RĒ-ko͞o	eːu'riːkuː
Euripides		
Greek tragedian	yu-RIP-uh-DĒZ	ju'ripəˌdiːz
Euro-		
combining form	YUR-ō, YUR-ō	'juroː, ˌjuroː
Euroa		
town, Australia	yu-RŌ-uh	ju'roːə
Euroclydon		
a wind	yu-RAHK-luh-DAHN	ju'rɑkləˌdɑn
Eurodollar		
US dollar credited to European bank	YUR-ō-DAHL-uhr, YUR-ō-DAHL-uhr	'juroːˌdɑləʳ, ˌjuroː'dɑləʳ
Europa		
mother of Minos by Zeus; satellite of Jupiter	yu-RŌ-puh	ju'roːpə
Europe		
continent	YUR-uhp	'jurəp

European
  pert. to Europe — YUR-uh-PĒ-uhn — ˌjurəˈpiːən

europium
  element — yu-RŌ-pē-uhm — juˈroːpiːəm

Europoort
  port, Netherlands — YUR-uh-PAWRT, YUR-ō-PAWRT — ˈjurəˌpɔːʳt, ˈjuroːˌpɔːʳt

Eurus
  the south-east or east wind in Roman mythology — YUR-uhs — ˈjurəs

Euryale
  Gorgon — yu-RĪ-uh-lē — juˈrɑiəliˑ

Eurycleia
  nurse of Odysseus — YUR-i-KLĀ-(y)uh, YUR-i-KLĒ-uh — ˌjuriˈkleː(j)ə, ˌjuriˈkliːə

Eurydice
  wife of Orpheus in Greek myth — yu-RID-uh-sē — juˈridəsiˑ

Eurylochus
  companion of Odysseus — yu-RIL-uh-kuhs — juˈriləkəs

Eurymachus
  suitor of Penelope — yu-RIM-uh-kuhs — juˈriməkəs

Eurymedon
  father of Prometheus; charioteer of Agamemnon — yu-RIM-uh-DAHN — juˈriməˌdɑn

Eurynome
  mother of the Graces — yu-RIN-uh-mē — juˈrinəmiˑ

Eurypylus
  king of Cyrene — yu-RIP-uh-luhs — juˈripələs

Eurysaces
  son of Telamon Ajax — yu-RIS-uh-KĒZ — juˈrisəˌkiːz

Eurystheus
  king who gave Heracles the Twelve Labors — yu-RIS-thē-uhs, yu-RIS-THO�templatēOS — juˈrisθiːəs, juˈrisˌθuːs

Eurythmics
  rock group — yu-RITH-miks — juˈriðmiks

Eurytus
  mythical archer — YUR-uht-uhs — ˈjurəʈəs

Eusden
  Laurence, *British poet laureate* — YO�§OZ-duhn — ˈjuːzdən

Eusebio
  1. pers. name, Italian — āu-ZEB-yō — eːuˈzebjoː
  2. Spanish — āu-SĀV-yō — eːuˈseːβjoː

Eusebius
  1. pope; Christian historian; pers. name — yō�§o-SĒB-ē-uhs — juːˈsiːbiːəs
  2. German — oi-ZĀB-yus, oi-ZĀ-bē-us — ɔiˈzeːbjus, ɔiˈzeːbiːus

Eustace
  pers. name — YO�§O-stuhs — ˈjuːstəs

Eustachian tube
  auditory canal — yu-STĀ-sh(ē-)uhn, yu-STĀ-kē-uhn — juˈsteːʃ(iː)ən, juˈsteːkiːən

Euterpe
  1. muse of the flute — yu-TUHR-pē — juˈtəʳpiˑ
  2. street, New Orleans — YO�§O-TUHRP, YO�§O-truhp — ˈjuːˌtəʳp, ˈjuːtrəp

Euthydemus
  king of Bactria; dialogue of Plato — YO�§O-thuh-DĒ-muhs, YO�§O-THID-uh-muhs — ˌjuːθəˈdiːməs, juːˈθidəməs

---

Foreign Sounds: **ue**: *Fr.* **rue**, *Ger.* **füllen** **uh(r)**: *Fr.* **boeuf**, *Ger.* **Höhle** <u>kh</u>: *Ger.* **ich**, *Scot.* lo<u>ch</u> **g̃**: *Sp.* amigo <u>v</u>: *Sp.* hablar **hl**: *Welsh* **Llanelli**. CAPITALS: primary stress. SMALL CAPS: secondary stress. (ⓢ): U.S. pron. (ⓔ): British pron.

Euthymus		
mythical hero of Temesa	YOO-thuh-muhs	ˈjuːθəməs
Euthyphro		
dialogue of Plato	YOO-thuh-FRŌ	ˈjuːθəˌfroː
Eutychian		
pope	yu-TIK-ē-uhn	juˈtikiːən
Eutychus		
Biblical name	YOOT-i-kuhs, yu-TĪ-kuhs	ˈjuːʈikəs, juˈˈtaikəs
Euxine [Black Sea]		
Sea, Europe, Asia	YOOK-suhn, YOOK-SĪN	ˈjuːksən, ˈjuːkˌsain
Eva		
1. pers. name	Ē-vuh, Ā-vuh	ˈiːvə, ˈeːvə
2. German	Ā-vah, Ā-fah	ˈeːva, ˈeːfa
3. Norwegian	Ā-vah	ˈeːva
Evadne		
mother of Iamus by Apollo	i-VAD-nē	iˈvædniˑ
Evan		
pers. name	EV-uhn	ˈevən
Evander		
mythical founder of Pallantium	i-VAN-duhr	iˈvændəʳ
Evangel		
College, MO	i-VAN-juhl	iˈvændʒəl
Evangeline		
pers. name	i-VAN-juh-LĒN, -LĬN, -luhn	iˈvændʒəˌliːn, -ˌlain, -lən
Evans		
Dame Edith, *English actress;* Mary Ann, *original name of* George Eliot	EV-uhnz	ˈevənz
Evanston		
city, IL	EV-uhn-stuhn	ˈevənstən
Evansville		
city, IN	EV-uhnz-VIL	ˈevənzˌvil
Evaristus		
pope	EV-uh-RIS-tuhs	ˌevəˈristəs
Eve		
pers. name	ĒV	ˈiːv
Evel		
pers. name (E. Knievel)	Ē-vuhl	ˈiːvəl
Evelyn		
pers. name	EV-(uh-)luhn, ⓔ ĒV-lin, EV-lin	ˈev(ə)lən, ⓔ ˈiːvlin, ˈevlin
Evenki		
lang., people, Siberia, China	uh-VENG-kē	əˈveŋkiˑ
Even [Lamut]		
lang., East Siberia	Ā-vuhn, Ē-vuhn	ˈeːvən, ˈiːvən
Evenus		
father of Marpessa	i-VĒ-nuhs	iˈviːnəs
Everest		
mtn., Himalayas	EV-(uh-)ruhst	ˈev(ə)rəst
Everett		
pers. name	EV-(uh-)ruht	ˈev(ə)rət
Everglades, The		
swamp, FL	EV-uhr-GLĀDZ	ˈevəʳˌgleːdz
Everly		
Don & Phil, *US singers, songwriters*	EV-uhr-lē	ˈevəʳliˑ

Key (col. 2):   a: f**a**d   ā: f**a**de   ah: f**a**ther   ar: m**a**rry   aw: l**a**w   e: f**e**d   ē: f**ee**d   er: m**e**rry   i: h**i**d   ī: h**i**de   ō: c**oa**t   o͞o: b**oo**t
oi: b**oy**   ow: n**ow**   u: p**u**t   uh: **a**bove   uhr: b**i**rd   ch: **ch**op   ng: ri**ng**   sh: **sh**ow   th: **th**ick   th: **th**is   zh: mea**s**ure

Evers
   Medger, *US civil rights activist*   EV-uhrz   'evə^{r}z
Evert
   Christine Marie (Chris), *US tennis*   EV-uhrt   'evə^{r}t
   player
Everyman
   morality play   EV-rē-MAN   'evri·,mæn
Evesham
   town, England   ĒV-shuhm   'iːvʃəm
Evgeni
   pers. name, Russian   yiv-GĀN-yē   jiv'geːnjiː
Evgenios
   pers. name, Mod. Greek   ev-YĀN-yaws   ev'jeːnjɔːs
Evi
   Biblical name   Ē-VĪ, ev-Ē   'iː,vɑi, ev'iː
Evian
   mineral water   ā-VYAH^n, Ⓢ EV-ē-uhn   eːvjɑ̃, Ⓢ 'eviːən
Evil-merodach
   Biblical name   Ē-vuhl-muh-RŌ-DAK, -MER-uh-DAK;   'iːvəlmə'roː,dæk,
       ev-ĒL-muh-raw-DAH<u>KH</u>   -'merə,dæk;
       ev'iːlmərɔː'dɑx
Evind
   pers. name, Finnish   Ā-vind   'eːvind
Evita
   1. pers. name   ā-VĒT-uh, uh-VĒT-uh   e·'viːțə, ə'viːțə
   2. Spanish   ā-<u>V</u>Ē-tah   eː'βiːta
Evonne
   pers. name   ē-VAHN   i·'vɑn
Évvoia [Euboea]
   island, Greece   EV-yah   'evjɑ
Ewa
   city, HI   EV-uh   ,evə
Ewa Beach
   city, HI   EV-uh BĒCH   ,evə 'biːtʃ
Ewald
   1. Johannes, Danish poet and   I-VAHL   'i,vɑl
   dramatist
   2. pers. name, German   Ā-VAHLT   'eː,vɑlt
Ewan
   pers. name   Y̅O̅O̅-uhn   'juːən
Ewe
   lang., people, Africa   Ā-WĀ, Ā-VĀ   'eː,weː, 'eː,veː
Ewell
   pers. name   Y̅O̅O̅-uhl   'juːəl
Ewen
   pers. name   Y̅O̅O̅-uhn   'juːən
Ewing
   Patrick, *US basketball player*   Y̅O̅O̅-ing   'juːiŋ
Ewry
   Ray C., *US athlete*   YUR-ē   'juri·
Ewok
   alien race in Star Wars   Ē-WAHK   'iː,wɑk
Excalibur
   King Arthur's sword   ek-SKAL-uh-buhr   ek'skæləbə^r

Foreign Sounds: ue: *Fr.* **rue**, *Ger.* **füllen**   uh(r): *Fr.* **boeuf**, *Ger.* **Höhle**   <u>kh</u>: *Ger.* **ich**, *Scot.* **loch**   g̃: *Sp.* **amigo**   <u>v</u>: *Sp.* **hablar**
hl: *Welsh* **Llanelli**.   CAPITALS: primary stress.   SMALL CAPS: secondary stress.   Ⓢ: U.S. pron.   Ⓔ: British pron.

Exe
   river, England   EKS   'eks

Exeter
   US pl. name; town, England; college,   EK-suht-uhr   'eksətə^r
      Oxford Univ.

Ex-lax
   tdmk for a laxative   EK-SLAKS   'ek‚slæks

Exmoor
   English moorland   EK-SMUR, EK-SMAWR   'ek‚smu^r, 'ek‚smɔː^r

Exmouth
   town, England   EK-smuhth, EK-SMOWTH   'eksməθ, 'ek‚smɑuθ

Exocet
   anti-ship missile   EK-suh-SET, EK-sō-SET   'eksə‚set, 'eksoː‚set

Exodus
   Old Testament book   EK-suhd-uhs, EG-zuhd-uhs 'eksədəs, 'egzədəs

Expos
   Montreal baseball team   EK-SPŌZ   'ek‚spoːz

Extremadura
   see Estremadura

Exuma and Cays
   island group, Bahamas   ik-S$\overline{OO}$-muh uhn(d) KĒZ,   ik'suːmə ən(d) 'kiːz,
                        ig-Z$\overline{OO}$-muh, KĀZ   ig'zuːmə, 'keːz

Exxon
   US oil co.   EK-SAHN   'ek‚san

Exxon Valdez
   former name, US tanker   EK-SAHN val-DĒZ   'ek‚san væl'diːz

Eydie
   pers. name (E. Gorme)   ĒD-ē   'iːdiˑ

Eyre
   salt lake, Australia   AR, ER   'æ^r, 'e^r

Eyvind
   pers. name, Norwegian, Swedish   Ā-vin   'eːvin

Ezbai
   Biblical name   EZ-bē-Ī, EZ-bī, ez-BĪ   'ezbiː‚ai, 'ezbai, ez'bai

Ezbon
   Biblical name   EZ-BAHN, EZ-BŌN, ets-BAWN 'ez‚ban, 'ez‚boːn, ets'bɔːn

Ezechiel
   pers. name, German   āt-S<u>ĀKH</u>-yel, -SE<u>KH</u>-ē-uhl eːt'seːçjel, -'seçiːəl

Ezechiel, Ezekiel
   Old Testament book; pers. name   i-ZĒK-yuhl, i-ZĒ-kē-uhl i'ziːkjəl, i'ziːkiːəl

Ezel
   Biblical name   Ē-zel, ET-SEL   'iːzel, 'et‚sel

Ezem
   Biblical name   Ē-zuhm, ET-SEM   'iːzəm, 'et‚sem

Ezer
   Biblical name   Ē-zuhr, ET-SER   'iːzə^r, 'et‚ser

Ezio
   pers. name, Italian   ETS-yō   'etsjoː

Ezion-geber, Ezion-gaber
   Biblical name   Ē-zē-AHN-GĀ-buhr, ets-YAWN-GEV-er 'iːziː‚an'geːbə^r, ets‚jɔːn'gever

Eznite
   Biblical name   EZ-NĪT   'ez‚nait

Ezra
   Old Testament book; pers. name   EZ-ruh   'ezrə

Key (col. 2): a: f**a**d ā: f**a**de ah: f**a**ther ar: m**a**rry aw: l**aw** e: f**e**d ē: f**ee**d er: m**e**rry i: h**i**d ī: h**i**de ō: c**oa**t $\overline{oo}$: b**oo**t
oi: b**oy** ow: n**ow** u: p**u**t uh: **a**bove uhr: b**ir**d ch: **ch**op ng: ri**ng** sh: **sh**ow th: **th**ick <u>th</u>: **th**is zh: mea**s**ure

Ezrahite

Biblical name   EZ-ruh-HĪT   'ezrə‚hɑit

Ezri

Biblical name   EZ-RĪ, ez-RĒ   'ez‚rɑi, ez'riː

F

Faber

pers. name   FĀ-buhr   'feːbəʳ

Fabergé

Peter Carl, *Russian jeweler;*   fah-ber-ZHĀ, Ⓢ FAB-uhr-ZHĀ,   fɑːberʒeː, Ⓢ ‚fæbəʳ'ʒeː,
decorative egg; perfume co.   FAB-uhr-ZHĀ   'fæbəʳ‚ʒeː

Fabian

pope; pers. name   FĀ-bē-uhn   'feːbiːən

Fabianism

theories of the Fabian society   FĀ-bē-uh-NIZ-uhm   'feːbiːə‚nizəm

Fabio

pers. name   FAHB-yō   'fɑbjoː

Fabiola

queen, Belgium   FAB-ē-Ō-luh   ‚fæbiː'oːlə

Fabius

1. Laurent, Prime minister of France   fahb-YUES   fɑːbjys
2. Roman cognomen   FĀ-bē-uhs   'feːbiːəs

Fabricius

1. pers. name, German   fah-BRĒT-sē-us   fɑ'briːtsiːus
2. Latin   fuh-BRISH(-ē)-uhs   fə'briʃ(iː)əs

Fabrizio

pers. name, Italian   fahb-RĒTS-yō   fɑb'riːtsjoː

Fadeyev

Aleksandr Aleksandrovich, *Russian*   fuhd-YĀ-yif   fəd'jeːjif
novelist

Faeroe, Faroe

Islands, *Atlantic*   FAR-ō, FER-ō   'færoː, 'feroː

Faeroese, Faroese

lang., people, Faeroe Islands   FAR-uh-WĒZ, -WĒS   ‚færə'wiːz, -'wiːs

Fafnir

dragon in Scandinavian myth   FAHF-NIR   'fɑf‚niʳ

Fagin

character in Oliver Twist, *C. Dickens*   FĀ-guhn   'feːgən

Fagunwa

Daniel O., *Nigerian novelist*   fah-GOON-wah   fɑ'guːnwɑ

Fahd

King, Saudi Arabia   FAHD   'fɑd

Fahd ibn Abdul Aziz al Saud

Saudi Arabian politician   FAHD IB-uhn ahb-DOOL ah-ZĒZ ahl   'fɑd ‚ibən ab'duːl ɑ'ziːz ɑːl
sah-OOD   sɑ'uːd

Fahrenheit
  temperature scale   FAR-uhn-HĪT   'færən‚hait

Faik
  pers. name,   FĪK   'faik

Fairbanks
  Douglas, *US actor; city, AK*   FAR-BANGKS, FER-BANGKS   'fær‚bæŋks, 'fer‚bæŋks

Fairleigh Dickinson
  University, *NJ*   FAR-lē DIK-uhn-suhn, FER-lē   'færli· 'dikənsən, 'ferli·

Faisal
  Saudi Arabian dynasty   FĪ-suhl   'faisəl

Faisalabad
  city, Pakistan   FĪ-SAHL-uh-BAHD, FĪ-SAL-uh-BAD   ‚fai‚salə'bad, ‚fai‚sælə'bæd

Faith
  pers. name   FĀTH   'fe:θ

Faiyum
  prov, Egypt   fā-(Y)OO̅M, fī-(Y)OO̅M   fe:'(j)u:m, fai'(j)u:m

Falange, Ph-
  party of Spain's Franco   FĀ-LANJ   'fe:‚lændʒ

Falangist, Ph-
  member of Spanish fascist political   fuh-LAN-juhst, FĀ-LAN-juhst   fə'lændʒəst, 'fe:‚lændʒəst
    party

Falasha
  Ethiopian people   fuh-LAHSH-uh   fə'laʃə

Falcon
  hawk genus   FAL-kuhn, FAW(L)-kuhn   'fælkən, 'fɔ:(l)kən

Falernian
  ancient Italian wine   fuh-LUHR-nē-uhn   fə'lərni:ən

Falerno
  Italian wine   fah-LER-nō   fa'lerno:

Falfurrias
  city, TX   fal-FYUR-ē-uhs   fæl'fjuri:əs

Falier [Faliero]
  Marino, *Doge of Venice*   fahl-YER   fal'jer

Faliero
  Marino, *Doge of Venice*   fahl-YER-ō   fal'jero:

Faliscan
  ancient Italian people   fuh-LIS-kuhn   fə'liskən

Falk
  Peter, *US actor*   FAW(L)K   'fɔ:(l)k

Falkland [Malvinas, Islas]
  Islands, *Atlantic*   FAW(L)K-luhnd   'fɔ:(l)klənd

Falla
  Manuel de, *Spanish composer*   FAH-yuh, FĪ-uh   'fajə, 'faiə

Fallas de San Jose
  Spanish festival   FAH-yahs t͟hā sahn hō-ZĀ   'fajas ðe: san ho:'ze:

Fallon
  county, MT; pers. name   FAL-uhn   'fælən

Fall River
  town, MA   FAWL RIV-uhr   ‚fɔ:l 'rivər

Falmouth
  city, MA; borough, England   FAL-muhth   'fælməθ

Falstaff
  Shakespearean character   FAWL-STAF, FAWL-STAHF   'fɔ:l‚stæf, 'fɔ:l‚sta:f

Falwell
  Jerry, *US TV evangelist*   FAWL-WEL, FAWL-wuhl   'fɔ:l‚wel, 'fɔ:lwəl

---

Key (col. 2):   a: fad   ā: fade   ah: father   ar: marry   aw: law   e: fed   ē: feed   er: merry   i: hid   ī: hide   ō: coat   oo̅: boot
oi: boy   ow: now   u: put   uh: above   uhr: bird   ch: chop   ng: ring   sh: show   th: thick   t͟h: this   zh: measure

Fames
   allegorical figure of hunger   FAM-ēz, FAHM-ēz   'fæmiːz, 'fɑmiːz

Faneuil Hall
   historic building, Boston, MA   FAN-yuhl, FAN-l, *locally sometimes* THAN-l   'fænjəl, 'fænl̩, *locally sometimes* 'θænl̩

Fanfani
   Amintore, *Italian statesman*   fahn-FAHN-ē   fɑn'fɑniˑ

Fang
   lang., Africa   FANG, FAHNG   'fæŋ, 'fɑŋ

Fang Lizhi
   Chinese dissident, physicist   FAHNG LĒ-JĒ   'fɑŋ 'liː'dʒiː

Fang Yi
   Chinese dissident   FAHNG YĒ   'fɑŋ 'jiː

Fannie, Fanny
   pers. name   FAN-ē   'fæniˑ

Fannius
   Roman name   FAN-ē-uhs   'fæniːəs

Fantin-Latour
   Ignace Henri, *French painter*   fahⁿ-TEⁿ-lah-TOOR   fɑ̃tẽlɑːtuːr

Fārābī, al- [Alpharabius, Avennasar]
   Tarkhān ibn Uzalagh, *Muslim philosopher*   AHL FAHR-ah-BĒ   ˌɑl ˌfɑrɑ'biː

Faraday
   Michael, *English physicist*   FAR-uh-DĀ, FER-uh-DĀ   'færəˌdeː, 'ferəˌdeː

Farah
   1. river, prov, town, Afghanistan   fuh-RAH   fə'rɑ
   2. US apparel co.   FAR-uh, FER-uh   'færə, 'ferə

Farallon Islands
   National Wildlife Refuge, CA   FAR-uh-LAHN, FER-   'færəˌlɑn, 'fer-

Farben, I.G.
   German corp.   Ē GĀ FAHR-buhn   ˌiː ˌgeː 'fɑʳbən

Farentino
   James, *US actor*   FAR-uhn-TĒ-nō   ˌfærən'tiːnoː

Fargo
   city, ND   FAHR-gō   'fɑʳgoː

Faribault
   county, MN   FAR-uh-BŌ   'færəˌboː

Farigoule [Romains]
   Louis Henri, *French writer*   fah-rē-GOOL   fɑːriːguːl

Farley
   Walter Lorimer, *US author*   FAHR-lē   'fɑʳliˑ

Farmer
   Philip Jose, *US author*   FAHR-muhr   'fɑʳməʳ

Farnese
   Italian family   fahr-NĀ-sā, -zā   fɑr'neːseː, -zeː

Farnese Palace
   Rome, Italy   fahr-NĀ-zā   fɑʳ'neːzeː

Faroe
   see Faeroe

Faroese
   see Faeroese

Farouk
   king, Egypt   fuh-ROOK   fə'ruːk

Foreign Sounds: ue: *Fr.* **rue**, *Ger.* **füllen**   uh(r): *Fr.* **boeuf**, *Ger.* **Höhle**   k͟h: *Ger.* **ich**, *Scot.* **loch**   g̱: *Sp.* **amigo**   v̱: *Sp.* **hablar** hl: *Welsh* **Llanelli**.   CAPITALS: primary stress.   SMALL CAPS: secondary stress.   ⓢ: U.S. pron.   ⓔ: British pron.

Farquhar
 George, *Irish dramatist*   FAHR-kuhr, FAHR-kwuhr, 'faᶜkəᶜ, 'faᶜkwəᶜ, 'faᶜˌkwaᶜ
              FAHR-KWAHR

Farquharson
 Scottish family name   FAHR-kuhr-suhn, Ⓢ *also* 'faᶜkəᶜsən, Ⓢ *also*
            FAHR-kwuhr-suhn   'faᶜkwəᶜsən

Farragut
 David, *militarist*   FAR-uh-guht   'færəgət

Farrah
 pers. name (F. Fawcett)   FAR-uh, FER-uh   'færə, 'ferə

Farrakhan
 Rev. Louis, *US political activist* FAR-uh-KAN, FAHR-uh-KAHN 'færəˌkæn, 'farəˌkan

Farrar
 1. Geraldine, *US singer*   fuh-RAHR   fə'raᶜ
 2. John Chipman, *US publisher and* FAR-uhr   'færəᶜ
  writer

Farrow
 Mia Villiers, *US actress*   FAR-ō   'færoː

Farsi
 lang., Middle East   FAHR-sē   'faᶜsiˑ

Fasching
 Austrian & German festival FAHSH-ing   'faʃiŋ

Fascisti
 members of the Italian Fascist party fah-SHḔ-stē, fa-SHIS-tē fa'ʃiːstiˑ, fæ'ʃistiˑ

Fasher, El [Al-Fashir]
 town, Sudan   el FASH-uhr   el 'fæʃəᶜ

Fashoda [Kodok]
 village, Sudan   fuh-SHŌD-uh   fə'ʃoːdə

Fasnacht
 Austrian & German festival FAHS-NAHKHT   'fasˌnaxt

Fasnet
 Austrian & German festival FAHS-nuht   'fasnət

Fassbinder
 Rainer Werner, *German film* FAHS-BIN-duhr   'fasˌbindəᶜ
  director

Fatehpur Sikri, Fathpur Sikri
 historic city, India   FAHT-uh-PUR SḔ-krē   'faʈəˌpuᶜ 'siːkriˑ

Fastelavn
 Danish festival   FAHST-l-ahv(-uh)n   'fastlav(ə)n

Fátima
 town, Portugal; pers. name FAT-uh-muh   'fæʈəmə

Fātimah
 daughter of Muhammad FAT-uh-muh   'fæʈəmə

Fātimid
 Muslim dynasty in North Africa FAT-uh-mid   'fæʈəmid

Fatum
 god of destiny   FAHT-uhm   'faʈəm

Faulk
 county, SD   FAWK   'fɔːk

Faulkner
 William, *US author (Nobel 1949)* FAWK-nuhr   'fɔːknəᶜ

Faulknerian
 pert. to Faulkner   fawk-NIR-ē-uhn, fawk-NER-ē-uhn fɔːk'niriːən, fɔːk'neriːən

---

Key (col. 2): a: fad ā: fade ah: father ar: marry aw: law e: fed ē: feed er: merry i: hid ī: hide ō: coat ōō: boot
oi: boy ow: now u: put uh: above uhr: bird ch: chop ng: ring sh: show th: thick <u>th</u>: this zh: measure

Fauna
  woodland goddess, sister and wife of   FAW-nuh   'fɔːnə
  Faunus (Roman god)
Fauntleroy
  Little Lord, Burnett novel   FAHNT-luh-ROI, FAWNT-luh-ROI   'fɑntlə‚rɔi, 'fɔːntlə‚rɔi
Faunus
  king of Latium; Roman woodland god   FAW-nuhs   'fɔːnəs
Fauquier
  county, VA   faw-KIR, FAW-KIR   fɔː'kiʳ, 'fɔː‚kiʳ
Faure
  Elie, French art historian   FAWR   fɔːr
Fauré
  Gabriel, French composer   faw-RĀ, fō-RĀ   fɔːreː, foːreː
Faust
  legendary German magician   FOWST   'faust
Faustinus
  companion of Evander   faw-STĪ-nuhs   fɔː'stainəs
Faustulus
  shepherd, guardian of Romulus and   FAWS-chuh-luhs   'fɔːstʃələs
  Remus
Faustus
  1. legendary German magician; pers.   FAWS-tuhs, FOWS-tuhs   'fɔːstəs, 'faustəs
  name
  2. Latin   FAWS-tuhs   'fɔːstəs
Fauve
  group of French artists   FŌV   foːv
Fauvism
  art movement   FŌ-VIZ-uhm   'foː‚vizəm
Faversham
  town, England   FAV-uhr-shuhm   'fævəʳʃəm
Favre
  Brett, US football player   FAHRV   'fɑʳv
Fawayid
  people, Africa   FAH-wī-(Y)ID   ‚fawai'(j)id
Fawcett
  Farrah Leni, US actress   FAW-suht   'fɔːsət
Fawkes
  Guy, English traitor   FAWKS   'fɔːks
Fay, Faye
  pers. name   FĀ   'feː
Fayette
  US pl. name   fā-ET, FĀ-uht   feː'et, 'feːət
Fayetteville
  city, AR   FĀ-uht-vuhl, FĀ-uht-VIL   'feːətvəl, 'feːət‚vil
Fayoum
  province, Egypt   fah-YOOM, fī-OOM   fɑ'juːm, fɑi'uːm
Feargus
  pers. name   FUHR-guhs   'fəʳgəs
Featherstonehaugh
  town, England; British family name   FETH-uhr-stuhn-HAW, FAN-SHAW,   'feðəʳstən‚hɔː, 'fæn‚ʃɔː,
                                             FEST-uhn-HAW, FĒ-suhn-HĀ,   'festən‚hɔː, 'fiːsən‚heː,
                                             FIR-stuhn-HAW   'fiʳstən‚hɔː
Febris
  goddess of fever   FĒ-bruhs   'fiːbrəs

Foreign Sounds: ue: *Fr.* **rue**, *Ger.* **füllen** uh(r): *Fr.* **boeuf**, *Ger.* **Höhle** kh: *Ger.* **ich**, *Scot.* **loch** g̅: *Sp.* **amigo** v: *Sp.* **hablar**
hl: *Welsh* **Llanelli**. CAPITALS: primary stress. SMALL CAPS: secondary stress. Ⓢ: U.S. pron. Ⓔ: British pron.

February		
month	FEB-yuh-WER-ē, FEB-uh-WER-ē, FEB-ruh-WER-ē	'febjə,weriˑ, 'febə,weriˑ, 'febrə,weriˑ
Februus		
Etruscan god of the Underworld	FEB-ruh-wuhs, FĒ-bruh-wuhs	'febrəwəs, 'fiːbrəwəs
Fecunditatis, Mare		
see Mare Fecunditatis		
Federico		
1. pers. name, Italian	FĀ-dā-RĒ-kō	,feːdeː'riːkoː
2. Spanish	fā-t͟hā-RĒ-kō, fā-dā-	feːðeː'riːkoː, feːdeː-
Fedor		
pers. name, German	FĀ-DŌR, FĀ-DAWR	'feː,doːʳ, 'feː,dɔːʳ
Fëdor, Fedor		
pers. name, Russian	FYAW-DAWR	'fjɔː,dɔːr
Fedorov		
Sergei, *Russian-born US hockey player*	FYAW-duh-RAWF, [$] FED-uh-RAWV, fuh-DAWR-uhv	'fjɔːdə,rɔːf, [$] 'fedə,rɔːv, fə'dɔːrəv
Feiffer		
Jules, *US cartoonist, writer*	FĪ-fuhr	'fɑifəʳ
Feininger		
Lyonel Charles Adrian, *US painter*	FĪ-ning-uhr	'fɑiniŋəʳ
Feinstein		
Diane, *US politician*	FĪN-STĪN	'fɑin,stɑin
Fejér		
Lipót, *Hungarian mathematician; theorem*	FE-YER	'fe,jeʳ
Feldberg		
mtn., Germany	FELT-BERK	'felt,beʳk
Felice		
1. pers. name	fuh-LĒS	fə'liːs
2. Italian	fā-LĒ-CHĀ	feː'liː,tʃeː
Felicia		
1. pers. name	fuh-LISH-(ē-)uh, fuh-LIS-ē-uh	fə'liʃ(iː)ə, fə'lisiːə
2. Spanish	fā-LĒS-yah, fā-LĒTH-yah	feː'liːsjɑ, feː'liːθjɑ
Felician		
College, *IL*	fuh-LISH-(ē-)uhn, fuh-LĒ-sh(ē-)uhn	fə'liʃ(iː)ən, fə'liːʃ(iː)ən
Feliciano		
Jose, *rock musician*	fā-LĒ-sē-AHN-ō, fuh-LISH-ē-AHN-ō	feː,liːsiː'ɑnoː, fə,liʃiː'ɑnoː
Feliks		
pers. name, Russian	FYĀL-yiks	'fjeːljiks
Felim		
pers. name	FĀ-lim	'feːlim
Felinfoel		
Welsh beer	VEL-uhn-VOIL	,velən'vɔil
Felipe		
pers. name	fā-LĒ-pā	feː'liːpeː
Felis		
former constellation	FĒ-luhs	'fiːləs
Felix		
1. pers. name	FĒ-liks	'fiːliks
2. Dutch, German	FĀ-liks	'feːliks
Félix, Felix		
pers. name, Russian	FYĀL-yiks	'fjeːljiks
Fellini		
Federico, *Italian film director*	fuh-LĒ-nē	fə'liːniˑ

Key (col. 2): a: **fad** ā: **fade** ah: **father** ar: **marry** aw: **law** e: **fed** ē: **feed** er: **merry** i: **hid** ī: **hide** ō: **coat** o͞o: **boot** oi: **boy** ow: **now** u: **put** uh: **above** uhr: **bird** ch: **chop** ng: **ring** sh: **show** th: **thick** t͟h: **this** zh: **measure**

Feltsman
    Vladimir, *Russian pianist*   FELT-smuhn   'feltsmən

Fénelon
    François, *French prelate, writer*   fān-LAW^n feːnlɔ̃

Fenian
    Irish revolutionary movement   FĒ-nē-uhn   'fiːniːən

Fenimore
    pers. name, (J. F. Cooper)   FEN-uh-MŌR, FEN-uh-MAWR   'fenəˌmoːr, 'fenəˌmɔːʳ

Fens, The
    district, England   t͟huh FENZ   ðə 'fenz

Fenway
    Park, *ballpark, Boston, MA*   FEN-wā   'fenweː

Feodor
    1. pers. name, German   FĀ-ō-DŌR, -DAWR   'feːoːˌdoːʳ, -ˌdɔːʳ
    2. Russian   fyi-AW-duhr   fjiˈɔːdər

Féraud
    Louis, *French designer*   fā-RŌ   feːroː

Ferber
    Edna, *US author*   FUHR-buhr   'fəʳbəʳ

Ferde
    pers. name (F. Grofé)   FUHRD-ē   'fəʳdiˑ

Fer-de-lance
    snake   FERD-l-AN(T)S, FERD-l-AHN(T)S   ˌfeʳdl̩ˈæn(t)s, ˌfeʳdl̩ˈɑn(t)s

Ferdinand
    1. pers. name   FUHRD-n-AND   'fəʳdn̩ˌænd
    2. Danish   FER-di-NAHN   'ferdiˌnɑːn
    3. Dutch   FER-dē-NAHNT   'ferdiːˌnɑnt
    4. French   fer-dē-NAH^n ferdiːnɑ̃
    5. German   FER-dē-NAHNT   'feʳdiːˌnɑnt

Ferdowsi
    see Firdawsī

Ferenc, Ferencz
    pers. name, Hungarian   FER-en(t)s   'feren(t)s

Ferengi
    Star Trek villains   fuh-RENG-gē, fuh-REN-gē   fəˈreŋgiˑ, fəˈrengiˑ

Fergie
    nickname, Duchess of York   FUHR-gē   'fəʳgiˑ

Fergus
    pers. name   FUHR-guhs   'fəʳgəs

Fergus Falls
    Community College, *MN*   FUHR-guhs FAWLZ   'fəʳgəs 'fɔːlz

Ferguson
    Maynard, *Canadian trumpet player*   FUHR-guh-suhn   'fəʳgəsən

Ferhat
    pers. name   fer-HAHT   ferˈhɑt

Feria de San Fermin
    Spanish holiday, 2nd week of July   FER-ē-ah t͟hā SAHN fer-MĒN   'feriːɑ ðeː ˌsɑn ferˈmiːn

Fermanagh
    administrative county, Northern Ireland   fuhr-MAN-uh   fəʳˈmænə

Fermat
    Pierre de, *French scientist*   fer-MAH   fermɑː

Fermi
    Enrico, *Italian-born US physicist* (Nobel 1938)   FER-mē   'feʳmiˑ

Foreign Sounds: ue: *Fr.* **rue**, *Ger.* **füllen** uh(r): *Fr.* **boeuf**, *Ger.* **Höhle** k͟h: *Ger.* **ich**, *Scot.* **loch** g̱: *Sp.* **amigo** v̱: *Sp.* **hablar**
hl: *Welsh* **Llanelli**. CAPITALS: primary stress. SMALL CAPS: secondary stress. Ⓢ: U.S. pron. Ⓑ: British pron.

fermium
element — FER-mē-uhm, FUHR-mē-uhm — 'fermiːəm, 'fərmiːəm

Fernam
pers. name, Portuguese — fuhr-NOWⁿ, fer-NOWⁿ — fər'naũ, fer'naũ

Fernandes
pers. name, Portuguese — fuhr-NAHⁿ-dish, fer-NAHⁿ-dis — fər'nãː(n)diʃ, fer'nãː(n)dis

Fernandez
1. pers. name — fuhr-NAN-DEZ — fəʳ'næn‚dez
2. Portuguese — fuhr-NAHⁿ-dish, fer-NAHⁿ-dis — fər'nãː(n)diʃ, fer'nãː(n)dis

Fernández
pers. name, Spanish — fer-NAHN-dāth, -dās — fer'nandeːθ, -deːs

Fernando
1. pers. name — fuhr-NAN-dō — fəʳ'nændoː
2. Italian — fer-NAHN-dō — fer'nandoː
3. Portuguese — fuhr-NAHⁿ-d$\overline{oo}$, fer- — fər'nãː(n)duː, fer-

Fernão
pers. name, Portuguese — fuhr-NOWⁿ, fer- — fər'naũ, fer-

Fernet Branca
Italian bitters — fer-NET BRAHNG-kuh — fer‚net 'braŋkə

Feronia
Roman goddess of spring — fi-RÕ-nē-uh — fi'roːniːə

Ferragamo
pers. name, Italian — FER-uh-GAHM-ō — ‚ferə'gamoː

Ferrante & Teicher
dual pianists — fuh-RANT-ē uhn(d) TĪ-kuhr — fə'rænti· ən(d) 'taikəʳ

Ferrara
prov & town, Italy — fuh-RAHR-uh — fə'rarə

Ferrari
Italian car — fuh-RAHR-ē — fə'rari·

Ferraris
Galileo, Italian scientist — fār-RAHR-ēs, ⑤ fer-AHR-uhs — feːr'rariːs, ⑤ fer'arəs

Ferraro
Geraldine, US politician — fuh-RAHR-ō — fə'raroː

Ferrer
Jose Vicente, Puerto Rican actor, producer, director — fuh-RER — fə'reʳ

Ferrigno
Lou, actor, bodybuilder — fuh-RIG-nō — fə'rignoː

Ferris wheel
amusement ride — FER-uhs (H)WĒL — 'ferəs ‚(h)wiːl

Ferruccio
pers. name, Italian — fār-R$\overline{OO}$T-chō, ⑤ fuh-R$\overline{OO}$-ch(ē-)ō — feːr'ruːttʃoː, ⑤ fə'ruːtʃ(iː)oː

Ferrum
College, VA — FER-uhm — 'ferəm

Fès [Fez]
city, Morocco — FES — 'fes

Fess
pers. name — FES — 'fes

Festa de Colete Encarnado
Portuguese festival — FES-tah dā KÕ-lā-tā EN-kahr-NAHD-$\overline{oo}$ — 'festa deː 'koːleːteː ‚enkar'naduː

Festival du Voyageur
Manitoban festival — fes-tē-VAHL due vwah-yah-ZHUHR — festiːvaːl dy vwaːjaːʒœːr

Festus
pers. name — fes-tuhs — festəs

Key (col. 2):   a: fad   ā: fade   ah: father   ar: marry   aw: law   e: fed   ē: feed   er: merry   i: hid   ī: hide   ō: coat $\overline{oo}$: boot
oi: boy   ow: now   u: put   uh: above   uhr: bird   ch: chop   ng: ring   sh: show   th: thick   <u>th</u>: this   zh: measure

Fête de la Madeleine, La
  see La Fête de la Madeleine
Fetzer
  winery, CA   FET-suhr   'fetsəʳ
Feuchtwanger
  Lion, *German novelist and dramatist*   FOI<u>KH</u>T-VAHNG-uhr, Ⓢ FOIKT-   'fɔiçtˌvaŋəʳ, Ⓢ 'fɔikt-
Feuerbach
  Ludwig Andreas, *philosopher*   FOI-uhr-BAH<u>KH</u>   'fɔiəʳˌbax
Feuerheerd Wearne
  Port wine   FOI-uhr-HERT VER-nuh   'fɔiəʳˌheʳt 'veʳnə
Feuillants
  political group, French Revolution   fuh(r)-YAHⁿN   fœjãn
Fevzi
  pers. name, Turkish   fev-ZĒ   fev'ziː
Feynman
  Richard Phillips, *US physicist (Nobel FĪN-muhn   'fainmən
  1965)*
Fez [Fès]
  city, Morocco   FEZ   'fez
Fianna Fail
  Irish political party   FĒ-uh-nuh FOIL   'fiːənə 'fɔil
Fiat
  Italian car co.   FĒ-AHT, FĒ-AT   'fiːˌat, 'fiːˌæt
Fibiger
  Johannes, *Danish pathologist*   FĒ-bē-guhr   'fiːbiːgəʳ
  (Nobel 1926)
Fibonacci
  Leonardo, *Italian mathematician;*   FĒ-bō-NAHT-chē, Ⓢ FIB-uh-NAHCH-ē   ˌfiːbɔː'nattʃiː, Ⓢ ˌfibə'natʃiˑ
  mathematical series
FICA
  Social Security tax act   FĪ-kuh   'faikə
Fichte
  J.G., *German philosopher*   FI<u>KH</u>-tuh   'fiçtə
Fichteanism
  philosophy of Fichte   FIK-tē-uh-NIZ-uhm,   'fiktiːəˌnizəm, 'fiçtiːəˌnizəm
                                          FI<u>KH</u>-tē-uh-NIZ-uhm
Ficino
  Marsilio, *Italian philosopher*   fē-CHĒ-nō   fiː'tʃiːnoː
Fidel
  1. pers. name   fi-DEL   fi'del
  2. Spanish   fē-<u>TH</u>EL   fiː'ðel
Fidelio
  pers. name   fē-DĀL-yō, fē-DĀ-lē-ō   fiː'deːljoː, fiː'deːliːoː
Fides
  personification of good faith   FĒD-ās   'fiːdeːs
Fido
  canine name   FĪD-ō   'faidoː
Fiedler
  Arthur, *US conductor*   FĒD-luhr   'fiːdləʳ
Fielding
  Henry, *English author; pers. name*   FĒL-ding   'fiːldiŋ
Fiennes
  William, *English Parliamentary*   FĪNZ   'fainz
  leader; Ralph, *US actor*

Foreign Sounds: ue: *Fr.* **rue**, *Ger.* **füllen** uh(r): *Fr.* **b**oeuf, *Ger.* **Höhle** <u>kh</u>: *Ger.* i**ch**, *Scot.* lo**ch** g̱: *Sp.* ami**g**o v: *Sp.* ha**b**lar
hl: *Welsh* **Ll**anelli. CAPITALS: primary stress. SMALL CAPS: secondary stress. Ⓢ: U.S. pron. Ⓔ: British pron.

Fiesole
  commune, Italy   fē-Ā-zuh-LĀ   fiːˈeːzəˌleː

Fiesta del Arbol
  Arbor Day (March 26), Spain   fē-ES-tah <u>th</u>el ahr-V<u>Ō</u>L   fiːˈesta ðel arˈβoːl

Fiesta de la Vendimia
  Spanish grape festival   fē-EST-ah <u>th</u>ā lah ven-DĒ-mē-ah   fiːˈesta ðeː la venˈdiːmiːa

FIFA
  international soccer organization   FĪ-fuh, FĒ-fuh   ˈfaifə, ˈfiːfə

Fifi
  pers. name   FĒ-fē, FĒ-FĒ   ˈfiːfiˑ, ˈfiːˌfiː

Figaro
  Marriage of, *opera, Mozart*   FIG-uh-RŌ   ˈfigəˌroː

Figueres Ferrer
  José, *president of Costa Rica*   fē-GER-es fe-RER   fiːˈgeres feˈrer

Fiji
  islands, Pacific; fraternity nickname   FĒ-jē   ˈfiːdʒiˑ

Fijian
  lang., Fiji   FĒ-jē-uhn   ˈfiːdʒiːən

Filbert
  nut   FIL-buhrt   ˈfilbəʳt

Filé
  sassafras   fuh-LĀ, fē-LĀ, FĒ-LĀ   fəˈleː, fiːˈleː, ˈfiːˌleː

Filene's
  US department store chain   fī-LĒNZ, FĪ-LĒNZ   faiˈliːnz, ˈfaiˌliːnz

Filioque clause
  clause, Nicene Creed   FĒ-lē-Ō-kwē KLAWZ, FĒ-lē-Ō-KWĀ   ˌfiːliːˈoːkwiˑ ˌklɔːz,
                                                                                           ˌfiːliːˈoːˌkweː

Filipina
  female native of the Philippines   FIL-uh-PĒ-nuh   ˌfiləˈpiːnə

Filipino
  male native of the Philippines   FIL-uh-PĒ-nō   ˌfiləˈpiːnoː

Filipovic
  Zlata, *Bosnian diarist*   FIL-uh-PAW-vits   ˌfiləˈpɔːvits

Filippino
  pers. name, Italian   fē-lēp-PĒ-nō, ⑤ FIL-uh-PĒ-nō   fiːliːpˈpiːnoː, ⑤ ˌfiləˈpiːnoː

Filippo
  pers. name, Italian   fē-LĒP-pō, ⑤ fuh-LĒP-ō   fiːˈliːppoː, ⑤ fəˈliːpoː

Fillmore
  Millard, *13th US president*   FIL-MŌR, FIL-MAWR   ˈfilˌmoːʳ, ˈfilˌmɔːʳ

Filofax
  tdmk for an organizer   FĪ-lō-FAKS, FĪ-luh-FAKS   ˈfailoːˌfæks, ˈfailəˌfæks

FINA
  US petroleum and natural gas co.   FĒ-nuh   ˈfiːnə

Findlay
  city, OH   FIN-(d)lē   ˈfin(d)liˑ

Fine Gael
  political party, Ireland   FĒ-nuh GĀL   ˈfiːnə ˈgeːl

Fingal
  pers. name   FING-guhl, FIN-guhl   ˈfiŋgəl, ˈfingəl

Finistère
  dept., France   fē-nē-STER   fiːniːster

Finisterre
  cape, Spain   fē-ni-STER   fiːniˈster

Finlandia
  symphony, Sibelius   fin-LAN-dē-uh   finˈlændiːə

Key (col. 2):   a: f**a**d   ā: f**a**de   ah: f**a**ther   ar: m**a**rry   aw: l**a**w   e: f**e**d   ē: f**ee**d   er: m**e**rry   i: h**i**d   ī: h**i**de   ō: c**oa**t   ōō: b**oo**t
oi: b**oy**   ow: n**ow**   u: p**u**t   uh: **a**bove   uhr: b**ir**d   ch: **ch**op   ng: ri**ng**   sh: **sh**ow   th: **th**ick   <u>th</u>: **th**is   zh: mea**s**ure

Finland [Suomi]
 republic, Europe FIN-luhnd 'finlənd
Finn
 European people; mythological Irish FIN 'fin
 hero
Finnair
 airline of Finland FIN-AR, FIN-ER 'fin₁æ^r, 'fin₁e^r
Finnbogadottir
 Vigdis, *president, Iceland* FIN-BŌ-guh-DAW-TIR ₁fin₁bo:gə'dɔ:₁ti^r
Finnegan's Wake
 novel, Joyce FIN-uh-guhnz WĀK ₁finəgənz 'we:k
Finney
 Albert, *British actor;* Ross Lee, *US* FIN-ē 'fini·
 composer
Finnish
 lang., Finland, Sweden, Russia FIN-ish 'finiʃ
Finno-Ugrian
 pert. to Finns and Ugrians FIN-ō-(Y)OO-grē-uhn ₁fino:'(j)u:gri:ən
Finno-Ugric
 lang. family FIN-ō-(Y)OO-grik ₁fino:'(j)u:grik
Finsen
 N. R., *Danish physician (Nobel* FIN-suhn 'finsən
 1903)
Finsteraarhorn
 mtn., Switzerland FIN(T)-stuhr-AHR-HAWRN ₁fin(t)stə^r'ɑ^{r}₁hɔ:^{r}n
Fiona
 pers. name fē-Ō-nuh, fī-Ō-nuh fi:'o:nə, fɑi'o:nə
Fionnula
 pers. name (F. M. Flanagan) fē-ŌN-yuh-luh fi:'o:njələ
Fior d'Alpi
 Italian liqueur fyawr DAHL-pē fjɔ:r 'dɑlpi·
Fiorello
 1. pers. name FĒ-uh-REL-ō ₁fi:ə'relo:
 2. Italian fyō-REL-lō fjo:'rello:
Fiore Sardo
 Italian cheese fē-ŌR-ā SAHR-dō, FYŌR-ā fi:₁o:re: 'sɑ^{r}do:, ₁fjo:re:
Firdawsī, Firdausi, Ferdowsi
 Persian poet fir-DOW-sē fir'dɑusi·
Firenze [Florence]
 prov & town, Italy fē-RENT-sā fi:'rentse:
Firmin
 pers. name, French fir-ME^n fir'mẽ
Fiscalini
 Field, *ballpark, San Bernardino, CA* FIS-kuh-LĒ-nē ₁fiskə'li:ni·
Fischer
 Emil, *German chemist (Nobel 1902);* FISH-uhr 'fiʃə^r
 Ernst Otto, *German inorganic*
 chemist (Nobel 1973); Hans,
 German chemist (Nobel 1930)
Fischer-Dieskau
 Dietrich, *German baritone/conductor* FISH-uhr-DĒ-SKOW ₁fiʃə^r'di:₁skɑu
Fitch
 Val L., *US physicist (Nobel 1980)* FICH 'fitʃ
Fitchburg
 city, MA FICH-BUHRG 'fitʃ₁bə^{r}g

Foreign Sounds: ue: *Fr.* **rue**, *Ger.* **füllen** uh(r): *Fr.* **boeuf**, *Ger.* **Höhle** <u>kh</u>: *Ger.* **ich**, *Scot.* **loch** g̅: *Sp.* **amigo** <u>v</u>: *Sp.* **hablar**
hl: *Welsh* **Llanelli**. CAPITALS: primary stress. SMALL CAPS: secondary stress. ⑤: U.S. pron. ⓔ: British pron.

Fitzgerald
  pers. name   fits-JER-uhld   fits'dʒerəld
Fitzwater
  Max Marlin, *US government official*   FIT-SWAWT-uhr   'fit,swɔːt̬əʳ
Fitzwilliam
  college, Cambridge Univ.   fit-SWIL-yuhm   fit'swiljəm
Fiume
  city, Croatia [Rijeka]; *former*   FYOO-mā   'fjuːmeː
    province, Italy
Fiumicino
  airport, Rome   FYOO-mi-CHĒ-nō   ,fjuːmi'tʃiːnoː
Fix
  Greek beer   FĒKS   'fiːks
Flaccus
  Roman cognomen   FLAK-uhs   'flækəs
Flacianism
  beliefs of Matthias Flacius Illyricus   FLĀ-sh(ē-)uh-NIZ-uhm   'fleːʃ(iː)ə,nizəm
Flageolet
  small flute   FLAJ-ē-uh-LET, FLAJ-ē-uh-LĀ   ,flædʒiːə'let, ,flædʒiːə'leː
Flagey-Echézeaux
  French wine   flah-ZHE-ā-shā-ZŌ   flɑːʒe-eːʃeːzoː
Flagler
  county, FL   FLAG-luhr   'flæɡləʳ
Flagstad
  Kirsten, *Norwegian opera star*   FLAHG-STAH, ⑤ FLAG-STAD   'flɑɡ,stɑ, ⑤ 'flæɡ,stæd
Flagstaff
  city, AZ   FLAG-STAF   'flæɡ,stæf
Flambeau
  river, WI   flam-BŌ   flæm'boː
Flamenco
  dance   fluh-MENG-kō   flə'meŋkoː
Flaminian Way [Via Flamina]
  ancient Roman road   fluh-MIN-ē-uhn WĀ   flə,miniːən 'weː
Flamininus
  Titus Quinctius, *Roman general*   FLAM-uh-NĪ-nuhs   ,flæmə'nɑinəs
Flaminius
  Gaius, *Roman general*   fluh-MIN-ē-uhs   flə'miniːəs
Flammarion
  Camille, *French scientist*   flah-mahr-YAWⁿ   flɑːmɑːrjɔ̃
Flanagan
  Fionnula Manon, *Irish actress*   FLAN-uh-guhn   'flænəgən
Flanders
  region, Belgium   FLAN-duhrz   'flændəʳz
Flandreau
  city, SD; Indian reservation, US   FLAN-droo   'flændruː
Flathead
  N. American people   FLAT-HED   'flæt,hed
Flaubert
  Gustave, *French author*   flō-BER   floːber
Flavel
  pers. name   fluh-VEL, FLĀ-vuhl   flə'vel, 'fleːvəl
Flavia
  pers. name   FLĀ-vē-uh   'fleːviːə
Flavian
  Roman imperial dynasty   FLĀ-vē-uhn   'fleːviːən

Key (col. 2):   a: fad   ā: fade   ah: father   ar: marry   aw: law   e: fed   ē: feed   er: merry   i: hid   ī: hide   ō: coat   oo: boot
oi: boy   ow: now   u: put   uh: above   uhr: bird   ch: chop   ng: ring   sh: show   th: thick   th̲: this   zh: measure

Flavius
   pers. name   FLĀ-vē-uhs   ˈfleːviːəs

Fleming
   Sir Alexander, *Scottish*   FLEM-ing   ˈflemɪŋ
     bacteriologist (Nobel 1945)

Flemish
   lang., W. Europe; pert. to Flanders   FLEM-ish   ˈflemɪʃ

Fletcher
   pers. name   FLECH-uhr   ˈfletʃəʳ

Fleur-de-lis
   French symbol   FLUHRD-l-Ē, FLURD-l-Ē   ˌfləʳdl̩ˈiː, ˌfluʳdl̩ˈiː

Fleurie
   French wine   fluhr-Ē   flœriː

Fleurs-de-lis
   plural of fleur-de-lis   FLUHRD-l-Ē(Z), FLURD-l-Ē(Z)   ˌfləʳdl̩ˈiː(z), ˌfluʳdl̩ˈiː(z)

Flewelling
   Ralph Tyler, *US philosopher*   fluh-WEL-ing   fləˈwelɪŋ

Flexner
   Stuart, *US lexicographer*   FLEK-snuhr   ˈfleksnəʳ

Fliegende Holländer, der
   opera, Wagner   der FLĒ-guhn-duh HAW-LEN-duhr   deʳ ˈfliːgəndə ˈhɔːˌlendəʳ

Flin Flon
   town, Canada   FLIN FLAHN   ˈflɪn ˌflɑn

Flintshire
   former county, Wales   FLINT-shuhr, -SHIR   ˈflɪntʃəʳ, -ˌʃiʳ

Flo
   pers. name   FLŌ   ˈfloː

Flora
   Roman flower goddess; pers name   FLŌR-uh, FLAWR-uh   ˈfloːrə, ˈflɔːrə

Floréal
   month, French Revolutionary   flaw-rā-AHL   flɔːreːɑːl
     calendar

Florence
   1. prov & town, Italy [Firenze]; *US*   FLAWR-uhn(t)s, FLAHR-uhn(t)s   ˈflɔːrən(t)s, ˈflɑrən(t)s
     pl. name; pers. name
   2. French   flaw-RAHⁿS   flɔːrãs

Florens
   1. pers. name, German   FLŌR-ens   ˈfloːrens
   2. Latin   FLŌR-enz   ˈfloːrenz

Florentine
   pert. to Florence; *served with*   FLAWR-uhn-TĒN, FLAWR-uhn-TĪN,   ˈflɔːrənˌtiːn, ˈflɔːrənˌtain,
     spinach   FLAHR-uhn-   ˈflɑrən-

Florenz
   pers. name (F. Ziegfeld)   FLAWR-uhn(t)s, FLAHR-uhn(t)s   ˈflɔːrən(t)s, ˈflɑrən(t)s

Flores
   island, Azores; island, sea, Indonesia   FLŌR-uhs, FLAWR-uhs   ˈfloːrəs, ˈflɔːrəs

Floresville
   city, TX   FLŌR-uhs-VIL, FLAWR-   ˈfloːʳəsˌvil, ˈflɔːr-

Florey
   Sir Howard W., *Australian-born*   FLŌR-ē, FLAWR-ē   ˈfloːriˑ, ˈflɔːriˑ
     British pathologist (Nobel 1945)

Florian
   1. pers. name   FLŌR-ē-uhn   ˈfloːriːən
   2. German   FLŌR-yahn, FLŌR-ē-ahn   ˈfloːʳjɑn, ˈfloːriːɑn

Foreign Sounds: ue: *Fr.* **rue**, *Ger.* füllen   uh(r): *Fr.* **boeuf**, *Ger.* Höhle   <u>kh</u>: *Ger.* **ich**, *Scot.* loch   ḡ: *Sp.* amigo   <u>v</u>: *Sp.* hablar
hl: *Welsh* **Llanelli.**   CAPITALS: primary stress.   SMALL CAPS: secondary stress.   Ⓢ: U.S. pron.   Ⓔ: British pron.

Florida

  1. state, US   FLAWR-uhd-uh, FLAHR-uhd-uh,   'flɔːrədə, 'flɑrədə, 'floːrədə
                                FLŌR-uhd-uh

  2. pl. name, S America; mtns., NM   flaw-RẼ-duh   flɔː'riːdə

Floridian

  pert. to Florida   fluh-RID-ē-uhn, flaw-RID-ē-uhn,   flə'ridiːən, flɔː'ridiːən,
                               flah-RID-ē-uhn   flɑ'ridiːən

Florio

  James, US politician; John, *English*   FLAWR-ē-Ō, FLŌR-ē-Ō   'flɔːriːˌoː, 'floːriːˌoː
    lexicographer

Florissant

  city, MO   FLŌR-uh-suhnt, FLAWR-   'floːrəsənt, 'flɔːr-

Florsheim

  US shoe store chain   FLAWR-SHĪM   'flɔːʳˌʃaim

Flory

  Paul J., US physical chemist (Nobel   FLŌR-ē, FLAWR-ē   'floːri·, 'flɔːri·
    1974)

Floyd

  pers. name   FLOID   'flɔid

Floydada

  town, TX   floi-DĀD-uh   flɔi'deːdə

Fluellen

  character in Henry V, *Shakespeare*   flo͞o-EL-uhn   fluː'elən

Fluor

  US engineering co.   FLUR   'fluʳ

fluorine

  element   FLUR-ĒN, FLU-uh-RĒN, FLŌR-ĒN,   'flurˌiːn, 'fluəˌriːn, 'floːrˌiːn,
                              FLAWR-ĒN   'flɔːrˌiːn

Fluvanna

  county, VA   flo͞o-VAN-uh   fluː'vænə

Flynt

  Larry Claxton, *US publisher*   FLINT   'flint

FNMA

  Federal National Mortgage   FAN-ē-MĀ   ˌfæni·'meː
    Association

Foch

  1. Ferdinand, French militarist   FAWSH   fɔːʃ
  2. Nina, US actress   FŌSH   'foːʃ

Fodor

  Eugene, *travel author*   FŌD-uhr   'foːdəʳ

Fogelberg

  Dan, *US recording artist*   FŌ-guhl-BUHRG   'foːgəlˌbəʳg

Fogerty

  John, *rock singer, guitarist,*   FŌ-guhrt-ē   'foːgəʳʈi·
    songwriter

Fogg

  pers. name   FAWG, FAHG   'fɔːg, 'fɑg

Foggia

  prov & town, Italy   FAWD-jah, Ⓢ FAW-juh   'fɔːddʒɑ, Ⓢ 'fɔːdʒə

Fohism

  Chinese Buddhism   FŌ-IZ-uhm   'foːˌizəm

Foix

  prov & town, France   FWAH   fwɑː

Fokine

  Michel, *US choreographer*   FAWK-yin, faw-KẼN   'fɔːkjin, fɔː'kiːn

---

Key (col. 2):   a: fad   ā: fade   ah: father   ar: marry   aw: law   e: fed   ē: feed   er: merry   i: hid   ī: hide   ō: coat   o͞o: boot
oi: boy   ow: now   u: put   uh: above   uhr: bird   ch: chop   ng: ring   sh: show   th: thick   th: this   zh: measure

Fokis [Phocis]
   ancient district, dept., Greece   fō-KĒS   fɔːˈkiːs

Fokker
   Anthony, *Dutch aircraft designer*   FAHK-uhr, FŌ-kuhr   ˈfɑkəʳ, ˈfoːkəʳ

Folger
   Shakespearean Library, Washington,   FŌL-juhr   ˈfoːldʒəʳ
   D. C.; pers. name

Folies Bergére
   music hall, Paris, French   faw-LĒ ber-ZHER   fɔːliː berʒer

Folkes
   pers. name   FŌLKS, FŌKS   ˈfoːlks, ˈfoːks

Folkestone
   resort, England   FŌK-stuhn   ˈfoːkstən

Folsom
   city, prison, CA; village, NM   FŌL-suhm   ˈfoːlsəm

Fomalhaut
   star   FŌ-muhl-HAWT, FŌ-muh-LAWT,   ˈfoːməlˌhoːt, ˈfoːməˌlɔːt,
              FŌ-muh-LŌ, FŌ-muhl-HŌT   ˈfoːməˌloː, ˈfoːməlˌhoːt

Fon
   lang., W. Africa   FAHN, FAWN   ˈfɑn, ˈfɔːn

Fonda
   US acting family   FAHN-duh   ˈfɑndə

Fond Du Lac
   city, county, WI; Indian reservation,   FAHN-dl-AK, FAHN-juh-LAK   ˈfɑndl̩ˌæk, ˈfɑndʒəˌlæk
   US

Fons
   Roman god of springs   FAHNZ, FŌNZ   ˈfɑnz, ˈfoːnz

Fonseca
   Gulf of, *Cen. America*   fahn-SĀ-kuh   fɑnˈseːkə

Fontaine
   1. Jean de la, *French writer*   fawⁿ-TEN   fɔ̃ten
   2. Joan, *US actress*   fahn-TĀN   fɑnˈteːn

Fontaine, La
   see La Fontaine

Fontainebleau
   palace, city, France   fawⁿ-ten-BLŌ, Ⓢ FAHNT-n-BLŌ   fɔ̃tenbloː, Ⓢ ˈfɑntn̩ˌbloː

Fontbonne
   College, *MO*   fahnt-BAHN, FAHNT-BAHN   fɑntˈbɑn, ˈfɑntˌbɑn

Fonteyn
   Dame Margot, *English ballet dancer*   fahn-TĀN, FAHN-TĀN   fɑnˈteːn, ˈfɑnˌteːn

Fontina
   Italian cheese   fahn-TĒ-nuh   fɑnˈtiːnə

Fonzie
   TV sitcom character   FAHN-zē   ˈfɑnziˑ

Foochow, Fuchau
   seaport, China   FŌŌ-JŌ, Ⓢ FŌŌ-CHOW   ˈfuːˈdʒoː, Ⓢ ˈfuːˈtʃau

Foote
   pers. name   FUT   ˈfut

Forbes
   Field, *ballpark, Pittsburgh, PA; US*   FAWRBZ   ˈfɔːʳbz
      publishing family

Ford
   Gerald R., *38th US president;*   FAWRD   ˈfɔːʳd
   Henry, *US industrialist; pers.*
   name

Foreign Sounds: ue: *Fr.* **rue**, *Ger.* **füllen**   uh(r): *Fr.* **boeuf**, *Ger.* **Höhle**   <u>kh</u>: *Ger.* **ich**, *Scot.* **loch**   ḡ: *Sp.* **amigo**   <u>v</u>: *Sp.* **hablar**
hl: *Welsh* **Llanelli**.   CAPITALS: primary stress.   SMALL CAPS: secondary stress.   Ⓢ: U.S. pron.   Ⓔ: British pron.

Fordham
University, *NY*	FAWRD-uhm	'fɔːʳdəm

Fordyce
pers. name	FAWR-DĪS	'fɔːʳˌdais

Forest
pers. name	FAWR-uhst, FAHR-uhst	'fɔːrəst, 'fɑrəst

Forester
pers. name	FAWR-uhs-tuhr, FAHR-	'fɔːrəstəʳ, 'fɑr-

Forman
Milos, *Czech film director*	FAWR-muhn	'fɔːʳmən

Formica
tdmk for plastic sheeting	fawr-MĪ-kuh	fɔːʳ'maikə

Formosa
prov, Argentina; former name of	fawr-MŌ-suh	fɔːʳ'moːsə
Taiwan		

Formosus
pope	fawr-MŌ-suhs	fɔːʳ'moːsəs

Fornax
Roman goddess of the bread oven;	FAWR-NAKS	'fɔːʳˌnæks
constellation		

Forrest
pers. name	FAWR-uhst, FAHR-uhst	'fɔːrəst, 'fɑrəst

Fors
Roman god of chance	FAWRS, FAWRZ	'fɔːʳs, 'fɔːʳz

Forssmann
Werner, *German physician (Nobel*	FAWR-SMAHN	'fɔːʳˌsmɑn
1956)		

Forster
pers. name	FAWR-stuhr	'fɔːʳstəʳ

Forsyth
county, GA, NC	FAWR-SĪTH, fawr-SĪTH	'fɔːʳˌsaiθ, fɔːʳ'saiθ

Forsythe
John, *US actor*	FAWR-SĪTH, fawr-SĪTH	'fɔːʳˌsaiθ, fɔːʳ'saiθ

Fortaleza
city, Brazil	FAWRT-l-Ā-zuh	ˌfɔːʳtl̩'eːzə

Fort Belknap
Indian reservation, US	FŌRT BEL-NAP, FAWRT	ˌfoːʳt 'belˌnæp, ˌfɔːʳt

Fort Belvoir
military post, VA	fōrt BEL-VAWR, FAWRT	foːʳt 'belˌvɔːʳ, ˌfɔːʳt

Fort Berthold
Indian reservation, US	FŌRT BUHR-TŌLD, FAWRT	ˌfoːʳt 'bəʳˌtoːld, ˌfɔːʳt

Fort Bidwell
Indian reservation, US	FŌRT BID-WEL, FAWRT, BID-wuhl	ˌfoːʳt 'bidˌwel, ˌfɔːʳt, 'bidwəl

Fort de Chartres
historic fort, IL	FŌRT duh CHAHR-tuhrz, FAWRT	'foːʳt də 'tʃɑʳtəʳz, 'fɔːʳt

Fort-de-France
town, Caribbean	FAWR-duh-FRAHⁿS	ˌfɔːʳdə'frɑs

Forth
river, Scotland; programming lang.	FŌRTH, FAWRTH	'foːʳθ, 'fɔːʳθ

Fortinbras
character in Hamlet, *Shakespeare*	FAWRT-n-BRAS	'fɔːʳtn̩ˌbræs

Fort Lauderdale
city, FL	FŌRT LAWD-uhr-DĀL, FAWRT	ˌfoːʳt 'lɔːdəʳˌdeːl, ˌfɔːʳt

Fort McDermitt
Indian reservation, US	FŌRT muhk-DUHR-muht, FAWRT	ˌfoːʳt mək'dəʳmət, ˌfɔːʳt

---

Key (col. 2):   a: fad   ā: fade   ah: father   ar: marry   aw: law   e: fed   ē: feed   er: merry   i: hid   ī: hide   ō: coat   ōō: boot
oi: boy   ow: now   u: put   uh: above   uhr: bird   ch: chop   ng: ring   sh: show   th: thick   th̲: this   zh: measure

Fort McDowell
   Indian reservation, US   FŌRT muhk-DOW(-uh)l, FAWRT   ˌfoːʳt məkˈdau(ə)l, ˌfɔːʳt

Fort Meigs
   historic fort, OH   FŌRT MEGZ, FAWRT, MĀGZ   ˌfoːʳt ˈmegz, ˌfɔːʳt, ˈmeːgz

Fort Moultrie
   historic fort, SC   FŌRT MŌŌL-trē, FAWRT, MŌL-trē   ˌfoːʳt ˈmuːltriː, ˌfɔːʳt, ˈmoːltri·

Fortnum & Mason
   exclusive retailer, London   FAWRT-nuhm uhn(d) MĀ-suhn   ˈfɔːʳtnəm ən(d) ˈmeːsən

Fort Pierre
   city, SD   FAWRT PĒR   ˌfɔːʳt ˈpiːʳ

Fort Qu'Appelle
   town, Saskatchewan, Canada   FŌRT kwah-PEL, FAWRT   ˌfoːʳt kwɑˈpel, ˌfɔːʳt

FORTRAN
   programming lang.   FAWR-TRAN   ˈfɔːʳˌtræn

Fort Steilacoom
   Community College, WA   FŌRT STĪ-luh-KŌŌM, FAWRT   ˌfoːʳt ˈstɑiləˌkuːm, ˌfɔːʳt

Fort Ticonderoga
   fort, NY   FŌRT TĪ-KAHN-duh-RŌ-guh, FAWRT   ˌfoːʳt ˌtaiˌkɑndəˈroːgə, ˌfɔːʳt

Fort Totten
   Indian reservation, US   FŌRT TAHT-n, FAWRT   ˌfoːʳt ˈtɑtn̩, ˌfɔːʳt

Fortuna
   city, CA; Roman goddess of fortune   fawr-T(Y)ŌŌ-nuh, fawr-CHŌŌ-nuh   fɔːʳˈt(j)uːnə, fɔːʳˈtʃuːnə

Fortunatus
   Biblical name   FAWR-chu-NĀT-uhs, FAWR-t(y)u-, -NAHT-uhs   ˌfɔːʳtʃuˈneːtəs, ˌfɔːʳt(j)u-, -ˈnɑtəs

Fort Victoria [Masvingo, Nyanda]
   city, Zimbabwe   FŌRT vik-TŌR-ē-uh, fawrt vik-TAWR-ē-uh   ˌfoːʳt vikˈtoːriːə, fɔːʳt vikˈtɔːriːə

Fort Yuma
   Indian reservation, US   FŌRT YŌŌ-muh, FAWRT   ˌfoːʳt ˈjuːmə, ˌfɔːʳt

Forum Romanum
   center of ancient Rome   FŌR-uhm rō-MAHN-uhm, FAWR-uhm   ˈfoːrəm roːˈmɑnəm, ˈfɔːrəm

Forza del Destino
   opera, Verdi   FAWRT-sah del des-TĒ-nō   ˈfɔːʳtsɑ del desˈtiːnoː

Fosbury
   Dick, *high jump champion*   FAHZ-BER-ē   ˈfɑzˌberi·

Foscari
   Francesco, *Doge of Venice*   faw-SKAHR-ē   fɔːˈskɑriː

Fosse
   1. Bob, *US director*   FAW-sē, FAHS-ē   ˈfɔːsi·, ˈfasi·
   2. pers. name   FAWS, FAHS, FAW-sē, FAHS-ē   ˈfɔːs, ˈfas, ˈfɔːsi·, ˈfasi·

Fossum
   Field, *ballpark, Aberdeen, SD*   FAHS-uhm   ˈfasəm

Fotomat
   US film processing co.   FŌT-uh-MAT   ˈfoːʈəˌmæt

Foucault
   Jean, *French physicist;* Michel, *French philosopher*   fŌŌ-KŌ   fuːkoː

Fouché
   Joseph, *French politician*   fŌŌ-SHĀ   fuːʃeː

Fourier
   Jean-Baptiste, *French mathematician*   fŌŌr-YĀ   fuːrjeː

Fourier

Charles, *French social theorist*   f͞oor-YĀ, Ⓢ FUR-ē-Ā   fuːrjeː, Ⓢ ˈfuriːˌeː

Fournier

Charles, *French socialist*   f͞oorn-YĀ   fuːrnjeː

Fou-shan

see Fushun

Fowkes

Robert, *US linguist*   FOWKS   ˈfɑuks

Fowler

Henry, *English lexicographer;*   FOW-luhr   ˈfɑuləʳ
    William A., *US physicist (Nobel 1983)*

Fowles

John, *British author*   FOWLZ   ˈfɑulz

Fox

N. American people; pers. name   FAHKS   ˈfɑks

Foyt

A.J., *US race car driver*   FOIT   ˈfɔit

Fra Angelico

Italian painter; liqueur   FRAH an-JEL-i-kō   ˌfrɑ ænˈdʒeliko

Fra Diavolo

Italian brigand   FRAH dē-AHV-uh-LŌ   ˌfrɑ diːˈɑvəˌlo

Fra Filippo Lippi

see Lippi

Fragonard

Jean-Honoré, *French artist*   frah-gaw-NAHR   frɑːgɔːnɑːr

Framingham

town, MA   FRĀ-ming-HAM   ˈfreːmiŋˌhæm

Frampton

Peter, *British rock musician*   FRAM(P)-tuhn   ˈfræm(p)tən

Fran

pers. name   FRAN   ˈfræn

Françaix

Jean, *French composer*   frahⁿ-SE   frɑse

France

1. *country, Europe; pers. name*   FRANS, FRAHNS, FRAHⁿS   ˈfræns, ˈfrɑːns, frɑs
2. Anatole *(pseudonym of J.-A. F.*   FRAHⁿS, Ⓢ FRANS   frɑs, Ⓢ ˈfræns
    Thibault*), French author (Nobel 1921)*

Frances

pers. name   FRAN-suhs   ˈfrænsəs

Francesca

1. *pers. name*   fran-CHES-kuh   frænˈtʃeskə
2. *Italian*   frahn-CHĀS-kah   franˈtʃeːska

Francescatti

Zino, *French violinist*   FRAHN-ches-KAHT-ē   ˌfrɑntʃesˈkɑtiˑ

Francesco

pers. name   frahn-CHĀS-kō   franˈtʃeːskoː

Franche-Comté

prov, France   frahⁿsh-kawⁿ-TĀ   frɑʃkõteː

Francia

José Gaspar Rodríguez de,   FRAHNS-yah   ˈfransjɑ
    Paraguayan dictator

Key (col. 2):   a: fad   ā: fade   ah: father   ar: marry   aw: law   e: fed   ē: feed   er: merry   i: hid   ī: hide   ō: coat   o͞o: boot
oi: boy   ow: now   u: put   uh: above   uhr: bird   ch: chop   ng: ring   sh: show   th: thick   t͟h: this   zh: measure

Francis		
1. pers. name	FRAN-suhs	ˈfrænsəs
2. Dutch	FRAHN-suhs	ˈfrɑnsəs
3. French	frah^n-SĒS	frɑ̃siːs
4. German	FRAHNT-sis	ˈfrɑntsis
5. Norwegian	FRAHN-sis	ˈfrɑnsis
Franciscans		
religious order	fran-SIS-kuhnz	frænˈsiskənz
Francisco		
1. pers. name	fran-SIS-kō	frænˈsiskoː
2. Portuguese	frah^n-SĒSH-ko͞o, -SĒS-ko͞o	frɑ̃ːˈsiːʃkuː, -ˈsiːskuː
3. Spanish	frahn-SĒS-kō, -THĒS-kō	frɑnˈsiːskoː, -ˈθiːskoː
Franciscus		
James, *US actor*	fran-SIS-kuhs	frænˈsiskəs
francium		
element	FRAN-sē-uhm	ˈfrænsiːəm
Franck		
1. César Auguste, *Belgian composer*	FRAH^{n}K, [$] FRAHNGK	frɑ̃k, [$] ˈfrɑŋk
2. James, *German-born US physicist (Nobel 1925)*	FRAHNGK	ˈfrɑŋk
Franco		
1. Francisco, *Spanish dictator; pers. name*	FRAHNG-kō, [$] FRANG-kō	ˈfrɑŋkoː, [$] ˈfræŋkoː
2. Italian	FRAHNG-kō	ˈfrɑŋkoː
François		
pers. name	frah^n-SWAH	frɑ̃swɑː
Françoise		
pers. name	frah^n-SWAHZ	frɑ̃swɑːz
Franconia		
town, NH; district, Germany	frang-KŌ-nē-uh, frang-KŌN-yuh	fræŋˈkoːniːə, fræŋˈkoːnjə
Franconian Forest [Frankenwald]		
mtn. range, Germany	frang-KŌ-nē-uhn FAWR-uhst, FAHR-uhst	fræŋˈkoːniːən ˈfɔːrəst, ˈfɑrəst
Francophile		
lover of things French	FRANG-kuh-FĪL	ˈfræŋkəˌfɑil
Francophobe		
hater of things French	FRANG-kuh-FŌB	ˈfræŋkəˌfoːb
Frangipani		
flowering tree	FRAN-juh-PAN-ē, FRAN-juh-PAHN-ē	ˌfrændʒəˈpæniː, ˌfrændʒəˈpɑniˑ
Franglais		
mixture of French & English	frahng-GLĀ	frɑŋˈgleː
Franjo		
pers. name (F. Tudjman)	FRAHN-yō	ˈfrɑnjoː
Frank		
1. Anne, *German Jewish diarist;* Ilya Mikhaylovich, *Soviet physicist (Nobel 1958)*	FRAHNGK, [$] FRANGK	ˈfrɑŋk, [$] ˈfræŋk
2. pers. name	FRANGK	ˈfræŋk
3. French	FRAH^{n}K	frɑ̃k
Frankenheimer		
John, *entertainer*	FRANG-kuhn-HĪ-muhr	ˈfræŋkənˌhaiməʳ
Frankenmuth		
city, MI; beer	FRANG-kuhn-MO͞OTH	ˈfræŋkənˌmuːθ

Foreign Sounds: ue: *Fr.* **rue**, *Ger.* **füllen** uh(r): *Fr.* **boeuf**, *Ger.* **Höhle** kh: *Ger.* **ich**, *Scot.* **loch** g̅: *Sp.* amigo v̲: *Sp.* hablar hl: *Welsh* **Llanelli**. CAPITALS: primary stress. SMALL CAPS: secondary stress. [$]: U.S. pron. [£]: British pron.

Frankenstein
  character in gothic novel by M.   FRANG-kuhn-STĪN   'fræŋkən,stɑin
  Shelley
Frankenthaler
  Helen, *US painter*   FRANG-kuhn-THAW-luhr, -THAHL-uhr   'fræŋkən,θɔːlə^r, -,θɑlə^r
Frankenwald [Franconian Forest]
  mtn. range, Germany   FRAHNG-kuhn-VAHLT   'frɑŋkən,vɑlt
Frankfort
  US pl. name   FRANGK-fuhrt   'fræŋkfə^rt
Frankfurt
  city, Germany   FRAHNGK-FURT, Ⓢ FRANGK-fuhrt   'frɑŋk,fu^rt, Ⓢ 'fræŋkfə^rt
Frankfurt/Main
  airport, Frankfurt   FRAHNGK-FURT-MĪN   'frɑŋk,fu^rt'mɑin
Frankfurter
  Felix, *US jurist*   FRANK-FUHRT-uhr   'fræŋk,fə^rtə^r
Frankie
  pers. name   FRANG-kē   'fræŋki·
Franklin, -lyn
  pers. name   FRANGK-luhn   'fræŋklən
Frans
  1. pers. name, Danish, Dutch   FRAHNS   'frɑns
  2. Finnish, Swedish   FRAHNS   'frɑːns
Franz
  1. pers. name   FRANS, FRANZ, FRAHNS   'fræns, 'frænz, 'frɑns
  2. French   FRAHⁿS   frɑ̃s
Franzia
  wine   FRAHN(T)-sē-uh, FRAN(T)-sē-uh   'frɑn(t)siːə, 'fræn(t)siːə
Franzikus
  German beer   FRAHN(T)-si-kus   'frɑn(t)sikus
Franz Josef Land
  Arctic archipelago   frahn(t)s YŌ-zuhf LAHNT; FRAN(T)S   frɑn(t)s 'joːzəf ,lɑnt; fræn(t)s
       JŌ-zuhf LAND, JŌ-suhf   'dʒoːzəf ,lænd, 'dʒoːsəf
Frascati
  wine   frahs-KAHT-ē   frɑs'kɑ̞i·
Fraser
  River, *Canada*   FRĀ-zuhr, FRĀ-zhuhr   'freːzə^r, 'freːʒə^r
Frau
  Mrs., *in German*   FROW   'frɑu
Frauen
  pl. of Frau   FROW-uhn   'frɑuən
Fräulein
  Miss, *in German*   FROI-LĪN   'frɔi,lɑin
Frazier
  June, *singer-songwriter;* Joe, *US*   FRĀ-zhuhr   'freːʒə^r
  prize fighter
Fred
  pers. name   FRED   'fred
Freda
  pers. name   FRĒD-uh, FRED-uh   'friːdə, 'fredə
Freddy
  pers. name   FRED-ē   'fredi·
Frederic
  1. pers. name   FRED(-uh)-rik   'fred(ə)rik
  2. Norwegian   FRED-rik   'fredrik

Key (col. 2):   a: fad ā: fade ah: father ar: marry aw: law e: fed ē: feed er: merry i: hid ī: hide ō: coat ōō: boot
oi: boy   ow: now   u: put   uh: above   uhr: bird   ch: chop   ng: ring   sh: show   th: thick   <u>th</u>: this   zh: measure

Frédéric
   pers. name, French   frā-dā-RĔK   freːdeːriːk

Frederica
   pers. name, German   FRĀ-dā-RĔ-kah   ˌfreːdeːˈriːkɑ

Frederici Honores
   former constellation   FRED-uh-RĔ-kē (h)ahn-ŌR-ĒZ,   ˌfredəˈriːkiˈ (h)ɑnˈoːrˌiːz,
                            (h)ahn-ŌR-uhs   (h)ɑnˈoːrəs

Frédérick
   French   frā-dā-RĔK   freːdeːriːk

Frederick
   1. pers. name   FRED(-uh)-rik   ˈfred(ə)rik
   2. Danish   FRI<u>TH</u>-rik   ˈfriðrik

Frederico
   pers. name, Italian   FRĀ-dā-RĔ-kō   ˌfreːdeːˈriːkoː

Fredericton
   city, New Brunswick, Canada   FRED-(uh-)rik-tuhn   ˈfred(ə)riktən

Frederika
   1. pers. name, Danish   fri<u>th</u>-RĔ-kah   friðˈriːkɑː
   2. Swedish   FRĀ-duh-RĔ-kah   ˌfreːdəˈriːkɑ

Fredonia
   city, KS; village, college, NY   frē-DŌ-nē-uh, frē-DŎN-yuh   friˈdoːniːə, friˈdoːnjə

Fredric
   1. pers. name   FRED-rik   ˈfredrik
   2. Swedish   FRĀ-drik   ˈfreːdrik

Fredrica
   pers. name   fred-RĔ-kuh   fredˈriːkə

Fredrik
   1. pers. name, Danish   FRI<u>TH</u>-rik   ˈfriðrik
   2. Dutch   FRĀ-druhk   ˈfreːdrək
   3. Finnish, Swedish   FRĀ-drik   ˈfreːdrik
   4. Norwegian   FRED-rik   ˈfredrik

Freeman
   pers. name   FRĒ-muhn   ˈfriːmən

Freemont
   pers. name   FRĒ-MAHNT   ˈfriːˌmɑnt

Freeport
   US pl. name; town, Bahamas   FRĒ-PŌRT, FRĒ-PAWRT   ˈfriːˌpoːʳt, ˈfriːˌpɔːʳt

Freer
   art gallery, Washington, DC   FRIR   ˈfriʳ

Freesia
   flower   FRĒ-zh(ē-)uh, FRĒ-zē-uh   ˈfriːʒ(iː)ə, ˈfriːziːə

Freetown
   town, Sierra Leone   FRĒ-TOWN   ˈfriːˌtɑun

Frege
   Gottlob, *German logician*   FREG-uh, FRĀ-guh   ˈfregə, ˈfreːgə

Freiburg
   city, Germany   FRĪ-BURK   ˈfrɑiˌbuʳk

Fremantle
   city, Australia   frē-MAN-tl   friˈmæntl̩

Fremont
   city, CA; pers. name   FRĒ-MAHNT   ˈfriːˌmɑnt

French
   lang., W. Europe   FRENCH   ˈfrentʃ

French Guiana

French overseas dept., S. America   FRENCH gē-AN-uh, gē-AHN-uh,   ˌfrentʃ giː'ænə, giː'ɑnə,
                                   gī-AN-uh   gɑi'ænə

French Guianese

pert. to French Guiana   GĪ-uh-NĒZ, GĒ-uh-, -NĒS   ˌgɑiə'niːz, ˌgiːə-, -'niːs

Frenchman

man from France   FRENCH-muhn   'frentʃmən

Freon

tdmk for fluorocarbon   FRĒ-AHN   'friːˌɑn

Fresnay

Pierre, *French actor*   fruh-NĀ   frəneː

Fresnel

Augustin Jean, *French physicist;*   frā-NEL, fre-NEL   freːnel, frenel
pers. name

Fresnel lens

focusing device   FREZ-nuhl, fruh-NEL, frā-NEL   'freznəl, frə'nel, freː'nel

Fresno

city, county, CA   FREZ-nō   'freznoː

Freud

Sigmund, *Austrian psychoanalyst*   FROID   'frɔid

Freudian

pert. to Freud   FROID-ē-uhn   'frɔidiːən

Frey

1. Scandinavian weather god   FRĀ   'freː
2. pers. name   FRĪ   'frɑi

Freya

pers. name   FRĀ-uh   'freːə

Freyja

Scandinavian fertility goddess   FRĀ-uh   'freːə

Freyr [Frey]

Scandinavian weather god   FRĀR, FRER, FRĀ   'freːʳ, 'freʳ, 'freː

Fribourg

city, Switzerland   frē-BUR   friːbur

Friday

day of the week   FRĪD-ē, FRĪD-ā   'frɑidiˑ, 'frɑideː

Frideric

pers. name (G. F. Handel)   FRĒD-rik   'friːdrik

Fridtjof

pers. name, Norwegian   FRICH-AWF   'fritʃˌɔːf

Fried

A. H., *Austrian pacifist, publicist*   FRĒT, FRĒD   'friːt, 'friːd
(Nobel 1911)

Frieda

1. pers. name   FRĒD-uh   'friːdə
2. German   FRĒ-dah   'friːdɑ

Friedan

Betty, *US feminist*   fri-DAN, frē-DAN   fri'dæn, friː'dæn

Friedman

Jerome I., *US physicist (Nobel*   FRĒD-muhn   'friːdmən
1990); Milton, *US economist*
(Nobel 1976)

Friedrich

1. pers. name   FRĒ-drik   'friːdrik
2. German   FRĒ-drikh   'friːdriç

Key (col. 2): a: fad ā: fade ah: father ar: marry aw: law e: fed ē: feed er: merry i: hid ī: hide ō: coat ōō: boot
oi: boy ow: now u: put uh: above uhr: bird ch: chop ng: ring sh: show th: thick th̲: this zh: measure

Friedrichshafen
  town, Germany — FRĒ-driks-HAHF-uhn — ˌfriːdriksˈhɑfən
Fries
  1. town, VA — FRĒZ — ˈfriːz
  2. pers. name — FRĒS — ˈfriːs
Friesche Eilanden [Frisian Islands]
  islands, North Sea — FRĒ-suh Ī-LAHN-duhn — ˌfriːsə ˈɑiˌlɑndən
Friese-Greene
  William, *English inventor* — FRĒZ-GRĒN — ˈfriːzˈgriːn
Friesian
  cattle — FRĒ-zhuhn — ˈfriːʒən
Friesland
  province, Netherlands — FRĒS-LAHNT — ˈfriːsˌlɑnt
Frietchie
  Barbara, *Civil War heroine* — FRICH-ē — ˈfritʃiˑ
Frigga [Frigg]
  Scandinavian fertility goddess — FRIG-uh — ˈfrigə
Frigg [Frigga]
  Scandinavian fertility goddess — FRIG — ˈfrig
Frigidaire
  tdmk for a refrigerator — FRIJ-uh-DAR, FRIJ-uh-DER, FRIJ-uh-DAR, FRIJ-uh-DER — ˌfridʒəˈdær, ˌfridʒəˈder, ˈfridʒəˌdær, ˈfridʒəˌder
Frigo
  cheese — FRĒ-gō — ˈfriːgoː
Frigoris, Mare
  see Mare Frigoris
Frimaire
  month, French Revolutionary calendar — frē-MER — friːmer
Friml
  Rudolf, *US composer* — FRIM-uhl — ˈfriməl
Frio
  river, county, TX — FRĒ-ō — ˈfriːoː
Friona
  city, TX — frē-Ō-nuh — friːˈoːnə
Frisbee
  tdmk for flying disk — FRIZ-bē — ˈfrizbiˑ
Frisch
  Karl von, *Austrian zoologist (Nobel 1973)*; Ragnar, *Norwegian economist (Nobel 1969)* — FRISH — ˈfriʃ
Frisch's
  US restaurant chain — FRISH-uhz — ˈfriʃəz
Frisian
  lang., Netherlands, Germany; Islands, North Sea — FRIZH-uhn, FRĒ-zhuhn — ˈfriʒən, ˈfriːʒən
Frissell, Mount
  mtn., CT — MOWNT fruh-ZEL — ˈmɑunt frəˈzel
Frito-Lay
  US snack foods co. — FRĒT-ō-LĀ, FRĒT-ō-LĀ — ˈfriːt̬oːˌleː, ˌfriːt̬oːˈleː
Frits
  pers. name, Dutch — FRITS — ˈfrits
Fritz
  pers. name — FRITS — ˈfrits

Friulian
  lang., people, North Italy frē-OO-lē-uhn fri:'u:li:ən

Frobisher
  Sir Martin, *English mariner* FRŌ-buh-shuhr 'froːbəʃərˡ

Froebel
  Friedrich, *German educator* FRUH(R)-buhl 'frœːbəl

Frohman
  pers. name FRŌ-muhn 'froːmən

Froissart
  Jean, *French poet* frwah-SAHR, ⓢ f(r)wah-SAHR frwɑːsɑːr, ⓢ f(r)wɑ'sɑˡ

Frome
  1. Lynette "Squeaky", US attempted assassin FRŌM 'froːm
  2. town, river, England FROOM 'fruːm

Fromm
  Erich, *US psychoanalyst* FRŌM, FRAHM 'froːm, 'frɑm

Fronsac
  French wine frawⁿ-SAHK frɔsɑːk

Frontenac
  1. Louis de, political leader frawⁿ-tuh-NAHK frɔtənɑːk
  2. city, KS; city, MO; county, Ont., Que., Canada FRAHNT-n-AK 'frɑntn̩ˌæk

Frontignac
  wine grape variety frawⁿ-tēn-YAHK frɔtiːnjɑːk

Frontignan
  commune, France frawⁿ-tēn-YAHⁿ frɔtiːnjɑ̃

Front National
  political party, France FRAWⁿ nahs-yaw-NAHL frɔ̃ nɑːsjɔːnɑːl

Froude
  James Anthony, *English historian;* Richard Hurrell, *Anglican clergyman* FROOD 'fruːd

Fructidor
  month, French Revolutionary calendar fruek-tē-DAWR fryːktiːdɔːr

Fructuoso
  pers. name frook-TWŌ-sō fruːk'twoːsoː

Fruehauf
  US truck-trailer co. FROO-HAWF, FROO-HAHF 'fruːˌhɔːf, 'fruːˌhɑf

Frydenlund
  Norwegian beer FRUED-n-LUND 'fryːdn̩ˌlund

FSLIC
  Federal Savings and Loan Insurance Corporation FIZ-lik, EF-es-EL-ī-SĒ 'fizlik, ˌefesˌelɑi'siː

Fthiótis
  see Phthiotis

Fuchau
  see Foochow

Fuegian
  pert. to Tierra del Fuego fyu-Ē-jē-uhn, fyu-Ā-gē-uhn fju'iːdʒiːən, fju'eːgiːən

Fuentes
  Carlos, *Mexican novelist & playwright* FWEN-tās 'fwenteːs

Fugard
  Athol, *South African playwright* F(Y)OO-GAHRD 'f(j)uːˌgɑˡd

---

Key (col. 2): a: fad ā: fade ah: father ar: marry aw: law e: fed ē: feed er: merry i: hid ī: hide ō: coat oo: boot
oi: boy ow: now u: put uh: above uhr: bird ch: chop ng: ring sh: show th: thick th: this zh: measure

Fugger
    German family of financiers and   FUG-uhr   'fugəʳ
        merchants
Fugue
    musical composition   FY$\overline{OO}$G   'fjuːg
Führer, der
    title, A. Hitler   der FUER-uhr; ⓈⓄ der FYUR-uhr,   deʳ 'fyːrəʳ; Ⓢ deʳ 'fjurəʳ,
                            duhr, FIR-uhr   dəʳ, 'firəʳ
Fujayrah, Al
    emirate, town, United Arab Emirates   ahl fuh-J$\overline{I}$-ruh, al   aːl fə'dʒaɪrə, æl
Fuji [Fujiyama]
    Mount, *sacred mtn., Japan*   F$\overline{OO}$-jē, FY$\overline{OO}$-jē   'fuːdʒiˑ, 'fjuːdʒiˑ
Fujian [Fukien]
    province, China   F$\overline{OO}$-jē-AHN   'fuːdʒiː'ɑn
Fujica
    Japanese camera co.   F$\overline{OO}$-ji-kuh   'fuːdʒikə
Fuji Hakone Izu
    park, Japan   f$\overline{oo}$-jē hah-kō-nā ē-z$\overline{oo}$ fuːdʒiː hɑkoːneː iːzuː
Fujimori
    Alberto, *president, Peru*   fu-<u>kh</u>ē-MAWR-ē, Ⓢ F$\overline{OO}$-jē-M$\overline{O}$R-ē,   fuxiː'mɔːriˑ,
                        -MAWR-ē   Ⓢ ˌfuːdʒiˑ'moːriˑ, -'mɔːriˑ
Fuji-san [Fuji]
    sacred mtn., Japan   f$\overline{oo}$-jē-sahn   fuːdʒiːsan
Fujitsu
    Japanese corp.   f$\overline{oo}$-jit-s$\overline{oo}$ fuːdʒitsuː
Fujiyama [Fuji]
    sacred mtn., Japan   f$\overline{oo}$-jē-ahm-ah, Ⓢ F$\overline{OO}$-jē-(Y)AHM-uh,   fuːdʒiːɑmɑ,
                        FY$\overline{OO}$-   Ⓢ ˌfuːdʒiː'(j)amə, ˌfjuː-
Fukien [Fujian]
    province, China   F$\overline{OO}$-KYEN, F$\overline{OO}$-kē-EN   'fuː'kjen, 'fuːkiː'en
Fukui
    Kenichi, *Japanese chemist (Nobel*   fu-ku-ē   fukuiˑ
        1981)
Fukuoka
    city, Japan   f$\overline{oo}$-k$\overline{oo}$-ō-kah   fuːkuːoːkɑ
Fula
    African people   F$\overline{OO}$-luh   'fuːlə
Fula
    lang., Africa   F$\overline{OO}$-LAHR   'fuːˌlɑʳ
Fulani [Ful, Fulfulde]
    lang., people, Africa   F$\overline{OO}$-LAHN-ē, f$\overline{oo}$-LAHN-ē   'fuːˌlɑniˑ, fuː'lɑniˑ
Fulbright
    James, *US politician; scholarship*   FUL-BR$\breve{I}$T   'fulˌbraɪt
Ful [Fulani]
    lang., people, Africa   F$\overline{OO}$L, FUL   'fuːl, 'ful
Fulfulde [Fulani]
    lang., people, West Africa   ful-FUL-dē   ful'fuldiˑ
Fulgencio
    pers. name   ful-$\bar{\text{G}}$AN-thyō, -syō   ful'ɣeːnθjoː, -sjoː
Fulmar
    bird   FUL-muhr   'fulməʳ
Fulvia
    wife of Mark Antony   FUL-vē-uh   'fulviːə
Fulvius
    pers. name, Latin   FUHL-vē-uhs, FUL-   'fəlviːəs, 'ful-

Foreign Sounds: ue: *Fr.* **rue**, *Ger.* füllen   uh(r): *Fr.* **boeuf**, *Ger.* Höhle   <u>kh</u>: *Ger.* **ich**, *Scot.* loch   ḡ: *Sp.* amigo   <u>v</u>: *Sp.* hablar
hl: *Welsh* **Ll**anelli.   CAPITALS: primary stress.   SMALL CAPS: secondary stress.   Ⓢ: U.S. pron.   Ⓔ: British pron.

Fulvius Flaccus
   Roman popular leader   FUHL-vē-uhs FLAK-uhs, FUL-   'fəlviːəs 'flækəs, 'ful-
Fulvus
   pers. name   FUHL-vuhs, FUL-vuhs   'fəlvəs, 'fulvəs
Funafuti
   atoll, Tuvalu   F(Y)OO-nuh-F(Y)OOT-ē   ˌf(j)uːnə'f(j)uːti·
Funchal
   port, Madeira   foon-SHAHL, fuhn-SHAHL   fuːn'ʃal, fən'ʃal
Fundy
   Bay of, *Atlantic inlet, Canada*   FUHN-dē   'fəndi·
Fung, El [Al-Fung]
   former province, Sudan   el FUNG   el 'fuŋ
Funicello
   Annette, *US entertainer*   FOO-nuh-CHEL-ō   ˌfuːnə'tʃeloː
Fuquay-Varina
   town, NC   F(Y)OO-KWĀ-vuh-RĪ-nuh   'f(j)uːˌkweːvə'rainə
Fur
   lang., Sudan, Chad   FUR, FUHR   'fuʳ, 'fəʳ
Furies
   Roman demons of the Underworld   FYUR-ēz   'fjuri·z
Furius
   Roman name   FYUR-ē-uhs   'fjuriːəs
Furman
   University, *SC*   FUHR-muhn   'fəʳmən
Furnas
   county, NE   FUHR-nuhs   'fəʳnəs
Furness
   Betty, *US journalist*   FUHR-NES   ˌfəʳ'nes
Furnivall
   Frederick James, *Englist philologist*   FUHR-nuh-vuhl   'fəʳnəvəl
Fürstenberg
   German beer   FUR-stuhn-BERK   'fyʳstən,berk
Fürstenberg
   German noble family   FUH(R)R-stuhn-BERK   'fœʳstən,beʳk
Furth
   George, *US actor, playwright*   FUHRTH   'fəʳθ
Furtwängler
   Wilhelm, *German conductor*   FURT-VENG-(g)luhr   'fuʳtˌveŋ(g)ləʳ
Fushun, Fou-shan
   city, China   FOO-SHUN   'fuː'ʃun
Futuna
   islands, Pacific   foo-TOO-nuh   fu·'tuːnə
Futunan
   pert. to Futuna   foo-TOO-nuhn   fu·'tuːnən
Futura
   type font   f(y)oo-T(Y)UR-uh, f(y)oo-CHUR-uh   f(j)uː't(j)urə, f(j)uː'tʃurə
Fuzhou
   city, China   FOO-JŌ   'fuː'dʒoː
Fyodor
   pers. name, Russian   FYAWD-uhr   'fjɔːdər

Key (col. 2):   a: fad   ā: fade   ah: father   ar: marry   aw: law   e: fed   ē: feed   er: merry   i: hid   ī: hide   ō: coat   ōō: boot
oi: boy   ow: now   u: put   uh: above   uhr: bird   ch: chop   ng: ring   sh: show   th: thick   th: this   zh: measure

G

Gā, Ga
   lang., people, Ghana, Togo, Benin   GAH   'gɑ

Ga-Adangbe
   lang., W. Africa   GAH-ah-DAHNG-bā   'gɑɑ'daŋbeː

Gaal
   Biblical name   GĀ(-uh)l, GAH-AHL   'geː(ə)l, 'gɑˌɑl

Gaash
   Biblical name   GĀ-ASH, GAH-AHSH   'geːˌæʃ, 'gɑˌɑʃ

Gabbai
   Biblical name   GAB-ē-Ī, gah-BĀ-Ī, gah-BĪ   'gæbiːˌɑi, gɑ'beːˌɑi, gɑ'bɑi

Gabbatha
   Biblical name   GAB-uh-thuh   'gæbəθə

Gabès
   town, oasis, gulf, Tunisia   GAHB-uhs, GAHB-ES   'gabəs, 'gabˌes

Gabon
   republic, Africa   ga-BAW^n gæ'bɔ̃

Gabonese
   pert. to Gabon   GAB-uh-NĒZ, -NĒS   ˌgæbə'niːz, -'niːs

Gabor
   1. Dennis, *Hungarian-born British*   GAHB-AWR, guh-BAWR   'gabˌɔː^r, gə'bɔː^r
      physicist (Nobel 1971)
   2. Eva, Zsa Zsa, *US entertainers*   guh-BAWR   gə'bɔː^r

Gábor
   pers. name, Hungarian   GAH-bawr   'gɑːbɔː^r

Gaboriau
   Emile, *French novelist*   gah-bawr-YŌ   gɑːbɔːrjoː

Gaborone
   city, Botswana   GAHB-uh-RŌ-nē   ˌgabə'roːniː

Gabriel
   1. pers. name   GĀ-brē-uhl   'geːbriːəl
   2. Dutch   GAHB-rē-el   'gɑːbriːel
   3. French   gah-brē-EL   gɑːbriːel
   4. German   GAHB-rē-el   'gabriːel
   5. Norwegian, Swedish   GAHB-rē-uhl   'gabriːəl
   6. Polish   GAHB-ryel, ⑤ GAHB-rē-el   'gɑːbrjel, ⑤ 'gɑːbriːel
   7. Portuguese   guh-brē-EL, gah-   gəbriː'el, gɑː-
   8. Spanish   gahv-rē-EL   gɑβriː'el

Gabriela
   1. pers. name, Polish   gahb-rē-Ā-lah   gɑːbriː'eːlɑː
   2. Spanish   gahv-rē-Ā-lah   gɑβriː'eːlɑ

Gabriele
   1. pers. name, German   GAHB-rē-Ā-luh   ˌgabriː'eːlə
   2. Italian   GAHB-rē-EL-ā   ˌgabriː'eleː

Foreign Sounds: ue: *Fr.* **rue**, *Ger.* **füllen**   uh(r): *Fr.* **boeuf**, *Ger.* **Höhle**   <u>kh</u>: *Ger.* i<u>ch</u>, *Scot.* lo<u>ch</u>   ḡ: *Sp.* ami**g**o   <u>v</u>: *Sp.* ha**b**lar
hl: *Welsh* **Ll**anelli.   CAPITALS: primary stress.   SMALL CAPS: secondary stress.   ⑤: U.S. pron.   ⓔ: British pron.

Gabrieli

  Andrea, Giovanni, *Italian*   GAHB-rē-EL-ē   ˌgɑbriːˈeliː

    composers

Gabrielino

  N. American people   GĀ-brē-uh-LĒ-nō   ˌgeːbriːəˈliːnoː

Gabriella

  pers. name   GAB-rē-EL-uh, GĀ-brē-EL-uh   ˌgæbriːˈelə, ˌgeːbriːˈelə

Gabrielle

  pers. name   GAHB-rē-EL, GAB-   ˌgɑbriːˈel, ˌgæb-

Gabrilowitsch

  Ossip, *Russian pianist*   guhv-ril-AWV-YICH,   gəvrilˈɔːvˌjitʃ,

       Ⓢ GAHB-ruh-LŌ-vich   Ⓢ ˌgɑbrəˈloːvitʃ

Gabrjel

  pers. name, Polish   GAHB-ryel, Ⓢ GAHB-rē-el   ˈgɑːbrjel, Ⓢ ˈgɑːbriːel

Gabrjela, -ryela

  pers. name, Polish   GAHB-RYEL-ah, Ⓢ GAHB-rē-EL-ah   ˌgɑːbˈrjelɑː, Ⓢ ˌgɑːbriːˈelɑː

Gad

  Biblical name   GAD, GAHD   ˈgæd, ˈgɑd

Gadara

  ancient city, Palestine   GAD-uh-ruh   ˈgædərə

Gadarene

  pert. to biblical Gadara   GAD-uh-RĒN, GAD-uh-RĒN   ˈgædəˌriːn, ˌgædəˈriːn

Gaddafi

  see Qadhafi

Gaddang

  lang., people, Philippine Islands   GAHD-AHNG, gah-DAHNG   ˈgadˌaŋ, gaˈdaŋ

Gaddi

  Biblical name   GAD-Ī, gahd-Ē   ˈgædˌai, gadˈiː

Gaddiel

  Biblical name   GAD-ē-uhl, GAHD-ē-EL   ˈgædiːəl, ˌgadiːˈel

Gadhafi

  see Qadhafi

Gadi

  Biblical name   GĀ-DĪ, gahd-Ē   ˈgeːˌdai, gadˈiː

Gadite

  Biblical name   GAD-ĪT   ˈgædˌait

gadolinium

  element   GAD-l-IN-ē-uhm   ˌgædl̩ˈiniːəm

Gadsden

  city, AL; county FL   GADZ-duhn   ˈgædzdən

Gadwall

  duck   GAD-WAWL   ˈgædˌwɔːl

Gaea [Gaia]

  Greek earth goddess   JĒ-uh   ˈdʒiːə

Gael

  Celtic inhabitant of Ireland, Scotland,   GĀL   ˈgeːl

    or the Isle of Man

Gaelic

  lang., Ireland, Scotland, Isle of Man   GĀ-lik   ˈgeːlik

Gaelic Mod

  Scots festival   GĀ-lik MAHD   ˈgeːlik ˈmɑd

Gaétan

  pers. name, French   gah-ā-TAH^n gɑːeːtɑ̃

Gaetana

  pers. name, Italian   GAH-ā-TAHN-ah   ˌgaeˈtɑnɑ

Key (col. 2):   a: fad   ā: fade   ah: father   ar: marry   aw: law   e: fed   ē: feed   er: merry   i: hid   ī: hide   ō: coat   ōō: boot
oi: boy   ow: now   u: put   uh: above   uhr: bird   ch: chop   ng: ring   sh: show   th: thick   th: this   zh: measure

Gaetano		
pers. name, Italian	GAH-ā-TAHN-ō	ˌgɑeːˈtɑnoː
Gaffar		
pers. name, Arabic	GAHF-AHR	ˈgɑfˌɑʳ
Gagarin		
Yuri, *cosmonaut, USSR*	guh-GAHR-yin, [$] guh-GAHR-uhn	gəˈgɑːrjin, [$] gəˈgɑrən
Gagliano		
Marco da, *Italian priest/composer*	gahl-YAH-nō	gɑlˈjɑnoː
Gaham		
Biblical name	GĀ-HAM, GĀ-uhm, GAH-KHAHM	ˈgeːˌhæm, ˈgeːəm, ˈgɑˌxɑm
Gahan		
pers. name	GĀ-uhn	ˈgeːən
Gahan		
Dave, *British rock star*	GĀ-uhn	ˈgeːən
Gahar		
Biblical name	GĀ-HAHR, GAH-khahr	ˈgeːˌhɑʳ, ˈgɑxɑr
Gaia [Gaea]		
the Earth, esp. personified as a Greek goddess	GĪ-(y)uh	ˈgɑi(j)ə
Gail		
pers. name	GĀL	ˈgeːl
Gaillard Cut		
section of Panama Canal	gil-YAHRD KUHT, GĀ-LAHRD	gilˈjɑʳd ˈkət, ˈgeːˌlɑʳd
Gaillardia		
flower	guh-LAHRD-ē-uh	gəˈlɑʳdiːə
Gainesville		
city, FL	GĀNZ-VIL, GĀNZ-vuhl	ˈgeːnzˌvil, ˈgeːnzvəl
Gainsborough		
Thomas, *English painter*	GĀNZ-BUH-ruh, GĀNZ-BUHR-uh, GĀNZ-b(uh-)ruh	ˈgeːnzˌbə-rə, ˈgeːnzˌbər-ə, ˈgeːnzb(ə)rə
Gairdner		
1. lake, South Australia	GARD-nuhr, GERD-nuhr	ˈgæʳdnəʳ, ˈgeʳdnəʳ
2. pers. name	GARD-nuhr, GERD-nuhr, GAHRD-nuhr	ˈgæʳdnəʳ, ˈgeʳdnəʳ, ˈgɑʳdnəʳ
Gaithersburg		
town, MD	GĀ-thuhrz-BUHRG	ˈgeːθəʳzˌbəʳg
Gaius		
Roman praenomen	GĀ-(y)uhs, GĪ-uhs	ˈgeː(j)əs, ˈgɑiəs
Gajdusek		
Daniel Carleton, *US virologist (Nobel 1976)*	GĪ-duh-SHEK	ˈgɑidəˌʃek
Gaki [Akutagawa Ryūnosuke]		
Japanese writer	gahk-ē	gɑkiˈ
Galahad		
Arthurian hero	GAL-uh-HAD	ˈgæləˌhæd
Galal		
Biblical name	GĀ-LAL, gah-LAHL	ˈgeːˌlæl, gɑˈlɑl
Galanos		
James, *US fashion designer*	guh-LAHN-ōs	gəˈlɑnoːs
Galápagos		
Pacific islands, Equador	guh-LAHP-uh-guhs, guh-LAP-uh-guhs	gəˈlɑpəgəs, gəˈlæpəgəs
Galatea		
daughter of Nereus, lover of Acis; mother of Leucippus	GAL-uh-TĒ-uh, GAL-uh-TĀ-uh	ˌgæləˈtiːə, ˌgæləˈteːə

Foreign Sounds: ue: *Fr.* **rue**, *Ger.* **füllen** uh(r): *Fr.* **boeuf**, *Ger.* **Höhle** kh: *Ger.* **ich**, *Scot.* **loch** g̃: *Sp.* **amigo** v̱: *Sp.* **hablar** hl: *Welsh* **Llanelli**. CAPITALS: primary stress. SMALL CAPS: secondary stress. [$]: U.S. pron. [£]: British pron.

Galates
  son of Heracles   GAL-uht-ēz   'gæləʈiːz
Galatia
  ancient country, Asia Minor   guh-LĀ-sh(ē-)uh   gə'leːʃ(iː)ə
Galatians
  New Testament book   guh-LĀ-shuhnz   gə'leːʃənz
Galax
  county, VA   GĀ-LAKS   'geːˌlæks
Galba
  Roman emperor   GAL-buh, GAWL-buh   'gælbə, 'gɔːlbə
Galbraith
  pers. name   GAL-BRĀTH   'gælˌbreːθ
Gale
  US publishing co.; pers. name   GĀL   'geːl
Galeed
  Biblical name   GAL-ē-uhd, gahl-ED   'gæliːəd, gɑl'ed
Galen
  Greek physician   GĀ-luhn   'geːlən
Galeotes
  son of Apollo and Themisto   GAL-ē-ŌT-ēz   ˌgæliː'oːʈiːz
Galerius
  Roman emperor   guh-LIR-ē-uhs   gə'liriːəs
Galiceño
  horse   GAL-uh-SĀN-yō   ˌgælə'seːnjoː
Galicia
  region, Spain   guh-LISH-(ē-)uh   gə'liʃ(iː)ə
Galician
  lang., Spain   guh-LISH-uhn   gə'liʃən
Galilean
  Biblical name   GAL-uh-LĒ-uhn, GAL-uh-LĀ-uhn   ˌgælə'liːən, ˌgælə'leːən
Galileans
  satellites of Jupiter   GAL-uh-LĒ-uhnz, -LĀ-uhnz   ˌgælə'liːənz, -'leːənz
Galilee [Tiberias]
  region, Israel; Sea of, *lake, Israel*   GAL-uh-LĒ, GAL-uh-LĒ   'gæləˌliː, ˌgælə'liː
Galilei
  Galileo, *Italian scientist*   gal-uh-LĀ-Ē   gælə'leːˌiː
Galileo
  1. pers. name   gal-uh-LĒ-ō, -LĀ-ō   gælə'liːoː, -'leːoː
  2. Italian   GAHL-ē-LE-ō   ˌgɑli:'leoː
Galinthias
  friend of Alcmene   guh-LIN-thē-uhs   gə'linθiːəs
Galla [Oromo]
  lang., people, Ethiopia, Kenya   GAL-uh, GAHL-uh   'gælə, 'gɑlə
Gallacian
  lang., Spain   guh-LĀTH-ē-uhn, guh-LĀ-shuhn   gə'leːθiːən, gə'leːʃən
Gallatin
  Albert, *US politician; US pl. name*   GAL-uht-n   'gælətn̩
Gallaudet
  College, *Washington, DC*   GAL-uh-DET, GAW-luh-DET   ˌgælə'det, ˌgɔːlə'det
Gallegos
  river, Argentina   gah(l)-YĀ-ǧuhs   gɑ(l)'jeːɣəs
Galleria Borghese
  see Borghese, Galleria
Gallia
  county, OH; ancient name of France   GAL-ē-uh   'gæliːə

Key (col. 2): a: fad ā: fade ah: father ar: marry aw: law e: fed ē: feed er: merry i: hid ī: hide ō: coat ōō: boot
oi: boy ow: now u: put uh: above uhr: bird ch: chop ng: ring sh: show th: thick th: this zh: measure

Galliano

  Italian liqueur — gahl-YAHN-ō, GAHL-ē-AHN-ō — gal'jɑnoː, ˌgɑliːˈɑnoː

Gallic

  pert. to Gaul *or* France — GAL-ik — ˈgælik

Gallicanism

  anti-papal movement — GAL-i-kuh-NIZ-uhm — ˈgælikəˌnizəm

Gallicism

  French idiom or expression — GAL-uh-SIZ-uhm — ˈgæləˌsizəm

Gallico

  Paul William, *US journalist and writer* — GAL-i-KŌ — ˈgæliˌkoː

Gallienus

  Roman emperor — GAL-ē-Ē-nuhs, GAL-ē-Ā-nuhs — ˌgæliːˈiːnəs, ˌgæliːˈeːnəs

Gallim

  Biblical name — GAL-im, gah-LĒM — ˈgælim, gɑˈliːm

Gallinule

  marsh bird — GAL-uh-N(Y)O̅O̅L — ˈgæləˌn(j)uːl

Gallio

  Biblical name — GAL-ē-Ō — ˈgæliːˌoː

Gallipoli

  port, Italy; port, Turkey — guh-LIP-uh-lē — gəˈlipəliˑ

Gallipolis

  city, OH — GAL-uh-puh-LĒS — ˌgæləpəˈliːs

gallium

  element — GAL-ē-uhm — ˈgæliːəm

Gallo

  US wine co. — GAL-ō — ˈgæloː

Galloway

  region, Scotland — GAL-uh-WĀ — ˈgæləˌweː

Gallup

  George, *US pollster* — GAL-uhp — ˈgæləp

Galop

  dance — GAL-uhp, ga-LŌ — ˈgæləp, gæˈloː

Galsworthy

  John, *English author (Nobel 1932)* — GAWLZ-WUHR-thē — ˈgɔːlzˌwəʳðiˑ

Galton

  Sir Francis, *English scientist* — GAWLT-n — ˈgɔːltn̩

Galungan

  Balinese New Year — guh-LUNG-(g)uhn — gəˈluŋ(g)ən

Galuppi

  Baldassare, *Italian composer* — gah-LOO̅P-pē — gɑˈluːppiˑ

Galvani

  Luigi, *Italian physiologist* — gahl-VAHN-ē, gal-VAHN-ē — gɑlˈvɑniˑ, gælˈvɑniˑ

Galveston

  1. city, TX — GAL-vuhs-tuhn — ˈgælvəstən

  2. town, IN — gal-VES-tuhn — gælˈvestən

Galway

  James, *Irish flutist; city, Irish Republic* — GAWL-WĀ — ˈgɔːlˌweː

Gamal

  pers. name, Arabic — guh-MAHL — gəˈmɑl

Gamaliel

  pers. name — guh-MĀ-lē-uhl, guh-MĀL-yuhl — gəˈmeːliːəl, gəˈmeːljəl

Gamarra

  Agustín, *president, Peru* — gah-MAHR-rah — gɑˈmɑrrɑ

Gambetta
  Léon-Michel, *French statesman*   gah^n-bā-TAH   gābeːtɑː

Gambia, The
  republic, river, Africa   <u>th</u>uh GAM-bē-uh, GAHM-   ðə 'gæmbiːə, 'gɑm-

Gambian
  pert. to the Gambia   GAM-bē-uhn, GAHM-   'gæmbiːən, 'gɑm-

Gambier
  village, OH; island group, S Pacific   GAM-BIR   'gæm͵bir
  Ocean

Gambrinus
  mythical Flemish king   gam-BRĪ-nuhs   gæm'brɑinəs

Gammadim
  Biblical name   GAM-uhd-im, GAHM-ah-DĒM   'gæmədim, ͵gɑmɑ'diːm

Gamow
  George, *US physicist*   GAM-AWF, -AHF   'gæm͵ɔːf, -͵ɑf

Gamul
  Biblical name   GĀ-muhl, gah-MOOL   'geːməl, gɑ'muːl

Gan
  lang., China   GAHN, GAN   'gɑn, 'gæn

Gananoque
  resort, Ontario, Canada   GAN-uh-NAHK-wē, -wā   ͵gænə'nɑkwiˑ, -weː

Ganda
  lang., people, Africa   GAN-duh, GAHN-duh   'gændə, 'gɑndə

Gander
  river, town, Canada   GAN-duhr   'gændər

Gandhara
  ancient region, India   guhn-DAHR-uh   gən'dɑrə

Gandhi
  Indira, *Indian prime minister;*   GAHN-dē, GAN-dē   'gɑndiˑ, 'gændiˑ
    Mohandas K., *Indian leader;*
    Rajiv, *Indian prime minister*

Gandolf
  Raymond, *US media correspondent*   GAN-DAWLF, GAN-DAHLF   'gæn͵dɔːlf, 'gæn͵dɑlf

Ganesh Chaturthi
  Indian festival   guh-NESH chuh-TUR-tē   gə'neʃ tʃə'turtiˑ

Ganga [Ganges]
  river, India; pers. name   GUHNG-guh   'gəŋgə

Ganges
  river, India   GAN-JĒZ   'gæn͵dʒiːz

Gani
  pers. name   GAHN-ē   'gɑniˑ

Gannet
  bird   GAN-uht   'gænət

Gannett
  1. US publishing co.   GAN-uht, guh-NET   'gænət, gə'net
  2. pers. name   GAN-uht   'gænət

Gannon
  University, *PA*   GAN-uhn   'gænən

Gansu, Kansu
  prov, China   GAHN-SOO, Ⓢ GAN-SOO, KAN-SOO   'gɑn'suː, Ⓢ 'gæn'suː,
    'kæn'suː

Ganymede
  cup-bearer to the Greek gods;   GAN-ē-MĒD   'gæniˑ͵miːd
    satellite of Jupiter

Key (col. 2):   a: f**a**d ā: f**a**de ah: f**a**ther ar: m**a**rry aw: l**a**w e: f**e**d ē: f**ee**d er: m**e**rry i: h**i**d ī: h**i**de ō: c**oa**t oo: b**oo**t
oi: b**oy** ow: n**ow** u: p**u**t uh: **a**bove uhr: b**i**rd ch: **ch**op ng: ri**ng** sh: **sh**ow th: **th**ick <u>th</u>: **th**is zh: mea**s**ure

Garagiola
Joe, *sports personality* GAR-uh-JŌ-luh, GAR-uh-jē-Ō-luh ˌgærəˈdʒɔːlə, ˌgærədʒiːˈoːlə
Garamond
Claude, *French type designer* gah-rah-MAW^n gɑːrɑːmɔ̃
Garand
John, *US inventor* guh-RAND, GAR-uhnd gəˈrænd, ˈgærənd
Garcia
1. *pers. name* gahr-SĒ-uh gɑ^{r}ˈsiːə
2. *Portuguese* guhr-SĒ-uh, gahr-SĒ-uh gərˈsiːə, gɑːrˈsiːə
García
Spanish gahr-SĒ-ah, gahr-THĒ-ah gɑrˈsiːɑ, gɑrˈθiːɑ
García Lorca
Federico, *Spanish poet* gahr-THĒ-ah LAWR-kah, gahr-SĒ-uh gɑrˈθiːɑ ˈlɔːrkɑ, gɑrˈsiːə
García Márquez
Gabriel, *Colombian author (Nobel 1982)* gahr-SĒ-uh MAHR-KĀS gɑ^{r}ˈsiːə ˈmɑ^{r}ˌkeːs
Garcia Robles
Alfonso, *Mexican diplomat (Nobel 1982)* gahr-SĒ-uh RŌ-v̲lās gɑ^{r}ˈsiːə ˈroːβleːs
Garda, Lago di
lake, Italy LAHG-ō dē GAHRD-ah, Ⓢ GAHRD-uh ˈlɑgoː diː ˈgɑ^{r}dɑ, Ⓢ ˈgɑ^{r}də
Gardena
city, CA gahr-DĒ-nuh gɑ^{r}ˈdiːnə
Gardenia
Vincent, *Italian actor* gahr-DĒN-yuh gɑ^{r}ˈdiːnjə
Gardiner
pers. name GAHRD-nuhr, GAHRD-n-uhr ˈgɑ^{r}dnə^r, ˈgɑ^{r}dn̩ə^r
Gareb
Biblical name GĀ-REB, GĀ-ruhb, gah-REV ˈgeːˌreb, ˈgeːrəb, gɑˈrev
Gareth
pers. name GAR-uhth, GER-uhth ˈgærəθ, ˈgerəθ
Garfield
James A., *20th US president; comic strip cat; pers. name* GAHR-FĒLD ˈgɑ^{r}ˌfiːld
Gargantua
novel, Rabelais gahr-GAN-chuh-wuh gɑ^{r}ˈgæntʃəwə
Garhwali
lang., India guhr-WAHL-ē gə^{r}ˈwɑliˑ
Garibaldi
Giuseppi, *Italian nationalist leader* GAH-rē-BAHL-dē, Ⓢ GAR-uh-BAWL-dē ˌgɑriːˈbɑldiˑ, Ⓢ ˌgærəˈbɔːldiˑ
Garland
Judy, *US entertainer; pers. name* GAHR-luhnd ˈgɑ^{r}lənd
Garmite
Biblical name GAHR-MĪT ˈgɑ^{r}ˌmait
Garnett
city, KS GAHR-nuht ˈgɑ^{r}nət
Garo
lang., people, India GAHR-ō ˈgɑroː
Garonne
river, France gah-RAWN, Ⓢ guh-RAHN, guh-RŌN gɑːrɔːn, Ⓢ gəˈrɑn, gəˈroːn
Garrard
county, KY GAR-uhd ˈgærəd
Garret, Garrett
pers. name GAR-uht ˈgærət

Foreign Sounds: ue: *Fr.* **rue**, *Ger.* füllen   uh(r): *Fr.* **boeuf**, *Ger.* Höhle   k̲h̲: *Ger.* ich, *Scot.* loch   ḡ: *Sp.* amigo   v̲: *Sp.* hablar
hl: *Welsh* Llanelli.   CAPITALS: primary stress.   SMALL CAPS: secondary stress.   Ⓢ: U.S. pron.   Ⓔ: British pron.

Garrick
   David, *English actor; pers. name*   GAR-ik   'gærik
Garrison
   pers. name   GAR-uh-suhn   'gærəsən
Garry
   pers. name   GAR-ē, GER-ē   'gæri·, 'geri·
Garth
   pers. name   GAHRTH   'gɑʳθ
Garvey
   marcus moziah, *Jamaican*   GAHR-vē   'gɑʳvi·
     black-nationalist leader; Steven,
     US baseball player
Garvey
   Marcus Moziah, *Jamaican*   GAHR-vē   'gɑʳvi·
     black-nationalist leader
Gary
   city, IN; pers. name   GAR-ē, GER-ē   'gæri·, 'geri·
Gasão
   pers. name   guh-SOWⁿ, gah-   gə'sɑ̃u, gɑː-
Gascogne [Gascony]
   prov, France   gahs-KAWN-yuh   gɑːskɔːɲ
Gascoigne
   George, *English poet*   GAS-KOIN   'gæs,kɔin
Gascon
   native of Gascony, France   gahs-KAWⁿ, GAS-kuhn   gɑːskɔ̃, 'gæskən
Gasconade
   county, MO   GAS-kuh-NĀD   ,gæskə'neːd
Gascony
   prov, France   GAS-kuh-nē   'gæskəni·
Gashmu
   Biblical name   GASH-M(Y)O͞O, gahsh-MO͞O   'gæʃ,m(j)uː, gɑʃ'muː
Gaspar
   1. pers. name   GAS-puhr   'gæspəʳ
   2. Latin   GAS-pahr   'gæspɑʳ
   3. Portuguese   guhsh-PAHR, gahs-PAHR   gəʃ'pɑːʳ, gɑːs'pɑːʳ
   4. Spanish   gahs-PAHR   gɑs'pɑr
Gaspard
   pers. name, French   gahs-PAHR   gɑːspɑːr
Gasparo
   pers. name, Italian   gahs-PAHR-ō   gɑs'pɑroː
Gaspé
   peninsula, Canada   ga-SPĀ   gæ'speː
Gasperi, De
   Alcide, *political leader*   duh gah-spā-RĒ   də gɑːspeːriː
Gassendi
   crater on Moon   guh-SEN-dē   gə'sendi·
Gasser
   H. S., *US physiologist (Nobel 1944)*   GAS-uhr   'gæsəʳ
Gassers
   Park, *former ballpark, Shreveport,*   GAS-uhrz   'gæsəʳz
     LA
Gastineau
   Marcus D., *US football player*   GAS-tuh-NŌ   ,gæstə'noː

Key (col. 2):   a: fad   ā: fade   ah: father   ar: **marry**   aw: **law**   e: fed   ē: feed   er: **merry**   i: hid   ī: hide   ō: coat   o͞o: boot
oi: **boy**   ow: **now**   u: **put**   uh: **above**   uhr: **bird**   ch: **chop**   ng: **ring**   sh: **show**   th: **thick**   <u>th</u>: **this**   zh: measure

Gaston
   1. county, NC; pers. name   GAS-tuhn   'gæstən
   2. French   gah-STAW^n gɑːstɔ̃
Gastonia
   city, NC   gas-TŌ-nē-uh, gas-TŌN-yuh   gæs'toːniːə, gæs'toːnjə
Gatam
   Biblical name   GĀ-TAM, GET-uhm, gah-TAHM   'geː,tæm, 'geţəm, gɑ'tɑm
Gately
   George, *US cartoonist*   GĀT-lē   'geːtliˑ
Gath
   city, Palestine   GATH   'gæθ
Gath-hepher [Gittah-hepher]
   Biblical name   gath-HĒ-fuhr, gi-TAH-<u>KH</u>EF-er   gæθ'hiːfə^r, gi,tɑ'xefer
Gath-rimmon
   Biblical name   gath-RIM-uhn, GAHT-ri-MŌN   gæθ'rimən, ,gɑtri'moːn
Gatling
   machine gun   GAT-ling   'gætliŋ
Gatsby
   Jay, *character in* The Great   GATS-bē   'gætsbiˑ
     Gatsby, *Fitzgerald*
Gatun
   lake, Panama   guh-TŌ͞ON   gə'tuːn
Gatwick
   airport, England   GAT-wik   'gætwik
GATX
   General American Transportation,   JĒ-Ā-TĒ-EKS   ,dʒiː,eː,tiː'eks
     US service co.
Gaudier-Brzeska
   Henri, *French sculptor*   gōd-YĀB-zhes-KAH   goːdjeːbʒeskɑ
Gaudí y Cornet
   Antonio, *Spanish architect*   gow-<u>TH</u>Ē ē kōr-NĀT   gɑu'ðiː iː koːr'neːt
Gaugamela
   ancient Assyrian village   GAW-guh-MĒ-luh   ,gɔːgə'miːlə
Gauguin
   Paul, *French painter*   gō-GE^n goːgẽ
Gaul
   Roman province   GAWL   'gɔːl
Gauley
   river, WV   GAW-lē   'gɔːliˑ
Gaulle, de
   see de Gaulle
Gaullism
   de Gaulle movement   GŌ-LIZ-uhm, GAW-LIZ-uhm   'goː,lizəm, 'gɔː,lizəm
Gaullist
   French political philosphy   GŌ-luhst, GAW-luhst   'goːləst, 'gɔːləst
Gauloise
   tdmk for French cigarette   gōl-WAHZ   goːlwɑːz
Gaumata
   ancient Persian revolutionary   gō-MAHT-uh   goː'mɑţə
Gauss
   Carl Friedrich, *German*   GOWS   'gɑus
     mathematician
Gaussian curve
   bell curve   GOW-sē-uhn, GOW-shuhn   'gɑusiːən, 'gɑuʃən

Gautama
  see Siddhartha Gautama

Gautier
1. Dick, *US actor*	gō-TYĀ	goːˈtjeː
2. Léon, *French literary scholar*	gō-TYĀ	goːtjeː

Gavarnie
  waterfall, France   gahv-ahr-NĒ, ⑤ GAV-uhr-NĒ   gɑːvɑːrniː, ⑤ ˌgævəʳniː

Gavilan
  College, *CA*   GAV-uh-LAN, -luhn   ˈgævəˌlæn, -lən

Gavin
  pers. name   GAV-uhn   ˈgævən

Gavriil
  pers. name, Russian   guhv-ri-ĒL   gəvr̩iˈiːl

Gavrilo
  pers. name, Serbo-Croatian   GAHV-rē-law   ˈgɑːvriːlɔː

Gawain
  a Knight of the Round Table   guh-WĀN, GAH-WĀN, GOW-uhn   gəˈweːn, ˈgɑˌweːn, ˈgauən

Gawin
  pers. name   GOW-uhn, GAH-wuhn   ˈgauən, ˈgawən

Gayle
  Crystal, *US singer*   GĀL   ˈgeːl

Gaylord
  pers. name   GĀ-LAWRD   ˈgeːˌlɔːʳd

Gay-Lussac
  Joseph, *French scientist*   ge-lue-SAHK, ⑤ GĀ-luh-SAK   gelyːsɑːk, ⑤ ˌgeːləˈsæk

Gaynor
  Mitzi, *US actress*   GĀ-nuhr   ˈgeːnəʳ

Gayo
  lang., people, North Sumatra   GĪ-ō, GAH-yō   ˈgaioː, ˈgajoː

Gaza
  strip of land, town, Mediterranean   GAHZ-uh, GAZ-uh   ˈgɑzə, ˈgæzə

Gazer [Gezer]
  Biblical name   GĀ-zuhr, GAHZ-er   ˈgeːzəʳ, ˈgɑzer

Gazez
  Biblical name   GĀ-ZEZ, gah-ZEZ   ˈgeːˌzez, gɑˈzez

Gazite
  Biblical name   GĀ-ZĪT   ˈgeːˌzait

Gazzam
  Biblical name   GAZ-uhm, gah-ZAHM   ˈgæzəm, gɑˈzɑm

Gazzara
  Ben, *US actor*   guh-ZAHR-uh, guh-ZAR-uh   gəˈzɑrə, gəˈzærə

Gbari
  lang., people, Nigeria   guh-BAHR-ē   gəˈbɑriˑ

Gbaya
  lang., Africa   guh-BĪ-uh, guh-BAH-yuh   gəˈbaiə, gəˈbajə

Gdańsk [Danzig]
  city, Poland   guh-DAHN(T)SK, guh-DAN(T)SK   gəˈdɑːn(t)sk, gəˈdæn(t)sk

Gdynia
  port, Poland   guh-DIN-ē-uh   gəˈdiniːə

Gê
  S. American people   ZHĀ   ˈʒeː

Geary
  county, KS   GIR-ē   ˈgiriˑ

Geauga
  county, OH   jē-AWG-uh   dʒiːˈɔːgə

Key (col. 2):   aː fad   āː fade   ahː father   arː marry   awː law   eː fed   ēː feed   erː merry   iː hid   īː hide   ōː coat   ōōː boot
oiː boy   owː now   uː put   uhː above   uhrː bird   chː chop   ngː ring   shː show   thː thick   <u>th</u>ː this   zhː measure

Geba
   Biblical name   JĒ-buh, GEV-ah   'dʒiːbə, 'gevɑ

Gebal
   Biblical name   JĒ-buhl, guh-VAHL   'dʒiːbəl, gə'vɑl

Gebalite
   Biblical name   JĒ-buh-LĪT   'dʒiːbə,lɑit

Gebel-Williams
   Gunther, *German animal trainer*   GĀ-buhl-WIL-yuhmz   'geːbəl'wiljəmz

Geber
   Biblical name   JĒ-buhr, GEV-er   'dʒiːbəʳ, 'gever

Gebhard
   pers. name, German   GEP-HAHRT   'gep,hɑʳt

Gebim
   Biblical name   GĀ-bim, JĒ-bim, gā-VĒM   'geːbim, 'dʒiːbim, geː'viːm

Geb [Keb, Seb]
   Egyptian earth god   GEB   'geb

Gedaliah
   Biblical name   GED-l-Ī-uh, guh-DAHL-YAH   ,gedl̩'ɑiə, gə,dɑl'jɑ

Gedda [Jedda]
   city, Saudi Arabia   JED-uh   'dʒedə

Geder
   Biblical name   GĀD-uhr, JĒ-duhr, GED-er   'geːdəʳ, 'dʒiːdəʳ, 'geder

Gederah
   Biblical name   gi-DIR-uh, guh-de-RAH   gi'dirə, gəde'rɑ

Gederathite
   Biblical name   gi-DIR-uh-THĪT   gi'dirə,θɑit

Gederite
   Biblical name   gi-DIR-ĪT   gi'dir,ɑit

Gederoth
   Biblical name   gi-DIR-AHTH, guh-der-ŌT   gi'dir,ɑθ, gəder'oːt

Gederothaim
   Biblical name   GED-uh-rō-THĀ-uhm,   ,gedəroː'θeːəm,
                                guh-DER-aw-TAH-yēm   gə,derɔ'tɑjiːm

Gedjensen
   Samuel, *US politician*   GĀD-n-suhn   'geːdn̩sən

Gedor
   Biblical name   GĀ-DAWR, JĒ-DAWR, guh-DŌR   'geː,dɔːʳ, 'dʒiː,dɔːʳ, gə'doːr

Geelong
   city, Australia   jē-LAHNG, jē-LAWNG   dʒi'laŋ, dʒi'lɔːŋ

Gehazi
   Biblical name   gi-HĀ-ZĪ, GĀ-khah-ZĒ   gi'heː,zɑi, ,geːxɑ'ziː

Gehenna
   valley of Hinom, Israel   guh-HEN-uh   gə'henə

Gehrig
   Lou, *US baseball player*   GER-ig   'gerig

Geiger
   Hans, *German physicist; counter,*   GĪ-guhr   'gɑigəʳ
     radiation detector

Geisel
   Theodore Seuss, *US author, aka*   GĪ-zuhl   'gɑizəl
     Dr. Seuss

Geissler
   Johann, *German glassblower*   GĪ-sluhr   'gɑisləʳ

Ge-Kayapo
   lang., S. America   ZHĀ-KĪ-uh-PŌ, ZHĀ-KĪ-uh-PŌ   'ʒeː,kɑiə'poː, 'ʒeː'kɑiə,poː

Foreign Sounds: ue: *Fr.* **rue**, *Ger.* **füllen**   uh(r): *Fr.* **boeuf**, *Ger.* **Höhle**   <u>kh</u>: *Ger.* i<u>ch</u>, *Scot.* lo<u>ch</u>   g̱: *Sp.* ami<u>g</u>o   v̲: *Sp.* ha<u>b</u>lar
hl: *Welsh* **Llanelli**.   CAPITALS: primary stress.   SMALL CAPS: secondary stress.   Ⓢ: U.S. pron.   Ⓔ: British pron.

Gelasius
  pope   juh-LĀ-shē-uhs, -zh(ē-)uhs, -zē-uhs   dʒəˈleːʃiːəs, -ʒ(iː)əs, -ziːəs
Gelbart
  Larry, *US TV producer*   GEL-BAHRT   ˈgelˌbaʳt
Gelderland
  prov, Netherlands   GEL-duhr-LAND   ˈgeldəʳˌlænd
Geldof
  Bob, *British rock promoter*   GEL-DAHF, GEL-DAWF   ˈgelˌdɑf, ˈgelˌdɔːf
Geliloth
  Biblical name   GEL-uh-LAHTH, gi-LĪ-LAHTH,   ˈgeləˌlɑθ, giˈlaiˌlɑθ, giˈlilˌɑθ,
                                 gi-LIL-AHTH, guh-LĒ-LŌT   gəˌliːˈloːt
Geller
  Uri, *US psychic*   GEL-uhr   ˈgeləʳ
Gell-Mann
  Murray, *US physicist (Nobel 1969)*   GEL-MAHN   ˈgelˌmɑn
Gemalli
  Biblical name   guh-MAL-Ī, guh-mah-LĒ   gəˈmælˌai, gəmɑˈliː
Gemara
  commentary on Jewish Mishna guh-MAHR-uh, guh-MAWR-uh,   gəˈmɑrə, gəˈmɔːrə, gəmɑrˈɑ
                                 guh-mahr-AH
Gemariah
  Biblical name   GEM-uh-RĪ-uh, guh-MAHR-YAH-hoo   ˌgeməˈraiə, gəˌmɑrˈjɑhuː
Gemayel
  Amin, *president, Lebanon*   juh-MĪ-uhl   dʒəˈmaiəl
Gemini
  constellation, sign of the zodiac   JEM-uh-nē, JEM-uh-NĪ, GEM-uh-NĒ ˈdʒeməniˑ, ˈdʒeməˌnai,
                                                                         ˈgeməˌniː
Geminids
  meteor shower   JEM-uh-nidz   ˈdʒemənidz
Gemma
  pers. name   JEM-uh   ˈdʒemə
Gemsbok
  national park, Botswana   GEMZ-BAHK   ˈgemzˌbɑk
Gena
  pers. name   JĒ-nuh   ˈdʒiːnə
Gene
  pers. name   JĒN   ˈdʒiːn
Genesee
  river; county, MI, NY; US beer   JEN-uh-SĒ   ˌdʒenəˈsiː
Geneseo
  College, *NY*   JEN-uh-SĒ-ō   ˌdʒenəˈsiːoː
Genesis
  Old Testament book   JEN-uh-suhs   ˈdʒenəsəs
Genet
  Jean, *French author*   zhuh-NE, Ⓢ zhuh-NĀ   ʒəne, Ⓢ ʒəˈneː
Geneva
  city, lake, Switzerland; US pl. name   juh-NĒ-vuh   dʒəˈniːvə
Genevanism
  Calvinism   juh-NĒ-vuh-NIZ-uhm   dʒəˈniːvəˌnizəm
Genève [Geneva]
  city, Switzerland   zhuh-NEV, zhuh-NĀV   ʒəˈnev, ʒəˈneːv
Genever
  Dutch gin   JEN-uh-vuhr   ˈdʒenəvəʳ
Genevieve
  pers. name   JEN-uh-VĒV   ˈdʒenəˌviːv

Key (col. 2):   a: fad ā: fade ah: father ar: marry aw: law e: fed ē: feed er: merry i: hid ī: hide ō: coat oo̅: boot
oi: boy   ow: now   u: put   uh: above   uhr: bird   ch: chop   ng: ring   sh: show   th: thick   <u>th</u>: this   zh: measure

Geneviève
  pers. name, French   zhuhn-VYEV   ʒənvjev
Genghis Khan [Temujin]
  Mongol leader   JENG-guhs KAHN, GENG-guhs   ˌdʒeŋgəs 'kan, ˌgeŋgəs
Genii
  Roman personification of being;   JĒ-nē-Ī   'dʒiːniːˌ,ɑi
    Manes
Genna
  Vince, Stadium, *Bend, OR*   VINS JEN-uh   'vins 'dʒenə
Gennadi
  pers. name, Russian   gyuh-NAHD-yē   gjə'nɑːdjiˑ
Gennadiyevich
  patronym, Russian   gyuh-NAHD-yiv-YICH   gjə'nɑːdjivˌjitʃ
Gennes
  Pierre-Gilles de, *French physicist*   ZHEN   ʒen
Gennesaret
  Biblical name   guh-NES-uh-RET   gə'nesəˌret
Genoa
  1. prov & town, Italy   JEN-uh-wuh   'dʒenəwə
  2. city, IL   juh-NŌ-uh   dʒə'noːə
Genoese
  pert. to Genoa   JEN-uh-WĒZ, JEN-uh-WĒS   ˌdʒenə'wiːz, ˌdʒenə'wiːs
Génoise
  Italian-style cake   zhen-WAHZ   ʒen'wɑːz
Genova [Genoa]
  prov & town, Italy   JEN-uh-vuh   'dʒenəvə
GenRad
  US software systems co.   JEN-RAD   'dʒenˌræd
Genscher
  Hans Dietrich, *German politician*   GEN-shuhr, GEN-chuhr   'genʃəʳ, 'gentʃəʳ
Genshi-Sai
  First Beginning holiday (Jan. 3),   gen-shē-sī   genʃiːsɑi
    Japan
Gent
  see Ghent
Gentile
  1. Giovanni, *Italian educator*   jān-TĒ-lā   dʒeːn'tiːleː
  2. non-Jew   JEN-tīl   'dʒentail
Gentoo
  a Hindu   JEN-tōō   'dʒentuː
Genubath
  Biblical name   guh-N(Y)OO-BATH, guh-NOO-VAHT gə'n(j)uːˌbæθ, gəˌnuː'vɑt
Geoffrey
  pers. name   JEF-rē   'dʒefriˑ
Geoffroi
  pers. name, French   zhaw-FRWAH   ʒɔːfrwɑ
Geoghegan
  family name   GĀ-guhn, guh-HĀ-guhn   'geːgən, gə'heːgən
Georg
  1. pers. name, Danish   gi-AWR(Ḡ)   gi'ɔːr(ɣ)
  2. Finnish   YE-AWRG   'jeˌɔːrg
  3. German   gā-AWRKH   geː'ɔʳx
  4. Norwegian   GĀ-AWRG   'geːˌɔːrg
  5. Swedish   YĀ-awr(-yuh)   'jeːɔːrj

Foreign Sounds: ue: *Fr.* rue, *Ger.* füllen uh(r): *Fr.* boeuf, *Ger.* Höhle <u>kh</u>: *Ger.* ich, *Scot.* loch ḡ: *Sp.* amigo <u>v</u>: *Sp.* hablar
hl: *Welsh* Llanelli. CAPITALS: primary stress. SMALL CAPS: secondary stress. Ⓢ: U.S. pron. Ⓔ: British pron.

George

1. pers. name	JAWRJ	'dʒɔːʳdʒ
2. French	ZHAWRZH	ʒɔːrʒ
3. German	ZHAWRSH	'ʒɔːʳʃ
4. Romanian	ZHURZH, YAWR-ye	'ʒurʒ, 'jɔːrje
5. Dutch	ZHAWR-zhuh	'ʒɔːrʒə

Georges

pers. name, French	ZHAWRZH	ʒɔːrʒ

Georgetown

city, Guyana; pl. name, US; University, *Washington, D. C.*	JAWRJ-TOWN	'dʒɔːʳdʒ,taun

Georgette

pers. name	jawr-JET	dʒɔːʳ'dʒet

Georgi

1. pers. name, Bulgarian	gā-AWR-gē	geː'ɔːrgiː
2. Russian	gyi-AWRG-yi	gji'ɔːrgjij

Georgia

state, US; republic, Caucasus Mts.; *pers. name*	JAWR-juh	'dʒɔːʳdʒə

Georgian

pert. to Georgia *or* King George	JAWR-juhn	'dʒɔːʳdʒən

Georgiana

pers. name	JAWR-jē-AN-uh, jawr-JAN-uh	ˌdʒɔːʳdʒiː'ænə, dʒɔːʳ'dʒænə

Georgie

pers. name	JAWR-jē	'dʒɔːʳdʒiˑ

Georgina

pers. name	jawr-JĒ-nuh	dʒɔːʳ'dʒiːnə

Georgios

pers. name, Mod. Greek	ye-AWR-yi-AWS	je'ɔːrjiˌɔːs

Georgius

1. pers. name, Latin	JAWR-j(ē-)uhs, jē-AWR-	'dʒɔːʳdʒ(iː)əs, dʒiː'ɔːr-
2. Swedish	ye-AWR-yi-uhs	je'ɔːrjiəs

Georgy

pers. name, Russian	gyi-AWRG-yi	gji'ɔːrgjij

Gephardt

Richard Andrew, *US politician*	GEP-HAHRT	'gep,hɑʳt

Gera

Biblical name	JIR-uh, JĒ-ruh, ger-AH	'dʒirə, 'dʒiːrə, ger'ɑ

Geraert

pers. name, Dutch	GĀ-RAHRT	'geːˌrɑːrt

Geraint

Arthurian hero; pers. name, Welsh	GER-ĪNT	'ger,ɑint

Gerald

1. pers. name	JER-uhld	'dʒerəld
2. French	zhā-RAHLD	ʒeːrɑːld

Geraldine

pers. name	JER-uhl-DĒN	'dʒerəlˌdiːn

Geraldo

pers. name (G. Rivera)	huh-RAHL-dō, huh-RAWL-dō	hə'rɑldoː, hə'rɔːldoː

Gerar

Biblical name	JIR-AHR, JĒ-RAHR, guh-RAHR-ah	'dʒirˌɑʳ, 'dʒiːˌrɑʳ, gə'rɑrɑ

Gérard

pers. name, French	zhā-RAHR	ʒeːrɑːr

Key (col. 2): a: **f**a**d** ā: **f**a**de** ah: **f**a**ther** ar: m**a**rry aw: l**a**w e: f**e**d ē: f**ee**d er: m**e**rry i: h**i**d ī: h**i**de ō: c**oa**t ōō: b**oo**t
oi: b**oy** ow: n**ow** u: p**u**t uh: **a**bove uhr: b**i**rd ch: **ch**op ng: ri**ng** sh: **sh**ow th: **th**ick t<u>h</u>: <u>th</u>is zh: mea**s**ure

Gerard
  1. pers. name juh-RAHRD dʒəˈrɑʳd
  2. Dutch GĀ-RAHRT ˈgeːˌrɑːrt
  3. German GĀ-RAHRT ˈgeːˌrɑʳt
Gerardus
  1. pers. name, Dutch gā-RAHR-dues geːˈrɑrdʏs
  2. Latin juh-RAHR-duhs dʒəˈrɑʳdəs
Gerasa [Gadarene]
  Biblical name GER-uh-suh ˈgerəsə
Gerasene [Gadarene]
  Biblical name GER-uh-SĒN ˈgerəˌsiːn
Gerasimov
  Gennadi, *Russian diplomat* ger-AHS-yē-MAWF gerˈɑːsjiːˌmɔːf
Gerber
  US baby food co. GUHR-buhr ˈgəʳbəʳ
Gerd
  1. Frey's wife in Scandinavian GERD, GER<u>TH</u> ˈgeʳd, ˈgerð
    mythology
  2. pers. name, German GERT ˈgeʳt
Gere
  Richard, *US actor* GIR ˈgiʳ
Gergesene [Gadarene]
  Biblical name GUHR-guh-SĒN ˈgəʳgəˌsiːn
Gerhard
  1. pers. name, Dutch GĀ-RAHRT ˈgeːˌrɑrt
  2. German GĀR-HAHRT ˈgeːrˌhɑʳt
  3. Norwegian GER-HAHRT ˈgerˌhɑrt
  4. Swedish YĀR-HAHRD ˈjeːrˌhɑːrd
Gerhardt
  pers. name GER-HAHRT ˈgerˌhɑʳt
Gerhart
  pers. name, German GĀR-HAHRT ˈgeːrˌhɑʳt
Geri
  Odin's wolf GER-ē ˈgeri·
Gering
  city, NE GIR-ing ˈgiriŋ
Gerizim
  Biblical name GER-uh-ZIM, guh-RĪ-zim, guh-riz-ĒM ˈgerəˌzim, gəˈrɑizim,
    gərizˈiːm
Germain
  pers. name, French zher-MEⁿ ʒermẽ
Germaine
  1. pers. name juhr-MĀN dʒəʳˈmeːn
  2. French zher-MEⁿ ʒermẽ
German
  lang., people, Europe JUHR-muhn ˈdʒəʳmən
Germán
  pers. name, Spanish kher-MAHN çerˈman
Germani
  ancient German tribe juhr-MAN-ē, juhr-MAHN-ē, dʒəʳˈmæni·, dʒəʳˈmɑni·,
    ger-MAHN-ē geʳˈmani·
Germanic
  lang. family juhr-MAN-ik dʒəʳˈmænik
Germanicus
  Roman general juhr-MAN-i-kuhs dʒəʳˈmænikəs

Foreign Sounds: ue: *Fr.* **rue**, *Ger.* **füllen** uh(r): *Fr.* **boeuf**, *Ger.* **Höhle** <u>kh</u>: *Ger.* **ich**, *Scot.* **loch** g̱: *Sp.* **amigo** v̱: *Sp.* **hablar**
hl: *Welsh* **Llanelli**. CAPITALS: primary stress. SMALL CAPS: secondary stress. Ⓢ: U.S. pron. Ⓔ: British pron.

germanium
  element   juhr-MĀ-nē-uhm   dʒəʳˈmeːniːəm

Germanna
  Community College, *VA*   juhr-MAN-uh   dʒəʳˈmænə

Germany
  republic, Europe   JUHR-muh-nē   ˈdʒəʳməniˑ

Germinal
  month, French Revolutionary   zher-mē-NAHL   ʒermiːnɑːl
    calendar

Gérôme
  pers. name, French   zhā-RAWM   ʒeːrɔːm

Geronimo
  1. Apache leader; pers. name   juh-RAHN-uh-MŌ   dʒəˈrɑnəˌmoː
  2. Italian   jā-RAW-nē-mō   dʒeːˈrɔːniːmoː

Gerónimo
  pers. name, Spanish   k͟hā-RŌ-nē-mō   çeːˈroːniːmoː

Gerousia
  Spartan council   juh-ROO-zh(ē-)uh   dʒəˈruːʒ(iː)ə

Gerry
  pers. name   GER-ē   ˈgeriˑ

Gerry
  Elbridge, *US politician, gave rise to*   GER-ē   ˈgeriˑ
    term "gerrymander"

Gershom
  Biblical name   GUHR-shuhm, ger-SHAWM   ˈgəʳʃəm, gerˈʃɔːm

Gershon
  Biblical name   GUHR-SHAHN, ger-SHAWN   ˈgəʳˌʃɑn, gerˈʃɔːn

Gershonite
  Biblical name   GUHR-shuh-NĪT   ˈgəʳʃəˌnɑit

Gershwin
  George, Ira, *US musicians*   GUHRSH-wuhn   ˈgəʳʃwən

Gersoppa [Jog Falls]
  waterfall, India   juhr-SAHP-uh   dʒəʳˈsɑpə

Gertrud
  1. pers. name, Danish   GER-tru̱th   ˈgertruð
  2. German   GER-TROOT   ˈgeʳˌtruːt

Gertrude
  pers. name   GUHR-TROOD   ˈgəʳˌtruːd

Gertrudis
  pers. name, Spanish   k͟her-TROO-thēs   çerˈtruːðiːs

Gerty
  1. pers. name   GUHRT-ē   ˈgəʳţiˑ
  2. Czech   GERT-ē   ˈgerţiˑ

Gervais
  pers. name, French   zher-VE   ʒerve

Gervase
  pers. name   juhr-VĀS, -VĀZ; JUHR-VĀS, -VĀZ   dʒəʳˈveːs, -ˈveːz; ˈdʒəʳˌveːs,
                                                                -ˌveːz

Geryon
  three-headed giant   JER-ē-uhn, JER-ē-AHN   ˈdʒeriːən, ˈdʒeriːˌɑn

Gerzean culture
  prehistoric Egyptian culture   GER-zē-uhn, GUHR-   ˈgeʳziːən, ˈgəʳ-

Gesell
  Arnold Lucius, *US psychologist and*   guh-ZEL   gəˈzel
    pediatrician

Key (col. 2):   a: **fad**   ā: **fade**   ah: **father**   ar: **marry**   aw: **law**   e: **fed**   ē: **feed**   er: **merry**   i: **hid**   ī: **hide**   ō: **coat**   oo: **boot**
oi: **boy**   ow: **now**   u: **put**   uh: **above**   uhr: **bird**   ch: **chop**   ng: **ring**   sh: **show**   th: **thick**   t͟h: **this**   zh: **measure**

Gesham [Geshan]
  Biblical name   GESH-uhm, JĒ-shuhm   'geʃəm, 'dʒiːʃəm
Geshan
  Biblical name   GESH-uhn, gesh-AHN   'geʃən, geʃ'ɑn
Geshem
  Biblical name   GESH-em, JĒ-shuhm, GESH-EM   'geʃem, 'dʒiːʃəm, 'geʃˌem
Geshur
  Biblical name   GESH-uhr, GĒ-shuhr, guh-SHUR 'geʃəʳ, 'giːʃəʳ, gə'ʃur
Geshuri
  Biblical name   guh-SHUR-Ĭ, guh-SHUR-Ē   gə'ʃur,ɑi, gə,ʃur'iː
Geshurite [Geshuri]
  Biblical name   GESH-uh-RĪT   'geʃəˌrɑit
Gestalt
  psychology, therapy   guh-SHTAWLT, guh-STAWLT   gə'ʃtɔːlt, gə'stɔːlt
Gestapo
  German secret police, WWII   guh-STAHP-ō   gə'stɑpoː
Gether
  Biblical name   GĒ-thuhr, GETH-uhr, GET-ER   'giːθəʳ, 'geθəʳ, 'getˌer
Gethsemane
  garden outside Jerusalem   geth-SEM-uh-nē   geθ'seməniˑ
Getty
  J. Paul, US industrialist   GET-ē   'getiˑ
Gettysburg
  town, PA   GET-ēz-BUHRG   'getiˑzˌbəʳg
Getz
  Stan, US saxophonist   GETS   'gets
Geuel
  Biblical name   gi-YOO-uhl, guh-OO-EL   gi'juːəl, gə,uː'el
Gewürztraminer
  German wine   guh-VURT-STRAM-uh-nuhr,   gə'vuʳt,stræmənəʳ,
                                     -STRAHM-uh-nuhr, -struh-MĒ-nuhr   -,stramənəʳ, -strə,miːnəʳ
Geysir
  geyser, Iceland   GĪ-zuhr   'gɑizəʳ
Géza
  pers. name, Hungarian   GĀ-zah   'geːzɑ
Gezer [Gazer]
  Biblical name   GĒ-zuhr, GĀ-zuhr, GEZ-ER   'giːzəʳ, 'geːzəʳ, 'gezˌer
Gezira, Al
  region, Sudan   AHL juh-ZIR-uh, AL   ,ɑːl dʒə'zirə, ,æl
Gezrite
  Biblical name   GEZ-RĪT   'gezˌrɑit
Ghana
  republic, Africa   GAHN-uh, GAN-uh   'gɑnə, 'gænə
Ghanaian
  pert. to Ghana   gah-NĀ-(y)uhn, ga-, -NĪ-uhn gɑ'neː(j)ən, gæ-, -'nɑiən
Ghats
  mtn. system, India   GAWTS   'gɔːts
Gheber
  Ghebre, Iranian Zoroastrian   GĀ-buhr   'geːbəʳ
Ghebre
  pers. name (G. Gheber)   GĀ-bruh   'geːbrə
Gheeraert
  pers. name, Dutch   ḠĀ-RAHRT   'ɣeːˌrɑːrt
Gheerardt
  pers. name, Dutch   ḠĀ-RAHRT   'ɣeːˌrɑrt

Foreign Sounds: ue: *Fr.* **rue**, *Ger.* **füllen** uh(r): *Fr.* **boeuf**, *Ger.* **Höhle** **kh**: *Ger.* **ich**, *Scot.* **loch** ḡ: *Sp.* **amigo** ɣ: *Sp.* **hablar** hl: *Welsh* **Llanelli**. CAPITALS: primary stress. SMALL CAPS: secondary stress. ⑤: U.S. pron. ⑥: British pron.

Ghent, Gent
　city, Belgium　　　　　　　　　GENT　　　　　　　　　　　　　'gent
Gheorghe
　pers. name, Romanian　　　　GYAWR-ge　　　　　　　　　　'gjɔːrge
Gheorghiu-Dej
　Gheorghe, *Romanian statesman*　GYAWR-gyōō-DĀ　　　　　'gjɔːˢgjuː'deː
Ghia
　Italian car designer　　　　　GĒ-uh　　　　　　　　　　　'giːə
Ghibelline
　Italian political party　　　　GIB-uh-LĒN, GIB-uh-LĪN　　'gibə,liːn, 'gibə,lain
Ghiberti
　Lorenzo, *Florentine sculptor*　gē-BERT-ē　　　　　　　　　giː'beˢʈi·
Ghirardelli
　square, San Francisco, CA　　GIR-ahr-DEL-ē　　　　　　　,giraˢ'deli·
Ghirlandajo
　Domenico, *Italian painter*　　GIR-luhn-DAH-yō, GIR-luhn-DĪ-ō　,giˢlən'dajoː, ,giˢlən'daioː
Ghislain
　pers. name, French　　　　　gē-LEⁿ　　　　　　　　　　　giːlē
Giacinto
　pers. name, Italian　　　　　jah-CHĒN-tō　　　　　　　　dʒa'tʃiːntoː
Giacobinids
　meteor shower　　　　　　　juh-KŌ-buh-nidz, ja-　　　　dʒə'koːbənidz, dʒæ-
Giacometti
　Alberto, *Swiss sculptor*　　　JAH-kō-MET-tē, ⑤ JAH-kuh-MET-ē　,dʒako:'mettiː,
　　　　　　　　　　　　　　　　　　　　　　　　　　　　⑤ ,dʒakə'meʈi·
Giacomo
　pers. name, Italian　　　　　JAHK-ō-mō　　　　　　　　　'dʒako:mo:
Giacopo
　pers. name, Italian　　　　　JAHK-ō-pō　　　　　　　　　'dʒako:po:
Giaever
　Ivar, *Norwegian-born US physicist*　YĀ-vuhr　　　　　　　　'jeːvəˢ
　(Nobel 1973)
Giah
　Biblical name　　　　　　　GĪ-uh, GĒ-uh, GĒ-AH<u>KH</u>　'gaiə, 'giːə, 'giː,ax
Giamatti
　A. Bartlett, *US educator, baseball*　j(ē-)uh-MAHT-ē　　　　dʒ(iː)ə'maʈi·
　commissioner
Giambattista
　pers. name, Italian　　　　　JAHM-baht-TĒS-tah　　　　,dʒambat'tiːsta
Gian
　pers. name, Italian　　　　　JAHN　　　　　　　　　　　'dʒan
Gianni
　pers. name, Italian　　　　　JAHN-nē　　　　　　　　　　'dʒanniː
Giano
　pers. name, Italian　　　　　JAHN-ō　　　　　　　　　　'dʒano:
Giants
　US sports teams; children of Gaia　JĪ-uhnts　　　　　　　'dʒaiənts
Giaour, The
　verse tale, Byron　　　　　JOWR　　　　　　　　　　　'dʒauˢ
Giauque
　W. F., *Canadian-born US chemist*　jē-ŌK　　　　　　　　　dʒiː'oːk
　(Nobel 1949)
Gibbar
　Biblical name　　　　　　　GIB-AHR, gi-BAHR　　　　　'gib,aˢ, gi'baˢ

Key (col. 2): 　a: fad　ā: fade　ah: father　ar: marry　aw: law　e: fed　ē: feed　er: merry　i: hid　ī: hide　ō: coat　ōō: boot
oi: boy　ow: now　u: put　uh: above　uhr: bird　ch: chop　ng: ring　sh: show　th: thick　<u>th</u>: this　zh: measure

Gibbethon
Biblical name   GIB-uh-THAHN, gib-TŌN   ˈgibəˌθan, gibˈtoːn

Gibbon
Edward, *English historian*   GIB-uhn   ˈgibən

Gibeah, Gibea
Biblical name   GIB-ē-uh, giv-AH   ˈgibiːə, givˈa

Gibeath-haaraloth
Biblical name   GIB-ē-ATH-hah-AHR-uh-LAHTH,   ˈgibiːˌæθhaˈarəˌlaθ,
                        giv-AHT-hah-AHR-ah-LŌT   givˌathaˌaraˈloːt

Gibeathite
Biblical name   GIB-ē-uh-THĪT   ˈgibiːəˌθait

Gibeon
town, Palestine   GIB-ē-uhn   ˈgibiːən

Gibeonite
Biblical name   GIB-ē-uh-NĪT   ˈgibiːəˌnait

Giblite
Biblical name   GIB-LĪT   ˈgibˌlait

Gibraltar
strait, rock, town, Spain   juh-BRAWL-tuhr   dʒəˈbrɔːltəʳ

Gibraltarian
one from Gibraltar   juh-BRAWL-TER-ē-uhn, JIB-RAWL-,   dʒəˌbrɔːlˈteriːən, ˌdʒibˌrɔːl-,
                        -TAR-ē-uhn   -ˈtæriːən

Gibran
Kahlil, *Syrian poet, author*   juh-BRAHN   dʒəˈbran

Gibson
Althea, *US tennis player;* Charles,   GIB-suhn   ˈgibsən
   US illustrator

Giddalti
Biblical name   gi-DAL-TĪ, gi-DAHL-tē   giˈdælˌtai, giˈdalti:

Giddel
Biblical name   GID-l, gi-DEL   ˈgidl̩, giˈdel

Gide
André, *French author (Nobel 1947)*   ZHĒD   ʒiːd

Gideon
1. *pers. name*   GID-ē-uhn   ˈgidiːən
2. *German*   GĒ-dā-AWN   ˈgiːdeːˌɔːn

Gideoni
Biblical name   GID-ē-Ō-NĪ, GID-aw-NĒ   ˌgidiːˈoːˌnai, ˌgidɔːˈniː

Gidom
Biblical name   GĪ-DAHM, gid-AWM   ˈgaiˌdam, gidˈɔːm

Gielgud
Sir Arthur John, *British actor*   GĒL-GUD   ˈgiːlˌgud

Gieseking
Walter Wilhelm, *German pianist*   GĒ-zuh-king   ˈgiːzəkiŋ

Giessbach
waterfall, Switz.   GĒS-BAHKH, GĒS-BAHK   ˈgiːsˌbax, ˈgiːsˌbak

Giessen
prov & town, Germany   GĒ-suhn   ˈgiːsən

GIGO
garbage in, garbage out   GĪ-GŌ, GĒ-GŌ   ˈgaiˌgoː, ˈgiːˌgoː

Gihon
Biblical name   GĪ-HAHN, GĒ-HŌN, gē-KHŌN   ˈgaiˌhan, ˈgiːˌhoːn, giːˈxoːn

---

Gil

1. pers. name	GIL	'gil
2. Portuguese	ZHIL	'ʒil
3. Spanish	KHĒL	'çiːl

Gila

| *river, US; county, AZ* | HĒ-luh | 'hiːlə |

Gila Bend

| *Indian reservation, US* | HĒ-luh BEND | 'hiːlə 'bend |

Gilalai

| *Biblical name* | GIL-uh-LĪ, GI-lah-LĪ | 'gilə͵lɑi, ͵gilə'lɑi |

Gila monster

| *venomous lizard* | HĒ-luh MAHN(T)-stuhr | 'hiːlə ͵mɑn(t)stə^r |

Gilbert

| *1.* Walter, *US molecular biologist (Nobel 1980);* Sir William S., *English poet; pers. name* | GIL-buhrt | 'gilbə^rt |
| *2. French* | zhēl-BER | ʒiːlber |

Gilbert [Kiribati]

| *islands, Pacific* | GIL-buhrt | 'gilbə^rt |

Gilbertese

| *lang., people, Kiribati* | GIL-buhrt-ĒZ, -ĒS | ͵gilbə^rţ'iːz, -'iːs |

Gilbertus

| *pers. name, Latin* | gil-BUHRT-uhs | gil'bə^rţəs |

Gilbey's

| *tdmk for gin* | GIL-bēz | 'gilbiˑz |

Gilboa

| Mount, *Israel* | gil-BŌ-uh | gil'boːə |

Gilboa

| *Biblical name* | gil-BŌ-uh | gil'boːə |

Gilchrist

| *pers. name* | GIL-krist | 'gilkrist |

Gilda

| *pers. name* | GIL-duh | 'gildə |

Gildersleeve

| *family name* | GIL-duhr-SLĒV | 'gildə^r͵sliːv |

Gilead

| *biblical mtn.* | GIL-ē-uhd | 'giliːəd |

Gileadite

| *Biblical name* | GIL-ē-uh-DĪT | 'giliːə͵dɑit |

Giles

| *county, VA; pers. name* | JĪLZ | 'dʒɑilz |

Gilgal

| *Biblical name* | GIL-GAL, gil-GAHL | 'gil͵gæl, gil'gɑl |

Gilgamesh

| *Sumerian epic hero* | GIL-guh-MESH | 'gilgə͵meʃ |

Gilgorov

| Kiro, *Macedonian president* | gil-GAWR-uhf, -AWV | gil'gɔː^rəf, -͵ɔːv |

Gilles

| *1. pers. name, Dutch* | ĞIL-uhs | 'ɣiləs |
| *2. French* | ZHĒL | ʒiːl |

Gillespie

| *pers. name* | guh-LES-pē | gə'lespiˑ |

Gillespie

| Dizzy, *US jazz musician* | guh-LES-pē | gə'lespiˑ |

Gillette
    Anita, *US actress;* King Camp, *US*   juh-LET   dʒəˈlet
      razor magnate; William, *US actor*
Gilliam
    Terry, *US animator, film director*   GIL-ē-uhm   ˈgiliːəm
Gillian
    pers. name   JIL-ē-uhn, JIL-yuhn   ˈdʒiliːən, ˈdʒiljən
Gillies
    pers. name   GIL-uhs, -uhz, -ēz   ˈgiləs, -əz, -iːz
Gillyflower
    flower   GIL-ē-FLOW(-uh)r   ˈgiliːˌflɑu(ə)ʳ
Gilman
    Charlotte Perkins, *US writer; city,*   GIL-muhn   ˈgilmən
      IL
Gilmer
    county, GA, WV; city, TX   GIL-muhr   ˈgilməʳ
Gilmore
    Artis, *US basketball player*   GIL-MŌR, GIL-MAWR   ˈgilˌmoːʳ, ˈgilˌmɔːʳ
Gilo, Giloh
    Biblical name   GĪ-lō, gi-LŌ   ˈgɑiloː, giˈloː
Gilonite
    Biblical name   GĪ-luh-NĪT, GIL-uh-   ˈgɑiləˌnɑit, ˈgilə-
Gilpin
    county, CO   GIL-puhn   ˈgilpən
Gilroy
    city, CA   GIL-ROI   ˈgilˌrɔi
Gilyak [Nivkh]
    lang., people, Russia   gil-YAHK, gil-YAK   gilˈjɑk, gilˈjæk
Gimbel
    Jacob & Isaac, *US merchants;*   GIM-buhl   ˈgimbəl
      Norman, *US lyricist, TV producer*
Gimlet
    alcoholic drink   GIM-luht   ˈgimlət
Gimson
    A.C., *British phonetician*   GIM(P)-suhn   ˈgim(p)sən
Gimzo
    Biblical name   GIM-zō, gim-ZŌ   ˈgimzoː, gimˈzoː
Gina
    pers. name   JĒ-nuh   ˈdʒiːnə
Ginath
    Biblical name   GĪ-NATH, gi-NAHT   ˈgɑiˌnæθ, giˈnɑt
Gingold
    Hermione, *entertainer*   GING-GŌLD   ˈgiŋˌgoːld
Gingrich
    Newt, *US politician*   GING-grich, GING-rich   ˈgiŋgritʃ, ˈgiŋritʃ
Ginn & Co.
    US publisher   GIN   ˈgin
Ginnetho
    Biblical name   GIN-uh-THŌ   ˈginəˌθoː
Ginnethoi [Ginnetho]
    Biblical name   GIN-uh-THOI, GIN-uh-TOI   ˈginəˌθɔi, ˌginəˈtɔi
Ginnethon [Ginnetho]
    Biblical name   GIN-uh-THAHN, GIN-uh-TŌN   ˈginəˌθɑn, ˌginəˈtoːn
Ginnie, Ginny
    pers. name   JIN-ē   ˈdʒiniˑ

Gino		
pers. name	JĒ-nō	'dʒiːnoː
Ginsberg		
1. Allen, *US poet*	GINZ-BUHRG	'ginzˌbəʳg
2. Asher, *Zionist leader (pseudonym* Ahad Ha-am*)*	GYINZ-BYIRG, Ⓢ GINZ-BUHRG	'gjinzˌbjirg, Ⓢ 'ginzˌbəʳg
Ginsburg		
Ruth Bader, *US Supreme Court justice*	GINZ-BUHRG	'ginzˌbəʳg
Ginza		
district, Japan	gin-zah	ginzɑ
Gioacchino		
pers. name, Italian	JŌ-uh-KĒ-nō	ˌdʒoːə'kiːnoː
Gioconda, La		
opera, Ponchielli; da Vinci painting (Mona Lisa)	LAH jō-KAHN-duh	ˌlɑ dʒoː'kɑndə
Gion Matsuri		
Japanese festival	gyawn maht-sur-ē	gjɔːn mɑtsuri·
Giordano		
pers. name, Italian	jawr-DAHN-ō	dʒɔːr'dɑnoː
Giorgio		
pers. name, Italian	JŌR-jō, JAWR-jō	'dʒoːrdʒoː, 'dʒɔːrdʒoː
Giörgio		
pers. name, Hungarian	DYUHRD-yō	'djœrdjoː
Giorgione		
Italian painter	jawr-JŌ-nā	dʒɔːʳ'dʒoːneː
Giorgios		
pers. name, Greek	YAWR-yaws	'jɔːrjɔːs
Giosuè		
pers. name, Italian	jōz-WE	dʒoːz'we
Giotto		
Italian painter	JAWT-tō, Ⓢ JAWT-ō, jē-AHT-ō	'dʒɔːttoː, Ⓢ 'dʒɔːt̬oː, dʒiː'ɑt̬oː
Giovanni		
pers. name, Italian	jō-VAHN-nē	dʒoː'vɑnniː
Gipsy		
pers. name	JIP-sē	'dʒipsi·
Giraf		
Danish beer	GĒ-RAHF	'giːˌrɑːf
Girard		
US pl. name	juh-RAHRD	dʒə'rɑʳd
Giraud		
pers. name, French	zhē-RŌ	ʒiːroː
Giraudoux		
Jean, *French writer*	zhē-rō-DOO	ʒiːroːduː
Girgashite		
Biblical name	GUHR-guh-SHĪT, GIR-	'gəʳgəˌʃait, 'giʳ-
Girja		
pers. name, Hindi	GIR-jah	'girdʒɑ
Girò di Cagliari		
Sardinian wine	zhē-RŌ dē kahl-YAHR-ē	ʒiː'roː diː kɑl'jɑriː
Girolamo		
pers. name, Italian	jē-RAW-lahm-ō	dʒiː'rɔːlɑmoː
Gironde		
French wine region	zhē-RAW^{n}D	ʒiːrɔ̃d

Key (col. 2): a: **fad** ā: **fade** ah: **father** ar: **marry** aw: **law** e: **fed** ē: **feed** er: **merry** i: **hid** ī: **hide** ō: **coat** oo: **boot** oi: **boy** ow: **now** u: **put** uh: **above** uhr: **bird** ch: **chop** ng: **ring** sh: **show** th: **thick** th: **this** zh: **measure**

Girondist
 member, French political party   juh-RAHN-duhst, zhi-RAHN-duhst   dʒəˈrɑndəst, ʒiˈrɑndəst
Girton
 college, Cambridge Univ.   GUHRT-n   ˈgəʳtn̩
Girzite
 Biblical name   GUHR-zĪT, GIR-   ˈgəʳˌzait, ˈgiʳ-
Gisborne
 town, New Zealand   GIZ-buhrn   ˈgizbəʳn
Giscard d'Estaing
 Valéry, president, France   zhis-KAHR des-TEⁿ   ʒiskɑːr destē
Giselle
 1. pers. name   juh-ZEL, zhi-ZEL   dʒəˈzel, ʒiˈzel
 2. French   zhē-ZEL   ʒiːzel
Gish
 Lillian, US actress   GISH   ˈgiʃ
Gishpa, Gispa
 Biblical name   GISH-puh, gish-PAH   ˈgiʃpə, giʃˈpɑ
Gitano
 US sportswear co.   gi-TAHN-ō   giˈtɑnoː
Gittah-hepher [Gath-hepher]
 Biblical name   GIT-uh-HĒ-fuhr, gi-TAH-KHEF-uhr   ˈgiṭəˈhiːfəʳ, giˌtɑˈxefər
Gittaim
 Biblical name   GIT-ā-uhm, gi-TĀ-im, gi-TAH-yim   ˈgiṭeːəm, giˈteːim, giˈtɑjim
Gittite
 Biblical name   GIT-ĪT   ˈgiṭˌait
Giucciardini
 Francesco, Italian historian   JŌŌT-chahr-DĒ-nē   ˌdʒuːttʃɑrˈdiːniː
Giuliani
 Rudolph, US politician   JŌŌ-lē-AHN-ē, jul-YAHN-ē   ˌdʒuːliːˈɑniˑ, dʒuˈlˈjaniˑ
Giuliano
 pers. name, Italian   jōōl-YAHN-ō   dʒuːlˈjanoː
Giulietta
 1. pers. name   JŌŌ-lē-ET-uh   ˌdʒuːliːˈeṭə
 2. Italian   jōōl-YET-tah   dʒuːlˈjettɑ
Giulio
 pers. name, Italian   JŌŌL-yō   ˈdʒuːljoː
Giuseppe
 pers. name, Italian   jōō-ZEP-pā   dʒuːˈzeppeː
Givenchy
 Hubert de, French fashion designer   zhē-vahⁿ-SHĒ   ʒiːvɑ̃ʃiː
Givry
 French wine   zhē-VRĒ   ʒiːvriː
Giza
 site of Egyptian pyramids   GĒ-zuh   ˈgiːzə
Gîza, El
 city, Egypt   el GĒ-zuh   el ˈgiːzə
Gizonite
 Biblical name   GĪ-zuh-NĪT   ˈgaizəˌnait
Gjellerup
 K. A., Danish author (Nobel 1917)   GIL-lā-RŌŌP, Ⓢ GEL-uh-RUP   ˈgilleːˌruːp, Ⓢ ˈgeləˌrup
Gladstone
 pers. name   GLAD-STŌN, Ⓔ GLAD-stuhn   ˈglædˌstoːn, Ⓔ ˈglædstən
Gladys
 pers. name   GLAD-uhs   ˈglædəs

Foreign Sounds: ue: *Fr.* **rue**, *Ger.* **füllen**   uh(r): *Fr.* **boeuf**, *Ger.* **Höhle**   <u>kh</u>: *Ger.* **ich**, *Scot.* **loch**   ğ: *Sp.* **amigo**   <u>v</u>: *Sp.* **hablar**   hl: *Welsh* **Llanelli.**   CAPITALS: primary stress.   SMALL CAPS: secondary stress.   Ⓢ: U.S. pron.   Ⓔ: British pron.

Glamis
  village, Scotland, scene of murder in   GLAHMZ, ⓢ GLAHM-uhs, GLAM-uhs   'glɑːmz, ⓢ 'glɑməs,
     Macbeth, *Shakespeare*   'glæməs

Glamorgan, Mid
  see Mid Glamorgan

Glamorgan, South
  see South Glamorgan

Glamorgan, West
  see West Glamorgan

Glamorganshire
  former county, Wales   gluh-MAWR-guhn-shuhr, -SHIR   glə'mɔːˈrgənʃəˈr, -ˌʃiˈr

Glarner
  Swiss beer   GLAHR-nuhr   'glɑˈrnəˈr

Glarus
  canton, Switzerland   GLAHR-uhs   'glɑrəs

Glaser
  D. A., US physicist (Nobel 1960)   GLĀ-zuhr   'gleːzəˈr

Glasgow
  city, Scotland; pers. name   GLAS-kō, -gō; GLAZ-gō; ⓔ   'glæskoː, -goː; 'glæzgoː; ⓔ
                             GLAHZ-gō, GLAHS-gō   'glɑːzgoː, 'glɑːsgoː

Glashow
  Sheldon L., US physicist (Nobel   GLASH-ō   'glæʃoː
  1979)

Glasnost
  Soviet policy of candor   GLAHS-nuhst, GLAHS-NAWST,   'glɑsnəst, 'glɑsˌnɔːst,
                       GLAHZ-NŌST   'glɑzˌnoːst

Glassboro
  State College, NJ   GLAS-b(uh-)ruh, GLAS-BUHR-ō   'glæsb(ə)rə, 'glæsˌbəroː

Glastonbury
  1. town, CT   GLAS-(t)uhn-BER-ē   'glæs(t)ənˌberi·
  2. borough, England   GLAS-tuhn-b(uh-)rē, GLAHS-   'glæstənb(ə)ri·, 'glɑːs-

Glaswegian
  inhabitant of Glasgow   glas-WĒ-juhn, ⓔ glahz-WĒ-juhn,   glæs'wiːdʒən, ⓔ
                      glaz-, glahs-, glas-   glɑːz'wiːdʒən, glæz-,
                                             glɑːs-, glæs-

Glauce
  daughter of King Creon; Creusa   GLAW-sē   'glɔːsi·

Glaucia
  Caius Servilius, Roman popular   GLAW-sh(ē-)uh   'glɔːʃ(iː)ə
     leader; mother of Scamander in
     Greek mythology

Glaucus
  Lycian commander in Trojan War;   GLAW-kuhs   'glɔːkəs
     son of Minos and Pasiphae; son of
     Sisyphus; sea god who courted
     Scylla

Glaxo
  British pharmaceutical co.   GLAK-sō   'glæksoː

Glazunoff
  Alexander K., Russian composer   GLAHZ-u-NAWF, ⓢ GLAZ-uh-NAWF,   ˌglɑːzu'nɔːf, ⓢ 'glæzəˌnɔːf,
                      -NAWV   -ˌnɔːv

Gleb
  pers. name, Russian   GLĀP   'gleːp

Glemp
  Józef, Polish cardinal   GLEMP   'glemp

Key (col. 2):   a: fad   ā: fade   ah: father   ar: marry   aw: law   e: fed   ē: feed   er: merry   i: hid   ī: hide   ō: coat   ōō: boot
oi: boy   ow: now   u: put   uh: above   uhr: bird   ch: chop   ng: ring   sh: show   th: thick   th: this   zh: measure

Glen, Glenn
  pers. name — GLEN — 'glen

Glenallachie
  Scotch whiskey — glen-AL-uh-kē, -k͟hē — glen'æləki·, -xi·

Glenda
  pers. name — GLEN-duh — 'glendə

Glendive
  city, MT — GLEN-DĪV — 'glen,daiv

Glendora
  city, CA — glen-DŌR-uh, -DAWR-uh — glen'doːrə, -'dɔːrə

Glendower [Glyndwr]
  Owen, *Welsh rebel* — glen-DOW(-uh)r — glen'dau(ə)ʳ

Glen Ellyn
  village, IL — glen EL-uhn — glen 'elən

Glenfiddich
  Scotch whiskey — glen-FID-ik, -i͟kh, -ich — glen'fidik, -ix, -itʃ

Glengarry
  valley, Scotland; county, Ontario, — glen-GAR-ē — glen'gæri·
  Canada

Glenlivet, The
  Scotch whiskey — t͟huh glen-LIV-uht — ðə glen'livət

Glenmorangie
  Scotch whisky — glen-MAHR-in-jē, -MAWR- — glen'mɑrindʒi·, -'mɔːr-

Glen of Imaal
  dog breed — GLEN uhv i-MAHL — 'glen əv i'mɑl

Gless
  Sharon, *US actress* — GLES — 'gles

Glimmerglass
  Opera, *NY* — GLIM-uhr-GLAS, -GLAHS — 'gliməʳ,glæs, -,glɑːs

Glinka
  Mikhail Ivanovitch, *Russian* — GLĒN-kuh, Ⓢ GLING-kuh — 'gliːnkə, Ⓢ 'gliŋkə
  composer

Glocester
  town, RI — GLAHS-tuhr, GLAW-stuhr — 'glɑstəʳ, 'glɔːstəʳ

Glockenspiel
  musical instrument — GLAHK-uhn-SHPĒL, GLAHK-uhn-SPĒL — 'glɑkən,ʃpiːl, 'glɑkən,spiːl

Gloria
  pers. name — GLŌR-ē-uh, GLAWR-ē-uh — 'gloːriːə, 'glɔːriːə

Gloucester
  US pl. name; city, England — GLAHS-tuhr, GLAW-stuhr — 'glɑstəʳ, 'glɔːstəʳ

Gloucestershire
  county, England — GLAHS-tuhr-shuhr, — 'glɑstəʳʃəʳ, 'glɔːstəʳʃəʳ, -,ʃiʳ
  GLAWS-tuhr-shuhr, -SHIR

Glouster
  village, OH — GLAHS-tuhr, GLAW-stuhr — 'glɑstəʳ, 'glɔːstəʳ

Glover
  pers. name — GLUHV-uhr — 'gləvəʳ

Gluck
  Alma, *US soprano* — GLUK — 'gluk

Gluyas
  pers. name — GLOO-yuhs — 'gluːjəs

Glyn
  pers. name — GLIN — 'glin

Glyndebourne
  town, festival, England — GLĪN(D)-BAWRN, GLĪM-BAWRN — 'glain(d),bɔːʳn, 'glaim,bɔːʳn

---

Foreign Sounds: ue: *Fr.* **rue**, *Ger.* füllen uh(r): *Fr.* **boeuf**, *Ger.* Höhle k͟h: *Ger.* ich, *Scot.* loch ğ: *Sp.* amigo v̱: *Sp.* hablar
hl: *Welsh* Llanelli. CAPITALS: primary stress. SMALL CAPS: secondary stress. Ⓢ: U.S. pron. Ⓛ: British pron.

Glyndwr [Glendower]
  Owain, *Welsh leader*   glin-DUR   glin'dur
Glynis
  pers. name   GLIN-uhs   'glinəs
Gnadenhutten
  village, former mission, OH   juh-NĀD-n-HUHT-n   dʒə'neːdn̩ˌhətn̩
Gnadenhutten
  village, OH   juh-NĀD-n-HUHT-n, guh-   dʒə'neːdn̩ˌhətn̩, gə-
Gnaeus, Gneius
  Roman praenomen   NĒ-uhs   'niːəs
GNMA
  Government National Mortgage   JIN-ē-MĀ   ˌdʒini·'meː
    Association
Gnostic
  adherent of Gnosticism   NAHS-tik   'nɑstik
Gnosticism
  beliefs of early Christian mystical NAHS-tuh-SIZ-uhm   'nɑstəˌsizəm
    cult
Goa
  state, India; city, Philippines GŌ-uh   'goːə
Goa, Daman and Diu
  former territory, India   GŌ-uh duh-MAN uhn(d) DĒ-ōō   'goːə də'mæn ən(d) 'diːuː
Goah
  Biblical name   GŌ-uh   'goːə
Goajiro
  S. American people   GŌ-uh-HĒ-rō   ˌgoːə'hiːroː
Goath [Goah]
  Biblical name   GŌ-ATH, GŌ-uh   'goːˌæθ, 'goːə
Gob
  Biblical name   GAHB, GŌV   'gɑb, 'goːv
Gobat
  C. A., Swiss politician, philanthropist gō-BAH   goː'bɑ
    (Nobel 1902)
Gobelin
  French family of tapestry makers gaw-BLE^n gɔːblẽ
Gobi
  desert, Asia   GŌ-bē   'goːbi·
Gobind
  pers. name (H. G. Khorana)   GŌ-BIND   'goːˌbind
Godard
  Jean Luc, *French film director* gaw-DAHR   gɔːdɑːr
Godavari
  river, India   guh-DAHV-uh-rē   gə'dɑvəri·
Goddard
  Robert, *US physicist; college, VT* GAHD-uhrd   'gɑdəʳd
Godden
  Rumer, *English novelist*   GAHD-n   'gɑdn̩
Godefroi, -froy
  pers. name, French   gawd-FRWAH   gɔːdfrwɑ
Godel, Gödel
  Kurt, *US mathematician*   GŌD-l, GUH(R)D-l   'goːdl̩, 'gœːdl̩
Goderich
  town, Ontario   GAHD-rich   'gɑdritʃ
Godfrey
  pers. name   GAHD-frē   'gɑdfri·

Key (col. 2):   a: fad   ā: fade   ah: father   ar: marry   aw: law   e: fed   ē: feed   er: merry   i: hid   ī: hide   ō: coat   ōō: boot
oi: boy   ow: now   u: put   uh: above   uhr: bird   ch: chop   ng: ring   sh: show   th: thick   th̲: this   zh: measure

Godiva
  Lady, *wife of Leofric, earl of Mercia*   guh-DĪ-vuh   gə'dɑivə

Godiva Chocolatier
  US gourmet candy co.   guh-DĪ-vuh SHAW-kuh-LAH-TYĀ   gə'dɑivə ˌʃɔːkəˌlɑ'tjeː

Godolphin Barb
  racehorse   guh-DAHL-fuhn BAHRB,   gə'dɑlfən 'bɑ^rb, gə'dɔːlfən
     guh-DAWL-fuhn

Godot
  character in Waiting for Godot, *S.*   guh-DŌ   gə'doː
    Beckett

Godoy
  pers. name   gō-THOI   goː'ðɔi

Godunov
  Boris, *Russian czar*   guh-doō-NAWF, Ⓢ GŌD-n-AWF,   gəduː'nɔːf, Ⓢ 'goːdn̩ˌɔːf,
     GAWD-n-AWF   'gɔːdn̩ˌɔːf

Godwin
  Mary Wollstonercraft, *English*   GAHD-wuhn   'gɑdwən
    author; William. *English*
    philosopher; pers. name

Godzilla
  movie monster   gahd-ZIL-uh   gɑd'zilə

Goebbels
  Paul Joseph, *Nazi propagandist*   GUH(R)B-uhls, Ⓢ GUHR-buhlz   'gœbəls, Ⓢ 'gə^rbəlz

Goeppert
  pers. name, German   GUH(R)P-uhrt   'gœpə^rt

Goering, Göring
  Hermann Wilhelm, *Nazi leader*   GUH(R)-ring, Ⓢ GER-ing, GUHR-ing   'gœːriŋ, Ⓢ 'geriŋ, 'gəriŋ

Goethals
  George, *US engineer*   GŌ-thuhlz   'goːθəlz

Goethe
  1. Johann Wolfgang von, *German*   GUH(R)-tuh   'gœːtə
    poet
  2. street, Chicago, IL   GŌ-ĒTH, gō-Ē-thē   'goːˌiːθ, goː'iːθiˑ

Goetz
  1. Hermann, *German composer*   GUH(R)TS   'gœts
  2. Bernhard, *New York City subway*   GETS   'gets
    assailant

Gog
  Biblical name   GAHG, GAWG   'gɑg, 'gɔːg

Gogebic
  lake, county, MI; iron range, MI,WI   gō-GĒ-bik   goː'giːbik

Gogh, Van
  see Van Gogh

Gogmagogs
  hills near Cambridge, England   GAHG-muh-GAHGZ   ˌgɑgmə'gɑgz

Gogo
  lang., people, Africa   GŌ-gō   'goːgoː

Gogol
  Nikolai, *Russian writer*   GAW-guhl, GŌ-GAWL   'gɔːgəl, 'goːˌgɔːl

Goidelic
  sub-branch of Celtic langs.   goi-DEL-ik, goi-DĒ-lik   gɔi'delik, gɔi'diːlik

Goiim
  Biblical city-state league   GOI-im, gaw-YIM   'gɔiim, gɔː'jim

Gola
  lang., people, Liberia, Sierra Leone   GŌ-luh   'goːlə

Foreign Sounds: ue: *Fr.* **rue**, *Ger.* **füllen**   uh(r): *Fr.* **boeuf**, *Ger.* **Höhle**   <u>kh</u>: *Ger.* **ich**, *Scot.* **loch**   g̱: *Sp.* **amigo**   v̱: *Sp.* **hablar**
hl: *Welsh* **Llanelli**.   CAPITALS: primary stress.   SMALL CAPS: secondary stress.   Ⓢ: U.S. pron.   Ⓔ: British pron.

Golan Heights

   hilly region, Syria, annexed by Israel   GŌ-LAHN HĪTS, GŌ-luhn   ˌgoːˌlɑn ˈhɑits, ˌgoːlən

Golconda

   town, IL; ruined city, India   gahl-KAHN-duh   gɑlˈkɑndə

gold

   element   GŌLD   ˈgoːld

Golda

   pers. name   GŌL-duh   ˈgoːldə

Goldberg

   Leonard, *US film and TV producer*   GŌL(D)-BUHRG   ˈgoːl(d)ˌbərg

Goldblum

   Jeff, *US actor*   GŌL(D)-BLO͞OM   ˈgoːl(d)ˌbluːm

Goldey Beacom

   College, *DE*   GŌL-dē BĒ-kuhm   ˈgoːldi· ˈbiːkəm

Gold Fassl

   Austrian beer   GAWLT FAHS-uhl   ˈgɔːlt ˈfɑsəl

Goldie

   pers. name   GŌL-dē   ˈgoːldi·

Goldilocks

   fairy tale character   GŌL-dē-LAHKS   ˈgoːldi·ˌlɑks

Golding

   William, *English author (Nobel 1983)*   GŌL-ding   ˈgoːldiŋ

Goldman

   Emma, *US anarchist*   GŌL(D)-muhn   ˈgoːl(d)mən

Goldoni

   Carlo, *Italian playwright*   gōl-DŌ-nē   goːlˈdoːni·

Goldstein

   Joseph L., *US molecular geneticist*   GŌL(D)-STĪN   ˈgoːl(d)ˌstain
     (Nobel 1985)

Goldsworthy

   pers. name   GŌL(D)Z-WUHR-<u>th</u>ē   ˈgoːl(d)z,wərði·

Goldwyn

   Samuel John, Jr., *US film producer*   GŌL-dwuhn   ˈgoːldwən

Golgi

   Camillo, *Italian physician (Nobel*   GAWL-jē   ˈgɔːldʒiː
     1906)

Golgotha [Calvary]

   site of Christ's crucifixion   GAHL-guh-thuh, gahl-GAHTH-uh   ˈgɑlgəθə, gɑlˈgɑθə

Goliad

   county, TX   GŌ-lē-AD   ˈgoːliːˌæd

Goliath

   Biblical giant   guh-LĪ-uhth   gəˈlɑiəθ

Gollancz

   Sir Victor, *British publisher and*   guh-LANTS   gəˈlænts
     writer

Golo

   Bantu people   GŌ-lō   ˈgoːloː

Gombei

   pers. name   GŌM-bā   ˈgoːmbeː

Gomer

   Biblical name   GŌ-muhr, GAW-mer   ˈgoːmər, ˈgɔːmer

Gomes

   1. Peter, *US theologian*   GŌMZ   ˈgoːmz
   2. pers. name, Portuguese   GŌ-mish, GŌ-mis   ˈgoːmiʃ, ˈgoːmis

---

Key (col. 2): a: fad ā: fade ah: father ar: marry aw: law e: fed ē: feed er: merry i: hid ī: hide ō: coat oͦo: boot
oi: boy ow: now u: put uh: above uhr: bird ch: chop ng: ring sh: show th: thick th: this zh: measure

Gómez		
pers. name, Spanish	GŌ-mās, GŌ-māth	'goːmeːs, 'goːmeːθ
Gomorrah		
Biblical city	guh-MŌR-uh, guh-MAWR-uh	gə'moːrə, gə'mɔːrə
Gompers		
Samuel, *US labor leader*	GAHM-puhrz	'gɑmpə^{r}z
Gonçalo		
pers. name, Portuguese	gaw^n-SAH-lo͞o	gõ'sɑːluː
Goncharov		
Ivan, *Russian novelist*	guhn-CHUH-RAWF	gənˌtʃə'rɔːf
Gond		
aboriginal people of India	GAHND	'gɑnd
Gondi		
lang., India	GAHN-dē	'gɑndiˑ
Gondwanaland		
Mesozoic supercontinent	gahn-DWAHN-uh-LAND	gɑn'dwɑnəˌlænd
Goneril		
character in King Lear, *Shakespeare*	GAHN-uh-RIL, GAHN-uh-ruhl	'gɑnəˌril, 'gɑnərəl
Gongola		
state, Nigeria	gahng-GŌ-luh	gɑŋ'goːlə
Gongorism		
deliberate literary obscurity	GAHNG-guh-RIZ-uhm, GAHN-guh-RIZ-uhm	'gɑŋgəˌrizəm, 'gɑngəˌrizəm
Gonville and Caius		
college, Cambridge Univ.	GAHN-VIL uhn(d) KĒZ, GAHN-vuhl	'gɑnˌvil ən(d) 'kiːz, 'gɑnvəl
Gonxha		
pers. name (A. G. Bojaxhiu)	gōn-KHAH	goːn'xɑ
Gonzaga		
University, *WA*	guhn-ZAHG-uh	gən'zɑgə
Gonzales		
1. city, county, TX; town, LA	guhn-ZAL-uhs, guhn-ZAHL-uhs	gən'zæləs, gən'zɑləs
2. pers. name, Dutch	ğawn-ZAHL-uhs	ɣɔːn'zɑləs
3. Spanish	gawn-SAHL-ās, gawn-THAHL-ās	gɔːn'sɑleːs, gɔːn'θɑleːs
González		
pers. name, Spanish	gawn-SAHL-ās, gawn-THAHL-āth	gɔːn'sɑleːs, gɔːn'θɑleːθ
Goodall		
Jane, *US zoologist; pers. name*	GUD-AWL	'gudˌɔːl
Gooden		
Dwight, *US baseball player*	GUD-n	'gudn̩
Goodenough		
island, Pacific	GUD-n-UHF	'gudn̩ˌəf
Goodhue		
pers. name	GUD-(h)yo͞o	'gud(h)juː
Goodman		
Benny, *US clarinetist*	GUD-muhn	'gudmən
Goodson		
Mark, *US TV producer*	GUD-suhn	'gudsən
Goolagong		
Evonne, *Australian tennis player*	GO͞O-luh-GAWNG	'guːləˌgɔːŋ
Goold		
pers. name	GO͞OLD	'guːld
Goondiwindi		
town, Australia	GUHN-duh-WIN-dē	ˌgəndə'windiˑ

Foreign Sounds: ue: *Fr.* **rue**, *Ger.* **füllen** uh(r): *Fr.* **boeuf**, *Ger.* **Höhle** kh: *Ger.* **ich**, *Scot.* **loch** ğ: *Sp.* amigo v: *Sp.* **hablar** hl: *Welsh* **Llanelli**. CAPITALS: primary stress. SMALL CAPS: secondary stress. [$]: U.S. pron. [£]: British pron.

Gopal

1. pers. name, Bengali	gō-PAWL(-aw)	goːˈpɔːl(ɔː)
2. Marathi	gō-PAHL(-uh)	goːˈpɑl(ə)

Gorazde

city, Bosnia	guh-RAHZH-duh	gəˈrɑʒdə

Gorbachev

Mikhail S., *political leader, USSR* *(Nobel 1990)*	GAWR-buh-CHAWF, GAWR-buh-CHAWV, GAWR-buh-CHAWF	ˈgɔːʳbəˌtʃɔːf, ˈgɔːʳbəˌtʃɔːv, ˌgɔːʳbəˈtʃɔːf

Gordeeva

Ekaterina, *Russian figure skater*	GAWR-duh-YĀ-vuh	ˌgɔːʳdəˈjeːvə

Gordian knot

knot cut by Alexander the Great	GAWRD-ē-uhn NAHT	ˌgɔːʳdiːən ˈnɑt

Gordias

Phrygian peasant who became king, *maker of the Gordian knot*	GAWRD-ē-uhs	ˈgɔːʳdiːəs

Gordimer

Nadine, *South African author*	GAWRD-uh-muhr	ˈgɔːʳdəməʳ

Gordium

ancient Phrygian city	GAWR-dē-uhm	ˈgɔːʳdiːəm

Gordon

pers. name	GAWRD-n	ˈgɔːʳdn̩

Gore

Albert, Jr., *US vice-president; pers.* *name*	GŌR, GAWR	ˈgoːʳ, ˈgɔːʳ

Gorgas

William C., *US physician*	GAWR-guhs	ˈgɔːʳgəs

Gorgias

dialogue of Plato	GAWR-jē-uhs	ˈgɔːʳdʒiːəs

Gorgones

Greek deities	gawr-GŌ-nēz	gɔːʳˈgoːniːz

Gorgons

snake-haired sisters: Stheno, Euryale, *and Medusa*	GAWR-guhnz	ˈgɔːʳgənz

Gorgonzola

cheese	GAWR-guhn-ZŌ-luh	ˌgɔːʳgənˈzoːlə

Gorham

town, NH; crystal; pers. name	GŌR-uhm, GAWR-uhm	ˈgoːrəm, ˈgɔːrəm

Gorkiy, Gorki, Gorky

city, Russia	GAWR-kē	ˈgɔːʳkiˑ

Gorky

Arshile, *US painter*	GAWR-kē	ˈgɔːʳkiˑ

Gorme

Eydie, *US entertainer*	gawr-MĀ	gɔːʳˈmeː

Gorno-Badakhshan

region, Tadzhikistan	GAWR-nō-BAHD-uhkh-SHAHN	ˌgɔːʳnoːˌbadəxˈʃɑn

Goronwy

pers. name, Welsh	gaw-RAWN-wē, Ⓢ guh-RAHN-wē	gɔːˈrɔːnwiˑ, Ⓢ gəˈrɑnwiˑ

Gorton

pers. name (G. Carruth)	GAWRT-n	ˈgɔːʳtn̩

Goscinny

René, *French cartoon author*	gaw-skē-NĒ, gaw-sē-NĒ	gɔːskiːniː, gɔːsiːniː

Goshen

biblical land, ancient Egypt; US pl. *name*	GŌ-shuhn	ˈgoːʃən

Key (col. 2):　a: fad　ā: fade　ah: father　ar: marry　aw: law　e: fed　ē: feed　er: merry　i: hid　ī: hide　ō: coat　ōō: boot
oi: boy　ow: now　u: put　uh: above　uhr: bird　ch: chop　ng: ring　sh: show　th: thick　th: this　zh: measure

Goshute, Gosiute		
N. American people	GŌ-SHO͞OT	'goːˌʃuːt
Gosplan		
Soviet planning organization	GAWS-PLAHN	'gɔːsˌplɑn
Gossage		
Richard Michael (Goose), *US baseball player*	GAHS-ij	'gɑsidʒ
Gosse		
Sir Edmund William, *English poet and man of letters*	GAWS, GAHS	'gɔːs, 'gɑs
Gösser		
Austrian beer	GUH(R)S-uhr	'gœsəʳ
Gösser Stiftsbräu		
Austrian beer	GUH(R)S-uhr STIFTS-BROI	'gœsəʳ 'stiftsˌbrɔi
Göteborg [Gothenburg]		
city, Sweden	YUH(R)-tuh-BAWR(-yuh)	'jœːtəˌbɔːr(jə)
Gotham		
1. nickname for New York City	GAHTH-uhm	'gɑθəm
2. town, England	GŌT-uhm, GAHT-uhm	'goːt̪əm, 'gɑt̪əm
Gothenburg		
city, NE	GAHTH-uhn-BUHRG	'gɑθənˌbəʳg
Gothenburg [Göteborg]		
city, Sweden	GAHTH-uhn-BUHRG, GAHT-uhn-BUHRG	'gɑθənˌbəʳg, 'gɑtənˌbəʳg
Gothic		
ancient lang., Europe; style of architecture, music, literature	GAHTH-ik	'gɑθik
Goths		
Teutonic tribe	GAHTHS	'gɑθs
Gotland		
island, county, Sweden	GAHT-LAND, GAHT-luhnd	'gɑtˌlænd, 'gɑtlənd
Götterdämmerung		
opera, R. Wagner	GUH(R)T-uhr-DEM-uh-RUNG	ˌgœtəʳ'deməˌruŋ
Gottfried		
1. pers. name, German	GAWT-FRĒT	'gɔːtˌfriːt
2. Swedish	GAWT-FRĒD	'gɔːtˌfriːd
Gotthold		
pers. name, German	GAWT-HAWLT	'gɔːtˌhɔːlt
Göttingen		
town, Germany	GUH(R)T-ing-uhn	'gœtiŋən
Gottlieb		
1. pers. name	GAHT-LĒB	'gɑtˌliːb
2. Finnish, Swedish	GAWT-LĒB	'gɔːtˌliːb
3. German	GAWT-LĒP	'gɔːtˌliːp
Gottlob		
pers. name, German	GAWT-LŌP	'gɔːtˌloːp
Gottschalk		
Louis, *US composer*	GAHCH-AWK, GAHT-SHAWK	'gɑtʃˌɔːk, 'gɑtˌʃɔːk
Gottschalks		
US department store chain	GAHCH-AWKS, GAHT-SHAWKS	'gɑtʃˌɔːks, 'gɑtˌʃɔːks
Goucher		
College, *MD*	GOW-chuhr	'gautʃəʳ
Gouda		
city, Netherlands; cheese	ḠOWD-uh, [$] GO͞OD-uh, GOWD-uh, HOWD-uh	'ɣaudə, [$] 'guːdə, 'gaudə, 'haudə

Gouden Carolus
  Belgian beer   G͞OOD-n KAHR-ō-lus   'guːdn̩ 'kɑroːlus

Goudy
  Frederic William, *US printer and*   GOWD-ē   'gaudiˑ
    type designer

Gough
  square, London; pers. name   GAWF   'gɔːf

Gould
  pers. name   G͞OOLD   'guːld

Goulet
  Robert, *entertainer*   g͞oo-LĀ   guːˈleː

Gounod
  Charles François, *French composer*   g͞oo-NŌ   guːnoː

Gouverneur
  pers. name   GUHV-uh-NUR, GUV-uh-NUR, -NUHR   ˌgəvəˈnuʳ, ˌguvəˈnuʳ, -ˈnəʳ

Govier
  pers. name   gō-VIR, guh-VIR   goːˈviʳ, gəˈviʳ

Govind
  pers. name, Punjabi   gō-VIND   goːˈvind

Govinda
  pers. name, Sanskrit   gō-VIN-duh   goːˈvində

Gowdy
  Curt, *US sportscaster*   GOWD-ē   'gaudiˑ

Gowen
  pers. name   GOW-uhn   'gauən

Gower
  John, *English poet*   GOW(-uh)r, GŌ(-uh)r, GAWR   'gau(ə)ʳ, 'goː(ə)ʳ, 'gɔːʳ

Goya
  Francisco, *Spanish painter*   GOI-(y)uh   'gɔi(j)ə

Gozan
  Biblical name   GŌ-ZAN, gō-ZAHN   'goːˌzæn, goːˈzɑn

Gozo
  island, Mediterranean   GAWT-sō   'gɔːtsoː

Gozzi
  Carlo, *Italian writer*   GAWT-sē   'gɔːtsiː

Gqoba
  William Wellington, *Bantu writer in*   KŌ-buh   'koːbə
    Cape Colony, South Africa

Graafian follicle
  ovum sac   GRAF-ē-uhn, Ⓔ GRAH-fē-uhn   'græfiːən, Ⓔ 'grɑːfiːən

Gracchi
  Roman reformers   GRAK-Ī   'grækˌai

Gracchus
  Roman political family   GRAK-uhs   'grækəs

Grace
  pers. name   GRĀS   'greːs

Graceland
  Elvis Presley's home   GRĀ-SLAND, GRĀ-sluhnd   'greːˌslænd, 'greːslənd

Graces
  Roman goddesses   GRĀ-suhz   'greːsəz

Gracey, Gracie
  pers. name   GRĀ-sē   'greːsiˑ

Graco
  US industrial equipment co.   GRĀ-kō   'greːkoː

Key (col. 2):   a: fad   ā: fade   ah: father   ar: marry   aw: law   e: fed   ē: feed   er: merry   i: hid   ī: hide   ō: coat   ō͞o: boot
oi: boy   ow: now   u: put   uh: above   uhr: bird   ch: chop   ng: ring   sh: show   th: thick   <u>th</u>: this   zh: measure

Grady
  pers. name — GRĀD-ē — 'greːdiˑ

Graeme
  pers. name — GRĀ-uhm, GRĀM — 'greːəm, 'greːm

Graf
  Steffi, *German tennis player* — GRAHF, ⓢ GRAF — 'grɑːf, ⓢ 'græf

Graham
  pers. name — GRĀ-uhm, GRAM — 'greːəm, 'græm

Graiae
  sisters of the Gorgons — GRĀ-Ē, GRĀ-Ī — 'greːˌiː, 'greːˌɑi

Graian Alps
  Alpine mtn. range — GRĀ-(y)uhn ALPS, GRĪ-(y)uhn — 'greː(j)ən 'ælps, 'grɑi(j)ən

Graig
  pers. name — GRĀG, GREG — 'greːg, 'greg

Grail
  legendary chalice — GRĀL — 'greːl

Grainger
  Percy, *US composer* — GRĀN-juhr — 'greːndʒəʳ

Grainne
  legendary Irish heroine — GROIN-yuh — 'grɔinjə

Gramercy
  Park, *New York City* — GRAM-uhr-sē — 'græməʳsiˑ

Grammy
  grandmother; music award — GRAM-ē — 'græmiˑ

Grampian
  hills, region, Scotland — GRAM-pē-uhn — 'græmpiːən

Granada
  prov., city, Spain; dept., city, — grah-NAH<u>TH</u>-ah, ⓢ gruh-NAHD-uh — grɑ'nɑðɑ, ⓢ grə'nɑdə
    Nicaragua

Granados
  Enrique, *Spanish composer* — grah-NAH<u>TH</u>-ōs, ⓢ gruh-NAHD-ōs — grɑ'nɑðoːs, ⓢ grə'nɑdoːs

Grana Padano
  Italian cheese — GRAHN-uh pah-DAHN-ō — ˌgrɑnə pɑ'dɑnoː

Granatelli
  Andy, *auto racing sponsor* — GRAN-uh-TEL-ē — ˌgrænə'teliˑ

Granbury
  city, TX — GRAHN-BER-ē, GRAN- — 'grɑnˌberiˑ, 'græn-

Gran Chaco
  region, S. America — grahn CHAHK-ō — grɑn 'tʃɑkoː

Grand Cayman
  island, Caribbean — gran(d) KĀ-MAN, KĀ-muhn, kā-MAN — græn(d) 'keːˌmæn, 'keːmən, keː'mæn

Grand Comore
  island, Mozambique Channel — GRAN(D) kuh-MAWR — ˌgræn(d) kə'mɔːʳ

Grand Coulee
  valley, city, WA — gran(d) KOO-lē — græn(d) 'kuːliˑ

Grande Champagne
  wine — GRAHⁿD shahⁿ-PAHN-yuh, GRAHⁿ-duh — grɑ̃d ʃɑ̃pɑːɲ , grɑ̃də

Grande Ronde
  river, OR — GRAN-DRAHND — 'græn'drɑnd

Grand Saline
  city, TX — GRAN(D) suh-LĒN — ˌgræn(d) sə'liːn

Grandes Marques
  wine — GRAHⁿD MAHRK, GRAHⁿ-duh — grɑ̃d mɑːrk, grɑ̃də

Foreign Sounds: ue: *Fr.* **rue**, *Ger.* **füllen**   uh(r): *Fr.* **boeuf**, *Ger.* **Höhle**   <u>kh</u>: *Ger.* **ich**, *Scot.* **loch**   ḡ: *Sp.* **amigo**   ᵛ: *Sp.* **hablar**
hl: *Welsh* **Llanelli**.   CAPITALS: primary stress.   SMALL CAPS: secondary stress.   ⓢ: U.S. pron.   ⓔ: British pron.

Grande-Terre
  islands, Caribbean   gran-TER   græn'te[r]
Grand Guignol
  horror drama   grah[n] gēn-YAWL, Ⓢ GRAHN gēn-YŌL   grɑ̃ giːnjɔːl, Ⓢ ˌgrɑn
                                                                             giːn'joːl

Grand Marais
  village, MN   GRAN(D) muh-RĀ   ˌgræn(d) mə're:
Grand Marnier
  liqueur   GRAH[n] mahrn-YĀ   grɑ̃ mɑːrnjeː
Grand Pré
  village, Nova Scotia   grah[n](n) PRĀ, Ⓢ GRAN PRĀ   grɑ̃(n) 'preː, Ⓢ 'græn 'preː
Grand Prix
  auto race   grah[n] PRĒ, gran(d) PRĒ   grɑ̃ 'priː, græn(d) 'priː
Grand Teton
  National Park, *Moose, WY*   gran(d) TĒ-TAHN   græn(d) 'tiːˌtɑn
Grand Traverse
  county, MI   gran(d) TRAV-uhrs   græn(d) 'trævə[r]s
Grandy
  Fred, *US actor, politician*   GRAN-dē   'grændi·
Grange, La
  see La Grange
Granit
  Ragnar, *Finnish-born Swedish*   grah-NĒT   grɑ'niːt
    physiologist (Nobel 1967)
Granma
  prov, Cuba   grahn-MAH   grɑn'mɑ
Grant
  Ulysses S., *18th US president; pers.* GRANT   'grænt
    name
Granta
  river, Cambridgeshire, England   GRANT-uh, Ⓔ GRAHNT-uh   'græntə, Ⓔ 'grɑːntə
Grantham
  town, England   GRAN-thuhm, GRANT-uhm   'grænθəm, 'græntəm
Grass
  Günter, *German writer*   GRAHS   'grɑs
Grasso
  Ella, *US politician*   GRAS-ō, GRAHS-ō   'græsˌoː, 'grɑsˌoː
Gratian
  Roman emperor   GRĀ-sh(ē-)uhn   'greːʃ(iː)ən
Gratiot
  county, MI   GRASH-uht   'græʃət
Grattan
  Henry, *Irish politician*   GRAT-n   'grætn̩
Grau
  Shirley Ann, *US writer*   GROW   'grɑu
Graubünden [Grisons]
  mtn. range, Switzerland   grow-BUEN-duhn, Ⓢ grow-BIN-duhn,   grɑu'byndən,
                                         grow-BUN-duhn   Ⓢ grɑu'bindən,
                                                                             grɑu'bundən
Grau San Martín
  Ramón, *president, Cuba*   GROW ꜱᴀʜɴ mahr-TĒN   'grɑu ˌsɑn mɑ[r]'tiːn
Graustark
  novel, G. B. McCutcheon   GROW-STAHRK   'grɑuˌstɑ[r]k

Key (col. 2):   a: fad   ā: fade   ah: father   ar: marry   aw: law   e: fed   ē: feed   er: merry   i: hid   ī: hide   ō: coat   ōō: boot
oi: boy   ow: now   u: put   uh: above   uhr: bird   ch: chop   ng: ring   sh: show   th: thick   th̲: this   zh: measure

Gravenstein
 apple   GRAV-uhn-STĒN, GRĀ-vuhn-STĪN,   'grævən‚sti:n, 'gre:vən‚stɑin,
                       -STĒN   -‚sti:n

Graves
 wine   GRAHV   'grɑv

Graz
 city, Austria   GRAHTS   'grɑts

Grazia
 pers. name, Italian   GRAHTS-yah   'grɑtsjɑ

Graziano
 Rocky, *US boxer*   GRAHT-sē-AHN-ō, GRAHS-ē-AHN-ō,   ‚grɑtsi:'ɑno:, ‚grɑsi:'ɑno:,
                       GRAHZ-ē-AHN-ō   ‚grɑzi:'ɑno:

Great Britain
 island, Europe   grāt BRIT-n   gre:t 'britn̩

Great Chazy
 river, NY   GRĀT SHĀ-zē   ‚gre:t 'ʃe:zi·

Great Pyrenees
 mts., France, Spain   PIR-uh-NĒZ   'pirə‚ni:z

Grebo
 lang., people, Liberia, Ivory Coast   GRĀ-bō   'gre:bo:

Grecia
 Biblical name   GRĒ-sh(ē-)uh   'gri:ʃ(i:)ə

Grecian
 pert. to Greece   GRĒ-shuhn   'gri:ʃən

Greco, El
 Doménikos, *Spanish painter*   el GREK-ō, el GRĀ-kō   el 'greko:, el 'gre:ko:

Greco-Roman
 pert. to ancient Greece and Rome   GREK-ō-RŌ-muhn   ‚greko:'ro:mən

Greece
 republic, Europe   GRĒS   'gri:s

Greek
 lang., Greece, Cyprus, Turkey   GRĒK   'gri:k

Greeley
 Horace, *US politician; US pl. name*   GRĒ-lē   'gri:li·

Green
 college, Oxford Univ.   GRĒN   'gri:n

Greenaway
 Kate, *English illustrator*   GRĒN-uh-WĀ   'gri:nə‚we:

Greenblatt
 Milton, *US psychiatrist*   GRĒN-BLAT   'gri:n‚blæt

Greenhow
 Rose, *US Confederate spy*   GRĒN-HOW   'gri:n‚hɑu

Greenland
 island, North America   GRĒN-luhnd, GRĒN-LAND   'gri:nlənd, 'gri:n‚lænd

Greenlander
 inhabitant of Greenland   GRĒN-luhn-duhr, -LAN-duhr   'gri:nləndəʳ, -‚lændəʳ

Greenlandic [Iniut]
 lang., Greenland, Canada, USA (AK)   grēn-LAN-dik, GRĒN-LAN-dik   gri:n'lændik, 'gri:n‚lændik

Greenleaf
 pers. name   GRĒN-LĒF   'gri:n‚li:f

Greenlee
 county, AZ   GRĒN-lē   'gri:nli·

Greenock
 port, Scotland   GRĒ-nuhk, GRIN-uhk, GREN-uhk   'gri:nək, 'grinək, 'grenək

---

Foreign Sounds: ue: *Fr.* **rue**, *Ger.* **füllen**   uh(r): *Fr.* **boeuf**, *Ger.* **Höhle**   <u>kh</u>: *Ger.* **ich**, *Scot.* **loch**   ḡ: *Sp.* amigo   y: *Sp.* hablar
hl: *Welsh* **Llanelli**.   CAPITALS: primary stress.   SMALL CAPS: secondary stress.   ⑤: U.S. pron.   ⑥: British pron.

Greenough
  pers. name   GRĒ-NŌ   'griː,noː

Greenpeace
  environmental organization   GRĒN-PĒS   'griːn,piːs

Greensboro
  city, NC   GRĒNZ-buhr-uh, GRĒNZ-buh-ruh   'griːnzbər-ə, 'griːnzbə-rə

Greenville
  US pl. name   GRĒN-vuhl, GRĒN-VIL   'griːnvəl, 'griːn,vil

Greenwich
  1. town, CT, RI   GREN-ich, GRĒN-WICH, GRIN-WICH   'grenitʃ, 'griːn,witʃ, 'grin,witʃ

  2. town, NY   GRĒN-WICH   'griːn,witʃ
  3. borough, London, England   GRIN-ij, GREN-ij, -ich   'grinidʒ, 'grenidʒ, -itʃ
  4. island, Shetland Islands   GREN-ich, GRIN-ich, -ij   'grenitʃ, 'grinitʃ, -idʒ

Greenwich Village
  area, New York City   GREN-ich VIL-ij, GREN-ij   'grenitʃ 'vilidʒ, 'grenidʒ

Greer
  Hershel, Stadium, *Nashville, TN*   GRIR   'grir

Greg
  pers. name   GREG, GRĀG   'greg, 'greːg

Grégoire
  pers. name, French   grā-GWAHR   greːgwɑːr

Gregor
  1. pers. name   GREG-uhr   'gregər
  2. German   GRĀ-GAWR, grā-GAWR   'greː,goːr, greː'goːr

Gregorian
  pert. to any Pope Gregory   gri-GAWR-ē-uhn, greg-AWR-ē-uhn   gri'goːriːən, greg'oːriːən

Gregório
  pers. name, Portuguese   grā-GAWR-yoo   greː'goːrjuː

Gregorio
  1. pers. name, Italian   grā-GAWR-yō   greː'goːrjoː
  2. Spanish   grā-ḠOR-yō   greː'ɣoːrjoː

Gregorius
  pers. name, Latin   gri-GAWR-ē-uhs, greg-AWR-ē-uhs   gri'goːriːəs, greg'oːriːəs

Gregory
  pers. name   GREG(-uh)-rē   'greg(ə)ri·

Grenache
  wine grape   gruh-NAHSH, gren-AHSH   grə'nɑʃ, gren'ɑʃ

Grenada
  island, West Indies; county, city, MS   gruh-NĀD-uh   grə'neːdə

Grenadian
  pert. to Grenada   gruh-NĀD-ē-uhn   grə'neːdiːən

Grenadine
  pomegranate syrup   GREN-uh-DĒN, GREN-uh-DĒN   ,grenə'diːn, 'grenə,diːn

Grenadines
  islands, West Indies   GREN-uh-DĒNZ   ,grenə'diːnz

Grendel
  monster in Beowulf   GREND-l   'grendl̩

Grenoble
  city, France   gruh-NAWBL, ⓢ gruh-NŌ-buhl   grənoːbl, ⓢ grə'noːbəl

Grenville
  pers. name; county, Ontario; town,   GREN-VIL, GREN-vuhl   'gren,vil, 'grenvəl
    Grenada

Grenzquell
  German beer   GRENTS-KVEL   'grents,kvel

Key (col. 2):   a: fad   ā: fade   ah: father   ar: marry   aw: law   e: fed   ē: feed   er: merry   i: hid   ī: hide   ō: coat   ōō: boot
oi: boy   ow: now   u: put   uh: above   uhr: bird   ch: chop   ng: ring   sh: show   th: thick   <u>th</u>: this   zh: measure

Gresham
   pers. name; city, OR   GRESH-uhm   'greʃəm

Gresham
   Sir Thomas, *English financier*   GRESH-uhm   'greʃəm

Greta
   1. pers. name   GRET-uh, GRĒT-uh   'greţə, 'griːţə
   2. Swedish   GRÃ-tah   'greːtɑː

Gretel
   pers. name   GRET-l   'gretļ

Gretna
   city, LA; district, Scotland   GRET-nuh   'gretnə

Gretna Green
   village, Scotland   GRET-nuh GRĒN   ˌgretnə 'griːn

Gretzky
   Wayne, *Canadian hockey player*   GRET-skē   'gretskiˑ

Grey
   pers. name   GRÃ   'greː

Grgich Hills
   winery, CA   GUHR-gich HILZ   'gəʳgitʃ 'hilz

Grieg
   Edvard, *Norwegian composer*   GRIG, ⑤ GRĒG   'grig, ⑤ 'griːg

Grier
   pers. name   GRIR   'griʳ

Griffin
   mythical beast; pers. name   GRIF-uhn   'grifən

Griffith
   pers. name   GRIF-uhth   'grifəθ

Griffiths
   pers. name   GRIF-uh(th)s   'grifə(θ)s

Griffon
   mythical beast; breed of dog   GRIF-uhn   'grifən

Grignard
   Victor, *French chemist (Nobel 1912)*   grēn-YAHR   griːnjɑr

Grigori, -ry
   pers. name, Russian   gri-GAWR-yi   gr�classicˑ — gri̯'gɔːrji̯j

Grimaldi
   royal family, Monaco; crater on   gruh-MAWL-dē, gruh-MAHL-dē,   grə'mɔːldiˑ, grə'mɑldiˑ,
     Moon   gruh-MAL-dē   grə'mældiˑ

Grimes
   pers. name; county, TX   GRĪMZ   'grɑimz

Grimm
   Jacob *and* Wilhelm, *German*   GRIM   'grim
     linguists, fairy tale collectors

Grimsby
   pers. name; town, Ontario; borough,   GRIMZ-bē   'grimzbiˑ
     England

Grindel [Éluard]
   Eugène, *French poet*   greⁿ-DEL   grɛ̃del

Grinkov
   Sergei, *Russian figure skater*   GRING-kuhf, -KAWF   'griŋkəf, -ˌkɔːf

Grinnell
   George, *US naturalist;* College, *IA;*   gruh-NEL   grə'nel
     pl. name, US, Canada

Gris
   Juan, *Spanish artist*   GRĒS   'griːs

Foreign Sounds: ue: *Fr.* **rue**, *Ger.* **füllen** uh(r): *Fr.* **boeuf**, *Ger.* **Höhle** k̲h̲: *Ger.* i**ch**, *Scot.* lo**ch** g̲: *Sp.* ami**g**o v̲: *Sp.* ha**b**lar
hl: *Welsh* **Ll**anelli. CAPITALS: primary stress. SMALL CAPS: secondary stress. ⑤: U.S. pron. ⓔ: British pron.

Grisham
  John, *US author*   GRISH-uhm   'griʃəm

Grisons [Graubünden]
  mtn. range, Switzerland   grē-ZAWⁿ   griːzɔ̃

Grissom
  Gus, *US astronaut*   GRIS-uhm   'grisəm

Griswold
  pers. name   GRIZ-wuhld, -WŌLD, -WAWLD   'grizwəld, -ˌwoːld, -ˌwɔːld

Grodin
  Charles, *US actor, writer, director*   GRŌD-n   'groːdn̩

Groening
  Matt, *US cartoonist*   GRĀ-ning   'greːniŋ

Groesbeck
  city, TX   GRŌS-bek   'groːsbek

Groesbeek
  commune, Netherlands   ḠRŌŌZ-BĀK   'ɣruːzˌbeːk

Grofé
  Ferde, *US composer*   GRŌ-FĀ   'groːˌfeː

Grogan
  Steven, *football player*   GRŌ-guhn   'groːgən

Grolier
  US publisher   GRŌL-yuhr, GRŌ-lē-uhr   'groːljəʳ, 'groːliːəʳ

Grolier de Servières
  Jean, *French bibliophile*   grawl-yā duh ser-VYER   grɔːljeː də servjer

Gromyko
  Andrei, *president, USSR*   gruh-MĒ-kō   grə'miːkoː

Gronchi
  Giovanni, *president, Italy*   GRAHNG-kē   'graŋkiˑ

Groningen
  prov & town, Netherlands   GRŌ-ning-uhn   'groːniŋən

Gropius
  Walter, *German architect*   GRŌ-pē-uhs   'groːpiːəs

Grosbeak
  songbird   GRŌS-BĒK   'groːsˌbiːk

Grosseteste
  Robert, *English prelate*   GRŌS-TEST   'groːsˌtest

Grosseto
  prov, Italy   grō-SĀT-ō   groː'seːtoː

Grossmont
  College, CA   GRŌ-smahnt   'groːsmɑnt

Grosvenor
  pers. name   GRŌV-nuhr, GRŌ-vuh-nuhr   'groːvnəʳ, 'groːvənəʳ

Gros Ventre
  N. American people   grō-VAHNT   groː'vɑnt

Grosz
  George, *US artist*   GRŌS   'groːs

Grotius
  Hugo, *Dutch statesman*   GRŌ-sh(ē-)uhs   'groːʃ(iː)əs

Groton
  town, CT, MA; village, NY   GRAHT-n   'grɑtn̩

Groucho
  pers. name (G. Marx)   GROW-chō   'grautʃoː

Groundsel
  plant   GROWN(D)-suhl   'graun(d)səl

Key (col. 2): a: fad ā: fade ah: father ar: marry aw: law e: fed ē: feed er: merry i: hid ī: hide ō: coat ōō: boot
oi: boy ow: now u: put uh: above uhr: bird ch: chop ng: ring sh: show th: thick t͟h: this zh: measure

Grover
  pers. name GRŌ-vuhr 'groːvəʳ

Grozny
  city, Russia GRAWZ-nē, GRAHZ-nē 'grɔːzniˑ, 'grɑzniˑ

Grudziądz
  city, Poland GROO-JAWⁿTS 'gruːˌdʒɔ̃ts

Gruffydd
  William John, *Welsh poet and* GRIF-ith 'grifið
    scholar; pers. name, Welsh

Grundig
  German radio co. GRUN-dig, GRUHN-dig 'grundig, 'grəndig

Grundy
  pl. name, US GRUHN-dē 'grəndiˑ

Grus
  constellation GROOS, GRUHS 'gruːs, 'grəs

Gruyère
  district, Switzerland; cheese groo-YER, grē-(Y)ER gruːˈjeʳ, griːˈ(j)eʳ

Gruzinian
  lang., Georgia groo-ZIN-ē-uhn, groo-ZIN-yuhn gruːˈziniːən, gruːˈzinjən

Grzegorz
  pers. name, Polish GZHEG-awsh 'gʒegɔːʃ

Gstaad
  city, Switzerland guh-SHTAHT gəˈʃtɑt

Guadalajara
  prov & town, Mexico; prov & town, gwahth-ah-lah-KHAHR-ah, gwaðalaˈxɑrɑ,
    Spain Ⓢ GWAHD-l-uh-HAHR-uh Ⓢ ˌgwɑdl̩əˈhɑrə

Guadalcanal
  island, Pacific GWAHD-l-kuh-NAL, ˌgwɑdl̩kəˈnæl, ˌgwɑdəkəˈnæl
    GWAHD-uh-kuh-NAL

Guadalquivir
  river, Spain gwahth-ahl-kē-VIR, Ⓢ GWAHD-l-ki-VIR gwaðalkiːˈβir,
    Ⓢ ˌgwɑdl̩kiˈviʳ

Guadalupe
  1. Mountains National Park, *TX;* GWAHD-l-OOP, GWAHD-l-OO-pē 'gwɑdl̩ˌuːp, ˌgwɑdl̩ˈuːpiˑ
    county, NM, TX
  2. pers. name, Spanish gwahth-ah-LOO-pā gwaðaˈluːpeː

Guadalupe Hidalgo
  city, Mexico GWAHTH-ah-LOO-pā ē-THAHL-ḡō, ˌgwaðaˈluːpeː iːˈðalɣoː,
    Ⓢ GWAHD-l-OOP(-ē) hi-DAL-gō Ⓢ 'gwɑdl̩ˌuːp(iˑ) hiˈdælgoː

Guadeloupe
  islands, West Indies GWAHD-l-OOP, GWAHD-l-OOP 'gwɑdl̩ˌuːp, ˌgwɑdl̩ˈuːp

Guadeloupian
  pert. to Guadeloupe GWAHD-l-OO-pē-uhn ˌgwɑdl̩ˈuːpiːən

Guadix
  city, Spain gwah-DĒKH, gwah-DĒKS gwɑˈdiːç, gwɑˈdiːks

Guahibo
  lang., Colombia, Venezuela gwah-(H)Ē-vō gwɑˈ(h)iːβoː

Guairá [Sete Quedas]
  waterfall, S. America gwī-RAH gwaiˈrɑ

Guam
  island, Pacific GWAHM 'gwɑm

Guan
  S. & Cen. American bird GWAHN 'gwɑn

Foreign Sounds: ue: *Fr.* **rue**, *Ger.* **füllen**   uh(r): *Fr.* **boeuf**, *Ger.* **Höhle**   kh: *Ger.* **ich**, *Scot.* **loch**   ḡ: *Sp.* **amigo**   v: *Sp.* **hablar**
hl: *Welsh* **Llanelli**.   CAPITALS: primary stress.   SMALL CAPS: secondary stress.   Ⓢ: U.S. pron.   Ⓔ: British pron.

Guanajuato
 state, city, Mexico   gwahn-ah-<u>KH</u>WAHT-ō,   gwɑnɑˈxwɑṭoː,
               ⑤ GWAHN-uh-(H)WAHT-ō   ⑤ ˌgwɑnəˈ(h)wɑṭoː

Guangdong, Kwangtung
 prov, China   GWAHNG-DUNG   ˈgwaŋˈduŋ

Guangxi [Kwangsi Chuang]
 region, China   GWAHNG-SĒ, GWAHNG-SHĒ ˈgwaŋˈsiː, ˈgwaŋˈʃiː

Guangzhou, Kwangchow [Canton]
 city, China   GWAHNG-JŌ   ˈgwaŋˈdʒoː

Guantánamo
 prov & bay, Cuba   gwahn-TAHN-uh-mō   gwɑnˈtɑnəmoː

Guaporé
 river, S. America   gwahp-uh-RĀ   gwɑpəˈreː

Guaraní
 lang., people, S. America   GWAHR-uh-NĒ   ˌgwɑrəˈniː

Guardi
 Francesco *and* Giovanni, *Italian* GWAHR-dē   ˈgwɑʳdiˑ
  painters

Guardia, La
 see La Guardia

Guarneri
 family of Italian violin makers gwahrn-YER-ē   gwɑʳnˈjeriˑ

Guarnerius
 Latin form of Guarneri   gwahr-NIR-ē-uhs   gwɑʳˈniriːəs

Guatemala
 republic, Cen. America   GWAHT-uh-MAHL-uh   ˌgwɑṭəˈmɑlə

Guatemalan
 pert. to Guatemala   GWAHT-uh-MAHL-uhn   ˌgwɑṭəˈmɑlən

Guató
 S. American people   gwah-TŌ   gwɑˈtoː

Guatimozin [Cuauh-témoc]
 last emperor of the Aztecs GWAHT-uh-MŌT-suhn   ˌgwɑṭəˈmoːtsən

Guayaná
 S. American people   GĪ-uh-NAH   ˌgɑiəˈnɑ

Guayaquil
 city, Ecuador   GWĪ-uh-KĒL   ˌgwɑiəˈkiːl

Guayas
 prov, Ecuador   GWĪ-uhs   ˈgwɑiəs

Guaymí
 Cen. American people   gwī-MĒ   gwɑiˈmiː

Gucci
 fashion designers   G<u>OO</u>-chē   ˈguːtʃiˑ

Gudea
 Sumerian ruler of Lagash g<u>oo</u>-DĒ-uh   guːˈdiːə

Guderian
 Heinz, *German militarist*   g<u>oo</u>-DER-ē-uhn   guːˈderiːən

Gudgodah
 Biblical name   guhd-GŌD-uh, GUHD-guh-duh, gədˈgoːdə, ˈgədgədə,
              gud-GAWD-ah   gudˈgɔːdɑ

Gudmund
 pers. name, Swedish   G<u>OO</u>D-MUHND   ˈguːdˌmənd

Gudmundur
 pers. name, Icelandic   GVUE<u>TH</u>-MUEN-duer   ˈgvyð̩ˌmyndyr

Gudrun
 wife of Sigurd & Atli in Norse myth GUD-R<u>OO</u>N   ˈgudˌruːn

---

Key (col. 2): a: **fad** ā: **fade** ah: **father** ar: **marry** aw: **law** e: **fed** ē: **feed** er: **merry** i: **hid** ī: **hide** ō: **coat** ōō: **boot**
oi: **boy** ow: **now** u: **put** uh: **above** uhr: **bird** ch: **chop** ng: **ring** sh: **show** th: **thick** <u>th</u>: **this** zh: **measure**

Guelph		
town, Canada	GWELF	'gwelf
Guenoc		
winery, CA	gwuh-NAHK	gwə'nɑk
Guérard		
Michel, *French chef*	gā-RAHR	geːrɑːr
Guerlain		
French perfume	ger-LE^{n}	gerlẽ
Guernica		
town, Spain; painting, Picasso	ger-NĒ-kuh, [S] GWER-ni-kuh, GER-ni-kuh	ge^{r}'niːkə, [S] 'gwe^{r}nikə, 'ge^{r}nikə
Guernsey		
island, English channel	GUHRN-zē	'gə^{r}nziˑ
Guerrero		
state, Mexico	ger-RER-ō	ger'reroː
Guevara		
Che, *Cuban revolutionary*	gā-V̲AHR-uh, [S] gwuh-VAHR-uh	geː'βɑrə, [S] gwə'vɑ^{r}ə
Guggenheim		
Solomon R., *museum, New York City*	GUG-uhn-HĪM, GO͞O-guhn-HĪM	'gugən,hɑim, 'guːgən,hɑim
Guglielmo		
pers. name, Italian	go͞ol-YEL-mō	guːl'jelmoː
Gui		
pers. name, French	GĒ	giː
Guiana		
region, S. America	gē-AN-uh, gē-AHN-uh, gī-AN-uh	giː'ænə, giː'ɑnə, gɑi'ænə
Guianese		
pert. to Guiana	GĪ-uh-NĒZ, GĒ-uh-, -NĒS	,gɑiə'niːz, ,giːə-, -'niːs
Guido		
1. pers. name	GĒD-ō, GWĒD-ō	'giːdoː, 'gwiːdoː
2. Dutch	G̲Ē-DŌ	'ɣiː,doː
3. Italian	GWĒ-dō	'gwiːdoː
4. German	go͞o-Ē-dō, GĒ-dō	guː'iːdoː, 'giːdoː
Guidry		
Ron, *US baseball player*	GID-rē	'gidriˑ
Guildenstern		
character in Hamlet, *Shakespeare*	GIL-duhn-STUHRN	'gildən,stə^{r}n
Guildford		
town, England	GIL-fuhrd	'gilfə^{r}d
Guilford		
county, college, NC; town, CT, ME	GIL-fuhrd	'gilfə^{r}d
Guilherme		
pers. name, Portuguese	gēl-YER-muh, -mā	giːl'jermə, -meː
Guilin, Kuei-lin, Kweilin		
city, China	GWĀ-LIN	'gweː'lin
Guillain-Barré		
medical syndrome	gē-YA^{n}-buh-RĀ	giː'jæ̃bə'reː
Guillaume		
1. C. E., *Swiss physicist (Nobel 1920)*	gē-YŌM	giː'joːm
2. Robert, *US entertainer*	gē-(Y)ŌM	giː'(j)oːm
3. pers. name, French	gē-YŌM	giːjoːm
Guillemin		
Roger C. L., *French-born US physiologist (Nobel 1977)*	gē-(yuh)-ME^{n}	giː(jə)mẽ

Foreign Sounds: ue: *Fr.* **rue**, *Ger.* **füllen** uh(r): *Fr.* **boeuf**, *Ger.* **Höhle** k̲h̲: *Ger.* **ich**, *Scot.* **loch** g̃: *Sp.* **amigo** v̲: *Sp.* **hablar** hl: *Welsh* **Llanelli**. CAPITALS: primary stress. SMALL CAPS: secondary stress. [S]: U.S. pron. [£]: British pron.

Guillemot
  sea bird   GIL-i-MAHT   'gili,mɑt

Guillermo
  1. pers. name, Spanish   gē(l)-YER-mō   giː(l)'jermoː
  2. in Argentina, Paraguay, Uruguay   gē-ZHER-mō, gē(l)-YER-mō   giː'ʒermoː, giː(l)'jermoː

Guillotin
  Joseph Ignace, *French physician*   gē-yaw-TE^n giːjɔːtē

Guinea
  region, republic, gulf, Africa   GIN-ē   'giniˑ

Guinea-Bissau
  country, Africa   GIN-ē-bis-OW   ‚giniˑbis'ɑu

Guinean
  pert. to Guinea   GIN-ē-uhn   'giniːən

Guinevere [Gwenhwyfar]
  Arthur's queen in legend   GWIN-uh-VIR, GWEN-   'gwinə,vi^r, 'gwen-

Guinness
  Irish stout   GIN-uhs   'ginəs

Guion
  David Wendel Fentress, *US songwriter*   GĪ-uhn   'gɑiən

Guipúzcoa
  prov, Spain   gē-P$\overline{OO}$TH-kuh-wuh, gē-P$\overline{OO}$S-kuh-wuh   giː'puːθkəwə, giː'puːskəwə

Guisborough
  town, England   GIZ-buh-ruh, GIZ-buhr-uh, GIZ-bruh   'gizbə-rə, 'gizbər-ə, 'gizbrə

Guise
  commune, France   GĒZ   giːz

Guiseley
  town, England   GĪZ-lē   'gɑizliˑ

Guisewite
  Cathy, *US cartoonist*   GĪZ-WĪT   'gɑiz,wɑit

Guislain
  pers. name, French   gēs-LE^n giːslē

Guiyang, Kuei-yang, Kweiyang
  city, China   GWĀ-YAHNG   'gweː'jaŋ

Guizhou, Kweichow
  prov, China   GWĀ-JŌ   'gweː'dʒoː

Gujarat
  state, India   G$\overline{OO}$-juh-RAHT, GUJ-uh-RAHT   ‚guːdʒə'rɑt, ‚gudʒə'rɑt

Gujarati
  lang., people, India   G$\overline{OO}$-juh-RAHT-ē, GUJ-uh-RAHT-ē   ‚guːdʒə'rɑtiˑ, ‚gudʒə'rɑtiˑ

GULAG
  USSR prison system   G$\overline{OO}$-LAHG   'guː,lɑg

Gulick
  Luther Halsey, *US educator*   G(Y)$\overline{OO}$-lik   'g(j)uːlik

Gulielmus
  pers. name, Latin   GY$\overline{OO}$-lē-EL-muhs   ‚gjuːliː'elməs

Gullah
  black Americans on coast of SC, GA, FL; their dialect of English   GUHL-uh   'gələ

Gulliver
  Lemuel, *hero of* Gulliver's Travels, *J. Swift*   GUHL-uh-vuhr   'gələvə^r

---

Key (col. 2):   a: **fad**   ā: **fade**   ah: **father**   ar: **marry**   aw: **law**   e: **fed**   ē: **feed**   er: **merry**   i: **hid**   ī: **hide**   ō: **coat**   ōō: **boot**
oi: **boy**   ow: **now**   u: **put**   uh: **above**   uhr: **bird**   ch: **chop**   ng: **ring**   sh: **show**   th: **thick**   <u>th</u>: **this**   zh: **measure**

Gullstrand

    Allvar, *Swedish ophthamologist*   GUHL-STRAHN(D)   'gəl͵strɑːn(d)
    (Nobel 1911)

Gulpener

    Dutch beer   ḠUL-puh-nuhr, GUL-   'ɣulpənər, 'gul-

Gum

    department store, Moscow   GOO̅M   'guːm

Gumbel

    Bryant, *US TV broadcaster*   GUHM-buhl   'gəmbəl

Gund

    US mfrs.   GUHND, GUND   'gənd, 'gund

Gundagai

    town, shire, Australia   GUHN-duh-GĪ   'gəndə͵gai

Gundel

    restaurant, Budapest, Hungary   GOO̅N-duhl   'guːndəl

Gunderson

    pers. name   GUHN-duhr-suhn   'gəndəʳsən

Gundlach-Bundschu

    winery, CA   GUND-lah<u>kh</u> BUND-SHO̅O̅   'gundlɑx 'bund͵ʃuː

Gunga Din

    Kipling character   GUHNG-guh DIN   ͵gəŋgə 'din

Guni

    Biblical name   G(Y)OO̅-nī, go̅o̅-NĒ   'g(j)uːnɑi, guːˈniː

Gunite

    Biblical name   G(Y)OO̅-NĪT   'g(j)uː͵nɑit

Gunnar

    1. pers. name, Icelandic   GUEN-nahr   'gynnɑr
    2. Norwegian   GUN-nahr   'gunnɑr
    3. Swedish   GUHN-nahr   'gənnɑːr

Gunnbjorn

    mtn., Greenland   GUN-BYUHRN, $ GUN-BYAWRN   'gun͵bjœːrn, $ 'gun͵bjɔːʳn

Gunnedah

    town, Australia   GUHN-uh-dah   'gənədɑː

Günter

    pers. name, German   GUEN-tuhr   'gyntəʳ

Gunther

    1. pers. name   GUHN-thuhr   'gənθəʳ
    2. German   GUN-tuhr   'guntəʳ

Günther

    pers. name, German   GUEN-tuhr   'gyntəʳ

Gunung Agung

    see Agung, Gunung

Gunung Awu

    see Awu, Gunung

Gur

    Biblical name   GUR, GOO̅R   'guʳ, 'guːr

Gurage

    lang., people, Ethiopia   go̅o̅-RAH-gā   guːˈrɑgeː

Guralnik

    David, *US lexicographer*   guh-RAL-nik   gəˈrælnik

Gur-baal

    Biblical name   guhr-BĀ(-uh)l, GO̅O̅R-BAH-AHL   gəʳˈbeː(ə)l, ͵guːrˈbɑ͵ɑl

Gurdjieff

    Armenian Sufi mystic in West   guhr-JEF, guhr-JĒF   gəʳˈdʒef, gəʳˈdʒiːf

---

Foreign Sounds: **ue**: *Fr.* **rue**, *Ger.* **füllen** **uh(r)**: *Fr.* **boeuf**, *Ger.* **Höhle** <u>kh</u>: *Ger.* **ich**, *Scot.* **loch** **ḡ**: *Sp.* **amigo** **y**: *Sp.* **hablar** **hl**: *Welsh* **Llanelli**. CAPITALS: primary stress. SMALL CAPS: secondary stress. $: U.S. pron. ©: British pron.

Gurkha
  Nepalese soldier in British or Indian   GUR-kuh, GUHR-kuh   ˈguᵊkə, ˈgəᵊkə
  army

Gurkhali [Nepali]
  lang., Nepal, Sikkim   gur-KAHL-ē, GUHR-KAHL-ē   guᵊˈkɑliˑ, ˌgəᵊˈkɑliˑ

Gurma
  lang., people, Togo, Burkina Faso   GUR-muh   ˈguᵊmə

Gursel
  Cemal, *president, Turkey*   guhr-SEL   gəᵊˈsel

Gus
  pers. name   GUHS   ˈgəs

Gusev, Gussev
  city, Russia   GŌO-suhf   ˈguːsəf

Gustaf
  1. pers. name, Finnish   GUS-TAHF   ˈgusˌtɑːf
  2. German   GUS-TAHF   ˈgusˌtɑf
  3. Swedish   GUHS-TAHV   ˈgəsˌtɑv

Gustav
  1. pers. name, Danish   GUS-TAHV   ˈgusˌtɑv
  2. German   GUS-TAHF   ˈgusˌtɑf
  3. Swedish   GUHS-TAHV   ˈgəsˌtɑv

Gustave
  1. pers. name   GUS-TAHV   ˈgusˌtɑv
  2. French   gue-TAHV   gyːtɑːv
  3. German   GUS-TAHV-uh   ˈgusˌtɑvə

Gustavo
  1. pers. name, Portuguese   gōosh-TAH-vōo, gōos-   guːʃˈtɑːvuː, guːs-
  2. Spanish   gōo-STAHV-ō   guːˈstɑvoː

Gustavus
  pers. name, Latin   guhs-TĀ-vuhs, gus-   gəsˈteːvəs, gus-

Gustavus Adolphus
  Swedish king; college, MN   guh-STAHV-uhs uh-DAHL-fuhs,   gəˈstɑvəs əˈdɑlfəs, əˈdɔːlfəs
       uh-DAWL-fuhs

Gustaw
  pers. name, Polish   GŌOS-tahf   ˈguːstɑːf

Gusztav
  pers. name, Hungarian   GUS-tahv   ˈgustɑv

Gutenberg
  Johannes, *German inventor of*   GŌOT-n-BERK, Ⓢ GŌOT-n-BUHRG   ˈguːtṇˌbeᵊk, Ⓢ ˈguːtṇˌbəᵊg
  printing

Guthrie
  Arlo, *folk singer;* Woody, *folk singer*   GUHTH-rē   ˈgəθriˑ
  & activist

Gutians
  ancient conquerors of Babylonia   GŌO-sh(ē-)uhnz   ˈguːʃ(iː)ənz

Gutierre
  pers. name, Spanish   gōo-TYER-ā   guːˈtjereː

Gutzon
  pers. name (G. Borglum)   GUHT-suhn   ˈgətsən

Guy
  1. pers. name   GĪ   ˈgɑi
  2. French   GĒ   giː

Guyana
  republic, S. America   gī-AHN-uh, gī-AN-uh   gɑiˈɑnə, gɑiˈænə

Key (col. 2):   a: fad   ā: fade   ah: father   ar: marry   aw: law   e: fed   ē: feed   er: merry   i: hid   ī: hide   ō: coat   ōō: boot
oi: boy   ow: now   u: put   uh: above   uhr: bird   ch: chop   ng: ring   sh: show   th: thick   th̲: this   zh: measure

Guyandotte
   river, WV   GĪ-uhn-DAHT   'gaiən‚dɑt

Guyanese
   pert. to Guyana   GĪ-uh-NĒZ, -NĒS   ‚gaiə'niːz, -'niːs

Guyenne
   prov, France   gē-EN   giːen

Guy Fawkes Day
   English celebration of capture of G.   GĪ FAWKS DĀ   ‚gai 'fɔːks ‚deː
   Fawkes, November 5

Guymon
   city, TX   GĪ-muhn   'gaimən

Guyra
   town, Australia   GĪ-ruh   'gairə

Guzmán Blanco
   Antonio, *Venezuelan politician*   go͞o-SMAHN BLAHNG-kō   guː'smɑn 'blaŋkoː

Gwalior
   city, India   GWAHL-ē-AWR   'gwaliː‚ɔːʳ

Gwen
   pers. name   GWEN   'gwen

Gwendolen, -lin, -lyn
   pers. name   GWEN-duh-luhn, GWEN-dl-uhn   'gwendələn, 'gwendḷən

Gwendoline
   pers. name   GWEN-duh-luhn, GWEN-dl-uhn,   'gwendələn, 'gwendḷən,
                            GWEN-duh-LĪN   'gwendə‚lain

Gwenhwyfar [Guinevere]
   Arthur's queen in Welsh legend   gwen-HUI-VAHR   gwen'hui‚vɑʳ

Gwenllïan
   pers. name, Welsh   gwen-HLĒ-ahn   gwen'ḷiːɑn

Gwent
   county, ancient kingdom, Wales   GWENT   'gwent

Gwerful Mechain
   Welsh poetess   GWER-vil MEKH-ĪN   'gweʳvil 'mex‚ain

Gwilym
   pers. name, Welsh   GWIL-im   'gwilim

Gwinnett
   county, GA   gwin-ET   gwin'et

Gwladys
   pers. name, Welsh   GWLAHD-is, ⑤ GLAD-uhs   'gwlɑdis, ⑤ 'glædəs

Gwyn
   pers. name   GWIN   'gwin

Gwynedd
   county, ancient kingdom, Wales   GWIN-eth, GWIN-uhth   'gwineð, 'gwinəð

Gwynedd-Mercy
   College, PA   GWIN-uhd-MUHR-sē, GWIN-uhth   'gwinəd'məʳsiˑ, 'gwinəð

Gwynne
   pers. name   GWIN   'gwin

Gyatso
   Tenzin, *Tibetan leader, the Dalai*   GYAHT-sō   'gjatsoː
   Lama (Nobel 1989)

Gyges
   king of Lydia   JĪ-JĒZ, GĪ-JĒZ   'dʒai‚dʒiːz, 'gai‚dʒiːz

Gymnasium
   1. Greek school   jim-NĀ-zē-uhm, -NĀ-zhuhm   dʒim'neːziːəm, -'neːʒəm
   2. German school   gim-NAHZ-ē-um   gim'nɑziːum

Foreign Sounds: ue: *Fr.* **rue**, *Ger.* **füllen**   uh(r): *Fr.* **boeuf**, *Ger.* **Höhle**   kh: *Ger.* **ich**, *Scot.* **loch**   ḡ: *Sp.* **amigo**   v: *Sp.* **hablar**
hl: *Welsh* **Llanelli**.   CAPITALS: primary stress.   SMALL CAPS: secondary stress.   ⑤: U.S. pron.   ⑥: British pron.

Gympie
   city, Australia   GIM-pē   ˈgimpi·

Gyo
   pers. name (G. Obata)   GYŌ   ˈgjoː

Gyöngyös
   city, Hungarian   DYUH(R)N-ᴅʏᴜʜ(ʀ)s,   ˈɖœːnˌɖœːs, Ⓢ ˈdʒəʳnˌdʒəʳs
                            Ⓢ JUHRN-ᴊᴜʜʀs

Győr
   city, Hungarian   DYUHR, Ⓢ JUHR   ˈɖœːʳ, Ⓢ ˈdʒəʳ

György
   pers. name, Hungarian DYUHRD, Ⓢ JUHR-jē   ˈɖœrɖ, Ⓢ ˈdʒəʳdʒi·

Gypsophila
   plant   jip-SAHF-uh-luh   dʒipˈsɑfələ

Gypsy [Romany]
   people, lang., South Asia, Near East, JIP-sē   ˈdʒipsi·
     Europe, USA

Gyrfalcon
   hawk   JUHR-FAL-kuhn, -FAWL-kuhn,   ˈdʒəʳˌfælkən, -ˌfɔːlkən,
                          -FAW-kuhn   -ˌfɔːkən

H

Ha
    lang., Africa   HAH   'hɑ

Haag, Den [Hague, The]
    city, Netherlands   duhn HAHḠ   dən 'hɑːɣ

Häagen-Dazs
    ice cream brand   HAHG-uhn-DAHZ, -DAHS   'hɑgən,dɑz, -,dɑs

Haahashtari
    Biblical name   HĀ-uh-HASH-tuh-RĪ,   ,heːə'hæʃtə,rɑi,
                hah-AHKH-AHSH-tah-RĒ   hɑ,ɑx,ɑʃtɑ'riː

Haakon
    county, SD   HAK-uhn   'hækən

Haarlem, Harlem
    city, Netherlands   HAHR-luhm   'hɑʳləm

Haavelmo
    Trygve, *Norwegian economist (Nobel*   HAHV-uhl-MŌ   'hɑvəl,moː
    1989)

Habacuc
    Old Testament book   HAB-uh-KUHK, -KUK; huh-BAK-uhk   'hæbə,kək, -,kuk; hə'bækək

Habaiah
    Biblical name   huh-BĀ-uh, huh-BĪ-uh, KHAH-vah-YAH   hə'beːə, hə'bɑiə, ,xɑvɑ'jɑ

Habakkuk
    1. Old Testament book, pers. name   HAB-uh-KUHK, -KUK; huh-BAK-uhk   'hæbə,kək, -,kuk; hə'bækək
    2. German   HAH-bah-KOO̅K, -KUK   'hɑbɑ,kuːk, -,kuk

Habaziniah, Habazziniah
    Biblical name   HAB-uh-zuh-NĪ-uh, KHAH-vaht-sin-YAH   ,hæbəzə'nɑiə, ,xɑvɑtsin'jɑ

Habdank
    pers. name, Polish   HAHB-DAHNGK   'hɑːb,dɑːŋk

Haber
    Fritz, *German chemist (Nobel 1918)*   HAHB-uhr   'hɑbəʳ

Habersham
    county, GA   HAB-uhr-SHAM, HAB-uhr-shuhm   'hæbəʳ,ʃæm, 'hæbəʳʃəm

Habib
    Philip Charles, *US foreign service*   hah-BĒB   hɑ'biːb
    officer; pers. name, Arabic

Habor
    Biblical name   HĀ-BAWR, khah-VŌR   'heː,bɔːʳ, xɑ'voːr

Habsburg, Hapsburg
    German royal house   HAHPS-BURK, Ⓢ HAPS-BUHRG   'hɑps,buʳk, Ⓢ 'hæps,bəʳg

Hacaliah, Hachaliah
    Biblical name   HAK-uh-LĪ-uh, KHAHKH-ahl-YAH   ,hækə'lɑiə, ,xɑxɑl'jɑ

Hachette
    Louis Christophe François, *French*   ah-SHET   ɑʃet
    editor and publisher

Foreign Sounds: ue: *Fr.* **rue**, *Ger.* **füllen**   uh(r): *Fr.* **boeuf**, *Ger.* **Höhle**   kh: *Ger.* **ich**, *Scot.* **loch**   ḡ: *Sp.* **amigo**   v: *Sp.* **hablar**
hl: *Welsh* **Llanelli**.   CAPITALS: primary stress.   SMALL CAPS: secondary stress.   Ⓢ: U.S. pron.   Ⓔ: British pron.

Hachilah
Biblical name   huh-KĪ-luh, HAK-uh-luh,   hə'kailə, 'hækələ, ˌxɑxiː'lɑ
                                   KHAHKH-ē-LAH

Hachiro
pers. name, Japanese   hah-chē-rō   hatʃiːroː
Hachmoni
Biblical name   HAK-muh-NĪ, hak-MŌ-nī,   'hækməˌnɑi, hæk'moːnɑi,
                                   KHAHKH-mō-NĒ   ˌxɑxmoː'niː

Hachmonite
Biblical name   HAK-muh-NĪT   'hækməˌnɑit
Hackensack
city, NJ   HAK-uhn-SAK   'hækənˌsæk
Hacker-Pschorr
German beer   HAHK-uhrp-SHAWR   'hakəʳpˌʃɔːʳ
Hackett
Buddy, *US comedian, actor*   HAK-uht   'hækət
Hackman
Gene, *US actor*   HAK-muhn   'hækmən
Hackney
borough, England; carriage   HAK-nē   'hæckniˑ
Hadad
Biblical name   HĀ-DAD, HAD-AD, huh-DAHD,   'heːˌdæd, 'hædˌæd, hə'dɑd,
                                   khah-DAHD   xɑ'dɑd

Hadad-ezer [Hadar-ezer]
Biblical name   HAD-AD-Ē-zuhr, HAD-uh-DĒ-;   'hædˌæd'iːzəʳ, ˌhædə'diː-;
                                   HAHD-AHD-EZ-er   ˌhɑdˌɑd'ezer

Hadad-rimmon
Biblical name   HĀ-DAD-RIM-uhn, HAH-DAHD-ri-MŌN   'heːˌdæd'rimən,
                                                                       'hɑˌdɑdri'moːn

Hadar
Biblical name   HĀ-DAHR, hah-DAHR   'heːˌdɑʳ, hɑ'dɑr
Hadar-ezer
Biblical name   HAD-AHR-Ē-zuhr, HAD-uh-RĒ-;   'hædˌɑr'iːzəʳ, ˌhædə'riː-;
                                   HAHD-AHR-EZ-er   ˌhɑdˌɑr'ezer

Hadashah
Biblical name   huh-DASH-uh, KHAHD-ah-SHAH   hə'dæʃə, ˌxɑdɑ'ʃɑ
Hadassah
1. *Jewish women's benevolent*   khuh-DAHS-uh, huh-DAHS-uh,   xə'dɑsə, hə'dɑsə, hɑ'dɑsə
   organization   hah-DAHS-uh
2. *Biblical name*   huh-DAS-uh, KHAHD-ah-SAH   hə'dæsə, ˌxɑdɑ'sɑ
Hadattah
Biblical name   huh-DAT-uh, KHAHD-ah-TAH   hə'dæt̪ə, ˌxɑdɑ'tɑ
Haddam
town, CT   HAD-uhm   'hædəm
Hades
Greek god of the Underworld; abode HĀD-ĒZ   'heːdˌiːz
   of dead, Hell
Hadid
pers. name   hah-DĒD   hɑ'diːd
Hadj [Hajj]
pilgrimage to Mecca   HAHJ   'hɑdʒ
Hadji
one who has made a pilgrimage to   HAHJ-ē   'hɑdʒiˑ
   Mecca

Key (col. 2):   a: fad   ā: fade   ah: father   ar: marry   aw: law   e: fed   ē: feed   er: merry   i: hid   ī: hide   ō: coat   ōō: boot
oi: boy   ow: now   u: put   uh: above   uhr: bird   ch: chop   ng: ring   sh: show   th: thick   th̲: this   zh: measure

Hadlai
  Biblical name — HAD-lā-Ī, <u>kh</u>ahd-LĪ — 'hædleːˌɑi, xɑd'lɑi
Hadoram
  Biblical name — huh-DAWR-AM, HAHD-ō-RAHM — hə'dɔːrˌæm, ˌhɑdoː'rɑm
Hadrach
  Biblical name — HĀ-DRAK, HA-DRAK, <u>kh</u>ah-DRAH<u>KH</u> — 'heːˌdræk, 'hæˌdræk, xɑ'drɑx
Hadrian
  Roman emperor — HĀ-drē-uhn — 'heːdriːən
Hadrianus
  pers. name, Dutch — HAH-drē-AHN-ues — ˌhɑdriː'ɑnys
Hadrosaurus
  dinosaur — HA-druh-SAWR-uhs — ˌhædrə'sɔːrəs
Haeckel
  Ernest, *German scientist* — HEK-uhl — 'hekəl
Haeckelism
  doctrines of Haeckel — HEK-uh-LIZ-uhm — 'hekəˌlizəm
Haeleph
  Biblical name — ha-Ē-LEF, HĀ-LEF, hah-EL-EF — hæ'iːˌlef, 'heːˌlef, hɑ'elˌef
Haemon
  son of Creon — HĒ-muhn — 'hiːmən
Haerhpin [Harbin]
  city, China — HAH-UHR-BIN, HAH-ER-BIN — 'hɑ'əʳ'bin, 'hɑ'eʳ'bin
Hafez
  pers. name, Arabic — <u>kh</u>ah-FEZ, hah-FEZ — xɑ'fez, hɑ'fez
Haflinger
  horse breed — HAF-ling-uhr — 'hæfliŋəʳ
hafnium
  element — HAF-nē-uhm — 'hæfniːəm
Hagab
  Biblical name — HĀ-GAB, <u>kh</u>ah-GAHV — 'heːˌgæb, xɑ'gɑv
Hagaba, Hagabah
  Biblical name — HAG-uh-buh, <u>KH</u>AHG-ah-VAH — 'hægəbə, ˌxɑgɑ'vɑ
Haganah
  Jewish underground militia — <u>KH</u>AHG-uh-NAH, HAHG-uh-NAH — ˌxɑgə'nɑ, ˌhɑgə'nɑ
Hagar
  pers. name — HĀ-guhr, HĀ-GAHR — 'heːgəʳ, 'heːˌgɑʳ
Hagarite
  Biblical name — HAG-uh-RĪT — 'hægəˌrɑit
Hagen
  Uta, *US Actress* — HAH-guhn — 'hɑgən
Hagerstown
  city, MD — HĀ-guhrz-TOWN — 'heːgəʳzˌtɑun
Hagerup
  pers. name, Norwegian — HAH-guh-rup — 'hɑgərup
Haggadah, the [Aggada]
  part of Jewish Talmud — HAHG-uh-DAH, huh-GAHD-uh, huh-GAWD-uh — ˌhɑgə'dɑ, hə'gɑdə, hə'gɔːdə
Haggai
  Old Testament book — HAG-ē-Ī, HAG-Ī — 'hægiːˌɑi, 'hægˌɑi
Haggard
  Sir Henry Rider, *English novelist;* HAG-uhrd — 'hægəʳd
  Merle, *US singer, songwriter*
Haggedolim
  Biblical name — HAG-uh-DŌ-lim, HAHG-uh-dō-LĒM — ˌhægə'doːlim, ˌhɑgədoː'liːm

---

Foreign Sounds: ue: *Fr.* **rue**, *Ger.* **füllen** uh(r): *Fr.* b**oeuf**, *Ger.* H**öhle** <u>kh</u>: *Ger.* i**ch**, *Scot.* lo**ch** g̱: *Sp.* ami**go** v: *Sp.* ha**b**lar
hl: *Welsh* **Ll**anelli. CAPITALS: primary stress. SMALL CAPS: secondary stress. Ⓢ: U.S. pron. Ⓔ: British pron.

Haggeri
   Biblical name   huh-JIR-Ī, hahg-RĒ   hə'dʒir₁ɑi, hɑg'riː

Haggerty
   Dan, *actor*   HAG-uhrt-ē   'hægə˞ʈiˑ

Haggi
   Biblical name   HAG-Ī, khah-GĒ   'hæg₁ɑi, xɑ'giː

Haggiah
   Biblical name   huh-GĪ-uh, KHAH-gē-YAH   hə'gɑiə, ₁xɑgiː'jɑ

Haggite
   Biblical name   HAG-ĪT   'hæg₁ɑit

Haggith
   Biblical name   HAG-uhth, khah-GĒT   'hægəθ, xɑ'giːt

Hagia Sophia [Santa Sophia, Aya Sofia]
   museum, mosque, church, Istanbul   HAHJ-ē-uh sō-FĒ-uh   ₁hɑdʒiːə soː'fiːə

Hagiographa
   a Jewish division of the Old   HAG-ē-AHG-ruh-fuh   ₁hægiː'ɑgrəfə
     Testament

Hagler
   Marvelous Marvin, *US boxer*   HAG-luhr   'hæglə˞

Hagman
   Larry, *US actor*   HAG-muhn   'hægmən

Hagri
   Biblical name   HAG-RĪ, hahg-RĒ   'hæg₁rɑi, hɑg'riː

Hagrite
   Biblical name   HAG-RĪT   'hæg₁rɑit

Hague, The
   city, Netherlands   thuh HĀG   ðə 'heːg

Hahn
   Otto, *German chemist (Nobel 1944)*   HAHN   'hɑn

Haida
   N. American people   HĪD-uh   'hɑidə

Haifa
   district, Israel   KHĪ-fuh, HĪ-fuh   'xɑifə, 'hɑifə

Haig
   pers. name   HĀG   'heːg

Haigh
   pers. name   HĀG, HĀ   'heːg, 'heː

Haight-Ashbury
   San Francisco hippie district   HĀT-ASH-BER-ē   'heːʈ'æʃ₁beriˑ

Haile Selassie [Ras Tafari]
   emperor of Ethiopia   HĪ-luh suh-lah-SĒ, Ⓢ HĪ-lē suh-LAS-ē,   'hɑilə sələ'siː, Ⓢ 'hɑiliː
                                 suh-LAHS-ē   sə'læsiː, sə'lɑsiː

Hailey
   Arthur, *British/Canadian author*   HĀ-lē   'heːliˑ

Haim
   pers. name, Hebrew   khī-(Y)IM, KHĪ-(y)im   xɑi'(j)im, 'xɑi(j)im

Hainan
   island, China   HĪ-NAHN   'hɑi'nɑn

Hainaut
   prov, Belgium   (h)ā-NŌ   (h)eː'noː

Haines
   division, AK; pers. name   HĀNZ   'heːnz

Haiphong
   seaport, Vietnam   HĪ-FAWNG, HĪ-FAHNG   'hɑi'fɔːŋ, 'hɑi'fɑŋ

Key (col. 2):   a: **fad**   ā: **fade**   ah: **father**   ar: **marry**   aw: **law**   e: **fed**   ē: **feed**   er: **merry**   i: **hid**   ī: **hide**   ō: **coat**   ōō: **boot**
oi: **boy**   ow: **now**   u: **put**   uh: **above**   uhr: **bird**   ch: **chop**   ng: **ring**   sh: **show**   th: **thick**   <u>th</u>: **this**   zh: **measure**

Haiti
republic, West Indies HĀT-ē 'heːʈiˑ
Haitian
lang., native, Haiti HĀ-shuhn, HĀT-ē-uhn 'heːʃən, 'heːʈiːən
Hajj [Hadj]
pilgrimage to Mecca HAHJ 'hɑdʒ
Hakeem
pers. name (H. Olajuwon) hah-KĒM hɑ'kiːm
Hakka
lang., China HAHK-AH, HAK-uh 'hɑk'ɑ, 'hækə
Hakkâri, Hakâri [Cölemerık]
town, Turkey HAHK-(y)ah-RĒ ˌhɑk(j)ɑ'riː
Hakkatan
Biblical name HAK-uh-TAN, HAHK-ah-TAHN 'hækəˌtæn, ˌhɑkɑ'tɑn
Hakkoz
Biblical name HAK-AHZ, hah-KŌTS 'hækˌɑz, hɑ'koːts
Hakluyt
Richard, *English geographer* HAK-LŌŌT, HAK-l-WIT, HAK-lit 'hækˌluːt, 'hæklˌwit, 'hæklit
Hakodate
island, Japan hahk-ō-daht-ā hɑkoːdateˑ
Hakupha
Biblical name huh-K(Y)ŌŌ-fuh, KHAH-kōō-FAH hə'k(j)uːfə, ˌxɑkuː'fɑ
Hal
pers. name HAL 'hæl
Halab, Haleb
city, Syria huh-LEB hə'leb
Halafian
prehistoric Near Eastern culture huh-LĀ-fē-uhn hə'leːfiːən
Halah
Biblical name HĀ-luh, khuh-LAHKH 'heːlə, xə'lɑx
Halak
Biblical name HĀ-LAK, khah-LAHK 'heːˌlæk, xɑ'lɑk
Halakah, Halachah
The, *part of Jewish Talmud* HAHL-uh-KHAH, hah-LAWKH-uh, ˌhɑlə'xɑ, hɑ'lɔːxə, hə'lɑxə
huh-LAHKH-uh
Halas
George, *sports personality* HAL-uhs 'hæləs
Halberstam
David, *US journalist, author* HAL-buhr-STAM 'hælbərˌstæm
Halb-und-Halb
orange liqueur HAHLP-unt-HAHLP 'hɑːlpunt'hɑːlp
Haldan
pers. name HAWL-duhn, HAL-duhn, HAHL-duhn 'hɔːldən, 'hældən, 'hɑldən
Haldane
J. B. S., *scientist; pers. name* HAWL-DĀN, HAWL-duhn 'hɔːlˌdeːn, 'hɔːldən
Haldeman
Harry R., *former US government* HAWL-duh-muhn 'hɔːldəmən
official; Joe William, *US novelist*
Haldeman
Harry Robbins (H. R.), *US* HAWL-duh-muhn 'hɔːldəmən
government official
Hale
pers. name HĀL 'heːl
Haleakala
National Park, *volcano, HI* HAHL-ē-AHK-uh-LAH ˌhɑliːˌɑkə'lɑ

Halevi

   pers. name   hah-LĀ-vē   ha'leːviˑ

Haley

   Alex, *US author; pers. name*   HĀ-lē   'heːliˑ

Halfdan

   1. pers. name, Danish   HAHLV-DAHN   'haːlvˌdɑːn

   2. Norwegian   HAHLV-DAHN   'halvˌdan

Halhul

   Biblical name   HAL-HUHL, k͟hahl-K͟HO͞OL   'hælˌhəl, xɑl'xuːl

Hali

   Biblical name   HĀ-LĪ, k͟hah-LĒ   'heːˌlai, xa'liː

Halicarnassus

   ancient city, Asia Minor   HAL-i-KAHR-NAS-uhs   ˌhæliˌkɑrˈnæsəs

Halifax

   city, Canada; borough, England; US   HAL-uh-FAKS   'hæləˌfæks
   pl. name

Halirrhothius

   son of Poseidon and Euryte   HAL-uh-RŌ-thē-uhs   ˌhæləˈroːθiːəs

Halldór

   pers. name, Icelandic   HAHD-l-DAWR   'hadl̩ˌdɔːr

Halle

   1. Morris, *US linguist; county, city,*   HAHL-uh   'halə
   Germany

   2. pers. name (H. Berry)   HAL-ē, HAHL-ē   'hæliˑ, 'haliˑ

Halley

   Edmund, *English astronomer*   HAL-ē, HĀ-lē, HAW-lē   'hæliˑ, 'heːliˑ, 'hɔːliˑ

Halley's

   comet   HAL-ēz, HĀ-lēz, HAW-lēz   'hæliˑz, 'heːliˑz, 'hɔːliˑz

Hallgrimur

   pers. name, Icelandic   HAHD-l-GRĒ-muer   'hadl̩ˌgriːmyr

Halliwell

   Park, *ballpark, Pocatello, ID*   HAL-uh-WEL, HAHL-uh-WEL, -wuhl   'hæləˌwel, 'haləˌwel, -wəl

Hallohesh

   Biblical name   huh-LŌ-HESH, HAHL-ō-K͟HESH   hə'loːˌheʃ, ˌhaloːˈxeʃ

Halloween

   October 31   HAL-uh-WĒN, HAHL-   ˌhæləˈwiːn, ˌhal-

Hallowell

   city, ME   HAHL-uh-WEL, -wuhl   'haləˌwel, -wəl

Hallstatt

   town, Austria; archaeological period HAWL-STAT, HAHL-SHTAHT   'hɔːlˌstæt, 'halˌʃtat

Halmahera

   island, sea, Pacific   HAL-muh-HER-uh, HAHL-   ˌhælməˈherə, ˌhal-

Hals

   Frans, *Dutch painter*   HAHLS   'hals

Halstead, -sted

   pers. name   HAWL-stuhd, -STED   'hɔːlstəd, -ˌsted

Ham

   Noah's son   HAM, K͟HAHM   'hæm, 'xam

Hamadān

   city, Iran   HAHM-uh-DAHN, HAM-uh-DAN,   ˌhaməˈdan, ˌhæməˈdæn,
                       HAHM-uh-DAHN   'haməˌdan

Hamadryad

   tree nymph   HAM-uh-DRĪ-uhd, -DRĪ-AD   ˌhæməˈdraiəd, -ˈdraiˌæd

Hamamatsu

   town, Japan   hahm-ah-maht-so͞o   hamamatsuː

Key (col. 2):   a: f**a**d   ā: f**a**de   ah: f**a**ther   ar: m**a**rry   aw: l**a**w   e: f**e**d   ē: f**ee**d   er: m**e**rry   i: h**i**d   ī: h**i**de   ō: c**oa**t   o͞o: b**oo**t
oi: b**oy**   ow: n**ow**   u: p**u**t   uh: **a**bove   uhr: b**ir**d   ch: **ch**op   ng: ri**ng**   sh: **sh**ow   th: **th**ick   t͟h: **th**is   zh: mea**s**ure

Haman
  Biblical name   HĀ-muhn   ˈheːmən

Hamar
  1. city, Norway   HAHM-AHR   ˈhɑmˌɑʳ
  2. pers. name   HĀ-muhr   ˈheːməʳ

Hamath
  Biblical name   HĀ-MATH, <u>kh</u>ah-MAHT   ˈheːˌmæθ, xɑˈmat

Hamathite
  Biblical name   HĀ-muh-THĪT   ˈheːməˌθɑit

Hamath-zobah
  Biblical name   HĀ-MATH-ZŌ-buh,   ˈheːˌmæθˈzoːbə,
           <u>kh</u>ah-MAHT-sō-VAH   xɑˈmatsoːˈva

Hambletonian
  horse   HAM-buhl-TŌ-nē-uhn   ˌhæmbəlˈtoːniːən

Hamburg
  1. city, Germany   HAHM-BURK, ⓢ HAM-BUHRG   ˈhɑmˌbuʳk, ⓢ ˈhæmˌbəʳg
  2. US pl. name   HAM-BUHRG   ˈhæmˌbəʳg

Hamel
  Veronica, *US actress*   HAM-uhl   ˈhæməl

Hamelin
  town, Germany   HAM-(uh-)luhn   ˈhæm(ə)lən

Hameln [Hamelin]
  town, Germany   HAHM-uhln   ˈhɑməln

Hamilcar
  Carthaginian general   huh-MIL-KAHR, HAM-uhl-KAHR   həˈmilˌkɑʳ, ˈhæməlˌkɑʳ

Hamill
  Dorothy, *US figure skater;* Mark, *US*   HAM-uhl   ˈhæməl
    actor

Hamilton
  Alexander, *US politician; pl. name;*   HAM-uhl-tuhn, HAM-uhlt-n   ˈhæməltən, ˈhæməltn̩
    pers. name

Hamish
  pers. name   HĀ-mish   ˈheːmiʃ

Hamite
  biblical tribe   HAM-ĪT   ˈhæmˌɑit

Hamito-Semitic
  Afroasiatic lang. group   HAM-uht-ō-suh-MIT-ik   ˌhæməṭoːsəˈmiṭik

Hamline
  University, *MN*   HAM-luhn   ˈhæmlən

Hamlisch
  Marvin, *US composer*   HAM-lish   ˈhæmliʃ

Hammacher Schlemmer
  NY retailers   HAM-uh-kuhr SHLEM-uhr   ˌhæməkəʳ ˈʃleməʳ

Hammarskjöld
  Dag, *Swedish statesman, U.N.*   HAHM-uhr-SHUHLD, HAM-, -SHULD,   ˈhɑməʳˌʃəld, ˈhæm-, -ˌʃuld,
    official (Nobel 1961)   -SHĒLD   -ˌʃiːld

Hammath
  Biblical name   HAM-uhth, <u>kh</u>ah-MAHT   ˈhæməθ, xɑˈmat

Hammedatha
  Biblical name   HAM-i-DĀ-thuh, hah-muh-DAH-tah   ˌhæmiˈdeːθə, hɑməˈdɑtɑ

Hammer
  Armand, *US oil co. executive*   HAM-uhr   ˈhæməʳ

Hammerfest
  port, Norway   HAHM-uhr-FEST, HAM-uhr-FEST   ˈhɑməʳˌfest, ˈhæməʳˌfest

---

Foreign Sounds: ue: *Fr.* **rue**, *Ger.* f**ü**llen   uh(r): *Fr.* b**oeu**f, *Ger.* H**ö**hle   <u>kh</u>: *Ger.* i**ch**, *Scot.* lo**ch**   g̱: *Sp.* ami**g**o   v̱: *Sp.* ha**b**lar
hl: *Welsh* L**l**anelli.   CAPITALS: primary stress.   SMALL CAPS: secondary stress.   ⓢ: U.S. pron.   ⓔ: British pron.

Hammersmith and Fulham
  borough, England   HAM-uhr-SMITH uhn(d) FUL-uhm   ˈhæməʳˌsmiθ ən(d) ˈfuləm
Hammerstein
  Oscar II, *US musical lyricist*   HAM-uhr-STĪN, -STĒN   ˈhæməʳˌstain, -ˌstiːn
Hammett
  Dashiell, *US writer*   HAM-uht   ˈhæmət
Hammolecheth, Hammoleketh
  Biblical name   hah-MAHL-uh-KETH,   haˈmaləˌkeθ, ˌhamɔːˈlexet
       HAH-maw-LEKH-et
Hammon
  Biblical name   HAM-uhn, khah-MŌN   ˈhæmən, xaˈmoːn
Hammonasset
  river, CT   HAM-uh-NAS-uht   ˌhæməˈnæsət
Hammond
  Jay Sterner, *US politician*   HAM-uhnd   ˈhæmənd
Hammoth-dor
  Biblical name   HAM-uhth-DAWR, khah-MAWT-DAWR   ˈhæməθˌdɔːʳ, xaˌmɔːtˈdɔːr
Hammurabi
  Babylonian king, lawgiver   HAM-uh-RAHB-ē, HAHM-   ˌhæməˈrabiˑ, ˌham-
Ham Nghi
  Vietnamese emperor   HAHM uhng-HĒ   ˈham əŋˈhiː
Hamonah
  Biblical name   huh-MŌ-nuh, HAHM-ō-NAH   həˈmoːnə, ˌhamoːˈna
Hamon-gog
  Biblical name   HĀ-muhn-GAHG, hah-MŌN-GŌG   ˈheːmənˈgag, haˈmoːnˈgoːg
Hamor
  Biblical name   HĀ-mawr, khah-MŌR   ˈheːmɔːʳ, xaˈmoːr
Hampden
  county, MA; town, ME   HAM-duhn   ˈhæmdən
Hampshire
  county, MA, WV, England   HAM(P)-shuhr, -SHIR   ˈhæm(p)ʃəʳ, -ˌʃiʳ
Hampstead
  London borough   HAM(P)-stid, HAM(P)-STED   ˈhæm(p)stid, ˈhæm(p)ˌsted
Hampton
  US pl. name; pers. name   HAM(P)-tuhn   ˈhæm(p)tən
Hampton Roads
  channel, VA   HAM(P)-tuhn RŌDZ   ˌhæm(p)tən ˈroːdz
Hamstrom
  1st Sunday of Feb., Switzerland   HAHM-STRAWM   ˈhamˌstrɔːm
Hamsun
  Knut, *(pseudonym of* Knut   HAHM-suhn   ˈhamsən
     Pedersen), *Norwegian author*
     (Nobel 1920)
Hamtramck
  city, MI   ham-TRAM-ik   hæmˈtræmik
Hamuel, Hammuel
  Biblical name   HAM-yuh-wuhl, KHAHM-oo-EL   ˈhæmjəwəl, ˌxamuːˈel
Hamul
  Biblical name   HĀ-muhl, khah-MOOL   ˈheːməl, xaˈmuːl
Hamulite
  Biblical name   HĀ-m(y)uh-LĪT, HAM-(y)uh-LĪT   ˈheːm(j)əˌlait, ˈhæm(j)əˌlait
Hamutal
  Biblical name   ham-YOOT-l, KHAHM-oo-TAHL   hæmˈjuːtl̩, ˌxamuːˈtal
Han
  river, people, China   HAHN, HAN   ˈhan, ˈhæn

Key (col. 2):   a: fad   ā: fade   ah: father   ar: marry   aw: law   e: fed   ē: feed   er: merry   i: hid   ī: hide   ō: coat   oo: boot
oi: boy   ow: now   u: put   uh: above   uhr: bird   ch: chop   ng: ring   sh: show   th: thick   th: this   zh: measure

Hanahan
    city, SC — HAN-uh-HAN, -huhn — ˈhænəˌhæn, -hən

Hana Matsuri
    Flower Festival (April 8), Japan — hah-nah maht-sur-ē — hɑnɑ mɑtsuriˑ

Hanamaulu
    village, HI — HAHN-uh-MAH-o͞o-LO͞O — ˌhɑnəˈmɑuːˌluː

Hanameel [Hanamel]
    Biblical name — HAN-uh-MĒL, huh-NAM-ē-EL, KHAHN-ah-MEL — ˈhænəˌmiːl, həˈnæmiːˌel, ˌxɑnɑˈmel

Hanamel
    Biblical name — HAN-uh-MEL, KHAHN-ah-MEL — ˈhænəˌmel, ˌxɑnɑˈmel

Hanan
    Biblical name — HĀ-NAN, khah-NAHN — ˈheːˌnæn, xɑˈnɑn

Hananeel
    Biblical name — HAN-uh-NĒL, huh-NAN-ē-EL, KHAHN-ah-NEL — ˈhænəˌniːl, həˈnæniːˌel, ˌxɑnɑˈnel

Hananel [Hananeel]
    Biblical name — HAN-uh-NEL, huh-NAN-EL, KHAHN-ah-NEL — ˈhænəˌnel, həˈnænˌel, ˌxɑnɑˈnel

Hanani
    Biblical name — huh-NĀ-NĪ, khah-NAHN-ē — həˈneːˌnɑi, xɑˈnɑniˑ

Hananiah
    Biblical name — HAN-uh-NĪ-uh, KHAHN-ahn-YAH — ˌhænəˈnɑiə, ˌxɑnɑnˈjɑ

Hanapepe
    town, HI — HAHN-uh-PĀ-pā — ˌhɑnəˈpeːpeː

Handel
    Georg Frideric, British composer — HAN-dl — ˈhændl̩

Handelian
    pert. to Handel — han-DĒ-lē-uhn, han-DEL-ē-uhn — hænˈdiːliːən, hænˈdeliːən

Handy
    William Christopher (W. C.), US musician and composer — HAN-dē — ˈhændiˑ

Haneda
    airport, Tokyo — hahn-uhd-uh, hah-nād-uh — hɑnədə, haneːdə

Hanes
    Biblical name — HĀ-nēz, khah-NES — ˈheːniːz, xɑˈnes

Hanford
    pers. name — HAN-fuhrd — ˈhænfəʳd

Hangchow, Hangzhou
    city, China — HAHNG-JŌ, ⓢ HANG-CHOW — ˈhɑŋˈdʒoː, ⓢ ˈhæŋˈtʃɑu

Haniel
    Biblical name — HAN-ē-EL, KHAHN-ē-EL — ˈhæniːˌel, ˌxɑniːˈel

Hank
    pers. name — HANGK — ˈhæŋk

Hankou, Hankow
    port, China — HAHNG-KŌ, HAHN-KŌ, ⓢ HANG-KOW — ˈhɑŋˈkoː, ˈhɑnˈkoː, ⓢ ˈhæŋˈkɑu

Han Lu
    Chinese festival — HAHN LO͞O — ˈhɑn ˈluː

Hanna, Hannah
    pers. name — HAN-uh — ˈhænə

Hanna-Barbera Productions, Inc.
    US entertainment co. — HAN-uh-bahr-BER-uh — ˈhænəbɑʳˈberə

Hannathon
    Biblical name — HAN-uh-THAHN, KHAHN-ah-TAWN — ˈhænəˌθɑn, ˌxɑnɑˈtɔːn

---

Hannes
    pers. name, Swedish   HAHN-is   'haːnis
Hannibal
    1. Carthaginian general; pers. name   HAN-uh-buhl   'hænəbəl
    2. Dutch   HAHN-i-bahl   'hɑnibɑl
Hanniel
    Biblical name   HAN-ē-EL, K͟HAHN-ē-EL   'hæniː‚el, ‚xɑniː'el
Hanno
    Carthaginian admiral   HAN-ō   'hænoː
Hannover
    prov, city, Germany   hah-NŌ-fuhr, hah-NŌ-vuhr,   hɑ'noːfəʳ, hɑ'noːvəʳ,
                     ⓢ HAN-ō-vuhr, HAN-uh-vuhr   ⓢ 'hæn‚oːvəʳ, 'hænəvəʳ
Hanns
    pers. name, German   HAHNS   'hans
Hanoch
    Biblical name   HĀ-NAHK, k͟hah-NŌK͟H   'heː‚nɑk, xɑ'noːx
Hanochite
    Biblical name   HĀ-nah-KĪT   'heːnɑ‚kait
Hanoi
    city, Vietnam   ha-NOI, huh-NOI   hæ'nɔi, hə'nɔi
Hanover
    British royal house; English form of   HAN-ō-vuhr, HAN-uh-vuhr   'hæn‚oːvəʳ, 'hænəvəʳ
    Hannover
Hanoverian
    pert. to Hanover *or* Hannover   HAN-uh-VIR-ē-uhn, HAN-uh-VER-ē-uhn   ‚hænə'viriːən, ‚hænə'veriːən
Hans
    1. pers. name   HAHNZ, HAHNS   'hanz, 'hans
    2. Danish, Swedish   HAHNS   'haːns
    3. Dutch, German, Norwegian   HAHNS   'hans
Hansa
    merchant guild; Norwegian beer   HAHN-suh   'hansə
Hansard
    parliamentary proceedings   HAN-SAHRD, HAN-suhrd   'hæn‚sɑʳd, 'hænsəʳd
Hansberry
    Lorraine, *US playwright*   HANZ-BER-ē, -b(uh-)rē   'hænz‚beriˑ, -b(ə)riˑ
Hanseatic League
    league of German towns   HAN-sē-AT-ik   ‚hænsiː'æʈik
Hansel
    pers. name   HAN(T)-suhl, HAN-zuhl   'hæn(t)səl, 'hænzəl
Hänsel and Gretel
    fairy tale   HAN(T)-suhl uhn(d) GRET-l,   'hæn(t)səl ən(d) 'gretļ,
                     HAN-zuhl   'hænzəl
Hansun
    Knute, *writer*   HAN-suhn, HAHN-suhn   'hænsən, 'hansən
Hants [Hampshire]
    county, England   HAN(T)S   'hæn(t)s
Hanukkah
    Jewish holiday   HAHN-uh-kuh, K͟HAHN-   'hanəkə, 'xan-
Hanun
    Biblical name   HĀ-nuhn, k͟hah-NO͞ON   'heːnən, xɑ'nuːn
Hanunóo
    lang., people, Philippine Islands   HAHN-uh-NŌ   ‚hanə'noː
Haole
    a non-Hawaiian   HOW-lē, HOW-lā   'hauliˑ, 'hauleː

Key (col. 2):   a: fad   ā: fade   ah: father   ar: **ma**rry   aw: **law**   e: fed   ē: feed   er: **me**rry   i: hid   ī: hide   ō: coat   o͞o: boot
oi: boy   ow: now   u: put   uh: above   uhr: bird   ch: chop   ng: ring   sh: show   th: thick   t͟h: this   zh: measure

Hapharaim
Biblical name   HAF-uh-RĀ-im, K̲H̲AHF-ah-RAH-yim   ˌhæfəˈreːim, ˌxɑfɑˈrɑjim

Hapi
Egyptian god of the Nile   HAHP-ē   ˈhɑpi·

Hapsburg
see Habsburg

Hara
Biblical name   HĀ-ruh, HAR-uh, hah-RAH   ˈheːrə, ˈhærə, hɑˈrɑ

Harabi
people, Africa   HAHR-ah-BĒ   ˌhɑrɑˈbiː

Haradah
Biblical name   huh-RĀD-uh, HAR-uhd-uh, K̲H̲AHR-ah-DAH   həˈreːdə, ˈhærədə, ˌxɑrɑˈdɑ

Harald
1. *pers. name, Danish, Norwegian*   HAHR-AHL   ˈhɑrˌɑl
2. *German*   HAH-RAHLT   ˈhɑˌrɑlt
3. *Swedish*   HAH-RAHLD   ˈhɑˌrɑːld

Haran
Biblical name   HĀ-ran, k̲h̲ah-RAHN   ˈheːræn, xɑˈrɑn

Harare
city, Zimbabwe   huh-RAH-RĀ   həˈrɑˌreː

Hararite
Biblical name   HĀ-ruh-RĪT, HAR-uh-RĪT   ˈheːrəˌrait, ˈhærəˌrait

Harbin [Haerhpin]
city, China   hahr-BIN, HAHR-buhn   hɑrˈbin, ˈhɑrbən

Harboe
Danish beer   HAHR-buh(r)   ˈhɑrbœ

Harbona, Harbonah
Biblical name   hahr-BŌ-nuh, k̲h̲ahr-vō-NAH   hɑrˈboːnə, xɑrvoːˈnɑ

Harcourt Brace Jovanovich
US publisher   HAHR-kuhrt BRĀS jō-VAHN-uh-VICH, HAHR-KAWRT   ˈhɑrkərt ˈbreːs dʒoːˈvɑnəˌvitʃ, ˈhɑrˌkɔːrt

Hard
pers. name   HAHRD   ˈhɑrd

Harden
Sir Arthur, English chemist (Nobel 1929)   HAHRD-n   ˈhɑrdn̩

Harding
Warren G., 29th US president   HAHRD-ing   ˈhɑrdiŋ

Hardin-Simmons
University, TX   HAHRD-n-SIM-uhnz   ˈhɑrdn̩ˈsimənz

Hardouin
pers. name, French   ahr-DWEⁿ   ɑːrdwē

Hare
N. American people   HAR, HER   ˈhær, ˈher

Harebell
flower   HAR-BEL, HER-BEL   ˈhærˌbel, ˈherˌbel

Hare Krishna
religious sect   HAHR-ē KRISH-nuh, HAR-ē, HER-ē   ˌhɑri· ˈkriʃnə, ˌhæri·, ˌheri·

Hareph
Biblical name   HĀ-REF, k̲h̲ah-REF   ˈheːˌref, xɑˈref

Hareth
Biblical name   HĀ-RETH, K̲H̲AH-ret   ˈheːˌreθ, ˈxɑret

Foreign Sounds: ue: *Fr.* **rue**, *Ger.* **füllen**   uh(r): *Fr.* **boeuf**, *Ger.* **Höhle**   k̲h̲: *Ger.* **ich**, *Scot.* **loch**   ğ: *Sp.* amigo   v̲: *Sp.* hablar
hl: *Welsh* **Llanelli**.   CAPITALS: primary stress.   SMALL CAPS: secondary stress.   Ⓢ: U.S. pron.   Ⓔ: British pron.

Harewood
1. village, England   HER-WUD, HAHR-WUD   'heʳˌwud, 'hɑʳˌwud
2. Earl of, English title   HAHR-WUD   'hɑʳˌwud

Hargreaves
James, English engineer   HAHR-GRĒVZ   'hɑʳˌgriːvz

Harhas
Biblical name   HAHR-HAS, <u>kh</u>ahr-<u>KH</u>AHS   'hɑʳˌhæs, xɑʳ'xɑs

Harhur
Biblical name   HAHR-HUHR, <u>kh</u>ahr-<u>KH</u>UR   'hɑʳˌhəʳ, xɑr'xur

Haricot
vegetable   HAR-i-KŌ, AR-i-KŌ   'hæriˌkoː, 'æriˌkoː

Hariett
pers. name   HAR-ē-uht   'hæriːət

Hari-Kuyo
Japanese festival   hahr-ē-kōō-yō   hɑri·kuːjoː

Harim
Biblical name   HĀ-ruhm, <u>kh</u>ah-RIM   'heːrəm, xɑ'rim

Haringey
borough, England   HAR-ing-gā   'hæriŋgeː

Hariph
Biblical name   HAHR-if, HER-if, <u>kh</u>ah-RĒF   'hɑrif, 'herif, xɑ'riːf

Haris
pers. name, Serbo-Croatian   HAHR-is   'hɑris

Harkin
Thomas R., US politician   HAHR-kuhn   'hɑʳkən

Harlan
pers. name   HAHR-luhn   'hɑʳlən

Harlech
village, Wales   HAHR-le<u>kh</u>, Ⓢ HAHR-luhk   'hɑrlex, Ⓢ 'hɑʳlək

Harleian
pert. to Harley   HAHR-lē-uhn   'hɑʳliːən

Harlem
river, NY; district, New York City   HAHR-luhm   'hɑʳləm

Harlequin
type of duck   HAHR-li-k(w)uhn   'hɑʳlik(w)ən

Harley
Sir Robert, English statesman; street,   HAHR-lē   'hɑʳli·
London; pers. name

Harley-Davidson
motorcycle co.   HAHR-lē-DĀ-vuhd-suhn   ˌhɑʳli·'deːvədsən

Harlingen
1. city, TX   HAHR-lin-juhn   'hɑʳlindʒən
2. seaport, Netherlands   HAHR-ling-uhn   'hɑʳliŋən

Harlow, Harlowe
pers. name   HAHR-lō   'hɑʳloː

Har-Magedon
Biblical name   HAHR-muh-GED-n   ˌhɑʳmə'gedn̩

Harmhab
Egyptian king   HAHRM-HAB   'hɑʳmˌhæb

Harmodio
pers. name, Spanish   ahr-MŌ<u>TH</u>-yō   ɑr'moːðjoː

Harmodius and Aristogiton
Athenian tyrannicides   hahr-MŌD-ē-uhs uhn(d)   hɑʳ'moːdiːəs ən(d)
    uh-RIS-tuh-JĪ-TAHN,   əˌristə'dʒɑiˌtɑn,
    AR-i-stuh-JĪ-TAHN   ˌæristə'dʒɑiˌtɑn

Key (col. 2):   a: fad   ā: fade   ah: father   ar: marry   aw: law   e: fed   ē: feed   er: merry   i: hid   ī: hide   ō: coat   ōō: boot
oi: boy   ow: now   u: put   uh: above   uhr: bird   ch: chop   ng: ring   sh: show   th: thick   <u>th</u>: this   zh: measure

Harmondsworth
town, England — HAHR-muhnz-WUHRTH — ˈhɑrmənz͵wərθ

Harmonia
wife of Cadmus — hahr-MŌ-nē-uh — hɑrˈmoːniːə

Harmost
Spartan governor — HAHRM-ōst — ˈhɑrmoːst

Harnepher
Biblical name — HAHR-nuh-fuhr, HAHR-NĒ-fuhr, khahr-NEF-er — ˈhɑrnəfər, ˈhɑr͵niːfər, xɑrˈnefer

Harod
Biblical name — HĀ-RAHD, khah-RAWD — ˈheː͵rɑd, xɑˈrɔːd

Harodite
Biblical name — HĀ-ruh-DĪT — ˈheːrə͵dɑit

Haroeh
Biblical name — huh-RŌ-uh, HAH-raw-E — həˈroːə, ͵hɑrɔːˈe

Harold
pers. name — HAR-uhld — ˈhærəld

Harorite
Biblical name — HĀ-ruh-RĪT — ˈheːrə͵rɑit

Harosheth
Biblical name — huh-RŌ-SHETH, khah-RAW-SHET — həˈroː͵ʃeθ, xɑˈrɔː͵ʃet

Harosheth-hagoiim,
Harosheth-hagoyim
Biblical name — huh-RŌ-SHETH-huh-GOI-im, khah-RAW-shet-HAHG-ō-YĒM — həˈroː͵ʃeθhəˈgɔiim, xɑˈrɔːʃet͵hagoːˈjiːm

Harpalyce
brigand daughter of King Harpalycus — hahr-PAL-uh-sē — hɑrˈpæləsiˑ

Harpalycus
king of Thrace — hahr-PAL-uh-kuhs — hɑrˈpæləkəs

Harpies
winged divinities who carried off or befouled things — HAHR-pēz — ˈhɑrpiˑz

Harpinna
mother of Oenomaus by Ares — hahr-PIN-uh — hɑrˈpinə

Harpocrates
Egyptian god, Horus depicted as a child — hahr-PAHK-ruht-ēz — hɑrˈpɑkrətiːz

Harrap
French publisher — HAR-uhp, HER-uhp — ˈhærəp, ˈherəp

Harricanaw
river, Canada — HAR-uh-KAN-aw — ͵hærəˈkænɔː

Harrier
marsh hawk — HAR-ē-uhr — ˈhæriːər

Harriet, -ett, -ette
pers. name — HAR-ē-uht — ˈhæriːət

Harriman
W. Averell, US statesman — HAR-uh-muhn, HER- — ˈhærəmən, ˈher-

Harrington
pers. name — HAR-ing-tuhn, HER- — ˈhæriŋtən, ˈher-

Harrison
Benjamin, 23rd US president;
William Henry, 9th US president;
pers. name — HAR-uh-suhn — ˈhærəsən

Harrogate
town, England — HAR-uh-guht, HAR-uh-GĀT, HER- — ˈhærəgət, ˈhærə͵geːt, ˈher-

---

Foreign Sounds: ue: *Fr.* **rue**, *Ger.* **füllen**   uh(r): *Fr.* **boeuf**, *Ger.* **Höhle**   <u>kh</u>: *Ger.* **ich**, *Scot.* **loch**   ğ: *Sp.* **amigo**   v̱: *Sp.* **hablar**
hl: *Welsh* **Llanelli**.   CAPITALS: primary stress.   SMALL CAPS: secondary stress.   Ⓢ: U.S. pron.   Ⓔ: British pron.

Harrovian *pert. to or a student at* Harrow	huh-RŌ-vē-uhn	hə'roːviːən
Harrow *borough & school, England*	HAR-ō	'hæroː
Harry *pers. name*	HAR-ē	'hæriˑ
Harsha *Biblical name*	HAHR-shuh, khahr-SHAH	'hɑʳʃə, xɑr'ʃɑ
Hart Lorenz, *US lyricist;* Moss, *US dramatist*	HAHRT	'hɑʳt
Harte Bret, *US author*	HAHRT	'hɑʳt
Hartford *city, CT*	HAHRT-fuhrd	'hɑʳtfəʳd
Hartlepool *town, England*	HAHRT-lē-PO͞OL	'hɑʳtliːˌpuːl
Hartley Mariette, *US actress*	HAHRT-lē	'hɑʳtliˑ
Hartline Haldan Keffer, *US biophysicist (Nobel 1967)*	HAHRT-LĪN	'hɑʳtˌlɑin
Hartmann *pers. name, German*	HAHRT-MAHN	'hɑʳtˌmɑn
Hartmut *pers. name* (H. Michel)	HAHRT-MUT	'hɑʳtˌmut
Hartsfield Henry Warren, Jr., *US astronaut*	HAHRTS-FĒLD	'hɑʳtsˌfiːld
Harum *Biblical name*	HĀ-ruhm, hah-RO͞OM	'heːrəm, hɑ'ruːm
Harumaph *Biblical name*	huh-RO͞O-MAF, KHAH-ro͞o-MAHF	hə'ruːˌmæf, ˌxɑruː'mɑf
Haruphite *Biblical name*	huh-RO͞O-FĪT	hə'ruːˌfɑit
Haruz *Biblical name*	HĀ-ruhz, HAR-uhz, HER-uhz, khah-RO͞OTS	'heːrəz, 'hærəz, 'herəz, xɑ'ruːts
Harvard *university, town, MA*	HAHR-vuhrd	'hɑʳvəʳd
Harvey *pers. name*	HAHR-vē	'hɑʳviˑ
Harwich *city, England*	HAR-ij, HAR-ich, [$] HAHR-wich	'hæridʒ, 'hæritʃ, [$] 'hɑʳwitʃ
Harwich Port *town, MA*	HAHR-wich PŌRT, PAWRT	'hɑʳwitʃ ˌpoːʳt, ˌpɔːʳt
Haryana *state, India*	HAHR-ē-AHN-uh	ˌhɑriː'ɑnə
Harz *mtn. group, Germany*	HAHRTS	'hɑʳts
Hasa, El [Al-Hasa] *province, Saudi Arabia*	el HAHS-uh	el 'hɑsə
Hasadiah *Biblical name*	HAS-uh-DĪ-uh, KHAH-sahd-YAH	ˌhæsə'dɑiə, ˌxɑsɑd'jɑ
Hasaniya Arabic *lang., Middle East*	hah-SAH-nē-(y)uh	hɑ'sɑniː(j)ə

Key (col. 2): a: fad ā: fade ah: father ar: marry aw: law e: fed ē: feed er: merry i: hid ī: hide ō: coat o͞o: boot oi: boy ow: now u: put uh: above uhr: bird ch: chop ng: ring sh: show th: thick th: this zh: measure

Hasbro
  toy co.   HAZ-brō   'hæzbroː

Hasbrouck Heights
  borough, NJ   HAZ-BRUK HĪTS   'hæz‚bruk 'haits

Hasdrubal
  Carthaginian general   HAZ-DRŌŌ-buhl, haz-DRŌŌ-buhl   'hæz‚druːbəl, hæz'druːbəl

Hašek
  Jaroslav, *Czech writer*   HAH-shek   'haːʃek

Hasenpfeffer
  rabbit stew   HAHZ-uhn-FEF-uhr, HAHS-   'hazən‚fefəʳ, 'has-

Hasenuah
  Biblical name   HAS-uh-N(Y)ŌŌ-uh, HAHS-uh-nŌŌ-AH   ‚hæsə'n(j)uːə, ‚hasənuː'a

Hashabiah
  Biblical name   HASH-uh-BĪ-uh, <u>KH</u>AHSH-ahv-YAH   ‚hæʃə'baiə, ‚xaʃav'ja

Hashabnah
  Biblical name   huh-SHAB-nuh, <u>KH</u>AHSH-vah-NAH   hə'ʃæbnə, ‚xaʃva'na

Hashabneiah
  Biblical name   HASH-uhb-NĒ-uh, <u>KH</u>AHSH-AHV-nuh-YAH   ‚hæʃəb'niːə, ‚xaʃ‚avnə'ja

Hashabniah [Hashabneiah]
  Biblical name   HASH-uhb-NĪ-uh, <u>KH</u>AHSH-AHV-nuh-YAH   ‚hæʃəb'naiə, ‚xaʃ‚avnə'ja

Hashbadana
  Biblical name   HASH-buh-DĀ-nuh, hash-BAD-n-uh, <u>KH</u>AHSH-bah-DAHN-ah   ‚hæʃbə'deːnə, hæʃ'bædn̩ə, ‚xaʃba'dana

Hashbaddana [Hashbadana]
  Biblical name   hash-BAD-n-uh, <u>KH</u>AHSH-bah-DAHN-ah   hæʃ'bædn̩ə, ‚xaʃba'dana

Hashem
  Biblical name   HĀ-SHEM, hah-SHEM   'heː‚ʃem, ha'ʃem

Hashemi
  pers. name (H. Rafsanjani)   HAHSH-uh-mē   'haʃəmiˑ

Hashemite
  member of an Arab dynasty   HASH-uh-MĪT   'hæʃə‚mait

Hashmonah
  Biblical name   hash-MŌ-nuh, <u>KH</u>AHSH-mō-NAH   hæʃ'moːnə, ‚xaʃmoː'na

Hashub [Hasshub]
  Biblical name   HASH-uhb, HĀ-shuhb, <u>kh</u>ah-SHŌŌV   'hæʃəb, 'heːʃəb, xa'ʃuːv

Hashubah
  Biblical name   huh-SHŌŌ-buh, <u>KH</u>AHSH-ōō-VAH   hə'ʃuːbə, ‚xaʃuː'va

Hashum
  Biblical name   HĀ-shuhm, <u>kh</u>ah-SHŌŌM   'heːʃəm, xa'ʃuːm

Hasid, Chasid, Hassid
  member of a Jewish sect   <u>KH</u>AHS-uhd, HAHS-uhd, <u>KH</u>AW-suhd   'xasəd, 'hasəd, 'xɔːsəd

Hasidic
  pert. to Hasidism   <u>kh</u>ah-SID-ik, hah-SID-ik, ha-SID-ik   xa'sidik, ha'sidik, hæ'sidik

Hasidim
  plural of Hasid   <u>kh</u>ah-SĒD-uhm, hah-SĒD-uhm   xa'siːdəm, ha'siːdəm

Hasidism
  beliefs of the Hasidim   <u>KH</u>AHS-uhd-IZ-uhm, HAHS-, HAS-   'xasəd‚izəm, 'has-, 'hæs-

Haslemere
  town, England   HĀ-zuhl-MIR   'heːzəl‚miʳ

Hasrah
  Biblical name   HAZ-ruh, <u>kh</u>ahs-RAH   'hæzrə, xas'ra

Foreign Sounds: ue: *Fr.* **rue**, *Ger.* **füllen**   uh(r): *Fr.* **boeuf**, *Ger.* **Höhle**   <u>kh</u>: *Ger.* **ich**, *Scot.* **loch**   g̲: *Sp.* **amigo**   v̲: *Sp.* **hablar**   hl: *Welsh* **Llanelli**.   CAPITALS: primary stress.   SMALL CAPS: secondary stress.   ⑤: U.S. pron.   ⑥: British pron.

Hass
   Robert, *US poet laureate*   HAHS   'hɑs

Hassam
   Childe, *US painter*   HAS-uhm   'hæsəm

Hassan II
   King of Morocco   hah-SAHN   hɑ'sɑn

Hassel
   Odd, *Norwegian physical chemist*   HAHS-uhl   'hɑsəl
   (Nobel 1969)

Hasselblad
   camera co.   HAHS-uhl-BLAHT, HAS-uhl-BLAD   'hɑsəl‚blɑt, 'hæsəl‚blæd

Hassenaah
   Biblical name   HAS-uh-NĀ-uh, HAHS-uh-nah-AH   ‚hæsə'neːə, ‚hɑsənɑ'ɑ

Hassenuah
   Biblical name   HAS-uh-N(Y)OO-uh, HAHS-uh-noo-AH   ‚hæsə'n(j)uːə, ‚hɑsənuː'ɑ

Hasshub [Hashub]
   Biblical name   HAS-shuhb, k͟hah-SHOOV   'hæsʃəb, xɑ'ʃuːv

Hassid
   see Hasid

Hastings
   pl. name   HĀ-stingz   'heːstiŋz

Hasupha
   Biblical name   huh-SOO-fuh, K͟HAHS-oo-FAH   hə'suːfə, ‚xɑsuː'fɑ

Hatach [Hathach]
   Biblical name   HĀ-TAK   'heː‚tæk

Hatchie
   river, MS, TN   HACH-ē   'hætʃiˑ

Hathach [Hatach]
   Biblical name   HĀ-THAK, hah-TAHK͟H   'heː‚θæk, hɑ'tɑx

Hathath
   Biblical name   HĀ-THATH, k͟hah-TAHT   'heː‚θæθ, xɑ'tɑt

Hathaway
   Anne, *Shakespeare's wife*   HATH-uh-WĀ   'hæθə‚weː

Hathor
   Egyptian sky goddess   HAH-TAWR, HAHTH-AWR   'hɑ‚tɔːʳ, 'hɑθ‚ɔːʳ

Hatikvah
   Israeli national anthem   hah-TIK-vah, -vuh   hɑ'tikvɑ, -və

Hatipha
   Biblical name   huh-TĪ-fuh, huh-TĒ-fuh, K͟HAH-tē-FAH   hə'taifə, hə'tiːfə, ‚xɑtiː'fɑ

Hatita
   Biblical name   huh-TĪT-uh, K͟HAH-tē-TAH   hə'taiţə, ‚xɑtiː'tɑ

Hatoyama
   Ichirō, *Japanese politician*   hah-tō-yah-mah   hɑtoːjɑmɑ

Hatra
   ancient fortress, Mesopotamia   HA-truh   'hætrə

Hatshepsut
   Egyptian pharoah-queen   hat-SHEP-SOOT, -suht   hæt'ʃep‚suːt, -sət

Hatteras
   cape, NC   HAT-uh-ruhs   'hæţərəs

Hattiesburg
   city, MS   HAT-ēz-BUHRG   'hæţiːz‚bəʳg

Hattil
   Biblical name   HAT-IL, HAT-uhl, k͟hah-TIL   'hæţ‚il, 'hæţəl, xɑ'til

Hattush
   Biblical name   HAT-uhsh, k͟hah-TOOSH   'hæţəʃ, xɑ'tuːʃ

Key (col. 2):   a: fad   ā: fade   ah: father   ar: marry   aw: law   e: fed   ē: feed   er: merry   i: hid   ī: hide   ō: coat   oo: boot
oi: boy   ow: now   u: put   uh: above   uhr: bird   ch: chop   ng: ring   sh: show   th: thick   th: this   zh: measure

Hatvan
  commune, Hungary   HAWT-VAWN   'hɔːt,vɔːn

Hauer
  Rutger, *entertainer*   HOW(-uh)r   'hɑu(ə)ʳ

Hauge
  pers. name, Norwegian   HOW-guh   'hɑugə

Haugesund
  port, Norway   HOW-guh-SUN   'hɑugə,sun

Haughey
  Charles, *Irish politician*   HAW<u>KH</u>-ē, HAW-hē   'hɔːxiˑ, 'hɔːhiˑ

Hauptman
  Herbert A., *US mathematical*   HOWP(T)-muhn   'hɑup(t)mən
    physicist (Nobel 1985)

Hauptmann
  Gerhart, *German author (Nobel* HOWP(T)-MAHN   'hɑup(t),mɑn
    1912)

Hauran
  Biblical name   HAW-RAN, <u>kh</u>ahv-RAHN   'hɔː,ræn, xɑv'rɑn

Hausa
  lang., people, Africa   HOW-suh, HOW-zuh   'hɑusə, 'hɑuzə

Haut Bailly
  wine   Ō bah-YĒ   oː baːjiː

Haut Batailley
  wine   Ō bah-tah-YE   oː baːtaːje

Haut Brion
  wine   Ō brē-AWⁿ   oː briːɔ̃

Haute-Garonne
  dept, France   ōt-gah-RAWN   oːtgaːrɔːn

Haute-Marne
  dept, France   ōt-MAHRN   oːtmaːrn

Haute-Normandie
  region, France   ōt-nawr-mahⁿ-DĒ   oːtnɔːrmãdiː

Haute-Savoie
  dept, France   ōt-sahv-WAH   oːtsaːvwaː

Hautes-Pyrénées
  dept, France   ōt-pē-rā-NĀ   oːtpiːreːneː

Haut-Rhin
  dept, France   ō-REⁿ   oːrẽ

Hauts-de-Seine
  dept, France   ōd(-uh)-SEN   oːd(ə)sen

Havana
  city, Cuba; cigar   huh-VAN-uh   hə'vænə

Havarti
  place, Denmark; cheese   huh-VAHRT-ē   hə'vɑʳʈiˑ

Havasupai
  N. American people   HAHV-uh-S͞OO-PĪ   ,hɑvə'suː,pai

Havel
  Vaclav, *Czech writer & politician* HAHV-uhl   'hɑvəl

Havelock
  pers. name   HAV-LAHK, HAV-luhk   'hæv,lɑk, 'hævlək

Haverford
  town, DE; College, *PA*   HAV-uhr-fuhrd, HAV-uh-fuhrd   'hævəʳfəʳd, 'hævəfərd

Haverhill
  city, MA; town, England   HĀ-v(uh-)ruhl   'heːv(ə)rəl

Foreign Sounds: ue: *Fr.* **rue**, *Ger.* **füllen**   uh(r): *Fr.* **boeuf**, *Ger.* **Höhle**   <u>kh</u>: *Ger.* **ich**, *Scot.* **loch**   g̃: *Sp.* **amigo**   v̲: *Sp.* **hablar**
hl: *Welsh* **Llanelli**.   CAPITALS: primary stress.   SMALL CAPS: secondary stress.   Ⓢ: U.S. pron.   Ⓔ: British pron.

Havering
  borough, England   HĀV(-uh)-ring   'heːv(ə)riŋ

Haversham
  pers. name   HAV-uhr-shuhm, HAHR-shuhm   'hævə^rʃəm, 'hɑ^rʃəm

Haverstraw
  village, NY   HAV-uhr-STRAW   'hævə^rˌstrɔː

Havilah
  Biblical name   HAV-uh-luh, hā-VĪ-luh, huh-VĒ-luh, KHAH-vē-LAH   'hævələ, heː'vailə, hə'viːlə, ˌxɑviː'lɑ

Haviland
  French china   HAV-uh-luhnd   ˌhævələnd

Havlicek
  John, *sports personality*   HAV-luh-CHEK   'hævlə,tʃek

Havoth-jair, Havvoth-jair
  Biblical name   HĀ-VAHTH-JĀ-ir, khah-VAWT-yah-IR   'heːˌvɑθ'dʒeːi^r, xɑ'vɔːtjɑ'ir

Havre
  city, MT   HAV-uhr   'hævə^r

Havre, Le
  see Le Havre

Havre de Grace
  city, MD   HAV-uhr duh GRĀS, GRAS   ˌhævə^r də 'greːs, 'græs

Haw
  river, NC   HAW   'hɔː

Hawaii, Hawai'i
  state, US   huh-WAH-(y)ē, huh-WĪ-(y)ē, huh-WAW-(y)ē   hə'wɑ-(j)iˑ, hə'wai-(j)iˑ, hə'wɔː(j)iˑ

Hawaiian
  pert. to Hawaii   huh-WAH-yuhn, huh-WĪ-(y)uhn, huh-WAW-yuhn   hə'wajən, hə'wai(j)ən, hə'wɔːjən

Hawarden
  1. *city, IA;* Viscount, *English peer*   HĀ-WAWRD-n   'heːˌwɔː^rdn̩
  2. *parish, castle, Wales; Barony of Gladstone*   HAHRD-n   'hɑ^rdn̩

Haweitat
  people, Africa   huh-WĀ-TAHT   hə'weːˌtɑt

Hawes
  pers. name   HAWZ   'hɔːz

Hawick
  burgh, Scotland   HAW-ik, HOIK   'hɔːik, 'hɔik

Hawke
  Robert J.L., *Prime minister of Australia*   HAWK   'hɔːk

Hawking
  Stephen, *British theoretical physicist*   HAW-king   'hɔːkiŋ

Hawkins
  pers. name   HAW-kuhnz   'hɔːkənz

Hawn
  Goldie, *US actress*   HAWN   'hɔːn

Haworth
  Sir Walter N., *English chemist (Nobel 1937); borough, NJ; village, England (Brontës' home)*   HAW(-uh)rth, HAW-wuhrth, HOW(-uh)rth, HAH-wuhrth   'hɔː(ə)^rθ, 'hɔːwə^rθ, 'hau(ə)^rθ, 'hawə^rθ

Hawthorne
  Nathaniel, *US writer*   HAW-THAWRN   'hɔːˌθɔː^rn

Haya de la Torre
  Victor, *Peruvian politician*   AH-yah <u>th</u>ā lah TAWR-rā   'aja ðeː la 'tɔːrreː

Hayakawa
  Sessue, *US politician, linguist*   HĪ-(y)uh-KOW-uh   ˌhɑi(j)ə'kauə

Hayashi
  Teru, *Japanese diplomat*   hah-yah-shē   hajaʃiː

Hayato
  pers. name, Japanese   hah-yah-tō   hajatoː

Hayden
  pers. name   HĀD-n   'heːdn̩

Haydn
  Franz Joseph, *Austrian composer*   HĪD-n   'hɑidn̩

Hayek
  Friedrich A. von, *Austrian-born British political economist (Nobel 1974)*   HĪ-(y)uhk   'hɑi(j)ək

Hayes
  Rutherford Birchard, *19th US president*   HĀZ   'heːz

Hayim
  pers. name, Hebrew   <u>kh</u>ī-(Y)IM, <u>KHĪ</u>-(y)im   xɑi'(j)im, 'xɑi(j)im

Hayley
  pers. name   HĀ-lē   'heːliˑ

Haym
  pers. name, Polish   HĪM   'hɑim

Haynes
  pers. name   HĀNZ   'heːnz

Hayti
  city, MO; town, SD   HĀ-TĪ   'heːˌtɑi

Hayyim
  pers. name, Hebrew   <u>kh</u>ī-(Y)IM, <u>KHĪ</u>-(y)im   xɑi'(j)im, 'xɑi(j)im

Hazael
  Biblical name   HAZ-ā-EL, huh-ZĀ-EL, <u>KH</u>AHZ-ah-EL   'hæzeːˌel, hə'zeːˌel, ˌxaza'el

Hazaiah
  Biblical name   huh-ZĪ-uh, huh-ZĀ-uh, <u>KH</u>AHZ-ah-YAH   hə'zɑiə, hə'zeːə, ˌxaza'ja

Hazar-addar
  Biblical name   HĀ-ZAHR-AD-AHR, <u>KH</u>AHT-SAHR-ah-DAHR   'heːˌzaʳˈædˌaʳ, 'xatˌsara'dar

Hazar-enan, Hazar-enon
  Biblical name   HĀ-zahr-Ē-nuhn, <u>KH</u>AHT-SAHR-ā-NAHN   'heːzaʳˈiːnən, 'xatˌsareː'nan

Hazar-gaddah
  Biblical name   HĀ-ZAHR-GAD-uh, <u>KH</u>AHT-SAHR-gah-DAH   'heːˌzaʳˈgædə, 'xatˌsarga'da

Hazar-maveth
  Biblical name   HĀ-ZAHR-MĀ-veth, <u>KH</u>AHT-SAHR-MAHV-et   'heːˌzaʳˈmeːveθ, 'xatˌsar'mavet

Hazar-shual
  Biblical name   HĀ-ZAHR-SHOO-uhl, <u>KH</u>AHT-SAHR-shoo-AHL   'heːˌzaʳˈʃuːəl, 'xatˌsarʃuː'al

Hazar-susah
  Biblical name   HĀ-ZAHR-SOO-suh, <u>KH</u>AHT-SAHR-soo-SAH   'heːˌzaʳˈsuːsə, 'xatˌsarsuː'sa

---

Hazar-susim
  plural of Hazar-susah

HĀ-ZAHR-SŌŌ-sim, KHAHT-SAHR-sōō-SIM

'heːˌzɑʳˈsuːsim, 'xɑtˌsɑrsuːˈsim

Hazazon-Tamar, Hazezon-tamar
  Biblical name

HAZ-uh-ZAHN-TĀ-MAHR, KHAHT-suht-SŌN-tah-MAHR

'hæzəˌzɑnˈteːˌmɑʳ, ˌxɑtsətˈsoːntɑˈmɑr

Hazelelponi, Hazzelponi
  Biblical name

HAZ-uh-LEL-PŌ-NĪ, HAHTS-LEL-pō-NĒ

ˌhæzəˌlelˈpoːˌnɑi, ˌhɑtsˌlelpoːˈniː

Hazeltine
  Louis Alan, *US electrical engineer;*
    US corporation

HĀ-zuhl-TĪN, -tin

'heːzəlˌtɑin, -tin

Hazer-Hatticon, Hazar-hatticon
  Biblical name

HĀ-ZAHR-HAT-i-KAHN, KHAHT-ser-HAHT-ē-KŌN

'heːˌzɑʳˈhæt̬iˌkɑn, 'xɑtseʳˌhɑtiːˈkoːn

Hazeroth
  Biblical name

huh-ZIR-AHTH, KHAHT-se-RŌT

həˈzirˌɑθ, ˌxɑtseˈroːt

Haziel
  Biblical name

HĀ-zē-EL, KHAHZ-ē-EL

'heːziːˌel, ˌxɑziːˈel

Hazlitt
  William, *English essayist*

HAZ-luht

'hæzlət

Hazo
  Biblical name

HĀ-zō, khah-ZŌ

'heːzoː, xɑˈzoː

Hazor
  Biblical name

HĀ-ZAWR, khaht-SŌR

'heːˌzɔːʳ, xɑtˈsoːr

Hazor-hadattah
  Biblical name

HĀ-ZAWR-huh-DAT-uh, khaht-SŌR-KHAHD-ah-TAH

'heːˌzɔːʳhəˈdæt̬ə, xɑtˈsoːrˌxɑdɑˈtɑ

Healy
  Timothy Michael, *Irish nationalist*
    and politician

HĒ-lē

'hiːliˑ

Heaney
  Seamus, *Irish poet*

HĒ-nē

'hiːniˑ

Hearn
  Lafcadio, *US writer*

HUHRN

'həʳn

Hearns
  Thomas, *US boxer*

HUHRNZ

'həʳnz

Hearst
  William R., *US publisher; pers. name*

HUHRST

'həʳst

Heath
  pers. name

HĒTH

'hiːθ

Heathcliff
  character in Wuthering Heights, *E.*
    Brontë; *cartoon cat*

HĒTH-KLIF

'hiːθˌklif

Heathcote
  pers. name

HĒTH-kuht, -KŌT

'hiːθkət, -ˌkoːt

Heather
  pers. name

HETH-uhr

'heðəʳ

Heathrow
  airport, London, England

HĒ-THRŌ, Ⓔ HĒTH-RŌ

'hiːˌθroː, Ⓔ ˌhiːθˈroː

Heaton
  Park, *stadium, Augusta, GA*

HĒT-n

'hiːtn̩

Heavener
  city, OK

HĒV-(uh-)nuhr

'hiːv(ə)nəʳ

Hebe
  Greek goddess of youth   HĒ-bē   'hiːbiˑ
Hebei [Hopeh]
  prov, China   HUH-BĀ   'hə'beː
Heber
  Biblical name   HĒ-buhr, <u>KH</u>EV-er   'hiːbəʳ, 'xever
Heber City
  city, UT   HĒ-buhr SIT-ē   'hiːbəʳ 'siṭiˑ
Heberite
  Biblical name   HEB-uh-RĪT   'hebəˌrɑit
Heber Springs
  city, AR   HĒ-buhr SPRINGZ   'hiːbəʳ 'spriŋz
Hébert
  Jacques-René, *French politician*   ā-BER   eːber
Hebraic
  pert. to Hebrew   hi-BRĀ-ik   hi'breːik
Hebraist
  scholar of Hebrew   HĒ-BRĀ-uhst   'hiːˌbreːəst
Hebrew
  Semitic lang., people, Israel, USA,   HĒ-bro͞o   'hiːbruː
  Europe
Hebrews
  New Testament book   HĒ-bro͞oz   'hiːbruːz
Hebrides
  islands, Scotland   HEB-ruh-DĒZ   'hebrəˌdiːz
Hebron
  city, Jordan   HĒ-bruhn   'hiːbrən
Hebronite
  Biblical name   HĒ-bruh-NĪT   'hiːbrəˌnɑit
Hecale
  hostess to Theseus   HEK-uh-lē   'hekəliˑ
Hecataeus
  Greek traveler, historian   HEK-uh-TĒ-uhs   ˌhekə'tiːəs
Hecate
  ancient Greek goddess of night and   HEK-uht-ē, HEK-uht   'hekəṭiˑ, 'hekət
  the Underworld
Hecatoncheires
  fifty-headed, hundred-armed giants   HEK-uh-TAHN-KĪ-rēz   ˌhekəˌtɑn'kɑiriːz
Hecht
  Anthony, *US poet;* Ben, *US writer*   HEKT   'hekt
Heckerism
  Catholic sect   HEK-uh-RIZ-uhm   'hekəˌrizəm
Heckler
  Margaret Mary, *US ambassador*   HEK-luhr   'hekləʳ
Hector
  1. Trojan hero; pers. name   HEK-tuhr   'hektəʳ
  2. French   ek-TAWR   ektɔːr
Héctor
  pers. name, Spanish   EK-tawr   'ektɔːr
Hecuba
  wife of Priam   HEK-yuh-buh   'hekjəbə
Hedgecock
  Roger Allan, *US politician*   HEJ-KAHK   'hedʒˌkɑk
Hedmark
  county, Norway   HED-MAHRK, HĀD-MAHRK   'hedˌmɑʳk, 'heːdˌmɑʳk

---

Foreign Sounds: **ue:** *Fr.* r**ue**, *Ger.* f**ü**llen **uh(r):** *Fr.* b**oeu**f, *Ger.* H**öh**le <u>kh</u>**:** *Ger.* i**ch**, *Scot.* lo**ch** **ḡ:** *Sp.* ami**g**o **v̱:** *Sp.* ha**b**lar
hl: *Welsh* **Ll**anelli. CAPITALS: primary stress. SMALL CAPS: secondary stress. Ⓢ: U.S. pron. Ⓔ: British pron.

Hedvig		
pers. name, Swedish	HED-vig	'hedvig
Hedwig		
pers. name, German	HĀT-vi<u>kh</u>	'heːtviç
Heffernan		
Nathan Stewart, *US jurist*	HEF-uhr-nuhn	'hefə^{r}nən
Heflin		
Howell Thomas, *US politician*	HEF-luhn	'heflən
Hefner		
Hugh, *US publisher*	HEF-nuhr	'hefnə^{r}
Hegai		
Biblical name	HĒ-GĪ, HEG-ē-Ī, he-GĪ	'hiːˌgɑi, 'hegiːˌɑi, he'gɑi
Hegel		
Georg Wilhelm Friedrich, *German philosopher*	HĀ-guhl	'heːgəl
Hegelian		
follower of Hegel	hā-GĀ-lē-uhn, huh-, -GĒ-lē-uhn	heː'geːliːən, hə-, -'giːliːən
Hegelianism		
philosophy of Hegel	hā-GĀ-lē-uh-NIZ-uhm, huh-, -GĒ-lē-uh-NIZ-uhm	heː'geːliːəˌnizəm, hə-, -'giːliːəˌnizəm
Hegira		
flight of Muhammad	hi-JĪ-ruh, HEJ-uh-ruh, hi-JĒ-ruh	hi'dʒɑirə, 'hedʒərə, hi'dʒiːrə
Hehe		
lang., people, Africa	HĀ-hā	'heːheː
Heidegger		
Martin, *German philosopher*	HĪD-i-guhr, HĪ-DEG-uhr	'hɑidigə^{r}, 'hɑiˌdegə^{r}
Heidelberg		
1. Germany	HĪD-uhl-BERK, 💲 HĪD-l-BUHRG, -BERG	'hɑidəlˌbe^{r}k, 💲 'hɑidl̩ˌbə^{r}g, -ˌbe^{r}g
2. town, PA, S. Africa; college, OH	HĪD-l-BUHRG	'hɑidl̩ˌbə^{r}g
Heidenstam		
Verner von, *Swedish author (Nobel 1916)*	HĀD-n-STAHM	'heːdn̩ˌstɑːm
Heidi		
pers. name	HĪD-ē	'hɑidiˑ
Heifetz		
Jascha, *US violinist*	HĪ-fuhts	'hɑifəts
Heijo [P'yŏngyang]		
city, N. Korea	hā-jō	heːdʒoː
Heike		
pers. name, Dutch	HĀ-kuh	'heːkə
Heikki		
pers. name, Finnish	HĀK-ki	'heːkki
Heilongjiang, Heilungkiang		
prov, China	HĀ-LUNG-jē-AHNG	'heː'luŋdʒiː'ɑŋ
Heimdall		
Scandinavian watchman of heaven	HĪM-DAWL, HĪM-DAHL	'hɑimˌdɔːl, 'hɑimˌdɑl
Heimlich maneuver		
anti-choking procedure	HĪM-lik	'hɑimlik
Heine		
Heinrich, *German writer; pers. name*	HĪ-nuh, 💲 HĪ-nē	'hɑinə, 💲 'hɑiniː
Heineken		
Dutch beer	HĪ-nuh-kuhn	'hɑinəkən

Key (col. 2): a: **fad** ā: **fade** ah: **father** ar: **marry** aw: **law** e: **fed** ē: **feed** er: **merry** i: **hid** ī: **hide** ō: **coat** o͞o: **boot** oi: **boy** ow: **now** u: **put** uh: **above** uhr: **bird** ch: **chop** ng: **ring** sh: **show** th: **thick** <u>th</u>: **this** zh: **measure**

Heinemann
  Julius, Stadium, *New Orleans;*   HĪ-nuh-muhn   ˈhaɪnəmən
  William, *British publisher*
Heinlein
  Robert, *US author*   HĪN-LĪN   ˈhaɪnˌlaɪn
Heinrich
  1. pers. name, Danish   HĪN-rēkh   ˈhaɪnriːç
  2. German   HĪN-rikh   ˈhaɪnriç
Heinz
  1. tdmk for food products; pers. name HĪNZ, HĪN(T)S   ˈhaɪnz, ˈhaɪn(t)s
  2. German   HĪNTS   ˈhaɪnts
Heisenberg
  Werner, *German physicist (Nobel* HĪ-zuhn-BERG, Ⓢ -BUHRG   ˈhaɪzənˌbeʳg, Ⓢ -ˌbəʳg
  1932)
Heisman
  John William, *US football coach;* HĪS-muhn   ˈhaɪsmən
  college football trophy
Heitor
  pers. name, Portuguese   Ā-TAWR   ˈeːˌtɔːʳ
Hejaz
  region, Saudi Arabia   he-JAZ, hij-AZ   heˈdʒæz, hidʒˈæz
Hekla
  Mount, *volcano, Iceland*   HEK-luh   ˈheklə
Hektemors
  Athenian farmers   hek-TĒ-MAWRZ   hekˈtiːˌmɔːʳz
Helah
  Biblical name   HĒ-luh, khe-LAH   ˈhiːlə, xeˈlɑ
Helam
  Biblical name   HĒ-luhm, HEL-AHM   ˈhiːləm, ˈhelˌɑm
Helbah
  Biblical name   HEL-buh, khel-BAH   ˈhelbə, xelˈbɑ
Helbon
  Biblical name   HEL-BAHN, HEL-buhn, khel-BŌN   ˈhelˌbɑn, ˈhelbən, xelˈboːn
Heldai
  Biblical name   HEL-DĪ, khel-DĪ   ˈhelˌdaɪ, xelˈdaɪ
Heleb
  Biblical name   HĒ-LEB, HĒ-luhb, KHEL-EV   ˈhiːˌleb, ˈhiːləb, ˈxelˌev
Heled
  Biblical names   HĒ-LED, HĒ-luhd, KHEL-ED   ˈhiːˌled, ˈhiːləd, ˈxelˌed
Helek
  Biblical name   HĒ-LEK, HĒ-lik, KHEL-EK   ˈhiːˌlek, ˈhiːlik, ˈxelˌek
Helekite
  Biblical name   HĒ-li-KĪT   ˈhiːliˌkaɪt
Helem
  Biblical name   HĒ-LEM, HĒ-luhm, HEL-EM   ˈhiːˌlem, ˈhiːləm, ˈhelˌem
Helen
  daughter of Zeus & Leda, wife of HEL-uhn   ˈhelən
  Menelaus, lover of Paris; pers.
  name
Helena
  1. city, MT   HEL-uh-nuh   ˈhelənə
  2. pers. name   HEL-uh-nuh, huh-LĒ-nuh, hel-Ā-nuh   ˈhelənə, həˈliːnə, helˈeːnə
  3. Dutch   hā-LĀ-nah   heːˈleːnɑː
  4. German   HĀ-lā-NAH   ˈheːleːˌnɑ

Foreign Sounds: ue: *Fr.* **rue**, *Ger.* **füllen** uh(r): *Fr.* **boeuf**, *Ger.* **Höhle** kh: *Ger.* **ich**, *Scot.* **loch** ğ: *Sp.* **amigo** v: *Sp.* **hablar**
hl: *Welsh* **Llanelli**. CAPITALS: primary stress. SMALL CAPS: secondary stress. Ⓢ: U.S. pron. Ⓔ: British pron.

Helene
 1. pers. name   huh-LĒN, huh-LĀN   hə'liːn, hə'leːn
 2. German   hā-LĀ-nuh   heː'leːnə
Hélène
 pers. name, French   ā-LEN   eːlen
Helenus
 1. son of Priam & Hecuba, twin of   HEL-uh-nuhs   'helənəs
  Cassandra
 2. pers. name, Swedish   he-LĀ-nuhs   he'leːnəs
Heleph
 Biblical name   HĒ-LEF, HĒ-luhf, <u>KH</u>EL-EF   'hiːˌlef, 'hiːləf, 'xelˌef
Helez
 Biblical name   HĒ-LEZ, <u>KH</u>EL-ETS   'hiːˌlez, 'xelˌets
Helga
 pers. name, Swedish   HEL-guh   'helgə
Helge
 pers. name, Danish   HEL-guh   'helgə
Helgoland [Heligoland]
 island, North Sea   HEL-gō-LAHNT, ⑤ HEL-gō-LAND   'helgoːˌlant, ⑤ 'helgoːˌlænd
Heli
 Biblical name   HĒ-LĪ   'hiːˌlɑi
Heliaea
 Athenian law courts   HEL-ē-Ē-uh   ˌheliː'iːə
Helianthus
 flower   HĒ-lē-AN-thuhs   ˌhiːliː'ænθəs
Helice
 guardian of Zeus   HEL-uh-sē   'heləsiˑ
Helicon
 Mount, abode of Muses   HEL-uh-KAHN, HEL-uh-kuhn   'heləˌkɑn, 'heləkən
Heligoland [Helgoland]
 island, North Sea   HEL-uh-gō-LAND   'heləgoːˌlænd
Heliogabalus
 Roman emperor   HĒ-lē-ō-GAB-uh-luhs   ˌhiːliːoː'gæbələs
Heliopolis
 ancient Egyptian city   HĒ-lē-AHP-uh-luhs   ˌhiːliː'ɑpələs
Helios
 Greek sun god   HĒ-lē-uhs, HĒ-lē-ŌS   'hiːliːəs, 'hiːliːˌoːs
helium
 element   HĒ-lē-uhm   'hiːliːəm
Helkai
 Biblical name   HEL-KĪ, hel-KĀ-Ī, <u>kh</u>el-KĪ   'helˌkɑi, hel'keːˌɑi, xel'kɑi
Helkath
 Biblical name   HEL-KATH, <u>kh</u>el-KAHT   'helˌkæθ, xel'kɑt
Helkath-hazzurim
 Biblical name   HEL-KATH-HAZ-YUR-im,   'helˌkæθˌhæz'jurim,
                                          <u>kh</u>el-KAHT-HAHT-s<u>oo</u>-RĒM   xel'kɑtˌhɑtsuː'riːm
Hellas
 ancient name of Greece   HEL-uhs   'heləs
Helle
 mythical Greek heroine drowned in   HEL-ē   'heliˑ
  the Hellespont
Hellen
 eponymous hero of the Greeks   HEL-uhn, HEL-ĒN   'helən, 'helˌiːn
Hellene
 a Greek   HEL-ĒN   'helˌiːn

Key (col. 2): a: fad ā: fade ah: father ar: marry aw: law e: fed ē: feed er: merry i: hid ī: hide ō: coat ōō: boot
oi: boy ow: now u: put uh: above uhr: bird ch: chop ng: ring sh: show th: thick <u>th</u>: this zh: measure

Hellenic
   pert. to ancient Greece   huh-LEN-ik, huh-LĒ-nik, hel-EN-ik,   hə'lenik, hə'liːnik, hel'enik,
                        hel-Ē-nik   hel'iːnik

Hellenism
   ancient Greek culture   HEL-uh-NIZ-uhm   'helə,nizəm

Hellenistic
   pert. to Greek civilization   HEL-uh-NIS-tik   ˌhelə'nistik

Hellenotamiae
   Athenian officials   HEL-uh-nō-TĀ-mē-Ī   ˌhelənoː'teːmiːˌɑi

Heller
   Joseph, *US writer*   HEL-uhr   'heləʳ

Hellespont [Dardanelles]
   strait, Turkey   HEL-uh-SPAHNT   'helə,spɑnt

Helmholtz
   Hermann von, *scientist*   HELM-HŌLTS   'helm,hoːlts

Helmond
   Katherine, *US actress*   HEL-muhnd   'helmənd

Helms
   Jesse, *US politician*   HELMZ   'helmz

Helmsley
   US hoteliers   HELMZ-lē, HEMZ-lē   'helmzliˑ, 'hemzliˑ

Helmut, -muth
   pers. name, German   HEL-MŌŌT   'hel,muːt

Heloise
   US columnist; pers. name   HEL-uh-WĒZ   'helə,wiːz

Héloïse
   French abbess, wife of Abelard   ā-law-ĒZ, Ⓢ EL-uh-WĒZ   eːlɔːiːz, Ⓢ 'elə,wiːz

Helon
   Biblical name   HĒ-LAHN, khe-LAWN   'hiːˌlɑn, xe'lɔːn

Helots
   Spartan serfs   HEL-uhts   'heləts

Helsingfors [Helsinki]
   city, Finland   HEL-sing-FAWRZ   'helsiŋ,fɔːʳz

Helsingør [Elsinore]
   seaport, Denmark   HEL-seng-UHR, Ⓢ HEL-sing-UHR   ˌhelseŋ'œːr, Ⓢ ˌhelsiŋ'əʳ

Helsinki
   city, Finland   HEL-SING-kē, hel-SING-kē   'hel,siŋkiˑ, hel'siŋkiˑ

Helvetia
   Latin name for Switzerland   hel-VĒ-sh(ē-)uh   hel'viːʃ(iː)ə

Helvetic
   pert. to Helvetia   hel-VET-ik   hel'veţik

Helvetica
   typeface   HEL-VET-i-kuh   ˌhel'veţikə

Helvetii
   ancient Celtic inhabitants of   hel-VĒ-shē-Ī   hel'viːʃiːˌɑi
     Switzerland

Helvidius Priscus
   Roman philosopher   hel-VID-ē-uhs PRIS-kuhs   hel'vidiːəs 'priskəs

Hemam
   Biblical name   HĒ-MAM, hā-MAHM   'hiːˌmæm, heː'mɑm

Hemdan
   Biblical name   HEM-DAN, khem-DAHN   'hem,dæn, xem'dɑn

Hémeenlinna
   city, Finland   HAM-ĀN-LIN-nuh   'hæm,eːn,linnə

Hemel Hempstead
  town, England   HEM-uhl HEM(P)-stuhd   ˌheməl 'hem(p)stəd

Hemera
  ancient Greek personification of the   HEM-uh-ruh   'hemərə
    day

Hemicynes
  legendary half-dogs   HEM-ē-SĪ-nēz   ˌhemiˑ'sɑiniːz

Hemingway
  Ernest, *US author (Nobel 1954);*   HEM-ing-WĀ   'hemiŋˌweː
    Margaux *and* Mariel, *US actresses*

Hempstead
  county, AR; town, NY; pers. name   HEM(P)-STED, HEM(P)-stuhd   'hem(p)ˌsted, 'hem(p)stəd

Hemsley
  Sherman, *US actor*   HEMZ-lē   'hemzliˑ

Hen
  Biblical name   HEN, KHEN   'hen, 'xen

Hena
  Biblical name   HĒ-nuh, hen-AH   'hiːnə, hen'ɑ

Henadad
  Biblical name   HEN-uh-DAD, KHEN-ah-DAHD   'henəˌdæd, ˌxenɑ'dɑd

Henan [Honan]
  prov, town, China   HUH-NAHN   'hə'nɑn

Hench
  Philip S., *US physician (Nobel 1950)*   HENCH   'hentʃ

Henderson
  Arthur, *British labor leader,*   HEN-duhr-suhn   'hendəʳsən
    politician (Nobel 1934)

Henderson
  pers. name   HEN-duhr-suhn   'hendəʳsən

Hendric
  pers. name   HEN-drik   'hendrik

Hendrick
  pers. name, Dutch   HEN-druhk   'hendrək

Hendricksz
  pers. name, Dutch   HEN-druhks   'hendrəks

Hendricus, Hendrikus
  pers. name, Dutch   hen-DRĒ-kues   hen'driːkys

Hendrik
  pers. name, Dutch   HEN-druhk   'hendrək

Hendrix
  Jimi, *rock musician*   HEN-driks   'hendriks

Heneage
  pers. name   HEN-ij   'henidʒ

Hengist
  pers. name   HENG-guhst, -GIST   'heŋgəst, -ˌgist

Hengwrt
  Chaucer manuscript   HEN-gurt, HENG-gurt   'henguʳt, 'heŋguʳt

Henie
  Sonja, *Norwegian-US figure skater*   HEN-ē   'heniˑ

Henleigh, -ley
  pers. name   HEN-lē   'henliˑ

Henley-on-Thames
  town, England   HEN-lē ahn TEMZ   'henliˑ ɑn 'temz

Key (col. 2):   a: fad   ā: fade   ah: father   ar: marry   aw: law   e: fed   ē: feed   er: merry   i: hid   ī: hide   ō: coat   ōō: boot
oi: boy   ow: now   u: put   uh: above   uhr: bird   ch: chop   ng: ring   sh: show   th: thick   th: this   zh: measure

Hennepin		
1. county, MN	HEN-uh-puhn	'henəpən
2. Louis, *Belgian explorer*	en-uh-PE^{n}, [$] HEN-uh-puhn	enəpẽ, [$] 'henəpən
Henner		
Marilu, *actress*	HEN-uhr	'henə^{r}
Hennessy		
tdmk for a cognac; pers. name	HEN-uh-sē	'henəsiˑ
Henning		
Doug, *Canadian magician*	HEN-ing	'heniŋ
Henninger		
German beer	HEN-ing-uhr	'heniŋə^{r}
Henoch		
Biblical name	HĒ-NAHK, khah-NŌKH	'hiː,nɑk, xɑ'noːx
Henri		
1. pers. name, Flemish	HAH^{n}-rē	'hɑ̃riː
2. French	ah^{n}-RĒ	ɑ̃riː
Henrich		
pers. name, German	HEN-rikh	'henriç
Henrico		
county, VA	hen-RĪ-kō	hen'rɑikoː
Henricus		
1. pers. name, Dutch	hen-RĒ-kues	hen'riːkys
2. Latin	hen-RĪ-kuhs, hen-RĒ-kuhs	hen'rɑikəs, hen'riːkəs
Henrietta		
pers. name	HEN-rē-ET-uh	,henriː'et̯ə
Henriette		
1. pers. name, French	ah^{n}r-YET	ɑ̃rjet
2. German	HEN-rē-ET-uh	,henriː'et̯ə
Henriëtte		
pers. name, Dutch	HEN-rē-ET-uh	,henriː'et̯ə
Henrik		
1. pers. name, Danish	HEN-rēk	'henriːk
2. Norwegian	HEN-rik	'henrik
Henrique		
1. pers. name, Portuguese	ān-RĒ-kuh, -kā	ẽːn'riːkə, -keː
2. Spanish	ān-RĒ-kā	eːn'riːkeː
Henriques		
pers. name, Portuguese	ān-RĒ-kish, -kis	ẽːn'riːkiʃ, -kis
Henry		
1. pers. name, English, German	HEN-rē	'henriˑ
2. Flemish	HAH^{n}-rē	'hɑ̃riː
3. French	ah^{n}-RĒ	ɑ̃riː
Henryk		
pers. name, Polish	HEN-rik	'henrik
Henslowe		
cape, Solomon Islands	HENZ-LŌ	'henz,loː
Henson		
Jim, *US puppeteer*	HEN(T)-suhn	'hen(t)sən
Hentiyn Nuruu		
mtn. range, Mongolia	hen-TĒN NUR-o͞o	hen'tiːn 'nuruː
Hen Wlad fy Nhadau		
Welsh national anthem	HEN WLAHD vuhn HAHD-ī	'hen ,wlɑd vən 'hɑdɑi
Hepatica		
flower	hi-PAT-i-kuh	hi'pæt̯ikə

Foreign Sounds: ue: *Fr.* **rue**, *Ger.* **füllen** uh(r): *Fr.* **boeuf**, *Ger.* **Höhle** kh: *Ger.* **ich**, *Scot.* **loch** ḡ: *Sp.* amigo v: *Sp.* hab**l**ar hl: *Welsh* **Llanelli**. CAPITALS: primary stress. SMALL CAPS: secondary stress. [$]: U.S. pron. [£]: British pron.

Hepatic Tanager
  songbird   hi-PAT-ik TAN-uh-juhr   hiˈpæʈik ˈtænədʒəʳ

Hepburn
  Audrey, *Belgian-born actress;*   HEP-BUHRN, ⓔ *also* HEB-uhrn   ˈhepˌbəʳn, ⓔ *also* ˈhebəʳn
    Katharine, *US actress; pers. name*

Hephaestus
  Greek god of fire   hi-FES-tuhs, hi-FĒ-stuhs   hiˈfestəs, hiˈfiːstəs

Hepher
  Biblical name   HĒ-fuhr, <u>KH</u>EF-er   ˈhiːfəʳ, ˈxefer

Hepherite
  Biblical name   HĒ-fuh-RĪT   ˈhiːfəˌraɪt

Hephzibah
  Biblical name   HEF-suh-BAH, HEF-suh-buh,   ˈhefsəˌba, ˈhefsəbə,
                        <u>KH</u>EFT-sē-BAH   ˌxeftsiːˈba

Hepplewhite
  furniture style   HEP-uhl-(H)WĪT   ˈhepəlˌ(h)waɪt

Heptateuch
  first seven books of Bible HEP-tuh-T(Y)O͞OK   ˈheptəˌt(j)uːk

Hepzibah
  pers. name   HEP-suh-BAH, HEP-suh-buh   ˈhepsəˌba, ˈhepsəbə

Hera
  Greek queen of the gods   HIR-uh, HER-uh, HĒ-ruh   ˈhirə, ˈherə, ˈhiːrə

Heraclean
  pert. to Heracles   HER-uh-KLĒ-uhn   ˌherəˈkliːən

Heracles, -kles [Hercules]
  mythical Greek hero   HER-uh-KLĒZ   ˈherəˌkliːz

Heraclids
  descendants of Heracles   HER-uh-KLIDZ   ˈherəˌklidz

Heraclitus
  Greek philosopher   HER-uh-KLĪT-uhs   ˌherəˈklaɪʈəs

Heraclius
  pers. name, Latin   huh-RAK-lē-uhs   həˈrækliːəs

Héraclius
  pers. name, French   ā-rah-klē-UES   eːraːkliːyːs

Heraklion
  dept & town, Greece   hi-RAK-lē-uhn   hiˈrækliːən

Herat
  prov, city, Afghanistan   he-RAHT, huh-RAHT   heˈrɑt, həˈrɑt

Hérault
  river, dept, France   ā-RŌ   eːroː

Herb
  pers. name   HUHRB   ˈhəʳb

Herbert
  1. pers. name   HUHR-buhrt, HUHR-buht   ˈhəʳbəʳt, ˈhəʳbət
  2. German   HER-BERT   ˈheʳˌbeʳt
  3. Swedish   HER-buhrt   ˈherbərt

Herbie
  pers. name   HUHR-bē   ˈhəʳbiˑ

Herblock
  penname of Herbert Lawrence Block, HUHR-BLAHK   ˈhəʳˌblɑk
    US cartoonist

Herculaneum
  ancient Roman town buried by HUHR-kyuh-LĀ-nē-uhm   ˌhəʳkjəˈleːniːəm
    Vesuvius

Key (col. 2):   a: fad   ā: fade   ah: father   ar: marry   aw: law   e: fed   ē: feed   er: merry   i: hid   ī: hide   ō: coat   o͞o: boot
oi: boy   ow: now   u: put   uh: above   uhr: bird   ch: chop   ng: ring   sh: show   th: thick   <u>th</u>: this   zh: measure

Hercule

  pers. name, French   er-KUEL   erkyːl

Herculean

  pert. to Hercules   HUHR-kyuh-LĒ-uhn,   ˌhəʳkjə'liːən, ˌhəʳ'kjuːliːən
                     HUHR-KY͞OO-lē-uhn

Hercules

  1. Latin form of Heracles;   HUHR-kyuh-LĒZ   'həʳkjəˌliːz
    constellation; pers. name

  2. Dutch   HER-kue-luhs   'herkyːləs

Herder

  Gerhard, *German ambassador*   HERD-uhr   'heʳdəʳ

Hereford

  1. town, England   HER-uh-fuhrd   'herəfəʳd

  2. breed of cattle   HUHR-fuhrd, HER-uh-fuhrd   'həʳfəʳd, 'herəfəʳd

  3. town, MD   HER-fuhrd   'herfəʳd

Herefordshire

  former county, England   HER-uh-fuhrd-shuhr, -SHIR;   'herəfəʳdʃəʳ, -ˌʃiʳ;
               Ⓢ HUHR-fuhrd-   Ⓢ 'həʳfəʳd-

Herennius

  pers. name, Latin   huh-REN-ē-uhs   hə'reniːəs

Herero

  lang., people, Africa   huh-RER-ō, HER-uh-RŌ   hə'reroː, 'herəˌroː

Heres

  Biblical name   HĒ-RES, HIR-ĒZ, KHER-es   'hiːˌres, 'hirˌiːz, 'xeres

Heresh

  Biblical name   HĒ-RESH, KHER-esh   'hiːˌreʃ, 'xereʃ

Hereth

  Biblical name   HĒ-reth   'hiːreθ

Herforder

  German beer   HER-FAWR-duhr   'herˌfɔːʳdəʳ

Herkimer

  county, NY   HUHR-kuh-muhr   'həʳkəməʳ

Herman

  1. pers. name   HUHR-muhn   'həʳmən

  2. Danish, Finnish   HER-MAHN   'herˌmɑːn

  3. Dutch, Norwegian   HER-MAHN   'herˌmɑn

  4. German   HER-MAHN   'heʳˌmɑn

Hermann

  1. pers. name   HUHR-muhn   'həʳmən

  2. Danish   HER-MAHN   'herˌmɑːn

  3. Dutch, Icelandic   HER-MAHN   'herˌmɑn

  4. French   er-MAHN   ermɑːn

  5. German   HER-MAHN   'heʳˌmɑn

Hermaphroditus

  androgynous Greek deity   huhr-MAF-ruh-DĪT-uhs   həʳˌmæfrə'daiţəs

Hermas [Hermes]

  Biblical name   HUHR-muhs   'həʳməs

Hermes

  1. Greek messenger god; asteroid;   HUHR-MĒZ   'həʳˌmiːz
    pers. name

  2. Portuguese   ER-mish, ER-mis   'ermiʃ, 'ermis

Hermès

  French fashion retailers   er-MES, HUHR-MĒZ   er'mes, 'həʳˌmiːz

---

Foreign Sounds: ue: *Fr.* **rue**, *Ger.* f**ü**llen   uh(r): *Fr.* b**oeuf**, *Ger.* H**öh**le   kh: *Ger.* i**ch**, *Scot.* lo**ch**   ğ: *Sp.* ami**g**o   v: *Sp.* ha**b**lar
hl: *Welsh* **Ll**anelli.   CAPITALS: primary stress.   SMALL CAPS: secondary stress.   Ⓢ: U.S. pron.   Ⓔ: British pron.

Hermes Trismegistus
  Thoth or Hermes as author of   HUHR-mēz TRIS-muh-JIS-tuhs   'hərˈmiːz ˌtrismə'dʒistəs
   magical works

Hermeticism
  Gnostic writings & teachings   HUHR-MET-uh-SIZ-uhm   ˌhərˈmeţəˌsizəm

Hermione
  1. daughter of Menelaus & Helen;   huhr-MĪ-uh-nē   hərˈmaiəni·
   pers. name
  2. French   erm-YAWN   ermjɔːn

Hermitage
  museum, Leningrad   er-mē-TAHZH   ermiːtɑːʒ

Hermogenes
  pers. name   huhr-MAHJ-uh-NĒZ   hərˈmɑdʒəˌniːz

Hermon
  mtn. between Lebanon & Syria   HUHR-muhn   'hərˈmən

Hermosa
  district, Philippines   er-MŌ-suh   eˈrˈmoːsə

Hernán
  pers. name, Spanish   er-NAHN   er'nɑn

Hernández
  pers. name, Spanish   er-NAHN-dās, -dāth   er'nɑndeːs, -deːθ

Hernando
  1. county, FL   huhr-NAN-dō   hərˈnændoː
  2. pers. name, Spanish   er-NAHN-dō   er'nɑndoː

Hero
  beloved of Leander in Greek   HĒ-rō, HIR-ō   'hiːroː, 'hiroː
   mythology

Herod
  Biblical ruler   HER-uhd   'herəd

Herodian
  Biblical name   huh-RŌD-ē-uhn, hir-ŌD-   həˈroːdiːən, hir'oːd-

Herodias
  Biblical name   huh-RŌD-ē-uhs   həˈroːdiːəs

Herodotus
  Greek historian   huh-RAHD-uht-uhs   həˈrɑdətəs

Herophile
  the second sibyl   hē-RAHF-uh-lē, hir-AHF-uh-lē   hiːˈrɑfəli·, hir'ɑfəli·

Herr
  Mr. in German   HER   'heʳ

Herrenbräu
  German beer   HER-uhn-BROI   'herənˌbrɔi

Herrenhäuser
  German beer   HER-uhn-HOI-zuhr   'herənˌhɔizəʳ

Herrenvolk
  master race   HER-uhn-FAWLK   'herənˌfɔːlk

Herrera
  José Joaquín, *Mexican general and*   er-RER-uh   er'rerə
   politician; province, Panama

Herrick
  Robert, *English poet*   HER-ik   'herik

Herriot
  1. James, British writer   HER-ē-uht   'heriːət
  2. Édouard, French politician   er-YŌ   erjoː

Herrmann
  pers. name, German   HER-MAHN   'heʳˌmɑn

Key (col. 2):   a: fad   ā: fade   ah: father   ar: marry   aw: law   e: fed   ē: feed   er: merry   i: hid   ī: hide   ō: coat   ōō: boot
oi: boy   ow: now   u: put   uh: above   uhr: bird   ch: chop   ng: ring   sh: show   th: thick   <u>th</u>: this   zh: measure

Herschbach

Dudley R., *US chemist (Nobel 1986)*   HUHRSH-BAK   ˈhərʃˌbæk

Herschel

Sir William, *British astronomer; pers.*   HUHR-shuhl   ˈhərʃəl
name

Herschel-Rigollet

comet   HUHR-shuhl-RIG-uh-LĀ   ˈhərʃəlˌrigəˈleː

Hersey

John, *US author*   HUHR-sē   ˈhərsi·

Hershel

pers. name   HUHR-shuhl   ˈhərʃəl

Hershey

Alfred D., *US biologist (Nobel 1969);*   HUHR-shē   ˈhərʃi·
city, PA; US candy co.

Hershler

Edgar J., *US politician*   HUHRSH-luhr   ˈhərʃlər

Hersholt

Jean, *Danish-born US actor;*   HUHR-SHŌLT, -SHAHLT   ˈhərˌʃoːlt, -ˌʃɑlt
Academy Award for
humanitarianism

Herstmonceux, Hurstmonceux

village, observatory site, England   HUHRST-muhn-S(Y)OO   ˌhərstmən's(j)uː

Hertford

1. county, town, NC   HUHRT-fuhrd   ˈhərtfərd
2. county, England; college, Oxford   HAHR-fuhrd, HAHRT-fuhrd   ˈhɑrfərd, ˈhɑrtfərd
Univ.
3. Marquess of, English peer   HAHR-fuhrd   ˈhɑrfərd

Hertfordshire

county, England   HAHR-fuhrd-shuhr,   ˈhɑrfərdʃər, ˈhɑrtfərdʃər,
     HAHRT-fuhrd-shuhr, -SHIR   -ˌʃir

Herts

Hertfordshire   HAHRTS   ˈhɑrts

Hertz

1. Gustav, German physicist (Nobel   HERTS, Ⓢ HUHRTS   ˈherts, Ⓢ ˈhərts
1925)
2. US car rental co.   HUHRTS   ˈhərts

Hertzog

James, *S. African prime minister*   HUHRT-SAWG, HUHRT-SAHG   ˈhərtˌsoːg, ˈhərtˌsɑg

Hertzsprung-Russel

astronomical diagram   HUHRT-SPRUNG-RUHS-uhl   ˈhərtˌspruŋˈrəsəl

Hervé

pers. name, French   er-VĀ   erveː

Hervey

pers. name   HUHR-vē, Ⓔ HAHR-vē   ˈhərvi·, Ⓔ ˈhɑrvi·

Herz

pers. name   HUHRTS   ˈhərts

Herzberg

Gerhard, *German-born Canadian*   HUHRTS-BUHRG   ˈhərtsˌbərg
physical chemist (Nobel 1971)

Herzegovina

region, Bosnia and Herzegovina   HERT-suh-gō-VĒ-nuh,   ˌhertsəgoːˈviːnə,
     HERT-suh-GŌ-vuh-nuh, HUHRT-   ˌhertsəˈgoːvənə, ˌhərt-

Herzl

Theodor, *Hungarian Zionist leader*   HERT-suhl   ˈhertsəl
in Vienna

Foreign Sounds: ue: *Fr.* **rue**, *Ger.* **füllen**   uh(r): *Fr.* **boeuf**, *Ger.* **Höhle**   kh: *Ger.* **ich**, *Scot.* **loch**   ḡ: *Sp.* **amigo**   v: *Sp.* **hablar**
hl: *Welsh* **Llanelli**.   CAPITALS: primary stress.   SMALL CAPS: secondary stress.   Ⓢ: U.S. pron.   Ⓔ: British pron.

Herzog		
1. Werner, *German film director*	HERT-ZAWK, Ⓢ HUHRT-SAWG, -SAHG	'hert,zɔːk, Ⓢ 'hə^{r}t,sɔːg, -,sɑg
2. Isaac Halevi, *Chief Rabbi of Israel*	HUHRT-SAWG, -SAHG	'hə^{r}t,sɔːg, -,sɑg
3. Émile Salomon Wilhelm, *(pseudonym* André Maurois*), French writer*	er-ZAWG, Ⓢ HUHRT-SAWG, -SAHG	erzɔːg, Ⓢ 'hə^{r}t,sɔːg, -,sɑg
Hesba		
pers. name	HEZ-buh	'hezbə
Hesed		
Biblical name	HĒ-SED, KHES-ed	'hiː,sed, 'xesed
Heseltine		
Michael, *English politician*	HES-uhl-TĪN, HEZ-uhl-TĪN	'hesəl,tɑin, 'hezəl,tɑin
Heshbon		
Biblical name	HESH-BAHN, khesh-BŌN	'heʃ,bɑn, xeʃ'boːn
Heshmon		
Biblical name	HESH-MAHN, HESH-muhn, khesh-MŌN	'heʃ,mɑn, 'heʃmən, xeʃ'moːn
Heshvan		
Jewish month	KHESH-vuhn, HESH-vuhn, HESH-VAHN	'xeʃvən, 'heʃvən, 'heʃ,vɑn
Hesiod		
Greek poet	HĒ-sē-uhd, HES-ē-uhd	'hiːsiːəd, 'hesiːəd
Hesione		
wife of Telamon	he-SĪ-uh-nē	he'sɑiəniˑ
Hesperia		
mythical West	he-SPIR-ē-uh	he'spiriːə
Hesperian		
pert. to Hesperia	he-SPIR-ē-uhn	he'spiriːən
Hesperides		
nymphs who guarded a tree of golden apples	he-SPER-uh-DĒZ	he'sperə,diːz
Hesperidin		
pigment	he-SPER-uhd-n	he'sperədn̩
Hesperus		
spirit of the evening star; schooner in Longfellow poem	HES-puh-ruhs	'hespərəs
Hess		
Rudolf, *German Nazi politician;* V. F., *Austrian-born US physicist (Nobel 1936);* Walter Rudolf, *Swiss physiologist (Nobel 1949)*	HES	'hes
Hesse		
1. Hermann, *German author (Nobel 1946)*	HES-uh	'hesə
2. *prov., Germany*	HES, HES-uh	'hes, 'hesə
Hesseman		
Howard, *US actor*	HES-muhn	'hesmən
Hessen [Hesse]		
prov., Germany	HES-n	'hesn̩
Hessian		
pert. to the German prov. Hesse	HESH-uhn	'heʃən
Hesston		
city, KS	HES-tuhn	'hestən

Key (col. 2): a: **fad** ā: **fade** ah: **father** ar: **marry** aw: **law** e: **fed** ē: **feed** er: **merry** i: **hid** ī: **hide** ō: **coat** o͞o: **boot** oi: **boy** ow: **now** u: **put** uh: **above** uhr: **bird** ch: **chop** ng: **ring** sh: **show** th: **thick** th: **this** zh: **measure**

Hester
   pers. name   HES-tuhr   'hestə^r

Hestia
   Greek goddess of the hearth   HES-tē-uh, HES-chuh, HESH-chuh   'hestiːə, 'hestʃə, 'heʃtʃə

Heston
   Charlton, *US actor*   HES-tuhn   'hestən

Heteroousian
   pert. to or member of an Arian sect.   HET-uh-rō-O͞O-sē-uhn,   ˌhet̬əroːˈuːsiːən,
    HET-uh-rō-O͞O-zh(ē-)uhn   ˌhet̬əroːˈuːʒ(iː)ən

Heth
   Biblical name   HETH, K͟HET   'heθ, 'xet

Hethlon
   Biblical name   HETH-LAHN, k͟het-LAWN   'heθˌlɑn, xetˈlɔːn

Het Kapittel Watou Prior
   Belgian beer   HET KAHP-i-tuhl VAH-TO͞O PRĒ-awr   ˌhet ˈkɑpitəl ˈvɑˌtuː ˈpriːɔːr

Hettinger
   county, ND   HET-uhn-juhr, HET-n-juhr   'het̬əndʒə^r, 'hetn̩dʒə^r

Hevesy
   Georg von, *Hungarian chemist*   HEV-ESH-ē; HEV-uh-shē   'hevˌeʃiˑ; 'hevəʃiˑ
   (Nobel 1943)

Hew
   pers. name   HY͞OO   'hjuː

Hewish
   Antony, *English radio astronomer*   HY͞OO-ish   'hjuːiʃ
   (Nobel 1974)

Hewitt
   pers. name   HY͞OO-uht   'hjuːət

Hewlett-Packard
   US computer co.   (H)Y͞OO-luht-PAK-uhrd   '(h)juːlətˈpækə^rd

Heyerdahl
   Thor, *Norwegian ethnologist*   HĀ-uhr-DAHL   'heːə^rˌdɑl

Heymans
   Corneille, *Belgian physiologist*   ā-MAHⁿS, ⑤ ā-MAHNS, ā-MANS   eːmɑ̃s, ⑤ eːˈmɑns, eːˈmæns
   (Nobel 1938)

Heyrovsky
   Jaroslav, *Czech physical chemist*   hā-RAWF-skē   heːˈrɔːfskiˑ
   (Nobel 1959)

Heyse
   Paul, *German author (Nobel 1910)*   HĪ-zuh   'hɑizə

Heyward
   DuBose, *US lyricist*   HĀ-wuhrd   'heːwə^rd

Hezbollah
   Palestinian military organization   HEZ-buh-LAH   ˌhezbəˈlɑ

Hezekiah
   pers. name   HEZ-uh-KĪ-uh   ˌhezəˈkɑiə

Hezion
   Biblical name   HĒ-zē-AHN, k͟hez-YŌN   'hiːziːˌɑn, xezˈjoːn

Hezir
   Biblical name   HĒ-zuhr, k͟he-ZIR   'hiːzə^r, xeˈzir

Hezrai
   Biblical name   HEZ-rē-Ī, k͟hets-RĪ   'hezriːˌɑi, xetsˈrɑi

Hezro
   Biblical name   HEZ-rō, k͟hets-RŌ   'hezroː, xetsˈroː

Hezron
   Biblical name   HEZ-RAHN, HEZ-ruhn, k͟hets-RŌN   'hezˌrɑn, 'hezrən, xetsˈroːn

---

Foreign Sounds: ue: *Fr.* **rue**, *Ger.* füllen   uh(r): *Fr.* **boeuf**, *Ger.* Höhle   k͟h: *Ger.* **ich**, *Scot.* loch   ḡ: *Sp.* amigo   v̲: *Sp.* hablar
hl: *Welsh* Llanelli.   CAPITALS: primary stress.   SMALL CAPS: secondary stress.   ⑤: U.S. pron.   ⑭: British pron.

Hezronite
  Biblical name   HEZ-ruh-NĪT   'hezrə‚naıt

Hialeah
  town, FL   HĪ-uh-LĒ-uh   ‚haıə'liːə

Hiawassee [Hiwassee]
  town, river, GA   HĪ-uh-WAHS-ē   ‚haıə'wasiˑ

Hiawatha
  legendary Onondaga chief   HĪ-uh-WAW-thuh, HĪ-uh-WAHTH-uh,   ‚haıə'wɔːθə, ‚haıə'waθə,
           HĒ-uh-   ‚hiːə-

Hibernia
  ancient Latin name of Ireland   hī-BUHR-nē-uh   haı'bəᵉniːə

Hibernian
  pert. to Hibernia   hī-BUHR-nē-uhn   haı'bəᵉniːən

Hickok
  James ("Wild Bill"), US   HIK-AHK   'hık‚ak
    frontiersman

Hicks
  Sir John R., English economist   HIKS   'hıks
    (Nobel 1972)

Hidalgo
  1. county, NM, TX   hid-AL-gō   hid'ælgoː
  2. state, Mexico   ē-T͟HAHL-ḡō   iː'ðalγoː

Hidatsa
  N. American people   hi-DAHT-suh, hi-DAT-suh   hi'datsə, hi'dætsə

Hiddai
  Biblical name   HID-ē-Ī, HID-Ī, hid-Ā-Ī, hi-DĪ   'hidiː‚aı, 'hid‚aı, hid'eːaı,
           hi'daı

Hiddekel
  Biblical name   HID-uh-kuhl, k͟hi-DEK-EL   'hidəkəl, xi'dek‚el

Hideki
  pers. name, Japanese   hē-dek-ē   hiːdekiː

Hideyo, Hideo
  pers. name, Japanese   hē-de-yō   hiːdejoː

Hiel
  Biblical name   HĪ-EL, k͟hē-EL   'haı‚el, xiː'el

Hiera
  wife of Telephus   HĪ-uh-ruh   'haıərə

Hierapolis
  Biblical name   HĪ-uh-RAHP-(uh-)lis   ‚haıə'rap(ə)lis

Hierax
  hero turned into a falcon   HĪ-uh-RAKS   'haıə‚ræks

Hiero
  tyrants of Syracuse   HĪ-uh-rō   ‚haıəroː

Hieronymus
  1. pers. name   HĪ-uh-RAHN-uh-muhs,   ‚haıə'ranəməs, hə'ranəməs
           huh-RAHN-uh-muhs
  2. Dutch   HĒ-uh-RŌ-nē-mues   ‚hiːə'roːniːmys
  3. German   HĒ-ā-RŌ-nue-mus   ‚hiːeː'roːnyːmus

Higgaion
  Biblical name   hi-GĀ-AHN, hi-GĪ-AHN, HIG-ah-YŌN   hi'geː‚an, hi'gaı‚an,
           ‚higa'joːn

Higginbotham
  Jay C., jazz musician   HIG-uhn-BAHTH-uhm   'higən‚baθəm

Higgins
  Jack, British author   HIG-uhnz   'higənz

Key (col. 2):   a: fad   ā: fade   ah: father   ar: marry   aw: law   e: fed   ē: feed   er: merry   i: hid   ī: hide   ō: coat   ōō: boot
oi: boy   ow: now   u: put   uh: above   uhr: bird   ch: chop   ng: ring   sh: show   th: thick   t͟h: this   zh: measure

Highgate
  1. town, VT HĪ-GĀT 'hɑiˌgeːt
  2. part of Haringey, *London,* HĪ-guht 'hɑigət
    England
Highland
  US pl. name; region, Scotland HĪ-luhnd 'hɑilənd
High Wycombe
  town, England HĪ WIK-uhm ˌhɑi 'wikəm
Hiiumaa
  island, Baltic Sea HĒ-uh-MAH 'hiːəˌmɑ
Hiko, Hyko
  Range, *mtn. range, NV* HĪ-kō 'hɑikoː
Hilaire
  pers. name hil-AR, hil-ER; Ⓔ *also* HIL-ER hil'æ\u02b3, hil'e\u02b3; Ⓔ *also* 'hilˌe\u02b3
Hilarius
  pope huh-LAR-ē-uhs hə'læriːəs
Hilarus
  pope HIL-uh-ruhs 'hilərəs
Hilary
  pers. name HIL-uh-rē 'hiləri·
Hilbert
  David, *German mathematician* HIL-buhrt 'hilbə\u02b3t
Hilburn
  Robert, *US music critic* HIL-BUHRN 'hilˌbə\u02b3n
Hilda
  pers. name HIL-duh 'hildə
Hildebrand
  1. pers. name HIL-duh-BRAND 'hildəˌbrænd
  2. Dutch, German HIL-duh-BRAHNT 'hildəˌbrɑnt
Hildegard
  pers. name, Finnish HIL-de-GAHRD 'hildeˌgɑrd
Hildegarde
  pers. name HIL-duh-GAHRD 'hildəˌgɑ\u02b3d
Hildegard of Bingen
  German nun, mystic, and composer HIL-duh-GAHRD uhv BING-uhn 'hildəˌgɑ\u02b3d əv 'biŋən
Hildesheim
  prov, Germany HIL-duhs-HĪM 'hildəsˌhɑim
Hilen
  Biblical name HĪ-LEN, khi-LEN 'hɑiˌlen, xi'len
Hiligaynon
  lang., people, Philippines HIL-uh-GĪ-nuhn ˌhilə'gɑinən
Hilkiah
  Biblical name hil-KĪ-uh, KHIL-ki-YAH hil'kɑiə, ˌxilki'jɑ
Hill
  A. V., *English physiologist (Nobel* HIL 'hil
    1922)
Hillary
  pers. name HIL-uh-rē 'hiləri·
Hillel
  Jewish scholar HIL-uhl, HIL-EL 'hiləl, 'hilˌel
Hiller
  Arthur, *Canadian film director;* HIL-uhr 'hilə\u02b3
    Wendy, *British actress*
Hillerman
  John, *US actor* HIL-uhr-muhn 'hilə\u02b3mən

Foreign Sounds: ue: *Fr.* **rue**, *Ger.* **füllen** uh(r): *Fr.* **boeuf**, *Ger.* **Höhle** <u>kh</u>: *Ger.* i**ch**, *Scot.* lo**ch** ḡ: *Sp.* ami**g**o v̱: *Sp.* ha**b**lar
hl: *Welsh* **Ll**anelli. CAPITALS: primary stress. SMALL CAPS: secondary stress. Ⓢ: U.S. pron. Ⓔ: British pron.

Hillingdon
  borough, England   HIL-ing-duhn   'hiliŋdən
Hilo
  city, HI   HĒ-lō   'hiːloː
Hilton
  Conrad, *US hotelier; pers. name*   HILT-n   'hiltn̩
Hilversum
  city, Netherlands   HIL-vuhr-suhm   'hilvəʳsəm
Himachal Pradesh
  state, India   huh-MAHCH-uhl pruh-DĀSH,   hə'matʃəl prə'deːʃ, prə'deʃ
                                      pruh-DESH
Himalayan
  pert. to the Himalayas; *cat*   HIM-uh-LĀ-uhn, huh-MAHL-(uh-)yuhn   ˌhimə'leːən, hə'mɑl(ə)jən
Himalayas
  The, *mts., Asia*   HIM-uh-LĀ-uhz, huh-MAHL-(uh-)yuhz   ˌhimə'leːəz, hə'mɑl(ə)jəz
Himalia
  satellite of Jupiter   huh-MĀ-lē-uh, huh-MĀL-yuh   hə'meːliːə, hə'meːljə
Himerus
  personification of sexual desire in HIM-uh-ruhs   'himərəs
  Greek mythology
Himmler
  Heinrich, *German Nazi leader*   HIM-luhr   'himləʳ
Himno Istmeño
  national anthem, Panama   ĒM-nō ēst-MĀN-yō   'iːmnoː iːst'meːnjoː
Hinano
  Tahitian beer   hē-NAHN-ō   hiː'nɑnoː
Hinayana [Theravada]
  branch of Buddhism   HĒ-nuh-YAHN-uh   ˌhiːnə'jɑnə
Hinayanism
  branch of Buddhism   HĒ-nuh-YAHN-ɪZ-uhm   ˌhiːnə'jɑnˌizəm
Hinckley
  John, Jr., *US convict, attempted* HING-klē   'hiŋkliˑ
  assassin
Hindemith
  Paul, *German composer*   HIN-duh-mit   'hindəmit
Hindenburg
  Paul von, *president, Germany;*   HIN-duhn-BURK, ⑤ HIN-duhn-BUHRG,   'hindən,buʳk,
  German airship   -BURG   ⑤ 'hindən,bəʳg, -,buʳg
Hindes
  pers. name   HĪN(D)Z   'hain(d)z
Hindi
  lang., India, Africa, Fiji, Surinam, HIN-dē   'hindiˑ
  Guyanas
Hindman
  city, KY   HĪN(D)-muhn   'hain(d)mən
Hinds
  county, MS   HĪN(D)Z   'hain(d)z
Hindu
  Indian culture   HIN-d͞o͞o   'hinduː
Hindu Kush
  mts., Asia   HIN-d͞o͞o KUSH, KUHSH   ˌhinduː 'kuʃ, 'kəʃ
Hindustani
  lang., N. India   HIN-d͞o͞o-STAN-ē, HIN-d͞o͞o-STAHN-ē   ˌhinduː'stæniˑ, ˌhinduː'stɑniˑ
Hinnom
  Biblical name   HIN-AHM, HIN-uhm, hi-NAWM   'hin,ɑm, 'hinəm, hi'nɔːm

---

Key (col. 2): a: fad ā: fade ah: father ar: marry aw: law e: fed ē: feed er: merry i: hid ī: hide ō: coat o͞o: boot
oi: boy ow: now u: put uh: above uhr: bird ch: chop ng: ring sh: show th: thick tẖ: this zh: measure

Hinshelwood
Sir Cyril N., *English chemist (Nobel*   HIN-chuhl-WUD   'hintʃəl,wud
1956)

Hippalus
Greek explorer   HIP-uh-luhs   'hipələs

Hipparchus
crater on Moon   hi-PAHR-kuhs   hi'paʳkəs

Hippe
daughter of Chiron   HIP-ē   'hipiˑ

Hippias
tyrant of Athens; Lesser *and*   HIP-ē-uhs   'hipiːəs
Greater, *dialogues of Plato*

Hipple
Eric, *US football player*   HIP-uhl   'hipəl

Hippocrates
Greek physician   hip-AHK-ruh-TĒZ   hip'ɑkrə,tiːz

Hippocratic
pert. to Hippocrates; *medical oath*   HIP-uh-KRAT-ik   ,hipə'kræţik

Hippocrene
fountain of inspiration created by   HIP-uh-KRĒN, HIP-uh-KRĒ-nē   'hipə,kriːn, ,hipə'kriːniˑ
Pegasus on Mt. Helicon

Hippodamia
wife of Pelops   HIP-uh-duh-MĪ-uh   ,hipədə'mɑiə

Hippodamus
Greek architect   hip-AHD-uh-muhs   hip'adəməs

Hippodrome
New York City theater   HIP-uh-DRŌM   'hipə,droːm

Hippogriff
fabulous creature   HIP-uh-GRIF   'hipə,grif

Hippolyta
queen of Amazons   hip-AHL-uht-uh   hip'aləţə

Hippolyte
pers. name, French   ē(p)-paw-LĒT   iː(p)pɔliːt

Hippolytus
son of Theseus   hip-AHL-uht-uhs   hip'aləţəs

Hippomedon
one of Seven against Thebes   hi-PAHM-uhd-uhn, hi-PAHM-uh-DAHN   hi'pamədən, hi'pamə,dan

Hippomenes
suitor of Atalanta   hi-PAHM-uh-NĒZ   hi'pamə,niːz

Hippotes
father of Aletes   HIP-uht-ĒZ   'hipəţ,iːz

Hirah
Biblical name   HĪ-ruh, khē-RAH   'hairə, xiː'rɑ

Hiram
township, OH; biblical ruler; pers.   HĪ-ruhm   'hairəm
name

Hirohito
emperor, Japan   HIR-uh-HĒT-ō   ,hirə'hiːţoː

Hiroshi
pers. name, Japanese   hē-rō-shē   hiːroːʃiː

Hiroshige
Ando, *Japanese painter*   hē-rō-shē-ge   hiːroːʃiːge

Hiroshima
city, Japan   hē-rō-shē-mah, Ⓢ HIR-uh-SHĒ-muh,   hiːroːʃiːmɑ, Ⓢ ,hirə'ʃiːmə,
huh-RŌ-shuh-muh   hə'roːʃəmə

Foreign Sounds: ue: *Fr.* **rue**, *Ger.* **füllen**   uh(r): *Fr.* **boeuf**, *Ger.* **Höhle**   kh: *Ger.* **ich**, *Scot.* **loch**   ḡ: *Sp.* **amigo**   ᵛ: *Sp.* **hablar** hl: *Welsh* **Llanelli.**   CAPITALS: primary stress.   SMALL CAPS: secondary stress.   Ⓢ: U.S. pron.   Ⓔ: British pron.

Hirsch
　Judd, *US actor* 　　　　　　　　HUHRSH　　　　　　　　　　　'hə^rʃ

Hirschfeld
　Al, *US cartoonist* 　　　　　　　HUHRSH-FELD　　　　　　　　'hə^rʃ,feld

Hirshhorn
　Joseph Herman, *US financier, art*　HUHRSH-HAWRN, HUHR-SHAWRN　'hə^rʃ,hɔː^rn, 'hə^r,ʃɔː^rn
　　collector; museum, Washington,
　　D.C.

Hispania
　Roman name for Spain 　　　　　his-PAN-yuh, his-PAN-ē-uh　　　his'pænjə, his'pæniːə

Hispanic
　pert. to Spain *and/or* Latin America　his-PAN-ik, *in running speech also*　his'pænik, *in running speech*
　　　　　　　　　　　　　　　　　is-PAN-ik　　　　　　　　　　*also* is'pænik

Hispaniola
　island, West Indies 　　　　　　HIS-puhn-YŌ-luh　　　　　　　,hispən'joːlə

Histiaeus
　tyrant of Miletus 　　　　　　　HIS-tuh-Ē-uhs　　　　　　　　,histə'iːəs

Hitachi
　Japanese corp. 　　　　　　　　hi-tahch-ē　　　　　　　　　　hitatʃiː

Hitchcock
　Sir Alfred Joseph, *English film*　HICH-KAHK　　　　　　　　　'hitʃ,kɑk
　　director

Hitchings
　George H., *US chemist (Nobel 1988)*　HICH-ingz　　　　　　　　'hitʃiŋz

Hitler
　Adolf, *Nazi dictator* 　　　　　　HIT-luhr　　　　　　　　　　'hitlə^r

Hitlerian
　pert. to Hitler 　　　　　　　　hit-LIR-ē-uhn, hit-LER-ē-uhn　hit'liriːən, hit'leriːən

Hitlerism
　adherence to practices of Nazi party　HIT-luh-RIZ-uhm　　　　　　'hitlə,rizəm

Hitlerite
　adherent of Hitlerism 　　　　　HIT-luh-RĪT　　　　　　　　　'hitlə,rait

Hittite
　ancient people of Asia Minor 　　HI-TĪT　　　　　　　　　　　'hi,tait

Hivite
　Biblical name 　　　　　　　　HĪ-VĪT　　　　　　　　　　　'hai,vait

Hiwassee
　river, US; college, dam, TN 　　hī-WAHS-ē　　　　　　　　　hai'wasi·

Hiwassee [Hiawassee]
　rivèr, SE United States 　　　　hī-WAHS-ē　　　　　　　　　hai'wasi·

Hizkiah, Hizkijah [Hezekiah]
　Biblical name 　　　　　　　　hiz-KĪ-uh, k͟hiz-ki-YAH　　　hiz'kaiə, xizki'ja

Hjalmar
　1. pers. name, Danish 　　　　YAHL-MAHR　　　　　　　　　'jaːl,mar
　2. Finnish, Swedish 　　　　　YAHL-MAHR　　　　　　　　　'jaːl,maːr
　3. Icelandic, Norwegian 　　　YAHL-MAHR　　　　　　　　　'jal,mar

Hler
　Scandinavian god 　　　　　　HLER　　　　　　　　　　　　'hle^r, 'le^r

Hmong [Miao]
　lang., people, China,Vietnam, Laos,　(H)MAWNG, (H)MAHNG　　　'(h)mɔːŋ, '(h)maŋ
　　Thailand

Ho
　Don, *US entertainer* 　　　　　HŌ　　　　　　　　　　　　　'hoː

Hoagy
　pers. name (H. Carmichael) 　　HŌ-gē　　　　　　　　　　　'hoːgi·

Key (col. 2):　a: fad　ā: fade　ah: father　ar: marry　aw: law　e: fed　ē: feed　er: merry　i: hid　ī: hide　ō: coat　oo: boot
oi: boy　ow: now　u: put　uh: above　uhr: bird　ch: chop　ng: ring　sh: show　th: thick　th: this　zh: measure

Hoatzin
   South American bird   wah(t)-SĒN   wɑ(t)'siːn

Hobab
   Biblical name   HŌ-BAB, <u>kh</u>ō-VAHV   'hoː,bæb, xoː'vɑv

Hobah
   Biblical name   HŌ-buh, <u>kh</u>ō-VAH   'hoːbə, xoː'vɑ

Hobart
   1. pers. name   HŌ-buhrt, HŌ-BAHRT, Ⓔ *also*   'hoːbəᴿt, 'hoː,bɑᴿt, Ⓔ *also*
           HUHB-uhrt   'həbəᴿt
   2. pl. name, IN   HŌ-buhrt   'hoːbəᴿt
   3. city, Tasmania   HŌ-BAHRT   'hoː,bɑᴿt

Hobbes
   Thomas, *British philosopher; comic*   HAHBZ   'hɑbz
    strip tiger

Hobbism
   philosophy of T. Hobbes   HAHB-IZ-uhm   'hɑb,izəm

Hoboken
   city, NJ; number designating F. J.   HŌ-bō-kuhn   'hoːboːkən
    Haydn compositions

Hobson-Jobson
   altered foreign borrowing   HAHB-suhn-JAHB-suhn   ,hɑbsən'dʒɑbsən

Hobson's choice
   no real alternative   HAHB-suhnz CHOIS   ,hɑbsənz 'tʃɔis

Hochheim
   commune, Germany   HŌ<u>KH</u>-HĪM, Ⓢ HAHK-HĪM, HŌK-,   'hoːx,haim, Ⓢ 'hak,haim,
           HAWK-   'hoːk-, 'hɔːk-

Hochi
   Honolulu newspaper   HŌ-chē   'hoːtʃiˑ

Ho Chi Minh
   president, N. Vietnam   HŌ chē MIN, HŌ shē MIN   ,hoː tʃiː 'min, ,hoː ʃiː 'min

Ho Chi Minh City [Saigon]
   city, Vietnam   HŌ chē MIN SIT-ē, shē   ,hoː tʃiː ,min 'siṭiˑ, ʃiː

Hod
   Biblical name   HAHD, HŌD   'had, 'hoːd

Hodaiah
   Biblical name   hō-DĀ-(y)uh, hō-DĪ-(y)uh,   hoː'deː(j)ə, hoː'dai(j)ə,
           HŌD-ah-YAH-ho͞o   ,hoːdɑ'jɑhuː

Hodaviah
   Biblical name   HŌD-uh-VĪ-uh, HŌ-DAHV-YAH   ,hoːdə'vaiə, ,hoː,dɑv'ja

Hodding
   pers. name   HAHD-ing   'hadiŋ

Hodesh
   Biblical name   HŌ-DESH, <u>KH</u>AW-DESH   'hoː,deʃ, 'xɔː,deʃ

Hodevah
   Biblical name   HŌD-uh-VAH, hō-DĒ-vuh, HŌD-i-VAH   'hoːdə,va, hoː'diːvə,
                                               ,hoːdi'va

Hodgkin
   Sir Alan Lloyd, *English physiologist*   HAHJ-kin   'hadʒkin
    (Nobel 1963); Dorothy Mary
    Crowfoot, *English chemist (Nobel*
    1964)

Hodgkin's disease
   lymphatic cancer   HAHJ-kinz di-ZĒZ   'hadʒkinz di,ziːz

Hodiah, Hodijah
   Biblical name   hō-DĪ-uh, HŌ-dē-YAH   hoː'daiə, ,hoːdiː'ja

---

Foreign Sounds: ue: *Fr.* **rue**, *Ger.* **füllen**   uh(r): *Fr.* **boeuf**, *Ger.* **Höhle**   <u>kh</u>: *Ger.* i**ch**, *Scot.* lo**ch**   g̱: *Sp.* ami**g**o   v: *Sp.* ha**b**lar
hl: *Welsh* **Ll**anelli.   CAPITALS: primary stress.   SMALL CAPS: secondary stress.   Ⓢ: U.S. pron.   Ⓔ: British pron.

Hodža
  Milan, *politician, prime minister,*   HAWJ-ah   'hɔːdʒɑ
  Czechoslovakia
Hoechst Celanese
  US chemical co.   HŌKST SEL-uh-NĒZ, SEL-uh-NĒS   'hoːkst ˌseləˈniːz, ˌseləˈniːs
Hoegaarden
  Belgian beer   H̄OO-GAHRD-n   'huːˌgɑːrdn̩
Hoek van Holland
  prov, Netherlands   H̄OOK vahn HŌ-LAHNT   'huːk van 'hoːˌlant
Hofbräu
  German beer   HAWF-BROI   'hɔːfˌbrɔi
Hoffa
  James Riddle (Jimmy), *US labor*   HAHF-uh, HAW-fuh   'hafə, 'hɔːfə
  leader
Hoffman
  Dustin, *US actor*   HAHF-muhn, HAWF-muhn   'hafmən, 'hɔːfmən
Hoffmann
  Roald, *Polish-born US chemist*   HAHF-muhn, HAWF-muhn   'hafmən, 'hɔːfmən
  (Nobel 1981)
Hofmannsthal
  Hugo von, *Austrian poet and*   HAWF-mahn-STAHL   'hɔːfmɑnˌstɑl
  playwright
Hofmark Wurzig
  German beer   HAWF-MAHRK VURT-siᴋʜ   'hɔːfˌmɑrk 'vurtsiç
Hofstadter
  Robert, *US physicist (Nobel 1961)*   HŌF-STAT-uhr, HAHF-, HAWF-   'hoːfˌstæʈərˈ, 'haf-, 'hɔːf-
Hofstra
  University, *NY*   HAHF-struh, HAWF-struh   'hafstrə, 'hɔːfstrə
Hogan
  Ben, *US golfer, business executive*   HŌ-guhn   'hoːgən
Hogarth
  William, *English artist*   HŌ-GAHRTH   'hoːˌgɑrˈθ
Hoggar [Ahaggar]
  mtn. range, Algeria   HAHG-uhr, HUH-GAHR   'hagər, ˌhəˈgar
Hoglah
  Biblical name   HAHG-luh, HAWG-luh, ᴋʜahg-LAH   'haglə, 'hɔːglə, xagˈla
Hogmanay
  Dec. 31, Scotland   HAHG-muh-NĀ   'hagməˌneː
Hoh
  N. American people   HŌ   'hoː
Hoham
  Biblical name   HŌ-HAM, HŌ-(h)uhm, hō-HAHM   'hoːˌhæm, 'hoː(h)əm,
      hoːˈham
Hohenzollern
  German royal family   HŌ-uhnt-SAWL-uhrn   'hoːəntˌsɔːlərˈn
Hohe Tauern
  Alpine mtn. range   HŌ-uh TOW-uhrn   ˌhoːə 'tauəˈrn
Hohokam
  Park, *stadium, Mesa, AZ*   hō-HŌ-kuhm   hoːˈhoːkəm
Ho-Ho-Kus
  borough, NJ   hō-HŌ-kuhs   hoːˈhoːkəs
Hojatolislam
  pers. name, Arabic   HŌ-yuh-T̄OO-lis-LAHM   ˌhoːjəˈtuːlisˌlam
Hokkaidō
  island, Japan   haw(k)-kī-dō, Ⓢ hah-KĪD-ō   hɔː(k)kaidoː, Ⓢ haˈkaidoː

Key (col. 2):   a: fad   ā: fade   ah: father   ar: marry   aw: law   e: fed   ē: feed   er: merry   i: hid   ī: hide   ō: coat   ōo: boot
oi: boy   ow: now   u: put   uh: above   uhr: bird   ch: chop   ng: ring   sh: show   th: thick   th: this   zh: measure

Hokkien
lang., China — HAWK-kē-EN — 'hɔːkkiːˈen

Hokusai Katsushika
Japanese artist — hō-kus-ī kaht-sush-ē-kah — hoːkusɑi kɑtsuʃiːkɑ

Hola
Hindu festival — HŌ-lah — 'hoːlɑ

Holbein
Hans, Jr. & Sr., *German painters* — HŌL-BĪN, HAWL-BĪN — 'hoːl,bain, 'hɔːl,bain

Holbrook
Hal, *US actor* — HŌL-BRUK — 'hoːl,bruk

Holder
Geoffrey, *West Indian dancer, actor* — HŌL-duhr — 'hoːldəʳ

Holderness
1. town, NH — HŌL-duhr-nuhs — 'hoːldəʳnəs
2. peninsula, England — HŌL-duhr-NES — ,hoːldəʳˈnes

Holi
Hindu festival — HŌ-lē — 'hoːliˑ

Holiness
title of the pope — HŌ-lē-nuhs — 'hoːliˑnəs

Holinshed
Raphael, *English chronicler* — HAHL-uhn-SHED, HAHL-uhnz-HED — 'halən,ʃed, 'halənz,hed

Holland
The Netherlands; town, MI — HAHL-uhnd — 'halənd

Hollandaise
egg-based sauce — HAHL-uhn-DĀZ — 'halən,deːz

Hollands
Dutch gin — HAHL-uhndz — 'haləndz

Hollerith
Herman, *US inventor* — HŌL-uh-rith — 'hoːləriθ

Holley
Robert W., *US biochemist (Nobel 1968)* — HAHL-ē — 'haliˑ

Holliman
Earl, *US actor* — HAHL-uh-muhn — 'haləmən

Hollings
Earnest Frederick, *US politician* — HAHL-ingz — 'haliŋz

Hollins College
town, college, VA — HAHL-uhnz — 'halənz

Hollis
pers. name — HAHL-uhs — 'haləs

Hollister
pers. name — HAHL-uhs-tuhr — 'haləstəʳ

Holloway
Stanley, *English entertainer* — HAHL-uh-WĀ — 'halə,weː

Holly
pers. name — HAHL-ē — 'haliˑ

Hollywood
city, CA; town, FL — HAHL-ē-WUD — 'haliˑ,wud

Holm
Celeste, *US actress* — HŌM — 'hoːm

Holmes
pers. name — HŌMZ — 'hoːmz

Holmes, Sherlock
fictional detective by A. Conan Doyle — SHUHR-luhk HŌMZ, SHUHR-LAHK, HŌLMZ — 'ʃəʳlək 'hoːmz, 'ʃəʳ,lak, 'hoːlmz

---

Foreign Sounds: ue: *Fr.* **rue**, *Ger.* **füllen** uh(r): *Fr.* **boeuf**, *Ger.* **Höhle** <u>kh</u>: *Ger.* **ich**, *Scot.* **loch** ḡ: *Sp.* **amigo** v̄: *Sp.* **hablar** hl: *Welsh* **Llanelli**. CAPITALS: primary stress. SMALL CAPS: secondary stress. Ⓢ: U.S. pron. Ⓔ: British pron.

holmium
  element — HŌ(L)-mē-uhm — 'hoː(l)miːəm
Holocene
  geologic epoch — HŌ-luh-SĒN, HAHL-uh- — 'hoːləˌsiːn, 'halə-
Holofernes
  1. Biblical general beheaded by — HAHL-uh-FUHR-NĒZ, HŌ-luh-FUHR-NĒZ — ˌhaləˈfəʳˌniːz, ˌhoːləˈfəʳˌniːz
  Judith
  2. schoolmaster in Love's Labour's — HAHL-uh-FAHR-NĒZ, HŌ-luh-FAHR-NĒZ, — ˌhaləˈfaʳˌniːz, ˌhoːləˈfaʳˌniːz,
  Lost, *Shakespeare* — -FUHR-NĒZ — -ˈfəʳˌniːz
Holon
  Biblical name — HŌ-LAHN, <u>kh</u>aw-LAWN — 'hoːˌlɑn, xɔːˈlɔːn
Holst
  Gustav, *English composer* — HŌLST — 'hoːlst
Holstein
  1. region, Germany — HŌL-SHTĪN, ⑤ HŌL-STĪN, HŌL-STĒN — 'hoːlˌʃtain, ⑤ 'hoːlˌstain, 'hoːlˌstiːn
  2. cattle — HŌL-STĒN, HŌL-STĪN — 'hoːlˌstiːn, 'hoːlˌstain
Holyhead
  town, Wales — HAHL-ē-HED — 'haliˑˌhed
Holyoke
  city, MA — HŌ-lē-ŌK, *locally* HŌ(L)-YŌK — 'hoːliːˌoːk, *locally* 'hoˑ(l)ˌjoːk
Holy Rood
  cross of Jesus — HŌ-lē R͞OOD — ˌhoːliˑ 'ruːd
Holyrood
  royal palace, Scotland — HAHL-ē-R͞OOD — 'haliˑˌruːd
Holy See
  papal court — HŌ-lē SĒ — ˌhoːliˑ 'siː
Holywell
  town, Wales — HAHL-ē-WEL, HAHL-ē-wuhl — 'haliːˌwel, 'haliˑwəl
Homam
  Biblical name — HŌ-MAM, hō-MAHM — 'hoːˌmæm, hoːˈmɑm
Homburg
  city, Germany — HAWM-BURK, ⑤ HAHM-BUHRG — 'hɔːmˌbuʳk, ⑤ 'hamˌbəʳg
Home
  Henry, Lord Kames, *Scottish jurist* — HY͞OOM — 'hjuːm
  and philosopher
Homer
  Greek epic poet; pers. name — HŌ-muhr — 'hoːməʳ
Homeric
  pert. to Homer — hō-MER-ik — hoːˈmerik
Homerton
  society, Cambridge Univ. — HAHM-uhrt-n — 'haməʳtn̩
Homoousian
  adherent of or pert. to the doctrine of — HŌ-mō-ŌO-sē-uhn, — ˌhoːmoːˈuːsiːən,
  the Nicene creed — HŌ-mō-ŌO-zh(ē-)uhn — ˌhoːmoːˈuːʒ(iː)ən
Homo sapiens
  human being — HŌ-mō SAP-ē-uhnz, SĀ-pē-uhnz — ˌhoːmoː 'sæpiːənz, 'seːpiːənz
Honan [Henan, Luoyang]
  prov, town, China — HUH-NAHN, ⑤ HŌ-NAHN — 'həˈnan, ⑤ 'hoːˈnan
Honda
  Japanese car co. — HAHN-duh — 'handə
Honduran
  pert. to Honduras — hahn-D(Y)UR-uhn — hɑnˈd(j)urən
Honduras
  republic, Cen. America — hahn-D(Y)UR-uhs — hɑnˈd(j)urəs

Key (col. 2):   a: **fad**   ā: **fade**   ah: **father**   ar: **marry**   aw: **law**   e: **fed**   ē: **feed**   er: **merry**   i: **hid**   ī: **hide**   ō: **coat**   ōo: **boot**
oi: **boy**   ow: **now**   u: **put**   uh: **above**   uhr: **bird**   ch: **chop**   ng: **ring**   sh: **show**   th: **thick**   <u>th</u>: **this**   zh: **measure**

Honecker
  Erich, *East German politician*   HŌ-nuh-kuhr   ˈhoːnəkəʳ

Honegger
  Arthur, *Swiss composer*   aw-nā-GER   ɔːneːger

Honeywell
  US corp.   HUHN-ē-WEL   ˈhəniˑˌwel

Hong Kong
  British colony, SE Asia   HAHNG-KAHNG, HAHNG-KAHNG,   ˈhaŋˌkaŋ, ˈhaŋˈkaŋ,
      HAWNG-KAWNG, HAWNG-KAWNG   ˈhɔːŋˌkɔːŋ, ˈhɔːŋˈkɔːŋ

Honiara
  town, Solomon Islands   HŌ-nē-AHR-uh   ˌhoːniːˈɑrə

Honolulu
  county, city, HI   HAHN-l-OO-loo, HŌN-l-OO-loo   ˌhanlˈuːluː, ˌhoːnlˈuːluː

Honor
  pers. name   AHN-uhr   ˈɑnəʳ

Honorat
  pers. name, French   aw-naw-RAH   ɔːnɔːrɑː

Honoré
  1. pers. name   AHN-uh-RĀ, AHN-uh-RĀ   ˌɑnəˈreː, ˈɑnəˌreː
  2. French   aw-naw-RĀ   ɔːnɔːreː

Honorius
  pope; pers. name, Latin   hō-NŌR-ē-uhs, huh-, -NAWR-ē-uhs   hoːˈnoːriːəs, hə-, -ˈnɔːriːəs

Honshū
  island, Japan   hawn-shoo, Ⓢ HAHN-shoo   hɔːnʃuː, Ⓢ ˈhanʃuː

Hooch, Hoogh
  Pieter de, *Dutch painter*   HŌKH   ˈhoːx

Hooghly
  river, India   HOO-glē   ˈhuːgliˑ

Hookham
  pers. name   HUK-uhm   ˈhukəm

Hoonah
  city, AK   HOO-nuh   ˈhuːnə

Hoopa
  N. American people   HOO-puh, HUP-uh   ˈhuːpə, ˈhupə

Hoosier
  someone from Indiana   HOO-zhuhr   ˈhuːʒəʳ

Hoover
  Herbert, *31st US president*   HOO-vuhr   ˈhuːvəʳ

Hooverville
  Depression shantytown   HOO-vuhr-VIL   ˈhuːvəʳˌvil

Hope
  town, AR; pers. name   HŌP   ˈhoːp

Hopeh [Hebei]
  prov, China   HUH-BĀ, Ⓢ HŌ-BĀ, HŌ-PĀ   ˈhəˈbeː, Ⓢ ˈhoːˈbeː, ˈhoːˈpeː

Hopfenperle
  Swiss beer   HAWP-fuhn-PER-luh   ˈhɔːpfənˌpeʳlə

Hophni
  Biblical name   HAHF-NĪ, khahf-NĒ   ˈhafˌnai, xafˈniː

Hopi
  N. American people   HŌ-pē   ˈhoːpiˑ

Hopkins
  Sir Frederick G., *English biochemist*   HAHP-kuhnz, -kinz   ˈhapkənz, -kinz
  (Nobel 1929); Gerard Manley,
  English poet; Johns, *US financier*

Hopkinsianism
   Christian sect   hahp-KIN-zē-uh-NIZ-uhm   hɑp'kinziːəˌnizəm

Hoplite
   Greek heavy-armed soldier   HAHP-LĪT   'hɑpˌlait

Hopper
   Dennis, *US actor, writer, film*   HAHP-uhr   'hɑpəʳ
       director

Hoquiam
   seaport, WA   HŌ-kwē-uhm   'hoːkwiːəm

Hor
   Egyptian god, aspect of Horus HAWR   'hɔːʳ

Hora, Horah
   Israeli and Romanian dance   HŌR-uh, HAWR-uh   'hoːrə, 'hɔːrə

Horace
   1. Roman poet; pers. name   HAWR-uhs, HAHR-uhs   'hɔːrəs, 'hɑrəs
   2. French   aw-RAHS   ɔːrɑːs

Horae
   Greek goddesses of the seasons HŌR-Ē, HAWR-Ē, HŌR-Ī, HAWR-Ī   'hoːrˌiː, 'hɔːrˌiː, 'hoːrˌai,
                                                        'hɔːrˌai

Horam
   Biblical name   HAWR-AM, HŌR-AM, hō-RAHM 'hɔːrˌæm, 'hoːrˌæm, hoː'rɑm

Horatian
   pert. to Horace   huh-RĀ-shuhn   hə're:ʃən

Horatii
   legendary Roman heros   huh-RĀ-shē-Ē   hə're:ʃiːˌiː

Horatio
   pers. name   huh-RĀ-sh(ē-)ō   hə're:ʃ(iː)oː

Horatius
   pers. name   huh-RĀ-sh(ē-)uhs   hə're:ʃ(iː)əs

Horeb [Sinai]
   mtn., Sinai peninsula   HŌR-EB, HAWR-EB   'hoːrˌeb, 'hɔːrˌeb

Horem
   Biblical name   HAWR-EM, HŌR-EM, <u>kh</u>aw-REM 'hɔːrˌem, 'hoːrˌem, xɔː'rem

Hor-hagidgad, Hor-haggidgad
   Biblical name   HAWR-huh-GID-GAD,   ˌhɔːʳhə'gidˌgæd,
                   <u>KH</u>AWR-hah-GID-GAHD   ˌxɔːrhaˌgid'gad

Hori
   Biblical name   HAWR-Ī, HŌR-Ī, <u>kh</u>aw-RĒ   'hɔːrˌai, 'hoːrˌai, xɔː'riː

Horite
   Biblical name   HAWR-ĪT, HŌR-ĪT   'hɔːrˌait, 'hoːrˌait

Horlicks
   tdmk for a malted milk powder HAWR-liks   'hɔːʳliks

Hormah
   Biblical name   HAWR-muh, <u>kh</u>awr-MAH   'hɔːʳmə, xɔːr'mɑ

Hormel
   US food products co.   hawr-MEL   hɔːʳ'mel

Hormisdas
   pope   hawr-MIZ-duhs   hɔːʳ'mizdəs

Hormuz
   strait, Persian Gulf   HAWR-muhz, hawr-MŌŌZ   'hɔːʳməz, hɔːʳ'muːz

Hornblende
   mineral   HAWRN-BLEND   'hɔːʳnˌblend

Hornell
   city, NY   hawr-NEL   hɔːʳ'nel

Key (col. 2):   a: fad ā: fade ah: father ar: marry aw: law e: fed ē: feed er: merry i: hid ī: hide ō: coat ōō: boot
oi: boy ow: now u: put uh: above uhr: bird ch: chop ng: ring sh: show th: thick th: this zh: measure

Hornsby
  Bruce, *singer, songwriter*   HAWRNZ-bē   'hɔːᵊnzbiˑ

Hornsby
  Rogers, *US baseball player*   HAWRNZ-bē   'hɔːᵊnzbiˑ

Hornung
  Paul, *sports personality*   HAWR-nuhng   'hɔːᵊnəŋ

Horologium
  constellation   HAWR-uh-LŌ-jē-uhm   ˌhɔːrə'loːdʒiːəm

Horonaim
  Biblical name   HAHR-uh-NĀ-im, HAWR-uh-;   ˌhɑrə'neːim, ˌhɔːrə-;
      KHAW-raw-NAH-yim   ˌxɔːrɔː'nɑjim

Horonite
  Biblical name   HAHR-uh-NĪT, HAWR-uh-NĪT   'hɑrəˌnɑit, 'hɔːrəˌnɑit

Horovitz
  Israel Arthur, *US playwright*   HAWR-uh-VITS, HAHR-uh-VITS   'hɔːrəˌvits, 'hɑrəˌvits

Horowitz
  Vladimir, *Russian pianist*   HAWR-uh-WITS, HAHR-uh-WITS   'hɔːrəˌwits, 'hɑrəˌwits

Horry
  county, SC   ō-RĒ, HAWR-ē   oː'riː, 'hɔːriˑ

Horsa
  Jutish chief; British WWII glider   HAWR-suh   'hɔːᵊsə

Horsley
  pers. name   HAWRZ-lē, HAWRS-lē   'hɔːᵊzliˑ, 'hɔːᵊsliˑ

Horst
  pers. name, German   HAWRST   'hɔːᵊst

Horsted Keynes
  village, England   HAWR-stuhd KĀNZ   ˌhɔːᵊstəd 'keːnz

Horst Wessel
  Nazi official song   HAWRST VES-uhl   'hɔːᵊst 'vesəl

Hortense
  1. pers. name   HAWR-TENS, HAWR-TENS   ˌhɔːᵊ'tens, 'hɔːᵊˌtens
  2. French   awr-TAHⁿS   ɔːrtɑ̃s

Hortensian Law
  Roman plebiscite law   hawr-TEN-sē-uhn, -TEN-shuhn   hɔːᵊ'tensiːən, -'tenʃən

Hortensius
  Roman name   hawr-TEN(T)-sē-uhs,   hɔːᵊ'ten(t)siːəs, hɔːᵊ'tentʃəs
      hawr-TEN-chuhs

Horus
  Egyptian sun god   HŌR-uhs, HAWR-uhs   'hoːrəs, 'hɔːrəs

Hosah
  Biblical name   HŌ-suh, khaw-SAH   'hoːsə, xɔː'sɑ

Hosea
  biblical prophet, Old Testament book   hō-ZĀ-uh, hō-ZĒ-uh   hoː'zeːə, hoː'ziːə

Hoshaiah
  Biblical name   hō-SHĪ-uh, hō-SHĀ-uh, HŌ-shah-YAH   hoː'ʃɑiə, hoː'ʃeːə, ˌhoːʃɑ'jɑ

Hoshama
  Biblical name   HAHSH-uh-muh, HŌ-shuh-muh,   'hɑʃəmə, 'hoːʃəmə,
      HŌ-shah-MAH   ˌhoːʃɑ'mɑ

Hoshea
  Biblical name   hō-SHĒ-uh, hō-SHĀ-ah   hoː'ʃiːə, hoː'ʃeˑɑ

Hosni
  pers. name, Arabic   HAWS-nē   'hɔːsniˑ

Hostius
  husband of Hersilia   HAHS-tē-uhs, HAHS-ch(ē-)uhs   'hɑstiːəs, 'hɑstʃ(iː)əs

---

Foreign Sounds: ue: *Fr.* **rue**, *Ger.* **füllen**   uh(r): *Fr.* **boeuf**, *Ger.* **Höhle**   <u>kh</u>: *Ger.* i**ch**, *Scot.* lo**ch**   ḡ: *Sp.* ami**g**o   <u>v</u>: *Sp.* ha**b**lar
hl: *Welsh* **Ll**anelli.   CAPITALS: primary stress.   SMALL CAPS: secondary stress.   ⑤: U.S. pron.   ⑥: British pron.

Hostos

Community College, *NY*	Ō-stōs	'ɔːstoːs
Hoth		
Scandinavian god	HAWTH	'hɔːθ
Hotham		
Biblical name	HŌ-THAM, <u>kh</u>ō-TAHM	'hoː,θæm, xoː'tɑm
Hothir		
Biblical name	HŌ-thuhr, hō-TIR	'hoːθə^r, hoː'tir
Hotpoint		
tdmk for home appliances	HAHT-POINT	'hɑt,pɔint
Hottentot		
S. African people	HAHT-n-TAHT	'hɑtn̩,tɑt
Houdini		
Harry, *US magician*	hoō-DĒ-nē	huː'diːniˑ
Hough		
Emerson, *US novelist*	HUHF	'həf
Houghton		
1. county, MI; college, NY	HŌT-n	'hoːtn̩
2. pers. name	HŌT-n, HOWT-n, HAWT-n	'hoːtn̩, 'hautn̩, 'hɔːtn̩
Houghton Mifflin		
US publishing house	HŌT-n MIF-luhn	ˌhoːtn̩ 'miflən
Houlton		
town, ME	HŌLT-n	'hoːltn̩
Houma		
city, LA	HŌ-muh, HOŌ-muh	'hoːmə, 'huːmə
Hounsfield		
Godfrey Newbold, *English electrical engineer (Nobel 1979)*	HOWNZ-FĒLD	'haunz,fiːld
Hounslow		
borough, England	HOWNZ-lō	'haunzloː
Housatonic		
river, MA, CT	HOŌ-suh-TAHN-ik, HOŌ-zuh-	ˌhuːsə'tɑnik, ˌhuːzə-
Houseman		
John, *US actor, producer, and director*	HOWS-muhn, HOWZ-	'hausmən, 'hauz-
Housman		
A.E., *British poet, scholar*	HOW-smuhn	'hausmən
Houssay		
B. A., *Argentine physiologist (Nobel 1947)*	oō-SĪ	uː'sai
Houston		
1. pers. name	(H)YOŌ-stuhn, HOŌ-stuhn	'(h)juːstən, 'huːstən
2. Sam, president of TX; pl. name, US	(H)YOŌ-stuhn	'(h)juːstən
3. street, New York City; county, GA	HOWS-tuhn	'haustən
Houyhnhnms		
race of intelligent horses in Gulliver's Travels, *J. Swift*	HOŌ-uh-nuhmz, HWIN-uhmz, hoō-IN-uhmz	'huːənəmz, 'hwinəmz, huː'inəmz
Hovey		
pers. name	HUHV-ē	'həviˑ
Hovhaness		
Alan, *US composer*	hō-VAHN-uhs	hoː'vɑnəs
Howard		
pers. name	HOW-uhrd	'hauə^rd

Key (col. 2): a: fad ā: fade ah: father ar: **marry** aw: **law** e: fed ē: feed er: **merry** i: hid ī: hide ō: coat oō: boot
oi: **boy** ow: **now** u: put uh: above uhr: bird ch: **chop** ng: **ring** sh: **show** th: thick <u>th</u>: this zh: measure

Howe
 Gordon, *Canadian hockey player*   HOW   ˈhɑu

Howell
 pers. name   HOW(-uh)l   ˈhɑu(ə)l

Howie
 pers. name   HOW-ē   ˈhɑui·

Howland
 Island, *Pacific Ocean*   HOW-luhnd   ˈhɑulənd

Hoxha
 Enver, *Albanian politician*   HAW-JAH   ˈhɔːˌdʒɑ

Hoyle
 card game rules; Fred, *English*   HOIL   ˈhɔil
  astronomer

Hoyt
 Dewey Lamarr, *baseball player;*   HOIT   ˈhɔit
  pers. name

Hrdlicka
 Ales, *US anthropologist*   HUHRD-LICH-kuh,   ˌhəʳdˈlitʃkə,

Hrvatska [Croatia]
 republic, E. Europe   huhr-VAHT-skah   həʳˈvatskɑ

Hsi
 see Xi

Hsia-men
 see Xiamen

Hsi Chiang
 see Xi Jiang

Hsin-hsiang
 see Xinxiang

Hsining
 see Xining

Hsüan Chiao
 Taoism   shue-AHN JOW   ʃyˈɑn ˈdʒɑu

Huachuca
 Fort, AZ   wah-CHOO-kuh   wɑˈtʃuːkə

Hua Guofeng, Hua Kuo-feng
 Chinese premier   HWAH GWŌ-FUHNG   ˈhwɑ ˈgwoːˈfəŋ

Hualapai
 N. American people   WAHL-uh-Pī   ˈwɑləˌpɑi

Huang He [Huang Ho]
 river, China   HWAHNG HUH   ˈhwɑŋ ˈhə

Huang Ho, Hwang Ho
 river, China   HWAHNG HUH, HWAHNG HŌ   ˈhwɑŋ ˈhə, ˈhwɑŋ ˈhoː

Huang-ti
 "Yellow Emperor" of China   HWAHNG-DĒ   ˈhwɑŋˈdiː

Huascarán
 mtn., Peru   WAHS-kuh-RAHN   ˌwɑskəˈrɑn

Huastec
 lang., Mexico   WAHS-TEK   ˈwɑsˌtek

Huave
 lang., people, Mexico   WAHV-ē   ˈwɑvi·

Hubble
 Edwin, *US astronomer; space*   HUHB-uhl   ˈhəbəl
  telescope

Hubbs
 pers. name   HUHBZ   ˈhəbz

Hubei, Hupeh		
prov, China	HOO-BĀ	'huːˈbeː
Hubel		
David H., *Canadian-born US neurophysiologist (Nobel 1981)*	(H)YOO-buhl	'(h)juːbəl
Huber		
Robert, *German chemist (Nobel 1988)*	HOO-buhr	'huːbəʳ
Hubert		
1. pers. name	HYOO-buhrt	'hjuːbəʳt
2. Dutch	HUE-buhrt	'hyːbərt
3. French	ue-BER	yːber
4. German	HOO-BERT	'huːˌbeʳt
Huck		
nickname for Huckleberry Finn	HUHK	'hək
Huckleberry Finn		
character, novel by Mark Twain	HUHK-uhl-BER-ē FIN	'həkəlˌberiˑ 'fin
Huddie		
pers. name	HUHD-ē	'hədiˑ
Huddleston		
Walter Darlington, *US politician*	HUHD-l-stuhn	'hədl̩stən
Hudibras		
poem, S. Butler	HYOOD-uh-BRAHS	'hjuːdəˌbrɑs
Hudnut		
William Herbert III, *US politician*	HUHD-NUHT	'hədˌnət
Hudson		
Henry, *English navigator; river, NY; bay, strait, Canada*	HUHD-suhn	'hədsən
Hué		
town, Vietnam	h(y)oo-Ā, (H)WĀ	h(j)uːˈeː, '(h)weː
Huelva		
prov, Spain	WEL-vah, ⑤ WEL-vuh	'welβɑ, ⑤ 'welvə
Hueneme [Port Hueneme]		
city, CA	wī-NĒ-mē	wɑiˈniːmiˑ
Huerfano		
river, county, CO	AWR-fuh-NŌ, WUHR-fuh-NŌ, WER-fuh-NŌ	'ɔːʳfəˌnoː, 'wəʳfəˌnoː, 'weʳfəˌnoː
Huerta		
Victoriano, *Mexican politician*	WER-tah	'weʳtɑ
Huesca		
prov, Spain	WES-kah	'weskɑ
Huey		
pers. name	HYOO-ē	'hjuːiˑ
Hufstedler		
Shirley Mount, *US jurist and cabinet member*	HUHF-sted-luhr	'həfstedləʳ
Huggins		
Charles Brenton, *Canadian-born US surgeon (Nobel 1966)*	HUHG-uhnz	'həgənz
Hugh		
pers. name	HYOO	'hjuː
Hugh Capet		
king of France	UEG kah-PE, ⑤ HYOO KĀ-puht, KAP-uht, ka-PĀ	yːg kɑːpe, ⑤ 'hjuː 'keːpət, 'kæpət, kæ'peː

Key (col. 2): a: fad ā: fade ah: father ar: marry aw: law e: fed ē: feed er: merry i: hid ī: hide ō: coat oo: boot
oi: boy ow: now u: put uh: above uhr: bird ch: chop ng: ring sh: show th: thick th̲: this zh: measure

Hughes
   Langston, *US writer; pers. name*   HY$\overline{OO}$Z, Y$\overline{OO}$Z   'hjuːz, 'juːz

Hughes Hall
   society, Cambridge Univ.   HY$\overline{OO}$Z HAWL   ˌhjuːz 'hɔːl

Hugo
   1. science fiction award; pers. name   HY$\overline{OO}$-gō   'hjuːgoː
   Victor Marie, *French writer; pers.*   ue-GŌ, ⑤ (H)Y$\overline{OO}$-GŌ   yːgoː, ⑤ '(h)juːˌgoː
   name
   2. Dutch   HUE-gō   'hygoː
   3. Finnish   HUG-ō   'hugoː
   4. German, Swedish   H$\overline{OO}$-gō   'huːgoː
   5. Polish   H$\overline{OO}$-gaw   'huːgɔː

Hugo

Huguenot
   French Protestant sect   HY$\overline{OO}$-guh-NAHT   'hjuːgəˌnɑt

Huguenotism
   beliefs of the Huguenots   HY$\overline{OO}$-guh-NAHT-IZ-uhm   'hjuːgəˌnɑtˌizəm

Hugues
   pers. name, French   UEG   yːg

Hui
   pers. name, Chinese   H$\overline{OO}$-ē, HWĒ   'huːiˑ, 'hwiː

Huidzong, Hui-tsung
   Chinese emperor   HWĀD-ZUNG   'hweːd'zuŋ

Huie
   William Bradford, *author*   HY$\overline{OO}$-ē   'hjuːiˑ

Huig
   pers. name, Dutch   HOIḠ   'hɔiɣ

Huila
   volcano, dept, Columbia   WĒ-lah   'wiːlɑ

Hui-tsung
   see Huidzong

Huizenga
   H. Wayne, *US entrepreneur*   (H)WĒ-zing-uh, HOI-zing-uh   '(h)wiːziŋə, 'hɔiziŋə

Huizenga
   Wayne, *US entrepreneur*   HĪ-zing-uh   'haiziŋə

Huizinga
   Johan, *Dutch scholar*   HOI-zing-uh, ⑤ (H)WĒ-zing-uh   'hɔiziŋə, ⑤ '(h)wiːziŋə

Huizinga
   Johan, *Dutch historian*   HUH(R)I-zing-ah, ⑤ (H)WĒ-zing-uh   'hœiziŋɑ, ⑤ '(h)wiːziŋə

Hull
   Cordell, *US statesman (Nobel 1945);*   HUHL   'həl
   city, England

Hukkok
   Biblical name   HUHK-AHK, kh$\overline{oo}$-KŌK   'həkˌɑk, xuː'koːk

Hukok
   Biblical name   (H)Y$\overline{OO}$-KAHK, H$\overline{OO}$-; kh$\overline{oo}$-KAWK   '(h)juːˌkɑk, 'huː-; xuː'kɔːk

Hul
   Biblical name   HUHL, KH$\overline{OO}$L   'həl, 'xuːl

Huldah
   Biblical name   HUHL-duh, kh$\overline{oo}$l-DAH   'həldə, xuːl'dɑ

Hulme
   Thomas, *English critic*   HY$\overline{OO}$M, Y$\overline{OO}$M   'hjuːm, 'juːm

Humbard
   Rex, *US TV evangelist*   HUHM-BAHRD   'həmˌbɑʳd

Foreign Sounds: **ue**: *Fr.* **rue**, *Ger.* **füllen**   **uh(r)**: *Fr.* **bœuf**, *Ger.* **Höhle**   **kh**: *Ger.* **ich**, *Scot.* **loch**   **ḡ**: *Sp.* **amigo**   **v**: *Sp.* **hablar**
hl: *Welsh* **Llanelli.**   CAPITALS: **primary stress.**   SMALL CAPS: secondary stress.   ⑤: U.S. pron.   ⑥: British pron.

Humber
  estuary, England; river, Canada   HUHM-buhr   'həmbə^r

Humberside
  county, England   HUHM-buhr-SĪD   'həmbə^rˌsaid

Humberto
  pers. name, Portuguese   o͞om-BER-to͞o   ūːmˈbertuː, uːm-

Humboldt
  1. Alexander von, *German naturalist*   HUM-BAWLT, Ⓢ HUHM-BŌLT   'humˌbɔːlt, Ⓢ 'həmˌboːlt
  2. State University, *CA; US pl.*   HUHM-BŌLT   'həmˌboːlt
    name

Humboldtianum, Mare
  see Mare Humboldtianum

Humboldt penguin
  bird   HUHM-BŌLT PEN-gwuhn,   'həmˌboːlt 'pengwən,
    PENG-gwuhn   'peŋgwən

Hume
  David, *Scottish philosopher; pers.*   HYo͞oM   'hjuːm
    name

Humorum, Mare
  see Mare Humorum

Humperdinck
  1. Engelbert, *German composer*   HUM-puhr-DINGK, HUHM-puhr-DINGK   'humpə^rˌdiŋk, 'həmpə^rˌdiŋk
  2. Engelbert, *US entertainer*   HUHM-puhr-DINGK   'həmpə^rˌdiŋk

Humphrey
  Hubert, *US politician; pers. name*   HUHM(P)-frē   'həm(p)friˑ

Humpty Dumpty
  Mother Goose character   HUHM(P)-tē DUHM(P)-tē   ˌhəm(p)tiˑ 'dəm(p)tiˑ

Humtah
  Biblical name   HUHM-tuh, kho͞om-TAH   'həmtə, xuːm'ta

Hunan
  prov, China   HO͞O-NAHN   'huːˈnan

Hungarian [Magyar]
  lang., people, Hungary   huhng-GAR-ē-uhn, huhng-GER-ē-uhn   həŋ'gæriːən, həŋ'geriːən

Hungary
  republic, Europe   HUHNG-g(uh-)rē   'həŋg(ə)riˑ

Hungnam
  port, N. Korea   hung-nahm   huŋnam

Hunsa
  lang., Africa   HUHN-suh   'hənsə

Huntingdonshire
  former county, England   HUHNT-ing-duhn-shuhr, -SHIR   'həntiŋdənʃə^r, -ˌʃi^r

Huntington
  Henry Edwards, *US railway*   HUHNT-ing-tuhn   'həntiŋtən
    executive & art collector; museum,
    library, CA

Hunyadi
  János, *Hungarian national hero*   HUN-yahd-ē   'hunjadiˑ

Huot
  pers. name, French   ue-Ō   yːoː

Hupa
  N. American people   HO͞O-puh   'huːpə

Hupeh
  see Hubei

Hupham
  Biblical name   (H)Yo͞o-FAM, HO͞O-; kho͞o-FAHM   '(h)juːˌfæm, 'huː-; xuː'fam

---

Key (col. 2):   aː fad   āː fade   ahː father   arː marry   awː law   eː fed   ēː feed   erː merry   iː hid   īː hide   ōː coat   o͞oː boot
oiː boy   owː now   uː put   uhː above   uhrː bird   chː chop   ngː ring   shː show   thː thick   th̲ː this   zhː measure

Huphamite
  Biblical name — (H)YŌO-fuh-MĪT, HŌO- — '(h)juːfə‚mait, 'huː-

Huppah
  Biblical name — HUHP-uh, khōo-PAH — 'həpə, xuː'pɑ

Huppim
  plural of Huppah — HUHP-im, khōo-PIM — 'həpim, xuː'pim

Hur
  Biblical name — HUHR, KHUR — 'həʳ, 'xur

Hurai
  Biblical name — (H)YUR-ē-Ī, (H)YUR-Ī, HUR-; (h)yu-RĀ-Ī, khōo-RĪ — '(h)juriː‚ai, '(h)jur‚ai, 'hur-; (h)ju'reːai, xuː'rai

Hural
  upper house of Mongolian Parliament — (H)YUR-uhl, (h)yur-AHL — '(h)jurəl, (h)jur'ɑl

Huram
  Biblical name — H(Y)UR-AM, hi-RAHM — 'h(j)ur‚æm, hi'rɑm

Huri
  Biblical name — H(Y)UR-Ī, khōo-RĒ — 'h(j)ur‚ai, xuː'riː

Hurley
  Kathy, *actress, playwright* — HUHR-lē — 'həʳliˑ

Hürlimann Stern
  Swiss beer — HUR-li-MAHN SHTERN — 'hyʳli‚mɑn 'ʃteʳn

Hurok
  Solomon, *US impresario* — (H)YUR-ahk — '(h)jurɑk

Huron
  pl. name, lake, people, N. America — (H)YUR-uhn, (H)YUR-AHN — '(h)jurən, '(h)jur‚ɑn

Hurrians
  ancient Middle Eastern people — HUR-ē-uhnz — 'huriːənz

Hurstmonceux
  see Herstmonceux

Hurston
  Zora Neale, *US writer* — HUHR-stuhn — 'həʳstən

Hus, Huss
  Jan, *Czech religious reformer* — HŌOS, Ⓢ HUS, HUHS — 'huːs, Ⓢ 'hus, 'həs

Husák
  Gustav, *Czech politician* — H(Y)ŌO-sahk — 'h(j)uːsɑk

Husch
  Vineyards, *winery, CA* — HUHSH — 'həʃ

Hushah
  Biblical name — H(Y)ŌO-shuh, khōo-SHAH — 'h(j)uːʃə, xuː'ʃɑ

Hushai
  Biblical name — H(Y)ŌO-SHĪ, khōo-SHĪ — 'h(j)uː‚ʃai, xuː'ʃai

Husham
  Biblical name — H(Y)ŌO-SHAM, khōo-SHAHM — 'h(j)uː‚ʃæm, xuː'ʃam

Hushathite
  Biblical name — H(Y)ŌO-shuh-THĪT — 'h(j)uːʃə‚θait

Hushim
  Biblical name — H(Y)ŌO-shim, khōo-SHĔM — 'h(j)uːʃim, xuː'ʃiːm

Hussein
  1. Ibrahim, *Kenyan marathoner;* Jordanian king; Saddam, *president, Iraq* — hōo-SĀN, hu-SĀN — huː'seːn, hu'seːn
  2. pers. name, Turkish — hue-SĀN — hyː'seːn

Husserl
  Edmund, *German philosopher* — HUHS-uhrl — 'həsəʳl

Foreign Sounds: ue: *Fr.* **rue**, *Ger.* **füllen** uh(r): *Fr.* **boeuf**, *Ger.* **Höhle** kh: *Ger.* **ich**, *Scot.* **loch** ḡ: *Sp.* amigo v̱: *Sp.* hablar hl: *Welsh* **Llanelli**. CAPITALS: primary stress. SMALL CAPS: secondary stress. Ⓢ: U.S. pron. Ⓔ: British pron.

Hussite
  adherent of Hussitism   HUHS-ĪT, HUS-ĪT   'həs,ait, 'hus,ait

Hussitism
  movement begun by Hus   HUHS-uht-ĬZ-uhm, HUS-   'həsət̬,izəm, 'hus-

Hussong's
  Mexican beer   HUS-AWNGZ, HŌŌ-SAWNGZ   'hus,ɔːŋz, 'huː,sɔːŋz

Huston
  John, Walter, & Anjelica, US entertainers   (H)YŌŌS-tuhn   '(h)juːstən

Huston-Tillotson
  College, TX   (H)YŌŌ-stuhn-TIL-uht-suhn   '(h)juːstən'tilətsən

Huszt [Khust]
  town, Ukraine   HUST   'hust

Hutterites
  Anabaptist sect   HUHT-uhr-ĪTS   'hət̬əʳ,aits

Huw
  pers. name, Welsh   HYŌŌ   'hjuː

Huxley
  Aldous, English writer; Andrew Fielding, *English physiologist (Nobel 1963);* Thomas Henry, *English biologist*   HUHKS-lē   'həksli·

Hu Yaobang
  Chinese Communist leader   HŌŌ YOW-BAHNG   'huː 'jau'baŋ

Huygens
  Christian, *Dutch mathematician*   HĪ-guhnz, HOI-guhnz   'haigənz, 'hoigənz

Huz
  Biblical name   HUHZ, ŌŌTS   'həz, 'uːts

Hwang Hai
  sea, China   HWAHNG HĪ   'hwaŋ 'hai

Hwang Ho
  see Huang Ho

Hyacinthe
  pers. name, French   yah-SEⁿT   jaːsẽt

Hyacinthids
  girls sacrificed for Athens   HĪ-uh-SIN-thidz   ,haiə'sinθidz

Hyacinthus
  beloved of Apollo   HĪ-uh-SIN-thuhs   ,haiə'sinθəs

Hyades
  nymphs who nursed Dionysus; star cluster in Taurus   HĪ-uh-DĒZ   'haiə,diːz

Hyannis
  town, MA; village, NE   hī-AN-uhs   hai'ænəs

Hyas
  brother of the Pleiades and Hyades   HĪ-uhs   'haiəs

Hyatt
  US hotel chain   HĪ-uht   'haiət

Hybris
  personification of insolence, hubris   HĪ-bruhs, HĒ-bruhs   'haibrəs, 'hiːbrəs

Hydaburg
  city, AK   HĪD-uh-BUHRG   'haidə,bəʳg

Hyde
  pers. name   HĪD   'haid

Hyderabad
  city, India   HĪD(-uh)-ruh-BAD, -BAHD   'haid(ə)rə,bæd, -,bad

---

Key (col. 2):   a: fad   ā: fade   ah: father   ar: marry   aw: law   e: fed   ē: feed   er: merry   i: hid   ī: hide   ō: coat   ōō: boot   oi: boy   ow: now   u: put   uh: above   uhr: bird   ch: chop   ng: ring   sh: show   th: thick   th: this   zh: measure

Hydra
island, Greece; constellation; HĪ-druh 'haidrə
nine-headed monster killed by
Heracles
hydrogen
element HĪ-druh-juhn 'haidrədʒən
Hydrus
constellation HĪ-druhs 'haidrəs
Hygeia, Hygiea
Greek goddess of health hī-JĒ-(y)uh hai'dʒiː(j)ə
Hyginus
pope huh-JĪ-nuhs hə'dʒainəs
Hyko
see Hiko
Hyksos
ancient nomadic people in Egypt HIK-SŌS, -SAHS 'hik,soːs, -,sɑs
Hyksos
Egyptian dynasty HIK-SŌS, HIK-SAHS 'hik,soːs, 'hik,sɑs
Hylaeus
Arcadian centaur HĪ-lē-uhs 'hailiːəs
Hylas
legendary youth, accompanied HĪ-luhs, HĒ-luhs 'hailəs, 'hiːləs
Heracles on the Argo
Hyllus
son of Heracles HIL-uhs 'hiləs
Hyman
Phyllis, soul singer; pers. name HĪ-muhn 'haimən
Hymen
Greek god of marriage; pers. name HĪ-muhn 'haimən
Hymenaeus
Greek personification of marriage; HĪ-muh-NĒ-uhs, HĪ-muh-NĀ-uhs ,haimə'niːəs, ,haimə'neːəs
Greek marriage song
Hymettus
mtn., Greece hī-MET-uhs hai'meṭəs
Hymie
pers. name HĪ-mē 'haimiˑ
Hymnus
Phrygian shepherd in Greek HIM-nuhs 'himnəs
mythology
Hypatia
Greek philosopher hī-PĀ-shuh hai'peːʃə
Hyperboreans
mythical northern race HĪ-puhr-BŌR-ē-uhnz, -BAWR-ē-uhnz ,haipərˈboːriːənz, -ˈbɔːriːənz
Hyperion
poem, Keats; titan in Greek hī-PIR-ē-uhn hai'piriːən
mythology; satellite of Saturn
Hypermestra
daughter of King Danaus HĪ-puhr-MES-truh ,haipərˈmestrə
Hypermnestra [Hypermestra]
daughter of King Danaus HĪ-puhrm-NES-truh ,haipərmˈnestrə
Hypnus
Greek god of sleep HIP-nuhs 'hipnəs
Hypolite
pers. name, French ē-paw-LĒT iːpɔːliːt

Foreign Sounds: ue: *Fr.* **rue**, *Ger.* **füllen** uh(r): *Fr.* **boeuf**, *Ger.* **Höhle** kh: *Ger.* **ich**, *Scot.* **loch** g̱: *Sp.* **amigo** v̱: *Sp.* **hablar** hl: *Welsh* **Llanelli**. CAPITALS: primary stress. SMALL CAPS: secondary stress. Ⓢ: U.S. pron. Ⓔ: British pron.

Hypsilophodon
  dinosaur   HIP-suh-LAHF-uh-DAHN   ͵hɪpsə'lɑfə͵dɑn
Hypsipyle
  mistress of Jason   hip-SIP-uh-lē   hɪp'sɪpəli·
Hypsistarianism
  Asian religious sect   HIP-suh-STAR-ē-uh-NIZ-uhm,   ͵hɪpsə'stæriːə͵nɪzəm,
                                          -STER-ē-uh-NIZ-uhm   -'steriːə͵nɪzəm
Hyracoidea
  hyraxes   HĪ-ruh-KOID-ē-uh   ͵haɪrə'kɔɪdiːə
Hyrax
  mammal   HĪ-RAKS   'haɪ͵ræks
Hyrcania
  ancient Persian province   HUHR-KĀ-nē-uh   ͵həʳ'keːniːə
Hyrieus
  father of Orion   HĪ-rē-uhs, hī-RĒ-uhs   'haɪriːəs, haɪ'riːəs
Hyundai
  Korean car co.   HUHN-DĀ   'hən͵deː

I

Iacchus
  god of the Eleusian mysteries   ī-AK-uhs   aɪ'ækəs
Iacocca
  Lee A., US businessman   Ī-uh-KŌ-kuh   ͵aɪə'koːkə
Iacopo
  pers. name, Italian   YAHK-ō-pō   'jɑkoːpoː
Iago
  1. character in Othello, *Shakespeare* ē-AHG-ō   iː'ɑgoː
  2. pers. name, Welsh   YAHG-ō   'jɑgoː
Ialemus
  personification of the funeral dirge ī-AL-uh-muhs   aɪ'æləməs
Ialmenus
  Argonaut, suitor of Helen   Ī-al-MĒ-nuhs, Ī-al-MEN-uhs   ͵aɪæl'miːnəs, ͵aɪæl'menəs
Iambe
  daughter of Pan and Echo   ī-AM-bē   aɪ'æmbi·
Iamus
  mythical founder of Olympic games   ī-Ā-muhs, ī-AM-uhs   aɪ'eːməs, aɪ'æməs
Ian
  pers. name   Ē-uhn   'iːən
Iapetus
  Titan, father of Atlas and   ī-AP-uht-uhs, ē-AP-uht-uhs   aɪ'æpəțəs, iː'æpəțəs
    Prometheus; satellite of Saturn
Iapyx
  Cretan hero   ī-Ā-piks   aɪ'eːpiks
Iarbas
  African king who loved Queen Dido   ī-AHR-buhs   aɪ'ɑʳbəs

Key (col. 2): a: fad ā: fade ah: father ar: marry aw: law e: fed ē: feed er: merry i: hid ī: hide ō: coat ōō: boot
oi: boy ow: now u: put uh: above uhr: bird ch: chop ng: ring sh: show th: thick <u>th</u>: this zh: measure

Iasi, Jassy, Yassy
  county, city, Romania   YAHSH(-ē)   'jaʃ(iˑ)

Iasion
  son of Zeus and Electra   ī-Ā-sē-uhn   ɑi'eːsiːən

Iasus
  king of Argos   ī-Ā-suhs   ɑi'eːsəs

Ibadan
  city, Africa   ē-BAHD-n   iː'bɑdn̩

Ibadhi [Islam]
  religion   uh-BAHD-ē   ə'bɑdiˑ

Ibanag
  lang., people, Philippine Islands   Ē-buh-NAHG, Ē-buh-NAHG   'iːbəˌnɑg, ˌiːbə'nɑg

Ibáñez
  Carlos, *Chilean soldier and*   ē-V̲AHN-yāth   iː'βɑnjeːθ
    politician

Iberia
  parish, LA; peninsula, Spain,   ī-BIR-ē-uh   ɑi'biriːə
    Portugal; airline, Spain

Iberian
  Peninsula, *Europe*   ī-BIR-ē-uhn   ɑi'biriːən

Ibhar
  Biblical name   IB-hahr, yiv-KHAHR   'ibhɑr, jiv'xɑr

Ibis
  shore bird   Ī-buhs   'ɑibəs

Ibiza, Iviza
  island, Mediterranean   ē-V̲Ē-thah, ē-V̲Ē-sah, i-V̲Ē-thuh,   iː'βiːθɑ, iː'βiːsɑ, i'viːθə,
        Ⓢ ē-V̲Ē-zuh   Ⓢ iː'viːzə

Ibiza hound
  breed of dog   i-V̲Ē-thuh   i'viːθə

Ibleam
  Biblical name   IB-lē-uhm, YIV-luh-AHM   'ibliːəm, ˌjivlə'ɑm

Iblis
  Devil   IB-luhs   'ibləs

Ibneiah
  Biblical name   ib-NĪ-uh, ib-NĒ-uh, YIV-nuh-YAH   ib'nɑiə, ib'niːə, ˌjivnə'jɑ

Ibnijah [Ibneiah]
  Biblical name   ib-NĪ-juh, yiv-nuh-YAH   ib'nɑidʒə, ˌjivnə'jɑ

Ibn Khaldūn
  Arab philosopher, historian, and   IB-uhn k̲h̲ahl-DO͞ON   ˌibən xɑl'duːn
    sociologist

Ibn Saud
  king, Saudi Arabia   IB-uhn sah-O͞OD   ˌibən sɑ'uːd

Ibo [Igbo]
  lang., people, Nigeria   Ē-bō   'iːboː

Ibrahim
  pers. name, Turkish   IB-rah-HIM   ˌibrɑ'him

Ibri
  Biblical name   IB-RĪ, IB-rē, iv-RĒ   'ibˌrɑi, 'ibriˑ, iv'riː

Ibsen
  Henrik, *Norwegian author*   IP-suhn, Ⓢ IB-suhn   'ipsən, Ⓢ 'ibsən

Ibzan
  Biblical name   IB-ZAN, iv-TSAHN   'ibˌzæn, iv'tsɑn

Icadius
  son of Apollo and Lycia   i-KĀD-ē-uhs, ī-KĀD-ē-uhs   i'keːdiːəs, ɑi'keːdiːəs

---

Foreign Sounds: ue: *Fr.* **rue**, *Ger.* **füllen**   uh(r): *Fr.* **boeuf**, *Ger.* **Höhle**   k̲h̲: *Ger.* **ich**, *Scot.* **loch**   g̲: *Sp.* **amigo**   v̲: *Sp.* **hablar**
hl: *Welsh* **Llanelli**.   CAPITALS: primary stress.   SMALL CAPS: secondary stress.   Ⓢ: U.S. pron.   Ⓔ: British pron.

Icahn
   Carl, *US businessman*   Ī-KAHN   ˈaɪˌkɑn

Icaria
   ancient name of Ikaria   ī-KER-ē-uh, ī-KAR-ē-uh, ik-ER-ē-uh,   aɪˈkeriːə, aɪˈkæriːə, ikˈeriːə,
                                 ik-AR-ē-uh   ikˈæriːə

Icarius
   father of Penelope   i-KAR-ē-uhs, ī-KAR-ē-uhs   iˈkæriːəs, aɪˈkæriːəs

Icarus
   son of Daedalus   IK-uh-ruhs   ˈikərəs

Iceland
   island country, Atlantic   Ī-sluhnd   ˈaɪslənd

Icelander
   inhabitant of Iceland   Ī-sluhn-duhr, Ī-SLAN-duhr   ˈaɪsləndəʳ, ˈaɪˌslændəʳ

Icelandic
   lang., Iceland   ī-SLAN-dik   aɪˈslændik

Iceni
   ancient Celtic tribe   ī-SĒ-nē   aɪˈsiːniˑ

Ichabod
   pers. name   IK-uh-BAHD   ˈikəˌbad

Ichihara
   city, Japan   ē-chē-hahr-ah   iːtʃiːhɑrɑ

Ichikawa
   city, Japan   ē-chē-kah-wah   iːtʃiːkɑwɑ

I Ching
   ancient Chinese book   Ē JING, Ⓢ ē CHING   ˈiː ˈdʒiŋ, Ⓢ iː ˈtʃiŋ

Ichiro
   pers. name, Japanese   ē-chē-rō   iːtʃiːroː

Ichitaro
   pers. name, Japanese   ē-chē-tahr-ō   iːtʃiːtaroː

Ichthyocentaurs
   fish centaurs   IK-thē-ō-SEN-TAWRZ   ˌikθiːoːˈsenˌtɔːʳz

Ickes
   Harold LeClair, *US administrator,*   IK-ēz, IK-uhs   ˈikiːz, ˈikəs
     politician

Iconium
   Biblical name   ī-KŌ-nē-uhm   aɪˈkoːniːəm

Ida
   mtn., Turkey; county, IA; guardian of   ĪD-uh   ˈaɪdə
    Zeus; pers. name

Idaho
   state, US   ĪD-uh-HŌ   ˈaɪdəˌhoː

Idahoan
   pert. to Idaho   ĪD-uh-HŌ-uhn   ˈaɪdəˌhoːən

'Id al-Adha
   Islamic festival   ID ahl-AH<u>TH</u>-ah   ˈidalˈɑðɑ

Idalah
   Biblical name   ID-l-uh, ĪD-l-uh, YID-ah-LAH   ˈidlə, ˈaɪdlə, ˌjidaˈla

'Id al-Fitr
   Islamic festival   ID ahl-FIT-uhr   ˈidalˈfitər

Idas
   Argonaut, killer of Castor   ĪD-uhs, ĒD-uhs   ˈaɪdəs, ˈiːdəs

Idbash
   Biblical name   ID-BASH, yid-BAHSH   ˈidˌbæʃ, jidˈbaʃ

Idd
   Moslem festival   ĒD   ˈiːd

Key (col. 2):   a: fad ā: fade ah: father ar: marry aw: law e: fed ē: feed er: merry i: hid ī: hide ō: coat ōō: boot
oi: boy ow: now u: put uh: above uhr: bird ch: chop ng: ring sh: show th: thick <u>th</u>: this zh: measure

Iddo
   Biblical name   ID-ō, i-DAW   'idoː, i'dɔː

Idhra [Hydra]
   island, Greece   Ē-<u>th</u>rah   'iːðrɑ

Idi
   pers. name (I. Amin)   ID-ē, ĒD-ē   'idiˑ, 'iːdiˑ

Iditarod
   dog sled race, AK   ī-DIT-uh-RAHD   ai'diṭəˌrɑd

Idleyld Park
   city, OR   ĪD-l-WĪLD PAHRK   'aidl̩ˌwaild 'paʳk

Idmon
   Argonaut; soothsayer   ID-muhn, ID-MAHN   'idmən, 'idˌmɑn

Ido
   revised form of Esperanto   Ē-dō   'iːdoː

Idomeneo
   opera, Mozart   Ē-dō-muh-NĀ-ō   ˌiːdoːmə'neːoː

Idomeneus
   king of Crete, suitor of Helen   ī-DAHM-uh-N(Y)O͞OS,   ai'dɑməˌn(j)uːs,
                                    ī-DAHM-uh-NĒ-uhs   ˌaiˌdɑmə'niːəs

Idumea
   Greek form of Edom   IJ-uh-MĒ-uh   ˌidʒə'miːə

Iðunn
   Scandinavian goddess of youth   I<u>TH</u>-un   'iðun

Idwal
   pers. name, Welsh   ID-wahl, ⑤ ID-wuhl   'idwaːl, ⑤ 'idwəl

Ieper [Ypres]
   town, Belgium   YĀ-puhr   'jeːpəʳ

Ieuan
   pers. name, Welsh   YĀ-yahn   'jeːjaːn

Iezer [Jeezer]
   Biblical name   ī-Ē-zuhr, ī-EZ-uhr, ē-EZ-uhr   ai'iːzəʳ, ai'ezəʳ, iː'ezəʳ

Ife
   town, Nigeria   Ē-fā   'iːfeː

Ifni
   Spanish prov., Morocco   ĒF-nē, IF-nē   'iːfniˑ, 'ifniˑ

Ifor
   1. pers. name   Ē-vuhr, Ī-vuhr   'iːvəʳ, 'aivəʳ
   2. pers. name, Welsh   Ē-vawr   'iːvɔr

Ifugao
   lang., people, Philippine Islands   Ē-fōō-GOW, Ē-fōō-GOW   'iːfuːˌgau, ˌiːfuː'gau

Igal
   Biblical name   Ī-GAL, i-GAHL, yi-GAHL   'aiˌgæl, i'gɑl, ji'gɑl

Igala
   lang., people, Nigeria, Benin   ē-GAHL-uh   iː'gɑlə

Igbirra
   lang., people, Nigeria   IG-buhr-uh   'igbərə

Igbo [Ibo]
   lang., people, Nigeria   IG-bō   'igboː

Igdaliah
   Biblical name   IG-duh-LĪ-uh, YIG-dahl-YAH-hōō   ˌigdə'laiə, ˌjigdɑl'jɑhuː

Igdrasil
   see Yggdrasil

Iggy
   pers. name   IG-ē   'igiˑ

Foreign Sounds: ue: *Fr.* **rue**, *Ger.* füllen   uh(r): *Fr.* **boeuf**, *Ger.* Höhle   <u>kh</u>: *Ger.* i<u>ch</u>, *Scot.* lo<u>ch</u>   ḡ: *Sp.* ami̅g̅o   v̲: *Sp.* ha̲b̲lar
hl: *Welsh* Llanelli.   CAPITALS: primary stress.   SMALL CAPS: secondary stress.   ⑤: U.S. pron.   Ⓔ: British pron.

Iglesias
   Julio, *entertainer*   ē-GLĀ-zē-uhs   iː'gleːziːəs
Ignace
   pers. name, French   ēn-YAHS   iːnjɑːs
Ignacio
   1. pers. name, Portuguese   ēg-NAHS-yōō   iːg'nɑːsjuː
   2. Spanish   ēḡ-NAHS-yō, -NAHTH-yō   iːɣ'nɑsjoː, -'nɑθjoː
Ignat
   pers. name, Russian   ēg-NAHT   iːg'nɑːt
Ignatian
   pert. to Ignatius   ig-NĀ-shuhn   ig'neːʃən
Ignatius
   pers. name   ig-NĀ-sh(ē-)uhs   ig'neːʃ(iː)əs
Ignatius Loyola
   Christian saint, Jesuit founder   ig-NĀ-sh(ē-)uhs loi-Ō-luh   ig'neːʃ(iː)əs lɔi'oːlə
Ignaz
   pers. name, German   IG-NAHTS, ig-NAHTS   'ig,nɑts, ig'nɑts
Ignazio
   pers. name, Italian   ēn-YAHT-syō   iːn'jɑtsjoː
Igor
   1. pers. name   Ē-GAWR   'iː,gɔːʳ
   2. Russian   Ē-guhr   'iːgəʳ
Igorot
   people of Malay stock, Philippines   IG-uh-RŌT   ,igə'roːt
Igraine
   mother of King Arthur   i-GRĀN   i'greːn
Iguana
   lizard   ig-WAHN-uh   ig'wɑnə
Iguanodon
   dinosaur   ig-WAHN-uh-DAHN   ig'wɑnə,dɑn
Iguassú
   river, Brazil   Ē-gwah-SŌŌ   ,iːgwɑ'suː
Iim
   Biblical name   Ī-(y)im, ē-YĒM   'ai(j)im, iː'jiːm
Ijaw
   lang., people, Nigeria   Ē-jaw   'iːdʒɔː
Ije-abarim
   Biblical name   Ī-juh-AB-uh-RIM, i-YĀ-ah-vah-RĒM   'aidʒə'æbə,rim, i'jeːɑvɑ'riːm
Ijo [Ijaw]
   lang., people, Nigeria   Ē-jō, Ē-jaw   'iːdʒoː, 'iːdʒɔː
Ijon
   Biblical name   Ī-JAHN, i-YŌN   'ai,dʒɑn, i'joːn
Ijssel
   tributary, Netherlands   Ī-suhl   'aisəl
Ijsselmeer
   inlet, Netherlands   Ī-suhl-MER   'aisəl,meʳ
Ikangaa
   Juma, *Tanzanian marathoner*   i-KAHNG-guh   i'kɑŋgə
Ikaria
   island, Greece   Ē-kuh-RĒ-uh   ,iːkə'riːə
Ike
   pers. name   ĪK   'aik
Ikeda
   Hayato, *Japanese statesman*   ē-kā-dah, ē-ked-ah   iːkeːdɑ, iːkedɑ

Key (col. 2):   a: fad   ā: fade   ah: father   ar: marry   aw: law   e: fed   ē: feed   er: merry   i: hid   ī: hide   ō: coat   ōō: boot
oi: boy   ow: now   u: put   uh: above   uhr: bird   ch: chop   ng: ring   sh: show   th: thick   <u>th</u>: this   zh: measure

Ikhnaton [Akhenaton]
   Egyptian king   ik-NAHT-n   ik'nɑtn̩
Ikkesh
   Biblical name   IK-ESH, i-KESH   'ik‚eʃ, i'keʃ
Ila
   lang., people, Africa   Ē-luh   'iːlə
Ilai
   Biblical name   Ī-lē-Ī, Ī-LĪ, ē-LĪ   'ɑiliː‚ɑi, 'ɑi‚lɑi, iː'lɑi
Ile-de-France
   prov, France   ēl-duh-FRAHⁿS   iːldəfrɑ̃s
I-li
   river, China, Kazakhstan   Ē-LĒ   'iː'liː
Iliad
   Greek epic poem   IL-ē-uhd, IL-ē-AD   'iliːəd, 'iliː‚æd
Ilia [Rhea Silvia]
   mother of Romulus and Remus   Ē-lē-uh, IL-ē-uh   'iːliːə, 'iliːə
Ilía [Elis]
   dept, Greece   ē-LĒ-uh   iː'liːə
Ilie
   pers. name, Romanian   Ē-lē-uh   'iːliːə
Iliescu
   Ion, *Romanian politician*   il-YES-ko͞o   il'jeskuː
Ilimbos
   mts., Greece   ē-LIM-bōs   iː'limboːs
Ilione
   daughter of Priam, wife of   IL-ē-Ō-nē   ‚iliː'oːniˑ
     Polymestor
Ilioneus
   Trojan killed by Diomedes   IL-ē-Ō-nē-uhs, IL-ē-ŌN-YO͞OS   ‚iliː'oːniːəs, ‚iliː'oːn‚juːs
Ilium [Troy]
   ancient city, Asia Minor   IL-ē-uhm   'iliːəm
Ill
   river, Austria   IL   'il
Illampu
   peak, Bolivia   ē-YAHM-po͞o   iː'jɑmpuː
Illia
   Arturo, *Argentinian politician*   ē-YĒ-ah   iː'jiːɑː
Illimani
   mtn., Bolivia   Ē-yuh-MAHN-uh   ‚iːjə'mɑnə
Illinois
   state, US ; N. American people; pers.   IL-uh-NOI, IL-uh-NOIZ   ‚ilə'nɔi, ‚ilə'nɔiz
     name
Illinoisan
   pert. to Illinois   IL-uh-NOI-uhn, IL-uh-NOIZ-n   ‚ilə'nɔiən, ‚ilə'nɔizn̩
Illuminati
   enlightened ones   il-O͞O-muh-NAHT-ē   il‚uːmə'nɑt̬iˑ
Illyria
   ancient country along Adriatic   il-IR-ē-uh   il'iriːə
Illyrian
   lang., people, pert. to Illyria   il-IR-ē-uhn   il'iriːən
Illyricum
   ancient Roman province, Balkan   il-IR-i-kuhm   il'irikəm
     Peninsula
Illyrius
   son of Cadmus   il-IR-ē-uhs   il'iriːəs

Foreign Sounds: ue: *Fr.* **rue**, *Ger.* füllen   uh(r): *Fr.* **boeuf**, *Ger.* Höhle   <u>kh</u>: *Ger.* i<u>ch</u>, *Scot.* lo<u>ch</u>   g̱: *Sp.* amigo   y: *Sp.* hablar
hl: *Welsh* Llanelli.   CAPITALS: primary stress.   SMALL CAPS: secondary stress.   Ⓢ: U.S. pron.   Ⓔ: British pron.

Ilmari
   pers. name, Finnish   IL-mah-rē   'ɪlmɑrɪ·

Ilmen
   lake, Russia   IL-muhn   'ɪlmən

Il Moro di Venezia
   Italian racing yacht   il MŌR-ō dē vuh-NET-sē-uh   il 'moːroː di· və'netsiːə

Ilocano
   lang., people, Philippine Islands   Ē-lō-KAHN-ō   ˌiːloː'kɑnoː

Ilocos Norte
   province, Philippines   i-LŌ-kōs NAWR-tā   i'loːkoːs 'nɔːrteː

Ilocos Sur
   province, Philippines   i-LŌ-kōs SUR   i'loːkoːs 'sur

Iloko [Ilocano]
   lang., Philippine Islands   ē-LŌ-kō   iː'loːkoː

Iloilo
   province, Philippines   Ē-lō-Ē-lō   ˌiːloː'iːloː

Il Penseroso
   poem, J. Milton   IL PEN-suh-RŌ-sō   ˌil ˌpensə'roːsoː

Ilse
   pers. name, German   IL-zuh   'ɪlzə

Ilson
   Robert, *US-born British*   IL-suhn   'ɪlsən
     lexicographer

Il Trovatore
   Italian opera, Verdi   ĒL trō-vuh-TŌR-ā, TRŌ-vuh-TAWR-ā   ˌiˑl troːvə'toːreː, ˌtroːvə'tɔːreː

Ilus
   founder of Troy   IL-uhs, Ē-luhs   'ɪləs, 'iːləs

Ilya
   pers. name, Russian   il-YAH   il'jɑː

Ilyich
   pers. name, Russian   il-YĒCH   il'jiːtʃ

Ilyushin
   Russian aircraft   il-YOO-shin   il'juːʃin

Imamu
   pers. name   i-MAHM-oo   i'mɑmuː

Iman
   Somali-born fashion model   Ē-mahn   'iːmɑn

Imbolc
   Celtic pagan festival   IM-BAWL(-uh)g   'imˌbɔːl(ə)g

Imbrium, Mare
   see Mare Imbrium

Imelda
   pers. name   i-MEL-duh   i'meldə

Imhotep
   Egyptian physician & sage   im-HŌ-TEP   im'hoːˌtep

Imla, Imlah
   Biblical name   IM-luh, yim-LAH   'imlə, jim'lɑ

Immanuel
   1. pers. name   i-MAN-yuh(-wuh)l   i'mænjə(wə)l
   2. Dutch   ē-MAHN-uh-wuhl   iː'mɑːnəwəl
   3. German   i-MAHN-oo-EL   i'mɑnuːˌel

Immer
   Biblical name   IM-uhr, i-MER   'iməʳ, i'mer

Imna, Imnah
   Biblical name   IM-nuh, yim-NAH   'imnə, jim'nɑ

Key (col. 2): a: fad ā: fade ah: father ar: marry aw: law e: fed ē: feed er: merry i: hid ī: hide ō: coat oo: boot
oi: boy ow: now u: put uh: above uhr: bird ch: chop ng: ring sh: show th: thick <u>th</u>: this zh: measure

Imnaha
  river, OR   im-NAW-haw, IM-nuh-HAW   imˈnɔːhɔː, ˈimnəˌhɔː

Imogen
  pers. name   IM-uh-juhn   ˈimədʒən

Imogene
  pers. name   IM-uh-JĒN   ˈiməˌdʒiːn

Imperator
  Roman title: commmander, emperor   IM-puh-RAHT-uhr, -RAH-TAWR   ˌimpəˈrɑtəʳ, -ˈrɑˌtɔːʳ

Imperium
  Roman term for official authority   im-PIR-ē-uhm   imˈpiriːəm

Imphal
  city, India   IMP-HUHL, IM-PUHL   ˈimpˌhəl, ˈimˌpəl

Imrah
  Biblical name   IM-ruh, yim-RAH   ˈimrə, jimˈrɑ

Imre
  pers. name, Hungarian   IM-re   ˈimre

Imrédy
  Béla, *Hungarian politician*   IM-red-ē   ˈimrediˑ

Imri
  Biblical name   IM-rē, IM-RĪ, im-RĒ   ˈimriˑ, ˈimˌrɑi, imˈriː

Imru' al-Qays
  Arab poet   IM-roo uhl-KĪS   ˈimruː əlˈkɑis

Ina
  pers. name   Ī-nuh, Ē-nuh   ˈɑinə, ˈiːnə

Inachus
  Greek river god, father of Io   IN-uh-kuhs   ˈinəkəs

Inagua
  island, British Virgin Islands   in-AHG-wuh   inˈɑgwə

Inaja-Cosmit
  N. American people   IN-uh-ZHAH-KAHZ-muht   ˈinəˌʒɑˈkɑzmət

Inca
  S. American people   ING-kuh   ˈiŋkə

Inchon
  city, S. Korea   IN-CHAHN   ˈinˌtʃɑn

Increase
  pers. name   IN-KRĒS, in-KRĒS   ˈinˌkriːs, inˈkriːs

Incubi
  plural of Incubus   ING-kyuh-BĪ, ING-kyuh-BĒ, IN-   ˈiŋkjəˌbɑi, ˈiŋkjəˌbiː, ˈin-

Incubus
  evil spirit of sleep   ING-kyuh-buhs, IN-kyuh-buhs   ˈiŋkjəbəs, ˈinkjəbəs

India
  subcontinent, republic, Asia   IN-dē-uh   ˈindiːə

Indian
  pert. to India; *Native American; ocean*   IN-dē-uhn   ˈindiːən

Indiana
  state, US   IN-dē-AN-uh   ˌindiːˈænə

Indianan
  pert. to Indiana   IN-dē-AN-uhn   ˌindiːˈænən

Indianapolis
  city, IN   IN-dē-uh-NAP-(uh-)luhs   ˌindiːəˈnæp(ə)ləs

Indic
  pert. to India   IN-dik   ˈindik

Indies
  islands (East and West)   IN-dēz   ˈindiːz

Foreign Sounds: ue: *Fr.* **rue**, *Ger.* **füllen**   uh(r): *Fr.* **boeuf**, *Ger.* **Höhle**   kh: *Ger.* **ich**, *Scot.* **loch**   g̱: *Sp.* amigo   v̱: *Sp.* hablar   hl: *Welsh* **Llanelli**.   CAPITALS: primary stress.   SMALL CAPS: secondary stress.   Ⓢ: U.S. pron.   Ⓔ: British pron.

Indigetes
  obscure Roman divinities   in-DIJ-uht-ĒZ   in'dɪdʒət͵iːz
Indira
  pers. name (I. Gandhi)   in-DIR-uh   in'dɪrə
indium
  element   IN-dē-uhm   'indiːəm
Indo-Aryan
  Indic culture   IN-dō-AR-ē-uhn, -ER-ē-uhn,   ͵indoː'æriːən, -'eriːən, -'ɑrjən
                                      -AHR-yuhn
Indochina
  peninsula, Asia   IN-dō-CHĪ-nuh   ͵indoː'tʃaɪnə
Indo-European
  prehistoric people of Eurasia; their IN-dō-YUR-uh-PĒ-uhn   ͵indoː͵jurə'piːən
  lang.
Indo-Iranian
  Indo-European lang. group   IN-dō-ir-Ā-nē-uhn   ͵indoːir'eːniːən
Indonesia
  republic, Asia   IN-duh-NĒ-zhuh, -shuh   ͵ində'niːʒə, -ʃə
Indonesian
  lang., Indonesia   IN-duh-NĒ-zhuhn, -NĒ-shuhn   ͵ində'niːʒən, -'niːʃən
Indore
  city, India   IN-DŌR, IN-DAWR   'in͵doːʳ, 'in͵dɔːʳ
Indra
  supreme Vedic god   IN-druh   'indrə
Indre
  dept, river, France   EⁿDR, ⑤ Aⁿ-druh   ẽdr, ⑤ 'æ(n)drə
Indurain
  Miguel, *Spanish bicycle racer*   ēn-DUR-ĪN   iːn'dur͵ain
Indus
  eponymous hero of India; river, Asia IN-duhs   'indəs
Indy, d'
  Vincent, *French composer*   deⁿ-DĒ, ⑤ dan-DĒ, DAN-dē   dẽdiː, ⑤ dæn'diː, 'dændiˑ
Inés
  pers. name, Spanish   ē-NĀS   iː'neːs
Inez
  1. Don Juan's mother; pers. name Ē-NEZ, Ī-NEZ, Ē-NEZ   'iː͵nez, 'ai͵nez, ͵iː'nez
  2. Spanish   ē-NĀS, ē-NĀTH   iː'neːs, iː'neːθ
Inga
  pers. name   ING-uh   'iŋə
Inge
  1. William, US playwright   INJ   'indʒ
  2. William, English prelate, author ING   'iŋ
Ingeborg
  1. pers. name, Danish   ĒNG-uh-BAWRğ   'iːŋə͵bɔːrɣ
  2. German   ING-uh-BAWR<u>KH</u>   'iŋə͵bɔʳx
Ingels
  Marty, *US agent, TV and film*   ING-guhlz   'iŋgəlz
    production executive
Ingenii, Mare
  see Mare Ingenii
Ingersoll
  Robert, *American orator*   ING-uhr-SAWL, ING-uhr-suhl   'iŋəʳ͵sɔːl, 'iŋəʳsəl
Ingmar
  pers. name, Swedish   ING-MAHR   'iŋ͵mɑʳ

Key (col. 2):   a: fad ā: fade ah: father ar: marry aw: law e: fed ē: feed er: merry i: hid ī: hide ō: coat ōō: boot
oi: boy   ow: now   u: put   uh: above   uhr: bird   ch: chop   ng: ring   sh: show   th: thick   <u>th</u>: this   zh: measure

Ingram

James, *US singer, songwriter*   ING-gruhm   'iŋgrəm

Ingres

Jean Auguste, *French painter*   EⁿGR   ĕgr

Ingrid

pers. name   ING-gruhd   'iŋgrəd

Ingush

lang., people, Kazakhstan   IN-GUSH, in-GUSH   'in‚guʃ, in'guʃ

Inigo

pers. name   IN-uh-gō   'inəgoː

Íñigo

pers. name, Spanish   ĒN-yē-g̃ō   'iːnjiːɣoː

Iniki

pers. name, Hawaiian   i-NĒ-kē   i'niːki·

Inkatha

South African politicial movement   in-KAHT-uh   in'kɑt̬ə

Innes

Scottish family name   IN-uhs   'inəs

Inno

national hymn, Vatican City   IN-nō   'innoː

Inno di Mameli

national anthem, Italy   IN-nō dē mah-MĀ-lē   'innoː diː ma'meːliː

Innoko

river, AK   IN-uh-KŌ   'inə‚koː

Innsbruck

city, Austria   IN(T)S-BRUK, INZ-BRUK   'in(t)s‚bruk, 'inz‚bruk

Ino

guardian of Dionysus; Leucothea   Ī-nō   'ɑinoː

İnönü

İsmet, president, Turkey   IN-uh(r)-NUE, ⑤ IN-uh-N(Y)OO   ‚inœːˈnyː, ⑤ ‚inəˈn(j)uː

Inouye

Daniel K., *US politician*   IN-uh-WĀ, i-NŌ-wā   'inə‚weː, i'noːweː

Insectivora

insect-eaters   IN-SEK-TIV-uh-ruh   ‚in‚sek'tivərə

Intel

US microprocessor co.   IN-TEL   'in‚tel

Intelsat

satellite consortium   IN-TEL-SAT   'in‚tel‚sæt

Interlaken

town, Switzerland   INT-uhr-LAH-kuhn   'intəʳ‚lɑkən

Interlochen

village, MI   INT-uhr-LAHK-uhn   'intəʳ‚lɑkən

Internationale

revolutionary anthem   INT-uhr-NASH-uh-NAHL   ‚intəʳ‚næʃə'nɑ·l

Internet

global computer network   INT-uhr-NET   'intəʳ‚net

Interpol

international police organization   INT-uhr-PŌL, INT-uhr-PAHL   'intəʳ‚poːl, 'intəʳ‚pɑl

Inuit

people, lang., N. America   IN-(y)uh-wuht   'in(j)əwət

Inuktitut [Inuit]

lang., Greenland, Canada, USA   i-NOOK-tuh-TUT   i'nuːktə‚tut

Inulin

carbohydrate   IN-yuh-luhn   'injələn

Foreign Sounds: ue: *Fr.* **rue**, *Ger.* **füllen**   uh(r): *Fr.* **boeuf**, *Ger.* **Höhle**   <u>kh</u>: *Ger.* **ich**, *Scot.* **loch**   g̃: *Sp.* amigo   y̠: *Sp.* hablar
hl: *Welsh* **Llanelli**.   CAPITALS: primary stress.   SMALL CAPS: secondary stress.   ⑤: U.S. pron.   ⓔ: British pron.

Inupiac [Inuit]
  lang., Greenland, Canada, USA   i-N$\overline{OO}$-pē-AK   i'nuːpiːˌæk
Inverell
  town, Australia   IN-vuh-REL, IN-vuh-REL   ˌinvə'rel, 'invəˌrel
Inver Hills
  Community College, *MN*   IN-vuhr HILZ   'invəʳ 'hilz
Inverness
  1. city, Scotland   IN-vuhr-NES   ˌinvəʳnes
  2. town, CA, FL, IL   IN-vuhr-NES, IN-vuhr-nuhs   'invəʳˌnes, 'invəʳnəs
INXS
  rock group   IN-ek-SES, IN-ik-SES   ˌinek'ses, ˌinik'ses
Inyo
  county, CA   IN-yō   'injoː
Io
  beloved of Zeus turned into a cow;   Ī-ō, Ē-ō   'aioː, 'iːoː
    satellite of Jupiter
Ioan
  1. pers. name, Romanian   YWAHN   'jwɑn
  2. Welsh   YŌ-ahn   'joːɑːn
Ioannes, Ioannis
  pers. name, Mod. Greek   yaw-AHN-yēs   jɔ'ɑnjiːs
Ioannina, Ioánnina
  department, Greece   yaw-AHN-ē-NAH, YAHN-ē-NAH   jɔː'aniːˌnɑː, 'janiːˌnɑː
Iobates
  father of Sthenboea   Ī-uh-BĀT-ēz   ˌaiə'beːʈiːz
Iobes
  son of Heracles and Certhe   ī-Ō-bēz   ai'oːbiːz
iodine
  element   Ī-uh-DĪN, Ī-uhd-n, Ī-uh-DĒN   'aiəˌdain, 'aiədn̩, 'aiəˌdiːn
Iola
  city, KS   ī-Ō-luh   ai'oːlə
Iolani
  palace, HI   Ē-uh-LAHN-ē   ˌiːə'lani·
Iolanthe
  operetta, Gilbert & Sullivan   Ī-uh-LAN-thē   ˌaiə'lænθi·
Iole
  captive of Hercules   Ī-uh-lē, ē-Ō-lē   'aiəli·, iː'oːli·
Iolo
  pers. name, Welsh   YŌ-lō   'joːloː
Ion
  1. dialogue of Plato; eponymous   Ī-uhn, Ī-AHN   'aiən, 'aiˌɑn
    ancestor of Ionians
  2. pers. name, Romanian   YAWN   'jɔːn
Iona
  island, Scotland; college, NY   ī-Ō-nuh   ai'oːnə
Ionesco
  Eugène, *French playwright*   yaw-nes-KŌ, ⑤ Ē-uh-NES-kō   jɔːneskoː, ⑤ ˌiːə'neskoː
Ionia
  ancient region, Asia Minor; county, ī-Ō-nē-uh   ai'oːniːə
    MI
Ionian
  sea, Mediterranean; architectural   ī-Ō-nē-uhn   ai'oːniːən
    order; musical mode; pert. to
    Ionia; Islands, *Greece*

Key (col. 2): a: fad ā: fade ah: father ar: marry aw: law e: fed ē: feed er: merry i: hid ī: hide ō: coat $\overline{oo}$: boot
oi: boy   ow: now   u: put   uh: above   uhr: bird   ch: chop   ng: ring   sh: show   th: thick   th̲: this   zh: measure

Ionic
    ancient Greek dialect; pert. to Ionian   ī-AHN-ik   aiˈɑnik
    order

Iora
    Asian songbird   ī-Ō-ruh, ē-Ō-ruh   aiˈoːrə, iːˈoːrə

Ios
    island, Greece   Ī-AHS, Ē-AWS   ˈɑiˌɑs, ˈiːˌɔːs

Iosco
    county, MI   ī-AHS-kō   aiˈɑskoː

Iosif
    pers. name, Russian   YAWS-yif, i-AWS-yif   ˈjoːsjif, iˈoːsjif

Iowa
    state, US ; river, IA; N. American   Ī-uh-wuh   ˈɑiəwə
    people

Iowan
    pert. to Iowa   Ī-uh-wuhn   ˈɑiəwən

Iphdeiah [Iphedeiah]
    Biblical name   if-DĒ-uh, YIF-duh-YAH   ifˈdiːə, ˌjifdəˈja

Iphedeiah
    Biblical name   IF-uh-DĪ-uh, IF-uh-DĒ-uh, YIF-duh-YAH   ˌifəˈdaiə, ˌifəˈdiːə, ˌjifdəˈja

Iphianassa [Iphigenia]
    daughter of Agamemnon   IF-ē-uh-NAS-uh   ˌifiːəˈnæsə

Iphicles
    twin brother of Heracles   IF-i-KLĒZ, Ē-fi-KLĒZ   ˈifiˌkliːz, ˈiːfiˌkliːz

Iphiclus
    Argonaut; conqueror of Phoenicians   IF-i-kluhs, Ē-fi-kluhs   ˈifikləs, ˈiːfikləs
    at Rhodes

Iphigenia, -neia
    daughter of Agamemnon and   IF-uh-juh-NĪ-uh, IF-uh-juh-NĒ-uh   ˌifədʒəˈnaiə, ˌifədʒəˈniːə
    Clytemnestra

Iphitus
    son of Eurytus   Ē-fuht-uhs   ˈiːfəṱəs

Iphtah
    Biblical name   IF-tuh, yif-TAHKH   ˈiftə, jifˈtax

Iphtah-el
    Biblical name   IF-tuh-EL, yif-TAHKH-EL   ˈiftəˌel, jifˌtaxˈel

I-pin
    former name of Suzhou   Ē-PIN, Ē-PĒN   ˈiːˈpin, ˈiːˈpiːn

Ipiros [Epirus]
    region, Greece   Ē-pi-RAWS   ˈiːpiˌrɔːs

Ippolito
    pers. name, Italian   ēp-PAW-lē-tō   iːpˈpɔːliːtoː

Ippolitov-Ivanov
    Mikhail, *Russian composer*   IP-uhl-YĒ-tuhf-yi-VAH-nuhf   ˌipəlˈjiːtəfjiˈvaːnəf

Ipsus
    ancient Phrygian village   IP-suhs   ˈipsəs

Ipswich
    US pl. name; borough, England; city,   IP-swich   ˈipswitʃ
    Australia

Ipuwer
    ancient Egyptian prophet   ē-PYOO-uhr   iːˈpjuːəʳ

Iqaluit
    town, Northwest Territories, Canada   i-KAHL-uh-wit   iˈkɑləwit

Iqbal
    Muhammad, *Pakistani poet*   ik-BAHL, Ⓢ IK-BAHL, IK-BAL   ikˈbɑl, Ⓢ ˈikˌbɑl, ˈikˌbæl

---

Foreign Sounds: ue: *Fr.* **r**u**e**, *Ger.* f**ü**llen   uh(r): *Fr.* b**oeu**f, *Ger.* H**öh**le   <u>kh</u>: *Ger.* i**ch**, *Scot.* lo**ch**   g̱: *Sp.* ami**g**o   v̱: *Sp.* ha**b**lar
hl: *Welsh* L**l**anelli.   CAPITALS: primary stress.   SMALL CAPS: secondary stress.   Ⓢ: U.S. pron.   Ⓔ: British pron.

Ir
  Biblical name   UHR, IR   'ɔʳ, 'iʳ

IRA
  1. Irish Republican Army   Ī-AHR-Ā   ˌɑiˌɑr'eː
  2. individual retirement account   Ī-AHR-Ā, Ī-ruh   ˌɑiˌɑʳ'eː, 'ɑirə

Ira
  pers. name   Ī-ruh   'ɑirə

Irad
  Biblical name   Ī-RAD, Ī-ruhd, ē-RAHD   'ɑiˌræd, 'ɑirəd, i·'rɑd

Iráklion
  dept & town, Greece   i-RAHK-lē-AWN   i'rɑkliːˌɔːn

Iram
  Biblical name   Ī-RAM, ē-RAHM   'ɑiˌræm, iː'rɑm

Iran
  country, SW Asia   i-RAHN, i-RAN, ī-RAN   i'rɑn, i'ræn, ɑi'ræn

Iranian
  pert. to Iran   i-RAHN-ē-uhn, i-RĀN-, i-RAN-, ī-RAN-   i'rɑniːən, i'reːn-, i'ræn-, ɑi'ræn-

Iraq
  country, Middle East   i-RAHK, i-RAK, ī-   i'rɑk, i'ræk, ɑi-

Iraqi
  pert. to Iraq   i-RAHK-ē, i-RAK-ē, ī-   i'rɑki·, i'ræki·, ɑi-

Iráya
  lang., people, Philippine Islands   i-RĪ-uh, i-RAH-yuh   i'rɑiə, i'rɑjə

Irazú
  volcano, Costa Rica   IR-uh-ZOO, IR-uh-SOO   ˌirə'zuː, ˌirə'suː

Irbid
  governorate, town, Jordan   ir-BID, IR-buhd   iʳ'bid, 'iʳbəd

Irbīl [Arbīl, Erbil]
  governorate, city, Iraq   UHR-BĒL   'ɔʳˌbiːl

Iredell
  county, NC   ĪR-DEL   'ɑirˌdel

Ireland [Eire]
  republic, Europe   ĪR-luhnd   'ɑiʳlənd

Irenaeus
  pers. name   Ī-ruh-NĒ-uhs   ˌɑirə'niːəs

Irene
  1. pers. name   ī-RĒN, ⓔ ī-RĒ-nē   ɑi'riːn, ⓔ ɑi'riːni·
  2. German   ē-RĀ-nā   iː'reːneː
  3. Latin   ī-RĒ-nē   ɑi'riːni·

Irène
  pers. name, French   ē-REN   iːren

Irénée
  pers. name, French   ē-rā-NĀ   iːreːneː

Irgun
  militant Zionist underground group   ir-GUN   iʳ'gun

Iri
  Biblical name   Ī-RĪ, ē-RĒ   'ɑiˌrɑi, iː'riː

Irian Jaya
  prov, Indonesia   IR-ē-AHN JĪ-uh   'iriːˌɑn 'dʒɑiə

iridium
  element   ir-ID-ē-uhm   ir'idiːəm

Iridum, Sinus
  see Sinus Iridum

Key (col. 2):   a: fad   ā: fade   ah: father   ar: marry   aw: law   e: fed   ē: feed   er: merry   i: hid   ī: hide   ō: coat   oo: boot
oi: boy   ow: now   u: put   uh: above   uhr: bird   ch: chop   ng: ring   sh: show   th: thick   <u>th</u>: this   zh: measure

Irijah
   Biblical name   ī-RĪ-juh, YIR-ē-YAH   αι'rɑidʒə, ˌjiriː'jɑ

Irion
   county, TX   IR-ē-uhn   'iriːən

Iris
   Greek goddess of the rainbow; pers.   Ī-ruhs   'αirəs
      name

Irish
   lang., people, Ireland   Ī-rish   'αiriʃ

Irish Free State [Ireland]
   republic, Europe   ĪR-ish FRĒ STĀT   ˌαiriʃ 'friː ˌsteːt

Irish Gaelic
   lang., Ireland   ĪR-ish GĀ-lik   'αiriʃ 'geːlik

Irkutsk
   city, Russia   ir-KŌŌTSK   iʳ'kuːtsk

Irma
   pers. name   UHR-muh   'əʳmə

Irminger
   current off west coast of Ireland   UHR-ming-uhr   'əʳmiŋəʳ

Ir-nahash
   Biblical name   UHR-NĀ-HASH, IR-nah-<u>KH</u>AHSH   ˌəʳ'neːˌhæʃ, ˌirnɑ'xɑʃ

iron
   element   Ī(-uh)rn   'αi(ə)ʳn

Irondequoit
   Bay, inlet, Lake Ontario; town, NY   ir-AHN-duh-KWOIT   ir'ɑndəˌkwɔit

Ironton
   city, MO; city, OH   Ī(-uh)rn-tuhn   'αi(ə)ʳntən

Iroquoian
   pert. to the Iroquois   IR-uh-KWOI-uhn   ˌirə'kwɔiən

Iroquois
   Native American confederacy   IR-uh-KWOI, IR-uh-KWAH   'irəˌkwɔi, 'irəˌkwɑ

Irpeel
   Biblical name   UHR-pē-EL, YIR-puh-EL   'əʳpiːˌel, ˌjirpə'el

Irra
   Babylonian god of disease   IR-uh   'irə

Irrawaddy
   river, Burma   IR-uh-WAHD-ē   ˌirə'wɑdi·

Irredentist
   advocate of historical or ethnic   IR-uh-DENT-uhst   ˌirə'dentəst
      political unity

Ir-shemesh
   Biblical name   UHR-SHĒ-MESH, IR-SHEM-ESH   ˌəʳ'ʃiːˌmeʃ, ˌir'ʃemˌeʃ

Irtish
   river, Kazakhstan, Russia   ir-TISH, uhr-TISH   iʳ'tiʃ, əʳ'tiʃ

Iru
   Biblical name   Ī-rōō, IR-ōō, Ē-rōō   'αiruː, 'iruː, 'iːruː

Irvine
   1. city, CA   UHR-VĪN   'əʳˌvαin
   2. city, KY; city, Scotland   UHR-vuhn   'əʳvən

Irving
   pers. name   UHR-ving   'əʳviŋ

Irwin
   Hale S., US golfer   UHR-wuhn   'əʳwən

Foreign Sounds: ue: *Fr.* **rue**, *Ger.* **füllen**   uh(r): *Fr.* **boeuf**, *Ger.* **Höhle**   <u>kh</u>: *Ger.* **ich**, *Scot.* **loch**   g̅: *Sp.* amigo   v̠: *Sp.* hablar
hl: *Welsh* **Llanelli**.   CAPITALS: primary stress.   SMALL CAPS: secondary stress.   ⑤: U.S. pron.   ⓔ: British pron.

Isaac
1. pers. name	Ī-zik, Ī-zuhk	'aɪzɪk, 'aɪzək
2. French	ē-ZAHK	iːzɑːk
3. German	Ē-zah-AHK, Ē-ZAHK	'iːzɑˌɑk, 'iːˌzɑk
4. Polish	Ē-sahk	'iːsɑːk
5. Russian	i-SAHK	i'sɑːk
6. Spanish	ē-sah-AHK	iːsɑ'ɑk

Isaacs
1. Isaac Alfred, *Australian jurist;* Katherine M., *US onomastician;* Rufus, *British politician*	Ī-zuhks, Ī-ziks	'aɪzəks, 'aɪzɪks
2. Jorge, *Colombian author*	ē-SAHKS, ē-SAH-ahks	iː'sɑks, iː'sɑ-ɑks

Isaak
1. Chris, *rock singer*	Ī-zik	'aɪzɪk
2. German	Ē-zah-AHK, Ē-ZAHK	'iːzɑˌɑk, 'iːˌzɑk

Isaäk, Isaak
pers. name, Dutch	Ē-sahk	'iːsɑk

Isabel
1. pers. name	IZ-uh-BEL	'izəˌbel
2. Spanish	ē-sah-BEL	iːsɑ'bel

Isabella
1. pers. name	IZ-uh-BEL-uh	ˌizə'belə
2. Dutch	Ē-sah-BEL-ah	ˌiːsɑː'belɑː
3. Italian	Ē-zah-BEL-lah	ˌiːzɑ'bellɑ

Isabelle
1. pers. name	IZ-uh-BEL	'izəˌbel
2. French	ē-zah-BEL	iːzɑːbel
3. German	Ē-zah-BEL-uh	ˌiːzɑ'belə

Isador, Isadore
pers. name	IZ-uh-DŌR, -DAWR	'izəˌdoː[r], -ˌdɔː[r]

Isadora
pers. name	IZ-uh-DŌR-uh, -DAWR-uh	ˌizə'doːrə, -'dɔːrə

Isagoras
Athenian politician	Ī-SAG-uh-ruhs	aɪ'sægərəs

Isaiah
biblical prophet; Old Testament book; pers. name	Ī-ZĀ-uh, ⓔ Ī-ZĪ-uh	aɪ'zeːə, ⓔ aɪ'zaɪə

Isaias
1. Old Testament book	Ī-ZĀ-uhs, ⓔ Ī-ZĪ-uhs	aɪ'zeːəs, ⓔ aɪ'zaɪəs
2. pers. name, Spanish	ē-sah-Ē-ahs	iːsɑ'iːɑs

Isak
pers. name, Dutch	Ē-SAHK	'iːˌsɑːk

Isanti
county, MN	i-SANT-ē	i'sænti·

Isar
Bavarian river	Ē-ZAHR	'iːˌzɑ[r]

Iscah
Biblical name	IS-kuh, yis-KAH	'iskə, jis'kɑ

Iscariot
see Judas Iscariot

Ischia
Italian island, west of Naples	IS-kē-uh	'iskiːə

Isenbeck
German beer	Ē-zuhn-BEK	'iːzənˌbek

Key (col. 2):   a: **fad**   ā: **fade**   ah: **father**   ar: **marry**   aw: **law**   e: **fed**   ē: **feed**   er: **merry**   i: **hid**   ī: **hide**   ō: **coat**   ōō: **boot**
oi: **boy**   ow: **now**   u: **put**   uh: **above**   uhr: **bird**   ch: **chop**   ng: **ring**   sh: **show**   th: **thick**   th: **this**   zh: **measure**

Iser
   Czech river   Ē-zuhr   'iːzəʳ

Isère
   river, dept, France   ē-ZER   iːzer

Iseult [Isolde]
   beloved of Tristram   is-O͞OLT, iz-O͞OLT   is'uːlt, iz'uːlt

Isfahan [Esfahān]
   prov & town, Iran   IS-fuh-HAHN   ˌisfə'hɑn

Ishbah
   Biblical name   ISH-buh, yish-BAH<u>KH</u>   'iʃbə, jiʃ'bɑx

Ishbak
   Biblical name   ISH-BAK, yish-BAHK   'iʃˌbæk, jiʃ'bɑk

Ishbi-benob
   Biblical name   ISH-BĪ-BĒ-NAHB, yish-BĒ-buh-NAWV   'iʃˌbai'biːˌnab, jiʃ'biːbə'nɔːv

Ishbosheth
   Biblical name   ish-BŌ-shuhth   iʃ'boːʃəθ

Isherwood
   Christopher, *English author*   ISH-uhr-WUD   'iʃəʳˌwud

Ishi
   Biblical name   ISH-Ī, yi-SHĒ   'iʃˌai, ji'ʃiː

Ishiah
   Biblical name   i-SHĪ-uh, YISH-i-YAH   i'ʃaiə, ˌjiʃi'ja

Ishijah
   Biblical name   i-SHĪ-juh, Ī-SHĪ-juh, YISH-i-YAH   i'ʃaidʒə, ai'ʃaidʒə, ˌjiʃi'ja

Ishikawa
   prefecture, Japan   ish-i-kah-wah   iʃikɑwɑ

Ishma
   Biblical name   ISH-muh, yish-MAH   'iʃmə, jiʃ'mɑ

Ishmael
   Biblical son of Abraham & Hagar; ISH-MĀ-uhl, ISH-mē-uhl   'iʃˌmeːəl, 'iʃmiːəl
     pers. name

Ishmaelite
   descendant of Ishmael   ISH-MĀ-uh-LĪT, ISH-mē-uh-LĪT   'iʃˌmeːəˌlait, 'iʃmiːəˌlait

Ishmaiah
   Biblical name   ish-MĪ-uh, ish-MĀ-uh,   iʃ'maiə, iʃ'meːə,
                              YISH-mah-YAH-ho͞o   ˌjiʃma'jahuː

Ishmerai
   Biblical name   ISH-muh-RĪ, YISH-muh-RĪ   'iʃməˌrai, ˌjiʃmə'rai

Ishod, Ishhod
   Biblical name   ISH-AHD, Ī-SHAHD, ēsh-HŌD   'iʃˌad, 'aiˌʃad, iːʃ'hoːd

Ishpah [Ispah]
   Biblical name   ISH-puh, yish-PAH   'iʃpə, jiʃ'pɑ

Ishpan
   Biblical name   ISH-PAN, yish-PAHN   'iʃˌpæn, jiʃ'pɑn

Ishpeming
   city, MI   ISH-puh-ming   'iʃpəmiŋ

Ishtar
   Assyrian and Babylonian fertility ISH-TAHR   'iʃˌtɑʳ
     goddess

Ishtar Terra
   highland on planet Venus   ISH-TAHR TER-uh   'iʃˌtɑʳ 'terə

Ishvah
   Biblical name   ISH-vuh, yish-VAH   'iʃvə, jiʃ'vɑ

Ishvi
   Biblical name   ISH-VĪ, yish-VĒ   'iʃˌvai, jiʃ'viː

Foreign Sounds: ue: *Fr.* **rue**, *Ger.* **füllen**   uh(r): *Fr.* **boeuf**, *Ger.* **Höhle**   <u>kh</u>: *Ger.* **ich**, *Scot.* **loch**   g̃: *Sp.* **amigo**   v: *Sp.* **hablar**
hl: *Welsh* **Llanelli**.   CAPITALS: primary stress.   SMALL CAPS: secondary stress.   Ⓢ: U.S. pron.   Ⓔ: British pron.

Ishvite
  Biblical name   ISH-VĪT   'iʃˌvɑit
Isidor, Isidore
  pers. name   IZ-uh-DŌR, -DAWR   'izəˌdoːᵘ, -ˌdɔːᵘ
Isin
  ancient Sumerian city   IS-n   'isn̩
Isis
  Egyptian queen of the gods   Ī-suhs   'aisəs
Ĭskenderun
  gulf, Mediterranean Sea   IS-KEN-duh-RO͞ON   ˌisˌkendə'ruːn
İskenderun [Alexandretta]
  gulf, Mediterranean Sea; city, Turkey   is-KEN-duh-RO͞ON   is'kendəˌruːn
Isla
  river, Scotland   Ī-luh   'ailə
Islam
  religion   is-LAHM, iz-LAHM, -LAM; IS-LAHM,   is'lɑm, iz'lɑm, -'læm;
                                                       IZ-LAHM, -LAM   'isˌlɑm, 'izˌlɑm, -ˌlæm
Islamabad
  city, Pakistan   is-LAHM-uh-BAHD, iz-LAM-uh-BAD   is'lɑməˌbɑd, iz'læməˌbæd
Islamic
  pert. to Islam   is-LAHM-ik, iz-LAHM-ik, is-LAM-ik,   is'lɑmik, iz'lɑmik, is'læmik,
                                                       iz-LAM-ik   iz'læmik
Islamorada
  resort, FL   Ī-luh-mawr-AHD-uh,   ˌailəmɔːr'ɑdə, ˌisləmə'rɑdə
                                                       IS-luh-muh-RAHD-uh
Island Carib
  lang., Honduras, Belize, Guatemala   Ī-luhnd KAR-uhb   'ailənd 'kærəb
Islay
  island, Scotland   Ī-luh, Ī-lā   'ailə, 'aileː
Isle
  river, France   ĒL   'iːl
Isle au Haut
  island, ME   Ī-luh-HŌ(T), Ē-luh-HŌ   ˌailə'hoː(t), ˌiːlə'hoː
Isle la Motte
  island, Lake Champlain   ĪL luh MAHT   ˌail lə 'mɑt
Isle of Wight
  see Wight, Isle of
Isles Dernieres
  island group, LA   ĒL dern-YER   ˌiːl deᵉn'jeᵉ
Isleta Pueblo
  Indian reservation, US   ēz-LĀT-uh po͞o-EB-lō, PWEB-lō,   iˑz'leːt̬ə puː'eblɔː, 'pweblɔː,
                                                       pyo͞o-EB-lō   pjuː'eblɔː
Islington
  borough, England   IZ-ling-tuhn   'izliŋtən
Islip
  town, NY; village, England   Ī-sluhp   'aisləp
Ismachiah
  Biblical name   IS-muh-KĪ-uh, YIS-mah<u>kh</u>-YAH-ho͞o   ˌismə'kaiə, ˌjismɑx'jɑhuː
Ismael
  1. pers. name, German   IS-mah-EL   'ismɑˌel
  2. Spanish   ēz-mah-ĀL   iːzmɑ'eːl
Ismaël
  pers. name, French   ēs-mah-EL   iːsmɑːel

Key (col. 2):   a: f**a**d   ā: f**a**de   ah: f**a**ther   ar: m**a**rry   aw: l**a**w   e: f**e**d   ē: f**ee**d   er: m**e**rry   i: h**i**d   ī: h**i**de   ō: c**oa**t   o͞o: b**oo**t
oi: b**oy**   ow: n**ow**   u: p**u**t   uh: **a**bove   uhr: b**i**rd   ch: **ch**op   ng: ri**ng**   sh: **sh**ow   th: **th**ick   <u>th</u>: **th**is   zh: mea**s**ure

Ismail
1. pers. name, Albanian	ēs-mah-ĒL	iːsmɑ'iːl
2. Russian	yis-MAH-(y)il	jis'mɑ(j)il

Isma'īl

pers. name, Arabic   is-mah-ĒL   ismɑ'iːl

Ismene

daughter of Oedipus and Jocasta   is-MĒ-nē   is'miːni·

Ĭsmet

pers. name   is-MET   is'met

Isobel

pers. name   IZ-uh-BEL   'izə,bel

Isocrates

Athenian orator   ī-SAHK-ruh-TĒZ   ɑi'sɑkrə,tiːz

Isolda

pers. name   i-SŌL-duh, i-ZŌL-duh, ⒠ i-ZAHL-duh   i'soːldə, i'zoːldə, ⒠ i'zɑldə

Isolde
1. beloved of Tristram [Iseult]; pers. name	i-SŌL-duh, ē-ZŌL-duh, i-SŌLD	i'soːldə, iː'zoːldə, i'soːld
2. German	i-ZAWL-duh	i'zɔːldə

I Solisti

chamber orchestras, Zagreb, Venice   Ē sō-LIS-tē   ,iː soː'listi·

Ispah [Ishpah]

Biblical name   IS-puh, yish-PAH   'ispə, jiʃ'pɑ

Israel
1. republic, ancient kingdom, eastern Mediterranean; pers. name	IZ-rē-uhl, IZ-rā-uhl, IZ-ruhl, IS-	'izriːəl, 'izreːəl, 'izrəl, 'is-
2. Dutch	IS-rah-EL	'israː,el
3. French	ēs-rah-EL	iːsraːel
4. Swedish	ĒS-rah-uhl	'iːsraːəl

Israel ben Eliezer [Ba'al Shem-Tov]

founder of Hasidism   IZ-rē-uhl BEN EL-ē-Ā-zuhr   'izriːəl ,ben ,eliː'eːzəʳ

Israeli

from or pert. to Israel   iz-RĀ-lē, IZ-ruh-Ā-lē   iz'reːli·, ,izrə'eːli·

Israelite

inhabitant of or pert. to Israel   IZ-r(ē-)uh-LĬT   'izr(iː)ə,lɑit

Issa

pers. name, Japanese   ē-sah   iːsɑ

Issachar

Biblical name   IS-uh-KAHR, yi-sahs-K̲H̲AHR   'isə,kɑʳ, jisɑs'xɑr

Issaquah

city, WA   IS-uh-KWAW   'isə,kwɔː

Issaquena

county, MS   IS-uh-KWĒ-nuh   ,isə'kwiːnə

Isshiah

Biblical name   is-SHĬ-uh, YISH-ē-YAH   is'ʃɑiə, ,jiʃiː'jɑ

Isshijah [Isshiah]

Biblical name   is-SHĬ-juh, yi-shē-YAH   is'ʃɑidʒə, ,jiʃiː'jɑ

Issus

ancient town, Asia Minor   IS-uhs   'isəs

Istanbul

province, city, Turkey   IS-tuhm-B̅O̅O̅L, -TAHM-, -TAM-, -TAHN-, -TAN-, -BUL   ,istəm'buːl, -,tɑm-, -,tæm-, -,tɑn-, -,tæn-, -'bul

---

Isthmian
  pert. to isthmus of Corinth *or*   IS-mē-uhn   'ismiːən
  Panama

Istra [Istria]
  peninsula, Croatia   Ē-struh   'iːstrə

Istranca
  mtn. range, Turkey   is-TRAHN-juh   is'trɑndʒə

Istria
  peninsula, Croatia   Ē-strē-uh, IS-trē-uh   'iːstriːə, 'istriːə

Istrus
  personification of the Danube River   IS-truhs   'istrəs

István
  pers. name, Hungarian   ISHT-vahn   'iʃtvɑːn

Isuzu
  Japanese car co.   i-SŌO-zōo   i'suːzuː

Itaípu
  city, Brazil   ē-TĪ-POO   iː'tɑi,puː

Italia [Italy]
  republic, Europe   ē-TAHL-yah, ē-TAHL-yuh   iː'taljɑ, iː'taljə

Italian
  lang., Europe   i-TAL-yuhn   i'tæljən

Italianate
  Italian in style   uh-TAL-yuh-NĀT, i-TAL-   ə'tæljə,neːt, i'tæl-

Italian spinone
  dog breed   i-TAL-yuhn spuh-NŌ-nä   i,tæljən spə'noːneː

Italo-
  combining form meaning Italian   IT-l-ō, uh-TAL-ō, i-TAL-ō   'itḷoː, ə'tæloː, i'tæloː

Italo
  pers. name, Italian   Ē-tahl-ō   'iːtɑloː

Italus
  hero of Italy   uh-TAL-uhs, i-TAL-uhs   ə'tæləs, i'tæləs

Italy
  republic, Europe   IT-l-ē   'itḷiˑ

Itar-Tass
  Russian news agency   Ē-TAHR-TAHS   'iː,tɑʳ'tas

Itasca
  lake, county, college, MN   ī-TAS-kuh   ɑi'tæskə

Itawamba
  county, MS   IT-uh-WAHM-buh   ,iṭə'wambə

Ithaca
  city, NY; island, Greece   ITH-i-kuh   'iθikə

Ithacus
  eponymous hero of Ithaca   ITH-i-kuhs   'iθikəs

Ithai
  Biblical name   Ī-thē-Ī, ITH-Ī, ē-TĪ   'ɑiθiː,ɑi, 'iθ,ɑi, iː'tɑi

Ithamar
  Biblical name   ITH-uh-MAHR, Ē-tah-MAHR   'iθə,mɑʳ, 'iːtɑ,mɑr

Ithome
  mtn., Greece   i-THŌ-mē   i'θoːmiˑ

Ito
  Lance, *US trial judge*   ĒT-ō   'iːṭoː

Ito Hirobumi
  Japanese statesman   ē-tō hir-ō-bōo-mē   iːtoː hiroːbuːmiː

Itta Bena
  town, MS   IT-uh BĒ-nuh   ,iṭə 'biːnə

Key (col. 2):   a: fad ā: fade ah: father ar: marry aw: law e: fed ē: feed er: merry i: hid ī: hide ō: coat ōo: boot
oi: boy ow: now u: put uh: above uhr: bird ch: chop ng: ring sh: show th: thick <u>th</u>: this zh: measure

Ittai
 Biblical name   IT-ē-Ī, i-TĀ-Ī, i-TĪ   'itiːˌɑi, i'teːˌɑi, i'tɑi
Ittmann
 Majorie McCullough, *Girl Scout*   IT-muhn   'itmən
      official
Ituraea
 Biblical name   IT-(y)uh-RĒ-uh, Ī-t(y)uh-RĒ-uh   ˌit(j)ə'riːə, ˌɑit(j)ə'riːə
Iturbi
 Jose, *Spanish musician*   ē-TŌOR-ve̱   iː'tuːrβiː
Ituri
 pers. name, Spanish   ē-TŌO-rē   iː'tuːriː
Itys
 son of Procne and Tereus   ĪT-uhs   'ɑițəs
Iuka
 town, MS   Ī-(Y)ŌO-kuh   ɑi'(j)uːkə
Iulus [Ascanius]
 son of Aeneas   YŌO-luhs   'juːləs
Ius auxilii
 Roman tribune's right of help   YŌOS owk-SIL-ē-Ē   'juːs ɑuk'siliːˌiː
Iuventas [Juventas]
 Roman goddess of youth   yōo-VENT-uhs   juː'ventəs
Ivah, Ivvah
 Biblical name   Ī-vuh, i-VAH   'ɑivə, i'vɑ
Ivan
 1. pers. name   ē-VAHN, Ī-vuhn   iː'vɑn, 'ɑivən
 2. Bulgarian   ē-VAHN   iː'vɑːn
 3. Russian   i-VAHN   i'vɑːn
 4. Serbo-Croatian, Swedish   Ē-vahn   'iːvɑːn
Ivana
 pers. name   i-VAHN-uh   i'vɑnə
Ivanhoe
 novel, Sir Walter Scott   Ī-vuhn-HŌ   'ɑivənˌhoː
Ivanovitch
 patronym, Russian   i-VAHN(-uhv)-YICH   i'vɑːn(əv)ˌjitʃ
Ivanovo
 city, Russia   i-VAHN-uh-vuh   i'vɑːnəvə
Ivar
 1. pers. name, Norwegian   Ē-vahr   'iːvɑr
 2. Swedish   Ē-vahr   'iːvɑːr
Iveco
 truck co.   uh-VĀ-kō, i-VĀ-kō   ə'veːkoː, i'veːkoː
Ives
 pers. name   ĪVZ   'ɑivz
Iviza
 see Ibiza
Ivo
 pers. name, Serbo-Croatian   Ē-vaw   'iːvɔː
Ivor
 pers. name   Ē-vuhr, Ī-vuhr   'iːvəʳ, 'ɑivəʳ
Ivorian
 inhabitant of the Ivory Coast   i-VŌR-ē-uhn, i-VAWR-ē-uhn   i'voːriːən, i'vɔːriːən
Ivory Coast
 republic, Africa   Ī-v(uh-)rē   'ɑiv(ə)riˑ
Ivy
 pers. name   Ī-vē   'ɑiviˑ

Foreign Sounds: ue: *Fr.* **rue**, *Ger.* **füllen**   uh(r): *Fr.* **boeuf**, *Ger.* **Höhle**   <u>kh</u>: *Ger.* **ich**, *Scot.* lo**ch**   ğ: *Sp.* ami**g**o   v: *Sp.* ha**b**lar
hl: *Welsh* **Ll**anelli.   CAPITALS: primary stress.   SMALL CAPS: secondary stress.   Ⓢ: U.S. pron.   Ⓔ: British pron.

Iwan

   1. pers. name, French   ē-VAH^n iːvɑ̃

   2. German   ē-VAHN, Ē-VAHN   iː'vɑn, 'iː,vɑn

   3. Welsh   YO͞O-ahn   'juːɑːn

Iwo Jima

   island, Pacific   Ē-wuh JĒ-muh, Ē-wō   ,iːwə 'dʒiːmə, ,iːwoː

Ixia

   flower   IK-sē-uh   'iksiːə

Ixil

   lang., people, Guatemala   ē-SHĒL   iː'ʃiːl

Ixion

   king of Thessaly, tortured on wheel in   ik-SĪ-uhn   ik'saiən
    Hades

Ixtaccihuatl, Iztaccíhuatl

   volcano, Puebla-México   ĒS-tahk-SĒ-WAHT-l   ,iːstɑk'siː,wɑtl̩

Ixtacihuatl [Ixtaccihuatl]

   volcano, Mexico   Ē-stah-SĒ-WAHT-l   ,iːstɑ'siː,wɑtl̩

Iyar

   Jewish month   Ē-YAHR   'iː,jɑr

Iyeabarim

   Biblical name   Ī(-ē)-AB-uhr-im, i-YĀ-ah-vah-RĒM   ,ai(iː)'æbərim, i'jeːɑvɑ'riːm

Izaak

   1. pers. name   Ī-zik, Ī-zuhk   'aizik, 'aizək

   2. Dutch   Ē-ZAHK   'iː,zɑk

Izard

   county, AR   IZ-uhrd   'izə^{r}d

Izehar [Izhar]

   Biblical name   Ī-zuh-HAHR, yits-HAHR   'aizə,hɑ^r, jits'hɑr

Izeharite

   Biblical name   IZ-uh-HAHR-ĪT   'izə,hɑr,ait

Izetbegovic

   Alija, Bosnian political leader   IZ-uht-BEG-uh-VICH, -BĀ-guh-   ,izət'begə,vitʃ, -'beːgə-

Izhar

   Biblical name   IZ-hahr, yits-HAHR   'izhɑ^r, jits'hɑr

Izharite

   Biblical name   IZ-huh-RĪT   'izhə,rait

Izliah

   Biblical name   iz-LĪ-uh, YIZ-lē-AH   iz'laiə, ,jizliː'ɑ

Îzmir [Smyrna]

   prov, Turkey   iz-MIR   iz'mi^r

İzmir [Smyrna]

   province, seaport, Turkey   iz-MIR   iz'mi^r

Izod Lacoste

   tdmk for sportswear   Ī-ZAHD luh-KAHST, luh-KAWST   ,ai,zad lə'kast, lə'kɔːst

Izrahiah

   Biblical name   IZ-ruh-HĪ-uh, yiz-rah<u>kh</u>-YAH   ,izrə'haiə, jizrɑx'jɑ

Izrahite

   Biblical name   IZ-ruh-HĪT   'izrə,hait

Izri

   Biblical name   IZ-RĪ, yits-RĒ   'iz,rai, jits'riː

Iztaccíhuatl

   see Ixtaccihuatl

Izvestia

   official Soviet newspaper   iz-VES-tē-uh, iz-VES-chē-uh   iz'vestiːə, iz'vestʃiːə

Key (col. 2):   a: **f**a**d** ā: **f**a**de** ah: **f**a**ther** ar: **marry** aw: **law** e: **fed** ē: **feed** er: **merry** i: **hid** ī: **hide** ō: **coat** o͞o: **boot**
oi: **boy** ow: **now** u: **put** uh: **above** uhr: **bird** ch: **chop** ng: **ring** sh: **show** th: **thick** <u>th</u>: **this** zh: **measure**

Izziah
Biblical name i-ZĪ-uh, YI-zē-YAH i'zɑiə, ˌjizi:'jɑ

J

Jaakan [Jakan]
Biblical name JĀ-uh-KAN, YAH-ah-KAHN 'dʒe:əˌkæn, ˌjɑ-ɑ'kɑn

Jaakobah
Biblical name JĀ-uh-KŌ-buh, YAH-ah-KAW-vah ˌdʒe:ə'ko:bə, ˌjɑ-ɑ'kɔ:vɑ

Jaala, Jaalah
Biblical name JĀ-uh-luh, jā-Ā-luh, YAH-uh-LAH 'dʒe:ələ, dʒe:'e:lə, ˌjɑə'lɑ

Jaalam [Jalam]
Biblical name JĀ-uh-LAM, juh-Ā-luhm, yah-LAHM 'dʒe:əˌlæm, dʒə'e:ləm, jɑ'lɑm

Jaanai [Janai, Jannai]
Biblical name JĀ-uh-NĪ, yah-NĪ 'dʒe:əˌnɑi, jɑ'nɑi

Jaare-oregim
Biblical name JĀ-uh-rē-ŌR-uh-GIM, -AWR-uh-GIM, yah-Ē-RAH-rah-GIM 'dʒe:əri:'o:rəˌgim, -'ɔ:rəˌgim, jɑ'i:ˌrɑrɑ'gim

Jaareshiah [Jaresiah]
Biblical name JĀ-uh-ri-SHĪ-uh, YAH-ah-resh-YAH ˌdʒe:əri'ʃɑiə, ˌjɑ-ɑreʃ'jɑ

Jaasau
Biblical name JĀ-uh-SAW, YAH-ah-SAW 'dʒe:əˌsɔ:, ˌjɑ-ɑ'sɔ:

Jaazaniah
Biblical name jā-AZ-uh-NĪ-uh, yuh-zahn-YAH-hoo dʒe:ˌæzə'nɑiə, jəzɑn'jɑhu:

Jaazer [Jazer]
Biblical name JĀ-uh-zuhr, jā-Ā-zuhr, yah-ZER 'dʒe:əzəʳ, dʒe:'e:zəʳ, jɑ'zer

Jaaziah
Biblical name JĀ-uh-ZĪ-uh, YAH-ah-zi-YAH-hoo ˌdʒe:ə'zɑiə, ˌjɑ-ɑzi'jɑhu:

Jaaziel
Biblical name jā-Ā-zē-EL, YAH-ah-zē-EL dʒe:'e:zi:ˌel, ˌjɑ-ɑzi:'el

Jabalpur
city, India JUHB-uhl-PUR 'dʒəbəlˌpuʳ

Jabberwocky
nonsense verse by Lewis Carroll JAB-uhr-WAHK-ē 'dʒæbəʳˌwɑki·

Jabbok
Biblical name JAB-uhk, -AHK; yah-BAWK 'dʒæbək, -ˌak; jɑ'bɔ:k

Jabel
Biblical name JĀ-buhl, yah-VAHL 'dʒe:bəl, jɑ'vɑl

Jabesh
Biblical name JĀ-BESH, yah-VESH 'dʒe:ˌbeʃ, jɑ'veʃ

Jabesh-gilead
Biblical name JĀ-BESH-GIL-ē-uhd, -ē-AD; yah-VESH-gil-AHD 'dʒe:ˌbeʃ'gili:əd, -i:ˌæd; jɑ'veʃgil'ɑd

Jabez
pers. name JĀ-buhz 'dʒe:bəz

Foreign Sounds: ue: *Fr.* **rue**, *Ger.* **füllen** uh(r): *Fr.* **boeuf**, *Ger.* **Höhle** kh: *Ger.* **ich**, *Scot.* **loch** ḡ: *Sp.* **amigo** v: *Sp.* **hablar**
hl: *Welsh* **Llanelli**. CAPITALS: primary stress. SMALL CAPS: secondary stress. ⑤: U.S. pron. ⑥: British pron.

Jabez		
Biblical name	JĀ-bez, yah-BETS	'dʒeːbez, jɑ'bets
Jabin		
Biblical name	JĀ-bin, yah-VĒN	'dʒeːbin, jɑ'viːn
Jabiru		
stork	ZHAB-uh-ROO	ˌʒæbə'ruː
Jabneel		
Biblical name	JAB-nē-EL, JAB-NĒL, YAHV-nuh-EL	'dʒæbniːˌel, 'dʒæbˌniːl, ˌjɑvnə'el
Jabneh		
Biblical name	JAB-nuh, yahv-NE	'dʒæbnə, jɑv'ne
Jabotinsky		
Vladimir, *Zionist leader*	yuh-BUHT-YĒN-skyiy, [$] YAB-uh-TIN-skē, YAHB-	jəˌbət'jiːnskjij, [$] ˌjæbə'tinskiˑ, ˌjɑb-
Jacaltec		
lang., people, Guatemala	HAHK-uhl-TĀK	ˌhɑkəl'teːk
Jacamar		
S. & Cen. American bird	ZHAK-uh-MAHR	'ʒækəˌmɑ^r
Jacan, Jachan		
Biblical name	JĀ-KAN, yah-KHĒN	'dʒeːˌkæn, jɑ'xiːn
Jaçana, Jacana		
wading bird	ZHAS-n-A^n, juh-KAHN-uh	ˌʒæsn̩'æ̃, dʒə'kɑnə
Jacaranda		
plant	JAK-uh-RAN-duh	ˌdʒækə'rændə
Jachin		
Biblical name	JĀ-kin, yah-KHĒN	'dʒeːkin, jɑ'xiːn
Jachinite		
Biblical name	JĀ-kuh-NĪT	'dʒeːkəˌnɑit
Jacint		
pers. name, Catalan	zhah-SĒNT	ʒɑː'siːnt
Jacinta		
1. pers. name	juh-SINT-uh	dʒə'sintə
2. Spanish	khah-SĒN-tah, khah-THĒN-tah	xɑ'siːntɑ, xɑ'θiːntɑ
Jacintha		
pers. name	juh-SIN-thuh	dʒə'sinθə
Jacinto		
pers. name, Spanish	khah-SĒN-tō, khah-THĒN-tō	xɑ'siːntoː, xɑ'θiːntoː
Jack		
pers. name	JAK	'dʒæk
Jackie		
pers. name	JAK-ē	'dʒækiˑ
Jackson		
pers. name	JAK-suhn	'dʒæksən
Jacob		
1. pers. name	JĀ-kuhb	'dʒeːkəb
2. Afrikaans, German, Norwegian, Swedish	YAH-KAWP	'jɑˌkɔːp
3. Danish, Dutch	YAH-KAWP	'jɑːˌkɔːp
4. François, *French biochemist (Nobel 1965); pers. name, French*	zhah-KAWB	ʒɑːkɔːb
Jacobean		
pert. to King James I of England	JAK-uh-BĒ-uhn	ˌdʒækə'biːən
Jacobi		
Derek, *British actor*	juh-KŌ-bē; JAK-uh-bē	dʒə'koːbiˑ; 'dʒækəbiˑ

Key (col. 2): a: fad ā: fade ah: father ar: marry aw: law e: fed ē: feed er: merry i: hid ī: hide ō: coat o͞o: boot oi: boy ow: now u: put uh: above uhr: bird ch: chop ng: ring sh: show th: thick th: this zh: measure

Jacobian
   mathematical determinant   juh-KŌ-bē-uhn, yah-KŌ-bē-uhn   dʒəˈkoːbiːən, jaˈkoːbiːən

Jacobin
   Dominican friar; political extremist   JAK-uh-buhn   ˈdʒækəbən

Jacobins Gueuze
   Belgian beer   YAH-kawb-uhns GUH(R)-zuh   ˈjakɔːbəns ˈɡœːzə

Jacobins Kriek
   Belgian beer   YAH-kawb-uhns KRĒK   ˈjakɔːbəns ˈkriːk

Jacobite
   English Tory party   JAK-uh-BĬT   ˈdʒækəˌbait

Jacobo
   pers. name; Spanish   k̲hah-KŌ-v̲ō   xaˈkoːβoː

Jacobus
   1. pers. name   juh-KŌ-buhs   dʒəˈkoːbəs
   2. Dutch   yah-KŌ-bues   jaˈkoːbys
   3. German   yah-KŌ-bus   jaˈkoːbus

Jacoby
   pers. name   juh-KŌ-bē   dʒəˈkoːbiˑ

Jacopo
   pers. name, Italian   YAHK-ō-pō   ˈjakoːpoː

Jacquard
   Joseph Marie Charles, French   zhah-KAHR, Ⓢ JAK-AHRD,   ʒaːkaːr, Ⓢ ˈdʒækˌaʳd,
   inventor   juh-KAHRD   dʒəˈkaʳd

Jacqueline
   1. pers. name   JAK-(w)uh-luhn, -LĒN   ˈdʒæk(w)ələn, -ˌliːn
   2. French   zhah-KLĒN   ʒaːkliːn

Jacquelyn
   pers. name   JAK-wuh-luhn, JAK-uh-luhn   ˈdʒækwələn, ˈdʒækələn

Jacquerie
   French peasant revolt   ZHAHK-uh-RĒ, ZHAK-uh-RĒ   ˌʒakəˈriː, ˌʒækəˈriː

Jacques
   1. pers. name, Dutch, German   ZHAHK   ˈʒak
   2. French   ZHAHK   ʒak

Jacquet
   Illinois, *jazz musician*   juh-KET   dʒəˈket

Jacquinot
   bay, Pacific Ocean   ZHAK-uh-NŌ   ˌʒækəˈnoː

Jacuzzi
   tdmk for a whirlpool bath or a pool   juh-KOO-zē   dʒəˈkuːziˑ

Jaeger
   sea bird   YĀ-guhr   ˈjeːɡəʳ

Jada
   Biblical name   JĀD-uh, yah-DAH   ˈdʒeːdə, jaˈda

Jaddua
   Biblical name   JAD-(y)uh-wuh, jad-(Y)OO-uh,   ˈdʒæd(j)əwə, dʒædˈ(j)uːə,
      YAH-d̄oo-ah   ˈjaduːa

Jadon
   Biblical name   JĀ-DAHN, yah-DŌN   ˈdʒeːˌdan, jaˈdoːn

Jael
   Biblical name   JĀ-(uh)l   ˈdʒeː(ə)l

Jaffa [Joppa]
   city, Israel   JAHF-uh, JAF-uh, YAHF-uh, YAF-uh   ˈdʒafə, ˈdʒæfə, ˈjafə, ˈjæfə

Jagang
   see Chagang

Foreign Sounds: ue: *Fr.* **rue**, *Ger.* **fü**llen   uh(r): *Fr.* **boeuf**, *Ger.* **Höhle**   k̲h: *Ger.* i**ch**, *Scot.* lo**ch**   g̲: *Sp.* ami**g**o   v̲: *Sp.* ha**b**lar
hl: *Welsh* **Ll**anelli.   CAPITALS: primary stress.   SMALL CAPS: secondary stress.   Ⓢ: U.S. pron.   Ⓔ: British pron.

Jägermeister
　German liqueur　　YĀ-guhr-MĪ-stuhr, YEG-uhr-　　'jeːgəʳˌmaistəʳ, 'jegəʳ-

Jägerwahl Das Bockbier
　US beer　　YĀ-guhr-WAHL dahs BAHK-BIR,　　'jeːgəʳˌwal das 'bakˌbiʳ,
　　　　　　　YĀ-guhr-VAHL　　　　　　　　　'jeːgəʳˌval

Jagger
　Mick, *British singer, songwriter*　　JAG-uhr　　'dʒægəʳ

Jaguar
　British car co.　　JAG(-yuh)-WAHR, JAG-wuhr, ⓔ　　'dʒæg(jə)ˌwaʳ, 'dʒægwəʳ, ⓔ
　　　　　　　JAG-yuh-wuhr　　　　　　　　'dʒægjəwəʳ

Jagur
　Biblical name　　JĀ-guhr, yah-GŌ͞OR　　'dʒeːgəʳ, jɑ'guːr

Jah
　shorter form of Jehovah　　JAH, YAH　　'dʒɑ, 'jɑ

Jahath
　Biblical name　　JĀ-HATH, YAH-khaht　　'dʒeːˌhæθ, 'jɑxɑt

Jahaz
　Biblical name　　JĀ-HAZ, YAHT-sah　　'dʒeːˌhæz, 'jɑtsɑ

Jahaza
　Biblical name　　juh-HĀ-zuh, YAHT-sah　　dʒə'heːzə, 'jɑtsɑ

Jahaziah
　Biblical name　　JĀ-huh-ZĪ-uh, YAHKH-zuh-YAH　　ˌdʒeːhə'zaiə, ˌjɑxzə'jɑ

Jahaziel
　Biblical name　　je-HĀ-zē-EL, -zē-uhl; YAH-khah-zē-EL　　dʒe'heːziːˌel, -ziːəl;
　　　　　　　　　　　　　　　　　　　　　　ˌjɑxɑziː'el

Jahdai
　Biblical name　　JAHD-ē-Ī, yah-DĪ　　'dʒɑdiːˌai, jɑ'dai

Jahdiel
　Biblical name　　JAHD-ē-EL, -ē-uhl; YAHKH-dē-EL　　'dʒɑdiːˌel, -iːəl; ˌjɑxdiː'el

Jahdo
　Biblical name　　JAHD-ō, yahkh-DŌ　　'dʒɑdoː, jɑx'doː

Jahleel
　Biblical name　　JAL-ē-EL, JAL-ÊL, YAHKH-luh-EL　　'dʒæliːˌel, 'dʒælˌiːl, ˌjɑxlə'el

Jahleelite
　Biblical name　　JAL-ē-uh-LĬT　　'dʒæliːəˌlait

Jahmai
　Biblical name　　JAM-ē-Ī, JAHM-Ī, yahkh-MĪ　　'dʒæmiːˌai, 'dʒamˌai,
　　　　　　　　　　　　　　　　　　　　　jɑx'mai

Jahveh
　see Yahweh

Jahzah
　Biblical name　　JAZ-uh, JAHZ-uh, YAH-tsah　　'dʒæzə, 'dʒazə, 'jɑtsɑ

Jahzeel
　Biblical name　　JAZ-ē-EL, yahkh-tsē-EL　　'dʒæziːˌel, jɑxtsiː'el

Jahzeelite
　Biblical name　　JAZ-ē-uh-LĬT　　'dʒæziːəˌlait

Jahzeiah
　Biblical name　　jaz-Ā-(y)uh, YAHKH-zuh-YAH　　dʒæz'eː(j)ə, ˌjɑxzə'jɑ

Jahzerah
　Biblical name　　JAZ-uh-ruh, YAHKH-zā-RAH　　'dʒæzərə, ˌjɑxze'rɑ

Jahziel
　Biblical name　　JAZ-ē-EL, YAHKH-tsē-EL　　'dʒæziːˌel, ˌjɑxtsiː'el

Jaime
　pers. name, Spanish　　KHĪ-mā　　'xaimeː

Key (col. 2):　a: fad　ā: fade　ah: father　ar: marry　aw: law　e: fed　ē: feed　er: merry　i: hid　ī: hide　ō: coat　ō͞o: boot
oi: boy　ow: now　u: put　uh: above　uhr: bird　ch: chop　ng: ring　sh: show　th: thick　th: this　zh: measure

Jain		
adherent of Jainism	JĪN	'dʒɑin
Jainat		
see Chainat		
Jainism		
religion	JĪ-NIZ-uhm	'dʒɑiˌnizəm
Jaipur		
city, India	JĪ-PUR	'dʒɑiˌpuʳ
Jair		
Biblical name	JĀ-uhr, JAR, JER, yah-ĒR	'dʒeːəʳ, 'dʒæʳ, 'dʒeʳ, jɑ'iːr
Jairite		
Biblical name	JĀ-uh-RĪT, JAR-ĪT, JER-ĪT	'dʒeːəˌrɑit, 'dʒærˌɑit, 'dʒerˌɑit
Jairus		
Biblical name	JĪ-ruhs, JĀ-uh-ruhs	'dʒɑirəs, 'dʒeːərəs
Jakan [Jaakan]		
Biblical name	JĀ-kuhn, YAH-ah-KAHN	'dʒeːkən, ˌjɑ-ɑ'kɑn
Jakarta		
see Djakarta		
Jakeh		
Biblical name	JĀ-kuh	'dʒeːkə
Jakim		
Biblical name	JĀ-kuhm, yah-KIM	'dʒeːkəm, jɑ'kim
Jakób		
pers. name, Polish	YAH-kōōp	'jɑːkuːp
Jakob		
1. pers. name, Danish, Dutch	YAH-KAWP	'jɑːˌkɔːp
2. German, Swedish	YAH-KAWP	'jɑˌkɔːp
Jakobson		
Roman, *US linguist*	YAHK-uhb-suhn	'jɑkəbsən
Jalālābād		
city, Afghanistan	juh-LAHL-uh-BAHD	dʒə'lɑləˌbɑd
Jalam [Jaalam]		
Biblical name	JĀ-luhm, yah-LAHM	'dʒeːləm, jɑ'lɑm
Jalap		
plant	JAL-uhp, JAHL-uhp	'dʒæləp, 'dʒɑləp
Jalapa		
dept, Guatemala; city, Mexico	k͟huh-LAHP-uh	xə'lɑpə
Jalisco		
state, Mexico	k͟hah-LĒ-skō	xɑ'liːskoː
Jalon		
Biblical name	JĀ-LAHN, JĀ-luhn, yah-LŌN	'dʒeːˌlɑn, 'dʒeːlən, jɑ'loːn
Jamaica		
island, Caribbean; area, New York City	juh-MĀ-kuh	dʒə'meːkə
Jamaican		
pert. to Jamaica	juh-MĀ-kuhn	dʒə'meːkən
Jamal		
pers. name	juh-MAHL	dʒə'mɑl
Jamberoo		
town, Australia	JAM-buh-ROO, JAM-buh-ROO	ˌdʒæmbə'ruː, 'dʒæmbəˌruː
Jambi		
see Djambi		
Jambres		
Biblical name	JAM-BRĒZ	'dʒæmˌbriːz

James
  1. New Testament book; pers. name,   JĀMZ   'dʒeːmz
    English, German
  2. French   JEMS   dʒems
Jamesian
  pert. to Henry James   JĀM-zē-uhn   'dʒeːmziːən
Jameson
  tdmk for an Irish whisky   JĀ-muh-suhn   'dʒeːməsən
Jamestown
  US pl. name   JĀMZ-TOWN   'dʒeːmz‚taun
Jamie
  pers. name   JĀ-mē   'dʒeːmiˑ
Jamin
  Biblical name   JĀ-muhn, yah-MIN   'dʒeːmən, jaˈmin
Jaminite
  Biblical name   JĀ-muh-NĪT   'dʒeːmə‚nait
Jamlech
  Biblical name   JAM-LEK, -lik; yahm-LEKH   'dʒæm‚lek, -lik; jamˈlex
Jammu-Kashmir
  state, India   JUHM-oo-KASH-MIR, -kash-MIR   'dʒəmuːˈkæʃ‚miʳ, -kæʃ'miʳ
Jan
  1. pers. name   JAN   'dʒæn
  2. Czech, Polish   YAHN   'jaːn
  3. Dutch, German, Latvian   YAHN   'jan
Janáček
  Leoš, *Czech composer*   YAHN-uh-CHEK   'janə‚tʃek
Janai [Jaanai, Jannai]
  Biblical name   JĀ-nē-Ī, yah-NĪ   'dʒeːniː‚ai, jaˈnai
Jane
  pers. name   JĀN   'dʒeːn
Janet
  1. pers. name   JAN-uht, juh-NET   'dʒænət, dʒəˈnet
  2. French   zhah-NE   ʒaːne
Janet
  Pierre Marie Félix, *French*   zhah-NE   ʒaːne
    psychologist and neurologist
Janice, Janis
  pers. name   JAN-uhs   'dʒænəs
Janis
  pers. name, Latvian   YAHN-uhs   'janəs
Janissary, Janizary
  soldier in Turkish army   JAN-uh-SER-ē, JAN-uh-ZER-ē   'dʒænə‚seriˑ, 'dʒænə‚zeriˑ
Janna
  Biblical name   JAN-uh   'dʒænə
Jannai [Jaanai, Janai]
  Biblical name   JAN(-ē)-Ī, juh-NĀ-Ī, yah-NĪ   'dʒæn(iː)‚ai, dʒəˈneː‚ai,
                                                           jaˈnai
Jannes
  Biblical name   JAN-ĒZ   'dʒæn‚iːz
Jannings
  Emil, *German actor*   YAH-ningz, ⑤ JAN-ingz   'janiŋz, ⑤ 'dʒæniŋz
Janoah
  Biblical name   juh-NŌ-uh, yah-NŌ-ahkh   dʒəˈnoːə, jaˈnoːax
Janohah
  Biblical name   juh-NŌ-(h)uh   dʒəˈnoː(h)ə

Key (col. 2):   a: fad   ā: fade   ah: father   ar: marry   aw: law   e: fed   ē: feed   er: merry   i: hid   ī: hide   ō: coat   ōō: boot
oi: boy   ow: now   u: put   uh: above   uhr: bird   ch: chop   ng: ring   sh: show   th: thick   th: this   zh: measure

János
   pers. name, Hungarian   YAH-nawsh   ˈjɑːnɔːʃ

Jansen
   1. Cornelis Otto, *Dutch theologian*   YAHN-suhn, ⑤ JAN(T)-suhn   ˈjɑnsən, ⑤ ˈdʒæn(t)sən
   2. tdmk for sportswear   JAN(T)-suhn   ˈdʒæn(t)sən

Jansenism
   doctrine of moral determinism   JAN-suh-NIZ-uhm   ˈdʒænsəˌnizəm

Jantzen
   US sportswear co.   JAN(T)-suhn   ˈdʒæn(t)sən

Januarius
   1. pers. name   JAN-yuh-WER-ē-uhs   ˌdʒænjəˈweriːəs
   2. German   YAHN-o͞o-AHR-yus, -AHR-ē-us   ˌjɑnuːˈɑrjus, -ˈɑriːus

January
   month   JAN-yuh-WER-ē   ˈdʒænjəˌweriˑ

Janum
   Biblical name   JĀ-nuhm, yah-NO͞OM   ˈdʒeːnəm, jɑˈnuːm

Janus
   Roman gateway god; satellite of   JĀ-nuhs   ˈdʒeːnəs
   Saturn; pers. name

Jap
   abbreviation for Japan or Japanese   JAP   ˈdʒæp

Japan
   nation, Asia   juh-PAN   dʒəˈpæn

Japanese
   lang., people, Asia   JAP-uh-NĒZ, -NĒS   ˌdʒæpəˈniːz, -ˈniːs

Japheth
   Biblical name   JĀ-fuhth   ˈdʒeːfəθ

Japhetic
   pert. to Japheth   jā-FET-ik   dʒeːˈfetik

Japhia
   Biblical name   juh-FĪ-uh, yah-FĒ-ah   dʒəˈfaiə, jɑˈfiːɑ

Japhlet
   Biblical name   JAF-LET, -luht; yahf-LET   ˈdʒæfˌlet, -lət; jɑfˈlet

Japhleti
   Biblical name   jaf-LET-ē, YAHF-le-TĒ   dʒæfˈletiˑ, ˌjɑfleˈtiː

Japhletite
   Biblical name   JAF-luh-TĪT   ˈdʒæfləˌtait

Japho
   Biblical name   JĀ-FŌ, yah-FŌ   ˈdʒeːˌfoː, jɑˈfoː

Japonica
   plant   juh-PAHN-i-kuh   dʒəˈpɑnikə

Japurá
   river, S. America   ZHAHP-uh-RAH   ˌʒɑpəˈrɑ

Jaques
   1. character in As You Like It,   ⓔ JĀ-kwiz, ⑤ JĀ-kwuhz, JĀ-KWĒZ   ⓔ ˈdʒeːkwiz, ⑤ ˈdʒeːkwəz,
   Shakespeare   ˈdʒeːˌkwiːz
   2. pers. name   JĀKS, JAKS   ˈdʒeːks, ˈdʒæks

Jarah
   Biblical name   JĀ-ruh, JAR-uh, yah-RAH   ˈdʒeːrə, ˈdʒærə, jɑˈrɑ

Jardines de la Reina
   island chain, Caribbean Sea   hahr-DĒ-nes dä lah RĀ-nah   hɑrˈdiːnes deː lɑ ˈreːnɑ

Jardins des Plantes
   botanical garden, Paris   zhahr-DEⁿ dä PLAHⁿT   ʒɑːrdẽ deˑ plɑ̃t

Jareb
   Biblical name   JĀ-REB, JAR-uhb, yah-REV   ˈdʒeːˌreb, ˈdʒærəb, jɑˈrev

---

Foreign Sounds: ue: *Fr.* **rue**, *Ger.* **füllen**   uh(r): *Fr.* **boeuf**, *Ger.* **Höhle**   <u>kh</u>: *Ger.* **ich**, *Scot.* **loch**   g̱: *Sp.* **amigo**   <u>v</u>: *Sp.* **hablar**
hl: *Welsh* **Llanelli**.   CAPITALS: primary stress.   SMALL CAPS: secondary stress.   ⑤: U.S. pron.   ⓔ: British pron.

Jared
  pers. name   JAR-uhd   'dʒærəd
Jaresiah [Jaareshiah]
  Biblical name   JAR-uh-SĪ-uh   ˌdʒærə'saiə
Jarha
  Biblical name   JAHR-huh, yahr-<u>KHAH</u>   'dʒɑʳhə, jɑr'xɑ
Jarib
  Biblical name   JĀ-ruhb, JAR-uhb, yah-RĒV   'dʒeːrəb, 'dʒærəb, jɑ'riːv
Jarl
  1. pers. name, Finnish   YAHRL   'jɑːrl
  2. Norwegian   YAHRL   'jɑrl
Jarmila
  pers. name, Czech   YAHR-mil-uh   'jɑːrmilə
Jarmo
  prehistoric village site, Iraq JAHR-mō   'dʒɑʳmoː
Jarmuth
  Biblical name   JAHR-muhth, yahr-M͞O͞OT   'dʒɑʳməθ, jɑr'muːt
Jaroah
  Biblical name   juh-RŌ-uh, yah-RAW-ah<u>kh</u> dʒə'roːə, jɑ'rɔːɑx
Jaromír
  pers. name, Czech   YAH-raw-MIR   'jɑːrɔːˌmir
Jaron
  pers. name   JAR-uhn, JER-uhn   'dʒærən, 'dʒerən
Jaroslav
  pers. name, Czech   YAH-raw-SLAHF   'jɑrɔːˌslɑːf
Jaroslaw
  pers. name, German   YAHR-aw-SLAHF   'jɑrɔːˌslɑf
Jarosław
  pers. name, Polish   yah-RAW-slahf   jɑː'rɔːsɫɑːf
Jarreau
  Al, *entertainer*   juh-RŌ   dʒə'roː
Jarrell
  Randall, *US writer*   juh-REL, ja-REL   dʒə'rel, dʒæ'rel
Jarrett
  Keith, *US pianist*   JAR-uht, JER-uht   'dʒærət, 'dʒerət
Jarriel
  Tom, *US TV journalist*   JAR-uhl, JER-uhl   'dʒærəl, 'dʒerəl
Jarrott
  Charles, *British film and TV director* JAR-uht, JER-uht   'dʒærət, 'dʒerət
Jarrow
  town, England   JAR-ō   'dʒæroː
Jarry
  Alfred, *French writer*   zhah-RĒ   ʒɑːriː
Jaruzelski
  Wojciech, *Polish political leader* YAHR-uh-ZEL-skē   ˌjɑrə'zelskiˑ
Järvi
  Neeme, *Estonian conductor*   YER-vē   'jerviˑ
Jarvik-7
  artificial heart   JAHR-vik SEV-uhn   'dʒɑʳvik 'sevən
Jarvis
  1. pers. name   JAHR-vuhs   'dʒɑʳvəs
  2. see Jervas
Jascha
  pers. name   YAHSH-uh   'jɑʃə

Key (col. 2): a: fad ā: fade ah: father ar: marry aw: law e: fed ē: feed er: merry i: hid ī: hide ō: coat o͞o: boot
oi: boy ow: now u: put uh: above uhr: bird ch: chop ng: ring sh: show th: thick <u>th</u>: this zh: measure

Jasenica
  city, Bosnia — YAHS-uh-NĒT-suh — ˌjasə'niːtsə

Jashen
  Biblical name — JĀ-shen, yah-SHEN — 'dʒeːʃen, ja'ʃen

Jasher, Jashur
  Biblical name — JASH-uhr, yah-SHAHR — 'dʒæʃəʳ, ja'ʃar

Jashobeam
  Biblical name — juh-SHŌ-bē-AM, YAH-shah-VAHM — dʒə'ʃoːbiːˌæm, ˌjaʃa'vam

Jashub
  Biblical name — JĀ-shuhb, JASH-uhb, yah-SHŌO̅V — 'dʒeːʃəb, 'dʒæʃəb, ja'ʃuːv

Jashubi-lehem
  Biblical name — juh-SHŌO̅-BĪ-LĒ-HEM, yah-SHŌO̅-vē-LE-khem — dʒə'ʃuːˌbai'liːˌhem, ja'ʃuːviː'lexem

Jashubite
  Biblical name — JĀ-shuh-BĪT, JASH-uh-BĪT — 'dʒeːʃəˌbait, 'dʒæʃəˌbait

Jashur
  see Jasher

Jasiel
  Biblical name — JAS-ē-EL, JĀ-sē-EL, -uhl; — 'dʒæsiːˌel, 'dʒeːsiːˌel, -əl;

Jasmine
  pers. name — JAZ-muhn, JAZ-MĪN — 'dʒæzmən, 'dʒæzˌmain

Jason
  leader of Argonauts, husband of Medea; pers. name — JĀS-n — 'dʒeːsn̩

Jaspar, Jasper
  pers. name — JAS-puhr — 'dʒæspəʳ

Jaspers
  Karl Theodor, *German psychiatrist and philosopher* — YAHS-puhrs — 'jaspəʳs

Jassy
  see Iasi

Jataka
  tales of Bhudda's births — JAHT-uh-kuh — 'dʒaṭəkə

Jathniel
  Biblical name — JATH-nē-EL, -nē-uhl; YAHT-nē-EL — 'dʒæθniːˌel, -niːəl; ˌjatniː'el

Jattir
  Biblical name — JAT-uhr, yah-TĒR — 'dʒæṭəʳ, ja'tiːr

Java
  Sea, *Asia* — JAHV-uh, JAV-uh — 'dʒavə, 'dʒævə

Java, Jawa, Djawa
  island, Indonesia — JAHV-uh, JAV-uh — 'dʒavə, 'dʒævə

Javan
  Biblical name — JĀ-VAN, yah-VAHN — 'dʒeːˌvæn, ja'van

Javanese
  lang., SE Asia — JAV-uh-NĒZ, JAHV-uh-NĒZ, -NĒS — ˌdʒævə'niːz, ˌdʒavə'niːz, -'niːs

Javel
  town, France — zhah-VEL — ʒaːvel

Javier
  pers. name, Spanish — khahv-YER — xav'jer

Javits
  Jacob, *US politician* — JAV-uhts — 'dʒævəts

Jawa
  see Java

Foreign Sounds: ue: *Fr.* **rue**, *Ger.* **füllen**   uh(r): *Fr.* **boeuf**, *Ger.* **Höhle**   kh: *Ger.* **ich**, *Scot.* **loch**   ḡ: *Sp.* amigo   v̱: *Sp.* hablar
hl: *Welsh* **Llanelli**.   CAPITALS: primary stress.   SMALL CAPS: secondary stress.   Ⓢ: U.S. pron.   Ⓔ: British pron.

Jawa Barat
   prov, Java   JAHV-uh buh-RAHT   ˌdʒɑvə bəˈrɑt
Jawaharlal
   pers. name, north India   juh-WAH-huhr-LAHL   dʒəˈwɑhərˌlɑl
Jawa Tengah
   prov, Java   JAHV-uh TENG-gah   ˌdʒɑvə ˈteŋgɑ
Jawa Timur
   prov, Java   JAHV-uh TĒ-MUR   ˌdʒɑvə ˈtiːˌmuʳ
Jaworski
   Leon, *US lawyer;* Ronald Vincent,   juh-WAWR-skē   dʒəˈwɔːʳskiˑ
      US football player
Jay
   pers. name   JĀ   ˈdʒeː
Jayabum
   see Chaiyaphum
Jayanath
   see Chainat
Jayapura
   city, Indonesia   JAH-(y)uh-PUR-uh   ˌdʒɑ(j)əˈpurə
Jaycee
   member of a junior chamber civic   JĀ-SĒ   ˌdʒeːˈsiː
      group
Jayhun
   Arabic name for Amu Darya   jī-HŌŌN   dʒaiˈhuːn
Jayne
   pers. name   JĀN   ˈdʒeːn
Jazer [Jaazer]
   Biblical name   JĀ-zuhr, yah-ZER   ˈdʒeːzəʳ, jaˈzer
Jaziz
   Biblical name   JĀ-ziz, yah-ZĒZ   ˈdʒeːziz, jaˈziːz
Jean
   1. pers. name   JĒN   ˈdʒiːn
   2. Finnish   ZHAHN   ˈʒɑːn
   3. Flemish, German   ZHAHⁿ   ˈʒɑ̃
   4. French   ZHAHⁿ   ʒɑ̃
Jean de Meun
   French poet   zhahⁿ duh MUH(R)ⁿ   ʒɑ̃ də mœ̃
Jeane
   pers. name   JĒN   ˈdʒiːn
Jeanerette
   town, LA   JEN-uh-RET   ˌdʒenəˈret
Jeanette
   pers. name   juh-NET   dʒəˈnet
Jeanie, Jeannie
   pers. name   JĒ-nē   ˈdʒiːniˑ
Jean Lassale
   watchmakers   ZHAHⁿ luh-SAHL, luh-SAL   ˌʒɑ̃ ləˈsɑːl, ləˈsæl
Jeanne
   1. pers. name   JĒN   ˈdʒiːn
   2. French   ZHAHN, ZHAHN   ʒɑn, ʒɑːn
Jeanne d' Arc
   French saint   zhahn DAHRK   ʒɑˈn dɑːrk
Jeanneret [Corbusier, Le]
   Charles Édouard, *Swiss architect*   zhahn(-uh)-RE   ʒɑːn(ə)re

---

Key (col. 2):   a: fad   ā: fade   ah: father   ar: marry   aw: law   e: fed   ē: feed   er: merry   i: hid   ī: hide   ō: coat   ōō: boot
oi: boy   ow: now   u: put   uh: above   uhr: bird   ch: chop   ng: ring   sh: show   th: thick   <u>th</u>: this   zh: measure

Jeannette
   pers. name   juh-NET   dʒə'net

Jeannot
   pers. name, French   zhah-NŌ   ʒɑːnoː

Jearim
   Biblical name   JĒ-uh-RIM, JIR-uhm, yuh-ah-RĒM   'dʒiːə,rim, 'dʒirəm, jə-a'riːm

Jeaterai
   Biblical name   jē-AT-uh-RĪ, yuh-AH-tuh-RĪ   dʒiː'æţə,rai, jə,atə'rai

Jeatherai [Jeaterai]
   Biblical name   jē-ATH-uh-RĪ, yuh-AH-tuh-RĪ   dʒiː'æθə,rai, jə,atə'rai

Jeb
   pers. name   JEB   'dʒeb

Jebel Toubkal
   see Toubkal, Jebel

Jeberechiah
   Biblical name   juh-BER-uh-KĪ-uh,   dʒə,berə'kaiə, jə,verex'jahuː
                    yuh-VER-e<u>kh</u>-YAH-hoo

Jebu
   West African people   JĒ-b(y)oo, JEB-(y)oo   'dʒiːb(j)uː, 'dʒeb(j)uː

Jebus
   Biblical name   JĒ-buhs, yuh-VOOS   'dʒiːbəs, jə'vuːs

Jebusa
   pers. name   juh-BYOO-suh, JEB-yu-suh   dʒə'bjuːsə, 'dʒebjusə

Jebusi
   Biblical name   JEB-yuh-SĪ, yuh-voo-SĒ   'dʒebjə,sai, jəvuː'siː

Jebusite
   Biblical name   JEB-yuh-SĪT   'dʒebjə,sait

Jecamiah
   Biblical name   JEK-uh-MĪ-uh, JĒ-kuh-   ,dʒekə'maiə, ,dʒiːkə-

Jecholiah, Jechiliah
   Biblical name   JEK-uh-LĪ-uh, yuh-<u>kh</u>ahl-YAH-hoo   ,dʒekə'laiə, jəxal'jahuː

Jechoniah
   Biblical name   JEK-uh-NĪ-uh, yuh-<u>kh</u>ahn-YAH   ,dʒekə'naiə, jəxan'ja

Jechonias
   Biblical name, Greek form of   JEK-uh-NĪ-uhs   ,dʒekə'naiəs
     Jechoniah

Jed
   pers. name   JED   'dʒed

Jedaiah
   Biblical name   juh-DĪ-uh, juh-DĀ-uh, yuh-dī-YAH   dʒə'daiə, dʒə'deːə, jədai'ja

Jedda [Jiddah, Gedda]
   city, Saudi Arabia   JED-uh   'dʒedə

Jedediah
   pers. name   JED-uh-DĪ-uh   ,dʒedə'daiə

Jedi
   knights in Star Wars films   JED-Ī   'dʒed,ai

Jediael
   Biblical name   juh-DĪ(-ē)-EL, yuh-DI-yah-EL   dʒə'dai(iː),el, jə,dija'el

Jedidah
   Biblical name   juh-DĪD-uh, yi-dē-DAH   dʒə'daidə, jidiː'da

Jedidiah
   pers. name   JED-uh-DĪ-uh   ,dʒedə'daiə

Jeduthun
   Biblical name   juh-D(Y)OO-thuhn, yuh-DOO-TOON   dʒə'd(j)uːθən, jə,duː'tuːn

---

Foreign Sounds: ue: *Fr.* **rue**, *Ger.* **füllen**   uh(r): *Fr.* **boeuf**, *Ger.* **Höhle**   <u>kh</u>: *Ger.* **ich**, *Scot.* **loch**   ḡ: *Sp.* **amigo**   v̲: *Sp.* **hablar**
hl: *Welsh* **Llanelli**.   CAPITALS: primary stress.   SMALL CAPS: secondary stress.   ⑤: U.S. pron.   Ⓔ: British pron.

Jeep
  tdmk for a vehicle JĒP 'dʒiːp

Jeeves
  character in novels of P. G. Wodehouse JĒVZ 'dʒiːvz

Jeezer [Iezer]
  Biblical name juh-Ē-zuhr, JĒ-zuhr, ē-EZ-er dʒəˈiːzəʳ, 'dʒiːzəʳ, iːˈezer

Jeezerite
  Biblical name juh-Ē-zuh-RĪT, JĒ-zuh-RĪT dʒəˈiːzəˌrait, 'dʒiːzəˌrait

Jeff
  pers. name JEF 'dʒef

Jefferson
  Thomas, *3rd US president; US pl. name; pers. name* JEF-uhr-suhn 'dʒefəʳsən

Jeffery
  pers. name JEF-(uh-)rē 'dʒef(ə)riˑ

Jegar-sahadutha
  Biblical name JĒ-GAHR-SĀ-huh-D(Y)OO-thuh, yi-GAHR-SAH-hah-doo-TAH 'dʒiːˌgaʳˌseːhəˈd(j)uːθə, jiˈgarˌsahaduːˈta

Jehaleleel
  Biblical name JĒ-huh-LĒ-lē-EL, yuh-HAH-lel-EL ˌdʒiːhəˈliːliːˌel, jəˌhalelˈel

Jehallelel
  Biblical name juh-HAL-uh-LEL, yuh-HAH-lel-EL dʒəˈhæləˌlel, jəˌhalelˈel

Jehan
  pers. name, French zhuh-AHN, -ZHAHN ʒəan, ʒan

Jehdeiah
  Biblical name juh-DĒ-uh, yekh-duh-YAH-hoo dʒəˈdiːə, jexdəˈjahuː

Jehezekel
  Biblical name juh-HEZ-uh-KEL, yuh-khez-KEL dʒəˈhezəˌkel, jəxezˈkel

Jehezkel [Jehezekel]
  Biblical name juh-HEZ-kel, yuh-khez-KEL dʒəˈhezkel, jəxezˈkel

Jehiah
  Biblical name juh-HĪ-uh, yuh-khē-YAH dʒəˈhaiə, jəxiːˈja

Jehiel
  Biblical name juh-HĪ-uhl, yuh-khē-EL dʒəˈhaiəl, jəxiːˈel

Jehieli
  Biblical name juh-HĪ-uh-lē, yuh-KHĒ-e-LĒ dʒəˈhaiəliˑ, jəˌxiːeˈliː

Jehizkiah
  Biblical name JĒ-HIZ-KĪ-uh, yuh-KHIZ-ki-YAH-hoo ˌdʒiːˌhizˈkaiə, jəˌxizkiˈjahuː

Jehoadah, Jehoaddah
  Biblical name juh-HŌ-uhd-uh, yuh-HŌ-ah-DAH dʒəˈhoːədə, jəˌhoːaˈda

Jehoaddan, Jehoaddin
  Biblical name JĒ-hō-AHD-n, JĒ-hō-AD-n, yuh-HŌ-ah-DAHN ˌdʒiːhoːˈadn̩, ˌdʒiːhoːˈædn̩, jəˌhoːaˈdan

Jehoahaz
  Biblical name juh-HŌ-uh-HAZ, yuh-HŌ-ah-KHAHZ dʒəˈhoːəˌhæz, jəˌhoːaˈxaz

Jehoash
  Biblical name juh-HŌ-ASH, yuh-hō-AHSH dʒəˈhoːˌæʃ, jəhoːˈaʃ

Jehohanan
  Biblical name JĒ-(h)uh-HĀ-NAN, -nuhn; yuh-HŌ-khah-NAHN ˌdʒiː(h)əˈheːˌnæn, -nən; jəˌhoːxaˈnan

Jehoiachin
  Biblical name juh-HOI-uh-kin, yuh-HŌ-yah-KHĒN dʒəˈhɔiəkin, jəˌhoːjaˈxiːn

Jehoiada
  Biblical name juh-HOI-uhd-uh, yuh-HŌ-yah-DAH dʒəˈhɔiədə, jəˈhoːjaˌda

Jehoiakim
  Biblical name   juh-HOI-uh-kuhm, -KIM   dʒə'hɔiəkəm, -ˌkim

Jehoiakim
  Biblical name   juh-HOI-uh-kim, yuh-HŌ-yah-KĒM   dʒə'hɔiəkim, jə'hoːjɑˌkiːm

Jehoiarib
  Biblical name   juh-HOI-uh-rib, yuh-HŌ-yah-RĒV   dʒə'hɔiərib, jə'hoːjɑˌriːv

Jehol
  region, city, China   juh-HŌL, RŌ-HŌ *[sic]*   dʒə'hoːl, 'roː'hoː *[sic]*

Jehonadab
  Biblical name   juh-HAHN-uh-DAB, yuh-HŌ-nah-DAHV   dʒə'hɑnəˌdæb, jə'hoːnɑˌdɑv

Jehonathan
  Biblical name   juh-HAHN-uh-thuhn, yuh-HAW-nah-TAHN   dʒə'hɑnəθən, jə'hɔːnɑˌtɑn

Jehoram
  Biblical name   juh-HŌR-uhm, -HAWR-uhm; yuh-hō-RAHM   dʒə'hoːrəm, -'hɔːrəm; jəho:'rɑm

Jehoshabeath
  Biblical name   JĒ-hō-SHAB-ē-ATH, yuh-HŌ-shah-VAHT   ˌdʒiːhoː'ʃæbiːˌæθ, jəˌhoːʃa'vɑt

Jehoshaphat
  pers. name   juh-HAHSH-uh-FAT, juh-HAHS-uh-FAT   dʒə'hɑʃəˌfæt, dʒə'hɑsəˌfæt

Jehosheba
  Biblical name   juh-HAHSH-uh-buh, yuh-hō-SHEV-ah   dʒə'hɑʃəbə, jəhoː'ʃeva

Jehoshua [Joshua]
  Biblical name   juh-HAHSH-(y)uh-wuh, yuh-hō-SHOO-ah   dʒə'hɑʃ(j)əwə, jəhoː'ʃuːɑ

Jehovah
  Old Testament name for God   juh-HŌ-vuh   dʒə'hoːvə

Jehovah-jireh
  Biblical name   juh-HŌ-vuh-JĪ-ruh   dʒəˌhoːvə'dʒɑirə

Jehovah-nissi
  Biblical name   juh-HŌ-vuh-NIS-Ī   dʒəˌhoːvə'nisˌɑi

Jehovah-shalom
  Biblical name   juh-HŌ-vuh-shah-LŌM   dʒəˌhoːvəʃa'loːm

Jehovism
  worship of Jehovah   juh-HŌ-VIZ-uhm   dʒə'hoːˌvizəm

Jehozabad
  Biblical name   juh-HAHZ-uh-BAD, yuh-HŌ-zah-VAHD   dʒə'hɑzəˌbæd, jə'hoːzɑˌvad

Jehozadak
  Biblical name   juh-HAHZ-uh-DAK, YŌT-sah-DAHK   dʒə'hɑzəˌdæk, ˌjoːtsɑ'dak

Jehu
  biblical ruler   JĒ-h(y)o͞o, JĒ-yo͞o, JĀ-   'dʒiːh(j)uː, 'dʒiːjuː, 'dʒeː-

Jehubbah
  Biblical name   juh-HUHB-uh, yuh-khah-BAH   dʒə'həbə, jəxɑ'ba

Jehucal
  Biblical name   juh-H(Y)o͞o-KAL, yuh-ho͞o-KHAHL   dʒə'h(j)uːˌkæl, jəhuː'xɑl

Jehud
  Biblical name   JĒ-ho͞oD, JĀ-; yuh-HOOD   'dʒiːˌhuːd, 'dʒeː-; jə'huːd

Jehuda
  pers. name   juh-HOOD-uh   dʒə'huːdə

Jehudi
  pers. name   juh-HOOD-ē   dʒə'huːdiˑ

Jehudijah
  Biblical name   JĒ-h(y)o͞o-DĪ-uh, JĒ-(y)o͞o-; yuh-HOO-di-YAH   ˌdʒiːh(j)uː'daiə, ˌdʒiː(j)uː-; jəˌhuːdi'ja

---

Foreign Sounds: ue: *Fr.* **rue**, *Ger.* **füllen**   uh(r): *Fr.* **boeuf**, *Ger.* **Höhle**   <u>kh</u>: *Ger.* **ich**, *Scot.* **loch**   g̱: *Sp.* **amigo**   v̱: *Sp.* **hablar**   hl: *Welsh* **Llanelli.**   CAPITALS: primary stress.   SMALL CAPS: secondary stress.   Ⓢ: U.S. pron.   Ⓔ: British pron.

Jehuel
Biblical name — juh-H(Y)OO-EL, ye-HOO-EL — dʒəˈh(j)uːˌel, jeˌhuːˈel

Jehush
Biblical name — juh-HUHSH, juh-HUSH, yuh-OOSH — dʒəˈhəʃ, dʒəˈhuʃ, jəˈuːʃ

Jeiel
Biblical name — jē-Ī-EL, -Ī-uhl; yuh-ē-EL — dʒiːˈɑiˌel, -ˈɑiəl; jəiːˈel

Jekabzeel
Biblical name — juh-KAB-ZĒL, −zē-EL; yuh-KAHV-tsē-EL — dʒəˈkæbˌziːl, -ziːˌel; jəˌkɑvtsiːˈel

Jekameam
Biblical name — juh-KAM-ē-AM, JEK-uh-MĒ-AM, yi-kahm-AHM — dʒəˈkæmiːˌæm, ˌdʒekəˈmiːˌæm, jikɑmˈɑm

Jekamiah
Biblical name — JEK-uh-MĪ-uh, yuh-kahm-YAH — ˌdʒekəˈmɑiə, jəkɑmˈjɑ

Jekuthiel
Biblical name — juh-K(Y)OO-thē-EL, — dʒəˈk(j)uːθiːˌel,

Jekyll
1. Henry, *character in* Dr. Jekyll and Mr. Hyde, *R. L. Stevenson* — JEK-uhl, JĒ-kuhl — ˈdʒekəl, ˈdʒiːkəl
2. island, GA — JEK-uhl — ˈdʒekəl

Jelenia Góra
province, Poland — yā-LEN-yuh GUR-uh — jeːˌlenjə ˈgurə

Jelly
pers. name, Hungarian — YELY, Ⓢ YEL-yuh — ˈjelj, Ⓢ ˈjeljə

Jemdet Nasr
Sumerian site — JEM-duht NAS-uhr — ˈdʒemdət ˈnæsər

Jemez
N. American people — HĀ-muhs — ˈheːməs

Jemima
pers. name — juh-MĪ-muh — dʒəˈmɑimə

Jemison
Mae, *US astronaut* — JEM-uh-suhn — ˈdʒeməsən

Jemuel
Biblical name — juh-M(Y)OO-EL, JEM-yuh-wuhl, yuh-moo-EL — dʒəˈm(j)uːˌel, ˈdʒemjəwəl, jəmuːˈel

Jena
city, Germany — YĀ-nuh — ˈjeːnə

Jena
town, LA — JĒ-nuh — ˈdʒiːnə

Jenever
Dutch gin — JEN-uh-vuhr — ˈdʒenəvər

Jenin
town, West Bank — juh-NĒN — dʒəˈniːn

Jenner
Edward, *British physician* — JEN-uhr — ˈdʒenər

Jennie, Jenny
pers. name — JEN-ē — ˈdʒeniˑ

Jennifer, Jenifer
pers. name — JEN-uh-fuhr — ˈdʒenəfər

Jennings
Peter, *US TV journalist; pers. name* — JEN-ingz — ˈdʒeniŋz

Jenő
pers. name, Hungarian — YEN-uh(r) — ˈjenœː

Jenolan
caves, Australia — juh-NŌ-luhn — dʒəˈnoːlən

Key (col. 2):   a: fad ā: fade ah: father ar: marry aw: law e: fed ē: feed er: merry i: hid ī: hide ō: coat oo: boot
oi: boy   ow: now   u: put   uh: above   uhr: bird   ch: chop   ng: ring   sh: show   th: thick   th̲: this   zh: measure

Jens
  1. Salome, *US entertainer*   JENZ   'dʒenz
  2. *pers. name, Danish, German,*   YENS   'jens
     Norwegian

Jensen
  1. J. Hans Daniel, *German physicist*   YEN-zuhn   'jenzən
     (Nobel 1963)
  2. Johannes Vilhelm, *Danish author*   YEN(T)-suhn, ⓢ JEN(T)-suhn   'jen(t)sən, ⓢ 'dʒen(t)sən
     (Nobel 1944)

Jephthae
  Biblical name   JEF-thē, yif-TAH<u>KH</u>   'dʒefθiː, jif'tɑx

Jephthah
  Biblical name   JEF-thuh, yif-TAH<u>KH</u>   'dʒefθə, jif'tɑx

Jephunneh
  Biblical name   juh-FUHN-uh, yuh-f͞oo-NE   dʒə'fənə, jəfuː'ne

Jeptha
  pers. name   JEP-thuh   'dʒepθə

Jerah
  Biblical name   JIR-uh, JĒ-ruh, YE-rah<u>kh</u>   'dʒirə, 'dʒiːrə, 'jerɑx

Jerahmeel
  Biblical name   juh-RAHM-ē-EL, yuh-RAH<u>KH</u>-mē-EL   dʒə'ramiˌel, jəˌraxmiː'el

Jerahmeelite
  Biblical name   juh-RAHM-ē-uh-LĪT   dʒə'ramiːəˌlait

Jerauld
  county, SD   juh-RAWLD   dʒə'rɔːld

Jered
  Biblical name   JER-uhd, JĒ-RED, YE-red   'dʒerəd, 'dʒiːˌred, 'jered

Jeremai
  Biblical name   JER-uh-MĪ, JER-uh-MĀ-Ī, yuh-rā-MĪ   'dʒerəˌmai, ˌdʒerə'meːˌai, jəre'mai

Jeremiah
  Old Testament book; pers. name   JER-uh-MĪ-uh   ˌdʒerə'maiə

Jeremias
  Old Testament book   JER-uh-MĪ-uhs   ˌdʒerə'maiəs

Jérémie
  pers. name, French   zhā-rā-MĒ   ʒeːreːmiː

Jeremoth
  Biblical name   JER-uh-MAHTH, -MAWTH;   'dʒerəˌmaθ, -ˌmɔːθ;
                                       yuh-rā-MAWT   jəre'mɔːt

Jeremy
  pers. name   JER-uh-mē   'dʒerəmiˑ

Jerez de la Frontera
  city, Spain   <u>kh</u>uh-RĀS t<u>h</u>ā lah frawn-TER-uh,   xə'reːs ðeː lɑ frɔːn'terə,
                                       ⓢ huh-RĀS duh luh-FRUHN-TER-uh   ⓢ hə'reːs də ləˌfrɛn'terə

Jeriah
  Biblical name   juh-RĪ-uh, Yɪ-ri-YAH-h͞oo   dʒə'raiə, ˌjiri'jɑhuː

Jeribai
  Biblical name   JER-i-BĀ-Ī, JER-uh-BĪ, yuh-rē-VĪ   ˌdʒeri'beːˌai, 'dʒerəˌbai, jəriː'vai

Jericho
  town, Jordan   JER-i-kō   'dʒerikoː

Jeriel
  Biblical name   JER-ē-EL, juh-RĪ-uhl, yuh-rē-EL   'dʒeriːˌel, dʒə'raiəl, jəriː'el

Jerijah
  Biblical name   juh-RĪ-uh, yuh-rē-YAH-h͞oo   dʒə'raiə, jəriː'jɑhuː

Foreign Sounds: ue: *Fr.* **rue**, *Ger.* **füllen**   uh(r): *Fr.* **boeuf**, *Ger.* **Höhle**   kh: *Ger.* **ich**, *Scot.* **loch**   g̱: *Sp.* **amigo**   v̱: *Sp.* **hablar**
hl: *Welsh* **Llanelli**. CAPITALS: primary stress. SMALL CAPS: secondary stress. ⓢ: U.S. pron. ⓔ: British pron.

Jerilderie
  town, Australia   juh-RIL-duh-rē   dʒəˈrildəriˑ
Jerimoth
  Biblical name   JER-uh-MAHTH, -MAWTH,   ˈdʒerəˌmɑθ, -ˌmɔːθ,
                                                   yuh-rē-MAWT   jəriːˈmɔːt
Jerioth
  Biblical name   JER-ē-AHTH, yuh-rē-ŌT   ˈdʒeriːˌɑθ, jəriːˈoːt
Jermaine
  pers. name   juhr-MĀN   dʒəʳˈmeːn
Jermyn
  Henry, *English courtier*   JUHR-muhn   ˈdʒəʳmən
Jerne
  Niels K., *Danish immunologist*   YER-nuh   ˈjeʳnə
  (Nobel 1984)
Jeroboam
  Hebrew king; pers. name; bottle   JER-uh-BŌ-uhm   ˌdʒerəˈboːəm
Jéroboam
  pers. name, French   zhā-raw-baw-AHM   ʒeːrɔːbɔːɑːm
Jeroham
  Biblical name   juh-RŌ-HAM, -RŌ-uhm;   dʒəˈroːˌhæm, -ˈroːəm;
                                                   yuh-raw-KHAHM   jərɔːˈxɑm
Jerome
  pers. name   juh-RŌM, ⒠ *also* JER-uhm   dʒəˈroːm, ⒠ *also* ˈdʒerəm
Jérôme
  pers. name, French   zhā-RŌM   ʒeːroːm
Jerônimo
  pers. name, Portuguese   zhuh-RAW-nē-mōo, zhā-   ʒəˈrɔːniːmuː, ʒeː-
Jerónimo
  pers. name, Spanish   khā-RŌ-nē-mō   xeːˈroːniːmoː
Jerry
  pers. name   JER-ē   ˈdʒeriˑ
Jersey
  county, IL; island, English Channel   JUHR-zē   ˈdʒəʳziˑ
Jerubbaal
  Biblical name   JER-uh-BĀ(-uh)l, yuh-roo-BAH-ahl   ˌdʒerəˈbeː(ə)l, jəruːˈbɑ-ɑl
Jerubbesheth
  Biblical name   juh-RUHB-uh-SHETH,   dʒəˈrəbəˌʃeθ, ˌdʒerəˈbiːˌʃeθ,
                                                   JER-uh-BĒ-SHETH, yuh-roo-BE-shet   jəruːˈbeʃet
Jeruel
  Biblical name   juh-ROO-uhl, JER-uh-WEL, yuh-roo-EL   dʒəˈruːəl, ˈdʒerəˌwel, jəruːˈel
Jerusalem
  holy city, Israel   juh-ROO-s(uh-)luhm,   dʒəˈruːs(ə)ləm,
                                                   juh-ROOZ-(uh-)luhm   dʒəˈruːz(ə)ləm
Jerusha
  pers. name   juh-ROO-shuh   dʒəˈruːʃə
Jerusha, Jerushah
  Biblical name   juh-ROO-shuh, yuh-roo-SHAH   dʒəˈruːʃə, jəruːˈʃɑ
Jervas, Jarvis
  Charles, *Irish painter and translator*   JAHR-vuhs, JUHR-   ˈdʒɑʳvəs, ˈdʒəʳ-
Jervis
  pers. name   JUHR-vuhs, ⒠ *also* JAHR-vis   ˈdʒəʳvəs, ⒠ *also* ˈdʒɑʳvis
Jerzy
  pers. name, Polish   YEZH-i   ˈjeʒi
Jesaiah
  Biblical name   juh-SĪ-uh, juh-SĀ-uh, yuh-shah-YAH   dʒəˈsaiə, dʒəˈseːə, jəʃɑˈjɑ

Key (col. 2):   a: **fad**   ā: **fade**   ah: **father**   ar: **marry**   aw: **law**   e: **fed**   ē: **feed**   er: **merry**   i: **hid**   ī: **hide**   ō: **coat**   o͞o: **boot**
oi: **boy**   ow: **now**   u: **put**   uh: **above**   uhr: **bird**   ch: **chop**   ng: **ring**   sh: **show**   th: **thick**   t͟h: **this**   zh: **measure**

Jesarelah
  Biblical name   JES-uh-RĒ-luh, yuh-sahr-EL-ah   ˌdʒesəˈriːlə, jəsarˈelɑ

Jeshaiah
  Biblical name   juh-SHĪ-uh, juh-SHĀ-uh,   dʒəˈʃaiə, dʒəˈʃeːə,
                          yuh-shah-YAH-hoo   jəʃaˈjɑhuː

Jeshanah
  Biblical name   juh-SHĀ-nuh, yuh-shah-NAH   dʒəˈʃeːnə, jəʃɑˈnɑ

Jesharelah
  Biblical name   JESH-uh-RĒ-luh, yuh-sahr-EL-ah   ˌdʒeʃəˈriːlə, jəsarˈelɑ

Jeshebeab
  Biblical name   juh-SHEB-ē-AB, YE-shev-AHV   dʒəˈʃebiːˌæb, jeʃevˈɑv

Jesher
  Biblical name   JĒ-shuhr, YESH-er   ˈdʒiːʃəʳ, ˈjeʃer

Jeshimon
  Biblical name   juh-SHĪ-muhn, JESH-uh-MAHN,   dʒəˈʃaimən, ˈdʒeʃəˌman,
                          yuh-shē-MŌN   jəʃiːˈmoːn

Jeshishai
  Biblical name   juh-SHISH-Ī, yuh-shē-SHĪ   dʒəˈʃiʃˌai, jəʃiːˈʃai

Jeshohaiah
  Biblical name   JESH-uh-HĪ-uh, -HĀ-uh,   ˌdʒeʃəˈhaiə, -ˈheːə,
                          yuh-SHŌ-<u>kh</u>ah-YAH   jəˌʃoːxaˈja

Jeshua, Jeshuah
  Biblical name   JESH-(y)uh-wuh, ye-SHOO-ah   ˈdʒeʃ(j)əwə, jeˈʃuːɑ

Jeshurun
  Biblical name   juh-SHUR-uhn, JESH-uh-ruhn,   dʒəˈʃurən, ˈdʒeʃərən,
                          yuh-shoo-ROON   jəʃuːˈruːn

Jesiah
  Biblical name   juh-SHĪ-uh, YI-shi-YAH-hoo   dʒəˈʃaiə, jiʃiˈjɑhuː

Jesimiel
  Biblical name   juh-SHIM-ē-EL, yi-SIM-ē-EL   dʒəˈʃimiːˌel, jiˈsimiːˌel

Jespersen
  Otto, *Danish philologist*   YES-puhr-suhn   ˈjespəʳsən

Jess
  pers. name   JES   ˈdʒes

Jessamine
  county, KY   JES-uh-muhn   ˈdʒesəmən

Jesse
  pers. name   JES-ē   ˈdʒesiˑ

Jessica
  pers. name   JES-i-kuh   ˈdʒesikə

Jessie
  pers. name   JES-ē   ˈdʒesiˑ

Jessore
  region, Bangladesh   je-SŌR, -SAWR   dʒeˈsoːʳ, -ˈsɔːʳ

Jesu
  literary term for Jesus   JĒ-zoo, JĀ-zoo, YĀ-zoo, -soo   ˈdʒiːzuː, ˈdʒeːzuː, ˈjeːzuː,
                                           -suː

Jesui
  Biblical name   JES-uh-WĪ, JESH-; yish-VĒ   ˈdʒesəˌwai, ˈdʒeʃ-; jiʃˈviː

Jesuite
  Biblical name   JES-uh-WĪT, JESH-   ˈdʒesəˌwait, ˈdʒeʃ-

Jesuitic
  pert. to the Jesuits   JEZH-uh-WIT-ik, JEZ-(y)uh-WIT-ik   ˌdʒeʒəˈwiţik, ˌdʒez(j)əˈwiţik

Jesuitism
  tenets of the Jesuits   JEZH-(uh-)wuht-IZ-uhm, JEZ-   ˈdʒeʒ(ə)wəţˌizəm, ˈdʒez-

---

Jesuits
  religious order   JEZH-uh-wuhts, JEZ-   'dʒeʒəwəts, 'dʒez-

Jesurun [Jeshurun]
  Biblical name   juh-SUR-uhn, JES-(y)uh-ruhn,   dʒə'surən, 'dʒes(j)ərən,
                   yuh-shoō-ROON   jəʃuː'ruːn

Jesus
  pers. name   JĒ-zuhs, JĒ-zuhz   'dʒiːzəs, 'dʒiːzəz

Jesús
  pers. name, Spanish   khā-SOOS, ⓢ hā-SOOS, HĀ-SOOS   xeː'suːs, ⓢ heː'suːs,
                                         'heː͵suːs

Jesus Christ
  Christian religious leader   JĒ-zuhs KRĪST, JĒ-zuhz   'dʒiːzəs 'kraist, 'dʒiːzəz

Jether
  Biblical name   JĒ-thuhr, YE-ter   'dʒiːθəʳ, 'jeter

Jetheth
  Biblical name   JĒ-THETH, yuh-TET   'dʒiː͵θeθ, jə'tet

Jethlah
  Biblical name   JETH-luh, yit-LAH   'dʒeθlə, jit'lɑ

Jethro
  pers. name   JETH-rō   'dʒeθroː

Jettora
  pers. name   JET-uh-ruh, juh-TAWR-uh   'dʒet̮ərə, dʒə'tɔːrə

Jetur
  Biblical name   JĒT-uhr, yuh-TOOR   'dʒiːt̮əʳ, jə'tuːr

Jeuel
  Biblical name   JOO-uhl, juh-YOO-uhl, yuh-oō-EL   'dʒuːəl, dʒə'juːəl, jəuː'el

Jeush
  Biblical name   JĒ-uhsh, yuh-OOSH   'dʒiːəʃ, jə'uːʃ

Jeuz
  Biblical name   JĒ-uhz, yuh-OOTS   'dʒiːəz, jə'uːts

Jever
  German beer   YĀ-vuhr   'jeːvəʳ

Jewett
  Sarah Orne, *US author*   JOO-uht   'dʒuːət

Jewish
  pert. to Judaism   JOO-ish   'dʒuːiʃ

Jewry
  Jewish people collectively   JUR-ē, JOO-rē   'dʒuriˑ, 'dʒuːriˑ

Jezaniah
  Biblical name   JEZ-uh-NĪ-uh, yuh-zahn-YAH-hoō   ͵dʒezə'naiə, jəzɑn'jɑhuː

Jezebel
  Biblical name   JEZ-uh-BUHL   'dʒezə͵bəl

Jezer
  Biblical name   JĒ-zuhr, YET-ser   'dʒiːzəʳ, 'jetser

Jezerite
  Biblical name   JĒ-zuh-RĪT   'dʒiːzə͵rait

Jeziah
  Biblical name   juh-ZĪ-uh, JEZ-yuh, YI-zē-YAH   dʒə'zaiə, 'dʒezjə, ͵jiziː'jɑ

Jeziel
  Biblical name   JĒ-zē-EL, yi-zē-EL   'dʒiːziː͵el, jiziː'el

Jezliah
  Biblical name   jez-LĪ-uh, yiz-lē-AH   dʒez'laiə, jizliː'ɑ

Jezoar
  Biblical name   juh-ZŌ-uhr, yuht-SŌ-khahr   dʒə'zoːəʳ, jət'soːxɑr

---

Key (col. 2):   a: **fad**   ā: **fade**   ah: **father**   ar: **marry**   aw: **law**   e: **fed**   ē: **feed**   er: **merry**   i: **hid**   ī: **hide**   ō: **coat**   oō: **boot**
oi: **boy**   ow: **now**   u: **put**   uh: **above**   uhr: **bird**   ch: **chop**   ng: **ring**   sh: **show**   th: **thick**   th: **this**   zh: **measure**

Jezrahiah
   Biblical name   JEZ-ruh-HĪ-uh, YIZ-rah<u>kh</u>-YAH   ˌdʒezrə'haiə, ˌjizrɑx'ja

Jezreel
   town, Samaria   JEZ-rē-EL, JEZ-RĒL   'dʒezriːˌel, 'dʒezˌriːl

Jezreelite
   Biblical name   JEZ-rē-uh-LĪT, JEZ-ruh-LĪT   'dʒezriːəˌlait, 'dʒezrəˌlait

Jhansi
   town, India   JAHN(T)-sē   'dʒɑn(t)siˑ

Jhelum
   river, Asia   JĀ-luhm   'dʒeːləm

Jiangsu, Kiang-Su
   prov, China   jē-AHNG-SO͞O   dʒiː'ɑŋ'suː

Jiang Qing, Chiang Ch'ing
   Chinese Communist leader   JAHNG CHING   'dʒɑŋ 'tʃiŋ

Jiangxi, Kiang-Si
   prov, China   jē-AHNG-SHĒ   dʒiː'ɑŋ'ʃiː

Jibsam
   Biblical name   JIB-SAM, yiv-SAHM   'dʒibˌsæm, jiv'sɑm

Jibuti
   see Djibouti

Jicarilla
   N. American people   HĒ-kuh-RĒ-(y)uh   ˌhiːkə'riː(j)ə

Jiddah [Jedda]
   city, Saudi Arabia   JID-uh   'dʒidə

Jidlaph
   Biblical name   JID-LAF, yid-LAHF   'dʒidˌlæf, jid'lɑf

Jihad
   Islamic Holy War   ji-HAHD, ji-HAD   dʒi'hɑd, dʒi'hæd

Jilin [Kirin]
   prov & town, China   JĒ-LIN   'dʒiː'lin

Jill
   pers. name   JIL   'dʒil

Jim
   pers. name   JIM   'dʒim

Jiménez
   Juan Ramón, *Spanish poet (Nobel 1956)*   <u>kh</u>ē-MĀ-nāth, -nās; Ⓢ hē-MĀ-nuhs   çiː'meːneːθ, -neːs; Ⓢ hiː'meːnəs

Jim Hogg
   county, TX   JIM HAWG, HAHG   'dʒim 'hɔːg, 'hɑg

Jimmy, Jimmie, Jimmi, Jimi
   pers. name   JIM-ē   'dʒimiˑ

Jimna, Jimnah
   Biblical name   JIM-nuh, yim-NAH   'dʒimnə, jim'nɑ

Jinan, Chi-nan, Tsinan
   prov, China   JĒ-NAHN   'dʒiː'nɑn

Jinghpo [Kachin]
   lang., China, Burma, India   JING-BŌ, JING-PŌ   'dʒiŋ'boː, 'dʒiŋ'poː

Jingmen
   city, China   JING-MUHN   'dʒiŋ'mən

Jinnah
   Mohammed Ali, *governor-general, Pakistan*   JIN-uh   'dʒinə

Jinnie, Jinny
   pers. name   JIN-ē   'dʒiniˑ

Foreign Sounds: ue: *Fr.* **rue**, *Ger.* f**ü**llen   uh(r): *Fr.* b**oeu**f, *Ger.* H**öh**le   <u>kh</u>: *Ger.* **ich**, *Scot.* lo**ch**   ḡ: *Sp.* ami**g**o   v̱: *Sp.* ha**b**lar
hl: *Welsh* L**l**anelli.   CAPITALS: primary stress.   SMALL CAPS: secondary stress.   Ⓢ: U.S. pron.   Ⓔ: British pron.

Jiphthah-el
  Biblical name — JIF-thuh-EL — ˈdʒifθəˌel

Jipijapa
  1. city, Ecuador — khē-pē-KHAH-pah, Ⓢ HĒ-pē-HAHP-uh — xiːpiːˈxɑpɑ, Ⓢ ˌhiːpiˈˈhɑpə
  2. plant — HĒ-pē-HAHP-uh — ˌhiːpiˈˈhɑpə

Jirajara
  S. American people — HIR-uh-HAHR-uh — ˌhirəˈhɑrə

Jiři
  pers. name, Czech — YIR-zhē — ˈjirʒiː

Jiro
  pers. name, Japanese — jē-rō — dʒiːroː

Ji Si
  Chinese year (Snake) — JUHR SĒ — ˈdʒɝ ˈsiː

Jívaro
  S. American people — HĒ-vuh-RŌ — ˈhiːvəˌroː

Jo
  1. pers. name — JŌ — ˈdʒoː
  2. Dutch — YŌ — ˈjoː

Joab
  Biblical name — JŌ-AB — ˈdʒoːˌæb

Joachim
  1. pers. name — YŌ-uh-kim, JŌ-uh-KIM — ˈjoːəkim, ˈdʒoːəˌkim
  2. Danish — YŌ-ah-kēm — ˈjoːɑːkiːm
  3. Dutch — YŌ-ah-khuhm — ˈjoːɑːxəm
  4. French — zhō-ah-KĒM — ʒoːɑːkiːm
  5. German — YŌ-ahkh-im — ˈjoːɑxim
  6. Norwegian — YŌ-ah-kim — ˈjoːɑkim
  7. Polish — yaw-AH-khēm — jɔːˈɑːçiːm

Joad
  Cyril, *British philosopher; family name, Steinbeck characters* — JŌD — ˈdʒoːd

Joah
  Biblical name — JŌ-uh, yō-AHKH — ˈdʒoːə, joːˈɑx

Joahaz
  Biblical name — JŌ-uh-HAZ, jō-Ā-HAZ, YŌ-ah-KHAHZ — ˈdʒoːəˌhæz, dʒoːˈeːˌhæz, joːɑˈxɑz

Joan
  1. pers. name — JŌN, jō-AN — ˈdʒoːn, dʒoːˈæn
  2. Spanish — khō-AHN — xoˈɑn

Joanna
  pers. name — jō-AN-uh — dʒoːˈænə

Joanne
  pers. name — jō-AN — dʒoːˈæn

Joannes
  1. pers. name — jō-AN-ēz, jō-AN-uhs — dʒoːˈæniːz, dʒoːˈænəs
  2. Dutch — yō-AHN-uhs — joːˈɑnəs
  3. Mod. Greek — yaw-AHN-yēs — jɔːˈɑnjiːs

João
  pers. name, Portuguese — ZHWOWⁿ — ˈʒwɑũ

Joash
  Biblical name — JŌ-ASH, yō-AHSH — ˈdʒoːˌæʃ, joːˈɑʃ

Joatham
  Biblical name — JŌ-uh-THAM, -thuhm — ˈdʒoːəˌθæm, -θəm

Joaquim
  pers. name, Portuguese — zhwuh-KIⁿ — ʒwəˈkĩ

Key (col. 2): a: fad ā: fade ah: father ar: marry aw: law e: fed ē: feed er: merry i: hid ī: hide ō: coat ōō: boot
oi: boy ow: now u: put uh: above uhr: bird ch: chop ng: ring sh: show th: thick th: this zh: measure

Joaquin
    pers. name   wah-KĒN   wɑˈkiːn

Joaquín
    pers. name, Spanish   <u>kh</u>wah-KĒN   xwɑˈkiːn

Joaquina
    pers. name, Spanish   <u>kh</u>wah-KĒ-nah   xwɑˈkiːnɑ

Job
    1. Old Testament book; pers. name   JŌB   ˈdʒoːb
    2. Dutch   YAWP   ˈjɔːp

Jobab
    Biblical name   JŌ-BAB, yō-VAHV   ˈdʒoːˌbæb, joːˈvɑv

Jobs
    Steven P., *US computer executive*   JAHBZ   ˈdʒɑbz

Jocasta
    wife and mother of Oedipus   jō-KAS-tuh   dʒoːˈkæstə

Jocelyn
    pers. name   JAHS-(uh-)luhn   ˈdʒɑs(ə)lən

Jochebed
    Biblical name   JAHK-uh-BED, yō-<u>KHE</u>-ved   ˈdʒɑkəˌbed, joːˈxeved

Jock
    pers. name   JAHK   ˈdʒɑk

Joda [Judah]
    Biblical name   JŌD-uh, yuh-ho͞o-DAH   ˈdʒoːdə, jəhuːˈda

Jodhpur
    city, India   JAHD-puhr, JAHD-PUR   ˈdʒɑdpəʳ, ˈdʒɑdˌpuʳ

Jodi, Jodie, Jody
    pers. name   JŌD-ē   ˈdʒoːdiˑ

Jodrell Bank
    site of radio telescope, England   JAHD-ruhl BANGK   ˌdʒɑdrəl ˈbæŋk

Joe
    pers. name   JŌ   ˈdʒoː

Joed
    Biblical name   JŌ-ED, yō-ED   ˈdʒoːˌed, joːˈed

Joel
    1. Old Testament book; pers. name   JŌ(-uh)l   ˈdʒoː(ə)l
    2. Finnish   YAW-el   ˈjɔːel

Joël
    pers. name, French   yaw-EL   jɔːel

Joelah
    Biblical name   jō-Ē-luh, YŌ-e-LAH   dʒoːˈiːlə, ˌjoːeˈlɑ

Jo Enlai
    see Chou En-Lai

Joey
    pers. name   JŌ-ē   ˈdʒoːiˑ

Joezer
    Biblical name   jō-Ē-zuhr, yō-E-zer   dʒoːˈiːzəʳ, joːˈezer

Joffe
    Charles, *US film producer*   JAHF-ē, JAW-fē   ˈdʒɑfiˑ, ˈdʒɔːfiˑ

Joffrey
    Robert, *US choreographer*   JAHF-rē, JAW-frē   ˈdʒɑfriˑ, ˈdʒɔːfriˑ

Jog Falls [Gersoppa]
    waterfall, India   JŌG   ˈdʒoːg

Jogjakarta
    autonomous district, Java   JAHG-yuh-KAHRT-uh,   ˌdʒɑgjəˈkɑʳʈə,
                JAWK-juh-KAHRT-uh   ˌdʒɔːkdʒəˈkɑʳʈə

Foreign Sounds: ue: *Fr.* **rue**, *Ger.* **füllen**   uh(r): *Fr.* **boeuf**, *Ger.* **Höhle**   <u>kh</u>: *Ger.* **ich**, *Scot.* **loch**   ḡ: *Sp.* amigo   ṿ: *Sp.* **hablar**
hl: *Welsh* **Llanelli**.   CAPITALS: primary stress.   SMALL CAPS: secondary stress.   Ⓢ: U.S. pron.   Ⓔ: British pron.

Jogli
  Biblical name   JAHG-lē, yahg-LĒ   'dʒɑgli·, jɑg'liː

Jogues
  Isaac, *French missionary*   ZHAWG, ZHŌG   ʒɔːg, ʒoːg

Joha
  Biblical name   JŌ-huh, yō-K͟HAH   'dʒoːhə, joː'xɑ

Johan
  1. pers. name, Danish   yu-HAHN   ju'hɑːn
  2. Dutch, Norwegian   yō-HAHN   joː'hɑn
  3. Estonian   YŌ-HAHN   'joː͵hɑn
  4. Finnish, Swedish   YO͞O-HAHN   'juː͵hɑn

Johanan [Johannan]
  Biblical name   jō-HĀ-nuhn, YŌ-k͟hah-nahn   dʒoː'heːnən, 'joːxɑnɑn

Johann
  1. pers. name   YŌ-HAHN   'joː͵hɑn
  2. Danish   yu-HAHN   ju'hɑːn
  3. Dutch, German   yō-HAHN   joː'hɑn
  4. Finnish, Swedish   YO͞O-HAHN   'juː͵hɑn

Jóhann
  pers. name, Icelandic   YŌ-HAHN   'joː͵hɑn

Johanna
  1. pers. name   jō-(H)AN-uh   dʒoː'(h)ænə
  2. Dutch   yō-HAHN-ah   joː'hɑnɑː
  3. German   yō-HAHN-ah   joː'hɑnɑ
  4. Swedish   yō-HAHN-nah   joː'hɑːnnɑː

Johannan [Johanan]
  Biblical name   jō-HAN-uhn, YŌ-k͟hah-nahn   dʒoː'hænən, 'joːxɑnɑn

Johannes
  1. pers. name   jō-HAN-uhs   dʒoː'hænəs
  2. Danish   yu-HAHN-uhs   ju'hɑːnəs
  3. Dutch, German   yō-HAHN-uhs   joː'hɑnəs
  4. Finnish   yu-HAHN-nes   ju'hɑːnnes
  5. French   zhaw-ah-NES   ʒɔɑːnes
  6. Swedish   yō-HAHN-nuhs   joː'hɑːnnəs

Johannesburg
  city, South Africa   jō-HAN-uhs-BUHRG,   dʒoː'hænəs͵bəᵊg,
                           jō-HAHN-uhs-BUHRG   dʒoː'hɑnəs͵bəᵊg

Johannine
  pert. to the apostle John   jō-HAN-uhn, jō-HAN-Īn   dʒoː'hænən, dʒoː'hæn͵ɑin

Johannisberg
  city, Germany   yō-HAHN-uhs-BERG   joː'hɑnəs͵beᵊg

Johbehah
  Biblical name   JAHG-buh-HAH, YAHG-buh-HAH   'dʒɑgbə͵hɑ, ͵jɑgbə'hɑ

John
  1. New Testament book; pers. name   JAHN   'dʒɑn
  2. French   YAWN, ZHAWN   jɔːn, ʒɔːn

John Bull
  personification for England   JAHN BUL   ͵dʒɑn 'bul

John Doe
  anonymous man   JAHN DŌ   ͵dʒɑn 'doː

Johnny, Johnnie
  pers. name   JAHN-ē   'dʒɑni·

John o' Groats
  northern point of Scotland   JAHN uh GRŌTS   ͵dʒɑn ə 'groːts

---

Key (col. 2):   a: fad   ā: fade   ah: father   ar: marry   aw: law   e: fed   ē: feed   er: merry   i: hid   ī: hide   ō: coat   o͞o: boot
oi: boy   ow: now   u: put   uh: above   uhr: bird   ch: chop   ng: ring   sh: show   th: thick   t͟h: this   zh: measure

Johns		
pers. name	JAHNZ	'dʒɑnz
Johnson		
1. pers. name	JAHN-suhn	'dʒɑnsən
2. Eyvind, *Swedish author (Nobel 1974)*	YO͞ON-sawn	'juːnsɔːn
Johnsonian		
pert. to Samuel Johnson	jahn-SŌ-nē-uhn, jahn-SŌN-yuhn	dʒɑn'soːniːən, dʒɑn'soːnjən
Johor, Johore		
state, Asia	juh-HŌR, juh-HAWR	dʒə'hoːʳ, dʒə'hɔːʳ
Johor Baharu		
city, Asia	juh-HŌR buh-HAHR-o͞o, juh-HAWR	dʒə'hoːʳ bə'hɑruː, dʒə'hɔːʳ
Joi		
pers. name	JOI	'dʒɔi
Joiada		
Biblical name	JOI-uhd-uh, YŌ-yah-DAH	'dʒɔiədə, ˌjoːjɑ'dɑ
Joiarib		
Biblical name	JOI-uh-RIB, YŌ-yah-RĒV	'dʒɔiəˌrib, ˌjoːjɑ'riːv
Jojo		
pers. name	JŌ-JŌ	'dʒoːˌdʒoː
Jojoba		
shrub	hō-HŌ-buh, huh-HŌ-buh	hoː'hoːbə, hə'hoːbə
Jókai		
Maurus, *Hungarian novelist*	YŌ-KOI	'joːˌkɔi
Jokdeam		
Biblical name	JAHK-dē-AM, -dē-uhm; YAHK-duh-AHM	'dʒɑkdiːˌæm, -diːəm; ˌjɑkdə'ɑm
Jokim		
Biblical name	JŌ-kuhm, yō-KĒM	'dʒoːkəm, joː'kiːm
Jokmeam		
Biblical name	JAHK-mē-AM, -mē-uhm; yahk-muh-AHM	'dʒɑkmiːˌæm, -miːəm; jɑkmə'ɑm
Jokneam		
Biblical name	JAHK-nē-AM, -nē-uhm; yahk-nuh-AHM	'dʒɑkniːˌæm, -niːəm; jɑknə'ɑm
Jokshan		
Biblical name	JAHK-SHAN, yahk-SHAHN	'dʒɑkˌʃæn, jɑk'ʃɑn
Joktan		
Biblical name	JAHK-TAN, yahk-TAHN	'dʒɑkˌtæn, jɑk'tɑn
Joktheel		
Biblical name	JAHK-thē-EL, JAHK-thēl, YAHK-tuh-EL	'dʒɑkθiːˌel, 'dʒɑkθiːl, ˌjɑktə'el
Joliet		
1. Louis, *French explorer*	zhawl-YĀ	ʒɔːl'jeː
2. city, IL	JŌ-lē-ET, *by outsiders also* JAHL-ē-ET	ˌdʒoːliː'et, *by outsiders also* ˌdʒɑliː'et
Joliette		
county, Quebec, Canada	ZHŌ-lē-ET	ˌʒoːliː'et
Joliot-Curie		
Frédéric & Irène, *French physicists (Nobel 1935)*	zhōl-YŌ-kue-RĒ, [$] -kyu-RĒ, -KYUR-ē	ʒoːljoːkyːriː, [$] -kju'riː, -'kjuriˑ
Jolla, La		
see La Jolla		
Jolo		
island, Philippines	K͟HŌ-lō, HŌ-lō	'xoːloː, 'hoːloː

Jolson
  Al, *US entertainer*   JŌL-suhn   'dʒoːlsən

Jomo
  pers. name (J. Kenyatta)   JŌ-mō   'dʒoːmoː

Jon
  1. pers. name   JAHN   'dʒɑn
  2. Norwegian   YŌN, YAWN   'joːn, 'jɔːn
  3. Romanian   YAWN   'jɔːn

Jonadab
  Biblical name   JAHN-uh-DAB, YŌ-nah-DAHV   'dʒɑnə,dæb, joːnɑ'dɑv

Jonah
  Old Testament book; pers. name   JŌ-nuh   'dʒoːnə

Jonan
  Biblical name   JŌ-NAN, -nuhn   'dʒoː,næn, -nən

Jonas
  1. Old Testament book; pers. name   JŌ-nuhs   'dʒoːnəs
  2. Dutch, German, Norwegian   YŌ-nahs   'joːnɑs
  3. Lithuanian   YAW-nahs   'jɔːnɑs
  4. Swedish   YOO-nahs   'juːnɑːs

Jónas
  pers. name, Icelandic   YŌ-NAHS   'joː,nɑs

Jonathan
  1. pers. name   JAHN-uh-thuhn   'dʒɑnəθən
  2. German   YŌ-nah-TAHN   'joːnɑ,tɑn

Jones
  family name   JŌNZ   'dʒoːnz

Jonestown
  former settlement, Guyana   JŌN-STOWN   'dʒoːn,stɑun

Jong
  Erica, *US writer*   JAWNG, ZHAWNG   'dʒɔːŋ, 'ʒɔːŋ

Joni
  pers. name   JŌ-nē   'dʒoːniˑ

Jöns
  pers. name, Swedish   YUH(R)NS   'jœns

Jonson
  Ben, *English author*   JAHN-suhn   'dʒɑnsən

Joos
  pers. name, Dutch   YŌS   'joːs

Joost
  pers. name   YŌST   'joːst

Joplin
  Scott, *US composer;* Janis, *US rock singer; town, MO*   JAHP-luhn   'dʒɑplən

Joppa
  ancient name of Jaffa   JAHP-uh   'dʒɑpə

Jorah
  Biblical name   JŌR-uh, JAWR-uh, yō-RAH   'dʒoːrə, 'dʒɔːrə, joː'rɑ

Jorai
  Biblical name   JŌR-ē-Ī, JAWR-ē-Ī, yō-RĪ   'dʒoːriː,ɑi, 'dʒɔːriː,ɑi, joː'rɑi

Joram
  Biblical name   JŌR-uhm, JAWR-uhm, yō-RAHM   'dʒoːrəm, 'dʒɔːrəm, joː'rɑm

Jordache
  clothing co.   JAWR-DASH   'dʒɔːʳ,dæʃ

Jordaens
  Jacob, *Flemish painter*   YAWR-dahns   'jɔːʳdɑːns

Key (col. 2):   a: fad   ā: fade   ah: father   ar: marry   aw: law   e: fed   ē: feed   er: merry   i: hid   ī: hide   ō: coat   ōō: boot
oi: boy   ow: now   u: put   uh: above   uhr: bird   ch: chop   ng: ring   sh: show   th: thick   <u>th</u>: this   zh: measure

Jordan

country, river, Middle East; pers.   JAWRD-n   'dʒɔːˈʳdṇ
name

Jordanian

pert. to Jordan   jawr-DĀ-nē-uhn   dʒɔːʳˈdeːniːən

Jörg

pers. name, German   YUHR<u>KH</u>   'jœʳx

Jorge

1. pers. name, Portuguese   ZHAWR-zhuh, ZHAWR-zhā   'ʒɔːrʒə, 'ʒɔːrʒeː
2. Spanish   <u>KH</u>AWR-ḡā, ⑤ HAWR-HĀ   'xɔːrɣeː, ⑤ 'hɔːʳˌheː

Jörgen, Jørgen

1. pers. name, Danish   YUHR-ḡuhn   'jœrɣən
2. Norwegian   YUHR-guhn   'jœrgən

Jorge Newbery Aeroparque

airport, Buenos Aires, Argentina   HAWR-hā N(Y)OO-buh-rē Ā-rō-PAHRK   'hɔːʳheː 'n(j)uːbəri·
                                                    'eːroːˌpɑʳk

Jorim

Biblical name   JŌR-uhm, JAWR-uhm   'dʒoːrəm, 'dʒɔːrəm

Jorkeam [Jorkoam]

Biblical name   JAWR-kē-AM, -kē-uhm,   'dʒɔːʳkiːˌæm, -kiːəm,
                 YAWR-kuh-AHM   ˌjɔːrkəˈɑm

Jorkoam

Biblical name   JAWR-kō-AM, -kō-uhm,   'dʒɔːʳkoːˌæm, -koːəm,
                 YAWR-kuh-AHM   ˌjɔːrkəˈɑm

Josabad

Biblical name   JAHS-uh-BAD, YŌ-zah-VAHD   'dʒɑsəˌbæd, ˌjoːzɑˈvad

José

1. pers. name   hō-ZĀ   hoːˈzeː
2. Portuguese   zhoo-ZE   ʒuːˈze
3. Spanish   <u>kh</u>ō-SĀ, hō-SĀ   xoːˈseː, hoːˈseː

Jose Cuervo

brand of tequila   hō-ZĀ KWER-vō   hoːˌzeː 'kweʳvoː

Josef

1. pers. name   JŌ-zuhf, JŌ-suhf   'dʒoːzəf, 'dʒoːsəf
2. Czech   YAW-SEF   'jɔːˌsef
3. Dutch   YŌ-SEF   'joːˌsef
4. German   YŌ-ZEF   'joːˌzef
5. Swedish   YOO-SEF   'juːˌsef

Joseph

1. pers. name   JŌ-zuhf, JŌ-suhf   'dʒoːzəf, 'dʒoːsəf
2. Dutch   YŌ-SEF   'joːˌsef
3. French   zhō-ZEF   ʒoːzef
4. German   YŌ-ZEF   'joːˌzef
5. Swedish   YOO-SEF   'juːˌsef

Josepha

pers. name   jō-SĒ-fuh   dʒoːˈsiːfə

Josephine

pers. name   JŌ-zuh-FĒN, JŌ-zuh-FĒN, JŌ-suh-FĒN,   'dʒoːzəˌfiːn, ˌdʒoːzəˈfiːn,
                 JŌ-suh-FĒN   'dʒoːsəˌfiːn, ˌdʒoːsəˈfiːn

Josephinism

Austrian sect   JŌ-zuh-fuh-NIZ-uhm,   'dʒoːzəfəˌnizəm,
                 JŌ-suh-fuh-NIZ-uhm, -FĒ-NIZ-uhm   'dʒoːsəfəˌnizəm,
                                                    -ˌfiːˌnizəm

---

Foreign Sounds: ue: *Fr.* **rue**, *Ger.* **füllen**   uh(r): *Fr.* **boeuf**, *Ger.* **Höhle**   <u>kh</u>: *Ger.* **ich**, *Scot.* **loch**   ḡ: *Sp.* **amigo**   <u>v</u>: *Sp.* **hablar**
hl: *Welsh* **Llanelli**.   CAPITALS: primary stress.   SMALL CAPS: secondary stress.   ⑤: U.S. pron.   ⑥: British pron.

Josephson
    Brian D., *Welsh physicist (Nobel*   JŌ-zuhf-suhn, JŌ-suhf-suhn   'dʒɔːzəfsən, 'dʒɔːsəfsən
    1973)
Josephus
    Flavius, *Jewish general/historian*   jō-SĒ-fuhs   dʒoː'siːfəs
Joses
    Biblical name   JAW-sēz, -zēz   'dʒɔːsiːz, -ziːz
Josh
    pers. name   JAHSH   'dʒaʃ
Joshah
    Biblical name   JAHSH-uh, yō-SHAH   'dʒaʃə, joː'ʃa
Joshaphat
    Biblical name   JAHSH-uh-FAT, YŌ-shah-FAHT   'dʒaʃə,fæt, ˌjoːʃa'fat
Joshaviah
    Biblical name   JAHSH-uh-VĪ-uh, yō-shahv-YAH   ˌdʒaʃə'vaiə, joːʃav'ja
Joshbekashah
    Biblical name   JAHSH-buh-KĀ-shuh,   ˌdʒaʃbə'keːʃə, ˌjaʃbə'kaʃa
                          YAHSH-buh-KAHSH-ah
Josheb-Basshebeth
    Biblical name   JŌ-shuh(b)-ba(s)-SHĒ-beth,   'dʒoːʃə(b)bæ(s)'ʃiːbeθ,
                          yō-SHEV-bah-SHE-bet   joː'ʃevba'ʃebet
Joshibiah
    Biblical name   JAHSH-uh-BĪ-uh, YŌ-shiv-YAH   ˌdʒaʃə'baiə, joːʃiv'ja
Joshua
    Old Testament book; pers. name   JAHSH-(uh-)wuh   'dʒaʃ(ə)wə
Josiah
    pers. name   jō-SĪ-uh, jō-ZĪ-uh   dʒoː'saiə, dʒoː'zaiə
Josibiah [Joshibiah]
    Biblical name   JAHS-uh-BĪ-uh, YŌ-shiv-YAH   ˌdʒasə'baiə, ˌjoːʃiv'ja
Josip
    pers. name, Serbo-Croatian   YAW-sēp   'jɔːsiːp
Josiphiah
    Biblical name   JAHS-uh-FĪ-uh, YŌ-sif-YAH   ˌdʒasə'faiə, ˌjoːsif'ja
Jostens
    US education products co.   JAHS-tuhnz   'dʒastənz
Josquin des Prez, Josquin
Desprez
    Franco-Flemish composer   zhaw-SKEⁿ dā PRĀ   ʒɔːskẽ deː preː
Josue
    Old Testament book   JAHSH-uh-wē   'dʒaʃəwiˑ
Jotbah
    Biblical name   JAHT-buh, yaht-VAH   'dʒatbə, jat'va
Jotbath
    Biblical name   JAHT-BATH, yaht-VAH-tah   'dʒat,bæθ, jat'vata
Jotbathah
    Biblical name   JAHT-buh-thuh, yaht-VAH-tah   'dʒatbəθə, jat'vata
Jotham
    Biblical name   JAW-thuhm, yō-TAHM   'dʒɔːθəm, joː'tam
Jotunheimen
    mtn. range, Norway   YŌT-n-HĀ-muhn   'joːtn̩ˌheːmən
Joual
    French Canadian dialect   ZHWAHL, zhōō-AHL   'ʒwaːl, ʒuˑ'al
Jou Enlai
    see Chou En-Lai

Jouhaux
  Léon, *French labor leader, politician* zhōō-Ō ʒuːoː
    (Nobel 1951)
Joule
  1. James Prescott, *English physicist* JOOL, JOWL, JŌL 'dʒuːl, 'dʒaul, 'dʒoːl
  2. unit of energy JOOL, JOWL 'dʒuːl, 'dʒaul
Jourdan
  Louis, *entertainer* zhur-DE^n ʒurdē
Jove
  supreme Roman god (Jupiter) JŌV 'dʒoːv
Jovian
  pert. to Jupiter JŌ-vē-uhn 'dʒoːviːən
Jowett
  Benjamin, *English scholar* JŌ-uht 'dʒoːət
Joyce
  James Augustine, *Irish writer; pers.* JOIS 'dʒɔis
    name
Joyner-Kersee
  Jackie, *US track and field athlete* JOI-nuhr-KUHR-zē 'dʒɔinə^r'kə^{r}ziˑ
Jozabad
  Biblical name JAHZ-uh-BAD, yō-zah-VAHD 'dʒazə,bæd, joːzɑ'vɑd
Jozachar
  Biblical name JAHZ-uh-KAHR, JAHZ-Ā-kuhr, 'dʒazə,kɑ^r, 'dʒaz,eːkə^r,
    JŌ-zuh-KAHR, yō-zah-<u>KH</u>AHR 'dʒoːzə,kɑ^r, joːzɑ'xɑr
Jozadak
  Biblical name JAHZ-uh-DAK, YŌT-sah-DAHK 'dʒazə,dæk, joːtsɑ'dak
Józef
  pers. name, Polish YŌŌ-zef 'juːzef
Juab
  county, UT JŌŌ-AB 'dʒuː,æb
Juan
  1. pers. name (H)WAHN '(h)wɑn
  2. French ZHWAH^n ʒ ɥ ã
  3. Spanish <u>KH</u>WAHN 'xwɑn
Juan Fernández
  islands, Pacific (H)WAHN fuhr-NAN-duhs ,(h)wɑn fə^r'nændəs
Juang
  lang., people, India (Orissa) JŌŌ-AHNG 'dʒuː,ɑŋ
Juanita
  1. pers. name wuh-NĒT-uh, wah-NĒT-uh wə'niːtə, wɑ'niːtə
  2. Spanish <u>kh</u>wah-NĒ-tah xwɑ'niːtɑ
Juan-les-Pins
  resort, France zhwah^n-lā-PE^n ʒ ɥ w ɑ̃ l e ː p ē
Juarez
  Benito, *Mexican political leader* <u>KH</u>WAHR-uhs 'xwɑrəs
Juárez, Ciudad
  town, Mexico syōō-<u>THAHTH</u> <u>KH</u>WAHR-es sjuː'ðɑð 'xwares
Juba
  river, Africa; town, Sudan JŌŌ-buh 'dʒuːbə
Jubal
  pers. name JŌŌ-buhl 'dʒuːbəl
Jubilate
  hymn; prayer yōō-buh-LAH-TĀ, JŌŌ-buh-LĀT-ē juːbə'lɑ,teː, ,dʒuːbə'leːtiˑ
Jucal
  Biblical name JŌŌ-KAL, yōō-<u>KH</u>AHL 'dʒuː,kæl, juː'xɑl

Juda
   Biblical name   JOOD-uh   ˈdʒuːdə

Judaea
   see Judea

Judaeo-German [Yiddish]
   European Jewish language   joo-DĀ-ō-JUHR-muhn   dʒuːˈdeːoːˈdʒəʳmən

Judah
   1. pers. name   JOOD-uh   ˈdʒuːdə
   2. Spanish   KHOO-thah   ˈxuːða

Judaic
   pert. to Judaism   joo-DĀ-ik   dʒuːˈdeːik

Judaica
   things pert. to Judaism   joo-DĀ-i-kuh   dʒuːˈdeːikə

Judaism
   Jewish religion   JOOD-uh-ɪZ-uhm, JOOD-ē-ɪZ-uhm   ˈdʒuːdə‚izəm, ˈdʒuːdiː‚izəm

Judas
   pers. name, French   zhue-DAH   ʒyːdɑ

Judas Iscariot
   apostle who betrayed Christ   JOOD-uhs is-KAR-ē-uht   ˈdʒuːdəs isˈkæriːət

Judd
   pers. name   JUHD   ˈdʒəd

Jude
   New Testament book; pers. name   JOOD   ˈdʒuːd

Judea, Judaea
   ancient region, Palestine   ju-DĒ-uh, JU-DĀ-uh   dʒuˈdiːə, ‚dʒuˈdeːə

Judeo-
   combining form, Judaic or Judaism   joo-DĀ-ō, joo-DĒ-ō   dʒuˈˈdeːoː, dʒuˈˈdiːoː

Judezmo [Ladino]
   lang., Sephardic Jews   joo-DES-mō, ju-DEZ-mō, hoo-DES-mō   dʒuˈdesmoː, dʒuˈdezmoː,
                                                   huˈdesmoː

Judges
   Old Testament book   JUHJ-uhz   ˈdʒədʒəz

Judi
   pers. name   JOOD-ē   ˈdʒuːdiˑ

Judith
   1. Old Testament book; pers. name   JOOD-uhth   ˈdʒuːdəθ
   2. Dutch   YUE-duht   ˈjyːdət
   3. French   zhue-DĒT   ʒyːdiːt
   4. German   YOO-dit   ˈjuːdit

Judy
   pers. name   JOOD-ē   ˈdʒuːdiˑ

Juggernaut
   idol of Krishna   JUHG-uhr-NAWT, -NAHT   ˈdʒəgəʳ‚nɔːt, -‚nɑt

Jugoslav
   see Yugoslav

Jugoslavia
   see Yugoslavia

Jugurtha
   king of Numidia   ju-GUHR-thuh   dʒuˈgəʳθə

Juilliard
   School, The, *music school, NY*   JOOL-YAHRD, JOO-lē-AHRD   ˈdʒuːl‚jɑʳd, ˈdʒuːliːˌɑʳd

Jui [Puyi]
   lang., China   JOO-Ē   ˈdʒuːˈiː

Jukes
   family, focus of a sociological study   JOOKS   ˈdʒuːks

Key (col. 2):   a: **fad**   ā: **fade**   ah: **father**   ar: **marry**   aw: **law**   e: **fed**   ē: **feed**   er: **merry**   i: **hid**   ī: **hide**   ō: **coat**   oo: **boot**
oi: **boy**   ow: **now**   u: **put**   uh: **above**   uhr: **bird**   ch: **chop**   ng: **ring**   sh: **show**   th: **thick**   <u>th</u>: **this**   zh: **measure**

Jule

pers. name	JOOL	'dʒuːl

Jules

1. pers. name	JOOLZ	'dʒuːlz
2. French	ZHUEL	ʒyːl

Julia

1. Raul, *US actor; pers. name*	JOOL-yuh, JOO-lē-uh	'dʒuːljə, 'dʒuːliːə
2. Dutch	YUE-lē-ah	'jyːliːɑː
3. Finnish	YOO-li-ah	'juːliɑː
4. French	zhuel-YAH	ʒyːljɑː

Julia Domna

Roman empress	JOOL-yuh DAHM-nuh	ˌdʒuːljə 'damnə

Julia Luperca

legendary Roman heroine	JOOL-yuh LOO-puhr-kuh	ˌdʒuːljə 'luːpərkə

Julia Maesa

sister of Julia Domna	JOOL-yuh MĪ-suh	ˌdʒuːljə 'maisə

Julia Mamaea

mother of Roman emperor Alexander Severus	JOOL-yuh mahm-Ē-uh, mahm-Ī-uh	ˌdʒuːljə mam'iːə, mam'aiə

Julian

1. pers. name	JOOL-yuhn	'dʒuːljən
2. German	YOO-lē-AHN, yool-YAHN	ˌjuːliː'an, juːl'jan
3. Polish	yool-YAHN	juːl'jaːn

Julián

pers. name, Spanish	khool-YAHN	xuːl'jan

Juliana

pers. name	JOO-lē-AN-uh	ˌdʒuːliː'ænə

Julian Alps

Alpine mtn. range	JOOL-yuhn ALPS	'dʒuːljən 'ælps

Julian the Apostate

Roman emperor	JOOL-yuhn thē uh-PAHS-TĀT	'dʒuːljən ðiˑ ə'pɑsˌteːt

Julie

1. pers. name	JOO-lē	'dʒuːliˑ
2. French	zhue-LĒ	ʒyːliː
3. German	YOO-lē-uh, YOOL-yuh	'juːliːə, 'juːljə

Julien

1. pers. name	JOOL-yuhn	'dʒuːljən
2. French	zhuel-YE[n]	ʒyːljẽ

Juliet

pers. name	JOOL-yuht, JOO-lē-ET, JOO-lē-ET	'dʒuːljət, ˌdʒuːliː'et, 'dʒuːliːˌet

Juliette

1. pers. name	JOO-lē-ET	ˌdʒuːliː'et
2. French	zhuel-YET	ʒyːljet

Julilla

Roman female name	juh-LIL-uh	dʒə'lilə

Julio

pers. name, Spanish	KHOOL-yō	'xuːljoː

Júlio

pers. name, Portuguese	ZHOOL-yoo	'ʒuːljuː

Julius

1. pers. name	YOOL-yuhs, JOO-lē-uhs	'juːljəs, 'dʒuːliːəs
2. Czech	YU-li-us	'julius
3. Danish, German	YOO-lē-us	'juːliːus
4. Dutch	YUE-lē-ues	'jyːliːys

Foreign Sounds: ue: *Fr.* **rue**, *Ger.* **füllen** uh(r): *Fr.* **boeuf**, *Ger.* **Höhle** kh: *Ger.* ich, *Scot.* lo**ch** ḡ: *Sp.* amigo v̱: *Sp.* hablar
hl: *Welsh* **Ll**anelli. CAPITALS: primary stress. SMALL CAPS: secondary stress. ⑤: U.S. pron. ⑥: British pron.

Julius Echter Hefe-Weissbier		
German beer	Y͞OO-lē-us E<u>KH</u>-tuhr HĀ-fuh-VĪS-BIR	'juːliːus 'eçtəʳ 'heːfəˌvɑisˌbiʳ
July		
month	juh-LĪ	dʒə'lɑi
Jumada		
Islamic month	ju-MAHD-uh	dʒu'mɑdə
Jumna [Yamuna]		
river, India	JUHM-nuh	'dʒəmnə
Jumporn		
see Chumpon		
Junco		
songbird	JUHNG-kō	'dʒəŋkoː
June		
month; pers. name	J͞OON	'dʒuːn
Juneau		
county, WI; division, AK	J͞OO-nō	'dʒuːnoː
Junee		
town, Australia	ju-NĒ, J͞OO-nē	dʒu'niː, 'dʒuːniˑ
Juneteenth		
June 19th celebrated in the US South as a day of freedom from slavery	j͞oon-TĒNTH	dʒuːn'tiːnθ
Jung		
Carl, *Swiss psychiatrist*	YUNG	'juŋ
Jungfrau		
mtn. peak, Switzerland	YUNG-FROW	'juŋˌfrɑu
Jungian		
pert. to Jung	YUNG-ē-uhn	'juŋiːən
Juniata		
county, PA	J͞OO-nē-AT-uh	ˌdʒuːniː'æt̬ə
Junípero		
pers. name, Spanish	<u>kh</u>͞oo-NĒ-pā-rō, [$] h͞oo-NIP-uh-ruh	xuː'niːpeːroː, [$] huː'nipərə
Junius		
pers. name	J͞OON-yuhs, J͞OO-nē-uhs	'dʒuːnjəs, 'dʒuːniːəs
Junker		
Prussian aristocrats	YUNG-kuhr	'juŋkəʳ
Juno		
Roman queen of the gods	J͞OO-nō	'dʒuːnoː
Junoesque		
stately, regal	J͞OO-nō-ESK	ˌdʒuːnoː'esk
Jupiter		
supreme Roman god; planet; pers. name	J͞OO-puht-uhr	'dʒuːpət̬əʳ
Juppé		
Alain, *French prime minister*	zhue-PĀ	ʒyːpeː
Jura		
1. mtn. range, dept, France	zhue-RAH, [$] JUR-uh	ʒyːrɑː, [$] 'dʒurə
2. island, Hebrides	JUR-uh	'dʒurə
Juraj		
pers. name, Serbo-Croatian	Y͞OO-RĪ	'juːˌrɑi
Jurassic		
geologic period	juh-RAS-ik, jur-AS-	dʒə'ræsik, dʒur'æs-
Jürgen		
1. pers. name, Danish	YUER-ḡuhn	'jyrɣən
2. German	YUR-guhn	'jyʳgən

Key (col. 2): a: **fad** ā: **fade** ah: **father** ar: **marry** aw: **law** e: **fed** ē: **feed** er: **merry** i: **hid** ī: **hide** ō: **coat** o͞o: **boot** oi: **boy** ow: **now** u: **put** uh: **above** uhr: **bird** ch: **chop** ng: **ring** sh: **show** th: **thick** <u>th</u>: **this** zh: **measure**

Jurgensen
　Christian Adolph III, *US sports*　　JUHR-guhn-suhn　　　　　　　'dʒəˈʳgənsən
　　commentator
Juris Doctor
　doctor of law, J.D.　　　　　　　JUR-uhs DAHK-TAWR, YUR-uhs,　　'dʒurəs 'dɑk,tɔːˈʳ, 'jurəs,
　　　　　　　　　　　　　　　　DAHK-tuhr　　　　　　　　　　'dɑktəʳ
Juruá
　river, S. America　　　　　　　ZHUR-uh-WAH, zhur-WAH　　　　,ʒurəˈwɑ, ʒuˈʳwɑ
Jushab-hesed
　Biblical name　　　　　　　　JOO-SHAB-HĒ-suhd,　　　　　'dʒuː,ʃæbˈhiːsəd,
　　　　　　　　　　　　　　　YOO-shahv-KHE-sed　　　　　　'juːʃɑvˈxesed
Justice
　pers. name　　　　　　　　　JUHS-tuhs　　　　　　　　　　'dʒəstəs
Justin
　1. pers. name　　　　　　　　JUHS-tuhn　　　　　　　　　　'dʒəstən
　2. French　　　　　　　　　　zhue-STEⁿ　　　　　　　　　　ʒyːstẽ
　3. German　　　　　　　　　yus-TĒN　　　　　　　　　　jusˈtiːn
Justine
　1. pers. name　　　　　　　　JUH-STĒN　　　　　　　　　　,dʒəˈstiːn
　2. French　　　　　　　　　　zhue-STĒN　　　　　　　　　　ʒyːstiːn
Justinian
　name, Eastern Roman emperors;　JUHS-TIN-ē-uhn　　　　　　　,dʒəsˈtiniːən
　　pers. name
Justus
　1. pers. name　　　　　　　　JUHS-tuhs　　　　　　　　　　'dʒəstəs
　2. Dutch　　　　　　　　　　YUES-tues　　　　　　　　　　'jystyːs
　3. German　　　　　　　　　YUS-tus　　　　　　　　　　'justus
Jutah, Juttah
　Biblical name　　　　　　　JUHT-uh, yoo-TAH　　　　　　'dʒəṭə, juːˈtɑ
Jute
　member of a continental Germanic　JOOT　　　　　　　　　　'dʒuːt
　　tribe
Jutish
　having characteristics of a Jute　JOOT-ish　　　　　　　　　'dʒuːṭiʃ
Jutland
　Danish peninsula　　　　　　JUHT-luhnd　　　　　　　　'dʒətlənd
Juturna
　Roman nymph of the springs　　ju-TUHR-nuh, yu-TUHR-nuh　dʒuˈtəʳnə, juˈtəʳnə
Juvenal
　Roman satirist　　　　　　　JOO-vuhn-l　　　　　　　　　'dʒuːvənḷ
Juventas [Iuventas]
　Roman goddess of youth　　　joo-VENT-uhs, yoo-VENT-uhs　dʒuːˈventəs, juːˈventəs
Juventius
　pers. name　　　　　　　　joo-VEN-sh(ē-)uhs　　　　　　dʒuːˈvenʃ(iː)əs
Juventus
　Italian soccer team　　　　　yoo-VEN-tuhs　　　　　　　juːˈventəs
Jylland [Jutland]
　Danish peninsula　　　　　　YOO-LAHN　　　　　　　　'juː,lɑːn

K

Kaaawa
   village, HI   KAH-AH-AH-wuh, KAH-uh-AH-wuh,   ˌkɑˌɑˈawə, ˌkɑəˈawə,
    kuh-AH-AH-wuh   kəˌɑˈawə

Kaaba
   Islamic sacred building   KAHB-uh   ˈkɑbə

Kaaterskill Creek
   creek, NY   KAHT-uhr-SKIL KRIK, KAWT-uhr-SKIL,   ˈkɑtəʳˌskil ˈkrik, ˈkɔːt̬ərˌskil,
    KRĒK   ˈkriːk

Kabardian
   lang., Caucasus Mts.   kuh-BAHR-dē-uhn   kəˈbɑʳdiːən

Kabuki
   Japanese drama   kah-boo̅-kē, ⑤ kuh-BOO̅-kē,   kɑbuːkiˈ, ⑤ kəˈbuːkiˈ,
    KAHB-u-kē   ˈkɑbukiˈ

Kabul
   river, city, prov, Afghanistan   kah-BOO̅L, KAHB-uhl   kɑˈbuːl, ˈkɑbəl

Kabyle
   lang., people, Algeria   kuh-BĪL, kuh-BĒL   kəˈbail, kəˈbiːl

Kabzeel
   Biblical name   KAB-zē-EL, KAB-ZĒL, KAHV-tsuh-EL   ˈkæbziːˌel, ˈkæbˌziːl,
    ˌkɑvtsəˈel

Kachina
   Pueblo ancestral spirit   kuh-CHĒ-nuh   kəˈtʃiːnə

Kachin [Jinghpo]
   lang., China, Burma, India   KAH-CHIN   ˈkɑˈtʃin

Kádár
   Janos, Hungarian political leader   KAH-DAHR   ˈkɑːˌdɑːʳ

Kaddish
   Jewish prayer for the dead   KAHD-ish   ˈkɑdiʃ

Kadesh
   ancient city, Syria   KĀ-DESH   ˈkeːˌdeʃ

Kadesh-barnea
   Biblical name   KĀD-uhsh-bahr-NĒ-uh,   ˈkeːdəʃbɑʳˈniːə,
    kah-DESH-bahr-NE-ah   kɑˈdeʃbɑrˈnea

Kadett
   tdmk for a German automobile   kuh-DET   kəˈdet

Kadmiel
   Biblical name   KAD-mē-EL, -uhl; KAHD-mē-EL   ˈkædmiːˌel, -əl; ˌkɑdmiːˈel

Kadmonit
   Biblical name   KAD-muh-NĪT   ˈkædməˌnait

Kaduna
   town, state, Nigeria   kuh-DOO̅-nuh   kəˈduːnə

Kael
   Pauline, US film critic   KĀL   ˈkeːl

Key (col. 2):   a: **fad**   ā: **fade**   ah: **father**   ar: **marry**   aw: **law**   e: **fed**   ē: **feed**   er: **merry**   i: **hid**   ī: **hide**   ō: **coat**   oo̅: **boot**
oi: **boy**   ow: **now**   u: **put**   uh: **above**   uhr: **bird**   ch: **chop**   ng: **ring**   sh: **show**   th: **thick**   <u>th</u>: **this**   zh: **measure**

Kaelin
Kato, *US personality*   KĀ-luhn   ˈkeːlən

Kaesŏng
town, N. Korea   KĀ-SAWNG   ˈkeːˌsɔːŋ

Kafa
lang., people, Ethiopia, Kenya   KAHF-uh, KAF-uh   ˈkɑfə, ˈkæfə

Kaffir, Kafir
Bantu people   KAF-uhr   ˈkæfəʳ

Kaffiyeh
Arab headdress   kah-FĒ-(y)uh, kuh-   kaˈfiː(j)ə, kə-

Kaffraria
region, S. Africa   kuh-FRAR-ē-uh, kuh-FRER-ē-uh   kəˈfræriːə, kəˈfreriːə

Kafka
Franz, *Austrian writer*   KAHF-kuh   ˈkɑfkə

Kafkaesque
pert. to Kafka   KAHF-kuh-ESK, KAF-   ˌkɑfkəˈesk, ˌkæf-

Kagawa
prefecture, Japan   kah-gah-wah   kɑgɑwɑ

Kagoshima
city, Japan   kah-gō-shē-mah   kagoːʃiːmɑ

Kahanamoku
Duke, *US surfer*   kuh-HAHN-uh-MŌ-k͞oo   kəˌhɑnəˈmoːkuː

Kahane
Meir, *activist rabbi*   kah-HAHN-uh, kuh-   kaˈhɑnə, kə-

Kahlil
pers. name   kuh-LĒL   kəˈliːl

Kahlo
Frida, *Mexican painter*   KAHL-ō   ˈkɑlˌoː

Kahlúa
liqueur   kuh-L͞OO-uh   kəˈluːə

Kahn
Michael, *US stage director*   KAHN   ˈkɑn

Kahn
Louis Isadore, *US architect*   KAHN   ˈkɑn

Kahuku
town, HI   kuh-H͞OO-k͞oo, kah-   kəˈhuːkuː, ka-

Kahului
city, airport, HI   KAH-h͞oo-L͞OO-ē   ˌkɑhuːˈluːiː

Kai
pers. name, Swedish   KĪ   ˈkɑi

Kaibab
National Forest, *Indian reservation,*   KĪ-BAB   ˈkɑiˌbæb
AZ

Kaibito
tableland, AZ   kī-BĒT-ō   kɑiˈbiːt̪oː

Kaieteur
waterfall, Guyana   KĪ-uh-TUR, KĪ-CHUR   ˈkɑiəˌtuʳ, ˈkɑiˌtʃuʳ

Kaifeng, K'ai-feng
city, China   KĪ-FUHNG   ˈkɑiˈfəŋ

Kaifu
Toshiki, *prime minister, Japan*   kī-f͞oo   kɑifuː

Kaikoura
mtn. range, New Zealand   kī-KAWR-uh, -KŌR-uh   kɑiˈkɔːrə, -ˈkoːrə

Kailas
mountain range, Tibet, China   kī-LAHS   kɑiˈlɑs

Foreign Sounds: ue: *Fr.* **rue**, *Ger.* **füllen**   uh(r): *Fr.* **boeuf**, *Ger.* **Höhle**   kh: *Ger.* **ich**, *Scot.* **loch**   g̃: *Sp.* **amigo**   v: *Sp.* **hablar**
hl: *Welsh* **Llanelli**.   CAPITALS: primary stress.   SMALL CAPS: secondary stress.   ⓢ: U.S. pron.   ⓔ: British pron.

Kailua
 town, HI   kī-L͞OO-uh   kaiˈluːə
Kaimanawa
 mountain range, New Zealand   kī-MAHN-uh-wuh   kaiˈmɑnəwə
Kaiser
 Henry John, *US industrialist; title*   KĪ-zuhr   ˈkaizəʳ
 for a German or Austrian emperor
Kaiserbräu Bamberg
 German beer   KĪ-zuhr-BROI BAHM-BERK   ˈkaizəʳˌbrɔi ˈbamˌberk
Kaiserdom
 German beer   KĪ-zuhr-DAWM   ˈkaizəʳˌdɔːm
Kaiserdom Rauchbier
 German beer   KĪ-zuhr-DAWM ROW<u>KH</u>-BIR   ˈkaizəʳˌdɔːm ˈrauxˌbiʳ
Kaiserslautern
 city, Germany   KĪ-zuhrz-LOWT-uhrn   ˌkaizəʳzˈlauʈəʳn
Kaiserstuhl
 mountain group, Germany   KĪ-zuhr-SHT͞OOL   ˈkaizəʳˌʃtuːl
Kai Tak
 airport, Hong Kong   KĪ TAHK, ⑤ KĪ TAK   ˈkai ˈtak, ⑤ ˈkai ˌtæk
Kake
 village, AK   KAK-ē, KAHK-ē   ˈkækiˑ, ˈkakiˑ
Kakinomoto no Hitomaro
 Japanese poet   kah-kē-nō-mō-tō nō hē-tō-mahr-ō   kakiːnoːmoːtoː noː
     hiːtoːmaroː
Kakuei
 Tanaka, *prime minister, Japan*   kah-k͞oo-ā   kakuːeː
Kalahari
 desert region, Africa   KAL-uh-HAHR-ē, KAHL-uh-HAHR-ē   ˌkæləˈhariˑ, ˌkaləˈhariˑ
Kalakaua
 avenue, Honolulu, HI   KAH-luh-KOW-uh   ˌkaləˈkauə
Kalakh
 ancient Assyrian city   KAHL-AH<u>KH</u>   ˈkalˌax
Kalamazoo
 river, city, county, MI   KAL-uh-muh-Z͞OO   ˌkæləməˈzuː
Kalambo
 waterfall, Africa   kuh-LAHM-bō   kəˈlamboː
Kalanchoe
 plant   KAL-uhn-KŌ-ē, kuh-LANG-kuh-wē   ˌkælənˈkoːiˑ, kəˈlæŋkəwiˑ
Kalashnikov
 Russian-designed automatic rifle   kuh-LAHSH-ni-KAWF, -KAWV, -KAHV   kəˈlaʃniˌkɔːf, -ˌkɔːv, -ˌkav
Kalat
 former Indian state, town, Pakistan   kuh-LAHT   kəˈlat
Kalaupapa
 leper colony, HI   kuh-LAH-u-PAHP-uh   kəˌlauˈpapə
Kalawao
 county, HI   KAHL-uh-WOW   ˌkaləˈwau
Kalb
 Marvin Leonard, *radio and TV news*   KALB   ˈkælb
 correspondent
Kalback
 Swedish beer   KAHL-BAHK   ˈkaːlˌbak
Kalevala
 national epic of Finland   KAHL-i-VAHL-uh   ˌkaliˈvalə
Kalgan
 city, China   KAHL-GAHN, ⑤ KAL-GAN   ˈkalˈgan, ⑤ ˈkælˈgæn

Key (col. 2):   a: fad   ā: fade   ah: father   ar: marry   aw: law   e: fed   ē: feed   er: merry   i: hid   ī: hide   ō: coat   o͞o: boot
oi: boy   ow: now   u: put   uh: above   uhr: bird   ch: chop   ng: ring   sh: show   th: thick   <u>th</u>: this   zh: measure

Kalgoorlie
   city, Australia   kal-GUR-lē   kæl'gu^rli·

Kalinga
   lang., people, Philippine Islands   kuh-LING-guh   kə'liŋgə

Kalinin
   city, Russia   kuhl-YĒN-yēn, Ⓢ kuh-LĒ-nuhn   kəl'jiːnjiːn, Ⓢ kə'liːnən

Kalispel
   N. American people   KAL-uh-SPEL, KAL-uh-SPEL   'kælə,spel, ,kælə'spel

Kalispell
   town, MT   KAL-uh-SPEL, KAL-uh-SPEL   'kælə,spel, ,kælə'spel

Kalisz
   prov, Poland   KAH-lēsh   'kaːliːʃ

Kalkaska
   county, MI   kal-KAS-kuh   kæl'kæskə

Kállay
   Miklós, *Hungarian politician*   KAHL-loi   'kaːllɔi

Kálmán
   pers. name, Hungarian   KAHL-mahn   'kaːlmaːn

Kalmuk [Kalmyk]
   lang., people, Russia   KAL-MUHK, kal-MUHK   'kæl,mək, kæl'mək

Kalmyk
   lang., people, Russia   KAL-mik   'kælmik

Kalpa Sutra
   Jain scripture   KUHL-puh SOO-truh   'kəlpə 'suːtrə

Kalpa Vruksha
   Hindu festival   KUHL-puhv RUHK-shuh   'kəlpəv 'rəkʃə

Kam
   lang., China   KAHM, KAM   'kam, 'kæm

Kamakura
   town, Japan   kahm-ah-kur-ah   kamakura

Kama Sutra
   Indian erotic text   KAHM-uh SOO-truh   ,kamə 'suːtrə

Kamba [Kikamba]
   lang., people, Africa   KAHM-buh   'kambə

Kamchatka
   peninsula, Russia   kahm-CHAHT-kuh, kam-CHAT-kuh   kam'tʃatkə, kæm'tʃætkə

Kamehameha
   King of Hawaii   kuh-MĀ-uh-MĀ-hah   kə,meːə'meːha

Kamehameha
   ruler of Hawaii   kuh-MĀ-uh-MĀ-uh, kah-MĀ-hah-MĀ-hah   kə,meːə'meːə, ka,meːha'meːha

Kamerlingh Onnes
   Heike, *Dutch physicist (Nobel 1913)*   KAHM-uhr-ling AWN-uhs   'kamə^rliŋ 'ɔːnəs

Kames
   Lord, Henry Hume, *Scottish jurist and philosopher*   KĀMZ   'keːmz

Kamia
   N. American people   KAHM-ē-uh   'kamiːə

Kamil
   pers. name, Polish   KAHM-yēl   'kaːmjiːl

Kamose
   Egyptian king   KAH-MŌS   'ka,moːs

Kampala
   capital, Uganda   kahm-PAHL-uh   kam'palə

Foreign Sounds: ue: *Fr.* rue, *Ger.* füllen   uh(r): *Fr.* boeuf, *Ger.* Höhle   <u>kh</u>: *Ger.* ich, *Scot.* loch   ḡ: *Sp.* amigo   v: *Sp.* hablar
hl: *Welsh* Llanelli.   CAPITALS: primary stress.   SMALL CAPS: secondary stress.   Ⓢ: U.S. pron.   Ⓔ: British pron.

Kamphaeng Phet, Kambaeng Petch
province, Thailand — kahm-PAHNG PET — kɑm'pɑŋ 'pet

Kampleman
Max M., *US ambassador* — KAM-puhl-muhn — 'kæmpəlmən

Kampot
province, Cambodia — KAHM-PAHT, -PŌT — 'kɑm'pɑt, -'poːt

Kampuchea [Cambodia]
republic, SE Asia — KAHM-puh-CHĒ-uh, KAM- — ˌkɑmpə'tʃiːə, ˌkæm-

Kampuchean
pert. to Kampuchea — KAHM-puh-CHĒ-uhn, KAM- — ˌkɑmpə'tʃiːən, ˌkæm-

Kanab
city, UT — kuh-NAB — kə'næb

Kanabec
county, MN — kuh-NĀ-bek, kuh-NAW-bek — kə'neːbek, kə'nɔːbek

Kanah
Biblical name — KĀ-nuh, kah-NAH — 'keːnə, kɑ'nɑ

Kanaka
Hawaiian "native" & derisive for "mainlander" — sg. kuh-NAHK-uh, pl. KAHN-uh-kuh — sg. kə'nɑkə, pl. 'kɑnəkə

Kananga
city, central Africa — kuh-NAHNG-guh — kə'nɑŋgə

Kanara
state, India — KAHN-uh-ruh — 'kɑnərə

Kanarese [Kannada]
lang., people, India — KAN-uh-RĒZ, -RĒS — ˌkænə'riːz, -'riːs

Kanawha
river, county, WV; Park, *ballpark, Charleston, SC* — kuh-NAW-(w)uh, kuh-NOI — kə'nɔː(w)ə, kə'nɔi

Kanazawa
port, Japan — kahn-ah-zah-wah — kɑnɑzɑwɑ

Kanchenjunga, Kangchenjunga [Kinchinjunga]
mtn., Himalaya — KAN-chuhn-JUHNG-guh, -JUNG-guh — ˌkæntʃən'dʒəŋgə, -'dʒuŋgə

Kanda
district, Japan — kahn-dah — kɑndɑ

Kāndāhār
prov & town, Pakistan — KAHN-duh-HAHR, KAN-duh-HAHR — 'kɑndəˌhɑʳ, 'kændəˌhɑʳ

Kandahār
prov, Afghanistan — KAHN-duh-HAHR — 'kɑndəˌhɑʳ

Kander
John, *US composer* — KAN-duhr — 'kændəʳ

Kandinsky
Wassily, *Russian painter* — kuhn-DYĒN-skyi, ⓢ kan-DIN(T)-skē — kən'djiːnskjij, ⓢ kæn'din(t)skiˑ

Kandiyohi
county, MN — KAN-duh-yō-HĪ — ˌkændəjoː'hɑi

Kandy
city, Sri Lanka — KAN-dē — 'kændiˑ

Kaneohe
city, HI — KAHN-ē-Ō-ē, KAHN-ē-Ō-hā — ˌkɑniː'oːiː, ˌkɑniː'oːheː

Kanesh [Kültepe]
ancient Assyrian city, Turkey — KAHN-uhsh, KAHN-ESH — 'kɑnəʃ, 'kɑnˌeʃ

Kangchenjunga
see Kanchenjunga

Key (col. 2):   a: fad ā: fade ah: father ar: marry aw: law e: fed ē: feed er: merry i: hid ī: hide ō: coat ōō: boot oi: boy   ow: now   u: put   uh: above   uhr: bIrd   ch: chop   ng: ring   sh: show   th: thick   th̲: this   zh: measure

Kangnŭng
  town, South Korea kahng-nuhng kɑŋnəŋ
KaNgwane
  state, South Africa kahng-(G)WAH-nā kɑŋˈ(g)wɑneː
Kang Wu
  Chinese year (Horse) KAHNG W͞OO ˈkɑŋ ˈwuː
Kanin
  peninsula, Barents Sea KAN-uhn ˈkænən
Kaniska, Kanishka
  king of India kuh-NISH-kuh kəˈniʃkə
Kanjobal, Kanhobal
  lang., people, Guatemala kahn-ō-V̲AHL kɑnoːˈβɑl
Kankakee
  river, US; city, county, IL KANG-kuh-KĒ ˌkæŋkəˈkiː
Kankanay
  lang., people, Philippine Islands KAHNG-kuh-NĪ, KAHNG-kuh-NĪ ˌkɑŋkəˈnɑi, ˈkɑŋkəˌnɑi
Kannada [Kanarese]
  lang., people, India KAHN-uhd-uh, KAN-uhd-uh ˈkɑnədə, ˈkænədə
Kannapolis
  town, NC kuh-NAP-(uh-)luhs kəˈnæp(ə)ləs
Kannon
  Japanese festival kahn-(n)awn kɑn(n)ɔːn
Kano
  state, city, Nigeria; school of painters KAHN-ō ˈkɑnoː
Kanpur
  city, India KAHN-PUR ˈkɑnˌpuʳ
Kansa
  N. American people KAN-zuh, KAN-suh ˈkænzə, ˈkænsə
Kansan
  pert. to Kansas KAN-zuhn ˈkænzən
Kansas
  state, river, US KAN-zuhs ˈkænzəs
Kansu
  see Gansu
Kant
  Immanuel, *German philosopher* KAHNT, KANT ˈkɑnt, ˈkænt
Kantian
  pert. to Kant KAHNT-ē-uhn, KANT-ē-uhn ˈkɑntiːən, ˈkæntiːən
Kantianism
  adherence to Kantian philosophy KANT-ē-uh-NIZ-uhm, ˈkæntiːəˌnizəm,
    KAHNT-ē-uh-NIZ-uhm, ˈkɑntiːəˌnizəm,
    KAN-chuh-NIZ-uhm, ˈkæntʃəˌnizəm,
    KAHN-chuh-NIZ-uhm ˈkɑntʃəˌnizəm
Kantner
  Paul, *US rock singer, songwriter* KANT-nuhr ˈkæntnəʳ
Kanto
  region, Japan kahn-tō kɑntoː
Kantorovich
  Leonid Vitaljevich, *Soviet economist,* KUHN-TAWR-uhv-yich, ˌkənˈtɔːrəvjitʃ,
    mathematician (Nobel 1975) ⓢ kan-TAWR-uh-VICH, ⓢ kænˈtɔːrəˌvitʃ,
    KANT-uh-RŌ-vich ˌkæntəˈroːvitʃ
Kantorowicz
  Hermann, *German jurist* kahn-TAWR-uh-VICH kɑnˈtɔːrəˌvitʃ
Kanuri
  lang., people, Nigeria, Niger kuh-NUR-ē kəˈnuriˑ

Foreign Sounds: **ue:** *Fr.* **rue**, *Ger.* **füllen** **uh(r):** *Fr.* **boeuf**, *Ger.* **Höhle** **k̲h̲:** *Ger.* **ich**, *Scot.* **loch** **ḡ:** *Sp.* **amigo** **v̲:** *Sp.* **hablar**
hl: *Welsh* **Llanelli.**   CAPITALS: primary stress.   SMALL CAPS: secondary stress.   ⓢ: U.S. pron.   ⓔ: British pron.

Kao-hsiung
   city, Taiwan   GOW-shē-UNG, GOW-SHUNG   'gauʃiː'uŋ, 'gau'ʃuŋ
Kaolan [Lanzhou]
   city, China   KOW-LAHN   'kau'lɑn
Kaoru
   pers. name, Japanese   kah-ō-rōō   kɑoːruː
Kapadokya [Cappadocia]
   region, Turkey   KAHP-ah-DAWK-yah   ˌkɑpɑ'dɔːkjɑ
Kapellmeister
   German for choirmaster   kuh-PEL-MĪ-stuhr, kah-   kə'pel͵maistəʳ, kɑ-
Kaplan
   Gabriel, *actor, comedian*   KAP-luhn   'kæplən
Kaposi's sarcoma
   skin disease   KAHP-ō-SHĒZ sahr-KŌ-muh,   ˌkɑpoːˌʃiːz sɑʳ'koːmə,
                    KAHP-uh-SĒZ, kuh-PŌ-sēz,   ˌkɑpəˌsiːz, kəˌpoːsiːz,
                    kuh-PŌ-shēz   kəˌpoːʃiːz
Kapunda
   town, Australia   kuh-PUHN-duh   kə'pəndə
Kapuskasing
   town, Ontario   KAP-uh-SKĀ-sing   ˌkæpə'skeːsiŋ
Kapuziner
   "Capuchin," German beer   KAH-PŌŌT-SĒ-nuhr   ˌkɑˌpuːt'siːnəʳ
Kara
   Sea, *Arctic*   KAHR-uh   'kɑrə
Karachai
   former autonomous oblast, USSR   KAR-uh-CHĪ   ˌkærə'tʃɑi
Karachay [Balkar]
   lang., people, Caucasus Mts.   KAR-uh-CHĪ, KAR-uh-CHĪ   ˌkærə'tʃɑi, 'kærəˌtʃɑi
Karachi
   city, Pakistan   kuh-RAHCH-ē   kə'rɑtʃiˑ
Karadeniz Boğazı [Bosporus]
   strait, Turkey   KAHR-uh-duh-NĒZ bō-ĞAHZ-ē   ˌkɑrədə'niːz boː'ɣɑziˑ
Karadzic
   Radovan, *Bosnian Serb political*   KAR-uh-JITS, KAHR-   'kærəˌdʒits, 'kɑr-
     leader
Karajan
   Herbert von, *Austrian conductor*   KAHR-uh-YAHN   'kɑrəˌjɑn
Karakalpak
   lang., republic, Uzbekistan   KAR-uhk-uhl-PAK, KAR-uhk-ahl-PAK   ˌkærəkəl'pæk, ˌkærəkɑl'pæk
Karakoram Range
   mtn. range, Asia   KAR-uh-KŌR-uhm, -KAWR-uhm   ˌkærə'koːrəm, -'kɔːrəm
Karakul
   sheep breed   KAR-uh-kuhl   'kærəkəl
Kara Kum, Qara Qum
   desert, Turkmenistan   KAR-uh KŌŌM, KAHR-uh KŌŌM   ˌkærə 'kuːm, ˌkɑrə 'kuːm
Karamanlis
   Constantine, *president of Greece*   KAHR-uh-MAHN-LĒS,   ˌkɑrəˌmɑn'liːs, ˌkɑrə'mɑnˌliːs
                    KAHR-uh-MAHN-LĒS
Karamazov
   see Brothers Karamazov, The
Karamchand
   pers. name, Gujarati   KUH-ruhm-CHUHND   'kərəmˌtʃənd
Karame
   Rashid, *Lebanese statesman*   KAHR-uh-MĀ   'kɑrəˌmeː

Key (col. 2):   a: fad   ā: fade   ah: father   ar: marry   aw: law   e: fed   ē: feed   er: merry   i: hid   ī: hide   ō: coat   ōō: boot
oi: boy   ow: now   u: put   uh: above   uhr: bird   ch: chop   ng: ring   sh: show   th: thick   <u>th</u>: this   zh: measure

Karamojong
  lang., people, Uganda, Kenya   KAR-uh-MŌ-JAHNG   ˌkærə'moːˌdʒaŋ

Karankawa
  N. American people   kuh-RANG-kuh-WAW   kə'ræŋkəˌwɔː

Karawanken [Caravanche]
  Alpine mtn. range   KAHR-uh-VAHNG-kuhn   ˌkarə'vaŋkən

Karbala [Kerbela]
  governorate, town, Iraq   KAHR-buh-luh   'karbələ

Kareah
  Biblical name   kuh-RĒ-uh, kah-RĀ-ah<u>kh</u>   kə'riːə, ka'reːax

Kareem
  pers. name   kuh-RĒM   kə'riːm

Karel
  1. pers. name, Czech   KAH-REL   'kaːˌrel
  2. Dutch   KAHR-uhl   'kaːrəl

Karelian
  lang., people, Russia   kuh-RĒ-lē-uhn, kuh-RĒL-yuhn   kə'riːliːən, kə'riːljən

Karen
  1. pers. name   KAR-uhn, KAHR-uhn   'kærən, 'karən
  2. Danish, Norwegian   KAHR-uhn   'karən
  3. lang., people, Burma, Thailand   kuh-REN   kə'ren

Karénina, Anna
  see Anna Karénina

Kareshkova
  Valentina, *cosmonaut, USSR*   kuh-RESH-kuh-vuh   kə'reʃkəvə

Kari
  lang., Chad, Cameroon, Central   KAR-ē, KAHR-ē   'kæriˑ, 'kariˑ
    African Rep.

Kariba
  dam, Zimbabwe, Zambia   kuh-RĒ-buh   kə'riːbə

Karimata
  Islands, *island group, Indonesia*   KAHR-uh-MAHT-uh   ˌkarə'maṭə

Karin
  pers. name   KAHR-uhn, KAR-uhn, KER-uhn,   'karən, 'kærən, 'kerən, kə'rin
    kuh-RIN

Karkaa
  Biblical name   KAHR-kā-uh, kahr-KAH-ah, kahr-KAH   'karkeːə, kar'ka-a, kar'ka

Karkor
  Biblical name   KAHR-KAWR, kahr-KAWR   'karˌkɔːr, kar'kɔːr

Karl
  1. pers. name, English, German   KAHRL   'karl
  2. Danish, Dutch, Norwegian,   KAHRL   'karl
    Swedish
  3. Finnish, Russian   KAHRL   'kaːrl
  4. French   KAHRL   kaːrl

Karle
  Jerome, *US physicist (Nobel 1985)*   KAHRL   'karl

Karlfeldt
  E. A., *Swedish poet (Nobel 1931)*   KAHRL-FELT   'karlˌfelt

Karlheinz
  pers. name, German   KAHRL-HĪNTS   'karlˌhaints

Karl Marx Stadt [Chemnitz]
  city, Germany   kahrl MAHRK SHTAHT   karl 'mark ˌʃtat

Karloff
  Boris, *US actor*   KAHR-LAWF, -LAHF, -luhf   'karˌlɔːf, -ˌlaf, -ləf

---

Foreign Sounds: ue: *Fr.* **rue**, *Ger.* **füllen** uh(r): *Fr.* **boeuf**, *Ger.* **Höhle** <u>kh</u>: *Ger.* **ich**, *Scot.* lo**ch** g̃: *Sp.* amigo v̱: *Sp.* hablar
hl: *Welsh* **Ll**anelli. CAPITALS: primary stress. SMALL CAPS: secondary stress. Ⓢ: U.S. pron. Ⓔ: British pron.

Karlovac
  city, Croatia   KAHR-luh-VAHTS   'kɑːᵣləˌvaːts
Karlovacko
  Yugoslavian beer   KAHR-lō-VAHT-skō   ˌkarloː'vatskoː
Karlsbad
  city, Czech republic   KAHRLZ-BAHT   'kɑᵣlzˌbɑt
Karlsruhe
  city, Germany   KAHRLZ-RŌŌ-uh   'kɑᵣlzˌruːə
Karmal
  Babrak, *president, Afghanistan*   KAHR-muhl   'kɑᵣməl
Karnaim
  Biblical name   kahr-NĀ-uhm, kahr-NAH-yim   kɑᵣ'neːəm, kɑr'nɑjim
Karnak
  village, temple, Egypt   KAHR-NAK   'kɑᵣˌnæk
Karnataka
  state, India   kahr-NAHT-uh-kuh   kɑᵣ'nɑtəkə
Karnische Alpen [Carnic Alps]
  Alpine mtn. range   KAHR-nish-uh AHL-puhn   'kɑᵣniʃə 'ɑlpən
Kärnten
  state, Austria   KERNT-n   'keᵣntn̩
Karok
  N. American people   kuh-RAHK   kə'rɑk
Karol
  pers. name   KAR-uhl, KER-uhl   'kærəl, 'kerəl
Károly
  pers. name, Hungarian   KAH-rōl(-yuh)   'kɑːroːlj
Karolyi
  Bela, *Hungarian gymnastics coach*   KAHR-uhl-yē, ⑤ kuh-RŌ-lē   'karəlji·, ⑤ kə'roːli·
Karpov
  Anatoly, *Russian chess master*   KAHR-PAWF   'kɑːᵣˌpɔːf
Karras
  Alex, *US actor*   KAR-uhs, KER-uhs   'kærəs, 'kerəs
Karrer
  Paul, *Swiss chemist (Nobel 1937)*   KAHR-uhr   'kɑrəᵣ
Karsavina
  Tamara, *Russian dancer*   KUHR-SAHV-yuh-nuh   ˌkəᵣ'saːvjənə
Kartah
  Biblical name   KAHRT-uh, kahr-TAH   'kɑᵣt̪ə, kɑr'tɑ
Kartan
  Biblical name   KAHR-TAN, kahr-TAHN   'kɑᵣˌtæn, kɑr'tɑn
Karuah
  river, Australia   kuh-RŌŌ-uh   kə'ruːə
Kasai
  river, Africa   kuh-SĪ   kə'sɑi
Kasamansa [Casamance]
  river, region, Senegal   KAHS-uh-MAHN-suh   ˌkasə'mɑnsə
Kasavubu
  Joseph, *Zairian political leader*   KAH-sah-VŌŌ-BŌŌ   ˌkasɑ'vuːˌbuː
Kasbah, Casbah
  Arab quarter of city, esp. Algiers   KAZ-BAH, KAHZ-BAH   'kæzˌbɑ, 'kɑzˌbɑ
Kasel
  German wine   KAH-suhl   'kɑːsəl
Kashmir, Cashmere
  region, India   KASH-MIR, KAZH-MIR, kash-MIR,   'kæʃˌmiᵣ, 'kæʒˌmiᵣ, kæʃ'miᵣ,
                                          kazh-MIR   kæʒ'miᵣ

Key (col. 2):   a: fad ã: fade ah: father ar: marry aw: law e: fed ē: feed er: merry i: hid ī: hide ō: coat ōō: boot
oi: boy   ow: now   u: put   uh: above   uhr: bird   ch: chop   ng: ring   sh: show   th: thick   th: this   zh: measure

Kashmiri
  lang., people, India & Pakistan   kazh-MIR-ē, kash-   kæʒˈmiriˑ, kæʃ-

Kashubian [Cassubian]
  lang., Europe   kash-OO-bē-uhn   kæʃˈuːbiːən

Kasim
  pers. name, Persian   KAHS-im   ˈkɑːsim

Kasimir
  pers. name, German   KAHZ-ē-MIR   ˈkɑziːˌmiʳ

Kasiwihara
  Ken, *TV journalist*   KAHS-uh-wuh-HAR-uh, -HAHR-uh   ˌkɑsəwəˈhærə, -ˈhɑrə

Kaska
  N. American people   KAS-kuh   ˈkæskə

Kaskaskia
  river, college, IL   kas-KAS-kē-uh   kæsˈkæskiːə

Kaspar
  1. pers. name, Danish   KAHS-PAHR   ˈkɑːsˌpɑr
  2. Dutch   KAHS-PAHR   ˈkɑsˌpɑr
  3. German   KAHS-PAHR   ˈkɑsˌpɑʳ
  4. Hungarian   KAHSH-PAHR   ˈkɑʃˌpɑr

Kasparov
  Gary, *Armenian chess player*   kuh-SPAHR-uhf, Ⓢ kuh-SPAHR-AWF, -AHF; KAS-puh-RAWF, -RAHF   kəˈspɑrəf, Ⓢ kəˈspɑrˌɔːf, -ˌɑf; ˈkæspəˌrɔːf, -ˌrɑf

Kassebaum
  Nancy, *US politician*   KAS-uh-BAWM, -BOWM   ˈkæsəˌbɔːm, -ˌbɑum

Kasserine
  village, Tunisia   KAHS-uh-RĒN   ˈkɑsəˌriːn

Kassites
  ancient people of Iran   KAS-ĪTS   ˈkæsˌɑits

Kasten
  Robert W., Jr., *US politician*   KAS-tuhn   ˈkæstən

Kastler
  Alfred, *French physicist (Nobel 1966)*   kahst-LER   kɑːstler

Kastrioti [Scanderbeg]
  George, *Albanian revolutionary leader*   KAHS-trē-ŌT-ē   ˌkɑstriːˈoːʈiˑ

Kastrup
  airport, Copenhagen   KAHS-trup   ˈkɑstrup

Katahdin, Ktaadn
  mtn., ME   kuh-TAHD-n   kəˈtɑdn̩

Katanga
  former name of Shaba, Zaire   kuh-TAHNG-guh, kuh-TANG-guh   kəˈtɑŋgə, kəˈtæŋgə

Katangese
  pert. to Katanga   kuh-tahng-GĒZ, -GĒS   kətɑŋˈgiːz, -ˈgiːs

Katarina
  pers. name, Russian   KAH-tah-RĒ-nah   ˌkɑːtɑːˈriːnɑː

Katayev
  Yevgeny Petrovich, *Russian writer* (pseudonym Yevgeny Petrov)   KUH-TAH-yuhf   ˌkəˈtɑjəf

Kate
  pers. name   KĀT   ˈkeːt

Katerina
  pers. name   KAT-uh-RĒ-nuh   ˌkæʈəˌriːnə

Katharevousa, Katharevusa
  Modern Greek literary lang.   KAHTH-uh-REV-oo-suh, KATH-   ˌkɑθəˈrevuːsə, ˌkæθ-

---

Foreign Sounds: ue: *Fr.* **rue**, *Ger.* **füllen**   uh(r): *Fr.* **boeuf**, *Ger.* **Höhle**   <u>kh</u>: *Ger.* **ich**, *Scot.* **loch**   g̱: *Sp.* **amigo**   v̱: *Sp.* **hablar**
hl: *Welsh* **Llanelli**.   CAPITALS: primary stress.   SMALL CAPS: secondary stress.   Ⓢ: U.S. pron.   Ⓔ: British pron.

Katharina

1. character in Taming of the   KAT-uh-RĒ-nuh, KATH-   ˌkæt̮əˈriːnə, ˌkæθ-
   Shrew, *Shakespeare; pers. name*

2. pers. name, German, Hungarian   KAHT-ah-RĒ-nah   ˌkɑtɑˈriːnɑ

Katharine

1. pers. name   KATH-(uh-)ruhn   ˈkæθ(ə)rən

2. German   KAHT-ah-RĒ-nuh   ˌkɑtɑˈriːnə

Käthe

pers. name, German   KET-uh   ˈketə

Katherine

1. river, town, Australia   KATH-uh-RĪN   ˈkæθəˌrɑin

2. pers. name   KATH-(uh-)ruhn   ˈkæθ(ə)rən

Kathie

pers. name   KATH-ē   ˈkæθiˑ

Kathleen

pers. name   kath-LĒN   kæθˈliːn

Kathryn

pers. name   KATH-ruhn   ˈkæθrən

Kathy

pers. name   KATH-ē   ˈkæθiˑ

Katie

pers. name   KĀT-ē   ˈkeːtiˑ

Katmai

National Park and Preserve, *King*   KAT-MĪ   ˈkætˌmɑi
   Salmon, AK

Katmandu

city, Nepal   KAT-man-DOO, KAHT-mahn-DOO,   ˌkætmænˈduː, ˌkɑtmɑnˈduː,
   -muhn-DOO   -mənˈduː

Kato

pers. name   KĀT-ō   ˈkeːt̮oː

Katoikiai

Seleucid rural colonies   kah-TOI-kē-Ī   kɑˈtɔikiːˌɑi

Katoomba

waterfall, Australia   kuh-TOOM-buh   kəˈtuːmbə

Katowice

city, Poland   KAHT-uh-VĒT-suh   ˌkɑːt̮əˈviːtsə

Katrina

pers. name   kuh-TRĒ-nuh, ka-TRĒ-nuh   kəˈtriːnə, kæˈtriːnə

Katrine

loch, Scotland   KA-truhn   ˈkætrən

Katsunori

pers. name, Japanese   kaht-su-nō-rē   kɑtsunoːriː

Katsunosuke

pers. name, Japanese   kaht-su-nō-su-ke   kɑtsunoːsuke

Katsushika

pers name, Japanese   kaht-soo-shē-kah   kɑtsuːʃiːkɑ

Kattath

Biblical name   KAT-ATH, kah-TAHT   ˈkæt̮ˌæθ, kɑˈtɑt

Kattegat, Cattegat

Sound & Belts, *North Sea*   KAT-i-GAT, KAHT-i-GAHT   ˈkæt̮iˌgæt, ˈkɑt̮iˌgɑt

Katy

city, TX; pers. name   KĀT-ē   ˈkeːtiˑ

Katz

Bernard, *German-born British*   KATS   ˈkæts
   biophysicist (Nobel 1970)

Key (col. 2):   a: f**a**d   ā: f**a**de   ah: f**a**ther   ar: m**arr**y   aw: l**aw**   e: f**e**d   ē: f**ee**d   er: m**err**y   i: h**i**d   ī: h**i**de   ō: c**oa**t   oo: b**oo**t
oi: b**oy**   ow: n**ow**   u: p**u**t   uh: **a**bove   uhr: b**ir**d   ch: **ch**op   ng: ri**ng**   sh: **sh**ow   th: **th**ick   <u>th</u>: **th**is   zh: mea**s**ure

Katzenjammer Kids
  comic strip   KAT-suhn-JAM-uhr   'kætsən͵dʒæməʳ
Kau
  division, HI   kah-O͞O   kɑ'uː
Kauai
  county, HI   KOW-Ī   'kɑu͵ɑi
Kaufman
  George S., *US dramatist*   KAWF-muhn   'kɔːfmən
Kaufmann's
  US department store chain   KAWF-muhnz, KAHF-muhnz, KOWF-   'kɔːfmənz, 'kɑfmənz, 'kɑuf-
Kaukauna
  city, WI; cheese spread   kaw-KAW-nuh   kɔː'kɔːnə
Kaunas [Kovno]
  city, Lithuania   KOW-nuhs, -NAHS   'kɑunəs, -͵nɑs
Kaunda
  Kenneth, *president, Zambia*   kah-O͞ON-duh   kɑ'uːndə
Kavanaugh
  Field, *ballpark, Little Rock, AR*   KAV-uh-NAW   'kævə͵nɔː
Kaváfis [Cavafy]
  Konstantínos Pétrou, *Greek poet*   kah-VAH-fēs   kɑ'vɑfiːs
Kavkaz [Caucasus]
  mtn. range, between Europe and Asia   KUHF-KAHZ   ͵kəf'kɑz
Kaw
  N. American people; usual Kansan   KAW   'kɔː
    name of Kansas River
Kawabata
  Yasunari, *Japanese author (Nobel*   kah-wah-bah-tah,   kɑwɑbɑtɑ, Ⓢ ͵kɑwə'bɑtə,
    1968)   Ⓢ KAH-wuh-BAHT-uh,   kə'wɑbətə
          kuh-WAHB-uht-uh
Kawaihae
  village, HI   KAH-wuh-HĪ   ͵kawə'hai
Kawasaki
  1. city, Japan   kah-wah-sahk-ē   kɑwɑsɑki·
  2. tdmk for a motorcycle   KAH-wuh-SAHK-ē, KOW-uh-SAHK-ē   ͵kɑwə'sɑki·, ͵kɑuə'sɑki·
Kazak, Kazakh
  lang., people, Kazakhstan, China,   kuh-ZAHK, kuh-ZAK   kə'zɑk, kə'zæk
    Mongolian PR, Afghanistan
Kazakh
  republic, Asia   kuh-ZAHK, kuh-ZAK   kə'zɑk, kə'zæk
Kazakhstan [Kazakh]
  republic, Asia   kuh-ZUHK͟H-STAHN, kuh-zahk-STAHN,   kə͵zəx'stɑn, kəzɑk'stɑn,
          kuh-zak-STAN   kəzæk'stæn
Kazakistan [Kazakh]
  republic, Asia   kuh-zahk-uh-STAHN,   kəzɑkə'stɑn, kəzækə'stæn
          kuh-zak-uh-STAN
Kazan
  1. Elia, US actor; river, Canada   kuh-ZAN   kə'zæn
  2. city, Russia   kuh-ZAHN(-yuh)   kə'zɑːn(jə)
Kazantzakis
  Nikos, *Greek writer*   KAHZ-ahn(t)-ZAHK-ēs,   ͵kɑzɑn(t)'zɑkiːs,
          KAHZ-ahn(t)-SAHK-ēs   ͵kɑzɑn(t)'sɑkiːs
Kazbek
  peak, Caucasus Mts.   kuhz-BYEK   kəz'bjek
Kazimierz
  pers. name, Polish   kah-ZĒM-yesh   kɑː'ziːmjeʃ

Foreign Sounds: **ue**: *Fr.* **rue**, *Ger.* f**ü**llen   **uh(r)**: *Fr.* b**oeuf**, *Ger.* H**ö**hle   <u>kh</u>: *Ger.* i**ch**, *Scot.* lo**ch**   <u>g</u>: *Sp.* ami**g**o   <u>v</u>: *Sp.* ha**b**lar
hl: *Welsh* **Ll**anelli.   CAPITALS: primary stress.   SMALL CAPS: secondary stress.   Ⓢ: U.S. pron.   Ⓔ: British pron.

Kazimir
  pers. name, Russian — kuhz-yim-YIR — kəzjim'jir
Kea
  parrot — KĒ-uh — 'kiːə
Keaau
  town, HI — KĀ-uh-OW, KĀ-uh-AH-ŌŌ — ˌkeːə'ɑu, ˌkeːə'ɑˌuː
Kéa [Keos]
  island, Greece — KĀ-uh, KĒ-uh — 'keːə, 'kiːə
Keach
  Stacy, Jr., *US entertainer* — KĒCH — 'kiːtʃ
Kean
  Edmund, *English actor;* Thomas — KĒN — 'kiːn
    H., *US politician*
Keanu
  pers. name (K. Reeves) — kē-AN-ŌŌ — kiː'ænuː
Kearney
  1. county, city, state college, NE — KAHR-nē — 'kɑʳniˑ
  2. street, San Francisco, CA — KUHR-nē — 'kəʳniˑ
Kearny
  county, KS; town, NJ — KAHR-nē — 'kɑʳniˑ
Keating
  Thomas Arthur, *US football player* — KĒT-ing — 'kiːʈiŋ
Keaton
  Diane, *US actress;* Michael, *US* — KĒT-n — 'kiːtn̩
    actor
Keaton
  Buster, *US comedian* — KĒT-n — 'kiːtn̩
Keaton
  Buster, *US comedian* — KĒT-n — 'kiːtn̩
Keats
  John, *English poet* — KĒTS — 'kiːts
Keatsian
  pert. to Keats — KĒT-sē-uhn — 'kiːtsiːən
Keb [Geb]
  Egyptian earth god — KEB — 'keb
Keble
  college, Oxford Univ. — KĒ-buhl — 'kiːbəl
Kedah
  state, Malaysia — KED-uh — 'kedə
Kedar
  Biblical name — KĒD-uhr — 'kiːdəʳ
Kedemah
  Biblical name — KED-uh-muh, KE-duh-MAH — 'kedəmə, 'kedəˌmɑ
Kedemoth
  Biblical name — KED-uh-MAHTH, kuh-DĒ-MAHTH, — 'kedəˌmɑθ, kə'diːˌmɑθ,
    -MAWTH; kuh-de-MŌT — -ˌmɔːθ; kəde'moːt
Kedesh
  Biblical name — KĒ-DESH, KED-esh — 'kiːˌdeʃ, 'kedeʃ
Kedron [Kidron]
  valley, Jordan — KED-ruhn, KĒ-druhn — 'kedrən, 'kiːdrən
Keebler
  US baking co. — KĒ-bluhr — 'kiːbləʳ
Keenen
  pers. name — KĒ-nuhn — 'kiːnən

Key (col. 2):   a: fad ā: fade ah: father ar: marry aw: law e: fed ē: feed er: merry i: hĭd ī: hīde ō: coat ōō: boot
oi: boy ow: now u: put uh: above uhr: bĭrd ch: chop ng: ring sh: show th: thick th̲: this zh: measure

Keeshond		
dog breed	KĀS-HAWNT	'keːs,hɔːnt
Keewatin		
district, Canada	kē-WĀT-n	kiː'weːtn̩
Kefallinía [Cephalonia]		
region, Greece	KEF-uh-lē-NĒ-uh	,kefəliː'niːə
Kefauver		
Estes, *US political leader*	KĒ-FAW-vuhr	'kiː,fɔːvəʳ
Keffer		
pers. name	KEF-uhr	'kefəʳ
Keflavik		
port, Iceland	KYEB-luh-VĒK, Ⓢ KEF-luh-VĒK	'kjeblə,viːk, Ⓢ 'keflə,viˑk
Kehelathah		
Biblical name	KĒ-(h)uh-LĀ-thuh, kuh-HĒ-luh-thuh, kuh-he-LAH-tah	,kiː(h)ə'leːθə, kə'hiːləθə, kəhe'lɑtɑ
Keighley		
town, borough, England	KĒTH-lē	'kiːθliˑ
Keijo		
Japanese for Seoul, *S. Korea*	kā-jō	keːdʒɔː
Keilah		
Biblical name	kē-Ī-luh, kuh-ē-LAH	kiː'ɑilə, kəiː'lɑ
Keillor		
Garrison, *US broadcaster*	KĒ-luhr	'kiːləʳ
Keir		
pers. name	KIR	'kiʳ
Keisha		
pers. name	KĒ-shuh	'kiːʃə
Keishiro		
pers. name, Japanese	kā-shē-rō	keːʃiːrɔː
Keisuke		
pers. name, Japanese	kā-suk-e	keːsuke
Keith		
pers. name	KĒTH	'kiːθ
Kekchi, Quekchi		
lang., people, Guatemala	KEK-chē	'kektʃiˑ
Kekkonen		
Urho, *president, Finland*	KEK-uh-NEN, KEK-uh-nuhn	'kekə,nen, 'kekənən
Kekulé von Stradonitz		
Friedrich August, *German chemist*	KĀ-ko͞o-LĀ fawn SHTRAHD-ō-nits	'keːkuː,leː fɔːn 'ʃtrɑdoːnits
Kelaiah		
Biblical name	kuh-LĪ-uh, kuh-LĀ-uh, KEL-ah-YAH	kə'lɑiə, kə'leːə, ,kelɑ'jɑ
Kelita		
Biblical name	kuh-LĪT-uh, KEL-uht-uh, kuh-lē-TAH	kə'lɑiţə, 'keləţə, kəliː'tɑ
Kelley, Kellie		
pers. name	KEL-ē	'keliˑ
Kellogg		
Frank B., *US jurist, statesman* (Nobel 1929); *US cereal co.*	KEL-AHG, KEL-AWG	'kel,ɑg, 'kel,ɔːg
Kells		
city, Ireland	KELZ	'kelz
Kelly		
pers. name	KEL-ē	'keliˑ
Kelson		
pers. name	KEL-suhn	'kelsən

Foreign Sounds: ue: *Fr.* **rue**, *Ger.* **füllen** uh(r): *Fr.* **boeuf**, *Ger.* **Höhle** kh: *Ger.* **ich**, *Scot.* **loch** g̱: *Sp.* **amigo** v̱: *Sp.* **hablar** hl: *Welsh* **Llanelli**. CAPITALS: primary stress. SMALL CAPS: secondary stress. Ⓢ: U.S. pron. Ⓔ: British pron.

Kelvin
   temperature scale; pers. name   KEL-vuhn   'kelvən

Kelvinator
   tdmk for home appliances   KEL-vuh-NĀT-uhr   'kelvə‚neːʈəʳ

Kemal Atatürk
   Turkish political leader   ke-MAHL AH-tah-TUERK, ⓢ kuh-MAL AT-uh-TUHRK   keˈmɑl ‚ɑtaˈtyːrk, ⓢ kəˈmæl ˈæʈə‚təʳk

Kemeny
   John George, *US mathematician, computer scientist, and educator*   KEM-uh-nē   'keməni·

Kemi
   river, port, Finland   KEM-ē   'kemi·

Kemmerer
   town, WY   KEM-uhr   'keməʳ

Kemp
   Jack F., *US politician*   KEMP   'kemp

Kempis
   Thomas à, *German ecclesiastic, author*   KEM-puhs   'kempəs

Kemuel
   Biblical name   kuhm-YOO-uhl, KEM-yuh-WEL, kuh-mOO-EL   kəmˈjuːəl, 'kemjə‚wel, kəmuːˈel

Ken
   pers. name   KEN   'ken

Kenai Fjords
   National Park, Kenai, AK   KĒ-NĪ FYAWRDZ   ‚kiː‚nɑi 'fjɔːʳdz

Kenai Peninsula
   division, AK   KĒ-NĪ   'kiː‚nɑi

Kenan
   Biblical name   KĒ-nuhn, kā-NAHN   'kiːnən, keːˈnɑn

Kenansville
   town, NC   KĒ-nuhnz-VIL   'kiːnənz‚vil

Kenath
   Biblical name   KĒ-NATH, kuh-NAHT   'kiː‚næθ, kəˈnɑt

Kenaz
   Biblical name   KĒ-NAZ, kuh-NAHZ   'kiː‚næz, kəˈnɑz

Kendall
   Edward C., *US chemist (Nobel 1950);* Henry W., *US physicist (Nobel 1990)*   KEN-dl   'kendl̩

Kendra
   pers. name   KEN-druh   'kendrə

Kendrew
   Sir John Cowdrey, *English biochemist (Nobel 1962)*   KEN-droo   'kendruː

Kendrick
   pers. name   KEN-drik   'kendrik

Keneally
   Thomas, *Australian novelist*   kuh-NĒL-ē   kəˈniːli·

Kenelm
   pers. name   KEN-ELM   'ken‚elm

Kenesaw
   pers. name   KEN-uh-SAW   'kenə‚sɔː

Kenezite
   Biblical name   KĒ-nuh-ZĪT   'kiːnə‚zɑit

Key (col. 2):   **a:** fad   **ā:** fade   **ah:** father   **ar:** marry   **aw:** law   **e:** fed   **ē:** feed   **er:** merry   **i:** hid   **ī:** hide   **ō:** coat   **ōō:** boot   **oi:** boy   **ow:** now   **u:** put   **uh:** above   **uhr:** bird   **ch:** chop   **ng:** ring   **sh:** show   **th:** thick   <u>th</u>: this   **zh:** measure

Kenichi
  pers. name, Japanese   ken-ē-chē   keni·tʃi·

Kenilworth
  town, England   KEN-l-WUHRTH   'kenl̩ˌwəʳθ

Kenite
  Biblical name   KEN-ĪT, KĒ-NĪT   'kenˌait, 'kiːˌnait

Kenizzite
  Biblical name   KEN-i-ZĪT   'keniˌzait

Kenji
  pers. name, Japanese   ken-jē   kendʒiː

Kennebec
  river, county, ME   KEN-uh-BEK, KEN-uh-BEK   ˌkenə'bek, 'kenəˌbek

Kennebunk
  town, ME   KEN-uh-BUHNGK, KEN-ē-;   'kenəˌbəŋk, 'keni·-;
                        KEN-uh-BUHNGK, KEN-ē-   ˌkenə'bəŋk, ˌkeni·-

Kennebunkport
  town, ME   KEN-uh-BUHNGK-PŌRT, KEN-ē-,   ˌkenə'bəŋkˌpoːʳt, ˌkeni·-,
                        -PAWRT   -ˌpoːʳt

Kennedale
  town, TX   KEN-uh-DĀL   'kenəˌdeːl

Kennedy
  Edward Moore, *US senator;* John   KEN-uhd-ē   'kenədi·
    F., *35th US president;* Robert F.,
    US attorney general

Kennesaw
  city, mtn., college, GA   KEN-uh-saw   'kenəsɔ·

Kenneth
  pers. name   KEN-uhth   'kenəθ

Kennewick
  city, WA   KEN-uh-wik   'kenəwik

Kenny
  pers. name   KEN-ē   'keni·

Kenogami
  river, lake, Canada   kuh-NAHG-uh-mē   kə'nagəmi·

Kenosha
  city, county, WI   kuh-NŌ-shuh   kə'noːʃə

Kensington
  pers. name   KEN-zing-tuhn   'kenziŋtən

Kensington and Chelsea
  borough, England   KEN-zing-tuhn uhn CHEL-sē   'kenziŋtən ən 'tʃelsi·

Kent
  county, England; pers. name   KENT   'kent

Kentaro
  pers. name, Japanese   ken-tah-rō   kentaroː

Kentucky
  state, US   kuhn-TUHK-ē, ken-TUHK-ē   kən'təki·, ken'təki·

Kenya
  mtn., republic, Africa   KEN-yuh, *(esp. before independence)*   'kenjə, *(esp. before*
                        KĒN-yuh   *independence)* 'kiːnjə

Kenyan
  adj.   KEN-yuhn, KĒN-yuhn   'kenjən, 'kiːnjən

Kenyapithecus Wickeri
  early hominid   KEN-yuh-PITH-i-kuhs WIK-uhr-ē,   ˌkenjə'piθikəs 'wikəri·,
                        KĒN-yuh-   ˌkiːnjə-

Foreign Sounds: ue: *Fr.* **rue,** *Ger.* f**ü**llen   uh(r): *Fr.* b**oeu**f, *Ger.* H**ö**hle   <u>kh</u>: *Ger.* i**ch**, *Scot.* lo**ch**   g̱: *Sp.* ami**g**o   v̱: *Sp.* ha**b**lar
hl: *Welsh* **Ll**anelli.   CAPITALS: primary stress.   SMALL CAPS: secondary stress.   Ⓢ: U.S. pron.   Ⓔ: British pron.

Kenyatta
Jomo, *president, Kenya*   ken-YAHT-uh   ken'jɑtə

Kenyon
John, *US phonetician*   KEN-yuhn   'kenjən

Keogh
savings plan   KĒ-ō   'kiːoː

Keohane
Nannerl O., *US college president*   kō-HĀN, kō-HAN   koː'heːn, koː'hæn

Keokuk
county, IA   KĒ-uh-KUHK   'kiːə‚kək

Keosauqua
town, IA   KĒ-uh-SAW-kwuh, -SAHK-wuh   ‚kiːə'soːkwə, -'sɑkwə

Keos [Kéa]
island, Greece   KĒ-AHS, KĒ-AWS   'kiː‚ɑs, 'kiː‚oːs

Kepler
Johannes, *German astronomer*   KEP-luhr   'keplər

Ker
William Paton, *British scholar*   KER, KUHR, KAHR   'ker, 'kər, 'kɑr

Kerak, El [Al-Karak, Kir Moab, Le Crac]
town, fortress, Jordan   el KAR-uhk, el KER-uhk   el 'kærək, el 'kerək

Kerala
state, India   KER-uh-luh   'kerələ

Kerang
lake district, Australia   kuh-RANG   kə'ræŋ

Kerbela [Karbala]
governorate, town, Iraq   KUHR-buh-luh   'kərbələ

Kerch
peninsula, port, Crimea   KERCH   'kertʃ

Keren-happuch
Biblical name   KER-uhn-HAP-uhk, KE-ren-hah-POOKH   'kerən'hæpək, 'kerenhɑ'puːx

Kerensky
Aleksandr Feodorovich, *Russian revolutionary*   KYER-yin-skyiy, ⑤ kuh-REN-skē   'kjerjinskjij, ⑤ kə'renski·

Keres
1. people, lang., N. America   KĀ-rās   'keːreːs
2. the Greek fates or destinies   KER-ēz   'keriːz

Keresan
N. American people   KER-uh-suhn   'kerəsən

Kerguelen
archipelago, Indian Ocean   KUHR-guh-luhn, KUHR-guh-LEN   'kərgələn, ‚kərgə'len

Kerioth
Biblical name   KIR-ē-AHTH, KER-; kuh-rē-ŌT   'kiriː‚ɑθ, 'ker-; kəriː'oːt

Kerioth-hezron
Biblical name   KIR-ē-AHTH-HEZ-RAHN, KER-; kuh-rē-ŌT-khets-RŌN   'kiriː‚ɑθ'hez‚rɑn, 'ker-; kəriː'oːtxets'roːn

Kérkira [Corfu]
island, Greece   KER-ki-ruh   'kerkirə

Kerman
city, CA   KUHR-muhn   'kərmən

Kermān [Kirman]
prov, city, Iran   kuhr-MAHN, ker-MAHN   kər'mɑn, ker'mɑn

Kermit
television and movie frog; pers. name   KUHR-muht, KUHR-MIT   'kərmət, 'kər‚mit

---

Key (col. 2):   a: f**a**d   ā: f**a**de   ah: f**a**ther   ar: m**ar**ry   aw: l**aw**   e: f**e**d   ē: f**ee**d   er: m**er**ry   i: h**i**d   ī: h**i**de   ō: c**oa**t   oo: b**oo**t
oi: b**oy**   ow: n**ow**   u: p**u**t   uh: **a**bove   uhr: b**ir**d   ch: **ch**op   ng: ri**ng**   sh: **sh**ow   th: **th**ick   <u>th</u>: **th**is   zh: mea**s**ure

Kermode
    Frank, *US literary critic*   KAHR-muhd-ē   'kɑʳmədiˑ

Kern
    Jerome, *US composer*   KUHRN   'kəʳn

Keros
    Biblical name   KIR-AHS, KER-; ke-RAWS   'kir‚ɑs, 'ker-; ke'rɔːs

Kerouac
    Jack, *US novelist*   KER-uh-WAK   'kerə‚wæk

Kerr
    1. Deborah, *US entertainer*   KAHR, KER, KUHR   'kɑʳ, 'keʳ, 'kəʳ
    2. pers. name   KUHR, ⓔ KUHR, KAHR, KER   'kəʳ, ⓔ 'kəʳ, 'kɑʳ, 'keʳ

Kerrigan
    Thomas Anthony, *US poet, editor,*   KER-uh-guhn   'kerəgən
        translator

Kerry
    pers. name   KAR-ē, KER-ē   'kæriˑ, 'keriˑ

Kershner
    Irvin, *film director*   KUHRSH-nuhr   'kəʳʃnəʳ

Kertész
    André, *US photographer*   kuhr-TEZ   kəʳ'tez

Kesey
    Ken, *US writer*   KĒ-zē   'kiːziˑ

Keswick
    town, England   KEZ-ik   'kezik

Keszthely
    commune, Hungary   KEST-HĀ   'kest‚heː

Ket
    lang., people, river, Russia   KET   'ket

Ketcham
    Henry King, *US cartoonist*   KECH-uhm   'ketʃəm

Ketchikan
    town, AK   KECH-i-KAN   'ketʃi‚kæn

Ketchwayo [Cetewayo]
    see Cetshwayo

Kettering
    city, OH   KET-uh-ring   'ketəriŋ

Keturah
    Biblical name   kuh-TUR-uh   kə'turə

Keuka
    lake, NY   KYOO-kuh, kā-YOO-kuh   'kjuːkə, keː'juːkə

Kevin
    pers. name   KEV-uhn   'kevən

Kew
    parish, gardens, London, England;   KYOO   'kjuː
        city, Australia

Kewanee
    city, IL   kuh-WAHN-ē   kə'wɑniˑ

Kewaunee
    county, WI   ki-WAHN-ē   ki'wɑniˑ

Keweenaw
    county, MI   KĒ-wuh-NAW   'kiːwə‚nɔː

Keya Paha
    river, county, NE   KĒ-(y)uh PAH-hah   'kiː(j)ə 'pɑhɑ

Keyes
    Frances Parkinson, *US novelist*   KĪZ   'kɑiz

Foreign Sounds: ue: *Fr.* **rue**, *Ger.* f**ü**llen   uh(r): *Fr.* b**oeu**f, *Ger.* H**öh**le   <u>kh</u>: *Ger.* i**ch**, *Scot.* lo**ch**   g̲: *Sp.* ami**g**o   v̲: *Sp.* ha**b**lar   hl: *Welsh* **Ll**anelli.   CAPITALS: primary stress.   SMALL CAPS: secondary stress.   ⓢ: U.S. pron.   ⓔ: British pron.

Keynes
  1. John, *English economist*   KĀNZ   'keːnz
  2. see Horsted Keynes, Milton
    Keynes
Keynesian
  pert. to J. Keynes   KĀN-zē-uhn   'keːnziːən
Keyser
  city, WV   KĪ-zuhr   'kɑizəʳ
Kezia, Keziah
  Biblical name   kuh-ZĪ-uh, kuht-sē-AH   kə'zɑiə, kətsiː'ɑ
Keziz
  Biblical name   KĒ-ziz, kuh-TSĒTS   'kiːziz, kə'tsiːts
Khabarovsk
  city, Russia   k͟huh-BAHR-uhfsk   xə'bɑːrəfsk
Khabarovsk Krai
  territory, Russia   k͟huh-BAHR-uhfsk KRĪ   xə'bɑːrəfsk 'krɑi
Khachaturian
  Aram, *Armenian composer*   KHUHCH-i-tur-YAHN,   ˌxətʃitur'jɑːn,
           ⑤ KAHCH-uh-TUR-ē-uhn, KACH-   ⑤ ˌkatʃə'turiːən, ˌkætʃ-
Khadafy
  see Qadhafi
Khakas, Khakass
  lang., people, region, Russia   k͟huh-KAHS, ⑤ kuh-KAS, kuh-KAHS   xə'kɑs, ⑤ kə'kæs, kə'kɑs
Khaled, King
  airport, Riyadh, Saudi Arabia   king k͟hah-LED, hah-LED   kiŋ xɑ'led, hɑ'led
Khālid
  king of Saudi Arabia   k͟hah-LĒD, K͟HAHL-ēd   xɑ'liːd, 'xɑliːd
Khalkha Mongol
  lang., Mongolia   KAL-kuh-MAHNG-guhl, MAHN-GŌL,   'kælkə'maŋgəl, 'man,goːl,
           MAHNG-GŌL   'maŋ,goːl
Khalkidhiki [Chalcidice]
  peninsula, Greece   K͟HAHL-kē-t͟hē-KĒ, KAHL-kuh-t͟hē-KĒ   ˌxɑlkiːðiː'kiː, ˌkɑlkəðiː'kiː
Khalkis [Chalcis]
  city, Greece   k͟hahl-KĒS, kahl-KĒS   xɑl'kiːs, kɑl'kiːs
Khamenei
  Hojatolislam Ali, *Iranian Islamic*   k͟hah-MĀ-nē, hah-MĒ-nē   xɑ'meːniˑ, hɑ'miːniˑ
    leader
Khan
  Asian title, Cen. Asian people   KAHN, K͟HAHN   'kɑn, 'xɑn
Khanaqin
  town, Iraq   K͟HAHN-uh-KĒN   ˌxɑnə'kiːn
Khandeshi
  lang., India   kahn-DĀ-shē   kɑn'deːʃiˑ
Khaniá [Canea]
  town, Greece   k͟hahn-YAH, kahn-YAH   xɑn'ja, kɑn'ja
Khanty [Ostyak]
  lang., Khanti-Mansi region, Russia   KAHNT-ē   'kɑːntiˑ
!Khara
  African people   KAHR-uh   'karə, 'ǀharə
Kharg [Khark]
  island, Iran   K͟HAHRG, KAHRG   'xɑʳg, 'kɑʳg
Kharia
  lang., people, India   KAHR-ē-uh   'kariːə
Khark [Kharg]
  island, Iran   K͟HAHRK   'xɑʳk

Key (col. 2):   a: f**a**d   ā: f**a**de   ah: f**a**ther   ar: m**a**rry   aw: l**a**w   e: f**e**d   ē: f**ee**d   er: m**e**rry   i: h**i**d   ī: h**i**de   ō: c**oa**t   ōō: b**oo**t
oi: b**oy**   ow: n**ow**   u: p**u**t   uh: **a**bove   uhr: b**ir**d   ch: **ch**op   ng: ri**ng**   sh: **sh**ow   th: **th**ick   t͟h: **th**is   zh: mea**s**ure

Kharkov

  city, Ukraine   K̲H̲AHR-kuhf, KAHR-KAWF,   'xɑrkəf, 'kɑʳˌkɔːf, 'kɑʳˌkɔːv,
                                       KAHR-KAWV, KAHR-kuhf   'kɑʳkəf

Khartoum

  capital, Sudan   kahr-TO͞OM   kɑr'tuːm

Khasi

  lang., India   KAHS-ē   'kɑsiˑ

Khattians

  pre-Hittite people of Anatolia   K̲H̲AHT-ē-uhnz, KAT-ē-uhnz   'xɑtiːənz, 'kætiːənz

Khattusha

  Hittite capital city   k̲h̲ah-TO͞O-shuh   xɑ'tuˑʃə

Khayyám

  see Omar Khayyám

Khe Sanh

  US marine outpost, Vietnam   kā sahn   keː sɑn

Khingan

  two mountain ranges, Asia   SHING-AHN   'ʃiŋ'ɑn

Khíos

  island, Greece   K̲H̲Ē-AWS, KĒ-AWS   'xiːˌɔːs, 'kiːˌɔːs

Khmer [Cambodian]

  lang., people, Indochina   kuh-MER   kə'meʳ

Khmer Rouge

  communist group, Cambodia   kuh-MER RO͞OZH, RO͞OJ   kə'meʳ 'ruːʒ, 'ruːdʒ

Khmu'

  lang., people, Laos, Thailand   kuh-MO͞O   kə'muː

Khnum

  Egyptian creator god   K̲H̲NUM, k̲h̲uh-NUM   'xnum, xə'num

Khnum-Re

  Egyptian god, aspect of Khnum   K̲H̲NUM-RĀ, k̲h̲uh-NUM-RĀ   'xnum're, xə'num're

Khoisan

  African lang. family   koi-SAHN, koi-SAN   kɔi'sɑn, kɔi'sæn

Khomeini

  Ruholla Mussaui, *Iranian ayatollah* k̲h̲ō-MĀ-nē, kō-, hō-; K̲H̲Ō-mā-NĒ   xoː'meːniˑ, koː-, hoː-;
                                                                        ˌxoːmeː'niː

Khorana

  H. Gobind, *Indian-born US*   kō-RAHN-uh   koː'rɑnə
  molecular chemist (Nobel 1968)

Khordad'sal

  Zoroastrian festival   KAWR-duhd-SAHL   'kɔːʳdədˌsɑl

Khrapovitshy

  Antony, *Russian cleric*   kruh-PUH-VICH-iy   krəˌpə'vitʃij

Khristian

  pers. name, Russian   k̲h̲rēs-ti-AHN   xriːsti'ɑːn

Khrushchev

  Nikita, *premier, USSR*   k̲h̲ro͞osh-CHAWF,   xruːʃ'tʃɔːf, Ⓢ kruːʃ'(tʃ)ɔːf,
                                       Ⓢ kro͞osh-(CH)AWF,   'kruːʃˌ(tʃ)ev
                                       KRO͞OSH-(CH)EV

Khufu [Cheops]

  Egyptian pharoah   KO͞O-FO͞O   'kuːˌfuː

Khulna

  region, Bangladesh   KUL-nuh   'kulnə

Khuri

  pers. name, Arabic   K̲H̲O͞O-rē   'xuːriː

Khust, Chust [Huszt]

  town, Ukraine   K̲H̲O͞OST   'xuːst

Foreign Sounds: ue: *Fr.* **rue**, *Ger.* füllen   uh(r): *Fr.* **boeuf**, *Ger.* Höhle   k̲h̲: *Ger.* i**ch**, *Scot.* lo**ch**   ḡ: *Sp.* ami**g**o   ṿ: *Sp.* ha**b**lar
hl: *Welsh* **Ll**anelli.   CAPITALS: primary stress.   SMALL CAPS: secondary stress.   Ⓢ: U.S. pron.   Ⓔ: British pron.

Khuzistan
 prov, Iran   KH͞OO-zuh-STAHN   ˌxuːzəˈstɑn
Khyber
 mtn. pass   KĪ-buhr   ˈkaibəʳ
Ki
 1. pers. name, Indonesian   KĒ   ˈkiː
 2. Japanese   kē   kiː
Kiamichi
 river, OK   KĪ-uh-MISH-ē   ˌkaiəˈmiʃiˑ
Kiangmai [Chiang Mai]
 province, Thailand   jē-AHNG-MĪ, kē-   dʒiːˈaŋˈmai, kiː-
Kiang-si
 see Jiangxi
Kiang-su
 see Jiangsu
Kiawah
 island, SC   KĒ(-uh)-WAW   ˈkiː(ə)ˌwɔː
Kibroth-hattaavah
 Biblical name   KIB-RAHTH-(h)uh-TĀ-uh-vuh,   ˈkibˌrɑθ(h)əˈteːəvə,
                                 kiv-RŌT-hah-TAH-AH-VAH   kivˈroːthɑˌtɑ-aˈvɑ
Kibzaim
 Biblical name   KIB-zā-uhm, kib-ZĀ-uhm,   ˈkibzeːəm, kibˈzeːəm,
                                 kiv-TSAH-yim   kivˈtsɑjim
Kickapoo
 N. American people   KIK-uh-P͞OO   ˈkikəˌpuː
Kiddush
 Jewish blessing over wine   KID-uhsh, KID-ish, kid-͞OOSH   ˈkidəʃ, ˈkidiʃ, kidˈuːʃ
Kidnis
 Igor, harpsichordist   KID-nuhs   ˈkidnəs
Kidron
 Biblical name   KID-ruhn, ki-DRŌN   ˈkidrən, kiˈdroːn
Kidron [Kedron]
 valley, Jordan   KID-ruhn, KĪ-druhn   ˈkidrən, ˈkaidrən
Kiefer
 pers. name   KĒ-fuhr   ˈkiːfəʳ
Kiel
 city, canal, Germany   KĒL   ˈkiːl
Kierkegaard
 Sören, Danish philosopher   KIR-kuh-GAHR(D), KIR-kuh-GAWR   ˈkiʳkəˌgɑʳ(d), ˈkiʳkəˌgɔːʳ
Kieran
 John Francis, US journalist   KIR-uhn   ˈkirən
Kieran [Ciaran]
 Irish saint   KYER-uhn, ⓢ KIR-uhn   ˈkjerən, ⓢ ˈkirən
Kiernan
 Edward J., labor union official   KIR-nuhn   ˈkiʳnən
Kieta
 district, Papua New Guinea   kē-ĀT-uh   kiːˈeːʈə
Kiev, Kiyev, Kiyiv
 city, Ukraine   KĒ-(Y)EF, KĒ-(Y)EV, KĒ-(y)uhf   ˈkiːˌ(j)ef, ˈkiːˌ(j)ev, ˈkiː(j)əf
Kigali
 capital, Rwanda   ki-GAHL-ē   kiˈgɑliˑ
Kiichi
 pers. name, Japanese   kē-ē-chē   kiːiːtʃiː
Kiichiro
 pers. name, Japanese   kē-ē-chē-rō   kiːiːtʃiːroː

Key (col. 2):   a: fad ā: fade ah: father ar: marry aw: law e: fed ē: feed er: merry i: hid ī: hide ō: coat ōō: boot
oi: boy   ow: now   u: put   uh: above   uhr: bird   ch: chop   ng: ring   sh: show   th: thick   th: this   zh: measure

Kijuro
   pers. name, Japanese   kē-ju-rō   kiːdʒuroː
Kikamba [Kamba]
   lang., Africa   ki-KAHM-buh   kiˈkɑmbə
Kikládhes [Cyclades]
   Aegean islands   ki-KLAH<u>TH</u>-is   kiˈklɑðis
Kikongo
   lang., Cen. Africa   kē-KAHNG-gō   kiˑˈkɑŋgoː
Kikujiro
   pers. name, Japanese   kē-kuj-ē-rō   kiːkudʒiːroː
Kikuyu
   lang., people, Africa   kē-K$\overline{OO}$-y$\overline{oo}$ kiˑˈkuːju
Kilauea
   Mount, *volcano, HI*   KĒ-LOW-Ā-uh, KIL-uh-WĀ-uh   ˌkiːˌlɑuˈeːə, ˌkiləˈweːə
Kildare
   county, Dublin   kil-DAR, kil-DER   kilˈdæʳ, kilˈdeʳ
Kilgore
   College, *TX*   KIL-GŌR, KIL-GAWR   ˈkilˌgoːʳ, ˈkilˌgɔːʳ
Kilimanjaro
   Mount, *Tanzania*   KIL-uh-muhn-JAHR-ō, -JAR-ō   ˌkiləmənˈdʒɑroː, -ˈdʒæroː
Kilkenny
   prov & town, Irish Republic   kil-KEN-ē   kilˈkeniˑ
Killanin
   Michael Morris, Lord, *Irish author*   kuh-LAN-uhn   kəˈlænən
Killarney
   town, Irish Republic   kil-AHR-nē   kilˈɑʳniˑ
Killebrew
   Gwendolyn, *US opera singer;*   KIL-uh-BR$\overline{OO}$ ˈkiləˌbruː
     Harmon, *US baseball player*
Killian
   pers. name, Dutch   KĒ-lē-AHN   ˈkiːliːˌɑːn
Killiecrankie
   mtn. pass, Scotland   KIL-ē-KRANG-kē   ˌkiliˑˈkræŋkiˑ
Killíni [Cyllene]
   mountain, Greece   kuh-LĒ-nē   kəˈliːniˑ
Kilmarnock
   burgh, Scotland   kil-MAHR-nuhk   kilˈmɑʳnək
Kim
   pers. name   KIM   ˈkim
Kimbanguist
   religion   kim-BAHNG-gwist   kimˈbɑŋgwist
Kimberly
   pers. name   KIM-buhr-lē   ˈkimbəʳliˑ
Kim Il-sung
   president, N. Korea   kim il-sung, kim il-suhng   kim ilsuŋ, kim ilsəŋ
Kimmochi
   pers. name, Japanese   kēm-mō-chē   kiːmmoːtʃiː
Kimpo
   airport, Seoul   kim-pō   kimpoː
Kinabalu
   mts., natl. park, Malaysia   KIN-uh-buh-L$\overline{OO}$ ˌkinəbəˈluː
Kinah
   Biblical name   KĪ-nuh, kē-NAH   ˈkɑinə, kiːˈnɑ
Kinchinjunga [Kanchenjunga]
   mtn., Himalaya   KIN-chuhn-JUHNG-guh, -JUNG-guh   ˌkintʃənˈdʒəŋgə, -ˈdʒuŋgə

Foreign Sounds: **ue**: *Fr.* **rue**, *Ger.* **füllen**   **uh(r)**: *Fr.* **boeuf**, *Ger.* **Höhle**   **kh**: *Ger.* i**ch**, *Scot.* lo**ch**   **ḡ**: *Sp.* ami**g**o   **v**: *Sp.* ha**b**lar   **hl**: *Welsh* **Ll**anelli.   CAPITALS: primary stress.   SMALL CAPS: secondary stress.   Ⓢ: U.S. pron.   Ⓔ: British pron.

Kindl
German beer KIND-l 'kindḷ

Kindrick
Legion Field, *ballpark, Helena, MT* KIN-drik 'kindrik

King
Martin Luther, Jr., *US civil rights* KING 'kiŋ
leader (Nobel 1964); pers. name

King Eider
duck king ĪD-uhr kiŋ 'aidəʳ

King's College
Cambridge Univ. KINGZ 'kiŋz

Kingsley
Ben, *British actor* KINGZ-lē 'kiŋzli·

Kingsley
Charles, *English clergyman, novelist* KINGZ-lē 'kiŋzli·

Kingston
pl. name KING-stuhn 'kiŋstən

Kingston-upon-Thames
borough, England KING-stuhn uh-PAHN TEMZ 'kiŋstən ə,pan 'temz

Kingstown
city, Ireland; city, St. Vincent & the KING-STOWN 'kiŋ,staun
Grenadines

Kingwana
lang., Zaire king-WAHN-uh kiŋ'wanə

Kingyarwanda [Rwanda]
lang., Africa KING-yuhr-WAHN-duh ,kiŋjəʳ'wandə

Kinkajou
mammal KING-kuh-JŌŌ 'kiŋkə,dʒuː

Kinki
island, Japan kin-kē, king-kē kinki·, kiŋki·

Kinloch
city, MO KIN-LAHK 'kin,lak

Kinnan
pers. name KIN-uhn 'kinən

Kinnock
Neil, *British politician* KIN-uhk 'kinək

Kinro-Kansha-No-Hi
Labor Thanksgiving Day (Nov. 23), kin-rō-kahn-shah-nō-hē kinroːkanʃanoːhiː
Japan

Kinsey
Alfred, *US sexologist, zoologist* KIN-zē 'kinzi·

Kinshasa
city, Zaire kin-SHAHS-uh kin'ʃasə

Kinski
Klaus & Nastassia, *entertainers* KIN-skē 'kinski·

Kinzua
Dam, *PA* kin-ZŌŌ-uh kin'zuːə

Kioga
see Kyoga

Kiowa
1. county, CO KĪ-uh-WAH 'kaiə,wa
2. N. American people KĪ-uh-WAW, -WAH, -WĀ 'kaiə,wɔː, -,wa, -,weː

Kipling
Rudyard, *English author (Nobel* KIP-ling 'kipliŋ
1907)

Key (col. 2): a: fad ā: fade ah: father ar: marry aw: law e: fed ē: feed er: merry i: hid ī: hide ō: coat ōō: boot
oi: boy ow: now u: put uh: above uhr: bird ch: chop ng: ring sh: show th: thick th̲: this zh: measure

Kiplingesque

    pert. to Kipling   KIP-ling-ESK   ˌkiplɪŋˈesk

Kippure

    mountain range, Ireland   kip-YUR   kipˈjuʳ

Kir

    alcoholic drink   KĒR, Ⓢ KIR   ˈkiːr, Ⓢ ˈkiʳ

Kirby

    pers. name   KUHR-bē   ˈkəʳbiˑ

Kirghiz, Kirgiz

    lang., people, republic, mtn. range,   kir-GĒZ   kiʳˈgiːz
      Asia

Kirghizia, Kirgizia

    republic, Europe   kir-GĒ-zh(ē-)uh, kir-GĒ-zē-uh   kiʳˈgiːʒ(iː)ə, kiʳˈgiːziːə

Kir-hareseth

    Biblical name   kuhr-HER-uh-SETH, KĒR-khah-RE-set   kəʳherəˌseθ, ˈkiːrxɑˈreset

Kir-haresh

    Biblical name   kuhr-HĀ-RESH, -HAR-ESH;   kəʳheːˌreʃ, -ˈhærˌeʃ;
                          KĒR-KHER-es   ˌkiːrˈxeres

Kir-heres

    Biblical name   kuhr-HIR-uhs, KĒR-KHE-res   kəʳhirəs, ˌkiːrˈxeres

Kiri

    pers. name (K. Te Kanawa)   KIR-ē   ˈkiriˑ

Kiriath [Kirioth, Kirjath]

    Biblical name   KIR-ē-ATH, KIR-yaht   ˈkiriːˌæθ, ˈkirjɑt

Kiriathaim [Kirjathaim]

    Biblical name   KIR-ē-uh-THĀ-uhm, KIR-yah-TAH-yēm   ˌkiriːəˈθeːəm, ˌkirjɑˈtɑjiːm

Kiriath-Arba

    Biblical name   KIR-ē-ATH-AHR-buh,   ˈkiriːˌæθˈɑʳbə, kirˈjɑtɑrˈbɑ
                          kir-YAHT-ahr-BAH

Kiriath-Arim

    Biblical name   KIR-ē-ATH-Ā-rim,   ˈkiriːˌæθˈeːrim,
                          kir-YAHT-yuh-ah-RĒM   kirˈjɑtjəɑˈriːm

Kiriath-Baal [Kirjath-baal]

    Biblical name   KIR-ē-ATH-BĀ(-uh)l,   ˈkiriːˌæθˈbeː(ə)l,
                          kir-YAHT-yuh-BAH-ahl   kirˈjɑtjəˈbɑ-al

Kiriath-Huzoth

    Biblical name   KIR-ē-ATH-H(Y)O͞O-ZAHTH,   ˈkiriːˌæθˈh(j)uːˌzɑθ,
                          kir-YAHT-kho͞ot-SŌT   kirˈjɑtxuːtˈsoːt

Kiriath-Jearim

    Biblical name   KIR-ē-ATH-JIR-im,   ˈkiriːˌæθˈdʒirim,
                          kir-YAHT-yuh-ah-RĒM   kirˈjɑtjəɑˈriːm

Kiriath-Sannah

    Biblical name   KIR-ē-ATH-SAN-uh, kir-YAHT-sah-NAH   ˈkiriːˌæθˈsænə, kirˈjɑtsɑˈnɑ

Kiriath-Sepher

    Biblical name   KIR-ē-ATH-SĀ-fuhr, kir-YAHT-SEF-er   ˈkiriːˌæθˈseːfəʳ, kirˈjɑtˈsefer

Kiribatian

    pert. to Kiribati   KIR-uh-BAS-ē-uhn *[sic]*   ˌkirəˈbæsiːən *[sic]*

Kiribati [Gilbert]

    islands, lang., people, Pacific   KIR-uh-BAS *[sic]*   ˈkirəˌbæs *[sic]*

Kiril

    pers. name, Bulgarian   kē-RĒL   kiːˈriːl

Kirill

    pers. name, Russian   kyir-YĒL   kjirˈjiːl

Kirin

    Japanese beer   kir-in   kirin

Foreign Sounds: ue: *Fr.* **rue**, *Ger.* füllen uh(r): *Fr.* **boeuf**, *Ger.* Höhle kh: *Ger.* **ich**, *Scot.* lo**ch** g̱: *Sp.* ami**g**o v̱: *Sp.* ha**b**lar
hl: *Welsh* **Ll**anelli. CAPITALS: primary stress. SMALL CAPS: secondary stress. Ⓢ: U.S. pron. Ⓔ: British pron.

Kirin [Jilin]
prov & town, China —　KĒ-RIN　—　'kiːˈrin
Kirioth [Kiriath]
Biblical name —　KIR-ē-AHTH, kir-YAHT　—　'kiriːˌɑθ, kirˈjɑt
Kiritimati Atoll [Christmas]
islands, Pacific —　kuh-RIS-muhs, ⑤ KRIS-muhs *[sic]*　—　kəˈrisməs, ⑤ 'krisməs *[sic]*
Kirjath [Kiriath]
Biblical name —　KIR-JATH, KIR-YATH, kir-YAHT　—　'kiʳˌdʒæθ, 'kiʳjæθ, kirˈjɑt
Kirjathaim [Kiriathaim]
Biblical name —　KIR-juh-THĀ-im, KIR-yah-TAH-yēm　—　ˌkirdʒəˈθeːim, ˌkirjɑˈtɑjiːm
Kirjath-arba [Kiriath-Arba]
Biblical name —　KIR-JATH-AHR-buh, kir-YAHT-ahr-BAH　—　'kiʳˌdʒæθ'ɑʳbə, kirˈjɑtɑrˈbɑ
Kirjath-arim [Kiriath-Arim]
Biblical name —　KIR-JATH-Ā-rim, kir-YAHT-yuh-ah-RĒM　—　'kiʳˌdʒæθ'eːrim, kirˈjɑtjə-ɑˈriːm
Kirjath-baal [Kiriath-Baal]
Biblical name —　KIR-JATH-BĀ(-uh)l, kir-YAHT-yuh-BAH-ahl　—　'kirˌdʒæθˈbeː(ə)l, kirˈjɑtjəˈbɑ-ɑl
Kirjath-huzoth [Kiriath-Huzoth]
Biblical name —　KIR-JATH-H(Y)OO-ZAHTH, kir-YAHT-khoo-TSŌT　—　'kiʳˌdʒæθ'h(j)uːˌzɑθ, kirˈjɑtxuːˈtsoːt
Kirjath-jearim [Kiriath-Jearim]
Biblical name —　KIR-JATH-JIR-im, kir-YAHT-yuh-ah-RĒM　—　'kiʳˌdʒæθ'dʒirim, kirˈjɑtjəɑˈriːm
Kirjath-sannah [Kiriath-Sannah]
Biblical name —　KIR-JATH-SAN-uh, kir-YAHT-sah-NAH　—　'kiʳˌdʒæθ'sænə, kirˈjɑtsɑˈnɑ
Kirjath-sepher [Kiriath-Sepher]
Biblical name —　KIR-JATH-SĀ-fuhr, kir-YAHT-SE-fer　—　'kiʳˌdʒæθ'seːfəʳ, kirˈjɑt'sefer
Kirk
James Tiberius, Star Trek captain; pers. name —　KUHRK　—　'kəʳk
Kirkcaldy
city, Scotland —　kuh-KAHD-ē, kuh-KAWD-ē, kuhr-; ⑤ kuhr-KAWL-dē　—　kəˈkɑdiˑ, kəˈkɔːdiˑ, kər-; ⑤ kəʳˈkɔːldiˑ
Kirkcudbright
town, Scotland —　kuhr-KOO-brē *[sic]*　—　kəʳˈkuːbriˑ *[sic]*
Kirke
pers. name —　KUHRK　—　'kəʳk
Kirkland
Gelsey, US ballet dancer —　KUHRK-luhnd　—　'kəʳklənd
Kirkpatrick
Jeane, US political scientist —　KUHRK-PA-trik, KUHR-PA-trik　—　ˌkəʳk'pætrik, ˌkəʳˈpætrik
Kirkuk
town, Iraq —　kir-KOOK　—　kiʳˈkuːk
Kirman [Kermān]
prov, city, Iran —　kuhr-MAHN, kir-MAHN　—　kəʳˈmɑn, kiʳˈmɑn
Kir Moab [Kerak, El]
town, fortress, Jordan —　KIR MŌ-ab　—　ˌkiʳ 'moːæb
Kiro
pers. name (K. Gilgorov) —　KĒ-rō　—　'kiːroː
Kirov
city, Russia —　KĒ-RAWF　—　'kiːˌrɔːf
Kirschwasser
cherry brandy —　KIRSH-VAHS-uhr　—　'kiʳʃˌvɑsəʳ

Key (col. 2):　a: fad　ā: fade　ah: father　ar: marry　aw: law　e: fed　ē: feed　er: merry　i: hid　ī: hide　ō: coat　oo: boot
oi: boy　ow: now　u: put　uh: above　uhr: bird　ch: chop　ng: ring　sh: show　th: thick　th: this　zh: measure

Kirsten		
1. Dorothy, *US soprano*	KUHR-stuhn	'kəʳstən
2. pers. name	KIRS-tuhn	'kiʳstən
3. Norwegian	KHYISH-tuhn, KHYIRS-tuhn, [$] KISH-tuhn	'xjiʃtən, 'xjirstən, [$] 'kiʃtən
Kirstie, Kirsty		
pers. name	KIR-stē, KUHR-stē	'kiʳstiˑ, 'kəʳstiˑ
Kirthar		
Range, *mtn. range, Pakistan*	kir-TAHR	kiʳ'tɑʳ
Kirundi		
lang., Burundi	kē-ROON-dē, kē-RUN-dē	kiˑ'ruːndiˑ, kiˑ'rundiˑ
Kisangani [Stanleyville]		
capital, Zaire	kē-SAHNG-GAHN-ē, KĒ-sahng-GAHN-ē	kiː'sɑŋˌgɑniˑ, ˌkiːsɑŋ'gɑniˑ
Kish		
ancient Sumerian & Akkadian city	KISH	'kiʃ
Kishi		
Nobusuke, *Japanese statesman*	kē-shē	kiːʃiˑ
Kishinev [Chişinău]		
capital, Moldova	KISH-uh-NEF, -NEV	'kiʃəˌnef, -ˌnev
Kishion		
Biblical name	KISH-ē-AHN, kish-YŌN	'kiʃiːˌɑn, kiʃ'joːn
Kishon		
Biblical name	KĪ-SHAHN, KISH-uhn, kē-SHŌN	'kɑiˌʃɑn, 'kiʃən, kiː'ʃoːn
Kishwaukee		
College, *IL*	kish-WAW-kē	kiʃ'wɔːkiˑ
Kiska		
island, AK	KIS-kuh	'kiskə
Kislev		
Jewish month	KIS-luhf, kē-SLEV	'kisləf, kiː'slev
Kislimu		
Babylonian month	KIS-lim-oo	'kislimuː
Kismet		
fate, destiny	KIZ-MET, KIZ-muht	'kizˌmet, 'kizmət
Kissimmee		
town, river, FL	kis-IM-ē	kis'imiˑ
Kissinger		
Henry A., *German-born US civil servant (Nobel 1973)*	KIS-n-juhr	'kisn̩dʒəʳ
Kistna [Krishna]		
river, India	KIS(T)-nuh	'kis(t)nə
Kiswahili		
lang., Africa	KIS-WAH-HĒ-lē	ˌkisˌwɑ'hiːliˑ
Kit		
pers. name	KIT	'kit
Kitagawa Utamaro		
Japanese artist	kē-tah-gah-wah ut-ah-mahr-ō	kiːtɑgɑwɑ ut̪ɑmɑroː
Kitchener		
Horatio H., *British militarist*	KICH-(uh-)nuhr	'kitʃ(ə)nəʳ
Kithlish		
Biblical name	KITH-lish, kit-LĒSH	'kiθliʃ, kit'liːʃ
Kitron		
Biblical name	KI-TRAHN, kit-RŌN	'kiˌtrɑn, kit'roːn
Kitsap		
county, WA	KIT-suhp	'kitsəp

Foreign Sounds: ue: *Fr.* **rue**, *Ger.* **füllen** uh(r): *Fr.* **boeuf**, *Ger.* **Höhle** kh: *Ger.* **ich**, *Scot.* **loch** g̃: *Sp.* **amigo** v̲: *Sp.* **hablar** hl: *Welsh* **Llanelli**. CAPITALS: primary stress. SMALL CAPS: secondary stress. [$]: U.S. pron. [£]: British pron.

Kittanning
  borough, PA   kuh-TAN-ing   kə'tæniŋ
Kittikachorn
  Thanom, *premier, Thailand*   KĒT-ē-kuh-CHAWRN   ˌkiːt̪iˈkəˈtʃɔːʳn
Kittim
  Biblical name   KIT-im, ki-TĒM   'kit̪im, ki'tiːm
Kittitas
  county, WA   KIT-i-tuhs   'kit̪itəs
Kittiwake
  sea bird (gull)   KIT-ē-WĀK   'kit̪iˑˌweːk
Kitto
  pers. name   KIT-ō   'kit̪oː
Kittsian
  person from St. Kitts   KIT-sē-uhn   'kitsiːən
Kitty
  pers. name   KIT-ē   'kit̪iˑ
Kitzbühel
  city, Austria   KITS-BUE-uhl, Ⓢ KITS-B(Y)O͞O(-uh)l   'kitsˌbyːəl, Ⓢ 'kitsˌb(j)uː(ə)l
Kiungchow [Ch'iung-shan]
  city, China   chē-UNG-JŌ   tʃiːˈuŋˈdʒoː
Kiungshan [Ch'iung-shan]
  city, China   chē-UNG-SHAHN   tʃiːˈuŋˈʃɑn
Kivu
  lake, province, Zaire   KĒ-vo͞o   'kiːvuː
Kiwanian
  member of Kiwanis club   kuh-WAHN-ē-uhn   kə'wɑniːən
Kiwanis
  business organization   kuh-WAHN-uhs   kə'wɑnəs
Kiwi
  New Zealand bird; fruit   KĒ-wē   'kiːwiˑ
Kiyev, Kiyiv
  see Kiev
Kiyoshi
  pers. name, Japanese   kē-yō-shē   kiːjoːʃiː
Kizzy
  pers. name   KIZ-ē   'kiziˑ
Klaberjass
  game   KLAHB-uhr-YAHS   'klɑbəʳjas
Klagenfurt
  city, Austria   KLAHG-uhn-FURT   'klɑgənˌfuʳt
Klallam
  see Clallam
Klamath
  county, OR; N. American people   KLAM-uhth   'klæməθ
Klaus
  pers. name, German   KLOWS   'klɑus
Klawock
  village, AK   KLAW-wuhk, KLOW-uhk   'klɔːwək, 'klɑuək
Kléber
  Jean, *French general*   klā-BER   kleːber
Kleberg
  county, TX   KLĀ-BUHRG   'kleːˌbəʳg
Klee
  Paul, *Swiss painter*   KLĀ   'kleː

Key (col. 2):   a: **f**a**d**   ā: **f**a**de**   ah: **f**a**ther**   ar: m**arry**   aw: l**aw**   e: **f**e**d**   ē: **f**ee**d**   er: m**erry**   i: h**i**d   ī: h**i**de   ō: c**oa**t   o͞o: b**oo**t
oi: b**oy**   ow: n**ow**   u: p**u**t   uh: **a**b**ove**   uhr: b**ir**d   ch: **ch**op   ng: ri**ng**   sh: **sh**ow   th: **th**ick   th̲: **th**is   zh: mea**s**ure

Kleenex
tdmk for a facial tissue	KLĒ-NEKS	'kliː,neks

Klein
Lawrence R., *US economist (Nobel 1980);* Melanie, *British psychoanalyst; bottle, single-sided surface*	KLĪN	'klɑin

Kleine Munsterlander
dog breed	KLĪ-nuh MUN-stuhr-LAHN-duhr	,klɑinə 'munstəʳ,landəʳ

Klemens
1. pers. name, German	KLĀ-MENS	'kleː,mens
2. Polish	KLEM-ens	'klemens

Klement
pers. name, Czech	KLEM-ent	'klement

Klemperer
Otto, *German conductor;* Werner, *US actor*	KLEM-puh-ruhr	'klempərəʳ

Kliban
Bernard, *US cartoonist*	KLĒ-BAN	'kliː,bæn

Klickitat
county, WA	KLIK-i-TAT	'kliki,tæt

Klikitat
N. American people	KLIK-uh-TAT	'klikə,tæt

Kliment
1. pers. name, Bulgarian	KLĒ-mänt	'kliːmeːnt
2. Russian	KLĒM-yint	'kl̡iːmjint

Klimenti, -ty
pers. name, Russian	klēm-YEN-ti	kl̡iːm'jent̡ij

Klimt
Gustav, *Austrian painter*	KLIM(P)T	'klim(p)t

Klingon
alien race, Star Trek	KLING-AHN	'kliŋ,ɑn

Klitzing
Klaus von, *German physicist (Nobel 1985)*	KLITS-ing	'klitsiŋ

Kljuc
city, Bosnia	KLYO̅O̅TS	'kljuːts

Klondike
region, river, Canada	KLAHN-DĪK	'klɑn,dɑik

Kloster
German beer	KLAWS-tuhr	'klɔːstəʳ

Klosters
resort, Switzerland	KLŌ-stuhrz	'kloːstəʳz

Klotz
Florence, *US costume designer*	KLAHTS	'klɑts

Kluckhohn
Clyde Kay Maben, *US anthropologist*	KLUHK-HŌN	'klək,hoːn

Klug
Aaron, *Lithuanian-born British biophysicist (Nobel 1982)*	KLO̅O̅G	'kluːg

Kluger
Richard, *US author, editor, critic*	KLOO-guhr	'kluːgəʳ

Klugman
Jack, *US actor*	KLUHG-muhn	'kləgmən

Knauer

Virginia Harrington, *US government official*   NOW(-uh)r   'nɑu(ə)ʳ

Kneller

Sir Godfrey, *British painter*   NEL-uhr   'neləʳ

Knesset

Israeli parliament   KNES-uht, kuh-NES-uht, KNES-et   'knesət, kə'nesət, 'kneset

Knickerbocker

a New Yorker   NIK-uhr-BAHK-uhr   'nikəʳˌbɑkəʳ

Knieval

Evel, *US daredevil*   kuh-NĒ-vuhl, KNĒ-vuhl   kə'niːvəl, 'kniːvəl

Knipperlé

wine grape variety   kuh-NIP-uhr-lē, -LĀ   kə'nipəʳliˑ, -ˌleː

Knockmealdown

mountain range, Ireland   nahk-MĒL-DOWN   nɑk'miːlˌdɑun

Knokke-Heist

resort, Belgium   KNAWK-uh-HĪST   'knɔːkə'hɑist

Knollys

Sir Francis, *Elizabethan courtier*   NŌLZ   'noːlz

Knopf, Alfred A.

US publishing co.   AL-fruhd Ā (kuh-)NAHPF, kuh-NUHPF   ˌælfrəd ˌeː (kə)'nɑpf, kə'nəpf

Knopf

Adolph, *US geologist*   (kuh-)NAHPF   (kə)'nɑpf

Knossos

city, Crete   NAHS-uhs   'nɑsəs

Knott

family name   NAHT   'nɑt

Knowles

John, *author*   NŌLZ   'noːlz

Knox

John, *Scottish religious reformer*   NAHKS   'nɑks

Knud

1. pers. name, Danish   KNO͞OTH   'knuːð

2. Norwegian   KNO͞OT   'knuːt

Knut

pers. name, Norwegian, Swedish   KNO͞OT   'knuːt

Knute

pers. name   NO͞OT   'nuːt

Koa

Biblical name   KŌ-uh, KŌ-ah   'koːə, 'koːɑ

Koala

marsupial   kō-AHL-uh, kuh-WAHL-uh   koː'ɑlə, kə'wɑlə

Koasati

N. American people   KŌ-uh-SAHT-ē   ˌkoːə'satiˑ

Kobarid

village, Slovenia   KŌ-buh-RĒD   'koːbəˌriːd

Kobbé

Gustave, *opera guide author*   kaw-BĀ   kɔː'beː

Kobe

city, Japan   kō-bā, ⓢ KŌ-bē, KŌ-bā   koːbeː, ⓢ 'koːbiˑ, 'koːbeː

København [Copenhagen]

Denmark   KUH(R)-buhn-HOWN   ˌkœːbən'hɑun

Koblenz, Coblenz

prov, Germany   KŌ-BLEN(T)S   'koːˌblen(t)s

Key (col. 2):   a: **fad**   ā: **fade**   ah: **father**   ar: **marry**   aw: **law**   e: **fed**   ē: **feed**   er: **merry**   i: **hid**   ī: **hide**   ō: **coat**   oo: **boot**
oi: **boy**   ow: **now**   u: **put**   uh: **above**   uhr: **bird**   ch: **chop**   ng: **ring**   sh: **show**   th: **thick**   <u>th</u>: **this**   zh: **measure**

Kobuk

division, AK   kō-BUK   koːˈbuk

Kobuk Valley

National Park, *AK*   kō-BUK   koːˈbuk

Koch

1. Edward I., *US politician*   KAHCH   ˈkɑtʃ

2. Robert, *German physician,*   KAWKH   ˈkɔːx
bacteriologist (Nobel 1905)

3. Bill, *US yachtsman*   KŌK   ˈkoːk

4. Frederick Henry, *US educator,*   KAHCH, KAHK   ˈkɑtʃ, ˈkɑk
theater founder

5. pers. name, US   KAHCH, KAHK, KUK, KŌK   ˈkɑtʃ, ˈkɑk, ˈkuk, ˈkoːk

Köchel

number, designation of Mozart   KUH(R)KH-uhl, ⓢ KUHR-shuhl,   ˈkœçəl, ⓢ ˈkəʳʃəl, ˈkəʳkəl
compositions   KUHR-kuhl

Kocher

Emil T., *Swiss surgeon (Nobel 1909)*   KŌKH-uhr   ˈkoːxəʳ

Kodachrome

tdmk for a positive color   KŌD-uh-KRŌM   ˈkoːdəˌkroːm
transparency

Kodagu [Coorg]

lang., people, India   KŌD-uh-GOO   ˈkoːdəˌguː

Kodak

tdmk for photographic supplies   KŌD-AK   ˈkoːdˌæk

Kodály

Zoltán, *Hungarian composer*   KAW-DĬ(-ē), KŌ-DĬ(-ē)   ˈkɔːˌdɑi(-iː), ˈkoːˌdɑi(-iː)

Kodiak

island, division, AL   KŌD-ē-AK   ˈkoːdiːˌæk

Kodok [Fashoda]

village, Sudan   KŌD-AHK   ˈkoːdˌɑk

Koestler

Arthur, *British writer*   KES(T)-luhr   ˈkes(t)ləʳ

Koff

Finnish beer   KAWF   ˈkɔːf

Kohath

Biblical name   KŌ-HATH, kuh-HAHT   ˈkoːˌhæθ, kəˈhɑt

Kohathite

Biblical name   KŌ-HATH-ĪT   ˈkoːˌhæθˌɑit

Kohinoor

diamond   KŌ-uh-NUR, KŌ-uh-NUR   ˈkoːəˌnuʳ, ˌkoːəˈnuʳ

Kohl

Helmut, *German Chancellor*   KŌL   ˈkoːl

Kohler

Georges J. F., *German*   KŌ-luhr   ˈkoːləʳ
immunologist (Nobel 1984)

Koil-Aligarh

city, India   KOIL-AHL-ē-GUHR   ˈkɔilˌɑliːˈgəʳ

Koine

Hellenistic Greek lang.; a   koi-NĀ, KOI-nē   kɔiˈneː, ˈkɔiniˑ
standardized dialect

Kojak

US television character   KŌ-JAK   ˈkoːˌdʒæk

Kojonup

town, Australia   KŌ-juh-NUHP   ˈkoːdʒəˌnəp

Foreign Sounds: ue: *Fr.* **rue**, *Ger.* **füllen**   uh(r): *Fr.* **boeuf**, *Ger.* **Höhle**   kh: *Ger.* **ich**, *Scot.* **loch**   ḡ: *Sp.* amigo   v̲: *Sp.* hablar
hl: *Welsh* **Llanelli**.   CAPITALS: primary stress.   SMALL CAPS: secondary stress.   ⓢ: U.S. pron.   ⓔ: British pron.

Kokama, Cocama
lang., Peru, Colombia, Brazil   kō-KAHM-uh   koː'kɑmə

Kokanee
Canadian beer   KŌ-kuh-nē, KŌ-kuh-nā   'koːkəniˑ, 'koːkəneˑ

Koko
Lord High Executioner in The Mikado; *US gorilla trained in sign lang.*   KŌ-kō   'koːkoː

Kokomo
city, IN   KŌ-kuh-MŌ   'koːkə,moː

Kokoschka
Oskar, *Austrian painter*   kuh-KAWSH-kuh   kə'koːʃkə

Koksoak
river, Canada   KAHK-suh-WAK   'kɑksə,wæk

Kolaiah, Koliah
Biblical name   kō-LĪ-uh, kō-LĀ-uh, KŌ-lah-YAH   koː'lɑiə, koː'leːə, 'koːlɑ,jɑ

Kolami
lang., India   kuh-LAHM-ē   kə'lɑmiˑ

Kolkhoz
collective farm in USSR   KUHL-<u>KH</u>AWZ, ⑤ kahl-KAWZ, kahl-KAWS   ˌkəl'xoːz, ⑤ kɑl'koːz, kɑl'koːs

Kolkhoznik
member of a kolkhoz   KUHL-<u>KH</u>AWZ-nik, ⑤ kahl-KAWZ-nik   ˌkəl'xoːznik, ⑤ kɑl'koːznik

Kolkhozy
pl. of Kolkhoz   KUHL-<u>KH</u>AW-zē, ⑤ kahl-KAW-zē   ˌkəl'xoːziˑ, ⑤ kɑl'koːziˑ

Kollwitz
Käthe, *German artist*   KAWL-VITS   'koːl,vits

Kolmar [Colmar]
city, France   KŌL-MAHR   'koːl,mɑʳ

Köln [Cologne]
city, Germany   KUH(R)LN   'kœln

Kol Nidre
Jewish prayer for Yom Kippur   kōl NID-rā, NID-ruh, nē-DRĀ, kawl   koːl 'nidreː, 'nidrə, niː'dreː, koːl

Koloa
division, village, HI   kō-LŌ-uh   koː'loːə

Kolyma
river, Russia   kuh-LĒ-muh   kə'liːmə

Komandorskiye [Commander]
Islands, *Bering Sea*   KAHM-uhn-DAWR-skē-yuh   ˌkɑmən'doːrskiːjə

Komárno
town, Slovakia   KAW-mahr-NAW   'koːmɑʳ,noː

Komarov
Vladimir Mikhaylovich, *Soviet cosmonaut*   kuh-MUH-RAWF   kə,mə'roːf

Komatsu
Japanese manufacturing co.   kō-maht-sōo   koːmɑtsuː

Kombu
seaweed   KAHM-bōo   'kɑmbuː

Komi [Zyryan]
lang., people, Russia   KŌ-mē   'koːmiˑ

Kommunizma, Pik
mtn. peak, Tadzhikistan   PĒK KAHM-yuh-NĒZ-muh   'piːk ˌkɑmjə'niːzmə

Komodo dragon
Indonesian lizard   kuh-MŌD-ō DRAG-uhn   kə,moːdoː 'drægən

Key (col. 2): a: fad ā: fade ah: father ar: marry aw: law e: fed ē: feed er: merry i: hid ī: hide ō: coat ōo: boot
oi: boy ow: now u: put uh: above uhr: bird ch: chop ng: ring sh: show th: thick <u>th</u>: this zh: measure

Komondor
dog breed — KAHM-uhn-DAWR, KŌ-muhn-DAWR — 'kamən,dɔːʳ, 'koːmən,dɔːʳ

Komsomol
communist youth organization, USSR — KUHM-suh-MAWL, ⑤ KAHM-suh-MAWL, -MŌL — ˌkəmsə'mɔːl, ⑤ 'kɑmsə,mɔːl, -ˌmoːl

Konakri
see Conakry

Konde [Makonde]
lang., people, Africa — KŌN-dā — 'koːndeː

Kondrati
pers. name, Russian — KUHN-DRAH-ti — ˌkən'drɑːtij

Kong Kristian
national anthem, Denmark — KAWNG KRĒST-yahn — 'kɔːŋ 'kriːstjɑn

Kongo
lang., people, Africa — KAHNG-gō — 'kɑŋgoː

Konica
tdmk for a camera — KAHN-i-kuh — 'kɑnikə

König-Pilsener
German beer — KUH(R)-nikh PIL-suh-nuhr — 'kœːniç 'pilsənəʳ

Konigsberg
Allen, orig. name of Woody Allen, *US filmmaker* — KŌ-nigz-BUHRG — 'koːnigz,bəʳg

Königsberg
city, Germany; city, region, Russia — KUH(R)-niks-BERK — 'kœːniks,beʳk

Koninck, De
see De Koninck

Kónitsa
commune, Greece — KAWN-yit-SAH — 'kɔːnjit,sɑ

Konkani
lang., India — KAHNG-kuh-nē, KAWNG-kuh-nē — 'kɑŋkəniˑ, 'kɔːŋkəniˑ

Konkow
N. American people — KAHNG-kō — 'kɑŋkoː

Kono
lang., people, Liberia, Mali, Sierra Leone — KŌ-nō — 'koːnoː

Konrád
pers. name, Icelandic — KAWN-ROWD — 'kɔːn,rɑud

Konrad
1. *pers. name, Danish* — KAWN-RAHD — 'kɔːn,rɑd
2. *German* — KAWN-RAHT — 'kɔːn,rɑt
3. *Polish* — KAWN-RAHT — 'kɔːn,rɑːt
4. *Romanian* — KAWN-RAHD — 'kɔːn,rɑd

Konstantin
1. *pers. name, Czech* — KAWN-stahn-CHIN — 'kɔːnstɑn,tʃin
2. *Danish* — KAWN-stahn-TĒN — ˌkɔːnstɑːn'tiːn
3. *Estonian* — KAWN-stahn-TIN — 'kɔːnstɑn,tin
4. *German* — KAWN-stahn-TĒN, KAWN-stahn-TĒN — ˌkɔːnstɑn'tiːn, 'kɔːnstɑn,tiːn
5. *Russian* — kuhn-STUHN-TĒN — kən,stən'tiːn

Konstantínos
pers. name, Greek — KAWN-stahn-DĒ-naws — ˌkɔːnstɑn'diːnɔːs

Konstanty
pers. name, Polish — kawn-STAHN-ti — kɔːn'stɑːnti

Konstanz, Constance
prov, Germany — KAWN-STAHN(T)S — 'kɔːn,stɑn(t)s

Kon Tiki
  raft, Thor Heyerdahl   kahn TĒ-kē   kɑn 'tiːkiˑ
Konya
  province, city, Turkey   KAWN-YAH, kawn-YAH   'kɔːn,jɑː, kɔːn'jɑː
Koochiching
  county, MN   KOO-chuh-CHING   'kuːtʃə,tʃiŋ
Kookaburra
  Australian bird   KUK-uh-BUHR-uh, KUK-uh-BUH-ruh   'kukə,bər-ə, 'kukə,bə-rə
Kookynie
  town, Australia   ku-KĪ-nē   ku'kɑiniˑ
Koolau
  Range, *mountain range, HI*   KŌ-ō-LAH-OO, KŌ-uh-LOW   ,koːoːˈlɑ,uː, ,koːəˈlɑu
Koolauloa
  division, HI   KŌ-ō-LAH-u-LŌ-uh   ,koːoː,lɑ-uˑˈloːə
Koolaupoko
  division, HI   KŌ-ō-LAH-u-PŌ-kō   ,koːoː,lɑ-uˑˈpoːkoː
Koopmans
  Tjalling C., *Dutch-born US*   KOOP-muhnz   'kuːpmənz
    economist (Nobel 1975)
Kooringa
  Australia   ku-RING-guh   ku'riŋgə
Kootenai
  1. county, ID   KOOT-n-Ā, KOOT-n-ē   'kuːtṇ,eː, 'kuːtṇiˑ
  2. *see* Kutenai
Kootenay, -ai
  river, N. America; lake, Canada   KOOT-n-ā, KOOT-n-ē   'kuːtṇeː, 'kuːtṇiˑ
Kopechne
  Mary Jo   kuh-PEK-nē   kə'pekniˑ
Kopernik [Copernicus]
  Mikołaj, *Polish astronomer*   kaw-PER-nēk   kɔːˈpeʳniːk
Kopet-Dag
  mountain range, Iran, Turkmenistan   KAW-pet-DAHG   ,kɔːpetˈdɑg
Kopit
  Arthur, *playwright*   KAHP-uht   'kapət
Koppel
  Ted, *US newscaster*   KAHP-uhl   'kapəl
Koppell
  Bernie, *actor*   KAHP-uhl   'kapəl
Koppernigk [Copernicus]
  Niklas, *Polish astronomer*   KAHP-uhr-nik   'kapəʳnik
Köprülü
  family of viziers, Turkey   kuh(r)-prue-LUE   kœːpry'ly
Korah
  Biblical name   KŌR-uh, KAWR-uh, KAW-rah<u>kh</u>   'koːrə, 'kɔːrə, 'kɔːrɑx
Korahite [Korhite]
  Biblical name   KŌR-uh-HĪT, KAWR-   'koːrə,hɑit, 'kɔːr-
Koran
  holy book of Islam   kuh-RAN, kuh-RAHN, KŌR-AN,   kə'ræn, kə'rɑn, 'koːr,æn,
                                            KAWR-AN   'kɔːr,æn
Koranic
  pert. to the Koran   kuh-RAN-ik, kawr-AN-ik   kə'rænik, kɔːr'ænik
Korathite
  Biblical name   KŌR-uh-THĪT, KAWR-   'koːrə,θɑit, 'kɔːr-
Korbel
  champagne winery, CA   kawr-BEL   kɔːʳ'bel

Key (col. 2):   a: fad   ā: fade   ah: father   ar: **marry**   aw: **law**   e: fed   ē: feed   er: **merry**   i: hid   ī: hide   ō: coat   oo: boot
oi: **boy**   ow: **now**   u: put   uh: **above**   uhr: **bird**   ch: **chop**   ng: **ring**   sh: **show**   th: **thick**   <u>th</u>: **this**   zh: measure

Korbut
   Olga, *sports personality*   KAWR-buht   'kɔːˤbət

Kordestān
   prov, Iran   KAWRD-uh-STAHN, -STAN   ˌkɔːˤdə'stɑn, -'stæn

Kore
   1. Biblical name   KŌR-uh, KAWR-uh, KAW-rah<u>kh</u>   'koːrə, 'kɔːrə, 'kɔːrɑx
   2. pers. name   KŌR-ē, KAWR-ē   'koːriˑ, 'kɔːriˑ

Korea
   country, Asia   kuh-RĒ-uh, kō-, kaw-   kə'riːə, koː-, kɔː-

Korean
   lang., people, Asia   kuh-RĒ-uhn, kō-, kaw-   kə'riːən, koː-, kɔː-

Korhite [Korahite]
   Biblical name   KAWR-HĪT   'kɔːˤˌhɑit

Kórinthos [Corinth]
   city, Greece   KŌ-rin-THAWS   'koːrinˌθɔːs

Korman
   Harvey, *US actor, comedian*   KAWR-muhn   'kɔːˤmən

Kornberg
   Arthur, *US biochemist (Nobel 1959)*   KAWRN-BUHRG   'kɔːˤnˌbəˤg

Kornelis
   pers. name, Dutch   kawr-NĀ-luhs   kɔːr'neːləs

Korney
   pers. name, Russian   kawrn-YĀ   kɔːˤn'jeː

Kornilov
   Lavrenti, *Russian militarist*   kawr-N(Y)Ē-luhf   kɔːˤ'n(j)iːləf

Korumburra
   town, Australia   KAHR-uhm-BUHR-uh   ˌkɑrəm'bərə

Koryak
   lang., people, region, Russia   KAWR-yak   'kɔːˤjæk

Korzeniowski
   Jósef, *orig. name of* Joseph Conrad, *British novelist*   KAW-zhen-YAWF-skē   ˌkɔːʒen'jɔːfskiˑ

Korzybski
   Alfred, *US semanticist*   kaw-ZHIP-skē, ⑤ kawr-ZIP-skē   kɔː'ʒipskiˑ, ⑤ kɔːˤ'zipskiˑ

Kós, Cos
   Greek island   KAHS, KAWS   'kɑs, 'kɔːs

Kosar
   Bernie, *football player*   KŌ-ZAHR   'koːˌzɑˤ

Kosciusko
   1. county, IN; city, MS   KAHS-ē-UHS-kō, KAHZ-ē-UHS-kō   ˌkɑsiː'əskoː, ˌkɑziː'əskoː
   2. Mount, Australia   KAHZ-ē-UHS-kō   ˌkɑziː'əskoː
   3. bridge, NY   KAHS-kē-UHS-kō   ˌkɑskiː'əskoː

Kosciuszko
   Tadeusz, *Polish militarist*   kawsh-CHUSH-kō, ⑤ KAHS-ē-UHS-kō, KAHZ-ē-UHS-kō   kɔːʃ'tʃuʃkoː, ⑤ ˌkɑsiː'əskoː, ˌkɑziː'əskoː

Košice
   city, Slovakia   KAW-shuht-SĀ   'kɔːʃətˌseː

Kosinski
   Jerzy, *Polish-born US writer*   kuh-ZIN(T)-skē   kə'zin(t)skiˑ

Kosovo
   province, Serbia   KAW-suh-VŌ   'kɔːsəˌvoː

Kossel
   Albrecht, *German physiological chemist (Nobel 1910)*   KAWS-uhl   'kɔːsəl

---

Foreign Sounds: **ue**: *Fr.* r**ue**, *Ger.* f**ü**llen   **uh(r)**: *Fr.* b**oeu**f, *Ger.* H**öh**le   <u>**kh**</u>: *Ger.* i**ch**, *Scot.* lo**ch**   ğ: *Sp.* ami**g**o   v̱: *Sp.* ha**b**lar
hl: *Welsh* **Ll**anelli.   CAPITALS: primary stress.   SMALL CAPS: secondary stress.   ⑤: U.S. pron.   ⓔ: British pron.

Kossuth

   1. county, IA — kuh-SŌŌTH — kə'suːθ

   2. Lajos, *Hungarian political leader* — KAW-SHUT, ⑤ KAHS-ŌŌTH, kah-SŌŌTH — 'kɔː,ʃut, ⑤ 'kɑs,uːθ, kɑ'suːθ

Kostelanetz

   Richard, *US writer, artist* — KAHS-tuh-LAHN-uhts — ,kɑstə'lɑnəts

Kosygin

   Alexei, *premier, USSR* — kuh-SIG-yin, ⑤ kuh-SĒ-guhn — kə'sigjin, ⑤ kə'siːgən

Kota

   lang., people, South India; lang., people, Africa — KŌT-uh — 'koːtə

Kota Kinabalu

   city, Malaysia — KŌT-uh KIN-uh-buh-LŌŌ — ,koːtə ,kinəbə'luː

Kotex

   tdmk for feminine hygiene products — KŌ-TEKS — 'koː,teks

Kotka

   port, Finland — KAWT-kuh — 'kɔːtkə

Kotoko

   lang., people, Chad — kuh-TŌ-kō — kə'toːkoː

Kotzebue

   1. August Friedrich Ferdinand von, *German dramatist;* Otto, *German naval officer and explorer* — KAHT-suh-B(Y)ŌŌ, KAWT- — 'kɑtsə,b(j)uː, 'kɔːt-

   2. city, AK — KAHT-suh-BYŌŌ — 'kɑtsə,bjuː

Koufax

   Sandy, *US baseball player* — KŌ-FAKS — 'koː,fæks

Kountze

   city, TX — KŌŌN(T)S — 'kuːn(t)s

Koussevitzky

   Serge, *US/Russian conductor* — KŌŌ-suh-VIT-skē — ,kuːsə'vitski·

Kovno [Kaunas]

   city, Lithuania — KAWV-nō — 'kɔːvnoː

Kowloon

   peninsula, Hong Kong — KOW-LŌŌN — 'kɑu'luːn

Koyukon

   N. American people — kō-YŌŌ-KAHN — koː'juː,kɑn

Koyukuk

   river, AK — KĪ-uh-KUHK — 'kɑiə,kək

Koz

   Biblical name — KAHZ, KŌTS — 'kɑz, 'koːts

Kpa

   lang., Africa — kuh-PAH — kə'pɑ

Kpelle

   lang., people, Liberia, Guinea — kuh-PEL-uh — kə'pelə

Kra

   Isthmus of, *Thailand* — KRAH — 'krɑ

Krafft

   pers. name — KRAFT — 'kræft

Krafft-Ebing

   Richard, *German neurologist* — KRAHFT-Ā-bing, KRAFT-Ā-bing, KRAFT-EB-ing — 'krɑft'eːbiŋ, 'kræft'eːbiŋ, 'kræft'ebiŋ

Kragerø

   port, Norway — KRAHG-uh-RUH(R) — 'krɑgə,rœː

Kragujevac

   city, former capital, Serbia — KRAH-gŌŌ-yuh-VAHTS — 'krɑːguˑjə,vɑːts

---

Key (col. 2): a: fad ā: fade ah: father ar: marry aw: law e: fed ē: feed er: merry i: hid ī: hide ō: coat ōō: boot
oi: boy ow: now u: put uh: above uhr: bird ch: chop ng: ring sh: show th: thick <u>th</u>: this zh: measure

Krahn
   lang., Liberia, Ivory Coast   KRAHN   'krɑn

Krajina
   region, Croatia   krah-YĒ-nuh   krɑːˈjiːnə

Krakatau, -tao [Krakatoa]
   island, volcano, Indonesia   KRAK-uh-TOW   ˌkrækəˈtɑu

Krakatoa
   island, volcano, Indonesia   KRAK-uh-TŌ-uh   ˌkrækəˈtoːə

Kraków, Cracow
   city, Poland   KRAH-KOŌF, ⓢ KRAHK-OW, KRAK-OW   'krɑːˌkuːf, ⓢ 'krɑkˌɑu, 'krækˌɑu

Krakus
   Polish beer   KRAH-kus   'krɑːkus

Kramer
   Stanley E., *US film maker*   KRĀ-muhr   'kreːmərᵣ

Krantz
   Judith, *US novelist*   KRAN(T)S   'kræn(t)s

Kraprayoon
   Suchinda, *Thai politician*   KRAHP-RĪ-(Y)OON   ˌkrɑpˌraiˈ(j)uːn

Krasnodar
   city, Russia   KRAHS-nuh-DAHR   'krɑsnəˌdɑrᵣ

Krasnoyarsk
   city, Russia   KRAHS-nuh-YAHRSK   ˌkrɑsnəˈjɑrᵣsk

Kravchuk
   Leonid Makarovich, *Ukrainian political leader*   KRAHV-chuk   'krɑvtʃuk

Krebs
   Sir Hans A., *German-born British biochemist (Nobel 1953)*   KREBZ   'krebz

Krefeld
   city, Germany   KRĀ-FELT   'kreːˌfelt

Kreisky
   Bruno, *Austrian chancellor*   KRĪ-skē   'krɑiskiˑ

Kreisler
   Fritz, *US violinist*   KRĪ-sluhr   'krɑislərᵣ

Kreps
   Juanita Morris, *US secretary of commerce*   KREPS   'kreps

Kreskin
   US mentalist   KRES-kuhn   'kreskən

Kreutzer
   Sonata, *Beethoven violin sonata*   KROIT-suhr   'krɔitsərᵣ

Kreymborg
   Alfred, *US writer*   KRĀM-BAWRG   'kreːmˌbɔːʳg

Krieg
   Dave, *football player*   KRĒG   'kriːg

Kriegspiel
   game   KRĒG-SHPĒL, KRĒG-SPĒL   'kriːgˌʃpiːl, 'kriːgˌspiːl

Kriemhild
   wife of Siegfried   KRĒM-HILD   'kriːmˌhild

Krimmler Wasserfälle
   waterfall, Austria   KRIM-luhr VAHS-uhr-FEL-uh   'krimlərᵣ 'vɑsəʳˌfelə

Krio
   lang., Sierra Leone   KRĒ-ō   'kriːoː

Foreign Sounds: ue: *Fr.* **rue**, *Ger.* füllen   uh(r): *Fr.* **boeuf**, *Ger.* Höhle   kh: *Ger.* ich, *Scot.* loch   ḡ: *Sp.* amigo   v̱: *Sp.* hablar
hl: *Welsh* Llanelli.   CAPITALS: primary stress.   SMALL CAPS: secondary stress.   ⓢ: U.S. pron.   ⓔ: British pron.

Kris		
pers. name	KRIS	ˈkris
Krishna		
Hindu incarnation of Vishnu; river, India; pers. name	KRISH-nuh	ˈkriʃnə
Krishnaism		
religion	KRISH-nuh-IZ-uhm	ˈkriʃnəˌizəm
Krista		
pers. name	KRIS-tuh	ˈkristə
Kristen		
pers. name	KRIS-tuhn	ˈkristən
Kristi, Kristie		
pers. name	KRIS-tē	ˈkristiˑ
Kristian		
1. pers. name, Danish	KRĒS-TYAHN	ˈkriːsˌtjɑn
2. Dutch	KRIS-tē-AHN	ˈkristiːˌɑn
3. Finnish	KRIS-ti-AHN	ˈkristiˌɑːn
Kristiansand		
port, Norway	KRIS-chuhn-SAN(D), KRISH-chuhn-SAN(D)	ˈkristʃənˌsæn(d), ˈkriʃtʃənˌsæn(d)
Kristiansen		
Ingrid, *Norwegian marathoner*	KRIST-yahn-suhn, [$] KRIS-chuhn-suhn	ˈkristjɑnsən, [$] ˈkristʃənsən
Kristiansund		
port, Norway	KRIS-chuhn-SUN(D), KRISH-chuhn-SUN(D)	ˈkristʃənˌsun(d), ˈkriʃtʃənˌsun(d)
Kristin		
pers. name	KRIS-tuhn	ˈkristən
Kristofer		
pers. name, Norwegian, Swedish	kris-TAW-fuhr	krisˈtɔːfər
Kristoffer		
1. pers. name, Danish	krēs-TAWF-uhr	kriːsˈtɔːfər
2. Norwegian, Swedish	kris-TAWF-fuhr	krisˈtɔːffər
Kristofferson		
Kris, *US entertainer*	kri-STAW-fuhr-suhn, kri-STAHF-uhr-suhn	kriˈstɔːfə^{r}sən, kriˈstɑfə^{r}sən
Kristy		
pers. name	KRIS-tē	ˈkristiˑ
Kríti [Crete]		
island, Greece	KRĒ-tē	ˈkriːtiˑ
Križanić		
Juraj, Croatian priest and scholar	KRĒ-zhah-NĒCH	ˈkriːʒɑːˌniːtʃ
Krk		
island, Croatia	KUHRK	ˈkə^{r}k
Krka		
river, Croatia	KUHR-kuh	ˈkə^{r}kə
Krnov		
town, Czech republic	KUHR-NAWF	ˈkə^{r}ˌnɔːf
Kroc		
Ray A., *US businessman*	KRAHK	ˈkrɑk
Kroeber		
Alfred L., *US anthropologist*	KRŌ-buhr	ˈkroːbə^{r}
Krogh		
S. A. S., *Danish physiologist (Nobel 1920)*	KRAWḠ	ˈkrɔːɣ

Key (col. 2): a: **fad** ā: **fade** ah: **father** ar: **marry** aw: **law** e: **fed** ē: **feed** er: **merry** i: **hid** ī: **hide** ō: **coat** o͞o: **boot** oi: **boy** ow: **now** u: **put** uh: **above** uhr: **bird** ch: **chop** ng: **ring** sh: **show** th: **thick** th: **this** zh: **measure**

Krona		
monetary unit, Sweden, Iceland, Faeroe Islands	KRO͞O-nah, [$] KRŌ-nuh	'kruːnaː, [$] 'kroːnə
Krone		
Danish monetary unit	KRŌ-nuh	'kroːnə
Kronen		
German beer	KRŌ-nuhn	'kroːnən
Kronenbourg		
French beer	kraw-ne^{n}-BO͞OR	krɔːnẽbuːr
Kronos		
Titan	KRŌ-nuhs, KRŌ-nōs	'kroːnəs, 'kroːnoːs
Kronstadt		
city, Romania	krahn-SHTAHT, [$] KRŌN-STAT	kran'ʃtat, [$] 'kroːnˌstæt
Kroonstad		
town, Orange Free State	KRŌN-STAT	'kroːnˌstæt
Kropf Edel		
German beer	KRAWPF ĀD-l	'krɔːpf 'eːdl̩
Kropotkin		
Pyotr, *Russian political leader*	kruh-PAHT-k(y)in	krə'patk(j)in
Krueger		
Freddy, *horror movie character*	KRO͞O-guhr	'kruːgə^{r}
Kruger		
1. Jerome, *US government official*	KRO͞O-guhr	'kruːgə^{r}
2. Paul, *S. African statesman*	KRUE-uhr, [$] KRO͞O-guhr	'kryːə^{r}, [$] 'kruːgə^{r}
Krugerrand		
gold coin, South Africa	KRO͞O-guh-RAND	'kruːgəˌrænd
Kru-Krawi		
lang., Liberia, Ivory Coast	KRO͞O-KROW-ē	'kruː'kraui·
Kru [Kru-Krawi]		
lang., Liberia, Ivory Coast	KRO͞O	'kruː
Krupa		
Gene, *US jazz drummer*	KRO͞O-puh	'kruːpə
Krupp		
German manufacturing co.	KRUP, KRUHP	'krup, 'krəp
Krups		
appliances	KRUHPS	'krəps
Krupske		
Danya, *US director, choreographer*	KRUHP-skē	'krəpski·
Kruševac		
town, Serbia	KRO͞O-shuh-VAHTS	'kruːʃəˌvaːts
Krutch		
Joseph Wood, *US critic and naturalist*	KRO͞OCH	'kruːtʃ
Krym [Crimea]		
peninsula, Ukraine	KRIM	'krim
Krypton		
fictional planet in Superman comics; element	KRIP-TAHN	'kripˌtan
Krzysztof		
pers. name, Polish (K. Penderecki)	KSHISH-tawf, [$] KRIS-tawf	'kʃiʃtɔːf, [$] 'kristɔːf
Krzyzewski		
Mike, *US college basketball coach*	shuh-SHEV-skē	ʃə'ʃevski·
Ktaadn		
see Katahdin		

Kuala Lumpur
  city, Malaysia   KWAHL-uh LUM-PUR, ku-AHL-uh,   ˌkwɑlə ˈlumˌpuʳ, kuˈɑlə,
                        LUHM-PUR, lum-PUR   ˈləmˌpuʳ, lumˈpuʳ

Kua [Makua]
  lang., people, Africa   KWAH   ˈkwɑ

Kubango
  river, Africa   ko͞o-BAHNG-gō   kuːˈbɑŋgoː

Kubek
  Tony, *US baseball player*   K(Y)O͞O-BEK   ˈk(j)uːˌbek

Kublai Khan
  Mongol leader   KO͞O-bluh KAHN, KO͞O-BLĪ KAHN   ˌkuːblə ˈkɑn, ˌkuːˌblai ˈkɑn

Kubler-Ross
  Elisabeth, *US physician & author*   KO͞O-bluhr-RAWS   ˈkuːbləʳˌrɔːs

Kubrick
  Stanley, *US film director*   K(Y)O͞O-brik   ˈk(j)uːbrik

Kučera
  Henry, *US linguist*   KO͞O-chuh-ruh   ˈkuːtʃərə

Kudzu
  vine   KUD-zo͞o   ˈkudzuː

Kuebler's
  Park, *St. Louis, MO*   K(Y)O͞OB-luhrz   ˈk(j)uːbləʳz

Kuei-lin
  see Guilin

Kuei-yang
  see Guiyang

Kufic
  Arabic script   K(Y)O͞O-fik   ˈk(j)uːfik

Kufow [Ch'ü-fou]
  town, China, residence of Confucius   CHUE-FŌ, KO͞O-   ˈtʃyːˈfoː, ˈkuː-

Kuhn
  Bowie, *US attorney, baseball*   K(Y)O͞ON   ˈk(j)uːn
    commissioner

Kui
  lang., people, India   KO͞O-ē   ˈkuːiˑ

Kuibyshev
  city, Russia   KWĒ-buh-SHEF, KO͞O-ē-buh-SHEF   ˈkwiːbəˌʃef, ˈkuːiːbəˌʃef

Kuiper
  Gerard (Gerrit), *Dutch-born US*   KĪ-puhr   ˈkaipəʳ
    astronomer

Ku Klux Klan
  white-supremacist organization   K(Y)O͞O KLUHKS KLAN, KLO͞O   ˌk(j)uː ˌkləks ˈklæn, ˌkluː

Kulmbacher Mönchshof
  German beer   KULM-BAHKH-uhr   ˈkulmˌbɑxəʳ ˈmœːnçsˌhɔːf
                  MUH(R)NKHS-HAWF

Kültepe [Kanesh]
  ancient Assyrian city, Turkey   KUL-tuh-PĀ   ˌkultəˈpeː

Kumbh Mela
  Indian festival   KUM-muh-LAH   ˈkumməˌlɑ

Kŭmgang
  Mountains, *North Korea*   kum-gahng   kumgɑŋ

Kumilla
  see Comilla

Kümmel
  liqueur   KIM-uhl, KUEM-uhl   ˈkiməl, ˈkyməl

Key (col. 2):   a: fad   ā: fade   ah: father   ar: marry   aw: law   e: fed   ē: feed   er: merry   i: hid   ī: hide   ō: coat   o͞o: boot
oi: boy   ow: now   u: put   uh: above   uhr: bird   ch: chop   ng: ring   sh: show   th: thick   th̲: this   zh: measure

Kumon
Range, *mtn. range, Burma*   K̄OO-MAWN   'kuː‚mɔːn

Kumyk
lang., people, Caucasus Mts.   k̄oo-MIK   kuː'mik

Kun
Béla, *Hungarian political leader*   K̄OON   'kuːn

Kunama
lang., Ethiopia   k̄oo-NAHM-uh   kuː'nɑmə

Kundera
Milan, *Czech-born French novelist*   kun-DER-uh   kun'derə

!Kung
African people   khuⁿ, Ⓢ KUNG   ꞔxũ, Ⓢ 'kuŋ

K'ung Fu-tzu [Confucius]
Chinese philosopher   KUNG F̄OOD-Z̄OO   'kuŋ 'fuːd'zuː

Kunimatsu
pers. name, Japanese   kun-ē-maht-su   kuniːmɑtsu

Kunin
Madeleine May, *US politician*   KȲOO-nuhn   'kjuːnən

Kunitz
Stanley, *US poet*   K̄OO-nits   'kuːnits

Kunming, K'ung-ming
city, China   KUN-MING   'kun'miŋ

Kuno
pers. name, German   K̄OO-nō   'kuːnoː

Kuomintang
political party, Taiwan   GW̄O-MIN-TAHNG   'gwoː'min'taŋ

Küppers Kölsch
German beer   KUEP-uhrs KUH(R)LSH   'kypəʳs 'kœlʃ

Kura
river, Turkey, Georgia, Azerbaijan   kuh-RAH, KUR-uh   kə'rɑ, 'kurə

Kurakin
Boris Ivanovich, *Russian diplomat*   k̄oo-RAHK-in   kuː'rɑkin

Kuralt
Charles, *US TV personality*   kuh-RAWLT, kuh-RAHLT   kə'rɔːlt, kə'rɑlt

Kurath
Hans, *US linguist*   KUR-AHT, KYUR-AHT   'kur‚ɑt, 'kjur‚ɑt

Kurd
1. *people, Middle East, Europe*   KUHRD, KURD   'kəʳd, 'kuʳd
2. *pers. name, German*   KURT   'kuʳt

Kurdish
lang., Middle East, Europe   KUHRD-ish, KURD-ish   'kəʳdiʃ, 'kuʳdiʃ

Kurdistan
region, Middle East; rug   KUHRD-uh-STAHN, KURD-uh-STAHN, -STAN   ‚kəʳdə'stɑn, ‚kuʳdə'stɑn, -'stæn

Kure
city, Japan   k̄oo-rā   kuːreː

Kuril
Islands, *Pacific*   KYUR-ĒL, kyu-RĒL   'kjur‚iːl, kju'riːl

Kuri [Lezghian]
lang., people, Caucasus Mts.   KUR-ē   'kuri·

Kuril'skiye Ostrova [Kuril]
Pacific   ku-RĒL-skuh-yuh AWS-truh-vuh   ku'riːlskəjə 'ɔːstrəvə

Kurku
lang., people, India   KUR-k̄oo   'kuʳkuː

Foreign Sounds: ue: *Fr.* **rue**, *Ger.* **füllen**   uh(r): *Fr.* **boeuf**, *Ger.* **Höhle**   kh: *Ger.* **ich**, *Scot.* **loch**   g̱: *Sp.* **amigo**   v: *Sp.* **hablar**
hl: *Welsh* **Llanelli**.   CAPITALS: primary stress.   SMALL CAPS: secondary stress.   Ⓢ: U.S. pron.   Ⓔ: British pron.

Kurosawa
Japanese film director	KUR-uh-SAH-wuh	ˌkurəˈsawə

Kurri Kurri
town, Australia	KUHR-ē KUHR-ē	ˈkəriˑ ˌkəriˑ

Kursk
city, Russia	KURSK	ˈkuʳsk

Kurt
1. pers. name	KUHRT	ˈkəʳt
2. German	KURT	ˈkuʳt
3. Swedish	KUHRT	ˈkərt

Kurukh
lang., people, India	KUR-uhk	ˈkurək

Kurukhi
lang., India	KUR-uh-kē	ˈkurəkiˑ

Kurumba
lang., people, Burkina Faso	kuh-ROOM-buh	kəˈruːmbə

Kurzweil
tdmk for optical scanning devices	KUHRT-SWĪL, KUHRZ-WĪL	ˈkəʳtˌswɑil, ˈkəʳzˌwɑil

Kusch
Polykarp, *German-born US physicist* (Nobel 1955)	KUSH	ˈkuʃ

Kush, Cush
ancient country on Nile	KUHSH, KUSH	ˈkəʃ, ˈkuʃ

Kushaiah
Biblical name	k(y)oo-SHĪ-uh, KOO-shah-YAH	k(j)uːˈʃaiə, ˌkuːʃaˈja

Kuskokwim
river, AK	KUHS-kuh-KWIM	ˈkəskəˌkwim

Kusu
lang., Africa	KOO-soo	ˈkuːsuː

Kutchin
N. American people	koo-CHIN	kuːˈtʃin

Kutenai, Kootenai
N. American people	KOOT-n-ā, KOOT-n-ē	ˈkuːtn̩eː, ˈkuːtn̩iˑ

Kutuzov
Mikhail, *Russian militarist*	koo-TOO-zuhf, -ZAWF, -ZAWV	kuːˈtuːzəf, -ˌzɔːf, -ˌzɔːv

Kutztown
borough, PA	KUTS-TOWN	ˈkutsˌtɑun

Kuvasz
dog breed	KOO-VAHS	ˈkuːˌvɑs

Kuwait
country, Persian Gulf	kuh-WĀT	kəˈweːt

Kuwaiti
pert. to Kuwait	kuh-WĀT-ē	kəˈweːṭiˑ

Kuybyshev
city, Russia	KOO-i-buh-SHEF	ˈkuːibəˌʃef

Kuzmich
pers. name, Russian	KOOZ-myēch	ˈkuːʐm̦iːtʃ

Kuznets
Simon, *Russian-born US economist* (Nobel 1971)	KUHZ-NETS	ˈkəzˌnets

Kuznetsk
former name of Novokuznetsk	kuz-NETSK	kuzˈnetsk

Kwaa
lang., Liberia	KWAH	ˈkwɑ

Key (col. 2):   a: fad   ā: fade   ah: father   ar: marry   aw: law   e: fed   ē: feed   er: merry   i: hid   ī: hide   ō: coat   oo: boot
oi: boy   ow: now   u: put   uh: above   uhr: bird   ch: chop   ng: ring   sh: show   th: thick   th̲: this   zh: measure

Kwajalein
    atoll, Marshall Islands   KWAHJ-uh-luhn, KWAHJ-uh-LĀN   'kwɑdʒələn, 'kwɑdʒəˌleːn

Kwak
    Belgian beer   KWAHK   'kwɑːk

Kwakiutl
    N. American people   KWAHK-ē-O͞OT-l, kwahk-YO͞OT-l   ˌkwɑkiː'uːtl̩, kwɑk'juːtl̩

Kwame
    pers. name (K. Nkrumah)   KWAHM-ā   'kwɑmeː

KwaNdebele
    state, South Africa   KWAHN-duh-BĀ-lā   ˌkwɑndə'beːleː

Kwangchow
    see Guangzhou

Kwango
    river, Africa   KWAHNG-gō   'kwɑŋgoː

Kwangsi Chuang [Guangxi]
    region, China   GWAHNG-SĒ chuh-WAHNG   'gwɑŋ'siː tʃə'wɑŋ

Kwangtung
    see Guangdong

Kwangwa
    African people   KWAHNG-gwuh   'kwɑŋgwə

Kwan-Ichi
    pers. name, Japanese   kwahn-ē-chē   kwɑniːtʃiː

Kwantung
    territory, China   GWAHN-DUNG   'gwɑn'duŋ

Kwanza
    see Cuanza

Kwanzaa, -za
    African-American festival   KWAHN-zuh   'kwɑnzə

Kwapa [Quapaw]
    N. American people   KWAW-PAW   'kwɔːˌpɔː

KwaZulu
    state, South Africa   kwah-ZO͞O-lo͞o   kwɑ'zuːlu

Kweichow
    see Guizhou

Kweilin
    see Guilin

Kweisi
    pers. name (K. Mfume)   KWĀ-sē, KWĀ-zē   'kweːsiˑ, 'kweːziˑ

Kweiyang
    see Guiyang

Kweni
    lang., Ivory Coast   KWĀ-nē   'kweːniˑ

Ky
    see Nguyen Cao Ky

Kyd
    Thomas, *English dramatist*   KID   'kid

Kyeretwi
    pers. name, Twi   KYER-e-TWĒ   'kjereˌtwiː

Kyle
    pers. name   KĪL   'kɑil

Kynuna
    town, Australia   kī-NO͞O-nuh   kɑi'nuːnə

Kyocera
    Japanese electronics co.   kē-ō-SER-uh   kiːoːˈserə

Foreign Sounds: ue: *Fr.* **rue**, *Ger.* **füllen**   uh(r): *Fr.* **boeuf**, *Ger.* **Höhle**   <u>kh</u>: *Ger.* **ich**, *Scot.* **loch**   g̃: *Sp.* **amigo**   v̲: *Sp.* **hablar**
hl: *Welsh* **Llanelli**.   CAPITALS: primary stress.   SMALL CAPS: secondary stress.   Ⓢ: U.S. pron.   Ⓔ: British pron.

Kyoga, Kioga
  lake, Uganda   kē-Ō-guh   kiːˈoːgə

Kyŏngju
  town, S. Korea   kē-AWNG-JOO   kiːˈɔːŋˈdʒuː

Kyoto, Kyōto
  city, Japan   kē-ō-tō, Ⓢ kē-ŌT-ō   kiːoːtoː, Ⓢ kiːˈoːṭoː

Kyowa Saitama
  Japanese bank   kē-ō-(w)ah sī-tahm-ah   kiːoː(w)ɑ sɑitɑmɑ

Kyrie eleison
  liturgical prayer, section of the Mass   KIR-ē-Ā uh-LĀ(-uh)-SAHN,   ˈkiriːˌeː əˈleː(ə)ˌsɑn,
                                   uh-LĀ(-uh)-suhn   əˈleː(ə)sən

Kyrillos
  pers. name, Mod. Greek   KYĒ-rē-LAWS   ˈkjiːriːˌlɔːs

Kyūshū
  island, Japan   kē-oo-shoo   kiːuːʃuː

Kyzylkum, Peski
  desert, Uzbekistan, Kazakhstan   PESH-kyē kuh-ZIL-KOOM   ˈpeʃkjiː kəˌzilˈkuːm

Kyzyl Kum, Qizil Qum
  desert, Uzbekistan, Kazakhstan   kuh-ZIL KOOM   kəˈzil ˈkuːm

---

Key (col. 2):   a: fad   ā: fade   ah: father   ar: marry   aw: law   e: fed   ē: feed   er: merry   i: hid   ī: hide   ō: coat   oo: boot
oi: boy   ow: now   u: put   uh: above   uhr: bird   ch: chop   ng: ring   sh: show   th: thick   th̲: this   zh: measure

L

Laadah
Biblical name LĀ-uhd-uh, lah-DAH 'leːədə, laˈdɑ

Laadan
Biblical name LĀ-uh-DAN, lah-DAHN 'leːə,dæn, laˈdɑn

La Araucanía
region, Chile lah ah-row-kah-NĒ-ah lɑ ɑrɑukaˈniːɑ

Laayoune [Aaiu'n, El]
town, W Sahara lī-OON lɑiˈuːn

Laban
Biblical name LĀ-buhn 'leːbən

Labatt
Canadian brewing co. luh-BAT ləˈbæt

La Bayamesa
national anthem, Cuba lah BAH-yah-mā-sah lɑ ˈbɑjameːsɑ

Labdacus
father of Laius LAB-duh-kuhs 'læbdəkəs

Labelle
Patti, *US singer* luh-BEL ləˈbel

La Belle Strasbourgeoise
French beer lah BEL strahs-boor-ZHWAHZ lɑː bel strɑːsbuːrʒwɑːz

Labette
Community College, *KS* luh-BET ləˈbet

L'Abidjanaise
national anthem, Ivory Coast lah-bēd-zhah-NEZ lɑːbiːdʒɑːnez

La Bohème
see Bohème, La

Laboure
Junior College, *MA* luh-BUR ləˈbuʳ

Labov
William, *US linguist* luh-BŌV, luh-BUHV ləˈboːv, ləˈbəv

Labovian
pert. to Labov luh-BŌ-vē-uhn, luh-BUHV-ē-uhn ləˈboːviːən, ləˈbəviːən

La Brabançonne
national anthem, Belgium lah brah-bahⁿ-SAWN lɑː brɑːbɑ̄sɔːn

Labrador
prov, Canada; dog breed LAB-ruh-DAWR 'læbrə,dɔːʳ

La Brea
Tar Pits, *CA* luh BRĀ-uh lə ˈbreːə

La Bruyère
Jean de, *French moralist* lah brue-YER lɑː bryjer

Labuan
island, Malaysia luh-BOO-uhn ləˈbuːən

Foreign Sounds: **ue**: *Fr.* **rue**, *Ger.* **füllen**   **uh(r)**: *Fr.* **boeuf**, *Ger.* **Höhle**   <u>kh</u>: *Ger.* i**ch**, *Scot.* lo**ch**   ḡ: *Sp.* ami**g**o   <u>v</u>: *Sp.* ha**b**lar   **hl**: *Welsh* **Ll**anelli.   CAPITALS: primary stress.   SMALL CAPS: secondary stress.   Ⓢ: U.S. pron.   Ⓔ: British pron.

Laburnum
 tree   luh-BUHR-nuhm   ləˈbəʳnəm
Lacandon
 rain forest, Mexico   lah-KAHN-dōn   lɑˈkɑndoːn
Laccadive [Lakshadweep]
 Islands, *Arabian Sea*   LAK-uh-DĪV   ˈlækəˌdɑiv
Lac Courte Oreilles
 Indian reservation, US   lahk KURT aw-RĀ(Y)   lɑk ˈkuʳt ɔːˈreː(j)
Lac Du Flambeau
 Indian reservation, US   LAHK dōō flam-BŌ   ˈlɑk duˑ flæmˈboː
Lacedaemonia
 ancient region, Greece   LAS-uhd-uh-MŌ-nē-uh   ˌlæsədəˈmoːniːə
Lacedaemon [Sparta]
 ancient city, country, Greece   LAS-uh-DĒ-muhn   ˌlæsəˈdiːmən
Lacerta
 constellation   luh-SUHRT-uh   ləˈsəʳtə
Lacey
 pers. name   LĀ-sē   ˈleːsiˑ
Laches
 dialogue of Plato   LĀ-KĒZ   ˈleːˌkiːz
Lachesis
 mythological Fate   LAK-uh-suhs   ˈlækəsəs
Lachine
 town, Canada   lah-SHĒN, ⑤ luh-SHĒN   lɑːʃiːn, ⑤ ləˈʃiːn
Lachish
 Biblical name   LĀ-kish, lah-<u>KH</u>ĒSH   ˈleːkiʃ, lɑˈxiːʃ
Lachlan
 pers. name   LAK-luhn, LAHK-luhn   ˈlæklən, ˈlɑklən
Lachryma Christi
 see Lacrima Christi
Lackawanna
 county, PA; city, NY   LAK-uh-WAHN-uh   ˌlækəˈwɑnə
Laclede
 county, MO; Park, *former ballpark,* luh-KLĒD, luh-KLED   ləˈkliːd, ləˈkled
  St. Louis, MO
La Concepción
 town, Panama   lah kawn-seps-YAWN   lɑ kɔːnsepsˈjɔːn
Lacon
 city, IL   LĀ-kuhn   ˈleːkən
Laconia
 city, NH; region, Greece   luh-KŌ-nē-uh, luh-KŌN-yuh   ləˈkoːniːə, ləˈkoːnjə
La Coruña
 prov & city, Spain   lah kuh-RŌŌN-yuh   lɑ kəˈruːnjə
Lac Qui Parle
 lake, county, MN   LAK ē PAHRL   ˌlæk iː ˈpɑʳl
Lacrima Christi, Lachryma Christi
 Italian wine   LAHK-ruh-muh KRIS-tē, LAK-   ˈlɑkrəmə ˈkristiˑ, ˈlæk-
La Crosse
 city, county, WI   luh KRAWS   lə ˈkrɔːs
Lactantius
 early Christian writer   lak-TAN-sh(ē-)uhs   lækˈtænʃ(iː)əs
Lac Vieux Desert
 lake, WI, MI   lahk VYŌŌ duh-ZAR, -ZER   lɑk ˌvjuː dəˈzæʳ, -ˈzeʳ
Lacy
 Beatrice Cates, *psychophysiologist*   LĀ-sē   ˈleːsiˑ

Key (col. 2):   a: f**a**d   ā: f**a**de   ah: f**a**ther   ar: m**a**rry   aw: l**a**w   e: f**e**d   ē: f**ee**d   er: m**e**rry   i: h**i**d   ī: h**i**de   ō: c**oa**t   ōō: b**oo**t
oi: b**oy**   ow: n**ow**   u: p**u**t   uh: **a**bove   uhr: b**i**rd   ch: **ch**op   ng: ri**ng**   sh: **sh**ow   th: **th**ick   <u>th</u>: **th**is   zh: mea**s**ure

Ladakh, Ladak
   district, Jammu and Kashmir   luh-DAHK   lə'dɑk
Lade
   island off Miletus   LAHD-ā   'lɑdeː
La Dessalinienne
   national anthem, Haiti   lah dā-sah-lēn-YEN   lɑː deːsɑːliːnjen
Lādhiqīyah, Al
   city, Syria   AHL LAH-tuh-KĒ-(y)uh, AL   ˌɑːl ˌlɑtə'kiː(j)ə, ˌæl
Ladin
   lang., Italy   luh-DĒN   lə'diːn
Ladino
   lang., Sephardic Jews   lah-<u>TH</u>Ē-nō, ⑤ luh-DĒ-nō   lɑ'ðiːnoː, ⑤ lə'diːnoː
Ladislas
   1. pers. name   LAD-uhs-luhs, LAD-uhs-LAHS   'lædəsləs, 'lædəsˌlɑs
   2. French   lah-dē-SLAHS   lɑːdiːslɑːs
Ladislaus
   pers. name, German   LAHD-is-LOWS   'lɑdisˌlɑus
Ladislav
   pers. name, Czech   LAHJ-is-LAHF   'lɑːdʒisˌlɑːf
Ladoga
   lake, Russia   LAHD-uh-guh, LAD-uh-guh   'lɑdəgə, 'lædəgə
Ladon
   dragon guarding the apples of the   LĀD-n, LĀ-DAHN   'leːdn̩, 'leːˌdɑn
     Hesperides; Greek river god
Ladozhskoye Ozero [Ladoga]
   lake, Russia   LAHD-uhsh-(s)kuh-yuh UHZ-YER-ō   'lɑːdəʃ(s)kəjə ˌəz'jeroː
Ladrones
   island group, Pacific Ocean   lah-<u>TH</u>RŌ-nās, ⑤ luh-DRŌNZ,   lɑ'ðroːneːs, ⑤ lə'droːnz,
      luh-DRŌ-NĀS   lə'droːˌneːs
Ladue
   city, MO   luh-D(Y)O͞O   lə'd(j)uː
Lady Margaret Hall
   college, Oxford Univ.   LĀD-ē MAHR-g(uh-)ruht HAWL   ˌleːdiˑ 'mɑʳg(ə)rət 'hɔːl
Lae
   port, New Guinea   LAH-Ā   'lɑˌeː
Lael
   Biblical name   LĀ(-uh)l, lah-EL   'leː(ə)l, lɑ'el
Laertes
   father of Odysseus; Ophelia's brother   lā-UHRT-ēz   leː'əʳʈiːz
     in Hamlet, *Shakespeare*
Laestrygonians
   giant cannibals met by Odysseus   LES-truh-GŌ-nē-uhnz   ˌlestrə'goːniːənz
Laetare Sunday
   4th Sunday of Lent   lā-TAHR-ē SUHN-dē, lā-TAR-ē,   leː'tɑʳiˑ 'sʌndiˑ, leː'tæriˑ,
      SUHN-dā   'sʌndeː
Laetitia
   pers. name   li-TISH-(ē-)uh   li'tiʃ(iː)ə
Laetrile
   controversial drug   LĀ-uh-TRIL, LĀ-uh-truhl, ⓔ   'leːəˌtril, 'leːətrəl, ⓔ
      LĀ-uh-TRĪL   'leːəˌtrail
La Farge
   Mme., character in Tale of Two   luh FAHRJ, luh FAHRZH, lah FAHRZH   lə 'fɑʳdʒ, lə 'fɑʳʒ, lɑ 'fɑʳʒ
      Cities, *Dickens*
La Fayette
   city, GA   luh-FET   lə'fet

Foreign Sounds: ue: *Fr.* **rue**, *Ger.* **füllen**   uh(r): *Fr.* **boeuf**, *Ger.* **Höhle**   <u>kh</u>: *Ger.* **ich**, *Scot.* **loch**   ḡ: *Sp.* **amigo**   <u>v</u>: *Sp.* **hablar**
hl: *Welsh* **Llanelli**.   CAPITALS: primary stress.   SMALL CAPS: secondary stress.   ⑤: U.S. pron.   ⓔ: British pron.

Lafayette

1. Marquis de, *French general*   lah-fah-YET, Ⓢ LAHF-ē-ET, LAF-ē-ET   laːfɑːjet, Ⓢ ˌlɑfiː'et, ˌlæfiː'et

2. US pl. name   LAHF-ē-ET, LAF-ē-ET, LAHF-ī-ET,   ˌlɑfiː'et, ˌlæfiː'et, ˌlɑfˌɑi'et,

LAF-Ī-ET, *esp. in southeastern US*   ˌlæfˌɑi'et, *esp. in*

LĀ-fē-ET, luh-FĀ(-uh)t   *southeastern US* ˌleːfiː'et,

lə'feː(ə)t

Lafcadio

pers. name   lahf-KAHD-ē-ō   lɑf'kɑdiːo

La Feria

city, TX   luh FER-ē-uh   lə 'feriːə

La Fête de la Madeleine

Provençal festival   lah FET duh lah mahd-LEN   lɑː fet də lɑː mɑːdlen

Lafferty

Perry Francis, *TV executive*   LAF-uhrt-ē   'læfər̩ʈiˑ

Laffite, Lafitte

Jean, *privateer and smuggler*   lah-FĒT, Ⓢ luh-FĒT   lɑːfiːt, Ⓢ lə'fiːt

Lafite

wine   lah-FĒT   lɑːfiːt

Lafite-Rothschild

wine   lah-FĒT-rawt-SHĒLD   lɑːfiːtrɔːtʃiːld

Lafleur

Guy, *sports personality*   luh-FLUHR   lə'fləʳ

LaFollette

Robert M., *US politician*   luh-FAHL-uht   lə'fɑlət

La Follette

city, TN   luh FAHL-uht   lə 'fɑlət

La Fontaine

Jean de, *French poet;* Henri,   lah fawⁿ-TEN; Ⓢ luh fahn-TĀN, luh   lɑː fɔ̃ten; Ⓢ lə fɑn'teːn, lə

Belgian politician (Nobel 1913)   FAHN-TĀN   'fɑnˌteːn

Lafourche

bayou, parish, LA   luh-FOOSH   lə'fuːʃ

Lagash

Sumerian city   LĀ-GASH   'leːˌgæʃ

Lag b'Omer

Jewish holiday   LAHG BŌ-muhr, buh-Ō-muhr,   'lɑg 'boːməʳ, bə'oːməʳ,

buh-Ō-mer   bə'oːmeʳ

Lagerfeld

Karl Otto, *European fashion designer*   LAHG-uhr-FELT   'lɑgəʳˌfelt

Lagerkvist

Pär F., *Swedish author (Nobel 1951)*   LAHG-uhrk-FIST   'lɑgəʳkˌfist

Lagerlöf

Selma, *Swedish author (Nobel 1909)*   LAH-guhr-LUH(R)V   'lɑːgəʳˌlœːv

La Gioconda

see Gioconda, La

Lagomorpha

hares & rabbits   LAG-uh-MAWR-fuh   ˌlægə'mɔːʳfə

Lagos

1. city, state, Nigeria   LĀ-GAHS, LAHG-ōs, LAHG-uhs   'leːˌgɑs, 'lɑgˌoːs, 'lɑgəs

2. town, Portugal   LAHG-o̅o̅sh   'lɑguːʃ

Lagos, Los

region, Chile   laws LAHG-ōs   lɔːs 'lɑgoːs

La Grange

pl. name, US   luh GRĀNJ   lə 'greːndʒ

Key (col. 2):   a: **fad** ā: **fade** ah: **father** ar: **marry** aw: **law** e: **fed** ē: **feed** er: **merry** i: **hid** ī: **hide** ō: **coat** o̅o̅: **boot**
oi: **boy** ow: **now** u: **put** uh: **above** uhr: **bird** ch: **chop** ng: **ring** sh: **show** th: **thick** <u>th</u>: **this** zh: **measure**

LaGrave

Field, *former ballpark, Fort Worth,*   luh-GRĀV   lə'greːv
TX

Lágrima

Spanish wine   LAHG-rē-muh   'lɑgriːmə

Lagthing, Lagting [Storting]

parliamentary body, Norway, Faeroe   LAHG-ting   'lɑgtiŋ
Islands

La Guardia

Fiorello, *New York City mayor;*   luh GWAHR-dē-uh   lə 'gwɑʳdiːə
airport, New York City

Laguna

1. pueblo, village, NM; N. American   luh-GŌŌ-nuh   lə'guːnə
people; Indian Reservation, US

2. city, Brazil; prov, Philippines   lah-GŌŌ-nah, ⓢ luh-GŌŌ-nuh   lɑ'guːnɑ, ⓢ lə'guːnə

Laguna Beach

city, CA   luh-GŌŌ-nuh BĒCH   lə,guːnə 'biːtʃ

Laguna Hills

city, CA   luh-GŌŌ-nuh HILZ   lə,guːnə 'hilz

Lahad

Biblical name   LĀ-HAD, LAH-hahd   'leː,hæd, 'lɑhɑd

Lahairoi

Biblical name   luh-HĪ-ROI, lah-<u>KH</u>Ī-raw-Ē   lə'hai,rɔi, lɑ,xairɔː'iː

Lahmam [Lahmas]

Biblical name   LA-MAM, LAH-MAM, lah<u>kh</u>-MAHS   'læ,mæm, 'lɑ,mæm, lɑx'mɑs

Lahmas [Lahmam]

Biblical name   LAHM-uhs, lah<u>kh</u>-MAHS   'lɑməs, lɑx'mɑs

Lahmi

Biblical name   LAM-Ī, LAHM-Ī, lah<u>kh</u>-MĒ   'læm,ai, 'lɑm,ai, lɑx'miː

Lahnda

lang., India, Pakistan   LAHN-duh   'lɑndə

Lahore

prov, Pakistan   luh-HŌR, luh-HAWR   lə'hoːʳ, lə'hɔːʳ

Lahr

Bert, *US comedian;* John, *US author*   LAHR   'lɑʳ

Laidlaw

William, *Scottish poet; US publisher*   LĀD-LAW   'leːd,lɔː

Laighton

pers. name   LĀT-n   'leːtn̩

Lailat al Miraj

Islamic festival   lī-LAHT ahl mir-AHZH, al   lai'lɑt ɑːl mir'ɑʒ, æl

Laine

Cleo, *British singer*   LĀN   'leːn

Laing

Ronald David, *Scottish psychiatrist*   LANG   'læŋ

Laird

pers. name   LARD, LERD   'læʳd, 'leʳd

Laish

Biblical name   LĀ-ish, lah-YĒSH   'leːiʃ, lɑ'jiːʃ

Laishah

Biblical name   LĀ-uh-shuh, LAH-yuh-SHAH   'leːəʃə, 'lɑjə,ʃɑ

Laius

father of Oedipus   LĀ-(y)uhs, LĪ-uhs   'leː(j)əs, 'laiəs

Foreign Sounds: ue: *Fr.* **r**ue, *Ger.* f**ü**llen   uh(r): *Fr.* b**œu**f, *Ger.* H**öh**le   <u>kh</u>: *Ger.* i**ch**, *Scot.* lo**ch**   g̱: *Sp.* ami**g**o   v̱: *Sp.* ha**b**lar
hl: *Welsh* **Ll**anelli.   CAPITALS: primary stress.   SMALL CAPS: secondary stress.   ⓢ: U.S. pron.   ⓔ: British pron.

Lajoie
 Napoleon (Larry), *US baseball*   LASH-uh-WĀ   'læʃəˌweː
  player
La Jolla
 resort area, CA   luh HOI-uh   lə 'hɔiə
Lajos
 pers. name, Hungarian   LAH-yawsh, LOI-ŌSH   'lajɔːʃ, 'lɔiˌoːʃ
La Junta
 city, CO   luh HUHNT-uh, luh HUN-tuh lə 'həntə, lə 'huntə
Lak, Lakh, Lakk
 lang., people, Caucasus Mts. LAHK, LAK   'lɑk, 'læk
Lake Havasu City
 city, AZ   LĀK HAV-uh-SOO SIT-ē ˌleːk 'hævəˌsuː 'siţiˑ
Lakeisha
 pers. name   luh-KĒ-shuh   lə'kiːʃə
Lake Orion
 village, MI   LĀK ŌR-ē-uhn, AWR-ē-uhn ˌleːk 'oːriːən, 'ɔːriːən
Lake Oswego
 city, OR   LĀK ahs-WĒ-GŌ   ˌleːk ɑs'wiːˌgoː
Lakin
 city, KS   LĀ-kuhn   'leːkən
Lakisha
 pers. name   luh-KĒ-shuh, luh-KISH-uh lə'kiːʃə, lə'kiʃə
Lakmé
 opera, Delibes   lahk-MĀ   lɑːkmeː
Lakonía [Laconia]
 region, Greece   LAHK-uh-NĒ-uh   ˌlɑkə'niːə
Lakshadweep [Laccadive]
 islands, Arabian Sea   luhk-SHAHD-WĒP   lək'ʃɑdˌwiːp
Lakshmi
 pers. name, Sanskrit   LUHK-shmē   'ləkʃmiˑ
Lakum, Lakkum
 Biblical name   LĀ-kuhm, LAK-uhm, lah-KOOM 'leːkəm, 'lækəm, lɑ'kuːm
Lal
 pers. name, Hindi   LAHL   'lɑl
Lalage
 character, Horatian ode   LAL-uh-gē, LAL-uh-jē 'læləgiˑ, 'lælədʒiˑ
LaLanne
 Jack, *US fitness expert*   luh-LĀN   lə'leːn
Lalas
 Alexi, *US soccer player*   LAL-uhs   'læləs
La Leche
 League for the promotion of lah LĀ-chā, lah LĀ-shā lɑ 'leːtʃeː, lɑ 'leːʃeː
  breast-feeding
Lalia
 lang., Africa   LĀ-lē-uh   'leːliːə
Lalique
 crystal   lah-LĒK   lɑ'liːk
Lallans
 Lowland Scots dialect   LAL-uhnz   'lælənz
L'Allegro
 poem, J. Milton   luh-LEG-rō, lah-   lə'legroː, lɑ-
Lalo
 Edouard Victor, *French composer* lah-LŌ   lɑːloː

Key (col. 2): a: f**a**d ā: f**a**de ah: f**a**ther ar: m**a**rry aw: l**a**w e: f**e**d ē: f**ee**d er: m**e**rry i: h**i**d ī: h**i**de ō: c**oa**t oo: b**oo**t
oi: b**oy** ow: n**ow** u: p**u**t uh: **a**bove uhr: b**ir**d ch: **ch**op ng: ri**ng** sh: **sh**ow th: **th**ick <u>th</u>: **th**is zh: mea**s**ure

Lamachus
   Athenian general   LAM-uh-kuhs   ˈlæməkəs

Lamade
   Stadium, *Williamsport, PA*   luh-MĀD   ləˈmeːd

La Madeleine
   city, France   lah mahd(-uh)-LEN, ⑤ luh-MAD-l-ĀN   laː maːd(ə)len,
                                                  ⑤ ləˌmædlˈeːn

Lamaism
   Tibetan Buddhism   LAHM-uh-IZ-uhm   ˈlaməˌizəm

Lamaistic Buddhism
   religion   LAHM-uh-IS-tik B̅O̅O̅D-IZ-uhm,   ˌlaməˌistik ˈbuːdˌizəm,
                BUD-IZ-uhm   ˈbudˌizəm

La Mancha
   region, Spain   luh MAHN-chuh   lə ˈmantʃə

La Manche [English Channel]
   strait between England & France   lah MAHⁿSH   laː mãʃ

Lamanism
   Buddhist sect   LĀ-muh-NIZ-uhm   ˈleːməˌnizəm

Lamar
   Community College, *CO;*   luh-MAHR   ləˈmɑʳ
     University, *TX; county, AL; pers.*
     name

Lamarck
   Jean Baptiste de, *French naturalist*   lah-MAHRK, ⑤ luh-MAHRK   laːmaːrk, ⑤ ləˈmɑʳk

Lamarckian
   pert. to Lamarckism   luh-MAHR-kē-uhn   ləˈmɑʳkiːən

Lamarckism
   theory of environmentally caused   luh-MAHR-KIZ-uhm   ləˈmɑʳˌkizəm
     evolutionary change

Lamarr
   pers. name   luh-MAHR   ləˈmɑʳ

La Marseillaise
   national anthem, France   lah mahr-se-YEZ   laː maːrsejez

Lamartine
   Alphonse de, *French writer*   lah-mahr-TĒN, ⑤ LAM-uhr-TĒN   laːmaːrtiːn, ⑤ ˌlæməʳˈtiːn

Lamas
   Fernando, *entertainer*   LAHM-uhs   ˈlaməs

Lamaze
   birthing method   luh-MAHZ   ləˈmɑz

Lamb
   Charles, *English essayist;* Willis E.,   LAM   ˈlæm
     Jr., *US physicist (Nobel 1955)*

Lamba
   lang., people, Africa   LAM-buh, LAHM-buh   ˈlæmbə, ˈlambə

Lambeosaurus
   dinosaur   LAM-bē-uh-SAWR-uhs   ˌlæmbiːəˈsɔːrəs

Lambert
   1. airport, St. Louis, MO; pers. name   LAM-buhrt   ˈlæmbəʳt
   2. Dutch   LAHM-buhrt   ˈlambərt
   3. French   lahⁿ-BER   lãber

Lambeth
   borough, England   LAM-buhth   ˈlæmbəθ

Lamborghini
   Italian car   LAM-buhr-GĒ-nē   ˌlæmbəʳˈgiːniˑ

Foreign Sounds: ue: *Fr.* **rue**, *Ger.* **füllen**   uh(r): *Fr.* **boeuf**, *Ger.* **Höhle**   <u>kh</u>: *Ger.* **ich**, *Scot.* lo**ch**   ḡ: *Sp.* ami**g**o   v̱: *Sp.* ha**b**lar
hl: *Welsh* **Ll**anelli.   CAPITALS: primary stress.   SMALL CAPS: secondary stress.   ⑤: U.S. pron.   ⑥: British pron.

Lambretta
  tdmk for an Italian motorbike   lam-BRET-uh   læmˈbreţə

Lambrusco
  Italian wine   lam-BRO͞OS-kō, lahm-   læmˈbruːskoː, lɑm-

Lambuth
  College, TN   LAM-buhth   ˈlæmbəθ

Lamech
  biblical patriarch   LAM-uhk   ˈlæmək

Lamedon
  king of Sicyon   LAM-uh-DAHN   ˈlæməˌdɑn ˈ

Lamentations
  Old Testament book   LAM-uhn-TĀ-shuhnz   ˌlæmənˈteːʃənz

La Mesa
  city, CA   luh MĀ-suh   lə ˈmeːsə

Lamesa
  city, TX   luh-MĒ-suh   ləˈmiːsə

Lamia
  mythical Greek woman who devoured   LĀ-mē-uh   ˈleːmiːə
    children; poem, Keats

Lamian War
  Greece, 4th cent. B.C.   luh-MĒ-uhn   ləˈmiːən

La Mirada
  city, CA   LAH muh-RAHD-uh   ˌlɑ məˈrɑdə

Lamm
  Richard Douglas, *US politician*   LAM   ˈlæm

Lammas
  English Christian festival, August 1st   LAM-uhs   ˈlæməs

Lammermuir Hills
  hills, Scotland   LAM-uhr-MYUR HILZ   ˌlæmərˌmjuʳ ˈhilz

Lamoille
  county, VT   luh-MOIL   ləˈmɔil

Lamont
  Corliss, *US philosophy educator,*   luh-MAHNT   ləˈmɑnt
    author

L'Amour
  Louis Dearborn, *US writer*   luh-MUR   ləˈmuʳ

La Moure
  county, ND   luh MUR   lə ˈmuʳ

Lampasas
  county, TX   lam-PAS-uhs   læmˈpæsəs

Lampedusa
  Giuseppe di, *Italian writer*   LAHM-pā-DO͞O-sah,   ˌlampeːˈduːsɑ,
       ⓢ LAM-puh-DO͞O-suh, -zuh   ⓢ ˌlæmpəˈduːsə, -zə

Lampung
  province, Indonesia   LAHM-PUNG   ˈlɑmˌpuŋ

Lamut [Even]
  lang., people, East Siberia   luh-MO͞OT   ləˈmuːt

LAN
  local area network   LAN   ˈlæn

Lanai
  island, HI   luh-NĪ   ləˈnɑi

Lanark
  county, Scotland; county, Ontario,   LAN-uhrk   ˈlænəʳk
    Canada

Key (col. 2):   a: **fad**   ā: **fade**   ah: **father**   ar: **marry**   aw: **law**   e: **fed**   ē: **feed**   er: **merry**   i: **hid**   ī: **hide**   ō: **coat**   o͞o: **boot**
oi: **boy**   ow: **now**   u: **put**   uh: **above**   uhr: **bird**   ch: **chop**   ng: **ring**   sh: **show**   th: **thick**   t̲h̲: **this**   zh: **measure**

Lancashire

  county, England   LANG-kuh-shuhr, -SHIR   'læŋkəʃəʳ, -,ʃiʳ

Lancaster

  1. US pl. name; town, England;   LANG-kuh-stuhr, LAN-KAS-tuhr,   'læŋkəstəʳ, 'læn,kæstəʳ,
    English noble family   LANG-KAS-tuhr   'læŋ,kæstəʳ

  2. Burt, US actor   LAN-KAS-tuhr, LANG-KAS-tuhr   'læn,kæstəʳ, 'læŋ,kæstəʳ

Lancastrian

  pert. to the house of Lancaster   lang-KAS-trē-uhn, lan-KAS-trē-uhn   læŋ'kæstriːən, læn'kæstriːən

Lance

  pers. name   LANS   'læns

Lancelot

  Arthurian hero; pers. name   LAN(T)-suh-LAHT, LAHN(T)-,   'læn(t)sə,lɑt, 'lɑn(t)-, -s(ə)lət
     -s(uh-)luht

Lanchow

  see Lanzhou

Lancia

  Italian car   LAN(T)-sē-uh   'læn(t)siːə

Lancome

  tdmk for cosmetics   lahng-KŌM   lɑŋ'koːm

Landau

  1. Lev Davidovich, Soviet physicist   LUHN-DOW   ,lən'dɑu

  2. Martin, US actor; Sidney, *US*   LAN-DOW   'læn,dɑu
    lexicographer

  3. city, Germany   LAHN-DOW   'lɑn,dɑu

Landers

  Ann, *US advice columnist*   LAN-duhrz   'lændəʳz

Landes

  department, France   LAHⁿD   'lɑ̃d

Landesberg

  Steve, *US actor*   LAN-duhs-BUHRG   'lændəs,bəʳg

Landis

  John, *US film writer, director*   LAN-duhs   'lændəs

Ländler

  dance   LENT-luhr   'lentləʳ

Landnámabók

  Icelandic "Book of Settlements"   LAHND-NAHM-uh-BŌK   'lɑnd,nɑmə,boːk

Lando

  pope   LAHN-dō   'lɑndoː

Landon

  Michael, *US actor, TV director*   LAN-duhn   'lændən

Landowska

  Wanda Louise, *Polish*   lahn-DAWF-skuh   lɑn'dɔːfskə
    harpsichordist

Land-Rover

  tdmk for a vehicle   LAND-RŌ-vuhr   'lænd,roːvəʳ

Landry

  Tom, *US football coach*   LAN-drē   'lændri·

Landsbergis

  Vytautas, *president, Lithuania*   LAHNZ-BER-guhs   'lɑnz,beʳgəs

Land's End

  cape, England; US clothing co.   LAN(D)Z END   'læn(d)z 'end

Landsteiner

  Karl, *Austrian-born US pathologist*   LAHNT-SHTĪ-nuhr,   'lɑnt,ʃtɑinəʳ,
    (Nobel 1930)   Ⓢ LAN(D)-STĪ-nuhr   Ⓢ 'læn(d),stɑinəʳ

Foreign Sounds: ue: *Fr.* **rue**, *Ger.* **füllen**   uh(r): *Fr.* **boeuf**, *Ger.* **Höhle**   <u>kh</u>: *Ger.* **ich**, *Scot.* **loch**   g̶: *Sp.* **amigo**   <u>v</u>: *Sp.* **hablar**   hl: *Welsh* **Llanelli**.   CAPITALS: primary stress.   SMALL CAPS: secondary stress.   Ⓢ: U.S. pron.   Ⓔ: British pron.

Lane
   pers. name   LĀN   'leːn

Lanett
   city, AL   luh-NET   lə'net

Lang
   1. Andrew, *Scottish folklorist, writer*   LANG   'læŋ
   2. Fritz, *US film director*   LAHNG   'laŋ

Lange
   1. C. L., *Norwegian pacifist (Nobel*   LAHNG-uh   'laŋə
     1921); pers. name, Norwegian
   2. Dorothea, *US photographer;*   LANG   'læŋ
     Jessica, *US actress*

Langella
   Frank, *US actor*   lan-JEL-uh   læn'dʒelə

Langerhans islets
   pancreatic cell clusters   LAHNG-uhr-HAHNZ Ī-luhts,   'laŋəʳˌhɑnz 'ailəts,
                        LAHNG-uhr-HAHN(T)S   'laŋəʳˌhɑn(t)s

Langfield
   Joanna, *radio talk show host*   LANG-FĒLD   'læŋˌfiːld

Langlade
   county, WI   LANG-LĀD   'læŋˌleːd

Langland
   William, *English poet*   LANG-luhnd   'læŋlənd

Langley
   Samuel, *US astronomer*   LANG-lē   'læŋliˑ

Langlois
   1. pers. name   LANG-LOIS   'læŋˌlɔis
   2. French   lahⁿg-LWAH   lãglwaː

Langmuir
   Irving, *US chemist (Nobel 1932)*   LANG-MYUR   'læŋˌmjuʳ

Lango
   lang., people, Uganda   LAHNG-gō   'laŋgoː

Langobardic
   pert. to Lombardy; *ancient Germanic*   LANG-gō-BAHRD-ik   ˌlæŋgoː'baʳdik
    lang.

Langston
   pers. name   LANG-stuhn   'læŋstən

Languedoc [Provençal]
   lang., prov, France   lahⁿg-DAWK, ⑤ lahng-DAWK   lãgdɔːk, ⑤ laŋ'dɔːk

Languedoc-Roussillon
   region, France   lahⁿg-DAWK-ro͞o-sē-YAWⁿ   lãgdɔːkruːsiːjɔ̃

Langue d'oïl
   medieval French dialect   lahng DOI(L), daw-ĒL,   laːŋ dɔi(l), dɔːiːl,
                       ⑤ lahng-DOI(L)   ⑤ laŋ'dɔi(l)

Lanier
   Sidney, *US poet; county, GA; pers.*   luh-NIR   lə'niʳ
    name

Lanneau
   pers. name   LAN-ō   'lænoː

Lanphier
   Park, *ballpark, Springfield, IL*   LAN-FIR   'lænˌfiʳ

Lansbury
   Angela, *British actress*   LANZ-b(uh-)rē, ⑤ LANZ-BER-ē   'lænzb(ə)riˑ, ⑤ 'lænzˌberiˑ

Lansdowne
   street, Boston   LANZ-DOWN   'lænzˌdaun

Key (col. 2):   a: **fad**   ā: **fade**   ah: **father**   ar: **marry**   aw: **law**   e: **fed**   ē: **feed**   er: **merry**   i: **hid**   ī: **hide**   ō: **coat**   o͞o: **boot**
oi: **boy**   ow: **now**   u: **put**   uh: **above**   uhr: **bird**   ch: **chop**   ng: **ring**   sh: **show**   th: **thick**   <u>th</u>: **this**   zh: **measure**

L'Anse
Indian reservation, US   LANS   'læns

Lansing
Robert Howell, US actor, director;   LAN(T)-sing   'læn(t)siŋ
city, MI

lanthanum
element   LAN(T)-thuh-nuhm   'læn(t)θənəm

Lantz
Walter, US cartoonist   LAN(T)S   'læn(t)s

Lanza
Mario, US entertainer   LAHN-zuh   'lanzə

Lanzhou, Lanchow [Kaolan]
city, China   LAHN-JŌ   'lan'dʒoː

Laoag
river, port, Philippines   luh-WAHG   lə'wɑg

Laocoön
Trojan priest   lā-AHK-uh-WAHN   leː'ɑkə͵wɑn

Laodamas
king of Thebes   lā-AHD-uh-muhs   leː'ɑdəməs

Laodamia
mother of Sarpedon by Zeus; wife of   LĀ-uhd-uh-MĪ-uh, -MĒ-(y)uh   ͵leːədə'mɑiə, -'miː(j)ə
Protesilaus

Laodice
daughter of Priam and Hecuba;   lā-AHD-uh-sē   leː'ɑdəsiˑ
daughter of Agamemnon and
Clytemnestra

Laodicea
ancient name of Latakia   lā-AHD-uh-SĒ-uh   leː͵adə'siːə

Laodocus
son of Apollo and Phthia   lā-AHD-uh-kuhs   leː'adəkəs

Lao [Laotian]
lang., people, Laos, Thailand   LOW, LAH-ō   'lau, 'lɑ-oː

Laoighis
county, Ireland   LĀSH, LĒSH   'leːʃ, 'liːʃ

Laomedon
father of Priam   lā-AHM-uh-DAHN   leː'amə͵dan

Laon, La
town, France   lah LAHⁿ   lɑː lã

Laos
republic, Asia   LOWS, LĀ-AHS, LAH-ōs   'laus, 'leː͵as, 'lɑ-oːs

Laotian [Lao]
lang., people, Laos, Thailand   LOW-shuhn, lā-Ō-shuhn,   'lauʃən, leː'oːʃən, lɑ'oːʃən
     lah-Ō-shuhn

Lao-tzu
Chinese philosopher   LOWD-ZU, LOWD-Z$\overline{\text{OO}}$ 'laud'zu, 'laud'zuː

La Paz
1. county, AZ   luh PAZ   lə 'pæz
2. S. American pl. name   luh PAHZ, luh PAHS, luh PAZ   lə 'paz, lə 'pas, lə 'pæz

Lapeer
county, MI   luh-PIR   lə'piʳ

Laphroaig
Scotch whiskey   luh-FROIG, la-FROIG   lə'frɔig, læ'frɔig

Lapidoth, Lappidoth
Biblical name   LAP-uh-DAHTH, lah-pē-DŌT   'læpə͵daθ, lɑpiː'doːt

---

Foreign Sounds: **ue**: *Fr.* **rue**, *Ger.* **füllen**   **uh(r)**: *Fr.* **boeuf**, *Ger.* **Höhle**   <u>kh</u>: *Ger.* **ich**, *Scot.* **loch**   g̃: *Sp.* **amigo**   v̱: *Sp.* **hablar**
hl: *Welsh* **Llanelli.**   CAPITALS: primary stress.   SMALL CAPS: secondary stress.   Ⓢ: U.S. pron.   Ⓔ: British pron.

Lapiths
mythological people of Thessaly   LĀ-puhths, LAP-uhths   'leːpəθs, 'læpəθs

Laplace
Pierre Simon, Marquis de, *French*   lah-PLAHS   lɑːplɑːs
    astronomer, mathematician

Lapland, Lappland
prov, Finland   LAP-LAND, LAP-luhnd   'læpˌlænd, 'læplənd

La Plata
county, CO   luh PLAT-uh, luh PLAHT-uh   lə 'plæt̬ə, lə 'plɑt̬ə

La Porte
county, IN   luh PŌRT, luh PAWRT   lə 'poːᶜt, lə 'pɔːᶜt

La Posta
Indian reservation, US   luh PŌ-stuh   lə 'poːstə

Lapp
lang., people, N. Europe   LAP   'læp

Lappi
prov, Finland   LAHP-pē   'lɑːppiˑ

Lappic [Lapp]
lang., N. Europe   LAP-ik   'læpik

Lappish [Lapp]
lang., N. Europe   LAP-ish   'læpiʃ

Lappland
see Lapland

Lapsang Souchong
tea   LAP-SANG SOO-CHAWNG   'læpˌsæŋ 'suːˌtʃɔːŋ

Laptev
Sea, *Arctic*   LAP-TEF, LAP-TEV   'læpˌtef, 'læpˌtev

La Puente
city, CA   lahp-WEN-TĀ, lahp-WENT-ē   lɑp'wenˌteː, lɑp'wentiˑ

Laputa
flying island in Gulliver's Travels, *J.*   luh-PYOOT-uh   lə'pjuːt̬ə
    Swift

Laputan
inhabitant of Laputa   luh-PYOOT-uhn   lə'pjuːtən

La Quinta
US motor inn chain   luh KĒN-tuh   lə 'kiːntə

Lar
singular of Lares   LAHR   'lɑᶜ

Lara
1. *mother of the Lares by Mercury*   LAR-uh   'lærə
2. *pers. name*   LAHR-uh, LAR-uh   'lɑrə, 'lærə

Laramie
river, US; city, county, WY   LAR-uh-mē, LER-uh-mē   'lærəmiˑ, 'lerəmiˑ

Lardner
Ring Wilmer, Jr., *US author*   LAHRD-nuhr   'lɑᶜdnəᶜ

La Realidad
city, Mexico   lah-rā-ahl-ē-THAHTH   lɑreːɑliː'ðɑð

La Realidad
city, Mexico   lah-rā-ahl-ē-THAHTH   lɑreːɑliː'ðɑð

Laredo
city, TX   luh-RĀD-ō   lə'reːdoː

La Renaissance
national anthem, Central African   lah ruh-nes-AHⁿS; lahr-nes-AHⁿS   lɑː rənesɑ̃s; lɑːrnesɑ̃s
    Republic

Key (col. 2):   a: fad   ā: fade   ah: father   ar: marry   aw: law   e: fed   ē: feed   er: merry   i: hid   ī: hide   ō: coat   ōō: boot
oi: boy   ow: now   u: put   uh: above   uhr: bird   ch: chop   ng: ring   sh: show   th: thick   th: this   zh: measure

Lares		
Roman household spirits	LĀ-RĒZ, LAR-ēz, LER-ēz	'leːˌriːz, 'læriːz, 'leriːz
La Riège [Ariège]		
river, department, France	lahr-YEZH, [S] LAH rē-EZH	larjeʒ, [S] ˌla riː'eʒ
Larisa		
pers. name	luh-RIS-uh	lə'risə
Larissa		
mother or daughter of Pelasgus; pers. name	luh-RIS-uh	lə'risə
Larnaca		
dist, Cyprus	LAHR-nuh-kuh	'laʳnəkə
La Roche		
College, *PA*	luh-RŌSH	lə'roːʃ
La Rochefoucauld		
François de, *French moralist*	lah rawsh-fo͞o-KŌ	laː rɔːʃfuːkoː
La Rochelle		
city, France	lah raw-SHEL	laː rɔːʃel
Larousse		
Pierre Athanase, *French grammarian, lexicographer; dictionary imprint*	lah-RO͞OS, [S] luh-RO͞OS	laːruːs, [S] lə'ruːs
Larousse Gastronomique		
cookery book	lah-RO͞OS gahs-traw-naw-MĒK, [S] luh-RO͞OS GAS-truh-NAHM-ĒK	laːruːs gaːstrɔːnɔːmiːk, [S] lə'ruːs ˌgæstrəˌnam'iːk
Larry		
pers. name	LAR-ē	'læri·
Lars		
1. pers. name	LAHRZ	'laʳz
2. Latin	LAHRZ, LAHRS	'laʳz, 'laʳs
3. Swedish	LAHZH, [S] LAHRZH, LAHRSH	'laʒ, [S] 'laʳʒ, 'laʳʃ
Larsa		
ancient Babylonian city	LAR-suh, LAHR-suh	'læʳsə, 'laʳsə
Larson		
Glen, *TV producer, writer*	LAHR-suhn	'laʳsən
Lars Porsena		
king of Clusium	lahrs PAWR-suh-nuh	laʳs 'pɔːʳsənə
Larvik		
port, Norway	LAHR-vik, LAHR-VĒK	'laʳvik, 'laʳˌviːk
La Salle		
University, *PA*	luh SAL	lə 'sæl
La Salle, Sieur de		
René Robert, *French explorer*	SYUH(R) duh lah SAHL, [S] SYUHR duh luh SAL	sjœʳ də laː saːl, [S] 'sjəʳ də lə 'sæl
Las Animas		
county, CO	las AN-uh-muhs, lahs	læs 'ænəməs, las
La Scala		
opera house, Milan	lah SKAHL-uh, luh	la 'skalə, lə
Lascăr		
pers. name, Romanian	LAHS-kuhr	'laskər
Lascaux		
cave with prehistoric paintings, France	lah-SKŌ, [S] las-KŌ	laːskoː, [S] læs'koː
Lascelles		
pers. name	LAS-uhlz	'læsəlz

Foreign Sounds: ue: *Fr.* **rue**, *Ger.* **füllen** uh(r): *Fr.* **boeuf**, *Ger.* **Höhle** kh: *Ger.* **ich**, *Scot.* lo**ch** g̱: *Sp.* ami**g**o v̱: *Sp.* ha**b**lar hl: *Welsh* **Ll**anelli. CAPITALS: primary stress. SMALL CAPS: secondary stress. [S]: U.S. pron. [£]: British pron.

Las Cruces		
city, NM	lahs KR$\overline{OO}$-suhs	lɑs 'kruːsəs
Lasea		
Biblical name	luh-SĒ-uh	lə'siːə
Lasell		
Junior College, *MA*	luh-SEL	lə'sel
Lasha		
Biblical name	LĀ-shuh, LAH-shah	'leːʃə, 'lɑʃɑ
Lashio		
town, Burma	LAHSH-ō, LAHSH-ē-ō	'lɑʃoː, 'lɑʃiːˌoː
Laski		
Harold Joseph, *English political scientist*	LAS-KĒ	'læsˌkiˑ
Lasorda		
Tom Charles, *US baseball team manager*	luh-SAWRD-uh	lə'sɔːʳdə
Las Palmas		
province, Spain	lahs PAHL-mahs, ⑤ lahs PAHL-muhs	lɑs 'pɑlmɑs, ⑤ lɑs 'pɑlməs
Las Palmas de Gran Canaria		
city, Spain	lahs PAHL-mahs <u>th</u>ā grahn kah-NAHR-yah	lɑs 'pɑlmɑs ðeː grɑn kɑ'nɑrjɑ
La Spezia		
prov, Italy	lah SPET-sē-uh	lɑ 'spetsiːə
Lassa fever		
African viral disease	LAS-uh FĒ-vuhr, LAH-suh	ˌlæsə 'fiːvəʳ, ˌlɑːsə
Lassen		
volcano, county, college, CA	LAS-uhn	'læsən
Lasser		
Louise, *US actress*	LAS-uhr	'læsəʳ
Lasseter		
John, *US film director*	LAS-uht-uhr	'læsət̬əʳ
Lassie		
young girl; fictional dog	LAS-ē	'læsiˑ
Lasso [Lassus]		
Orlando di, *Flemish composer*	LAHS-SŌ	'lasˌsoː
L'Assomption		
river, county, Canada	lah-saw^{n}p-SYAW^n, ⑤ luh-SUHM(P)-shuhn	lɑːsɔ̃psjɔ̃, ⑤ lə'səm(p)ʃən
Lassus [Lasso]		
Flemish composer	LAHS-uhs	'lasəs
Lasswell		
Fred, *US cartoonist*	LAS-WEL	'læsˌwel
La Sueur		
county, MN	luh SUR	lə 'suʳ
Las Vegas		
city, NV	lahs VĀ-guhs	lɑs 'veːgəs
László		
pers. name, Hungarian	LAHS-lō	'lɑːsloː
Latah		
county, ID	LĀ-TAH, luh-TAH	'leːˌtɑ, lə'tɑ
Latakia		
port, governorate, Syria	LAT-uh-KĒ-uh	ˌlætə'kiːə
Latasha		
pers. name	luh-TAHSH-uh, luh-TASH-uh	lə'tɑʃə, lə'tæʃə

Key (col. 2):   a: f**a**d   ā: f**a**de   ah: f**a**ther   ar: m**a**rry   aw: l**a**w   e: f**e**d   ē: f**ee**d   er: m**e**rry   i: h**i**d   ī: h**i**de   ō: c**oa**t $\overline{oo}$: b**oo**t
oi: b**oy**   ow: n**ow**   u: p**u**t   uh: **a**bove   uhr: b**i**rd   ch: **ch**op   ng: ri**ng**   sh: **sh**ow   th: **th**ick   <u>th</u>: **th**is   zh: mea**s**ure

La Tène
  archaeological site, Switzerland   lah TEN, lah TĀN   lɑ 'ten, lɑ 'teːn
Lateran, St. John
  church in Rome   sānt JAHN LAT-uh-ruhn, suhnt   seːnt 'dʒɑn 'læṱərən, sənt
Latham
  pers. name   LĀ-thuhm, LĀ-<u>th</u>uhm   'leːθəm, 'leːðəm
Lathrop
  pers. name   LĀ-thruhp   'leːθrəp
Latifundia
  Roman plantations   LAT-uh-FUHN-dē-uh   ˌlæṱə'fəndiːə
Latimer
  Hugh, *English Protestant bishop;*   LAT-uh-muhr   'læṱəməʳ
  pers. name
Latin
  lang. of Romans   LAT-n   'lætn̩
Latinate
  pert. to Latin   LAT-n-ĀT   'lætn̩ˌeːt
Latino
  person of Hispanic descent   la-TĒ-nō, luh-TĒ-nō   læ'tiːnoː, lə'tiːnoː
Latinus
  eponymous king of the Latins   luh-TĪ-nuhs   lə'tɑinəs
Latinus Silvius
  son of Aeneas Silvius   luh-TĪ-nuhs SIL-vē-uhs   ləˌtɑinəs 'silviːəs
Latisha
  pers. name   luh-TISH-uh, luh-TĒ-shuh   lə'tiʃə, lə'tiːʃə
Latium [Lazio]
  ancient country, autonomous region,   LĀ-sh(ē-)uhm   'leːʃ(iː)əm
  Italy
Latonya
  pers. name   luh-TAHN-yuh   lə'tɑnjə
Latour
  pers. name, French   lah-TOOR   lɑːtuːr
Latoya
  pers. name   luh-TOI-uh   lə'tɔiə
Latrobe
  city, Pennsylvania   luh-TRŌB   lə'troːb
Latvia
  Baltic republic   LAT-vē-uh   'lætviːə
Latvian
  lang., Latvia   LAT-vē-uhn   'lætviːən
Latviskaya
  Russian form of Latvia   LUHT-VĒ-skuh-yuh   ˌlət'viːskəjə
L'Aube Nouvelle
  national anthem, Benin   LŌB noo-VEL   loːb nuːvel
Lauder
  Estee, *see* Estée Lauder
Lauderdale
  county, AL, MS, TN   LAWD-uhr-DĀL   'lɔːdəʳˌdeːl
Laudianism
  doctrines of Laud   LAWD-ē-uh-NIZ-uhm   'lɔːdiːəˌnizəm
Laue
  Max von, *German physicist (Nobel*   LOW-uh   'lauə
  1914)
Laughton
  Charles, *British actor*   LAWT-n   'lɔːtn̩

Foreign Sounds: ue: *Fr.* **rue**, *Ger.* **füllen**   uh(r): *Fr.* **boeuf**, *Ger.* **Höhle**   <u>kh</u>: *Ger.* **ich**, *Scot.* **loch**   g̊: *Sp.* amigo   v̥: *Sp.* hablar
hl: *Welsh* **Llanelli**.   CAPITALS: primary stress.   SMALL CAPS: secondary stress.   Ⓢ: U.S. pron.   Ⓔ: British pron.

Launcelot		
pers. name	LAWN-suh-LAHT, LAHN-, LAN-, -s(uh-)luht	'lɔːnsəˌlɑt, 'lɑn-, 'læn-, -s(ə)lət
Laupahoehoe		
village, HI	LAH-o͞o-pah-HŌ-uh-HŌ-uh	ˌlɑuːpɑˌhoːə'hoːə
Lauper		
Cyndi, *rock musician*	LOW-puhr	'lɑupə^{r}
Laura		
1. pers. name	LAWR-uh, LAHR-uh	'lɔːrə, 'lɑrə
2. Italian	LOW-rah	'lɑurɑ
3. Swedish	LOW-rah	'lɑurɑː
Laurasia		
Mesozoic supercontinent	lawr-Ā-zhuh, lawr-Ā-shuh	lɔːr'eːʒə, lɔːr'eːʃə
Laurasian		
pert. to Laurasia	lawr-Ā-zhuhn, lawr-Ā-shuhn	lɔːr'eːʒən, lɔːr'eːʃən
Laure		
pers. name, French	LAWR	lɔːr
Laurel		
pers. name	LAWR-uhl, LAHR-uhl	'lɔːrəl, 'lɑrəl
Lauren		
1. pers. name	LAWR-uhn, LAHR-uhn	'lɔːrən, 'lɑrən
2. Ralph, *fashion designer*	LAWR-uhn, LAHR-uhn, luh-REN, law-REN	'lɔːrən, 'lɑrən, lə'ren, lɔː'ren
Laurence		
pers. name	LAWR-uhn(t)s, LAHR-uhn(t)s	'lɔːrən(t)s, 'lɑrən(t)s
Laurencin		
Marie, *French artist*	law-rah^{n}-SE^{n}	lɔːrɑ̃sẽ
Laurens		
1. county, GA, SC; city, SC	LAWR-uhnz, LAHR-uhnz	'lɔːrənz, 'lɑrənz
2. pers. name	LAWR-uhnz, LAHR-uhnz, -uhn(t)s	'lɔːrənz, 'lɑrənz, -ən(t)s
Laurent		
pers. name, French	law-RAH^{n}	lɔːrɑ̃
Laurentian		
hills, Canada; pert. to Laurence, Laurentius, *or* Lawrence	law-REN-chuhn, luh-	lɔː'rentʃən, lə-
Laurentius		
1. pers. name, Latin	law-REN-sh(ē-)uhs	lɔː'renʃ(iː)əs
2. Swedish	low-RENT-sē-uhs	lɑu'rentsiːəs
Lauretta		
pers. name	luh-RET-uh, lawr-ET-uh	lə'ret̬ə, lɔːr'et̬ə
Laureum		
site of Athenian silver mines	LAWR-ē-uhm, LAHR-ē-uhm	'lɔːriːəm, 'lɑriːəm
Lauri		
pers. name, Finnish	LOW-rē	'lɑuriː
Laurie		
pers. name	LAWR-ē, LAHR-ē	'lɔːriˑ, 'lɑriˑ
Laurier		
Sir Wilfrid, *Canadian prime minister*	lawr-YĀ, [$] LAW-rē-Ā	lɔːrjeː, [$] 'lɔːriːˌeː
Laurits, Lauritz		
1. pers. name, Danish	LOW-rēts	'lɑuriːts
2. Norwegian	LOW-rits	'lɑurits
Lauro		
pers. name, Italian	LOW-rō	'lɑuroː
Lausanne		
resort, Switzerland	lō-ZAHN, lō-ZAN	loː'zɑn, loː'zæn

Key (col. 2): a: **fad** ā: **fade** ah: **father** ar: **marry** aw: **law** e: **fed** ē: **feed** er: **merry** i: **hid** ī: **hide** ō: **coat** o͞o: **boot** oi: **boy** ow: **now** u: **put** uh: **above** uhr: **bird** ch: **chop** ng: **ring** sh: **show** th: **thick** t͟h: **this** zh: **measure**

Lavaca
  county, TX   luh-VAK-uh   lə'vækə

Laval
  1. Pierre, *French politician; town,*   lah-VAHL   lɑːvɑːl
    France
  2. town, Canada   lah-VAHL, luh-VAL   lɑːvɑːl, lə'væl
  3. pers. name   luh-VAL   lə'væl

Lavalleja
  Juan Antonio, *Uruguayan*   LAHV-ah(l)-YĀ-hah   ˌlɑvɑ(l)'jeːhɑ
    revolutionary; department,
    Uruguay

Laver
  seaweed   LAHV-uhr, LĀ-vuhr   'lɑvəʳ, 'leːvəʳ

Laveran
  C. L. A., *French physician (Nobel* lah-vuh-RAHⁿ, lahv-RAHⁿ   lɑːvərɑ̃, lɑːvrɑ̃
    1907)

Lavern, Laverne
  pers. name   luh-VUHRN   lə'vəʳn

La Verne
  University of, *CA; pers. name*   luh-VUHRN   lə'vəʳn

Lavin
  Linda, *US actress*   LAV-uhn   'lævən

Lavinia
  1. wife of Aeneas; pers. name   luh-VIN-ē-uh   lə'viniːə
  2. Italian   lah-VĒN-yah   lɑ'viːnjɑ

Lavoisier
  Antoine, *French scientist*   lahv-wahz-YĀ, ⓢ luhv-WAHZ-ē-Ā lɑːvwɑːzjeː, ⓢ ləv'wɑziːˌeː

Lavrenti
  pers. name, Russian   LUHV-REN-ti   ˌləv'ṛenṭij

Lawrence
  D. H., *English writer;* E. O., *US* LAWR-uhn(t)s, LAHR-uhn(t)s 'lɔːrən(t)s, 'lɑrən(t)s
    physicist (Nobel 1939); T(homas)
    E(dward), *British adventurer &*
    writer; pers. name

lawrencium
  element   law-REN(T)-sē-uhm   lɔː'ren(t)siːəm

Lawrentian
  pert. to D. H. Lawrence   law-REN-chuhn, luh-   lɔː'rentʃən, lə-

Laxalt
  Paul, *US politician*   LAK-SAWLT   'lækˌsɔːlt

Laxness
  Halldór K., *Icelandic author (Nobel* LAHK-snuhs, LAHK-snes 'lɑksnəs, 'lɑksnes
    1955)

Layamon
  English poet   LĪ-uh-muhn, LĀ-uh-muhn   'lɑiəmən, 'leːəmən

Layton
  Joe, *US director, choreographer* LĀT-n   'leːtn̩

Lazar
  pers. name, Russian   LAH-zuhr   'lɑːzəṛ

Lázár
  pers. name, Hungarian   LAH-zahr   'lɑːzɑːr

Lazare
  pers. name, French   lah-ZAHR   lɑːzɑːr

Lázaro
  pers. name, Spanish   LAHS-ahr-ō, LAHTH-ahr-ō   'lɑsɑroː, 'lɑθɑroː

Foreign Sounds: ue: *Fr.* **rue**, *Ger.* **füllen**   uh(r): *Fr.* **boeuf**, *Ger.* **Höhle** <u>kh</u>: *Ger.* i**ch**, *Scot.* lo**ch** ḡ: *Sp.* ami**g**o <u>v</u>: *Sp.* ha**b**lar
hl: *Welsh* **Ll**anelli. CAPITALS: primary stress. SMALL CAPS: secondary stress. ⓢ: U.S. pron. ⓔ: British pron.

Lazarus
    Biblical name; Mell, *US cartoonist;*   LAZ-uh-ruhs   'læzərəs
    pers. name

LA-Z-Boy
    US chair co.   LĀ-zē-BOI   'leːziˑˌbɔi

Lazio [Latium]
    autonomous region, Italy   LAHT-sē-Ō   'lɑtsiːˌoː

Lazuli Bunting
    songbird   LAZ-uh-lē BUHNT-ing, LAZ-uh-LĪ   'læzəliˑ 'bəntiŋ, 'læzəˌlɑi

Lazzaro
    pers. name, Italian   LAHD-dźahr-ō   'lɑddzɑroː

L-dopa
    anti-Parkinson's disease drug   el-DŌ-puh   el'doːpə

Leach
    Robin, *TV host*   LĒCH   'liːtʃ

Leachman
    Cloris, *US actress*   LĒCH-muhn   'liːtʃmən

Lead
    city, SD   LĒD   'liːd

lead
    element   LED   'led

Leadbelly [Ledbetter]
    US singer   LED-BEL-ē   'ledˌbeliˑ

Leah
    Biblical name; pers. name   LĒ-uh   'liːə

Leahy
    Patrick Joseph, *US politician;*   LĀ-hē, LĀ-ē   'leːhiː, 'leːiː
    William Daniel, *US naval officer*

Leakey
    Louis, Mary, & Richard, *British*   LĒ-kē   'liːkiˑ
    anthropologists

Leamington
    town, Canada   LĒ-ming-tuhn   'liːmiŋtən

Leamington Spa
    resort, England   LEM-ing-tuhn SPAH   'lemiŋtən 'spɑ

Leander
    1. beloved of Hero in Greek myth;   lē-AN-duhr   liː'ændəʳ
    pers. name
    2. German   lā-AHN-duhr   leː'ɑndəʳ

Leandro
    pers. name, Italian, Spanish   lā-AHN-drō   leː'ɑndroː

Leanne
    pers. name   lē-AN   liː'æn

Lear
    Edward, *English poet;* Norman, *US*   LIR   'liʳ
    film, TV writer, producer;
    Shakespearean character

Learned
    pers. name   LUHR-nuhd   'ləʳnəd

Leary
    Timothy, *US psychologist, author*   LIR-ē   'liriˑ

Leavenworth
    city, county, KS; US penitentiary   LEV-uhn-WUHRTH   'levənˌwəʳθ

Key (col. 2):   a: fad   ā: fade   ah: father   ar: marry   aw: law   e: fed   ē: feed   er: merry   i: hid   ī: hide   ō: coat   ōō: boot
oi: boy   ow: now   u: put   uh: above   uhr: bird   ch: chop   ng: ring   sh: show   th: thick   th̲: this   zh: measure

Leavis
  Frank Raymond *and* Queenie   LĒ-vuhs   ˈliːvəs
    Dorothy, *English literary critics*
Leavitt
  pers. name   LEV-it   ˈlevit
Leavitt
  Henrietta Swan, *US astronomer*   LĒ-vuht   ˈliːvət
Lebana, Lebanah
  Biblical name   luh-BĀ-nuh, luh-vah-NAH   ləˈbeːnə, ləvɑˈnɑ
Lebanese
  pert. to Lebanon   leb-uh-NĒZ, -NĒS   lebəˈniːz, -ˈniːs
Lebanon
  republic, Middle East   LEB-uh-nuhn, -NAHN   ˈlebənən, -ˌnɑn
Lebaoth
  Biblical name   luh-BĀ-AHTH, luh-vah-ŌT   ləˈbeːˌɑθ, ləvɑˈoːt
Lebbeus
  Biblical name   luh-BĒ-uhs   ləˈbiːəs
Lebensraum
  additional territory wanted by a   LĀ-buhnz-ROWM, LĀ-buhn(t)s-ROWM   ˈleːbənzˌrɑum,
    nation   ˈleːbən(t)sˌrɑum
Leberecht
  pers. name, German   LĀ-buh-REKHT   ˈleːbəˌreçt
Lebonah
  Biblical name   luh-BŌ-nuh, luh-vō-NAH   ləˈboːnə, ləvoːˈnɑ
Le Bourget
  city, France   luh bur-ZHE   lə burʒe
Lebrecht
  1. pers. name, Danish   LIB-REKHT   ˈlibˌreçt
  2. German   LĀ-PREKHT, LĀ-BREKHT   ˈleːˌpreçt, ˈleːˌbreçt
Lebrija
  commune, Spain   lā-BRĒ-khah   leːˈbriːxɑ
Le Brun
  Charles, *French painter, architect*   luh BRUH(R)ⁿ   lə brœ̃
Lebrun
  Albert, *French politician*   luh-BRUH(R)ⁿ   ləbrœ̃
Lecah
  Biblical name   LĒ-kuh, le-KHAH   ˈliːkə, leˈxɑ
Le Carré
  John, *pseudonym of* D. J. M.   Ⓔ luh KAR-Ā, Ⓢ luh kahr-Ā   Ⓔ lə ˈkærˌeː, Ⓢ lə kɑrˈeː
    Cornwall, *British writer*
Lech
  pers. name, Polish   LEKH, Ⓢ LEK   ˈlex, Ⓢ ˈlek
Lechtal Alps
  mtn. range, Austria   LEKH-tuhl, LEKH-TAHL   ˈlextəl, ˈlexˌtɑl
Lecithin
  food ingredient   LES-uh-thuhn   ˈlesəθən
Le Claire
  pers. name   luh KLAR, luh KLER   lə ˈklærʳ, lə ˈklerʳ
Le Clerc, Leclerc
  pers. name, French   luh-KLER   ləkler
Le Corbusier
  see Corbusier, Le
Lęczyca
  commune, Poland   leⁿ-CHIT-suh, Ⓢ len-CHIT-suh   lẽˈtʃitsə, Ⓢ lenˈtʃitsə

Foreign Sounds: ue: *Fr.* **rue**, *Ger.* **füllen**   uh(r): *Fr.* **boeuf**, *Ger.* **Höhle**   <u>kh</u>: *Ger.* **ich**, *Scot.* **loch**   ḡ: *Sp.* **amigo**   <u>v</u>: *Sp.* **hablar**
hl: *Welsh* **Llanelli.**   CAPITALS: primary stress.   SMALL CAPS: secondary stress.   Ⓢ: U.S. pron.   Ⓔ: British pron.

Leda
   beloved of Zeus in Greek myth;   LĒD-uh   'liːdə
     satellite of Jupiter
Ledbetter
   Huddie, *US singer, known as*   LED-BET-uhr   'led‚beţəʳ
     Leadbelly
Lederberg
   Joshua, *US biologist, geneticist*   LĀD-uhr-BUHRG   'leːdəʳ‚bəʳg
     (Nobel 1958)
Lederle
   US pharmaceutical co.   LED-uhr-lē   'ledəʳliˑ
Lederman
   Leon M., *US physicist (Nobel 1988)*   LED-uhr-muhn   'ledəʳmən
Le Duc Tho
   Vietnamese statesman (Nobel 1973)   LĀ DUHK TŌ   ‚leː ‚dək 'toː
Ledyard
   town, CT   LED-yuhrd, LEJ-uhrd   'ledjəʳd, 'ledʒəʳd
Lee
   pers. name   LĒ   'liː
Leeds
   town, England   LĒDZ   'liːdz
Lee Kuan Yew
   prime minister, Singapore   LĒ KWAHN YŌŌ   'liː 'kwɑn 'juː
Leelanau
   county, MI   LĒ-luh-NAW   'liːlə‚nɔː
Lee Tsung-Dao
   Chinese physicist (Nobel 1957)   LĒ DZUNG-DOW   'liː 'dzuŋ'dɑu
Leeuw
   Dutch beer   LĀ-ŌŌ   'leːuː
Leeuw
   Gerardus van der, *Dutch Reformed*   LĀ-ŌŌ   'leːuː
     theologian
Leeuwarden
   city, Netherlands   LĀ-VAHRD-n   'leː‚vɑʳdn̩
Leeuwenhoek
   Antonie von, *Dutch scientist*   LĀ-ŌŌ-vuhn-HŌŌK, ⑤ LĀ-vuhn-HUK   'leːuːvən‚huːk,
                                           ⑤ 'leːvən‚huk
Leevi
   pers. name, Finnish   LĀ-vi   'leːvi
Leeward
   Islands, *Pacific, Caribbean*   LĒ-wuhrd, LŌŌ-uhrd   'liːwəʳd, 'luːəʳd
Le Fanu
   Sheridan, *Irish writer, editor*   LEF-uhn-yŌŌ, luh-FAHN-yŌŌ   'lefənjuː, lə'fɑˑnjuː
Lefebvre
   Marcel François, *French schismatic*   luh-FEVR, ⑤ luh-FEV(-ruh)   ləfevr, ⑤ lə'fev(rə)
     Roman Catholic prelate
Le Fèvre
   1. pers. name   luh FĀV(-ruh), luh FEV   lə 'feːv(rə), lə 'fev
   2. French   luh FEVR   lə fevr
Leffe Blonde
   Belgian beer   LEF-uh BLAWⁿD   'lefə 'blɔ̃d
Le Gallienne
   Eva, *English actress;* Richard,   luh GAL-yuhn, luh GAL-YEN   lə 'gæljən, lə 'gæl‚jen
     English writer

Key (col. 2):   a: fad ā: fade ah: father ar: marry aw: law e: fed ē: feed er: merry i: hid ī: hide ō: coat ōō: boot
oi: boy ow: now u: put uh: above uhr: bird ch: chop ng: ring sh: show th: thick th̲: this zh: measure

Legaré
Hugh Swinton, *US laywer*   luh-GRĒ, luh-GRĀ   lə'griː, lə'greː
Léger
Alexis St.-Léger, *French poet,*   lā-ZHĀ   leːʒeː
diplomat (Nobel 1960)
Legh
pers. name   LĒ   'liː
Leghorn [Livorno]
prov, Italy   LEG-HAWRN   'legˌhɔːʳn
Légier
pers. name, French   lāzh-YĀ   leːʒjeː
Lego
tdmk for toy building blocks   LEG-ō, LĀ-gō   'legoː, 'leːgoː
Legree
Simon, *character in* Uncle Tom's   luh-GRĒ   lə'griː
Cabin, *H. B. Stowe*
Le Guin
Ursula, *US writer*   luh GWIN   lə 'gwin
Legum Baccalaureus
bachelor of laws, LL.B.   LĀ-guhm BAK-uh-LŌR-ē-uhs,   'leːgəm ˌbækə'loːriːəs,
   -LAWR-ē-uhs   -'lɔːriːəs
Lehabim
Biblical name   LĒ-HĀ-bim, lē-HĀ-bim, luh-hah-VĒM   'liːˌheːbim, li·'heːbim,
   ləhɑ'viːm
Lehár
Franz, *Hungarian composer*   LĀ-HAHR   'leːˌhɑʳ
Le Havre
seaport, France   luh HAHV(-ruh)   lə hɑv(rə)
Lehi
Biblical name   LĒ-HĪ, LE<u>KH</u>-ē   'liːˌhai, 'lexiː
Lehi
city, UT   LĒ-HĪ   'liːˌhai
Lehigh
river, county, university, PA   LĒ-HĪ   'liːˌhai
Lehman
1. Christopher M., *US government*   LĀ-muhn   'leːmən
official
2. Herbert Henry, *US banker and*   LĒ-muhn, LĀ-muhn   'liːmən, 'leːmən
politician
3. Lilli, *German soprano;* Lotte,   LĀ-MAHN, ⓢ LĀ-muhn   'leːˌmɑn, ⓢ 'leːmən
German-born American soprano
Lehn
Jean-Marie, *French chemist (Nobel*   LEⁿ   lē(n)
1987)
Lehrer
Jim, *US newscaster;* Tom, *US*   LER-uhr, LER   'lerəʳ, 'leʳ
mathematician & entertainer
Leibman
Ron, *US actor*   LĒB-muhn   'liːbmən
Leibnitz, Leibniz
Gottfried, *German philosopher*   LĪP-nits, ⓢ LĪB-nuhts   'laipnits, ⓢ 'laibnəts
Leibnizianism
philosophy of Leibnitz   līp-NIT-sē-uh-NIZ-uhm   laip'nitsiːəˌnizəm
Leica
brand of 35mm camera   LĪ-kuh   'laikə

Foreign Sounds: ue: *Fr.* **rue**, *Ger.* **fü**llen uh(r): *Fr.* **b**oeuf, *Ger.* **Hö**hle <u>kh</u>: *Ger.* i**ch**, *Scot.* lo**ch** g̱: *Sp.* ami**g**o v̱: *Sp.* ha**b**lar hl: *Welsh* **Ll**anelli. CAPITALS: primary stress. SMALL CAPS: secondary stress. ⓢ: U.S. pron. ⓔ: British pron.

Leicester
   town, MA; city, England   LES-tuhr   'lestə^r

Leicestershire
   county, England   LES-tuhr-shuhr, -SHIR   'lestə^{r}ʃə^r, -ˌʃi^r

Leiden, Leyden
   city, Netherlands   LĀ-yuh, LĀD-n, Ⓢ LĪD-n   'leːjə, 'leːdn̩, Ⓢ 'lɑidn̩

Leif
   pers. name   LĒF, LĀF   'liːf, 'leːf

Leigh
   pers. name   LĒ   'liː

Leighton
   pers. name   LĀT-n   'leːtn̩

Leighton Buzzard
   town, England   LĀT-n buh-ZAHRD, BUHZ-uhrd   ˌleːtn̩ bə'zɑ^{r}d, 'bəzə^{r}d

Leila
   pers. name   LĒ-luh, LĀ-luh   'liːlə, 'leːlə

Leinsdorf
   Erich, *US conductor*   LĪNZ-DAWRF, LĪN(T)S-DAWRF   'lɑinzˌdɔː^{r}f, 'lɑin(t)sˌdɔː^{r}f

Leinster
   1. prov., Ireland   LEN-stuhr   'lenstə^r
   2. Duke of, British title   LIN-stuhr   'linstə^r

Leipsic
   town, DE   LĪP-sik   'lɑipsik

Leipzig
   city, Germany   LĪPT-si<u>kh</u>, Ⓢ LĪP-sig, LĪP-sik   'lɑiptsiç, Ⓢ 'lɑipsig, 'lɑipsik

Leith
   port, Scotland   LĒTH   'liːθ

Leland
   pers. name   LĒ-luhnd   'liːlənd

Lele
   lang., Africa   LĀ-lā   'leːleˑ

Leloir
   Luis Federico, *French-born*   lā-LWAHR   leː'lwɑr
      Argentine biochemist (Nobel 1970)

Lely
   Sir Peter, *Dutch painter*   LĀ-lē, Ⓢ LĒ-lē   'leːliˑ, Ⓢ 'liːliˑ

Léman, Lac [Geneva]
   lake, Switzerland   lahk lā-MAH^n lɑːk leːmã

Le Mans
   city, auto race, France   luh MAH^n, Ⓢ luh MAHN   lə mã, Ⓢ lə 'mɑn

Lemass
   Sean, *prime minister, Ireland*   luh-MAHS   lə'mɑˑs

Lemay
   town, MO   LĒ-MĀ   'liːˌmeː

Lemhi
   county, ID   LEM-HĪ   'lemˌhɑi

Lemieux
   Mario, *Canadian hockey player*   luh-MYUH(R)   lə'mjœː

Lemmon
   Jack, *US actor*   LEM-uhn   'lemən

Lemnitzer
   Lyman, *US militarist*   LEM-nuht-suhr   'lemnətsə^r

Lemnos [Límnos]
   island, Greece   LEM-NAHS, LEM-nuhs   'lemˌnɑs, 'lemnəs

Key (col. 2):   a: f**a**d ā: f**a**de ah: f**a**ther ar: m**a**rry aw: l**a**w e: f**e**d ē: f**ee**d er: m**e**rry i: h**i**d ī: h**i**de ō: c**oa**t ōō: b**oo**t
oi: b**oy** ow: n**ow** u: p**u**t uh: **a**bove uhr: b**i**rd ch: **ch**op ng: ri**ng** sh: **sh**ow th: **th**ick <u>th</u>: **th**is zh: mea**s**ure

LeMond
    Greg, *US bicycle racer*   luh-MAHND   ləˈmɑnd

Le Moyne
    College, *NY*   luh MOIN   lə ˈmɔin

Lemuel
    pers. name   LEM-yuh(-wuh)l   ˈlemjə(wə)l

Lemures
    Roman spirits of the dead   LEM-uh-RĀS, LEM-yuh-RĒZ   ˈleməˌreːs, ˈlemjəˌriːz

Lena
    1. pers. name   LĒ-nuh   ˈliːnə
    2. river, Russia   LĀ-nuh, LĒ-nuh   ˈleːnə, ˈliːnə

Lenape
    see Lenni-Lenape

Lenard
    Philipp, *German physicist (Nobel*   LĀ-NAHRT   ˈleːˌnɑᶠt
    1905)

Lenawee
    county, MI   LEN-uh-WĒ   ˈlenəˌwiː

Lenca
    Cen. American people   LENG-kuh   ˈleŋkə

Lendl
    Ivan, *Czech.-born US tennis player*   LEN-dl   ˈlendl̩

Lendu
    lang., people, Uganda, Zaire   LEN-do͞o   ˈlenduː

L'Enfant
    Pierre, *designer of Washington, DC*   lahⁿ-FAHⁿ   lãfã

L'Engle
    Madeleine, *US writer*   LENG-guhl   ˈleŋgəl

Lenglen
    Suzanne, *French tennis player*   lahⁿ-GLEN, Ⓢ LENG-(g)luhn, LANG-(g)luhn   lãglen, Ⓢ ˈleŋ(g)lən, ˈlæŋ(g)lən

Leni
    pers. name   LEN-ē   ˈleniˑ

Lenin
    premier, USSR; orig. Vladimir Ilyich   LĀN-yin, Ⓢ LEN-uhn   ˈl̪eːnjin, Ⓢ ˈlenən
    Ulyanov

Leningrad [St. Petersburg]
    city, Russia   LUHN-yin-GRAHT, Ⓢ LEN-uhn-GRAD   ˌlənjinˈgrɑt, Ⓢ ˈlenənˌgræd

Leninism
    form of Communism taught by Lenin   LEN-uh-NIZ-uhm   ˈlenəˌnizəm

Lennie
    pers. name   LEN-ē   ˈleniˑ

Lenni-Lenape
    N. American people   LEN-ē luh-NAHP-ē, LEN-ē LEN-uh-pē   ˌleniˑ ləˈnɑpiˑ, ˌleniˑ ˈlenəpiˑ

Lennon
    John, *& his son* Julian, *British*   LEN-uhn   ˈlenən
    musicians

Lennox
    city, CA, SD; family name   LEN-uhks, LEN-iks   ˈlenəks, ˈleniks

Lenny
    pers. name   LEN-ē   ˈleniˑ

Leno
    Jay, *US entertainer*   LEN-ō   ˈlenoː

Lenoir
    county, NC; pers. name   luh-NŌR, luh-NAWR   ləˈnoːᶠ, ləˈnɔːᶠ

Lenoir-Rhyne		
College, *NC*	luh-NŌR-RĪN, luh-NAWR-	ləˌnoː^{r}'rɑin, ləˌnɔː^{r}-
Lenore		
pers. name	luh-NŌR, luh-NAWR	lə'noː^{r}, lə'nɔː^{r}
Lenox		
town, MA; tdmk for china	LEN-uhks, LEN-iks	'lenəks, 'leniks
Lentulus		
Roman cognomen	LEN-chuh-luhs, LENT-yuh-luhs	'lentʃələs, 'lentjələs
Lenya		
Lotte, *entertainer*	LEN-yuh	'lenjə
Leo		
1. constellation; pers. name	LĒ-ō	'liːoː
2. Dutch, German	LĀ-ō	'leːoː
3. Finnish	LE-aw	'leɔː
4. Italian	LE-ō	'leoː
Léo		
pers. name, French	lā-Ō	leːoː
Leofric		
pers. name	lā-AHF-rik, lā-Ō-frik	leː'ɑfrik, leː'oːfrik
Leo Minor		
constellation	LĒ-ō MĪ-nuhr	'liːoː 'mɑinə^{r}
Leominster		
1. city, MA	LEM-uhn-stuhr	'lemənstə^{r}
2. borough, England	LEM(P)-stuhr, LEM-uhn-stuhr	'lem(p)stə^{r}, 'lemənstə^{r}
Leon		
1. pers. name	LĒ-AHN, LĒ-uhn	'liːˌɑn, 'liːən
2. Italian	lā-ŌN	leː'oːn
León		
1. town, Mexico; pers. name, Spanish	lā-AWN	leː'ɔːn
2. pers. name, French	lā-AW^{n}	leːɔ̃
Leona		
pers. name	lē-Ō-nuh	liː'oːnə
Leonard		
1. pers. name	LEN-uhrd	'lenə^{r}d
2. Dutch	LĀ-ō-NAHRT	'leːoːˌnɑrt
3. German	LĀ-ō-NAHRT	'leːoːˌnɑ^{r}t
4. Polish	le-AW-nahrt	le'ɔːnɑːrt
5. Swedish	LĀ-aw-NAHRD	'leːɔːˌnɑːrd
Léonard		
pers. name, French	lā-aw-NAHR	leːɔːnɑːr
Leonardo		
1. pers. name, Italian	LĀ-ō-NAHR-dō, [$] LĒ-uh-NAHRD-ō, LĀ-uh-	ˌleːoː'nɑrdoː, [$] ˌliːə'nɑ^{r}doː, ˌleːə-
2. Spanish	lā-ō-NAHR-thō	leːoː'nɑrðoː
Leonardo da Vinci		
Italian scientist, artist	LĀ-uh-NAHRD-ō duh VĒN-chē, LĒ-uh-NAHRD-ō, VIN-chē	ˌleːə'nɑ^{r}doː də 'viːntʃiˑ, ˌliːə'nɑ^{r}doː, 'vintʃiˑ
Leonberger		
dog breed	LĀ-ahn-BER-guhr	'leːɑnˌbe^{r}gə^{r}
Leoncavallo		
Ruggero, *Italian composer*	LĀ-ŌN-kuh-VAHL-ō	ˌleːˌoːnkə'vɑloː
Leone		
pers. name, Italian	lā-Ō-nā	leː'oːneː

Leonhard
   1. pers. name, German — LĀ-awn-HAHRT — ˈleːɔːnˌhaʳt
   2. Swedish — LĀ-aw-NAHRD — ˈleːɔːˌnɑːrd

Leonid
   pers. name, Russian — li-UHN-YĒT, ⑤ LĀ-uh-nid, LĒ-uh-nid — l̡iˌənˈjiːt, ⑤ ˈleːənid, ˈliːənid

Leonidas
   1. king of Sparta; pers. name — lē-AHN-uhd-uhs — liːˈɑnədəs
   2. Spanish — lā-ō-NĒ-thahs — leːɔːˈniːðɑs

Léonide
   pers. name, French — lā-aw-NĒD — leːɔːniːd

Leonides
   meteor shower — lē-AHN-uh-DĒZ — liːˈɑnəˌdiːz

Leonids
   meteor shower — LĒ-uh-nuhdz — ˈliːənədz

Léonie
   1. pers. name — LĒ-uh-nē — ˈliːəniˑ
   2. French — lā-aw-NĒ — leːɔːniː

Leonor
   pers. name — LĒ-uh-NŌR, -NAWR — ˈliːəˌnoːʳ, -ˌnɔːʳ

Leonora
   pers. name — LĒ-uh-NŌR-uh, -NAWR-uh — ˌliːəˈnoːrə, -ˈnɔːrə

Leonov
   Aleksei Arkhipovich, Soviet cosmonaut — lyi-AW-nuhf, ⑤ lē-Ō-NAWF, -NAHF, -nuhf — l̡jiˈɔːnəf, ⑤ liːˈoːˌnɔːf, -ˌnɑf, -nəf

Leonteus
   chief of the Lapiths — lē-AHNT-ē-uhs — liːˈɑntiːəs

Leontief
   Wassily, Russian-born US economist (Nobel 1973) — lē-AWNT-yuhf — liːˈɔːntjəf

Leontius
   emperor of the Eastern Roman Empire — lē-AHN-sh(ē-)uhs — liːˈɑnʃ(iː)əs

Leontyne
   pers. name — lē-AHN-TĒN, LĒ-uhn-TIN, LĀ-uhn-TĒN — liːˈɑnˌtiːn, ˈliːənˌtin, ˈleːənˌtiːn

Leopardi
   Giacomo, Italian poet — LĀ-uh-PAHRD-ē — ˌleːəˈpaʳdiˑ

Leopold
   1. pers. name — LĒ-uh-PŌLD — ˈliːəˌpoːld
   2. Dutch, German — LĀ-ō-PAWLT — ˈleːoːˌpɔːlt
   3. Finnish — LE-aw-PAWLT — ˈleɔːˌpɔːlt
   4. Polish — le-AW-pawlt — leˈɔːpɔːlt
   5. Belgian beer — LĀ-ō-PAWLT — ˈleːoːˌpɔːlt

Léopold
   pers. name, French — lā-aw-PAWL(D) — leːɔːpɔːl(d)

Leopoldo
   1. pers. name, Italian — LĀ-ō-PAWL-dō — ˌleːoːˈpɔːldoː
   2. Spanish — lā-ō-PAWL-dō — leːoːˈpɔːldoː

Léopoldville
   former name for Kinshasa — LĒ-uh-PŌLD-VIL, LĀ-uh-PŌLD-VIL — ˈliːəˌpoːldˌvil, ˈleːəˌpoːldˌvil

Leos
   son of Orpheus — LĒ-AHS — ˈliːˌɑs

Leoš
   pers. name, Czech — LE-AWSH — ˈleˌɔːʃ

Foreign Sounds: ue: *Fr.* **rue**, *Ger.* **füllen** uh(r): *Fr.* **boeuf**, *Ger.* **Höhle** <u>kh</u>: *Ger.* **ich**, *Scot.* **loch** ḡ: *Sp.* **amigo** v: *Sp.* **hablar** hl: *Welsh* **Llanelli.** CAPITALS: primary stress. SMALL CAPS: secondary stress. ⑤: U.S. pron. ⓔ: British pron.

Lepanto		
port, gulf, Greece	luh-PAHN-tō, luh-PAN-tō	lə'pɑntoː, lə'pæntoː
Le Pen		
Jacques, *French politician*	luh PE^{n}	lə pẽ
Lepidus		
Roman family name (cognomen)	LEP-uhd-uhs	'lepədəs
Lepini		
mtn. range, Italy	lā-PĒ-nē	leː'piːniː
Lepontine Alps		
Alpine mtn. range	li-PAHN-TĪN, LEP-uhn-TĪN	li'pɑnˌtɑin, 'lepənˌtɑin
Leppard		
Raymond, *English conductor*	LEP-AHRD	'lepˌɑ^{r}d
Leptis Magna		
Roman seaport, Africa	LEP-tuhs MAG-nuh	'leptəs 'mægnə
Lepus		
constellation	LĒ-puhs, LEP-uhs	'liːpəs, 'lepəs
Le Puy		
city, France	luh PWĒ, [S] luh PWĒ	lə pɥiː, [S] lə 'pwiː
Lermontov		
Mikhail, *writer*	LYER-muhn-tuhf	'ljermәntәf
Lerner		
Louis Abraham, *US ambassador, newspaper publisher;* Alan Jay, *US lyricist*	LUHR-nuhr	'lə^{r}nə^{r}
Leroy, Le Roy		
pers. name	li-ROI, LĒ-ROI	li'rɔi, 'liːˌrɔi
Les		
pers. name	LES	'les
Lesage		
Alain-René, *French writer*	lā-SAHZH	leːsɑːʒ
Lesbos		
island, dept, Greece	LEZ-BAHS, LEZ-buhs	'lezˌbɑs, 'lezbəs
Lescaze		
William, *US architect*	les-KAHZ	les'kɑz
Leschetizky, Leszetycki		
Theodor, *Polish pianist*	LESH-ā-TIT-skē	ˌleʃeˑ'titskiˑ
Leshem		
Biblical name	LĒ-SHEM, LE-shem	'liːˌʃem, 'leʃem
Les Invalides		
soldiers' home, tomb of Napoleon, Paris, France	lez e^{n}-vah-LĒD	lez ẽvɑːliːd
Lesley, Leslie		
pers. name	LES-lē, LEZ-lē	'lesliˑ, 'lezliˑ
Lesotho [Basutoland]		
country, S. Africa	luh-SŌŌ-tōō, luh-SŌ-tō	lə'suːtuː, lə'soːtoː
Lespedeza		
plant	LES-puh-DĒ-zuh	ˌlespə'diːzə
Lesseps		
Ferdinand de, *French political leader*	lā-SEPS, les-EPS [S] LES-uhps	leːseps, leseps [S] 'lesəps
Lessing		
Gotthold, *German writer*	LES-ing	'lesiŋ
Lester		
pers. name	LES-tuhr	'lestə^{r}

Key (col. 2): a: **fad** ā: **fade** ah: **father** ar: **marry** aw: **law** e: **fed** ē: **feed** er: **merry** i: **hid** ī: **hide** ō: **coat** ōō: **boot** oi: **boy** ow: **now** u: **put** uh: **above** uhr: **bird** ch: **chop** ng: **ring** sh: **show** th: **thick** th: **this** zh: **measure**

Les Trois Glorieuses
national anthem, Congo lā TRWAH glawr-YUH(R)Z leː trwɑː glɔːrjœːz

Le Sueur
county, city, MN luh SUR lə ˈsuʳ

Lésvos [Lesbos]
island, dept, Greece LEZ-VAWS ˈlezˌvɔːs

Leszetycki
see Leschetizky

Leta
pers. name LĒT-uh ˈliːtə

Lethbridge
city, Canada LETH-brij ˈleθbridʒ

Lethe
river of forgetfulness in Hades LĒ-thē ˈliːθiˑ

Letitia
pers. name li-TISH-(ē-)uh liˈtiʃ(iː)ə

Letizia
pers. name, Italian lā-TĒT-syah leːˈtiːtsjɑ

Leto
mother of Apollo and Artemis LĒT-ō ˈliːt̮oː

LeTourneau
University, TX luh-TUR-NŌ, luh-TUR-NŌ ləˈtuʳˌnoː, ləˌtuʳˈnoː

Letterman
David, US TV personality LET-uhr-muhn ˈlet̮əʳmən

Lettie
pers. name LET-ē ˈlet̮iˑ

Lettish
pert. to the Letts LET-ish ˈlet̮iʃ

Letushim
Biblical name luh-T(Y)OO-shim, luh-tōō-SHIM ləˈt(j)uːʃim, lətuːˈʃim

Letzebuergesch [Luxemburgish]
lang., Luxemburg LET-suh-BUR-guhsh ˈletsəˌbyʳɡəʃ

Leucadius
son of Icarius and Polycaste lōō-KĀD-ē-uhs luːˈkeːdiːəs

Leucaria
wife of King Italus lōō-KAR-ē-uh luːˈkæriːə

Leuce
nymph loved by Hades LOO-sē ˈluːsiˑ

Leucippe
mother of Priam lōō-SIP-ē luːˈsipiˑ

Leucippidae
daughters of Leucippus lōō-SIP-uhd-ē luːˈsipədiˑ

Leucippus
king of Messina lōō-SIP-uhs luːˈsipəs

Leucippus
Greek philosopher lōō-SIP-uhs luːˈsipəs

Leucothea
Greek sea-goddess LOO-kuh-THĒ-uh ˌluːkəˈθiːə

Leuctra
ancient village, Greece LOOK-truh ˈluːktrə

Leucus
foster-child and betrayer of LOO-kuhs ˈluːkəs
Idomeneus

Leummim
Biblical name lē-UHM-im, luh-ōō-MĒM liːˈəmim, ləuːˈmiːm

Leuven [Louvain]
   city, Belgium   LUH(R)-vuhn   'lœːvən
Lev
   pers. name, Russian   lef   l̯ef
Levant
   Oscar, *US pianist and composer*   luh-VANT   lə'vænt
Levant, The
   eastern Mediterranean shores   t̲huh luh-VANT   ðə lə'vænt
Levantine
   pert. to the Levant   LEV-uhn-TĪN, luh-VAN-TĪN, -TĒN   'levən‚tɑin, lə'væn‚tɑin, -‚tiːn
Levar
   pers. name   luh-VAHR   lə'vɑʳ
Leven, Loch
   see Loch Leven
Leventhal
   Harold, *talent manager, producer*   LEV-uhn-THAWL, LEV-uhn-THAHL   'levən‚θɔːl, 'levən‚θɑl
Leverkusen
   city, Germany   LĀ-vuhr-KO͞O-zuhn   'leːvəʳ‚kuːzən
Levertov
   Denise, *US poet*   LEV-uhr-TAWF, -TAHF   'levəʳ‚tɔːf, -‚tɑf
Leveson-Gower
   Granville George & *his uncle*   LO͞O-suhn-GAWR   'luːsən'gɔːʳ
     George Granville, *English*
     politicians
Levesque
   Rene, *Canadian political leader*   luh-VEK   ləvek
Levi
   1. Jacob's son; Hebrew tribe; pers.   LĒ-VĪ   'liː‚vɑi
     name
   2. Carlo, Italian writer, artist,   LĀ-vē   'leːviˑ
     physician
   3. family name   LEV-ē, LĒ-vē   'leviˑ, 'liːviˑ
Levice
   town, Slovakia   LEV-uht-SĀ   'levət‚seː
Levi-Montalcini
   Rita, *Italian-born US neurobiologist*   LEV-ē-MAHNT-l-SĒ-nē   ‚leviˑ‚mɑntl̩'siːniˑ
     (Nobel 1986)
Levin
   1. pers. name   LEV-uhn   'levən
   2. German   LĀ-vuhn   'leːvən
Levin
   Gerald, *US media executive*   LEV-uhn   'levən
Levine
   James, *US opera director*   luh-VĪN   lə'vɑin
Levi's
   tdmk for clothing   LĒ-VĪZ   'liː‚vɑiz
Levisa Fork
   river, KY; river, Canada   luh-VĪ-suh FAWRK   lə'vɑisə 'fɔːʳk
Lévis-Lauzon
   College, *Canada*   lā-VĒ-lō-ZAWⁿ   leː‚viːloː'zɔ̃
Levi Strauss
   US clothing co.   LĒ-VĪ STROWS   ‚liː‚vɑi 'strɑus
Lévi-Strauss
   Claude, *French anthropologist*   lā-vē-STROWS   leːviːstrɑus

---

Key (col. 2):   a: **f**a**d**   ā: **f**a**de**   ah: **f**a**ther**   ar: **marry**   aw: **law**   e: **f**e**d**   ē: **feed**   er: **merry**   i: **h**i**d**   ī: **hide**   ō: **coat**   o͞o: **boot**
oi: **boy**   ow: **now**   u: **put**   uh: **above**   uhr: **b**i**rd**   ch: **chop**   ng: **ring**   sh: **show**   th: **thick**   t̲h: **this**   zh: **measure**

Levite
  descendant of Levi   LĒ-VĪT   'liː‚vɑit

Levitical
  pert. to the Levites   luh-VIT-i-kuhl   lə'vitikəl

Leviticus
  Old Testament book   luh-VIT-i-kuhs   lə'viṭikəs

Levittown
  town, NY   LEV-uht-TOWN   'levət‚tɑun

Levitz
  US furniture corp.   LEV-uhts   'levəts

Levulin
  carbohydrate   LEV-yuh-luhn   'levjələn

Levy
  1. Louis, *US chess master*   LEV-ē   'levi·
  2. pers. name   LEV-ē, LĒ-vē   'levi·, 'liːvi·

Lévy-Bruhl
  Lucien, *French philosopher*   lā-vē-BRUEL   leːviːbryːl

Lew
  pers. name   LOO   'luː

Lewellyn
  pers. name   luh-WEL-uhn   lə'welən

Lewes
  George Henry, *English philosopher;*   LOO-uhs   'luːəs
    town, DE

Lewin
  Kurt, *US psychologist*   LOO-uhn   'luːən

Lewis
  Meriwether, *US explorer;* Sinclair,   LOO-uhs   'luːəs
    US novelist; C.S., *British writer;*
    pers. name

Lewis
  Meriwether, *US explorer;* Sinclair,   LOO-is   'luːis
    US novelist

Lewisham
  borough, England   LOO-uh-shuhm   'luːəʃəm

Lex
  pers. name   LEKS   'leks

Lexan
  tdmk for synthetic resin   LEK-SAN   'lek‚sæn

Lex Canuleia
  Roman marriage law   LEKS KAN-yuh-LĀ-uh   'leks ‚kænjə'leːə

Lex Frumentaria
  Roman grain law   LEKS FROO-muhn-TAR-ē-uh,   'leks ‚fruːmən'tæriːə, -'teriːə
                         -TER-ē-uh

Lexington
  city, KY; town, MA   LEK-sing-tuhn, LEK-suhn-tuhn   'leksiŋtən, 'leksəntən

Lex Provinciae
  Roman provincial charter   LEKS pruh-VIN-sē-Ī   'leks prə'vinsiː‚ɑi

Leyden
  1. town, MA   LĪD-n   'lɑidn̩
  2. see Leiden

Leyden jar
  electrical condenser   LĪD-n JAHR   'lɑidn̩ 'dʒɑʳ

Leyland
  town, England   LĀ-luhnd   'leːlənd

Leyte
  gulf, island, Philippines — LĀT-ē, LĀT-ā — 'leːt̬iˑ, 'leːt̬eː
Lezghian [Kuri]
  lang., people, Caucasus Mts. — LEZ-gē-uhn — 'lezgiːən
Lezgi
  lang., people, Daghestan, Georgia, Azerbaijan — LEZ-gē — 'lezgiˑ
Lhasa
  city, Tibet — LAHS-uh, LAS-uh — 'lasə, 'læsə
Lhasa apso
  dog breed — LAHS-uh AHP-sō, LAS-uh AP-sō — ˌlasə 'apsoː, ˌlæsə 'æpsoː
Lhévinne
  Josef, *Russian pianist* — lā-VEN — leː'viːn
Lhotse
  Mount, *Himalayas* — (H)LŌT-SĀ — '(h)loːt'seː
Lhuyd
  Edward, *Welsh antiquarian* — HLU-ēd — 'l̩uiˑd
Li
  lang., people, China — LĒ — 'liː
Liam
  pers. name — LĒ-uhm — 'liːəm
Liamine
  pers. name, — lyah-MĒN — lja:miːn
Liao
  river, China — lē-OW — liː'au
Liaoning
  prov, China — lē-OW-NING — liː'au'niŋ
Liao-yang
  city, China — lē-OW-YAHNG — liː'au'jaŋ
Liard
  river, Canada — LĒ-AHRD, lē-AHRD — 'liːˌaʳd, liː'aʳd
Libbie
  pers. name — LIB-ē — 'libiˑ
Libby
  W. F., *US chemist (Nobel 1960); pers. name* — LIB-ē — 'libiˑ
Liber
  Roman wine god — LĒ-buhr, LĒ-BER — 'liːbəʳ, 'liːˌbeʳ
Liberace
  US entertainer — LIB-uh-RAHCH-ē — ˌlibə'ratʃiˑ
Liberia
  republic, Africa — lī-BIR-ē-uh — lai'biriːə
Liberian
  pert. to Liberia — lī-BIR-ē-uhn — lai'biriːən
Liberius
  pope — lī-BIR-ē-uhs — lai'biriːəs
Libitina
  Roman goddess of rites for the dead — LIB-uh-TĪ-nuh, LIB-uh-TĒ-nuh — ˌlibə'tainə, ˌlibə'tiːnə
Libnah
  Biblical name — LIB-nuh, liv-NAH — 'libnə, liv'na
Libni
  Biblical name — LIB-NĪ, LIB-nē, liv-NĒ — 'libˌnai, 'libniˑ, liv'niː
Libnite
  Biblical name — LIB-NĪT — 'libˌnait

Key (col. 2): a: fad ā: fade ah: father ar: marry aw: law e: fed ē: feed er: merry i: hid ī: hide ō: coat ōō: boot oi: boy ow: now u: put uh: above uhr: bird ch: chop ng: ring sh: show th: thick th̲: this zh: measure

Libra		
constellation, sign of the zodiac	LĒ-bruh	'liːbrə
Libreville		
city, Gabon	LĒ-bruh-VIL	'liːbrə,vil
Librium		
tdmk for a drug	LIB-rē-uhm	'libriːəm
Libya		
republic, Africa	LIB-ē-uh	'libiːə
Libyan		
pert. to Libya	LIB-ē-uhn	'libiːən
Licania		
plant	li-KĀ-nē-uh, lī-KĀ-nē-uh	li'keːniːə, lɑi'keːniːə
Lichfield		
town, England	LICH-FĒLD	'litʃ,fiːld
Lichtenstein		
Roy, *US painter*	LIK-tuhn-STĒN	'liktən,stiːn
Li Chun		
Chinese spring observance	LĒ CHO͞ON	'liː 'tʃuːn
Licinian-Sextian		
Roman Laws, 367 B.C.	lī-SIN-ē-uhn-SEK-stē-uhn	lɑi'siniːən'sekstiːən
Licinius		
Roman emperor; pers. name, Latin	li-SIN-ē-uhs	li'siniːəs
Licorice		
spice; candy	LIK-(uh-)rish, LIK-(uh-)ruhs	'lik(ə)riʃ, 'lik(ə)rəs
Liddell		
Henry, *English classical scholar; his daughter* Alice, *the inspiration for* Alice in Wonderland	LID-l	'lidl̩
Lidice		
1. village, Czechoslovakia	LĒ-duht-SĀ, LID-yuht-SĀ	'liːdət,seː, 'lidjət,seː
2. village, IL	LID-uh(t)-sē, LID-uh(t)-SĀ	'lidə(t)siˑ, 'lidə(t),seː
Lidiya		
pers. name, Russian	LĒ-dē-yah	'l̥iːd̥iːjɑː
Lido		
Adriatic resort	LĒD-ō	'liːdoː
Lie		
Trygve Halvdan, *Norwegian secretary general, United Nations*	LĒ	'liː
Liebfraumilch		
wine	LĒP-FROW-MILKH, [$] -MILK	'liːp,frɑu,milx, [$] -,milk
Liebmann		
pers. name, German	LĒP-MAHN	'liːp,mɑn
Liechtenstein		
principality, Europe	LIKH-tuhn-SHTĪN; [$] LIK-tuhn-STĪN, -SHTĪN	'liçtən,ʃtɑin; [$] 'liktən,stɑin, -,ʃtɑin
Liechtensteiner		
pert. to Liechtenstein	LIKH-tuhn-SHTĪ-nuhr; [$] LIK-tuhn-STĪ-nuhr, -SHTĪ-nuhr	'liçtən,ʃtɑinə^{r}; [$] 'liktən,stɑinə^{r}, -,ʃtɑinə^{r}
Liederkranz		
cheese	LĒD-uhr-KRAN(T)S, LĒD-uhr-KRAHN(T)S	'liːdə^{r},kræn(t)s, 'liːdə^{r},krɑn(t)s
Liège		
prov, Belgium	LYEZH, [$] lē-ĀZH, lē-EZH	ljeʒ, [$] liː'eːʒ, liː'eʒ
Ligonier		
city, IN; borough, PA	LIG-uh-NIR	,ligə'ni^{r}

Liguria
    autonomous region, Italy   luh-GYUR-ē-uh   lə'gjuriːə

Ligurian
    Alps, *Alpine mtn. range;* Sea,   li-GYUR-ē-uhn   li'gjuriːən
       branch of Mediterranean

Lihue
    division, city, HI   lē-H͞OO-ē   liː'huːiː

Like-Like
    highway, Oahu, HI   LĒ-kē-LĒ-kē   ˌliːkiː'liːkiː

Likhi
    Biblical name   LIK-HĪ, lik-<u>KH</u>Ē   'likˌhɑi, lik'xiː

Likud
    political party, Israel   li-K͞OOD   li'kuːd

Lili
    1. pers. name, French   lē-LĒ   liːliː
    2. German   LIL-ē   'liliː

Lilian
    pers. name   LIL-ē-uhn, LIL-yuhn   'liliːən, 'liljən

Lilith
    mythological female demon; Adam's   LIL-uhth   'liləθ
       first wife

Liliuokalani
    queen, Hawaii   li-LĒ-uh-WŌ-kuh-LAHN-ē   li,liːə,woːkə'lɑni·

Lille
    city, France   LĒL   liːl

Lillehammer
    city, Norway   LIL-uh-HAHM-uhr, -HAM-uhr 'lilə,hɑmər

Lilli
    pers. name, German   LIL-ē   'liliː

Lillian
    pers. name   LIL-ē-uhn, LIL-yuhn   'liliːən, 'liljən

Lillibullero
    English tune   LIL-ē-buh-LER-ō   ,lili·bə'leroː

Lillie
    pers. name   LIL-ē   'lili·

Lilliput
    island in Gulliver's Travels, *J. Swift* LIL-i-puht   'lilipət

Lilliputians
    tiny inhabitants of Lilliput   LIL-uh-PY͞OO-shuhnz   ,lilə'pjuːʃənz

Lillooet
    river, Canada   LIL-uh-WET   'lilə,wet

Lilly
    pers. name   LIL-ē   'lili·

Lilly, Eli
    US pharmaceutical firm   Ē-LĪ LIL-ē   ,iːˌlɑi 'lili·

Lilongwe
    city, Malawi   li-LAWNG-wā   li'lɔːŋweː

Lily
    1. pers. name, English, German LIL-ē   'lili·
    2. French   lē-LĒ   liːliː

Lima
    1. city, OH   LĪ-muh   'lɑimə
    2. city, Peru   LĒ-muh   'liːmə

Limba
    lang., people, Guinea, Sierra Leone LIM-buh   'limbə

Key (col. 2):   a: **fad** ā: **fade** ah: **father** ar: **marry** aw: **law** e: **fed** ē: **feed** er: **merry** i: **hid** ī: **hide** ō: **coat** o͞o: **boot**
oi: **boy** ow: **now** u: **put** uh: **above** uhr: **bird** ch: **chop** ng: **ring** sh: **show** th: **thick** <u>th</u>: **this** zh: **measure**

Limbaugh
  Rush, *US conservative radio*   LIM-baw, LIM-bō   'limbɔː, 'limboː
    personality
Limburger
  cheese   LIM-BUHR-guhr   'lim‚bəʳgəʳ
Limerick
  city, Irish Republic   LIM-(uh-)rik   'lim(ə)rik
Limes
  Roman fortified frontier   LĪ-MĒZ   'lɑi‚miːz
Limites
  plural of Limes   LIM-uh-TĒZ   'limə‚tiːz
Límnos [Lemnos]
  island, Greece   LĒM-NAWS   'liːm‚nɔːs
Limoges
  town, France   lē-MŌZH   liːmoːʒ
Limousin
  prov, France   lē-moo-ZEⁿ   liːmuːzē
Limpopo
  river, Africa   lim-PŌ-pō   lim'poːpoː
Lina
  pers. name   LĒ-nuh   'liːnə
Linacre
  college, Oxford Univ.   LIN-uh-kuhr   'linəkəʳ
Linate
  airport, Milan   lē-NAH-tā   liː'nɑːteː
Lincoln
  Abraham, *16th US president; city,*   LING-kuhn   'liŋkən
    NE
Lincolnshire
  county, England   LING-kuhn-shuhr, -SHIR   'liŋkənʃəʳ, -‚ʃiʳ
Linda
  pers. name   LIN-duh   'lində
Lindbergh
  Charles, *US aviator; his wife* Anne,   LIN(D)-BUHRG   'lin(d)‚bəʳg
    US writer
Lindemans Faro
  Belgian beer   LIN-duh-MAHNS FAHR-ō   'lində‚mɑns 'fɑroː
Linden
  Hal, *US actor*   LIN-duhn   'lindən
Lindesay
  pers. name   LIN(D)-zē   'lin(d)ziˑ
Lindisfarne
  island, England   LIN-duhs-FAHRN   'lindəs‚fɑʳn
Lindsay
  pers. name   LIN(D)-zē   'lin(d)ziˑ
Lindsborg
  city, KS   LINZ-buhrg   'linzbəʳg
Lindsey
  Benjamin, *US jurist; pers. name*   LIN(D)-zē   'lin(d)ziˑ
Lindy
  jitterbug dance   LIN-dē   'lindiˑ
Lingala
  lang., Cen. Africa   ling-GAHL-uh   liŋ'gɑlə
Lingayen
  gulf, city, Philippines   LING-gah-YEN   ‚liŋgɑ'jen

Foreign Sounds: ue: *Fr.* **rue**, *Ger.* füllen   uh(r): *Fr.* **boeuf**, *Ger.* Höhle   kh: *Ger.* ich, *Scot.* loch   ğ: *Sp.* amigo   v: *Sp.* hablar
hl: *Welsh* Llanelli.   CAPITALS: primary stress.   SMALL CAPS: secondary stress.   Ⓢ: U.S. pron.   ⓒ: British pron.

Linguaphone
   tdmk for a language-teaching system   LING-gwuh-FŌN   'liŋgwə,foːn

Linkletter
   Art, Canadian radio, TV broadcaster   LING-KLET-uhr   'liŋ,kleʈəʳ

Linlithgow
   former name of West Lothian   lin-LITH-gō   lin'liθgoː

Linnaean
   pert. to Linnaeus   luh-NĒ-uhn, luh-NĀ-uhn   lə'niːən, lə'neːən

Linnaeus
   Carolus, *Latin name of* Carl von   luh-NĒ-uhs, luh-NĀ-uhs   lə'niːəs, lə'neːəs
   Linné, *Swedish botanist; pers.*
   name

Linné [Linnaeus]
   Carl von, *Swedish botanist*   lin-Ā   lin'eː

Linnell
   pers. name   luh-NEL   lə'nel

Linnet
   songbird   LIN-uht   'linət

Linneus
   city, MO   LIN-ē-uhs   'liniːəs

Lino Lakes
   village, MN   LĪ-nō LĀKS   'lainoː 'leːks

Linotype
   typesetting machine   LĪ-nuh-TĪP   'lainə,taip

Lin Piao
   Chinese politician   LIN bē-OW   'lin biː'ɑu

Linus
   pope; son of Psamathe & Apollo in   LĪ-nuhs   'lainəs
   Greek myth; comic strip character;
   pers. name

Lin Yutang
   Chinese author   LIN YŌŌ-TAHNG   'lin 'juː'tɑŋ

Linz
   town, Austria   LIN(T)S   'lin(t)s

Linzer torte
   sweet filled pastry   LIN(T)-suhr TAWRT, LIN(D)-zuhr   'lin(t)səʳ ,tɔːʳt, 'lin(d)zəʳ

Lion
   pers. name, German   LĒ-awn   'liːɔːn

Lionel
   1. pers. name   LĪ-uhn-l, LĪ-uh-NEL   'laiənl̩, 'laiə,nel
   2. tdmk for toy trains   LĪ-uh-NEL, LĪ-uhn-l   ,laiə'nel, 'laiənl̩

Lipan
   N. American people   lē-PAHN   li·'pɑn

Lipari
   island group, Tyrrhenian Sea   LIP-uh-rē   'lipəri·

Liparus
   son of Auson   LIP-uh-ruhs   'lipərəs

Lipe
   S. American people   LĒ-pā   'liːpeː

Li Peng
   premier, China   LĒ PUHNG   'liː 'pəŋ

Lipmann
   F. A., German-born US biochemist   LIP-muhn   'lipmən
   (Nobel 1953)

Key (col. 2):   a: fad   ā: fade   ah: father   ar: marry   aw: law   e: fed   ē: feed   er: merry   i: hid   ī: hide   ō: coat   ōō: boot
oi: boy   ow: now   u: put   uh: above   uhr: bird   ch: chop   ng: ring   sh: show   th: thick   <u>th</u>: this   zh: measure

Li Po [Li Tai Po]
   Chinese poet   LĒ BŌ   ˈliː ˈboː

Lipót
   pers. name, Hungarian   LIP-ōt   ˈlipoːt

Lippard
   pers. name   LIP-AHRD   ˈlip͵ɑʳd

Lippe
   river, state, Germany   LIP-uh   ˈlipə

Lippi
   Fra Filippo *& his son* Filippo *or*   LIP-ē   ˈlipiˑ
   Filippino, *Florentine painters*

Lippizaner
   horse breed   LIP-uh-ZAHN-uhr   ˈlipə͵zɑnəʳ

Lippman
   Gabriel, *French physicist (Nobel*   lēp-MAHN   liːpmɑːn
   1908)

Lippmann
   Walter, *US journalist*   LIP-muhn   ˈlipmən

Lippo
   pers. name, Italian   LĒP-pō   ˈliːppoː

Lipscomb
   Mance, *US blues guitarist;* William   LIP-skuhm   ˈlipskəm
   Nunn, *US inorganic chemist*
   (Nobel 1976)

Lipton
   Sir Thomas, *Scottish merchant; US*   LIP-tuhn   ˈliptən
   tea & food co.

Lisa
   1. pers. name   LĒ-suh, LĪ-zuh   ˈliːsə, ˈlaizə
   2. German, Italian   LĒ-zah   ˈliːzɑ

Lisbeth
   pers. name, German   LĒS-bet   ˈliːsbet

Lisboa [Lisbon]
   city, Portugal   lēzh-VŌ-uh   liːʒˈvoːə

Lisbon
   city, Portugal   LIZ-buhn   ˈlizbən

Lise
   pers. name, German   LĒ-zuh   ˈliːzə

Lisle
   1. city, France   LĒL, LIL   liːl, lil
   2. village, IL; pers. name   LĪL   ˈlail

Lister
   Joseph, *English surgeon*   LIS-tuhr   ˈlistəʳ

Listerine
   tdmk for a mouthwash   LIS-tuh-RĒN, LIS-tuh-RĒN   ͵listəˈriːn, ˈlistə͵riːn

Lisu
   lang., people, China   LĒ-SOO, LĒ-SOO   ˈliːˈsuː, ˈliː͵suː

Liszt
   Franz, *Hungarian composer*   LIST   ˈlist

Li Tai Po [Li Po]
   Chinese poet   LĒ TĪ BŌ   ˈliː ˈtai ˈboː

Litchfield
   town, county, CT   LICH-FĒLD   ˈlitʃ͵fiːld

Lithgow
   John, *US actor*   LITH-GŌ   ˈliθ͵goː

Foreign Sounds: **ue**: *Fr.* **rue**, *Ger.* **füllen**   **uh(r)**: *Fr.* **boeuf**, *Ger.* **Höhle**   **kh**: *Ger.* **ich**, *Scot.* **loch**   **g̃**: *Sp.* **amigo**   **v̲**: *Sp.* **hablar**
hl: *Welsh* **Llanelli**.   CAPITALS: primary stress.   SMALL CAPS: secondary stress.   ⓢ: U.S. pron.   ⓔ: British pron.

Lithium
   anti-depressant drug; element   LITH-ē-uhm   'liθiːəm

Lithuania
   republic, Europe   LITH-(y)uh-WĀ-nē-uh, -nyuh   ˌliθ(j)ə'weːniːə, -njə

Lithuanian
   lang., Lithuania   LITH-(y)uh-WĀ-nē-uhn, -nyuhn   ˌliθ(j)ə'weːniːən, -njən

Litsea
   plant   LIT-sē-uh   'litsiːə

Litterarum Baccalaureus
   bachelor of letters   LIT-uh-RAR-uhm BAK-uh-LŌR-ē-uhs, -LAWR-ē-uhs   ˌlitə'rærəm ˌbækə'loːriːəs, -'loːriːəs

Litterarum Doctor
   doctor of letters, Litt.D.   LIT-uh-RAR-uhm DAHK-TAWR   ˌlitə'rærəm 'dɑkˌtoːʳ

Litterarum Humaniorum Doctor
   doctor of humanities, L.H.D.   LIT-uh-RAR-uhm h(y)u-MAN-ē-AWR-uhm, yu-MAN-   ˌlitə'rærəm h(j)uˌmæniː'oːrəm, juˌmæn-

Little Chute
   village, WI   LIT-l SHŌŌT   'litl̩ ˌʃuːt

Little Rock
   city, AR   LIT-l RAHK   'litl̩ ˌrɑk

Litton
   US manufacturing co.   LIT-n   'litn̩

Litva [Lithuania]
   republic, Europe   LIT-vuh   'litvə

Litvinov
   Maxim, *Russian political leader*   lyit-VYĒ-nuhf, ⑤ lit-VĒ-nuhf   ljit'vjiːnəf, ⑤ lit'viːnəf

Liu Shao-chi
   Chinese politician   lē-ŌŌ SHOW-JĒ   liː'uː 'ʃɑu'dʒiː

Liv
   pers. name, Swedish   LĒV, LIV   'liːv, 'liv

Liverpool
   seaport, England   LIV-uhr-PŌŌL   'livəʳˌpuːl

Liverpudlian
   pert. to Liverpool   LIV-uhr-PUHD-lē-uhn, *locally* LIV-uhr-PUD-lē-uhn   ˌlivəʳ'pədliːən, *locally* ˌlivəʳ'pudliːən

Livia
   wife of Roman emperor Augustus; pers. name   LIV-ē-uh   'liviːə

Livingstone
   David, *Scottish missionary and explorer*   LIV-ing-stuhn   'liviŋstən

Livius
   pers. name, Latin   LIV-ē-uhs   'liviːəs

Livonia
   city, MI   luh-VŌ-nē-uh, luh-VŌN-yuh   lə'voːniːə, lə'voːnjə

Livorno [Leghorn]
   prov, Italy   lē-VAWR-nō   liː'voːʳnoː

Livy
   Roman historian   LIV-ē   'liviˑ

Li Xiannian
   Chinese politician   LĒ shē-AHN-YAHN   'liː ʃiː'ɑn'jɑn

Liz
   pers. name   LIZ   'liz

Key (col. 2):   a: fad   ā: fade   ah: father   ar: marry   aw: law   e: fed   ē: feed   er: merry   i: hid   ī: hide   ō: coat   ōō: boot
oi: boy   ow: now   u: put   uh: above   uhr: bird   ch: chop   ng: ring   sh: show   th: thick   <u>th</u>: this   zh: measure

Liza
   pers. name   LĪ-zuh   'laizə

Lizzie
   pers. name   LIZ-ē   'lizi·

Ljubljana
   city, Slovenia   LYO͞OB-lyah-nah,   'ljuːbljɑnɑ, ⓢ liːˌuːbliːˈanə,
                          ⓢ lē-O͞O-blē-AHN-uh,   liːˈuːbliːəˌnɑ
                          lē-O͞O-blē-uh-NAH

Ljubomir
   pers. name, Serbo-Croatian   LYO͞O-baw-MĒR   'ljuːbɔːˌmiːr

Ljudevit
   pers. name, Serbo-Croatian   LYO͞O-de-VĒT   'ljuːdeˌviːt

Lladró
   Spanish porcelain   (L)YAHTH-rō   '(l)jaðroː

Llanberis
   village, mtn. pass, Wales   hlahn-BER-is   ɬanˈberis

Llanelli
   town, Wales   hlah-NEHL-ē   ɬaˈneɬi·

Llanera
   commune, Spain   (l)yah-NĀ-ruh   (l)jaˈneːrə

Llanfairpwllgwyngyll
   village, Wales (short form)   HLAHN-vīr-PUHL-GWIN-gihl   ˌɬanvairˈpuɬˌgwingiɬ

Llanfairpwll-
gwyngyllgogery-
chwyrndrobwll-
llandysiliogogogoch
   village, Wales (full form)   HLAHN-vīr-PUHL-   ˌɬanvairˈpuɬ-
                          GWIN-gihl-GŌ-ger-uh-   ˌgwingiɬˌgoːgerə-
                          KHWUHRN-DRŌ-buhl-HLAHN   'xwərnˈdroːbuɬˌɬ-
                          -duh-SIL-yō-GŌ-gō-GŌKH   andəˈsiljoːˌgoːgoːˈgoːx

Llangollen
   town, Wales   hlahn-GAWHL-en   ɬanˈgɔːɬen

Llano
   river, county, TX   LAN-ō   'lænoː

Llareggub
   fictional Welsh town in Under Milk   hlah-REG-ib   ɬaˈregib
        Wood, *D. Thomas*

Llewelyn
   pers. name, Welsh   hle-WEL-in, hlyo͞o-EL-in   ɬeˈwelin, ɬjuːˈelin

Llewelyn, Llewellyn
   pers. name   luh-WEL-uhn   ləˈwelən

Lleyn
   peninsula, Wales   HLĒN   'ɬiːn

Lloyd
   pers. name   LOID   'lɔid

Llull
   Ramón, *Catalan poet*   LYO͞OL   'ljuːɬ

Llullaillaco
   volcano, Chile   yo͞o-yī-YAHK-ō   juːjaiˈjakoː

Llwchwr [Loughor]
   urban district, Wales   HLO͞O-khur   'ɬuːxur

Llywelyn
   1. pers. name   luh-WEL-uhn   ləˈwelən
   2. Welsh   hlyo͞o-EL-in   ɬjuːˈelin

Foreign Sounds: **ue**: *Fr.* **rue**, *Ger.* **füllen**   **uh(r)**: *Fr.* **boeuf**, *Ger.* **Höhle**   **kh**: *Ger.* **ich**, *Scot.* **loch**   **g̃**: *Sp.* **amigo**   **v**: *Sp.* **hablar**
hl: *Welsh* **Llanelli**.   CAPITALS: primary stress.   SMALL CAPS: secondary stress.   ⓢ: U.S. pron.   ⓔ: British pron.

Llywelyn ap Gruffydd
Welsh prince　　　hlyo͞o-EL-in ahp GRIF-i<u>th</u>　　　ḷjuːˈelin ɑp ˈɡrifið

Loa
town, UT; river, Chile　　　LŌ-uh　　　ˈloːə

Loammi
Biblical name　　　lō-AM-Ī, LŌ-ah-MĒ　　　loːˈæmˌɑi, ˌloːɑˈmiː

Löb
pers. name, German　　　LUH(R)P　　　ˈlœːp

Lobachevsky
Nikolai Ivanovich, *Russian*　　　luh-BUH-CHEF-skyiy,　　　lǝˌbǝˈtʃefskjij,
　　mathematician　　　Ⓢ LŌ-buh-CHEF-skē　　　Ⓢ ˌloːbǝˈtʃefskiˑ

Lobelia
plant　　　lō-BĒL-yuh, lō-BĒ-lē-uh　　　loːˈbiːljǝ, loːˈbiːliːə

Lobito
port, Angola　　　lō-BĒT-ō　　　loːˈbiːʈoː

Locarno
commune, Switzerland　　　lō-KAHR-nō　　　loːˈkɑʳnoː

Lochinvar
romantic suitor in Marmion, *Sir*　　　LAH<u>KH</u>-uhn-VAHR, LAHK-uhn-VAHR　　　ˌlaxǝnˈvɑʳ, ˌlakǝnˈvɑʳ
　　Walter Scott

Loch Leven
lake, Scotland　　　LAH<u>KH</u> LĒ-vuhn, LAHK　　　ˌlax ˈliːvǝn, ˌlak

Loch Lomond
lake, Scotland　　　lah<u>kh</u> LŌ-muhnd, lahk　　　lax ˈloːmǝnd, lak

Loch Morar
lake, Scotland　　　LAH<u>KH</u> MAWR-uhr, LAHK　　　ˌlax ˈmɔːrǝʳ, ˌlak

Loch Ness
lake, Scotland　　　LAH<u>KH</u> NES, LAHK　　　ˌlax ˈnes, ˌlak

Loch Rannoch
lake, Scotland　　　LAH<u>KH</u> RAN-uh<u>kh</u>, RAN-uhk, LAHK　　　ˌlax ˈrænǝx, ˈrænǝk, ˌlak

Locke
John, *English philosopher;* Sondra,　　　LAHK　　　ˈlak
　　US actress

Lockerbie
town, Scotland　　　LAHK-uhr-bē　　　ˈlakǝʳbiˑ

Lockhart
pers. name　　　LAHK-HAHRT, LAHK-uhrt　　　ˈlakˌhɑʳt, ˈlakǝʳt

Lockheed
US aircraft manufacturer　　　LAHK-ĒD, LAHK-HĒD　　　ˈlakˌiːd, ˈlakˌhiːd

Locris
district, Greece　　　LŌ-kruhs　　　ˈloːkrǝs

Locrus
builder of Thebes　　　LŌ-kruhs　　　ˈloːkrǝs

Lod
Biblical name　　　LŌD, LAWD　　　ˈloːd, ˈlɔːd

Lo-debar
Biblical name　　　lō-DĒ-BAHR, LŌD-uh-VAHR　　　loːˈdiːˌbɑʳ, ˌloːdǝˈvɑr

Lodewijk, -wyck
pers. name, Dutch　　　LŌ-duh-VĪK　　　ˈloːdǝˌvɑik

Lodge
Henry Cabot, *US politician*　　　LAHJ　　　ˈladʒ

Lodi
1. city, CA, NJ　　　LŌ-DĪ　　　ˈloːˌdɑi
2. commune, Italy　　　LAWD-ē　　　ˈlɔːdiˑ

Key (col. 2):　a: fad　ā: fade　ah: father　ar: marry　aw: law　e: fed　ē: feed　er: merry　i: hid　ī: hide　ō: coat　o͞o: boot
oi: boy　ow: now　u: put　uh: above　uhr: bird　ch: chop　ng: ring　sh: show　th: thick　<u>th</u>: this　zh: measure

Lodovico		
pers. name, Italian	LŌ-dō-VĒ-kō	ˌloːdoːˈviːkoː
Łódź		
city, Poland	LOOJ, [$] LAHDZ	ˈɫuːdʒ, [$] ˈlɑdz
Łódź		
province, city, Poland	LOOCH, [$] LUJ, LAHDZ	ˈɫuːtʃ, [$] ˈludʒ, ˈlɑdz
Loeb		
1. classical text series; pers. name	LŌB	ˈloːb
2. German	LUH(R)P	ˈlœːp
Loeffler		
Charles Martin Tornov, *US composer*	LEF-luhr	ˈleflə^{r}
Loesser		
Frank, *US composer*	LES-uhr	ˈlesə^{r}
Loew		
US theater chain	LŌ, LŌ-ē	ˈloː, ˈloːiˑ
Loewi		
Otto, *German-born US pharmacologist (Nobel 1936)*	LŌ-ē	ˈloːiˑ
Lofoten		
island group, Norway	LŌ-FŌT-n	ˈloːˌfoːtn̩
Lofsöngur		
national anthem, Iceland	LAWF-SUH(R)NG-guhr	ˈlɔːfˌsœŋgər
Lofton		
James David, *US football player*	LAWF-tuhn	ˈlɔːftən
Logan		
pers. name; US pl. name	LŌ-guhn	ˈloːgən
Loggia		
Robert, *US actor*	LŌ-j(ē-)uh	ˈloːdʒ(iː)ə
Loggins		
Kenny, *US singer, songwriter*	LAW-guhnz, LAHG-uhnz	ˈlɔːgənz, ˈlɑgənz
Logo		
lang., Sudan, Zaire	LŌ-gō	ˈloːgoː
Logroño		
town, Spain	lō-GRŌN-yō	loːˈgroːnjoː
Lohengrin		
knight in German legend; opera, R. Wagner	LŌ-uhn-GRIN	ˈloːənˌgrin
Lohrer		
German beer	LŌR-uhr, LAWR-uhr	ˈloːrə^{r}, ˈlɔːrə^{r}
Loir		
river, France	LWAHR, [$] luh-WAHR	lwɑr, [$] ləˈwɑ^{r}
Loire		
river, region, dept, France	LWAHR, [$] luh-WAHR	lwɑːr, [$] ləˈwɑ^{r}
Loire-Atlantique		
dept, France	LWAHR-aht-lah^{n}-TĒK	lwɑrɑːtlɑ̃tiːk
Loire-et-Cher		
dept, France	LWAHR-ā-SHER	lwɑreːʃer
Loiret		
dept, France	lwah-RE	lwɑːre
Lois		
pers. name	LŌ-uhs	ˈloːəs
Loki		
Scandinavian adversary of the gods	LŌ-kē	ˈloːkiˑ

Lok Sabha
　lower house of Indian parliament　　LAHK SAHB-uh, LAWK　　　'lɑk 'sɑbə, 'lɔːk

Lola
　pers. name　　LŌ-luh　　　'loːlə

Lolita
　novel, V. Nabokov　　lō-LĒT-uh　　　loː'liːtə

Lollard
　English or Scottish follower of J.　　LAHL-uhrd, ⑤ LAHL-AHRD　　　'lɑləʳd, ⑤ 'lɑlˌɑʳd
　Wyclif

Lollardism
　teachings of J. Wyclif　　LAHL-uhr-DIZ-uhm　　　'lɑləʳˌdizəm

Lollobrigida
　Gina, *entertainer*　　LŌ-luh-BRIJ-uhd-uh　　　ˌloːlə'bridʒədə

Loma
　lang., people, Liberia, Guinea　　LŌ-muh　　　'loːmə

Loma Linda
　city, CA　　LŌ-muh LIN-duh　　　ˌloːmə 'lində

Lomax
　John Avery & *his son*, Alan, *US*　　LŌ-MAKS　　　'loːˌmæks
　folklorists

Lombard
　Carol, *US actress*; Longobard;　　LAHM-BAHRD, LAHM-buhrd　　　'lɑmˌbɑʳd, 'lɑmbəʳd
　person from Lombardy

Lombardi
　Vince, *US coach*　　luhm-BAHRD-ē, lahm-　　　ləm'bɑʳdiˑ, lɑm-

Lombardia [Lombardy]
　prov, Italy　　LAHM-buhr-DĒ-uh　　　ˌlɑmbəʳ'diːə

Lombardo
　Guy Albert, *US bandleader*　　luhm-BAHR-DŌ, lahm-　　　ləm'bɑʳˌdoː, lɑm-

Lombardy
　prov, Italy　　LAHM-BAHRD-ē, LAHM-buhrd-ē　　　'lɑmˌbɑʳdiˑ, 'lɑmbəʳdiˑ

Lombok
　island, Indonesia　　LAHM-BAHK　　　'lɑmˌbɑk

Lombrosian
　pert. to C. Lombroso　　lahm-BRŌ-zē-uhn, lahm-BRŌ-sē-uhn　　　lɑm'broːziːən, kɑm'broːsiːən

Lombroso
　Cesare, *Italian criminologist*　　lahm-BRŌ-sō　　　lɑm'broːsoː

Lomé
　city, Togo　　lō-MĀ　　　loː'meː

Lomita
　city, CA　　lō-MĒT-uh　　　loː'miːtə

Lomond, Loch
　see Loch Lomond

Lompoc
　city, CA　　LAHM-PAHK　　　'lɑmˌpɑk

Lon
　pers. name　　LAHN　　　'lɑn

Londinium
　ancient name of London　　LUHN-DIN-ē-uhm, lahn-DIN-ē-uhm　　　ˌlən'diniːəm, lɑn'diniːəm

London
　city, England　　LUHN-duhn　　　'ləndən

Londonderry
　city, Ireland　　LUHN-duhn-DER-ē, LUHN-duhn-DER-ē　　　ˌləndən'deriˑ, 'ləndənˌderiˑ

Londoner
　inhabitant of London　　LUHN-duh-nuhr　　　'ləndənəʳ

Key (col. 2):　a: fad　ā: fade　ah: father　ar: marry　aw: law　e: fed　ē: feed　er: merry　i: hid　ī: hide　ō: coat　ōō: boot
oi: boy　ow: now　u: put　uh: above　uhr: bird　ch: chop　ng: ring　sh: show　th: thick　th: this　zh: measure

Long Beach
   city, NJ, CA   LAWNG BĒCH   'lɔːŋ ˌbiːtʃ
Longfellow
   Henry Wadsworth, *US poet*   LAWNG-FEL-ō, -FEL-uh   'lɔːŋˌfeloː, -ˌfelə
Longinus
   Dionysius, *Greek philosopher*   lahn-JĪ-nuhs, lawn-JĪ-nuhs   lɑn'dʒɑinəs, lɔːn'dʒɑinəs
Long Island
   island, NY   lawng Ī-luhnd, *locally also* lawng GĪ-luhnd   lɔːŋ 'ailənd, *locally also* lɔːŋ 'gailənd
Longisquamata
   dinosaur   LAHN-juh-SKWAHM-uht-uh   ˌlɑndʒə'skwɑmət̬ə
Longman
   English family of book publishers   LAWNG-muhn   'lɔːŋmən
Longobard
   one of an ancient German tribe in Italy   LAWNG-guh-BAHRD, LAHNG-guh-BAHRD   'lɔːŋgəˌbaʳd, 'laŋgəˌbaʳd
Longobardi
   plural of Longobard   LAWNG-guh-BAHRD-Ī, LAHNG-guh-BAHRD-Ī, -BAHRD-ē   ˌlɔːŋgə'baʳdˌai, ˌlaŋgə'baʳdˌai, -'baʳdiˑ
Long Sault
   scenic parkway, Ontario   LAWNG SŌŌ   'lɔːŋ 'suː
Longueuil
   town, Canada   lawng-GĀL   lɔːŋ'geːl
Longueville
   pers. name   LAWNG-VIL   'lɔːŋˌvil
Longus
   Greek author   LAHNG-guhs, LAWNG-guhs   'laŋgəs, 'lɔːŋgəs
Lon Morris
   College, *TX*   LAHN MAWR-uhs, MAHR-uhs   'lɑn 'mɔːrəs, 'mɑrəs
Lonnie
   pers. name   LAHN-ē   'lɑniˑ
Lonoke
   county, AR   LŌ-NŌK   'loːˌnoːk
Loomis
   pers. name   LŌŌ-mis   'luːmis
Loos
   Adolph, *US architect;* Anita, *US writer*   LŌŌS   'luːs
Lope
   pers. name, Spanish   LŌ-pā   'loːpeː
Lope de Vega Carpio
   Félix, *Spanish writer*   LŌ-pā thā VĀ-ḡah KAHR-pē-ō   'loːpeː ðeː 'βeːɣa 'karpiːoː
Lopes
   pers. name, Portuguese   LŌ-pēsh, LŌ-pēs   'loːpiːʃ, 'loːpiːs
López
   pers. name, Spanish   LŌ-pās, LŌ-pāth   'loːpeːs, 'loːpeːθ
Lopez-Cobos
   Jesus, *Spanish conductor*   lō-pāth-KŌ-v̠ōs, lō-PĀS-   loːpeːθ'koːβoːs, loːˈpeːs-
López Mateos
   Adolfo, *president, Mexico*   LŌ-pās mah-TĀ-ōs   'loːpeːs ma'teːoːs
López Portillo y Pacheco
   José, *Mexican politician*   LŌ-pās pawr-TĒ-yō ē pah-CHĀ-kō   'loːpeːs pɔːr'tiːjoː iː pa'tʃeːkoː
López Pumarejo
   Alfonso, *Columbian politician*   LŌ-pās pōō-mah-RĀ-hō   'loːpeːs puːma'reːhoː

Foreign Sounds: ue: *Fr.* **rue**, *Ger.* **füllen**   uh(r): *Fr.* **boeuf**, *Ger.* **Höhle**   kh: *Ger.* **ich**, *Scot.* lo**ch**   ḡ: *Sp.* ami**g**o   v̠: *Sp.* ha**b**lar
hl: *Welsh* **Ll**anelli.   CAPITALS: primary stress.   SMALL CAPS: secondary stress.   ⑤: U.S. pron.   ⑥: British pron.

Lora
  pers. name   LŌR-uh, LAWR-uh   'lo:rə, 'lɔ:rə
Lorain
  town, county, OH   luh-RĀN, law-RĀN   lə'reːn, lɔ:'reːn
Loral
  US defense electronics co.   lōr-AL, lawr-AL   lo:r'æl, lɔːr'æl
Loran
  tdmk for a long range navigational system   LŌR-AN, LAWR-AN   'lo:r,æn, 'lɔːr,æn
Lorber
  Jeff, *recording artist*   LAWR-buhr   'lɔːʳbəʳ
Lorca
  1. city, Spain   LAWR-kuh   'lɔːʳkə
  2. see García Lorca
Lord's Prayer
  prayer, "Our Father"   LAWRDZ PRAR, PRER   ˌlɔːʳdz 'præʳ, 'preʳ
L'Oreal
  tdmk for cosmetics   LŌR-ē-AL, LAWR-ē-AL   ˌloːriː'æl, ˌlɔːriː'æl
Loredana
  pers. name, Italian   LAWR-e-DAHN-ah   ˌlɔːre'dɑnɑ
Lorelei
  nymph of the Rhine; pers. name   LŌR-uh-LĪ, LAWR-uh-LĪ   'loːrəˌlɑi, 'lɔːrəˌlɑi
Loren
  1. pers. name   LŌR-uhn, LAWR-uhn, LAHR-uhn   'loːrən, 'lɔːrən, 'lɑrən
  2. Sophia, *Italian actress*   luh-REN, law-REN   lə'ren, lɔ:'ren
Lorentz
  1. H. A., Dutch physicist (Nobel 1902)   LŌR-EN(T)S, LAWR-EN(T)S   'loːr,en(t)s, 'lɔːr,en(t)s
  2. pers. name, Danish   LAWR-uhns   'lɔːrəns
  3. Norwegian   LŌR-uhns   'loːrəns
Lorenz
  Konrad, *Austrian zoologist, ethologist (Nobel 1973); pers. name*   LŌ-rens, ⓢ LŌR-EN(T)S, LAWR-EN(T)S   'loːrens, ⓢ 'loːr,en(t)s, 'lɔːr,en(t)s
Lorenzo
  1. pers. name   luh-REN-zō   lə'renzoː
  2. Italian   lō-RENT-sō   lo:'rentsoː
  3. Spanish   lō-RĀN-sō, -thō   lo:'reːnsoː, -θoː
  4. Swedish   law-RENT-sō   lɔ:'rentsoː
Loreto
  pers. name, Italian   lō-RĀ-tō   lo:'reːtoː
Loretta
  pers. name   luh-RET-uh   lə'reʈə
Lori, Lorie
  pers. name   LAWR-ē   'lɔːriˑ
Lorica
  port, Colombia   luh-RĒ-kuh   lə'riːkə
L'Orignal
  village, Canada   law-rēn-YAHL, ⓢ lawr-NEL, LAWR-in-YAHL   lɔːriːnjɑːl, ⓢ lɔːʳnel, ˌlɔːrin'jɑl
Lorikeet
  parrot   LAWR-i-KĒT, LAHR-i-KĒT   'lɔːriˌkiːt, 'lɑriˌkiːt
Lorimer
  pers. name   LAWR-uh-muhr, LŌR-   'lɔːrəməʳ, 'loːr-

Key (col. 2):   a: fad   ā: fade   ah: father   ar: marry   aw: law   e: fed   ē: feed   er: merry   i: hid   ī: hide   ō: coat   ōō: boot
oi: boy   ow: now   u: put   uh: above   uhr: bird   ch: chop   ng: ring   sh: show   th: thick   <u>th</u>: this   zh: measure

Lorin
   pers. name   LŌR-uhn, LAWR-uhn   ˈlɔːrən, ˈlɔːrən

Loring
   pers. name   LŌ-ring, LAWR-ing   ˈlɔːrɪŋ, ˈlɔːrɪŋ

Lorna
   pers. name   LAWR-nuh   ˈlɔːʳnə

Lorrain, Lorraine
   pers. name   luh-RĀN, law-RĀN   ləˈreɪn, lɔːˈreɪn

Lorraine
   prov., France   law-REN, Ⓢ luh-RĀN   lɔːren, Ⓢ ləˈreɪn

Lorre
   Peter, *US actor*   LAWR-ē, LAHR-ē   ˈlɔːriˑ, ˈlɑriˑ

Lo-ruhamah
   Biblical name   LŌ-roo-HAHM-uh, LŌ-roo-KHAHM-ah   ˌlɔːruːˈhɑmə, ˌlɔːruːˈxɑmɑ

Lory
   parrot   LŌR-ē, LAWR-ē   ˈlɔːriˑ, ˈlɔːriˑ

Los Alamos
   county, town, NM   laws AL-uh-MŌS   lɔːs ˈæləˌmoːs

Los Altos
   city, CA   laws AL-TŌS, AL-tuhs, lahs   lɔːs ˈælˌtoːs, ˈæltəs, lɑs

Los Andes [Andes]
   mtn. range, S. America   laws AHN-dās   lɔːs ˈɑndeːs

Los Angeles
   1. city, CA   laws AN-juh-luhs, AN-juh-LĒZ, ANG-g(uh-)luhs   lɔːs ˈændʒələs, ˈændʒəˌliːz, ˈæŋg(ə)ləs
   2. city, Chile   laws AHNG-hel-ās   lɔːs ˈɑŋheleːs

Los Baños
   municipality, Philippines   laws BAHN-yōs   lɔːs ˈbɑnjoːs

Los Banos
   city, CA   laws BAN-uhs, lahs   lɔːs ˈbænəs, lɑs

Los Coyotes
   Indian reservation, US   LAWS kī-ŌT-ēz, laws KĪ-ŌT-ēz   ˌlɔːs kaiˈoːtiˑz, lɔːs ˈkaiˌoːtiˑz

Los Gatos
   city, CA   laws GAT-uhs   lɔːs ˈgæṭəs

Los Lobos
   rock band   laws LŌ-bōs, lahs   lɔːs ˈloːboːs, lɑs

Lot
   1. Ferdinand, *French historian*   LAWT   lɔːt
   2. Biblical name   LAHT, LŌT   ˈlɑt, ˈloːt

Lotan
   Biblical name   LŌ-TAN, lō-TAHN   ˈloːˌtæn, loːˈtɑn

Lotario
   pers. name, Italian   lō-TAHR-yō   loːˈtɑrjoː

Lot-et-Garonne
   department, France   lawt-ā-gah-RAWN   lɔːteːgarɔːn

Lothar
   pers. name, German   lō-TAHR, LŌ-TAHR   loːˈtɑʳ, ˈloːˌtɑʳ

Lotharingia
   early European kingdom   LŌ-thuh-RIN-j(ē-)uh   ˌloːθəˈrindʒ(iː)ə

Lothario
   seducer; character in The Fair Penitent, *N. Rowe*   lō-THAR-ē-ō, lō-THER-ē-Ō, lō-THAHR-ē-Ō   loːˈθæriːˌoː, loːˈθeriːˌoː, loːˈθɑriːˌoː

Lothian
   region, Scotland   LŌ-thē-uhn   ˈloːðiːən

Foreign Sounds: ue: *Fr.* **rue**, *Ger.* f**ü**llen   uh(r): *Fr.* b**oeu**f, *Ger.* H**öh**le   kh: *Ger.* i**ch**, *Scot.* lo**ch**   g̠: *Sp.* ami**g**o   v̠: *Sp.* ha**b**lar
hl: *Welsh* **Ll**anelli.   CAPITALS: primary stress.   SMALL CAPS: secondary stress.   Ⓢ: U.S. pron.   Ⓔ: British pron.

Loti
Pierre, *French novelist*	lō-TĒ	loːtiː

Lotis
nymph loved by Priapus	LŌT-uhs	ˈloːţəs

Lotophagi
lotus-eaters, hosts of Odysseus	LŌT-uh-FĀ-JĪ	ˌloːţəˈfeːˌdʒɑi

Lotta
1. pers. name	LAHT-uh	ˈlaţə
2. Finnish	LAWT-tah	ˈlɔːttɑ

Lotte
pers. name, German	LAWT-uh	ˈlɔːţə

Lottie
pers. name	LAHT-ē	ˈlaţiˑ

Lotuko
lang., people, Sudan	luh-TŌŌ-kō	ləˈtuːkoː

Lou
pers. name	LŌŌ	ˈluː

Loudon
county, TN; pers. name	LOWD-n	ˈlaudn̩

Loudoun
county, VA	LOWD-n	ˈlaudn̩

Louella
pers. name	luh-WEL-uh	ləˈwelə

Louganis
Greg, *US Olympic diver*	lōō-GĀ-nuhs, lōō-GAHN-uhs	luːˈgeːnəs, luːˈganəs

Loughborough
town, England	LUHF-b(uh-)ruh, LUHF-BUH-ruh, LUHF-BUHR-uh	ˈləfb(ə)rə, ˈləfˌbə-rə, ˈləfˌbər-ə

Lough Derg
lake, Ireland	lawkh DYERG̃, ⓢ lahkh DUHRG, lahk	lɔːx ˈdjerɣ, ⓢ lax ˈdəʳg, lak

Loughlin
family name	LAHK-luhn, LAHKH-luhn	ˈlaklən, ˈlaxlən

Loughor [Llwchwr]
urban district, Wales	LUHKH-uhr	ˈləxəʳ

Loughrea
town, Ireland	lahkh-RĀ, lahk-RĀ	laxˈreː, lakˈreː

Louiche
pers. name, French	LWĒSH	lwiːʃ

Louie
pers. name	LŌŌ-ē	ˈluːiˑ

Louis
1. pers. name	LŌŌ-uhs, LŌŌ-ē	ˈluːəs, ˈluːiˑ
2. Dutch	lōō-Ē	luːˈiː
3. French	LWĒ	lwiː
4. German, Swedish	LŌŌ-ē	ˈluːiː
5. Norwegian	LŌŌ-ē, LŌŌ-is	ˈluːiː, ˈluːis

Louisa
1. city, KY; county, VA; pers. name	luh-WĒ-zuh	ləˈwiːzə
2. county, IA	luh-WĪ-zuh	ləˈwaizə
3. pers. name, Dutch	lōō-Ē-zuh	luːˈiːzə

Louise		
1. lake, Canada; pers. name	luh-WĒZ, lu-ĒZ	lə'wiːz, lu'iːz
2. Danish	lu-Ē-suh	lu'iːsə
3. Dutch	lo͞o-Ē-suh	luː'iːsə
4. French	LWĒZ	lwiːz
5. German	lo͞o-Ē-zuh	luː'iːzə
Louisiana		
state, US	lo͞o-Ē-zē-AN-uh, LO͞O-uh-zē-AN-uh, LO͞O-zē-AN-uh	lu'ˌiːziː'ænə, ˌluːəziː'ænə, ˌluːziː'ænə
Louis Philippe		
king of France	LWĒ fē-LĒP	lwiː fiːliːp
Louis Quatorze		
pert. to French king Louis XIV	lwē kah-TAWRZ, [S] LO͞O-ē kuh-TAWRZ, luh-WĒ	lwiː kaːtɔːrz, [S] ˌluːi' kə'tɔː^{r}z, ləˌwiː
Louis Quinze		
pert. to French king Louis XV	lwē KE^{n}Z, [S] LO͞O-ē KA^{n}Z, luh-WĒ, KANZ	lwiː kẽz, [S] ˌluːi' 'kæ̃(n)z, ləˌwiː, 'kænz
Louis Seize		
pert. to French king Louis XVI	lwē SEZ, [S] LO͞O-ē SEZ, luh-WĒ	lwiː 'sez, [S] ˌluːi' 'sez, ləˌwiː
Louis Treize		
pert. to French king Louis XIII	lwē TREZ, [S] LO͞O-ē TREZ, luh-WĒ	lwiː 'trez, [S] ˌluːi' 'trez, ləˌwiː
Louisville		
city, KY	LO͞O-i-VIL, LO͞O-i-vuhl, lo͞o-uh-vuhl	'luːiˌvil, 'lu'ivəl, lu'əvəl
Loup		
river, county, NE	LO͞OP	'luːp
Lourdes		
1. town, France	LURD, [S] LURD(Z)	lurd, [S] 'lu^{r}d(z)
2. College, *OH*	LURD(Z)	'lu^{r}d(z)
Lourenço		
pers. name, Portuguese	lō-RE^n-so͞o	loː'rẽːsuː
Louth		
1. county, Ireland	LOWT͟H, LOWTH	'lauð, 'lauθ
2. town, England	LOWTH	'lauθ
Louvain [Leuven]		
city, Belgium	lo͞o-VE^n	luːvẽ
Louvre		
museum, art gallery, Paris, France	LO͞OVR, [S] LO͞OV(-ruh)	luːvr, [S] 'luːv(rə)
Loveland		
city, CO	LUHV-luhnd	'ləvlənd
Lovell		
pers. name	LUHV-uhl	'ləvəl
Lovell		
James, *US astronaut*	LUHV-uhl	'ləvəl
Lowchen		
dog breed	LŌ-CHUHN, -CHEN	'loː'tʃən, -'tʃen
Lowe		
Arthur, *English actor;* E. Nobles, *US lawyer;* Rob, *US actor*	LŌ	'loː
Lowell		
Amy, *US poet;* James Russell, *US writer;* Robert, *US poet; city, MA; pers. name*	LŌ-uhl	'loːəl

Lowenbrau, Löwenbräu
  US beer   LŌ-uhn-BROW   ˈloːən‚brɑu

Löwenbräu
  Swiss, German beers   LUH(R)-vuhn-BROI, Ⓢ LŌ-uhn-BROW   ˈlœːvən‚brɔi, Ⓢ ˈloːən‚brɑu

Lower Brule
  Indian reservation, US   BRŌŌL, BRŌŌ-lē   ˈbruːl, ˈbruːliˑ

Lower Elwah
  Indian reservation, US   EL-WAH   ˈel‚wɑ

Lowestoft
  town, England   LŌ-STAWFT, LŌ-stuhf(t), LŌ-i-   ˈloː‚stɔːft, ˈloːstəf(t), ˈloːi-

Lowndes
  county, AL, GA, MS   LOWN(D)Z   ˈlɑun(d)z

Lowrie, Lowry
  pers. name   LOWR-ē   ˈlɑuriˑ

Lowthers, The
  mountain range, Scotland   thuh LOW-thuhrz   ðə ˈlɑuðəʳz

Lowthian
  pers. name   LŌ-thē-uhn, LŌTH-yuhn   ˈloːθiːən, ˈloːθjən

Lowville
  village, NY   LOW-VIL   ˈlɑu‚vil

Lowy
  Jay Stanton, US music publisher   LŌ-ē   ˈloːiˑ

Loxahatchee
  National Wildlife Refuge, FL   LAHK-suh-HACH-ē   ‚lɑksəˈhætʃiˑ

Loy
  Myrna, US actress   LOI   ˈlɔi

Lo-yang
  see Luoyang

Loy Krathong
  Thai festival   LOI KRAH-tawng   ˈlɔi ˈkrɑtɔːŋ

Loyola
  University, LA, IL; College, MD   loi-Ō-luh   lɔiˈoːlə

Lozère
  department, France   law-ZER   lɔːzer

Lozi
  lang., people, Africa   LŌ-zē   ˈloːziˑ

Lua
  Roman goddess of plague or   LŌŌ-uh   ˈluːə
    defilement

Luanda
  city, Angola   lōō-AHN-duh, lōō-AN-duh   luːˈɑndə, luːˈændə

Luang
  pers. name, Thai   lōō-AHNG   luːˈɑŋ

Luang Prabang
  prov & town, Laos   lōō-AHNG pruh-BAHNG   luː‚ɑŋ prəˈbɑŋ

Luba
  lang., people, Africa   LŌŌ-buh   ˈluːbə

Luba-Lulua
  lang., people, Africa   LŌŌ-buh-LŌŌ-lōō-uh   ‚luːbəˈluːluːə

Lubang
  group of islands, Philippines   lōō-BAHNG   luːˈbɑŋ

Lubavitcher
  Jewish Hassidic movement   lōō-BAHV-uh-chuhr   luˈbɑvətʃəʳ

Lubec
  town, ME   lōō-BEK   luːˈbek

Key (col. 2):   a: fad   ā: fade   ah: father   ar: marry   aw: law   e: fed   ē: feed   er: merry   i: hid   ī: hide   ō: coat   ōō: boot
oi: boy   ow: now   u: put   uh: above   uhr: bird   ch: chop   ng: ring   sh: show   th: thick   th: this   zh: measure

Lubbock
 city, TX   LUHB-uhk   ˈləbək
Lübeck
 seaport, Germany   LUE-BEK   ˈlyːˌbek
Lubim
 Biblical name   LŌO-bim, lōo-VĒM   ˈluːbim, luːˈviːm
Lubitsch
 Ernst, *US film director*   LŌO-bich   ˈluːbitʃ
Lübke
 Heinrich, *president, W. Germany*   LUEP-kuh   ˈlypkə
Lublin
 city, Poland   LŌO-bluhn, LŌO-BLĒN   ˈluːblən, ˈluːˌbliːn
Lubor
 pers. name, Czech   LŌO-bawr   ˈluːbɔːr
Lubrizol
 US chemical co.   LŌO-bruh-ZAWL, -ZAHL   ˈluːbrəˌzɔːl, -ˌzɑl
Lubu
 lang., East Sumatra   LŌO-bōo   ˈluːbuː
Luc
 pers. name, French   LUEK   lyːk
Luca
 ancient Roman colony, Italy   LŌO-kuh   ˈluːkə
Lucan
 Roman poet   LŌO-kuhn   ˈluːkən
Lucania
 Mount, *Canada*   lōo-KĀ-nē-uh, lōo-KĀN-yuh   luːˈkeːniːə, luːˈkeːnjə
Lucas
 1. pers. name   LŌO-kuhs   ˈluːkəs
 2. Dutch   LUE-KAHS   ˈlyːˌkɑs
 3. French   lue-KAH   lyːkɑ
 4. German   LŌO-KAHS   ˈluːˌkɑs
 5. Spanish   LŌO-kahs   ˈluːkɑs
Lucayo
 Bahamian people   lōo-KĪ-ō, lōo-KĀ-ō   luːˈkɑioː, luːˈkeːoː
Lucazi
 lang., Africa   lōo-KAHZ-ē   luːˈkɑziˑ
Lucca
 prov, Italy   LŌO-kuh   ˈluːkə
Lucci
 Susan, *US actress*   LŌO-chē   ˈluːtʃiˑ
Luce
 1. Henry *and* Clare B., *US*   LŌOS   ˈluːs
   publishers; county, MI; pers. name
 2. river, France; pers. name, French LUES   lyːs
Lučenec
 town, Slovakia   LUCH-uh-NETS   ˈlutʃəˌnets
Lucerne [Luzern]
 lake, canton, city, Switzerland   lōo-SUHRN   luːˈsəʳn
Lucia
 1. pers. name   LŌO-sh(ē-)uh   ˈluːʃ(iː)ə
 2. Italian   lōo-CHĒ-ah   luːˈtʃiːɑ

Foreign Sounds: **ue:** *Fr.* **rue**, *Ger.* **füllen**   **uh(r):** *Fr.* **b**o**euf**, *Ger.* **Höhle**   **kh:** *Ger.* **ich**, *Scot.* **loch**   **ǧ:** *Sp.* **amigo**   **v̱:** *Sp.* **hablar**
hl: *Welsh* **Llanelli**.   CAPITALS: primary stress.   SMALL CAPS: secondary stress.   ⑤: U.S. pron.   ⓔ: British pron.

Lucian
1. Greek satirist; pers. name	LOO-shuhn	'luːʃən
2. German	LOOT-sē-AHN, loots-YAHN	ˌluːtsiːˈɑn, luːtsˈjɑn
3. Polish	LOOTS-yahn	'luːtsjɑːn
4. Romanian	loo-CHAHN	luːˈtʃɑn

Luciano
1. pers. name, Italian	loo-CHAHN-ō	luːˈtʃɑnoː
2. Portuguese	loos-YAH-noo	luːsˈjɑːnuː
3. Spanish	loos-YAHN-ō, looth-	luːsˈjɑnoː, luːθ-

Lucie
1. pers. name	LOO-sē	'luːsi˙
2. French	lue-SĒ	lyːsiː

Lucien
1. pers. name	LOO-shuhn	'luːʃən
2. French	lues-YE[n]	lyːsˈjẽ

Lucifer
Satan; planet Venus when a morning *star*	LOO-suh-fuhr	'luːsəfə[r]

Lucilius
Roman name	lu-SIL-ē-uhs	luˈsiliːəs

Lucille
pers. name	loo-SĒL	luːˈsiːl

Lucina
Roman goddess of birth; midwife	loo-SĪ-nuh	luːˈsɑinə

Lucinda
pers. name	loo-SIN-duh	luːˈsində

Lucinde
pers. name, French	lue-SE[n]D	lyːsẽd

Lucite
tdmk for a clear plastic	LOO-sīt	'luːˌsɑit

Lucius
Roman praenomen; pers. name	LOO-sh(ē-)uhs	'luːʃ(iː)əs

Łuck
see Lutsk

Lucknow
city, India	LUHK-NOW	'lək̩nɑu

Lucrece, The Rape of
poem, Shakespeare	loo-KRĒS, LOO-KRĒS	luːˈkriːs, 'luːˌkriːs

Lucrecia
pers. name, Spanish	loo-KRĀS-yah, loo-KRĀTH-	luːˈkreːsjɑ, luːˈkreːθ-

Lucretia
Roman matron, pers. name	loo-KRĒ-sh(ē-)uh	luːˈkriːʃ(iː)ə

Lucretius
Roman philosopher	loo-KRĒ-sh(ē-)uhs	luːˈkriːʃ(iː)əs

Lucrezia
pers. name, Italian	loo-KRET-syah	luːˈkretsjɑ

Lucullan
pert. to Lucullus	loo-KUHL-uhn	luːˈkələn

Lucullus
Lucius Licinius, *Roman epicure &* *general*	loo-KUHL-uhs	luːˈkələs

Lucy
pers. name	LOO-sē	'luːsi˙

Lucy Cavendish
College, *Cambridge Univ.*	LOO-sē KAV-uhn-dish	'luːsi˙ 'kævəndiʃ

Key (col. 2):   a: fad   ā: fade   ah: father   ar: marry   aw: law   e: fed   ē: feed   er: merry   i: hid   ī: hide   ō: coat   oo: boot
oi: boy   ow: now   u: put   uh: above   uhr: bird   ch: chop   ng: ring   sh: show   th: thick   th̲: this   zh: measure

Lud
   Biblical name   LUHD, LOOD   'ləd, 'luːd

Luddite
   one opposed to technological change   LUHD-ĪT   'ləd‚ait

Ludim
   Biblical name   LOOD-im, loo-DĒM   'luːdim, luː'diːm

Ludington
   city, MI   LUHD-ing-tuhn   'lədiŋtən

Ludlow
   town, England; town, MA   LUHD-lō   'lədloː

Ludmilla
   pers. name, German   loot-MIL-ah   luːt'milɑ

Ludovic
   1. pers. name   LOOD-uh-VIK   'luːdə‚vik
   2. French   lue-daw-VĒK   lyːdɔːviːk

Ludovico
   pers. name, Italian   LOO-dō-VĒ-kō   ‚luːdoː'viːkoː

Ludowici
   city, GA   LOOD-uh-WIS-ē   ‚luːdə'wisi·

Ludvig
   1. pers. name, Danish   LOOTH-vē   'luːðviː
   2. Swedish   LUHD-vig   'lədvig

Ludwig
   1. pers. name   LUHD-wig, LOOD-wig   'lədwig, 'luːdwig
   2. Danish   LOOTH-vē   'luːðviː
   3. German   LOOT-vikh   'luːtviç
   4. Swedish   LUHD-vig   'lədvig

Ludwik
   pers. name, Polish   LOOD-vēk   'luːdviːk

Lufthansa
   German airline   LUFT-HAHN-suh, -zuh   'luft‚hansə, -zə

Luftwaffe
   German airforce, WWII   LUFT-VAHF-uh, Ⓢ LUFT-WAHF-uh   'luft‚vɑfə, Ⓢ 'luft‚wɑfə

Lug, Lugh
   Celtic hero-god   LOOG, LUḠ   'luːg, 'luɣ

Lugal
   title, Sumerian kings   LOO-guhl   'luːgəl

Lugalzaggisi
   Mesopotamian king, 24th c. BC   LOO-guhl-ZAG-uh-sē   ‚luːgəl'zægəsi·

Luganda
   Bantu lang., Africa   loo-GAHN-duh, loo-GAN-duh   luː'gɑndə, luː'gændə

Lugandan
   lang., Africa   loo-GAHN-duhn, loo-GAN-duhn   luː'gɑndən, luː'gændən

Lugano
   town, Switzerland; lake, Italy, Switzerland   loo-GAHN-ō   luː'gɑnoː

Lugar
   Richard G., US politician   LOO-guhr   'luːgəʳ

Lugbara
   lang., people, Uganda, Zaire   lug-BAHR-uh   lug'bɑrə

Lugdunum [Lyons]
   Roman city   lug-DOO-nuhm, LUHG-   lug'duːnəm, ‚ləg-

Luger
   German pistol   LOO-guhr   'luːgəʳ

Foreign Sounds: ue: *Fr.* **r**ue, *Ger.* f**ü**llen   uh(r): *Fr.* b**oeu**f, *Ger.* H**öh**le   kh: *Ger.* i**ch**, *Scot.* lo**ch**   ḡ: *Sp.* ami**g**o   v: *Sp.* ha**b**lar
hl: *Welsh* **Ll**anelli.   CAPITALS: primary stress.   SMALL CAPS: secondary stress.   Ⓢ: U.S. pron.   Ⓔ: British pron.

Lugh
  see Lug

Lughnasa, Dancing at
  Broadway play   lug-NAHS-uh, L$\overline{OO}$-nuhs-uh   lug'nɑsə, 'luːnəsə

Lugosi
  Bela, *US actor*   luh-G$\overline{O}$-sē, lu-   lə'goːsiˑ, lu-

Luhith
  Biblical name   L$\overline{OO}$-HITH, l$\overline{oo}$-<u>KH</u>ĒT   'luːˌhiθ, luː'xiːt

Luigi
  pers. name   l$\overline{oo}$-Ē-jē   luː'iːdʒiˑ

Luis
  1. pers. name, Portuguese   l$\overline{oo}$-ĒSH, l$\overline{oo}$-ĒS   luː'iːʃ, luː'iːs
  2. Spanish   l$\overline{oo}$-ĒS   luː'iːs

Luís
  pers. name, Portuguese   l$\overline{oo}$-ĒSH, l$\overline{oo}$-ĒS   luː'iːʃ, luː'iːs

Luisa
  pers. name, Italian   l$\overline{oo}$-Ē-zah   luː'iːzɑ

Luise
  1. pers. name, Danish   lu-Ē-suh   lu'iːsə
  2. German   l$\overline{oo}$-Ē-zuh   luː'iːzə

Luiseño
  N. American people   L$\overline{OO}$-ē-SĀN-yō   ˌluːiˑ'seːnjoː

Luis Muñoz Marin
  Airport, *San Juan, Puerto Rico*   l$\overline{oo}$-ĒS m$\overline{oo}$n-YŌS mah-RĒN   luː'iːs muːn'joːs mɑ'riːn

Luitpold
  pers. name, German   L$\overline{OO}$-it-PAWLT   'luːitˌpɔːlt

Lukács
  George, *Hungarian literary critic,*   L$\overline{OO}$-KAHCH   'luːˌkɑtʃ
    philosopher

Luke
  Christian apostle; New Testament   L$\overline{OO}$K   'luːk
    book; pers. name

Luken
  Charles, *US politician*   L$\overline{OO}$-kuhn   'luːkən

Lukl
  pers. name, Czech   L$\overline{OO}$-kuhl   'luːkəl

Łuków
  commune, Poland   L$\overline{OO}$-K$\overline{OO}$F   'ɫuːˌkuːf

Lulu
  pers. name   L$\overline{OO}$-L$\overline{OO}$ 'luːˌluː

Lumet
  Sidney, *entertainer*   l$\overline{oo}$-MET, luh-MET   luˑ'met, lə'met

Lumière
  Louis Jean *and* Auguste, *French*   luem-YER   lymjer
    inventors, motion picture pioneers

Lumm
  Herman Tsui Fai, *US jurist*   LUHM   'ləm

Lummi
  N. American people   LUHM-ē   'ləmiˑ

Lumumba
  Patrice, *politician, Zaire*   luh-MUHM-buh, luh-MUM-buh   lə'məmbə, lə'mumbə

Luna
  Roman moon goddess   L$\overline{OO}$-nuh   'luːnə

Lund
  city, Sweden   LUHND   'lənd

Key (col. 2):   a: fad   ā: fade   ah: father   ar: marry   aw: law   e: fed   ē: feed   er: merry   i: hid   ī: hide   ō: coat $\overline{oo}$: boot
oi: boy   ow: now   u: put   uh: above   uhr: bird   ch: chop   ng: ring   sh: show   th: thick   <u>th</u>: this   zh: measure

Lunda
  lang., people, Africa — L̅OO̅N-duh, LUN-duh — 'luːndə, 'lundə

Lunden
  Joan, *TV host* — LUHN-duhn — 'ləndən

Lundu
  lang., Africa — L̅OO̅N-d̅oo̅, LUN-d̅oo̅ — 'luːnduː, 'lunduː

Lüneburg
  prov & town, Germany — LUE-nuh-BURK, Ⓢ L̅OO̅-nuh-BURG — 'lyːnə͵buʳk, Ⓢ 'luːnə͵buʳg

Lunenburg
  county, VA; town, MA; county, town,
    Canada — L̅OO̅-nuhn-BUHRG — 'luːnən͵bəʳg

Lungkiang
  former name of Qiqihar — LUNG-jē-AHNG — 'luŋdʒiːˈaŋ

Luo
  lang., people, Kenya, Tanzania — luh-Wō — ləˈwoː

Luoyang, Lo-yang [Honan]
  town, China — L̅OO̅-YAHNG, Ⓢ Lō-YAHNG — 'luːˈjaŋ, Ⓢ 'loːˈjaŋ

Lupercal
  cave near Rome — L̅OO̅-puhr-KAL — 'luːpəʳ͵kæl

Lupercalia
  ancient Roman fertility festival — L̅OO̅-puhr-KĀL-yuh, -KĀ-lē-uh — ͵luːpəʳˈkeːljə, -ˈkeːliːə

Luperci
  Roman priests of Faunus Lupercus — l̅oo̅-PUHR-SĪ, l̅oo̅-PUHR-KĪ — luːˈpəʳ͵sai, luːˈpəʳ͵kai

Lupercio
  pers. name, Spanish — lu-PER-syō, -thyō — luˈpersjoː, -θjoː

Lupine
  plant — L̅OO̅-puhn, L̅OO̅-PĪN — 'luːpən, 'luː͵pain

Lupus
  constellation — L̅OO̅-puhs — 'luːpəs

Luray
  town, VA — L̅OO̅-rā — 'luːreː

Lurcher
  dog breed — LUHR-chuhr — 'ləʳtʃəʳ

Lurex
  tdmk for a metallic yarn — LUR-EKS, Ⓔ LYUR-EKS — 'lur͵eks, Ⓔ 'ljur͵eks

Luria
  A. R., *Russian neuropsychologist;*
    Salvador E., *Italian-born US*
    biologist (Nobel 1969) — LUR-ē-uh — 'luriːə

Lurleen
  pers. name — luhr-LĒN — ləʳˈliːn

Lusaka
  city, Zambia — l̅oo̅-SAHK-uh — luːˈsɑkə

Lusatia
  region, Germany, Poland — l̅oo̅-SĀ-sh(ē-)uh — luːˈseːʃ(iː)ə

Lusatian [Sorbian]
  lang., Germany — l̅oo̅-SĀ-shuhn — luːˈseːʃən

Lushai
  lang., people, Burma — L̅OO̅-SHĪ, l̅oo̅-SHĪ — 'luː͵ʃai, luːˈʃai

Lusitania
  Roman province, Europe; Cunard
    liner sunk 1915 — L̅OO̅-suh-TĀ-nē-uh, -TĀN-yuh — ͵luːsəˈteːniːə, -ˈteːnjə

Lutatius
  pers. name — l̅oo̅-TĀ-sh(ē-)uhs — luːˈteːʃ(iː)əs

Lute
  musical instrument   LO͞OT   'luːt
Lutece
  French restaurant, New York City   lue-TES, l(y)o͞o-TES   lyːtes, l(j)uːˈtes
Lutetia
  ancient name of Paris, *France*   lo͞o-TĒ-sh(ē-)uh   luːˈtiːʃ(iː)ə
lutetium
  element   lo͞o-TĒ-sh(ē-)uhm   luːˈtiːʃ(iː)əm
Luther
  Martin, *German religious reformer;*   LO͞O-thuhr   'luːθəʳ
  pers. name
Lutheran
  pert. to Luther; *member of Lutheran*   LO͞O-th(uh-)ruhn   'luːθ(ə)rən
  Church
Lutheranism
  doctrines of Luther & his followers   LO͞O-th(uh-)ruh-NIZ-uhm   'luːθ(ə)rə,nizəm
Luthuli
  Albert J., *South African activist*   lo͞o-TO͞O-lē, lo͞o-THO͞O-lē   luːˈtuːliˑ, luːˈθuːliˑ
  (Nobel 1960)
Lutomer
  Yugoslavian wine   L(Y)O͞OT-uh-muhr   'l(j)uːtəməʳ
Lutsk, Łuck
  city, Ukraine   LO͞OTSK   'luːtsk
Lutyens
  Sir Edwin L., *English architect*   LUHT-yuhnz, LUHCH-uhnz   'lətjənz, 'lətʃənz
Luwi
  ancient Anatolian people   LO͞O-wē   'luːwiˑ
Luwian
  ancient Anatolian lang.   LO͞O-ē-uhn   'luːiːən
Luxembourg, -burg
  grand duchy, city, Europe   LUHK-suhm-BUHRG, LUK-suhm-BURG   'ləksəm,bəʳg, 'luksəm,buʳg
Luxembourger, -burger
  pert. to Luxembourg   LUHK-suhm-BUHR-guhr,   'ləksəm,bəʳgəʳ,
                                                LUK-suhm-BUR-guhr   'luksəm,buʳgəʳ
Luxemburgish
  lang., Luxembourg   LUHK-suhm-BUHR-gish,   'ləksəm,bəʳgiʃ,
                                                LUK-suhm-BUR-gish   'luksəm,buʳgiʃ
Luxor
  town, Egypt   LUHK-SAWR, LUK-SAWR   'lək,sɔːʳ, 'luk,sɔːʳ
Luz
  Biblical name   LUHZ, LO͞OZ   'ləz, 'luːz
Luzerne
  county, town, PA   lu-ZUHRN   luˈzəʳn
Luzern [Lucerne]
  lake, canton, city, Switzerland   lo͞ot-SERN   luːtˈseʳn
Luzon
  island, Philippines   lo͞o-ZAHN   luːˈzɑn
Lvov [Lwów]
  city, Ukraine   LVAWF, Ⓢ luh-VAWF, luh-VAWV   'lvɔːf, Ⓢ ləˈvɔːf, ləˈvɔːv
Lwena
  lang., people, Africa   luh-WĀ-nuh   ləˈweːnə
Lwo, Lwoo
  lang., Uganda   luh-WŌ   ləˈwoː

Key (col. 2):   a: fad   ā: fade   ah: father   ar: marry   aw: law   e: fed   ē: feed   er: merry   i: hid   ī: hide   ō: coat   o͞o: boot
oi: boy   ow: now   u: put   uh: above   uhr: bird   ch: chop   ng: ring   sh: show   th: thick   <u>th</u>: this   zh: measure

Lwoff
André, *French biochemist (Nobel 1965)* — LVAWF, ⑤ LWAWF, luh-WAWF — lvɔːf, ⑤ 'lwɔːf, lə'wɔːf

Lwów
Polish name for Lvov — LVOOF, ⑤ luh-VOOF, luh-VOOV — 'lvuːf, ⑤ lə'vuːf, lə'vuːv

Lycaon
son of Pelasgus — lī-KĀ-uhn — lɑi'keːən

Lycaonia
ancient country, Asia Minor — LIK-ā-Ō-nē-uh, LĪ-kā-Ō-nē-uh — ˌlikeː'oːniːə, ˌlɑikeː'oːniːə

Lycastus
son of Ares and Phylonome — lī-KAS-tuhs — lɑi'kæstəs

Lyceum
educational institution, esp. that of Aristotle — lī-SĒ-uhm — lɑi'siːəm

Lycia
ancient district, Asia Minor — LISH-(ē-)uh — 'liʃ(iː)ə

Lycian
pert. to Lycia — LISH-(ē-)uhn — 'liʃ(iː)ən

Lycidas
elegy, J. Milton — LIS-uhd-uhs, ⓔ LIS-i-DAS — 'lisədəs, ⓔ 'lisiˌdæs

Lycomedes
Dolopian king; host of Achilles — LĪ-kuh-MĒD-ēz — ˌlɑikə'miːdiːz

Lycoming
county, PA — lī-KŌ-ming — lɑi'koːmiŋ

Lycra
tdmk for an elastic cloth — LĪ-kruh — 'lɑikrə

Lycurgus
Spartan lawgiver; Athenian orator; king of Thrace — lī-KUHR-guhs — lɑi'kəʳgəs

Lycus
founder of the cult of Lycian Apollo — LĪ-kuhs — 'lɑikəs

Lydda
Biblical name — LID-uh — 'lidə

Lydgate
John, *English monk, poet, translator* — LID-GĀT, LIG-ĀT — 'lidˌgeːt, 'ligˌeːt

Lydia
1. ancient country, Asia Minor; pers. name — LID-ē-uh — 'lidiːə
2. German — LUED-yah, LUE-dē-ah — 'lyːdjɑ, 'lyːdiːɑ

Lydian
musical mode — LID-ē-uhn — 'lidiːən

Lyell
pers. name — LĪL — 'lɑil

Lyell
Sir Charles, *British geologist* — LĪ-uhl — 'lɑiəl

Lyle
pers. name — LĪL — 'lɑil

Lyly
John, *English author* — LIL-ē — 'liliˑ

Lyman
pers. name — LĪ-muhn — 'lɑimən

Lyme
town, CT; disease — LĪM — 'lɑim

Lymington
seaport, England — LIM-ing-tuhn — 'limiŋtən

Foreign Sounds: ue: *Fr.* **rue**, *Ger.* **füllen**   uh(r): *Fr.* **boeuf**, *Ger.* **Höhle**   kh: *Ger.* **ich**, *Scot.* **loch**   g̱: *Sp.* **amigo**   v̱: *Sp.* **hablar**   hl: *Welsh* **Llanelli**.   CAPITALS: primary stress.   SMALL CAPS: secondary stress.   ⑤: U.S. pron.   ⓔ: British pron.

Lymphae
 Latin divinities of springs LIM(P)-fē   'lim(p)fiˑ

Lympne
 village, England   LIM   'lim

Lynceus
 husband of Hypermestra LING-kē-uhs   'liŋkiːəs

Lynch
 William Dennis, Jr., *US broadcast* LINCH   'lintʃ
  journalist

Lynde
 pers. name   LIND   'lind

Lyndhurst
 town, NJ; city, OH LIND-HUHRST   'lind,həʳst

Lyndon
 pers. name   LIN-duhn   'lindən

Lynen
 Feodor, *German biochemist (Nobel* LUE-nuhn   'lyːnən
  1964)

Lynette
 pers. name   luh-NET   lə'net

Lynley
 Carol Ann, *US actress* LIN-lē   'linliˑ

Lynn, Lynne
 pers. name   LIN   'lin

Lynsey
 pers. name   LIN-zē   'linziˑ

Lynx
 constellation   LINGKS   'liŋks

Lynyrd Skynyrd
 rock group   LIN-uhrd SKIN-uhrd 'linəʳd 'skinəʳd

Lyon
 pl. name, US; pers. name LĪ-uhn   'lɑiən

Lyonel
 pers. name   LĪ-uhn-l, LĪ-uh-NEL 'lɑiənl̩, 'lɑiə,nel

Lyon [Lyons]
 city, France   LYAWⁿ   ljɔ̃

Lyonnais
 prov, France lyaw-NE, Ⓢ LĒ-uh-NĀ ljɔːne, Ⓢ ˌliːə'neː

Lyonnaise
 brown onion sauce LĪ-uh-NĀZ, LĒ-uh-NĀZ, -NEZ ˌlɑiə'neːz, ˌliːə'neːz, -'nez

Lyonnesse
 mythical region in Arthurian legend LĪ-uh-NES ˌlɑiə'nes

Lyons
 1. city, France LYAWⁿ, Ⓢ lē-AWⁿ, LĪ-uhnz ljɔ̃, Ⓢ liː'ɔ̃, 'lɑiənz
 2. pl. name, US; family name LĪ-uhnz   'lɑiənz

Lyra
 constellation   LĪ-ruh   'lɑirə

Lyrebird
 Australian bird   LĪR-BUHRD   'lɑiʳ,bəʳd

Lys
 French-Belgian river LĒS   'liːs

Lysander
 Spartan military commander; pers. lī-SAN-duhr lɑi'sændəʳ
  name

Key (col. 2): a: f**a**d ā: f**a**de ah: f**a**ther ar: m**a**rry aw: l**a**w e: f**e**d ē: f**ee**d er: m**e**rry i: h**i**d ī: h**i**de ō: c**oa**t ōō: b**oo**t
oi: b**oy** ow: n**ow** u: p**u**t uh: **a**bove uhr: b**i**rd ch: **ch**op ng: ri**ng** sh: **sh**ow th: **th**ick <u>th</u>: **th**is zh: mea**s**ure

Lysanias		
Biblical name	lī-SĀ-nē-uhs	lɑi'seːniːəs
Lysenko		
Trofim, *Russian biologist*	lī-SENG-kuh	lɑi'seŋkə
Lysias		
Athenian orator	LIS-ē-uhs, LIS-ē-AS	'lisiːəs, 'lisiːˌæs
Lysidice		
daughter of Pelops	lī-SID-uh-sē	lɑi'sidəsiˑ
Lysippus		
Greek sculptor	lī-SIP-uhs	lɑi'sipəs
Lysis		
dialogue of Plato	LĪ-suhs	'lɑisəs
Lysistrata		
comedy, Aristophanes	LIS-uh-STRAHT-uh, lī-SIS-truht-uh	ˌlisə'strɑt̬ə, lɑi'sistrət̬ə
Lysithea		
satellite of Jupiter	lī-SITH-ē-uh	lɑi'siθiːə
Lysol		
tdmk for a disinfectant	LĪ-SAWL, LĪ-SAHL	'lɑiˌsɔːl, 'lɑiˌsɑl
Lystra		
town, Asia Minor	LIS-truh	'listrə
Lytham St. Anne's		
town, England	LĪ-thuhm suhnt ANZ, sānt	'lɑiðəm sənt 'ænz, seːnt
Lytton		
pers. name	LIT-n	'litn̩

M

Ma		
Yo-Yo, *US cellist*	MAH	'mɑ
Maacah		
Biblical name	MĀ-uh-kuh, MAH-ah-KHAH	'meːəkə, ˌmɑ-ɑ'xɑ
Maacathite		
Biblical name	MĀ-AK-uh-THĪT, mā-AK-uh-THĪT	'meːˌækəˌθɑit, meː'ækəˌθɑit
Maachah		
Biblical name	MĀ-uh-kuh, MAH-ah-KHAH	'meːəkə, ˌmɑ-ɑ'xɑ
Maadai		
Biblical name	MĀ-uh-DĀ-Ī, MĀ-uh-DĪ, MAH-ah-DĪ	ˌmeːə'deːˌɑi, 'meːəˌdɑi, 'mɑ-ɑˌdɑi
Maadiah		
Biblical name	MĀ-uh-DĪ-uh, MAH-ahd-YAH	ˌmeːə'dɑiə, ˌmɑ-ɑd'jɑ
Maai		
Biblical name	mā-Ā-Ī, MĀ-Ī, mah-Ī	meː'eːˌɑi, 'meːˌɑi, mɑ'ɑi
Maaleh-acrabbim		
Biblical name	MĀ-uh-le-uh-KRAB-im, MAH-ah-LE-ah-krah-BĒM	'meːəleə'kræbim, ˌmɑ-ɑ'leɑkrɑ'biːm

Foreign Sounds: ue: *Fr.* **rue**, *Ger.* **füllen** uh(r): *Fr.* **boeuf**, *Ger.* **Höhle** kh: *Ger.* **ich**, *Scot.* **loch** g̃: *Sp.* **amigo** v̱: *Sp.* **hablar** hl: *Welsh* **Llanelli**. CAPITALS: primary stress. SMALL CAPS: secondary stress. [$]: U.S. pron. [£]: British pron.

Maarath
   Biblical name   MĀ-uh-RATH, MAH-ah-RAHT   'meːə,ræθ, ˌmɑ-ɑ'rɑt

Maareh-geba
   Biblical name   MĀ-uh-re-JĒ-buh, MAH-ah-RE-GE-vah   'meːəre'dʒiːbə,
                                                    ˌmɑ-ɑˌre'gevɑ

Maarten
   pers. name, Dutch   MAHR-tuhn   'mɑːrtən

Maas
   Dutch name for river Meuse   MAHS   'mɑs

Maasai
   see Masai

Maaseiah
   Biblical name   MĀ-uh-SĪ-uh, -SĒ-uh; MAH-ah-se-YAH   ˌmeːə'saiə, -'siːə; ˌmɑ-ɑse'jɑ

Maastricht
   city, Netherlands; European   MAH-STRI<u>K</u>HT   'mɑːˌstrixt
     Community treaty site

Maath
   Biblical name   MĀ-ATH   'meːˌæθ

Maaz
   Biblical name   MĀ-AZ, MAH-ahts   'meːˌæz, 'mɑ-ɑts

Maazel
   Lorin, *US conductor*   mah-ZEL   mɑ'zel

Maaziah
   Biblical name   MĀ-uh-ZĪ-uh, MAH-ahz-YAH-ho͞o   ˌmeːə'zaiə, ˌmɑ-ɑz'jɑhuː

Mab
   fairy queen of English and Irish   MAB   'mæb
     folklore

Mabel
   pers. name   MĀ-buhl   'meːbəl

Mabinogi
   medieval Welsh story cycle   MAB-uh-NAWG-ē   ˌmæbə'nɔːgiˑ

Mabinogion
   collection of Welsh tales   MAB-uh-NAWG-ē-uhn   ˌmæbə'nɔːgiːən

Mac-
   see also Mc-

Macalester
   College, *MN*   muh-KAL-uhs-tuhr   mə'kæləstəʳ

Macanese
   pert. to Macao   MAK-uh-NĒZ, -NĒS   ˌmækə'niːz, -'niːs

Macao, Macau
   colony, Portugal   muh-KOW   mə'kɑu

Macapagal
   Diosdado, *president, Philippines*   MAHK-uh-puh-GAHL   ˌmɑkəpə'gɑl

Macarena
   Mountains, *mountain range,*   MAHK-uh-RĀ-nuh, MAK-   ˌmɑkə're:nə, ˌmæk-
     Colombia; *dance*

MacArthur
   Douglas, *US general;* James, *US*   muh-KAHR-thuhr   mə'kɑʳθəʳ
     actor

Macassarese
   lang., Asia   muh-KAS-uh-RĒZ, -RĒS   mə,kæsə'riːz, -'riːs

Macassar oil
   hairdressing preparation   muh-KAS-uhr OIL   mə'kæsəʳ ˌɔil

Macau
   see Macao

Key (col. 2):   a: fad   ā: fade   ah: father   ar: **marry**   aw: **law**   e: fed   ē: feed   er: **merry**   i: hid   ī: hide   ō: coat   o͞o: boot
oi: **boy**   ow: **now**   u: put   uh: above   uhr: bird   ch: **chop**   ng: **ring**   sh: **show**   th: thick   <u>th</u>: **this**   zh: measure

Macaulay, -ley
  pers. name   muh-KAW-lē   məˈkɔːliˑ

Macaw
  parrot   muh-KAW   məˈkɔː

Macbannai, Machbanai, Machbannai
  Biblical name   MAK-buh-NĪ, MAHKH-bah-NĪ   ˈmækbəˌnɑi, ˌmɑxbaˈnɑi

Macbenah, Machbena, Machbenah
  Biblical name   mak-BĒ-nuh, MAHKH-bē-NAH   mækˈbiːnə, ˌmɑxbiːˈnɑ

Macbeth
  play, Shakespeare; pers. name   muhk-BETH   məkˈbeθ

MacBride
  Seán, *Irish civil rights activist (Nobel 1974); pers. name*   muhk-BRĪD   məkˈbraid

Maccabaean, -bean
  pert. to Maccabaeus *or* Maccabees   MAK-uh-BĒ-uhn   ˌmækəˈbiːən

Maccabaeus
  Judas, *Judean patriot*   MAK-uh-BĒ-uhs   ˌmækəˈbiːəs

Maccabees
  Apocryphal book   MAK-uh-BĒZ   ˈmækəˌbiːz

Macchio
  Ralph, *US actor*   MAHK-ē-ō   ˈmɑkiːɔː

Macclesfield
  town, district, England   MAK-uhlz-FĒLD   ˈmækəlzˌfiːld

Macdonald
  pers. name   muhk-DAHN-uhld   məkˈdɑnəld

MacDougal
  pers. name   muhk-DŌŌ-guhl   məkˈduːgəl

Macdhui, Ben
  see Ben Macdhui

Macédoine
  fruit dessert   MAS-uh-DWAHN   ˌmæsəˈdwɑn

Macedon
  ancient country, NW of Aegean Sea   MAS-uhd-uhn, MAS-uh-DAHN   ˈmæsədən, ˈmæsəˌdɑn

Macedonia [Macedon]
  country, Europe; region, Greece; ancient country, NW of Aegean Sea   MAS-uh-DŌ-nē-uh, -DŌN-yuh   ˌmæsəˈdoːniːə, -ˈdoːnjə

Macedonian
  pert. to Macedon; *Balkan lang*   MAS-uh-DŌ-nē-uhn, MAS-uh-DŌN-yuhn   ˌmæsəˈdoːniːən, ˌmæsəˈdoːnjən

Macedonianism
  Christian heresy   MAS-uh-DŌ-nē-uh-NIZ-uhm   ˌmæsəˈdoːniːəˌnizəm

Macedonio
  pers. name, Italian   MAH-chä-DAWN-yō   ˌmatʃeːˈdɔːnjoː

Macfarlane
  pers. name   muhk-FAHR-luhn   məkˈfɑʳlən

Macgillycuddy's Reeks
  mtn. range, Ireland   MAG-li-KUHD-ēz RĒKS, ⓢ *also* muh-GIL-uh-KUHD-ēz RĒKS   ˌmægliˌkədiˑz ˈriːks, ⓢ *also* məˌgiləˌkədiˑz ˈriːks

MacGraw
  Ali, *US actress*   muh-GRAW   məˈgrɔː

Macgregor
  pers. name   muh-GREG-uhr   məˈgregəʳ

Mach

Ernst, *Austrian physicist; supersonic scale*   MAH<u>KH</u>, MAHK   'mɑx, 'mɑk

Machabees

Old Testament book   MAK-uh-bēz   'mækəbiːz

Machado

1. Antonio, Manuel, *Spanish poets*   mah-CHAH<u>TH</u>-ō   mɑ'tʃaðoː
2. Bernardino Luís, *Portuguese politician*   muh-SHAH<u>TH</u>-o͞o   mə'ʃaðuː

Machado de Assis

Joaquim Maria, *Brazilian novelist*   muh-SHAH-t<u>h</u>o͞o t<u>h</u>ē ah-SĒS   mə'ʃaːðuː ði: ɑː'siːs

Machado y Morales

Gerardo, *Cuban politician*   mah-CHAH<u>TH</u>-ō ē mō-RAHL-ās   mɑ'tʃaðoː iː moː'rɑleːs

Machaon

son of Asclepius   muh-KĀ-uhn, muh-KĀ-AHN   mə'keːən, mə'keːˌɑn

Machaut

Guillaume de, *French composer*   mah-SHŌ   mɑ'ʃoː

Machbanai, Machbannai

see Macbannai

Machbena, Machbenah

see Macbenah

Machel

Samora Moisés, *president, Mozambique*   mah-SHEL   mɑ'ʃel

Machi

Biblical name   MĀ-KĪ, mah-<u>KH</u>Ē   'meːˌkɑi, mɑ'xiː

Machias

town, ME   muh-CHĪ-uhs   mə'tʃaiəs

Machiavelli

Niccolò, *Italian political writer*   MAK-ē-uh-VEL-ē, MAHK-   ˌmækiːə'veliˑ, ˌmɑk-

Machiavellian

pert. to Machiavelli   MAK-ē-uh-VEL-ē-uhn, MAHK-, -VEL-yuhn   ˌmækiːə'veliːən, ˌmɑk-, -'veljən

Machiguenga

lang., people, Peru   MAH<u>CH</u>-uh-GENG-guh   ˌmɑtʃə'geŋgə

Machir

Biblical name   MĀ-kir, mah-<u>KH</u>IR   'meːkiʳ, mɑ'xir

Machirite

Biblical name   MĀ-kir-ĪT   'meːkirˌait

Machnadebai

Biblical name   mak-NAD-uh-BĪ, mah<u>kh</u>-NAH-duh-VĪ   mæk'nædəˌbai, mɑx,nadə'vai

Machpelah

Biblical name   mak-PĒ-luh, MAK-pē-LAH, MAH<u>KH</u>-pe-LAH   mæk'piːlə, 'mækpiːˌlɑ, ˌmɑxpe'lɑ

Macquarie

river, Australia   muh-KWAHR-ē, muh-KWAWR-ē   mə'kwɑriˑ, mə'kwɔːriˑ

Machu Picchu

ruined Inca city, Peru   MAH<u>CH</u>-o͞o PĒK-cho͞o, PĒ-cho͞o   ˌmɑtʃuː 'piːktʃuː, 'piːtʃuː

Machynlleth

town, Wales   muh-<u>KH</u>UHN-hluhth   mə'xənɬəθ

Maciej

pers. name, Polish   MAH-chā   'mɑːtʃeː

Key (col. 2):   a: **fad**   ā: **fade**   ah: **father**   ar: **marry**   aw: **law**   e: **fed**   ē: **feed**   er: **merry**   i: **hid**   ī: **hide**   ō: **coat**   o͞o: **boot** oi: **boy**   ow: **now**   u: **put**   uh: **above**   uhr: **bird**   ch: **chop**   ng: **ring**   sh: **show**   th: **thick**   <u>th</u>: **this**   zh: **measure**

Maciejowice
commune, Poland   MAHT-suh-yaw-VĒT-suh,   ˌmɑːtsəjɔːˈviːtsə,
                    MAHCH-uh-yaw-VĒT-suh   ˌmɑːtʃəjɔːˈviːtsə

MacInnes
Helen, *British writer*   muh-KIN-uhs   məˈkinəs

Macintosh
family name; tdmk for computers   MAK-uhn-TAHSH   ˈmækənˌtɑʃ

Mack
pers. name; US truck co.   MAK   ˈmæk

Mackay
pers. name   muh-KĪ, muh-KĀ, MAHK-ē   məˈkai, məˈkeː, ˈmɑkiˑ

Mackenzie
pers. name   muh-KEN-zē   məˈkenziˑ

Mackie
Bob, *US costume and fashion*   MAK-ē   ˈmækiˑ
designer

Mackinac
1. island, straits, MI   MAK-uh-NAK, MAK-uh-NAW   ˈmækəˌnæk, ˈmækəˌnɔː
2. county, MI   MAK-uh-NAW   ˈmækəˌnɔː

Mackinaw
river, IL   MAK-uh-NAW   ˈmækəˌnɔː

Mackintosh
pers. name   MAK-uhn-TAHSH   ˈmækənˌtɑʃ

Macklin
pers. name   MAK-luhn   ˈmæklən

Maclaine
Shirley, *US actress, author*   muh-KLĀN   məˈkleːn

MacLean
pers. name   muh-KLĀN   məˈkleːn

MacLeish
Archibald, *US poet*   muh-KLĒSH   məˈkliːʃ

MacLeod
J. J. R., *Scottish physiologist (Nobel*   muh-KLOWD   məˈklɑud
1923); pers. name

Macmillan
publishing house; pers. name   muhk-MIL-uhn   məkˈmilən

MacMurray
Fred, *US actor*   muhk-MUHR-ē, muhk-MUH-rē   məkˈmər-iˑ, məkˈmə-riˑ

MacNamara
Donal Eoin Joseph, *US*   MAK-nuh-MAR-uh   ˈmæknəˌmærə
criminologist

Macnamara
Robert, *US statesman*   MAK-nuh-MAR-uh, -MER-uh   ˈmæknəˌmærə, -ˌmerə

Macnee
Patrick, *British actor*   muhk-NĒ   məkˈniː

Macneil
Robert, *Canadian broadcast*   muhk-NĒL   məkˈniːl
journalist

Macomb
pl. name, US   muh-KŌM   məˈkoːm

Macon
pl. name; pers. name   MĀ-kuhn   ˈmeːkən

Mâcon
city, France   mah-KAW^n mɑkɔ̃

Foreign Sounds: ue: *Fr.* **rue**, *Ger.* **füllen**   uh(r): *Fr.* **bœuf**, *Ger.* **Höhle**   <u>kh</u>: *Ger.* **ich**, *Scot.* **loch**   g̱: *Sp.* **amigo**   v̱: *Sp.* **hablar**
hl: *Welsh* **Llanelli**.   CAPITALS: primary stress.   SMALL CAPS: secondary stress.   ⒮: U.S. pron.   ⒠: British pron.

Mâconnais
French wine   mah-kaw-NE   mɑkɔːne

Macoupin
county, IL   muh-K͞OO-puhn   məˈkuːpən

Macquarie
Lachlan, *Scottish soldier, colonial governor*   muh-KWAHR-ē, Ⓢ *also* muh-KWAWR-ē   məˈkwɑriˑ, Ⓢ *also* məˈkwɔːriˑ

MacRae
Gordon, *singer, actor*   muh-KRĀ   məˈkreː

Macready
pers. name   muh-KRĒD-ē   məˈkriːdiˑ

Macrinus
Roman emperor   muh-KRĪ-nuhs   məˈkrɑinəs

Macris
guardian of Dionysus   MAK-ruhs   ˈmækrəs

Macrobius
Ambrosius, *Latin grammarian*   muh-KRŌ-bē-uhs   məˈkroːbiːəs

Macú
S. American people   mah-K͞OO, muh-K͞OO   mɑˈkuː, məˈkuː

Macy's
US department store   MĀ-sēz   ˈmeːsiˑz

Madagascan
pert. to Madagascar   MAD-uh-GAS-kuhn   ˌmædəˈgæskən

Madagascar
island, country, Indian Ocean   MAD-uh-GAS-kuhr   ˌmædəˈgæskəʳ

Madai
Biblical name   MĀ-DĪ, MAD-ē-Ī, mah-DĪ   ˈmeːˌdɑi, ˈmædiːˌɑi, mɑˈdɑi

Madame
French term of address for a married woman   mah-DAHM, Ⓢ MAD-uhm, muh-DAHM, muh-DAM   mɑˈdɑːm, Ⓢ ˈmædəm, məˈdɑm, məˈdæm

Madang
dist, New Guinea   MAHD-AHNG   ˈmɑdˌɑŋ

Madawaska
river, Canada   MAD-uh-WAHS-kuh   ˌmædəˈwɑskə

Madden
John, *US TV sports commentator*   MAD-n   ˈmædn̩

Maddock
pers. name   MAD-uhk   ˈmædək

Madeira
islands, Atlantic; river, Brazil; wine   muh-DIR-uh, muh-DER-uh   məˈdirə, məˈderə

Madeleine
1. pers. name   MAD-l-uhn   ˈmædl̩ən
2. French   mahd-LEN   mɑːdlen

Madeleine, La
see La Madeleine

Madeleine, La Fête de la
see La Fête de la Madeleine

Madeline
pers. name   MAD-l-uhn   ˈmædl̩ən

Mademoiselle
French term of address for an unmarried woman   mahd-mwah-ZEL, mahn-mwah-ZEL, Ⓢ MAD-uh-m(w)uh-ZEL, MAD-m(w)uh-ZEL   mɑːdmwɑːzel, mɑːnmwɑːzel, Ⓢ ˌmædəm(w)əˈzel, ˌmædm(w)əˈzel

---

Key (col. 2):   a: fad   ā: fade   ah: father   ar: marry   aw: law   e: fed   ē: feed   er: merry   i: hid   ī: hide   ō: coat   o͞o: boot
oi: boy   ow: now   u: put   uh: above   uhr: bird   ch: chop   ng: ring   sh: show   th: thick   th: this   zh: measure

Madera
  1. county, CA   muh-DER-uh   mə'derə
  2. town, Mexico; volcano, Nicaragua   mah-THĀ-rah   mɑ'ðeːrɑ
Madge
  pers. name   MAJ   'mædʒ
Madhya Bharat
  state, India   MUHD-yuh BUH-ruht, BUHR-uht   ˌmədjə 'bə-rət, 'bər-ət
Madhya Pradesh
  state, India   MUHD-yuh pruh-DĀSH, pruh-DESH   ˌmədjə prə'deːʃ, prə'deʃ
Madi
  lang., people, Uganda, Sudan   MAHD-ē   'mɑdi·
Madian
  Biblical name   MĀD-ē-uhn, muh-DĪ-uhn   'meːdiːən, mə'dɑiən
Madill
  city, OK   muh-DIL   mə'dil
Madīnah, Al [Medina]
  city, Saudi Arabia   AHL mah-DĒ-nuh, AL ma-DĒ-nuh   ˌɑːl mɑ'diːnə, ˌæl mæ'diːnə
Madison
  James, 4th US president; US pl.   MAD-uh-suhn   'mædəsən
  name
Madlock
  William, Jr., US baseball player   MAD-LAHK   'mædˌlɑk
Madmannah
  Biblical name   mad-MAN-uh, MAHD-mah-NAH   mæd'mænə, ˌmɑdmɑ'nɑ
Madoc
  pers. name, Welsh   MAH-dawg   'mɑːdɔːg
Madon
  Biblical name   MĀ-DAHN, mah-DŌN   'meːˌdɑn, mɑ'doːn
Madonna
  the Virgin Mary; US singer, actress   muh-DAHN-uh   mə'dɑnə
Madras
  1. city, India   muh-DRAS, muh-DRAHS   mə'dræs, mə'drɑs
  2. city, OR   MA-druhs   'mædrəs
  3. fabric   MA-druhs, muh-DRAS, muh-DRAHS   'mædrəs, mə'dræs, mə'drɑs
Madrid
  1. city, province, Spain   mah-THRĒTH, ⑤ muh-DRID   mɑ'ðriːð, ⑤ mə'drid
  2. city, IA   MAD-ruhd   'mædrəd
Madrid Hurtado
  see de la Madrid Hurtado
Madrigal
  song   MAD-ri-guhl   'mædrigəl
Madrilène
  consommé   MAD-ruh-LEN, MAD-ruh-LĀN   ˌmædrə'len, ˌmædrə'leːn
Madura
  1. city, India   MAHJ-uh-ruh, MAJ-uh-ruh   'mɑdʒərə, 'mædʒərə
  2. island, Indonesia   muh-DUR-uh   mə'durə
Madurese
  lang., people, Madura, Indonesia   MAD-uh-RĒZ, MAJ-uh-RĒZ, -RĒS   ˌmædə'riːz, ˌmædʒə'riːz,
                                                                                      -'riːs
Mae
  pers. name   MĀ   'meː
Maecenas
  Roman statesman, literary patron   mī-SĒ-nuhs   mɑi'siːnəs
Maecilius
  pers. name   mē-SIL-ē-uhs   miː'siliːəs

Foreign Sounds: ue: *Fr.* **r**ue, *Ger.* f**ü**llen   uh(r): *Fr.* b**oeu**f, *Ger.* H**öh**le   kh: *Ger.* i**ch**, *Scot.* lo**ch**   ḡ: *Sp.* ami**g**o   ṿ: *Sp.* ha**b**lar
hl: *Welsh* **Ll**anelli.   CAPITALS: primary stress.   SMALL CAPS: secondary stress.   ⑤: U.S. pron.   ⓔ: British pron.

Máel
   pers. name, Irish Gaelic   MOIL   'mɔil

Maelstrom
   current, whirlpool, Norwegian Sea   MĀL-struhm, MĀL-STRAHM   'meːlstrəm, 'meːlˌstrɑm

Maenads
   female followers of Dionysus   ME̅-NADZ   'miːˌnædz

Maenalus
   son of Lycaon or Arcas   ME̅N-l-uhs   'miːnl̩əs

Maeon
   ancestor of Homer   ME̅-AHN   'miːˌɑn

Maera
   dog of Icarius; constellation   ME̅-ruh, MIR-uh   'miːrə, 'mirə

Maeterlinck
   Maurice, *Belgian author (Nobel 1911)*   MĀT-uhr-LINGK, MET-, MAT-   'meːtərˌliŋk, 'met-, 'mæt-

Mae West
   inflatable lifejacket   MĀ WEST   ˌmeː 'west

Mafeking
   town, S. Africa   MAF-uh-king   'mæfəkiŋ

Maffeo
   pers. name, Italian   mahf-FE̅-ō   mɑf'feoː

Mafia
   criminal organization   MAHF-ē-uh, MAF-ē-uh   'mɑfiːə, 'mæfiːə

Magahi
   lang., India   MAG-uh-hē   'mægəhiˑ

Magallanes [Punta Arenas]
   city, Chile   mah-g̅ah-YAH-nās   mɑɣɑ'janeːs

Magbish
   Biblical name   MAG-bish, mahg-BE̅SH   'mægbiʃ, mɑg'biːʃ

Magda
   pers. name, Romanian   MAHG-dah   'mɑgdɑ

Magdala
   ancient town, Palestine   MAG-duh-luh   'mægdələ

Magdalen
   college, Oxford Univ.   MAWD-luhn   'mɔːdlən

Magdalen
   Islands, *Canada*   MAG-duh-luhn   'mægdələn

Magdalena
   1. river, dept., Colombia; island, Pacific   MAG-duh-LĀ-nuh   ˌmægdə'leːnə
   2. village, NM   MAG-duh-LE̅-nuh   ˌmægdə'liːnə
   3. pers. name, German   MAHG-dah-LĀ-nah   ˌmɑgdɑ'leːnɑ

Magdalene
   college, Cambridge Univ.   MAWD-luhn   'mɔːdlən

Magdalenian
   Paleolithic culture   MAG-duh-LE̅-nē-uhn   ˌmægdə'liːniːən

Magdeburg
   city, Germany   MAHG-duh-BURK, Ⓢ MAG-duh-BUHRG   'mɑgdəˌbuʳk, Ⓢ 'mægdəˌbəʳg

Magdiel
   Biblical name   MAG-dē-EL, MAHG-dē-EL   'mægdiːˌel, ˌmɑgdiː'el

Magellan
   Ferdinand, *Portuguese navigator*   muh-JEL-uhn   mə'dʒelən

---

Key (col. 2):   a: fad ā: fade ah: father ar: marry aw: law e: fed ē: feed er: merry i: hid ī: hide ō: coat ōō: boot
oi: boy ow: now u: put uh: above uhr: bird ch: chop ng: ring sh: show th: thick <u>th</u>: this zh: measure

Magellanic cloud
  galaxy   MAJ-uh-LAN-ik KLOWD, Ⓔ   'mædʒə,lænik 'klɑud, Ⓔ
                      MAG-uh-LAN-ik   ,mægə,lænik

Magellanic penguin
  bird   MAJ-uh-LAN-ik PEN-gwuhn,   'mædʒə,lænik 'pengwən,
                      PENG-gwuhn, Ⓔ MAG-uh-LAN-ik   'peŋgwən, Ⓔ ,mægə,lænik

Magen David, Mogen David
  hexagram symbol of Judaism   MAW-guhn DAW-vuhd, MAHG-uhn   ,mɔːgən 'dɔːvəd, ,mɑgən
                      DAHV-uhd, mah-GEN dah-VĒD   'davəd, mɑ'gen dɑ'viːd

Maggie
  pers. name   MAG-ē   'mægi·

Maggiore
  lake, Italy, Switzerland   mahd-JŌR-ā, Ⓢ muh-JŌR-ē,   mɑd'dʒoːreː, Ⓢ mə'dʒoːri·,
                      muh-JAWR-ē   mə'dʒɔːri·

Magherafelt
  administrative county, Northern   MAHR-uh-FELT, MAH<u>KH</u>-uh-ruh-FELT   'mɑrə,felt, 'mɑxərə,felt
  Ireland

Magh Mela
  Hindu pilgrimage   MAHG MĀ-luh   'mɑg 'meːlə

Maghreb, Maghrib
  northwestern Africa   MUHG-ruhb   'məgrəb

Magi
  Biblical visitors of Christ child;   MĀ-JĪ, MAJ-Ī   'meː,dʒɑi, 'mædʒ,ɑi
  plural of Magus

Magill
  pers. name   muh-GIL   mə'gil

Magindanao
  Moro people of Mindanao,   muh-GĒN-duh-NOW,   mə,giːndə'nɑu,
  Philippines   muh-GĒN-duh-NAH-ō   mə,giːndə'nɑoː

Maginot
  André, *French war minister*   mah-zhē-NŌ   mɑːʒiːnoː

Maginot Line
  French defensive line, WWII   MAZH-uh-NŌ LĪN, MAJ-uh-NŌ   'mæʒə,noː 'lɑin, 'mædʒə,noː

Maglie
  Sal, Stadium, *Niagara Falls, NY*   MAG-lē   'mægli·

Magna Carta
  English charter of liberties   MAG-nuh KAHRT-uh   ,mægnə 'kɑʳtə

Magna cum laude
  with great praise   MAHG-nuh KUM LOWD-uh, MAG-nuh   ,mɑgnə ,kum 'lɑudə, ,mægnə
                      KUHM LAWD-ē   ,kəm 'lɔːdi·

Magna Graecia
  Greek settlements in southern Italy   MAG-nuh GRĒ-shuh   ,mægnə 'griːʃə

Magnani
  Anna, *Italian actress*   mahn-YAHN-ē   mɑn'jɑni·

Magnavox
  tdmk of a radio/TV mfg co   MAG-nuh-VAHKS   'mægnə,vɑks

Magnes
  Judah Leon, *US religious leader*   MAG-nuhs   'mægnəs
  and educator

Magnesia
  ancient city, Asia Minor   mag-NĒ-zhuh, mag-NĒ-shuh   mæg'niːʒə, mæg'niːʃə

magnesium
  element   mag-NĒ-zē-uhm, mag-NĒ-zhuhm   mæg'niːziːəm, mæg'niːʒəm

---

Foreign Sounds: ue: *Fr.* **rue**, *Ger.* **füllen** uh(r): *Fr.* **boeuf**, *Ger.* **Höhle** <u>kh</u>: *Ger.* **ich**, *Scot.* lo**ch** ḡ: *Sp.* a**m**igo <u>v</u>: *Sp.* ha**b**lar
hl: *Welsh* **Ll**anelli. CAPITALS: primary stress. SMALL CAPS: secondary stress. Ⓢ: U.S. pron. Ⓔ: British pron.

Magnificat
  canticle; hymn of praise   mag-NIF-i-KAT, mag-NIF-i-KAHT,   mæg'nifi‚kæt, mæg'nifi‚kat,
                             mahn-YIF-i-KAHT   man'jifi‚kat

Magnifico
  chianti bottle   mahg-NIF-ē-kō, mag-   mɑg'nifiːkoː, mæg-

Magnitogorsk
  city, Russia   muhg-NYI-tuh-GAWRSK,   məg‚njitə'gɔːrsk,
                       Ⓢ mag-NĒT-uh-GAWRSK   Ⓢ mæg'niːțə‚gɔːʳsk

Magor-missabib
  Biblical name   MĀ-GAWR-mi-SĀ-bib,   'meːˌgɔːʳmi'seːbib,
                       mah-GŌR-mi-sah-VĒV   mɑ'goːrmisɑ'viːv

Magnus
  1. pers. name   MAG-nuhs   'mægnəs
  2. Danish   MAHĜ-nus   'maɣnus
  3. German   MAHG-nus   'magnus
  4. Norwegian   MANG-nus   'mæŋnus
  5. Swedish   MAHNG-nus   'mɑːŋnus

Magoffin
  county, KY   muh-GAHF-uhn   mə'gafən

Magog
  Biblical people descended from   MĀ-GAHG   'meːˌgag
    Japheth

Magpiash
  Biblical name   MAG-pē-ASH, mag-PĪ-ASH,   'mægpiːˌæʃ, mæg'paiˌæʃ,
                       mahg-pē-AHSH   mɑgpiː'aʃ

Magritte
  René, *Belgian painter*   muh-GRĒT   mə'griːt

Magsaysay
  Ramón, *president, Philippines*   mahg-SĪ-SĪ, mahg-SĪ-SĪ   mɑg'saiˌsai, mɑgˌsai'sai

Mag Tured
  site of mythological Irish battle   moi T(Y)UR-uh   mɔi 't(j)urə

Magus
  Zoroastrian priest   MĀ-guhs   'meːgəs

Magyar [Hungarian]
  people, lang., Hungary   MAG-YAHR, MAHG-YAHR,   'mægˌjaʳ, 'magˌjaʳ, 'madˌjaʳ,
                       MAHD-YAHR, MAHJ-AHR   'madʒˌaʳ

Magyarorszag [Hungary]
  republic, Europe   MAHD-yahr-AWR-SAHG,   'madjarˌɔːʳˌsag,
                       MAHJ-AHR-AWR-SAHG   'madʒˌarˌɔːʳˌsag

Mahabharata
  epic poem of India   muh-HAH-BAHR-uh-tuh   məˌhɑ'barətə

Mahalah
  Biblical name   muh-HĀ-luh, MĀ-(h)uh-luh,   mə'heːlə, 'meː(h)ələ, mɑx'lɑ
                       mah<u>kh</u>-LAH

Mahalaleel
  Biblical name   muh-HĀ-luh-LĒ(-uh)l,   mə'heːləˌliː(ə)l,
                       MĀ-huh-LĀ-LĒ(-uh)l,   ˌmeːhə'leːˌliː(ə)l,
                       MAH-hah-lahl-EL   ˌmɑhɑlɑl'el

Mahalath
  Biblical name   MĀ-(h)uh-LATH, MAH-<u>kh</u>ah-LAHT   'meː(h)əˌlæθ, ˌmɑxɑ'lɑt

Mahalath-leannoth
  Biblical name   MĀ-(h)uh-LATH-lē-AN-ahth,   'meː(h)əˌlæθliː'ænɑθ,
                       MAH-<u>kh</u>ah-LAHT-luh-ah-NŌT   ˌmɑxɑ'lɑtləɑ'noːt

Mahali
  Biblical name   MĀ-(h)uh-LĪ, mah<u>kh</u>-LĒ   'meː(h)əˌlai, mɑx'liː

Key (col. 2):   a: fad   ā: fade   ah: father   ar: marry   aw: law   e: fed   ē: feed   er: merry   i: hid   ī: hide   ō: coat   ōō: boot
oi: boy   ow: now   u: put   uh: above   uhr: bird   ch: chop   ng: ring   sh: show   th: thick   <u>th</u>: this   zh: measure

Mahalia
pers. name — muh-HĀL-yuh — məˈheːljə

Mahanaim
Biblical name — MĀ-(h)uh-NĀ-im, MAH-<u>kh</u>ah-NAH-yim — ˌmeː(h)əˈneːim, ˌmɑxɑˈnɑjim

Mahaneh-dan
Biblical name — MĀ-(h)uh-nuh-DAN, mah-HAH-ne-DAN, MAH-<u>kh</u>ah-ne-DAHN — ˈmeː(h)ənəˌdæn, məˈhɑneˌdæn, ˌmɑxɑneˈdɑn

Mahanoy City
borough, PA — MAH-huh-NOI SIT-ē — ˈmɑhəˌnɔi ˈsiti·

Maharai
Biblical name — muh-HAR-ē-Ī, MAH-hah-RĪ, MAH-huh-RĪ — məˈhæriːˌai, ˈmɑhɑˌrɑi, ˌmɑhəˈrɑi

Maharashtra
state, India — MAH-huh-RAHSH-truh — ˌmɑhəˈrɑʃtrə

Maharbanji
pers. name, Parsi — MUH-huhr-BAHN-jē — ˌməhərˈbɑndʒi·

Maharishi
Hindu teacher — MAH-huh-RĒ-shē, muh-HAHR-ē-SHĒ — ˌmɑhəˈriːʃiː, məˈhɑri·ˌʃiː

Mahashivarati
Hindu festival — muh-HAH-SHIV-uh-RAH-tē — məˌhɑˌʃivəˈrɑti·

Mahaska
county, IA — muh-HAS-kuh — məˈhæskə

Mahath
Biblical name — MĀ-HATH, MAH-<u>kh</u>aht — ˈmeːˌhæθ, ˈmɑxɑt

Mahatma
Brahman sage — muh-HAHT-muh, muh-HAT-muh — məˈhɑtmə, məˈhætmə

Mahavira
Jain teacher — mah-hah-VĒ-ruh — mɑhɑˈviːrə

Mahavira Jayanti
Jain festival — muh-hah-VĒ-ruh JĪ-(Y)AHN-tē — məhɑˈviːrə ˈdʒɑiˌ(j)ɑnti·

Mahavite
Biblical name — MĀ-huh-VĪT — ˈmeːhəˌvɑit

Mahayana
branch of Buddhism — MAH-huh-YAHN-uh — ˌmɑhəˈjɑnə

Mahayanism
tenets of Mahayana Buddhism — MAH-huh-YAHN-IZ-uhm — ˌmɑhəˈjɑnˌizəm

Mahazioth
Biblical name — muh-HĀ-zē-AHTH, MAH-<u>kh</u>aht-sē-ŌT — məˈheːziːˌɑθ, ˈmɑxɑtsiːˌoːt

Mahdi
Muslim messiah — MAHD-ē — ˈmɑdi·

Mahendra Bir Bikram Shah Deva
king, Nepal — muh-HEN-druh BIR bi-KRUHM SHAH dē-VAH — məˈhendrə ˈbiʳ biˈkrəm ˈʃɑ diːˈvɑ

Maher
1. Frank A., US psychologist; Field, *ballpark, Roanoke, VA* — MĀ(-uh)r, MER, MAHR, MAH-huhr — ˈmeː(ə)ʳ, ˈmeʳ, ˈmɑʳ, ˈmɑhəʳ
2. John, US drug rehabilitation worker — MAH-huhr — ˈmɑhəʳ

Maher-shalal-hashbaz
Biblical name — MĀ-(h)uhr-SHAL-ahl-HASH-BAZ, mah-HER-shah-LAHL-<u>kh</u>ahsh-BAHZ — ˈmeː(h)əʳˈʃælalˈhæʃˌbæz, mɑˈherʃɑˈlɑlxɑʃˈbɑz

Mahfouz
Naguib, *Egyptian author (Nobel 1988)* — MAH-FO͞OZ — ˈmɑˌfuːz

---

Mahican
  N. American people   muh-HĒ-kuhn   mə'hiːkən
Mahlah
  Biblical name   MAL-uh, mah<u>kh</u>-LAH   'mælə, mɑx'lɑ
Mahler
  Donald, *US ballet master;* Gustav,   MAHL-uhr   'mɑləʳ
    Austrian composer
Mahli
  Biblical name   MAL-Ī, mah<u>kh</u>-LĒ   'mæl,ɑi, mɑx'liː
Mahlite
  Biblical name   MAL-ĪT   'mæl,ɑit
Mahlon
  Biblical name   MAL-AHN, mah<u>kh</u>-LŌN   'mæl,ɑn, mɑx'loːn
Mahol
  Biblical name   MĀ-HAHL, mah-<u>KH</u>ŌL   'meː,hɑl, mɑ'xoːl
Mahmud
  pers. name, Turkish   mah-MOOD   mɑ'muːd
Mahnomen
  county, MN   maw-NŌ-muhn   mɔː'noːmən
Mahomet
  pers. name   muh-HŌ-muht   mə'hoːmət
Mahon
  Derek, *Irish poet*   MAHN, ⑤ MAN   'mɑːn, ⑤ 'mæn
Mahoney
  J. Daniel, *US judge; pers. name* muh-HŌ-nē   mə'hoːni·
Mahoning
  county, OH   muh-HŌ-ning   mə'hoːniŋ
Mahopac
  village, NY   MĀ-uh-PAK   'meː,ə,pæk
Mahore
  island, Indian Ocean   muh-HŌR, muh-HAWR   mə'hoːʳ, mə'hɔːʳ
Mahorian
  lang., Comoros Islands   muh-HŌR-ē-uhn, muh-HAWR-ē-uhn   mə'hoːriːən, mə'hɔːriːən
Mahratti, Mahrati
  see Marathi
Mahtomedi
  village, MN   MAHT-uh-MĒD-Ī   ,mɑt̬ə'miːd,ɑi
Mahukona
  village, HI   MAH-hoo-KŌ-nuh   ,mɑhuː'koːnə
Maia
  mother of Hermes   MĪ-uh   'mɑiə
Maiasaurus
  dinosaur   MĪ-uh-SAWR-uhs   ,mɑiə'sɔːrəs
Maida
  pers. name   MĀD-uh, MĪD-uh   'meːdə, 'mɑidə
Maidanek
  Nazi concentration camp, Poland MĪD-uh-NEK   'mɑidə,nek
Maidstone
  town, England   MĀD-stuhn, MĀD-STŌN   'meːdstən, 'meːd,stoːn
Maidu
  N. American people   MĪD-oo   'mɑiduː
Maigret
  Inspector, *fictional detective of G.* me-GRE, ⑤ mā-GRĀ, Ⓔ MĀ-GRĀ   megre, ⑤ meː'greː, Ⓔ
    Simenon   'meː,greː

Key (col. 2):   a: fad   ā: fade   ah: father   ar: **marry**   aw: **law**   e: fed   ē: feed   er: **merry**   i: hid   ī: hide   ō: coat   oo: boot
oi: boy   ow: now   u: put   uh: above   uhr: bird   ch: chop   ng: ring   sh: show   th: thick   <u>th</u>: this   zh: measure

Mailer		
Norman, *US author*	MĀ-luhr	ˈmeːləʳ
Mailgram		
tdmk for electronic mail	MĀL-GRAM	ˈmeːlˌgræm
Maili		
city, HI	MĪ-lē	ˈmɑiliˑ
Maillol		
Aristide, *French sculptor*	mah-YAWL	mɑːjɔːl
Maimonides		
Jewish philosopher	mī-MAHN-uh-DĒZ	mɑiˈmɑnəˌdiːz
Main		
river, Germany	MĪN	ˈmɑin
Mainbocher		
US fashion designer	me^{n}-bō-SHĀ, MEN-bō-SHĀ	mẽboːʃeː, ˌmenboːˈʃeː
Maine		
1. state, US	MĀN	ˈmeːn
2. river, France	MEN	men
Maintenon [Aubigné]		
Françoise d'Aubigné, Madame de, *French noblewoman*	me^{n}t-NAW^{n}	mẽtnɔ̃
Mainwaring		
British family name	MAN-uh-ring, MĀN-WER-ing, MĀN-wuh-ring	ˈmænəriŋ, ˈmeːnˌweriŋ, ˈmeːnwəriŋ
Mainz		
city, Germany	MĪN(T)S	ˈmɑin(t)s
Mair		
1. pers. name	MAR, MER	ˈmæʳ, ˈmeʳ
2. Welsh	MĪR	ˈmɑir
Mairead		
pers. name, Irish	MOI-ruh	ˈmɔirə
Màiri		
pers. name, Scots Gaelic	MAHR-uh	ˈmɑʳə
Maisel		
German beer	MĪ-zuhl	ˈmɑizəl
Maiselbräu		
German beer	MĪ-zuhl-BROI	ˈmɑizəlˌbrɔi
Maithili		
lang., India, Nepal	MĪT-uh-lē, MĪT-l-ē	ˈmɑitəliˑ, ˈmɑitl̩iˑ
Maitland		
Frederic W., *English jurist*	MĀT-luhnd	ˈmeːtlənd
Maius Imperium		
Roman term for higher authority	MĪ-uhs im-PIR-ē-uhm, -PER-ē-uhm	ˈmɑiəs imˈpiriːəm, -ˈperiːəm
Majlis		
parliamentary chamber, Iran, Iraq	maj-LIS, MAHJ-lis	mædʒˈlis, ˈmɑːdʒlis
Majolica		
earthenware	muh-JAHL-i-kuh	məˈdʒɑlikə
Major		
John, *British prime minister*	MĀ-juhr	ˈmeːdʒəʳ
Majorca		
pers. name	muh-YAWR-kuh, muh-JAWR-kuh, mī-AWR-kuh	məˈjɔːʳkə, məˈdʒɔːʳkə, mɑiˈɔːʳkə
Majorca [Mallorca]		
island, Spain	mah-YAWR-kah, [$] muh-JAWR-kuh, mī-AWR-kuh	mɑˈjɔːrkɑ, [$] məˈdʒɔːʳkə, mɑiˈɔːʳkə

Majulah Singapura
   national anthem, Singapore   MAHJ-ul-ah SING-(g)ah-PUR-ah   'madʒulɑ ˌsiŋ(g)ɑ'purɑ
Makah
   N. American people   MAH-kah   'mɑkɑ
Makaha
   city, HI   muh-KAH-huh   mə'kɑhə
Makakilo City
   town, HI   MAHK-uh-KĒ-lō SIT-ē   ˌmakə'kiːloː 'siti·
Makalu
   Mount, *Himalayas*   MUHK-uh-LŌŌ   'məkəˌluː
Makara Sankranti
   Indian festival   MAHK-uh-ruh sahn-KRAHN-tē,   'makərə san'kranti·,
        sahng-KRAHN-tē   saŋ'kranti·
Makarios III
   Cypriot political leader   mah-KAHR-yaws   mɑ'karjɔːs
Makarova
   Natalia, *USSR-born ballerina*   muh-KAHR-uh-vuh   mə'karəvə
Makarovich
   patronym, Ukrainian   muh-KAHR(-uhv)-yich   mə'kar(əv)jitʃ
Makaz
   Biblical name   MĀ-KAZ, MAH-kahts   'meːˌkæz, 'makɑts
Makedhonia [Macedonia]
   region, Greece   MAHK-uh-<u>th</u>uh-NĒ-uh   ˌmakəðə'niːə
Makepeace
   pers. name, (William M. Thackeray)   MĀK-PĒS   'meːkˌpiːs
Makhachkala
   city, Russia   muh-<u>KHAHCH</u>-kuh-LAH   məˌxɑːtʃkə'lɑ
Makheloth
   Biblical name   MAK-HĒ-LAHTH, MAK-uh-LAHTH,   'mækˌhiːˌlɑθ, 'mækəˌlɑθ,
        MAHK-he-LAWT   ˌmakhe'lɔːt
Makkah [Mecca]
   city, Saudi Arabia   MAK-uh   'mækə
Makkedah
   Biblical name   ma-KĒD-uh, mah-ke-DAH   mæ'kiːdə, make'dɑ
Makonde [Konde]
   lang., people, Africa   muh-KŌN-dā   mə'koːndeː
Makoto
   pers. name, Japanese   mah-kō-tō   makoːtoː
Maksim
   pers. name, Russian   MUHK-SYĒM   ˌmək'sjiːm
Maksimilian
   pers. name, Russian   MUHK-syēm-yēl-YAHN   ˌməksjiːmjiːl'jaːn
Maktesh
   Biblical name   MAK-TESH, mah<u>kh</u>-TESH   'mækˌteʃ, max'teʃ
Makua [Kua]
   lang., people, Africa   muh-KWAH   mə'kwɑ
Malabar
   district, India   MAL-uh-BAHR   'mæləˌbaʳ
Malabo
   town, Equatorial Guinea   muh-LAHB-ō   mə'laboː
Malacca
   Strait of, *Asia*   muh-LAHK-uh, muh-LAK-uh   mə'lakə, mə'lækə
Malachi
   Old Testament book; pers. name   MAL-uh-KĪ   'mæləˌkai

Key (col. 2):   a: fad   ā: fade   ah: father   ar: marry   aw: law   e: fed   ē: feed   er: merry   i: hid   ī: hide   ō: coat   ōō: boot
oi: boy   ow: now   u: put   uh: above   uhr: bird   ch: chop   ng: ring   sh: show   th: thick   <u>th</u>: this   zh: measure

Malachias
  Old Testament book   MAL-uh-KĪ-uhs   ˌmælə'kaɪəs
Malad City
  city, ID   muh-LAD SIT-ē   mə'læd 'sɪt̬i·
Málaga
  prov., city, Spain; wine   MAHL-uh-ḡuh, Ⓢ MAL-uh-guh   'maləɣə, Ⓢ 'mæləgə
Malagasy
  lang., people, Madagasar   MAL-uh-GAS-ē, MAHL-uh-GAHS-ē   ˌmælə'gæsi·, ˌmalə'gasi·
Malagueña
  dance   MAL-uh-GĀN-yuh, MAHL-   ˌmælə'geːnjə, ˌmal-
Malahide
  town, Irish Republic   MAL-uh-HĪD   'mæləˌhaid
Malamud
  Bernard, *US novelist*   MAL-uh-MUHD, MAL-uh-muhd   'mæləˌməd, 'mæləməd
Malamute
  dog breed   MAL-uh-MYO͞OT   'mæləˌmjuːt
Malaprop
  Mrs., *character in* The Rivals,   MAL-uh-PRAHP   'mæləˌprap
  Sheridan
Malathion
  insecticide   MAL-uh-THĪ-uhn, -THĪ-AHN   ˌmælə'θaɪən, -'θaiˌan
Malawi [Nyasa]
  country, lake, Africa   muh-LAH-wē, muh-LOW-ē   mə'lawi·, mə'laui·
Malawian
  pert. to Malawi   muh-LAH-wē-uhn, muh-LOW-ē-uhn   mə'lawiːən, mə'lauiːən
Malay
  Archipelago, *island group, Pacific &*   muh-LĀ, MĀ-lā   mə'leː, 'meːleː
  Indian Oceans; lang., people,
  Malaysia
Malaya
  part of Malaysia   muh-LĀ-uh   mə'leːə
Malayalam
  lang., India   MAHL-uh-YAHL-uhm,   ˌmalə'jaləm, ˌmaliː'aləm
            MAHL-ē-AHL-uhm
Malayan
  lang., Malaysia   muh-LĀ-uhn   mə'leːən
Malaysia
  federation, Asia   muh-LĀ-zh(ē-)uh, -sh(ē-)uh   mə'leːʒ(iː)ə, -ʃ(iː)ə
Malaysian
  pert. to Malaysia   muh-LĀ-zh(ē-)uhn, -sh(ē-)uhn   mə'leːʒ(iː)ən, -ʃ(iː)ən
Malcam, Malcham
  Biblical name   MAL-KAM, mahl-KAHM   'mælˌkæm, mal'kam
Malchiah
  Biblical name   mal-KĪ-uh, MAL-kē-uh, mahl-kē-YAH   mæl'kaiə, 'mælkiːə, malkiː'ja
Malchiel
  Biblical name   MAL-kē-EL, MAHL-kē-EL   'mælkiːˌel, ˌmalkiː'el
Malchielite
  Biblical name   MAL-kē-uh-LĪT   'mælkiːəˌlait
Malchijah
  Biblical name   mal-KĪ-uh, mahl-kē-YAH   mæl'kaiə, malkiː'ja
Malchiram
  Biblical name   mal-KĪ-RAM, mahl-kē-RAHM   mæl'kaiˌræm, malkiː'ram
Malchishua
  Biblical name   MAL-KĪ-SHO͞O-uh, MAHL-kē-SHO͞O-ah   ˌmælˌkai'ʃuːə, ˌmalkiː'ʃuːa

---

Foreign Sounds: ue: *Fr.* **rue,** *Ger.* **füllen** uh(r): *Fr.* **boeuf,** *Ger.* **Höhle** kh: *Ger.* **ich,** *Scot.* **loch** ḡ: *Sp.* **amigo** v: *Sp.* **hablar** hl: *Welsh* **Llanelli.** CAPITALS: primary stress. SMALL CAPS: secondary stress. Ⓢ: U.S. pron. Ⓔ: British pron.

Malchus
   Biblical name   MAL-kuhs, MAWL-   'mælkəs, 'mɔːl-
Malcolm
   pers. name   MAL-kuhm   'mælkəm
Malden
   Karl, US actor; city, MA, MO   MAWL-duhn   'mɔːldən
Maldives
   islands, Indian Ocean   MAWL-DĒVZ, MAWL-DĪVZ   'mɔːl,diːvz, 'mɔːl,daivz
Maldivian
   lang., Maldives   mawl-DIV-ē-uhn, mawl-DĒ-vē-uhn   mɔːl'diviːən, mɔːl'diːviːən
Maldon
   borough, battlesite, England   MAWL-duhn   'mɔːldən
Male
   1. lang., people, Ethiopia   MAHL-ā, MAHL-ē   'maleː, 'mali·
   2. atoll, city, Maldives   MAHL-ē   'mali·
Malecite
   N. American people   MAL-uh-SĒT, MAL-uh-SĒT   'mælə,siːt, ,mælə'siːt
Maleleel
   Biblical name   muh-LĒ-lē-EL   mə'liːliː,el
Malenkov
   Georgi, premier, USSR   MUHL-yin-KAWF, ⓢ MAL-uhn-KAWF,   ,məljin'kɔːf, ⓢ ,mælən'kɔːf,
                      MAHL-   ,mɑl-
Malesherbes
   pers. name   MAL-ZUHRB   ,mæl'zəʳb
Maletsunyane
   river, falls, Lesotho   MAHL-uht-sun-YAHN-ē   ,malətsun'jani·
Malfi, The Duchess of
   play by Webster   MAL-fē   'mælfi·
Malheur
   river, county, OR   mal-HUR   mæl'huʳ
Mali
   republic, Africa   MAHL-ē, MAL-ē   'mɑli·, 'mæli·
Malian
   pert. to Mali   MAHL-ē-uhn, MAL-ē-uhn   'mɑliːən, 'mæliːən
Malibu
   beach, California   MAL-uh-BOO   'mælə,buː
Malik
   pers. name, Arabic   MAH-lēk   'mɑliːk
Malines [Mechelen]
   city, Belgium   mah-LĒN   maliːn
Malinka [Malinke]
   lang., people, West Africa   muh-LING-kuh   mə'liŋkə
Malinke [Malinka, Mandingo]
   lang., people, West Africa   muh-LING-kā, muh-LING-kuh·   mə'liŋkeː, mə'liŋkə
Malinowski
   Bronislaw, Polish anthropologist   MAL-uh-NAWF-skē, MAHL-, -NAWV-skē   ,mælə'nɔːfski·, ,mɑl-,
                                         -'nɔːvski·
Maliseet
   N. American people   MAL-uh-SĒT, MAL-uh-SĒT   'mælə,siːt, ,mælə'siːt
Malkovich
   John, US actor   MAL-kuh-VICH, MAWL-kuh-VICH   'mælkə,vitʃ, 'mɔːlkə,vitʃ
Mall
   London district   MAL   'mæl
Mallacoota
   township, Australia   MAL-uh-KOOT-uh   ,mælə'kuːtə

Key (col. 2):   a: fad ā: fade ah: father ar: marry aw: law e: fed ē: feed er: merry i: hid ī: hide ō: coat ōō: boot
oi: boy ow: now u: put uh: above uhr: bird ch: chop ng: ring sh: show th: thick <u>th</u>: this zh: measure

Mallarmé
Stéphane, *French writer* — mah-lahr-MĀ — mɑːlɑːrmeː

Malle
Louis, *French film director* — MAHL — mɑːl

Mallorca [Majorca]
island, Spain — mah(l)-YAWR-kuh, muh(l)-YAWR-kuh, mī-YAWR-kuh — mɑ(l)ˈjɔːʳkə, mə(l)ˈjɔːʳkə, mɑiˈjɔːʳkə

Mallory
pers. name — MAL-(uh-)rē — ˈmæl(ə)riˑ

Mallothi
Biblical name — MAL-uh-THĪ, ma-LŌ-THĪ, mah-LŌ-tē — ˈmæləˌθɑi, mæˈloːˌθɑi, mɑˈloːtiː

Malluch
Biblical name — MAL-uhk, mah-LO͞OKH — ˈmælək, mɑˈluːx

Malluchi [Malachi]
Biblical name — MAL-uh-KĪ, MAHL-ah-KHĒ — ˈmæləˌkɑi, ˌmɑlɑˈxiː

Malmédy
commune, Belgium — mahl-mā-DĒ — mɑːlmeːdiː

Malmesbury
borough, England — MAHMZ-b(uh-)rē, MAH(L)MZ-b(uh-)rē — ˈmɑːmzb(ə-)riˑ, ˈmɑ(l)mzb(ə-)riˑ

Malmö
city, Sweden — MAHL-muh(r) — ˈmɑlmœː

Malmsey
wine — MAH(L)M-zē, MAHM-zē — ˈmɑ(l)mziˑ, ˈmɑːmziˑ

Malone
Moses, *US basketball player* — muh-LŌN — məˈloːn

Malope
plant — MAL-uh-pē — ˈmæləpiˑ

Malory
Sir Thomas, *English author* — MAL-uh-rē, MAL-rē — ˈmæləriˑ, ˈmælriˑ

Malpas
Robert, *English business executive* — MAL-puhs — ˈmælpəs

Malpighi
Marcello, *Italian anatomist* — mahl-PĒ-gē, mal- — mɑlˈpiːgiˑ, mæl-

Malpighian
pert. to Malpighi — mal-PIG-ē-uhn, mal-PĒ-gē-uhn — mælˈpigiːən, mælˈpiːgiːən

Malraux
André, *French writer* — mahl-RŌ, Ⓢ mal-RŌ — mɑːlroː, Ⓢ mælˈroː

Malta
island state, Mediterranean — MAWL-tuh — ˈmɔːltə

Maltaise
orange sauce — mawl-TEZ — mɔːlˈtez

Maltan
pert. to Malta — MAWL-tuhn — ˈmɔːltən

Maltese
lang., Malta — mawl-TĒZ, mawl-TĒS — mɔːlˈtiːz, mɔːlˈtiːs

Malthus
Thomas Robert, *English economist* — MAL-thuhs, MAWL-thuhs — ˈmælθəs, ˈmɔːlθəs

Malthusian
pert. to Malthus — mal-TH(Y)O͞O-zhuhn, mawl-TH(Y)O͞O-zhuhn — mælˈθ(j)uːʒən, mɔːlˈθ(j)uːʒən

Malto
lang., people, India — MAL-tō — ˈmæltoː

Maluku [Moluccas]		
islands, Indonesia	muh-L͞OO-k͞oo	məˈluːkuː
Malvern		
1. US pl. name	MAL-vuhrn	ˈmælvəʳn
2. urban area, England	MAW(L)-vuhrn	ˈmɔː(l)vəʳn
3. city, Australia	MAWL-vuhrn	ˈmɔːlvəʳn
Malvern Hills		
urban area, England	MAW(L)-vuhrn HILZ	ˌmɔː(l)vəʳn ˈhilz
Malvi		
lang., India	MAL-vē	ˈmælviˑ
Malvina		
pers. name	mal-VĒ-nuh	mælˈviːnə
Malvinas, Islas [Falkland]		
islands, Atlantic	ĒZ-lahs mahl-V͟Ē-nahs	ˈiːzlɑs mɑlˈβiːnɑs
Malvolio		
character in Twelfth Night,	mal-VŌ-lē-Ō	mælˈvoːliˑˌoː
Shakespeare		
Mam		
lang., people, Guatemala, Mexico	MAHM	ˈmɑm
Mama		
informal for mother	MAHM-uh, ⓔ muh-MAH	ˈmɑmə, ⓔ məˈmɑː
Mamaroneck		
city, NY	muh-MAR-uh-NEK, muh-MAR-uh-nik	məˈmærəˌnek, məˈmærənik
Mamba		
snake	MAHM-buh, MAM-buh	ˈmɑmbə, ˈmæmbə
Mambo		
dance	MAHM-bō	ˈmɑmboː
Mameluke [Mamlūk]		
Egyptian and Syrian dynasty of	MAM-uh-L͞OOK	ˈmæməˌluːk
warriors		
Mamelukes		
military class that controlled Turkey	MAM-uh-L͞OOKS	ˈmæməˌluːks
Mamenchisaurus		
dinosaur	MAM-EN-kī-SAWR-uhs	ˌmæmˌenkaiˈsɔːrəs
Mamercus		
Roman praenomen	MAHM-uhr-kuhs	ˈmɑməʳkəs
Mamie		
pers. name	MĀ-mē	ˈmeːmiˑ
Mamilius		
pers. name, Latin	muh-MIL-ē-uhs	məˈmiliːəs
Mamlūk [Mameluke]		
Egyptian and Syrian dynasty of	MAM-L͞OOK	ˈmæmˌluːk
warriors		
Mamma Leone's		
restaurant, New York City	MAHM-uh lē-Ō-nēz	ˌmɑmə liːˈoːniˑz
Mammon		
greed or riches personified	MAM-uhn	ˈmæmən
Mamre		
Biblical name	MAM-ruh, MAHM-ruh, mahm-RE	ˈmæmrə, ˈmɑmrə, mɑmˈre
Mamurius		
shield-maker for Numa	mam-(Y)UR-ē-uhs	mæmˈ(j)uriːəs
Manaen		
Biblical name	MAN-uh-EN, MAN-ē-EN	ˈmænəˌen, ˈmæniːˌen
Managua		
city, dept, Nicaragua	mah-NAHG̱-wah, Ⓢ muh-NAHG-wuh	mɑˈnɑɣwɑ, Ⓢ məˈnɑgwə

Key (col. 2): a: f**a**d ā: f**a**de ah: f**a**ther ar: m**a**rry aw: l**a**w e: f**e**d ē: f**ee**d er: m**e**rry i: h**i**d ī: h**i**de ō: c**oa**t ōō: b**oo**t
oi: b**oy** ow: n**ow** u: p**u**t uh: **a**bove uhr: b**ir**d ch: **ch**op ng: ri**ng** sh: **sh**ow th: **th**ick t͟h: **th**is zh: mea**s**ure

Manahath
Biblical name   MAN-uh-HATH, mah-NAH-khaht   'mænəˌhæθ, mɑ'nɑxɑt
Manama
town, Bahrain   muh-NAM-uh   mə'næmə
Manaslu
mtn., Himalayas   muh-NAHS-lōo   mə'nɑsluː
Manasquan
borough, NJ   MAN-uh-SKWAHN   'mænəˌskwɑn
Manassas
county, VA   muh-NAS-uhs   mə'næsəs
Manasseh
Prayer of, *Apocryphal book; pers.*   muh-NAS-uh   mə'næsə
   name
Manasses
Prayer of, *Apocryphal book*   muh-NAS-uhs, muh-NAS-ēz   mə'næsəs, mə'næsiːz
Manatee
county, FL   MAN-uh-TĒ, MAN-uh-TĒ   ˌmænə'tiː, 'mænəˌtiː
Mance
pers. name (M. Lipscomb)   MAN(T)S   'mæn(t)s
Mancha, La
see La Mancha
Manche
dept, France   MAHⁿSH   mɑ̃ʃ
Manchester
US pl. name; borough, England   MAN-CHES-tuhr, MAN-chuh-stuhr   'mænˌtʃestərˢ, 'mæntʃəstərˢ
Manchu
dynasty, China; ancient lang., China   man-CHŌO   mæn'tʃuː
Manchukuo
former state, Asia   MAHN-CHŌO-KWŌ   'mɑn'tʃuː'kwoː
Manchuria
region, China   man-CHUR-ē-uh   mæn'tʃuriːə
Mancini
Henry, *composer*   man-SĒ-nē   mæn'siːniˑ
Manco Capac, Manqo Qhapaq
traditional founder of Inca dynasty,   MAHNG-kō KAH-PAHK   'mɑŋkoː 'kɑˌpak
   Peru
Mancunian
pert. to Manchester, *England*   man-KYŌO-nē-uhn,   mæn'kjuːniːən,
   mang-KYŌO-nē-uhn   mæŋ'kjuːniːən
Mancuso
Nick, *actor, director*   man-KŌO-sō, man-KŌO-zō   mæn'kuːsoː, mæn'kuːzoː
Mandala
Hindu symbol   MUHN-duh-luh   'məndələ
Mandalay
city, division, Burma   MAN-duh-LĀ   ˌmændə'leː
Mandan
N. American people   MAN-DAN, MAN-duhn   'mænˌdæn, 'mændən
Mandarin
lang., China   MAN-duh-ruhn   'mændərən
Mandé
pers. name   mahⁿ-DĀ   mɑ̃deː
Mandela
Nelson, *S. African political leader*   man-DEL-uh   mæn'delə
Mandelbrot
Benoit B., *French mathematician*   mahn-del-BRAW, ⓢ MAN-dl-BRŌ   mɑndelbrɔː, ⓢ 'mændlˌbroː

Foreign Sounds: ue: *Fr.* **rue**, *Ger.* **füllen**   uh(r): *Fr.* **boeuf**, *Ger.* **Höhle**   kh: *Ger.* **ich**, *Scot.* **loch**   ḡ: *Sp.* **amigo**   v: *Sp.* **hablar**
hl: *Welsh* **Llanelli**.   CAPITALS: primary stress.   SMALL CAPS: secondary stress.   ⓢ: U.S. pron.   Ⓔ: British pron.

Mandell
  pers. name   MAN-dl, man-DEL   'mændļ, mæn'del
Mandelstam
  Osip, *Russian writer*   MUHN-dyil-SHTAHM   ˌməndjil'ʃtɑːm
Mandeville
  Sir John, *fictional 14th-century*   MAN-duh-VIL   'mændəˌvil
    traveler; town, LA
Mandingo [Malinke]
  lang., people, Africa   man-DING-gō   mæn'diŋgoː
Mandinka
  lang., W. Africa   man-DING-kuh   mæn'diŋkə
Mandrell
  Barbara, *US country singer*   man-DREL   mæn'drel
Mandy
  pers. name   MAN-dē   'mændiˑ
Manes
  1. husband of Callirhoe in Roman   MĀ-nēz   'meːniːz
    mythology
  2. Roman souls of the dead   MAHN-ĀS, MĀ-NĒZ   'mɑnˌeːs, 'meːˌniːz
Manes [Mani, Manichaeus]
  Persian religious leader   MĀ-NĒZ   'meːˌniːz
Manet
  Edouard, *French painter*   mah-NE, Ⓢ ma-NĀ, mah-NĀ   mɑːne, Ⓢ mæ'neː, mɑ'neː
Manfred
  1. pers. name   MAN-fruhd   'mænfrəd
  2. German   MAHN-FRĀT   'mɑnˌfreːt
Manfredo
  pers. name, Italian   mahn-FRĀ-dō   mɑn'freːdoː
Mangalore
  seaport, India   MAHNG-guh-LAWR   'mɑŋgəˌlɔːʳ
manganese
  element   MANG-guh-NĒZ, MANG-guh-NĒS   'mæŋgəˌniːz, 'mæŋgəˌniːs
Mangano
  Silvana, *Italian entertainer*   mahn-GAHN-ō   mɑn'gɑnoː
Mangbetu
  lang., people, Uganda, Zaire   mahng-BE-to͞o   mɑŋ'betuː
Mangione
  Chuck, *US musician*   MAN-jē-Ō-nē, man-JŌ-nē   ˌmændʒiˑ'oːniˑ, mæn'dʒoːniˑ
Mangosuthu
  pers. name, S. Africa   MAHNG-gō-SO͞O-to͞o   ˌmɑŋgoːˈsuːtuː
Manhattan
  island, NY   man-HAT-n, muhn-HAT-n   mæn'hætṇ, mən'hætṇ
Mani [Manes]
  Persian religious leader   MAHN-ē   'mɑniˑ
Mania
  personification of madness   MĀ-nē-uh, MĀN-yuh   'meːniːə, 'meːnjə
Manichaean
  adherent of Manichaeanism   MAN-uh-KĒ-uhn   ˌmænəˈkiːən
Manichaeanism [Manichaeism]
  religious or philosophical dualism   MAN-i-KĒ-uh-NIZ-uhm   ˌmæniˈkiːəˌnizəm
Manichaeism [Manichaeanism]
  religious or philosophical dualism   MAN-i-kē-IZ-uhm   'mæniki:ˌizəm
Manichaeus [Manes]
  Persian religious leader   MAN-uh-KĒ-uhs   ˌmænəˈkiːəs

Key (col. 2):   aː fad   āː fade   ahː father   arː **ma**rry   awː law   eː fed   ēː feed   erː **me**rry   iː hid   īː hide   ōː coat   o͞oː boot
oiː boy   owː now   uː put   uhː above   uhrː bird   chː chop   ngː ring   shː show   thː thick   <u>th</u>ː this   zhː measure

Manicouagan
  river, Canada   MAN-uh-KWAHG-uhn   ˌmænəˈkwɑgən

Manila
  city, Philippines   muh-NIL-uh   məˈnilə

Manilow
  Barry, US entertainer   MAN-l-ō   ˈmænl̩ˌoː

Manipur
  river, Burma; state, India   MUHN-uh-PUR, MAHN-uh-PUR, MAN-uh-PUR   ˌmənəˈpuʳ, ˌmɑnəˈpuʳ, ˌmænəˈpuʳ

Manipuri [Meithei]
  lang., people, India   MUHN-uh-PUR-ē, MAHN-uh-PUR-ē, MAN-uh-PUR-ē   ˌmənəˈpuriˑ, ˌmɑnəˈpuriˑ, ˌmænəˈpuriˑ

Manischewitz
  kosher food & wine co.   MAN-uh-SHEV-uhts   ˌmænəˈʃevəts

Manistee
  river, county, MI   MAN-uh-STĒ   ˌmænəˈstiː

Manistique
  river, MI   MAN-uh-STĒK   ˌmænəˈstiːk

Manitoba
  lake, province, Canada   MAN-uh-TŌ-buh   ˌmænəˈtoːbə

Manitou Springs
  town, CO   MAN-uh-TOO SPRINGZ   ˈmænəˌtuː ˈspriŋz

Manitoulin
  Islands, Lake Huron   MAN-uh-TOO-luhn   ˌmænəˈtuːlən

Manitowoc
  city, county, WI   MAN-uht-uh-WAHK   ˈmænətəˌwɑk

Manius
  pers. name, Latin   MĀ-nē-uhs   ˈmeːniːəs

Mankato
  city, MN   man-KĀT-ō   mænˈkeːtoː

Mankiewicz
  Joseph Leo, US film director, writer, and producer   MANG-kuh-WITS   ˈmæŋkəˌwits

Manley
  pers. name   MAN-lē   ˈmænliˑ

Manlius
  pers. name   MAN-lē-uhs   ˈmænliːəs

Mann
  1. Horace, US education reformer   MAN   ˈmæn
  2. Thomas, German author (Nobel 1929)   MAHN   ˈmɑn

Manne
  pers. name, Swedish   MAHN-ne   ˈmɑːnne

Mannerheim
  Baron Carl Gustav, Finnish politician   MAHN-uhr-HĀM, -HĪM   ˈmɑnəʳˌheːm, -ˌhaim

Mannes
  College of Music, NY   MANZ   ˈmænz

Mannheim
  1. Karl, Hungarian historian   MAHN-HĪM   ˈmɑnˌhaim
  2. port, Germany   MAHN-HĪM, Ⓢ MAN-HĪM   ˈmɑnˌhaim, Ⓢ ˈmænˌhaim

Mano
  lang., people, Liberia, Guinea   MAHN-ō   ˈmɑnoː

Manoah
  Biblical name   muh-NŌ-uh   məˈnoːə

Manoel
  pers. name, Portuguese   muhn-WEL, mahn-WEL   mən'wel, mɑːn'wel
Manolete
  cognomen of Manuel Rodriguez   mahn-ō-LĀ-tā   mɑno:'leːteː
    Sánchez, *Spanish bullfighter*
Manon
  pers. name, French   mah-NAWⁿ   mɑːnɔ̃
Manon Lescaut
  opera, Puccini   mah-NAWⁿ les-KŌ   mɑːnɔ̃ leskoː
Manqo Qhapaq
  see Manco Capac
Mans, Le
  see Le Mans
Mansi [Vogul]
  lang., people, Russia   MAHN-sē   'mɑnsiˑ
Manson
  Charles, *US mass murderer*   MAN-suhn   'mænsən
Mansur
  pers. name, Persian   mahn-SOOR   mɑːn'suːr
Mansūra, El [Al-Mansūra]
  city, Egypt   EL mahn-SUR-uh   ˌel mɑn'surə
Mantegna
  Andrea, *Italian painter*   mahn-TEN-yah   mɑn'tenja
Manti
  city, UT   MAN-tī   'mænˌtai
Mantinea
  ancient village, Greece   MANT-n-Ē-uh   ˌmæntn̩'iːə
Mantle
  Mickey, *US baseball player*   MANT-l   'mæntl̩
Manto
  prophetic daughter of Tiresias   MAN-tō   'mæntoː
Mantoux
  TB test   mahⁿ-TOO, mahn-TOO   mãtuː, mɑn'tuː
Mantova [Mantua]
  prov, Italy   MAHNT-uh-vuh   'mɑntəvə
Mantovani
  Annunzio, *US entertainer*   MAHNT-uh-VAHN-ē   ˌmɑntə'vɑniˑ
Mantua
  1. prov, Italy   MAN-chuh-wuh, MANT-uh-wuh   'mæntʃəwə, 'mæntəwə
  2. city, Cuba   MAHN-twuh   'mɑntwə
Manuel
  1. pers. name   MAN-yuh(-wuh)l, MAN-yuh-WEL   'mænjə(wə)l, 'mænjəˌwel
  2. Portuguese   muhn-WEL, mahn-WEL   mən'wel, mɑːn'wel
  3. Spanish   mahn-WEL   mɑn'wel
Manx
  Celtic lang. of Isle of Man   MANGKS   'mæŋks
Man [Yao]
  lang.; people, SE Asia   MAHN   'mɑn
Manzanillo
  port, Cuba   MAHN-zuh-NĒ-(y)ō   ˌmɑnzə'niː(j)oː
Manzanita
  N. American people; shrub   MAN-zuh-NĒT-uh   ˌmænzə'niːt̬ə
Maoch
  Biblical name   MĀ-AHK, mah-ŌKH   'meːˌɑk, mɑ'oːx

Key (col. 2):   a: fad ā: fade ah: father ar: marry aw: law e: fed ē: feed er: merry i: hid ī: hide ō: coat ōō: boot
oi: boy   ow: now   u: put   uh: above   uhr: bird   ch: chop   ng: ring   sh: show   th: thick   th: this   zh: measure

Maoism
  political philosophy of Mao Zedong MOW-ɪz-uhm ˈmɑuˌizəm
Maoist
  follower of Maoism MOW-uhst ˈmɑuəst
Maoke Range
  mts., Indonesia MOW-kā ˈmɑukeː
Maon
  Biblical name MĀ-AHN, mah-ŌN ˈmeːˌɑn, mɑˈoːn
Maonite
  Biblical name MĀ-uh-NĬT ˈmeːəˌnɑit
Maori
  New Zealand people MOWR-ē ˈmɑuri·
Maotai
  town, China MOW-TĪ ˈmɑuˈtɑi
Mao Tse Tung
  see Mao Zedong
Mao Zedong, Mao Tse Tung
  Chinese leader MOWD-ZUH-DUNG ˈmɑudˈzəˈduŋ
Mapplethorpe
  Robert, *US photographer* MĀ-puhl-THAWRP ˈmeːpəlˌθɔːʳp
Mapuche [Araucanian]
  lang., S. America muh-PŌŌ-chā məˈpuːtʃeː
Maputo
  river, prov, Mozambique muh-PŌŌT-ō məˈpuːtoː
Maquis
  French resistance group, WWII mah-KĒ, ⓢ muh-KĒ, mah-KĒ mɑːkiː, ⓢ məˈkiː, mɑˈkiː
Maquoketa
  river, city, IA muh-KŌ-kuht-uh məˈkoːkətə
Mara
  1. evil Hindu god MAHR-uh ˈmɑrə
  2. pers. name MAR-uh, MAHR-uh ˈmærə, ˈmɑrə
Marabou
  bird MAR-uh-BŌŌ ˈmærəˌbuː
Maracaibo
  lake, city, Venezuela MAR-uh-KĪ-bō ˌmærəˈkɑiboː
Marah
  Biblical name MAHR-uh, MĀ-ruh, mah-RAH ˈmɑrə, ˈmeːrə, mɑˈrɑ
Marais des Cygnes
  river, KS, MO MERD-uh-ZĒN, -SĒN ˈmeʳdəˌziːn, -ˌsiːn
Marajó
  island, Amazon River MAR-uh-ZHŌ ˌmærəˈʒoː
Maralah
  Biblical name MAHR-uh-luh, MAHR-ah-LAH ˈmɑrələ, ˌmɑrɑˈlɑ
Maranatha
  Biblical name MAHR-uh-NATH-uh ˌmɑrəˈnæθə
Maraschino
  preserved cherry MAR-uh-SKĒ-nō, -SHĒ-nō ˌmærəˈskiːnoː, -ˈʃiːnoː
Mărăsești
  commune, Romania MUHR-uh-SHEST(-ē) ˌmərəˈʃest(i·)
Marat
  Jean Paul, *French political leader* mah-RAH mɑːrɑː
Maratha
  people, India muh-RAHT-uh məˈrɑtə
Marathi, Mahratti, Mahrati
  Indic lang. muh-RAHT-ē məˈrɑti·

Foreign Sounds: ue: *Fr.* **rue,** *Ger.* füllen uh(r): *Fr.* **b**oeuf, *Ger.* Höhle kh: *Ger.* i**ch,** *Scot.* lo**ch** ḡ: *Sp.* ami**g**o v̱: *Sp.* ha**b**lar
hl: *Welsh* **Ll**anelli. CAPITALS: primary stress. SMALL CAPS: secondary stress. ⓢ: U.S. pron. ⓔ: British pron.

Marathon
  plain & ancient town, Greece   MAR-uh-THAHN, MAR-uh-thuhn   'mærə͵θɑn, 'mærəθən
Marattia
  plant   muh-RAT-ē-uh   mə'ræṭiːə
Marawi
  municipality, Philippines   muh-RAH-wē   mə'rɑwiˑ
Marbella
  port, Spain   mahr-BĀ(L)-yah   mɑr'beː(l)jɑ
Marburg
  city, Germany   MAHR-BURK, ⑤ MAHR-BURG, MAHR-BUHRG   'mɑʳ͵buʳk, ⑤ 'mɑʳ͵burg, 'mɑʳ͵bəʳg
Marc
  1. pers. name   MAHRK   'mɑʳk
  2. French   MAHRK   mɑːrk
Marceau
  Marcel, *French mime*   mahr-SŌ   mɑːrsoː
Marcel
  1. pers. name   mahr-SEL   mɑʳ'sel
  2. French   mahr-SEL   mɑːrsel
Marcellinus
  pope   MAHR-suh-LĪ-nuhs   ͵mɑʳsə'lɑinəs
Marcello
  pers. name, Italian   mahr-CHEL-lō   mɑr'tʃelloː
Marcellus
  1. pope; pers. name   mahr-SEL-uhs   mɑʳ'seləs
  2. Dutch   mahr-SEL-ues   mɑr'selys
March
  month   MAHRCH   'mɑʳtʃ
Marchand
  Nancy, *US actress*   mahr-SHAND, mahr-SHAHND   mɑʳ'ʃænd, mɑʳ'ʃɑnd
Marcha Real
  national anthem, Spain   MAHR-chah rā-AHL   'mɑrtʃɑ reː'ɑl
Marcia
  pers. name   MAHR-shuh   'mɑʳʃə
Marcial
  pers. name, Spanish   mahr-SYAHL, mahr-THYAHL   mɑr'sjɑl, mɑr'θjɑl
Marciano
  Rocco "Rocky," *US boxer*   MAHR-sē-AN-ō, MAHR-shē-AN-ō, -AHN-ō   ͵mɑʳsiː'ænoː, ͵mɑʳʃiː'ænoː, -'ɑnoː
Marcia Pontificale
  national anthem, Vatican City   MAHR-chah PAWN-tē-fē-KAH-lā   'mɑrtʃɑ ͵pɔːntiːfiːˈkɑːleː
Marcionism
  Gnostic sect   MAHR-suh-NIZ-uhm   'mɑʳsə͵nizəm
Marcius
  pers. name, Latin   MAHR-sh(ē-)uhs   'mɑʳʃ(iː)əs
Marco
  1. pers. name   MAHR-kō   'mɑʳkoː
  2. French   mahr-KŌ   mɑːrkoː
  3. Italian, Spanish   MAHR-kō   'mɑrkoː
Marconi
  Guglielmo, *Italian physicist, inventor* (Nobel 1909)   mahr-KŌ-nē   mɑʳ'koːniˑ

Key (col. 2):   a: f**a**d   ā: f**a**de   ah: f**a**ther   ar: m**a**rry   aw: l**a**w   e: f**e**d   ē: f**ee**d   er: m**e**rry   i: h**i**d   ī: h**i**de   ō: c**oa**t   ōō: b**oo**t
oi: b**oy**   ow: n**ow**   u: p**u**t   uh: **a**bove   uhr: b**i**rd   ch: **ch**op   ng: ri**ng**   sh: **sh**ow   th: **th**ick   <u>th</u>: **th**is   zh: mea**s**ure

Marcos

  1. Philippine political family; pers.   MAHR-kōs   'mɑʳkoːs
    name, Spanish

  2. Portuguese   MAHR-kōōsh   'mɑːrkuːʃ

Marcus

  1. pers. name   MAHR-kuhs   'mɑʳkəs

  2. Dutch   MAHR-kues   'mɑrkys

  3. German   MAHR-kus   'mɑʳkus

  4. Norwegian   MAHR-kus   'mɑrkus

  5. Swedish   MAHR-kuhs   'mɑːrkəs

Marcus Aurelius

  Roman emperor & philosopher   MAHR-kuhs aw-RĒL-yuhs,   'mɑʳkəs ɔː'riːljəs, ɔː'riːliːəs
                                       aw-RĒ-lē-uhs

Marcuse

  Herbert, *US political philosopher*   mahr-KŌŌ-zuh   mɑʳ'kuːzə

Marcy

  pers. name   MAHR-sē   'mɑʳsiˑ

Mardi Gras

  New Orleans festival   MAHRD-ē GRAH, GRAW   'mɑʳdiˑ ˌgrɑ, ˌgrɔː

Mardonius

  Persian general   mahr-DŌ-nē-uhs   mɑʳ'doːniːəs

Marduk

  supreme Babylonian god   MAHR-DŌŌK   'mɑʳˌduːk

Mare Australe

  'sea' on Moon   MAHR-ā aw-STRĀ-lē, ahs-TRĀ-   ˌmɑreː ɔː'streːliˑ, ɑs'treː-

Mare Crisium

  'sea' on Moon   MAHR-ā KRIS-ē-uhm, KRĒ-sē-uhm,   'mɑreː 'krisiːəm, 'kriːsiːəm,
                               KRISH-(ē-)uhm   'kriʃ(iː)əm

Maredudd, -dydd

  pers. name, Welsh   me-RED-ith   me'redi ð

Mare Fecunditatis

  'sea' on Moon   MAHR-ā fuh-KUHN-duh-TAHT-uhs   'mɑreː fəˌkəndə'tɑţəs

Mare Frigoris

  'sea' on Moon   MAHR-ā fri-GŌR-uhs, -GAWR-uhs   'mɑreː fri'goːrəs, -'gɔːrəs

Mare Humboldtianum

  'sea' on Moon   MAHR-ā HUHM-BŌL-tē-Ā-nuhm   'mɑreː ˌhəmˌboːltiː'eːnəm

Mare Humorum

  'sea' on Moon   MAHR-ā (H)YŌŌ-MŌR-uhm,   'mɑreː ˌ(h)juː'moːrəm,
                               -MAWR-uhm   -'mɔːrəm

Mare Imbrium

  'sea' on Moon   MAHR-ā IM-brē-uhm   'mɑreː 'imbriːəm

Mare Ingenii

  'sea' on Moon   MAHR-ā in-JEN-ē-Ē, -ē-Ī   'mɑreː in'dʒeniːˌiː, -iːˌɑi

Mare Marginis

  'sea' on Moon   MAHR-ā mahr-JĪ-nuhs   'mɑreː mɑʳ'dʒɑinəs

Maremma

  Italian sheepdog   muh-REM-uh   mə'remə

Mare Moscoviense

  'sea' on Moon   MAHR-ā MAHS-kōv-YEN-sē   'mɑreː ˌmɑskoːv'jensiˑ

Mare Nectaris

  'sea' on moon   MAHR-ā NEK-tuh-ruhs   'mɑreː 'nektərəs

Marengo

  1. county, AL; chicken dish   muh-RENG-gō   mə'reŋgoː

  2. village, Italy   mah-RENG-gō   mɑ'reŋgoː

Mare Nubium
'sea' on Moon   MAHR-ā N(Y)O͞O-bē-uhm   'mɑreː 'n(j)uːbiːəm

Mare Orientale
'sea' on Moon   MAHR-ā AWR-ē-uhn-TĀ-lē   'mɑreː ˌɔːriːən'teːliː

Mare Serenitatis
'sea' on Moon   MAHR-ā suh-REN-uh-TAHT-uhs   'mɑreː səˌrenə'tɑtəs

Mareshah
Biblical name   muh-RĒ-shuh, MAH-re-SHAH   məˈriːʃə, ˌmɑreˈʃɑ

Mare Smythii
'sea' on Moon   MAHR-ā SMITH-ē-Ē   'mɑreː 'smiθiːˌiː

Mare Tranquillitatis
'sea' on Moon   MAHR-ā TRAN-kwil-uh-TAHT-uhs   'mɑreː ˌtrænkwilə'tɑtəs

Mare Undarum
'sea' on Moon   MAHR-ā UHN-DAHR-uhm   'mɑreː ˌən'dɑrəm

Mare Vaporum
'sea' on Moon   MAHR-ā vā-PŌR-uhm, -PAWR-uhm   'mɑreː veː'poːrəm, -'poːrəm

Marfeh
Mideast Christian festival   MAHR-fe   'mɑʳfe

Margaret
pers. name   MAHR-g(uh-)ruht   'mɑʳg(ə)rət

Margareta
pers. name, Swedish   MAHR-gah-RĀ-tah   ˌmɑːrgɑːˈreːtɑː

Margarete
pers. name, German   MAHR-guh-RĀ-tuh   ˌmɑʳgəˈreːtə

Margaretha
pers. name, Dutch   MAHR-gah-RĀ-tah   ˌmɑrgɑ'reːtɑ

Margaretta
pers. name   MAHR-guh-RET-uh   ˌmɑʳgəˈreţə

Margarita
cocktail; pers. name   MAHR-guh-RĒT-uh   ˌmɑʳgəˈriːţə

Margaux
French wine; pers. name   mahr-GŌ   mɑːrgoː

Marge
pers. name   MAHRJ   'mɑʳdʒ

Margery
pers. name   MAHR-juh-rē, MAHRJ-rē   'mɑʳdʒəriˑ, 'mɑʳdʒriˑ

Margherita
pers. name, Italian   MAHR-gā-RĒ-tah   ˌmɑrgeːˈriːtɑ

Margi
lang., sub-Saharan Africa   MAHR-gē   'mɑʳgiˑ

Margie
pers. name   MAHR-jē, MAHR-gē   'mɑʳdʒiˑ, 'mɑʳgiˑ

Marginis, Mare
see Mare Marginis

Margo
pers. name   MAHR-gō   'mɑʳgoː

Margot
1. pers. name   MAHR-gō, MAHR-guht   'mɑʳgoː, 'mɑʳgət
2. French   mahr-GŌ   mɑrgoː

Marguerite
1. pers. name   MAHR-guh-RĒT   ˌmɑʳgəˈriːt
2. French   mahr-guh-RĒT   mɑːrgəriːt

Mari
lang., people, Russia [Cheremis]*;*   MAHR-ē   'mɑriˑ
ancient Mesopotamian city

Key (col. 2):   a: fad   ā: fade   ah: father   ar: marry   aw: law   e: fed   ē: feed   er: merry   i: hid   ī: hide   ō: coat   o͞o: boot
oi: boy   ow: now   u: put   uh: above   uhr: bird   ch: chop   ng: ring   sh: show   th: thick   th̲: this   zh: measure

Maria		
1. pers. name	muh-RĒ-uh, muh-RĪ-uh	mə'riːə, mə'rɑiə
2. Dutch, Finnish	mah-RĒ-ah	mɑː'riːɑː
3. German, Italian	mah-RĒ-ah	mɑ'riːɑ
4. Polish	MAHR-yah	'mɑːrjɑː
5. Portuguese	muh-RĒ-uh, mah-RĒ-ah	mə'riːə, mɑː'riːɑː
6. Russian	MUHR-YĒ-(y)uh	ˌmər'jiː(j)ə
7. Swedish	mah-RĒ-ah	mɑː'riːɑː
María		
pers. name, Spanish	mah-RĒ-ah	mɑ'riːɑ
Mariah		
pers. name	muh-RĪ-uh	mə'rɑiə
Marian		
pers. name	MER-ē-uhn, MAR-ē-uhn	'meriːən, 'mæriːən
Mariana		
Trench, *Pacific; pers. name*	MAR-ē-AN-uh, MER-ē-AN-uh, MAHR-ē-AHN-uh	ˌmæriː'ænə, ˌmeriː'ænə, ˌmɑriː'ɑnə
Marianas		
islands, Pacific	MAR-ē-AN-uhz, MER-ē-AN-uhz, MAHR-ē-AHN-uhz	ˌmæriː'ænəz, ˌmeriː'ænəz, ˌmɑriː'ɑnəz
Marianism		
Christian veneration of Mary	MER-ē-uh-NIZ-uhm, MAR-ē-, MĀ-rē-	'meriːəˌnizəm, 'mæriː-, 'meːriː-
Marianna		
pers. name, Portuguese	muh-rē-AH-nuh, mah-rē-AH-nah	məriː'ɑːnə, mɑːriː'ɑːnɑː
Marianne		
1. pers. name	MER-ē-AN, MAR-	ˌmeriː'æn, ˌmær-
2. German	MAHR-ē-AHN-uh, mahr-YAHN-uh	ˌmɑriː'ɑnə, mɑ^{r}'jɑnə
Mariano		
pers. name, Italian, Spanish	mahr-YAHN-ō	mɑr'jɑnoː
Maribor		
city, Slovenia	MAHR-i-BAWR	'mɑriˌbɔː^{r}
Maricopa		
county, mtn. range, AZ; N. American people	MAR-uh-KŌ-puh	ˌmærə'koːpə
Marie		
1. pers. name	muh-RĒ, [£] *also* MAHR-ē, MAR-ē	mə'riː, [£] *also* 'mɑriˑ, 'mæriˑ
2. Danish, German	mah-RĒ(-uh)	mɑ'riː(ə)
3. Dutch, Swedish	mah-RĒ	mɑː'riː
4. French	mah-RĒ	mɑːriː
5. Norwegian	mah-RĒ-uh	mɑ'riːə
Marie Antoinette		
queen of France, wife of Louis XVI	mah-RĒ ah^{n}-twah-NET, [$] muh-RĒ AN-twuh-NET, AN-tuh-NET	mɑːriː ɑ̃twɑːnet, [$] məˌriː ˌæntwə'net, ˌæntə'net
Mariel		
pers. name (M. Hemingway)	MAR-ē-uhl, MER-ē-uhl	'mæriːəl, 'meriːəl
Maries		
county, MO	MAR-ēz	'mæriˑz
Marietta		
1. pers. name	MER-ē-ET-uh, MAR-	ˌmeriː'etə, ˌmær-
2. Italian	MAHR-ē-ĀT-tah	ˌmɑriː'eːttɑ
Mariette		
pers. name	MAR-ē-ET, MER-ē-ET, MAR-ē-ET, MER-ē-ET	ˌmæriː'et, ˌmeriː'et, 'mæriːˌet, 'meriːˌet

Marilu
   pers. name (M. Henner)   MAR-ē-L$\overline{OO}$, MER-ē-L$\overline{OO}$ ˌmæriˈluː, ˌmeriˈluː

Marilyn
   pers. name   MAR-uh-luhn, MER-uh-luhn   ˈmærələn, ˈmerələn

Marimba
   musical instrument   muh-RIM-buh   məˈrimbə

Marin
   1. county, CA   muh-RIN   məˈrin
   2. pers. name, Serbo-Croatian   MAHR-in   ˈmɑːrin

Marín
   commune, Spain   muh-RĒN   məˈriːn

Marinelli
   Field, *ballpark, Rockford, IL*   MAR-uh-NEL-ē   ˌmærəˈneliˑ

Marinette
   county, WI   MAR-uh-NET, MER-   ˌmærəˈnet, ˌmer-

Marino
   pers. name, Italian   mah-RĒ-nō   mɑˈriːnoː

Marinus
   pope   muh-RĪ-nuhs   məˈrainəs

Mario
   1. pers. name   MER-ē-ō, MAR-   ˈmeriːoː, ˈmær-
   2. French   mahr-YŌ   mɑːrjoː
   3. Italian, Spanish   MAHR-yō   ˈmɑrjoː

Mário
   pers. name, Portuguese   MAHR-y$\overline{oo}$ ˈmɑːrjuː

Mariolatry
   veneration of the Virgin Mary   MER-ē-AHL-uh-trē, MAR-ē-, MĀ-rē-   ˌmeriːˈɑlətriˑ, ˌmæriː-, ˌmeːriː-

Mariology
   doctrine relating to the Virgin Mary   MER-ē-AHL-uh-jē, MAR-ē-, MĀ-rē-   ˌmeriːˈɑlədʒiˑ, ˌmæriː-, ˌmeːriː-

Marion
   pl. name, US; pers. name   MER-ē-uhn, MAR-   ˈmeriːən, ˈmær-

Mariposa
   county, CA   MAR-uh-PŌ-suh, -PŌ-zuh   ˌmærəˈpoːsə, -ˈpoːzə

Maris
   Roger, *US baseball player*   MAR-uhs   ˈmærəs

Marist
   Roman Catholic religious order   MAR-uhst, MER-uhst   ˈmærəst, ˈmerəst

Maritain
   Jacques, *French diplomat*   mah-rē-TE[n]   mɑːriːtē

Maritime Alps
   Alpine mtn. range   MAR-uh-TĪM   ˈmærəˌtaim

Marius
   1. Gaius, Roman general; pers. name   MER-ē-uhs, MAR-   ˈmeriːəs, ˈmær-
   2. Dutch   MAH-rē-ues   ˈmɑːriːys
   3. French   mahr-YUES   mɑːrjyːs
   4. German   MAHR-yus, MAH-rē-us   ˈmɑ[r]jus, ˈmariːus
   5. Norwegian   MAH-rē-us   ˈmɑriːus

Mariveles
   municipality, Philippines   MAHR-uh-VĀ-luhs   ˌmɑ[r]əˈveːləs

Mariya
   pers. name, Russian   MUHR-YĒ-(y)uh   ˌmərˈjiː(j)ə

Marjoribanks
   British family name   MAHRCH-BANGKS   ˈmɑ[r]tʃˌbæŋks

Key (col. 2): a: **fad** ā: **fade** ah: **father** ar: **marry** aw: **law** e: **fed** ē: **feed** er: **merry** i: **hid** ī: **hide** ō: **coat** $\overline{oo}$: **boot**
oi: **boy** ow: **now** u: **put** uh: **above** uhr: **bird** ch: **chop** ng: **ring** sh: **show** th: **thick** <u>th</u>: **this** zh: **measure**

Marjorie, Marjory
   pers. name   MAHR-juh-rē, MAHRJ-rē   'mɑʳdʒəri·, 'mɑʳdʒri·
Mark
   1. New Testament book; pers. name   MAHRK   'mɑʳk
   2. Dutch   MAHRK   'mɑrk
   3. Russian   MAHRK   'mɑːrk
Markos
   pers. name, Mod. Greek   MAHR-kaws   'mɑrkɔːs
Markova
   1. Alicia, English ballet dancer   mahr-KŌ-vuh   mɑʳ'koːvə
   2. Olga, Russian marathoner   MAHR-kuh-vuh   'mɑːʳkəvə
Markov process
   statistical procedure   MAHR-KAWF PRAHS-ES, PRŌ-SES   'mɑʳˌkɔːf ˌprɑsˌes, ˌproːˌses
Markowitz
   Harry M., *US economist (Nobel 1990)*   MAHRK-uh-WITS   'mɑʳkəˌwits
Marlboro, Marlborough
   pers. name; pl. name   MAHRL-BUHR-uh, MAHRL-BUH-ruh, MAHRL-bruh   'mɑʳlˌbər-ə, 'mɑʳlˌbə-rə, 'mɑʳlbrə
Marlene
   1. pers. name   mahr-LĒN   mɑʳ'liːn
   2. German   mahr-LÃ-nuh   mɑʳ'leːnə
Marley
   Bob, *Jamaican reggae musician*   MAHR-lē   'mɑʳli·
Marlin
   pers. name   MAHR-luhn   'mɑʳlən
Marlon
   pers. name   MAHR-luhn   'mɑʳlən
Marlow, Marlowe
   pers. name   MAHR-LŌ   'mɑʳˌloː
Marmaduke
   pers. name   MAHR-muh-D(Y)OOK   'mɑʳməˌd(j)uːk
Marmara
   Sea of, *Turkey*   MAHR-muh-ruh   'mɑʳmərə
Marmara Denizi
   sea, Turkey   MAHR-muh-RAH DEN-i-ZĒ   'mɑrməˌrɑ ˌdeni'ziː
Marmax
   suitor of Hippodamia   MAHR-MAKS   'mɑʳˌmæks
Marmoset
   monkey   MAHR-muh-SET, MAHR-muh-ZET   'mɑʳməˌset, 'mɑʳməˌzet
Marmot
   rodent   MAHR-muht   'mɑʳmət
Marne
   river, France   MAHRN   mɑːrn
Marnie
   pers. name   MAHR-nē   'mɑʳni·
Maronism
   Uniat sect   MAR-uh-NIZ-uhm, MER-   'mærəˌnizəm, 'mer-
Maronite
   religion   MAR-uh-NĪT   'mærəˌnɑit
Maroth
   Biblical name   MÃ-RAHTH, mah-RŌT   'meːˌrɑθ, mɑ'roːt
Marpessa
   beloved of Idas and Apollo   mahr-PES-uh   mɑʳ'pesə

Foreign Sounds: ue: *Fr.* **rue**, *Ger.* **füllen**   uh(r): *Fr.* **boeuf**, *Ger.* **Höhle**   kh: *Ger.* **ich**, *Scot.* **loch**   ğ: *Sp.* **amigo**   v̦: *Sp.* **hablar** hl: *Welsh* **Llanelli.**   CAPITALS: primary stress.   SMALL CAPS: secondary stress.   Ⓢ: U.S. pron.   Ⓔ: British pron.

Marquand
  John Philips, *US author*   mahr-KWAHND   mɑʳkwɑnd

Marques
  pers. name, Portuguese   MAHR-kēsh, -kēs   'mɑːrkiːʃ, -kiːs

Marquesan
  lang., Oceania   mahr-KĀ-zuhn, mahr-KĀ-suhn   mɑʳkeːzən, mɑʳkeːsən

Marquesas
  islands, Pacific   mahr-KĀ-zuhz, -zuhs, -suhz, -suhs   mɑʳkeːzəz, -zəs, -səz, -səs

Marquette
  1. county, MI, WI; univ., WI; city, MI   mahr-KET   mɑʳket
  2. Jacques, *French explorer*   mahr-KET   mɑːrket

Márquez
  pers. name, Spanish; see also García   MAHR-kās, MAHR-kāth   'mɑrkeːs, 'mɑrkeːθ
  Márquez

Marquis
  1. title   MAHR-kwuhs, mahr-KĒ   'mɑʳkwəs, mɑʳkiː
  2. French title   mahr-KĒ   mɑːrkiː

Marquis
  Don, *US journalist and humorist*   MAHR-kwis   'mɑʳkwis

Marquises, Îles [Marquesas]
  islands, Pacific   ēl mahr-KĒZ   iːl mɑːrkiːz

Marquita
  pers. name   mahr-KĒT-uh   mɑʳkiːtə

Marrakech, -kesh
  city, Morocco   MAR-uh-KESH, MAR-uh-KESH,   'mærə,keʃ, ,mærə'keʃ,
       muh-RAHK-ish   mə'rɑkiʃ

Marriott
  US food service and hotel co.   MAR-ē-uht, MAR-ē-AHT, MER-   'mæriːət, 'mæriː,ɑt, 'mer-

Marron
  chestnut   ma-RŌⁿ   mæ'rõː

Mars
  Roman god of war; planet   MAHRZ   'mɑʳz

Marsala
  seaport, Sicily; wine   mahr-SAHL-uh   mɑʳsɑlə

Marsalis
  Wynton *and* Branford, *US musicians*   mahr-SAL-uhs   mɑʳsæləs

Marseillaise, La
  see La Marseillaise

Marseille [Massilia]
  city, France   mahr-SE   mɑːrsej

Marseilles
  1. English form of Marseille   mahr-SĀ, mahr-SĀLZ   mɑʳseː, mɑʳseːlz
  2. city, IL   mahr-SĀLZ   mɑʳseːlz

Marsena
  Biblical name   mahr-SĒ-nuh, MAHR-suh-NAH   mɑʳsiːnə, ,mɑrsə'nɑ

Marshall
  George C., *US army officer,*   MAHR-shuhl   'mɑʳʃəl
    statesman (Nobel 1953); John, *US*
    chief justice; Thurgood, *US jurist;*
    Pacific islands; pers. name

Marshallese
  lang., Marshall Islands   MAHR-shuh-LĒZ, -LĒS   ,mɑʳʃə'liːz, -'liːs

Marsilio
  pers. name, Italian   mahr-SĒL-yō   mɑʳsiːljoː

Key (col. 2):   a: f**a**d   ā: f**a**de   ah: f**a**ther   ar: m**a**rry   aw: l**aw**   e: f**e**d   ē: f**ee**d   er: m**e**rry   i: h**i**d   ī: h**i**de   ō: c**oa**t   ōō: b**oo**t
oi: b**oy**   ow: n**ow**   u: p**u**t   uh: **a**bove   uhr: b**ir**d   ch: **ch**op   ng: ri**ng**   sh: **sh**ow   th: **th**ick   <u>th</u>: **th**is   zh: mea**s**ure

Marsupialia
  pouched animals   mahr-sōō-pē-Ā-lē-uh   mɑʳˌsuːpiːˈeːliːə
Marsyas
  mythical inventor of the double flute   MAHR-sē-uhs   ˈmɑʳsiːəs
Martaban
  town, Burma   MAHRT-uh-BAHN, MAHRT-uh-BAN   ˌmɑʳʈəˈbɑn, ˌmɑʳʈəˈbæn
Martell
  cognac brand   mahr-TEL   mɑʳˈtel
Martha
  pers. name   MAHR-thuh   ˈmɑʳθə
Marti
  pers. name   MAHRT-ē   ˈmɑʳʈiˑ
Martial
  Roman poet   MAHR-shuhl   ˈmɑʳʃəl
Martian
  pert. to Mars; *alien*   MAHR-shuhn   ˈmɑʳʃən
Martic
  Milan, *Krajina Serb political leader*   MAHR-tits   ˈmɑʳtits
Martim
  pers. name, Portuguese   muhr-TIⁿ, mahr-TIⁿ   mərˈtĩ, mɑːrˈt ̃ĩ
Martin
  1. A. J. P., English biochemist   MAHRT-n   ˈmɑʳtn̩
    (Nobel 1952); pers. name
  2. Danish, Norwegian   MAHR-tēn   ˈmartiːn
  3. Dutch   MAHR-tuhn, mahr-TĪN   ˈmartən, mɑrˈtain
  4. Finnish, Swedish   MAHR-tin   ˈmaːrtin
  5. French   mahr-TEⁿ   mɑːrtẽ
  6. German   MAHR-tēn   ˈmɑʳtiːn
Martín
  pers. name, Spanish   mahr-TĒN   mɑrˈtiːn
Martina
  pers. name   mahr-TĒ-nuh   mɑʳˈtiːnə
Martin du Gard
  Roger, *French author (Nobel 1937)*   mahr-TEⁿ due GAHR   mɑːrtẽ dyː gɑːr
Martine
  pers. name, French   mahr-TĒN   mɑːrtiːn
Martinez
  city, CA   mahr-TĒ-nuhs, -nuhz   mɑʳˈtiːnəs, -nəz
Martínez
  pers. name, Spanish   mahr-TĒ-nās, -nāth   mɑrˈtiːneːs, -neːθ
Martini
  Louis M., *winery, CA; alcoholic*   mahr-TĒ-nē   mɑʳˈtiːniˑ
    drink
Martiniquais
  pert. to Martinique   MAHR-TĒ-ni-KE   ˌmɑʳˌtiːniˈke
Martiniquaise
  fem. of Martiniquais   MAHR-TĒ-ni-KEZ   ˌmɑʳˌtiːniˈkez
Martinique
  island, West Indies   MAHRT-n-ĒK   ˌmɑʳtn̩ˈiːk
Martinmas
  November 11 festival for St. Martin   MAHRT-n-muhs   ˈmɑʳtn̩məs
Martins
  pers. name, Portuguese   muhr-TIⁿS, mahr-TIⁿS   mərˈtĩs, mɑːrˈt ̃ĩs
Martinson
  Harry, *Swedish author (Nobel 1974)*   MAHR-tēn-sawn   ˈmɑʳtiːnsɔːn

---

Foreign Sounds: ue: *Fr.* **rue**, *Ger.* **füllen**   uh(r): *Fr.* **boeuf**, *Ger.* **Höhle**   <u>kh</u>: *Ger.* i**ch**, *Scot.* lo**ch**   ḡ: *Sp.* ami**g**o   <u>v</u>: *Sp.* ha**b**lar
hl: *Welsh* **Ll**anelli.   CAPITALS: primary stress.   SMALL CAPS: secondary stress.   Ⓢ: U.S. pron.   Ⓔ: British pron.

Martinus
1. pers. name	mahr-TĪ-nuhs	mɑrˈtɑinəs
2. Dutch	mahr-TĒ-nues	mɑrˈtiːnys

Marty
pers. name	MAHRT-ē	ˈmɑrt̬iˑ

Marvel
tdmk for comic books	MAHR-vuhl	ˈmɑrvəl

Marvell
Andrew, *English poet*	MAHR-vuhl	ˈmɑrvəl

Marvin
pers. name	MAHR-vuhn	ˈmɑrvən

Marwari [Rajasthani]
lang., India, Pakistan	mahr-WAHR-ē	mɑrˈwariˑ

Marx
Karl, *German political and economic theorist;* Groucho, Harpo, Chico, Zeppo, *US comedians*	MAHRKS	ˈmɑrks

Marxism
philosophy of Karl Marx	MAHRK-sɪz-uhm	ˈmɑrkˌsizəm

Marxist
pert. to Marx	MAHRK-suhst, MAHRK-sist	ˈmɑrksəst, ˈmɑrksist

Mary
pers. name	MER-ē, MAR-ē, MÃ-rē	ˈmeriˑ, ˈmæriˑ, ˈmeːriˑ

Maryland
state, US	MER-uh-luhnd	ˈmerələnd

Marylebone
1. district, London	MAR-uh-luh-buhn, MAR-uh-luh-BŌN, MAR-uh-buhn, MAHR-luh-buhn	ˈmærələbən, ˈmærələˌboːn, ˈmærəbən, ˈmɑrləbən
2. St., parish church, London	MAR-uh-luh-buhn	ˈmærələbən

Marylhurst
College for Lifelong Learning	MAR-uhl-HUHRST, MER-uhl-	ˈmærəlˌhərst, ˈmerəl-

Marymount Palos Verdes
College, *CA*	MAR-ē-MOWNT PAL-uhs VUHRD-ēz, MER-ē-, MÃ-rē-	ˈmæriˑˌmɑunt ˌpæləs ˈvərdiːz, ˈmeriˑ-, ˈmeːriˑ-

Masa
lang., Chad, Cameroon	MAHS-uh	ˈmɑsə

Masada
mountaintop fortress in Israel	muh-SAHD-uh	məˈsɑdə

Masai, Maasai
lang., people, Tanzania, Kenya	muh-SĪ	məˈsɑi

Masaryk
Tomáš, *president, Czechoslovakia*	MAH-sah-rik	ˈmɑːsɑːrik

Masa's
restaurant, San Francisco, CA	MAHS-uhz, MAS-uhz	ˈmɑsəz, ˈmæsəz

Masayoshi
pers. name, Japanese	mah-sah-yō-shē	mɑsɑjoːʃiː

Masbate
island, prov, Philippines	mahs-BAHT-ē	mɑsˈbɑt̬iˑ

Mascagni
Pietro, *Italian composer*	mahs-KAHN-yē	mɑsˈkɑnjiˑ

Mas Canosa
Jorge, *Cuban activist*	mahs kah-NŌ-sah	mɑs kɑˈnoːsɑ

Mascara
dept, Algeria	MAS-kuh-ruh	ˈmæskərə

Key (col. 2):   a: fad   ā: fade   ah: father   ar: marry   aw: law   e: fed   ē: feed   er: merry   i: hid   ī: hide   ō: coat   ōō: boot
oi: boy   ow: now   u: put   uh: above   uhr: bird   ch: chop   ng: ring   sh: show   th: thick   <u>th</u>: this   zh: measure

Mascerene
islands, Indian Ocean MAS-kuh-RĒN ˌmæskəˈriːn

Maschil, Maskil
designation for certain Biblical MAHS-KĒL, mahs-KĒL ˈmɑsˌkiːl, mɑsˈkiːl
psalms

Mascoutah
city, IL mas-K͞OOT-uh mæsˈkuːʈə

Masefield
John, English poet MĀS-FĒLD, MĀZ-FĒLD ˈmeːsˌfiːld, ˈmeːzˌfiːld

Masekela
Hugh, South African musician MAS-uh-KĀ-luh ˌmæsəˈkeːlə

Maserati
Italian car marque MAHZ-uh-RAHT-ē, MAZ-uh-RAT-ē ˌmɑzəˈrɑʈiˑ, ˌmæzəˈræʈiˑ

Maseru
town, Lesotho MAHZ-uh-R͞OO ˈmɑzəˌruː

Mash
Biblical name MASH, MAHSH ˈmæʃ, ˈmɑʃ

Mashal
Biblical name MĀ-SHAL, mah-SHAHL ˈmeːˌʃæl, mɑˈʃɑl

Mashantucket Pequot
N. American people MASH-uhn-TUHK-uht PĒ-KWAHT ˌmæʃənˈtəkət ˈpiːˌkwɑt

Masharbrum, Masherbrum
peak, Himalayas MUHSH-uhr-BRUM ˈməʃərˌbrum

Mashhad
city, Iran muh-SHAD məˈʃæd

Masinissa
king of Numidia MAS-uh-NIS-uh ˌmæsəˈnisə

Maso
pers. name, Italian MAHZ-ō ˈmɑzoː

Mason
pers. name MĀS-n ˈmeːsn̩

Mason-Dixon line
boundary between PA and MD MĀS-n-DIK-suhn LĪN ˌmeːsn̩ˈdiksən ˌlɑin

Masonic
pert. to the Freemasons muh-SAHN-ik məˈsɑnik

Masonite
tdmk for a hardboard MĀS-n-ĪT ˈmeːsn̩ˌɑit

Masora, Masorah
critical notes on Hebrew Old muh-SŌR-uh, muh-SAWR-uh məˈsoːrə, məˈsɔːrə
Testament

Masorete, Massorete
one versed in the Masora MAS-uh-RĒT ˈmæsəˌriːt

Masotho
plural of Basotho mah-SŌT-ō, mah-S͞OOT-͞oo mɑˈsoːʈoː, mɑˈsuːʈuː

Masqat
city, Oman MUHS-KAHT ˈməsˌkɑt

Masrekah
Biblical name MAS-ruh-kuh, mas-RĒ-kuh, ˈmæsrəkə, mæsˈriːkə,
MAHS-re-KAH ˌmɑsreˈkɑ

Mass
Christian liturgy MAS ˈmæs

Massa, Massah
Biblical name MAS-uh, mah-SAH ˈmæsə, mɑˈsɑ

Massac
county, IL MAS-AK, MAS-uhk ˈmæsˌæk, ˈmæsək

Massachuset [Massachusetts]

  N. American people   MAS-uh-CH$\overline{OO}$-suht, -zuht, *esp. in SE*   ˌmæsə'tʃuːsət, -zət, *esp. in*
                                             US -TY$\overline{OO}$-   SE US -'tjuː-

Massachusetts

  state, US; N. American people   MAS-uh-CH$\overline{OO}$-suhts,   ˌmæsə'tʃuːsəts,
                                           MAS-uh-CH$\overline{OO}$-zuhts, *esp. in SE US*   ˌmæsə'tʃuːzəts, *esp. in SE*
                                         MAS-uh-TY$\overline{OO}$-suhts   US ˌmæsə'tjuːsəts

Massapequa

  town, NY   MAS-uh-P$\overline{E}$-kwuh   ˌmæsə'piːkwə

Massasoit

  Community College, lake, MA; N.   MAS-uh-SOI-it, MAS-uh-SOIT,   ˌmæsə'sɔi-it, 'mæsəˌsɔit,
    American people   MAS-uh-SOIT   ˌmæsə'sɔit

Massenet

  Jules, French composer   mah-SNE, ⑤ MAS-n-$\overline{A}$, mas-N$\overline{A}$ maːsne, ⑤ ˌmæsn̩'eː,
                                                                      mæs'neː

Massif Central

  ancient rocks, France   mah-S$\overline{E}$F sah^n-TRAHL   maːsiːf sɑ̃traːl

Massilia

  ancient name of Marseilles   muh-SIL-ē-uh   mə'siliːə

Massillon

  town, OH   MAS-uh-luhn, MAS-uh-LAHN   'mæsələn, 'mæsəˌlɑn

Massine

  Léonide, Russian ballet dancer/   MUHS-Y$\overline{E}$N   ˌməs'jiːn
    choreographer

Masson, Paul

  winery, CA   PAWL muh-SAHN, ma-SAHN   ˌpɔːl mə'sɑn, mæ'sɑn

Massorete

  see Masorete

Mastaba

  Egyptian tomb   MAS-tuh-buh   'mæstəbə

MasterCard

  tdmk for a bank credit card   MAS-tuhr-KAHRD, MAH-stuh-KAHD   'mæstə^{r}ˌkɑ^{r}d, 'mɑːstəˌkɑːd

Mastrantonio

  Mary Elizabeth, US actress   MAHS-trahn-T$\overline{O}$-nē-ō, -T$\overline{O}$N-yō   ˌmɑstrɑn'toːniːˌoː, -'toːnjoː

Mastroianni

  Marcello, Italian actor   MAHS-troi-AHN-ē   ˌmɑstrɔi'ɑniˑ

Masur

  Kurt, German conductor   MAHZ-UR, mah-ZUR   'mɑzˌu^r, mɑ'zu^r

Masvingo [Fort Victoria, Nyanda]

  city, Zimbabwe   mahz-VING-gō   mɑz'viŋgoː

Matabele

  Bantu people, lang.   MAT-uh-B$\overline{A}$-lā, MAT-uh-B$\overline{E}$-lē   ˌmætə'beːleː, ˌmætə'biːliˑ

Mataco

  S. American people   muh-TAHK-ō   mə'tɑkoː

Matagalpa

  dept, Nicaragua   maht-ah-$\overline{G}$AHL-pah,   mɑtɑ'ɣɑlpɑ, ⑤ ˌmæţə'gælpə
                                     ⑤ MAT-uh-GAL-puh

Matagorda

  county, TX   MAT-uh-GAWRD-uh   ˌmæţə'gɔː^{r}də

Mata Hari

  cognomen of Margaretha Zelle   MAHT-uh HAHR-ē, MAT-uh HAR-ē   ˌmɑţə 'hɑriˑ, ˌmæţə 'hæriˑ
    MacLeod, Dutch dancer & spy

Matamoros

  town, Mexico   MAT-uh-M$\overline{O}$R-uhs, MAT-uh-MAWR-uhs ˌmæţə'moːrəs, ˌmæţə'mɔːrəs

---

Key (col. 2): a: fad ā: fade ah: father ar: marry aw: law e: fed ē: feed er: merry i: hid ī: hide ō: coat ōō: boot
oi: boy ow: now u: put uh: above uhr: bird ch: chop ng: ring sh: show th: thick <u>th</u>: this zh: measure

Matane
  county, Quebec   muh-TAN   mə'tæn

Matanuska-Susitna
  division, AK   MAT-uh-NŌŌ-skuh-su-SIT-nuh   ˌmæṭə'nuːskəsu'sitnə

Matanzas
  prov, Cuba   muh-TAN-zuhs   mə'tænzəs

Matapan
  cape, Greece   MAT-uh-PAN   'mæṭəˌpæn

Matawan
  borough, NJ   MAT-uh-WAHN   'mæṭəˌwɑn

Maté
  plant   MAH-TĀ   'mɑˌteː

Matecumbe, Upper
  key, FL   MAT-uh-KUHM-bē   ˌmæṭə'kəmbi·

Mateo
  pers. name, Spanish   mah-TĀ-ō   mɑ'teːoː

Mater Dei
  College, NY   MAHT-uhr DĀ-ē   'mɑṭəʳ 'deːiː

Mathäus
  pers. name, German   mah-TE-us   mɑ'teus

Mather
  Richard, Increase, Cotton, *US*   MA<u>TH</u>-uhr   'mæðəʳ
  clergymen; pers. name

Matheson
  Scott M., *US lawyer, politician*   MATH-uh-suhn   'mæθəsən

Mathew
  pers. name   MATH-yōō   'mæθjuː

Mathewson
  Christy, *US baseball player*   MATH-(y)uh-suhn   'mæθ(j)əsən

Mathias
  1. pers. name   muh-THĪ-uhs   mə'θɑiəs
  2. German, Norwegian   mah-TĒ-ahs   mɑ'tiːɑs
  3. Portuguese   muh-TĒ-uhsh, mah-TĒ-ahs   mə'tiːəʃ, mɑ'tiːɑːs
  4. French   mah-TYAHS   mɑːtjɑːs

Mathieu
  pers. name, French   mah-TYUH(R)   mɑːtjœː

Mathilde
  1. pers. name, French   mah-TĒLD   mɑːtiːld
  2. German   mah-TIL-duh   mɑ'tildə
  3. Russian   muh-TIL-duh   mə'ṭildə

Mathis
  Johnny, *US singer*   MATH-uhs   'mæθəs

Mathusala [Methuselah]
  Biblical name   muh-THŌŌ-suh-luh   mə'θuːsələ

Matilda
  1. pers. name   muh-TIL-duh   mə'tildə
  2. Italian   mah-TĒL-dah   mɑ'tiːldɑ

Matilde
  pers. name, French   mah-TĒLD   mɑːtiːld

Matisse
  Henri, *French artist*   mah-TĒS   mɑːtiːs

Mato Grosso
  plateau, state, Brazil   MAT-uh GRŌ-sō   ˌmæṭə 'groːsoː

Matosinhos, -zinhos
  parish, Portugal   MAHT-uh-ZĒN-yōōsh   ˌmɑːṭə'ziːnjuːʃ

Foreign Sounds: ue: *Fr.* **rue**, *Ger.* **füllen**   uh(r): *Fr.* **boeuf**, *Ger.* **Höhle**   <u>kh</u>: *Ger.* **ich**, *Scot.* **loch**   ğ: *Sp.* **amigo**   <u>v</u>: *Sp.* **hablar**
hl: *Welsh* **Llanelli**.   CAPITALS: primary stress.   SMALL CAPS: secondary stress.   Ⓢ: U.S. pron.   Ⓔ: British pron.

Matreyevna
   patronym, Russian   MUH-TRĀ-yev-nuh   ˌməˈtreːjevnə

Matred
   Biblical name   MĀ-TRED, MĀ-truhd, mah-TRED   ˈmeːˌtred, ˈmeːtrəd, mɑˈtred

Matri
   Biblical name   MĀ-TRĪ, maht-RĒ   ˈmeːˌtrɑi, mɑtˈriː

Matrūh
   city, Egypt   muh-TR͞OO, MA-tr͞oo   məˈtruː, ˈmætruː

Ma-tsu
   island, China   MAHT-S͞OO   ˈmɑtˈsuː

Matsuo [Basho]
   Munefusa, *Japanese poet*   maht-s͞oo-ō   mɑtsuːoː

Matsuoka
   Yōsuke, *Japanese statesman*   maht-su-ō-kah   mɑtsuoːkɑ

Matsushima
   Satoshi, *US astronomer, educator*   mat-S͞OO-shim-uh, MAT-s͞oo-SHĒ-muh   mætˈsuːʃimə, ˌmætsuːˈʃiːmə

Matsushita
   Japanese corp.   maht-su-shi-tah, Ⓢ MAT-s͞oo-SHĒT-uh   mɑtsuʃitɑ, Ⓢ ˌmætsuˈʃiːtə

Matswana
   plural of Tswana or Batswana   maht-SWAHN-uh   mɑtˈswɑnə

Matt
   pers. name   MAT   ˈmæt

Mattamuskeet Lake
   lake, NC   MAT-uh-muh-SKĒT LĀK   ˌmæṭəməˈskiːt ˈleːk

Mattan
   Biblical name   MAT-n, mah-TAHN   ˈmætn̩, mɑˈtɑn

Mattaniah
   Biblical name   MAT-n-Ī-uh, MAH-tahn-YAH   ˌmætn̩ˈɑiə, ˌmɑtɑnˈjɑ

Mattapony
   N. American people   MAT-uh-PŌ-nē, MAT-uh-PŌ-nē   ˈmæṭəˌpoːniˑ, ˌmæṭəˈpoːniˑ

Mattatha
   Biblical name   MAT-uh-thuh, MAH-tah-TAH   ˈmæṭəθə, ˌmɑtɑˈtɑ

Mattatuck
   Community College, *CT*   MAT-uh-TUHK   ˈmæṭəˌtək

Mattawamkeag
   river, ME   MAT-uh-WAHM-KEG   ˌmæṭəˈwɑmˌkeg

Mattel
   US toy co.   muh-TEL   məˈtel

Mattenai
   Biblical name   MAT-n-Ī, MAT-n-Ā, mah-tuh-NĪ   ˈmætn̩ˌɑi, ˌmætn̩ˈeː, mɑtəˈnɑi

Matteo
   pers. name, Italian   maht-TE-ō   mɑtˈteoː

Matterhorn
   mtn., Switzerland, Italy   MAT-uhr-HAWRN, MAHT-   ˈmæṭərˌhɔːʳn, ˈmɑṭ-

Matterhorn Peak
   mtn., CO   MAT-uhr-HAWRN PĒK   ˌmæṭərˌhɔːʳn ˈpiːk

Matteson
   village, IL   MAT-suhn   ˈmætsən

Matthan
   Biblical name   MAT-THAN, MA-THAN   ˈmætˌθæn, ˈmæˌθæn

Matthat
   Biblical name   MAT-THAT, MA-THAT   ˈmætˌθæt, ˈmæˌθæt

Matthau
   Walter, *US actor*   MATH-OW   ˈmæθˌɑu

Key (col. 2): a: **fad** ā: **fade** ah: **father** ar: **marry** aw: **law** e: **fed** ē: **feed** er: **merry** i: **hid** ī: **hide** ō: **coat** ō͞o: **boot**
oi: **boy** ow: **now** u: **put** uh: **above** uhr: **bird** ch: **chop** ng: **ring** sh: **show** th: **thick** th̲: **this** zh: **measure**

Matthäus
  pers. name, Dutch, German   mah-TE-us   mɑ'teus
Matthes
  François Emile, *US geologist*   MAHT-uhs, MAT-uhs   'mɑʈəs, 'mæʈəs
Matthew
  New Testament book; pers. name   MATH-y͞oo   'mæθjuː
Matthias
  1. pers. name   muh-THĪ-uhs   mə'θɑiəs
  2. Finnish   mah-TĒ-ahs   mɑ'tiːɑːs
  3. German, Norwegian   mah-TĒ-ahs   mɑ'tiːɑs
Matthías
  pers. name, Icelandic   MAHT-TĒ-ahs   'mɑt,tiːɑs
Mattie
  pers. name   MAT-ē   'mæʈiˑ
Mattingly
  Mack F., *US politician;* Don,   MAT-ing-lē   'mæʈiŋliˑ
    baseball player
Mattithiah
  Biblical name   MAT-uh-THĪ-uh, MAH-tit-YAH   ˌmæʈə'θɑiə, ˌmɑtit'jɑ
Mattoon
  city, IL   muh-T͞OON   mə'tuːn
Mauchline
  town, Scotland   MAWK-luhn   'mɔːklən
Maud, Maude
  pers. name   MAWD   'mɔːd
Maugham
  Somerset, *English author*   MAWM   'mɔːm
Maui
  island, county, HI   MOW-ē   'mɑuiˑ
Mauldin
  Bill, *US cartoonist*   MAWL-duhn   'mɔːldən
Mau Mau
  Kikuyu rebels in Kenya   MOW MOW   'mɑu ˌmɑu
Maumee
  city, OH; river, IN, OH   maw-MĒ, MAW-mē   mɔː'miː, 'mɔːmiˑ
Mauna Kea
  extinct volcano, HI   MOW-nuh KĀ-uh, MAW-nuh   ˌmɑunə 'keːə, ˌmɔːnə
Mauna Loa
  volcano, HI   MOW-nuh LŌ-uh, MAW-nuh   ˌmɑunə 'loːə, ˌmɔːnə
Maundy Thursday
  Christian holy day   MAWN-dē THUHRZ-dē, THUHRZ-dā   'mɔːndiˑ 'θəʳzdiˑ, 'θəʳzdeː
Maupassant
  Guy de, *French writer*   mō-pah-SAHⁿ   moːpɑːsɑ̃
Maupertuis
  Pierre Louis Moreau de, *French*   mō-per-TWĒ   moːpertwiː
    mathematician
Maur
  pers. name   MAWR   'mɔːʳ
Maureen
  pers. name   maw-RĒN, muh-RĒN   mɔː'riːn, mə'riːn
Mauretania
  ancient country, Africa   MAWR-uh-TĀ-nē-uh, MAHR-, -TĀN-yuh   ˌmɔːrə'teːniːə, ˌmɑr-, -'teːnjə
Mauriac
  François, *French author (Nobel*   mawr-YAHK   mɔːrjɑːk
    1952)

Foreign Sounds: ue: *Fr.* **rue**, *Ger.* **füllen**   uh(r): *Fr.* **boeuf**, *Ger.* **Höhle**   kh: *Ger.* **ich**, *Scot.* **loch**   ḡ: *Sp.* **amigo**   v: *Sp.* **hablar**
hl: *Welsh* **Llanelli**.   CAPITALS: primary stress.   SMALL CAPS: secondary stress.   Ⓢ: U.S. pron.   Ⓔ: British pron.

Maurice

　1. pers. name　　　　　　　MAWR-uhs, MAHR-uhs, maw-RĒS　　'mɔːrəs, 'mɑrəs, mɔː'riːs

　2. French　　　　　　　　　maw-RĒS　　　　　　　　　　　mɔːriːs

Mauritania

　republic, Africa　　　　　MAWR-uh-TĀ-nē-uh, MAHR-, -nyuh　ˌmɔːrə'teːniːə, ˌmɑr-, -njə

Mauritanian

　pert. to Mauritania　　　MAWR-uh-TĀ-nē-uhn, MAHR-, -nyuhn　ˌmɔːrə'teːniːən, ˌmɑr-, -njən

Mauritian

　pert. to Mauritius　　　maw-RISH-(ē-)uhn　　　　　　mɔː'riʃ(iː)ən

Mauritius

　island, Indian Ocean　　maw-RISH-(ē-)uhs　　　　　　mɔː'riʃ(iː)əs

Maurits

　pers. name, Dutch　　　MOW-rits　　　　　　　　　　'mɑurits

Mauritz

　pers. name, Dutch, Norwegian,　MOW-rits　　　　　　　'mɑurits
　Swedish

Maurizio

　pers. name, Italian　　　mow-RĒT-syō　　　　　　　mɑu'riːtsjoː

Maurois

　André, *pseudonym of* Émile Herzog　mawr-WAH　　　　mɔːrwɑ

Mauser

　German gun　　　　　MOW-zuhr　　　　　　　　　'mɑuzər

Mausoleum

　tomb of Mausolus at Halicarnassus　MAW-suh-LĒ-uhm, MAW-zuh-　ˌmɔːsə'liːəm, ˌmɔːzə-

Mausolus

　Persian satrap of Caria　maw-SŌ-luhs　　　　　　　mɔː'soːləs

Mauss

　Marcel, *French sociologist and*　MŌS　　　　　　　　　'moːs
　anthropologist

Mavrokordátos

　Aléxandros, Prince, *Greek*　MAHV-rō-kawr-THAH-taws　ˌmɑvroːkɔːr'ðɑtɔːs
　politician and patriot

Mawlid al-Nabi

　Islamic festival　　　MOW-lid ahl-NAHB-ē, al-　　'mɑulid ɑl'nɑbiˑ, æl-

Max

　1. pers. name　　　　MAKS　　　　　　　　　　　'mæks

　2. Dutch, German　　MAHKS　　　　　　　　　　'mɑks

　3. French　　　　　　MAHKS　　　　　　　　　　mɑːks

Maxim

　pers. name, Russian　MUHK-SYĒM　　　　　　　ˌmək'sjiːm

Maxime

　1. pers. name　　　　mak-SĒM　　　　　　　　　mæk'siːm

　2. French　　　　　　mahk-SĒM　　　　　　　　mɑːksiːm

Maximianus

　Roman emperor　　　MAK-SIM-ē-Ā-nuhs　　　ˌmækˌsimiː'eːnəs

Maximilian

　1. pers. name　　　　MAK-suh-MIL-yuhn　　　ˌmæksə'miljən

　2. German　　　　　MAHK-sē-MĒL-yahn, -MĒ-lē-ahn　ˌmɑksiː'miːljɑn, -'miːliːɑn

　3. Norwegian　　　　MAHK-sē-MĒ-lē-AHN　　ˌmɑksiːˌmiːliˑ'ɑn

　4. Polish　　　　　　MAHK-si-MĒL-yahn　　　ˌmɑːksi'miːljɑːn

Maximilien

　pers. name　　　　　mahk-sē-mēl-YEⁿ　　　mɑːksiːmiːljẽ

Maximinus

　name, Roman emperors　MAK-suh-MĒ-nuhs　　ˌmæksə'miːnəs

Key (col. 2): 　a: fad　ā: fade　ah: father　ar: marry　aw: law　e: fed　ē: feed　er: merry　i: hid　ī: hide　ō: coat　ōō: boot
oi: boy　ow: now　u: put　uh: above　uhr: bird　ch: chop　ng: ring　sh: show　th: thick　th: this　zh: measure

Maximus		
pers. name, Latin	MAK-suh-muhs	'mæksəməs
Maxine		
pers. name	mak-SĒN	mæk'siːn
Maxwell		
pers. name	MAK-SWEL, MAK-swuhl	'mækˌswel, 'mækswəl
May		
month; pers. name	MĀ	'meː
Mayacamas		
winery, CA	MĪ-(y)uh-KAHM-uhs	ˌmɑi(j)ə'kɑməs
Mayaguana		
island, British Virgin Islands	MĀ-uh-GWAHN-uh	ˌmeːə'gwɑnə
Mayagüez		
city, Puerto Rico	mī-uh-G̃WĀS	mɑiə'ɣweːs
Mayakovsky		
Vladimir, *writer*	MAH-yuh-KAWF-skē, MĪ-uh-	ˌmɑjə'kɔːfskiˑ, ˌmɑiə-
Mayall		
John, *English blues musician*	MĀ-AWL	'meːˌɔːl
Mayan		
pert. to the Maya	MĪ-(y)uhn	'mɑi(j)ən
Maya [Yucatec]		
lang., people, Guatemala, Mexico, British Honduras; pers. name	MĪ-(y)uh	'mɑi(j)ə
Mayberry		
pers. name	MĀ-BER-ē	'meːˌberiˑ
Mayenne		
dept & river, France	mah-YEN	mɑːjen
Mayer		
1. Maria Goeppert, *German-born US physicist (Nobel 1963)*	MĪ(-uh)r	'mɑi(ə)ʳ
2. pers. name	MĪ-uhr, MĀ-uhr	'mɑiəʳ, 'meːəʳ
3. German	MĪ-uhr	'mɑiəʳ
Mayet [Ma'at]		
Egyptian goddess of truth and justice	MAH-yuht, MĪ-uht	'mɑjət, 'mɑiət
Mayfair		
district, London, England	MĀ-FAR, MĀ-FER	'meːˌfæʳ, 'meːˌfeʳ
Mayflower		
Pilgrim ship	MĀ-FLOW(-uh)r	'meːˌflɑu(ə)ʳ
Mayim		
pers. name	MĪ-im	'mɑiim
Maynard		
pers. name	MĀ-nuhrd, MĀ-NAHRD	'meːnəʳd, 'meːˌnɑʳd
Mayo		
1. Charles H., William J., *US surgeons; clinic, MN*	MĀ-ō	'meːoː
2. county, Irish Republic	MĀ-ō, *in Ireland also* mā-Ō	'meːoː, *in Ireland also* meː'oː
3. mtn., Chile; river, Mexico	MĪ-ō	'mɑioː
Mayodan		
town, NC	mā-Ō-DAN	meː'oːˌdæn
Mayon		
volcano, Philippines	mah-YŌN	mɑ'joːn
Mayonnaise		
condiment	MĀ-uh-NĀZ, MĀ-uh-NĀZ	'meːəˌneːz, ˌmeːə'neːz

Foreign Sounds: ue: *Fr.* **rue**, *Ger.* **füllen** uh(r): *Fr.* **boeuf**, *Ger.* **Höhle** k̲h̲: *Ger.* **ich**, *Scot.* **loch** g̃: *Sp.* **amigo** v̲: *Sp.* **hablar** hl: *Welsh* **Llanelli**. CAPITALS: primary stress. SMALL CAPS: secondary stress. [$]: U.S. pron. [£]: British pron.

Mayotte
　island, Indian Ocean　　　mah-YAWT　　　　　　　mɑˈjɔːt

Mays
　Willie, *US baseball player*　　MĀZ　　　　　　　　ˈmeːz

Mazahua
　lang., people, Mexico　　muh-ZAH-wuh　　　　　məˈzɑwə

Mazarin
　Jules, *French political leader*　mah-zah-REⁿ　　　　　mɑːzɑːrē

Mazatec
　lang., people, Mexico　　MAHZ-uh-TEK, MAHZ-uh-TEK　ˈmɑzəˌtek, ˌmɑzəˈtek

Mazateco [Mazatec]
　lang., people, Mexico　　MAHZ-uh-TĀ-kō　　　　ˌmɑzəˈteːkoː

Mazatlán
　seaport, Mexico　　　　MAHZ-uh-TLAHN　　　　ˌmɑzəˈtlɑn

Mazda
　Japanese car co.　　　　MAHZ-duh　　　　　　ˈmɑzdə

Mazda, Ahura
　see Ahura Mazda

Mazdaism
　religion　　　　　　MAZ-duh-IZ-uhm, MAHZ-　ˈmæzdəˌizəm, ˈmɑz-

Mazowiecki
　Tadeusz, *Polish politician*　MAHZ-uhv-YET-skē　　　ˌmɑzəvˈjetskiˑ

Mazurka
　dance　　　　　　muh-ZUHR-kuh, muh-ZUR-kuh　məˈzəʳkə, məˈzuʳkə

Mazzaroth
　Biblical name　　　　MAZ-uh-RAHTH, mah-zah-RŌT　ˈmæzəˌrɑθ, mɑzɑˈroːt

Mazzini
　Giuseppe, *Italian philosopher*　maht-SĒ-nē, mahd-ZĒ-nē　mɑtˈsiːniˑ, mɑdˈziːniˑ

Ma'at
　Egyptian goddess of truth and justice　MAH-AHT　　ˈmɑˌɑt

Mba
　lang., Congo　　　　m-BAH, uhm-BAH, em-BAH　m̩ˈbɑ, əmˈbɑ, emˈbɑ

Mbaama
　lang., Africa　　　　m-BAHM-uh, uhm-BAHM-uh,　m̩ˈbɑmə, əmˈbɑmə,
　　　　　　　　　em-BAHM-uh　　　　　emˈbɑmə

Mbabane
　town, Swaziland　　　m-buh-BAHN, EM-buh-BAHN　m̩bəˈbɑn, ˌembəˈbɑn

Mbai
　lang., Chad, Central African Republic　m-BĪ, uhm-BĪ, em-BĪ　m̩ˈbɑi, əmˈbɑi, emˈbɑi

Mbati
　lang., Africa　　　　m-BAHT-ē, uhm-BAHT-ē, em-BAHT-ē　m̩ˈbɑtiˑ, əmˈbɑtiˑ, emˈbɑtiˑ

Mbaya
　S. American people　　m-buh-YAH, EM-buh-YAH　m̩bəˈjɑ, ˌembəˈjɑ

Mbete
　lang., Africa　　　　m-BĀT-ā, uhm-BĀT-ā, em-BĀT-ā　m̩ˈbeˑt̬eː, əmˈbeˑt̬eː,
　　　　　　　　　　　　　　　　　　　emˈbeˑt̬eː

Mbimu
　lang., Africa　　　　m-BĒ-mōō, uhm-BĒ-mōō, em-BĒ-mōō　m̩ˈbiːmuː, əmˈbiːmuː,
　　　　　　　　　　　　　　　　　　emˈbiːmuː

Mbo
　lang., Africa　　　　m-BŌ, uhm-BŌ, em-BŌ　m̩ˈboː, əmˈboː, emˈboː

Mbole
　lang., Africa　　　　m-BŌ-lā, uhm-BŌ-lā, em-BŌ-lā　m̩ˈboːleː, əmˈboːleː,
　　　　　　　　　　　　　　　　　　emˈboːleː

Key (col. 2):　a: fad　ā: fade　ah: father　ar: marry　aw: law　e: fed　ē: feed　er: merry　i: hid　ī: hide　ō: coat　ōō: boot
oi: boy　ow: now　u: put　uh: above　uhr: bird　ch: chop　ng: ring　sh: show　th: thick　th̲: this　zh: measure

Mboya
Tom, *Kenyan political leader* — m-BOI-uh, uhm-BOI-uh, em-BOI-uh — m̩'bɔiə, əm'bɔiə, em'bɔiə

Mbunda
lang., Africa — m-BOON-duh, uhm-BOON-duh, em-BOON-duh — m̩'buˑndə, əm'buˑndə, em'buˑndə

Mbundu [Ovimbundu]
lang., people, Africa — m-BOON-doo, uhm-BOON-doo, em-BOON-doo — m̩'buˑnduː, əm'buˑnduː, em'buˑnduː

Mbwera
lang., Africa — m-BWER-uh, uhm-BWER-uh, em-BWER-uh — m̩'bwerə, əm'bwerə, em'bwerə

Mc-
see also Mac-

McAdam
John Loudon, *British engineer* — muh-KAD-uhm — mə'kædəm

McAdoo
Bob, *basketball player* — MAK-uh-DOO — 'mækə,duː

McCaffrey
Anne, *US author* — muh-KAF-rē — mə'kæfriˑ

McCallum
David, *British actor* — muh-KAL-uhm — mə'kæləm

McCamey
city, TX — muh-KĀ-mē — mə'keːmiˑ

McCarthy
Eugene, *US writer, politician;* — muh-KAHR-thē, muh-KAHRT-ē — mə'kɑʳθiˑ, mə'kɑʳʈiˑ
Joseph, *US politician*

McCarthyism
political intolerance — muh-KAHR-thē-ɪZ-uhm, muh-KAHRT-ē-ɪZ-uhm — mə'kɑʳθiː,izəm, mə'kɑʳʈiː,izəm

McCartney
Paul, *British musician, songwriter* — muh-KAHRT-nē — mə'kɑʳtniˑ

McCauley
Mary, *American Revolutionary* — muh-KAW-lē — mə'kɔːliˑ
heroine, known as Molly Pitcher

McClanahan
Rue, *US actress* — muh-KLAN-uh-HAN — mə'klænə,hæn

McClintock
Barbara, *US geneticist, biologist* — muh-KLIN-tuhk — mə'klintək
(Nobel 1983); Jessica, *US fashion designer*

McClure
James A., *US politician;* Doug, *US* — muh-KLUR — mə'kluʳ
actor

McConnell
Addison Mitchell, Jr., *US politician* — muh-KAHN-l — mə'kɑnl̩

McCormack
Cyrus, *US industrialist;* Richard — muh-KAWR-mik — mə'kɔːʳmik
Thomas Fox, *US government official*

McCovey
Willie, *US baseball player* — muh-KUHV-ē — mə'kəviˑ

McCown's longspur
bird — muh-KOWNZ LAWNG-SPUHR — mə'kɑunz 'lɔːŋ,spəʳ

McCoy
pers. name — muh-KOI — mə'kɔi

Foreign Sounds: **ue:** *Fr.* **rue**, *Ger.* **füllen** **uh(r):** *Fr.* **boeuf**, *Ger.* **Höhle** **kh**: *Ger.* **ich**, *Scot.* **loch** **ḡ**: *Sp.* **amigo** **v**: *Sp.* **hablar** **hl**: *Welsh* **Llanelli**. CAPITALS: primary stress. SMALL CAPS: secondary stress. ⑤: U.S. pron. ⑥: British pron.

McCrae, McCrea
   family name   muh-KRĀ   mə'kreː

McCullers
   Carson, *US author*   muh-KUHL-uhrz   mə'kələʳz

McCulloch, McCullough
   pers. name   muh-KUHL-uhk, muh-KUHL-uh<u>kh</u>   mə'kələk, mə'kələx

McDermott
   pers. name   muhk-DUHR-muht   mək'dəʳmət

McDiarmid
   Hugh, *Scottish poet*   muhk-DUHR-muhd,   mək'dəʳməd, mək'dəʳmət
                            muhk-DUHR-muht

McDonagh
   Donagh, *Irish dramatist;* Thomas,   muhk-DAHN-uh   mək'dɑnə
     Irish poet

McDonald
   pers. name   muhk-DAHN-uhld   mək'dɑnəld

McDonough
   family name   muhk-DUHN-uh, muhk-DAHN-uh   mək'dənə, mək'dɑnə

McDowell
   Roddy, *British actor*   muhk-DOW(-uh)l   mək'dɑu(ə)l

McElroy
   family name   MAK-uhl-ROI, muh-KEL-ROI   'mækəl₁rɔi, mə'kel₁rɔi

McEnroe
   John, *US tennis player*   MAK-uhn-RŌ   'mækən₁roː

McEntire
   Reba, *US country western singer*   MAK-uhn-TĪR   'mækən₁tɑiʳ

McEvoy
   family name   MAK-uh-VOI   'mækə₁vɔi

McEwan, McEwen
   family name   muh-KYO͞O-uhn   mə'kjuːən

McGavin
   Darren, *US actor*   muh-GAV-uhn   mə'gævən

McGee
   Willie, *US baseball player* muh-GĒ   mə'giː

McGehee
   city, AR   muh-GĒ   mə'giː

McGhee
   Walter Brownie, *blues singer,* muh-GĒ   mə'giː
     guitarist

McGillivray
   Alexander, *Creek chief*   muh-GIL-uh-VRĀ   mə'gilə₁vreː

McGovern
   George, *US politician*   muh-GUHV-uhrn   mə'gəvəʳn

McGraw
   John J., *US baseball manager* muh-GRAW   mə'grɔː

McGregor
   pers. name   muh-GREG-uhr   mə'gregəʳ

McGuffey
   William Holmes, *US educator* muh-GUHF-ē   mə'gəfiˑ

McGuigan
   family name   muh-GWĒ-guhn, muh-GWIG-uhn   mə'gwiːgən, mə'gwigən

McGuire
   Dorothy, *US actress*   muh-GWĪR   mə'gwɑiʳ

Key (col. 2):   a: fad ā: fade ah: father ar: marry aw: law e: fed ē: feed er: merry i: hid ī: hide ō: coat o͞o: boot
oi: boy ow: now u: put uh: above uhr: bird ch: chop ng: ring sh: show th: thick <u>th</u>: this zh: measure

McIntosh

    1. pers. name; apple; US pl. name   MAK-uhn-TAHSH   'mækən,taʃ

    2. county, GA   MAK-uhn-tuhsh, MAK-uhn-TAHSH   'mækəntəʃ, 'mækən,taʃ

McKay

    Jim, US TV sports commentator   muh-KĀ   mə'keː

McKean

    Michael, US actor   muh-KĒN   mə'kiːn

McKechnie

    Field, ballpark, Bradenton, FL   muh-KEK-nē   mə'kekni·

McKendree

    College, IL   muh-KEN-drē   mə'kendri·

McKinley [Denali]

    Mount, AK   muh-KIN-lē   mə'kinli·

McKinley

    William, 25th US president; pers.   muh-KIN-lē   mə'kinli·

      name

McKinsey, McKinzey

    pers. name   muh-KIN-zē   mə'kinzi·

McKuen

    Rod, US poet, composer, author   muh-KY͞OO-uhn   mə'kjuːən

McLaglen

    pers. name   muh-KLAHK-luhn, muh-GLAHK-luhn   mə'klaklən, mə'glaklən

McLaughlin

    John, English musician   muh-KLAHK-luhn, muh-GLAHK-luhn,   mə'klaklən, mə'glaklən,

                                    muh-KLAH<u>KH</u>-luhn,   mə'klaxlən, mə'glaxlən

                                    muh-GLAH<u>KH</u>-luhn

McLeod

    county, MN; pers. name   muh-KLOWD   mə'klaud

McLuhan

    Marshall, Canadian educator and   muh-KL͞OO-uhn   mə'kluːən

      philosopher

McIver, McIvor

    family name   muh-KĪ-vuhr   mə'kaivəʳ

McMahon

    1. Ed, US TV personality   muhk-MAN   mək'mæn

    2. pers. name   muhk-MĀ-uhn, muhk-MAN,   mək'meːən, mək'mæn,

                                    muhk-MAH(-uh)n   mək'ma(ə)n

McManus

    William J., US political organization   muhk-MAN-uhs   mək'mænəs

      executive

McMillan

    Edwin M., US physical chemist   muhk-MIL-uhn   mək'milən

      (Nobel 1951)

McNamara

    Robert, US government official   MAK-nuh-MAR-uh, MAK-nuh-MER-uh   'mæknə,mærə, 'mæknə,merə

McNearney

    Stadium, Schenectady, NY   muhk-NIR-nē   mək'nirni·

McNeil

    Freeman, football player   muhk-NĒL   mək'niːl

McNichol

    Kristy, US actress   muhk-NIK-uhl   mək'nikəl

McPherson

    Aimée Semple, US evangelist;   muhk-FUHR-suhn   mək'fəʳsən

      James, Scottish poet

McRae

    Milton Alexander, *US newspaper*   muh-KRĀ   mə'kreː
      publisher

McRaney

    Gerald, *US actor*   muh-KRĀ-nē   mə'kreːniˑ

McVay, McVeagh, McVeigh, McVey

    family name   muhk-VĀ   mək've

McVie

    Christine Perfect, *British musician,*   muhk-VĒ   mək'viː
      singer; John, *musician*

McWethy

    John, *US journalist*   muh-KWETH-ē   mə'kweθiˑ

Mdina

    town, Malta   muh-DĒ-nuh   mə'diːnə

Mélník

    town, Czech republic   MYEL-NYĒK, MEL-nik   'mjel‚njiːk, 'melnik

Mead

    Margaret, *US anthropologist*   MĒD   'miːd

Meade

    George Gordon, *US general;*   MĒD   'miːd
      James E., *English economist*
      (Nobel 1977)

Meagher

    county, MT   MAHR   'mɑ^r

Meah

    Biblical name   MĒ-uh, me-AH   'miːə, me'ɑ

Meany

    George, *US labor leader*   MĒ-nē   'miːniˑ

Meara

    Anne, *US actress*   MIR-uh   'mirə

Mearah

    Biblical name   mē-Ā-ruh, muh-ah-RAH   miː'eːrə, məɑ'rɑ

Mearns's gilded flicker

    bird   MUHRN-zuhz GILD-uhd FLIK-uhr ‚mə^{r}nzəz ‚gildəd 'flikə^r

Mearns's quail

    bird   MUHRN-zuhz KWĀL   ‚mə^{r}nzəz 'kweːl

Mears

    Rick, *US race car driver*   MIRZ   'mi^{r}z

Mebane

    town, NC   MEB-uhn   'mebən

Mebunnai

    Biblical name   muh-BUHN-ī, muh-voo̅-NĪ   mə'bən‚ɑi, məvuː'nɑi

Mecca

    city, Saudi Arabia, center of Islam MEK-uh   'mekə

Mechain

    1. Pierre, *French astronomer*   me-SHE^n meʃẽ
    2. see Gwerful Mechain

Mechant, Lake

    lake, LA   LĀK muh-SHAHN   ‚leːk mə'ʃɑn

Mechelen [Malines]

    city, Belgium   MEKH-uh-luh(n)   'mexələ(n)

Mechlin

    English form of Mechelen   MEK-luhn   'meklən

Key (col. 2):   a: fad ā: fade ah: father ar: marry aw: law e: fed ē: feed er: merry i: hid ī: hide ō: coat oo̅: boot
oi: boy ow: now u: put uh: above uhr: bird ch: chop ng: ring sh: show th: thick <u>th</u>: this zh: measure

Mecklenburg
- *1. county, NC, VA* — MEK-luhn-BUHRG — 'meklən,bəʳg
- *2. former German state* — MEK-luhn-BURK, -BURG — 'meklən,buʳk, -,buʳg

Mecosta
- *county, MI* — mi-KAHS-tuh, mi-KAWS-tuh — mi'kɑstə, mi'kɔːstə

Medaglia d'Oro
- *tdmk of a coffee co* — muh-DAL-yuh DŌR-ō, DAWR-ō — mə'dæljə 'doːroː, 'dɔːroː

Medaille
- College, *NY* — muh-DĀL — mə'deːl

Medan
- *Biblical name* — MĒ-DAN, muh-DAHN — 'miː,dæn, mə'dɑn

Medawar
- *P. B., British zoologist, immunologist (Nobel 1960)* — MED-uh-wuhr — 'medəwəʳ

Medb
- *Irish goddess of war* — ME<u>TH</u>V, ⑤ MEV, māv — 'meðv, ⑤ 'mev, meːv

Mede
- *ancient Persian* — MĒD — 'miːd

Medea
- *wife of Jason; tragedy, Euripides* — muh-DĒ-uh — mə'diːə

Medeba
- *Biblical name* — MED-uh-buh, ME-duh-VAH — 'medəbə, 'medə,vɑ

Médecine Sans Frontière
- *international medical aid group* — med-SIN sahⁿ frawⁿ-TYER — medsin sã frɔ̃tjer

Medellín
- *city, Colombia* — mā-<u>th</u>uh-YĒN, ⑤ MED-uh-YĒN, MED-l-(Y)ĒN — meːðə'jiːn, ⑤ ,medə'jiːn, ,medl̩'(j)iːn

Medger
- *pers. name* (M. Evers) — MED-guhr — 'medgəʳ

Media
- *ancient country, Asia* — MĒD-ē-uh — 'miːdiːə

Medici
- *Florentine family* — MĀ-dē-chē, ⑤ MED-uh-chē, muh-DĒ-chē — 'meːdiːtʃiː, ⑤ 'medətʃiˑ, mə'diːtʃiˑ

Medicinae Doctor
- *Doctor of Medicine, M.D.* — MED-uh-SĒ-NĪ DAHK-TAWR — ,medə'siː,nɑi 'dɑk,tɔːʳ

Medii, Sinus
- *see* Sinus Medii

Medina
- *1. city, county, OH; character in* Faerie Queen, *Spenser* — muh-DĪ-nuh — mə'dɑinə
- *2. river, county, TX; city, Saudi Arabia* — muh-DĒ-nuh — mə'diːnə

MEDIQ
- *US healthcare services co.* — MED-ik — 'medik

Mediterranean
- *Sea* — MED-uh-tuh-RĀ-nē-uhn, -RĀN-yuhn — ,medətə'reːniːən, -'reːnjən

Médoc
- *district, France; wine variety* — mā-DAWK — meːdɔːk

Medusa
- *Gorgon* — muh-D(Y)O͞O-suh — mə'd(j)uːsə

Meerendal
- *S. African wine* — MER-uhn-DAHL, -DAL — 'meʳən,dɑl, -,dæl

Meese
- Edwin, III, *US government official* — MĒS — 'miːs

Foreign Sounds: **ue**: *Fr.* **rue**, *Ger.* f**ü**llen   **uh(r)**: *Fr.* b**oeuf**, *Ger.* H**öh**le   **kh**: *Ger.* i**ch**, *Scot.* lo**ch**   **ḡ**: *Sp.* ami**g**o   **v**: *Sp.* ha**b**lar   **hl**: *Welsh* **Ll**anelli.   CAPITALS: primary stress.   SMALL CAPS: secondary stress.   ⑤: U.S. pron.   Ⓔ: British pron.

Meg
　pers. name　　　　　　MEG　　　　　　　　　　　　　'meg

Megacles
　Athenian politician　　MEG-uh-KLĒZ　　　　　　　'megə‚kliːz

Megaera
　one of the Greek Furies　muh-GIR-uh　　　　　　　mə'girə

Megalosaurus
　dinosaur　　　　　　　MEG-uh-lō-SAWR-uhs　　　‚megəloː'soːrəs

Megan
　1. pers. name　　　　MEG-uhn, MĀ-guhn, MĒ-guhn　'megən, 'meːgən, 'miːgən
　2. Welsh　　　　　　MEG-ahn　　　　　　　　　'megɑːn

Megara
　daughter of Creon; ancient city, state,　MEG-uh-ruh　　　'megərə
　　Africa

Mégara, Megara
　city, Greece　　　　　MEG-uh-ruh　　　　　　　'megərə

Megasthenes
　Greek explorer　　　muh-GAS-thuh-NĒZ　　　　mə'gæsθə‚niːz

Meghan
　pers. name　　　　　MEG-uhn　　　　　　　　'megən

Megiddo
　archaeological site, Israel　mi-GID-ō　　　　　　mi'gidoː

Megiddon
　Biblical name　　　　muh-GID-n, muh-gi-DŌN　　mə'gidn̩, məgi'doːn

Meharry
　Medical College, *TN*　muh-HAR-ē, muh-HER-ē　　mə'hæriˑ, mə'heriˑ

Mehemed, Mehemet
　pers. name, Turkish　me-MET　　　　　　　　me'met

Meherrin
　river, VA, NC　　　　muh-HER-uhn　　　　　　mə'herən

Mehetabeel
　Biblical name　　　　muh-HET-uh-BĒL, muh-HĀ-tah-VEL　mə'heţə‚biːl, mə‚heːtɑ'vel

Mehetabel
　Biblical name　　　　muh-HET-uh-BEL, muh-HĀ-tah-VEL　mə'heţə‚bel, mə‚heːtɑ'vel

Mehida
　Biblical name　　　　muh-HĪD-uh, muh-<u>kh</u>ē-DAH　mə'hɑidə, məxiː'dɑ

Mehir
　Biblical name　　　　MĒ-(h)uhr, muh-<u>KHĒR</u>　　'miː(h)əʳ, mə'xiːr

Mehitabel
　literary cat　　　　　muh-HIT-uh-BEL　　　　　mə'hiţə‚bel

Mehmed
　1. pers. name, Serbo-Croatian　MEM-ed　　　　'memed
　2. Turkish　　　　　me-MET　　　　　　　　me'met

Mehmet
　pers. name, Albanian, Turkish　me-MET　　　　　me'met

Meholathite
　Biblical name　　　　muh-HŌ-luh-THĪT　　　　mə'hoːlə‚θɑit

Mehta
　Zubin, *US conductor*　MĀT-uh　　　　　　　　'meːţə

Mehujael
　Biblical name　　　　muh-H(Y)OO-YĀ-EL,　　　mə'h(j)uːˌjeːˌel, məˌxuːjɑ'el
　　　　　　　　　　　muh-<u>KH</u>OO-yah-EL

Mehuman
　Biblical name　　　　muh-HYOO-muhn, muh-hoo-MAHN　mə'hjuːmən, məhuː'mɑn

---

Key (col. 2):　a: **fad**　ā: **fade**　ah: **father**　ar: **marry**　aw: **law**　e: **fed**　ē: **feed**　er: **merry**　i: **hid**　ī: **hide**　ō: **coat**　oo: **boot**
oi: **boy**　ow: **now**　u: **put**　uh: **above**　uhr: **bird**　ch: **chop**　ng: **ring**　sh: **show**　th: **thick**　<u>th</u>: **this**　zh: **measure**

Meier
  pers. name   MĪ-uhr   'mɑiəʳ

Meiggs
  Henry, *US businessman*   MEGZ   'megz

Meigs
  county, OH, TN   MEGZ   'megz

Me-jarkon
  Biblical name   MĒ-JAHR-kuhn, MĀ-yahr-KŌN   'miː'dʒɑʳkən, ˌmeːjɑr'koːn

Meiji
  district, Japan   mā-jē   meːdʒiː

Meiklejohn
  Alexander, *US educator*   MIK-uhl-JAHN, MĪ-kuhl-JAHN   'mikəlˌdʒɑn, 'mɑikəlˌdʒɑn

Meineke
  US muffler co.   MĪ-nuh-kē   'mɑinəkiˑ

Meinen
  Field, *ballpark, Peoria, IL*   MĪ-nuhn   'mɑinən

Mein Kampf
  autobiography, Adolf Hitler   mīn KAHM(P)F   mɑin 'kɑm(p)f

Meir
  Golda, *Israeli prime minister; pers. name, Hebrew*   me-IR   me'iʳ

Meissen
  town, Germany; porcelain   MĪS-n   'mɑisn̩

Meister Bräu
  US beer   MĪ-stuhr BROW, MĪ-stuhr BROI   'mɑistəʳ ˌbrɑu, 'mɑistəʳ ˌbrɔi

Meistersinger
  member of a German poetry & music guild   MĪ-stuhr-SING-uhr, -ZING-uhr   'mɑistəʳˌsiŋəʳ, -ˌziŋəʳ

Meithei [Manipuri]
  lang., people, India   MĀ-THĀ   'meːˌθeː

Meitner
  Lise, *Austrian nuclear physicist*   MĪT-nuhr   'mɑitnəʳ

Mekele
  city, Ethiopia   MĀ-kuh-LĀ   'meːkəˌleː

Meklong
  river, Thailand   MĀ-KLAWNG   'meː'klɔːŋ

Meknès
  city, Morocco   mek-NES   mek'nes

Mekonah
  Biblical name   mi-KŌ-nuh, muh-<u>kh</u>aw-NAH   mi'koːnə, məxɔː'nɑ

Mekong
  river, Asia   MĀ-KAWNG, MĀ-KAHNG   'meː'kɔːŋ, 'meː'kɑŋ

Mel
  pers. name   MEL   'mel

Melampus
  Greek prophet   muh-LAM-puhs   mə'læmpəs

Melanchthon
  Philipp, *German scholar*   mā-LAHN<u>KH</u>-tawn   meː'lɑnxtɔːn

Melanchthon, Melancthon
  pers. name   muh-LANG(K)-thuhn, -tuhn   mə'læŋ(k)θən, -tən

Melanesia
  Pacific islands   MEL-uh-NĒ-zhuh, MEL-uh-NĒ-shuh   ˌmelə'niːʒə, ˌmelə'niːʃə

Melanesian
  pert. to Melanesia   MEL-uh-NĒ-zhuhn, MEL-uh-NĒ-shuhn   ˌmelə'niːʒən, ˌmelə'niːʃən

---

Melanie
  pers. name   MEL-uh-nē   'meləni·
Melanippe
  sister of Queen Hippolyta; daughter   MEL-uh-NIP-ē   ˌmelə'nipi·
    of Hippe and Aeolus
Melanippus
  killer of Tydeus, killed by Amphiaraus   MEL-uh-NIP-uhs   ˌmelə'nipəs
Melantho
  mother of Delphus by Poseidon   muh-LAN(T)-thō   mə'læn(t)θoː
Melanthus
  killer of Xanthus   muh-LAN(T)-thuhs   mə'læn(t)θəs
Melatiah
  Biblical name   MEL-uh-TĪ-uh, muh-laht-YAH   ˌmelə'taiə, məlat'ja
Melba
  pers. name   MEL-buh   'melbə
Melbourne
  1. city, Australia; town, FL   MEL-buhrn, *by outsiders or*   'melbəʳn, *by outsiders or*
                                                    non-Australians also MEL-BAWRN   *non-Australians also*
                                                                                               'melˌbɔːʳn
  2. town, England   MEL-bawrn   'melbɔːʳn
Melcher
  John, US politician   MEL-chuhr   'meltʃəʳ
Melchi
  Biblical name   MEL-KĪ   'melˌkai
Melchiades
  pope   mel-KĪ-uh-DĒZ   mel'kaiəˌdiːz
Melchiah
  Biblical name   mel-KĪ-uh, MAHL-kē-YAH   mel'kaiə, ˌmalkiː'ja
Melchior
  1. Lauritz, US tenor; pers. name   MEL-kē-awr   'melkiːɔːʳ
  2. French   mel-KYAWR   melkjɔːr
  3. German   MEL<u>KH</u>-yawr   'melçjɔːʳ
Melchizedek, Melchisedec
  Biblical priest-king of Jerusalem   mel-KIZ-uh-DEK, mel-KĒ-zuh-DEK   mel'kizəˌdek, mel'kiːzəˌdek
Melchizedek
  Biblical name   mel-KIZ-uh-DEK, MAHL-kēt-SED-ek   mel'kizəˌdek, ˌmalkiːt'sedek
Melea
  Biblical name   MĒ-lē-uh   'miːliːə
Meleager
  killer of the Calydonian boar   MEL-ē-Ā-guhr   ˌmeliː'eːgəʳ
Meleagrids
  sisters of Meleager   MEL-ē-Ā-gridz   ˌmeliː'eːgridz
Melech
  Biblical name   MĒ-LEK, MEL-e<u>kh</u>   'miːˌlek, 'melex
Meles
  Athenian loved by Timagoras   MĒ-lēz   'miːliːz
Meliads
  nymphs of the ash tree   MĒ-lē-ADZ, MĒ-lē-uhdz   'miːliːˌædz, 'miːliːədz
Melian
  Dialogue *on power, Thucydides*   MĒ-lē-uhn, MĒL-yuhn   'miːliːən, 'miːljən
Meliboea
  daughter of Niobe; beloved of Alexis   MEL-uh-BĒ-uh   ˌmelə'biːə
Meliboeus
  guardian of Oedipus   MEL-uh-BĒ-uhs   ˌmelə'biːəs

Key (col. 2):   a: fad   ā: fade   ah: father   ar: marry   aw: law   e: fed   ē: feed   er: merry   i: hid   ī: hide   ō: coat   ōō: boot
oi: boy   ow: now   u: put   uh: above   uhr: bird   ch: chop   ng: ring   sh: show   th: thick   <u>th</u>: this   zh: measure

Melicertes

    son of Ino, deified as Palaemon   MEL-uh-SUHRT-ēz   ˌmelə'sərˌʧiːz

Melilla

    port, Morocco   mā-LĒ-(y)uh   meː'liː(j)ə

Melina

    pers. name   muh-LĒ-nuh   mə'liːnə

Melissa

    pers. name   muh-LIS-uh   mə'lisə

Melisseus

    king of Crete   muh-LIS-ē-uhs, muh-LIS-(Y)O͞OS   mə'lisiːəs, mə'lisˌ(j)uːs

Mell

    pers. name   MEL   'mel

Mellencamp

    John Cougar, *rock musician*   MEL-uhn-KAMP   'melənˌkæmp

Mellette

    county, SD   muh-LET   mə'let

Mellon

    Andrew, *US financier*   MEL-uhn   'melən

Melnick

    Daniel, *US film producer*   MEL-nik   'melnik

Melos [Mílos, Milo]

    island, Aegean   MĒ-LAHS   'miːˌlɑs

Melpomene

    1. muse of tragedy   mel-PAHM-uh-nē   mel'pɑməni·

    2. street, New Orleans   MEL-puh-MĒN, mel-PAHM-uh-nē   'melpəˌmiːn, mel'pɑməni·

Melrose

    city, Massachusetts; village, Scotland   MEL-RŌZ   'melˌroːz

Melton Mowbray

    town, England   MELT-n MŌ-brā, MŌ-brē   'meltn̩ 'moːbreː, 'moːbri·

Melus

    friend of Adonis   MĒ-luhs   'miːləs

Melvil

    pers. name   MEL-VIL, MEL-vuhl   'melˌvil, 'melvəl

Melville

    Herman, *US writer*   MEL-VIL, MEL-vuhl   'melˌvil, 'melvəl

Melvin

    pers. name   MEL-vuhn   'melvən

Memel

    river, city, Lithuania   MĀ-muhl   'meːməl

Memmius

    Roman name   MEM-ē-uhs   'memiːəs

Memnon

    Ethiopian ally of the Trojans   MEM-NAHN   'memˌnɑn

Memphian

    resident of Memphis, *TN*   MEM(P)-fē-uhn   'mem(p)fiːən

Memphis

    city, TN; ancient capital of Egypt   MEM(P)-fuhs   'mem(p)fəs

Memphremagog

    lake, VT, Quebec   MEM-fri-MĀ-GAHG   ˌmemfri'meːˌgɑg

Memucan

    Biblical name   mi-M(Y)O͞O-KAN, -kuhn;   mi'm(j)uːˌkæn, -kən;

        muh-mo͞o-KHAHN   məmuː'xɑn

Menachem

    pers. name, Hebrew   muh-NAHKH-uhm   mə'nɑxəm

Foreign Sounds: ue: *Fr.* **rue**, *Ger.* **füllen** uh(r): *Fr.* **boeuf**, *Ger.* **Höhle** kh: *Ger.* **ich**, *Scot.* **loch** g̅: *Sp.* **amigo** v: *Sp.* **hablar**
hl: *Welsh* **Llanelli**. CAPITALS: primary stress. SMALL CAPS: secondary stress. Ⓢ: U.S. pron. Ⓔ: British pron.

Menahem
   pers. name, German   MĀ-nah-HEM, mā-NAH-hem   'meːnɑˌhem, meːˈnɑhem
Menai
   strait, bridge between Anglesey and   MEN-Ī   'menˌɑi
   Welsh mainland
Menam, Me Nam
   English name of Chao Phraya   mā-NAHM   meːˈnɑm
Menander
   Greek dramatist   muh-NAN-duhr   məˈnændəʳ
Menands
   village, NY   muh-NAN(D)Z   məˈnæn(d)z
Menard
   county, IL, TX   muh-NAHRD   məˈnɑʳd
Menard
   John Willis, *US politician*   MĀ-nuhrd, MĀ-NAHRD, muh-NAHRD   'meːnəʳd, 'meːˌnɑʳd,
                                                     məˈnɑʳd
Menchú
   Rigoberta, *Guatemalan activist*   men-CHOO   men'tʃuː
   (Nobel, 1992)
Mencius [Meng-tzu]
   Chinese philosopher   MEN-ch(ē-)uhs   'mentʃ(iː)əs
Mencken
   H.L., *US writer*   MENG-kuhn   'meŋkən
Mende
   1. lang., people, Africa   MEN-dē   'mendiˑ
   2. town, France   MAHⁿD   mɑ̃d
Mendel
   Gregor, *Austrian botanist*   MEN-dl   'mendl̩
Mendele Mokher Sefarim
   pseudonym of S.J. Abramovich   MEND-l-uh MAW-khuhr SFAWR-im   'mendl̩ə 'mɔːxəʳ 'sfɔːrim
mendelevium
   element   MEN-duh-LĒ-vē-uhm,   ˌmendə'liːviːəm,
                      MEN-duh-LĀ-vē-uhm   ˌmendə'leːviːəm
Mendeleyev, -leev
   Dmitri Ivanovitch, *Russian chemist*   MEN-duh-LĀ-uhf   ˌmendə'leːəf
Mendelian
   pert. to G. Mendel   men-DĒ-lē-uhn, men-DĒL-yuhn   men'diːliːən, men'diːljən
Mendelssohn-Bartholdy
   Felix, *German composer*   MEN-dl-suhn-bahr-TAWL-dē   'mendl̩sənbɑʳ'tɔːldiˑ
Menderes
   Turkish political leader; river, Asia   MEN-duh-RES   ˌmendə'res
   Minor
Mendes
   Sergio, *Brazilian entertainer*   MEN-DEZ, men-DĀS   'menˌdez, men'deːs
Méndez, Mendez
   1. pers. name   MEN-DEZ, men-DEZ   'menˌdez, men'dez
   2. Spanish   MĀN-dās, MĀN-dāth   'meːndeːs, 'meːndeːθ
Mendip Hills
   hill range, England   MEN-DIP HILZ   'menˌdip 'hilz
Mendocino
   county, CA   MEN-duh-SĒ-nō   ˌmendə'siːnoː
Mendota
   city, CA; city, IL; lake, WI   men-DŌT-uh   men'doːʈə
Mendoza
   river, prov, town, Argentina   men-DŌ-zuh, men-DŌ-sah   men'doːzə, men'doːsɑ

Key (col. 2):   a: f**a**d   ā: f**a**de   ah: f**a**ther   ar: m**a**rry   aw: l**a**w   e: f**e**d   ē: f**ee**d   er: m**e**rry   i: h**i**d   ī: h**i**de   ō: c**oa**t   o͞o: b**oo**t
oi: b**oy**   ow: n**ow**   u: p**u**t   uh: **a**bove   uhr: b**i**rd   ch: **ch**op   ng: ri**ng**   sh: **sh**ow   th: **th**ick   <u>th</u>: **th**is   zh: mea**s**ure

Menelaus
king of Sparta & husband of Helen   MEN-l-Ā-uhs   ˌmenl̩ˈeːəs

Menelik
emperor, Ethiopia   MĀ-nuh-lik, MEN-l-ik   ˈmeːnəlik, ˈmenl̩ik

Menem
Carlos Saul, *president, Brazil*   MEN-eⁿ   ˈmenēː

Menes
1st king of Egypt, 3100 BC   MĒ-nēz   ˈmiːniːz

Menestheus
legendary Athenian leader   muh-NES-thē-uhs,   məˈnesθiːəs, məˈnesˌθ(j)uːs
                                 muh-NES-TH(Y)O͞OS

Menexenus
dialogue of Plato   muh-NEK-suh-nuhs, me-NEK-   məˈneksənəs, meˈnek-

Mengele
Joseph, *Nazi officer*   MENG-guh-luh   ˈmeŋgələ

Mengistu Haile Mariam
Ethiopian dictator   meng-GIS-tōō HĪ-lē MAHR-ē-uhm   meŋˈgistuː ˈhailiˑ ˈmariˑəm

Meng-tzu [Mencius]
Chinese philosopher   MUHNG-DZU, MUHNG-DZO͞O   ˈməŋˈdzu, ˈməŋˈdzuː

Ménière's
disease of the ear   MEN-ē-uhrz, MEN-yuhrz, muhn-YERZ   ˈmeniːəʳz, ˈmenjəʳz, mənˈjeʳz

Menifee
county, KY   MEN-uh-fē   ˈmenəfiˑ

Menindie
Australia   muh-NIN-dē   məˈnindiˑ

Menippus
Greek cynic philosopher and satirist   muh-NIP-uhs   məˈnipəs

Menjou
Adolphe, *actor*   mahⁿ-ZHO͞O, MAHN-zhōō   mãʒuː, ˈmanʒuː

Menkaure
king of Egypt   men-KOW-rā   menˈkaureː

Menlo
College, *CA*   MEN-lō   ˈmenloː

Menlo Park
city, CA   MEN-lō PAHRK   ˌmenloː ˈpaʳk

Menna
pers. name, Welsh; Biblical name   MEN-uh   ˈmenə

Menninger
Karl Augustus, *US psychiatrist;*   MEN-ing-uhr   ˈmeniŋəʳ
   clinic

Menno
pers. name, Dutch   MEN-ō   ˈmenoː

Mennonite
Christian sect   MEN-uh-NĪT   ˈmenəˌnait

Meno
dialogue of Plato   MĒ-nō   ˈmiːnoː

Menoetes
herdsman of the flocks of Hades   MEN-uh-WĒT-ēz   ˌmenəˈwiːt̪iːz

Menoetius
Argonaut   MEN-uh-WĒ-sh(ē-)uhs   ˌmenəˈwiːʃ(iː)əs

Menominee
county, MI, WI   muh-NAHM-uh-nē   məˈnaməniˑ

Menominee, -ni
S. American people   muh-NAHM-uh-nē   məˈnaməniˑ

Foreign Sounds: ue: *Fr.* **rue**, *Ger.* **füllen**   uh(r): *Fr.* **boeuf**, *Ger.* **Höhle**   <u>kh</u>: *Ger.* i**ch**, *Scot.* lo**ch**   g̃: *Sp.* ami**g**o   <u>v</u>: *Sp.* ha**b**lar
hl: *Welsh* **Ll**anelli.   CAPITALS: primary stress.   SMALL CAPS: secondary stress.   Ⓢ: U.S. pron.   Ⓔ: British pron.

Menomonee Falls
　town, WI　　　　　　　　　muh-NAHM-uh-nē FAWLZ　　　　mə'nɑməni· 'fɔːlz
Menomonie
　city, WI　　　　　　　　　muh-NAHM-uh-NĒ　　　　　　　mə'nɑmə,niː
Menorah
　Jewish candelabrum　　　muh-NŌR-uh, muh-NAWR-uh　　mə'noːrə, mə'nɔːrə
Menorca [Minorca]
　island, Balearic Islands　mā-NAWR-kuh　　　　　　　　meː'nɔː˞kə
Menotti
　Gian Carlo, *Italian composer; pers.*　mā-NAWT-tē　　　　　　meː'nɔːtti·
　　name, Italian
Mensa
　constellation; high IQ organization　MEN-suh　　　　　　　'mensə
Menshevik
　member of party opposing Bolsheviks　MEN-chuh-VIK　　　　　'mentʃə,vik
Mensheviki
　plural of Menshevik　　　MEN-chuh-VĒ-kē, -VIK-ē　　　,mentʃə'viːki·, -'viki·
Menshikov
　Aleksandr Danilovich, *Russian*　MYĀN-shi-kuhf　　　　　'mjeːnʃikəf
　　soldier
Menthe
　nymph loved by Hades　MEN-thē　　　　　　　　　　'menθi·
Menthu-Hotep
　name, kings of Egypt　　MEN-tōo-HŌ-TEP　　　　　　'mentuː'hoː,tep
Mentone
　village, TX　　　　　　　MEN-TŌN　　　　　　　　　　'men,toːn
Mentor
　friend of Odysseus; pers. name　MEN-TAWR, MENT-uhr　　'men,tɔː˞, 'mentə˞
Menuhin
　Yehudi, *US violinist*　　MEN-yuh-wuhn　　　　　　　'menjəwən
Menuhoth
　Biblical name　　　　　　men-(Y)ŌO-HAHTH muh-nōo-KHŌT　men'(j)uː,hɑθ mənuː'xoːt
Menzies
　1. British family name　MEN-ZĒZ, MEN-ziz; *in Scotland*　'men,ziːz, 'menziz; *in*
　　　　　　　　　　　　　　MING-is, -iz　　　　　　　　　　*Scotland* 'miɲis, -iz
　2. Sir Robert G., Australian prime　MEN-zēz　　　　　　　'menzi·z
　　minister
Meo
　see Miao
Meonenim
　Biblical name　　　　　　mē-AHN-uh-NIM, muh-Ō-nuh-NĒM　miː'ɑnə,nim, mə,oːnə'niːm
Meonothai
　Biblical name　　　　　　mē-AHN-uh-THĪ, mē-Ō-nuh-THĪ,　miː'ɑnə,θai, miː'oːnə,θai,
　　　　　　　　　　　　　　muh-Ō-naw-TĪ　　　　　　　　mə,oːnɔː'tai
Mephaath
　Biblical name　　　　　　me-FĀ-AHTH, -ATH; me-FAH-aht　me'feː,ɑθ, -,æθ; me'fɑɑt
Mephibosheth
　Biblical name　　　　　　muh-FIB-uh-SHETH, muh-fi-VŌ-shet　mə'fibə,ʃeθ, məfi'voːʃet
Mephisto
　a devil　　　　　　　　　muh-FIS-tō　　　　　　　　　mə'fistoː
Mephistophelean
　pert. to Mephisto *or*　MEF-uh-STAHF-uh-LĒ-uhn,　,mefə,stɑfə'liːən,
　　Mephistopheles　　　　muh-FIS-tuh-FĒ-lē-uhn　　　mə,fistə'fiːliːən
Mephistopheles
　a devil　　　　　　　　　MEF-uh-STAHF-uh-LĒZ　　　,mefə'stɑfə,liːz

Key (col. 2):　a: fad　ā: fade　ah: father　ar: **marry**　aw: **law**　e: fed　ē: feed　er: **merry**　i: hid　ī: hide　ō: coat　ōo: boot
oi: **boy**　ow: **now**　u: put　uh: above　uhr: **bird**　ch: **chop**　ng: **ring**　sh: **show**　th: **thick**　th̲: **this**　zh: measure

Mequon
   city, WI   MEK-WAHN   'mek‚wɑn

Merab
   Biblical name   MĒ-RAB, MIR-AB, me-RAHV   'miː‚ræb, 'mir‚æb, me'rɑv

Meraiah
   Biblical name   muh-RĪ-uh, muh-RĀ-uh,   mə'rɑiə, mə'reːə, mərɑ'jɑ
                           muh-rah-YAH

Meraioth
   Biblical name   muh-RĀ-AHTH, muh-RĪ-AHTH,   mə'reː‚ɑθ, mə'rɑi‚ɑθ,
                           muh-rah-YŌT   mərɑ'joːt

Meramec
   river, MO   MER-uh-MAK   'merə‚mæk

Merari
   Biblical name   muh-RĀ-RĪ, muh-rah-RĒ   mə'reː‚rɑi, mərɑ'riː

Merarite
   Biblical name   muh-RĀ-RĪT   mə'reː‚rɑit

Merathaim
   Biblical name   MER-uh-THĀ-im, muh-rah-TAH-yim   ‚merə'θeːim, mərɑ'tɑjim

Mercator
   Gerardus, *Flemish cartographer;*   muhr-KĀT-uhr   məʳ'keːʈəʳ
     map projection

Merced
   river, city, county, CA   muhr-SED   məʳ'sed

Mercedes
   city, TX   muhr-SĀD-ēz   məʳ'seːdiːz

Mercedes-Benz
   German car marque   muhr-SĀD-ēz-BENZ, -BEN(T)S   məʳ‚seːdiːz'benz, -'ben(t)s

Mercer
   University, *GA*   MUHR-suhr   'məʳsəʳ

Mercia
   Anglo-Saxon kingdom   MUHR-shuh   'məʳʃə

Mercian
   pert. to Mercia   MUHR-shuhn   'məʳʃən

Mercier
   pers. name, French   mers-YĀ   mersjeː

Merck, Sharp, & Dohme
   division of Merck & Co., US   MUHRK SHAHRP uhn DŌM   'məʳk 'ʃɑʳp ən 'doːm
    pharmaceuticals co.

Mercouri
   Melina, *Greek actress*   muhr-K(Y)UR-ē   məʳ'k(j)uri·

Mercurius
   pers. name, Dutch   mer-KUE-rē-ues   mer'kyːriːys

Mercurius
   Biblical name   muhr-KYUR-ē-uhs   məʳ'kjuriːəs

Mercurochrome
   tdmk for an antiseptic   muhr-KYUR-uh-KRŌM   məʳ'kjurə‚kroːm

Mercury
   Roman messenger god; planet;   MUHR-kyuh-rē   'məʳkjəri·
    element

Mercutio
   character in Romeo and Juliet,   muhr-KYOO-shē-Ō, muhr-KYOO-shō   məʳ'kjuːʃiː‚oː, məʳ'kjuːʃoː
    Shakespeare

Mercy
   pers. name   MUHR-sē   'məʳsi·

Foreign Sounds: ue: *Fr.* **rue**, *Ger.* **füllen**   uh(r): *Fr.* **boeuf**, *Ger.* **Höhle**   <u>kh</u>: *Ger.* **ich**, *Scot.* **loch**   g̃: *Sp.* amigo   v: *Sp.* hablar
hl: *Welsh* **Llanelli**.   CAPITALS: primary stress.   SMALL CAPS: secondary stress.   Ⓢ: U.S. pron.   Ⓔ: British pron.

Mercyhurst
  College, *PA*   MUHR-sē-HUHRST   'mə*r*si·ˌhə*r*st

Mered
  Biblical name   MĒ-RED, MIR-ED, ME-red   'miːˌred, 'mirˌed, 'mered

Meredith
  Burgess, *US actor; pers. name*   MER-uhd-uhth, *in Wales* muh-RED-ith   'merədəθ, *in Wales* mə'rediθ

Meredydd
  pers. name, Welsh   me-RED-i<u>th</u>   me'redi ð

Meremoth
  Biblical name   MER-i-MAHTH, muh-re-MŌT   'meriˌmɑθ, məre'moːt

Merengue
  dance   muh-RENG-gā   mə'reŋgeː

Meres
  Biblical name   MĒ-ruhs, MIR-uhs, MĒ-rēz, ME-res   'miːrəs, 'mirəs, 'miːriːz,
                                                        'meres

Merfyn
  pers. name   MUHR-vuhn   'mə*r*vən

Mergenthaler
  Ottmar, *US inventor*   MUHR-guhn-THAHL-uhr,   'mə*r*gənˌθɑlə*r*, 'mergənˌtɑlə*r*
                                    MER-guhn-TAHL-uhr

Meribah
  Biblical name   MER-uh-BAH, muh-rē-VAH   'merəˌbɑ, məriː'vɑ

Merib-baal
  Biblical name   MER-i(b)-BĀ(-uh)l, muh-RIV-BAH-ahl   ˌmeri(b)'beː(ə)l, məˌriv'bɑ-al

Mérida
  city, Mexico; commune, Spain; state,   MĀ-rē-<u>th</u>ah, ⓢ MER-uhd-uh   'meːriːðɑ, ⓢ 'merədə
    Venezuela

Meriden
  city, CT   MER-uhd-n, MER-uhd-uhn   'merədn̩, 'merədən

Mérimée
  Prosper, *French writer*   mā-rē-MĀ, ⓢ MER-uh-MĀ   meːriːmeː, ⓢ 'merəˌmeː

Merino
  sheep breed   muh-RĒ-nō   mə'riːnoː

Meriones
  companion of Idomeneus   MER-ē-Ō-nēz   ˌmeri'oːniːz

Merionethshire
  former county, Wales   MER-ē-AHN-uhth-shuhr, -SHIR   ˌmeri'ɑnəθʃə*r*, -ˌʃir

Meriwether
  pers. name   MER-i-WE<u>TH</u>-uhr   'meriˌweðə*r*

Merle
  pers. name   MUHRL, MUHR-uhl   'mə*r*l, 'mərəl

Merlin
  wizard in Arthurian legend; pers.   MUHR-luhn   'mə*r*lən
    name

Merlot
  wine   mer-LŌ   merloː

Merneptah
  king of Egypt   MUHR-NEP-TAH   'mə*r*ˌnepˌtɑ

Merodach
  Biblical name   muh-RŌ-DAK, MER-uh-DAK,   mə'roːˌdæk, 'merəˌdæk,
                                    muh-rō-DAH<u>KH</u>   məro'dɑx

Merodach-baladan
  Biblical name   mi-RŌ-DAK-BAL-uh-DAN,   mi'roːˌdæk'bæləˌdæn,
                                    muh-rō-DAH<u>KH</u>-bahl-ah-DAHN   məroː'dɑxbɑlɑ'dɑn

---

Key (col. 2):   a: fad ā: fade ah: father ar: marry aw: law e: fed ē: feed er: merry i: hid ī: hide ō: coat ōō: boot
oi: boy ow: now u: put uh: above uhr: bird ch: chop ng: ring sh: show th: thick <u>th</u>: this zh: measure

Meroë
  capital city, ancient Ethiopia   MER-uh-WĒ   'merə͵wi·

Merom
  Biblical name   MĒ-RAHM, MIR-AHM, me-RŌM   'miː͵rɑm, 'mir͵ɑm, me'roːm

Merope
  wife of Sisyphus; one of the Pleiades   MER-uh-pē   'merəpi·

Merovingian
  Frankish dynasty   MER-uh-VIN-jē-uhn   ͵merə'vindʒiːən

Meroz
  Biblical name   MĒ-RAHZ, MIR-AHZ, me-RŌZ   'miː͵rɑz, 'mir͵ɑz, me'roːz

Merrifield
  R. Bruce, *US organic chemist (Nobel 1984)*   MER-uh-FĒLD   'merə͵fiːld

Merrimack
  town, county, NH; river, NH, MA   MER-uh-MAK   'merə͵mæk

Merriwether
  Lee, *US actress*   MER-i-WE<u>TH</u>-uhr   'meri͵weðəʳ

Mersey
  river, England   MUHR-zē   'məʳzi·

Merseyside
  county, England   MUHR-zē-SĪD   'məʳzi·͵said

Merthyr Tydvil
  county borough, Wales   MUHR-thuhr TID-VIL   ͵məʳθəʳ 'tid͵vil

Merton
  borough, England; college, Oxford Univ.; pers. name   MUHRT-n   'məʳtņ

Mervin, -vyn
  pers. name   MUHR-vuhn   'məʳvən

Merwanji
  pers. name, Parsi   mār-VAHN-jē   meːr'vɑndʒiː

Meryl
  pers. name   MER-uhl, MERL   'merəl, 'merl

Mesa
  county, CO; town, AZ   MĀ-suh   'meːsə

Mesa, La
  see La Mesa

Mesabi
  iron range, college, MN   muh-SAHB-ē   mə'sɑbi·

Mesa Grande
  Indian reservation, US   MĀ-suh GRAHN-dē   ͵meːsə 'grɑndi·

Mesa Verde
  National Park, *CO*   MĀ-suh VUHRD, VUHR-dē   ͵meːsə 'vəʳd, 'vəʳdi·

Mescalero
  N. American people   MES-kuh-LER-ō   ͵meskə'leroː

Mesdames
  French, plural of Madame   mā-DAHM, Ⓢ mā-DAHM, mā-DAM   meːdɑːm, Ⓢ meː'dɑm, meː'dæm

Mesdemoiselles
  French, plural of Mademoiselle   mād-mwah-ZEL, Ⓢ MĀD-uh-m(w)uh-ZEL, MĀD-m(w)uh-ZEL   meːdmwɑːzel, Ⓢ ͵meːdəm(w)ə'zel, ͵meːdm(w)ə'zel

Mesech [Meshech]
  Biblical name   MĒ-sek, ME-she<u>kh</u>   'miːsek, 'meʃex

Mesha
  Biblical name   MĒ-shuh, me-SHAH   'miːʃə, me'ʃɑ

Foreign Sounds: **ue:** *Fr.* **rue**, *Ger.* **füllen**   **uh(r):** *Fr.* **boeuf**, *Ger.* **Höhle**   **kh:** *Ger.* **ich**, *Scot.* **loch**   **g̃:** *Sp.* **amigo**   **v:** *Sp.* **hablar**
hl: *Welsh* **Llanelli**.   CAPITALS: primary stress.   SMALL CAPS: secondary stress.   Ⓢ: U.S. pron.   Ⓔ: British pron.

Meshach
   Biblical name   MĒ-SHAK   'miːˌʃæk

Meshech
   Biblical name   MĒ-shek, ME-she<u>kh</u>   'miːʃek, 'meʃex

Meshelemiah
   Biblical name   muh-SHEL-uh-MĪ-uh,   məˌʃeləˈmɑiə, məˌʃelemˈjɑ
                       muh-SHE-lem-YAH

Meshezabeel [Meshezabel]
   Biblical name   muh-SHEZ-uh-BĒL, muh-SHĀ-zah-BEL   məˈʃezəˌbiːl, məˌʃeːzɑˈbel

Meshezabel
   Biblical name   muh-SHEZ-uh-BEL, muh-SHĀ-zah-BEL   məˈʃezəˌbel, məˌʃeːzɑˈbel

Meshillemith
   Biblical name   muh-SHIL-uh-MITH, -muhth   məˈʃiləˌmiθ, -məθ

Meshillemoth
   Biblical name   muh-SHIL-uh-MAHTH,   məˈʃiləˌmɑθ, məˌʃileˈmoːt
                       muh-SHI-le-MŌT

Meshobab
   Biblical name   muh-SHŌ-BAHB, muh-shō-VAHV   məˈʃoːˌbɑb, məʃoːˈvɑv

Meshullam
   Biblical name   muh-SHUL-uhm, muh-shōō-LAHM   məˈʃuləm, məʃuːˈlɑm

Meshullemeth
   Biblical name   muh-SHUL-uh-METH,   məˈʃuləˌmeθ, məʃuːˈlemet
                       muh-shōō-LE-met

Mesilla
   town, NM   mā-SĒ-(y)uh   meːˈsiː(j)ə

Mesmer
   Franz, *German physician*   MEZ-muhr, MES-muhr   'mezməʳ, 'mesməʳ

Mesoamerica
   region of Mexico & Cen. America   MEZ-ō-uh-MER-i-kuh, MĒ-zō-   ˌmezoːəˈmerikə, ˌmiːzoː-

Mesogeia
   Attic plain   MES-ō-GĀ-uh, MEZ-   ˌmesoːˈgeːə, ˌmez-

Mesolithic
   geologic era   MEZ-uh-LITH-ik, MĒZ-, MES-, MĒS-   ˌmezəˈliθik, ˌmiːz-, ˌmes-,
                                                            ˌmiːs-

Meson
   subatomic particle   MEZ-AHN, MES-AHN; MĀ-ZAHN,   'mezˌɑn, 'mesˌɑn; 'meːˌzɑn,
                       MĒ-ZAHN, -SAHN   'miːˌzɑn, -ˌsɑn

Mesopotamia
   region of early civilization, Near East   MES-(uh-)puh-TĀ-mē-uh, -TĀM-yuh   ˌmes(ə)pəˈteːmiːə, -ˈteːmjə

Mesozoic
   geologic era   MEZ-uh-ZŌ-ik, MĒZ-, MES-, MĒS-   ˌmezəˈzoːik, ˌmiːz-, ˌmes-,
                                                            ˌmiːs-

Mesquite
   town, TX   muh-SKĒT, me-SKĒT   məˈskiːt, meˈskiːt

Messalim
   king of Lagash   MES-uh-luhm, MES-uh-LIM   'mesələm, 'mesəˌlim

Messalina
   Valeria, *third wife of Claudius I*   MES-uh-LĪ-nuh, MES-uh-LĒ-nuh   ˌmesəˈlɑinə, ˌmesəˈliːnə

Messana [Messina]
   seaport, Sicily   muh-SAHN-uh   məˈsɑnə

Messenia
   region of ancient Greece   muh-SĒ-nē-uh, muh-SĒN-yuh   məˈsiːniːə, məˈsiːnjə

Messerschmitt
   German WWII fighter plane   MES-uhr-SHMIT   'mesəʳˌʃmit

Key (col. 2):   a: fad   ā: fade   ah: father   ar: marry   aw: law   e: fed   ē: feed   er: merry   i: hid   ī: hide   ō: coat   ōō: boot
oi: boy   ow: now   u: put   uh: above   uhr: bird   ch: chop   ng: ring   sh: show   th: thick   <u>th</u>: this   zh: measure

Messiaen		
Oliver, *French composer and organist*	mās-YAH^{n}	meˈsjɑ̃
Messiah		
Jewish deliverer; Jesus Christ	muh-SĪ-uh	məˈsɑiə
Messianic		
pert. to a messiah	MES-ē-AN-ik	ˌmesiːˈænik
Messidor		
month, French Revolutionary calendar	mā-sē-DAWR	meˈsiːdɔːr
Messier		
Mark, *Canadian hockey player*	mes-YĀ	mesˈjeː
Messieurs		
French, plural of Monsieur	mā-SYUH(R), [$] muhsh-YUHRZ, muhs-YUHRZ, muh-SIRZ, mās-YUHRZ	meːsjœː, [$] məʃˈjə^{r}z, məsˈjə^{r}z, məˈsi^{r}z, meːsˈjə^{r}z
Messina		
seaport, Sicily	muh-SĒ-nuh	məˈsiːnə
Messius		
pers. name, Latin	MES-ē-uhs	ˈmesiːəs
Messrs.		
gentlemen, plural of Mr.	MES-uhrz	ˈmesə^{r}z
Mestra		
daughter of Erysichthon	MES-truh	ˈmestrə
Meštrović		
Ivan, *Croatian-born American sculptor*	MESH-traw-VĒT, [$] MESH-truh-VICH, MES-	ˈmeʃtrɔːˌviːt̪ , [$] ˈmeʃtrəˌvitʃ, ˈmes-
Meta		
1. river, Colombia	MĀT-uh	ˈmeːt̪ə
2. pers. name	MĒT-uh	ˈmiːt̪ə
Metabus		
father of Camilla	MET-uh-buhs	ˈmet̪əbəs
Metallica		
rock group	muh-TAL-i-kuh	məˈtælikə
Metanira		
employer of Demeter	MET-uh-NĪ-ruh	ˌmet̪əˈnɑirə
Metairie		
urban area, LA	MET-uh-rē	ˈmet̪əriˑ
Metaxa		
tdmk for a Greek brandy	me-TAK-suh, muh-TAK-suh, muh-TAHK-suh	meˈtæksə, məˈtæksə, məˈtɑksə
Metaxas		
Ioannis, *Greek dictator*	MET-ahk-SAHS, [$] me-TAHK-SAHS	ˌmet̪ɑkˈsɑs, [$] meˌtɑkˈsɑs
Metchnikoff		
Elie, *Russian-born French zoologist, bacteriologist (Nobel 1908)*	MECH-ni-KAWF	ˈmetʃniˌkɔːf
Metellus		
prominent Roman family	muh-TEL-uhs	məˈteləs
Meteor		
French beer	mā-tā-AWR	meːteːɔːr
Metheg-ammah		
Biblical name	METH-uh-GAM-uh, ME-teg-ah-MAH	ˈmeθəˈgæmə, ˈmetegɑˈmɑ
Methodism		
doctrines of the Methodists	METH-uhd-IZ-uhm	ˈmeθədˌizəm

Foreign Sounds: ue: *Fr.* **rue**, *Ger.* **füllen** uh(r): *Fr.* **boeuf**, *Ger.* **Höhle** kh: *Ger.* **ich**, *Scot.* **loch** g̃: *Sp.* **amigo** v̲: *Sp.* **hablar** hl: *Welsh* **Llanelli**. CAPITALS: primary stress. SMALL CAPS: secondary stress. [$]: U.S. pron. [£]: British pron.

Methodist		
religion	METH-uhd-uhst	'meθədəst
Methodius		
saint, apostle of the Slavs	me-THŌD-ē-uhs	me'θoːdiːəs
Methow		
river, WA	MET-HOW	'met,hau
Methuen		
1. town, MA	muh-TH(Y)O͞O-uhn	mə'θ(j)uːən
2. pers. name	METH-yuh-wuhn	'meθjəwən
Methuen		
Sir Algernon Methuen Marshall, *English publisher*	METH-yuh-wuhn	'meθjəwən
Methusael [Methushael]		
Biblical name	muh-TH(Y)O͞O-sē-EL, -zē-EL; muh-TO͞O-shah-EL	mə'θ(j)uːsiː,el, -ziː,el; mə,tuːʃɑ'el
Methuselah		
elderly ancestor of Noah; large wine bottle	muh-TH(Y)O͞OZ(-uh)-luh	mə'θ(j)uːz(ə)lə
Methushael		
Biblical name	mi-TH(Y)O͞O-shuh-EL, muh-TO͞O-shah-EL	mi'θ(j)uːʃə,el, mə,tuːʃɑ'el
Metics		
aliens in Athens	MET-iks	'meţiks
Metinic		
island, ME	muh-TIN-ik	mə'tinik
Metis		
Greek goddess of wisdom	MĒT-uhs	'miːţəs
Metlakatla		
village, AK	MET-luh-KAT-luh	,metlə'kætlə
Metoac		
N. American people	muh-TŌ-AK	mə'toː,æk
Metonic		
cycle, *19-year cycle of the moon*	muh-TAHN-ik, me-TAHN-ik	mə'tɑnik, me'tɑnik
Metternich		
Clemens Wenzel, *Austrian statesman*	MET-uhr-nikh, MET-uhr-nik	'metəʳnix, 'metəʳnik
Metuchen		
city, NJ	muh-TUHCH-uhn	mə'tətʃən
Metz		
town, France	MES, [$] METS	mes, [$] 'mets
Metzenbaum		
Howard, *US politician*	MET-suhn-BAWM, -BOWM	'metsən,bɔːm, -,baum
Meun, de		
see Jean de Meun		
Meunier		
Constantin, *Belgian sculptor*	muh(r)n-YĀ	mœːnjeː
Meunim		
Biblical name	mē-YO͞O-nim, muh-o͞o-NĒM	miː'juːnim, məuː'niːm
Meunites		
Biblical name	mē-(Y)O͞O-NĪTS	miː'(j)uː,nɑits
Meursault		
French wine	muhr-SŌ	mœrsoː
Meurthe		
river, France	MUHRT	mœrt

Key (col. 2): a: **fad** ā: **fade** ah: **father** ar: **marry** aw: **law** e: **fed** ē: **feed** er: **merry** i: **hid** ī: **hide** ō: **coat** o͞o: **boot** oi: **boy** ow: **now** u: **put** uh: **above** uhr: **bird** ch: **chop** ng: **ring** sh: **show** th: **thick** th: **this** zh: **measure**

Meurthe-et-Moselle
  dept, France   MUHR-tã-mō-ZEL   mœrteːmoːzel

Meuse
  river, Europe; dept., France   MUH(R)Z, ⑤ MYŌOZ   mœːz, ⑤ 'mjuːz

Mewari [Rajasthani]
  lang., India, Pakistan   muh-WAHR-ē   mə'wɑriˑ

Me-Wuk
  N. American people   MĒ-WUHK   'miːˌwək

Mexia
  city, TX   muh-HĀ-uh *[sic]*   mə'heːə *[sic]*

Mexicali
  city, Mexico   MEK-si-KAL-ē   ˌmeksi'kæliˑ

Mexican
  pert. to Mexico   MEK-si-kuhn   'meksikən

Mexico, México
  republic, N. America   MĀ-hē-kō, ⑤ MEK-si-KŌ   'meˑhiːkoː, ⑤ 'meksiˌkoː

Mextitlaneca
  N. American people   MEK-STĒT-luh-NĀ-kuh   ˌmekˌstiːtlə'neːkə

Meyer
  pers. name   MĪ-uhr   'mɑiəʳ

Meyerbeer
  Giacomo, *German composer*   MĪR-BĀR, ⑤ MĪR-BIR   'mɑiʳˌbeːʳ, ⑤ 'mɑiʳˌbiʳ

Meyerhof
  Otto, *German physiologist (Nobel*   MĪ-uhr-HŌF   'mɑiəʳˌhoːf
  1922)

Meyerhoff
  concert hall, Baltimore   MĪ-ER-hawf   'mɑiˌeʳhɔːf

Meynell
  Wilfrid, *English journalist and writer;*   MEN-l   'menl̩
  Alice Christiana Gertrude, *poet*
  and essayist

Mezada
  mountaintop, Israel   muh-ZAHD-uh   mə'zɑdə

Mezahab
  Biblical name   MEZ-uh-HAB, MĀ-zah-HAHV   'mezəˌhæb, ˌmeːzɑ'hɑv

Mezentius
  Etruscan king defeated by Aeneas   muh-ZEN-sh(ē-)uhs,   mə'zenʃ(iː)əs, mə'zentʃ(iː)əs
                                    muh-ZEN-ch(ē-)uhs

Mezobaite
  Biblical name   muh-ZŌ-bē-ĪT   mə'zoːbiːˌɑit

Mezzogiorno
  region, Italy   MET-sō-JAWR-nō   ˌmetso'dʒɔːʳnoː

Mfume
  Kweisi, *US politician, civil rights*   em-FŌO-mã, m-   em'fuːmeː, m̩-
  leader

MIA
  soldier listed as missing in action   EM-Ī-Ā   ˌemˌɑi'eː

Mia
  pers. name   MĒ-uh   'miːə

Miami
  river, OH; city, FL; N. American   mī-AM-ē, mī-AM-uh   mɑi'æmiˑ, mɑi'æmə
  people

Miamin
  Biblical name   MĪ-uh-MIN, mē-AHM-uhn, mi-yah-MIN   'mɑiəˌmin, miː'ɑmən,
                                                                       mijɑ'min

---

Foreign Sounds: ue: *Fr.* **rue**, *Ger.* **füllen**   uh(r): *Fr.* **boeuf**, *Ger.* **Höhle**   kh: *Ger.* **ich**, *Scot.* **loch**   g̃: *Sp.* ami**g**o   v̱: *Sp.* ha**b**lar
hl: *Welsh* **Ll**anelli.   CAPITALS: primary stress.   SMALL CAPS: secondary stress.   ⑤: U.S. pron.   ⑥: British pron.

Mianus
   village, river, CT   mī-AN-uhs   mɑiˈænəs

Miao, Meo [Hmong]
   lang., people, China, Vietnam, Laos,   mē-OW   miːˈɑu
     Thailand

Mibhar
   Biblical name   MIB-HAHR, miv-<u>KH</u>AHR   ˈmibˌhɑ^r, mivˈxɑr

Mibsam
   Biblical name   MIB-SAM, miv-SAHM   ˈmibˌsæm, mivˈsɑm

Mibzar
   Biblical name   MIB-ZAHR, miv-TSAHR   ˈmibˌzɑ^r, mivˈtsɑr

Mica, Micah
   Biblical name   MĪ-kuh, mē-<u>KH</u>AH   ˈmɑikə, miːˈxɑ

Micah
   Old Testament book; pers. name   MĪ-kuh   ˈmɑikə

Micaiah, Michaiah
   Biblical name   mī-KĪ-uh, -KĀ-uh; MĒ-<u>kh</u>ah-YAH   mɑiˈkɑiə, -ˈkeːə; ˌmiːxɑˈjɑ

Micawber
   Wilkins, *character in* David   mi-KAWB-uhr, mi-KAHB-uhr   miˈkɔːbə^r, miˈkɑbə^r
    Copperfield, *Dickens*

Miccosukee
   N. American people   MIK-uh-S͞OO-kē   ˌmikəˈsuːkiˑ

Michael
   1. pers. name   MĪ-kuhl   ˈmɑikəl
   2. Danish   mi-KAHL, MĒK-kuhl   miˈkɑːl, ˈmiːkkəl
   3. Dutch   MĒ-<u>kh</u>ah-EL   ˈmiːxɑːˌel
   4. Finnish   MĒ-kah-EL   ˈmiːkɑːˌel
   5. German   MI<u>KH</u>-ah-EL   ˈmiçɑˌel
   6. Norwegian   mē-KAHL   miːˈkɑl
   7. Serbo-Croatian   MĒ-<u>kh</u>ah-el   ˈmiːxɑːel

Michaela
   pers. name   muh-KĀ-luh   məˈkeːlə

Michaelmas
   feast of St. Michael the Archangel,   MIK-uhl-muhs   ˈmikəlməs
    Sept. 29th

Michaiah
   see Micaiah

Michal
   Biblical name   MĪ-kuhl, mē-<u>KH</u>AHL   ˈmɑikəl, miːˈxɑl

Micheas
   Old Testament book   MĪ-kē-uhs, mī-KĒ-uhs   ˈmɑikiːəs, mɑiˈkiːəs

Michel
   1. Hartmut, *German biochemist*   MI<u>KH</u>-uhl   ˈmiçəl
    (Nobel 1988)
   2. pers. name   MĪ-kuhl   ˈmɑikəl
   3. French   mē-SHEL   miːʃel
   4. German   MI<u>KH</u>-uhl   ˈmiçəl

Michel Angelo, Michelangelo
   1. Italian artist; pers. name   MĪ-kuh-LAN-juh-LŌ, MIK-uh-, MĒ-kuh-   ˌmɑikəˈlændʒəˌloː, ˌmikə-, ˌmiːkə-
   2. Italian   MĒ-kā-LAHN-jā-LŌ   ˌmiːkeːˈlɑndʒeːˌloː

Michele
   1. pers. name   mi-SHEL   miˈʃel
   2. Italian   mē-KEL-ā   miːˈkeleː

Key (col. 2):   a: fa**d**   ā: fa**de**   ah: f**a**ther   ar: m**a**rry   aw: l**a**w   e: f**e**d   ē: f**ee**d   er: m**e**rry   i: h**i**d   ī: h**i**de   ō: c**oa**t   o͞o: b**oo**t
oi: b**oy**   ow: n**ow**   u: p**u**t   uh: **a**bove   uhr: b**i**rd   ch: **ch**op   ng: ri**ng**   sh: **sh**ow   th: **th**ick   <u>th</u>: **th**is   zh: mea**s**ure

Michelin
  French tire manufacturer; travel   MISH-(uh-)luhn, MICH-uh-luhn   'mɪʃ(ə)lən, 'mɪtʃələn
  guide
Michelle
  1. pers. name   mi-SHEL   mi'ʃel
  2. French   mē-SHEL   miːʃel
Michelob
  US beer   MIK-uh-LŌB   'mɪkəˌloːb
Michelson
  Albert A., German-born US physicist   MĪ-kuhl-suhn   'mɑikəlsən
  (Nobel 1907)
Michener
  James, US novelist   MICH-nuhr   'mɪtʃnəʳ
Michigamme
  river, MI   MISH-uh-GAHM-ē, -GAM-ē   ˌmɪʃə'gɑmiˑ, -'gæmiˑ
Michigan
  lake, state, US   MISH-i-guhn   'mɪʃigən
Michigander
  inhabitant of Michigan   MISH-i-GAN-duhr   ˌmɪʃi'gændəʳ
Michiganite
  inhabitant of Michigan   MISH-i-guh-NĪT   'mɪʃigəˌnɑit
Michio
  pers. name, Japanese   mē-chē-ō   miːtʃiːoː
Michmas [Michmash]
  Biblical name   MIK-muhs, mikh-MAHS   'mɪkməs, mix'mɑs
Michmash
  Biblical name   MIK-MASH, mikh-MAHSH   'mɪkˌmæʃ, mix'mɑʃ
Michmethah [Michmethath]
  Biblical name   MIK-muh-thuh, MIKH-muh-TAHT   'mɪkməθə, ˌmixmə'tɑt
Michmethath
  Biblical name   MIK-muh-THATH, MIKH-muh-TAHT   'mɪkməˌθæθ, ˌmixmə'tɑt
Michoacán
  state, Mexico   mē-chuh-wah-KAHN   miːtʃəwɑ'kɑn
Michri
  Biblical name   MIK-RĪ, mikh-RĒ   'mɪkˌrɑi, mix'riː
Mick
  pers. name   MIK   'mɪk
Mickey
  pers. name   MIK-ē   'mɪkiˑ
Mickey Finn
  drugged drink   MIK-ē FIN   ˌmɪkiˑ 'fɪn
Micmac
  N. American people   MIK-MAK   'mɪkˌmæk
MicroGeneSys
  US biotechnology co.   MĪ-krō-JEN-uh-suhs   ˌmɑikroː'dʒenəsəs
Micronesia
  islands of the western Pacific   MĪ-kruh-NĒ-zhuh, -NĒ-shuh   ˌmɑikrə'niːʒə, -'niːʃə
Micronesian
  pert. to Micronesia   MĪ-kruh-NĒ-zhuhn, -NĒ-shuhn   ˌmɑikrə'niːʒən, -'niːʃən
Microscopium
  constellation   MĪ-kruh-SKŌ-pē-uhm   ˌmɑikrə'skoːpiːəm
Midas
  king of Phrygia with golden touch   MĪD-uhs   'mɑidəs
Middin
  Biblical name   MID-n, mi-DĒN   'mɪdn̩, mi'diːn

Middlebury
  town, CT, VT; College, *VT*   MID-l-BER-ē   'midļ‚beri·

Middlemarch
  novel, George Eliot   MID-l-MAHRCH   'midļ‚maᵉtʃ

Middlesex
  former county, England; county, CT, MID-l-SEKS   'midļ‚seks
    MA, NJ, VA

Middletown
  town, NJ, CT, NY   MID-l-TOWN   'midļ‚taun

Mid Glamorgan
  county, Wales   MID gluh-MAWR-guhn   ‚mid glə'mɔːᵉgən

MIDI
  Musical Instrument Digital Interface MID-ē   'midi·

Midi
  south of France   mē-DĒ   miːdiː

Midian
  Biblical name   MID-ē-uhn, mid-YAHN   'midiːən, mid'jan

Midianite
  ancient Arabian people   MID-ē-uh-NĪT   'midiːə‚nait

Midi-Pyrénées
  region, France   mē-dē-pē-rā-NĀ   miːdiːpiːreːneː

Midler
  Bette, *US entertainer*   MID-luhr   'midləᵉ

Midlothian
  1. town, IL   mid-LŌ-thē-uhn   mid'loːθiːən
  2. county, Scotland   mid-LŌ-th͟e-uhn   mid'loːðiːən

Midori
  US violinist; melon liqueur   muh-DŌR-ē, muh-DAWR-ē   mə'doːri·, mə'dɔːri·

Midrash
  Hebrew scriptural interpretation   MID-RAHSH   'mid‚raʃ

Midrashim
  pl. of Midrash   mid-RAHSH-uhm   mid'raʃəm

Midsummer Day
  June 24   MID-SUHM-uhr DĀ   ‚mid‚səməᵉ 'deː

Midwest
  region, central US   mid-WEST   mid'west

Midwestern
  pert. to the Midwest   mid-WES-tuhrn   mid'westəᵉn

Midwesterner
  inhabitant of the Midwest   mid-WES-tuhr-nuhr   mid'westəᵉnəᵉ

Mieczysław
  pers. name, Polish   mye-CHIS-lahf   mje'tʃisɫaːf

Mielziner
  Jo, *US theatrical designer*   mēl-ZĒ-nuhr, mel-   miːl'ziːnəᵉ, mel-

Miesian
  pert. to Mies van der Rohe   MĒ-sē-uhn, MĒ-shuhn   'miːsiːən, 'miːʃən

Mies van der Rohe
  Ludwig, *US architect*   MĒS VAHN duh RŌ-uh, MĒZ   ‚miːs ‚van də 'roːə, ‚miːz

Mifune
  Toshiro, *Japanese entertainer*   mē-fun-e   miːfune

MiG
  Russian fighter aircraft   MIG   'mig

Migdal-Eder
  Biblical name   MIG-DAL-ĒD-uhr, mig-DAHL-E-der   'mig‚dæl'iːdəᵉ, mig‚dal'eder

---

Key (col. 2):   a: fad ā: fade ah: father ar: marry aw: law e: fed ē: feed er: merry i: hid ī: hide ō: coat ōō: boot
oi: boy ow: now u: put uh: above uhr: bird ch: chop ng: ring sh: show th: thick t͟h: this zh: measure

Migdal-el
    Biblical name   MIG-DAL-EL, mig-DAHL-EL   'mig,dæl,el, mig,dɑl'el

Migdal-gad
    Biblical name   MIG-DAL-GAD, mig-DAHL-GAHD   'mig,dæl,gæd, mig,dɑl'gɑd

Migdol
    Biblical name   MIG-DAHL, mig-DAWL   'mig,dɑl, mig'dɔːl

Mignonette
    flower   MIN-yuh-NET   ˌminjə'net

Migron
    Biblical name   MIG-RAHN, mig-RŌN   'mig,rɑn, mig'roːn

Miguel
    1. pers. name, Portuguese   mē-GEL   miːˈgel
    2. Spanish   mē-ḠEL   miːˈɣel

Mihai
    pers. name, Romanian   mē-HĪ   miːˈhɑi

Mihail
    pers. name, Romanian   MĒ-hah-EL   ˌmiːhɑ'el

Mihály
    pers. name, Hungarian   MI-hahl   'mihɑːl̦

Mijamin
    Biblical name   MIJ-uh-MIN, MI-yah-MIN   'midʒə,min, ˌmijɑ'min

Mikado
    operetta, Gilbert & Sullivan   mi-KAHD-ō   mi'kado:

Mike
    pers. name   MĪK   'mɑik

Mikhail
    1. pers. name, Bulgarian   MĒ-<u>kh</u>ah-ĒL, Ⓢ mi-KĪL   ˌmiːxɑ'iːl, Ⓢ mi'kɑil
    2. Russian   MI<u>KH</u>-UH-ĒL, Ⓢ mi-KĪL   ˌmi̦ç,ə'iːl, Ⓢ mi'kɑil

Mikhailovich
    patronym, Russian   myi-<u>KHĪ</u>L(-uhv)-YICH,   mji'xɑil(əv),jitʃ,
                           Ⓢ mi-KĪ-luh-VICH   Ⓢ mi'kɑilə,vitʃ

Miki
    Takeo, *Japanese politician*   mē-kē   miːkiː

Miklós
    pers. name, Hungarian   MIK-LŌSH   'mik,loːʃ

Mikloth
    Biblical name   MIK-LAHTH, mik-LŌT   'mik,lɑθ, mik'loːt

Mikneiah
    Biblical Names   mik-NĪ-uh, mik-NĒ-uh,   mik'nɑiə, mik'niːə,
                       MIK-ne-YAH-hoo   ˌmikne'jahuː

Mikołaj
    pers. name, Polish   mē-KAWL-Ī   miːˈkɔːł,ɑi

Míkonos, Mykonos
    island, Greece   MĒ-kuh-NAWS   'miːkə,nɔːs

Mikoyan
    Anastas, *Soviet political leader*   MYĒ-kō-YAHN   ˌmjiːkoːˈjɑːn

Milalai
    Biblical name   MIL-uh-LĪ, MIL-uh-LĀ-Ī, MI-lah-LĪ   'milə,lɑi, ˌmilə'leːˌɑi,
                          ˌmilɑ'lɑi

Milan
    1. city, Italy   muh-LAN, muh-LAHN   mə'læn, mə'lɑn
    2. US pl. name   MĪ-luhn   'mɑilən
    3. pers. name, Czech   MIL-AHN   'mil,ɑːn

Milanese
    pert. to Milan   MIL-uh-NĒZ, -NES   ˌmilə'niːz, -'niːs

Foreign Sounds: ue: *Fr.* **rue**, *Ger.* füllen   uh(r): *Fr.* **boeuf**, *Ger.* Höhle   <u>kh</u>: *Ger.* i**ch**, *Scot.* lo**ch**   ḡ: *Sp.* ami**g**o   <u>v</u>: *Sp.* ha**b**lar
hl: *Welsh* **Ll**anelli.   CAPITALS: primary stress.   SMALL CAPS: secondary stress.   Ⓢ: U.S. pron.   Ⓔ: British pron.

Milano [Milan]
   city, Italy   mē-LAHN-ō   mi:'lɑnoː
Milcah
   Biblical name   MIL-kuh, mil-KAH   'milkə, mil'kɑ
Milcom
   Biblical name   MIL-KAHM, mil-KAWM   'mil‚kɑm, mil'kɔːm
Mildred
   pers. name   MIL-druhd   'mildrəd
Mildura
   city, Australia   mil-DYUR-uh   mil'djurə
Miles
   pers. name   MĪLZ   'mɑilz
Milesian
   pert. to Miletus   mī-LĒ-zhuhn, mī-LĒ-shuhn   mɑi'liːʒən, mɑi'liːʃən
Miletus
   ancient city, Asia Minor   mī-LĒT-uhs, muh-LĒT-uhs   mɑi'liːțəs, mə'liːțəs
Milhaud
   Darius, French composer   mē-YŌ   mi:joː
Milhous
   pers. name   MIL-HOWS   'mil‚hɑus
Millard
   pers. name   MIL-uhrd   'miləʳd
Millay
   Edna St. Vincent, US poet   mil-Ā   mil'eː
Mille Lacs
   lake, county, Indian reservation, MN;   mil (L)AK(S)   mil '(l)æk(s)
     lake, Canada
Millet
   Jean François, French painter   mē-YE, mē-LE   mi:je, mi:le
Millicent
   pers. name   MIL-uh-suhnt   'miləsənt
Millie
   former First Dog; pers. name   MIL-ē   'mili·
Milligan
   College, TN   MIL-uh-guhn   'miləgən
Millikan
   Robert A., US physicist (Nobel 1923)   MIL-i-kuhn   'milikən
Millikin
   University, IL   MIL-i-kuhn   'milikən
Millington
   pers. name   MIL-ing-tuhn   'miliŋtən
Milli Vanilli
   lip-synching rock group   MIL-ē vuh-NIL-ē   ‚mili· və'nili·
Millo
   Biblical name   MIL-ō, mi-LŌ   'mil‚oː, mi'loː
Millsaps
   College, MS   MIL-SAPS   'mil‚sæps
Milly
   pers. name   MIL-ē   'mili·
Milne
   A. A., British author; pers. name   MILN, MIL   'miln, 'mil
Milner
   pers. name   MIL-nuhr   'milnəʳ
Milo
   pers. name   MĪ-lō   'mɑiloː

Key (col. 2):   a: **fad**   ā: **fade**   ah: **father**   ar: **marry**   aw: **law**   e: **fed**   ē: **feed**   er: **merry**   i: **hid**   ī: **hide**   ō: **coat**   ōō: **boot**
oi: **boy**   ow: **now**   u: **put**   uh: **above**   uhr: **bird**   ch: **chop**   ng: **ring**   sh: **show**   th: **thick**   <u>th</u>: **this**   zh: **measure**

Milo [Melos]
 island, Aegean   MḖ-lō   'miːloː
Milos
 pers. name, Czech   MIL-aws   'milɔːs
Mílos [Melos]
 island, Aegean   MḖ-LAHS, MḖ-LAWS 'miːˌlɑs, 'miːˌlɔːs
Milošević
 Slobodan, *Serbian politician* muh-LAW-shuh-VICH məˈlɔːʃəˌvitʃ
Miłosz
 Czesław, *Lithuanian-born US poet,* MḖ-lawsh   'miːɫɔːʃ
  author (Nobel 1980)
Milovan
 pers. name, Serbo-Croatian MḖ-law-VAHN   'miːlɔːˌvɑːn
Milpitas
 city, CA   mil-PḖT-uhs   milˈpiːʈəs
Milquetoast
 Caspar, *comic strip character by H.* MILK-TŌST   'milkˌtoːst
  T. Webster; timid person
Milsap
 Ronnie, *US country musician* MIL-SAP   'milˌsæp
Milstein
 Cesar, *Argentine-born British* MIL-STĪN   'milˌstɑin
  molecular biologist (Nobel 1984)
Milt
 pers. name   MILT   'milt
Miltiades
 Athenian politician, general; pope mil-TĪ-uh-DĒZ   milˈtɑiəˌdiːz
Milton
 John, *English poet; pers. name* MILT-n   'miltn̩
Milton Keynes
 town, England   MILT-n KĒNZ   ˌmiltn̩ 'kiːnz
Milvian Bridge
 ancient battle site north of Rome MIL-vē-uhn BRIJ 'milviːən 'bridʒ
Milwaukee
 city, WI   mil-WAW-kē   milˈwɔːkiˑ
Milwaukie
 city, OR   mil-WAW-kē   milˈwɔːkiː
Mimas
 satellite of Saturn   MĪ-muhs   'mɑiməs
Mimbres
 river, mtn. range, village, NM MIM-bruhs   'mimbrəs
Mimi
 1. lang., Sudan; pers. name MḖ-mē   'miːmiˑ
 2. French   mē-MḖ   miːmiː
Mimieux
 Yvette, *US entertainer* mēm-YUH(R)   miːmjœː
Min
 Egyptian fertility god; lang., China MIN   'min
Mina
 lang., Togo   MḖ-nuh   'miːnə
Minamata
 disease, mercury poisoning MIN-uh-MAHT-uh ˌminəˈmɑʈə
Minan
 lang., China   MḖ-nuhn   'miːnən

Foreign Sounds: ue: *Fr.* **rue**, *Ger.* **füllen** uh(r): *Fr.* **boeuf**, *Ger.* **Höhle** <u>kh</u>: *Ger.* i**ch**, *Scot.* lo**ch** g̱: *Sp.* ami**g**o v̱: *Sp.* ha**b**lar
hl: *Welsh* **Ll**anelli. CAPITALS: primary stress. SMALL CAPS: secondary stress. $), US. pron. £): British pron.

Minangkabau
   lang., people, West Sumatra   MĒ-NAHNG-kuh-BOW   ˌmiːˌnaŋkəˈbau
Minas Gerais
   state, Brazil   MĒ-nuhs zhuh-RĪS   ˌmiːnəs ʒəˈrais
Minchia [Pai]
   lang., people, China   MIN-jē-AH   ˈmindʒiːˈa
Mindanao
   island, Philippines   MIN-duh-NAH-ō, MIN-duh-NOW   ˌmindəˈnaoː, ˌmindəˈnau
Mindoro
   island, Philippines   min-DŌR-ō, min-DAWR-ō   minˈdoːroː, minˈdɔːroː
Mindy
   pers. name   MIN-dē   ˈmindiˑ
Mineola
   village, NY; city, TX   MIN-ē-Ō-luh   ˌminiːˈoːlə
Minerva
   Roman goddess of wisdom; pers.   muh-NUHR-vuh   məˈnəʳvə
   name
Minestrone
   soup   MIN-uh-STRŌ-nē   ˌminəˈstroːniˑ
Ming
   Chinese dynasty   MING   ˈmiŋ
Minge
   pers. name   MINJ   ˈmindʒ
Mingus
   Charles, US jazz musician   MING-guhs   ˈmiŋgəs
Minho
   river, Europe; prov., Portugal   MĒN-yoo   ˈmiːnjuː
Miniamin
   Biblical name   mi-NĪ-uh-MIN, MIN-ī-uh-MIN, miˈnaiəˌmin, ˈminaiəˌmin,
                                            min-yah-MIN   minjaˈmin
Minidoka
   county, ID   MIN-uh-DŌ-kuh   ˌminəˈdoːkə
Minié
   Claude-Étienne, French militarist   mēn-YĀ, Ⓢ MIN-ē-Ā   miːnjeː, Ⓢ ˈminiːˌeː
Minié ball
   muzzle-loading bullet   MIN-ē BAWL, MIN-ē-Ā BAWL   ˈminiˑ ˌbɔːl, ˈminiːˌeː ˈbɔːl
Ministerium für Staatssicherheit
[Stasi]
   East German security organization   MIN-is-TER-yum fuer   ˌminisˈteʳjum fyːʳ
                                            SHTAHT-ZIKH-uhr-HĪT   ˈʃtatˌziçəʳˌhait
Miniver
   pers. name   MIN-uh-vuhr   ˈminəvəʳ
Minivet
   bird   MIN-uh-VET   ˈminəˌvet
Minmi
   Australia   MIN-MĪ   ˈminˌmai
Minneapolis
   city, MN   MIN-ē-AP-(uh-)luhs   ˌminiːˈæp(ə)ləs
Minnehaha
   county, SD   MIN-ē-HAH-HAH   ˌminiːˈhaˌha
Minnelli
   Liza, US entertainer; Vincent, *(her* muh-NEL-ē   məˈneliˑ
   father) US director
Minnesota
   state, US   MIN-uh-SŌT-uh   ˌminəˈsoːʈə

Key (col. 2):   a: fad ā: fade ah: father ar: marry aw: law e: fed ē: feed er: merry i: hid ī: hide ō: coat oo: boot
oi: boy ow: now u: put uh: above uhr: bird ch: chop ng: ring sh: show th: thick <u>th</u>: this zh: measure

Minnesotan
    pert. to Minnesota; *inhabitant of*   MIN-uh-SŌT-n   ˌminəˈsoːtn̩
    Minnesota

Minnetonka
    lake, MN   MIN-uh-TAHNG-kuh   ˌminəˈtaŋkə

Minni
    Biblical name for Armenia   MIN-Ī, mi-NĒ   ˈminˌai, miˈniː

Minnie, -ny
    pers. name   MIN-ē   ˈmini·

Minnith
    Biblical name   MIN-uhth, mi-NĒT   ˈminəθ, miˈniːt

Minoan
    ancient Cretan culture, lang.   muh-NŌ-uhn   məˈnoːən

Minolta
    Japanese camera co.   muh-NŌL-tuh, muh-NAHL-tuh   məˈnoːltə, məˈnaltə

Minonk
    city, IL   mi-NAHNGK, mi-NUHNGK   miˈnaŋk, miˈnəŋk

Minorca
    island, Balearic Islands   muh-NAWR-kuh   məˈnɔːʳkə

Minoru
    pers. name, Japanese   mē-nō-r͞oo   miːnoːruː

Minos
    legendary Cretan king   MĪ-nuhs   ˈmainəs

Minot
    1. city, ND   MĪ-NAHT   ˈmaiˌnat
    2. G. R., US physician (Nobel 1934);   MĪ-nuht   ˈmainət
    pers. name

Minotaur
    half-man, half-bull of Greek myth   MIN-uh-TAWR, MĪ-nuh-TAWR   ˈminəˌtɔːʳ, ˈmainəˌtɔːʳ

Minsk
    city, Belorussia   MIN(T)SK   ˈmin(t)sk

Minucius
    Roman name   muh-N(Y)͞OO-shē-uhs   məˈn(j)uːʃiːəs

Minuet
    dance   MIN-yuh-WET   ˌminjəˈwet

Minuit
    Peter, *Dutch colonist*   MIN-yuh-wuht   ˈminjəwət

Minuteman
    Revolutionary War militia; US   MIN-uht-MAN   ˈminətˌmæn
    ballistic missile

Minya, El [Al-Minya]
    city, Egypt   el MIN-yuh   el ˈminjə

Minyads
    Minyas' daughters who offended   MIN-YADZ, MIN-ē-ADZ   ˈminˌjædz, ˈminiːˌædz
    Dionysus

Minyas
    king of Orchomenus   MIN-yuhs   ˈminjəs

Mio
    village, MI   MĪ-ō   ˈmaiˌoː

Miocene
    geologic epoch   MĪ-uh-SĒN   ˈmaiəˌsiːn

Miphkad
    Biblical name   MIF-KAD, mif-KAHD   ˈmifˌkæd, mifˈkad

MIPS
    million instructions per second   MIPS   ˈmips

Foreign Sounds: ue: *Fr.* **rue**, *Ger.* **fü**llen   uh(r): *Fr.* b**oeuf**, *Ger.* H**öh**le   kh: *Ger.* i**ch**, *Scot.* lo**ch**   ḡ: *Sp.* ami**g**o   v: *Sp.* ha**b**lar
hl: *Welsh* **Ll**anelli.   CAPITALS: primary stress.   SMALL CAPS: secondary stress.   Ⓢ: U.S. pron.   Ⓔ: British pron.

Miquelon		
see Saint-Pierre & Miquelon		
Mira		
pers. name (M. Sorvino)	MIR-uh, MĪ-ruh	'mirə, 'mɑirə
Mirabeau		
pers. name	MIR-uh-BŌ	'mirə,boː
Mira Costa		
College, *CA*	MIR-uh KAHS-tuh	'mirə 'kɑstə
Miraflores		
village, lake, Panama	MIR-uh-FLŌR-uhs, MIR-uh-FLAWR-uhs	,mirə'floːrəs, ,mirə'flɔːrəs
Miramar		
city, FL	MIR-uh-MAHR	'mirə,mɑʳ
Miramichi		
river, Canada	MIR-uh-muh-SHĒ	,mirəmə'ʃiː
Miranda		
satellite of Uranus; US Supreme Court ruling; pers. name	muh-RAN-duh	mə'rændə
Mirani		
Australia	mir-AN-ē	mir'æniˑ
Mircea		
pers. name (M. Eliade)	MUHR-shuh	'məʳʃə
Miriam		
pers. name	MIR-ē-uhm	'miriːəm
Mirma, Mirmah		
Biblical name	MUHR-muh, MIR-muh, mir-MAH	'məʳmə, 'miʳmə, mir'mɑ
Miró		
Joan, *Spanish artist*	mē-RŌ	miː'roː
Mirro		
tdmk for cookware	MIR-ō	'miroː
MIRV		
multiple independently targetable reentry vehicle	MUHRV	'məʳv
Misbourne		
river, England	MIS-buhrn, MIZ-buhrn	'misbəʳn, 'mizbəʳn
Mischa		
pers. name, Russian	MĒ-shuh	'miːʃə
Misenum		
headland on Bay of Naples	mī-SĒ-nuhm	mɑi'siːnəm
Misenus		
trumpeter drowned by Triton in the Aeneid	mī-SĒ-nuhs	mɑi'siːnəs
Misérables, Les		
novel, V. Hugo	lā mē-zā-RAHBL, [S] LĀ MIZ-uh-RAHB(-luh)	leː miːzeːrɑːbl, [S] ,leː ,mizə'rɑb(lə)
Miserere		
prayer, Latin "have mercy"	MIZ-uh-RIR-ē, MIZ-uh-RER-ē, MIZ-uh-RĀ-rā	,mizə'riri˙, ,mizə'reri˙, ,mizə'reːreː
Misgab		
Biblical name	MIS-GAB, mis-GAHV	'mis,gæb, mis'gɑv
Mishael		
Biblical name	MISH-ē-EL, MĪ-shē-uhl, MĒ-shah-EL	'miʃiː,el, 'mɑiʃiːəl, ,miːʃɑ'el
Mishal		
Biblical name	MĪ-SHAL, mē-SHAHL	'mɑi,ʃæl, miː'ʃɑl
Misham		
Biblical name	MĪ-SHAM, mish-AHM	'mɑi,ʃæm, miʃ'ɑm

Key (col. 2): a: **fad** ā: **fade** ah: **father** ar: **marry** aw: **law** e: **fed** ē: **feed** er: **merry** i: **hid** ī: **hide** ō: **coat** ōō: **boot** oi: **boy** ow: **now** u: **put** uh: **above** uhr: **bird** ch: **chop** ng: **ring** sh: **show** th: **thick** th̲: **this** zh: **measure**

Mishawaka
 city, IN — MISH-uh-WAHK-uh, -WAW-kuh — ˌmɪʃəˈwɑkə, -ˈwɔːkə

Mishma
 Biblical name — MISH-muh, mish-MAH — ˈmɪʃmə, mɪʃˈmɑ

Mishmannah
 Biblical name — mish-MAN-uh, MISH-mah-NAH — mɪʃˈmænə, ˌmɪʃmɑˈnɑ

Mishna, -nah
 Jewish oral law — MISH-nuh — ˈmɪʃnə

Mishraite
 Biblical name — MISH-rē-ĪT — ˈmɪʃriːˌɑit

Miskito [Mosquito]
 Cen. American people — muh-SKĒT-ō — məˈskiːtoː

Mispereth
 Biblical name — MIS-puh-RETH, mis-PER-et — ˈmɪspəˌreθ, mɪsˈperet

Misrephoth-maim
 Biblical name — MIS-ruh-FAHTH-MĀ-uhm, MIS-ruh-FŌT-MAH-yim — ˈmɪsrəˌfɑθˈmeːəm, ˌmɪsrəˌfoːtˈmɑjim

Miss
 form of address for an unmarried woman — MIS, mis, muhs — ˈmɪs, mɪs, məs

Missa Brevis
 Latin "short mass" — MIS-uh BREV-uhs — ˌmɪsə ˈbrevəs

Missa Solemnis
 Latin "solemn mass" — MIS-uh suh-LEM-nuhs — ˌmɪsə səˈlemnəs

Missaukee
 county, MI — mi-SAW-kē — mɪˈsɔːkiˑ

Missenden
 former name of the Misbourne River, *England* — MIS-n-duhn — ˈmɪsn̩dən

Missinaibi
 river, Canada — MIS-uh-NĪ-bē — ˌmɪsəˈnɑibiˑ

Mission Haut Brion, La
 wine — lah mēs-YAWⁿ ō brē-AWⁿ — lɑː miːsjɔ̃ oː briːɔ̃

Missisquoi
 river, United States, Canada — muh-SIS-KWOI — məˈsɪsˌkwɔi

Mississagi
 river, Canada — MIS-uh-SAHG-ē — ˌmɪsəˈsɑgiˑ

Mississauga
 town, Canada — MIS-uh-SAW-guh — ˌmɪsəˈsɔːgə

Mississippi
 river, state, US — MIS-(uh-)SIP-ē — ˌmɪs(ə)ˈsipiˑ

Mississippian
 geologic period; pert. to Mississippi — MIS-(uh-)SIP-ē-uhn — ˌmɪs(ə)ˈsipiːən

Missoula
 city, county, MT — muh-ZOO-luh — məˈzuːlə

Missouri
 state, US; N. American people — muh-ZUR-ē, muh-ZUR-uh — məˈzuriˑ, məˈzurə

Missourian
 pert. to Missouri; *inhabitant of* Missouri — muh-ZUR-ē-uhn — məˈzuriːən

Missy
 pers. name — MIS-ē — ˈmɪsiˑ

Mistassini
 river, Canada — MIS-tuh-SĒ-nē — ˌmɪstəˈsiːniˑ

Foreign Sounds: ue: *Fr.* **rue**, *Ger.* füllen uh(r): *Fr.* **boeuf**, *Ger.* Höhle k͟h: *Ger.* i**ch**, *Scot.* lo**ch** ḡ: *Sp.* ami**g**o v̲: *Sp.* ha**b**lar
hl: *Welsh* **Ll**anelli. CAPITALS: primary stress. SMALL CAPS: secondary stress. Ⓢ: U.S. pron. Ⓔ: British pron.

Mister

   form of address for a man MIS-tuhr, MIS-tuhr 'mistə^r, ˌmistə^r

Misti, El

   volcano, Peru el MĒ-stē, el MIS-tē el 'miːstiː, el 'mistiˑ

Mistral

   1. Frédéric, *Provençal poet (Nobel 1904)* mē-STRAHL miːstrɑːl

   2. Gabriela, *Chilean poet, diplomat (Nobel 1945)* mē-STRAHL miːˈstrɑl

   3. wind MIS-truhl 'mistrəl

Mita

   tdmk for a photocopying machine MĒT-uh 'miːt̬ə

Mitanni

   ancient Mesopotamian people muh-TAN-ē məˈtæniˑ

Mitch

   pers. name MICH 'mitʃ

Mitchell

   Peter, *English biochemist (Nobel 1978); pers. name* MICH-uhl 'mitʃəl

Mitchum

   Robert, *US actor* MICH-uhm 'mitʃəm

Mithkah

   Biblical name MITH-kuh, mi-KAH 'miθkə, miˈkɑ

Mithnite

   Biblical name MITH-NĪT 'miθˌnait

Mithraism

   ancient cult of Mithras MITH-ruh-IZ-uhm, MITH-RĀ-IZ-uhm 'miθrəˌizəm, 'miθˌreːˌizəm

Mithras

   supreme Persian god MITH-ruhs 'miθrəs

Mithredath

   Biblical name MITH-ruh-DATH, mit-ruh-DAHT 'miθrəˌdæθ, mitrəˈdɑt

Mithridates

   king of Parthia MITH-ruh-DĀT-ēz ˌmiθrəˈdeːt̬iːz

Mitla

   ancient city, Mexico MĒT-lah 'miːtlɑ

Mitsubishi

   Japanese corp. MIT-su-BĒ-shē ˌmitsuˈbiːʃiˑ

Mitsui

   Japanese trading co MIT-soo-ē 'mitsuːiˑ

Mittagong

   town, Australia MIT-uh-GAHNG, -GAWNG 'mit̬əˌgaŋ, -ˌgɔːŋ

Mittelfranken

   prov, Germany MIT-l-FRAHNG-kuhn 'mitl̩ˌfraŋkən

Mittelheim

   German wine MIT-l-HĪM 'mitl̩ˌhaim

Mittelmosel

   German wine MIT-l-MŌ-zuhl 'mitl̩ˌmoːzəl

Mittelrhein

   German wine MIT-l-RĪN 'mitl̩ˌrain

Mitterrand

   François, *president, France* mē-ter-AHⁿ miːterɑ̃

Mitty

   Walter, *Thurber character* MIT-ē 'mit̬iˑ

Mitylene

   see Mytilene

Key (col. 2):   a: **fad** ā: **fade** ah: **father** ar: **marry** aw: **law** e: **fed** ē: **feed** er: **merry** i: **hid** ī: **hide** ō: **coat** oo: **boot**
oi: **boy** ow: **now** u: **put** uh: **above** uhr: **bird** ch: **chop** ng: **ring** sh: **show** th: **thick** th: **this** zh: **measure**

Mitzi
  pers. name   MIT-sē   'mitsi·

Mixe
  lang., people, Mexico   MĒ-HĀ   'miː‚heː

Mixolydian
  musical mode   MIK-suh-LID-ē-uhn   ‚miksə'lidiːən

Mixtec [Mixteco]
  N. American people   MĒ-STEK   'miː‚stek

Mixteco [Mixtec]
  N. American people   mē-STĀ-kō, mē-STEK-ō   miː'steːkoː, miː'stekoː

Miyazawa
  Kiichi, *Japanese prime minister*   mē-ah-zah-wah, ⓢ MĒ-uh-ZAH-wuh   miːɑzɑwɑ, ⓢ ‚miːə'zɑwə

Mizar
  Biblical name   MĪ-ZAHR, mit-SAHR   'mɑi‚zɑ^r, mit'sɑr

Mizpah
  towns, Palestine   MIZ-PAH, MIZ-puh   'miz‚pɑ, 'mizpə

Mizpeh [Mizpah]
  Biblical name   MIZ-puh, mits-PE   'mizpə, mits'pe

Mizraim
  Biblical name for Egypt   MIZ-rē-uhm, mits-RAH-yim   'mizriːəm, mits'rɑjim

Mizzah
  Biblical name   MIZ-uh, mi-ZAH   'mizə, mi'zɑ

Mladá Boleslav
  town, Czech republic   MLAHD-uh BAW-luh-SLAHF,   ‚mlɑdə 'bɔːlə‚slaf,
         ⓢ uhm-LAHD-uh   ⓢ əm‚lɑdə

Mmabatho
  town, S. Africa   mah-BAH-tō   mɑ'bɑtoː

Mnason
  Biblical name   (muh-)NĀ-suhn   (mə)'neːsən

Mnemon
  servant of Achilles   NĒ-MAHN, NĒ-muhn   'niː‚mɑn, 'niːmən

Mnemosyne
  Greek goddess of memory, mother of   ni-MAHS-n-ē, ni-MAHZ-n-ē   ni'mɑsni·, ni'mɑzni·
    the Muses

Mnestheus
  companion of Aeneas   NES-thē-uhs, NES-th(y)o͞os   'nesθiːəs, 'nesθ(j)uːs

Mo
  pers. name   MŌ   'moː

Moab
  ancient kingdom, Middle East; city,   MŌ-AB   'moː‚æb
    UT

Moabite
  native or inhabitant of Moab   MŌ-uh-BĪT   'moːə‚bɑit

Moadiah
  Biblical name   MŌ-uh-DĪ-uh, MŌ-ahd-YAH   ‚moːə'dɑiə, ‚moːad'jɑ

Moammar
  pers. name, Arabic   MŌ-uh-MAHR   'moːə‚mɑ^r

Moana
  Municipal Stadium, *Reno, NV*   mō-AN-uh   moː'ænə

Moapa
  Indian reservation, NV   mō-AP-uh   moː'æpə

Moberly
  city, MO   MŌ-buhr-lē   'moːbə^rli·

Mobil
  US oil co.   MŌB-uhl   'moːbəl

Mobile
  river, city, county, AL   mō-BĒL, MŌ-BĒL   moːˈbiːl, ˈmoːˌbiːl

Möbius
  band or strip, one-sided surface   MUH(R)-bē-uhs, MŌ-bē-uhs   ˈmœːbiːəs, ˈmoːbiːəs

Mobutu Sese Seko
  president, Zaire   muh-BOO-too SĀ-sā SĀ-kō   məˈbuːtu ˈseːseː ˈseːkoː

Moby Dick
  novel, H. Melville   MŌ-bē DIK   ˌmoːbiˈ ˈdik

Mocha
  1. seaport, Yemen; chocolate/coffee   MŌ-kuh   ˈmoːkə
    drink
  2. island, Pacific   MŌ-chuh   ˈmoːtʃə

Moctezuma [Montezuma]
  Aztec emperor   MAHK-tuh-ZOO-muh   ˌmɑktəˈzuːmə

Modelo Especial
  Mexican beer   mō-THĀ-lō es-pes-YAHL   moːˈðeːloː espesˈjɑl

Modem
  computer peripheral   MŌD-uhm, MŌ-DEM   ˈmoːdəm, ˈmoːˌdem

Modena
  prov & town, Italy   MAW-den-AH, ⓢ MAWD-n-uh,   ˈmɔːdenˌɑ, ⓢ ˈmɔːdn̩ə,
     MAWD-n-AH   ˈmɔːdn̩ˌɑ

Moderatus
  pers. name, Latin   MAHD-uh-RĀT-uhs   ˌmɑdəˈreːt̬əs

Modest
  pers. name, Russian   MUHD-YEST   ˌmədˈjest

Modeste
  pers. name, French   maw-DEST   mɔːdest

Modesto
  1. city, CA   muh-DES-tō   məˈdestoː
  2. pers. name, Spanish   mō-THĀ-stō   moːˈðeːstoː

Modigliani
  Amedeo, Italian artist; Franco,   MŌ-dēl-YAHN-ē, MAWD-l-YAHN-ē   ˌmoːdiːlˈjaniˈ, ˌmɔːdl̩ˈjaniˈ
    Italian-born US economist (Nobel
    1985)

Modius Fabidius
  son of the Sabine god Quirinus   MŌD-ē-uhs fuh-BID-ē-uhs   ˌmoːdiːəs fəˈbidiːəs

Modjeska
  Helena, US actress   muh-JES-kuh   məˈdʒeskə

Modoc
  county, CA; N. American people   MŌD-AHK   ˈmoːdˌɑk

Modred [Mordred]
  Arthurian villain   MŌ-druhd   ˈmoːdrəd

Modrow
  Hans, German politican   MŌ-DRŌ   ˈmoːˌdroː

Moerae [Moirae]
  the Greek fates   MOI-RĪ   ˈmɔiˌrai

Moesia
  ancient country of southern Europe   MĒ-shuh, MĒ-sē-uh   ˈmiːʃə, ˈmiːsiːə

Moët & Chandon
  champagne   maw-ET ā shahⁿ-DAWⁿ, MWET   mɔːet eː ʃɑ̃dɔ̃, mwet

Mofaddaliyat
  see Mufaddaliyat

Moffat
  Donald, British actor; pers. name   MAHF-uht   ˈmɑfət

Key (col. 2):   a: fad ā: fade ah: father ar: marry aw: law e: fed ē: feed er: merry i: hid ī: hide ō: coat ōō: boot
oi: boy ow: now u: put uh: above uhr: bird ch: chop ng: ring sh: show th: thick <u>th</u>: this zh: measure

Mofolo
Thomas Mokopu, *Bantu novelist*   mō-FŌ-lō   moː'foːloː

Mogadishu
city, Somalia   MAHG-uh-DISH-o͞o, MAWG-, -DĒSH-o͞o   ˌmɑgə'diʃuː, ˌmɔːg-, -'diːʃuː

Mogador
former name of Essaouira   MAHG-uh-DŌR, MAHG-uh-DAWR   ˌmɑgə'doːʳ, ˌmɑgə'dɔːʳ

Mogadore
village, OH   MAHG-uh-DŌR, -DAWR   'mɑgəˌdoːʳ, -ˌdɔːʳ

Mogen David
1. *kosher food co.*   MAW-guhn DAW-vuhd, MŌ-guhn   ˌmɔːgən 'dɔːvəd, ˌmɔːgən
    DAHV-uhd, DĀ-vuhd   'dɑvəd, 'deːvəd

2. *see* Magen David

Mogollon
mtn. range, AZ   MUHG-ē-ŌN, MŌ-guh-YŌN   ˌməgiː'oːn, ˌmoːgə'joːn

Mogul, Moghul
Indian Muslim of Mongol origin   MŌ-guhl, mō-GUHL   'moːgəl, moː'gəl

Mohács
city, Hungary   MŌ-HAHCH   'moːˌhɑtʃ

Mohammed
1. *pers. name*   mō-HAM-uhd, mō-HAHM-uhd   moː'hæməd, moː'hɑməd
2. *Afghan*   mō-HUHM-muhd   moː'həmməd
3. *Arabic*   mu-HAM-muhd   mu'hæmməd
4. *Persian*   maw-HAHM-mahd   mɔː'hɑːmmɑːd

Mohammedan
see Muhammedan

Mohammedanism
see Muhammedanism

Mohammed Zahir
king, Afghanistan   mō-HUHM-muhd zah-IR,   moː'həmməd zɑ'iʳ,
    Ⓢ mō-HAM-uhd, mō-HAHM-uhd   Ⓢ moː'hæməd,
        moː'hɑməd

Mohan
pers. name   mō-HAHN   moː'hɑn

Mohandas
pers. name, Gujarati   MŌ-huhn-DAHS   'moːhənˌdɑs

Mohave
county, AZ   muh-HAHV-ē, mō-   mə'hɑviˈ, moː-

Mohave, Mojave
desert, CA; N. American people   muh-HAHV-ē, mō-   mə'hɑviˈ, moː-

Mohawk
N. American people   MŌ-HAWK   'moːˌhɔːk

Mohegan
N. American people   mō-HĒ-guhn   moː'hiːgən

Mohenjo-daro
prehistoric city, Pakistan   mō-HEN-jō-DAHR-ō   moːˌhendʒoː'dɑroː

Mohican
N. American people; river, OH   mō-HĒ-kuhn   moː'hiːkən

Moholy-Nagy
László, *Hungarian artist*   MAW-HOI-NAHD,   'mɔːˌhɔi'nɑɖ,
    Ⓢ MAW-HOI-NAHZH, -NAHJ   Ⓢ 'mɔːˌhɔi'nɑʒ, -'nɑdʒ

Mohorovičić
Andrija, *Croatian physicist*   maw-HAWR-uh-VĒ-CHĒCH,   mɔːˌhɔːrə'viːˌtʃiːtʃ,
    Ⓢ MŌ-huh-RŌ-vuh-CHICH   Ⓢ ˌmoːhə'roːvəˌtʃitʃ

Mohs' scale
scale of hardness   MŌZ SKĀL, MŌS, MŌ-zuhz   'moːz ˌskeːl, 'moːs, 'moːzəz

---

Foreign Sounds: ue: *Fr.* **rue**, *Ger.* **füllen**   uh(r): *Fr.* **boeuf**, *Ger.* **Höhle**   <u>kh</u>: *Ger.* **ich**, *Scot.* **loch**   g̃: *Sp.* **amigo**   v̲: *Sp.* **hablar**
hl: *Welsh* **Llanelli**.   CAPITALS: primary stress.   SMALL CAPS: secondary stress.   Ⓢ: U.S. pron.   Ⓔ: British pron.

Moi

Daniel arap, *Kenyan leader*	MOI	'mɔi
Moira		
pers. name	MOI-ruh	'mɔirə
Moirae, Moirai		
the Fates	MOI-RĪ	'mɔi͵rai
Moïse		
pers. name, French	maw-ĒZ	mɔːiːz
Moisés		
pers. name	MOI-shās	'mɔiʃeːs
Moisie		
river, Canada	mwah-ZĒ	mwɑ'ziː
Moissan		
Henri, *French chemist (Nobel 1906)*	mwah-SAHⁿ	mwɑːsɑ̃
Mojave		
see Mohave		
Moji		
city, Japan	mō-jē	moːdʒiˑ
Mojo		
S. American people	MÕ-HÕ	'moːˌhoː
Mokelumne		
river, CA	muh-KAHL-uh-MĒ, muh-KEL-uh-mē	mə'kɑləˌmiː, mə'keləmiˑ
Moktar		
pers. name, Arabic	MAHK-TAHR	'mɑkˌtɑʳ
Moladah		
Biblical name	mō-LĀD-uh, maw-lah-DAH	moː'leːdə, mɔːlɑ'dɑ
Moldau		
river, E. Europe; region, Romania	MAWL-DOW, MŌL-DOW	'mɔːlˌdɑu, 'moːlˌdɑu
Moldavia		
republic, Europe; province, Romania	mahl-DĀ-vē-uh, -vyuh	mɑl'deːviːə, -vjə
Moldavian		
pert. to Moldavia	mahl-DĀ-vē-uhn, -vyuhn	mɑl'deːviːən, -vjən
Moldova [Moldavia]		
Eastern European republic	muhl-DŌ-vuh	məl'doːvə
Molech		
Biblical name	MÕ-LEK, MÕ-lekh	'moːˌlek, 'moːlex
Mole-Dagbani		
lang., Ghana	MÕ-lā-DAHG-BAHN-ē	ˌmoːleːˌdɑg'bɑniˑ
Molid		
Biblical name	MÕ-lid, mō-LĒD	'moːlid, moːˈliːd
Molière		
Jean Baptiste, *French playwright*	mawl-YER, ⓢ mōl-YER, MŌL-YER	mɔːljer, ⓢ moːl'jeʳ, 'moːlˌjeʳ
Molina		
city, Chile	muh-LĒ-nuh	mə'liːnə
Moline		
town, IL	mō-LĒN	moː'liːn
Molinism		
Christian sect	MÕ-luh-NIZ-uhm, MAHL-	'moːləˌnizəm, 'mɑl-
Molionidae		
twin brothers, Eurytus and Cteatus	MÕ-lē-AHN-uh-DĒ	ˌmoːliː'ɑnəˌdiː
Mollie, Molly		
pers. name	MAHL-ē	'mɑliˑ
Möllnir		
Thor's hammer in Scandinavian myth	MUH(R)D-l-NIR, MUH(R)L-nir	'mœdlˌniʳ, 'mœlniʳ

Key (col. 2): a: fad ā: fade ah: father ar: marry aw: law e: fed ē: feed er: merry i: hid ī: hide ō: coat ōō: boot
oi: boy ow: now u: put uh: above uhr: bird ch: chop ng: ring sh: show th: thick <u>th</u>: this zh: measure

Mollweide

    projection, map projection   MAWL-VĪD-uh, MŌL-WĪD-uh   'mɔːl‚vaidə, 'moːl‚waidə

Molly

    see Mollie

Mollymauk

    sea bird (albatross)   MAHL-ē-MAWK   'mɑliˑ‚mɔːk

Molnár

    Ferenc, *Hungarian writer*   MŌL-NAHR, MAWL-NAHR   'moːl‚nɑr, 'mɔːl‚nɑr

Moloch

    Canaanite god   MAHL-uhk, MŌ-LAHK   'mɑlək, 'moː‚lak

Molokai

    island, HI   MAHL-uh-KĪ, MŌ-luh-KĪ   ‚mɑlə'kai, ‚moːlə'kai

Molong

    town, Australia   MŌ-LAHNG, MŌ-LAWNG   'moː‚lɑŋ, 'moː‚lɔːŋ

Molossus

    son of Andromache and Neoptolemus   mō-LAHS-uhs   moː'lasəs

Molotov cocktail

    crude bomb   MAHL-uh-TAWF KAHK-TĀL, MAW-luh-TAWF, MŌ-luh-TAWF, -TAWV   ‚mɑlə‚tɔːf 'kak‚teːl, ‚mɔːlə‚tɔːf, ‚moːlə‚tɔːf, -‚tɔːv

Moltke

    Helmuth von, *Prussian militarist*   MŌLT-kuh   'moːltkə

Molucca

    Sea, *Asia*   muh-LUHK-uh   mə'ləkə

Moluccas [Maluku]

    islands, Indonesia   muh-LUHK-uhz   mə'ləkəz

molybdenum

    element   muh-LIB-duh-nuhm   mə'libdənəm

Molyneux

    pers. name   MAHL-uhn-Y$\overline{OO}$(KS), MUHL-   'mɑlənˌjuː(ks), 'məl-

Mom

    informal for mother   MAHM, MUHM   'mɑm, 'məm

Momaday

    Navarre Scott, *US writer*   MAHM-uh-DĀ   'mɑmə‚deː

Mombasa

    island, city, Kenya   mahm-BAHS-uh   mɑm'bɑsə

Momence

    city, IL   mō-MEN(T)S   moː'men(t)s

Momma

    informal for mother   MAHM-uh, MUHM-uh   'mɑmə, 'məmə

Mommsen

    Theodor, *German historian (Nobel 1902)*   MŌM-zuhn   'moːmzən

Mommy

    informal for mother   MAHM-ē, MUHM-ē   'mɑmiˑ, 'məmiˑ

Momus

    personification of sarcasm or mockery   MŌ-muhs   'moːməs

Mon [Talaing]

    lang., people, Burma, Thailand   MŌN   'moːn

Mona

    pers. name   MŌ-nuh   'moːnə

Monacan

    pert. to Monaco   MAHN-uh-KUHN, muh-NAHK-uhn   'mɑnə‚kən, mə'nɑkən

---

Monaco
principality, Europe MAHN-uh-KŌ, muh-NAHK-ō 'manə‚koː, mə'nɑkoː
Monaco-Ville
city, Monaco MAHN-uh-KŌ-VĒL, muh-NAHK-ō- ‚manə‚koː'viːl, mə‚nɑkoː-
Monadnock
peak, NH muh-NAD-NAHK mə'næd‚nɑk
Monaghan
county, Ireland MAHN-uh-huhn, ⑤ MAHN-uh-HAN 'manəhən, ⑤ 'manə‚hæn
Monahans
city, TX MAHN-uh-HANZ 'manə‚hænz
Mona Lisa [La Gioconda]
da Vinci painting MŌ-nuh LĒ-suh ‚moːnə 'liːsə
Monarch
butterfly species MAHN-uhrk, MAHN-AHRK 'manəʳk, 'man‚ɑʳk
Monarchianism
early Christian anti-Trinitarian muh-NAHR-kē-uh-NIZ-uhm mə'nɑʳkiːə‚nizəm
    teachings
Monashee
Mountains, mtn. range, Canada muh-NASH-ē mə'næʃiˑ
Mönchengladbach
city, Germany MUH(R)N-<u>kh</u>uhn-GLAHT-BAH<u>KH</u> ‚mœnçən'glat‚bax
Mönchshof
German beer MUH(R)N<u>KHS</u>-HAWF 'mœːnçs‚hɔːf
Monck
George, English soldier MUHNGK 'məŋk
Moncrief
Sidney, US basketball player mahn-KRĒF, MAHN-KRĒF man'kriːf, 'man‚kriːf
Moncton
town, Canada MUHNG(K)-tuhn 'məŋ(k)tən
Mondale
Walter, US politician MAHN-DĀL 'man‚deːl
Mondavi
Robert, California vintner mahn-DAHV-ē man'daviˑ
Monday
day of the week MUHN-dē, MUHN-dā 'məndiˑ, 'məndeː
Mondovi
city, WI mahn-DŌ-vē man'doːviˑ
Mondrian
Piet, Dutch artist MAWN-drē-AHN 'mɔːndriː‚an
Monegasque
people of Monaco MAHN-uh-GASK, MŌ-nuh-GAHSK ‚manə'gæsk, ‚moːnə'gaˑsk
Monel
tdmk for a metal alloy mō-NEL moː'nel
Monessen
city, PA muh-NES-uhn, mō- mə'nesən, moː-
Monet
Claude, French painter maw-NE, ⑤ muh-NĀ mɔːne, ⑤ mə'neː
Moneta
1. E. T., Italian journalist, pacifist mō-NĀT-uh moː'neːʈə
    (Nobel 1907)
2. title of Juno mō-NĒT-uh, mō-NĀT-uh, muh- moː'niːʈə, moː'neːʈə, mə-
Monett
city, MO MŌ-NET, mō-NET 'moː‚net, moː'net

Key (col. 2): a: fad ā: fade ah: father ar: marry aw: law e: fed ē: feed er: merry i: hid ī: hide ō: coat ōō: boot
oi: boy ow: now u: put uh: above uhr: bird ch: chop ng: ring sh: show th: thick <u>th</u>: this zh: measure

Mongol		
people, Asia	MAHNG-guhl, MAHN-GŌL, MAHNG-GŌL	ˈmɑŋgəl, ˈmɑnˌgoːl, ˈmɑŋˌgoːl
Mongolia		
region, Asia	mahn-GŌL-yuh, mahng-, -GŌ-lē-uh	mɑnˈgoːljə, mɑŋ-, -ˈgoːliːə
Mongolian		
pert. to Mongols or Mongolia	mahn-GŌL-yuhn, mahng-, -GŌ-lē-uhn	mɑnˈgoːljən, mɑŋ-, -ˈgoːliːən
Mongoloid		
resembling the Mongols	MAHNG-guh-LOID	ˈmɑŋgəˌlɔid
Monguor		
lang., people, China	MAHN-GWAWR, MAHNG-GWAWR	ˈmɑnˌgwɔːʳ, ˈmɑŋˌgwɔːʳ
Monica		
pers. name	MAHN-i-kuh	ˈmɑnikə
Monique		
pers. name	muh-NĒK, mō-NĒK	məˈniːk, moːˈniːk
Moniteau		
county, MO	MAHN-uh-TŌ	ˈmɑnəˌtoː
Moniz		
see Egas Moniz		
Monk		
Thelonious, *US jazz pianist and composer*	MUHNGK	ˈməŋk
Mon-Khmer		
Austroasiatic lang. family	MŌN-kuh-MER	ˌmoːnkəˈmeʳ
Mon-Lei		
Chinese beer	MAHN-LĀ, MŌN-LĀ	ˈmɑnˈleː, ˈmoːnˈleː
Monmouth		
pl. name, US & Britain	MAHN-muhth, MUHN-muhth	ˈmɑnməθ, ˈmənməθ
Monmouthshire		
former county, England or Wales	MAHN-muhth-shuhr, MUHN-muhth-shuhr, -SHIR	ˈmɑnməθʃəʳ, ˈmənməθʃəʳ, -ˌʃiʳ
Monnet		
Jean, *French economist*	maw-NE, Ⓢ muh-NĀ	mɔːne, Ⓢ məˈneː
Mono		
county, CA; river, Togo; island, Pacific; N. American people	MŌ-nō	ˈmoːnoː
Monoceros		
constellation	muh-NAHS-uh-ruhs	məˈnɑsərəs
Monoclonius		
dinosaur	MAHN-uh-KLŌ-nē-uhs	ˌmɑnəˈkloːniːəs
Monod		
Jacques, *French biochemist (Nobel 1965)*	maw-NŌ	mɔːnoː
Monona		
county, IA; lake, WI	muh-NŌ-nuh	məˈnoːnə
Monongah		
town, VA	muh-NAHNG-guh	məˈnɑŋgə
Monongahela		
river, WV, PA	muh-NAHN-guh-HĒ-luh, muh-NAHNG-guh-, -HĀ-luh	məˌnɑngəˈhiːlə, məˌnɑŋgə-, -ˈheːlə
Monongalia		
county, WV	MAHN-uhn-GĀ-lē-uh, MAHN-uhng-GĀ-lē-uh, -GĀL-yuh, *locally also* MAHN-guh-HĀL-ē(-uh)	ˌmɑnənˈgeːliːə, ˌmɑnəŋˈgeːliːə, -ˈgeːljə, *locally also* ˌmɑngəˈheːliː(ə)

Foreign Sounds: ue: *Fr.* **rue**, *Ger.* **füllen** uh(r): *Fr.* **boeuf**, *Ger.* **Höhle** <u>kh</u>: *Ger.* i**ch**, *Scot.* lo**ch** g̃: *Sp.* ami**g**o v̧: *Sp.* ha**b**lar
hl: *Welsh* **Ll**anelli. CAPITALS: primary stress. SMALL CAPS: secondary stress. Ⓢ: U.S. pron. Ⓔ: British pron.

Monophysite
  adherent of Monophysitism   muh-NAHF-uh-SĪT   məˈnɑfəˌsɑit

Monophysitism
  doctrine of Christ's total divinity   muh-NAHF-uh-SIT-IZ-uhm   məˈnɑfəˌsiţizəm

Monosodium glutamate
  food additive   MAHN-uh-SŌD-ē-uhm GLŌ͞OT-uh-MĀT   ˌmɑnəˈsoːdiːəm ˈgluːţəˌmeːt

Monothelitism
  7th-century heresy   muh-NAHTH-uh-līt-IZ-uhm   məˈnɑθəlɑiţˌizəm

Monotremata
  egg-laying mammals   MAHN-uh-TREM-uht-uh,   ˌmɑnəˈtreməţə,
      MAHN-uh-TRĒ-muht-uh   ˌmɑnəˈtriːməţə

Monotype
  tdmk for a typesetting machine   MAHN-uh-TĪP   ˈmɑnəˌtɑip

Monroe
  James, *5th US president;* Marilyn,   muhn-RŌ, MUHN-RŌ   mənˈroː, ˈmənˌroː
  US actress; US pl. name; pers.
  name

Monrovia
  city, Liberia   muhn-RŌ-vē-uh   mənˈroːviːə

Mons
  city, Belgium   MAWⁿS   ˈmɔ̃s

Monsanto
  US chemical co.   mahn-SAN-tō   manˈsæntoː

Monsarrat
  Nicholas, *English novelist*   MAHN-suh-RAHT, MAHN-suh-RAT, ⓔ   ˌmɑnsəˈrɑt, ˌmɑnsəˈræt, ⓔ
      MAHN-suh-RAT   ˈmɑnsəˌræt

Monseigneur
  French title of honor   mawⁿ-sen-YUHR ⓢ mawⁿ-SĀN-yuhr   mɔ̃seɲ œr, ⓢ mɔ̃ˈseːnjəʳ

Monsieur
  French form of address for a man   muhs-YUH(R), ⓢ muhsh-YUHR,   məsjœː, ⓢ məʃˈjəʳ, məsˈjəʳ,
      muhs-YUHR, muh-SIR   məˈsiʳ

Monsignor
  title for certain prelates   mahn-SĒN-yuhr, muhn-SĒN-yuhr   manˈsiːnjəʳ, mənˈsiːnjəʳ

Monson
  town, MA   MUHN(T)-suhn   ˈmən(t)sən

Montagnais
  N. American people   MAHN-tuhn-YĀ   ˌmɑntənˈjeː

Montagu
  Lady Mary Wortley, *English poet;*   MAHNT-uh-GYŌ͞O   ˈmɑntəˌgjuː
  pers. name

Montague
  1. *family name of Romeo in* Romeo   MAHNT-uh-GYŌ͞O   ˈmɑntəˌgjuː
  and Juliet, *Shakespeare; town,*
  MA; island, AK; pers. name
  2. *county, TX*   mahn-TĀG, MAHN-TĀG   manˈteːg, ˈmanˌteːg

Montaigne
  Michel, *French essayist*   mawⁿ-TEN-yuh   mɔ̃teɲ

Montalban
  Ricardo, *US actor*   mōn-tahl-V̲AHN, ⓢ MAHNT-l-BAHN   moːntalˈβan, ⓢ ˌmantl̩ˈban

Montalbana
  Italian chianti   MAWN-tahl-BAHN-uh   ˌmɔːntalˈbanə

Montale
  Eugenio, *Italian poet (Nobel 1975)*   mōn-TAHL-ā   moːnˈtɑleː

Montana
  state, US; Joe, *US football player*   mahn-TAN-uh   manˈtænə

Key (col. 2): a: fad ā: fade ah: father ar: marry aw: law e: fed ē: feed er: merry i: hid ī: hide ō: coat ō͞o: boot
oi: boy ow: now u: put uh: above uhr: bird ch: chop ng: ring sh: show th: thick t̲h̲: this zh: measure

Montand		
Yves, *French actor and singer*	maw^{n}-TAH^{n}, [$] mahn-TAHND, -TAHN	mɔ̃tɑ̃, [$] mɑn'tɑnd, -'tɑn
Montanism		
Christian heresy	MAHN-tuh-NIZ-uhm	'mɑntəˌnizəm
Montauk Point		
eastern point of Long Island, NY	MAHN-TAWK POINT	ˌmɑnˌtɔːk 'pɔint
Mont Blanc		
mtn., France; mfrs.	maw^{n} BLAH^{n}	mɔ̃ blɑ̃
Montcalm		
county, MI	mahnt-KAHM	mɑnt'kɑm
Montcalm		
Louis Joseph de, *French general*	maw^{n}-KAHLM, [$] mahnt-KAHM	mɔ̃'kɑːlm, [$] mɑnt'kɑm
Mont Cervin		
see Cervin, Mont		
Monte Albán		
ancient ruins, Mexico	MAWN-te ahl-BAHN	'mɔːnte ɑl'bɑn
Monte Carlo		
tourist resort, Monaco	MAHNT-ē KAHR-lō	ˌmɑnti· 'kɑɾloː
Monte Cassino		
abbey, Italy	MAHNT-ē kuh-SĒ-nō	ˌmɑntiː kə'siːnoː
Monte Cervino		
see Cervino, Monte		
Monte Cristo		
1. island, Italy	MAWN-tā KRĒ-stō, [$] MAHN-tē KRIS-tō	ˌmɔːnteː 'kriːstoː, [$] ˌmɑnti· 'kristoː
2. sandwich	MAHN-tē KRIS-tō	ˌmɑnti· 'kristoː
Montefiascone		
commune, Italy	MAWN-tā-fyah-SKŌ-nā, [$] MAHNT-ē-fyah-SKŌ-nē	ˌmɔːnteːfjɑ'skoːneː, [$] ˌmɑntiːfjɑ'skoːni·
Montefiore		
Sir Moses Haim, *British philanthropist*	MAHNT-uh-FYAWR-ē, -fē-ŌR-ē, -fē-AWR-ē	ˌmɑntə'fjɔːri·, -fiː'oːri·, -fiː'ɔːri·
Montego Bay		
city, Jamaica	mahn-TĒ-gō BĀ	mɑn'tiːgoː 'beː
Monteith		
pers. name	mahn-TĒTH	mɑn'tiːθ
Montenegrin		
pert. to Montenegro	MAHNT-uh-NĒ-gruhn, -NEG-ruhn, -NĀ-gruhn	ˌmɑntə'niːgrən, -'negrən, -'neːgrən
Montenegro [Crna Gora]		
republic, E. Europe (former kingdom)	MAHNT-uh-NĒ-grō, -NEG-rō, -NĀ-grō	ˌmɑntə'niːgroː, -'negroː, -'neːgroː
Montepulciano		
commune, Italy	MAWNT-ā-pul-CHAHN-ō	ˌmɔːnteːpul'tʃɑnoː
Monterey		
city, county, CA	MAHNT-uh-RĀ	ˌmɑntə'reː
Monterrey		
city, Mexico	MAHNT-uh-RĀ	ˌmɑntə'reː
Montesquieu		
Baron de, Charles-Louis de Secondat, *French philosopher*	maw^{n}-tes-KYUH(R), [$] MAHNT-uhs-KYO͞O	mɔ̃teskjœː, [$] ˌmɑntəs'kjuː
Montessori		
Maria, *Italian educator; teaching method*	MAHNT-uh-SŌR-ē, MAHNT-uh-SAWR-ē	ˌmɑntə'soːri·, ˌmɑntə'sɔːri·

Foreign Sounds: ue: *Fr.* **rue**, *Ger.* **füllen** uh(r): *Fr.* **boeuf**, *Ger.* **Höhle** kh: *Ger.* **ich**, *Scot.* **loch** g̱: *Sp.* amigo v̱: *Sp.* hablar hl: *Welsh* **Llanelli**. CAPITALS: primary stress. SMALL CAPS: secondary stress. [$]: U.S. pron. [£]: British pron.

Montevallo		
town, AL	MAHNT-uh-VAL-ō	ˌmɑntə'væloː
Monteverdi		
Claudio, *Italian composer*	MAHNT-uh-VERD-ē,	ˌmɑntə'veʳdiˑ, ˌmɑntə'vəʳdiˑ
	MAHNT-uh-VUHRD-ē	
Montevideo		
1. dept, city, Uruguay	MAHNT-uh-vuh-DĀ-ō, -VID-ē-ō	ˌmɑntəvə'deːoː, -'vidiːoː
2. city, MN	MAHNT-uh-VID-ē-Ō	ˌmɑntə'vidiːˌoː
Montezuma [Moctezuma]		
Aztec emperor	MAHNT-uh-ZŌŌ-muh	ˌmɑntə'zuːmə
Montfort		
1. pers. name	MAHNT-fuhrt	'mɑntfəʳt
2. Simon de, French leader	mawⁿ-FAWR, ⓢ MAHNT-fuhrt	mɔ̃fɔːr, ⓢ 'mɑntfəʳt
Montgolfier		
Joseph Michel *and* Jacques	mawⁿ-gawl-FYĀ,	mɔ̃gɔːlfjeː, ⓢ mɑnt'gɑlfiːəʳ
Étienne, *French aviation pioneers*	ⓢ mahnt-GAHL-fē-uhr	
Montgomerie, Montgomery		
pers. name	muhn(t)-GUHM-(uh-)rē, mahn(t)-,	mən(t)'gəm(ə)riˑ, mɑn(t)-,
	-GAHM-(uh-)rē	-'gɑm(ə)riˑ
Montgomery		
Sir Bernard Law, 1st Viscount, *of*	muhn(t)-GUHM-(uh-)rē, mahn(t)-,	mən(t)'gəm(ə)riˑ, mɑn(t)-,
Alamein, British Soldier; US pl.	-GAHM-(uh-)rē	-'gɑm(ə)riˑ
name; borough, Wales		
Montgomeryshire		
former county, Wales	muhnt-GUHM-(uh-)rē-shuhr, -SHIR	mənt'gəm(ə)riˑʃəʳ, -ˌʃiʳ
Month		
Egyptian war god	MAHNT, MAWNT	'mɑnt, 'mɔːnt
Monticello		
Jefferson's home; US pl. name	MAHNT-uh-SEL-ō, -CHEL-ō	ˌmɑntə'seloː, -'tʃeloː
Montmartre		
section, Paris, France	mawⁿ-MAHRTR	mɔ̃mɑrtr
Montmorency		
1. county, MI; river, Canada	MAHNT-muh-REN(T)-sē	ˌmɑntmə'ren(t)siˑ
2. commune, France	mawⁿ-maw-rahⁿ-SĒ	mɔ̃mɔːrɑ̃siː
Montour		
county, PA	mahn-TUR	mɑn'tuʳ
Montoya		
Carlos, *Spanish guitarist*	mahn-TOI-(y)uh	mɑn'tɔi(j)ə
Montparnasse		
quarter, Paris	mawⁿ-pahr-NAHS	mɔ̃pɑrnɑs
Montpelier		
city, VT	mahnt-PĒL-yuhr	mɑnt'piːljəʳ
Montpellier		
city, France	mawⁿ-pel-YĀ	mɔ̃peljeː
Montrachet		
wine	mawⁿ-rah-SHE	mɔ̃rɑːʃe
Montreal		
city, Canada	mawⁿ-re-AHL, ⓢ MAHN-trē-AWL,	mɔ̃reaːl, ⓢ ˌmɑntriː'ɔːl,
	MUHN-	ˌmən-
Montreux		
town, Switzerland	mawⁿ-TRUH(R), ⓢ mahn-TRŌ,	mɔ̃trœː, ⓢ mɑn'troː,
	MAHN-trō	'mɑntroː
Mont-Saint-Michel		
islet near French coast; abbey and	mawⁿ-seⁿ-mē-SHEL,	mɔ̃sēmiːʃel,
fortress	ⓢ MŌN-san-mē-SHEL	ⓢ ˌmoːnsænmiˑ'ʃel

Key (col. 2):   a: f**a**d   ā: f**a**de   ah: f**a**ther   ar: m**a**rry   aw: l**a**w   e: f**e**d   ē: f**ee**d   er: m**e**rry   i: h**i**d   ī: h**i**de   ō: c**oa**t   ōō: b**oo**t
oi: b**o**y   ow: n**o**w   u: p**u**t   uh: **a**bove   uhr: b**i**rd   ch: **ch**op   ng: ri**ng**   sh: **sh**ow   th: **th**ick   <u>th</u>: **th**is   zh: mea**s**ure

Montserrat

  1. island, West Indies   MAHNT-suh-RAT, *locally*   ˌmɑntsəˈræt, *locally*
                                    MAHNT-suh-RAT   ˈmɑntsəˌræt

  2. mtn., Spain   mōnt-sä-RAHT, Ⓢ MAHNT-suh-RAT   mɔːntseːˈrɑt, Ⓢ ˌmɑntsəˈræt

Mont Tremblant

  park, Quebec   mawⁿ trahⁿ-BLAHⁿ   mɔ̃ trɑ̃blɑ̃

Montu [Month]

  Egyptian war god   MAHN-tōo, MAWN-tōo   ˈmɑntuː, ˈmɔːntuː

Montu-Re [Month]

  Egyptian war god   MAHN-tōo-RÄ, MAWN-tōo-RÄ   ˈmɑntuːˈreː, ˈmɔːntuːˈreː

Monty

  pers. name   MAHNT-ē   ˈmɑntiˑ

Monty Python

  British comedy troupe   MAHNT-ē PĪ-THAHN   ˌmɑntiˑ ˈpaiˌθɑn

Monza

  city, Italy   MŌNT-sah, MAHN-zuh   ˈmɔːntsɑ, ˈmɑnzə

Mooers

  Field, *ballpark, Richmond, VA*   MURZ, MŌRZ, MAWRZ   ˈmuʳz, ˈmoːʳz, ˈmɔːʳz

Moog

  tdmk for a music synthesizer   MŌG, MŌOG   ˈmoːg, ˈmuːg

Moon

  Sun Myung, *see* Sun Myung Moon

Moonachie

  borough, NJ   mōo-NACH-ē   muːˈnætʃiˑ

Moonbi

  mtn. range, Australia   MŌON-bē   ˈmuːnbiˑ

Moonie

  follower of S. M. Moon *(derogatory)*   MŌO-nē   ˈmuːniˑ

Moor

  Arab & Berber conquerors of Spain   MUR   ˈmuʳ

Moore

  Henry, *British sculptor;* Marianne,   MŌR, MAWR, MUR   ˈmoːʳ, ˈmɔːʳ, ˈmuʳ
  US *poet;* Stanford, *US biochemist*
  (Nobel 1972); pers. name

Moorish

  pert. to the Moors   MUR-ish   ˈmuriʃ

Moosup

  town, CT   MŌO-suhp   ˈmuːsəp

Mopsus

  Argonaut; grandson of Tiresias MAHP-suhs   ˈmɑpsəs

Mór

  pers. name, Hungarian   MAWR   ˈmɔːʳ

Mora

  county, NM   MŌR-uh, MAWR-uh   ˈmoːrə, ˈmɔːrə

Moraine

  city, OH   muh-RÄN   məˈreːn

Moran

  family name   MAWR-uhn, MAHR-uhn, muh-RAN   ˈmɔːrən, ˈmɑrən, məˈræn

Morar, Loch

  see Loch Morar

Morarji

  pers. name, Bengali   mawr-AHR-jē   mɔːrˈɑʳdʒiˑ

Morava

  river, prov, Czech republic   MAWR-uh-vuh   ˈmɔːrəvə

Foreign Sounds: ue: *Fr.* **rue**, *Ger.* **füllen**   uh(r): *Fr.* **boeuf**, *Ger.* **Höhle**   kh: *Ger.* **ich**, *Scot.* **loch**   g̱: *Sp.* **amigo**   v̱: *Sp.* **hablar**
hl: *Welsh* **Llanelli**.   CAPITALS: primary stress.   SMALL CAPS: secondary stress.   Ⓢ: U.S. pron.   Ⓔ: British pron.

Moravia		
1. Alberto, *Italian writer*	maw-RAHV-yah, [$] muh-RĀ-vē-uh, muh-RAHV-ē-uh	mɔː'rɑvjɑː, [$] mə're:viːə, mə'rɑviːə
2. prov, Czech republic	muh-RĀ-vē-uh	mə're:viːə
Moravian		
College, *PA*	muh-RĀ-vē-uhn	mə're:viːən
Moray		
eel	muh-RĀ, MAWR-ā	mə'reː, 'mɔːreː
Morbihan		
dept, France	mawr-bē-AH^{n}	mɔːrbiːɑ̃
Mordecai		
pers. name	MAWRD-i-KĪ	'mɔː^{r}di,kɑi
Mordred [Modred]		
Arthurian villain	MAWR-druhd	'mɔː^{r}drəd
Mordva		
lang., Russia	MAWRD-vuh	'mɔː^{r}dvə
Mordvin		
European people	MAWRD-vin	'mɔː^{r}dvin
Mordvinian		
European people	mawrd-VIN-ē-uhn, mawrd-VIN-yuhn	mɔː^{r}d'viniːən, mɔː^{r}d'vinjən
More		
Sir Thomas, *English humanist, statesman, saint*	MŌR, MAWR	'moː^{r}, 'mɔː^{r}
Moré [Mossi]		
lang., Ghana, Burkina Faso	muh-RĀ	mə'reː
Morea [Peloponnese]		
peninsula, Greece	muh-RĒ-uh	mə'riːə
Moreau		
1. pers. name	mawr-Ō, MŌR-ō, MAWR-ō	mɔːr'oː, 'moːroː, 'mɔːroː
2. French	maw-RŌ	mɔːroː
Morecambe		
town, England	MAWR-kuhm	'mɔː^{r}kəm
Moree		
town, Australia	mawr-Ē	mɔːr'iː
Moreh		
Biblical name	MŌR-uh, MAWR-uh, mō-RE	'moːrə, 'mɔːrə, moː're
Moreing		
Field, *ballpark, Sacramento, CA*	MŌR-ing, MAWR-ing	'moːriŋ, 'mɔːriŋ
Morelia		
city, Mexico	muh-RĀL-yuh	mə'reːljə
Morelos		
state, Mexico	muh-RĀ-luhs	mə'reːləs
Moreno		
Rita, *Puerto Rican actress*	maw-RĀ-nō, muh-RĒ-nō	mɔː'reːnoː, mə'riːnoː
Moresheth-gath		
Biblical name	MŌR-uh-SHETH-GATH, MAWR-; mō-RE-shet-GAHT	'moːrə,ʃeθ'gæθ, 'mɔːr-; moː'reʃet'gɑt
Moretti		
Italian beer	mōr-ET-ē, mawr-ET-ē	moːr'etiˑ, mɔːr'etiˑ
Morgan		
John Pierpont *(father & son), US financiers;* Thomas H., *US geneticist (Nobel 1933); pers. name*	MAWR-guhn	'mɔː^{r}gən

Key (col. 2): a: **fad** ā: **fade** ah: **father** ar: **marry** aw: **law** e: **fed** ē: **feed** er: **merry** i: **hid** ī: **hide** ō: **coat** o͞o: **boot** oi: **boy** ow: **now** u: **put** uh: **above** uhr: **bird** ch: **chop** ng: **ring** sh: **show** th: **thick** th: **this** zh: **measure**

Morgenthau
Henry, Jr., *US Secretary of the Treasury*   MAWR-guhn-THAW   ˈmɔːʳgənˌθɔː

Moriah
Biblical name   muh-RĪ-uh, MAW-ri-YAH   məˈraiə, ˈmɔːriˌjɑ

Moriah, Mount
peak, NH   MOWNT muh-RĪ-uh   ˌmaunt məˈraiə

Moriarty
Michael, *US actor;* Professor, *opponent of Sherlock Holmes*   MAWR-ē-AHRT-ē   ˌmɔːriːˈɑʳṭiˑ

Moriches
village, NY   muh-RICH-uhz   məˈritʃəz

Morisot
Berthe, *French painter*   maw-rē-SŌ   mɔːriːsoː

Moritz
pers. name, German   MŌ-rits   ˈmoːrits

Morley
pers. name   MAWR-lē   ˈmɔːʳliˑ

Mormon
member of the Church of Jesus Christ of Latter-day Saints   MAWR-muhn   ˈmɔːʳmən

Mormonism
religion   MAWR-muh-NIZ-uhm   ˈmɔːʳməˌnizəm

Mornay
white sauce with cheese   mawr-NĀ   mɔːʳˈneː

Moro
Philippine Muslim   MŌR-ō, MAWR-ō   ˈmoːroː, ˈmɔːroː

Moro
Aldo, *Italian politician*   MŌR-ō   ˈmoːroː

Moroccan
pert. to Morocco   muh-RAHK-uhn   məˈrakən

Morocco
kingdom, Africa   muh-RAHK-ō   məˈrakoː

Morón
city, Argentina, Spain; town, Cuba   muh-RŌN   məˈroːn

Moroni
town, Comoro Islands   maw-RŌ-nē   mɔːˈroːniˑ

Morpheus
Greek god of dreams   MAWR-fē-uhs, MAWR-F(Y)O͞OS   ˈmɔːʳfiːəs, ˈmɔːʳˌf(j)uːs

Morris
1. dance; pers. name   MAWR-uhs, MAHR-uhs   ˈmɔːrəs, ˈmarəs
2. Danish   MAWR-ēs   ˈmɔːriːs

Morrison
Toni, *US writer (Nobel 1993);* Van, *Irish singer, composer*   MAWR-uh-suhn, MAHR-uh-suhn   ˈmɔːrəsən, ˈmarəsən

Morse
Samuel, *US inventor*   MAWRS   ˈmɔːʳs

Mort
pers. name   MAWRT   ˈmɔːʳt

Morta
Roman goddess of fate   MAWRT-uh   ˈmɔːʳṭə

Mortimer
pers. name   MAWRT-uh-muhr   ˈmɔːʳṭəməʳ

Mortis, Lacus
'lake' on Moon   LAHK-uhs MAWRT-uhs   ˈlakəs ˈmɔːʳṭəs

Foreign Sounds: ue: *Fr.* **rue**, *Ger.* **füllen**   uh(r): *Fr.* **boeuf**, *Ger.* **Höhle**   <u>kh</u>: *Ger.* **ich**, *Scot.* **loch**   g̱: *Sp.* **amigo**   <u>v</u>: *Sp.* **hablar**
hl: *Welsh* **Llanelli**.   CAPITALS: primary stress.   SMALL CAPS: secondary stress.   Ⓢ: U.S. pron.   Ⓔ: British pron.

Morton		
pers. name	MAWRT-n	'mɔːʳtn̩
Mort Subite Kriek		
Belgian beer	MAWRT S͞OO-bi-TĀ KRĒK	'mɔːrt 'suːbiˌteː 'kriːk
Moru		
lang., people, Sudan	MŌ-r͞oo, MAWR-͞oo	'moːruː, 'mɔːruː
Moruya		
town, Australia	muh-R͞OO-yuh	mə'ruːjə
Mosaddeq		
see Mossadegh		
Mosby		
pers. name	MŌZ-bē	'moːzbiˑ
Moscatel		
sweet wine	maw-skah-TEL	mɔːskɑːtel
Moscato		
Italian wine	maw-SKAHT-ō	mɔː'skɑtoː
Moschus		
Greek pastoral poet	MAHS-kuhs	'mɑskəs
Moscoviense, Mare		
see Mare Moscoviense		
Moscow		
1. city, Russia	MAHS-KOW, MAHS-kō	'mɑsˌkɑu, 'mɑskoː
2. city, ID	MAHS-KŌ	'mɑsˌkoː
Mosel		
river, France, Germany; dept., France; wine	MŌ-zuhl	'moːzəl
Moseley		
Mark, *US football player*	MŌZ-lē	'moːzliˑ
Moselle [Mosel]		
river, France, Germany	mō-ZEL	moː'zel
Moserah		
Biblical name	mō-SIR-uh, MŌ-se-RAH	moː'sirə, ˌmoːse'rɑ
Moses		
1. Hebrew prophet; pers. name	MŌ-zuhz, MŌ-zuhs	'moːzəz, 'moːzəs
2. German	MŌ-zes	'moːzes
Moshe		
pers. name, Yiddish, Hebrew	MŌ-shuh, mō-SHE	'moːʃə, moː'ʃe
Moshoeshoe		
king, Lesotho	mō-SH͞OO-sh͞oo	moː'ʃuːʃuː
Moskva		
Russian for Moscow	MUHSK-VAH, [S] mahsk-VAH	ˌməsk'vɑː, [S] mɑsk'vɑ
Moslem [Muslim]		
pert. to Islam; *adherent of Islam*	MAHZ-luhm, MAHS-luhm	'mɑzləm, 'mɑsləm
Mosonmagyaróvár [Altenburg]		
town, Hungary	MAW-shawn-MAHD-yuh-RŌ-VAHR	'mɔːʃɔːnˌmɑdjəˌroːˌvɑːʳ
Mosquero		
village, NM	mahs-KER-ō	mɑs'keroː
Mosquito [Miskito]		
Cen. American people	muh-SKĒT-ō	mə'skiːt̬oː
Mosquito Coast		
region, Honduras, Nicaragua	muh-SKĒT-ō KŌST	məˌskiːt̬oː 'koːst
Moss		
pers. name	MAWS, MAHS	'mɔːs, 'mɑs
Mossadegh, Mosaddeq		
Mohammed, *premier, Iran*	MAWS-uh-DEK	'mɔːsəˌdek

Key (col. 2): a: **fad** ā: **fade** ah: **father** ar: **marry** aw: **law** e: **fed** ē: **feed** er: **merry** i: **hid** ī: **hide** ō: **coat** ͞oo: **boot** oi: **boy** ow: **now** u: **put** uh: **above** uhr: **bird** ch: **chop** ng: **ring** sh: **show** th: **thick** t͟h: **this** zh: **measure**

Mössbauer

R. L., *German-born US physicist (Nobel 1961);* effect, *gamma radiation* — MUH(R)S-BOW(-uh)r, ⑤ MAWS-BOW(-uh)r — ˈmœsˌbau(ə)ʳ, ⑤ ˈmɔːsˌbau(ə)ʳ

Mossi [Moré]

lang., people, Ghana, Burkina Faso — MAHS-ē — ˈmɑsiˑ

Mossmorran

region, Scotland — maws-MAWR-uhn — mɔːsˈmɔːrən

Mostel

Zero, *US entertainer* — muh-STEL, mahs-TEL — məˈstel, mɑsˈtel

Mosul

city, Iraq — mō-SOOL, MŌ-suhl — moːˈsuːl, ˈmoːsəl

Mota

Rosa, *Portuguese marathoner* — MAW-tah — ˈmɔːtɑː

Motilal

pers. name, Kashmiri — MŌ-ti-LAHL — ˈmoːtiˌlɑl

Motilón

S. American people — MŌT-uh-LŌN, MŌT-l-ŌN — ˌmoːtʃəˈloːn, ˌmoːtl̩ˈoːn

Motilónes

plural of Motilón — MŌT-uh-LŌ-NĀS, MŌT-l-Ō-NĀS — ˌmoːtʃəˈloːˌneːs, ˌmoːtl̩ˈoːˌneːs

Motley Crue

rock band — MAHT-lē KROO — ˌmɑtliˑ ˈkruː

Motown

nickname for Detroit; musical style — MŌ-TOWN — ˈmoːˌtɑun

Mott

J. R., *US religious leader (Nobel 1946);* Sir Nevill F., *English physicist (Nobel 1977)* — MAHT — ˈmɑt

Mottelson

Benjamin Roy, *US-born Danish physicist (Nobel 1975)* — MŌT-l-suhn, -sawn — ˈmoːtl̩sən, -sɔːn

Motu

Papuan people, lang. — MŌ-too — ˈmoːtuː

Motzu

Chinese philosopher — MŌD-ZU — ˈmoːdˈzuˑ

Mouache Ute

N. American people — moo-AHCH-ā YOOT — muːˈatʃeː ˈjuːt

Moulin à Vent

French wine — moo-LEⁿ ah VAHⁿ — muːlē ɑː vɑ̃

Moulinex

tdmk for housewares — MOOL-uh-NEKS — ˈmuːləˌneks

Moulis

French wine region — moo-LĒ — muːliˑ

Moulmein

port, Burma — mool-MĀN, mōl-MĀN, -MIN — muːlˈmeːn, moːlˈmeːn, -ˈmin

Moulton

pers. name — MŌLT-n, MŌL-tuhn — ˈmoːltn̩, ˈmoːltən

Moultrie

county, IL; city, GA — MŌL-trē — ˈmoːltriˑ

Mount Aloysius

Junior College — MOWNT AL-uh-WISH-uhs — ˌmɑunt ˌæləˈwiʃəs

Mount Athos

mtn., theocratic republic, Greece — mownt ATH-AHS, Ā-THAHS — mɑunt ˈæθˌɑs, ˈeːˌθɑs

Mountbatten

Louis, *British militarist* — mownt-BAT-n — mɑuntˈbætn̩

Foreign Sounds: ue: *Fr.* **rue**, *Ger.* **füllen** uh(r): *Fr.* **boeuf**, *Ger.* **Höhle** kh: *Ger.* **ich**, *Scot.* **loch** g̱: *Sp.* **amigo** v: *Sp.* **hablar** hl: *Welsh* **Llanelli.** CAPITALS: primary stress. SMALL CAPS: secondary stress. ⑤: U.S. pron. ⑥: British pron.

Mount Desert
   island, ME   MOWNT duh-ZUHRT, DEZ-uhrt   ˌmɑunt dəˈzərt, ˈdezərt

Mount Holyoke
   College, *MA*   mownt HŌ-lē-ŌK, *locally* HŌ(L)-YŌK   mɑunt ˈhoːliːˌoːk, *locally* ˈhoˑ(l)ˌjoːk

Mountrail
   county, ND   MOWNT-RĀL   ˈmɑuntˌreːl

Mount Senario
   College, *WI*   MOWNT suh-NAR-ē-ō, suh-NER-ē-ō   ˌmɑunt səˈnæriːoː, səˈneriːoː

Mount Vernon
   estate, VA, home of George   mownt VUHR-nuhn   mɑunt ˈvərnən
    Washington

Mount Wachusett
   Community College, *MA*   MOWNT wah-CHOO-suht   ˌmɑunt wɑˈtʃuːsət

Moure, La
   see La Moure

Mousehole
   town, Cornwall, England   MOWZ-l   ˈmɑuzl̩

Moussorgsky
   see Mussorgsky

Mousterian
   Paleolithic culture   moo-STIR-ē-uhn   muːˈstiriːən

Mouton Baron Philippe
   wine   moo-TAWⁿ bah-RAWⁿ fē-LĒP   muːtɔ̃ barɔ̃ fiːliːp

Mouton Cadet
   wine   moo-TAWⁿ kah-DE   muːtɔ̃ kɑːde

Mouton Rothschild
   wine   moo-TAWⁿ rawt-SHÊLD   muːtɔ̃ rɔːtʃiːld

Movado
   fashion designers   muh-VAHD-ō, mō-VAHD-ō   məˈvadoː, moːˈvadoː

Movimento Popular de Libertaçao de Angola
   (MPLA), political party, Angola   MŌ-vē-MÃ(N)-too PUH-poo-LAHR thā   ˌmoːviːˈmẽː(n)tuː ˌpəpuːˈlɑːr
                         LÊ-ber-tah-SOWⁿ thā ahng-GŌ-lah   ðeː ˌliːbertɑˈsaũ ðeː
                                                aŋˈgoːlɑː

Mowbray
   pers. name   MŌ-BRĀ, MŌ-brē   ˈmoːˌbreː, ˈmoːbriˑ

Mower
   county, MN   MOW-uhr   ˈmɑuər

Mowgli
   character in Jungle Books, *R.*   MOW-glē, MŌ-glē   ˈmɑugliˑ, ˈmoːgliˑ
    Kipling

Moynihan
   1. Daniel P., US politician   MOI-nuh-HAN   ˈmɔinəˌhæn
   2. Berkeley George Andrew,   MOIN-yuhn, MOI-nē-uhn,   ˈmɔinjən, ˈmɔiniːən,
    English surgeon   Ⓢ MOI-nuh-HAN   Ⓢ ˈmɔinəˌhæn

Moyra
   pers. name   MOI-ruh   ˈmɔirə

Mozah
   Biblical name   MŌ-zuh, mawt-SAH   ˈmoːzə, mɔːtˈsɑ

Mozambican
   pert. to Mozambique   MŌ-zuhm-BĒ-kuhn, MŌ-ZAM-BĒ-kuhn   ˌmoːzəmˈbiːkən, ˌmoːˌzæmˈbiːkən

Mozambique
   channel, country, Africa   MŌ-zuhm-BĒK, MŌ-ZAM-BĒK   ˌmoːzəmˈbiːk, ˌmoːˌzæmˈbiːk

---

Key (col. 2):   a: fad   ā: fade   ah: father   ar: marry   aw: law   e: fed   ē: feed   er: merry   i: hid   ī: hide   ō: coat   oo: boot
oi: boy   ow: now   u: put   uh: above   uhr: bird   ch: chop   ng: ring   sh: show   th: thick   th̲: this   zh: measure

Mozart
   Wolfgang Amadeus, *Austrian*   MŌT-SAHRT   'moːtˌsɑʳt
     composer

Mozzarella
   cheese   MAHT-suh-REL-uh   ˌmɑtsə'relə

Mpumalanga
   city, S. Africa   em-pōōm-uh-LANG-guh   empuːmə'læŋgə

Mqhayi
   Samuel Edward Krune, *South*   uhm-KĪ, uhm-KAH-YĒ   əm'kɑi, əm'kɑˌjiː
    African writer

Mr.
   form of address to a man   MIS-tuhr, MIS-tuhr, *in rapid speech esp.*   'mistəʳ, ˌmistəʳ, *in rapid*
                                    before a title mis(t)   *speech esp. before a title*
                                                               mis(t)

Mrs.
   form of address to a married woman   MIS-iz, MIS-is, *in rapid speech* MIZ,   'misiz, 'misis, *in rapid*
                                 MIS; *esp. southern US* MIZ-iz, MIZ-is   *speech* ˌmiz, ˌmis; *esp.*
                                                               southern US 'miziz, 'mizis

Ms.
   magazine; form of address to a   MIZ, MIZ   'miz, ˌmiz
    woman

MS-DOS
   tdmk for a microcomputer operating   EM-ES-DAHS, -DAWS   ˌemˌes'dɑs, -'dɔːs
    system

Msta
   river, Russia   uhm-STAH   əm'stɑː

Mstislav
   pers. name, Russian   sti-SLAHV; Ⓢ MIS-tuh-SLAHV   sti'slɑːv; Ⓢ 'mistəˌslɑv

Muallaqat
   anthology of Arabic poetry   mōō-AHL-lah-KAHT   muːˌɑllɑ'kɑt

Muammar
   pers. name, Arabic   MŌŌ-uh-MAHR   'muːəˌmɑʳ

Mubarak
   Hosni, *president, Egypt*   mu-BAHR-uhk   mu'bɑrək

Mucius
   pers. name, Latin   M(Y)ŌŌ-sh(ē-)uhs   'm(j)uːʃ(iː)əs

Mucius Scaevola
   Roman who fought Etruscans   MYŌŌ-shuhs SEV-uh-luh   ˌmjuːʃəs 'sevələ

Muckleshoot
   N. American people   MUHK-uhl-SHŌŌT   'məkəlˌʃuːt

Mudgee
   town, Australia   MUHJ-ē   'məʤiˑ

Muenchen
   airport, Munich   MUEN-<u>kh</u>uhn   'mynçən

Muenster
   cheese   MUHN-stuhr, M(Y)ŌŌN-stuhr,   'mənstəʳ, 'm(j)uːnstəʳ,
                             MUN-stuhr   'munstəʳ

Mufaddaliyat, Mofaddaliyat
   anthology of Arabic poetry   mōō-FAHD-duh-lē-YAHT   muːˌfɑddəliː'jɑt

Muffy
   pers. name   MUHF-ē   'məfiˑ

Mufti
   Muslim religious leader   MUHF-tē, MUF-tē   'məftiˑ, 'muftiˑ

Mugabe
   Robert, *prime minister, Zimbabwe*   mu-GAHB-ē   mu'gɑbiˑ

Foreign Sounds: ue: *Fr.* **rue**, *Ger.* **füllen**   uh(r): *Fr.* **boeuf**, *Ger.* **Höhle**   <u>kh</u>: *Ger.* **ich**, *Scot.* **loch**   ḡ: *Sp.* **amigo**   <u>v</u>: *Sp.* **hablar**
hl: *Welsh* **Llanelli.**   CAPITALS: primary stress.   SMALL CAPS: secondary stress.   Ⓢ: U.S. pron.   Ⓔ: British pron.

Muhammad
1. founder of Islam; pers. name,	mu-KHAM-muhd	mu'xæmməd
Arabic		
2. Persian	mō-KHAHM-mahd	moː'xɑːmmɑːd
3. Elijah, US cleric	mōō-HAHM-uhd	muˑ'hɑməd

Muhammedan, Mohammedan
pert. to Muhammad *or* Islam;	mō-HAM-uhd-uhn,	moː'hæmədən,
adherent of Islam	mō-HAHM-uhd-uhn, mōō-	moː'hɑmədən, muˑ-

Muhammedanism,
Mohammedanism
religion	mō-HAM-uhd-uh-NIZ-uhm,	moː'hæmədə‚nizəm,
	mō-HAHM-uhd-uh-NIZ-uhm, mōō-	moː'hɑmədə‚nizəm, muˑ-

Muharram
Islamic month	mōō-HAHR-uhm	muː'hɑrəm

Muhlenberg
county, KY; college, PA	MYŌŌ-luhn-BUHRG	'mjuːlən‚bərg

Mühlhausen
town, Germany	MUEL-HOW-zuhn	'myːl‚hauzən

Muir
Edwin, *Scottish poet and critic;*	MYUR, MYŌŌ-uhr	'mjur, 'mjuːər
John, *US naturalist; glacier, AK;*		
pers. name		

Mujeres, Isla
island, Caribbean	ĒZ-lah mōō-KHER-ās	'iːzlɑ muː'xereːs

Mukačevo, Mukachevo
town, Ukraine	MUK-uh-CHEV-ō	'mukə‚tʃevoː

Mukden
city, China	MUK-duhn, MUHK-duhn, muk-DEN	'mukdən, 'məkdən, muk'den

Mukhā, Al
seaport, Yemen	ahl mu-KHAH, al	ɑːl mu'xɑ, æl

Mulcahy
Richard James, *Irish politician*	muhl-KĀ-hē	məl'keːhiˑ

Muldaur
Diana, *US actress;* Maria, *US singer*	MUHL-DOWR, MUHL-DAWR	'məl‚daur, 'məl‚dɔːr

Muldoon
Robert, *prime minister, New Zealand*	MUHL-DŌŌN	‚məl'duːn

Mulgrew
Kate, *US actress*	MUHL-GRŌŌ	‚məl'gruː

Mulhacén
Mount, *Spain*	MŌŌ-lah-SĀN, -SEN	‚muːlɑ'seːn, -'sen

Mülhausen [Mulhouse]
port, France	MUEL-HOW-zuhn	'myl‚hauzən

Mulhouse
port, France	mue-LŌŌZ	myːluːz

Müller
K. Alex, *Swiss physicist (Nobel*	MUEL-uhr; ⑤ MYŌŌ-luhr, MIL-uhr,	'mylər; ⑤ 'mjuːlər, 'milər,
1987); Max, *German philologist;*	MUHL-uhr	'mələr
Paul H., *Swiss chemist (Nobel*		
1948)		

Muller
H. J., *US geneticist (Nobel 1946)*	MUHL-uhr	'mələr

Mullewa
township, Australia	MUHL-uh-WAW	'mələ‚wɔː

Mulligan
Richard, *US actor*	MUHL-uh-guhn	'mələgən

Key (col. 2):   a: fad   ā: fade   ah: father   ar: marry   aw: law   e: fed   ē: feed   er: merry   i: hid   ī: hide   ō: coat   ōō: boot
oi: boy   ow: now   u: put   uh: above   uhr: bird   ch: chop   ng: ring   sh: show   th: thick   th̲: this   zh: measure

Mulligatawny
   soup   MUHL-i-guh-TAW-nē, -TAHN-ē   ˌməligə'tɔːni·, -'tɑni·

Mulliken
   Robert S., *US chemist, physicist*   MUHL-i-kuhn   'məlikən
   (Nobel 1966)

Mullumbimby
   town, Australia   MUHL-uhm-BIM-bē   ˌmələm'bimbi·

Mulroney
   Brian, *prime minister, Canada*   MUHL-RŌ-nē, MUHL-ROO-nē   ˌməl'roːni·, ˌməl'ruːni·

Multnomah
   county, OR; Stadium, *Portland, OR*   MUHLT-NŌ-muh   ˌməlt'noːmə

Mumford
   Lewis, *US educator*   MUHM-fuhrd   'məmfəʳd

Munch
   Edvard, *Norwegian painter*   MUNGK   'muŋk

Munch, Münch
   Charles, *French conductor*   MUENSH   'mynʃ

Munchausen
   anglicization of Münchhausen   MUHN-CHOWZ-n, MUN-CHOWZ-n,   'mənˌtʃɑuzn̩, 'munˌtʃɑuzn̩,
                               -CHAWZ-n   -ˌtʃɔːzn̩

München [Munich]
   city, Germany   MUEN-khuhn, ⓢ MUN-chuhn,   'mynçən, ⓢ 'muntʃən,
                   MIN-chuhn   'mintʃən

Münchhausen
   Karl F. Hieronymus, *Baron von,*   MUENKH-HOWZ-n   'mynçˌhɑuzn̩
   German soldier

Muncie
   city, IN   MUHN(T)-sē   'mən(t)si·

Mundari
   lang., India   MUHN-DAHR-ē   ˌmən'dɑri·

Mundelein
   College, *IL*   MUHN-duh-LĪN   'məndəˌlɑin

Mundulla
   Australia   MUHN-DUHL-uh   ˌmən'dələ

Mundurucú
   S. American people   MOON-doo-roo-KOO   ˌmuːnduːruː'kuː

Munefusa
   pers. name, Japanese   moo-ne-foo-sah   muːnefuːsɑ

Mungo
   pers. name   MUHNG-gō   'məŋgoː

Mungunyah
   Australia   MUHN-GUHN-yuh   ˌmən'gənjə

Muni
   Paul, *Austrian-born US actor*   MYOO-nē   'mjuːni·

Munich
   city, Germany   MYOO-nik, MYOO-nikh   'mjuːnik, 'mjuːnix

Munich-Riem
   airport, Munich   MYOO-nik-RĒM, MYOO-nikh-   ˌmjuːnik'riːm, ˌmjuːnix-

Munichus
   king of Molossians   MYOO-ni-kuhs   'mjuːnikəs

Munising
   city, MI   MYOO-nuh-SING   'mjuːnəˌsiŋ

Munitus
   son of Laodice and Acamas   MYOO-nuht-uhs   'mjuːnətəs

Foreign Sounds: ue: *Fr.* **rue**, *Ger.* **füllen**   uh(r): *Fr.* **boeuf**, *Ger.* **Höhle**   <u>kh</u>: *Ger.* **ich**, *Scot.* **loch**   ḡ: *Sp.* **amigo**   v̱: *Sp.* **hablar**
hl: *Welsh* **Llanelli.**   CAPITALS: primary stress.   SMALL CAPS: secondary stress.   ⓢ: U.S. pron.   Ⓔ: British pron.

Muñoz Marín

  Luis, *governor, Puerto Rico*   mo͞on-YŌS mah-RĒN   muːnˈjoːs maˈriːn

Munro, Munroe

  pers. name   muhn-RŌ, MUHN-RŌ   mənˈroː, ˈmənˌroː

Munroe [Saki]

  Hector Hugh, *Scottish writer*   muhn-RŌ   mənˈroː

Munsee

  N. American people   MUHN-sē   ˈmənsiˑ

Munsell

  pers. name   MUHN-suhl   ˈmənsəl

Munson

  Thurman, *US baseball player; pers.*   MUHN-suhn   ˈmənsən
    name

Munster

  prov, Ireland; town, IN; cartoon   MUHN(T)-stuhr   ˈmən(t)stəʳ
    family

Münster

  city, Germany   MUEN-stuhr, ⑤ MIN(T)-stuhr,   ˈmynstəʳ, ⑤ ˈmin(t)stəʳ,
                 MUN(T)-stuhr, MUHN(T)-stuhr   ˈmun(t)stəʳ, ˈmən(t)stəʳ

Münsterhof

  French beer   MUEN-stuhr-HAWF   ˈmynstəʳˌhoːf

Munthe

  pers. name   MUN-tuh   ˈmuntə

Mu'ò'ng, Muong

  lang., people, North Vietnam   MWAHNG, muh-WAHNG   ˈmwɑŋ, məˈwɑŋ

Muon

  subatomic particle   MYo͞o-AHN   ˈmjuːˌɑn

Muppets

  puppet characters   MUHP-uhts   ˈməpəts

Muppim

  Biblical name   MUHP-im, mo͞o-PĒM   ˈməpim, muːˈpiːm

Mura

  S. American people   Mo͞o-ruh   ˈmuːrə

Murasaki

  Shikibu, *Japanese poet*   mur-ah-sahk-ē   murɑsɑkiˑ

Murat

  1. Joachim, French militarist   mue-RAH, ⑤ myu-RAH, m(y)uh-RAT   myːrɑː, ⑤ mjuˈrɑ, m(j)əˈræt
  2. pers. name   m(y)uh-RAT   m(j)əˈræt
  3. river, Turkey   mu-RAHT   muˈrɑt

Murcia

  prov & town, Spain   MURTH-yah, ⑤ MUHR-sh(ē-)uh   ˈmurθja, ⑤ ˈməʳʃ(iː)ə

Murdoch

  Iris, *British writer;* Rupert,   MUHR-duhk, MUHR-DAHK   ˈməʳdək, ˈməʳˌdɑk
    Australian entrepreneur

Murfreesboro

  city, TN   MUHR-f(r)ēz-BUHR-uh, -BUH-ruh   ˈməʳf(r)iːz,bər-ə, -ˌbə-rə

Muriel

  pers. name   MYUR-ē-uhl   ˈmjuriːəl

Murillo

  Bartolomé Esteban, *Spanish painter*   mo͞o-RĒ(L)-yō, ⑤ m(y)u-RIL-ō,   muːˈriː(l)joː, ⑤ m(j)uˈriloː,
                 m(y)u-RĒ-ō   m(j)uˈriːoː

Murmansk

  city, Russia   mur-MAHN(T)SK, mur-MAN(T)SK   muʳˈmɑːn(t)sk, muʳˈmæn(t)sk

Murmi [Bhutia]

  lang., India (Sikkim), Nepal   MUR-mē, MUHR-mē   ˈmuʳmiˑ, ˈməʳmiˑ

Key (col. 2):   a: fad   ā: fade   ah: father   ar: marry   aw: law   e: fed   ē: feed   er: merry   i: hid   ī: hide   ō: coat   o͞o: boot
oi: boy   ow: now   u: put   uh: above   uhr: bird   ch: chop   ng: ring   sh: show   th: thick   th̲: this   zh: measure

Murnane
Field, *ballpark, Utica, NY*   muhr-NĀN, MUHR-NĀN   məʳ'neːn, 'məʳ‚neːn

Murnau
F.W., *pseudonym of* Friedrich W.   MUR-NOW   'muʳ‚nɑu
  Plumpe, *German film director*

Murphy
W. P., *US physician (Nobel 1934);*   MUHR-fē   'məʳfiˑ
  pers. name

Murray
Sir James A. H., *British*   MUHR-ē, MUH-rē   'mər-iˑ, 'mə-riˑ
  lexicographer; Joseph E., *US*
  surgeon (Nobel 1990); pers. name

Murre
sea bird   MUHR   'məʳ

Murree
Pakistani beer   m(y)u-RĀ, M(Y)UR-Ā   m(j)u'reː, 'm(j)ur‚eː

Murrelet
sea bird   MUHR-luht   'məʳlət

Murrough
pers. name   MUHR-ō, MUH-RŌ   'məroː, 'mə‚roː

Murrow
Edward R., *US journalist*   MUH-RŌ, MUHR-Ō   'mə-roː, 'mər-oː

Murrumbidgee
river, Australia   MUHR-uhm-BIJ-ē   ‚mərəm'bidʒiˑ

Murrumburrah
town, Australia   MUHR-uhm-BUHR-uh   ‚mərəm'bərə

Murrurundi
town, Australia   MUHR-uh-RUHN-DĪ   ‚mərə'rən‚dɑi

Mururoa
atoll, Pacific   MOO-roo-RŌ-uh   ‚muˑruˑ'roːə

Murwillumbah
town, Australia   muhr-WIL-uhm-buh   məʳ'wiləmbə

Musaeus
legendary Greek musician and seer   myoo-ZĒ-uhs   mjuː'ziːəs

Musburger
Brent, *US sportscaster*   MUHS-BUHR-guhr   'məs‚bəʳgəʳ

Musca
constellation   MUHS-kuh   'məskə

Muscadelle
wine grape   mue-skah-DEL   myːskɑːdel

Muscadet
wine grape   mue-skah-DE, Ⓢ MUHS-kuh-DĀ   myːskɑːde, Ⓢ ‚məskə'deː

Muscadine
wine grape   MUHS-kuh-DĒN, -DĪN   'məskə‚diːn, -‚dɑin

Muscat
1. *city, Oman*   MUHS-KAHT, MUHS-kuht   'məs‚kɑt, 'məskət
2. *wine*   mue-SKAH, Ⓢ MUHS-KAT, -KAHT,   myːskɑː, Ⓢ 'məs‚kæt, -‚kɑt,
      -kuht   -kət

Muscat de Beaumes de Venise
wine   mue-SKAH duh BŌM duh vuh-NĒZ   myːskɑː də boːm də vəniːz

Muscatel
wine   MUHS-kuh-TEL   ‚məskə'tel

Muscatine
city, county, IA   MUHS-kuh-TĒN   ‚məskə'tiːn

Foreign Sounds: ue: *Fr.* **rue**, *Ger.* **füllen**   uh(r): *Fr.* **boeuf**, *Ger.* **Höhle**   <u>kh</u>: *Ger.* **ich**, *Scot.* **loch**   g̃: *Sp.* **amigo**   v̲: *Sp.* **hablar**
hl: *Welsh* **Llanelli.**   CAPITALS: primary stress.   SMALL CAPS: secondary stress.   Ⓢ: U.S. pron.   Ⓔ: British pron.

Muscogee
county, GA muh-SKŌ-GĒ məˈskoːˌgiː

Musconetcong
river, NJ MUHS-kuh-NET-KAHNG ˌməskəˈnetˌkaŋ

Muscovite
person from Moscow MUHS-kuh-VĪT ˈməskəˌvait

Muscovy
former principality centered on MUHS-kuh-vē ˈməskəviˑ
Moscow; duck

Muse
one of nine Greek inspirational MYO͞OZ ˈmjuːz
nymphs

Musgu
lang., people, Chad, Cameroon MUHS-GO͞O ˈməsˌguː

Mushi
Biblical name M(Y)O͞O-SHĪ, mōo-SHĒ ˈm(j)uːˌʃai, muːˈʃiː

Mushite
Biblical name M(Y)O͞O-SHĪT ˈm(j)uːˌʃait

Musial
Stan, US baseball player MYO͞O-zē-uhl, -zh(ē-)uhl ˈmjuːziːəl, -ʒ(iː)əl

Musica Antiqua Köln
early music ensemble, Germany MO͞O-zēk-uh an-TĒ-kwuh KUH(R)LN ˈmuːziˑkə ænˈtiːkwə ˈkœln

Muskegat
island, channel, MA muh-SKĒ-guht məˈskiːgət

Muskego
city, WI muhs-KĒ-GŌ məsˈkiːˌgoː

Muskegon
city, county, MI muh-SKĒ-guhn məˈskiːgən

Muskie
Edmund, US politician MUHS-kē ˈməskiˑ

Muskingum
river, county, OH muh-SKING-guhm, muh-SKING-uhm məˈskiŋgəm, məˈskiŋəm

Muskogean
N. American lang. family muh-SKŌ-gē-uhn məˈskoːgiːən

Muskogee
city, county, OK; N. American people muh-SKŌ-gē məˈskoːgiˑ

Muskoka
Lake, Canada muh-SKŌ-kuh məˈskoːkə

Muslim [Moslem]
pert. to Islam; adherent of Islam MUHZ-luhm, MUS-luhm, MUZ-luhm ˈməzləm, ˈmusləm, ˈmuzləm

Mussaui
pers. name, Persian muh-SOW-ē məˈsauiˑ

Musset
Alfred de, French writer mue-SE, Ⓢ myōo-SĀ myːse, Ⓢ mjuːˈseː

Mussolini
Benito, Italian leader MO͞O-suh-LĒ-nē, MUS-uh-LĒ-nē ˌmuːsəˈliːniˑ, ˌmusəˈliːniˑ

Mussorgsky, Moussorgsky
Modest, Russian composer mu-SAWRG-skē, mu-ZAWRG-skē muˈsɔːʳgskiˑ, muˈzɔːʳgskiˑ

Mustafa, Mustapha
1. pers. name, Arabic MUS-tah-fah ˈmustafɑ
2. Turkish mus-tah-FAH mustɑˈfɑ

Mut
Egyptian sky goddess MUT ˈmut

Muti
Riccardo, US conductor MO͞OT-ē ˈmuːt̬iˑ

Key (col. 2): a: fad ā: fade ah: father ar: marry aw: law e: fed ē: feed er: merry i: hid ī: hide ō: coat o͞o: boot
oi: boy ow: now u: put uh: above uhr: bird ch: chop ng: ring sh: show th: thick <u>th</u>: this zh: measure

Mutsuhito
   emperor, Japan   mut-su-hē-tō   mutsuhiːtoː

Muybridge
   Eadweard, *US motion-picture*   MĪ-BRIJ   'mɑiˌbridʒ
   pioneer

Muzak
   tdmk for recorded background music   MYO͞O-ZAK   'mjuːˌzæk

Muzio
   pers. name, Italian   MO͞OT-syō   'muːtsjoː

Mwami
   pers. name, Kirundi   MWAHM-ē   'mwɑmiˑ

Mwanbutsa
   Mwami, *king, Burundi*   mwahn-BO͞OT-suh   mwɑn'buːtsə

Mwanga
   lang., Africa   MWAHNG-guh   'mwɑŋgə

Mwera
   lang., Africa   MWER-uh   'mwerə

Mweru
   lake, Zaire, Zambia   MWER-o͞o   'mweruː

Myanmar [Burma]
   republic, Asia   myahn-MAH, mē-ahn-MAHR   mjɑn'mɑ, miːɑn'mɑʳ

Myaungmya
   town, district, Burma   MYOWNG-MYAH   'mjɑuŋ'mja

Mycale
   ancient promontory, Asia Minor   MIK-uh-lē   'mikəliˑ

Mycenae
   ancient city, Greece   mī-SĒ-nē   mɑi'siːniˑ

Mycenaean
   Bronze age culture   MĪ-suh-NĒ-uhn   ˌmɑisə'niːən

Myceneus
   founder of Mycenae   mī-SĒ-nē-uhs   mɑi'siːniːəs

Mygdon
   Phrygian king, ally of Priam MIG-duhn, MIG-DAHN   'migdən, 'migˌdɑn

Mykonos
   see Míkonos

Mýkonos
   Greek island   MĒ-kuh-NAWS, Ⓢ MIK-uh-NAHS,   'miːkəˌnɔːs, Ⓢ 'mikəˌnɑs,
                        MIK-uh-nuhs   'mikənəs

My Lai
   village, Vietnam   MĒ LĪ   'miː 'lɑi

Myles
   pers. name   MĪLZ   'mɑilz

Mynheer
   Dutch form of address for a man muh-NER   mə'neʳ

Myra
   pers. name   MĪ-ruh   'mɑirə

Myrdal
   Alva, *Swedish peace activist (Nobel* MUER-DAHL, Ⓢ MUHR-DAHL, 'myrˌdɑl, Ⓢ 'məʳˌdɑl,
   1982); Gunnar *(her husband),*   MIR-DAHL   'miʳˌdɑl
   Swedish economist (Nobel 1974)

Myrina
   Amazon queen who fought the   muh-RĪ-nuh   mə'rɑinə
   Gorgons

Myristica
   nutmeg   muh-RIS-ti-kuh, mī-RIS-ti-kuh   mə'ristikə, mɑi'ristikə

Myrmex
   girl changed into ant by Athena   MUHR-MEKS   'mə^{r}ˌmeks

Myrmidon
   subjects of Peleus & Achilles   MUHR-muh-DAHN, MUHR-muhd-uhn   'mə^{r}məˌdɑn, 'mə^{r}mədən

Myrna
   pers. name   MUHR-nuh   'mə^{r}nə

Myron
   Greek sculptor; pers. name   MĪ-ruhn   'mɑirən

Myrsus
   son of Aretus   MUHR-suhs   'mə^{r}səs

Myrtilus
   son of Hermes; charioteer   MUHRT-l-uhs   'mə^{r}tləs
   constellation

Myrtle
   pers. name   MUHRT-l   'mə^{r}tl̩

Myrto
   sister of Patroclus   MUHRT-ō   'mə^{r}t̬oː

Mysia
   Biblical name   MIS-ē-uh   'misiːə

Mysore
   city, India   mī-SÕR, mī-SAWR   mɑi'soː^r, mɑi'sɔː^r

Mystic
   town, CT; river, CT, MA   MIS-tik   'mistik

Mytilene, Mitylene [Lesbos]
   island, city, Greece   MIT-l-Ē-nē   ˌmitl̩'iːniˑ

Key (col. 2):   a: fad ā: fade ah: father ar: **marry** aw: **law** e: fed ē: feed er: **merry** i: hid ī: hide ō: coat ōō: boot
oi: **boy** ow: **now** u: put uh: above uhr: bird ch: chop ng: ring sh: show th: thick <u>th</u>: this zh: measure

N

NAACP
  National Assoc. for the Advancement   EN DUHB-uhl Ā SĒ PĒ   ˌen ˌdəbəl ˌeː ˌsiː ˈpiː
  of Colored People
Naam
  Biblical name   NĀ-uhm, NAH-ahm   ˈneːəm, ˈnɑ-ɑm
Naamah
  Biblical name   NĀ-uh-muh, NAH-ah-mah   ˈneːəmə, ˈnɑ-ɑmɑ
Naaman
  Biblical name   NĀ-uh-muhn, NAH-ah-MAHN   ˈneːəmən, ˈnɑ-ɑˌmɑn
Naamathite
  Biblical name   NĀ-uh-muh-THĪT   ˈneːəməˌθɑit
Naamite
  Biblical name   NĀ-uh-MĪT   ˈneːəˌmɑit
Naarah
  Biblical name   NĀ-uh-ruh, NAH-ah-RAH   ˈneːərə, ˈnɑ-ɑˌrɑ
Naarai
  Biblical name   NĀ-uh-RĪ, NAH-ah-RĪ   ˈneːəˌrɑi, ˌnɑ-ɑˈrɑi
Naarai [Paarai]
  Biblical name   NĀ-uh-RĪ, NAH-ah-RĪ   ˈneːəˌrɑi, ˌnɑ-ɑˈrɑi
Naaran
  Biblical name   NĀ-uh-RAN, NAH-ah-RAHN   ˈneːəˌræn, ˌnɑ-ɑˈrɑn
Naashon
  Biblical name   NĀ-ASH-AHN, nā-ASH-AHN,   ˈneːˌæʃˌɑn, neːˈæʃˌɑn,
       nahkh-SHŌN   nɑxˈʃoːn
Nabal
  Biblical name   NĀ-BAL, nah-VAHL   ˈneːˌbæl, nɑˈvɑl
Nabataean
  ancient Arab people   NAB-uh-TĒ-uhn   ˌnæbəˈtiːən
Nabisco
  US food products co.   nuh-BIS-kō   nəˈbiskoː
Nablus
  district, Israel   NAHB-luhs, NAB-luhs   ˈnɑbləs, ˈnæbləs
Nabokov
  Vladimir, *Russian American writer*   nuh-BAW-kuhf, NAB-uh-KAWF   nəˈbɔːkəf, ˈnæbəˌkɔːf
Nabonidus
  king of Babylonia   NAB-uh-NĪD-uhs   ˌnæbəˈnɑidəs
Nabopolassar
  king of Babylonia   NAB-uh-puh-LAS-uhr   ˌnæbəpəˈlæsəʳ
Nabors
  Jim, *US actor, singer*   NĀ-buhrz   ˈneːbəʳz
Naboth
  Biblical name   NĀ-BAHTH   ˈneːˌbɑθ

Foreign Sounds: ue: *Fr.* **rue**, *Ger.* **füllen**   uh(r): *Fr.* **boeuf**, *Ger.* **Höhle**   <u>kh</u>: *Ger.* **ich**, *Scot.* lo**ch**   ğ: *Sp.* ami**g**o   v: *Sp.* ha**b**lar
hl: *Welsh* **Ll**anelli.   CAPITALS: primary stress.   SMALL CAPS: secondary stress.   Ⓢ: U.S. pron.   Ⓔ: British pron.

Naches
  river, WA   NACH-ēz   'nætʃˌiːz
Nachman
  pers. name, Hebrew   NAH<u>KH</u>-mahn   'nɑːxmɑn
Nacogdoches
  city, county, TX   NAK-uh-DŌ-chuhz   ˌnækə'doːtʃəz
Nachon
  Biblical name   NĀ-KAHN, nah-<u>KH</u>ŌN   'neːˌkɑn, nɑ'xoːn
Nachor [Nahor]
  Biblical name   NĀ-KAWR, nuh-KAWR, nah-<u>KH</u>ŌR   'neːˌkɔːʳ, nə'kɔːʳ, nɑ'xoːr
Nacon
  Biblical name   NAH-KAHN, nah-<u>KH</u>ŌN   'nɑˌkɑn, nɑ'xoːn
Nadab
  Biblical name   NĀ-DAB, NAD-AB, nah-DAHV   'neːˌdæb, 'nædˌæb, nɑ'dɑv
Na-Dene, Na-Déné
  N. American lang. family   NAH-DEN-ē, NAH-DEN-Ā   ˌnɑ'deniˑ, ˌnɑ'denˌeː
Nader
  Ralph, *US consumer advocate*   NĀD-uhr   'neːdəʳ
Nadia
  1. pers. name   NAHD-yuh, NAHD-ē-uh   'nɑdjə, 'nɑdiːə
  2. French   nahd-YAH   nɑːdjɑː
Nadine
  pers. name   nā-DĒN   neː'diːn
Naera
  pers. name, Maori   nah-Ā-rah   nɑ'eːrɑ
Naevius
  Gnaeus, *Roman writer; pers. name,*   NĒ-vē-uhs   'niːviːəs
  Latin
NAFTA
  North American Free Trade   NAF-tuh   'næftə
  Agreement
Naftali
  1. pers. name, French   nahf-tah-LĒ   nɑːftɑːliː
  2. Hebrew   nahf-TAH-lē   nɑːf'tɑːliː
Nafūd
  desert, Arabian Peninsula   nuh-F͞OOD   nə'fuːd
Naga
  lang., India, Burma; municipality,   NAHG-uh   'nɑgə
  Philippines
Nagambie
  town, Australia   nuh-GAM-bē   nə'gæmbiˑ
Nagasaki
  city, Japan   nahg-uh-sahk-ē, ⑤ NAHG-uh-SAHK-ē,   nɑgəsɑkiˑ, ⑤ ˌnɑgə'sɑkiˑ,
                                     NAG-uh-SAK-ē   ˌnægə'sækiˑ
Nagasaki Takoage
  Japanese kite contest   nahg-uh-sahk-ē tahk-ō-ahg-ā   nɑgəsɑkiˑ tɑkoːageː
Nagel
  pers. name, Norwegian   NAHG-uhl   'nɑgəl
Nagge
  Biblical name   NAG-uh   'nægə
Nagorno-Karabakh
  region, Azerbaijan   nuh-GAWR-nō-KAR-uh-BAH<u>KH</u>   nə'gɔːʳnoːˌkærə'bɑx
Nagoya
  city, Japan   nuh-GOI-uh, NAHG-uh-yah   nə'goiə, 'nɑgəja

Key (col. 2):   a: **f**a**d**   ā: **f**a**de**   ah: **f**a**ther**   ar: **marry**   aw: **law**   e: **fed**   ē: **feed**   er: **merry**   i: **hid**   ī: **hide**   ō: **coat**   o͞o: **boot**
oi: **boy**   ow: **now**   u: **put**   uh: **above**   uhr: **bird**   ch: **chop**   ng: **ring**   sh: **show**   th: **thick**   <u>th</u>: **this**   zh: **measure**

Nagpur		
city, India	NAHG-PUR	'nɑgˌpuʳ
Naguib		
pers. name, Arabic	NAH-GĒB, nah-GĒB	'nɑˌgiːb, nɑ'giːb
Nagy		
Imre, *Hungarian political leader*	NAHD, [$] NAHZH, NAHJ	'nɑɖ, [$] 'nɑʒ, 'nɑdʒ
Naha		
city, Okinawa	NAH-hah	'nɑhɑ
Nahalal		
Biblical name	nuh-HAL-uhl, NA-huh-LAL, NAH-hah-LAHL	nə'hæləl, 'næhəˌlæl, ˌnɑhɑ'lɑl
Nahaliel		
Biblical name	nuh-HĀ-lē-EL, nuh-HAL-ē-EL, -ē-uhl; NAH-khah-lē-EL	nə'heːliːˌel, nə'hæliːˌel, -iːəl; ˌnɑxɑliː'el
Nahalol		
Biblical name	NĀ-huh-LAHL, NAH-hah-LAWL	'neːhəˌlɑl, ˌnɑhɑ'lɔːl
Naham		
Biblical name	NĀ-uhm, NAH-khahm	'neːəm, 'nɑxɑm
Nahamani		
Biblical name	NĀ-huh-MĀ-NĪ, NAH-khah-MAH-nē	ˌneːhə'meːˌnɑi, ˌnɑxɑ'mɑniː
Nahant		
town, bay, MA	nuh-HANT	nə'hænt
Naharai		
Biblical name	NĀ-(h)uh-RĪ, nahkh-RĪ	'neː(h)əˌrɑi, nɑx'rɑi
Nahash		
Biblical name	NĀ-HASH, nah-KHAHSH	'neːˌhæʃ, nɑ'xɑʃ
Nahath		
Biblical name	NĀ-HATH, NAH-khaht	'neːˌhæθ, 'nɑxɑt
Nahbi		
Biblical name	NAB-Ī, nahkh-BĒ	'næbˌɑi, nɑx'biː
Nahor		
biblical patriarch	nuh-HAWR	nə'hɔːʳ
Nahshon		
Biblical name	NA-SHAHN, NAHSH-AHN, nahkh-SHŌN	'næˌʃɑn, 'nɑʃˌɑn, nɑx'ʃoːn
Nahua		
ancient Central American people	NAH-wuh	'nɑwə
Nahuatl		
people, lang., Cen. America	NAH-WAHT-l	'nɑˌwɑtl̩
Nahuatlan		
lang. family, N. America	nah-WAHT-luhn	nɑ'wɑtlən
Nahum		
1. Old Testament book; pers. name	NĀ-(h)uhm, NĀ-HUHM	'neː(h)əm, 'neːˌhəm
2. German	NAH-HUM	'nɑˌhum
3. Hebrew	NAHKH-um	'nɑxum
Nahum		
Biblical name	NĀ-uhm, nah-KHOOM	'neːəm, nɑ'xuːm
Naiad		
water nymph	NĀ-uhd, NĪ-uhd, NĀ-AD, NĪ-AD	'neːəd, 'nɑiəd, 'neːˌæd, 'nɑiˌæd
Naiades		
plural of Naiad	NĀ-uh-DĒZ, NĪ-uh-DĒZ	'neːəˌdiːz, 'nɑiəˌdiːz
Nain		
Biblical name	NĀN, NĪN, NĀ-in	'neːn, 'nɑin, 'neːin
Naioth		
Biblical name	NĀ-AHTH, NĪ-AHTH, nah-YŌT	'neːˌɑθ, 'nɑiˌɑθ, nɑ'joːt

Foreign Sounds: ue: *Fr.* **rue**, *Ger.* **füllen** uh(r): *Fr.* **boeuf**, *Ger.* **Höhle** kh: *Ger.* **ich**, *Scot.* **loch** g̃: *Sp.* **amigo** v̱: *Sp.* **hablar** hl: *Welsh* **Llanelli**. CAPITALS: primary stress. SMALL CAPS: secondary stress. [$]: U.S. pron. [£]: British pron.

Naipaul
   V.J., *Trinidadian novelist*   nī-PAWL   nɑi'pɔːl

Nairobi
   city, Kenya   nī-RŌ-bē   nɑi'roːbiˑ

Naismith
   James, *Canadian-born US*   NĀ-smith   'neːsmiθ
     originator of basketball

Najd [Nejd]
   prov, Saudi Arabia   NAJD   'nædʒd

Najibullah
   Mohammad, *Afghan president* NAHJ-ē-bu-LAH   ,nɑdʒiˑbu'lɑ

Nakasone
   Yasuhiro, *prime minister, Japan* nahk-ah-sō-nā   nɑkɑsoːneː

Nakhichevan
   town, Azerbaijan   NAHK-i-chuh-VAHN   ,nɑkitʃə'vɑn

Nam, 'Nam
   informal reference to Vietnam NAHM, NAM   'nɑm, 'næm

Nama
   lang., people, Namibia   NAHM-uh   'nɑmə

Namaqualand
   region, Southern Africa   nuh-MAHK-wuh-LAND   nə'mɑkwə,lænd

Namath
   Joe, *US football player*   NĀ-muhth   'neːməθ

Nambe Pueblo
   Indian reservation, US   NAHM-bā po͞o-EB-lō, PWEB-lō,   'nambeː puː'ebloː, 'pwebloː,
                               py͞oo-EB-lō   pju:'ebloː

Nambicuara
   S. American people   NAM-bē-KWAHR-uh, NAHM-   ,næmbiˑ'kwɑrə, ,nɑm-

Nambucca
   river, Australia   nam-BUHK-uh   næm'bəkə

Namib
   desert, Africa   NAHM-ib   'nɑmib

Namibia
   territory, Africa   nuh-MIB-ē-uh   nə'mibiːə

Namoi
   river, Australia   NAM-OI   'næm,ɔi

Nampula
   prov, Mozambique   nam-PO͞O-luh   næm'puːlə

Namur
   commune, prov, Belgium   nah-MUR   nɑ'muʳ

Nan
   pers. name   NAN   'næn

Nanaian
   pert. to Nanays   na-NĪ-uhn   næ'nɑiən

Nanakuli
   city, HI   NAH-nah-KO͞O-lē   ,nɑnɑ'kuːliː

Nanango
   town, Australia   nuh-NANG-gō   nə'næŋgoː

Nanchang, Nan-ch'ang
   city, China   NAHN-CHAHNG   'nɑn'tʃɑŋ

Nancy
   1. pers. name   NAN-sē   'nænsiˑ
   2. city, France   nahⁿ-SĒ, Ⓢ NAN-sē   nɑ̃siː, Ⓢ 'nænsiˑ

Nanda Devan
   Indian festival   NAHN-duh DĀ-vuhn   'nɑndə 'deːvən

Key (col. 2): a: fad ā: fade ah: father ar: marry aw: law e: fed ē: feed er: merry i: hid ī: hide ō: coat o͞o: boot
oi: boy ow: now u: put uh: above uhr: bird ch: chop ng: ring sh: show th: thick <u>th</u>: this zh: measure

Nandi		
lang., people, Kenya, Uganda, Tanzania	NAHN-DĒ	'nɑn,diː
Nanette		
pers. name	nan-ET, nuh-NET	næn'et, nə'net
Nanga Parbat		
mtn., Himalayas	NUHNG-guh PUHR-buht	,nəŋgə 'pə^{r}bət
Nanjing [Nanking]		
city, China	NAHN-JING	'nɑn'dʒiŋ
Nanking		
city, China	NAHN-KING, [$] NAN-KING	'nɑn'kiŋ, [$] 'næn'kiŋ
Nannacus		
king of Phrygia	NAN-uh-kuhs	'nænəkəs
Nannerl		
pers. name, German	NAHN-uhrl	'nɑnə^{r}l
Nansemond		
stream, former county, VA	NAN(T)-sē-MUHN(D)	,næn(t)siˑ'mən(d)
Nansen		
1. Fridtjof, *Norwegian explorer, zoologist, statesman (Nobel 1922)*	NAHN-suhn	'nɑnsən
2. Sound, *strait, Canada*	NAN-suhn	'nænsən
Nantahala		
river, NC	NANT-uh-HĀ-luh, -lē	,næntə'heːlə, -liˑ
Nantes		
city, France	NAH^{n}T	nɑ̃t
Nanticoke		
river, MD; city, PA; N. American people	NANT-i-KŌK	'nænti,koːk
Nantucket		
island, county, MA	nan-TUHK-uht	næn'təkət
Nanuet		
town, NY	NAN-yuh-WET	,nænjə'wet
Naomi		
pers. name	nā-Ō-mē	neː'oːmiˑ
Naotake		
pers. name, Japanese	nā-ō-tah-ke	neːoːtɑke
NAPA		
auto parts chain	NAP-uh	'næpə
Napa		
city, county, valley, CA	NAP-uh	'næpə
Naphish		
Biblical name	NĀ-fish, nah-FĒSH	'neːfiʃ, nɑ'fiːʃ
Naphtali		
1. pers. name	NAF-tuh-LĪ	'næftə,lɑi
2. Russian	NUHF-TAHL-yi	,nəf'tɑljij
Naphtali		
one of the twelve tribes of Israel	NAF-tuh-LĪ, nahf-tah-LĒ	'næftə,lɑi, nɑftɑ'liː
Naphtuhim		
Biblical name	NAF-t(y)o͞o-HIM, nahf-to͞o-KHIM	'næft(j)uː,him, nɑftuː'xim
Napier		
pers. name	NĀ-pē-uhr, NĀ-PIR, nuh-PIR	'neːpiːə^{r}, 'neː,pi^{r}, nə'pi^{r}
Naples		
city, FL; city, prov, Italy	NĀ-puhlz	'neːpəlz

Foreign Sounds: ue: *Fr.* **rue**, *Ger.* **füllen** uh(r): *Fr.* **boeuf**, *Ger.* **Höhle** kh: *Ger.* **ich**, *Scot.* **loch** g̃: *Sp.* amigo v̱: *Sp.* hablar hl: *Welsh* **Llanelli**. CAPITALS: primary stress. SMALL CAPS: secondary stress. [$]: U.S. pron. [£]: British pron.

Napoleon
   1. custard-filled pastry; pers. name   nuh-PŌ-lē-uhn, nuh-PŌL-yuhn   nə'poːliːən, nə'poːljən
   2. German   nah-PŌ-lā-awn, nah-PŌ-lā-awⁿ   nɑ'poːleːɔːn, nɑ'poːleːɔ̃
Napoléon
   French emperor   nah-paw-lā-AWⁿ, Ⓢ nuh-PŌ-lē-uhn   nɑːpɔːleːɔ̃, Ⓢ nə'poːliːən
Napoleonic
   pert. to Napoléon   nuh-PŌ-lē-AHN-ik   nə,poːliː'ɑnik
Napoli [Naples]
   city, prov., Italy   NAHP-uh-lē   'nɑpəliˑ
Nappanee
   city, IN   NAP-uh-NĒ   'næpə,niː
Nara
   1. city, Japan   nahr-ah   nɑrɑ
   2. lang., Ethiopia   NAHR-uh   'nɑrə
Narada Falls
   waterfall, WA   nuh-RAD-uh FAWLZ   nə'rædə 'fɔːlz
Naram-Sin
   king of Akkad   nah-RAHM-SIN   nɑ'rɑm'sin
Narasimha
   pers. name, Hindi   nuh-RAHS-im-HAH   nə'rɑsim,hɑ
Narayan
   pers. name   NAH-rī-(Y)AHN   ,nɑrai'(j)ɑn
Narbada [Narmada]
   river, India   nuhr-BUHD-uh   nə^r'bədə
Narbo
   ancient name of Narbonne   NAHR-bō   'nɑ^rboː
Narbonensis
   region of Gaul   NAHR-buh-NEN-suhs   ,nɑ^rbə'nensəs
Narbonne
   commune, France   nahr-BAWN   nɑːrbɔːn
Narciso
   pers. name, Spanish   nahr-SĒ-sō, nahr-THĒ-sō   nɑr'siːsoː, nɑr'θiːsoː
Narcissus
   handsome youth in Greek myth   nahr-SIS-uhs   nɑ^r'sisəs
Narita
   airport, Tokyo   nahr-ē-tah   nɑriːtɑ
Narmada [Narbada]
   river, India   nuhr-MUHD-uh   nə^r'mədə
Narmer
   king of Egypt   NAHR-mer   'nɑ^rme^r
Naropa
   Institute, *college, CO*   nuh-RŌ-puh   nə'roːpə
Narrabri
   town, Australia   NAR-uh-BRĪ   'nærə,brai
Narraganset
   N. American people   NAR-uh-GAN-suht, NER-   ,nærə'gænsət, ,ner-
Narrandera
   town, Australia   nuh-RAN-druh   nə'rændrə
Narva
   river, city, Estonia   NAHR-vuh   'nɑ^rvə
Narvik
   city, Norway   NAHR-vik, NAHR-VĒK   'nɑ^rvik, 'nɑ^r,viːk
NASA
   US space agency   NAS-uh   'næsə

Key (col. 2):   a: fad   ā: fade   ah: father   ar: marry   aw: law   e: fed   ē: feed   er: merry   i: hid   ī: hide   ō: coat   ōō: boot
oi: boy   ow: now   u: put   uh: above   uhr: bird   ch: chop   ng: ring   sh: show   th: thick   <u>th</u>: this   zh: measure

Nasca
   see Nazca

Nashua

city, NH	NASH-uh-wuh, NASH-uh-WĀ	ˈnæʃəwə, ˈnæʃəˌweː

Nashville

city, TN	NASH-VIL, NASH-vuhl	ˈnæʃˌvil, ˈnæʃvəl

Nasica

Roman cognomen	NAHS-i-kuh	ˈnɑsikə

Naskapi

N. American people	NAS-kuh-pē	ˈnæskəpiˑ

Nassau

1. county, FL, NY; city, Bahamas; pers. name	NAS-aw	ˈnæsɔː
2. region, Germany	NAHS-OW	ˈnɑsˌɑu

Nasser

Gamal Abdel, *president, Egypt*	NAHS-uhr	ˈnɑsəʳ

Nastase

Ilie, *Romanian tennis player*	nahs-TAHZ-ē	nɑsˈtɑziˑ

Nastassja

pers. name (N. Kinski)	nuh-STAHS-yuh	nəˈstɑsjə

Nat

pers. name	NAT	ˈnæt

Natal

port, Brazil; prov, S. Africa	nah-TAHL, nuh-TAL	nɑːˈtɑːl, nəˈtæl

Natalia, Natalya

pers. name	nuh-TAHL-yuh	nəˈtɑljə

Natalie

pers. name	NAT-l-ē	ˈnætl̩iˑ

Natasha

pers. name	nuh-TASH-uh, nuh-TAHSH-uh	nəˈtæʃə, nəˈtɑʃə

Natashquan, Natashkwan

river, Canada	nuh-TASH-kwuhn	nəˈtæʃkwən

Natchaug

river, CT	nuh-CHAWG	nəˈtʃɔːg

Natchez

city, MS; N. American people	NACH-uhz	ˈnætʃəz

Natchitoches

city, parish, LA	NAK-uh-TAHSH, NAK-(uh-)tuhsh	ˈnækəˌtɑʃ, ˈnæk(ə)təʃ

Nathan

1. pers. name	NĀ-thuhn	ˈneːθən
2. German	NAH-tahn	ˈnɑtɑn
3. Swedish	NAH-tahn	ˈnɑtɑːn

Nathan-melech

Biblical name	NĀ-thuhn-MĒ-LEK, nuh-TAHN-ME-lekh	ˈneːθənˈmiːˌlek, nəˌtɑnˈmelex

Nathanael

1. pers. name	nuh-THAN-ā-uhl, nuh-THAN-ē-uhl	nəˈθæneːəl, nəˈθæniːəl
2. German	nah-TAHN-ah-EL	nɑˈtɑnɑˌel

Nathaniel

pers. name	nuh-THAN-yuhl	nəˈθænjəl

Nathans

Daniel, *US microbiologist (Nobel 1978)*	NĀ-thuhnz	ˈneːθənz

Natick

town, MA; village, RI	NĀT-ik	ˈneːt̬ik

Foreign Sounds: **ue**: *Fr.* **rue**, *Ger.* **füllen** **uh(r)**: *Fr.* **boeuf**, *Ger.* **Höhle** <u>kh</u>: *Ger.* **ich**, *Scot.* **loch** g̅: *Sp.* **amigo** v̲: *Sp.* **hablar**
hl: *Welsh* **Llanelli**. CAPITALS: primary stress. SMALL CAPS: secondary stress. Ⓢ: U.S. pron. Ⓔ: British pron.

Nationalrat

Austrian parliament   NAHTS-yō-NAHL-RAHT   ˌnatsjoːˈnalˌrat

NATO

North Atlantic Treaty Organization   NĀT-ō, NĀ-TŌ   ˈneːt̥oː, ˈneːˌtoː

Natrona

county, WY   nuh-TRŌ-nuh   nəˈtroːnə

Natta

Giulio, Italian chemist (Nobel 1963)   NAHT-tah   ˈnatta

Natty

pers. name   NAT-ē   ˈnætiˑ

Natufian

Mesolithic culture in Palestine   nuh-TOO-fē-uhn   nəˈtuːfiːən

Natzler

Otto, US ceramic artist   NAT-sluhr   ˈnætsləʳ

Naucratis, Naukratis

ancient Greek city, Egypt   NAW-kruht-uhs   ˈnɔːkrətəs

Naugahyde

tdmk for a vinyl upholstery fabric   NAW-guh-HĪD, NAHG-uh-HĪD   ˈnɔːgəˌhaid, ˈnagəˌhaid

Naugatuck

town, CT   NAW-guh-TUHK   ˈnɔːgəˌtək

Naupactus

ancient seaport, Greece   naw-PAK-tuhs   nɔːˈpæktəs

Nauplia

town, Greece   NAW-plē-uh   ˈnɔːpliːə

Nauplion

see Návplion

Nauplius

father of Palamedes   NAW-plē-uhs   ˈnɔːpliːəs

Nauru

island   nah-OO-roo   naˈuːruː

Nauruan

lang., Nauru   NAH-OO-ROO-uhn, NOW-ROO-uhn   ˌnaˌuːˈruːən, ˌnauˈruːən

Nauset

N. American people   NAW-suht   ˈnɔːsət

Nausicaa

daughter of Alcinous   NAW-si-kuh   ˈnɔːsikə

Nautes

companion of Aeneas in Italy   NAW-TĒZ   ˈnɔːˌtiːz

Nautilus

submarine   NAWT-l-uhs, NAHT-l-uhs   ˈnɔːtl̩əs, ˈnatl̩əs

Nauvoo

city, IL   naw-VOO, NAW-voo   nɔːˈvuː, ˈnɔːvuː

Navajo, Navaho

county, AZ; N. American people   NAV-uh-HŌ, NAHV-uh-HŌ   ˈnævəˌhoː, ˈnavəˌhoː

Navarra [Navarre]

region, Spain   nah-VAHR-rah   naˈvarra

Navarre

ancient kingdom, region, Spain   nuh-VAHR, *French* nah-VAHR   nəˈvaʳ, *French* naːvaːr

Navarro

county, TX   nuh-VAHR-ō   nəˈvaroː

Navasota

river, TX   NAV-uh-SŌT-uh   ˌnævəˈsoːt̥ə

Návplion, Nauplion

town, Greece   NAHF-plē-AWN   ˈnafpliːˌɔːn

Key (col. 2):   a: fad   ā: fade   ah: father   ar: **marry**   aw: **law**   e: fed   ē: feed   er: **merry**   i: hid   ī: hide   ō: coat   oo: boot
oi: **boy**   ow: **now**   u: put   uh: **above**   uhr: **bird**   ch: **chop**   ng: **ring**   sh: **show**   th: **thick**   th: **this**   zh: measure

Navratilova
   Martina, *sports personality* NAV-ruh-tuh-LŌ-vuh, NAHV- ˌnævrətəˈloːvə, ˌnɑv-

Naxi
   lang., China NAH-SĒ, NAH-SHĒ ˈnɑˈsiː, ˈnɑˈʃiː

Náxos
   island, Greece NAHK-SAWS, ⑤ NAK-suhs, NAK-SAHS ˈnɑkˌsɔːs, ⑤ ˈnæksəs, ˈnækˌsɑs

Nayarit
   state, Mexico NĪ-uh-RĒT ˌnɑiəˈriːt

Nazarbayev
   Nursultan, *Kazakhstanian political leader* NAHZ-uhr-BĪ-(y)uhf ˌnɑzərˈbɑi(j)əf

Nazaré
   town, Portugal NAHZ-uh-RĀ ˌnɑzəˈreː

Nazarene
   native or inhabitant of Nazareth NAZ-uh-RĒN ˌnæzəˈriːn

Nazareth
   town, Israel; borough, PA NAZ-(uh-)ruhth ˈnæz(ə)rəθ

Nazca, Nasca
   Peruvian Indian culture NAS-kuh ˈnæskə

Nazi
   member of German fascist party NAHT-sē, NAT-sē ˈnɑtsiˑ, ˈnætsiˑ

Naziism
   principles or methods of the Nazis NAHT-sē-IZ-uhm, NAT-sē-IZ-uhm ˈnɑtsiːˌizəm, ˈnætsiːˌizəm

Nazism
   principles or methods of the Nazis NAHT-SIZ-uhm, NAT-SIZ-uhm ˈnɑtˌsizəm, ˈnætˌsizəm

Ndali
   lang., Africa n-DAHL-ē, uhn-DAHL-ē, en- n̩ˈdɑliˑ, ənˈdɑliˑ, en-

Ndamba
   lang., Africa n-DAHM-buh, uhn-DAHM-buh, en- n̩ˈdɑmbə, ənˈdɑmbə, en-

Ndandi
   lang., Africa n-DAHN-dē, uhn-DAHN-dē, en- n̩ˈdɑndiˑ, ənˈdɑndiˑ, en-

Ndebele
   people, Africa n-duh-BĒ-lē, EN-duh-BĒ-lē n̩dəˈbiːliˑ, ˌendəˈbiːliˑ

Ndeti
   Cosmas, *Kenyan marathoner* n-DET-ē, en- n̩ˈdetiˑ, en-

N'Djamena
   city, Chad n-juh-MĀ-nuh, EN-juh-, -MĒ-nuh, -MEN-uh n̩dʒəˈmeːnə, ˌendʒə-, -ˈmiːnə, -ˈmenə

Ndo
   lang., Uganda, Zaire n-DŌ, en- n̩ˈdoː, en-

Ndonde
   lang., Africa n-DŌN-dā, uhn-DŌN-dā, en-, -DAHN-dā n̩ˈdoːndeː, ənˈdoːndeː, en-, -ˈdandeː

Neagh Windermere, Lough
   N. Ireland LAHK NĀ WIN-duhr-MIR, LAHKH ˈlɑk ˈneː ˈwindərˌmirˑ, ˈlɑx

Neah
   Biblical name NĒ-uh, ne-AH ˈniːə, neˈɑ

Neahwa
   Park, *former name for* Damaschke Field, *Oneonta, NY* NĒ-uh-WAW, NĒ-uh-WAH, NĒ-uh-wuh ˈniːəˌwɔː, ˈniːəˌwɑ, ˈniːəwə

Neal, Neale
   pers. name NĒL ˈniːl

Foreign Sounds: ue: *Fr.* **rue**, *Ger.* **füllen** uh(r): *Fr.* **boeuf**, *Ger.* **Höhle** kh: *Ger.* **ich**, *Scot.* **loch** g̱: *Sp.* **amigo** v̱: *Sp.* **hablar** hl: *Welsh* **Llanelli**. CAPITALS: primary stress. SMALL CAPS: secondary stress. ⑤: U.S. pron. ⑥: British pron.

Neanderthal
  Paleolithic human subspecies nē-AN-duhr-THAWL, -TAWL; niːˈændərˌθɔːl, -ˌtɔːl;
                                  nā-AHN-duhr-TAHL   neːˈandərˌtɑl
Neapolis
  ancient name of Naples   nē-AP-uh-luhs   niːˈæpələs
Neapolitan
  pert. to Naples   NĒ-uh-PAHL-uht-n   ˌniːəˈpɑlətn̩
Nearchus
  Macedonian soldier, explorer nē-AHR-kuhs   niːˈɑrkəs
Neariah
  Biblical name   NĒ-uh-RĪ-uh, nuh-ahr-YAH   ˌniːəˈraiə, nəarˈja
Nebai
  Biblical name   NĒ-BĪ, NEB-ā-Ī, nuh-VĪ   ˈniːˌbai, ˈnebeːˌai, nəˈvai
Nebaioth
  Biblical name   ni-BĪ-AHTH, ni-BĀ-AHTH, -uhth; niˈbaiˌɑθ, niˈbeːˌɑθ, -əθ;
                                  nuh-vah-YŌT   nəvaˈjoːt
Nebajoth [Nebaioth]
  Biblical name   nuh-BĀ-JAHTH, nuh-vah-YŌT   nəˈbeːˌdʒɑθ, nəvaˈjoːt
Neballat
  Biblical name   nuh-BAL-uht, nev-ah-LAHT   nəˈbælət, nevaˈlat
Nebat
  Biblical name   NĒ-BAT, nuh-VAHT   ˈniːˌbæt, nəˈvat
Nebbiolo
  Italian wine grape   neb-BYŌ-lō   nebbjoːloː
Nebo
  Mount, *Jordan*   NĒ-bō   ˈniːboː
Nebraska
  state, US   nuh-BRAS-kuh   nəˈbræskə
Nebuchadnezzar
  king of Babylon   NEB-(y)uh-kuhd-NEZ-uhr   ˌneb(j)əkədˈnezər
Nebuchadrezzar
  alternate form of Nebuchadnezzar NEB-(y)uh-kuh-DREZ-uhr ˌneb(j)əkəˈdrezər
Nebularum, Palus
  see Palus Nebularum
Nebushasban, Nebushazban
  Biblical name   NEB-(y)uh-SHAS-BAN, -SHAZ-BAN; ˌneb(j)əˈʃæsˌbæn, -ˈʃæzˌbæn;
                                  nuh-VOO-shahz-BAHN   nəˌvuːʃazˈban
Nebuzaradan
  Biblical name   NEB-(y)uh-ZAHR-Ā-DAN,   ˌneb(j)əˌzarˈeːˌdæn,
                                  -ZAHR-uh-DAN;   -ˈzarəˌdæn;
                                  nuh-VOO-zahr-ah-DAHN   nəˌvuːzarɑˈdan
NEC
  Japanese electronics co.   NEK, EN-Ē-SĒ   ˈnek, ˌenˌiːˈsiː
Necaxa
  river, Mexico   nuh-KAH-hah   nəˈkɑːhaː
Necchi
  sewing machine co.   NEK-ē   ˈnekiˑ
Nechako
  river, Canada   ni-CHAH-kō   niˈtʃakoː
Neches
  river, TX   NECH-uhz   ˈnetʃəz
Necho
  Egyptian pharaoh   NĒ-kō   ˈniːkoː

Key (col. 2): a: f**a**d ā: f**a**de ah: f**a**ther ar: m**ar**ry aw: l**aw** e: f**e**d ē: f**ee**d er: m**er**ry i: h**i**d ī: h**i**de ō: c**oa**t o͞o: b**oo**t
oi: b**oy** ow: n**ow** u: p**u**t uh: **a**bove uhr: b**ir**d ch: **ch**op ng: ri**ng** sh: **sh**ow th: **th**ick <u>th</u>: **th**is zh: mea**s**ure

Necker
    Jacques, *18th-cent. French financier*   ne-KER, ⓢ NEK-uhr   neker, ⓢ 'nekəʳ
    and statesman

Neco, Necho
    Biblical name   NĒ-KŌ, nuh-K̲H̲Ō   'niːˌkoː, nə'xoː

Necronomicon
    ancient occult text, H.P. Lovecraft   NEK-ruh-NAHM-i-KAHN   ˌnekrə'nɑmiˌkɑn

Nectaris, Mare
    see Mare Nectaris

Ned
    pers. name   NED   'ned

Nedabiah
    Biblical name   NED-uh-BĪ-uh, nuh-dahv-YAH   ˌnedə'baiə, nədav'ja

Neðri Deild
    Icelandic legis. body   NET̲H̲-rē DĀLD   'neðriˑ 'deːld

Nederland [Netherlands]
    1. kingdom, Europe   NĀD-uhr-LAHNT   'neːdəʳˌlant
    2. city, TX   NĒD-uhr-LAND   'niːdəʳˌlænd

Needham
    Hal, *US film writer; town, MA*   NĒD-uhm   'niːdəm

Néel
    Louis Eugène, *French physicist*   nā-EL   neːel
    (Nobel 1970)

Neeme
    pers. name, Estonian   nyi-ĀM-yuh, ⓢ NĒ-muh   nji'eːmjə, ⓢ 'niːmə

Nefertiti
    Egyptian queen   NEF-uhr-TĒT-ē   ˌnefəʳ'tiːʈiˑ

Neftalí
    pers. name, Spanish   nef-tah-LḖ   neftɑ'liː

Negev
    desert, Israel   NEG-EV   'negˌev

Neginoth
    Biblical name   NEG-uh-NAHTH, nuh-gē-NŌT   'negəˌnɑθ, nəgiː'noːt

Negra Modelo
    Mexican beer   NĀ-grah mō-DĀ-lō   'neːgrɑ moː'deːloː

Negress
    (formerly) woman of black African   NĒ-gruhs   'niːgrəs
    race

Negrillo
    Pygmy   ni-GRḖ-(y)ō, ni-GRIL-ō   ni'griː(j)oː, ni'griloː

Negri Sembilan
    state, Malaysia   nuh-GRḖ sem-BḖ-luhn   nəˌgriː sem'biːlən

Negrito
    small-statured people, Asia   nuh-GRḖT-ō   nə'griːʈoː

Negro
    1. member of black African race   NĒ-grō   'niːgroː
    2. Rio, *river, S. America*   NĀ-ḡrō, ⓢ NEG-rō   'neːɣroː, ⓢ 'negroː

Negroid
    pert. to Negro *people*   NĒ-GROID   'niːˌgrɔid

Negros
    island, Philippines   NĀ-grōs, NEG-rōs   'neːgroːs, 'negroːs

Negus
    title of sovereign in Ethiopia   NĒ-guhs   'niːgəs

Nehelamite
    Biblical name   nuh-HEL-uh-MĪT   nə'heləˌmɑit

Nehemiah
pers. name   NĒ-(h)uh-MĪ-uh   ˌniː(h)əˈmaɪə

Neher
Edwin, *German physicist (Nobel 1991)*   NĀ-uhr, NER   ˈneːərˌ, ˈnerˌ

Nehiloth
Biblical name   NĒ-(h)uh-LAHTH, nuh-hē-LŌT   ˈniː(h)əˌlɑθ, nəhiːˈloːt

Nehru
Jawaharlal, *Indian leader*   NER-ōō, NĀ-rōō   ˈneruːˌ, ˈneːruː

Nehum
Biblical name   NĒ-(h)uhm, nuh-KHŌŌM   ˈniː(h)əm, nəˈxuːm

Nehushta
Biblical name   nuh-HUHSH-tuh, nuh-khōōsh-TAH   nəˈhəʃtə, nəxuːʃˈtɑ

Nehushtan
Biblical name   nuh-HUHSH-TAN, -tuhn; nuh-khōōsh-TAHN   nəˈhəʃˌtæn, -tən; nəxuːʃˈtɑn

Neiel
Biblical name   NĀ-EL, nē-Ī-EL, -uhl; nuh-ē-EL   ˈneːˌel, niːˈɑiˌel, -əl; nəiːˈel

Neil
pers. name   NĒL   ˈniːl

Neilson
William Allen, *US educator*   NĒL-suhn   ˈniːlsən

Neiman
Leroy, *US artist*   NĒ-muhn   ˈniːmən

Neiman-Marcus
department store, US   NĒ-muhn-MAHR-kuhs   ˌniːmənˈmɑrkəs

Nei-Meng-Gu, Nei-Meng-Ku, Nei Mongol
Inner Mongolia, China   NĀ MUHNG-GŌŌ   ˈneː ˈməŋˈguː

Nei Mongol
autonomous region, China   NĀ MAHNG-guhl, MAHN-GŌL, MAHNG-GŌL   ˈneː ˈmaŋgəl, ˈmanˌgoːl, ˈmaŋˌgoːl

Neineva
governorate, Iraq   NĀ-nuh-vuh   ˈneːnəvə

Neith
Egyptian war goddess   NĀT, NĀTH   ˈneːt, ˈneːθ

Nejd [Najd]
prov, Saudi Arabia   NEJD   ˈnedʒd

Nekeb
Biblical name   NĒ-KEB, NEK-EB, NEK-ev   ˈniːˌkeb, ˈnekˌeb, ˈnekev

Nekhbet
Egyptian guardian goddess   NEKH-buht   ˈnexbət

Nekhebet [Nekhbet]
Egyptian guardian goddess   NEKH-uh-buht   ˈnexəbət

Nekoda
Biblical name   nuh-KŌD-uh, nuh-kō-DAH   nəˈkoːdə, nəkoːˈdɑ

Nektar
Yugoslavian beer   NEK-TAHR   ˈnekˌtɑr

Neleus
son of Tyro and Poseidon   NĒ-lē-uhs, NĒ-L(Y)ŌŌS   ˈniːliːəs, ˈniːˌl(j)uːs

Neligh
city, NE   NĒL-Ē   ˈniːlˌiː

Nell
pers. name   NEL   ˈnel

Key (col. 2):   a: fad   ā: fade   ah: father   ar: marry   aw: law   e: fed   ē: feed   er: merry   i: hid   ī: hide   ō: coat   ōō: boot
oi: boy   ow: now   u: put   uh: above   uhr: bird   ch: chop   ng: ring   sh: show   th: thick   th: this   zh: measure

Nellie, Nelly
   pers. name   NEL-ē   'neli·
Nelligan
   Kate, *Canadian actress*   NEL-uh-guhn   'neləgən
Nelson
   pers. name   NEL-suhn   'nelsən
Nemaha
   river, US; county, KS, NE   NEM-uh-HAW, NĒ-muh-HAW   'nemə,hɔː, 'niːmə,hɔː
Neman
   river, Belorussia, Lithuania, Russia   NEM-uhn   'nemən
Nembutal
   tdmk for pentobarbital   NEM-byuh-TAWL   ,nembjə'tɔːl
Nemea
   valley, ancient Greece   NĒ-mē-uh   'niːmiːə
Nemean
   pert. to Nemea   ni-MĒ-uhn, NEM-ē-uhn, NĒ-mē-uhn   ni'miːən, 'nemiːən, 'niːmiːən
Nemencha
   Mountains, *mtn. range, Algeria*   nuh-MEN-chuh   nə'mentʃə
Nemerov
   Howard, *US poet laureate*   NEM-uh-RAWV   'nemə,rɔːv
Nemesis
   Greek goddess of divine vengeance   NEM-uh-suhs   'neməsəs
Nemetz
   Nathaniel Theodore, *Canadian*   NEM-uhts   'neməts
      jurist
Nemi
   lake, Italy   NĀ-mē, NEM-ē   'neːmi·, 'nemi·
Nemo
   Captain, *character in 20,000*   NĒ-mō   'niːmoː
      Leagues Under the Sea, *Jules*
      Verne
Nemuel
   Biblical name   NEM-yuh-wuhl, nuh-m$\overline{oo}$-EL   'nemjəwəl, nəmuː'el
Nemuelite
   Biblical name   NEM-yuh-wuh-LĬT   'nemjəwə,lait
Nenana
   city, AK   nē-NAN-uh   niː'nænə
Nene
   1. English river   NĒN, NEN   'niːn, 'nen
   2. Hawaiian goose   NĀ-nā   'neːneː
Nenets [Yurak]
   lang., region, Russia   nyuhn-YETS   njən'jets
Neocene
   geologic era   NĒ-uh-SĒN, NĒ-uh-SĒN   ,niːə'siːn, 'niːə,siːn
Neodesha
   city, KS   nē-ŌD-uh-SHĀ, nē-ŌD-uh-SHĀ   niː'oːdə,ʃeː, niː,oːdə'ʃeː
neodymium
   element   NĒ-ō-DIM-ē-uhm   ,niːoː'dimiːəm
Neogaea
   biogeographical division, the   NĒ-uh-JĒ-uh   ,niːə'dʒiːə
      Neotropical region
Neogene
   geologic period   NĒ-uh-JĒN   'niːə,dʒiːn
Neolithic
   prehistoric age   NĒ-uh-LITH-ik   ,niːə'liθik

Foreign Sounds: ue: *Fr.* **rue**, *Ger.* **füllen**   uh(r): *Fr.* **boeuf**, *Ger.* **Höhle**   <u>kh</u>: *Ger.* **ich**, *Scot.* **loch**   ḡ: *Sp.* **amigo**   ᴠ: *Sp.* **hablar**
hl: *Welsh* **Llanelli**.   CAPITALS: primary stress.   SMALL CAPS: secondary stress.   Ⓢ: U.S. pron.   Ⓔ: British pron.

Neo-Melanesian [Tok Pisin]
  lang., Papua New Guinea   NĒ-ō-MEL-uh-NĒ-zhuhn, -NĒ-shuhn   ˌniːoːˌmeləˈniːʒən, -ˈniːʃən
neon
  element   NĒ-AHN   ˈniːˌɑn
Neoplatonism
  modified Platonism   NĒ-ō-PLĀT-n-IZ-uhm   ˌniːoːˈpleːtn̩ˌizəm
Neoptolemus
  son of Achilles and Deidamia NĒ-uhp-TAHL-uh-muhs   ˌniːəpˈtɑləməs
Neosho
  river, county, KA   nē-Ō-shō, nē-Ō-shuh   niːˈoːʃoː, niːˈoːʃə
Nepal
  kingdom, Asia   nuh-PAWL, -PAHL, -PAL   nəˈpɔːl, -ˈpɑl, -ˈpæl
Nepalese
  people, lang. Nepal   NEP-uh-LĒZ, -LĒS   ˌnepəˈliːz, -ˈliːs
Nepali [Gurkhali]
  lang., Nepal, Sikkim   nuh-PAW-lē, nuh-PAHL-ē   nəˈpɔːliˑ, nəˈpɑliˑ
Nepaug
  river, CT   NĒ-PAWG, -PAHG   ˈniːˌpɔːg, -ˌpɑg
Nepean
  river, Australia   nuh-PĒ-uhn   nəˈpiːən
Nepheg
  Biblical name   NĒ-FEG, NEF-EG   ˈniːˌfeg, ˈnefˌeg
Nephele
  Greek mythical figure   NEF-uh-lē   ˈnefəliˑ
Nephelococcygia
  Cloud-cuckoo-land (Aristophanes) NEF-uh-LŌ-kuh-SIJ-ē-uh,   ˌnefəˌloːkəˈsidʒiːə,
                                NEF-uh-LŌ-kuh-KIJ-ē-uh   ˌnefəˌloːkəˈkidʒiːə
Nephi
  city, UT   NĒ-FĪ   ˈniːˌfɑi
Nephishesim
  Biblical name   nuh-FISH-uh-SIM, nuh-FĒ-shuh-SĒM   nəˈfiʃəˌsim, nəˌfiːʃəˈsiːm
Nephthalim
  Biblical name   NEF-thuh-LIM   ˈnefθəˌlim
Nephtoah
  Biblical name   nef-TŌ-uh, nef-TŌ-AHKH   nefˈtoːə, nefˈtoːˌɑx
Nephthys
  Egyptian goddess of the dead NEP-tuhs, NEF-thuhs   ˈneptəs, ˈnefθəs
Nephusim
  Biblical name   nuh-F(Y)OO-SIM, nuh-foo-SĒM   nəˈf(j)uːˌsim, nəfuːˈsiːm
Nepomuk
  pers. name, Czech, German   NĀ-pō-MUK   ˈneːpoːˌmuk
Neptun
  Danish beer   nep-TUH(R)N   nepˈtœn
Neptune
  Roman god of the sea; planet NEP-T(Y)OON   ˈnepˌt(j)uːn
Neptunian
  pert. to Neptune   nep-T(Y)OO-nē-uhn   nepˈt(j)uːniːən
neptunium
  element   nep-T(Y)OO-nē-uhm   nepˈt(j)uːniːəm
Ner
  Biblical name   NUHR, NER   ˈnərʳ, ˈnerʳ
Nereid
  sea nymph; satellite of Neptune NIR-ē-uhd   ˈniriːəd
Nereids
  sea deities, daughters of Nereus NIR-ē-uhdz   ˈniriːədz

Key (col. 2): a: f**a**d ā: f**a**de ah: f**a**ther ar: m**a**rry aw: l**a**w e: f**e**d ē: f**ee**d er: m**e**rry i: h**i**d ī: h**i**de ō: c**oa**t o͞o: b**oo**t
oi: b**oy** ow: n**ow** u: p**u**t uh: **a**bove uhr: b**i**rd ch: **ch**op ng: ri**ng** sh: **sh**ow th: **th**ick th̲: **th**is zh: mea**s**ure

Nereus

  sea-god in Greek mythology   NIR-ē-uhs   ˈniriːəs

Nereus

  Biblical name   NĒ-RŌŌS, NIR-ē-uhs, NĒ-rē-uhs   ˈniːˌruːs, ˈniriːəs, ˈniːriːəs

Nergal

  Biblical name   NUHR-GAL, GAHL; ner-GAHL   ˈnəʳˌgæl, -ˌgal; nerˈgal

Nergal-sarezer

  Biblical name   NUHR-GAHL-suh-RĒ-zuhr,   ˈnəʳˌgalsəˈriːzəʳ,
                     ner-GAHL-sahr-ET-ser   nerˈgalsarˈetser

Nergal-sharezer [Nergal-sarezer]

  Biblical name   NUHR-GAHL-shuh-RĒ-zuhr   ˈnəʳˌgalʃəˈriːzəʳ

Neri

  Biblical name   NIR-Ī, NĒ-RĪ   ˈnirˌai, ˈniːˌrai

Neriah

  Biblical name   nuh-RĪ-uh, NE-ri-YAH   nəˈraiə, ˌneriˈja

Nerio

  personification of valor   NIR-ē-Ō   ˈniriːˌoː

Nerites

  son of Nereus   nir-ĪT-ēz   nirˈaiṭiːz

Nernst

  Walther, *German physicist, chemist*   NERNST   ˈneʳnst
  (Nobel 1920)

Nero

  Roman emperor   NĒ-rō, NIR-ō   ˈniːroː, ˈniroː

Neruda

  1. Pablo, *Chilean poet, diplomat*   nā-RŌŌ-thah, Ⓢ nā-RŌŌD-uh   neːˈruːða, Ⓢ neˑˈruːdə
  (Nobel 1971)

  2. Jan, *Czech poet*   NER-ud-AH   ˈnerudˌaː

Nerva

  Roman emperor   NUHR-vuh   ˈnəʳvə

Nescafe, Nescafé

  tdmk for coffee   NES-kuh-FĀ, NES-kuh-FĀ   ˈneskəˌfeː, ˌneskəˈfeː

Neshoba

  county, MS   nuh-SHŌ-buh   nəˈʃoːbə

Ness, Loch

  see Loch Ness

Nesselrode

  1. Count Karl Robert, *Russian*   nyis-il-RAW-duh, Ⓢ NES-uhl-RŌD   njisilˈrɔːdə, Ⓢ ˈnesəlˌroːd
  diplomat

  2. fruit-nut mixture   NES-uhl-RŌD   ˈnesəlˌroːd

Nessus

  centaur   NES-uhs   ˈnesəs

Nesta

  pers. name   NES-tuh   ˈnestə

Nestlé

  Swiss food products co.   NES-lē, Ⓔ NES-uhl, NES-LĀ   ˈnesliˑ, Ⓔ ˈnesəl, ˈnesˌleː

Néstor

  pers. name, Spanish   NĀ-stawr   ˈneːstɔːr

Nestor

  1. long-winded king of Pylos in   NES-tuhr, NES-TAWR   ˈnestəʳ, ˈnesˌtɔːʳ
  Greek mythology; pers. name

  2. Finnish   NES-TAWR   ˈnesˌtɔːr

  3. French   nes-TAWR   nestɔːr

Nestorian

  pert. to Nestor   nes-TŌR-ē-uhn, nes-TAWR-ē-uhn   nesˈtoːriːən, nesˈtɔːriːən

---

Netanyahu
  Binyamin, *Israeli political leader*   NE-tuhn-YAH-hoo͞, NET-n-YAH-hoo͞   ˌnetənˈjɑhuː, ˌnetn̩ˈjɑhuː

Nethaneel
  Biblical name   nuh-THAN-ē-EL, -THAN-yuhl,   nəˈθæniː‚el, -ˈθænjəl,
    -THAN-ĒL; nuh-tahn-EL   -ˈθænˌiːl; nətanˈel

Nethaniah
  Biblical name   NETH-uh-NĪ-uh, NUH-tahn-YAH   ˌneθəˈnaiə, ˌnətanˈjɑ

Netherlander
  inhabitant of the Netherlands   NETH-uhr-LAN-duhr, -luhn-duhr   ˈneðərˌlændərˌ, -ləndər

Netherlandic [Dutch]
  lang., Netherlands, Belgium,   NETH-uhr-LAN-dik, NETH-uhr-LAN-dik   ˈneðərˌlændik, ˌneðərˈlændik
  Suriname, Antilles

Netherlands [Nederland]
  kingdom, Europe   NETH-uhr-luhn(d)z   ˈneðərˌlən(d)z

Netherlands Antillean
  pert. to Netherlands Antilles   NETH-uhr-luhn(d)z an-TIL-ē-uhn   ˈneðərˌlən(d)z ænˈtiliːən

Netherlands Antilles
  islands, West Indies   NETH-uhr-luhn(d)z an-TIL-ēz   ˈneðərˌlən(d)z ænˈtiliːz

Nethinims
  Biblical name   NETH-uh-NIMZ, nuh-tē-NĒM   ˈneθəˌnimz, nətiːˈniːm

Netophah
  Biblical name   nuh-TŌ-fuh, NET-uh-fuh, nuh-tō-FAH   nəˈtoːfə, ˈnetˌəfə, nətoːˈfɑ

Netophathi
  Biblical name   nuh-TAHF-uh-THĪ, nuh-TŌ-fah-TĒ   nəˈtɑfəˌθai, nəˌtoːfɑˈtiː

Netophathite
  Biblical name   nuh-TAHF-uh-THĪT   nəˈtɑfəˌθait

Nettleton
  Lois, *US actress*   NET-l-tuhn   ˈnetl̩tən

Netzahualcóyotl
  city, Mexico   nāt-SAH-wahl-KŌ-YŌT-l   neːtˌsɑwɑlˈkoːˌjoːtl̩

Neuburger
  Austrian wine grape   NOI-BURG-uhr, -BUHRG-uhr   ˈnɔiˌburgər, -ˌbərgər

Neuchâtel
  town, canton, Switzerland   nuh(r)-shah-TEL   nœːʃatel

Neuenburg [Neuchâtel]
  town, Switzerland   NOI-uhn-BURK   ˈnɔiənˌburk

Neufchâtel
  town, France; cheese   nuh(r)-shah-TEL,   nœːʃatel, Ⓢ ˌn(j)uːʃəˈtel
    Ⓢ N(Y)OO͞-shuh-TEL

Neufeldt
  Victoria, *US lexicographer*   N(Y)OO͞-FELD, N(Y)OO͞-FELT   ˈn(j)uːˌfeld, ˈn(j)uːˌfelt

Neuilly-sur-Seine
  suburb, Paris   nuh(r)-YĒ-suer-SEN   nœjiːsyːrsen

Neumann
  1. John N., *Czech-born US*   N(Y)OO͞-muhn   ˈn(j)uːmən
    clergyman, saint
  2. family name, German   NOI-MAHN   ˈnɔiˌmɑn

Neuse
  river, NC   N(Y)OO͞S   ˈn(j)uːs

Neusiedlersee
  lake, Austria, Hungary   NOI-ZĒD-luhr-ZĀ   ˈnɔiˌziːdlərˌzeː

Neuth [Nut]
  Egyptian sky goddess   N(Y)OO͞T, N(Y)OO͞TH   ˈn(j)uːt, ˈn(j)uːθ

Neutrino
  subatomic particle   n(y)oo͞-TRĒ-nō   n(j)uːˈtriːnoː

Key (col. 2): a: f**a**d ā: f**a**de ah: f**a**ther ar: m**a**rry aw: l**aw** e: f**e**d ē: f**ee**d er: m**e**rry i: h**i**d ī: h**i**de ō: c**oa**t oo͞: b**oo**t
oi: b**oy** ow: n**ow** u: p**u**t uh: **a**bove uhr: b**i**rd ch: **ch**op ng: ri**ng** sh: **sh**ow th: **th**ick <u>th</u>: **th**is zh: mea**s**ure

Neva
  river, Russia   NĒ-vuh, NĀ-vuh   ˈniːvə, ˈneːvə

Nevada
  1. state, US   nuh-VAD-uh, nuh-VAHD-uh   nəˈvædə, nəˈvɑdə
  2. city, IA; city, MO   nuh-VĀD-uh   nəˈveːdə

Nevil, Neville
  pers. name   NEV-uhl, NEV-il   ˈnevəl, ˈnevil

Nevins
  Allan, *US historian & biographer*   NEV-uhnz   ˈnevənz

Nevis
  one of the Leeward Islands, West Indies   NĒ-vuhs, NEV-uhs   ˈniːvəs, ˈnevəs

Nevis, Ben
  see Ben Nevis

Nevisian
  pert. to Nevis   NEV-uh-SĒ-uhn   ˌnevəˈsiːən

Newari
  lang., Central Nepal   nuh-WAHR-ē   nəˈwɑriˑ

Newark
  1. city, CA, NJ, OH; village, NY; borough, England   N(Y)OO-uhrk, N(Y)U(-uh)rk   ˈn(j)uːəʳk, ˈn(j)u(ə)ʳk
  2. city, DE   N(Y)OO-AHRK   ˈn(j)uːˌɑʳk

Newaygo
  county, MI   ni-WĀ-gō   niˈweːgoː

Newbold
  pers. name   N(Y)OO-BŌLD   ˈn(j)uːˌboːld

New Braunfels
  city, TX   N(Y)OO BROWN-fuhlz   ˌn(j)uː ˈbraunfəlz

New Brunswick
  city, NJ; province, Canada   n(y)oo BRUHNZ-wik   n(j)uˑ ˈbrənzwik

Newburgh
  city, NY   N(Y)OO-BUHRG   ˈn(j)uːˌbəʳg

New Caledonia
  island, French territory, Pacific   N(Y)OO KAL-uh-DŌ-nē-uh   ˌn(j)uː ˌkæləˈdoːniːə

New Caledonian
  pert. to New Caledonia   N(Y)OO KAL-uh-DŌ-nē-uhn   ˌn(j)uː ˌkæləˈdoːniːən

Newcastle
  pl. name, US, England   N(Y)OO-KAS-uhl, n(y)oo-KAS-uhl   ˈn(j)uːˌkæsəl, n(j)uːˈkæsəl

New College
  college, Oxford Univ.   N(Y)OO KAHL-ij   ˈn(j)uː ˌkɑlidʒ

New Delhi
  city, India   n(y)oo DEL-ē   n(j)uˑ ˈdeliˑ

New England
  region, Northeast US   n(y)oo ING-gluhnd, ING-luhnd   n(j)uˑ ˈiŋglənd, ˈiŋlənd

New Englander
  inhabitant of New England   n(y)oo ING-gluhn-duhr, ING-luhn-duhr   n(j)uˑ ˈiŋgləndəʳ, ˈiŋləndəʳ

Newfie
  slang, inhabitant of Newfoundland   N(Y)OO-fē   ˈn(j)uːfiˑ

Newfoundland
  island, province, Canada; dog breed   N(Y)OO-fuhn(d)-luhnd, N(Y)OO-fuhn(d)-LAND, n(y)oo-FOWN(D)-luhnd; *in Canada usually* N(Y)OO-fuhn(d)-LAND   ˈn(j)uːfən(d)lənd, ˈn(j)uːfən(d)ˌlænd, n(j)uːˈfaun(d)lənd; *in Canada usually* ˌn(j)uːfən(d)ˈlænd

---

Foreign Sounds: ue: *Fr.* **rue**, *Ger.* füllen   uh(r): *Fr.* **boeuf**, *Ger.* Höhle   kh: *Ger.* i**ch**, *Scot.* lo**ch**   ḡ: *Sp.* amigo   v̱: *Sp.* hablar   hl: *Welsh* Llanelli.   CAPITALS: primary stress.   SMALL CAPS: secondary stress.   Ⓢ: U.S. pron.   Ⓔ: British pron.

Newfoundlander *inhabitant of Newfoundland*	N(Y)O͞O-fuhn(d)-luhn-duhr, N(Y)O͞O-fuhn(d)-LAN-duhr, n(y)o͞o-FOWN(D)-luhn-duhr; *in Canada usually* N(Y)O͞O-fuhn(d)-LAN-duhr	ˈn(j)uːfən(d)ləndəʳ, ˈn(j)uːfən(d)ˌlændəʳ, n(j)uːˈfaun(d)ləndəʳ; *in Canada usually* ˌn(j)uːfən(d)ˈlændəʳ
Newgrange *prehistoric burial site, Ireland*	n(y)o͞o-GRĀNJ	n(j)uˑˈgreːndʒ
New Guinea *island, Pacific*	n(y)o͞o GIN-ē	n(j)uˑ ˈginiˑ
New Hall *college, Cambridge Univ.*	n(y)o͞o HAWL	n(j)uː ˈhɔːl
Newham *borough, England*	N(Y)O͞O-uhm	ˈn(j)uːəm
New Hampshire *state, US*	n(y)o͞o HAM(P)-shuhr, HAM(P)-SHIR	n(j)uˑ ˈhæm(p)ʃəʳ, ˈhæm(p)ˌʃiʳ
New Hanover *county, NC*	N(Y)O͞O han-Ō-vuhr; n(y)o͞o HAN-Ō-vuhr, HAN-uh-vuhr	ˌn(j)uː hænˈoːvəʳ; n(j)uː ˈhænˌoːvəʳ, ˈhænəvəʳ
Newhart Bob, *US actor*	N(Y)O͞O-HAHRT	ˈn(j)uːˌhaʳt
New Haven *city, county, CT*	n(y)o͞o HĀ-vuhn, N(Y)O͞O HĀ-vuhn	n(j)uˑ ˈheːvən, ˈn(j)uː ˌheːvən
Newhaven *port, England*	n(y)o͞o-HĀ-vuhn, N(Y)O͞O-HĀ-vuhn	n(j)uˑˈheːvən, ˈn(j)uːˌheːvən
Ne Win *Burmese leader*	NĀ WIN	ˈneː ˈwin
New Jersey *state, US*	n(y)o͞o JUHR-zē	n(j)uˑ ˈdʒəʳziˑ
Newley Anthony, *British actor, singer*	N(Y)O͞O-lē	ˈn(j)uːliˑ
Newlin Michael H., *US ambassador*	N(Y)O͞O-luhn	ˈn(j)uːlən
New Madrid *county, city, MO; earthquake fault, US*	n(y)o͞o MAD-ruhd	n(j)uˑ ˈmædrəd
New Mexico *state, US*	n(y)o͞o MEK-si-KŌ	n(j)uˑ ˈmeksiˌkoː
Newnes Sir George, *English publisher*	N(Y)O͞ONZ	ˈn(j)uːnz
Newnham college, *Cambridge Univ.*	N(Y)O͞O-nuhm	ˈn(j)uːnəm
New Orleans *city, LA*	n(y)o͞o AWR-lē-uhnz, AWRL-(y)uhnz; *mostly by outsiders* N(Y)O͞O awr-LĒNZ	n(j)uˑ ˈɔːʳliˑənz, ˈɔːʳl(j)ənz; *mostly by outsiders* ˌn(j)uː ɔːʳˈliːnz
New Paltz *town, NY*	N(Y)O͞O PAWLTS	ˈn(j)uː ˌpɔːlts
Newport *city, RI*	N(Y)O͞O-PŌRT, N(Y)O͞O-PAWRT	ˈn(j)uːˌpoːʳt, ˈn(j)uːˌpɔːʳt
Newport News *city, VA*	N(Y)O͞O-PŌRT N(Y)O͞OZ, N(Y)O͞O-PAWRT, N(Y)O͞O-puhrt	ˌn(j)uːˌpoːʳt ˈn(j)uːz, ˌn(j)uːˌpɔːʳt, ˌn(j)uːpəʳt

Key (col. 2): a: **fad** ā: **fade** ah: **father** ar: **marry** aw: **law** e: **fed** ē: **feed** er: **merry** i: **hid** ī: **hide** ō: **coat** o͞o: **boot** oi: **boy** ow: **now** u: **put** uh: **above** uhr: **bird** ch: **chop** ng: **ring** sh: **show** th: **thick** t͟h: **this** zh: **measure**

New Prague
    city, MN   N(Y)O͞O PRĀG   ˌn(j)uː ˈpreːg

New Rochelle
    town, NY   N(Y)U ruh-SHEL, N(Y)O͞O rō-SHEL   ˌn(j)u rəˈʃel, ˌn(j)uː roːˈʃel

New South Wales
    state, Australia   N(Y)O͞O SOWTH WĀLZ   ˌn(j)uː ˌsɑuθ ˈweːlz

Newt
    pers. name   N(Y)O͞OT   ˈn(j)uːt

Newton
    Sir Isaac, English philosopher,   N(Y)O͞OT-n   ˈn(j)uːtn̩
      mathematician; city, MA

Newtonian
    pert. to Newton *or his theories*   n(y)o͞o-TŌ-nē-uhn   n(j)uːˈtoːniːən

New York
    state, city, US   n(y)o͞o YAWRK   n(j)uˑ ˈjɔːʳk

New Zealand
    island nation, Pacific   n(y)o͞o ZĒ-luhnd   n(j)uˑ ˈziːlənd

New Zealander
    inhabitant of New Zealand   n(y)o͞o ZĒ-luhn-duhr   n(j)uˑ ˈziːləndəʳ

Ney
    Michel, French militarist   NE, Ⓔ NĀ   ne, Ⓔ ˈneː

Neziah
    Biblical name   nuh-ZĪ-uh, NEZ-ē-uh, nuht-SĒ-AHKH   nəˈzɑiə, ˈneziːə, nətˈsiːˌɑx

Nezib
    Biblical name   NĒ-zuhb, nuht-SĒV   ˈniːzəb, nətˈsiːv

Nez Perce
    county, ID; mtn., WY   NEZ PUHRS   ˈnez ˈpəʳs

Nezperce
    village, ID   NEZ-PUHRS   ˈnezˈpəʳs

Nez Percé
    1. N. American people   NEZ PUHRS, PERS   ˈnez ˈpəʳs, ˈpeʳs
    2. French   nā per-SĀ   neː perseː

Ngadju, Ngaju
    lang., people, South Borneo   NGAHJ-o͞o, Ⓔ uhng-GAHJ-o͞o   ˈŋadʒuː, Ⓔ əŋˈgadʒuː

Ngaio
    pers. name   NĪ-ō   ˈnɑioː

Ngo Dinh Diem
    president, South Vietnam   NŌ DIN dē-EM, NGŌ   ˈnoː ˈdin diːˈem, ŋoː

Ngoni
    lang., people, Africa   NGŌ-nē, Ⓔ uhng-GŌ-nē, eng-   ˈŋoːniː, Ⓔ əŋˈgoːniˑ, eŋ-

Ngorongoro
    crater, Tanzania   NGŌR-ōng-GŌR-ō,   ˌŋoːroːŋˈgoːroː,
         Ⓔ eng-GŌR-ōng-GŌR-ō,   Ⓔ eŋˌgoːroːŋˈgoːroː,
         eng-GAWR-ōng-GAWR-ō   eŋˌgɔːroːŋˈgɔːroː

Nguni
    lang., people, Africa   NGO͞O-nē, Ⓔ uhng-GO͞O-nē, eng-   ˈŋuːniˑ, Ⓔ əŋˈguːniˑ, eŋ-

Nguyen Cao Ky
    military official, South Vietnam   NO͞O-yen KOW KĒ, NGO͞O-yen   ˈnuːjen ˈkɑu ˈkiː, ˈŋuːjen

Nguyen Van Thieu
    president, South Vietnam   NO͞O-yen VAN TO͞O, NGO͞O-yen   ˈnuːjen ˈvæn ˈtuː, ˈŋuːjen

Niagara
    river, N. America; county, NY   nī-AG(-uh)-ruh   nɑiˈæg(ə)rə

Niagara Falls
    falls, N. America; town, Canada   nī-AG(-uh)-ruh FAWLZ   nɑiˌæg(ə)rə ˈfɔːlz

---

Foreign Sounds: ue: *Fr.* **rue**, *Ger.* **füllen**   uh(r): *Fr.* **boeuf**, *Ger.* **Höhle**   k̲h̲: *Ger.* **ich**, *Scot.* **loch**   g̅: *Sp.* **amigo**   v̲: *Sp.* **hablar** hl: *Welsh* **Llanelli**.   CAPITALS: primary stress.   SMALL CAPS: secondary stress.   Ⓢ: U.S. pron.   Ⓔ: British pron.

Niall
   king of Ireland; pers. name, Irish   NĒL   'niːl
    Gaelic

Niamey
   city, Niger   nē-AHM-ā   niː'ɑmeː

Niantic
   stream, inlet, town division, CT   nī-ANT-ik   nɑi'æntik

Nias
   island, lang., Indian Ocean   NĒ-AHS   'niː,ɑs

Nibelung
   dwarf in German legend; follower of   NĒ-buh-LUNG   'niːbə,luŋ
    Siegfried

Nibelungenlied
   medieval German legend   NĒ-buh-LUNG-uhn-LĒD   ,niːbə'luŋən,liːd

Nibhaz
   Biblical name   NIB-HAZ, niv-<u>KH</u>AHZ   'nib,hæz, niv'xɑz

Nibshan
   Biblical name   NIB-SHAN, niv-SHAHN   'nib,ʃæn, niv'ʃɑn

Nicaea
   ancient city, empire, Asia Minor;   nī-SĒ-uh   nɑi'siːə
    naiad pursued by Dionysus

Nicanor
   Biblical name   nuh-KĀ-nawr, nī-   nə'keːnɔːʳ, nɑi-

Nicaragua
   republic, Cen. America   nē-kah-RAHḠ-wah,   niːkɑ'rɑɣwɑ,
                        Ⓢ NIK-uh-RAHG-wuh, Ⓔ   Ⓢ ,nikə'rɑgwə, Ⓔ
                        NIK-uh-RAG-yuh-wuh   ,nikə'rægjəwə

Nicaraguan
   pert. to Nicaragua   NIK-uh-RAHG-wuhn   ,nikə'rɑgwən

Niccolò
   pers. name, Italian   NĒK-kō-LAW   ,niːkkoː'lɔː

Nice
   resort, France   NĒS   niːs

Nicene
   pert. to Nicaea *or to church council*   NĪ-SĒN, nī-SĒN   'nɑi,siːn, nɑi'siːn
    held there

Nicene Creed
   statement of Christian belief   NĪ-SĒN KRĒD   ,nɑi,siːn 'kriːd

Nicephorus
   Byzantine emperor   nī-SEF-uhr-uhs   nɑi'sefərəs

Niceto
   pers. name, Spanish   nē-THĀ-tō, nē-SĀ-tō   niː'θeːtoː, niː'seːtoː

Nichol
   William, *British physicist*   NIK-uhl   'nikəl

Nicholas
   pers. name   NIK-(uh-)luhs   'nik(ə)ləs

Nicholson
   Ben, *English artist;* Jack, *US actor*   NIK-uhl-suhn   'nikəlsən

Nicias
   Athenian general   NIS-ē-uhs, NISH-ē-uhs   'nisiːəs, 'niʃiːəs

Nick
   pers. name   NIK   'nik

nickel
   element   NIK-uhl   'nikəl

Key (col. 2):   a: fad   ā: fade   ah: father   ar: marry   aw: law   e: fed   ē: feed   er: merry   i: hid   ī: hide   ō: coat   ōō: boot
oi: boy   ow: now   u: put   uh: above   uhr: bird   ch: chop   ng: ring   sh: show   th: thick   <u>th</u>: this   zh: measure

Nicki
  pers. name   NIK-ē   'niki·

Nicklaus
  Jack, *US golfer*   NIK-luhs   'nikləs

Nickleby
  Nicholas, *character by Dickens*   NIK-uhl-bē   'nikəlbi·

Nickles
  Don, *US politician*   NIK-uhlz   'nikəlz

Nicky
  pers. name   NIK-ē   'niki·

Nicobar
  Islands, *Bay of Bengal*   NIK-uh-BAHR   'nikə‚bɑʳ

Nicobarese
  lang., people, Nicobar Islands   NIK-uh-bahr-ĒZ, -ĒS   ‚nikəbar'iːz, -'iːs

Nicodemus
  1. pers. name   NIK-uh-DĒ-muhs   ‚nikə'diːməs
  2. Swedish   NIK-ō-DĀ-muhs   ‚nikoː'deːməs

Niçoise
  salad   nē-SWAHZ   niː'swɑz

Nicol
  pers. name   NIK-uhl   'nikəl

Nicola
  1. pers. name   NIK-uh-luh   'nikələ
  2. Italian   nē-KAW-lah   niː'kɔːla
  3. see Nikola

Nicolaas
  see Nikolaas

Nicolae
  pers. name, Romanian   NĒ-kō-LĪ   ‚niːkoː'lai

Nicolai
  1. pers. name, Danish   NĒ-kuh-LĪ   ‚niːkə'lai
  2. Dutch   NĒ-kō-LAH-ē   ‚niːkoː'laːiː
  3. German   NĒ-kō-LAH-ē, NĒ-kō-LĪ   ‚niːkoː'la-iː, 'niːkoː‚lai

Nicolaitans
  Biblical name   NIK-uh-LĀ-uht-nz, -LĀT-nz   ‚nikə'leːətn̩z, -'leːtn̩z

Nicolas
  1. pers. name   NIK-(uh-)luhs   'nik(ə)ləs
  2. Dutch   NĒ-kuh-lahs   'niːkəlaːs
  3. French   nē-kaw-LAH   niːkɔːla

Nicolás
  pers. name, Spanish   nē-kō-LAHS   niːkoː'las

Nicolaus
  pers. name, Latin   NIK-uh-LĀ-uhs   ‚nikə'leːəs

Nicole
  1. pers. name   ni-KŌL   ni'koːl
  2. French   nē-KAWL   niːkɔːl

Nicolet
  Canada   NĒ-kuh-LĀ   ‚niːkə'leː

Nicolette
  pers. name   NIK-uh-LET   ‚nikə'let

Nicolle
  C. J. H., *French bacteriologist*   nē-KAWL   niːkɔːl
  (*Nobel 1928*)

Foreign Sounds: ue: *Fr.* **rue**, *Ger.* **füllen**   uh(r): *Fr.* **boeuf**, *Ger.* **Höhle**   <u>kh</u>: *Ger.* **ich**, *Scot.* **loch**   g̱: *Sp.* amigo   v̱: *Sp.* hablar
hl: *Welsh* **Llanelli**.   CAPITALS: primary stress.   SMALL CAPS: secondary stress.   Ⓢ: U.S. pron.   Ⓔ: British pron.

Nicollet
county, MN; Park, *former ballpark,*   NIK-uh-LET   'nikə,let
Minneapolis, MN
Nicolò
pers. name, Italian   NĒ-kō-LAW   ˌniːkoːˈlɔː
Nicoma Park
town, OK   nuh-KŌ-muh PAHRK   nəˈkoːmə ˈpɑʳk
Nicomachean Ethics
Aristotelian treatise   NĪ-KAHM-uh-KĒ-uhn ETH-iks   ˌnɑiˌkɑməˈkiːən ˈeθiks
Nicomedia
ancient city, Asia Minor   NIK-uh-MĒD-ē-uh   ˌnikəˈmiːdiːə
Nicopolis
ancient city, Greece; town, Bulgaria   ni-KAHP-uh-luhs, nī-   niˈkapələs, nɑi-
Nicosia
city, district, Cyprus   NIK-uh-SĒ-uh   ˌnikəˈsiːə
Nicostratus
son of Helen and Menelaus   nī-KAHS-truht-uhs   nɑiˈkastrəʈəs
Niebuhr
1. Barthold Georg, *German*   NĒ-BŌŌR   ˈniːˌbuˑʳ
historian
2. Rheinhold, *US theologian*   NĒ-BUR, NĒ-buhr   ˈniːˌbuʳ, ˈniːbəʳ
Niedere Tauern
mtn. range, Austria   NĒD-uhr-uh TOW-uhrn   ˌniːdərə ˈtɑuəʳn
Niederösterreich
state, Austria   NĒD-uh-RUH(R)-stuhr-RĪKH   ˌniːdəˈrœːstəʳˌraiç
Niedersachsen
prov, Germany   NĒD-uhr-SAHK-suhn   ˈniːdəʳˌsaksən
Niels
1. pers. name, Danish   NILS   ˈnils
2. Norwegian   NĒLS   ˈniːls
nielsbohrium
element   nēlz-BŌR-ē-uhm, nēlz-BAWR-   niːlzˈboːriːəm, niːlzˈbɔːr-
Nielsen
1. Carl August, *Danish composer*   NIL-suhn, Ⓢ NĒL-suhn   ˈnilsən, Ⓢ ˈniːlsən
2. A.C., *TV ratings firm;* Erik H.,   NĒL-suhn   ˈniːlsən
Canadian politician
Niemeyer
German publishing co.   NĒ-MĪ(-uh)r   ˈniːˌmɑi(ə)ʳ
Niemeyer
Oscar, *Brazilian architect*   NĒ-MĪ(-uh)r   ˈniːˌmɑi(ə)ʳ
Niemöller
Martin, *German Protestant*   NĒ-MUH(R)L-uhr   ˈniːˌmœləʳ
theologian
Niepce
Joseph Nicéphore, *French*   NYEPS   njeps
photographic pioneer
Nietzsche
Friedrich Wilhelm, *German*   NĒ-chuh, NĒ-chē   ˈniːtʃə, ˈniːtʃiˑ
philosopher
Nietzscheism
philosophy of Nietzsche   NĒ-chē-IZ-uhm   ˈniːtʃiːˌizəm
Nigel
pers. name   NĪ-juhl   ˈnɑidʒəl

Key (col. 2):   a: fad ā: fade ah: father ar: marry aw: law e: fed ē: feed er: merry i: hid ī: hide ō: coat ōō: boot
oi: boy   ow: now   u: put   uh: above   uhr: bird   ch: chop   ng: ring   sh: show   th: thick   th: this   zh: measure

Niger
  1. river, Africa; Roman general   NĪ-juhr   ˈnɑidʒəʳ
  2. republic, Africa   nē-ZHER, NĪ-juhr   niːˈʒeʳ, ˈnɑidʒəʳ
Nigeria
  republic, Africa   nī-JIR-ē-uh   nɑiˈdʒiriːə
Nigerian
  pert. to Nigeria   nī-JIR-ē-uhn   nɑiˈdʒiriːən
Nigerois
  inhabitant of Niger   nē-zher-WAH   niːʒerwɑː
Nightingale
  Florence, *English nurse*   NĪT-n-GĀL, NĪT-ing-GĀL   ˈnaitn̩ˌgeːl, ˈnaitin̩ˌgeːl
Nihoa
  islet, HI   nē-HŌ-uh   niːˈhoːə
Nihon
  Japanese name for Japan   nē-hawn   niːhɔːn
Niihau
  island, HI   NĒ-HOW, NĒ-ē-HOW   ˈniːˌhɑu, ˈniːiːˌhɑu
Nijinksky
  Vaslav, *Russian ballet dancer*   nuh-ZHIN-skē, nuh-JIN-skē   nəˈʒinskiˑ, nəˈdʒinskiˑ
Nijmegen
  city, Netherlands   NĪ-MĀ-ḡuh(n)   ˈnaiˌmeːɣə(n)
Nike
  Greek goddess of victory; sportswear   NĪ-kē   ˈnaikiˑ
    mfrs.
Nikita
  pers. name, Russian   nyik-YĒ-tuh, Ⓢ ni-KĒT-uh   njikˈjiːtə, Ⓢ niˈkiːt̬ə
Nikkei Dow
  Japanese stock index   NĒ-KĀ DOW   ˌniːˌkeː ˈdɑu
Nikki
  pers. name   NIK-ē   ˈnikiˑ
Niklas
  pers. name, German   NĒ-klahs   ˈniːklɑs
Nikodemus
  pers. name, German   NĒ-kō-DĀ-mus   ˌniːkoːˈdeːmus
Nikola, Nicola
  pers. name, Serbo-Croatian   NĒ-kaw-LAH   ˈniːkɔːˌlɑː
Nikolaas, Nicolaas
  pers. name, Dutch   NĒ-kuh-LAHS   ˈniːkəˌlɑːs
Nikolai
  1. pers. name, Danish   NĒ-kuh-LĪ   ˌniːkəˈlai
  2. Russian   nyik-uh-LĪ   njikəˈlai
Nikolaos
  pers. name, Greek   nyē-KAW-lah-aws   njiˑˈkɔːlɑɔːs
Nikon
  Japanese camera co.   NĒ-KAHN, NĪ-KAHN, NIK-AHN   ˈniːˌkɑn, ˈnɑiˌkɑn, ˈnikˌɑn
Nikos
  pers. name, Greek   NĒ-KAWS   ˈniːˌkɔːs
Niksicko Pivo
  Yugoslavian beer   NIK-SHIT-skō PĒ-vō   ˈnikˌʃitskoː ˈpiːvoː
Nile
  river, Africa   NĪL   ˈnail
Nilo-Hamitic
  lang., Africa   NĪ-lō-ha-MIT-ik   ˌnailoːhæˈmit̬ik

Foreign Sounds: **ue**: *Fr.* **r**u**e**, *Ger.* f**ü**llen   **uh(r)**: *Fr.* b**oeu**f, *Ger.* H**öh**le   kh: *Ger.* i**ch**, *Scot.* lo**ch**   ḡ: *Sp.* ami**g**o   v: *Sp.* ha**b**lar
hl: *Welsh* **Ll**anelli.   CAPITALS: primary stress.   SMALL CAPS: secondary stress.   Ⓢ: U.S. pron.   Ⓔ: British pron.

Nilo-Saharan
   African lang. family   NĪ-lō-suh-HAR-uhn, -suh-HER-uhn,   ˌnaɪloːsəˈhærən, -səˈherən,
                                 -suh-HAHR-uhn   -səˈharən

Nilotic
   lang., pert. to the Nile   nī-LAHT-ik   naɪˈlɑtʃik

Nils
   1. pers. name, Danish, Swedish   NILS   ˈnils
   2. Norwegian   NĒLS   ˈniːls

Nilsson
   1. Birgit, *Swedish soprano*   NĒL-sawn   ˈniːlsɔːn
   2. Harry, *US singer, songwriter*   NIL-suhn, NĒL-suhn   ˈnilsən, ˈniːlsən

Nilus
   god of the Nile River   NĪ-luhs, NĒ-luhs   ˈnaɪləs, ˈniːləs

NIMBY
   not in my back yard   NIM-bē   ˈnimbiˑ

Nimeiry, al-
   Gaffar Mohammed, *president,*   AHL ni-MER-ē, AL   ˌɑːl niˈmeriˑ, ˌæl
     Sudan

Nîmes
   town, France   NĒM   niːm

Nimitz
   Chester W., *US admiral*   NIM-its   ˈnimits

Nimmitabel
   town, Australia   NIM-uht-uh-BEL   ˈnimətəˌbel

Nimoy
   Leonard, *US actor, director*   NĒ-MOI   ˈniːˌmɔi

Nimrah
   Biblical name   NIM-ruh, nim-RAH   ˈnimrə, nimˈrɑ

Nimrim
   Biblical name   NIM-rim, nim-RĒM   ˈnimrim, nimˈriːm

Nimrod
   great-grandson of Noah; great hunter   NIM-RAHD   ˈnimˌrɑd

Nimrud
   modern name, site of ancient Kalakh   nim-ROOD   nimˈruːd

Nimshi
   Biblical name   NIM-SHĪ, nim-SHĒ   ˈnimˌʃai, nimˈʃiː

Nin
   Anaïs, *US author*   NĒN, NIN   ˈniːn, ˈnin

Nina
   1. pers. name   NĒ-nuh, NĪ-nuh   ˈniːnə, ˈnainə
   2. Russian   NYĒ-nuh   ˈnjiːnə

Nineveh
   capital of Assyria   NIN-uh-vuh   ˈninəvə

Ninevite
   Biblical name   NIN-uh-VĪT   ˈninəˌvait

Ningxia Huizu
   admin. division, China   NING-shē-AH HWĀ-ZOO   ˈniŋʃiːˈɑ ˈhweːˈzuː

Ninian
   pers. name   NIN-ē-uhn   ˈniniːən

Nino
   pers. name   NĒ-nō   ˈniːnoː

Niño
   Pedro Alonzo, Spanish explorer   NĒN-yō   ˈniːnjoː

Nintendo
   Japanese computer game co.   nin-TEN-dō   ninˈtendoː

Key (col. 2):   a: fad ā: fade ah: father ar: marry aw: law e: fed ē: feed er: merry i: hid ī: hide ō: coat ōō: boot
oi: boy ow: now u: put uh: above uhr: bird ch: chop ng: ring sh: show th: thick th: this zh: measure

Ninus
  founder of Nineveh and Babylonian   NĪ-nuhs   'naɪnəs
    Empire
Niobe
  mother of Argos and Pelasgus   NĪ-uh-bē, NĪ-Ō-bē   'naɪəbiˑ, 'naɪˌoːbiˑ
niobium
  element   nī-Ō-bē-uhm   naɪ'oːbiːəm
Niobrara
  county, WY   NĪ-uh-BRAR-uh, NĪ-uh-BRER-uh   ˌnaɪə'brærə, ˌnaɪə'brerə
Niort
  town, France   NYAWR   njɔːr
Nipissing
  Canada   NIP-uh-SING   'nɪpəˌsɪŋ
Nipmuc
  N. American people   NIP-MUHK   'nɪpˌmək
Nippon [Japan]
  nation, Asia   nip-ahn   nɪpɑn
Nippondenso
  Japanese electronics co.   NIP-ahn-DEN(T)-sō   ˌnɪpɑn'den(t)soː
Nipponese
  Japanese   NIP-uh-NĒZ, -NĒS   ˌnɪpə'niːz, -'niːs
Nippur
  ancient Sumerian/Babylonian city   nip-UR   nɪp'uʳ
Nirenberg
  Marshall W., *US biochemist (Nobel*   NIR-uhn-BUHRG   'nɪrənˌbəʳg
    1968)
Niš, Nish
  city, Serbia   NĒSH   'niːʃ
Nisan
  Jewish month   NIS-n, nē-SAHN   'nɪsn̩, niː'sɑn
Nisanu
  Babylonian month   nē-SAHN-o͞o   niː'sɑnuː
Nisei
  Japanese-American or -Canadian   nē-SĀ, NĒ-SĀ   niː'seː, 'niːˌseː
Nishapur
  town, Iran   NĒ-shuh-PUR   ˌniːʃə'puʳ
Nisqually
  N. American people   ni-SKWAHL-ē, niz-KWAHL-ē   nɪ'skwɑliˑ, nɪz'kwɑliˑ
Nisroch
  Biblical name   NIS-RAHK, -ruhk; nis-RAW<u>KH</u>   'nɪsˌrɑk, -rək; nɪs'rɔːx
Nissan
  1. Japanese car co.   NĒ-SAHN, NIS-AHN   'niːˌsan, 'nɪsˌɑn
  2. river, Sweden   NIS-AHN   'nɪsˌɑn
Nissen
  prefabricated hut   NIS-n   'nɪsn̩
Nisus
  father of Scylla   NĪ-suhs   'naɪsəs
Nita
  pers. name   NĒT-uh   'niːt̬ə
Nitro
  city, WV   NĪ-trō   'naɪtroː
nitrogen
  element   NĪ-truh-juhn   'naɪtrədʒən
Niue
  island, Pacific Ocean   nē-o͞o-(w)ā   niː'uː(w)eː

Foreign Sounds: ue: *Fr.* **rue**, *Ger.* **füllen**   uh(r): *Fr.* **boeuf**, *Ger.* **Höhle**   <u>kh</u>: *Ger.* **ich**, *Scot.* **loch**   ğ: *Sp.* amigo   v̱: *Sp.* hablar
hl: *Welsh* **Llanelli**. CAPITALS: primary stress. SMALL CAPS: secondary stress. (Ⓢ): U.S. pron. (Ⓔ): British pron.

Niuean
   lang., people, Niue   n(y)o͞o-(W)Ā-uhn   n(j)uːˈ(w)eːən

Nivea
   tdmk for a cosmetic cream   NIV-ē-uh   ˈniviːə

Niven
   David, *English actor*   NIV-uhn   ˈnivən

Nivkh [Gilyak]
   lang., people, Russia   NIVKH   ˈnivx

Nivôse
   month, French Revolutionary   nē-VŌZ   niːvoːz
     calendar

Nixon
   Richard Milhous, *37th US president* NIK-suhn   ˈniksən

Njörð
   Scandinavian sea god   NYUHRTH   ˈnjœrð

Nkore [Nyankole]
   lang., people, Africa   (uh)ng-KŌR-ā, eng-   (ə)ŋˈkoːreː, eŋ-

Nkrumah
   Kwame, *president, Ghana*   ng-KRO͞O-muh, en-KRO͞O-muh ŋˈkruːmə, enˈkruːmə

Noadiah
   Biblical name   NŌ-uh-DĪ-uh, NŌ-ahd-YAH ˌnoːəˈdɑiə, ˌnoːɑdˈjɑ

Noah
   pers. name   NŌ-uh   ˈnoːə

Noailles
   pers. name, French   naw-AHY, ⑤ nō-Ī   nɔːɑj, ⑤ noːˈɑi

Noam
   pers. name   NŌ(-uh)m   ˈnoː(ə)m

Noamon
   Biblical name   nō-Ā-MAHN, NAW-ah-MŌN noːˈeːˌmɑn, ˌnɔːɑˈmoːn

Noatak
   river, village, AK   nō-AHT-uhk   noːˈɑʈək

Nob
   Biblical name   NAHB, NAWV   ˈnɑb, ˈnɔːv

Nobah
   Biblical name   NŌ-buh, NAW-BAHKH   ˈnoːbə, ˈnɔːˌbɑx

Nobel
   Alfred, *Swedish engineer*   nō-BEL   noːˈbel

Nobelist
   winner of a Nobel Prize   nō-BEL-uhst   noːˈbeləst

nobelium
   element   nō-BĒ-lē-uhm   noːˈbiːliːəm

Nobel Prize
   annual prize established by A. Nobel nō-BEL PRĪZ, NŌ-BEL noːˌbel ˈprɑiz, ˈnoːˌbel

Nobles
   pers. name (E. N. Lowe)   NŌ-buhlz   ˈnoːbəlz

Noblia
   watchmakers   NŌ-blē-uh   ˈnoːbliːə

Noboru
   pers. name, Japanese   nō-bō-ro͞o   noːboːruː

Nobusuke
   pers. name, Japanese   nō-bu-suk-e   noːbusuke

Noche Buena
   Mexican beer   NŌ-chā BWĀ-nah   ˈnoːtʃeː ˈbweːnɑ

Nod
   Biblical land where Cain dwelt NAHD, NŌD   ˈnɑd, ˈnoːd

Key (col. 2): a: f**a**d ā: f**a**de ah: f**a**ther ar: m**a**rry aw: l**a**w e: f**e**d ē: f**ee**d er: m**e**rry i: h**i**d ī: h**i**de ō: c**oa**t o͞o: b**oo**t
oi: b**oy** ow: n**ow** u: p**u**t uh: **a**bove uhr: b**ir**d ch: **ch**op ng: ri**ng** sh: **sh**ow th: **th**ick th: **th**is zh: mea**s**ure

Nodab
Biblical name   NŌ-DAB, nō-DAHV   'noːˌdæb, noː'dɑv

Nodaway
county, MO   NAHD-uh-WĀ   'nɑdəˌweː

Noe [Noah]
Biblical name   NŌ-uh   'noːə

Noël
pers. name, French   naw-EL   nɔːel

Noel, Noël
  1. pers. name   NŌ-uhl   'noːəl
  2. Christmas; Christmas carol   nō-EL   noː'el

Noel-Baker
Philip J., English statesman (Nobel 1959)   NŌ-uhl-BĀ-kuhr   ˌnoːəl'beːkəʳ

Nogah
Biblical name   NŌ-guh, NAW-gah   'noːgə, 'nɔːgɑ

Nogai
lang., people, Caucasus Mts.   NŌ-GĪ   'noːˌgɑi

Nogales
city, AZ; town, Mexico   nō-GAL-uhs, nō-GAHL-uhs, *Spanish* nō-ḠAHL-ās   noː'gæləs, noː'gɑləs, *Spanish* noː'ɣɑleːs

Noguchi
Hideyo, US bacteriologist   nō-GOO-chē   noː'guːtʃiˑ

Nohah
Biblical name   NŌ-(h)uh, nō-KHAH   'noː(h)ə, noː'xɑ

Noilly Prat
wine   n(uh-)wah-YĒ PRAHT   n(ə)wɑːjiː prɑːt

Noir de Pressac
wine   nwahr duh pres-AHK   nwɑːr də presɑːk

Nola
pers. name   NŌ-luh   'noːlə

Nolan
pers. name   NŌ-luhn   'noːlən

Nolichucky
river, NC, TN   NAHL-uh-CHUHK-ē   ˌnɑlə'tʃəkiˑ

Nolte
Nick, US actor   NŌL-tē   'noːltiˑ

Nomalacki
N. American people   NŌ-muh-LAK-ē   ˌnoːmə'lækiˑ

Nomalaki-Wailaki
N. American people   NŌ-muh-LAK-ē-WĪ-LAK-ē   ˌnoːmə'lækiˑˌwai'lækiˑ

Nomaoi Matsuri
Japanese festival   nō-mah-oi maht-sur-ē   noːmɑɔi mɑtsuriˑ

Nomarch
ancient Egyptian magistrate   NAHM-AHRK   'nɑmˌɑʳk

Nome
division, city, AK; ancient Egyptian administrative unit   NŌM   'noːm

Non [Nun]
Biblical name   NAHN, NUHN, NŌN   'nɑn, 'nən, 'noːn

Nonius
Roman name   NŌ-nē-uhs   'noːniːəs

Nooksack
N. American people   NUK-SAK   'nukˌsæk

Foreign Sounds: ue: *Fr.* **rue**, *Ger.* **füllen**   uh(r): *Fr.* **boeuf**, *Ger.* **Höhle**   kh: *Ger.* **ich**, *Scot.* **loch**   ḡ: *Sp.* **amigo**   v: *Sp.* **hablar**
hl: *Welsh* **Llanelli**.   CAPITALS: primary stress.   SMALL CAPS: secondary stress.   Ⓢ: U.S. pron.   Ⓔ: British pron.

Noord Brabant		
prov, Netherlands	NŌRT bruh-BAHNT	ˌnoːʳt brəˈbɑnt
Noord Holland		
prov, Netherlands	nōrt HŌ-lahnt	noːʳt ˈhoːlɑnt
Nootka		
N. American people	NUT-kuh, NŌŌT-kuh	ˈnutkə, ˈnuːtkə
Nophah		
Biblical name	NŌ-fuh, NAW-FAHKH	ˈnoːfə, ˈnɔːˌfɑx
Noquet		
N. American people	NŌ-kwā	ˈnoːkweː
Nora		
pers. name	NŌR-uh, NAWR-uh	ˈnoːrə, ˈnɔːrə
NORAD		
air defense system	NŌR-AD, NAWR-AD	ˈnoːrˌæd, ˈnɔːrˌæd
Norbert		
1. pers. name	NAWR-buhrt	ˈnɔːʳbəʳt
2. Czech	NAWR-bert	ˈnɔːrbert
3. French	nawr-BER	nɔːrber
4. German	NAWR-bert	ˈnɔːʳbeʳt
Nord		
dept, France	NAWR	nɔːr
Nordahl		
pers. name, Norwegian	NAWR-dahl	ˈnɔːrdɑl
Nordeste		
region, Brazil	nawr-DES-tā	nɔːʳˈdesteː
Nordik Wölf		
Swedish beer	NAWR-dik VUH(R)LF	ˈnɔːrdik ˈvœlf
Nordiques		
Quebec hockey team	nawr-DĒKS	nɔːʳˈdiːks
Nord-Pas-de-Calais		
region, France	nawr-PAH-duh-kah-LE	nɔːrpɑdəkɑle
Nordrhein-Westfalen		
prov, Germany	nōrt-RĪN-vest-FAHL-uhn	noːʳtˌrɑinvestˈfɑlən
Nordstrom		
US department store	NAWRD-struhm	ˈnɔːʳdstrəm
Noreen		
pers. name	nōr-ĒN, nawr-ĒN	noːrˈiːn, nɔːrˈiːn
Norell		
tdmk, perfume	nawr-EL	nɔːrˈel
Norfolk		
city, NE, VA; county, MA; county, England	NAWR-fuhk, [S] *also* NAWR-FAWK	ˈnɔːʳfək, [S] *also* ˈnɔːʳˌfɔːk
Norgay		
Tenzing, *Sherpa mountaineer*	NAWR-gā	ˈnɔːʳgeː
Norge [Norway]		
kingdom, Europe	NAWR-guh	ˈnɔːʳgə
Noric		
Alps, *Alpine mtn. range*	NŌR-ik, NAWR-ik	ˈnoːrik, ˈnɔːrik
Noriega		
Manuel, *Panamanian leader*	nawr-YĀ-guh, NAWR-ē-Ā-guh	nɔːʳˈjeːgə, ˌnɔːriːˈeːgə
Noriker		
German horse breed	NŌR-i-kuhr, NAWR-	ˈnoːrikəʳ, ˈnɔːr-
Norische Alpen [Noric Alps]		
Alpine mtn. range	NŌ-rish-uh AHL-puhn	ˈnoːriʃə ˈɑlpən

Noritake
  brand of china NŌR-uh-TAHK-ē, NAWR-uh-TAHK-ē ˌnoːrə'taki·, ˌnɔːrə'taki·

Norm
  pers. name NAWRM 'nɔːʳm

Norma
  constellation; pers. name NAWR-muh 'nɔːʳmə

Norman
  inhabitant of Normandy; pers. name NAWR-muhn 'nɔːʳmən

Normande, potée
  three-meat dish paw-TÃ nawr-MAHⁿD pɔːteː nɔːrmãd

Normandie [Normandy]
  prov, France nawr-mahⁿ-DĒ nɔːrmãdiː

Normandy
  prov, France NAWR-muhn-dē 'nɔːʳməndi·

Norodom Sihanouk
  Cambodian chief of state NŌR-uh-DUM SĒ-uh-NUK ˌnoːrə'dum 'siːə,nuk

Noroton
  village, CT naw-RŌT-n nɔː'roːtn̩

Norrish
  Ronald George Wreyford, *English* NAWR-ish 'nɔːriʃ
    chemist (Nobel 1967)

Norse
  lang., N. Europe; pert. to ancient NAWRS 'nɔːʳs
    Scandinavia; Norwegian

Northampton
  US pl. name; town, England nawr-THAM(P)-tuhn, nɔːʳ'θæm(p)tən,
    nawrth-HAM(P)-tuhn nɔːʳθ'hæm(p)tən

Northamptonshire
  county, England nawr-THAM(P)-tuhn-shuhr, nɔːʳ'θæm(p)tənʃəʳ,
    nawrth-HAM-tuhn-shuhr, -SHIR nɔːʳθ'hæmtənʃəʳ, -ˌʃiʳ

Northanger Abbey
  novel, J. Austen nawr-THANG-uhr AB-ē, nɔːʳˌθæŋəʳ 'æbi·, ˌnɔːʳθæŋəʳ
    NAWR-thang-uhr

North Berwick
  1. town, ME NAWRTH BUHR-wik ˌnɔːʳθ 'bəʳwik
  2. royal burgh, parish, Scotland NAWRTH BER-ik ˌnɔːʳθ 'berik

North Carolina
  state, US NAWRTH KAR-uh-LĪ-nuh, kuhr-LĪ-nuh, ˌnɔːʳθ ˌkærə'lainə, kəʳ'lainə,
    kar-LĪ-nuh kæʳ'lainə

North Catasauqua
  borough, PA NAWRTH KAT-uh-SAW-kwuh ˌnɔːʳθ ˌkæt̬ə'sɔːkwə

North Dakota
  state, US NAWRTH duh-KŌT-uh ˌnɔːʳθ də'koːt̬ə

Northern Sotho
  lang., Africa NAWR-thuhrn SŌ-thō, SŌT-ō 'nɔːʳðəʳn 'soːθoː, 'soːtoː

Northrop
  J. H., *US biochemist (Nobel 1946);* NAWR-thruhp 'nɔːʳθrəp
    pers. name

North Slope
  division, AK nawrth SLŌP nɔːʳθ 'sloːp

Northumberland
  1. county, England; county, PA nawr-THUHM-buhr-luhnd nɔːʳ'θəmbəʳlənd
  2. county, VA nawr-THUHM-uhr-luhn(d), nɔːʳ'θəməʳlən(d),
    nawr-THUHM-buhr-luhnd nɔːʳ'θəmbəʳlənd

Foreign Sounds: ue: *Fr.* **rue**, *Ger.* **füllen** uh(r): *Fr.* **boeuf**, *Ger.* **Höhle** kh: *Ger.* **ich**, *Scot.* **loch** ḡ: *Sp.* **amigo** v̲: *Sp.* **hablar**
hl: *Welsh* **Llanelli**. CAPITALS: primary stress. SMALL CAPS: secondary stress. Ⓢ: U.S. pron. Ⓔ: British pron.

Northumbria *early English kingdom*	nawr-THUHM-brē-uh	nɔː^{r}'θəmbriːə
North Yorkshire *county, England*	nawrth YAWRK-shuhr, -SHIR	nɔː^{r}θ 'jɔː^{r}kʃə^{r}, -ˌʃi^{r}
Norton *pers. name*	NAWRT-n	'nɔː^{r}tn̩
Norval *pers. name*	NAWR-vuhl	'nɔː^{r}vəl
Norwalk *river, city, CT; city, CA*	NAWR-WAWK	'nɔː^{r}ˌwɔːk
Norway *kingdom, Europe*	NAWR-WĀ	'nɔː^{r}ˌweː
Norwegian *lang., Norway*	nawr-WĒ-juhn	nɔː^{r}'wiːdʒən
Norwegian buhund *dog breed*	nawr-WĒ-juhn BO͞O-HUNT	nɔː^{r}ˌwiːdʒən 'buːˌhunt
Norwich *1. town, CT, NY*	NAWR-wich, NAHR-wich	'nɔː^{r}witʃ, 'nɑ^{r}witʃ
2. town, England	NAWR-ij, NAWR-ich	'nɔːridʒ, 'nɔːritʃ
Nosferatu *fictional vampire*	NAWS-fuh-RAH-TO͞O, NAHS-	ˌnɔːsfə'rɑˌtuː, ˌnɑs-
Nostradamus *French astrologer*	NAHS-truh-DĀ-muhs, NAWS-truh-DAHM-uhs	ˌnɑstrə'deːməs, ˌnɔːstrə'dɑməs
Notimex *Mexican news agency*	NŌT-uh-MEKS	'noːt̬əˌmeks
Notre Dame University, *IN; bay, Newfoundland*	NŌT-uhr DĀM	ˌnoːt̬ə^{r} 'deːm, -'dɑːm
Notre-Dame *cathedral, Paris, France*	naw-truh-DAHM, Ⓢ NŌ-truh-DĀM, NŌT-uhr-DĀM, -DAHM	nɔːtrədɑːm, Ⓢ ˌnoːtrə'deːm, ˌnoːt̬ə^{r}'deːm, -'dɑːm
Nottaway *river, Canada*	NAHT-uh-WĀ	'nɑt̬əˌweː
Nottely *stream, GA, NC*	NAHT-lē	'nɑtliˑ
Nottingham *town, England*	NAHT-ing-uhm	'nɑt̬iŋəm
Nottinghamshire *county, England*	NAHT-ing-uhm-shuhr, -SHIR	'nɑt̬iŋəmʃə^{r}, -ˌʃi^{r}
Nottoway *river, county, VA*	NAHT-uh-WĀ	'nɑt̬əˌweː
Notts [Nottinghamshire] *county, England*	NAHTS	'nɑts
Notus *Greek god of the south wind*	NŌT-uhs	'noːt̬əs
Nouakchott *city, Mauritania*	nu-AHK-SHAHT	nu'ɑkˌʃɑt
Nouméa *town, New Caledonia*	no͞o-MĀ-uh	nuː'meːə
Novak Kim, *US actress*	NŌ-VAK	'noːˌvæk
Nova Scotia *prov, Canada*	NŌ-vuh SKŌ-shuh	ˌnoːvə 'skoːʃə
Novatian *antipope*	nō-VĀ-shuhn	noː'veːʃən

Key (col. 2): a: **fad** ā: **fade** ah: **father** ar: **marry** aw: **law** e: **fed** ē: **feed** er: **merry** i: **hid** ī: **hide** ō: **coat** o͞o: **boot** oi: **boy** ow: **now** u: **put** uh: **above** uhr: **bird** ch: **chop** ng: **ring** sh: **show** th: **thick** t͟h: **this** zh: **measure**

Novationism *early Christian schism*	no-VĀ-shuh-NIZ-uhm	no'veːʃəˌnizəm
Novato *city, CA*	nuh-VAHT-ō	nə'vɑt̬oː
Novaya Zemlya *islands, Russia*	NŌ-vuh-yuh ZEM-lē-AH	'noːvəjə ˌzemliː'ɑː
Novello *1. pers. name* *2. Italian*	 nuh-VEL-ō, nō- nō-VEL-lō	 nə'veloː, noː- noː'velloː
November *month*	nō-VEM-buhr, nuh-VEM-buhr	noː'vembəʳ, nə'vembəʳ
Nové Zámky [Érsekújvár] *town, Slovakia*	NŌ-vā ZAHM(P)-kē	ˌnoːveː 'zɑm(p)kiˑ
Novgorod *city, Russia*	NAHV-guh-RAHD	'nɑvgəˌrɑd
Novi *village, MI*	NŌ-VĪ	'noːˌvɑi
Novi Sad *city, Serbia*	NŌ-vē SAHD	ˌnoːviˑ 'sɑːd
Novocaine *tdmk for procaine*	NŌ-vuh-KĀN	'noːvəˌkeːn
Novorossisk *port, Russia*	NŌ-vuh-ruh-SĒSK	ˌnoːvərə'siːsk
Novosibirsk *city, Russia*	NŌ-vuh-suh-BIRSK, NUH-vuh-	ˌnoːvəsə'biʳsk, ˌnəvə-
Novotný Antonin, *president, Czechoslovakia*	NAW-vawt-nē	'nɔːvɔːtniˑ
Novy Frederick George, *US bacteriologist*	NŌ-vē	'noːviˑ
Nowa Huta *suburb of Kraków, Poland*	NŌ-vuh HO͞O-tuh	'noːvə ˌhuːtə
Nowata *county, OK*	nō-WAHT-uh	noː'wɑt̬ə
Nox *Roman goddess of the night*	NAHKS	'nɑks
Noxubee *river, county, MS*	NAHK-shuh-bē	'nɑkʃəbiˑ
Nu [Nun] *Egyptian god or goddess, source of all life*	NO͞O	'nuː
Nuadu *Irish god, former leader of the Tuatha de Danaan*	NO͞O-uh-tho͞o	'nuːəðuː
Nuba *mts., Sudan*	N(Y)O͞O-buh	'n(j)uːbə
Nubia *region in Nile valley*	N(Y)O͞O-bē-uh	'n(j)uːbiːə
Nubian *lang., desert, Africa*	N(Y)O͞O-bē-uhn	'n(j)uːbiːən
Nubium, Mare *see* Mare Nubium		
Nuckolls *county, NE*	NUHK-uhlz	'nəkəlz
Nueces *river, county, TX*	n(y)u-Ā-suhs	n(j)u'eːsəs

Foreign Sounds: ue: *Fr.* **rue**, *Ger.* **füllen** uh(r): *Fr.* **boeuf**, *Ger.* **Höhle** kh: *Ger.* **ich**, *Scot.* **loch** g̃: *Sp.* **amigo** v: *Sp.* **hablar** hl: *Welsh* **Llanelli**. CAPITALS: primary stress. SMALL CAPS: secondary stress. [$]: U.S. pron. [£]: British pron.

Nuer
lang., people, Sudan, Ethiopia — NŌŌ-uhr, NUR — 'nuːəʳ, 'nuʳ

Nuevo León
state, Mexico — nu-Ā-vō lā-ŌN — nuˌeːvoː leː'oːn

Nuffield
college, Oxford Univ. — NUHF-ĒLD — 'nəfˌiːld

Nugent
pers. name — N(Y)ŌŌ-juhnt — 'n(j)uːdʒənt

Nuit
Egyptian god — N(Y)ŌŌT, N(Y)ŌŌ-uht — 'n(j)uːt, 'n(j)uːət

Nuits-Saint-Georges
wine — nwē-seⁿ-ZHAWRZH, — nɥiːsẽʒɔːrʒ,
Ⓢ nuh-WĒ-SĀNT-JAWRJ, NWĒ- — Ⓢ nəˌwiːˌseːnt'dʒɔːʳdʒ, ˌnwiː-

Nukualofa
city, Tonga — NŌŌ-kuh-wuh-LAW-fuh, -LŌ-fuh — ˌnuːkəwə'lɔːfə, -'loːfə

Nuku Hiva
island, Marquesas — NŌŌ-kuh HĒ-vuh — ˌnuːkə 'hiːvə

Nulato
city, AK — nu-LAHT-ō — nu'laʈoː

Nullarbor Plain
plateau, Australia — NUHL-uh-BAWR PLĀN, NUHL-uhr-BAWR — ˌnələˌbɔːʳ 'pleːn, ˌnələrˌbɔːr

Numantia
ancient city, Spain — n(y)ōō-MAN-ch(ē-)uh — n(j)uˈmæntʃ(iː)ə

Numa Pompilius
legendary 2nd king of Rome — N(Y)ŌŌ-muh pahm-PIL-ē-uhs — 'n(j)uːmə pɑm'piliːəs

Numbers
Old Testament book — NUHM-buhrz — 'nəmbəʳz

Numeri
formations of the Roman army — N(Y)ŌŌ-muh-RĪ, N(Y)ŌŌ-muh-rē — 'n(j)uːməˌrai, 'n(j)uːməri·

Numidia
ancient country, Africa — n(y)ōō-MID-ē-uh — n(j)uˈmidiːə

Numitor
grandfather of Romulus and Remus — N(Y)ŌŌ-muht-uhr, N(Y)ŌŌ-muh-TAWR — 'n(j)uːməʈəʳ, 'n(j)uːməˌtɔːʳ

Nun [Nu]
Egyptian god or goddess, source of all life — NUN, NUHN — 'nun, 'nən

Nun [Non]
Biblical name — NUHN, NŌŌN — 'nən, 'nuːn

Nunc Dimittis
canticle — NUHNGK duh-MIT-uhs, NUNGK — ˌnəŋk də'miʈəs, ˌnuŋk

Nuñez
pers. name — NŌŌN-yāth, NŌŌN-yās — 'nuːnjeːθ, 'nuːnjeːs

Nung
lang., people, Vietnam, South China — NUNG — 'nuŋ

Nunn
Sam, US politician; pers. name — NUHN — 'nən

Nupe
lang., people, Nigeria — NŌŌ-pā — 'nuːpeː

Nuremberg
city, Germany — N(Y)UR-uhm-BUHRG — 'n(j)urəmˌbəʳg

Key (col. 2): a: fad ā: fade ah: father ar: marry aw: law e: fed ē: feed er: merry i: hid ī: hide ō: coat ōō: boot oi: boy ow: now u: put uh: above uhr: bird ch: chop ng: ring sh: show th: thick th: this zh: measure

Nureyev
Rudolf, *Russian ballet dancer*   nur-YĀ-yif, Ⓢ nur-Ā-(y)uhf, nur-Ā-(y)ev, NUR-ē-EF   nur'jeːjif, Ⓢ nur'eː(j)əf, nur'eː(j)ev, 'nuriːˌef

Nurmi
Paavo, *Finnish athlete*   NUR-mē   'nuʳmiˑ

Nürnberg [Nuremberg]
city, Germany   NUERN-BERK   'nyːʳnˌbeʳk

Nursultan
pers. name (N. Nazarbayev)   nur-SUL-tahn, nur-sul-TAHN   nuʳ'sultɑn, nuʳsul'tɑn

Nut
Egyptian sky goddess   NUT, NOOT, NUHT   'nut, 'nuːt, 'nət

NutraSweet
tdmk for aspartame, a sweetener   NOO-truh-SWĒT   'nuːtrəˌswiːt

Nuwara-Eliya
city, Sri Lanka   NOO-wuh-ruh-Ā-lē-(y)uh   ˌnuːwərə'eːliː(j)ə

Nuyen
France, *US entertainer*   noo-YEN   nuˑ'jen

Nuzi
archaeological site, Iraq   NOO-zē   'nuːziˑ

Nyack
town, NY   NĪ-AK   'nɑiˌæk

Nyamwesi
lang., people, Africa   nyahm-WĀ-zē   njɑm'weːziˑ

Nyanda [Masvingo, Fort Victoria]
city, Zimbabwe   NYAHN-duh, Ⓢ nī-AN-duh   'njɑndə, Ⓢ nɑi'ændə

Nyanga
lang., Africa   NYAHN-guh   'njɑngə

Nyanja [Chewa]
lang., people, Africa   NYAHN-juh   'njɑndʒə

Nyankole [Nkore]
lang., people, Africa   nyahng-KŌ-lā   njɑŋ'koːleː

Nyasa [Malawi]
lake, Africa   nī-AS-uh, nē-AS-uh   nɑi'æsə, niː'æsə

Nyborg
town, Denmark   NUE-BAWRG̃   'nyːˌbɔːrɣ

Nycteus
father of Antiope   NIK-tē-uhs   'niktiːəs

Nyctimus
son of Lycaon   NIK-tuh-muhs   'niktəməs

Nyerere
Julius, *president, Tanzania*   nyuh-RER-ā   njə'rereː

Nyeri
town, Kenya   nē-ER-ē   niː'eriˑ

Nygaarsdvold
Johan, *prime minister, Norway*   NĪ-gawrs-VAWL   'nɑigɔːʳsˌvɔːl

Nyíreghyháza
city, Hungary   NĒ-REJ-HAHZ-aw   'niːˌredʒˌhɑzɔː

Nyköping
city, Sweden   NUE-KUH(R)-ping   'nyːˌkœːpiŋ

Nymphas
Biblical name   NIM(P)-fuhs   'nim(p)fəs

Nymphs
Greek deities   NIM(P)FS   'nim(p)fs

NYNEX
US telecommunications co.   NĪ-NEKS   'nɑiˌneks

Nyngan
   town, Australia   NING-guhn   'niŋgən

Nyoro
   lang., people, Africa   NYŌR-ō   'njoːroː

Nysa
   nursemaid of Dionysus; pers. name   NĒ-suh, NĪ-suh   'niːsə, 'nɑisə

Nysus
   adoptive father of Dionysus   NĪ-suhs   'nɑisəs

Nyx
   Greek goddess of night   NIKS   'niks

O

Oahe
   dam, lake, SD   ō-AH-hē   oːˈɑhiˑ

Oahu
   island, HI   uh-WAH-hōō, ō-AH-hōō   əˈwɑhuː, oːˈɑhuː

Oakley
   Annie, *US markswoman;* Robert, *US*   Ō-klē   'oːkliˑ
      ambassador

Oates
   John, *US musician;* Joyce Carol,   ŌTS   'oːts
      US writer; Titus, *British traitor*

Oaxaca
   state, Mexico   wah-K̲H̲AH-kah, Ⓢ wuh-HAHK-uh   waˈxɑkɑ, Ⓢ wəˈhɑkə

Ob
   1. river, Russia   AHB, AWB   'ab, 'ɔːb
   2. Korean beer   ŌB, AHB   'oːb, 'ab

Obadiah
   Old Testament book; pers. name   ō-buh-DĪ-uh   ˌoːbəˈdaiə

Obata
   Gyo, *US architect*   ō-BAHT-uh   oːˈbɑțə

Obal
   Biblical name   Ō-buhl, ō-VAHL   'oːbəl, oːˈval

Obed
   pers. name   Ō-buhd   'oːbəd

Obed-edom
   Biblical name   Ō-buhd-ĒD-uhm, aw-VED-ED-awm   'oːbədˈiːdəm, ɔːˌvedˈedɔːm

Obeid, El
   town, Sudan   EL ō-BĀD   ˌel oːˈbeːd

Oberammergau
   resort, Passion play, Germany   ō-buh-RAHM-uhr-GOW,   ˌoːbəˈramərˌgau,
                      Ⓢ ō-buh-RAM-uhr-GOW   Ⓢ ˌoːbəˈræmərˌgau

Oberbayern
   prov, Germany   Ō-buhr-BĪ-uhrn   'oːbəʳˌbaiəʳn

Key (col. 2):   a: **fad** ā: **fade** ah: **father** ar: **marry** aw: **law** e: **fed** ē: **feed** er: **merry** i: **hid** ī: **hide** ō: **coat** ōō: **boot**
oi: **boy** ow: **now** u: **put** uh: **above** uhr: **bird** ch: **chop** ng: **ring** sh: **show** th: **thick** <u>th</u>: **this** zh: **measure**

Oberdorfer
    German beer   Ō-buhr-DAWR-fuhr   'oːbəʳˌdɔːʳfəʳ

Oberfranken
    prov, Germany   Ō-buhr-FRAHNG-kuhn   'oːbəʳˌfraŋkən

Oberland
    mtn. region, Switzerland   Ō-buhr-LAHNT, Ō-buhr-LAND   'oːbəʳˌlant, 'oːbəʳˌlænd

Oberlin
    city, college, OH   Ō-buhr-luhn   'oːbəʳlən

Oberon
    Merle, *US entertainer; fairy king;*   Ō-buh-RAHN, -ruhn   'oːbəˌran, -rən
      satellite of Uranus

Oberösterreich
    state, Austria   Ō-buh-RUH(R)-stuhr-RĪ<u>KH</u>   ˌoːbəˈrœːstəʳˌraiç

Oberpfalz
    prov, Germany   Ō-buhr-FAHLTS   'oːbəʳˌfalts

Obey
    David, *US politician*   Ō-bē   'oːbiˑ

Obie
    off-Broadway award   Ō-bē   'oːbiˑ

Obil
    Biblical name   Ō-buhl, ō-VĒL   'oːbəl, oːˈviːl

Obion
    river, county, TN   ō-BĪ-uhn   oːˈbaiən

Ob-Irtysh
    river, Russia   AWB UHR-TISH, ir-TISH   'ɔːb ˌərˈtiʃ, irˈtiʃ

Oblate
    College, *Washington, DC*   AHB-LĀT   'abˌleːt

Oblomov
    novel by Ivan Goncharov   uh-BLAW-mawf, AHB-luh-MAWF   əˈblɔːmɔːf, 'abləˌmɔːf

Oboe
    musical instrument   Ō-bō   'oːboː

O-Bon
    Japanese festival   ō-bōn   oːboːn

Oboth
    Biblical name   Ō-BAHTH, Ō-BŌTH, Ō-buhth,   'oːˌbaθ, 'oːˌboːθ, 'oːbəθ,
       aw-VAWT   ɔːˈvɔːt

Obote
    Milton, *president, Uganda*   aw-BAW-TĀ   ɔːˈbɔːˌteː

Obregón
    Alvaro, *president, Mexico*   ō-v̲rā-ḠŌN   oːβreːˈɣoːn

O'Brien
    pers. name   ō-BRĪ-uhn   oːˈbraiən

Ocala
    city, FL   ō-KAL-uh   oːˈkælə

Ocarina
    musical instrument   AHK-uh-RĒ-nuh   ˌakəˈriːnə

O'Casey
    Sean, *Irish playwright*   ō-KĀ-sē   oːˈkeːsiˑ

Occam, Ockham
    William of, *English philosopher*   AHK-uhm   'akəm

Occam's razor
    principle of logic   AHK-uhmz RĀ-zuhr   ˌakəmz 'reːzəʳ

Occident
    western hemisphere   AHK-suhd-uhnt, AHK-suh-DENT   'aksədənt, 'aksəˌdent

---

Foreign Sounds: ue: *Fr.* **rue**, *Ger.* **füllen**   uh(r): *Fr.* **boeuf**, *Ger.* **Höhle**   <u>kh</u>: *Ger.* **ich**, *Scot.* **loch**   g̃: *Sp.* **amigo**   v̲: *Sp.* **hablar**
hl: *Welsh* **Llanelli**.   CAPITALS: primary stress.   SMALL CAPS: secondary stress.   Ⓢ: U.S. pron.   Ⓔ: British pron.

Occidental

  pert. to the western hemisphere   AHK-si-DENT-l   ,ɑksi'dentl̩

Occitan [Provençal]

  lang., France   awk-sē-TAH^n ɔːksiːtɑ̃

Oceana

  county, MI   Ō-shē-AN-uh   ,oːʃiː'ænə

Oceania

  Pacific islands   Ō-shē-AN-ē-uh, O-shē-Ā-nē-uh   ,oːʃiː'æniːə, ,oʃiː'eːniːə

Oceanica [Oceania]

  Pacific islands   Ō-shē-AN-i-kuh, Ō-shē-Ā-ni-kuh   ,oːʃiː'ænikə, ,oːʃiː'eːnikə

Oceanids

  mythological daughters of Oceanus   ō-SĒ-uh-nidz, ō-SHĒ-uh-nidz   oː'siːənidz, oː'ʃiːənidz
  and Tethys

Oceanus

  Titan who rules the earth-encircling   ō-SĒ-uh-nuhs   oː'siːənəs
  river

Ochiltree

  county, TX   AHK-uhl-TRĒ   'ɑkəl,triː

Ochoa

  Severo, *Spanish-born US biochemist*   ō-CHŌ-uh   oː'tʃoːə
  (Nobel 1959)

Ochs

  Phil, *US folksinger*   ŌKS   'oːks

Ochlockonee

  river, GA   ahk-LAHK-uh-nē   ɑk'lɑkəniː

Ochozias [Ahaziah]

  Biblical king   AHK-uh-ZĪ-uhs   ,ɑkə'zɑiəs

Ochs

  Peter, *Swiss politician*   ŌKS   'oːks

Ockeghem

  Jean d', *Flemish composer*   AHK-uh-guhm   'ɑkəgəm

Ockham

  see Occam

Ocmulgee

  1. National Monument, *river, GA*   ōk-MUHL-gē   oːk'məlgiˑ
  2. see Okmulgee

Ocnus

  rope-maker in Hades   AHK-nuhs   'ɑknəs

Ocoee [Toccoa]

  river, GA, TN; city, FL   ō-KŌ-ē   oː'koːiˑ

Oconee

  county, GA, SC   ō-KŌ-nē   oː'koːniˑ

O'Connor

  John, *US Roman Catholic cardinal;*   ō-KAHN-uhr   oː'kɑnər
  Sandra Day, *US Supreme Court*
  justice

Oconomowoc

  city, WI   uh-KAHN-uh-muh-WAWK, -WAHK   ə'kɑnəmə,wɔːk, -,wɑk

O'Conor

  pers. name   ō-KAHN-uhr   oː'kɑnər

Oconto

  county, WI   ō-KAHN-tō   oː'kɑntoː

Ocracoke

  island, inlet, NC   Ō-kruh-KŌK, Ō-kuhr-KŌK   'oːkrə,koːk, 'oːkər,koːk

---

Key (col. 2):   a: fad ā: fade ah: father ar: marry aw: law e: fed ē: feed er: merry i: hid ī: hide ō: coat ōō: boot
oi: boy   ow: now   u: put   uh: above   uhr: bird   ch: chop   ng: ring   sh: show   th: thick   <u>th</u>: this   zh: measure

Ocran
  Biblical name   AHK-ruhn, ah<u>kh</u>-RAHN   ˈɑkrən, ɑxˈrɑn

Octans
  constellation   AHK-TANZ   ˈɑkˌtænz

Octavia
  Roman matron (Augustus' sister),   ahk-TĀ-vē-uh   ɑkˈteːviːə
  pers. name

Octavian
  1. Roman emperor, pers. name   ahk-TĀ-vē-uhn   ɑkˈteːviːən
  2. Romanian   AWK-tahv-YAHN   ˌɔːktɑvˈjɑn

Octavio
  pers. name, German   awk-TAHV-yō, awk-TAHV-ē-ō   ɔːkˈtɑvjoː, ɔːkˈtɑviːoː

Octavius
  Roman politician, emperor, pers.   ahk-TĀ-vē-uhs   ɑkˈteːviːəs
  name

October
  month   ahk-TŌ-buhr   ɑkˈtoːbəʳ

Ocyrrhoe
  daughter of Chiron   ō-SIR-uh-wē   oːˈsirəwiˑ

Odd
  pers. name, Norwegian   AWD   ˈɔːd

Oddone
  pers. name, Italian   ōd-DŌ-nā   oːdˈdoːneː

Oded
  Biblical name   ŌD-ED, ō-DED   ˈoːdˌed, oːˈded

Odell, Odelle
  pers. name   ō-DEL   oːˈdel

Odelsting
  Norwegian parliament   ŌD-l-STING   ˈoːdl̩ˌstiŋ

Odense
  town, Denmark   U-uhn-zuh *(local pron.)*, ŌD-n-suh   ˈuənzə *(local pron.)*, ˈoːdn̩sə

Odeon
  tdmk for cognac, perfume; recording   ŌD-ē-uhn   ˈoːdiːən
  label

Oder
  river, Baltic   ŌD-uhr   ˈoːdəʳ

Oder-Neisse Line
  boundary between Poland and   ŌD-uhr-NĪ-suh LĪN   ˌoːdəʳˈnɑisə ˌlɑin
  Germany

Odessa
  city, TX; city, Ukraine   ō-DES-uh   oːˈdesə

Odet
  pers. name, French   aw-DE   ɔːde

Odets
  Clifford, writer   ō-DETS   oːˈdets

Odetta
  US folk singer; pers. name   ō-DET-uh   oːˈdet̬ə

Odette
  pers. name, French   aw-DET   ɔːdet

Odeum
  hall or theater   ŌD-ē-uhm   ˈoːdiːəm

Odilon
  pers. name, French   aw-dē-LAW^n ɔːdiːlɔ̃

Odin
  supreme Scandinavian god   ŌD-n, Ō-<u>th</u>uhn   ˈoːdn̩, ˈoːðən

---

Foreign Sounds: ue: *Fr.* **rue**, *Ger.* **füllen**   uh(r): *Fr.* **boeuf**, *Ger.* **Höhle**   <u>kh</u>: *Ger.* **ich**, *Scot.* **loch**   ḡ: *Sp.* **amigo**   v̲: *Sp.* **hablar**
hl: *Welsh* **Llanelli**.   CAPITALS: primary stress.   SMALL CAPS: secondary stress.   Ⓢ: U.S. pron.   Ⓔ: British pron.

Oðinn [Odin]
   supreme Scandinavian god　Ō-<u>th</u>uhn　'oːðən

Odo
   pers. name　ŌD-ō　'oːdoː

Odoacer
   barbarian king of Italy　ō-duh-WĀ-suhr　ˌoːdə'weːsə^r

Odysseus [Ulysses]
   mythical Greek hero　ō-DIS-ē-uhs, ō-DIS-yuhs, ō-DISH-uhs,　oːˈdisiːəs, oːˈdisjəs, oːˈdiʃəs,
        ō-DISH-ōōS　oːˈdiʃˌuːs

Odyssey
   epic poem, Homer　AHD-uh-sē　'adəsiˑ

Oedipal
   pert. to Oedipus　ED-uh-puhl, ĒD-uh-puhl　'edəpəl, 'iːdəpəl

Oedipus
   legendary king of Thebes　ED-uh-puhs, ĒD-uh-puhs　'edəpəs, 'iːdəpəs

Oekist
   founder of a Greek colony　Ē-kuhst　'iːkəst

Oeneus
   king of Calydon　Ē-nē-uhs, ĒN-YŌŌS　'iːniːəs, 'iːnˌjuːs

Oenomaus
   father of Hippodamia　Ē-nuh-MĀ-uhs　ˌiːnə'meːəs

Oenone
   wife of Paris, abandoned for Helen　ē-NŌ-nē　iːˈnoːniˑ

Oenopion
   son of Ariadne　ē-NŌ-pē-uhn　iːˈnoːpiːən

Oeonus
   cousin and companion of Heracles　ē-Ō-nuhs　iːˈoːnəs

O-erh-ku-na [Argun]
   river, Asia, between China & Russia　Ō-UHR-KŌŌ-NAH, Ō-ER-　'oːˈə^rˈkuːnɑ, 'oːˈe^r-

Oersted, Ørsted
   Hans Christian, *Danish physicist*　UH(R)R-sti<u>th</u>, ⑤ UHR-stuhd　'œrstið, ⑤ 'ə^rstəd
      and chemist

O'Faoláin
   Seán, *Irish writer*　ō-FĀ-luhn, ō-FAL-uhn　oːˈfeːlən, oːˈfælən

Offa
   1. king of Mercia　AW-fuh　'ɔːfə
   2. town, Nigeria　AHF-uh　'afə

Offenbach
   1. city, Germany　AW-fuhn-BAH<u>KH</u>, ⑤ AW-fuhn-BAHK　'ɔːfənˌbax, ⑤ 'ɔːfənˌbak
   2. Jacques, French composer　aw-fen-BAHK, AW-fuhn-BAHK, -BAH<u>KH</u>　ɔːfenbɑːk, 'ɔːfənˌbak, -ˌbax

O'Flaherty
   Liam, *Irish novelist*　ō-FLAH-huhrt-ē, ⑤ ō-FLĀ-uhrt-ē,　oːˈflaːhə^rti·, ⑤ oːˈfleːə^rti·,
      ō-FLART-ē　oːˈflæ^rti·

Og
   Biblical name　AHG, AWG, ŌG　'ag, 'ɔːg, 'oːg

Ogallala
   city, NE　Ō-guh-LAHL-uh　ˌoːgə'lalə

Ogasawara-shotō
   islands, Pacific Ocean　ō-GAHS-uh-WAHR-uh-SHŌ-tō　oːˌgasə'warə'ʃoːtoː

Ogbomosho
   city, Nigeria　AHG-buh-MŌ-shō　ˌagbə'moːʃoː

Ogden
   city, UT; pers. name　AHG-duhn　'agdən

Ogeechee
   river, GA　ō-GĒ-chē　oːˈgiːtʃiˑ

Key (col. 2):　a: fad　ā: fade　ah: father　ar: marry　aw: law　e: fed　ē: feed　er: merry　i: hid　ī: hide　ō: coat　ōō: boot
oi: boy　ow: now　u: put　uh: above　uhr: bird　ch: chop　ng: ring　sh: show　th: thick　<u>th</u>: this　zh: measure

Ogemaw
   county, MI — Ō-guh-MAW — 'oːgə͵mɔː

Ogilvie
   mtn. range, Canada — Ō-guhl-vē — 'oːgəlviˑ

Ogilvy
   pers. name — Ō-guhl-vē — 'oːgəlviˑ

Oglala
   N. American people — ahg-LAHL-uh, ō-GLAHL-uh — ag'lalə, oː'glalə

Oglala Lakota
   N. American people — ahg-LAHL-uh luh-KŌT-uh, ō-GLAHL-uh — ag'lalə lə'koːʈə, oː'glalə

Oglala Sioux
   N. American people — ahg-LAHL-uh SOO̅, ō-GLAHL-uh — ag'lalə 'suː, oː'glalə

Oglethorpe
   James, English colonizer of GA; county, city, GA — Ō-guhl-THAWRP — 'oːgəl͵θɔːʳp

Ogoki
   river, Canada — ō-GŌ-kē — oː'goːkiˑ

O'Gorman
   Juan, Mexican architect and muralist — ō-GAWR-mahn — oː'gɔːrman

Oglio
   river, Italy — ŌL-yō — 'oːljoː

Ohad
   Biblical name — Ō-HAD, AW-HAHD — 'oː͵hæd, 'ɔː͵had

O'Hara
   pers. name — ō-HAR-uh, ō-HER-uh — oː'hærə, oː'herə

O'Hare
   pers. name — ō-HAR, ō-HER — oː'hæʳ, oː'heʳ

Ohel
   Biblical name — Ō-HEL, AW-HEL — 'oː͵hel, 'ɔː͵hel

Ohio
   river, state, US; county, IN, KY, WV — ō-HĪ-ō, uh-HĪ-uh — oː'haioː, ə'haiə

Ohira
   Masayoshi, prime minister, Japan — ō-hē-rah — oːhiːra

Ohlin
   Bertil, Swedish economist, politician (Nobel 1977) — Ō-lin — 'oːlin

Ohm
   Georg S., German physicist; electrical unit — ŌM — 'oːm

Ohoopee
   river, GA — ō-HOO̅-pē — oː'huːpiˑ

Ohrid
   lake, Albania, Macedonia — ŌKH-RĒD, Ō-KRĒD — 'oːx͵riːd, 'oː͵kriːd

Oireachtas
   Irish parliament — AWR-yuhkh-tuhs — 'ɔːrjəxtəs

Oise
   river, dept, France — WAHZ — waːz

Oistrakh
   David Fyodorovich, Russian violinist — OI-STRAHKH, OI-STRAHK — 'ɔi͵strax, 'ɔi͵strak

Ojai
   city, CA — Ō-HĪ — 'oː͵hai

Ojibwa [Chippewa]
   N. American people — ō-JIB-wā, -wuh — oː'dʒibweː, -wə

Foreign Sounds: ue: *Fr.* **rue**, *Ger.* **füllen**   uh(r): *Fr.* **boeuf**, *Ger.* **Höhle**   <u>kh</u>: *Ger.* **ich**, *Scot.* **loch**   g̱: *Sp.* **amigo**   v̱: *Sp.* **hablar** hl: *Welsh* **Llanelli.**   CAPITALS: primary stress.   SMALL CAPS: secondary stress.   Ⓢ: U.S. pron.   Ⓔ: British pron.

Ojos del Salado
　mtn., Argentina　　Ō-hōz <u>th</u>el sah-LAH-<u>th</u>ō, Ⓢ Ō-hōz　'oːhoːz ðel saˈlaðoː,
　　　　　　　　　　　DEL suh-LAHD-ō　　　　　　　　Ⓢ 'oːhoːz ˌdel səˈladoː

Okaloosa
　county, FL　　Ō-kuh-LOO̅-suh　　ˌoːkəˈluːsə

Okaloosa-Walton
　junior college, FL　　Ō-kuh-LOO̅-suh-WAWLT-n, -WAHLT-n　　ˌoːkəˈluːsəˈwɔːltn̩, -ˈwaltn̩

Okanagan
　lake, college, Canada; river, Canada　　Ō-kuh-NAHG-uhn　　ˌoːkəˈnagən
　　& US

Okanogan
　county, WA; US spelling of　　Ō-kuh-NAHG-uhn　　ˌoːkəˈnagən
　　Okanagan

Okavango
　river, Africa　　Ō-kuh-VANG-gō　　ˌoːkəˈvæŋgoː

Okayama
　city, Japan　　ō-kah-yahm-ah　　oːkajama

Okeechobee
　lake, county, FL　　Ō-kuh-CHŌ-bē　　ˌoːkəˈtʃoːbiˑ

O'Keefe
　Miles, *actor*　　ō-KĒF　　oːˈkiːf

O'Keeffe
　Georgia, *US artist*　　ō-KĒF　　oːˈkiːf

Okefenokee
　swamp land, wildlife refuge, GA　　Ō-kē-fuh-NŌ-kē　　ˌoːkiˑfəˈnoːkiˑ

Okfuskee
　county, OK　　ōk-FUHS-kē　　oːkˈfəskiˑ

Okhotsk
　sea, Russia　　UH-<u>KH</u>AWTSK, ō-<u>KH</u>AHTSK,　　ˌəˈxɔːtsk, oːˈxatsk,
　　　　　　　　　Ⓢ ō-KAHTSK　　　　　　　　　Ⓢ oːˈkatsk

Oki
　Japanese electronics co.　　Ō-kē　　'oːkiˑ

Okie
　native or inhabitant of Oklahoma　　Ō-kē　　'oːkiˑ

Okinawa
　island, Pacific　　Ō-kuh-NAH-wuh　　ˌoːkəˈnawə

Okinawan
　pert. to Okinawa　　Ō-kuh-NAH-wuhn　　ˌoːkəˈnawən

Oklahoma
　state, US　　Ō-kluh-HŌ-muh　　ˌoːkləˈhoːmə

Oklawaha
　river, FL　　AHK-luh-WAW-haw　　ˌakləˈwɔːhɔː

Okmulgee
　1. city, county, OK　　ōk-MUHL-gē　　oːkˈməlgiˑ
　2. see Ocmulgee

Okoboji
　East, West, *lakes, IA*　　Ō-kuh-BŌ-jē　　ˌoːkəˈboːdʒiˑ

Okobojo Creek
　river, SD　　Ō-kuh-BŌ-jō KRĒK, KRIK　　ˌoːkəˈboːdʒoː 'kriːk, 'krik

Okocim
　Polish beer　　aw-KAW-chēm　　ɔːˈkɔːtʃiːm

Okolona
　city, MS　　Ō-kuh-LŌ-nuh　　ˌoːkəˈloːnə

Oksana
　pers. name (O. Baiul)　　ahk-SAHN-uh　　akˈsanə

Key (col. 2):　a: fad　ā: fade　ah: father　ar: marry　aw: law　e: fed　ē: feed　er: merry　i: hid　ī: hide　ō: coat　oo̅: boot
oi: boy　ow: now　u: put　uh: above　uhr: bird　ch: chop　ng: ring　sh: show　th: thick　<u>th</u>: this　zh: measure

Oktibbeha
   county, MS   ahk-TIB-uh-HAW   ɑk'tibə‚hɔː

Oktoberfest
   German festival   ahk-TŌ-buhr-FEST   ɑk'toːbə^r‚fest

Olaf
   1. pers. name   Ō-luhf, Ō-luhv   'oːləf, 'oːləv
   2. Danish   Ō-LAHF   'oː‚lɑːf
   3. Norwegian   Ō-LAHF   'oː‚lɑf
   4. Swedish   OO̅-lahf, OO̅-lahv   'uːlɑːf, 'uːlɑːv

Olajuwon
   Hakeem, *Nigerian basketball player*   ō-LĪ-juh-wahn   oː'lɑidʒəwɑn

Olathe
   city, KS   ō-LĀ-thuh   oː'leːθə

Olaus
   1. pers. name, Danish ō-LOWS   oː'lɑus
   2. German   ō-LAH-us, Ō-LOWS   oː'lɑ-us, 'oː‚lɑus
   3. Latin   uh-LĀ-uhs, ō-LĀ-uhs ə'leːəs, oː'leːəs
   4. Swedish   oo̅-LAH-uhs   u'lɑəs

Olav
   pers. name, Norwegian Ō-LAHV, Ō-LAHF   'oː‚lɑv, 'oː‚lɑf

Oldham
   town, England   ŌL-duhm   'oːldəm

Oldsmobile
   US automobile co. ŌL(D)Z-mō-BĒL, ŌL(D)Z-muh-BĒL   'oːl(d)zmoː‚biːl,
                                                       'oːl(d)zmə‚biːl

Oldsquaw
   duck   ŌL(D)-SKWAW   'oːl(d)‚skwɔː

Olduvai
   Gorge, *Tanzania*   ŌL-duh-WĀ, ŌL-duh-VĀ   'oːldə‚weː, 'oːldə‚veː

Ole
   pers. name, Danish, Norwegian Ō-luh   'oːlə

Olean
   city, NY   ō-lē-AN, Ō-lē-AN   ‚oːliː'æn, 'oːliː‚æn

Oleander
   plant   Ō-lē-AN-duhr, ō-lē-AN-duhr   'oːliː‚ændə^r, ‚oːliː'ændə^r

Oleg
   pers. name, Russian AW-leg   'ɔːleg

Oléron, Ile d'
   island, France   ēl daw-lā-RAW^n iːl dɔːleːrɔ̃

Olga
   1. pers. name   AWL-guh, AHL-guh, ŌL-guh   'ɔːlgə, 'ɑlgə, 'oːlgə
   2. Russian   AWL-guh   'ɔːlgə

Oligocene
   geologic epoch   AHL-i-gō-SĒN, Ō-li-gō-, uh-LIG-uh-   'ɑligoː‚siːn, 'oːligoː-, ə'ligə-

Olimbia [Olympia]
   village, Greece   ō-LIM-bē-uh   oː'limbiːə

Olin
   US defense products co. Ō-luhn   'oːlən

Oliphant
   Pat, *US cartoonist*   AHL-uh-fuhnt   'ɑləfənt

Olivaceous
   flycatcher   AHL-uh-VĀ-shuhs   ‚ɑlə'veːʃəs

Olive
   pers. name   AHL-iv, AHL-uhv   'ɑliv, 'ɑləv

Oliver
  pers. name   AHL-uh-vuhr   'ɑləvəʳ

Olivet
  1. city, MI   AHL-uh-VET   ,ɑlə'vet
  2. town, SD   Ō-luh-VET   'oːlə,vet
  3. Biblical name   AHL-uh-VET   'ɑlə,vet

Olivette
  city, MO   AHL-uh-VET   'ɑlə,vet

Olivetti
  Italian manufacturing co. AHL-uh-VET-ē   ,ɑlə'veṭiˑ

Olivia
  pers. name   uh-LIV-ē-uh, ō-   ə'liviːə, oː-

Olivier
  1. Sir Laurence, British actor; pers. ō-LIV-ē-Ā, uh-LIV-ē-Ā   oː'liviː,eː, ə'liviː,eː
    name
  2. Dutch   Ō-li-VIR   'oːli,vir
  3. French   aw-lēv-YĀ   ɔːliːvjeː

Ollie
  pers. name   AHL-ē   'ɑliˑ

Olmec
  N. American people   AHL-MEK, ŌL-MEK, AWL-MEK   'ɑl,mek, 'oːl,mek, 'ɔːl,mek

Olmos
  Edward James, *US actor*   ŌL-muhs   'oːlməs

Olmsted
  Frederick Law, *US landscape* ŌM-stuhd, ŌM-STED, AHM-   'oːmstəd, 'oːm,sted, 'ɑm-
    architect

Olney
  city, IL; city, TX   AHL-nē   'ɑlniˑ

Olof
  pers. name, Swedish   O̅O̅-lawv, O̅O̅-lawf, ⑤ Ō-luhf, Ō-LAHF   'uːlɔːv, 'uːlɔːf, ⑤ 'oːləf,
                                                          'oː,lɑf

Oloroso
  type of sherry   ō-luh-RŌ-sō   oːlə'roːsoː

Olsen
  Merlin, *US sports analyst, football* ŌL-suhn   'oːlsən
    player

Olus
  giant in Etruscan legend   Ō-luhs   'oːləs

Olustee
  village, FL   ō-LUHS-tē   oː'ləstiˑ

Olympe
  pers. name, French   aw-LEⁿP   ɔːlẽp

Olyphant
  borough, PA   AW-luh-fuhnt, Ō-luh-fuhnt   'ɔːləfənt, 'oːləfənt

Olympia
  city, WA; village, ancient city, uh-LIM-pē-uh, ō-   ə'limpiːə, oː-
    Greece; pers. name

Olympiad
  four-year period between Olympic ō-LIM-pē-uhd, ō-LIM-pē-AD   oː'limpiːəd, oː'limpiː,æd
    games

Olympian
  pert. to Mount Olympus   ō-LIM-pē-uhn   oː'limpiːən

Olympias
  Macedonian queen   uh-LIM-pē-uhs, ō-   ə'limpiːəs, oː-

Key (col. 2):   a: fad ā: fade ah: father ar: marry aw: law e: fed ē: feed er: merry i: hid ī: hide ō: coat o̅o̅: boot
oi: boy ow: now u: put uh: above uhr: bird ch: chop ng: ring sh: show th: thick th: this zh: measure

Olympic
   pert. to Olympic Games *or to*   ō-LIM-pik   oː'limpik
     Olympia

Olympus
   mtn., Greece, home of Greek gods   uh-LIM-puhs, ō-   ə'limpəs, oː-

Olympus Mons
   mtn., Mars, highest in solar system   uh-LIM-puhs MAHNZ, ō-LIM-puhs,   ə'limpəs 'mɑnz, oː'limpəs,
                                MŌNZ   'moːnz

Olynthus
   Macedonian town   ō-LIN-thuhs   oː'linθəs

Om
   Hindu mantra   ŌM   'oːm

Om
   river, Russia   AWM   'ɔːm

Omagh
   administrative county, Northern   Ō-MAH, Ō-muh   'oːˌmɑː, 'oːmə
     Ireland

Omagua
   S. American people   ō-MAH(G)-wuh, ō-MAHḠ-wah   oː'mɑ(g)wə, oː'mɑɣwɑ

Omaha
   city, NE; beach, France; N. American   Ō-muh-HAW, Ō-muh-HAH   'oːməˌhɔː, 'oːməˌhɑ
     people

Omak
   lake, city, WA   Ō-MAK   'oːˌmæk

Oman
   sultanate, Asia; Gulf of, *arm of*   ō-MAHN, ō-MAN   oː'mɑn, oː'mæn
     Arabian Sea

Omani
   pert. to Oman   ō-MAHN-ē, ō-MAN-ē   oː'mɑniˑ, oː'mæniˑ

Omar
   1. pers. name   Ō-MAHR   'oːˌmɑr
   2. French   aw-MAHR   ɔːmɑːr

Omar Khayyám
   Persian writer, astronomer   Ō-MAHR KĪ-(Y)AHM, KĪ-(Y)AM   ˌoːˌmɑr ˌkɑiˈ(j)ɑm,
                                            ˌkɑiˈ(j)æm

Omdurman
   city, Sudan   AHM-duhr-MAN   ˌɑmdəʳˈmæn

Omega
   last letter of the Greek alphabet   ō-MEG-uh, ō-MĒ-guh, ō-MĀ-guh   oː'megə, oː'miːgə, oː'meːgə

Omer
   49 days from Passover to Shabuoth   Ō-muhr, Ō-MER, ō-MER   'oːməʳ, 'oːˌmeʳ, oː'meʳ

Omisoka
   Grand Last Day (Dec. 31), Japan   ō-mis-ō-kah   oːmisoːkɑ

Omizutori
   Japanese ritual   ō-mē-zoo-tōr-ē   oːmiːzuːtoːriˑ

O-Mizutori Matsuri
   Japanese festival   ō-mē-zoo-tōr-ē maht-sur-ē   oːmiːzuːtoːriˑ mɑtsuriˑ

Omnigraphics
   US publishing co.   AHM-ni-GRAF-iks   ˌɑmni'græfiks

Omoo
   novel, H. Melville   Ō-MOO   'oːˌmuː

Omphale
   wife of Heracles   AHM-fuh-lē   'ɑmfəliˑ

Ompompanoosuc
   river, VT   ahm-PAHM-puh-NOO-suhk   ɑmˌpɑmpə'nuːsək

Foreign Sounds: ue: *Fr.* **rue**, *Ger.* f**ü**llen   uh(r): *Fr.* b**oeu**f, *Ger.* H**öh**le   <u>kh</u>: *Ger.* i**ch**, *Scot.* lo**ch**   ḡ: *Sp.* ami**g**o   ᴠ: *Sp.* ha**b**lar
hl: *Welsh* **Ll**anelli.   CAPITALS: primary stress.   SMALL CAPS: secondary stress.   ⑤: U.S. pron.   ⓔ: British pron.

Omri
  Biblical name   AHM-RĬ, -RĒ; ahm-RĒ   'am͵rɑi, -͵riː; am'riː
Omro
  city, WI   AHM-RŌ   'am͵roː
OMRON
  Japanese co.   ŌM-RAHN   'oːm͵rɑn
Omsk
  city, Russia   AWM(P)SK, AHM(P)SK   'ɔːm(p)sk, 'am(p)sk
Omsk
  city, Siberian Russia   AWM(P)SK, AHM(P)SK   'ɔːm(p)sk, 'am(p)sk
On
  Biblical name   AHN, AWN, ŌN   'an, 'ɔːn, 'oːn
Ona
  S. American people   Ō-nuh   'oːnə
Onam
  Hindu festival   Ō-nuhm   'oːnəm
Onan
  Biblical character, son of Judah   Ō-NAN, Ō-nuhn   'oː͵næn, 'oːnən
Onassis
  Jacqueline Bouvier Kennedy, *US*   ō-NAS-uhs   oː'næsəs
    editor; Greek/US shipping family
Onawa
  city, IA   AHN-uh-WAH, -wuh   'anə͵wa, -wə
Oncoba
  plant   AHNG-kuh-buh, AHN-kuh-buh   'aŋkəbə, 'ankəbə
Ondine
  play, Giraudoux   awⁿ-DĒN   ɔ̃diːn
Oneco
  urban community, FL   ō-NĒ-KŌ   oː'niː͵koː
Onega
  lake, Europe   ōn-YEG-uh   oːn'jegə
Oneida
  US pl. name; N. American people   ō-NĪD-uh   oː'nɑidə
O'Neill
  Eugene, *US playwright (Nobel*   ō-NĒL   oː'niːl
    1936)
Oneiros
  dream demon sent by Zeus to   ō-NĪ-ruhs   oː'nɑirəs
    Agamemnon
Oneonta
  city, AL, NY   Ō-nē-AHNT-uh   ͵oːniː'antə
Onesimus
  Biblical name   ō-NES-uh-muhs   oː'nesəməs
Onezhskoye, Ozero [Onega]
  lake, Europe   UHZ-YER-ō UHN-YESH-kuh-yuh   ͵əz'jeroː ͵ən'jeʃkəjə
Onida
  city, SD   ō-NĪD-uh   oː'nɑidə
Onions
  Charles T., *English lexicographer*   UHN-yuhnz   'ənjənz
    and philologist
Onnes
  see Kamerlingh Onnes
Ono
  1. Yoko, *US artist*   Ō-nō   'oːnoː
  2. Biblical name   Ō-nō, ō-NŌ   'oːnoː, oː'noː

Key (col. 2):   a: fad ā: fade ah: father ar: marry aw: law e: fed ē: feed er: merry i: hid ī: hide ō: coat ōō: boot
oi: boy   ow: now   u: put   uh: above   uhr: bird   ch: chop   ng: ring   sh: show   th: thick   th̲: this   zh: measure

Onondaga
  lake, county, NY; N. American people   AHN-uh(n)-DAHG-uh, -DĀ-guh   ˌɑnə(n)'dɑgə, -'deːgə
Onsager
  Lars, *US chemist (Nobel 1968)*   AWN-SAHG-uhr, AHN-   'ɔːnˌsɑgəʳ, 'ɑn-
Ons Hémécht
  national anthem, Luxembourg   AWNS HĀ-māk̲h̲t   'ɔːns 'heːmeːxt
Onslow
  county, NC   AHNZ-lō   'ɑnzloː
Ontario
  province, Canada; county, NY   ahn-TER-ē-ō, ahn-TAR-ē-ō   ɑn'teriːoː, ɑn'tæriːoː
Ontonagon
  county, MI   AHN-tuh-NAW-guhn,   ˌɑntə'nɔːgən, ˌɑntə'nɑgən
      AHN-tuh-NAHG-uhn
Oodnadatta
  township, Australia   ŌŌD-nuh-DAT-uh   ˌuˑdnə'dætə
Oona, Oonagh
  pers. name   ŌŌ-nuh   'uːnə
Oort Cloud
  'cloud' of comets   AWRT KLOWD, ŌRT   'ɔːʳt ˌklɑud, 'oːʳt
Oostanaula
  river, GA   ŌŌ-stuh-NAW-luh   ˌuːstə'nɔːlə
Oostende [Ostend]
  prov & town, Belgium   ō-STEN-duh   oː'stendə
Opa-Locka
  city, FL   Ō-puh-LAHK-uh   ˌoːpə'lɑkə
Opatija
  town, Croatia   ō-ṖAHT-ē-(y)uh   oː'paṭiː(j)ə
OPEC
  Organization of Petroleum Exporting   Ō-PEK   'oːˌpek
    Countries
Opel
  tdmk for a German car   Ō-puhl   'oːpəl
Opelika
  city, AL   Ō-puh-LĪ-kuh   ˌoːpə'lɑikə
Opelousas
  city, LA   AHP-uh-LŌŌ-suhs   ˌɑpə'luːsəs
Opequon
  village, creek, VA   ō-PEK-uhn   oː'pekən
Opéra
  French for opera   aw-pā-RAH   ɔːpeːrɑː
Ophel
  Biblical name   Ō-FEL, Ō-fuhl, AW-fel   'oːˌfel, 'oːfəl, 'ɔːfel
Ophelia
  character in Hamlet, Shakespeare   ō-FĒL-yuh   oː'fiːljə
Ophir
  Biblical land rich in gold   Ō-fuhr   'oːfəʳ
Ophism
  Gnostic serpent worship   AHF-IZ-uhm, Ō-FIZ-uhm   'ɑfˌizəm, 'oːˌfizəm
Ophiuchids
  meteor shower   Ō-fē-(Y)ŌŌ-kidz, AHF-ē-   ˌoːfiː'(j)uːkidz, ˌɑfiː-
Ophiuchus
  constellation   Ō-fē-(Y)ŌŌ-kuhs, AHF-ē-   ˌoːfiː'(j)uːkəs, ˌɑfiː-
Ophni
  Biblical name   AHF-NĪ, ahf-NĒ   'ɑfˌnɑi, ɑf'niː

Foreign Sounds: ue: *Fr.* **rue**, *Ger.* **füllen** uh(r): *Fr.* **boeuf**, *Ger.* **Höhle** k̲h̲: *Ger.* **ich**, *Scot.* **loch** g̲: *Sp.* **amigo** v̲: *Sp.* **hablar** hl: *Welsh* **Llanelli**. CAPITALS: primary stress. SMALL CAPS: secondary stress. Ⓢ: U.S. pron. Ⓔ: British pron.

Ophrah
   Biblical name   AHF-ruh, Ō-fruh, ahf-RAH   'afrə, 'oːfrə, afˈrɑ

Opimius
   Lucius, *Roman politician*   ō-PIM-ē-uhs   oːˈpimiːəs

Opinaca, Opinaka
   river, Canada   ō-PIN-uh-KAW   oːˈpinəˌkɔː

Oporto [Porto]
   port city, Portugal   ō-PŌRT-ō, ō-PAWRT-ō   oːˈpoːˡtoː, oːˈpɔːˡtoː

Oppenheimer
   J. Robert, *US physicist*   AHP-uhn-HĪ-muhr   'apən,haiməˡ

Oprah
   pers. name (O. Winfrey)   Ō-pruh   'oːprə

Ops
   Roman goddess of plenty   AHPS   'ɑps

Optacon
   tdmk for reading machines for the AHP-tuh-KAHN, AHP-tuh-kuhn   'aptəˌkɑn, 'aptəkən
   blind

Optimates
   Roman senatorial faction   AHP-tuh-MĀT-ēz   ˌaptəˈmeːʈiːz

Optimator
   German beer   AWP-ti-MAH-tawr   ˌɔptiˈmatəˡ

Oquirrh
   mtn. range, UT   Ō-kuhr   'oːkəˡ

Oradea
   city, Romania   aw-RAHD-yah   ɔːˈrɑdjɑ

Oradell
   borough, NJ   ŌR-uh-DEL, AWR-   'oːrəˌdel, 'ɔːr-

Oran
   seaport, Algeria   ō-RAHN   oːˈrɑn

Orange
   1. city, France   aw-RAHⁿZH   ɔːrɑ̃ʒ
   2. pl. name, US   AHR-inj, AHR-uhnj, AHRNJ, AWR-inj,   'arindʒ, 'arəndʒ, 'aˡndʒ,
                           AWR-uhnj, AWRNJ   'ɔːrindʒ, 'ɔːrəndʒ, 'ɔːˡndʒ

Orangutan
   type of ape   uh-RANG-uh-TANG, uh-RANG-uh-TAN   ə'ræŋəˌtæŋ, ə'ræŋəˌtæn

Oranjeboom
   Dutch beer   aw-RAHN-yuh-BŌM   ɔːˈranjəˌboːm

Oraoni [Kurukh]
   lang., people, India   ō-RAH-Ō-nē   oːˈrɑˌoːniˑ

Oraon [Kurukh]
   lang., people, India   ō-RAH-ŌN   oːˈrɑˌoːn

Orazio
   pers. name, Italian   ō-RAHT-syō   oːˈratsjoː

Orbison
   Roy, *rock musician*   AWR-buh-suhn   'ɔːˡbəsən

Orca
   killer whale   AWR-kuh   'ɔːˡkə

Orcadian
   inhabitant of the Orkney Islands awr-KĀD-ē-uhn   ɔːˡˈkeːdiːən

Orcus [Dis]
   Roman god of the Underworld   AWR-kuhs   'ɔːˡkəs

Key (col. 2):   a: fad ā: fade ah: father ar: marry aw: law e: fed ē: feed er: merry i: hid ī: hide ō: coat ōō: boot
oi: boy ow: now u: put uh: above uhr: bird ch: chop ng: ring sh: show th: thick <u>th</u>: this zh: measure

Orczy
    Emmuska Magdalena Rosalia   AWRT-sē   'ɔːʳtsiˑ
    Marie Josepha Barbara,
    Baroness, *Hungarian-born British*
    novelist and playwright

Ordoñez
    Antonio, *Spanish bullfighter;*   awr-THAWN-yāth   ɔːr'ðɔːnjeːθ
    Bartolomé, *Spanish sculptor*

Ordovician
    geologic period   awrd-uh-VISH-uhn   ɔːʳdə'viʃən

Ordzhonikidze
    city, Russia   AWR-JAHN-uh-KID-zuh   ˌɔːʳˌdʒɑnə'kidzə

Oreb
    Biblical name   ŌR-EB, AWR-EB, –uhb; ō-REV   'oːrˌeb, 'ɔːrˌeb, -əb; oː'rev

Oregon
    state, US   AWR-uh-guhn, AHR-uh-guhn; *by*   'ɔːrəgən, 'ɑrəgən; *by*
                        outsiders often AWR-uh-GAHN, AHR-   *outsiders often* 'ɔːrəˌgɑn,
                                                                  'ɑr-

Oregonian
    pert. to Oregon   AWR-i-GŌ-nē-uhn, AHR-i-GŌ-nē-uhn,   ˌɔːri'goːniːən, ˌɑri'goːniːən,
                              -GŌN-yuhn   -'goːnjən

Orel
    Russian port   awr-YAWL, aw-REL   ɔːʳjɔːl, ɔː'rel

Orem
    town, UT   ŌR-uhm, AWR-uhm   'oːrəm, 'ɔːrəm

Oren
    pers. name   Ō-ruhn, AWR-uhn   'oːrən, 'ɔːrən

Orenthal
    pers. name (O.J. Simpson)   AWR-uhn-THAWL, ŌR-, -THAHL   'ɔːrənˌθɔːl, 'oːr-, -ˌθɑl

Orense
    prov, Spain   ō-REN(T)-sā   oː'ren(t)seː

Oreo
    tdmk for a sandwich cookie   ŌR-ē-Ō, AWR-ē-Ō   'oːriːˌoː, 'ɔːriːˌoː

Oreopithicus
    genus of fossil primate   AWR-ē-uh-PITH-i-kuhs   ˌɔːriːə'piθikəs

Orest
    pers. name, Russian   UHR-YĀST   ˌər'jeːst

Oreste
    pers. name, Italian   ō-RES-tā   oː'resteː

Oresteia
    tragic trilogy, Aeschylus   AWR-uh-STĪ-uh, AWR-uh-STĀ-uh,   ˌɔːrə'staiə, ˌɔːrə'steːə,
                              AWR-uh-STĒ-uh   ˌɔːrə'stiːə

Orestes
    son of Agamemnon and   uh-RES-tēz, aw-RES-tēz   ə'restiːz, ɔː'restiːz
    Clytemnestra; tragedy, Euripides;
    pers. name

Orff
    Carl, *German composer*   AWRF   'ɔːʳf

Oriel
    college, Oxford Univ.   AWR-ē-uhl   'ɔːriːəl

Orient
    Eastern hemisphere   ŌR-ē-uhnt, AWR-ē-uhnt, -ENT   'oːriːənt, 'ɔːriːənt, -ˌent

Oriental
    pert. to the Orient   ŌR-ē-ENT-l, AWR-ē-ENT-l   ˌoːriː'entl̩, ˌɔːriː'entl̩

Foreign Sounds: ue: *Fr.* **rue**, *Ger.* **füllen**   uh(r): *Fr.* **boeuf**, *Ger.* **Höhle**   kh: *Ger.* **ich**, *Scot.* **loch**   ḡ: *Sp.* **amigo**   v: *Sp.* **hablar**
hl: *Welsh* **Llanelli**.   CAPITALS: primary stress.   SMALL CAPS: secondary stress.   Ⓢ: U.S. pron.   Ⓔ: British pron.

Orientale, Mare
   see Mare Orientale
Oriente
   prov, Cuba   ōr-ē-EN-tā, ⑤ ŌR-ē-ENT-ē,   oːriː'enteː, ⑤ ˌoːriː'enti·,
                                 AWR-ē-ENT-ē   ˌɔːriː'enti·

Origen
   Christian theologian   AWR-i-juhn, AHR-i-juhn   'ɔːridʒən, 'aridʒən
Origenism
   adherence to the teachings of Origen   AWR-uh-juh-NIZ-uhm, AHR-,   'ɔːʳədʒəˌnizəm, 'aʳ-,
                                   -JEN-IZ-uhm   -,dʒenˌizəm
Orinda
   community, CA   uh-RIN-duh, aw-RIN-duh   ə'rində, ɔː'rində
Orinoco
   river, Venezuela   ŌR-uh-NŌ-kō, AWR-   ˌoːrə'noːkoː, ˌɔːr-
Oriole
   songbird   ŌR-ē-ŌL, AWR-, -ē-uhl   'oːriːˌoːl, 'ɔːr-, -iːəl
Orion
   giant Boeotian hunter; constellation   uh-RĪ-uhn, aw-RĪ-uhn   ə'raiən, ɔː'raiən
Orionids
   meteor shower   AWR-ē-AHN-idz, uh-RĪ-uh-nidz   ˌɔriː'anidz, ə'raiənidz
Oriskany
   village, NY   aw-RIS-kuh-nē   ɔː'riskəni·
Orissa
   state, India   aw-RIS-uh   ɔː'risə
Oriya
   lang., people, India   aw-RĒ-(y)uh   ɔː'riː(j)ə
Orizaba [Citlaltépetl]
   mtn., city, Mexico   AWR-ē-SAH<u>V</u>-ah, ⑤ ŌR-uh-ZAHB-uh,   ˌɔːriː'saβa, ⑤ ˌoːrə'zabə,
                           AWR-   ˌɔːr-
Orkney
   islands, Scotland   AWRK-nē   'ɔːʳkni·
Orlando
   1. city, FL; pers. name   awr-LAN-dō, awr-LAHN-dō   ɔːʳ'lændoː, ɔːʳ'landoː
   2. Italian   ōr-LAHN-dō   oːr'landoː
Orléannais
   prov, France   awr-lā-ah-NE   ɔːrleːaːne
Orleans
   1. parish, LA   AWR-lē-uhnz, AWRL-(y)uhnz   'ɔːʳli·ənz, 'ɔːʳl(j)ənz
   2. county, NY   AWR-lēnz   'ɔːʳliːnz
   3. county, VT; town, MA   awr-LĒNZ   ɔːʳ'liːnz
Orléans
   town, France   awr-lā-AHⁿ   ɔːrleːã
Orlich
   Francisco, *president, Costa Rica*   awr-LĒCH   ɔːʳ'liːtʃ
Orlon
   tdmk for a synthetic acrylic   AWR-LAHN   'ɔːʳˌlan
Orlov trotter
   horse breed   AWR-LAHF, AWR-LAWF, awr-LAWF   'ɔːʳˌlaf, 'ɔːʳˌlɔːf, ɔːʳ'lɔːf
Orly
   city, airport, France   awr-LĒ   ɔːrliː
Ormandy
   Eugene, *US conductor*   AWR-muhn-dē   'ɔːʳməndi·
Ormazd
   Zoroastrian god   AWR-MAHZD   'ɔːʳˌmazd

Key (col. 2): a: f**a**d ā: f**a**de ah: f**a**ther ar: m**a**rry aw: l**a**w e: f**e**d ē: f**ee**d er: m**e**rry i: h**i**d ī: h**i**de ō: c**oa**t ōō: b**oo**t
oi: b**oy** ow: n**ow** u: p**u**t uh: **a**bove uhr: b**ir**d ch: **ch**op ng: ri**ng** sh: **sh**ow th: **th**ick <u>th</u>: **th**is zh: mea**s**ure

Ornan
  Biblical name   AWR-nuhn, AWR-NAN, ahr-NAHN   'ɔːʳnən, 'ɔːʳˌnæn, ɑr'nɑn
Orne
  1. river, dept, France   AWRN   ɔːrn
  2. pers. name (S. O. Jewett)   AWRN   'ɔːʳn
Ornithischia
  dinosaur order   AWR-nuh-THIS-kē-uh   ˌɔːʳnəˈθiskiːə
Ornitholestes
  dinosaur   AWR-nuh-thō-LES-TĒZ   ˌɔːʳnəθoːˈlesˌtiːz
Ornithomimus
  dinosaur   AWR-nuh-thō-MĪ-muhs   ˌɔːʳnəθoːˈmaiməs
Ornithopoda
  dinosaur suborder   AWR-nuh-THAHP-uhd-uh   ˌɔːʳnəˈθapədə
Ornithosuchus
  dinosaur   AWR-nuh-THŌ-si-kuhs   ˌɔːʳnəˈθoːsikəs
Orofino
  city, ID   AWR-uh-FĒ-nō   ˌɔːrəˈfiːnoː
Orokaiva
  lang., people, New Guinea   AWR-uh-KĪ-vuh   ˌɔːrəˈkaivə
Orominga
  lang., Ethiopia   AWR-uh-MING-guh   ˌɔːrəˈmiŋgə
Oromo [Galla]
  lang., Ethiopia, Kenya   ŌR-uh-MŌ, AWR-uh-MŌ   'oːrəˌmoː, 'ɔːrəˌmoː
Orontes
  mtn., Iran; river, Syria; Hindu hero   awr-AHN-TĒZ, ō-RAHN-TĒZ   ɔːrˈanˌtiːz, oːˈranˌtiːz
  wounded by Dionysus
Oroville
  city, dam, CA; town, WA   AWR-uh-VIL   'ɔːrəˌvil
Orozco
  José Clemente, Mexican painter   ō-RŌS-kō, ⓢ ō-RAWS-kō   oːˈroːskoː, ⓢ oːˈrɔːskoː
Orpah
  Biblical name   AWR-puh, ahr-PAH   'ɔːʳpə, ɑrˈpɑː
Orphean
  pert. to Orpheus   AWR-fē-uhn   'ɔːʳfiːən
Orpheus
  mythogical Greek musician; pers.   AWR-FYOOS, AWR-fē-uhs   'ɔːʳˌfjuːs, 'ɔːʳfiːəs
  name
Orphic
  pert. to Orpheus, his music, or cult   AWR-fik   'ɔːʳfik
  of Dionysus
Orphism
  mystic Greek religion   AWR-FIZ-uhm   'ɔːʳˌfizəm
Orpington
  breed of fowl   AWR-ping-tuhn   'ɔːʳpiŋtən
Orr
  1. Robert G. (Bobby), Canadian   AWR   'ɔːʳ
  hockey player
  2. see Boyd Orr
Orren
  pers. name   AWR-uhn, AHR-uhn   'ɔːrən, 'arən
Orson
  pers. name   AWR-suhn   'ɔːʳsən
Ørsted
  see Oersted

Foreign Sounds: ue: *Fr.* **rue**, *Ger.* **füllen**   uh(r): *Fr.* **boeuf**, *Ger.* **Höhle**   <u>kh</u>: *Ger.* **ich**, *Scot.* **loch**   ğ: *Sp.* **amigo**   <u>v</u>: *Sp.* **hablar**
hl: *Welsh* **Llanelli**.   CAPITALS: primary stress.   SMALL CAPS: secondary stress.   ⓢ: U.S. pron.   ⓔ: British pron.

Ortega
 Saavedra Daniel, *president,*   awr-TĀ-ḡah, ⓢ awr-TĀ-guh   ɔːrˈteːɣɑ, ⓢ ɔːˈrteːgə
 Nicaragua

Ortega y Gasset
 Jose, *Spanish philosopher*   awr-TĀ-ḡah ē ḡah-SET   ɔːrˈteːɣɑ iː ɣɑˈset

Orthagoras
 tyrant of Sicyon   awr-THAG-uh-ruhs   ɔːˈrθæɡərəs

Orthopolis
 king of Sicyon   awr-THAHP-uh-luhs   ɔːˈrθɑpələs

Orthros
 dog of Geryon   AWR-THRŌS   ˈɔːrˌθroːs

Ortón
 river, Peru, Bolivia   awr-TŌN   ɔːrˈtoːn

Orton
 Joe, *British playwright*   AWR-tn   ˈɔːrtn̩

Oruro
 dept, Bolivia   aw-RUR-ō   ɔːˈruroː

Orust
 island, Sweden   O͞O-RUHST   ˈuːˌrəst

Orval
 Belgian beer   AWR-vahl   ˈɔːrvɑl

Orvieto
 commune, Italy   AWR-vē-ĀT-ō   ˌɔːrviːˈeːtoː

Orville
 pers. name   AWR-vuhl   ˈɔːrvəl

Orvon
 pers. name (O. G. Autry)   AWR-vuhn, AWR-VAHN   ˈɔːrvən, ˈɔːrˌvɑn

Orwell
 George, *English writer*   AWR-WEL, AWR-wuhl   ˈɔːrˌwel, ˈɔːrwəl

Osage
 river, MO; county, KS, MO, OK;   ō-SĀJ, Ō-SĀJ   oːˈseːdʒ, ˈoːˌseːdʒ
 Plains, *geographic feature, US; N.*
 American people

Osaka
 city, Japan   ō-sahk-ah, ⓢ ō-SAHK-uh   oːsɑkɑ, ⓢ oːˈsɑkə

Osami
 pers. name, Japanese   ō-sah-mē   oːsɑmiː

Osawatomie
 city, KS   Ō-suh-WAHT-uh-mē   ˌoːsəˈwɑt̬əmiˑ

Osbourne
 Ozzy, *rock singer*   AHZ-BAWRN, AHZ-BUHRN   ˈɑzˌbɔːrn, ˈɑzˌbərn

Oscan
 ancient people, Italy   AHS-kuhn   ˈɑskən

Oscar
 1. pers. name   AHS-kuhr   ˈɑskər
 2. French   aws-KAHR   ɔːskɑːr
 3. German   AWS-KAHR   ˈɔːsˌkɑr
 4. Norwegian   AWS-KAHR   ˈɔːsˌkɑr
 5. Polish, Swedish   AWS-KAHR   ˈɔːsˌkɑːr
 6. Russian   AWS-kuhr   ˈɔːskər

Óscar
 pers. name, Spanish   Ō-skahr   ˈoːskɑr

Oscar de la Renta
 see de la Renta

Key (col. 2):   a: **fad** ā: **fade** ah: **father** ar: **marry** aw: **law** e: **fed** ē: **feed** er: **merry** i: **hid** ī: **hide** ō: **coat** o͞o: **boot**
oi: **boy**   ow: **now**   u: **put**   uh: **above**   uhr: **bird**   ch: **chop**   ng: **ring**   sh: **show**   th: **thick**   <u>th</u>: **this**   zh: **measure**

Oscar Mayer

US food co. AHS-kuhr MĪ(-uh)r ˌɑskəʳ ˈmɑi(ə)ʳ

Osceola

US pl. name; N. American people Ō-sē-Ō-luh, AHS-ē-Ō-luh ˌoːsiːˈoːlə, ˌɑsiːˈoːlə

Oscoda

county, MI ahs-KŌD-uh ɑsˈkoːdə

Osco-Umbrian

ancient Italic lang. family AHS-kō-UHM-brē-uhn ˌɑskoːˈəmbriːən

Osee

Old Testament book Ō-ZĒ, ō-ZĀ-uh ˈoːˌziː, oːˈzeːə

Osgood

Charles, US broadcast journalist; AHZ-GUD ˈɑzˌgud
pers. name

Oshawa

town, Canada AHSH-uh-wuh, AHSH-uh-WAH, ˈɑʃəwə, ˈɑʃəˌwɑ, ˈɑʃəˌwɔː
AHSH-uh-WAW

Osha Peak

mountain, NM Ō-shuh PĒK ˈoːʃə ˈpiːk

Oshea

Biblical name ō-SHĒ-uh, hō-SHĀ-ah oːˈʃiːə, hoːˈʃeːɑ

Oshima [Amami]

island group, Japan ō-shē-mah oːʃiːmɑ

Oskaloosa

city, IA; city, KS AHS-kuh-LOO-suh ˌɑskəˈluːsə

Oshkosh

city, WI; tdmk for clothing AHSH-KAHSH ˈɑʃˌkɑʃ

Osijek

city, Croatia Ō-sē-(Y)EK ˈoːsiːˌ(j)ek

Osip

pers. name, Russian AWS-yip ˈɔːsjip

Osiris

Egyptian god of the Underworld ō-SĪ-ruhs oːˈsɑirəs

Oskar

1. pers. name AHS-kuhr ˈɑskəʳ

2. Finnish, Swedish AWS-KAHR ˈɔːsˌkɑːr

3. German AWS-KAHR ˈɔːsˌkɑʳ

4. Norwegian AWS-KAHR ˈɔːsˌkɑr

Osler

William, Canadian physician AHS-luhr, AHZ-luhr, Ō-sluhr ˈɑsləʳ, ˈɑzləʳ, ˈoːsləʳ

Oslo

city, Norway AHZ-lō, AHS-lō ˈɑzloː, ˈɑsloː

Osman

Turkish emir, founder of Ottoman AHZ-muhn, AHS-muhn, -MAHN ˈɑzmən, ˈɑsmən, -ˌmɑn
dynasty

Osmanli

an Ottoman; lang. of the Ottoman ahz-MAN-lē, ahs- ɑzˈmænliˑ, ɑs-
Turks

osmium

element AHZ-mē-uhm ˈɑzmiːəm

Osmond

Donny, Marie, US singers AHZ-muhnd ˈɑzmənd

Osnabruck, Osnabrück

city, Germany AWS-nuh-BRUEK, Ⓢ AHZ-nuh-BRUK ˈɔːsnəˌbryk, Ⓢ ˈɑznəˌbruk

Ossa

mtn., Greece AHS-uh ˈɑsə

Foreign Sounds: ue: *Fr.* **rue**, *Ger.* **füllen** uh(r): *Fr.* **boeuf**, *Ger.* **Höhle** kh: *Ger.* **ich**, *Scot.* **loch** ḡ: *Sp.* **amigo** v̱: *Sp.* **hablar** hl: *Welsh* **Llanelli**. CAPITALS: primary stress. SMALL CAPS: secondary stress. Ⓢ: U.S. pron. Ⓔ: British pron.

Ossetia
  region, Caucasus Mts.   ah-SĒ-sh(ē-)uh   ɑ'siːʃ(iː)ə
Ossetic
  lang., Caucasus Mts.   uh-SET-ik   ə'setik
Ossian
  Irish legendary hero; pers. name   AHSH-uhn, AHS-ē-uhn, AWSH-uhn   'aʃən, 'asiːən, 'ɔːʃən
Ossietzky
  Carl von, *German pacifist, author*   aws-YET-skē   ɔːs'jetski·
  (Nobel 1935)
Ossining
  town, NY   AHS-uh-ning, AW-suh-ning   'asəniŋ, 'ɔːsəniŋ
Ossip
  pers. name, Russian   AWS-yip   'ɔːsjip
Ossipee
  river, town, NH   AHS-uh-PĒ   'asə͵piː
Ostend
  prov & town, Belgium   ahs-TEND, AHS-TEND   ɑs'tend, 'ɑs͵tend
Österreich [Austria]
  republic, Europe   UH(R)-stuh-RĪ<u>KH</u>   'œːstə͵raiç
Ostia
  port, Italy   AHS-tē-uh, AW-stē-uh   'astiːə, 'ɔːstiːə
Ostian Way
  road from Rome to Ostia   AHS-tē-uhn WĀ, AW-stē-uhn   ͵astiːən 'weː, ͵ɔːstiːən
Ostrava
  city, Czech republic   AW-struh-vuh   'ɔːstrəvə
Ostrogoth
  easterly division of Goths   AHS-truh-GAHTH   'astrə͵gɑθ
Ostrowiec
  commune, site of WWII concentration aw-STRAWV-YETS   ɔː'strɔːv͵jets
  camp, Poland
Ostwald
  Friedrich Wilhelm, *German chemist*   AWST-VAHLT, Ⓢ AHST-WAWLD   'ɔːst͵vɑlt, Ⓢ 'ast͵wɔːld
  (Nobel 1909)
Ostyak [Khanty]
  lang., Khanti-Mansi region, Russia   AHS-tē-AK   'astiː͵æk
Ostyak Samoyed [Selkup]
  lang., Khanti-Mansi region, Russia   AHS-tē-AK SAM-uh-YED, SAM-OI-ED,   'astiː͵æk 'sæmə͵jed,
                                         suh-MOI-(y)uhd   'sæm͵ɔi͵ed, sə'mɔi(j)əd
Oswald
  1. pers. name   AHZ-wuhld, AHZ-WAWLD   'azwəld, 'az͵wɔːld
  2. German   AWS-VAHLT   'ɔːs͵vɑlt
Oswaldo
  pers. name, Portuguese   awzh-WAHL-do͞o, awz-   ɔːʒ'wɑlduː, ɔːz-
Oswego
  pl. name, US   ahs-WĒ-gō   ɑs'wiːgoː
Oswegatchie
  river, NY   AHS-wuh-GAHCH-ē   ͵aswə'gatʃi·
Oświęcim [Auschwitz]
  commune, site of WWII concentration awsh-VYEⁿT-sēm   ɔːʃ'vjētsiːm
  camp, Poland
Osyth
  Christian saint   Ō-zuhth, Ō-suhth   'oːzəθ, 'oːsəθ
Otero
  county, CO, NM   ō-TER-ō   oː'teroː

Key (col. 2): a: fad ā: fade ah: father ar: marry aw: law e: fed ē: feed er: merry i: hid ī: hide ō: coat o͞o: boot
oi: boy ow: now u: put uh: above uhr: bird ch: chop ng: ring sh: show th: thick <u>th</u>: this zh: measure

Othello
  play, Shakespeare   uh-THEL-ō, ō-THEL-ō   ə'θelo:, o:'θelo:
Othmar
  pers. name, German   AWT-MAHR   'ɔ:t,maʳ
Othni
  Biblical name   AHTH-NĪ, aht-NĒ   'aθ,nai, at'ni:
Othniel
  Biblical name   AHTH-nē-EL, -nē-uhl; AHT-nē-EL   'aθni:,el, -ni:əl; ,atni:'el
Otho
  Roman emperor; pers. name   Ō-thō   'o:θo:
Othon
  pers. name, French   aw-TAWⁿ   ɔ:tɔ̃
Otis
  pers. name   ŌT-uhs   'o:təs
Otmar
  pers. name, German   AWT-MAHR   'ɔ:t,maʳ
Oto, Otoe
  N. American people   ŌT-ō   'o:ʈo:
Otoe
  county, NE   ŌT-ō   'o:ʈo:
Otoe Missouria
  N. American people   ŌT-ō muh-ZUR-ē-uh   'o:ʈo: mə'zuri:ə
Otomí
  N. American people   ŌT-uh-MĒ   ,o:ʈə'mi:
Oton
  pers. name, French   aw-TAWⁿ   ɔ:tɔ̃
Otranto
  town, Italy   ō-TRAN-tō, AW-truhn-TŌ   o:'trænto:, 'ɔ:trən,to:
Otsego
  county, MI, NY   aht-SĒ-gō   at'si:go:
Ottavio
  pers. name, Italian   ōt-TAHV-yō   o:t'tavjo:
Ottawa
  city, Canada; N. American people AHT-uh-wuh, -WAH, -WAW   'aʈəwə, -,wɑ, -,wɔ:
Otterbein
  University, OH   AHT-uhr-BĪN   'aʈəʳ,bain
Ottmar
  pers. name, German   AWT-MAHR   'ɔ:t,maʳ
Otto
  1. pers. name   AHT-ō   'ato:
  2. Danish, Dutch, German   AW-tō   'ɔ:to:
  3. Estonian, Norwegian   AWT-tō   'ɔ:tto:
  4. Finnish   AWT-taw   'ɔ:ttɔ:
  5. Swedish   AWT-tu   'ɔ:ttu
Ottoman
  pert. to Turks or Turkey   AHT-uh-muhn   'aʈəmən
Ottorino
  pers. name, Italian   ŌT-tō-RĒ-nō   ,o:tto:'ri:no:
Ottumwa
  city, IA   ah-TUHM-wuh, uh-TUHM-wuh   ɑ'təmwə, ə'təmwə
Ouachita
  river, mts., lake, pl. name, US WAHSH-uh-TAW   'waʃə,tɔ:
Ouadai, Wadai
  prefecture, Chad   WAH-DĪ   ,wa'dai

Foreign Sounds: ue: *Fr.* **rue**, *Ger.* **füllen** uh(r): *Fr.* **boeuf**, *Ger.* **Höhle** kh: *Ger.* **ich**, *Scot.* **loch** g̃: *Sp.* **amigo** v: *Sp.* **hablar**
hl: *Welsh* **Llanelli**. CAPITALS: primary stress. SMALL CAPS: secondary stress. ⑤: U.S. pron. ⓔ: British pron.

Ouagadougou
   city, Burkina Faso   WAHG-uh-D$\overline{OO}$-g$\overline{oo}$ ˌwɑgə'duːguː

Oudenaarde
   prov, Belgiuim   OWD-n-AHRD-uh   ˌaudn̩'ɑʳdə

Ouessant, Ile d' [Ushant]
   island, France   ēl dwe-SAH^n iːl dwesɑ̃

Ouida
   pen name of Louise de la Ramée;   WĒD-uh   'wiːdə
   pers. name

Ouija
   tdmk for a board game   WĒ-juh, WĒ-jē   'wiːdʒə, 'wiːdʒiˑ

Ouimet
   Francis, *US golfer*   WĒ-MET   'wiːˌmet

Oulu
   river, city, prov, Finland   OW-l$\overline{oo}$ 'auluː

Our
   river, Belgium   UR   'uʳ

Ouray
   county, CO $\overline{oo}$-RĀ   uː'reː

Ourthe
   river, Belgium   URT   'uʳt

Ouse
   river, England $\overline{OO}$Z   'uːz

Ouspenskaya
   Maria, *entertainer* $\overline{OO}$-SPEN-SKĪ-uh   ˌuːˌspen'skaiə

Outagamie
   county, WI   OWT-uh-GAM-ē   ˌautə'gæmiˑ

Outardes
   river, Canada $\overline{oo}$-TAHRD   uː'tɑʳd

Outer Hebrides
   islands, Scotland   OWT-uhr HEB-ruh-DĒZ   ˌautəʳ 'hebrəˌdiːz

Ouzel
   songbird $\overline{OO}$-zuhl   'uːzəl

Ovaltine
   tdmk for a malt flavoring   Ō-vuhl-TĒN   'oːvəlˌtiːn

Ovambo [Ambo]
   lang., people, Angola, Namibia   ō-VAHM-bō   oː'vamboː

Ovamboland
   region, Africa   ō-VAHM-bō-LAND   oː'vamboːˌlænd

Overijsell
   prov, Netherlands   Ō-vuh-RĪ-suhl   ˌoːvə'raisəl

Ovett
   Steve, *English runner*   ō-VET   oː'vet

Ovid
   1. Roman poet; pers. name   AHV-uhd   'avəd
   2. village, NY   Ō-vuhd   'oːvəd

Ovide
   pers. name, French   aw-VĒD   ɔːviːd

Ovidian
   pert. to Ovid   ō-VID-ē-uhn, ah-VID-ē-uhn   oː'vidiːən, ɑ'vidiːən

Oviedo
   prov, Spain   Ō-vē-Ā-t͟hō   ˌoːviː'eːðoː

Ovimbundu [Mbundu]
   lang., people, Africa   Ō-vuhm-B$\overline{OO}$N-d$\overline{oo}$ ˌoːvəm'buˑnduː

Key (col. 2):   a: fad   ā: fade   ah: father   ar: marry   aw: law   e: fed   ē: feed   er: merry   i: hid   ī: hide   ō: coat $\overline{oo}$: boot
oi: boy   ow: now   u: put   uh: above   uhr: bird   ch: chop   ng: ring   sh: show   th: thick   t͟h: this   zh: measure

Owain
   pers. name, Welsh   Ō-WĪN, Ⓢ Ō-īn, Ō-uhn, Ō-ān   'oː‚wɑin, Ⓢ 'oːɑin, 'oːən, 'oːeːn

Owasso
   town, OK   ō-WAHS-ō   oː'wɑsoː

Owatonna
   city, MN   Ō-wuh-TAHN-uh   ‚oːwə'tɑnə

Owego
   village, NY   ō-WĒ-gō   oː'wiːgoː

Owen
   pers. name   Ō-uhn   'oːən

Owosso
   city, MI   ō-WAH-sō   oː'wɑːsoː

Owsley
   county, KY   OWZ-lē   'ɑuzliˑ

Owyhee
   county, ID   ō-WĪ-(h)ē   oː'wɑi(h)iː

Oxbridge
   Oxford or Cambridge University, or   AHKS-brij, AHKS-BRIJ   'ɑksbridʒ, 'ɑks‚bridʒ
   both

Oxenstierna
   Count Axel Gustaffson, Swedish   UK-suhn-SHER-nah   'uksən‚ʃeʳnɑː
   statesman

Oxford
   town, university, England   AHKS-fuhrd   'ɑksfəʳd

Oxfordshire
   county, England   AHKS-fuhrd-shuhr, -SHIR   'ɑksfəʳdʃəʳ, -‚ʃiʳ

Oxnard
   city, CA   AHK-SNAHRD   'ɑk‚snɑʳd

Oxon
   abbr. for Oxoniensis "of Oxford"   AHK-SAHN   'ɑk‚sɑn

Oxonian
   pert. to Oxford   ahk-SŌ-nē-uhn   ɑk'soːniːən

Oxus
   ancient name of Amu Darya   AHK-suhs   'ɑksəs

Oxydol
   tdmk for a detergent   AHK-suh-DAWL, -DAHL   'ɑksə‚dɔːl, -‚dɑl

oxygen
   element   AHK-suh-juhn   'ɑksədʒən

Oxynius
   son of Hector   ahk-SIN-ē-uhs   ɑk'siniːəs

Oxynthes
   king of Athens   ahk-SIN-THĒZ   ɑk'sin‚θiːz

Oxyrhynchus
   archaeological site, Egypt   AHK-si-RING-kuhs   ‚ɑksi'riŋkəs

Oyo
   state, Nigeria   Ō-yō   'oːjoː

Oyvind
   pers. name, Norwegian   OI-vind   'ɔivind

Oz
   Frank, *British puppeteer, actor;*   AHZ   'ɑz
   fictional land, Baum; Australian
   slang for Australia

Ozark
   county, MO; city, AL, AR; mtns., US   Ō-ZAHRK   'oː‚zɑʳk

Foreign Sounds: ue: *Fr.* **rue**, *Ger.* **füllen**   uh(r): *Fr.* **boeuf**, *Ger.* **Höhle**   kh: *Ger.* **ich**, *Scot.* lo**ch**   ḡ: *Sp.* amiḡo   ṿ: *Sp.* haḇlar
hl: *Welsh* **Llanelli.**   CAPITALS: primary stress.   SMALL CAPS: secondary stress.   Ⓢ: U.S. pron.   Ⓔ: British pron.

Ozaukee
   county, WI   ō-ZAW-kē   ɔːˈzɔːkiˑ

Ozawa
   Seiji, *Japanese conductor*   ō-ZAH-wuh   ɔːˈzɑwə

Ozem
   Biblical name   Ō-ZEM, Ō-zuhm, AWT-sem   ˈɔːˌzem, ˈɔːzəm, ˈɔːtsem

Ozero Baykal
   see Baykal, Ozero

Ozero Onezhskoye
   see Onezhskoye, Ozero

Ozette
   lake, Indian reservation, WA   ō-ZET   ɔːˈzet

Ozias
   Biblical name   ō-ZĪ-uhs   ɔːˈzaiəs

Ozick
   Cynthia, *US writer*   Ō-zik   ˈɔːzik

Ozni
   Biblical name   AHZ-NĪ, ahz-NĒ   ˈazˌnai, azˈniː

Oznite
   Biblical name   AHZ-NĪT   ˈazˌnait

Ozona
   town, TX   ō-ZŌ-nuh   ɔːˈzoːnə

Ozu
   Yasujirō, *Japanese film director*   ō-zu   ɔːzu

Ozymandias
   sonnet by Shelley   AHZ-i-MAN-dē-uhs   ˌaziˈmændiːəs

Ozzie, Ozzy
   pers. name   AHZ-ē   ˈaziˑ

P

Paarai [Naarai]
   Biblical name   PĀ-uh-RĪ, PAH-ah-RĪ   ˈpeːəˌrai, ˌpɑːɑːˈrai

Paavo
   pers. name, Finnish   PAH-VAW   ˈpɑˌvɔː

Pablo
   pers. name, Spanish   PAHV̲-lō   ˈpaβloː

Pabst
   1. US beer   PABST, PAPST   ˈpæbst, ˈpæpst
   2. George Wilhelm, German film   PAHPST   ˈpɑpst
      director

Pacaraima, Sierra
   mtn. range, S. America   sē-ER-uh PAK-uh-RĪ-muh   siːˌerə ˌpækəˈraimə

Pachaug
   lake, river, CT   PACH-AWG   ˈpætʃˌɔːg

Key (col. 2): a: fad ā: fade ah: father ar: marry aw: law e: fed ē: feed er: merry i: hid ī: hide ō: coat ōō: boot
oi: boy ow: now u: put uh: above uhr: bird ch: chop ng: ring sh: show th: thick th̲: this zh: measure

Pachelbel

Johann, *German composer*   pah<u>kh</u>-EL-BEL, PAH<u>KH</u>-uhl-BEL,   pɑx'el¡bel, 'pɑxəl¡bel,
                              PAHK-uhl-BEL   'pɑkəl¡bel

Pachistima

plant   puh-KIS-tuh-muh   pə'kistəmə

Pachuca

city, Mexico   puh-CHŌŌ-kuh   pə'tʃuːkə

Pachycephalosaurus

dinosaur   PAK-uh-SEF-uh-lō-SAWR-uhs   ¡pækə¡sefəloː'sɔːrəs

Pachyderm

thick-skinned, hoofed mammal   PAK-i-DUHRM   'pæki¡dəʳm

Pacifica

city, CA   puh-SIF-i-kuh   pə'sifikə

Pacifico

Mexican beer   pah-SĒ-fē-kō   pɑ'siːfiːkoː

Pacino

Al, *US actor*   puh-CHĒ-nō   pə'tʃiːnoː

Packard

US car co.   PAK-uhrd   'pækəʳd

Pac-man

tdmk for a video game   PAK-MAN   'pæk¡mæn

Pactolus

river in Asia Minor   pak-TŌ-luhs   pæk'toːləs

Padang

island, city, Sumatra   PAHD-AHNG   'pɑd¡ɑŋ

Padan [Paddan]

Biblical name   PĀD-n, PAD-n, pah-DAHN   'peːdn̩, 'pædn̩, pɑ'dɑn

Padan-aram

Biblical name   PĀD-n-Ā-RAM, PAD-n-AR-uhm,   'peːdn̩'eː¡ræm, 'pædn̩'ærəm,
                 pah-DAHN-ah-RAHM   pɑ'dɑnɑ'rɑm

Paddan [Padan]

Biblical name   PAD-n, pah-DAHN   'pædn̩, pɑ'dɑn

Paddan-aram

Biblical name   PAD-n-AR-uhm, -Ā-RAM;   'pædn̩'ærəm, -'eː¡ræm;
                 pah-DAHN-ah-RAHM   pɑ'dɑnɑ'rɑm

Paddy

pers. name   PAD-ē   'pædiˑ

Paden City

town, WV   PĀD-n SIT-ē   'peːdn̩ 'siṭiˑ

Paderewski

Ignace, *Polish composer &*   PAHD-uh-REF-skē, PAD-uh-REV-skē   ¡pɑdə'refskiˑ, ¡pædə'revskiˑ
   statesman

Padouca

N. American people   puh-D(Y)ŌŌ-kuh   pə'd(j)uːkə

Padova [Padua]

city, prov, Italy   PAHD-uh-vuh   'pɑdəvə

Padraic, Padhraic, Padraig

1. pers. name   PAH-drig, PAHD-rik, PAH<u>TH</u>-rig   'pɑdrig, 'pɑdrik, 'pɑðrig
2. Irish Gaelic   PAWR-ig, PAW<u>TH</u>-rig, PAH-rig   'pɔːrig, 'pɔːðrig, 'pɑrig

Padre

Island, *TX*   PAHD-rē, PAD-rē   'pɑdriˑ, 'pædriˑ

Padua

city, Italy   PAJ-uh-wuh   'pædʒəwə

Paducah

city, KY   puh-D(Y)ŌŌ-kuh   pə'd(j)uːkə

Foreign Sounds: ue: *Fr.* **rue**, *Ger.* **füllen**   uh(r): *Fr.* **boeuf**, *Ger.* **Höhle**   <u>kh</u>: *Ger.* **ich**, *Scot.* **loch**   ḡ: *Sp.* **amigo**   ṿ: *Sp.* **hablar**
hl: *Welsh* **Llanelli**.   CAPITALS: primary stress.   SMALL CAPS: secondary stress.   ⑤: U.S. pron.   ⑥: British pron.

Paean
  Greek god of healing; epithet of   PĒ-uhn   'piːən
  Apollo
Paeon
  grandson of Nestor   PĒ-uhn, PĒ-AHN   'piːən, 'piːˌɑn
Paestum
  ancient city, Italy   PES-tuhm, PĒ-stuhm   'pestəm, 'piːstəm
Paez
  lang., people, Colombia, Panama   pah-EZ   pɑ'ez
Pagan
  temple city, Burma; island, Pacific   puh-GAHN   pə'gɑn
Paganini
  Niccolo, *Italian composer*   PAHG-uh-NĒ-nē, PAG-uh-NĒ-nē   ˌpɑgə'niːniˑ, ˌpægə'niːniˑ
Paget
  pers. name   PAJ-uht   'pædʒət
Pagiel
  Biblical name   PĀ-gē-EL, PĀ-jē-EL, -uhl; PAHG-ē-EL   'peːgiːˌel, 'peːdʒiːˌel, -əl;
                                                  ˌpɑgiː'el
Paglia
  Camille, *US writer*   PAHL-yuh, PAHG-lē-uh, PAG-lē-uh   'pɑljə, 'pɑgliːə, 'pægliːə
Pagliacci
  opera, Leoncavallo   pahl-YAHCH-ē   pɑl'jɑtʃiˑ
Pago Pago, Pango Pango
  town, American Samoa   PAHNG-(g)ō PAHNG-(g)ō, PAHG-ō   ˌpɑŋ(g)oː 'pɑŋ(g)oːˌ, ˌpɑgoː
                        PAHG-ō   'pɑgoː
Pahang
  river, state, Malaysia   puh-HAHNG   pə'hɑŋ
Pahath-moab
  Biblical name   PĀ-(H)ATH-MŌ-AB,   'peːˌ(h)æθ'moːˌæb,
                pah-<u>KH</u>AHT-mō-AHV   pɑ'xɑtmoː'ɑv
Pahlavi
  Iranian lang.   PAHL-uh-vē, PAL-uh-vē   'pɑləviˑ, 'pæləviˑ
Pahoa
  town, HI   pah-HŌ-uh   pɑ'hoːə
Pahokee
  town, FL   puh-HŌ-kē   pə'hoːkiˑ
Pahranagat
  mtn. range, NV   puh-RAN-uh-GAT   pə'rænəˌgæt
Pahrock, Pahroc
  mtn. range, NV   puh-RAHK   pə'rɑk
Pahute Mesa, Paiute Mesa
  tableland, NV   PAH-yo͞ot MĀ-suh, PĪ-yo͞ot   'pajuːt 'meːsə, 'paijuːt
Pai [Bai, Minchia]
  lang., China   BĪ, PĪ   'bai, 'pai
Paige
  pers. name   PĀJ   'peːdʒ
Päijänne
  lake, Finland   PĀ-YAHN-ne   'peːˌjɑnne
Paisley
  Ian, *N. Irish politician; city,*   PĀZ-lē   'peːzliˑ
  Scotland; pattern
Pais Vasco
  region, Spain   pīs <u>V</u>AHS-kō   pais 'βaskoː
Paiute
  N. American people   PĪ-(Y)O͞OT   'pai,(j)uːt

Key (col. 2):   a: f**a**d ā: f**a**de ah: f**a**ther ar: m**a**rry aw: l**a**w e: f**e**d ē: f**ee**d er: m**e**rry i: h**i**d ī: h**i**de ō: c**oa**t o͞o: b**oo**t
oi: b**oy** ow: n**ow** u: p**u**t uh: **a**bove uhr: b**ir**d ch: **ch**op ng: ri**ng** sh: **sh**ow th: **th**ick <u>th</u>: **th**is zh: mea**s**ure

Paiwan
  lang., Taiwan   pī-WAHN   paɪˈwɑn
Pajjusana
  Jain penitential period   pah-J͞O͞O-sahn-uh   pʌˈdʒuːsɑnə
Pajonism
  Christian sect   PAJ-uh-NIZ-uhm   ˈpædʒəˌnizəm
Pakenham
  1. Sir Edward M., British soldier   PAK-(uh-)nuhm   ˈpæk(ə)nəm
  2. town, England   PĀ-kuh-nuhm, PĀK-nuhm   ˈpeːkənəm, ˈpeːknəm
Pakhto [Pashto]
  lang., Afghanistan, Pakistan   PUHKH-tō   ˈpəxtoː
Pakistan
  republic, Asia   PAK-i-STAN, PAHK-i-STAHN, PAK-i-STAN   ˌpækiˈstæn, ˌpɑkiˈstɑn, ˈpækiˌstæn
Pakistani
  pert. to Pakistan   PAK-i-STAN-ē, PAHK-i-STAHN-ē   ˌpækiˈstæniˑ, ˌpɑkiˈstɑniˑ
Pál
  pers. name, Hungarian   PAHL   ˈpɑːl
Pala
  Indian reservation, CA   PAL-uh   ˈpælə
Palacios
  town, TX   puh-LASH-uhz   pəˈlæʃəz
Palade
  George Emil, Romanian-born US cell biologist (Nobel 1974)   puh-LAHD-ē   pəˈlɑdiˑ
Palaemon
  son of Heracles; Argonaut   pal-Ē-muhn   pælˈiːmən
Palaeologus
  Greek dynasty of the Byzantine Empire   PĀ-lē-AHL-uh-guhs, PAL-   ˌpeːliːˈɑləgəs, ˌpæl-
Palaestra
  Greek or Roman wrestling school   puh-LES-truh   pəˈlestrə
Palais-Royal
  French 'royal palace'   pah-LE-raw-YAHL   pɑːlerɔːjɑːl
Palal
  Biblical name   PĀ-LAL, -luhl; pah-LAHL   ˈpeːˌlæl, -ləl; pɑˈlɑl
Palamedes
  legendary inventor in Greek mythology   PAL-uh-MĒD-ēz   ˌpæləˈmiːdiːz
Palamon
  lover in The Knight's Tale, *Chaucer*   PAL-uh-MAHN, PAL-uh-muhn   ˈpæləˌmɑn, ˈpæləmən
Palatinate
  district, Germany   puh-LAT-n-ĀT   pəˈlætn̩ˌeːt
Palatine
  hill, Rome, Italy; village, IL   PAL-uh-TĪN   ˈpæləˌtain
Palatka
  city, FL   puh-LAT-kuh   pəˈlætkə
Palau [Belau]
  islands, Pacific   puh-LOW   pəˈlau
Palaung
  lang., people, Burma   puh-LOWNG   pəˈlauŋ
Palaung-Wa
  division of Mon-Khmer lang. group   puh-LOWNG-WAH   pəˈlauŋˈwɑ
Palawan
  island, Philippines   puh-LAH-wuhn   pəˈlawən

Palazzo Venezia
  museum, Rome, Italy   puh-LAHT-sō vuh-NET-sē-uh   pəˈlɑtsoː vəˈnetsiːə
Palembang
  prov., Indonesia   PAHL-uhm-BAHNG   ˌpaləmˈbaŋ
Palencia
  prov., Spain   puh-LEN-ch(ē-)uh   pəˈlentʃ(iː)ə
Palenque
  city, Mexico   puh-LEN-kā   pəˈlenkeː
Paleocene
  geologic epoch   PĀ-lē-uh-SĒN, Ⓔ PAL-ē-uh-   ˈpeːliːəˌsiːn, Ⓔ ˈpæliːə-
Paleogene
  geologic period   PĀ-lē-uh-JĒN, Ⓔ PAL-ē-uh-   ˈpeːliːəˌdʒiːn, Ⓔ ˈpæliːə-
Paleolithic
  prehistoric age   PĀ-lē-uh-LITH-ik, Ⓔ PAL-ē-uh-   ˌpeːliːəˈliθik, Ⓔ ˌpæliːə-
Paleozoic
  geologic era   PĀ-lē-uh-ZŌ-ik, Ⓔ PAL-ē-uh-   ˌpeːliːəˈzoːik, Ⓔ ˌpæliːə-
Palermo
  prov., Sicilia   puh-LER-mō, puh-LUHR-mō   pəˈleʳmoː, pəˈləʳmoː
Pales
  Roman guardian spirit of flocks   PĀ-LĒZ   ˈpeːˌliːz
Palestine
  1. ancient country, site of Holy Land   PAL-uh-STĪN, -STĒN   ˈpæləˌstɑin, -ˌstiːn
  2. city, TX   PAL-uh-STĒN   ˈpæləˌstiːn
Palestinian
  pert. to Palestine   PAL-uh-STIN-ē-uhn, PAL-uh-STIN-yuhn   ˌpæləˈstiniːən, ˌpæləˈstinjən
Palestrina
  Giovanni Pierluigi da, *Italian*   PAH-lā-STRĒ-nah,   ˌpɑleːˈstriːnɑ,
    composer; commune, Italy   ⓈPAL-uh-STRĒ-nuh   Ⓢ ˌpæləˈstriːnə
Paley
  William S., *US broadcasting*   PĀ-lē   ˈpeːliˑ
    executive
Pali
  lang., India   PAHL-ē   ˈpɑliˑ
Palin
  Michael, *British writer, comedian*   PĀ-luhn   ˈpeːlən
Palinurus
  pilot of Aeneas   PAL-uhn-YUR-uhs   ˌpælənˈjurəs
Palisades
  line of cliffs, NY, NJ   PAL-uh-SĀDZ   ˌpæləˈseːdz
Palladian
  pert. to Palladio or Athena   puh-LĀD-ē-uhn, puh-LAHD-ē-uhn   pəˈleːdiːən, pəˈlɑdiːən
Palladio
  Andrea, *Italian architect*   pah-LAHD-yō   pɑˈlɑdjoː
Palladium
  statue of Pallas Athena which   puh-LĀD-ē-uhm   pəˈleːdiːəm
    protected Troy; element
Pallantidae
  fifty sons of Pallas   puh-LANT-uh-DĒ   pəˈlæntəˌdiː
Pallas
  1. epithet of Athena   PAL-uhs   ˈpæləs
  2. grandfather of Evander   PAL-uhs, PAL-AS, PAL-AHS   ˈpæləs, ˈpælˌæs, ˈpælˌɑs
Pallas Athena
  Greek goddess, protective aspect of   PAL-uhs uh-THĒ-nuh   ˈpæləs əˈθiːnə
    Athena; asteroid

Key (col. 2): a: fad ā: fade ah: father ar: **marry** aw: **law** e: fed ē: feed er: **merry** i: hid ī: hide ō: coat ōō: boot
oi: **boy** ow: **now** u: put uh: **above** uhr: **bird** ch: **chop** ng: **ring** sh: **show** th: thick <u>th</u>: this zh: measure

Pallene
  daughter of Sithon   puh-LĒ-nē   pə'liːniˑ

Pall Mall
  1. street, London, England   PAL MAL, *formerly* PEL MEL, ⑤ PAWL MAWL   ˌpæl 'mæl, *formerly* ˌpel 'mel, ⑤ 'pɔːl 'mɔːl

  2. brand of cigarettes   PAWL MAWL, PEL MEL   'pɔːl 'mɔːl, ˌpel 'mel

Pallu
  Biblical name   PAL-O͞O, pah-LO͞O   'pælˌuː, pa'luː

Palluite
  Biblical name   PAL-(y)uh-WĪT   'pæl(j)əˌwait

Palma de Mallorca
  city, Spain   PAHL-muh t̲h̲ā mah(l)-YAWR-kuh   'palmə ðeː ma(l)'jɔːʳkə

Palme
  Olof, *prime minister, Sweden*   PAHL-muh   'paːlmə

Palmer
  Arnold, *US golfer; pers. name*   PAHM-uhr, PAHL-muhr   'paˑməʳ, 'paˑlməʳ

Palmolive
  tdmk for a soap   pah(l)-MAHL-uhv   pa(l)'maləv

Palmyra
  ancient city, Syria; pl. name, US   pal-MĪ-ruh   pæl'mairə

Palo Alto
  city, CA   PAL-ō AL-tō   ˌpæloː 'æltoː

Palomar
  Mount, *mtn., observatory, CA*   PAL-uh-MAHR   'pæləˌmaʳ

Palomino
  horse breed   PAL-uh-MĒ-nō   ˌpælə'miːnoː

Palos
  port, Spain   PAHL-ōs   'paloːs

Palos Verdes Estates
  city, CA   PAL-uhs VUHRD-ēz i-STĀTS, VUHRD-uhs   'pæləs 'vəʳdiːz i'steːts, 'vəʳdəs

Palouse, Pelouse
  river, ID, WA   puh-LO͞OS   pə'luːs

Palti
  Biblical name   PAL-TĪ, pahl-TĒ   'pælˌtai, pal'tiː

Paltiel
  Biblical name   PAL-tē-EL, -uhl; PAHL-tē-EL   'pæltiːˌel, -əl; ˌpaltiː'el

Paltite
  Biblical name   PAL-TĪT   'pælˌtait

Palus Nebularum
  feature on Moon   PĀ-luhs NEB-yuh-LAHR-uhm   'peːləs ˌnebjə'larəm

Palus Putredinis
  feature on Moon   PĀ-luhs pyo͞o-TRED-n-uhs   'peːləs pjuː'tredn̩əs

Palus Somnii
  feature on Moon   PĀ-luhs SAHM-nē-Ē   'peːləs 'samniːˌiː

Pam
  pers. name   PAM   'pæm

Pama-Nyungan
  Australian aboriginal lang. family   PAHM-uh-NYUNG-guhn   ˌpamə'njuŋgən

Pamela
  pers. name   PAM-uh-luh   'pæmələ

Pamfilo
  pers. name, Italian   PAHM-fē-lō   'pamfiːloː

Pamirs
  mtn. range, Asia   puh-MIRZ   pə'miʳz

Foreign Sounds: ue: *Fr.* **rue**, *Ger.* **füllen**   uh(r): *Fr.* **boeuf**, *Ger.* **Höhle**   k̲h̲: *Ger.* **ich**, *Scot.* **loch**   g̅: *Sp.* amigo   v̲: *Sp.* hablar
hl: *Welsh* **Llanelli**.   CAPITALS: primary stress.   SMALL CAPS: secondary stress.   ⑤: U.S. pron.   Ⓔ: British pron.

Pamlico
　river, county, sound, NC　　　PAM-li-KŌ　　　　　　　'pæmli,koː

Pampa, La
　prov., Argentina　　　lah PAHM-puh　　　　　　　lɑ 'pɑmpə

Pamphile
　pers. name, French　　　pahⁿ-FĒL, *in Canada* pahⁿ-FIL　　　pãfiːl, *in Canada* pãfil

Pamphylia
　ancient country, Asia Minor　　　pam-FIL-ē-uh　　　　　　　pæm'filiːə

Pamplona
　prov., Spain　　　pam-PLŌ-nuh　　　　　　　pæm'ploːnə

Pamunkey
　N. American people　　　puh-MUHNG-kē　　　　　　　pə'məŋki·

Pan
　Greek god of shepherds & flocks　　　PAN　　　　　　　'pæn

Pana
　city, IL　　　PĀ-nuh　　　　　　　'peːnə

Panacea
　Greek goddess of herbal healing　　　PAN-uh-SĒ-uh　　　　　　　,pænə'siːə

Panadol
　tdmk for an analgesic　　　PAN-uh-DAWL, PAN-uh-DAHL　　　'pænə,dɔːl, 'pænə,dɑl

Pan Am
　former US airline　　　pan AM　　　　　　　pæn 'æm

Panama
　republic, C. America　　　PAN-uh-MAH, -MAW; PAN-uh-MAH, -MAW　　　'pænə,mɑ, -,mɔː; ,pænə'mɑ, -'mɔː

Panamanian
　pert. to Panama　　　PAN-uh-MĀ-nē-uhn　　　　　　　,pænə'meːniːən

Panasonic
　electronics co.　　　PAN-uh-SAHN-ik, PAN-uh-SAHN-ik　　　,pænə'sɑnik, 'pænə,sɑnik

Panathenaea
　ancient Athenian festival　　　PAN-ATH-uh-NĒ-uh　　　　　　　,pæn,æθə'niːə

Panathenaic
　festival, ancient Athens　　　PAN-ATH-uh-NĀ-ik　　　　　　　,pæn,æθə'neːik

Panavision
　trademark, film technique　　　PAN-uh-VIZH-uhn　　　　　　　'pænə,viʒən

Panay
　Philippine island　　　puh-NĪ　　　　　　　pə'nɑi

Panchatantra
　collection of Sanskrit animal fables　　　PUHN-chuh-TUHN-truh　　　,pəntʃə'təntrə

Panchayat
　council of elders or elected officials, India　　　PUHN-CHĪ-(y)uht　　　,pən'tʃai(j)ət

Pancho
　pers. name, Spanish　　　PAHN-chō　　　　　　　'pɑntʃoː

Pancratis
　sister of the Aloadae　　　pan-KRĀT-uhs, pang-KRĀT-uhs　　　pæn'kreːʈəs, pæŋ'kreːʈəs

Pandareus
　father of girls killed by harpies　　　pan-DAR-ē-uhs　　　　　　　pæn'dæriːəs

Pandarus
　Lycian who broke the truce at Troy　　　PAN-duh-ruhs　　　　　　　'pændərəs

Pandect
　Roman law; digest　　　PAN-DEKT　　　　　　　'pæn,dekt

Pandemonium
　capital of Hell in Paradise Lost*, Milton*　　　PAN-duh-MŌ-nē-uhm　　　,pændə'moːniːəm

---

Key (col. 2):　a: fad　ā: fade　ah: father　ar: marry　aw: law　e: fed　ē: feed　er: merry　i: hid　ī: hide　ō: coat　ōō: boot
oi: boy　ow: now　u: put　uh: above　uhr: bird　ch: chop　ng: ring　sh: show　th: thick　th: this　zh: measure

Pandion
  father of Philomela and Procne   pan-DĪ-uhn   pæn'daiən

Pandit
  Vijaya Lakshmi, *Indian stateswoman*   PAHN-dit   'pɑndit

Pandora
  Greek mythical figure   pan-DŌR-uh, pan-DAWR-uh   pæn'doːrə, pæn'dɔːrə

Pandrosus
  daughter of Cecrops and Aglaurus   pan-DRŌ-suhs   pæn'droːsəs

Pánfilo
  pers. name, Spanish   PAHM-fē-lō   'pɑmfiːloː

Pangaea
  Paleozoic supercontinent   pan-JĒ-uh   pæn'dʒiːə

Pangaion Oros
  region, Greece   pahng-GĀ-uhn AWR-uhs   pɑŋ,geːən 'ɔːrəs

Pangasinan
  lang., people, Philippine Islands   PAHN-GAHS-ē-NAHN   ,pɑn,gɑsiː'nɑn

Pangloss
  character, Voltaire   PAN-GLAHS, PAN-GLAWS   'pæn,glɑs, 'pæn,glɔːs

Panglossian
  pert. to Pangloss   pan-GLAHS-ē-uhn, pan-GLAW-sē-uhn   pæn'glɑsiːən, pæn'glɔːsiːən

Pangong, Panggong
  mtn. range, lake, Tibet, China   PUHN-GAWNG, PUHNG-   'pən,gɔːŋ, 'pəŋ-

Pango Pango
  see Pago Pago

Panguingue
  game   pahng-GING-gē, pahng-GĒNG-gē   pɑŋ'giŋgiˑ, pɑŋ'giːŋgiˑ

Panguitch
  city, UT   PAN-GWICH   'pæn,gwitʃ

Panhellenism
  spirit of unity among ancient Greeks   PAN-HEL-uh-NIZ-uhm   ,pæn'helə,nizəm

Panic
  Milan, *Yugoslav prime minister*   PAHN-ēts   'paniːts

Panides
  poetry judge who chose Hesiod over   PAN-e-DĒZ   'pæne,diːz
  Homer

Panini, Pānini
  Sanskrit grammarian   PAHN-uh-nē, PAHN-yuh-nē   'panəniˑ, 'panjəniˑ

Panjab
  see Punjab

Panjabi
  see Punjabi

Pankhurst
  Emmeline *and* Christabel, *English*   PANGK-HUHRST   'pæŋk,həʳst
  suffragists

Pankush
  Hittite assembly   pan-KUSH, pang-KUSH   pæn'kuʃ, pæŋ'kuʃ

Panmunjom
  community between N. & S. Korea   pahn-mun-juhm   pɑnmundʒəm

Pannonia
  ancient country and Roman province,   puh-NŌ-nē-uh   pə'noːniːə
  Europe

Pano
  S. American people   PAHN-ō   'pɑnoː

Panofsky
  Erwin, *US art historian*   puh-NAWF-skē, pan-AWF-   pə'nɔːfskiˑ, pæn'ɔːf-

---

Foreign Sounds: ue: *Fr.* **rue**, *Ger.* **füllen**   uh(r): *Fr.* **boeuf**, *Ger.* **Höhle**   kh: *Ger.* **ich**, *Scot.* **loch**   ḡ: *Sp.* amigo   v̱: *Sp.* hablar
hl: *Welsh* **Llanelli.**   CAPITALS: primary stress.   SMALL CAPS: secondary stress.   Ⓢ: U.S. pron.   Ⓔ: British pron.

Panola
  county, MS   puh-NŌ-luh   pə'noːlə
Panopeus
  twin brother of Crisus   pa-NŌ-pē-uhs   pæ'noːpiːəs
Pansatanism
  Gnostic doctrine   pan-SĀT-n-ɪz-uhm̀   pæn'seːtn̩ˌizəm
Pantages
  Theater, *Los Angeles, CA*   pan-TĀ-juhz   pæn'teːdʒəz
Pantagruel
  giant in Pantagruel, *Rabelais*   pah^n-tah-grue-EL,   pātaːgryːel,
      Ⓢ PANT-uh-GRŌŌ(-uh)l,   Ⓢ ˌpæntə'gruː(ə)l,
      pan-TAG-ruh-WEL, -ruh-wuhl   pæn'tægrəˌwel, -rəwəl
Pantagruelian
  pert. to Pantagruel   PANT-uh-grŌŌ-EL-ē-uhn,   ˌpæntəgru·'eliːən,
      PAN-TAG-ruh-WEL-ē-uhn   ˌpænˌtægrə'weliːən
Pantelleria
  island, Italy   PAN-TEL-uh-RĒ-uh   ˌpænˌtelə'riːə
Pantheon
  ancient Roman building   PAN-thē-AHN   'pænθiːˌɑn
Panthéon
  national monument, Paris, France   pah^n-tā-AW^n, Ⓢ PAN(T)-thē-AHN,   pāteːɔ̃, Ⓢ 'pæn(t)θiːˌɑn,
      PAN(T)-thē-uhn   'pæn(t)θiːən
Panurge
  character in Pantagruel, *Rabelais*   pah-NUERZH, Ⓢ PAN-UHRJ,   paːnyːrʒ, Ⓢ 'pæn,ə^{r}dʒ,
      pa-NURZH   pæ'nu^{r}ʒ
Panza
  see Sancho Panza
Panzer
  German tank, WW II   PAN-zuhr, PAHN(T)-suhr   'pænzə^r, 'pɑn(t)sə^r
Pao-an [Santa]
  lang., China   POW-AHN   'pɑu'ɑn
Paola
  city, KS   pā-Ō-luh   peː'oːlə
Paoli
  1. Pasquale, *Corsican patriot*   PAH-ō-lē   'pɑoːliː
  2. town, IN, PA   pā-Ō-lē   peː'oːli·
Paolo
  pers. name, Italian   PAH-ō-lō   'pɑ-oːloː
Papa
  father   PAHP-uh, Ⓔ puh-PAH   'pɑpə, Ⓔ pə'pɑː
Papadopoulos
  George, *Greek colonel and political*   PAHP-ah-THAW-pŌŌ-laws,   ˌpɑpa'ðɔːpuːlɔːs,
    leader   Ⓢ PAHP-uh-DAHP-uh-luhs   Ⓢ ˌpapə'dɑpələs
Papago
  N. American people   PAP-uh-GŌ, PAHP-uh-GŌ   'pæpəˌgoː, 'pɑpəˌgoː
Papaikou
  town, HI   pah-PAH-ē-KŌ-ŌŌ   pɑˌpaiː'koːuː
Papandreou
  Andreas, *prime minister, Greece*   PAHP-ahn-DRĀ-ŌŌ   ˌpɑpɑn'dreːuː
Papeete
  port, Tahiti   PAHP-ē-ĀT-ē, puh-PĒT-ē   ˌpɑpiː'eːṭi·, pə'piːṭi·
Papen
  Franz von, *German political leader*   PAHP-uhn   'pɑpən
Paphlagonia
  ancient region, Asia Minor   PAF-luh-GŌ-nē-uh   ˌpæflə'goːniːə

Key (col. 2):   a: fad   ā: fade   ah: father   ar: marry   aw: law   e: fed   ē: feed   er: merry   i: hid   ī: hide   ō: coat   ōō: boot
oi: boy   ow: now   u: put   uh: above   uhr: bird   ch: chop   ng: ring   sh: show   th: thick   th̲: this   zh: measure

Paphos
   district, Cyprus   PĀ-FAHS   'peːˌfɑs

Papiamento [Papiamentu]
   lang., Dutch Antilles   PAHP-yuh-MEN-tō   ˌpɑpjə'mentoː

Papiamentu [Papiamento]
   lang., Dutch Antilles   PAHP-yuh-MEN-t$\overline{oo}$ ˌpɑpjə'mentuː

Papillion
   city, NE   puh-PIL-yuhn   pə'piljən

Papillon
   dog breed   PAHP-ē-(Y)AW^n, PAP-   ˌpɑpiː'(j)ɔ̃, ˌpæp-

Papirius
   Lucius, *Roman consul, dictator*   puh-PIR-ē-uhs   pə'piriːəs

Papp
   Joseph, *US director and producer*   PAP   'pæp

Paragould
   city, AR   PAR-uh-G$\overline{OO}$LD   'pærəˌguːld

Papua New Guinea
   nation, island group, Pacific   PAHP-uh-wuh N(Y)$\overline{OO}$ GIN-ē,   'pɑpəwə ˌn(j)uˈ 'gini',
                                   PAP-yuh-wuh   'pæpjəwə

Papua New Guinean
   pert. to Papua New Guinea   PAHP-uh-wuh N(Y)$\overline{OO}$ GIN-ē-uhn,   'pɑpəwə ˌn(j)uˈ 'giniːən,
                                   PAP-yuh-wuh   'pæpjəwə

Pär
   pers. name, Swedish   PER   'pe^r

Paracelsus
   Swiss physician, alchemist   PAR-uh-SEL-suhs   ˌpærə'selsəs

Paraclete
   Holy Spirit   PAR-uh-KLĒT   'pærəˌkliːt

Paradise
   garden of Eden   PAR-uh-DĪS, PAR-uh-DĪZ   'pærəˌdɑis, 'pærəˌdɑiz

Paraguay
   republic, S. America   PAR-uh-GWĪ, -GWĀ   'pærəˌgwɑi, -ˌgweː

Paraguayan
   pert. to Paraguay   PAR-uh-GWĪ-uhn, -GWĀ-uhn   'pærəˌgwɑiən, -ˌgweːən

Parah
   Biblical name   PĀ-ruh, PAR-uh, pah-RAH   'peːrə, 'pærə, pɑ'rɑ

Paralipomenon
   Old Testament book   PAR-uh-luh-PAHM-uh-NAHN,   ˌpærələ'pɑməˌnɑn,
                                 PAR-uh-LĪ-PAHM-uh-NAHN   ˌpærəˌlɑi'pɑməˌnɑn

Paramaribo
   city, Suriname   PAR-uh-MAR-uh-BŌ   ˌpærə'mærəˌboː

Paramus
   city, NJ   puh-RAM-uhs   pə'ræməs

Paran
   Biblical name   PĀ-ruhn, PAR-uhn, pah-RAHN   'peːrən, 'pærən, pɑː'rɑn

Paraná
   river; state, Brazil; city, Argentina   PAR-uh-NAH   ˌpærə'nɑ

Paranaíba
   river, Brazil   PAHR-uh-nah-Ē-buh,   ˌpɑːrənɑ'iːbə,
                  Ⓢ PAR-uh-nuh-Ē-buh   Ⓢ ˌpærənə'iːbə

Paraquat
   toxic herbicide   PAR-uh-KWAHT   'pærəˌkwɑt

Parasaurolophus
   dinosaur   PAR-uh-saw-RAHL-uh-fuhs   ˌpærəsɔː'rɑləfəs

Foreign Sounds: ue: *Fr.* **rue**, *Ger.* **füllen**   uh(r): *Fr.* **boeuf**, *Ger.* **Höhle**   <u>kh</u>: *Ger.* i**ch**, *Scot.* lo**ch**   ḡ: *Sp.* ami**g**o   <u>v</u>: *Sp.* ha**b**lar <br> hl: *Welsh* **Ll**anelli.   CAPITALS: primary stress.   SMALL CAPS: secondary stress.   Ⓢ: U.S. pron.   Ⓔ: British pron.

Parbar
  Biblical name   PAHR-ʙᴀʜʀ, pahr-BAHR   'paʳˌbaʳ, paɾ'bar
Parcae
  Roman goddesses of destiny   PAHR-ᴋĪ, PAHR-sē   'paʳˌkɑi, 'paʳsi·
Parcheesi
  tdmk for a board game   pahr-CHḖ-zē   paʳ't ʃiːzi·
Pardalote
  Australian bird   PAHRD-l-ŌᴛT   'paʳdl̩ˌoːt
Pardo
  Don, US broadcasting announcer   PAHRD-ō   'paʳdoː
Pardo Bazán
  Emilia de, Condesa, Spanish   PAHR-thō vah-THAHN   'parðoː βa'θan
  novelist and critic
Pare
  mtn. range, Tanzania   PAHR-ā   'pareː
Pareto
  Vilfredo, Italian economist   puh-RĀT-ō   pə'reːtoː
Paria
  river, UT, AZ   puh-RḖ-uh   pə'riːə
Parian
  pert. to Páros; marble   PAR-ē-uhn   'pæriːən
Paricutín
  volcano, former village, Mexico   puh-RḖ-kōō-TḔN   pəˌriːkuˈtiːn
Parinarium
  plant   PAR-uh-NAR-ē-uhm   ˌpærə'næriːəm
Paris
  1. city, France   pah-RḖ, ⓢ PAR-uhs   paːriː, ⓢ 'pærəs
  2. Trojan who abducted Helen; US   PAR-uhs   'pærəs
  pl. name
Parisian
  pert. to Paris   puh-RḖ-zhuhn, puh-RIZH-uhn,   pə'riːʒən, pə'riʒən, pə'riziːən
       puh-RIZ-ē-uhn
Park Chung Hee
  president, S. Korea   pahrk chuhng hē   paʳk tʃəŋ hiː
Parke-Bernet
  auction gallery   ᴘAHRK-BUHR-nuht   ˌpaʳk'bəʳnət
Parker
  Dorothy, US writer; Charlie, US jazz   PAHR-kuhr   'paʳkəʳ
  musician; pers. name
Parkinson
  C. N., English historian; James,   PAHR-kuhn-suhn   'paʳkənsən
  English physician
Parkman
  Francis, US historian   PAHRK-ᴍᴜʜɴ   'paʳkˌmən
Parliament
  legislative assembly of Great Britain   PAHR-luh-muhnt, PAHR-lyuh-   'paʳləmənt, 'paʳljə-
Parlier
  city, CA   PAHR-luhr   'paʳləʳ
Parma
  prov, Italy; city, OH   PAHR-muh   'paʳmə
Parmashta
  Biblical name   pahr-MASH-tuh, pahr-MAHSH-tah   paʳ'mæʃtə, paɾ'maʃta
Parmenas
  Biblical name   PAHR-muh-nuhs   'paʳmənəs

Key (col. 2):   a: fad   ā: fade   ah: father   ar: marry   aw: law   e: fed   ē: feed   er: merry   i: hid   ī: hide   ō: coat   ōō: boot
oi: boy   ow: now   u: put   uh: above   uhr: bird   ch: chop   ng: ring   sh: show   th: thick   t̲h̲: this   zh: measure

Parmenides
   Greek philosopher; dialogue of Plato   pahr-MEN-uh-DĒZ   pɑrˈmenəˌdiːz

Parmenio
   Macedonian general   pahr-MĒ-nē-ō, pahr-MĒN-yō   pɑrˈmiːniːˌoː, pɑrˈmiːnjoː

Parmentier
   food prepared or served with potatoes   PAHR-muhn-TYĀ   ˌpɑrmənˈtjeː

Parmesan
   pert. to Parma; *cheese*   PAHR-muh-ZAHN, PAHR-muh-ZHAHN, PAHR-muh-zuhn, PAHR-muh-ZAN   ˈpɑrməˌzɑn, ˈpɑrməˌʒɑn, ˈpɑrməzən, ˈpɑrməˌzæn

Parmigiana
   made with Parmesan cheese   PAHR-mi-JAHN-uh, PAHR-mi-ZHAHN, PAHR-mi-ZHAHN   ˌpɑrmiˈdʒɑnə, ˈpɑrmiˌʒɑn, ˌpɑrmiˈʒɑn

Parmigiano Reggiano
   Italian cheese   PAHR-mi-ZHAHN-ō rej-AHN-ō   ˌpɑrmiˈʒɑnoː redʒˈɑnoː

Parnach
   Biblical name   PAHR-NAK, pahr-NAHKH   ˈpɑrˌnæk, pɑrˈnɑx

Parnassian
   pert. to Parnassus, *to poetry, to a school of French poets*   pahr-NAS-ē-uhn   pɑrˈnæsiːən

Parnassus
   mtn., Greece   pahr-NAS-uhs   pɑrˈnæsəs

Parnell
   Charles Stewart, *Irish nationalist leader; pers. name*   pahr-NEL, PAHR-nl   pɑrˈnel, ˈpɑrn̩

Parnu
   bay, river, port, Estonia   PAHR-noo   ˈpɑrnuː

Páros
   Greek island noted for white marble   PAH-RAWS, ⑤ PAR-AHS, PER-AHS   ˈpɑˌrɔːs, ⑤ ˈpærˌɑs, ˈperˌɑs

Parosh [Pharosh]
   Biblical name   PĀ-RAHSH, PAR-AHSH, pahr-AWSH   ˈpeːˌrɑʃ, ˈpærˌɑʃ, pɑrˈɔːʃ

Parowan
   city, UT   PAR-uh-WAN, PAR-uh-WAN   ˈpærəˌwæn, ˌpærəˈwæn

Parrhasius
   Greek painter, 5th cent., BC   puh-RĀ-zh(ē-)uhs, puh-RĀ-sh(ē-)uhs   pəˈreːʒ(iː)əs, pəˈreːʃ(iː)əs

Parsee
   Indian Zoroastrian descended from Persians   pahr-SĒ, PAHR-sē   pɑrˈsiː, ˈpɑrsiˈ

Parshandatha
   Biblical name   PAHR-shan-DĀ-thuh, pahr-SHAN-duh-thuh, PAHR-shahn-DAH-tah   ˌpɑrʃænˈdeːθə, pɑrˈʃændəθə, ˌpɑrʃanˈdɑtɑ

Parsi
   follower of Zoroastrianism; Iranian dialect   PAHR-sē   ˈpɑrsiˈ

Parsifal
   opera, R. Wagner; Arthurian romance hero   PAHR-suh-VAHL, PAHR-suh-vuhl   ˈpɑrsəˌvɑl, ˈpɑrsəvəl

Parsiism
   religion   PAHR-SĒ-IZ-uhm   ˈpɑrˌsiːˌizəm

Parsippany-Troy Hills
   township, NJ   pahr-SIP-uh-nē-TROI HILZ   pɑrˈsipəniːˈtrɔi ˈhilz

Partch
   Harry, *US composer*   PAHRCH   ˈpɑrtʃ

Parthenon
  Athenian temple PAHR-thuh-NAHN 'pɑᵳθəˌnɑn
Parthenopaeus
  one of the Seven against Thebes PAHR-thuh-nō-PĒ-(y)uhs ˌpɑᵳθənoːˈpiː(j)əs
Parthenope
  a siren in Greek mythology pahr-THEN-uh-pē pɑᵳˈθenəpiˑ
Parthenos
  epithet of Athena PAHR-thuh-NŌS 'pɑᵳθəˌnoːs
Parthia
  ancient country, Asia PAHR-thē-uh 'pɑᵳθiːə
Parthians
  inhabitants of Parthia PAHR-thē-uhnz 'pɑᵳθiːənz
Partido Revolucionario Institucional
  political party, Mexico pahr-TĒ-thō rā-yō-lo͞os-yō-NAHR-yō in-stē-to͞os-yō-NAHL pɑrˈtiːðoː reːβoːluːsjoːˈnɑrjoː instiˑˈtuːsjoːˈnɑl
Parti Québecois
  Canadian provincial political party pahr-TĒ kā-bek-WAH pɑrtiː keːbekwɑ
Parton
  Dolly, *US singer, actress* PAHRT-n 'pɑᵳtn̩
Paruah
  Biblical name puh-RO͞O-uh, pah-RO͞O-AHKH pəˈruːə, pɑˈruːˌɑx
Parvaim
  Biblical name pahr-VĀ-im, pahr-VAH-yim pɑᵳˈveːim, pɑrˈvɑjim
Parzival [Parsifal]
  Arthurian romance hero PAHRT-suh-FAHL 'pɑᵳtsəˌfɑl
Pas, The
  town, Manitoba thuh PAH, thuh PAW ðə 'pɑ, ðə 'pɔː
Pasach
  Biblical name PĀ-SAHK, PĀ-SAK, pah-SAHKH 'peːˌsɑk, 'peːˌsæk, pɑ'sɑx
Pasadena
  city, CA, MD PAS-uh-DĒ-nuh ˌpæsəˈdiːnə
Pasargadae
  ruined city, Persia puh-SAHR-guh-DĒ pəˈsɑᵳgəˌdiː
Pascagoula
  river, city, MS PAS-kuh-GO͞O-luh ˌpæskəˈguːlə
Pascal
  1. Blaise, *French philosopher* pahs-KAHL, Ⓢ pas-KAL pɑːskɑːl, Ⓢ pæsˈkæl
  2. programming lang. pas-KAL, pahs-KAHL pæsˈkæl, pɑːsˈkɑːl
Paschal
  antipope pas-KAL, pahs-KAHL pæsˈkæl, pɑsˈkɑl
Pascoag
  community, RI PAS-KŌG 'pæsˌkoːg
Pasco-Hernando
  Community College, *FL* PAS-kō-(h)er-NAHN-dō, -huhr-NAN-dō 'pæskoː(h)eᵳˈnɑndoː, -həᵳˈnændoː
Pascua, Isla de
  Easter Island ĒZ-lah thā PAHS-kwah 'iːzlɑ ðeː 'pɑskwɑ
Pascual
  pers. name, Spanish pahs-KWAHL pɑsˈkwɑl
Pascua Yaqui
  N. American people PAS-kwuh YAHK-ē 'pæskwə 'jɑkiˑ
Pas-dammim
  Biblical name pas-DAM-uhm, PAHS-dah-MĒM pæsˈdæməm, ˌpɑsdɑˈmiːm

---

Key (col. 2):   a: fad   ā: fade   ah: father   ar: marry   aw: law   e: fed   ē: feed   er: merry   i: hid   ī: hide   ō: coat   o͞o: boot
oi: boy   ow: now   u: put   uh: above   uhr: bird   ch: chop   ng: ring   sh: show   th: thick   th̲: this   zh: measure

Pas-de-Calais
dept, France — pah-duh-kah-LE — pɑːdəkɑːle

Paseah
Biblical name — puh-SĒ-uh, puh-SĀ-uh, pah-SE-ah<u>kh</u> — pə'siːə, pə'seːə, pɑ'seɑx

Pasha
Turkish title — PAHSH-uh, PASH-uh, puh-SHAH — 'pɑʃə, 'pæʃə, pə'ʃɑ

Pashto
lang., Afghanistan, Pakistan — PUHSH-tō — 'pəʃtoː

Pashtu [Pashto]
lang., Afghanistan, Pakistan — PASH-t͞oo, PAHSH-t͞oo — 'pæʃtuː, 'pɑʃtuː

Pashur, Pashhur
Biblical name — PASH-uhr, PAHSH-UR, pahsh-<u>KH͞OO</u>R — 'pæʃəʳ, 'pɑʃˌuʳ, pɑʃ'xuːr

Pasiphaë
wife of Minos, mother of the Minotaur; satellite of Jupiter — puh-SIF-uh-Ē — pə'sifəˌiː

Paso Doble
dance — PAHS-ō DŌ-blā — ˌpɑsoː 'doːbleː

Pasolini
Pier Paolo, *Italian writer and film director* — PAHS-ō-LĒ-nē, Ⓢ PAS-uh-LĒ-nē — ˌpɑsoː'liːniː, Ⓢ ˌpæsə'liːni·

Paso Robles [El Paso de Robles]
city, CA — PAS-uh RŌ-buhlz — ˌpæsə 'roːbəlz

Pasquale
pers. name, Italian — pahs-KWAHL-ā — pɑs'kwɑleː

Pasqueflower
flower — PASK-FLOW-uhr — 'pæskˌflɑuəʳ

Pasquotank
county, NC — PAS-kwuh-TANGK — 'pæskwəˌtæŋk

Passaic
river, city, county, NJ — puh-SĀ-ik — pə'seːik

Passamaquoddy
lang., people, N America — PAS-uh-muh-KWAHD-ē — ˌpæsəmə'kwɑdi·

Passat
tdmk for a German automobile — pa-SAHT, puh-SAT — pæ'sɑt, pə'sæt

Passau
city, Germany — PAHS-OW — 'pɑsˌɑu

Passerine
bird genus (English name) — PAS-uh-RĪN — 'pæsəˌrɑin

Passiontide
Passion Sunday to Holy Saturday — PASH-uhn-TĪD — 'pæʃənˌtɑid

Passon
Field, *former ballpark, Philadelphia, PA* — PAS-uhn — 'pæsən

Passover
Jewish holiday — PAS-Ō-vuhr — 'pæsˌoːvəʳ

Passumpsic
river, VT — puh-SUHM(P)-sik — pə'səm(p)sik

Passy
Frédéric, *French economist, author (Nobel 1901)* — pah-SĒ — pɑːsiː

Pasternak
Boris L., *Russian author (Nobel 1958)* — PAS-tuhr-NAK — 'pæstəʳˌnæk

Pasteur
Louis, *French scientist* — pahs-TUHR, Ⓢ pas-TUHR — pɑːstœːr, Ⓢ pæs'təʳ

Foreign Sounds: ue: *Fr.* rue, *Ger.* füllen   uh(r): *Fr.* boeuf, *Ger.* Höhle   <u>kh</u>: *Ger.* ich, *Scot.* loch   g̱: *Sp.* amigo   v̱: *Sp.* hablar
hl: *Welsh* Llanelli.   CAPITALS: primary stress.   SMALL CAPS: secondary stress.   Ⓢ: U.S. pron.   Ⓔ: British pron.

Pasto
  city, Colombia   PAHS-tō   'pɑstoː
Pastorale
  type of musical work   PAS-tuh-RAHL, PAS-tuh-RAL,   ˌpæstə'rɑl, ˌpæstə'ræl,
                             PAS-tuh-RAHL-ē   ˌpæstə'rɑliˑ
Pat
  pers. name   PAT   'pæt
Patagonia
  prov., Argentina   PAT-uh-GŌ-nē-uh, PAT-uh-GŌN-yuh   ˌpæṭə'goːniːə, ˌpæṭə'goːnjə
Patagonian Desert
  S. America   PAT-uh-GŌ-nē-uhn, -GŌN-yuhn   ˌpæṭə'goːniːən, -'goːnjən
Patapsco
  river, MD   puh-TAP-skō   pə'tæpskoː
Patara
  Biblical name   PAT-uh-ruh   'pæṭərə
Patarinism
  Christian heresy   PAT-uh-ruh-NIZ-uhm, -uh-RĒ-NIZ-uhm   'pæṭərəˌnizəm, -əˌriːˌnizəm
Patavium
  Latin form of Padua   puh-TĀ-vē-uhm   pə'teːviːəm
Patchogue
  village, NY   PACH-AWG   'pætʃˌɔːg
Pate
  Jerome Kendrick, *US golfer*   PĀT   'peːt
Pater
  1. Walter H., *English author*   PĀT-uhr   'peːṭəʳ
  2. British term for father   PĀT-uhr   'peːṭəʳ
  3. see Pater Noster
Pater Noster
  Lord's Prayer   PAHT-uhr NAHS-tuhr, PAT-uhr   ˌpɑṭəʳ 'nɑstəʳ, 'pæṭəʳ ˌnɑstəʳ,
                       NAHS-tuhr, PAH-TER NAHS-TER   'pɑˌteʳ 'nɑsˌteʳ
Paterson
  city, NJ   PAT-uhr-suhn   'pæṭəʳsən
Pathé
  Charles *and* Emile, *French film*   pah-TĀ   pateː
    executives
Pathetiqué
  sonata, Beethoven   PAH-thā-TĒK   ˌpɑθeː'tiːk
Pathet Lao
  communist group, Laos   PAHT-uht LOW, LAH-ō   'pɑṭət 'lau, 'laoː
Pathros
  Biblical name   PATH-ruhs, pah-TRŌS   'pæθrəs, pɑ'troːs
Pathrusim
  Biblical name   path-RŌŌ-sim, PAHT-rōō-SĒM   pæθ'ruːsim, ˌpɑtruː'siːm
Patiala
  city, India   PUHT-ē-AHL-uh   ˌpəṭiː'ɑlə
Patinkin
  Mandy, *US actor*   puh-TING-kin   pə'tiŋkin
Patmos
  Biblical name   PAT-muhs   'pætməs
Pátmos, Patmos
  island, Greece   PAHT-maws, Ⓢ PAT-muhs   'pɑtmɔːs, Ⓢ 'pætməs
Patna
  city, India   PUHT-nuh   'pətnə
Patoka
  river, IN   puh-TŌ-kuh   pə'toːkə

Key (col. 2):   a: fad   ā: fade   ah: father   ar: marry   aw: law   e: fed   ē: feed   er: merry   i: hid   ī: hide   ō: coat   ōō: boot
oi: boy   ow: now   u: put   uh: above   uhr: bird   ch: chop   ng: ring   sh: show   th: thick   <u>th</u>: this   zh: measure

Paton

    Alan, *S. African novelist; pers. name*   PĀT-n   'peːtn̩

Patos

    lake, Argentina   PAH-tōs   'pɑtoːs

Patrae

    ancient form of Patras   PĀ-trē   'peːtri·

Pátrai

    town, Greece   PAH-trā   'pɑtreː

Patras

    town, Greece   puh-TRAS, PA-truhs   pə'træs, 'pætrəs

Patrice

    pers. name, French   pah-TRĒS   pɑːtriːs

Patricia

    pers. name   puh-TRISH-uh, puh-TRĒ-shuh   pə'triʃə, pə'triːʃə

Patricians

    Roman aristocratic class   puh-TRISH-uhnz   pə'triʃənz

Patricio

    pers. name, Spanish   pah-TRĒS-yō, pah-TRĒTH-yō   pɑ'triːsjoː, pɑ'triːθjoː

Patrick

    pers. name   PA-trik   'pætrik

Patrimonium

    Roman emperor's private estate   PA-truh-MŌ-nē-uhm   ˌpætrə'moːniːəm

Patripassianism

    Christian heresy   PA-truh-PAS-ē-uh-NIZ-uhm,   ˌpætrə'pæsiːəˌnizəm,

        PA-truh-PĀ-sē-uh-NIZ-uhm   ˌpætrə'peːsiːəˌnizəm

Patrizier

    German beer   pah-TRĒTS-yuhr   pɑ'triːtsjəʳ

Patrobas

    Biblical name   PA-truh-buhs   'pætrəbəs

Patroclus

    friend of Achilles   puh-TRŌ-kluhs   pə'troːkləs

Patsy

    pers. name   PAT-sē   'pætsi·

Pattala

    ancient city, Indus river delta   puh-TAHL-uh   pə'tɑlə

Patterson

    Floyd, *US boxer, athletic commissioner*   PAT-uhr-suhn   'pæṭəʳsən

Patti, Pattie, Patty

    pers. name   PAT-ē   'pæṭi·

Patton

    Gen. George Smith, *US general*   PAT-n   'pætn̩

Patuxent

    river, MD   puh-TUHK-suhnt   pə'təksənt

Pau

    city, France   PŌ   poː

Pauillac

    French wine   paw-YAHK, pō-YAHK   pɔːjɑːk, poːjɑːk

Paul

1. Wolfgang, *German physicist (Nobel 1989)*	POWL	'paul
2. US pers. name	PAWL	'pɔːl
3. Afrikaans	PŌ-ul	'poːul
4. Danish, Dutch, German, Norwegian, Swedish	POWL	'paul
5. French	PAWL	pɔːl

Paula

1. pers. name	PAW-luh	'pɔːlə
2. German, Spanish	POW-lah	'paula
3. Portuguese	POW-luh, POW-lah	'paulə, 'paulaː

Paulaner

German beer	POW-LAHN-uhr	'pau,lanəʳ

Paule

pers. name, French	PAWL	pɔːl

Paulette

pers. name	paw-LET	pɔːˈlet

Pauley

Jane, *US TV journalist*	PAW-lē	'pɔːliˑ

Pauli

Wolfgang, *Austrian-born US physicist (Nobel 1945)*	POW-lē	'pauliˑ

Pauline

1. pers. name	paw-LĒN, ⓔ PAW-LĒN	pɔːˈliːn, ⓔ 'pɔː,liːn
2. Dutch, German	pow-LĒ-nuh	pau'liːnə
3. French	paw-LĒN	pɔːliːn
4. pert. to St. Paul; *pupil of St. Paul's School, London*	PAW-LĪN	'pɔː,lain

Pauling

Linus C., *US chemist (Nobel 1954), pacifist (Nobel 1962)*	PAW-ling	'pɔːliŋ

Paulinism

doctrines of St. Paul	PAW-luh-NIZ-uhm	'pɔːlə,nizəm

Paulinus

pers. name	paw-LĪ-nuhs	pɔːˈlainəs

Paulo

pers. name, Portuguese	POW-loo	'pauluː

Paulo Afonso

waterfalls, Brazil	POW-loo uh-FŌN-soo	'pauluː əˈfõːnsuː

Paulus

1. pers. name, Afrikaans	PŌ-ul-uh(r)s	'poːulœs
2. German	POW-lus	'paulus

Paulus, Paullus

pers. name, Latin	PAW-luhs	'pɔːləs

Paung-daw-U

Burmese festival	POWNG-DOW-OO	'pauŋ'dau'uː

Pausanias

Spartan general	paw-SĀ-nē-uhs	pɔːˈseːniːəs

Pavane

dance	puh-VAHN, puh-VAN	pəˈvan, pəˈvæn

Pavarotti

Luciano, *Italian tenor*	PAHV-ah-RAWT-tē, ⓢ PAHV-uh-RAHT-ē, PAV-	ˌpavaˈrɔːttiː, ⓢ ˌpavəˈraṭiˑ, ˌpæv-

---

Key (col. 2): a: f**a**d   ā: f**a**de   ah: f**a**ther   ar: m**a**rry   aw: l**a**w   e: f**e**d   ē: f**ee**d   er: m**e**rry   i: h**i**d   ī: h**i**de   ō: c**oa**t   oo: b**oo**t
oi: b**oy**   ow: n**ow**   u: p**u**t   uh: **a**bove   uhr: b**i**rd   ch: **ch**op   ng: ri**ng**   sh: **sh**ow   th: **th**ick   th: **th**is   zh: mea**s**ure

Pavel
    1. pers. name, Czech   PAH-VEL, PAHV-uhl   'pɑːˌvel, 'pɑːvəl
    2. Russian   PAHV-yil   'pɑːvjil

Pavese
    Cesare, *Italian writer*   pah-VĀ-zā   pɑ'veːzeː

Pavia
    prov., Italy   puh-VĒ-uh   pə'viːə

Pavillon Blanc
    wine   pah-vē-yaw^n BLAH^n pɑːviːjɔ̃ blɑ̃

Pavlos
    pers. name, Mod. Greek   PAHV-laws   'pɑvlɔːs

Pavlov
    Ivan Petrovich, *Russian physiologist* (Nobel 1904)   PAHV-LAWF, PAV-LAWF, -LAWV   'pɑvˌlɔːf, 'pævˌlɔːf, -ˌlɔːv

Pavlova
    Anna Matreyevna, *Russian ballet dancer*   PAHV-luh-vuh, ⓢ PAV-luh-vuh, pav-LŌ-vuh   'pɑːvləvə, ⓢ 'pævləvə, pæv'loːvə

Pavlovian
    pert. to Pavlov; *learned response*   pav-LAW-vē-uhn, pav-LŌ-vē-uhn   pæv'lɔːviːən, pæv'loːviːən

Pavlovich
    patronym, Russian   puhv-LAWV-yich   pəv'lɔːvjitʃ

Pavo
    constellation   PĀ-vō, PAHV-ō   'peːvoː, 'pɑvoː

Pawcatuck
    river, RI   PAW-kuh-TUHK   'pɔːkəˌtək

Pawhuska
    city, OK   paw-HUHS-kuh   pɔː'həskə

Pawnee
    N. American people   paw-NĒ, pah-NĒ   pɔː'niː, pɑ'niː

Pawtucket
    city, RI   puh-TUHK-uht, paw-TUHK-uht   pə'təkət, pɔː'təkət

Pawtuxet
    river, RI   paw-TUHK-suht, puh-   pɔː'təksət, pə-

Pax
    Roman personification of peace   PAKS, PAHKS   'pæks, 'pɑks

Pax Christi
    Latin for 'Peace of Christ'   paks KRIS-tē, pahks   pæks 'kristiˑ, pɑks

Pax Romana
    Roman political peace   PAKS rō-MAHN-uh, PAHKS   'pæks roː'mɑnə, 'pɑks

Paxton
    Tom, *US songwriter*   PAK-stuhn   'pækstən

Payaguá
    S. American people   PĪ-(y)uh-GWAH   ˌpɑi(j)ə'gwɑ

Payette
    river, county, ID   pā-ET   peː'et

Pays de la Loire
    region, France   pād lahl WAHR   peːd laːl waːr

Payton
    Walter, *US football player*   PĀT-n   'peːtn̩

Paz
    1. Octavio, *Mexican poet (Nobel 1990)*   PAHS, ⓢ PAHZ   'pɑs, ⓢ 'pɑz
    2. pers. name, Spanish   PAHS, PAHTH   'pɑs, 'pɑθ

Paz, La
    see La Paz

Foreign Sounds: ue: *Fr.* **rue**, *Ger.* **füllen**   uh(r): *Fr.* **boeuf**, *Ger.* **Höhle**   kh: *Ger.* **ich**, *Scot.* **loch**   ḡ: *Sp.* amigo   v: *Sp.* hablar
hl: *Welsh* **Llanelli**.   CAPITALS: primary stress.   SMALL CAPS: secondary stress.   ⓢ: U.S. pron.   ⓔ: British pron.

Paz Estenssoro
   Victor, *president, Bolivia*   PAHS es-ten-SAWR-ō   ˌpɑs esten'sɔːroː

Peabody
   town, MA   PĒ-BAHD-ē, *esp. locally* PĒ-buhd-ē   'piːˌbɑdiˑ, *esp. locally* 'piːbədiˑ

Peale
   Norman Vincent, *US clergyman*   PĒL   'piːl

Peano
   Giuseppe, *Italian mathematician*   pā-AHN-ō   peː'ɑnoː

Pear
   British family name   PIR   'piʳ

Pearce
   pers. name   PIRS   'piʳs

Pearisburg
   town, VA   PER-is-BUHRG   'perisˌbəʳg

Pearl
   pers. name   PUHRL, PUHR-uhl   'pəʳl, 'pərəl

Pears
   1. Sir Peter, *British tenor*   PIRZ   'piʳz
   2. brand of soap   PERZ   'peʳz

Pearsall
   city, Texas   PIR-SAWL   'piʳˌsɔːl

Pearse
   pers. name   PIRS   'piʳs

Pearson
   Lester B., *Canadian politician*   PIRS-n   'piʳsn̩
   (Nobel 1957); airport, Toronto

Peary
   Robert E., *US admiral, explorer*   PIR-ē   'piriˑ

Pecksniff
   Seth, *character in* Martin   PEK-SNIF   'pekˌsnif
   Chuzzlewit, *Dickens*

Pecksniffian
   pert. to Pecksniff; *a hypocrite*   pek-SNIF-ē-uhn   pek'snifiːən

Peconic Bay
   inlet, NY   pi-KAHN-ik BĀ   pi'kɑnik 'beː

Pecorino Romano
   Italian cheese   PEK-uh-RĒ-nō rō-MAHN-ō   ˌpekə'riːnoː roː'mɑnoː

Pecos
   river, NM, TX; city, county, TX;   PĀ-kuhs   'peːkəs
   National Monument, *NM*

Pécs
   city, Hungary   PĀCH   'peːtʃ

Pedahel
   Biblical name   PED-uh-HEL, puh-dah-EL   'pedəˌhel, pədɑ'el

Pedahzur
   Biblical name   puh-DAHZ-uhr, puh-daht-SOOR   pə'dazəʳ, pədɑt'suːr

Pedaiah
   Biblical name   puh-DĪ-uh, puh-DĀ-uh, puh-dah-YAH   pə'daiə, pə'deːə, pədɑ'jɑ

Peder
   pers. name, Danish   PI-thuhr   'piðər

Pedernales
   1. river, TX   PUHRD-n-AL-uhs *[sic]*   ˌpəʳdn̩'æləs *[sic]*
   2. province, Dominican Republic   PED-er-NAH-les   ˌpeder'nɑles

---

Key (col. 2):   a: **fad**   ā: **fade**   ah: **father**   ar: **marry**   aw: **law**   e: **fed**   ē: **feed**   er: **merry**   i: **hid**   ī: **hide**   ō: **coat**   ōō: **boot**
oi: **boy**   ow: **now**   u: **put**   uh: **above**   uhr: **bird**   ch: **chop**   ng: **ring**   sh: **show**   th: **thick**   <u>th</u>: **this**   zh: **measure**

Pedersen
   1. Charles J., *US chemist (Nobel*   PED-uhr-suhn, PĒD-uhr-suhn   'pedəʳsən, 'piːdəʳsən
   1987)
   2. Knut, *Norwegian writer,*   PĀ-duhr-suhn   'peːdəʳsən
   pseudonym Knut Hamsun *(Nobel*
   1920)
Pedro
   1. pers. name, Portuguese   PĀ-th<u>r</u>oo, ⓢ PĀ-drō   'peːðruː, ⓢ 'peːdroː
   2. Spanish   PĀ-th<u>r</u>ō, ⓢ PĀ-drō   'peːðroː, ⓢ 'peːdroː
Pee Dee, Pedee
   river, NC, SC   PĒ DĒ   'piː ˌdiː
Pedroncelli
   J., winery, CA   PED-ruhn-CHEL-ē   ˌpedrən'tʃeliˑ
Pedro Ximenez
   wine grape   PĀ<u>TH</u>-rō hē-MĀ-neth   'peːðroː hiː'meːneθ
Pegasus
   mythical flying horse; constellation   PEG-uh-suhs   'pegəsəs
Peggy
   pers. name   PEG-ē   'pegiˑ
Pehr
   pers. name, Finnish, Swedish   PER   'per
Pei
   I. M., *US architect;* Mario, *US*   PĀ   'peː
   linguist
Peiping [Beijing]
   city, China   PĀ-PING   'peː'piŋ
Peipus
   lake, Estonia, Russia   PĪ-puhs   'paipəs
Peiraeus
   see Piraeus
Peisistratus, Pisistratus
   Athenian tyrant   pi-SIS-truht-uhs, puh-   pi'sistrəṭəs, pə-
Pekah
   Biblical name   PĒ-kuh, PE-kah<u>kh</u>   'piːkə, 'pekɑx
Pekahiah
   Biblical name   PEK-uh-HĪ-uh, puh-kah<u>kh</u>-YAH   ˌpekə'haiə, pəkɑx'jɑ
Pekin
   city, IL   PĒ-kuhn, PĒ-KIN   'piːkən, 'piːˌkin
Peking [Beijing]
   city, China   PĒ-KING, PĀ-KING   'piː'kiŋ, 'peː'kiŋ
Pekingese
   pert. to Peking; *dog breed*   PĒ-kuh-NĒZ, -NĒS; PĒ-king-ĒZ, -ĒS   ˌpiːkə'niːz, -'niːs; ˌpiːkiŋ'iːz, -'iːs
Pekod
   Biblical name   PĒ-KAHD, puh-KŌD   'piːˌkɑd, pə'koːd
Pelagian
   pert. to or a follower of Pelagius   puh-LĀ-jē-uhn   pə'leːdʒiːən
Pelagianism
   denial of original sin   puh-LĀ-jē-uh-NIZ-uhm   pə'leːdʒiːəˌnizəm
Pelagio
   pers. name, Spanish   pā-LAH-ḡyō   peː'lɑɣjoː
Pelagius
   pope   puh-LĀ-j(ē-)uhs   pə'leːdʒ(iː)əs
Pelaiah
   Biblical name   puh-LĪ-uh, puh-LĀ-uh, puh-lah-YAH   pə'laiə, pə'leːə, pəlɑ'jɑ

Pelaliah
  Biblical name   PEL-uh-LĪ-uh, puh-lahl-YAH   ˌpelə'laiə, pəlal'ja

Pelasgus
  founder of the Pelasgians   puh-LAS-guhs   pə'læsgəs

Pelatiah
  Biblical name   PEL-uh-TĪ-uh, puh-laht-YAH   ˌpelə'taiə, pəlat'ja

Pele
  Hawaiian volcano goddess   PĀ-lā   'peːleː

Pelé
  Brazilian soccer player   PĀ-lā   'peːleː

Pelée
  volcano, Martinique   puh-LĀ   pə'leː

Peleg
  Biblical name   PĒ-LEG, PEL-EG,   'piːˌleg, 'pelˌeg,

Peleliu
  island, Pacific   PEL-uh-LĒ-o͞o   ˌpelə'liːuː

Pelet
  Biblical name   PĒ-LET, PEL-ET   'piːˌlet, 'pelˌet

Peleth
  Biblical name   PĒ-LETH, PEL-ET   'piːˌleθ, 'pelˌet

Pelethite
  Biblical name   PĒ-luh-THĪT, PEL-uh-THĪT   'piːləˌθait, 'peləˌθait

Peleus
  father of Achilles   PĒ-lē-uhs, PĒL-YO͞OS   'piːliːəs, 'piːlˌjuːs

Pelham
  US pl. name; pers. name   PEL-uhm   'peləm

Pelias
  uncle of Jason   PEL-ē-uhs   'peliːəs

Pelion
  mtn., Greece   PĒ-lē-uhn   'piːliːən

Pelon
  Biblical name   PEL-uhn, PĒ-luhn, puh-LAWN   'pelən, 'piːlən, pə'lɔːn

Peloncillo
  mtn. range, NM   PEL-uhn-SĒ-(y)ō   ˌpelən'siː(j)oː

Pelonite
  Biblical name   PĒ-luh-NĪT, PEL-uh-NĪT   'piːləˌnait, 'peləˌnait

Pelopia
  mother of Aegisthus   puh-LŌ-pē-uh   pə'loːpiːə

Pelopidas
  Theban general   puh-LAHP-uhd-uhs   pə'lapədəs

Peloponnese
  peninsula, Greece   PEL-uh-puh-NĒZ, -NĒS   'peləpəˌniːz, -ˌniːs

Peloponnesian
  pert. to the Peloponnesus   PEL-uh-puh-NĒ-zhuhn, -shuhn ˌpeləpə'niːʒən, -ʃən

Peloponnesus
  peninsula, Greece   PEL-uh-puh-NĒ-suhs   ˌpeləpə'niːsəs

Pelopónnisos [Peloponnesus]
  peninsula, Greece   pel-uh-PAWN-uh-saws   pelə'pɔːnəsɔːs

Pelops
  father of Atreus   PĒ-LAHPS, PEL-AHPS   'piːˌlaps, 'pelˌaps

Pelouse
  see Palouse

Peltier
  effect, *electrical temperature change*   pel-TYĀ, PEL-tē-Ā   pel'tjeː, 'peltiːˌeː

Key (col. 2):   a: fad ā: fade ah: father ar: ma**rr**y aw: law e: fed ē: feed er: me**rr**y i: hid ī: hide ō: coat o͞o: boot
oi: boy ow: now u: put uh: above uhr: bird ch: chop ng: ring sh: show th: thick th: this zh: measure

Pelvoux, Massif du
　mtn., France　　mah-SĒF due pel-VOO　　mɑːsiːf dyː pelvuː
Pemba
　island, Indian Ocean; town,　　PEM-buh　　ˈpembə
　　Mozambique
Pembina
　county, ND　　PEM-buh-nuh, PEM-buh-NAW　　ˈpembənə, ˈpembəˌnɔː
Pembroke
　1. town, Wales; college, Oxford Univ.,　　PEM-bruk, PEM-bruhk, PEM-BRŌK　　ˈpembruk, ˈpembrək,
　　Cambridge Univ.　　　　　　　　　　　　　　　　　　　　　ˈpemˌbroːk
　2. pl. name, US　　PEM-BRŌK, PEM-BRUK　　ˈpemˌbroːk, ˈpemˌbruk
Pembrokeshire
　former county, Wales　　PEM-bruk-shuhr, PEM-bruhk-, -SHIR　　ˈpembrukʃəʳ, ˈpembrək-, -ˌʃiʳ
Pemigewasset
　river, NH　　PEM-uh-juh-WAHS-uht　　ˌpemədʒəˈwɑsət
Pemiscot
　county, MO　　PEM-i-SKAHT, PEM-i-SKŌ　　ˈpemiˌskɑt, ˈpemiˌskoː
Penang
　state, Malaysia　　puh-NANG　　pəˈnæŋ
Pen Argyl
　borough, PA　　PEN AHR-juhl　　ˌpen ˈɑʳdʒəl
Penates
　Roman household gods　　puh-NĀT-ēz, puh-NAHT-ēz　　pəˈneːṭiːz, pəˈnɑṭiːz
Penderecki
　Krzysztof, *Polish composer*　　PEN-duh-RET-skē　　ˌpendəˈretskiˑ
Pendergrass
　Teddy, *US musician, singer,*　　PEN-duhr-GRAS　　ˈpendəʳˌgræs
　　songwriter
Pendleton
　1. Austin, *US actor, director*　　PEN-dl-tuhn　　ˈpendl̩tən
　2. county, WV　　PEN-dl-tuhn, PEN-l-tuhn　　ˈpendl̩tən, ˈpenl̩tən
Pend Oreille
　county, WA　　PAHN duh-RĀ　　ˌpɑn dəˈreː
Pendragon
　title of Uther, King Arthur's father　　pen-DRAG-uhn, PEN-DRAG-uhn　　penˈdrægən, ˈpenˌdrægən
Penelope
　faithful wife of Odysseus; pers. name　　puh-NEL-uh-pē　　pəˈneləpiˑ
Penetanguishene
　city, Ontario　　PEN-uh-TANG-gwuh-SHĒN　　ˌpenəˈtæŋgwəˌʃiːn
Peneus
　ancient name of Salambria　　puh-NĒ-uhs　　pəˈniːəs
Peng-hu
　islands, Taiwan　　PUHNG-HOO　　ˈpəŋˈhuː
P'eng-hu Lieh-tao [Pescadores]
　islands, Taiwan　　PENG-HOO lē-E-DOW　　ˈpeŋˈhuː liːˈeˈdɑu
Peniel
　Biblical name　　puh-NĪ-uhl, PEN-ē-uhl, -EL; puh-nē-EL　　pəˈnɑiəl, ˈpeniːəl, -ˌel;
　　　　　　　　　　　　　　　　　　　　　　　　　　　　　　pəniːˈel
Penina
　pers. name　　pen-Ē-nuh, puh-NĒ-nuh　　penˈiːnə, pəˈniːnə
Peninnah
　Biblical name　　puh-NIN-uh, puh-nē-NAH　　pəˈninə, pəniːˈnɑ
Pennacook
　N. American people　　PEN-uh-KUK　　ˈpenəˌkuk

Foreign Sounds:　ue: *Fr.* **rue**, *Ger.* **füllen**　uh(r): *Fr.* **boeuf**, *Ger.* **Höhle**　kh: *Ger.* **ich**, *Scot.* **loch**　ǥ: *Sp.* **amigo**　ʋ: *Sp.* **hablar**
hl: *Welsh* **Llanelli**.　CAPITALS: primary stress.　SMALL CAPS: secondary stress.　Ⓢ: U.S. pron.　Ⓔ: British pron.

Pennine
   Alps, *Alpine mtn. range*   PEN-ĪN   'pen‚aın

Pennines, The
   mts., England   PEN-ĪNZ   'pen‚aınz

Pennsauken
   township, NJ   pen-SAW-kuhn   pen'sɔːkən

Pennsylvania
   state, US   PEN(T)-suhl-VĀ-nyuh, -VĀ-nē-uh   ‚pen(t)səl've:njə, -'ve:ni:ə

Pennsylvanian
   geologic period   PEN-suhl-VĀ-nyuhn, -nē-uhn   ‚pensəl've:njən, -ni:ən

Penny, Penney, Pennie
   pers. name   PEN-ē   'peni·

Penobscot
   river, bay, ME; N. American people   puh-NAHB-skuht, -SKAHT   pə'nɑbskət, -‚skɑt

Penrhyn
   pers. name   PEN-rin, pen-RIN   'penrin, pen'rin

Pensacola
   city, FL; N. American people   PEN(T)-suh-KŌ-luh   ‚pen(t)sə'koːlə

Pentagon
   US Defense Dept bldg.   PENT-uh-GAHN   'pentə‚gɑn

Pentateuch
   first five books of Bible   PENT-uh-T(Y)O͞OK   'pentə‚t(j)uːk

Pentax
   tdmk for a Japanese camera   PEN-TAKS   'pen‚tæks

Pentecost
   Christian holy day   PENT-uh-KAWST, -KAHST   'penṭə‚kɔːst, -‚kɑst

Penthesilea
   Amazon who fought Achilles   PEN-thuh-suh-LĒ-uh   ‚penθəsə'liːə

Pentheus
   king of Thebes   PEN-thē-uhs, PEN-TH(Y)O͞OS   'penθiːəs, 'pen‚θ(j)uːs

Pentothal
   tdmk for an anesthetic   PENT-uh-THAWL   'pentə‚θɔːl

Pentstemon
   plant   pent-STĒ-muhn, PEN(T)-stuh-muhn   pent'stiːmən, 'pen(t)stəmən

Penuel
   Biblical name   PEN-(y)uh-wuhl, puh-nO͞O-EL   'pen(j)əwəl, pənuː'el

Penutian
   N. American lang. group   puh-N(Y)O͞O-sh(ē-)uhn,   pə'n(j)uːʃ(iː)ən,
                                puh-N(Y)O͞OT-ē-uhn   pə'n(j)uːṭiːən

Penzance
   town, England   pen-ZAN(T)S, puhn-ZAN(T)S   pen'zæn(t)s, pən'zæn(t)s

Penzias
   Arno A., *German-born US*   PEN(T)-sē-uhs   'pen(t)siːəs
     astrophysicist (Nobel 1978)

Peor
   Biblical name   PĒ-AWR, -ŌR; puh-ŌR   'piː‚ɔːʳ, -‚oːʳ; pə'oːr

Peoria
   city, IL; N. American people   pē-ŌR-ē-uh, pē-AWR-ē-uh   piː'oːriːə, piː'ɔːriːə

Pepe
   1. pers. name   PEP-Ā, PEP-ē   'pep‚eː, 'pepi·
   2. Spanish   PĀ-pā   'peːpeː

Pepin
   1. Frankish king, father of   PEP-uhn   'pepən
    Charlemagne
   2. county, WI   PIP-uhn, PEP-uhn   'pipən, 'pepən

Key (col. 2): a: fad ā: fade ah: father ar: marry aw: law e: fed ē: feed er: merry i: hid ī: hide ō: coat o͞o: boot
oi: boy ow: now u: put uh: above uhr: bird ch: chop ng: ring sh: show th: thick th: this zh: measure

Peppard
  George, *US actor*   pep-AHRD, puh-PAHRD   pep'aʳd, pə'paʳd

Pepperdine
  University, *CA*   PEP-uhr-DĪN   'pepəʳˌdɑin

Pepperidge Farm
  US food co.   PEP-(uh-)rij FAHRM   ˌpep(ə)ridʒ 'fɑʳm

Pepsi-Cola
  tdmk for a soft drink   PEP-sē-KŌ-luh   ˌpepsiˑ'koːlə

Pepsodent
  tdmk for dental care products   PEP-suhd-uhnt, PEP-suh-DENT   'pepsədənt, 'pepsəˌdent

Pepys
  1. Samuel, *English diarist*   PĒPS   'piːps
  2. current British family name   PEP-is, PEPS   'pepis, 'peps

Pequannock
  river, village, NJ   pi-KWAHN-uhk   pi'kwɑnək

Pequonnock
  river, city, CT   pi-KWAHN-uhk   pi'kwɑnək

Pequot
  N. American people   PĒ-KWAHT   'piːˌkwɑt

Per
  pers. name, Swedish   PER   'per

Perahia
  Murray, *US pianist*   puh-RĪ-uh   pə'rɑiə

Perak
  river, state, Malaysia   PER-uh, PIR-uh *[sic]*   'perə, 'pirə *[sic]*

Perazim
  Biblical name   PER-uh-ZIM, puh-RĀ-zim, puh-raht-SĒM   'perəˌzim, pə'reːzim, pərɑt'siːm

Perceval
  pers. name   PUHR-suh-vuhl   'pəʳsəvəl

Percheron
  draft horse   PUHR-chuh-RAHN, PUHR-shuh-RAHN   'pəʳtʃəˌrɑn, 'pəʳʃəˌrɑn

Percival
  pers. name   PUHR-suh-vuhl   'pəʳsəvəl

Percy
  pers. name   PUHR-sē   'pəʳsiˑ

Perdiccas
  Macedonian king, general   puhr-DIK-uhs   pəʳ'dikəs

Perdue
  US food products co.   PUHR-D(Y)OO   ˌpəʳ'd(j)uː

Perdido
  river, AL   puhr-DĒD-ō   pəʳ'diːdoː

Peregrine
  pers. name   PER-uh-gruhn, -GRĒN, -GRIN   'perəgrən, -ˌgriːn, -ˌgrin

Pereira
  1. William, *US architect*   puh-RĀ-ruh, puh-RER-uh   pə're:rə, pə'rerə
  2. pers. name, Portuguese   puh-RĀ-ruh   pə're:rə

Perelman
  S. J., *US author*   PER-uhl-muhn *(his own pron.)*, PUHR-uhl-muhn, PUHRL-muhn   'perəlmən *(his own pron.)*, 'pər-əlmən, 'pəʳlmən

Peres
  Shimon, *Israeli politician*   PER-EZ   'perˌez

Peresh
  Biblical name   PIR-ESH, PER-ESH   'pirˌeʃ, 'perˌeʃ

Foreign Sounds: ue: *Fr.* **rue**, *Ger.* **füllen**   uh(r): *Fr.* **boeuf**, *Ger.* **Höhle**   kh: *Ger.* **ich**, *Scot.* **loch**   g̱: *Sp.* **amigo**   v̱: *Sp.* **hablar** hl: *Welsh* **Llanelli**.   CAPITALS: primary stress.   SMALL CAPS: secondary stress.   Ⓢ: U.S. pron.   Ⓔ: British pron.

Peretz, Perez
  Isaac Leip, *Polish Jewish poet*   PER-uhts, PER-ets   'perəts, 'perets
Perey
  Marguerite, *French physicist*   pe-RĀ   pereː
Pérez
  pers. name, Spanish   PĀ-rās, PĀ-rāth   'peːreːs, 'peːreːθ
Perez
  Biblical name   PIR-EZ, PER-EZ, PER-ETS   'pir‚ez, 'per‚ez, 'per‚ets
Pérez de Cuellar
  Javier, *UN Secretary General*   PĀ-rās <u>th</u>ā KWĀ-(y)ahr   'peːreːs ðeː 'kweː(j)aʳ
Perezite
  Biblical name   PIR-uh-ZĪT, PER-   'pirə‚zɑit, 'per-
Perez-uzzah, Perez-uzza
  Biblical name   PIR-EZ-UHZ-uh, PER-et-sōō-ZAH   'pir‚ez'əzə, 'peretsuː'zɑː
Perfect
  pers. name (C. P. McVie)   PUHR-fikt   'pəʳfikt
Perga
  Biblical name   PUHR-guh   'pəʳgə
Pergamon
  town, Turkey   PUHR-guh-MAHN   'pəʳgə‚mɑn
Pergamos
  Biblical name   PUHR-guh-MAHS, MAWS, -muhs, puhr-GAM-uhs   'pəʳgə‚mɑs, -‚mɔːs, -məs, pəʳ'gæməs
Pergamum
  city, ancient Greek kingdom, Asia Minor   PUHR-guh-muhm   'pəʳgəməm
Pergamus
  son of Andromache and Neoptolemus   PUHR-guh-muhs   'pəʳgəməs
Pergolesi
  Giovanni Battista, *Italian composer*   PER-gō-LĀ-sē   ‚peʳgoː'leːsi·
Periander
  Greek statesman   PER-ē-AN-duhr   ‚periː'ændəʳ
Peribonca
  river, Canada   PER-uh-BAHNG-kuh   ‚perə'baŋkə
Periclean
  pert. to Pericles   PER-i-KLĒ-uhn   ‚peri'kliːən
Pericles
  Athenian statesman   PER-i-KLĒZ   'peri‚kliːz
Perida
  Biblical name   puh-RĪD-uh, puh-rē-DAH   pə'rɑidə, pəriː'dɑ
Périgord
  prov, France   pā-rē-GAWR   peːriːgɔːr
Périgueux
  town, France; sauce with truffles   pā-rē-GUH(R)   peːriːgœː
Perikles
  pers. name, Mod. Greek   per-ē-KLĒS   periː'kliːs
Perilla
  plant   puh-RIL-uh   pə'rilə
Perioeci
  free inhabitants of Laconia   PER-ē-Ē-SĪ   ‚periː'iː‚sɑi
Peripatetic
  pert. to the Aristotelian school of philosophy   PER-uh-puh-TET-ik   ‚perəpə'teţik
Peripateticism
  Aristotelianism   PER-uh-puh-TET-uh-SIZ-uhm   ‚perəpə'teţə‚sizəm

---

Key (col. 2):   a: f**a**d   ā: f**a**de   ah: f**a**ther   ar: m**a**rry   aw: l**a**w   e: f**e**d   ē: f**ee**d   er: m**e**rry   i: h**i**d   ī: h**i**de   ō: c**oa**t   ōō: b**oo**t
oi: b**oy**   ow: n**ow**   u: p**u**t   uh: **a**bove   uhr: b**ir**d   ch: **ch**op   ng: ri**ng**   sh: **sh**ow   th: **th**ick   <u>th</u>: **th**is   zh: mea**s**ure

Periphetes
  brigand slain by Theseus   PER-uh-FĒT-ēz   ˌperəˈfiːt̬iːz
Perissodactyla
  hoofed animals   puh-RIS-uh-DAK-tuh-luh   pəˌrisəˈdæktələ
Perizzite
  Biblical name   PER-uh-ZĪT   ˈperəˌzɑit
Perkin
  pers. name   PUHR-kuhn   ˈpərᵏkən
Perkins
  Anthony, *US actor*   PUHR-kuhnz   ˈpərᵏkənz
Perlis
  state, Malaysia   PER-luhs   ˈperᵏləs
Perlman
  Rhea, *US actress*   PUHRL-muhn   ˈpərᵏlmən
Perm
  city, Russia   PYERM, Ⓢ PUHRM, PERM   ˈpjerm, Ⓢ ˈpərᵏm, ˈperᵏm
Permian
  geologic period   PUHR-mē-uhn   ˈpərᵏmiːən
Pernambuco
  state, Brazil   PER-nuhm-B͞O͞O-kō,   ˌperᵏnəmˈbuːkoː,
                                    PUHR-nuhm-B(Y)͞O͞O-kō   ˌpərᵏnəmˈb(j)uːkoː
Pernod
  tdmk for a liqueur   per-NŌ   perᵏˈnoː
Perón
  Juan *and* Evita, *Argentine political* pā-RŌN, puh-RŌN   peːˈroːn, pəˈroːn
  leaders
Peroni
  Italian beer   pā-RŌ-nē   peːˈroːniː
Perot
  H. Ross, *US business executive* puh-RŌ, PIR-ō   pəˈroː, ˈpiroː
Perpignan
  town, France   per-pēn-YAHⁿ   perpiːnjɑ̃
Perquimans
  county, NC   puhr-KWIM-uhn(t)s   pərᵏˈkwimən(t)s
Perrault
  Charles, *French poet, author of fairy* pe-RŌ, Ⓢ puh-RŌ, per-Ō   peroː, Ⓢ pəˈroː, perˈoː
  tales
Perrier
  tdmk for mineral water   PER-ē-Ā, per-YĀ   ˈperiːˌeː, perˈjeː
Perrin
  1. pers. name   PER-uhn   ˈperən
  2. J. B., French physicist (Nobel pe-REⁿ   perẽ
  1926)
Perrine
  Valerie, *US actress*   puh-RĪN   pəˈrɑin
Perry
  pers. name   PER-ē   ˈperiˑ
Perse
  St.-John, *pseudonym of* Alexis   PERS, Ⓢ PUHRS   ˈpers, Ⓢ ˈpərᵏs
  St.-Léger Léger
Perseids
  meteor shower   PUHR-sē-uhdz   ˈpərᵏsiːədz
Persephone
  Greek goddess of the Underworld puhr-SEF-uh-nē   pərᵏˈsefəniˑ

Foreign Sounds: ue: *Fr.* **rue**, *Ger.* **füllen** uh(r): *Fr.* **boeuf**, *Ger.* **Höhle** kh: *Ger.* **ich**, *Scot.* **loch** ḡ: *Sp.* **amigo** v̇: *Sp.* **hablar**
hl: *Welsh* **Llanelli**. CAPITALS: primary stress. SMALL CAPS: secondary stress. Ⓢ: U.S. pron. Ⓔ: British pron.

Persepolis		
ancient Persian city	puhr-SEP-uh-luhs	pəʳˈsepələs
Perses		
father of Hecate	PUHR-sēz	ˈpəʳsiːz
Perseus		
mythological Greek hero; constellation; pers. name	PUHR-sē-uhs, PUHR-S(Y)O͞OS	ˈpəʳsiːəs, ˈpəʳˌs(j)uːs
Pershing		
John, *US general*	PUHR-shing, PUHR-zhing	ˈpəʳʃiŋ, ˈpəʳʒiŋ
Persia		
former name for Iran	PUHR-zhuh, PUHR-shuh	ˈpəʳʒə, ˈpəʳʃə
Persian		
pert. to Persia; *lang., Middle East*	PUHR-zhuhn, PUHR-shuhn	ˈpəʳʒən, ˈpəʳʃən
Persis		
Biblical name	PUHR-sis	ˈpəʳsis
Perth		
city, Australia; city, Scotland	PUHRTH	ˈpəʳθ
Perth Amboy		
city, NJ	PUHRTH AM-BOI	ˌpəʳθ ˈæmˌbɔi
Pertinax		
Roman emperor	PUHRT-n-AKS	ˈpəʳtn̩ˌæks
Peru		
1. republic, S. America	pā-RO͞O, [S] puh-RO͞O	peːˈruː, [S] pəˈruː
2. city, IL; city, IN	PĒ-RO͞O, puh-RO͞O	ˈpiːˌruː, pəˈruː
Peruda		
Biblical name	puh-RO͞OD-uh, puh-ro͞o-DAH	pəˈruːdə, pəruːˈdɑ
Perugia		
prov, Italy	puh-RO͞O-j(ē-)uh	pəˈruːdʒ(iː)ə
Perugino		
Italian painter	PER-o͞o-JĒ-nō	ˌperuːˈdʒiːnoː
Perutz		
M. F., *Austrian-born British biochemist (Nobel 1962)*	puh-RO͞OTS	pəˈruːts
Peruvian		
pert. to Peru	puh-RO͞O-vē-uhn	pəˈruːviːən
Pesach, Pesah [Passover]		
Jewish holiday	PĀ-SAHKH, PES-AHKH	ˈpeːˌsɑx, ˈpesˌɑx
Pescadores		
islands, Taiwan	PES-kuh-DŌR-ēz, -DAWR-ēz	ˌpeskəˈdoːriːz, -ˈdɔːriːz
Peshawar		
prov, Pakistan	puh-SHAH-wuhr, puh-SHOW(-uh)r	pəˈʃɑwəʳ, pəˈʃɑu(ə)ʳ
Peshtigo		
river, city, WI	PESH-ti-GŌ	ˈpeʃtiˌgoː
Pessoa		
Fernando António Nogueira, *Portuguese poet*	PES-wah, PES-o͞o-ah	ˈpeswɑː, ˈpesuːɑː
Pest		
county, Hungary	PESHT, [S] PEST	ˈpeʃt, [S] ˈpest
Pestalozzi		
Johann H., *Swiss educational reformer*	PES-tuh-LAHT-sē	ˌpestəˈlɑtsiˑ
Petach Tikva		
town, Israel	PE-TAHKH TIK-vah [S] PET-uhk TIK-vuh	ˈpeˌtɑx ˈtikvɑ [S] ˈpet̬ək ˈtikvə

Key (col. 2): a: **fad** ā: **fade** ah: **father** ar: **marry** aw: **law** e: **fed** ē: **feed** er: **merry** i: **hid** ī: **hide** ō: **coat** o͞o: **boot** oi: **boy** ow: **now** u: **put** uh: **above** uhr: **bird** ch: **chop** ng: **ring** sh: **show** th: **thick** th: **this** zh: **measure**

Pétain

Henri Philippe, *French militarist*   pā-TE^n peːtẽ

Petaluma

city, CA   PET-l-OO-muh   ˌpeʈlˈuːmə

Petar

pers. name, Serbo-Croatian   PE-tahr   ˈpetɑːr

Pete

pers. name   PĒT   ˈpiːt

Peter

1. New Testament book; pers. name   PĒT-uhr   ˈpiːʈə^r

2. Danish   PI-tuhr   ˈpitər

3. Dutch, Norwegian, Swedish   PĀ-tuhr   ˈpeːtər

4. German   PE-tuhr   ˈpetə^r

Péter

pers. name, Hungarian   PĀ-ter   ˈpeːter

Peterhouse

college, Cambridge Univ.   PĒT-uhr-HOWS   ˈpiːʈə^{r}ˌhɑus

Petersham

town, England; heavy woolen cloth for coats   PĒT-uhr-shuhm, -SHAM   ˈpiːʈə^{r}ʃəm, -ˌʃæm

Pethahiah

Biblical name   PETH-uh-HĪ-uh, puh-tah<u>kh</u>-YAH   ˌpeθəˈhɑiə, pətɑxˈjɑ

Pethor

Biblical name   PĒ-THAWR, PĒ-THŌR, puh-TŌR   ˈpiːˌθɔː^r, ˈpiːˌθoː^r, pəˈtoːr

Pethuel

Biblical name   puh-TH(Y)OO-uhl, puh-too-EL   pəˈθ(j)uːəl, pətuːˈel

Petit

pers. name   PET-uht   ˈpeʈət

Petite Champagne

wine   puh-TĒT shah^n-PAHN-yuh   pətiːt ʃɑ̃pɑːɲ

Petite Sirah

wine grape   puh-TĒT suh-RAH   pəˌtiːt səˈrɑ

Petits pois

peas   puh-tē PWAH   pətiː ˈpwɑ

Petit Village

wine   puh-TĒ vē-LAHZH   pətiː viːlɑːʒ

Petőfi

Sándor, *Hungarian poet*   PET-uh(r)-fē, Ⓢ PET-uh-fē   ˈpetœːfiˑ, Ⓢ ˈpeʈəfiˑ

Petoskey

city, MI   puh-TAHS-kē   pəˈtɑskiˑ

Petr

1. pers. name, Czech   PET-uhr   ˈpeʈər

2. Russian   PYAW-tuhr   ˈpjɔːtər

Pëtr

pers. name, Russian   PYAW-tuhr   ˈpjɔːtər

Petra

1. ruined city, Jordan   PĒ-truh, PE-truh   ˈpiːtrə, ˈpetrə

2. pers. name   PE-truh   ˈpetrə

Petrarch

Italian poet, scholar   PĒ-TRAHRK, PE-TRAHRK   ˈpiːˌtrɑ^{r}k, ˈpeˌtrɑ^{r}k

Petrarchan

pert. to Petrarch; type of sonnet   pē-TRAHR-kuhn, pe-TRAHR-kuhn   piˑˈtrɑ^{r}kən, peˈtrɑ^{r}kən

Petri

J. R., *German bacteriologist; bacteria culture dish*   PĒ-trē, PE-trē   ˈpiːtriˑ, ˈpetriˑ

Foreign Sounds: ue: *Fr.* **rue**, *Ger.* f**ü**llen uh(r): *Fr.* b**oeu**f, *Ger.* H**öh**le <u>kh</u>: *Ger.* i**ch**, *Scot.* lo**ch** ḡ: *Sp.* ami**g**o <u>v</u>: *Sp.* ha**b**lar
hl: *Welsh* L**l**anelli. CAPITALS: primary stress. SMALL CAPS: secondary stress. Ⓢ: U.S. pron. Ⓔ: British pron.

Petrie		
Sir William Matthew Flinders, *English archaeologist*	PĒ-trē	ˈpiːtriˑ
Petrofina		
Belgian petroleum firm	PE-trō-FĒ-nuh	ˌpetroːˈfiːnə
Petrograd		
former name of St. Petersburg, *Russia*	pyi-TRUH-GRAHT, $ PE-truh-GRAD	pjiˌtrəˈgrɑːt, $ ˈpetrəˌgræd
Petronius		
Roman writer; pers. name, Latin	puh-TRŌ-nē-uhs	pəˈtroːniːəs
Petropavlovsk		
city, Kazakhstan	PYI-truh-PAHV-luhfsk, $ PE-truh-PAV-LAWFSK	ˌpjitrəˈpɑvləfsk, $ ˌpetrəˈpævˌlɔːfsk
Petrópolis		
town, Brazil	puh-TRAHP-uh-luhs	pəˈtrɑpələs
Petros		
town, Romania	PE-truh-SHAHN(-ē)	ˌpetrəˈʃɑn(iˑ)
Pétrou		
pers. name, Greek	PĀ-tro͞o	ˈpeːtruː
Petrouchka		
ballet, Stravinsky	pe-TRO͞OCH-kuh, puh-TRO͞OSH-kuh	peˈtruːtʃkə, pəˈtruːʃkə
Petrov		
Yevgeny, *pseudonym of* Yevgeny Katayev	PYĀ-truhf	ˈpjeːtrəf
Petrovna		
pers. name, Russian	pyi-TRAWV-nuh	pjiˈtrɔːvnə
Petrozavodsk		
city, Russia	PE-truh-suh-VAHTSK	ˌpetrəsəˈvɑːtsk
Petruccio		
1. pers. name	puh-TRO͞O-chē-ō, puh-TRO͞O-chō	pəˈtruːtʃiːˌoː, pəˈtruːtʃoː
2. Italian	pā-TRO͞OT-chō	peːˈtruːttʃoː
Petruchio		
character in Taming of the Shrew, *Shakespeare*	puh-TRO͞O-kē-ō, puh-TRO͞O-chē-ō, puh-TRO͞O-chō	pəˈtruːkiːoː, pəˈtruːtʃiːˌoː, pəˈtruːtʃoː
Petrus		
1. pers. name, Dutch	PĀ-trues	ˈpeːtrys
2. Latin	PĒ-truhs	ˈpiːtrəs
3. Swedish	PĀ-truhs	ˈpeːtrəs
Pétrus		
pers. name, French	pā-TRUES	peːtrys
Petsamo		
territory, Russia	PET-suh-MŌ	ˈpetsəˌmoː
Petula		
pers. name	puh-T(Y)O͞O-luh	pəˈt(j)uːlə
Peugeot		
French car co.	puh(r)-ZHŌ, $ p(y)o͞o-ZHŌ	pœːʒoː, $ p(j)uːˈʒoː
Peullethai [Peulthai]		
Biblical name	pē-UH-luh-THĪ, puh-ul-TĪ	piːˈələˌθai, pəulˈtai
Peulthai		
Biblical name	pē-UHL-THĪ, puh-ul-TĪ	piːˈəlˌθai, pəulˈtai
Pewaukee		
village, WI	pi-WAW-kē	piˈwɔːkiˑ
Pewee		
bird	PĒ-WĒ	ˈpiːˌwiː

Key (col. 2): a: **fad** ā: **fade** ah: **father** ar: **marry** aw: **law** e: **fed** ē: **feed** er: **merry** i: **hid** ī: **hide** ō: **coat** o͞o: **boot** oi: **boy** ow: **now** u: **put** uh: **above** uhr: **bird** ch: **chop** ng: **ring** sh: **show** th: **thick** t͟h: **this** zh: **measure**

Peyton		
pers. name	PĀT-n	'peːtn̩
Pfaff		
Johann, *German mathematician; sewing machine co.*	PFAHF	'pfɑf
Pfeiffer		
Michelle, *US actress;* College, *NC*	FĪ-fuhr	'fɑifəʳ
Pfizer		
US chemical co.	FĪ-zuhr	'fɑizəʳ
Pforzheim		
city, Germany	PFAWRTS-HĪM, [$] FAWRTS-(H)ĪM	'pfɔːʳts,hɑim, [$] 'fɔːʳts,(h)ɑim
Phaeacians		
mythical sailors	fē-Ā-shuhnz	fiː'eːʃənz
Phaedo		
Greek philosopher; dialogue of Plato	FĒD-ō	'fiːdoː
Phaedra		
wife of Theseus	FĒ-druh, FE-druh, FĀ-druh	'fiːdrə, 'fedrə, 'feːdrə
Phaedrus		
Greek philosopher; dialogue of Plato	FĒ-druhs, FE-druhs, FĀ-druhs	'fiːdrəs, 'fedrəs, 'feːdrəs
Phaestus		
1. ancient city, Crete	FES-tuhs, FĒ-stuhs	'festəs, 'fiːstəs
2. son of Heracles	FĒ-stuhs	'fiːstəs
Phaëthon		
son of Helios	FĀ-uht-n, FĀ-uh-tuhn, FĀ-uh-THAHN	'feːətn̩, 'feːətən, 'feːə,θɑn
Phaidon		
Cultural Guides, *imprint for a book series*	FĪD-n	'fɑidn̩
Phainopepla		
songbird	fā-Ī-nuh-PEP-luh, FĪN-uh-PEP-luh	feː,ɑinə'peplə, ,fɑinə'peplə
Phalange, Phalangist		
see Falange, Falangist		
Phalanx		
brother of Arachne	FĀ-LANGKS, [£] FAL-ANGKS	'feː,læŋks, [£] 'fæl,æŋks
Phalarope		
shore bird	FAL-uh-RŌP	'fælə,roːp
Pham Van Dong		
prime minister, Vietnam	FAHM VAHN DAHNG	,fɑm ,vɑn 'dɑŋ
Phanerozoic		
eon that includes Paleozoic, Mesozoic, Cenozoic eras	FAN-uhr-uh-ZŌ-ik	,fænərə'zoːik
Phanuel		
Biblical name	fuh-N(Y)OO-uhl, FAN-yuh(-wuh)l	fə'n(j)uːəl, 'fænjə(wə)l
Phaon		
legendary ferryman of Lesbos	FĀ-uhn, FĀ-AHN	'feːən, 'feː,ɑn
Pharaoh		
Egyptian ruler	FER-ō, FAR-ō, FĀ-rō	'feroː, 'færoː, 'feːroː
Pharaoh-hophra		
Biblical name	FER-ō-HAHF-ruh, FAR-ō-, FĀ-rō-; pahr-Ō-khahf-RAH	'feroː'hɑfrə, 'færoː-, 'feːroː-; pɑr'oːxɑf'rɑː
Pharaoh-necho		
Biblical name	FER-ō-NĒ-kō, FAR-ō-, FĀ-rō-, -NEK-ō; pahr-Ō-nuh-KHŌ	'feroː'niːkoː, 'færoː-, 'feːroː-, -'nekoː; pɑr'oːnə'xoː
Pharaonic		
like a Pharoah	FER-ā-AHN-ik, FAR-ā-AHN-ik	,fereː'ɑnik, ,færeː'ɑnik

Phares
  Biblical name   FĀ-RĒZ, FAHR-ES   'feːˌriːz, 'fɑrˌes
Pharez
  Biblical name   FĀ-REZ, FAR-EZ, PER-ets   'feːˌrez, 'færˌez, 'perets
Pharisaic
  pert. to Pharisees   FAR-uh-SĀ-ik   ˌfærə'seːik
Pharisee
  Jewish sect   FAR-uh-sē   'færəsiː
Phariseeism
  tenets of the Pharisees   FAR-uh-SĒ-ız-uhm, FER-   'færəˌsiːˌizəm, 'fer-
Pharos
  ancient lighthouse, Alexandria; pilot FAR-AHS, FER-AHS   'færˌɑs, 'ferˌɑs
    for Helen & Menelaus
Pharosh [Parosh]
  Biblical name   FĀ-RAHSH, FAR-AHSH, pahr-AWSH   'feːˌrɑʃ, 'færˌɑʃ, pɑr'ɔːʃ
Pharpar
  river, Damascus   FAHR-puhr   'fɑrpər
Pharsalia
  epic poem, Lucan   fahr-SĀ-lē-uh, fahr-SĀL-yuh   fɑr'seːliːə, fɑr'seːljə
Pharsalus
  battlesite, Greece   fahr-SĀ-luhs   fɑr'seːləs
Pharzite
  Biblical name   FAHR-ZĪT   'fɑrˌzɑit
Phebe
  Biblical name   FĒ-bē   'fiːbiˑ
Pheidias [Phidias]
  Greek sculptor   FID-ē-uhs, FĪD-ē-uhs   'fidiːəs, 'fɑidiːəs
Pheidippides
  Greek runner from Sparta to Athens   fī-DIP-uhd-ĒZ   fɑi'dipədˌiːz
    before battle of Marathon
Pheidon
  king of Argos   FĪ-DAHN   'fɑiˌdɑn
Phelim
  pers. name, Irish Gaelic   FYĀ-lyim, Ⓢ FĀ-lim   'fjeːljim, Ⓢ 'feːlim
Phenice
  Biblical name   fuh-NĪ-suh, FĒ-nuh-SĒ   fə'nɑisə, 'fiːnəˌsiˑ
Phenix City
  city, AL   FĒ-niks SIT-ē   ˌfiːniks 'sitiˑ
Phenomenology
  study of awareness; classification of fi-NAHM-uh-NAHL-uh-jē   fiˌnɑmə'nɑlədʒiˑ
    phenomena
Pheops
  name, Egyptian kings   FĒ-AHPS   'fiːˌɑps
Pheres
  son of Medea and Jason   FER-ĒZ   'ferˌiːz
Phibeseth [Pibeseth]
  Biblical name   FĪ-buh-SETH, FIB-uh-SETH, fī-BĒ-SETH,   'fɑibəˌseθ, 'fibəˌseθ,
                                           fē-BES-et   fɑi'biːˌseθ, fiː'beset
Phi Beta Kappa
  academic honor society   FĪ BĀT-uh KAP-uh   ˌfɑi ˌbeːtə 'kæpə
Phicol, Phichol
  Biblical name   FĪ-KAHL, FĒ-; fē-KAWL   'fɑiˌkɑl, 'fiː-; fiː'kɔːl
Phidias [Pheidias]
  Greek sculptor   FID-ē-uhs   'fidiːəs

Key (col. 2): a: fad ā: fade ah: father ar: marry aw: law e: fed ē: feed er: merry i: hid ī: hide ō: coat ōō: boot
oi: boy ow: now u: put uh: above uhr: bird ch: chop ng: ring sh: show th: thick th: this zh: measure

Phil

pers. name	FIL	'fil

Philadanco

dance co., PA	FIL-uh-DANG-kō, FIL-uh-DAN-kō	ˌfilə'dæŋkoː, ˌfilə'dænkoː

Philadelphia

city, PA	FIL-uh-DEL-fyuh, -fē-uh	ˌfilə'delfjə, -fiːə

Philammon

legendary poet and seer	fuh-LAM-uhn	fə'læmən

Philander

1. pers. name	fuh-LAN-duhr	fə'lændəʳ
2. Dutch	fē-LAHN-duhr	fiː'lɑndər
3. German	fē-LAHN-duhr	fiː'lɑndəʳ

Philéas

pers. name, French	fē-lā-AHS	fiːleːɑs

Philebus

dialogue of Plato	fuh-LĒ-buhs, fī-LĒ-buhs	fə'liːbəs, fɑi'liːbəs

Philemon

New Testament book; pers. name	fuh-LĒ-muhn, fī-	fə'liːmən, fɑi-

Philetus

Biblical name	fuh-LĒT-uhs	fə'liː̪təs

Philharmonia

orchestra	FIL-uhr-MŌ-nē-uh,	ˌfiləʳ'moːniːə,
	FIL-(H)AHR-MŌ-nē-uh	ˌfilˌ(h)ɑʳ'moːniːə

Philharmonia Virtuosi

symphony, NY	FIL-uhr-MŌ-nē-uh vuhr-chuh-WŌ-sē,	ˌfiləʳ'moːniːə vəʳtʃə'woːsiˑ,
	FIL-(H)AHR-MŌ-nē-uh	ˌfilˌ(h)ɑʳ'moːniːə

Philip

1. pers. name	FIL-uhp	'filəp
2. Dutch	FĒ-luhp	'fiːləp
3. German	FĒ-lip, FIL-ip	'fiːlip, 'filip
4. Swedish	FĒ-lip	'fiːlip

Philipp

1. pers. name	FIL-uhp	'filəp
2. German	FĒ-lip, FIL-ip	'fiːlip, 'filip
3. Russian	fyil-YĒP	fjil'jiːp
4. Swedish	FĒ-lip	'fiːlip

Philippa

pers. name	FIL-uh-puh, FI-LI-puh	'filəpə, ˌfi'lipə

Philippe

pers. name, French	fē-LĒP	fiː'liːp

Philippi

1. ancient town, Macedonia	FIL-uh-PĪ, fuh-LIP-Ī	'filəˌpɑi, fə'lipˌɑi
2. Civil War battle site, WV	FIL-uh-pē	'filəpiː

Philippians

New Testament book	fuh-LIP-ē-uhnz	fə'lipiːənz

Philippics

speeches of Demosthenes	fuh-LIP-iks	fə'lipiks

Philippines

island nation, Pacific	FIL-uh-PĒNZ, FIL-uh-PĒNZ	ˌfilə'piːnz, 'filəˌpiːnz

Philippism

doctrines of Philip Melanchthon	FIL-uh-PIZ-uhm	'filəˌpizəm

Philippus

pers. name	fi-LIP-uhs	fi'lipəs

Philistia

ancient region, Palestine	fuh-LIS-tē-uh	fə'listiːə

Philistine
  inhabitant of Philistia   FIL-uh-STĒN, -STĪN; fuh-LIS-tuhn,   'filə,sti:n, -,stɑin; fə'listən,
                                     FIL-uh-stuhn   'filəstən

Phillip
  pers. name   FIL-uhp   'filəp

Phillips
  pers. name   FIL-uhps   'filəps

Philly
  nickname for Philadelphia   FIL-ē   'fili·

Philo
  pers. name   FĪ-lō   'failo:

Philoctetes
  keeper of the bow and arrow of   fi-LAHK-tuh-TĒZ, FIL-ahk-TĒT-ēz   fi'lɑktə,ti:z, ,filɑk'ti:ʈi:z
    Heracles

Philologus
  Latin bestiary; Biblical name   fuh-LAHL-uh-guhs   fə'lɑləgəs

Philomel
  poetic Latin name for the nightingale   FIL-uh-MEL   'filə,mel

Philomela
  sister of Procne   FIL-uh-MĒ-luh   ,filə'mi:lə

Philomena
  Christian saint   FIL-uh-MĒ-nuh   ,filə'mi:nə

Philosophiae Baccalaureus
  bachelor of philosophy, Ph.B.   fil-AHS-uh-FĒ-Ī BAK-uh-LŌR-ē-uhs,   fil,asə'fi:,ai ,bækə'lo:ri:əs,
                                    -LAWR-ē-uhs   -'lɔ:ri:əs

Philosophiae Doctor
  doctor of philosophy, Ph.D.   fil-AHS-uh-FĒ-Ī DAHK-TAWR   fil,asə'fi:,ai 'dɑk,tɔ:ʳ

Philostratus
  Greek sophist at Rome   fuh-LAHS-truht-uhs   fə'lɑstrəʈəs

Philyra
  mother of Chiron by Cronus   fil-Ī-ruh   fil'airə

Phineas
  pers. name   FIN-ē-uhs   'fini:əs

Phinehas
  Biblical name   FIN-ē-uhs, PĒN-<u>KH</u>AHS   'fini:əs, 'pi:n,xɑs

Phineus
  uncle of Andromeda; king of Thrace   FIN-ē-uhs   'fini:əs

pHisoDerm
  tdmk for a medicated soap   FĪ-suh-DUHRM, FĪ-zuh-DUHRM   'faisə,dəʳm, 'faizə,dəʳm

Phix
  the Sphinx   FIKS   'fiks

Phlegethon
  river of Hades   FLEG-uh-THAHN   'flegə,θɑn

Phlias
  Argonaut   FLĒ-uhs   'fli:əs

Phlegon
  Biblical name   FLĒ-GAHN   'fli:,gɑn

Phlox
  flower   FLAHKS   'flɑks

Phnom Penh
  city, Cambodia   (puh-)NAHM PEN   (pə)'nɑm 'pen

Phobos
  "Fear," son of Ares; satellite of Mars   FŌ-BŌS, FŌ-buhs   'fo:,bo:s, 'fo:bəs

Phocaea
  ancient city, Asia Minor   fō-SĒ-uh   fo:'si:ə

Key (col. 2):   a: fad   ā: fade   ah: father   ar: marry   aw: law   e: fed   ē: feed   er: merry   i: hid   ī: hide   ō: coat   ōō: boot
oi: boy   ow: now   u: put   uh: above   uhr: bird   ch: chop   ng: ring   sh: show   th: thick   <u>th</u>: this   zh: measure

Phocas
  pers. name, Latin   FŌ-kuhs   'foːkəs
Phocis [Fokis]
  ancient district, dept., Greece   FŌ-suhs   'foːsəs
Phocus
  father of Callirhoe   FŌ-kuhs   'foːkəs
Phoebe
  Titaness in Greek myth; songbird;   FĒ-bē   'fiːbi·
    satellite of Saturn; pers. name
Phoebus
  epithet of Apollo; pers. name   FĒ-buhs   'fiːbəs
Phoenice
  ancient city, Epirus   fi-NĪ-sē   fi'nɑisi·
Phoenicia
  ancient country, Syria   fi-NISH-(ē-)uh, fi-NĒ-sh(ē-)uh   fi'niʃ(iː)ə, fi'niːʃ(iː)ə
Phoenician
  lang., native of Phoenicia   fi-NISH-(ē-)uhn, fi-NĒ-sh(ē-)uhn   fi'niʃ(iː)ən, fi'niːʃ(iː)ən
Phoenicids
  meteor shower   FĒ-nuh-sidz   'fiːnəsidz
Phoenix
  city, AZ; mythical bird; companion of   FĒ-niks   'fiːniks
    Achilles; eponymous founder of
    Phoenicia; constellation
Pholidota
  pangolins   FAHL-uh-DŌT-uh   ˌfɑlə'doːʈə
Pholus
  centaur, host of Heracles   FŌ-luhs   'foːləs
Phorcys
  Greek sea god, husband of Ceto   FAWR-kuhs   'fɔːʳkəs
Phosphorus
  morning star personified in Greek   FAHS-f(uh-)ruhs   'fɑsf(ə)rəs
    myth; element
Photinianism
  Christian heresy   fō-TIN-ē-uh-NIZ-uhm   foː'tiniːəˌnizəm
Phraortes
  king of Media   frā-AWRT-ēz   freːˈɔːʳtiːz
Phra [Re]
  Egyptian sun god   PRAH, FRAH   'prɑ, 'frɑ
Phratry
  Greek "fraternal" group   FRĀ-trē   'freːtri·
Phrixus
  brother of Helle   FRIK-suhs   'friksəs
Phrygia
  ancient country, Asia Minor   FRIJ-(ē-)uh   'fridʒ(iː)ə
Phrygian
  pert. to Phrygia; *musical mode*   FRIJ-ē-uhn   'fridʒiːən
Phrygius
  king of Miletus   FRIJ-ē-uhs   'fridʒiːəs
Phrynichus
  Athenian tragedian   FRIN-uh-kuhs   'frinəkəs
Phthah
  see Ptah
Phthiotis, Fthiótis
  dept, Greece   thī-ŌT-uhs   θɑi'oːtəs

Foreign Sounds: ue: *Fr.* **rue**, *Ger.* **fü**llen   uh(r): *Fr.* **boeuf**, *Ger.* **Hö**hle   <u>kh</u>: *Ger.* i<u>ch</u>, *Scot.* lo<u>ch</u>   g̱: *Sp.* ami**g**o   y̱: *Sp.* ha**b**lar   hl: *Welsh* **Ll**anelli.   CAPITALS: primary stress.   SMALL CAPS: secondary stress.   Ⓢ: U.S. pron.   Ⓔ: British pron.

Phuket
  island near Thailand — P$\overline{OO}$-KET — ˌpuːˈket

Phurah
  Biblical name — F(Y)UR-uh, p$\overline{oo}$-RAH — ˈf(j)urə, puːˈrɑ

Phut [Put]
  Biblical name — FUT, F$\overline{OOT}$ — ˈfut, ˈfuːt

Phuvah
  Biblical name — F$\overline{OO}$-vuh, f$\overline{oo}$-VAH — ˈfuːvə, fuːˈvɑ

Phygelus, Phygellus
  Biblical name — fuh-JEL-uhs, fī-G$\overline{E}$-luhs — fəˈdʒeləs, faiˈgiːləs

Phyfe
  Duncan, *US cabinetmaker* — F$\overline{I}$F — ˈfaif

Phylas
  opponent of Heracles — F$\overline{I}$-luhs — ˈfailəs

Phyle
  Greek tribe — F$\overline{I}$-lē — ˈfailiˑ

Phyleus
  son of Augeas — F$\overline{I}$-lē-uhs, F$\overline{I}$-L$\overline{OO}$S — ˈfailiːəs, ˈfaiˌluːs

Phyllis
  pers. name — FIL-uhs — ˈfiləs

Phylloxera vastatrix
  grapevine pest — fī-LAHK-suh-ruh VAS-tuh-TRIKS — faiˈlaksərə ˈvæstəˌtriks

Pia
  pers. name (P. Zadora) — P$\overline{E}$-uh — ˈpiːə

Piacenza
  prov, Italy — pyah-CHEN(T)-suh, -sah — pjaˈtʃen(t)sə, -sɑ

Piaf
  Edith, *French singer* — PYAHF, Ⓢ P$\overline{E}$-AHF — pjɑːf, Ⓢ ˈpiːˌɑf

Piaget
  Jean, *Swiss psychologist* — pyah-ZH$\overline{A}$ — pjaˈʒeː

Piagetian
  pert. to theories of Jean Piaget — P$\overline{E}$-uh-ZH$\overline{A}$-uhn — ˌpiːəˈʒeːən

Piatigorsky
  Gregor, *US cellist* — PYAHT-i-GAWR-skē, PYAT- — ˌpjatiˈgɔːʳskiˑ, ˌpjæt-

Piatt
  county, IL — P$\overline{I}$-uht — ˈpaiət

Piazza Venezia
  central square, Rome, Italy — pē-AHT-suh vuh-NET-sē-uh — piːˈatsə vəˈnetsiːə

Piazzi
  1. pers. name — pē-AZ-ē — piːˈæziˑ
  2. Italian — PYAHT-tsē — ˈpjattsiː

Pibeseth [Phibeseth]
  Biblical name — P$\overline{I}$-buh-SETH, pī-B$\overline{E}$-SETH, fē-BES-et — ˈpaibəˌseθ, paiˈbiːˌseθ, fiːˈbeset

Pibroch
  see Piobaireachd

Picard
  Jean, *French astronomer* — pē-KAHR — piːkɑːr

Picardie
  prov, France — pē-kahr-D$\overline{E}$ — piːkɑːrdiː

Picardy
  prov, France — PIK-uhr-dē — ˈpikəʳdiˑ

Picasso
  Pablo, *Spanish artist* — pi-KAHS-ō, pi-KAS-ō — piˈkasoː, piˈkæsoː

Key (col. 2): a: fad ā: fade ah: father ar: marry aw: law e: fed ē: feed er: merry i: hid ī: hide ō: coat $\overline{oo}$: boot
oi: boy ow: now u: put uh: above uhr: bird ch: chop ng: ring sh: show th: thick <u>th</u>: this zh: measure

Picayune Rancheria		
Indian reservation, US	PIK-ē-(Y)O͞ON RAN-chuh-RĒ-uh, PIK-uh-YO͞ON	ˌpikiːˈ(j)uːn ˌræntʃəˈriːə, ˌpikəˈjuːn
Piccadilly Circus		
landmark, London, England	PIK-uh-DIL-ē SUHR-kuhs	ˌpikəˌdiliˑ ˈsəʳkəs
Piccard		
Auguste, *Swiss physicist*	pē-KAHR	piːkɑːr
Piccolo		
musical instrument	PIK-uh-LŌ	ˈpikəˌloː
Picenum		
ancient Roman province	pī-SĒ-nuhm	pɑiˈsiːnəm
Pichincha		
volcano, province, Ecuador	pē-CHĒN-chah, [$] puh-CHIN-chuh	piːˈtʃiːntʃɑ, [$] pəˈtʃintʃə
Pickaway		
county, OH	PIK-uh-WĀ	ˈpikəˌweː
Pickett		
George E., *Confederate general*	PIK-uht	ˈpikət
Pickwick		
Samuel, *Dickens character*	PIK-wik	ˈpikwik
Pickwickian		
pert. to Pickwick	pik-WIK-ē-uhn	pikˈwikiːən
Pico		
volcano, Azores	PĒ-kō	ˈpiːkoː
Pico Rivera		
city, CA	PĒ-kō ri-VER-uh, ri-VIR-uh	ˌpiːkoː riˈverə, riˈvirə
Pict		
ancient people, northern Britain	PIKT	ˈpikt
Pictish		
pert. to the Picts; *lang. of the Picts*	PIK-tish	ˈpiktiʃ
Pictor		
constellation	PIK-tuhr	ˈpiktəʳ
Piculet		
woodpecker	PIK-yuh-LUHT	ˈpikjəˌlət
Picuris Pueblo		
Indian reservation, US	pi-KYUR-uhs po͞o-EB-lō, PWEB-lō, pyo͞o-EB-lō	piˈkjuʳəs puːˈebloː, ˈpwebloː, pjuːˈebloː
Picus		
legendary 1st king of Italy	PĒ-kuhs, PĪ-kuhs	ˈpiːkəs, ˈpɑikəs
Piebald		
horse	PĪ-BAWLD	ˈpɑiˌbɔːld
Piedmont		
plateau region, US; region, Italy	PĒD-MAHNT	ˈpiːdˌmɑnt
Piedmontese		
pert. to the Piedmont, Italy	PĒD-muhn-TĒZ, PĒD-mahn-TĒZ, -TĒS	ˌpiːdmənˈtiːz, ˌpiːdmɑnˈtiːz, -ˈtiːs
Pied Piper		
German legendary character	PĪD PĪ-puhr	ˌpɑid ˈpɑipəʳ
Piegan		
N. American people	pē-GAN	piːˈgæn
Pie Jesu		
hymn	PĒ-Ā YĀ-zo͞o, YĀ-so͞o	ˌpiːˌeː ˈjeːzuː, ˈjeːsuː
Piels		
US beer	PĒLZ	ˈpiːlz
Piemonte [Piedmont]		
region, Italy	pyā-MAWN-tā	pjeːˈmɔːnteː

Foreign Sounds: ue: *Fr.* **rue**, *Ger.* **füllen** uh(r): *Fr.* **boeuf**, *Ger.* **Höhle** kh: *Ger.* **ich**, *Scot.* **loch** g̃: *Sp.* **amigo** v̱: *Sp.* **hablar** hl: *Welsh* **Llanelli**. CAPITALS: primary stress. SMALL CAPS: secondary stress. [$]: U.S. pron. [£]: British pron.

Pier
   1. pers. name, Danish   PIR   'pɪr
   2. Italian   PYER   'pjer

Pierce
   Franklin, *14th US president*   PIRS, PUHRS *(his own pron.)*   'pɪʳs, pəʳs

Piercy
   Marge, *US writer*   PIR-sē   'pɪʳsiˑ

Pierfrancesco
   pers. name, Italian   PYER-frahn-CHĀS-kō   ˌpjerfrɑn'tʃeːskoː

Pieria
   dept, Greece   pī-IR-ē-uh   pɑi'iriːə

Pierian
   pert. to the Muses   pī-IR-ē-uhn, pī-ER-ē-uhn   pɑi'iriːən, pɑi'eriːən

Pierides
   nine maidens changed to magpies by pē-ER-uhd-ĒZ   piː'erədˌiːz
    Muses

Pierluigi
   pers. name, Italian   PYER-l͞oo-Ē-jē   ˌpjerluː'iːdʒiː

Piero
   pers. name, Italian   PYĀ-rō   'pjeːroː

Piero de' Franceschi
   Italian renaissance painter   PYĀ-rō DĀ frahn-CHĀ-skē   'pjeːroː ˌdeː fran'tʃeːskiˑ

Piero della Francesca [Piero de' Franceschi]
   Italian renaissance painter   PYĀ-rō DĀL-lah frahn-CHĀ-skah   'pjeːroː ˌdeːllɑ fran'tʃeːskɑ

Pierpont
   pers. name   PIR-PAHNT   'pɪʳˌpɑnt

Pierre
   1. city, SD   PĒR   'piːʳ
   2. pers. name   pē-ER, PIR   piː'eʳ, 'pɪʳ
   3. Flemish   PYER   'pjer
   4. French   PYER   pjer

Pierres Dorés
   wine region   PYER daw-RĀ   pjer dɔːreː

Pierrot
   French pantomine character   pye-RŌ, Ⓢ PĒ-uh-RŌ   pjeroː, Ⓢ 'piːəˌroː

Piers
   pers. name   PIRZ   'pɪʳz

Piers Plowman
   Middle English poem, Langland PIRZ PLOW-muhn   'pɪʳz 'plɑumən

Piešťany
   town, Slovakia   PYESH-tuh-nē   'pjeʃtəniˑ

Piet
   pers. name, Dutch   PĒT   'piːt

Pietà
   Mary mourning the dead Christ, esp. PĒ-Ā-TAH, PYĀ-TAH   ˌpiːˌeː'tɑ, ˌpjeː'tɑ
    Michelangelo's sculpture

Pietas
   Roman sense of duty   PĒ-uh-TAHS   'piːəˌtɑs

Pieter
   pers. name, Dutch   PĒ-ter   'piːter

Pietermaritzburg
   town, S. Africa   PĒT-uhr-MAR-uhts-BUHRG   ˌpiːt̬əʳ'mærətsˌbəʳg

Pietro
   pers. name, Italian   PYE-trō   'pjetroː

Key (col. 2):   a: fad ā: fade ah: father ar: marry aw: law e: fed ē: feed er: merry i: hid ī: hide ō: coat o͞o: boot
oi: boy   ow: now   u: put   uh: above   uhr: bird   ch: chop   ng: ring   sh: show   th: thick   tẖ: this   zh: measure

Pigalle
square in Paris, France   pē-GAHL   piːgɑːl

Pigmy
see Pygmy

Pignola
pine nut   pēn-YŌ-luh   piːnˈjoːlə

Pihahiroth, Pi-hahiroth
Biblical name   PĪ-(h)uh-HĪ-RAHTH, RAWTH, -ruhth;   ˌpɑi(h)əˈhɑiˌrɑθ, -ˌrɔːθ, -rəθ;
       PĒ-HAH-hē-RAWT   ˈpiːˌhɑhiːˈrɔːt

Pila
lang., Benin   PĒ-luh   ˈpiːlə

Pila-pila
lang., Benin   PĒ-luh-PĒ-luh   ˌpiːləˈpiːlə

Pilarczyk
Daniel, archbishop of Cincinnati   puh-LAHR-chik   pəˈlɑʳtʃik

Pilate
Pontius, Roman procurator of Judea   PĪ-luht   ˈpɑilət

Pilatus
mtn. peak, Swiss Alps   pē-LAH-TUS, Ⓢ puh-LAHT-uhs   piːˈlɑːˌtus, Ⓢ pəˈlɑṭəs

Pilcomayo
river, S. America   PIL-kuh-MĪ-ō   ˌpilkəˈmɑioː

Pildash
Biblical name   PIL-DASH, pil-DAHSH   ˈpilˌdæʃ, pilˈdɑʃ

Pileha [Pilha]
Biblical name   PIL-ē-HAH, PĪ-lē-HAH, pil-<u>KH</u>AH   ˈpiliːˌhɑ, ˈpɑiliːˌhɑ, pilˈxɑ

Pilgrim
English Puritan settler in MA   PIL-gruhm   ˈpilgrəm

Pilha [Pileha]
Biblical name   PIL-HAH, pil-<u>KH</u>AH   ˈpilˌhɑ, pilˈxɑ

Pilipino [Tagalog]
lang., Philippine Islands   PIL-uh-PĒ-nō   ˌpiləˈpiːnoː

Pillsbury
US food products co.   PILZ-BER-ē, PILZ-b(uh-)rē   ˈpilzˌberiˑ, ˈpilzb(ə)riˑ

Pilnyak
Boris, pseudonym of Boris Vogau   pyil-NYAHK   pjilˈnjɑk

Pilobolus
US dance troupe   pi-LAHB-uh-luhs   piˈlɑbələs

Pilsen
1. city, Czech republic   PIL-zuhn   ˈpilzən
2. Peruvian beer   PIL-suhn, PIL-zuhn   ˈpilsən, ˈpilzən

Pilsner Urquell
Czech beer   PILZ-nuhr URK-vel   ˈpilznər ˈurkvel

Piłsudski
Jósef, Polish political leader   pēl-SOOT-skē   piːɫˈsuːtskiː

Piltai
Biblical name   PIL-TĪ, pil-TĪ   ˈpilˌtɑi, pilˈtɑi

Piltdown
site of fraudulent early human bone   PILT-DOWN   ˈpiltˌdɑun
    fragments, England

Pilumnus
Roman protector of newborn babies   puh-LUHM-nuhs   pəˈləmnəs

Pima
county, AZ; N. American people   PĒ-muh   ˈpiːmə

Pima-Papago
lang., people, US , Mexico   PĒ-muh-PAHP-uh-GŌ, -PAP-uh-GŌ   ˈpiːməˈpɑpəˌgoː, -ˈpæpəˌgoː

Foreign Sounds: ue: *Fr.* **rue**, *Ger.* **füllen**   uh(r): *Fr.* **boeuf**, *Ger.* **Höhle**   <u>kh</u>: *Ger.* **ich**, *Scot.* **loch**   ḡ: *Sp.* **amigo**   v: *Sp.* **hablar**
hl: *Welsh* **Llanelli.**   CAPITALS: primary stress.   SMALL CAPS: secondary stress.   Ⓢ: U.S. pron.   Ⓔ: British pron.

Pimento
  allspice   puh-MENT-ō   pə'mentoː

Pimiento
  vegetable   puh-MENT-ō, puhm-YENT-ō   pə'mentoː, pəm'jentoː

Pimlico
  district, London; race course, MD   PIM-li-KŌ   'pimli‚koː

Pimpernel
  plant   PIM-puhr-NEL, PIM-puhr-nuhl   'pimpə‌ʳ‚nel, 'pimpə‌ʳnəl

Piña Colada
  alcoholic drink   PĒN-yuh kuh-LAHD-uh   'piːnjə kə'ladə

Pinal
  county, AZ   puh-NAL   pə'næl

Pinaleno
  mtn. range, AZ   PIN-l-Ā-nō   ‚pinḷ'eːnoː

Pinatubo
  Mount, volcano, Philippines   PIN-uh-T͞OO-bō   ‚pinə'tuːboː

Pinchas
  pers. name   PING-kuhs, PIN-k͟huhs   'piŋkəs, 'pinxəs

Pindar
  Greek lyric poet   PIN-duhr, PIN-DAHR   'pində‌ʳ, 'pin‚daʳ

Pinchot
  Gifford, US conservationist &   PIN-SHŌ, PIN-chō   'pin‚ʃoː, 'pintʃoː
   politician

Pindaric
  pert. to the style of Pindar   pin-DAR-ik, pin-DAHR-ik   pin'dærik, pin'darik

Pindus
  mtn. range, Greece; son of Macedon   PIN-duhs   'pindəs

Pinellas
  county, FL   pī-NEL-uhs   pai'neləs

Pinero
  Sir Arthur W., English playwright,   puh-NIR-ō, puh-NER-ō   pə'niroː, pə'neroː
   actor

Pine Siskin
  songbird   PĪN SIS-kuhn   'pain 'siskən

Piniella
  Louis Victor, US baseball player   pin-EL-uh   pin'elə

Pinkerton
  Allan, US detective   PING-kuhr-tuhn, PING-kuhr-tn   'piŋkə‌ʳtən, 'piŋkə‌ʳtṇ

Pinkham
  pers. name   PING-kuhm   'piŋkəm

Pinkiang
  former name of Harbin   BIN-jē-AHNG, BING-jē-AHNG   'bindʒiː'aŋ, 'biŋdʒiː'aŋ

Pinkus
  German beer   PING-kuhs   'piŋkəs

Pinnipedia
  seals & walruses   PIN-uh-PĒD-ē-uh   ‚pinə'piːdiːə

Pinocchio
  fairy tale wooden puppet   puh-NŌ-kē-Ō   pə'noːkiː‚oː

Pinochet Ugarte
  Augusto, president, Chile   pē-nō-CHET ͞oo-G̅AHR-tā   piːnoː'tʃet uː'ɣarteː

Pinochle
  game   PĒ-NUHK-uhl   'piː‚nəkəl

Piñon, Pinyon
  pine nut   PIN-YŌN, pin-YŌN, PIN-YAHN,   'pin‚joːn, pin'joːn, 'pin‚jan,
                         PIN-yuhn   'pinjən

Key (col. 2):   a: fad   ā: fade   ah: father   ar: marry   aw: law   e: fed   ē: feed   er: merry   i: hid   ī: hide   ō: coat   ōō: boot
oi: boy   ow: now   u: put   uh: above   uhr: bird   ch: chop   ng: ring   sh: show   th: thick   th: this   zh: measure

Piñon jay
   bird   PIN-YŌN JĀ, PIN-YAHN, PIN-yuhn   'pin,jo:n 'dʒe:, 'pin,jɑn, 'pinjən

Pinot
   wine; pers. name, French   pē-NŌ   pi:no:

Pinot Noir
   wine variety   pē-nō NWAHR   pi:no: nwɑ:r

Pinta
   one of Columbus' ships   PĒN-tah, ⓈPINT-uh, PIN-tuh   'pi:ntɑ, Ⓢ 'pint-ə, 'pin-tə

Pinter
   Harold, *British playwright*   PINT-uhr   'pintər

Pinteresque
   pert. to Pinter *or his style*   PINT-uh-RESK   ,pintə'resk

Pinyin
   transliteration system for Chinese   PIN-YIN   'pin'jin

Pinza
   Ezio, *Italian singer*   PĒN-zuh   'pi'nzə

Pinzgauer
   Austrian horse breed   PIN(T)S-GOWR   'pin(t)s,gɑur

Piobaireachd, Pibroch
   style of Scottish bagpipe music   PĒ-BRAH<u>KH</u>, -BRAW<u>KH</u>   'pi:,brɑx, -,bro:x

Pioche
   village, NV   pē-ŌCH   pi:'o:tʃ

Piotr
   pers. name, Polish, Russian   PYAW-tuhr   'pjo:tər

Piper
   pers. name   PĪ-puhr   'pɑipər

Pippa
   pers. name   PIP-uh   'pipə

Piqua
   city, OH   PIK-wā, PIK-wuh   'pikwe:, 'pikwə

Piquet
   game   pē-KĀ   pi'ke:

Piracicaba
   town, Brazil   PIR-uh-si-KAHB-uh   ,pirəsi'kɑbə

Piraeus, Peiraeus
   seaport, Greece   pī-RĒ-uhs, pi-RĀ-uhs   pɑi'ri:əs, pi're:əs

Piraiévs [Piraeus]
   port, Greece   PĒ-re-EFS   ,pi:re'efs

Piram
   Biblical name   PĪ-RAM, -ruhm; pir-AHM   'pɑi,ræm, -rəm; pir'ɑm

Pirandello
   Luigi, *Italian author (Nobel 1934)*   PIR-uhn-DEL-ō   ,pirən'delo:

Piranesi
   Giambattista, *Italian architect, artist*   PIR-uh-NĀ-zē   ,pirə'ne:zi'

Pirathon
   Biblical name   pī-RĀ-THAHN, PIR-uh-THAHN, PIR-ah-TAWN   pɑi're:,θɑn, 'pirə,θɑn, ,pirɑ'to:n

Pirathonite
   Biblical name   pī-RĀ-thuh-NĪT, puh-RATH-uh-   pɑi're:θə,nɑit, pə'ræθə-

Pire
   Dominique Georges, *Belgian priest (Nobel 1958)*   PIR   pir

Pirene
   mother of Leches and Cenchrias   pī-RĒ-nē   pɑi'ri:ni'

Pirenne

Henri, *Belgian historian*   pē-REN   pɪːren

Pirithous

friend of Theseus   pī-RITH-o͞os, PIR-uh-THo͞oS   pɑɪˈriθuːs, ˈpirə,θuːs

Piro

lang., Peru; lang., US & Mexico   PIR-ō   ˈpiroː

Pisa

prov & town, Italy   PĒ-sah, ⑤ PĒ-zuh   ˈpiːsɑ, ⑤ ˈpiːzə

Pisanello

Italian renaissance medalist   PĒ-sah-NEL-lō   ˌpiːsɑˈnelloː

Pisano

Andrea, *Italian sculptor;* Nicola, *Italian sculptor;* Giovanni, *Italian sculptor, architect*   pē-SAHN-ō   piˈsɑnoː

Piscataqua

river, ME, NH   pis-KAT-uh-KWAW   pisˈkæʈə,kwɔː

Piscataquis

county, ME   pis-KAT-uh-kwis   pisˈkæʈəkwis

Piscataway

village, NJ   pis-KAT-uh-WĀ   pisˈkæʈə,weː

Piscean

pert. to the constellation Pisces   PĪ-sē-uhn, PIS-ē-uhn, PIS-kē-uhn   ˈpɑɪsiːən, ˈpisiːən, ˈpiskiːən

Pisces

constellation, sign of the zodiac   PĪ-SĒZ   ˈpɑɪ,siːz

Piscis Austrinus

constellation   PĪ-suhs aw-STRĪ-nuhs   ˈpɑɪsəs ɔːˈstrɑɪnəs

Pisco

seaport, Peru   PĒ-skō   ˈpiːskoː

Piscopo

Joseph Charles, *US actor, comedian*   PIS-kuh-pō   ˈpiskəpoː

Piseco

lake, NY   puh-SĒ-kō   pəˈsiːkoː

Pisgah

Mount, *NY; mtn. ridge, Jordan*   PIZ-guh   ˈpizgə

Pishon

Biblical name   PĪ-SHAHN, pē-SHŌN   ˈpɑɪ,ʃɑn, piːˈʃoːn

Pisidia

ancient Roman province, Asia Minor   pī-SID-ē-uh   pɑɪˈsidiːə

Pisidia

Biblical name   puh-SID-ē-uh   pəˈsidiːə

Pisistratus

see Peisistratus

Piso

L. Calpurnius, *Roman politician*   PĪ-sō   ˈpɑɪsoː

Pison [Pishon]

Biblical name   PĪ-SAHN, pē-SHŌN   ˈpɑɪ,sɑn, piːˈʃoːn

Pispa, Pispah

Biblical name   PIS-puh, PIZ-puh, pis-PAH   ˈpispə, ˈpizpə, pisˈpɑ

Pissarro

Camille, *French painter*   pē-sah-RŌ, ⑤ puh-SAHR-ō   piːsɑːroː, ⑤ pəˈsaroː

Pitcairn

Island, *Pacific*   PIT-KARN, PIT-KERN   ˈpit,kæʳn, ˈpit,keʳn

Pitchblende

uraninite   PICH-BLEND   ˈpitʃ,blend

Key (col. 2):   a: fad   ā: fade   ah: father   ar: marry   aw: law   e: fed   ē: feed   er: merry   i: hid   ī: hide   ō: coat   o͞o: boot
oi: boy   ow: now   u: put   uh: above   uhr: bird   ch: chop   ng: ring   sh: show   th: thick   <u>th</u>: this   zh: measure

Pitcher

    Molly, *sobriquet of* Mary McCauley   PICH-uhr   'pitʃəʳ

Pithecanthropus

    hominid genus   PITH-i-KAN-thruh-puhs,   ˌpiθi'kænθrəpəs,

        PITH-i-KAN-THRŌ-puhs   ˌpiθiˌkæn'θroːpəs

Pithom

    Biblical name   PĪ-THAHM, pi-TAWM   'paiˌθam, pi'tɔːm

Pithon

    Biblical name   PĪ-THAHN, pē-TŌN   'paiˌθan, piː'toːn

Pitlochry

    town, Scotland   pit-LAH<u>KH</u>-rē   pit'laxriˑ

Pitney Bowes

    US manufacturing co.   PIT-nē BŌZ   ˌpitniˑ 'boːz

Pitons, The

    mts., Caribbean   pē-TAW^n piː'tɔ̃

Pitot tube

    flow measuring device   PĒ-TŌ, pē-TŌ   'piːˌtoː, piː'toː

Pitri

    Hindu legendary figure   PI-trē   'pitriˑ

Pitta

    songbird   PIT-uh   'pitə

Pitti

    gallery, Florence, Italy   PIT-ē   'pitiˑ

Pitts

    Zasu, *entertainer; aerobatic airplane*   PITS   'pits

        marque

Pittsburgh

    city, PA; county, OK   PITS-BUHRG   'pitsˌbəʳg

Pius

    name of 12 popes   PĪ-uhs   'paiəs

Piute

    county, UT   pī-(Y)O͞OT   pai'(j)uːt

Pizarro

    Francisco, *Spanish conquistador*   puh-ZAHR-ō   pə'zaʳoː

Piz Bernina

    see Bernina, Piz

Placentia

    city, CA   pluh-SEN-ch(ē-)uh   plə'sentʃ(iː)ə

Placid, Lake

    lake, village, NY   lāk PLAS-uhd   leːk 'plæsəd

Placide

    pers. name, French   plah-SĒD   plaːsiːd

Plácido

    pers. name, Spanish   PLAHS-ē-<u>th</u>ō, PLAHTH-ē-<u>th</u>ō,   'plasiːðoː, 'plaθiːðoː,

        Ⓢ PLAHS-uh-dō   Ⓢ 'plasədoː

Plaid Cymru

    Welsh nationalist political party,   PLĪD KUHM-rē   ˌplaid 'kəmriˑ

        United Kingdom

Plaistow

    1. town, NH   PLAS-tō   'plæstoː

    2. various towns, England   PLĀ-stō, PLAS-tō, PLAHS-tō   'pleːstoː, 'plæstoː, 'plaːstoː

Planck

    Max Karl Ernst, *German physicist*   PLAHNGK   'plaŋk

        (Nobel 1918)

Foreign Sounds: ue: *Fr.* **rue**, *Ger.* **füllen** uh(r): *Fr.* **boeuf**, *Ger.* **Höhle** <u>kh</u>: *Ger.* **ich**, *Scot.* **loch** ḡ: *Sp.* **amigo** v: *Sp.* **hablar**
hl: *Welsh* **Llanelli**. CAPITALS: primary stress. SMALL CAPS: secondary stress. Ⓢ: U.S. pron. Ⓔ: British pron.

Planck's
   mathematical constant   PLANGKS, PLAHNGKS   'plæŋks, 'plɑŋks
Plano
   town, TX   PLĀ-nō   'pleːnoː
Plantagenet
   English ruling dynasty   plan-TAJ-uh-nuht   plæn'tædʒənət
Plaquemines
   parish, LA   PLAK-(uh-)muhnz   'plæk(ə)mənz
Plassey
   village, India   PLAS-ē   'plæsiˑ
Plasticine
   tdmk for a synthetic modeling   PLAS-tuh-SĒN   'plæstə,siːn
     material
Plata, La
   1. prov, Argentina   lah PLAHT-ah   lɑ 'plɑtɑ
   2. see La Plata
Plata, Río de la
   estuary, S. America   RĒ-ō thā lah PLAHT-ah   ˌriːoˑ ðeː lɑ 'plɑtɑ
Plataea
   ancient city, Greece   pluh-TĒ-uh   plə'tiːə
Plate [Plata, Río de la]
   river, South America   PLĀT   'pleːt
Plateau
   N. American people   pla-TŌ   plæ'toː
Plateosaurus
   dinosaur   PLAT-ē-uh-SAWR-uhs   ˌplætiːə'soːrəs
Plath
   Sylvia, *US poet*   PLATH   'plæθ
platinum
   element   PLAT-nuhm, PLAT-n-uhm   'plætnəm, 'plætn̩əm
Plato
   Greek philosopher   PLĀT-ō   'pleːṭoː
Platonic
   pert. to Plato   pluh-TAHN-ik, plā-TAHN-ik   plə'tɑnik, pleː'tɑnik
Platonism
   philosophy of Plato   PLĀT-n-IZ-uhm   'pleːtn̩,izəm
Plattdeutsch
   Low German dialects   PLAHT-DOICH   'plɑt,dɔitʃ
Platte
   rivers, US   PLAT   'plæt
Plautus
   Roman playwright   PLAWT-uhs   'plɔːṭəs
Plaza Lasso
   Galo, *president, Ecuador*   PLAHS-ah LAHS-ō   'plɑsɑ 'lɑsoː
Pleasence
   Donald, *British actor*   PLEZ-uhn(t)s   'plezən(t)s
Plebeians
   Roman lower class   pluh-BĒ-uhnz, plē-BĒ-uhnz   plə'biːənz, pliː'biːənz
Pleiades
   daughters of Atlas; star cluster in   PLĒ-uh-DĒZ, PLĀ-, Ⓔ PLĪ-   'pliːə,diːz, 'pleː-, Ⓔ 'plɑi-
     Taurus
Pleiku
   city, Vietnam   plā-ko͞o   pleːkuː
Pleisthenes
   son of Pelops   PLĪS-thuh-NĒZ   'plɑisθə,niːz

Key (col. 2):   a: fad   ā: fade   ah: father   ar: marry   aw: law   e: fed   ē: feed   er: merry   i: hid   ī: hide   ō: coat   o͞o: boot
oi: boy   ow: now   u: put   uh: above   uhr: bird   ch: chop   ng: ring   sh: show   th: thick   th̲: this   zh: measure

Pleistocene
   geologic epoch   PLĪ-stuh-SĒN   'plaistə,siːn

Plekhanov
   Georgi, *Russian political leader*   pluh-KAHN-uhf, -AWF, -AWV   plə'kanəf, -,ɔːf, -,ɔːv

Plexiglas
   tdmk for a thermoplastic polymer   PLEK-sē-GLAS   'pleksi·,glæs

Plimpton
   George, *US author, editor*   PLIM(P)-tuhn   'plim(p)tən

Plimsoll
   Samuel, *English reformer*   PLIM-suhl, SŌL   'plimsəl, -,soːl

Pliny
   name of two Roman authors   PLIN-ē   'plini·

Pliocene
   geologic epoch   PLĪ-uh-SĒN   'plaiə,siːn

Plisetskaya
   Maya, *ballet dancer, USSR*   pli-SET-skuh-yuh   pli'setskəjə

Ploies
   city, Romania   plaw-YESHT(-ē)   plɔ'jeʃt(i·)

Plotinus
   Roman philosopher   plō-TĪ-nuhs   plo'tainəs

Plotius
   Roman name   PLŌT-ē-uhs   'ploːʈiːəs

Plotz-Brau
   German beer   PLAWTS-BROW   'plɔːts,brau

Plough
   star cluster in Great Bear   PLOW   'plau
     constellation; US pharmaceutical
     co.

Plovdiv
   prov, Bulgaria   PLAWV-DIF, PLAWV-DIV   'plɔːv,dif, 'plɔːv,div

Plumas
   county, CA   PLOO-muhs   'pluːməs

Plumbago
   flower   PLUHM-BĀ-gō   ,pləm'beːgoː

Plumbeous gnatcatcher
   gnatcatcher   PLUHM-bē-uhs   'pləmbiːəs

Plummer
   Christopher, *Canadian actor*   PLUHM-uhr   'pləməʳ

Plumpe
   Friedrich W., *German film director*   PLUM-puh   'plumpə

Plunkett
   James William, Jr., *US football*   PLUHNG-kuht   'pləŋkət
     player

Plutarch
   Greek biographer   PLOO-TAHRK   'pluː,taʳk

Plutarco
   pers. name, Spanish   ploo-TAHR-kō   pluː'taʳkoː

Pluto
   Roman god of the Underworld;   PLUT-ō   'pluʈoː
     planet

Pluton
   title of Hades, god of the Underworld   PLOO-TAHN   'pluː,tan

Plutonian
   pert. to Pluto *or the lower world*   ploo-TŌ-nē-uhn   pluː'toːniːən

---

Foreign Sounds: ue: *Fr.* **rue**, *Ger.* **füllen**   uh(r): *Fr.* **boeuf**, *Ger.* **Höhle**   <u>kh</u>: *Ger.* i**ch**, *Scot.* lo**ch**   ğ: *Sp.* ami**g**o   v: *Sp.* ha**b**lar
hl: *Welsh* **Ll**anelli.   CAPITALS: primary stress.   SMALL CAPS: secondary stress.   ⑤: U.S. pron.   ⓔ: British pron.

plutonium
element　　　ploo-TŌ-nē-uhm　　　plu:'to:ni:əm

Plutus
personification of wealth　　　PLOOT-uhs　　　'plu:ʈəs

Pluviôse
month, French Revolutionary calendar　　　pluev-YŌZ　　　ply:vjo:z

Plymouth
port, England; US pl. name; US car make　　　PLIM-uhth　　　'pliməθ

Plzeň
city, Czech Republic　　　PUHL-ZEN(-yuh)　　　'pəl‚zen(jə)

Pnyx
hill, Athens, Greece　　　NIKS　　　'niks

Po
river, Italy　　　PŌ　　　'po:

Poarch Band
N. American people (Creek)　　　PŌRCH, PAWRCH　　　'po:ʳtʃ, 'pɔ:ʳtʃ

Pobeda
peak between Kirghiz and China　　　puh-B(Y)ED-uh　　　pə'b(j)edə

Pocahontas
American Indian princess; county, IA, WV　　　PŌ-kuh-HAHNT-uhs, -HUHNT-uhs　　　‚po:kə'hɑntəs, -'həntəs

Pocatello
city, Idaho　　　PŌ-kuh-TEL-ō　　　‚po:kə'telo:

Pochereth
Biblical name　　　PAHK-uh-RETH, PŌ-kuh-; paw-KHE-ret　　　'pɑkə‚reθ, 'po:kə-; pɔ:'xeret

Pochereth-hazzebaim, Pokereth-Hazzebaim
Biblical name　　　PAHK-uh-RETH-HAZ-uh-BĀ-im, PŌ-kuh-; paw-KHE-ret-hahts-vī-YĒM　　　'pɑkə‚reθ‚hæzə'be:im, 'po:kə-; pɔ:'xerethɑtsvɑi'ji:m

Pocola
town, OK　　　puh-KŌ-luh　　　pə'ko:lə

Pocomoke
river, MD　　　PŌ-kuh-MŌK　　　'po:kə‚mo:k

Poconos
mtns., PA　　　PŌ-kuh-NŌZ　　　'po:kə‚no:z

Pocotopaug
Lake, CT　　　PŌ-kuht-uh-PAWG　　　'po:kəʈə‚pɔ:g

Podgorica
former name for Titograd　　　PAHD-guh-RĒT-suh　　　'pɑdgə‚ri:tsə

Podgorny
Nikolai, *president, USSR*　　　pahd-GAWR-nē　　　pɑd'gɔ:ʳni·

Podhoretz
Norman, *US editor and essayist*　　　pahd-HAWR-uhts　　　pɑd'hɔ:rəts

Podocarpus
plant　　　PAHD-uh-KAHR-puhs　　　‚pɑdə'kɑʳpəs

Podokesaurus
dinosaur　　　puh-DŌ-kuh-SAWR-uhs　　　pə‚do:kə'sɔ:rəs

Podunk
village, CT　　　PŌ-DUHNGK　　　'po:‚dəŋk

Poe
Edgar A., *US author*　　　PŌ　　　'po:

Key (col. 2):　a: fad　ā: fade　ah: father　ar: marry　aw: law　e: fed　ē: feed　er: merry　i: hid　ī: hide　ō: coat　oo: boot
oi: boy　ow: now　u: put　uh: above　uhr: bird　ch: chop　ng: ring　sh: show　th: thick　th: this　zh: measure

Poggio Bracciolini
  Gian Francesco, *Italian humanist*   PAWD-jō BRAHT-chō-LḔ-nē   'pɔːddʒoː ˌbrɑttʃoːˈliːniˑ

Po Hai, Bohai [Chihli]
  gulf, Yellow Sea   BŌ HĪ   'boː 'hɑi

Pohl
  Frederick, *US writer*   PŌL   'poːl

Pohlman
  Harry C., Field, *ballpark, Beloit, WI*   PŌL-muhn   'poːlmən

Poincaré
  Jules Henri, *French mathematician,*   pweⁿ-kah-RĀ   pwĕkɑːreː
  physicist, author

Poinciana
  festival, Miami, FL   POIN-sē-AN-uh, P(W)AHN-   ˌpɔinsiːˈænə, ˌp(w)ɑn-

Poinciano
  pers. name, Spanish   poin-SYAHN-ō, -THYAHN-ō   pɔinˈsjɑnoː, -ˈθjɑnoː

Poinsett
  county, AR   POIN-SET, POIN-sit   'pɔinˌset, 'pɔinsit

Poinsettia
  plant   poin-SET-ē-uh, poin-SET-uh   pɔinˈsetiːə, pɔinˈsetə

Pointe a la Hache
  village, LA   POINT-AL-uh-HASH   'pɔintˌæləˈhæʃ

Pointe Coupée
  parish, LA   POINT kōō-PḖ   'pɔint kuːˈpiː

Pointe-Noire
  city, Congo   pweⁿt-NWAHR   pwĕtnwɑːr

Point Pelee
  National Park, *Ontario*   point PḔ-lē   pɔint 'piːliː

Poire Williams
  brand of pear liqueur   PWAHR WIL-yuhmz   'pwɑʳ 'wiljəmz

Poirot
  Hercule, *Agatha Christie's detective*   pwah-RŌ   pwɑˈroː

Poisson
  S. D., *French mathematician,*   pwah-SAWⁿ Ⓢ pwah-SŌN,   pwɑːsɔ̃ Ⓢ pwɑˈsoːn,
  physicist   pwah-SAHN   pwɑˈsɑn

Poitier
  Sidney, *US actor*   pwaht-YĀ, PWAHT-ē-Ā   pwɑtˈjeː, 'pwɑ̧iːˌeː

Poitiers
  city, France   pwah-TYĀ   pwɑːtjeː

Poitou-Charentes
  region, France   pwah-tōō-shah-RAHⁿT   pwɑːtuːʃɑːrɑ̃t

Pojoaque Pueblo
  Indian reservation, US   pō-(H)WAHK-ē pōō-EB-lō, PWEB-lō,   poːˈ(h)wɑkiˑ puːˈebloː,
  pyōō-EB-lō   'pwebloː, pjuːˈebloː

Pokereth-Hazzebaim
  see Pochereth-hazzebaim

Pokhara
  valley, Nepal   PŌ-kuh-ruh   'poːkərə

Pokomam [Pokoman]
  lang., Cen. America   PŌ-kō-MAHM   ˌpoːkoːˈmɑm

Pokoman
  lang., Cen. America   PŌ-kō-MAHN   ˌpoːkoːˈmɑn

Pokomo
  lang., people, Africa   puh-KŌ-mō   pəˈkoːmoː

Pokonchi
  lang., people, Guatemala   puh-KAHN-chē   pəˈkɑntʃiˑ

Polabian
> *ancient Slavic people of Germany;*   pō-LÃ-bē-uhn, puh-   po:ˈleːbiːən, pə-
> *extinct language*

Poland
> *republic, Europe*   PŌ-luhnd   ˈpoːlənd

Polanski
> Roman, *US filmmaker*   puh-LAN-skē   pəˈlænskiˑ

Polanyi
> John C., *Canadian chemist (Nobel*   puh-LAN-yē   pəˈlænjiˑ
> *1986)*

Polari
> *English argot of theater and circus*   puh-LAHR-ē   pəˈlariˑ

Polaris
> *1. star Alpha Ursae Minoris*   puh-LAR-uhs, puh-LAHR-uhs   pəˈlærəs, pəˈlarəs
> *2. submarine missile*   puh-LAR-uhs   pəˈlærəs

Polaroid
> *tdmk for an instant camera*   PŌ-luh-ROID   ˈpoːləˌrɔid

Pole
> *inhabitant of Poland*   PŌL   ˈpoːl

Poleis
> *plural of* Polis   PŌ-LĪS   ˈpoːˌlais

Polemarch
> *Athenian general*   PAHL-uh-MAHRK   ˈpaləˌmaᵊk

Polhymnia [Polyhymnia]
> *muse of mime; street, New Orleans*   puh-LIM-nē-uh   pəˈlimniːə

Policarpo
> *pers. name, Spanish*   pō-lē-KAHR-pō   poːliːˈkarpoː

Poli-Grip
> *tdmk for a denture adhesive*   PAHL-ē-GRIP   ˈpaliˑˌgrip

Polis
> *Greek city-state*   PŌ-luhs   ˈpoːləs

Polish
> *lang., Poland*   PŌ-lish   ˈpoːliʃ

Politburo
> *Communist executive committee*   PAHL-uht-BYUR-ō, PŌ-luht-BYUR-ō,   ˈpalətˌbjuroː, ˈpoːlətˌbjuroː,
>   puh-LIT-BYUR-ō   pəˈlitˌbjuroː

Politian [Ambrogini]
> *Italian poet & scholar*   puh-LISH-uhn   pəˈliʃən

Poliziano [Ambrogini]
> Angelo, *Italian poet & scholar*   PŌ-lēts-YAHN-ō   ˌpoːliːtsˈjanoː

Polk
> James K., *11th US president*   PŌK   ˈpoːk

Polka
> *dance*   PŌL-kuh, PŌ-kuh   ˈpoːlkə, ˈpoːkə

Pollack
> Sydney, *US film director*   PAHL-uhk   ˈpalək

Pollaiuolo
> Jacopo, Antonio, Piero, Simone,   PŌL-lī-WAW-lō   ˌpoːllaiˈwɔːloː
> *family of Florentine artists*

Pollio
> *pers. name, Latin*   PAHL-ē-Ō, PAHL-yō   ˈpaliːˌoː, ˈpaljoː

Pollock
> Jackson, *artist*   PAHL-uhk   ˈpalək

Pollux
> *twin of Castor; star Beta Geminorum*   PAHL-uhks   ˈpaləks

---

Key (col. 2):   a: fad   ā: fade   ah: father   ar: marry   aw: law   e: fed   ē: feed   er: merry   i: hid   ī: hide   ō: coat   ōō: boot
oi: boy   ow: now   u: put   uh: above   uhr: bird   ch: chop   ng: ring   sh: show   th: thick   <u>th</u>: this   zh: measure

Polly
   pers. name   PAHL-ē   ˈpɑliˑ

Pollyanna
   character, Eleanor Porter   PAHL-ē-AN-uh   ˌpɑliːˈænə

Pollyannaish
   excessively optimistic, as Pollyanna   PAHL-ē-AN-uh-ISH   ˌpɑliːænəˌiʃ

Polo
   Marco, *Italian explorer*   PŌ-lō   ˈpoːloː

Polonaise
   dance; butter-crumb sauce   PAHL-uh-NĀZ, PŌ-luh-NĀZ   ˌpɑləˈneːz, ˌpoːləˈneːz

polonium
   element   puh-LŌ-nē-uhm   pəˈloːniːəm

Polonius
   character in Hamlet, *Shakespeare*   puh-LŌ-nē-uhs, puh-LŌN-yuhs   pəˈloːniːəs, pəˈloːnjəs

Pol Pot
   Cambodian dictator   PAHL PAHT, PŌL PAHT   ˌpɑl ˈpɑt, ˌpoːl ˈpɑt

Poltava
   city, Ukraine   puhl-TAHV-uh   pəlˈtɑvə

Polybius
   Greek historian   puh-LIB-ē-uhs   pəˈlibiːəs

Polybus
   king of Thebes in Egypt; foster father   PAHL-uh-buhs   ˈpɑləbəs
     of Oedipus

Polycarp
   1. Christian saint   PAHL-ē-KAHRP   ˈpɑliˑˌkɑʳp
   2. pers. name, German   PŌ-lue-KAHRP   ˌpoːlyːˈkɑʳp

Polycarpe
   pers. name, French   paw-lē-KAHRP   pɔːliːkɑːrp

Polycaste
   daughter of Nestor; mother of   PAHL-i-KAS-tē   ˌpɑliˈkæstiˑ
     Penelope

Polyclitus, Polycleitus
   Greek sculptor   PAHL-i-KLĪT-uhs   ˌpɑliˈklaiţəs

Polycrates
   tyrant of Samos   puh-LIK-ruh-TĒZ   pəˈlikrəˌtiːz

Polycrite
   heroine of Naxos   PAHL-i-KRĪT-ē   ˌpɑliˈkraiţiˑ

Polydectes
   man who sent Perseus for head of   PAHL-uh-DEK-tēz   ˌpaləˈdektiːz
     Medusa

Polydora
   daughter of Peleus   PAHL-uh-DŌR-uh, PAHL-uh-DAWR-uh   ˌpaləˈdoːrə, ˌpaləˈdɔːrə

Polydore
   1. pers. name   PAHL-i-DAWR   ˈpɑliˌdɔːʳ
   2. French   paw-lē-DAWR   pɔːliːdɔːr

Polydorus
   Greek sculptor; son of Priam; son of   PAHL-uh-DŌR-uhs,   ˌpaləˈdoːrəs, ˌpaləˈdɔːrəs
     Cadmus and Harmonia   PAHL-uh-DAWR-uhs

Polygnotus
   Greek painter   PAHL-ig-NŌT-uhs   ˌpaligˈnoːţəs

Polyhymnia
   1. muse of mime   PAHL-ē-HIM-nē-uh   ˌpaliˑˈhimniːə
   2. street, New Orleans   puh-LIM-nē-uh   pəˈlimniːə

Polykarp
   pers. name   PAHL-ē-KAHRP   ˈpaliˑˌkɑʳp

Polymede
> *mother of Jason*   PAHL-uh-MĒD-ē   ˌpɑlə'miːdi·

Polymestor
> *king of Thrace*   PAHL-uh-MES-tuhr   ˌpɑlə'mestə^r

Polymnus
> *Dionysus's guide to the Underworld*   puh-LIM-nuhs   pə'limnəs

Polynesia
> *central Pacific islands*   PAHL-uh-NĒ-zhuh, -shuh   ˌpɑlə'niːʒə, -ʃə

Polynesian
> *pert. to* Polynesia   PAHL-uh-NĒ-zhuhn, -shuhn   ˌpɑlə'niːʒən, -ʃən

Polynices
> *son of Oedipus*   PAHL-uh-NĪ-sēz   ˌpɑlə'nɑisiːz

Polyphemus
> *Cyclops blinded by Odysseus;*   PAHL-i-FĒ-muhs   ˌpɑli'fiːməs
> *Argonaut*

Polyphonte
> *girl changed into night bird by Ares*   PAHL-uh-FAHNT-ē   ˌpɑlə'fɑnti·

Polypody
> *plant*   PAHL-ē-PŌD-ē   'pɑli·ˌpoːdi·

Polyxena
> *daughter of Priam*   puh-LIK-suh-nuh   pə'liksənə

Polyxenus
> *son of Jason and Medea*   puh-LIK-suh-nuhs   pə'liksənəs

Polyxo
> *wife of Tlepolemus*   puh-LIK-sō   pə'liksoː

Pomarine jaeger
> *sea bird*   PAHM-uh-RĪN YĀ-guhr   'pɑməˌrɑin 'jeːgə^r

Pomerania
> *region, Europe*   PAHM-uh-RĀ-nē-uh, -RĀN-yuh   ˌpɑmə're:niːə, -'re:njə

Pomeranian
> *pert. to* Pomerania; *dog breed*   PAHM-uh-RĀ-nē-uhn   ˌpɑmə're:niːən

Pomerol
> *French wine*   pawm-RAWL   pɔːmrɔːl

Pomeroy
> *pers. name*   PAHM-(uh-)ROI, PUHM-(uh-)ROI   'pɑm(ə)ˌrɔi, 'pəm(ə)ˌrɔi

Pommard
> *red wine variety*   paw-MAHR   pɔːmɑːr

Pomo
> *N. American people*   PŌ-mō   'poːmoː

Pomona
> *Roman goddess of fruit; city, CA*   puh-MŌ-nuh   pə'moːnə

Pomo-Patwin
> *N. American people*   PŌ-mō-PAT-wuhn   'poːmoː'pætwən

Pompadour
> Jeanne Antoinette Poisson Le   pawⁿ-pah-DOOR, ⓢ PAHM-puh-DŌR,   põpaduːr, ⓢ 'pɑmpəˌdoː^r,
> Normant d'Étoiles, Marquise de,   -DAWR, -DUR   -ˌdɔː^r, -ˌdu^r
> *mistress of Louis XV*

Pompano Beach
> *town, FL*   PAHM-puh-NŌ BĒCH, PUHM-puh-NŌ   ˌpɑmpəˌnoː 'biːtʃ,
>   ˌpəmpəˌnoː

Pompei
> *commune, Italy*   pahm-PĀ(-Ē)   pɑm'peː(ˌiː)

Pompeian, Pompeiian
> *pert. to* Pompeii *or its culture*   pahm-PĀ-uhn   pɑm'peːən

---

Key (col. 2): a: fad ā: fade ah: father ar: marry aw: law e: fed ē: feed er: merry i: hid ī: hide ō: coat ōō: boot
oi: boy   ow: now   u: put   uh: above   uhr: bird   ch: chop   ng: ring   sh: show   th: thick   <u>th</u>: this   zh: measure

Pompeii
ancient city, Italy — pahm-PĀ, pahm-PĀ-Ē — pɑmˈpeː, pɑmˈpeːˌiː

Pompeius
pers. name, Latin — pahm-PĒ-uhs — pɑmˈpiːəs

Pompeo
pers. name, Italian — pōm-PE-Ō — poːmˈpe-oː

Pompey
Roman statesman — PAHM-pē — ˈpɑmpi·

Pompey, Sextus
son of Pompey — SEK-stuhs PAHM-pē — ˈsekstəs ˈpɑmpi·

Pompidou
Georges, president, France — pawⁿ-pē-D$\overline{OO}$ — pɔ̃piːduː

Pomponius
pers. name, Latin — pahm-PŌ-nē-uhs — pɑmˈpoːniːəs

Ponapean
lang., people, Micronesia — PŌ-nuh-PĀ-uhn, PAHN-uh-PĀ-uhn — ˌpoːnəˈpeːən, ˌpɑnəˈpeːən

Ponca
city, NE; N. American people — PAHNG-kuh — ˈpɑŋkə

Ponca City
city, OK — PAHNG-kuh SIT-ē — ˌpɑŋkə ˈsiti·

Ponce
1. city, Puerto Rico — PAWN(T)-sā — ˈpɔːn(t)seː
2. pers. name, French — PAWⁿS — pɔ̃s

Ponce
Manuel María, Mexican composer — PŌN-sā — ˈpoːnseː

Ponce de Leon
Juan, Spanish explorer — PAHN(T)S duh LĒ-uhn, PAHN(T)-suh dā lē-ŌN — ˌpɑn(t)s də ˈliːən, ˌpɑn(t)sə deː liːˈoːn

Ponchatoula
town, LA — PAHN-chuh-T$\overline{OO}$-luh — ˌpɑntʃəˈtuːlə

Ponchielli
Amilcare, Italian composer — PAWNG-kē-EL-lē — ˌpɔːŋkiːˈelli·

Pondera
county, MT — PAHN-duh-RĀ — ˌpɑndəˈreː

Pondicherry
territory, India — PAHN-duh-CHER-ē, PAHN-duh-SHER-ē — ˌpɑndəˈtʃeri·, ˌpɑndəˈʃeri·

Ponselle
Rosa, US operatic soprano — pahn-SEL — pɑnˈsel

Ponta Delgada
port, Azores — PAHNT-uh del-GAHD-uh — ˌpɑntə delˈgɑdə

Pontchartrain
lake, LA — PAHN-chuhr-TRĀN, PAHN-chuhr-TRĀN — ˈpɑntʃəʳˌtreːn, ˌpɑntʃəʳˈtreːn

Pontefract
town, England — PAHNT-uh-FRAKT, *locally also* PUHM-fruht — ˈpɑntəˌfrækt, *locally also* ˈpəmfrət

Pontiac
city, MI, IL; N. American people; US car make — PAHNT-ē-AK — ˈpɑntiːˌæk

Pontian
pope — PAHN-sh(ē-)uhn — ˈpɑnʃ(iː)ən

Pontifex maximus
Roman high priest — PAHNT-uh-FEKS MAK-suh-muhs — ˈpɑntəˌfeks ˈmæksəməs

Pontifices
Roman priests — pahn-TIF-uh-SĒZ — pɑnˈtifəˌsiːz

Foreign Sounds: ue: *Fr.* **rue**, *Ger.* **füllen**   uh(r): *Fr.* **boeuf**, *Ger.* **Höhle**   kh: *Ger.* i**ch**, *Scot.* lo**ch**   ḡ: *Sp.* ami**g**o   v̥: *Sp.* ha**b**lar   hl: *Welsh* **Ll**anelli.   CAPITALS: primary stress.   SMALL CAPS: secondary stress.   ⓢ: U.S. pron.   ⓔ: British pron.

Pontine Marshes
   marshy area near Rome, now drained   PAHN-TĬN MAHR-shuhz   ˌpɑnˌtain 'mɑʳʃəz

Pontius
   pers. name, Latin   PAHN-chuhs, PUHN-chuhs   'pɑntʃəs, 'pəntʃəs

Pontius Pilate
   biblical Roman procurator, Judea   PAHN-chuhs PĪ-luht, PUHN-chuhs   ˌpɑntʃəs 'pailət, ˌpəntʃəs

Pont Neuf
   bridge, Paris, France   pawⁿ NUH(R)F   pɔ̃ nœf

Pontoise
   town, France   pawⁿ-TWAHZ   pɔ̃twɑːz

Pontoppidan
   Henrik, *Danish author (Nobel 1917)*   pahn-TAHP-uh-DAHN   pɑn'tɑpəˌdɑːn

Pontormo
   Jacopo da, *Florentine painter*   pōn-TAWR-mō   poːn'tɔːrmoː

Pontotoc
   county, MS, OK   PAHNT-uh-TAHK   'pɑntəˌtak

Pontus
   ancient country, Asia Minor;   PAHN-tuhs, PAHNT-uhs   'pɑn-təs, 'pɑnt-əs
     personification of the sea

Pooh-Bah
   character in the Mikado, *Gilbert and*   P‾OO-BAH   'puːˌbɑ
     Sullivan; a high official

Poona, Pune
   city, India   P‾OO-nuh   'puːnə

Poospatuck
   N. American people   p‾oo-SPAT-uhk   puː'spætək

Pop
   informal for father   PAHP   'pɑp

Popayán
   city, Columbia   PŌ-puh-YAHN   ˌpoːpə'jɑn

Popeil
   Ron, *US TV merchandiser*   pō-PĒL   poː'piːl

Popeye
   cartoon character   PAHP-Ī   'pɑpˌai

Popo Agie
   river, WY   puh-PŌ-zhuh, puh-PŌ-zē-uh   pə'poːʒə, pə'poːziːə

Popocatepetl
   volcano, Mexico   PŌ-puh-KAT-uh-PET-l   ˌpoːpəˌkæʈə'petl̩

Popoloca
   lang., people, Mexico   PŌ-puh-LŌ-kuh   ˌpoːpə'loːkə

Popoluca
   lang., people, Mexico   PŌ-puh-LUHK-uh, PŌ-puh-L‾OO-kuh   ˌpoːpə'ləkə, ˌpoːpə'luːkə

Popov
   vodka brand   PAHP-AWF, PAHP-AWV   'pɑpˌɔːf, 'pɑpˌɔːv

Poppa
   informal for father   PAHP-uh   'pɑpə

Poppaea
   Sabina, *2nd wife of Nero*   pahp-Ē-uh   pɑp'iːə

Populares
   Roman popular leaders   PAHP-yuh-LĀ-rēz   ˌpɑpjə'leːriːz

Poquoson
   county, VA   puh-KWAW-suhn   pə'kwɔːsən

Poratha
   Biblical name   puh-RĀ-thuh; PAWR-uh-thuh, PŌR-;   pə're:θə; 'pɔːrəθə, 'poːr-;
      pō-RAH-tah   poː'rɑtɑ

Key (col. 2):   a: fad   ā: fade   ah: father   ar: marry   aw: law   e: fed   ē: feed   er: merry   i: hid   ī: hide   ō: coat   o͞o: boot
oi: boy   ow: now   u: put   uh: above   uhr: bird   ch: chop   ng: ring   sh: show   th: thick   th̲: this   zh: measure

Porcella *Roman cognomen*	pawr-SEL-uh	pɔːʳˈselə
Porcia, Portia *Roman woman, wife of Brutus*	PŌR-sh(ē-)uh, PAWR-	ˈpoːʳʃ(iː)ə, ˈpɔːʳ-
Porcius *pers. name, Latin*	PAWR-sh(ē-)uhs	ˈpɔːʳʃ(iː)əs
Porcius-Festus *Biblical name*	PAWR-sh(ē-)uhs-FES-tuhs	ˈpɔːʳʃ(iː)əsˈfestəs
Poretti *Italian beer*	pō-RET-tē	poːˈrettiː
Porgy *character in* Porgy & Bess, *Gershwin*	PAWR-gē	ˈpɔːʳgiˑ
Pori *port, Finland*	PAWR-ē	ˈpɔːriˑ
Porsche *German car make*	PAWR-shuh, PAWRSH	ˈpɔːʳʃə, ˈpɔːʳʃ
Porsena, Lars *see* Lars Porsena		
Portales *city, NM*	pawr-TAL-uhs	pɔːʳˈtæləs
Port-au-Prince *city, Haiti*	pawr-tō-PRE^{n}S; [S] PŌRT-ō-PRINS, PAWRT-, -PRANS	pɔːrtoːprẽs; [S] ˌpoːʳtoːˈprins, ˌpɔːʳt-, -ˈpræns
Port-de-Paix *town, Haiti*	PAWR-duh-PĀ	ˌpɔːʳdəˈpeː
Port du Salut *Trappist monastery, France; cheese*	pawr due sah-LUE, [S] PAWR duh suhl-(Y)O͞O	pɔːr dyː sɑːlyː, [S] ˌpɔːʳ də səlˈ(j)uː
Porte, La *see* La Porte		
Porteño *Spanish for one who lives on the coast*	pawr-TĀN-yō	pɔːʳˈteːnjoː
Porteous John, *Scottish soldier; riots*	PAWRT-ē-uhs, PAWR-chuhs	ˈpɔːʳt̬iːəs, ˈpɔːʳtʃəs
Porter *pers. name*	PŌRT-uhr, PAWRT-uhr	ˈpoːʳt̬əʳ, ˈpɔːʳt̬əʳ
Port Gentil *city, Gabon*	pawr zhah^{n}-TĒ	pɔːr ʒɑ̃tiː
Port Harcourt *city, Nigeria*	pōrt HAHR-kuhrt, pawrt	poːʳt ˈhɑʳkəʳt, pɔːʳt
Porthos *character in* The Three Musketeers, *A. Dumas*	pawr-TŌS, [S] PAWR-THŌS	pɔːrtoːs, [S] ˈpɔːʳˌθoːs
Port Hueneme [Hueneme] *city, CA*	PŌRT wī-NĒ-mē, PAWRT	ˌpoːʳt wɑiˈniːmiˑ, ˌpɔːʳt
Portia *pers. name*	PAWR-shuh	ˈpɔːʳʃə
Portinari *1.* Beatrice, *Florentine noblewoman, Dante's inspiration*	PŌR-tē-NAHR-ē, PAWR-	ˌpoːrtiːˈnɑriː, ˌpɔːʳ-
2. Candido, *Brazilian painter*	PAWR-tē-nah-RĒ	ˌpɔːrtiːnɑːˈriː
Portland *US pl. name*	PŌRT-luhnd, PAWRT-luhnd	ˈpoːʳtlənd, ˈpɔːʳtlənd

Portlaoighise
city, Ireland   pawrt-LÃ-uh-shuh, pawrt-LĒSH   pɔːʳt'leːǝʃǝ, pɔːʳt'liːʃ

Port Louis
city, Mauritius   pōrt LOO-uhs, pawrt, LOO-ē, lu-Ē   poːʳt 'luːǝs, pɔːʳt, 'luːiˑ, lu'iː

Port Moresby
city, New Guinea   pōrt MŌRZ-bē, pawrt MAWRZ-   poːʳt 'moːʳzbiˑ, pɔːʳt 'mɔːʳz-

Port Natal
seaport, Brazil   PŌRT nah-TAHL, PAWRT   ˌpoːʳt naˈtal, ˌpɔːʳt

Porto [Oporto]
port city, Portugal   PŌR-too   'poːʳtuː

Pôrto Alegre
city, Brazil   PAWR-too uh-LÃG-ruh, PŌR-too   ˌpɔːʳtuː ǝ'leˑgrǝ, ˌpoːʳtuː

Port-of-Spain
city, Trinidad   PŌRT-uhv-SPÃN, PAWRT-   ˌpoːʳt̬ǝv'speːn, ˌpɔːʳt̬-

Portola Valley
city, CA   pawr-TŌ-luh VAL-ē   pɔːʳ'toːlǝ 'væliˑ

Porto-Novo
port city, Benin   PŌRT-ō-NŌ-vō, PAWRT-   ˌpoːʳtoːˈnoːvoː, ˌpɔːʳt-

Porto Rico
former name of Puerto Rico   PAWRT-uh RĒ-kō   ˌpɔːʳt̬ǝ 'riːkoː

Pôrto Velho
town, Brazil   PAWR-too VEL-yoo   'pɔːrtuː 'veljuː

Port Pirie
port, South Australia   pōrt PIR-ē, pawrt   poːʳt 'piriˑ, pɔːʳt

Port Said
seaport, Egypt   PŌRT sah-ĒD, PAWRT, SĪD   ˌpoːʳt saˈiːd, ˌpɔːʳt, 'said

Portsmouth
city, England; city, NH, OH, VA   PŌRT-smuhth, PAWRT-smuhth   'poːʳtsmǝθ, 'pɔːʳtsmǝθ

Portugal
republic, Europe   PŌR-chi-guhl, PAWR-   'poːʳtʃigǝl, 'pɔːʳ-

Portuguese
lang., Portugal, Brazil, parts of Africa   PŌR-chuh-GĒZ, PAWR-, -GĒS   ˌpoːʳtʃǝ'giːz, ˌpɔːʳ-, -'giːs

Portulaca
plant   PAWR-chuh-LAK-uh   ˌpɔːʳtʃǝ'lækǝ

Portunus
Roman god of doors or harbors   pawr-T(Y)OO-nuhs   pɔːʳ't(j)uːnǝs

Porus
Indian king   PŌR-uhs   'poːrǝs

Posada
Nine Days of, 3rd week of Dec., Mexico   pō-SAHTH-ah   poː'saðɑ

Posavina
Corridor, area, Bosnia   PŌ-suh-VĒ-nuh   ˌpoːsǝ'viːnǝ

Poseidon
Greek god of the sea   puh-SĪD-n   pǝ'saidn̩

Posen
1. city, Poland   PŌ-zuhn   'poːzǝn
2. village, IL   PŌ-zuhn, PŌS-n   'poːzǝn, 'poːsn̩

Positron
nuclear particle   PAHZ-uh-TRAHN   'pɑzǝˌtrɑn

Posner
Vladimir, Russian commentator   PŌZ-nuhr   'poːznǝʳ

Posta, La
see La Posta

Key (col. 2):   a: fad   ã: fade   ah: father   ar: marry   aw: law   e: fed   ē: feed   er: merry   i: hid   ī: hide   ō: coat   oo: boot
oi: boy   ow: now   u: put   uh: above   uhr: bird   ch: chop   ng: ring   sh: show   th: thick   th: this   zh: measure

Poston
Tom, *US actor* — PŌ-stuhn — 'poːstən

Postumius
pers. name, Latin — pahs-T(Y)OŌ-mē-uhs — pɑs't(j)uːmiːəs

Postumus
Roman cognomen — PAHS-chuh-muhs — 'pɑstʃəməs

potassium
element — puh-TAS-ē-uhm — pə'tæsiːəm

Potawatomi
N. American people — PAHT-uh-WAHT-uh-mē — ˌpɑtə'wɑtəmi·

Poteau
river, city, OK — PŌ-TŌ — 'poːˌtoː

Potemkin
Grigori, *Russian nobleman* — puh-TYAWM-kyin, Ⓢ pō-TEM(P)-kuhn — pə'tjɔːmkjin, Ⓢ poː'tem(p)kən

Pothos
personification of love and desire — PŌ-THŌS, PŌ-THAHS — 'poːˌθoːs, 'poːˌθɑs

Potidaea
ancient city, Macedonia — PAHT-uh-DĒ-uh — ˌpɑtə'diːə

Potiphar
Biblical name — PAHT-uh-fuhr, PAHT-uh-FAHR — 'pɑtəfəʳ, 'pɑtəˌfɑʳ

Potiphera, Potipherah
Biblical name — pō-TIF-uh-ruh, PŌ-tē-FER-ah — poː'tifərə, 'poːtiː'ferɑ

Potomac
river, US — puh-TŌ-muhk, puh-TŌ-mik — pə'toːmək, pə'toːmik

Potoo
S. & Cen. American bird — pō-TOŌ — poː'tuː

Potosi
city, MO; mtn., NV, CO — puh-TŌ-sē — pə'toːsi·

Potosí
dept, city, Bolivia — PŌT-uh-SĒ — ˌpoːtə'siː

Potsdam
county, Germany — PAHTS-DAM — 'pɑtsˌdæm

Pottawatomie
county, KA, OK — PAHT-uh-WAHT-uh-mē — ˌpɑtə'wɑtəmi·

Pottawattamie
county, IA — PAHT-uh-WAHT-uh-mē — ˌpɑtə'wɑtəmi·

Poughkeepsie
city, NY — puh-KIP-sē, pō-KIP-sē — pə'kipsi·, poː'kipsi·

Pouilly Fuissé
wine — poō-YĒ fwē-SÃ, Ⓢ poō-YĒ fwē-SÃ — puːjiː fɥiːseː, Ⓢ puː'jiː fwiː'seː

Pouilly Fumé
wine — poō-YĒ fue-MÃ, Ⓢ poō-YĒ foō-MÃ — puːjiː fyːmeː, Ⓢ puː'jiː fuː'meː

Poul
pers. name, Danish — POWL, PŌL — 'paul, 'poːl

Poulenc
Francis, *French composer* — poō-LEⁿK, Ⓢ POŌ-LANGK — puːlẽk, Ⓢ 'puːˌlæŋk

Poulsbo
city, WA — PAWLZ-BŌ — 'pɔːlzˌboː

Poultney
river, town, VT — PŌLT-nē — 'poːltni·

Poussin
Nicolas, *French painter* — poō-SEⁿ — puːsẽ

Foreign Sounds: ue: *Fr.* **rue**, *Ger.* **füllen** uh(r): *Fr.* **boeuf**, *Ger.* **Höhle** kh: *Ger.* **ich**, *Scot.* **loch** g̱: *Sp.* **amigo** v̱: *Sp.* **hablar** hl: *Welsh* **Llanelli**. CAPITALS: primary stress. SMALL CAPS: secondary stress. Ⓢ: U.S. pron. Ⓔ: British pron.

Powel
pers. name	POW(-uh)l, ⒺΘ *also* PŌ-uhl	'paʊ(ə)l, ⒺΘ *also* 'poːəl

Powell
1. Adam Clayton, *US politician;* Colin, *US general;* Lewis Franklin, *US jurist*	POW(-uh)l	'paʊ(ə)l
2. Anthony, *British writer;* C. F., *English physicist (Nobel 1950)*	PŌ-uhl, POW(-uh)l	'poːəl, 'paʊ(ə)l

Poweshiek
county, IA	POW-uh-SHĒK	'paʊəˌʃiːk

Powhatan
1. American Indian leader; N. American people	POW-uh-TAN, POW-uh-TAN, pow-HAT-n	'paʊəˌtæn, ˌpaʊə'tæn, paʊ'hætn̩
2. county, VA	POW-uh-TAN	ˌpaʊə'tæn
3. town, AR	pow-HAT-n, POW-uh-TAN	paʊ'hætn̩, ˌpaʊə'tæn

Powis
pers. name	PŌ-uhs, POW-uhs	'poːəs, 'paʊəs

Powys
1. county, ancient kingdom, Wales	PŌ-is, PUH-wis	'poːis, 'pəwis
2. family name	POW-uhs, PŌ-uhs	'paʊəs, 'poːəs
3. John Cowper, *English writer*	PŌ-uhs	'poːəs

Požarevac
town, Serbia	pō-ZHAHR-uh-VAHTS	poː'ʒɑːrəˌvɑːts

Požega
town, Croatia	PAW-zhuh-guh	'pɔːʒəgə

Poznán
city, Poland	PŌZ-NAHN-yuh, Ⓢ PŌZ-NAN(-yuh)	'poːzˌnɑːɲ , Ⓢ 'poːzˌnæn(jə)

Prabhashankar
pers. name, Hindi	PRUH-buh-SHUHNG-kuhr	ˌprəbə'ʃəŋkər

Prado
museum, Madrid, Spain	PRAH<u>TH</u>-ō, PRAHD-ō	'praðoː, 'prɑdoː

Praetorian guard
bodyguards of the ancient Roman emperors	prē-TŌR-ē-uhn GAHRD, prē-TAWR-	priːˌtoːriːən 'gɑrd, priːˌtɔːr-

Praetorium
Biblical name	pri-TŌR-ē-uhm, pri-TAWR-	pri'toːriːəm, pri'tɔːr-

Praetorius
Michael, *German composer*	pri-TŌR-ē-uhs, pri-TAWR-ē-uhs	pri'toːriːəs, pri'tɔːriːəs

Prague
city, Czech republic	PRAHG	'prɑg

Praha
Czech name for Prague	PRAH-hah	'prɑhɑ

Praia
city, Cape Verde Islands	PRĪ-uh	'praiə

Prairial
month, French Revolutionary calendar	prer-YAHL	prerjɑːl

Prajadhipok
king, Siam	PRĪ-ahd-ē-PAWK	ˌpraiɑdiː'pɔːk

Prakrit
Indic lang.	PRAHK-rit	'prɑkrit

praseodymium
element	PRĀ-zē-ō-DIM-ē-uhm, PRĀ-sē-	ˌpreːziːoː'dimiːəm, ˌpreːsiː-

Prather
pers. name	PRA<u>TH</u>-uhr	'præðərʳ

Key (col. 2): a: f**a**d ā: f**a**de ah: f**a**ther ar: m**a**rry aw: l**a**w e: f**e**d ē: f**ee**d er: m**e**rry i: h**i**d ī: h**i**de ō: c**oa**t ōō: b**oo**t
oi: b**oy** ow: n**ow** u: p**u**t uh: **a**bove uhr: b**ir**d ch: **ch**op ng: ri**ng** sh: **sh**ow th: **th**ick <u>th</u>: **th**is zh: mea**s**ure

Pratincole

   wading bird   PRAT-n-KŌL, PRAT-ing-KŌL, PRĀT-   ˈprætn̩ˌkoːl, ˈprætiŋˌkoːl, ˈpreːt-

Pratt

   pers. name   PRAT   ˈpræt

Pratt & Whitney

   US machine tools co.   PRAT n (H)WIT-nē   ˌpræt n̩ ˈ(h)witniˑ

Pravda

   official Communist newspaper, USSR   PRAHV-duh   ˈprɑvdə

Praxede

   pers. name, German   prahk-SĀ-duh   prɑkˈseːdə

Práxedes

   pers. name, Spanish   PRAHK-sā-<u>th</u>ās   ˈprɑkseːðeːs

Praxiteles

   Greek sculptor   prak-SIT-l-ĒZ   prækˈsitl̩ˌiːz

Precambrian

   geologic period   prē-KAM-brē-uhn, PRĒ-KAM-brē-uhn, -KĀM-brē-uhn   priːˈkæmbriːən, ˈpriːˈkæmbriːən, -ˈkeːmbriːən

pre-Columbian

   pert. to the Americas before arrival of Columbus   PRĒ-kuh-LUHM-bē-uhn   ˌpriːkəˈləmbiːən

Pregl

   Fritz, Austrian chemist (Nobel 1923)   PRĀ-guhl   ˈpreːgəl

Prelog

   Vladimir, Yugoslav-born Swiss organic chemist (Nobel 1975)   PREL-ŌG   ˈprelˌoːg

Prelude, The

   poem, Wordsworth   PREL-yo͞od, PRĀ-L(Y)O͞OD   ˈpreljuːd, ˈpreːˌl(j)uːd

Premières Côtes de Bordeaux

   wine   pruhm-YER KŌT duh bawr-DŌ   prəmjer koːt də bɔːrdoː

Premont

   city, TX   PRĒ-MAHNT   ˈpriːˌmɑnt

Prendergast

   Maurice Brazil, US painter   PREN-duhr-GAST   ˈprendərˌgæst

Pre-Raphaelite

   member of a group of English artists   prē-RAF-(ē-)uh-LĪT, prē-RĀ-fē-uh-LĪT   priːˈræf(iː)əˌlait, priːˈreːfiːəˌlait

Presbyterian

   Protestant church   PREZ-buh-TIR-ē-uhn, PRES-   ˌprezbəˈtiriːən, ˌpres-

Presbyterianism

   Christian religion   PREZ-buh-TIR-ē-uh-NIZ-uhm, PRES-   ˌprezbəˈtiriːəˌnizəm, ˌpres-

Prescott

   pers. name; US pl. name   PRES-kuht   ˈpreskət

Preserved

   pers. name   pri-ZUHR-vuhd   priˈzərvəd

Presidente

   Dominican beer   prā-zi-DEN-tā   preːziˈdenteː

Presidente Hayes

   dept, Paraguay   PRES-uh-<u>THEN</u>-tā ĪS   ˌpresəˌðenteː ˈais

Presidio

   military post, San Francisco, CA; county, TX   pruh-SID-ē-ō   prəˈsidiːoː

Presley

   Elvis, US musician; pers. name   PREZ-lē, PRES-lē   ˈprezliˑ, ˈpresliˑ

Foreign Sounds: ue: *Fr.* **rue**, *Ger.* **füllen**   uh(r): *Fr.* **boeuf**, *Ger.* **Höhle**   <u>kh</u>: *Ger.* **ich**, *Scot.* **loch**   ğ: *Sp.* **amigo**   v: *Sp.* **hablar**
hl: *Welsh* **Llanelli**.   CAPITALS: primary stress.   SMALL CAPS: secondary stress.   Ⓢ: U.S. pron.   Ⓔ: British pron.

Presocratics
  Greek philosophers before Socrates   PRĒ-suh-KRAT-iks   ˌpriːsəˈkrætiks
Prester John
  legendary Christian priest   PRES-tuhr JAHN   ˈprestəʳ ˈdʒɑn
Presque Isle
  1. peninsula, bay, Lake Erie; city, ME presk ĪL   presk ˈɑil
  2. county, MI   presk ĒL   presk ˈiːl
Pressler
  Larry, *US politician*   PRES-luhr   ˈpresləʳ
Preston
  pers. name; US pl. name   PRES-tuhn   ˈprestən
Prestonpans
  seaside resort, Scotland   PRES-tuhn-PANZ   ˌprestənˈpænz
Prestwick
  airport, Scotland   PREST-wik   ˈprestwik
Pretoria
  city, S. Africa   pri-TŌR-ē-uh, pri-TAWR-ē-uh   priˈtoːriːə, priˈtɔːriːə
Pretorius
  Andries, *S. African colonizer*   pri-TŌR-ē-uhs, pri-TAWR-ē-uhs   priˈtoːriːəs, priˈtɔːriːəs
Prevert
  Jacques, *French poet and*   prā-VER   preːver
    screenwriter
Previn
  André, *US musician*   PREV-uhn   ˈprevən
Prévost
  Eugène Marcel, *French novelist*   prā-VŌ   preːvoː
Priam
  king of Troy   PRĪ-uhm, PRĪ-AM   ˈprɑiəm, ˈprɑiˌæm
Priapus
  Greek god of fertility   prī-Ā-puhs, PRĪ-uh-puhs,   prɑiˈeːpəs, ˈprɑiəpəs,
                                            PRĒ-uh-puhs   ˈpriːəpəs
Pribilof
  islands, Bering Sea   PRIB-uh-LAWF   ˈpribəˌlɔːf
Prichard
  pers. name   PRICH-uhrd   ˈpritʃəʳd
Prideaux
  pers. name   prē-DŌ, PRID-ō   priːˈdoː, ˈpridoː
Priene
  Ionian city   prī-Ē-nē   prɑiˈiːniˑ
Priestley
  J. B., *English writer;* Joseph,   PRĒST-lē   ˈpriːstliˑ
    English theologian and scientist
Prigogine
  Ilya, *Russian-born Belgian chemist*   pri-GAW-zhuhn, pri-gaw-ZHĒN   priˈgɔːʒən, prigɔːˈʒiːn
    (Nobel 1977)
Prijedor
  city, Bosnia   PRĒ-uh-DAWR, -DŌR   ˈpriːəˌdɔːʳ, -ˌdoːʳ
Primo
  pers. name, Spanish   PRĒ-mō   ˈpriːmoː
Primo de Rivera y Orbaneja
  Miguel, *Spanish general and*   PRĒ-mō thā rē-V̲Ā-rah ē   ˈpriːmoː ðeː riːˈβeːrɑ iː
    politician   ōr-v̲ah-NEK̲H-ah   oːrβɑˈnexɑ
Prince Edward
  1. county, VA   prin(t)s ED-(w)uhrd   prin(t)s ˈed(w)əʳd
  2. county, Ontario, Canada   prin(t)s ED-wuhrd   prin(t)s ˈedwəʳd

---

Key (col. 2):   a: f**a**d   ā: f**a**de   ah: f**a**ther   ar: m**a**rry   aw: l**a**w   e: f**e**d   ē: f**ee**d   er: m**e**rry   i: h**i**d   ī: h**i**de   ō: c**oa**t   ōō: b**oo**t
oi: b**o**y   ow: n**o**w   u: p**u**t   uh: **a**bove   uhr: b**i**rd   ch: **ch**op   ng: ri**ng**   sh: **sh**ow   th: **th**ick   t̲h̲: **th**is   zh: mea**s**ure

Prince Edward Island		
island province, Canada	prin(t)s ED-wuhrd Ī-luhnd	prin(t)s ˌedwə^{r}d 'ɑilənd
Prince Gustaf Adolf		
Sea, *arm of the Arctic Ocean, Canada*	prin(t)s GOO͞S-tahf Ā-DAHLF SĒ, AD-AHLF	prin(t)s ˌgu'stɑf ˌeːˌdɑlf 'siː, ˌædˌɑlf
Prince of Wales-Outer Ketchikan		
division, AK	PRIN(T)S uhv WĀLZ OWT-uhr KECH-i-KAN	ˌprin(t)s əv ˌweːlz ˌɑut̬ə^{r} 'ketʃiˌkæn
Princeps		
term for Roman emperor	PRIN-SEPS, PRING-KEPS	'prinˌseps, 'priŋˌkeps
Princeton		
river, city, university, NJ	PRIN(T)-stuhn	'prin(t)stən
Príncipe		
island, São Tomé & Príncipe	PRI(N)-suh-puh, [$] PRIN(T)-suh-puh	'prĩ(n)səpə, [$] 'prin(t)səpə
Principes		
plural of Princeps	PRIN-suh-PĒZ, PRING-kuh-PĀS	'prinsəˌpiːz, 'priŋkəˌpeːs
Principia		
College, *IL*	prin-SIP-ē-uh	prin'sipiːə
Principia Mathematica		
scientific work, Newton	prin-SIP-ē-uh MATH-uh-MAT-i-kuh	prin'sipiːə ˌmæθə'mæt̬ikə
Prine		
John, *US singer, songwriter*	PRĪN	'prɑin
Prinknash		
district, Gloucestershire, England	PRIN-ij *[sic]*	'prinidʒ *[sic]*
Prior		
Matthew, *English poet and diplomat*	PRĪ(-uh)r	'prɑi(ə)^{r}
Pripet		
river, Belorussia, Ukraine	PRIP-ET, PRIP-uht	'pripˌet, 'pripət
Prisca		
Biblical name	PRIS-kuh	'priskə
Priscian		
Latin grammarian	PRISH-(ē-)uhn	'priʃ(iː)ən
Priscilla		
pers. name	pruh-SIL-uh	prə'silə
Priscillian		
Spanish religious reformer	pruh-SIL-ē-uhn, pruh-SIL-yuhn	prə'siliːən, prə'siljən
Priscillianism		
teachings of Priscillian	pruh-SIL-yuh-NIZ-uhm, -SIL-ē-uh-NIZ-uhm	prə'siljəˌnizəm, -'siliːəˌnizəm
Pritchard		
pers. name	PRICH-uhrd	'pritʃə^{r}d
Pritchett		
Victor Sawdon, *English writer*	PRICH-it	'pritʃit
Privet		
bush	PRIV-uht	'privət
Proboscidea		
elephants	PRŌ-buh-SID-ē-uh, prō-BAHS-uh-DĒ-uh	ˌproːbə'sidiːə, proːˌbɑsə'diːə
Probus		
Roman emperor	PRŌ-buhs	'proːbəs
Procellarum, Oceanus		
'ocean' on Moon	Ō-shē-AN-uhs PRŌ-suh-LAHR-uhm, -LAR-uhm	ˌoːʃiː'ænəs ˌproːsə'lɑrəm, -'lærəm
Prochorus, Procorus		
Biblical name	PRAHK-uh-ruhs, PRŌ-kuh-ruhs	'prɑkərəs, 'proːkərəs

Foreign Sounds: ue: *Fr.* **rue**, *Ger.* **füllen** uh(r): *Fr.* **boeuf**, *Ger.* **Höhle** kh: *Ger.* **ich**, *Scot.* **loch** g̃: *Sp.* amigo v̲: *Sp.* hablar hl: *Welsh* **Llanelli**. CAPITALS: primary stress. SMALL CAPS: secondary stress. [$]: U.S. pron. [£]: British pron.

Procne
  sister of Philomela   PRAHK-nē   ˈprɑkniˑ
Procofieff
  pers. name, Russian   PRUH-KAWF-yif   ˌprəˈkɔːfjif
Procopius
  Greek historian   pruh-KŌ-pē-uhs   prəˈkoːpiːəs
Procris
  daughter of Erechtheus   PRŌ-kruhs   ˈproːkrəs
Procrustean
  pert. to Procrustes *and his bed*   p(r)uh-KRUHS-tē-uhn,   p(r)əˈkrəstiːən, proːˈkrəstiːən
                                           prō-KRUHS-tē-uhn
Procrustes
  cruel son of Poseidon   p(r)uh-KRUHS-tēz, prō-KRUHS-tēz   p(r)əˈkrəstiːz, proːˈkrəstiːz
Procter
  Bryan, *(pseudonym* Barry Cornwall*)*,   PRAHK-tuhr   ˈprɑktəʳ
  English poet
Procter & Gamble
  US co.   PRAHK-tuhr uhn(d) GAM-buhl   ˈprɑktəʳ ən(d) ˈgæmbəl
Procul Harum
  rock group   PRŌ-kuhl HAR-uhm, HER-uhm   ˈproːkəl ˈhærəm, ˈherəm
Procyon
  star   PRŌ-sē-AHN   ˈproːsiːˌɑn
Prof.
  abbreviation of Professor   PRAHF   ˈprɑf
Professor
  academic title   pruh-FES-uhr, *in rapid speech*   prəˈfesəʳ, *in rapid speech*
                                           puh-FES-uhr   pəˈfesəʳ
Profumo
  John, *English politician*   pruh-FY͞OO-mō   prəˈfjuːmoː
Prokhorov
  Alexander Mikhailovich, *Russian*   PRAW-k͟huh-RAWF   ˌprɔːxəˈrɔːf
  physicist (Nobel 1964)
Prokofiev
  Sergei, *Russian composer*   pruh-KAWF-yuhf, pruh-KAWF-YEF,   prəˈkɔːfjəf, prəˈkɔːfˌjef,
                                           pruh-KAWF-YEV   prəˈkɔːfˌjev
Prokopyevsk
  city, Russia   pruh-KAWP-yuhfsk   prəˈkɔːpjəfsk
PROLOG
  programming lang.   PRŌ-LAWG, PRŌ-LAHG   ˈproːˌlɔːg, ˈproːˌlɑg
PROM
  programmable read-only memory   PRAHM   ˈprɑm
  (computer chip)
Promethean
  pert. to Prometheus   pruh-MĒ-thē-uhn   prəˈmiːθiːən
Prometheus
  Titan who championed humankind;   pruh-MĒ-thē-uhs, pruh-MĒ-TH(Y)O͞OS   prəˈmiːθiːəs, prəˈmiːˌθ(j)uːs
  pers. name
promethium
  element   pruh-MĒ-thē-uhm, prō-   prəˈmiːθiːəm, proː-
Propertius
  Roman poet   prō-PUHR-sh(ē-)uhs   proːˈpəʳʃ(iː)əs
Propontis
  sea, Turkey   prō-PAHNT-uhs   proːˈpɑntəs
Propylaea
  entrance to Acropolis   PRŌ-puh-LĒ-uh, PRAHP-uh-LĒ-uh   ˌproːpəˈliːə, ˌprɑpəˈliːə

Key (col. 2): a: fad ā: fade ah: father ar: marry aw: law e: fed ē: feed er: merry i: hid ī: hide ō: coat o͞o: boot
oi: boy   ow: now   u: put   uh: above   uhr: bird   ch: chop   ng: ring   sh: show   th: thick   t͟h: this   zh: measure

Prosauropoda
dinosaur infraorder   PRŌ-suh-RAHP-uhd-uh   ˌproːsəˈrɑpədə
Proserpina
Roman goddess of Underworld   pruh-SUHR-puh-nuh   prəˈsərˌpənə
Proserpine
anglicization of Proserpina   PRAHS-uhr-PĪN   ˈprasərˌpɑin
Proskynesis
Persian ceremony of prostration   PRAHS-KĪ-NĒ-suhs   ˌprasˌkaiˈniːsəs
Prosper
1. pers. name   PRAHS-puhr   ˈpraspər
2. French   praws-PER   prɔːsper
3. German   PRAWS-puhr   ˈprɔːspər
Prospero
1. Shakespearean enchanter; pers.   PRAHS-puh-rō   ˈpraspəroː
name
2. Italian   PRAWS-pā-rō   ˈprɔːspeːroː
Próspero
pers. name, Spanish   PRŌ-spā-rō   ˈproːspeːroː
Prostigmin
tdmk for neostigmine   prō-STIG-muhn   proːˈstigmən
protactinium
element   PRŌT-AK-TIN-ē-uhm   ˌproːtˌækˈtiniːəm
Protagoras
Greek philosopher; dialogue of Plato   prō-TAG-uh-ruhs   proːˈtægərəs
Protean
pert. to Proteus   PRŌT-ē-uhn, prō-TĒ-uhn   ˈproːtiːən, proːˈtiːən
Proterozoic
geologic era   PRAHT-uh-ruh-ZŌ-ik, PRŌT-   ˌpratərəˈzoːik, ˌproːt-
Protesilaus
first Greek killed by Trojans   PRŌT-uh-suh-LĀ-(y)uhs   ˌproːtəsəˈleː(j)əs
Protestant
type of Christian   PRAHT-uh-stuhnt   ˈpratəstənt
Protestantism
branch of Christianity   PRAHT-uh-stuhnt-IZ-uhm   ˈpratəstəntˌizəm
Proteus
Greek sea god; pers. name   PRŌT-ē-uhs, PRŌ-T(Y)ŌŌS   ˈproːtiˑəs, ˈproːˌt(j)uːs
Prothonotary warbler
bird   prō-THAHN-uh-TER-ē WAWR-bluhr,   proːˈθanəˌteriˑ ˈwɔːrblər,
                                         PRŌ-thuh-NŌT-uh-rē   ˌproːθəˈnoːtəriˑ
Protoceratops
dinosaur   PRŌT-ō-SER-uh-TAHPS   ˌproːtɔːˈserəˌtaps
Proto-Indo-European
prehistoric parent lang. of   PRŌT-ō-IN-dō-YUR-uh-PĒ-uhn   ˌproːtɔːˌindoːˌjurəˈpiːən
Indo-European
Proudhon
Pierre Joseph, *French socialist*   prōō-DAWⁿ   pruːdɔ̃
Proulx
W. Annie, *US author*   PRŌŌ   ˈpruː
Proust
Marcel, *French writer*   PRŌŌST   pruːst
Proustian
pert. to Proust   PRŌŌ-stē-uhn   ˈpruːstiːən
Provençal [Languedoc, Occitan]
lang., France   praw-vahⁿ-SAHL   prɔːvãsal

Foreign Sounds: **ue**: *Fr.* **rue**, *Ger.* **füllen**   **uh(r)**: *Fr.* **boeuf**, *Ger.* **Höhle**   **kh**: *Ger.* **ich**, *Scot.* **loch**   **g̵**: *Sp.* **amigo**   **v**: *Sp.* **hablar**
hl: *Welsh* **Llanelli**.   CAPITALS: primary stress.   SMALL CAPS: secondary stress.   Ⓢ: U.S. pron.   Ⓔ: British pron.

Provence
  prov, France   praw-VAH^nS   prɔːvɑ̃s

Proverbs
  Old Testament book   PRAHV-UHRBZ   'prɑv,əʳbz

Providence
  divine guidance; US pl. name   PRAHV-uhd-uhn(t)s,   'prɑvədən(t)s, 'prɑvədn̩(t)s,
                                    PRAHV-uhd-n(t)s,   'prɑvə,den(t)s
                                    PRAHV-uh-DEN(T)S

Provincetown
  town, MA   PRAHV-uhn-STOWN   'prɑvən,stɑun

Provincias Vascongadas
  region, Spain   prō-VIN-sē-ahs   proːˈvinsiːɑs βaskɔːnˈgaðas
                                    v̲ahs-kawn-GAH T̲H-ahs

Provo
  city, UT   PRŌ-vō   'proːvoː

Provolone
  cheese   PRŌ-vuh-LŌ-nē, PRŌ-vuh-LŌN   ,proːvəˈloːniˑ, ,proːvəˈloːn

Prowers
  county, CO   PRŌ-uhrz   'proːəʳz

Proxima Centauri
  star in Centaurus   PRAHK-sim-uh sen-TAWR-ē   'prɑksimə senˈtɔːriˑ

Proxmire
  William, US politician   PRAHK-SMĪR   'prɑk,smaiʳ

Prozac
  tdmk for anti-depressant drug   PRŌ-ZAK   'proː,zæk

Prudence
  pers. name   PROOD-ns   'pruːdn̩s

Prudencio
  pers. name, Spanish   proo-T̲H̲ĀN-syō, -thyō   pruːˈðeˑnsjoː, -θjoː

Prudential-Bache
  US financial co.   pru-DEN-chuhl-BĀSH   pruˈdentʃəlˈbeːʃ

Prudhoe
  bay, AK   PRUHD-(h)ō, PROOD-ō   'prəd(h)oː, 'pruːdoː

Prud'hon
  Pierre Paul, *French painter*   prue-DAW^n   pryːdɔ̃

Prufrock
  J. Alfred, *character in poem of T. S.*   PROO-FRAHK   'pruː,frɑk
  Eliot

Prussia
  former German state   PRUHSH-uh   'prəʃə

Prussian
  pert. to Prussia   PRUHSH-uhn   'prəʃən

Pruszków
  commune, Poland   PROOSH-koof   'pruːʃkuːf

Prut, Pruth
  river, Romania   PROOT   'pruːt

Prynne
  Hester, *Hawthorne character*   PRIN   'prin

Pryor
  David Hampton, *US politician;*   PRĪ(-uh)r   'prai(ə)ʳ
  Richard, *US comedian*

Prytany
  panel of Athenian Council of 500   PRIT-n-ē   'pritn̩iˑ

Key (col. 2): a: fad ā: fade ah: father ar: marry aw: law e: fed ē: feed er: merry i: hid ī: hide ō: coat ōō: boot
oi: boy ow: now u: put uh: above uhr: bird ch: chop ng: ring sh: show th: thick t̲h̲: this zh: measure

Przybysz		
Polish family name	PSHI-bish, [$] SHĒ-bish, PRIZ-bē, PRIZ-BIZ	'pʃibiʃ, [$] 'ʃiːbiʃ, 'prizbiˑ, 'priz,biz
Psalms		
Old Testament book	SAHMZ, SAHLMZ	'sɑˑmz, 'sɑlmz
Psalter		
book of Psalms	SAWL-tuhr	'sɔːltəʳ
Psaltery		
the Psalter	SAWL-tuh-rē, SAWL-trē	'sɔːltəriˑ, 'sɔːltriˑ
Psammetichus		
name, kings of Egypt	suh-MET-i-kuhs	sə'metikəs
Psittacosaurus		
dinosaur	SIT-uh-kō-SAWR-uhs	,sitəkoː'sɔːrəs
Psyche		
wife of Eros in Roman myth	SĪ-kē	'sɑikiˑ
Ptah, Phthah		
Egyptian creator god	(P)TAH, puh-TAH	'(p)tɑ, pə'tɑ
Pterodactyl		
prehistoric, bird-like reptile	TER-uh-DAK-tl	,terə'dæktl̩
Pterosauria		
reptilian order	TER-uh-SAWR-ē-uh	,terə'sɔːriːə
Ptolemais [Accho, Acre]		
ancient city, Israel	TAHL-uh-MĀ-uhs	,tɑlə'meːəs
Ptolemaeus		
crater on Moon	TAHL-uh-MĀ-uhs	,tɑlə'meːəs
Ptolemaic		
pert. to Ptolemy	TAHL-uh-MĀ-ik	,tɑlə'meːik
Ptolemy		
name, kings of Egypt; Alexandrian astronomer	TAHL-uh-mē	'tɑləmiˑ
Ptuj		
town, Slovenia	PTOO-ē, puh-TOO-ē	'ptuːiˑ, pə'tuːiˑ
Pua		
Biblical name	P(Y)OO-uh, poo-VAH	'p(j)uːə, puː'vɑ
Puah		
Biblical name	P(Y)OO-uh, poo-AH	'p(j)uːə, puː'ɑ
Publicani		
Roman tax collectors	PUHB-li-KĀ-nē, -KĀ-NĪ	,pəbli'keːniˑ, -'keː,nɑi
Publilius		
pers. name, Latin	PUHB-LIL-ē-uhs	,pəb'liliːəs
Publius		
pers. name, Latin	PUHB-lē-uhs	'pəbliːəs
Pucci		
Emilio, *Italian fashion designer*	POO-chē	'puːtʃiˑ
Puccini		
Giacomo, *Italian composer*	poo-CHĒ-nē	puː'tʃiːniˑ
Puebla		
state, Mexico	PWEV-lah	'pweβlɑ
Pueblo		
city, county, CO; N. American people	poo-EB-lō, PWEB-lō, pyoo-EB-lō	puː'ebloː, 'pwebloː, pjuː'ebloː
Pudens		
Biblical name	P(Y)OO-DENZ	'p(j)uː,denz

Foreign Sounds: ue: *Fr.* **rue**, *Ger.* **fü**llen uh(r): *Fr.* **boeuf**, *Ger.* **Hö**hle kh: *Ger.* i**ch**, *Scot.* lo**ch** g̱: *Sp.* ami**g**o v̱: *Sp.* ha**b**lar hl: *Welsh* **Ll**anelli. CAPITALS: primary stress. SMALL CAPS: secondary stress. [$]: U.S. pron. [£]: British pron.

Pudovkin
   Vsevolod Ilarionovich, *Russian film*   pōō-DAWF-kyin   pu:ˈdɔːfkjin
   director

Puelche
   S. American people   PWEL-chē   ˈpweltʃiˑ

Puente
   Tito, *US musician and bandleader*   PWEN-TĀ   ˈpwenˌteː

Puerco
   river, NM   PWER-kō   ˈpweʳkoː

Puerto De la Cruz
   resort, Canary Islands   PWER-tō <u>th</u>ā lah KRŌŌTH   ˌpwerto: ðeː la ˈkruːθ

Puerto Plata
   prov, Dominican Republic   PWER-tō PLAHT-ah   ˌpwerto: ˈplata

Puerto Presidente Stroessner
   town, Paraguay   PWER-tō PREZ-i-<u>THEN</u>-tā STRES-nuhr   ˌpwerto: ˌpreziˌðenteː
                                                                   ˈstresnəʳ

Puerto Rican
   pert. to or inhabitant of Puerto Rico   PŌRT-uh RĒ-kuhn, PAWRT-uh,   ˌpoːʳtə ˈriːkən, ˌpɔːʳtə,
                                  PWERT-ō   ˌpweʳʈoː

Puerto Rico
   island, West Indies   PŌRT-uh RĒ-kō, PAWRT-uh, PWERT-ō   ˌpoːʳtə ˈriːkoː, ˌpɔːʳtə,
                                                                    ˌpweʳʈoː

Puerto Vallarta
   resort, Mexico   PWERT-ō vah-YAHRT-uh   ˌpweʳʈoː vaˈjaʳʈə

Puget
   sound, WA   PYŌŌ-juht   ˈpjuːdʒət

Pugh
   Robert L., *US ambassador*   PYŌŌ   ˈpjuː

Puglia
   prov, Italy   POOL-yah   ˈpuːlja

Pukapuka
   coral atoll, Cook Islands, Pacific   PŌŌ-kuh-PŌŌ-kuh   ˌpuːkəˈpuːkə

Pukaskwa
   National Park, *Ontario*   pōō-KAHS-kwuh   puːˈkaskwə

Pul
   Biblical name   PUL, PŌŌL   ˈpul, ˈpuːl

Pulaski
   1. Kazimierz, *Polish nobleman*   pōō-LAHS-kē, Ⓢ puh-LAS-kē,   puːˈlaskiˑ, Ⓢ pəˈlæskiˑ,
                                  pyu-LAS-kē   pjuˈlæskiˑ
   2. pl. name, US   puh-LAS-kē, pyu-LAS-kē   pəˈlæskiˑ, pjuˈlæskiˑ

Pulcher
   Roman cognomen   PUHL-kuhr   ˈpəlkəʳ

Puli
   dog breed   PUL-ē, P(Y)ŌŌ-lē   ˈpuliˑ, ˈp(j)uːliˑ

Puligny-Montrachet
   French wine   pue-lēn-YĒ-mawⁿ-trah-SHE   pyːliːnjiːmõtraːʃe

Pulitzer
   Joseph, *US journalist; literary/music*   PUL-uht-suhr *(family's usual pron.)*,   ˈpulətsəʳ *(family's usual*
   prize   PYŌŌ-luht-suhr   *pron.*), ˈpjuːlətsəʳ

Pullman
   George, *US inventor; tdmk for a*   PUL-muhn   ˈpulmən
   railroad sleeping car

Pulteney
   pers. name   PUHLT-nē   ˈpəltniˑ

Key (col. 2):   a: fad ā: fade ah: father ar: marry aw: law e: fed ē: feed er: merry i: hid ī: hide ō: coat ōō: boot
oi: boy ow: now u: put uh: above uhr: bird ch: chop ng: ring sh: show th: thick <u>th</u>: this zh: measure

Pułtusk

   commune, Poland   POOL-TOOSK   'puːɫˌtuːsk

Punchinello

   puppet show character   PUHN-chuh-NEL-ō   ˌpəntʃə'neloː

Pune

   see Poona

Pungwe

   river, waterfall, Mozambique   PUNG-gwuh   'puŋgwə

Punic

   Carthaginian (adj.)   PYOO-nik   'pjuːnik

Punite

   Biblical name   P(Y)OO-NĪT   'p(j)uːˌnɑit

Punjab, Panjab

   prov, India & Pakistan   PUHN-JAHB, PUHN-JAHB   ˌpən'dʒɑb, 'pənˌdʒɑb

Punjabi, Panjabi

   lang., native of Punjab   PUHN-JAHB-ē   ˌpən'dʒɑbiˑ

Punon

   Biblical name   P(Y)OO-NAHN, poo-NAWN   'p(j)uːˌnɑn, puː'nɔːn

Punt

   ancient name for part of Africa   PUNT   'punt

Punta, Cerro de

   island, Puerto Rico   SER-ō thā POON-tuh   ˌseroː ðeː 'puːntə

Punta Arenas [Magallanes]

   city, Chile   POON-tuh uh-RĀ-nuhs   ˌpuːntə ə'reːnəs

Punt e Mes

   Italian vermouth   PUNT ē MES   ˌpunt iː 'mes

Puntigam

   Austrian beer   PUN-ti-GAHM, PUN-ti-GAHM   'puntiˌgɑm, ˌpunti'gɑm

Punxsutawney

   borough, PA   PUHNGK-suh-TAW-nē   ˌpəŋksə'tɔːniˑ

Puppis

   constellation   PUHP-uhs   'pəpəs

Pur

   Biblical name   PUR, POOR   'puʳ, 'puːr

Puran

   pers. name   poo-RAHN   puː'rɑn

Purcell

   1. E. M., US physicist (Nobel 1952); city, OK   puhr-SEL   pəʳ'sel

   2. Henry, *English composer*   PUHR-suhl, puhr-SEL   'pəʳsəl, pəʳ'sel

Purdue

   University, *IN*   puhr-D(Y)OO   pəʳ'd(j)uː

Purgatoire

   river, CO   PUHR-guh-TWAHR, PIK-it-WĪR   'pəʳgəˌtwɑʳ, 'pikitˌwɑiʳ

Purim

   Jewish holiday   PUR-uhm, POO-ruhm, pu-RIM   'purəm, 'puːrəm, pu'rim

Purina

   tdmk for pet food   pyur-Ē-nuh   pjur'iːnə

Puritan

   English Protestant group   PYUR-uht-n   'pjurətn̩

Puritanism

   beliefs of the Puritans   PYUR-uht-n-IZ-uhm   'pjurətn̩ˌizəm

Purolator Courier

   US corp.   PYUR-uh-LĀT-uhr KUR-ē-uhr, KUHR-ē-uhr, KUH-rē-uhr   'pjurəˌleːʈəʳ 'kuriːəʳ, 'kər-iːəʳ, 'kə-riːəʳ

Purus		
river, S. America	puh-RO̅O̅S	pə'ruːs
Purvis		
John, *US lawyer*	PUHR-vuhs	'pəʳvəs
Pusan		
city, S. Korea	po̅o̅-sahn	puːsɑn
Pusey		
Edward B., *English theologian*	PYO̅O̅-zē	'pjuːziˑ
Puseyism		
the theology of Pusey	PYO̅O̅-zē-IZ-uhm, PYO̅O̅-sē-	'pjuːziːˌizəm, 'pjuːsiː-
Puseyite		
follower of Pusey (Oxford Movement)	PYO̅O̅-zē-ĪT	'pjuːziːˌɑit
Pushkin		
Alexander S., *Russian author*	PO̅O̅SH-kyin, [S] PUSH-kin	'puːʃkjin, [S] 'puʃkin
Pushmataha		
county, OK	PUSH-muh-TAH-hah, -HAW	ˌpuʃmə'tɑhɑ, -ˌhɔː
Pushto [Pashto]		
lang., Afghanistan, Pakistan	PUSH-tō, PO̅O̅SH-tō	'puʃtoː, 'puːʃtoː
Pushtu [Pashto]		
lang., Afghanistan, Pakistan	PUSH-to̅o̅, PO̅O̅SH-to̅o̅	'puʃtuː, 'puːʃtuː
Put [Phut]		
Biblical name	PUT, PO̅O̅T	'put, 'puːt
Puteoli		
ancient town near Naples	PO̅O̅-tā-Ō-lē	ˌpuːteː'oːliˑ
Puthite		
Biblical name	PO̅O̅-THĪT	'puːˌθɑit
Putiel		
Biblical name	P(Y)O̅O̅T-ē-EL, PO̅O̅-tē-EL	'p(j)uːt̪iːˌel, ˌpuːtiː'el
Puti tai nobio		
flower	PO̅O̅T-i TĪ NŌ-bē-ō	ˌpuːt̪i ˌtɑi 'noːbiːoː
Putnam		
US publishing co.	PUHT-nuhm	'pətnəm
Putredinis, Palus		
see Palus Putredinis		
Putumayo		
river, S. America	PO̅O̅T-uh-MĪ-ō	ˌpuːt̪ə'mɑioː
Puyallup		
N. American people	pyo̅o̅-AL-uhp	pjuː'æləp
Puyang		
city, China	PO̅O̅-YAHNG	'puː'jɑŋ
Puy-de-Dôme		
dept, France	pwēd(-uh)-DŌM	pɥiːd(ə)doːm
Puyi [Buyi, Chung-chia, Jui]		
lang., China	BO̅O̅-YĒ, PO̅O̅-YĒ	'buː'jiː, 'puː'jiː
Puzo		
Mario, *US writer*	PO̅O̅-zō	'puːzoː
Pwani		
region, Tanzania	PWAHN-ē	'pwɑniˑ
Pycnanthus		
plant	pik-NAN-thuhs	pik'nænθəs
Pydna		
town, Greece	PID-nuh	'pidnə
Pygmalion		
legendary sculptor & king of Cyprus; play, G. B. Shaw	pig-MĀL-yuhn, pig-MĀ-lē-uhn	pig'meːljən, pig'meːliːən

Key (col. 2): a: **fad** ā: **fade** ah: **father** ar: **marry** aw: **law** e: **fed** ē: **feed** er: **merry** i: **hid** ī: **hide** ō: **coat** o̅o̅: **boot** oi: **boy** ow: **now** u: **put** uh: **above** uhr: **bird** ch: **chop** ng: **ring** sh: **show** th: **thick** t̲h̲: **this** zh: **measure**

Pygmy, Pigmy

people, equatorial Africa or SE Asia   PIG-mē   'pigmi·

Pylades

friend of Orestes   PĪ-luh-DĒZ   'pɑilə,diːz

Pylas

king of Megara   PĪ-luhs   'pɑiləs

Pyle

Denver, *actor*   PĪL   'pɑil

Pylos, Pylus

ancient Greek city   PĪ-luhs   'pɑiləs

Pynchon

Thomas, *US writer;* Park, *ballpark,*   PIN-chuhn   'pintʃən
    Springfield, MA

Pyongyang

city, N. Korea   PYUHNG-YAHNG, PYUHNG-YANG   ˌpjəŋ'jɑŋ, ˌpjəŋ'jæŋ

P'yŏngyang [Heijo]

city, N. Korea   pyuhng-yahng   pjəŋjɑŋ

Pyote

city, TX   PĪ-ōt   'pɑioːt

Pyotr

pers. name, Russian   PYAW-tuhr   'pjɔːtər

Pyramus

mythological lover of Thisbe   PIR-uh-muhs   'pirəməs

Pyrene

victim of Heracles   pī-RĒ-ne   pɑi'riːni·

Pyrenean

pert. to the Pyrenees   PIR-uh-NĒ-uhn   ˌpirə'niːən

Pyrenees

mts., France, Spain   PIR-uh-NĒZ   'pirə,niːz

Pyrénées-Atlantiques

dept, France   pē-rā-nā-zaht-lahⁿ-TĒK   piːreːneːzɑːtlɑ̃tiːk

Pyrénées-Orientales

dept, France   pē-rā-nā-zawr-yahⁿ-TAHL   piːreːneːzɔːrjɑ̃tɑːl

Pyrex

tdmk for heat resistant glassware   PĪ-REKS   'pɑi,reks

Pyrrha

wife of Deucalion; Horace's beloved   PIR-uh   'pirə

Pyrrhic

pert. to Pyrrhus   PIR-ik   'pirik

Pyrrhic victory

costly victory   PIR-ik VIK-t(uh-)rē   ˌpirik 'vikt(ə)ri·

Pyrrho

Greek philosopher   PIR-ō   'piroː

Pyrrhus

king of Epirus   PIR-uhs   'pirəs

Pythagoras

Greek philosopher, mathematician   puh-THAG-uh-ruhs, pī-   pə'θægərəs, pɑi-

Pythagoreanism

doctrines of Pythagoras &   puh-THAG-uh-RĒ-uh-NIZ-uhm   pə,θægə'riːə,nizəm
    Pythagoreans

Pythagoreans

followers of Pythagoras   puh-THAG-uh-RĒ-uhnz   pə,θægə'riːənz

Pytheas

Greek explorer   PITH-ē-uhs, PĪ-thē-uhs, Ⓔ *also*   'piθiːəs, 'pɑiθiːəs, Ⓔ *also*
    PITH-ē-AS   'piθiːˌæs

Foreign Sounds: ue: *Fr.* **rue,** *Ger.* **füllen**   uh(r): *Fr.* **boeuf,** *Ger.* **Höhle**   kh: *Ger.* **ich,** *Scot.* **loch**   ḡ: *Sp.* **amigo**   v: *Sp.* **hablar**
hl: *Welsh* **Llanelli.**   CAPITALS: primary stress.   SMALL CAPS: secondary stress.   Ⓢ: U.S. pron.   Ⓔ: British pron.

Pythia
  priestess of Apollo at Delphi   PITH-ē-uh   'piθiːə
Pythian
  pert. to Delphi *or* Pythia   PITH-ē-uhn   'piθiːən
Pythias
  friend of Damon in Greek legend   PITH-ē-uhs, ⒺＥ *also* PITH-ē-AS   'piθiːəs, Ⓔ *also* 'piθiːˌæs
Python
  dragon and oracle in Greek myth   PĪ-THAHN, PĪ-thuhn   'paiˌθan, 'paiθən
Pythonesque
  pert. to Monty Python   PĪ-THAHN-ESK, PĪ-thuh-NESK   ˌpaiˌθan'esk, ˌpaiθə'nesk
Pyxis
  constellation   PĪK-suhs, PIK-suhs   'paiksəs, 'piksəs

Q

Qadhafi, Qaddafi
  Moammar, *Libyan leader*   kuh-DAHF-ē   kə'dafiˑ
Qâhira, Al [Cairo]
  city, Egypt   ahl KAH-hē-RAW, al   aːl 'kahiːˌrɔː, æl
Qaidam Pendi
  basin, China   CHĪ-DAHM PUHN-DĒ   'tʃai'dam 'pən'diː
Qājār
  Iranian dynasty   KAHJ-AHR   'kadʒˌaʳ
Qalqilya
  town, West Bank   kahl-KĒL-yuh   kal'kiˑljə
Qalyûbîya
  governorate, Egypt   KAHL-yu-BĒ-(y)uh   ˌkalju'biː(j)ə
Qantas
  Australian airline   K(W)AHNT-uhs   'k(w)antəs
Qara Dagh
  mountain range, Iran, Iraq   KAHR-ah DAH(G)   ˌkara 'da(g)
Qara Qum
  see Kara Kum
Qatar
  sheikdom on Persian Gulf   KAHT-uhr, GAHT-uhr, GUHT-uhr,   'kaṭəʳ, 'gaṭəʳ, 'gəṭəʳ, kə'taʳ
                                           kuh-TAHR
Qatari
  pert. to Qatar   KAHT-uh-rē, GAHT-uh-rē,   'kaṭəriˑ, 'gaṭəriˑ, 'gəṭəriˑ,
                                           GUHT-uh-rē, kuh-TAHR-ē   kə'tariˑ
Qattara
  Depression, *geographical feature,*   kuh-TAHR-uh   kə'tarə
    Egypt
Qeshm
  island, Iran   KESH-uhm   'keʃəm
Qian Qichen
  Chinese politician   chē-AHN CHĒ-CHEN   tʃiː'an 'tʃiː'tʃen

Key (col. 2): a: f**a**d ā: f**a**de ah: f**a**ther ar: m**a**rry aw: l**a**w e: f**e**d ē: f**ee**d er: m**e**rry i: h**i**d ī: h**i**de ō: c**oa**t ōō: b**oo**t
oi: b**oy** ow: n**ow** u: p**u**t uh: **a**bove uhr: b**i**rd ch: **ch**op ng: ri**ng** sh: **sh**ow th: **th**ick <u>th</u>: <u>th</u>is zh: mea**s**ure

Qilian Shan
  mtn. range, China   CHIL-YAHN SHAHN   'tʃil'jɑn 'ʃɑn
Qingdao, Tsingtao
  city, China   CHING-DOW   'tʃiŋ'dɑu
Qinghai, Tsinghai, Chinghai
  prov, China   CHING-HĪ   'tʃiŋ'hai
Qiqihar, Ch'i-ch'i-ha-erh, Tsitsihar
  prov, China   CHI-CHI-HAH(-UH)R   'tʃi'tʃi'hɑ('ə)ʳ
Qizil Qum
  see Kyzyl Kum
Qom
  town, Iran   KŌM   'koːm
Quaalude
  tdmk for methaqualone   KWĀ-LO͞OD   'kweː‚luːd
Quaboag
  river, MA   KWĀ-BAHG   'kweː‚bɑg
Quadragesima
  1st Sunday in Lent   KWAHD-ruh-JES-uh-muh   ‚kwɑdrə'dʒesəmə
Quadrans Muralis
  former constellation   KWAHD-ruhnz myu-RĀ-luhs, myu-RAL-uhs   'kwɑdrænz mju'reːləs, mju'ræləs
Quadrantids
  meteor shower   kwah-DRANT-uhdz   kwa'dræntədz
Quahog
  clam   KŌ-HAWG, KWAW-HAWG, KWŌ-HAWG, -HAHG   'koː‚hɔːg, 'kwɔː‚hɔːg, 'kwoː‚hɔːg, -‚hɑg
Quaid
  Dennis, *US actor*   KWĀD   'kweːd
Quai d'Orsay
  French Ministry of Foreign Affairs   kā dawr-SE   keː dɔːrse
Quaker
  member of Religious Society of Friends   KWĀ-kuhr   'kweːkəʳ
Quakerism
  Quaker beliefs   KWĀ-kuh-RIZ-uhm   'kweːkə‚rizəm
Quanah
  city, TX   KWAHN-uh   'kwɑnə
Quant
  Mary, *British designer*   KWAHNT   'kwɑnt
Quantico
  town, VA   KWAHNT-i-KŌ   'kwɑnti‚koː
Quantrill
  William Clark, *Confederate soldier*   KWAHN-truhl   'kwɑntrəl
Quapaw [Kwapa]
  N. American people   KWAW-PAW   'kwɔː‚pɔː
Qu'Appelle
  river, Canada   kwah-PEL   kwa'pel
Quara
  lang., Ethiopia   K(W)AHR-uh   'k(w)ɑrə
Quaraí
  river, Uruguay, Brazil   KWAH-rah-Ē   ‚kwɑra'iː
Quarles
  pers. name   KWAWRLZ, KWAHRLZ   'kwɔːʳlz, 'kwɑʳlz
Quarnero
  gulf in Adriatic Sea   kwuhr-NER-ō   kwəʳ'neroː

Foreign Sounds: **ue**: *Fr.* **rue**, *Ger.* **füllen**   **uh(r)**: *Fr.* **boeuf**, *Ger.* **Höhle**   <u>kh</u>: *Ger.* **ich**, *Scot.* **loch**   ḡ: *Sp.* **amigo**   <u>v</u>: *Sp.* **hablar**   hl: *Welsh* **Llanelli**.   CAPITALS: primary stress.   SMALL CAPS: secondary stress.   Ⓢ: U.S. pron.   Ⓔ: British pron.

Quartus
  Biblical name   KWAWRT-uhs   'kwɔːʳʈəs

Quasar
  distant star-like object; electronics   KWĀ-ZAHR, KWĀ-SAHR   'kweːˌzɑʳ, 'kweːˌsɑʳ
  brand

Quasimodo
  1. Salvatore, *Italian poet, critic*   KWAH-zē-MAW-dō   ˌkwɑziːˈmɔːdoː
  (Nobel 1959)
  2. the Sunday after Easter; fictional   KWAHZ-ē-MŌD-ō   ˌkwɑziːˈmoːdoː
  hunchback

Quaternary
  geologic period   KWAHT-uh(r)-NER-ē,   'kwɑʈə(r)ˌneriˑ, kwəˈtəʳnəriˑ
         kwuh-TUHR-nuhr-ē

Quathlamba [Drakensberg]
  mtn. range, S. Africa   kwaht-LAM-buh   kwɑtˈlæmbə

Quattro Stagioni
  classical vocal quartet   KWAH-trō stahg-YŌ-nē   'kwɑtroː stɑgˈjoːniˑ

Quay
  county, NM   KWĀ   'kweː

Quayle
  James Danforth, *US vice president*   KWĀL   'kweːl

Québec, Quebec
  prov, Canada   kā-BEK, ⓢ kwi-BEK, ki-BEK   keːbek, ⓢ kwiˈbek, kiˈbek

Quebecer
  inhabitant of Quebec   kwi-BEK-uhr, ki-BEK-uhr   kwiˈbekəʳ, kiˈbekəʳ

Québecois
  inhabitant of Québec   KĀ-buh-KWAH, KĀ-BE-KWAH   ˌkeːbəˈkwɑ, ˌkeːˌbeˈkwɑ

Quechan
  people, N. America   KECH-uhn   'ketʃən

Quechua
  people, lang., S. America   KECH-wuh   'ketʃwə

Queensberry
  Sir John S. Douglas, *Scottish*   KWĒNZ-b(uh-)rē, ⓢ KWĒNZ-BER-ē   'kwiːnzb(ə)riˑ,
  Marquis; boxing rules   ⓢ 'kwiːnzˌberiˑ

Queensland
  state, Australia   KWĒNZ-luhnd, -LAND   'kwiːnzlənd, -ˌlænd

Quekchi
  see Kekchi

Quelpart
  former name of Cheju, *S. Korea*   KWEL-PAHRT   'kwelˌpɑʳt

Queluz
  town, Portugal   ki-LŌŌZH   kiˈluːʒ

Quemoy
  island, Formosa Strait   k(w)i-MOI, KWĒ-MOI   k(w)iˈmɔi, 'kwiːˌmɔi

Quentin
  1. pers. name   KWENT-n   'kwentn̩
  2. Dutch   KVIN-tuhn, KVEN-; kvin-TIN, kven-   'kvintən, 'kven-; kvinˈtin, kven-
  3. French   kahⁿ-TEⁿ   kɑ̃tẽ

Querandí
  S. American people   KĀ-ruhn-DĒ   ˌkeːrənˈdiː

Querétaro
  state, Mexico   kuh-RĀT-uh-RŌ   kəˈreˑʈəˌroː

Quesnay
  Francois, *French economist*   kā-NE, ⓢ kā-NĀ   keːne, ⓢ keːˈneː

Key (col. 2):   aː **fad**   āː **fade**   ahː **father**   arː **marry**   awː **law**   eː **fed**   ēː **feed**   erː **merry**   iː **hid**   īː **hide**   ōː **coat**   ōōː **boot**
oiː **boy**   owː **now**   uː **put**   uhː **above**   uhrː **bird**   chː **chop**   ngː **ring**   shː **show**   thː **thick**   <u>th</u>ː **this**   zhː **measure**

Questel

   Mae, *US actress*   KWES-tl   'kwestl̩

Quetta

   town, Pakistan   KWET-uh   'kweţə

Quetzal

   Central American bird   ket-SAHL, ket-SAL   ket'sɑl, ket'sæl

Quetzalcoatl

   Aztec & Toltec creator god   ket-SAHL-KWAHT-l,   ket'sɑl,kwatl̩, ket'sɑlkə,watl̩
                           ket-SAHL-kuh-WAHT-l

Quezon City

   city, Philippines   KĀ-SŌN SIT-ē   'keː,soːn 'siţiˑ

Quiche

   1. S. American people   KĒ-chā   'kiːtʃeː
   2. custard pie   KĒSH   'kiːʃ

Quiche Lorraine

   quiche with cheese & bacon or ham KĒSH luh-RĀN, luh-REN, law-REN ,kiːʃ lə'reːn, lə'ren, lɔː'ren

Quiche-Mayan

   lang., C. America   KĒ-chā-MĪ-uhn   'kiːtʃeː'maiən

Quidde

   Ludwig, *German historian, politician* KFID-uh, Ⓢ KWID-uh   'kfidə, Ⓢ 'kwidə
   (Nobel 1927)

Quileute

   N. American people   KWIL-uh-YŌŌT   'kwilə,juːt

Quiller-Couch

   Sir Arthur T., *English author* KWIL-uhr-KŌŌCH   ,kwiləʳ'kuːtʃ

Quilmes

   city, Argentina   KĒL-mes   'kiːlmes

Quimper

   city, France   keⁿ-PER   kẽper

Quinault

   N. American people   kwuh-NUHLT   kwə'nəlt

Quinctius

   pers. name, Latin   KWING(K)-sh(ē-)uhs   'kwiŋ(k)ʃ(iː)əs

Quincy

   1. city, FL, IL; town, WA; village, CA KWIN(T)-sē   'kwin(t)siˑ
   2. city, MA   KWIN-zē   'kwinziˑ
   3. pers. name   KWIN-zē, KWIN(T)-sē   'kwinziˑ, 'kwin(t)siˑ

Quinebaug

   river, MA, CT   KWIN-uh-BAWG   'kwinə,bɔːg

Quinn

   Aidan, *actor;* Anthony, *US actor* KWIN   'kwin

Quinnipiac

   river, CT   KWIN-uh-pē-AK   ,kwinəpiː'æk

Quinquagesima

   Sunday before Lent   KWING-kwuh-JES-uh-muh,   ,kwiŋkwə'dʒesəmə,
                           -JĀ-zuh-muh   -'dʒeːzəmə

Quinsigamond

   Community College, *lake, MA* kwin-SIG-uh-muhnd   kwin'sigəmənd

Quintana Roo

   state, Mexico   kēn-TAHN-ah RŌŌ   kiːn,tɑnɑ 'ruː

Quintilian

   Roman rhetorician   kwin-TIL-ē-uhn   kwin'tiliːən

Quintilianus

   pers. name, Latin   kwin-TIL-ē-Ā-nuhs   kwin,tiliː'eːnəs

Foreign Sounds: ue: *Fr.* **rue**, *Ger.* **füllen**   uh(r): *Fr.* **boeuf**, *Ger.* **Höhle**   <u>kh</u>: *Ger.* **ich**, *Scot.* **loch**   ḡ: *Sp.* **amigo**   <u>v</u>: *Sp.* **hablar**
hl: *Welsh* **Llanelli**.   CAPITALS: primary stress.   SMALL CAPS: secondary stress.   Ⓢ: U.S. pron.   Ⓔ: British pron.

Quintilius

   pers. name, Latin   kwin-TIL-ē-uhs, kwin-TIL-yuhs   kwin'tiliːəs, kwin'tiljəs

Quintius

   pers. name, Latin   KWIN-sh(ē-)uhs, KWINT-ē-uhs   'kwinʃ(iː)əs, 'kwintiːəs

Quintus

   pers. name, Latin   KWINT-uhs   'kwintəs

Quirinal

   hill, Rome, Italy   KWIR-uhn-l   'kwirənl̩

Quirindi

   town, Australia   kwuh-RIN-DĪ   kwə'rin‚dɑi

Quirino

   pers. name, Italian   kwē-RĒ-nō   kwiː'riːnoː

Quirinus

   1. Sabine/Roman god of war   kwuh-RĪ-nuhs, kwuh-RĒ-nuhs   kwə'rɑinəs, kwə'riːnəs

   2. pers. name, Dutch   kvē-RĒ-nues   kviː'riːnys

   3. German   kvē-RĒ-nus   kviː'riːnus

Quirites

   citizens of ancient Rome   kwuh-RĪT-ēz   kwə'rɑiṭiːz

Quisenberry

   Dan, *US baseball player*   KWIZ-uhn-BER-ē   'kwizən‚beriˑ

Quisling

   Vidkun, *Norwegian army officer &*   KFIS-ling, KWIZ-ling   'kfisliŋ, 'kwizliŋ
   Nazi politician

Quito

   city, Ecuador   KĒ-tō   'kiːtoː

Qum

   town, Iran   KUM   'kum

Qunaytirah, El

   governorate, Syria   EL kōō-NĀ-truh   ‚el kuˑ'neːtrə

Quonset

   naval base, RI; tdmk for a   KWAHN(T)-suht, KWAHN-zuht   'kwɑn(t)sət, 'kwɑnzət
   prefabricated shelter

Quo Vadis

   novel, Henry Sienkiewicz   kwō VAHD-uhs   kwoː 'vadəs

Qur'ân, al- [Koran]

   holy book of Islam   ahl kuh-RAN, al, kuh-RAHN, kur-AN,   ɑːl kə'ræn, æl, kə'rɑn,
                     kur-AHN   kur'æn, kur'ɑn

QwaQwa

   state, South Africa   KWAH-KWAH   'kwɑ'kwɑ

QWERTY

   standard keyboard layout   KWUHRT-ē   'kwəʳṭiˑ

Key (col. 2):   a: fad   ā: fade   ah: father   ar: marry   aw: law   e: fed   ē: feed   er: merry   i: hid   ī: hide   ō: coat   ōō: boot
oi: boy   ow: now   u: put   uh: above   uhr: bird   ch: chop   ng: ring   sh: show   th: thick   <u>th</u>: this   zh: measure

R

Ra [Re]
  Egyptian sun god   RAH   'rɑ
Raama, Raamah
  Biblical name   RĀ-uh-muh, RAHM-uh, rah-MAH   'reːəmə, 'rɑmə, rɑ'mɑ
Raamiah
  Biblical name   RĀ-uh-MĪ-uh, RAH-ahm-YAH   ˌreːə'maiə, ˌrɑɑm'jɑ
Raamses
  Biblical form of Ramses   RAM-sēz, rā-AM-sēz, rahm-SES   'ræmsiːz, reː'æmsiːz, rɑm'ses
Rab [Abba Arika]
  Babylonian rabbi   RAHV, RUHV, RAHB   'rɑv, 'rəv, 'rɑb
Raban
  pers. name   RĀ-BAN   'reːˌbæn
Rabat
  city, Morocco; town, Malta   ruh-BAHT   rə'bɑt
Rabaul
  town, New Guinea   ruh-BOWL   rə'baul
Rabb
  Ellis, *US actor, director, writer*   RAB   'ræb
Rabbah
  Biblical name   RAB-uh, rah-BAH   'ræbə, rɑ'bɑ
Rabbath
  Biblical name   RAB-uhth, rah-BAHT   'ræbəθ, rɑ'bɑt
Rabbith
  Biblical name   RAB-uhth, rah-BĒT   'ræbəθ, rɑː'biːt
Rabboni
  Biblical name   ruh-BŌ-NĪ   rə'boːˌnɑi
Rabelais
  Françoise, *French writer*   rah-BLE, Ⓢ RAB-uh-LĀ, RAB-uh-LĀ   rɑːble, Ⓢ ˌræbə'leː, 'ræbəˌleː
Rabelaisian
  pert. to Rabelais   RAB-uh-LĀ-zhuhn, RAB-uh-LĀ-zē-uhn   ˌræbə'leːʒən, ˌræbə'leːziːən
Rabi
  1. I. I., *Austrian-born US physicist* RAHB-ē   'rɑbi·
     (Nobel 1944)
  2. *Islamic month*   RUHB-ē   'rəbi·
Rabi Al-Awal
  Islamic holiday   RUHB-ē ahl-AH-wahl   'rəbiː ɑl'awɑl
Rabin
  Yitzhak, *prime minister, Israel*   rah-BĒN   rɑ'biːn
Rabindranath
  pers. name, Bengali   ruh-BIN-druh-NAHT   rə'bindrəˌnɑt
Rabinowitz
  Sholem, *US author, aka* Shalom   ruh-BIN-uh-WITS   rə'binəˌwits
  Aleichem

Foreign Sounds: **ue**: *Fr.* **rue**, *Ger.* f**ü**llen   **uh(r)**: *Fr.* b**oeu**f, *Ger.* H**ö**hle   <u>kh</u>: *Ger.* i**ch**, *Scot.* lo**ch**   ḡ: *Sp.* ami**g**o   v̲: *Sp.* ha**b**lar
hl: *Welsh* **Ll**anelli.   CAPITALS: primary stress.   SMALL CAPS: secondary stress.   Ⓢ: U.S. pron.   Ⓔ: British pron.

Rab-mag
  Biblical name — RAB-MAG, rahv-MAHG — 'ræb₁mæg, rɑv'mɑg

Rab-saris
  Biblical name — RAB-suh-ris, RAB-SAR-uhs, RAHV-sah-RĒS — 'ræbsəris, 'ræb₁særəs, ₁rɑvsɑ'riːs

Rab-shakeh
  Biblical name — RAB-SHAK-uh, RAHV-shah-KE — 'ræb₁ʃækə, ₁rɑvʃɑ'ke

Rabun
  county, GA — RĀ-buhn — 'reːbən

Raca
  Biblical name — RAHK-uh, RĀ-kuh — 'rɑkə, 'reːkə

Racal
  British communications co. — RĀ-KAWL — 'reː₁kɔːl

Rachab [Rahab]
  Biblical name — RĀ-KAB, rah-KHAHV — 'reː₁kæb, rɑ'xɑv

Rachel
  1. pers. name — RĀ-chuhl — 'reːtʃəl
  2. Dutch — RAH-KHEL — 'rɑː₁xel
  3. French — rah-SHEL — rɑːʃel
  4. Hebrew — rah-KHEL — rɑ'xel

Rachins
  Alan, *US actor* — RĀ-shuhnz — 'reːʃənz

Rachmaninoff
  Sergei, *Russian composer* — RUHKH-MAHN-yi-nuhf, ⓢ rahk-MAHN-uh-NAWF — ₁rəx'mɑːnjinəf, ⓢ rɑk'mɑnə₁nɔːf

Racine
  1. city, county, WI — ruh-SĒN, rā-SĒN — rə'siːn, reː'siːn
  2. Jean Baptiste, French playwright — rah-SĒN, ⓢ ra-SĒN, ruh-SĒN — rɑːsiːn, ⓢ ræ'siːn, rə'siːn

Racine, Hector
  Stadium, *Montreal, Canada* — ek-TAWR ra-SĒN, HEK-tuhr ruh-SĒN — ek'tɔːʳ ræ'siːn, 'hektəʳ rə'siːn

Rackham
  Arthur, *English illustrator* — RAK-uhm — 'rækəm

Racovianism
  Christian heresy — ruh-KŌ-vē-uh-NIZ-uhm — rə'koːviːə₁nizəm

Rădăut
  town, Romania — RAHD-uh-O͞OTS, RAHD-uh-O͞OT-sē — ₁rɑdə'uːts, ₁rɑdə'uːtsiˑ

Radcliffe
  College, *MA* — RAD-klif — 'rædklif

Raddai
  Biblical name — RAD-ē-Ī, RAD-Ī, rah-DĪ — 'rædiː₁ɑi, 'ræd₁ɑi, rɑ'dɑi

Radeberger
  German beer — RAHD-uh-BER-guhr — 'rɑdə₁beʳgəʳ

Radhakrishnan
  Sarvepalli, *president, India* — RAHD-uh-KRISH-nuhn — ₁rɑdə'kriʃnən

radium
  element — RĀD-ē-uhm — 'reːdiːəm

Radko
  pers. name, Bulgarian — RAHT-kō — 'rɑːtkoː

Radner
  Gilda, *US comedienne* — RAD-nuhr — 'rædnəʳ

Radnor
  town, PA; former county, Wales — RAD-nuhr — 'rædnəʳ

Radnorshire
  former county, Wales — RAD-nuhr-shuhr, -SHIR — 'rædnəʳʃəʳ, -₁ʃiʳ

Key (col. 2):   a: fad ā: fade ah: father ar: marry aw: law e: fed ē: feed er: merry i: hid ī: hide ō: coat o͞o: boot
oi: boy ow: now u: put uh: above uhr: bird ch: chop ng: ring sh: show th: thick th̲: this zh: measure

Radó
   pers. name, Hungarian   RAH-dō   'rado:

Radom
   province, city, Poland   RAHD-AWM   'ra:d,ɔ:m

Radomir
   pers. name, Serbo-Croatian   RAH-daw-MĒR   'ra:dɔ:,mi:r

radon
   element   RĀ-DAHN   're:,dɑn

Radovan
   pers. name (R. Karadzic)   RAHD-uh-VAHN   'radə,vɑn

Rae
   Charlotte, *US actress; pers. name* RĀ   're:

Rafael
   pers. name, Spanish   rahf-ah-EL   rɑfɑ'el

Rafah
   district, occupied West Bank, Israel RAHF-uh   'rafə

Raffaello
   pers. name, Italian   RAHF-fah-EL-lō   ,rɑffɑ'ello:

Raffi
   US children's singer   RAF-ē, RAHF-ē   'ræfi·, 'rɑfi·

Raffin
   Deborah, *actress*   RAF-uhn   'ræfən

Raffo
   Italian beer   RAHF-fō   'rɑffo:

Rafkin
   Alan, *US TV director*   RAF-kuhn   'ræfkən

Rafsanjani
   Hashemi, *president, Iran*   RAHF-suhn-JAHN-ē   ,rɑfsən'dʒɑni·

Ragbrai
   Iowa bicycle ride   RAG-BRĀ   'ræg,bre:

Ragau
   Biblical name   RĀ-GAW, RĀ-GOW   're:,gɔ:, 're:,gɑu

Ragnar
   pers. name, Swedish   RAHNG-nahr   'ra:ŋna:r

Ragnarök
   fall of the gods in Scandinavian myth RAHG-nuh-RUH(R)K,   'ragnə,rœk, Ⓢ 'rægnə,rɑk,
                                   Ⓢ RAG-nuh-RAHK, -ruhk   -rək

Ragu
   US food brand   rag-O͞O   ræg'u:

Raguel
   Biblical name   RAG-yuh-wuhl, ruh-GYO͞O-EL,   'rægjəwəl, rə'gju:,el, rəu:'el
                              ruh-o͞o-EL

Ragusa
   prov, Italy   ruh-GO͞O-zuh   rə'gu:zə

Rahab [Rachab]
   Biblical name   RĀ-HAB, rah-<u>KH</u>AHV   're:,hæb, rɑ'xɑv

Raham
   Biblical name   RĀ-HAM, RĀ-uhm, RAH-<u>kh</u>ahm 're:,hæm, 're:əm, 'rɑxɑm

Rahel [Rachel]
   Biblical name   RĀ-(h)uhl, rah-<u>KH</u>EL   're:(h)əl, rɑ'xel

Rahman
   Omar Abdel, *Sheik, Muslim terrorist* RAH<u>KH</u>-MAHN, -muhn   'rɑx,mɑn, -mən

Rahway
   town, NJ   RAW-WĀ, RAH-WĀ   'rɔ:,we:, 'rɑ,we:

Foreign Sounds: ue: *Fr.* **rue**, *Ger.* **füllen** uh(r): *Fr.* **boeuf**, *Ger.* **Höhle** <u>kh</u>: *Ger.* **ich**, *Scot.* **loch** g̱: *Sp.* **amigo** v̱: *Sp.* **hablar**
hl: *Welsh* **Llanelli**. CAPITALS: primary stress. SMALL CAPS: secondary stress. Ⓢ: U.S. pron. Ⓔ: British pron.

Raimond
   pers. name, French   re-MAWⁿ   remɔ̃

Raimondo
   pers. name, Italian   rī-MŌN-dō   raiˈmoːndoː

Raimund
   pers. name, German   RĪ-munt   ˈraimunt

Raimundo
   1. pers. name, Portuguese   rī-M$\overline{OO}$(N)-d$\overline{oo}$ raiˈmũː(n)duː
   2. Spanish   rī-M$\overline{OO}$N-dō   raiˈmuːndoː

Raine
   pers. name   RĀN   ˈreːn

Rainer
   1. pers. name, Dutch   RĪ-nuhr   ˈrainər
   2. German   RĪ-nuhr   ˈrainəʳ

Raines
   Tim, *US baseball player*   RĀNZ   ˈreːnz

Rainier
   1. mtn., WA   ruh-NIR, rā-NIR   rəˈniʳ, reːˈniʳ
   2. prince of Monaco; pers. name   ren-YĀ, ⓢ rā-NIR   renjeː, ⓢ reːˈniʳ

Rainwater
   James, *US physicist (Nobel 1975)*   RĀN-WAWT-uhr, RĀN-WAHT-uhr   ˈreːnˌwɔːʈəʳ, ˈreːnˌwɑʈəʳ

Raisa
   pers. name, Russian   ruh-Ē-suh, ⓢ rī-Ē-suh, rā-Ē-suh   rəˈiːsə, ⓢ raiˈiːsə, reːˈiːsə

Raïssa
   pers. name, French   rah-ē-SAH   raːiːsaː

Raitt
   Bonnie, *US singer*   RĀT   ˈreːt

Raj
   pers. name, Hindi   RAHJ, RAHZH   ˈrɑdʒ, ˈrɑʒ

Rajab
   Islamic month   ruh-JAB   rəˈdʒæb

Rajahmundry
   city, India   RAHJ-uh-MUHN-drē   ˌrɑdʒəˈməndriˑ

Rajasthan
   state, India   RAHJ-uh-STAHN   ˈrɑdʒəˌstɑn

Rajasthani [Marwari, Mewari]
   lang., India, Pakistan   RAHJ-uh-STAHN-ē   ˌrɑdʒəˈstaniˑ

Rajiv
   pers. name, India   RAHJ-iv, rahj-ĒV   ˈrɑdʒiv, rɑdʒˈiːv

Rajput
   people, India   RAHJ-PUT, RAHZH-PUT   ˈrɑdʒˌput, ˈrɑʒˌput

Rajputana
   region, India   RAHJ-puh-TAHN-uh   ˌrɑdʒpəˈtɑnə

Rajshahi
   region, Bangladesh   rahj-SHAH-hē   rɑdʒˈʃɑhiˑ

Rakem
   Biblical name   RĀ-KEM, REK-em   ˈreːˌkem, ˈrekem

Rakhine [Arakan]
   state, Burma   rah-KĒN   rɑˈkiːn

Rakkath
   Biblical name   RAK-uhth, rah-KAHT   ˈrækəθ, rɑˈkat

Rakkon
   Biblical name   RAK-AHN, RAHK-AHN, rah-KŌN   ˈrækˌan, ˈrɑkˌan, rɑˈkoːn

Raksha Bandha
   Indian festival   RUHK-shuh BUHN-duh   ˈrəkʃə ˈbəndə

Key (col. 2):   a: fad   ā: fade   ah: father   ar: marry   aw: law   e: fed   ē: feed   er: merry   i: hid   ī: hide   ō: coat   o͞o: boot
oi: boy   ow: now   u: put   uh: above   uhr: bird   ch: chop   ng: ring   sh: show   th: thick   <u>th</u>: this   zh: measure

Raleigh

  1. Sir Walter, *English courtier, poet,*   RAW-lē, RAHL-ē, RAL-ē   'rɔːliˑ, 'rɑliˑ, 'ræliˑ
    explorer; pers. name

  2. pl. name, NC, WV   RAW-lē, RAHL-ē   'rɔːliˑ, 'rɑliˑ

  3. British bicycle co.   RAW-lē, RAHL-ē, Ⓔ RAL-ē   'rɔːliˑ, 'rɑliˑ, Ⓔ 'ræliˑ

Ralph

  pers. name   RALF, Ⓔ RALF, RĀF   'rælf, Ⓔ 'rælf, 'reːf

Ralston

  city, NE   RAWL-stuhn   'rɔːlstən

Ralston Purina

  US food co.   RAWL-stuhn pyu-RĒ-nuh   ˌrɔːlstən pjuˈriːnə

RAM

  random-access memory   RAM   'ræm

Ram

  Biblical name   RAM, RAHM   'ræm, 'rɑm

Rama

  incarnation of Vishnu; pers. name,   RAHM-uh   'rɑmə
    Sanskrit

Rama, Ramah

  Biblical name   RĀ-muh, RAHM-uh, rah-MAH   'reːmə, 'rɑmə, rɑˈmɑ

Ramachandra

  hero of the Ramayana   RAHM-uh-CHUHN-druh   ˌrɑməˈtʃəndrə

Ramada

  US hotel chain   ruh-MAHD-uh   rəˈmɑdə

Ramadan

  Islamic month   RAHM-uh-DAHN, RAM-uh-DAN   'rɑməˌdɑn, 'ræməˌdæn

Ramah

  N. American people   RAHM-uh   'rɑmə

Ramaism

  worship of Rama   RAHM-uh-IZ-uhm   'rɑməˌizəm

Ramallah

  district, Israel   ruh-MAHL-uh   rəˈmɑlə

Raman

  Sir Chandrasekhara V., *Indian*   RAHM-uhn   'rɑmən
    physicist (Nobel 1930)

Ramapo

  river, mts., NJ, NY   RAM-uh-PŌ   'ræməˌpoː

Ramaswami

  pers. name, Sanskrit   RAHM-uh-SWAHM-ē   ˌrɑməˈswɑmiˑ

Ramat Gan

  town, Israel   ruh-MAHT GAHN, RAHM-aht GAHN   rəˈmat 'gan, 'rɑmat 'gan

Ramath

  Biblical name   RĀ-MATH, RĀ-muhth, rah-MAHT   'reːˌmæθ, 'reːməθ, rɑˈmɑt

Ramathaim

  Biblical name   RĀ-muh-THĀ-im, RAHM-uh-;   ˌreːməˈθeːim, ˌrɑmə-;
     RAH-mah-TAH-yim   ˌrɑmaˈtɑjim

Ramathaim-zophim

  Biblical name   RĀ-muh-THĀ-im-ZŌ-fim, RAHM-uh-;   ˌreːməˈθeːimˈzoːfim, ˌrɑmə-;
     RAH-mah-TAH-yim-tsō-FĒM   ˌrɑmaˈtɑjimtsoːˈfiːm

Ramathite

  Biblical name   RĀ-muh-THĪT, RAHM-uh-THĪT   'reːməˌθɑit, 'rɑməˌθɑit

Ramath-lehi

  Biblical name   RĀ-muhth-LĒ-HĪ, RAH-maht-LE-khē   'reːməθ'liːˌhɑi, 'rɑmat'lexiˑ

Foreign Sounds: ue: *Fr.* **rue**, *Ger.* **füllen**   uh(r): *Fr.* **boeuf**, *Ger.* **Höhle**   <u>kh</u>: *Ger.* **ich**, *Scot.* **loch**   g̃: *Sp.* **amigo**   v̱: *Sp.* **hablar**
hl: *Welsh* **Llanelli**.   CAPITALS: primary stress.   SMALL CAPS: secondary stress.   Ⓢ: U.S. pron.   Ⓔ: British pron.

Ramath-Mizpah, Ramath-mizpeh

Biblical name   RĀ-ᴍᴀᴛʜ-ᴍɪᴢ-puh, RĀ-muhth-;   'reːˌmæθ'mizpə, 'reːməθ-;
     rah-ᴍᴀʜᴛ-hah-mit-ꜱᴘᴇ   rɑ'mɑthɑmit'spe

Ramayana

Indian epic   ruh-ᴍᴀʜ-yuh-nuh,   rə'majənə, ˌrɑmə'janə,
     ʀᴀʜᴍ-uh-ʏᴀʜɴ-uh, ruh-ᴍῙ-uh-nuh   rə'mɑiənə

Rambo

Stallone film character   ʀᴀᴍ-ʙō   'ræmˌboː

Rambouillet

1. town, France   rahⁿ-b͞oo-ʏᴇ   rãbuːje

2. sheep breed   ʀᴀᴍ-buh-ʟĀ, ʀᴀᴍ-b͞oo-ʏĀ   ˌræmbə'leː, ˌræmbuː'jeː

Rambouillet [Angennes]

Marquise de, *French hostess*   rahⁿ-b͞oo-ʏᴇ   rãbuːje

Ramchandra

pers. name, Sanskrit   ruhm-ᴄʜᴜʜɴ-druh   rəm'tʃəndrə

Ramée [Ouida]

Louise de la, *English novelist*   ruh-ᴍĀ   rə'meː

Rameses [Ramses]

Egyptian king   ʀᴀᴍ-uh-ꜱĒᴢ   'ræməˌsiːz

Ramiah

Biblical name   ruh-ᴍῙ-uh, rahm-ʏᴀʜ   rə'mɑiə, rɑm'jɑ

Ramírez

pers. name, Spanish   rah-ᴍĒ-res, -reth   rɑ'miːres, -reθ

Ramism

doctrines of Ramée   RĀ-ᴍɪᴢ-uhm   'reːˌmizəm

Ramji

pers. name, Marathi   ʀᴀʜᴍ-jē   'rɑmdʒiˑ

Ramla

district, Israel   ʀᴀʜᴍ-luh   'rɑmlə

Ramón

pers. name, Spanish   rah-ᴍᴀᴡɴ, Ⓢ ruh-ᴍŌɴ   rɑ'mɔːn, Ⓢ rə'moːn

Ramona

pers. name   ruh-ᴍŌ-nuh   rə'moːnə

Ramón y Cajal

Santiago, *Spanish physician,*   rah-ᴍᴀᴡɴ ē kah-ᴋʜᴀʜʟ,   rɑ'mɔːn iː kɑ'xɑl,
histologist (Nobel 1906)   Ⓢ ruh-ᴍŌɴ ē kuh-ʜᴀʜʟ   Ⓢ rə'moːn iː kə'hɑl

Ramoth

Biblical name   RĀ-ᴍᴀʜᴛʜ, -ᴍᴀᴡᴛʜ, -muhth;   'reːˌmɑθ, -ˌmɔːθ, -məθ;
     rah-ᴍŌᴛ   rɑ'moːt

Ramoth-gilead

Biblical name   RĀ-ᴍᴀʜᴛʜ-ɢɪʟ-ē-ᴀᴅ, -ɢɪʟ-ē-uhd,   'reːˌmɑθ'giliːˌæd, -'giliːəd,
     RĀ-ᴍᴀᴡᴛʜ-, RĀ-muhth-;   'reːˌmɔːθ-, 'reːməθ-;
     rah-ᴍŌᴛ-gil-ᴀʜᴅ   rɑ'moːtgil'

Ramoth-Negev

Biblical name   RĀ-ᴍᴀʜᴛʜ-ɴᴇɢ-ev, RĀ-ᴍᴀᴡᴛʜ-,   'reːˌmɑθ'negev, 'reːˌmɔːθ-,
     RĀ-muhth-; rah-ᴍŌᴛ-ne-ɢᴇᴠ   'reːməθ-; rɑ'moːtne'gev

Rampal

Jean-Pierre, *French flautist*   rahⁿ-ᴘᴀʜʟ   rãpɑːl

Ramsay

Sir William, *Scottish chemist (Nobel*   ʀᴀᴍ-zē   'ræmziˑ
1904); pers. name

Ramses [Rameses]

Egyptian king   ʀᴀᴍ-sēz   'ræmsiːz

Key (col. 2):   a: **fad**   ā: **fade**   ah: **father**   ar: **marry**   aw: **law**   e: **fed**   ē: **feed**   er: **merry**   i: **hid**   ī: **hide**   ō: **coat**   o͞o: **boot**
oi: **boy**   ow: **now**   u: **put**   uh: **above**   uhr: **bird**   ch: **chop**   ng: **ring**   sh: **show**   th: **thick**   <u>th</u>: **this**   zh: **measure**

Ramsey
    Norman F., Jr., *US physicist (Nobel*   RAM-zē   'ræmziˑ
    1989)

Ramsgate
    town, England   RAMZ-GĀT, RAMZ-guht   'ræmz͵geːt, 'ræmzgət

Rancagua
    prov, Chile   rahn-KAHḠ-wuh, rahng-KAHḠ-wuh   rɑn'kɑɣwə, rɑŋ'kɑɣwə

Ranchhodji
    pers. name, Bengali   ruhn-CHŌ-jē   rən'tʃoːdʒiˑ

Rancho Palos Verdes
    city, CA   RAN-chō PAL-uhs VUHRD-ēz   ͵ræntʃoː 'pæləs 'vəʳdiːz

Randal, Randall
    pers. name   RAN-dl   'rændl̩

Randers
    seaport, Denmark   RAHN-uhrz   'rɑnəʳz

Randolph
    pers. name   RAN-DAHLF, RAN-DAWLF   'ræn͵dɑlf, 'ræn͵dɔːlf

Randolph-Macon
    College, *VA*   RAN-DAHLF-MĀ-kuhn, RAN-DAWLF-   ͵ræn͵dɑlf'meːkən, ͵ræn͵dɔːlf-

Randstad
    conurbation, Netherlands   RAHN-STAHD   'rɑn͵stɑd

Randy
    pers. name   RAN-dē   'rændiˑ

Rangel
    Charles B., *US politician*   RANG-guhl   'ræŋgəl

Rangoon
    river, city, Burma   ran-GOON, rang-   ræn'guːn, ræŋ-

Rangpur
    region, Bangladesh   RUHNG-PUR   'rəŋ͵puʳ

Ranjan
    pers. name, Bengali   RUHN-juhn   'rəndʒən

Rank
    Otto, *Austrian psychoanalyst*   RAHNGK   'rɑŋk

Rannoch, Loch
    see Loch Rannoch

Ransom
    pers. name   RAN-suhm   'rænsəm

Ranulf, Ranulph
    pers. name   RĀ-nuhlf, RAN-uhlf   'reːnəlf, 'rænəlf

Rao
    P.V. Narasimha, *Indian prime*   ROW   'rɑu
    minister

Rao, Rau
    Santha Rama, *Indian writer*   ROW   'rɑu

Raoul
    1. pers. name, French   rah-OOL   rɑːuːl
    2. German, Spanish   rah-OOL   rɑ'uːl

Rapallo
    port, Italy   ruh-PAHL-ō   rə'pɑloː

Rapha, Raphah
    Biblical name   RĀ-fuh, rah-FAH   'reːfə, rɑ'fɑ

Raphael

   1. Italian painter   RAF-ē-uhl, RĀ-fē-uhl, RAHF-ē-uhl,   'ræfiːəl, 'reːfiːəl, 'rɑfiːəl,
                               RAHF-ī-EL   ˌrɑfɑi'el

   2. archangel; pers. name   RĀ-fē-uhl, RAF-ē-uhl, RAF-Ā-uhl,   'reːfiːəl, 'ræfiːəl, 'ræfˌeːəl,
                               RĀF-yuhl   'reːfjəl

   3. Dutch   RAH-FEL   'rɑːˌfel

   4. French   rah-fah-EL   rɑːfɑːel

   5. German   RAH-fah-EL   'rɑfɑˌel

Raphia

   ancient town, Gaza & Egypt   ruh-FĪ-uh   rə'fɑiə

Raphu

   Biblical name   RĀ-fuh, RĀ-F(Y)O͞O, rah-FO͞O   'reːfə, 'reːˌf(j)uː, rɑ'fuː

Rapidan

   river, VA   RAP-uh-DAN   ˌræpə'dæn

Rapides

   parish, LA   rah-PĒD   rɑ'piːd

Rappahannock

   river, county, VA   RAP-uh-HAN-uhk   ˌræpə'hænək

Rapunzel

   fairy tale character   ruh-PUHN-zuhl   rə'pənzəl

Raquel

   1. pers. name   rah-KEL, ra-KEL   rɑ'kel, ræ'kel

   2. Spanish   rah-KEL   rɑ'kel

Raquette

   river, NY   RAK-uht   'rækət

Raritan

   river, borough, NJ   RAR-uht-n   'rærətn̩

Rarotonga

   island, Cook Islands   RAR-uh-TAHNG-guh   ˌrærə'tɑŋgə

Ras al-Khaimah

   emirate, United Arab Emirates   RAHS al-KĪ-mah   'rɑs æl'kɑimɑ

Ra's al Khaymah

   emirate, United Arab Emirates   RAHS ahl <u>KH</u>Ī-muh, al   ˌrɑs ɑːl 'xɑimə, æl

Rashi

   French Hebrew scholar   rah-SHĒ   rɑːʃiː

Rashid

   pers. name   rah-SHĒD, ra-SHĒD   rɑ'ʃiːd, ræ'ʃiːd

Rask

   Rasmus, *Danish philologist*   RAHSG, Ⓢ RASK, RAHSK   'rɑːsg, Ⓢ 'ræsk, 'rɑsk

Rasmus

   pers. name, Danish, Norwegian   RAHS-mus   'rɑsmus

Rasmussen

   Knud, *Danish explorer*   RAHS-MUS-n, Ⓢ RAS-muh-suhn   'rɑsˌmusn̩, Ⓢ 'ræsməsən

Rasputin

   Grigori, *Russian mystic*   ruh-SPO͞OT-yin, Ⓢ ra-SP(Y)O͞OT-n,   rə'spuːtjin, Ⓢ ræ'sp(j)uːtn̩,
                               ra-SPUT-n   ræ'sputn̩

Ras Shamra

   site of Ugarit   RAHS SHAM-rah   ˌrɑs 'ʃæmrɑ

Rastafari

   pert. to Rastafarianism   RAS-tuh-FAR-ē, RAHS-, -FER-ē, -FAHR-ē   ˌræstə'færiˑ, ˌrɑs-, -'feriˑ,
                                                        -'fɑriˑ

Ras Tafari [Haile Selassie]

   emperor of Ethiopia   RAHS tuh-fah-RĒ   ˌrɑs təfɑ'riː

Key (col. 2):   a: fad ā: fade ah: father ar: marry aw: law e: fed ē: feed er: merry i: hid ī: hide ō: coat o͞o: boot
oi: boy   ow: now   u: put   uh: above   uhr: bird   ch: chop   ng: ring   sh: show   th: thick   <u>th</u>: this   zh: measure

Rastafarian
  pert. to Rastafarianism   RAS-tuh-FAR-ē-uhn, RAHS-,   ˌræstə'færiːən, ˌrɑs-,
                                     -FER-ē-uhn, -FAHR-ē-uhn   -'feriːən, -'fɑriːən

Rastafarianism
  religion   RAS-tuh-FAR-ē-uh-NIZ-uhm, RAHS-,   ˌræstə'færiːəˌnizəm, ˌrɑs-,
                                     -FER-ē-uh-NIZ-uhm,   -'feriːəˌnizəm,
                                     -FAHR-ē-uh-NIZ-uhm   -'fɑriːəˌnizəm

Rastus
  pers. name   RAS-tuhs   'ræstəs

Ratatouille
  vegetable dish   RA-TA-T$\overline{OO}$-ē, RAH-TAH-T$\overline{OO}$-ē,   ˌræˌtæ'tuːiˑ, ˌrɑˌtɑ'tuːiˑ,
                                     RAT-uh-TWĒ   ˌræt̬ə'twiː

Ratcliffe
  pers. name   RAT-KLIF   'rætˌklif

Rathbone
  pers. name   RATH-BŌN, RATH-buhn   'ræθˌboːn, 'ræθbən

Rathlin
  island, Ireland   RATH-luhn   'ræθlən

Rätische Alpen [Rhaetian Alps]
  Alpine mtn. range   RĀ-tish-uh AHL-puhn   ˌreːtiʃə 'ɑlpən

Raton
  city, NM   ruh-TŌN, ra-, -T$\overline{OO}$N   rə'toːn, ræ-, -'tuːn

Rau
  see Rao

Rauber Skat
  game   ROI-buhr SKAHT, ROW-buhr SKAT   'rɔibəʳ 'skɑt, 'raubəʳ 'skæt

Rauchenfels
  German beer   ROW-khuhn-FELS   'rauxənˌfels

Raúl
  pers. name, Spanish   rah-$\overline{OO}$L   rɑ'uːl

Rauschenberg
  Robert, *US artist*   ROW-shuhn-BUHRG   'rauʃənˌbəʳg

Ravalli
  county, MT   ruh-VAL-ē   rə'væliˑ

Ravel
  Maurice, *French composer*   rah-VEL, Ⓢ ruh-VEL   rɑːvel, Ⓢ rə'vel

Ravenna
  prov, city, Italy   ruh-VEN-uh   rə'venə

Ravindranatha
  pers. name, Sanskrit   ruh-VIN-druh-NAH-tah   rə'vindrəˌnɑtɑ

Rawalpindi
  prov, Pakistan   RAH-wuhl-PIN-dē, rowl-PIN-dē   ˌrɑwəl'pindiˑ, rɑul'pindiˑ

Rawlings
  Lester, *US actor;* Marjorie Kinnan,   RAW-lingz   'rɔːliŋz
  US author; US sporting goods co.

Rawlins
  city, WY   RAW-luhnz, RAHL-uhnz   'rɔːlənz, 'rɑlənz

Rawls
  Lou, *US singer*   RAWLZ   'rɔːlz

Ray
  1. Satyajit, *Indian film maker*   RĪ, RĀ   'rai, 'reː
  2. pers. name   RĀ   'reː

Ray-Ban
  tdmk for sunglasses   RĀ-BAN   'reːˌbæn

Rayburn
  Gene, *US TV performer*   RĀ-BUHRN   'reːˌbərn
Rayleigh
  J. W. S., *English physicist (Nobel*   RĀ-lē   'reːliˑ
  1904)
Raymond
  1. pers. name   RĀ-muhnd   'reːmənd
  2. French   re-MAWⁿ   remɔ̃
Raymund
  pers. name, German   RĪ-munt   'rɑimunt
Raymundo
  pers. name, Portuguese   rī-MŌŌ(N)-dōō   rɑi'mūː(n)duː
Rayovac
  US corp.   RĀ-ō-VAK, RĀ-uh-VAK   'reːoːˌvæk, 'reːəˌvæk
Re
  Egyptian sun god   RĀ   'reː
Rea
  pers. name   RĀ   'reː
Reading
  railroad, US; city, PA; city, England   RED-ing   'rediŋ
Reagan
  1. Ronald, 40th US president   RĀ-guhn; *now rarely* RĒ-guhn   'reːgən; *now rarely* 'riːgən
  2. county, TX   RĀ-guhn   'reːgən
Reaiah
  Biblical name   rē-Ī-uh, rē-Ā-uh, ruh-ah-YAH   riː'ɑiə, riː'eːə, rəɑ'jɑ
Real
  county, TX   RĒ-AWL   'riːˌɔːl
Real Madrid
  Spanish soccer team   rā-AHL mah-THRĒTH   reː'ɑl mɑ'ðriːð
Reasoner
  Harry, *US TV news reporter*   RĒZ-nuhr, RĒ-zuh-nuhr   'riːznər, 'riːzənər
Reate
  ancient form of Rieti   rē-ĀT-ē   riː'eːțiˑ
Reba
  pers. name (R. McEntire)   RĒ-buh   'riːbə
Rebecca, Rebekah
  pers. name   ri-BEK-uh   ri'bekə
Rechab
  Biblical name   RĒ-KAB, re-KHAHV   'riːˌkæb, re'xɑv
Rechabite
  Biblical name   RĒ-kuh-BĪT, REK-uh-   'riːkəˌbɑit, 'rekə-
Rechah
  Biblical name   RĒ-kuh, re-KHAH   'riːkə, re'xɑ
Recife
  city, Brazil   ruh-SĒ-fuh   rə'siːfə
Red
  pers. name   RED   'red
Redbridge
  borough, England   RED-BRIJ   'redˌbridʒ
Reddy
  Helen, *Australian singer*   RED-ē   'rediˑ
Redemptorist
  religious order   ruh-DEM(P)-t(uh-)ruhst   rə'dem(p)t(ə)rəst
Redenbacher
  Orville, *US popcorn magnate*   RED-n-BAK-uhr, RED-n-BAHK-uhr   'redn̩ˌbækər, 'redn̩ˌbɑkər

---

Key (col. 2): a: fad ā: fade ah: father ar: marry aw: law e: fed ē: feed er: merry i: hid ī: hide ō: coat ōō: boot
oi: boy   ow: now   u: put   uh: above   uhr: bird   ch: chop   ng: ring   sh: show   th: thick   th: this   zh: measure

Redfern
  pers. name — RED-FUHRN — ˈredˌfərn

Redford
  Robert, *US actor, director* — RED-fuhrd — ˈredfərd

Redgrave
  British acting family — RED-GRĀV — ˈredˌgreːv

Redjang
  lang., people, Sumatra — rä-ZHAHNG, rä-ZHANG — reːˈʒɑŋ, reːˈʒæŋ

Redlands
  city, CA — RED-luhn(d)z — ˈredlən(d)z

Redon
  Odilon, *French artist* — ruh-DAWⁿ — rədɔ̃

Redondo Beach
  city, CA — ri-DAHN-dō BĒCH — riˌdɑndoː ˈbiːtʃ

Reebok
  US footwear co. — RĒ-BAHK — ˈriːˌbɑk

Reelaiah
  Biblical name — RĒ-uh-LĪ-uh, -LĀ-uh; ruh-EL-ah-YAH — ˌriːəˈlɑiə, -ˈleːə; rəˌelɑˈjɑ

Reese
  Della, *US singer* — RĒS — ˈriːs

Reeve
  Christopher, *US actor* — RĒV — ˈriːv

Reeves
  Keanu, *US actor* — RĒVZ — ˈriːvz

Refugio
  county, town, TX — ruh-F(Y)UR-ē-ō *[sic]* — rəˈf(j)uriːoː *[sic]*

Reg
  pers. name — REJ — ˈredʒ

Regan
  Donald, *US government official;* — RĒ-guhn — ˈriːgən
    character in King Lear,
    Shakespeare

Regem
  Biblical name — RĒ-JEM, RE-gem — ˈriːˌdʒem, ˈregem

Regem-melech
  Biblical name — RĒ-JEM-MĒ-LEK, -MEL-ek, — ˈriːˌdʒemˈmiːˌlek, -ˈmelek,
    RE-gem-ME-lekh — ˈregemˈmelex

Régence
  style of French furnishings — rä-ZHAHⁿS — reːʒɑ̃s

Regency
  pert. to styles of 1811-20; genre of — RĒ-juhn-sē — ˈriːdʒənsiˑ
    romance novel

Regensburg
  city, Germany — RĀ-guhnz-BURK, Ⓢ RĀ-guhnz-BUHRG — ˈreːgənzˌburk,
    Ⓢ ˈreːgənzˌbərg

Regenstein
  Joseph, Library, *Chicago* — RĀ-guhn-STĪN, REG-uhn-STĪN — ˈreːgənˌstɑin, ˈregənˌstɑin

Reggie
  pers. name — REJ-ē — ˈredʒiˑ

Reggio di Calabria
  prov & town, Italy — RED-j(ē-)ō DĒ kah-LAHB-rē-ah — ˈreddʒ(iː)oː ˌdiː kɑˈlɑbriːɑ

Reggio nell'Emilia
  prov, Italy — RED-j(ē-)ō NEL le-MĒL-yah — ˈreddʒ(iː)oː ˌnel leˈmiːljɑ

Regia
  Roman home of Numa Pompilius — RĒ-jē-uh — ˈriːdʒiːə

Foreign Sounds: ue: *Fr.* **rue**, *Ger.* **füllen** uh(r): *Fr.* **boeuf**, *Ger.* **Höhle** kh: *Ger.* **ich**, *Scot.* **loch** ḡ: *Sp.* **amigo** v̱: *Sp.* **hablar**
hl: *Welsh* **Llanelli**. CAPITALS: primary stress. SMALL CAPS: secondary stress. Ⓢ: U.S. pron. Ⓔ: British pron.

Regina		
1. city, Canada	ri-JĪ-nuh	ri'dʒɑinə
2. pers. name	ri-JĒ-nuh, (£) ri-JĪ-nuh	ri'dʒiːnə, (£) ri'dʒɑinə
3. Italian	rā-JĒ-nah	reː'dʒiːnɑ
Reginald		
pers. name	REJ-uhn-ld	'redʒənl̩d
Régine		
pers. name, French	rā-ZHĒN	reːʒiːn
Regis		
College, *CO, MA; pers. name*	RĒ-juhs	'riːdʒəs
Régis		
pers. name, French	rā-ZHĒS	reːʒiːs
Regius		
royal professorship	RĒ-j(ē-)uhs	'riːdʒ(iː)əs
Regulus		
Roman hero	REG-yuh-luhs	'regjələs
Rehabiah		
Biblical name	RĒ-(h)uh-BĪ-uh, ruh-khahv-YAH	ˌriː(h)ə'bɑiə, rəxɑv'jɑ
Rehnquist		
William Hubbs, *US Supreme Court justice*	REN-kwist, RENG-kwist	'renkwist, 'reŋkwist
Rehob		
Biblical name	RĒ-HAHB, ruh-KHAWV	'riːˌhɑb, rə'xɔːv
Rehoboam		
king of Judah	RĒ-(h)uh-BŌ-uhm	ˌriː(h)ə'boːəm
Rehoboth		
US pl. name	ri-HŌ-buhth	ri'hoːbəθ
Rehoboth-Ir		
Biblical name	ri-HŌ-buhth-IR, -UHR; ruh-khaw-VAWT-ĒR	ri'hoːbəθ'i^{r}, -'ə^{r}; rəxɔː'vɔːt'iːr
Rehovot		
district, Israel	ruh-KHAW-VAWT, ($) RĀ-hō-VŌT	rə'xɔːˌvɔːt, ($) 'reːhoːˌvoːt
Rehum		
Biblical name	RĒ-(h)uhm, ruh-KHOOM	'riː(h)əm, rə'xuːm
Rei		
Biblical name	RĒ-Ī, RĀ-Ī, re-Ē	'riːˌɑi, 'reːˌɑi, re'iː
Reich		
German regime	RĪKH, ($) RĪK	'rɑiç, ($) 'rɑik
Reichenbach		
waterfall, Switzerland	RĪ-khuhn-BAHKH, ($) RĪ-kuhn-BAHK	'rɑiçənˌbɑx, ($) 'rɑikənˌbɑk
Reichstag		
German parliament	RĪKH-STAHK, ($) RĪK-STAHG	'rɑiçˌstɑk, ($) 'rɑikˌstɑg
Reichstein		
Tadeus, *Polish-born Swiss chemist (Nobel 1950)*	RĪKH-SHTĪN, ($) RĪK-STĪN	'rɑiçˌʃtɑin, ($) 'rɑikˌstɑin
Reid		
Kate, *British actress*	RĒD	'riːd
Reigate		
suburb of London, England	RĪ-GĀT, RĪ-git	'rɑiˌgeːt, 'rɑigit
Reijiro		
pers. name, Japanese	rā-jē-rō	reːdʒiːroː
Reilly		
pers. name	RĪ-lē	'rɑiliˑ
Reims, Rheims		
town, France	RE^{n}S, ($) RĒMZ	rẽs, ($) 'riːmz

Reina Adelaida
  Archipelago of, *island group, Pacific*   RĀ-nuh AHD-l-ĪD-uh   ˈreːnə ˌadḷˈaidə
    Ocean

Reiner
  Carl, *US comedian, writer, & his son*   RĪ-nuhr   ˈrainərʳ
    Rob, *US actor, writer*

Reinhard
  pers. name, German   RĪN-HAHRT   ˈrainˌhɑʳt

Reinhardt
  Django, *French jazz musician;*   RĪN-HAHRT   ˈrainˌhɑʳt
    College, *GA*

Reinhart
  pers. name, Dutch   RĪN-HAHRT   ˈrainˌhart

Reinheitsgebot
  German beer purity laws   RĪN-HĪTS-guh-BŌT   ˈrainˌhaitsgəˌboːt

Reinhold
  1. pers. name   RĪN-HŌLD   ˈrainˌhoːld
  2. German   RĪN-HAWLT   ˈrainˌhɔːlt

Rek
  lang., Sudan, Ethiopia   RĀK   ˈreˑk

Rekem
  Biblical name   RĒ-KEM, -kuhm; RE-kem   ˈriːˌkem, -kəm; ˈrekem

Religio Medici
  meditative writings of Sir Thomas   rē-LIJ-ē-ō MED-uh-chē   riˑˈlidʒiːoː ˈmedətʃiˑ
    Browne

REM
  rapid eye movement   REM, AHR-Ē-EM   ˈrem, ˌɑrˌiːˈem

Remaliah
  Biblical name   REM-uh-LĪ-uh, ruh-mahl-YAH-hoo   ˌreməˈlaiə, rəmɑlˈjɑhuː

Remarque
  Erich, *German novelist*   ruh-MAHRK   rəˈmɑʳk

Rembrandt
  1. pers. name   REM-BRANT   ˈremˌbrænt
  2. Dutch   REM-BRAHNT   ˈremˌbrɑnt

Rembrandt van Rijn
  Dutch painter   REM-BRAHNT vahn RĪN,   ˈremˌbrɑnt vɑn ˈrain,
     Ⓢ REM-BRANT van RĪN   Ⓢ ˈremˌbrænt væn ˈrain

Remeth
  Biblical name   RĒ-METH, REM-ETH, REM-et   ˈriːˌmeθ, ˈremˌeθ, ˈremet

Remfan
  Biblical name   REM-FAN   ˈremˌfæn

Remi
  1. pers. name, French   ruh-MĒ, rā-MĒ   rəmiː, reːmiː
  2. ancient Gaulish people   RĒ-MĪ   ˈriːˌmai
  3. lang., Africa   RĀ-mē   ˈreːmiˑ

Remick
  Lee, *US actress*   REM-ik   ˈremik

Remigio
  pers. name, Spanish   rā-MĒG̃-yō   reːˈmiːɣjoː

Remigius
  pers. name, German   rā-MĒG-yus, rā-MĒ-gē-us   reːˈmiːgjus, reːˈmiːgiːus

Remington
  Frederic, *US painter; US rifle*   REM-ing-tuhn   ˈremiŋtən
    manufacturer

Remmon [Rimmon]
  Biblical name   REM-AHN, REM-uhn, ri-MŌN   'rem͵ɑn, 'remən, ri'moːn
Remmon-methoar
  Biblical name   REM-AHN-muh-THŌ-AHR,   'rem͵ɑnmə'θoː͵ɑ^r,
                               -METH-uh-WAHR, REM-uhn-;   -'meθə͵wɑ^r, 'remən-;
                               ri-MŌN-hahm-uh-taw-AHR   ri'moːnhɑmətɔː'ɑr
Remus
  1. twin brother of Romulus; pers.   RĒ-muhs   'riːməs
  name
  2. German   RĀ-mus   'reːmus
Rémy
  pers. name, French   rā-MĒ   reːmiː
Remy Martin
  cognac   ruh-MĒ mahr-TEⁿ, ⓢ REM-ē   rəmiː mɑːrtẽ, ⓢ 'remi·
                               MAHRT-n   'mɑ^rtn̩
Renaissance
  period of intellectual & artistic   REN-uh-SAHN(T)S, -ZAHN(T)S, -SAHⁿS,   'renə͵sɑn(t)s, -͵zɑn(t)s, -͵sɑ̃s,
  activity   -ZAHⁿS, ⓔ ri-NĀS-n(t)s   -͵zɑ̃s, ⓔ ri'neːsn̩(t)s
Renaissance, La
  see La Renaissance
Renata
  pers. name   ruh-NAHT-uh   rə'nɑtə
Renato
  pers. name   ri-NAHT-ō, rā-   ri'nɑtoː, reː-
Renatus
  pers. name, Latin   ri-NĀT-uhs   ri'neːtəs
Renaud
  pers. name, French   ruh-NŌ   rənoː
Renault
  1. French automobile   ruh-NŌ; ⓢ ruh-NŌ, ruh-NAWLT   rənoː; ⓢ rə'noː, rə'nɔːlt
  2. Louis, French jurist, pacifist   ruh-NŌ   rənoː
  (Nobel 1907)
Rene
  pers. name   ruh-NĀ, ⓔ REN-Ā, RUHN-Ā, REN-ē   rə'neː, ⓔ 'ren͵eː, 'rən͵eː,
                                                                           'reni·
René
  1. pers. name, English, German   ruh-NĀ, ⓔ REN-Ā, RUHN-Ā, REN-ē   rə'neː, ⓔ 'ren͵eː, 'rən͵eː,
                                                                           'reni·
  2. French   ruh-NĀ   rəneː
Renée
  1. pers. name   ruh-NĀ   rə'neː
  2. French   ruh-NĀ   rəneː
Reni
  Guido, *Italian painter*   REN-ē   'reni·
Rennes
  city, France   REN   ren
Rennie
  pers. name   REN-ē   'reni·
Reno
  1. city, NV; county, KS; pers. name   RĒ-nō   'riːnoː
  2. river, Italy   RĀ-nō, REN-ō   'reːnoː, 'renoː
Renoir
  Jean, *French film director, son of*   ruhn-WAHR, ⓢ REN-WAHR,   rənwɑːr, ⓢ 'ren͵wɑ^r,
  Pierre Auguste, *French painter*   ruhn-WAHR   rən'wɑ^r

Key (col. 2):   a: fad   ā: fade   ah: father   ar: marry   aw: law   e: fed   ē: feed   er: merry   i: hid   ī: hide   ō: coat   ōō: boot
oi: boy   ow: now   u: put   uh: above   uhr: bird   ch: chop   ng: ring   sh: show   th: thick   <u>th</u>: this   zh: measure

Rensselaer
   1. town, Polytechnic Institute, *NY*   REN(T)-suh-LIR, REN(T)-s(uh-)luhr   ˌren(t)səˈliʳ, ˈren(t)s(ə)ləʳ
   2. pers. name   REN(T)-suh-LIR   ˈren(t)səˌliʳ

Rephah
   Biblical name   RĒ-fuh, REF-ah<u>kh</u>   ˈriːfə, ˈrefɑx

Rephaiah
   Biblical name   ruh-FĪ-uh, ruh-FĀ-uh, ruh-fah-YAH   rəˈfɑiə, rəˈfeːə, rəfɑˈjɑ

Rephaim
   Biblical name   REF-ā-im, ruh-fah-ĒM   ˈrefeːim, rəfɑˈiːm

Rephael
   Biblical name   REF-ā-EL, REF-ē-EL, ruh-fah-EL   ˈrefeːˌel, ˈrefiːˌel, rəfɑˈel

Rephidim
   Biblical name   REF-uhd-im, ruh-FĪD-im, ruh-fē-DĒM   ˈrefədim, rəˈfɑidim, rəfiːˈdiːm

Repsol
   Spanish oil co.   REP-SŌL   ˈrepˌsoːl

Republican
   US political party   ri-PUHB-li-kuhn   riˈpəblikən

République
   French for republic   rā-pue-BLĒK   reːpyːbliːk

Requiem
   mass for the dead   REK-wē-uhm, RĀ-kwē-uhm   ˈrekwiːəm, ˈreːkwiːəm

Resen
   Biblical name   RĒ-suhn, RES-en   ˈriːsən, ˈresen

Res gestae
   autobiography of Augustus   RĀS JES-TĪ, GES-TĪ   ˈreːs ˈdʒesˌtɑi, ˈgesˌtɑi

Resheph
   Biblical name   RĒ-SHEF, RESH-EF   ˈriːˌʃef, ˈreʃˌef

Resighini Rancheria
   Indian reservation, US   RES-uh-GĒ-nē RAN-chuh-RĒ-uh   ˌresəˈgiːniˑ ˌræntʃəˈriːə

Respighi
   Ottorino, *Italian composer*   ruh-SPĒ-gē, res-PĒ-gē   rəˈspiːgiˑ, resˈpiːgiˑ

Restigouche
   river, Canada   RES-ti-GŌŌSH   ˈrestiˌguːʃ

Reston
   James, *Scottish-born US journalist;*   RES-tuhn   ˈrestən
   city, VA

Reticulum
   constellation   ri-TIK-yuh-luhm   riˈtikjələm

Retsina
   Greek resinated wine   ret-SĒ-nuh   retˈsiːnə

Reu
   Biblical name   RĒ-o͞o, ruh-o͞o   ˈriːuː, rəˈuː

Reuben
   sandwich; pers. name   RO͞O-buhn   ˈruːbən

Reubenite
   Biblical name   RO͞O-buh-NĪT   ˈruːbəˌnɑit

Reuel
   1. pers. name (J. R. R. Tolkien)   RO͞O-uhl   ˈruːəl
   2. Biblical name   RO͞O-uhl, ruh-o͞o-EL   ˈruːəl, rəuːˈel

Reumah
   Biblical name   RO͞O-muh, ruh-o͞o-MAH   ˈruːmə, rəuːˈmɑ

Réunion
   island, Indian Ocean   rē-YO͞ON-yuhn   riˑˈjuːnjən

Foreign Sounds: **ue**: *Fr.* **rue**, *Ger.* f**ü**llen **uh(r)**: *Fr.* b**oeu**f, *Ger.* H**öh**le <u>kh</u>: *Ger.* i**ch**, *Scot.* lo**ch** **g̱**: *Sp.* ami**g**o **v**: *Sp.* ha**b**lar
hl: *Welsh* **Ll**anelli. CAPITALS: primary stress. SMALL CAPS: secondary stress. Ⓢ: U.S. pron. Ⓔ: British pron.

Reunionese
  lang., pert. to Réunion   rē-YŌŌN-yuh-NĒZ, -NĒS   ri·ˌjuːnjəˈniːz, -ˈniːs
Reuters
  British news agency   ROIT-uhrz   ˈrɔiʈəʳz
Reuther
  Walter, *US labor leader*   RŌŌ-thuhr   ˈruːθəʳ
Revelation
  New Testament book   REV-uh-LĀ-shuhn   ˌrevəˈleːʃən
Revere
  Paul, *American patriot; town, MA*   ri-VIR   riˈviʳ
Reverend
  title for a member of the clergy   REV-(uh-)ruhnd, REV-uhrnd   ˈrev(ə)rənd, ˈrevəʳnd
Revlon
  US cosmetics co.   REV-LAHN   ˈrevˌlɑn
Rex
  pers. name   REKS   ˈreks
Reye's
  syndrome, medical disorder   RĪZ, RĀZ   ˈraiz, ˈreːz
Reykjavik
  city, Iceland   RĀK-yuh-VIK, -VĒK   ˈreːkjəˌvik, -ˌviːk
Reymont
  Władysław Stanisław, *Polish*   RĀ-MAHNT   ˈreːˌmɑnt
  author (Nobel 1924)
Reynaldo
  pers. name, Spanish   rā-NAHL-dō   reːˈnɑldoː
Reynard
  fox in medieval stories   RĀ-nuhrd, REN-uhrd, RĀ-NAHR(D)   ˈreːnəʳd, ˈrenəʳd, ˈreːˌnɑʳ(d)
Reynaud
  Paul, *French political leader*   re-NŌ   renoː
Reynella
  Australian wine   ren-EL-uh   renˈelə
Reynolds
  Burt, *US actor;* Debbie, *US actress*   REN-l(d)z   ˈrenl̩(d)z
Reza Shah Pahlavi
  shah, Iran   ri-ZAH SHAH PAHL-uh-vē   riˈzɑ ˈʃɑ ˈpɑləviˑ
Rezeph
  Biblical name   RĒ-ZEF, RET-sef   ˈriːˌzef, ˈretsef
Rezia
  Biblical name   ri-ZĪ-uh, RĒ-zē-uh, rits-YAH   riˈzaiə, ˈriːziːə, ritsˈjɑ
Rezin
  Biblical name   RĒ-zuhn, ruht-SĒN   ˈriːzən, rətˈsiːn
Rezon
  Biblical name   RĒ-ZAHN, RĒ-zuhn, ruht-SŌN   ˈriːˌzɑn, ˈriːzən, rətˈsoːn
Rhadamanthine
  pert. to Rhadamanthys   RAD-uh-MAN(T)-thuhn,   ˌrædəˈmæn(t)θən,
          RAD-uh-MAN-THĪN   ˌrædəˈmænˌθain
Rhadamanthys, -thus
  judge of the Underworld in Greek   RAD-uh-MAN(T)-thuhs   ˌrædəˈmæn(t)θəs
  mythology
Rhaetia
  ancient Roman province, Europe   RĒ-sh(ē-)uh   ˈriːʃ(iː)ə
Rhaetian
  lang., Switzerland, Italy, Austria;   RĒ-sh(ē-)uhn   ˈriːʃ(iː)ən
  Alps, *mtn. range*

Key (col. 2):   a: fad   ā: fade   ah: father   ar: marry   aw: law   e: fed   ē: feed   er: merry   i: hid   ī: hide   ō: coat   ōō: boot
oi: boy   ow: now   u: put   uh: above   uhr: bird   ch: chop   ng: ring   sh: show   th: thick   <u>th</u>: this   zh: measure

Rhaetic
   pert. to Rhaetia   RĒT-ik   'riːţik
Rhaeto-Romanic
   Romance lang.   RĒT-ō-rō-MAN-ik   ˌriːţoːroː'mænik
Rhea
   1. Greek goddess, mother of Zeus;   RĒ-uh   'riːə
     satellite of Saturn; S. American
     flightless bird
   2. pers. name   RĒ, RĀ, RĒ-uh   'riː, 'reː, 'riːə
Rhea Silvia [Ilia]
   mother of Romulus and Remus   RĒ-uh SIL-vē-uh   ˌriːə 'silviːə
Rhee
   Syngman, *Korean political leader*   RĒ   'riː
Rhegium
   Biblical name   RĒ-jē-uhm   'riːdʒiːəm
Rheims
   see Reims
Rhein
   see Rhine
Rheingold, Das
   opera, R. Wagner   dahs RĪN-GŌLD   dɑs 'rain,goːld
Rheinhessen-Pfalz
   prov, Germany   RĪN-HES-uhn-(P)FAHLTS   ˌrain,hesən'(p)falts
Rheinisches Schiefergebirge
   plateau, Germany   RĪ-nuh-shuhs SHĒ-fuhr-guh-BIR-guh   'rainəʃəs 'ʃiːfəʳgəˌbiʳgə
Rheinland-Pfalz
   prov, Germany   RĪN-LAHNT-(P)FAHLTS   'rain,lant'(p)falts
Rheinpfalz
   prov, Germany   RĪN-(P)FAHLTS   'rainˌ(p)falts
Rhenish
   pert. to the Rhine   REN-ish   'reniʃ
Rhenish Slate
   plateau, Germany   REN-ish SLĀT   'reniʃ 'sleːt
rhenium
   element   RĒ-nē-uhm   'riːniːəm
Rhenus
   Latin name of the Rhine   RĒ-nuhs   'riːnəs
Rhesa
   Biblical name   RĒ-suh   'riːsə
Rhesus
   mythical Thracian; monkey genus   RĒ-suhs   'riːsəs
Rhett
   pers. name   RET   'ret
Rhin [Rhine]
   river, Europe; dept, France   REⁿ   rẽ
Rhine, Rhein, Rijn
   river, Europe   RĪN   'rain
Rhineland
   region, Germany   RĪN-luhnd, -LAND   'rainlənd, -ˌlænd
Rhineland-Palatinate
   prov, Germany   RĪN-luhnd-puh-LAT-n-uht   'rainləndpə'lætn̩ət
Rhoda
   pers. name   RŌD-uh   'roːdə
Rhodanus
   Latin name of the Rhone   RAHD-n-uhs   'radn̩əs

Rhode Island		
state, US	rōd Ī-luhnd, ruh-DĪ-luhnd	roːd 'ɑilənd, rə'dɑilənd
Rhodes		
Cecil John, *British financier; island, Aegean*	RŌDZ	'roːdz
Rhodesia		
region, central Africa, now Zambia and Zimbabwe	rō-DĒ-zh(ē-)uh	roː'diːʒ(iː)ə
rhodium		
element	RŌD-ē-uhm	'roːdiːəm
Rhodolite		
garnet	RŌD-l-ĪT	'roːdḷˌɑit
Rhodonite		
mineral	RŌD-n-ĪT	'roːdṇˌɑit
Rhodope		
1. region, Greece; mtn. range, Europe	RAHD-uh-pē	'rɑdəpiˑ
2. legendary Ephesian heroine	rō-DŌ-pē, ruh-DŌ-pē	roː'doːpiˑ, rə'doːpiˑ
Rhodus		
wife of Helios	RŌD-uhs	'roːdəs
Rhön		
mtn. range, Germany	RUH(R)N	'rœːn
Rhonda		
pers. name	RAHN-duh	'rɑndə
Rhondda		
valley, district, Wales	HRAHN-thuh, [S] RAHN-thuh	'r̥ɑnðə, [S] 'rɑnðə
Rhône		
river, Europe	RŌN	'roːn
Rhône-Alpes		
region, France	RŌN-AHLP	roːnɑːlp
Rhumba		
see Rumba		
Rhymney, Rhymni		
river, Wales	HRUHM-nē, [S] RUHM-nē	'r̥əmniˑ, [S] 'rəmniˑ
Rhys		
1. pers. name	RĒS	'riːs
2. Welsh	HRĒS, [S] RĒS	'r̥iːs, [S] 'riːs
Rialto		
1. city, CA	rē-AL-tō	riː'æltoː
2. street, Venice	rē-AHL-tō, [S] rē-AL-tō	riː'ɑltoː, [S] riː'æltoː
Ribai		
Biblical name	RĪ-bē-Ī, ri-BĀ-Ī, rē-VĪ	'rɑibiːˌɑi, ri'beːˌɑi, riː'vɑi
Ribbonism		
precepts of an Irish secret society opposing landlords	RIB-uh-NIZ-uhm	'ribəˌnizəm
Riblah		
Biblical name	RIB-luh, riv-LAH	'riblə, riv'lɑ
Ricardo		
1. David, *British economist*	ri-KAHR-dō	ri'kɑʳdoː
2. pers. name, Spanish	rē-KAHR-thō	riː'kɑrðoː
Riccardo		
1. pers. name	rik-AHRD-ō	rik'ɑʳdoː
2. Italian	rēk-KAHR-do	riːk'kɑrdo

Key (col. 2): a: **fad** ā: **fade** ah: **father** ar: **marry** aw: **law** e: **fed** ē: **feed** er: **merry** i: **hid** ī: **hide** ō: **coat** ōō: **boot** oi: **boy** ow: **now** u: **put** uh: **above** uhr: **bird** ch: **chop** ng: **ring** sh: **show** th: **thick** th: **this** zh: **measure**

Ricci		
Marco, *Italian painter;* Nina, *Italian designer;* Sebastiano, *Italian painter*	RĒT-chē, [$] RĒ-chē	ˈriːttʃiˑ, [$] ˈriːtʃiˑ
Rice		
University, *TX; pers. name*	RĪS	ˈrɑis
Rice-a-Roni		
tdmk for rice and stuffing mixes	RĪ-suh-RŌ-nē	ˌrɑisəˈroːniˑ
Rich		
pers. name	RICH	ˈritʃ
Richard		
1. pers. name	RICH-uhrd	ˈritʃəʳd
2. Dutch	RĒ-SHAHRT	ˈriːˌʃɑrt
3. French	rē-SHAHR	riːʃɑːr
4. German	RI<u>KH</u>-AHRT	ˈriçˌɑʳt
Richards		
D. W., Jr., *US physician (Nobel 1956);* T. W., *US chemist (Nobel 1914)*	RICH-uhrdz	ˈritʃəʳdz
Richardson		
Sir Owen W., *English physicist (Nobel 1928);* Sir Ralph, *English actor*	RICH-uhrd-suhn	ˈritʃəʳdsən
Richelieu		
1. Duc de, *French cardinal*	rē-shuh-LYUH(R), [$] RISH-uhl-(Y)O͞O	riːʃəljœː, [$] ˈriʃəlˌ(j)uː
2. river, Canada	RISH-uhl-(Y)O͞O	ˈriʃəlˌ(j)uː
Richet		
C. R., *French physiologist (Nobel 1913)*	rē-SHĀ	riːʃeː
Richie		
Lionel B., Jr., *US singer*	RICH-ē	ˈritʃiˑ
Richmond		
pl. name; pers. name	RICH-muhnd	ˈritʃmənd
Richmond-upon-Thames		
borough, England	RICH-muhn-duh-puhn-TEMZ	ˈritʃməndəpənˈtemz
Richter		
Burton, *US particle physicist (Nobel 1976);* Francis, *US seismologist; earthquake scale*	RIK-tuhr	ˈriktəʳ
Rick		
pers. name	RIK	ˈrik
Rickenbacker		
Edward, *US military aviator*	RIK-uhn-BAK-uhr	ˈrikənˌbækəʳ
Rickles		
Don, *US comedian*	RIK-uhlz	ˈrikəlz
Rickover		
Hyman, *US admiral*	RIK-Ō-vuhr	ˈrikˌoːvəʳ
Ricky, Rickey, Ricki, Rickie		
pers. name	RIK-ē	ˈrikiˑ
Rico		
pers. name	RĒ-kō	ˈriːkoː
Ricoh		
tdmk for watches	RĒ-kō	ˈriːkoː
Ricotta		
cheese	ri-KAHT-uh	riˈkɑt̬ə

Foreign Sounds: ue: *Fr.* **rue**, *Ger.* **füllen** uh(r): *Fr.* **boeuf**, *Ger.* **Höhle** <u>kh</u>: *Ger.* **ich**, *Scot.* **loch** g̃: *Sp.* **amigo** <u>v</u>: *Sp.* **hablar** hl: *Welsh* **Llanelli**. CAPITALS: primary stress. SMALL CAPS: secondary stress. [$]: U.S. pron. [£]: British pron.

Rideau
  lake, river, canal, Canada   ri-DŌ   ri'doː

Rider
  pers. name   RĪD-uhr   'rɑidəʳ

Ridley
  pers. name   RID-lē   'ridliˑ

Riegle
  Donald W., Jr., *US politician*   RĒ-guhl   'riːgəl

Riemann
  Bernhard, *German mathematician*   RĒ-MAHN   'riː‚mɑn

Riesling
  wine   RĒZ-ling, RĒ-sling   'riːzliŋ, 'riːsliŋ

Rieti
  city, Italy   rē-ĀT-ē, rē-ET-ē   riː'eːțiˑ, riː'ețiˑ

Riff
  lang., Algeria, Morocco   RIF   'rif

Riga
  city, Latvia; gulf, Baltic Sea   RĒ-guh   'riːgə

Rigakushi
  pers. name, Japanese   rē-gah-kōō-shē   riːgɑkuːʃiː

Rigby
  Cathy, *US gymnast*   RIG-bē   'rigbiˑ

Rigel
  star   RĪ-juhl, RĪ-guhl   'rɑidʒəl, 'rɑigəl

Rigoberta
  pers. name (R. Menchú)   rē-gō-VER-tah, Ⓢ RIG-uh-BERT-uh   riːɣoː'βertɑ, Ⓢ ‚rigə'beʳțə

Rigoletto
  opera, Verdi   RIG-uh-LET-ō   ‚rigə'lețoː

Rigsdag
  former Parliament, Denmark   RIGZ-DAHG   'rigz‚dɑg

Rig-Veda
  Hindu book of hymns   rig-VĀD-uh   rig'veːdə

Riis
  Jacob, *US reformer*   RĒS   'riːs

Rijeka [Fiume]
  city, Croatia   rē-YEK-uh   riː'jekə

Rijks
  museum, Amsterdam, Netherlands   RĪKS   'rɑiks

Rijn
  see Rhine

Rikki
  pers. name   RIK-ē   'rikiˑ

Rikki-Tiki-Tavi
  fictional mongoose, Kipling   RIK-ē-TIK-ē-TAHV-ē, -TĀ-vē, -TAV-ē   ‚rikiˑ‚tikiˑ'tɑviˑ, -'teːviˑ, -'tæviˑ

Riksdag
  parliament, Sweden   RĒKS-DAHG   'riːks‚dɑːg

Riley
  James Whitcomb, *US poet;* Pat, *US*   RĪ-lē   'rɑiliˑ
   basketball coach

Rilke
  Rainer Maria, *German poet*   RIL-kuh   'rilkə

Rima
  pers. name   RĒ-muh   'riːmə

Key (col. 2):   a: fad   ā: fade   ah: father   ar: marry   aw: law   e: fed   ē: feed   er: merry   i: hid   ī: hide   ō: coat   ōō: boot
oi: boy   ow: now   u: put   uh: above   uhr: bird   ch: chop   ng: ring   sh: show   th: thick   th̲: this   zh: measure

Rimbaud		
Arthur, *French writer*	re^{n}-BŌ, Ⓢ ram-BŌ, RAM-bō	rɛ̃boː, Ⓢ ræm'boː, 'ræmboː
Rimini		
port, Italy	RIM-uh-nē, RĒ-muh-nē	'riməniˑ, 'riːməniˑ
Rimmon [Remmon]		
Biblical name	RIM-uhn, ri-MŌN	'rimən, ri'moːn
Rimmon-parez [Rimmon-perez]		
Biblical name	RIM-uhn-PER-ĒZ, -PAR-ĒZ, -EZ; ri-MŌN-PE-rets	'rimən'perˌiːz, -'pærˌiːz, -ˌez; ri'moːn'perets
Rimmon-perez		
Biblical name	RIM-uhn-PĒ-REZ, -PER-EZ, ri-MŌN-PE-rets	'rimən'piːˌrez, -'perˌez, ri'moːn'perets
Rimouski		
city, Canada	ruh-MO͞O-skē	rə'muːskiˑ
Rimsky-Korsakov		
Nikolai, *Russian composer*	RĒM-ski-KAWR-suh-KUHF, Ⓢ RIM(P)-skē-KAWR-suh-KAWF, -KAWR-suh-KAWF	'ṛiːmsḳij'kɔː^{r}səˌkəf, Ⓢ ˌrim(p)skiˑ'kɔː^{r}səˌkɔːf, -ˌkɔː^{r}sə'kɔːf
Rina		
pers. name	RĒ-nuh	'riːnə
Rinaldo		
1. pers. name	ri-NAHL-dō, ri-NAL-dō	ri'nɑldoː, ri'nældoː
2. Italian	rē-NAHL-dō	riː'nɑldoː
Rincon		
Indian reservation, US	RING-kahn, ring-KŌN	'riŋkɑn, riŋ'koːn
Ring		
pers. name	RING	'riŋ
Ringnes		
Norwegian beer	RING-nuhs	'riŋnəs
Rinnah		
Biblical name	RIN-uh, ri-NAH	'rinə, ri'nɑ
Rio Amazonas [Amazon]		
river, S. America	RĒ-o͞o AHM-uh-ZŌ-nuhs	'riːuː ˌɑmə'zoːnəs
Rio Arriba		
county, NM	RĒ-ō uh-RĒ-buh	ˌriːoː ə'riːbə
Rio Blanco		
county, CO	RĒ-ō BLANG-kō	ˌriːoː 'blæŋkoː
Rio Bravo		
Mexican name for Rio Grande	RĒ-ō BRAHV-ō	ˌriːoː 'brɑβoː
Rio Chama		
river, CO, NM	RĒ-ō CHAHM-uh	ˌriːoː 'tʃɑmə
Rio de Janeiro		
state, city, Brazil	RĒ-ō DĀ zhuh-NER-ō, DĒ, juh-NER-ō	'riːoː ˌdeː ʒə'neroː, ˌdiː, dʒə'neroː
Rio de Oro		
bay, Sahara	RĒ-ō dē ŌR-ō, AWR-ō	ˌriːoː diː 'oːroː, 'ɔːroː
Rio Gallegos		
port, Argentina	RĒ-ō gah-ZHĀ-gōs, Ⓢ RĒ-ō gah-YĀ-guhs, gī-Ā-guhs	ˌriːoː gɑ'ʒeːɣoːs, Ⓢ ˌriːoː gɑ'jeːgəs, gɑi'eːgəs
Rio Grande		
1. county, CO	RĒ-ō GRAND(-ē), RĪ-ō GRAND	ˌriːoː 'grænd(iˑ), ˌrɑioː 'grænd
2. river, Africa; river, Brazil	RĒ-o͞o GRAHN-duh	ˌriːuː 'grɑndə

Foreign Sounds: ue: *Fr.* **rue**, *Ger.* **fü**llen uh(r): *Fr.* **boeu**f, *Ger.* H**ö**hle kh: *Ger.* i**ch**, *Scot.* lo**ch** g: *Sp.* ami**g**o v: *Sp.* ha**b**lar hl: *Welsh* **Ll**anelli. CAPITALS: primary stress. SMALL CAPS: secondary stress. Ⓢ: U.S. pron. [£]: British pron.

Río Grande, Rio Grande
   river, US & Mexico   RĒ-ō GRAND(-ē), RĪ-ō GRAND   ˌriːoː ˈgrænd(iˑ), ˌraioː
                                                              ˈgrænd

Rio Hondo
   College, CA   RĒ-ō (H)AHN-dō   ˌriːoː ˈ(h)ɑndoː

Rioja, La
   region, Spain; wine variety   lah rē-AW-hah   lɑ riːˈɔːhɑ

Rio Muni
   prov, Equatorial Guinea   RĒ-ō MOO-nē   ˌriːoː ˈmuːniˑ

Riordan
   family name   RIRD-n   ˈriʳdn̩

Riphath
   Biblical name   RĪ-FATH, rē-FAHT   ˈraiˌfæθ, riːˈfɑt

Ripon
   town, England   RIP-uhn   ˈripən

RISC
   reduced instruction set [computer]   RISK   ˈrisk
     chip

Risë
   pers. name   RĒ-suh   ˈriːsə

Rison
   city, AR   RĪ-zuhn   ˈraizən

Risorgimento
   political movement, Italy   rē-ZAWR-ji-MEN-tō, rē-SAWR-   riːˌzɔːʳdʒiˈmentoː, riːˌsɔːʳ-

Risotto
   cooked rice dish   ri-SAWT-ō, ri-ZAWT-ō, ri-ZAHT-ō   riˈsɔːt̪oː, riˈzɔːt̪oː, riˈzɑt̪oː

Rissah
   Biblical name   RIS-uh, ri-SAH   ˈrisə, riˈsɑ

Rissole
   small pastry   RIS-ŌL   ˈrisˌoːl

Rita
   pers. name   RĒT-uh   ˈriːt̪ə

Ritchie
   pers. name   RICH-ē   ˈritʃiˑ

Rithmah
   Biblical name   RITH-muh, rit-MAH   ˈriθmə, ritˈmɑ

Ritter
   John, US actor; German beer   RIT-uhr   ˈrit̪əʳ

Ritz
   César, Swiss founder of luxury hotels   RITS   ˈrits

Riva
   Belgian beer   RĒ-vuh   ˈriːvə

Rivanna
   river, VA   ruh-VAN-uh   rəˈvænə

Rivas
   dept, town, Nicaragua   RĒ-vahs   ˈriːβas

Rivera
   Chita, US actress, singer; Geraldo,   ruh-VER-uh   rəˈverə
     US TV interviewer

Rivier
   College, NH   ri-VIR   riˈviʳ

Riviera, The
   region, Mediterranean   RIV-ē-ER-uh   ˌriviːˈerə

Rivière
   pers. name, French   rē-VYER   riːvjer

Key (col. 2):   a: fad   ā: fade   ah: father   ar: marry   aw: law   e: fed   ē: feed   er: merry   i: hid   ī: hide   ō: coat   ōō: boot
oi: boy   ow: now   u: put   uh: above   uhr: bird   ch: chop   ng: ring   sh: show   th: thick   <u>th</u>: this   zh: measure

Rivoli's
hummingbird	RIV-uh-lēz	'rivəli·z

Riyadh
city, Saudi Arabia	rē-(Y)AHD	riː'(j)ɑd

Rizal
prov, Philippines	ri-ZAHL, ri-SAHL	ri'zɑl, ri'sɑl

Rizos
pers. name, Mod. Greek	RI-zaws	'rizɔːs

Rizpah
Biblical name	RIZ-puh, rit-SPAH	'rizpə, rit'spɑ

Rizzoli
bookstore, publisher, New York City	ri-ZŌ-lē	ri'zoːli·

Roald
pers. name, Norwegian	RŌ-ahl	'roːɑl

Roanoke
river, city, county, VA; island, NC; N. American people	RŌ-(uh-)-NŌK	'roː(ə),noːk

Roanoke-Chowan
Technical College, *NC*	RŌ-(uh-)-NŌK-chuh-WAHN	'roː(ə),noːktʃə'wɑn

Rob
pers. name	RAHB	'rɑb

Robards
Jason, *US actor*	RŌ-BAHRDZ	'roː,bɑᵣdz

Robb
Charles Spittal, *US politician*	RAHB	'rɑb

Robbie
pers. name	RAHB-ē	'rɑbi·

Robbins
F. C., *US physiologist, pediatrician (Nobel 1954)*	RAHB-uhnz	'rɑbənz

Robert
1. pers. name	RAHB-uhrt	'rɑbəᵣt
2. Danish	RŌ-BERT	'roː,bert
3. Dutch	RAWB-uhrt	'rɔːbərt
4. Finnish	RAW-BERT	'rɔː,bert
5. French	rō-BER	roːber
6. German	RŌ-BERT	'roː,beᵣt
7. Russian	RUHB-YERT, RAWB-yirt	ˌrəb'jert, 'rɔːbjirt
8. Swedish	RAWB-buhrt	'rɔːbbərt

Roberta
pers. name	ruh-BUHRT-uh	rə'bəᵣʈə

Roberto
1. pers. name, Italian	rō-BER-tō	roː'bertoː
2. Spanish	rō-VER-tō	roː'βertoː

Robertson
Cliff, *US actor, writer*	RAHB-uhrt-suhn	'rɑbəᵣtsən

Robeson
1. Paul, US singer, actor	RŌB-suhn	'roːbsən
2. county, NC	RAHB-uh-suhn	'rɑbəsən

Robespierre
Maximilien, *French revolutionary*	raw-bes-PYER, ⓢ RŌBZ-PIR, RŌBZ-PYER	rɔːbespjer, ⓢ 'roːbz,piᵣ, 'roːbz,pjeᵣ

Robigo
Roman divinity of wheat	rō-BĪ-gō, rō-BĒ-gō	roː'bɑigoː, roː'biːgoː

Foreign Sounds: ue: *Fr.* **rue**, *Ger.* **fü**llen   uh(r): *Fr.* **boeuf**, *Ger.* **Höhle**   kh: *Ger.* i**ch**, *Scot.* lo**ch**   ḡ: *Sp.* ami**g**o   v̱: *Sp.* ha**b**lar
hl: *Welsh* **Ll**anelli.   CAPITALS: primary stress.   SMALL CAPS: secondary stress.   ⓢ: U.S. pron.   ⓔ: British pron.

Robin
   pers. name   RAHB-uhn   'rabən

Robinson
   college, Cambridge Univ.; pers. name   RAHB-uhn-suhn   'rabənsən

Robinson Crusoe
   character, novel, Defoe   RAHB-uhn-suhn KR$\overline{OO}$-sō, KR$\overline{OO}$-zō   ˌrabənsən 'kruːsoː, 'kruːzoː

Robur Carolinum
   former constellation   RŌ-buhr KAR-uh-LĪ-nuhm, RŌ-bur   'roːbə^r ˌkærə'lainəm, 'roːbu^r

Rocco
   pers. name   RAHK-ō   'rakoː

Rocha
   city, dept, Uruguay   RAW-chuh   'rɔːtʃə

Rochambeau
   Conte de, *French general*   raw-shah^n-BŌ   rɔːʃãboː

Rochdale
   borough, England   RAHCH-DĀL   'ratʃˌdeːl

Roche
   pers. name   RAWSH, RŌSH, RŌCH   'rɔːʃ, 'roːʃ, 'roːtʃ

Roche, La
   see La Roche

Rochefoucauld, La
   see La Rochefoucauld

Rochelle, La
   see La Rochelle

Rochester
   pl. name, England, US   RAHCH-uh-stuhr, RAHCH-ES-tuhr   'ratʃəstə^r, 'ratʃˌestə^r

Rockefeller
   noted US family   RAHK-uh-FEL-uhr, RAHK-FEL-uhr   'rakəˌfelə^r, 'rakˌfelə^r

Rockies
   mtn. range, N. America   RAHK-ēz   'rakiˑz

Rockingham
   county, NC, NH, VA   RAHK-ing-HAM   'rakiŋˌhæm

Rockne
   Knute, *US football coach*   RAHK-nē   'rakniˑ

Rockwell
   Norman, *US painter; pers. name*   RAHK-WEL, RAHK-wuhl   'rakˌwel, 'rakwəl

Rocky
   Mountains, *mtn. range, N. America;*   RAHK-ē   'rakiˑ
   pers. name

Rococo
   ornate style of art and music   ruh-KŌ-kō, RŌ-kuh-KŌ   rə'koːkoː, ˌroːkə'koː

Rod, Rodd
   pers. name   RAHD   'rad

Rodanim
   Biblical name   RAHD-n-im, RŌ-dah-NĒM   'radn̩im, ˌroːdɑ'niːm

Roddy
   pers. name   RAHD-ē   'radiˑ

Rodenbach
   Belgian beer   RŌD-n-BAH<u>KH</u>   'roːdn̩ˌbax

Rodentia
   gnawing mammals   rō-DEN-ch(ē-)uh, rō-DENT-ē-uh   roː'dentʃ(iː)ə, roː'dentiːə

Roderic, -ick
   pers. name   RAHD-uhr-ik, RAHD-rik   'radərik, 'radrik

Roderich
   pers. name, German   RŌ-duh-ri<u>kh</u>   'roːdəriç

Key (col. 2):   a: fad   ā: fade   ah: father   ar: marry   aw: law   e: fed   ē: feed   er: merry   i: hid   ī: hide   ō: coat   ō̄o: boot
oi: boy   ow: now   u: put   uh: above   uhr: bird   ch: chop   ng: ring   sh: show   th: thick   <u>th</u>: this   zh: measure

Rodgers
  Richard, *US composer*   RAHJ-uhrz   'rɑdʒəʳz
Rodham
  pers. name (Hillary R. Clinton)   RAHD-uhm   'rɑdəm
Ródhos [Rhodes]
  island, Greece   RAW-T͟HAWS   'rɔːˌðɔːs
Rodin
  Auguste, *French sculptor*   raw-DEⁿ, Ⓢ RŌ-DA(N)   rɔːdẽ, Ⓢ 'rɔːˌdæ(n)
Rodney
  pers. name   RAHD-nē   'rɑdni·
Rodolfo
  1. pers. name, Italian   rō-DAWL-fō   roː'dɔːlfoː
  2. Spanish   rō-T͟HAWL-fō   roː'ðɔːlfoː
Rodolphe
  pers. name, French   raw-DAWLF   rɔːdɔːlf
Rodôpi [Rhodope]
  region, Greece   raw-T͟HAW-pē   rɔː'ðɔːpi·
Rodrigo
  1. pers. name   rahd-RĒ-gō   rɑd'riːgoː
  2. Italian   rō-DRĒ-gō   roː'driːgoː
  3. Spanish   rō-T͟HRĒ-g̃ō   roː'ðriːɣoː
Rodrigues
  pers. name, Portuguese   ro͞o-DRĒ-gish, -gis   ruː'driːgiʃ, -gis
Rodríguez
  pers. name, Spanish   raw-T͟HRĒ-gās, -gāth; Ⓢ rahd-RĒ-gez   rɔː'ðriːgeːs, -geːθ; Ⓢ rɑd'riːgez
Rodriguez Sánchez [Manolete]
  Manuel, *Spanish bullfighter*   rawt͟h-RĒ-g̃āth SAHN-chāth   rɔːð'riːɣeːθ 'sɑntʃeːθ
Roebling
  John Augustus, *US engineer*   RŌ-bling   'roːbliŋ
Roentgen, Röntgen
  Wilhelm Conrad von, *German*   RUH(R)NT-guhn, Ⓢ RENT-guhn,   'ræntgən, Ⓢ 'rentgən,
    physicist (Nobel 1901)   RUHNT-guhn, REN-chuhn   'rəntgən, 'rentʃən
Roethke
  Theodore, *US writer*   RET-kē, RETH-kē   'retki·, 'reθki·
Rogelim
  Biblical name   RŌ-guh-LIM, rō-JĒ-luhm, rawg-LĒM   'roːgəˌlim, roː'dʒiːləm, rɔːg'liːm
Roger
  1. pers. name   RAHJ-uhr   'rɑdʒəʳ
  2. French   raw-ZHĀ   rɔːʒeː
Roget
  Peter Mark, *English thesaurus*   rō-ZHĀ, RŌ-ZHĀ   roː'ʒeː, 'roːˌʒeː
    compiler
Rogue
  Community College, *OR*   RŌG   'roːg
Rohgah
  Biblical name   RŌ-guh, rah-GAH   'roːgə, rɑ'gɑ
Rohnert Park
  city, CA   RŌ-nuhrt PAHRK   'roːnəʳt 'pɑʳk
Rohrer
  Heinrich, *Swiss physicist (Nobel 1986)*   RAWR-uhr   'rɔːrəʳ
Roh Tae Woo
  S. Korean leader   nō tā wo͞o *[sic]*   noː teː wuː *[sic]*

Foreign Sounds: ue: *Fr.* **rue**, *Ger.* **füllen**   uh(r): *Fr.* **boeuf**, *Ger.* **Höhle**   kh: *Ger.* **ich**, *Scot.* **loch**   g̃: *Sp.* **amigo**   v̲: *Sp.* **hablar**
hl: *Welsh* **Llanelli**.   CAPITALS: primary stress.   SMALL CAPS: secondary stress.   Ⓢ: U.S. pron.   Ⓔ: British pron.

Roissy [Charles de Gaulle]
  airport, Paris   rwah-SĒ   rwɑːsiː
Rokusai Nembutsu
  Japanese festival   rō-k$\overline{oo}$-sī nem-b$\overline{oo}$t-s$\overline{oo}$ roːkuːsɑi nembuːtsuː
Roland
  1. pers. name   RŌ-luhnd   'roːlənd
  2. French   raw-LAH^n rɔːlɑ̃
  3. German; beer   RŌ-LAHNT   'roː,lɑnt
Rolando
  pers. name, Italian   rō-LAHN-dō   roː'lɑndoː
Rolette
  county, ND   rō-LET   roː'let
Rolex
  tdmk for watches   RŌ-LEKS   'roː,leks
Rolf
  pers. name   RAHLF, RAWLF   'rɑlf, 'rɔːlf
Rolla
  city, MO, ND   RAHL-uh   'rɑlə
Rolland
  Romain, *French musicologist, author*   raw-LAH^n rɔːlɑ̃
    (Nobel 1915)
Rollei
  tdmk for photographic equipment   RŌ-LĪ   'roː,lɑi
Rollo
  pers. name   RAHL-ō   'rɑloː
Rolls-Royce
  tdmk for an English car   RŌLZ-ROIS   ,roːlz'rɔis
Rolo
  tdmk for a candy   RŌ-lō   'roːloː
Rolodex
  tdmk for a rotary card file system   RŌ-luh-DEKS   'roːlə,deks
Rölvaag
  Ole, *US novelist*   RŌL-VAHG   'roːl,vɑg
ROM
  read-only memory   RAHM   'rɑm
Rom
  gypsy man or boy   RŌM, RAHM   'roːm, 'rɑm
Roma [Rome]
  city, Italy   RŌ-muh   'roːmə
Romaic
  modern Greek vernacular   rō-MĀ-ik   roː'meːik
Romain
  pers. name, French   raw-ME^n rɔːmɛ̃
Romaine
  lettuce; pers. name   rō-MĀN   roː'meːn
Romains
  Jules, *pen name of* Louis Farigoule,   raw-ME^n rɔːmɛ̃
    French writer
Romamtiezer
  Biblical name   RŌ-MAM-TĪ-Ē-zuhr, rō-MAHM-tē-EZ-er   ,roː,mæm,tɑi'iːzəʳ,
                                                                                       roː,mɑmtiː'ezer

---

Key (col. 2): a: fad ā: fade ah: father ar: marry aw: law e: fed ē: feed er: merry i: hid ī: hide ō: coat $\overline{oo}$: boot
oi: boy   ow: now   u: put   uh: above   uhr: bird   ch: chop   ng: ring   sh: show   th: thick   <u>th</u>: this   zh: measure

Roman

   1. pert. to Rome *or the* Roman   RŌ-muhn   ˈroːmən
     Catholic Church; *pers. name*

   2. Polish   RAW-MAHN   ˈrɔːˌmaːn

   3. Russian   RUH-MAHN   ˌrəˈmaːn

Romanesque

   architectural style   RŌ-muh-NESK   ˌroːməˈnesk

Romania

   republic, Europe   rō-MĀ-nē-uh, -nyuh   roːˈmeːniːə, -njə

Romanian

   lang., Romania   rō-MĀ-nē-uhn, -nyuhn   roːˈmeːniːən, -njən

Romanic

   derived from Latin   rō-MAN-ik   roːˈmænik

Romanism

   Roman Catholicism   RŌ-muh-NIZ-uhm   ˈroːməˌnizəm

Romano

   cheese   ruh-MAHN-ō, rō-MAHN-ō   rəˈmɑnoː, roːˈmɑnoː

Romanov, Romanoff

   Russian dynasty   ruh-MAHN-uhf, Ⓢ rō-MAHN-AWF,   rəˈmɑːnəf, Ⓢ roːˈmɑnˌɔːf,
                          RŌ-muh-NAWF   ˈroːməˌnɔːf

Romans

   New Testament book   RŌ-muhnz   ˈroːmənz

Romansch, -sh, -tsch

   lang., Switzerland, Italy   rō-MAHNCH, rō-MANCH   roːˈmɑntʃ, roːˈmæntʃ

Romanus

   pope   rō-MĀ-nuhs   roːˈmeːnəs

Romany, Romani [Gypsy]

   people, lang., South Asia, Near East,   RAHM-uh-nē, RŌ-muh-nē   ˈrɑməniˑ, ˈroːməniˑ
     Europe, USA

Rome

   city, Italy   RŌM   ˈroːm

Romeo

   Shakespearean character; pers. name   RŌ-mē-ō   ˈroːmiːoː

Romero

   1. Cesar, *entertainer*   rō-MER-ō, ruh-   roːˈmeroː, rə-

   2. pers. name, Spanish   rō-MĀ-rō, Ⓢ ruh-MER-ō   roːˈmeːroː, Ⓢ rəˈmeroː

Romish

   pert. to Rome *as center of the Roman*   RŌ-mish   ˈroːmiʃ
     Catholic Church

Rommel

   Erwin, *German general*   RAHM-uhl   ˈrɑməl

Romolo

   pers. name, Italian   RŌ-mō-LŌ   ˈroːmoːˌloː

Romulan

   alien race, Star Trek   RAHM-yuh-luhn   ˈrɑmjələn

Romulo

   Carlos, *Philippine diplomat*   RAHM-yuh-LŌ   ˈrɑmjəˌloː

Romulus

   eponymous founder of Rome; pers.   RAHM-yuh-luhs   ˈrɑmjələs
     name

Romulus Augustulus

   last Western Roman emperor   RAHM-yuh-luhs aw-GUHS-chuh-luhs   ˈrɑmjələs ɔːˈgəstʃələs

Ron

   1. lang., Nigeria   RŌN, RAHN   ˈroːn, ˈrɑn

   2. pers. name   RAHN   ˈrɑn

Foreign Sounds: ue: *Fr.* **rue**, *Ger.* **füllen**   uh(r): *Fr.* **boeuf**, *Ger.* **Höhle**   <u>kh</u>: *Ger.* i**ch**, *Scot.* lo**ch**   ğ: *Sp.* ami**g**o   <u>v</u>: *Sp.* ha**b**lar
hl: *Welsh* **Ll**anelli.   CAPITALS: primary stress.   SMALL CAPS: secondary stress.   Ⓢ: U.S. pron.   Ⓔ: British pron.

Rona
  pers. name   RŌ-nuh   'roːnə

Ronald
  1. pers. name   RAHN-ld   'rɑn|d
  2. Norwegian   RŌ-NAHL(D)   'roː‚nɑl(d)
  3. Portuguese   roo̅-NAHLD   ruː'nɑld

Roncesvalles
  village, Spain   rawn(t)-suhs-VAH(L)-YĀS   rɔːn(t)səs'vɑ(l)‚jeːs

Roncevaux
  French for Roncesvalles   rawⁿs(-uh)-VŌ   rɔ̃s(ə)voː

Ronceverte
  city, WV   RAHN(T)-suh-VUHRT   'rɑn(t)sə‚vəʳt

Ronga
  lang., people, Africa   RAHNG-guh   'rɑŋgə

Ronnie, Ronny
  pers. name   RAHN-ē   'rɑniˑ

Ronsard
  Pierre de, *French writer*   rawⁿ-SAHR   rɔ̃sɑr

Ronstadt
  Linda, *US singer*   RAHN-STAT   'rɑn‚stæt

Röntgen
  see Roentgen

Roodepoort-Maraisburg
  city, S. Africa   ROO̅D-uh-PURT-mah-RĀ-BURK   'ruːdə‚puʳtmɑ're ː‚buʳk

Roone
  pers. name   ROO̅N   'ruːn

Rooney
  Mickey, *US actor; pers. name*   ROO̅-nē   'ruːniˑ

Roosevelt
  Eleanor, *US humanitarian (wife of FDR);* Franklin Delano, *32d US president;* Theodore, *26th US president (Nobel 1906); pers. name*   RŌ-zuh-vuhlt *(family's usual pron.),* RŌ-zuh-VELT, ROO̅-   'roːzəvəlt *(family's usual pron.),* 'roːzə‚velt, 'ruː-

Root
  Elihu, *US jurist, statesman (Nobel 1912)*   ROO̅T, RUT   'ruːt, 'rut

Roquefort
  1. town, France   rawk-FAWR   rɔːkfɔːr
  2. tdmk for a cheese   RŌK-fuhrt   'roːkfəʳt

Roris, Sinus
  see Sinus Roris

Rorschach test
  psychological inkblot test   RAWR-SHAHK   'rɔːʳ‚ʃɑk

Rory
  pers. name   RŌR-ē, RAWR-ē   'roːriˑ, 'rɔːriˑ

Ros
  1. pers. name, short for Rosalind, Rosaline   RAHZ   'rɑz
  2. family name   RAWS, RAHS   'rɔːs, 'rɑs

Rosa
  1. pers. name   RŌ-zuh   'roːzə
  2. French   rō-ZAH   roːzɑː
  3. German   RŌ-zah   'roːzɑ
  4. Italian   RAW-zah   'rɔːzɑ
  5. Spanish   RŌ-sah   'roːsɑ

Key (col. 2):   a: f**a**d   ā: f**a**de   ah: f**a**ther   ar: m**a**rry   aw: l**aw**   e: f**e**d   ē: f**ee**d   er: m**e**rry   i: h**i**d   ī: h**i**de   ō: c**oa**t   oo̅: b**oo**t
oi: b**oy**   ow: n**ow**   u: p**u**t   uh: **a**bove   uhr: b**ir**d   ch: **ch**op   ng: ri**ng**   sh: **sh**ow   th: **th**ick   <u>th</u>: **th**is   zh: mea**s**ure

Rosalie
  1. pers. name   RŌ-z(uh-)lē   ˈroːz(ə)liˑ
  2. French   raw-zah-LĒ   rɔːzɑːliː
Rosalind
  pers. name   RAHZ-(uh-)lind, RŌZ-(uh-)lind, -LĪND   ˈraz(ə)lind, ˈroːz(ə)lind, -ˌlaind
Rosaline
  pers. name   RAHZ-(uh-)lin, RŌZ-(uh-)lin, -LĪN   ˈraz(ə)lin, ˈroːz(ə)lin, -ˌlain
Rosalyn, Rosalynn
  pers. name   RŌZ-(uh-)luhn, RAHZ-   ˈroːz(ə)lən, ˈraz-
Rosamond, -mund
  pers. name   RAHS-(uh-)muhnd, RŌZ-   ˈras(ə)mənd, ˈroːz-
Rosanna
  pers. name   rō-ZAN-uh   roːˈzænə
Rosanne
  pers. name   rō-ZAN   roːˈzæn
Rosario
  city, Argentina   rō-SAHR-ē-ō, rō-ZAHR-ē-ō   roːˈsɑriːoː, roːˈzɑriːoː
Roscoe
  pers. name   RAHS-kō   ˈrɑskoː
Roscommon
  county, MI; county, Ireland   rah-SKAHM-uhn   rɑˈskɑmən
Rose
  1. pers. name   RŌZ   ˈroːz
  2. French   RŌZ   roːz
Rosé
  wine   rō-ZĀ   roːˈzeː
Roseau
  county, MN   rō-ZŌ   roːˈzoː
Rosecrans
  pers. name   RŌZ-KRANS   ˈroːzˌkræns
Rosemarie
  pers. name   RŌZ-muh-RĒ, RŌZ-muh-RĒ   ˌroːzməˈriː, ˈroːzməˌriː
Rosemary
  pers. name   RŌZ-MER-ē, RŌZ-MAR-ē, RŌZ-MĀ-rē   ˈroːzˌmeri, ˈroːzˌmæriˑ, ˈroːzˌmeːriˑ
Rosemonde
  pers. name, French   rawz-MAWⁿD   rɔːzmɔ̃d
Rosemontag
  German festival   RŌ-zuh-MŌN-TAHK   ˈroːzəˌmoːnˌtɑːk
Rosencrantz
  character in Hamlet, *Shakespeare*   RŌ-zuhn-KRAN(T)S   ˈroːzənˌkræn(t)s
Rosetta
  Stone, *ancient inscribed tablet*   rō-ZET-uh   roːˈzeʈə
Rosh
  Biblical name   RAHSH, RŌSH, RAWSH   ˈraʃ, ˈroːʃ, ˈrɔːʃ
Rosh Hashanah
  Jewish New Year   RAWSH hah-shuh-NAH, RŌSH (h)uh-SHAW-nuh, RAHSH, RUHSH, (h)uh-SHAHN-uh   ˌrɔːʃ haʃəˈnɑ, ˌroːʃ (h)əˈʃɔːnə, ˌraʃ, ˌrəʃ, (h)əˈʃɑnə
Rosiclare
  city, IL   RŌ-zuh-KLAR, -KLER   ˈroːzəˌklæʳ, -ˌkleʳ
Rosicrucian
  member of an esoteric spiritual movement   RŌ-zuh-KROO-shuhn, RAHZ-uh-KROO-shuhn   ˌroːzəˈkruːʃən, ˌrazəˈkruːʃən

---

Foreign Sounds: ue: *Fr.* **rue,** *Ger.* **füllen**   uh(r): *Fr.* **boeuf,** *Ger.* **Höhle**   kh: *Ger.* **ich,** *Scot.* **loch**   g̱: *Sp.* amigo   v: *Sp.* hablar   hl: *Welsh* **Llanelli.**   CAPITALS: primary stress.   SMALL CAPS: secondary stress.   Ⓢ: U.S. pron.   Ⓔ: British pron.

Rosicrucianism
   tenets of the Rosicrucians   RŌ-zuh-KRŌŌ-shuh-NIZ-uhm,   ˌroːzəˈkruːʃəˌnizəm, ˌrɑzə-
                            RAHZ-uh-

Rosie
   pers. name   RŌ-zē   ˈroːziˑ

Rosillos
   mtn. range, TX   rō-SĒ-(y)uhs   roːˈsiː(j)əs

Rosinante
   Don Quixote's horse   RAHZ-uh-NANT-ē, RŌ-zuh-NANT-ē   ˌrɑzəˈnæntiˑ, ˌroːzəˈnæntiˑ

Rosita
   pers. name   rō-ZĒT-uh   roːˈziːʈə

Roskilde
   prov & town, Denmark   RUHS-KIL-uh   ˈrəsˌkilə

Roslyn
   pers. name   RAHZ-luhn   ˈrɑzlən

Rosminianism
   philosophy   rahz-MIN-ē-uh-NIZ-uhm,   rɑzˈminiːəˌnizəm,
                 rahz-MĒ-nē-uh-NIZ-uhm   rɑzˈmiːniːəˌnizəm

Ross
   pers. name   RAWS, RAHS   ˈrɔːs, ˈrɑs

Rossano
   pers. name, Italian   rō-SAHN-ō   roːˈsɑnoː

Rossellini
   Roberto, *Italian film director*   RŌS-sāl-LĒ-nē   ˌroːsseːlˈliːniˑ

Rosser
   John B., *US mathematician*   RAHS-uhr   ˈrɑsəʳ

Rossetti
   Dante Gabriel, *English painter, poet;*   rō-ZET-ē, rō-SET-ē   roːˈzeʈiˑ, roːˈseʈiˑ
      Christina, *English poet*

Rossignol
   ski manufacturer   RAHS-ēn-YŌL, RAHS-ig-NAHL   ˌrɑsiːnˈjoːl, ˈrɑsigˌnɑl

Rossini
   Gioacchino, *Italian composer*   raw-SĒ-nē, ruh-SĒ-nē   rɔːˈsiːniˑ, rəˈsiːniˑ

Rossiyskaya
   SSR, Russian republic, USSR   raw-SĒ-skuh-yuh   rɔːˈsiːskəjə

Rostand
   Edmond, *French playwright*   raw-STAHⁿ, Ⓢ RAHS-TAND   rɔːstɑ̃, Ⓢ ˈrɑsˌtænd

Rostenkowski
   Dan, *US politician*   RAHS-tuhn-KOW-skē   ˌrɑstənˈkɑuskiˑ

Rostock
   county, Germany   RAHS-TAHK, RAW-STAWK   ˈrɑsˌtɑk, ˈrɔːˌstɔːk

Rostock-Warnemünde
   city, Germany   RAHS-TAHK-VAHR-nuh-MUEN-duh,   ˌrɑsˌtɑkˌvaʳnəˈmyndə,
              RAW-STAWK-   ˌrɔːˌstɔːk-

Rostov
   principality, town, Russia   ruh-STAWF, ruh-STAWV   rəˈstɔːf, rəˈstɔːv

Rostropovich
   Mstislav, *Russian cellist/conductor*   ruhs-TRUH-PAWV-yech,   rəsˌtrəˈpɔːvjiˑtʃ,
              Ⓢ RAHS-truh-PŌ-vich   Ⓢ ˌrɑstrəˈpoːvitʃ

Rotarian
   member of Rotary Club   rō-TAR-ē-uhn, rō-TER-ē-uhn   roːˈtæriːən, roːˈteriːən

Rotary
   business club   RŌT-uh-rē   ˈroːʈəriˑ

Key (col. 2): a: fad ā: fade ah: father ar: marry aw: law e: fed ē: feed er: merry i: hid ī: hide ō: coat ōō: boot
oi: boy ow: now u: put uh: above uhr: bird ch: chop ng: ring sh: show th: thick <u>th</u>: this zh: measure

Roth
David Lee, *rock singer;* Philip, *US writer*   RAWTH, RAHTH   'rɔːθ, 'rɑθ

Rothko
Mark, *Russian-born US painter*   RAHTH-kō   'rɑθkoː

Rothschild
European family financial dynasty   RAWTHS-CHĪLD, RAWTH-CHĪLD, RAWS-, *German* RŌT-SHILT   'rɔːθs,tʃaild, 'rɔːθ,tʃaild, 'rɔːs-, *German* 'roːt,ʃilt

Roto-Rooter
US co.   RŌT-ō-RŌŌT-uhr, RŌT-ō-RŌŌT-uhr   ˌroːtoː'ruːt̬əʳ, 'roːtoːˌruːt̬əʳ

Rototiller
tdmk for a rotary cultivator   RŌT-uh-TIL-uhr   'roːt̬əˌtiləʳ

Rotterdam
city, Netherlands   RAHT-uhr-DAM   'rɑt̬əʳˌdæm

Rottweiler
dog breed   RAHT-WĪ-luhr, RAWT-VĪ-luhr   'rɑtˌwailəʳ, 'rɔːtˌvailəʳ

Rouault
Georges, *French artist*   RWŌ, Ⓢ rōō-Ō   rwoː, Ⓢ ruː'oː

Roubaix
city, France   rōō-BE   ruːbe

Rouen
city, France   RWAHⁿ, Ⓢ ru-AHⁿ, ru-AHN   rwɑ̃, Ⓢ ru'ɑ̃, ru'ɑn

Rouget de Lisle
Claude Joseph, *French composer*   rōō-ZHE duh LĒL   ruːʒe də liːl

Rough Tor
granite hill, Cornwall, England   ROW TAWR   'rau ˌtɔːʳ

Roundhead
member of Parliamentary Party, English Civil War   ROWND-HED   'raundˌhed

Rous
Francis Peyton, *US pathologist (Nobel 1966)*   ROWS   'raus

Rousseau
Jean Jacques, *French philosopher*   rōō-SŌ   ruːsoː

Roussillon
prov, France   rōō-sē-YAWⁿ   ruːsiːjɔ̃

Routledge
British publishing co.   RUHT-lij, ROWT-lij   'rətlidʒ, 'rautlidʒ

Routt
county, CO   ROWT   'raut

Rovno
town, Ukraine   RAWV-nuh   'rɔːvnə

Rowan
1. tree   RŌ-uhn, ROW-uhn   'roːən, 'rauən
2. pers. name   RŌ-uhn, RŌ-AN   'roːən, 'roːˌæn

Rowayton
village, CT   rō-WĀT-n   roː'weitn̩

Rowe
Nicholas, *English poet, dramatist*   RŌ   'roː

Rowena
pers. name   rō-Ē-nuh   roː'iːnə

Rowenta
tdmk for cookware   rō-ENT-uh   roː'entə

Rowland
pers. name   RŌ-luhnd   'roːlənd

Foreign Sounds: ue: *Fr.* **rue**, *Ger.* **füllen** uh(r): *Fr.* **bœuf**, *Ger.* **Höhle** <u>kh</u>: *Ger.* **ich**, *Scot.* lo**ch** g̃: *Sp.* ami**g**o <u>v</u>: *Sp.* ha**b**lar
hl: *Welsh* **Ll**anelli. CAPITALS: primary stress. SMALL CAPS: secondary stress. Ⓢ: U.S. pron. Ⓔ: British pron.

Rowley
   pers. name   ROW-lē, RŌ-lē   'rɑuliˑ, 'roːliˑ

Roxana
   pers. name   rahk-SAN-uh   rɑk'sænə

Roxanna
   pers. name   rahk-SAN-uh   rɑk'sænə

Roxanne
   pers. name   rahk-SAN   rɑk'sæn

Roxburgh
   pers. name   RAHKS-buhr-uh, RAHKS-buh-ruh,   'rɑksbər-ə, 'rɑksbə-rə,
                               RAHKS-bruh   'rɑksbrə

Roxy
   pers. name   RAHK-sē   'rɑksiˑ

Roy
   pers. name   ROI   'rɔi

Roz
   pers. name   RAHZ   'rɑz

Rozelle
   Pete, *US football commissioner*   rō-ZEL   roː'zel

Ruadh
   pers. name, Scots Gaelic   R‾OO-uhth   'ruːəð

Ruaidhri
   pers. name, Irish Gaelic   R‾OO-uh-rē   'ruːəriˑ

Ruanda
   former name of Rwanda   ruh-WAHN-duh, ru-AHN-duh   rə'wɑndə, ru'ɑndə

Ruanda-Urundi
   former territory, Africa   r‾oo-AHN-duh-u-R‾OON-dē   ruː'ɑndəu'ruːndiˑ

Ruapehu
   volcano, New Zealand   R‾OO-uh-PĀ-h‾oo   ˌruːə'peːhuː

Rubaiyat
   poem, Omar Khayyam   R‾OO-bē-AHT, R‾OO-BĪ-AHT, -AT   'ruːbiːˌɑt, 'ruːˌbɑiˌɑt, -ˌæt

Rub al Khālī
   desert, Saudi Arabia   RUB ahl KHAHL-ē, al KAHL-ē   ˌrub ɑːl 'xɑːliˑ, æl 'kɑliˑ

Rubbia
   Carlo, *Italian-born US physicist*   R‾OOB-bē-uh   'ruːbbiːə
     (Nobel 1984)

Rube
   pers. name   R‾OOB   'ruːb

Rubén
   pers. name, Spanish   r‾oo-V‾AN   ruː'βeːn

Rubens
   Peter Paul, *Flemish painter*   RUE-buhns, ⑤ R‾OO-buhnz   'ryːbəns, ⑤ 'ruːbənz

Rubicon
   river, Italy   R‾OO-bi-KAHN   'ruːbiˌkɑn

rubidium
   element   r‾oo-BID-ē-uhm   ruː'bidiːəm

Rubik
   Erno, *Hungarian mathematician*   R‾OO-bik   'ruːbik

Rubik's cube
   puzzle   R‾OO-biks   'ruːbiks

Rubin
   pers. name   R‾OO-buhn   'ruːbən

Rubino
   Italian wine   r‾oo-BĒ-nō   ruː'biːnoː

Key (col. 2):   a: f**a**d   ā: f**a**de   ah: f**a**ther   ar: m**a**rry   aw: l**a**w   e: f**e**d   ē: f**ee**d   er: m**e**rry   i: h**i**d   ī: h**i**de   ō: c**oa**t   ōō: b**oo**t
oi: b**oy**   ow: n**ow**   u: p**u**t   uh: **a**bove   uhr: b**i**rd   ch: **ch**op   ng: ri**ng**   sh: **sh**ow   th: **th**ick   t̲h̲: **th**is   zh: mea**s**ure

Rubinstein

   1. Anton, *Russian pianist &*   R͞OOB-yin-SHTĪN, ⑤ R͞OO-buhn-STĪN   ˌruːbjinˈʃtain,

   composer   ⑤ ˈruːbənˌstain

   2. Artur, *US pianist*   R͞OO-buhn-STĪN   ˈruːbənˌstain

Ruby

   pers. name   R͞OO-bē   ˈruːbiˑ

Rudbeckia

   flower   RUHD-BEK-ē-uh, r͞ood-BEK-ē-uh   ˌrədˈbekiːə, ruːdˈbekiːə

Rüdesheim

   German wine   RUE-duhs-HĪM   ˈryːdəsˌhaim

Rudi

   pers. name   R͞OOD-ē   ˈruːdiˑ

Rüdiger

   pers. name, German   RUE-di-guhr   ˈryːdigəʳ

Rudman

   Warren Bruce, *US politician*   RUHD-muhn   ˈrədmən

Rudolf

   1. pers. name   R͞OO-DAHLF, R͞OO-DAWLF   ˈruːˌdɑlf, ˈruːˌdɔːlf

   2. Czech, Finnish   RUD-AWLF   ˈrudˌɔːlf

   3. Dutch   RUE-dawlf   ˈryːdɔːlf

   4. German, Swedish   R͞OO-DAWLF   ˈruːˌdɔːlf

Rudolph

   1. pers. name   R͞OO-DAHLF, R͞OO-DAWLF   ˈruːˌdɑlf, ˈruːˌdɔːlf

   2. Dutch   RUE-dawlf   ˈryːdɔːlf

   3. German, Norwegian   R͞OO-DAWLF   ˈruːˌdɔːlf

Rudolphe

   pers. name, French   rue-DAWLF   ryːdɔːlf

Rudy

   pers. name   R͞OOD-ē   ˈruːdiˑ

Rudyard

   pers. name   RUHD-yuhrd   ˈrədjəʳd

Rue

   pers. name   R͞OO   ˈruː

Rueil-Malmaison

   suburb, France   rwel-mahl-me-ZAWⁿ   rɥelmaːlmezɔ̃

Rue Morgue

   Murders in the, *story, E. A. Poe*   R͞OO MAWRG   ˈruː ˈmɔːʳg

Rufino

   pers. name, Spanish   r͞oo-FĒ-nō   ruːˈfiːnoː

Rufinus

   Roman cognomen   r͞oo-FĪ-nuhs   ruːˈfainəs

Rufus

   pers. name   R͞OO-fuhs   ˈruːfəs

Rugby

   town, school, England; ball game   RUHG-bē   ˈrəgbiˑ

Ruggero, Ruggiero

   pers. name, Italian   r͞ood-JER-ō   ruːdˈdʒeroː

Ruhamah

   Biblical name   r͞oo-HAHM-uh, r͞oo-HĀ-muh,   ruːˈhɑmə, ruːˈheːmə,

                                     r͞oo-KHAH-mah   ruːˈxɑːmaː

Ruhollah

   pers. name, Persian   ru-HŌ-luh   ruˈhoːlə

Ruhr

   river, industrial area, Germany   RUR   ˈruʳ

Foreign Sounds: ue: *Fr.* **rue**, *Ger.* **füllen** uh(r): *Fr.* **boeuf**, *Ger.* **Höhle** <u>kh</u>: *Ger.* **ich**, *Scot.* **loch** g̃: *Sp.* **amigo** v̱: *Sp.* **hablar**
hl: *Welsh* **Llanelli**. CAPITALS: primary stress. SMALL CAPS: secondary stress. ⑤: U.S. pron. ⓔ: British pron.

Rui
  pers. name, Portuguese, Spanish   R$\overline{OO}$-i   'ruːi
Ruiz
  pers. name, Spanish   r$\overline{oo}$-ĒS, r$\overline{oo}$-ĒTH   ruːˈiːs, ruːˈiːθ
Rukeyser
  Louis, *television economist*   R$\overline{OO}$-KĪ-zuhr, RUK-Ī-zuhr   'ruːˌkɑizəʳ, 'rukˌɑizəʳ
Rumah
  Biblical name   R$\overline{OO}$-muh, r$\overline{oo}$-MAH   'ruːmə, ruːˈmɑ
Rumanian [Romanian]
  lang., Romania   r$\overline{oo}$-MĀ-nē-uhn   ruˈˈmeːniːən
Rumantsch [Romansch]
  lang., Switzerland, North Italy   r$\overline{oo}$-MANCH, r$\overline{oo}$-MAHNCH   ruˈˈmæntʃ, ruˈˈmɑntʃ
Rumba, Rhumba
  dance   RUHM-buh, RUM-buh, R$\overline{OO}$M-buh   'rəmbə, 'rumbə, 'ruːmbə
Rumelia
  division of the Turkish Empire   r$\overline{oo}$-MĒL-yuh, r$\overline{oo}$-MĒ-lē-uh   ruːˈmiːljə, ruːˈmiːliːə
Rumer
  pers. name   R$\overline{OO}$-muhr   'ruːməʳ
Rumpelstiltskin
  fairytale character   RUHM-puhl-STIL(T)-skuhn   ˌrəmpəl'stil(t)skən
Runcie
  Robert, *archbishop of Canterbury*   RUHN(T)-sē   'rən(t)siˈ
Rundgren
  Todd, *US musician, record producer*   RUHN(D)-gruhn, RUHNG-gruhn   'rən(d)grən, 'rəŋgrən
Rundi
  lang., people, Africa   R$\overline{OO}$N-dē   'ruːndiˈ
Rundstedt
  Karl von, *German militarist*   RUN(T)-SHTET   'run(t)ˌʃtet
Runnemede
  borough, NJ   RUHN-ē-MĒD   'rəniːˌmiːd
Runnymede
  meadow, England   RUHN-ē-MĒD   'rəniˈˌmiːd
Runyon
  Damon, *US author*   RUHN-yuhn   'rənjən
Rupert
  1. pers. name   R$\overline{OO}$-puhrt   'ruːpəʳt
  2. German   R$\overline{OO}$-PERT   'ruːˌpeʳt
  3. Swedish   R$\overline{OO}$-puhrt   'ruːpərt
Ruppert
  Stadium, *Kansas City, MO*   R$\overline{OO}$-puhrt   'ruːpəʳt
Rurik, Ryurik
  Scandinavian founder of Russian   RY$\overline{OO}$R-yik, Ⓢ RUR-ik   'rjuːrjik, Ⓢ 'rurik
  dynasty
Ruritania
  fictional country in The Prisoner of   RUR-uh-TĀ-nē-uh, -TĀN-yuh   ˌrurə'teːniːə, -'teːnjə
  Zenda, *A. Hope; state ruled by*
  reactionary court
Rush
  pers. name   RUHSH   'rəʃ
Rushdi
  pers. name, Turkish   ruesh-TUE, Ⓢ RUHSH-dē   ryːʃ'tyː, Ⓢ 'rəʃdiˈ
Rushdie
  Salman, *British author*   RUHSH-dē, RUSH-dē *(his own pron.)*   'rəʃdiˈ, 'ruʃdiˈ *(his own pron.)*

Key (col. 2):   a: f**a**d   ā: f**a**de   ah: f**a**ther   ar: m**a**rry   aw: l**a**w   e: f**e**d   ē: f**ee**d   er: m**e**rry   i: h**i**d   ī: h**i**de   ō: c**oa**t $\overline{oo}$: b**oo**t
oi: b**oy**   ow: n**ow**   u: p**u**t   uh: **a**bove   uhr: b**ir**d   ch: **ch**op   ng: ri**ng**   sh: **sh**ow   th: **th**ick   <u>th</u>: <u>th</u>is   zh: mea**s**ure

Rushmore
  Mount, *National Memorial, SD*   RUHSH-MŌR, RUHSH-MAWR   'rəʃˌmoːʳ, 'rəʃˌmɔːʳ

Rusk
  Dean, *US educator, government*   RUHSK   'rəsk
  official

Ruska
  Ernest, *German physicist (Nobel*   RUS-kuh   'ruskə
  1986)

Ruskin
  John, *English author*   RUHS-kuhn   'rəskən

Russ
  Viking people   RUHS, ROŌS, RUS   'rəs, 'ruːs, 'rus

Russel
  pers. name   RUHS-uhl   'rəsəl

Russell
  Bertrand, *British intellectual (Nobel*   RUHS-uhl   'rəsəl
  1950); pers. name

Russia
  republic, Europe, Asia   RUHSH-uh   'rəʃə

Russian
  pert. to Russia   RUHSH-uhn   'rəʃən

Russification
  process of making Russian   RUHS-uh-fi-KĀ-shuhn   ˌrəsəfi'keːʃən

Russo-
  combining form, Russia or Russian   RUHS-uh, RUHS-uh, RUHSH-uh,   ˌrəsə, 'rəsə, ˌrəʃə, 'rəʃə, -oː
                                     RUHSH-uh, -ō

Russophile
  lover of Russia   RUHS-uh-FĪL, RUHSH-uh-FĪL   'rəsəˌfail, 'rəʃəˌfail

Russophobe
  hater of Russia   RUHS-uh-FŌB, RUHSH-uh-FŌB   'rəsəˌfoːb, 'rəʃəˌfoːb

Rustin
  Bayard, *US activist*   RUHS-tuhn   'rəstən

Rust-Oleum
  US corp.   RUHST-Ō-lē-uhm   ˌrəst'oːliːəm

Rustom
  pers. name   ROŌ-stuhm, RUHS-tuhm   'ruːstəm, 'rəstəm

Rutger
  pers. name   RUHT-guhr   'rətgəʳ

Rutgers
  University, NJ   RUHT-guhrz   'rətgəʳz

Ruth
  Old Testament book; pers. name   ROŌTH   'ruːθ

Ruthenia
  region, E. Europe   roō-THĒN-yuh, roō-THĒ-nē-uh   ruː'θiːnjə, ruː'θiːniːə

ruthenium
  element   roō-THĒ-nē-uhm   ruː'θiːniːəm

Rutherford
  borough, NJ; pers. name   RUHTH-uhr-fuhrd, RUHTH-   'rəðəʳfəʳd, 'rəθ-

Ruthven
  village, Scotland   RIV-uhn, ROŌTH-vuhn, RUHTH-vuhn   'rivən, 'ruːθvən, 'rəθvən

Rutilius
  Roman name   roō-TIL-ē-uhs   ruː'tiliːəs

Rutland
  town, VT; former county, England   RUHT-luhnd   'rətlənd

Foreign Sounds: ue: *Fr.* **rue**, *Ger.* f**ü**llen   uh(r): *Fr.* b**oeu**f, *Ger.* H**öh**le   kh: *Ger.* i**ch**, *Scot.* lo**ch**   ḡ: *Sp.* ami**g**o   v: *Sp.* ha**b**lar
hl: *Welsh* **Ll**anelli.   CAPITALS: primary stress.   SMALL CAPS: secondary stress.   Ⓢ: U.S. pron.   Ⓔ: British pron.

Rutuli
   tribe of Turnus   rōō-TŌŌ-lē   ruˈtuːliˑ

Ruwenzori
   mts., Uganda, Zaire   RŌŌ-(w)uhn-ZŌR-ē,   ˌruː(w)ənˈzoːriˑ,
                          RŌŌ-(w)uhn-ZAWR-ē   ˌruː(w)ənˈzɔːriˑ

Ruy
   1. pers. name, Portuguese   RŌŌ-ē   ˈruːiː
   2. Spanish   rōō-Ē   ruːˈiː

Ružička
   Leopold, *Yugoslav chemist (Nobel*   RŌŌ-ZHICH-kuh, RŌŌ-ZICH-kuh,   ˈruːˌʒitʃkə, ˈruːˌzitʃkə,
   1939)   RŌŌ-ZHITS-kuh   ˈruːˌʒitskə

Rwanda
   country, lang., Africa   ruh-WAHN-duh, ru-AHN-duh, ⒺⒸ   rəˈwɑndə, ruˈɑndə, ⒺⒸ
                          ru-AN-duh   ruˈændə

Rwandan
   pert. to Rwanda   ruh-WAHN-duhn, ru-AHN-duhn, ⒺⒸ   rəˈwɑndən, ruˈɑndən, ⒺⒸ
                          ru-AN-duhn   ruˈændən

Ry
   pers. name (R. Cooder)   RĪ   ˈrɑi

Ryan
   pers. name   RĪ-uhn   ˈrɑiən

Ryazan
   city, Russia   RĒ-uh-ZAHN(-yuh)   ˌriːəˈzɑːn(jə)

Ryle
   Martin, *English radio astronomer*   RĪL   ˈrɑil
   (Nobel 1974)

Ryokei
   pers. name, Japanese   ryō-kā   rjoːkeː

Ryther
   pers. name   RĪ-<u>th</u>uhr   ˈrɑiðəʳ

Ryukyu
   islands, Pacific   rē-(Y)ŌŌ-k(y)ōō   riːˈ(j)uːk(j)uː

Rzeszów
   city, Poland   ZHESH-ŌŌF   ˈʒeʃˌuːf

S

Saab
   Swedish automobile   SAHB   ˈsɑb

Saad
   pers. name, Arabic   sah-AHD   sɑˈɑd

Saale
   river, Germany   ZAHL-uh, SAHL-uh   ˈzɑlə, ˈsɑlə

Saarbrücken
   city, Germany   zahr-BRUEK-uhn, sahr-   zɑʳˈbrykən, sɑʳ-

Key (col. 2):   a: **fad**   ā: **fade**   ah: **father**   ar: **marry**   aw: **law**   e: **fed**   ē: **feed**   er: **merry**   i: **hid**   ī: **hide**   ō: **coat**   ōō: **boot**
oi: **boy**   ow: **now**   u: **put**   uh: **above**   uhr: **bird**   ch: **chop**   ng: **ring**   sh: **show**   th: **thick**   <u>th</u>: **this**   zh: **measure**

Saarinen
    Eero, *US architect*   SAHR-uh-nuhn   'sɑrənən
Saarland
    prov., Germany   ZAHR-LAHNT, ⑤ ZAHR-LAND,   'zɑrˌlɑnt, ⑤ 'zɑrˌlænd,
                                     SAHR-LAND   'sɑrˌlænd
Saar [Sarre]
    European river   SAHR, ZAHR   'sɑr, 'zɑr
Saatchi & Saatchi
    British advertising co.   SAH-chē uhn(d) SAH-chē   ˌsɑːtʃiˑ ən(d) 'sɑːtʃiˑ
Saavedra Lamas
    Carlos, *Argentine jurist (Nobel 1936)* sah-VĀTH-rah LAHM-ahs,   sɑ've:ðrɑ 'lɑmɑs,
                                     ⑤ suh-VĀ-druh LAHM-uhs   ⑤ sə've:drə 'lɑməs
Saba
    island, Netherland Antilles   SĀ-buh, SAHB-uh   'se:bə, 'sɑbə
Šabac
    town, Serbia   SHAH-BAHTS   'ʃɑːˌbɑːts
Sabaean
    pert. to Saba   suh-BĒ-uhn, SĀ-bē-uhn, SAHB-ē-uhn sə'bi:ən, 'se:bi:ən, 'sɑbi:ən
Sabaoth
    1. Biblical name   SAB-ē-AHTH, SAB-ā-AHTH, sa-BĀ-uhth 'sæbi:ˌɑθ, 'sæbe:ˌɑθ,
                                                                        sæ'be:əθ
    2. Sabbath   SAH-bah-ōt   'sɑbɑo:t
Sabaragamuwa
    prov., Sri Lanka   SAHB-uh-ruh-GAHM-o͞o-vuh   ˌsɑbərə'gɑmuˑvə
Sabatier
    Paul, *French chemist (Nobel 1912)* sah-bah-TYĀ   sɑːbɑːtjeː
Sabatini
    Rafael, *English writer;* Gabriela, SAB-uh-TĒ-nē, SAHB-uh-TĒ-nē ˌsæbə'ti:niˑ, ˌsɑbə'ti:niˑ
    tennis player
Sabato
    1. pers. name   suh-BAT-ō, SAB-uht-ō   sə'bæʈo:, 'sæbəʈo:
    2. Italian   SAH-bah-tō   'sɑbato:
Sabazius
    Phrygian god of agriculture   suh-BĀ-zē-uhs   sə'be:zi:əs
Sabbath
    day of worship & rest   SAB-uhth   'sæbəθ
Sabbatical
    pert. to the Sabbath   suh-BAT-i-kuhl   sə'bæʈikəl
Sabean
    Biblical name   suh-BĒ-uhn, SAH-vah-ĒM   sə'bi:ən, ˌsɑvɑ'i:m
Sabellian
    group of early Italian peoples & suh-BEL-ē-uhn   sə'beli:ən
    langs.
Sabellianism
    early Christian theological doctrine suh-BEL-ē-uh-NIZ-uhm   sə'beli:əˌnizəm
Sabena
    Belgian airline   suh-BĒ-nuh, suh-BĀ-nuh   sə'bi:nə, sə'be:nə
Sabetha
    city, KS   suh-BETH-uh   sə'beθə
Sabianism
    star-worshipping religion   SĀ-bē-uh-NIZ-uhm   'se:bi:əˌnizəm
Sabin
    polio vaccine   SĀ-buhn   'se:bən
Sabina
    pers. name, Latin   suh-BĒ-nuh   sə'bi:nə

Foreign Sounds: ue: *Fr.* **rue**, *Ger.* **füllen** uh(r): *Fr.* **boeuf**, *Ger.* **Höhle** kh: *Ger.* **ich**, *Scot.* **loch** ḡ: *Sp.* amigo v̲: *Sp.* hablar
hl: *Welsh* **Llanelli**. CAPITALS: primary stress. SMALL CAPS: secondary stress. ⑤: U.S. pron. ⑤: British pron.

Sabine

  1. river, US; county, TX; parish, LA   suh-BĒN   sə'biːn

  2. ancient people of the Apennines   SĀ-BĬN, ⓔ SAB-ĬN   'seːˌbain, ⓔ 'sæbˌɑin

  3. pers. name   SĀ-BĬN, SĀ-buhn, ⓢ SAB-ĬN, SAB-uhn   'seːˌbain, 'seːbən,

                                              ⓢ 'sæbˌɑin, 'sæbən

  4. French   sah-BĒN   sɑːbiːn

Sabinian

  pope   suh-BIN-ē-uhn   sə'biniːən

Sabinus

  pers. name, Latin   suh-BĪ-nuhs, suh-BĒ-nuhs   sə'bainəs, sə'biːnəs

Sables Saint Émilion

  wine   SAHB-luh SEⁿ tā-mēl-YAWⁿ   sɑːblə sē teːmiːljɔ̃

Sabra

  refugee camp, Lebanon; native Israeli   SAHB-ruh, SAHB-rah   'sɑbrə, 'sɑbrɑ

Sabrina

  pers. name   suh-BRĒ-nuh, suh-BRĪ-nuh   sə'briːnə, sə'brainə

Sabta, Sabtah

  Biblical name   SAB-tuh, sahv-TAH   'sæbtə, sɑv'tɑ

Sabteca, Sabtecah

  Biblical name   SAB-TĒ-kuh, sab-TĒ-kuh,   'sæbˌtiːkə, sæb'tiːkə,

                SAHV-tuh-<u>KHAH</u>   ˌsɑvtə'xɑ

Sabus

  son of Sancus   SĀ-buhs   'seːbəs

Sac

  N. American people   SAK   'sæk

Sac

  county, IA   SAWK   'sɔːk

Sacagawea, -jawea

  Shoshone interpreter   SAK-uh-juh-WĒ-uh, -WĀ-uh;   ˌsækədʒə'wiːə, -'weːə;

                SAK-uh-JAH-wē-uh   ˌsækə'dʒawiːə

Sacandaga

  river, NY   SAK-uhn-DAW-guh, -DAHG-uh   ˌsækən'dɔːgə, -'dɑgə

Sacar, Sachar

  Biblical name   SĀ-KAHR, sah-<u>KH</u>AHR   'seːˌkɑr, sɑ'xɑr

Saccharin

  artificial sweetener   SAK-(uh-)ruhn   'sæk(ə)rən

Sacco

  Nicola, *Italian anarchist executed in*   SAK-ō   'sækoː

  US

Sacha

  pers. name, French   sah-SHAH   sɑːʃɑː

Sacher torte, Sachertorte

  chocolate-apricot cake   ZAH<u>KH</u>-uhr-TAWR-tuh,   'zaxəʳˌtɔːʳtə, ⓢ 'zakəʳˌtɔːʳt,

                ⓢ ZAHK-uhr-TAWRT,   'sakəʳˌtɔːʳt

                SAHK-uhr-TAWRT

Sacheverell

  pers. name   suh-SHEV(-uh-)ruhl   sə'ʃev(ə)rəl

Sachs

  Hans, *German Meistersinger;* Nelly,   ZAHKS, SAKS   'zɑks, 'sæks

  German-born Swedish author

  (Nobel 1966)

Sackville

  pers. name   SAK-vuhl, SAK-VIL   'sækvəl, 'sækˌvil

Saco

  river, NH, ME; city, ME   SAW-kō, SAHK-ō   'sɔːkoː, 'sakoː

Key (col. 2):   a: **fad**   ā: **fade**   ah: **father**   ar: **marry**   aw: **law**   e: **fed**   ē: **feed**   er: **merry**   i: **hid**   ī: **hide**   ō: **coat**   ōō: **boot**
oi: **boy**   ow: **now**   u: **put**   uh: **above**   uhr: **bird**   ch: **chop**   ng: **ring**   sh: **show**   th: **thick**   <u>th</u>: **this**   zh: **measure**

Sacrae Theologiae Baccalaureus
   bachelor of sacred theology, S.T.B.   SA-KRĒ THĒ-uh-LŌ-jē-Ē   'sæˌkriː ˌθiːəˈloːdʒiːˌiː
                                  BAK-uh-LŌR-ē-uhs, -LAWR-ē-uhs   ˌbækəˈloːriːəs, -ˈlɔːriːəs

Sacramento
   city, CA   SAK-ruh-MENT-ō   ˌsækrəˈmentoː

Sacré Cœur
   basilica, Paris, France   sah-krā KUHR   saːkreː kœr

Sadakichi
   pers. name, Japanese   sah-dah-kē-chē   sɑdɑkiːtʃiː

Sadao
   pers. name, Japanese   sah-dah-ō   sɑdɑ-oː

Sadat, al-
   Anwar, Egyptian statesman (Nobel   AHL-suh-DAHT, AL-suh-DAHT,   ˌɑːlsəˈdɑːt, ˌælsəˈdɑt,
     1978)   AL-suh-DAT   ˌælsəˈdæt

Saddam
   pers. name, Arabic   sahd-AHM, ⑤ suh-DAHM, SAD-uhm,   saːdˈɑm, ⑤ səˈdɑm, ˈsædəm,
                                    SAHD-uhm   ˈsɑdəm

Sadduccee
   Jewish sect   SAJ-uh-SĒ, SAD-yuh-SĒ   ˈsædʒəˌsiː, ˈsædjəˌsiː

Sadducean
   pert. to Sadducees   SAJ-uh-SĒ-uhn, SAD-yuh-SĒ-uhn   ˌsædʒəˈsiːən, ˌsædjəˈsiːən

Sadduceeism
   tenets of the Sadduccees   SAJ-uh-SĒ-IZ-uhm, SAD-yuh-SĒ-   ˈsædʒəˌsiːˌizəm, ˈsædjəˌsiːˌ-

Sade
   Marquis de, French novelist   SAHD   sɑːd

Sadie
   pers. name   SĀD-ē   ˈseːdiˈ

Sadoc
   Biblical name   SĀ-DAHK, tsah-DŌK   ˈseːˌdɑk, tsɑˈdoːk

Sadowa
   village, Czech republic   SAHD-uh-VAH   ˈsɑdəˌvɑ

Safar
   Islamic month   suh-FAHR   səˈfɑr

Safer
   Morley, Canadian-born TV journalist   SĀ-fuhr   ˈseːfər

Safid Rud
   river, Iran   sa-FĒD RŌŌD   sæˈfiːd ˈruːd

Safire
   William, US columnist   SAF-ĪR   ˈsæfˌair

Sagadahoc
   county, ME   SAG-uhd-uh-HAHK   ˌsægədəˈhɑk

Sagaing
   city, Burma   suh-GĪNG   səˈgaiŋ

Sagan
   1. Carl, US astronomer   SĀ-guhn   ˈseːgən
   2. Françoise, French writer   sah-GAH[n]   sɑːgɑ̃

Saginaw
   city, county, MI   SAG-uh-NAW   ˈsægəˌnɔː

Sagitta
   constellation   suh-JIT-uh, SAJ-uht-uh   səˈdʒițə, ˈsædʒəțə

Sagittarius
   constellation, sign of the zodiac   SAJ-uh-TER-ē-uhs   ˌsædʒəˈteriːəs

Sagres
   Portuguese beer   SAH-grish, SHAH-gris   ˈsɑːgriʃ, ˈʃɑːgris

---

Saguache
  county, CO   suh-WAHCH   sə'watʃ
Saguaro
  cactus   suh-WAHR-uh, suh-(G)WAHR-ō   sə'warə, sə'(g)warɑː
Saguenay
  river, Canada   SAG-uh-NĀ, SAG-uh-NĀ   'sægə‚neː, ‚sægə'neː
Saguenay-Lac-St.-Jean
  College, Canada   SAG-uh-NĀ-LAHK-se^n-ZHAH^n ‚sægə'neː‚lɑ·ksẽ'ʒɑ̃
Saguntum
  Greek settlement, Spain   suh-GUHN-tuhm   sə'gəntəm
Sahachiro
  pers. name, Japanese   sah-hah-chē-rō   sɑhɑtʃiːroː
Sahara
  desert, Africa   suh-HAR-uh, suh-HER-uh,   sə'hærə, sə'herə, sə'hɑrə
                           suh-HAHR-uh
Sahel
  desert, Africa   suh-HĀL, suh-HĒL, SAH-HEL   sə'heːl, sə'hiːl, 'sɑ‚hel
Sahl
  Mort, *Canadian comedian*   SAHL, SAWL   'sɑl, 'sɔːl
Saïda [Sidon]
  city, Lebanon   SĪD-uh   'sɑidə
Said Mohamed Djohar
  Comoran president   shah-ĒD mō-HAHM-uhd JŌ-HAHR   ʃɑ'iːd moː'hɑməd 'dʒoː‚hɑ^r
Saigon [Ho Chi Minh City]
  city, Vietnam   sī-GAHN, SĪ-GAHN   sɑi'gɑn, 'sɑi‚gɑn
Sailer
  German beer   ZĪ-luhr   'zɑilə^r
Sainsbury
  British retailers   SĀNZ-b(uh-)rē, ⓢ SĀNZ-BER-ē   'seːnzb(ə)ri·, ⓢ 'seːnz‚beri·
Saint, St.
  as an element in US & British names   ⓢ *usually* SĀNT; ⓔ *usually* suhnt   ⓢ *usually* ‚seːnt; ⓔ *usually* sənt
St. Albans
  town, England   suhnt AWL-buhnz, ⓢ sānt   sənt 'ɔːlbənz, ⓢ seːnt
Saint Alphonsus
  College, CT   SĀNT al-FAHN-suhs   ‚seːnt æl'fɑnsəs
Saint Ambrose
  College, IA   sānt AM-BRŌZ   seːnt 'æm‚broːz
St. Andrews
  town, Scotland   suhnt AN-drōōz, ⓢ sānt   sənt 'ændruːz, ⓢ seːnt
St. Anne's
  college, Oxford Univ.   suhnt ANZ, ⓢ sānt   sənt 'ænz, ⓢ seːnt
Saint Anthony's fire
  skin disease   SĀNT AN(T)-thuh-nēz FĪR, ⓔ   ‚seːnt ‚æn(t)θəni·z 'fɑi^r, ⓔ
                           AN-tuh-nēz   ‚æntəni·z
St. Antony's
  college, Oxford Univ.   suhnt AN-tuh-nēz, ⓢ sānt ANT-n-ēz   sənt 'æntəni·z, ⓢ seːnt
                                                   'æntṇi·z
St. Asaph
  city, cathedral, Wales   suhnt AS-uhf, sānt   sənt 'æsəf, seːnt
St. Augustine
  1. early Christian philosopher   SĀNT AW-guhs-TĒN, suhnt,   ‚seːnt 'ɔːgəs‚tiːn, sənt,
                           aw-GUHS-tuhn, uh-GUHS-tuhn   ɔː'gəstən, ə'gəstən
  2. city, FL   SĀNT AW-guhs-TĒN, suhnt   ‚seːnt 'ɔːgəs‚tiːn, sənt

---

Key (col. 2):   a: fad   ā: fade   ah: father   ar: marry   aw: law   e: fed   ē: feed   er: merry   i: hid   ī: hide   ō: coat   ōō: boot
oi: boy   ow: now   u: put   uh: above   uhr: bird   ch: chop   ng: ring   sh: show   th: thick   <u>th</u>: this   zh: measure

St. Austell *town, England*	suhnt AWS-tl, [$] sānt	sənt ˈɔːstl̩, [$] seːnt
Saint Bernard *dog breed*	SĀNT buhr-NAHRD	ˌseːnt bə^{r}ˈnɑ^{r}d
Saint Bonaventure University, *NY*	sānt BAHN-uh-VEN-chuhr	seːnt ˈbɑnəˌventʃə^{r}
St. Catharine's *college, Cambridge Univ.*	suhnt KATH-(uh-)ruhnz, [$] sānt	sənt ˈkæθ(ə)rənz, [$] seːnt
St. Catherine's *college, Oxford Univ.*	suhnt KATH-(uh-)ruhnz, [$] sānt	sənt ˈkæθ(ə)rənz, [$] seːnt
Saint Christopher-Nevis *independent state, West Indies*	sānt KRIS-tuh-fuhr-NĒ-vuhs, suhnt, -NEV-uhs	seːnt ˈkristəfə^{r}ˈniːvəs, sənt, -ˈnevəs
Saint Clair, St. Clair *pers. name*	sānt KLAR, KLER; [£] suhnt KLER, SING-KLER, SIN-KLER	seːnt ˈklæ^{r}, ˈkle^{r}; [£] sənt ˈkle^{r}, ˈsiŋˌkle^{r}, ˈsinˌkle^{r}
St. Cloud *1. city, MN*	sānt KLOWD, suhnt	seːnt ˈklaud, sənt
2. city, France	se^{n} KLOO, [$] sang KLOO	sẽ kluː, [$] sæŋ ˈkluː
St. Croix *island, West Indies; county, WI*	sānt KROI, suhnt	seːnt ˈkrɔi, sənt
St. Cross *college, Oxford Univ.*	suhnt KRAWS, [$] sānt	sənt ˈkrɔːs, [$] seːnt
St. Denis *city, France; city, Réunion Island*	se^{n}d-NĒ, se^{n}-duh-NĒ, [$] SAN duh-NĒ	sẽdniː, sẽdəniː, [$] ˌsæn dəˈniː
St. Dogmaels *village, Wales*	suhnt DAWG-muhlz, sānt, DAHG-muhlz	sənt ˈdɔːgməlz, seːnt, ˈdɑgməlz
St. Donat's *village, Wales*	suhnt DAHN-uhts, sānt	sənt ˈdɑnəts, seːnt
St. Edmund Hall *college, Oxford Univ.*	suhnt ED-muhnd HAWL, [$] sānt	sənt ˈedmənd ˈhɔːl, [$] seːnt
St. Edmund's House *college, Cambridge Univ.*	suhnt ED-muhn(d)z HOWS, [$] sānt	sənt ˈedmən(d)z ˌhaus, [$] seːnt
Sainte Foy *town, Canada*	se^{n}t FWAH	sẽt ˈfwɑː
Saint Elias *mtn. range, N. America*	SĀNT-l-Ī-uhs	ˌseːntl̩ˈɑiəs
Saint Elmo's fire *electrical discharge in storms*	SĀNT EL-mōz FĪR	ˌseːnt ˌelmoːz ˈfɑi^{r}
Saint Émilion *wine*	se^{n} tā-mēl-YAW^{n}	sẽ teːmiːljɔ̃
Saintes, Îles des *islands, Caribbean*	ēl duh SE^{n}T	iːl də sẽt
St.-Étienne *town, France*	se^{n}-tā-TYEN	sẽteːtjen
Saint-Exupéry Antoine de, *French writer*	se^{n}-tāg-zue-pā-RĒ	sẽteːgzyːpeːriː
St. Francois *county, MO*	sānt FRAN(T)-suhs	seːnt ˈfræn(t)səs
St. Gall *canton, Switzerland*	sānt GAWL, suhnt, GAHL	seːnt ˈgɔːl, sənt, ˈgɑl

St. Gallen [St Gall]
  canton, Switzerland   zahng(k)t GAHL-uhn   zaŋ(k)t 'galən

Saint-Gaudens
  Augustus, *US sculptor*   sānt-GAWD-nz   seːnt'gɔːdn̩z

Ste. Genevieve
  county, MO   sānt JEN-uh-VĒV, suhnt   seːnt 'dʒenə,viːv, sənt

Saint Georges
  town, Grenada   sānt JAWR-juhz, suhnt   seːnt 'dʒɔː^{r}dʒəz, sənt

St. Gotthard
  mtn. range, Switzerland   se^n guh-TAHR, Ⓢ sānt GAHT-uhrd, suhnt   sē gətɑːr, Ⓢ seːnt 'gatə^{r}d, sənt

St. Helena
  island, Atlantic; parish, LA; city, CA   SĀNT-l-Ē-nuh, SĀNT-huh-LĒNUH   ˌseːnt]'iːnə, ˌseːnthə'liːnə

St. Helens
  Mount, *volcano, WA*   SĀNT HEL-uhnz   ˌseːnt 'helənz

St. Helier
  city, Channel Islands   suhnt HEL-yuhr, Ⓢ sānt   sənt 'heljə^r, Ⓢ seːnt

St. Hilda's
  college, Oxford Univ.   suhnt HIL-duhz, Ⓢ sānt   sənt 'hildəz, Ⓢ seːnt

St. Hugh's
  college, Oxford Univ.   suhnt HYO͞OZ, Ⓢ sānt   sənt 'hjuːz, Ⓢ seːnt

Saint-Hyacinthe
  College, *MA*   sānt-HĪ-uh-SINTH, suhnt-   seːnt'haiəˌsinθ, sənt-

Saint Ignace
  city, MI   SĀNT IG-nuhs   ˌseːnt 'ignəs

St. Ives
  town, England   suhnt ĪVZ, Ⓢ sānt   sənt 'aivz, Ⓢ seːnt

Saint Jérôme
  Canada   SE^n zhā-RŌM   ˌsē ʒeː'roːm

St. John
  pers. name   sānt-JAHN, Ⓔ SIN-juhn   seːnt'dʒɑn, Ⓔ 'sindʒən

Saint John's
  city, Canada; University, *NY*   sānt JAHNZ, suhnt   seːnt 'dʒɑnz, sənt

St. John's
  college, Oxford Univ., Cambridge Univ.   suhnt JAHNZ, Ⓢ sānt   sənt 'dʒɑnz, Ⓢ seːnt

St. Kitts-Nevis
  state, Caribbean   sānt KITS-NĒ-vuhs, suhnt, -NEV-uhs   seːnt 'kits'niːvəs, sənt, -'nevəs

St. Laurent
  see Yves Saint Laurent

Saint-Laurent
  city, Canada   SE^n luh-RAH^n, SANT law-RENT   ˌsē lə'rɑ̃, ˌsænt lɔː'rent

St. Lawrence
  county, NY; river, US & Canada   sānt LAWR-uhn(t)s, LAHR-uhn(t)s, suhnt   seːnt 'lɔːrən(t)s, 'larən(t)s, sənt

St. Leger
  1. pers. name   sānt LEJ-uhr, Ⓔ suhnt LEJ-uhr   seːnt 'ledʒə^r, Ⓔ sənt 'ledʒə^r
  2. family name   sānt LEJ-uhr, Ⓔ suhnt LEJ-uhr, SEL-in-juhr   seːnt 'ledʒə^r, Ⓔ sənt 'ledʒə^r, 'selindʒə^r

St. Léonard
  town, Canada   se^n lā-aw-NAHR; sānt LEN-uhrd, suhnt   sē leːɔːnɑːr; seːnt 'lenə^{r}d, sənt

St.-Lô
  town, France   se^n-LŌ   sēloː

Key (col. 2):   a: **fad**   ā: **fade**   ah: **father**   ar: **marry**   aw: **law**   e: **fed**   ē: **feed**   er: **merry**   i: **hid**   ī: **hide**   ō: **coat**   o͞o: **boot**
oi: **boy**   ow: **now**   u: **put**   uh: **above**   uhr: **bird**   ch: **chop**   ng: **ring**   sh: **show**   th: **thick**   <u>th</u>: **this**   zh: **measure**

St. Louis

   1. city, MO; river, MN   sānt LŌŌ-uhs, suhnt   seːnt ˈluːəs, sənt

   2. city, France; city, Réunion; city,   se^n LWĒ   sē lwiː

     Senegal

St. Louis encephalitis

   a viral encephalitis   SĀNT LŌŌ-uhs in-SEF-uh-LĪT-uhs   ˌseːnt ˌluːəs inˌsefəˈlaiţəs

Saint Lucia

   island, West Indies   sānt LŌŌ-shuh, suhnt; SĀNT   seːnt ˈluːʃə, sənt; ˌseːnt

      lŌŌ-SĒ-uh   luːˈsiːə

Saint Lucian

   pert. to St. Lucia   sānt LŌŌ-shuhn, suhnt; SĀNT   seːnt ˈluːʃən, sənt; ˌseːnt

      lŌŌ-SĒ-uhn   luːˈsiːən

St. Lucie

   county, FL   sānt LŌŌ-sē, suhnt   seːnt ˈluːsiˈ, sənt

St.-Malo

   seaport, France   se^n-mah-LŌ   sēmɑːloː

Saint Maries

   city, ID   SĀNT muh-RĒZ   ˌseːnt məˈriːz

St. Martin

   island, Caribbean; parish, LA   sānt MAHRT-n, suhnt   seːnt ˈmɑ^{r}tn̩, sənt

Saint-Maurice

   river, Canada   SE^n-muh-RĒS, SĀNT-muh-RĒS,   ˌsē məˈriːs, ˌseːntməˈriːs,

      -MAWR-is, -MAHR-is, suhnt-   -ˈmɔːris, -ˈmɑris, sənt-

Saint Meinrad

   College, IN   SĀNT MĪN-RAD   ˌseːnt ˈmainˌræd

St.-Mihiel

   commune, France   se^n-mē-EL, se^n-MYEL   sēmiːel, sēmjel

St.-Moritz

   commune, Switzerland   se^n-maw-RĒTS, Ⓢ SĀNT muh-RITS   sēmɔːriːts, Ⓢ ˌseːnt məˈrits

St.-Nazaire

   town, France   se^n-nah-ZER   sēnɑːzer

St. Neots

   town, England   suhnt NĒTS, Ⓢ sānt   sənt ˈniːts, Ⓢ seːnt

Saint Olaf

   College, MN   SĀNT Ō-luhf, Ō-luhv   ˌseːnt ˈoːləf, ˈoːləv

St. Olaves

   village, England   suhnt AHL-uhvz, Ⓢ sānt   sənt ˈɑləvz, Ⓢ seːnt

St.-Ouen

   commune, France   se^n-TWAH^n, se^n-TWE^n sētwã, sētwē

St. Pancras

   Christian saint; former borough,   suhnt PANG-kruhs, Ⓢ sānt   sənt ˈpæŋkrəs, Ⓢ seːnt

     London, England

St. Pauli Girl

   beer   sānt PAW-lē GUHRL   seːnt ˈpɔːliˈ ˈgə^{r}l

St. Peter's

   church, Vatican City; college, Oxford   sānt PĒT-uhrz, suhnt   seːnt ˈpiːţə^{r}z, sənt

     Univ.

St. Petersburg

   city, FL; city, Russia [Leningrad]   sānt PĒT-uhrz-BUHRG, suhnt   seːnt ˈpiːţə^{r}zˌbə^{r}g, sənt

St.-Pierre

   town, Réunion   se^n-PYER, Ⓢ sānt-PIR, suhnt-PIR,   sēpjer, Ⓢ seːnt'pi^r, sənt'pi^r,

      SĀNT-pē-ER   ˌseːntpiːˈe^r

Foreign Sounds: ue: *Fr.* **rue**, *Ger.* f**ü**llen   uh(r): *Fr.* b**oeu**f, *Ger.* H**öh**le   <u>kh</u>: *Ger.* i**ch**, *Scot.* lo**ch**   g̃: *Sp.* ami**g**o   <u>v</u>: *Sp.* ha**b**lar
hl: *Welsh* **Ll**anelli.   CAPITALS: primary stress.   SMALL CAPS: secondary stress.   Ⓢ: U.S. pron.   Ⓔ: British pron.

Saint-Pierre & Miquelon

islands, N Atlantic — se^n-PYER ã mē-KLAW^n, ⑤ sãnt-PIR uhn(d) MIK-uh-LAHN, suhnt, pē-ER — sẽpjer eː miːklɔ̃, ⑤ seːnt'pir ən(d) 'mikə,lan, sənt, piː'er

Saint-Saëns

Camille, French composer — se^n-SAH^{n}S — sẽsãs

St. Sixtus

Belgian beer — sãnt SIK-stuhs — seːnt 'sikstəs

St.-Tropez

resort, France — se^n-traw-PÃ — sẽtrɔːpeː

Saint Vincent and the Grenadines

nation, West Indies — sãnt VIN(T)-suhnt uhn(d) thuh GREN-uh-DĒNZ, suhnt — seːnt 'vin(t)sənt ən(d) ðə ˌgrenə'diːnz, sənt

Saint Vincentian

pert. to Saint Vincent — SÃNT vin-SENT-ē-uhn, suhnt, vin-SEN-shuhn — ˌseːnt vin'sentiːən, sənt, vin'senʃən

St. Weonards

town, England — suhnt WEN-uhrdz — sənt 'wenə^{r}dz

Saipan

island, Pacific — sī-PAN, sī-PAHN, SĪ-PAN, SĪ-PAHN — sai'pæn, sai'pan, 'sai,pæn, 'sai,pan

Sait

pers. name, Turkish — SĪT — 'sait

Sakalava

people, Madagascar — SAHK-uh-LAHV-uh — ˌsakə'lavə

Sakhalin

island, Sea of Okhotsk — SUHKH-UHL-YĒN, ⑤ SAK-uh-LĒN, SAK-uh-luhn, SAK-uh-LĒN — ˌsəx,əl'jiːn, ⑤ 'sækə,liːn, 'sækələn, ˌsækə'liːn

Sakharov

Andrei D., Russian physicist, dissident (Nobel 1975) — SAHKH-uh-RAWF, SAHK-, -RAWV — 'saxə,rɔːf, 'sak-, -,rɔːv

Saki

pen name of H.H. Munro — SAHK-ē — 'saki·

Sakmann

Bert, German physician (Nobel 1991) — ZAHK-muhn, ZAHK-mahn — 'zakmən, 'zakman

Sakonnet River

inlet, RI — suh-KAHN-uht RIV-uhr — sə'kanət 'rivə^r

Sakura

Japanese bank — sah-kur-ah, ⑤ suh-KUR-uh — sakura, ⑤ sə'kurə

Sala

pers. name — SAL-uh — 'sælə

Salacia

Roman sea goddess — suh-LÃ-sh(ē-)uh — sə'leːʃ(iː)ə

Saladillo

rivers, Argentina — SAL-uh-DĒ-yaw — ˌsælə'diːjɔː

Saladin

Muslim hero & sultan — SAL-uhd-n, SAL-uh-DIN — 'sælədn̩, 'sælə,din

Salado

river, Cuba; river, Mexico — suh-LAHTH-ō — sə'laðoː

Salado, Río

rivers, Argentina — RĒ-ō suh-LAHTH-ō — ˌriːoː sə'laðoː

Salam

Abdus, Pakistani physicist (Nobel 1979) — sah-LAHM — sa'lam

Key (col. 2): a: fad ã: fade ah: father ar: marry aw: law e: fed ē: feed er: merry i: hid ī: hide ō: coat ōō: boot
oi: boy ow: now u: put uh: above uhr: bird ch: chop ng: ring sh: show th: thick th̲: this zh: measure

Salamanca
   1. city, university, Spain; prov &   SAHL-uh-MAHNG-kuh,   ˌsɑləˈmɑŋkə, ˌsæləˈmæŋkə
      town, Mexico   SAL-uh-MANG-kuh
   2. city, NY   SAL-uh-MANG-kuh   ˌsæləˈmæŋkə
Salambria
   river, Greece   SAHL-ahm-BRĒ-uh, suh-LAM-brē-uh   ˌsɑlamˈbriːə, səˈlæmbriːə
Salamis
   island, town, Aegean; ancient city,   SAL-uh-muhs   ˈsæləməs
      Cyprus
Salamonie
   river, IN   SAL-uh-MŌ-nē   ˈsæləˌmoːniː
Salang
   island, Taiwan   sah-LAHNG   sɑˈlɑŋ
Salathiel
   Biblical name   suh-LĀ-thē-EL, -uhl; shuh-AHL-tē-EL   səˈleːθiːˌel, -əl; ʃəˌɑltiːˈel
Salazar
   Alberto, US runner   SAL-uh-ZAHR   ˈsæləˌzɑʳ
Salcah, Salchah
   Biblical name   SAL-kuh, SAHL-<u>KH</u>AH   ˈsælkə, ˈsɑlˌxɑ
Salecah [Salcah]
   Biblical name   SAL-uh-kuh   ˈsæləkə
Salem
   US pl. name   SĀ-luhm   ˈseːləm
Salerno
   prov & town, Italy   suh-LER-nō, suh-LUHR-nō   səˈleʳnoː, səˈləʳnoː
Salesian
   religious order   suh-LĒ-zhuhn, sā-   səˈliːʒən, seː-
Salian Franks
   ancient Frankish people   SĀ-lē-uhn FRANGKS   ˌseːliːən ˈfræŋks
Salic
   pert. to Salian Franks   SĀ-lik, SAL-ik   ˈseːlik, ˈsælik
Salida
   city, CO   suh-LĪD-uh   səˈlaidə
Salieri
   Antonio, Italian composer   sahl-YER-ē   sɑlˈjeriˑ
Salim
   Biblical name   SĀ-luhm   ˈseːləm
Salina
   1. city, KS   suh-LĪ-nuh   səˈlainə
   2. island, Tyrrhenian Sea   suh-LĒ-nuh   səˈliːnə
Salinan
   N. American people   suh-LĒ-nuhn   səˈliːnən
Salinas
   river, city, CA   suh-LĒ-nuhs   səˈliːnəs
Saline
   pl. name, US   suh-LĒN   səˈliːn
Salinger
   J.D., US writer   SAL-uhn-juhr   ˈsæləndʒəʳ
Salinger
   Pierre, US journalist   SAL-uhn-juhr   ˈsæləndʒəʳ
Salisbury
   city, England; pl. name, US; pers.   SAWLZ-BER-ē, SAWLZ-b(uh-)rē, SALZ-   ˈsɔːlzˌberiˑ, ˈsɔːlzb(ə)riˑ,
      name   ˈsælz-
Salish
   people, lang., N. America   SĀ-lish   ˈseːliʃ

Foreign Sounds: ue: *Fr.* **rue**, *Ger.* **füllen**   uh(r): *Fr.* **boeuf**, *Ger.* **Höhle**   <u>kh</u>: *Ger.* **ich**, *Scot.* **loch**   ḡ: *Sp.* **amigo**   <u>v</u>: *Sp.* **hablar**
hl: *Welsh* **Llanelli**.   CAPITALS: primary stress.   SMALL CAPS: secondary stress.   Ⓢ: U.S. pron.   Ⓔ: British pron.

Salishan
　N. American lang. family　　SĀ-lish-uhn　　　　　'seːliʃən

Salius
　companion of Aeneas　　SĀ-lē-uhs　　　　　'seːliːəs

Salk
　Jonas, *US physician, scientist*　　SAW(L)K　　　　　'sɔː(l)k

Salkehatchie
　river, SC　　SAWL-kuh-HACH-ē　　　　　ˌsɔːlkə'hætʃiˑ

Sallai
　Biblical name　　SAL-ē-Ī, suh-LĀ-Ī, SAL-Ī, sah-LĪ　　　　　'sæliːˌai, sə'leːˌai, 'sælˌai, sɑ'lai

Salle, La
　see La Salle

Salle, Sieur de La
　see La Salle, Sieur de

Sallisaw
　city, OK　　SAL-uh-SAW　　　　　'sæləˌsɔː

Sallu
　Biblical name　　SAL-o͞o, sah-LO͞O　　　　　'sæluː, sɑ'luː

Sallust
　Roman historian　　SAL-uhst　　　　　'sæləst

Sally
　pers. name　　SAL-ē　　　　　'sæliˑ

Salma, Salmah
　Biblical name　　SAL-muh, SAHL-muh, sahl-MAH　　　　　'sælmə, 'sɑlmə, sɑl'mɑ

Salman
　pers. name　　SAL-muhn　　　　　'sælmən

Salmon
　1. river, CT; river, ID　　SAM-uhn　　　　　'sæmən
　2. pers. name　　SAL-muhn　　　　　'sælmən
　3. French　　sahl-MAW^n　　　　　sɑːlmɔ̃

Salmone
　Biblical name　　sal-MŌ-nuh　　　　　sæl'moːnə

Salmoneus
　father of Tyro　　sal-MŌ-nē-uhs, sal-MŌ-n(y)o͞os　　　　　sæl'moːniːəs, sæl'moːn(j)uːs

Salomé
　opera, R. Strauss　　ZAHL-ō-mā　　　　　'zɑloːmeː

Salome
　niece of Herod Antipas; pers. name　　suh-LŌ-mē　　　　　sə'loːmiˑ

Salomon
　1. pers. name, Dutch　　SAH-lō-MAWN　　　　　'sɑːloːˌmɔːn
　2. French　　sah-law-MAW^n　　　　　sɑːlɔːmɔ̃
　3. German　　ZAH-lō-MAWN　　　　　'zɑloːˌmɔːn
　4. Swedish　　SAH-lo͞o-MAWN　　　　　'sɑluːˌmɔːn

Salonica, -ika
　city, Greece　　suh-LAHN-i-kuh, SAL-uh-NĒ-kuh　　　　　sə'lɑnikə, ˌsælə'niːkə

Salop [Shropshire]
　former county, England　　SAL-uhp　　　　　'sæləp

Salopian
　pert. to Salop　　suh-LŌ-pē-uhn　　　　　sə'loːpiːən

Salsify
　plant　　SAL-suh-fē, SAL-suh-FĪ　　　　　'sælsəfiˑ, 'sælsəˌfai

SALT
　Strategic Arms Limitation Treaty　　SAWLT　　　　　'sɔːlt

Key (col. 2):　a: fad　ā: fade　ah: father　ar: marry　aw: law　e: fed　ē: feed　er: merry　i: hid　ī: hide　ō: coat　o͞o: boot
oi: boy　ow: now　u: put　uh: above　uhr: bird　ch: chop　ng: ring　sh: show　th: thick　th̲: this　zh: measure

Salta
prov & town, Argentina	SAHL-tuh	ˈsɑltə

Saltillo
city, Mexico	sahl-TĒ-(y)ō	salˈtiː(j)oː

Salto
prov & town, Uruguay	SAHL-tō	ˈsɑltoː

Salton Sea
lake, CA	SAWLT-n SĒ	ˌsɔːltn̩ ˈsiː

Saltopus
dinosaur	SAWL-tuh-puhs	ˈsɔːltəpəs

Salu
Biblical name	SĀ-lōō, sah-LŌŌ	ˈseːluː, sɑˈluː

Saluda
river, county, SC	suh-LŌŌD-uh	səˈluːdə

Saluki
dog breed	suh-LŌŌ-kē	səˈluːkiˑ

Salus
Roman goddess, protector of health	SĀ-luhs	ˈseːləs

Salut, Îles du
islands, S. America	ēl due sah-LUE	iːl dyː sɑːlyː

Salvador
1. city, Brazil	SAL-vuh-DAWR, SAL-vuh-DAWR	ˈsælvəˌdɔːʳ, ˌsælvəˈdɔːʳ
2. pers. name, Spanish	sahl-vah-THAWR, ⓢ SAL-vuh-DAWR	sɑlvɑˈðɔːr, ⓢ ˈsælvəˌdɔːʳ

Salvador, El
see El Salvador

Salvadoran
pert. to Salvador	SAL-vuh-DAWR-uhn	ˌsælvəˈdɔːrən

Salvator
pers. name, Italian	SAHL-vah-TŌR	ˌsɑlvɑˈtoːr

Salvatore
pers. name, Italian	SAHL-vah-TŌ-rā	ˌsɑlvɑˈtoːreː

Salve Regina
College, *MA*	SAL-vā ruh-JĪ-nuh	ˈsælveː rəˈdʒainə

Salween
river, Asia	SAL-WĒN	ˈsælˌwiːn

Salyut
Soviet space station	SUHL-YŌŌT, sal-YŌŌT	ˌsəlˈjuːt, sælˈjuːt

Salzburg
state, city, Austria	ZAHLTS-BURK; ⓢ SAWLZ-BUHRG, SAHLZ-, -BURG	ˈzalts,buʳk; ⓢ ˈsɔːlz,bəʳg, ˈsɑlz-, -,buʳg

Salzkammergut
Alpine region, Austria	ZAHLT-SKAHM-uhr-GŌŌT	ˈzalt,skaməʳ,guːt

SAM
surface-to-air missile	SAM, ES-ā-EM	ˈsæm, ˌeseːˈem

Sam
pers. name	SAM	ˈsæm

Samanala [Adam's Peak]
sacred mtn., Sri Lanka	SUHM-uh-nuh-luh	ˈsəmənələ

Samangān [Āybak]
city, Afghanistan	SAHM-ahn-GAHN	ˌsamanˈgan

Samantha
pers. name	suh-MAN-thuh	səˈmænθə

Samar
island, Philippines	SAHM-AHR	ˈsam,aʳ

Samaranch
  Juan Antonio, *president,*   SAHM-uh-RAHNCH   ˌsɑməˈrɑntʃ
  International Olympic Committee
Samaria
  ancient city, region, Palestine   suh-MAR-ē-uh, suh-MER-ē-uh   səˈmæriːə, səˈmeriːə
Samaritan
  lang., people, Samaria; generous   suh-MAR-uht-n, suh-MER-uht-n   səˈmærətn̩, səˈmerətn̩
  helper
Samaritanism
  religious doctrine of the Samaritans   suh-MAR-uht-n-IZ-uhm, suh-MER-   səˈmærətn̩ˌizəm, səˈmer-
samarium
  element   suh-MER-ē-uhm, suh-MAR-ē-uhm   səˈmeriːəm, səˈmæriːəm
Samarkand
  city, Uzbekistan   suh-MUHR-KAHNT, ⑤ SAM-uhr-KAND,   səˌmərˈkɑnt,
      SAM-uhr-KAND   ⑤ ˈsæmərˌkænd,
      ˌsæmərˈkænd
Samarra
  town, Iraq   suh-MAHR-uh   səˈmɑrə
Samba
  dance   SAHM-buh   ˈsɑmbə
Sambuca Romana
  liqueur   sam-BŌŌ-kuh rō-MAHN-uh   sæmˈbuːkə roːˈmɑnə
Samgar-nebo
  Biblical name   SAM-GAHR-NĒ-BŌ,   ˈsæmˌgɑrˈniːˌboː,
      SAHM-gahr-nuh-VŌ   ˈsɑmgɑrnəˈvoː
Samgar-nebu [Samgar-nebo]
  Biblical name   SAM-GAHR-NĒ-BUH, -NĒ-BŌŌ;   ˈsæmˌgɑrˈniːˌbə, -ˈniːˌbuː;
      SAHM-gahr-nuh-VŌ   ˈsɑmgɑrnəˈvoː
Samhain
  Celtic pagan festival   SOW-uhn   ˈsauən
Samhita
  Hindu prayers & hymns   SUHM-hi-TAH   ˌsəmhiˈtɑ
Samian
  pert. to Samos   SĀ-mē-uhn   ˈseːmiːən
Samichlaus
  "Santa Claus," Swiss beer   ZAHM-ikh-LOWS   ˈzɑmiçˌlaus
Samlah
  Biblical name   SAM-luh, sahm-LAH   ˈsæmlə, samˈla
Sammy, Sammie
  pers. name   SAM-ē   ˈsæmiˑ
Samnite
  ancient people of Samnium   SAM-NĪT   ˈsæmˌnait
Samnium
  ancient country, central Italy   SAM-nē-uhm   ˈsæmniːəm
Samoa
  island, Pacific   suh-MŌ-uh   səˈmoːə
Samoan
  lang., Samoa Islands, New Zealand,   suh-MŌ-uhn   səˈmoːən
  USA
Samora
  pers. name, Kirundi   sah-MAWR-uh   sɑˈmɔːrə
Sámos, Samos
  island, Greece   SAH-MAWS, ⑤ SĀ-MAHS   ˈsɑˌmɔːs, ⑤ ˈseːˌmɑs

---

Key (col. 2):   a: fad ā: fade ah: father ar: marry aw: law e: fed ē: feed er: merry i: hid ī: hide ō: coat ōō: boot
oi: boy ow: now u: put uh: above uhr: bird ch: chop ng: ring sh: show th: thick th: this zh: measure

Samothrace

island, Aegean Sea — SAM-uh-THRĀS, *in ancient context* SAM-uh-THRĀ-sē — 'sæmə‚θreːs, *in ancient context* ‚sæmə'θreːsiˑ

Samothracia [Samothrace]

Biblical name — SAM-uh-THRĀ-shuh — ‚sæmə'θreːʃə

Samothráki [Samothrace]

island, Aegean Sea — SAHM-ō-THRAHK-ē — ‚samoː'θrakiˑ

Samoyed [Selkup]

lang., Khanti-Mansi region, Russia; dog breed — SAM-uh-YED, SAM-OI-ED, SAM-uh-YED, SAM-OI-ED, suh-MOI-(y)uhd — 'sæmə‚jed, 'sæm‚ɔi‚ed, ‚sæmə'jed, ‚sæm‚ɔi'ed, sə'mɔi(j)əd

Sampang

town, Indonesia — SAHM-PAHNG — 'sam‚paŋ

Samphire

plant — SAM(P)-FĪR — 'sæm(p)‚faiʳ

Sampras

Pete, *US tennis player* — SAHM-pruhs, SAM-pruhs — 'samprəs, 'sæmprəs

Sampson

pers. name — SAM(P)-suhn — 'sæm(p)sən

Samson

1. *pers. name* — SAM(P)-suhn — 'sæm(p)sən
2. *German* — ZAHM-ZAWN — 'zam‚zɔːn

Samson Agonistes

drama, J. Milton — SAM-suhn AG-uh-NIS-TĒZ — 'sæmsən ‚ægə'nis‚tiːz

Samsonite

tdmk for luggage — SAM(P)-suh-NĪT — 'sæm(p)sə‚nait

Samsonov

Aleksandr, *Russian militarist* — SUHM-SAW-nuhf — ‚səm'sɔːnəf

Samsun

prov & town, Turkey — sahm-SOON — sam'suːn

Samsung

tdmk of a Korean electronics firm — sahm-sawng, Ⓢ SAM-SUHNG, SAM-suhng — saːmsɔːŋ, Ⓢ 'sæm‚səŋ, 'sæmsəŋ

Samuel

1. *Old Testament book; pers. name* — SAM-yuh(-wuh)l — 'sæmjə(wə)l
2. *Dutch* — SAH-mue-EL — 'saːmyː‚el
3. *French* — sah-MWEL — saːmɥel
4. *German* — ZAHM-oo-EL — 'zamuː‚el
5. *Polish* — sah-MOO-el — saː'muːel
6. *Spanish* — sahm-WEL — sam'wel

Samuelson

Paul A., *US economist (Nobel 1970)* — SAM-yuh(-wuh)l-suhn — 'sæmjə(wə)lsən

Samuelsson

Bengt I., *Swedish medical chemist (Nobel 1982)* — SAHM-uh-wuhl-SAWN — 'saməwəl‚sɔːn

San [Bushman]

lang., people, Angola — SAHN — 'san

San [Zan]

lang., people, Caucasus Mts., Georgia, Turkey — SAHN — 'san

Sanaa

city, Saudi Arabia — san-AH, SAN-AH — sæn'a, 'sæn‚a

San Agustín

cape, Philippines — SAN AHG-u-STĒN — ‚sæn ‚agu'stiːn

San Andreas
village, CA — SAN an-DRĀ-uhs — ˌsæn ænˈdreːəs

San Andreas Fault
geological fault line, CA — SAN an-DRĀ-uhs FAWLT — ˌsæn ænˌdreːəs ˈfɔːlt

San Andrés
island, town, Caribbean — SAN uhn-DRES — ˌsæn ənˈdres

San Angelo
city, TX — san AN-juh-lō — sæn ˈændʒəloː

San Anselmo
town, CA — SAN an-SEL-mō — ˌsæn ænˈselmoː

San Antonio
river, city, TX — SAN an-TŌ-nē-ō, uhn-TŌ-nē-ō — ˌsæn ænˈtoːniːoː, ənˈtoːniːoː

San Augustine
county, TX — san AW-guh-STĒN — sæn ˈɔːgəˌstiːn

Sanballat
Biblical name — san-BAL-uht, sahn-vah-LAHT — sænˈbælət, sɑnvaˈlɑt

San Benito
county, CA — SAN buh-NĒT-ō — ˌsæn bəˈniːt̮oː

San Bernardino
city, county, CA — SAN BUHR-nuh(r)-DĒ-nō, BUHR-nuhr-DĒ-nō — ˌsæn ˌbərnə(r)ˈdiːnoː, ˌbərˈnərˈdiːnoː

San Blas, Cordillera de
mountain range, Panama — kawr-dē(l)-YER-ah thā sahn BLAHS — kɔːʳdiː(l)ˈjerɑ ðeː sɑn ˈblɑs

Sanborn
David, *singer, songwriter* — SAN-BAWRN — ˈsænˌbɔːʳn

San Bruno
city, CA — san BROO-nō — sæn ˈbruːnoː

San Buenaventura
city, CA — SAN BWEN-uh-ven-T(Y)UR-uh — ˌsæn ˌbwenəvenˈt(j)urə

San Carlos
river, AZ; N. American people; city, CA, Philippines — san KAHR-luhs, KAHR-LŌS — sæn ˈkɑʳləs, ˈkɑʳˌloːs

San Carlos de Ancud [Ancud]
port, Chile — sahn KAHR-lōs thā ahng-KOOTH — sɑn ˈkɑrloːs ðeː ɑŋˈkuːð

Sánchez
pers. name, Spanish — SAHN-chās, SAHN-chāth — ˈsɑntʃeːs, ˈsɑntʃeːθ

Sancho Panza
character in Don Quixote, *Cervantes* — SAHN-chō PAHN-zuh — ˌsɑntʃoː ˈpɑnzə

San Clemente
city, CA — SAN kluh-MENT-ē — ˌsæn kləˈmentiˑ

San Cristóbal
Latin American pl. name — sahn krē-STŌ-vahl, Ⓢ SAN kris-TŌ-buhl — sɑn kriːˈstoːβɑl, Ⓢ ˌsæn krisˈtoːbəl

Sancti Spiritus
prov & town, Cuba — SAHNG(K)-tē SPIR-uh-TOOS — ˌsɑŋ(k)tiˑ ˈspirəˌtuːs

Sanctus
Christian liturgical hymn, part of the Mass — SANG(K)-tuhs, SAHNG(K)-tuhs, SAHNG(K)-TOOS — ˈsæŋ(k)təs, ˈsɑŋ(k)təs, ˈsɑŋ(k)ˌtuːs

Sancus
Sabine god of oath-keeping — SANG-kuhs — ˈsæŋkəs

Sand
George, *pseudonym of* A. Dudevant, *French writer* — sahⁿd, sahⁿ, Ⓢ SAND — sɑ̃d, sɑ̃, Ⓢ ˈsænd

Sandarac
tree — SAN-duh-RAK — ˈsændəˌræk

Key (col. 2): a: fad ā: fade ah: father ar: marry aw: law e: fed ē: feed er: merry i: hid ī: hide ō: coat oo: boot
oi: boy ow: now u: put uh: above uhr: bird ch: chop ng: ring sh: show th: thick th̲: this zh: measure

Sandawe
  lang., people, Tanzania   sahn-DAH-wā   sɑn'dɑwe·

Sandefjord
  port, Norway   SAHN-uh-FYUR   'sɑnə‚fjuʳ

Sandeman
  Port wine   SAHN-duh-mahn, ⑤ SAN-duh-muhn   'sɑndəmɑn, ⑤ 'sændəmən

Sanders
  Richard, *US actor*   SAN-duhrs   'sændəʳs

Sandhurst
  Royal Military Academy, *England*   SAND-HUHRST   'sænd‚həʳst

Sandia
  N. American people   san-DĒ-uh   sæn'diːə

San Diego
  city, county, CA   SAN dē-Ā-gō   ‚sæn diː'eːgoː

San Diego Miramar
  College, *CA*   SAN dē-Ā-gō MIR-uh-MAHR   ‚sæn diː'eːgoː 'mirə‚mɑʳ

San Dimas
  city, CA   san DĒ-muhs   sæn 'diːməs

Sandinista
  political party, Nicaragua   sahn-dē-NĒ-stah, ⑤ SAN-duh-NĒ-stuh   sɑndiː'niːstɑ, ⑤ ‚sændə'niːstə

Sandino
  Augusto César, *Nicaraguan revolutionary*   sahn-DĒ-nō, san-DĒ-nō   sɑn'diːnoː, sæn'diːnoː

Sandø
  pers. name, Danish   SAHN-nuh(r)   'sɑːnnœː

Sándor
  pers. name, Hungarian, Serbo-Croatian   SHAHN-dawr   'ʃɑːndɔːʳ

Sandoval
  county, NM   SAN-duh-VAHL, san-DŌ-vuhl   'sændə‚vɑl, sæn'doːvəl

Sandra
  pers. name   SAN-druh, SAHN-druh   'sændrə, 'sɑ·ndrə

Sandringham
  village, royal residence, England   SAN-dring-uhm   'sændriŋəm

Sandro
  pers. name, Italian   SAHN-drō   'sɑndroː

Sandusky
  river, city, county, OH   suhn-DUHS-kē, san-DUHS-kē   sən'dəski·, sæn'dəski·

Sandvic
  Swedish manufacturing co.   SAHND-vik, ⑤ SAN(D)-vik   'sɑːndvik, ⑤ 'sæn(d)vik

Sandy
  pers. name   SAN-dē   'sændi·

Sandys
  Edwin, *British prelate;* George, *English colonist, poet*   SAN(D)Z   'sæn(d)z

San Eugenio del Cuareim [Artigas]
  town, Uruguay   sahn āu-KHĀN-yō t̲h̲el kwah-RĀM   sɑn eːu'çeːnjoː ðel kwɑ'reːm

San Fernando
  pl. name   SAN fuhr-NAN-dō   ‚sæn fəʳ'nændoː

Sanford
  Isabel, *US actress; pers. name*   SAN-fuhrd   'sænfəʳd

San Francisco
  city, county, CA   SAN fruhn-SIS-kō, fran-SIS-kō   ‚sæn frən'siskoː, fræn'siskoː

San Francisco, Rio
  river, NM, AZ   RĒ-ō SAN fruhn-SIS-kō, fran-SIS-kō   'riːoː ˌsæn frənˈsiskoː,
                                                                           frænˈsiskoː

San Francisco de Macorís
  town, Dominican Republic   SAN fruhn-SIS-kō dā MAHK-uh-RIS,   ˌsæn frənˈsiskoː deː
                              fran-SIS-kō   ˌmakəˈris, frænˈsiskoː

San Francisco Gotera
  city, El Salvador   SAN fruhn-SIS-kō gō-TĀ-ruh,   ˌsæn frənˈsiskoː goːˈteːrə,
                              fran-SIS-kō   frænˈsiskoː

San Gabriel
  river, city, CA   san GĀ-brē-uhl   sæn ˈgeːbriːəl

Sangamon
  State University, *river, county, IL*   SANG-guh-muhn   ˈsæŋgəmən

San Gennaro
  Italian name for St. Januarius   SAN je-NAR-ō, je-NER-ō   ˌsæn dʒeˈnæroː, dʒeˈnero

Sanger
  1. Frederick, *English biochemist*   SANG-uhr   ˈsæŋərʳ
    (Nobel 1958, 1980); Margaret, *US*
    women's rights leader
  2. pers. name   SANG-uhr, SANG-guhr   ˈsæŋərʳ, ˈsæŋgərʳ

Sangir
  lang., people, Sangihe, Talaud,   SAHNG-IR   ˈsaŋˌiʳ
    Philippine Islands

Sango
  lang., Africa   SAHNG-gō   ˈsaŋgoː

Sangre
  alcoholic drink   SAHNG-grā   ˈsaŋgreː

Sangre de Cristo
  mtn. range, CO, NM   SANG-grē duh KRIS-tō   ˌsæŋgriː də ˈkristoː

Sangria
  alcoholic drink   sang-GRĒ-uh, sahng-   sæŋˈgriːə, saŋ-

Sanhedrin
  ancient Jewish council   san-HED-ruhn, sahn-HED-ruhn,   sænˈhedrən, sanˈhedrən,
                              san-HĒ-druhn   sænˈhiːdrən

Sanilac
  county, MI   SAN-l-AK   ˈsænl̩ˌæk

Sanibel
  Island, *FL*   SAN-uh-buhl, SAN-uh-BEL   ˈsænəbəl, ˈsænəˌbel

San Ildefonso
  N. American people   SAN IL-duh-FAHN(T)-sō   ˌsæn ˌildəˈfan(t)soː

San Jacinto
  US pl. name   SAN juh-SINT-ō, SAN huh-SINT-ō,   ˌsæn dʒəˈsintoː, ˌsæn
                              -SINT-uh   həˈsintoː, -ˈsintə

San Joaquin
  river, valley, county, CA   SAN wah-KĒN, san waw-KĒN   ˌsæn waˈkiːn, sæn wɔːˈkiːn

San Jorge
  Latin American pl. name   sahn KHAWR-ḡā, Ⓢ san HAWR-hä   san ˈxɔːrɣeː, Ⓢ sæn ˈhɔːʳheː

San José
  1. city, CA   SAN ō-ZĀ, SAN uh-ZĀ   ˌsæn oːˈzeː, ˌsæn əˈzeː
  2. prov, city, Costa Rica; dept.,   sahn haw-SĀ, Ⓢ SAN ō-ZĀ, SAN   san hɔːˈseː, Ⓢ ˌsæn oːˈzeː,
    Uruguay   uh-ZĀ   ˌsæn əˈzeː

San Juan
  pl. name   san (H)WAHN   sæn ˈ(h)wan

Sankhya
  system of Hindu philosophy   SAHNGK-yuh   ˈsaŋkjə

Key (col. 2): a: fad ā: fade ah: father ar: marry aw: law e: fed ē: feed er: merry i: hid ī: hide ō: coat ōō: boot
oi: boy ow: now u: put uh: above uhr: bird ch: chop ng: ring sh: show th: thick th̲: this zh: measure

San Leandro
   city, CA   SAN lē-AN-drō   ˌsæn liːˈændroː

San Lucas, Cabo
   southernmost point of Baja   KAH-v̠ō sahn LŌŌ-kahs   ˌkaβoː san ˈluːkas
   California, Mexico

San Luis
   1. prov & town, Argentina; city, Cuba   sahn lu-ĒS   san luˈiːs
   2. city, CO   san LŌŌ-uhs   sæn ˈluːəs

San Luiseño
   Band, N. American people   SAN LŌŌ-i-SĀN-yō   ˌsæn ˌluːiˈseːnjoː

San Luis Obispo
   city, county, CA   SAN LŌŌ-uhs uh-BIS-pō   ˌsæn ˌluːəs əˈbispoː

San Luis Potosí
   state, Mexico   SAHN lu-ĒS PŌT-uh-SĒ   ˌsan luˌiːs ˌpoːt̠əˈsiː

San Manuel
   Indian reservation, US   SAN muhn-WEL, mahn-WEL   ˌsæn mənˈwel, manˈwel

San Marcos
   1. city, CA, TX   san MAHR-kuhs   sæn ˈmɑʳkəs
   2. Guatemala   sahn MAHR-kōs   san ˈmarkoːs

San Marinese, Sanmarinese
   pert. to San Marino   SAN-MAR-uh-NĒZ, -NĒS   ˌsæn,mærəˈniːz, -ˈniːs

San Marino
   repuplic, city, Europe   SAN muh-RĒ-nō   ˌsæn məˈriːnoː

San Martín
   town, Argentina   SAN mahr-TĒN   ˌsæn mɑʳˈtiːn

San Mateo
   city, county, CA   SAN muh-TĀ-ō   ˌsæn məˈteːoː

San Miguel
   1. river, CO; county, CO, NM   SAN muh-GIL   ˌsæn məˈgil
   2. city, El Salvador; island,   sahn mē-ǦEL, Ⓢ SAN muh-GEL   san miːˈɣel, Ⓢ ˌsæn məˈgel
   Philippines; Philippine beer

San Pasqual
   Indian reservation, US   SAN puh-SKWAWL, puh-SKWAHL   ˌsæn pəˈskwɔːl, pəˈskwal

San Patricio
   county, TX   SAN puh-TRISH-ē-Ō   ˌsæn pəˈtriʃiːˌoː

Sanpete
   county, UT   SAN-PĒT   ˈsæn,piːt

San Quentin
   prison, town, CA   san KWENT-n, sang   sæn ˈkwentn̩, sæŋ

San Rafael
   1. city, CA; river, UT   SAN ruh-FEL   ˌsæn rəˈfel
   2. town, Argentina; national park,   SAN RAH-fē-EL   ˌsæn ˌrafiːˈel
   Chile

San Remo
   1. port, Italy   sahn RĀ-mō, san RĒ-mō   san ˈreːmoː, sæn ˈriːmoː
   2. community, NY   san RĒ-mō   sæn ˈriːmoː

San Saba
   county, TX   san SAB-uh   sæn ˈsæbə

San Salvador
   island, Bahamas   sahn sahl-vah-THAWR, Ⓢ san   san salvaˈðɔːr, Ⓢ sæn
                             SAL-vuh-DAWR   ˈsælvəˌdɔːʳ

Sansannah
   Biblical name   san-SAN-uh, SAHN-sahn-AH   sænˈsænə, ˌsansanˈɑː

Foreign Sounds: ue: *Fr.* **rue**, *Ger.* füllen   uh(r): *Fr.* **boeuf**, *Ger.* Höhle   <u>kh</u>: *Ger.* i<u>ch</u>, *Scot.* lo<u>ch</u>   ḡ: *Sp.* ami**g**o   v̠: *Sp.* ha**b**lar
hl: *Welsh* **Ll**anelli.   CAPITALS: primary stress.   SMALL CAPS: secondary stress.   Ⓢ: U.S. pron.   Ⓔ: British pron.

San Sebastián
   pl. name   SAN suh-bast-YAHN, SAN   ˌsæn səbæst'jɑn, ˌsæn
                             suh-BAS-chuhn   sə'bæstʃən

Sanskrit
   ancient lang., India   SAN-SKRIT, SAN-skruht   'sænˌskrit, 'sænskrət

Sanskritic
   pert. to Sanskrit   san-SKRIT-ik   sæn'skriţik

Santa
   1. see Santa Claus
   2. pers. name, Italian, Spanish   SAHN-tah   'sɑntɑ

Santa [Pao-an]
   lang., China   SAHN-TAH   'sɑn'tɑ

Santa Ana
   1. city, CA; strong, hot wind in CA   SANT-uh AN-uh   ˌsæntə 'ænə
   2. prov & town, El Salvador   SAHNT-uh AHN-uh   ˌsɑntə 'ɑnə

Santa Barbara
   city, county, CA   SANT-uh BAHR-b(uh-)ruh   ˌsæntə 'bɑʳb(ə)rə

Santa Catalina
   islands, CA   SANT-uh KAT-l-Ē-nuh   ˌsæntə ˌkætļ'iːnə

Santa Clara
   1. river, city, county, CA; N.   SANT-uh KLAR-uh, KLER-uh   ˌsæntə 'klærə, 'klerə
     American people
   2. city, Cuba   sahn-tah KLAHR-ah   sɑntɑ 'klɑrɑ

Santa Claus
   Christmas folk figure   SANT-uh KLAWZ, SANT-ē KLAWZ   'sæntə ˌklɔːz, 'sæntiˑ ˌklɔːz

Santa Cruz
   1. river, AZ; county, AZ, CA; city, CA   SANT-uh KRŌŌZ, SANT-uh KRŌŌZ   'sæntə ˌkruːz, ˌsæntə 'kruːz
   2. pl. name, S. America, Philippines;   sahn-tah KRŌŌS   sɑntɑ 'kruːs
     islands, Pacific

Santa Cruz de Mayo
   Philippine festival   SAHN-tah KRŌŌS thā MĪ-ō   ˌsɑntɑ 'kruːs ðeː 'mɑioː

Santa Cruz de Tenerife
   prov, Canary Islands   SAHN-tah KRŌŌS thā TEN-uh-RĒ-fā   ˌsɑntɑ 'kruːs ðeː ˌtenə'riːfeː

Santa Fe
   city, NM   SANT-uh FĀ, SANT-uh FĀ   ˌsæntə 'feː, 'sæntə ˌfeː

Santali
   lang., India   SUHN-TAHL-ē   ˌsən'tɑliˑ

Santa María
   pl. name   SANT-uh muh-RĒ-uh   ˌsæntə mə'riːə

Santa Monica
   city, CA   SANT-uh MAHN-i-kuh   ˌsæntə 'mɑnikə

Santana
   Carlos, *rock guitarist*   san-TAN-uh   sæn'tænə

Santander
   prov & town, Colombia   SAHN-tahn-DER   ˌsɑntɑn'der

Santarém
   prov & town, Brazil   SAHNT-uh-REM   ˌsɑntə'rem

Santa Rosa
   city, CA   SANT-uh RŌ-zuh   ˌsæntə 'roːzə

Santa Sophia [Hagia Sophia, Aya Sofia]
   museum, mosque, church, Istanbul   SAHN-tuh sō-FĒ-uh   ˌsɑntə soː'fiːə

Santayana
   George, *Spanish philosopher*   SANT-uh-YAHN-uh, SANT-ē-AHN-uh,   ˌsæntə'jɑnə, ˌsæntiː'ɑnə,
                                 SAHNT-   ˌsɑnt-

Key (col. 2): a: fad ā: fade ah: father ar: marry aw: law e: fed ē: feed er: merry i: hid ī: hide ō: coat ōō: boot
oi: boy ow: now u: put uh: above uhr: bird ch: chop ng: ring sh: show th: thick th: this zh: measure

Santa Ynez

Band, *N. American people* — SANT-uh ē-NEZ — ˌsæntə iːˈnez

Santee

N. American people — san-TĒ — sænˈtiː

Santeria

Voodoo sect — SAHNT-uh-RĒ-uh — ˌsɑntəˈriːə

Santha

pers. name, Bengali — SHAHN-tuh — ˈʃɑntə

Santiago

1. city, Chile — sahn-TYAHḠ-ō, Ⓢ SAHNT-ē-AHG-ō, SANT-ē-AHG-ō — sɑnˈtjɑɣoː, Ⓢ ˌsɑntiːˈɑgoː, ˌsæntiːˈɑgoː

2. pers. name, Spanish — sahn-TYAHḠ-ō — sɑnˈtjɑɣoː

Santiago de Cuba

prov & town, Cuba — sahn-TYAHḠ-ō t͟hā KOO-buh, Ⓢ SANT-ē-AHG-ō duh KYOO-buh — sɑnˈtjɑɣoː ðeː ˈkuːbə, Ⓢ ˌsæntiːˈɑgoː də ˈkjuːbə

Santiago Fiesta

Puerto Rican festival — SANT-ē-AHG-ō fē-EST-uh — ˌsæntiːˈɑgoː fiːˈestə

Santiam

river, OR — SANT-ē-AM — ˌsæntiːˈæm

Santo Domingo

city, Dominican Republic — sahn-tō t͟haw-MING-gō, Ⓢ SANT-uh duh-MING-gō — sɑntoː ðɔːˈmiŋgoː, Ⓢ ˌsæntə dəˈmiŋgoː

Santorin [Thera]

island, Greece — SANT-uh-RĒN — ˌsæntəˈriːn

Santoríni [Thera]

island, Greece — SANT-uh-RĒ-nē — ˌsæntəˈriːniˑ

Santos

1. city, Brazil — SAHN-tōs, Ⓢ SANT-uhs — ˈsɑntoːs, Ⓢ ˈsæntəs

2. pers. name, Spanish — SAHN-tōs — ˈsɑntoːs

San Vicente

dept, El Salvador — sahn bē-THĀN-tā, bē-SĀN-tā, Ⓢ SAN vuh-SENT-ē — sɑn biːˈθeːnteː, biːˈseːnteː, Ⓢ ˌsæn vəˈsentiˑ

San Xavier

Indian reservation, US — SAN hahv-YER, sahn k͟hahv-YER — ˌsæn hɑvˈjeʳ, sɑn xɑvˈjer

Sanyo

Japanese electronics co. — sahn-yō, Ⓢ SAN-yō — sɑnjoː, Ⓢ ˈsænjoː

São Francisco

island, river, city, Brazil — SOW(M) fruhn-SIS-koo — ˌsɑū(m) frənˈsiskuː

São Luis

island, seaport, Brazil — SOWⁿ lu-ĒS — ˌsɑū luˈiːs

São Miguel

island, Azores — SOWⁿ mi-GEL — ˌsɑū miˈgel

Saône

river, France — SŌN — soːn

São Paulo

state, city, Brazil — sow(m) POW-loo, -lō — sɑū(m) ˈpɑuluː, -loː

Saorstat Eireann

Gaelic name for Irish Free State — SĀR-STAWT ER-(y)uhn — ˌseːʳˌstɔːt ˈer(j)ən

São Salvador

port, Brazil — SOWⁿ sahl-vuh-DAWR, sowⁿ SAHL-vuh-DAWR — ˌsɑū sɑːlvəˈdɔːʳ, sɑū ˈsɑːlvəˌdɔːʳ

São Tiago

islands, Cape Verde — sowⁿ(n) TYAHG-oo — sɑū(n) ˈtjɑguː

São Tomé

island, Africa — SOWⁿ(N) tuh-MĀ — ˌsɑū(n) təˈmeː

Foreign Sounds: ue: *Fr.* **rue**, *Ger.* **füllen** uh(r): *Fr.* **boeuf**, *Ger.* **Höhle** k͟h: *Ger.* i**ch**, *Scot.* lo**ch** ḡ: *Sp.* ami**g**o v: *Sp.* ha**b**lar hl: *Welsh* **Ll**anelli. CAPITALS: primary stress. SMALL CAPS: secondary stress. Ⓢ: U.S. pron. Ⓔ: British pron.

Sao Tomean
  pert. to São Tomé   SOWⁿ(N) tuh-MĀ-uhn   ˌsaũ(n) təˈmeːən

Sao Tome and Principe
  republic, Africa   SOWⁿ(N) tuh-MĀ uhn(d)   ˌsaũ(n) təˈmeː ən(d)
                 PRIN-suh-puh   ˈprinsəpə

São Tomé e Príncipe
  republic, Africa   SOWⁿ(N) tuh-ME ā PRIⁿ(N)-suh-puh   ˌsaũ(n) təˈme eː ˈpr(n)səpə

Saph
  Biblical name   SAF, SAHF   ˈsæf, ˈsɑf

Saphir
  Biblical name   SĀ-fuhr, shah-FĒR   ˈseːfəʳ, ʃɑˈfiːr

Sapir
  Edward, *US anthropologist, linguist*   suh-PIR   səˈpiʳ

Sapodilla
  tree   SAP-uh-DIL-uh, SAP-uh-DĒ-(y)uh   ˌsæpəˈdilə, ˌsæpəˈdiː(j)ə

Sapphic
  pert. to Sappho   SAF-ik   ˈsæfik

Sapphira
  Biblical name   suh-FĪ-ruh   səˈfairə

Sappho
  Greek poet   SAF-ō   ˈsæfoː

Sapporo
  city, Japan; tdmk for a Japanese beer   sahp-pōr-ō   sɑppoːroː

Saqqara
  village, Egypt   suh-KAHR-uh   səˈkɑrə

Sara
  1. African people   SAHR-uh   ˈsɑʳə
  2. pers. name   SER-uh, SAR-uh, SĀ-ruh   ˈserə, ˈsærə, ˈseːrə
  3. French   sah-RAH   sɑːrɑː

Saracen
  nomadic people, Syria, Arabia;   SAR-uh-suhn   ˈsærəsən
    former name for Arabs

Saracenic
  pert. to the Saracens   SAR-uh-SEN-ik   ˌsærəˈsenik

Saracoğlu
  Šükrü, *Turkish politician*   suh-RAHJ-ō-GLUE   səˈrɑdʒoːˌglyː

Saragossa
  prov, city, Spain   SAR-uh-GAHS-uh   ˌsærəˈgɑsə

Sarah
  1. pers. name   SER-uh, SAR-uh, SĀ-ruh   ˈserə, ˈsærə, ˈseːrə
  2. French   sah-RAH   sɑːrɑː

Sarai [Sarah]
  Biblical name   SĀ-RĪ, SER-Ī, sah-RĪ   ˈseːˌrai, ˈserˌai, sɑˈrai

Sarajevo
  city, Bosnia and Herzegovina   SAHR-uh-ye-VAW, Ⓢ SAR-uh-YĀ-vō   ˈsɑrɑjeˌvɔː, Ⓢ ˌsærəˈjeːvoː

Sarakole
  African people   SAR-uh-KŌL, SAR-uh-KŌL   ˌsærəˈkoːl, ˈsærəˌkoːl

Saranac
  river, lakes, NY   SAR-uh-NAK   ˈsærəˌnæk

Sarandon
  Susan, *US actress;* Chris, *US actor*   suh-RAN-duhn   səˈrændən

Saraph
  Biblical name   SĀ-RAF, SER-AF, sah-RAHF   ˈseːˌræf, ˈserˌæf, sɑˈrɑf

Sarasota
  city, FL   SAR-uh-SŌT-uh   ˌsærəˈsoːʈə

Key (col. 2):   aː **fad**   āː **fade**   ahː **father**   arː **marry**   awː **law**   eː **fed**   ēː **feed**   erː **merry**   iː **hid**   īː **hide**   ōː **coat**   ōōː **boot**
oiː **boy**   owː **now**   uː **put**   uhː **above**   uhrː **bird**   chː **chop**   ngː **ring**   shː **show**   thː **thick**   <u>th</u>ː **this**   zhː **measure**

Saratoga
  city, CA; race track, NY SAR-uh-TŌ-guh ˌsærə'toːgə
Saratov
  city, region, Russia suh-RAHT-uhf sə'rɑːʈəf
Sarawak
  state, Malaysia suh-RAH-wah(k), suh-RAH-WAK sə'rɑwɑ(k), sə'rɑˌwæk
Sarbanes
  Paul Spyros, *US politician* SAHR-BĀNZ 'sɑʳˌbeːnz
Sardanapalian
  pert. to Sardanapalus SAHRD-n-uh-PĀ-lē-uhn, SAHR-duh-nuh- ˌsɑʳdn̩ə'peːliːən, ˌsɑʳdənə-
Sardanapalus
  legendary decadent Assyrian king SAHRD-n-AP-uh-luhs, ˌsɑʳdn̩'æpələs,
    SAHR-duh-NAP-uh-luhs   ˌsɑʳdə'næpələs
Sardar
  pers. name, Afghan SAHR-DAHR 'sɑʳˌdɑʳ
Sardegna [Sardinia]
  island, Mediterranean sahr-DĀN-yuh sɑʳ'deːnjə
Sardes
  ancient city, Asia Minor SAHRD-ēz 'sɑʳdiːz
Sardinia
  island, Mediterranean sahr-DIN-ē-uh, sahr-DIN-yuh sɑʳ'diniːə, sɑʳ'dinjə
Sardinian
  pert. to Sardinia sahr-DIN-ē-uhn, sahr-DIN-yuhn sɑʳ'diniːən, sɑʳ'dinjən
Sardis
  ancient city, Asia Minor SAHRD-uhs 'sɑʳdəs
Sardite
  Biblical name SAHR-DĪT 'sɑʳˌdɑit
Sarepta
  Biblical name suh-REP-tuh sə'reptə
Sargasso Sea
  region of Atlantic Ocean sahr-GAS-ō SĒ sɑʳˌgæsoː 'siː
Sargeant, Sargent
  pers. name SAHR-juhnt 'sɑʳdʒənt
Sargon
  ruler of Akkad; king of Assyria SAHR-GAHN, SAHR-guhn 'sɑʳˌgɑn, 'sɑʳgən
Sarid
  Biblical name SĀ-rid, SAR-id, sah-RĒD 'seːrid, 'særid, sɑ'riːd
Sarita
  village, TX suh-RĒT-uh sə'riːʈə
Sarmatia
  ancient region, eastern Europe sahr-MĀ-shuh sɑʳ'meːʃə
Sarmatian
  pert. to Sarmatia sahr-MĀ-shuhn sɑʳ'meːʃən
Sarnia
  port, Ontario, Canada SAHR-nē-uh 'sɑʳniːə
Saron
  Biblical name SĀ-RAHN 'seːˌrɑn
Saronic
  pert. to saros, 18-year astronomical suh-RAHN-ik sɔ'rɑnik
    period
Saroyan
  William, *US writer* suh-ROI-(y)uhn sə'rɔi(j)ən
Sarpedon
  Lycian hero in Odyssey sahr-PĒD-n sɑʳ'piːdn̩

Foreign Sounds: **ue:** *Fr.* **rue**, *Ger.* füllen **uh(r):** *Fr.* **boeuf**, *Ger.* Höhle **kh:** *Ger.* **ich**, *Scot.* lo**ch** ḡ: *Sp.* amigo v: *Sp.* hablar
hl: *Welsh* Llanelli. CAPITALS: primary stress. SMALL CAPS: secondary stress. Ⓢ: U.S. pron. Ⓔ: British pron.

Sarre		
French name of Saar	SAHR	sɑːr
Sarsechim, Sar-sekim		
Biblical name	SAHR-suh-kim, SAHR-SĒ-kim, SAHR-suh-KHĒM	'sɑʳsəkim, ˌsɑʳ'siːkim, ˌsɑrsə'xiːm
Sarsi		
N. American people	SAHR-sē	'sɑʳsi·
Sarto, del		
Andrea, *Florentine artist*	del SAHR-tō	del 'sɑʳtoː
Sartre		
Jean Paul, *French philosopher (Nobel 1964)*	SAHRTR, [S] SAHRT, SAHR-truh	sɑːrtr, [S] 'sɑʳt, 'sɑʳtrə
Saruch		
Biblical name	SĀ-ruhk, SER-uhk, SAR-uhk	'seːrək, 'serək, 'særək
Sarvepalli		
pers. name, Hindi	SUHR-vuh-PUHL-lē	ˌsəʳvə'pəlli·
SASE		
self-addressed stamped envelope	ES-Ā-ES-Ē, SĀ-zē	ˌesˌeːˌes'iː, 'seːzi·
Sasha		
pers. name	SAHSH-uh, SASH-uh	'sɑʃə, 'sæʃə
Saskatchewan		
river, province, Canada	suh-SKACH-uh-wuhn, sas-KACH-, -uh-WAHN	sə'skætʃəwən, sæs'kætʃ-, -əˌwɑn
Saskatoon		
town, Canada	SAS-kuh-TO͞ON	ˌsæskə'tuːn
Sasquatch [Big Foot]		
legendary manlike creature	SAS-KWACH, SAS-KWAHCH	'sæsˌkwætʃ, 'sæsˌkwɑtʃ
Sassanid		
Persian dynasty	suh-SAHN-uhd, suh-SAN-uhd, SAS-uh-nid	sə'sɑnəd, sə'sænəd, 'sæsənid
Sassari		
prov & town, Sardinia	SAHS-uh-rē	'sɑsəri·
Sassenach		
Irish/Scots disparaging term for English	SAH-suh-nuhkh, [S] SAS-n-AK, SAS-n-AHKH	'sɑːsənəx, [S] 'sæsn̩ˌæk, 'sæsn̩ˌɑx
Sassoon		
Siegfried, *English author;* Vidal, *British hair styling executive*	suh-SO͞ON, sa-SO͞ON	sə'suːn, sæ'suːn
Satan		
adversary of God, devil	SĀT-n	'seːtn̩
Satanic		
pert. to Satan	suh-TAN-ik, sā-TAN-ik	sə'tænik, seː'tænik
Satanism		
worship of Satan	SĀT-n-IZ-uhm	'seːtn̩ˌizəm
Satanist		
worshipper of Satan	SĀT-n-uhst	'seːtn̩əst
Sathanas		
the Devil	SAT-uh-nuhs, SĀT-n-uhs	'sæt̬ənəs, 'seːtn̩əs
Satie		
Erik, *French composer*	sah-TĒ	sɑːtiː
Satilla		
river, GA	suh-TIL-uh	sə'tilə
Satis		
Egyptian goddess	SAHT-uhs, SĀT-uhs	'sɑt̬əs, 'seːt̬əs

Key (col. 2): a: **fad** ā: **fade** ah: **father** ar: **marry** aw: **law** e: **fed** ē: **feed** er: **merry** i: **hid** ī: **hide** ō: **coat** o͞o: **boot** oi: **boy** ow: **now** u: **put** uh: **above** uhr: **bird** ch: **chop** ng: **ring** sh: **show** th: **thick** th: **this** zh: **measure**

Sato
Eisaku, *Japanese politician (Nobel 1974)* — sah-tō — sɑtoː

Satoshi
pers. name, Japanese — sah-tō-shē — sɑtoːʃiː

Satsuma
prov, Japan; porcelain; tree — saht-sōō-mah, ⑤ sat-SŌŌ-muh, SAT-suh-muh — sɑtsuːmɑ, ⑤ sæt'suːmə, 'sætsəmə

Sattui
V., winery, CA — suh-TŌŌ-ē — sə'tuːiˑ

Saturday
day of the week — SAT-uhr-dē, SAT-uhr-dā, *rapidly also* SAR-dē, SAD-dē — 'sæt̬ərdiˑ, 'sæt̬ərdeː, *rapidly also* 'særdiˑ, 'sæddiˑ

Saturn
Roman god, father of Jupiter; planet — SAT-uhrn — 'sæt̬ərn

Saturnalia
Roman festival — SAT-uhr-NĀL-yuh, -NĀ-lē-uh — ˌsæt̬ərˈneːljə, -'neːliːə

Saturnian
pert. to Saturn — sa-TUHR-nē-uhn, suh- — sæ'təʳniːən, sə-

Saturninus
Roman politician — SAT-uhr-NĪ-nuhs — ˌsæt̬ərˈnɑinəs

Satyagraha
passive resistance, India — suh-TYAHG-ruh-huh — sə'tjɑgrəhə

Satyendra
pers. name, Bengali — sawt-YĀN-draw, ⑤ suht-YEN-druh — sɔːt'jeːndrɔː, ⑤ sət'jendrə

Satyendranath
pers. name, Bengali — sawt-YĀN-druh-nuht — sɔːt'jeːndrənət

Satyrs
Greek sylvan deities — SĀT-uhrz, SAT-uhrz — 'seːt̬əʳz, 'sæt̬əʳz

Saud
royal family, Saudi Arabia — sah-ŌŌD — sɑ'uːd

Saudi
pert. to Saudi Arabia — SOWD-ē, SAWD-ē, sah-ŌŌD-ē — 'sɑudiˑ, 'sɔːdiˑ, sɑ'uːdiˑ

Saudi Arabia
kingdom, Arabian Peninsula — SOWD-ē uh-RĀ-bē-uh, SAWD-ē, sah-ŌŌD-ē — ˌsɑudiː ə'reːbiːə, ˌsɔːdiː, sɑˌuːdiː

Saudi Arabian
pert. to Saudi Arabia — SOWD-ē uh-RĀ-bē-uhn, SAWD-ē, sah-ŌŌD-ē — ˌsɑudiː ə'reːbiːən, ˌsɔːdiː, sɑˌuːdiː

Saugatuck
river, CT — SAW-guh-TUHK — 'sɔːgəˌtək

Saugerties
village, NY — SAW-guhr-TĒZ, SAW-guhrt-ēz — 'sɔːgəʳˌtiːz, 'sɔːgəʳt̬iːz

Saugus
town, MA — SAW-guhs, SAHG-uhs — 'sɔːgəs, 'sɑgəs

Sauk
county, WI; N. American people — SAWK — 'sɔːk

Sauk-Fox
Indian reservation, US — SAWK-FAHKS — 'sɔːk'fɑks

Sauk-Suiattle
Indian reservation, US — SAWK-SŌŌ-ē-AT-l — 'sɔːkˌsuːiːˈæt̬l̩

Saul
king of Israel; pers. name — SAWL — 'sɔːl

Sault Ste. Marie
city, MI; N. American people — SŌŌ SĀNT muh-RĒ — ˌsuː ˌseːnt mə'riː

Foreign Sounds: ue: *Fr.* **rue**, *Ger.* **füllen** uh(r): *Fr.* **boeuf**, *Ger.* **Höhle** <u>kh</u>: *Ger.* **i<u>ch</u>**, *Scot.* lo**<u>ch</u>** ḡ: *Sp.* amiḡo <u>v</u>: *Sp.* hablar hl: *Welsh* **Ll**anelli. CAPITALS: primary stress. SMALL CAPS: secondary stress. ⑤: U.S. pron. ⓔ: British pron.

Saunders
   pers. name   SAWN-duhrz, SAHN-duhrz   'sɔːndəʳz, 'sɑndəʳz

Saurashtra
   state, India   sow-RAHSH-truh   sɑu'raʃtrə

Saurischia
   dinosaur order   saw-RIS-kē-uh   sɔː'riskiːə

Saurolophus
   dinosaur   saw-RAHL-uh-fuhs   sɔː'rɑləfəs

Sauropoda
   dinosaur infraorder   saw-RAHP-uhd-uh   sɔː'rɑpədə

Sauropodomorpha
   dinosaur suborder   saw-RAHP-uhd-uh-MAWR-fuh   sɔː,rɑpədə'mɔːʳfə

Sausalito
   city, CA   SAW-suh-LĒT-ō   ,sɔːsə'liːt̠ɔː

Saussure
   Ferdinand de, *Swiss linguist* sō-SUER, ⑤ sō-SIR, sō-SUR   sɔːsyːr, ⑤ sɔː'siʳ, sɔː'suʳ

Saussurean, Saussurian
   pert. to Saussure   sō-SIR-ē-uhn, sō-SUR-ē-uhn,   sɔː'siriːən, sɔː'suriːən,
                         sō-SHUR-ē-uhn   sɔː'ʃuriːən

Sauternes
   wine   sō-TERN, ⑤ sō-TUHRN, saw-   sɔːtern, ⑤ sɔː'təʳn, sɔː-

Sauvignon Blanc
   wine   sō-vēn-yawⁿ BLAHⁿ   sɔːviːnjɔ̃ blɑ̃

Sava, Save
   river, Serbia   SAHV-uh   'sɑvə

Savaii, Savai'i
   island, Samoa   suh-VĪ-ē   sə'vaiiː

Savalas
   Telly, *US entertainer*   suh-VAL-uhs, suh-VAHL-uhs   sə'væləs, sə'vɑləs

Savanna
   city, IL   suh-VAN-uh   sə'vænə

Savannah
   city, GA   suh-VAN-uh   sə'vænə

Savarin
   flavored cake; brand of coffee SAV-uh-ruhn   'sævərən

Savigny-sur-Orge
   commune, France   sah-vēn-YĒ-suer-AWRZH   sɑviːnjiːsyːrɔːrʒ

Savile, Saville
   pers. name   SAV-uhl, SAV-il   'sævəl, 'sævil

Savile Row
   street, London, England   SAV-uhl RŌ, SAV-il RŌ   ,sævəl 'roː, ,sævil 'roː

Savin
   US copier co.   SAV-uhn, SĀ-vuhn   'sævən, 'seːvən

Savinien
   pers. name, French   sah-vēn-YEⁿ   sɑviːnjẽ

Savoie [Savoy]
   region, France, Italy   sahv-WAH, ⑤ sav-WAH, suh-VOI sɑːvwɑː, ⑤ sæv'wɑ, sə'vɔi

Savona
   prov & town, Italy   suh-VŌ-nuh   sə'voːnə

Savonarola
   Girolamo, *Italian religious leader* SAV-uh-nuh-RŌ-luh,   ,sævənə'roːlə, sə,vɑnə'roːlə
                         suh-VAHN-uh-RŌ-luh

Key (col. 2): a: fad ā: fade ah: father ar: marry aw: law e: fed ē: feed er: merry i: hid ī: hide ō: coat ōō: boot
oi: boy ow: now u: put uh: above uhr: bird ch: chop ng: ring sh: show th: thick th̲: this zh: measure

Savoy

theatre, street, London, England;   suh-VOI   sə'vɔi
anglicization of Savoie; Alps,
mtn. range

Savoyard

inhabitant of or pert. to Savoy; *fan*   SAV-OI-AHRD, suh-VOI-AHRD,   ˌsæv͵ɔi'ɑ͏ʳd, sə'vɔi͵ɑ͏ʳd,
of Gilbert & Sullivan operas   SAV-wah-YAHR(D)   ˌsævwa'jɑ͏ʳ(d)

Savoyarde

cookery preparation   SAV-OI-AHRD, suh-VOI-AHRD,   ˌsæv͵ɔi'ɑ͏ʳd, sə'vɔi͵ɑ͏ʳd,
                           SAV-wah-YAHRD   ˌsævwa'jɑ͏ʳd

Savusavu

city, Fiji   SAHV-o͞o-SAHV-o͞o   ˌsɑvuː'sɑvuː

Sawatch

mtn. range, CO   suh-WAHCH   sə'wɑtʃ

Sawu Sea, Savu Sea

region of Indian Ocean   SAHV-o͞o SĒ   ˌsɑvuː 'siː

Saw-whet

owl   SAW-(H)WET   'sɔː͵(h)wet

Sawyer

Diane, *US TV journalist; pers. name*   SAW-yuhr, SOI(-uh)r   'sɔːjə͏ʳ, 'sɔi(ə)͏ʳ

Saxe-Coburg-Gotha

British royal family   SAKS-KŌ-BUHRG-GŌ-thuh   ˌsæks͵koː͵bəʳg'goːθə

Saxifrage

plant   SAK-suh-frij, SAK-suh-FRĀJ   'sæksəfridʒ, 'sæksə͵freːdʒ

Saxo Grammaticus

Danish historian, poet   SAK-sō gruh-MAT-i-kuhs   'sæksoː grə'mætikəs

Saxon

a Germanic people   SAK-suhn   'sæksən

Saxony

state, Germany   SAK-suh-nē   'sæksəniˑ

Saxophone

musical instrument   SAK-suh-FŌN   'sæksə͵foːn

Sayan

mtn. range, Russia   suh-YAHN   sə'jɑn

Sayer

Leo, *musician, singer*   SĀ(-uh)r   'seː(ə)͏ʳ

Sazerac

tdmk for a cocktail   SAZ-uh-RAK   'sæzə͵ræk

Sbarro

US restaurant chain   SPAHR-ō   'spɑroː

Scaasi

Arnold, *US fashion designer*   SKAHS-ē, SKAHZ-ē   'skɑsiˑ, 'skɑziˑ

Scabious

flower   SKĀ-bē-uhs, SKAB-ē-uhs   'skeːbiːəs, 'skæbiːəs

Scaevola

Roman cognomen   SĒ-vuh-luh, SEV-uh-luh   'siːvələ, 'sevələ

Scafell

mtn., England   SKAW-FEL   'skɔː͵fel

Scaggs

Boz, *US musician*   SKAGZ   'skægz

Scala, La

see La Scala

Scaldis

Belgian beer   SKAHL-duhs   'skɑldəs

Scaliger
   J. C., *Italian scholar in France; his*   SKAL-uh-juhr   'skæləd$\mathrm{\zi}$ə$^\mathrm{r}$
   son, J. J., *French scholar*

Scamander
   river of Troy   skuh-MAN-duhr   skə'mændə$^\mathrm{r}$

Scammony
   plant   SKAM-uh-nē   'skæməni·

Scanderbeg [Kastrioti]
   Albanian revolutionary leader   SKAHN-duhr-BEG, SKAN-   'skandə$^\mathrm{r}$ˌbeg, 'skæn-

Scandia
   Danish beer   SKAHN-dē-uh, ⓢ SKAN-dē-uh   'skandiːə, ⓢ 'skændiːə

Scandian
   a Scandinavian   SKAN-dē-uhn   'skændiːən

Scandinavia
   region, North Europe   SKAN-duh-NĀ-vē-uh, -NĀV-yuh   ˌskændə'neːviːə, -'neːvjə

scandium
   element   SKAN-dē-uhm   'skændiːəm

Scapa Flow
   area of water, Orkney Islands   SKAP-uh FLŌ   ˌskæpə 'floː

Scaramouch, -che
   braggart character in Commedia   SKAR-uh-MŌŌSH, -MŌŌCH, -MOWCH   'skærəˌmuːʃ, -ˌmuːtʃ,
   dell' Arte   -ˌmautʃ

Scaramuccia
   pers. name, Italian   SKAHR-ah-MŌŌT-chah   ˌskara'muːttʃa

Scarborough
   town, England   SKAHR-BUHR-uh, -BUH-ruh, -bruh   'ska$^\mathrm{r}$ˌbər-ə, -ˌbə-rə, -brə

Scarlatti
   Alessandro, *Italian composer*   skahr-LAHT-ē   ska$^\mathrm{r}$'laţi·

Scarlett
   pers. name   SKAHR-luht   'ska$^\mathrm{r}$lət

Scarritt
   College for Christian Education,   SKAR-uht, SKER-uht   'skærət, 'skerət
   TN

Scarry
   Richard, *US children's author*   SKER-ē, SKAR-ē   'skeri·, 'skæri·

Scaup
   duck   SKAWP   'skɔːp

Scaurus
   Roman cognomen   SKŌR-uhs, SKAWR-uhs   'skoːrəs, 'skɔːrəs

Scawen
   pers. name   SKŌ-uhn   'skoːən

Scelidosaurus
   dinosaur   SEL-uhd-uh-SAWR-uhs   ˌselədə'sɔːrəs

Sceva
   Biblical name   SĒ-vuh   'siːvə

Schacht
   Hjalmar, *German economist*   SHAH<u>KH</u>T   'ʃaxt

Schaffhausen
   canton, Switzerland   shahf-HOWZ-n   ʃaf'hauzn̩

Schafkopf
   game   SHAHF-KAWPF   'ʃafˌkɔːpf

Schally
   Andrew V., *Polish-born US*   SHAL-ē   'ʃæli·
   biochemist (Nobel 1977)

Key (col. 2):   a: fad ā: fade ah: father ar: marry aw: law e: fed ē: feed er: merry i: hid ī: hide ō: coat ōō: boot
oi: boy ow: now u: put uh: above uhr: bird ch: chop ng: ring sh: show th: thick <u>th</u>: this zh: measure

Schaumburg
   village, IL   SHAWM-BUHRG   ˈʃɔːmˌbəʳg

Schawlow
   Arthur, *US physicist (Nobel 1981)*   SHAW-lō   ˈʃɔːloː

Scheherazade, Sh-
   symphonic suite, Rimsky-Korsakov   shuh-HER-uh-ZAHD-uh, -ZAHD   ʃəˌheraˈzadə, -ˈzad

Scheidemann
   Philipp, *German political leader*   SHĪD-uh-MAHN   ˈʃaidəˌman

Schelde
   river, Europe   SKEL-duh   ˈskeldə

Scheldt [Schelde]
   river, Europe   SKELT   ˈskelt

Schell
   Maximilian, *Australian actor*   SHEL   ˈʃel

Schelling
   Friedrich Wilhelm, *German*   SHEL-ing   ˈʃeliŋ
     philosopher

Schellingism
   philosophy of F. W. Schelling   SHEL-ing-IZ-uhm   ˈʃeliŋˌizəm

Schenectady
   city, county, NY   skuh-NEK-tuhd-ē   skəˈnektədiˑ

Schenkel
   Chris, *US sportscaster*   SHENG-kuhl   ˈʃeŋkəl

Schering-Plough
   US drug co.   SHIR-ing-PLOW   ˈʃiriŋˌplau

Schermerhorn
   1. Kenneth, *US conductor*   SHUHR-muhr-HAWRN   ˈʃəʳməʳˌhɔːʳn
   2. street, New York City   SKUHR-muhr-HAWRN, SKER-   ˈskəʳməʳˌhɔːʳn, ˈskeʳ-

Scherzo
   musical passage   SKERT-sō   ˈskeʳtsoː

Schiaparelli
   Elsa, *fashion designer*   SKYAHP-uh-REL-ē, SKAP-, SHAP-   ˌskjapəˈreliˑ, ˌskæp-, ˌʃæp-

Schiava
   Italian wine grape   skē-AHV-uh   skiːˈavə

Schick
   test for diphtheria; razor mfr.   SHIK   ˈʃik

Schickel
   Richard, *US writer*   SHIK-uhl   ˈʃikəl

Schickele
   1. Peter, *US composer, aka "P.D.Q.*   SHIK-uh-lē   ˈʃikəliˑ
     Bach"
   2. René, *German writer*   SHIK-uh-luh   ˈʃikələ

Schieffer
   Bob, *US journalist*   SHĒ-fuhr   ˈʃiːfəʳ

Schiele
   Egon, *Austrian painter*   SHĒ-luh   ˈʃiːlə

Schiff
   pers. name   SHIF   ˈʃif

Schild
   US beer   SHILD, SHILT   ˈʃild, ˈʃilt

Schildkraut
   Joseph & Rudolf, *German actors*   SHILT-KROWT   ˈʃiltˌkraut

Schiller
   Friedrich von, *German writer*   SHIL-uhr   ˈʃiləʳ

Foreign Sounds: ue: *Fr.* **rue**, *Ger.* **füllen**   uh(r): *Fr.* **boeuf**, *Ger.* **Höhle**   <u>kh</u>: *Ger.* **ich**, *Scot.* **loch**   ḡ: *Sp.* **amigo**   <u>v</u>: *Sp.* **hablar**
hl: *Welsh* **Llanelli.**   CAPITALS: primary stress.   SMALL CAPS: secondary stress.   Ⓢ: U.S. pron.   Ⓔ: British pron.

Schindler's List		
movie	SHIN-(d)luhrz-LIST	ˈʃin(d)ləʳzˈlist
Schiphol		
airport, Amsterdam	SHIP-ŌL	ˈʃipˌoːl
Schipperke		
dog breed	SKIP-uhr-kē, SHIP-, -uhrk, -uhr-kuh	ˈskipəʳkiˑ, ˈʃip-, -əʳk, -əʳkə
Schippers		
Thomas, *US conductor*	SHIP-uhrz	ˈʃipəʳz
Schlafly		
Phyllis, *US author, activist*	SHLAF-lē	ˈʃlæfliˑ
Schlage		
lock	SHLĀG, SLĀG, SLĀJ, SHLĀJ	ˈʃleːg, ˈsleːg, ˈsleːdʒ, ˈʃleːdʒ
Schlegel		
A. W. von, *German author;* F. von,	SHLĀ-guhl	ˈʃleːgəl
German author		
Schleicher		
county, TX	SHLĪ-kuhr, SLĪ-kuhr	ˈʃlaikəʳ, ˈslaikəʳ
Schlesinger		
1. Arthur Meier *(father & son), US*	SHLĀ-zing-uhr	ˈʃleːziŋəʳ
historians		
2. James, *US cabinet officer*	SLES-ing-(g)uhr, SLES-in-juhr	ˈslesiŋ(g)əʳ, ˈslesindʒəʳ
Schleswig-Holstein		
prov, Germany	SHLES-vi<u>kh</u>-HŌL-SHTĪN,	ˈʃlesviç'hoːlˌʃtain,
	⑤ SLES-vig-HŌL-STĪN	⑤ ˈslesvig'hoːlˌstain
Schley		
county, GA	SLĪ	ˈslai
Schliemann		
Heinrich, *German archaeologist*	SHLĒ-MAHN	ˈʃliːˌmɑn
Schmidt		
Helmut, *German chancellor;*	SHMIT	ˈʃmit
Michael, *US baseball player; pers.*		
name		
Schmierkase		
cheese	SHMIR-KĀ-zuh, SHMIR-KĀS	ˈʃmiʳˌkeːzə, ˈʃmiʳˌkeːs
Schmitt		
Harrison Hagan, *US astronaut,*	SHMIT	ˈʃmit
politician		
Schnapps		
liquor	SHNAPS, SHNAHPS	ˈʃnæps, ˈʃnɑps
Schnauzer		
dog breed	SHNOW-zuhr, SNOW-; SHNOWT-suhr	ˈʃnauzəʳ, ˈsnau-; ˈʃnautsəʳ
Schnitzel		
meat cutlet	SHNIT-suhl, SNIT-suhl	ˈʃnitsəl, ˈsnitsəl
Schoene		
Field, *airport, Germany*	SHUH(R)-nuh	ˈʃœnə
Schoenling		
US beer	SHEN-ling	ˈʃenliŋ
Schoharie		
county, NY	skō-HAR-ē	skoːˈhæriˑ
Scholasticism		
medieval philosophical system	skuh-LAS-tuh-SIZ-uhm	skəˈlæstəˌsizəm
Schopenhauer		
Arthur, *German philosopher*	SHŌ-puhn-HOW-uhr	ˈʃoːpənˌhauəʳ
Schorling		
Park, *former ballpark, Chicago, IL*	SHAWR-ling	ˈʃɔːʳliŋ

Key (col. 2):   a: f**a**d   ā: f**a**de   ah: f**a**ther   ar: m**a**rry   aw: l**a**w   e: f**e**d   ē: f**ee**d   er: m**e**rry   i: h**i**d   ī: h**i**de   ō: c**oa**t   ōō: b**oo**t
oi: b**o**y   ow: n**ow**   u: p**u**t   uh: **a**bove   uhr: b**i**rd   ch: **ch**op   ng: ri**ng**   sh: **sh**ow   th: **th**ick   <u>th</u>: **th**is   zh: mea**s**ure

Schottische		
dance	SHAHT-ish, shah-TĒSH	ˈʃɑʈɪʃ, ʃaˈtiːʃ
Schramberg		
city, Germany	SHRAHM-BERK	ˈʃrɑmˌbeʳk
Schramsberg		
winery, CA	SHRAMZ-BUHRG	ˈʃræmzˌbəʳg
Schreiffer		
John Robert, US physicist (Nobel 1972)	SHRĒ-fuhr, SRĒ-fuhr	ˈʃriːfəʳ, ˈsriːfəʳ
Schreiner		
College, TX	SHRĪ-nuhr	ˈʃrɑinəʳ
Schrödinger		
Erwin, Austrian physicist (Nobel 1933)	SHRUH(R)D-ing-uhr, Ⓢ SHRĀD-ing-uhr, SHRŌD-ing-uhr, SRĀD-, SRŌD-	ˈʃrœːdiŋəʳ, Ⓢ ˈʃreːdiŋəʳ, ˈʃroːdiŋəʳ, ˈsreːd-, ˈsroːd-
Schroeder		
Patricia, US politician	SHRŌD-uhr	ˈʃroːdəʳ
Schroon		
river, lake, NY	SKRŌŌN	ˈskruːn
Schubert		
Franz, Austrian composer	SHŌŌ-buhrt, SHŌŌ-BERT	ˈʃuːbəʳt, ˈʃuːˌbeʳt
Schulenburg		
city, TX	SHŌŌ-luhn-BUHRG	ˈʃuːlənˌbəʳg
Schuller		
Gunther, US composer	SHUL-uhr	ˈʃuləʳ
Schultz		
Theodore W., US economist (Nobel 1979)	SHULTS	ˈʃults
Schulz		
Charles, US cartoonist	SHULTS	ˈʃults
Schumacher		
pers. name, Danish	SHŌŌ-mahkh-uhr	ˈʃuːmɑːxər
Schumann		
Robert, German composer	SHŌŌ-MAHN, SHŌŌ-muhn	ˈʃuːˌman, ˈʃuːmən
Schumpeter		
Joseph, US economist	SHUM-PĀT-uhr	ˈʃumˌpeːʈəʳ
Schuschnigg		
Kurt von, Austrian politician	SHUSH-nik	ˈʃuʃnik
Schutz		
French beer	SHUTS	ʃuts
Schutzenburger		
French beer	shut-suhn-bŌŌr-GER, SHUT-suhn-BUR-guhr	ʃutsənbuːrger, ˈʃutsənˌburgəʳ
Schutzenfeste		
German festival	SHUT-suhn-FES-tuh	ˈʃutsənˌfestə
Schutzstaffel		
elite Nazi military unit	SHUT-STAHF-uhl	ˈʃutˌstɑfəl
Schuyler		
county, IL, MO, NY; pers. name	SKĪ-luhr	ˈskɑiləʳ
Schuylkill		
river, county, PA	SKŌŌL-KIL, SKŌŌ(L)-kuhl	ˈskuːlˌkil, ˈskuː(l)kəl
Schwaben [Swabia]		
prov, Germany	SHFAHB-uhn	ˈʃfɑbən

Foreign Sounds: ue: *Fr.* **rue**, *Ger.* **füllen**   uh(r): *Fr.* **boeuf**, *Ger.* **Höhle**   kh: *Ger.* **ich**, *Scot.* **loch**   g̃: *Sp.* **amigo**   v̧: *Sp.* **hablar**
hl: *Welsh* **Llanelli**.   CAPITALS: primary stress.   SMALL CAPS: secondary stress.   Ⓢ: U.S. pron.   Ⓔ: British pron.

Schwann
  1. Theodor, *German zoologist*   SHFAHN, Ⓢ SHWAHN   'ʃfɑn, Ⓢ 'ʃwɑn
  2. music catalogue   SHWAHN   'ʃwɑn

Schwartz
  Melvin, *US physicist (Nobel 1988)*   SHWAWRTS   'ʃwɔːʳts

Schwarzenegger
  Arnold, *Austrian actor in US*   SHWAWRT-suh-NEG-uhr, -NĀ-guhr   'ʃwɔːʳtsə,negəʳ, -,neːgəʳ

Schwarzkopf
  Norman, *US general*   SHWAWRTS-KAW(P)F,   'ʃwɔːʳts,kɔː(p)f,
         SHWAWRTS-KAH(P)F, SWAWRTS-   'ʃwɔːʳts,kɑ(p)f, 'swɔːʳts-

Schwarzwald
  Black Forest, Germany   SHFAHRTS-VAHLT   'ʃfɑʳts,vɑlt

Schweitzer
  Albert, *Alsatian doctor (Nobel 1952)*   SHFĪT-suhr, Ⓢ SHWĪT-suhr   'ʃfaitsəʳ, Ⓢ 'ʃwaitsəʳ

Schweizerhofbrau
  German beer   SHFĪT-suhr-HAWF-BROW   'ʃfaitsəʳ,hɔːf,brau

Schweiz [Switzerland]
  republic, Europe   SHFĪTS   'ʃfaits

Schwenkfeld
  Kaspar von, *German religious*   SHFENGK-FELT   'ʃfeŋk,felt
    leader

Schweppes
  soft drink co.   SHWEPS, SWEPS   'ʃweps, 'sweps

Schwerin
  county, Germany   shfā-RĒN   ʃfeː'riːn

Schwinger
  Julian Seymour, *US physicist (Nobel*   SHWING-uhr   'ʃwiŋəʳ
  1965)

Schwinn
  US bicycle co.   SHWIN   'ʃwin

Schwyz
  mtn., canton, Switzerland   SHFĒTS   'ʃfiːts

Scientology
  tdmk for a US group   SĪ-uhn-TAHL-uh-jē   ,saiən'tɑlədʒiˑ

Scilly
  Isles of, *islands, England*   SIL-ē   'siliˑ

Scioto
  river, county, OH   sī-ŌT-uh   sai'oːʈə

Scipio Aemilianus Africanus
  Roman general   SIP-ē-ō i-MIL-ē-Ā-nuhs AF-ri-KĀ-nuhs,   'sipiː,oː i,miliː'eːnəs
         SKIP-ē-ō   ,æfri'keːnəs, 'skipiː,oː

Scipio Africanus
  Roman general   SIP-ē-ō AF-ri-KĀ-nuhs, SKIP-ē-ō   'sipiː,oː ,æfri'keːnəs,
         'skipiː,oː

Scipion
  pers. name, French   sēp-YAWⁿ   siːpjɔ̃

Sciron
  brigand killed by Theseus   SKĪ-ruhn, SKĪ-RAHN, SKIR-uhn,   'skairən, 'skai,ran, 'skirən,
         SKIR-AHN   'skir,an

Scituate
  town, MA   SICH-(uh-)wuht   'sitʃ(ə)wət

Scleromochlus
  dinosaur   SKLER-uh-MAHK-luhs   ,sklerə'mɑkləs

Scofield
  Paul, *English actor*   SKŌ-FĒLD   'skoː,fiːld

Key (col. 2):   a: f**a**d   ā: f**a**de   ah: f**a**ther   ar: m**a**rry   aw: l**a**w   e: f**e**d   ē: f**ee**d   er: m**e**rry   i: h**i**d   ī: h**i**de   ō: c**oa**t   o͞o: b**oo**t
oi: b**oy**   ow: n**ow**   u: p**u**t   uh: **a**bove   uhr: b**ir**d   ch: **ch**op   ng: ri**ng**   sh: **sh**ow   th: **th**ick   <u>th</u>: **<u>th</u>is**   zh: mea**s**ure

Scone
Stone of, *Scottish coronation stone* SK$\overline{OO}$N 'skuːn
Sconset
local name for Siasconset SKAWN-SET, SKAHN-suht 'skɔːn‚set, 'skɑnsət
Scopas
Greek sculptor SK$\overline{O}$-puhs 'skoːpəs
Scorpio
sign of the zodiac SKAWR-pē-$\overline{O}$ 'skɔːˈpiː‚oː
Scorpius
constellation SKAWR-pē-uhs 'skɔːˈpiːəs
Scorsese
Martin, *entertainer* skawr-S$\overline{A}$-zē skɔːˈseːziˑ
Scot
inhabitant of Scotland SKAHT 'skɑt
Scotch
pert. to Scotland *or* Scots; *whiskey;* SKAHCH 'skɑtʃ
tdmk for adhesive tape
Scotch-Irish
mixed Scottish and Irish descent skahch-Ī-rish skɑtʃˈɑiriʃ
Scoter
duck SK$\overline{O}$T-uhr 'skoːʈəˈ
Scotia Sea
region, South Atlantic ocean SK$\overline{O}$-shuh S$\overline{E}$ ‚skoːʃə 'siː
Scotism
doctrines of Duns Scotus SK$\overline{O}$T-IZ-uhm 'skoːʈ‚izəm
Scotland
northern part of Great Britain SKAHT-luhnd 'skɑtlənd
Scots
form of English spoken in Scotland SKAHTS 'skɑts
Scott
pers. name SKAHT 'skɑt
Scotticism
Scots term SKAHT-uh-SIZ-uhm 'skɑʈə‚sizəm
Scottish
pert. to Scotland SKAHT-ish 'skɑʈiʃ
Scottish Gaelic
lang., Scotland SKAHT-ish G$\overline{A}$-lik 'skɑʈiʃ 'geːlik
Scottsdale
city, AZ SKAHTS-D$\overline{A}$L 'skɑts‚deːl
Scotty
pers. name SKAHT-ē 'skɑʈiˑ
Scotus
pers. name, Latin SK$\overline{O}$T-uhs 'skoːʈəs
Scowcroft
Brent, *US politician* SK$\overline{O}$-KRAWFT 'skoː‚krɔːft
Scrabble
tdmk for a board game SKRAB-uhl 'skræbəl
Scranton
William, *US politician; city, PA* SKRANT-n 'skræntn̩
Screven
county, GA SKRIV-uhn 'skrivən
Scriabin
Aleksandr, *Russian composer* SKRYAHB-yin, skrē-AHB-uhn 'skrjɑːbjin, skriːˈɑbən
Scrooge
Ebenezer, *Dickens character* SKR$\overline{OO}$J 'skruːdʒ

Foreign Sounds: ue: *Fr.* **rue**, *Ger.* **füllen** uh(r): *Fr.* **boeuf**, *Ger.* **Höhle** kh: *Ger.* **ich**, *Scot.* **loch** ğ: *Sp.* **amigo** v: *Sp.* **hablar**
hl: *Welsh* **Llanelli**. CAPITALS: primary stress. SMALL CAPS: secondary stress. Ⓢ: U.S. pron. Ⓔ: British pron.

SCSI
   small computer system interface   SKUHZ-ē   'skəzi·

Scud
   missile   SKUHD   'skəd

Scudamore
   pers. name   SKUHD-uh-MŌR, -MAWR   'skədə͵moːʳ, -͵mɔːʳ

Scully
   Vin, *US sportscaster*   SKUHL-ē   'skəli·

Sculptor
   constellation   SKUHLP-tuhr   'skəlptəʳ

Scuppernong
   river, lake, NC; grape; wine   SKUHP-uhr-NAWNG, -NAHNG, -NUHNG   'skəpəʳ͵nɔːŋ, -͵nɑŋ, -͵nəŋ

Scutari
   lake, Europe   SKOOT-uh-rē   'skuːţəri·

Scutum
   constellation   SK(Y)OOT-uhm   'sk(j)uːţəm

Scylax
   Greek explorer   SĪ-LAKS   'sɑi͵læks

Scylla
   sea monster   SIL-uh   'silə

Scythia
   ancient regions of Europe & Asia   SITH-ē-uh, S<u>ITH</u>-ē-uh   'siθiːə, 'siðiːə

Scythian
   inhabitant of Scythia   SITH-ē-uhn, S<u>ITH</u>-ē-uhn   'siθiːən, 'siðiːən

Seaborg
   Glenn T., *US nuclear chemist (Nobel 1951)*   SĒ-BAWRG   'siː͵bɔːʳg

Seagal
   Steven, *US actor*   si-GAHL, si-GAL   si'gɑl, si'gæl

Seagram
   liquor co.   SĒ-gruhm   'siːgrəm

Sealyham
   terrier breed   SĒ-lē-HAM, ⒺSĒ-lē-uhm   'siːli·͵hæm, Ⓔ'siːliːəm

Seamus
   pers. name, Irish   SHĀ-muhs   'ʃeːməs

Sean, Seán
   pers. name, Irish Gaelic   SHAWN, SHAHN   'ʃɔːn, 'ʃɑn

Seaned Eireann
   Irish legislative body   SHAH-nuh<u>th</u> ER-(y)uhn   ͵ʃɑːnəð 'er(j)ən

Searcy
   city, county, AR   SUHR-sē   'səʳsi·

Sears Roebuck
   US retail chain   SIRZ RŌ-BUHK, RŌ-buhk   ͵siʳz 'roː͵bək, 'roːbək

Sea-Tac
   airport, Seattle-Tacoma, WA   SĒ-TAK   'siː͵tæk

SEATO
   South-East Asian Treaty Organization   SĒT-ō   'siːţoː

Seattle
   city, WA   sē-AT-l   siː'ætl̩

Seaver
   Tom, *US baseball player*   SĒ-vuhr   'siːvəʳ

Seb
   pers. name   SEB   'seb

Seb [Geb]
   Egyptian earth god   SEB   'seb

Key (col. 2): a: fad ā: fade ah: father ar: marry aw: law e: fed ē: feed er: merry i: hid ī: hide ō: coat ōō: boot
oi: boy ow: now u: put uh: above uhr: bird ch: chop ng: ring sh: show th: thick <u>th</u>: this zh: measure

Seba
Biblical name   SĒ-buh, suh-VAH   'siːbə, sə'vɑ

Sebam [Shebam]
Biblical name   SĒ-BAM, suh-VAHM   'siːˌbæm, sə'vɑm

Sebastian
1. pers. name   suh-BAS-chuhn, suh-BASH-chuhn   sə'bæstʃən, sə'bæʃtʃən
2. Dutch, Norwegian   sā-BAHS-tē-ahn   seː'bɑstiːɑn
3. German   zā-BAHS-tyahn, -tē-ahn   zeː'bɑstjɑn, -tiːɑn
4. Polish   se-BAHS-tyahn   se'bɑːstjɑːn

Sebastián
pers. name, Spanish   sā-ṿahs-TYAHN   seː'βɑs'tjɑn

Sebastiani
winery   suh-BAS-tē-AHN-ē   səˌbæstiː'ɑniˑ

Sebastiano
pers. name, Italian   SĀ-bahs-TYAH-nō   ˌseːbɑs'tjɑnoː

Sebastianus
pers. name, Latin   suh-BAS-chē-Ā-nuhs, suh-BASH-   səˌbæstʃiː'eːnəs, səˌbæʃ-

Sebastião
pers. name, Portuguese   suh-buhsh-TYOWⁿ, sā-bahs-TYOWⁿ   səbəʃ'tjɑũ, seːbɑːs'tjɑũ

Sebastopol
1. city, CA   suh-BAS-tuh-PŌOL, -PŌL   sə'bæstəˌpuːl, -ˌpoːl
2. see Sevastopol

Sebat [Shebat]
Jewish month   SĒ-BAT, shuh-VAHT, shvaht   'siːˌbæt, ʃə'vɑt, ʃvɑt

Sebek, Sebeq
Egyptian crocodile god   SEB-uhk, SĀ-buhk   'sebək, 'seːbək

Sebeok
Thomas, *US linguist*   SĒ-bē-AHK   'siːbiːˌɑk

Sebring
city, FL   SĒ-bring   'siːbriŋ

Sebuano, Cebuano [Bisaya]
lang., people, Philippine Islands   sā-BWAHN-ō   seː'bwɑnoː

Secaucus
town, NJ   si-KAW-kuhs   si'kɔːkəs

Secacah
Biblical name   suh-KĀ-kuh, SEK-uh-kuh, suh-ḵhah-ḴHAH   sə'keːkə, 'sekəkə, səxɑ'xɑː

Secessio
Roman plebeian walkout   suh-SESH-ō   sə'seʃoː

Seconal
tdmk for secobarbital   SEK-uh-NAWL, SEK-uhn-l   'sekəˌnɔːl, 'sekənl̩

Secondat
pers. name, French   suh-gawⁿ-DAH   səgɔ̃dɑː

Secu, Sechu
Biblical name   SĒ-K(Y)OO, SEḴH-oo   'siːˌk(j)uː, 'sexuː

Secunderabad
town, India   si-KUHN-duhr-uh-BAHD, -BAD   si'kəndərəˌbɑd, -ˌbæd

Secundus
pers. name, Latin   si-KUHN-duhs, si-KUN-duhs   si'kəndəs, si'kundəs

Sedaka
Neil, *rock musician*   suh-DAK-uh   sə'dækə

Sedalia
city, MO   si-DĀL-yuh   si'deːljə

Sedan
city, KS   si-DAN   si'dæn

Foreign Sounds: ue: *Fr.* **rue**, *Ger.* **füllen**   uh(r): *Fr.* **boeuf**, *Ger.* **Höhle**   ḵh: *Ger.* **ich**, *Scot.* **loch**   ḡ: *Sp.* **amigo**   ṿ: *Sp.* **hablar**
hl: *Welsh* **Llanelli**.   CAPITALS: primary stress.   SMALL CAPS: secondary stress.   Ⓢ: U.S. pron.   Ⓔ: British pron.

Sedang
  lang., people, South Vietnam   sā-DAHNG, suh-DANG   seː'dɑŋ, sə'dæŋ
Seder
  Passover meal   SĀD-uhr   'seːdəʳ
Sedgwick
  pers. name   SEJ-wik   'sedʒwik
Sedro Wooley
  city, WA   SĒ-drō WUL-ē   ˌsiːdroː 'wuliˑ
Sedum
  plant   SĒD-uhm   'siːdəm
Seebohm
  pers. name   SĒ-BŌM   'siːˌboːm
Seeger
  family of US musicologists, singers   SĒ-guhr   'siːgəʳ
Seekonk
  river, RI; town, MA   SĒ-KAHNGK   'siːˌkɑŋk
Seferiades
  Giorgios Stylianou, *orig. name of*   SEF-ER-YAH<u>TH</u>-ēs   ˌsefˌer'jɑðiːs
  George Seferis
Seferis
  George (*pseudonym of* G. S.   se-FER-ēs   se'feriːs
  Seferiades), *Greek poet, diplomat*
  (Nobel 1963)
Sega
  tdmk for video games   SĀ-guh   'seːgə
Segal
  George, *US actor;* Erich, *US author* SĒ-guhl   'siːgəl
Segesta
  ancient city, Sicily   si-JES-tuh   si'dʒestə
Sego
  lily   SĒ-gō   'siːgoː
Segovia
  prov, Spain; Andrés, *Spanish*   sā-GŌ-<u>v</u>yah, ⑤ si-GŌ-vē-uh   seː'ɣoːβjɑ, ⑤ si'goːviːə
  guitarist
Segrè
  Emilio, *Italian-born US physicist*   suh-GRĀ, sā-GRĀ   sə'greː, seː'greː
  (Nobel 1959)
Segub
  Biblical name   SĒ-guhb, suh-GŌŌV   'siːgəb, sə'guːv
Seguidilla
  dance   SEG-uh-DĒ-(y)uh, SEG-uh-DĒL-yuh   ˌsegə'diː(j)ə, ˌsegə'diːljə
Seguin
  city, TX   suh-GĒN   sə'giːn
Seidlitz
  laxative powders   SED-luhts   'sedləts
Seifert
  Jaroslav, *writer*   SĪ-fuhrt   'sɑifəʳt
Seihin
  pers. name, Japanese   sā-hin   seːhin
Seiichiro
  pers. name, Japanese   sā-ē-chē-rō   seːiːtʃiːroː
Seiji
  pers. name, Japanese   sā-jē   seːdʒiˑ
Seiko
  tdmk, Japanese watches   SĀ-kō   'seːkoː

Key (col. 2): a: **fad** ā: **fade** ah: **father** ar: **marry** aw: **law** e: **fed** ē: **feed** er: **merry** i: **hid** ī: **hide** ō: **coat** ōō: **boot**
oi: **boy** ow: **now** u: **put** uh: **above** uhr: **bird** ch: **chop** ng: **ring** sh: **show** th: **thick** <u>th</u>: **this** zh: **measure**

Seim, Sejm, Seym *river, Russia*	SĀM	'seːm
Seine *river, France*	SEN, [$] SĀN, SEN	sen, [$] 'seːn, 'sen
Seine-et-Marne *dept, France*	sen-ā-MAHRN	seneːmaːrn
Seine-Maritime *dept, France*	sen-mah-rē-TĒM	senmaːriːtiːm
Seine-Saint-Denis *dept, France*	sen-se^{n}d-NĒ	sensẽdniː
Seinfeld Jerry, *US actor, comedian*	SĪN-FELD	'sain,feld
Seir *Biblical name*	SĒ-uhr, SIR, se-ĒR	'siːə^{r}, 'si^{r}, se'iːr
Seirah *Biblical name*	SĒ-uh-ruh, SIR-uh, sē-Ī-ruh, suh-ē-RAH	'siːərə, 'sirə, siː'airə, səiː'raː
Seirath *Biblical name*	sē-Ī-RATH, SĒ-uh-RATH, SIR-ATH, suh-ē-RAH-tah	siː'ai,ræθ, 'siːə,ræθ, 'sir,æθ, səiː'rata
Seisachtheia *Solon's debt cancellation*	SĪ-suhk-THĀ-(y)uh	,saisək'θeː(j)ə
Seishiro *pers. name, Japanese*	sā-shē-rō	seːʃiːroː
Sejanus *Roman conspirator*	si-JĀ-nuhs	si'dʒeːnəs
Sejm *see* Seim		
Seker Bayrami *Turkish festival*	SĀ-kuhr bī-RAHM-ē	'seːkə^{r} bai'ramiˑ
Sekhet [Sekhmet] *Egyptian goddess of war*	SEKH-uht, SEK-uht	'sexət, 'sekət
Sekhmet *Egyptian goddess of war*	SEKH-muht, SEK-, -met	'sexmət, 'sek-, -met
Sela [Selah] *Biblical name*	SĒ-luh, SEL-ah	'siːlə, 'sela
Selah *pers. name*	SĒ-luh	'siːlə
Sela-hammahlekoth *Biblical name*	SĒ-luh-huh-MAHL-uh-KAHTH, -KAWTH; SE-lah-HAH-mahkh-luh-KAWT	'siːləhə'malə,kaθ, -,kɔːθ; 'sela,hamaxlə'kɔːt
Selangor *state, Malaysia*	suh-LANG-uhr	sə'læŋə^{r}
Selassie *see* Haile Selassie		
Seled *Biblical name*	SĒ-LED, SEL-ED	'siː,led, 'sel,ed
Selena *pers. name*	suh-LĒ-nuh	sə'liːnə
Selena *Tejano entertainer*	suh-LĀ-nuh, suh-LĒ-nuh	sə'leːnə, sə'liːnə
Selene *Greek goddess of the moon*	suh-LĒ-nē	sə'liːniˑ
selenium *element*	suh-LĒ-nē-uhm	sə'liːniːəm

Seles
  Monica, *Romanian-born tennis* .... SEL-uhs .... 'seləs
    player
Seleucia
  ancient city, Asia Minor .... suh-LOO-sh(ē-)uh .... sə'luːʃ(iː)ə
Seleucid
  Greek dynasty in Syria .... suh-LOO-suhd, suhl-YOO-suhd .... sə'luːsəd, səl'juːsəd
Seleucus
  Seleucid king .... suh-LOO-kuhs .... sə'luːkəs
Selig
  1. pers. name .... SĒ-lig .... 'siːlig
  2. German .... ZĀ-li<u>kh</u> .... 'zeːliç
Selim
  1. pers. name .... SĒ-luhm .... 'siːləm
  2. Finnish .... SĀ-lim .... 'seːlim
Selina
  pers. name .... suh-LĒ-nuh, suh-LĪ-nuh .... sə'liːnə, sə'lainə
Seljuk
  pert. to a Turkish dynasty .... SEL-JOOK, sel-JOOK .... 'sel͵dʒuːk, sel'dʒuːk
Selkirk
  mts., Canada; burgh, Scotland .... SEL-KUHRK .... 'sel͵kəʳk
Selkup
  lang., Khanti-Mansi region, Russia .... SEL-KUHP .... 'sel͵kəp
Selleck
  Tom, *US actor* .... SEL-ik .... 'selik
Selma
  1. city, AL; pers. name .... SEL-muh .... 'selmə
  2. Swedish .... SEL-mah .... 'selmɑː
Selwyn
  pers. name .... SEL-wuhn, SEL-win .... 'selwən, 'selwin
Selznick
  David O., *US film producer* .... SELZ-nik .... 'selznik
Semarang
  port, Java .... suh-MAHR-AHNG .... sə'mɑr͵ɑŋ
Sem [Shem]
  Biblical name .... SEM .... 'sem
Semachiah, Semakiah
  Biblical name .... SEM-uh-KĪ-uh, suh-mah<u>kh</u>-YAH-hoo .... ͵semə'kɑiə, səmɑx'jɑhuː
Semei
  Biblical name .... SEM-ē-Ī .... 'semiː͵ɑi
Semein
  Biblical name .... SEM-ē-uhn .... 'semiːən
Semele
  mother of Dionysus by Zeus .... SEM-uh-lē .... 'seməliˑ
Semen, Semën
  pers. name, Russian .... syim-YAWN .... sjim'jɔːn
Semenov
  Nikolai N., *Russian physicist (Nobel* .... syim-YAWN-uhf .... sjim'jɔːnəf
    1956)
Semichi
  Islands, *island group, AK* .... suh-MĒ-chē Ī-luhndz .... sə͵miːtʃiˑ 'ɑiləndz
Seminole
  N. American people .... SEM-uh-NŌL .... 'semə͵noːl

---

Key (col. 2):　a: fad　ā: fade　ah: father　ar: marry　aw: law　e: fed　ē: feed　er: merry　i: hid　ī: hide　ō: coat　oō: boot
oi: boy　ow: now　u: put　uh: above　uhr: bird　ch: chop　ng: ring　sh: show　th: thick　<u>th</u>: this　zh: measure

Semi-Pelagianism
  doctrine that man needs God's   SEM-ē-puh-LĀ-jē-uh-NIZ-uhm, SEM-Ī-   ˌsemiˈpəˈleːdʒiːəˌnizəm,
    special help   ˌsemˌɑi-

Semiramis
  Assyrian queen   suh-MIR-uh-muhs   səˈmirəməs

Semite
  Semitic people; descendant of Shem   SEM-ĪT, Ⓔ SĒ-MĪT   ˈsemˌait, Ⓔ ˈsiːˌmait

Semitic
  lang. family; pert. to Semites, *esp.*   suh-MIT-ik   səˈmiṭik
    Jews

Semitics
  study of Semitic peoples & langs.   suh-MIT-iks   səˈmiṭiks

Semitism
  Semitic characteristics   SEM-uh-TIZ-uhm   ˈseməˌtizəm

Semitist
  Semitic scholar   SEM-uht-uhst   ˈseməṭəst

Semple
  pers. name (A. S. McPherson)   SEM-puhl   ˈsempəl

Sempronius
  pers. name, Latin   sem-PRŌ-nē-uhs   semˈproːniːəs

Semyon
  pers. name, Russian   syim-YAWN   sjimˈjɔːn

Senaah
  Biblical name   suh-NĀ-uh, SEN-Ā-uh, suh-nah-AH   səˈneːə, ˈsenˌeːə, sənɑˈɑː

Senatobia
  town, MS   SEN-uh-TŌ-bē-uh, -TŌB-yuh   ˌsenəˈtoːbiːə, -ˈtoːbjə

Senatus consultum ultimum
  final decree of the Roman Senate   suh-NĀT-uhs kuhn-SUHL-tuhm   səˈneːṭəs kənˈsəltəm
                                    UHL-tuh-muhm   ˈəltəməm

Sendai
  city, Japan   sen-dī   sendɑi

Sendak
  Maurice, *US author, illustrator*   SEN-dak   ˈsendæk

Seneca
  Roman writer; N. American people   SEN-i-kuh   ˈsenikə

Senecan
  pert. to Seneca   SEN-i-kuhn   ˈsenikən

Senegal
  republic, Africa   SEN-i-GAWL   ˌseniˈgɔːl

Senegalese
  pert. to Senegal   SEN-i-guh-LĒZ, -LĒS   ˌsenigəˈliːz, -ˈliːs

Senegambia
  confederation, Africa   SEN-i-GAHM-bē-uh, SEN-i-GAM-bē-uh   ˌseniˈgɑmbiːə, ˌseniˈgæmbiːə

Seneh
  Biblical name   SĒ-nuh, SĒ-NE, SEN-uh, SEN-e   ˈsiːnə, ˈsiːˌne, ˈsenə, ˈsene

Senghor
  Leopold, *president, Senegal*   sahⁿ-GAWR, sen-GAWR   sɑ̃ˈgɔːʳ, senˈgɔːʳ

Senir
  Biblical name   SĒ-NIR, suh-NĒR   ˈsiːˌniʳ, səˈniːr

Senlac
  hill, England   SEN-LAK   ˈsenˌlæk

Sennacherib
  Assyrian king   suh-NAK-uh-ruhb, -RIB   səˈnækərəb, -ˌrib

Sennacherib
  Biblical name   suh-NAK-uh-RIB, sahn-kher-ĒV   səˈnækəˌrib, sɑnxerˈiːv

---

Foreign Sounds: ue: *Fr.* **rue**, *Ger.* **füllen**   uh(r): *Fr.* **boeuf**, *Ger.* **Höhle**   <u>kh</u>: *Ger.* i**ch**, *Scot.* lo**ch**   g̃: *Sp.* ami**g**o   v̲: *Sp.* ha**b**lar
hl: *Welsh* **Ll**anelli.   CAPITALS: primary stress.   SMALL CAPS: secondary stress.   Ⓢ: U.S. pron.   Ⓔ: British pron.

Señor
Spanish form of address for a man   sän-YAWR, sen-YAWR   seːnˈjɔːʳ, senˈjɔːʳ

Señora
Spanish form of address for a   sän-YŌR-ah, sän-YAWR-uh, sen-   seːnˈjoːrɑ, seːnˈjɔːrə, sen-
married woman

Señores
plural of Señor   sän-YŌR-äs, sän-YAWR-äs, sen-   seːnˈjoːreːs, seːnˈjɔːreːs, sen-

Señorita
Spanish form of address for an   sän-yaw-RĒ-tah, ⓢ SĀN-yuh-RĒT-uh,   seːnjɔːˈriːtɑ, ⓢ ˌseːnjəˈriːʈə,
unmarried woman   SEN-   ˌsen-

Sensodyne
tdmk for toothpaste   SEN(T)-suh-DĪN   ˈsen(t)səˌdɑin

Sentinum
ancient town, Italy   sen-TĪ-nuhm   senˈtɑinəm

Senuah
Biblical name   suh-N(Y)O͞O-uh, SEN-(y)uh-wuh,   səˈn(j)uːə, ˈsen(j)əwə,
    suh-no͞o-AH   sənuːˈɑː

Seorim
Biblical name   sē-AWR-im, -ŌR-im; suh-aw-RĒM   siːˈɔːrim, -ˈoːrim; səɔːˈriːm

Seoul
city, S. Korea   sōl   soːl

Sephar
Biblical name   SĒ-FAHR, suh-FAHR   ˈsiːˌfɑʳ, səˈfɑr

Sepharad
Biblical name   suh-FAR-AD, SEF-uh-RAD,   səˈfærˌæd, ˈsefəˌræd,
    suh-fah-RAHD, sfah-RAHD   səfɑːˈrɑd, sfɑːˈrɑd

Sephardi
Jew from Spain, Portugal, or N.   suh-FAHRD-ē   səˈfɑʳdiˑ
Africa

Sephardic
pert. to the Sephardim   suh-FAHRD-ik   səˈfɑʳdik

Sephardim
plural of Sephardi   suh-FAHRD-im   səˈfɑʳdim

Sepharvaim
Biblical name   SĒ-fahr-VĀ-im, SEF-AHR-;   ˌsiːfɑʳˈveːim, ˌsefˌɑʳ-;
    suh-FAHR-vah-YIM   səˌfɑrvɑˈjim

Sepharvite
Biblical name   suh-FAHR-VĪT, SEF-AHR-VĪT   səˈfɑʳˌvɑit, ˈsefˌɑʳˌvɑit

Sepik
river, New Guinea   SĀ-pik   ˈseːpik

Septante
French beer   sep-TAHⁿT   septɑ̃t

September
month   sep-TEM-buhr   sepˈtembəʳ

Sept-Îles
city, Canada   se-TĒL   seˈtiːl

Septimius
pers. name, Latin   sep-TIM-ē-uhs   sepˈtimiːəs

Septimius Severus
Roman emperor   sep-TIM-ē-uhs suh-VIR-uhs   sepˈtimiːəs səˈvirəs

Septimus
pers. name, Latin   SEP-tuh-muhs   ˈseptəməs

Septuagesima
3rd Sunday before Lent   SEP-tuh-wuh-JES-uh-muh,   ˌseptəwəˈdʒesəmə,
    -JĀ-zuh-muh   -ˈdʒeːzəmə

Key (col. 2):   a: fad   ā: fade   ah: father   ar: marry   aw: law   e: fed   ē: feed   er: merry   i: hid   ī: hide   ō: coat   o͞o: boot
oi: boy   ow: now   u: put   uh: above   uhr: bird   ch: chop   ng: ring   sh: show   th: thick   <u>th</u>: this   zh: measure

Septuagint
Greek version of the Old Testament sep-T(Y)OO̅-uh-juhnt, sep't(j)uːədʒənt,
SEP-tuh-wuh-JINT 'septəwə,dʒint

Sepúlveda
Juan Gines de, Spanish historian sā-POO̅L-vā-thah, seː'puːlβeːða, ⓢ sə'pulvədə,
ⓢ suh-PUL-vuhd-uh, sə'pəlvədə
suh-PUHL-vuhd-uh

Sepulveda
Boulevard, Los Angeles, CA suh-PUHL-vuhd-uh, suh-PUL-vuhd-uh sə'pəlvədə, sə'pulvədə

Sequatchie
river, county, TN si-KWAHCH-ē si'kwɑtʃiˑ

Sequim
town, WA SKWIM, suh-KWIM 'skwim, sə'kwim

Sequoia
Cherokee scholar; park, CA si-KWOI-(y)uh si'kwɔi(j)ə

Sequoyah
county, OK si-KWOI-(y)uh si'kwɔi(j)ə

Serafin
Barry, US TV news correspondent SER-uh-fin, SER-uh-fuhn 'serəfin, 'serəfən

Serafino
pers. name, Italian SĀ-rah-FĒ-nō ˌseːrɑ'fiːnoː

Serah
Biblical name SIR-uh, SĒ-ruh, SE-rahkh 'sirə, 'siːrə, 'serɑx

Seraiah
Biblical name suh-RĪ-uh, suh-rah-YAH sə'rɑiə, sərɑ'jɑ

Seram
see Ceram

Serang
island, town, Indonesia SĀ-RAHNG 'seːˌrɑŋ

Seraphim
order of angels SER-uh-FIM 'serəˌfim

Séraphin
pers. name, French sā-rah-FEⁿ seːrɑːfẽ

Seraphina
seraphine, reed instrument SER-uh-FĒ-nuh ˌserə'fiːnə

Séraphine
pers. name, French sā-rah-FĒN seːrɑːfiːn

Serapis
Ptolemaic Egyptian god suh-RĀ-puhs sə'reːpəs

Serb
a native of Serbia SUHRB 'səʳb

Serban
pers. name, Romanian sher-BAHN ʃeʳ'bɑn

Serbia
republic, E. Europe SUHR-bē-uh 'səʳbiːə

Serbian
pert. to Serbia SUHR-bē-uhn 'səʳbiːən

Serbo-Croatian
Slavonic lang., Europe SUHR-bō-KRŌ-Ā-shuhn ˌsəʳboːˌkroː'eːʃən

Sered
Biblical name SIR-ED, SIR-uhd, SER-ed 'sirˌed, 'sirəd, 'sered

Seredite
Biblical name SIR-uh-DĪT, SĒ-ruh- 'sirəˌdɑit, 'siːrə-

Serengeti
natl. park, Tanzania SER-uhn-GET-ē ˌserən'geti̇ˑ

Foreign Sounds: ue: *Fr.* **rue**, *Ger.* **füllen**   uh(r): *Fr.* b**oeuf**, *Ger.* H**öhle**   kh: *Ger.* i**ch**, *Scot.* lo**ch**   ḡ: *Sp.* ami**g**o   v: *Sp.* ha**b**lar
hl: *Welsh* **Ll**anelli.   CAPITALS: primary stress.   SMALL CAPS: secondary stress.   ⓢ: U.S. pron.   ⓔ: British pron.

Serenitatis, Mare
  see Mare Serenitatis
Serer
  lang., people, Senegal, Gambia   suh-RER   səˈreʳ
Serestus
  companion of Aeneas   suh-RES-tuhs   səˈrestəs
Serge
  1. pers. name   SUHRJ, SERZH, SERJ   ˈsəʳdʒ, ˈseʳʒ, ˈseʳdʒ
  2. French   SERZH   serʒ
Sergei, Sergey
  pers. name, Russian   syir-GYĀ(-ē), ⑤ ser-GĀ, SER-gā   sjirˈgjeː(iː), ⑤ seʳˈgeː, ˈseʳgeː

Sergestus
  companion of Aeneas   suhr-JES-tuhs   səʳˈdʒestəs
Sergio
  pers. name   SER-<u>kh</u>yō, ⑤ SUHR-jē-ō   ˈserxjoː, ⑤ ˈsəʳdʒiːoː
Sergius
  pope   SUHR-jē-uhs   ˈsəʳdʒiːəs
Sergius-Paulus
  Biblical name   SUHR-jē-uh-SPAW-luhs   ˈsəʳdʒiːəˈspɔːləs
Seriema
  South American bird   SER-ē-Ē-muh, SER-ē-Ā-muh   ˌseriːˈiːmə, ˌseriːˈeːmə
Seringapatam
  town, Karnataka, India   suh-RING-guh-puh-TAHM, -TAM   səˌriŋgəpəˈtɑm, -ˈtæm
Seriphos
  island, Greece   si-RĪ-fuhs, SER-i-FAWS   siˈrɑifəs, ˈseriˌfɔːs
Serkin
  Rudolf, *Austrian-born US pianist*   SUHR-kuhn   ˈsəʳkən
Serov
  city, Russia   SER-uhf   ˈserəf
Serpens
  constellation   SUHR-puhnz, SUHR-PENZ   ˈsəʳpənz, ˈsəʳˌpenz
Serra
  Junípero, *Spanish missionary in*   SER-rah, ⑤ SER-uh   ˈserrɑ, ⑤ ˈserə
  California
Sertorius
  Roman general   SUHR-TŌR-ē-uhs, SUHR-TAWR-ē-uhs   ˌsəʳˈtoːriːəs, ˌsəʳˈtɔːriːəs
Serug
  Biblical name   SIR-uhg, suh-ROOG   ˈsirəg, səˈruːg
Servian Reform
  Roman reorganization, 6th cent., BC   SUHR-vē-uhn   ˈsəʳviːən
Servilia
  pers. name, Latin   suhr-VIL-ē-uh   səʳˈviliːə
Servilius
  pers. name, Latin   suhr-VIL-ē-uhs, suhr-VIL-yuhs   səʳˈviliːəs, səʳˈviljəs
Servius
  pers. name, Latin   SUHR-vē-uhs   ˈsəʳviːəs
Servius Tullius
  sixth king of Rome   SUHR-vē-uhs TUHL-ē-uhs   ˈsəʳviːəs ˈtəliːəs
Sesame Street
  TV program   SES-uh-mē STRĒT   ˈsesəmiˑ ˌstriːt
Seshat
  Egyptian goddess of writing   SESH-uht   ˈseʃət
Sesostris
  king of Egypt   suh-SAHS-truhs   səˈsɑstrəs

Key (col. 2):   a: fad   ā: fade   ah: father   ar: marry   aw: law   e: fed   ē: feed   er: merry   i: hid   ī: hide   ō: coat   ōō: boot
oi: boy   ow: now   u: put   uh: above   uhr: bird   ch: chop   ng: ring   sh: show   th: thick   <u>th</u>: this   zh: measure

Sesotho
   Bantu lang., Lesotho   suh-S͞O͞OT-o͞o, suh-S͞O͞O-to͞o   sə'suːțuː, sə'suːtuː
Sessue
   pers. name   SES-(y)o͞o   'ses(j)uː
Set [Seth]
   evil Egyptian god   SET   'set
Setekh [Seth]
   evil Egyptian god   SET-uhkh, SET-uhk   'sețəx, 'sețək
Sete Quedas [Guairá]
   waterfall, S. America   SĀT-uh KĀ-thuhsh   ˌseːțə 'keːðəʃ
Setesh [Seth]
   evil Egyptian god   SET-uhsh   'sețəʃ
Seth
   1. *evil Egyptian god; pers. name*   SETH   'seθ
   2. *German*   ZĀT   'zeːt
Sethur
   Biblical name   SĒ-THUR, suh-T͞O͞OR   'siːˌθuʳ, sə'tuːr
Seti
   king of Egypt   SET-ē   'sețiˑ
Seton
   Elizabeth, US educator   SĒT-n   'siːtn̩
Seto Naikai
   Inland Sea, Japan   se-tō nī-kī   setoː nɑikɑi
Seton Hall
   University, NJ   SĒT-n HAWL   ˌsiːtn̩ 'hɔːl
Setsubun
   Bean-throwing Festival (Feb. 3), Japan   set-so͞o-bun   setsuːbun
Setswana [Tswana]
   lang., Africa   set-SWAHN-uh   set'swɑnə
Setúbal
   prov & town, Portugal   suh-T͞O͞O-buhl   sə'tuːbəl
Seurat
   Georges, French painter   suh(r)-RAH   sœːrɑː
Seuss
   Dr., pseudonym of Theodore Geisel, *US writer*   S͞O͞OS   'suːs
Sevareid
   Eric, US journalist   SEV-uh-RĪD   'sevəˌrɑid
Sevastopol, Sebastopol
   port, Ukraine   SYEV-uh-STAW-puhl, Ⓢ suh-VAS-tuh-PŌL, -PAWL   ˌsjevə'stɔːpəl̩, Ⓢ sə'væstəˌpoːl, -ˌpɔːl
Seve
   pers. name, Spanish   SĀ-vā   'seːβeː
Sevechorus
   grandfather of Gilgamesh   suh-VEK-uh-ruhs   sə'vekərəs
Seveneh
   Biblical name   suh-VEN-uh, SEV-uh-nuh, suh-ven-E   sə'venə, 'sevənə, səven'e
Severan Dynasty
   Roman imperial dynasty   suh-VIR-uhn   sə'virən
Severinsen
   Doc, US musician   SEV-(uh-)ruhn-suhn   'sev(ə)rənsən
Severinus
   pope; pers. name, Latin   SEV-uh-RĪ-nuhs   ˌsevə'rɑinəs

Foreign Sounds: ue: *Fr.* **rue**, *Ger.* **füllen** uh(r): *Fr.* **boeuf**, *Ger.* **Höhle** kh: *Ger.* **ich**, *Scot.* **loch** ḡ: *Sp.* **amigo** v̱: *Sp.* **hablar** hl: *Welsh* **Llanelli**. CAPITALS: primary stress. SMALL CAPS: secondary stress. Ⓢ: U.S. pron. Ⓔ: British pron.

Severn
   river, Gt. Britain — SEV-uhrn — ˈsevəʳn

Severnaya Zemlya
   island group, Arctic Ocean — SEV-uhr-nuh-YAH ZEM-lē-AH — ˈsevəʳnəˌja ˌzemliːˈɑ

Severo
   pers. name, Spanish — sā-V̱Ā-rō — seːˈβeːroː

Severus Alexander
   Roman emperor — se-VIR-uhs AL-ig-ZAN-duhr, EL-ig- — seˈvirəs ˌæligˈzændəʳ, ˌelig-

Sevier
   river, UT; county, AR, TN, UT — suh-VIR — səˈviʳ

Sevilla
   city, prov, Spain — sā-V̱Ē(L)-yah — seːˈβiː(l)jɑ

Seville [Sevilla]
   city, prov, Spain — suh-VIL — səˈvil

Sèvres
   commune, France — SEVR — sevr

Sewanee
   town, TN — suh-WAW-nē, suh-WAH-nē — səˈwɔːniˑ, səˈwɑːniˑ

Seward
   1. William Henry, US politician; US — SO͞O-uhrd, SURD — ˈsuːəʳd, ˈsuʳd
   pl. name
   2. pers. name — SO͞O-uhrd, SURD, Ⓔ *also* SĒ-wuhrd — ˈsuːəʳd, ˈsuʳd, Ⓔ *also* ˈsiːwəʳd

Sewickley
   borough, PA — suh-WIK-lē — səˈwikliˑ

Sexagesima
   2nd Sunday before Lent — SEK-suh-JES-uh-muh — ˌseksəˈdʒesəmə

Sextans
   constellation — SEK-STANZ, -stuhnz — ˈsekˌstænz, -stənz

Sextus
   pers. name, Latin — SEK-stuhs — ˈsekstəs

Seychelles
   islands, Indian Ocean — sā-SHEL(Z) — seːˈʃel(z)

Seychellois
   inhabitant(s) of Seychelles — sā-shel-WAH — seːʃelwɑː

Seym
   see Seim

Seymour
   family name; pers. name — SĒ-MŌR, SĒ-MAWR, Ⓔ SĒ-muhr, SĒ-MAWR, SĀ-muhr — ˈsiːˌmoːʳ, ˈsiːˌmɔːʳ, Ⓔ ˈsiːməʳ, ˈsiːˌmɔːʳ, ˈseːməʳ

Sforza
   ruling family of Milan, Italy — SFAWRT-sah — ˈsfɔːʳtsɑ

Sgaw
   lang., people, Burma, Thailand — SKAW — ˈskɔː

's-Gravenhage [Hague, The]
   city, Netherlands — S(K)RAHV-uhn-HAH-g̱uh — ˌs(k)rɑvənˈhɑɣə

Shaalabbin
   Biblical name — SHĀ-uh-LAB-in, shā-AL-uh-bin, SHAH-ah-lah-BĒN — ˌʃeːəˈlæbin, ʃeːˈæləbin, ˌʃɑɑlɑˈbiːn

Shaalbim
   Biblical name — shā-AL-bim, SHAH-ahl-VĒM — ʃeːˈælbim, ˌʃɑɑlˈviːm

Shaalbon
   Biblical name — shā-AL-buhn, SHAH-ahl-VAWN — ʃeːˈælbən, ˌʃɑɑlˈvɔːn

Shaalbonite
   Biblical name — SHĀ-AL-buh-NĪT — ˌʃeːˈælbəˌnɑit

Key (col. 2):   a: fad   ā: fade   ah: father   ar: marry   aw: law   e: fed   ē: feed   er: merry   i: hid   ī: hide   ō: coat   o͞o: boot
oi: boy   ow: now   u: put   uh: above   uhr: bird   ch: chop   ng: ring   sh: show   th: thick   <u>th</u>: this   zh: measure

Shaalim
Biblical name   SHĀ-uh-LIM, SHAH-ah-LIM   'ʃeːəˌlim, ˌʃɑɑ'lim

Shaanxi
see Shanxi

Shaaph
Biblical name   SHĀ-AF, SHAH-ahf   'ʃeːˌæf, 'ʃɑɑf

Shaaraim
Biblical name   SHĀ-uh-RĀ-im, SHAH-ah-RAH-yim   ˌʃeːə'reːim, ˌʃɑɑ'rɑjim

Shaashgaz
Biblical name   shā-ASH-GAHZ, SHAH-ahsh-GAHZ   ʃeː'æʃˌgɑz, ˌʃɑɑʃ'gɑz

Shaba [Katanga]
prov, Zaire   SHAHB-uh   'ʃɑbə

Sha'ban
Islamic month   shuh-BAHN   ʃə'bɑn

Shabatu
Babylonian month   shuh-BAHT-o͞o   ʃə'bɑṭuː

Shabbat
Jewish Sabbath   shuh-BAHT, SHAHB-uhs   ʃə'bɑt, 'ʃɑbəs

Shabbethai
Biblical name   SHAB-uh-THĪ, shahb-TĪ   'ʃæbəˌθɑi, ʃɑb'tɑi

Shabuoth, Shavuoth
Jewish festival   SHAHV-o͞o-AWT, shuh-VO͞O-ŌT, shuh-VO͞O-ŌTH, shuh-VO͞O-ŌS, shuh-VO͞O-uhs   ˌʃɑvuː'ɔːt, ʃə'vuːˌoːt, ʃə'vuːˌoːθ, ʃə'vuːˌoːs, ʃə'vuːəs

Shachia
Biblical name   shuh-KĪ-uh, SHAK-ē-uh, sahkh-YAH   ʃə'kɑiə, 'ʃækiːə, sɑx'jɑ

Shackelford
Ted, US actor   SHAK-uhl-fuhrd   'ʃækəlfərd

Shaddai
Hebrew name for God inscribed in a mezuzah   SHAHD-Ī   'ʃɑdˌɑi

Shadrach
pers. name   SHAD-RAK   'ʃædˌræk

SHAEF
Supreme Headquarters, Allied Expeditionary Force   SHĀF   'ʃeːf

Shaeffer
Peter, English playwright; US pen co.   SHĀ-fuhr   'ʃeːfər

Shaemas
pers. name, Irish Gaelic   SHĀ-muhs   'ʃeːməs

Shafi'i
school of Islam   SHAF-ē-Ē, SHAHF-ē-Ē   'ʃæfiːˌiː, 'ʃɑfiːˌiː

Shaftesbury
Earl of, British reformer   SHAHF(T)S-b(uh-)rē, Ⓢ SHAF(T)S-b(uh-)rē   'ʃɑːf(t)sb(ə)riˑ, Ⓢ 'ʃæf(t)sb(ə)riˑ

Shage
Biblical name   SHĀ-guh, shah-GE   'ʃeːgə, ʃɑ'ge

Shagee [Shage]
Biblical name   SHĀ-gē, SHĀ-jē, shah-GE   'ʃeːgiˑ, 'ʃeːdʒiˑ, ʃɑ'ge

Shage
Biblical name   SHĀ-guh, shah-GE   'ʃeːgə, ʃɑ'ge

Shagee [Shage]
Biblical name   SHĀ-gē, SHĀ-jē, shah-GE   'ʃeːgiˑ, 'ʃeːdʒiˑ, ʃɑ'ge

---

Foreign Sounds: **ue**: *Fr.* **rue**, *Ger.* **füllen**   **uh(r)**: *Fr.* **boeuf**, *Ger.* **Höhle**   **kh**: *Ger.* **ich**, *Scot.* **loch**   **g̱**: *Sp.* **amigo**   **v**: *Sp.* **hablar**   **hl**: *Welsh* **Llanelli**.   CAPITALS: primary stress.   SMALL CAPS: secondary stress.   Ⓢ: U.S. pron.   Ⓔ: British pron.

Shahada
  Islamic profession of faith   shuh-HAHD-uh   ʃəˈhadə

Shaharaim
  Biblical name   SHĀ-(h)uh-RĀ-im,   ˌʃeː(h)əˈreːim, ˌʃaxaˈrajim
       SHAH-<u>kh</u>ah-RAH-yim

Shahazimah
  Biblical name   SHĀ-(h)uh-ZĪ-muh,   ˌʃeː(h)əˈzaimə, ˌʃaxatˈsiːmaː
       SHAH-<u>kh</u>aht-SĒ-mah

Shahazumah [Shahazimah]
  Biblical name   SHĀ-(h)uh-ZOO-muh   ˌʃeː(h)əˈzuːmə

Shahjahanpur
  city, India   SHAH-juh-HAHN-PUR, SHAW-   ˌʃadʒəˈhanˌpuʳ, ˌʃɔː-

Shaitan
  evil jinni or spirit   shā-TAHN, shī-TAHN   ʃeːˈtan, ʃaiˈtan

Shakerism
  religion   SHĀ-kuh-RIZ-uhm   ˈʃeːkəˌrizəm

Shakespeare
  William, *English poet; pers. name*   SHĀK-SPIR   ˈʃeːkˌspiʳ

Shakespearean
  pert. to Shakespeare   shāk-SPIR-ē-uhn   ʃeːkˈspiriːən

Shakespeareana
  things pert. to Shakespeare   SHĀK-SPIR-ē-AN-uh, -AHN-uh   ˌʃeːkˌspiriːˈænə, -ˈɑːnə

Shakopee Mdewakanton Sioux
  N. American people   SHAK-uh-pē EM-duh-WAW-kuhn-TŌN   ˈʃækəpiˑ ˌemdəˈwɔːkənˌtoːn
       SOO, MED-uh-WAW-kuhn-TŌN   ˈsuː, ˌmedəˈwɔːkənˌtoːn

Shakta
  adherent of Shaktism   SHAHK-tuh   ˈʃaktə

Shakti
  Hindu embodiment of female creative   SHAHK-tē   ˈʃaktiˑ
    energy; cosmic energy

Shaktism
  Hindu worship of Shakti   SHAHK-TIZ-uhm   ˈʃakˌtizəm

Shalala
  Donna, *US political figure*   shuh-LĀ-luh   ʃəˈleːlə

Shalem
  Biblical name   SHĀ-luhm, shah-LEM   ˈʃeːləm, ʃaˈlem

Shalim [Shaalim]
  Biblical name   SHĀ-lim   ˈʃeːlim

Shalisha, Shalishah
  Biblical name   SHAL-uh-SHAH, shuh-LĪ-shuh,   ˈʃæləˌʃaː, ʃəˈlaiʃə, ʃaˈliːʃa
       shah-LĒ-shah

Shalit
  Gene, *US TV commentator*   SHAL-uht   ˈʃælət

Shallecheth, Shalleketh
  Biblical name   SHAL-uh-KETH, shuh-LEK-eth,   ˈʃæləˌkeθ, ʃəˈlekeθ, ʃaːˈlexet
       shah-LE-<u>kh</u>et

Shallum
  Biblical name   SHAL-uhm, shah-LOOM   ˈʃæləm, ʃaˈluːm

Shallun
  Biblical name   SHAL-uhn, shah-LOON   ˈʃælən, ʃaˈluːn

Shalmai
  Biblical name   SHAL-mē-Ī, SHAL-MĪ, shahl-MĪ   ˈʃælmiːˌai, ˈʃælˌmai, ʃalˈmai

Shalman
  Biblical name   SHAL-muhn, SHAHL-mahn   ˈʃælmən, ˈʃalman

Key (col. 2):   a: fad   ā: fade   ah: father   ar: marry   aw: law   e: fed   ē: feed   er: merry   i: hid   ī: hide   ō: coat   ōō: boot
oi: boy   ow: now   u: put   uh: above   uhr: bird   ch: chop   ng: ring   sh: show   th: thick   <u>th</u>: this   zh: measure

Shalmaneser *king of Assyria*	SHAL-muh-NĒ-zuhr	ˌʃælməˈniːzəʳ
Shalom *pers. name, Hebrew*	shah-LŌM, *for S. Aleichem often* SHAW-luhm	ʃɑˈloːm, *for S. Aleichem often* ˈʃɔːləm
Shama *Biblical name*	SHĀ-muh, shah-MAH	ˈʃeːmə, ʃɑˈmɑ
Shamanism *religion*	SHAHM-uh-NIZ-uhm, SHĀ-muh-NIZ-uhm, SHAM-uh-NIZ-uhm	ˈʃɑməˌnizəm, ˈʃeːməˌnizəm, ˈʃæməˌnizəm
Shamariah *Biblical name*	SHAM-uh-RĪ-uh, shuh-mahr-YAH	ˌʃæməˈrɑiə, ʃəmɑrˈjɑː
Shamed *Biblical name*	SHĀ-MED, SHĀ-muhd, SHEM-ed	ˈʃeːˌmed, ˈʃeːməd, ˈʃemed
Shamer *Biblical name*	SHĀ-muhr, SHEM-er	ˈʃeːməʳ, ˈʃemer
Shamgar *Biblical name*	SHAM-GAHR, shahm-GAHR	ˈʃæmˌgɑʳ, ʃɑmˈgɑr
Shamhuth *Biblical name*	SHAM-(h)uhth, shahm-HOOT	ˈʃæm(h)əθ, ʃɑmˈhuːt
Shamir Yitzhak, *Israeli prime minister*	shah-MIR, shuh-MIR	ʃɑˈmiʳ, ʃəˈmiʳ
Shamir *Biblical name*	SHĀ-muhr, shah-MIR	ˈʃeːməʳ, ʃɑˈmir
Shamma, Shammah *Biblical name*	SHAM-uh, shah-MAH	ˈʃæmə, ʃɑˈmɑ
Shammai *Biblical name*	SHAM-ē-Ī, SHAM-Ī, shah-MĪ	ˈʃæmiːˌɑi, ˈʃæmˌɑi, ʃɑˈmɑi
Shammoth *Biblical name*	SHAM-AHTH, -AWTH, -uhth; shah-MŌT	ˈʃæmˌɑθ, -ˌɔːθ, -əθ; ʃɑˈmoːt
Shammua, Shammuah *Biblical name*	SHAM-(y)uh-wuh, shah-MOO-ah	ˈʃæm(j)əwə, ʃɑˈmuːɑː
Shamokin *city, PA*	shuh-MŌ-kuhn	ʃəˈmoːkən
Shamsherai *Biblical name*	SHAM-shuh-RĪ, SHAHM-shuh-RĪ	ˈʃæmʃəˌrɑi, ˌʃɑmʃəˈrɑi
Shan *S. Asian people*	SHAHN, SHAN	ˈʃɑn, ˈʃæn
Shandong *prov, peninsula, China*	SHAHN-DUNG	ˈʃɑnˈduŋ
Shang *dynasty, China*	SHAHNG, SHANG	ˈʃɑŋ, ˈʃæŋ
Shanghai *city, China*	shang-HĪ, SHANG-HĪ	ʃæŋˈhɑi, ˈʃæŋˌhɑi
Shangri-La *imaginary paradise*	SHANG-gri-LAH	ˌʃæŋgriˈlɑ
Shankar Ravi, *Indian sitar player*	SHAHNG-KAHR	ˈʃɑŋˌkɑʳ
Shannon *river, Ireland; pers. name*	SHAN-uhn	ˈʃænən
Shansi *see* Shanxi		

Foreign Sounds: ue: *Fr.* **rue**, *Ger.* **füllen** uh(r): *Fr.* **boeuf**, *Ger.* **Höhle** kh: *Ger.* **ich**, *Scot.* **loch** g: *Sp.* **amigo** v: *Sp.* **hablar** hl: *Welsh* **Llanelli**. CAPITALS: primary stress. SMALL CAPS: secondary stress. [$]: U.S. pron. [£]: British pron.

Shanti		
pers. name	SHAHN-tē	ˈʃɑnti·
Shanxi, Shaanxi, Shansi		
prov, China	SHAHN-SHĒ, SHAHN-SĒ	ˈʃanˈʃiː, ˈʃanˈsiː
Shapham		
Biblical name	SHĀ-FAM, shah-FAHM	ˈʃeːˌfæm, ʃaˈfɑm
Shaphan		
Biblical name	SHĀ-FAN, shah-FAHN	ˈʃeːˌfæn, ʃaˈfɑn
Shaphat		
Biblical name	SHĀ-FAT, shah-FAHT	ˈʃeːˌfæt, ʃaˈfɑt
Shapher		
Biblical name	SHĀ-fuhr, SHE-fer	ˈʃeːfərʳ, ˈʃefer
Shaphir		
Biblical name	SHĀ-fuhr, shah-FĒR	ˈʃeːfərʳ, ʃaːˈfiːr
Shapur		
Persian king	shah-POOR, shuh-PUR	ʃaːˈpuːrʳ, ʃəˈpurʳ
Shaqra [Ash-Shaqra]		
town, Saudi Arabia	shuh-KRAH	ʃəˈkrɑ
Shaquille		
pers. name	shah-KĒL	ʃaˈkiːl
Shara		
a Mongol people	SHAHR-uh	ˈʃɑrə
Sharai		
Biblical name	SHAR-Ī, SHER-Ī, shah-RĪ	ˈʃærˌai, ˈʃerˌai, ʃaˈrai
Sharaim [Shaaraim]		
Biblical name	shuh-RĀ-im	ʃəˈreːim
Sharar		
Biblical name	SHAR-uhr, SHER-uhr, shah-RAHR	ˈʃærərʳ, ˈʃerərʳ, ʃaˈrɑr
Sharezer		
Biblical name	shuh-RĒ-zuhr, shahr-ET-ser	ʃəˈriːzərʳ, ʃarˈetser
Shari		
see Chari		
Sharif		
Omar, *Egyptian actor*	shuh-RĒF	ʃəˈriːf
Sharjah		
emirate, town, United Arab Emirates	SHAHR-zhuh, SHAHR-juh	ˈʃɑrʒə, ˈʃɑrdʒə
Sharon		
1. *district, Israel; US pl. name; pers. name*	SHAR-uhn, SHER-uhn	ˈʃærən, ˈʃerən
2. Ariel, *Israeli politician*	shah-RŌN	ʃaˈroːn
Sharonite		
Biblical name	SHAR-uh-NĪT, SHER-	ˈʃærəˌnait, ˈʃer-
Sharpe		
William F., *US economist (Nobel 1990)*	SHAHRP	ˈʃɑrp
Shar Pei		
dog breed	shahr PĀ	ʃɑrʳ ˈpeː
Sharpeville		
prov, South Africa	SHAHRP-VIL	ˈʃɑrpˌvil
Sharuhen		
Biblical name	shuh-ROO-HEN, SHAH-roo-KHEN	ʃəˈruːˌhen, ˌʃaːruːˈxen
Shashai		
Biblical name	SHĀ-SHĪ, shah-SHĪ	ˈʃeːˌʃai, ʃaˈʃai
Shashak		
Biblical name	SHĀ-SHAK, shah-SHAHK	ˈʃeːˌʃæk, ʃaˈʃɑk

Key (col. 2): a: fad ā: fade ah: father ar: marry aw: law e: fed ē: feed er: merry i: hid ī: hide ō: coat ōō: boot
oi: boy ow: now u: put uh: above uhr: bird ch: chop ng: ring sh: show th: thick <u>th</u>: this zh: measure

Shasta
  N. American people; Mount, *volcano,*   SHAS-tuh   'ʃæstə
  CA

Shatner
  William, *Canadian-born actor,*   SHAT-nuhr   'ʃætnəʳ
  director

Shatt al'Arab
  river channel, Iraq   SHAHT ahl-AHR-ahb, SHAT al-AR-uhb   ˌʃɑːt ɑːlˈɑːrɑːb, ˌʃæt ælˈærəb

Shaul [Saul]
  Biblical name   SHĀ-uhl, shah-O͞OL   'ʃeːəl, ʃɑˈuːl

Shaulite
  Biblical name   SHĀ-uh-LĪT   'ʃeːəˌlait

Shaun
  pers. name   SHAWN, SHAHN   'ʃɔːn, 'ʃɑn

Shaveh
  Biblical name   SHĀ-vuh, shah-VE   'ʃeːvə, ʃɑˈve

Shaveh-kiriathaim
  Biblical name   SHĀ-vuh-KIR-ē-uh-THĀ-im,   'ʃeːvəˌkiriːəˈθeːim,
    shah-VE-KIR-yah-TAH-yim   ʃɑˈveˌkirjɑˈtɑjim

Shavian
  pert. to G. B. Shaw   SHĀ-vē-uhn   'ʃeːviːən

Shavonne
  pers. name   shuh-VAHN   ʃəˈvɑn

Shavsha
  Biblical name   SHAV-shuh, shahv-SHAH   'ʃævʃə, ʃɑvˈʃɑː

Shavuoth
  see Shabuoth

Shaw
  G. B., *Irish author (Nobel 1925)*   SHAW   'ʃɔː

Shawangunk Mountains
  mtn. range, NY   SHAHNG-guhm MOWNT-nz *[sic]*   ˌʃɑŋgəm 'mɑuntn̩z *[sic]*

Shawano
  county, WI   SHAW-nō   'ʃɔːnoː

Shawinigan
  city, Canada   shuh-WIN-uh-guhn   ʃəˈwinəgən

Shawn
  pers. name   SHAWN   'ʃɔːn

Shawnee
  N. American people; US pl. name;   shaw-NĒ, shah-NĒ   ʃɔːˈniː, ʃɑˈniː
  college, IL

Shawwal
  Islamic month   shuh-WAHL   ʃəˈwɑl

Shcharansky
  Anatoly, *mathematician, USSR*   sh(ch)uh-RAHN-skē   ʃ(tʃ)əˈrɑːnskiˑ

Shcherbakov
  city, Russia   SH(CH)ER-buh-KAWF   ˌʃ(tʃ)eʳbəˈkɔːf

She
  Chinese people   SHUH, SHĀ, SHĒ   'ʃə, 'ʃeː, 'ʃiː

Shea
  1. William A., Stadium, *New York*   SHĀ   'ʃeː
  City
  2. tree; pers. name   SHĒ, SHĀ   'ʃiː, 'ʃeː

Sheal
  Biblical name   SHĀ-uhl, shuh-AHL   'ʃeːəl, ʃəˈɑl

Foreign Sounds: ue: *Fr.* **rue**, *Ger.* **füllen**   uh(r): *Fr.* **boeuf**, *Ger.* **Höhle**   kh: *Ger.* **ich**, *Scot.* **loch**   ḡ: *Sp.* **amigo**   v̠: *Sp.* **hablar**
hl: *Welsh* **Llanelli.**   CAPITALS: primary stress.   SMALL CAPS: secondary stress.   Ⓢ: U.S. pron.   Ⓔ: British pron.

Shealtiel
   Biblical name   shē-AL-tē-EL, shuh-AHL-tē-EL   ʃiːˈæltiːˌel, ʃəˌɑltiːˈel

Sheariah
   Biblical name   SHĒ-uh-RĪ-uh, shuh-ahr-YAH   ˌʃiːəˈraiə, ʃɑərˈja

Shearing
   George, *US pianist, composer*   SHIR-ing   ˈʃiriŋ

Shear-jashub
   Biblical name   SHĒ-AHR-JĀ-shuhb,   ˈʃiːˌɑrˈdʒeːʃəb, ʃəˌɑrjaˈʃuːv
                               shuh-AHR-yah-SHOO̅V

Shearson Lehman Brothers
   US financial co.   SHIR-suhn LĀ-muhn   ˌʃirsən ˈleːmən

Sheba
   ancient country, Arabian Peninsula SHĒ-buh   ˈʃiːbə

Shebam
   Biblical name   SHĒ-BAM, SHĒ-buhm, shuh-BAM,   ˈʃiːˌbæm, ˈʃiːbəm, ʃəˈbæm,
                                 shuh-VAHM   ʃəˈvam

Shebaniah
   Biblical name   SHEB-uh-NĪ-uh, shuh-vahn-YAH   ˌʃebəˈnaiə, ʃəvanˈja

Shebarim
   Biblical name   SHEB-uh-rim, shuh-vah-RĒM   ˈʃebərim, ʃəvaˈriːm

Shebat, Shevat
   Jewish month   shuh-BAHT, shuh-VAHT   ʃəˈbɑt, ʃəˈvɑt

Shebelle, -bele, -beli
   river, Africa   shuh-BEL-ē   ʃəˈbeliˑ

Sheber
   Biblical name   SHĒ-buhr, shev-ER   ˈʃiːbər, ʃevˈer

Shebna, Shebnah
   Biblical name   SHEB-nuh, shev-NAH   ˈʃebnə, ʃevˈnɑ

Sheboygan
   city, county, WI   shi-BOI-guhn   ʃiˈbɔigən

Shebuel
   Biblical name   SHEB-yuh-wuhl, shuh-B(Y)OO̅-uhl, ˈʃebjəwəl, ʃəˈb(j)uːəl,
                                shuh-voo̅-EL   ʃəvuːˈel

Shechem
   Biblical name   SHEK-uhm, SHĒ-kuhm, shuh-KHEM ˈʃekəm, ˈʃiːkəm, ʃəˈxem

Shechemite
   Biblical name   SHEK-uh-MĪT, SHĒ-kuh-MĪT   ˈʃekəˌmait, ˈʃiːkəˌmait

Shechinah
   manifestation of God's presence on shuh-KHĒ-nuh, shuh-KĒ-nuh,   ʃəˈxiːnə, ʃəˈkiːnə, ʃəˈkainə
    Earth in Judaism   shuh-KĪ-nuh

Shedeur
   Biblical name   SHED-ē-uhr, shuh-dā-OO̅R   ˈʃediːər, ʃədeːˈuːr

Sheehan
   David, *US entertainment critic; pers.* SHĒ-uhn   ˈʃiːən
    name

Sheen
   Martin, *US actor*   SHĒN   ˈʃiːn

Sheena
   pers. name   SHĒ-nuh   ˈʃiːnə

Sheerah
   Biblical name   SHĒ-uh-ruh, SHIR-uh, SHE-e-rah   ˈʃiːərə, ˈʃirə, ˈʃeerɑ

Sheetrock
   tdmk for a plasterboard   SHĒT-RAHK   ˈʃiːtˌrɑk

Key (col. 2):   a: fad ā: fade ah: father ar: marry aw: law e: fed ē: feed er: merry i: hid ī: hide ō: coat oo̅: boot
oi: boy ow: now u: put uh: above uhr: bird ch: chop ng: ring sh: show th: thick <u>th</u>: this zh: measure

Sheffield		
William Jennings, *US politician; city, AL; city, England*	SHEF-ēld	'ʃefiːld
Shehariah		
Biblical name	SHĒ-(h)uh-RĪ-uh, SHE-huh-; shuh-khahr-YAH	ˌʃiː(h)ə'raiə, ˌʃehə-; ʃəxar'ja
Sheherazade		
see Scheherazade		
Shehu		
Mehmet, *Albanian politician*	she-HO͞O	ʃe'huː
Sheila		
pers. name	SHĒ-luh	'ʃiːlə
Shel		
pers. name	SHEL	'ʃel
Shelah		
Biblical name	SHĒ-luh, she-LAH	'ʃiːlə, ʃe'laː
Shelanite		
Biblical name	SHĒ-luh-NĪT	'ʃiːləˌnait
Sheldon		
pers. name	SHEL-duhn	'ʃeldən
Sheldonian		
Theatre, *Oxford University, England*	shel-DŌ-nē-uhn	ʃel'doːniːən
Shelemiah		
Biblical name	SHEL-uh-MĪ-uh, SHEL-em-YAH-ho͞o	ˌʃelə'maiə, ˌʃelem'jahuː
Sheleph		
Biblical name	SHĒ-LEF, SHEL-EF, SHE-lef	'ʃiːˌlef, 'ʃelˌef, 'ʃelef
Shelesh		
Biblical name	SHĒ-LESH, SHEL-ESH	'ʃiːˌleʃ, 'ʃelˌeʃ
Sheliff [Chéliff]		
river, Algeria	shuh-LĒF	ʃə'liːf
Shelley		
Mary Wollstonecraft, *English writer;* Percy Bysshe, *English poet; pers. name*	SHEL-ē	'ʃeliˑ
Shelomi		
Biblical name	shuh-LŌ-MĪ, SHEL-uh-MĪ, shuh-law-MĒ	ʃə'loːˌmai, 'ʃeləˌmai, ʃəlɔː'miː
Shelomith		
Biblical name	shuh-LŌ-muhth, shuh-law-MĒT	ʃə'loːməθ, ʃəlɔː'miːt
Shelomoth		
Biblical name	shuh-LŌ-MAHTH, -muhth; shuh-law-MŌT	ʃə'loːˌmɑθ, -məθ; ʃəlɔː'moːt
Shelumiel		
Biblical name	shuh-LO͞O-mē-EL, shuh-LO͞O-mē-EL	ʃə'luːmiːˌel, ʃəˌluːmiː'el
Shem		
Biblical name, eldest son of Noah	SHEM	'ʃem
Shema		
Biblical name	SHĒ-muh, shuh-MAH, SHEM-ah	'ʃiːmə, ʃə'ma, 'ʃema
Shemaah		
Biblical name	shuh-MĀ-uh, SHEM-ā-uh, shuh-mah-AH	ʃə'meːə, 'ʃemeːə, ʃəmaː'aː
Shemaiah		
Biblical name	shuh-MĀ-uh, shuh-MĪ-uh, shuh-mī-YAH	ʃə'meːə, ʃə'maiə, ʃəmai'ja

Foreign Sounds: ue: *Fr.* **rue**, *Ger.* **füllen** uh(r): *Fr.* **boeuf**, *Ger.* **Höhle** kh: *Ger.* **ich**, *Scot.* **loch** g̱: *Sp.* **amigo** v̱: *Sp.* **hablar** hl: *Welsh* **Llanelli**. CAPITALS: primary stress. SMALL CAPS: secondary stress. [$]: U.S. pron. [£]: British pron.

Shemariah		
Biblical name	SHEM-uh-RĪ-uh, shuh-mahr-YAH	ˌʃemə'raɪə, ʃəmɑr'jɑ
Shemeber		
Biblical name	shem-Ē-buhr, shem-EV-er	ʃem'iːbəʳ, ʃem'ever
Shemer		
Biblical name	SHĒ-muhr, SHEM-er	'ʃiːməʳ, 'ʃemer
Shemida, Shemidah		
Biblical name	shuh-MĪD-uh, SHEM-uhd-uh, shuh-mē-DAH	ʃə'maɪdə, 'ʃemədə, ʃəmiː'dɑː
Shemidaite		
Biblical name	shuh-MĪD-uh-ĪT, -ē-ĪT	ʃə'maɪdəˌaɪt, -iːˌaɪt
Sheminith		
Biblical name	SHEM-uh-nuhth, shuh-mē-NĒT	'ʃemənəθ, ʃəmiː'niːt
Shemini Atzereth		
Jewish holiday	shuh-MĒ-nē aht-SER-uht, SHMĒ-nē, aht-SER-uhth, -uhs	ʃə'miːni ɑt'serət, 'ʃmiːniː, ɑt'serəθ, -əs
Shemiramoth		
Biblical name	shuh-MIR-uh-MAHTH, -MAWTH, -muhth, shuh-MĪ-ruh-; shuh-MĒ-rah-MAWT	ʃə'mirəˌmɑθ, -ˌmɔːθ, -məθ, ʃə'mairə-; ʃə'miːrɑˌmɔːt
Shemtob, Shem Tov		
pers. name, Hebrew	shem-TŌV, shem-TAWV	ʃem'toːv, ʃem'tɔːv
Shemuel [Samuel]		
Biblical name	shuh-M(Y)OO-el, SHEM-(y)uh-wuhl, shuh-moo-EL	ʃə'm(j)uːel, 'ʃem(j)əwəl, ʃəmuː'el
Shen		
Biblical name	SHEN	'ʃen
Shenandoah		
river, VA, WV; US pl. name	SHEN-uhn-DŌ-uh, SHAN-uhn-DŌ-uh	ˌʃenən'doːə, ˌʃænən'doːə
Shenango		
river, PA	shuh-NANG-GŌ	ʃə'næŋˌgoː
Shenazar, Shenazzar		
Biblical name	shuh-NĀ-ZAHR, shuh-NAZ-AHR, SHEN-uh-ZAHR, SHEN-aht-SAHR	ʃə'neːˌzɑʳ, ʃə'næzˌɑʳ, 'ʃenəˌzɑʳ, ˌʃenɑt'sɑr
Shenir		
Biblical name	SHĒ-nuhr, suh-NĒR	'ʃiːnəʳ, sə'niːr
Shenyang		
city, China	SHUHN-YAHNG	'ʃən'jɑŋ
Sheol		
Hebrew abode of the dead	shē-ŌL, SHĒ-ŌL	ʃiː'oːl, 'ʃiːˌoːl
Shepard, Shepherd		
pers. name	SHEP-uhrd	'ʃepəʳd
Shepaug		
river, CT	shuh-PAWG	ʃə'pɔːg
Shepham		
Biblical name	SHĒ-FAM, SHEF-AM, shuh-FAHM	'ʃiːˌfæm, 'ʃefˌæm, ʃə'fɑm
Shephatiah		
Biblical name	SHEF-uh-TĪ-uh, shuh-faht-YAH-hoo	ˌʃefə'taɪə, ʃəfɑt'jɑhuː
Shephi		
Biblical name	SHĒ-FĪ, shuh-FĒ	'ʃiːˌfaɪ, ʃə'fiː
Shepho		
Biblical name	SHĒ-FŌ, shuh-FŌ	'ʃiːˌfoː, ʃə'foː
Shephuphan		
Biblical name	shuh-FOO-FAN, shuh-foo-FAHN	ʃə'fuːˌfæn, ʃəfuː'fɑn

Key (col. 2): a: f**a**d ā: f**a**de ah: f**a**ther ar: m**a**rry aw: l**a**w e: f**e**d ē: f**ee**d er: m**e**rry i: h**i**d ī: h**i**de ō: c**oa**t ōō: b**oo**t
oi: b**oy** ow: n**ow** u: p**u**t uh: **a**bove uhr: b**i**rd ch: **ch**op ng: ri**ng** sh: **sh**ow th: **th**ick <u>th</u>: **th**is zh: mea**s**ure

Sherah [Sheerah]
  Biblical name   SHIR-uh   ˈʃirə
Sheraton
  Thomas, *English furniture designer;*   SHER-uht-n   ˈʃerətn̩
    US hotel chain
Sheremetyevo
  airport, Moscow   SHER-yuhm-yuh-TYĀ-vō   ˌʃerjəmjəˈtjeːvoː
Sherebiah
  Biblical name   SHER-uh-BĪ-uh, she-REV-yah   ˌʃerəˈbaiə, ʃeˈrevja
Sherente
  S. American people   shuh-RĀN-tā   ʃəˈreːnteː
Sheresh
  Biblical name   SHIR-ESH, SHER-esh   ˈʃirˌeʃ, ˈʃereʃ
Sheri, Sheree
  pers. name   SHER-ē   ˈʃeriˑ
Sheridan
  Philip Henry, *US general;* Richard   SHER-uhd-n   ˈʃerədn̩
    B., *Irish dramatist; pers. name*
Sherlock
  pers. name (S. Holmes)   SHUHR-luhk, SHUHR-LAHK   ˈʃərlək, ˈʃərˌlɑk
Sherman
  William T., *US general; pers. name*   SHUHR-muhn   ˈʃərmən
Sherpa
  people of Tibet   SHER-puh, SHUHR-puh   ˈʃerpə, ˈʃərpə
Sherr
  Lynn, *US journalist*   SHUHR   ˈʃər
Sherri, Sherree
  pers. name   SHER-ē   ˈʃeriˑ
Sherrington
  Sir Charles, *English physiologist*   SHER-ing-tuhn   ˈʃeriŋtən
    (Nobel 1932)
Sherry
  pers. name; wine   SHER-ē   ˈʃeriˑ
's-Hertogenbosch
  city, Netherlands   SER-tō-ḡuh(n)-BAWS   ˈsertoːɣə(n)ˌbɔːs
Sherwin
  pers. name   SHUHR-wuhn   ˈʃərwən
Sherwood
  pers. name   SHUHR-WUD, SHER-WUD   ˈʃərˌwud, ˈʃerˌwud
Sheryl
  pers. name   SHER-uhl   ˈʃerəl
Sheshach, Sheshak
  Biblical name   SHĒ-SHAK, she-SHAH<u>KH</u>   ˈʃiːˌʃæk, ʃeˈʃɑx
Sheshai
  Biblical name   SHĒ-SHĪ, she-SHĪ   ˈʃiːˌʃai, ʃeˈʃai
Sheshan
  Biblical name   SHĒ-SHAN, she-SHAHN   ˈʃiːˌʃæn, ʃeˈʃan
Sheshbazzar
  Biblical name   shesh-BAZ-uhr, shes-;   ʃeʃˈbæzər, ʃes-; ˌʃeʃbatˈsɑr
                                     SHESH-baht-SAHR
Sheth
  Biblical name   SHETH, SHET   ˈʃeθ, ˈʃet
Shethar
  Biblical name   SHĒ-THAHR, she-TAHR   ˈʃiːˌθɑr, ʃeˈtɑr

Foreign Sounds: **ue**: *Fr.* **rue**, *Ger.* **füllen**   **uh(r)**: *Fr.* **boeuf**, *Ger.* **Höhle**   **kh**: *Ger.* **ich**, *Scot.* **loch**   **ḡ**: *Sp.* **amigo**   **v**: *Sp.* **hablar** **hl**: *Welsh* **Llanelli**.   CAPITALS: primary stress.   SMALL CAPS: secondary stress.   Ⓢ: U.S. pron.   Ⓔ: British pron.

Shethar-Bozenai
  Biblical name   SHĒ-THAHR-BAHZ-uh-NĪ,   ˈʃiːˌθɑʳˈbazəˌnai,
           shuh-TAHR-BŌZ-NĪ   ʃəˈtɑrˈboːzˌnai

Shethar-boznai
  Biblical name   SHĒ-THAHR-BAHZ-NĪ, SHETH-AHR-;   ˈʃiːˌθɑʳˈbazˌnai, ˈʃeθˌɑr-;
           shuh-TAHR-BŌZ-NĪ   ʃəˈtɑrˈboːzˌnai

Shetland
  islands, Scotland   SHET-luhnd   ˈʃetlənd

Shetucket
  river, CT   she-TUHK-uht   ʃiːˈtəkət

Sheva
  Biblical name   SHĒ-vuh, shuh-VAH   ˈʃiːvə, ʃəˈvɑ

Shevardnadze
  Eduard, foreign minister, USSR   SHEV-uhrd-NAHD-zuh   ˌʃevəʳdˈnɑdzə

Shevat
  see Shebat

Sheyenne
  river, ND   shī-EN, shī-AN   ʃaiˈen, ʃaiˈæn

Shi'a
  branch of Islam   SHĒ-ah, SHĒ-uh   ˈʃiːɑ, ˈʃiːə

Shiawassee
  river, county, MI   SHĒ-uh-WAW-sē, SHĒ-uh-WAHS-ē   ˌʃiːəˈwɔːsiˑ, ˌʃiːəˈwasiˑ

Shibah
  Biblical name   SHIB-uh, SHIV-uh, shiv-AH   ˈʃibə, ˈʃivə, ʃivˈɑː

Shibboleth [Sibboleth]
  Hebrew word for "stream," used to   SHIB-uh-luhth, -LETH; shi-BAW-let   ˈʃibələθ, -ˌleθ; ʃiˈbɔːlet
    identify Ephraimites in Judges
    12:6.

Shibe
  Park, former ballpark, Philadelphia,   SHĪB   ˈʃaib
    PA

Shibmah
  Biblical name   SHIB-muh, SHIV-mah   ˈʃibmə, ˈʃivmɑ

Shigionoth
  Biblical name   SHIG-ē-Ō-NAHTH, shuh-GĪ-uh-NAHTH,   ˌʃigiˈoːˌnɑθ, ʃəˈgaiəˌnɑθ,
           -NAWTH, -nuhth; SHIG-yaw-NŌT   -ˌnɔːθ, -nəθ; ˌʃigjɔːˈnoːt

Shih Hwang-ti [Cheng, Ch'in Shih
Huang T:]
  Chinese emperor   SHIR HWAHNG-DĒ   ˈʃiʳ ˈhwaŋˈdiː

Shihor [Sihor]
  Biblical name   SHĪ-(H)AWR, -(H)ŌR; she-KHŌR   ˈʃai(h)ɔːʳ, -ˌ(h)oːʳ; ʃiːˈxoːr

Shihor-libnath
  Biblical name   SHĪ-(H)AWR-LIB-NATH, SHĪ-(H)ŌR-;   ˈʃai(h)ɔːʳˈlibˌnæθ,
           she-KHŌR-liv-NAHT   ˈʃai(h)oːʳ-; ʃiːˈxoːrlivˈnɑt

Shih Tzu
  dog breed   SHĒD ZOO, SHIRD ZOO, SHI TSOO   ˈʃiːd ˈzuː, ˈʃiʳd ˈzuː, ˈʃit ˈsuː

Shiism
  tenets of Shi'a   SHĒ-IZ-uhm   ˈʃiːˌizəm

Shiite
  adherent of Shi'a   SHĒ-ĪT   ˈʃiːˌait

Shikibu
  pers. name, Japanese   she-kē-bu   ʃiːkiːbu

Shikoku
  island, Japan   shi-kō-koo   ʃikoːkuː

Key (col. 2):   a: fad   ā: fade   ah: father   ar: marry   aw: law   e: fed   ē: feed   er: merry   i: hid   ī: hide   ō: coat   oo: boot
oi: boy   ow: now   u: put   uh: above   uhr: bird   ch: chop   ng: ring   sh: show   th: thick   <u>th</u>: this   zh: measure

Shilelagh
village, Ireland   shuh-LÃ-lē, -luh   ʃə'leːliˑ, -lə

Shilhi
Biblical name   SHIL-HĪ, shil-<u>KH</u>Ī   'ʃil͵hai, ʃil'xai

Shilhim
Biblical name   SHIL-HIM, SHIL-uhm, shil-<u>KH</u>ĒM   'ʃil͵him, 'ʃiləm, ʃil'xiːm

Shillem
Biblical name   SHIL-uhm, shi-LEM   'ʃiləm, ʃi'lem

Shillemite
Biblical name   SHIL-uh-MĪT   'ʃilə͵mait

Shiloah
Biblical name   shī-LŌ-uh, shi-LŌ-ah<u>kh</u>   ʃai'loːə, ʃi'loːax

Shillong
city, India   shi-LAWNG   ʃi'lɔːŋ

Shilluk
lang., people, Sudan   shuh-LO͞OK   ʃə'luːk

Shiloh
ancient ruins; site of Civil War battle, TN   SHĪ-lō   'ʃailoː

Shiloni
Biblical name   shī-LŌ-NĪ, shuh-; SHIL-aw-NĒ   ʃai'loː͵nai, ʃə-; ͵ʃilɔː'niː

Shilonite
Biblical name   SHĪ-luh-NĪT   'ʃailə͵nait

Shilshah
Biblical name   SHIL-SHAH, shil-SHAH   'ʃil͵ʃaː, ʃil'ʃaː

Shimea, Shimeah
Biblical name   SHIM-ē-uh, shim-AH   'ʃimiːə, ʃim'aː

Shimeam
Biblical name   SHIM-ē-AM, -uhm; shim-AHM   'ʃimiː͵æm, -əm; ʃim'am

Shimeath
Biblical name   SHIM-ē-ATH, -uhth; shim-AHT   'ʃimiː͵æθ, -əθ; ʃim'at

Shimeathite
Biblical name   SHIM-ē-uh-THĪT   'ʃimiːə͵θait

Shimei
Biblical name   SHIM-ē-Ī, shim-Ē   'ʃimiː͵ai, ʃim'iː

Shimeites
Biblical name   SHIM-ē-ĪTS   'ʃimiː͵aits

Shimeon
Biblical name   SHIM-ē-uhn, shim-ŌN   'ʃimiːən, ʃim'oːn

Shimer
College, IL   SHĪ-muhr   'ʃaimər

Shimhi
Biblical name   SHIM-HĪ, shim-Ē   'ʃim͵hai, ʃim'iː

Shimite
Biblical name   SHIM-ĪT   'ʃim͵ait

Shimizu
port, Japan   shim-ē-zo͞o   ʃimiːzuː

Shimma
Biblical name   SHIM-uh, shim-AH   'ʃimə, ʃim'a

Shimon
pers. name (S. Peres)   shi-MŌN   ʃi'moːn

Shimonoseki
port, Japan   shim-ō-nō-sek-ē   ʃimoːnoːsekiˑ

Shimrath
Biblical name   SHIM-RATH, shim-RAHT   'ʃim͵ræθ, ʃim'rat

Foreign Sounds: ue: *Fr.* **rue**, *Ger.* **füllen**   uh(r): *Fr.* **boeuf**, *Ger.* **Höhle**   <u>kh</u>: *Ger.* i**ch**, *Scot.* lo**ch**   g̱: *Sp.* ami**g**o   v̱: *Sp.* ha**b**lar   hl: *Welsh* **Ll**anelli.   CAPITALS: primary stress.   SMALL CAPS: secondary stress.   Ⓢ: U.S. pron.   Ⓔ: British pron.

Shimri
　Biblical name　　　　SHIM-RĪ, shim-RĒ　　　　'ʃimˌrai, ʃim'riː

Shimrith
　Biblical name　　　　SHIM-rith, shim-RĒT　　　　'ʃimriθ, ʃim'riːt

Shimrom [Shimron]
　Biblical name　　　　SHIM-RAHM　　　　'ʃimˌram

Shimron
　Biblical name　　　　SHIM-RAHN, shim-RŌN　　　　'ʃimˌran, ʃim'roːn

Shimronite
　Biblical name　　　　SHIM-ruh-NĪT　　　　'ʃimrəˌnait

Shimron-meron
　Biblical name　　　　SHIM-ruhn-MIR-uhn,　　　　'ʃimrən'mirən,
　　　　　　　　　　　　shim-RŌN-muh-RAWN　　　　ʃim'roːnməˈrɔːn

Shimshai
　Biblical name　　　　SHIM-SHĪ, shim-SHĪ　　　　'ʃimˌʃai, ʃim'ʃai

Shinab
　Biblical name　　　　SHĪ-NAB, shin-AHV　　　　'ʃaiˌnæb, ʃin'av

Shinar
　Biblical name　　　　SHĪ-NAHR, shin-AHR　　　　'ʃaiˌnaʳ, ʃin'ar

Shinichiro
　pers. name, Japanese　　　　shēn-ē-chē-rō　　　　ʃi'niːtʃiːroː

Shinnecock
　N. American people　　　　SHIN-uh-KAHK　　　　'ʃinəˌkak

Shintaro
　pers. name, Japanese　　　　shin-tahr-ō　　　　ʃintaroː

Shinto
　Japanese religion　　　　SHIN-tō　　　　'ʃintoː

Shintoism
　Japanese religion　　　　SHIN-tō-IZ-uhm　　　　'ʃintoːˌizəm

Shiphi
　Biblical name　　　　SHĪ-FĪ, SHIF-Ī, shif-Ē　　　　'ʃaiˌfai, 'ʃifˌai, ʃif'iː

Shiphmite
　Biblical name　　　　SHIF-MĪT　　　　'ʃifˌmait

Shiphrah
　Biblical name　　　　SHIF-ruh, shif-RAH　　　　'ʃifrə, ʃif'ra

Shiphtan
　Biblical name　　　　SHIF-tuhn, shif-TAHN　　　　'ʃiftən, ʃif'tan

Shīrāz
　city, Iran　　　　shi-RAHZ　　　　ʃi'raz

Shire, Shiré
　river, Malawi, Mozambique　　　　SHIR-Ā　　　　'ʃirˌeː

Shirley
　pers. name　　　　SHUHR-lē　　　　'ʃəʳliˑ

Shisha
　Biblical name　　　　SHĪ-shuh, shē-SHAH　　　　'ʃaiʃə, ʃiː'ʃa

Shishak
　Biblical name　　　　SHĪ-SHAK, shē-SHAHK　　　　'ʃaiˌʃæk, ʃiː'ʃak

Shitrai
　Biblical name　　　　shi-TRĀ-Ī, SHI-trē-Ī, SHI-TRĪ, shir-TĪ　　　　ʃi'treːˌai, 'ʃitriːˌai, 'ʃiˌtrai,
　　　　　　　　　　　　　　　　　　　　　　　　ʃir'tai

Shittim
　Biblical name　　　　SHIT-uhm, shi-TIM　　　　'ʃiʈəm, ʃi'tim

Shiva
　see Siva

Shizuoka
city, Japan — shiz-o͞o-ō-kah — ˈʃizuːoːkɑ

Shlomo
pers. name — SHLŌ-mō — ˈʃloːmoː

Shluh
lang., people, Morocco, Mauritania — SHLOO, shuh-LOO — ˈʃluː, ʃəˈluː

Shmuel
pers. name — SHMOO-uhl, SHMOO-EL — ˈʃmuːəl, ˈʃmuːˌel

Shoa
Biblical name — SHŌ-uh, sho-AH — ˈʃoːə, ʃoˈɑː

Shobab
Biblical name — SHŌ-BAB, shō-VAHV — ˈʃoːˌbæb, ʃoːˈvɑv

Shobach
Biblical name — SHŌ-BAK, -BAKH; shō-VAHKH — ˈʃoːˌbæk, -ˌbæx; ʃoːˈvɑx

Shobai
Biblical name — SHŌ-bē-ī, SHŌ-BĪ, shaw-VĪ — ˈʃoːbiːˌɑi, ˈʃoːˌbai, ʃɔːˈvai

Shobal
Biblical name — SHŌ-BAL, -buhl; shō-VAHL — ˈʃoːˌbæl, -bəl; ʃoːˈvɑl

Shobek
Biblical name — SHŌ-BEK, shō-VEK — ˈʃoːˌbek, ʃoːˈvek

Shobi
Biblical name — SHŌ-BĪ, shaw-VĒ — ˈʃoːˌbai, ʃɔːˈviː

Shockley
W. B., English-born US physicist (Nobel 1956) — SHAHK-lē — ˈʃɑkliˈ

Shoco, Shocho, Shochoh [Socho]
Biblical name — SHŌ-kō, shō-KHŌ — ˈʃoːkoː, ʃoːˈxoː

Shoham
Biblical name — SHŌ-HAM, SHŌ-uhm, SHAW-hahm — ˈʃoːˌhæm, ˈʃoːəm, ˈʃɔːhɑm

Shoko
pers. name, Japanese — shō-kō — ʃoːkoː

Sholapur
city, India — SHŌ-luh-PUR — ˈʃoːləˌpuʳ

Sholem
pers. name, Yiddish — SHŌ-luhm — ˈʃoːləm

Sholokhov
Mikhail A., Russian author (Nobel 1965) — SHAW-luh-KHAWF, ⓢ SHAW-luh-KAWF, -KAWV — ˈʃɔːləˌxɔːf, ⓢ ˈʃoːləˌkɔːf, -ˌkɔːv

Sholom
pers. name, Hebrew — SHŌ-luhm — ˈʃoːləm

Shomer
Biblical name — SHŌ-muhr, shō-MER — ˈʃoːməʳ, ʃoːˈmer

Shona
lang., southern Africa — SHŌ-nuh — ˈʃoːnə

Shophach
Biblical name — SHŌ-FAK, -FAKH; shō-FAHKH — ˈʃoːˌfæk, -ˌfæx; ʃoːˈfɑx

Shophan
Biblical name — SHŌ-FAN, shō-FAHN — ˈʃoːˌfæn, ʃoːˈfɑn

Shor
lake, Asia — SHAWR — ˈʃɔːʳ

Shoreham
port, England — SHŌR-uhm, SHAWR-uhm — ˈʃoːrəm, ˈʃɔːrəm

Shoshana
pers. name, Hebrew — shō-SHAHN-uh — ʃoːˈʃɑnə

Foreign Sounds: ue: *Fr.* **rue**, *Ger.* **füllen** uh(r): *Fr.* **boeuf**, *Ger.* **Höhle** kh: *Ger.* **ich**, *Scot.* **loch** g̱: *Sp.* **amigo** v̱: *Sp.* **hablar** hl: *Welsh* **Llanelli.** CAPITALS: primary stress. SMALL CAPS: secondary stress. ⓢ: U.S. pron. ⓔ: British pron.

Shoshanim-eduth
  Biblical name   shō-SHAN-uhm-ĒD-uhth,   ʃoːˈʃænəmˈiːdəθ,
                           SHAW-shah-NĒM-e-DŌOT   ˌʃɔːʃaˈniːmeˈduːt

Shoshone, -ni
  N. American people   shuh-SHŌ-nē, shō-SHŌ-nē   ʃəˈʃoːniˑ, ʃoːˈʃoːniˑ

Shoshonean
  lang., N. America   shō-SHŌ-nē-uhn, SHŌ-shuh-NĒ-uhn ʃoːˈʃoːniːən, ˌʃoːʃəˈniːən

Shostakovich
  Dmitri, *Russian composer;* Maxim,   shuhs-tuh-KAWV-yich,   ʃəstəˈkɔːvjitʃ,
    Russian conductor   ⓢ SHAHS-tuh-KŌ-vich,   ⓢ ˌʃastəˈkoːvitʃ,
                           SHAW-stuh-KAW-vich   ˌʃɔːstəˈkɔːvitʃ

Shoyu
  soy sauce   SHŌ-yoo   ˈʃoːju

Shreveport
  city, LA   SHRĒV-PŌRT, SHRĒV-PAWRT, *esp.* ˈʃriːvˌpoːʳt, ˈʃriːvˌpɔːʳt, *esp.*
                         southeastern US SRĒV-   *southeastern US* ˈsriːv-

Shrewsbury
  1. US pl. name   SHROOZ-BER-ē, *esp. southeastern US* ˈʃruːzˌberiˑ, *esp. southeastern*
                         SROOZ-BER-ē   *US* ˈsruːzˌberiˑ
  2. borough, England   SHRŌZ-b(uh-)rē, SHROOZ-b(uh-)rē, ˈʃroːzb(ə)riˑ, ˈʃruːzb(ə)riˑ,
                        ⓢ SHROOZ-BER-ē, *esp. southeastern* ⓢ ˈʃruːzˌberiˑ, *esp.*
                        US SROOZ-BER-ē   *southeastern US*
                                                ˈsruːzˌberiˑ

Shriver
  Maria, *US newscaster;* Pamela, *US* SHRĪ-vuhr, *esp. southeastern US* ˈʃraivəʳ, *esp. southeastern*
    tennis player   SRĪ-vuhr   *US* ˈsraivəʳ

Shropshire
  county, England   SHRAHP-shuhr, -SHIR, *esp.*   ˈʃrapʃəʳ, -ˌʃiʳ, *esp.*
                         southeastern US SRAHP-   *southeastern US* ˈsrap-

Shrove Tuesday
  day before Ash Wednesday   SHRŌV, *esp. southeastern US* SRŌV ˈʃroːv, *esp. southeastern US*
                                                  ˈsroːv

Shrovetide
  the three days before Ash Wednesday SHRŌV-TĪD, *esp. southeastern US* ˈʃroːvˌtaid, *esp. southeastern*
                         SRŌV-TĪD   *US* ˈsroːvˌtaid

Shu
  Egyptian god of the air   SHOO   ˈʃuː

Shua
  Biblical name   SHOO-uh, SHOO-ah   ˈʃuːə, ˈʃuːaː

Shuah
  Biblical name   SHOO-uh, SHOO-ah, shoo-AHKH   ˈʃuːə, ˈʃuːaː, ʃuːˈax

Shual
  Biblical name   SHOO-uhl, shoo-AHL   ˈʃuːəl, ʃuːˈal

Shubael
  Biblical name   SHOO-bē-EL, -BĀL; SHOO-vah-EL   ˈʃuːbiːˌel, -ˌbeːl; ˌʃuːvaˈel

Shughni
  lang., Afghanistan   SHUG-nē   ˈʃugniˑ

Shuhah [Shuah]
  Biblical name   SHOO-HAH, shoo-AHKH   ˈʃuːˌhaː, ʃuːˈax

Shuham
  Biblical name   SHOO-HAM, shoo-KHAHM   ˈʃuːˌhæm, ʃuːˈxam

Shuhamite
  Biblical name   SHOO-ham-ĪT, SHOO-(h)uh-MĪT   ˈʃuːhæmˌait, ˈʃuː(h)əˌmait

Shuhite
  Biblical name   SHOO-HĪT   ˈʃuːˌhait

Key (col. 2): a: fad ā: fade ah: father ar: marry aw: law e: fed ē: feed er: merry i: hid ī: hide ō: coat ōō: boot
oi: boy ow: now u: put uh: above uhr: bird ch: chop ng: ring sh: show th: thick th̲: this zh: measure

Shuji Tsushima
Japanese novelist (pseudonym Dazai shoō-jēt-soō-shē-mah ʃuːdʒiːtsuːʃiːma
Osamu)

Shula
Don, *US football coach* SHOO-luh ˈʃuːlə

Shulam
Biblical name SHOO-LAM, SHOO-lahm ˈʃuːˌlæm, ˈʃuːlɑm

Shulamit
pers. name, Hebrew shoo-LAHM-it, shoo-LAHM-is ʃuːˈlɑmit, ʃuːˈlɑmis

Shulamite
Biblical name SHOO-luh-MĪT ˈʃuːləˌmait

Shulgi
Sumerian king SHUL-gē ˈʃulgiˑ

Shultheiss
German beer SHULT-HĪS ˈʃultˌhais

Shultz
George Pratt, *US government* SHULTS ˈʃults
official

Shumathite
Biblical name SHOO-muh-THĪT ˈʃuːməˌθait

Shunammite
Biblical name SHOO-nuh-MĪT ˈʃuːnəˌmait

Shunem
Biblical name SHOO-NEM, -nuhm; shoo-NEM ˈʃuːˌnem, -nəm; ʃuːˈnem

Shuni
Biblical name SHOO-NĪ, shu-NĒ ˈʃuːˌnai, ʃuˈniː

Shunite
Biblical name SHOO-NĪT ˈʃuːˌnait

Shunroku
pers. name, Japanese shun-rō-koō ʃunroːkuː

Shupham [Shuppim]
Biblical name SHOO-FAM, shoo-PIM ˈʃuːˌfæm, ʃuːˈpim

Shuphamite
Biblical name SHOO-FAM-ĪT, SHOO-fuh-MĪT ˈʃuːˌfæmˌait, ˈʃuːfəˌmait

Shuppiluliumash
Hittite king shuh-PIL-oō-LĒ-oō-MAHSH ʃəˌpiluːˈliːuˑˌmaʃ

Shuppim
Biblical name SHUP-im, shoo-PIM ˈʃupim, ʃuːˈpim

Shur
Biblical name SHUR, SHOOR ˈʃuʳ, ˈʃuːr

Shushan
Biblical name SHOO-SHAN, shoo-SHAHN ˈʃuːˌʃæn, ʃuːˈʃɑn

Shushkevich
Stanislav, *Belorussian political* SHUSH-kyuhv-YICH ˈʃuʃkjəvˌjitʃ
leader

Shuthela
Biblical name SHOO-thuh-luh, shoo-THĒ-luh, ˈʃuːθələ, ʃuːˈθiːlə, ʃuːˈtalax
shoo-TAHL-ahkh

Shuzo
pers. name, Japanese SHUZ-ō ˈʃuzoː

Shylock
character in Merchant of Venice, SHĪ-LAHK ˈʃaiˌlak
Shakespeare

Si
see Xi

Foreign Sounds: ue: *Fr.* **rue**, *Ger.* **füllen** uh(r): *Fr.* **boeuf**, *Ger.* **Höhle** kh: *Ger.* **ich**, *Scot.* **loch** g̃: *Sp.* **amigo** v: *Sp.* **hablar**
hl: *Welsh* **Llanelli**. CAPITALS: primary stress. SMALL CAPS: secondary stress. Ⓢ: U.S. pron. Ⓔ: British pron.

Sia
Biblical name   SĪ-uh, sē-AH   'saɪə, siː'ɑː

Siaha
Biblical name   SĪ-uh-huh, SĒ-uh-HAH   'saɪəhə, ˌsiːə'hɑ

Sialkot
city, India   sē-AHL-KŌT   siː'al̩koːt

Siam
former name of Thailand   sī-AM   saɪ'æm

Siamese
pert. to Siam   SĪ-uh-MĒZ, -MĒS   ˌsaɪə'miːz, -'miːs

Sian
1. pers. name   SHAHN   'ʃɑ·n
2. see Xian

Siasconset [Sconset]
resort, Nantucket Island, MA SĪ-uh-SKAWN-SET, -SKAHN-suht   ˌsaɪə'skɔːn̩set, -'skɑnsət

Sibbecai, Sibbechai
Biblical name   SIB-uh-KĪ, si-buh-KHĪ   'sibəˌkaɪ, sibə'xaɪ

Sibboleth [Shibboleth]
Ephraimite pronunciation of   SIB-uh-LETH, -luhth; si-BAW-let   'sibəˌleθ, -ləθ; si'bɔːlet
Shibboleth

Sibelius
Jean, composer   suh-BĀL-yuhs, suh-BĀ-lē-uhs   sə'beːljəs, sə'beːliːəs

Siberia
region, Russia   sī-BIR-ē-uh   saɪ'biriːə

Sibert
pers. name   SĪ-buhrt   'saɪbəʳt

Sibmah
Biblical name   SIB-muh, siv-MAH   'sibmə, siv'mɑː

Sibraim
Biblical name   SIB-rā-uhm, -rē-uhm, sib-RĀ-uhm,   'sibreːəm, -riːəm, sib'reːəm,
                                siv-RAH-yim   siv'rajim

Sibyl
ancient priestess; pers. name SIB-uhl   'sibəl

Sibylla
pers. name, German   zē-BUEL-ah   ziː'bylɑ

Sibylle
pers. name, French   sē-BĒL   siːbiːl

Sichuan [Szechuan]
prov, China   SICH-WAHN   'sitʃ'wɑn

Sichuan Pendi
basin, China   SICH-WAHN PUHN-DĒ   'sitʃ'wɑn 'pən'diː

Sicilia [Sicily]
island, Mediterranean   *Ital.* sē-CHĒL-yah, *Lat.* si-KIL-yuh,   *Ital.* siː'tʃiːlja, *Lat.* si'kiljə,
                                si-SIL-yuh   si'siljə

Sicilian
pert. to Sicily   si-SIL-yuhn   si'siljən

Sicily
island, Mediterranean   SIS-(uh-)lē   'sis(ə)li·

Siculus
Roman cognomen   SIK-yuh-luhs   'sikjələs

Sicyon
ancient city, Greece   SIS-ē-AHN, SISH-ē-AHN, SIK-ē-AHN   'sisiːˌɑn, 'siʃiːˌɑn, 'sikiːˌɑn

Sid
pers. name   SID   'sid

Key (col. 2): a: fad ā: fade ah: father ar: marry aw: law e: fed ē: feed er: merry i: hid ī: hide ō: coat ōō: boot
oi: boy ow: now u: put uh: above uhr: bird ch: chop ng: ring sh: show th: thick <u>th</u>: this zh: measure

Siddhartha Gautama
  the Buddha   si-DAHRT-uh GOWT-uh-muh,   si'dɑˤʈə 'gauʈəmə, 'gɔːʈəmə
                                  GAWT-uh-muh

Siddim
  Biblical name   SID-im, si-DĒM   'sidim, si'diːm

Sīdī Barrāni
  village, Egypt   SĒD-ē buh-RAHN-ē   ˌsiːdiˑ bə'rɑniˑ

Sidney
  pers. name   SID-nē   'sidniˑ

Sidney Sussex
  college, Cambridge Univ.   SID-nē SUHS-uhks   'sidniˑ 'səsəks

Sidon
  city, Lebanon   SĪD-n   'sɑidn̩

Sidonian
  pert. to Sidon   sī-DŌ-nē-uhn   sɑi'doːniːən

Sidonie
  1. pers. name, French   sē-daw-NĒ   siːdɔːniː
  2. German   zē-DŌ-nē-uh   ziː'doːniːə

Sidra
  gulf, Libya   SID-ruh   'sidrə

Siefert
  Jaroslav, *Czech author (Nobel 1984)*   SĒ-FERT   'siːˌfeˤt

Siegbahn
  Kai Manne, *Swedish physicist (Nobel*   SĒG-BAHN   'siːgˌbɑn
  1981); Karl Manne Georg,
  Swedish physicist (Nobel 1924)

Siegen
  city, Germany   ZĒ-guhn   'ziːgən

Siegfried
  1. dragon-slayer in German   SIG-FRĒD, SĒG-FRĒD   'sigˌfriːd, 'siːgˌfriːd
  mythology; pers. name
  2. German   ZĒ<u>KH</u>-FRĒT   'ziːçˌfriːt

Sieglinde
  mother of Siegfried in German ZĒ<u>KH</u>-LIN-duh   'ziːçˌlində
  mythology

Siegmund
  pers. name, German   ZI<u>KH</u>-MUNT   'ziçˌmunt

Siemens
  Ernst Werner von, *German*   ZĒ-muhnz, Ⓢ SĒ-muhnz   'ziːmənz, Ⓢ 'siːmənz
  industrialist; German electronics
  co.

Siena
  commune, Italy; college, NY   sē-EN-uh   siː'enə

Sienkiewicz
  Henryk, *Polish author (Nobel 1905)*   shen-KYĀ-vich   ʃen'kjeːvitʃ

Sierra
  county, CA, NM   sē-ER-uh   siː'erə

Sierra de Juárez
  mountain range, CA   sē-ER-uh dā HWAHR-ES, -WAHR-uhz   siː'erə deː 'hwɑrˌes, -'wɑrəz

Sierra Gallinas
  mountain range, NM   sē-ER-uh guh-YĒ-nuhs, guh-LĒ-nuhs   siː'erə gə'jiːnəs, gə'liːnəs

Sierra Leone
  republic, Africa   sē-ER-uh lē-ŌN, SIR-uh   siːˌerə liː'oːn, ˌsirə

Sierra Leonean
  pert. to Sierra Leone   sē-ER-uh lē-Ō-nē-uhn, SIR-uh   siːˌerə liː'oːniːən, ˌsirə

Sierra Madre
   mts., WY; city, CA   sē-ER-uh MAHD-rē, MAHD-rā   si:ˌerə 'mɑdriˑ, 'mɑdreː

Sierra Nevada
   1. mts., CA   sē-ER-uh nuh-VAD-uh, nuh-VAHD-uh   si:ˌerə nə'vædə, nə'vɑdə
   2. mts., Spain   sē-ER-ah nā-VAH<u>TH</u>-ah   si:ˌerɑ neː'vaða

Sierra Popoloca
   lang., Mexico   sē-ER-uh PŌ-puh-LŌ-kuh   si:ˌerə ˌpoːpə'loːkə

Sieur de La Salle
   see La Salle, Sieur de

Sigbjörn
   pers. name, Norwegian   SIG-byuhrn   'sigbjœːrn

Sigfrid
   pers. name, German   Z<u>ĒKH</u>-FRĒT   'ziːçˌfriːt

Sighişoara
   city, Romania   SĒ-guh-SHWAHR-uh   ˌsiːgə'ʃwɑrə

Sigismond
   pers. name, French   sē-zhēs-MAWⁿ   si:ʒiːsmɔ̃

Sigismund
   pers. name, German   ZĒ-gis-munt   'ziːgismunt

Sigmund
   1. pers. name   SIG-muhnd   'sigmənd
   2. German   Z<u>ĒKH</u>-munt   'ziːçmunt

Signor
   Italian form of address for a man   sēn-YAWR, SĒN-YAWR   siːn'jɔːʳ, 'siːnˌjɔːʳ

Signora
   Italian form of address for a married   sēn-YŌR-uh, sēn-YAWR-uh   siːn'joːrə, siːn'jɔːrə
      woman

Signoret
   Simone, *entertainer*   SĒN-yuh-RĀ   ˌsiːnjə'reː

Signorina
   Italian form of address for an   SĒN-yaw-RĒ-nuh, SĒN-yuh-RĒ-nuh   ˌsiːnjɔː'riːnə, ˌsiːnjə'riːnə
      unmarried woman

Sigourney
   1. town, IA   SIG-uhr-nē   'sigəʳniˑ
   2. pers. name   si-GUHR-nē, si-GAWR-nē   si'gəʳniˑ, si'gɔːʳniˑ

Sigrid
   1. pers. name, German   ZĒ-grit, ZĒ-GRĒT   'ziːgrit, 'ziːˌgriːt
   2. Norwegian   SIG-rē   'sigriˑ
   3. Swedish   SĒ-grid   'siːgrid

Sigurð [Sigurd]
   legendary Scandinavian hero   SIG-ur<u>th</u>   'sigurð

Sigurd
   1. legendary Scandinavian hero   SIG-urd, SIG-uhrd   'siguʳd, 'sigəʳd
   2. pers. name, Norwegian   SIG-urd   'sigurd

Sihanouk
   see Norodom Sihanouk

Sihon
   Biblical name   SĪ-HAHN, sē-<u>KH</u>AWN   'sɑiˌhan, siː'xɔːn

Sihor [Shihor]
   Biblical name   SĪ-HAWR, -HŌR; shē-<u>KH</u>ŌR   'sɑiˌhɔːʳ, -ˌhoːʳ; ʃiː'xoːr

Sikandarabad
   town, India   si-KUHN-duh-ruh-BAHD, -BAD   si'kəndərəˌbad, -ˌbæd

Sikh
   adherent of Sikhism   SĒK   'siːk

Key (col. 2):   a: f**a**d   ā: f**a**de   ah: f**a**ther   ar: m**a**rry   aw: l**a**w   e: f**e**d   ē: f**ee**d   er: m**e**rry   i: h**i**d   ī: h**i**de   ō: c**oa**t   ōō: b**oo**t
oi: b**oy**   ow: n**ow**   u: p**u**t   uh: **a**bove   uhr: b**ir**d   ch: **ch**op   ng: ri**ng**   sh: **sh**ow   th: **th**ick   <u>th</u>: **th**is   zh: mea**s**ure

Sikhism		
religion	SĒ-KIZ-uhm	'siːˌkizəm
Sikhote-Alin		
mtn. range, Russia	SYĒ-khō-TĀ uh-LĒN	ˌsjiːxoːˌteː ə'liːn
Sikinos		
island, Greece	SIK-uh-NAWS, -NAHS	'sikəˌnɔːs, -ˌnɑs
Sikkim		
state, India	SIK-uhm	'sikəm
Sikorsky		
1. Igor, *Russian-born US aeronautical inventor*	syi-KAWR-skyi, [S] suh-KAWR-skē	sji'kɔːrskjij, [S] sə'kɔːrskiˑ
2. US helicopter co.	suh-KAWR-skē	sə'kɔːrskiˑ
Silajdzic		
Haris, *Bosnian prime minister*	suh-LAHJ-its, -ich	sə'lɑdʒits, -itʃ
Silas		
pers. name	SĪ-luhs	'sɑiləs
Silenus		
satyr who reared Dionysus	sī-LĒ-nuhs	sɑi'liːnəs
Siles		
Hernan, *president, Bolivia*	SĒ-lās	'siːleːs
Silesia		
region, central Europe	sī-LĒ-zh(ē-)uh, sī-LĒ-sh(ē-)uh, suh-	sɑi'liːʒ(iː)ə, sɑi'liːʃ(iː)ə, sə-
Silesian		
pert. to Silesia	sī-LĒ-zh(ē-)uhn, sī-LĒ-sh(ē-)uhn, suh-	sɑi'liːʒ(iː)ən, sɑi'liːʃ(iː)ən, sə-
Siletz		
Indian reservation, US	SĪ-luhts	'sɑiləts
silicon		
element	SIL-i-kuhn, SIL-uh-KAHN	'silikən, 'siləˌkɑn
Silla		
Biblical name	SIL-uh, si-LAH	'silə, si'lɑː
Sillanpää		
Frans Eemil, *Finnish author (Nobel 1939)*	SIL-ahn-PAH, [S] SIL-uhn-PA	'silɑːnˌpɑ, [S] 'silənˌpæ
Sillus		
grandson of Nestor	SIL-uhs	'siləs
Siloam		
spring near Jerusalem	sī-LŌ-uhm	sɑi'loːəm
Siloam Springs		
city, AR	SĪ-lōm SPRINGZ, SĪ-luhm	ˌsɑiloːm 'spriŋz, ˌsɑiləm
Silurian		
geologic period	suh-LUR-ē-uhn, sī-	sə'luriːən, sɑi-
Silvan		
pers. name	SIL-vuhn	'silvən
Silvana		
pers. name, Italian	sēl-VAHN-uh	siːl'vɑnə
Silvanus		
Roman divinity of the woods; pers. name	sil-VĀ-nuhs	sil'veːnəs
silver		
element	SIL-vuhr	'silvər
Silverius		
pope	sil-VIR-ē-uhs	sil'viriːəs
Silverstein		
Shel, *US humorist*	SIL-vuhr-STĪN, -STĒN	'silvərˌstɑin, -ˌstiːn

Foreign Sounds: ue: *Fr.* **rue**, *Ger.* **füllen** uh(r): *Fr.* **boeuf**, *Ger.* **Höhle** kh: *Ger.* **ich**, *Scot.* **loch** g: *Sp.* amigo v: *Sp.* hablar hl: *Welsh* **Llanelli**. CAPITALS: primary stress. SMALL CAPS: secondary stress. [S]: U.S. pron. [£]: British pron.

Silvester
   pers. name   sil-VES-tuhr   sil'vestə[r]

Silvestre
   1. pers. name, French   sēl-VESTR   siːlvestr
   2. Spanish   sēl-V<u>Ā</u>-strä   siːl'βeːstreː

Silvestro
   pers. name, Italian   sēl-VES-trō   siːl'vestroː

Silvia
   pers. name   SIL-vē-uh   'silviːə

Silvio
   1. pers. name   SIL-vē-ō   'silviːoː
   2. German   ZIL-vyō, ZIL-vē-ō   'zilvjoː, 'zilviːoː
   3. Italian   S<u>Ē</u>L-vyō   'siːlvjoː

Silvius
   king of Alba   SIL-vē-uhs   'silviːəs

Simanu
   Babylonian month   suh-MAHN-o͞o   sə'manuː

Simão
   pers. name, Portuguese   sē-MOW[n]   siː'maũ

Simbirsk [Ulyanovsk]
   city, Russia   syim-BYIRSK   sjim'bji[r]sk

Simchas Torah
   Jewish festival   sim-<u>KH</u>AHT tawr-AH, SIM-<u>kh</u>uhs   sim'xɑt tɔːr'ɑ, ˌsimxəs 'toːrə,
                        T<u>Ō</u>R-uh, TAWR-uh   'tɔːrə

Simenon
   Georges, *French writer*   sē-me-NAW[n]   siːmenɔ̃

Simeon
   1. pers. name   SIM-ē-uhn   'simiːən
   2. Russian   syim-yi-AWN   sjimji'ɔːn
   3. Spanish   sē-mä-<u>Ō</u>N   siːmeː'oːn

Siméon
   pers. name, French   sē-mä-AW[n]   siːmeːɔ̃

Simeonite
   Biblical name   SIM-ē-uh-N<u>Ī</u>T   'simiːəˌnɑit

Simferopol
   city, Ukraine   S(Y)IM(P)-fuh-RAW-puhl,   ˌs(j)im(p)fə'rɔːpəl,
                        SIM(P)-fuh-R<u>Ō</u>-puhl   ˌsim(p)fə'roːpəl

Simi Valley
   city, CA   si-M<u>Ē</u> VAL-ē   si,miː 'væliˑ

Simmel
   George, *German sociologist*   ZIM-uhl   'ziməl

Simmons
   College, *MA*   SIM-uhnz   'simənz

Simon
   1. Herbert A., *US economist (Nobel*   S<u>Ī</u>-muhn   'sɑimən
     1978); pers. name
   2. Claude, *French author (Nobel*   sē-MAW[n]   siːmɔ̃
     1985); pers. name, French
   3. German   Z<u>Ē</u>-mawn   'ziːmɔːn
   4. Russian   SY<u>Ē</u>-muhn   'sjiːmən
   5. Serbo-Croatian   S<u>Ē</u>-mawn   'siːmɔːn

Simón
   pers. name, Spanish   sē-MAWN   siː'mɔːn

Key (col. 2):   a: fad ā: fade ah: father ar: marry aw: law e: fed ē: feed er: merry i: hid ī: hide ō: coat o͞o: boot
oi: boy ow: now u: put uh: above uhr: bird ch: chop ng: ring sh: show th: thick <u>th</u>: this zh: measure

Simon & Schuster		
US publisher	SĪ-muhn uhn(d) SHO͞O-stuhr, SHUS-tuhr	ˌsaimən ən(d) 'ʃu:stə^{r}, 'ʃustə^{r}
Simón Bolívar Maiquetia		
airport, Caracas, Venezuela	sē-MŌN bō-LĒ-v̱ahr mī-KĀT-yah	si:'mo:n bo:'li:βar mai'ke:tja
Simone		
1. pers. name	si-MŌN	si'mo:n
2. French	sē-MAWN	si:mɔ:n
3. Italian	sē-MŌ-nā	si:'mo:ne:
Simonides		
Greek poet	sī-MAHN-uhd-ĒZ	sai'manədˌi:z
Simpatico		
German beer	zim-PAHT-i-kō	zim'pat̪iko:
Simplice		
pers. name, French	se^{n}-PLĒS	sẽpli:s
Simplicius		
pope	sim-PLISH-(ē-)uhs	sim'pliʃ(i:)əs
Simplon Pass		
Alpine pass	SIM-PLAHN PAS	'simˌplan 'pæs
Simpson		
Alan K., *US politician*	SIM(P)-suhn	'sim(p)sən
Simri		
Biblical name	SIM-rē, shim-RĒ	'simri·, ʃim'ri:
Sin		
Biblical name	SIN, SĒN	'sin, 'si:n
Sinai [Horeb]		
peninsula, mtn., desert, Egypt	SĪ-NĪ	'saiˌnai
Sinaloa		
state, Mexico	SĒ-nuh-LŌ-uh	ˌsi:nə'lo:ə
Sinanthropus		
early hominid, "Peking man"	sī-NAN-thruh-puhs, SĪ-nan-THRŌ-puhs	sai'nænθrəpəs, ˌsainæn'θro:pəs
Sinarquist		
member of a Mexican political movement	SIN-AHR-kist	'sinˌa^{r}kist
Sinarquista		
Spanish form of Sinarquist	sin-ahr-KĒ-stah	sinar'ki:sta
Sinatra		
Frank, *US singer, actor*	suh-NAH-truh	sə'natrə
Sinbad		
hero, Arabian Nights	SIN-BAD	'sinˌbæd
Sinclair		
pers. name	SIN-KLAR, SIN-KLER, SING-; sin-KLAR, sin-KLER, sing-	'sinˌklæ^{r}, 'sinˌkle^{r}, 'siŋ-; sin'klæ^{r}, sin'kle^{r}, siŋ-
Sind, Sindh		
prov, Pakistan	SIND	'sind
Si Ndebele		
lang., Africa	SĒN-duh-BĒ-lē, SĒ EN-duh-BĒ-lē	ˌsi:ndə'bi:li·, ˌsi: ˌendə'bi:li·
Sindhi		
people, lang., India	SIN-dē	'sindi·
Sinéad		
pers. name, Irish	SHIN-Ā-uh, [$] shuh-NĀD, shuh-NĀ-uhd	'ʃinˌe:ə, [$] ʃə'ne:d, ʃə'ne:əd

Foreign Sounds: ue: *Fr.* **rue**, *Ger.* **füllen** uh(r): *Fr.* **boeuf**, *Ger.* **Höhle** kh: *Ger.* **ich**, *Scot.* **loch** g̃: *Sp.* amigo v̱: *Sp.* **hablar** hl: *Welsh* **Llanelli.** CAPITALS: primary stress. SMALL CAPS: secondary stress. [$]: U.S. pron. [£]: British pron.

Singapore
  republic, city, Asia   SING-(g)uh-PÕR, -PAWR   'sɪŋ(g)ə͵pɔːʳ, -͵pɔːʳ
Singaporean
  pert. to Singapore   SING-(g)uh-PÕR-ē-uhn, -PAWR-ē-uhn   ͵sɪŋ(g)ə'pɔːriːən, -'pɔːriːən
Singaraja, Singaradja
  town, Bali   SING-guh-RAHJ-uh   ͵sɪŋgə'radʒə
Singer
  Isaac Bashevis, *Polish-born US author (Nobel 1978)*   SING-uhr   'sɪŋəʳ
Singh
  pers. name   SING   'sɪŋ
Singha
  Thai beer   SING-HAH, SING-(h)uh   'sɪŋ'ha, 'sɪŋ(h)ə
Singhalese
  see Sinhalese
Singhji
  pers. name, Hindi   SING-jē   'sɪŋdʒiˑ
Singleton
  pers. name   SING-guhl-tuhn   'sɪŋgəltən
Sinhala
  Sri Lankan New Year   SIN-huh-luh   'sɪnhələ
Sinhalese, Singhalese
  Sri Lankan people, lang.   SING-guh-LĒZ, SIN-(h)uh-LĒZ, -LĒS   ͵sɪŋgə'liːz, ͵sɪn(h)ə'liːz, -'liːs
Sinicism
  characteristic of the Chinese   SĪ-nuh-SIZ-uhm, SIN-uh-SIZ-uhm   'saɪnə͵sɪzəm, 'sɪnə͵sɪzəm
Sinim
  Biblical name   SĪ-nim, sē-NĒM   'saɪnɪm, siː'niːm
Sinite
  Biblical name   SĪ-NĪT   'saɪ͵naɪt
Sinitic
  pert. to the Chinese   sī-NIT-ik, suh-NIT-ik   saɪ'nɪt̪ɪk, sə'nɪt̪ɪk
Sinkiang
  see Xinjiang
Sinkiang Uighur
  see Xingjiang Uygur
Sinn Fein
  Irish political party   SHIN FĀN   ͵ʃɪn 'feɪn
Sino-
  combining form meaning 'Chinese'   SĪ-nō, SĪ-nuh, SĪ-nō   'saɪnoː, 'saɪnə, ͵saɪnoː
Sinology
  study of things Chinese   sī-NAHL-uh-jē, suh-NAHL-uh-jē   saɪ'nalədʒiˑ, sə'nalədʒiˑ
Sinon
  Greek spy at Troy   SĪ-NAHN, SĪ-nuhn   'saɪ͵nan, 'saɪnən
Sinope
  ancient seaport, Turkey; satellite of Jupiter   suh-NŌ-pē   sə'noːpiˑ
Sino-Tibetan
  S. Asian lang. family   SĪ-nō-tuh-BET-n   ͵saɪnoːtə'betn̩
Sinte Gleska
  College, SD   SINT-uh GLES-kuh   ͵sɪntə 'gleskə
Sint-Niklaas
  prov, Belgium   sint-NĒ-kluhs   sɪnt'niːkləs
Sinuhe
  Egyptian politician   SIN-(y)uh-HĀ   'sɪn(j)ə͵heː

Key (col. 2):   a: fad   ā: fade   ah: father   ar: marry   aw: law   e: fed   ē: feed   er: merry   i: hid   ī: hide   ō: coat   oo: boot
oi: boy   ow: now   u: put   uh: above   uhr: bird   ch: chop   ng: ring   sh: show   th: thick   <u>th</u>: this   zh: measure

Sinus Iridum		
'bay' on Moon	SĪ-nuhs IR-uh-duhm	'saɪnəs 'ɪrədəm
Sinus Medii		
'bay' on Moon	SĪ-nuhs MED-ē-Ē, MED-ē-Ī	'saɪnəs 'mediːˌiː, 'mediːˌaɪ
Sinus Roris		
'bay' on moon	SĪ-nuhs RŌR-uhs, RAWR-uhs	'saɪnəs 'roːrəs, 'rɔːrəs
Siobhan		
pers. name, Irish	shuh-VAHN	ʃə'vɑn
Siôn		
pers. name, Welsh	SYAWN, ⑤ SHAWN, SHAHN	'sjɔːn, ⑤ 'ʃɔːn, 'ʃɑn
Siouan		
pert. to the Sioux	SOO-uhn	'suːən
Sioux		
N. American people	SOO	'suː
Siphmoth		
Biblical name	SIF-MAHTH, -MAWTH, -muhth; sif-MŌT	'sifˌmɑθ, -ˌmɔːθ, -məθ; sif'moːt
Sippai		
Biblical name	SIP-ē-Ī, SIP-Ī, si-PĪ	'sipiːˌaɪ, 'sipˌaɪ, si'paɪ
Siqueiros		
David, *Mexican painter*	sē-KĀ-rōs	siː'keːroːs
Sirah		
Biblical name	SĪ-ruh, si-RAH	'saɪrə, si'rɑː
Siracusa		
prov, Italy	SIR-uh-KOO-zuh	ˌsirə'kuːzə
Sirenia		
dugongs & manatees	sī-RĒ-nē-uh	saɪ'riːniːə
Sirens		
Greek legendary sea demons	SĪ-ruhnz	'saɪrənz
Siret		
river, Europe	sē-RET	siː'ret
Sirhan		
Sirhan, *US assassin; pers. name*	sir-HAHN, SIR-HAHN	siʳ'hɑn, 'siʳˌhɑn
Siricius		
pope	suh-RISH-(ē-)uhs	sə'riʃ(iː)əs
Sirimavo		
pers. name, Sinhalese	SIR-uh-MAHV-ō	ˌsirə'mɑvoː
Sirion		
Biblical name	SIR-ē-AHN, suh-RĪ-uhn, sir-YŌN	'siriːˌɑn, sə'raɪən, sir'joːn
Sirionó		
S. American people	SIR-ē-uh-NŌ	ˌsiriːə'noː
Sirius		
star Alpha Canis Majoris	SIR-ē-uhs	'siriːəs
Síros		
island, Greece	SĒ-RAWS	'siːˌrɔːs
Sirte		
gulf, Africa; town, Libya	SIR-TĀ	'siʳˌteː
Sisamai [Sismai]		
Biblical name	SIS-uh-MĪ, sis-MĪ	'sisəˌmaɪ, sis'maɪ
Sisera		
Biblical name	SIS-uh-ruh, SĒ-suh-RAH	'sisərə, ˌsiːsə'rɑ
Sisinnius		
pope	suh-SIN-ē-uhs	sə'siniːəs
Siskel		
Gene, *US film critic*	SIS-kuhl	'siskəl

Foreign Sounds: ue: *Fr.* **rue**, *Ger.* **füllen**   uh(r): *Fr.* **b**o**euf**, *Ger.* **Höhle**   kh: *Ger.* i**ch**, *Scot.* lo**ch**   g̃: *Sp.* ami**g**o   v: *Sp.* ha**b**lar
hl: *Welsh* **Ll**anelli.   CAPITALS: primary stress.   SMALL CAPS: secondary stress.   ⑤: U.S. pron.   ⑥: British pron.

Siskiyou
   county, CA; mts., US　　SIS-ki-YŌO　　'siski‚juː

Siskiyous
   College of the, *CA*　　SIS-ki-YŌOZ　　'siski‚juːz

Sismai
   Biblical name　　SIS-MĪ, sis-MĪ　　'sis‚mɑi, sis'mɑi

Sisseton
   N. American people　　SIS-uht-n　　'sisətn̩

Sissy
   pers. name　　SIS-ē　　'sisiˑ

Sistine
   Chapel, *the Vatican*　　SIS-TĒN　　'sis‚tiːn

Sisto
   pers. name, Italian　　SĒS-tō　　'siːstoː

siSwati [Swazi]
   lang., Africa　　si-SWAHT-ē　　si'swɑtiˑ

Sisyphean
   pert. to Sisyphus *or his labors*　　suh-SIF-ē-uhn, SIS-uh-FĒ-uhn　　sə'sifiːən, ‚sisə'fiːən

Sisyphus
   man condemned to roll rock uphill in Hades　　SIS-uh-fuhs　　'sisəfəs

Sitar
   musical instrument　　si-TAHR, SI-TAHR　　si'tɑr, 'si‚tɑr

Sitka
   city, division, AK; N. American people　　SIT-kuh　　'sitkə

Sithri [Zithri]
   Biblical name　　SITH-RĪ, si-TRĒ　　'siθ‚rɑi, si'triː

Sitnah
   Biblical name　　SIT-nuh, sit-NAH　　'sitnə, sit'nɑː

Sittang
   river, Burma　　SI-TAHNG　　'si‚tɑŋ

Sitting Bull
   N. American Indian warrior　　SIT-ing BUL　　‚siţiŋ 'bul

Sittwe [Akyab]
   town, Burma　　SIT-wē　　'sitwiˑ

Siut [Asyūt]
   governorate, Egypt　　SYŌOT　　'sjuːt

Siva, Shiva
   Hindu god, member of the supreme triad　　SHIV-uh, SHĒ-vuh　　'ʃivə, 'ʃiːvə

Sivaism
   worship of Siva　　SHIV-uh-IZ-uhm, SHĒ-vuh-IZ-uhm　　'ʃivə‚izəm, 'ʃiːvə‚izəm

Sivan
   Jewish month　　SIV-uhn, SĒ-VAHN　　'sivən, 'siː‚vɑn

Sivas
   city, prov, Turkey　　si-VAHS　　si'vɑs

Siwa
   town, Egypt　　SĒ-wuh　　'siːwə

Sixtine
   pert. to Pope Sixtus *or to* Sistine Chapel　　SIK-STĒN　　'sik‚stiːn

Sixtus
   pope　　SIK-stuhs　　'sikstəs

Key (col. 2):   a: fad ā: fade ah: father ar: marry aw: law e: fed ē: feed er: merry i: hid ī: hide ō: coat ōo: boot
oi: boy ow: now u: put uh: above uhr: bird ch: chop ng: ring sh: show th: thick th̲: this zh: measure

Sjælland [Zealand]		
island, Denmark	SHEL-AHN	ˈʃelˌɑn
Skaði		
Scandinavian goddess	SKAH<u>TH</u>-ē	ˈskaðiˑ
Skagen		
town, Denmark	SKAHG-uhn	ˈskɑgən
Skagerrak		
arm of North Sea	SKAG-uh-RAK	ˈskægəˌræk
Skaggs		
Ricky, *US country musician*	SKAGS	ˈskægs
Skagit		
river, bay, county, WA; N. American people	SKAJ-uht	ˈskædʒət
Skagway-Yakutat-Angoon		
division, AK	SKAG-WĀ-YAK-uh-TAT-ang-ḠOON	ˈskægˌweːˈjækəˌtæʈæŋˈguːn
Skamania		
county, WA	skuh-MĀN-yuh	skəˈmeːnjə
Skaneateles		
town, NY	SKIN-ē-AT-luhs, SKAN-ē-AT-luhs	ˌskiniːˈætləs, ˌskæniːˈætləs
Skara Brae		
excavated Neolithic village, Orkney Islands	SKAR-uh BRĀ	ˌskærə ˈbreː
Skeat		
Walter, *English philologist, lexicographer*	SKĒT	ˈskiːt
Skeena		
river, Canada	SKĒ-nuh	ˈskiːnə
Skene		
pers. name	SKĒN	ˈskiːn
Skíathos, Skiathos		
island, Greece	SKĒ-uh-THAWS, ⑤ SKĪ-uh-THAHS	ˈskiːəˌθɔːs, ⑤ ˈskɑiəˌθas
Skiatook		
town, OK	SKĪ(-uh)-T̄OOK, -TUK	ˌskɑi(ə)ˈtuːk, -ˈtuk
Skinner		
Burrhus Frederic, *US psychologist, educator*	SKIN-uhr	ˈskinəʳ
Skinnerian		
pert. to Skinner or behaviorist theories	ski-NIR-ē-uhn, ski-NER-ē-uhn	skiˈniriːən, skiˈneriːən
Skíros		
island, Greece	SKĒ-RAWS	ˈskiːˌrɔːs
Skoda, Škoda		
J., *Austrian physician;* Emil von, *Czech engineer*	SHKŌ-dah, ⑤ SKŌD-uh, SHKŌD-uh	ˈʃkoːdɑː, ⑤ ˈskoːdə, ˈʃkoːdə
Skokie		
town, IL	SKŌ-kē	ˈskoːkiˑ
Skokomish		
N. American people	skō-KŌ-mish	skoːˈkoːmiʃ
Skol		
tdmk for vodka, tobacco	SKŌL, SKAWL	ˈskoːl, ˈskɔːl
Skopje		
city, Macedonia	SKAWP-ye, SKAWP-yā	ˈskɔːpje, ˈskɔːpjeː
Skoplje [Skopje]		
city, Macedonia	SKAWP-lye, SKAWP-lē-Ā	ˈskɔːplje, ˈskɔːpliːˌeː

Foreign Sounds: ue: *Fr.* **rue**, *Ger.* **füllen**   uh(r): *Fr.* **boeuf**, *Ger.* **Höhle**   <u>kh</u>: *Ger.* **ich**, *Scot.* **loch**   g̱: *Sp.* **amigo**   v̱: *Sp.* **hablar**
hl: *Welsh* **Llanelli**.   CAPITALS: primary stress.   SMALL CAPS: secondary stress.   ⑤: U.S. pron.   ⑥: British pron.

Skua
   sea bird   SKYOO-uh   'skjuːə

Skye
   island, Scotland   SKĪ   'skɑɪ

Skykomish
   river, WA   skī-KŌ-mish   skɑɪ'koːmiʃ

Skylab
   US space station   SKĪ-LAB   'skɑɪˌlæb

Slatkin
   Leonard, *US conductor*   SLAT-kin   'slætkin

Slaughter
   pers. name   SLAWT-uhr   'slɔː̬tərʳ

Slav
   European ethnic group   SLAHV   'slɑv

Slave
   river, Canada; N. American people   SLĀV   'sleːv

Slavic
   pert. to Slavs; *branch of*   SLAHV-ik   'slɑvik
     Indo-European langs.

Slavonia
   region, Croatia   sluh-VŌN-yuh, sluh-VŌ-nē-uh   slə'voːnjə, slə'voːniːə

Slavonic
   Slavic   sluh-VAHN-ik   slə'vɑnik

Slavophile
   admirer of the Slavs   SLAV-uh-FĪL, SLAHV-uh-FĪL   'slævəˌfɑil, 'slɑvəˌfɑil

Slavophobe
   hater of the Slavs   SLAV-uh-FŌB, SLAHV-uh-FŌB   'slævəˌfoːb, 'slɑvəˌfoːb

Slayton
   Donald Kent, *US astronaut*   SLĀT-n   'sleːtn̩

Slazenger
   tdmk for sport racquets   SLĀ-zuhn-juhr   'sleːzəndʒərʳ

Sleigh
   pers. name   SLĀ   'sleː

Slezak
   Leo, *Czech tenor;* Walter, *US actor*   SLEZ-AHK, Ⓢ SLĀ-ZAK   'slezˌɑːk, Ⓢ 'sleːˌzæk

Slidell
   pers. name   SLĪD-l, slī-DEL   'slɑidl̩, slɑi'del

Sligh
   pers. name   SLĪ   'slɑi

Sligo
   pers. name   SLĪ-gō   'slɑigoː

Slivovitz
   Balkan plum brandy   SLIV-uh-VITS, SLĒ-vuh-VITS,   'slivəˌvits, 'sliːvəˌvits,
                       SHLIV-uh-VITS, -WITS   'ʃlivəˌvits, -ˌwits

Slobodan
   pers. name, Serbo-Croatian   slaw-BAW-dahn   slɔː'bɔːdɑːn

Slobodan
   pers. name,   slaw-BAW-dahn, Ⓢ SLŌ-buh-DAHN,   slɔː'bɔːdɑn, Ⓢ 'sloːbəˌdɑn,
                       sluh-BŌD-AHN   slə'boːdˌɑn

Slough
   town, England   SLOW   'slɑu

Slough of Despond
   bog in Pilgrim's Progress, *J.*   SLOW uhv di-SPAHND, Ⓢ *also* SLOO   ˌslɑu əv di'spɑnd, Ⓢ *also*
    Bunyan; *depression*   ˌsluː

Key (col. 2):   a: fad   ā: fade   ah: father   ar: marry   aw: law   e: fed   ē: feed   er: merry   i: hid   ī: hide   ō: coat   ōō: boot
oi: boy   ow: now   u: put   uh: above   uhr: bird   ch: chop   ng: ring   sh: show   th: thick   <u>th</u>: this   zh: measure

Slovak
  lang., people, E. Europe   SLŌ-VAHK, SLŌ-VAK   'sloːˌvɑk, 'sloːˌvæk

Slovakia
  republic, E. Europe   slō-VAHK-ē-uh, slō-VAK-ē-uh   sloː'vɑkiːə, sloː'vækiːə

Slovene
  lang., people, Slovenia   SLŌ-VĒN   'sloːˌviːn

Slovenia
  republic, E. Europe   slō-VĒN-yuh, slō-VĒ-nē-uh   sloː'viːnjə, sloː'viːniːə

Slovenian [Slovene]
  lang., Slovenia   slō-VĒ-nē-uhn, slō-VĒN-yuhn   sloː'viːniːən, sloː'viːnjən

Slovenija [Slovenia]
  republic, E. Europe   slō-VEN-ē-(Y)AH   sloː'veniːˌ(j)ɑ

Slovensko [Slovakia]
  republic, E. Europe   slō-VEN-skō   sloː'venskoː

Smedley
  pers. name   SMED-lē   'smedliˑ

Smenkhare
  king of Egypt   smeng-KAHR-uh   smeŋ'kɑrə

Smerdis
  Persian noble   SMUHR-duhs   'sməʳdəs

Smetana
  Bedřich, *Czech composer*   SMET-n-uh   'smetn̩ə

Smith
  pers. name   SMITH   'smiθ

Smithson
  James, *English chemist, mineralogist*   SMITH-suhn   'smiθsən

Smithsonian
  Institution, *US natl. museum*   smith-SŌ-nē-uhn   smiθ'soːniːən

Smolensk
  city, Russia   SMUHL-YEN(T)SK, ⑤ smō-LEN(T)SK   ˌsməl'jen(t)sk, ⑤ smoː'len(t)sk

Smollett
  Tobias G., *English author*   SMAHL-uht   'smɑlət

Smothers
  Dick *and* Tom, *US comedians*   SMUHTH-uhrz   'sməðəʳz

Smucker's
  US jam co.   SMUHK-uhrz   'sməkəʳz

Smuts
  Jan, *South African statesman*   SMUETS, ⑤ SMUHTS   'smyːts, ⑤ 'sməts

Smyrna
  mother of Adonis in Greek myth;   SMUHR-nuh   'sməʳnə
  ancient city, Asia Minor; prov,
  Turkey; pl. name, US

Smyth
  1. pers. name   SMITH, SMĪTH   'smiθ, 'smaiθ
  2. county, VA   SMĪTH   'smaiθ

Smythe
  pers. name   SMĪTH, SMĪTH   'smaið, 'smaiθ

Smythii, Mare
  see Mare Smythii

Smyth-sewn
  bookbinding   SMITH-SŌN, SMĪTH-SŌN   'smiθˌsoːn, 'smaiθˌsoːn

SNCC
  Student Non-Violent Coordinating   SNIK   'snik
  Committee

Foreign Sounds: ue: *Fr.* **rue**, *Ger.* **füllen**   uh(r): *Fr.* **boeuf**, *Ger.* **Höhle**   kh: *Ger.* **ich**, *Scot.* **loch**   ğ: *Sp.* amigo   y: *Sp.* hablar
hl: *Welsh* **Llanelli**.   CAPITALS: primary stress.   SMALL CAPS: secondary stress.   ⑤: U.S. pron.   ⓔ: British pron.

Snead

  Sam, *US golfer*   SNĒD   'sniːd

Snell

  George D., *US immunologist (Nobel*   SNEL   'snel
  1980)

SNET

  Southern New England Telephone Co.   ES-EN-Ē-TĒ, SNET   ˌesˌenˌiː'tiː, 'snet

SNOBOL

  programming lang.   SNŌ-BAWL   'snoːˌbɔːl

Snohomish

  river, county, WA; N. American   snō-HŌ-mish   snoː'hoːmiʃ
  people

Snoopy

  cartoon beagle   SNOOP-ē   'snuːpiˑ

Snoqualmie

  river, WA   snō-KWAHL-mē   snoː'kwɑlmiˑ

Snowdonia

  region, natl. park, Wales   snō-DŌN-yuh, snō-DŌ-nē-uh   snoː'doːnjə, snoː'doːniːə

So

  Biblical name   SŌ   'soː

Soame

  pers. name   SŌM   'soːm

Soave

  wine   SWAHV-ā, suh-WAHV-ā   'swɑveː, sə'wɑveː

Sobek-Re

  Egyptian god   SAWB-uhk-RĀ, SAHB-uhk-RĀ   'sɔːbək'reː, 'sɑbək'reː

Sobhuza

  king of Swaziland   sō-BOO-zuh   soː'buːzə

Sobk [Sebek]

  Egyptian crocodile god   SAHB-uhk, SAWB-uhk   'sɑbək, 'sɔːbək

Soboba

  Band, *N. American people*   sō-BŌ-buh   soː'boːbə

Sochi

  port, Russia   SŌ-chē   'soːtʃiˑ

Socho, Socoh, Sochoh

  Biblical name   SŌ-KŌ, shō-KHŌ   'soːˌkoː, ʃoː'xoː

Socinian

  follower of Socinus   suh-SIN-ē-uhn   sə'siniːən

Socinianism

  religious beliefs of Socinus   suh-SIN-ē-uh-NIZ-uhm   sə'siniːəˌnizəm

Socinus

  Faustus, *Protestant theologian*   sō-SĪ-nuhs, suh-SĪ-nuhs   soː'sainəs, sə'sainəs

Socorro

  county, NM   suh-KAWR-ō   sə'kɔːroː

Socotra

  island, Indian Ocean   suh-KŌ-truh   sə'koːtrə

Socrates

  1. Greek philosopher; pers. name   SAHK-ruh-TĒZ   'sɑkrəˌtiːz
  2. Mod. Greek   saw-KRAH-tēs   sɔː'krɑtiːs

Socratic

  pert. to Socrates   suh-KRAT-ik, sō-KRAT-ik   sə'kræṭik, sɔː'kræṭik

Socraticism

  a characteristic of Socrates   suh-KRAT-uh-SIZ-uhm   sə'kræṭəˌsizəm

Socratism

  philosophy or method of Socrates   SAHK-ruh-TIZ-uhm   'sɑkrəˌtizəm

---

Key (col. 2):   a: fad   ā: fade   ah: father   ar: marry   aw: law   e: fed   ē: feed   er: merry   i: hid   ī: hide   ō: coat   oo: boot
oi: boy   ow: now   u: put   uh: above   uhr: bird   ch: chop   ng: ring   sh: show   th: thick   th: this   zh: measure

Soddy
  Frederick, *English chemist (Nobel*   SAHD-ē   'sɑdi·
  1921)
Söderblom
  Nathan, *Swedish churchman (Nobel*   SUH(R)D-uhr-BLŌŌM   'sœːdəʳˌbluːm
  1930)
Sodi
  Biblical name   SŌD-Ī, sō-DĒ   'soːdˌɑi, soː'diː
sodium
  element   SŌD-ē-uhm   'soːdiːəm
Sodom
  Biblical city   SAHD-uhm   'sɑdəm
Sodomite
  inhabitant of Sodom   SAHD-uh-MĪT   'sɑdəˌmɑit
Sodus
  village, NY   SŌD-uhs   'soːdəs
Soerabaja
  see Surabaja
Sofia
  1. pers. name   suh-FĒ-uh, suh-FĪ-uh, sō-FĒ-uh   sə'fiːə, sə'fɑiə, soː'fiːə
  2. Swedish   su-FĒ-ah   su'fiːɑː
Sofonisba
  pers. name, Italian   SŌ-fō-NĒZ-bah   ˌsoːfoː'niːzbɑ
Soga
  lang., people, Africa   SŌ-guh   'soːgə
Sogdian
  extinct Iranian lang.   SAHG-dē-uhn   'sɑgdiːən
Sogdiana
  region, Uzbekistan   SAHG-dē-AHN-uh, SAHG-dē-AN-uh,   ˌsɑgdiː'ɑnə, ˌsɑgdiː'ænə,
                                               SAHG-dē-Ā-nuh   ˌsɑgdiː'eːnə
Soho, SoHo
  district, NY & London, England   SŌ-HŌ   'soːˌhoː
Soissons
  city, France   swah-SAW[n]   swɑsɔ̃
Sojourner
  pers. name   SŌ-JUHR-nuhr, sō-JUHR-nuhr   'soːˌdʒəʳnəʳ, soː'dʒəʳnəʳ
Sojourner-Douglas
  College, *MD*   SŌ-JUHR-nuhr-DUHG-luhs,   'soːˌdʒəʳnəʳ'dəgləs,
                                               sō-JUHR-nuhr-   soː'dʒəʳnəʳ-
Sokagoan Chippewa
  N. American people   sō-kuh-GŌ-uhn CHIP-uh-WAW, -WAH,   ˌsoːkə'goːən 'tʃipəˌwɔː,
                                               -WĀ, -wuh   -ˌwɑ, -ˌweː, -wə
Sokar
  Egyptian god of the dead   SAWK-uhr, SAHK-uhr   'sɔːkəʳ, 'sɑkəʳ
Sol
  Roman sun god   SAWL, SAHL, SŌL   'sɔːl, 'sɑl, 'soːl
Solano
  county, CA   suh-LAHN-ō   sə'lɑnoː
Solāpur
  city, India   sō-LAH-PUR   soː'lɑˌpuʳ
Soldotna
  city, AK   sahl-DAHT-nuh   sɑl'dɑtnə

Foreign Sounds: ue: *Fr.* **rue**, *Ger.* **füllen**   uh(r): *Fr.* **boeuf**, *Ger.* **Höhle**   <u>kh</u>: *Ger.* **ich**, *Scot.* **loch**   ḡ: *Sp.* **amigo**   v̲: *Sp.* **hablar**
hl: *Welsh* **Llanelli**.   CAPITALS: primary stress.   SMALL CAPS: secondary stress.   Ⓢ: U.S. pron.   Ⓔ: British pron.

Soledad

   1. city, CA   SAHL-uh-DAD, SŌ-luh-DAD   'sɑlə‚dæd, 'soːlə‚dæd

   2. town, Colombia   SAW-luh-<u>TH</u>AH(TH)   ‚sɔːlə'ðɑ(ð)

   3. city, Mexico   SAW-luh-DAHD, SAW-luh-<u>TH</u>AH(TH)   ‚sɔːlə'dad, ‚sɔːlə'ðɑ(ð)

Solent, The

   channel between Isle of Wight &   <u>th</u>uh SŌ-luhnt   ðə 'soːlənt
     England

Sol Especial

   Mexican beer   SŌL es-pes-YAHL   'soːl espes'jɑl

Soli

   lang., Africa   SŌ-lē   'soːliˑ

Solidarnosc

   "Solidarity" political party, Poland   SAWL-ē-DAHR-NAWSH   ‚soːliː'daːr‚nɔːʃ

Solingen

   city, Germany   ZŌ-ling-uhn, SŌ-ling-uhn   'zoːliŋən, 'soːliŋən

Solo

   river, Indonesia; former name of   SŌ-lō   'soːloː
     Surakarta; Han, *hero of Star Wars*

Sologne

   basin, France   saw-LAWN-yuh   sɔːlɔːɲ

Solomon

   king of Israel; Islands, *Pacific; pers.*   SAHL-uh-muhn   'sɑləmən
     name

Solon

   Athenian statesman; pers. name   SŌ-luhn, SŌ-LAHN   'soːlən, 'soː‚lɑn

Solothurn

   canton, Switzerland   ZŌ-luh-TURN, SŌ-luh-TURN   'zoːlə‚tuᵣn, 'soːlə‚tuᵣn

Solow

   Robert M., *US economist (Nobel*   SŌ-lō   'soːloː
     1987)

Solti

   Sir Georg, *Hungarian conductor*   SHŌL-tē   'ʃoːltiˑ

Solvay

   1. Ernest, *Belgian chemist*   sawl-VE, Ⓢ SAHL-VĀ   sɔːlve, Ⓢ 'sɑl‚veː

   2. village, NY   SAHL-VĀ   'sɑl‚veː

Solway Firth

   arm of Irish Sea   SAHL-wā FUHRTH   ‚sɑlweː 'fəᵣθ

Solzhenitsyn

   Alexandr I., *Russian author (Nobel*   SAWL-zhuhn-YĒT-syin,   ‚sɔːlʒən'jiːtsjin,
     1970)   Ⓢ SŌL-zhuh-NĒT-suhn, SAWL-   Ⓢ ‚soːlʒə'niːtsən, ‚sɔːl-

Somali

   people, lang., Africa   suh-MAHL-ē, sō-   sə'mɑliˑ, soː-

Somalia

   republic, Africa   sō-MAHL-ē-uh, suh-, -MAHL-yuh   soː'mɑliːə, sə-, -'mɑlj

Somaliland

   region, Africa   sō-MAHL-ē-LAND, suh-   soː'mɑliˑ‚lænd, sə-

Somers

   John, *1st Baron, English statesman;*   SUHM-uhrz   'səməᵣz
     Suzanne, *US actress*

Somerset

   county, England; pers. name   SUHM-uhr-SET, SUHM-uhr-suht   'səməᵣ‚set, 'səməᵣsət

Somerville

   town, MA, NJ, TN; college, Oxford   SUHM-uhr-VIL   'səməᵣ‚vil
     Univ.

Key (col. 2):　a: fad　ā: fade　ah: father　ar: marry　aw: law　e: fed　ē: feed　er: merry　i: hid　ī: hide　ō: coat　ōō: boot
oi: boy　ow: now　u: put　uh: above　uhr: bird　ch: chop　ng: ring　sh: show　th: thick　<u>th</u>: this　zh: measure

Somme		
river, dept., France	SAWM, [$] SUHM, SAHM	sɔːm, [$] 'səm, 'sam
Sommer		
Elke, *German actress*	ZAWM-uhr, [$] SUHM-uhr	'zɔːmə^{r}, [$] 'səmə^{r}
Somnii, Palus		
see Palus Somnii		
Somniorum, Lacus		
feature on Moon	LAHK-uhs SAHM-nē-AWR-uhm	'lakəs ˌsamniː'ɔːrəm
Somnus		
Roman personification of sleep	SAHM-nuhs	'samnəs
Somoza		
Nicaraguan political family	suh-MŌ-suh, suh-MŌ-zuh	sə'moːsə, sə'moːzə
Sønderborg		
town, Denmark	SUH(R)N-uhr-BAWRḠ	'sœnə^{r}ˌbɔː^{r}ɣ
Sondheim		
Stephen, *US composer*	SAHND-HĪM	'sandˌhaim
Sondra		
pers. name	SAHN-druh	'sandrə
Songhai		
lang., people, Africa	sahng-GĪ	saŋ'gai
Songkran		
Buddhist New Year	SAWNG-KRAHN	'sɔːŋˌkran
Songo		
lang., Africa	SAHNG-gō, SAWNG-gō	'saŋgoː, 'sɔːŋgoː
Sonia, Sonja, Sonya		
1. pers. name	SŌN-yuh, SAHN-yuh	'soːnjə, 'sanjə
2. Russian	SAWN-yuh	'sɔːnjə
Sonnambula, La		
opera, Bellini	LAH saw-NAHM-byu-lah, LAH suh-NAM-byuh-luh	ˌla sɔː'nambjula, ˌla sə'næmbjələ
Sonny		
pers. name	SUHN-ē	'səniˑ
Sonoma		
county, CA	suh-NŌ-muh	sə'noːmə
Sonora		
city, CA, TX; river, state, Mexico	suh-NŌR-uh, suh-NAWR-uh	sə'noːrə, sə'nɔːrə
Sony		
Japanese corp.	SŌ-nē	'soːniˑ
Sonya		
see Sonja		
Soochow		
see Suzhou		
Sopater		
Biblical name	SAHP-uht-uhr	'sapət̬ə^{r}
Sophereth		
Biblical name	SAHF-uh-RETH, SŌ-fuh-, -ruhth; so-FE-ret	'safəˌreθ, 'soːfə-, -rəθ; so'feret
Sophia		
1. pers. name	suh-FĒ-uh, suh-FĪ-uh, sō-FĒ-uh, SŌ-fē-uh	sə'fiːə, sə'faiə, soː'fiːə, 'soːfiːə
2. Danish, Swedish	su-FĒ-ah	su'fiːaː
3. German	zō-FĒ-ah	zoː'fiːa
4. Russian	SAWF-yuh	'sɔːfjə

Foreign Sounds: ue: *Fr.* **rue**, *Ger.* **füllen** uh(r): *Fr.* **boeuf**, *Ger.* **Höhle** kh: *Ger.* **ich**, *Scot.* **loch** ḡ: *Sp.* amigo v̱: *Sp.* hablar hl: *Welsh* **Llanelli**. CAPITALS: primary stress. SMALL CAPS: secondary stress. [$]: U.S. pron. [£]: British pron.

Sophianism

   Orthodox Christian sect   sō-FĒ-uh-NIZ-uhm, SŌ-fē-uh-,   soːˈfiːə͵nizəm, ˈsoːfiːə-,
                                   SAHF-ē-uh-   ˈsɑfiːə-

Sophie

   1. pers. name   SŌ-fē   ˈsoːfiˑ

   2. French   saw-FĒ   sɔːfiː

   3. German   zō-FĒ(-uh)   zoːˈfiː(ə)

   4. Swedish   su-FĒ   suˈfiː

Sophist

   dialogue of Plato   SAHF-uhst   ˈsɑfəst

Sophistic

   ancient Greek rhetorical movement   sah-FIS-tik, suh-   sɑˈfistik, sə-

Sophoclean

   pert. to Sophocles   SAHF-uh-KLĒ-uhn   ͵safəˈkliːən

Sophocles

   1. Greek playwright; pers. name   SAHF-uh-KLĒZ   ˈsafə͵kliːz

   2. Mod. Greek   saw-faw-KLĒS   sɔːfɔːˈkliːs

Sophonias

   Old Testament book   SAHF-uh-NĪ-uhs, SŌ-fuh-NĪ-uhs   ͵safəˈnɑiəs, ͵soːfəˈnɑiəs

Sophonisba

   pers. name   SAHF-uh-NIZ-buh, SŌ-fuh-   ͵safəˈnizbə, ͵soːfə-

Sophronia

   Roman wife of Maxentius   suh-FRŌ-nē-uh   səˈfroːniːə

Sophy

   pers. name   SŌ-fē   ˈsoːfiˑ

Sopron

   city, Hungary   SHŌ-PRŌN   ˈʃoː͵proːn

Sopwith

   British-designed aircraft   SAHP-with   ˈsɑpwiθ

Sora

   bird   SŌR-uh, SAWR-uh   ˈsoːrə, ˈsɔːrə

Sorata

   mtn., village, Bolivia   sō-RAHT-uh   soːˈrɑt̪ə

Sorbian [Lusatian]

   lang., Germany   SAWR-bē-uhn   ˈsɔːʳbiːən

Sorbonne

   university, Paris, France   sawr-BAWN, ⑤ sawr-BUHN,   sɔːrbɔːn, ⑤ sɔːʳˈbən,
                                   sawr-BAHN   sɔːʳˈban

Sorek

   Biblical name   SŌR-ek, sō-REK   ˈsoːr͵ek, soːˈrek

Søren, Sören

   pers. name, Danish   SUH(R)-ruhn   ˈsœrən

Sorensen

   Theodore, *US public figure*   SAWR-uhn-suhn, SAHR-uhn-suhn   ˈsɔːrənsən, ˈsɑrənsən

Soroptimist

   member of an international women's   saw-RAHP-tuh-muhst,   sɔːˈrɑptəməst, sɔːˈrɑptə͵mist
     organization   saw-RAHP-tuh-MIST

Sorrel

   plant   SAWR-uhl, SAHR-uhl   ˈsɔːrəl, ˈsɑrəl

Sorrento

   port, Italy   suh-REN-tō   səˈrentoː

Sorvino

   Paul, *US actor*   sawr-VĒ-nō   sɔːʳˈviːnoː

Sorvino

   Mira, *US actress*   sawr-VĒ-nō   sɔːʳˈviːnoː

Key (col. 2):   a: fad ā: fade ah: father ar: marry aw: law e: fed ē: feed er: merry i: hid ī: hide ō: coat ōō: boot
oi: boy ow: now u: put uh: above uhr: bird ch: chop ng: ring sh: show th: thick th̲: this zh: measure

Sosipater
  Biblical name   sō-SIP-uht-uhr   soː'sipəṭəʳ

Sosnowiec
  city, Poland   saw-SNŌV-YETS   sɔː'snoːvˌjets

Sosthenes
  Biblical name   SAHS-thuh-NĒZ   'sɑsθəˌniːz

Sotai
  Biblical name   SŌT-ē-Ī, SŌ-TĪ, saw-TĪ   'soːṭiːˌai, 'soːˌtai, sɔː'tai

Soter
  pope   SŌT-uhr   'soːṭəʳ

Sotheby
  auction house, London & New York   SUHTH-uh-bē   'səðəbi·
    City

Sotho
  Bantu lang. group, Africa   SŌ-thō, SŌT-ō   'soːθoː, 'soːṭoː

Souphanouvong
  president, Laos   su-FAHN-o͞o-VAWNG   su'fɑnu·ˌvɔːŋ

Soûr [Tyre]
  fishing port, Lebanon   SUR   'suʳ

Souris
  river, Manitoba   SUR-uhs   'surəs

Sousa
  John Philip, *US composer*   SO͞O-zuh   'suːzə

Sousaphone
  musical instrument   SO͞O-zuh-FŌN   'suːzəˌfoːn

Souter
  David, *US Supreme Court Justice*   SO͞OT-uhr   'suːṭəʳ

South Africa
  republic, Africa   sowth AF-rik-uh   sɑuθ 'æfrikə

South African
  pert. to South Africa   sowth AF-rik-uhn   sɑuθ 'æfrikən

Southall
  1. British family name   SUHTH-AWL, SUHTH-uhl   'səðˌɔːl, 'səðəl
  2. location, London, England   SOW-THAWL   'sauˌθɔːl

Southampton
  1. city, former county, England   sowth-HAM(P)-tuhn,   sɑuθ'hæm(p)tən,
                      sow-THAM(P)-tuhn,   sau'θæm(p)tən,
                      suh-THAM(P)-tuhn,   sə'θæm(p)tən,
                      suh-THAM(P)-tuhn   sə'ðæm(p)tən
  2. pl. name, US   sowth-HAM(P)-tuhn,   sɑuθ'hæm(p)tən,
                      sow-THAM(P)-tuhn   sau'θæm(p)tən

South Carolina
  state, US   SOWTH KAR-uh-LĪ-nuh, kuhr-LĪ-nuh,   ˌsɑuθ ˌkærə'lɑinə, kəʳ'lɑinə,
                 kar-LĪ-nuh   kæʳ'lɑinə

Southcote
  pers. name   SOWTH-kuht, SOWTH-KŌT   'sauθkət, 'sauθˌkoːt

South Dakota
  state, US   SOWTH duh-KŌT-uh   ˌsɑuθ də'koːṭə

Southend-on-Sea
  town, England   SOW-THEN-dawn-SĒ   ˌsɑuˌθendɔːn'siː

Southern Sotho
  lang., Africa   SUHTH-uhrn SŌ-thō, SŌT-ō   'səðəʳn 'soːθoː, 'soːṭoː

Southey
  Robert, *English poet*   SOW-thē, SUHTH-ē   'sauði·, 'səði·

Foreign Sounds: ue: *Fr.* **rue**, *Ger.* **füllen**   uh(r): *Fr.* **boeuf**, *Ger.* **Höhle**   <u>kh</u>: *Ger.* **ich**, *Scot.* **loch**   g̶: *Sp.* **amigo**   v̲: *Sp.* **hablar**
hl: *Welsh* **Llanelli**.   CAPITALS: primary stress.   SMALL CAPS: secondary stress.   Ⓢ: U.S. pron.   Ⓔ: British pron.

South Glamorgan
county, Wales — SOWTH gluh-MAWR-guhn — ˌsɑuθ glə'mɔːʳgən

South Nahanni
river, Canada — SOWTH nuh-HAN-ē — ˌsɑuθ nə'hæni·

Southwark
borough, England — SUH<u>TH</u>-uhrk, ⑤ SOWTH-WUHRK — 'səðəʳk, ⑤ 'sɑuθˌwəʳk

Southwick
1. *town, MA* — SOWTH-wik — 'sɑuθwik
2. *town, England* — SOWTH-wik, SUH<u>TH</u>-ik — 'sɑuθwik, 'səðik

South Yorkshire
county, England — sowth YAWRK-shuhr, -SHIR — sɑuθ 'jɔːʳkʃəʳ, -ˌʃiʳ

Souvanna Phouma
premier, Laos — sōō-VAHN-uh POO-muh — su·'vɑnə 'puːmə

Souverain Cellars
winery, CA — SOO-vuh-RĀN SEL-uhrz — 'suːvəˌreːn 'seləʳz

Soviet
Russian Communist system — SŌ-vē-ET, SAHV-ē-, -uht — 'soːviːˌet, 'sɑviː-, -ət

Sowerby
pers. name — SŌ-uhr-bē — 'soːəʳbi·

Soweto
prov, South Africa — suh-WET-ō, suh-WĀT-ō — sə'weṭoː, sə'weːṭoː

Soyinka
Wole, *Nigerian author (Nobel 1986)* — swoi-(Y)ING-kuh — swɔi'(j)iŋkə

Soyuz
Soviet spacecraft — SUH-YOOS, ⑤ soi-OOZ, SOI-OOZ — ˌsə'juːs, ⑤ sɔi'uːz, 'sɔiˌuːz

Spaatz
Carl, *US militarist* — SPAHTS — 'spɑts

Spacek
Sissy, *US actress* — SPĀ-SEK — 'speːˌsek

Spain
kingdom, Europe — SPĀN — 'speːn

Spalding
Albert, *US violinist; US sporting goods co.* — SPAWL-ding — 'spɔːldiŋ

Spam
tdmk for a meat product — SPAM — 'spæm

Spandau
city, Germany — SHPAHN-DOW, ⑤ SPAN-DOW — 'ʃpɑnˌdɑu, ⑤ 'spænˌdɑu

Spaniard
inhabitant of Spain — SPAN-yuhrd — 'spænjəʳd

Spanish
lang., Spain, the Americas — SPAN-ish — 'spæniʃ

Sparta [Lacedaemon]
ancient city, country, Greece; pl. name, US — SPAHRT-uh — 'spɑʳṭə

Spartacus
Roman rebel slave — SPAHRT-uh-kuhs — 'spɑʳṭəkəs

Spartoi
mythical men from dragon's teeth — SPAHR-TOI — 'spɑʳˌtɔi

Spassky
Tower, *Moscow* — SPAHS-kyuh, ⑤ SPAS-kē — 'spɑskjəi, ⑤ 'spæski·

Spaten
German beer — SHPAHT-n — 'ʃpɑtn̩

Spector
Phil, *US record producer* — SPEK-tuhr — 'spektəʳ

Speidel
tdmk for watchbands	spī-DEL	spɑiˈdel

Speke
John, *British explorer*	SPĒK	ˈspiːk

Spelman
College, *GA*	SPEL-muhn	ˈspelmən

Spemann
Hans, *German zoologist (Nobel 1935)*	SHPĀ-MAHN	ˈʃpeːˌmɑn

Spencer
Herbert, *English philosopher; British noble family; pers. name*	SPEN(T)-suhr	ˈspen(t)sərᵣ

Spencerianism
philosophy of Herbert Spencer	spen-SIR-ē-uh-NIZ-uhm	spenˈsiriːəˌnizəm

Spener
Phillip Jacob, *German theologian*	SHPĀ-nuhr	ˈʃpeːnərᵣ

Spenerism
teaching of P. J. Spener	SHPĀ-nuh-RIZ-uhm, SPĀ-	ˈʃpeːnəˌrizəm, ˈspeː-

Spengler
Oswald, *German philosopher*	SHPENG-gluhr, SPENG-gluhr	ˈʃpeŋglərᵣ, ˈspeŋglərᵣ

Spenser
Edmund, *English poet; pers. name*	SPEN(T)-suhr	ˈspen(t)sərᵣ

Spenserian
pert. to Spenser	spen(t)-SIR-ē-uhn, spen(t)-SER-ē-uhn	spen(t)ˈsiriːən, spen(t)ˈseriːən

Sperry
Roger W., *US neurobiologist (Nobel 1981)*	SPER-ē	ˈsperiˑ

Spertus
College of Judaica, *IL*	SPUHRT-uhs	ˈspərᵣʈəs

Spes
Roman goddess of hope	SPĀS, SPĀZ	ˈspeːs, ˈspeːz

Spezia, La
see La Spezia

Sphacteria
island, Greece	sfak-TIR-ē-uh	sfækˈtiriːə

Sphaerus
charioteer of Pelops	SFĒ-ruhs, SFIR-uhs	ˈsfiːrəs, ˈsfirəs

Sphinx
mythical riddler; Egyptian stone colossus	SFINGKS	ˈsfiŋks

Spica
star	SPĪ-kuh	ˈspɑikə

Spiegel
US mail order co.; pers. name	SPĒ-guhl	ˈspiːgəl

Spiegel, Der
see Der Spiegel

Spielberg
Steven, *US film maker*	SPĒL-BUHRG	ˈspiːlˌbərᵣg

Spillane
Mickey, *US writer*	spuh-LĀN	spəˈleːn

Spinelli
Jerry, *US children's author*	spuh-NEL-ē	spəˈneliˑ

Spinifex
Australian songbird	SPĪ-nuh-FEKS, SPIN-uh-FEKS	ˈspɑinəˌfeks, ˈspinəˌfeks

---

Foreign Sounds: ue: *Fr.* **rue**, *Ger.* **füllen**   uh(r): *Fr.* **boeuf**, *Ger.* **Höhle**   <u>kh</u>: *Ger.* **ich**, *Scot.* **loch**   ḡ: *Sp.* **amigo**   v̲: *Sp.* **hablar**   hl: *Welsh* **Llanelli**.   CAPITALS: primary stress.   SMALL CAPS: secondary stress.   Ⓢ: U.S. pron.   Ⓔ: British pron.

Spinks
  Michael, *US boxer*　　　　　　SPINCKS　　　　　　　　　'spiŋks
Spinoza
  Benedict (Baruch), *Dutch*　　spi-NŌ-zuh　　　　　　　spi'noːzə
    philosopher
Spinozism
  philosophy of Spinoza　　　　spuh-NŌ-ZIZ-uhm　　　　spə'noːˌzizəm
Spirea
  plant　　　　　　　　　　　spī-RĒ-uh　　　　　　　　spɑi'riːə
Spiridon
  see Spyridon
Spiro
  pers. name　　　　　　　　SPIR-ō, SPĪ-rō　　　　　　'spiroː, 'spɑiroː
Spitsbergen
  archipelago, Arctic Ocean　　SPITS-BUHR-guhn　　　　'spitsˌbəʳgən
Spittal
  pers. name　　　　　　　　SPIT-l　　　　　　　　　　'spitl̩
Spitteler
  C. F. G., *Swiss author (Nobel 1919)*　SHPIT-l-uhr, SHPIT-luhr　　'ʃpitləʳ, 'ʃpitləʳ
Split
  city, Croatia　　　　　　　SPLIT　　　　　　　　　　'split
Spock
  Benjamin, *US physician;* Mr.,　SPAHK　　　　　　　　　'spɑk
    character, Star Trek
Spode
  tdmk for china　　　　　　SPŌD　　　　　　　　　　'spoːd
Spokane
  river, city, county, WA; N. American　spō-KAN　　　　　　　spoː'kæn
    people
Spoleto
  town, Italy; music festival, SC　spuh-LĀT-ō　　　　　　　spə'leːt̩oː
Sporades
  islands, Greece　　　　　　SPAWR-uh-DĒZ, SPAHR-uh-DĒZ　'spoːrəˌdiːz, 'spɑrəˌdiːz
Sporádhes [Sporades]
  islands, Greece　　　　　　spaw-RAH-<u>th</u>ās　　　　　spoː'rɑðeːs
Spotsylvania
  county, village, VA　　　　SPAHT-suhl-VĀN-yuh　　　ˌspɑtsəl've̠ːnjə
Sprague
  pers. name　　　　　　　　SPRĀG　　　　　　　　　　'spreːg
Springboks
  South African rugby team　　SPRING-BAHKS　　　　　　'spriŋˌbɑks
Springsteen
  Bruce, *US rock musician*　　SPRING-STĒN　　　　　　　'spriŋˌstiːn
Spruance
  Raymond, *US militarist*　　SPROO-uhn(t)s　　　　　'spruːən(t)s
Spruille
  pers. name　　　　　　　　SPROO-uhl　　　　　　'spruːəl
Spurius
  pers. name, Latin　　　　　SPUR-ē-uhs　　　　　　　　'spuriːəs
Sputnik
  Soviet space satellite　　　SPUT-nik, SPUHT-nik, SPOOT-nik　'sputnik, 'spətnik, 'spuːtnik
Spuyten Duyvil
  creek, NY; district, New York City　SPĪT-n DĪ-vuhl　　　　　'spɑit̩n ˌdɑivəl
Spyridon, Spiridon
  pers. name, Mod. Greek　　spē-RĒ-<u>th</u>awn　　　　　spiː'riːðɔːn

---

Key (col. 2):　a: fad　ā: fade　ah: father　ar: marry　aw: law　e: fed　ē: feed　er: merry　i: hid　ī: hide　ō: coat　o͞o: boot
oi: boy　ow: now　u: put　uh: above　uhr: bird　ch: chop　ng: ring　sh: show　th: thick　<u>th</u>: this　zh: measure

Spyro Gyra
   rock group   SPĪ-rō JĪ-ruh   ˌspɑɪroː ˈdʒɑɪrə
Spyros
   pers. name, Greek   SPĒ-raws, SPĒ-rōs   ˈspiːrɔːs, ˈspiːroːs
Squab
   bird   SKWAHB   ˈskwɑb
Squacco
   heron   SKWAHK-ō, SKWAW-kō   ˈskwɑkoː, ˈskwɔːkoː
Squapan
   lake, ME   SKWAW-PAN   ˈskwɔːˌpæn
Squaxin Island
   Indian reservation, US   SKWAHK-suhn   ˈskwɑksən
Sranan Tongo
   lang., S. America   SRAHN-uhn TAWNG-gō, TAHNG-gō   ˌsrɑnən ˈtɔːŋoː, ˈtɑŋoː
Srbija [Serbia]
   republic, E. Europe   SUHR-bē-AH   ˈsərbiːˌɑ
Srebrenica
   city, Bosnia   SREB-ruh-NĒT-suh, -NIT-suh   ˌsrebrəˈniːtsə, -ˈnitsə
Sri
   Hindu prosperity goddess; pers. name   SHRĒ, SRĒ   ˈʃriː, ˈsriː
Sri-Jayawardenapura
   city, Sri Lanka   SRĒ-JĪ-uh-wuhr-duhn-uh-PUR-uh, SHRĒ-   ˈsriːˌdʒɑɪəwəᵊdənəˈpurə, ˈʃriː-
Sri Lanka [Ceylon]
   island state, Indian Ocean   srē LAHNG-kuh, shrē   sriː ˈlɑŋkə, ʃriː
Sri Lankan
   pert. to Sri Lanka   srē LAHNG-kuhn, shrē   sriː ˈlɑŋkən, ʃriː
Srinagar
   city, India   sri-NUHG-uhr, shri-   sriˈnəgəᵊ, ʃri-
Srinivasa
   pers. name   SRĒ-nuh-VAHS-uh, SHRĒ-   ˌsriːnəˈvɑsə, ˌʃriː-
St.
   see under Saint
Staatliche Weinbaudomäne
   German wine concern   SHTAHT-li<u>kh</u>-uh VĪN-BOW-dō-MEN-uh   ˈʃtatliçə ˈvainˌbaudoːˌmenə
Stabat Mater
   Latin hymn   STAHB-AHT MAHT-uhr   ˈstabˌat ˈmɑţəᵊ
Stabler
   Kenny, *US football player*   STĀ-bluhr   ˈsteːbləᵊ
Stacey, Stacy
   pers. name   STĀ-sē   ˈsteːsi·
Stachys
   Biblical name   STĀ-kuhs   ˈsteːkəs
Stade Olympique
   stadium, Montreal, Canada   STAHD aw-leⁿ-PĒK   stɑːd ɔːlēpiːk
Stafford
   Robert Theodore, *US politician; borough, England; US pl. name*   STAF-uhrd   ˈstæfəᵊd
Staffordshire
   county, England   STAF-uhrd-shuhr, -SHIR   ˈstæfəᵊdʃəᵊ, -ˌʃiᵊ
Stahl
   Lesley, *US journalist*   STAHL   ˈstɑl
Stakhanovism
   Soviet system to increase production   stuh-KAHN-uh-VIZ-uhm   stəˈkɑnəˌvizəm

---

Foreign Sounds: ue: *Fr.* **rue**, *Ger.* fűllen   uh(r): *Fr.* boeuf, *Ger.* Höhle   <u>kh</u>: *Ger.* **ich**, *Scot.* loch   g̃: *Sp.* amigo   y: *Sp.* hablar
hl: *Welsh* Llanelli.   CAPITALS: primary stress.   SMALL CAPS: secondary stress.   Ⓢ: U.S. pron.   Ⓔ: British pron.

Stakhanovite
  Soviet worker who surpasses quotas   stuh-KAHN-uh-VĪT   stə'kɑnə͵vait

Stalin
  Joseph, *leader, USSR*   STAHL-yin, Ⓢ STAHL-uhn, STAHL-ĔN, STAL-uhn   'stɑːljin, Ⓢ 'stɑlən, 'stɑl͵iːn, 'stælən

Stalinabad
  former name of Dushanbe   STAHL-in-uh-BAHD   ͵stɑlinə'bɑd

Stalingrad [Volgograd]
  city, Russia   STUHL-yin-GRAHT, Ⓢ STAHL-uhn-GRAD, -GRAHD   ͵stəljin'grɑt, Ⓢ 'stɑlən͵græd, -͵grɑd

Stalinism
  communist principles associated with Stalin   STAHL-uh-NIZ-uhm, STAL-   'stɑlə͵nizəm, 'stæl-

Stalinist
  pert. to Stalin; *advocate of Stalinism*   STAHL-uh-nuhst   'stɑlənəst

Stallone
  Sylvester, *US actor*   stuh-LŌN   stə'loːn

Stamboul, Stambul
  part of Istanbul, Turkey   stahm-BO͞OL, stam-BO͞OL   stɑm'buːl, stæm'buːl

Stamford
  city, CT   STAM-fuhrd   'stæmfəʳd

Stan
  pers. name   STAN   'stæn

Stanburrough
  pers. name   STAN-BUHR-uh, STAN-bruh   'stæn͵bərə, 'stænbrə

Standish
  pers. name   STAN-dish   'stændiʃ

Stanford
  University, *CA; pers. name*   STAN-fuhrd   'stænfəʳd

Stanford-Binet
  psychological test   STAN-fuhrd-buh-NĀ   ͵stænfəʳdbə'neː

Stanislas
  1. pers. name   STAN-uh-SLAWS, -SLAHS   'stænə͵slɔːs, -͵slɑs
  2. French   stah-nē-SLAHS   stɑːniːslas

Stanislaus
  1. pers. name   STAN-uh-SLAWS, -SLOWS   'stænə͵slɔːs, -͵slaus
  2. German   SHTAHN-is-LOWS, STAHN-   'ʃtanis͵laus, 'stan-

Stanislav
  pers. name, Czech   STAHN-yis-LAHF   'stɑːnjis͵lɑːf

Stanislavski, -sky
  Konstantin, *Russian actor, producer, director*   STUHN-yi-SLAHF-ski, Ⓢ STAN-uh-SLAHV-skē   ͵stənji'slɑːfskjj, Ⓢ ͵stænə'slavski·

Stanisław
  pers. name, Polish   stah-NĒ-slahf   stɑː'niːsɫɑːf

Stanko
  pers. name, Serbo-Croatian   STAHNG-kaw   'stɑːŋkɔː

Stanley
  pers. name; tdmk for tools   STAN-lē   'stænli·

Stanleyville [Kisangani]
  capital, Zaire   STAN-lē-VIL   'stænli·͵vil

Stanovoi
  mtn. range, Russia   STAHN-uh-VOI, STAN-uh-VOI   'stɑnə͵vɔi, 'stænə͵vɔi

Stansfield
  pers. name (S. Turner)   STANZ-FĒLD   'stænz͵fiːld

Key (col. 2): a: fad ā: fade ah: father ar: marry aw: law e: fed ē: feed er: merry i: hid ī: hide ō: coat o͞o: boot
oi: boy ow: now u: put uh: above uhr: bird ch: chop ng: ring sh: show th: thick <u>th</u>: this zh: measure

Stanton
  pers. name   STANT-n, ⓔ STAN-tuhn   'stæntn̩, ⓔ 'stæntən

Stanwyck
  Barbara, *US actress*   STAN-wik   'stænwik

Staples
  pers. name   STĀ-puhlz   'steːpəlz

Stapleton
  Jean, *US actress*   STĀ-puhl-tuhn   'steːpəltən

Stark
  Johannes, *German physicist (Nobel 1919)*   SHTAHRK   'ʃtɑʳk

Starkað
  legendary Scandinavian hero STAHR-KAH<u>TH</u>, STAHR-kuh<u>th</u>   'stɑʳ‚kað, 'stɑʳkəð

Stasi [Ministerium für Staatssicherheit]
  East German security organization SHTAHZ-ē   'ʃtɑziˑ

Stassen
  Harold E., *US politician*   STAS-uhn   'stæsən

Staten Island
  borough, New York City   STAT-n Ī-luhnd   ‚stætn̩ 'ɑilənd

Statius
  Roman poet   STĀ-sh(ē-)uhs   'steːʃ(iː)əs

Statler
  Brothers, *country music group; hotel, New York City* STAT-luhr   'stætləʳ

Staubach
  Roger, *US football player* STOW-BAHK   'stau‚bak

Staubbach
  waterfall, Switzerland SHTOWP-BAH<u>KH</u>, ⓢ STOWP-BAHK 'ʃtaup‚bax, ⓢ 'staup‚bak

Stauder
  German beer   SHTOWD-uhr   'ʃtaudəʳ

Staudinger
  Hermann, *German organic chemist (Nobel 1953)* SHTOWD-ing-uhr   'ʃtaudiŋəʳ

Staunton
  1. city, IL   STAWNT-n, STAHNT-n   'stɔːntn̩, 'stɑntn̩
  2. city, VA   STANT-n   'stæntn̩

Stavanger
  port, Norway   stuh-VAHNG-uhr   stə'vɑŋəʳ

Stavropol [Tol'yatti]
  city, Russia   stahv-RAW-puhl, stahv-RŌ-puhl stɑːv'rɔːpəl, stav'roːpəl

Stearns
  pers. name   STUHRNZ   'stəʳnz

Steele
  pers. name   STĒL   'stiːl

Steen
  1. Jan, Dutch painter   STĀN   'steːn
  2. Marguerite, English novelist STĒN   'stiːn
  3. pers. name, Danish   STIN   'stin

Steenburgen
  Mary, *US actress*   STĒN-BUHR-guhn   'stiːn‚bəʳgən

Stefan
  1. pers. name, Bulgarian, Polish STEF-ahn   'stefɑːn
  2. German   SHTEF-ahn   'ʃtefɑn

Stefán
   pers. name, Icelandic   STE-FOWN   ˈsteˌfɑun

Ştefan
   pers. name, Romanian   shte-FAHN   ʃteˈfɑn

Stefanie
   see Stephanie

Stefano
   pers. name, Italian   STĀ-fahn-ō, STEF-ahn-ō   ˈsteːfɑnoː, ˈstefɑnoː

Steffi
   pers. name   SHTEF-ē   ˈʃtefiˑ

Steffl
   Austrian beer   SHTEF-uhl   ˈʃtefəl

Steger
   village, IL   STĀ-guhr   ˈsteːgəʳ

Stegner
   pers. name   STEG-nuhr   ˈstegnəʳ

Stegosauria
   dinosaur suborder   STEG-uh-SAWR-ē-uh   ˌstegəˈsɔːriːə

Stegosaurus
   dinosaur   STEG-uh-SAWR-uhs   ˌstegəˈsɔːrəs

Steichen
   Edward, *US photographer*   STĪ-kuhn   ˈstɑikən

Steilacoom
   town, WA   STIL-uh-kuhm   ˈstiləkəm

Steiermark
   state, Austria   SHTĪR-MAHRK   ˈʃtɑiʳˌmɑʳk

Steiger
   Rod, *US actor*   STĪ-guhr   ˈstɑigəʳ

Stein
   1. Gertrude, *US writer;* William   STĪN   ˈstɑin
     Howard, *US biochemist (Nobel*
     1972); pers. name
   2. Norwegian   STĀN   ˈsteːn

Steinbeck
   John, *US author (Nobel 1962)*   STĪN-BEK   ˈstɑinˌbek

Steinberg
   David, *Canadian comedian, actor*   STĪN-BUHRG   ˈstɑinˌbəʳg

Steinberger
   Jack, *German-born US physicist*   STĪN-BUHR-guhr   ˈstɑinˌbəʳgəʳ
     (Nobel 1988)

Steinbrenner
   George, *US businessman*   STĪN-BREN-uhr   ˈstɑinˌbrenəʳ

Steinem
   Gloria, *US feminist, writer, editor*   STĪ-nuhm   ˈstɑinəm

Steinhäuser
   German beer   SHTĪN-HOI-zuhr   ˈʃtɑinˌhɔizəʳ

Steinlager
   New Zealand beer   STĪN-LAH-guhr, SHTĪN-   ˈstɑinˌlɑˑgəʳ, ˈʃtɑin-

Steinway
   piano manufacturer   STĪN-WĀ   ˈstɑinˌweː

Stella Artois
   Belgian beer   STEL-uh ahr-TWAH   ˈstelə ɑʳˈtwɑ

Stellenbosch
   town, South Africa   STEL-uhn-BAWS, STEL-uhn-BUSH   ˈstelənˌbɔːs, ˈstelənˌbuʃ

Key (col. 2):   a: fad   ā: fade   ah: father   ar: marry   aw: law   e: fed   ē: feed   er: merry   i: hid   ī: hide   ō: coat   ōō: boot
oi: boy   ow: now   u: put   uh: above   uhr: bird   ch: chop   ng: ring   sh: show   th: thick   <u>th</u>: this   zh: measure

Sten

   pers. name, Norwegian, Swedish   STĀN   'steːn

Stendhal

   pseudonym of Marie Henri Beyle   steⁿ-DAHL, ⑤ sten-DAHL, stan-DAHL   stĕdaːl, ⑤ sten'dɑl, stæn'dɑl

Stengel-Huggins

   Field, *former ballpark, St. Petersburg, FL*   STENG-guhl-HUHG-uhnz   'steŋgəl'həgənz

Stennis

   John Cornelius, *US politician*   STEN-uhs   'stenəs

Stentor

   Thracian herald in Trojan War   STEN-TAWR, STENT-uhr   'sten,tɔːʳ, 'stentəʳ

Stepan

   1. pers. name, Russian   styi-PAHN   stji'paːn

   2. Serbo-Croatian   STEP-ahn   'stepaːn

Stephan

   1. pers. name, German   SHTEF-ahn   'ʃtefɑn

   2. Norwegian   STĀ-fahn   'steːfɑn

Stephanas

   Biblical name   STEF-uh-nuhs   'stefənəs

Stéphane

   pers. name, French   stā-FAHN   steːfaːn

Stéphanie

   pers. name, French   stā-fah-NĒ   steːfaːniː

Stephanie, Stefanie

   pers. name   STEF-uh-nē   'stefəniˑ

Stephanopoulos

   George, *US government official*   STEF-uh-NAHP-uh-luhs   ˌstefə'nɑpələs

Stephanos

   pers. name, Mod. Greek   STEF-ah-naws   'stefanɔːs

Stephanus

   pers. name, Dutch   stā-FAHN-ues   steː'faːnys

Stephen

   1. pers. name   STĒ-vuhn   'stiːvən

   2. French   stā-FEN   steːfen

   3. German   SHTEF-uhn   'ʃtefən

Stéphen

   pers. name, French   stā-FEN   steːfen

Sterculia

   plant   stuhr-K(Y)OO-lē-uh   stəʳ'k(j)uːliːə

Sterling

   pers. name   STUHR-ling   'stəʳliŋ

Stern

   1. Isaac, *US violinist;* Otto, *German-born US physicist (Nobel 1943)*   STUHRN   'stəʳn

   2. Daniel (*pseudonym of* Marie Catherine Sophie d' Agoult), *French writer*   STERN   stern

   3. German beer   SHTERN   'ʃteʳn

Sterne

   Laurence, *English writer*   STUHRN   'stəʳn

Sterner

   pers. name   STUHR-nuhr   'stəʳnəʳ

Foreign Sounds: **ue:** *Fr.* **rue,** *Ger.* **füllen**   **uh(r):** *Fr.* **boeuf,** *Ger.* **Höhle**   **kh:** *Ger.* **ich,** *Scot.* **loch**   **g̱:** *Sp.* **amigo**   **v̱:** *Sp.* **hablar** **hl:** *Welsh* **Llanelli.**   CAPITALS: primary stress.   SMALL CAPS: secondary stress.   ⑤: U.S. pron.   ⓔ: British pron.

Sterope
   mother of Oenomaus; star in   STER-uh-pē, STIR-uh-pē   'sterəpi·, 'stirəpi·
   Pleiades

Steropes
   a Cyclops   STER-uh-PĒZ, STIR-uh-PĒZ   'sterə‚piːz, 'stirə‚piːz

Stesemann
   Gustav, *political leader*   SHTĀ-zuh-MAHN   'ʃteːzə‚mɑn

Stetson
   tdmk for a hat; pers. name   STET-suhn   'stetsən

Stettin
   German form of Szczecin   shte-TĒN   ʃte'tiːn

Stettinius
   Edward R., Jr., *US political leader*   stuh-TIN-ē-uhs, ste-   stə'tiniːəs, ste-

Steuben
   1. county, IN, NY; pers. name   st(y)o͞o-BEN, ST(Y)O͞O-buhn   st(j)uː'ben, 'st(j)uːbən
   2. US glassmakers   st(y)o͞o-BEN   st(j)uː'ben
   3. Friedrich von, Baron, *Prussian*   SHTOI-buhn   'ʃtɔibən
   soldier in US

Steubenville
   city, OH   ST(Y)o͞o-buhn-VIL   'st(j)uːbən‚vil

Stevan
   pers. name, Serbo-Croatian   STEV-ahn   'stevɑːn

Steve
   pers. name   STĒV   'stiːv

Steven
   pers. name   STĒ-vuhn   'stiːvən

Stevie
   pers. name   STĒ-vē   'stiːvi·

Stewart
   pers. name   ST(Y)o͞o-uhrt, ST(Y)U-uhrt,   'st(j)uːəʳt, 'st(j)uəʳt, 'st(j)uʳt
        ST(Y)URT

Sthenelas
   son of Evadne   STHEN-l-uhs   'sθenl̩əs

Sthenelus
   companion of Heracles; son of   STHEN-l-uhs   'sθenl̩əs
   Perseus and Andromeda

Stheno
   Gorgon   STHEN-ō   'sθenoː

Stich
   Michael, *German tennis player*   SHTĒ<u>KH</u>, ⑤ STĒK   'ʃtiːç, ⑤ 'ʃtiːx, 'stiːk

Stieglitz
   Alfred, *US photographer*   STĒG-luhts   'stiːgləts

Stieng
   lang., people, South Vietnam   STĒNG   'stiːŋ

Stiers
   David Ogden, *US actor*   STĪRZ   'staiʳz

Stigler
   George J., *US economist (Nobel*   STIG-luhr   'stigləʳ
   1982)

Stigwood
   Robert, *Australian film, record*   STIG-WUD, STIG-wuhd   'stig‚wud, 'stigwəd
   producer

Stijn
   pers. name, Dutch   STĪN   'stain

Key (col. 2):   a: fad   ā: fade   ah: father   ar: marry   aw: law   e: fed   ē: feed   er: merry   i: hid   ī: hide   ō: coat   o͞o: boot
oi: boy   ow: now   u: put   uh: above   uhr: bIrd   ch: chop   ng: ring   sh: show   th: thick   <u>th</u>: this   zh: measure

Stillaguamish
    Indian reservation, US   STIL-uh-GWAHM-ish   ˌstilə'gwɑmiʃ

Stiller
    Jerry, *US actor*   STIL-uhr   'stilərᵣ

Stillingia
    plant   stuh-LING-ē-uh, stuh-LIN-j(ē-)uh   stə'liŋiːə, stə'lindʒ(iː)ə

Stillwell, Stilwell
    pers. name   STIL-WEL, STIL-wuhl   'stilˌwel, 'stilwəl

Stilton
    English cheese   STILT-n   'stiltn̩

Stinnett
    town, TX   sti-NET   sti'net

Stith
    pers. name   STITH   'stiθ

Stoa
    Greek colonnade   STŌ-uh   'stoːə

Stockard
    pers. name (S. Channing)   STAHK-uhrd   'stɑkərᵣd

Stockholm
    city, Sweden   STAHK-HŌ(L)M   'stɑkˌhoː(l)m

Stockton
    Dick, *US sports broadcaster; city, CA*   STAHK-tuhn   'stɑktən

Stoddard
    Brandon, *US TV and film co.*   STAHD-uhrd   'stɑdərᵣd
       executive

Stoic
    adherent of Stoicism   STŌ-ik   'stoːik

Stoicism
    philosophy of Zeno of Citium   STŌ-uh-SIZ-uhm   'stoːəˌsizəm

Stojan
    pers. name, Serbo-Croatian   STAW-yahn   'stɔːjɑːn

Stokowski
    Leopold, *US conductor*   stuh-KAWF-skē, stuh-KAWV-skē,   stə'kɔːfski·, stə'kɔːvski·,
                                  stuh-KOW-skē   stə'kɑuski·

STOL
    short takeoff and landing   STAHL, ES-tahl   'stɑl, 'estɑl

Stolichnaya
    vodka brand   stuh-LICH-nuh-yuh,   stə'litʃnəjə, ˌstəlitʃ'nɑi(j)ə
                              STUHL-ich-NĪ-(y)uh

Stone
    Sir Richard, *English economist*   STŌN   'stoːn
       (Nobel 1984)

Stonehenge
    megalithic monument, England   STŌN-HENJ   'stoːnˌhendʒ

Stoppard
    Tom, *Czech-born British playwright*   STAHP-AHRD, STAHP-uhrd   'stɑpˌɑᵣd, 'stɑpərᵣd

Store Bededag
    Danish prayer day   STŌR-uh BĀD-uh-DAHK   'stoːrə 'beːdəˌdɑk

Storting [Lagthing]
    parliament, Norway   STAWR-ting   'stɔːᵣtiŋ

Stouffer
    US food products co.   STŌ-fuhr   'stoːfərᵣ

Stoughton
    city, MA   STŌT-n   'stoːtn̩

Foreign Sounds: ue: *Fr.* **rue**, *Ger.* füllen   uh(r): *Fr.* **boeuf**, *Ger.* Höhle   kh: *Ger.* ich, *Scot.* loch   ḡ: *Sp.* amigo   v̱: *Sp.* hablar
hl: *Welsh* Llanelli.   CAPITALS: primary stress.   SMALL CAPS: secondary stress.   Ⓢ: U.S. pron.   Ⓔ: British pron.

Stour
1. *river, Suffolk & Essex, England* — STUR — 'stuʳ
2. *river, Kent, England* — STUR, STOWR — 'stuʳ, 'stauʳ
3. *river, Warwickshire, England* — STOWR, STŌR — 'stauʳ, 'stoːʳ
4. *other rivers, England* — *usually* STOWR — *usually* 'stauʳ

Stow
town, MA; city, OH — STŌ — 'stoː

Stowe
urban area, PA; city, VT — STŌ — 'stoː

Stow-on-the-Wold
town, England — STŌ-AHN-thuh-WŌLD — ˌstoːˌɑndə'woːld

Stoyan
pers. name, Bulgarian — staw-YAHN — stɔː'jɑːn

Strabo
Greek geographer — STRĀ-bō — 'streːboː

Strachan
pers. name — STRAWN, STRAHKH-uhn — 'strɔːn, 'strɑxən

Strachey
Lytton, English writer — STRĀ-chē — 'streːtʃiˑ

Stradivari
Antonio, Italian violin maker — STRAHD-uh-VAHR-ē, STRAD-uh-VAR-ē, STRAD-uh-VER-ē — ˌstrɑdə'vɑˡiˑ, ˌstrædə'væriˑ, ˌstrædə'veri

Stradivarius
Antonius, Latin form of A. Stradivari — STRAD-uh-VAR-ē-uhs, STRAD-uh-VER-ē-uhs — ˌstrædə'værˡiːəs, ˌstrædə'veriːəs

Stram
Hank Louis, US football coach, commentator — STRAM — 'stræm

Strasberg
Susan, US actress — STRAS-BUHRG, STRAHS-BUHRG — 'stræsˌbəʳg, 'strɑsˌbəʳg

Strasbourg
city, France — strahs-BOOR, ⑤ STRAHS-BURG, STRAHZ- — strɑːsbuːr, ⑤ 'strɑsˌbuʳg, 'strɑz-

Strasbourgeoise, La Belle
see La Belle Strasbourgeoise

Strasbrau
German beer — SHTRAHS-BROW — 'ʃtrɑsˌbrɑu

Strassburg
German form of Strassbourg — SHTRAHS-BURK — 'ʃtrɑsˌbuʳk

Strategia
Athenian generalship — stra-TĒ-jē-uh — stræ'tiːdʒiːə

Stratford-on-Avon
town, England — STRAT-fuhrd-AHN-Ā-vuhn, ⑤ -Ā-VAHN — ˌstrætfəʳd͵ɑn'eːvən, ⑤ -'eːˌvɑn

Stratford-upon-Avon
town, England — STRAT-fuhrd-uh-PAHN-Ā-vuhn, ⑤ -Ā-VAHN — ˌstrætfəʳdə͵pɑn'eːvən, ⑤ -'eːˌvɑn

Strathclyde
medieval Celtic kingdom; region, Scotland — strath-KLĪD — stræθ'klɑid

Strauss
1. *family of Austrian composers* — SHTROWS — 'ʃtrɑus
2. *Levi, US clothing manufacturer; Peter, US actor* — STROWS — 'strɑus

---

Key (col. 2): a: fad ā: fade ah: father ar: marry aw: law e: fed ē: feed er: merry i: hid ī: hide ō: coat ōō: boot
oi: boy ow: now u: put uh: above uhr: bird ch: chop ng: ring sh: show th: thick th: this zh: measure

Stravinsky
  Igor, *US composer*   struhv-YĒN-skyi, Ⓢ struh-VIN(T)-skē   strəv'jiːnskjij,
                                                  Ⓢ strə'vin(t)ski·

Streator
  city, IL   STRĒT-uhr   'striːʈəʳ

Středočeský
  region, Czech republic   STRED-uh-CHES-kē   'stredə,tʃeski·

Streep
  Meryl, *US actress*   STRĒP   'striːp

Strega
  tdmk for a liqueur   STRĀ-guh   'streːgə

Streisand
  Barbra, *US singer, actress*   STRĪ-zuhnd, STRĪ-ZAND   'strɑizənd, 'strɑi,zænd

Stresemann
  Gustav, *German statesman (Nobel*   SHTRĀ-zuh-MAHN   'ʃtreːzə,mɑn
    1926)

Strindberg
  August, *Swedish writer*   STRIN-BER, Ⓢ STRIN(D)-BUHRG,   'strin,beʳ, Ⓢ 'strin(d),bəʳg,
                         STRIN-BER-ē   'strin,beri·

Stroessner
  Alfredo, *president, Paraguay*   STRES-nuhr   'stresnəʳ

Stroganoff
  beef dish   STRŌ-guh-NAWF   'stroːgə,nɔːf

Stroheim
  see Von Stroheim

Stroh's
  US beer   STRŌZ   'stroːz

Strom
  pers. name   STRAHM   'strɑm

Stromboli
  island, volcano, Italy   strahm-BŌ-lē   strɑm'boːli·

strontium
  element   STRAHN-ch(ē-)uhm,   'strantʃ(iː)əm, 'strantiːəm
                 STRAHNT-ē-uhm

Strophanthus
  plant   struh-FAN-thuhs   strə'fænθəs

Strophius
  son of Crisus   STRŌ-fē-uhs   'stroːfiːəs

Stroud
  city, OK   STROWD   'strɑud

Struthers
  pers. name   STRUH<u>TH</u>-uhrz   'strəðəʳz

Struthiomimus
  dinosaur   STROO-thē-ō-MĪ-muhs   ,struːθiːoːˈmɑiməs

Stu
  pers. name   STOO   'stuː

Stuart
  pers. name   ST(Y)OO-uhrt, ST(Y)U-uhrt,   'st(j)uːəʳt, 'st(j)uəʳt, 'st(j)uʳt
                 ST(Y)URT

Stubai Alps
  mtn. range, Austria   st(y)oo-BĪ, shtoo-BĪ   st(j)uːˈbɑi, ʃtuːˈbɑi

Stubaier Alpen
  mtn. range, Austria (German)   shtoo-BĪ-uhr AHL-puhn   ʃtuːˈbɑiər 'ɑlpən

Studebaker
  US car   STOOD-uh-BĀ-kuhr   'stuːdə,beːkəʳ

Foreign Sounds: ue: *Fr.* **rue**, *Ger.* **füllen**   uh(r): *Fr.* **boeuf**, *Ger.* **Höhle**   <u>kh</u>: *Ger.* **ich**, *Scot.* **loch**   g̅: *Sp.* **amigo**   v̱: *Sp.* **hablar**
hl: *Welsh* **Llanelli**.   CAPITALS: primary stress.   SMALL CAPS: secondary stress.   Ⓢ: U.S. pron.   Ⓔ: British pron.

Studs
   pers. name   STUHDZ   'stədz

Stuka
   German warplane   SHTOO-kuh, STOO-kuh   'ʃtuːkə, 'stuːkə

Stumpf
   Field, former ballpark, Lancaster, PA   STUHM(P)F   'stəm(p)f

Stundism
   evangelical Russian protestant movement   SHTUN-DIZ-uhm, STUN-, STUHN-   'ʃtun‚dizəm, 'stun-, 'stən-

Sturm und Drang
   style of German literature   SHTURM unt DRAHNG, STURM   ‚ʃtuʳm unt 'draŋ, ‚stuʳm

Sturtevant
   Alfred H., US geneticist   STUHRT-uh-vuhnt   'stəʳʈəvənt

Stuttgart
   1. prov & town, Germany   SHTUT-GAHRT, Ⓢ STUHT-GAHRT, STOOT-GAHRT   'ʃtut‚gaʳt, Ⓢ 'stət‚gaʳt, 'stuːt‚gaʳt
   2. city, AR   STUHT-GAHRT, STUHT-guhrt   'stət‚gaʳt, 'stətgəʳt

Stuyvesant
   1. Peter, Dutch official in America   STUH(R)-vuh-SAHNT, Ⓢ STĪ-vuh-suhnt   'stœivə‚sant, Ⓢ 'staivəsənt
   2. pers. name   STĪ-vuh-suhnt   'staivəsənt

Stygian
   pert. to the river Styx *or* Hades   STIJ-ē-uhn   'stidʒiːən

Stylian
   pers. name, Albanian   STĒL-yahn   'stiːljɑn

Stylianou
   pers. name, Greek   stil-YAHN-oo   stil'jɑnuː

Styne
   Jule, US composer, producer   STĪN   'stain

Styr
   river, Ukraine   STIR   'stiʳ

Styracosaurus
   dinosaur   stuh-RAK-uh-SAWR-uhs, STĪ-RAK-uh-SAWR-uhs   stə‚rækə'sɔːrəs, ‚stai‚rækə'sɔːrəs

Styrofoam
   tdmk for expanded plastic   STĪ-ruh-FŌM   'stairə‚foːm

Styx
   stream, Greece; Underworld river in Greek myth   STIKS   'stiks

Suah
   Biblical name   SOO-uh, SOO-ahkh   'suːə, 'suːɑx

Suakin
   port, Sudan   SWAHK-uhn   'swɑkən

Suarez
   Xavier Louis, US politician   SWAHR-ĀS, SWAHR-EZ   'swɑr‚eːs, 'swɑr‚ez

Subang
   airport, Kuala Lumpur, Malaysia   soo-BAHNG   suː'baŋ

Subanun
   lang., people, Philippine Islands   soo-BAH-NOON   suː'bɑ‚nuːn

Subaru
   tdmk of a Japanese car co.   SOO-buh-ROO   'suːbə‚ruː

Subhas
   pers. name, Bengali   shub-HAHSH, sub-HAHSH   ʃub'haʃ, sub'haʃ

Subic
   bay, city, Philippines   SOO-bik   'suːbik

Key (col. 2):   a: **fad**   ā: **fade**   ah: **father**   ar: **marry**   aw: **law**   e: **fed**   ē: **feed**   er: **merry**   i: **hid**   ī: **hide**   ō: **coat**   oo: **boot** oi: **boy**   ow: **now**   u: **put**   uh: **above**   uhr: **bird**   ch: **chop**   ng: **ring**   sh: **show**   th: **thick**   <u>th</u>: **this**   zh: **measure**

Sublette
   county, WY   suh-BLET   sə'blet

Subotica, Subotitsa
   city, Serbia   SOO-buh-TĒT-suh   'suːbəˌtiːtsə

Subrahmanyan
   pers. name (S. Chandrasekhar)   SUB-ruh-MAHN-yuhn   ˌsubrə'mɑnjən

Subura
   district of ancient Rome   SUHB-(y)uh-ruh   'səb(j)ərə

Sucathite, Suchathite
   Biblical name   SOO-kuh-THĪT   'suːkəˌθɑit

Succoth
   see Sukkoth

Suceava
   river, county, town, Romania   soo-CHAHV-uh   suː'tʃɑvə

Suchinda
   pers. name, Thai   su-CHIN-duh   su'tʃində

Suchos [Sebek]
   Egyptian crocodile god   SUKH-uhs, SOO-khuhs   'suxəs, 'suːxəs

Su-chou, Suchow
   see Suzhou

Sucre
   city, Bolivia   SOO-krā   'suːkreː

Sudan
   region, republic, Africa   soo-DAN, soo-DAHN   suː'dæn, suː'dɑn

Sudanese
   pert. to Sudan *or to the Republic of*   SOOD-n-ĒZ, -ĒS   ˌsuːdn̩'iːz, -'iːs
      Sudan

Sudanic
   former lang. family   soo-DAN-ik, soo-DAHN-ik   suː'dænik, suː'dɑnik

Sudbury
   1. town, Canada, England   SUHD-b(uh-)rē   'sədb(ə)riˑ
   2. town, MA   SUHD-BER-ē, SUHD-b(uh-)rē   'sədˌberiˑ, 'sədb(ə)riˑ

Sudeste
   region, Brazil   soo-DES-tā   suː'desteː

Sudeten
   mountainous region, Europe   soo-DĀT-n   suː'deːtn̩

Sudetenland
   mountainous region, Europe   soo-DĀT-n-LAHNT, Ⓢ soo-DĀT-n-LAND   suː'deːtn̩ˌlɑnt,
                                             Ⓢ suː'deːtn̩ˌlænd

Sudetes
   mtn. range, Czech republic   soo-DIT-ēz   suː'diṭiˑz

Sue
   pers. name   SOO   'suː

Suetonius
   Roman historian   swē-TŌ-nē-uhs, SOO-uh-TŌ-nē-uhs   swiː'toːniːəs, ˌsuːə'toːniːəs

Sueur, La
   see La Sueur

Suez
   gulf, canal, isthmus, city, Middle East   soo-EZ, SOO-EZ, Ⓔ SOO-iz   suː'ez, 'suːˌez, Ⓔ 'suːiz

Suffolk
   county, England; county, MA, NY   SUHF-uhk, Ⓢ *also* SUHF-AWK   'səfək, Ⓢ *also* 'səfˌɔːk

Sufi
   member, Muslim sect   SOO-fē   'suːfiˑ

Sufiism
   religion   SOO-fē-IZ-uhm   'suːfiːˌizəm

Foreign Sounds: ue: *Fr.* **rue**, *Ger.* **füllen**   uh(r): *Fr.* **boeuf**, *Ger.* **Höhle**   kh: *Ger.* i**ch**, *Scot.* lo**ch**   g̱: *Sp.* ami**g**o   v: *Sp.* ha**b**lar
hl: *Welsh* **Ll**anelli.   CAPITALS: primary stress.   SMALL CAPS: secondary stress.   Ⓢ: U.S. pron.   Ⓔ: British pron.

Sufism		
religion	S$\overline{OO}$-FIZ-uhm	ˈsuːˌfizəm
Suharo		
pers. name, Japanese	s$\overline{oo}$-hahr-ō	suːhɑroː
Suharto		
president, Indonesia	su-HAHRT-ō	suˈhɑ^rʈoː
Suisse, La [Switzerland]		
republic, Europe	lah SWĒS	lɑː sɥiːs
Sukarno		
Indonesian political leader	su-KAHR-nō	suˈkɑ^rnoː
Sukenori		
pers. name, Japanese	suk-en-ō-rē	sukenoːriː
Sukhothai		
city, Thailand	SUK-uh-TĪ	ˈsukəˈtɑi
Sukiro		
pers. name, Japanese	suk-ē-rō	sukiːroː
Sukkiim		
Biblical name	SUK-ē-im, S$\overline{OO}$-kē-ĒM	ˈsukiːim, ˌsuːkiːˈiːm
Sukkoth, Succoth		
Jewish holiday	SUK-uhs, SUK-ōt, SUK-ōs, s$\overline{oo}$-KŌS, s$\overline{oo}$-KAWT	ˈsukəs, ˈsukoːt, ˈsukoːs, suˈˈkoːs, suˈˈkoːt
Šükrü		
pers. name, Turkish	shue-KRUE	ʃyːˈkryː
Suku		
lang., people, Africa	suh-K$\overline{OO}$	səˈkuː
Sukuma		
lang., people, Africa	suh-K$\overline{OO}$-muh	səˈkuːmə
Sul		
region, Brazil	S$\overline{OO}$L	ˈsuːl
Sulawesi [Celebes]		
island, Indonesia	S$\overline{OO}$-luh-WĀ-sē	ˌsuːləˈweːsiˈ
Sulawesi Selatan		
prov, Indonesia	S$\overline{OO}$-luh-WĀ-sē sā-LAH-TAHN	ˌsuːləˈweːsiˈ seːˈlɑˌtɑn
Sulawesi Tengah		
prov, Indonesia	S$\overline{OO}$-luh-WĀ-sē TENG-guh	ˌsuːləˈweːsiˈ ˈteŋgə
Sulawesi Tenggara		
prov, Indonesia	S$\overline{OO}$-luh-WĀ-sē TENG-guh-ruh	ˌsuːləˈweːsiˈ ˈteŋgərə
Sulawesi Utara		
prov, Indonesia	S$\overline{OO}$-luh-WĀ-sē $\overline{OO}$T-uh-ruh	ˌsuːləˈweːsiˈ ˈuːtərə
Suleiman		
pers. name, Turkish	sue-lā-MAHN	syːleːˈmɑn
sulfur		
element	SUHL-fuhr	ˈsəlfə^r
Sulla		
Roman politician	SUHL-uh, SUL-uh	ˈsələ, ˈsulə
Sullivan		
family name	SUHL-uh-vuhn	ˈsələvən
Sully-Prudhomme		
R. F. A., French poet (Nobel 1901)	suel-LĒ-prue-DAWM	syːlliːpryːdɔːm
Sulpicia		
pers. name, Latin	suhl-PISH-(ē-)uh	səlˈpiʃ(iː)ə
Sulpicius		
pers. name, Latin	suhl-PISH-(ē-)uhs	səlˈpiʃ(iː)əs
Sul Ross		
State University, TX	SUHL RAWS, RAHS	ˈsəl ˈrɔːs, ˈrɑs

Key (col. 2): a: fad ā: fade ah: father ar: marry aw: law e: fed ē: feed er: merry i: hid ī: hide ō: coat $\overline{oo}$: boot
oi: boy ow: now u: put uh: above uhr: bird ch: chop ng: ring sh: show th: thick th̲: this zh: measure

Sultan
  sovereign of Turkey SUHLT-n, SUHL-tuhn 'səltn̩, 'səltən

Sulu
  archipelago, sea, Philippines; SOO-loo 'suːluː
  Hikaru, *character, Star Trek*

Sumac
  Yma, *entertainer* SOO-MAK, SHOO-MAK 'suːˌmæk, 'ʃuːˌmæk

Sumatra
  island, Indonesia su-MAH-truh su'matrə

Sumba
  island, Indonesia SOOM-buh 'suːmbə

Sumbawa
  island, Indonesia soom-BAH-wuh suːm'bawə

Sumer
  ancient kingdom, Asia SOO-muhr 'suːməʳ

Sumerian
  native of Sumer; ancient lang. soo-MER-ē-uhn, soo-MIR-ē-uhn suː'meriːən, suː'miriːən

Sumitomo
  Japanese bank soo-mē-tō-mō suːmiːtoːmoː

Summa cum laude
  with highest praise SUM-uh KUM LOWD-uh, SUHM-uh ˌsumə ˌkum 'laudə, ˌsəmə
    KUHM LAWD-ē, SOO-muh, LOWD-ē ˌkəm 'lɔːdiˈ, ˌsuːmə,
      'laudiˈ

Summerall
  Pat, *US sportscaster* SUHM-uh-RAWL 'səməˌrɔːl

Sumner
  J. B., *US biochemist (Nobel 1946)* SUHM-nuhr 'səmnəʳ

Sumter
  county, AL SUHM(P)-tuhr 'səm(p)təʳ

Sunda
  Deep, *Indian Ocean* SUHN-duh, SOON-duh 'səndə, 'suːndə

Sundanese
  lang., West Java SUHN-duh-NĒZ, -NĒS ˌsəndə'niːz, -'niːs

Sunday
  day of the week SUHN-dē, SUHN-dā 'səndiˈ, 'səndeː

Sune
  pers. name, Swedish SOO-nuh 'suːnə

Sung
  Chinese dynasty SUNG, SUHNG 'suŋ, 'səŋ

Sunkist
  US food products co. SUHN-KIST 'sənˌkist

Sun Lik
  Hong Kong beer SUN LIK, SUHN 'sun 'lik, 'sən

Sun Myung Moon
  Korean religious group leader SUHN MYUHNG MOON 'sən 'mjəŋ 'muːn

Sunna
  traditional Muslim law SUN-uh, SUHN-uh 'sunə, 'sənə

Sunni
  adherents of a branch of Islam SUN-(n)ē 'sun(n)iˈ

Sunnism
  religious tenets of the Sunni SUN-IZ-uhm 'sunˌizəm

Sunnite
  pert. to the Sunni SUN-(N)ĪT 'sunˌ(n)ait

Sunny
  pers. name SUHN-ē 'səniˈ

Foreign Sounds: ue: *Fr.* **rue**, *Ger.* **füllen** uh(r): *Fr.* **boeuf**, *Ger.* **Höhle** kh: *Ger.* **ich**, *Scot.* **loch** ḡ: *Sp.* amigo v: *Sp.* hablar
hl: *Welsh* **Llanelli**. CAPITALS: primary stress. SMALL CAPS: secondary stress. Ⓢ: U.S. pron. Ⓔ: British pron.

Sunnyvale
  city, CA — SUHN-ē-VĀL — 'səniˑˌveːl

SUNOCO
  Sun Oil Co., US — suh-NŌ-kō — sə'noːkoː

Suntory
  Japanese beverage co. — sun-tō-rē, sun-tawr-ē — suntoːriː, suntɔːriː

Sununu
  John H., US politician — suh-NOO-noo — sə'nuːnuː

SUNY
  State University of New York — SOO-nē — 'suːniˑ

Sun Yat-sen
  Chinese leader — SUN YAHT-SEN, SUHN YAT-SEN — 'sun 'jɑt'sen, 'sən 'jæt'sen

Suomenlinna
  fortress, Helsinki, Finland — SWAW-muhn-LIN-nuh — 'swɔːmənˌlinnə

Suomi
  College, MI — suh-WAW-mē, SWAW-mē — sə'wɔːmiˑ, 'swɔːmiˑ

Suomi [Finland]
  republic, Europe — SWAW-mē — 'swɔːmiˑ

Superior
  lake, N. America; city, WI — su-PIR-ē-uhr — su'piriːəʳ

Suph
  Biblical name — SOOF — 'suːf

Suphah
  Biblical name — SOO-fuh, soo-FAH — 'suːfə, suː'fɑ

Suquamish
  N. American people — suh-KWAHM-ish, SKWAHM-ish, suh-KWAW-mish, SKWAW-mish — sə'kwɑmiʃ, 'skwɑmiʃ, sə'kwɔːmiʃ, 'skwɔːmiʃ

Sur
  Biblical name — SUR, SOOR — 'suʳ, 'suːr

Sura
  lang., Nigeria; section of the Koran — SUR-uh — 'surə

Surabaja, Soerabaja, Surabaya
  seaport, Java, Indonesia — SUR-uh-BĪ-uh — ˌsurə'bɑiə

Surakarta
  native principality, city, Java — SUR-uh-KAHRT-uh — ˌsurə'kɑʳʈə

Surat
  city, Gujarat, India — SUR-uht, suh-RAT — 'surət, sə'ræt

Surendranath
  1. pers. name, Bengali — su-RĀN-draw-NAWT, -druh-NAHT — su're:ndrɔːˌnɔːt, -drəˌnɑt
  2. Hindi — suh-REN-druh-NAHT — sə'rendrəˌnɑt

Suribachi
  volcano, Iwo Jima — SUR-uh-BAHCH-ē — ˌsurə'bɑtʃiˑ

Surinam [Suriname]
  republic, S. America — SUR-uh-NAM — 'surəˌnæm

Suriname
  river, republic, S. America — SUR-uh-NAHM-uh, SUR-uh-NAM — ˌsurə'nɑmə, ˌsurə'næm

Surinamer
  inhabitant of Suriname — SUR-uh-NAM-uhr, SUR-uh-NAHM-uhr — 'surəˌnæməʳ, ˌsurə'nɑməʳ

Surinamese
  pert. to Suriname — SUR-uh-nuh-MĒZ, -MĒS — ˌsurənə'miːz, -'miːs

Surrey
  county, England — SUHR-ē, SUH-rē — 'sər-iˑ, 'sə-riˑ

Surridge
  pers. name — SUHR-ij — 'səridʒ

Key (col. 2): a: fad ā: fade ah: father ar: marry aw: law e: fed ē: feed er: merry i: hid ī: hide ō: coat ōō: boot
oi: boy ow: now u: put uh: above uhr: bird ch: chop ng: ring sh: show th: thick th: this zh: measure

Surry
pl. name, US   SUHR-ē, SUH-rē   'sər-iˑ, 'sə-riˑ

Sursum Corda
exhortation to worship in the mass   SUR-suhm KAWRD-uh, KAWR-DAH   ˌsuʳsəm 'kɔːʳdə, 'kɔːʳˌdɑ

Surtees
pers. name   SUHR-TĒZ   'səʳˌtiːz

Susa
ancient city, Iran   SOO-suh, SOO-zuh   'suːsə, 'suːzə

Susan
pers. name   SOO-zuhn   'suːzən

Susanchite
Biblical name   SOO-SAN-KĬT   'suːˌsænˌkɑit

Susanna, -nah
Apocryphal book; pers. name   soo-ZAN-uh   suː'zænə

Susanne
pers. name, German   zoo-ZAHN-uh   zuː'zɑnə

Susi
Biblical name   SOO-SĪ, soo-SĒ   'suːˌsɑi, suː'siː

Susie, Susy
pers. name   SOO-zē   'suːziˑ

Susitna
river, AK   soo-SIT-nuh   suː'sitnə

Suslov
Mikhail, government official, USSR   SUS-LAWF   'susˌlɔːf

Susquehanna
river, US; N. American people;   SUHS-kwuh-HAN-uh   ˌsəskwə'hænə
county, univ., PA

Susse Chalet
US hotel chain   SOOS sha-LĀ   ˌsuːs ʃæ'leː

Sussex
former county, England   SUHS-iks   'səsiks

Susskind
David, TV, film, theater producer   SUHS-KĪND   'səsˌkɑind

Susu
lang., people, Africa   SOO-SOO   'suːˌsuː

Susumu
pers. name, Japanese   sus-um-u   susumu

Sutherland
pers. name   SUHTH-uhr-luhnd   'səðəʳlənd

Sutlej
river, India   SUHT-LEJ   'sətˌledʒ

Sutter
Howard, US baseball player   SUHT-uhr   'sət̬əʳ

Suttner
Baroness Bertha von, Austrian   ZUT-nuhr, SUT-nuhr   'zutnəʳ, 'sutnəʳ
author, pacifist (Nobel 1905)

Sutton
Don, US baseball player; borough,   SUHT-n   'sətn̩
England

Suva
town, Fiji   SOO-vuh   'suːvə

Suvorov
island, Pacific Ocean   su-VAWR-uhf   su'vɔːrəf

Suwannee [Swanee]
river, GA, FL; county, FL   suh-WAHN-ē, SWAHN-ē   sə'wɑniˑ, 'swɑniˑ

Foreign Sounds: ue: *Fr.* **rue**, *Ger.* **füllen**   uh(r): *Fr.* **boeuf**, *Ger.* **Höhle**   <u>kh</u>: *Ger.* **ich**, *Scot.* **loch**   g̅: *Sp.* amigo   v̲: *Sp.* hablar
hl: *Welsh* **Llanelli**.   CAPITALS: primary stress.   SMALL CAPS: secondary stress.   Ⓢ: U.S. pron.   Ⓔ: British pron.

Suwŏn
  town, S. Korea   sōō-wuhn   suːwən
Suzan
  pers. name   SŌŌ-zuhn   'suːzən
Suzanna, Suzannah
  pers. name   sōō-ZAN-uh   suːˈzænə
Suzanne
  1. pers. name   sōō-ZAN   suːˈzæn
  2. French   sue-ZAHN   syːzɑːn
Suzette
  pers. name   sōō-ZET   suːˈzet
Suzhou, Su-chou, Suchow,
  Soochow
  city, China   SŌŌ-JŌ, ⓢ SŌŌ-CHOW   'suːˈdʒoːˌ, ⓢ 'suːˈtʃɑu
Suzie, Suzy
  pers. name   SŌŌ-zē   'suːziˑ
Suzuki
  1. Japanese motor vehicle co.; pers.   suz-uk-ē, ⓢ suh-ZŌŌ-kē   suzukiː, ⓢ səˈzuːkiˑ
  name, Japanese
  2. method of music instruction   suh-ZŌŌ-kē   səˈzuːkiˑ
Suzy
  see Suzie
Svalbard
  islands, Arctic   SFAHL-BAHR   'sfɑlˌbɑʳ
Svan
  lang., people, Caucasus Mts.   SFAHN, SVAHN   'sfɑn, 'svɑn
Svedberg
  Theodor, *Swedish physical chemist*   SFED-BER, ⓢ SFED-BUHRG, -BER-ē   'sfedˌbeɹ, ⓢ 'sfedˌbəʳg,
  (Nobel 1926)   -ˌberiˑ
Svein
  pers. name, Norwegian   SVĀN   'sveːn
Sveinbjörn
  pers. name, Icelandic   SVĀN-BYUH(R)D-n   'sveːnˌbjœdn̩
Sveinn
  pers. name, Icelandic   SVĀD-n   'sveːdn̩
Sven
  pers. name, Danish, Norwegian,   SVEN   'sven
  Swedish
Svengali
  evil dominator   sfeng-GAHL-ē, sfen-GAHL-ē   sfeŋˈgɑliˑ, sfenˈgɑliˑ
Svenska [Sweden]
  kingdom, Europe   SFEN-skah   'sfenskɑː
Svenson
  Bo, *US actor*   SFEN-suhn   'sfensən
Sverdlovsk
  city, region, Russia   sferd-LAWFSK   sfeʳdˈloːfsk
Sverdrup
  Islands, *island group, Canada*   SFER-druhp, SVER-   'sfeʳdrəp, 'sveʳ-
Sverige [Sweden]
  kingdom, Europe   SFAR-yuh   'sfærjə
Svetlana
  pers. name, Russian   sfet-LAHN-uh   sfetˈlɑːnə
Svizzera [Switzerland]
  republic, Europe   ZVĒT-tsā-rah   'zviːttseːrɑ

Key (col. 2):   a: fad   ā: fade   ah: father   ar: marry   aw: law   e: fed   ē: feed   er: merry   i: hid   ī: hide   ō: coat   ōō: boot
oi: boy   ow: now   u: put   uh: above   uhr: bird   ch: chop   ng: ring   sh: show   th: thick   th̲: this   zh: measure

Swabia
  medieval duchy, prov, Germany   SWĀ-bē-uh   'sweːbiːə

Swabian Jura
  mtn. range, Germany   SWĀ-bē-uhn JUR-uh   ˌsweːbiːən 'dʒurə

Swadeshi
  political independence movement,   swah-DĀ-shē, swah-DESH-ē   swɑ'deːʃiˑ, swɑ'deʃiˑ
  India

Swaggart
  Jimmy, *US TV evangelist*   SWAG-uhrt   'swægəʳt

Swahili
  lang., people, Africa   swah-HĒ-lē   swɑ'hiːliˑ

Swainson's
  hawk   SWĀN-suhnz   'sweːnsənz

Swanee [Suwannee]
  river, GA, FL   SWAHN-ē   'swɑniˑ

Swansea
  city, Wales; town, IL, MA   SWAHN-zē, SWAHN(T)-sē   'swɑnziˑ, 'swɑn(t)siˑ

SWAPO
  South-West Africa People's   SWAHP-ō   'swɑpoː
  Organization, political party,
  Namibia

Swaraj
  national or local home rule, India   swuh-RAHJ   swə'rɑdʒ

Swarthmore
  College, *town, PA*   SWAWRTH-MŌR, SWAHTH-, -MAWR   'swɔːʳθˌmoːʳ, 'swɑθ-, -ˌmɔːʳ

SWAT
  Special Weapons and Tactics police   SWAHT   'swɑt
  team

Swat
  river, region, Pakistan   SWAHT   'swɑt

Swati [Swazi]
  lang., people, South Africa,   SWAHT-ē   'swɑṭiˑ
  Swaziland

Swayne
  Noah H., Field, *former ballpark,*   SWĀN   'sweːn
  Toledo, OH

Swayze
  Patrick, *US actor;* John Cameron,   SWĀ-zē   'sweːziˑ
  US broadcaster

Swazi
  lang., people, South Africa,   SWAHZ-ē   'swɑziˑ
  Swaziland

Swaziland
  kingdom, Africa   SWAHZ-ē-LAND   'swɑziˑˌlænd

Swede
  inhabitant of Sweden   SWĒD   'swiːd

Sweden
  kingdom, Europe   SWĒD-n   'swiːdn̩

Swedenborg
  Emanuel, *Swedish mystic*   SVĀ-duhn-BAWR-yuh,   'sveːdənˌbɔːrj,
      ⓢ SWĒD-n-BAWRG   ⓢ 'swiːdn̩ˌbɔːʳg

Swedenborgian
  pert. to teachings of Swedenborg   SWĒD-n-BAWR-jē-uhn,   ˌswiːdn̩'bɔːʳdʒiːən,
      SWĒD-n-BAWR-gē-uhn   ˌswiːdn̩'bɔːʳgiːən

Foreign Sounds: ue: *Fr.* **rue**, *Ger.* **füllen**   uh(r): *Fr.* **boeuf**, *Ger.* **Höhle**   kh: *Ger.* **ich**, *Scot.* **loch**   ḡ: *Sp.* **amigo**   v: *Sp.* **hablar** hl: *Welsh* **Llanelli**.   CAPITALS: primary stress.   SMALL CAPS: secondary stress.   ⓢ: U.S. pron.   Ⓔ: British pron.

Swedish
  lang., Scandinavia; pert. to Sweden   SWĒD-ish   'swiːdiʃ
Swinburne
  A.C., *English poet*   SWIN-BUHRN   'swin,bərn
Swinkels
  Dutch beer   SVING-kuhls   'sviŋkəls
Swinomish
  N. American people   swuh-NŌ-mish   swə'noːmiʃ
Swiss
  pert. to Switzerland   SWIS   'swis
Swissair
  Swiss airline co.   SWIS-AR, SWIS-ER, swis-AR, swis-ER   'swis,ær, 'swis,er, swis'ær, swis'er
Swithin, Swithun
  English saint   SWITH-uhn   'swiðən
Switzerland
  republic, Europe   SWIT-suhr-luhnd   'switsərlənd
Sybaris
  ancient city, Italy   SIB-uh-ruhs   'sibərəs
Sybarite
  inhabitant of Sybaris; *sensualist*   SIB-uh-RĪT   'sibə,rɑit
Sybaritic
  pert. to Sybaris *or* Sybarites; *luxurious*   SIB-uh-RIT-ik   ,sibə'riṭik
Sybil
  pers. name   SIB-uhl   'sibəl
Sychar
  Biblical name   SĪ-KAHR   'sɑi,kɑr
Sycuan
  Band, *N. American people*   si-KYOO-uhn   si'kjuːən
Sydney
  city, Australia; pers. name   SID-nē   'sidniˑ
Syene
  Biblical name   sī-Ē-nē, suh-ve-NE *[sic]*   sɑi'iːniˑ, səve'ne *[sic]*
Sylacauga
  city, AL   SIL-uh-KAW-guh   ,silə'kɔːgə
Sylphides, Les
  ballet, Chopin   lā sēl-FĒD   leː siːlfiːd
Sylvanus
  pers. name   sil-VĀ-nuhs   sil've:nəs
Sylvester
  pers. name   sil-VES-tuhr   sil'vestər
Sylvestre
  pers. name, French   sēl-VESTR   siːlvestr
Sylvia
  pers. name   SIL-vē-uh   'silviːə
Sylvio
  pers. name   SIL-vē-ō   'silviːoː
Syme
  Sir Ronald, *New Zealand historian*   SĪM   'sɑim
Symington
  W. Stuart, *US senator*   SĪ-ming-tuhn   'sɑimiŋtən
Symmachus
  Roman politician; pope   SIM-uh-kuhs   'siməkəs

Key (col. 2): a: fad ā: fade ah: father ar: marry aw: law e: fed ē: feed er: merry i: hid ī: hide ō: coat ōō: boot
oi: boy ow: now u: put uh: above uhr: bird ch: chop ng: ring sh: show th: thick <u>th</u>: this zh: measure

Symms
    Steven Douglas, *US politician*   SIMZ   'simz

Symonds
    John Addington, *English poet,*   SIM-uhn(d)z   'simən(d)z
        essayist, critic

Symons
    Arthur, *British poet, critic*   SIM-uhn(d)z   'simən(d)z

Symposium
    dialogue of Plato   sim-PŌ-zē-uhm   sim'poːziːəm

Syng
    pers. name   SING   'siŋ

Synge
    John Millington, *Irish writer;*   SING   'siŋ
        Richard Laurence Millington,
        English biochemist (Nobel 1952);
        pers. name

Syngman
    pers. name, Korean   SING-muhn, SIG-muhn   'siŋmən, 'sigmən

Syntychi
    Biblical name   SINT-uh-KĒ   'sintə‚kiː

Syracusan
    pert. to Syracuse; *native or*   SIR-uh-KYŌŌ-zuhn, Ⓔ   ‚sirə'kjuːzən, Ⓔ
        inhabitant of Syracuse   SĪR-uh-KYŌŌ-zuhn   ‚sairə'kjuːzən

Syracuse
    1. city, Sicily   SIR-uh-KYŌŌS, -KYŌŌZ, Ⓔ   'sirə‚kjuːs, -‚kjuːz, Ⓔ
         SĪ-ruh-KYŌŌS   'sairə‚kjuːs
    2. city, county, NY   SIR-uh-KYŌŌS, -KYŌŌZ, *locally often*   'sirə‚kjuːs, -‚kjuːz, *locally*
         SER-   *often* 'ser-

Syr Darya
    river, Kazakhstan, Kirghiz,   sir DAHR-yuh   siʳ 'daʳjə
        Uzbekistan

Syria
    1. country, Middle East   SIR-ē-uh   'siriːə
    2. town, VA   sī-RĒ-uh   sai'riːə

Syriac
    literary & liturgical form of Aramaic   SIR-ē-AK   'siriː‚æk

Syrian
    pert. to Syria   SIR-ē-uhn   'siriːən

Syringa
    flower   suh-RING-guh   sə'riŋgə

Syrinx
    hamadryad loved by Pan   SIR-ingks   'siriŋks

Syro-Hittites
    ancient peoples, Cilicia & Syria   SĪ-rō-HI-TĪTS, SIR-Ō-   ‚sairoː'hi‚taits, ‚siroː-

Syrophenician, Syrophoenician
    Biblical name   SĪ-rō-fi-NĒ-sh(ē-)uhn, -NISH-(ē-)uhn,   ‚sairoːfi'niːʃ(iː)ən,
         SIR-Ō-   -'niʃ(iː)ən, ‚siroː-

Syros
    island, Greece   SĪ-RAHS   'sai‚ras

Syrtis
    area in northern hemisphere of Mars   SUHRT-uhs   'səʳţəs

SYSOP
    system operator   SIS-AHP   'sis‚ap

Syssition
    Spartan military unit   sī-SIT-ē-uhn   sai'sitiːən

Foreign Sounds: **ue**: *Fr.* **rue**, *Ger.* **füllen**   **uh(r)**: *Fr.* **boeuf**, *Ger.* **Höhle**   <u>**kh**</u>: *Ger.* **ich**, *Scot.* **loch**   <u>ḡ</u>: *Sp.* amigo   <u>v</u>: *Sp.* hablar
<u>hl</u>: *Welsh* **Llanelli**.   CAPITALS: primary stress.   SMALL CAPS: secondary stress.   Ⓢ: U.S. pron.   Ⓔ: British pron.

Szczęsny
　　pers. name, Polish　　　　　　SHCHEⁿS-ni　　　　　　　　'ʃtʃē̃sni

Szczecin
　　prov, seaport, Poland　　　　SHCHET-SĒN　　　　　　　　'ʃtʃet͵siːn

Szechuan, Szechwan [Sichuan]
　　prov, China; regional cookery style　SECH-WAHN　　　　　　'setʃ'wɑn

Szeged
　　city, Hungary　　　　　　　SEG-ED　　　　　　　　　　'seg͵ed

Szell
　　George, *US conductor*　　　SEL, ZEL　　　　　　　　　'sel, 'zel

Szent-Györgyi
　　Albert von, *Hungarian-born US*　sānt-JAWRJ(-ē)　　　　　seːnt'dʒɔːʳdʒ(iˑ)
　　　biochemist (Nobel 1937)

Szilard
　　Leo, *US physicist*　　　　　ZIL-AHRD, zuh-LAHRD, SIL-AHRD　'zil͵ɑʳd, zə'lɑʳd, 'sil͵ɑʳd

Szoka
　　Edmund Cardinal, *archbishop,*　SHŌ-kuh　　　　　　　　'ʃoːkə
　　　Detroit

Szold
　　Henrietta, *US Zionist*　　　ZŌLD　　　　　　　　　　'zoːld

Szolnok
　　county, city, Hungary　　　SHŌL-NŌK　　　　　　　　'ʃoːl͵noːk

Szombathely
　　city, Hungary　　　　　　SŌM-BAWT-HĀ *[sic]*　　　'soːm͵bɔːt͵heː *[sic]*

Szymon
　　pers. name, Polish　　　　SHIM-awn　　　　　　　　'ʃimɔːn

Key (col. 2):　a: fad　ā: fade　ah: father　ar: marry　aw: law　e: fed　ē: feed　er: merry　i: hid　ī: hide　ō: coat　ōō: boot
oi: boy　ow: now　u: put　uh: above　uhr: bird　ch: chop　ng: ring　sh: show　th: thick　tẖ: this　zh: measure

T

Taal
   1. volcano, city, Philippines   tah-AHL, TAHL   tɑˈɑl, ˈtɑl
   2. Afrikaans   TAHL   ˈtɑl

Taanach
   Biblical name   TĀ-uh-NAK, tah-NAH<u>KH</u>   ˈteːəˌnæk, tɑˈnɑx

Taanath-shiloh
   Biblical name   TĀ-uh-NATH-SHĪ-LŌ,   ˈteːəˌnæθˈʃɑiˌloː,
          TAH-ah-NAHT-shē-LAW   ˌtɑɑˈnɑtʃiːˈlɔː

Ta'anit Esther
   Jewish fast day   TAH-uh-NĒT es-TER, TAHN-it ES-tuhr,   ˌtɑəˈniːt esˈteʳ, ˈtɑnit ˈestəʳ,
          TAHN-is   ˈtɑnis

Tabar
   Islands, island group, Pacific Ocean   tuh-BAHR   təˈbɑʳ

Tabasco
   1. river, state, Mexico   tah-<u>V</u>AHS-kō, Ⓢ tuh-BAS-kō   tɑˈβɑskoː, Ⓢ təˈbæskoː
   2. tdmk for a hot pepper sauce   tuh-BAS-kō   təˈbæskoː

Tabaski
   Islamic festival   tah-BAHS-kē   tɑˈbɑskiˑ

Tabbaoth
   Biblical name   TAB-ē-AHTH, -AWTH, -uhth, tuh-BĀ-;   ˈtæbiːˌɑθ, -ˌɔːθ, -əθ, təˈbeː-;
          TAH-bah-ŌT   ˌtɑbɑˈoːt

Tabbath
   Biblical name   TAB-uhth, tah-BAHT   ˈtæbəθ, tɑˈbɑt

Tabeal
   Biblical name   TĀ-bē-uhl, tahv-EL   ˈteːbiːəl, tɑvˈel

Tabeel
   Biblical name   TAB-uhl, TAB-ē-EL, TĀB-; tahv-EL   ˈtæbəl, ˈtæbiːˌel, ˈteːb-; tɑvˈel

Taberah
   Biblical name   TAB(-uh)-ruh, TAHV-e-RAH   ˈtæb(ə)rə, ˌtɑveˈrɑː

Tabitha, Tabatha
   pers. name   TAB-uh-thuh   ˈtæbəθə

Tabor
   1. biblical mtn.; college, KS   TĀ-buhr   ˈteːbəʳ
   2. Czech republic   TAHB-AWR   ˈtɑbˌɔːʳ

Tab-rimon, Tab-rimmon
   Biblical name   tab-RIM-uhn, TAHV-ri-MAWN   tæbˈrimən, ˌtɑvriˈmɔːn

Tabrīz
   city, Iran   tuh-BRĒZ   təˈbriːz

Tabuleiros
   Portuguese festival   TAHB-yu-LĀ-ro͞os   ˌtɑbjuˈleːruːs

Tache
   N. American people   TASH, TACH-ē   ˈtæʃ, ˈtætʃiˑ

Foreign Sounds: ue: *Fr.* **rue**, *Ger.* **füllen**   uh(r): *Fr.* **boeuf**, *Ger.* **Höhle**   <u>kh</u>: *Ger.* **ich**, *Scot.* **loch**   g̱: *Sp.* **amigo**   <u>v</u>: *Sp.* **hablar**
hl: *Welsh* **Llanelli**.   CAPITALS: primary stress.   SMALL CAPS: secondary stress.   Ⓢ: U.S. pron.   Ⓔ: British pron.

Taché
   Étienne Paschal, *Canadian*   tah-SHĀ   tɑːˈʃeː
    statesman

Tachmonite
   Biblical name   TAK-muh-NĬT   ˈtækməˌnɑit

Tacitus
   Roman historian   TAS-uht-uhs   ˈtæsəṭəs

Tacna
   town, Chile; dept., Peru   TAHK-nah, Ⓢ TAK-nuh   ˈtɑknɑ, Ⓢ ˈtæknə

Tacoma
   city, WA   tuh-KŌ-muh   təˈkoːmə

Taconic
   mtn. range, northeast US   tuh-KAHN-ik   təˈkɑnik

Tacubaya
   district, Mexico City   tah-ko͞o-BAH-yah   tɑkuːˈbɑjɑ

Taddeo
   pers. name, Italian   tahd-DE-ō   tadˈdeoː

Tadeo
   pers. name, Spanish   tah-<u>TH</u>Ā-ō   tɑˈðeːoː

Tadeus
   pers. name, German   tah-DĀ-us   tɑˈdeːus

Tadeusz
   pers. name, Polish   tah-DE-o͞osh   tɑːˈdeuːʃ

Tadmor
   Biblical name   TAD-MAWR, -MŌR; tahd-MAWR   ˈtædˌmɔːʳ, -ˌmoːʳ; tɑdˈmɔːr

Tadmur
   ancient city, Syria   TAD-MUR, TAD-muhr   ˈtædˌmuʳ, ˈtædməʳ

Tadzhik
   lang., people, central Asia   tah-JIK, tah-JĒK, tuh-   tɑˈdʒik, tɑˈdʒiːk, tə-

Tadzhikistan, Tajikistan
   republic, central Asia   tah-JIK-i-STAHN, tah-JĒK-i-STAHN,   tɑˌdʒikiˈstɑn, tɑˌdʒiːkiˈstɑn,
                  -STAN   -ˈstæn

Taegu
   city, S. Korea   tag-o͞o   tæguː

Taejŏn
   city, S. Korea   taj-awn   tædʒɔːn

Taft
   William Howard, *27th US president*   TAFT   ˈtæft

Tagakaolo
   lang., people, Philippine Islands   TAHG-uh-KOW-lō   ˌtɑgəˈkɑuloː

Tagalog [Pilipino]
   lang., people, Philippine Islands   tuh-GAHL-uhg, tuh-GAHL-AWG,   təˈgaləg, təˈgalˌɔːg,
                  tuh-GAHL-AHG   təˈgalˌɑg

Taganrog
   seaport, Russia   TAG-uhn-RAHG   ˈtægənˌrɑg

Tagbanuwa
   lang., people, Philippines   TAHG-bahn-uh-WAH   ˌtɑgbanəˈwɑ

Tage
   pers. name, Swedish   TAHG-uh   ˈtɑgə

Tages
   Etruscan prophet   TĀ-jēz   ˈteːdʒiːz

Tagliabue
   Paul, *US football commissioner*   TAG-lē-uh-BO͞O   ˈtægliːəˌbuː

Key (col. 2):   a: fad   ā: fade   ah: father   ar: marry   aw: law   e: fed   ē: feed   er: merry   i: hid   ī: hide   ō: coat   o͞o: boot
oi: boy   ow: now   u: put   uh: above   uhr: bird   ch: chop   ng: ring   sh: show   th: thick   <u>th</u>: this   zh: measure

Tagore
Sir Rabindranath, *Indian author,*   tuh-GŌR, tuh-GAWR   tə'goːʳ, tə'gɔːʳ
  philosopher (Nobel 1913)

Tagus [Tajo, Tejo]
river, Spain, Portugal   TĀ-guhs   'teːgəs

Tahan
Biblical name   TĀ-HAN, TAH-khahn   'teːˌhæn, 'tɑxɑn

Tahanite
Biblical name   TĀ-(h)uhn-ĪT   'teː(h)ənˌɑit

Tahapanes [Tahpanhes]
Biblical name   tuh-HAP-uh-NĒZ, TAHKH-pahn-KHES   tə'hæpəˌniːz, ˌtɑxpɑn'xes

Tahath
Biblical name   TĀ-HATH, TAH-khaht   'teːˌhæθ, 'tɑxɑt

Taheiho [Ai-hui]
town, China   TAH-HĀ-HŌ   'tɑ'heː'hoː

Tahini
sesame paste   tuh-KHĒ-nuh, Ⓢ tuh-HĒ-nē   tə'xiːnə, Ⓢ tə'hiːni·

Tahiti
island, Pacific   tuh-HĒT-ē   tə'hiːt̬i·

Tahitian
pert. to Tahiti   tuh-HĒ-shuhn   tə'hiːʃən

Tahoe
lake, CA, NV   TAH-HŌ   'tɑˌhoː

Tai
Asian lang. family; pers. name   TĪ   'tɑi

T'ai-chung
city & town, Taiwan   TĪ-CHUNG   'tɑi'tʃuŋ

Ta'if, At
town, Saudi Arabia   aht TAH-if   ɑt 'tɑ-if

Tahlequah
city, OK   TAL-uh-KWAW   'tæləˌkwɔː

Tahmah
Biblical name   TAHM-uh, TAH-mahkh   'tɑmə, 'tɑmɑx

Tahoka
city, TX   tuh-HŌ-kuh   tə'hoːkə

Tahpanhes
Biblical name   TAP-uhn-HĒZ, -uh-NĒZ; tuh-PAN-(H)ĒZ,   'tæpənˌhiːz, -əˌniːz;
    TAHKH-pahn-KHES   tə'pænˌ(h)iːz, ˌtɑxpɑn'xes

Tahpenes
Biblical name   TAP-uh-NĒZ, tahkh-puh-NES   'tæpəˌniːz, tɑxpə'nes

Tahrea
Biblical name   tuh-RĒ-uh, tahkh-RĀ-ah   tə'riːə, tɑx'reːɑ

Tahtim-hodshi
Biblical name   TAT-uhm-HAHD-shē,   'tæt̬əm'hɑdʃi·,
    tahkh-TĒM-khahd-SHĒ   tɑx'tiːmxɑd'ʃiː

Taimyr, Taimir
district, peninsula, Russia   TĪ-MIR   ˌtɑi'miʳ

T'ai-nan [Tainan]
city, Taiwan   TĪ-NAHN   'tɑi'nɑn

Tainan
city, Taiwan   TĪ-NAHN, DĪ-NAHN   'tɑi'nɑn, 'dɑi'nɑn

Táin Bó Cuailnge
ancient Irish epic   TOIN BŌ KŌŌ-ling-uh *[sic]*   'tɔin 'boː 'kuːliŋə *[sic]*

Taine
Hippolyte, *French historian*   TEN   ten

Foreign Sounds: ue: *Fr.* **rue**, *Ger.* **füllen**   uh(r): *Fr.* **boeuf**, *Ger.* **Höhle**   kh: *Ger.* **ich**, *Scot.* **loch**   g̃: *Sp.* **amigo**   v: *Sp.* **hablar**
hl: *Welsh* **Llanelli**.   CAPITALS: primary stress.   SMALL CAPS: secondary stress.   Ⓢ: U.S. pron.   Ⓔ: British pron.

Taino
   West Indian people   TĪ-nō   'taino:

Taipei
   city, Taiwan   TĪ-PĀ, -BĀ   'tai'pe:, -'be:

Taiping
   river, China, Burma; city, Malaysia   TĪ-PING, TĪ-BING   'tai'piŋ, 'tai'biŋ

Tairona
   S. American people   TAH-Ē-RŌ-nuh   ˌtɑ-iː'roːnə

Taisho
   reign of Emperor Yoshihito of Japan   tī-shō   taiʃoː

Taittinger
   champagne brand   te-teⁿ-ZHĀ   tetẽʒeː

Taiwan
   island nation, SE Asia   TĪ-WAHN, tī-WAHN   'tai'wɑn, tai'wɑn

Taïyetos Oros
   mtn. range, Greece   TĪ-ye-TAWS AW-RAWS   'taije,tɔːs 'ɔːˌrɔːs

Taiyo
   Japanese fishing co.   tī-(y)ō   tai(j)oː

Taiyuan
   city, China   TĪ-yo͞o-AHN   'taiju:'ɑn

Taizz
   city, Yemen   ta-IZ   tæ'iz

Tajik [Tadzhik]
   people, Tadzhikistan, Afghanistan,   tah-JIK, tah-JĒK   tɑ'dʒik, tɑ'dʒiːk
   Turkestan

Tajikistan
   see Tadzhikistan

Taj Mahal
   mausoleum, India; Indian beer; US   TAHZH MUH-HAHL, TAHJ   ˌtaʒ mə'hɑl, ˌtadʒ
   musician

Tajo [Tagus]
   river, Spain, Portugal   TAH-hō, TAH-k̲h̲ō   'tɑ·hoː, 'tɑxoː

Takamatsu
   port, Japan   tahk-ah-maht-so͞o   takɑmatsuː

Takamori
   pers. name, Japanese   tah-kah-mō-rē   takamoːri

Takao
   city, Taiwan   tah-KAH-ō, tah-KOW   tɑ'kɑoː, tɑ'kɑu

Takashi
   pers. name, Japanese   tah-kah-shē   takaʃiː

Takeda
   Japanese chemical co.   tah-kā-dah, ⑤ tuh-KĀD-uh   takeːda, ⑤ tə'keːdə

Takehito
   pers. name, Japanese   tah-ke-hē-tō   takehiːtoː

Takeo
   pers. name, Japanese   tahk-ā-ō   takeːoː

Takeshita
   Noboru, *Japanese prime minister*   tah-ke-shē-tah   takeʃiːta

Takkakaw
   waterfall, Canada   TAK-uh-KAW   'tækəˌkɔː

Takla Makan
   desert, China   TAHK-luh muh-KAHN   ˌtaklə mə'kɑn

Talaing [Mon]
   lang., people, Burma, Thailand   tah-LĪNG   tɑ'laiŋ

Key (col. 2):   a: fad   ā: fade   ah: father   ar: marry   aw: law   e: fed   ē: feed   er: merry   i: hid   ī: hide   ō: coat   o͞o: boot   oi: boy   ow: now   u: put   uh: above   uhr: bird   ch: chop   ng: ring   sh: show   th: thick   t̲h̲: this   zh: measure

Talamanca, Cordillera de
  mtn. range, Central America   kawr-dē(l)-YER-ah dā   kɔːˈdiː(l)ˈjerɑ deː
                       tahl-ah-MAHNG-kah   tɑlɑˈmaŋkɑ

Talassio
  ritual cry at ancient Roman   tuh-LAS-ē-ō, tuh-LAHS-ē-ō   təˈlæsiːoː, təˈlɑsiːoː
  marriages

Talber
  pers. name   TAWL-buhr, TAL-buhr   ˈtɔːlbəʳ, ˈtælbəʳ

Talbot
  pers. name   TAWL-buht, TAL-buht   ˈtɔːlbət, ˈtælbət

Talbots
  US apparel co.   TAWL-buhts, TAL-buhts   ˈtɔːlbəts, ˈtælbəts

Talcahuano
  port, Chile   TAHL-kuh-<u>KH</u>WAHN-ō   ˌtɑlkəˈxwɑnoː

Taliaferro
  1. county, GA   TAHL-uh-vuhr   ˈtɑləvəʳ
  2. pers. name   TAHL-uh-vuhr, TAHL-yuh-FER-ō   ˈtɑləvəʳ, ˌtɑljəˈferoː

Taliesin
  Welsh bard; home of Frank Lloyd   tahl-YES-in, TAL-ē-ES-uhn   tɑlˈjesin, ˌtæliːˈesən
  Wright

Talitha-cumi
  Biblical name   tuh-LĒ-thuh-KOO-mē, TAL-i-   təˈliːθəˈkuːmiˈ, ˈtæli-

Talladega
  city, county, AL   TAL-uh-DĒ-guh, TAL-uh-DĀ-guh   ˌtæləˈdiːgə, ˌtæləˈdeːgə

Tallahassee
  city, FL   TAL-uh-HAS-ē   ˌtæləˈhæsiˈ

Tallahatchie
  river, county, MS   TAL-uh-HACH-ē   ˌtæləˈhætʃiˈ

Tallapoosa
  river, county, AL   TAL-uh-POO-suh   ˌtæləˈpuːsə

Tallassee
  city, AL   TAL-uh-SĒ   ˈtæləˌsiː

Talleyrand Périgord
  Charles Maurice de, French   tah-le-RAHⁿ pā-rē-GAWR   tɑːlerɑ̃ peːriːgɔːr
  statesman

Tallinn
  city, Estonia   TAHL-yin, ⑤ TAL-uhn, TAHL-uhn   ˈtɑljin, ⑤ ˈtælən, ˈtɑlən

Tallis
  Thomas, English composer   TAL-uhs   ˈtæləs

Tallulah
  pers. name   tuh-LOO-luh   təˈluːlə

Talmadge
  pers. name   TAL-mij   ˈtælmidʒ

Talmai
  Biblical name   TAL-MĪ, tahl-MĪ   ˈtælˌmai, tɑlˈmai

Talmon
  Biblical name   TAL-muhn, tahl-MAWN   ˈtælmən, tɑlˈmɔːn

Talmud
  Jewish rabbinical law   TAHL-MUD, TAL-muhd   ˈtɑlˌmud, ˈtælməd

Talmudic
  pert. to Jewish law   tahl-MUD-ik, tal-M(Y)OOD-ik   tɑlˈmudik, tælˈm(j)uːdik

Taloga
  town, OK   tuh-LŌ-guh   təˈloːgə

Talos
  mythical guardian of Crete   TAL-uhs   ˈtæləs

Foreign Sounds: ue: *Fr.* **rue**, *Ger.* **füllen** uh(r): *Fr.* **boeuf**, *Ger.* **Höhle** <u>kh</u>: *Ger.* **ich**, *Scot.* **loch** ḡ: *Sp.* **amigo** v̲: *Sp.* **hablar**
hl: *Welsh* **Llanelli**. CAPITALS: primary stress. SMALL CAPS: secondary stress. ⑤: U.S. pron. Ⓔ: British pron.

Talysh
  lang., Iran, Azerbaijan　　　tuh-LISH　　　　　　　　tə'liʃ
Tama
  lang., Sudan, Chad　　　TAHM-uh　　　　　　　'tɑmə
Tama
  county, IA　　　TÄ-muh　　　　　　　'teːmə
Tamaqua
  borough, PA　　　tuh-MAK-wuh　　　　　　　tə'mækwə
Tamar
  Biblical name　　　TÄ-muhr　　　　　　　'teːmə^r
Tamara
  1. pers. name　　　TAM-uh-ruh　　　　　　　'tæmərə
  2. Russian　　　tuh-MAH-ruh　　　　　　　tə'mɑːrə
Tamari
  soy sauce　　　tuh-MAHR-ē　　　　　　　tə'mɑri·
Tamashek [Tuareg]
  lang., N Africa　　　TAM-uh-SHEK　　　　　　　'tæmə‚ʃek
Tamatave
  port, Madagascar　　　TAHM-uh-TAHV, TAM-uh-TAHV　　　‚tɑmə'tɑv, ‚tæmə'tɑv
Tamaulipas
  1. state, Mexico　　　tahm-ow-LĒ-pahs　　　　　　　tɑmɑu'liːpɑs
  2. thrush, songbird　　　tuh-MAW-luh-puhs　　　　　　　tə'mɔːləpəs
Tamayo
  Rufino, *Mexican painter*　　　tah-MAH-yō　　　　　　　tɑ'mɑjoː
Tamazight
  lang., Morocco　　　TAHM-uh-ZIKHT　　　　　　　'tɑmə‚ziçt
Tambora
  Mount, *volcano, Indonesia*　　　TAHM-buh-ruh　　　　　　　'tɑmbərə
Tamburlaine [Tamerlane, Timur]
  Tartar conqueror　　　TAM-(b)uhr-LĀN　　　　　　　'tæm(b)ə^r‚leːn
Tamerlane [Tamburlaine]
  Tartar conqueror　　　TAM-uhr-LĀN　　　　　　　'tæmə^r‚leːn
Tamil
  lang., people, Asia　　　TAHM-uhl, TAM-uhl, -il　　　　　　　'tɑməl, 'tæməl, -il
Tamil Nadu
  state, India　　　TAHM-uhl NAHD-ōō, TAM-uhl, -il　　　‚tɑməl 'nɑduː, ‚tæməl, -il
Tamkarum
  Babylonian trader　　　tam-KAHR-uhm　　　　　　　tæm'kɑrəm
Tamm
  Igor Yevgenyevich, *Soviet physicist*　　　TAHM　　　　　　　'tɑm
  (Nobel 1958)
Tammany Hall
  corrupt Democratic political　　　TAM-uh-nē HAWL　　　　　　　‚tæməni· 'hɔːl
  organization
Tammuz
  Jewish month　　　TAHM-UZ　　　　　　　'tɑm‚uz
Tammy
  pers. name　　　TAM-ē　　　　　　　'tæmi·
Tam o' Shanter
  1. poem, R. Burns　　　TAM uh SHANT-uhr　　　　　　　‚tæm ə 'ʃæntə^r
  2. Scottish cap　　　TAM uh SHANT-uhr　　　　　　　'tæm ə ‚ʃæntə^r
Tampa
  city, FL　　　TAM-puh　　　　　　　'tæmpə
Tampere
  city, Finland　　　TAHM-puh-ruh, TAM-puh-ruh　　　　'tɑmpərəː, 'tæmpərəː

Key (col. 2):　　a: fad　ā: fade　ah: father　ar: marry　aw: law　e: fed　ē: feed　er: merry　i: hid　ī: hide　ō: coat　ōō: boot
oi: boy　ow: now　u: put　uh: above　uhr: bird　ch: chop　ng: ring　sh: show　th: thick　th: this　zh: measure

Tampico
  city, IL; port, Mexico   tam-PĒ-kō   tæm'pi:ko:

Tamworth
  city, Australia   TAM-WUHRTH   'tæm,wəʳθ

Tana [Tsana]
  lake, Ethiopia; river, Kenya   TAHN-uh   'tɑnə

Tanach [Taanach]
  Biblical name   TĀ-NAK, tah-NAHKH   'te:,næk, tɑ'nɑx

Taney
  Roger Brooke, *chief justice, US* TAW-nē   'tɔ:ni·
    Supreme Court

Tanager
  songbird   TAN-uh-juhr   'tænədʒəʳ

Tanagra
  town, ancient Greece   TAN-uh-gruh   'tænəgrə

Tanaina
  N. American people   tuh-NĪ-nuh   tə'nainə

Tanaka
  pers. name, Japanese   tahn-ahk-ah   tɑnɑkɑ

Tanakh, Tanach
  Hebrew scriptures   tah-NAHKH   tɑ'nɑx

Tanana
  1. Frank, US baseball player   tuh-NAN-uh   tə'nænə
  2. river, city, AK   TAN-uh-NAW   'tænə,nɔ:

Tananarive
  former name of Antananarivo   tuh-NAN-uh-RĒV   tə'nænə,ri:v

Tancred
  Norman crusader; king of Sicily TANG-kruhd   'tæŋkrəd

Tancrède
  pers. name, French   tahⁿ-KRED   tãkred

Tandy
  Jessica, *British actress*   TAN-dē   'tændi·

Tanesha
  pers. name   tuh-NĒ-shuh   tə'ni:ʃə

Tang
  Chinese dynasty   TAHNG   'tɑŋ

Tanganyika
  lake, Africa   TAN-guhn-YĒ-kuh,   ,tæŋgən'ji:kə, ,tæŋgən'ji:kə,
                                    TANG-guhn-YĒ-kuh, -guh-NĒ-kuh -gə'ni:kə

Tanger [Tangier]
  seaport, Morocco   *French* tahⁿ-ZHĀ, *German* TAHN-juhr, *French* tãʒe:, *German*
                                    TAHNG-uhr   'tandʒəʳ, 'tɑŋəʳ

Tangier
  seaport, Morocco   tan-JIR   tæn'dʒiʳ

Tangiers [Tangier]
  seaport, Morocco   tan-JIRZ   tæn'dʒiʳz

Tangipahoa
  parish, LA   TAN-juh-puh-HŌ(-uh)   ,tændʒəpə'ho:(ə)

Tangshan, T'angshan
  city, China   TAHNG-SHAHN   'tɑŋ'ʃɑn

Tanguy
  Yves, *French painter*   tahⁿ-GĒ   tãgi:

Tanhumeth
  Biblical name   tan-H(Y)OO-METH, tahn-KHOO-met tæn'h(j)u:,meθ, tɑn'xu:met

---

Tania
  pers. name　　　　　　　TAHN-yuh　　　　　　　ˈtɑnjə
Tanis
  city, Egypt　　　　　　　TĀ-nuhs　　　　　　　ˈteːnəs
Tannhäuser
  opera, R. Wagner　　　　TAHN-HOI-zuhr　　　　ˈtɑnˌhɔizərᵣ
Tannu Tuva
  region, Russia　　　　　TAHN-o͞o TO͞O-vuh　　　ˌtɑnuː ˈtuːvə
Tano-Tewa
  N. American people　　　TAHN-ō-TĒ-wuh, TAHN-ō-TĀ-wuh　　　ˌtɑnoːˈtiːwə, ˌtɑnoːˈteːwə
Tano-Tigua
  N. American people　　　TAHN-ō-TĒ-wuh　　　ˌtɑnoːˈtiːwə
Tanqueray
  tdmk for gin　　　　　TANG-kuh-RĀ　　　　ˈtæŋkəˌreː
tantalum
  element　　　　　　　TANT-l-uhm　　　　ˈtæntl̩əm
Tantalus
  son of Zeus condemned to eternal thirst　　　TANT-l-uhs　　　ˈtæntl̩əs
Tantra
  Hindu doctrine　　　　TAHN-truh, TUHN-truh, TAN-truh　　　ˈtɑntrə, ˈtəntrə, ˈtæntrə
Tantrism
  school of Mahayana Buddhism　　　TUHN-TRIZ-uhm　　　ˈtənˌtrizəm
Tanzania
  republic, Africa　　　TAN-zuh-NĒ-uh, TAHN-　　　ˌtænzəˈniːə, ˌtɑːn-
Tanzanian
  pert. to Tanzania　　　TAN-zuh-NĒ-uhn, TAHN-　　　ˌtænzəˈniːən, ˌtɑːn-
Tao
  a doctrine of Taoism　　DOW　　　　ˈdɑu
Taoiseach
  Irish prime minister　　THĒ-shuhkh, TĒ-shuhkh, TĒ-shuhk　　　ˈθiːʃəx, ˈtiːʃəx, ˈtiːʃək
Taoism
  religion　　　　　　　DOW-IZ-uhm, TOW-IZ-uhm　　　ˈdɑuˌizəm, ˈtɑuˌizəm
Taos
  town, county, NM; N. American people; Indian reservation, US　　TOWS, TAH-ōs　　　ˈtɑus, ˈtɑoːs
Tao-te-ching
  basic text of Taoism　　DOW-DĀ-JING　　　ˈdɑuˈdeːˈdʒiŋ
Tapaculo
  S.American songbird　　TAP-uh-KO͞O-lō　　　ˌtæpəˈkuːloː
Tapajós, Tapajoz
  river, Brazil　　　　　TAHP-uh-ZHAWS, -ZHAWSH　　　ˌtɑpəˈʒɔːs, -ˈʒɔːʃ
Taphath
  Biblical name　　　　　TĀ-FATH, tah-FAHT　　　ˈteːˌfæθ, tɑˈfɑt
Tappan
  1. village, NY　　　　tap-AN　　　　tæpˈæn
  2. US appliance co.　　tap-AN, TAP-uhn　　　tæpˈæn, ˈtæpən
Tappan Zee Bridge
  Hudson River, NY　　TAP-an ZĒ BRIJ, TAP-uhn ZĒ　　　ˌtæpæn ˌziː ˈbridʒ, ˌtæpən ˌziː
Tappuah
  Biblical name　　　　ta-P(Y)O͞O-uh, TAP-(y)uh-wuh, tah-PO͞O-ahkh　　　tæˈp(j)uːə, ˈtæp(j)əwə, tɑˈpuːɑx

---

Key (col. 2):　a: fad　ā: fade　ah: father　ar: marry　aw: law　e: fed　ē: feed　er: merry　i: hid　ī: hide　ō: coat　o͞o: boot
oi: boy　ow: now　u: put　uh: above　uhr: bird　ch: chop　ng: ring　sh: show　th: thick　t͟h: this　zh: measure

Tara
  1. *ancient Irish capital; plantation in*   TAR-uh, TER-uh, TAHR-uh   'tærə, 'terə, 'tɑrə
     Gone with the Wind*; pers. name*
  2. *lang., Central Sulawesi (Celebes)*   TAHR-uh   'tɑrə
Tarabulus
  see Trâblous
Tarahumara
  lang., people, Mexico   TAHR-uh-hōō-MAHR-uh   ˌtɑrəhuː'mɑrə
Taralah
  Biblical name   TAHR-uh-luh, TAR-; tahr-ah-LAH   'tɑrələ, 'tær-; tɑrɑ'lɑ
Tarantino
  Quentin, *US screenwriter*   TAR-uhn-TĒ-nō   ˌtærən'tiːnoː
Taranto
  prov & town, Italy   TAHR-uhn-TŌ, tuh-RANT-ō   'tɑrənˌtoː, tə'rænto:
Tarascan
  N. American people   tuh-RAS-kuhn, tuh-RAHS-kuhn   tə'ræskən, tə'rɑskən
Tarasco
  lang., Mexico   tuh-RAHS-kō, tuh-RAS-kō   tə'rɑskoː, tə'ræskoː
Tarawa
  atoll, Kiribati   tuh-RAH-wuh, TAR-uh-WAH   tə'rɑwə, 'tærəˌwɑ
Tarbell
  Ida Minerva, *US author*   TAHR-buhl   'tɑʳbəl
Tarea
  Biblical name   TAR-ē-uh, tuh-RĒ-uh, tah-RĀ-ah   'tæriːə, tə'riːə, tɑ'reːɑ
Taree
  town, Australia   tah-RĒ   tɑː'riː
Tarentum
  ancient seaport, Italy   tuh-RENT-uhm   tə'rentəm
Targum
  Aramaic translation of the Old   TAHR-GUM, TAHR-GŌŌM   'tɑʳˌgum, 'tɑʳˌguːm
     Testament
Tarim He
  river, China   DAH-RĒM HUH, TAH-RĒM   'dɑ'riːm 'hə, 'tɑ'riːm
Tarim Pendi
  basin, China   DAH-RĒM PUHN-DĒ, TAH-RĒM   'dɑ'riːm 'pən'diː, 'tɑ'riːm
Tariq
  pers. name, Arabic   tah-RĒK   tɑ'riːk
Tarkanian
  Jerry, *US basketball coach*   tahr-KĀ-nē-uhn   tɑʳ'keːniːən
Tarkenton
  Fran, *US football player, sportscaster*   TAHR-kuhn-tuhn   'tɑʳkəntən
Tarkhān
  pers. name, Arabic   tahr-<u>KH</u>AHN, tahr-KAHN   tɑʳ'xɑn, tɑʳ'kɑn
Tarkio
  pl. name, US   TAHR-kē-ō   'tɑʳkiːoː
Tarkington
  Newton Booth, *US author*   TAHR-king-tuhn   'tɑʳkiŋtən
Tarleton
  pers. name   TAHRL-tuhn, TAHRLT-n   'tɑʳltən, 'tɑʳltn̩
Tarpeia
  legendary Roman traitor   tahr-PĒ-uh   tɑʳ'piːə
Tarpeian Rock
  Roman execution site   tahr-PĒ-uhn RAHK   tɑʳ'piːən 'rɑk
Tarpelite
  Biblical name   TAHR-puh-LĪT   'tɑʳpəˌlait

Foreign Sounds: ue: *Fr.* **rue**, *Ger.* **füllen**   uh(r): *Fr.* **boeuf**, *Ger.* **Höhle**   <u>kh</u>: *Ger.* **ich**, *Scot.* **loch**   ḡ: *Sp.* **amigo**   v̱: *Sp.* **hablar**
hl: *Welsh* **Llanelli**.   CAPITALS: primary stress.   SMALL CAPS: secondary stress.   Ⓢ: U.S. pron.   Ⓔ: British pron.

Tarquin
  king of Rome   TAHR-kwin   'tɑʳkwin

Tarquinii
  ancient town, Italy   tahr-KWIN-ē-Ī   tɑʳˈkwiniːˌɑi

Tarquinius
  name of two early Roman kings   tahr-KWIN-ē-uhs   tɑʳˈkwiniːəs

Tarragona
  prov & town, Spain   TAR-uh-GŌ-nuh   ˌtærəˈgoːnə

Tarrant
  county, TX   TAR-uhnt   'tærənt

Tarrytown
  town, NY   TAR-ē-TOWN, TER-ē-TOWN   'tæriːˌtɑun, 'teriːˌtɑun

Tarshish
  Biblical name   TAHR-shish   'tɑʳʃiʃ

Tarsus
  town, Turkey   TAHR-suhs   'tɑrsəs

Tartak
  Biblical name   TAHR-TAK, tahr-TAHK   'tɑʳˌtæk, tɑrˈtɑk

Tartan
  Biblical name   TAHR-TAN, TAHR-tn, tahr-TAHN   'tɑʳˌtæn, 'tɑʳtn̩, tɑrˈtɑn

Tartar
  Asian tribal people   TAHRT-uhr   'tɑʳʈəʳ

Tartarus
  portion of Hades in Roman myth   TAHRT-uh-ruhs   'tɑʳʈərəs

Tartary
  region overrun by Tatars, Europe and Asia   TAHRT-uh-rē   'tɑʳʈəriˑ

Tartessus
  ancient kingdom, Spain   tahr-TES-uhs   tɑʳˈtesəs

Tartikoff
  Brandon, *US entertainment executive*   TAHRT-i-KAWF, TAHRT-i-KAHF   'tɑʳʈiˌkɔːf, 'tɑʳʈiˌkɑf

Tartu
  city, Estonia   TAHR-tōō   'tɑʳtuː

Tartuffe
  comedy, Molière   tahr-TUEF, ⓢ tahr-TUF, tahr-TŌŌF   tɑːrtyːf, ⓢ tɑʳˈtuf, tɑʳˈtuːf

Tarzan
  character, E. R. Burroughs   TAHR-zuhn, TAHR-ZAN   'tɑʳzən, 'tɑʳˌzæn

Tasaday
  indigenous people, Philippines   TAS-uhd-Ā, tuh-SAHD-Ī   'tæsədˌeː, təˈsadˌɑi

Tasha
  pers. name   TAHSH-uh, ⓔ TASH-uh   'tɑʃə, ⓔ 'tæʃə

Tashkent, Tashkend
  city, Uzbekistan   tash-KENT, tash-KEND, tahsh-   tæʃˈkent, tæʃˈkend, tɑʃ-

Tashritu
  Babylonian month   tahsh-RĒ-tōō   tɑʃˈriːtuː

Tasman
  Sea, *between New Zealand & Australia*   TAZ-muhn   'tæzmən

Tasmania
  island, state, Australia   taz-MĀ-nē-uh, taz-MĀN-yuh   tæzˈmeːniːə, tæzˈmeːnjə

Tasmanian devil
  marsupial   taz-MĀ-nē-uhn DEV-uhl, taz-MĀN-yuhn   tæzˌmeːniːən 'devəl, tæzˈmeːnjən

Tass
  news agency, USSR   TAHS, TAS   'tɑs, 'tæs

Key (col. 2):   a: fad   ā: fade   ah: father   ar: **marry**   aw: **law**   e: fed   ē: feed   er: **merry**   i: hid   ī: hide   ō: coat   ōō: boot
oi: **boy**   ow: **now**   u: put   uh: above   uhr: **bird**   ch: **chop**   ng: **ring**   sh: **show**   th: **thick**   <u>th</u>: **this**   zh: measure

Tasso
    Torquato, *Italian poet*   TAHS-sō, ⓢ TAS-ō   ˈtɑssoː, ⓢ ˈtæsoː

Tat
    lang., people, Caucasus Mts.   TAHT   ˈtɑt

Tatar
    lang., people, Eurasia   TAHT-uhr   ˈtɑʈəʳ

Tate
    pers. name   TĀT   ˈteːt

Tatiana
    pers. name   tah-TYAHN-uh   tɑˈtjɑnə

Tatius
    second king of Rome   TĀ-sh(ē-)uhs   ˈteːʃ(iː)əs

Tatler
    British periodical by Steele, Addison,   TAT-luhr   ˈtætləʳ
    and Swift

Tatnai [Tattenai]
    Biblical name   TAT-NĪ, TAH-tuh-NĪ   ˈtæt͵nɑi, ͵tɑtəˈnɑi

Tatra
    mts., E. Europe   TAH-truh   ˈtɑtrə

Tatry [Tatra]
    mts., E. Europe   TAH-trē   ˈtɑtriˑ

Tattenai
    Biblical name   TAT-n-Ī, TAH-tuh-NĪ   ˈtætn͵ɑi, ͵tɑtəˈnɑi

Tattnall
    county, GA   TAT-nl   ˈtætnḷ

Tatum
    E. L., *US biochemist (Nobel 1958);*   TĀT-uhm   ˈteːʈəm
    pers. name

Tatum
    Arthur, *US musician*   TĀT-uhm   ˈteːʈəm

Ta-t'ung
    see Datong

Taube
    Henry, *Canadian-born US inorganic*   TAWB, TOWB   ˈtɔːb, ˈtɑub
    chemist (Nobel 1983)

Taulipang
    S. American people   TOW-luh-PAHNG, TOW-luh-PAHNG   ˈtɑulə͵pɑŋ, ͵tɑuləˈpɑŋ

Taumotu
    archipelago, Pacific   tow-MŌ-tōo   tɑuˈmoːtuː

Taungthu
    lang., people, Burma, Thailand   TOWNG-TU   ˈtɑuŋ͵tu

Taunus
    mtn. range, Germany   TOW-nuhs   ˈtɑunəs

Taurids
    meteor shower   TAWR-idz   ˈtɔːridz

Taurt [Taweret]
    Egyptian goddess of childbirth   TOWRT   ˈtɑuʳt

Taurus
    constellation, sign of the zodiac; mts.,   TAWR-uhs   ˈtɔːrəs
    Turkey

Taussig
    Frank W., *US economist*   TOW-sig   ˈtɑusig

Taussig
    Helen Brooke, *US pediatrician*   TOW-sig   ˈtɑusig

Foreign Sounds: ue: *Fr.* **rue**, *Ger.* **füllen**   uh(r): *Fr.* **boeuf**, *Ger.* **Höhle**   kh: *Ger.* i**ch**, *Scot.* lo**ch**   g̲: *Sp.* ami**g**o   v̲: *Sp.* ha**b**lar
hl: *Welsh* **Ll**anelli.   CAPITALS: primary stress.   SMALL CAPS: secondary stress.   ⓢ: U.S. pron.   Ⓔ: British pron.

Tavares
city, FL   tuh-VAR-ēz, tuh-VER-ēz   tə'væriːz, tə'veriːz

Tawas City
city, MI   TAW-wuhs SIT-ē   'tɔːwəs 'siṭiˑ

Tawe
river, Wales   TAH-wā, Ⓢ , Ⓔ TOW-ē   'tɑːweː, Ⓢ , Ⓔ 'tauiˑ

Taweret [Taurt]
Egyptian goddess of childbirth   TOW(-uh)r-uht   'tau(ə)rət

Tawney
Richard Henry, *English historian*   TAW-nē, TĀ-nē   'tɔːniˑ, 'teːniˑ

Taxco
city, Mexico   TAHS-kō   'taskoː

Taxila
ancient town, Indus valley   TAK-suh-luh   'tæksələ

Taxiles
king of Taxila   TAK-suh-lēz   'tæksəliːz

Tay
river, Scotland   TĀ   'teː

Ta Yü [Yü]
Chinese emperor, *legendary*   TAH YUE   'tɑ 'jy
founder of the first dynasty

Tayal [Atayal]
Malayasian people, lang.   tuh-YAHL   tə'jɑl

Tayback
Vic, *US actor*   TĀ-BAK   'teːˌbæk

Taygete
mother of Lacedaemon by Zeus   tā-IJ-uht-ē   teː'idʒəṭiˑ

Taygetus
mtn. range, Greece   tā-IJ-uht-uhs   teː'idʒəṭəs

Taylor
pers. name   TĀ-luhr   'teːləʳ

Tay-Sachs
disease   TĀ-SAKS   'teː'sæks

Tayside
region, Scotland   TĀ-SĪD   'teːˌsaid

Tazewell
county, VA   TAZ-ᴡᴇʟ, TAZ-wuhl   'tæzˌwel, 'tæzwəl

Tbilisi [Tiflis]
city, Georgia   tuh-bil-Ē-sē, tuh-BIL-uh-sē   təbil'iːsiˑ, tə'biləsiˑ

Tchaikovsky, Tsch-
Peter Ilyich, *Russian composer*   chī-KAWF-skē, chī-KAWV-skē   tʃai'kɔːfskiˑ, tʃai'kɔːvskiˑ

Tchelitchew
Pavel, *Russian-US painter*   CHIL-uh-ᴄʜᴇғ   'tʃiləˌtʃef

Tchibanga
city, Gabon   CHĒ-BAHNG-GAH   ˌtʃiːˌbaŋ'ga

Tczew
commune, Poland   CHEF   'tʃef

Teasdale
Sara, *US poet*   TĒZ-ᴅᴀʟ   'tiːzˌdeːl

Tebah
Biblical name   TĒ-buh, TE-vahkh   'tiːbə, 'tevɑx

Tebaldi
Renata, *Italian soprano*   tā-BAHL-dē, Ⓢ tuh-BAWL-dē   teː'baldiˑ, Ⓢ tə'bɔːldiˑ

Tebaliah
Biblical name   TEB-uh-LĪ-uh, tuh-vahl-YAH-hoo   ˌtebə'laiə, təval'jahuː

Key (col. 2):   a: fad   ā: fade   ah: father   ar: marry   aw: law   e: fed   ē: feed   er: merry   i: hid   ī: hide   ō: coat   oo: boot
oi: boy   ow: now   u: put   uh: above   uhr: bird   ch: chop   ng: ring   sh: show   th: thick   <u>th</u>: this   zh: measure

Tebet, Tevet
   Jewish month   tā-VET, TĀ-VĀS, TĀ-VĀT   teː'vet, 'teː͵veːs, 'teː͵veːt

Tebetu
   Babylonian month   tā-BĀ-too̅   teː'beːtuː

Tecate
   Mexican beer   tā-KAHT-ā   teː'kaṭeː

Teche, Bayou
   stream, LA   BAH-yoo̅ TESH, BĪ-ō   ͵baju: 'teʃ, ͵baio:

technetium
   element   tek-NĒ-sh(ē-)uhm   tek'niːʃ(iː)əm

Technicolor
   tdmk for a color motion picture   TEK-ni-KUHL-uhr   'tekni͵kələʳ
    system

Tecmessa
   girl abducted by Great Ajax   tek-MES-uh   tek'mesə

Tecumseh
   Shawnee leader; pers. name   tuh-KUHM-suh, -sē   tə'kəmsə, -si·

Ted
   pers. name   TED   'ted

Teda
   lang., people, Chad, Libya   TĀD-uh   'teːdə

Teddy, Teddie
   pers. name   TED-ē   'tedi·

Te Deum
   Christian hymn of praise   tā DĀ-uhm, tē DĒ-uhm   teː 'deːəm, tiː 'diːəm

Teej
   Indian festival   TĒJ   'tiːdʒ

Teena
   pers. name   TĒ-nuh   'tiːnə

Tees
   river, England   TĒZ   'tiːz

TEFL
   Teaching English as a Foreign   TEF-uhl   'tefəl
    Language

Teflon
   tdmk for a synthetic resin   TEF-LAHN   'tef͵lɑn

Tefnut, Tefnet
   Egyptian rain goddess   TEF-nuht   'tefnət

Tegal
   port, Java   tā-GAHL   teː'gɑl

Tegeates
   mythical son of Lycaon & founder of   tuh-JĒ-uht-ēz   tə'dʒiːəṭiːz
    Tegea

Tegel
   airport, Germany   TĀ-guhl   'teːgəl

Tegucigalpa
   dept, city, Honduras   tā-goo̅-sē-ḠAHL-pah,   teːɣuːsiː'ɣɑlpɑ,
                          ⓢ tuh-GOO̅-suh-GAL-puh,   ⓢ tə͵guːsə'gælpə, -'gɑlpə
                          -GAHL-puh

Tehachapi
   mtn. range, city, CA   tuh-HACH-uh-pē   tə'hætʃəpi·

Tehama
   county, CA   ti-HĀ-muh   ti'heːmə

Tehaphnehes [Tahpanhes]
   Biblical name   tuh-HAF-nuh-HĒZ, TAHKH-pahn-KHES   tə'hæfnə͵hiːz, ͵tɑxpɑn'xes

---

Foreign Sounds: ue: *Fr.* **rue**, *Ger.* **füllen**   uh(r): *Fr.* **boeuf**, *Ger.* **Höhle**   <u>kh</u>: *Ger.* i<u>ch</u>, *Scot.* lo<u>ch</u>   ḡ: *Sp.* ami**g**o   y: *Sp.* ha**b**lar
hl: *Welsh* **Ll**anelli.   CAPITALS: primary stress.   SMALL CAPS: secondary stress.   ⓢ: U.S. pron.   ⓔ: British pron.

Teheran, Tehran
  city, Iran   TĀ(-uh)-RAN, TĀ(-uh)-RAHN   ˌteː(ə)'ræn, ˌteː(ə)'rɑn

Tehinnah
  Biblical name   tuh-HIN-uh, tuh-<u>khi</u>-NAH   tə'hinə, təxi'nɑ

Tehipite Dome
  mountain peak, CA   tuh-HIP-uht-ē DŌM   tə,hipət̬iˑ 'doːm

Tehuantepec
  town, Mexico   tā-<u>KH</u>WAHN-tā-pek,   teː'xwɑnteːpek,
                              ⓢ tuh-(H)WAHN-tuh-PEK   ⓢ tə'(h)wɑntə,pek

Tehuelche
  S. American people   tuh-WEL-chē, te-WEL-chā   tə'weltʃiˑ, te'weltʃeː

Teicher
  see Ferrante & Teicher

Teide, Teyde
  mtn., Canary Islands   TĀD-ē   'teːdiˑ

Teign
  river, England   TIN, TĒN   'tin, 'tiːn

Teignmouth
  town, England   TIN-muhth, TĒN-muhth, TIM-uhth   'tinməθ, 'tiːnməθ, 'timəθ

Teilhard de Chardin
  Pierre, *French philosopher*   tā-YAHR duh shahr-DEⁿ   teːjɑːr də ʃɑːrdẽ

Teixeira
  pers. name, Portuguese   tā-SHĀ-ruh, -rah   teːˈʃeːrə, -rɑː

Tejano
  US-Mexico border culture tā-HAHN-ō, tā-<u>KH</u>AHN-ō   teːˈhɑnoː, teːˈxɑnoː

Tejo [Tagus]
  river, Spain, Portugal   TĀ-zho͞o   'teːʒuː

Tekamah
  city, NE   tuh-KĀ-muh   tə'keːmə

Te Kanawa
  Kiri, *New Zealand soprano* tā KAHN-uh-wuh, tuh   teː 'kɑnəwə, tə

Tekoa, Tekoah
  Biblical name   ti-KŌ-uh, tuh-KŌ-ah   ti'koːə, tə'koːɑː

Tekoite
  Biblical name   ti-KŌ-ĪT   ti'koːˌɑit

Tel-abib [Tel Aviv]
  Biblical name   tel-Ā-BIB, TEL-ah-VĒV   tel'eːˌbib, ˌtelɑ'viːv

Telah
  Biblical name   TĒ-luh, TE-lah<u>kh</u>   'tiːlə, 'telɑx

Telaim
  Biblical name   tuh-LĀ-im, TEL-ā-im, tuh-lah-ĒM   tə'leːim, 'teleːim, təlɑ'iːm

Telamon
  father of Great Ajax and Teucer   TEL-uh-MAHN   'telə,mɑn

Telassar
  Biblical name   tuh-LAS-uhr, tuh-lah-SAHR   tə'læsəʳ, təlɑ'sɑr

Tel Aviv
  city, Israel   TEL uh-VĒV   ˌtel ə'viːv

Tel Aviv-Jaffa
  cities, Israel   TEL UH-VĒV-JAHF-uh, -YAHF-uh   ˌtel ə'viːv'dʒɑfə, -'jɑfə

Tel Aviv-Yafo
  cities, Israel   TEL uh-VĒV-YAH-fō   ˌtel ə'viːv'jɑfoː

Telecleia
  mother of Hecuba   TEL-uh-KLĒ-uh, TEL-uh-KLĪ-uh   ˌtelə'kliːə, ˌtelə'klɑiə

Teledyne
  US co.   TEL-uh-DĪN   'telə,dɑin

Key (col. 2):   a: fad ā: fade ah: father ar: marry aw: law e: fed ē: feed er: merry i: hid ī: hide ō: coat o͞o: boot
oi: boy   ow: now   u: put   uh: above   uhr: bird   ch: chop   ng: ring   sh: show   th: thick   <u>th</u>: this   zh: measure

Teléfonos de Mexico
  Mexican phone co. tel-Ā-fō-nōs thā MĀ-hē-kō tel'eːfoːnoːs ðeː 'meˑhiːkoː
Telegonus
  son of Odysseus and Circe tuh-LEG-uh-nuhs təˈlegənəs
Telemachus
  son of Odysseus and Penelope tuh-LEM-uh-kuhs təˈleməkəs
Telem
  Biblical name TĒ-luhm, TEL-uhm, TEL-em ˈtiːləm, ˈteləm, ˈtelem
Telemann
  Georg Philipp, *German composer* TĀ-luh-MAHN ˈteːlə͵mɑn
Telemark
  region, county, Norway TEL-uh-MAHRK ˈtelə͵mɑʳk
Telephassa
  mother of Cadmus, Europa, Cilix, TEL-uh-FAS-uh ͵teləˈfæsə
  Phoenix
Telephus
  son of Heracles TEL-uh-fuhs ˈteləfəs
Telescopium
  constellation TEL-uh-SKŌ-pē-uhm ͵teləˈskoːpiːəm
Telesphorus
  pope tuh-LES-fuh-ruhs təˈlesfərəs
Tel-harsa [Tel-harsha]
  Biblical name tel-HAHR-suh, TEL-khahr-SHAH telˈhɑʳsə, ͵telxarˈʃɑ
Tel-harsha
  Biblical name tel-HAHR-shuh, TEL-khahr-SHAH telˈhɑʳʃə, ͵telxarˈʃɑ
Teller
  Edward, *US physicist* TEL-uhr ˈteləʳ
Telluride
  city, CO TEL-(y)uh-RĪD ˈtel(j)ə͵raid
tellurium
  element tuh-LUR-ē-uhm, te-LUR-ē-uhm təˈluriːəm, teˈluriːəm
Tellus
  Roman earth goddess TEL-uhs ˈteləs
Telly
  pers. name TEL-ē ˈteliˑ
Tel-melah
  Biblical name tel-MĒ-luh, TEL-MEL-ahkh telˈmiːlə, ͵telˈmelɑx
TelPrompTer
  tdmk for a TV cueing device TEL-(uh)-PRAHM(P)-tuhr ˈtel(ə)͵prɑm(p)təʳ
Telstar
  tdmk for a communication satellite TEL-STAHR ˈtel͵stɑʳ
Telugu
  lang., people, India, Malaysia TEL-uh-GOO ˈtelə͵guː
Tem
  lang., Ghana, Benin, Togo TEM ˈtem
Tem [Atum]
  Egyptian creator god TEM ˈtem
Tema
  Biblical name TĒ-muh, tā-MAH ˈtiːmə, teːˈmɑː
Temah
  Biblical name TĒ-muh, tā-MAH ˈtiːmə, teːˈmɑː
Teman
  Biblical name TĒ-MAN, TĒ-muhn, tā-MAHN ˈtiː͵mæn, ˈtiːmən, teːˈmɑn
Temani [Temanite]
  Biblical name TĒ-muh-NĪ, TEM-uh-; TĀ-mah-NĒ ˈtiːmə͵nai, ˈtemə-; ͵teːmɑˈniː

Foreign Sounds: ue: *Fr.* **rue**, *Ger.* **füllen** uh(r): *Fr.* **boeuf**, *Ger.* **Höhle** kh: *Ger.* **ich**, *Scot.* **loch** ḡ: *Sp.* **amigo** v̱: *Sp.* **hablar**
hl: *Welsh* **Llanelli**. CAPITALS: primary stress. SMALL CAPS: secondary stress. ⑤: U.S. pron. ⑥: British pron.

Temanite
  Biblical name   TĒ-muh-NĪT, TEM-uh-   'tiːməˌnɑit, 'temə-

Temeni
  Biblical name   TĒ-muh-NĪ, TE-; TĀ-muh-NĒ   'tiːməˌnɑi, 'te-; ˌteːmə'niː

Temenus
  a Heraclid, conqueror of Argos   TEM-uh-nuhs   'temənəs

Temin
  Howard M., *US virologist (Nobel 1975)*   TEM-uhn   'temən

Temne
  people, lang., Africa   TEM-nē   'temniˑ

Te-Moak
  N. American people   TĀ-MŌ-uhk   ˌteː'moːək

Tempe
  1. city, AZ   tem-PĒ   tem'piː
  2. valley, Greece   TEM-pē   'tempiˑ

Templar
  member of a religious military order   TEM-pluhr   'templəʳ

Temuco
  city, Chile   tā-MOO-kō   teː'muːkoː

Temujin [Genghis Khan]
  Mongol leader   TEM-yuh-juhn   'temjədʒən

Tenafly
  borough, NJ   TEN-uh-FLĪ   'tenəˌflɑi

Tène, La
  see La Tène

Tenebrae
  morning services during Christian Holy Week   TEN-uh-BRĀ, TEN-uh-BRĪ, TEN-uh-BRĒ   'tenəˌbreː, 'tenəˌbrɑi, 'tenəˌbriː

Tenedos
  ancient name of Bozcaada   TEN-uh-DAHS   'tenəˌdɑs

Tenerife, Teneriffe
  largest Canary Island   TEN-uh-RĒ-fē, TEN-uh-RĒ-fā, TEN-uh-RIF, TEN-uh-RĒF   ˌtenə'riːfiˑ, ˌtenə'riːfeˑ, ˌtenə'rif, ˌtenə'riːf

Tenes
  son of Procleia   TĒ-nēz, TĒ-nēs   'tiːniːz, 'tiːniːs

Teng Hsiao-p'ing, Teng Hsiao-ping
  see Deng Xiaoping

Teniers
  David & *his son* David, *Flemish painters*   tuh-NĒRS, ⓢ TEN-yuhrz   tə'niːrs, ⓢ 'tenjəʳz

Tennant
  Victoria, *actress*   TEN-uhnt   'tenənt

Tenneco
  US corp.   TEN-uh-KŌ   'tenəˌkoː

Tennessean, Tennesseean
  pert. to Tennessee; *native of* Tennessee   TEN-uh-SĒ-uhn, TEN-uh-SĒ-uhn   ˌtenə'siːən, 'tenəˌsiːən

Tennessee
  river, state, US; pers. name (T. Williams)   TEN-uh-SĒ, TEN-uh-SĒ   ˌtenə'siː, 'tenəˌsiː

Tenney
  pers. name   TEN-ē   'teniˑ

Ten Nhat
  Vietnamese New Year   ten HAHT   ten 'hɑt

Key (col. 2): a: f**a**d ā: f**a**de ah: f**a**ther ar: m**a**rry aw: l**a**w e: f**e**d ē: f**ee**d er: m**e**rry i: h**i**d ī: h**i**de ō: c**oa**t ōō: b**oo**t
oi: b**oy** ow: n**ow** u: p**u**t uh: **a**bove uhr: b**i**rd ch: **ch**op ng: ri**ng** sh: **sh**ow th: **th**ick <u>th</u>: **th**is zh: mea**s**ure

Tenniel
Sir John, *British illustrator*   TEN-ē-uhl   'teniːəl

Tennille
Toni, *US entertainer*   tuh-NĒL   təˈniːl

Tennyson
Alfred, Lord, *English poet; pers.*   TEN-uh-suhn   'tenəsən
    name

Tennysonian
pert. to Tennyson   TEN-uh-SŌ-nē-uhn   ˌtenəˈsoːniːən

Tensas
river, AL; parish, LA   TEN-SAW   'tenˌsɔː

Tenzin
pers. name, Tibetan   TEN-zin, TEN-sin   'tenzin, 'tensin

Tenzing
pers. name, Nepalese   TEN-zing, TEN-sing   'tenziŋ, 'tensiŋ

Teobaldo
pers. name, Italian   TĀ-ō-BAHL-dō   ˌteːoːˈbɑldoː

Teodor
1. pers. name, Polish   te-AW-dawr   teˈɔːdɔːr
2. Swedish   TĀ-aw-DAWR   'teːɔːˌdɔːr

Teodoro
1. pers. name, Italian   TĀ-ō-DAWR-ō   ˌteːoːˈdɔːroː
2. Spanish   tā-ō-<u>TH</u>ŌR-ō   teːoːˈðoːroː

Teofil
pers. name, Polish   tā-AW-fēl   teːˈɔːfiːl

Teófilo
pers. name, Portuguese   tā-AW-fē-loo   teːˈɔːfiːlu

Teofilo
pers. name, Italian   tā-AW-fē-lō   teːˈɔːfiːloː

Teófilo Otoni
city, Brazil   tā-AW-fi-LOO uh-TAW-nē   teːˈɔːfiˌluː əˈtɔːniː

Teotihuacán
town, Toltec ruins, Mexico   TĀ-uh-TĒ-wah-KAHN   ˌteːəˌtiːwɑˈkɑn

Terah
Biblical name   TIR-uh, TER-ah<u>kh</u>   'tirə, 'terɑx

Teraphim
Biblical household gods   TER-uh-fim, tuh-rah-FĒM   'terəfim, tərɑˈfiːm

terbium
element   TUHR-bē-uhm   'təʳbiːəm

Ter Borch, Terborch
Gerard, *Dutch portrait painter*   tuhr BAWR<u>KH</u>   təʳ 'bɔːʳx

Terbrugghen
Hendrik, *Dutch painter*   tuhr-BROO-guhn   təʳˈbruːgən

Terceira
island, Azores   tuhr-SIR-uh, tuhr-SER-uh   təʳˈsirə, təʳˈserə

Terence
Roman playwright; pers. name   TER-uhn(t)s   'terən(t)s

Terentius
pers. name, Latin   tuh-REN-sh(ē-)uhs   təˈrenʃ(iː)əs

Teresa
1. Mother, Albanian religious (Nobel   tuh-RĒ-suh, tuh-RĀ-suh   təˈriːsə, təˈreːsə
    1979); pers. name
2. Italian   tā-REZ-ah   teːˈrezɑ
3. Spanish   tā-RĀ-sah   teːˈreːsɑ

Foreign Sounds: ue: *Fr.* **rue**, *Ger.* **füllen**   uh(r): *Fr.* **boeuf**, *Ger.* **Höhle**   <u>kh</u>: *Ger.* **ich**, *Scot.* **loch**   ḡ: *Sp.* amigo   <u>v</u>: *Sp.* hablar
hl: *Welsh* **Llanelli**.   CAPITALS: primary stress.   SMALL CAPS: secondary stress.   Ⓢ: U.S. pron.   Ⓔ: British pron.

Terese
   pers. name   tuh-RĒZ, tuh-RĀZ   təˈriːz, təˈreːz

Teresh
   Biblical name   TIR-ESH, TE-resh   ˈtirˌeʃ, ˈtereʃ

Tereshkova
   Valentina, *cosmonaut, USSR*   TUHR-(y)uhsh-KAW-vuh, TER-   ˌtər(j)əʃˈkoːvə, ˌter-

Terfel
   Bryn, *Welsh baritone*   TER-vuhl   ˈteʳvəl

Terkel
   Studs, *US writer*   TUHR-kuhl   ˈtəʳkəl

Terman
   Lewis Madisohn, *US psychologist*   TUHR-muhn   ˈtəʳmən

Terminus
   Roman god of the boundaries of   TUHR-muh-nuhs   ˈtəʳmənəs
     fields

Ternate
   island, Indonesia   tuhr-NAHT-ē   təʳˈnɑṭiˑ

Terpander
   Greek musician & poet   tuhr-PAN-duhr   təʳˈpændəʳ

Terpsichore
   1. muse of light verse & dance   tuhrp-SIK-uh-rē   təʳpˈsikəriˑ
   2. street, New Orleans   TUHRP-si-KŌR, -KAWR   ˈtəʳpsiˌkoːʳ, -ˌkɔːʳ

Terpsichorean
   pert. to Terpsichore   TUHRP-sik-uh-RĒ-uhn,   ˌtəʳpsikəˈriːən,
                        TUHRP-si-KŌR-ē-uhn,   ˌtəʳpsiˈkoːriːən,
                        TUHRP-si-KAWR-ē-uhn   ˌtəʳpsiˈkɔːriːən

Terra
   Latin for 'earth' or 'land'   TER-uh   ˈterə

Terramycin
   tdmk for oxytetracycline   TER-uh-MĪS-n   ˌterəˈmɑisn̩

Terrance
   pers. name   TER-uhns   ˈterəns

Terre Adélie [Adélie]
   region, Antarctica   ter ah-dā-LĒ   ter ɑdeːliː

Terrebonne
   parish, LA; county, town, Quebec,   TER-uh-BAHN   ˈterəˌbɑn
     Canada

Terre Haute
   city, IN   TER-uh HŌT, TER-ē, HUHT, HAWT   ˌterə ˈhoːt, ˌteriˑ, ˈhət, ˈhɔːt

Terremare
   culture, Italian Bronze Age   TER-uh-MAHR-ā   ˌterəˈmɑreː
     settlements

Terri, Terry
   pers. name   TER-ē   ˈteriˑ

Tertiary
   geologic period   TUHR-shē-ER-ē, TUHR-shuh-rē   ˈtəʳʃiːˌeriˑ, ˈtəʳʃəriˑ

Tertius
   Roman name   TUHR-sh(ē-)uhs   ˈtəʳʃ(iː)əs

Tertullian
   Latin Church Father   TUHR-TUHL-yuhn, TUHR-TUHL-ē-uhn   ˌtəʳˈtəljən, ˌtəʳˈtəliːən

Tertullianism
   teachings of Tertullian   TUHR-TUHL-ē-uh-NIZ-uhm,   ˌtəʳˈtəliːəˌnizəm, təʳˈtuːliː-
                        tuhr-TOO-lē-

Tertullus
   Biblical name   tuhr-TUHL-uhs   təʳˈtələs

Key (col. 2):   a: fad   ā: fade   ah: father   ar: marry   aw: law   e: fed   ē: feed   er: merry   i: hid   ī: hide   ō: coat   ōō: boot
oi: boy   ow: now   u: put   uh: above   uhr: bird   ch: chop   ng: ring   sh: show   th: thick   th̲: this   zh: measure

Teru
  pers. name, Japanese   ter-u   teru

Teshekpuk
  lake, AK   tuh-SHEK-PŌOK   tə'ʃek‚puːk

TESL
  Teaching English as a Second   TES-uhl   'tesəl
    Language

Tesla
  Nikola, *US inventor*   TES-luh   'teslə

Teso
  lang., people, Uganda   TĀ-sō   'teːsoː

TESOL
  Teaching English to Speakers of   TĒ-SAWL, TĒ-SAHL, TES-AWL, TES-uhl   'tiː‚sɔːl, 'tiː‚sɑl, 'tes‚ɔːl,
    Other Languages   'tesəl

Tess
  pers. name   TES   'tes

Tessa
  pers. name   TES-uh   'tesə

Tessie
  pers. name   TES-ē   'tesiˑ

Tessin [Ticino]
  canton, Switzerland   te-SE^n tesē

Tesuque
  N. American people   tuh-SŌO-kē   tə'suːkiˑ

Tet
  Vietnamese New Year   TET   'tet

Tethys
  Greek sea divinity; satellite of Saturn   TĒ-thuhs   'tiːθəs

Tetley
  Glen, *US modern dancer; tea*   TET-lē   'tetliˑ
    manufacturer

Teton
  river, MT; mtn. range, WY; county,   TĒ-TAHN, TĒT-n   'tiː‚tɑn, 'tiːtn̩
    ID, MT, WY; N. American people

Tetradenia
  plant   TE-truh-DĒ-nē-uh   ‚tetrə'diːniːə

Tetragrammaton
  the 4 letters YHWH, a Hebrew name   TE-truh-GRAM-uh-TAHN   ‚tetrə'græmə‚tɑn
    of God

Tetrazzini
  1. baked dish in cream sauce   TE-truh-ZĒ-nē   ‚tetrə'ziːniˑ
  2. Luisa, *Italian soprano*   TĀ-traht-TSĒ-nē   ‚teːtrɑt'tsiːniˑ

Tetuán
  city, Morocco   tā-TWAHN, tuh-TWAHN   teː'twɑn, tə'twɑn

Teucer
  Trojan ancestor   T(Y)ŌO-suhr   't(j)uːsəʳ

Teucher
  Swiss chocolate mfrs.   TOI-shuhr   'tɔiʃəʳ

Teutarus
  teacher of archery to Heracles   T(Y)ŌOT-uh-ruhs   't(j)uːt̬ərəs

Teuton
  early European people; a German   T(Y)ŌOT-n   't(j)uːtn̩

Teutones
  Latin name of Teutons   t(y)ōo-TŌ-nēz   t(j)uː'toːniːz

Foreign Sounds: ue: *Fr.* **rue**, *Ger.* **füllen**   uh(r): *Fr.* **boeuf**, *Ger.* **Höhle**   <u>kh</u>: *Ger.* **ich**, *Scot.* **loch**   ḡ: *Sp.* **amigo**   <u>v</u>: *Sp.* **hablar**
hl: *Welsh* **Llanelli**.   CAPITALS: primary stress.   SMALL CAPS: secondary stress.   Ⓢ: U.S. pron.   Ⓔ: British pron.

Teutonic
  pert. to Teutons; *Germanic*   t(y)o͞o-TAHN-ik   t(j)uːˈtɑnik
Tevere [Tiber]
  river, Italy   TĀ-vā-rā   ˈteːveːreː
Tevet
  see Tebet
Tevfik
  Mehmed, *Turkish poet*   tāv-FIK   teːvˈfik
Tewa
  N. American people   TĀ-wuh, TĒ-wuh   ˈteːwə, ˈtiːwə
Tewkesbury
  borough, England   T(Y)O͞OKS-b(uh-)rē,   ˈt(j)uːksb(ə)riˈ,
    Ⓢ T(Y)O͞OKS-BER-ē   Ⓢ ˈt(j)uːksˌberiˈ
Tewksbury
  town, MA   TUKS-b(uh-)rē, *by outsiders often*   ˈtuksb(ə)riˈ, *by outsiders*
    T(Y)O͞OKS-BER-ē   *often* ˈt(j)uːksˌberiˈ
Tex
  abbreviation for Texan or Texas;   TEKS   ˈteks
    pers. name
Texaco
  US oil co.   TEK-si-KŌ   ˈteksiˌkoː
Texan
  pert. to Texas; *inhabitant of* Texas   TEK-suhn   ˈteksən
Texarkana
  twin cities, AK, TX   TEK-sahr-KAN-uh, TEK-suhr-KAN-uh   ˌteksɑrˈkænə, ˌteksərˈkænə
Texas
  state, US   TEK-suhs, TEK-siz   ˈteksəs, ˈteksiz
Tex-Mex
  Texas-Mexican culture   TEK-SMEKS   ˈtekˈsmeks
Tey
  Josephine *(pseudonym of* Elizabeth   TĀ   ˈteː
    Mackintosh*), British mystery*
    writer
Teyde
  see Teide
Tezcatlipoca
  Aztec warrior god   tez-KAT-luh-PŌ-kuh   tezˈkætləˌpoːkə
Thackeray
  William Makepeace, *English*   THAK-(uh-)rē, THAK-uh-RĀ   ˈθæk(ə)riˈ, ˈθækəˌreː
    novelist
Thad
  pers. name   THAD   ˈθæd
Thaddeus, Thadeus
  pers. name   THAD-ē-uhs   ˈθædiːəs
Thadingyut
  Buddhist penitential period   tah-DING-GYO͞OT   tɑˈdiŋˌgjuːt
Thahash
  Biblical name   THĀ-HASH, TAH-<u>kh</u>ahsh   ˈθeːˌhæʃ, ˈtɑxɑʃ
Thai
  lang., people, SE Asia   TĪ   ˈtɑi
Thailand
  kingdom, Asia   TĪ-LAND, TĪ-luhnd   ˈtɑiˌlænd, ˈtɑilənd
Thaipusam
  Hindu festival   TĪ-PO͞O-juhm, TĪ-PO͞O-suhm   ˈtɑiˌpuːdʒəm, ˈtɑiˌpuːsəm

Key (col. 2): a: fad ā: fade ah: father ar: marry aw: law e: fed ē: feed er: merry i: hid ī: hide ō: coat o͞o: boot
oi: boy ow: now u: put uh: above uhr: bird ch: chop ng: ring sh: show th: thick <u>th</u>: this zh: measure

Thaïs
  1. Athenian courtesan   THĀ-uhs   'θeːəs
  2. opera, Massenet   tah-ĒS   tɑːiːs
Thalberg
  Irving, *film executive; Academy*   THAHL-BUHRG, TAHL-   'θɑl‚bəʳg, 'tɑl-
  Award for special achievement
Thales
  Greek philosopher   THĀ-LĒZ   'θeː‚liːz
Thalhimers
  US department store chain   TAWL-HĪ-muhrz   'tɔːl‚hɑiməʳz
Thalia
  1. muse of comedy; one of the Graces   thuh-LĪ-uh   θə'lɑiə
  2. street, New Orleans   THĀ-lē-uh   'θeːliːə
  3. pers. name   THĀ-lē-uh, THAL-yuh, THAHL-yuh   'θeːliːə, 'θæljə, 'θɑljə
thallium
  element   THAL-ē-uhm   'θæliːəm
Thamah
  Biblical name   THĀ-muh, TAH-mahkh   'θeːmə, 'tɑmɑx
Thamar
  Biblical name   THĀ-MAHR   'θeː‚mɑʳ
Thames
  1. rivers, England, Canada   TEMZ   'temz
  2. river, CT; street, Newport, RI   THĀMZ, TEMZ, TĀMZ   'θeːmz, 'temz, 'teːmz
  3. pers. name   THĀMZ   'θeːmz
Thamyris
  mythical Thracian musician   THAM-uh-ruhs   'θæmərəs
Thanatos
  Greek personification of death   THAN-uh-TAHS, -TŌS   'θænə‚tɑs, -‚toːs
Thanet
  Isle of, *region, England*   THAN-uht   'θænət
Thanksgiving
  November holiday, US; October   thangks-GIV-ing   θæŋks'giviŋ
  holiday, Canada
Thanom
  pers. name, Thai   tah-NAWM   tɑ'nɔːm
Thant
  U, *former UN Secretary General*   THAHNT, THANT   'θɑnt, 'θænt
Thapsus
  ancient town, Tunisia   THAP-suhs   'θæpsəs
Thar
  desert region, India, Pakistan   TAHR, TUHR   'tɑʳ, 'təʳ
Thara [Terah]
  Biblical name   THAR-uh, THER-uh   'θærə, 'θerə
Tharp
  Twyla, *US dancer, choreographer*   THAHRP   'θɑʳp
Tharshish
  Biblical name   THAHR-shish, tahr-SHĒSH   'θɑʳʃiʃ, tɑʳ'ʃiːʃ
Thásos
  island, Greece   THAH-SAWS, ⑤ THĀ-SAHS   'θɑ‚sɔːs, ⑤ 'θeː‚sɑs
Thasus
  brother of Cadmus and Europa   THĀ-suhs   'θeːsəs
Thatcher
  Margaret, *British politician*   THACH-uhr   'θætʃəʳ
Thatcherism
  policies of M. Thatcher   THACH-uh-RIZ-uhm   'θætʃə‚rizəm

Foreign Sounds: **ue:** *Fr.* **rue**, *Ger.* **füllen**   **uh(r):** *Fr.* **boeuf**, *Ger.* **Höhle**   **kh:** *Ger.* **ich**, *Scot.* **loch**   **ḡ:** *Sp.* **amigo**   **v:** *Sp.* **hablar**
hl: *Welsh* **Llanelli.**   CAPITALS: primary stress.   SMALL CAPS: secondary stress.   ⑤: U.S. pron.   Ⓔ: British pron.

Thaumas
   primordial sea divinity   THAW-muhs   'θɔːməs

Thayendanegea [Brant]
   Mohawk Indian chief   THĪ-en-DAHG-ē   ,θai-en'dɑgiˑ

Thayer
   pers. name   THER, THĀ-uhr   'θeʳ, 'θeːəʳ

Thea
   1. pers. name   THĒ-uh   'θiːə
   2. German   TĀ-ah   'teːɑ

Theaetetus
   dialogue of Plato   thē-ĒT-uht-uhs, THĒ-uh-TĒT-uhs   θiː'iːt̬ətəs, ,θiːə'tiːt̬əs

Theatines
   religious order   THĒ-uh-tuhnz, THĒ-uh-TĒNZ   'θiːətənz, 'θiːə,tiːnz

Thebaid
   epic poem, Statius   thuh-BĪ-uhd   θə'baiəd

Theban
   pert. to Thebes   THĒ-buhn   'θiːbən

Thebe
   wife of Heracles; satellite of Jupiter   THĒ-bē   'θiːbiˑ

Thebes
   ancient city, Egypt; ancient city,   THĒBZ   'θiːbz
     Greece

Thebez
   Biblical name   THĒ-BEZ, te-VETS   'θiː,bez, te'vets

Thecodontia
   reptilian order   THĒ-kuh-DAHN-chuh   ,θiːkə'dɑntʃə

Theda
   pers. name   THĀD-uh, THĒD-uh   'θeːdə, 'θiːdə

Theia
   mother of Helios, Eos, and Selene   THĒ-uh, THĪ-uh   'θiːə, 'θaiə

Theias
   father of Adonis   THĒ-uhs, THĪ-uhs   'θiːəs, 'θaiəs

Theiler
   Max, *South African-born US*   TĪ-luhr   'tailəʳ
    bacteriologist (Nobel 1951)

Themis
   Greek goddess, personification of   THĒ-muhs   'θiːməs
    justice

Thelasar [Telassar]
   Biblical name   thuh-LĀ-suhr, tuh-lah-SAHR   θə'leːsəʳ, təlaˈsɑʳ

Thelonious
   pers. name (T. Monk)   thuh-LŌ-nē-uhs   θə'loːniːəs

Themisto
   wife of Athamas   thuh-MIS-tō   θə'mistoː

Themistocles
   1. Athenian statesman; pers. name   thuh-MIS-tuh-KLĒZ   θə'mistə,kliːz
   2. Mod. Greek   the-mē-staw-KLĒS   θemiːstɔːˈkliːs

Theo
   1. pers. name   THĒ-ō   'θiːoː
   2. Dutch   TĀ-ō   'teːoː

Théobald
   pers. name, French   tā-aw-BAHLD   teːɔːbaːld

Theobald
   pers. name   THĒ-uh-BAWLD, TIB-uhld   'θiːə,bɔːld, 'tibəld

---

Key (col. 2): a: f**a**d ā: f**a**de ah: f**a**ther ar: m**a**rry aw: l**a**w e: f**e**d ē: f**ee**d er: m**e**rry i: h**i**d ī: h**i**de ō: c**o**at ōō: b**oo**t
oi: b**o**y ow: n**ow** u: p**u**t uh: **a**bove uhr: b**ir**d ch: **ch**op ng: ri**ng** sh: **sh**ow th: **th**ick <u>th</u>: **th**is zh: mea**s**ure

Theocritus
   Greek poet   thē-AHK-ruht-uhs   θiːˈɑkrətəs
Theoderic
   antipope   thē-AHD-uh-rik   θiːˈadərik
Théodor
   pers. name, French   tã-aw-DAWR   teːɔːdɔːr
Theodor
   1. pers. name   THĒ-uh-DŌR, THĒ-uh-DAWR,   ˈθiːəˌdoːʳ, ˈθiːəˌdɔːʳ, ˈθiːədəʳ
                             THĒ-uhd-uhr
   2. Danish, Dutch   TĀ-ō-DAWR   ˈteːoːˌdɔːr
   3. German   TĀ-ō-DŌR   ˈteːoːˌdoːʳ
   4. Norwegian   TĀ-ō-DŌR   ˈteːoːˌdoːr
   5. Swedish   TĀ-aw-DAWR   ˈteːɔːˌdɔːr
Theodora
   Byzantine empress; pers. name   THĒ-uh-DŌR-uh, THĒ-uh-DAWR-uh   ˌθiːəˈdoːrə, ˌθiːəˈdɔːrə
Théodore
   pers. name, French   tã-aw-DAWR   teːɔːdɔːr
Theodore
   pers. name   THĒ-uh-DŌR, THĒ-uh-DAWR,   ˈθiːəˌdoːʳ, ˈθiːəˌdɔːʳ, ˈθiːədəʳ
                             THĒ-uhd-uhr
Theodoric
   pers. name   thē-AHD-uh-rik   θiːˈadərik
Theodorus
   pers. name, Latin   THĒ-uh-DŌR-uhs, THĒ-uh-DAWR-uhs   ˌθiːəˈdoːrəs, ˌθiːəˈdɔːrəs
Theodosia
   pers. name   THĒ-uh-DŌ-shuh   ˌθiːəˈdoːʃə
Theodosius
   1. the Great, Roman emperor   THĒ-uh-DŌ-sh(ē-)uhs   ˌθiːəˈdoːʃ(iː)əs
   2. pers. name, German   TĀ-ō-DŌZ-yus, -DŌ-zē-us   ˌteːoːˈdoːzjus, -ˈdoːziːus
Theodric
   pers. name   thē-AHD-rik   θiːˈadrik
Theognis
   Greek poet   thē-AHG-nuhs   θiːˈagnəs
Theoni
   pers. name, Greek   thã-AW-nē   θeːˈɔːniː
Theopaschitism
   Christian heresy   THĒ-uh-PAS-KĪT-IZ-uhm   ˌθiːəˈpæsˌkɑiṭˌizəm
Theophane
   mother of ram with golden fleece   thē-AHF-uh-nē   θiːˈafəniˑ
Théophile
   pers. name, French   tã-aw-FĒL   teːɔːfiːl
Theophilus
   1. crater on Moon   thē-AHF-uh-luhs, tã-AHF-   θiːˈafələs, teːˈaf-
   2. pers. name   thē-AHF-uh-luhs   θiːˈafələs
   3. Danish   tē-Ō-fē-lus   tiːˈoːfiːlus
   4. German   tã-Ō-fē-lus   teːˈoːfiːlus
Théophraste
   pers. name, French   tã-aw-FRAHST   teːɔːfrɑːst
Theophrastus
   1. Greek philosopher   THĒ-uh-FRAS-tuhs   ˌθiːəˈfræstəs
   2. pers. name, German   TĀ-ō-FRAHS-tus   ˌteːoːˈfrɑstus
Theorell
   A. H. T., Swedish biochemist (Nobel   TE-u-REL, Ⓢ TĀ-uh-REL   ˌteuˈrel, Ⓢ ˌteːəˈrel
   1955)

Foreign Sounds: ue: *Fr.* **rue**, *Ger.* **füllen**   uh(r): *Fr.* **boeuf**, *Ger.* **Höhle**   <u>kh</u>: *Ger.* **ich**, *Scot.* **loch**   g̃: *Sp.* **amigo**   <u>v</u>: *Sp.* **hablar**
hl: *Welsh* **Llanelli.**   CAPITALS: **primary stress.**   SMALL CAPS: secondary stress.   Ⓢ: U.S. pron.   Ⓔ: British pron.

Theosophism
  belief in Theosophy   thē-AHS-uh-FIZ-uhm   θiːˈɑsəˌfizəm

Theosophy
  system of esoteric thought   thē-AHS-uh-fē   θiːˈɑsəfiˑ

Theotocopoulos [Greco, El]
  Doménikos, *Cretan-born Spanish*   THĀ-ō-tō-KŌ-poo-lōs   ˌθeːoːtoːˈkoːpuːloːs
  artist

Thera, Thíra [Santoríni]
  island, Greece   THIR-uh   ˈθirə

Theramenes
  Athenian politician   thi-RAM-uh-NĒZ   θiˈræməˌniːz

Theras
  descendant of Oedipus   THIR-uhs   ˈθirəs

Theravada [Hinayana]
  branch of Buddhism   THER-uh-VAHD-uh   ˌθerəˈvɑdə

Thérésa
  pers. name, French   tā-rā-ZAH   teːreːzɑː

Theresa
  pers. name   tuh-RĒ-suh, tuh-RĒ-zuh   təˈriːsə, təˈriːzə

Thérèse
  pers. name, French   tā-REZ   teːrez

Therese
  pers. name, German   tā-RĀ-zuh   teːˈreːzə

Thermidor
  month, French Revolutionary   ter-mē-DAWR   termiːdɔːr
  calendar

Thermopolis
  town, WY   thuhr-MAHP-uh-luhs   θəʳˈmɑpələs

Thermopylae
  pass, battle site, Greece   THUHR-MAHP-uh-lē   ˌθəʳˈmɑpəliˑ

Theropoda
  dinosaur suborder   thi-RAHP-uhd-uh   θiˈrɑpədə

Theroux
  Paul, *US writer*   thuh-ROO   θəˈruː

Thersander
  one of the Epigoni   thuhr-SAN-duhr   θəʳˈsændəʳ

Thersites
  ugliest and most abusive Greek at   thuhr-SĪT-ēz   θəʳˈsɑiti̧ːz
  Troy

Theseus
  mythological king of Athens   THĒ-sē-uhs, THĒ-S(Y)OOS   ˈθiːsiːəs, ˈθiːˌs(j)uːs

Thesmothetai
  Athenian magistrates   THES-mō-THĒ-TĪ   ˌθesmoːˈθiːˌtɑi

Thespiae
  ancient town, Greece   THES-pē-Ē   ˈθespiːˌiː

Thespian
  pert. to Thespiae, Thespis, *or to*   THES-pē-uhn   ˈθespiːən
  drama

Thespis
  Greek poet   THES-puhs   ˈθespəs

Thespius
  king of Boeotia   THES-pē-uhs   ˈθespiːəs

Thessalia [Thessaly]
  region, Greece   THĀ-suh-LĒ-uh   ˌθeːsəˈliːə

Key (col. 2):   a: fad ā: fade ah: father ar: marry aw: law e: fed ē: feed er: merry i: hid ī: hide ō: coat oo: boot
oi: boy   ow: now   u: put   uh: above   uhr: bird   ch: chop   ng: ring   sh: show   th: thick   th: this   zh: measure

Thessalian
  pert. to Thessaly — the-SĀ-lē-uhn — θe'seːliːən

Thessalonians
  New Testament book — THES-uh-LŌN-yuhnz, -LŌ-nē-uhnz — ˌθesə'loːnjənz, -'loːniːənz

Thessalonica
  official name of Salonika — THES-uh-luh-NĪ-kuh, THES-uh-LAHN-i-kuh — ˌθesələ'nɑikə, ˌθesə'lɑnikə

Thessaloníki
  region, Greece — THES-ah-law-NĒ-kē — ˌθesɑlɔː'niːkiˑ

Thessaly
  region, Greece — THES-uh-lē — 'θesəliˑ

Thestor
  father of Calchas, Leucippe, and Theonoe — THES-tuhr, THES-TAWR — 'θestəʳ, 'θesˌtɔːʳ

Thetes
  Athenian lowest class — THĒT-ēz — 'θiːṭiːz

Thetis
  Greek sea goddess, mother of Achilles — THĒT-uhs — 'θiːṭəs

Theudas
  Biblical name — TH(Y)O͞O-duhs — 'θ(j)uːdəs

Thibodaux
  city, LA — TIB-uh-DŌ — 'tibəˌdoː

Thiel
  College, *PA* — TĒL, THĒL — 'tiːl, 'θiːl

Thierry
  pers. name, French — tye-RĒ — tjeriː

Thiers
  Louis, *president, France; city, France* — tē-ER — tiːer

Thieu
  see Nguyen Van Thieu

Thimnathah
  Biblical name — THIM-nuh-thuh, thim-NĀ-thuh, tim-NAH-tah — 'θimnəθə, θim'neːθə, tim'nɑtɑː

Thimphu
  city, Butan — thim-PO͞O — θim'puː

Thingvellir
  plain, Iceland (site of Althing, 930-1880) — THING(G)-VET-LIR — 'θiŋ(g)ˌvetˌliʳ

Thingyan
  Burmese festival — THING-GYAHN — 'θiŋˌgjɑn

Thiokol
  tdmk for synthetic rubber products — THĪ-uh-KAWL, -KŌL — 'θɑiəˌkɔːl, -ˌkoːl

Thíra
  see Thera

Thisbe
  mythological lover of Pyramus — THIZ-bē — 'θizbiˑ

Thívai [Thebes]
  town, Greece — THĒ-vā — 'θiːveː

Tho
  lang., people, Vietnam — TŌ — 'toː

Thoas
  son of Ariadne — THŌ-uhs — 'θoːəs

Foreign Sounds: ue: *Fr.* **rue**, *Ger.* **füllen** uh(r): *Fr.* **boeuf**, *Ger.* **Höhle** kh: *Ger.* **ich**, *Scot.* **loch** ḡ: *Sp.* amigo v̱: *Sp.* hablar
hl: *Welsh* **Llanelli**. CAPITALS: primary stress. SMALL CAPS: secondary stress. ⑤: U.S. pron. ⓔ: British pron.

Thohoyandou
 capital city, Venda   tuh-HOI-AHN-dōō   tə'hɔɪˌɑnduː

Thom
 pers. name   TAHM   'tɑm

Thomas
 1. pers. name   TAHM-uhs   'tɑməs
 2. Danish   TAW-MAHS   'tɔːˌmɑːs
 3. Dutch, German   TŌ-MAHS   'toːˌmɑs
 4. French   taw-MAH   tɔmɑ
 5. Norwegian   TAWM-AHS   'tɔːmˌɑs
 6. Swedish   TŌŌ-MAHS   'tuːˌmɑːs

Thomasena, Thomasina
 pers. name   TAHM-uh-SĒ-nuh   ˌtɑmə'siːnə

Thomasin
 pers. name   TAHM-uh-suhn   'tɑməsən

Thomism
 philosophy of Thomas Aquinas   TŌ-MIZ-uhm   'toːˌmizəm

Thom McAn
 US shoe co.   TAHM muh-KAN   ˌtɑm mə'kæn

Thompson
 James Robert, *US politician*   TAHM(P)-suhn   'tɑm(p)sən

Thomson
 Sir George P., *English physicist (Nobel 1937); his father* Sir Joseph, *English physicist (Nobel 1906)*   TAHM(P)-suhn   'tɑm(p)sən

Thor
 1. Scandinavian god of thunder   THAWR   'θɔːʳ
 2. pers. name, Icelandic   THAWR   'θɔːr

Thorazine
 tdmk for a tranquilizer   THŌR-uh-ZĒN, THAWR-   'θoːrəˌziːn, 'θɔːr-

Thoreau
 Henry David, *US writer*   thuh-RŌ, thaw-RŌ, THAWR-ō   θə'roː, θɔː'roː, 'θɔːroː

thorium
 element   THŌR-ē-uhm, THAWR-ē-uhm   'θoːriːəm, 'θɔːriːəm

Thornburgh
 Dick Lewis, *US politician*   THAWRN-BUHRG   'θɔːʳnˌbəʳg

Thorndike
 Edward, *US educator*   THAWRN-DĪK   'θɔːʳnˌdɑik

Thornton
 pers. name   THAWRNT-n   'θɔːʳntn̩

Thorpe
 Jim, *US athlete*   THAWRP   'θɔːʳp

Thorshavn
 capital, Faroe Islands   tawrs-HOWN   tɔːʳs'hɑun

Thorstein
 pers. name   THAWR-STĪN   'θɔːʳˌstɑin

Thorvald
 pers. name, Danish   TUR-VAHL   'tuʳˌvɑːl

Thorvaldsen, Thorwaldsen
 Albert Bertel, *Danish sculptor*   TUR-VAHL-suhn   'tuʳˌvɑlsən

Thorvaldur
 pers. name, Icelandic   THAWR-vahl-duer   'θɔːʳvɑldyːr

Thoth
 Egyptian god of wisdom   TŌT, TŌTH, THŌTH   'toːt, 'toːθ, 'θoːθ

Key (col. 2): a: f**a**d ā: f**a**de ah: f**a**ther ar: m**a**rry aw: l**a**w e: f**e**d ē: f**ee**d er: m**e**rry i: h**i**d ī: h**i**de ō: c**oa**t ōō: b**oo**t
oi: b**oy** ow: n**ow** u: p**u**t uh: **a**bove uhr: b**i**rd ch: **ch**op ng: ri**ng** sh: **sh**ow th: **th**ick th: **th**is zh: mea**s**ure

Thothmes

    name, Egyptian pharoahs   TŌT-muhs, TAHT-muhs,   'toːtməs, 'tatməs, tə'hɑtməs
                   tuh-HUHT-muhs

Thrace

    region, Greece   THRĀS, *in ancient context* THRĀ-sē   'θreːs, *in ancient context* 'θreːsi·

Thracian

    pert. to Thrace   THRĀ-shuhn   'θreːʃən

Thraco-Phrygian

    hypothetical branch of Indo-European   THRĀ-kō-FRIJ-ē-uhn   ˌθreːkoː'fridʒiːən
      lang.

Thráki [Thrace]

    region, Greece   THRAHK-(y)ē   'θrɑk(j)i·

Thrale

    Hester L., *Welsh author*   THRĀL   'θreːl

Thrasyboulos

    Athenian general   thras-IB-uh-luhs   θræs'ibələs

Thrasymedes

    son of Nestor   thruh-SIM-uhd-ēz   θrə'simədiːz

Threefin Blenny

    Icelandic skeptic   THRĀ-fin BLED-nue   'θreːfin 'bledny ː

Thucydidean

    pert. to Thucydides   TH(Y)OO-SID-uh-DĒ-uhn   ˌθ(j)uːˌsidə'diːən

Thucydides

    Greek historian   th(y)oo-SID-uh-DĒZ   θ(j)uː'sidəˌdiːz

Thue

    Axel, *Norwegian mathematician*   TOO-uh   'tuːə

Thule

    ancient northern world; settlement,   T(Y)OO-lē, TH(Y)OO-lē, TH(Y)OOL   't(j)uːli·, 'θ(j)uːli·, 'θ(j)uːl
      Greenland; N. American Eskimo
      culture

thulium

    element   TH(Y)OO-lē-uhm   'θ(j)uːliːəm

Thummim

    Biblical name of ornaments in the   THUHM-im, too-MĒM   'θəmim, tuː'miːm
      high priest's breastplate; see Urim

Thun

    lake, commune, Switzerland   TOON   'tuːn

Thuner See

    lake, Switzerland   TOO-nuhr ZĀ   'tuːnəʳ ˌzeː

Thunor [Thor]

    Scandinavian god of thunder   THUN-AWR   'θunˌɔːʳ

Thurber

    James, *US humorist*   THUHR-buhr   'θəʳbəʳ

Thurgood

    pers. name   THUHR-GUD   'θəʳˌgud

Thurii

    Athenian colony, Italy   TH(Y)UR-ē-Ī   'θ(j)uriːˌɑi

Thüringer Wald

    Thuringian Forest   TUE-ring-uhr VAHLT   'tyːriŋəʳ ˌvɑlt

Thuringia

    former state, Germany   th(y)ur-IN-j(ē-)uh   θ(j)ur'indʒ(iː)ə

Thuringian

    Forest, *region, Germany*   th(y)u-RIN-j(ē-)uhn   θ(j)u'rindʒ(iː)ən

---

Foreign Sounds: ue: *Fr.* **rue**, *Ger.* **füllen**   uh(r): *Fr.* **boeuf**, *Ger.* **Höhle**   <u>kh</u>: *Ger.* **ich**, *Scot.* **loch**   g̱: *Sp.* **amigo** <u>v</u>: *Sp.* **hablar** hl: *Welsh* **Llanelli**.   CAPITALS: primary stress.   SMALL CAPS: secondary stress.   Ⓢ: U.S. pron.   Ⓔ: British pron.

Thurlow		
pers. name	THUHR-lō	'θə^{r}loː
Thurman		
pers. name	THUHR-muhn	'θə^{r}mən
Thurmond		
Strom, *US politician*	THUHR-muhnd	'θə^{r}mənd
Thursday		
day of the week	THUHRZ-dē, THUHRZ-dā	'θə^{r}zdiˑ, 'θə^{r}zdeː
Thurston		
pers. name	THUHR-stuhn	'θə^{r}stən
Thutmose		
Egyptian ruler	thōōt-MŌ-suh, tuh-HUT-muh-suh	θuːt'moːsə, tə'hutməsə
Thyatira		
ancient city, Asia Minor	THĪ-uh-TĪ-ruh	ˌθɑiə'tɑirə
Thyestean		
pert. to Thyestes	thī-ES-tē-uhn	θɑi'estiːən
Thyestes		
twin brother of Atreus	thī-ES-tēz	θɑi'estiːz
Thymoetes		
husband of Cilla	THĪ-muh-WĒT-ēz	ˌθɑimə'wiːt̬iːz
Thyone		
mother of Dionysus	thī-Ō-nē	θɑi'oːniˑ
Thyssen		
Fritz, *German industrialist*	TUES-uhn, [S] TĒ-suhn	'tysən, [S] 'tiːsən
Tia		
pers. name	TĒ-uh	'tiːə
Tiahuanaco		
ancient ruin, Bolivia	TĒ-uh-wuh-NAHK-ō	ˌtiːəwə'nɑkoː
Tia Juana		
city, Mexico	TĒ-uh WAHN-uh	ˌtiːə 'wɑnə
Tia Maria		
tdmk for a liqueur	TĒ-uh muh-RĒ-uh	ˌtiːə mə'riːə
Tiananmen		
Square, *public square, Beijing*	TYEN-uh(n)-MEN, tē-EN-uh(n)-muhn, tē-AHN-uh(n)-MEN	'tjenə(n)ˌmen, tiː'enə(n)mən, tiː'ɑnə(n)ˌmen
Tianjin [Tientsin]		
city, China	tē-AHN-JIN, tē-EN-JIN	tiː'ɑn'dʒin, tiː'en'dʒin
Tian Shan [Tien Shan]		
mts., Asia	tē-AHN SHAHN, tē-EN SHAHN	tiː'ɑn 'ʃɑn, tiː'en 'ʃɑn
Tiber		
river, Italy	TĪ-buhr	'tɑibə^{r}
Tiberias [Galilee]		
sea, city, Israel	tī-BIR-ē-uhs	tɑi'biriːəs
Tiberinus		
eponymous hero of the Tiber River	TĪ-buh-RĪ-nuhs	ˌtɑibə'rɑinəs
Tiberius		
1. Roman emperor; pers. name	tī-BIR-ē-uhs	tɑi'biriːəs
2. Dutch	tē-BĀ-rē-ues	tiː'beːriːys
Tibet		
region, China	tuh-BET	tə'bet
Tibetan		
pert. to Tibet	tuh-BET-n	tə'betn̩
Tibhath		
Biblical name	TIB-HATH, TIB-uhth, tiv-<u>KH</u>AHT	'tibˌhæθ, 'tibəθ, tiv'xɑt

Key (col. 2): a: fad ā: fade ah: father ar: marry aw: law e: fed ē: feed er: merry i: hid ī: hide ō: coat ōō: boot oi: boy ow: now u: put uh: above uhr: bird ch: chop ng: ring sh: show th: thick <u>th</u>: this zh: measure

Tibni
  Biblical name   TIB-NĪ, tiv-NĒ   'tibˌnɑi, tiv'niː

Tibullus
  Roman poet   tuh-BUHL-uhs   tə'bələs

Tiburon
  peninsula, city, CA   TIB-uh-RAHN   'tibəˌrɑn

Ticino [Tessin]
  canton, Switzerland   ti-CHĒ-nō   ti'tʃiːnoː

Ticonderoga
  fort, former village, NY   TĪ-KAHN-duh-RŌ-guh   ˌtɑiˌkɑndə'roːgə

Tidal
  Biblical name   TĪ-DAL, TĪD-l, tid-AHL   'tɑiˌdæl, 'tɑidl̩, tid'ɑl

Tiegs
  Cheryl, *US fashion model*   TĒGZ   'tiːgz

T'ien-Ching
  city, China   tē-EN-JING   tiː'en'dʒiŋ

Tien Shan
  mts., Asia   tē-EN SHAHN   tiː'en 'ʃɑn

Tientsin [Tianjin]
  city, China   tē-EN(T)-SIN, TIN(T)-SIN   tiː'en(t)'sin, 'tin(t)'sin

T'ien-ts'ung
  Manchu reign of emperor Abahai   tē-ENT-SUNG   tiː'ent'suŋ

Tierney
  pers. name   TIR-nē   'tiʳniˑ

Tiepolo
  Giovanni, *Italian painter*   TYEP-uh-lō   'tjepəloː

Tierra Amarilla
  village, NM   tē-ER-uh AM-uh-RIL-uh   tiːˌerə ˌæmə'rilə

Tierra del Fuego
  island territory, Argentina   tē-ER-uh del FWĀ-gō   tiː'erə del 'fweːgoː

Tietjens
  Eunice Strong, *US author*   TĒ-juhnz   'tiːdʒənz

Tieton
  river, WA   TĪ-uht-n   'tɑiətn̩

Tiffany
  US jewelry co.; pers. name   TIF-uh-nē   'tifəniˑ

Tiflis [Tbilisi]
  city, Georgia   TIF-luhs, tuh-FLĒS   'tifləs, tə'fliːs

Tigard
  city, OR   TĪ-guhrd   'tɑigəʳd

Tigellinus
  Roman politician, adviser of Nero   TIJ-uh-LĪ-nuhs   ˌtidʒə'lɑinəs

Tiglath-Pileser
  Assyrian king   TIG-LATH-pī-LĒ-zuhr   'tigˌlæθpɑi'liːzəʳ

Tigray
  see Tigre

Tigre
  river, S. America; city, Argentina   TĒ-ḡrā   'tiːɣreː

Tigre, Tigray
  lang., region, Ethiopia   ti-GRĀ   ti'greː

Tigrinya
  Semitic lang.   tuh-GRĒN-yuh   tə'griːnjə

Tigris
  river, Asia Minor   TĪ-gruhs   'tɑigrəs

Tigua
　N. American people　　TĒ-wuh, TĒG-wuh　　　　'tiːwə, 'tiːɣwə

Tijuana
　town, Baja California Norte, Mexico　　tē-HWAHN-ah, ⓢ TĒ-uh-WAHN-uh, ti-WAHN-uh　　　　tiː'hwɑnɑ, ⓢ ˌtiːə'wɑnə, ti'wɑnə

Tijuca
　mtn., Brazil; Brazilian beer　　ti-ZHOO-kuh　　　　ti'ʒuːkə

Tikvah
　Biblical name　　TIK-vuh, tik-VAH　　　　'tikvə, tik'vɑː

Tikvath [Tokhath]
　Biblical name　　TIK-VATH　　　　'tikˌvæθ

Tilburg
　city, Netherlands　　TIL-BUHRG　　　　'tilˌbəʳg

Tilden
　Bill, *US tennis player;* Samuel, *US political leader*　　TIL-duhn　　　　'tildən

Tilgath-pilneser
　Biblical name　　TIL-GATH-pil-NĒ-zuhr, til-GAHT-pil-NES-er　　　　'tilˌgæθpil'niːzəʳ, til'gɑtpil'neser

Tillamook
　county, OR; N. American people　　TIL-uh-muhk, TIL-uh-MUK　　　　'tiləmək, 'tiləˌmuk

Till Eulenspiegel
　German lengendary character　　TIL OI-luhn-SHPĒ-guhl　　　　'til 'ɔilən,ʃpiːgəl

Tillich
　Paul, *US philosopher*　　TIL-ikh, ⓢ TIL-ik　　　　'tiliç, ⓢ 'tilik

Tillinghast
　pers. name　　TIL-ing-HAST　　　　'tiliŋˌhæst

Tillis
　Melvin, *US musician, songwriter*　　TIL-uhs　　　　'tiləs

Tilon
　Biblical name　　TĪ-LAHN, tē-LŌN　　　　'taiˌlɑn, tiː'loːn

Tilsit
　cheese　　TIL-suht, TIL-zuht　　　　'tilsət, 'tilzət

Tim
　pers. name　　TIM　　　　'tim

Timaeus
　Greek astronomer; dialogue of Plato　　tī-MĒ-uhs　　　　tai'miːəs

Timaeus
　Biblical name　　tī-MĒ-uhs, tī-MĀ-uhs, tuh-MĀ-uhs　　　　tai'miːəs, tai'meːəs, tə'meːəs

Timandra
　mother of Evander　　tuh-MAN-druh　　　　tə'mændrə

Timba-Sha
　Indian reservation, US　　TIM-buh-SHAH　　　　'timbə'ʃɑ

Timbira
　S. American people　　tim-BĒ-ruh　　　　tim'biːrə

Timbuktu
　ancient city, town, Mali　　TIM-BUHK-TOO　　　　ˌtimˌbək'tuː

Times-Picayune
　newspaper, New Orleans, LA　　TĪMZ PIK-ē-YOON　　　　'taimz ˌpiki'juːn

Timex
　US watch co.　　TĪ-MEKS　　　　'taiˌmeks

Timişoara
　city, Romania　　TĒ-mish-WAHR-uh　　　　ˌtiːmiʃ'wɑrə

Timna
　Biblical name　　TIM-nuh, tim-NAH　　　　'timnə, tim'nɑː

Key (col. 2):　a: fad　ā: fade　ah: father　ar: marry　aw: law　e: fed　ē: feed　er: merry　i: hid　ī: hide　ō: coat　ōō: boot
oi: boy　ow: now　u: put　uh: above　uhr: bird　ch: chop　ng: ring　sh: show　th: thick　th: this　zh: measure

Timnah
  Biblical name   TIM-nuh, tim-NAH   'timnə, tim'nɑː

Timnath
  Biblical name   TIM-NATH, -nuhth; tim-NAHT   'tim‚næθ, -nəθ; tim'nɑt

Timnath-heres
  Biblical name   TIM-NATH-HĒ-RĒZ, TIM-nuhth-; tim-NAHT-<u>KH</u>ER-es   'tim‚næθ'hiː‚riːz, 'timnəθ-; tim'nɑt'xeres

Timnath-serah
  Biblical name   TIM-NATH-SIR-uh, TIM-nuhth-; tim-NAHT-SER-ah<u>kh</u>   'tim‚næθ'sirə, 'timnəθ-; tim'nɑt'serɑx

Timnite
  Biblical name   TIM-NĪT   'tim‚nait

Timoleon
  Greek statesman   tuh-MŌ-lē-uhn, tī-   tə'moːliːən, tɑi-

Timon
  Shakespearean character   TĪ-muhn   'tɑimən

Timor
  island, sea, Indonesia   TĒ-MAWR, tē-MAWR   'tiː‚mɔːʳ, tiː'mɔːʳ

Timor Timur
  eastern half of Timor island, Indonesia   TĒ-MAWR TĒ-MUR, tē-MAWR tē-MUR   ‚tiː‚mɔːʳ 'tiː‚muʳ, tiː‚mɔːʳ tiː'muʳ

Timoshenko
  Semyon, *Russian militarist*   tyim-uh-SHENG-kō   tjimə'ʃeŋkoː

Timothée
  pers. name, French   tē-maw-TĀ   tiːmɔːteː

Timotheus
  Biblical name   ti-MŌ-thē-uhs, TIM-uh-THĒ-uhs   ti'moːθiːəs, ‚timə'θiːəs

Timothy
  New Testament book; pers. name   TIM-uh-thē   'timəθiˑ

Timpahute
  Range, *mtn. range, NV*   TIM-puh-Y̅O̅O̅T   ‚timpə'juːt

Timpanogos, Mount
  mtn. peak, UT   MOWNT TIM-puh-NŌ-guhs   ‚mɑunt ‚timpə'noːgəs

Timucua
  N. American people   TIM-uh-K̅O̅O̅-uh   ‚timə'kuːə

Timur [Tamburlaine]
  Tartar conqueror   TIM-UR, TĒ-MUR   'tim‚uʳ, 'tiː‚muʳ

tin
  element   TIN   'tin

T'in, Tin
  lang., people, Laos, Thailand   TIN   'tin

Tina
  1. pers. name   TĒ-nuh   'tiːnə
  2. German   TĒ-nah   'tiːnɑ

Tinamou
  South American bird   TIN-uh-M̅O̅O̅   'tinə‚muː

Tinbergen
  Jan, *Dutch economist (Nobel 1969); his brother* Nikolaas, *Dutch zoologist (Nobel 1973)*   TIN-BER-ḡuh(n)   'tin‚beʳɣə(n)

Tindale, Tyndale
  William, *English New Testament translator*   TIN-dl, TIN-DĀL   'tindl̩, 'tin‚deːl

---

Foreign Sounds: ue: *Fr.* **rue**, *Ger.* füllen   uh(r): *Fr.* **boeuf**, *Ger.* Höhle   <u>kh</u>: *Ger.* **ich**, *Scot.* loch   ḡ: *Sp.* amigo   v: *Sp.* hablar hl: *Welsh* **Llanelli**.   CAPITALS: primary stress.   SMALL CAPS: secondary stress.   Ⓢ: U.S. pron.   Ⓔ: British pron.

Ting
   Samuel Chao Chung, *US physicist*   TING   'tiŋ
   (Nobel 1976)
Tinggian
   lang., people, Philippine Islands   TING-gē-AHN   ,tiŋgiː'ɑn
Tinian
   island, Pacific   TIN-ē-AN, TIN-ē-uhn   ,tiniː'æn, 'tiniːən
Tintagel Head
   cape, England   tin-TAJ-uhl HED   tin'tædʒəl 'hed
Tintern
   ruined abbey, England   TIN-tuhrn   'tintəʳn
Tintoretto
   Jacopo, *Italian painter*   TIN-tuh-RET-ō   ,tintə'reṭoː
Tioga
   river, county, NY, PA   tī-Ō-guh   tai'oːgə
Tiomkin
   Dimitri, *US composer*   TYAWM-kyin, ⑤ tē-AHM(P)-kuhn 'tjɔːmkjin, ⑤ tiː'ɑm(p)kən
Tionesta
   borough, PA   TĪ-uh-NES-tuh   ,taiə'nestə
Tiphsah
   Biblical name   TIF-suh, tif-SAH<u>KH</u>   'tifsə, tif'sɑx
Tiphys
   pilot of the Argo   TĪ-fuhs, TĒ-fuhs   'taifəs, 'tiːfəs
Tippah
   county, MS   TIP-uh   'tipə
Tippecanoe
   river, county, IN   TIP-uh-kuh-NOO   ,tipəkə'nuː
Tipperary
   prov & town, Irish Republic TIP-uh-RER-ē   ,tipə'reri·
Tippetarius
   Queen of Oz   TIP-uh-TAR-ē-uhs, TIP-uh-TER-ē-uhs ,tipə'tæriːəs, ,tipə'teriːəs
Tippett
   Sir Michael, *English composer* TIP-uht   'tipət
Tirana, Tiranë
   city, Albania   ti-RAHN-uh   ti'rɑnə
Tiras
   Biblical name   TĪ-ruhs, tē-RAHS   'tairəs, tiː'rɑs
Tirathite
   Biblical name   TĪ-ruhth-ĪT, tuh-RATH-ĪT 'tairəθ,ait, tə'ræθ,ait
Tiresias
   soothsayer at Thebes   tī-RĒ-sē-uhs, tī-RĒ-zē-uhs tai'riːsiːəs, tai'riːziːəs
Tirhakah
   Biblical name   tuhr-HĀ-kuh, TIR-(h)uh-kuh,   təʳ'heːkə, 'tir(h)əkə,
                          tir-HAH-kah   tir'hɑːkɑ
Tirhanah
   Biblical name   tuhr-HĀ-nuh, TIR-(h)uh-nuh,   təʳ'heːnə, 'tir(h)ənə,
                          tir-<u>kh</u>ah-NAH   tirxɑ'nɑː
Tiria
   Biblical name   TIR-ē-uh, TĪ-rē-uh, TĒR-yah 'tiriːə, 'tairiːə, 'tiːrjɑ
Tirol, Tyrol
   state, Austria   tuh-RŌL, TĪ-RŌL, tī-RŌL, TIR-uhl tə'roːl, 'tai,roːl, tai'roːl, 'tirəl
Tiros
   satellites   TĪ-RŌS   'tai,roːs
Tirpitz
   Alfred von, *German militarist* TIR-puhts   'tiʳpəts

Key (col. 2): a: fad ā: fade ah: father ar: marry aw: law e: fed ē: feed er: merry i: hid ī: hide ō: coat ōō: boot
oi: boy ow: now u: put uh: above uhr: bird ch: chop ng: ring sh: show th: thick th: this zh: measure

Tirshatha		
Biblical name	tir-SHAHTH-uh, tir-SHAH-tah	tir'ʃɑθə, tir'ʃɑːtɑ
Tiruray		
lang., people, Philippine Islands	TIR-uh-RĪ, TIR-uh-RĪ	'tirə,rɑi, ,tirə'rɑi
Tiryns		
ancient city, Greece	TIR-uhnz, TĪ-ruhnz	'tirənz, 'tɑirənz
Tirzah		
ancient Canaanite town	TUHR-zuh	'təʳzə
Tirzah		
Biblical name	TUHR-zuh, tirt-SAH	'təʳzə, tirt'sɑː
Tisch		
Preston, *US government official*	TISH	'tiʃ
Tiselius		
Arne, *Swedish chemist (Nobel 1948)*	tuh-SĀ-lē-uhs, tuh-ZĀ-lē-uhs	tə'seːliːəs, tə'zeːliːəs
Tish Ab B'ab		
Jewish holiday	TISH uh BAHV, BAWV	'tiʃ ə ,bɑv, ,bɔːv
Tishah Be'av		
Jewish holiday	TISH-uh buh-AHV, buh-AWV	'tiʃə bə'ɑv, bə'ɔːv
Tishbe		
Biblical name	TISH-BĒ, tish-BĒ	'tiʃ,biː, tiʃ'biː
Tishbite		
Biblical name	TISH-BĪT	'tiʃ,bɑit
Tishomingo		
county, MS	TISH-uh-MING-gō	,tiʃə'miŋgoː
Tishri		
Jewish month	TISH-rē, TISH-rā	'tiʃriˑ, 'tiʃreˑ
Tisiphone		
one of the Greek Furies	tī-SIF-uh-nē, tuh-SIF-uh-nē	tɑi'sifəniˑ, tə'sifəniˑ
Tisza		
river, Europe	TIS-AW	'tis,ɔː
Titan		
giant in Greek myth; satellite of Saturn	TĪT-n	'tɑitn̩
Titania		
fairy queen in A Midsummer Night's Dream, *Shakespeare; satellite of Uranus*	tuh-TĀN-yuh, tuh-TAHN-yuh, tī-TĀN-yuh	tə'teːnjə, tə'tɑnjə, tɑi'teːnjə
Titanic		
British ocean liner	tī-TAN-ik	tɑi'tænik
Titanides		
daughters of Uranus and Gaia	tī-TAN-uh-DĒZ	tɑi'tænə,diːz
titanium		
element	tī-TĀ-nē-uhm, tuh-, -TAN-ē-uhm	tɑi'teːniːəm, tə-, -'tæniːəm
Titanosaurus		
dinosaur	TĪ-TAN-uh-SAWR-uhs, TĪT-n-uh-SAWR-uhs	,tɑi,tænə'sɔːrəs, ,tɑitn̩ə'sɔːrəs
Tithonus		
brother of Priam	tī-THŌ-nuhs	tɑi'θoːnəs
Titian		
Italian painter; pers. name	TISH-uhn	'tiʃən
Titicaca		
lake, Peru	TIT-i-KAHK-uh, TĒT-ē-KAHK-uh	,tit̪i'kɑkə, ,tiːt̪iː'kɑkə
Titius		
Roman name	TISH-uhs	'tiʃəs

Foreign Sounds: ue: *Fr.* **rue**, *Ger.* **füllen** uh(r): *Fr.* **boeuf**, *Ger.* **Höhle** kh: *Ger.* **ich**, *Scot.* **loch** ḡ: *Sp.* amigo v̲: *Sp.* ha**b**lar hl: *Welsh* **Ll**anelli. CAPITALS: primary stress. SMALL CAPS: secondary stress. [$]: U.S. pron. [£]: British pron.

Tito

1. Josip Broz, *Yugoslav leader*   TĒ-taw, ⑤ TĒT-ō   'tiːtɔː, ⑤ 'tiːʈɔː

2. pers. name, Italian   TĒ-tō   'tiːtoː

Titograd [Podgorica]

city, Montenegro   TĒT-ō-GRAD, -GRAHD   'tiːʈɔːˌgræd, -ˌgrɑd

Tittabawassee

river, MI   TIT-uh-buh-WAHS-ē   ˌtiʈəbə'wɑsiˑ

Titus

New Testament book; Roman   TĪT-uhs   'taitəs
emperor; pers. name

Titus Andronicus

play, Shakespeare   TĪT-uhs an-DRAHN-i-kuhs   'taiʈəs æn'drɑnikəs

Tityus

son of Zeus who attacked Leto   TIT-ē-uhs   'tiʈiːəs

Tiv

lang., people, Nigeria   TIV   'tiv

Tivoli

1. town, Roman resort, Italy   TĒ-vō-lē, ⑤ TIV-uh-lē   'tiːvoːliˑ, ⑤ 'tivəliˑ

2. entertainment park, Copenhagen   TIV-uh-lē   'tivəliˑ

Tiy

Queen of Egypt   TĒ   'tiː

Tiziano

pers. name, Italian   tēts-YAHN-ō   tiːts'jɑnoː

Tizite

Biblical name   TĪ-ZĪT   'taiˌzait

Tjalling

pers. name, Dutch   TYAHL-ing   'tjɑliŋ

Tjilatjap

seaport, Indonesia   chē-LAHCH-ahp   tʃiː'lɑtʃap

Tlapanec

lang., people, Mexico   TLAHP-uh-ɴᴇᴋ, ᴛʟᴀʜᴘ-uh-ɴᴇᴋ   'tlapəˌnek, ˌtlapə'nek

Tlaxcala

state, Mexico   tlah-SKAHL-uh   tlaˈskɑlə

Tlemcen

mtn. range, town, dept, Algeria   tlem-SEN   tlemˈsen

Tlepolemus

son of Heracles   tlep-AHL-uh-muhs   tlepˈɑləməs

Tlingit

N. American people   TLING-(g)uht, TLING-kuht   'tliŋ(g)ət, 'tliŋkət

Toah

Biblical name   TŌ-uh, TŌ-ah<u>kh</u>   'toːə, 'toːɑx

Toano

Range, *mtn. range, NV*   TŌ-uh-ɴŌ   'toːəˌnoː

Tob

Biblical name   TAHB, TŌB, TŌV   'tab, 'toːb, 'toːv

Toba

lang., people, Sumatra [Batak]; lang.,   TŌ-buh   'toːbə
people, Argentina

Tob-adonijah

Biblical name   TAHB-ahd-n-Ī-uh, TŌB-;   ˌtabadn̩'aiə, ˌtoːb-;
TŌ-vah-DŌ-ni-YAH   ˌtoːvaˌdoːni'jɑː

Tobago

see Trinidad and Tobago

Key (col. 2):   a: fad   ā: fade   ah: father   ar: marry   aw: law   e: fed   ē: feed   er: merry   i: hid   ī: hide   ō: coat   ōō: boot
oi: boy   ow: now   u: put   uh: above   uhr: bird   ch: chop   ng: ring   sh: show   th: thick   <u>th</u>: this   zh: measure

Tobagonian
  pert. to Tobago; *native or inhabitant*   TŌ-buh-GŌ-nē-uhn   ,toːbəˈgoːniːən
    of Tobago

Tobiah
  Biblical name   tuh-BĪ-uh   təˈbɑiə

Tobias
  1. Old Testament book, pers. name   tuh-BĪ-uhs   təˈbɑiəs
  2. Dutch, German   tō-BĒ-ahs   toːˈbiːɑs
  3. Swedish   tu-BĒ-ahs   tuˈbiːɑːs

Tobijah
  Biblical name   tuh-BĪ-uh, TŌ-vē-YAH-hoo   təˈbɑiə, ,toːviːˈjɑːhuː

Tobin
  James, *US economist (Nobel 1981);*   TŌ-buhn   ˈtoːbən
    pers. name

Tobit
  Apocryphal book   TŌ-buht   ˈtoːbət

Toblerone
  tdmk for a candy bar   TŌ-bluh-RŌN, TAHB-luh-RŌN   ,toːbləˈroːn, ,tɑbləˈroːn

Tobruk
  prov, Libya   TŌ-BRUK, tō-BRUK   ˈtoː,bruk, toːˈbruk

Toby
  pers. name   TŌ-bē   ˈtoːbiˑ

Tocai [Tokay]
  wine   TŌ-kī   ˈtoːkɑi

Tocantins
  river, Brazil   TŌ-kuhn-TIⁿS   ,toːkənˈtʲs

Toccoa [Ocoee]
  river, city, falls, GA   tuh-KŌ-uh   təˈkoːə

Toch
  Ernst, *US composer*   TAW<u>KH</u>   ˈtɔːx

Tocharian, Tokharian
  ancient Asian people, lang.   tō-KAR-ē-uhn, tō-KER-ē-uhn,   toːˈkæriːən, toːˈkeriːən,
                              tō-KAHR-ē-uhn   toːˈkɑriːən

Tochen
  Biblical name   TŌ-kuhn, TAW-<u>kh</u>en   ˈtoːkən, ˈtɔːxen

Tocqueville, de
  Alexis, *French writer*   duh tawk-VĒL   də tɔːkviːl

Tod
  pers. name   TAHD   ˈtad

Toda
  1. lang., people, South India   TŌD-uh   ˈtoːdə
  2. Japanese construction co.   tō-dah   toːda

Todd
  Sir Alexander R., *Scottish chemist*   TAHD   ˈtad
    (Nobel 1957); pers. name

Todor
  pers. name (T. Zhivkov)   TAW-DAWR   ˈtɔː,dɔːʳ

Tody
  Caribbean bird   TŌD-ē   ˈtoːdiˑ

TOEFL
  Test of English as a Foreign   TŌ-fuhl   ˈtoːfəl
    Language

Togarmah
  Biblical name   tō-GAHR-muh, TAW-gahr-MAH   toːˈgɑʳmə, ,tɔːgɑrˈmɑː

Togo
  republic, Africa   TŌ-gō   'toːgoː

Togolese
  pert. to Togo   TŌ-guh-LĒZ, -LĒS   ˌtoːgə'liːz, -'liːs

Tōhoku
  mtn. region, Japan   tō-hō-ko͞o   toːhoːkuː

Tohono O'odham
  N. American people   tō-HŌ-nō ō-ŌD-uhm   toː'hoːnoː oː'oːdəm

Tohopekaliga
  lake, FL   tuh-HŌP-uh-KAL-uhg-uh   təˌhoːpə'kæləgə

Toi
  Biblical name   TŌ-Ī, taw-Ē   'toːˌɑi, tɔː'iː

Toiyabe
  mountain range, NV   toi-(Y)AHB-ē   tɔi'(j)ɑbiˑ

Tojolabal
  lang., people, Mexico   TŌ-kho͞-luh-BAHL   ˌtoːxoːlə'bɑl

Tokai
  Japanese bank   tō-kī   toːkɑi

Tokhath [Tikvath]
  Biblical name   TAHK-(H)ATH, tahk-HAHT   'tɑkˌ(h)æθ, tɑk'hɑt

Tokaj [Tokay]
  town, Hungary   TAW-KĪ   'tɔːˌkɑi

Tokay
  1. town, Hungary   TAW-KĪ, Ⓢ TŌ-KĪ, TŌ-KĀ, tō-KĀ   'tɔːˌkɑi, Ⓢ 'toːˌkɑi, 'toːˌkeː, toː'keː

  2. wine   tō-KĀ, TŌ-KĀ, TŌ-KĪ   toː'keː, 'toːˌkeː, 'toːˌkɑi

Tokay d'Alsace
  wine   taw-KE dahl-SAHS   tɔːke dɑːlsɑːs

Tokelau
  islands, Pacific   TŌ-kuh-LOW   'toːkəˌlɑu

Tokelauan
  pert. to Tokelau   TŌ-kuh-LOW-uhn   ˌtoːkə'lɑuən

Tokharian
  see Tocharian

Toklas
  Alice B., *US author*   TŌ-kluhs   'toːkləs

Tok Pisin [Neo-Melanesian]
  lang., Papua New Guinea   TAWK PĒ-suhn, TAHK   'tɔːk 'piːsən, 'tɑk

Tokushima
  city, Japan   tō-ko͞o-shē-mah   toːkuːʃiːmɑ

Tokyo
  city, Japan   TŌ-kē-Ō, TŌ-kyō   'toːkiːˌoː, 'toːkjoː

Tola
  Biblical name   TŌ-luh, tō-LAH   'toːlə, toː'lɑː

Tolad
  Biblical name   TŌ-LAD, tō-LAHD   'toːˌlæd, toː'lɑd

Tolaite
  Biblical name   TŌ-lā-ĪT, TŌ-lē-ĪT   'toːleːˌɑit, 'toːliːˌɑit

Toland
  John, *US author*   TAHL-uhnd   'tɑlənd

Tolbert
  William, *president of Liberia*   TŌL-buhrt, TAWL-   'toːlbəʳt, 'tɔːl-

---

Key (col. 2):   a: fad   ā: fade   ah: father   ar: marry   aw: law   e: fed   ē: feed   er: merry   i: hid   ī: hide   ō: coat   o͞o: boot
oi: boy   ow: now   u: put   uh: above   uhr: bird   ch: chop   ng: ring   sh: show   th: thick   th̲: this   zh: measure

Toledo
1. US pl. name	tuh-LĒD-ō, tuh-LĒD-uh	təˈliːdoː, təˈliːdə
2. prov & town, Spain; district,	tō-LÃ-thō, ⓢ tuh-LĒD-ō, tuh-LĒD-uh	toːˈleːðoː, ⓢ təˈliːdoː,
Belize		təˈliːdə

Tolkien
J.R.R., English writer	TAHL-KĒN, ⓢ TŌL-KĒN	ˈtɑlˌkiːn, ⓢ ˈtoːlˌkiːn

Tolland
county, town, CT	TAHL-uhnd	ˈtɑlənd

Toller
Ernst, *German expressionist*	TAW-luhr, ⓢ TAHL-uhr	ˈtoːləʳ, ⓢ ˈtɑləʳ

Tolstoy, Tolstoi
Lev (Leo), *Russian novelist*	TUHL-STOI, ⓢ TAWL-STOI, TŌL-, TAHL-	ˌtəlˈstɔi, ⓢ ˈtoːlˌstɔi, ˈtoːl-, ˈtɑl-

Toltec
N. American people	TŌL-TEK, TAHL-TEK	ˈtoːlˌtek, ˈtɑlˌtek

Toluca
city, volcano, Mexico	tuh-LOO-kuh	təˈluːkə

Tol'yatti [Stavropol]
city, Russia	tawl-YAHT-ē	tɔːlˈjaːʈiˑ

Tom
pers. name	TAHM	ˈtɑm

Toma
pers. name, Romanian	TAW-mah	ˈtoːmɑ

Tomah
city, WI	TŌ-muh	ˈtoːmə

Tomales Bay
inlet, CA	tuh-MAHL-ēz BÃ, tuh-MAHL-uhs	təˌmaliːz ˈbeː, təˌmaləs

Tomáš
pers. name, Czech	TAW-MAHSH	ˈtɔːˌmaʃ

Tomás
pers. name, Spanish	tō-MAHS	toːˈmas

Tomaso
pers. name, Italian	tō-MAHS-ō	toːˈmasoː

Tomasz
pers. name, Polish	TAW-mahsh	ˈtɔmɑːʃ

Tomaz
pers. name, Portuguese	too-MAHSH	tuːˈmɑːʃ

Tombigbee
river, MS, AL	tahm-BIG-bē	tɑmˈbigbiˑ

Tombouctou [Timbuktu]
town, Mali	tawⁿ-book-TOO	tõbuːktuː

Tombstone
city, AZ	TOOM-STŌN	ˈtuːmˌstoːn

Tomini
Gulf of, Molucca Sea	tō-MẼ-nē	toːˈmiːniˑ

Tomlin
Lily, *US actress*	TAHM-luhn	ˈtɑmlən

Tommaso
pers. name, Italian	tōm-MAHZ-ō	toːmˈmazoː

Tommy, Tommie
pers. name	TAHM-ē	ˈtamiˑ

Tomomi
pers. name, Japanese	tō-mō-mē	toːmoːmiː

Foreign Sounds: ue: *Fr.* **rue**, *Ger.* **füllen**   uh(r): *Fr.* **boeuf**, *Ger.* **Höhle**   kh: *Ger.* **ich**, *Scot.* **loch**   ğ: *Sp.* **amigo**   v: *Sp.* **hablar** hl: *Welsh* **Llanelli**.   CAPITALS: primary stress.   SMALL CAPS: secondary stress.   ⓢ: U.S. pron.   ⓔ: British pron.

Tomonaga
  Shinichiro, *Japanese physicist (Nobel*   tō-mō-nahg-ah   to:mo:nɑgɑ
    1965)
Tomoyuki
  pers. name, Japanese   tō-mō-yuk-ē   to:mo:juki:
Tomoyushi
  pers. name, Japanese   tō-mō-yush-ē   to:mo:juʃi:
Tonawanda
  town, NY   TAHN-uh-WAHN-duh   ˌtanə'wandə
Tonegawa
  Susumu, *Japanese biologist (Nobel*   tō-nā-gah-wah   to:ne:gawɑ
    1987)
Tonga
  1. island kingdom, Pacific   TAHNG-(g)uh, TAWNG-(g)uh   'tɑŋ(g)ə, 'tɔ:ŋ(g)ə
  2. lang., people, Africa   TAHNG-guh, TAWNG-guh   'tɑŋgə, 'tɔ:ŋgə
Tongan
  lang., people, Tonga   TAHNG-(g)uhn   'tɑŋ(g)ən
Tongan-Samoan
  lang., Polynesia   TAHNG-(g)uhn-suh-MŌ-uhn   'tɑŋ(g)ənsə'mo:ən
Toni
  pers. name   TŌ-nē   'to:ni·
Tonia
  pers. name   TŌN-yuh   'to:njə
Tonka
  tdmk for toys   TAWNG-kuh, TAHNG-kuh   'tɔ:ŋkə, 'tɑŋkə
Tonkawa
  N. American people   TAHNG-kuh-wuh   'tɑŋkəwə
Tonkin
  gulf, China Sea; region, Vietnam   TAHNG-kuhn, TAHN-KIN, TAHNG-KIN   'tɑŋkən, 'tan'kin, 'tɑŋ'kin
Tonle Sap
  lake, Cambodia   TAHN-lā SAHP, SAP   ˌtanle: 'sɑp, 'sæp
Tonopah
  community, NV   TŌ-nuh-PAH   'to:nəˌpɑ:
Tonowanda
  N. American people   TAHN-uh-WAHN-duh   ˌtanə'wandə
Tønsberg
  port, Norway   TUH(R)NZ-BER-yuh, Ⓢ TUHRNZ-BAR   'tœ:nzˌberj, Ⓢ 'təʳnzˌbæʳ
Tonto
  river, Mexico; Lone Ranger's   TAHN-tō   'tanto:
    companion
Tony
  1. pers. name   TŌ-nē   'to:ni·
  2. French   taw-NĒ   tɔ:ni:
Tooele
  county, UT   tu-EL-uh, tuh-WEL-uh   tu'elə, tə'welə
Toomer
  Jean, *African-American writer*   TOO-muhr   'tu:məʳ
Toowoomba
  city, Australia   tuh-WUM-buh   tə'wumbə
Topa'zio
  Portuguese beer   tō-PAHZ-yō   to:'pɑ:zjo:
Topeka
  city, KS   tuh-PĒ-kuh   tə'pi:kə
Topham
  pers. name   TAHP-uhm   'tɑpəm

Key (col. 2):   a: fad ā: fade ah: father ar: marry aw: law e: fed ē: feed er: merry i: hid ī: hide ō: coat ōō: boot
oi: boy   ow: now   u: put   uh: above   uhr: bird   ch: chop   ng: ring   sh: show   th: thick   th̲: this   zh: measure

Tophel *Biblical name*	TŌ-FEL, tō-FEL	'toːˌfel, toː'fel
Tophet *Biblical place*	TŌ-fuht, TŌ-FET	'toːfət, 'toːˌfet
Topheth *Biblical name*	TŌ-FETH, TAW-fet	'toːˌfeθ, 'tɔːfet
Toppan *Japanese printing co.*	tō-pahn	toːpɑn
Toppenish *city, WA*	TAHP-uh-nish	'tɑpəniʃ
Topsham *town, ME*	TAHP-suhm	'tɑpsəm
Tor *pers. name, Swedish*	TO͞OR	'tuːʳ
Torah *Jewish scripture & law*	TŌR-uh, TAWR-uh, TOI-ruh, taw-RAH	'toːrə, 'tɔːrə, 'tɔirə, tɔː'rɑ
Torbay *borough, England*	TAWR-BĀ	ˌtɔːʳ'beː
Torcuato *pers. name, Spanish*	tawr-KWAH-tō	tɔːr'kwɑtoː
Tordesillas *village, Spain*	tawr-thā-SĒ(L)-yahs, [$] TAWRD-uh-SĒ-(y)uhs, TAWRD-uh-SĒL-yuhs	tɔːrðeː'siː(l)jɑs, [$] ˌtɔːʳdə'siː(j)əs, ˌtɔːʳdə'siːljəs
Torii *Shinto symbol*	TŌR-ē(-Ē), TAWR-ē(-Ē)	'toːriː(ˌiː), 'tɔːriː(ˌiː)
Torino [Turin] *prov & town, Italy*	tō-RĒ-nō	toː'riːnoː
Torme Mel, *US entertainer*	tawr-MĀ	tɔːʳ'meː
Torne *river, Sweden*	TAWR-nuh	'tɔːʳnə
Tornio *port, Finland*	TAWR-nē-Ō	'tɔːʳniːˌoː
Toro *lang., Africa*	TŌR-ō, TAWR-ō	'toːroː, 'tɔːroː
Toronto *1. city, Canada* *2. city, OH*	tuh-RAHNT-ō, -uh; TRAHN(T)-ō tuh-RAHNT-ō, -uh	tə'rɑntoː, -ə; 'trɑn(t)oː tə'rɑntoː, -ə
Torosaurus *dinosaur*	TAWR-uh-SAWR-uhs	ˌtɔːrə'sɔːrəs
Toros Dağları [Taurus] *mtn. range, Turkey*	taw-RAWS DAHĞ-lah-RĒ	tɔːˌrɔːs ˌdɑɣlɑ'riː
Torquato *pers. name, Italian*	tawr-KWAH-tō	tɔːʳ'kwɑtoː
Torquay *former borough, England, now part of Torbay*	tawr-KĒ	tɔːʳ'kiː
Torquemada Juan de, *Spanish inquisitor*	tawr-kā-MAH-thah	tɔːʳkeː'mɑðɑ
Torrance *city, CA; county, NM*	TAWR-uhn(t)s, TAHR-uhn(t)s	'tɔːrən(t)s, 'tɑrən(t)s
Torremolinos *town, Spain*	tawr-rā-mō-LĒ-nōs, [$] TAWR-uh-muh-LĒ-nōs	tɔːrreːmoː'liːnoːs, [$] ˌtɔːrəmə'liːnoːs

Foreign Sounds: ue: *Fr.* **rue**, *Ger.* **füllen** uh(r): *Fr.* **boeuf**, *Ger.* **Höhle** kh: *Ger.* **ich**, *Scot.* **loch** ğ: *Sp.* **amigo** v: *Sp.* **hablar** hl: *Welsh* **Llanelli**. CAPITALS: primary stress. SMALL CAPS: secondary stress. [$]: U.S. pron. [£]: British pron.

Torrens
  lake, Australia   TAWR-uhnz, TAHR-uhnz   'tɔːrənz, 'tɑrənz
Torres
  Islands, *island group, Pacific Ocean*   TAWR-uhs Ī-luhn(d)z   'tɔːʳəs 'ɑilən(d)z
Torres-Martinez
  N. American people   TAWR-ās-mahr-TĒ-nez   ˌtɔːreːsmɑʳ'tiːnez
Torres Vedras
  town, Portugal   TAWR-uhs VĀ-druhs   ˌtɔːrəs 'veːdrəs
Torrey
  pers. name   TAWR-ē   'tɔːriˑ
Torrijos Herrera
  Omar, *Panamanian general*   tawr-RĒ-khōs er-RĀ-rah   tɔːr'riːxoːs er'reːrɑ
Torsten
  pers. name, Swedish   TAWR-stuhn   'tɔːʳstən
Tortola
  island, British Virgin Islands   tawr-TŌ-luh   tɔːʳ'toːlə
Tortolita
  mtn. range, AZ   TAWRT-l-ĒT-uh   ˌtɔːʳtl̩'iːtə
Tortoni
  dessert   tawr-TŌ-nē   tɔːʳ'toːniˑ
Tortuga
  island, Haiti   tawr-TOO-guh   tɔːʳ'tuːgə
Tory
  political party, England & Canada;   TŌR-ē, TAWR-ē   'toːriˑ, 'tɔːriˑ
  pers. name
Toscana [Tuscany]
  region, Italy   tō-SKAHN-uh, taw-SKAHN-uh   toː'skɑnə, tɔː'skɑnə
Toscanini
  Arturo, *Italian conductor*   TAHS-kuh-NĒ-nē, TAWS-   ˌtɑskə'niːniˑ, ˌtɔːs-
Toshiba
  Japanese electronics co.   tuh-SHĒ-buh   tə'ʃiːbə
Toshiki
  pers. name, Japanese   tō-shē-kē   toːʃiːkiː
Toshiro
  pers. name, Japanese   tō-shē-rō   toːʃiːroː
Toshkent [Tashkent]
  city, Uzbekistan   tuhsh-KYENT, ⑤ tahsh-KENT   təʃ'kjent, ⑤ tɑʃ'kent
Tosk
  lang., Albania   TAHSK   'tɑsk
Toto
  pop music group; dog in The Wizard   TŌT-ō   'toːʈoː
  of Oz, *F. Baum*
Totonac
  N. American people   TŌT-n-AHK   ˌtoːtn̩'ɑk
Totowa
  city, NJ   TŌT-uh-wuh   'toːʈəwə
Tottel
  Richard, *English publisher*   TAHT-l   'tɑtl̩
Tottenham
  former borough, England   TAHT-n-uhm, TAHT-nuhm   'tɑtn̩əm, 'tɑtnəm
Tou
  Biblical name   TŌ-OO, TAW-oo   'toːˌuː, 'tɔːuː
Toubkal, Jebel
  mtn., Morocco   JEB-uhl toob-KAHL   ˌdʒebəl tuːb'kɑl

Key (col. 2):   a: fad ā: fade ah: father ar: marry aw: law e: fed ē: feed er: merry i: hid ī: hide ō: coat oo: boot
oi: boy   ow: now   u: put   uh: above   uhr: bird   ch: chop   ng: ring   sh: show   th: thick   th̲: this   zh: measure

Toucouleur, Tukulör
   people, lang., Africa   TŌŌ-kuh-LUHR   ˌtuːkə'ləʳ

Toulon
   1. city, France   tōō-LAWⁿ   tuːlɔ̃
   2. city, IL   TŌŌ-LAHN   'tuːˌlɑn

Toulouse
   city, France   tu-LŌŌZ   tuluːz

Toulouse-Lautrec
   Henri de, *French painter*   tu-lōōz-lō-TREK   tuluːzloːtrek

Toungoo
   district, town, Burma   TOWNG-(G)ŌŌ   'tauŋˌ(g)uː

Touraine
   prov., France   tōō-REN   tuːren

Tour Blanche, La
   wine   lah tōōr BLAHⁿSH   lɑ tuːr blɑ̃ʃ

Tour de France
   French bicycle race   tōōr duh FRAHⁿS, Ⓢ TUR duh   tuːr də frɑ̃s, Ⓢ ˌtuʳ də 'frɑ̃s,
                        FRAHⁿS, TUR duh FRAN(T)S   ˌtuʳ də 'fræn(t)s

Tour Haut Brion, La
   wine   lah TŌŌR ō brē-AWⁿ   lɑ tuːr oː briːɔ̃

Tour Martillac, La
   wine   lah TŌŌR mahr-tē-YAHK   lɑ tuːr mɑːrtiːjɑːk

Tournai
   district, Belgium   tur-NĀ   tuʳneː

Tourneau
   jewelers   tur-NŌ   tuʳnoː

Tourneur
   Cyril, *English dramatist*   TUHR-nuhr   'təʳnəʳ

Touro
   College, *NY*   TUR-ō   'turoː

Tours
   city, France   TŌŌR   tuːr

Tours-sur-Marne
   town, France   TŌŌR-suer-MAHRN   tuːrsyːrmɑːrn

Toushi
   fermented black beans   TŌŌ-shē   'tuːʃiˑ

Toussaint
   pers. name, French   tōō-SEⁿ   tuːsɛ̃

Toussaint L'Ouverture
   François, *Haitian political leader*   tōō-seⁿ lōō-ver-TUER   tuːsɛ̃ luːvertyːr

Toutle
   river, WA   TŌŌT-l   'tuːtl̩

Tower Hamlets
   borough, England   TOW(-uh)r HAM-luhts   'tau(ə)ʳ 'hæmləts

Towhee
   songbird   TŌ-HĒ, TŌ-ē, tō-HĒ   'toːˌhiː, 'toːiː, toː'hiː

Townes
   Charles Hard, *US physicist (Nobel*   TOWNZ   'taunz
   1964)

Townsend
   Francis E., *US physician*   TOWN-zuhnd   'taunzənd

Townshend
   family of British politicians; Peter,   TOWN-ZEND, TOWN-zuhnd   'taunˌzend, 'taunzənd
   British rock musician

Foreign Sounds: ue: *Fr.* **rue**, *Ger.* f**ü**llen uh(r): *Fr.* b**oeu**f, *Ger.* H**öh**le k̲h̲: *Ger.* i**ch**, *Scot.* lo**ch** g̱: *Sp.* ami**g**o v̱: *Sp.* ha**b**lar
hl: *Welsh* **Ll**anelli. CAPITALS: primary stress. SMALL CAPS: secondary stress. Ⓢ: U.S. pron. Ⓔ: British pron.

Towong
  Australia   tuh-WAHNG, tuh-WAWNG   təˈwaŋ, təˈwɔːŋ
Towson
  town, MD   TOWS-n   ˈtɑusn̩
Towy
  see Tywi
Toya, Toyah
  pers. name   TOI-uh   ˈtɔiə
Toynbee
  Arnold, *British historian*   TOIN-bē   ˈtɔinbiˑ
Toyota
  Japanese car co.   toi-ŌT-uh   tɔiˈoːt̺ə
Toys "R" Us
  US toy co.   TOI-ZAHR-UHS, TOI-zuh-RUHS   ˌtɔiˌzɑrˈəs, ˌtɔizəˈrəs
Trâblous, Tarabulus [Tripoli]
  city, Lebanon   tuh-RAHB-uh-luhs   təˈrɑbələs
Trabzon [Trebizond]
  province, city, Turkey   trahb-ZAWN   trɑbˈzɔːn
Tracey
  pers. name   TRĀ-sē   ˈtreːsiˑ
Trachodon
  dinosaur   trak-uh-DAHN, TRĀ-kuh-DAHN   trækəˌdɑn, ˈtreːkəˌdɑn
Trachonitis
  Biblical name   TRAK-uh-NĪT-is   ˌtrækəˌnɑit̺is
Tractarian
  supporter of Tractarianism   trak-TAR-ē-uhn   trækˈtæriːən
Tractarianism
  Oxford Movement toward   trak-TAR-ē-uh-NIZ-uhm   trækˈtæriːəˌnizəm
    Anglo-Catholicism
Tracy
  US pl. name; pers. name   TRĀ-sē   ˈtreːsiˑ
Trafalgar
  Square, *London, England*   truh-FAL-guhr   trəˈfælgəʳ
Trafalgar, Cabo
  cape, Spain   KAHV̲-ō trah-fahl-ḠAHR   ˈkaβoː trafalˈɣar
Traherne
  Thomas, *English author*   truh-HUHRN   trəˈhəʳn
Traill's flycatcher
  bird   TRĀLZ   ˈtreːlz
Train à Grand Vitesse
  high-speed French train   TREN ah GRAHⁿ vē-TES   trēn ɑː grɑ̃ viːtes
Trajan
  Roman emperor   TRĀ-juhn   ˈtreːdʒən
Trakehner
  wine   truh-KĀ-nuhr   trəˈkeːnəʳ
Tralee
  seaport, Ireland   truh-LĒ   trəˈliː
Tralles
  ancient city, Lydia, now Aydın,   TRAHL-ēz   ˈtraliːz
    Turkey
Traminer
  wine   TRAM-uh-nuhr, TRAHM-uh-nuhr,   ˈtræmənəʳ, ˈtramənəʳ,
                                           truh-MĒ-nuhr   trəˈmiːnəʳ
Tramore
  town, Ireland   truh-MAWR   trəˈmɔːʳ

Key (col. 2): a: fad ā: fade ah: father ar: marry aw: law e: fed ē: feed er: merry i: hid ī: hide ō: coat ōō: boot
oi: boy ow: now u: put uh: above uhr: bird ch: chop ng: ring sh: show th: thick t̲h̲: this zh: measure

Tranquillitatis, Mare
  see Mare Tranquillitatis

Transcaucasia

region, Caucasus Mts.	TRAN(T)S-kaw-KĀ-zh(ē-)uh, TRANZ-	ˌtræn(t)skɔːˈkeːʒ(iː)ə, ˌtrænz-

Transcendentalism

philosophical movement	TRAN-SEN-DENT-l-iz-uhm, TRAN-suhn-	ˌtrænˌsenˈdentl̩izəm, ˌtrænsən-

Transjordan

part of kingdom of Jordan	tranz-JAWRD-n, tran(t)s-	trænzˈdʒɔːʳdn̩, træn(t)s-

Transkei

independent territory, South Africa	tran(t)-SKĪ, -SKĀ; tranz-KĪ, -KĀ	træn(t)ˈskɑi, -ˈskeː; trænzˈkɑi, -ˈkeː

Trans-Siberian

across Siberia, Russia, esp. the railroad	tran(z)-sī-BIR-ē-uhn	træn(z)sɑiˈbiriːən

Transvaal

prov, South Africa	tran(t)s-VAHL, tranz-VAHL	træn(t)sˈvɑl, trænzˈvɑl

Transylvania

prov, Romania; county, NC	TRAN-suhl-VĀ-nē-uh, TRAN-suhl-VĀN-yuh	ˌtrænsəlˈveːniːə, ˌtrænsəlˈveːnjə

Trapani

prov, port, Sicily	TRAHP-uh-nē	ˈtrɑpəniˑ

Trapier

pers. name	truh-PIR	trəˈpiʳ

Trappist

religious order	TRAP-uhst	ˈtræpəst

Trasimene

lake, central Italy	TRAS-uh-MĒN	ˈtræsəˌmiːn

Trasimeno [Trasimene]

lake, central Italy	TRAHZ-i-MĀ-nō	ˌtrɑziˈmeːnoː

Traubel

Helen, *US soprano*	TROW-buhl	ˈtrɑubəl

Traugott

1. pers. name	TROW-guht	ˈtrɑugət
2. German	TROW-GAWT	ˈtrɑuˌgɔːt

Traun

river, Austria	TROWN	ˈtrɑun

Traun See

lake, Austria	TROWN ZĀ	ˈtrɑun ˌzeː

Travancore

former state, India	TRAV-uhn-KAWR, TRAV-uhn-KAWR	ˌtrævənˈkɔːʳ, ˈtrævənˌkɔːʳ

Travelodge

tdmk for a US hotel/motel chain	TRAV-uh-LAHJ	ˈtrævəˌlɑdʒ

Traverse

county, MN; lake, SD, MI	TRAV-uhrs	ˈtrævəʳs

Traviata, La

opera, Verdi	lah TRAHV-ē-AHT-uh	lɑ ˌtraviːˈɑt̬ə

Travis

pers. name	TRAV-uhs	ˈtrævəs

Travolta

John, *US actor*	truh-VŌL-tuh	trəˈvoːltə

Treat

pers. name	TRĒT	ˈtriːt

Trebbiano

Italian wine	treb-YAHN-ō	trebˈjɑnoː

Foreign Sounds: ue: *Fr.* **rue**, *Ger.* **füllen**   uh(r): *Fr.* **boeuf**, *Ger.* **Höhle**   <u>kh</u>: *Ger.* **ich**, *Scot.* **loch**   ḡ: *Sp.* **amigo**   v̱: *Sp.* **hablar**
hl: *Welsh* **Llanelli.**   CAPITALS: primary stress.   SMALL CAPS: secondary stress.   Ⓢ: U.S. pron.   Ⓔ: British pron.

Trebizond
  province, city, Turkey; Greek empire TREB-uh-ZAHND   'trebə‚zɑnd
Treblinka
  Nazi concentration camp, Poland truh-BLING-kuh   trə'bliŋkə
Trefethen
  winery, CA truh-FETH-uhn   trə'feθən
Trego
  county, KA TRĒ-gō   'triːgoː
Treitschke
  Heinrich von, German historian TRĪCH-kuh   'traitʃkə
Trelawney
  pers. name tri-LAW-nē   tri'lɔːniˑ
Trematoda
  class of flatworms truh-MAT-uhd-uh   trə'mæt̪ədə
Tremayne
  pers. name truh-MĀN   trə'meːn
Tremiti Islands
  prov. & islands, Italy TRĀ-muht-ē, TREM-uht-ē   'treːmət̪iˑ, 'tremət̪iˑ
Tremonton
  city, UT TRĒ-MAHNT-n   'triː‚mɑntn̩
Trempealeau
  river, county, WI TREM-puh-LŌ   'trempə‚loː
Trengganu
  river, state, Malaysia treng-GAHN-o͞o   treŋ'gɑnuː
Trent
  river, NC, Canada, England; city, Italy TRENT   'trent
Trenton
  city, NJ TRENT-n   'trentn̩
Tres Equis (XXX)
  Mexican beer trās Ā-kēs   treːs 'eːkiːs
Treutlen
  county, GA TRO͞OT-luhn   'truːtlən
Trevelyan
  George, British historian; pers. name tri-VIL-yuhn, truh-VEL-yuhn   tri'viljən, trə'veljən
Trèves
  French name for Trier TREV   trev
Treves
  English name for Trier TRĒVZ   'triːvz
Trevi, Fontana di
  fountain, Rome, Italy fōn-TAHN-uh dē TRĀ-vē   foːn'tɑnə diː 'treːviˑ
Trevino
  Lee, US golfer truh-VĒ-nō   trə'viːnoː
Trevithick
  Richard, English engineer TREV-uh-thik   'trevəθik
Trevor
  pers. name TREV-uhr   'trevəʳ
Triangulum
  constellation trī-ANG-gyuh-luhm   trɑi'æŋgjələm
Triangulum Australe
  constellation trī-ANG-gyuh-luhm aw-STRĀ-lē, ahs-TRĀ-lē   trɑi'æŋgjələm ɔː'streːliˑ, ɑs'treːliˑ
Triassic
  geologic period trī-AS-ik   trɑi'æsik

Key (col. 2): a: fad ā: fade ah: father ar: marry aw: law e: fed ē: feed er: merry i: hid ī: hide ō: coat o͞o: boot
oi: boy ow: now u: put uh: above uhr: bird ch: chop ng: ring sh: show th: thick th̲: this zh: measure

Tribeca, TriBeCa
    neighborhood, Manhattan, New York City   trī-BĒ-kuh   trɑɪˈbiːkə

Triceratops
    dinosaur   trī-SER-uh-TAHPS   trɑɪˈserə‚tɑps

Tricia
    pers. name   TRISH-uh   ˈtriʃə

Tridentine
    pert. to city of Trent; pert. to Council of Trent   trī-DEN-TĪN, -TĒN, -tuhn   trɑɪˈden‚tɑin, -‚tiːn, -tən

Trier
    city, Germany   TRIR   ˈtriʳ

Trieste
    prov & town, Italy   trē-EST, trē-ES-tē   triːˈest, triːˈestiˑ

Trigère
    Pauline, *US fashion designer*   tri-ZHER   triˈʒeʳ

Trigonella
    herb   TRIG-uh-NEL-uh   ‚trigəˈnelə

Trilby
    novel, G. Du Maurier; hat   TRIL-bē   ˈtrilbiˑ

Trilling
    Lionel, *US critic*   TRIL-ing   ˈtriliŋ

Trillo
    Manny, *Venezuelan baseball player*   TRĒ-(y)ō, TRĒL-yō   ˈtriː(j)oː, ˈtriːljoː

Trimurti
    Hindu trinity   tri-MURT-ē   triˈmuʳtiˑ

Trina
    pers. name   TRĒ-nuh   ˈtriːnə

Trinacria
    ancient name for Sicily   tri-NAK-rē-uh, trī-NAK-rē-uh   triˈnækriːə, trɑɪˈnækriːə

Trincomalee
    city, Sri Lanka   TRING-kō-muh-LĒ   ‚triŋkoːməˈliː

Trinidad and Tobago
    islands, West Indies   TRIN-uh-DAD uhn(d) tuh-BĀ-gō   ˈtrinə‚dæd ən(d) təˈbeːgoː

Trinidadian
    pert. to Trinidad   TRIN-uh-DĀD-ē-uhn, -DAD-ē-uhn   ‚trinəˈdeːdiːən, -ˈdædiːən

Trinity
    Christian godhead   TRIN-uht-ē   ˈtrinəʈiˑ

Triple sec
    liqueur   TRIP-uhl SEK   ˈtripəl ‚sek

Tripoli
    city, Lebanon; city, Libya; region, Africa   TRIP-uh-lē   ˈtripaliˑ

Tripolis
    Phoenician colony, Africa   TRIP-uh-luhs   ˈtripələs

Tripolitania [Tripoli]
    region, Africa   trip-AHL-uh-TĀN-yuh, TRIP-uh-luh-TĀN-yuh, -TĀ-nē-uh   trip‚ɑləˈteːnjə, ‚tripələˈteːnjə, -ˈteːniːə

Triptolemus
    Eleusian hero favored by Demeter   trip-TAHL-uh-muhs   tripˈtɑləməs

Tripura
    state, India   TRIP-uh-ruh   ˈtripərə

Trish
    pers. name   TRISH   ˈtriʃ

Foreign Sounds: **ue:** *Fr.* **rue**, *Ger.* **füllen**   **uh(r):** *Fr.* **boeuf**, *Ger.* **Höhle**   <u>kh</u>: *Ger.* i<u>ch</u>, *Scot.* lo<u>ch</u>   **ḡ:** *Sp.* ami**g**o   v: *Sp.* ha**b**lar
hl: *Welsh* **Ll**anelli.   CAPITALS: primary stress.   SMALL CAPS: secondary stress.   Ⓢ: U.S. pron.   Ⓔ: British pron.

Tristán
   pers. name, Spanish   trē-STAHN   triː'stɑn

Tristan
   1. pers. name   TRIS-tuhn, TRIS-TAHN, TRIS-TAN   'tristən, 'tris,tɑn, 'tris,tæn
   2. French   tre-STE^n   triːstē
   3. Romanian   tre-STAHN   triː'stɑn

Tristan da Cunha
   island, Atlantic   TRIS-tuhn duh KOO-nuh   ,tristən də 'kuːnə

Tristão
   pers. name, Portuguese   trēsh-TOW^n, trēs-   triːʃ'taū, triːs-

Tristram
   pers. name   TRIS-truhm, TRIS-tuhm   'tristrəm, 'tristəm

Triton
   Greek sea god; satellite of Neptune;   TRĪT-n   'trɑitn̩
     College, IL

Triumvirate
   ancient Roman ruling board of three   trī-UHM-vuhr-uht, -vuh-RĀT   trɑi'əmvərət, -və,reːt
    men

Trivandrum
   city, India   truh-VAN-druhm   trə'vændrəm

Trixie
   pers. name   TRIK-sē   'triksi·

Trnava
   town, Slovakia   TUHR-nuh-vuh   'təʳnəvə

Troad
   region around ancient Troy   TRŌ-AD   'troː,æd

Troas
   region around ancient Troy   TRŌ-AS   'trōː,æs

Trobriand
   Islands, *New Guinea*   TRŌ-brē-AND   'troːbriː,ænd

Trobriander
   a person from the Trobriand Islands   TRŌ-brē-AN-duhr   'troːbriː,ændəʳ

Trocaire
   College, *NY*   trō-KAR, trō-KER   .roː'kæʳ, troː'keʳ

Trochilus
   son of Io   TRŌ-kuh-luhs   'troːkələs

Troezen
   ancient town, Greece   TRĒ-zuhn   'triːzən

Trofim
   pers. name, Russian   TRUHF-YĒM   ,trəf'jiːm

Trogon
   bird   TRŌ-GAHN   'troː,gɑn

Trogyllium
   Biblical name   trō-JIL-ē-uhm, trō-GIL-   troː'dʒiliːəm, troː'gil-

Troilus
   Trojan hero & lover   TROI-luhs   'trɔiləs

Trois Gymnopédie
   piano pieces, E. Satie   T(R)WAH ZHIM-nō-pā-DĒ   ,t(r)wɑ ,ʒimnoːpeː'diː

Trois-Rivières
   Canada   TRWAH-rēv-YER   ,trwɑriːv'jer

Trojan
   inhabitant of Troy; *tdmk for condoms* TRŌ-juhn   'troːdʒən

Trollope
   Anthony, *British writer*   TRAHL-uhp   'trɑləp

Key (col. 2): a: fad ā: fade ah: father ar: marry aw: law e: fed ē: feed er: merry i: hid ī: hide ō: coat ōō: boot
oi: boy ow: now u: put uh: above uhr: bird ch: chop ng: ring sh: show th: thick <u>th</u>: this zh: measure

Troms
county, Norway   TRUM(P)S   'trum(p)s

Tromsø
seaport, Norway   TRUM-SUH(R), Ⓢ TRAHM-SŌ   'trum‚sœ:, Ⓢ 'trɑm‚soː

Trondheim
city, Norway   TRUN-HĬM, Ⓢ TRAHN-HĀM   'trun‚hɑim, Ⓢ 'trɑn‚heːm

Trophimus
Biblical name   TRAHF-uh-muhs   'trɑfəməs

Trophonius
legendary Greek architect   truh-FŌ-nē-uhs, truh-FŌN-yuhs   trə'foːniːəs, trə'foːnjəs

Tros
Trojan hero; father of Ilus   TRŌS   'troːs

Trossachs
valley, Scotland   TRAHS-uhks, TRAHS-AKS   'trɑsəks, 'trɑs‚æks

Trotsky
Leon, Russian revolutionary   TRAWTS-kyi, Ⓢ TRAHT-skē, TRAWT-skē   'trɔːtskjij, Ⓢ 'trɑtski·, 'trɔːtski·

Trotskyite
pert. to or supporter of Trotsky   TRAHT-skē-ĪT   'trɑtskiː‚ɑit

Troupial
South American songbird   TRŌŌ-pē-uhl   'truːpiːəl

Trousdale
county, TN   TRŌŌZ-DĀL   'truːz‚deːl

Trouville
port, France   troo-VĒL   truːviːl

Troy
ancient city, Asia Minor; pl nam   US   TROI   'trɔi

Troyes
city, France   TRWAH, Ⓢ truh-WAH   trwɑː, Ⓢ trə'wɑ

Trucial Oman
former name of United Arab Emirates   TRŌŌ-shuhl ō-MAHN   ‚truːʃəl oː'mɑn

Trucial States
former name of United Arab Emirates   TRŌŌ-shuhl STĀTS   ‚truːʃəl 'steːts

Truckee
river, NV   TRUHK-ē   'trəki·

Trudeau
Garry, US cartoonist; Pierre, Canadian politician   troo-DŌ   truː'doː

Truett McConnell
College, GA   TRU-uht muh-KAHN-l   'truət mə'kɑnḷ

Truffaut
François, French film director   true-FŌ, Ⓢ troo-FŌ   tryːfoː, Ⓢ truˑ'foː

Trujillo
1. city, Peru; city, state, Venezuela   troo-KHĒ(L)-yō, Ⓢ troo-HĒ-(y)ō   truː'çiː(l)joː, Ⓢ truˑ'hiː(j)oː
2. see Ciudad Trujillo

Trujillo Molina
Rafael L., Dominican political leader   troo-KHĒ(L)-yō mō-LĒ-nah, Ⓢ troo-HĒ-(y)ō   truˑ'çiː(l)joː moː'liːnɑ, Ⓢ truˑ'hiː(j)oː

Truk
Islands, Pacific   TRUHK, TRUK   'trək, 'truk

Trukese
lang., Polynesia   tru-KĒZ, troo-KĒZ, -KĒS   tru'kiːz, truː'kiːz, -'kiːs

---

Foreign Sounds: ue: *Fr.* **rue**, *Ger.* **füllen** uh(r): *Fr.* **boeuf**, *Ger.* **Höhle** kh: *Ger.* **ich**, *Scot.* **loch** ğ: *Sp.* **amigo** v: *Sp.* **hablar**
hl: *Welsh* **Llanelli**. CAPITALS: primary stress. SMALL CAPS: secondary stress. Ⓢ: U.S. pron. Ⓔ: British pron.

Truman
   Harry S., *33rd US president; pers.*   TR$\overline{OO}$-muhn   'truːmən
    name

Trumbull
   pers. name   TRUHM-buhl   'trʌmbəl

Trümmelbach
   waterfall, Switzerland   TRUEM-uhl-BAH<u>KH</u>   'tryməl,bɑx

Trung-Thu
   Vietnamese festival   TRUNG-T$\overline{OO}$ 'truŋ'tuː

Truong
   pers. name, Vietnamese   TR$\overline{OO}$-awng   'truːɔːŋ

Truro
   town, Nova Scotia; town, MA; city,   TRUR-$\overline{o}$ 'truroː
    England

Truva [Troy]
   city, Turkey; brandy   TR$\overline{OO}$-vuh   'truːvə

Tryggve, Trygve
   pers. name, Norwegian   TRUEG-vuh, ⑤ TRIG-v$\bar{e}$ 'trygvə, ⑤ 'trigvi·

Tryon
   Thomas, *US author; village, NE*   TR$\overline{I}$-uhn   'traiən

Tryphaena, Tryphena
   Biblical name   tr$\overline{i}$-F$\bar{E}$-nuh   trai'fiːnə

Tryphosa
   Biblical name   tr$\overline{i}$-F$\bar{O}$-suh   trai'foːsə

Tsaiwa
   lang., China   CH$\overline{I}$-WAH   'tʃai'wɑ

Tsala Apopka
   lake, FL   (tuh-)SAL-uh uh-PAHP-kuh (tə)'sælə ə'pɑpkə

Tsana [Tana]
   lake, Ethiopia; river, Kenya   (T)SAHN-uh   '(t)sanə

Tsao Chun
   Chinese festival   CHOW J$\overline{OO}$N   'tʃau 'dʒuːn

Tsavo
   river, Africa   (T)SAHV-$\overline{o}$ '(t)savoː

Tschaikovsky
   see Tchaikovsky

Tsezar
   pers. name, Russian   TSEZ-uhr   'tsezər

Tshiluba
   African trade lang.   chi-L$\overline{OO}$-buh   tʃi'luːbə

Tshombe
   Moise K., *African political leader*   CHAWM-b$\bar{a}$ 'tʃɔːmbe·

Tsimshatsui
   business section, Kowloon, Hong   (T)SIM-SHAHT-S$\overline{OO}$-$\bar{e}$ '(t)sim'ʃat'su·i·
    Kong

Tsimshian
   N. American people   CHIM-sh$\bar{e}$-uhn, TSIM-sh$\bar{e}$-uhn 'tʃimʃiːən, 'tsimʃiːən

Tsinan
   see Jinan

Tsing Hai, Ching Hai
   lake, China   CHING H$\overline{I}$ 'tʃiŋ 'hai

Tsinghai
   see Qinghai

Tsingtao
   see Qingdao

Key (col. 2): a: fad $\bar{a}$: fade ah: father ar: marry aw: law e: fed $\bar{e}$: feed er: merry i: hid $\bar{i}$: hide $\bar{o}$: coat $\overline{oo}$: boot
oi: boy ow: now u: put uh: above uhr: bird ch: chop ng: ring sh: show th: thick <u>th</u>: this zh: measure

Tsing Tao, Tsingtao
  Chinese beer   CHING DOW   'tʃiŋ 'dɑu
Tsinling Shan
  mtn. range, China   CHIN-LING SHAHN   'tʃin'liŋ 'ʃɑn
Tsitsihar
  see Qiqihar
Tso-lin
  see Zhang Zuolin
Tsonga
  lang., Africa   (T)SAWNG-guh   '(t)sɔːŋgə
Tsongas
  Paul, US politician   SAWNG-guhs, SAHNG-guhs   'sɔːŋgəs, 'sɑŋgəs
Tsugaru
  strait, Japan   (t)su-gahr-o͞o   (t)sugɑruː
Tsui Fai
  pers. name, Chinese   (T)SUĒ FĪ   '(t)suiˑ 'fɑi
Tsuneo
  pers. name, Japanese   (t)sun-e-ō   (t)suneoː
Tsuruga
  port, Japan   (t)so͞o-ro͞o-gah   (t)suːruːgɑ
Tsushima
  island, Japan   (t)so͞o-shē-mah   (t)suːʃiːmɑ
Tsuyoshi
  pers. name, Japanese   (t)su-yō-shē   (t)sujoːʃiː
Tsvetayeva, Tsvetaeva
  Marina Ivanovna, Russian poet tsfi-TAH-yuh-vuh   tsfi'tɑːjəvə
Tswa
  lang., people, Africa   TSWAH, SWAH, CHWAH, chuh-WAH   'tswɑ, 'swɑ, 'tʃwɑ, tʃə'wɑ
Tswana
  people, lang., Africa   (T)SWAHN-uh, CHWAHN-uh,   '(t)swɑnə, 'tʃwɑnə, tʃə'wɑnə
                                   chuh-WAHN-uh
Tuamotu
  islands, Pacific; kingfisher   TO͞O-uh-MŌ-to͞o   ˌtuːə'moːtuː
Tuan Wu
  Chinese festival   TWAHN WO͞O   'twɑn 'wuː
Tuapse
  port, Russia   tu-AHP-SĀ   tuˌɑp'seː
Tuareg [Tamashek]
  lang., N Africa   TWAHR-EG   'twɑrˌeg
Tuatha Dé Danann
  Irish gods   TO͞O-uh-huh DĀ DAHN-ahn,   'tuːəhə 'deː 'dɑnɑn, 'tuːəθə
                                   TO͞O-uh-thuh
Tubal
  Biblical name   T(Y)O͞O-buhl, to͞o-VAHL   't(j)uːbəl, tuː'vɑl
Tubal-cain
  Biblical name   T(Y)O͞O-buhl-KĀN, TO͞O-vahl-KAH-yin 't(j)uːbəlˌkeːn, 'tuːvɑl'kɑjin
Tübingen
  city, Germany   TUE-bing-uhn, Ⓢ T(Y)O͞O-bing-uhn   'tyːbiŋən, Ⓢ 't(j)uːbiŋən
Tubman
  Harriet, African-American   TUHB-muhn   'təbmən
    abolitionist
Tubruq [Tobruk]
  prov, Libya   tu-BRO͞OK   tu'bruːk

Foreign Sounds: **ue:** *Fr.* **rue,** *Ger.* **füllen uh(r):** *Fr.* **boeuf,** *Ger.* **Höhle   kh:** *Ger.* **ich,** *Scot.* **loch   g̃:** *Sp.* **amigo   v̰:** *Sp.* **hablar
hl:** *Welsh* **Llanelli.   CAPITALS: primary stress.   SMALL CAPS: secondary stress.   Ⓢ: U.S. pron.   Ⓔ: British pron.**

Tubulidentata
   aardvarks   T(Y)O͞O-byuh-luh-den-TAHT-uh,   ˌt(j)uːbjələdenˈtaʈə, -ˈteːʈə
                          -TĀT-uh

Tucana
   constellation   to͞o-KĀ-nuh, tu-KAN-uh   tuːˈkeːnə, tuˈkænə

Tucher
   German beer   TO͞O-k͟huhr   ˈtuːxəʳ

Tuchmann
   Barbara, *US historian, writer*   TUHK-muhn   ˈtəkmən

Tuckaseigee
   river, NC   TUHK-uh-SĒ-jē   ˌtəkəˈsiːdʒiˑ

Tucker
   Richard, *US tenor*   TUHK-uhr   ˈtəkəʳ

Tucson
   city, AZ   TO͞O-SAHN, to͞o-SAHN   ˈtuːˌsɑn, tuːˈsɑn

Tucumcari
   city, NM   TO͞O-kuhm-KAR-ē   ˈtuːkəmˌkæriˑ

Tudjman
   Franjo, *Croatian politician*   TO͞OJ-mahn   ˈtuːdʒmɑːn

Tudor
   royal family, England, 1485-1603   T(Y)O͞OD-uhr, CHO͞OD-uhr   ˈt(j)uːdəʳ, ˈtʃuːdəʳ

Tuesday
   day of the week; pers. name   T(Y)O͞OZ-dē, T(Y)O͞OZ-dā   ˈt(j)uːzdiˑ, ˈt(j)uːzdeː

Tufts
   University, *MA*   TUHF(T)S   ˈtəf(t)s

Tugaloo, Tugalo
   river, GA   TUG-uh-LŌ   ˈtugəˌloː

Tugela
   river, falls, S. Africa   to͞o-GĀ-luh   tuːˈgeːlə

Tuguegarao
   municipality, Philippines   TO͞O-gā-guh-ROW   ˌtuːgeːgəˈrɑu

Tuileries
   gardens, Paris, France   twēl-RĒ, ⓢ TWĒ-luh-RĒ   tɥiːlriː, ⓢ ˌtwiːləˈriː

Tukulör
   see Toucouleur

Tula
   lang., Nigeria; city, Russia   TO͞O-luh   ˈtuːlə

Tulagi
   island, Solomon Islands   to͞o-LAHG-ē   tuːˈlɑgiˑ

Tulalip
   Indian reservation, US   to͞o-LAHL-uhp   tuːˈlɑləp

Tulare
   county, CA   to͞o-LAR-ē, to͞o-LER-ē, to͞o-LAR,   tuːˈlæriˑ, tuːˈleriˑ, tuːˈlæʳ,
                          to͞o-LER   tuːˈleʳ

Tulkarm
   town, West Bank   to͞ol-KAHRM   tuːlˈkɑʳm

Tullius
   pers. name, Latin   TUHL-ē-uhs   ˈtəliːəs

Tully
   British name for Roman Cicero;   TUHL-ē   ˈtəliˑ
   pers. name

Tulsa
   city, OK   TUHL-suh   ˈtəlsə

Tulu
   lang., people, India   TO͞O-lo͞o   ˈtuːluː

Key (col. 2):   a: fad   ā: fade   ah: father   ar: marry   aw: law   e: fed   ē: feed   er: merry   i: hid   ī: hide   ō: coat   o͞o: boot
oi: boy   ow: now   u: put   uh: above   uhr: bird   ch: chop   ng: ring   sh: show   th: thick   t͟h: this   zh: measure

Tumacacori
National Monument, *AZ*   T͞OO-muh-KAHK-uh-rē   ˌtuːməˈkɑkəriˑ

Tum [Atum]
Egyptian creator god   TUM   ˈtum

Tumi
mfrs.   T(Y)͞OO-mē   ˈt(j)uːmiˑ

tungsten
element   TUHNG-stuhn   ˈtəŋstən

Tung-t'ing Hu
see Dongting Hu

Tungus
lang., people, Asia   tung-G͞OOZ, TUHNG-G͞OOZ   tuŋˈguːz, ˌtəŋˈguːz

Tungusic
lang. family, Manchuria and Siberia   tung-GUS-ik, tung-G͞OO-zik   tuŋˈgusik, tuŋˈguːzik

Tunguska
river, Siberia   tung-G͞OO-skuh, TUHNG-G͞OO-skuh   tuŋˈguːskə, ˌtəŋˈguːskə

Tunica
county, MS   T(Y)͞OO-ni-kuh   ˈt(j)uːnikə

Tunica-Biloxi
N. American people   T(Y)͞OO-nuh-kuh-buh-LUHK-sē, -buh-LAHK-sē   ˈt(j)uːnəkəbəˈləksiˑ, -bəˈlɑksiˑ

Tunis
city, Tunisia   T(Y)͞OO-nis   ˈt(j)uːnis

Tunisia
country, Africa   t(y)͞oo-NĒ-zh(ē-)uh, -NIZH-(ē-)uh   t(j)uːˈniːʒ(iː)ə, -ˈniʒ(iː)ə

Tunisian
pert. to Tunisia *or* Tunis   t(y)͞oo-NĒ-zh(ē-)uhn, -NIZH-(ē-)uhn   t(j)uːˈniːʒ(iː)ən, -ˈniʒ(iː)ən

Tunney
Gene, *US boxer*   TUHN-ē   ˈtəniˑ

Tunxis
Community College, *CT*   TUHNG(K)-suhs   ˈtəŋ(k)səs

Tuohey, Tuohy
family name   T͞OO-ē, T͞OO-hē   ˈtuːiˑ, ˈtuːhiˑ

Tuolumne
river, mtn., county, CA   t͞oo-AHL-uh-mē   tuːˈɑləmiˑ

Tuolumne Rancheria
Indian reservation, US   t͞oo-AHL-uh-mē RAN-chuh-RĒ-uh   tuːˈɑləmiˑ ˌræntʃəˈriːə

Tupamaro
S. American people   T͞OO-puh-MAHR-ō   ˌtuːpəˈmɑroː

Tupelo
city, MS; tree   T(Y)͞OO-puh-LŌ   ˈt(j)uːpəˌloː

Tupí
lang., people, S America   T͞OO-pē, t͞oo-PĒ   ˈtuːpiˑ, tuːˈpiː

Tupí-Guaraní
S. American people   t͞oo-PĒ-GWAH-rah-NĒ   tuːˈpiːˌgwɑrɑˈniː

Tupina
S. American people   T͞OO-pē-NAH   ˌtuːpiˑˈnɑ

Tupinambá
S. American people   T͞OO-pē-NAM-buh, T͞OO-pē-NAM-BAH   ˌtuːpiˑˈnæmbə, ˌtuːpiˑˌnæmˈbɑ

Turaco
African bird   TUR-uh-kō   ˈturəkoː

Turandot
Puccini opera   TUR-uhn-DAHT   ˈturənˌdɑt

Foreign Sounds: ue: *Fr.* **rue**, *Ger.* **füllen**   uh(r): *Fr.* **boeuf**, *Ger.* **Höhle**   <u>kh</u>: *Ger.* **ich**, *Scot.* **loch**   g̅: *Sp.* **amigo**   v̲: *Sp.* **hablar**
hl: *Welsh* **Llanelli**.   CAPITALS: primary stress.   SMALL CAPS: secondary stress.   Ⓢ: U.S. pron.   Ⓔ: British pron.

Turanian		
Ural-Altaic lang., people	t(y)u-RĀ-nē-uhn, t(y)u-RAHN-ē-uhn	t(j)u'reːniːən, t(j)u'rɑniːən
Turgenev, Turgeniev		
Ivan, *Russian novelist*	tur-GYĀN-yuhf, [$] tur-GĀN-yuhf, tur-GEN-yuhf	tur'gjeːnjəf, [$] tuʳ'geːnjəf, tuʳ'genjəf
Turin		
prov & town, Italy	T(Y)UR-uhn, t(y)u-RIN	't(j)urən, t(j)u'rin
Turing		
Alan, *English computer theorist*	T(Y)UR-ing	't(j)uriŋ
Turkana		
lang., people, Sudan, Kenya, Ethiopia; lake, Kenya	tur-KAHN-uh, tur-KAN-uh	tuʳ'kɑnə, tuʳ'kænə
Turkestan		
region, desert, Asia	TUHR-kuh-STAN, -STAHN	ˌtəʳkə'stæn, -'stɑn
Turkey		
country, Europe, Asia	TUHR-kē	'təʳkiˑ
Turki		
people, lang., Asia	TUHR-kē, TUR-kē	'təʳkiˑ, 'tuʳkiˑ
Turkic		
Asian lang. family	TUHR-kik	'təʳkik
Turkish		
lang., Turkey, Bulgaria	TUHR-kish	'təʳkiʃ
Turkism, Turcism		
customs of the Turks	TUHR-KIZ-uhm	'təʳˌkizəm
Turkmen		
lang., people, Asia	TUHRK-muhn	'təʳkmən
Turkmenistan		
republic, Asia	tuhrk-MEN-uh-STAN, TUHRK-MEN-uh-STAHN, TUHRK-MEN-uh-STAN	təʳk'menəˌstæn, ˌtəʳkˌmenə'stɑn, ˌtəʳkˌmenə'stæn
Turkmenskaya		
SSR, *Turkmen republic, USSR*	turk-MEN-skuh-yuh	tuʳk'menskəjə
Turkoman		
people, Asia	TUHR-kuh-muhn	'təʳkəmən
Turks and Caicos		
islands, West Indies	TUHRKS uhn(d) KĀ-kuhs	'təʳks ən(d) 'keːkəs
Turku		
port, Finland	TUR-ko͞o	'tuʳkuː
Turlogh, Turlough		
1. pers. name	TUHR-lō, TUR-lō	'təʳloː, 'tuʳloː
2. Irish Gaelic	THUR-luh(g̃)	'θurlə(ɣ)
Turmeric		
spice	TUHR-muh-rik, T(Y)O͞O-muh-rik	'təʳmərik, 't(j)uːmərik
Turner		
Kathleen, *US actress; pers. name*	TUHR-nuhr	'təʳnəʳ
Turnhout		
prov & town, Belgium	TURN-HOWT	'tuʳnˌhɑut
Turnus		
king of the Rutuli in the Aeneid, *Virgil*	TUHR-nuhs, TUR-nuhs	'təʳnəs, 'tuʳnəs
Turnverein		
gymnastic club	TURN-fer-ĪN, [$] TUHRN-vuh-RĪN	'tuʳnferˌɑin, [$] 'təʳnvəˌrɑin
Turow		
Scott, *US novelist*	T(Y)UR-ō	't(j)uroː

Key (col. 2): a: **fad** ā: **fade** ah: **father** ar: **marry** aw: **law** e: **fed** ē: **feed** er: **merry** i: **hid** ī: **hide** ō: **coat** o͞o: **boot** oi: **boy** ow: **now** u: **put** uh: **above** uhr: **bird** ch: **chop** ng: **ring** sh: **show** th: **thick** th: **this** zh: **measure**

Tuscaloosa
city, county, AL TUHS-kuh-L$\overline{OO}$-suh ˌtəskə'luːsə

Tuscan
pert. to Tuscany TUHS-kuhn 'təskən

Tuscany
region, Italy TUHS-kuh-nē 'təskəniˑ

Tuscarawas
river, county, OH TUHS-kuh-RAW-(w)uhs ˌtəskə'rɔː(w)əs

Tuscarora
mts., PA, NV; people, lang., N. TUHS-kuh-R$\overline{O}$R-uh, -RAWR-uh ˌtəskə'roːrə, -'rɔːrə
America

Tuscola
county, MI tuhs-K$\overline{O}$-luh təs'koːlə

Tusculum
ancient town, Italy; college, TN TUHS-k(y)uh-luhm 'təsk(j)ələm

Tuscumbia
city, AL tuh-SKUHM-bē-uh tə'skəmbiːə

Tuskegee
Institute, *college, AL; N. American* TUH-SK$\overline{E}$-gē ˌtə'skiːgiˑ
people

Tussaud
Marie, *London waxworks founder* tue-S$\overline{O}$, ⓢ T$\overline{OO}$-sō, tuh-SAWD, tyːsoː, ⓢ 'tuːsoː, tə'sɔːd,
  tuh-S$\overline{O}$D tə'soːd

Tutankhamen
king of Egypt T$\overline{OO}$-TANG-KAHM-uhn, T$\overline{OO}$-TAHNG- ˌtuːˌtæŋ'kamən, ˌtuːˌtaŋ-

Tutchone
N. American people t$\overline{oo}$-CH$\overline{O}$-nē tuː'tʃoːniˑ

Tutelo
N. American people t$\overline{oo}$-T$\overline{A}$-lō tuː'teːloː

Tutsi [Watusi]
people, Rwanda, Burundi TUT-sē, T$\overline{OO}$T-sē 'tutsiˑ, 'tuːtsiˑ

Tutu
Desmond, *South African prelate* T$\overline{OO}$-T$\overline{OO}$ 'tuːˌtuː
(Nobel 1984)

Tutuila
island, American Samoa T$\overline{OO}$T-uh-W$\overline{E}$-luh ˌtuːt̮ə'wiːlə

Tuva [Tuvinian]
lang., Russia, Mongolian PR T$\overline{OO}$-vuh 'tuːvə

Tuvalu
islands, Pacific t$\overline{oo}$-VAHL-$\overline{oo}$, t$\overline{oo}$-VAHR-$\overline{oo}$ tuː'valuː, tuː'varuː

Tuvaluan
pert. to Tuvalu t$\overline{oo}$-VAHL-$\overline{oo}$-uhn, t$\overline{oo}$-VAHR-$\overline{oo}$-uhn tuː'valuːən, tuː'varuːən

Tuvinian [Tuva]
lang., Russia, Mongolian PR t$\overline{oo}$-VIN-ē-uhn tuː'viniːən

Tuzla
city, Bosnia TUZ-luh, T$\overline{OO}$Z-luh 'tuzlə, 'tuːzlə

Twain
Mark, *pseudonym of* Samuel TW$\overline{A}$N 'tweːn
Clemens, *US writer*

Tweedledee
character in Through the Looking TW$\overline{E}$D-l-D$\overline{E}$ ˌtwiːdl̩'diː
Glass, *Lewis Carroll*

Tweedledum
companion of Tweedledee TW$\overline{E}$D-l-DUHM ˌtwiːdl̩'dəm

---

Foreign Sounds: ue: *Fr.* **rue**, *Ger.* **füllen**   uh(r): *Fr.* **boeuf**, *Ger.* **Höhle**   kh: *Ger.* **ich**, *Scot.* **loch**   ḡ: *Sp.* **amigo**   v: *Sp.* **hablar**
hl: *Welsh* **Llanelli**.   CAPITALS: primary stress.   SMALL CAPS: secondary stress.   ⓢ: U.S. pron.   ⓔ: British pron.

Tweedsmuir
   provincial park, Canada   TWĒDZ-MYUR   'twiːdzˌmjuʳ

Twi [Akan]
   lang., Ghana, Ivory Coast   TWĒ   'twiː

Twickenham
   former borough, England   TWIK-uh-nuhm   'twikənəm

Twining
   Nathan F., *US general; tdmk for a*   TWĪ-ning   'twɑiniŋ
     British tea

Twitty
   Conway, *US country singer*   TWIT-ē   'twiţiˑ

Twohy
   family name   TOO-ē, TOO-hē   'tuːiˑ, 'tuːhiˑ

Twomey
   family name   TOO-mē   'tuːmiˑ

Twyla
   pers. name   TWĪ-luh   'twɑilə

Txukahamei
   S. American people   CHOO-kuh-HAHM-Ī   ˌtʃuːkə'hɑmˌɑi

Ty
   1. pers. name   TĪ   'tɑi
   2. Egyptian queen   TĒ, TĪ   'tiː, 'tɑi

Tybalt
   character in Romeo & Juliet,   TIB-uhlt   'tibəlt
    Shakespeare

Tyburn
   execution site, London, England   TĪ-buhrn   'tɑibəʳn

Tyche
   Greek goddess of fortune   TĪ-kē   'tɑikiˑ

Tychicus
   Biblical name   TIK-i-kuhs   'tikikəs

Tychius
   shieldmaker for Ajax   TĪ-kē-uhs   'tɑikiːəs

Tycho
   1. crater on Moon   TĪ-kō   'tɑikoː
   2. pers. name, Danish   TUE-kō, Ⓢ TĪ-kō, TĒ-kō   'tyːkoː, Ⓢ 'tɑikoː, 'tiːkoː
   3. German   TUE-k͟hō   'tyːçoː

Tydeus
   father of Diomedes   TĪD-ē-uhs   'tɑidiːəs

Tyldesley
   town, England   TILZ-lē, TILDZ-lē   'tilzliˑ, 'tildzliˑ

Tygart
   river, WV   TĪ-guhrt   'tɑigəʳt

Tylenol
   tdmk for acetaminophen   TĪ-luh-NAWL, TĪ-luh-NAHL   'tɑiləˌnɔːl, 'tɑiləˌnɑl

Tyler
   John, *10th US president; pers. name*   TĪ-luhr   'tɑiləʳ

Tyndale
   see Tindale

Tyndale, Tyndall
   pers. name   TIN-dl   'tindl̩

Tyndareus
   father of Dioscuri, Helen,   tin-DAR-ē-uhs   tin'dæriːəs
    Clytemnestra

Key (col. 2):   a: fad ā: fade ah: father ar: marry aw: law e: fed ē: feed er: merry i: hid ī: hide ō: coat ōō: boot
oi: boy ow: now u: put uh: above uhr: bird ch: chop ng: ring sh: show th: thick t͟h: this zh: measure

Tyne
river, England; pers. name   TĪN   'taɪn

Tyne and Wear
county, England   TĪN uhn(d) WIR   'taɪn ən(d) 'wɪʳ

Tynemouth
port, England   TĪN-MOWTH, TĪN-muhth   'taɪnˌmaʊθ, 'taɪnməθ

Tyneside
urban area, England   TĪN-SĪD   'taɪnˌsaɪd

Typee
novel, H. Melville   tī-PĒ   taɪ'piː

Typhoeus [Typhon]
monster son of Gaia & Tartarus   tī-FĒ-uhs, tī-FŌ-YOŌS   taɪ'fiːəs, taɪ'foːˌjuːs

Typhon
monster son of Gaia & Tartarus   TĪ-FAHN   'taɪˌfɑn

Tyr
Scandinavian battle god   TIR   'tiʳ

Tyrannius
pers. name, Latin   ti-RAN-ē-uhs   ti'ræniːəs

Tyrannosaurus
dinosaur   tuh-RAN-uh-SAWR-uhs,   tə,rænə'sɔːrəs,
          TĪ-RAN-uh-SAWR-uhs   ˌtaɪˌrænə'sɔːrəs

Tyrannus
Biblical name   tī-RAN-uhs   taɪ'rænəs

Tyre
fishing port, Lebanon; Phoenician   TĪR   'taɪʳ
   capital

Tyrell
pers. name   TIR-uhl   'tɪrəl

Tyrian
pert. to ancient Tyre   TIR-ē-uhn   'tɪriːən

Tyro
mother of Pelias   TĪ-rō   'taɪroː

Tyrol
see Tirol

Tyrolean, Tyrolian
pert. to the Tirol   tuh-RŌ-lē-uhn, tī-RŌ-lē-uhn   tə'roːliːən, taɪ'roːliːən

Tyrolese
pert. to the Tirol   TIR-uh-LĒZ, -LĒS   ˌtɪrə'liːz, -'liːs

Tyrone
1. borough, PA   TĪ-RŌN   'taɪˌroːn
2. former county, N. Ireland   tir-ŌN   tɪr'oːn
3. pers. name   TĪ-RŌN, ti-RŌN, tir-ŌN   'taɪˌroːn, ti'roːn, tɪr'oːn

Tyrrell
county, NC   TIR-uhl, TER-uhl   'tɪrəl, 'terəl

Tyrrhenian
Sea, Mediterranean   tuh-RĒ-nē-uhn   tə'riːniːən

Tyrrhenus
hero of the Tyrrhenians or Etruscans   tī-RĒ-nuhs   taɪ'riːnəs

Tyrtaeus
Spartan poet   TUHR-TĒ-uhs   ˌtəʳ'tiːəs

Tyrwhitt
Thomas, English scholar; pers.   TIR-uht   'tɪrət
   name

Tyson
pers. name   TĪS-n   'taɪsn̩

Foreign Sounds: ue: *Fr.* **rue**, *Ger.* **füllen**   uh(r): *Fr.* **boeuf**, *Ger.* **Höhle**   <u>kh</u>: *Ger.* **ich**, *Scot.* **loch**   g̲: *Sp.* **amigo**   v̲: *Sp.* **hablar**
hl: *Welsh* **Llanelli**.   CAPITALS: primary stress.   SMALL CAPS: secondary stress.   Ⓢ: U.S. pron.   Ⓔ: British pron.

Tyus
　Wyomia, *sports personality*　　　TĪ-uhs　　　　　　　'tɑɪəs
Tywi, Towy
　river, Wales　　　　　　　　　TUH-wē　　　　　　'təwiˑ
Tzeltal
　lang., people, Mexico　　　　(t)sel-TAHL　　　　　(t)sel'tɑl
Tzigane
　pert. to gypsies or to Romany　(t)sē-GAHN　　　　　(t)siː'gɑn
Tzotzil
　lang., people, Mexico　　　　(t)sōt-SĒL　　　　　(t)soːt'siːl
Tz'u Hsi
　dowager empress of China　　TSŌŌ SHĒ　　　　'tsuː 'ʃiː
Tzutuhil
　lang., people, Guatemala　　(T)SŌŌT-uh-WĒL　　ˌ(t)suːt̬ə'wiːl

U

U
　Burmese title　　　　　　　ŌŌ　　　　　　　　　'uː
U2
　rock group　　　　　　　　YŌŌ-TŌŌ　　　　　'juː'tuː
Ubaid
　Bronze Age culture　　　　ōō-BĀD, ōō-BĪD　　uː'beːd, uː'baid
Ubaldino
　pers. name, Italian　　　　ŌŌ-bahl-DĒ-nō　　ˌuːbɑl'diːnoː
Ubaldo
　pers. name, Italian　　　　ŌŌ-BAHL-dō　　uː'bɑldoː
Ubangi
　river, Africa　　　　　　　(y)ōō-BANG-(g)ē　(j)uː'bæŋ(g)iˑ
Ubangi-Shari
　former name of Central African　(y)ōō-BANG-(g)ē-SHAHR-ē　(j)uːˌbæŋ(g)iˑ'ʃariˑ
　Republic
Ubeda
　commune, Spain　　　ŌŌ-vā-THAH, ⑤ ŌŌ-buh-DAH　'uːβeːˌðɑ, ⑤ 'uːbəˌdɑ
Ubertino
　pers. name, Italian　　　ŌŌ-ber-TĒ-nō　　ˌuːber'tiːnoː
Uberto
　pers. name, Italian　　　ōō-BER-tō　　uː'bertoː
Ubykh
　lang., Turkey　　　　　ŌŌ-bikh　　　'uːbix
Ucalegon
　counsellor of Priam　　(y)ōō-KAL-uh-GAHN　(j)uː'kælə,gɑn
Ucal
　Biblical name　　　YŌŌ-KAL, ōō-KHAHL　'juːˌkæl, uː'xɑl
Ucayali
　river, Peru　　　　ŌŌ-kuh-YAHL-ē　　ˌuːkə'jaliˑ

Key (col. 2):　a: **fad**　ā: **fade**　ah: **father**　ar: **marry**　aw: **law**　e: **fed**　ē: **feed**　er: **merry**　i: **hid**　ī: **hide**　ō: **coat**　ōō: **boot**
oi: **boy**　ow: **now**　u: **put**　uh: **above**　uhr: **bird**　ch: **chop**　ng: **ring**　sh: **show**　th: **thick**　th̲: **this**　zh: **measure**

Uccello
  Paolo, *Italian painter* · o͞o-CHEL-ō · uːˈtʃeloː

UConn
  nickname for U. Connecticut · YO͞O-KAHN · ˈjuːˌkɑn

Udaipur
  former state, India · o͞o-DĪ-PUR, o͞o-dī-PUR · uːˈdɑiˌpuʳ, ˌuːdɑiˈpuʳ

Udall
  Morris K., *US politician* · YO͞OD-AWL · ˈjuːdˌɔːl

Udmurt [Votyak]
  lang., Russia · ud-MURT · udˈmuʳt

U Dub
  nickname for U. Wisconsin, Washington · YO͞O DUHB · ˌjuː ˈdəb

Ueberroth
  Peter, *US businessman* · YO͞O-buh-RAWTH · ˈjuːbəˌrɔːθ

Uecker
  Bob, *US entertainer* · YO͞O-kuhr · ˈjuːkəʳ

Uel
  Biblical name · YO͞O-EL, o͞o-EL · ˈjuːˌel, uːˈel

Uele
  river, Africa · WEL-ē · ˈweliˑ

Ufa
  river, city, Russia · o͞o-FAH · uːˈfɑ

Uffizi
  gallery, Florence, Italy · o͞o-FIT-sē, o͞o-FĒT-sē · uːˈfitsiˑ, uːˈfiːtsiˑ

UFOlogy
  study of UFO's · yo͞o-FAHL-uh-jē · juːˈfɑlədʒiˑ

Uganda
  republic, Africa · (y)o͞o-GAN-duh, -GAHN-duh · (j)uːˈgændə, -ˈgɑˑndə

Ugandan
  pert. to Uganda · (y)o͞o-GAN-duhn, -GAHN-duhn · (j)uːˈgændən, -ˈgɑˑndən

Ugarit [Ras Shamra]
  ancient city, Syria · o͞o-guh-RĒT · ˌuːgəˈriːt

Ugaritic
  lang., pert. to Ugarit · (Y)o͞o-guh-RIT-ik · ˌ(j)uːgəˈriṭik

Uggams
  Leslie, *US entertainer* · UHG-uhmz · ˈəgəmz

Ugni Blanc
  wine · o͞on-yē BLAHⁿ · uːnjiː blɑ̃

Ugo
  pers. name, Italian · O͞O-gō · ˈuːgoː

Ugolino
  pers. name, Italian · O͞O-gō-LĒ-nō · ˌuːgoːˈliːnoː

Ugrian
  eastern Finno-Ugric people · (Y)O͞O-grē-uhn · ˈ(j)uːgriːən

Ugric
  branch of Uralic langs. · (Y)O͞O-grik · ˈ(j)uːgrik

Uhrichsville
  city, OH · YUR-iks-VIL · ˈjuriksˌvil

Uhura
  Lt., *character, Star Trek* · u-HUR-uh · uˈhurə

Uighur, Uigur
  lang., people, China, Uzbekistan · wē-GUR, WĒ-guhr · wiːˈguʳ, ˈwiːgəʳ

Uillean pipes
  Irish bagpipe · IL-uhn, IL-yuhn · ˈilən, ˈiljən

Foreign Sounds: ue: *Fr.* **rue**, *Ger.* **füllen**   uh(r): *Fr.* **boeuf**, *Ger.* **Höhle**   <u>kh</u>: *Ger.* **ich**, *Scot.* **loch**   ḡ: *Sp.* **amigo**   v̱: *Sp.* **hablar**
hl: *Welsh* **Llanelli**.   CAPITALS: primary stress.   SMALL CAPS: secondary stress.   ⑤: U.S. pron.   ⑥: British pron.

Uinta
  river, mts., UT; county, WY   yo͞o-INT-uh   juːˈintə
Uintah
  county, UT   yo͞o-INT-uh   juːˈintə
Ujiji
  town, Tanzania   o͞o-JĒ-jē   uːˈdʒiːdʒiː
Ujpest
  suburb, Budapest, Hungary   O͞O-ē-PESHT   ˈuːiːˌpeʃt
Ukiah
  city, CA   yu-KĪ-uh   juˈkɑiə
Ukraine
  republic, Europe   yo͞o-KRĀN, yo͞o-KRĪN, YO͞O-KRĀN   juːˈkreːn, juːˈkrɑin, ˈjuːˌkreːn
Ukrainian
  lang., pert. to Ukraine   yo͞o-KRĀ-nē-uhn, yo͞o-KRĀN-yuhn   juˈˈkreːniːən, juˈˈkreːnjən
Ukrainskaya
  SSR, Ukrainian republic, USSR   o͞o-krah-ĒN-skuh-yuh   uːkrɑˈiːnskəjə
Ulaanbaatar
  city, Mongolia   O͞O-LAHN-BAH-TAHR, -TAWR   ˌuːˌlɑnˈbɑˌtɑʳ, -ˌtɔːʳ
Ulai
  Biblical name   (Y)O͞O-LĪ, (Y)O͞O-lē-Ī, o͞o-LĪ   ˈ(j)uːˌlɑi, ˈ(j)uːliːˌɑi, uːˈlɑi
Ulan Bator [Ulaanbaatar]
  city, Mongolia   O͞O-LAHN BAH-TAWR   ˌuːˌlɑn ˈbɑˌtɔːʳ
Ulanov
  see Ulyanov
Ulan-Ude
  city, Russia   O͞O-LAHN-u-DĀ   ˌuːˌlɑːnuˈdeː
Ulf
  pers. name, Swedish   O͞OLF   ˈuːlf
Ulises
  pers. name, Spanish   o͞o-LĒ-sās   uːˈliːseːs
Ulisse
  pers. name, Italian   o͞o-LĒS-sā   uːˈliːsseː
Ulithi
  islands, Pacific   o͞o-LĒ-thē   uːˈliːθiˑ
Ull
  Scandinavian hunter god   UL   ˈul
Ullman
  Tracy, *English actress*   UHL-muhn   ˈəlmən
Ullmann
  Liv, *Swedish actress*   UL-MAHN   ˈulˌmɑːn
Ulm
  city, Germany   ULM   ˈulm
Ulpius
  pers. name, Latin   UHL-pē-uhs   ˈəlpiːəs
Ulrich
  1. pers. name   UHL-rik   ˈəlrik
  2. French   uel-RĒK   yːlriːk
  3. German   UL-ri<u>kh</u>   ˈulriç
Ulster
  county, NY; prov, Eire   UHL-stuhr   ˈəlstəʳ
Ultbanerisches
  German beer   ult-BAHN-uhr-ISH-uhs   ultˈbɑnərˌiʃəs
Ultima Thule
  the farthest land   UHL-tuh-muh TO͞O-lē, UL-tuh-muh,   ˌəltəmə ˈtuːliˑ, ˌultəmə,
                                       TH O͞O-lē   ˈθuːliˑ

Key (col. 2): a: fad ā: fade ah: father ar: marry aw: law e: fed ē: feed er: merry i: hid ī: hide ō: coat o͞o: boot
oi: boy ow: now u: put uh: above uhr: bird ch: chop ng: ring sh: show th: thick <u>th</u>: this zh: measure

Ult-Münchner
  German beer   ult-MUE<u>NKH</u>-nuhr   ult'mynçnə^r

Ululu
  Babylonian month   O͞O-lo͞o-LO͞O, o͞o-LO͞O-lo͞o   'uːluː,luː, uː'luː,luː

Uluru
  aboriginal name for Ayers Rock;   O͞O-luh-RO͞O   ,uːlə'ruː
  natl. park, Australia

Ulyanov, Ulanov
  Vladimir Ilyich, *former name of*   o͞ol-YAHN-uhf   uːl'jɑːnəf
  Lenin

Ulyanovsk [Simbirsk]
  city, Russia   o͞ol-YAHN-uhfsk   uːl'jɑːnəfsk

Ulysse
  pers. name, French   ue-LĒS   yːliːs

Ulysses
  1. Latin-derived form of Odysseus;   yu-LIS-ēz   ju'lisiːz
  novel, J. Joyce; pers. name
  2. German   o͞o-LUES-es   uː'lyses

UMass
  nickname for U. Massachusetts   yo͞o-MAS   juː'mæs

Umatilla
  N. American people; river, county,   YO͞O-muh-TIL-uh   ,juːmə'tilə
  OR

Umberto
  pers. name, Italian   o͞om-BER-tō   uːm'bertoː

Umbria
  region, Italy   UHM-brē-uh   'əmbriːə

Umbrian
  pert. to Umbria   UHM-brē-uhn   'əmbriːən

Umbriel
  satellite of Uranus   UHM-brē-uhl   'əmbriːəl

UMIST
  U. Manchester Institute of Science   YO͞O-mist   'juːmist
  and Technology

Umma
  Sumerian city   UHM-uh   'əmə

Ummah
  Biblical name   UHM-uh, o͞o-MAH   'əmə, uː'mɑː

Umm al Qaywayn
  states, United Arab Emirates   O͞OM ahl kī-WĪN   'uːm ɑːl kɑi'wɑin

Umpqua
  river, OR   UHM(P)-KWAW   'əm(p),kwɔː

Umtata
  river, town, S. Africa   um-TAHT-uh   um'tɑʈə

Una
  pers. name   YO͞O-nuh, O͞O-nuh   'juːnə, 'uːnə

Unaka
  mtn. range, TN   yu-NĀ-kuh   ju'neːkə

Unalaska
  Aleutian island, city, bay, AK   UHN-uh-LAS-kuh, UHN-l-AS-kuh   ,ənə'læskə, ,ən̩'æskə

Unamuno y Jugo
  Miguel de, *Spanish philosopher*   o͞o-nah-MO͞O-nō ē <u>KH</u>O͞O-gō   uːnɑ'muːnoː iː 'xuːgoː

Uncas
  first chief of the Mohegans   UHNG-kuhs   'əŋkəs

Foreign Sounds: ue: *Fr.* **rue**, *Ger.* **füllen** uh(r): *Fr.* **b**oeuf, *Ger.* **Höhle** kh: *Ger.* **ich**, *Scot.* **loch** ḡ: *Sp.* ami**g**o v: *Sp.* ha**b**lar
hl: *Welsh* **Ll**anelli. CAPITALS: primary stress. SMALL CAPS: secondary stress. Ⓢ: U.S. pron. Ⓔ: British pron.

Undarum, Mare
see Mare Undarum

Undine
water nymph   UHN-DĒN   ˌənˈdiːn

Undset
Sigrid, *Norwegian author (Nobel*   UN-SET   ˈunˌset
1928)

UNESCO
UN agency   yu-NES-kō   juˈneskoː

Uniat
member of Eastern church   YOO-nē-uht, YOO-nē-AT   ˈjuːniːət, ˈjuːniːˌæt

Uniate [Uniat]
member of Eastern church   YOO-nē-uht, YOO-nē-ĀT   ˈjuːniːət, ˈjuːniːˌeːt

Uniatism
religion   YOO-nē-uh-TIZ-uhm   ˈjuːniːəˌtizəm

Unicef, UNICEF
United Nations International   YOO-nuh-SEF   ˈjuːnəˌsef
Children's Fund

Unicoi
county, TN   YOO-nuh-KOI   ˈjuːnəˌkɔi

Unicorn
mythical beast; constellation   YOO-ni-KAWRN   ˈjuːniˌkɔːʳn

Unilever
US corp.   YOO-nuh-LĒ-vuhr   ˈjuːnəˌliːvəʳ

Uniroyal
US tire co.   YOO-nuh-ROI(-uh)l   ˈjuːnəˌrɔi(ə)l

Unisys
US computer co.   YOO-nuh-SIS   ˈjuːnəˌsis

UNITA
Angolan political organization   yu-NĒT-uh   juˈniːʈə

Unitarian
religious group   YOO-nuh-TAR-ē-uhn,   ˌjuːnəˈtæriːən, ˌjuːnəˈteriːən
                     YOO-nuh-TER-ē-uhn

Unitas
Johnny, *US football player*   yu-NĪT-uhs   juˈnɑiʈəs

United Arab Emirates
country, Arabia   EM-uh-ruhts, -RĀTS; i-MIR-uhts   ˈemərəts, -ˌreːts; iˈmirəts

United States
republic, N. America   yu-NĪT-uhd STĀTS, *esp. southeastern*   juˌnɑiʈəd ˈsteːts, *esp.*
            US YOO-NĪT-uhd STĀTS, *in rapid*   *southeastern US*
            speech often yuh-NĪD STĀTS   ˈjuːˌnɑiʈəd ˈsteːts, *in rapid*
                                           speech often jəˌnɑid ˈsteːts

UNIVAC
UN agency   YOO-nuh-VAK   ˈjuːnəˌvæk

Univac
tdmk for an early computer   YOO-nuh-VAK   ˈjuːnəˌvæk

UNIX
computer operating system   YOO-niks   ˈjuːniks

Unni
Biblical name   UHN-Ī, OO-NĒ   ˈənˌɑi, uːˈniː

Unocal
US oil co.   YOO-nuh-KAL   ˈjuːnəˌkæl

UNRWA
United Nations Relief and Works   UHN-ruh   ˈənrə
        Agency

Key (col. 2): a: **fad** ā: **fade** ah: **father** ar: **marry** aw: **law** e: **fed** ē: **feed** er: **merry** i: **hid** ī: **hide** ō: **coat** oo: **boot**
oi: **boy**   ow: **now**   u: **put**   uh: **above**   uhr: **bird**   ch: **chop**   ng: **ring**   sh: **show**   th: **thick**   <u>th</u>: **this**   zh: **measure**

Unter den Linden
   main avenue, Berlin, Germany   UN-tuhr den LIN-duhn   ˌuntəʳ den ˈlindən

Unterseeboot
   German for submarine   UN-tuhr-ZĀ-BŌT   ˈuntəʳˌzeːˌboːt

Unwin
   pers. name   UHN-wuhn   ˈənwən

Upanishads
   basic text of Hinduism   o͞o-PAHN-i-SHAHDZ,   uːˈpaniˌʃadz, juːˈpænəˌʃædz
                 yo͞o-PAN-uh-SHADZ

Updike
   John, US writer; pers. name   UHP-DĪK   ˈəpˌdaik

Upham
   pers. name   UHP-uhm   ˈəpəm

Uphaz
   Biblical name   YO͞O-FAZ, o͞o-FAHZ   ˈjuːˌfæz, uːˈfaz

Upland
   city, CA   UHP-luhnd   ˈəplənd

Upolu
   island, Samoa   o͞o-PŌ-lo͞o   uːˈpoːluː

Upper Volta
   former name of Burkina Faso   UHP-uhr VAHL-tuh, VŌL-, VAWL-   ˌəpəʳ ˈvaltə, ˈvoːl-, ˈvɔːl-

Upper Voltan
   pert. to Upper Volta   UHP-uhr VAHL-tuhn, VŌL-, VAWL-   ˌəpəʳ ˈvaltən, ˈvoːl-, ˈvɔːl-

Uppsala
   county, city, Sweden   UHP-suh-LAH, UHP-SAHL-uh,   ˈəpsəˌla, ˈəpˌsala, əpˈsala
                 uhp-SAHL-uh

Upsala
   College, *NJ*   UHP-suh-luh, UHP-suh-LAH,   ˈəpsələ, ˈəpsəˌla, əpˈsala
                 uhp-SAHL-uh

Upshaw
   Gene, *US football executive*   UHP-SHAW   ˈəpˌʃɔː

Upton
   pers. name   UHP-tuhn   ˈəptən

Ur
   ancient Sumerian city   UHR, UR   ˈəʳ, ˈuʳ

Ural
   river, mtn. range, Russia   YUR-uhl   ˈjurəl

Ural-Altaic
   pert. to Ural *and* Altai Mts.; *lang.*   YUR-uhl-AL-TĀ-ik   ˌjurəlˌælˈteːik
   families

Uralian
   pert. to Ural Mts. *or their inhabitants*   yu-RĀ-lē-uhn   juˈreːliːən

Uralic
   pert. to Finno-Ugric *and* Samoyed   yu-RAL-ik   juˈrælik
   langs.

Uralskiy Khrebet
   mtn. range, Russia   yu-RAHL-skyi <u>kh</u>reb-YET   juˈraːl̩skjij xr̩ebˈjet

Urania
   muse of astronomy; street, New   yu-RĀ-nē-uh, yu-RĀN-yuh   juˈreːniːə, juˈreːnjə
   Orleans

uranium
   element   yu-RĀ-nē-uhm   juˈreːniːəm

Uranus
   Greek sky god; planet   YUR-uh-nuhs, yuh-RĀ-nuhs,   ˈjurənəs, jəˈreːnəs, ˈurənəs
                 UR-uh-nuhs

Foreign Sounds: ue: *Fr.* **rue**, *Ger.* **füllen** uh(r): *Fr.* **boeuf**, *Ger.* **Höhle** <u>kh</u>: *Ger.* **ich**, *Scot.* **loch** ḡ: *Sp.* **amigo** v̲: *Sp.* **hablar**
hl: *Welsh* **Llanelli**. CAPITALS: primary stress. SMALL CAPS: secondary stress. Ⓢ: U.S. pron. Ⓔ: British pron.

Urartu
　ancient Assyrian kingdom　　ur-AHR-TŌŌ　　　　　　ur'ɑˤˌtuː

Urban
　pope　　UHR-buhn　　　　　　'əˤbən

Urbana
　city, IL, OH　　UHR-BAN-uh　　　　　　ˌəˤ'bænə

Urbano
　pers. name, Italian　　ōōr-BAHN-ō　　　　　　uːr'bɑnoː

Urbanus
　Biblical name　　uhr-BĀ-nuhs　　　　　　əˤ'beːnəs

Urdu
　Indic lang.　　UR-dōō, UHR-dōō　　　　'uˤduː, 'əˤduː

Urey
　Harold C., *US physical chemist*　　YUR-ē　　　　'juri·
　(Nobel 1934)

Urfa
　prov., city, Turkey　　ur-FAH　　　　uˤ'fɑ

Urga
　former name for Ulaanbaatar　　UR-guh　　　　'uˤgə

Urho
　pers. name, Finnish　　UR-haw　　　　'urhɔː

Uri
　1. Swiss commune　　UR-ē　　　　'uri·
　2. pers. name (U. Geller)　　UR-ē, YUR-ē　　　　'uri·, 'juri·

Uria, Uriah
　Bathsheba's husband; pers. name　　yuh-RĪ-uh　　　　jə'rɑiə

Urian
　pers. name　　YUR-ē-uhn　　　　'juriːən

Urich
　Robert, *US actor*　　YUR-ik　　　　'jurik

Uriel
　1. pers. name, Portuguese　　ōōr-YEL　　　　uːr'jel
　2. Biblical name　　YUR-ē-uhl, ŌŌ-rē-EL　　'juriːəl, ˌuːriː'el

Urijah
　Biblical name　　yuh-RĪ-uh, ŌŌ-rē-YAH　　jə'rɑiə, ˌuːriː'jɑː

Urim
　Biblical name of ornaments in the　　YUR-im, ōō-RĒM　　'jurim, uː'riːm
　high priest's breastplate; see
　Thummim

Uris
　Leon, *US author*　　YUR-uhs　　　　'jurəs

Ur-Marzen
　German beer　　UR-MAHRT-suhn　　　　'uˤˌmɑˤtsən

Urmia
　lake, Iran　　UR-mē-uh　　　　'uˤmiːə

Ur-Nammu
　king of Ur　　UHR-NAHM-ŌŌ, UR-　　ˌəˤ'nɑmˌuː, 'uˤ-

Urquhart
　family name　　UHR-kuhrt, UHR-KAHRT　　'əˤkəˤt, 'əˤˌkɑˤt

Ursa Major
　constellation　　UHR-suh MĀ-juhr　　　　ˌəˤsə 'meːdʒəˤ

Ursa Minor
　constellation　　UHR-suh MĪ-nuhr　　　　ˌəˤsə 'mɑinəˤ

Ursids
　meteor shower　　UHR-sidz　　　　'əˤsidz

Key (col. 2):　a: fad　ā: fade　ah: father　ar: **marry**　aw: **law**　e: fed　ē: **feed**　er: **merry**　i: hid　ī: hide　ō: coat　ōō: **boot**
oi: **boy**　ow: **now**　u: put　uh: **above**　uhr: **bird**　ch: **chop**　ng: **ring**　sh: **show**　th: **thick**　th̲: **this**　zh: measure

Ursinus
   antipope; college, PA   UHR-SĪ-nuhs   ,əʳˈsaɪnəs

Ursprache
   reconstructed parent lang.   UR-SHPRAHKH-uh   ˈuʳˌʃprɑxə

Ursula
   1. Christian saint; pers. name UHR-s(y)uh-luh   ˈəʳs(j)ələ
   2. Italian   o͞or-SO͞O-lah   uːrˈsuːlɑ

Ursuline
   College, OH   UHR-suh-luhn, UHR-suh-LĬN,   ˈəʳsələn, ˈəʳsəˌlaɪn, ˈəʳsəˌliːn
                      UHR-suh-LĔN

Ursulines
   religious order   UHR-s(y)uh-luhnz, -LĬNZ, -LĔNZ   ˈəʳs(j)ələnz, -ˌlaɪnz, -ˌliːnz

Urtyp 1634
   German beer   UR-TUEP TOW-zuht SEKHS   ˈur,tyːp ˈtauzənt ˈseçs
                      HUN-duhrt FIR unt DRĪ-sikh   ˈhundəʳt ˈfir unt ˈdraɪsiç

Uru
   S. American people   O͞O-ro͞o, o͞o-RO͞O   ˈuːruː, uːˈruː

Uruguay
   republic, S. America   (Y)UR-uh-GWĪ, YUR-uh-GWĀ   ˈ(j)urəˌgwaɪ, ˈjurəˌgweː

Uruguayan
   pert. to Uruguay   (Y)UR-uh-GWĪ-uhn, YUR-uh-GWĀ-uhn ,(j)urəˈgwaɪən, ˌjurəˈgweːən

Uruk
   Sumerian city   O͞O-RUK   ˈuːˌruk

Urukagina
   Sumerian reformer   O͞O-ruk-AJ-uh-nuh   ,uːrukˈædʒənə

Ürümqi, Urumchi
   city, China   UE-RUEM-CHĒ, Ⓢ u-RUM-chē   ˈyːˈryːmˈtʃiː, Ⓢ uˈrumtʃiˑ

Urundi
   former name of Burundi   u-RO͞ON-dē   uˈruːndiˑ

Ushant [Ouessant, Ile d']
   island, France   UHSH-uhnt   ˈəʃənt

Ushas
   Vedic dawn goddess   O͞OSH-uhs   ˈuˑʃəs

Ushuaia
   city, Argentina   o͞o-SWĀ-yuh   uːˈsweːjə

Usk
   river, Wales, England   UHSK   ˈəsk

Uspallata
   mtn. pass, Andes   *in Chile* o͞o-spah-YAHT-ah, *in*   *in Chile* uːspaˈjaṭa, *in*
                      Argentina o͞o-spah-ZHAHT-ah   *Argentina* uːspaˈʒaṭa

Usquaebach
   Scotch whisky   UHS-kwuh-BAH(KH), -BAW(KH)   ˈəskwəˌbɑ(x), -ˌbɔː(x)

Ussuri
   river, Asia   u-SUR-ē   uˈsuriˑ

Ustinov
   1. Peter, entertainer   (Y)O͞O-stuh-NAWF, -NAWV   ˈ(j)uːstəˌnɔːf, -ˌnɔːv
   2. city, Russia   O͞O-sti-NAWF   ˈuːsṭiˌnɔːf

Utah
   state, US   YO͞O-TAW, YO͞O-TAH   ˈjuːˌtɔː, ˈjuːˌtɑ

Utahan, Utahn
   pert. to or inhabitant of Utah YO͞O-TAHN   ˈjuːˌtɑn

Utamaro
   pers. name, Japanese; see **Kitagawa** ut-ah-mahr-ō   uṭamaroː
     Utamaro

Foreign Sounds: ue: *Fr.* **rue**, *Ger.* füllen   uh(r): *Fr.* **boeuf**, *Ger.* Höhle   kh: *Ger.* ich, *Scot.* loch   ğ: *Sp.* amigo   v̩: *Sp.* hablar
hl: *Welsh* Llanelli.   CAPITALS: primary stress.   SMALL CAPS: secondary stress.   Ⓢ: U.S. pron.   Ⓔ: British pron.

Ute
  N. American people   YŌŌT   'juːt

Uthai
  Biblical name   (Y)ŌŌ-THĪ, (Y)ŌŌ-thē-Ī, ōō-TĪ   '(j)uː,θɑi, '(j)uːθiː,ɑi, uː'tɑi

Uther Pendragon
  father of King Arthur   (Y)ŌŌ-thuhr PEN-DRAG-uhn, pen-DRAG-uhn   '(j)uːθəʳ 'pen,drægən, pen'drægən

Utica
  city, NY; ancient N. African city   YŌŌT-i-kuh   'juːțikə

Utley
  Garrick, *TV personality*   UHT-lē   'ətliˑ

Uto-Aztecan
  American lang. family   YŌŌT-ō-AZ-TEK-uhn   ˌjuːțoː'æzˌtekən

Utopia
  book, Sir Thomas More; ideal place   yu-TŌ-pē-uh   ju'toːpiːə

Utrecht
  prov & town, Netherlands   ŌŌ-TREK<u>H</u>T, Ⓢ YŌŌ-TREKT   'uːˌtreçt, Ⓢ 'juːˌtrekt

Utrillo
  Maurice, *French painter*   ue-trē-YŌ, Ⓢ yōō-TRĒ-ō, yōō-TRIL-ō   yːtriːjoː, Ⓢ juː'triːoː, juː'triloː

Uttar Pradesh
  state, India   UT-uhr pruh-DĀSH, pruh-DESH   ˌuțəʳ prə'deːʃ, prə'deʃ

Utu
  Sumerian sun god   (Y)ŌŌT-ōō   '(j)uːtuː

Uusikaupunki
  port, Finland   ŌŌ-si-KAH-PUNG-kē   'uːsi'kɑˌpuŋkiˑ

Uvalde
  county, TX   yu-VAL-dē   ju'vældiˑ

Uxbridge
  town, England   UHKS-brij   'əksbridʒ

Uxmal
  ancient Mayan city, Mexico   ōōs-MAHL   uːs'mɑl

Uz
  Biblical name   ŌŌZ, UHZ, ŌŌTS   'uːz, 'əz, 'uːts

Uzai
  Biblical name   (Y)ŌŌ-ZĪ, (Y)ŌŌ-zē-Ī, ōō-ZĪ   '(j)uːˌzɑi, '(j)uːziːˌɑi, uː'zɑi

Uzal
  Biblical name   (Y)ŌŌ-ZAL, ōō-ZAHL   '(j)uːˌzæl, uː'zɑl

Uzbek
  lang., people, Asia   UZ-BEK, UHZ-BEK, uz-BEK   'uzˌbek, 'əzˌbek, uz'bek

Uzbekistan
  republic, Asia   uz-BEK-i-STAHN, -STAN; uz-BEK-i-STAHN, -STAN   uzˌbeki'stɑn, -'stæn; uz'bekiˌstɑn, -ˌstæn

Uzbekskaya
  SSR, *Uzbek republic, USSR*   ōōz-BEK-skuh-yuh   uˑz'bekskəjə

Uzi
  Israeli-designed machine gun   ŌŌ-zē   'uːziˑ

Uzza
  Biblical name   UHZ-uh, ōō-ZAH   'əzə, uː'zɑː

Uzzen-sheerah, Uzzen-sherah
  Biblical name   UHZ-in-SHĒ-(uh-)ruh, ōō-ZEN-she-e-RAH   'əzin'ʃiː(ə)rə, uː'zenʃee'rɑː

Uzzi
  Biblical name   UHZ-Ī, ōō-ZĒ   'əzˌɑi, uː'ziː

Key (col. 2):   a: fad   ā: fade   ah: father   ar: **marry**   aw: **law**   e: fed   ē: feed   er: **merry**   i: hid   ī: hide   ō: coat   ōō: boot
oi: **boy**   ow: **now**   u: put   uh: above   uhr: **bird**   ch: **chop**   ng: **ring**   sh: **show**   th: **thick**   <u>th</u>: **this**   zh: measure

Uzzia
   Biblical name   uh-ZĪ-uh, ōō-zē-YAH   əˈzaiə, uːziːˈjɑː

Uzziah
   Biblical name   uh-ZĪ-uh, ŌŌ-zē-YAH-hōō   əˈzaiə, ˌuːziːˈjɑhuː

Uzziel
   Biblical name   uh-ZĪ-uhl, ōō-zē-EL   əˈzaiəl, uːziːˈel

Uzzielite
   Biblical name   uh-ZĪ-LĬT, UHZ-ē-uh-LĬT   əˈzaiˌlait, ˈəziːəˌlait

V

Vaal
   South African river   VAHL   ˈvɑl

Vaasa
   prov & town, Finland   VAHS-ah   ˈvɑsɑː

Vaccaro
   Brenda, *US actress*   vuh-KAR-ō, vuh-KAHR-ō   vəˈkæroː, vəˈkaroː

Vachel
   pers. name   VĀ-chuhl   ˈveːtʃəl

Václav
   pers. name, Czech   VAHT-SLAHF   ˈvatˌslɑf

Vacuna
   ancient Sabine goddess of leisure   va-K(Y)ŌŌ-nuh   væˈk(j)uːnə

Vadim
   1. Roger, *French director*   vah-DĒM   vɑːdiːm
   2. pers. name, Russian   VAHD-yēm   ˈvɑːdjiːm

Vaduz
   city, Liechtenstein   fah-DŌŌTS   fɑˈduːts

Vai
   lang., people, Liberia, Sierra Leone   VĪ   ˈvai

Vaiden
   town, MS   VĀD-n   ˈveːdn̩

Vaikunth
   Indian festival   VĪ-KUNT   ˈβaiˌkunt

Vaillant
   George, *US archaeologist*   vuh-LAHNT   vəˈlɑnt

Vaishnavism
   worship of Vishnu   VĪSH-nuh-VIZ-uhm   ˈvaiʃnəˌvizəm

Vaizatha
   Biblical name   VĪ-zuh-thuh, VAH-yuh-ZAH-tah   ˈvaizəθə, ˌvajəˈzɑːtɑː

Vajezatha [Vaizatha]
   Biblical name   vuh-JEZ-uh-thuh, VA-juh-ZĀ-thuh,   vəˈdʒezəθə, ˌvædʒəˈzeːθə,
                VAH-yuh-ZAH-tah   ˌvajəˈzɑːtɑː

Val
   pers. name   VAL   ˈvæl

Foreign Sounds: ue: *Fr.* **rue**, *Ger.* **füllen**   uh(r): *Fr.* **boeuf**, *Ger.* **Höhle**   <u>kh</u>: *Ger.* **ich**, *Scot.* **loch**   g̅: *Sp.* **amigo**   y: *Sp.* **hablar**   hl: *Welsh* **Llanelli**.   CAPITALS: primary stress.   SMALL CAPS: secondary stress.   Ⓢ: U.S. pron.   Ⓔ: British pron.

Valais		
canton, Switzerland	vah-LE, Ⓢ va-LĀ	vɑːle, Ⓢ væ'leː
Valdai		
hills, Russia	vahl-DĪ	vɑl'dɑi
Valdemar		
1. king, Denmark; pers. name, Danish; fictional country, M. Lackey	VAHL-duh-MAHR	'vɑːldə,mɑ^r
2. Swedish	VAHL-duh-MAHR	'vɑːldə,mɑː^r
Val-de-Marne		
dept, Ile-de-France	vahl-duh-MAHRN	vɑːldəmɑːrn
Valdepeñas		
commune, Spain	bahl-dā-PĀN-yahs	bɑldeː'peːnjɑs
Valdés		
peninsula, Argentina	vahl-DES	vɑl'des
Valdez		
port, AK	val-DĒZ	væl'diːz
Valdez-Cordova		
division, AK	val-DĒZ-kawr-DŌ-vuh	væl'diːzkɔː^r'doːvə
Val-d'Oise		
dept, Ile-de-France	vahl-DWAHZ	vɑːldwɑːz
Valdosta		
city, GA	val-DAHS-tuh	væl'dɑstə
Valencia		
1. county, NM	vuh-LEN-ch(ē-)uh, vuh-LEN(T)-sē-uh	və'lentʃ(iː)ə, və'len(t)siːə
2. region, Spain	vah-LEN-thyah	vɑ'lenθjɑ
Valenciennes		
city, France	vah-lah^{n}s-YEN	vɑːlɑ̃sjen
Valens		
1. Roman emperor	VĀ-luhnz, VĀ-LENZ, VĀ-luhns	'veːlənz, 'veː,lenz, 'veːləns
2. pers. name, German	VAHL-ens	'vɑlens
Valentín		
pers. name, Spanish	bahl-ān-TĒN	bɑleːn'tiːn
Valentin		
1. pers. name, French	vah-lah^n-TE^n	vɑːlɑ̃tẽ
2. German	VAHL-en-TĒN	'vɑlen,tiːn
3. Serbo-Croatian	VAHL-en-TĒN	'vɑːlen,tiːn
Valentina		
pers. name, Russian	VUHL-yin-TĒN-uh	,vəljin't̪iːnə
Valentine		
1. saint; sweetheart; pers. name	VAL-uhn-TĪN	'vælən,tɑin
2. German	VAH-len-TĒ-nuh	,vɑlen'tiːnə
Valentinian		
Roman emperor	VAL-uhn-TIN-ē-uhn, -TIN-yuhn	,vælən'tiniːən, -'tinjən
Valentinianism		
form of Gnosticism	VAL-uhn-TIN-ē-uh-NIZ-uhm	,vælən'tiniːə,nizəm
Valentino		
1. Rudolph, *US actor*	VAL-uhn-TĒ-nō	,vælən'tiːnoː
2. pers. name, Italian	VAHL-ān-TĒ-nō	,vɑleːn'tiːnoː
Valenzuela		
Fernando, *Mexican baseball player*	VAL-uhnz-WĀ-luh	,vælənz'weːlə
Valera, de		
Eamon, *Irish statesman*	DEV-uh-LER-uh	,devə'lerə
Valeri		
pers. name, Russian	VUHL-YER-yi	,vəl'jerjij

Key (col. 2): a: **fad** ā: **fade** ah: **father** ar: **marry** aw: **law** e: **fed** ē: **feed** er: **merry** i: **hid** ī: **hide** ō: **coat** o͞o: **boot** oi: **boy** ow: **now** u: **put** uh: **above** uhr: **bird** ch: **chop** ng: **ring** sh: **show** th: **thick** t͟h: **this** zh: **measure**

Valeria
pers. name — vuh-LIR-ē-uh — və'liːriːə
Valerian
1. *Roman emperor* — vuh-LIR-ē-uhn — və'liːriːən
2. *pers. name, Russian* — VUHL-yir-YAHN — ˌvəljir'jaːn
Valeriano
pers. name, Spanish — bahl-ār-YAHN-ō — bɑleːr'janoː
Valerianus
pers. name, Latin — vuh-LIR-ē-Ā-nuhs — vəˌliriː'eːnəs
Valerie
pers. name — VAL-(uh-)rē — 'væl(ə)ri·
Valérie
pers. name, French — vah-lā-RĒ — vɑːleːriː
Valerius
1. *pers. name, German* — vah-LĀ-rē-us — vɑ'leːriːus
2. *Latin* — vuh-LIR-ē-uhs — və'liriːəs
Valéry
pers. name, French — vah-lā-RĒ — vɑːleːriː
Valga
town, Estonia — VAL-guh — 'vælgə
Valhalla
hall of the slain in Norse myth — val-HAL-uh, vahl-HAHL-uh — væl'hælə, vɑl'hɑlə
Valium
tdmk for diazepam — VAL-ē-uhm — 'væliːəm
Valjean
Jean, *hero of* Les Misérables, *V. Hugo* — vahl-ZHAH^n — vɑːlʒɑ̃
Valkyrie
Scandinavian mythical maidens — val-KIR-ē, VAL-kuh-rē — væl'kiri·, 'vælkəri·
Valla
Lorenzo, *Italian humanist* — VAHL-lah — 'vɑllɑ
Vallabhbhai
pers. name, Gujarati — VUHL-luhb-BAH-ē — ˌvəlləb'bɑ-iː
Valladolid
prov, city, Spain; town, Mexico; city, Philippines — bah(l)-yah-<u>thō</u>-LĒ(<u>TH</u>), ⓢ VAL-uh-duh-LID, -LĒD — bɑ(l)jɑðoː'liː(ð), ⓢ ˌvælədə'lid, -'liːd
Vallandigham
Clement Laird, *US political leader* — vuh-LAN-duh-guhm — və'lændəgəm
Vallauris
commune, France — vah-law-RĒS, vah-lō-RĒS — vɑːlɔːriːs, vɑːloːriːs
Valle Crucis
abbey, Wales — VAL-ē KROO-suhs — 'væli· 'kruːsəs
Valle d'Aosta
region, Italy — VAHL-ā dah-AW-stuh — ˌvaleː dɑ'ɔːstə
Vallejo
city, CA — vuh-LĀ-ō — və'leːoː
Valletta
city, Malta — vuh-LET-uh — və'lețə
Valli
Frankie, *US singer* — VAL-ē — 'væli·
Vallombrosa
resort, Italy — VAL-uhm-BRŌ-suh — ˌvæləm'broːsə
Valmiera
town, Latvia — VAHL-MYER-uh — 'valˌmjerə

Valois
  duchy, France   vahl-WAH   vɑːlwɑː

Valparaíso
  region, city, Chile; city, Mexico   bahl-pah-rah-Ē-sō, Ⓢ VAL-puh-RĀ-zō,   bɑlpɑrɑ'iːsoː,
                   -RĪ-zō   Ⓢ ˌvælpə'reːzoː, -'rɑizoː

Valparaiso
  1. town, FL   VAL-puh-RĪ-zō   ˌvælpə'rɑizoː
  2. town, IN   VAL-puh-RĀ-zō   ˌvælpə'reːzoː

Valpolicella
  wine   VAHL-PŌ-luh-CHEL-uh, VAL-   ˌvɑlˌpoːlə'tʃelə, ˌvæl-

Val Verde
  county, TX   val VUHRD-ē   væl 'vəʳdiˑ

Valvoline
  US oil co.   VAL-vuh-LĒN   'vælvəˌliːn

Van
  pers. name   VAN   'væn

vanadium
  element   vuh-NĀD-ē-uhm   və'neːdiːəm

Van Allen
  James, US physicist; radiation belt   van AL-uhn   væn 'ælən
    above Earth

Van Ark
  Joan, actress   van AHRK   væn 'ɑʳk

Van Allsburg
  Chris, US author   van-AWLZ-BUHRG   væn'ɔːlzˌbəʳg

Vanbrugh
  Sir John, English dramatist and   VAN-BRUK, VAN-bruh, van-BR͞OO   'vænˌbruk, 'vænbrə, væn'bruː
    architect

Van Buren
  Martin, 8th US president; Abigail,   van BYUR-uhn, vuhn   væn 'bjurən, vən
    US advice columnist; pers. name

Van Cleef
  Lee, US actor   van KLĒF   væn 'kliːf

Vancouver
  city, Canada; city, WA   van-K͞OO-vuhr   væn'kuːvəʳ

Vandalia
  city, IL   van-DĀL-yuh   væn'deːljə

Vandals
  ancient Germanic people   VAN-duhlz   'vændəlz

Van de Graaf
  Robert J., US physicist   VAN-duh GRAF, VAN duh GRAF   'vændə ˌgræf, ˌvæn də 'græf

Vandenberg
  Hoyt S., US general; US air force   VAN-duhn-BUHRG, VAN-duhm-BUHRG   'vændənˌbəʳg, 'vændəmˌbəʳg
    base

Van Depoele
  Charles Joseph, US inventor   VAN duh-P͞OOL   'væn dəˌpuːl

Vanderbilt
  US family name   VAN-duhr-BILT   'vændəʳˌbilt

van der Meere
  Simon, Dutch physicist (Nobel 1984)   VAHN duhr MER   ˌvɑn dəʳ 'meʳ

van der Waals
  J. D., Dutch physicist (Nobel 1910)   VAHN DUHR VAHLS, Ⓢ VAN duhr   ˌvɑn dəʳ 'vɑls, Ⓢ ˌvæn dəʳ
                WAWLZ   'wɔːlz

Van Devere
  Trish, US actress   VAN duh-VIR   ˌvæn də'viʳ

Key (col. 2):   a: fad   ā: fade   ah: father   ar: marry   aw: law   e: fed   ē: feed   er: merry   i: hid   ī: hide   ō: coat   o͞o: boot
oi: boy   ow: now   u: put   uh: above   uhr: bird   ch: chop   ng: ring   sh: show   th: thick   <u>th</u>: this   zh: measure

Vandross
   Luther, *US entertainer*   van-DRAWS   væn'drɔːs

Van Dyck, Vandyke
   Sir Anthony, *Flemish painter; pers.*   vahn DĪK, ⓢ van DĪK, vuhn DĪK   vɑn 'dɑik, ⓢ væn 'dɑik, vən
     name   'dɑik

Vane
   Sir John R., *English biochemist*   VĀN   'veːn
     (Nobel 1982)

Vanessa
   pers. name   vuh-NES-uh   və'nesə

Van Eyck
   Hubert *and* Jan, *Flemish painters*   vahn ĀK, ⓢ van ĪK   vɑn 'eːk, ⓢ væn 'ɑik

Vanga
   insectivorous bird   VAHNG-guh   'vɑŋgə

Van Gogh
   Vincent, *Dutch painter*   vahn ĠAWĠ, ⓢ van GŌ, van GAH<u>KH</u>   vɑn 'ɣɔːɣ, ⓢ væn 'goː, væn
      'gɑx

Van Heusen
   James, *US composer; brand of*   van HY$\overline{\text{OO}}$-zuhn   væn 'hjuːzən
     clothing

Vaniah
   Biblical name   vuh-NĪ-uh, vahn-YAH   və'nɑiə, vɑn'jɑː

Vanier
   city, Canada   va^{n}NYĀ, VAN-YĀ   væ'njeː, 'væn͵jeː

Vanir
   Scandinavian fertility gods   VAHN-IR   'vɑn͵i^r

Vanna
   pers. name (V. White)   VAN-uh   'vænə

Van Ness
   street, San Francisco, CA; pers.   van-(N)ES   væn'(n)es
     name

Vannevar
   pers. name   vuh-NĒ-VAHR   və'niː͵vɑ^r

Van Nostrand
   David, *US publisher*   van NŌ-struhnd   væn 'noːstrənd

Van Nuys
   region, Los Angeles, CA   van NĪZ   væn 'nɑiz

Vanocur
   Sander, *US newsman*   van-Ō-kuhr   væn'oːkə^r

Van Patten
   Dick, *US actor*   van PAT-n   væn 'pætn̩

Van Rensselaer
   Stephen, *US politician*   van REN(T)-suh-LĒR,   væn ͵ren(t)sə'liː^r, 'ren(t)sələ^r
      REN(T)-suh-luhr

Van Riebeeck Day
   holiday, S. Africa   vahn RĒ-BĀK   vɑn 'riː͵beːk

Vantaa
   city, airport, Finland   VAHN-tah   'vɑːntɑ

van't Hoff
   Jacobus Hendricus, *Dutch chemist*   vahnt HAWF   vɑnt 'hɔːf
     (Nobel 1901)

Vanua Levu
   island, Pacific Ocean   vuh-N$\overline{\text{OO}}$-uh LEV-$\overline{\text{oo}}$ və'nuːə 'levuː

Foreign Sounds: ue: *Fr.* **rue**, *Ger.* **füllen**   uh(r): *Fr.* **boeuf**, *Ger.* **Höhle**   <u>kh</u>: *Ger.* **ich**, *Scot.* **loch**   ḡ: *Sp.* **amigo**   v: *Sp.* **hablar**
hl: *Welsh* **Llanelli**.   CAPITALS: primary stress.   SMALL CAPS: secondary stress.   ⓢ: U.S. pron.   ⓔ: British pron.

Vanuatu
  islands, Pacific   VAHN-(y)uh-WAH-TŌŌ,   ˌvɑn(j)ə'wɑˌtuː, ˌvænə'wɑtuː
                                        VAN-uh-WAHT-ōō

Vanuatuan
  pert. to Vanuatu   VAHN-(y)uh-WAH-TŌŌ-uhn,   ˌvɑn(j)ə'wɑˌtuːən,
                                        VAN-(y)uh-WAHT-uh-wuhn   ˌvæn(j)ə'wɑtəwən

Van Vechten
  Carl, *US author*   van VEK-tuhn   væn 'vektən

Van Vleck
  John H., *US physicist (Nobel 1977)* van VLEK   væn 'vlek

Van Wert
  county, OH   van WUHRT   væn 'wəʳt

van Wijk
  pers. name, Dutch   vahn VĀK   vɑn 'veːk

Van Wyck
  pers. name   van WĪK, van WIK   væn 'wɑik, væn 'wik

Vanya
  pers. name   VAHN-yuh, VAN-yuh   'vɑnjə, 'vænjə

Van Zandt
  county, TX   van ZANT   væn 'zænt

Vanzetti
  Bartolomeo, *Italian anarchist*   van-ZET-ē   væn'zeʈiˑ
    executed in US

Vaporum, Mare
  see Mare Vaporum

Varanasi [Benares]
  city, India   vuh-RAHN-uh-sē   və'rɑnəsiˑ

Varèse
  Edgard, *US composer*   vuh-RĀZ, vuh-REZ   və'reːz, və'rez

Varese
  prov, city, Italy   vahr-Ā-sā, ⑤ vuh-RĀ-sē   vɑr'eːseˑ, ⑤ və'reːsiˑ

Varig
  Brazilian airline   VAHR-ig, VAR-ig   'vɑrig, 'værig

Varius
  pers. name, Latin   VAR-ē-uhs   'væriːəs

Varley
  John Herbert, *US author*   VAHR-lē   'vɑʳliˑ

Varmus
  Harold E., *US microbiologist (Nobel* VAHR-muhs   'vɑʳməs
    1989)

Varna
  prov, Bulgaria   VAHR-nuh   'vɑʳnə

Varro
  Marcus, *Roman scholar*   VAR-ō   'væroː

Varsa
  Buddhist penitential period   V̲AHR-shuh   'βɑʳʃə

Vartanantz Day
  Armenian commemoration   VAHR-tuh-NAHNTS   'vɑʳtəˌnɑnts

Varuna
  supreme Vedic god   VUR-un-uh, VAHR-uh-nuh   'vurunə, 'vɑrənə

Vasco
  1. *pers. name, Portuguese*   VAHSH-kōō, VAHS-kōō   'vɑːʃkuː, 'vɑːskuː
  2. *Spanish*   BAHS-kō, ⑤ VAS-kō   'bɑskoː, ⑤ 'væskoː

Key (col. 2):   a: fad ā: fade ah: father ar: marry aw: law e: fed ē: feed er: merry i: hid ī: hide ō: coat ōō: boot
oi: boy   ow: now   u: put   uh: above   uhr: bird   ch: chop   ng: ring   sh: show   th: thick   t̲h̲: this   zh: measure

Vasco da Gama
Portuguese navigator   VAHSH-ko͞o thuh ḠAH-muh,   ˌvɑːʃkuː ðə ˈɣɑːmə,
                                Ⓢ VAHS-kō duh GAHM-uh,   Ⓢ ˌvɑskoː də ˈɡɑmə,
                                GAH-muh; VAS-kō duh GAM-uh   ˈɡɑːmə; ˌvæskoː də ˈɡæmə

Vaseline
tdmk for petrolatum   VAS-uh-LĒN, VAS-uh-LĒN   ˈvæsəˌliːn, ˌvæsəˈliːn

Vashni
Biblical name   VASH-NĪ, VAHSH-nē, vahsh-NĒ   ˈvæʃˌnai, ˈvɑʃniː, vɑʃˈniː

Vashti
Biblical name   VAHSH-tē, VAHSH-TĪ   ˈvɑʃtiˑ, ˈvɑʃˌtai

Vasil
pers. name, Bulgarian   vah-SĒL   vɑːˈsiːl

Vasile
pers. name, Romanian   vah-SĒ-le   vɑˈsiːle

Vasili, -ly
pers. name, Russian   VUHS-YĒL-yi   ˌvəsˈjiːljij

Vaslav
pers. name, Russian   VUHT-SLAHF   ˌvətˈslɑːf

Vásquez
pers. name, Spanish   BAHS-kās, -kāth; Ⓢ VAS-K(W)EZ,   ˈbɑskeːs, -keːθ;
                                VAHS-   Ⓢ ˈvæsˌk(w)ez, ˈvɑs-

Vassar
College, *NY*   VAS-uhr   ˈvæsəʳ

VAT
value-added tax   VAT, VĒ-Ā-TĒ   ˈvæt, ˌviːˌeːˈtiː

Vatican
papal state, Rome   VAT-i-kuhn   ˈvæṭikən

Vaticanism
doctrine of supremacy of the pope   VAT-i-kuh-NIZ-uhm   ˈvæṭikəˌnizəm

Vaucluse
dept, France   vō-KLO͞OZ   voːkluːz

Vaud
canton, Switzerland   VŌ   voː

Vaughan, Vaughn
pers. name   VAWN, VAHN   ˈvɔːn, ˈvɑn

Vaughan Williams
Ralph, *composer*   RĀF VAWN WIL-yuhmz   ˈreːf ˌvɔːn ˈwiljəmz

Vaux
English beer   VAWKS, VAHKS   ˈvɔːks, ˈvɑks

Vaux
Calvert, *US landscape architect*   VAWZ, VAWKS, VAHKS, VŌKS   ˈvɔːz, ˈvɔːks, ˈvɑks, ˈvoːks

Vauxhall
pers. name   VAHK-SAWL, VAHKS-HAWL   ˈvɑkˌsɔːl, ˈvɑksˌhɔːl

Vaux's
swift   VAWK-suhz, VAHK-suhz   ˈvɔːksəz, ˈvɑksəz

VAX
tdmk for computer hardware   VAKS   ˈvæks

Veadar [Adar Sheni]
Jewish month   VĀ-AHD-AHR, VĀ-uh-DAHR, VĒ-   ˈveːˌadˌɑʳ, ˈveːəˌdɑʳ, ˈviː-

Veblen
Thorstein B., *US economist*   VEB-luhn   ˈveblən

Vecelli [Titian]
Tiziano, *Italian painter*   vā-CHEL-lē   veːˈtʃelliˑ

Veda
Hindu sacred writings   VĀD-uh   ˈveːdə

Vedaism *religion*	VĀD-uh-IZ-uhm	'veːdəˌizəm
Vedanta *Hindu philosophy*	vā-DAHNT-uh, vā-DANT-uh, vuh-	veː'dɑntə, veː'dæntə, və-
Vedantism *religion*	vā-DAHN-TIZ-uhm, vuh-DAN-	veː'dɑnˌtizəm, və'dæn-
Vedic *pert. to the* Veda	VĀD-ik	'veːdik
Vega Suzanne, *US singer; star; stringed instrument mfrs.*	VĒ-guh, VĀ-guh	'viːgə, 'veːgə
Vega Lope de, *Spanish dramatic poet*	V̲E-ḡah	'βeɣɑ
Veii *ancient city, central Italy*	VĒ-(Y)Ī, VĀ-(y)ē	'viːˌ(j)ɑi, 'veː(j)iː
Vela *constellation*	VĒ-luh	'viːlə
Velasco *pers. name, Spanish*	bā-LAHS-kō, [S] vuh-LAS-kō	beː'lɑskoː, [S] və'læskoː
Velázquez Diego, *Spanish painter*	bā-LAHTH-kāth, [S] vuh-LAS-kuhs, vuh-LAS-K(W)EZ	beː'lɑθkeːθ, [S] və'læskəs, və'læsˌk(w)ez
Velcro *tdmk for fasteners*	VEL-krō	'velkroː
Velia *ridge between Palatine and Oppian hills, Rome*	VĒ-lē-uh	'viːliːə
Velleius Paterculus *Roman historian*	vuh-LĒ-uhs puh-TUHR-kyuh-luhs	və'liːəs pə'tə^{r}kjələs
Vellelus *pers. name, Latin*	ve-LĒ-luhs	ve'liːləs
Velma *pers. name*	VEL-muh	'velmə
Venable *pers. name*	VEN-uh-buhl	'venəbəl
Venables *pers. name*	VEN-uh-buhlz	'venəbəlz
Venancio *pers. name, Spanish*	bā-NAHN-syō, -thyō, [S] vā-NAHN-sē-Ō	beː'nɑnsjoː, -θjoː, [S] veː'nɑnsiːˌoː
Venango *county, PA*	vi-NANG-gō	vi'næŋgoː
Venda *lang., people, Africa; independent homeland, S. Africa*	VEN-duh	'vendə
Vendée *river, dept, France*	vah^{n}-DĀ	vɑ̃deː
Vendémiaire *month, French Revolutionary calendar*	vah^{n}-dām-YER	vɑ̃deːmjer
Venelin *pers. name, Bulgarian*	ve-ne-LĒN	vene'liːn
Venetia *region, Italy*	vi-NĒ-sh(ē-)uh	vi'niːʃ(iː)ə

Venetian
    pert. to Venice   vuh-NĒ-shuhn   vəˈniːʃən

Venetic
    Indo-European lang., Italy   vuh-NET-ik   vəˈneţik

Veneto
    region, Italy   VĀ-nuh-TŌ, VEN-uh-TŌ   ˈveːnəˌtoː, ˈvenəˌtoː

Venezia [Venice]
    city, Italy   vuh-NET-sē-uh   vəˈnetsiːə

Venezuela
    republic, S. America   VEN-uhz(-uh)-WĀ-luh, -WĒ-luh   ˌvenəz(ə)ˈweːlə, -ˈwiːlə

Venezuelan
    pert. to Venezuela   VEN-uhz(-uh)-WĀ-luhn, -WĒ-luhn   ˌvenəz(ə)ˈweːlən, -ˈwiːlən

Venice
    city, Italy; city, CA, FL, IL   VEN-uhs   ˈvenəs

Venite
    liturgical chant   vuh-NĪT-ē, vuh-NĒ-TĀ, VE-   vəˈnɑiṭiˑ, vəˈniːˌteː, ve-

Venn
    John, *English logician*   VEN   ˈven

Venta
    river, Latvia, Lithuania   VEN-tuh   ˈventə

Ventnor
    street, Atlantic City, NJ   VENT-nuhr   ˈventnəʳ

Ventôse
    month, French Revolutionary   vahⁿ-TŌZ   vɑ̃toːz
        calendar

Ventris
    Michael, *British linguist*   VEN-tris, ⑤ VEN-truhs   ˈventris, ⑤ ˈventrəs

Ventspils
    port, Latvia   VENT-SPILS   ˈventˌspils

Ventura
    1. city, CA; computer software, US   ven-TYUR-uh, ven-CHUR-uh   venˈtjurə, venˈtʃurə
    2. pers. name, Spanish   bān-TOO-rah, ⑤ ven-TYUR-uh,   beːnˈtuːrɑ, ⑤ venˈtjurə,
        ven-CHUR-uh   venˈtʃurə

Venturi
    G. B., *Italian physicist;* Ken, *US*   ven-TUR-ē, ven-TYUR-ē, ven-CHUR-ē   venˈturiˑ, venˈtjuriˑ, venˈtʃuriˑ
        golfer

Venus
    Roman goddess of love; planet   VĒ-nuhs   ˈviːnəs

Venus de Milo
    statue of Aphrodite   VĒ-nuhs duh MĪ-lō   ˌviːnəs də ˈmɑiloː

Venusian
    pert. to Venus   vuh-NOO-zhuhn, vuhn-YOO-zhuhn   vəˈnuːʒən, vənˈjuːʒən

Venus's-flytrap
    insectivorous plant   VĒ-nuhs(-uhz)-FLĪ-TRAP   ˌviːnəs(əz)ˈflɑiˌtræp

Venustiano
    pers. name, Spanish   bā-noos-TYAHN-ō   beːnuːsˈtjɑnoː

Veps
    lang., people, Russia, Europe   VEPS   ˈveps

Vepsian [Veps]
    lang., Russia, Europe   VEP-sē-uhn   ˈvepsiːən

Vera
    pers. name   VIR-uh, VER-uh   ˈvirə, ˈverə

Veracruz
    seaport, state, Mexico   VER-uh-KROOS, VER-uh-KROOZ   ˌverəˈkruːs, ˌverəˈkruːz

---

Foreign Sounds: ue: *Fr.* **rue**, *Ger.* **füllen** uh(r): *Fr.* **boeuf**, *Ger.* **Höhle** <u>kh</u>: *Ger.* **ich**, *Scot.* **loch** ḡ: *Sp.* **amigo** v: *Sp.* **hablar**
hl: *Welsh* **Llanelli**. CAPITALS: primary stress. SMALL CAPS: secondary stress. ⑤: U.S. pron. Ⓔ: British pron.

Vercingetorix
  Gallic chieftain   VUHR-suhn-JET-uh-riks   ˌvəʳsən'dʒeţəriks
Verde
  1. river, AZ   VUHRD-ē, VERD-ē   'vəʳdi·, 've ʳdi·
  2. river, Brazil   VERD-uh   've ʳdə
  3. cape, Senegal   VUHRD   'vəʳd
Verdelho
  wine   ver-DEL-yōō   veʳ'deljuː
Verdi
  Giuseppe, *Italian composer*   VERD-ē   've ʳdi·
Verdicchio
  wine   ver-DIK-ē-ō   veʳ'dikiːoː
Verdigris
  river, KS, OK   VUHR-duh-gruhs   'vəʳdəgrəs
Verdin
  songbird   VUHRD-n   'vəʳdn̩
Verdun
  city, France; city, Canada   ver-DUHⁿ, Ⓢ vuhr-DUHN   verdœ̃, Ⓢ vəʳ'dən
Vereen
  Ben, *US actor, singer, dancer*   vuh-RĒN   və'riːn
Vereeniging
  city, South Africa   fuh-RĒ-ni-KING   fə'riːniˌkiŋ
Verein
  German union association   fer-ĪN   fer'ɑin
Vergennes
  1. Charles, *French statesman* ver-ZHEN   verʒen
  2. city, VT   vuhr-JENZ   vəʳ'dʒenz
Vergil, Virgil
  Roman poet; pers. name   VUHR-juhl   'vəʳdʒəl
Vergilian, Virgilian
  pert. to Vergil   vuhr-JIL-ē-uhn   vəʳ'dʒiliːən
Verlaine
  Paul, *French poet*   ver-LEN, Ⓢ vuhr-LĀN   verlen, Ⓢ vəʳ'leːn
Vermeer
  Jan, *Dutch painter*   vuhr-MER, vuhr-MIR   vəʳ'meʳ, vəʳ'miʳ
Vermilion
  pl. name, US   vuhr-MIL-yuhn   vəʳ'miljən
Vermont
  state, US   vuhr-MAHNT   vəʳ'mɑnt
Vermonter
  inhabitant of Vermont   vuhr-MAHNT-uhr   vəʳ'mɑntəʳ
Verna
  pers. name   VUHR-nuh   'vəʳnə
Vernal
  city, UT   VUHRN-l   'vəʳn̩
Verne
  1. Jules, *French writer*   VERN, Ⓢ VUHRN   vern, Ⓢ 'vəʳn
  2. pers. name   VUHRN   'vəʳn
Verne, La
  see La Verne
Verner
  1. Karl, *Danish philologist*   VER-nuhr, Ⓢ VUHR-nuhr   'veʳnəʳ, Ⓢ 'vəʳnəʳ
  2. pers. name   VUHR-nuhr   'vəʳnəʳ
  3. Swedish   VER-nuhr   'veʳnəʳ

Key (col. 2):   a: fad   ā: fade   ah: father   ar: marry   aw: law   e: fed   ē: feed   er: merry   i: hid   ī: hide   ō: coat   ōō: boot
oi: boy   ow: now   u: put   uh: above   uhr: bird   ch: chop   ng: ring   sh: show   th: thick   th: this   zh: measure

Vernier

Pierre, *French mathematician; scale*   vern-YĀ, Ⓢ VUHR-nē-uhr   vernjeː, Ⓢ 'vəʳniːəʳ

Vernon

pers. name   VUHRN-uhn   'vəʳnən

Verona

prov, town, Italy   vuh-RŌ-nuh   və'roːnə

Veronese

1. Paolo, *cognomen of* P. Caliari,   VĀ-rō-NĀ-zā   ˌveːroː'neːzeː
     Venetian painter

2. *pert. to* Verona   VER-uh-NĒZ, -NĒS   ˌverə'niːz, -'niːs

Veronica

pers. name   vuh-RAHN-i-kuh   və'rɑnikə

Verrazano

Giovanni de, *Italian navigator*   VER-uh-ZAHN-ō, VER-uht-SAHN-ō   ˌverə'zɑnoː, ˌverət'sɑnoː

Verrazano Narrows

bridge, New York City   VER-uh-ZAHN-ō NAR-ōz   ˌverə'zɑnoː 'næroːz

Verres

Roman politician   VER-ĒZ   'verˌiːz

Verrius

pers. name, Latin   VER-ē-uhs   'veriːəs

Verrocchio

Andrea del, *Florentine sculptor*   ver-RŌK-yō   ver'roːkjoː

Versailles

1. *city, France*   ver-SAH-yuh, Ⓢ vuhr-SĪ, ver-SĪ   versɑːj, Ⓢ vəʳ'sɑi, veʳ'sɑi

2. *US pl. name*   vuhr-SĀLZ   vəʳ'seːlz

Vertebrata

subphylum of vertebrates   VUHRT-uh-BRAHT-uh,   ˌvəʳtə'brɑtə, ˌvəʳtə'breːtə
     VUHRT-uh-BRĀT-uh

Vertumnus

Etruscan/Roman god of change   vuhr-TUHM-nuhs   vəʳ'təmnəs

Verulam

Baron, *title of* Francis Bacon   VER-(y)uh-luhm   'ver(j)ələm

Verulamium

ancient name of St. Albans   VER-(y)uh-LĀ-mē-uhm   ˌver(j)ə'leːmiːəm

Verus

Lucius, *Roman co-emperor with* M.   VIR-uhs, VER-uhs   'virəs, 'verəs
     Aurelius

Verwoerd

Hendrik, *prime minister, S. Africa*   fuhr-VO͞ ORT   fəʳ'vuˑʳt

Vesak

Buddhist holiday   V̲Ā-SHAHK   'βeːˌʃɑk

Vesalius

Andreas, *Flemish anatomist*   vuh-SĀ-lē-uhs, vuh-SĀL-yuhs,   və'seːliːəs, və'seːljəs,
     vuh-ZĀ(L)-yuhs   və'zeː(l)jəs

Vesey

pers. name   VĒ-zē   'viːziˑ

Vespa

Italian motor scooter co.   VES-puh   'vespə

Vespasian

Roman emperor; pers. name   ves-PĀ-zh(ē-)uhn   ves'peːʒ(iː)ən

Vespucci

Amerigo, *Italian explorer*   ves-PO͞ O-chē   ves'puːtʃiˑ

Vesta

Roman goddess of the hearth;   VES-tuh   'vestə
     wooden match; pers. name

Vestal Virgins
   Roman virgins in temple of Vesta   VES-tuhl VUHR-juhnz   ˌvestəl ˈvəʳdʒənz

Vestavia Hills
   city, AL   ves-TĀ-vē-uh HILZ   vesˌteːviːə ˈhilz

Vestine
   Ernest Harry, *US geophysicist*   VES-TĪN   ˈvesˌtɑin

Vestmannaeyjar [Westman]
   islands, Iceland   VEST-MAHN-uh-Ā-YAHR   ˈvestˌmanəˈeːˌjaʳ

Vesuvianite
   mineral   vuh-SOO-vē-uh-NĪT   vəˈsuːviːəˌnɑit

Vesuvio [Vesuvius]
   volcano, Italy   vā-ZOOV-yō   veːˈzuːvjoː

Vesuvius
   volcano, Italy   vuh-SOO-vē-uhs   vəˈsuːviːəs

Vettisfoss
   waterfall, Norway   VET-uhs-FAWS   ˈvetəsˌfɔːs

Vettius
   Roman name   VET-ē-uhs   ˈveʈiːəs

Via Aemilia
   ancient Roman road   VĪ-uh ē-MIL-ē-uh, VĒ-uh   ˌvɑiə iːˈmiliːə, ˌviːə

Via Appia
   ancient Roman road   VĪ-uh AP-ē-uh, VĒ-uh   ˌvɑiə ˈæpiːə, ˌviːə

Viacom
   US communications co.   VĪ-uh-KAHM   ˈvɑiəˌkɑm

Via Dolorosa
   Christ's route to Golgotha   VĒ-uh DAHL-uh-RŌ-suh, DŌ-luh-RŌ-suh   ˌviːə ˌdɑləˈroːsə, ˌdoːləˈroːsə

Via Flamina
   ancient Roman road   VĪ-uh FLAM-uh-nuh, VĒ-uh   ˌvɑiə ˈflæmənə, ˌviːə

Via Lata
   ancient Roman road   VĪ-uh LAHT-uh, VĒ-uh   ˌvɑiə ˈlɑʈə, ˌviːə

Via Latina
   ancient Roman road   VĪ-uh luh-TĪ-nuh, VĒ-uh luh-TĒ-nuh   ˌvɑiə ləˈtɑinə, ˌviːə ləˈtiːnə

Via Nova
   ancient Roman road   VĪ-uh NŌ-vuh, VĒ-uh   ˌvɑiə ˈnoːvə, ˌviːə

Via Sacra
   ancient Roman road   VĪ-uh SAK-ruh, VĒ-uh, SĀ-kruh   ˌvɑiə ˈsækrə, ˌviːə, ˈseːkrə

Via Veneto
   ancient Roman road   VĪ-uh VEN-uht-ō, VĒ-uh   ˌvɑiə ˈvenəʈoː, ˌviːə

Vibram
   tdmk for shoe soles   VĪ-bruhm   ˈvɑibrəm

Viburnum
   plant   vī-BUHR-nuhm   vɑiˈbəʳnəm

Vic, Vick
   pers. name   VIK   ˈvik

Vicary
   pers. name   VIK-(uh-)rē   ˈvik(ə)riˑ

Vicente
   pers. name, Spanish   bē-SĀN-tā, bē-THĀN-tā   biːˈseːnteː, biːˈθeːnteː

Vicenzo
   pers. name, Italian   vē-CHENT-sō   viːˈtʃentsoː

Vichy
   1. town, France   vē-SHĒ, Ⓢ VISH-ē, VĒ-shē   viːʃiː, Ⓢ ˈviʃiˑ, ˈviːʃiˑ
   2. mineral water   VISH-ē   ˈviʃiˑ

Key (col. 2):   a: fad   ā: fade   ah: father   ar: marry   aw: law   e: fed   ē: feed   er: merry   i: hid   ī: hide   ō: coat   ōō: boot
oi: boy   ow: now   u: put   uh: above   uhr: bird   ch: chop   ng: ring   sh: show   th: thick   t̲h̲: this   zh: measure

Vichyssoise
  cream of potato soup   VISH-ē-SWAHZ, VĒ-shē-SWAHZ   ˌviʃiː'swɑz, ˌviːʃiː'swɑz
Vicki
  1. pers. name   VIK-ē   'vikiˑ
  2. German   VIK-ē   'vikiː
Vickie, Vicky
  pers. name   VIK-ē   'vikiˑ
Vicksburg
  city, MS   VIKS-BUHRG   'viksˌbəʳg
Vico
  Giovanni, *Italian historian*   VĒ-kō   'viːkoː
Victoire
  pers. name, French   vēk-TWAHR   viːktwɑːr
Víctor
  pers. name, Spanish   BĒK-tawr   'biːktɔːr
Victor
  1. pers. name   VIK-tuhr   'viktəʳ
  2. Danish   VĒK-TAWR   'viːkˌtɔːr
  3. French   vēk-TAWR   viːktɔːr
  4. German   VIK-TAWR   'vikˌtɔːʳ
  5. Romanian   vēk-TAWR   viːk'tɔːr
Victoria
  1. Roman personification of victory;   vik-TŌR-ē-uh, vik-TAWR-ē-uh   vik'tɔːriːə, vik'tɔːriːə
     Queen of England; pers. name
  2. French   vēk-tawr-YAH   viːktɔːrjɑː
  3. German   vik-TŌR-ē-ah   vik'tɔːriːɑ
  4. Swedish   vik-TOO-rē-ah   vik'tuːriːɑː
Victorian
  pert. to Queen Victoria *or her reign*   vik-TŌR-ē-uhn, vik-TAWR-ē-uhn   vik'tɔːriːən, vik'tɔːriːən
Victoriana
  things pert. to Queen Victoria *or her*   vik-TŌR-ē-AN-uh, vik-TAWR-ē-AN-uh,   vik'tɔːriː'ænə, vik'tɔːriː'ænə,
     reign   -AHN-uh, -Ā-nuh   -'ɑnə, -'eːnə
Victoriano
  pers. name, Spanish   bēk-tōr-YAHN-ō   biːktɔːr'jɑnoː
Victrola
  tdmk for phonographs   vik-TRŌ-luh   vik'troːlə
Vida
  pers. name   VĒD-uh, VĪD-uh   'viːdə, 'vaidə
Vidal
  Gore, *US writer*   vi-DAHL, vi-DAWL   vi'dɑl, vi'dɔːl
Vidalia
  city, GA; town, LA; onion variety   vuh-DĀL-yuh, vuh-DĀ-lē-uh, vī-   və'deːljə, və'deːliːə, vai-
Vidal Sassoon
  haircare products co.   vi-DAL sa-SOON, vi-DAHL   vi'dæl sæ'suːn, vi'dɑl
Vidkun
  pers. name, Norwegian   VID-kun   'vidkun
Vidmar
  pers. name   VID-MAHR   'vidˌmɑʳ
Vidor
  King Wallis, *US motion-picture*   VĒ-DŌR, -DAWR   'viːˌdoːʳ, -ˌdɔːʳ
     director
Vieira
  pers. name, Portuguese   VYĀ-ruh   'vjeːrə
Viejas
  Indian reservation, US   VYĀ-HAHS, vē-Ā-HAHS   'vjeːˌhɑs, viː'eːˌhɑs

---

Foreign Sounds: ue: *Fr.* **rue**, *Ger.* **füllen**   uh(r): *Fr.* **boeuf**, *Ger.* **Höhle**   <u>kh</u>: *Ger.* **ich**, *Scot.* **loch**   ḡ: *Sp.* amigo   <u>v</u>: *Sp.* hablar
hl: *Welsh* **Llanelli**.   CAPITALS: primary stress.   SMALL CAPS: secondary stress.   Ⓢ: U.S. pron.   Ⓔ: British pron.

Vienna
  1. city, Austria   vē-EN-uh   viː'enə
  2. city, GA   vī-EN-uh   vɑi'enə

Vienne
  river, dept, France   VYEN   vjen

Viennese
  pert. to Vienna   VĒ-uh-NĒZ, VĒ-uh-NĒS   ˌviːə'niːz, ˌviːə'niːs

Vientiane
  city, Laos   vyen-TYAHN   vjen'tjɑn

Vierwaldstätter See [Lucerne]
  lake, Switzerland   fir-VAHLT-SHTET-uhr ZĀ   fiʳ'vɑlt,ʃtetəʳ ˌzeː

Vietcong
  Communist guerrillas, Vietnam   vē-ET-KAWNG, vyet-KAWNG,   viːˌet'kɔːŋ, vjet'kɔːŋ,
                                 VĒ-uht-KAWNG, vēt-KAWNG,   ˌviːət'kɔːŋ, viːt'kɔːŋ,
                                 -KAHNG   -'kɑŋ

Viet Minh
  Vietnamese faction   vē-ET MIN, vyet, VĒ-uht, vēt   viː'et 'min, vjet, ˌviːət, viːt

Vietnam
  country, Asia   vē-ET-NAHM, vyet-, VĒ-uht-, vēt-,   viːˈet'nɑm, vjet-, ˌviːət-,
                         -NAM   viːt-, -'næm

Vietnamese
  lang., people, Indochina   VĒ-ET-nuh-MĒZ, VYET-, VĒT-, -na-MĒZ,   ˌviːˌetnə'miːz, ˌvjet-, ˌviːt-,
                         -nah-MĒZ, -MĒS   -næ'miːz, -nɑ'miːz, -'miːs

Vieux Carré
  French Quarter, New Orleans   VYŌŌ KAHR-Ā, VŌŌ   ˌvjuː kɑr'eː, ˌvuː

Vieux Montréal
  College, Canada   vyuh(r) mawⁿ-re-AHL, ⑤ VYUHR   vjœː mõreɑːl, ⑤ ˌvjəʳ
                         MAHN-trē-AWL, MUHN-   ˌmɑntriː'ɔːl, ˌmən-

Vigan
  municipality, Philippines   VĒ-GAHN   'viːˌgɑn

Vigdis
  pers. name, Icelandic   VIG-DĒS   'vig,diːs

Vigilius
  antipope   vuh-JIL-ē-uhs   və'dʒiliːəs

Vignola
  Giacomo da, *Renaissance Italian*   vēn-YŌ-lah   viːn'joːlɑ
    architect

Vigo
  1. prov, Spain   BĒ-ḡō, ⑤ VĒ-gō   'biːɣoː, ⑤ 'viːgoː
  2. county, IN   VĒ-gō, VĪ-gō   'viːgoː, 'vɑigoː

Vigoda
  Abe, *US actor*   vuh-GŌD-uh   və'goːdə

Vijag
  Armenian festival   VĒ-(Y)AHG   'viːˌ(j)ɑg

Vijaya
  pers. name, Hindi   vi-JĪ-(y)uh   vi'dʒɑi(j)ə

Vijayawada
  city, India   VIJ-uh-yuh-WAHD-uh   ˌvidʒəjə'wɑdə

Vikenti, -ty
  pers. name, Russian   vēk-YENT-yi   viːk'jentjij

Viking
  Scandinavian pirate   VĪ-king   'vɑikiŋ

Vikki
  pers. name   VIK-ē   'vikiˑ

Key (col. 2):   a: fa**d**   ā: fa**de**   ah: f**a**ther   ar: m**a**rry   aw: l**aw**   e: f**e**d   ē: f**ee**d   er: m**e**rry   i: h**i**d   ī: h**i**de   ō: c**oa**t   ōō: b**oo**t
oi: b**oy**   ow: n**ow**   u: p**u**t   uh: **a**bove   uhr: b**ir**d   ch: **ch**op   ng: ri**ng**   sh: **sh**ow   th: **th**ick   <u>th</u>: <u>th</u>is   zh: mea**s**ure

Viktor
    1. pers. name, Czech, German,   VIK-TAWR   'vik‚tɔːr
    Swedish
    2. Russian   VYĒK-tuhr   'vjiːktər
Viktoria
    pers. name, German   vik-TŌR-ē-ah   vik'toːriːɑ
Vila
    seaport, Vanuatu   VĒ-luh   'viːlə
Vila Real
    prov & town, Portugal   VĒ-luh rē-AHL   ‚viːlə riː'ɑl
Vilas
    county, WI   VĪ-luhs   'vɑiləs
Vilfredo
    pers. name, Italian   vēl-FRĀD-ō   viːl'freːdoː
Vilhelm
    1. pers. name, Danish, Norwegian   VIL-HELM   'vil‚helm
    2. Swedish   VIL-(h)uhlm   'vil(h)əlm
Vilhjálmur
    pers. name, Icelandic   VIL-HYOWL-muhr   'vil‚hjɑulmər
Viljandi
    town, Estonia   VIL-YAHN-dē   'vil‚jɑndiˑ
Villa
    Pancho, *Mexican revolutionary &*   VĒ-(y)uh   'viː(j)ə
    outlaw
Villahermosa
    city, Mexico   <u>v</u>ē-yah-er-MŌ-sah   βiːjɑer'moːsɑ
Villa-Lobos
    Heitor, *Brazilian composer*   VĒ-lah-LŌ-bush, ⑤ VĒ-luh-LŌ-bōs   ‚viːlɑ'loːbuʃ, ⑤ ‚viːlə'loːboːs
Villanovan
    Iron age culture   VIL-uh-NŌ-vuhn, VĒ-luh-NŌ-vuhn   ‚vilə'noːvən, ‚viːlə'noːvən
Ville de Paris
    dept, France   vēl duh pah-RĒ   viːl də pɑːriː
Villella
    Edward, *US ballet dancer*   vuh-LEL-uh   və'lelə
Ville Platte
    town, LA   vēl PLAT   viːl 'plæt
Villiers
    pers. name   VIL-yuhrz   'viljərz
Villius
    pers. name, Latin   VIL-ē-uhs   'viliːəs
Villon
    François, *French writer*   vē-YAWⁿ   viːjɔ̃
Vilmos
    pers. name, Hungarian   VIL-mawsh   'vilmɔːʃ
Vilna [Vilnius]
    city, Lithuania   VIL-nuh   'vilnə
Vilnius
    city, Lithuania   VIL-nē-uhs   'vilniːəs
Viminal
    hill, Rome, Italy   VIM-uhn-l   'vimənḷ
Viña
    pers. name   VĒN-yuh   'viːnjə
Viña del Mar
    town, Chile   VĒN-yuh <u>th</u>el MAHR   'viːnjə ðel 'mɑʳ

Foreign Sounds: ue: *Fr.* **rue,** *Ger.* **füllen**   uh(r): *Fr.* **boeuf,** *Ger.* **Höhle**   <u>kh</u>: *Ger.* **ich,** *Scot.* **loch**   g̃: *Sp.* amigo   <u>v</u>: *Sp.* hablar
hl: *Welsh* **Llanelli.**   CAPITALS: primary stress.   SMALL CAPS: secondary stress.   ⑤: U.S. pron.   ⑥: British pron.

Vinayak
   pers. name, Hindi   VIN-ī-(Y)AHK   ˌvinɑi'(j)ɑk
Vincas
   pers. name, Lithuanian   VINT-sahs   'vintsɑs
Vincennes
   1. commune, France   veⁿ-SEN   vẽsen
   2. city, IN; US navy warship   vin-SENZ   vin'senz
Vincent
   1. pers. name, English, Norwegian   VIN-suhnt   'vinsənt
   2. Dutch   vin-SENT   vin'sent
   3. French   veⁿ-SAHⁿ   vẽsɑ̃
Vincente
   pers. name, Spanish   bēn-THĀN-tā, bēn-SĀN-tā,   biːn'θeːnteː, biːn'seːnteː,
                      Ⓢ vin-SEN-tā, vin-SENT-ē   Ⓢ vin'senteː, vin'senti·
Vincentian
   religious order   vin-SENT-ē-uhn, SEN-shuhn   vin'sentiːən, -'senʃən
Vincentius
   pers. name, Latin   vin-SEN-sh(ē-)uhs   vin'senʃ(iː)əs
Vincenzo
   pers. name, Italian   vēn-CHENT-sō   viːn'tʃentsoː
Vinci, da
   see Leonardo da Vinci
Vindhya
   mtn. range, India   VIND-yuh, VIN-dē-uh   'vindjə, 'vindiːə
Vingt-et-un
   game   VAN-TĀ-UHN   ˌvænˌteː'ən
Vinho verde
   wine   VĒN-yo͞o VERD-uh, Ⓢ VĒ-nō VERD-ē   ˌviːnjuː 'veʳdə, Ⓢ ˌviːnoː
                                                  'veʳdi·
Vinita
   city, OK   vuh-NĒT-uh   və'niːţə
Vinita Park
   city, MO   vuh-NĒT-uh PAHRK   və'niːţə 'pɑʳk
Vinland
   region, eastern N. America   VIN-luhnd, VIN-LAND   'vinlənd, 'vinˌlænd
Vinnie
   pers. name   VIN-ē   'vini·
Vinogradoff
   Sir Paul Gavrilovitch, *British jurist*   VĒ-nuh-GRAHD-uhf   ˌviːnə'grɑdəf
     and historian
Vinogradov
   Ivan Matveyevich, *Soviet*   VYI-nuh-GRAHD-uhf   ˌvjinə'grɑːdəf
    mathematician
Vinson Massif
   mtn. range, Antarctica   VIN-suhn ma-SĒF   'vinsən mæ'siːf
Vintilă
   pers. name, Romanian   vēn-TĒ-luh   viːn'tiːlə
Vinton
   Bobby, *US entertainer*   VINT-n   'vintn̩
Viola
   pers. name   vī-Ō-luh, vē-Ō-luh, VĪ-uh-luh,   vai'oːlə, viː'oːlə, 'vaiələ,
                      VĒ-uh-luh   'viːələ
Violet
   pers. name   VĪ-(uh-)luht   'vai(ə)lət

Key (col. 2):   a: fad   ā: fade   ah: father   ar: marry   aw: law   e: fed   ē: feed   er: merry   i: hid   ī: hide   ō: coat   o͞o: boot
oi: boy   ow: now   u: put   uh: above   uhr: bird   ch: chop   ng: ring   sh: show   th: thick   th̲: this   zh: measure

Vipsania
   pers. name, Latin   vip-SĀ-nē-uh, vip-SĀN-yuh   vipˈseːniːə, vipˈseːnjə

Vipsanius
   pers. name, Latin   vip-SĀ-nē-uhs, vip-SĀN-yuhs   vipˈseːniːəs, vipˈseːnjəs

Virbius
   demon, resurrection of Hippolytus   VUHR-bē-uhs, VIR-bē-uhs   ˈvəʳbiːəs, ˈviʳbiːəs

Virden
   city, IL   VUHRD-n   ˈvəʳdn̩

Vireo
   songbird   VIR-ē-ō   ˈviriːoː

Virgen del Pilar
   Spanish festival   bir-Ḡ̄AN del pē-LAHR   birˈɣeːn del piːˈlɑr

Virgil
   1. pers. name   VUHR-juhl   ˈvəʳdʒəl
   2. see Vergil

Virgile
   pers. name, French   vēr-ZHĒL   viːrʒiːl

Virgilian
   see Vergilian

Virginia
   1. state, US; pers. name   vuhr-JIN-yuh, vuhr-JIN-ē-uh   vəʳˈdʒinjə, vəʳˈdʒiniːə
   2. Italian   vēr-JĒN-yah   viːrˈdʒiːnjɑ

Virginie
   pers. name, French   vēr-zhē-NĒ   viːrʒiːniː

Virginius
   pers. name   vuhr-JIN-yuhs, vuhr-JIN-ē-uhs   vəʳˈdʒinjəs, vəʳˈdʒiniːəs

Virgo
   constellation, sign of the zodiac   VUHR-gō, VIR-gō   ˈvəʳgoː, ˈviʳgoː

Virgoan
   person born under sign of Virgo   VUHR-GŌ-uhn, VIR-GŌ-uhn   ˈvəʳˌgoːən, ˈviʳˌgoːən

Viroqua
   city, WI   vī-RŌ-kwuh   vɑiˈroːkwə

Virtanen
   Arturi Ilmari, *Finnish biochemist*   VIR-tuh-NEN   ˈviʳtəˌnen
   (Nobel 1945)

Visa
   tdmk for a credit card   VĒ-zuh, VĒ-suh   ˈviːzə, ˈviːsə

Visalia
   city, CA   vi-SĀL-yuh, vī-SĀL-yuh   viˈseːljə, vɑiˈseːljə

Visayan
   Malay people   vuh-SĪ-uhn   vəˈsɑiən

Visby
   city, Sweden   VIZ-bē   ˈvizbiˑ

Visconti
   Italian family name   vēs-KŌN-tē, Ⓢ vis-KAHNT-ē   viːsˈkoːntiˑ, Ⓢ visˈkɑntiˑ

Vishakhapatnam
   city, India   vi-SHAHK-uh-PUHT-nuhm   viˌʃɑkəˈpətnəm

Vishniac
   Roman, *Russian-US biologist*   VISH-nē-AK   ˈviʃniːˌæk

Vishnu
   Hindu god, member of the supreme   VISH-n‾oo   ˈviʃnuː
   triad

Visigoth
   westerly division of the Goths   VIZ-uh-GAHTH   ˈvizəˌgɑθ

Foreign Sounds: ue: *Fr.* **rue**, *Ger.* **füllen**   uh(r): *Fr.* **boeuf**, *Ger.* **Höhle**   kh: *Ger.* **ich**, *Scot.* **loch**   ḡ: *Sp.* **amigo**   v: *Sp.* **hablar**   hl: *Welsh* **Llanelli.**   CAPITALS: primary stress.   SMALL CAPS: secondary stress.   Ⓢ: U.S. pron.   Ⓔ: British pron.

Vistritsa [Aliákmon]
  river, Greece, Macedonia   vis-TRĒT-suh   vis'triːtsə

Vistula
  river, Poland   VIS-chuh-luh, VIS-tuh-luh   'vistʃələ, 'vistələ

Vital
  pers. name, French   vē-TAHL   viːtaːl

Vitalian
  pope   vuh-TĀ-lē-uhn, vuh-TĀL-yuhn   və'teːliːən, və'teːljən

Vítézslav
  pers. name, Czech   VĒ-ches-LAHF   'viːtʃes͵laːf

Vitebsk
  city, Belorussia   VĒ-TEPSK, VĒ-TEBSK, vi-TEPSK   'viː͵tepsk, 'viː͵tebsk, vi'tepsk

Vitellius
  Roman emperor   vuh-TEL-ē-uhs   və'teliːəs

Viterbo
  1. College, WI   vi-TER-bō, vi-TUHR-bō   vi'teʳboː, vi'təʳboː
  2. prov, Italy   vē-TER-bō   viː'teʳboː

Viti Levu
  island, Fiji   VĒT-ē LEV-o͞o   ͵viːṭi· 'levuː

Vitis vinifera
  grape vine   VĪT-uhs vuh-NIF-uh-ruh   'vaiṭəs və'nifərə

Vito
  pers. name, Italian   VĒ-tō, ⓢ VĒT-ō   'viːtoː, ⓢ 'viːṭoː

Vitruvius
  Roman architect, author   vuh-TRO͞O-vē-uhs   və'truːviːəs

Vittore
  pers. name, Italian   vēt-TŌ-rä   viːt'toːreː

Vittoria
  pers. name, Italian   vēt-TŌR-yah   viːt'toːrja

Vittorio
  pers. name, Italian   vēt-TŌR-yō   viːt'toːrjoː

Vitus
  1. Christian saint   VĪT-uhs   'vaiṭəs
  2. pers. name, Danish   VĒ-tus   'viːtus

Vivaldi
  Antonio, *Italian composer*   vi-VAHL-dē, vi-VAWL-dē   vi'vɑldi·, vi'vɔːldi·

Vivant
  pers. name, French   vē-VAHⁿ   viːvɑ̃

Vivian, Vivien
  pers. name   VIV-ē-uhn, VIV-yuhn   'viviːən, 'vivjən

Vivienne
  pers. name   VIV-ē-uhn, VIV-ē-EN   'viviːən, ͵viviː'en

Vizcaya
  prov, Spain   bēth-KAH-yah, ⓢ vis-KĪ-(y)uh, vith-KĪ-(y)uh   biːθ'kɑjɑ, ⓢ vis'kai(j)ə, viθ'kai(j)ə

Vlaanderen [Flanders]
  region, Belgium   VLAHN-duh-ruh(n)   'vlaːndərə(n)

Vlad
  1. pers. name   VLAD   'vlæd
  2. Romanian   VLAHD   'vlaːd

Vladimír
  pers. name, Czech   VLAH-jim-ĒR   'vlaːdʒim͵iːr

Key (col. 2):   a: fad   ā: fade   ah: father   ar: marry   aw: law   e: fed   ē: feed   er: merry   i: hid   ī: hide   ō: coat   o͞o: boot
oi: boy   ow: now   u: put   uh: above   uhr: bird   ch: chop   ng: ring   sh: show   th: thick   th: this   zh: measure

Vladimir
1. pers. name	VLAD-uh-MIR, vluh-DĒ-MIR	'vlædə‚mir, vlə'diː‚mir
2. Russian	VLUH-DĒM-yir	‚vlə'ḏiːmjir
3. Serbo-Croatian	VLAHD-ē-MĒR	'vlaːdiː‚miːr

Vladislav
1. pers. name, Czech	VLAH-jis-LAHF	'vlaːdʒis‚laːf
2. Russian	vluh-di-SLAHF	vlə‚ḏi'slaːf

Vladivostok
city, Russia	VLUHD-yi-vuh-STAWK,	‚vlədjivə'stɔːk,
	ⓢ VLAD-uh-vuh-STAHK,	ⓢ ‚vlædəvə'stak,
	VLAD-uh-VAHS-TAHK	‚vlædə'vas‚tak

Vlaminck
Maurice de, *French painter*	vlah-MEⁿK, ⓢ vluh-MANGK	vlaːmẽk, ⓢ vlə'mæŋk

Vlasic
US pickle co.	VLAS-ik	'vlæsik

Vlastimil
pers. name, Czech	VLAHS-chim-IL	'vlaːstʃim‚il

Vogau
Boris Andreyevich, *Russian novelist* (*pseudonym* Boris Pilnyak)	VAW-GOW	'vɔː‚gau

Vogul [Mansi]
lang., people, Russia	VŌ-gul	'voːgul

Voight
Jon, *US actor*	VOIT	'vɔit

Voigt
Cynthia, *US author*	VOIT	'vɔit

Vojtéch
pers. name, Czech	VOI-CHEKH	'vɔi‚tʃeç

Volans
constellation	VŌ-luhnz	'voːlənz

Volapuk
artificial lang.	VŌ-luh-PUK, VAHL-uh-PUK	'voːlə‚puk, 'valə‚puk

Volcker
Paul, *US economist*	VŌ(L)-kuhr	'voː(l)kər

Volga
river, Russia	VAHL-guh, VAWL-guh, VŌL-guh	'valgə, 'vɔːlgə, 'voːlgə

Volgograd [Stalingrad]
city, Russia	VUHL-guh-GRAHT,	‚vəlgə'grat, ⓢ 'valgə‚græd,
	ⓢ VAHL-guh-GRAD, VAWL-, VŌL-	'vɔːl-, 'voːl-

Volk
German for 'people'	FAWLK	'fɔːlk

Volkswagen
German car	FAWLKS-VAHG-uhn,	'fɔːlks‚vagən,
	ⓢ VŌK-SWAG-uhn,	ⓢ 'voːk‚swægən,
	VŌKS-VAHG-uhn	'voːks‚vagən

Volla
Alessandro, *scientist*	VŌL-lah	'voːlla

Volnay
wine	vawl-NE	vɔːlne

Vologda
city, region, Russia	VAW-luhg-duh	'vɔːləgdə

Volpone
play, Jonson	vahl-PŌ-nē	val'poːniˑ

Volsci
ancient people, Italy	VAHL-SĪ, VAHL-shē	'val‚sai, 'valʃiˑ

Volscian
  lang., pert. to the Volsci   VAHL-shuhn   'vɑlʃən
Volstead
  Andrew John, *US politician*   VAHL-STED, VŌL-   'vɑl,sted, 'vɔːl-
Volsunga
  Icelandic saga   VAWL-SUNG-(g)uh   'vɔːl,suŋ(g)ə
Volta
  1. Alessandro, *Italian physicist*   VŌL-tuh, VAHL-tuh, VAWL-tuh   'voːltə, 'vɑltə, 'vɔːltə
  2. *river, lake, Ghana*   VAHL-tuh, VŌL-tuh, VAWL-tuh   'vɑltə, 'voːltə, 'vɔːltə
Voltaire
  François Marie Arouet de, *French*   vawl-TER, ⑤ vōl-TAR, vahl-, vawl-,   vɔːlter, ⑤ voːl'tæʳ, vɑl-,
    philosopher   -TER   vɔːl-, -'teʳ
Volturno
  river, Italy   vahl-TUR-nō, vōl-, vawl-   vɑl'tuʳnoː, voːl-, vɔːl-
Volturnus
  Roman divinity, father of Juturna   vahl-TUR-nuhs, vōl-, vawl-   vɑl'tuʳnəs, voːl-, vɔːl-
Volusia
  county, FL   vuh-LOO-shuh   və'luːʃə
Volvo
  tdmk for a Swedish car   VAHL-vō, VAWL-vō, VŌL-vō   'vɑlvoː, 'vɔːlvoː, 'voːlvoː
von Braun
  Wernher, *German-US rocket*   fuhn BROWN, ⑤ vahn BROWN   fən 'brɑun, ⑤ vɑn 'brɑun
    engineer
Von Bulow
  Claus, *US socialite*   vahn BYOO-lō   vɑn 'bjuːloː
Vondel
  Joost van den, *Dutch poet and*   VAHN-dl   'vɑndl̩
    dramatist
Vonnegut
  Kurt, Jr., *US writer*   VAHN-uh-guht   'vɑnəgət
von Neumann
  John, *US mathematician*   vahn NOI-MAHN, NOI-muhn   vɑn 'nɔi,mɑn, 'nɔimən
Von Stade
  Frederica, *US mezzo-soprano*   fawn SHTAHD-uh, vahn STAHD-uh   fɔːn 'ʃtɑdə, vɑn 'stɑdə
Von Sternberg
  Josef, *US film director*   vahn STUHRN-BUHRG   vɑn 'stəʳn,bəʳg
Von Stroheim
  Erich, *US film director, actor*   fawn SHTRŌ-HĪM, vahn, STRŌ-HĪM   fɔːn 'ʃtroː,hɑim, vɑn,
                                                                                                 'stroː,hɑim
Von Sydow
  Max, *Swedish actor*   fawn SUE-DAWF, ⑤ vahn SĪD-ō   fɔːn 'syː,dɔːf, ⑤ vɑn 'sɑidoː
Voorhees
  College, *SC*   VUR-HĒZ, VUR-HĒS   'vuʳ,hiːz, 'vuʳ,hiːs
Vophsi
  Biblical name   VAHF-SĪ, vahf-SĒ   'vaf,sɑi, vaf'siː
Voronezh
  river, city, region, Russia   vuh-RAW-nish   və'rɔːniʃ
Vörösmarty
  Mihály, *Hungarian poet*   VUH(R)R-uh(r)sh-MAHRT(Y)   'vœrœʃ,mɑrt(j)
Vorster
  Balthazar Johannes, *South African*   FAWR-stuhr   'fɔːʳstəʳ
    politician
Vosges
  mts., dept, France   VŌZH   voːʒ

Key (col. 2): a: fad ā: fade ah: father ar: marry aw: law e: fed ē: feed er: merry i: hid ī: hide ō: coat ōō: boot
oi: boy ow: now u: put uh: above uhr: bird ch: chop ng: ring sh: show th: thick th: this zh: measure

Vosne-Romanée
wine — VŌN-raw-mah-NĀ — voːnrɔːmaːneː

Vostock
  1. scientific station, Antarctica — VAHS-TAHK — 'vɑsˌtɑk
  2. island, Kiribati — vuh-STAHK — vəˈstɑk

Vostok 1
first manned spaceflight, 1961 — VAHS-TAHK, VAWS-TAWK — 'vɑsˌtɑk, 'vɔːsˌtɔːk

Votyak [Udmurt]
lang., Russia — VŌ-TYAHK, VŌT-ē-AK — 'voːˌtjɑːk, 'voːʈiːˌæk

Vouli
wine — VŌ-lē, VOO-lē — 'voːliˑ, 'vuːliˑ

Vouvray
wine — voov-RE — vuːvre

Voyageurs
National Park, *Kabetogama, MN* — VWAH-YAH-ZHUHR, VOI-uh-JUHR, VOI-uh-ZHUHR — ˌvwɑˌjaˈʒərᵣ, ˌvɔiəˈdʒərᵣ, ˌvɔiəˈʒərᵣ

Vsevolod
pers. name, Russian — FSYEV-uh-luht — 'fsjevələt

VTOL
vertical takeoff and landing — VĒ-TAWL, VĒ-TAHL — 'viːˌtɔːl, 'viːˌtɑl

Vuelta Abajo
region, Cuba — BWEL-tah ah-VAH-khō, Ⓢ VWEL-tuh uh-BAH-hō — 'bwelta aˈβaxoː, Ⓢ 'vwelta əˈbahoː

Vuillard
Édouard, *French painter* — vwē-YAHR — vwiːjaːr

Vuitton
tdmk for handbags and luggage — vwē-TAWⁿ, Ⓢ vwē-TAHN, vwē-TAWN — vɥiːtɔ̃, Ⓢ vwiːˈtan, vwiːˈtɔːn

Vukovar
city, Croatia — VOO-kuh-VAHR — 'vuːkəˌvɑʳ

Vulcan
Roman fire god; alien race, Star Trek — VUHL-kuhn — 'vəlkən

Vulgate
Latin version of the Bible — VUHL-GĀT, VUHL-guht — 'vəlˌgeːt, 'vəlgət

Vulpecula
constellation — VUHL-PEK-yuh-luh — ˌvəlˈpekjələ

Vulso
Manlius, *Roman general* — VUL-sō, VUHL-sō — 'vulsoː, 'vəlsoː

Vung Tau
town, Vietnam — VUNG TOW — 'vuŋ 'tau

Vyacheslav
pers. name, Russian — vyi-chis-LAHF — vjitʃisˈlaːf

Vyatka
river, city, Russia — VYAHT-kuh, vē-AHT-kuh — 'vjɑtkə, viːˈatkə

Vyazma
town, Russia — VYAHZ-muh, vē-AHZ-muh — 'vjɑzmə, viːˈazmə

Vyborg
port, Russia — VĒ-BAWRG — 'viːˌbɔːʳg

Vychegda
river, Russia — VICH-uhg-duh — 'vitʃəgdə

Vycpálek
Ladislav, *Czech composer* — VIT-spahl-ek — 'vitspɑlek

Vyshinsky
Andrey Yanuaryevich, *Soviet diplomat and politician* — vyi-SHIN-skyiy, Ⓢ vuh-SHIN-skē — vjiˈʃinskjij, Ⓢ vəˈʃinskiˑ

Foreign Sounds: ue: *Fr.* **rue**, *Ger.* **füllen**   uh(r): *Fr.* **boeuf**, *Ger.* **Höhle**   kh: *Ger.* **ich**, *Scot.* **loch**   ḡ: *Sp.* **amigo**   v: *Sp.* **hablar**
hl: *Welsh* **Llanelli.**   CAPITALS: primary stress.   SMALL CAPS: secondary stress.   Ⓢ: U.S. pron.   Ⓔ: British pron.

Vytautas
pers. name, Lith.   vē-TOWT-uhs   viːˈtɑuʈəs

W

Waal
  river, Netherlands   VAHL   'vɑl

Waals
  Johannes Diderik van der, *Dutch*   VAHLS   'vɑls
    physicist (Nobel 1910)

Wabash
  river, US; county, IN, IL; college, IN   WAW-BASH   'wɔːˌbæʃ

Wabasha
  county, MN   WAW-buh-SHAW   'wɔːbəˌʃɔː

Wabaunsee
  county, KA   wah-BAWN-sē   wɑ'bɔːnsiˑ

WAC
  Women's Army Corp.,US   WAK   'wæk

Waccamaw
  river, NC   WAHK-uh-MAW   'wɑkəˌmɔː

Waccasassa Bay
  inlet, Gulf of Mexico   WAW-kuh-SAS-uh BĀ   ˌwɔːkəˌsæsə 'beː

Wach
  Joachim, *US theologian*   VAH<u>KH</u>   'vɑx

Wachovia
  region, NC; US bank   wah-CHŌ-vē-uh   wɑ'tʃoːviːə

Wachusett
  mtn., reservoir, MA   wah-CHO͞O-suht   wɑ'tʃuːsət

Wackenhut
  US security services co.   WAK-uhn-HUHT   'wækənˌhət

Wacław
  pers. name, Polish   VAHCH-LAHF   'vɑːtʃˌłɑːf

Waco
  city, TX   WĀ-kō   'weːkoː

Wadai
  see Ouadai

Waddel, Waddell
  pers. name   wah-DEL   wɑ'del

Waddenzee
  inlet, Netherlands   VAHD-n-ZĀ   'vɑdn̩ˌzeː

Wade
  pers. name   WĀD   'weːd

Wade-Giles
  transliteration system for Chinese   WĀD-JĪLZ   ˌweːd'dʒɑilz

Wade Hampton
  division, AK   WĀD HAM(P)-tuhn   ˌweːd 'hæm(p)tən

Wadena
  county, MN   waw-DĒ-nuh   wɔː'diːnə

Foreign Sounds: ue: *Fr.* **rue**, *Ger.* **füllen**   uh(r): *Fr.* **boeuf**, *Ger.* **Höhle**   <u>kh</u>: *Ger.* **ich**, *Scot.* **loch**   ḡ: *Sp.* **amigo**   <u>v</u>: *Sp.* **hablar**
hl: *Welsh* **Llanelli.**   CAPITALS: primary stress.   SMALL CAPS: secondary stress.   Ⓢ: U.S. pron.   Ⓔ: British pron.

Wadham
　college, Oxford Univ.　　　WAHD-uhm　　　　　'wɑdəm
Wadleigh
　pers. name　　　WAHD-lē　　　　　'wɑdli·
Wadsworth
　pers. name　　　WAHDZ-wuhrth　　　　　'wɑdzwəʳθ
Wafd
　political party, Egypt　　　WAHFT　　　　　'wɑft
Wagga Wagga
　city, Australia　　　WAHG-uh WAHG-uh　　　　　'wɑgə ˌwɑgə
Wagner
　1. US family name　　　WAG-nuhr　　　　　'wægnəʳ
　2. Richard, German composer　　　VAHG-nuhr　　　　　'vɑgnəʳ
Wagnerian
　pert. to Richard Wagner　　　vahg-NIR-ē-uhn, vahg-NER-ē-uhn　　　　　vɑg'niriːən, vɑg'neriːən
Wagner-Jauregg
　Julius, *Austrian neurologist,*　　　VAHG-nuhr-YOW-REK　　　　　'vɑgnəʳjɑuˌrek
　　psychiatrist (Nobel 1927)
Wagoner
　Porter, *US country music singer*　　　WAG-(uh-)nuhr　　　　　'wæg(ə)nəʳ
Wahconah
　Park, *ballpark, Pittsfield, MA*　　　wah-KŌ-nuh, wuh-KŌ-nuh　　　　　wɑ'koːnə, wə'koːnə
Wahhabi
　Muslim sect　　　wuh-HAHB-ē, wah-　　　　　wə'hɑbi·, wɑ-
Wahhabism
　beliefs of the Wahhabis　　　wuh-HAHB-ɪz-uhm, wah-　　　　　wə'hɑbˌizəm, wɑ-
Wahiawa
　division, HI　　　WAH-hē-uh-WAH　　　　　ˌwɑhiːə'wɑ
Wahkiakum
　county, WA　　　waw-KĪ-uh-kuhm　　　　　wɔː'kɑiəkəm
Wahlbündis '90
　political party, Germany　　　VAHL-BUEN-duhs NOINT-si<u>kh</u>　　　　　'vɑlˌbyndəs 'nɔintsiç
Wahoo
　plant　　　WAH-HŌŌ, WAW-HŌŌ　　　　　'wɑˌhuː, 'wɔːˌhuː
Wahpeton Sioux
　N. American people　　　WAW-puht-uhn SŌŌ　　　　　'wɔːpəʈən 'suː
Wahroonga
　town, Australia　　　wuh-RUNG-guh　　　　　wə'ruŋgə
Waialeale
　mtn., HI　　　wī-AHL-ä-AHL-ä　　　　　wɑiˌaleː'aleː
Waialua
　division, bay, HI　　　WĪ-uh-LŌŌ-uh　　　　　ˌwɑiə'luːə
Waianae
　division, mountain range, city, HI　　　WĪ-uh-NĪ　　　　　ˌwɑiə'nɑi
Waicuri
　N. American people　　　wī-KUR-ē　　　　　wɑi'kuri·
Waikiki Beach
　resort, HI　　　WĪ-kuh-KĒ BĒCH　　　　　ˌwɑikəˌkiː 'biːtʃ
Wailuku
　division, city, HI　　　wī-LŌŌ-koo　　　　　wɑi'luːkuː
Waimea
　division, bay, town, HI　　　wī-MĀ-uh　　　　　wɑi'meːə
Wainwright
　Jonathan Mayhew, *US general*　　　WĀN-RĪT　　　　　'weːnˌrɑit

Key (col. 2):　a: fad　ā: fade　ah: father　ar: marry　aw: law　e: fed　ē: feed　er: merry　i: hid　ī: hide　ō: coat　ōō: boot
oi: boy　ow: now　u: put　uh: above　uhr: bird　ch: chop　ng: ring　sh: show　th: thick　<u>th</u>: this　zh: measure

Waipahu
  city, HI   wī-PAH-hōō   waiˈpɑhuː
Waite
  Ralph, *US actor*   WĀT   ˈweːt
Waits
  Thomas Alan, *US composer, singer*   WĀTS   ˈweːts
Wakame
  seaweed   WAHK-uh-mē   ˈwɑkəmiˑ
Wakashan
  N. American lang. family   waw-KASH-uhn, WAW-KASH-uhn   wɔːˈkæʃən, ˈwɔːˌkæʃən
Wakayama
  port, Japan   wah-kah-yahm-ah   wɑkɑjɑmɑ
Waksman
  S. A., *Russian-born US biochemist (Nobel 1952)*   WAHK-smuhn, WAK-smuhn   ˈwɑksmən, ˈwæksmən
Wakulla
  county, FL   wah-KUHL-uh   wɑˈkələ
Walachia, Wallachia
  region, Romania   wah-LĀ-kē-uh   wɑˈleːkiːə
Walcha
  town, Australia   WAHL-kuh, WAWL-kuh   ˈwɑlkə, ˈwɔːlkə
Walcott
  Derek, *West Indian poet*   WAWL-kuht   ˈwɔːlkət
Wald
  George, *US biochemist (Nobel 1967)*; Lillian, *US social worker*   WAWLD, WAHLD   ˈwɔːld, ˈwɑld
Waldbaum
  US grocery store chain   WAWL(D)-BOWM   ˈwɔːl(d)ˌbɑum
Waldemar
  1. king, Denmark; pers. name, Danish   VAHL-duh-MAHR   ˈvɑːldəˌmɑʳ
  2. German   VAHL-duh-MAHR   ˈvaldəˌmɑʳ
  3. Swedish   VAHL-duh-MAHR   ˈvɑːldəˌmɑːʳ
Walden
  town, Ontario, Canada; Pond, *MA*   WAWL-duhn   ˈwɔːldən
Waldenses [Waldensians]
  Protestant religious sect   wawl-DEN-SĒZ, wahl-   wɔːlˈdenˌsiːz, wɑl-
Waldensians
  Protestant religious sect   wawl-DEN(T)-sē-uhnz, wahl-   wɔːlˈden(t)siːənz, wɑl-
Waldheim
  Kurt, *UN Secy. Genl.*   VAHLT-HĪM, ⑤ VAWLD-HĪM, WAWLD-HĪM   ˈvaltˌhaim, ⑤ ˈvɔːldˌhaim, ˈwɔːldˌhaim
Waldmeister
  plant   WAWLD-MĪ-stuhr, VAHLT-MĪ-stuhr   ˈwɔːldˌmaistəʳ, ˈvaltˌmaistəʳ
Waldo
  pers. name   WAWL-dō, WAHL-dō   ˈwɔːldoː, ˈwaldoː
Waldorf
  hotel, New York City; salad   WAWL-DAWRF   ˈwɔːlˌdɔːʳf
Wałęsa
  Lech, *Polish president (Nobel 1983)*   vah-LEⁿ-suh, ⑤ vuh-LEN-suh, vuh-WEN-suh   vɑːˈɫẽsə, ⑤ vəˈlensə, vəˈwensə
Wales [Cymru]
  principality, Gt. Britain   WĀLZ   ˈweːlz
Walgett
  town, Australia   WAHL-guht, WAWL-guht   ˈwɑlgət, ˈwɔːlgət

Walken
  Christopher, *US actor*   WAW(L)-kuhn   'wɔː(l)kən
Walker
  pers. name   WAWK-uhr   'wɔːkər
Walkman
  tdmk for a portable cassette player   WAWK-muhn, WAHK-muhn   'wɔːkmən, 'wɑkmən
Walküre, Die
  see Die Walküre
Wallace
  pers. name   WAHL-uhs   'wɑləs
Wallach
  1. Eli, US actor   WAHL-uhk   'wɑlək
  2. Otto, German chemist (Nobel   VAHL-ah<u>kh</u>, ⑤ VAHL-uhk, WAHL-uhk   'vɑlɑx, ⑤ 'vɑlək, 'wɑlək
  1910)
Wallachia
  see Walachia
Walla Walla
  river, city, WA; N. American people   WAHL-uh WAHL-uh, WAHL-uh   ˌwɑlə 'wɑlə, 'wɑlə ˌwɑlə
                                            WAHL-uh
Wallenberg
  Raoul, *Swedish diplomat and hero of*   VAHL-uhn-BER(Y),   'vɑlənˌber(j), ⑤ 'wɑlənˌbərg
  the Holocaust   ⑤ WAHL-uhn-BUHRG
Wallenda
  Karl, *German-born US circus*   vah-LEN-dah, ⑤ wuh-LEN-duh   vɑ'lendɑ, ⑤ wə'lendə
  performer
Wallenpaupack
  lake, PA   WAH-luhn-PAW-PAK   ˌwɑlən'pɔːˌpæk
Wallensis
  pers. name   waw-LEN-suhs, wah-   wɔː'lensəs, wɑ-
Waller
  pers. name   WAHL-uhr   'wɑlər
Wallerawang
  town, Australia   wuh-LER-uh-WANG   wə'lerəˌwæŋ
Wallis
  pers. name   WAHL-uhs   'wɑləs
Wallis and Futuna
  islands, Pacific   WAHL-uhs uhn(d) foo-TOO-nuh   'wɑləs ən(d) fuˈ'tuːnə
Wallisian
  pert. to Wallis Islands   wahl-ISH-uhn   wɑl'iʃən
Wallonia
  region, Belgium   wah-LŌ-nē-uh   wɑ'loːniːə
Walloon
  people, Belgium, France; French   wah-LOON, wuh-, waw-   wɑ'luːn, wə-, wɔː-
  dialect
Wallops
  island, VA   WAHL-uhps   'wɑləps
Wallowa
  river, lake, mts., county, OR   wah-LOW-uh   wɑ'lauə
Wallo [Welo]
  region, Ethiopia   WAWL-ō   'wɔːloː
Wal-Mart
  US retail chain   WAWL-MAHRT   'wɔːlˌmɑrt
Walpole
  city, MA; British family   WAWL-PŌL   'wɔːlˌpoːl

Key (col. 2):   a: f**a**d   ā: f**a**de   ah: f**a**ther   ar: m**a**rry   aw: l**a**w   e: f**e**d   ē: f**ee**d   er: m**e**rry   i: h**i**d   ī: h**i**de   ō: c**oa**t   oō: b**oo**t
oi: b**oy**   ow: n**ow**   u: p**u**t   uh: **a**bove   uhr: b**i**rd   ch: **ch**op   ng: ri**ng**   sh: **sh**ow   th: **th**ick   <u>th</u>: **th**is   zh: mea**s**ure

Walpurgisnacht
  Walpurgis Night   vahl-PUR-guhs-NAHKHT   vɑlˈpuʳgəsˌnɑxt
Walpurgis Night
  April 30th holiday, Germany   vahl-PUR-guhs, val-PUHR-juhs   vɑlˈpuʳgəs, vælˈpəʳdʒəs
Walsh
  family name   WAWLSH   ˈwɔːlʃ
Walsingham
  1. Sir Francis, *Elizabethan statesman*   WAWL-sing-uhm   ˈwɔːlsiŋəm
  2. town, England   WAWL-zing-uhm   ˈwɔːlziŋəm
  3. cape, Canada   WAWL-sing-HAM   ˈwɔːlsiŋˌhæm
Walston
  Ray, *US actor*   WAWL-stuhn   ˈwɔːlstən
Walt
  pers. name   WAWLT, WAHLT   ˈwɔːlt, ˈwɑlt
Walter
  1. pers. name   WAWL-tuhr   ˈwɔːltəʳ
  2. German   VAHL-tuhr   ˈvɑltəʳ
Walter
  Bruno, *German-born US conductor*   VAHL-tuhr, Ⓢ WAWL-tuhr   ˈvɑltəʳ, Ⓢ ˈwɔːltəʳ
Waltham
  1. city, MA   WAWL-THAM, *by non-residents often*   ˈwɔːlˌθæm, *by non-residents*
                                   WAWL-thuhm   *often* ˈwɔːlθəm
  2. pl. name, England   WAWL-thuhm, WAWL-tuhm   ˈwɔːlθəm, ˈwɔːltəm
Waltham Forest
  borough, England   WAWL-thuhm FAWR-uhst,   ˌwɔːlθəm ˈfɔːrəst, ˌwɔːltəm,
                                   WAWL-tuhm, FAHR-uhst   ˈfɑrəst
Walther
  1. pers. name, French   vahl-TER   vɑːlter
  2. German   VAHL-tuhr   ˈvɑltəʳ
Walton
  Ernest T., *Irish physicist (Nobel*   WAWLT-n   ˈwɔːltn̩
  1951); Izaak, *British writer*
Walvis
  Bay, *west coast of Africa*   WAWL-vuhs   ˈwɔːlvəs
Wambaugh
  Joseph, *US writer*   WAHM-BOW   ˈwɑmˌbɑu
Wamego
  city, KS   wah-MĒ-gō   wɑˈmiːgoː
Wampanoag
  N. American people   WAHM-puh-NŌ-AG, WAWM-   ˌwɑmpəˈnoːˌæg, ˌwɔːm-
Wanamaker
  John, *US merchant;* Sam, *US actor,*   WAHN-uh-MĀ-kuhr   ˈwɑnəˌmeːkəʳ
  director
Wanaque
  borough, NJ   wuh-NAHK-(w)ē; WAHN-uh-KYOO, -KĒ   wəˈnɑk(w)iˑ; ˈwɑnəˌkjuː,
                                                                    -ˌkiː
Wanda
  1. pers. name   WAHN-duh   ˈwɑndə
  2. Polish   VAHN-dah   ˈvɑːndɑː
Wanderjahr
  a year of travel   VAHN-duhr-YAHR   ˈvɑndəʳˌjɑʳ
Wandsworth
  borough, England   WAHN(D)Z-wuhrth   ˈwɑn(d)zwəʳθ
Wang
  An, *US computer engineer*   WANG   ˈwæŋ

Foreign Sounds: ue: *Fr.* **rue,** *Ger.* **füllen**   uh(r): *Fr.* **boeuf,** *Ger.* **Höhle**   kh: *Ger.* **ich,** *Scot.* **loch**   g̃: *Sp.* amigo   v: *Sp.* hablar
hl: *Welsh* **Llanelli.** CAPITALS: primary stress. SMALL CAPS: secondary stress. Ⓢ: U.S. pron. Ⓔ: British pron.

Wankel		
1. Felix, *German engineer*	VAHNG-kuhl	ˈvɑŋkəl
2. engine	WANG-kuhl, VAHNG-kuhl	ˈwæŋkəl, ˈvɑŋkəl
Wanne-Eickel		
city, Germany	VAHN-uh-Ī-kuhl	ˈvɑnəˈɑikəl
Wantage		
Community, *religious order*	WAHNT-ij, WUHNT-ij	ˈwɑntidʒ, ˈwəntidʒ
Wantagh		
town, NY	WAHN-TAW	ˈwɑnˌtɔː
Wapakoneta		
city, OH	WAW-puh-kuh-NET-uh	ˌwɔːpəkəˈneţə
Wapato		
city, WA	WAW-puht-ō, WAHP-uht-ō	ˈwɔːpəţˌoː, ˈwɑpəţoː
Wapello		
county, IA	WAHP-uh-LŌ	ˈwɑpəˌloː
Wapiti		
town, WY; elk	WAHP-uht-ē	ˈwɑpəţiˑ
Wapping		
district, England	WAHP-ing	ˈwɑpiŋ
Wappinger		
N. American people	WAHP-uhn-juhr	ˈwɑpəndʒə^{r}
Wappingers Falls		
town, NY	WAHP-uhn-juhrz FAWLZ	ˌwɑpəndʒə^{r}z ˈfɔːlz
Wapsipinicon		
river, IA, MN	WAHP-suh-PIN-i-kuhn	ˌwɑpsəˈpinikən
Warangal		
city, India	WAWR-uhng-guhl	ˈwɔːrəŋgəl
Warbeck		
Perkin, *pretender to the English throne*	WAWR-BEK	ˈwɔː^{r}ˌbek
Warburg		
Otto H., *German biochemist (Nobel 1931)*	VAHR-BUR<u>KH</u>, [$] WAWR-BUHRG	ˈvɑ^{r}ˌbu^{r}x, [$] ˈwɔː^{r}ˌbə^{r}g
Warcup		
pers. name	WAWR-kuhp, WAWR-KUHP	ˈwɔː^{r}kəp, ˈwɔː^{r}ˌkəp
Ward		
pers. name	WAWRD	ˈwɔː^{r}d
Wardell		
pers. name	wawr-DEL	wɔː^{r}ˈdel
Wareham		
town, England	WER-uhm, WAR-uhm	ˈwerəm, ˈwærəm
Warhol		
Andy, *US artist*	WAWR-HAWL, WAWR-HŌL	ˈwɔː^{r}ˌhɔːl, ˈwɔː^{r}ˌhoːl
Waring		
tdmk. for small appliances; pers. name	WAR-ing, WER-ing	ˈwæriŋ, ˈweriŋ
Warner		
John William, *US politician*	WAWR-nuhr	ˈwɔː^{r}nə^{r}
Warragamba		
river, Australia	WAHR-uh-GAM-buh	ˌwɑrəˈgæmbə
Warrawee		
town, Australia	WAHR-uh-wē	ˈwɑrəwiˑ
Warren		
pers. name	WAWR-uhn, WAHR-uhn	ˈwɔːrən, ˈwɑrən

Warrick
  Ruth, *actress*   WAWR-ik, WAHR-ik   'wɔːrik, 'wɑrik
Warsaw
  city, prov, Poland; pl. name, US   WAWR-SAW   'wɔːrˌsɔː
Warsteiner
  German beer   VAHR-SHTĪ-nuhr   'vɑrˌʃtainər
Warszawa [Warsaw]
  city, prov, Poland   vahr-SHAHV-uh   vɑːrˈʃɑːvə
Wartburg
  castle, Germany   VAHRT-BURK, Ⓢ WAWRT-BUHRG   'vɑrtˌburk, Ⓢ 'wɔːrtˌbərg
Warwick
  1. pl. name, Australia, Canada,   WAHR-ik, WAWR-ik   'wɑrik, 'wɔːrik
     England
  2. city, RI   WAWR-wik, WAWR-ik, WAHR-ik   'wɔːrwik, 'wɔːrik, 'wɑrik
  3. pers. name   WAHR-ik, WAWR-ik, WAWR-wik   'wɑrik, 'wɔːrik, 'wɔːrwik
Warwickshire
  county, England   WAHR-ik-shuhr, -SHIR;   'wɑrikʃər, -ˌʃɪr;
                                           Ⓢ WAWR-(w)ik-   Ⓢ 'wɔːr(w)ik-
Wasabi
  horseradish   WAHS-uh-bē, wuh-SAHB-ē   'wɑsəbiˑ, wəˈsɑbiˑ
Wasatch
  county, UT; mtn. range, US   WAW-SACH   'wɔːˌsætʃ
Wasco
  county, OR   WAHS-kō   'wɑskoː
Waseca
  county, MN   wah-SĒ-kuh   wɑˈsiːkə
Washakie
  county, WY   WAHSH-uh-kē   'wɑʃəkiˑ
Washington
  Booker T., *US educator;* George,   WAWSH-ing-tuhn, WAHSH-ing-tuhn,   'wɔːʃiŋtən, 'wɑʃiŋtən, *esp.*
     1st US president; state, pl. name,   *esp. in US Midlands*   *in US Midlands*
     US   WAWR-shing-tuhn,   'wɔːrʃiŋtən, 'wɑrʃiŋtən
                                           WAHR-shing-tuhn
Washita
  river, US; county, AR, OK   WAHSH-uh-TAW, WAWSH-uh-TAW   'wɑʃəˌtɔː, 'wɔːʃəˌtɔː
Washoe
  county, NV; N. American people   WAHSH-ō   'wɑʃoː
Washtenaw
  county, MI   WAHSH-tuh-NAW   'wɑʃtəˌnɔː
WASP
  white Anglo-Saxon Protestant   WAHSP, WAWSP   'wɑsp, 'wɔːsp
Wassermann
  diagnostic test for syphilis   WAHS-uhr-muhn   'wɑsərmən
Wassily
  pers. name, Russian   VAHS-yil-yi   'vɑːsjiljij
Watanabe
  Michio, *Japanese statesman*   wah-tah-nah-bā, Ⓢ WAHT-n-AHB-ā,   watanabeˑ, Ⓢ ˌwatn̩ˈabeː,
                                           WAHT-n-AHB-ē   ˌwatn̩ˈabiˑ
Watauga
  river, US; county, NC   wah-TAW-guh   wɑˈtɔːgə
Waterbury
  US pl. name   WAWT-uhr-BER-ē, WAHT-uhr-BER-ē   'wɔːt̬ərˌberiˑ, 'wat̬ərˌberiˑ
Waterford
  county, Ireland; town, CT   WAWT-uhr-fuhrd, WAHT-uhr-fuhrd   'wɔːt̬ərᶠfərd, 'wat̬ərᶠfərd

---

Foreign Sounds: ue: *Fr.* **rue**, *Ger.* **füllen**   uh(r): *Fr.* **boeuf**, *Ger.* **Höhle**   <u>kh</u>: *Ger.* **ich**, *Scot.* **loch**   ḡ: *Sp.* **amigo**   v̱: *Sp.* **hablar**
hl: *Welsh* **Llanelli**.   CAPITALS: primary stress.   SMALL CAPS: secondary stress.   Ⓢ: U.S. pron.   Ⓔ: British pron.

Watergate
   hotel, DC; US political scandal   WAWT-uhr-GĀT, WAHT-uhr-GĀT   'wɔːʈəʳˌgeːt, 'waʈəʳˌgeːt

Waterloo
   1. US & Canadian pl. name   WAWT-uhr-LŌŌ, WAWT-uhr-LŌŌ,   ˌwɔːʈəʳˈluː, 'wɔːʈəʳˌluː,
                        WAHT-uhr-LŌŌ, WAHT-uhr-LŌŌ   ˌwaʈəʳˈluː, 'waʈəʳˌluː

   2. commune, battlesite, Belgium   VAHT-uhr-LŌ, Ⓢ *as above*   'vaʈəʳˌloː, Ⓢ *as above*

Waterston
   Samuel Atkinson, *US actor*   WAWT-uhr-stuhn, WAHT-uhr-stuhn   'wɔːʈəʳstən, 'waʈəʳstən

Watervliet
   city, NY   WAWT-uhr-VLĒT, WAHT-uhr-   'wɔːʈəʳˌvliːt, 'waʈəʳ-

Watford
   district, England   WAHT-fuhrd   'watfəʳd

Watkin
   pers. name   WAHT-kuhn   'watkən

Watonga
   city, OK   wuh-TAHNG-guh   wə'taŋgə

Watonwan
   county, MN   WAHT-n-WAHN   'watn̩ˌwan

Watrous
   village, NM   WAW-truhs, WAH-   'wɔːtrəs, 'wa-

WATS
   wide-area telephone service   WAHTS   'wats

Watseka
   city, IL   waht-SĒ-kuh   wat'siːkə

Watson
   family name   WAHT-suhn   'watsən

Watt
   James, *Scottish inventor*   WAHT   'wat

Watteau
   Antoine, *French painter*   vah-TŌ   vaːtoː

Watusi [Tutsi]
   people, Rwanda, Burundi; dance   wah-TŌŌ-sē   waˈtuːsi·

Watutsi [Tutsi]
   people, Rwanda, Burundi   wah-TŌŌT-sē   waˈtuːtsi·

Wauchope
   town, Australia   WAW-HŌP   'wɔˌhoːp

Wauchula
   city, FL   waw-CHŌŌ-luh   wɔːˈtʃuːlə

Waugh
   Alec, Evelyn, *English writers*   WAW   'wɔː

Waukegan
   city, IL   waw-KĒ-guhn   wɔːˈkiːgən

Waukesha
   city, county, WI   WAW-ki-SHAW   'wɔːkiˌʃɔː

Waukon
   city, IA   waw-KAHN   wɔːˈkan

Waupaca
   county, WI   waw-PAK-uh   wɔːˈpækə

Waurika
   city, OK   waw-RĒ-kuh   wɔːˈriːkə

Waupun
   city, WI   waw-PAHN *[sic]*   wɔːˈpɑn *[sic]*

Wausau
   city, WI   WAW-SAW   'wɔːˌsɔː

Key (col. 2): a: fad ā: fade ah: father ar: **m**arry aw: **l**aw e: fed ē: feed er: **m**erry i: hid ī: hide ō: coat ōō: boot
oi: **b**oy ow: **n**ow u: put uh: above uhr: **b**ird ch: **ch**op ng: ring sh: **sh**ow th: **th**ick <u>th</u>: **th**is zh: measure

Wauseon
village, OH WAW-sē-AHN 'wɔːsiːˌɑn

Waushara
county, WI waw-SHAR-uh, waw-SHER-uh wɔːˈʃærə, wɔːˈʃerə

Wautoma
city, WI waw-TŌ-muh wɔːˈtoːmə

Wauwatosa
city, WI WAW-wuh-TŌ-suh ˌwɔːwəˈtoːsə

Wavell
Archibald, *British militarist* WĀ-vuhl 'weːvəl

Wawrzyniec
pers. name, Polish vahv-ZHIN-yets vɑːvˈʒinjets

Wayans
Keenen Ivory, *US entertainer* WĀ-uhnz 'weːənz

Wayne
pers. name WĀN 'weːn

Wayzata
city, MN wī-ZET-uh wɑiˈzeʈə

Waziristan
mtn. tract, Pakistan wuh-ZIR-i-STAN, -STAHN wəˌziriˈstæn, -ˈstɑn

Weald, The
wooded district, England thuh WĒLD ðə 'wiːld

Weaver
Sigourney, *entertainer* WĒ-vuhr 'wiːvəʳ

Webber
Robert, *US actor* WEB-uhr 'webəʳ

Weber
1. family name, English WEB-uhr 'webəʳ
2. German VĀ-buhr 'veːbəʳ
3. river, county, UT WĒ-buhr 'wiːbəʳ

Webern
Anton von, *Austrian composer* VĀ-buhrn 'veːbəʳn

Webster
Daniel, *US statesman;* Noah, *US* WEB-stuhr 'webstəʳ
  lexicographer; pers. name

Wechsler
David, *US psychologist* WEK-sluhr 'weksləʳ

Weddell Sea
arm of Atlantic wuh-DEL, WED-l wəˈdel, 'wedl̩

Wedekind
Frank, *German dramatist* VĀD-uh-KINT 'veːdəˌkint

Wedemeyer
Albert Goady, *US army officer* WED-uh-MĪ-er, WĒD- 'wedəˌmɑieʳ, 'wiːd-

Wedgeworth
Ann, *US actress* WEJ-WUHRTH 'wedʒˌwəʳθ

Wedgwood
tdmk for ceramic ware WEJ-WUD 'wedʒˌwud

Wednesday
day of the week WENZ-dē, WENZ-dā, Ⓔ *sometimes* 'wenzdiˑ, 'wenzdeː, Ⓔ
  WED-nz-dē, WED-nz-dā *sometimes* 'wedn̩zdiˑ,
  'wedn̩zdeː

Wedowee
town, AL wē-DOW-ē, wuh- wiːˈdɑuiˑ, wə-

Foreign Sounds: ue: *Fr.* **rue**, *Ger.* **füllen** uh(r): *Fr.* **boeuf**, *Ger.* **Höhle** <u>kh</u>: *Ger.* **ich**, *Scot.* **loch** ḡ: *Sp.* **amigo** v: *Sp.* **hablar** hl: *Welsh* **Llanelli**. CAPITALS: primary stress. SMALL CAPS: secondary stress. Ⓢ: U.S. pron. Ⓔ: British pron.

Weeghman
  Charles, Park, *former name for*   WĒG-muhn, WIG-muhn   'wiːgmən, 'wigmən
  Wrigley Field, *Chicago, IL*

Weehawken
  town, NJ   wē-HAW-kuhn   wiːˈhɔːkən

Weejuns
  tdmk for shoes   WĒ-juhnz   'wiːdʒənz

Weeks, Weekes
  pers. name   WĒKS   'wiːks

Weelkes
  Thomas, *English composer*   WĒLKS   'wiːlks

Weems
  Mason Locke, *US author*   WĒMZ   'wiːmz

Wee Waa
  town, Australia   WĒ WAW   'wiː ˌwɔː

Weicker
  Lowell Palmer, Jr., *US politician*   WĪ-kuhr   'wɑikəʳ

Weidman
  Charles, *US modern dancer*   WĪD-muhn   'wɑidmən

Weifang
  city, China   WĀ-FAHNG   'weːˈfaŋ

Weigela
  bush   wī-JĒ-luh   wɑiˈdʒiːlə

Weihai
  port, China   WĀ-HĪ   'weːˈhɑi

Weil
  Simone, *French writer*   VE-yuh, Ⓢ VĀ, VĪL   vej, Ⓢ 'veː, 'vɑil

Weill
  Kurt, *US composer*   VĪL, WĪL   'vɑil, 'wɑil

Weimar
  city, Germany; Republic, *German*   VĪ-MAHR, Ⓢ WĪ-MAHR   'vɑiˌmɑʳ, Ⓢ 'wɑiˌmɑʳ
  regime

Weimaraner
  dog breed   VĪ-muh-RAHN-uhr, WĪ-;   ˌvɑiməˈrɑnəʳ, ˌwɑi-;
          VĪ-muh-RAHN-uhr, WĪ-   'vɑiməˌrɑnəʳ, 'wɑi-

Weinberg
  Steven, *US physicist (Nobel 1979)*   WĪN-BUHRG   'wɑinˌbəʳg

Weinberger
  1. Casper Willard, *US government*   WĪN-BUHR-guhr   'wɑinˌbəʳgəʳ
  official
  2. Jaromír, *Czech-born US composer*   VĀN-BER-ger, Ⓢ WĪN-BUHR-guhr   'veːnˌberger, Ⓢ 'wɑinˌbəʳgəʳ

Weiner
  Edmund, *British lexicographer*   VĪ-nuhr   'vɑinəʳ

Weippe
  prairie, ID   WĒ-ī-pē   'wiːɑipiˑ

Weir
  Julian Alden, *US painter*   WIR   'wiʳ

Weiser
  city, ID   WĒ-suhr, WĒ-zuhr   'wiːsəʳ, 'wiːzəʳ

Weiss
  Donald Logan, *US football executive*   WĪS   'wɑis

Weiss
  Pierre, *French physicist; magneton*   VES   ves

Weissmuller
  Johnny, *US actor*   WĪ-SMUHL-uhr   'wɑiˌsmələʳ

Key (col. 2): a: fad ā: fade ah: father ar: marry aw: law e: fed ē: feed er: merry i: hid ī: hide ō: coat ōō: boot
oi: boy ow: now u: put uh: above uhr: bird ch: chop ng: ring sh: show th: thick <u>th</u>: this zh: measure

Weizenkrone
  German beer   VĪT-suhn-KRŌ-nuh   'vaitsən,kroːnə

Weizmann
  Chaim, *Israeli political leader*   VĪT-smuhn   'vaitsmən

Welch
  Raquel, *US actress*   WELCH   'weltʃ

Welega
  mtn. range, Africa   we-LĀ-guh   we'leːgə

Welland
  city, prov, canal, Canada   WEL-uhnd   'welənd

Weller
  T. H., *US physiologist (Nobel 1954)*   WEL-uhr   'welə^r

Welles
  Gideon, *US politician;* Orson, *US*   WELZ   'welz
    film director

Wellesley
  College, *town, MA*   WELZ-lē   'welzli·

Wellington
  pers. name   WEL-ing-tuhn   'weliŋtən

Wells
  Herbert George, *English author and*   WELZ   'welz
    social thinker

Welo [Wallo]
  region, Ethiopia   WĀ-lō   'weːloː

Welsh
  lang., people, Wales   WELSH   'welʃ

Weltanschauung
  'world view'   VEL-TAHN-SHOW-uhng,   'vel,tan,ʃauəŋ,
         VEL-tuhn-SHOW(-uh)ng   'veltən,ʃau(ə)ŋ

Weltpolitik
  'world politics'   VELT-PAW-luh-tik   'velt,pɔːlətik

Weltschmerz
  depression; sentimental sorrow   VELT-SHMERTS   'velt,ʃme^{r}ts

Welty
  Eudora, *US writer*   WEL-tē   'welti·

Welwyn Garden City
  town, England   WEL-uhn   'welən

Wembley
  stadium, London   WEM-blē   'wembli·

Wemyss
  region, Scotland   WĒMZ   'wiːmz

Wenatchee
  river, lake, city, WA; N. American   wuh-NACH-ē   wə'nætʃi·
    people

Wenceslao
  pers. name, Spanish   bān-sā-SLAH-ō, wān-, bān-thā-   beːnseː'slɑ-oː, weːn-,
         beːnθeː-

Wenceslas
  pers. name   WEN-suh-SLAHS, -SLAWS   'wensə,slɑːs, -,slɔːs

Wenceslaus
  1. pers. name   WEN-suh-SLAHS, -SLAWS   'wensə,slɑːs, -,slɔːs
  2. German   VENT-suh-SLOWS   'ventsə,slɑus

Wen-chou, Wenchow
  see Wenzhou

Foreign Sounds: ue: *Fr.* **rue**, *Ger.* **füllen**   uh(r): *Fr.* **boeuf**, *Ger.* **Höhle**   <u>kh</u>: *Ger.* **ich**, *Scot.* **loch**   ḡ: *Sp.* amigo   <u>v</u>: *Sp.* hablar
hl: *Welsh* **Llanelli**.   CAPITALS: primary stress.   SMALL CAPS: secondary stress.   Ⓢ: U.S. pron.   Ⓔ: British pron.

Wend
  Slavic people of Germany   WEND   'wend

Wendel
  1. pers. name   WEN-duhl   'wendəl
  2. German   VEN-duhl   'vendəl

Wendelin
  pers. name, German   VEN-duh-LĒN   'vendə‚liːn

Wendell
  pers. name   WEN-duhl   'wendəl

Wendish [Sorbian]
  lang., Germany   WEN-dish   'wendiʃ

Wendy
  pers. name   WEN-dē   'wendi·

Weni
  Egyptian governor   WĀ-nē   'weːni·

Wenrohronon
  N. American people   WEN-RŌ-RŌ-NAHN   ‚wen‚roː'roː‚nɑn

Wenzel
  pers. name, German   VENT-suhl   'ventsəl

Wenzeslaus
  pers. name, German   VENT-suh-SLOWS   'ventsə‚slɑus

Wenzhou, Wen-chou, Wenchow
  port, China   WEN-JŌ   'wen'dʒoː

Werner
  1. Alfred, German-born Swiss   VER-nuhr   'veʳnəʳ
    inorganic chemist (Nobel 1913)
  2. pers. name   WUHR-nuhr, VUHR-nuhr   'wəʳnəʳ, 'vəʳnəʳ
  3. German   VER-nuhr   'veʳnəʳ
  4. Swedish   VUHR-nuhr   'vərnər

Wernher
  pers. name, German   VER-nuhr, Ⓢ WUHR-nuhr   'veʳnəʳ, Ⓢ 'wəʳnəʳ

Wernicke
  Carl, German neurologist   VER-nik-uh   'veʳnikə

Wernicke's
  area of the human brain   VER-ni-kuhz, VER-ni-kēz   'veʳnikəz, 'veʳnikiːz

Wertheimer
  Max, German psychologist and   VERT-HĪ-muhr   'veʳt‚hɑiməʳ
    philosopher

Wertmuller
  Lina, Italian film director   VUHRT-MUL-uhr, WUHRT-   'vəʳt‚muləʳ, 'wəʳt-

Weser
  river, Germany   VĀ-zuhr, Ⓢ WĒ-zuhr   'veːzəʳ, Ⓢ 'wiːzəʳ

Wesley
  John and Charles, English religious   WES-lē, WEZ-lē   'wesli·, 'wezli·
    leaders; pers. name

Wesleyan
  college & univ. name, US   WEZ-lē-uhn   'wezliːən

Wessex
  medieval British kingdom; fictional   WES-iks   'wesiks
    county, Hardy

West Bromwich
  town, England   wes(t) BRUHM-ij, BRUHM-ich   wes(t) 'brəmidʒ, 'brəmitʃ

Westcott
  pers. name   WES(T)-kuht   'wes(t)kət

Key (col. 2):   a: fad   ā: fade   ah: father   ar: marry   aw: law   e: fed   ē: feed   er: merry   i: hid   ī: hide   ō: coat   ōō: boot
oi: boy   ow: now   u: put   uh: above   uhr: bird   ch: chop   ng: ring   sh: show   th: thick   <u>th</u>: this   zh: measure

West Covina
  city, CA   WES(T) kō-VĒ-nuh   ˌwes(t) koːˈviːnə
Western Samoa
  independent state, Pacific   WES-tuhrn suh-MŌ-uh   ˌwestəʳn səˈmoːə
Western Scheldt
  estuary, Netherlands   WEST-uhrn SKELT   ˌwestəʳn ˈskelt
Westerschelde
  estuary, Netherlands   VES-tuhr-SKEL-duh   ˈvestəʳˌskeldə
Westfalen
  German beer   VEST-FAHL-uhn   ˈvestˌfɑlən
West Feliciana
  parish, LA   WEST fuh-LISH-ē-AN-uh   ˌwest fəˌliʃiːˈænə
West Glamorgan
  county, Wales   WES(T) gluh-MAWR-guhn   ˌwes(t) gləˈmɔːʳgən
West Haverstraw
  village, NY   west HAV-uhr-STRAW   west ˈhævəʳˌstrɔː
Westinghouse
  George, *US inventor*   WES-ting-HOWS   ˈwestiŋˌhɑus
Westley
  pers. name   WES(T)-lē   ˈwes(t)liˑ
Westman
  Islands, *Iceland*   WES(T)-muhn   ˈwes(t)mən
West Midlands
  county, England   wes(t) MID-luhn(d)z   wes(t) ˈmidlən(d)z
Westminster
  city of, borough, England; abbey   WES(T)-MIN(T)-stuhr   ˈwes(t)ˌmin(t)stəʳ
Westmoreland
  1. William, *US general*   WES(T)-MŌR-luhnd,   ˈwes(t)ˌmoːʳlənd,
                                    WES(T)-MAWR-luhnd,   ˈwes(t)ˌmɔːʳlənd,
                                    wes(t)-MŌR-luhnd,   wes(t)ˈmoːʳlənd,
                                    wes(t)-MAWR-luhnd   wes(t)ˈmɔːʳlənd
  2. county, PA; city, KS   wes(t)-MŌR-luhnd,   wes(t)ˈmoːʳlənd,
                                  wes(t)-MAWR-luhnd   wes(t)ˈmɔːʳlənd
  3. county, VA   WES(T)-mōr-luhn(d),   ˈwes(t)moːʳlən(d),
                        WES(T)-mawr-luhn(d),   ˈwes(t)mɔːʳlən(d),
                        WES(T)-muhr-luhn(d)   ˈwes(t)məʳlən(d)
Westmorland
  former county, England   WES(T)-muhr-luhnd;   ˈwes(t)məʳlənd;
                                 ⑤ WES(T)-MŌR-luhnd,   ⑤ ˈwes(t)ˌmoːʳlənd,
                                 -MAWR-luhnd   -ˌmɔːʳlənd
Weston
  Jack, *actor*   WES-tuhn   ˈwestən
Westover
  city, WV; air force base, MA   WES-TŌ-vuhr   ˈwesˌtoːvəʳ
Westphalia
  former prov of Prussia   wes(t)-FĀL-yuh, wes(t)-FĀ-lē-uh   wes(t)ˈfeːljə, wes(t)ˈfeːliːə
West Sussex
  county, England   wes(t) SUHS-iks   wes(t) ˈsəsiks
Westvaco
  US paper and chemical co.   wes(t)-VĀ-kō   wes(t)ˈveːkoː
West Virginia
  state, US   WES(T) VUHR-JIN-yuh, vuhr-JIN-ē-uh   ˌwes(t) vəʳˈdʒinjə,
                                                             vəʳˈdʒiniːə
Westwego
  city, LA   wes-TWĒ-gō   wesˈtwiːgoː

Foreign Sounds: ue: *Fr.* **rue**, *Ger.* **füllen**   uh(r): *Fr.* **boeuf**, *Ger.* **Höhle**   kh: *Ger.* **ich**, *Scot.* **loch**   g̱: *Sp.* **amigo**   v̱: *Sp.* **hablar**
hl: *Welsh* **Llanelli**.   CAPITALS: primary stress.   SMALL CAPS: secondary stress.   ⑤: U.S. pron.   ⑥: British pron.

West Yorkshire
　county, England　　west YAWRK-shuhr, -SHIR　　west ˈjɔːᵗkʃəᵗ, -ˌʃiᵗ
Wetherbee
　pers. name　　WETH-uhr-bē　　ˈweðəᵗbiˑ
Wetterhorn
　peak, Bernese Alps　　VET-uhr-HAWRN　　ˈveʈəᵗˌhɔːᵗn
Wetumka
　city, OK　　wi-TUHM-kuh　　wiˈtəmkə
Wetumpka
　city, AL　　wi-TUHM(P)-kuh　　wiˈtəm(p)kə
Wewahitchka
　town, FL　　WĒ-wuh-HICH-kuh　　ˌwiːwəˈhitʃkə
Wewoka
　city, OK　　wē-WŌ-kuh　　wiːˈwoːkə
Wey
　river, England　　WĀ　　ˈweː
Weyden
　Roger van der, *Flemish painter*　　VĪD-n　　ˈvɑidn̩
Weyerhaeuser
　US paper products co.　　WER-HOW-zuhr, WĪ(-uh)r-HOW-zuhr　　ˈweᵗˌhɑuzəᵗ, ˈwɑi(ə)ᵗˌhɑuzəᵗ
Weymouth
　town, MA; town, England　　WĀ-muhth　　ˈweːməθ
Whalen
　pers. name　　(H)WĀ-luhn　　ˈ(h)weːlən
Wharton
　Edith, *US writer; county, city, TX;*　　(H)WAWRT-n　　ˈ(h)wɔːᵗtn̩
　pers. name
Whatcom
　county, town, WA　　(H)WAHT-kuhm　　ˈ(h)wɑtkəm
Whatmough
　family name　　(H)WAHT-MŌ　　ˈ(h)wɑtˌmoː
Wheatley
　Phillis, *US poet*　　(H)WĒT-lē　　ˈ(h)wiːtliˑ
Wheaton
　pers. name　　(H)WĒT-n　　ˈ(h)wiːtn̩
Wheeling
　city, OH, WV　　(H)WĒ-ling　　ˈ(h)wiːliŋ
Wheelock
　pers. name　　(H)WĒ-LAHK　　ˈ(h)wiːˌlɑk
Whig
　US & British political parties　　(H)WIG　　ˈ(h)wig
Whipple
　G. H., *US pathologist (Nobel 1934)*　　(H)WIP-uhl　　ˈ(h)wipəl
Whistler
　James, *US painter*　　(H)WIS-luhr　　ˈ(h)wisləᵗ
Whitaker
　pers. name　　(H)WIT-uh-kuhr　　ˈ(h)wiʈəkəᵗ
Whitbread
　tdmk for a beer　　(H)WIT-BRED　　ˈ(h)witˌbred
Whitcomb
　pers. name　　(H)WIT-kuhm　　ˈ(h)witkəm
White
　family name　　(H)WĪT　　ˈ(h)wɑit
Whitefield
　pers. name　　(H)WIT-FĒLD, (H)WĪT-FĒLD　　ˈ(h)witˌfiːld, ˈ(h)wɑitˌfiːld

---

Key (col. 2):　a: fad　ā: fade　ah: father　ar: marry　aw: law　e: fed　ē: feed　er: merry　i: hid　ī: hide　ō: coat　oo̅: boot
oi: boy　ow: now　u: put　uh: above　uhr: bird　ch: chop　ng: ring　sh: show　th: thick　th̲: this　zh: measure

Whitehall
  former palace, London; pert. to   (H)WĪT-HAWL   '(h)wɑit‚hɔːl
    British government
Whitehead
  pers. name   (H)WĪT-HED   '(h)wɑit‚hed
Whitehorse
  city, Yukon Territory   (H)WĪT-HAWRS   '(h)wɑit‚hɔːʳs
Whitley
  pers. name   (H)WIT-lē   '(h)witliˑ
Whitman
  pers. name   (H)WIT-muhn   '(h)witmən
Whitmore
  James, *US actor*   WIT-MAWR   'wit‚mɔːʳ
Whitney
  pers. name   (H)WIT-nē   '(h)witniˑ
Whitsunday
  Christian holy day   (H)WIT-SUHN-dē, (H)WIT-suhn-DĀ   ‚(h)wit'səndiˑ, '(h)witsən‚deː
Whitsuntide
  week beginning 7th Sunday after   (H)WIT-suhn-TĪD   '(h)witsən‚tɑid
    Easter
Whittier
  College, *CA; city, CA; pers. name*   (H)WIT-ē-uhr   '(h)witִiːəʳ
Whittingham
  pers. name   (H)WIT-ing-uhm, (H)WIT-n-juhm   '(h)witִiŋəm, '(h)witn̩dʒəm
Whorf
  Benjamin Lee, *US linguist*   (H)WAWRF   '(h)wɔːʳf
Whyalla
  city, Australia   (h)wī-AL-uh   (h)wɑi'ælə
Whydah
  African bird   (H)WID-uh   '(h)widə
Wibaux
  county, MT   WĒ-bō   'wiːboː
Wichita
  river, county, TX; city, county, KS; N.   WICH-uh-TAW, -TAH   'witʃə‚tɔː, -‚tɑ
    American people
Wickham
  pers. name   WIK-uhm   'wikəm
Wicklow
  county, Eire   WIK-lō   'wikloː
Wicküler
  German beer   VIK-UE-luhr   'vik‚yːləʳ
Wicomico
  county, MD   wi-KAHM-i-KŌ   wi'kɑmi‚koː
Widener
  univ., PA; library, Harvard Univ.,   WĪD-nuhr   'wɑidnəʳ
    MA; pers. name
Widmark
  Richard, *US actor*   WID-MAHRK   'wid‚mɑʳk
Wiedenmeyer
  Park, *former ballpark, Newark, NJ*   WĒD-n-MĪ(-uh)r   'wiːdn̩‚mɑi(ə)ʳ
Wieland
  Heinrich, *German organic chemist*   VĒ-LAHNT   'viː‚lɑnt
    (Nobel 1927)

Foreign Sounds: ue: *Fr.* **rue**, *Ger.* **füllen**   uh(r): *Fr.* **boeuf**, *Ger.* **Höhle**   <u>kh</u>: *Ger.* **ich**, *Scot.* **loch**   ḡ: *Sp.* **amigo**   <u>v</u>: *Sp.* **hablar**
hl: *Welsh* **Llanelli**.   CAPITALS: primary stress.   SMALL CAPS: secondary stress.   Ⓢ: U.S. pron.   Ⓔ: British pron.

Wien
  Wilhelm, *German physicist (Nobel*   VĒN   'viːn
  1911)
Wien/Schwechat
  airport, Vienna   VĒN-SHVĀ-<u>kh</u>aht   'viːn'ʃveːxɑt
Wiener
  1. Norbert, *US founder of*   WĒ-nuhr   'wiːnəʳ
  cybernetics
  2. pers. name   WĒ-nuhr, WĪ-nuhr   'wiːnɑʳ, 'wainəʳ
Wiener schnitzel
  veal cutlet   VĒ-nuhr SHNIT-suhl   'viːnəʳ ˌʃnitsəl
Wien [Vienna]
  city, Austria   VĒN   'viːn
Wiesbaden
  city, Germany   VĒS-BAHD-n, VIS-BAHD-n   'viːs,bɑdn̩, 'vis,bɑdn̩
Wiesel
  1. Elie, *Romanian-born US author,*   vē-ZEL, VĒ-zuhl, wi-ZEL   viː'zel, 'viːzəl, wi'zel
  educator (Nobel 1986)
  2. Torsten N., *Swedish*   VĒ-zuhl   'viːzəl
  neurobiologist (Nobel 1981)
Wiesenthal
  Simon, *Nazi hunter*   VĒ-zuhn-TAHL, ⑤ WĒ-zuhn-THAWL,   'viːzən,tɑl, ⑤ 'wiːzən,θɔːl,
                             -THAHL   -ˌθɑl
Wigan
  borough, England   WIG-uhn   'wigən
Wigeon
  bird   WIJ-uhn   'widʒən
Wight, Isle of
  island, England; county, VA   ĪL uh(v) WĪT   ˌail ə(v) 'wait
Wigner
  Eugene Paul, *Hungarian-born US*   WIG-nuhr   'wignəʳ
  physicist (Nobel 1963)
Wilbarger
  county, TX   WIL-BAHR-guhr   'wil,bɑʳgəʳ
Wilber
  pers. name   WIL-buhr   'wilbəʳ
Wilberforce
  William, *British abolitionist*   WIL-buhr-FAWRS   'wilbəʳˌfɔːʳs
Wilbur
  pers. name   WIL-buhr   'wilbəʳ
Wilcox
  county, AL, GA; pers. name   WIL-KAHKS   'wil,kɑks
Wilde
  Cornel, *US actor;* Oscar, *Irish wit*   WĪLD   'waild
  & writer
Wilder
  pers. name   WĪL-duhr   'waildəʳ
Wilds
  pers. name   WĪL(D)Z   'wail(d)z
Wiles
  pers. name   WĪLZ   'wailz
Wilfred
  pers. name   WIL-fruhd   'wilfrəd
Wilfrid Laurier
  University, *Canada*   WIL-fruhd lawr-YĀ   'wilfrəd lɔːr'jeː

Key (col. 2):   a: f**a**d   ā: f**a**de   ah: f**a**ther   ar: m**a**rry   aw: l**aw**   e: f**e**d   ē: f**ee**d   er: m**e**rry   i: h**i**d   ī: h**i**de   ō: c**oa**t   ōō: b**oo**t
oi: b**oy**   ow: n**ow**   u: p**u**t   uh: **a**bove   uhr: b**ir**d   ch: **ch**op   ng: ri**ng**   sh: **sh**ow   th: **th**ick   <u>th</u>: **th**is   zh: mea**s**ure

Wilfried		
pers. name, German	VIL-FRĒT	'vil‚friːt
Wilhelm		
1. pers. name	WIL-HELM	'wil‚helm
2. Danish, German, Norwegian	VIL-HELM	'vil‚helm
3. Swedish	VIL-(h)uhlm	'vil(h)əlm
Wilhelmina		
1. pers. name	WIL-hel-MĒ-nuh	‚wilhel'miːnə
2. Dutch	VIL-hel-MĒ-nah	‚vilhel'miːnɑː
3. German	VIL-hel-MĒ-nah	‚vilhel'miːnɑ
Wilhelm Meister		
novel, Goethe	VIL-HELM MĪ-stuhr	'vil‚helm 'maistəʳ
Wilhelmshaven		
port, Germany	VIL-helms-HAHF-uhn	‚vilhelms'hɑfən
Wilhelmstrasse		
street, Berlin, Germany	VIL-helm-SHTRAHS-uh	'vilhelm‚ʃtrɑsə
Wilhelmus		
pers. name, Dutch	vil-HEL-mues	vil'helmys
Wilibald		
pers. name, German	VIL-ē-BAHLT	'viliː‚bɑlt
Wilkes		
Charles, *US naval officer;* John,	WILKS	'wilks
English politician		
Wilkes-Barre		
city, PA	WILKS-BAR-uh, WILKS-BAR-ē,	'wilks‚bærə, 'wilks‚bæriˑ,
	WILKS-BAR	'wilks‚bæʳ
Wilkins		
M. H. F., *British physicist (Nobel*	WIL-kuhnz	'wilkənz
1962); Roy, *US civil rights leader;*		
pers. name		
Wilkinson		
Sir Geoffrey, *English inorganic*	WIL-kuhn-suhn	'wilkənsən
chemist (Nobel 1973)		
Will		
pers. name	WIL	'wil
Willa		
pers. name	WIL-uh	'wilə
Willacy		
county, TX	WIL-uh-sē	'wiləsiˑ
Willamette		
river, OR	wuh-LAM-uht	wə'læmət
Willapa Bay		
bay, WA	WIL-uh-PAW BĀ, WIL-uh-PAH	‚wilə‚pɔː 'beː, ‚wilə‚pɑ
Willard		
pers. name	WIL-uhrd	'wiləʳd
Willem		
pers. name, Dutch	VIL-uhm	'viləm
Willemstad		
port, Curaçao	VIL-uhm-STAHT	'viləm‚stɑt
Willesden		
former borough, England	WILZ-duhn	'wilzdən
Willi		
pers. name, German	VIL-ē	'viliː
William		
pers. name	WIL-yuhm	'wiljəm

Foreign Sounds: ue: *Fr.* **rue**, *Ger.* füllen   uh(r): *Fr.* **boeuf**, *Ger.* Höhle   <u>kh</u>: *Ger.* i<u>ch</u>, *Scot.* lo<u>ch</u>   ḡ: *Sp.* ami**g**o   <u>v</u>: *Sp.* ha**b**lar
hl: *Welsh* **Ll**anelli.   CAPITALS: primary stress.   SMALL CAPS: secondary stress.   ⑤: U.S. pron.   ⑥: British pron.

Williams
   1. family name   WIL-yuhmz   'wiljəmz
   2. Ralph Vaughan, *see Vaughan*
     Williams

Williamsburg
   city, VA   WIL-yuhmz-BUHRG   'wiljəmzˌbəʳg

Willibald
   pers. name, German   VIL-ē-BAHLT   'viliːˌbɑlt

Willie
   pers. name   WIL-ē   'wili·

Willimantic
   town, river, CT   WIL-uh-MANT-ik   ˌwilə'mæntik

Willis
   Bruce, *US actor; pers. name* WIL-uhs   'wiləs

Willkie
   Wendell Lewis, *US political leader* WIL-kē   'wilki·

Willoughby
   city, OH; pers. name   WIL-uh-bē   'wiləbi·

Willowick
   city, OH   WIL-uh-WIK   'wiləˌwik

Willstätter
   Richard, *German organic chemist* VIL-SHTET-uhr   'vilˌʃteṭəʳ
    (Nobel 1915)

Willy
   1. pers. name   WIL-ē   'wili·
   2. German   VIL-ē   'vili·

Wilma
   pers. name   WIL-muh   'wilmə

Wilmer
   pers. name   WIL-muhr   'wilməʳ

Wilmette
   town, IL   wil-MET   wil'met

Wilmington
   city, DE, NC   WIL-ming-tuhn   'wilmiŋtən

Wilmot
   pers. name   WIL-muht   'wilmət

Wilshere
   pers. name   WIL-shuhr, WIL-SHIR   'wilʃəʳ, 'wilˌʃiʳ

Wilson
   Thomas Woodrow, *28th US*   WIL-suhn   'wilsən
    president; family name

Wilsonian
   pert. to Woodrow Wilson wil-SŌ-nē-uhn, wil-SŌN-yuhn wil'soːniːən, wil'soːnjən

Wilton
   pers. name   WILT-n   'wiltn̩

Wiltshire
   county, England   WIL-chuhr, WILT-shuhr, WILT-SHIR 'wil-tʃəʳ, 'wilt-ʃəʳ, 'wiltˌʃiʳ

Wilts [Wiltshire]
   county, England   WILTS   'wilts

Wima'kwari
   Mexican festival   WĒ-muh-KWAHR-ē   ˌwiːmə'kwɑri·

Wimbledon
   section of London; tennis tournament, WIM-buhl-duhn   'wimbəldən
    England

Wiminuche Ute		
N. American people	WIM-uh-N(Y)OO-chā YOOT	ˌwiməˈn(j)uːtʃeː ˈjuːt
Wimpole		
street, London	WIM-PŌL	ˈwimˌpoːl
Winamac		
town, IN	WIN-uh-MAK	ˈwinəˌmæk
Wincent		
pers. name, Polish	VĒNT-sent	ˈviːntsent
Wincenty		
pers. name, Polish	vēnt-SEN-ti	viːntˈsenti
Winchell		
Walter, *US journalist*	WIN-chuhl	ˈwintʃəl
Winchester		
1. city , England	WIN-chuh-stuhr	ˈwintʃəstəʳ
2. pl. name, US; pers. name	WIN-CHES-tuhr, WIN-chuh-stuhr	ˈwinˌtʃestəʳ, ˈwintʃəstəʳ
Windaus		
Adolf, *German chemist (Nobel 1928)*	VIN-DOWS	ˈvinˌdɑus
Winder		
city, GA	WĪN-duhr	ˈwɑindəʳ
Windermere		
lake, town, England	WIN-duhr-MIR, WIN-duh-MIR	ˈwindəʳˌmiʳ, ˈwindəˌmiʳ
Windham		
county, CT, VT	WIN-duhm	ˈwindəm
Windhoek		
city, Namibia	VINT-HUK	ˈvintˌhuk
Windom		
William, *US actor*	WIN-duhm	ˈwindəm
Windsor		
pl. name; pers. name	WIN-zuhr	ˈwinzəʳ
Windward		
Islands, *Caribbean*	WIN-dwuhrd	ˈwindwəʳd
Winegar		
pers. name	WĪ-nuh-GAHR	ˈwɑinəˌgɑʳ
Winfield		
Paul Edward, *US actor;* Dave, *US baseball player; pers. name*	WIN-FĒLD	ˈwinˌfiːld
Winfred		
pers. name	WIN-fruhd	ˈwinfrəd
Winfrey		
Oprah, *US entertainer*	WIN-frē	ˈwinfriˑ
Winifred		
pers. name	WIN-uh-fruhd	ˈwinəfrəd
Winkler		
Henry, *US actor*	WING-kluhr	ˈwiŋkləʳ
Winnebago		
US pl. name; tdmk for campers; N. American people	WIN-uh-BĀ-gō	ˌwinəˈbeːgoː
Winnemucca		
city, NV	WIN-uh-MUHK-uh	ˌwinəˈməkə
Winneshiek		
county, IA	WIN-uh-SHĒK	ˈwinəˌʃiːk
Winnetka		
village, IL	wuh-NET-kuh	wəˈnetkə
Winnibigoshish		
lake, MN	WIN-uh-buh-GŌ-shish	ˌwinəbəˈgoːʃiʃ

Foreign Sounds: **ue:** *Fr.* **rue,** *Ger.* **füllen   uh(r):** *Fr.* **boeuf,** *Ger.* **Höhle   <u>kh</u>:** *Ger.* **i<u>ch</u>,** *Scot.* **lo<u>ch</u>   ḡ:** *Sp.* **ami<u>g</u>o   <u>v</u>:** *Sp.* **ha<u>b</u>lar hl:** *Welsh* **Llanelli.   CAPITALS:** primary stress.   SMALL CAPS: secondary stress.   ⑤: U.S. pron.   ⓔ: British pron.

Winnipeg		
river, lake, city, Canada	WIN-uh-PEG	'winə‚peg
Winnipegosis		
lake, Canada	WIN-uh-puh-GŌ-suhs	‚winəpə'goːsəs
Winnipesaukee		
lake, NH	WIN-uh-puh-SAW-kē, -SAHK-ē	‚winəpə'sɔːkiˑ, -'sɑkiˑ
Winona		
city, MN; pers. name (W. Ryder)	wuh-NŌ-nuh	wə'noːnə
Winooski		
river, city, VT	wuh-NOO-skē	wə'nuːskiˑ
Winslow		
pers. name	WINZ-lō	'winzloː
Winston		
pers. name	WIN-stuhn	'winstən
Winston-Salem		
city, NC	WIN(T)-stuhn-SĀ-luhm	'win(t)stən'seːləm
Winterthur		
1. town, Switzerland	VINT-uhr-TUR	'vintəʳ‚tuʳ
2. museum, DE	WINT-uhr-THUR, WINT-uhr-thuhr	'wintəʳ‚θuʳ, 'wintəʳθəʳ
Winthrop		
John, *American colonist*	WIN-thruhp	'winθrəp
Wintun		
N. American people	win-TOON	win'tuːn
Winwood		
Stephen Lawrence, *British musician*	WIN-WUD, WIN-wuhd	'win‚wud, 'winwəd
Wirt		
county, WV; pers. name	WUHRT	'wəʳt
Wirth		
Louis, *US sociologist*	VIRT	'viʳt
Wisbech		
borough, England	WIZ-BĒCH	'wiz‚biːtʃ
Wisconsin		
state, US	wis-KAHN(T)-suhn	wis'kɑn(t)sən
Wisconsinite		
inhabitant of Wisconsin	wis-KAHN(T)-suh-NĪT	wis'kɑn(t)sə‚nɑit
Wisła [Vistula]		
river, Poland	VĒ-slah	'viːsła
Wissota		
lake, WI	wi-SŌT-uh	wi'soːṭə
Withlacoochee		
river, FL	WITH-luh-KOO-chē	‚wiθlə'kuːtʃiˑ
Withycombe		
family name	WI<u>TH</u>-i-kuhm	'wiðikəm
Witoto		
S. American people	wuh-TŌT-ō	wə'toːṭoː
Witt		
Katarina, *German figure skater*	VIT	'vit
Wittekop		
Belgian beer	VIT-uh-KAWP, -KAHP	'viṭə‚kɔːp, -‚kɑp
Wittenberg		
1. town, Germany	VIT-n-BERK, ⑤ VIT-n-BUHRG, WIT-n-BUHRG	'vitn̩‚beʳk, ⑤ 'vitn̩‚bəʳg, 'witn̩‚bəʳg
2. mtn., NY	WIT-n-BUHRG	'witn̩‚bəʳg

Key (col. 2):   a: fad ā: fade ah: father ar: merry aw: law e: fed ē: feed er: merry i: hid ī: hide ō: coat oo: boot
oi: boy   ow: now   u: put   uh: above   uhr: bird   ch: chop   ng: ring   sh: show   th: thick   <u>th</u>: this   zh: measure

Wittgenstein		
Ludwig, *Austrian philosopher*	VIT-guhn-SHTĪN, [$] -STĪN	ˈvitgənˌʃtain, [$] -ˌstain
Wittig		
Georg, *German organic chemist (Nobel 1979)*	VIT-ikh	ˈvit̬iç
Witwatersrand		
region, South Africa	WIT-WAWT-uhrz-RAHND, -RAND	ˈwitˌwɔːt̬əʳzˌrɑnd, -ˌrænd
Wjeprz		
river, Poland	VYEPSH	ˈvjepʃ
Wladimir		
pers. name, German	vlah-DĒ-mir	vlɑˈdiːmiʳ
Władysław		
pers. name, Polish	vlah-DIS-lahf	vɫɑːˈdisɫɑːf
Włodzimierz		
pers. name, Polish	vlaw-JĒM-yesh	vɫɔːˈdʒiːmjeʃ
Wobegon		
Lake, *fictional place, G. Keillor*	WŌ-bi-GAWN, -GAHN	ˈwoːbiˌgɔːn, -ˌgɑn
Woburn		
1. city, MA	WO͞O-buhrn, WŌ-buhrn	ˈwuːbəʳn, ˈwoːbəʳn
2. parish, England	WO͞O-buhrn	ˈwuːbəʳn
Wodehouse		
P. G., *English author; pers. name*	WUD-HOWS	ˈwudˌhɑus
Woden, Wodan [Odin]		
supreme Scandinavian god	WŌD-n	ˈwoːdn̩
Wojciech		
pers. name, Polish	VOI-chekh	ˈvɔitʃeç
Wojtyla		
Karol (Pope John Paul II)	voi-TIL-ah	vɔiˈtilɑː
Woking		
town, England	WŌ-king	ˈwoːkiŋ
Wokingham		
town, England	WŌ-king-uhm	ˈwoːkiŋəm
Woldemar		
1. pers. name, Finnish	WAWL-de-MAHR	ˈwɔːldeˌmɑːʳ
2. German	VAWL-de-MAHR	ˈvɔːldeˌmɑʳ
Wolds Way		
footpath, England	WŌDZ WĀ	ˌwoːdz ˈweː
Wole		
pers. name, West Africa	WŌ-lā, WAW-lā	ˈwoːleː, ˈwɔːleː
Wolf		
1. pers. name	WULF	ˈwulf
2. German	VAWLF	ˈvɔːlf
Wölfbräu		
German beer	VUH(R)LF-BROI	ˈvœlfˌbrɔi
Wolfe, Wolff		
pers. name	WULF	ˈwulf
Wolfgang		
pers. name, German	VAWLF-GAHNG	ˈvɔːlfˌgɑŋ
Wolfram		
Walt, *US linguist; former name for* tungsten	WUL-fruhm	ˈwulfrəm
Wolfram von Eschenbach		
German poet	VAWL-FRAHM fawn ESH-uhn-BAHKH	ˈvɔːlˌfrɑm fɔːn ˈeʃənˌbɑx

Wolfsberg
town, Austria VAWLFS-BERK, ⑤ WULFS-BUHRG, -BERG 'vɔːlfs‚be^rk, ⑤ 'wulfs‚bə^rg, -‚be^rg

Wolfsburg
city, Germany VAWLFS-BURK, ⑤ WULFS-BUHRG, -BURG 'vɔːlfs‚bu^rk, ⑤ 'wulfs‚bə^rg, -‚bu^rg

Wolfson
college, Oxford Univ., Cambridge Univ. WULF-suhn 'wulfsən

Wollaston
pers. name WUL-uhs-tuhn 'wuləstən

Wollongong
city, Australia WUL-uhng-GAHNG, -GAWNG 'wuləŋ‚gɑŋ, -‚gɔːŋ

Wollstonecraft
pers. name (M. W. Shelley) WUL-stuhn-KRAFT, -KRAHFT 'wulstən‚kræft, -‚krɑːft

Wolof
lang., people, Africa WŌ-LAHF, WŌ-LAWF 'woː‚lɑf, 'woː‚lɔːf

Wolsey
Thomas, *English prelate and statesman* WUL-zē 'wulziˑ

Wolters Kluwer
Dutch publishing co. VAWL-tuhrs KLOO-uhr, ⑤ WŌL-tuhrz KLU(-uh)r ‚vɔːltə^rs 'kluːə^r, ⑤ ‚woːltə^rz 'klu(ə)^r

Wolverhampton
town, England WUL-vuhr-HAM(P)-tuhn 'wulvə^r‚hæm(p)tən

Wonsan
port, N. Korea wuhn-sahn wənsɑn

Wood
pers. name WUD 'wud

Woodbury
pers. name WUD-BER-ē, WUD-buhr-ē, -brē 'wud‚beriˑ, 'wudbəriˑ, -briˑ

Woodhull
Victoria, *US journalist* WUD-HUHL 'wud‚həl

Woodrow
pers. name WUD-rō 'wudroː

Woodruff
pers. name WUD-ruhf 'wudrəf

Woodward
1. Robert Burns, *US chemist (Nobel 1965);* Robert, *US journalist* WUD-wuhrd 'wudwə^rd
2. city, county, OK WUD-wuhrd, WUD-uhrd 'wudwə^rd, 'wudə^rd
3. pers. name WUD-wuhrd, ⓔ WUD-uhrd 'wudwə^rd, ⓔ 'wudə^rd

Woolworth
Frank Winfield, *US merchant; dept. store chain* WUL-wuhrth 'wulwə^rθ

Woody
pers. name WUD-ē 'wudiˑ

Woolf
Virginia, *English writer; pers. name* WULF 'wulf

Woollcott
Alexander, *US writer* WUL-kuht 'wulkət

Woolloomooloo
Australia WUL-uh-muh-LOO, WUL-uh-muh-LOO ‚wuləmə'luː, 'wuləmə‚luː

Woolsey
pers. name WUL-zē 'wulziˑ

Key (col. 2):   a: **fad** ā: **fade** ah: **father** ar: **marry** aw: **law** e: **fed** ē: **feed** er: **merry** i: **hid** ī: **hide** ō: **coat** ōō: **boot**
oi: **boy**   ow: **now**   u: **put**   uh: **above**   uhr: **bird**   ch: **chop**   ng: **ring**   sh: **show**   th: **thick**   <u>th</u>: **this**   zh: **measure**

Woolwich
  former borough, England   WUL-ij, WUL-ich   'wulidʒ, 'wulitʃ
Woomera
  township, Australia   WUM-uh-ruh   'wumərə
Woonsocket
  city, RI, SD   wo͞on-SAHK-uht, WO͞ON-SAHK-uht   wuːn'sɑkət, 'wuːn,sɑkət
Woosnam
  Ian, *Welsh golfer*   WO͞OZ-nuhm   'wuːznəm
Wooster
  city, OH; pers. name   WUS-tuhr   'wustəʳ
Worcester
  city, MA, England; county, MA, MD; WUS-tuhr   'wustəʳ
  pers. name
Worcestershire
  1. former county, England   WUS-tuhr-SHIR, WUS-tuhr-shuhr   'wustəʳ,ʃiʳ, 'wustəʳʃəʳ
  2. sauce   WUS-tuhr-SHIR, WUS-tuhr-shuhr,   'wustəʳ,ʃiʳ, 'wustəʳʃəʳ,
                                     WUS-tuhr [sic]   'wustəʳ [sic]
Wordsworth
  William, *English poet; pers. name*   WUHRDZ-WUHRTH   'wəʳdz,wəʳθ
Wordsworthian
  pert. to William Wordsworth   WUHRDZ-WUHR-the̅-uhn,   ,wəʳdz'wəʳθiːən,
                                     WUHRDZ-WUHR-the̅-uhn   ,wəʳdz'wəʳðiːən
Worms
  port, Germany   VAWRM(P)S, Ⓢ WUHRMZ   'vɔːʳm(p)s, Ⓢ 'wəʳmz
Worthing
  town, England   WUHR-thing   'wəʳðiŋ
Wortis [Avi]
  Avi, *US children's author*   WAWRT-uhs, WUHRT-uhs   'wɔːʳtəs, 'wəʳtəs
Wortley
  pers. name   WUHRT-le̅   'wəʳtliˑ
Worzel
  pers. name   WUHRT-suhl   'wəʳtsəl
Wotan [Odin]
  supreme Scandinavian god   VO̅-TAHN   'voː,tɑn
Wotton
  Sir Henry, *English diplomat and poet* WAHT-n   'wɑtn̩
Wotton-under-Edge
  village, England   WUT-n-UHN-drij, WUT-n-UHN-duh-REJ   ,wutn̩'əndridʒ,
                                                                  ,wutn̩,əndə'redʒ
Wouk
  Herman, *US writer*   WO̅K, WO͞OK   'woːk, 'wuːk
Wovoka
  Paiute mystic, also known as Jack   wuh-VO̅-kuh   wə'voːkə
  Wilson
Wozzeck
  opera, A. Berg   VAWT-SEK   'vɔːt,sek
Wrangel
  Ferdinand Petrovich von, *Russian*   VRAHN-gyil, Ⓢ RANG-guhl   'vrɑːngjil, Ⓢ 'ræŋgəl
  explorer; island, Arctic
Wrangell-Petersburg
  division, AK   RANG-guhl-PE̅T-uhrz-BUHRG   'ræŋgəl'piːtəʳz,bəʳg
Wrangell-St Elias
  National Park and Preserve, AK   RANG-guhl-SA̅NT-l-I̅-uhs   'ræŋgəl,seːntl̩'aiəs
Wrexham
  city, Wales; Welsh beer   REK-suhm   'reksəm

Foreign Sounds: **ue**: *Fr.* **rue**, *Ger.* **füllen uh(r)**: *Fr.* **boeuf**, *Ger.* **Höhle kh**: *Ger.* **ich**, *Scot.* **loch g̱**: *Sp.* **amigo v̱**: *Sp.* **hablar
hl**: *Welsh* **Llanelli. CAPITALS**: primary stress. SMALL CAPS: secondary stress. Ⓢ: U.S. pron. Ⓔ: British pron.

Wreyford
  pers. name   RĀ-fuhrd   ˈreːfərd
Wright
  pers. name   RĪT   ˈrɑit
Wrigley
  tdmk for a chewing gum; Field,   RIG-lē   ˈrigliˑ
    ballpark, Chicago
Wriothesley
  Henry, *Shakespearean patron*   RĪ-uhth-slē, RAHT-(uh-)slē, RITH-lē,   ˈrɑiəθsliˑ, ˈrɑt(ə)sliˑ, ˈriθliˑ,
                                         RIZ-lē   ˈrizliˑ
Wrocław [Breslau]
  city, voivodship, Poland   VRAWT-SLAHF   ˈvrɔːtˌsɫaf
Wrotham
  village, England   RŌŌT-uhm   ˈruːʈəm
Wu
  lang.; pers. name, Chinese   WŌŌ   ˈwuː
Wuchang, Wuch'ang
  city, China   WŌŌ-CHAHNG   ˈwuːˈtʃɑŋ
Wu Chen
  Chinese year (Dragon)   WŌŌ CHUHN   ˈwuː ˈtʃən
Wuhan, Wu-han
  port, China   WŌŌ-HAHN   ˈwuːˈhɑn
Wundt
  Wilhelm, *German physiologist*   VUNT   ˈvunt
Wuppertal
  city, Germany   VUP-uhr-TAHL, ⑤ WUP-   ˈvupərˌtɑl, ⑤ ˈwup-
Wurlitzer
  US jukebox mfr.   WUHR-luht-suhr   ˈwərlətsər
Württemberg
  region, Germany   VURT-uhm-BERK;   ˈvyrtəmˌberk;
                                         ⑤ WUHRT-uhm-BUHRG,   ⑤ ˈwərtəmˌbərg,
                                         VIRT-uhm-BUHRG   ˈvirtəmˌbərg
Würzburg
  city, Germany   VUERTS-BURK, ⑤ WUHRTS-BUHRG,   ˈvyːrtsˌburk, ⑤ ˈwərtsˌbərg,
                                         VIRTS-BURG   ˈvirtsˌburg
Würzburger
  German beer   VUERTS-BUR-guhr   ˈvyːrtsˌburgər
Wüsthof
  German mfr.   VUEST-HAWF   ˈvyːstˌhɔːf
Wu Yue
  mtns., China   WŌŌ yōō-Ā   ˈwuː juːˈeː
Wyalusing
  town, WI   WĪ-uh-LŌŌ-sing   ˌwɑiəˈluːsiŋ
Wyandot
  county, OH   WĪ-uhn-DAHT   ˈwɑiənˌdɑt
Wyandotte
  city, MI; county, KS; N. American   WĪ-uhn-DAHT, WĪN-DAHT   ˈwɑiənˌdɑt, ˈwɑinˌdɑt
    people
Wyatt
  pers. name   WĪ-uht   ˈwɑiət
Wycherley
  William, *English dramatist*   WICH-uhr-lē   ˈwitʃərliˑ
Wyckoff
  town, NJ   WĪ-KAWF   ˈwɑiˌkɔːf

Key (col. 2):   a: fad ā: fade ah: father ar: marry aw: law e: fed ē: feed er: merry i: hid ī: hide ō: coat ōō: boot
oi: boy   ow: now   u: put   uh: above   uhr: bird   ch: chop   ng: ring   sh: show   th: thick   th: this   zh: measure

Wycliffe
  pers. name   WIK-LIF, WIK-luhf   'wik͵lif, 'wikləf
Wye
  river, Wales, England   WĪ   'wɑi
Wyeth
  family of US painters   WĪ-uhth   'wɑiəθ
Wyeth-Ayerst
  US pharmaceutical co.   WĪ-uhth Ā-uhrst, ERST   ͵wɑiəθ 'eːəʳst, 'eʳst
Wykeham
  William of, *founder, Winchester*   WIK-uhm   'wikəm
    College, Oxford
Wykehamist
  student of Winchester College WIK-uh-muhst   'wikəməst
Wylacki Pomo
  N. American people   wī-LAK-ē PŌ-mō   wɑi'læki· 'poːmoː
Wyld, Wylde
  family name   WĪLD   'wɑild
Wylie
  pers. name   WĪ-lē   'wɑili·
Wyman
  Jane, *US actress*   WĪ-muhn   'wɑimən
Wymondham
  1. town, Leicestershire, England WĪ-muhn-duhm   'wɑiməndəm
  2. town, Norfolk, England   WIN-duhm, WIM-uhn-duhm   'windəm, 'wiməndəm
Wyndham
  pers. name   WIN-duhm   'windəm
Wynette
  Tammy, *US singer*   wī-NET   wɑi'net
Wynkyn
  pers. name   WING-kuhn   'wiŋkən
Wynne
  pers. name   WIN   'win
Wynona
  pers. name (W. Judd)   wī-NŌ-nuh   wɑi'noːnə
Wynooche
  river, WA   wī-NŌO-chē   wɑi'nuːtʃi·
Wynter
  Dana, *British actress*   WINT-uhr   'wintəʳ
Wynton
  pers. name (W. Marsalis)   WINT-n   'wintṇ
Wyomia
  pers. name (W. Tyus)   wī-Ō-mē-uh   wɑi'oːmiːə
Wyoming
  state, US   wī-Ō-ming   wɑi'oːmiŋ
Wyomingite
  inhabitant of Wyoming   wī-Ō-ming-ĪT   wɑi'oːmiŋ͵ɑit
Wyomissing
  borough, PA   WĪ-uh-MIS-ing   ͵wɑiə'misiŋ
WYSIWYG
  "what you see is what you get" WIZ-ē-WIG, WIZ-ē-WIG   'wizi·͵wig, ͵wizi·'wig
Wystan
  pers. name   WIS-tuhn   'wistən
Wyszyński
  Stefan, *Polish cardinal*   vish-IN-yuh-skē, Ⓢ vuh-SHIN-skē   viʃ'iɲ ski·, Ⓢ və'ʃinski·

Wythe

George, *US jurist, statesman;*   WITH   'wiθ
county, VA

X

X-acto

tdmk for a graphics knife   ig-ZAK-tō, ek-SAK-tō   ig'zæktoː, ek'sæktoː

Xanadu

place in Kubla Khan, *Coleridge;*   ZAN-uh-D(Y)O͞O   'zænə,d(j)uː
house in film Citizen Kane

Xanthe

pers. name   ZAN-thē   'zænθiˑ

Xanthippe, Xantippe

wife of Socrates   zan-TIP-ē, zan-THIP-ē   zæn'tipiˑ, zæn'θipiˑ

Xanthus

pers. name   ZAN-thuhs   'zænθəs

Xantus's murrelet

sea bird   ZAN-tuhs-uhz MUHR-luht   'zæntəsəz 'məʳlət

Xau

lake, Botswana   KSAH-o͞o, KSOW   'ksɑuː, 'ksɑu

Xaverian Brothers

Roman Catholic teaching order   zā-VIR-ē-uhn BRU<u>TH</u>-uhrz   zeː'viriːən ˌbrəðəʳz

Xavier

1. University, *OH, LA;* Christian   ZĀ-vē-uhr, ig-ZĀ-vē-uhr, -vyuhr   'zeːviːəʳ, ig'zeːviːəʳ, -vjəʳ
saint; pers. name

2. French   gzahv-YĀ   gzɑːvjeː

3. Portuguese   shuhv-YĀR, shahv-YĀR   ʃəv'jeːr, ʃɑːv'jeːr

4. Spanish   <u>kh</u>ahv-YER   xɑv'jer

Xaviero

pers. name, Italian   ksahv-YER-ō   ksɑv'jeroː

Xenia

city, OH   ZĒN-yuh, ZĒ-nē-uh   'ziːnjə, 'ziːniːə

Xenocrates

Greek philosopher   zuh-NAHK-ruh-TĒZ   zə'nɑkrə,tiːz

xenon

element   ZĒ-NAHN   'ziː,nɑn

Xenophanes

Greek philosopher   zi-NAHF-uh-NĒZ   zi'nɑfə,niːz

Xenophon

Greek historian   ZEN-uh-fuhn   'zenəfən

Xeres

former name of Jerez   SHER-ēz, <u>KH</u>ER-es   'ʃeriːz, 'xeres

Xerox

tdmk for a photocopier; US corp.   ZIR-AHKS, ZĒ-RAHKS   'zir,ɑks, 'ziː,rɑks

---

Key (col. 2): a: fad ā: fade ah: father ar: marry aw: law e: fed ē: feed er: merry i: hid ī: hide ō: coat o͞o: boot
oi: boy ow: now u: put uh: above uhr: bird ch: chop ng: ring sh: show th: thick <u>th</u>: this zh: measure

Xerxes [Ahasuerus]

   Persian king   ZUHRK-SĒZ   ˈzəʳkˌsiːz

Xhosa, Xosa

   Kaffir people, lang.   HAW-sah, KAW-suh, KŌ-suh   ˈɔhɔːsɑː, ˈkɔːsə, ˈkoːsə

Xi, Hsi, Si

   river, China   SHĒ   ˈʃiː

Xiamen, Hsia-men [Amoy]

   city, China   shē-AH-MUHN   ʃiːˈɑˈmən

Xian, Xi'an, Sian [Changan]

   city, China   SHĒ-AHN   ˈʃiːˈɑn

Xiang

   lang., China   shē-AHNG   ʃiːˈɑŋ

Xi Jiang, Hsi Chiang [Xi]

   river, China   SHĒ jē-AHNG   ˈʃiː dʒiːˈɑŋ

Xingu

   river, park, beer, Brazil   shēng-G͞O͞O, shing-G͞O͞O   ʃiːŋˈguː, ʃiŋˈguː

Xining, Hsining

   city, China   SHĒ-NING   ˈʃiːˈniŋ

Xinjiang, Sinkiang

   region, China   SHIN-jē-AHNG   ˈʃindʒiːˈɑŋ

Xinjiang Uygur, Sinkiang Uighur

   division, China   SHIN-jē-AHNG WĒ-GUR   ˈʃindʒiːˈɑŋ ˈwiːˈguʳ

Xinxiang, Hsin-hsiang

   city, China   SHIN-shē-AHNG   ˈʃinʃiːˈɑŋ

Xiquets de Valls

   Spanish festival   k͟hē-KETS t͟hā VAHLS   xiːˈkets ðeː ˈvɑls

Xizang

   region, Tibet   SHĒT-SAHNG   ˈʃiːtˈsɑŋ

Xmas

   abbreviation for Christmas   KRIS-muhs, EK-smuhs   ˈkrisməs, ˈeksməs

Xochimilco

   lake, city, Mexico   SŌ-chē-MĒL-kō, SŌ-shē-, -MIL-kō   ˌsoːtʃiːˈmiːlkoː, ˌsoːʃiː-, -ˈmilkoː

Xosa

   see Xhosa

X-Pert

   Dutch beer   EK-SPERT, Ⓢ EK-SPUHRT   ˈekˌspert, Ⓢ ˈekˌspəʳt

Xu Shiyou

   city, China   SH͞O͞O SHUH(R)-Y͞O͞O   ˈʃuː ˈʃə(r)ˈjuː

Xystus

   pope   SIS-tuhs, ZIS-tuhs   ˈsistəs, ˈzistəs

Foreign Sounds: ue: *Fr.* **rue**, *Ger.* füllen   uh(r): *Fr.* b**oeuf**, *Ger.* Höhle   k͟h: *Ger.* i**ch**, *Scot.* lo**ch**   g̃: *Sp.* ami**g**o   v: *Sp.* ha**b**lar
hl: *Welsh* **Ll**anelli.   CAPITALS: primary stress.   SMALL CAPS: secondary stress.   Ⓢ: U.S. pron.   Ⓔ: British pron.

Y

Yaakov
  see Yakov

Yablonoi
  mts., Russia   YAHB-luh-NOI   ˌjɑːbləˈnɔi

Yablonovy
  mts., Russia   YAHB-luh-nuh-VĒ   ˌjɑːblənəˈviː

Yachats
  town, river, OR   YAH-hahts   ˈjɑhɑts

Yadkin
  river, county, NC   YAD-kuhn   ˈjædkən

Yagua
  S. American people   YAHG-wuh, YAHḠ-wuh   ˈjɑgwə, ˈjɑɣwə

Yahgan
  S. American people   YAHG-uhn   ˈjɑgən

Yahoo
  brutes in Gulliver's Travels, *Swift*   YAH-hoo, YĀ-hoo   ˈjɑhuː, ˈjeːhuː

Yahweh, Yahveh, Jahveh
  Hebrew name of God   YAH-WĀ, YAH-VĀ   ˈjɑˌweː, ˈjɑˌveː

Yajur Veda
  Hindu book of hymns   YAHJ-ur VĀD-uh   ˈjɑdʒuʳ ˈveːdə

Yakima
  1. river, city, county, WA   YAK-uh-MAW   ˈjækəˌmɔː
  2. N. American people   YAK-uh-MAW, YAK-uh-muh   ˈjækəˌmɔː, ˈjækəmə

Yakov
  pers. name, Russian   YAH-kuhf   ˈjɑːkəf

Yakov, Yaakov
  pers. name, Hebrew   YAHK-awv   ˈjɑkɔːv

Yakumo
  pers. name, Japanese   yah-ku-mō   jɑkumoː

Yakut
  Siberian people   yuh-KOOT   jəˈkuːt

Yakutat
  city, AK   YAK-uh-TAT   ˈjækəˌtæt

Yakutsk
  town, Russia   yuh-KOOTSK   jəˈkuːtsk

Yale
  univ., CT; pers. name   YĀL   ˈjeːl

Yalobusha
  river, county, MS   YAL-uh-BUSH-uh   ˌjæləˈbuʃə

Yalow
  Rosalyn S., US physiologist (Nobel   YAL-ō   ˈjæloː
  1977)

Key (col. 2):   a: fad   ā: fade   ah: father   ar: marry   aw: law   e: fed   ē: feed   er: merry   i: hid   ī: hide   ō: coat   oo: boot
oi: boy   ow: now   u: put   uh: above   uhr: bird   ch: chop   ng: ring   sh: show   th: thick   th̲: this   zh: measure

Yalta		
town, Ukraine	YAWL-tuh	'jɔːltə
Yalu		
river, China	YAH-L̄OO	'jɑ'luː
Yalung		
river, China	YAH-LUNG	'jɑ'luŋ
Yamaguchi		
Kristi, *US figure skater*	YAHM-uh-ḠOO-chē	ˌjɑmə'guːtʃiˑ
Yamaha		
Japanese corp.	YAHM-uh-HAH	'jɑməˌhɑ
Yamaichi		
Japanese financial services co.	yah-mah-ē-chē	jɑmɑiːtʃiː
Yamamadi		
S. American people	YAHM-uh-MAHD-ē	ˌjɑmə'mɑdiˑ
Yamani		
Ahmed Zaki, *Saudi official*	yuh-MAHN-ē, yah-	jə'mɑniˑ, jɑ-
Yamasaki		
Minoru, *US architect*	YAHM-uh-SAHK-ē	ˌjɑmə'sɑkiˑ
Yamasee		
N. American people	YAHM-uh-sē	'jɑməsiˑ
Yamhill		
county, OR	YAM-HIL	'jæmˌhil
Yamuna [Jumna]		
river, India	YAH-muh-nuh	'jɑmənə
Yan'an, Yenan		
town, China	YEN-AHN	'jen'ɑn
Yanco		
town, creek, Australia	YANG-kō	'jæŋkoː
Yáñez		
pers. name, Spanish	YAHN-yās, YAHN-yāth	'jɑnjeːs, 'jɑnjeːθ
Yang Chen Ning		
Chinese-born US physicist (Nobel 1957)	YAHNG JUHN NING	'jɑŋ 'dʒən 'niŋ
Yangchow		
see Yangzhou		
Yangtze [Chang Jiang]		
river, China	YANG-SĒ, YANG(K)T-SĒ	'jæŋ'siː, 'jæŋ(k)t'siː
Yangzhou, Yangchow		
city, China	YAHNG-JŌ	'jɑŋ'dʒoː
Yankton		
N. American people	YANG(K)-tuhn	'jæŋ(k)tən
Yanni		
Greek-born US musician	YAHN-ē	'jɑniˑ
Yao		
lang., people, Africa; lang., people, SE Asia [Man]	YOW	'jɑu
Yaoundé		
city, Cameroon	yown-DĀ	jɑun'deː
Yap [Caroline Islands]		
federated state, Pacific	YAP, YAHP	'jæp, 'jɑp
Yaphank		
town, NY	YAP-ANGK, YAP-HANGK	'jæpˌæŋk, 'jæpˌhæŋk
Yaqui		
N. American people	YAHK-ē	'jɑkiˑ

Foreign Sounds:　ue: *Fr.* **rue**, *Ger.* **füllen**　uh(r): *Fr.* **boeuf**, *Ger.* **Höhle**　<u>kh</u>: *Ger.* **ich**, *Scot.* lo**ch**　g̃: *Sp.* ami**g**o　ⱴ: *Sp.* ha**b**lar
hl: *Welsh* **Ll**anelli.　CAPITALS: primary stress.　SMALL CAPS: secondary stress.　Ⓢ: U.S. pron.　Ⓔ: British pron.

Yarborough

  William, *US stock car racer*   YAHR-BUHR-ō, YAHR-brō   ˈjɑʳˌbərɔː, ˈjɑʳbrɔː

Yaren

  district, Nauru   YAHR-uhn   ˈjɑrən

Yarmouth

  city, MA; city, England   YAHR-muhth   ˈjɑʳməθ

Yaroslavl

  city, Russia   YAHR-uh-SLAHV-uhl   ˌjɑːrəˈslɑːvəl

Yarrawonga

  town, Australia   YAR-uh-WAHNG-guh, -WAWNG-guh   ˌjærəˈwɑŋgə, -ˈwɔːŋgə

Yarrow

  Peter, *US folk singer*   YAR-ō   ˈjærɔː

Yasir

  pers. name, Arabic   YAHS-IR, ⓢ YAS-uhr   ˈjɑsˌir, ⓢ ˈjæsəʳ

Yasmin

  pers. name   YAS-muhn, YAZ-muhn   ˈjæsmən, ˈjæzmən

Yassy

  see Iasi

Yasuga

  pers. name, Japanese   yah-sug-ah   jɑsugɑ

Yasuhiro

  pers. name, Japanese   yah-su-hē-rō   jɑsuhiːrɔː

Yasuhito

  pers. name, Japanese   yah-su-hē-tō   jɑsuhiːtɔː

Yasujirō

  pers. name, Japanese   yah-suj-ē-rō   jɑsudʒiːrɔː

Yasukini Matsuri

  Japanese memorial   yah-su-kē-nē maht-sur-ē   jɑsukiːniː mɑtsuriˑ

Yasunari

  pers. name, Japanese   yah-su-nahr-ē   jɑsunɑriː

Yasuo

  pers. name, Japanese   yah-sōō-ō   jɑsuːɔː

Yathrib

  former name of Medina   YATH-ruhb   ˈjæθrəb

Yavapai

  1. county, AZ   YAV-uh-PĪ   ˈjævəˌpai

  2. N. American people   YAHV-uh-PĪ, YAV-uh-PĪ   ˌjɑvəˈpai, ˈjævəˌpai

Yazoo

  river, county, MS   ya-ZŌŌ   jæˈzuː

Ybor

  Vicente Martínez, *cigar*   Ē-bawr   ˈiːbɔːʳ
    manufacturer

Yeadon

  1. town, PA   YĀD-n   ˈjeːdn̩

  2. town, England   YĒD-n, YĀD-n   ˈjiːdn̩, ˈjeːdn̩

  3. family name   YĒD-n, YĀD-n, YED-n   ˈjiːdn̩, ˈjeːdn̩, ˈjedn̩

Yeager

  Chuck, *US air force pilot;* Jeana,   YĀ-guhr   ˈjeːgəʳ
    US pilot

Yeats

  W. B., *Irish poet, playwright (Nobel*   YĀTS   ˈjeːts
    1923)

Yehudi

  pers. name   yuh-HŌŌD-ē   jəˈhuːdiˑ

Key (col. 2):   a: fad   ā: fade   ah: father   ar: marry   aw: law   e: fed   ē: feed   er: merry   i: hid   ī: hide   ō: coat   ōō: boot
oi: boy   ow: now   u: put   uh: above   uhr: bird   ch: chop   ng: ring   sh: show   th: thick   th: this   zh: measure

Ye Jiangying
  Chinese communist leader   YUH jē-AHNG-YING   ˈjə dʒiːˈɑŋˈjiŋ

Yekaterinburg, Ekaterinburg [Sverdlovsk]
  city, Russia   yi-KUHT-yir-yin-BURK,   ji͵kətjirjinˈburk,
       Ⓢ yuh-KAT-uh-ruhn-BUHRG   Ⓢ jəˈkæʈərən͵bəʳg

Yellowknife
  river, town, Canada; N. American people   YEL-uh-NĪF, YEL-ō-NĪF   ˈjelə͵nɑif, ˈjeloː͵nɑif

Yeltsin
  Boris, *Russian politician*   YELTS-yin, Ⓢ YELT-suhn   ˈjeltsjin, Ⓢ ˈjeltsən

Yemen
  republic, Arabian Peninsula   YEM-uhn, YĀ-muhn   ˈjemən, ˈjeːmən

Yemeni
  pert. to Yemen   YEM-uh-nē, YĀ-muh-nē   ˈjeməniˑ, ˈjeːməniˑ

Yenan
  see Yan'an

Yenisey, -sei
  river, Russia   YEN-uh-SĀ   ͵jenəˈseː

Yeovil
  town, England   YŌ-VIL   ˈjoː͵vil

Yerba Buena
  city, CA   YUHR-buh BWĀ-nuh   ͵jəʳbə ˈbweːnə

Yerba maté
  plant   YER-buh MAH-TĀ, YUHR-buh   ͵jeʳbə ˈmɑ͵teː, ͵jəʳbə

Yerevan
  city, Armenia   YER-uh-VAHN   ͵jerəˈvɑn

Yerkes
  Charles, *US financier;* Robert, *US psychologist*   YUHR-kēz   ˈjəʳkiːz

Yeu, Ile d'
  island, France   ēl DYUH(R)   iːl djœː

Yevgeni, Yevgeny
  pers. name, Russian   yiv-GYĀN-yi   jivˈgjeːnjij

Yevtushenko
  Yevgeni, *Russian poet*   YEV-tuh-SHENG-kō   ͵jevtəˈʃeŋkoː

Yggdrasill
  tree in Scandinavian myth   IG-druh-SIL   ˈigdrə͵sil

YHWH [Yahweh]
  a Hebrew name of God   YAH-WĀ, YAH-VĀ   ˈjɑ͵weː, ˈjɑ͵veː

Yi
  lang., China, Burma, Tibet   YĒ   ˈjiː

Yi
  Korean dynasty, ruling family; river, Uruguay   YĒ   ˈjiː

Yi Chou
  Chinese year (Ox)   YĒ JŌ   ˈjiː ˈdʒoː

Yiddish
  European Jewish lang.   YID-ish   ˈjidiʃ

Yin Yang
  Taoist symbol   YIN YANG   ˈjin ˈjæŋ

Yitzhak
  pers. name, Hebrew   YITS-khahk, Ⓢ YIT-sahk   ˈjitsxɑk, Ⓢ ˈjitsɑk

Yizkor
  Jewish memorial service   YIZ-KAWR   ˈjiz͵kɔːʳ

Foreign Sounds: ue: *Fr.* **rue**, *Ger.* **füllen**   uh(r): *Fr.* **boeuf**, *Ger.* **Höhle**   kh: *Ger.* **ich**, *Scot.* **loch**   g̃: *Sp.* **amigo**   v: *Sp.* **hablar** hl: *Welsh* **Llanelli.**   CAPITALS: primary stress.   SMALL CAPS: secondary stress.   Ⓢ: U.S. pron.   Ⓔ: British pron.

Yma

pers. name — Ē-muh — 'iːmə

Ymir

Norse giant — Ē-MIR — 'iː‚miʳ

Ynys Môn [Anglesey]

island, Wales — UHN-is MAWN — ‚ənis 'mɔːn

Yoakam

Dwight, *US country musician* — YŌ-kuhm — 'joːkəm

Yogi

cartoon bear; pers. name (Y. Berra) — YŌ-gē — 'joːgi·

Yogism

Yoga philosophy — YŌ-GIZ-uhm — 'joː‚gizəm

Yoknapatawpha

fictional MS county, Faulkner — YAHK-nuh-puh-TAW-fuh — ‚jɑknəpə'tɔːfə

Yoko

pers. name (Y. Ono) — YŌ-kō — 'joːkoː

Yokohama

city, Japan — yō-kō-hahm-ah, Ⓢ YŌ-kuh-HAHM-uh — joːkoːhɑmɑ, Ⓢ ‚joːkə'hɑmə

Yokosuka

port, Japan — yō-kō-suk-ah — joːkoːsukɑ

Yokozuna

sumo wrestling Grand Champion — yō-kō-zun-ah — joːkoːzunɑ

Yolanda

pers. name — yō-LAN-duh, yō-LAHN-duh — joː'lændə, joː'lɑndə

Yolande

pers. name, French — yaw-LAHⁿD — jɔːlɑ̃d

Yomba

Indian reservation, US — YAWM-buh, YAHM-buh — 'jɔːmbə, 'jɑmbə

Yom Ha' Azma'ut

Jewish holiday — YAWM HAH AHT-smah-O͞OT, YŌM, YAHM — ‚jɔːm hɑ ‚ɑtsmɑ'uːt, ‚joːm, ‚jɑm

Yom Hashoa

Jewish memorial day — YAWM HAHSH-ō-AH, YŌM, YAHM — ‚jɔːm ‚hɑʃoː'ɑ, ‚joːm, ‚jɑm

Yom Kippur

Jewish fast day — YAWM KI-PUR, YŌM, YAHM, KIP-uhr, KIP-UR — ‚jɔːm ki'puʳ, ‚joːm, ‚jɑm, 'kipəʳ, 'kip‚uʳ

Yonge

street, Toronto, Ontario — YUHNG — 'jəŋ

Yonkers

town, NY — YAHNG-kuhrz — 'jɑŋkəʳz

Yoplait

yogurt brand — yō-PLĀ, YŌ-PLĀ — joː'pleː, 'joː‚pleː

Yorba Linda

city, CA — YŌR-buh LIN-duh, YAWR-buh — ‚joːʳbə 'lində, jɔːʳbə

Yorick

character in Hamlet *and* Tristram Shandy — YAWR-ik, YAHR-ik — 'jɔːrik, 'jɑrik

Yorkshire

former county, England — YAWRK-shuhr, -SHIR — 'jɔːʳkʃəʳ, -‚ʃiʳ

Yorktown

town, VA — YAWRK-TOWN — 'jɔːʳk‚tɑun

Yoruba

people, lang., Africa — YAWR-uh-buh — 'jɔːrəbə

Yosemite

waterfall, valley, National Park, CA — yō-SEM-uht-ē — joː'seməti·

Key (col. 2): a: fad ā: fade ah: father ar: marry aw: law e: fed ē: feed er: merry i: hid ī: hide ō: coat o͞o: boot
oi: boy ow: now u: put uh: above uhr: bird ch: chop ng: ring sh: show th: thick th̲: this zh: measure

Yoshihito
emperor, Japan   yō-shē-hē-tō   joːʃiːhiːtoː

Yoshisuke
pers. name, Japanese   yō-shē-suk-e   joːʃiːsuke

Yosuke
pers. name, Japanese   yō-suk-e   joːsuke

Yothers
Tina, actress   YUH<u>TH</u>-uhrz   ˈjəðəʳz

Youghal
town, Ireland   YAWL   ˈjɔːl

Youghiogheny
river, MD, PA   YAHK-uh-GĀ-nē   ˌjɑkəˈgeːniˑ

Youngstown
city, OH   YUHNGZ-TOWN   ˈjəŋzˌtɑun

Yo-Yo
pers. name (Y, Ma)   YŌ-YŌ   ˈjoːˌjoː

Ypres [Ieper]
town, Belgium   ĒPR, Ē-pruh, Ⓔ WĪ-puhrz   iːpr, iːprə, Ⓔ ˈwaipəʳz

Ypsilanti
city, MI   IP-suh-LANT-ē   ˌipsəˈlæntiˑ

Yreka
town, CA   wī-RĒ-kuh   waiˈriːkə

Yrjö
pers. name, Finnish   O͞OR-yuh(r)   ˈuːrjœː

Yser
Belgian river   ē-ZER   iːˈzeʳ

Ysleta del Sur Pueblo
Indian reservation, US   ēz-LĀT-uh <u>th</u>el SUR po͞o-EB-lō, del, PWEB-lō, pyo͞o-EB-lō   iˑzˈleːʈə ðel ˈsuʳ puːˈebloː, del, ˈpwebloː, pjuːˈebloː

ytterbium
element   i-TUHR-bē-uhm   iˈtəʳbiːəm

yttrium
element   I-trē-uhm   ˈitriːəm

Yü [Ta Yü]
Chinese emperor, legendary founder of the first dynasty   YUE   ˈjy

Yuan
dynasty, China; pers. name   yo͞o-AHN   juːˈɑn

Yuan, Yüan
see Yuen

Yucatán
state, Mexico   YO͞O-kuh-TAHN, -TAN   ˌjuːkəˈtɑn, -ˈtæn

Yucatec [Maya]
lang., people, Guatemala, Mexico, British Honduras   YO͞O-kuh-TEK   ˈjuːkəˌtek

Yucatecan
pert. to Yucatec *or* Yucatán   YO͞O-kuh-TEK-uhn   ˌjuːkəˈtekən

Yuchi
N. American people   YO͞O-chē   ˈjuːtʃiˑ

Yuchuan
Chinese beer   YO͞O-jo͞o-AHN   ˈjuːdʒuːˈɑn

Yue [Cantonese]
lang., China   yo͞o-Ā   juːˈeː

Yuen, Yüan, Yuan
river, China   yo͞o-EN, yo͞o-AHN   juːˈen, juːˈɑn

Foreign Sounds: ue: *Fr.* **rue**, *Ger.* **füllen**   uh(r): *Fr.* **boeuf**, *Ger.* **Höhle**   <u>kh</u>: *Ger.* **ich**, *Scot.* **loch**   ḡ: *Sp.* **amigo**   v̲: *Sp.* **hablar**   hl: *Welsh* **Llanelli.**   CAPITALS: primary stress.   SMALL CAPS: secondary stress.   Ⓢ: U.S. pron.   Ⓔ: British pron.

Yuga
  Hindu age YUG-uh, YOO-guh 'jugə, 'juːgə
Yugo
  automobile YOO-gō 'juːgoː
Yugoslav, Jugoslav
  pert. to Yugoslavia YOO-gō-SLAHV, -SLAV ˌjuːgoː'slɑv, -'slæv
Yugoslavia, Jugoslavia
  republic, Europe YOO-gō-SLAHV-ē-uh ˌjuːgoː'slɑviːə
Yukaghir
  lang., people, Russia YOO-kuh-GIR juːkə'giɾ
Yukawa
  Hideki, *Japanese physicist (Nobel 1949)* yoo-kah-wah juːkɑwɑ
Yuki
  N. American people YOO-kē 'juːkiˑ
Yukon
  river, N. America; territory, Canada YOO-KAHN 'juːˌkɑn
Yukon-Koyukuk
  division, AK YOO-KAHN-KĪ-uh-KUHK 'juːˌkɑn'kɑiə̯ˌkək
Yul
  pers. name YOOL, YUL 'juːl, 'jul
Yule
  Christmas season YOOL 'juːl
Yuma
  city, AZ; county, AZ, CO; N. American people YOO-muh 'juːmə
Yunnan [Kunming]
  prov, city, China YOO-NAHN 'juː'nɑn
Yupik
  people, lang., AK YOO-pik 'juːpik
Yurak [Nenets]
  lang., people, Russia yuh-RAK jə'ræk
Yuri
  pers. name, Russian YOOR-yi 'juːrjij
Yurok
  N. American people YUR-AHK, YUR-uhk 'jurˌɑk, 'jurək
Yussuf
  pers. name YUS-uf, YUS-uhf 'jusuf, 'jusəf
Yves
  pers. name, French ĒV iːv
Yves Saint Laurent
  French fashion designer ĒV seⁿ law-RAHⁿ iːv sɛ̃ lɔːrɑ̃
Yvette
  pers. name ē-VET iː'vet
Yvon
  pers. name, French ē-VAWⁿ iːvɔ̃
Yvonne
  1. pers. name i-VAHN, ē-VAHN i'vɑn, iː'vɑn
  2. French ē-VAWN iːvɔːn
Yvor
  pers. name Ē-vuhr, Ī-vuhr, Ī-VAWR 'iːvəɾ, 'ɑivəɾ, 'ɑiˌvɔːɾ

Key (col. 2): a: fad ā: fade ah: father ar: marry aw: law e: fed ē: feed er: merry i: hid ī: hide ō: coat oo: boot
oi: boy ow: now u: put uh: above uhr: bird ch: chop ng: ring sh: show th: thick <u>th</u>: this zh: measure

Z

Zaanaim [Zaanannim]
Biblical name   ZĀ-uh-NĀ-im, TSAH-ah-nah-NĒM   ˌzeːəˈneːim, ˌtsɑːɑnɑˈniːm

Zaanan
Biblical name   ZĀ-uh-NAN, TSAH-ah-NAHN   ˈzeːəˌnæn, ˌtsɑːɑːˈnɑn

Zaanannim
Biblical name   ZĀ-uh-NAN-im, TSAH-ah-nah-NĒM   ˌzeːəˈnænim, ˌtsɑːɑnɑˈniːm

Zaavan
Biblical name   ZĀ-uh-VAN, ZAH-ah-VAHN   ˈzeːəˌvæn, ˌzɑːɑˈvɑn

Zabad
Biblical name   ZĀ-BAD, zah-VAHD   ˈzeːˌbæd, zɑˈvɑd

Zabar's
delicatessen, New York City   ZĀ-BAHRZ   ˈzeːˌbɑʳz

Zabbai
Biblical name   ZAB-Ī, ZAB-ē-Ī, zah-BĪ   ˈzæbˌai, ˈzæbiːˌai, zɑˈbai

Zabbud [Zaccur]
Biblical name   ZAB-uhd   ˈzæbəd

Zabdi
Biblical name   ZAB-DĪ, zahv-DĒ   ˈzæbˌdai, zɑvˈdiː

Zabdiel
Biblical name   ZAB-dē-uhl, ZAHV-dē-EL   ˈzæbdiːəl, ˌzɑvdiːˈel

Zabud
Biblical name   ZĀ-buhd, zah-VOOD   ˈzeːbəd, zɑˈvuːd

Zabulon [Zebulon]
Biblical name   ZAB-yuh-LAHN   ˈzæbjəˌlɑn

Zacatecas
state, city, Mexico   zahk-ah-TĀ-kahs   zɑkɑˈteːkɑs

Zaccai
Biblical name   ZAK-Ī, ZAK-ē-Ī, za-KĀ-Ī, zah-KĪ   ˈzækˌai, ˈzækiːˌai, zæˈkeːˌai, zɑˈkai

Zacchaeus, Zaccheus
Biblical name   za-KĒ-uhs   zæˈkiːəs

Zaccur, Zachur [Zabbud]
Biblical name   ZAK-uhr, zah-KHOOR   ˈzækəʳ, zɑˈxuːr

Zachariah
pers. name   ZAK-uh-RĪ-uh   ˌzækəˈraiə

Zacharias
1. Old Testament book; pope; pers. name   ZAK-uh-RĪ-uhs   ˌzækəˈraiəs
2. Dutch   ZAH-khah-RĒ-ahs   ˌzɑːxɑːˈriːɑs
3. German   TSAHKH-ah-RĒ-ahs   ˌtsɑxɑˈriːɑs

Zacharie
pers. name, French   zah-kah-RĒ   zɑːkɑːriː

Zachary
  pers. name   ZAK-(uh-)rē   'zæk(ə)ri·
Zacher
  Biblical name   ZĀ-kuhr, ZE<u>KH</u>-er   'zeːkə^r, 'zexer
Zachris
  pers. name, Swedish   SAHK-ris   'saːkris
Zack
  pers. name   ZAK   'zæk
Zacynthus
  ancient name of Zante   zuh-SIN(T)-thuhs   zə'sin(t)θəs
Zadok
  Biblical name   ZĀD-AHK, tsah-DŌK   'zeːdˌɑk, tsɑ'doːk
Zadokites
  Biblical name   ZĀD-uh-KĪTS   'zeːdəˌkaits
Zadora
  Pia, *US actress*   zuh-DŌR-uh, zuh-DAWR-uh   zə'doːrə, zə'dɔːrə
Zagat
  restaurant guidebooks   zuh-GAT   zə'gæt
Zagazig
  city, Egypt   ZAG-uh-ZIG   'zægəˌzig
Zagreb
  city, Croatia   ZAH-GREB   'zɑːˌgreb
Zagreus
  son of Zeus and Persephone   ZAG-rē-uhs, ZAG-ROOS   'zægriːəs, 'zægˌruːs
Zagros
  mtn. range, Iran   ZAG-ruhs   'zægrəs
Zaham
  Biblical name   ZĀ-HAM, ZAH-hahm   'zeːˌhæm, 'zɑhɑm
Zaharias
  Babe Didrikson, *US athlete*   zuh-HAR-ē-uhs   zə'hæriːəs
Zair
  Biblical name   ZĀ(-uh)r, tsah-ĒR   'zeː(ə)^r, tsɑ'iːr
Zaire
  republic, Africa   zah-IR, ZĪR   zɑ'i^r, 'zai^r
Zairian, Zairean
  pert. to Zaire   zah-IR-ē-uhn, ZĪR-ē-uhn   zɑ'iriːən, 'zairiːən
Zak
  pers. name   ZAK   'zæk
Zaki
  pers. name, Arabic   ZAHK-ē   'zɑki·
Zákinthos [Zante]
  island, Greece   ZAHK-ēn-THAWS,   'zɑkiːnˌθɔːs, Ⓢ zə'kin(t)θəs
                       Ⓢ zuh-KIN(T)-thuhs
Zalaph
  Biblical name   ZĀ-LAF, ZĀ-luhf, tsah-LAHF   'zeːˌlæf, 'zeːləf, tsɑ'lɑf
Zalmon
  Biblical name   ZAL-muhn, ZAHL-; tsahl-MŌN   'zælmən, 'zɑl-; tsɑl'moːn
Zalmonah
  Biblical name   zal-MŌ-nuh, tsahl-MAW-nah   zæl'moːnə, tsɑl'mɔːnɑː
Zama
  ancient town, Africa   ZĀ-muh   'zeːmə
Zambezi, Zambesi
  river, Africa   zam-BĒ-zē   zæm'biːzi·
Zambézia
  prov, Mozambique   zam-BĒ-zē-uh   zæm'biːziːə

Key (col. 2): **a**: f**a**d **ā**: f**a**de **ah**: f**a**ther **ar**: m**ar**ry **aw**: l**aw** **e**: f**e**d **ē**: f**ee**d **er**: m**err**y **i**: h**i**d **ī**: h**i**de **ō**: c**oa**t **ōō**: b**oo**t
oi: b**oy** **ow**: n**ow** **u**: p**u**t **uh**: **a**bove **uhr**: b**ir**d **ch**: **ch**op **ng**: ri**ng** **sh**: **sh**ow **th**: **th**ick <u>**th**</u>: <u>**th**</u>is **zh**: mea**s**ure

Zambia
  republic, Africa ZAM-bē-uh 'zæmbiːə

Zambian
  pert. to Zambia ZAM-bē-uhn 'zæmbiːən

Zamboanga
  port, Philippines ZAM-buh-WAHNG-guh ˌzæmbə'waŋgə

Zamfir
  Gheorghe, *Romanian panpiper* ZAHM-FIR 'zɑmˌfiʳ

Zamora
  river, town, Ecuador; prov., city, Spain zuh-MŌR-uh, zuh-MAWR-uh zə'moːrə, zə'mɔːrə

Zampieri [Domenichino]
  Domenico, *Bolognese painter* tsahm-PYER-ē tsɑm'pjeri·

Zamuco
  S. American people zuh-M$\overline{\text{OO}}$-kō, suh- zə'muːkoː, sə-

Zamzummim
  Biblical name zam-ZUHM-im, -Z$\overline{\text{OO}}$-mim; zæm'zəmim, -'zuːmim;
    ZAHM-z$\overline{\text{oo}}$-MĒM ˌzɑmzu'miːm

Zan
  lang., people, Caucasus ZAHN 'zɑn

Zande [Azande]
  lang., people, Africa ZAN-dē 'zændi·

Zander
  pers. name ZAN-duhr 'zændəʳ

Zandra
  pers. name ZAN-druh 'zændrə

Zane
  pers. name ZĀN 'zeːn

Zangwill
  Israel, *English writer* ZANG-(G)WIL 'zæŋˌ(g)wil

Zanoah
  Biblical name zuh-NŌ-uh, ZAH-nō-AH<u>KH</u> zə'noːə, ˌzɑnoː'ɑx

Zante
  island, Greece ZAN-tē 'zæntiː

Zanuck
  Darryl F., *US film producer* ZAN-uhk 'zænək

Zanzibar
  island, Tanzania ZAN-zuh-BAHR 'zænzəˌbaʳ

Zanzibari
  lang., native of Zanzibar ZAN-zuh-BAHR-ē ˌzænzə'bari·

Zaozhuang
  city, China JOW-zh$\overline{\text{oo}}$-AHNG 'dʒɑuʒuː'aŋ

Zapata
  1. Emiliano, *Mexican political* sah-PAHT-ah, Ⓢ zuh-PAHT-uh sɑ'pața, Ⓢ zə'pațə
    leader; swamp, Cuba
  2. county, TX zuh-PAHT-uh zə'pațə

Zaphenath-paneah
[Zaphnath-paaneah]
  Biblical name zuhf-Ē-NATH-pan-Ē-uh, zəf'iːˌnæθpæn'iːə,
    tsahf-NAHT-pah-NĀ-ahkh tsɑf'nɑtpaː'neːɑx

Zaphnath-paaneah
  Biblical name ZAF-NATH-PĀ-uh-NĒ-uh, 'zæfˌnæθˌpeːə'niːə,
    tsahf-NAHT-pah-NĀ-ahkh tsɑf'nɑtpaː'neːɑx

Zaphon
  Biblical name ZĀ-FAHN, tsah-FŌN 'zeːˌfɑn, tsɑ'foːn

Foreign Sounds: ue: *Fr.* **r**ue, *Ger.* f**ü**llen uh(r): *Fr.* b**oeu**f, *Ger.* H**öh**le <u>kh</u>: *Ger.* i**ch**, *Scot.* lo**ch** ḡ: *Sp.* ami**g**o v̱: *Sp.* ha**b**lar hl: *Welsh* **Ll**anelli. CAPITALS: primary stress. SMALL CAPS: secondary stress. Ⓢ: U.S. pron. Ⓔ: British pron.

Zaporozhe
  city, Ukraine   ZAHP-uh-RAW-zhuh   ˌzɑpəˈrɔːʒə

Zapotec
  N. American people   ZAHP-uh-TEK, SAHP-uh-TEK   ˈzɑpəˌtek, ˈsɑpəˌtek

Zara
  Italian province   ZAHR-uh   ˈzɑrə

Zaragoza [Saragossa]
  prov, city, Spain; city, Mexico   thah-rah-GŌ-thah, sah-rah-GŌ-sah   θɑrɑˈgoːθɑ, sɑrɑˈgoːsɑ

Zarathustra [Zoroaster]
  Persian religious teacher   ZAR-uh-T͞HOO-struh, ZER-   ˌzærəˈθuːstrə, ˌzer-

Zareah [Zorah]
  Biblical name   ZER-ē-uh, ZAR-ē-uh, zuh-RĒ-uh,   ˈzeriːə, ˈzæriːə, zəˈriːə,
              tsah-RAH   tsɑˈrɑː

Zareathite
  Biblical name   ZAR-ē-uh-THĪT, ZER-; zuh-RĒ-uh-THĪT   ˈzæriːəˌθait, ˈzer-;
                                     zəˈriːəˌθait

Zared [Zered]
  Biblical name   ZAR-ED, ZAR-uhd, ZE-red   ˈzærˌed, ˈzærəd, ˈzered

Zarephath
  Biblical name   ZAR-uh-FATH, ZER-; tsahr-FAHT   ˈzærəˌfæθ, ˈzer-; tsɑrˈfɑt

Zaretan
  Biblical name   ZAR-uh-TAN, ZER-, tsahr-TAHN   ˈzærəˌtæn, ˈzer-, tsɑrˈtɑn

Zarethan
  Biblical name   ZAR-uh-THAN, -thuhn, ZER-;   ˈzærəˌθæn, -θən, ˈzer-;
              tsahr-TAHN   tsɑrˈtɑn

Zareth-shahar
  Biblical name   ZĀ-RETH-SHĀ-HAHR,   ˈzeːˌreθˈʃeːˌhɑr,
              TSE-ret-hah-SHAH-khahr   ˈtseretˌhaˈʃɑxɑr

Zarhite
  Biblical name   ZAHR-HĪT   ˈzɑrˌhait

Zarthan [Zarethan]
  Biblical name   ZAHR-THAN, -thuhn; tsahr-TAHN   ˈzɑrˌθæn, -θən; tsɑrˈtɑn

Zasu
  pers. name (Z. Pitts)   ZAHZ-o͞o, ZAZ-o͞o   ˈzɑzuː, ˈzæzuː

Žatec
  town, Czech republic   ZHAH-TETS   ˈʒɑˌtets

Zattu
  Biblical name   ZAT-o͞o, zah-T͞OO   ˈzæʈuː, zɑˈtuː

Zavala
  county, TX   zuh-VAHL-uh   zəˈvɑlə

Zavan [Zaavan]
  Biblical name   ZĀ-VAN, ZAH-ah-VAHN   ˈzeːˌvæn, ˌzɑːɑˈvɑn

Zaventem
  Bruxelles National Airport   zah-ven-TEM   zɑvenˈtem

Zaza
  Biblical name   ZĀ-zuh, ZAHZ-uh, zah-ZAH   ˈzeːzə, ˈzɑzə, zɑˈzɑː

Zbigniew
  pers. name, Polish   ZBĒG-nyef, Ⓢ ZBIG-nē-o͞o   ˈzbiːgnjef, Ⓢ ˈzbigniːˌuː

Zdeněk
  pers. name, Czech   ZDEN-yek   ˈzdenjek

Zdenko
  pers. name, Czech   ZDENG-kō   ˈzdeŋkoː

Zea
  Francisco Antonio, Colombian   SĀ-ah   ˈseːɑ
    revolutionary

Key (col. 2):   a: f**a**d   ā: f**a**de   ah: f**a**ther   ar: m**a**rry   aw: l**a**w   e: f**e**d   ē: f**ee**d   er: m**e**rry   i: h**i**d   ī: h**i**de   ō: c**oa**t   o͞o: b**oo**t
oi: b**oy**   ow: n**ow**   u: p**u**t   uh: **a**bove   uhr: b**i**rd   ch: **ch**op   ng: ri**ng**   sh: **sh**ow   th: **th**ick   <u>th</u>: **th**is   zh: mea**s**ure

Zealand [Sjælland] *island, Denmark*	ZĒ-luhnd	'ziːlənd
Zebadiah *Biblical name*	ZEB-uh-DĪ-uh, zuh-vahd-YAH	ˌzebə'daiə, zəvad'ja
Zebah *Biblical name*	ZĒ-buh, ZE-vahkh	'ziːbə, 'zevax
Zebaim *Biblical name*	zi-BĀ-im, tsuh-vah-YĒM	zi'beːim, tsəva'jiːm
Zebedee *biblical name*	ZEB-uhd-ē	'zebədiˑ
Zebina *Biblical name*	zi-BĪ-nuh, zuh-BĒ-nuh, zuh-vē-NAH	zi'bainə, zə'biːnə, zəviː'naː
Zeboiim *Biblical name*	zuh-BOI-(y)im, tsuh-vaw-YIM	zə'bɔi(j)im, tsəvɔː'jim
Zeboim *Biblical name*	zuh-BŌ-im, tsuh-vō-ĒM	zə'boːim, tsəvoː'iːm
Zebudah *Biblical name*	zuh-BYO͞OD-uh, zuh-vo͞o-DAH	zə'bjuːdə, zəvuː'daː
Zebul *Biblical name*	ZĒ-buhl, zuh-VO͞OL	'ziːbəl, zə'vuːl
Zebulon *pers. name*	ZEB-yuh-luhn	'zebjələn
Zebulonite, Zebulunite *Biblical name*	ZEB-yuh-luh-NĪT	'zebjələˌnait
Zebulun [Zebulon] *Biblical name*	ZEB-yuh-luhn, zuh-vo͞o-LO͞ON	'zebjələn, zəvuː'luːn
Zechariah *Old Testament book; pers. name*	ZEK-uh-RĪ-uh	ˌzekə'raiə
Zecher *Biblical name*	ZĒ-kuhr, ZEKH-er	'ziːkəʳ, 'zexer
Zedad *Biblical name*	ZĒ-DAD, tsuh-DAHD	'ziːˌdæd, tsə'dad
Zedekiah *king of Judah*	ZED-uh-KĪ-uh	ˌzedə'kaiə
Zedillo Ernesto, *Mexican president*	zuh-DĒ-(y)ō	zə'diː(j)oː
Zeeb *Biblical name*	ZĒ-EB, zuh-EV	'ziːˌeb, zə'ev
Zeebrugge *port, Belgium*	ZĀ-BRUEKH-uh, [$] ZĀ-BRUG-uh	'zeːˌbryxə, [$] 'zeːˌbrugə
Zeeland *prov, Netherlands*	ZĀ-LAHNT, [$] ZĒ-luhnd, ZĀ-luhnd	'zeːˌlant, [$] 'ziːlənd, 'zeːlənd
Zeeman Pieter, *Dutch physicist (Nobel 1902)*	ZĀ-MAHN, ZĀ-muhn	'zeːˌman, 'zeːmən
Zeffirelli Franco, *Italian film director*	ZEF-uh-REL-ē	ˌzefə'reliˑ
Zeigler *pers. name*	ZIG-luhr	'zigləʳ
Zeiss *tdmk for binoculars*	TSĪS, [$] ZĪS	'tsais, [$] 'zais
Zeitgeist *spirit of the time*	TSĪT-GĪST, ZĪT-GĪST	'tsaitˌgaist, 'zaitˌgaist
Zeitschrift *German for magazine*	TSĪT-SHRIFT	'tsaitˌʃrift

Foreign Sounds: ue: *Fr.* **rue**, *Ger.* **füllen** uh(r): *Fr.* **boeuf**, *Ger.* **Höhle** kh: *Ger.* **ich**, *Scot.* **loch** g̃: *Sp.* **amigo** v: *Sp.* **hablar** hl: *Welsh* **Llanelli**. CAPITALS: primary stress. SMALL CAPS: secondary stress. [$]: U.S. pron. [£]: British pron.

Zeitung
  German for newspaper   TSĪ-tung   'tsɑituŋ
Zelah, Zela
  Biblical name   ZĒ-luh, tse-LAH   'ziːlə, tse'lɑː
Zelda
  pers. name   ZEL-duh   'zeldə
Zelek
  Biblical name   ZĒ-LEK, TSE-lek   'ziː,lek, 'tselek
Zelle
  pers. name, Dutch   ZEL-uh   'zelə
Zelophehad
  Biblical name   zuh-LŌ-fuh-HAD, zuh-LAHF-uh-;   zə'loːfə,hæd, zə'lɑfə-;
                            tsuh-LAH-fuh-<u>KH</u>AHD   tsə,lɑfə'xɑd
Zelotes
  Biblical name   zuh-LŌ-TĒZ   zə'loː,tiːz
Zelus
  personification of zeal ZĒ-luhs, ZEL-uhs   'ziːləs, 'zeləs
Zelzah
  Biblical name   ZEL-zuh, tsel-TSAH<u>KH</u>   'zelzə, tsel'tsɑx
Zemaraim
  Biblical name   ZEM-uh-RĀ-im, tsuh-mah-RAH-yim   ,zemə're:im, tsəmɑ'rɑːjim
Zemarite
  Biblical name   ZEM-uh-RĪT   'zemə,rɑit
Zemeckis
  Robert, *US film director* zuh-MEK-uhs   zə'mekəs
Zemira, Zemirah
  Biblical name   zuh-MĪ-ruh, zuh-mē-RAH   zə'mɑirə, zəmiː'rɑː
Zemlya Frantsa-Iosifa [Franz Josef Land]
  archipelago, Arctic   ZYIM-lah FRAHNT-sah-YŌS-yi-fah   'zjimlɑ ,frɑntsa'joːsjifɑ
Zen
  religion   ZEN   'zen
Zena
  pers. name   ZĒ-nuh   'ziːnə
Zenan
  Biblical name   ZĒ-NAN, tsuh-NAHN   'ziː,næn, tsə'nɑn
Zenas
  Biblical name   ZĒ-nuhs   'ziːnəs
Zend
  translation of the Avesta ZEND   'zend
Zend-Avesta
  Zoroastrian holy books ZEN-duh-VES-tuh   ,zendə'vestə
Zener diode
  semiconductor diode   ZĒ-nuhr DĪ-ŌD, ZEN-uhr   ,ziːnə^r 'dɑi,oːd, ,zenə^r
Zenger
  John Peter, *US printer* ZENG-(g)uhr   'zeŋ(g)ə^r
Zengo
  pers. name, Japanese   zeng-gō   zeŋgoː
Zenith
  US electronics co.   ZĒ-nuhth   'ziːnəθ
Zeno
  Greek philosopher   ZĒ-nō   'ziːnoː
Zénobe
  pers. name, French   zā-NAWB   zeːnɔːb

Key (col. 2):   a: fad   ā: fade   ah: father   ar: marry   aw: law   e: fed   ē: feed   er: merry   i: hid   ī: hide   ō: coat   ōō: boot
oi: boy   ow: now   u: put   uh: above   uhr: bird   ch: chop   ng: ring   sh: show   th: thick   <u>th</u>: this   zh: measure

Zenobia
  queen of Palmyra   zuh-NŌ-bē-uh   zə'noːbiːə
Zenobio
  pers. name, Italian   dzā-NAWB-yō   dzeː'nɔːbjoː
Zenobius
  pers. name   zi-NŌ-bē-uhs   zi'noːbiːəs
Zenón
  pers. name, Spanish   sā-NAWN, thā-NAWN   seː'nɔːn, θeː'nɔːn
Zenon
  1. dance co., MN   ZĒ-NAHN   'ziːˌnɑn
  2. pers. name, Polish   ZEN-AWN   'zenˌɔːn
Zephaniah
  Old Testament book; pers. name ZEF-uh-NĪ-uh   ˌzefə'nɑiə
Zephath
  Biblical name   ZĒ-FATH, tsuh-FAHT   'ziːˌfæθ, tsə'fɑt
Zephathah
  Biblical name   ZEF-uh-thuh, tsuh-FAH-tah, TSFAHT   'zefəθə, tsə'fɑːtɑː, 'tsfɑt
Zephi
  Biblical name   ZĒ-FĪ, tsuh-FĒ, TSFĒ   'ziːˌfɑi, tsə'fiː, 'tsfiː
Zepho
  Biblical name   ZĒ-FŌ, tsuh-FŌ, TSFŌ   'ziːˌfoː, tsə'foː, 'tsfoː
Zephon
  Biblical name   ZĒ-FAHN, tsuh-FŌN   'ziːˌfɑn, tsə'foːn
Zephonite
  Biblical name   ZĒ-fuh-NĪT, ZEF-uhn-ĪT   'ziːfəˌnɑit, 'zefənˌɑit
Zephyrinus
  pope   ZEF-uh-RĪ-nuhs   ˌzefə'rɑinəs
Zephyrus
  personification of west wind   ZEF-uh-ruhs   'zefərəs
Zeppelin
  German-designed dirigible   TSEP-uh-LĒN, ⑤ ZEP-uh-luhn,   'tsepəˌliːn, ⑤ 'zepələn,
                                   ZEP-luhn   'zeplən
Zer
  Biblical name   ZUHR, TSER   'zəʳ, 'tser
Zerah
  pers. name   ZĒ-ruh   'ziːrə
Zerahiah
  Biblical name   ZER-uh-HĪ-uh, zuh-rah<u>kh</u>-YAH   ˌzerə'hɑiə, zərax'jɑː
Zerahite
  Biblical name   ZIR-uh-HĪT   'zirəˌhɑit
Zered [Zared]
  Biblical name   ZIR-ED, ZE-RED   'zirˌed, 'zeˌred
Zereda, Zeredah
  Biblical name   ZER-uhd-uh, zuh-RĒD-uh,   'zerədə, zə'riːdə, tsɑre'dɑː
                                   tsuh-re-DAH
Zeredathah
  Biblical name   ZER-uh-DĀ-thuh, zuh-RED-uh-thuh,   ˌzerə'deːθə, zə'redəθə,
                                   tsuh-re-DAH-tah   tsɑre'dɑːtɑː
Zererah
  Biblical name   ZER-uh-ruh, tse-re-RAH   'zerərə, tsere'rɑː
Zererath [Zererah]
  Biblical name   ZER-uh-RATH, tsuh-re-RAH-tah   'zerəˌræθ, tsɑre'rɑːtɑː
Zeresh
  Biblical name   ZIR-ESH, ZER-ESH, ZE-resh   'zirˌeʃ, 'zerˌeʃ, 'zereʃ

Foreign Sounds: ue: *Fr.* **rue**, *Ger.* **füllen** uh(r): *Fr.* **boeuf**, *Ger.* **Höhle** <u>kh</u>: *Ger.* **ich**, *Scot.* **loch** ğ: *Sp.* **amigo** v̵: *Sp.* **hablar**
hl: *Welsh* **Llanelli**. CAPITALS: primary stress. SMALL CAPS: secondary stress. ⑤: U.S. pron. Ⓔ: British pron.

Zereth
  Biblical name — ZIR-ETH, ZER-ETH, TSE-ret — 'zir‚eθ, 'zer‚eθ, 'tseret
Zereth-shahar
  Biblical name — ZIR-ETH-SHĀ-HAHR, ZER-ETH-; TSE-ret-hah-SHAH-<u>kh</u>ahr — 'zir‚eθ'ʃeː‚haʳ, 'zer‚eθ-; 'tseretha'ʃaːxɑr
Zeri
  Biblical name — ZIR-Ī, tsuh-RĒ, TSRĒ — 'zir‚ɑi, tsə'riː, 'tsriː
Zeria
  see Ziria
Zermatt
  village, Switzerland — (t)ser-MAHT — (t)seʳ'mɑt
Zernike
  Frits, *Dutch physicist (Nobel 1953)* — ZER-ni-kuh, ZUHR-ni-kuh — 'zeʳnikə, 'zəʳnikə
Zero
  pers. name (Z. Mostel) — ZĒ-rō, ZIR-ō — 'ziːroː, 'ziroː
Zeror
  Biblical name — ZIR-AWR, tsuh-RŌR — 'zir‚ɔːʳ, tsə'roːr
Zeroual
  Liamine, *Algerian president* — zer-WAHL — zerwɑːl
Zeruah
  Biblical name — zuh-R͞OO-uh, tsuh-r͞oo-AH — zə'ruːə, tsəruː'ɑː
Zerubbabel
  Biblical name — zuh-RUHB-uh-buhl, zuh-R͞OO-bah-VEL — zə'rəbəbəl, zə‚ruːbɑː'vel
Zeruiah
  Biblical name — ZER-͞OO-Ī-uh, tsuh-r͞oo-YAH — ‚zeruː'ɑiə, tsəruː'jɑː
Zetham
  Biblical name — ZĒ-THAM, ZĒ-thuhm, ze-TAHM — 'ziː‚θæm, 'ziːθəm, ze'tɑm
Zethan
  Biblical name — ZĒ-THAN, ZĒ-thuhn, zā-TAHN — 'ziː‚θæn, 'ziːθən, zeː'tɑn
Zethar
  Biblical name — ZĒ-THAHR, ze-TAHR — 'ziː‚θɑʳ, ze'tɑr
Zeus
  supreme Greek god — Z͞OOS — 'zuːs
Zeuxippe
  mother of Erechtheus and Butes — z͞ook-SIP-ē — zuˑk'sipiˑ
Zeuxis
  Greek painter — Z͞OOK-suhs, Z͞OOK-sis — 'zuːksəs, 'zuːksis
Zevi
  1. pers. name — ZEV-ē — 'zeviˑ
  2. Hebrew — TSVĒ — 'tsviː
  3. Russian — ZYĀ-vyi — 'zjeːvji
Zgusta
  Ladislav, *Czech-born lexicographer* — ZUH-GUS-tuh — ‚zə'gustə
Zhang Zuolin, Chang Tso-lin
  Chinese general — JAHNG DZU-LIN — 'dʒɑŋ 'dzu'lin
Zhao Ziyang
  premier, China — JOW jē-YAHNG — 'dʒɑu dʒiˑ'jɑŋ
Zhejiang, Chekiang
  prov, China — JUH-jē-AHNG — 'dʒədʒiː'ɑŋ
Zhengzhou, Chengchow
  city, China — JUHNG-JŌ — 'dʒəŋ'dʒoː
Zhenjiang, Chen-chiang
  city, China — JUHN-jē-AHNG — 'dʒəndʒiː'ɑŋ
Zhivago
  see Doctor Zhivago

Key (col. 2): a: fad ā: fade ah: father ar: marry aw: law e: fed ē: feed er: merry i: hid ī: hide ō: coat ōō: boot
oi: boy ow: now u: put uh: above uhr: bird ch: chop ng: ring sh: show th: thick <u>th</u>: this zh: measure

Zhivkov
Todor, *president, Bulgaria*   ZHĒV-KAWF   ˈʒiːvˌkɔːf

Zhongshan
city, China   JUNG-SHAHN   ˈdʒuŋˈʃɑn

Zhou Enlai
see Chou En-Lai

Zhukov
Georgi, *Russian militarist*   ZHOO̅-kuhf, -KAWF, -KAWV   ˈʒuːkəf, -ˌkɔːf, -ˌkɔːv

Zia
N. American people   ZĒ-uh, SĒ-uh   ˈziːə, ˈsiːə

Zia
Biblical name   ZĪ-uh, ZĒ-ah   ˈzaiə, ˈziːɑː

Zia-ul-Haq
Mohammad, *Pakistani leader*   ZĒ-uh-ul-HAHK   ˌziːəulˈhɑk

Ziba
Biblical name   ZĪ-buh, tsē-VAH   ˈzaibə, tsiːˈvɑː

Zibeon
Biblical name   ZIB-ē-uhn, tsiv-ŌN   ˈzibiːən, tsivˈoːn

Zibia, Zibiah
Biblical name   ZIB-ē-uh, ZĪ-bē-uh, zi-BĪ-uh, tsiv-YAH   ˈzibiːə, ˈzaibiːə, ziˈbaiə, tsivˈjɑː

Zibo
city, China   JĒ-BOO̅   ˈdʒiːˈbuː

Zichri
Biblical name   ZIK-RĪ, zikh-RĒ   ˈzikˌrai, zixˈriː

Ziddim
Biblical name   ZID-im, tsi-DĒM   ˈzidim, tsiˈdiːm

Zidkijah
Biblical name   zid-KĪ-uh, TSID-ki-YAH   zidˈkaiə, ˌtsidkiˈjɑː

Zidovudine [AZT]
AIDS drug   zī-DŌ-vyoo̅-DĒN   zaiˈdoːvjuːˌdiːn

Ziebach
county, SD   ZĒ-BAHK, zē-BAH, zē-BAW   ˈziːˌbak, ziːˈbɑ, ziːˈbɔː

Ziegfeld
Florenz, *US theatrical producer*   ZIG-FELD, ZĒG-FĒLD   ˈzigˌfeld, ˈziːgˌfiːld

Ziegler
Karl, *German chemist (Nobel 1963)*   TSĒ-gluhr, ⓢ ZĒ-gluhr   ˈtsiːglərʳ, ⓢ ˈziːglərʳ

Ziha
Biblical name   ZĪ-(h)uh, tsē-KHAH   ˈzai(h)ə, tsiːˈxɑː

Ziklag
Biblical name   ZIK-LAG, tsik-LAHG   ˈzikˌlæg, tsikˈlag

Zillah
Biblical name   ZIL-uh, tsi-LAH   ˈzilə, tsiˈlɑː

Zillertal Alps
mtn. range, Italy   TSIL-uhr-TAHL, ZIL-uhr-TAHL   ˈtsilərʳˌtal, ˈzilərʳˌtal

Zilpah
pers. name   ZIL-puh   ˈzilpə

Zilthai
Biblical name   ZIL-THĪ, tsil-TĪ   ˈzilˌθai, tsilˈtai

Zimba
lang., Africa   ZIM-buh   ˈzimbə

Zimbabwe
republic, Africa   zim-BAHB-wā, -wē   zimˈbabweː, -wiˑ

Zimbabwean
pert. to Zimbabwe   zim-BAHB-wā-uhn, -wē-uhn   zimˈbabweːən, -wiːən

---

Foreign Sounds: ue: *Fr.* **r**ue, *Ger.* f**ü**llen   uh(r): *Fr.* b**œu**f, *Ger.* H**ö**hle   kh: *Ger.* i**ch**, *Scot.* lo**ch**   ḡ: *Sp.* ami**g**o   v: *Sp.* ha**b**lar   hl: *Welsh* **Ll**anelli.   CAPITALS: primary stress.   SMALL CAPS: secondary stress.   ⓢ: U.S. pron.   ⓔ: British pron.

Zimbalist
  Efrem, Jr., *US actor;* Stephanie, *US*   ZIM-buh-luhst   ˈzimbələst
    actress
Zimmah
  Biblical name   ZIM-uh, zi-MAH   ˈzimə, ziˈmɑː
Zimran
  Biblical name   ZIM-RAN, ZIM-ruhn, zim-RAHN   ˈzimˌræn, ˈzimrən, zimˈrɑn
Zimri
  Biblical name   ZIM-RĪ, zim-RĒ   ˈzimˌrɑi, zimˈriː
Zin
  Biblical name   ZIN, TSIN   ˈzin, ˈtsin
Zina
  Biblical name   ZĪ-nuh, zē-NAH   ˈzɑinə, ziːˈnɑː
zinc
  element   ZINGK   ˈziŋk
Zindel
  Paul, *US author*   ZIN-duhl, zin-DEL   ˈzindəl, zinˈdel
Zinfandel
  wine variety   ZIN-fuhn-DEL   ˈzinfənˌdel
Zinka
  pers. name, Russian   ZYING-kuh   ˈzjiŋkə
Zinman
  David, *US conductor*   ZIN-muhn   ˈzinmən
Zino
  pers. name   zē-NŌ, ZĒ-nō   ziːˈnoː, ˈziːnoː
Zinsser
  Hans, *US bacteriologist*   ZIN(T)-suhr   ˈzin(t)səʳ
Zion
  hill, stronghold, Jerusalem; city, IL   ZĪ-uhn   ˈzɑiən
Zionism
  Jewish movement   ZĪ-uh-NIZ-uhm   ˈzɑiəˌnizəm
Zior
  Biblical name   ZĪ-AWR, -ŌR; tsē-AWR   ˈzɑiˌɔːʳ, -ˌoːʳ; tsiːˈɔːr
Ziph
  Biblical name   ZIF, ZĒF   ˈzif, ˈziːf
Ziphah
  Biblical name   ZĪ-fuh, zē-FAH   ˈzɑifə, ziːˈfɑː
Ziphims
  Biblical name   ZIF-imz, zē-FĒM   ˈzifimz, ziːˈfiːm
Ziphion
  Biblical name   ZIF-ē-AHN, -uhn; tsif-YŌN   ˈzifiːˌɑn, -ən; tsifˈjoːn
Ziphites [Ziphims]
  Biblical name   ZIF-ĪTS   ˈzifˌɑits
Ziphron
  Biblical name   ZIF-RAHN, -ruhn; zif-RAWN   ˈzifˌrɑn, -rən; zifˈrɔːn
Zippor
  Biblical name   ZIP-AWR, -ŌR; tsi-PŌR   ˈzipˌɔːʳ, -ˌoːʳ; tsiˈpoːr
Zipporah
  1. wife of Moses   ZIP-(uh-)ruh, zuh-PŌR-uh,   ˈzip(ə)rə, zəˈpoːrə, zəˈpɔːrə
                                                zuh-PAWR-uh
  2. pers. name, Hebrew   tsē-PAWR-ah   tsiˈpɔːrɑ
zirconium
  element   ZUHR-KŌ-nē-uhm   ˌzəʳˈkoːniːəm
Ziria, Zeria [Cyllene]
  mountain, Greece   ZIR-ē-uh   ˈziriːə

Zithri		
Biblical name	ZITH-RĪ, sit-RĒ	'ziθˌrɑi, sit'riː
Ziz		
Biblical name	ZIZ, TSĒTS	'ziz, 'tsiːts
Ziza, Zizah		
Biblical name	ZĪ-ZUH, zē-ZAH	'zɑiˌzə, ziː'zɑː
Zlata		
pers. name, Serbo-Croatian (Z.	ZLAHT-uh	'zlɑt̪ə
Filipovic)		
Zmeskal		
Kim, *US gymnast*	zuh-MES-kuhl	zə'meskəl
Zoan		
Biblical name	ZŌ-uhn, TSAW-ahn	'zoːən, 'tsɔːɑn
Zoar		
Biblical name	ZŌ-uhr, TSAW-ahr	'zoːəʳ, 'tsɔːɑr
Zoba, Zobah		
Biblical name	ZŌ-buh, tsō-VAH	'zoːbə, tsoː'vɑː
Zobebah		
Biblical name	zō-BĒ-buh, TSAW-ve-VAH	zoː'biːbə, ˌtsɔːve'vɑː
Zoé		
pers. name, French	zaw-Ā	zɔːeː
Zoë, Zoe		
pers. name	ZŌ-ē	'zoːiˑ
Zofia		
pers. name, Polish	ZAWF-yah	'zɔːfjɑː
Zohar		
Jewish medieval mystical	ZŌ-HAHR, TSAW-khahr	'zoːˌhɑʳ, 'tsɔːxɑr
interpretation of the Torah;		
Biblical name		
Zoheleth		
Biblical name	ZŌ-(h)uh-luhth, tsaw-KHE-let	'zoː(h)ələθ, tsɔː'xelet
Zoheth		
Biblical name	ZŌ-HETH, tsō-KHET	'zoːˌheθ, tsoː'xet
Zola		
Emile, *French writer*	zaw-LAH, ⓢ ZŌ-luh, ZŌ-lah, zō-LAH	zɔːlɑː, ⓢ 'zoːlə, 'zoːlɑ, zoː'lɑ
Zollverein		
union of German states	TSAWL-fer-ĪN	'tsɔːlferˌɑin
Zoltán		
pers. name, Hungarian	ZAWL-tahn	'zɔːltɑːn
Zomba		
city, Malawi	ZAHM-buh	'zɑmbə
Zombie, Zombi		
voodoo snake deity; walking dead;	ZAHM-bē	'zɑmbiˑ
religious group		
Zombiism		
beliefs of Zombi	ZAHM-bē-IZ-uhm	'zɑmbiːˌizəm
Zonta		
international women's organization	ZAHNT-uh	'zɑntə
Zontian		
member of Zonta	ZAHNT-ē-uhn	'zɑntiːən
Zophah		
Biblical name	ZŌ-fuh, tsō-FAHKH	'zoːfə, tsoː'fɑx
Zophai [Zuph]		
Biblical name	ZŌ-FĪ, tsō-FĪ	'zoːˌfɑi, tsoː'fɑi

Foreign Sounds: ue: *Fr.* **rue**, *Ger.* **füllen**   uh(r): *Fr.* **boeuf,** *Ger.* **Höhle**   <u>kh</u>: *Ger.* **i<u>ch</u>,** *Scot.* **lo<u>ch</u>**   ğ: *Sp.* **amigo**   <u>v</u>: *Sp.* **hablar**
hl: *Welsh* **Llanelli.**   CAPITALS: primary stress.   SMALL CAPS: secondary stress.   ⓢ: U.S. pron.   ⓔ: British pron.

Zophar
Biblical name   ZŌ-FAHR, tsō-FAHR   'zoː͵faʳ, tsoːˈfɑr

Zophim
Biblical name   ZŌ-fim, tsaw-FĒM   'zoːfim, tsɔːˈfiːm

Zoque
N. American people   SŌ-kā   'soːkeː

Zora, Zorah
pers. name   ZŌR-uh, ZAWR-uh   'zoːrə, 'zɔːrə

Zorach
William, US scultpor   ZAWR-AHK, -AH<u>KH</u>, ZŌR-   'zɔːr͵ak, -͵ax, 'zoːr-

Zorah [Zareah]
Biblical name   ZAWR-uh, ZŌR-uh, tsahr-AH   'zɔːrə, 'zoːrə, tsɑrˈɑː

Zorathite
Biblical name   ZAWR-uh-THĪT, ZŌR-   'zɔːrə͵θait, 'zoːr-

Zorinsky
Edward, US politician   zuh-RIN-skē   zəˈrinski·

Zorite
Biblical name   ZAWR-ĪT, ZŌR-   'zɔːr͵ait, 'zoːr-

Zoroaster [Zarathustra]
Persian religious leader   ZŌR-ō-AS-tuhr, ZAWR-   'zoːroː͵æstəʳ, 'zɔːr-

Zoroastrianism
religion   ZŌR-ō-AS-trē-uh-NIZ-uhm, ZAWR-   ͵zoːroːˈæstriːə͵nizəm, ͵zɔːr-

Zorrilla y Moral
José, Spanish romantic dramatist   thaw-RĒ(L)-yah ē mō-RAHL, sō-RĒ-yah   θɔːˈriː(l)jɑ iː moːˈrɑl, soːˈriːjɑ

Zosimo
pers. name, Italian   DZAW-zē-mō   'dzɔːziːmoː

Zosimus
pope   ZŌ-suh-muhs, ZAHS-uh-muhs   'zoːsəməs, 'zɑsəməs

Zouave
body of infantry, French army   zo͞o-AHV   zuˈˈɑv

Zsa Zsa
pers. name, Hungarian (Z. Gabor)   ZHAH ZHAH   'ʒɑ ͵ʒɑ

Zsigmond
pers. name, Hungarian   ZHIG-mawnd   'ʒigmɔːnd

Zsigmondy
Richard, German chemist (Nobel 1925)   ZHIG-MAWN-dē   'ʒig͵mɔːndi·

Zsolt
pers. name, Hungarian   ZHAWLT   'ʒɔːlt

Zuar
Biblical name   ZOO-uhr, tsoo-AHR   'zuːəʳ, tsuːˈɑr

Zubin
pers. name   ZOO-buhn   'zuːbən

Zuerich
airport, Zürich   TSUE-ri<u>kh</u>, Ⓢ ZUR-ik   'tsyːriç, Ⓢ 'zurik

Zug
canton, Switzerland   TSOOK, Ⓢ SOOK, ZOOG   'tsuːk, Ⓢ 'suːk, 'zuːg

Zugspitze
mtn., Germany   TSOOK-SHPIT-suh   'tsuːk͵ʃpitsə

Zuider Zee
inlet, Netherlands   ZĪD-uhr ZĀ, Ⓢ ZĪD-uhr ZĒ   ͵zaidəʳ 'zeː, Ⓢ ͵zaidəʳ 'ziː

Zuid Holland
province, Netherlands   zoit HAWL-AHNT   zɔit 'hɔːl͵ɑnt

Key (col. 2):   a: fad   ā: fade   ah: father   ar: marry   aw: law   e: fed   ē: feed   er: merry   i: hid   ī: hide   ō: coat   o͞o: boot
oi: boy   ow: now   u: put   uh: above   uhr: bird   ch: chop   ng: ring   sh: show   th: thick   <u>th</u>: this   zh: measure

Zukerman		
Pinchas, *Israeli-born US violinist*	ZUK-uhr-muhn, ZO͞O-kuhr-muhn	ˈzukə^{r}mən, ˈzuːkə^{r}mən
Zukor		
Adolph, *US movie producer*	ZO͞O-kuhr	ˈzuːkə^{r}
Zuleika		
character in Zuleika Dobson, *Beerbohm*	zo͞o-LĒ-kuh, zo͞o-LĀ-kuh, zo͞o-LĪ-kuh	zuˑˈliːkə, zuˑˈleːkə, zuˑˈlɑikə
Zuléma		
pers. name, French	zo͞o-lā-MAH	zuːleːmɑː
Zulu		
African people	ZO͞O-lo͞o	ˈzuːluː
Zululand		
territory, Republic of South Africa	ZO͞O-lo͞o-LAND	ˈzuːluˑˌlænd
Zumwalt		
Elmo, III, *US admiral*	ZUM-WAWLT, ZUHM-WAWLT	ˈzumˌwɔːlt, ˈzəmˌwɔːlt
Zuñi		
N. American people	ZO͞O-nē, ZO͞ON-yē	ˈzuːniˑ, ˈzuːnjiˑ
Zuolin		
see Zhang Zuolin		
Zuph [Zophai]		
Biblical name	ZUF, TSO͞OF	ˈzuf, ˈtsuːf
Zuppke		
Bob, *US football coach*	ZUHP-kē	ˈzəpkiˑ
Zur		
Biblical name	ZUHR, ZUR, TSO͞OR	ˈzə^{r}, ˈzu^{r}, ˈtsuːr
Zürich, Zurich		
canton, city, Switzerland	TSUE-rikh, [$] ZUR-ik	ˈtsyːriç, [$] ˈzurik
Zuriel		
Biblical name	ZUR-ē-uhl, TSO͞O-rē-EL	ˈzuriːəl, ˌtsuːriːˈel
Zuri-shaddai		
Biblical name	ZUR-ē-SHAD-ē-Ī, -SHAD-Ī; tsu-RĒ-shah-DĪ	ˈzuriːˈʃædiːˌɑi, -ˈʃædˌɑi; tsuˌriːʃɑˈdɑi
Zuzim		
Biblical name	ZO͞O-ZIM, zo͞o-ZĒM	ˈzuːˌzim, zuːˈziːm
Zwickau		
city, Germany	TSVIK-OW	ˈtsvikˌɑu
Zwingli		
Ulrich, *Swiss Protestant reformer*	TSFING-lē, [$] ZWING-(g)lē, SWING-(g)lē	ˈtsfiŋliˑ, [$] ˈzwiŋ(g)liˑ, ˈswiŋ(g)liˑ
Zwinglianism		
beliefs of Zwingli *& his followers*	TSFING-lē-uh-NIZ-uhm, ZWING-(g)lē-, SWING-lē-	ˈtsfiŋliːəˌnizəm, ˈzwiŋ(g)liː-, ˈswiŋliː-
Zwolle		
1. city, Netherlands	SFAWL-uh	ˈsfɔːlə
2. town, LA	ZWAHL-ē	ˈzwɑliˑ
Zworykin		
Vladimir, *Russian-born physicist*	ZVAWR-kyin, [$] ZWAWR-i-kuhn	ˈzvɔːɾkjin, [$] ˈzwɔːrikən
Zygmunt		
pers. name, Polish	ZIG-mo͞ont	ˈzigmuːnt
Zyryan [Komi]		
lang., people, Russia	ZIR-ē-uhn	ˈziriːən
Zyuganov		
Gennadi A., *Russian politician*	z(y)o͞o-GAHN-uhf, -AWF	z(j)uːˈgɑnəf, -ˌɔːf
Zywiec		
town, Poland; Polish beer	ZHIV-uhts	ˈʒivəts

Foreign Sounds: ue: *Fr.* **rue**, *Ger.* **füllen** uh(r): *Fr.* **boeuf**, *Ger.* **Höhle** kh: *Ger.* **ich**, *Scot.* **loch** g: *Sp.* **amigo** v: *Sp.* **hablar** hl: *Welsh* **Llanelli**. CAPITALS: primary stress. SMALL CAPS: secondary stress. [$]: U.S. pron. [£]: British pron.

Simplified Pronunciation Symbols

(See the Introduction for detailed explanation)

Symbol	Example	as in
a A	FAD, ASK	fad, ask
ā Ā	FĀD	fade
ah AH	BAH-thuhr, KAHT;	bother, cot;
	FAH-thuhr, AHSK	father, ask
aw AW	KAWT, LAW	caught, law
b B	BID	bid
ch CH	CHIP	chip
d D	DID	did
e E	FED	fed
ē Ē	BĒD	bead
f F	FIT	fit
g G	GET	get
ḡ Ḡ	ah-ME-ḡō	Span. amigo (*Anglicized alternative* g)
h H	HED	head
hl HL	hlah-NEHL-ē	Welsh Llanelli (*Anglicized alternative* l *or* thl)
hw HW	HWET, HWICH	whet, which
i I	BID	bid
ī Ī	BĪ, RĪD, LĪ	buy, ride, lie
j J	JET	jet
k K	KIK, KUK	kick, cook
kh KH	BAHKH, IKH, LAHKH	Ger. Bach, ich, Scottish loch.
l L	LEG, MID-l	leg, middle
m M	MEN	men
n N	NET, KIT-n	net, kitten
ng NG	RING, RINGK	ring, rink
ō Ō	KŌT	coat
oi OI	BOI, KOIN	boy, coin
oo OO	MOOD	mood
ow OW	OWT, NOW	out, now
p P	PIN, LIP	pin, lip
r R	RED, KAHRD	red, card
s S	SIT	sit
t T	TŌ, SIT-ing	toe, sitting
th TH	THIN	thin
th TH	THIS	this
u U	GUD, PUT, PUR	good, put, poor
ue UE	RUE, FUE-luhn;	Fr. rue, Ger. fühlen;
	FUEL-uhn	Ger. füllen
uh UH	buh-NAN-uh, BUHD	banana, bud
uhr UHR	BET-uhr, BUHRD	better, bird
uh(r) UH(R)	BUH(R)F,	*Anglicization of* Fr. boeuf, Ger. Hölle.
	HUH(R)L-uh	
	FUH(R),	*Anglicization of* Fr. feu, Ger. Höhle.
	HUH(R)-luh	
v V	VET	vet
v V	ahv-LAHR	Span. hablar (*Anglicized alternative* b *or* v)
w W	WET, WICH	wet, witch
y Y	YES	yes
z Z	ZIP	zip
zh ZH	MEZH-uhr	measure